NEW CATHOLIC
ENCYCLOPEDIA

*An International Work of Reference
on the Teachings, History, Organization,
and Activities of the Catholic Church,
and on All Institutions, Religions,
Philosophies, and Scientific and Cultural
Developments Affecting the Catholic Church
from Its Beginning to the Present.*

*Prepared by an Editorial Staff at
The Catholic University of America,
Washington, District of Columbia.*

McGRAW-HILL BOOK COMPANY   NEW YORK   ST LOUIS

Volume II

Baa to Cam

NEW CATHOLIC
ENCYCLOPEDIA

SAN FRANCISCO   TORONTO   LONDON   SYDNEY

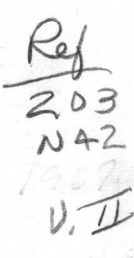

Nihil Obstat:
John P. Whalen, M.A., S.T.D.
Censor Deputatus

Imprimatur:
✠ Patrick A. O'Boyle, D.D.
Archbishop of Washington
August 5, 1966

NEW CATHOLIC ENCYCLOPEDIA

Samson, detail (actual size) of a 6th- or 7th-century
Egyptian silk compound twill fabric.

B

BAADER, FRANZ XAVER VON

Social philosopher, lay theologian, and mining engineer; b. Munich, March 27, 1765; d. Munich, May 23, 1841. Baader was a leading member of the "Munich circle" of romantic Catholics who did so much to advance the renewal of Catholicism in the 19th century. Through his influence on *Schelling, *Döllinger, E. von Lasaulx, *Kierkegaard, *Solov'ev, and *Berdîaev, he affected intellectual developments extending well beyond his century.

Baader first studied medicine at Ingolstadt and Vienna. His intellectual formation was strongly influenced by J. M. *Sailer and the French mystic L. C. Saint-Martin. Abandoning medical practice after a short time, he turned to the study of mining engineering at Freiberg (1788–92). While serving as an engineer in England and Scotland (1792–96) he studied at firsthand the impact of the industrial revolution, the liberal economic theory of Adam *Smith, and the sensational psychology of *Hume. About the same time he undertook the study and criticism of *Kant and German idealistic philosophy. His rejection of rationalistic philosophy, liberal economics, and the revolutionary transformation of the social order were rooted in these experiences and studies. He distinguished himself in his profession from the time of his return to Bavaria in 1799 until his retirement from engineering in 1820. Then he began intensive work and publication in the field of speculative theology and in 1826 was appointed professor of philosophy at Munich. Here, in association with *Görres and the younger members of the "Munich circle," he published the journal *Eos*. Although his literary style was cloudy and aphoristic he was regarded as one of the most brilliant conversationalists and lecturers in Germany.

Baader, in the years between 1814 and 1822, laid the basis for modern ecumenicism. He was responsible for the establishment of the Holy Alliance, which he conceived as a bridge not only between political entities but between Protestantism, Orthodoxy, and Catholicism. In 1822 he founded an ecumenical academy in St. Petersburg. Although these ventures were failures, Baader's efforts at reunion lived on in the thought of Döllinger and the South German school.

Baader's theosophical thought, colored by Neoplatonism and gnostic tendencies, aimed at a reconciliation of reason and authority. On this account he is frequently described as a neoscholastic although his fantastic thought structures frequently verged on heterodoxy. More immediately important was his social teaching, which, like his epistemology, was a return to authority. Highly critical of liberal politics and economics, he proposed a corporative social structure based upon principles of authority, hierarchy, subordination, and status. His corporativist ideas became commonplaces of European social thought in the century that followed his death.

See also SOCIAL MOVEMENTS, CATHOLIC, 3.

Bibliography: *Sämtliche Werke,* ed. F. HOFFMANN et al., 16 v. (Leipzig 1850–60); newly repr. (Aalen 1963–); *Lettres inédites,* ed. E. SUSINI (Paris 1943). Literature. H. GRASSL, NDB 1:474–476, extensive bibliog. D. BAUMGARDT, *Franz von Baader und die philosophische Romantik* (Halle 1927). E. SUSINI, *Franz von Baader et le romantisme mystique,* 2 v. (Paris 1943). For an introduction to Baader's social theory see R. BOWEN, *German Theories of the Corporative State* (New York 1947) 46–53. For Baader's relationship to romantic Catholicism see T. STEINBÜCHEL, "Romantisches Denken im Katholizismus mit besonderer Berücksichtigung der romantischen Philosophie Franz von Baaders," *Romantik: Ein Zyklus Tübinger Vorlesungen,* ed. T. STEINBÜCHEL (Tübingen 1948).

[S. J. TONSOR]

BAAL

Chief god of the Canaanites, son or grandson of the sky god *El, and consort of *Asera (Asherah). Baal was the most popular god of the Canaanite pantheon, since he was the administrator of divine favors, the high god El being treated as a shadowy and distant figurehead. In the mythology of *Ugarit, Baal was the champion of the gods in their fight against the sea *dragon Yam; when he killed him, he was acclaimed king and hailed as Zabul, "the exalted lord of the earth," and Baal Samen, "lord of the heavens." He was likewise known as "the rider of the clouds" (an OT title of Yahweh also) and "the lord of the storm," whose voice was thunder. Thus, he was the god who controlled the rain. Since the Canaanites were entirely dependent on the rain for the growth of their crops, they fervently sought the good will of Baal. Later he was identified

"Baal of the Lightning," limestone relief from Ras Shamra, c. 1900 to 1750 B.C., height 55 inches.

with the storm god Hadad (Adad). In Akkadian, Baal was pronounced as *Bel.

The Canaanite word *ba'al* (lord, master, owner, husband) was originally one of Baal's titles, but by the 15th or 14th century B.C. it was used almost exclusively as his proper name. Since Yahweh was the lord and master (and even husband) of His people Israel, the early Israelites often called Him *ba'al;* but when they indulged in the fertility cult of the Canaanite Baal, this appellation for Yahweh was forbidden (Os 2.18–19).

Before this time many Israelite names were formed with *ba'al* as a title for Yahweh, e.g., *Meri-Baal, a son of Saul (2 Sam 21.8) and a son of Jonathan (2 Sm 4.4); *Is-Baal (Ish-Baal), another son of Saul (1 Chr 8.33); and Baaliada, a daughter of David (1 Chr 14.7). Later scribes changed *ba'al* in some of these names to *bōšet* (shame). Place names were likewise formed with *ba'al,* e.g., Baala in northern Juda (Jos 15.9), Baal-Gad (Jos 11.17), Baal-Hermon (Jgs 3.3), etc.; but most, if not all, of these place names went back to the Canaanites, and their full form was probably as in Beth-Baal-Maon (house, i.e., sanctuary of the Lord of Maon; cf. Nm 32.38 with Jos 13.17).

The OT (Jgs 2.11; 8.33; 10.10) speaks of Baals (in the plural), not because there were many different Baals but because the same god was worshiped at different sanctuaries, e.g., at Baal-Phogor (Dt 4.3; Os 9.10) and at the temple of Baal-Berith (the lord of the covenant) in Sichem (Jgs 8.33; 9.4). The commingling of the Israelites with the Canaanites led to more and more religious syncretism. Even among the Israelites, Baal had his high places (Jer 19.5; 32.35), his altars (Jgs 6.25–30), his sacred *stones (4 Kgs 11.18; 2 Chr 23.17), and his prophets (3 Kgs 18.19, 22). The struggle between Yahweh and Baal came to a climax under King *Achab of Israel and his wife *Jezabel, who built a temple in Baal's honor at Samaria and supported 450 of his prophets (3 Kgs 16.32). Elia successfully challenged these prophets on Mt. Carmel (3 Kgs 18.20–40). Although almost eradicated by Jehu (4 Kgs 10.18–28), the cult revived and remained until the destruction of the Northern Kingdom of Israel (4 Kgs 17.10). Promoters of the Baal cult in Juda were Achab's daughter Athalia, who was married to King Joram of Juda (4 Kgs 11.18), and King Manasse (4 Kgs 21.3). Although strenuously opposed by the Prophets Jeremia (Jer. 2.23; 11.13) and Ezechiel (Ez 6.4–6), the cult continued in Juda until the destruction of the Southern Kingdom. Many of the attributes of Baal are paralleled by those applied to Yahweh, and perhaps some of the Psalms were influenced by the cultic hymns of Baal worship [e.g., Ps 28(29)].

Bibliography: EncDictBibl 182–183. A. S. KAPELRUD, *Baal in the Ras Shamra Texts* (Copenhagen 1952). G. R. DRIVER, *Canaanite Myths and Legends* (Edinburgh 1956). J. GRAY, *The Legacy of Canaan: The Ras Shamra Texts and Their Relevance to the Old Testament* (VetTest Suppl. 5; 2d ed. 1964). R. DUSSAUD, "Le Vrai nom de Ba'al," RevHistRel 113 (1936) 5–20. **Illustration credit:** Musée du Louvre.

[H. MUELLER]

BABISM

An ultra-Shī'ite (Shiites) sect founded in Shiraz, Persia, in 1844 by a dissenting theologian, Muḥammad 'Alī (1819–50), who assumed the title of al-Bāb (Ar., short for Bāb-al-Dīn, "the gateway to religion"). Al-Bāb built on foundations laid in Persia by a native of eastern Arabia, al-Shaykh Aḥmad Aḥsa'i (d. 1828), whose followers (Shaykhis) held the 12 *imām descendants of *Ali in excessive veneration and emphasized the cult of al-Mahdī [the (divinely) guided one]. The *Mahdī, according to the major body of the *Shiites, is the 12th hidden imām who, in the fullness of time, will reappear and, messiahlike, lead his followers to a new era of justice and prosperity. When on a pilgrimage to Kerbela (Karbalā'), Iraq, al-Bāb made the acquaintance of a Shaykhi missionary from whom he received instruction, and when he was on another pilgrimage to *Mecca, he developed the doctrine that he was the door to esoteric knowledge and the inner veiled meaning of the scriptures. His ideas were formulated in a "revealed" book al-Bayān (the manifestation), where Koranic laws were abrogated and an allegorical interpretation (ta'wīl) was so applied to the Koran and ḥadīth (*Islamic traditions) as to be viewed as a threat to Shī'ism, the state religion, as well as to the state itself. The new teaching abolished the veil, circumcision, and ritual ablution. The law on usury was likewise repealed, but not that against drinking. Furthermore, the innovator proclaimed himself the mirror in which God was reflected and in which his adherents could see Him. Following neo-Pythagorean precedent, he gave the number 19 a mystical meaning. The year was divided into 19 months and the month into 19 days; the daily reading of 19 verses from al-Bayān, written in the style of the Koran, was enjoined on all believers. The name of God was to be prayerfully repeated 361 times a day.

As al-Bāb went from place to place preaching his new gospel, he was jailed, and his followers were persecuted. Among his disciples was a beautiful, intelligent poetess, Qurrat al-'Ayn (the satisfaction of the eye), whose missionary activity was especially successful. Despite civil and governmental opposition, adherents increased. The movement became a rallying center for political, economic, and spiritual malcontents. At the accession of Shah Nāṣir-al-Dīn (1848), the Bābis, fearing intensified persecution, took up arms. Disturbances spread in Mashhad, Zanjān, Tabriz, and other towns of Persia. In the capital, Teheran, the insurgents routed the first contingents sent against them, but were later surrounded, starved, and destroyed. In July 1850 al-Bāb was executed in the public square of Tabriz, and his body was thrown into a ditch. Two years later Bābis were charged with conspiring to murder the Shah. Another persecution followed in which Qurrat-al-'Ayn was strangled. In all about 20,-000 lost their lives at the hands of the mob, religious leaders, or soldiers.

A disciple of al-Bāb was accepted as the manifestation of the Diety for whom the Bāb had prepared the way. He assumed the title of Bahā'-Allāh (splendor of God). The cycle of 19 years (1844–63), was completed. Shaykhism led to Babism, and Babism ended in *Baha'ism. All three movements represented spiritual ferment and political turbulence in 19th-century Persia. But while Shaykhism remained within the fold of Islam, its outgrowths moved to the periphery.

Bibliography: C. HUART, *La Religion de Bāb* (Paris 1889). ALĪ MUHAMMAD, SHĪRĀZĪ, *A Traveller's Narrative Written to Illustrate the Episode of the Bāb*, tr. and ed. E. G. BROWNE (Cambridge, Eng. 1891). E. G. BROWNE, comp., *Materials for the Study of the Bābī Religion* (Cambridge, Eng. 1918). NABÍL-I-A'ZAM, *The Dawn Breakers*, tr. SHOGHI EFFENDI (2d ed. Wilmette, Ill. 1953).

[P. K. HITTI]

BABITS, MIHÁLY, Hungarian poet, novelist, translator, and literary scholar; b. Szekszárd, Oct. 23, 1883; d. Budapest, Aug. 5, 1941. He graduated from the Cistercians' Gymnasium at Pécs and continued his studies at the University of Budapest, where he became a close friend of two eminent poets: Desiderius Kosztolányi and Julius Juhász. From 1905 to 1916, while teaching Latin and Hungarian, he wrote highly intellectual, largely impersonal lyric poems that were published under the title *Recitative* (1916). Ernő Osvát recognized in Babits a virtuoso of form and made him coeditor of *Nyugat* (Occident), a literary magazine with strong Western orientation. He lectured (1919) on Hungarian and world literature at the University of Budapest; in 1921 he married Ilona Tanner, the poetess known as Sophie Török. In 1940 Babits received the Italian San Remo Prize for his scholarly and poetic translation of Dante's *Divina Commedia*. In the same year he was chosen a member of the Hungarian Academy. Babits began his career as a symbolist poet. His autobiographical novels, *A gólyakalifa* (1916, The Stork Caliph), *Timár Virgil fia* (1922, The Son of Virgil Timár), and *Kártyavár* (1924, House of Cards), reveal the conflicting aspirations of an intellectual who longs for communion with God and the world. In his *History of European Literature* (1934–35) and translations of medieval Latin hymns, *Amor sanctus,* 1932, he is the great humanist with a strong Catholic faith reaffirming the Catholic basis of European culture. During his last years, he found a mode of expression that borders on the language of the mystics, such as in his long poem entitled *Jonás Könyve* (1939, Book of Jonas).

Bibliography: M. BABITS, *Összes versei* (Budapest 1942), collected poetry; *Összes novellai* (Budapest 1938), novels; *Összes müvei*, 10 v. (Budapest 1937–38), essays. J. REMÉNYI, "The Passing of Mihály Babits," *Books Abroad* 16 (1942) 36.

[O. J. EGRES]

BABYLON, CITY OF

Capital of *Babylonia and one of the most famous cities of antiquity. Its original name was perhaps the Akkadian term *bābu ellu* (holy gate)—which term had been transferred from its processional gate to the section of the city near the gate and then to the whole city—or it was a pre-Semitic, non-Sumerian word; but at an early period this name was changed by folk etymology to *bāb-ilim*ᵏⁱ [gate of the god (*Marduk)]. The latter name appeared in Hebrew as *bābel* and was translated into Sumerian as *ká-dingir-ra*ᵏⁱ. Other neo-Sumerian names of the city were *tin-tir*ᵏⁱ (park of life) and *e*ᵏⁱ (canal city). In Gn 11.9 the Hebrew name *bābel* is explained by folk etymology as if the city were thus called because Yahweh there "confused" (*bālal*) the language of the builders of the *Tower of Babel. From the neo-Babylonian name of the city *bāb-ilāni* (gate of the gods) is derived its Greek name Βαβυλών.

The ruins of the ancient city lie about 60 miles south of Baghdad, near the Hilla Canal of the Euphrates. About 12 miles to the east are the ruins of the much more ancient Sumerian city of Kish, which was once on the Euphrates. When the Euphrates changed its bed westward (probably in the 3d millennium B.C.), Babylon took the place of Kish as the chief city of middle Mesopotamia. The Euphrates has since then moved further to the west and is now about 10 miles west of the site of Babylon.

Despite the descriptions of the city given in cuneiform documents and by classical authors, its topography is not entirely clear. But the excavations made by German archeologists under the direction of R. Koldewey have revealed the main features of the an-

The Ishtar Gate of Babylon showing mythical dragons embossed in colored tilework on its brick walls.

cient city, especially its walls, its chief temple (the *é-sag-illa*, "the house that raises high its head") and ziggurat, or temple tower (the *é-tem-an-ki*, "the house of the foundation of heaven and earth"), and its magnificent processional "Ishtar Gate." Most of the surface ruins come from the neo-Babylonian period.

The earliest mention of Babylon comes from the time of the Dynasty of Akkad (2360–2180). But the city was not important until it was taken and made the capital of a small kingdom by the *Amorrite founder of the First Dynasty of Babylon, Sumu-abum (1830–1817). The sixth king of this dynasty, *Hammurabi (1728–1686), extended the sway of Babylon over all of Mesopotamia and made the city the capital of an empire. Thereafter the history of the city of Babylon is intimately connected with the history of Babylonia. (*See* MESOPOTAMIA, ANCIENT, 2.) Although it always retained its cultural leadership, it did not regain its political hegemony until the time of the Neo-Babylonian Empire (626–539), when, especially under *Nabuchodonosor (Nebuchadrezzar), it reached its greatest glory. After it fell to Cyrus the Great in 539 B.C., it was merely one, and not the most important one, of the several administrative centers of the Persian Empire. With the founding of *Seleucia-Ctesiphon (about 45 miles to the north) as the political center of Mesopotamia toward the end of the 4th century B.C., Babylon quickly decayed, so that by the end of the 2d century B.C., especially after it had been sacked by the Parthians (127 B.C.), it had become a heap of ruins.

In the Bible Babylon looms large with the rise of the Neo-Babylonian Empire, and several oracles of the Prophets predict its doom because of its wickedness and its hostility toward Israel (e.g., Is 13.1–14.23; 21.1–10; Jer 50.1–51.64). In the NT the name Babylon is a symbolic term for Rome (Apocalypse ch. 17–18; 1 Pt 5.13).

Bibliography: R. KOLDEWEY, *Das wieder erstehende Babylon* (4th ed. Leipzig 1925). W. VON SODEN, RGG³ 1:808–810. E. UNGER, ReallexAssyr 1:330–339. H. JUNKER, LexThK² 1:1165–67. F. SPADAFORA, EncCatt 2:636–638. EncDictBibl 184–188. **Illustration credit:** The Matson Photo Service, Los Angeles, California.

[J. S. CONSIDINE]

BABYLON OF THE CHALDEANS, PATRIARCHATE OF (BABYLONENSIS CHALDAEORUM)

Patriarchate of the *Chaldean rite, located in *Baghdad, *Iraq. In 1963 it had 11 parishes, 16 secular and 5 religious priests, 76 sisters in 3 convents, 3,005 pupils in 6 schools, and 100,000 Catholics in a population of 1,450,000; it is 646 square miles in area. Under the patriarchate are the metropolitanates of Baghdad (the patriarchal see), *Kirkuk, *Sanandaj, and *Rizaiyeh, and the archbishopric of *Basra. Suffragan to Baghdad are five sees, which had 86 parishes, 53 secular and 9 religious priests, 56 sisters, and 52,440 Catholics in a population of some 500,000: Algosh (created in 1960), Amadiyah (*c.* 1785), Aqra (separated from Amadiyah in 1850 but reunited to it 1895–1910), *Mosul (1960), and Zakho (separated from Amadiyah in 1850).

The name Chaldean, of Western origin in the 15th century when the Syriac language was called Chaldean, has been used to describe those Christians of the Sassanid Empire who became *Nestorian but returned to union with Rome. Nestorians called themselves Assyrians.

The apostolate of St. *Thomas the Apostle in the area was mentioned by *Origen (185–253), and a tradition attributes the evangelization to St. *Addai and his disciples. The gospel is said to have come by way of *Edessa before the Sassanid dynasty (226), and the region thus had ties, however weak, with the Patriarchate of *Antioch. Bishop Mar Papa of *Seleucia-Ctesiphon, the Sassanid capital, organized the relatively independent bishops of the region under Seleucia (*c.* 300). Persecution by the Sassanids (340–*c.* 380), who had made *Zoroastrianism the state religion and were constantly at war first with Rome and then with Byzantium, claimed martyrs, including St. *Simeon Barsabae (d. 344) and other bishops. The school of theology at *Nisibis, where the Persian clergy studied, moved to Edessa when Nisibis came under Persian rule (363). With Yazdegerd I (399–420) persecution ceased and a council in Seleucia under *Maruthas of Martyropolis, a Byzantine archbishop and ambassador, accepted the canons of the Council of *Nicaea I and organized the Sassanid episcopacy under the *catholicos of Seleucia-Ctesiphon (410). Persecution returned at the end of Yazdegerd's reign to last until peace with Byzantium (422). In 424 the Synod of Markabta decreed that the catholicos thenceforth was subject to judgment by Christ alone, and the Persian Church became independent of the "Western Fathers" (Church of Antioch?). Nestorian influence entered the Persian Church from Nisibis, to which the school of theology returned in 457, and at the Council of Seleucia (486) the Persian Church became Nestorian officially. Councils in 497 and 544 strengthened Nestorianism further.

Christians in Persia, closer to the Arabs in race and language than to the Iranians, were relieved of religious persecution by the arrival of the Arabs (637), and many apostatized to Islam. The seat of the catholicate moved to Baghdad (c. 777), which had become the seat of the Abbasid caliphate (c. 750). Nestorian clergy, notably Catholicos *Timotheus I (780–823), served the Caliphs; and Nestorian Christianity spread to India, central Asia, and China. After the embassy of the Dominican William of Montferrat to the Nestorian catholicos in 1235, *John of Monte Corvino in 1289 brought from Pope Nicholas IV a letter for Catholicos Yaballaha III (1281–1317), a Mongolian, resident in Maragheh, who was favorable to Catholics. When the Mongol rulers of Persia became Moslem, however, Nestorian Christians there suffered severe persecution, and little is heard of them from the early 14th to the 16th century.

In 1553, when the Nestorian patriarchate was located in Mosul, John Sulaqa was proclaimed in Rome as patriarch of the Chaldeans. However, his successors subsequently moved the patriarchate to Kotchanes. A Chaldean patriarchate of Christians remained united with Rome and was confirmed by the Holy See (1681). These patriarchs, who took the name Joseph, resided in Diarbekr. From 1780 they were administrators rather than patriarchs, inasmuch as Rome still was seeking the conversion of the two Nestorian patriarchates (Kotchanes and Rabban-Hormizd). Metropolitan John IX Hormizd (d. 1838) of Mosul, who had become Catholic in 1778, was confirmed by Rome in 1830 as patriarch of Babylon of the Chaldeans, the only patriarchate of Chaldeans recognized by Rome; his seat was in Mosul. Patriarch Joseph V Audo (1847–78) gained many conversions and disputed with Rome about his jurisdiction in Malabar.

American (1834), Anglican (1876), and Russian (1898) non-Catholic missions became active in the patriarchate but had little success. Nestorians of the Patriarchate of Kotchanes suffered dispersion after World War I; their patriarch moved his official residence to Chicago, Ill. (1940). Recently Nestorians have declined considerably in numbers. Many of them resettled in Iraq and became Catholic. Chaldean Catholics, on the other hand, have increased from 50,000 to 200,000 since World War I. Inasmuch as 75,000 of them live in Baghdad, the seat of the patriarchate was moved there from Mosul (1947), which became a diocese (1960). There is also a Nestorian bishopric in Baghdad.

The archbishopric of the *Syrian rite, created in 1790 as the See of Babylon (Baghdad, Mosul, and Basra), was divided into the Archdioceses of Baghdad and Mosul in 1862. In 1962 Baghdad had 5 parishes, 10 secular priests, 400 pupils in one school, and 11,000 Catholics in a population of 3,500,000; it is 130,888 square miles in area. There was a *Jacobite bishop of Baghdad in the early 9th century.

The Latin Archdiocese of Babylon (Baghdad) was created as a bishopric in 1632 for the Carmelite coadjutor bishop of *Isfahan; in 1638 the see was restricted to resident bishops of French birth, but there was no resident bishop before 1722. In 1848 Baghdad became an archdiocese with Isfahan as a suffragan

(1848–1910). Latin prelates of Baghdad generally functioned as apostolic delegates to Churches of the Eastern rites. In 1963 the Latin see, 142,857 square miles in area, had 6 parishes, 67 religious priests in 7 houses, 189 sisters in 17 convents, 8,935 pupils in 19 schools, and 3,000 Catholics in a population of 6 million.

The archdiocese of the *Armenian rite, the only Armenian see in Iraq, was created in 1954. In 1963 it had 3 parishes, 3 secular and one religious priest, 9 sisters in one convent, 850 pupils in 6 schools, and 3,000 Catholics in a population of 6 million; it is 142,857 square miles in area.

Bibliography: W. DE VRIES, LexThK² 1:1169–70; 2:1004–05. *Église vivante* 10 (1958) 259–261. OrientCatt 359–377. AnnPont (1965) 6, 47–48.

[J. A. DEVENNY]

BABYLONIA, ancient country in southern Mesopotamia, on the lower courses of the Tigris and Euphrates Rivers (see MESOPOTAMIA, ANCIENT, 1). It was so named by the Greeks of the Hellenistic period after its capital city, *Babylon; the Babylonians themselves called the land Sumer and Akkad, after its southern and northern portions, respectively. In the OT the land is termed Sennaar (Gn 10.10; Is 11.11; Dn 1.2; Za 5.11) or the land of the Chaldeans (Jer 24.5; Ez 12.13) after its later Aramaic-speaking conquerors [see CHALDEANS (IN THE BIBLE)]. A richly fertile land, Babylonia was the site of the earliest civilization known, that of the Sumerians, and remained a cultural center of the Near East throughout the pre-Christian period. It rose to political dominance under *Hammurabi (Hammurapi) in the 18th century B.C., and again under *Nabuchodonosor (Nebuchadrezzar) and the other kings of the Neo-Babylonian Empire (626–539 B.C.). Besides Babylon, other famous cities of Babylonia were *Nippur, *Ur, and *Uruk. For a more detailed history of Babylonia, see MESOPOTAMIA, ANCIENT, 2. On the languages of Babylonia, see SUMERIAN LANGUAGE AND LITERATURE; AKKADIAN LANGUAGE AND LITERATURE; ARAMAIC LANGUAGE, 1.

Bibliography: B. MEISSNER, *Babylonien und Assyrien*, 2 v. (Heidelberg 1920–25); ReallexAssyr 1:369–384. EncDictBibl 187–191. M. A. BEEK, *Atlas of Mesopotamia*, tr. D. R. WELSH (London 1962).

[R. I. CAPLICE]

BACH, JOHANN CHRISTIAN, preclassical composer, referred to as the "Milan Bach" and the "London Bach"; b. Leipzig, Sept. 5, 1735; d. London, Jan. 1, 1782. He was the youngest son of J. S. *Bach and his second wife, Anna Magdalena. Only 15 at his father's death, he was taken to Berlin by his half-brother, Carl Philipp Emanuel Bach, who taught him for 5 years. In 1756 he went to Milan with an introduction to Count Litta, who financed further study with G. B. ("Padre") *Martini, under whose tutelage he composed several church works. In 1760 he was appointed Milan cathedral organist, but opera commissions from Turin and Naples in the same year necessitated prolonged absence from his duties. The strained situation resulting was terminated by his appointment to the King's Theatre, London, for the opera season 1762 to 1763. *Orione* (1763) was so successful that Christian was appointed music master to Queen Charlotte and retained this post as long as he lived. His

Johann Christian Bach, portrait by Gainsborough.

copious works in the rococo (late baroque) idiom exerted a strong influence on the Viennese classical style, conspicuously on the boy *Mozart, who visited Christian in London in 1764 and profited immensely from his interest and generous, practical advice.

Christian's conversion to Catholicism soon after his arrival in Italy was resented by his brothers. Several biographers have judged it merely an expedient act to gain church posts, but the fact that he adhered to his faith in Protestant England argues his sincerity. His Catholic church music (1756–62) reflects the prevailing style of Neapolitan opera, each work consisting of arias, duets, and choruses, and accompanied by an orchestra of strings, oboes, organ, and horns (or trumpets). Among his church works are two Glorias and Magnificats, a Requiem, Lessons and Responsories, *Miserere*, and *Te Deum*, this last described by a contemporary poet and musician, C. F. D. Schubart (1739–91), as "one of the most beautiful we have in Europe."

Bibliography: C. S. TERRY, *John Christian Bach* (Oxford 1929). K. GEIRINGER, *The Bach Family* (New York 1954). H. WIRTH, MusGG 1:942–954. R. G. PAULY, *Music in the Classic Period* (Englewood Cliffs, N.J. 1965). W. S. NEWMAN, *The Sonata in the Classic Era* (Chapel Hill, N.C. 1963). Láng Mus WC. Grout HistOp. Modern eds. of several works are available. **Illustration credit:** Liceo Musicale, Bologna.

[A. MILNER]

BACH, JOHANN SEBASTIAN

Preeminent composer who brought the baroque style in music to a close; b. Eisenach, Germany, March 21, 1685; d. Leipzig, July 28, 1750.

Life. Bach was the most illustrious member of a family of successful musicians, all of whom, until Sebastian's youngest son Johann Christian *Bach became a Catholic, were Lutheran. Sebastian was only 10 when his father, a musician in the Eisenach town band, died; thereafter he received most of his musical training from his elder brother, Johann Christof, in Ohrdruf. In 1703 he entered his first post as organist of the New Church at Arnstadt, transferring in 1707 to a similar post at St. Blasius, Mühlhausen, where he married his cousin Maria Barbara Bach. A year later he became court organist to the Duke of Weimar and was later (1714) promoted to the post of concertmaster (i.e., director of the orchestra). In 1717 he became *Kapellmeister* (director of music) to Prince Leopold of Cöthen. His wife died in 1720, and a year later he married Anna Magdalena Wülcken. In 1723 he was appointed to one of the chief musical posts in Germany, music director in Leipzig at two principal churches, St. Thomas and St. Nicholas, as well as the Pauliner-Kirche of the University, and cantor (choir director) at the Thomasschüle. He retained this post until his death. Nine of his twenty children survived him, four sons possessing outstanding musical talent: Wilhelm Friedmann and Carl Philipp Emmanuel (children of Maria Barbara), and Johann Christoph Friedrich and Johann Christian (children of Anna Magdalena). Philipp Emmanuel and Johann Christian became more famous than their father during their lifetimes.

Religious Music. Sebastian's fame was chiefly that of a virtuoso organist and a learned but old-fashioned contrapuntist; his music never had the success of *Handel's because it was not addressed to the public audiences of the opera houses and choral concerts. If, like Handel, he had depended on popular approval for his livelihood, he might have adopted more of the newer compositional techniques; but since he remained all his life a paid employee of either prince or town council, he was under no urgent compulsion to please the public ear. Whereas Handel's music looks outward, every note designed to make an immediate impression on its audience, Bach's is introspective, full of detail that can be perceived only through careful listening and sympathetic understanding. Though he wrote much instrumental music, he designed the bulk of his work for use in the

Johann Sebastian Bach.

Lutheran church. In notes on thorough-bass playing dictated to his student Niedt, he said: "The aim and final reason of all music should be none else but the glory of God and the recreation of the mind. Where this is not observed, there will be no music but only a devilish hubbub."

Bach wrote 295 church cantatas (5 yearly cycles of 59 each) during the first 6 years of his Leipzig cantorate, of which some 200 are extant. To study them profitably it is important to remember their intimate connection with the liturgy of the Lutheran Sunday morning or festal service: their texts frequently contain quotations from, or reference to, the Epistle and Gospel of the day; and the concluding chorale is always that of the particular Sunday or feast day. The music is full of symbolism, allusion, and word painting that become clear only when the works are viewed in their liturgical context. Most of the cantatas commence with a large-scale movement, frequently blended with the Italian concerto style; but where Handel would have a largely homophonic texture, Bach develops the chorus in elaborate counterpoint, e.g., in the Ascension cantata (No. 11). Sometimes this is combined with a chorale *cantus firmus* in the top chorus voice (*Wachet auf,* No. 140). The first movement may also be built on a French overture (No. 61) or preceded by it (No. 119). Several cantatas use a chorale melody as a thematic basis for all movements, but treated very freely. Only one of these preserves the melody intact throughout—*Christ lag in Todesbanden* (No. 4). Cantatas having two or more chorales are generally narrative cantatas, e.g., the six constituting the *Christmas Oratorio.* Similar variety of style and form is found in the solo arias, duets, and trios that form the middle section of cantatas.

The Mass in B minor is a composite work: the first two movements were heard as a Lutheran *missa* when the Elector of Saxony visited Leipzig in 1733. The *Gloria* uses material from an earlier cantata (No. 191). The other movements, from the *Credo* onward, are now known to date from the very last years of Bach's life as far as their present form is concerned: most of them are built on materials, sections, and movements from other works. As court composer to the Elector (who was a Catholic) Bach compiled the Mass, but it was never intended for Catholic or for any liturgy in its complete form. Each of the sections has something of the plan of a cantata but also follows the shape of contemporary Masses by Austrian and Italian composers.

The Passions according to St. John (1724) and St. Matthew (1729) represent a compromise between the earlier "dramatic" and the newer "opera" forms of Passion composition (*see* PASSION OF CHRIST, MUSIC OF). Bach retained the complete relevant Gospel portions in both works, adding chorales of his own selection. For the solo arias and accompanied recitatives of *St. John* he drew on a text by Heinrich Brockes, and for *St. Matthew* his libretto was prepared by a Leipzig poet, Picander. *St. John* is more obviously dramatic by reason of the fewer lyrical interruptions to the narrative and the extended "crowd" sections; *St. Matthew,* though it has dramatic moments, is more meditative and leisurely in its progress. Bach's treatment of the Gospel narrative is peculiarly his own: he abandoned every trace of the old chant intonations, substituting a vocal line ostensibly based on the *secco recitativo* but with a lyrical turn of phrase not to be found there, an effect that conformed entirely to the requirements of the German language and to the expressiveness required by the subject. In the Passions, as in all his religious music, Bach's devotion and deep feeling for religion are manifest.

Bach, fragment of the autograph manuscript of Cantata No. 10, "Meine Seel' erhebt den Herrn."

See also MUSIC, SACRED, HISTORY OF, 5; ORGAN MUSIC; CHOIR MUSIC; CANTATA; PASSION OF CHRIST, MUSIC OF.

Bibliography: *Werke,* ed. Bach-Gesellschaft, 61 v. in 47 (Leipzig 1851–1926; repr. Ann Arbor 1947); *Briefe,* ed. E. H. MÜLLER VON ASOW (2d ed. Regensburg 1950). P. SPITTA, *Johann Sebastian Bach,* tr. C. BELL and J. A. FULLER-MAITLAND, 3 v. (London 1884; 2d ed. New York 1951). C. S. TERRY, *Bach* (2d ed. London 1933). A. SCHWEITZER, *J. S. Bach,* tr. E. NEWMAN, 2 v. (New York 1911; reissue London 1923), new Ger. ed. (Wiesbaden 1955). A. PIRRO, *Johann Sebastian Bach,* tr. M. SAVILL (London 1959). H. T. DAVID and A. MENDELS, eds., *A Bach Reader* (New York 1954). K. and I. GEIRINGER, *The Bach Family* (New York 1954). N. DUFOURCQ, *Jean-Sébastian Bach: Le Maître de l'orgue* (Paris 1948). J. B. CONNOR, *Gregorian Chant and Medieval Hymn Tunes in the Works of J. S. Bach* (Washington 1957). F. BLUME, MusGG 1:962–1047. H. C. COLLES, Grove DMM 1:293–321. Buk MsB. Láng MusWC. **Illustration credits:** Fig. 1, Museo Teatrale Alla Scala. Fig. 2, From the Collections of the Library of Congress, Whitehall Foundation Collection.

[A. MILNER]

BACH, JOSEPH, theologian; b. Aislingen, Bavaria, March 4, 1833; d. Munich, Sept. 22, 1901. He was ordained in 1856. He taught pedagogy and philosophy (1872) at the University of Munich and apologetics and the history of dogmas (1888) after the suppression of the philosophical faculty. His chief work was *Die Dogmengeschichte des Mittelalters* (2 v. Vienna 1873–75), which is still very useful. Other books were *Meister*

Eckhart (Vienna 1864), *Des Albertus Magnus Verhalten zur Erkenntnislehre der Griechen, Lateiner, Araber und Juden* (Vienna 1881).

Bibliography: A. SCHMID, *Lebens-Bild des hochwürdigen Herrn Dr. Joseph Bach* (Kempten 1902). V. ZOLLINI, EncCatt 2:653. J. GRISAR, DHGE 6:55–56.

[M. SCHMAUS]

BACHA, CONSTANTINE,

modern historian of the Melchite Church; b. Douma (Batroun, Lebanon), Feb. 3, 1870; d. Holy Savior's Monastery (Saida, Lebanon), Oct. 12, 1948. After his early studies at Holy Savior's Seminary (Saida), Bacha (al-Bāša) became a Salvatorian religious in 1886 and was ordained in 1893. Wherever he served as pastor, teacher, or administrator, he devoted all his leisure time to research in Church history. He visited every library he could, especially those of Rome and Paris. In 1925 he retired to Holy Savior's Monastery, where he devoted the rest of his life to writing a history of the Melchite Church.

Holy Savior's library lists 40 works as translated, composed, or published by him. His magistral work is the *Ṭārîh Ṭāifat ar-Rūm al-Malakîyat war Rahbānîat al-Muhallişîat* (*History of the Catholic Melchite Community and of the Salvatorian Order*) in two volumes. The first volume, published in 1938, is dedicated to Metropolitan Euthymios *Saifi, and the second, published in 1945, to Patriarch Cyril Ṭanas. The extensive and varied sources used make this work a rich mine of information as well as a history of note. The manuscripts gathered by him for his research are preserved in the archives department of Holy Savior's Monastery and continue to be the richest collection of material on this subject to be found anywhere.

Bibliography: L. MALOUF in *Ar-Risālat al-Muhallişîat* (Sidon, Leb. 1948) 705–718. J. CHAMMAS, *Hulāṣat Ṭārîh al-Kanîsat al-Malakîyat*, 3 v. (Sidon, Leb. 1952) 231–237.

[L. MALOUF]

BACHEM, JULIUS

German lawyer and journalist; b. Mülheim, July 2, 1845; d. Cologne, Jan. 22, 1918. He was descended from an old Cologne family of publishers and book dealers. The most prominent member of the family before Julius was Joseph (1821–93), founder (1860) of the *Kölner Blätter,* which became (1869) the *Kölnische Volkszeitung.* A publishing house (established 1818) and a printing press, both of which Joseph had taken over from the family, enabled him to risk founding the newspaper. Toward the end of 1869, Joseph put the management of the *Kölnische Volkszeitung* in the hands of his nephew Julius, who had first embarked on the study of modern languages but then turned to jurisprudence. Even while attending school, however, he had been on the editorial staff of the newspaper, and he later gave up law completely in favor of journalism. Together with the historian Hermann Cardauns, he made the *Kölnische Volkszeitung* the leading organ of German Catholicism. Bachem specialized in constitutional and socio-political questions and in national and local politics; he became well known as the author of many political pamphlets and brochures, such as *Die Sünden des Liberalismus* (1872), *Vor den Wahlen* (1873), *Das Zentrum im Landtag und im Reichstag* (1874), and *Strafrechtspflege und Politik* (1877)—all appearing anonymously as *von einem rhein-preussischen Juristen* (by a Rhenish-Prussian jurist). His chief concerns were to balance the rights of the monarchy and those of the people and to lead Catholics from mere defense of their rights to total political activity. He treated the question of equality (*Paritätsfrage*) in numerous articles (e.g., *Die Parität in Preussen*) and declared himself in favor of fair distribution of governmental posts between Protestants and Catholics alike.

Bachem was elected (1875) to the municipal assembly of Cologne and as representative (1876) to the Prussian Parliament (Landtag). Like *Windthorst, he regarded the (Catholic) *Center party not as denominational but as political. In his epoch-making appeal, "Wir müssen aus dem Turm heraus" (*Historische Politische Blätter,* 1906), he attempted to win non-Catholics for the Center party. He sought assurance that Parliament would keep hands off specifically church affairs and matters of faith, and thus made many enemies within his own ranks. A dispute between factions in Cologne and Berlin (where the group was more integrated) was eventually settled by party declarations in 1909 and 1914 favoring Bachem's views as expressed in *Das Zentrum, wie es war, ist, und bleibt* (1913). During the *Kulturkampf, Bachem, with a group of Rhenish-Westphalian jurists, fought against Prussia's prejudicial legislation and for the rights of the Church in *Preussen und die katholische Kirche* (1884) and *Die kirchenpolitischen Kämpfe in Preussen* (1910), written in collaboration with Karl Bachem. Julius Bachem continued his scholarly work through the *Görres-Gesellschaft,* of which he was a founding member (1876), and exercised lasting influence on public opinion through the publication of the *Staatslexikon.* As a member of the *Augustinus-Verein zur Pflege der katholischen Presse,* he contributed to the advancement and improvement of Catholic journalism.

Bibliography: J. BACHEM, *Erinnerungen eines alten Publizisten und Politikers* (Cologne 1913). K. BACHEM, *Joseph Bachem: Seine Familie und die Firma J. P. Bachem,* 2 v. (Cologne 1912); *Vorgeschichte, Geschichte, und Politik der deutschen Zentrumspartei,* 9 v. (Cologne 1927–32). K. BUCHHEIM, *Geschichte der christlichen Parteien in Deutschland* (Munich 1953). H. CARDAUNS, *Julius Bachem* (München-Gladbach 1918); *Julius Bachem und die Görres-Gesellschaft* (Cologne 1919). M. SPAHN, *Hochland* 15 (1918) 17–21. A. RITTHALER, NDB 1:493–494.

[O. B. ROEGELE]

BACHIARIUS,

4th-century monk and theologian; b. probably in Galicia, Spain, c. 350; d. time and place unknown. He became a monk, was suspected of *Priscillianism, and had to leave Spain (c. 380). He was the author of two books: *Libellus fidei,* written probably in Rome in 383 or 384 as a profession of faith to refute the accusation of heresy; and *De reparatione lapsi,* in which he pleaded for a monk who had sinned but was now repentant, and in so doing gave an excellent presentation of the Spanish penitential system (*see* PENITENTIALS). His explanations of the Trinity, the Incarnation, and the perpetual virginity of Mary are admired for their clarity and orthodoxy. G. *Morin regards him as the author of two letters on asceticism. Bachiarius's style has been compared to that of *Jerome, and *Gennadius calls him a "Christian philosopher" (*De vir. ill.* c. 24).

Bibliography: J. MADOZ, *Revista Española de Teología* 1 (1941) 457–488. G. MORIN, "Pages inédites de deux Pseudo-

Jérômes," RevBén 40 (1928) 289–318. H. RAHNER, LexThK² 1:1180. F. X. MURPHY, "Bachiarius," *Leaders of Iberian Christianity,* ed. J. M. F. MARIQUE (Boston 1962) 121–126. A. LAMBERT, DHGE 6:58–68.

[S. J. MC KENNA]

BACHILLER Y MORALES, ANTONIO,

Cuban scholar, bibliographer, and historian; b. Havana, 1812; d. there, 1889. He graduated from the University of Havana in civil and Canon Law and became a professor there and dean of the school of philosophy. He was also professor of political economy of the San Carlos Seminary. In 1863 the Institute of Secondary Instruction of Havana was established under his direction, and he held the chair of political economy and mercantile law. At the same time he practiced law. He was secretary of the Sociedad Económica de Amigos del País and director of the Liceo de la Habana. He held the post of syndic of the municipal government of Havana and later was elected councilman (1860). As an opponent of the colonial Spanish regime, during the war of 1868 he lived in exile in the U.S., where he became a citizen. He did not renounce his American citizenship when he returned to Cuba. His chief work as bibliographer and historian is *Apuntes para la historia de las letras y de la instrucción pública en la Isla de Cuba* (3 v. 1859–61). It is an invaluable source of information. The first part is devoted to an analysis of primary instruction; the second, to secondary and university instruction; the third, to printing, periodicals, and literary history (poetry, songs, drama, history); the fourth consists of 13 biographies and a catalogue of books and pamphlets. Other writings include: *Cuba, monografía histórica que comprende desde la pérdida de la Habana hasta la restauración española* (1883); *Los Negros* (1887); and *Cuba primitiva* (1883).

Bibliography: F. PERAZA SARACUSA, *Antonio Bachiller y Morales: El padre de la bibliografía cubana* (Havana 1937). J. M. PÉREZ CABRERA, *Historiografía de Cuba* (Mexico City 1962).

[F. DOMINGUEZ-COMPAÑY]

BACKER, AUGUSTIN DE,

bibliographer; b. Antwerp, Belgium, July 18, 1809; d. Liège, Belgium, Dec. 1, 1873. He joined the *Jesuits (1835), went to Louvain to study theology (1840), and was ordained (1843). With the encouragement of his religious superiors, he remained in Louvain and continued the bibliography of writings by Jesuits published by Pedro de Ribadeneira in 1608 and 1613, by Philippe de Alegambe in 1643, and by Nathaniel Southwell in 1676. With the help of his brother Alois (1823–83) from 1850, he published *Bibliothèque des écrivains de la Compagnie de Jésus* (7 v. 1853–61). With Charles Ruelens he edited *Annales Plantiniennes depuis la fondation de l'imprimerie jusqu'à la mort de Christophe Plantin* (1865–66). Aided by Carlos *Sommervogel he published a second edition of his *Bibliothèque* (3 v. 1869–76), which contained 11,000 names of Jesuit writers, together with information about their lives, works, editions, translations, manuscripts, etc. After the death of the De Backer brothers, Sommervogel continued the work.

Bibliography: V. VAN TRICHT, *La Bibliothèque des écrivains de la Compagnie de Jésus et le P. Augustin De Backer* (Louvain 1875). Sommervogel 1:753–755. E. LAMALLE, DHGE 6:73–75. Koch JesLex 1:145–146. B. SCHNEIDER, LexThK² 1:1181–82.

É. DE MOREAU, *Biographie nationale de Belgique,* v.29 (Brussels 1956) 176–178.

[M. DIERICKX]

BACON, DAVID WILLIAM,

first bishop of Portland, Maine; b. Brooklyn, N.Y., Sept. 15, 1813; d. New York City, Nov. 5, 1874. He was the son of William and Elizabeth (Redmond) Bacon. After study at the Sulpician College, Montreal, Canada, and Mt. St. Mary's Seminary, Emmitsburg, Md., he was ordained by Abp. Samuel Eccleston on Dec. 13, 1838. Following parish assignments in northern New York and in New Jersey, he was sent to Brooklyn to organize the new parish of the Assumption of Our Lady, where he was pastor from 1841 to 1855. He was appointed bishop of Portland, and was consecrated by Abp. John Hughes in St. Patrick's Cathedral, New York City, on April 22, 1855. His diocese, which included Maine and New Hampshire, was aided by Jesuits who served Catholics in central Maine and by priests from Quebec, Canada, who ministered to Franco-Americans in northern Maine. Educational and charitable needs were met by the Sisters of Mercy, who established their first house in Manchester, N.H. (1858), and extended their work in Maine to Bangor (1865), Whitefield (1871), and Portland (1873). Bacon was a notable pulpit orator. He built the Cathedral of the Immaculate Conception, and he attended Vatican Council I. By the time of his death, his diocese possessed 52 priests, and its Catholic population, mainly Irish-Americans and Franco-Americans, had doubled to about 80,000.

Bibliography: W. L. LUCEY, *The Catholic Church in Maine* (Francestown, N.H. 1957).

[W. L. LUCEY]

BACON, FRANCIS

Statesman and philosopher, b. London, Jan. 22, 1561; d. London, April 9, 1626. He was educated in the classics at Cambridge and in law at Gray's Inn. He sought and obtained public offices in range from that of member of Parliament to the lord chancellorship, and became a knight, Baron Verulam, and Viscount St. Albans. Another object of Bacon's ambition was the reform of human learning through the advancement of a nontraditional, anti-Aristotelian philosophy. This undertaking was impeded by large expenditures of time on political and legal tasks. Of the 30-odd writings on philosophical and scientific topics that were begun, only 7 were developed sufficiently for publication by the author. These are the *Advancement of Learning* (1605) and a Latin version with amendments of the same (1623), critical examinations of "ancient" opinions, disputational practices, and "bookish" preoccupations within the universities; *De sapientia veterum* (1609), a statement by way of interpretation of poetic fables of the basic principles of a naturalistic philosophy; *Novum organum* (1620), a confessedly incomplete description of a "new logic" of induction; and, hastily compiled in the last years of the author's life, three inconclusive works on natural history.

Sciences and Causes. In expounding his "new philosophy" Bacon rejects Aristotle's classification of independent sciences with their several segregating axioms. He refuses to separate physics or the science of nature from knowledge in the arts, and denies mathematics an independent status. He also transfers certain of Aris-

Effigy of Sir Francis Bacon, Viscount St. Albans, in St. Michael's Church, St. Albans.

totle's metaphysical and ethical subjects, including the being and the nature of God on the one hand and the governing rules for human conduct on the other, to the province of revealed theology. The base of Bacon's own scheme of science, or philosophy, is natural history; above this in a "pyramid" of knowledge lies physics, and at the apex metaphysics or universal physics. Physics contains the more limited axioms or principles of causal explanation, and metaphysics the more general. The primary task of science, for Bacon, is the discovery of forms, the components of and the causes within the particulars of nature. These forms are inseparable from matter, which is itself formed, active, and causal. All natural causes, then, are material causes—there are no final causes in nature.

Induction and Axioms. The sole method for discovering forms is an induction that relies on a constant and perpetual adduction of particulars. This induction begins with particulars sorted within natural history, in a preliminary response to a query put, as a "prenotion," to nature, and ascends through the less inclusive to the more general axiom. It proceeds by the examination of three sorts of instance, those of "presence," of "absence," and of "deviation." The first or affirmative sort are examples in which the form or cause or nature under investigation is present—form, cause, and nature are, for Bacon, convertible terms. The second or negative sort of instances are examples from which the form is lacking. The third are examples that manifest severally varied degrees of the form's activity—the degrees of deviation, comparable to deflection in the compass needle, being dependent upon the operations severally of other conjunct forms, as causes, within the particulars under observation and experiment. The negative instances, long disregarded in inductive theory, are of especial consequence because of their agency in refuting such misleading axioms as may be too hastily derived from an examination of positive instances alone.

All axioms, whether suggested by particulars or by lesser axioms, are established through sense observation. No explanation that asserts a wider range of causation within particulars than testing by experiments can verify is ever to be deemed true; and always it is sense that must try the experiment. There is to be no adding to the content of science by the employment of deductive, syllogistic devices or through the introduction, at any stage, of so-called "first principles." The most general or metaphysical axioms or principles of science are inductive pronouncements upon causal operation within the whole of nature. And since whatever in science is cause is also in nature operation, metaphysical knowledge enables the scientist to produce inventions in great array for the "relief of man's estate"; and this, indeed—and not Aristotle's "meditation"—is both the supreme warranty and the final goal of inductive metaphysics.

Evaluation. Because of his stress on induction Bacon has often been hailed as the "prophet" of "experimental discovery." He has provided, also, an example for those who would equate the findings of experimental science with the principles of metaphysics; but few of his followers in this regard have thought it possible to establish or to pursue a science of physical nature, let alone an ontology, by the sole use of his inductive method. Bacon's philosophy has long been recognized as a definite antithesis to Aristotelianism. Certainly the two are opposites that do not readily lend themselves either to compromise or to transformation within a synthesis.

See also INDUCTION; FIRST PRINCIPLES; PHILOSOPHY, HISTORY OF.

Bibliography: *Works,* ed. J. Spedding et al., 14 v. (London 1857–74); 15 v. (New York 1869); *Novum Organum,* ed. T. Fowler (2d ed. Oxford 1889); *The New Organon and Related Writings,* ed. F. H. Anderson (New York 1960). F. H. Anderson, *The Philosophy of Francis Bacon* (Chicago 1948); *Francis Bacon, His Career and His Thought* (Los Angeles 1962). C. D. Broad, *The Philosophy of Francis Bacon* (Cambridge, Eng. 1926). R. W. Church, *Bacon* (London 1884). K. Fischer, *Francis Bacon of Verulam,* tr. J. Oxenford (London 1857). A. Levi, *Il pensiero di Francesco Bacone* (Turin 1925). C. F. M. de Rémusat, *Bacon: Sa vie, son temps, sa philosophie . . .* (Paris 1857). **Illustration credit:** National Portrait Gallery, London.

[F. H. ANDERSON]

BACTERIA

Bacteria are primitive unicellular organisms that are microscopic in size and possess a rigid cell wall. There are three main types: spherical (*cocci*), cylindrical (*bacilli*), and helical (*spirilla*). Bacteria vary in diameter or width from 0.5 microns (1/25,000 inch) to 1–2 microns, and from 1–2 to 8–10 microns in length.

The bacterial cell is surrounded by a slime layer, underlying which is a supporting structure the rigid cell wall. Internal to the wall is the cytoplasmic membrane that regulates the flow of materials into and out of the cell.

Classification and Reproduction. The hereditary material of the cell, deoxyribonucleic acid, exists within the cytoplasm as loose packets of fibrillar material that do not possess nuclear membranes. The cytoplasm also contains ribosomes, composed of ribonucleic acid, that are the sites of protein synthesis. Cytoplasmic derivatives having a lamellar structure, termed mesosomes, exist in some bacteria. Photosynthetic bacteria possess chromatophores that house the photosynthetic apparatus; motile bacteria possess flagella that originate in the cytoplasm; and certain genera form resistant bodies termed spores.

Taxonomists usually place bacteria in the plant kingdom as members of the class Schizomycetes (fission fungi). However, some modern taxonomists group the protozoa, algae, and fungi into a separate kingdom, the Protista. They further subdivide the Protista to form a more primitive group containing the bacteria and blue-green algae, as these organisms possess neither a nuclear membrane nor chloroplasts.

Bacterial reproduction is predominantly asexual and bacteria are ordinarily haploid. (*See* CELL DIVISION.) True sexual reproduction does not occur, but bacteria possess three mechanisms—conjugation, transformation, and transduction—by which they can exchange a portion of their genetic material. Conjugation involves the temporary fusion of a donor cell with a recipient cell during which a portion of the genetic material of the donor is transferred to the recipient. Transformation is the process in which the free genetic material of one organism enters another organism by as yet unknown means. In transduction a portion of the hereditary material of one bacterium is "carried" into a second bacterium by a bacteriophage (bacterial virus).

Growth and Nutrition. Bacterial growth is considered to be an increase in numbers and occurs in a definite cycle. Bacteria, upon inoculation into a fresh medium, enter a lag phase in which the cells adapt to the medium but do not increase in numbers. The cells then start to multiply and soon reach a stage of maximum and constant increase (phase of logarithmic growth). The duration of this phase is determined by the concentration of nutrients and the degree of accumulation of toxic end-products. The rate of increase then diminishes, and the culture enters a stationary phase in which the number of viable organisms remains constant. The bacteria then start to decrease in numbers until a phase of logarithmic death is reached. The duration of the various phases depends upon the species of bacterium and the environmental conditions.

Oxygen exerts a great influence on bacterial growth. It is required by aerobic bacteria and prevents the growth of anaerobic bacteria; facultative types grow in the presence or absence of oxygen. Each species of bacteria has an optimum growth temperature. The optimum growth range for psychrophilic bacteria is from 0 to 20°C, for mesophilic, from 20 to 40°C, and for strict thermophilic types, from 55 to 75°C. Each bacterial species grows over a relatively narrow range of acidity or alkalinity. Most bacteria exhibit optimum growth near neutrality (pH 6 to 8); however, certain species have their optimum growth range at lower or higher pH values. High osmotic pressure inhibits the growth of most bacteria but halophilic and saccharophilic strains may grow in solutions containing as much as 25 per cent salt or sugar.

The nutritional requirements of bacteria vary widely. Autotrophic bacteria require only inorganic compounds for growth since they contain all the enzymes necessary to catalyze the reactions involved; heterotrophic types cannot synthesize their protoplasm from inorganic compounds alone. The most fastidious organisms require amino acids, vitamins, and an oxidizable carbohydrate. A spectrum of nutritional types exists between these extremes.

Bacteria respond to changing environmental conditions by physiological or genetic adaptation involving their metabolic activities. These processes play important roles in the development of bacteria that are resistant to chemical disinfection and antibiotic treatment. Because of their nutritional variation and adaptive ability, bacteria are found in practically all environments. The corollary of this is the fact that a bacterium can be isolated that will attack practically any organic compound.

Functions of Bacteria. Bacteria play important roles in the nitrogen, carbon, sulfur, and phosphorus cycles. In the nitrogen cycle, saprophytic bacteria break down dead plant and animal matter to release ammonia that is oxidized to nitrates by autotrophic bacteria. Other bacteria fix free nitrogen by converting it into a form that is available for plant life. In all these cycles, bacteria make possible a continual turnover of the elements that have become bound up in organic matter.

A few species of bacteria cause infectious diseases. Three attributes contribute to their pathogenicity: the production of exotoxins that attack plant or animal tissues, the possession of a capsule that renders them resistant to the host's defense mechanisms, and the production of an invasive factor that facilitates their penetration into tissues.

Bacteria are utilized in industrial fermentations to produce organic compounds from inexpensive natural substances. Pharmaceuticals, antibiotics, and solvents are produced in this manner. Bacteria cause industrial problems that range from metallic corrosion to the destruction of organic materials. The recent realization that such metabolically diverse organisms exist has made possible a fundamental attack on the problems of corrosion, decay, and spoilage.

Bibliography: Soc. of Amer. Bacteriologists, *Birgey's Manual of Determinative Bacteriology,* by R. S. BREED, et al. (7th ed. Baltimore 1957). M. FROBISHER, *Fundamentals of Microbiology* (7th ed. Philadelphia 1962). I. C. GUNSALUS and R. Y. STANIER, eds., *The Bacteria,* 5 v. (New York 1960–63). S. C. PRESCOTT and C. G. DUNN, *Industrial Microbiology* (3d. ed. rev. New York 1959). R. Y. STANIER, et al., *Microbial World* (2d ed. Englewood Cliffs, N.J. 1963).

[K. E. ANDERSON]

BADET, ARNOLD, Dominican, mystical theologian, inquisitor in Languedoc; b. Limoux, France, *c.* 1475; d. Toulouse, 1536. Badet spent most of his life in Languedoc, especially in *Toulouse, where he had a reputation as a preacher and teacher. He was associated with Jean Caturce and other French humanists, many of whom were sympathetic to the new religious movements. Having been made a master in theology in 1530, he was appointed inquisitor for Toulouse (1531). The appointment of Badet, as well as his association with Caturce, prompted some of the members of the

Dominican congregation of Toulouse to denounce him (1535) to the Parlement of Toulouse for heresy. Badet evidently had little trouble in refuting the charges, for he retained his position as inquisitor until his death in 1536.

See also INQUISITION.

Bibliography: Works. *Breviarium de mirabilibus mundi et ejus compositione* (Avignon 1499); *Margarita virorum illustrium* (Lyons 1527); *Destructorium haeresum* (Paris 1532). Literature. Quétif-Échard 2.1:96. G. LOIRETTE, DHGE 6:140–141. Archives de l'Aude, H. 418.

[P. M. STARRS]

BADIA, TOMMASO, theologian and cardinal; b. Modena, 1493 (1483?); d. Rome, Sept. 6, 1547. He was a Dominican from the province of Lombardy, a brilliant professor in Ferrara, Venice, and Bologna and Master of the Sacred Palace. Badia was strict in condemning heterodoxy but lenient with regard to persons. From 1536 he belonged to the reform group of Cardinal Gasparo *Contarini. He endorsed the *Consilium de emendanda ecclesia* and the *Consilium quattuor delectorum* in 1537, and became a member of the commission for the proposed council at Mantua. Paul III approved the Society of Jesus in 1539 on his recommendation. Badia wrote a letter to Contarini in the diet of Worms of 1540 and the next year was advisor to the cardinal-legate at the diet of Regensburg. He was made a cardinal in 1542 and then a member of the Inquisition. Although in 1543–44 he was a member of the deputation for the Council of Trent, he remained in Rome. Badia has been widely known for learning and virtue, but his writings, letters and treatises on philosophy and theology, have yet to be studied.

Bibliography: M. T. DISDIER, DHGE 6:145. A. WALZ, LexThK² 1:1187–88. A. DUVAL, *Catholicisme* 1:1161–62. A. WALZ, *I domenicani al concilio di Trento* (Rome 1961).

[A. M. WALZ]

BADIN, STEPHEN THEODORE, missionary; b. Orléans, France, July 17, 1768; d. Cincinnati, Ohio, April 19, 1853. In 1792, because of the Revolution, he left the Sulpician seminary in France for America and became one of the first students at St. Mary's Seminary, Baltimore, Md. He was ordained by Bp. John Carroll on May 25, 1793, the first priest ordained in the U.S.

From 1793 to 1811 Badin was Carroll's vicar-general in the Old West. Generally alone, and never with more than six priests to aid him, he served the scattered Catholics of Kentucky, Ohio, Indiana, Illinois, Michigan, and Tennessee. He was chiefly responsible for the designation of the see at Bardstown, Ky., and the selection of Benedict J. Flaget as its first bishop.

Because of difficulties with Flaget over church property, Badin returned to France in 1819 and remained there acting as agent for various American bishops until 1826. On his return to the U.S., he joined the Cincinnati diocese and was sent by Bp. Edward D. Fenwick to the Pottawatomie Indian mission in Indiana. He founded the first orphan asylum in that state near South Bend, and bought the land on which the University of Notre Dame now stands. After the Indian mission closed he served the Irish laborers building the Wabash canal and purchased tracts for Catholic churches along this route. From 1835 on he traveled over the Ohio Valley assisting the bishops and pastors of the area.

Badin possessed a keen wit and a sharp humor. Although tolerant with Protestants, he was very strict with his own flock. His writings included several Latin poems, religious tracts, and two books on Catholic doctrine. Martin J. Spalding's sketches on the missions of early Kentucky were largely based on Badin's notes and reminiscences.

Stephen Badin.

After 60 years of missionary labors on frontier lands, Badin died in his 85th year and was buried in the cathedral crypt in Cincinnati. In 1904 his remains were transferred to Notre Dame University and are in the Badin chapel there. At this university Badin Hall is named after him; there is a monument to him at the motherhouse of the Sisters of Loretto in Kentucky, the location of his headquarters in that state. His work earned him the right to be called "the Apostle of Kentucky."

Bibliography: J. H. SCHAUINGER, *Stephen T. Badin* (Milwaukee 1956). M. J. SPALDING, *Sketches of the Early Catholic Missions of Kentucky, 1787–1827* (Louisville 1844). B. J. WEBB, *The Centenary of Catholicity in Kentucky* (Louisville, 1884). **Illustration credit:** The Filson Club, Louisville, Kentucky.

[J. H. SCHAUINGER]

BAEUMKER, CLEMENS, historian of medieval philosophy; b. Paderborn, Sept. 16, 1853; d. Munich, Oct. 7, 1924. After studying at Paderborn and Münster, where he obtained his doctorate in philosophy in 1877, he taught at the Gymnasium in Münster before being appointed professor of philosophy in the universities of Breslau in 1883, Bonn in 1900, Strassburg in 1903, and Munich, where he succeeded G. von *Hertling in 1912. Through his numerous writings and lectures he was one of the leading figures in the revival of Thomism in Germany. As a medievalist he was a pioneer in the study and editing of philosophical texts, notably those of Avicebron, Alfarabi, Alfred of Shareshel, and Siger of Brabant. His greatest service was the founding of the *Beiträge zur Geschichte der Philosophie des Mittelalters* (Münster 1891–   ), which he directed until his death and in which he published his important monograph on *Witelo. The most influential of his works was *Die christliche Philosophie des Mittelalters,* of which there were three editions (Berlin-Leipzig 1909, 1913, 1923). His library passed to the Albertus Magnus Institut in Cologne.

Bibliography: A. A. BOGDANSKI, *The Significance of Clemens Baeumker in Neo-Scholastic Philosophy* (Milwaukee 1942). "C. Baeumker," in *Die Philosophie der Gegenwart in Selbstdarstellungen,* ed. R. SCHMIDT (Leipzig 1922–   ) 2:31–60, autobiography and bibliog. M. GRABMANN, "Clemens Baeumker und die

Erforschung der Geschichte der mittelalterlichen Philosophie," BeitrGeschPhilMA 25 (1927) 1–38. G. BRUNI, EncCatt 2:680–681. C. MAZZANTINI, EncFil 1:559–561.

[A. M. WALZ]

BAGHDAD

Center of the ancient Baghdad Caliphate, capital of modern Iraq, a diocesan center for Churches in communion with the Apostolic See and separated Churches. In A.D. 762 Mansur, second caliph of the 'Abbāsid dynasty, founded Baghdad on the west bank of the Tigris about 30 miles from the ancient Sassanid *Seleucia-Ctesiphon, from which building materials were taken for the new city. Originally called Madinat as-Salam (city of peace), it was known also by its Greek name Eirenopolis; Baghdad is the popular name, meaning probably Garden of Dat. A village of Christians was already in existence in the near vicinity in 762.

Under the 'Abbāsids Baghdad became the intellectual and cultural center of the highly developed Arab Empire. Religious tolerance toward Christians, Jews, and Zoroastrians generally prevailed, although some caliphs, as "deputies of God," occasionally harassed non-Moslems. Churches were built for Christians captured in campaigns against the Byzantine Empire. In the 11th century, Baghdad fell temporarily under the rule of the Seljuk Turks. In 1256 the Mongols under Hulagu captured and destroyed a great part of the city. The Persians conquered and rebuilt it (1517), and in 1638 Baghdad became part of the Ottoman Empire. At the end of World War I it became the capital of an independent Arab state (Iraq).

The official title of the Churches in communion with the Apostolic See is *Ecclesia Babylonensis,* a name that rests on the erroneous belief once held in the West that Baghdad was built on the site of ancient Babylon.

As early as 1628 some Capuchins arrived in Baghdad, and in 1632 the first titular Latin bishop of Baghdad was appointed, but he died before assuming office. A second titular bishop, designated in 1634, refused the appointment. On June 6, 1638, *Urban VIII issued the bull *Super universas* (BullRom 14:652–654) establishing the Diocese of Baghdad, which became an archbishopric (*Ecclesia Babylonensis Latinorum*) in 1848. In 1963 the Latin jurisdiction numbered 3,000 souls in 6 parishes and had 67 religious priests. American Jesuits of the New England province (19 priests, 1 scholastic, 1 lay brother), assisted by 16 lay professors, staffed Al-Hikma University (enrollment 475). Baghdad College was conducted by the same Jesuit province (30 priests, 30 lay instructors) with an enrollment of 1,000.

The Chaldean Patriarchate (*Ecclesia Babylonensis Chaldaeorum*) was established in Baghdad in 1834. Some Nestorians in 1553 united with the Apostolic See and formed the Chaldean Church, but this communion came to an end about a century later. Efforts for reunion (begun c. 1783) were successful, and John Hormez was enthroned as patriarch of Babylon in 1834. This jurisdiction had 100,000 communicants in 11 parishes served by 21 priests (1963).

In 1862 Baghdad became the seat of the Syrian Archdiocese (*Ecclesia Babylonensis Syrorum*), which numbered 11,000 in 5 parishes served by 10 priests (1962). The Armenian Archdiocese (*Ecclesia Babylonensis Armenorum*) was established in 1954; this archdiocese, in

1963, had 3,000 in 3 parishes ministered to by 4 priests. The apostolic delegation for Iraq and Arabia is in Baghdad. The Nestorian bishop has his residence in Baghdad, and in 1964 the Jacobites had one parish in the city.

Bibliography: E. HONIGMANN, Pauly-Wiss RE suppl. 4 (1924) 1118. AMBROSIUS A S. THERESIA, AnalOCarmD 8 (1933) 31–46; 9 (1934) 52–56. R. JANIN, DHGE 6:198–201. T. ARNOLD, CMedH 4:274–298. *Catalogus Provinciae Novae Angliae Societatis Jesu* (Boston 1964) 63–67. AnnPont (1964) 47–48, 957. W. DE VRIES, LexThK² 1:1188–89.

[H. DRESSLER]

BAGLEY, WILLIAM CHANDLER, American educator, opponent of progressive education popular in the 1930s; b. Detroit, Mich., March 19, 1874; d. New York, N.Y., July 1, 1946. He graduated from Michigan Agricultural College (later Michigan State) in 1895, attained his M.S. in experimental psychology at the University of Wisconsin, Madison, in 1898, and his Ph.D. at Cornell University, Ithaca, N.Y., in 1900. From 1908 to 1917 he was professor of education at the University of Illinois, Urbana, and from 1917 to 1940, head of the department of teacher education at Teachers College, Columbia University.

Bagley was a prolific author; his first book, *The Educative Process* (1905) brought him prestige both at home and abroad. *The Professional Preparation of Teachers for American Public Schools* (1919), which he wrote in collaboration with W. S. Learned, represents the chief interest of his professional life. In 1935, he headed a small group of educators called the Essentialist Committee whose purpose was to defend systematic instruction in the fundamentals, a position diametrically opposed to the then prevailing emphasis on incidental learning through activities and experience. *See* ESSENTIALIST MOVEMENT (EDUCATION). Bagley also championed the view that intelligence as measured by test scores is greatly affected by schooling. He enlarged upon this conviction in *Determinism in Education* (1925). Throughout his career he often served as editor for professional periodicals; at the time of his death he was editor of *School and Society.*

Bagley contributed to American education by his insistence on adequate preparation of teachers, and by his fearless challenging of innovations that he deemed detrimental to true progress in education in a democracy.

From a Catholic viewpoint, Bagley must be classified with the naturalistic school of thought. A firm believer in the perfectibility of man, he attributed its source to man himself, and its manifestation to "emergent evolution." As a materialistic monist he failed to recognize the distinction between God and the world, and the essential distinction in man between the spiritual principle, the soul, and the material element, the body. Although he affirmed the existence of certain nonmaterial "qualities" or "functions" he did not posit a spiritual principle as their source.

Bibliography: I. L. KANDEL, *William Chandler Bagley* (New York 1961). J. N. BROWN, *Educational Implications of Four Conceptions of Human Nature* (Washington 1940).

[M. G. KECKEISSEN]

BAGSHAW, CHRISTOPHER, priest and controversialist; b. Lichfield?, c. 1552; d. Paris?, c. 1625. From Oxford he received his B.A. (July 12, 1572) and M.A. (June 21, 1575) degrees; he became principal of Gloucester Hall in 1579, but resigned and went to

France in 1582. After his conversion to Catholicism, he began his studies at the English College, Rome, on Oct. 1, 1583. In January 1585 he was expelled as "unwilling to take the oath" (*Liber Ruber*). He "did not behave well." Passing through Italy to France he acquired a doctorate at Padua; hence his nickname "Doctor per saltum." He arrived at Douai on April 2, 1585, and was sent to England on May 27. Captured on landing, he was imprisoned in the Tower, and then in Wisbich (Wisbech, Wisbeach) from 1588? until November 1601 when, with the approval of the bishop of London, and the Privy Council, he passed with other appellants to Paris en route to Rome. He remained in Paris, a controversial figure, difficult to friends, and irreconcilable to the Jesuits. He was the author, most probably, of *A True Relation of the Faction begun at Wisbich by Fa: Edmonds, alias Weston, a Jesuit, 1595 . . .* (London 1601); *Relatio compendiosa Turbarum quas Jesuitae Angli una cum D. Georgio Blackwello . . . concivere* (Rouen 1601); *An Answer . . . to certain points of a libell called an Apologie of the subordination in England* (Paris 1601); and *A sparing discoverie of our English Jesuits, and of Fa: Parsons . . .* (London 1601).

Bibliography: A. à WOOD, *Athenae Oxonienses,* ed. P. BLISS, 5 v. (London 1813–20) 2:389–390. T. G. LAW, ed., *The Archpriest Controversy,* 2 v. (Camden Society 56, 58; London 1896–98). "Liber Ruber," ed. W. KELLY (CathRecSoc 37; 1940) 43. P. RENOLD, "The Wisbech Stirs," (*ibid.* 51; 1958). A. H. BULLEN, DNB 1:872–873. DictEngCath 1:100–101.

[F. EDWARDS]

BAHA'ISM

A religion founded by Mīrzā Ḥusayn 'Alī Nūrī, called Bahā'Ullāh (the splendor of God), who was born in Teheran, Iran, in 1817. According to Baha'i tradition, Bahā'Ullāh received no formal education. He became one of the early disciples of 'Alī Muḥammad of Shīrāz, called "al-Bāb" (the gateway), who had proclaimed himself as "al-*Mahdī" in 1844. Al-Bāb was executed in 1850 by the order of Naṣir-al-Dīn Shah, who was determined to eradicate the Bābi sect because of the disorders that its propaganda had caused throughout Iran. Bahā'Ullāh was imprisoned in Teheran for 4 months in 1852–53, and while in prison he experienced his first call to a prophetic mission. He was banished to Iraq with other Bābis and lived in Baghdad for a year and then in Kurdistan as a dervish from 1854 to 1856. During the following years in Baghdad he increased his spiritual influence over the Bābi exiles, whose numbers had swelled, until the Persian government formally requested his exile to Constantinople. Shortly before his departure in April 1863 he declared himself to a small number of followers as *man yuzhiruhu 'llāh* (he whom God shall manifest), whom al-Bāb had predicted.

Bahā'Ullāh and some of his followers spent a few months in Constantinople in 1863 before being transferred to Edirne. There he openly proclaimed his prophethood and sent letters to various sovereigns inviting them to accept Baha'ism. Most of the Bābis accepted Bahā'Ullāh's claim, but a minority group loyal to his half brother Mīrzā Yaḥyā precipitated such disturbances within the sect that the Ottoman authorities decided to exile the Baha'is to Acre and Cyprus. Bahā'Ullāh and his family were imprisoned in Acre between 1868 and 1877, and during that time they were allowed to live under house arrest at nearby

Mazra'a. From 1871 to 1873 Bahā'Ullāh was engaged in writing the fundamental scripture of his faith, *Kitāb-i Aqdas* (the most holy book). In 1880 he moved nearer Acre to Bahji, where he died on May 29, 1892.

The greatest apostle of Baha'ism was 'Abbās Effendi, Bahā'Ullāh's eldest son, who was known as 'Abd-al-Bahā'. He was born in 1844 and accompanied his father on his journeys and exile and was recognized by most Baha'is as the authoritative interpreter of his father's teachings. However, a rival party, gathered around his brother Muḥammad 'Alī, brought about his imprisonment in 1908. Two years later he was granted amnesty by the Young Turks and set out on three missionary journeys to Egypt (1910), Europe (1911), and America (1912–13). These journeys had the effect of discrediting his brother's organization and of winning an international following for Baha'ism. 'Abd-al-Bahā' returned to Palestine, was knighted by the British government in 1920 for his philanthropic services during the war, and died the next year. By his testament his oldest grandson Shoghi Effendi was named "Guardian of the Cause of God." From 1923 on Shoghi Effendi made his home in Haifa, Israel, thereafter the principal center of the Baha'i religion. He had studied at Oxford and in 1936 married a Canadian, Mary Maxwell.

Baha'ism propounds a body of doctrine that clearly originated in *Shiïte Islam, but closely resembles Unitarianism and Ramakrishnan Hinduism. It is syncretistic and universalist. It declares that God is unknowable except through His "manifestations" the prophets, including Bahā'Ullāh himself, who perpetuate themselves among mankind and are the "mirrors" of God. It holds a doctrine of creation and at the same time the "eternal" world of Greco-Islamic philosophy. Its eschatology is regarded as entirely symbolic. It aims to establish a unity of the human race, of all religions, and of science and advocates universal education, world peace through social equality and opposition to all forms of prejudice, equal rights for the sexes, an international language, and an international tribunal. It follows a calendar that

Baha'i house of worship in Wilmette, Illinois.

is a revision of the Bābi calendar and elects local assemblies, but there is no public ritual nor even private rites of a sacred character. Its temples are designed in such fashion as to symbolize the unity of the "great" world religions. The headquarters of Baha'ism in the U.S. is located at Wilmette, Ill.

Bibliography: BAHĀ'ULLĀH, *Bahai World Faith* (Wilmette, Ill. 1943); *Kitáb-i-íqán (The Book of Certitude)*, tr. SHOGHI EFFENDI (Wilmette, Ill. 1950); *Selected Writings of Bahā'u'lláh*, tr. SHOGHI EFFENDI (Wilmette, Ill. 1942). NABÍL-I-A'ZAM, *Dawn Breakers,* tr. SHOGHI EFFENDI (2d ed. London 1953). SHOGHI EFFENDI, *God Passes By* (Wilmette, Ill. 1944).

[J. KRITZECK]

BAHAMAS

On Oct. 12, 1492, Christopher Columbus landed on a remote island in the Atlantic known as Guanahani to its Indian inhabitants. This island, renamed San Salvador by Columbus, is one of the archipelago of the Bahamas. Here the first Mass was offered in the New World. The Bahamas include some 3,000 islands and cays covering an area of approximately 90,000 square miles. Since most of the land is of coral formation and consequently unproductive, possessing neither gold, silver, nor precious stones, it was of little interest to the Spaniards. The aboriginal population of the Bahamas, a gentle people of the Taino culture, was pressed into service in the mines of Haiti and Cuba. In a short time, under unaccustomed conditions of forced labor, they were wiped out.

Political History. In the century and a half after Columbus, three attempts were made to wrest control of the Bahamas from Spain. In 1578 Elizabeth I granted to Sir Humphrey Gilbert (half brother of Sir Walter Raleigh) lands "not actually possessed of any Christian prince or people." Charles I in 1629 granted to Sir Robert Heath the Lucayan Island of "Veajus (Abaco) and Bahama." In 1633 through Cardinal Richelieu, France granted to Guillaume de Caen a barony that included part of the Bahamas, and especially Guanahani. But in each case circumstances prevented colonization, and the claims were fruitless. Finally, Captain William Sayle, former governor of Bermuda, obtained a grant from Charles II in 1647. Early in the following year, with a small band of Puritans in search of religious freedom, he landed on a Bahamian island, which he named "Eleuthera" (from the Greek word *Eleutherios,* meaning freedom). The island of New Providence, on which Nassau is located, was settled about 20 years later by survivors of the first colonists, and it became the seat of government. Proximity to the Spanish Main and shipping lanes, the many protected harbors by means of which pirates and shipwreckers could elude pursuit, and occasional treasure finds from wrecked Spanish galleons were factors attracting the adventurous to the Bahamas. Among the most famous English pirates who frequented Bahamian waters were Sir Henry Morgan and Bill Teach, otherwise known as "Blackbeard."

This phase of Bahamian history officially ended when in 1718 Capt. Woodes Rogers was appointed governor and given naval backing to restore order. The motto "Expulsis Piratis, Restituta Commercia," incorporated in the Seal of the Bahamas, memorializes his efforts. Constitutional government was established in 1728 when King George II, by order-in-council, created the House of Assembly with powers similar to those

Cathedral of St. Francis Xavier, Nassau, Bahamas.

of the House of Commons. During the American War of Independence, Nassau was captured and occupied by American forces for 1 day in 1776 and for 3 days in 1783. For just less than a year—May 8, 1782, to April 1783—Spanish forces occupied the town of Nassau. On Jan. 7, 1964, Great Britain granted a new constitution to the Bahamas, bestowing internal self-government within the British Commonwealth. Great Britain, through a royal governor, still maintained control of civil service, internal security, and foreign affairs.

Ecclesiastical Organization. In 1858 Rome placed the Bahamas under the ecclesiastical jurisdiction of the Diocese of Charleston, South Carolina. Catholic priests visited Nassau sporadically until 1885 when in February, Archbishop Corrigan of New York sent Rev. George O'Keefe to reside in the Bahamas. On July 28 of that same year Cardinal Simeoni of the Propaganda transferred the Bahamas to the ecclesiastical jurisdiction of New York. On Feb. 14, 1887, Corrigan dedicated the first Catholic church under the patronage of St. Francis Xavier. This church, now greatly enlarged, serves as the cathedral. The missions of the Church in the Bahama Islands date from October 1889, when Mother Ambrosia and four Sisters of Charity from Mt. St. Vincent on the Hudson in New York arrived in Nassau to establish St. Francis Xavier Academy on November 6. In January 1890 the sisters opened St. Francis Xavier Primary School.

At the invitation of Archbishop Corrigan, St. John's Benedictine Abbey, Collegeville, Minn., undertook responsibility for the mission. On Feb. 2, 1891, Chrysostom Schreiner, OSB, was appointed vicar forane by the archbishop of New York. Father Chrysostom, the "Apostle of the Bahamas," spent the rest of his life in the islands and died in 1928 at San Salvador, where he is buried. The non-Catholic population with its Established Church was militantly anti-Catholic. Yet in a few short years he had established Sacred Heart church in Nassau and several mission churches at Andros. Gabriel Roerig, OSB, who spent his 56 years in the priesthood in the Bahamas, received the decoration of M.B.E. from the government in recognition of his work. The decree *Constans apostolicae sedis* established the island as a prefecture apostolic on March

Holy Cross Church in San Salvador of the Bahamas, built in 1938.

21, 1929. On Feb. 7, 1932, John Bernard Kevenhoerster, OSB, was installed as the first prefect apostolic. In 1941 the prefecture was raised to a vicariate apostolic and Bishop Bernard was named its first vicar. Paul Leonard Hagarty, OSB, was appointed vicar apostolic June 25, 1950. On July 5, 1960, when the Bahamas was erected into the Diocese of Nassau, he was appointed its first bishop.

The Church in the 1960s. Ethnically the population of the Bahamas is 85 per cent African origin. Most are descendants of former slaves or of Africans who were freed by the British navy while on their way to be sold into slavery. Their descendants are active participants in all phases of social, political, and religious life in the Bahamas. It has been among them that the missionary work of the Church has been most effective. In 1964 the Catholic population was estimated at 23,374. Among the 43 priests working in the missionary diocese, 5 were colored Bahamians; 26 Bahamian sisters were Benedictines, and 7 others belonged to other orders teaching in the Bahamas. The schools and clinics were staffed by 78 sisters from 7 orders. The 15 grammar and 3 high schools registered 5,008 students. Attached to the diocese were 9 secular priests; the others were members of 4 religious orders. They cared for 66 parishes and missions and staffed St. Augustine's Monastery School. There were 4 Papal Knights of St. Gregory, among them Etienne Dupuch, editor of a leading daily newspaper, a convert, and the first Catholic member of the legislature.

Bibliography: J. H. LEFROY, *Memorials of the Discovery and Early Settlement of the Bermudas or Somers Islands,* 2 v. (Bermuda 1932). R. A. CURRY, *Bahamian Lore* (Paris 1930). M. MOSELEY, *The Bahamas Handbook* (Nassau 1926). C. J. BARRY, *Worship and Work: St. John's Abbey and University, 1856–1956* (Collegeville, Minn. 1956). **Illustration credit:** Bahamas Ministry of Tourism.

[B. F. FORSYTH]

BAHÍA BLANCA, ARCHDIOCESE OF (SINUS ALBI).

Bahía Blanca was made a diocese in 1934 from the territory of the Archdiocese of La Plata. It was raised to an archdiocese in 1957 with the suffragan dioceses of Comodoro Rivadavia (1957), Santa Rosa (1957), Viedma (1934), and Río Gallegos (1961) under its jurisdiction. In 1963 Bahía Blanca was one of the most thriving cities of Argentina, and Comodoro Rivadavia one of the most heavily populated areas. In addition, the important cities of Pigüé, Tres Arroyos, Puán, Carmen de Patagones, and Santa Rosa were all located within the archdiocese. Therefore, the proportion of clergy—only 50 in the archdiocese—was very low. There were, in addition, about 100 priests belonging to religious orders, mostly Salesians, who were in charge of the majority of parishes except for those in Bahía Blanca itself. There were 20 communities of religious women, maintaining 42 convents; 1 institute of higher education; 2 secondary and 6 primary schools for boys, and 9 secondary and 23 grade schools for girls. The sisters also staffed 17 hospitals, sanitariums, and asylums.

See also ARGENTINA; LA PLATA, ARCHDIOCESE OF.

[G. FURLONG]

BAHIRA LEGEND

A tale widely circulated in medieval times concerning a meeting between *Mohammed and a Christian monk or hermit named Bahira (Aramaic *baḥīrā,* "the chosen"). The most common Moslem version of the legend is included in the principal biographies of Mohammed by Ibn-Sa‘d and Ibn-Isḥāq, confirmed by Ibn-Hishām and Al-Ṭabari and regarded as fact by most later Moslem biographers of Mohammed. According to this version Mohammed, when 12 years old, accompanied his uncle Abū Ṭālib (some accounts say Abū Bakr, Mohammed's father-in-law and the first caliph) on a caravan trip to Syria. When the caravan was near or already in the town of Bosra, a Christian monk or hermit, noting what he regarded as a miraculous movement of a cloud (or branch) shading it, invited the caravan to dine with him. All accounts agree that the monk on that occasion foretold the young man's prophetic destiny. Some of them also assert that Bahira had foreknowledge of Mohammed's advent, from certain "unadulterated" (*tabdīl*) Christian Scriptures in his possession; some mention an exchange of questions and answers between Bahira and Mohammed; most include Bahira's admonition to Abū Ṭālib to preserve the lad against the malice of the Jews and the violence of the Byzantines. The name of the monk Bahira is lacking in the oldest versions of the legend, and is given in others as Sergius, Georgius, Nestor, or Nicholas. Within the Moslem tradition this legend supplied Islam with a prediction and guarantee of the prophet's mission, and had a considerable polemical value against Christianity.

On the other hand in its Christian form, the Bahira legend was regarded as confirmation of the falsity of Mohammed's prophetic claim. Bahira was portrayed as a renegade heretic, most often a Nestorian, but in some cases a Jacobite (PG 104:1446) or an Arian (PG 108:192; 130:1333c), and an accomplice in or even an instigator of items of Islamic doctrine and the production of the *Koran. Bahira is mentioned quite early in Byzantine historical and polemical literature under the name Sergius, and the two names were ultimately conjoined in that and other later Christian tradition. He is mentioned by Theophanes [ed. C. de Boor, 2 v. (Leipzig 1883–85) 333, 1209] with this name, but in such a way as to identify him more or less clearly with Waraqah ibn-Nawfal, a cousin of Mohammed's wife Khadījah. After the 9th century the name Bahira, with slight variations in form, was well known to Byzantine apologists such as Bartholomew of Edessa (PG 104: 1429). The legend is included also in the famous Christian Arabic apology of 'Abd al-Masiḥ ibn-Isḥāq al-*Kindi. But the chief Christian form taken by the legend is that of the *Apocalypse of Bahira,* which, it is agreed, combines elements of earlier Christian literature of the same genre with some echoes of specifically Moslem lore and doctrine. In the Christian form of the legend generally, Bahira is credited with having provided whatever authentic information from Scripture is to be found in the Koran. A "monastery of Bahira" is still shown as a curiosity to travelers, at Bosra in Syria.

Bibliography: J. BIGNAMI-ODIER and G. LEVI DELLA VIDA, "Une Version latine de l'Apocalypse syro-arabe de Serge-Bahira," *Mélanges d'Archéologie et d'Histoire* (École Française de Rome 1950) 125. R. GOTTHEIL, "A Christian Bahira Legend," *Zeitschrift für Assyriologie* 13 (1898) 189–242; 14 (1899) 203–268. IBN-ISHÂQ, *Sîrat Rasûl Allâh* (*The Life of Muhammad*), tr. A. GUILLAUME (London 1955). A. ABEL, EncIslam² 1:922–923.

[J. KRITZECK]

BAHREIN ISLANDS, called in Arabic Al-Baḥrayn (the two seas), an independent sheikhdom comprising several islands about 13 miles east of the Dhahran area (northeast *Saudi Arabia). The largest island, Al-Manâmah, and the second in importance, Al-Muḥarraq (northeast of the preceding), have each their main city bearing the same name. The present (1965) ruling family has been in power since 1782. The population of about 110,000 Moslems is composed mostly of Arabs. In ancient times, Al-Manâmah, called Tylos and later Awâl, was renowned for its pearls; Al-Muḥarraq was then called Arados. Through the centuries until recent times, the principal economic factor was the pearl industry. Oil, which was discovered there in 1932, is the source of a continuously progressing modernization of the islands.

Bibliography: *Bilan du Monde* 2:119–120. G. DALYELL, "The Persian Gulf," *The Scottish Geographical Magazine* 57 (1941) 58–65.

[A. JAMME]

BAILLY, VINCENT DE PAUL, French journalist; b. Berteaucourt-les-Thennes, Dec. 2, 1832; d. Paris, Dec. 2, 1912. His grandfather had preserved the MSS of St. *Vincent de Paul during the Revolution, and his uncle and future mother had transported the body of the saint to Paris for interment. This heritage and the Christian atmosphere of his large family doubtless determined his vocation. His father, one of the founders of the Conférences St. Vincent de Paul, operated a boarding home for students in Paris and was active in all religious movements. Leading Catholics frequented the Bailly home, notably the Abbé Emmanuel d'*Alzon, the founder of the Augustinian Congregation of the Assumption (the *Assumptionists). Bailly entered the Paris École Polytechnique at 20, and after graduation he served for some years as a civil servant in the Post Office Department. In 1860, after a retreat at Nîmes, he decided to enter the Assumptionists. He was ordained at Rome in 1863 and became superior of the congregation's college at Nîmes (1863–

67). He was chaplain to the French forces that defended the Holy See in 1867 and again at Metz during the war of 1870.

Bailly was deeply concerned with the welfare of the

Vincent de Paul Bailly.

people. He aided in founding various Catholic associations and organized the first lay pilgrimages to La Salette, Lourdes, and Paray-le-Monial. In 1876 he took over the direction of *Le Pèlerin,* the journal devoted to promoting the pilgrimages, and transformed it into a lively popular weekly that was at the same time militantly Catholic. By 1879 *Le Pèrelin* had 80,000 subscribers and ably combatted the nonsectarian but anticlerical press. In 1883 he founded the daily *La Croix,* also designed as a popular and simple defense of the Church at a time when the successive governments of the Third Republic were either openly interdicting or rendering extremely difficult the existence of religious congregations.

The vigor of Bailly's polemics sometimes took him beyond a point sanctioned by Rome and incurred the hatred of his adversaries, but his sense of prayer and obedience balanced his excesses. In November 1899 the Assumptionists were suppressed by law, and Bailly left France for Rome, where he lived until 1906. He founded houses in Belgium and England and finally returned to Paris. His achievement lay not only in the foundation of a great daily paper, a popular weekly, and a score of other publications connected with them, but more especially in the vision that led to the establishment of the publishing house, La Bonne Presse, at a time when such coordination of publishing was indispensable for the success of Catholic journalism.

See also CATHOLIC PRESS, WORLD SURVEY, 10.

Bibliography: E. LACOSTE, *Le Père Vincent de Paul Bailly* (Paris 1913). R. KOKEL, *Le Père Vincent de Paul Bailly* (Paris 1943).

[G. HOURDIN]

BAIN, ALEXANDER, Scottish psychologist credited with being the first to make psychology his life work; b. Aberdeen, 1818; d. there, Sept. 18, 1903. The precocious son of a weaver, Bain graduated from Marischal College in 1840. In 1851, he began to write a systematic psychology text, publishing consecutively two volumes, *The Senses and the Intellect* (Oxford 1855) and *The Emotions and the Will* (Oxford 1859). Partly as a result of his writing, he was appointed in 1860 to a chair of logic at the University of Aberdeen. He published also *Mind and Body* (Oxford 1860), and, in 1864, founded the periodical *Mind,* the first psychological journal in any country. Although Bain is not considered original or profound, he nevertheless performed a valuable service in elucidating general principles and relating them to what was previously known. He was an associationist and a psychophysical parallelist; he recognized the importance for psychology of the brain and nervous system. He anticipated later psychology while representing a culmination of earlier forms; in short, he determined the form in which psychological doctrine was to be cast.

See also ASSOCIATIONISM; PSYCHOLOGY, HISTORY OF.

Bibliography: Boring HistExpPsych. J. C. FLÜGEL, *A Hundred Years of Psychology, 1833–1933* (New York 1939).

[M. G. KECKEISSEN]

BAINBRIDGE, CHRISTOPHER, cardinal archbishop of York, civil servant; b. Hilton, near Appleby, Westmorland, England, between 1462 and 1464; d. Rome, Italy, July 13 or 14, 1514. His family were gentry, and he was a nephew of Thomas Langton, Bishop of Winchester. In 1479 he received a papal dispensation that allowed him to receive any benefice, with or without cure of souls, once he turned 16 years old. At Oxford he was a master of arts by 1486, after which he studied in Italy, at Ferrara (1487–88) and at Bologna, where he was admitted doctor of civil law (1492); by 1498 he was also a doctor of Canon Law. He incorporated as a doctor of civil law at Cambridge (1503–04); in 1505 he became a student of English *common law at Lincoln's Inn. Meanwhile he had become provost of Queen's College, Oxford, in 1496 (until 1508); successively prebend in several cathedral churches; and dean of York in 1503. While dean he was concurrently master of the Rolls (1504–07) and then bishop of *Durham by papal *provision (1507–08). In 1508 he was translated to *York as archbishop, largely *in absentia.* *Henry VIII sent him in 1509 as his orator to Rome, where he remained until his death. Pope *Julius II created him cardinal priest in 1511 and entrusted him with siege operations at Ferrara. An intense rivalry developed between Bainbridge, who was anti-French, and Silvestre Gigli, absentee bishop of Worcester and resident English ambassador at Rome, who was pro-French. Possibly as a result of Gigli's machinations, Bainbridge was poisoned by one of his Italian chaplains, Rinaldo de Modena, who confessed under torture that he had acted on Gigli's orders. Bainbridge was buried in what has since become the English College at Rome, where his fine tomb with recumbent effigy remains.

Bibliography: Emden 1:91–93. LeNeveFastEcclAngli v.6. D. S. CHAMBERS, *Cardinal Bainbridge in the Court of Rome, 1509–1514* (London 1965).

[H. S. REINMUTH, JR.]

BAINES, PETER AUGUSTINE, titular bishop of Siga; b. Kirkby, Lancashire, Jan. 25, 1787; d. Prior Park, Bath, July 6, 1843. He was educated at the monastery in Lampspring, Germany (1798–1802) and at Ampleforth in England. After his profession in the *Benedictines (1804), he held many important offices at *Ampleforth Abbey. He took charge of the Benedictine mission at Bath (1817), and was appointed (1823) coadjutor to Bishop Collingridge, Vicar Apos-

tolic of the Western District of England, whom he succeeded (1829). Baines found that his district was the only one without a seminary, and in trying to remedy this, fell into acrimonious dispute with the Benedictines at *Downside, because they were unwilling to agree to his plan, and resisted his coercive measures. Much bitterness ensued but the problem was eventually solved when four Ampleforth monks left the order, as did Baines, and put the seminary plan into effect at Prior Park, a magnificent mansion near Bath purchased by Baines. Lay students were also taught, and Baines indulged in dreams of a Catholic university. But the bishop was a man in advance of his times. Prior Park never achieved the success he had forecast.

Bibliography: J. S. ROCHE, *A History of Prior Park College and Its Founder Bishop Baines* (London 1931). DictEngCath 1:105–110.

[V. A. MC CLELLAND]

BAINI, GIUSEPPE, titular abbot, composer, and music historian whose writings fostered a renewed interest in *Palestrina; b. Rome, Oct. 21, 1775; d. Rome, May 21, 1844. While still a student at the Seminario Romano, Baini, because of his rich bass voice, was admitted to the pontifical choir (1795). He was ordained in 1798. It is possible that he studied with his uncle, Lorenzo Baini, but the strongest musical influences in his life came from F. Bianchini, S. Silveyra, and G. Jannaconi. From 1818 until his death Baini was annually reelected by the members of the pontifical choir as their director. His musical interests centered on the 16th century, and his compositions reflected this preoccupation. A *Miserere* in 10 parts, sung for the first time during Holy Week of 1821, is his most famous composition. He had no use for, nor understanding of, contemporary idioms. Enthusiastic by nature, he poured forth his passion for the *cinquecento* in a two-volume study, *Memorie storico-critiche della vita e delle opere di Giovanni Pierluigi da Palestrina* (Rome 1828). Although its inaccuracies and the lack of critical historical perspective created many false legends about Palestrina, the work gave impetus to renewed scholarship about, and performances of, Palestrina's works, and his enthusiasm for Palestrina was caught by his distinguished pupils J. *Lafage, O. Nicolai, K. *Proske, and F. X. *Haberl.

Bibliography: O. URSPRUNG, MusGG 1:1089–90. Baker 75. E. H. PEMBER, Grove DMM 1:357–358. Lang MusWC 233. F. HILLER, "Erinnerungen an den Abbate Baini," *Musica Sacra* 1 (1868) 36–40.

[R. G. WEAKLAND]

BAINVEL, JEAN VINCENT, theologian; b. Plougoumelen, France, Aug. 4, 1858; d. Jan. 29, 1937. In 1877 he became a Jesuit, and in 1900 was named professor of fundamental theology at the Institut Catholique de Paris, where he worked until 1925. His works include the following: *La Foi et l'acte de foi* (Paris 1908), *La Vie intime du catholique* (Paris 1916), *La Dévotion au Sacré Coeur de Jésus* (Paris 1919), *Le Saint Coeur de Marie* (Paris 1919), *Naturel et Surnaturel* (Paris 1920), and *Marie, mère de Dieu* (Paris 1921). His courses at the Institut were published successively under the titles: *De magisterio vivo, et traditione* (Paris 1905), *De Scriptura Sacra* (Paris 1919), and *De Ecclesia Christi* (Paris 1925).

Bibliography: J. LEBRETON, Catholicisme 1:1168–69. E. LAMALLE, EncCatt 2:704–705.

[G. MOLLAT]

BAIUS AND BAIANISM

Baius (de Bay, Michel), theologian; b. Mélin l'Évêque (Hennegau), Belgium, 1513; d. Louvain, Sept. 16, 1589. This article will present a summary of his life, an account of his doctrine, and a list of his chief errors.

Life. Baius began his philosophical studies at the University of Louvain in 1533, and became a master of arts in 1535. His theological studies occupied the years from 1536 to 1541. From 1544 to 1550, he taught philosophy at the University, and during this period received his licentiate (1545) and master's degree (1550) in theology. In 1551 he was named Regius Professor of Sacred Scripture.

With his friend, Jan Hessels, he inaugurated new methods in theology. Neglecting the doctrine on original sin and justification of the great scholastics and of the fifth (1546) and sixth (1547) sessions of the Council of Trent, they laid almost exclusive emphasis on Scripture, as they understood it in their interpretation of the anti-Pelagian writings of St. Augustine. Conflict arose between Baius and Hessels, on the one hand, and older colleagues such as Ruard Tapper and Josse Ravesteyn on the other. The new methods were combined with new doctrinal positions. On June 27, 1560, the Sorbonne condemned 18 theses extracted from notes taken by Baius's students. Baius's reply and defense broadened the conflict. The Cardinal Legate, Giovanni Commendone, sought the intervention of Rome, but Pius IV merely imposed silence on both sides. In 1563 Baius and Hessels were sent as theologians of the King of Spain to the Council of Trent, but did not exercise a prominent role.

Between 1563 and 1566 Baius published various opuscula that contain his essential doctrine and system. Excerpts from these works were condemned by the Universities of Alcalá and Salamanca. The Spanish condemnations caused grave concern in Rome. After a thorough examination of these writings, Pius V on Oct. 1, 1567, condemned 79 propositions (Denz 1901–79) in the papal bull *Ex omnibus afflictionibus. These condemned theses are contained, for the most part, in Baius's works, but the bull did not mention him by name. The formal condemnation following the 79 theses was written without punctuation and proclaimed: ". . . quas quidem sententias stricto coram Nobis examine ponderatas quamquam nonnullae aliquo pacto sustineri possent in rigore et proprio sensu ab assertoribus intento haereticas erroneas . . . damnamus." According to whether a comma is placed after "possent" or after "intento," the condemnation has two quite different meanings. With the comma placed after "possent," it has the following meaning: "We condemn as heretical, erroneous, etc., in the sense intended by their authors and according to the strict use of the terms employed, the aforesaid opinions, after a close scrutiny of them has been conducted in our presence, even though some of them might in one way or another be defended." If the comma is placed after "intento," the clause ". . . in the sense intended by their authors and according to the strict use of the terms employed . . ." should be placed at the end of the whole sentence. This is the famous problem of the *comma pianum, which has never been settled. Modern research tends to show that the Pope, while certainly condemning the 79 theses, did not wish to embarrass Baius and to make his submission more difficult [cf. É. van Eijl, "L'Interprétation de la Bulle

de Pie V portant condamnation de Baius," RHE 50 (1955) 499–542].

Baius at first submitted, but in 1569 he sent a protest to the Pope. After a new hearing, Pius reiterated his first condemnation of the 79 theses. Baius was ordered not only to submit, but to express a formal disavowal of all the condemned propositions. In 1575 he became chancellor of the University. In 1580 Pope Gregory XIII published the bull *Provisionis nostrae* confirming the condemnation of Pius V. The new papal condemnation was promulgated solemnly at Louvain by Cardinal Toletus, March 21, 1580. Baius and the entire faculty of Louvain submitted. To put an end to any further controversy, the faculty, at the instigation of the papal nuncio, Bonomini, composed a document entitled *Doctrinae eius (quam certorum articulorum damnatio postulare visa est) brevis et quoad fieri potest ordinata et cohaerens explicatio* (1586). This document is a clear exposition of the positive doctrine opposed to the condemned propositions, and, after 4 centuries, still remains an excellent source for understanding correctly the exact meaning of the condemnation.

In the last years of Baius's life, the renowned controversy between the faculty of Louvain and the Jesuits arose. It is difficult to establish whether, or to what extent, Baius contributed to the composition of the faculty's censure against Leonard Lessius, SJ, in 1587, but he certainly had a share in its wide diffusion. Baius died in union with the Church.

Doctrine. An accurate understanding of the principal truths of Christianity depends, according to Baius, on a correct answer to two questions: (1) What was the nature of the first man's original integrity before his fall from original justice? (2) What is to be thought of the so-called virtues of sinners and infidels among Adam's posterity? For, without exact answers to these questions, one will neither recognize the corruption of human nature by original sin, nor will one be able to evaluate properly the restoration of human nature through Christ (*De prima hominis iustitia, Praefatio*).

Original Integrity. Baius answers that according to Sacred Scripture the first man was created in the image and likeness of God and was adorned with all virtues (*ibid.* ch. 1, 2). The integrity of Adam consisted not only in complete knowledge of the divine law and in full submission to his Creator, but also in the fact that the lower powers of man were subject to his higher faculties, and all the members of his body and their movements were submissive to his will, which was free with true liberty of choice (*ibid.* ch. 3). Furthermore, man's initial integrity was not an undue (i.e., supernatural) elevation of his nature. For, according to Baius, all perfections that pertain to any class of beings in their origin are natural (*ibid.* ch. 4). Thus he considers the lack of integrity in fallen man to be an evil; but evil in his view is the privation of what is natural. Hence the evils derived from original sin in Adam's posterity can be termed natural, but only in a very loose sense; namely, inasmuch as they are the result of the transmission through generation of a corrupt nature (*ibid.* ch. 5, 6). Conversely, if, and to whatever extent, the natural endowments, lost in Adam's sin, are restored to fallen human nature through Christ, they can be called supernatural, but again, only in the loose sense whereby one may designate as supernatural anything derived from a special benefit of God (for example, the miraculous restoration of sight to one who had been blinded), not however, in the sense that this restored integrity is itself supernatural (*ibid.* ch. 7–10).

Although Baius calls the endowments of man's original state natural, he does not mean that they emanate from the nature of man, considered as a composite of body and soul, as the faculties of intellect and will emanate from the soul; rather, they are communicated directly by God. Nevertheless, he maintains, they belong to man's nature and are demanded by man's natural constitution of soul and body, in this sense, that their lack would be an evil for human nature itself. They are, then, just as natural to man as his soul, which is not the product of the generative act of parents as efficient causes, but must be infused directly by God through creation (*ibid.* ch. 11).

Adam's Reward. Created in this state of natural integrity, Adam was obliged to obey his Creator, and thus to merit eternal life, i.e., the unending and immediate vision of God. Even as God's unchangeable wisdom established eternal death as the proportionate punishment of human disobedience and sin, the same wisdom established that the first man would have received eternal life as the natural and just recompense for his obedience to God. Thus, the reward of eternal life would have been man's natural end and would have been due solely to man's natural merit, and in no way to grace. Similarly the good angels after their trial received eternal life, not as a grace nor as in any wise unowed, but as the just reward of their obedience (*De meritis operum,* ch. 1–3).

From this, Baius concludes that God could not have created man without endowing him with integrity and without destining him uniquely to the beatific vision. He thus maintains that a state of pure nature, in which man would have been ordained by God to an end inferior to the direct and immediate vision of God and would have lacked the perfection of integrity, is impossible and chimerical. [See Pius XII, *Humani generis* ActApS 42 (1950) 570: "Alii veram 'gratuitatem' ordinis supernaturalis corrumpunt, cum autument Deum entia intellectu praedita condere non posse quin eadem ad beatificam visionem ordinet et vocet."]

Original Sin. Through his sin, Adam lost his integrity, and thereby the possibility of attaining his unique end. His sin with these two consequences was transmitted to all his descendants by the vitiated and disordered generative act whereby all men are conceived (*De peccato originis,* ch. 1, 2). Original sin consists in the malice of a will that does not love God and His justice, in the rebellion of fallen man's lower nature against his spirit and in ignorance (*ibid.* ch. 3). Because of original sin, all men, even infants, are subject to the wrath of God and to eternal death. Even as Adam was created in God's favor through no merit of his own, so the newborn infant is the object of God's loathing; because of original sin alone, and not because of any personal commitment, the newborn baby stands in opposition to God and to His law (*ibid.* ch. 4).

Baius teaches that sin is essentially opposition to the law of God and disobedience to His commands. The question whether sin should be voluntary has nothing to do with its essence, but only with its origin. Whatever is contrary to the law of God is a sin in whomsoever it exists, and is justly imputed as sin by God, merely because it exists (*ibid.* ch. 7). In the state of integrity Adam could have fulfilled the law easily and with true freedom of choice (*De libero hominis arbitrio,* ch. 9). By original sin this power was lost completely (*ibid.* ch. 11).

Fallen Man. Nothing more deplorable than the moral condition of fallen man in the system of Baius can be imagined. Even man's indeliberate and inoperative desires, being infringements of the law of God *non concupisces* (Rom 7.7, "Thou shalt not lust"), are actual sins worthy of eternal punishment (*De peccato originis,* ch. 2). Every sin deserves eternal punishment, because all sins are by their very nature mortal sins (*De meritis operum,* ch. 2). There is no certainty that God will give the power to perform what He commands. On the contrary, the opinion that God commands nothing impossible finds no support in Augustine, but derives from Pelagius (*De peccato originis,* ch. 12). The general conclusion, so well summed up in the words of the condemned proposition: "All the works of unbelievers are sins" (Denz 1925), is defended by Baius in his *De virtutibus impiorum:* there is, he says, only one possible end of man, which is the intuitive vision of God, and one way only of loving God, which is charity. Therefore without charity (which presupposes faith) there is only sin (*ibid.* ch. 5, 8).

Redemption and Justification. Christ came to restore to fallen man the spiritual state that was his due in creation, but which, owing to original sin, is now "grace." Just as fallen man is wholly characterized and determined, before Redemption, by evil concupiscence, so that his every movement and impulse is sin, so redeemed man lives and merits the beatific vision by charity. Charity is ". . . that motion of the soul whereby we love God and our neighbor" (*De charitate,* ch. 2), and proceeds immediately from "the touch of God, who is charity" (*ibid.* ch. 3).

Justification in the sense of "fulfilling all justice" means no more than "having charity," and this proceeds from actual grace; charity may also precede the remission of sins, which is conferred by the Sacraments of Baptism and Penance; charity bears no relation to a habitual state of formal, intrinsic, and permanent justification, as proposed by the scholastics (*ibid.* ch. 7). The scholastic insistence on charity as a permanent gift was quite mistaken. The origin of charity is a transitory impulse received from God, and this is all that matters, because such an impulse, indefinitely repeated, enables us to live in perfect justice (*ibid.* ch. 2). Perfect charity is not to be understood by reference "to any sacrament or permanent state" (*ibid.* ch. 9; cf. Denz 1931–33). Similarly justification is really a continuous process, wherein man performs more and more good works under actual impulses of God, and overcomes more and more the evil desires of concupiscence, i.e., makes progress "toward the remission of sins" (*De justificatione,* ch. 1).

Merit. This denial of the significance, if not of the existence, of habitual or sanctifying grace, has an important bearing upon Baius's notion of merit, which is solely and exclusively the execution of God's commands, the fulfillment of the law of God. According to Baius, man's operation of itself and alone, i.e., apart from any freedom of choice and apart from the influx of habitual grace and of the infused virtues, merits heaven or hell: heaven if it proceeds from charity, i.e., from a transitory impulse of God, stronger than any opposing evil desire, which brings about the fulfillment of God's law; hell, if it proceeds from the evil desires of concupiscence, which effects the violation of God's law. The patristic and scholastic belief solemnly defined by the Council of Trent (Denz 1545–47), that it is our adoption by God as living members of Christ, sharing in His divine nature, which enables us to merit eternal life freely, with true freedom of choice (*ibid.* 1525–27, 1574), seemed to Baius to be entirely erroneous (*De meritis operum,* ch. 2). Consequently there is no need for man to be in the state of grace in order that his works be meritorious (*ibid.*).

The pharisaism of Baius's doctrine of justification and merit in fallen man is a sharp contrast to the Pelagianism of his doctrine on innocent man before the Fall, and reveals that extraordinary singularity that makes it impossible to call his system by any other name than his own. In endeavoring to set aside all subsequent tradition, even the authentic teaching of the Church, in order to rediscover the pure spirit of St. Augustine, he fell into a disastrous eclecticism.

Chief Errors. (1) Baius set up the anti-Pelagian treatises of Augustine, against the whole body of post-Augustinian thought, as the sole repository of orthodox teaching on grace. (2) He professed to mistrust any attempt to interpret, develop, or modify the doctrine of Augustine by the use of exegetical, historical, philosophical, or psychological progress in human intelligence. (3) He was not afraid, but rather glad, to arrive at conclusions, in matters of faith and morals, that were in open contradiction with all contemporary Catholic views.

The most important of his erroneous opinions are the following: (1) The state of pure nature is a useless fiction of scholastics and involves an insoluble contradiction. (2) The justice and merits of man in the state of original innocence were natural and did not proceed from grace. (3) Fallen man is determined to evil whenever he is not drawn by charity into holiness. (4) God may and does command man to do the impossible without any injustice. (5) Charity, which is the transitory impulse of God, is the only and infallible source of good works and of merit. (6) Man is not now free under the influence of grace.

It was the method of Baius and the conclusions just enumerated that laid the foundations for the much more important heresy of Jansenism.

See also AUGUSTINE, ST.; AUGUSTINIANISM; AUGUSTINIANISM, THEOLOGICAL SCHOOL OF; ELEVATION OF MAN; FREE WILL AND GRACE; GRACE; GRACE AND NATURE; JANSENISM; JUSTICE OF MEN; ORIGINAL JUSTICE; ORIGINAL SIN; PELAGIUS AND PELAGIANISM; PURE NATURE, STATE OF; SUPERNATURAL.

Bibliography: M. BAIUS, *Opera . . . studio A. P. theologi* (1696). N. J. ABERCROMBIE, *The Origins of Jansenism* (Oxford 1936). J. ALFARO, "Sobrenatural y pecado original en Bayo," *Revista española de teología* 12 (1952) 3–75. X. M. LE BACHELET, DTC 2.1:38–111. L. CEYSSENS, "Un Échange de lettres entre Michel Baius et Henri Gravius," EphemThLov 26 (1950) 59–86. F. CLAEYS-BOUUAERT, "Un Épisode peu connu de la procédure instituée contre le Baianisme à Louvain," *ibid.* 28 (1952) 277–284; "La soumission de Michel Baius, fut-elle sincère?" *ibid.* 30 (1954) 457–464. E. VAN EIJL, "Les Censures des Universités d'Alcalà et de Salamanque et la censure du Pape Pie V contre M. Baius, 1565–1567," RHE 48 (1953) 719–776. M. R. GAGNEBET, "L'Enseignement du Magistère et le problème du surnaturel," RevThom 53 (1953) 5–27. R. GUELLUY, "L'Évolution des méthodes théologiques à Louvain d'Érasme à Jansénius," RHE 37 (1941) 31–144. F. X. JANSEN, *Baius et le Baianisme* (Louvain 1927). A. LANZ, "Dottrina di Michele Baio sul Romano Pontefice," CivCatt 90.2 (1939) 29–44, 507–521. H. DE LUBAC, "Deux Augustiniens fourvoyés, Baius et Jansenius," RechScRel 21 (1931) 422–443; 513–540. F. X. LINSENMANN, *Michael Baius und die Grundlegung des Jansenismus* (Tübingen 1867). J. MARTÍNEZ DE RIPALDA, "Adversus Baium et Baianos," v. 5 and 6 of his *De ente supernaturali,* 8 v. (Paris 1871–72). M. J. SCHEEBEN, "Zur Geschichte des Baianismus," *Katholik* NS 19 (1868) 281–308. F. SUAREZ, *Opera Omnia,* v.7 *De gratia Dei, prolegomena* 6, ch. 2 (Paris 1857).

[P. J. DONNELLY]

BAKER, DAVID AUGUSTINE

Benedictine spiritual writer; b. Abergavenny, Wales, Dec. 9, 1575; d. London, Aug. 9, 1641. He was brought up a Protestant, studied law in London, and became recorder of Abergavenny (1598). In 1600 a narrow escape from drowning turned his thoughts to religion from what was apparently a practical atheism. As a result he was received into the Church in 1603. He met some English Benedictine fathers of the Cassinese congregation, and in 1605 decided to join the order. In Padua, where he entered the novitiate at St. Justina's, his health suffered and he was sent back to England before making his profession. Early in 1607 he was professed on the English mission and subsequently joined the English congregation when it was refounded in 1619, and became a member of St. Laurence's, Dieulouard, now Ampleforth.

The outstanding feature of Baker's life as a religious was his great attraction for contemplative prayer, which appears to have been innate, for he tells that he received no instruction on it in his novitiate, and it was long before he discovered books on the subject. Soon after his profession, however, while at the house of Sir Nicholas Fortescue in Worcestershire, he gave himself up to the practice of internal prayer for as much as 5 or 6 hours a day. He reached what he considered his highest experience in it, which amounted apparently to some sort of intellectual vision. But so uninstructed was he that, when this was succeeded by a period of desolation, he gave up the practice of mental prayer and fell back into relative tepidity, which lasted for 12 years, until 1620. During this time he was ordained priest in France but lived mostly in England, where he did some notable historical research, which was afterward incorporated in the volume *Apostolatus Benedictinorum in Anglia* (1626). In 1620 he discovered the literature of contemplation and took up again the intensive practice of mental prayer, which he maintained for the rest of his life.

In 1624 he was recalled to France and made assistant chaplain to the English Benedictine nuns at Cambrai (now Stanbrook). There he gave spiritual conferences to the nuns and started to write his treatises on prayer. He left more than 60 treatises, though some of them were historical or were translations. He wrote without any idea of publication and in a style that is often diffuse and rambling, though sometimes attractively naïve. The treatises as a whole do not form any coherent treatment of the spiritual life; they reflect his reading, which was assiduous. His aim was always the achievement of contemplation, and he reacted against methodical meditation in favor of an affective prayer that tended to become purely contemplative. This reaction against meditation, then recently and highly developed, was resented by the official English Benedictine chaplain to the Cambrai nuns; and Baker was involved in something of a controversy over it. In the end his views were vindicated by the authorities of the congregation, but he was withdrawn to the monastery of St. Gregory at Douai (now Downside) in 1633, where he continued to write for another 5 years. In 1638 a difference of opinion with his superior led to his return to England.

Bibliography: Works. *Sancta Sophia,* ed. S. CRESSY (New York 1857); *Holy Wisdom,* ed. G. SITWELL (London 1964), not authoritative on higher forms of mystical prayer, but admirable on the mortifications and on the affective prayer of acts; *The Confessions of Venerable Father Augustine Baker,* ed. P. J. McCANN (London 1922), his spiritual autobiography extracted from Baker's treatise on *The Cloud of Unknowing,* ed. P. McCANN (5th ed. London 1947). Studies. P. J. McCANN and R. H. CONNOLLY, eds., *Memorials of Father Augustine Baker* (CathRecSoc 33; London 1933). P. SALVIN and S. CRESSY, *The Life of Father Augustine Baker,* ed. P. J. McCANN (London 1933). D. KNOWLES, *The English Mystical Tradition* (New York 1961). E. I. WATKIN, *Poets and Mystics* (New York 1953) 188–237.

[G. SITWELL]

BAKER, FRANCIS ASBURY, Paulist missionary; b. Baltimore, Md., March 30, 1820; d. New York City, April 4, 1865. Baker, the son of Sarah (Dickens) and Dr. Samuel Baker, both Methodists, joined the Episcopal Church shortly after his graduation from Princeton College (later University), and in 1846 was ordained to the ministry. At St. Paul's church, his first assignment, and later as rector of St. Luke's church in Baltimore, he was considered one of the city's outstanding preachers. Under the influence of the *Oxford Movement, he resigned his pulpit, and in 1853 he embraced Catholicism and entered the Redemptorist community. On Sept. 21, 1856, he was ordained in the Baltimore Cathedral (now basilica) and a month later joined four other American Redemptorist converts, Isaac Hecker, Augustine F. Hewit, George Deshon, and Clarence A. Walworth, in their missionary work throughout the U.S. When Pius IX released the five missionaries from their Redemptorist vows in 1858, Baker united with Hecker, Hewit, and Deshon to form the Society of Missionary Priests of St. Paul the Apostle (*see* PAULISTS). While continuing his missionary career, he took a prominent part in inaugurating and establishing the Paulist tradition of ceremonial dignity in liturgical services.

Bibliography: J. McSORLEY, *Father Hecker and His Friends* (2d ed. St. Louis 1953). V. F. HOLDEN, *The Yankee Paul: Isaac Thomas Hecker* (Milwaukee 1958).

[V. F. HOLDEN]

BAKER, NELSON HENRY; b. Buffalo, N.Y., Feb. 16, 1841; d. Lackawanna, N.Y., July 29, 1936. After his early education in public schools he went into business, but in 1868 resumed his education at Canisius College, Buffalo, as one of its first students. He entered Our Lady of Angels Seminary at Niagara University, N.Y., in 1870, and was ordained on March 19, 1876. For 5 years he served as assistant pastor at Lackawanna, then as curate in Corning, N.Y. (then part of the Buffalo diocese). In 1882 he was recalled to Lackawanna to succeed Rev. Vincent Hines as superintendent of the institution destined to become Our Lady of Victory Homes of Charity, with an orphanage, industrial school, home for infants, and maternity hospital. Baker was named vicar general of the Buffalo diocese (1902), made a domestic prelate (1905), and later raised to the rank of prothonotary apostolic. The Basilica of Our Lady of Victory was consecrated in 1926, and, with the adjacent homes of charity, was administered by Baker for the rehabilitation of countless underprivileged men, women, and children.

Bibliography: F. ANDERSON, *Father Baker* (Milwaukee 1960).

[P. J. RIGA]

BAKER, DIOCESE OF (BAKERIENSIS), suffragan of the metropolitan See of Portland, Ore., comprising 18 counties of Oregon east of the Cascade Mountain Range, an area of 55,826 square miles. In 1963, there were 22,524 Catholics in a total population of 270,815.

The area, originally in the vicariate apostolic of Oregon and then part of the Diocese of Walla Walla (suppressed in 1850), later was placed under the care of the archbishop of Oregon City. It was erected a diocese by Leo XIII on June 19, 1903, and the first bishop, Charles J. O'Reilly, pastor of the Church of Mary Immaculate, Portland, was installed on Sept. 1, 1903. He governed the see until March 20, 1918, when he was transferred to the Diocese of Lincoln, Nebr. His successor, Joseph F. McGrath, was installed at St. Francis Cathedral, Baker, April 1, 1919, and ruled until his death on April 12, 1950. The third bishop, Francis P. Leipzig, was pastor of St. Mary's Church, Eugene, Ore., until his appointment to Baker, July 18, 1950.

When the diocese was erected there were 2,350 Catholics and 13 priests, 10 diocesan and 3 religious. By the time of the arrival of Bishop McGrath in 1919 the Catholic population had increased to 6,809 and there were 25 priests, 15 diocesan and 10 religious, as well as 123 sisters and 3 seminarians. By 1950, there were 23 parishes, 38 priests, 136 sisters, and 9 seminarians for a Catholic population of 15,065. Thirteen years later, there were 51 priests, 46 diocesan and 5 religious, serving in 29 parishes and 34 missions. Five religious communities provided 118 sisters who staffed 2 secondary and 6 elementary schools, and directed 5 hospitals and 2 homes for the aged. An official diocesan newspaper, the *Catholic Sentinel,* is published weekly.

The Confraternity of Christian Doctrine, established by Bishop McGrath on Feb. 11, 1935, is directed by two Sisters of St. Francis, who have offices in Baker and give full time to this work. Every parish has a well-trained corps of teachers to help the priests instruct the children. In every parish and in the larger missions of the diocese, religious vacation schools are held for 2 weeks each year after the closing of the public schools.

Bibliography: Chancery Office Records, Diocese of Baker. D. O'CONNOR, *Brief History of the Diocese of Baker City* (Baker, Ore. 1930).

[P. J. GAIRE]

BAKÓCZ, TAMÁS, cardinal, prince primate of Hungary; b. Erdoed (Szatmar), *c.* 1442; d. June 15, 1521. He received his education in Hungary, Poland, and the Italian cities of Ferrara and Padua, where he obtained a doctor's degree. Returning to Hungary in 1470, he became secretary and confidant to King Matthias (Hunyadi). He was appointed bishop of Györ and member of the royal council in 1490, bishop of Eger and archbishop of Esztergom in 1497, cardinal in 1500, and titular patriarch of Constantinople 10 years later.

Bakócz was Hungary's principal statesman until his death, and his policies were not free of the intrigue and bribery typical of Renaissance diplomacy. Invited by Julius II to attend the general Roman synod of 1512, he became influential in the committee for the reform of the Church and the Roman Curia. In the conclave in 1513 he was supported by Emperor Maximilian and by Venice, but his chance of election failed because the Italian cardinals feared that Bakócz as pope would devote his power exclusively to the destruction of the Ottoman menace. The new pope, Leo X, appointed him legate *a latere* for Hungary with a bull for a new crusade. George Dózsa was commissioned to form an army, but the opposition of the nobles turned the plan into a futile and bloody peasant revolt. Discredited, Bakócz retired from public life in 1516. He was a noted and generous patron of the arts, and built the famous Bakócz chapel, one of the few remaining masterpieces of the Hungarian Renaissance, in the original basilica of his primatial see in Esztergom.

Bibliography: V. FRAKNÓI, *Ungarn vor der Schlacht bei Mohacs, 1524–1526*, tr. J. H. SCHWICKER (Budapest 1886). S. DOMANOVSZKY, ed., *Magyar művelődéstörténet*, 5 v. (Budapest 1939–42) v.2, Magyar Renaissance. B. HOMAN and G. SZEKFÜ, *Magyar történet*, 5 v. (Budapest 1935–36). L. TOTH, DHGE 6: 291–292. A. ALESSANDRINI, EncCatt 2:715. *Wetzer und Welte Kirchenlexicon*, v.1 (2d ed. Freiburg 1882) 1862–67.

[G. C. PAIKERT]

BALAAM, Oriental seer summoned by Balac, King of Moab, to curse the invading Israelites who threatened to overrun Moab (Nm 22.1–7). Balaam came from "the land of the Amauites," a region in northern Syria, to the west of the Euphrates, between Aleppo and *Carchemish. The story of how Balaam's attempts to curse Israel were turned by Yahweh into blessings for Israel teaches the truth that even the pagan seer is subject to Israel's God; he is but the minister of God's word, and he can say only what God permits (Nm 23.12; 24.13). The OT concept of the intrinsic power of the spoken word in a *curse or a *blessing is taken for granted in the story. *Yahwist and *Elohist traditions have been merged in the narrative, causing some discrepancies in the account.

A highlight in the story is the folk tale of Balaam's talking ass (Nm 22.22–35). The popular story makes the point that God's control over all nature, animate and inanimate, is so complete that He can use any form of nature as the instrument of His powerful revealing word. In this case He spoke through a harassed beast of burden, as later He would continue to utter His mighty word through a pagan diviner. Even a non-believer could serve temporarily as His prophet.

The hopes of King Balac were dashed when each attempt of Balaam to curse Israel misfired and turned into a blessing. The seer uttered three oracles at the request of the King, each time at a different location. But neither the new place nor the prepared ritual could thwart the protective care of Yahweh over His people. Balac finally gave up in despair and sent Balaam northward to his homeland.

The seer's fourth and final oracle, unsolicited by Balac, was a message to the enraged King predicting a smashing Israelite triumph over Moab. Part of this prophecy (Nm 24.17–18) was fulfilled in the Davidic triumph over Moab and Edom (2 Sm 8.2, 13–14), and it is possibly involved in the symbolism of the story of the Magi (Mt 2.1–12; *see* INFANCY GOSPEL). It does not follow from this, however, that all the oracles of Balaam in Nm 23–24 date from the 10th century B.C., the time of David. They are now ascribed by many competent scholars to the late 13th or early 12th century B.C., since

they contain many archaic grammatical and stylistic features that are absent in later poetry.

Balaam is described in an entirely different light in Nm 31.8, 16; Jos 13.22. Here he is instrumental in leading the Israelites into infidelity and is executed by them. In the NT, therefore, he becomes a type for false teachers (2 Pt 2.16; Jude 11; Ap 2.14). Rabbinical sources have generally treated him with similar disdain.

Bibliography: EncDictBibl 192–193. W. F. ALBRIGHT, "The Oracles of Balaam," JBiblLit 63 (1944) 207–233.

[F. L. MORIARTY]

BALASSA, BÁLINT, Hungarian soldier-poet; b. Kékkő, 1551; d. Esztergom, May 26, 1594. His education was supervised by Peter Bornemisza, court chaplain at the Balassas' baronial estate. Balassa's life was a succession of stormy adventures—of heroic deeds and audacious highway robberies. One day he was the ideal *miles christianus* practicing the vows of a monk, the next day he was accused of incest and was involved in endless lawsuits. In 1574 he fought against the Turks at Eger, and after an escape to Transylvania and Poland he resumed his personal war against them. In 1584 he married his cousin, Christine Dobó, but the marriage was nullified 2 years later when Balassa became a Catholic. In 1594 he fought at Esztergom, and almost in the midst of clashing arms he translated Edmund *Campion's *Decem Rationes,* a pamphlet defending Catholic teaching. During the siege he received a mortal wound; his last words were: "My God, I have been Thy soldier." His poems fall into three categories: religious hymns, martial songs, and love poems. For beauty, sincerity, and expression of passion there is nothing to match them in 16th-century Hungarian literature. He was also the inventor of new verse forms.

Bibliography: B. BALASSA, *Minden munkái,* ed. L. Dézsi, 2 v. (Budapest 1923). J. REMÉNYI, *Three Hungarian Poets: Bálint Balassa, Miklós Zrinyi, Mihály Csokonai Vitéz* (Washington 1955).

[O. J. EGRES]

BALBI, GIROLAMO (ACCELLINI), bishop, Italian humanist; b. Venice, mid-15th century; d. 1535?. When orphaned and adopted by his maternal grandfather, he gave up his original surname, Accellini Azalini, in favor of his mother's family name. He studied belles-lettres in Rome at the school of *Pomponius Laetus and then jurisprudence at Padua, though he was forced to discontinue. In 1485 he was in Paris and in 1489 was asked to lecture in the humanities at the University of Paris. A violent and bitter polemicist, he soon became embroiled with the local humanists, especially William Tardif and Publio Fausto *Andrelini, and had to leave France suddenly; he went to England after a brief stay in Germany. Emperor *Maximilian I called him to Vienna in January 1493, and there he successfully held the new chairs in Roman law and humanities. But his quarrelsome and ambitious nature soon led to clashes with his colleagues in Vienna, and he went to Prague, where his lectures were a great success. After he left Prague c. 1501, there is little information about him. Balbi is known to have become a priest and to have settled in Hungary, where he held various positions and was active in the diplomatic service of Hungary and Austria. Consecrated bishop of Gurk in 1523, he resigned in 1529. In 1524 he returned to Italy (Padua and Venice) and spent several years as domestic prelate at the court of Pope Clement VII. Balbi was a man of vast culture, but his diverse literary output (except for his poetry) is superficial and of little value. He is most important as one of the disseminators of humanistic culture throughout *Renaissance Europe. His works were published in the two-volume *Hieronimi Balbi . . . opera poetica, oratoria ac politico-moralia quae collegit et praefatus est Josephus de Retzer* (Vienna 1791). The collection includes (1:vii–lxxxviii) a Latin translation of his biography by J. von Retzer, *Nachrichten von dem Leben und den Schriften des ehemaligen Bischofs von Gurk Hieronimus Balbi . . .* (Vienna 1790).

Bibliography: G. DEGLI AGOSTINI, *Notizie istorico-critiche intorno la vita e le opere degli scrittori Viniziani,* 2 v. (Venice 1752–54) 2:240–280. G. M. MAZZUCHELLI, *Gli scrittori d'Italia,* 2 v. (Brescia 1753–63) 2.1:83. P. S. ALLEN, "Hieronymus Balbus in Paris," EngHistRev 17 (1902) 417–428. G. BAUCH, *Die Reception des Humanismus in Wien* (Breslau 1903). A. FAVARO, *Un "conservatore" dello studio di Padova eletto dal consiglio dei Dieci nel 1524* (Venice 1917). DizBiogItal 5:370. Cosenza DictItHum 1:367.

[M. MONACO]

BALBIN, BOHUSLAV, Bohemian Jesuit historian; b. Hradec Králové (Königgrätz), Dec. 4, 1621; d. Prague, Nov. 29, 1688. He entered the Society of Jesus on Sept. 8, 1636, and taught at Prague, Brno, and elsewhere until 1662, when he turned his full attention to the study of Bohemian history. He assiduously collected Bohemian historical documents and edited old chronicles; his writings have become part of the heritage of Bohemian intellectual life and national consciousness. Neither banishment from Prague by the Hapsburg government nor physical paralysis, which seized him in 1683, turned him from his interests. Of his more than 30 works, the following are the most important: *Epitome rerum bohemicarum seu historia Boleslaviensis* (Prague 1677); *Miscellanea historica regni Bohemiae* (6 v. Prague 1679–88), an extensive collection of historical and genealogical information; and *Disputatio apologetica pro lingua slavonica, praecipue bohemica* (Prague 1775), a defense of the Bohemian language and a warning against Germanic influences. The 18th-century publication of the *Disputatio* heightened the controversy over the Hapsburg policy of reforming the monarchy and eliminating the Bohemian language from education.

Bibliography: A. REJZEK, *B. Balbin: Jeho život a práce* (Prague 1908). E. LAMALLE, DHGE 6:316–319, bibliog. Sommervogel 1:792–808; 8:1729–30.

[T. T. HELDE]

BALBO, CESARE, historian and statesman; b. Turin, Italy, Nov. 21, 1789; d. Turin, June 3, 1853. As the son of Prospero Balbo, a nobleman, ambassador of Sardinia to France, Cesare was deeply influenced by the events of the French Revolution and its aftermath. Between 1807 and 1814 he served the Napoleonic regime in Italy in various capacities, and he reluctantly acted as secretary of the Consulta that reorganized Rome after Napoleon's annexation of the *States of the Church. From 1824 to 1848 Balbo devoted most of his efforts to historical research and writing, especially on Italian history. His publications made him one of the leaders of the school of moderate liberalism. His most significant contribution to *Risorgimento literature was *Le Speranze d'Italia* (1844), which advocated independence, but met a hostile reception in Catholic circles.

Although he dedicated this work to Vincenzo *Gioberti, Balbo did not share Gioberti's view that the pope could be simultaneously head of the Church and president of an Italian confederation. For some months during 1848 Balbo acted as the first premier of the constitutional regime established in Piedmont by King Charles Albert of Sardinia. Although he was unsuccessful in his attempts to win Pius IX to the cause of Italian unification (1849), he opposed the Siccardi bills, which sought changes in the Italian ecclesiastical establishment, and he insisted on negotiations with the papacy. He devoted the last few years of his life to study.

Bibliography: A. VISMARA, *Bibliografia di C. Balbo* (Florence 1882). E. RICOTTI, *Della vita e degli scritti del conte Cesare Balbo* (Florence 1856). A. M. GHISALBERTI, EncCatt 2:727–729; "Reazione di cattolici alle *Speranze d'Italia,*" ArchStorIt 112 (1954) 195–216. E. PASSERIN D'ENTRÈVES, DizBiogItal 5:395–405.

[E. A. CARRILLO]

BALBOA, MIGUEL CABELLO DE, b. Málaga, Spain, between 1530 and 1535; d. *c.* 1608. As a soldier he visited the Low Countries and France. In 1564 he returned to Spain and 2 years later went to America, where in Bogotá he met the conquistador Gonzalo Jiménez de Quesada. In 1571 he was ordained in Quito. He joined Gen. Bartolomé Marín in his discoveries of new provinces and in 1572 took part in expeditions to Chocó and Quijos. He was the pastor at Funes and there started writing his *Miscelánea antártica* in 1576, renewing his travels the following year. Between 1578 and 1580 he twice visited the province of the Jumbos, without neglecting his parish. On his way to Lima in 1580 he visited Lambayeque and lived in Túcume where he gathered the history of the Naylamp and obtained genealogical data from a member of the Indian nobility. He was present at the Third Council of Lima and was pastor of Ica where he continued to write his *Miscelánea*. Further travels took him to Trujillo, and in 1593 he was in upper Peru where he made more trips in the jungle. In 1596 he wrote his *Orden y traza para descubrir y poblar la tierra de los Chunchos y otras provincias*. A summary of his *Miscelánea* was published in French by Henri Termaux Compans, and the Spanish translation appeared in the Colección Urtega-Romero. One copy of the manuscript is at the New York Public Library and another at the University of Texas; both copies come from the Icazbalceta collection and formerly belonged to the Conde-Duque de Olivares's library.

[C. D. VALCÁRCEL]

BALBOA, VASCO NÚÑEZ DE, discoverer of the Pacific; b. Jerez de los Caballeros, Spain, *c.* 1475; d. Acla, near Darien, probably Jan. 12, 1517. He sailed with Rodrigo de Bastidas and Juan de la Cosa in their explorations of the coasts of Colombia and Panama (1501) and settled in Hispaniola (Haiti), where he ran into debt as a planter. To escape his creditors, he hid in a supply vessel carrying Martín Fernández de Enciso to the new Colombian colony of San Sebastián, founded in 1509 by Alonzo de Ojeda (Hojeda). Ojeda was nearly slain with a poisoned arrow; the remnants of his colony had abandoned San Sebastián and were rescued by the reinforcing party. Balboa proposed the foundation of a new settlement on the Isthmus of Darien, which was named Santa María de la Antigua del Darien (1510). In the struggle for leadership, Enciso proved an inept administrator and was sent back to Spain by Balboa, who assumed command and was appointed acting governor by King Ferdinand on Dec. 11, 1511. With 190 Spaniards and many Indians Balboa began an expedition across the Isthmus, and on Sept. 25, 1513, from a mountain peak he saw the "South Sea"; he reached San Miguel Bay 4 days later. Meanwhile in Spain Balboa had been condemned on the complaints of Enciso, and a successor as governor, Pedro Arias de Ávila (Pedrarias Dávila), was en route to Colombia. The King appointed Balboa to explore the shores of the South Sea, but Arias withheld the commission. Jealousy, incompetence, and bad advice combined to arrange the judicial murder of Balboa. He was arrested, convicted, and decapitated by order of Arias.

Bibliography: J. WINSOR, ed., *Narrative and Critical History of America,* 8 v. (Boston 1884–89). E. G. BOURNE, *Spain in America* (New York 1904). C. L. G. ANDERSON, *Life and Letters of Vasco Núñez de Balboa* (New York 1941).

[J. B. HEFFERNAN]

BALDACHINO, overhanging used as a mark of honor, named after Baghdad whence came the cloth originally used for this purpose. The more generic term for this covering is canopy. There are two chief forms of the fixed canopy: (1) the civory (*ciborium*), a structure in stone, metal, or wood consisting of four or more columns, united by an arch or architrave, roofed, highly decorated, and built over an altar; (2) the baldachin (*baldachino*) or tester, which is simpler in form and consists of a smaller, lighter structure of metal or wood (carved and gilded, and often adorned with textiles) either hung over an altar, or attached to the wall behind, like a bracket, or supported at the back by two pillars so that it juts over the altar like the canopy of a throne. A canopy of some form is obligatory over the high altar of at least a greater church and over the altar of the Blessed Sacrament, and has been used as a mark of distinction over altars since the 4th century.

Another type of canopy is that placed over the throne of a "greater prelate," i.e., a cardinal anywhere, or a nuncio, apostolic delegate, archbishop, bishop, or abbot in the place of his jurisdiction, as a mark of honor and a sign of authority.

A portable canopy—a collapsible, ornamental awning of silk or other precious material—sustained by four, six, or eight poles, or in the form of a large ornamental umbrella, is borne as a mark of honor over the Blessed Sacrament in procession, as well as over the pope, a cardinal legate at his solemn entry into the place of his legacy, and a bishop for his first solemn entry into his cathedral or other church of his diocese.

For illustrations, see following page.

Bibliography: G. F. VOLBACH and S. MATTEI, EncCatt 2:730. J. B. O'CONNELL, *Church Building and Furnishing* (Notre Dame, Ind. 1955) 183–186. J. BRAUN, *I Paramenti sacri,* tr. G. ALLIOD (Turin 1914) 180–182, 215–217. Righetti 1:313–316. **Illustration credit:** Fig. 1, Photo Archives, Maria Laach.

[J. B. O'CONNELL]

BALDE, JAKOB, Jesuit neo-Latin lyrical poet; b. Ensisheim, Alsace, Jan. 4, 1604; d. Neuburg Aug. 9, 1668. He was educated in the classics and rhetoric in the town of his birth, and later in law and philosophy at the University of Ingolstadt. Here he entered the Society of Jesus on July 1, 1624. Balde taught classics and rhetoric at the colleges of Munich and Innsbruck. He was ordained in 1633 and then appointed professor of eloquence at Ingolstadt. His fame reached Munich, and he was summoned to educate the sons of Duke Albert of Bavaria. He then became court preacher and historian to the Duke in 1638. Twelve years later he went to Landshut, then Amberg, and in 1654, because of failing health, he went as court preacher to Count Philip Wilhelm at Neuburg. Balde's works include satires, lyrics, letters, and epic and dramatic verse. They are characterized by naturalism, patriotism, humor, and a sound religious spirit. He was much admired by *Herder, who translated many of his works, such as the *Carmina lyrica* and *Silvae,* in the periodical *Terpsichore.* Herder revived Balde's fame and as a result he became known as the "German Horace."

Bibliography: G. WESTERMAYER, *Jakob Balde* (Munich 1868). J. BACH, *Jakob Balde* (St. Louis 1904). A. HENRICH, "Die lyrischen Dichtungen J. Baldes," *Quellen und Forschungen zur Sprach- u. Kulturgeschichte der germanischen Völker* 122 (1915). M. SCHUSTER, "Jakob Balde und die Horazische Dichtung," *Zeitschrift für deutsche Geistesgeschichte* 1 (1935) 194–206. F. W. WENTZLAFF-EGGEBERT, NDB 1:549.

[C. L. HOHL, JR.]

BALDINUCCI, ANTONIO, BL., Jesuit and preacher of popular missions; b. Florence, June 19, 1665; d. Pofio, Nov. 7, 1717 (feast, Nov. 7). Baldinucci entered the famous Jesuit novitiate of Sant'Andrea, Rome, on April 21, 1681. He was ordained on Oct. 28, 1695. His precarious health led his superiors to refuse his repeated requests to labor as a missionary in India. Instead he was assigned in 1697 to mission work in the Italian provinces of Abruzzi and Romagna. During his remaining 20 years Baldinucci preached 448 popular missions, 1 to 2 weeks in length, traveling on foot (usually barefoot) from town to town. His preaching manner was dramatic, impassioned, and extraordinarily successful. He always carried with him a miraculous picture of the Madonna, and frequently preached laden with chains or bearing a heavy cross. At times he scourged himself publicly until blood flowed to obtain the conversion of hardened sinners. His techniques, while startling, were effective for the audiences of his day. He collapsed in October 1717 while serving the sick of his famine-stricken area. Leo XIII beatified him in 1893.

Bibliography: F. J. CORLEY and R. J. WILLMES, *Wings of Eagles: The Jesuit Saints and Blessed* (Milwaukee 1941). C. TESTORE, EncCatt 2:735–736. E. LAMALLE, DHGE 6:337–339. Sommervogel 1:828–829; 8:1733. ActSS Nov. 3:723–742.

[F. A. SMALL]

BALDINUCCI, FILIPPO, 17th-century Italian connoisseur, writer on art, and curator of Cardinal Leopold de' Medici's drawing collection; b. Florence, 1625; d. Florence, 1696. Baldinucci's most important book is his *Notizie de' professori del disegno da Cimabue* (pub. 1702), in which more than 600 biographies of artists from 1260 through the baroque period are arranged in chronological order according to decades. It was his stated intention to modernize *Vasari's *Lives* and to write a comprehensive history of art. Although heavily biased toward Florentine art, Baldinucci was the first Italian writer to give serious consideration to the Flemish and Dutch schools. The value of the *Notizie,* particularly for the late periods, lies in the completeness of its documentation. Though he frequently included moralizing anecdotes, Baldinucci refrained from making value judgments beyond his predi-

Fig. 2. Baldachino, Annunciation Priory, Bismarck, N.Dak.; architect Marcel Breuer.

BALDACHINO

Fig. 1. Ciborium over main altar, Maria Laach Abbey, Germany.

Fig. 3. Processional Canopy, Holy Rood Guild, St. Joseph's Abbey, Spencer, Mass.

lection for Florentine art. The one exception to his brevity with regard to non-Tuscan artists is his indispensable *Life of Bernini* (pub. 1682). In his personal collection of drawings, now at the Louvre and one of the rare examples of a 17th-century collection that has survived intact, Florentine artists from the later 16th century on are best represented. The work in the collection is of the highest quality. Baldinucci's basic historical orientation is shown by his inclusion of examples attributed by him to the Tuscan 14th and 15th centuries.

Bibliography: *Opera di Filippo Baldinucci,* 14 v. (Milan 1808–12). Musée National du Louvre, *Dessins florentins de la collection de Filippo Baldinucci* (Paris 1958).

[M. M. SCHAEFER]

BALDUS DE UBALDIS, Roman lawyer, canonist; b. Perugia, *c.* 1320; d. Pavia, April 28, 1400. About 1344 he received a doctoral degree in law from the University of Perugia, under the guidance of *Bartolo of Sassoferrato. After a brief stay in Siena, he moved to Bologna, where he was probably given a teaching assignment. He returned to his native city in 1351 in order to teach at the university, and he remained there until 1390, save for periods spent in Pisa in 1356–57, in Florence from 1358 to 1364, and in Padua from 1376 to 1380. He took an interest not only in teaching, but also in the public affairs of the country, as well as in the events that tormented the Catholic Church and Italy as a result of the Roman Curia's exile to Avignon and of the Great Schism of the West. In 1390 he left Perugia and moved to Pavia in order to teach at the *studium,* where he remained until his death.

Baldus, exponent of the juridical thought that was later attributed to the "Commentators," continued the great tradition initiated 3 centuries earlier by *Irnerius and the glossators and adapted it to the practical and cultural needs of his time. (*See* GLOSSES, ROMAN LAW.) He was such a distinguished representative that he later deserved the title of φιλοσοφώτατος for his unique force of argumentation and for his skill in arriving at prime principles from the various norms of the *Corpus Iuris Civilis.* Baldus's research, which has been preserved in his writings (of which, unfortunately, there are only editions of the 15th and 16th centuries without any commentary), had as its object the entire Justinian corpus, on which he accomplished a monumental complex of commentaries, fruit of his university lectures. He was also a prominent canonist and wrote a commentary on the *decretals. In addition, he devoted attention to feudal law, as attested by his commentary on the *Usus feudorum,* and his great activity as adviser and lawyer is amply documented by his *Consilia.*

It is practically impossible to trace even a summary profile of the various doctrines advocated by Baldus. It is sufficient to remember, for example, the theoretic justification that he gave of the *potestas statuendi* of Italy's free communes (*In Dig. Vet.* 1.1, *De iust. et iure* 1.9.n.4) and to compare it with what had been said and written before him, to recognize his scholarly greatness and his worthiness of his high fame. For his extraordinary mind and talent, Baldus can rightfully be considered one of the greatest jurists of all time. Among the Commentators he was perhaps second only to his master, Bartolo of Sassoferrato.

Bibliography: Savigny 6:208–248 and *passim.* I. TARDUCCI, *L'Opera di Baldo per cura dell'Università di Perugia nel V centenario della morte del grande giureconsulto* (Annali dell'Università di Perugia, Facoltà di Giurisprudenza 10–11; 1900–01), pub. sep. 1901. F. CALASSO, *Medio evo del diritto* 1 (Milan 1954) 577–578.

[U. SANTARELLI]

BALDWIN, KING OF JERUSALEM

Five kings of the Crusaders' Kingdom of *Jerusalem bore the name Baldwin.

Baldwin I, King of Jerusalem (1100–18). Born Baldwin of Boulogne, brother of *Godfrey of Bouillon, founder of the first Crusaders' principality in Edessa (*see* CRUSADERS' STATES). On his brother's death he was welcomed in Jerusalem by the Lorraine party, and Godfrey's vassals swore allegiance. The Patriarch Daimbert of Pisa was constrained to crown him king (Dec. 25, 1100), and Daimbert's ambitions to establish a church-state were ultimately thwarted. Baldwin inherited a desperate economic and military situation, but within 10 years, with the aid of the Genoese, whom he rewarded handsomely, he had occupied the ports of Arsuf, Caesarea, Acre, Beirut, and Sidon, the last-named with assistance from a Norwegian expedition. Meanwhile, he had beaten back Egyptian attacks, resisted pressure from the north and east, and aided in the capture of Tripoli (1109). Castles had been built at Toron in Galilee and Montréal (Shaubak), south of the Dead Sea, and the kingdom's boundaries had been extended to Ailah on the Gulf of Aqaba. Baldwin terrorized his enemies but was tolerant toward his native subjects. He died April 2, 1118, the real founder of the feudal kingdom of Jerusalem.

Baldwin II, King of Jerusalem (1118–31). Formerly of Le Bourg, cousin of Baldwin I and count of Edessa. After Roger of Antioch's death in the great defeat of June 27, 1119, the new King, already an experienced crusader, was able to stabilize the military situation. Although he was captured in April 1123 and not released until Aug. 29, 1124, Tyre was taken (July 7, 1124) with the aid of a Venetian fleet, which the King had earlier requested. During Baldwin II's reign the feudal structure of the kingdom was further developed, the Knights *Templars were established, and the Knights of St. John (*Knights of Malta), militarized. An important Church council was held at Nablus in 1120. Under Baldwin II the authority of the King of Jerusalem over the other crusaders' states reached a point not to be maintained afterward. His suzerainty was recognized, and he frequently acted as regent. In 1128 he took steps to prepare for the succession to the throne by sending to France. Fulk V of Anjou was selected and married the King's daughter, Melisend. Baldwin II was the last of the original crusaders. His death (Aug. 21, 1131) marked the end of an era in the Latin Orient.

Baldwin III, King of Jerusalem (1143–63). Son of King Fulk and Melisend. Since Baldwin was only 13 when his father died, the barons decided that he and his mother, Melisend, should be crowned jointly. The young ruler soon proved his courage and skill and grew to be a highly respected King of engaging personality, wide interests, and considerable administrative and diplomatic ability. His early years were troubled by the fall of Edessa (1144), the failure of the Second *Crusade, in which he participated, and the rise of Nur eddin. Since the joint rule with his mother had not worked well, Baldwin, acting on the advice of the barons, was crowned alone in 1151. In 1153 he achieved his greatest success, the capture of Ascalon, the last port still in Moslem hands. This operation foreshadowed a southward orientation of the kingdom's military effort, which coincided with the decline of the Fatimid caliphate in Egypt. The success was, however, somewhat offset by Nur ed-din's taking of Damascus in the following year and the largely ineffective countermoves on the part of the crusaders. Another feature of Baldwin III's reign that foreshadowed future policies was the move toward rapprochement with Byzantium. In September 1158 the King married Theodora, niece of the Emperor *Manuel I Comnenus. On April 12, 1159, the Emperor entered Antioch with great ceremony. Plans for joint action against the Moslems did not materialize as Manuel, to the dismay of the Latins, accepted Nur ed-din's offer to negotiate. Nevertheless, the Emperor did not then press the demands that he had previously made on Antioch or break with the crusaders. In fact, on Dec. 25, 1161, he married Maria of Antioch. That the Latin kingdom had achieved a status in European affairs seems evident in Pope *Alexander III's seeking its declaration against the antipope. When Baldwin III died (Feb. 10, 1163) he was mourned by friend and foe alike. The historian *William of Tyre eulogized him as the ideal king.

Baldwin IV, King of Jerusalem (1174–85), and Baldwin V. Nephew of Baldwin III, son of King Amalric I. He was only 13 at the time of his father's death. He had been tutored by William of Tyre, and he possessed a keen intelligence. Despite the affliction of leprosy he displayed heroic fortitude in carrying on his duties. The state of his health necessitated frequent regencies, and these in turn gave rise to internal dissension just at the time *Saladin was completing the union of Egypt and Syria. In 1183 he had his 5-year old nephew, Baldwin, crowned; and shortly afterward arrangements were made for the guardianship in the event of his own death. Baldwin IV died early in 1185. The death of the boy-king, Baldwin V, only a few months later in 1186 was the prelude to the fall of the kingdom.

Bibliography: For the early period, esp. Baldwin I, see FULCHER OF CHARTRES, *Historia Hierosolymitana,* ed. H. HAGENMEYER (Heidelberg 1913). For the later period, esp. after 1127, WILLIAM OF TYRE, *Historia rerum in partibus transmarinis gestarum (Recueil des historiens des croisades: Historiens occidentaux* 1; Paris 1844); Eng. *A History of Deeds Done beyond the Sea,* ed. and tr. E. A. BABCOCK and A. C. KREY, 2 v. (New York 1943). J. L. LA MONTE, *Feudal Monarchy in . . . Jerusalem . . .* (Cambridge, Mass. 1932). S. RUNCIMAN, *A History of the Crusades,* 3 v. (Cambridge, Eng. 1951–54). K. M. SETTON, ed., *A History of the Crusades* (Philadelphia 1955–   ).

[M. W. BALDWIN]

BALDWIN OF BRANDENBURG, canonist; b. Brandenburg, 1230. Few details of his life are known. He studied theology in Paris, and was assigned to write a brief chronicle of the Franciscans. While engaged in teaching in one of the seminaries of the order in Germany, between 1265 and 1270, he wrote a *Summa titulorum* on Canon Law, which from the standpoint of comprehensiveness is scarcely inferior to the similar work by *Hostiensis, from which it is independent. This fine work is concerned primarily with practical questions on Canon Law. Because of the complete success of the *Summa* by Hostiensis, however, it did not find a very wide reception.

Bibliography: Schulte 2:498–503. B. KURTSCHEID, "De studio iuris canonici in Ordine Fratrum Minorum saeculo XIII," *Antonianum* 2 (1927) 174–182.

[R. WEIGAND]

BALDWIN OF CANTERBURY, Cistercian archbishop of Canterbury, canonist; b. Diocese of Exeter, England; d. Acre, Nov. 19 or 20, 1190. Born of humble stock, Baldwin was a learned product of the school of Exeter, perhaps a pupil of *Robert Pullen, and later himself a master of the school. Baldwin first emerges clearly as tutor to Gratian (the later *Cardinalis*), nephew of Pope *Innocent II, at Ferentino (Italy) after November 1150. Appointed archdeacon of Totnes (near Exeter) by *Bartholomew of Exeter, soon after the latter's consecration in 1161, he was much immersed in diocesan administration in the following years. The protégé of Bartholomew and a friend of the canonist Bp. *Roger of Worcester and of *John of Salisbury, Baldwin was an emphatic supporter of Thomas *Becket in his dispute with King *Henry II from 1163. At the height of the conflict he retired to the *Cistercian abbey of Ford (c. 1169) and by 1175 was its abbot. He succeeded Roger as bishop of *Worcester (Aug. 10, 1180) and *Richard of Canterbury as archbishop of Canterbury (December 1184). His rule at Worcester was marked by pastoral care and zealous administration, but that at Canterbury, while revealing similar characteristics, was marred by a long and bitter strife with the monks in which he enjoyed the support of King Henry II, but lacked that of the Popes (successively *Urban III, *Gregory VIII, and *Clement III). Baldwin visited the Welsh Church as legate in 1187 and preached the Third *Crusade in Wales in 1188, having taken the cross at Geddington on February 11 of that year. He died while on the Crusade.

An ascetic and spiritual prelate, whose character and temperament have been variously assessed, Baldwin was a distinguished scholar. His works included *De commendatione fidei, De sacramento altaris,* and 16 extant sermons. An eminent canonist, he was appointed judge delegate by Pope Alexander III on several occasions while still at Ford, and later as bishop and archbishop he left a remarkable imprint in the primitive English decretal collections from c. 1179 (*see* DECRETALISTS; DECRETISTS; DECRETALS, COLLECTIONS OF).

Bibliography: Works. PL 204:401–774; 202:1533. *Chronicles and Memorials of the Reign of Richard I,* ed. W. STUBBS, 2 v. (RollsS 38; 1864–65), v.2. P. GUÉBIN, "Deux sermons inédits . . .," JThSt 13 (1911–12) 571–574. *Baudouin de Ford: Le Sacrement de l'autel,* ed. J. MORSON, Fr. tr. E. DE SOLMS, 2 v. (Paris 1963), introd. J. LECLERCQ. Literature. B. E. A. JONES, *The Acta of Archbishops Richard and Baldwin: 1174–90* (Doctoral diss. unpub. London 1964). W. HUNT, DNB 1:952–954. J. M. CANIVEZ, DHGE 6:1415–16; DictSpirAscMyst 1:1285–86. R. FOREVILLE, *L'Église et la royauté en Angleterre sous Henri II Plantagenet* (Paris 1943) 533–554. Knowles MOE 316–322. C. DUGGAN, *Twelfth-Century Decretal Collections and Their Importance in English History* (London 1963) 110–115.

[C. DUGGAN]

BALDWIN, JAMES MARK, American philosopher and psychologist; b. Columbia, S.C., Jan. 12, 1861; d. Paris, Nov. 8, 1934. Baldwin received his A.B. (1884) and Ph.D. (1889) from Princeton, where he began his teaching career (1886) and later founded the psychology department (1893). He taught also at other institutions in the U.S. and in Europe. He was the founder of the American Psychological Association (1892) and its first president. In 1894 he and J. M. Cattell founded the *Psychological Review,* which he continued to edit until 1909. Profoundly influenced by Darwin, Baldwin developed a theory of emergent or genetic evolution that extended from the biological into the social order and was used to explain both the growth of an individual's mind and the evolution of mind in general. In psychology Baldwin was a functionalist. He is remembered primarily for the contributions he made to the development of child and social psychology.

Baldwin's works include *Handbook of Psychology* (2 v. New York 1890), *Mental Development in the Child and in the Race* (New York 1896), *Social and Ethical Interpretations in Mental Development* (New York 1898), and the editing and publishing of the *Dictionary of Philosophy and Psychology* (3 v. New York 1901–05).

Bibliography: G. TAMPIERI, EncFil 1:564–565. H. S. LANGFELD, DAB 21 [suppl. 1] 49–50. M. W. URBAN, PsychRev 42 (1935) 303–306. J. JASTROW, *Science* 80 (1934) 497–498.

[J. P. DOUGHERTY]

BALL, FRANCES MARY TERESA, foundress of the Irish branch of the Ladies of *Loretto (Institute of the Blessed Virgin Mary); b. Dublin, Jan. 6, 1794; d. Dublin, May 19, 1861. Her father, a wealthy Dublin silk weaver, sent her to the Institute of the Blessed Virgin Mary, Micklegate Bar, York, England, for her education. In 1814 Bp. (later Abp.) Daniel *Murray of Dublin, hoping to introduce the Institute into Ireland, arranged for her to make her novitiate at York. In 1822 Frances, now Mother Teresa, established Loretto House, the first Irish branch of the Institute, at Rathfarnham, Dublin. After Catholic *Emancipation (1829), which afforded new opportunities for Catholic education, she opened boarding, day, and free schools in rapid succes-

Mother Frances Mary Teresa Ball.

sion. Guided by Peter Kenny, SJ, Tom Bourke, OP, and Abp. D. Murray, she sent her sisters to India to found the first Loretto (or Loreto) foreign mission (1841). There were 34 Loretto convents in Ireland, England, Spain, Canada, India, Mauritius, and Gibraltar by 1861. Before 1900 the Institute had spread to Australia and Africa.

Bibliography: H. J. COLERIDGE, *Life of Mother Frances Mary Teresa Ball* (London 1881). *Joyful Mother of Children* by a Loreto Sister (Dublin 1961). **Illustration credit:** Rex Roberts Studios Ltd., Dublin.

[M. M. SHANAHAN]

BALL, JOHN, priest, leader of the English Peasants' Revolt; d. Saint Albans, *c.* July 15, 1381. First heard of at York, where he was probably attached to the Benedictine abbey of St. Mary's, he later removed to Colchester. *Simon Islip, Archbishop of Canterbury, excommunicated him sometime between 1362 and 1366, and Archbishops *Simon Langham (1366) and *Simon of Sudbury (1376) confirmed the sentence, but Ball nevertheless continued to preach both in churches and out of doors and to circulate rhyming letters embodying radical views. Arrested in 1381, he was in the archbishop's prison at Maidstone, Kent, when the peasants' revolt started. Released by the rebels, he proceeded with them to Canterbury, Rochester, and Blackheath, where he incited them to murder nobles and lawyers, using the text, "When Adam delved and Eve span, who was then the gentleman?" His advocacy of complete social equality probably inspired some of the peasants' demands. Ball was among those who entered the Tower of London and murdered Sudbury. He was present at the young King *Richard II's interview with Wat Tyler at *Smithfield. Subsequently he fled, was captured at Coventry, brought before Richard, condemned for treason, and executed. Modern writers question Ball's sanity. His views were partly John *Wyclif's, especially on withholding *tithes from unworthy clergy, but his confession linking Wyclif with the revolt is unquestionably fraudulent.

Bibliography: THOMAS WALSINGHAM, *Historia Anglicana*, ed. H. T. RILEY, 2 v. (RollsS 28.1; 1863–64) 2:32–34. *Fasciculi zizaniorum*, ed. W. W. SHIRLEY, (*ibid.* 5; 1858). J. GAIRDNER, DNB 1:993–994. H. B. WORKMAN, DHGE 6:392. G. M. TREVELYAN, *England in the Age of Wycliffe* (new ed. London 1909; repr. 1948) 183–255. G. R. OWST, *Literature and Pulpit in Medieval England* (2d ed. New York 1961), *passim.* A. B. STEEL, *Richard II* (Cambridge, Eng. 1941; repr. 1963) 58–91. W. L. WARREN, "The Peasants' Revolt," *History Today* 12 (1962) 845–853; 13 (1963) 44–51.

[R. W. HAYS]

BALLAD

In a broad sense, a ballad is a short verse story meant to be sung. It includes: (1) the folk ballad, (2) the broadside ballad, (3) the drawingroom ballad, and (4) the literary ballad. The first is the ballad proper: a narrative folk song traditional in form, shaped by oral transmission. It is marked by impersonality of tone, concentration on a single situation, a dramatic use of action and dialogue, and a distinctive stanzaic structure. European balladry manifests a common folk culture with roots in still older Eastern cultures. Ballads travel widely, carrying similar themes and techniques into many countries. Verse structure varies, however, as does the name of the genre, e.g., Spanish, *romancero;* Danish, *vise;* Russian, *bylini.* The English name (from *ballare*, to dance) was given to the folk ballad proper only in the late 16th century.

Style and Melody. In all languages this form of folk story is marked by stark poignancy of emotion; by the leaping and lingering movement of the narrative; by parallelism in thought and phrase; by incremental repetition, refrains, and conventional epithets. Abruptness, understatement, and brilliant flashes of color lend a shock of surprise to the familiar. The imagery is frequently symbolic, with overtones of myth and folklore. Among the subjects treated are preternatural events, involving ghosts and fairies, magic and riddling; tales of romance and tragedy turning on love, loyalty, courage, warfare, crime, and revenge; legends drawn from the Bible or from saints' lives. In general, ballads are starkly areligious and amoral, even fatalistic in tone, including those that have Christian elements or a historic basis.

The melodies are traditional, too. They differ from those of art-song in being monodic and without harmony or counterpoint. They are not based on the 7-tone scale of classical music but on the modes, a series of gapped scales, frequently pentatonic. These modes are probably of Greek origin, and their use in ballads is parallel to (and possibly derived from) Gregorian plainchant. These melodies change little in the course of repetition and are thus a strong element in perpetuating the ballad tradition.

Origin of Ballads. The question of ballad origins has been hotly debated. German scholars, such as the Grimm brothers (Jacob, 1785–1863; Wilhelm, 1786–1859), formulated the romantic 19th-century theory of folk art in the phrase "Das Volk dichtet." This stand for communal authorship was defended by Francis B. Gummere (1855–1919), but was attacked by the advocates of the theory of individual authorship. All agreed, however, that a continuous "re-creating" of the ballad by oral transmission is of its essence.

Gordon H. Gerould (1877–1953) harmonized all the evidence into the most accepted theory of ballad origins. He showed that from what is now known of primitive folkways, it can be postulated that behind the ballad are earlier forms of group singing. At all times, the power and habit of verse-making are most vigorous among peoples of simple and homogeneous culture who meet for entertainment and sing stories (often accompanied by dancing) under some definite stimulus. Conditions such as these existed under the manorial system in the Middle Ages. Story-poems composed by some gifted individual would be taken up by the crowd of folk and sung to a known melody, one to which they danced or one that they sang as a hymn in church. The recurrent melody, of itself, tended to fix the poetic shape of the words, thus producing a stanzaic text and forcing the story into the centralized, dramatic, and repetitive form essential to the ballad. As the song was repeated over the years and traveled to other areas, it underwent the stylization common to long memory-traditions, while at the same time it produced as many variants as there were times, places, and singers.

Other factors were the itinerant noncourtly minstrels who sang in the villages; the ecclesiastics who used communal singing for instruction and edification on Church feast days; and the constant, uneven "two-way traffic" between the literate and the illiterate levels of society. Thus the ballad proper is a medieval form, originating not earlier than the 12th century and reaching its height in the 15th; most of the extant texts are from the 16th, when the ballad had already begun to decline after the coming of printing.

English and American Ballads. Ballads in English form a clearly defined corpus, generally known as "the Child Ballads" from the American scholar Francis

Printed broadside of a ballad, London, 1745.

A New *SONG*,
By Mr Rann one of his *Majeftys* Forrefters at *Windfer*.
Tune King Georges **March**,

FROM London to fcotland
    with fpeed the Duke did flye
All for to face the Rebels
    or make them for to fly,
But when he came to fterling
    no Rebels there could find,
Their Magazine blew up
    and their Cannon leaft behind,
Then fcotland did Rejoice,
    O that the Youth was come,
The Glory of the Nation
    King George's Youngeft Son,
Refolved like a briton
    to conquer or to Dye,
He march'd to Aberdeen
    but before him they did fly.
He croff'd the River Spey
    a battle did Enfue,
But few were left alive
    Rebellion to purfue,
Then Britons all rejoice
    O that the Youth is come,
The Glory of the Nation
    King Georges Youngeft fon.
Now Peace and Plenty
amongeft us all will Reign,
In fpite of a Pretender, Dupe,
    to France and Spain,
French foupes we do difpife
    it fuiteth not our blood,
Brown bear and good roft beef
    is holfome britifh food,
Then britons all Rejoice
    O that the Youth is come,
The Deliverer of his Country
    King George's Youngeft Son.

James Child (1825–96), who in 1898 printed 305 of them, with more than 1,000 variants, under the title *English and Scottish Popular Ballads*. Child grouped them according to subject matter that frequently overlaps: preternatural (*Lady Isabel and the Elf Knight*); romance and tragedy (*Fair Annie, Edward*); semi-historical, such as those dealing with the Scottish border warfare (*Chevy Chase*); the Robin Hood cycle; and comic tales (*Get up and Bar the Door*). The oldest known ballad is *Judas,* from a 13th-century manuscript.

English colonists brought these ballads to America in the 17th century, and traditional ballad singing persisted in rural areas such as the Appalachian Mountains. Oral transmission produced American variants in the texts while the music remained more stable (*Barbara Allen*). By the 19th century social conditions among "the folk" in a rapidly expanding country were such that indigenous ballads with distinctive metrical forms were created: on the cowboy ranges (*Old Chisolm Trail*), in the Negro cabins (*Boll Weevil*), in the lumberjack camps (*The Jamb on Jerry's Rocks*), and among migrant railroad workers (*John Henry*). The movement was arrested by over-rapid industrial development.

Ballads in a Wider Sense. The other forms to which the name "ballad" is given show the influence of oral poetry upon written. In the 16th century the broadside ballads arose, narrative poems printed on single sheets. They claimed to give "news," but old forms and themes persisted in these debased texts through the 18th century. Drawingroom ballads, overrefined and sentimental tales sung in Victorian parlors, are at the other extreme.

The literary ballad (the only type without music) is the work of an educated poet using ballad techniques for his own artistic purposes. It is not an outgrowth of folkways; rather it reflects an aesthetic interest in the relation of "primitive" to "cultivated" forms of art. The appearance of Percy's *Reliques of Ancient English Poetry* (1765) and of Scott's *Minstrelsey of the Scottish Border* (1802–03) advanced the Romantic movement.

Ballad-making goes on in rural areas (such as the hills of Yugoslavia) even today. Printing, recording, and broadcasting have not only preserved old traditional ballads but have also fostered communal singing, creating a "folk sense" under far from primitive conditions. The appeal of the true folk ballad springs from the blend of a good story, ancient oral forms, archetypal images, and the direct utterance of emotion by "ancestral voices."

See also LITERATURE, ORAL TRANSMISSION OF; FOLK-LORE; CAROL; TROUBADOUR; MEISTERSINGER; MINNE-SINGER.

Bibliography: F. J. CHILD, ed. *English and Scottish Ballads,* 5 v. in 3 (New York 1883–98; reprint 1956). W. J. ENTWISTLE, *European Balladry* (Oxford 1939). A. B. FRIEDMAN, *The Ballad Revival* (Chicago 1961). C. J. SHARP, comp. and ed., *English Folk Songs from the Southern Appalachians,* 2 v. (London 1932). G. H. GEROULD, *The Ballad of Tradition* (Oxford 1932). F. B. GUMMERE, *The Popular Ballad* (Boston 1907; reprint Dover Pub., New York 1959). M. J. HODGART, *The Ballads* (2d ed. New York 1962). L. SHEPARD, *The Broadside Ballad* (Hatboro, Pa. 1962). **Illustration credit:** From A. S. Turberville, *English Men and Manners in the 18th Century* (Clarendon Press, Oxford).

[M. WILLIAMS]

BALLERINI, ANTONIO, Jesuit moral theologian; b. Medicina, near Bologna, Oct. 10, 1805; d. Rome, Nov. 27, 1881. He entered the Society of Jesus in 1826 and became professor of Church history at the Gregorian University in Rome in 1844 and then professor of moral theology in 1855. Among his early writing was *Sylloge monumentorum ad mysterium conceptionis Immaculatae Virginis Deiparae illustrandum* (2v. Rome 1854–56), an historic work. Turning to moral theology, he published *De morali systemate s. Alphonsi M. de Ligorio* (Rome 1863) and then contributed annotations to the 17th edition of J. P. Gury's *Compendium theologiae moralis* (2 v. Rome 1866), which added to the value and to the further widespread use of that work. Ballerini was a strong defender of probabilism, and his interpretation of certain Alphonsian doctrines brought him into controversy with some of the Redemptorists. His last great work, *Opus theologicum morale in Busembaum medullam,* was nearly completed at the time of his death, and the last volume was written by D. Palmieri (7 v. Prato 1889–93). Ballerini was outstanding among his contemporaries for his contribution to the restoration and progress of moral theology.

Bibliography: Sommervogel 1:843–848, 8:1733–34. R. BROUILLARD, DHGE 6:398–399. C. SOMMERVOGEL, DTC 2.1:130–131. Hurter Nomencl 5.2:1793–95.

[J. C. WILLKE]

BALLERINI, PIETRO AND GIROLAMO, patristic scholars and theologians; Pietro, b. Sept. 7, 1698, d. March 28, 1769; Girolamo, b. Jan. 29, 1702, d. Feb. 23, 1781. The brothers, sons of a surgeon, were born and educated in Verona. Pietro was ordained in 1722 and became the principal of a classical school in Verona. Several propositions in his book on usury were condemned by Benedict XIV in the bull *Vix pervenit* (1745). But together with Girolamo (ordained 1725), Pietro opposed the Jansenists (*see* JANSENISM), and the Febronian party, which questioned the administrative power of the pope. The Ballerinis' primary service to scholarship consisted in a close collaboration in editing ecclesiastical works, particularly the writings of several Fathers of the Church. Between 1729 and 1732, they published four volumes of the historical and other writings of Cardinal Henry Noris, a Veronese compatriot. In quick succession, but with careful scholarship, they brought out *S. Zenonis, Episcopi Veronensis, Sermones* (with notes, 1739); *S. Antonini, Archiepiscopi Florentini, Summa Theologica* (with a life of the author, 4 parts, 1740–41); and *Ratherii, Episcopi Veronensis, Opera* (1765). At the request of Benedict XIV they prepared a new edition of the works of St. Leo the Great to replace that of the Gallican-tainted Pasquier *Quesnel (1675); theirs is still the standard edition (complete with notes, 3 v., Venice 1753–57; reprinted PL v. 54–56). Pietro published a history of probabilism, *Saggio della Storia del Probabilismo* (Verona 1736); *De vi et ratione Primatus Romanorum Pontificum* (1766); and *De Potestate Ecclesiastica Summorum Pontificum et Conciliorum Generalium* (1765).

Bibliography: A. DE MEYER, DHGE 6:399–401. W. TELFER, "The Codex Verona LX (58) Note B," HarvThRev 36 (1943) 231–232. C. VERSCHAFFEL, DTC 2.1:131–132.

[F. X. MURPHY]

BALMACEDA, FRANCISCO, Chilean ascetic; b. Ibscache, Oct. 2, 1772; d. Santiago, Nov. 2, 1842. He studied at the Convictorio Carolino and was ordained by Bishop Marán. Heir to a great fortune, he personally administered his hacienda in Ibscache. According to one of his biographers, "he took special care of the moral and physical well-being of its tenants"; he taught them prayers, reading, writing, and arithmetic; he also provided them with seeds and farming tools. Many families in Santiago lived on the crops from his hacienda. Upon his mother's death he gave away to the San Borja Hospital, among other smaller donations, his farm in Ibscache and a second one he had acquired for that purpose. He kept nothing for himself except 1,000 pesos per year and the modest house in which he lived. A tall, strong man, inflamed with zeal, he had great self-control and practiced asceticism to the point of appearing strange. During hot weather he wore heavy garments; when it rained he used to walk in the middle of the street unmindful of the rain. For many years he lived on boiled vegetables. On the morning of Nov. 2, 1842, on his way to the chapel of some neighboring nuns where he used to say Mass, he collapsed in agony on his own doorstep. Some considered him an eccentric; yet the majority of the people of his time, particularly the poor, thought him a saint.

Bibliography: F. DE P. TAFORÓ, "Don Francisco Balmaceda," *Revista de Sud-América* 3 (Valparaíso 1862) 735–741. E. BALMACEDA VALDÉS, *La familia Balmaceda* (Santiago 1919) 107–117.

[A. M. ESCUDERO]

BALMERINO, ABBEY OF, former *Cistercian abbey on the south bank of the Tay in Fifeshire, Scotland, in the old Diocese of Saint Andrews. It was founded and richly endowed by King Alexander II and his mother, Queen Ermengarde, *c.* 1227 and colonized by monks from *Melrose on Dec. 13, 1229. The abbey was dedicated to St. Mary and St. Edward the Confessor. After it had been sacked and burned by the English under Admiral Wyndham on Dec. 25, 1547, and desecrated by Reformers in 1559, the Abbey was erected into a temporal lordship by the royal charters of 1603 and 1607 for Sir James Elphinstone, first Lord Balmerino. Only ruins now remain.

Bibliography: W. B. TURNBULL, ed., *The Chartularies of Balmerino and Lindores* (Edinburgh 1841). J. M. CANIVEZ, ed., *Statuta capitulorum generalium ordinis cisterciensis ab anno 1116 ad annum 1786,* 8 v. (Louvain 1933–41) 2:63. J. WILKIE, *The Benedictine Monasteries of Northern Fife* (Edinburgh 1927). Easson 62.

[L. MACFARLANE]

BALMES, JAIME LUCIANO

Spanish secular priest and philosopher; b. Vich, Catalonia, Aug. 28, 1810; d. there, July 9, 1848. He studied in the seminary at Vich (1817–26) and at the University of Cervera (1826–35). He was ordained in 1834 and received his degree in theology the following year. Returning to Vich, he taught mathematics in the seminary. The next 8 years witnessed his prodigious expansion of activity devoted to the apologetical, philosophical, sociological, and political aspects of current problems. In Barcelona he founded and directed *La Civilización* (1841–43) and *La Sociedad* (1843–44). In Madrid he edited *El Pensamiento de la nación* (1844–46) and *El Conciliador* (1845). He made his entry into politics in 1840 by writing forcefully against the ambitions of General Espartero in *Consideraciones políticas sobre la situación de España* (Barcelona 1840). In answer to the general thesis of F. Guizot, he wrote *El Protestantismo comparado con el Catolicismo en sus relaciones con la civilización europea* (4 v. Barcelona 1842–44). This is actually a philosophy of history and,

at the same time, a basic sociology that considers the various influences of Catholicism on society. Some of the very last works he published are also apologetical in character: *Cartas a un escéptico* (Barcelona 1864) and *Pio IX* (Madrid 1847).

His second and more philosophical period of development began with the bombardment of Barcelona, when, protected in the Prat de Dalt (1843), he spent a month and a half writing *El Criterio* (Barcelona 1845), in which the right use of reason is described as good sense and clear thinking. In *Filosofía fundamental* (4 v. Barcelona 1846) he tried to protect youth from the errors of modern philosophy, namely, sensism, materialism, rationalism, idealism, and skepticism. As a textbook for students he provided *Filosofía elemental* (4 v. Madrid 1847); this was translated into many languages, including Latin. The basic qualities of his thought are realism, objectivity, order and clarity, and naturalness and simplicity. He eliminated useless questions and complicated technicalities. A sensitive observer and analyst, he considered also the totality of things. He was profoundly human, balanced, and independent in spirit.

Balmes thought highly of St. *Thomas Aquinas, whose *Summa* he studied for 4 years at Cervera, but he himself was bound to no school. He did not accept fundamental Thomistic doctrines such as the real distinction between essence and existence, potency and act, substance and accidents, hylomorphism, the agent intellect, and impressed species. Under the influence of P. Buffier he treated the problem of certitude on a subjective and psychological level; this teaching would influence the school of Louvain. His confident intuitionism was rooted in "common sense" or an "intellectual instinct," upon which were established three fundamental truths: a first fact ("that I think"), a first principle (contradiction), and a first condition (evidence).

Balmes prepared the way for the resurgence of Christian philosophy. Not so much a precursor of the scholastic revival, he is better enumerated among the Catholic apologists of the early 19th century as one who excelled in solidity of thought, in philosophical formation, and in historical erudition. *Leo XIII, whom Balmes had known in Brussels, described him as "the foremost political talent of the 19th century and one of the greatest in the history of political writers."

Bibliography: *Obras Completas,* ed. I. CASANOVAS, 33 v. (Barcelona 1925–27); also in 8 v. in BiblAutCrist (Madrid 1948–50). I. CASANOVAS, *Balmes: La Seva vida, el seu temps, les sevas obres,* 3 v. (Barcelona 1932); "Balmes en el primer centenario de su muerte, 1848–1948," *Pensamiento* 3 (1947). M. BATLLORI, Enc Catt 2:753–755.

[G. FRAILE]

BALSAMON, THEODORE, 12th-century Byzantine canonist; b. Constantinople, *c.* 1105; d. there, *c.* 1195. Of a Constantinopolitan family, Theodore was a deacon in the church of *Hagia Sophia and served the patriarch as his chief legal adviser, or chartophylax. He was elected patriarch of Antioch in his eighties (between 1185 and 1191), but he remained in Constantinople until his death.

His chief work is his commentary on the Photian Nomocanon of 14 titles that he composed at the suggestion of Emperor *Manuel I Comnenus and Patriarch Michael of Anchialos. This was an attempt to solve the difficulties raised by contradictory Church laws and conflicting ecclesiastical and civil legislation. Besides the 14 titles, he clarified the whole collection of Byzantine law, relying strongly on the earlier canonist *Zonaras. His principal interest for the historian is the number of documents he cites, frequently verbatim, that would be otherwise unknown.

In 1195 Patriarch Marcus of Alexandria directed some 60 questions to the permanent synod (*synodos endemousa*) at Constantinople. Balsamon gave the answers; but recent investigation has shown that a second recension of these answers was most probably due to the Metropolitan John of Chalcedon, a contemporary of Balsamon.

A series of canonical monographs that clarify the inner organization of Byzantine ecclesiastical offices in relation to the patriarchate are also the work of Balsamon. He defended the position of the legal adviser to the patriarch against the encroachments of the protecticos, the curial official who presided over lesser legal cases. Balsamon aided the patriarch in composing a series of synodal acts, including that dealing with the translation of Patriarch Dositheus to the See of Constantinople (1190). Several MSS attribute to his authorship scholia on the OT prophets; and *Fabricius credits him with an account of the martyrdom of SS. Theodore and Claudius.

Bibliography: PG 119:904–909, 1162–1224, monographs; v.137–138. G. A. Rhalles and M. Potles, *Syntagma tōn theiōn kai hierōn kanonōn*, 6 v. (Athens 1852–59) in Gr. L. Petit, DTC 2.1:135–137. E. Herman, DDC 2:76–83. V. Narbekov, *Der Nomokanon des Photios mit der Erklärung Balsamons*, 2 v. (Kazan 1888–89), in Russ. S. P. Lampros, ByzZ 5 (1896) 565–566. V. Grumel, RevÉtByz 1 (1943) 239–249, tr. Beck KTLBR 70–73, 657–658, bibliog.

[F. X. Murphy]

BALTHASAR OF ST. CATHERINE OF SIENA,

Discalced Carmelite and mystical writer; b. Bologna, Aug. 24, 1597; d. Bologna, Aug. 23, 1673. He was a descendant of Niccolò Machiavelli. Balthasar was attracted to the Teresian Reform while taking part in the celebrations of St. Teresa's beatification. He took the habit at the novitiate of La Scala in Rome (Nov. 21, 1614), where he was later professed (Nov. 11, 1615).

After his ordination, he was appointed professor at the Seminary for the Missions, then at St. Paul of the Quirinale. He filled various positions of administrative responsibility in his order: provincial, general definitor, procurator general.

The most important of his writings include a pastoral letter to the religious of his own Lombardy Province; the Italian translation of the work of Father Joseph of Jesus Mary (Quiroga), *Subida del Alma a Dios* (Rome 1664); his commentary on the *Mansions* of St. Teresa, entitled *Splendori Riflessi di Gloria Celeste* (Bologna 1671–94), is representative of the Carmelite school (see Gabriel, bibliography). The work is important because he harmonized the teaching of St. Teresa, which prevailed in the Teresian carmel of the Italian congregation, with that of St. John of the Cross, then less known than St. Teresa in Italy. If these works have not been translated into other languages, it is primarily because the author's style is artificial and diffuse, after the fashion of his age. His interpretation of St. Teresa is, nevertheless, known among the representatives of the Teresian Carmelite school, and is often quoted.

Bibliography: Graziano della Croce, "Patrimonio espiritual de la Cong. de S. Elías," *El Monte Carmelo* 70 (1962) 228–229, 243–245. Gabriel de Sainte Marie Madeleine, DictSpirAsc Myst 1.1:1210–17.

[O. Rodriguez]

BALTIC RELIGION,

the religion, typically agricultural, of the Baltic peoples (Latvians, Lithuanians, and Old Prussians). Among the high gods primacy was enjoyed by the gods of heaven. Dievs (Heaven), through etymology directly connected with Dyāus, Zeus, and Jupiter, was the most important of these. In his concrete form he was regarded as a great farmer who worked his fields in the same manner as the modern Latvian peasant. Generally, he was the arbiter of welfare and prosperity. Only Saule (the Sun, a goddess) could compete in importance with Dievs. She was usually regarded as the patroness of fertility, and numerous myths of the courtship of gods were associated with her. A prominent place was allotted also to Pērkons (Thunder), a god of fertility, and Mēness (Moon, a male deity), in whom one can discern traits of a god of war.

Much clearer in her functions was the earth goddess (called Mother Earth). She was patron of fertility, but, at the same time, seems to have been the source of a number of mythical figures of chthonic character. Of the feminine deities, however, Laima, the goddess of Fate, was the most fully developed. She belonged to the Indo-European group of arbiters of fate or destiny, and had a central place in Baltic religion.

Beside these higher deities there were numerous mythological figures who were generally connected with the different phases of agricultural life. The functions of these lower beings and those of the higher gods were not strictly delimited.

The higher gods received a definite cult, which was connected especially with important occasions in human life, and with annual feasts. There were birth and wedding rites; the summer solstice and the harvest were celebrated with special solemnity.

Bibliography: H. Biezais, "Baltische Religion," RGG³ 1:856–859, with bibliog.; *Die Hauptgöttinnen der alten Letten* (Uppsala 1955); *Die Gottesgestalt der lettischen Volksreligion* (Uppsala 1961).

[H. Biezais]

BALTICUS, MARTINUS,

humanist and educator; b. Munich, Germany, c. 1532; d. Ulm, 1600. He began his early studies in Greek and Latin in Bruck under the direction of the local pastor, Zachary Weichsner. Subsequently Balticus spent 6 years in studies under Johann Mathesius (d. 1565) and a shorter period of instruction under *Melanchthon in *Wittenberg. In 1553 the young humanist returned to Munich and succeeded Jerome Ziegler as the director of the Latin *Poetenschule*. However, his *Lutheran sympathies cut short his stay in Munich, which he left in 1559. In the same year he received his appointment as director of the Latin school in Ulm, a position he filled with distinction till 1592. He was the author of Latin elegies and epigrams, which show genuine poetic skill (*Poematum libri tres*, Augsburg c. 1556), and of several dramas written in Latin for staging in the schools: *Adelphopolae* (1556), translated into German by Balticus himself, *Daniel* (1558), and *Christogonia* (1589). After completing his teaching career he wrote a paraphrase in elegiacs of the Sunday Epistles and Gospels (*Evangeliorum et epistolarum . . . sensus genuinus*, Tübingen 1593).

Bibliography: W. Scherer, ADB 2:32–33. A. Roersch, DHGE 6:431. U. Thürauf, NDB 1:568–569. H. Bender, Lex ThK² 1:1213.

[H. Dressler]

BALTIMORE, ARCHDIOCESE OF
(BALTIMORENSIS)

Senior metropolitan see of the U.S., comprising Baltimore city and Baltimore, Allegany, Anne Arundel, Carroll, Frederick, Garrett, Harford, Howard, and Washington counties, an area of 4,801 square miles, with an estimated total population in 1965 of 2,300,000, including 500,000 Catholics. The diocese was established Nov. 6, 1789; the archdiocese, April 8, 1808.

Origins. Catholicism was brought to Maryland (1634) by the first English settlers, among whom were three Jesuit missionaries whose successors continued the work of ministering to the colonists and converting the Indians. The area comprising the present Baltimore archdiocese was probably served by itinerant priests including Benedict Neale, who visited Harford county in 1747. In 1755 a group of exiled French Catholic refugees from Acadia (Nova Scotia) settled in Edward Fotterell's abandoned house on Calvert and Fayette Streets, Baltimore. From 1756 to 1763 Jesuits from the White Marsh mission, 25 miles southwest, periodically conducted services first in Fotterell's house and after 1775, in St. Peter's. This small church was built by laymen on a lot purchased by the Jesuit superior from Charles Carroll of Annapolis and located near the northwest corner of the later Charles and Saratoga Streets. By 1784, when the first resident pastor, Charles Sewall, SJ, arrived, the church had been enlarged to more than twice its original size, and a rectory had been added. There the vicar apostolic of the new Republic, John *Carroll, took up residence in 1786 and remained until his death there in 1815. By then, three more city churches had been added as the Catholic population increased to an estimated 10,000—St. Patrick's (1795); St. John's (1799), on the site of the later St. Alphonsus; and St. Mary's Seminary Chapel (1808), a Gothic structure designed by Maximilian *Godefroy.

Ecclesiastical Jurisdiction. From 1688 to 1784 the English colonies seemingly were under the jurisdiction of the vicar apostolic of the London District in the home country. Before 1688 priests in the colonies (mostly Jesuits) apparently received all necessary faculties from the superiors of their religious communities. From 1784 to 1789 John Carroll as prefect apostolic exercised limited jurisdiction over the Church in the new Republic of the U.S. After his appointment as bishop on Nov. 6, 1789, and his consecration in Lulworth Castle chapel, Dorset, England, on Aug. 15, 1790, Carroll assumed full responsibility for his vast Diocese of Baltimore, which was until 1808 the only see in the U.S. It extended from the Atlantic Ocean to the Mississippi River and from Canada to Florida, an area of about 890,000 square miles, later comprising 25 states. The record of its territorial contraction as a diocese or archdiocese and as a province is, therefore, unique. In 1808, with the establishment of the suffragan Sees of Boston, Mass., New York, N.Y., Philadelphia, Pa., and Bardstown (later Louisville), Ky., and the creation of Baltimore as a metropolitan see, the Archdiocese of Baltimore was confined to what are now the District of Columbia, Maryland, West Virginia, Virginia, North and South Carolina, Georgia, Alabama, and Mississippi, an area of 317,610 square miles. The archdiocese, which remained the only metropolitan see in the U.S. until 1846, was subsequently reduced in area by four main

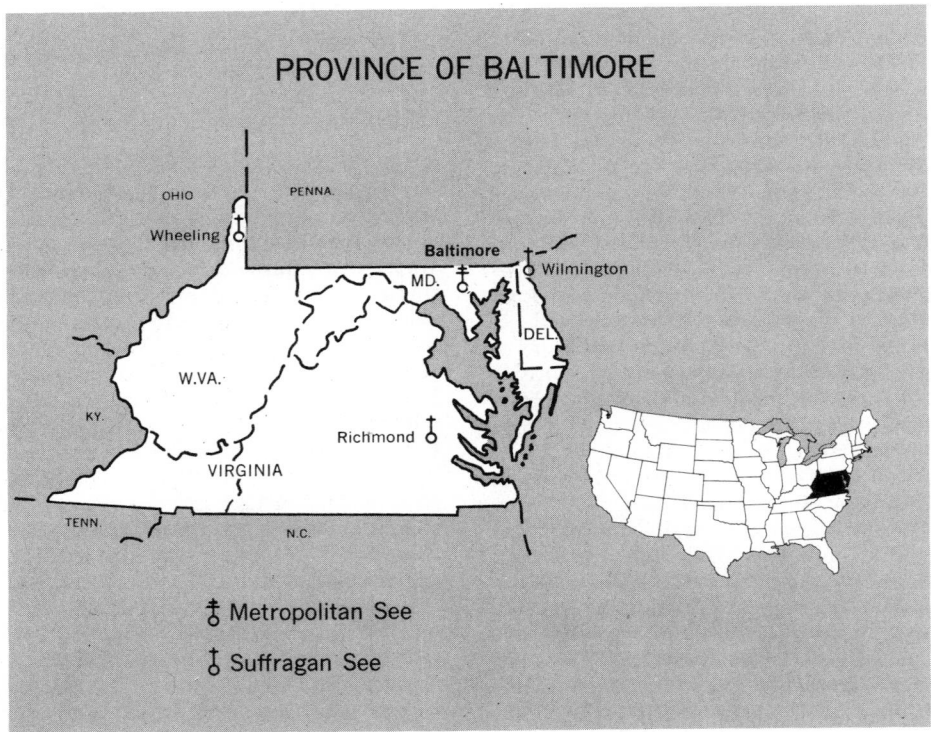

Fig. 1. *Province of Baltimore, comprising the Archdiocese of Baltimore, known as the metropolitan see, and three dioceses called suffragan sees. The archbishop has metropolitan jurisdiction over the province.*

subdivisions. In 1820 it lost West Virginia and Virginia to the Diocese of Richmond, although the archbishops of Baltimore administered the see when it was vacant from 1822 to 1841. North Carolina, South Carolina, and Georgia also were separated in 1820 to form the Diocese of Charleston, S.C.; these divisions left the two remaining parts of the archdiocese separated by more than 500 miles. In 1825 Mississippi and Alabama were severed when each became a vicariate apostolic; the latter included Florida, recently ceded to the U.S. by Spain. When the Diocese of Wilmington, Del., was created in 1868, Baltimore lost all of Maryland's eastern shore counties (nine) to the new see. In 1939 the District of Columbia was made an archdiocese, although its archbishop was simultaneously archbishop of Baltimore until 1947, when it was given its own archbishop and an additional five Maryland counties previously governed by Baltimore.

The Province of Baltimore was, in practice, coterminous with the Republic from 1808 to 1846, when Oregon City (now Portland, Ore.) became the second U.S. province. Between 1847 (when the Archdiocese of St. Louis, Mo., was erected) and 1850 (when the Provinces of New York, New Orleans, La., and Cincinnati, Ohio, were set up) the senior province was greatly reduced in size, losing Alabama and Mississippi, once part of the Baltimore archdiocese, to the New Orleans province. Delaware, never a part of the archdiocese as such, remained in the province when the state of Delaware was detached from the Diocese of Philadelphia and made part of the new Diocese of Wilmington (1868). West Florida, which had become part of the province in 1819, was transferred to the New Orleans province in 1850, but East Florida remained in that of Baltimore. The state of Pennsylvania also remained part of the Baltimore province until 1875, when the Province of Philadelphia was erected. Since then Baltimore has lost the District of Columbia and the five Maryland counties (1947) included in the Archdiocese of Washington, which belongs to no province. In 1962 the establishment of the new Province of Atlanta took the states of Georgia, North and South Carolina, and the eastern part of Florida, leaving the Province of Baltimore with all of Maryland except five counties, and Delaware, Virginia, and West Virginia, with suffragan sees at Richmond, Va., Wheeling, W.Va., and Wilmington, Del.

Prominent Leaders and Developments. Baltimore's ordinaries, beginning with the renowned John Carroll, who ruled the see from 1789 to 1815, have included many outstanding prelates. Carroll's successor was his coadjutor, Leonard *Neale, whose brief administration terminated with his death in 1817. He was followed by the French-born Sulpician Ambrose *Maréchal (1817–28); English-born James *Whitfield (1828–34); the Sulpician Samuel *Eccleston, a native of Maryland (1834–51); Irish-born Francis Patrick *Kenrick, who had served as bishop in Philadelphia, Pa., before his appointment to Baltimore (1851–63); Martin John *Spalding, born in Kentucky and auxiliary (1848–52) and bishop (1852–64) of Louisville, Ky., before his appointment as archbishop of Baltimore (1864–72); New York-born James Roosevelt *Bayley (1872–77); James *Gibbons, who became the second U.S. cardinal (1877–1921); Michael Joseph *Curley, Irish-born bishop of St. Augustine, Fla., when chosen for Baltimore (1921–47); Francis Patrick *Keough (1947–61);

and Baltimore-born Lawrence Joseph Shehan, who was named auxiliary of the archbishop of Baltimore and Washington in 1945 while serving as pastor of St. Patrick's, Washington. In 1948 he became auxiliary to the archbishop of Baltimore, where he took up residence as pastor of SS. Philip and James. Made first bishop of Bridgeport, Conn., in 1953, he was named to Baltimore in July 1961 as coadjutor archbishop and succeeded to the see at Keough's death on December 8 of that year. In February 1965 Shehan was raised to the College of Cardinals by Paul VI.

Under its episcopal leaders, Baltimore assumed an important role in U.S. Catholic history that was both enhanced and reflected by the many important meetings of Church leaders held in the see city. As early as 1791 Carroll had called a meeting of his clergy (22 attended) at which a number of regulations were decreed for observance throughout the diocese. These decrees were reaffirmed and amplified in 1810, when Carroll met informally with Neale, his coadjutor, and his newly consecrated suffragans Michael Egan of Philadelphia, Jean Cheverus of Boston, and Benedict Flaget of Bardstown. The First Provincial Council of Baltimore was held in 1829, followed by others in 1833, 1837, 1840, 1843, 1846, 1849, 1855, 1858, and 1869. Of these, the first seven—like the meetings of 1791 and 1810—were nationwide in scope and hence plenary in effect. Three other Councils of Baltimore were plenary in the strict sense, since they were presided over by an apostolic delegate (in each case, the incumbent archbishop of Baltimore) and the nation had by then been divided into additional provinces, each headed by a metropolitan archbishop. Held in 1852, 1866, and 1884, these meetings were epochal in character (see BALTIMORE, COUNCILS OF). Baltimore held also nine diocesan synods (i.e., meetings of the archbishop and his diocesan clergy concerning strictly diocesan regulations), which besides the national synod of 1791 included those held in 1831, 1853, 1857, 1863, 1865, 1868, 1875, and 1886.

When the diocese was created, Baltimore had only one church, St. Peter's, which served as procathedral for Carroll, Neale, and Maréchal until 1821. The first synod in the U.S. was held there, as was also the first ordination (Stephen T. *Badin, 1793), and the first episcopal consecration (Leonard Neale, 1800). In use until 1841, it was razed the following year to make room for Calvert Hall, a boys' school conducted there (1845–91) by the Brothers of the Christian Schools. To carry on the name of St. Peter's, another city parish of that name was established in 1842. On land purchased from the estate of the Revolutionary hero and Maryland governor, John Eager Howard, the old Cathedral of the Assumption of the Blessed Virgin Mary was begun on July 7, 1806, when Carroll laid the cornerstone. (Contrary to later development, this stone designated the church under the name of Jesus and Mary.) The Romanesque-Byzantine structure designed by the British-born non-Catholic Benjamin Henry Latrobe, one of the architects of the national capitol, was dedicated on May 31, 1821, but it remained in debt and unconsecrated until May 25, 1876. The building escaped the fires of 1873 and 1904; its location placed it (1964) on the northern edge of the city's 22-acre Charles Center redevelopment area. The old cathedral, important for its historical associations, became the nation's fourth minor basilica on Sept. 1, 1937. Within its

Fig. 2. Basilica of the Assumption of the Blessed Virgin Mary, Baltimore, Md., designed by Benjamin Henry Latrobe, dedicated May 31, 1821.

walls all of Baltimore's great councils were solemnized. Beneath its altar lie all the archbishops of Baltimore except Neale, Bayley, and Keough. At its altar more than 30 bishops have been consecrated, and 2,000 priests ordained. On Sept. 21, 1959, the basilica ceased to be the metropolitan cathedral, but was accorded the status of a cocathedral. The Cathedral of Mary Our Queen was built from funds bequeathed by Thomas J. O'Neill (1849–1919), an Irish-born Baltimore merchant. Ground was broken by Keough on Oct. 10, 1954, and the cornerstone was laid the following May. The building was consecrated Oct. 13, 1959, and solemnly opened November 15.

Religious Communities. A number of religious communities established their first U.S. foundations under the ordinaries of Baltimore: the Carmelites at Port Tobacco, Md. (1790); the Sulpicians at Baltimore (1791);

Fig. 3. Home of Elizabeth Seton on the grounds of St. Mary's Seminary, North Paca St., Baltimore.

the Visitation nuns (1799) and the restored Jesuits (1806), both at Georgetown, D.C.; the Christian Brothers (1845), the Josephites (1871), and the Bon Secour Sisters (1881), all at Baltimore. In addition three new communities for women were founded within the archdiocese. In 1809 the Sisters of St. Joseph, as they were originally called, founded by (Bl.) Elizabeth *Seton, established St. Joseph's Academy at Emmitsburg, Md. The Oblate Sisters of Providence were founded in Baltimore in 1829 by the Sulpician Jacques Joubert. This community of Negro sisters is dedicated to the education of Negro children. The Mission Helpers of the Sacred Heart began in 1891, when Mary Cunningham (later Mother Demetrias) joined with a group of Baltimore women in helping the Josephites with their catechetical and missionary work among the Negro missions. With headquarters in Towson, Md., they engage in general and special catechetics.

Within the archdiocese the Sulpicians, Josephites, Pallottines, and Trinitarians have their national headquarters; Baltimore is also a provincial center for the Friars Minor Conventuals, Jesuits, and Xaverian Brothers, as well as for the Daughters of Charity, Franciscan Sisters of Baltimore City, Franciscans Sisters of the Third Order, Good Shepherd Sisters, Notre Dame de Namur Sisters, Oblate Sisters of Providence, Religious Sisters of Mercy, and the School Sisters of Notre Dame.

Education. In the document establishing the diocese of Baltimore, the Holy See urged upon Carroll the necessity of establishing "an episcopal seminary either in the same city [Baltimore] or elsewhere, as he shall judge most expedient." By the time the new bishop issued the nation's first pastoral letter in 1792, he was able "to return God thanks for having conducted to our assistance a number of learned and exemplary clergymen, devoted by choice, and formed by experience to the important function of training young Ecclesiastics to all the duties of the ministry." These clergymen were the *Sulpicians, who had arrived in Baltimore in July 1791. Three months after their arrival, and under the direction of Father Nagot, four Sulpicians and the five students who accompanied them from Europe had begun the pioneer U.S. Seminary, St. Mary's, at Paca Street, Baltimore. The lack of native candidates to the priesthood during the Sulpicians' first 13 years nearly caused the closing of the seminary, and only the express wish of Pius VII saved the project. Since 1929 only the philosophy department has continued at Paca Street; the theology school was transferred to Roland Park in suburban Baltimore. In 1963 the combined faculty numbered 34, and the student body totaled 612 from 53 dioceses, including sees in Japan, Canada, and the Philippines. On property in Ellicott City donated by Charles Carroll, a signer of the Declaration of Independence, the Sulpicians in 1831 established a permanent minor seminary, St. Charles, the oldest preparatory seminary in the U.S. The original school was destroyed by fire in 1911; since then St. Charles has been located at Catonsville, in southwest Baltimore. In 1963 it had a faculty of 26 and an enrollment of 398 high school and junior college students.

Another training school for the diocesan priesthood, the seminary department of Mt. St. Mary's College, Emmitsburg, was established in 1808 by the Sulpician John Dubois, later third bishop of New York. Mt. St. Mary's was from the start both a seminary and a lay college. Since ending its association with the Sulpicians in 1826, the college has been directed by an association of secular priests from various dioceses, with the archbishop of Baltimore as ex officio president. Its graduates include many bishops and the first U.S. Cardinal, John McCloskey. In 1963 the seminary department had a faculty of 14 and an enrollment of 129 seminarians. Religious communities of men with houses of training for their members in the archdiocese included: the Capuchins, Friars Minor Conventuals, Jesuits, Passionists, Paulists, Redemptorists, and Trinitarians; and those of women, the Bon Secours, Daughters of Charity, Franciscans of Baltimore City, Good Shepherd Sisters, Mercy Sisters, Notre Dame de Namur Sisters, Oblate Sisters of Providence, School Sisters of Notre Dame, Servants of Mary Immaculate, and Visitation Sisters. There were also cloistered convents of the Carmelites, Dominican Nuns of the Perpetual Rosary, and Visitation Nuns.

The archdiocese has two Catholic colleges for men and four for women. The men's colleges, Mt. St. Mary's and Loyola, Baltimore (1852), are directed respectively by secular priests and Jesuits. From 1803 to 1852 another college, St. Mary's, adjoined the seminary in Baltimore. Founded by the Sulpician Louis Du Bourg and managed by his community, it was both a day and a boarding school, admitting students of all creeds. Despite its success, it was closed when the growth of priestly vocations recalled the Sulpicians to their proper work. A college at Rock Hill, Ellicott City, was opened by the Christian Brothers in 1857 and conducted by them until the fire of 1923. Women's colleges in Baltimore are under the direction of the Sisters of Mercy at Mt. St. Agnes (1867) and the School Sisters of Notre Dame at Notre Dame of Maryland (1873). In Stevenson the Notre Dame de Namur Sisters conduct Villa Julie, a junior college (1952), and the Daughters of Charity, St. Joseph's (1809), at Emmitsburg. In addition, there were 39 high schools (13,783 students) and 116 elementary schools (62,673 students) in the archdiocese under Catholic auspices in 1963. A home for problem girls is conducted by the Good Shepherd Sisters; and a day school for retarded children, by the Franciscan Sisters of Baltimore City.

Religious communities teaching in the archdiocese include the School Sisters of Notre Dame, Franciscans, Sisters of Mercy, Daughters of Charity, Notre Dame de Namur, Sisters of St. Joseph, Oblate Sisters of Divine Providence, Religious of the Holy Union of the Sacred Heart, Servants of the Immaculate Heart of Mary, Ursulines, Visitandines, Christian Brothers, Franciscans of Baltimore City, Franciscans of St. Joseph, Good Shepherd Sisters, Sisters of Providence of St. Mary-of-the-Woods, Sisters of St. Casimir, Xaverian Brothers, Charity Sisters from Seton Hill, Christian Charity Sisters, Divine Providence Sisters of Kentucky, Felicians, Filippini, Handmaids of the Sacred Heart, Holy Cross Sisters, Holy Family of Nazareth Sisters, Jesuits, Pallottines, and Sisters of St. Dominic.

Charitable Works. In 1963 there were five general hospitals: Sacred Heart, Cumberland (Daughters of Charity, 1911), and four in Baltimore: St. Agnes (Daughters of Charity, 1862), St. Joseph (Sisters of St. Francis of Philadelphia, 1864), Mercy (Sisters of Mercy, 1874), and Bon Secours (Bon Secours Sisters, 1919). Baltimore's two other specialized hospitals are

conducted by the Daughters of Charity: Jenkins Memorial (1926), for the Incurable, and Seton Psychiatric Institute (originally Mt. St. Vincent's, 1841). Homes for the aged and the convalescent in Baltimore include one under the Little Sisters of the Poor (1869), Mercy Villa (Sisters of Mercy, 1920), Kirkleigh Villa (Daughters of Charity, 1926), St. Joseph Nursing Home (Sisters Servants of Mary Immaculate, 1959), and, in Towson, Md., Stella Maris Hospice (Sisters of Mercy, 1953). An infirmary for their own sisters, conducted by the School Sisters of Notre Dame, is located at Villa Marie (Notch Cliff, 1909); a similar infirmary is conducted by the Daughters of Charity at Villa St. Michael (1952). In 1960 Villa Maria in Towson was opened by the Sisters of Mercy to replace six older institutions in Baltimore for the care of boys and girls. St. Mary's Industrial School for Boys (Xaverian Brothers, 1866) was closed in 1950 and a new coinstructional high school has been constructed on the site. Young people were also cared for by the Catholic Youth Organization (9,500 members) and the units of the Veterans Mission Crusade. Staffed by the Daughters of Charity, St. Vincent's Infant Home (Baltimore, 1865) moved to new quarters (1964), where it cares for needy preschool children. Many of these charitable institutions are affiliated with Associated Catholic Charities, Inc., of Baltimore. An outgrowth of the St. Vincent De Paul Society, this corporation began in 1923 as the Bureau of Catholic Charities. In 1941 Archbishop Curley instituted the Confraternity of the Laity, which conducted a yearly appeal for funds, and Curley's successors have continued to sponsor an annual charity appeal.

Catholic Press. The short-lived *Metropolitan,* founded in Baltimore by Peter *Blenkinsop in 1830, is credited with being the pioneer Catholic magazine in the U.S. In 1842 Rev. Charles I. *White of Baltimore began a monthly called the *Religious Cabinet.* Renamed the *U.S. Catholic Magazine* in 1843, in became a weekly in 1849 and was succeeded in 1850 by the *Catholic Mirror,* a weekly newspaper. Except for a brief period during the Civil War when its publisher was imprisoned for southern sympathies, it continued as Baltimore's archdiocesan paper until 1908. When White relinquished its editorship in 1853, he began another monthly under the old name of the *Metropolitan* and continued it until 1857. It died out shortly after a new editor took over in 1858. Since 1913 the official weekly organ of the archdiocese has been the *Baltimore Catholic Review.* Between 1944 and 1952 there were separate Baltimore and Washington editions. (Since then Washington has had its own paper.)

Other Developments. The Third Plenary Council of Baltimore (1884) established a committee of bishops to draw up a catechism for use in elementary religious instruction throughout the U.S. The first edition of the so-called Baltimore Catechism appeared in April 1885; it was chiefly the work of Bp. John L. Spalding of Peoria, Ill., and Msgr. J. V. De Concilio of St. Michael's parish, Jersey City, N.J. This original edition became the No. 2 catechism, No. 1 being a simplified version and No. 3 an amplified one. In 1941 a considerably revised edition was published.

Baltimore possesses a storehouse of documents "ranking first among the archives of the Catholic Church in the United States," according to John Tracy Ellis, American Church historian. Located in the new (1965) Cath-

Fig. 4. Cathedral of Mary Our Queen, Baltimore.

olic Center, these documents are catalogued chiefly according to the administrations of the successive arch-bishops. A few documents antedate the American Revolution. There are autographed letters from ten popes (beginning with Pius VII in 1817) and sixteen American presidents (beginning with Washington in 1790).

The principal patron of the archdiocese is the Blessed Virgin Mary, Assumed into Heaven (synod of 1791); St. Ignatius Loyola was chosen as the secondary patron (synod of 1886), since the Jesuits established the first missions in Maryland (1634). His Spanish name still identifies one of the oldest towns in the state (St. Inigoes, St. Mary's county, 1634) and its historic church. To him is dedicated also the Mission of St. Ignatius at St. Thomas Manor (Chapel Point, Charles County); it was established in 1641, and the cornerstone of its church was laid by Carroll in 1798. Finally there is St. Ignatius parish, at Hickory (Harford County), which was established in 1792.

By 1965 the archdiocese had 129 parishes, 23 missions, and 177 chapels; it was served by 881 priests, of whom 530 were religious. Also working in the archdiocese were 162 brothers and 2,739 sisters. Since 1913 two Ukrainian Catholic churches of the Byzantine rite have been located in Baltimore, St. Michael and SS. Peter and Paul. The Catholic Interracial Council and general activities on behalf of the Negro have grown in importance with the *Civil Rights movement and the increase of Catholic Negroes in the archdiocese, particularly in the city of Baltimore. Other organizations active in archdiocesan life include the Archdiocesan Commission for Christian Unity (the nation's first), the Liturgical Commission, the Cursillo Retreat Movement, Newman Clubs, the Spanish apostolate, the Confraternity of Christian Doctrine, and the Christian Family Movement.

Bibliography: No adequate history of Catholicism in Maryland or in the archdiocese has been written. Partial sources include J. D. G. SHEA, *A History of the Catholic Church within the Limits of the United States,* 4 v. (New York 1886–92). M. E. STANTON, *A Century of Growth: The History of the Church in Western Maryland,* 2 v. (Baltimore 1891). M. J. RIORDAN, *Cathedral Records from the Beginning of Catholicism in Baltimore* (Baltimore 1906). P. K. GUILDAY, *Life and Times of John Carroll: Archbishop of Baltimore, 1735–1815,* 2 v. (New York 1927). J. T. ELLIS, *Life of James Cardinal Gibbons: Archbishop of Baltimore, 1834–1921,* 2 v. (Milwaukee 1952). A. M. MEL-VILLE, *John Carroll of Baltimore* (New York 1955). By 1965 The Catholic University of America library contained studies of all Baltimore's archbishops from Carroll through Gibbons. Other valuable sources are the Archives of the Archdiocese of Baltimore, the Maryland Historical Society, and the Maryland Room of the Pratt Library.

[J. J. GALLAGHER]

BALTIMORE, COUNCILS OF

Although the Council of Trent (1545–63) decreed that diocesan synods were to be held everywhere each year and that provincial councils should meet every 3 years, this regulation was rarely, if ever, followed to the letter in any part of the world. The Code of Canon Law (1918) prescribes the holding of diocesan synods every 10 years and of provincial councils every 20 years. Provision is also made in the Code for plenary councils, in which the bishops of more than one ecclesiastical province meet. In a plenary council, laws are promulgated that bind the dioceses in the area represented in the council; the decrees of a provincial council are binding within the territory of the province; and in a synod, diocesan statutes are laid down.

Regulations have been made for the Church in the U.S. in all three types of assembly. From 1789 to 1808, the whole territory of the U.S. belonged to the Diocese of Baltimore, Md., and from 1808 to 1846, the Province of Baltimore was the only one in the country. Although Oregon City became a metropolitan see in 1846 and St. Louis, in 1847, the bishops who met in 1849 for the Seventh Provincial Council of Baltimore represented the entire nation. Since that time, three plenary councils of the U.S. Church have been held, all at Baltimore. Before the establishment of the first U.S. diocese in 1789, the clergy had met also in several general chapters at Whitemarsh, Md. Although these meetings did not fall within the strict canonical categories of synod and council, brief mention of them will be included in this article, which is divided as follows: (1) general chapters of the clergy (1783–89); (2) Baltimore diocesan synod (1791); (3) meeting of the American bishops (1810); (4) first seven provincial councils of Baltimore (1829–49); (5) the three plenary councils of Baltimore (1852–84).

General Chapters of the Clergy (1783–89). Until 1773 care of the Church in the English colonies on the Eastern Seaboard of the present U.S. was left almost entirely to missionaries of the Society of Jesus. There was no ecclesiastical organization except that which the internal Jesuit structure provided. From 1721 on, the colonies came under the tenuous supervision of the English vicar apostolic of the London district, a supervision that became more formal after 1757 but was never really effective. In 1773 the Society of Jesus was suppressed, but most of its missionaries in the English colonies continued their work there under the direction of the last superior of the mission, Rev. John Lewis. The American Revolution ended all possibility of ecclesiastical government from England, and for 10 years no attempt at formal organization of the U.S. Church was made.

In 1782, Rev. John Carroll, one of the former Jesuits, proposed the creation of a provisional chapter of the clergy in order to preserve the property that had belonged to the Jesuit order and also to see to other problems of ecclesiastical administration. Three meetings of the General Chapter were held at Whitemarsh: in

1783–84, 1786, and 1789. Decisions were made touching on the preservation of the Jesuit estates, the foundation of an academy at Georgetown (later Georgetown University, Washington, D.C.), the need for educating a native clergy, and the erection of the Diocese of Baltimore. In 1784, the chapter voted against the creation of a bishopric in the U.S., but 2 years later the members changed their minds and petitioned the Holy See for the foundation of a diocese and the right to elect the first bishop. This was conceded by Rome. In 1789, Carroll, who had been superior of the mission by papal appointment since 1784, was chosen by the clergy as the first bishop in the U.S. With the creation of the Diocese of Baltimore on Nov. 6, 1789, the general chapters of the clergy ceased to perform their quasi-conciliar function in the U.S. Church.

Synod of Baltimore (1791). When John Carroll was consecrated first bishop of Baltimore on Aug. 15, 1790, his jurisdiction extended over the entire area of what was then the U.S. From Nov. 7 to 10, 1791, Carroll held a diocesan synod in St. Peter's procathedral, Baltimore. It was the only such formal meeting in his 18 years as bishop and 7 years as archbishop (1790–1815). Twenty-two priests attended, most of them from Maryland and Pennsylvania. Boston was represented, but there were no delegates from New York, Philadelphia, Kentucky, the Northwest, or the South.

Twenty-four statutes were promulgated. The Blessed Virgin Mary was declared patroness of the diocese and August 15 was fixed as its principal feast day. In the remaining regulations, the administration of the Sacraments was standardized, the precept of paschal Communion was emphasized, mixed marriages were discouraged, and non-Catholic partners in such marriages were to be required to promise in the presence of witnesses that they would not oppose the education of their children in the Catholic faith. An order of Sunday services also was prescribed. Mass was to be preceded by the Litany of Loretto and followed by recitation of the prayer for the civil authorities that Carroll had composed, the Gospel of the day in the vernacular, notices, and a short sermon. Vespers and Benediction of the Blessed Sacrament were to be held in the afternoon. Provision was made also for catechism classes, to be conducted after Mass.

One of the principal problems confronting the infant U.S. Church was that of *trusteeism. Although the decrees of the Baltimore Synod made no explicit reference to the efforts of some laymen to usurp control of various congregations, regulations were laid down concerning the collection and distribution of parish funds, and it was made clear that no priest could function in the diocese or change his place of residence without authorization from the bishop. Carroll also discussed with his priests the method to be adopted for electing future bishops. He issued two letters, one dealing with Christian marriage and the other a pastoral (May 28, 1792) that treated Catholic education, priestly vocations, support of pastors and the Church, Mass attendance, prayers for the dead, and devotion to the Blessed Virgin Mary. The synodal statutes were submitted to Rome and, in 1794, were approved, with only minor changes, by the Congregation for the Propagation of the Faith.

Meeting of American Bishops (1810). On April 8, 1808, Pius VII made Baltimore a metropolitan see with suffragans at Boston, New York, Philadelphia, and

Bardstown, Ky. Bp. Richard L. Concanen, OP, who was consecrated in Rome as first bishop of New York, died in Naples without ever reaching the U.S. The three other bishops were consecrated in Baltimore between October 28 and November 4: John Cheverus, of Boston; Michael Egan, OFM, of Philadelphia; and Benedict J. Flaget, SS, of Bardstown.

After the consecration ceremonies, the new bishops met for 2 weeks with Archbishop Carroll and his coadjutor, Leonard Neale. Two series of resolutions were issued and made binding throughout the province. The bishops decided to defer calling a provincial council until 1812, and they resolved to advise the Holy See that the canonical prescriptions of annual synods and diocesan visitations were impractical in the U.S. and should be left to the discretion of each bishop. They also warned pastors and the faithful not to allow unauthorized priests to exercise the sacred ministry; discouraged frequent theater-going, dancing, and uncontrolled reading, particularly of novels; forbade the Sacraments to known Freemasons; ordered that Baptism should, as far as possible, be administered in church and not in private homes; and recommended that the same be done for Matrimony.

The bishops suggested to the Holy See that future episcopal nominations for their country be made by the U.S. hierarchy; they urged religious superiors not to transfer those of their subjects who held parochial offices without the consent of the local ordinary; and they ordered that the Douay Bible be used as the English version of Scripture in public worship and in devotional books. Although as early as 1787 Carroll had advocated introduction of a complete vernacular liturgy, the bishops' meeting of 1810 decreed that Latin should be used in the Mass and for the form of the Sacraments; all other prayers in the sacramental ceremonies might be in English. They promised to publish a ritual that would standardize liturgical practice. No pastoral letter was issued.

First Seven Provincial Councils. The War of 1812, the imprisonment of Pius VII by Napoleon, the difficulties of travel, and the lack of any outstanding problems demanding conciliar action were some of the factors that combined to postpone the council scheduled for 1812. Carroll had summoned the bishops to Baltimore in a letter sent out in June 1812, but the following September they were notified that the council would not be held. The archbishop died in 1815, and his successor, the ailing Leonard Neale, succumbed in 1817 without taking any action in regard to a council.

First Provincial Council (1829). Ambrose Maréchal, SS, third archbishop of Baltimore (1817–28), was unwilling to call a provincial council despite the insistent demands of Bp. John England of Charleston, S.C., that one be held. Maréchal remained convinced that there were no compelling reasons for a council; he also objected to the growing Irish influence in the U.S. Church and had no intention of giving Irish-born prelates like England a wider forum for their opinions.

Abp. James Whitfield succeeded Maréchal in 1828, and on December 18 of that year he announced that a provincial council would meet in October 1829. After a preparatory meeting on September 30 in the archbishop's house, 13 private, 13 public, and 3 solemn sessions were held in the Baltimore cathedral (Oct. 3–18, 1829). Six bishops and the apostolic administrator of

Philadelphia attended; three bishops were absent and Bishop Conwell was not admitted to a vote, a fact that he protested to the Congregation of the Propaganda. Three lawyers, including the future chief justice of the U.S., Roger B. Taney, were invited as guests of the Council to advise on legal matters. Thirty-eight decrees were promulgated and sent to Rome for approval. The bishops also sent two letters to Pius VIII and another to the Society for the Propagation of the Faith at Lyons. These letters of gratitude to mission societies were to be a regular feature of all the Baltimore councils.

The first eight decrees of the First Provincial Council dealt with the stability of priests in the parishes assigned to them and with various aspects of trusteeism. Other decrees ordered the use of the Douay Version of the Bible and the Roman Ritual, although vernacular translations might be employed in administering the Sacraments after the Latin had been read. Several decrees called for a tightening of discipline in the administration of the Sacraments and in the life of the clergy. It was announced that a uniform catechism and ceremonial would be prepared, and the bishops asserted that it was "absolutely necessary" that Catholic schools be established. A tract society for publication of Catholic literature was established. Two pastoral letters were signed by the fathers of the Council, one to the clergy and one to the laity. Both were composed by Bishop England. The decrees of the Council were sent to Rome, where Bp. John Dubois of New York and Rev. Anthony Kohlmann, SJ, former administrator of the same diocese, were charged with their examination by the Propaganda. The decrees were finally approved by Pius VIII in 1830 and promulgated in 1831. The net result of the First Provincial Council was a strengthening of ties with Rome and greater uniformity of practice among the several American dioceses.

Second Provincial Council (1833). The next council should have been held in 1832, but Whitfield was reluctant to issue the necessary summons. England, Bp. Joseph Rosati, of St. Louis, and Francis P. Kenrick, coadjutor of Philadelphia, enlisted the support of the Congregation of the Propaganda, and the archbishop was finally forced to call a council that met from Oct. 20 to 27, 1833, in the Baltimore cathedral. Nine bishops and the archbishop were present. Eleven decrees were adopted. Three of these dealt with the territorial distribution of the dioceses, another proposed that the selection of future bishops be kept in the hands of the hierarchy, and two assigned to the Jesuits the Indian missions and the mission that it was hoped would be founded in Liberia. The presidents of St. Mary's Seminary, Baltimore; Mt. St. Mary's College, Emmitsburg, Md.; and Georgetown College were appointed to supervise publication of Catholic textbooks, and the bishops were encouraged to establish seminaries along the lines prescribed by the Council of Trent.

The bishops revoked an agreement made in 1810 according to which priests who had faculties in one diocese also had them in neighboring dioceses. A new edition of the Roman Ritual for the use of missionaries was also commissioned. England's suggestion of an American national seminary to be located in Ireland was not adopted. The pastoral letter of the Council, again composed by England, contained an appeal for a more vigorous sacramental life. It dealt also with Catholic education, priestly vocations, the laws of fast and abstinence, and, for the first time, with attacks that were

being made on Catholics as the great tide of immigration to the United States began.

Third Provincial Council (1837). This was the first of five provincial councils presided over by Abp. Samuel Eccleston, SS. It met (April 16–23) at a time when Nativist anti-Catholic agitation was at its height. Nine of the fourteen American bishops participated. Eleven disciplinary decrees were enacted, including regulations on ordinations, provision for the care of aged and infirm priests, directions for safeguarding legal ownership of church property, and prohibitions against bringing ecclesiastical cases before civil courts and collecting alms without written permission from the bishop. In liturgical matters, the Ceremonial commissioned by the first provincial council (and approved in 1841 by the Holy See) was made normative. Sacred music was to be regulated, and vernacular hymns were forbidden at Mass and solemn Vespers.

The bishops also petitioned the Holy See for abrogation of the obligation to hear Mass on Easter and Pentecost Mondays, and of the fast on Wednesdays and Fridays in Advent. In a letter to Gregory XVI, the fathers asked that new dioceses be erected to cope with the flow of immigrants and that Rome support their requests for bishops from religious orders when it was found necessary to nominate them. The lengthy pastoral letter of 1837 outlined the persecution to which Catholics were being subjected, counseled patience and attention to religious duties, and included a ringing assertion of the loyalty of Catholics to the civil government. It also discussed trusteeism, the need for religious and clerical vocations, Catholic publications, education, and the support of the clergy.

Fourth Provincial Council (1840). John England, the father of the conciliar tradition in the U.S Church, attended his last council in Baltimore from May 17 to 24, 1840. (He died in 1842.) The 12 U.S. bishops present at the Council admitted to their deliberations Bp. Charles de Forbin-Janson of Nancy and Toul, France, who was in the U.S. at the time. International affairs were given considerable attention. An unsuccessful plea was made that the prelates interest themselves in the educational controversy that was then occupying the Irish hierarchy. Gregory XVI's apostolic letter condemning the slave trade, *In supremo apostolatus,* was read. Letters of sympathy were sent to Archbishops Clemens von Droste-Vischering of Cologne and Martin von Dunin of Gnesen-Posen, who were then engaged in the dispute with the Prussian government over mixed marriages. Previous conciliar decrees on Matrimony, preaching, and the catechism were reiterated, and temperance societies were commended.

The Protestant orientation of U.S. public schools was stressed, and Catholics were urged to assert their civil rights in the matter. Nothing was said about the establishment of parochial schools. Membership in secret societies was forbidden to Catholics. The final decree of the Council was an exhortation to the clergy to lead lives worthy of their vocation. The pastoral letter of 1840 touched upon the usual topics of anti-Catholicism, religious education, vocations, and marriage, but also included an exhortation to conscientious exercise of the right to vote in civil elections, and sections on secret societies, intemperance, and the dangers of wealth.

Fifth Provincial Council (1843). Sixteen bishops and the apostolic administrator of Charleston, S.C., met for the Fifth Provincial Council at Baltimore, from May 14 to 21, 1843. The Province of Baltimore then included 15 suffragan sees. Among those who attended the Council was the vicar apostolic of the Republic of Texas, Bp. Claude Dubuis. The 11 decrees dealt with matrimonial legislation, financial arrangements, ownership of church property, encouragement of Catholic printing houses, visitation of the sick, and the obligation to use the Latin prayers of the Roman Ritual, although prayers in English might be added. The pastoral letter treated Catholic education, secret societies, temperance, the missions in Liberia and among the Indians, obedience to the civil government, the fruits in both England and the U.S. of the Oxford Movement, and the evils of divorce. One of the decrees of the Council imposed excommunication on those who attempted marriage after civil divorce.

Sixth Provincial Council (1846). Archbishop Eccleston and 23 bishops met in Baltimore from May 10 to 17, 1846. Although these were the peak Nativist years, neither the decrees nor the pastoral letter of the Council made any reference to the fact. Only four decrees were issued. The Blessed Virgin was declared patroness of the U.S., under the title of the Immaculate Conception; the Holy See was asked to forbid clerics in Sacred Orders from entering religious orders without the permission of their bishop; the proclamation of the banns of Matrimony was insisted upon; and priests were forbidden to administer Baptism and Matrimony to those who were not their proper subjects. The pastoral letter dealt with the same topics as in previous years, with the addition of a paragraph announcing the Council's action in naming the Mother of God, under the title of the Immaculate Conception, as patroness of the U.S.

Seventh Provincial Council (1849). Oregon City had been made a metropolitan see in 1846, and 1 year later the same was done for St. Louis. By 1849 there were 29 U.S. dioceses. At the Council that met in Baltimore from May 6 to 13, 1849, Archbishops Eccleston and Peter R. Kenrick, of St. Louis, and 23 bishops were present. The archbishop of Oregon City and his suffragans did not attend. Despite the presence of Kenrick, Eccleston presided; the Council was not plenary in nature.

The fathers petitioned Pius IX to define the Immaculate Conception of the Blessed Virgin. They drafted regulations concerning the destination of alms, transfer of priests from one diocese to another, and the method of selecting bishops. They also asked permission to hold a national council in 1850 and petitioned the Holy See, unsuccessfully, to grant to the archbishop of Baltimore the title of primate. The pastoral letter dealt with only two topics: the pope and his office, and the Immaculate Conception. Pius IX was at the time in Gaeta, a refugee from the Roman Revolution of 1848, and Bp. Michael Portier of Mobile, Ala., was commissioned to carry the acts and decrees of the Council to him there and to visit Lyons also to thank the Society for the Propagation of Faith for its help to the U.S. Church.

Three Plenary Councils. Although a plenary council had been planned for 1850, it did not meet until May 9, 1852.

First Plenary Council (1852). Six archbishops and twenty-seven U.S. bishops attended this Council, as did the Canadian bishop of Toronto. Its sessions lasted from May 9 to 20, with Francis P. Kenrick, the new arch-

bishop of Baltimore, serving as apostolic delegate. Twenty-five decrees were promulgated. The first was a formal acknowledgement of the pope as successor of St. Peter, Vicar of Christ, head of the whole Church, and father and teacher of all Christians, with universal authority to rule and govern. The second decree expressly declared that the legislation of the seven Provincial Councils of Baltimore extended to all the dioceses of the U.S. Some provisions of that legislation were explicitly restated in the decrees of the Plenary Council. Bishops were also urged to organize chancery offices and to appoint consultors and censors of books, and it was recommended that there be at least one major seminary in each province. The Council likewise urged the erection of parochial schools. The 19th decree included a tribute to the wise noninterference of U.S. civil authority in religious matters, and urged bishops to see to it, prudently, that members of the Army and Navy were not required to attend non-Catholic services. Although the national crisis over slavery was mounting, the fathers made no statement on the subject. They petitioned once more that the primacy be granted to Baltimore, but it was not until 1858 that "prerogative of place" was granted to the occupant of that see.

The decrees of the Council were approved in Rome on Sept. 26, 1852, but a private letter was sent to Archbishop Kenrick in which he was warned that the asking of exceptions to general Church law should be kept to a minimum, lest the U.S. church take on the appearance of a national church. The pastoral letter of 1852, written by Kenrick, began with an explanation of the nature of episcopal authority and its relation to the papacy. Passages then followed on the administration of church property, obedience to ecclesiastical authority, the needs of the Church in the U.S., Catholic education, vocations, and civil allegiance. The letter ended with separate exhortations to priests, sisters, and laity.

Second Plenary Council (1866). In the interim between the first two Plenary Councils, the slavery crisis had come to a head and the nation had undergone the Civil War. Martin J. Spalding had succeeded Archbishop Kenrick in Baltimore, and nearly half of the U.S. bishops had been appointed since 1852. There were in all 7 metropolitan sees with 40 suffragan dioceses. On March 19, 1866, Spalding, as apostolic delegate, announced the forthcoming council and gave as the principal reason for it "that at the close of the national crisis, which had acted as a dissolvent on all sectarian ecclesiastical institutions, the Catholic Church might present to the country and the world a striking proof of the strong bond of unity with which her members are knit together."

An instruction on the agenda for the Council had been sent by the Propaganda on Jan. 31, 1866. It proposed as topics the care of the recently freed Negroes, the method of selecting bishops, the problem of unattached priests, the erection of seminaries, feasts, fasts and holydays of obligation, legal arrangements for the holding of church property, and the relation of bishops to religious orders in the same matter. The Congregation of the Propaganda asked the fathers to take up also the question of an increase in the number of dioceses. Spalding, one of the leading scholars in the Church, saw the 1866 assembly as an opportunity to include, for the first time in U.S. conciliar decrees, a doctrinal exposition on current heresies and errors, and to codify existing disciplinary legislation.

Third Plenary Council of Baltimore, 1884—from Clarke's "History of the Catholic Church in the United States."

The Council met (Oct. 7–20, 1866) in the Baltimore cathedral and was the largest such meeting in the history of the U.S. Church to that time. Thousands of onlookers gathered for the opening procession, in which 7 archbishops, 38 bishops, 3 abbots, and 120 theologians participated. The first order of business after the opening solemnities was the cabling of a greeting and good wishes to Pius IX.

The legislation of the Council was set down in 14 titles: on orthodox faith, hierarchy and government of the Church, ecclesiastical persons, church property, Sacraments, divine worship, promotion of disciplinary uniformity, regulars and nuns, education of youth, more efficacious promotion of the salvation of souls, books and newspapers, secret societies, erection of new sees and choice of episcopal candidates, and the more effective execution of the decrees of the Council. The decrees resumed previous U.S. legislation and included directives received from the Holy See, as well as ideas taken from other provincial councils that had been held in the U.S. and elsewhere. An entire chapter was devoted to the care of Negroes, and it was stated that segregated churches might be provided for them if the local situation demanded it. Although Spalding had hoped that a Catholic university might be authorized by the Council, the decree contented itself with a velleity on the point. Secret societies were condemned, but labor unions were specifically excluded from this prohibition. President Andrew Johnson attended the final solemn session of the Council.

The usual letters were sent by the fathers; the one to Pius IX was so phrased that it was later used at Vatican Council I (1869–70) in arguing that the Second Council of Baltimore had at least implicitly affirmed

papal infallibility. This was denied by several of the signers, including Archbishops Kenrick and Purcell. The conciliar decrees were not approved until 1868, partly because several bishops, including Kenrick, had protested to Rome that insufficient time had been allowed for discussion, and that the text as adopted did not reflect accurately the wishes of the fathers. Nevertheless, the Council became a model for similar assemblies in other countries. A lengthy pastoral letter explained the conciliar legislation to the clergy and laity.

Third Plenary Council (1884). By 1884 the Church in the U.S. was increasing by about 2 million members every decade, largely as a result of immigration. The impetus for a council came chiefly from the West. The archbishops of the country were called to Rome in 1883 to plan the assembly. Since Cardinal John McCloskey of New York was too feeble to preside, Roman authorities intended to send an Italian archbishop as apostolic delegate. They were, however, persuaded to substitute Abp. James Gibbons of Baltimore, and it was he who organized and directed the Council.

Seventy-two prelates attended the sessions, which lasted from November 9 to December 7. The 12 titles of the conciliar decrees included Catholic faith, ecclesiastical persons, divine worship, Sacraments, clerical education, education of Catholic youth, Christian doctrine, zeal for souls, church property, ecclesiastical trials, and Christian burial. Much of the legislation repeated previous law, and it was stated that enactments of the Second Plenary Council remained in force unless revoked. In the first title, the decrees of Vatican Council I were explicitly accepted, and mention was made of errors condemned in the encyclicals of the reigning Pope, Leo XIII. Priests were given a voice in the choice of bishops, through diocesan consultors. One of a series of regulations on clerical discipline made the Roman collar obligatory. Relations between bishops and regulars were to be governed according to the constitution *Romanos pontifices* (1881). The Council once more urged erection of parochial schools, and a committee was set up to arrange for the creation of a Catholic university. Other committees were commissioned to prepare what became the Baltimore Catechism, to look after missions among Negroes and Indians, and to pass upon secret societies.

The Council had wide influence in the English-speaking world, especially because of the way in which it set up diocesan organization. The 1884 pastoral letter explained the decrees of the Council and exhorted clergy and laity to fulfillment of them. It was remarkable as a clear assertion of the fathers' belief that American institutions were most propitious to the growth of the Catholic Church.

From the Third Plenary Council of Baltimore until the formation of the *National Catholic Welfare Conference, the archbishops of the U.S. met annually, but their discussions were not conciliar in form. The same has been true of the annual meetings of the hierarchy that have taken place regularly since the formation of the NCWC.

Bibliography: P. GUILDAY, ed., *A History of the Councils of Baltimore, 1791–1884* (New York 1932); *The National Pastorals of the American Hierarchy, 1792–1919* (Washington 1923). CollLac 3. J. D. BARRETT, *A Comparative Study of the Councils of Baltimore and the Code of Canon Law* (Washington 1932). *Concilia provincialia, Baltimori habita ab anno 1829, usque ad annum 1840* (Baltimore 1842). T. F. CASEY, *The Sacred Congregation de Propaganda Fide and the Revision of the First Provincial Council of Baltimore, 1829–30* (AnalGreg 88; Rome 1957). *Concilium plenarium totius Americae Septentrionalis Foederatae Baltimori habitum anno 1852* (Baltimore 1853). J. T. ELLIS, "The Centennial of the First Plenary Council of Baltimore," *Perspectives in American Catholicism* (Baltimore 1963). ActDecrConcPlenBaltII. J. L. SPALDING, *The Life of the Most Reverend M. J. Spalding* (New York 1873), for the Second Plenary Council. ActDecrConPlenBaltIII. J. T. ELLIS, *The Life of James Cardinal Gibbons, Archbishop of Baltimore, 1834–1921* (Milwaukee 1952), for the Third Plenary Council.

[J. HENNESEY]

BALUFFI, GAETANO, first internuncio to South America; b. Ancona, Italy, 1788; d. Imola, Italy, Nov. 11, 1866. In 1835 Gregory XVI recognized the independence of New Granada and sent Baluffi, then bishop of Bagnorea, as his first internuncio there. In 1837 Baluffi began his mission to the government of General Santander, and then extended it to several South American countries, whose relations with the Holy See had previously been conducted through Madrid. His lack of knowledge of the environment led him into unfortunate attitudes, influenced by the sectarian Catholic Society. This society was hostile to Abp. Manuel José Mosquera of Bogotá, whose policy was approved by Rome. Baluffi drafted a good proposal for a concordat, which was not approved. In 1841 he was named bishop of Camerino and apostolic administrator of Treja, and Pius IX named him bishop of Imola and a cardinal. He was the author of *La iglesia romana, conocida por su caridad al prójimo como verdadera iglesia de Jesucristo,* and *La América un tiempo española, considerada por su aspecto religioso, desde su descubrimiento hasta 1843.* The latter work was intended to make known to Europeans the political and religious situation of the republics that had won independence from Spain, but the work went down only to the causes of the revolution of 1810, and included nothing based on the author's personal experience. A book of history and apologetics, it is a bibliographical curiosity.

Bibliography: A. M. PINILLA COTE, *La internunciature de Mons. Cayetano Baluffi en Bogotá, primera en Hispanoamérica, 1837–1842* (Rome 1953). J. RESTREPO POSADA, "La obra de Mons. B.," *Conferencias de la Academia Colombiana de Historia* (Bogotá 1947).

[R. GÓMEZ HOYOS]

BALUZE, ÉTIENNE

French scholar; b. Tulle, Nov. 24, 1630; d. Paris, July 28, 1718. At 15 he was a cleric in a college in Toulouse, but he never went beyond tonsure. Ecclesiastical benefices permitted him to devote himself entirely to study. In 1652 and 1654 he had to retire to Tulle to regain his health. In 1652 he published an attack on P. Frizon's history of French cardinals (1638) that gained him scholarly recognition. He left Tulle in 1656 and went to Paris to be secretary and assistant to the archbishop of Paris, Pierre de *Marca, from whom he gained a rich knowledge of Church history and a sympathy for *Gallicanism. When De Marca died in 1662, Baluze served the archbishop of Auch briefly, leaving because he did not share the prelate's admiration of scholasticism. After sustaining nine theses of Canon Law, Gallican in sympathy, at the Sorbonne in 1665, he became librarian for J. B. *Colbert in 1667. The library of rare MSS that Baluze collected for Colbert from all Europe, later enriched the Bibliothèque Nationale. Baluze accurately transcribed about 80 volumes of material from MSS. In 1671 he had to stop

Étienne Baluze, portrait by Hyacinthe Rigaud in the Musée de Tours.

work a third time because of an eye illness. Louis XIV made him professor of Canon Law at the Collège de France in 1689. Baluze resigned as librarian for Colbert in 1700 and withdrew outside Paris. In 1710 Louis XIV exiled him from the capital because Baluze had insisted on publicizing in his *Histoire généalogique de la maison d'Auvergne* in 1709 the descent of Cardinal *Bouillon from the Dukes of Aquitaine and the Counts of Auvergne, much to the displeasure of the King. In Tours, Baluze made copies of a wealth of documents later destroyed by fire. In 1713 he was allowed to return to Paris, but without position or pension. After his death the 10,000 printed works in his library were auctioned separately, but the King purchased the 1,500 MSS, today in the Bibliothèque Nationale. Baluze was one of the greatest scholars of the age of Louis XIV.

The collection and classification of Baluze's writings, mostly in Latin, is itself a task of historical research. His 1663 Latin version of a work of Cardinal de Marca, the *De concordia sacerdotii et imperii seu de libertatibus ecclesiae gallicanae*, was put on the Index but went through five more editions. Baluze edited the works of Salvian of Marseilles; Vincent of Lerins; Lupus of Ferrières; Agobard, Leidradus, Amulo, and Florus of Lyons; Caesarius of Arles; Regino of Prüm; Antonio Agustín; Lactantius; letters of Innocent III (incomplete); and Cyprian of Carthage (completed 1726 by P. Maran). His capitularies of the French kings (2 v. 1677), in the 1780 edition of P. de Chiniac, was incorporated into Mansi's *Concilia*. In 1683 Baluze published the first volume of a new collection of councils but, perhaps fearing that his Gallican ideas might jeopardize his position, carried the work no further. In this volume he called attention to certain early councils not noted previously and, on the basis of MSS, published the most critical texts available. The mass of variant readings are useless, but the notes are exceptionally good. His lives of the Avignon popes (2 v. 1693), whom he accused of introducing immorality into Avignon, was put on the Index. G. Mollat has reedited the work (4 v. 1914–28) in line with later research and Baluze's own notes. Baluze's letters, many in French, are to important men about important matters, and some amount to official pronouncements.

Bibliography: Autobiography in *Capitularia regum Francorum* (Paris 1780). J. MARTIN, DTC 2.1:138–139. G. MOLLAT, DHGE 6:439–452; *Catholicisme* 1:1197. **Illustration credit:** Archives Photographiques.

[W. E. LANGLEY]

BALZAC, HONORÉ DE

French novelist; b. Tours, France, May 20, 1799; d. Paris, Aug. 18, 1850. He was the third child of a prosperous middle-class family, and suffered from his mother's partiality for a younger brother. From his father he inherited his exuberant and imaginative temperament. Sent to the Collège de Vendôme in 1807, he read widely, and at the time of his First Communion, seems to have experienced some sort of mystical exaltation. Moving to Paris with his parents (1814), he continued his studies and read law (1816–19), gaining practical experience in the office of Guyonnet de Merville, the model for Derville in *La Comédie humaine*. His real ambition, however, was to become a writer, and in 1819 he rented an attic room and tried his hand at literature. A vivid account of those days of struggle is included in

several of his novels. In 1822 he fell ardently in love with a woman 22 years his senior, Mme. de Berny, who exercised a decisive influence on his intellectual and moral development and remained his devoted friend until her death in 1836.

Honoré de Balzac, bronze by Auguste Rodin.

Under various pseudonyms, Balzac turned out (1821–27) a series of potboilers and sought financial success by becoming in turn a publisher, a printer, and a type founder. Failure in these ventures made him a lifelong debtor, and he turned again to literature to meet his obligations. His first important work was the historical novel *Les Chouans* (1829). It was followed by the sensational *La Physiologie du mariage* (1830), a cynical but often penetrating essay on marriage and infidelity. After the great success of *La Peau de chagrin* (1831) and until his death, Balzac devoted himself to the other novels that were to compose *La Comédie humaine*. His fame had spread throughout Europe, and in March 1832 he received a letter from an admirer who signed herself *l'Étrangère*. She turned out to be the Polish Countess Éveline Hanska. They first met in Neuchâtel, Switzerland, in 1833, and thereafter carried on an ardent correspondence in which *l'Étrangère* became his inspiration and confidante.

The Beginnings of Balzac's Masterpiece. In 1834 Balzac published *Le Père Goriot*, the keystone, as it were, of his vast edifice. The following year he conceived the fruitful idea of linking his novels by means of reappearing characters. In the famous "Avant-Propos" (1842) of *La Comédie Humaine* he not only developed this important idea but also outlined the philosophic basis, the political and religious foundations, and the organic structure of his great cycle. Three main parts—*Études de moeurs, Études philosophiques, Études analytiques*—constitute the main divisions of his ambitious project. The first and most important part is subdivided into six *Scènes*, designed to show every aspect of French life, private and political, provincial and Parisian, military and rustic.

The same *Avant-Propos* contains Balzac's vehement denial of being a materialist. "I write," he states, "in the light of two eternal truths: Religion and Monarchy.

Christianity, and especially Catholicism, being a complete system of repression of the depraved tendencies of man, is the greatest element of social order." True, as late as 1840 Balzac affirmed Swedenborgianism as his religion, and his works reflect his belief that occult mysticism and Catholicism are not contradictory (*see* SWEDENBORG, EMANUEL). But this did not satisfy him, and later he placed his hopes in the Church for which he had so often expressed admiration. He is not anticlerical, although he often misunderstands or misinterprets the role of the priest. His last novel, *L'Envers de l'histoire contemporaine* (1842–48), shows a fine understanding of the meaning of Christian charity. Further study of the religious element in his works may lead to a reconsideration of the fact that all his love stories ("omnes fabulae amatoriae") are on the Index.

The death of Count Hanska made marriage with his aristocratic mistress possible, and he worked with renewed vigor to provide her with luxury. He spent the winter (1848–49) in the Ukraine, where his marriage was celebrated in 1850. He had begun to feel great fatigue in 1844; after reaching Paris with his bride in May 1850, the heart trouble detected in 1848 proved fatal and he succumbed after receiving Extreme Unction.

Precursor of Realism. Balzac was long classed as a romantic, but 20th-century critics consider him the great precursor of the realistic school. He lacks objectivity; though his novels (many of them with fantastic themes) often reflect the influence of the tale of terror and of melodrama, their realistic qualities predominate. A powerful imagination, wedded to a rare ability to observe, enabled him to create living characters. Many of them are monomaniacs, but the intensity of their passions makes them real. His long expositions are often tedious, but they serve as a solid foundation for the action.

Balzac's style is often cumbersome and occasionally rhetorical. His descriptions and dialogues are sometimes cluttered with technical terms, but there is nearly always a harmony between subject matter and style. The style, like the structure of the novels, is solid.

The breadth and scope of Balzac's monumental work is hardly surpassed in fiction. *The Human Comedy* is a true and vivid document on the customs of a people from 1799 to 1846, and a penetrating and intensely dramatic study of human nature. Balzac's characters are at once typical and eternally true. Vautrin, the archcriminal; Goriot, Balzac's Lear; and the miser Grandet are comparable to Shakespeare's immortal creations.

Bibliography: H. DE BALZAC, *Oeuvres complètes*, ed. Société des Études balzaciennes (Paris 1956–); *La Comédie humaine*, ed. M. BOUTERON, 11 v. (Bibliothèque de la Pléiade 26–27, 30–32, 35, 38–39, 41–42, 141; Paris 1935–59). C. V. DE SPOELBERCH DE LOVENJOUL, *Histoire des oeuvres de H. de Balzac* (3d ed. rev. Paris 1888). A. BILLY, *Vie de Balzac*, 2 v. (Paris 1944). M. BARDÈCHE, *Balzac romancier* (Paris 1950). S. ROGERS, *Balzac and the Novel* (Madison 1953). W. H. ROYCE, *A Balzac Bibliography* (Chicago 1929); *Indexes to a Balzac Bibliography* (Chicago 1930). A. MAUROIS, *Prometheus: The Life of Balzac* (New York 1966). **Illustration credit:** Courtesy of the Cleveland Museum of Art.

[J. C. ALCIATORE]

BALZAC, JEAN LOUIS GUEZ DE, French writer and critic; b. Angoulême, *c.* 1595; d. Angoulême, Feb. 18, 1654. Educated in Paris and Leyden, Balzac became a disciple of the poet François de Malherbe. While representing the archbishop of Toulouse in Rome

in 1621–22, he began to write the letters for which he is most famous. The first selections were published in 1624. In *Le Prince* (1631) and *Aristippe* (1658) Balzac progressed toward a Machiavellian concept of the ruler, although he denounced wars of conquest and held men to be primarily citizens of the world, thus foreshadowing subsequent peace movements. The influence of his *Socrate chrétien* (1652) is apparent in Pascal's *Provincial Letters*. Unable to find a position at court upon his return to France from Rome, he retired to his estate near Angoulême, where he spent the rest of his life. He continued to write letters and essays, gaining the support and admiration of Richelieu and the literary and intellectual elite of Paris who met at the Hôtel Rambouillet. Balzac was one of the first members of the French Academy, and also one of the most eminent precursors of French classicism; he did for French prose what Malherbe did for French poetry. Through his criticism he formulated a prose style as orderly as that of the Romans. His own writing retained many of the florid characteristics of the 16th century, but lucidity and discipline were its dominant characteristics.

Bibliography: G. GUILLAUMIE, *Jean-Louis Guez de Balzac et la prose française* (Paris 1927). R. PINTARD, *Le Libertinage érudit dans la première moitie du XVIIᵉ siècle* (Paris 1943).

[J. M. HAYDEN]

BAMAKO, ARCHDIOCESE OF (BAMAKOËNSIS), metropolitan see since 1955, in southwest *Mali, west Africa. In 1963 it had 7 parishes, 32 priests (6 African), 51 sisters (18 African), and 15,000 Catholics and catechumens in a population of 700,000; it is 29,807 square miles in area. The suffragan See of Ségou was created in 1962, Kayes and Sikasso in 1963, and San and Mopti in 1964. In 1883 the French built a fort on the Niger River at Bamako, now the terminus of a railroad from *Dakar and capital of Mali. In 1921 the Vicariate of the French Sudan (1901), detached from the Vicariate of Sahara-Sudan (1891), was divided into the Vicariates of Bamako (until 1955) and *Ouagadougou (*Upper Volta). Later ecclesiastical jurisdictions in Mali have been detached from that of Bamako. The parish of Bamako was founded in 1923 by dividing the old mission of Kati, the first post in the Sudan (1897). In 1963 the see had 110 catechists, 11 primary schools, 2 secondary schools, a minor seminary, a technical school, 2 schools of home economics, a center of rural education, and a school for catechists; sisters cared for 4 dispensaries and a leprosarium. The laity are organized in the Legion of Mary, Family Catholic Action, and Catholic Agricultural Youth. The archbishop is a native of Mali.

Bibliography: MissCattol 108–111. G. B. TRAGELLA, EncCatt 2:766–767. AnnPont (1965) 50.

[J. R. DE BENOIST]

BAMBERG, ARCHDIOCESE OF (BAMBERGENSIS)

Metropolitan see since 1817, in Upper and Middle Franconia, with the suffragan Sees of *Eichstätt, *Speyer, and *Würzburg. It includes about 4,000 square miles in Upper and Middle Franconia. It was founded by Emperor Henry II with papal approval, Nov. 1, 1007, within the older Diocese of Würzburg. Apart from his piety, Henry was moved by the need for Christian missionary work among the immigrant Slav popu-

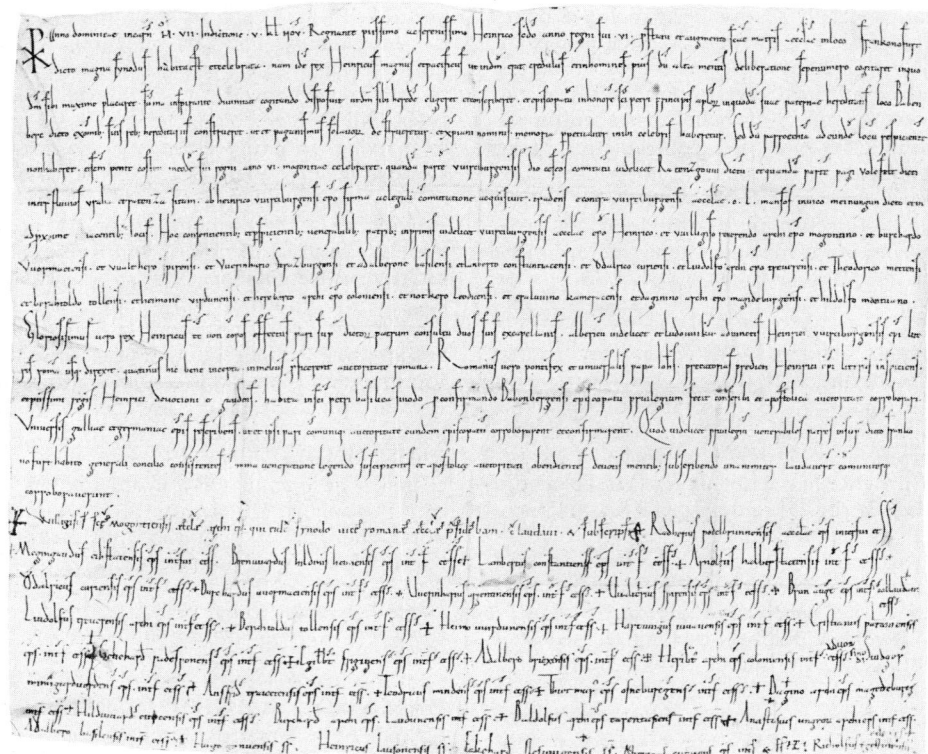

Original document creating the Diocese of Bamberg, signed at Frankfurt, Nov. 1, 1007, now in the Allgemeines Staatsarchiv, Munich (MS Bamberg Ur. 21).

lation and the need to create a political territory on the upper Main. With the Empress, Bl. *Kunigunde, he endowed the diocese, which numbered about 30 parishes, with a rich income and provided the new churches and monasteries with art treasures and valuable libraries, a good part of which are still preserved in the cathedral and the Staatsbibliothek of Bamberg. In 1053 the bishop first received the pallium. Thereafter the bishops of Bamberg filled high offices in the empire, as the see rose to prominence in the German church. Full exemption from the Archdiocese of Mainz came in the 13th century. The secular authority of the bishop of Bamberg (*Hochstift*) in the Middle Ages was about half of his spiritual jurisdiction. Noteworthy medieval bishops were Suidger, later Pope Clement II (1040–47), St. *Otto (1102–39), and *Lupold of Bebenburg (1353–63). Durandus of Liège (d. 1025), Meinhard (1065), St. *Anno of Cologne (d. 1075), Ulrich (d. 1128), *Frutolf of Michelsberg (d. 1103), Ezzo (1063), and Williram (d. 1084) studied and taught in Bamberg.

The status of the diocese was seriously threatened in the Reformation when 85 parishes outside the secular authority of the bishop were lost. A turning point was reached, however, and Catholic teaching attained its full strength under Bp. J. G. von Aschhausen (1609–22), who invited the Jesuits into the diocese. Buildings of baroque splendor arose under bishops of the House of Schönborn, Lothar Franz (1693–1729) and Friedrich Karl (1729–46), who was also vice chancellor of the empire. The reforms of Franz Ludwig von Erthal (1779–95) came to an end with the secularization of 1803, which terminated the secular authority of bishops and gave their territory to the kingdom of *Bavaria.

The see was vacant from 1805 until the Concordat of 1817, when the Church in Bavaria was reorganized. Bamberg then became an archbishopric with a larger territory. Archbishop J. Hauck (1912–43) built churches and successfully organized the pastoral care of Catholics living in Protestant areas. After 1945, in addition to rebuilding destroyed churches and providing for pastoral care, the diocese had to deal with difficulties resulting from World War II, the shifting of populations, and the proximity of the Iron Curtain. In 1955 Abp. Joseph Schneider became the 72d bishop.

The cathedral, consecrated in its present form in 1237 and built in a style transitional from Romanesque to Gothic, houses excellent works of art: the famous equestrian statue and many other pieces of sculpture (1200–50), works by T. Riemenschneider (tomb of Henry II and Kunigunde) and Veit Stoss, as well as the tombs of Clement II and Emperor Conrad III. Other important buildings are the monastery of Michelsberg (St. Otto's tomb), the old and new residence, the monastery of Banz, and the Gothic churches of St. Lorenz and St. Sebald in Nürnberg. The churches of Vierzehnheiligen and Gössweinstein (both by Balthasar *Neumann) are centers of pilgrimage.

In 1962 the archdiocese had 798,492 Catholics (39.5 per cent of the population) in 258 parishes, 575 secular and 158 religious priests, 270 men in 25 religious houses, 2,217 women in 225 convents. The diocese is administered under the archbishop by a 12-member chapter with an auxiliary bishop. The clergy is trained in a state Hochschule for philosophy and theology, the successor to the academy (1648–1773) and the university (1773–1803). There are many diocesan charitable in-

Exterior, east choir, 13th-century cathedral of Bamberg.

stitutions and Catholic organizations, as well as two journals. In 1948 the archdiocese established a foundation for the construction of dwellings.

Bibliography: J. Looshorn, *Die Geschichte des Bistums Bamberg,* 7 v. (Bamberg 1886–1910). W. R. Valentiner, *The Bamberg Rider* (Los Angeles 1956). J. Kist, *Fürst- und Erzbistum Bamberg* (Bamberg 1962); LexThK² 1:1215–17. H. Burkard, DHGE 6:457–471. *Schematismus der Geistlichkeit des Bistums Bamberg* (1963), every 2 years. AnnPont (1964) 51. **Illustration credits:** Fig. 1, Allgemeines Staatsarchiv, Munich. Fig. 2, German Information Center.

[F. DRESSLER]

BAN (ANATHEMA). The Hebrew word *ḥerem,* commonly translated "anathema" or "ban," was connected with the idea of holiness and exclusion. Whatever was *ḥerem* was withdrawn from ordinary use and consecrated to God. From the same root, the Arabic word *ḥarām* signifies what is set aside as sacred, e.g., the Temple area in Jerusalem, the precincts of Mecca. In the Septuagint *ḥerem* is rendered by ἀνάθημα.

Originally *ḥerem* belonged to the ritual of the holy war [*see* WAR (IN THE BIBLE)], whence it gradually took on different shades of meaning. *Ḥerem,* as a part of holy war, meant consecrating to God the fruits of victory in return for God's help in conquering the enemy (Nm 21.1–3; Jos 6.17–21; 7.1, 10–26; Jgs 1.17; 1 Sm 15.1–33). Yahweh was the Lord of the armies of Israel (1 Sm 17.45); Israel's wars were, thus, those of Yahweh (Ex 17.16; 1 Sm 25.28; Jgs 5.23).

Complete *ḥerem* demanded the disposal of all living (Dt 20.16) and non-living things (Dt 13.17). Achan's transgression of a complete *ḥerem* brought death to himself and his entire family (Jos 7.10–25). In 1 Sm 15.16–33, Samuel berated Saul for not observing the *ḥerem* against the *Amalecites. Sometimes exempted

from the destruction imposed by the ban were women and children (Nm 31.7–12; Dt 21.10–14), virgins (Nm 31.17–18; Jgs 21.11–12), and farm animals (Dt 2.34–35; 3.6–7).

In prophetic circles of the Northern Kingdom and in Deuteronomy *ḥerem* was given a new theological meaning: it referred to the destruction of God's enemies in order to safeguard the religious purity of Yahwism. Thus, the reason for *ḥerem,* according to the *Deuteronomists, was to preclude temptations to idolatry and syncretism by the extermination of the Canaanites (Dt 7.1–6; 20.15–18). Similarly, individuals (Ex 22.19) and even cities (Dt 13.13–19) were to be destroyed for fear of religious pollution. Because of this theological reinterpretation many scholars doubt whether such a severe penalty was always exacted.

Ban as a vow differed from an ordinary vow in that the vowed object became so completely God's that it could not be exchanged for a monetary equivalent (Lv 27.28); the banned object could, however, be used by the clergy (Lv 27.21; Nm 18.14; Ez 44.29).

In postexilic times *ḥerem* came to signify confiscation of goods and exclusion from the community (Ezr 10.7–8). This idea later developed, in Judaism and the Christian Church, into the concept basic to *excommunication.

Bibliography: De Vaux AncIsr 258–265. EncDictBibl 195–197. H. Gross, LexThK² 1:1225–27. F. Horst, RGG³ 1:860–861. B. Mariani, EncCatt 1:1159. F. Vigouroux, DB 1.1:545–550. J. Behm, Kittel ThW 1:356–357.

[E. J. CIUBA]

BANDELIER, ADOLPH, archeologist, author; b. Berne, Switzerland, Aug. 6, 1840; d. Seville, Spain, March 18, 1914. His father was a Swiss soldier and jurist; his mother was Russian. In 1855, after the family had immigrated (1848) to a Swiss community at Highland, Ill., Bandelier returned to study at the University of Berne. Back in Highland, he worked in a bank founded by his father until the 1870s, when he took up the study of anthropology and became associated with the Peabody Museum at Harvard University. He produced a series of works on ancient Mexico: *Art of War and Mode of Warfare* (1877), *Distribution and Tenure of Land* (1878), and *Social Organization and Mode of Government* (1879). In 1880 the newly organized Archaeological Institute sent him to New Mexico, where his study of Indian society and culture led to the publication of his *Indians of the Southwestern U.S.* (2 v. 1890–92) and *Contributions of the Southwestern Portions of the U.S.* (1890). These pioneer studies and his investigations in Peru and Bolivia laid the foundations for later research in American archeology. In 1891 he was converted to Catholicism, and 2 years later he married Fanny Ritter of Zurich, Switzerland.

After 10 years (1893–1903) of exploring in the highlands of Peru, investigating Bolivian archives, and studying in the private libraries of La Paz, Bandelier returned to the U.S. to work in the Museum of Natural History, New York City, and to lecture on Spanish-American literature at Columbia University. After becoming almost totally blind with cataracts, he produced his last books, *The Islands of Titicaca and Koati* (1910) and *The Ruins of Tiahuanaca in Bolivia* (1912), with the aid of his wife. In 1911 he was appointed research associate for archival research in Spain. He carried out preliminary work in Mexico before going to Seville, where he died.

Bandelier depended chiefly on archival sources, checked against a thorough study of archeological materials and the collection of legendary data from surviving aborigines. His work tended to discredit romantic conceptions of American Indian history and led the way to critical scientific research. Later scholars, however, have largely rejected Bandelier's own conclusions on many points, including the nature of Aztec society and government.

Bibliography: A. V. KIDDER, DAB (1928) 1:571–572.

[J. L. MORRISON]

BÁÑEZ AND BAÑEZIANISM

Domingo Báñez (originally Banes or Vañez) was a Spanish Dominican theologian of major stature. The son of Juan Báñez of Mondragon, he was born on Feb. 29, 1528, in Valladolid; at an early age he moved with his family to Medina del Campo in what was then Old Castile, and died there on Oct. 22, 1604. He began his studies in the arts and philosophy at Salamanca at the age of 15; and there, 3 years later, in the spring of 1546, he received the Dominican habit at San Esteban's, where, on May 3, 1547, he made his religious profession. At Salamanca he studied under such renowned theologians as Bartolomé de Medina and Melchior Cano, was for a time master of students, and began his teaching career under Domingo de Soto as prior and regent. From 1561 to 1566 Báñez taught at Avila; in 1567 he occupied the chair of theology at Alcalá. He returned to Salamanca during 1572–73 and was regent of San Gregorio's at Valladolid from 1573 until 1577. Then, when De Medina advanced to the chief professorship, he assumed the so-called Durandus chair of theology at Salamanca from 1577 to 1580; on De Medina's death in 1580, Báñez was appointed his successor, a position he held for 20 years.

Relationship with St. Teresa of Avila. Of major significance in the life of Báñez is the influence he exerted upon St. *Teresa of Avila. He first came in contact with her in 1562, and thenceforward, until her death in 1582, he served as her confessor and spiritual director. How meaningful this relationship was, St. Teresa suggests in her own words, saying of Báñez that ". . . it is with him that she has held, and still holds, the most frequent communication" [*The Spiritual Relations* 4, in *The Complete Works of St. Teresa of Avila*, 3 v., tr. E. A. Peers (New York 1946) 1:323–324]. Even before actually meeting the saint, Báñez alone defended her first reform foundation, that of San José in Avila, when civil and ecclesiastical authorities had summoned a *junta,* which was on the verge of recommending dissolution of the new convent. Teresa herself writes, "There was only one of them, a Presentado of the Order of St. Dominic, who was not opposed to the convent, though he objected to its poverty: he said that there was no reason for dissolving it . . ." (*Life of the Holy Mother Teresa of Jesus by Herself,* in *op. cit.* 1:254). Báñez's own words are quoted from the *Cronica carmelitana* by F. Martin, OP [*Santa Teresa y la Orden de Predicadores* (Ávila 1909) 275–277].

Nearly all the correspondence between them has been lost; only four letters of the saint to Báñez and one of his letters to her are extant. He did carefully read over her *Vida,* or autobiography; and when years after its completion it was denounced to the Holy Office in Madrid in 1574, Báñez sent his own copy to the Holy Office with a vigorous vindication appended to the blank pages at the end of the volume, which judgment the Holy Office made its own. It was also at Báñez's suggestion that the saint wrote her *Way of Perfection.* He also gave deposition to the preparatory commission for Teresa's canonization. This holy association most probably accounts for a Thomistic cast of mind that underlies her spirituality. At any rate, Báñez did discern the work of God in her in spite of her exaggerated accounts of her own sins and his own acknowledged suspicions concerning her mystical visions and locutions. The image of him that emerges from St. Teresa's writings is of a learned man who was at the same time discreet and judicious, inclined to be firm and unbending with her, and counseling above all patience and charity toward those who persecuted her.

Disputes on Grace. The late 15th and the 16th centuries saw a revival of *scholasticism, especially in Spain, where Renaissance culture and the religious ferment of the Reformation were not strongly felt. The revival was dominated for the most part by illustrious Dominican theologians such as F. de Vitoria, M. Cano, D. de Soto, B. de Medina, and finally Báñez; it received further impetus from the Council of Trent, summoned in 1545. In 1540 the Society of Jesus was founded, and, officially adopting the theological system of St. Thomas, the society soon entered into the academic life of the period. In Salamanca in 1582 the first phase in an unrivaled theological controversy occurred. In a public disputation conducted by the Mercederian priest Francisco Zumel, Prudentius Montemayor, a Jesuit, defended the proposition that Christ, acting in obedience to His Father's command, died neither freely nor meritoriously. (*See* MANDATE, PROBLEM OF.) Supporting him on this was an Augustinian, Louis of León. This occasioned a strong reaction from the faculty at Salamanca, in particular from Báñez. Further debate resulted, culminating in the matter's being brought before the Inquisition, where on Feb. 3, 1584, judgment was pronounced against Montemayor and León. By this time the area of disagreement had broadened and 16 distinct propositions were condemned, among which were the following:

6. "God is not the cause of the free operation but only causes the cause to be."

9. "The providence of God does not determine the human will or any other particular cause to operate well, but rather the particular cause determines the act of divine providence."

13. "The impious man in his justification determines the sufficient help of God to actual use by his own will."

The second phase of the controversy occurred in 1588 with the publication in Lisbon of the first edition of the *Concordia liberi arbitrii cum gratiae donis, divina praescientia, providentia, praedestinatione et reprobatione* of Luis de *Molina, SJ. The Inquisitor General of Portugal, Cardinal Albert of Austria, withheld distribution of the book pending the theological evaluation of Báñez, whom he had appointed as censor. It was the latter's opinion that Molina was giving restatement to six of the already condemned propositions of the pre-Molinists. Presented with these objections, Molina wrote a defense of himself, and in August 1589 the *Concordia* was given an imprimatur and published with the defense as an appendix. The resulting agitations grew to alarming proportions, especially in the public debates between the Jesuits and Dominicans in March and May of 1594 in Valladolid, until in August of that year the papal nuncio at Madrid imposed silence on the disputants and delated the matter to Rome. Molina sought to defend himself by denouncing Báñez to the Inquisition at Castile. Báñez replied with the publication in 1595 of *Apologia fratrum praedicatorum in provincia hispaniae sacrae theologiae professorum, adversus novas quasdam assertiones cuiusdam doctoris Ludovici Molinae nuncupati,* in joint authorship with P. Herrera and D. Alvarez, both Dominicans. This was followed by the *Libellus supplex* in October 1597, a letter (for text see De Meyer) addressed by Báñez to Pope Clement VIII seeking dissolution of the silence imposed in 1594. This was granted in February 1598 in a letter of Cardinal C. Madruzzi writing in behalf of the Pope to the nuncio. Báñez's active participation ceased at this point; the *Congregatio de Auxiliis,* begun in Rome in 1598, extended over two pontificates until 1607, 3 years after Báñez's death. It failed to resolve the dispute, choosing not to define either position as the true doctrine of the Church and granting each side freedom to teach in accord with its own interpretation.

The Charge of Bañezianism. Molina's central doctrinal assertion was that God's graces are rendered efficacious (*see* GRACE, EFFICACIOUS) by the actual consent of the human will. God's infallible foreknowledge is safeguarded by recourse to a hypothesis, admittedly original with himself, namely, that there is in God a *scientia media,* or intermediate knowledge, whereby God foreknows what every man will choose in varying circumstances, before the will determines itself and independently of any divine *predetermination. Primary among the conclusions flowing from this is that God predestines those whom He foresees as consenting to His grace.

Báñez took immediate exception to this, seeing therein a rejection of the traditional teaching, founded in St. Augustine and St. Thomas, wherein grace is intrinsically efficacious as itself effecting the will's free consent, so that predestination is ultimately gratuitous rather than dependent upon foreseen merits. *See* PREDESTINATION (IN CATHOLIC THEOLOGY).

Historically, the countercharge was made that Báñez himself was an innovator; that such concepts as physical *premotion, intrinsically efficacious grace, and predestination completely apart from foreseen merits represent but one interpretation of St. Thomas; and that such Thomism is in reality Bañezianism [cf. G. Schneemann, SJ, *Controversiarum de divinae gratiae liberique arbitrii concordia initia et progressus* (Freiburg 1881) and T. de Régnon, SJ, *Báñez et Molina* (Paris 1883)]. This allegation has been rigorously refuted [cf. A. M. Dummermuth, OP, *Defensio doctrinae s. Thomae* (Louvain and Paris, 1895); and Cardinal T. Zigliara, OP, *Summa philosophica* (Paris 1898) 2:525]. The attribution to Báñez even among authors of the Molinist school is by no means universal; F. Suárez points rather to De Medina as the author of physical premotion (*De auxiliis* 7.2; Vivès 11:183), even at one point assigning the doctrine to St. Thomas (*De concursu Dei cum voluntate* 11.6; Vivès 11:50); Victor Frins, SJ, in his reply to Dummermuth traces the teaching back to F. de Vitoria.

With the waning of the controversy, there seems little doubt on the point of Báñez's fidelity to St. Thomas.

His own intentions were very clear as is evident from his autobiographical prologue to his commentary on the *Prima pars.* The judgment of Cardinal Madruzzi corroborates this: "His teaching seems to be deduced from the principles of St. Thomas and to flow wholly from St. Thomas's doctrine, though he differs somewhat in his mode of speaking" (J. H. Serry, appendix 89). The equivalent of what he taught can be found in St. Thomas, as, for example, the intrinsic efficacy of grace (*De ver.* 6.2 ad 11). The very difficulties raised by the Molinist position and the new doctrines of the reformers, as well as Báñez's polemical intentions, account for the variations in language. Contemporary Thomistic thought does tend to mitigate somewhat the rigidity of his vocabulary [e.g., F. Marín-Sola, OP, *Concordia tomista entre la mocion divina y la libertad creada,* 3 v. (Salamanca 1958) and F. P. Muñiz, OP, "Es posible una predestinación gratuita post praevisa merita?" *La ciencia tomista* 73 (1947) 105–115], but this is a matter of emphasis and development, not rejection. Doctrinally, he stands in the main stream of Thomism linked both to his predecessors and to his successors.

Viewed from the vantage point of 400 years of history, two reflections suggest themselves: (1) that the disputes were excessively negative and partisan, perhaps hindering intellectual effort of a more positive nature; and (2) that, on the other hand, questions of great import and urgency were raised that had to be dealt with and that were profoundly clarified, if not resolved.

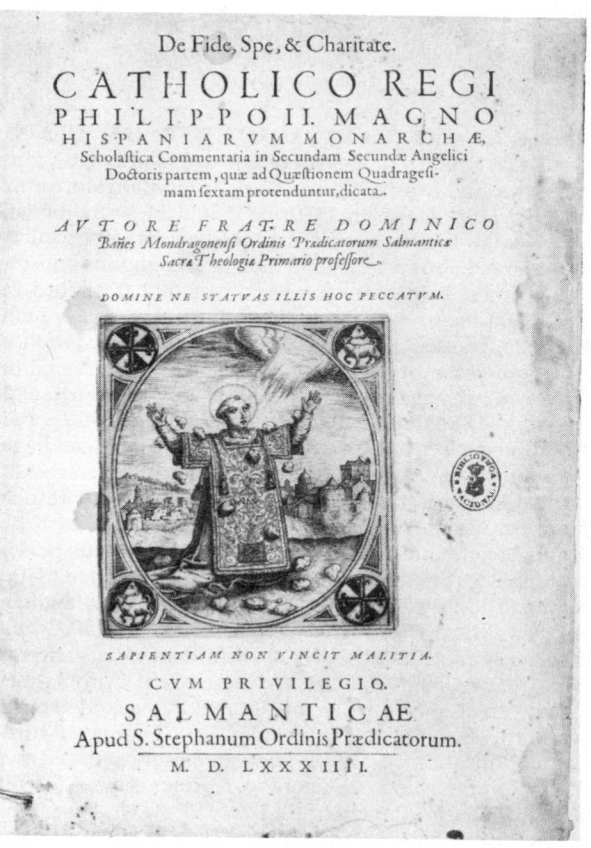

Title page of Domingo Báñez's "De fide, spe, et charitate," a commentary on St. Thomas Aquinas's ST 2a2ae. The page features a dedication to King Philip II and a picture of the martyrdom of St. Stephen, patron of the Dominican foundation in Salamanca, publisher of the volume.

Báñez's Writings. Báñez's depth and clarity earn him a deserved place in the forefront of St. Thomas's great commentators, a reputation that rests largely upon the following works. Scholastic commentaries: *In 1am Partem divi Thomae,* qq. 1–64 (Salamanca 1584); qq. 65–119 (1588); *In 2am2ae Partem,* qq. 1–46 (1584); qq. 47–189 (1594); (the following commentaries have been newly translated by V. Beltrán de Heredia, OP) *In 1am2ae Partem—De fine ultimo et de actibus humanis, De vitiis et peccatis, De gratia* (Salamanca 1942–48); *In 3am Partem—De Verbo incarnato, De sacramentis* (Salamanca 1951–53). Other works: *Relectio de merito et augmento caritatis* (Salamanca 1590); *Institutiones minoris dialecticae* (Salamanca 1599); *Comment. in Libros de generatione et corruptione* (Salamanca 1585).

See also CONGRUISM; FREE WILL AND GRACE; FREE WILL AND PROVIDENCE; FUTURIBLE; GRACE, ARTICLES ON; GRACE, CONTROVERSIES ON; MOLINISM; OMNISCIENCE; PERSEVERANCE, FINAL; PREDEFINITION; REPROBATION; WILL OF GOD.

Bibliography: P. MANDONNET, DTC 2.1:140–145. A. DUVAL, *Catholicisme* 1:1202–04. C. VELECKY, Davis CDT 1:227–228. U. VIGLINO, EncCatt 2:784–785. L. DE MEYER, *Historia controversiarum de divinae gratiae auxiliis* (Venice 1742). N. DEL PRADO, *De gratia et libero arbitrio,* 3 v. (Fribourg 1907). R. GARRIGOU-LAGRANGE, *God: His Existence and His Nature,* tr. B. ROSE, 2 v. (St. Louis 1934–36), see app. T. DE LEMOS, *Panoplia gratiae,* 4 v. in 2 (Liège 1676). M. LÉPÉE, *Báñez et Ste. Thérèse* (Paris 1947). Quétif-Échard 2.1:352–353. J. H. SERRY, *Historia congregationum de auxiliis divinae gratiae* (Venice 1740). D. BÁÑEZ, *Scholastica commentaria in primam partem* (Madrid 1934), prologue to 4 v. ed. of L. URBANO. V. BELTRÁN DE HEREDIA, LexThK² 1:1219–20; in *La ciencia tomista* 25–28 (1922–23); 37–39 (1928–29); 47 (1933). **Illustration credit:** MAS, Barcelona.

[W. J. HILL]

BANGALORE, ARCHDIOCESE OF (BANGALORENSIS), metropolitan see since 1953, in Mysore state, south *India. The city of Bangalore was taken by the British in 1791. In 1962 the archdiocese, 9,056 square miles in area, had 42 parishes, 94 secular and 136 religious priests, 203 men in 10 religious houses, 718 women in 47 convents, and 105,000 Catholics in a population of 6 million. Its four suffragans, which had 325 priests, 1,226 sisters, and 257,000 Catholics in a population of 10 million, were: Bellary (created in 1949), Chikmagalur (1963), Mangalore (1886), and Mysore (1886). Although Dominicans (*c.* 1350) and Franciscans (*c.* 1600) visited Mysore and may have come to Bangalore, the first Christian converts of Bangalore were made in the south and west by Jesuits from Mysore (1644) and in the north and east by Jesuits from the Carnatic (1702). During the persecution of Christians by the anti-British Sultan Tipu Sahib (1782–99), the *Paris Foreign Mission Society entered. Missionary activity increased after 1850, when Bangalore was made part of the new Vicariate of Mysore, detached from the Vicariate of the Coromandel Coast. In 1940 the See of Bangalore was detached from the See of Mysore; under Bp. Thomas Pothacamury (1942–   ) Indian secular clergy replaced the Paris Foreign Mission Society. A regional synod (1887) and a plenary council of India (1950) were held in Bangalore, which has a major and a minor seminary and two university colleges.

Bibliography: T. POTHACAMURY, *The Church in Independent India* (Bombay 1961). *The Catholic Directory of India, 1962* (Allahabad, India 1962). AnnPont (1965) 52.

[E. R. HAMBYE]

BANGOR, ABBEYS OF, three former Celtic abbeys of this name.

Bangor Fawr yn Arfon, on the eastern side of Menai Straits, Caernarvonshire, Wales, was founded by St. Deiniol in the 6th century and became the seat of the ancient See of *Bangor.

Bangor-ys-coed, in Powys, Wales, on the river Dee, some 12 miles south of Chester, England, is noted for its abbot Dunot (Donatus), who was one of the 7 native British bishops who met *Augustine of Canterbury in the second conference held between the Christian Britons and the missionaries from Rome. The meeting was a failure, and *Bede (*Hist. eccl.* 2.2) relates that the monks of Bangor were massacred by the Saxons under King Ethelfrid of Northumbria, in what was for the Britons the disastrous Battle of Chester (616). The number of monks slain is given at 1,200, which indicates a monastery of exceptional size and importance. However, it had a far more modest status in the succeeding centuries.

Bangor in the Ards of Ulster, County Down, Ireland, was founded *c.* 555 by St. *Comgall, who received his religious formation from St. *Fintan of Clonenagh in Leix. The observance in Clonenagh was noted for its severity, and it was this exceptionally hard rule that, through Bangor and *Luxeuil, became the Irish rule known on the Continent of Europe. It was Comgall who helped (St.) *Columba of Iona convert the Picts of Scotland and then sent (St.) *Columban with 12 companions to help restore religious life in Merovingian Gaul. The writings of Columban and the liturgical manuscript known as the Antiphonary of Bangor (compiled 680–691), now in the Ambrosian Library, Milan, bear witness to the excellence of the monastic school. The Antiphonary contains *Sancti venite, Christi corpus sumite,* said to be the oldest Eucharistic hymn in existence. Comgall's vita claims that the Bangor community numbered 3,000, a statement repeated by *Bernard of Clairvaux in his life of St. *Malachy of Armagh (d. 1148). Bangor suffered severely at the hands of the Vikings; Malachy's revival met with only limited success. Later, Franciscans and Augustians occupied the buildings. Only ruins remain.

Bibliography: *The Antiphonary,* ed. F. E. WARREN, 2 v. (HBradshSoc 4; 1893–95). *The Annals of Ulster,* ed. and tr. W. M. HENNESSEY and B. MACCARTHY, 4 v. (Dublin 1887–1901). R. GRAHAM, DHGE 6:502. F. O'BRIAIN, *ibid.* 6:497–502.

[J. RYAN]

BANGOR, ANCIENT SEE OF, one of the four ancient Welsh dioceses growing out of the monastery of *Bangor, Caernarvonshire, traditionally founded by St. Deiniol in the 6th century. Because *Wales was converted by Celtic monk missionaries of the "Age of Saints," Bangor, like other Welsh dioceses, was at first nonterritorial in character and depended on the affiliation of daughter churches to monastic mother churches in Gwynedd (northwest Wales). Chance very largely determined which of the leading Welsh monasteries should become permanent ecclesiastical sees. In 768 Elfodd, often called bishop of Bangor (more strictly, chief bishop of Gwynedd), took the lead in securing recognition of papal authority by the Welsh Church. After the Norman Conquest the boundaries of Bangor, which covered, broadly speaking, the modern counties of Anglesey, Caernarvon, and Merioneth, were delimited; and there were attempts to get Norman bishops elected and an oath of canonical obedience made to

*Canterbury. But the counter influence of the powerful native princes of Gwynedd usually sufficed to ensure the election of their own Welsh nominees. Even after the Edwardian Conquest (1282–83), and until late in the 14th century, the bishops chosen, often by papal *provision, were usually Welsh. Thereafter, the bishops were ordinarily royal nominees, frequently royal confessors and friars. The cathedral at Bangor was rebuilt by Bishop Anian (1267–1305), who cooperated closely with Abp. *John Peckham. A fine *pontifical belonging to Anian is still preserved at Bangor, and bishops' registers survive from the 16th century. The cathedral was partly destroyed during the Glyn Dŵr Rebellion (1400–10). It remained in ruinous condition for most of the 15th century, when successive bishops complained of the extreme poverty of the see, rated in *Valor ecclesiasticus* at £131—the poorest in England and Wales. Bp. Henry *Deane began the work of rebuilding, which was completed by Bishop Skeffington (1509–33). In 1558 Bangor's last Roman Catholic bishop-elect, Morys Clynnog, went into exile in Italy. Today Bangor is one of the six dioceses of the Church of Wales.

See also LLANDAFF, ANCIENT SEE OF; SAINT ASAPH, ANCIENT SEE OF; SAINT DAVIDS, ANCIENT SEE OF.

Bibliography: *A Bibliography of the History of Wales* (2d ed. Cardiff 1962). J. C. DAVIES, *Episcopal Acts Relating to Welsh Dioceses, 1066–1272,* 2 v. (Cardiff 1946–48). G. WILLIAMS, *The Welsh Church from Conquest to Reformation* (Cardiff 1962).

[G. WILLIAMS]

BANGUI, ARCHDIOCESE OF (BANGUENSIS)

BANGUI, ARCHDIOCESE OF (BANGUENSIS), metropolitan see since 1955, in southeast *Central African Republic, central Africa. In 1963 it had 13 secular and 54 religious priests, 74 men in 24 religious houses, 103 women in 19 convents, and 100,000 Catholics in a population of 500,000; it is 124,251 square miles in area. Its suffragans are Bangassou (created in 1964), Berberati (1955), and Bossangoa (1964). Bangui, on the right bank of the Ubangi River, the capital of the country, doubled its population to 80,000 (1951–63). From the Vicariate of the Upper Congo and Ubangi (1894), now *Brazzaville, was detached the Prefecture of Ubangi-Chari (1909), made a vicariate (1937–55), called Bangui when the Capuchin Prefecture of Berberati was detached (1940). Prosper Augouard, the great missionary-explorer of the Congo, founded a mission near Bangui in hostile country raided by slave traders (1894); but missions did not penetrate north until 1914 and began to thrive only after World War I.

Bibliography: MissCattol 127. G. TRAGELLA, EncCatt 2:788. AnnPont (1964) 52. *Bilan du Monde* 2.206–210.

[J. LE GALL]

BANKRUPTCY

Generally understood to be the process of reducing all the assets of an insolvent debtor to cash and the payment of such cash, after deducting expenses, to the creditors of the debtor in the order of their legal entitlement. Usually, such payments—if there be any at all—are a small fraction of the debt owed. Moreover, the debtor is absolved of further legal responsibility to pay debts properly discharged in bankruptcy.

Bankruptcy laws of the U.S. may be traced to England, where in 1542 during the reign of Henry VIII, the first bankruptcy act was enacted. The U.S. Constitution, in Article 1, section 8, clause 4, specifically gives Congress the power to legislate uniformly concerning bankruptcy throughout the U.S. Originally, the U.S. laws, patterned after the English statutes, provided only for creditor seizure of assets for equitable distribution among creditors, but in its development, the U.S. law has increasingly been concerned with debtor rehabilitation, reorganization, or discharge procedures.

The U.S. has a comprehensive Federal Bankruptcy Act covering voluntary and involuntary proceedings relating to individuals, corporations, and other legal persons; it also includes, among others, chapters on liquidation of assets, corporate reorganization, compositions and arrangements, wage-earner plans, and railroad reorganizations.

Depressions brought many debtor-creditor cases to the Bankruptcy Courts, and court decisions provided refinements in the statutory scheme or showed defects in the law. Inevitably, major changes in bankruptcy law were made after depressions, the last having appeared in 1938. Amendments since that time have been relatively minor.

The bankruptcy law is a device for creditors to seize and divide a debtor's assets swiftly, rather than see them dissipated, and thus it is founded in the virtue of justice. At the same time a procedure is provided for the relief and rehabilitation of persons in financial distress, and as such, the law is founded in charity. Thus, it is a law for the benefit of both creditors and debtors.

Moral theologians have stated that the legal discharge from debts relieves the debtor also of moral obligation in the matter. Fathers Healey and Meara, for example, state:

> The civil law also extinguishes such debts *in conscience* because the law is enacted for the common good and businessmen know the law and willingly assume the risk of losses because of the bankruptcy of those with whom they deal. [*Moral Guidance,* 210.]

In general, it may be said that bankruptcy laws are social laws having as their purpose the protection of creditors and debtors and the facilitation of credit and commercial transactions by assuring fairness to both parties in the event of financial distress.

Bibliography: *United States Code Annotated,* Title 11, *Bankruptcy* (St. Paul 1953). AmJur 9 (1963) *Bankruptcy.* H. REMINGTON, *A Treatise on the Bankruptcy Laws of the United States* (6th ed. Rochester, N.Y. 1955–) kept up to date with pocket supplements. E. F. HEALEY, *Moral Guidance,* rev. J. F. MEARA (Chicago 1960). H. DAVIS, *Moral and Pastoral Theology,* rev. and enl. L. W. GEDDES, 4 v. (New York 1958) v.2.

[J. L. HAWKINS]

BANNER

Like the Latin *vexillum,* the word "banner" denotes two types of emblem: a recognition sign in battle or a symbol of victory, investiture, and power. Perhaps the older of the two is derived from the classical *signum* and its Christianized equivalent, the *labarum* of *Constantine I the Great: a staff tipped by a plastic figure (cross or statue) with a short oblong of cloth fastened to a traverse bar below it. It can be recognized in the *crux altissima in quodam plaustro erecto et rubeo vexillo decorata,* under which "the faithful of St. Peter" fought against *Henry IV (1086) and in the banner of St. Peter (see below), described by *Simeon of Durham (1138). The second type is the early medieval gonfalon or flag, frequently with tails or, later, streamers, whereby the side edge of the cloth is immediately attached to the staff. It occurs several times on the *Bayeux tapestry (*c.* 1080). Ancient Christianity recognized only the

Blessing of banners, miniature in a 15th-century English manuscript (MS Tiberius B.VIII, fol. 73r).

cross as the sign of Christ's victory over the world; hence throughout the Middle Ages *vexillum* was frequently used for the cross alone. By the 9th century the *Ecclesia* was represented holding a banner, and soon so also was the risen Christ. Blessing of battle banners was customary in Byzantium before it was recorded in the West. Church banners go back to at least the 10th century; an early miniature occurs in the Prümm troper (*c.* 1000), now in the Bibliothèque Nationale, Paris. Banners symbolized victory and the protection of a saint—*Benedict, *Denis of Paris (oriflamme), *George, Hermachoras of Venice, *James the Elder (Zebedee), *Martin of Tours—and were used for processions of all kinds, on gravesides, and as decoration of altars and churches. Early references occur in the testament of Leofric of Exeter (1072) and in the decreta of *Lanfranc (1067–89).

The banner of the Apostolic See (*vexillum s. Petri*) has a special place in the history of Western Christianity. It is first mentioned under *Benedict IX in 1044 for the campaign of *Henry III against the pagan reaction in Hungary. In presenting his own banner to the emperor, the Pope made this campaign into a holy war, a kind of crusade. With the reign of *Nicholas II begins the long list of papal gonfaloniers (*vexilliferi*), opening in 1059 with William of Montreuil. *Alexander II presented three banners: to *Roger I of Sicily to encourage him in his struggle against the Saracens, to *Erlembald, captain of Milan and leader of the reform party (d. 1075), and to *William I the Conqueror for his expedition to England. They were all banners of the gonfalon type with tails. The type is depicted twice on the Bayeux tapestry: a yellow or gold cross formée on a white or silver ground, cantoned by four disks, and a border. A schola or guild of *bandularii* is mentioned from the late 12th century in the *ordines* of Albinus, Savelli, Stefaneschi, etc. At papal processions 12 banners (*bandora*) were carried before the pope's cross.

A new development of the papal standard took place during the reign of *Innocent III, who sent his flag to the Czar of the Bulgars and Vlacks with a letter explaining its symbolism. Henceforth the papal flag bore a cross and the keys of St. Peter. Papal banners of this type can still be seen on the loggia of the pope's palace (1267) and on a diploma by Bernardo Cucuico (1316), both at Viterbo. The blessing of banners is found in many medieval Pontificals, including those of the papal court and of William *Duranti the Elder, and in the Roman Pontifical of Clement VIII, etc., almost always in connection with the blessing of a knight. By recognizing only procession banners of the first type, the modern *Rituale Romanum* is unrepresentative of the practice of both the past and present.

Bibliography: J. BRAUN, *Die liturgischen Paramente* (2d ed. Freiburg 1924). D. L. GALBREATH, *Papal Heraldry,* v.1 of *A Treatise on Ecclesiastical Heraldry* (Cambridge, Eng. 1930–   ). C. ERDMANN, "Das Wappen und die Fahne der römischen Kirche," QuellForschItalArchBibl 22 (1930–31) 227–255; "Kaiserliche und päpstliche Fahnen im hohen Mittelalter," *ibid.* 25 (1933–34) 1–48). A. GÜTTICH, *Zur Geschichte der Fahnen und Flaggen* (Cologne 1939). P. E. SCHRAMM, "Sacerdotium und Regnum . . .," StGreg 2 (1947) 403–457; *Herrschaftszeichen und Staatssymbolik,* 3 v. (Schriften der Monumenta Germaniae Historica 13; Stuttgart 1954–56) 2:643–673. **Illustration credit:** Courtesy of the Trustees of the British Museum.

[S. J. P. VAN DIJK]

BANNISTER, HENRY MARRIOTT, hymnologist, authority on medieval music notation and *sequence; b. Oxford, England, March 18, 1854; d. Oxford, Feb. 16, 1919. After studies at Epsom College and at Pembroke College, Oxford (M.A. 1877), he was ordained Anglican deacon in 1877 and priest, 1878. Following several pastoral appointments in England and in Queensland, Australia (1887–92), he concentrated on medieval music, working at Oxford and in Rome, where he was especially close to the Vatican librarian, Achille Ratti (later Pope *Pius XI). During World War I he remained at Oxford, and took the D.Litt. degree in 1915 while serving as sublibrarian of the Bodleian. He published many scholarly articles, edited *Monumenti vaticani di paleografia musicale latina* (1913) and *Missale Gothicum* (1917–19), and was co-editor of volumes 40 to 55 of *Analecta Hymnica Medii Aevi,* whose last volume (55) contains a tribute by Clemens *Blume (xii–xiii). Bannister's investigations demonstrated that the original home of the sequence was in northern France [see introduction to v.53, *Analecta Hymnica;* also *Anglo-French Sequelae,* ed. A. Hughes from the papers of Bannister (1934)]. His papers, including well over 1,100 sequences, are preserved in the Bodleian.

Bibliography: B. STÄBLEIN, MusGG 1:1213–15. Y. DELAPORT, RevGrég 5 (1920) 73–76. Baker 82–83.

[L. ELLINWOOD]

BANNON, JOHN B., military chaplain, Confederate commissioner; b. Roosky, County Roscommon, Ireland, Dec. 28, 1829; d. Dublin, Ireland, July 14, 1913. Following his ordination at Maynooth, Ireland, in 1853, he came to St. Louis, Mo., where he served at St. Louis Cathedral and the Immaculate Conception Church. In 1858 he was made pastor of St. John's parish and immediately began the construction of a new church, which was completed in 1860. With the outbreak of the Civil War, St. Louis was divided in its loyalty. Many of Bannon's parishioners joined the Confederate forces under Gen. Sterling Price at Springfield, Mo. Without obtaining permission from his bishop, Bannon left his newly built church and in January 1862 began serving as a chaplain to the Confederate forces under Price. He was on the battlefields of Pea Ridge, Iuka, Corinth, Fort Gibson, and Vicksburg, winning the respect of all religious groups. He was granted a commission as chaplain, Feb. 12, 1863. Later in the same year, he was released from the Confederate army and appointed Confederate commissioner to Ireland. His task was to win friends for the South among the Irish. He enjoyed some success in explaining the Confederate cause as he wrote letters to the leading newspapers, prepared articles for magazines, and distributed thousands of handbills throughout Ireland. When Bp. Patrick Lynch of Charleston, S.C., visited Europe as Confederate commissioner in 1864, Bannon accompanied him to Rome. Their efforts to obtain papal recognition of the Confederacy were unsuccessful. After returning to Ireland, Bannon entered the Society of Jesus on Jan. 9, 1865, and made his final vows on Feb. 2, 1876. He served at St. Ignatius University College Church, Dublin, and St. Francis Xavier, Dublin, where for a while he was superior.

Bibliography: J. E. ROTHENSTEINER, *History of the Archdiocese of St. Louis,* 2 v. (St. Louis 1928). L. F. STOCK, "Catholic Participation in the Diplomacy of the Southern Confederacy," Cath HistRev 16 (1930) 1–18.

[A. PLAISANCE]

BANNS (CANON LAW)

The banns of Matrimony are public announcements made by the parish priest to his congregation that two clearly identified persons intend to contract marriage with one another. The purpose of this publication is to uncover any impediment that might exist to the proposed marriage. If any one of the faithful is aware of any such impediment he has a serious obligation to make this known before the marriage takes place. This obligation does not bind if knowledge of the impediment comes from information received in the confessional or from other information that is the subject of natural or professional secrecy. Furthermore, one would not be obligated to disclose an impediment if by doing so he would incur serious personal harm (CIC c.1027; CrebAllat c.17).

The banns are to be announced on three successive Sundays, intervening holy days being counted as Sundays, in the parish churches in which the parties have either a domicile or a quasi-domicile. *See* DOMICILE (CANON LAW). If deemed prudent, the bishop can order that the banns also be published in any or every parish in which either of the parties has lived for 6 months after reaching the age of puberty. The announcements are made orally during Mass or during some church service that a large number of parishioners attend. Within his own territory, however, a bishop can allow, in substitution of the oral announcements, that the banns be published by a written public notice posted at the entrance of the church. In such a case, the written notice must remain posted for at least 8 days with at least 2 days of obligatory attendance at Mass included in that period (CIC cc.1022–25; CrebAllat cc.12–15).

A pastor is not to perform a marriage until 3 days have elapsed since the publication of the last bann, but any good reason excuses him from this provision of the law. If a proposed marriage does not take place within 6 months after the banns have been published, they are to be published again unless the bishop decides otherwise (CIC c.1030; CrebAllat c.20).

Banns are announced only for the marriage of two Catholics and not for mixed marriages. If the bishop thinks it advisable to publish banns for a mixed marriage, he may allow it to be done provided that a dispensation from the impediment of mixed religion or disparity of cult has been granted for the marriage and that no mention of the religion of the non-Catholic be made in the announcements. These banns would be announced only in the proper parish of the Catholic party and not in that of the non-Catholic (CIC c.1026; CrebAllat c.16).

For a legitimate reason the bishop can dispense from the publication of one, two, or all three of the banns, not only from those that should be made within his own territory but also from those that should be made outside of his territory. If more than one bishop has jurisdiction in this matter, the right of dispensing belongs to the one in whose territory the wedding is to be celebrated. Some valid reasons for dispensing from the banns would be: the pregnancy of the woman, the fact that the parties have already attempted marriage invalidly, the fact that one of the parties has been invalidly married, the lack of time to announce the banns when the marriage could not reasonably be postponed, the justifiable fear that publication of the marriage would bring ridicule, abuse, or serious difficulty to the parties.

The Canon Law on banns for Oriental Churches is the same as that for the Latin Church except that the Oriental Code prescribes the banns only if the particular law of an individual Oriental Church demands them. The banns are prescribed in the particular Canon Law of the Ruthenian, Italo-Albanian, Russian, Rumanian, Maronite, Malakar, and Malabar Churches (CrebAllat c.12).

In addition to the banns for Matrimony, Canon Law prescribes that banns be announced for the reception of any Sacred Order, unless the person receiving the Order is a religious who has already taken perpetual vows. The public announcement that a certain person is to receive a Sacred Order is made in the candidate's parish church at Mass, on one Sunday or holy day, or on any other day and hour when a greater part of the faithful come to the church. If the ordination is delayed for more than 6 months after the announcement of the bann, the publication is to be repeated. For any good reason the bishop can dispense from the banns of ordination. He can also, on the other hand, require that the publication be made in other churches as well as the candidate's parish church. In lieu of the oral announcement the bishop can allow the publication to be made by written public notice posted at the entrance of the church for a few days, including 1 day of obligation. The faithful have the same obligation to disclose a known impediment to ordination as they have to disclose an impediment to Matrimony (CIC c.998–999).

See MARRIAGE, CANON LAW OF, 2.

Bibliography: Abbo 2:198–205. Conte Coron Sac v.3. J. B. ROBERTS, *The Banns of Marriage* (CUA CLS 64; Washington 1931). R. P. ROBERTS, *Matrimonial Legislation in Latin and Oriental Canon Law* (Westminster, Md. 1961).

[J. J. MC GRATH]

BAPST, JOHN, Jesuit missionary and educator; b. LaRoche, Switzerland, Dec. 7, 1815; d. Baltimore, Md., Nov. 2, 1887. A prosperous farmer's son, Bapst attended St. Michael's College, Fribourg, Switzerland, entered the Society of Jesus in 1835, and was ordained in 1846. As one of a group of exiled Swiss Jesuits assigned to the U.S., he arrived in New York in May 1848. Although highly qualified for the classroom and disinclined to the missions, Bapst was immediately assigned to reside with the Indians on Indian Island in the newly established mission in north central Maine. He and a few companions organized a circuit covering 33 towns and serving, until recalled in 1859, about 9,000 people—Irish, Canadians, and the Indians on two reservations. The opposition of *Know-Nothingism in Ellsworth, Maine, ended in a brutal attack on him Oct. 14, 1853, when he was tarred and feathered. Horrified Protestants of Bangor, Maine, honored him after his recovery. He was rector of the Boston, Mass., Jesuit seminary (1860–63), the first president of Boston College (1864–69), and superior of the New York–Canadian Mission (1869–73). His health had failed by 1881, and during the last years of his life his mind was haunted by the Ellsworth outrage.

Bibliography: Archives, Woodstock College, Md., J. Bapst correspondence. "Fr. J. B., a Sketch," *Woodstock Letters* 17 (1888); 18 (1889); 20 (1891), contains many letters from the preceding reference. W. L. LUCEY, *The Catholic Church in Maine* (Francestown, N.H. 1957). D. R. DUNIGAN, *A History of Boston College* (Milwaukee 1947).

[W. L. LUCEY]

BAPTISM (IN THE BIBLE)

Described in the NT as the sacramental entrance into the people of God, Baptism was foreshadowed in the OT by *circumcision and typified by the crossing of the *Red Sea. Baptism into Christ, when received in faith, effects forgiveness of sin, bestows the Holy Spirit, and unites the believer to Christ's Mystical Body [*see* CHURCH, I (IN THE BIBLE)]. As a providential preparation for the Baptism instituted by Christ, a widespread use of ablutions and washings appeared in the religious sects of the pagan and Jewish world in the age preceding Christ; this preparation was climaxed in proselyte baptism of the Jews and the ministry of the Baptist. This article treats Baptism in three main sections: terminology, pre-Christian practices, and Baptism in the NT.

Terminology. The name baptism came from the Greek noun βάπτισμα, "the dipping, washing," less commonly βαπτισμός, stemming from the verb βάπτω, "to dip" or "immerse." In the NT this verb is used only in the literal sense (Lk 16.24; Jn 13.26; Ap 19.13). From this form is derived the iterative form βαπτίζω which, in classical Greek, was used in the literal sense of "dipping" and in the figurative sense of "being overwhelmed" with sufferings and miseries. The latter figurative meaning occurs in the NT where Christ and his Apostles are described as "baptized" with suffering (Mk 10.38–39). For the rest of the NT, however, the verb βαπτίζω has its technical sense signifying the religious ceremony of Baptism. The nouns, also, are used in a technical religious sense: βαπτισμός designates the act of baptizing; βάπτισμα, used only in the NT and by later Christian writers, signifies Baptism as an institution; and, ὁ βαπτιστής (the baptizer) became the title of John the Baptist. This development of technical terminology demonstrates that Baptism was considered something special, something new; therefore, these technical terms were merely transliterated, not translated, into the Latin alphabet as *baptizo, baptisma,* and *baptista.*

Pre-Christian Practices. Christian Baptism is an external rite that signifies what it effects. The rite of washing had long been used as a religious practice; the signification attributed to it in Christian times builds

Fig. 1. John the Baptist baptizing in the desert; bronze, panel on the south door of the baptistery of St. John the Baptist at Florence, Andrea Pisano, 14th century.

upon these earlier usages, and so an investigation of them will be useful to the present study.

In the Pagan World. In the ancient world the waters of the Ganges in India, Euphrates in Babylonia, and Nile in Egypt were used for sacred baths; the sacred bath was known also in the Hellenistic mystery cults. And in the Attis and Mithra cults sacred initiation included a blood bath. A twofold effect was attributed to these baths: first, a cleansing from ritual and, more rarely, moral impurities that, according to primitive notions, could be washed away like bodily dirt; secondly, a bestowal of immortality and an increase of vital strength. The latter idea developed especially in Egypt where a person who drowned in the Nile became divinized. Mystery baths and baptisms are only a further step; in symbolic rite the initiate dies, and his death results in divinization. Cleansing and vivification, however, are understood more in the merely ritual or magic than in the moral sense. This deficiency in their religion was sensed even by the pagans.

In the Old Testament and Judaism. The Hebrew verb ṭābal, which the Septuagint (LXX) regularly translates by βάπτω, means "to dip" into a liquid, e.g., a morsel into wine (Ru 2.14), the feet into the river (Jos 3.15), and ritually defiled objects into water. In the OT, ṭābal becomes a technical term connected with removal of ritual impurity: dipping (ṭābal, βάπτω) hyssop into blood and sprinkling it upon a leper who has been healed is part of the ritual by which he is pronounced clean (Lv 14.6–7). Later Judaism multiplied prescriptions of ritual purity referred to in the Gospels as "washing [βαπτισμός] of cups and pots" (Mk 7.4) and "bathing [ἐβαπτίσθη] before eating" (Lk 11.38).

Baths were prescribed also by the Torah for the removal of various kinds of ritual impurities; one must bathe after being cured of leprosy (Lv 14.8–9), after contracting personal uncleanness (Lv 15.11, 13, 16, 18,

27), and after touching a corpse (Nm 19.19). But in all these instances, not the term *ṭābal,* but *rāḥaṣ (bammayim),* "to wash (in water)," is used, equivalent to a sort of sponge bath. Only once, in a clear case of immersion, does the LXX translate *ṭābal* with βαπτίζω: "He [Naaman] went down, and washed in the Jordan seven times" (4 Kgs 5.14). In later times, *ṭābal* and, therefore, βαπτίζω became the technical terms for such bathing to remove ritual uncleanness: "Each night she [Judith] went out to the ravine of Bethulia, where she washed herself [ἐβαπτίζετο] at the spring of the camp" (Jdt 12.7). But these Jewish practices of washing and bathing were intended merely as ritual purifications and had no direct moral purpose.

An extension of the general custom of ritual washings and the simple bath of purification was proselyte baptism, which in later Judaism was prescribed for Gentile converts; *see* PROSELYTES (BIBLICAL). Slowly it developed into a recognized rite of initiation consisting of three parts: circumcision, baptism, and sacrifice. It seems that this ritual rose from Jewish consciousness of the necessity for a Gentile proselyte to repeat the triple experience of the Israelites who had participated in the Sinaitic covenant: they were circumcised "a second time" (Jos 5.2), they were baptized in the desert (Ex 19.10 reads "sanctify," but Jewish tradition understood this in a baptismal sense; cf. 1 Cor 10.2), and they shared the covenant sacrifice (Ex 24.3–8). Thus it was through circumcision and baptism that the non-Jew entered the covenant and became a full-fledged Israelite. All this, however, was concerned primarily with legal purity and juridical incorporation. As for the origin of proselyte baptism it must have been practiced in Judaism prior to Christianity; it is hardly likely that the Jews would have borrowed the practice of baptism from a sect they looked upon with animosity.

In the New Testament. By Christian Baptism one enters into the kingdom of God and into the sphere of the saving work of Christ. John the Baptist proclaimed the advent of the kingdom and administered a baptism of penance by which those who received it proclaimed their willingness to enter the kingdom; his ministry, then, presents a good transition from earlier baptismal practices to those which were specifically Christian in character.

Baptism of John. From the middle of the 2d century B.C. until *c.* A.D. 300 there was a great deal of baptismal activity in Syria and Palestine, especially along the upper Jordan, among many different groups (see J. Thomas). But the different forms of ablution, whether the lustrations of Hellenistic syncretism, the baptism of the Mandaeans (a Gnostic sect of the Christian era; *see* MANDAEAN RELIGION), the bath of the *Essenes, or finally, proselyte baptism of late Judaism, are insufficient to account fully for the baptism of John; they fall short of the ethical and messianic implications of his baptism. Providentially, by the earlier baptismal movements, the people were disposed more immediately for John's baptism and ultimately for that of Christ. The fact that John came to be known as "baptizer" or the "Baptist" (even Flavius Josephus mentions him by this title in *Jewish Antiquities* 18.5.2 par. 116–117) shows that his activity must have been considered as something special and, at least partly, something new. This title was obviously first given him, not by Christians, but by pre-Christian popular consent.

In the mystery religions the lustrations and baptisms were conceived of as working magically; in Judaism proselyte baptism was derived from a legalistic conception of uncleanness; in contrast, John's baptism had an explicitly moral character. It was the visible sign of μετάνοια (repentance; *see* CONVERSION, I), a change of heart necessary for the remission of sins ("There came John . . . preaching a baptism of repentance for the forgiveness of sins": Mk 1.4; see also Acts 13.24; 19.4). Soon after John, the mightier One, the Messiah, was to come. John's baptism prepared for the eschatological kingdom: "Repent, for the kingdom of heaven is at hand" (Mt 3.1).

The Prophets had already used the symbolism of bathing to express the idea of interior, moral purification [Is 1.16; Ez 36.25; Za 13.1; Ps 50(51).9]. Although John's baptism was administered by divine command ("Was the baptism of John from heaven or from men?" Mk 11.30–33), it was a baptism with water lacking full messianic efficacy; it was a figure and a preparation for the Baptism instituted by Christ, a symbol of the right disposition for the coming kingdom.

John's baptism posed a crisis for the piety of contemporary Judaism. His baptism implied that the Law and all efforts to observe it could not produce the sanctity envisioned and foretold by the Prophets. One greater than John must come who would baptize "with the Holy Spirit and with fire" (Mt 3.11). The Messiah would pour forth the Holy Spirit and with that (according to the Baptist) a coinciding eschatological judgment. In Acts it is emphasized that the baptism of John, in contrast to that of Jesus, did not confer the Spirit (Acts 1.5; 11.15–16; 19.1–6). The baptism of John, unlike proselyte baptism, was administered primarily to Jews (Mk 1.5). Between John and those he baptized, a community that lasted beyond his death was established (Acts 19.1–4).

The lustral practices of the Essenes attest to the widespread concern for ritual purity in later Judaism. The bath of the *Qumran community shows similarities to John's baptism: both demand a conversion to God as a condition for the forgiveness of sin: both occur more or less in an eschatological context (see J. Gnilka, 205).

Fig. 2. Baptism of Christ, mosaic, dome of Orthodox baptistery at Ravenna, c. 450. The figure to the right of Christ is a personification of the Jordan.

John's baptism, however, stands more in the tradition of the Prophets both in its demand for moral reform and as the climactic preparation for the imminent messianic kingdom, whereas the bath of the Essenes is inspired more by the tradition of the Law, especially in its emphasis on ritual purity as a precondition to participation in community cult. The practice of the Essenes was exclusive, whereas John's baptism was open to all. Moreover, the bath of Qumran neither symbolized nor effected entrance into the community; it is not regarded as an initiation rite by the *Manual of Discipline*.

Jesus also baptized during His public life (Jn 3.22), not personally, but through His disciples (Jn 4.2). In this pre-Passion baptism St. Augustine and St. Thomas saw the Christian Sacrament, but this is improbable ("The Spirit had not yet been given, since Jesus had not yet been glorified": Jn 7.39).

Jesus Baptized by John. The Synoptic Gospels (Mk 1.9–11 and parallels) record and the Fourth Gospel (Jn 1.32–34) presumes that Jesus accepted baptism from the hands of John. In this baptism Jesus is symbolically and actually commissioned as Servant of Yahweh (*see* SERVANT OF THE LORD ORACLES). Other Jews came to the Jordan to be baptized by John for their own sins. Jesus was baptized not for His own sins, but for those of the whole people; He is the one whom Isaia prophesied must suffer vicariously for the sins of the people. The words, "Thou art my beloved Son; in thee I am well pleased" (Mk 1.11), bring to mind Is 42.1, 4: "Here is my servant [LXX παῖς] whom I uphold, my chosen one with whom I am pleased, upon whom I have put my spirit; he shall bring forth justice to the nations, . . . establish justice on the earth." The Greek term παῖς means both servant and son, two titles of Christ. And this allusion is meant to recall the wider context of the other Servant of Yahweh Oracles, especially Is 53.4–7: "It was our infirmities that he bore, our sufferings that he endured. . . . The Lord laid upon him the guilt of us

Fig. 3. Baptism of Christ; gold medallion from Palestine, 6th to early 7th century, diameter 3.7 centimeters.

all. He was harshly treated . . .; like a lamb led to the slaughter . . ., he opened not his mouth." Jesus was baptized in view of His death that effected the forgiveness of sins for all men. For this reason Jesus must unite Himself in solidarity with His whole people; "all justice must be fulfilled" (Mt 3.15). Thus the baptism of Jesus points forward to the cross, in which alone all Baptism will find its fulfillment.

At His baptism in the Jordan Jesus also received the fullness of the Spirit. His full possession of the Spirit was to be joined to His redemptive suffering as the Servant of God: "I have put my Spirit upon him [the Servant of God]; he shall bring forth justice to the nations" (Is 42.1). Consequently, in Jesus' baptism in the Jordan, the prototype of every Christian Baptism, the effects of the later Sacrament are foreshadowed, i.e., "justice to the nations [forgiveness of sins]" and possession of the Spirit. *See* BAPTISM OF CHRIST.

In the Apostolic Church. To Nicodemus Jesus clearly stated the necessity of Baptism for salvation: "Unless a man be born again he cannot see the kingdom of God," and more specifically, "Unless a man be born again of water and the Spirit, he cannot enter into the kingdom of God" (Jn 3.3, 5). The author of the Fourth Gospel viewed the *washing of the feet of the Apostles by Jesus as a symbol of the cleansing of Baptism; this is suggested by the words of Christ: "If I do not wash thee, thou shalt have no part with me" (Jn 13.8).

After His Resurrection Jesus gave His disciples the commission to preach the Gospel to all nations and to "baptize them in the name of the Father, and of the Son, and of the Holy Spirit, teaching them to observe all that I have commanded you" (Mt 28.19–20). To this, Mk 16.16 adds the necessary condition of faith for Baptism and thus for salvation. Since the command to baptize is one of His most important commissions, Jesus refers to the eschatological Lordship that empowers Him to give such a command. Although the explicit formula of Baptism in Mt 28.19 may derive from the liturgy of the Church, the central meaning of Baptism and the command to baptize derive from Christ. It is to be noted, too, that the clearly formulated necessity of Baptism found in the Fourth Gospel is due to the fact that the final form of this Gospel reflects the actual experience and practice of the Apostolic Church. This does not contradict the teaching that Jesus spoke explicitly about the necessity of Baptism and that He gave the commission to baptize. If He had not, one could not explain why, from the very outset, starting with Pentecost, the Apostolic Church preached the absolute need of Baptism for salvation, admonishing all to do penance, to believe in Jesus, and to be baptized (Acts 2.38, 41; 8.12–13, 16, 36, 38; 9.18; 10.47; 19.3–5). References in the Epistles also prove that Baptism was a well-established institution forming the climax of preaching and its acceptance by faith (Rom 6.3; 1 Cor 12.13). Although St. Paul says that Christ did not send him to baptize but to preach (1 Cor 1.17), this does not argue against the necessity of Baptism. No writer in the NT stresses the need for Baptism more than St. Paul; he knows no unbaptized Christian (Rom 6.3).

It is evident that Baptism in the early Church was by immersion. This is implicit in terminology and context: "Let us draw near . . . having . . . the body washed with clean water" (Heb 10.22), and the account of the Ethiopian chamberlain, who, to be baptized, "went down

Fig. 4. St. Philip baptizing the Ethiopian eunuch; American, embroidery and collage, first half of the 19th century.

into the water" and "came up out of the water" (Acts 8.38–39). St. Paul sees in Baptism a burial with Christ and a rising with Him (Rom 6.3–4; Col 2.12). The term λουτρόν (Eph 5.26; Ti 3.5), finally, can mean only "bath." The *Didache for the first time clearly advises Baptism of infusion in case of necessity, "If you have no running water . . ., pour water on the head" (7.2–3). The NT does not explicitly mention infusion. Yet one might wonder if the Apostles did not use it in cases where a great number of people were baptized (3,000 on the first Pentecost: Acts 2.41), or when circumstances hardly allowed immersion, as in the case of the nocturnal baptism in Philippi of the jailer and his family (Acts 16.33). The NT defines neither the exact rite of Baptism nor the exact formulas. That some formula was pronounced by the minister in Baptism is certain from Christ's command (Mt 28.19) and is perhaps alluded to in Ephesians when St. Paul says that Christ shall sanctify His Church "cleansing her in the bath of water by means of the word" (Eph 5.26). Yet, possibly, "the word" may refer to the confession of faith of the one baptized. Despite baptismal traditions evident in 1 Peter, the exact reconstruction of the baptismal rite remains problematic, as attempts of H. Preisker, R. Perdelwitz, and M. E. Boismard show. Besides the formula of Matthew in explicit Trinitarian form (Mt 28.19), the NT refers also to Baptism "into Christ" and "into the name of Christ" (Acts 2.38; 8.16; 10.48; 19.5). It is not clear whether either short phrase represents a formal, established baptismal formula. To baptize in the name of Jesus may mean to baptize by the authority of Jesus in distinction from any other baptism. The Didache in one place quotes the Trinitarian formula, "baptize as follows: after first explaining all these points, baptize in the name of the Father, and of the Son, and of the Holy Spirit" (7.3) and in another place states that only "those baptized in the name of the Lord" (9.5) shall eat and drink of the Eucharist. The frequent use of εἰς

(into) in this context, however, probably expresses the new relationship into which one enters with Christ through Baptism; one enters into the sphere of His saving activity, becomes His property.

The recipient of Baptism made a profession of faith, as evidenced from Acts 22.16, which was essentially an expression of belief in Jesus as Son of God, Lord, and Messiah (see also Rom 10.9; 1 Cor 12.3; Phil 2.11), of belief in God as the one who raised up Jesus from the dead, and in the Holy Spirit as Him whom Jesus in His exaltation possesses and imparts (Acts 2.32–39). It seems that the phrase often occurring in the context of Baptism, "What prevents [i.e., baptism]"—τί κωλύει (Acts 8.36; 10.47; 11.17; see also Mt 3.13) refers to the prebaptismal examination that sought to determine whether any hindrance existed and whether the candidate had really fulfilled the preliminary conditions. Texts treating Baptism furnish primary sources for the profession-of-faith formulas used in the early Church (Rom 10.9; 1 Cor 10.1–6; Heb 6.2).

Theological Significance. Christian Baptism is the NT fulfillment and replacement of circumcision (Col 2.11). Just as Jewish circumcision meant reception into the Old Covenant, so too Christian Baptism means reception into the New. Circumcision was the seal (σφραγίς) of the faith of Abraham. Rightly understood, circumcision is of the heart (Rom 2.29) and leads directly to Christian Baptism. Christian Baptism is "the circumcision of Christ" (Col 2.11) by which the tyranny of "the flesh" is categorically repudiated; henceforth life is "in the Spirit" since the baptized is sealed [ἐσφραγίσθητε] with the Holy Spirit (Eph 1.13). Baptism is the seal, the climax of preaching and of the reception of preaching by faith. Faith is required for Baptism and there is no true faith that does not lead to Baptism (cf. Gal 3.25–27). Even the visible outpouring of the Holy Spirit does not remove the necessity of receiving Baptism as a rite of initiation (Acts 10.48).

Baptism is the initiation rite for all those who want to belong to Christ. They who "have been baptized into Christ, have put on Christ" (Gal 3.27), they have become a new man "in Christ," and they are "conformed" (σύμμορφοι) to Christ (Rom 8.29). Baptism initiates into the Christian community: "All [believers] are baptized into one body" (1 Cor 12.13), i.e., into the body, which is Christ's Church (Eph 1.23). Baptism brings one into the community that knows no barriers between different nations (Eph 2.14); all are one in Christ, whether Jew or Greek, slave or free man, male or female (Gal 3.28). They are one body through the one Spirit (1 Cor 12.13), namely, the "Body of Christ" (1 Cor 12.27). Thus Baptism has a great importance for both the local and world community since it symbolizes and at the same time brings about unity and harmony in society.

The full messianic efficacy of the Baptism instituted by Christ became possible only through His death on the cross and His Resurrection. Only after Christ's death and Resurrection does the Church become the sphere of activity of the Holy Spirit (Jn 7.39). The baptismal rite of immersion suggests dying and rising with Christ. Being buried with Him means forgiveness of sins, and the emergence from this burial with Him means walking "in newness of life" (Rom 6.4; cf. Col 2.12), or walking "in the Spirit" (Gal 5.16). Both effects are essentially bound up with one another as is the death of Christ with His Resurrection. The baptism of John the Baptist was only an outward sign of contrition that cleansed according to the degree of contrition; Christian Baptism, however, when received with faith, "washes sins away" (Acts 2.38; 3.19); it is a moral purification effected by the power of Christ's redemptive action (Heb 10.19–22). Thus it demands a decisive turning from evil and the reception of the gospel of Christ (Acts 2.38–41; 3.17–19).

Baptism effects justice, holiness, and sinlessness (Rom 6.1–14; 1 Cor 6.11; Eph 5.26–27) through the operation of the Holy Spirit, the eschatological gift of God (Acts 2.17–21, 33) given to all who are baptized (Acts 2.38). It makes man a child of God, forming him to the image of Christ (Gal 3.26–27), who is "the firstborn among many brethren" (Rom 8.29), and "the firstborn from the dead" (Col 1.18; see also 1 Cor 15.20). To have died to sin and to have risen with Christ to a new life imposes the obligation on the Christian of becoming morally what he is ontologically (1 Thes 4.3–8). Baptism does not magically effect sanctification, but requires conscious struggle against unruly passions (Rom 6.12–14, 19; Gal 5.24). The Christian life is a progressive laying hold of and appropriation of what was rendered accessible by baptism (Eph 5.6–14; Phil 2.15; Col 3.12–17).

In their endeavor to describe the baptismal mystery, the NT writers, besides drawing directly on Jesus' earthly career, have recourse also to the wonderful acts of God in the OT. St. Paul sees Baptism as a new life, a second creation (Eph 2.10). Since the creation of light was most impressive and mysterious (Gn 1.3), it is fitting that the divine Word should be called "the true light" (Jn 1.4), and faith and Baptism in His name an enlightenment (2 Cor 4.6; see also Heb 6.4–6). St. Peter saw baptismal symbolism in the waters of the flood and in the ark in which Noe was saved (1 Pt 3.20–21). The typology of the crossing of the Red Sea presents Bap-

tism as an incorporation by immersion, as it were, into Christ (1 Cor 10.1–5).

Bibliography: J. COPPENS and A. D'ALÈS, DBSuppl 1:852–924. A. OEPKE, Kittel ThW 1:527–543. J. THOMAS, *Le Mouvement baptiste en Palestine et Syrie* (Gembloux 1935). H. G. MARSH, *The Origin and Significance of the N. T. Baptism* (Manchester, Eng. 1941). F. J. LEENHARDT, *Le Baptême chrétien, son origine, sa signification* (Neuchâtel 1944). W. F. FLEMINGTON, *The N.T. Doctrine of Baptism* (New York 1949). J. CREHAN, *Early Christian Baptism and the Creed* (London 1950). R. SCHNACKENBURG, *Das Heilsgeschehen bei der Taufe nach dem Apostel Paulus* (Munich 1950). H. SCHWARZMANN, *Zur Tauftheologie des hl. Paulus in Röm. 6* (Heidelberg 1950). G. W. H. LAMPE, *The Seal of the Spirit* (London 1951). G. F. VICEDOM, *Die Taufe unter den Heiden* (Munich 1960). O. CULLMANN, *Baptism in the N.T.*, tr. J. K. S. REID (Studies in Biblical Theology 1; London 1961). G. R. BEASLEY-MURRAY, *Baptism in the N.T.* (New York 1962). A. GEORGE et al., *Baptism in the N.T.*, tr. D. ASKEW (Baltimore 1964). W. MICHAELIS, "Zum jüdischen Hintergrund der Johannestaufe," *Judaica* 7 (1951) 81–120. N. A. DAHL, "The Origin of Baptism," *Norsk Teologisk Tidsskrift* 56 (1955) 36–52. M. E. BOISMARD, "Une Liturgie baptismale dans la Prima Petri," RevBibl 63 (1956) 182–208; 64 (1957) 161–183. D. M. STANLEY, "Baptism in the N.T.," *Scripture* 8 (1956) 44–57; "The N.T. Doctrine of Baptism: An Essay in Biblical Theology," ThSt 18 (1957) 169–215. O. BETZ, "Die Proselytentaufe der Qumransekte und die Taufe im N.T.," Rev Qum 1 (1958–59) 213–234. J. GNILKA, "Die essenischen Tauchbäder und die Johannestaufe," *ibid.* 3 (1961–62) 185–207. **Illustration credits:** Fig. 1, Alinari-Art Reference Bureau. Fig. 2, R. V. Schoder, SJ. Fig. 3, Courtesy of the Dumbarton Oaks Collection. Fig. 4, Courtesy of Smithsonian Institution—Museum of History and Technology.

[H. MUELLER]

BAPTISM (LITURGY OF)

The Church has sought to express in many different ways her faith in the Lord's institution of Baptism as a birth to supernatural life and an incorporation into Christ's Mystical Body. Here we investigate the ritual of Baptism: the manner of its administration, the formula used, and the ceremonies surrounding the essential action, the development of the modern ritual, and reminders of Baptism.

Manner of Administration. Baptism is discussed extensively in St. Paul's epistles, and this sheds some light on the baptismal rite. That Baptism took place by immersion is evidenced by Paul's presenting it as a "being buried with Christ" (Rom 6.3–4; Col 2.12). The same is true of his description of Baptism as a bath (λουτρόν, Eph 5.26; Ti 3.5; see also Heb 10.22), which leaves open the question whether or not a complete submersion is meant so that the head must also disappear under the water. The form of the bath also manifests itself in the manner in which the Ethiopian was baptized (Acts 8.36–38), and finally in the word that is generally used for this, βαπτίζειν (A. Oepke, "βάπτω," Kittel ThW 1:527–544).

According to the Didache, pouring the water was permissible; if immersion was not feasible, one could "pour water on the head three times, in the name of the Father and of the Son and of the Holy Spirit" (7; Quasten MonE 10). It is clear from this that from the very beginning there was great freedom with regard to immersion. The activity of the minister was emphasized throughout; it seems to have consisted either in pouring water on the head of the candidate, or at least in touching the candidate with a slight pressure suggesting the motion of immersion.

Iconography seems to favor this latter notion. The pictorial representations of the baptism of Christ beginning with the 2d century generally show John the Baptist placing his hand upon the Lord. However, this touch can also signify a washing with the moistened hand. By means of the pouring or sprinkling the (more or less complete) bath was made an "immersion." Extant baptisteries from a few centuries later (see DACL 2:382–409) show, by the very shallowness of the water receptacle, that an immersion for adults was no longer considered the general rule, and that therefore the pouring of water must have rounded out a partial bath. By comparison, the full immersion even for adults was still used by Otto of Bamberg (d. 1139), the apostle of Pomerania (*Vita* 2.15; DACL 2.1:398–399). A complete immersion for infants must have remained in use longer, for St. Thomas acknowledged it to have been the more common practice (ST 3a, 66.7).

Formula. With regard to the form used for Baptism in the early Church, there is the difficulty that although Matthew (28.19) speaks of the Trinitarian formula, which is now used, the Acts of the Apostles (2.38; 8.16; 10.48; 19.5) and Paul (1 Cor 1.13; 6.11; Gal 3.27; Rom 6.3) speak only of Baptism "in the Name of Jesus." It has been proposed that we assume that the one being baptized had to confess the name of Jesus and that then the minister pronounced a Trinitarian formula (Crehan 76, 81). This remains, however, an arbitrary conjecture.

While it is more obvious in the Matthaean formula (Mt 28.19) that Baptism establishes a relationship to the triune God, it is no less true when Baptism is given "in the name of Jesus." Since Baptism is an incorporation into Christ, it bestows at the same time the Holy Spirit (Acts 2.38; Eph 1.13; Gal 3.14; 4.6) and makes men children of the Father (Gal 4.6). It is conceivable that "in the name of Jesus" meant nothing more than that the candidate was given over to Christ, consecrated to Him, and submerged in Him (in His death). Though there is no clear proof that this phase was really used as a liturgical formula, the possibility of its being used thus even as late as the 3d century cannot be excluded (Stenzel 88–93). After all, the validity of Baptism "in the name of Jesus" was still accepted in the age of scholasticism.

An explicit reference to the Trinitarian formula of Baptism cannot be found in the first centuries. The Didache, for instance, merely repeats Mt 28.19. In the East, St. John Chrysostom (d. 407) is the first to report it: "N. is baptized in the name of the Father and of the Son and of the Holy Spirit" [*Baptismal Instructions* 2.26; ed. P. Harkins, AncChrWr 31 (Westminster, Md. 1963) 52–53]. We find it in the West already in Hippolytus's (d. 236) *Apostolic Tradition* (21; Botte LQF 48–51).

However, ancient Christian tradition until the 4th century (Western-Roman tradition until the 8th) shows that the baptismal formula was spoken as questions that the candidate answered.

It was natural to expect the candidate for Baptism to make a confession of his Christian faith—all the more necessary in view of the fact that at that time other groups had a baptism, e.g., the baptism of John (Acts 19.3). The Ethiopian chamberlain, for instance, had first to make a confession of his faith: "I believe that Jesus Christ is the Son of God" (Acts 8.37). The confession could be more or less explicit. As a matter of fact, the Christological part of the Apostles' Creed came into use first (1 Cor 15.3–4). Trinitarian formulas,

Fig. 1. Fresco, Baptism of Christ, from the Cemetery of St. Calixtus, Rome, end of the 2d century. This faded painting is one of our earliest representations of the baptismal act, and was painted on the wall of a tomb.

however, also spread at an early time, and they could have appeared as an extension of Christological formulas (see the formula Paul uses for the greeting at the beginnings of his letters).

By the 3d century there is evidence that this confession of faith was the baptismal formula. Thus, Hippolytus reports that the minister places his hand on the candidate's head and asks: "Do you believe in God, the Father almighty?" The candidate answers: "I believe." Then he baptizes (immerses?) him once. The minister asks again: "Do you believe in Jesus Christ, the Son of God, who was born of the Holy Spirit and the Virgin Mary, suffered under Pontius Pilate, died, and on the third day arose from the dead?" The candidate answers: "I believe," and is baptized a second time. The minister once again asks: "Do you believe in the Holy Spirit, the Holy Church and the resurrection of the body?" The candidate replies: "I believe," and is baptized the third time.

This baptismal formula in question form is found again and again in the West until the Gelasian Sacramentary [1.44; ed. H. Wilson (Oxford 1894) 86]. But then a change occurs.

In the East, a 5th-century Syrian adaptation of Hippolytus's *Apostolic Tradition*, the *Canons of Hippolytus*, adds that the minister says each time he immerses the candidate: "I baptize you in the name of the Father and of the Son and of the Holy Spirit" (19.133 DACL 2.1:262). This is the first time that a declarative formula accompanied the threefold immersion. Apparently in reaction to *Arianism a single immersion was adopted in Spain, (Gregory the Great, *Epist.* 1.43; PL 77:497–498), and the Eastern use of a single declarative formula was followed, since it tied in so well with the single immersion (Andrieu OR 3:87–90).

The first Western books to report our present declarative formula were the Gallican Sacramentaries [e.g., the 8th-century *Missale Gothicum* 260; ed. H. Bannister, HBradshSoc 52 (London 1917) 17]. From among the books of the Roman rite, the Hadrian recension (end

Fig. 2. The Baptism of Constantine by Pope St. Sylvester, fresco of the 12th century, in the chapel of St. Sylvester, Church of the Santi Quattro Coronati, Rome. Although the Emperor is known to have been baptized in the baths of the Lateran Palace, he is shown here receiving the Sacrament in a large font of the late medieval type.

of 8th century) of the Gregorian Sacramentary was the first to reproduce it [*Das Sakramentarium Gregorianum* 206.3; ed. H. Lietzmann (Münster 1921) 124]. While these documents do not indicate the number of times the immersion and formula were repeated, some manuscripts of this period seem to vacillate between the threefold interrogatory formula and the single declarative one. A Sacramentary written in Prague shortly before 794 contains the threefold interrogation and immersion but adds that the minister may say: "I baptize you . . ." without indicating whether this latter formula is to be repeated or not [*Das Prager Sakramentar*, ed. A. Dold and L. Eizenhöfer (Beuron 1949) 98.12]. On the other hand, other books, such as the Sacramentary of Gellone (end of 8th century), insist that the formula is spoken only once (P. de Puniet, DACL 2.1:305).

A consideration of these historical facts forces us to conclude with De Puniet (*ibid.* 342) that the tradition of the Church until the 8th century was to accept the threefold Trinitarian question and answer as the baptismal formula.

Surrounding Ceremonies. The baptismal act has from ancient times been enlarged with preparatory and concluding rites. Tertullian spoke of a renunciation of Satan, his pomps and his angels by means of three questions and answers [*De spect.* 4; *De corona militis* 3; *De anima* 35 (PL 1:635; 2:79; 2:710)].

According to Hippolytus (*Apostolic Tradition* 20–21; Botte LQF 42–53), besides fasting and renunciation of Satan, there were also a preliminary anointing with oil that was exorcized beforehand (later, oil of catechumens) and an anointing after Baptism with oil over which a thanksgiving prayer had been spoken (later, chrism). The baptismal water was supposed to be blessed ahead of time (Tertullian, *De baptismo* 4; PL 1:1205).

A special practice, which lasted for but a few centuries, was the offering of a drink of milk and honey to the newly baptized before the reception of the chalice in the first celebration of the Eucharist on the part of the neophyte [Tertullian, *De corona militis* 3 (PL 2:99); Hippolytus, *Apostolic Tradition* 21 (Botte LQF 56–57); Jerome, *Adv. Luciferianos* 8 (PL 23:172); John the Deacon, *Epist. ad Senarium* 12 (PL 59:405)]. This drink harkened back to the promise made to the Chosen People in the desert that they would inherit a land flowing with milk and honey, an inheritance that the candidate was now to enjoy. From the 4th century there is evidence of the white clothing received by the newly baptized to symbolize the innocence of his new life (Ambrose, *De mysteriis* 7; Quasten MonE 129). About the same time a presentation of a burning candle to the neophyte is reported (Pseudo-Ambrosius, *De lapsu virginis* 5; PL 16:372), a reminder of his purity of soul. The anointing of the head of the newly baptized [Hippolytus, *Apostolic Tradition* 21 (Botte LQF 51); Ambrose, *De sacramentis* 3.1.1 (Quasten MonE 151)] is to symbolize his configuration to Christ, the anointed priest.

The early Church took great care to bring out the fact that Baptism was the great event by which the Christian life takes hold of man. For this reason it was linked with the celebration of the Easter Vigil. The whole community, therefore, took part in it, not by being present during the baptismal act which took place in the form of an immersion in the baptistery, but by fasting beforehand with the candidates, and by bringing them into the church immediately after Baptism to celebrate the communal Eucharist. It was because reception into the Church is sealed with the Eucharist that the Communion of newly baptized infants was retained even as late as the 12th century.

While infants were baptized either immediately or on Holy Saturday without any preparation (Cyprian, *Epist.* 64; CSEL 3.1:720), adult candidates had to undergo a *catechumenate of varying length before they could receive Baptism. At an early date the administration of the Sacrament was normally restricted to the Easter or Pentecost Vigil. *Lent thus served as a period of final intensified instruction and interior preparation for reception of Baptism. Those catechumens who were ready to make the step were enrolled in the ranks of the *competentes,* those "seeking" Baptism; and exercises, called scrutinies, were held for them. The candidates on these occasions received many *exorcisms, the exsufflation or blowing out of the devil, the *imposition of hands, *salt; they were taught and had to repeat the Apostles' Creed and Our Father, the essential part of the rites for the *competentes.*

Modern Ritual. When at the start of the Middle Ages adult Baptism became more rare, the rites of the catechumenate were used for infant candidates. Their Baptism was even restricted to Easter and Pentecost; so strictly was this followed in Spain (Ildephonse, *De cognitione baptismi* 107; PL 96:156) and elsewhere that the baptistery was locked during Lent. Such a transfer to infant Baptism of customs designed for adults was impossible without abbreviations and loss of meaning.

Infant Baptism. The ritual for infant Baptism thus came into existence. It contains a reception into the catechumenate by means of the sign of the cross, and exsufflation, the imposition of hands, and the giving of salt; the exorcism with the oration *Aeternam* coming from the catechumenate (*Ordo Romanus* 11.21, 24; Andrieu OR 2:423); and lastly, inside the church, the recitation of the Apostles' Creed and Our Father. There follows the threefold renunciation of Satan separated from the confession of faith, as was often done in ancient times, by the anointing with oil of catechumens. The threefold immersion, bound up in earlier times with the three baptismal questions, left its vestige in the triple pouring of water that now accompanies the single indicative Trinitarian formula.

Baptism of Adults. The ritual for Baptism of adults is basically nothing else but a more prolix rite for infant Baptism that originated in the declining Middle Ages. Instead of the single exorcism a whole series of them was introduced. The ceremony for reception into the catechumenate was lengthened by mere repetition of already existing rites. An insufflation (breathing the Holy Spirit into the candidate) was added to the exsufflation. Finally the whole ritual was outfitted with an introduction consisting of psalms.

On April 16, 1962, the Holy See, wishing to make the ceremonies of adult Baptism a more meaningful introduction to the Christian life, published a new Ordinal allowing for the celebration of the rites of the catechumenate in a series of services prior to the actual conferring of the Sacrament [ActApS 54 (1962) 310–338]. Vatican Council II also insisted on separating the adult baptismal rites into several distinct steps (*Constitution on the Sacred Liturgy* 3:64); but it went further and decreed a full revision of both adult and infant rites (3:66–70), for it is clear that a genuine reform is not achieved by a mere extension of such ceremonies over a longer period of time.

Reminders of Baptism. Not only was the celebration of Baptism extended for 8 days till Low Sunday, *dominica in albis,* but its anniversary—the *pascha annotinum,* the Monday after Low Sunday—was celebrated by means of a community Mass with those who had been baptized the previous year. Although the use of holy water did not result from reflections on Baptism, the *Asperges* before the services on Sunday was regarded in the early Middle Ages as a remembrance of Baptism. The blessing of dwellings with holy water, still common today, can also be understood in the same sense.

Godparents are a higher kind of remembrance of Baptism. The present institution combines the godparent's original function of witness on behalf of the catechumen (in the case of adults), that of sponsor (in the case of infants, in whose place he pronounces the renunciation of Satan and confession of faith), and that of helper during the Baptism itself. The latter duty was especially important when the one being baptized was a woman. For this, moreover, *deaconesses were provided; in Syria they had to see to the anointing of the woman's body [*Didascalia Apostolorum* 3.12.2–4 (Funk DidConst 1:208–210); *Apostolic Constitutions* 8.28.6 (*ibid.* 1.531)].

Fig. 3. Baptism, detail of the ivory cover of the Sacramentary of Bishop Drogo of Metz, c. 855 (Paris, Bibl. Nat. MS Lat. 9428).

Other reminders of Baptism are the baptismal *name, given to the candidate since the late Middle Ages, and the ritual of *religious profession which reflects the ceremonial of Baptism because it was regarded as a "second Baptism."

Bibliography: P. DE PUNIET, DACL 2.1:251–346. J. H. CREHAN, *Early Christian Baptism and the Creed* (London 1950). J. QUASTEN, "Baptismal Creed and Baptismal Act in St. Ambrose's 'De

Mysteriis' and 'De Sacramentis,' " *Mélanges de Ghellinck,* 2 v. (Gembloux 1951) 1:223–234. A. STENZEL, *Die Taufe* (Innsbruck 1958). ANDRIEU OR. E. DICK, "Das Pateninstitut im altchristlichen Katechumenate," ZKathTh 68 (1939) 1–49. M. DUJARIER, *Le Parrainage des adultes aux trois premiers siècles de l'Église* (Paris 1962). T. MAERTENS, *Histoire et pastorale du rituel du catéchuménat et du baptême* (Bruges 1963). H. RAHNER, "*Pompa Diaboli;* Ein Beitrag zur Bedeutungsgeschichte des Wortes πομπή-pompa in der urchristlichen Taufliturgie," ZKathTh 55 (1931) 239–273. B. FISCHER, "Formen gemeinschaftlicher Tauferinnerung im Abendland," LiturgJb 9 (1959) 87–93; "Formen privater Tauferinnerung im Abendland," *ibid.* 156–166. Miller FundLit 433–448. **Illustration credits:** Fig. 1, Pontificia Commissione di Archeologia Sacra. Fig. 2, Alinari-Art Reference Bureau. Fig. 3, Photo Archives-Maria Laach.

[J. A. JUNGMANN]

BAPTISM (THEOLOGY OF)

The word "baptism" is derived from the Greek, βαπτίζω meaning "plunge" or "dip" (as in Jn 13.26). Our word "baptism" has come to mean "purify" or "cleanse"; it is helpful, in seeking an understanding of the mystery of Baptism, to recall the original meaning of the term. The Council of Florence (Denz 1314) stated: "Holy Baptism holds the first place among all the Sacraments because it is the door of the spiritual life. By it we are made members of Christ and of His body, the Church."

Baptism is the sacramental representation of the death and resurrection of Jesus Christ. By this action of the Church the person baptized dies to sin and is regenerated with the life of God or grace. He thus bears in himself a share in the victory that Christ has won over sin and death and can look forward, if he is faithful, to his own resurrection and ultimate glorification at the parousia. St. Paul in Rom 6.3–5 states: "Do you know that all we who have been baptized into Christ Jesus have been baptized into his death? For we were buried with him by means of Baptism into death, in order that, just as Christ has arisen from the dead through the glory of the Father, so we also may walk in newness of life. For if we have been united with him in the likeness of his death, we shall be so in the likeness of his resurrection also." This article will treat the following: pagan and Old Testament antecedents of Baptism, its institution by Christ, the necessity of Baptism,

Fig. 1. Administration of Baptism, relief on the campanile of the cathedral at Florence, Andrea Pisano, 14th century.

the sacramental sign, the effects of Baptism, the minister, the recipient, and sponsors.

Pagan and Old Testament Antecedents. Other religions besides Christianity had baptismal rites. There were the sanctifying baths in the Isis mystery, the taurobolium of the Cybele-Attis cult and many others. The idea of pagan baptismal rites should not be disturbing to Christians. It suggests that religion has roots in human nature and Christianity is not a thing inhumanly apart. At one time it was asserted that there was an actual relation of dependence between Christianity and the pagan mystery religions, but this has been disproved. H. Rahner has summarized the theories of dependence and genetic derivation with numerous references to studies of them [*Greek Myths and Christian Mystery* (London 1963) 7–28]. He states that in the actual situation there was a distinct development, on the one hand, of the fundamental Christian attitudes formulated by Paul and early Christian writers, and, on the other hand, of the stand taken by the later fully developed Christian Church in regard to the mystery cults of late antiquity.

Paul's concept of mystery (Eph 3.9; Rom 16.25; Col 1.26) is basically that of the Old Testament and is the supernatural mystery of salvation. "Mystery" means, for Paul, God's decision to save man separated from Him by sin. This decision, made from all eternity, is hidden in the Godhead and at the same time is manifested in the God-man, Christ, who brings the gift of life to all men. Christianity is distinguished from the pagan religions by its historical character and the wholly different significance ascribed to the appearance and death of the Christian Redeemer. Rahner admits, however, that there is in Paul and even Ignatius (d. *c.* 110) and others an undeniable tendency to adapt to their own uses a kind of subdued mystery language. The 3d century was the age in which pagan mystery religions flourished and at that time there were divergent attitudes within Christianity toward adaptation to the pagan culture. Tertullian (d. after 220) opposed the mysteries entirely. Clement (d. *c.* 215) freely used verbal images from them familiar to the time in order to put strangers at ease. Eventually things taken from mystery religions passed into full Christian possession acquiring a different significance and new glory.

The Old Testament antecedents of Baptism include the ablutions and baths of ritual purification (e.g., Lv 11.32; Dt 23.10–11; 2 Sm 12.20), proselyte baptism, the baptism of John the Baptist, the baptism of the Essenes and other sects on the fringe of Judaism, and events and things of the Old Testament which were considered by the Apostles and the Fathers as types of Baptism, such as Paradise, the flood, the dove at Noah's ark and at Christ's baptism, the departure from Egypt, and the crossing of the Jordan.

Two kinds of ablution must be distinguished in Judaism: one that came to be mainly a ritual cleansing of the body; the other a solemn act signifying cleansing from death and sin such as the cleansing of priests before offering sacrifice. At this time they were both baptized in water and sprinkled with blood. Christian Baptism should perhaps be understood not in terms of the ritual bath of late Judaism, but of the cleansing effected by the blood of the covenant shed for remission of sins. The fulfillment of the ancient rites of atonement in the death of Christ meant the abrogation of those rites.

There is no model for John's baptism. The rite resembled proselyte initiation, but John's prophetic consciousness gave it originality. John's baptism was not just a ritual purification of flesh but a spiritual purification of sin. It was offered to all people to aggregate them into a community that expected the Messiah, an expectation which John saw realized. It seems, contrary to the opinion of Augustine, that the baptism practiced by the Apostles in Our Lord's lifetime was John's and not the Sacrament.

The types of Baptism mentioned above have been traced in detail through the Fathers by Jean Daniélou. The traditional typology that appears in the baptismal catecheses and commentaries of the Fathers shows a common tradition. Biblical types of the Sacraments were an integral part of the early Christian mentality. The theology of the Exodus [as seen in 1 Cor 10.2–11, in chapters 8 and 9 of Tertullian's *De baptismo*, CSEL 20:207–208, and in the *De mysteriis* of St. Ambrose (d. 397), 3.13, CSEL 73:94] teaches that what God did once by the mystery of water to free an earthly people from an earthly tyrant that they might pass from Egypt into the desert, He still does by the mystery of water when He frees a spiritual people from a spiritual tyrant and leads them from the world into the Kingdom of God.

Institution by Christ. Older studies of Baptism often presume some particular situation in Our Lord's life when the Sacrament was instituted, although they admit that there is nothing in the text directly on institution. Many of the Fathers, and St. Thomas, thought that the institution occurred at the baptism of Our Lord in the Jordan. Hugh of Saint-Victor (d. 1096) thought that Baptism was established in a universal manner only on the day of the Ascension (*De sacramentis* 2.5–6). Alexander of Hales (d. 1245) connected it with Mt 28.19. Some say that it was probably instituted in the commission to the Apostles recorded in John 3 and 4; Matthew 28 would have been the solemn proclamation. According to this theory, the death of Christ was the meritorious cause of perfection of the Sacrament, but not its institution.

Modern writers point out that there is a dogma that Jesus Christ instituted the Sacrament but there is nothing of faith about how. According to A. M. Roguet the dogma that Christ instituted the Sacraments is not on the historical plane at all [*Christ Acts through the Sacraments* (Collegeville, Minn. 1954) 13–14]. K. Rahner explains more specifically that in the early Church there was no concept of Sacrament as such (42–43). The institution of a Sacrament can follow simply from the fact that Christ founded the Church with its sacramental nature. E. Schillebeeckx also holds that the Church as primordial Sacrament and as community of worship is already the fundamental institution of the seven Sacraments by Christ (116–117). But this is not sufficient. Christ must have directed the meaning in some way. He must have established the sevenfold direction of grace, of which the visible act of the Church is medium. This may have been implicit and unparticularized but nevertheless it was a real manifestation. There are scriptural data for Baptism which would have been established in power only by Christ's death and resurrection. Christ did in some way determine the actual shape for certain Sacraments such as Baptism. Baptism was one of the common religious archetypes, but Christ instituted it also as a Sacrament by telling the Apostles to baptize and by indicating that it should be with water. That the material rite was practiced in the Church can be seen from Acts 2.38–41; 8.12–13, 16; 9.18.

Necessity of the Sacrament. Christ said "Unless a man be born again of water and the Holy Spirit he cannot enter into the Kingdom of God" (Jn 3.5). The Council of Trent declared: "If anyone says that baptism is optional, that is, not necessary for salvation, let him be anathema" (Denz 1618). The Council also indicated that "Since the Gospel was promulgated this passing [justification] cannot take place without the water of regeneration or the desire for it as it is written in Jn 3.5" (Denz 1524).

That the Church, as far back as the 2d century, possessed the truth that Baptism is necessary for salvation can be seen from the debate about the Baptism of the Apostles. There was a tradition (Tertullian, *De baptismo* 7.12; CSEL 20:210–211) that Christ baptized Peter, who then baptized Andrew, James, and John; they, in turn, baptized the others. Today it is said that the contact that the apostles had with the primordial Sacrament, Christ, made it unnecessary for them to receive Baptism. The doctrine of the necessity of Baptism was attacked during the early period of the Church by the Pelagians, who, not accepting original sin, did not require Baptism (Augustine, *Enchir.* 13.43; PL 40:253).

St. Thomas (ST 3.68.2), interpreting patristic treatment of such catechumens as Valentinian, said that salvation without the actual water of Baptism was considered in similar circumstances possible. However, since the Church does not know exactly what is the fate of the unbaptized, even while she is aware that desire and martyrdom may substitute for the Sacrament in the case of adults, she takes the safer practical course and urges that Baptism be administered whenever possible.

Baptism of Desire and Blood. The question with regard to Baptism of desire for adults is whether the effect of a Sacrament in desire really is an anticipation of the effect of the desired Sacrament and thus a sacramental grace in the strict sense, or is it a bestowal of grace outside of the Sacraments. It is acknowledged that Baptism of desire cleanses from original sin and remits all personal sins. It does not give the character peculiar to Baptism or incorporate the person into the Church with the ability to receive the other Sacraments. According to Schillebeeckx, the person is imperfectly a member of the ecclesial community (143). Baptism of desire can be a more vital experience at times than the reception of the actual Sacrament, but it does not have the same effect. This presacramental bestowal of grace cannot occur without at least implicit desire of the Sacrament, and so it is sacramental but not a true anticipated effect of the future ecclesial symbolic act.

J. Crehan states that the earliest plain acknowledgement of martyrdom as equivalent to Baptism is made by Melito of Sardis (Davis CDT 235). St. Thomas says that, as in Baptism one is assimilated to Christ through death for Him, the death of Christ produces the same effect apart from the Sacrament of Water (ST 3.66.11). Martyrdom, then, is a participation in the Passion, not sacramentally but really. Sacramental participation is real but through the intermediary of symbol. The other is participation by imitation and reproduction.

Fate of Unbaptized Infants. Many theories have been offered concerning the fate of infants who die without Baptism. The most common opinion until now has been that, since Baptism is necessary for salvation, unbaptized infants who die cannot enjoy supernatural happiness. The dilemma consists in two truths that must be held together: the universality of the salvific design of God in Christ, and the unequal participation of men in this design. Journet stresses that though the unbaptized infant is not capable of reaching heaven, he does benefit from Christ's redemptive work by receiving a reward of natural happiness in *Limbo, the restoration of the fullness of human nature. Journet supports his theory from the Council of Carthage (Denz 219), which regarded unbaptized infants as excluded from heaven, and from a statement of Pius XII to a gathering of midwives [Oct. 29, 1951; ActApS 43 (1951) 841] that, as things are at present, no other way besides Baptism is seen of imparting the life of Christ to little children. Other theologians have said that at the moment of death there is a moment of grace in which a choice is made. Y. M. Congar [*The Wide World My Parish* (Baltimore 1961) 152] thinks that, though exploration has been made in this direction, our present knowledge about consciousness in the newly born or our knowledge about death does not demand that a change be made in views that can be regarded today as traditional or classical. The door is to be kept open to the two ways: Baptism and moral choice.

G. Dyer has written a historical study (141–154) of the doctrine of Limbo (which is not a defined truth) and the salvation of unbaptized children. He notes that Augustine thought that these children would go into eternal fire. Anselm (d. 1109), who taught that original sin is privative, was followed by Abelard (d. 1142) who concluded that its punishment was also privative. The idea was taken up by Peter Lombard (d. 1322), and Albert the Great (d. 1280) seems to have been the one who coined the name "Limbo." Dyer comments that Journet's theory is disquieting, for it means that a large segment of the race was never destined for the vision of God.

Another modern writer, V. Wilkin, has written an impassioned plea for the salvation of these children. He argues that infants have been loosed from their solidarity with Adam since the death of Christ. They may be in Limbo but Limbo is the "baptistery of heaven."

In this matter Schillebeeckx again has some original observations to make (146). The Church teaches that whoever dies in original sin cannot inherit heaven, but this is quite different from maintaining that whoever dies without Baptism is by the very fact excluded from heaven. For adults this is obviated by Baptism of desire, which is sufficient for salvation, although the actual reception of the Sacrament remains necessary and is not rendered meaningless. So also for infants God's grace can take the initiative, although we do not know whether in actual fact it does. We need not fear that in agreeing to the possibility of heaven for children who die without Baptism we will be making the need for the Sacrament relative. Pius XII's statement (Oct. 29, 1951) was directed to the nurse's responsibility to baptize in emergency and not to the possibility of salvation for children apart from the Sacrament. He does suggest that the fate of such children is still an open question.

Protestant Position. Robert McAfee Brown may be taken as giving a representative Protestant opinion on the necessity of Baptism (147). He states that few Protestants would hold that one who is cut off from the Sacraments is denied the possibility of salvation. On the other hand, few would assert that Baptism is merely optional to the Christian life. The Sacraments are necessary for Church proclamation but not for individual salvation. Salvation is conferred by God and not by the Sacraments, which ratify but do not guarantee or control God's work.

The Sacramental Sign. The sacramental sign can be considered under three aspects: its relation to the paschal mystery, Baptism as Sacrament of initiation, and the essence of the sign according to the division of matter and form.

Rite of Initiation. The meaning of Christian Baptism is indicated by the ceremony in which the unbaptized person is plunged in water by a kind of burial that is an image of the entombment of Christ. The symbol is efficacious and transmits to us the effect that God intended by the death of His Son. The burial of Jesus was subordinate to the resurrection. Accordingly, Baptism has for its purpose to give us complete change, a new life, for we have conquered sin in union with the risen Christ. St. Paul describes not just a state of soul but something that affects the very being of the Christian by assimilating it to a past event that first existed in Christ. L. Cerfaux (303–309) attempts to distinguish the relationship to the death-resurrection of Christ in Baptism from that in the Eucharist. He asks whether Rom 6.3–13 might not be considered a dramatization representing the burial of Christ between His crucifixion and resurrection and suggesting both. On the other hand, 1 Cor 11.17–34 suggests a dramatized proclamation analogous to that of Baptism, but this time the symbolic idea is clearly surpassed. The reproduction is so real that we are confronted with not just material nourishment but the body and blood of the Lord, with His real death toward which we must take a stand.

St. Thomas also speaks of the configuration in Baptism to the passion and death of Christ (ST 3.66.9 ad 5; 3.79.5 ad 1; 3.86.4 ad 3; *Ad Rom.* 6.1). In *4 Sent.* 4.1.2.2 ad 3, Baptism is considered not only symbolic reproduction by the rite of immersion (relating directly to the burial) but reproduction by intimate communion in the passion itself and the death of the Savior. This is a realization in the sacramental order, a participation in the mystery as the death of sin. It is profound and real in the Baptism of water, though not bloody; it is so real and total that there cannot be rebaptism.

E. Kilmartin has given a resumé of the doctrine of Baptism in the works of the Fathers. He shows that during the 2d century writers such as Ignatius (d. *c.* 110) and Irenaeus (d. *c.* 202) speak of a presence of the Incarnate Word in the soul of the baptized but do not draw on the Pauline doctrine (Rom 6) of configuration to the death and resurrection of Jesus. Origen (d. *c.* 253) is outstanding in the 3d century for his doctrine that the Christian lives out of the mystery of Baptism as a mystical death with Christ (e.g., *In Rom. comm.* 5.8; PG 14:1040). The ideas of Origen became common in the mystagogical catecheses of the 4th century. Kilmartin concludes that the Fathers of the Church did not, as in later theology, consider the work of redemption complete or the sacramental system merely an application of its effects. Rather, for the Fathers as for Scripture, the economy of salvation is presented as a process of redemption still in progress. Thus the rite of initiation does not so much bestow on us the fruit of the cross as crucify us with Christ. Salvation, while completed in Christ, must be realized in the individual and in the whole Church.

Paul says that Baptism is a rite of initiation or of entrance into the Church (1 Cor 12.13; 10.21). There is only one Baptism as there is only one Christ (Eph 4.5). The soul puts on Christ (Gal 3.27) and lives mystically the death and resurrection of the Savior (Rom 6.3–4). A spiritual imprint of the Holy Spirit (2 Cor 1.21–22; Eph 1.13; 4.30) seems to have designated a determined act that, following upon preaching and the awareness of the faith, aggregated pagans to the Church. Recipients were added not only to a group but to the Lord Himself (Acts 11.24).

Matter and Form. We have no precise information about the exact rite of Christian Baptism in the New Testament. Old Testament covenant rites and earliest Christian evidence would lead us to believe that both total immersion and affusion were in use and sometimes both together. The Didache (7.3; Quasten MonE 10) and Cyprian (*Epist.* 64; CSEL 3:717–721) are generally cited as the earliest evidence (Acts 16.33 being inadequate to prove affusion) for the allowance of affusion instead of full immersion, but the two practices are not entirely distinct. The neophyte descended into the water and the baptizer with him; the latter plunged him totally, head and body, or if the depth was not sufficient, after having plunged him half-way, took in hand water which he poured over his head. Baptism by sprinkling is admitted by the present discipline of the Church as valid, but is not encouraged and has no ancient warrant (CIC c.758).

The matter of Baptism is true and natural water (Denz 1615). In solemn Baptism blessed water is used for licit administration. In the beginning Baptism consisted of a triple ablution. Today the Roman ritual prescribes a triple affusion but this does not involve validity. The change from immersion to affusion is not so much a change as a reduction of the ritual act, which is the complete matter. Unless washing is signified by the flowing of the water the Baptism must be conferred again conditionally (CIC c.758).

The form makes precise the meaning of the matter. The Trinitarian formula is attested by Didache (7.1; Quasten MonE 9), Justin (1 *Apologia* 61.3; Quasten MonE 14), Tertullian (*De baptismo* 13; CSEL 20.212–213), and Cyprian (*Epist.* 74.5; CSEL 3:802–803). The Latin ritual has kept the words of Mt 28.19. The Greek has a passive form such as "By my hands this one is baptized in the name of the Father, and of the Son, and of the Holy Spirit."

The Church has not held absolutely to the materiality of the words but it is necessary that they express the act that is accomplished and that each of the persons of the Holy Trinity be invoked. In conditional Baptism the formula varies according to the thing doubted, e.g., "If you are alive," or, "If you have not already been baptized." Many ancient documents do not indicate the baptismal formula but do describe a triple profession of faith and triple immersion. Since its condemnation by Alexander VI such a practice would not be permitted.

The Acts of the Apostles (2.38; 8.16; 10.48; 19.5) mentions Baptism "in the name of Jesus," which seems contrary to the Trinitarian formula of Mt 28.19 given by Jesus Himself. Possibly the meaning of the term in Acts is that the candidate invoked or confessed the name and was then baptized for the sake and worship of Jesus but with a Trinitarian formula. D. M. Stanley, on the other hand ["Liturgical Influences on the Formation of the Four Gospels," CathBiblQuart, 21 (1959) 28–29], comments in the light of form criticism that the inspired writer has probably made Jesus' command to baptize more explicit by introducing the words familiarly used in administering the Sacrament. He thinks that to assume that Our Lord Himself would have used such a precise allusion to the Trinity before the Pentecostal Revelation is to shut one's eyes to the historical process by which Christian dogma was gradually imparted to the Apostolic Church.

Effects of the Sacrament. Baptism incorporates the recipient into the Church, which is the Body of Christ. Both Catholics and Protestants see this as a decisive act by which God claims man and which cannot be repeated. The Church formally teaches that Baptism is an incorporation into the Church (Denz 632, 1314, 1621; CIC c.87). K. Rahner goes beyond this to assert that this incorporation is the *sacramentum et res* of this Sacrament of Christian initiation (88–89). Full membership in the new people of God brings with it all the other effects of Baptism.

Sacramental Character. This does not contradict the idea of the character as the *sacramentum et res*. The character is the power to share in the priestly function of Christ, but it is the Church in the world of time and space and not only in the depth of the conscience sanctified by grace which continues the priestly function of Christ the high priest (*see* SACRAMENTAL CHARACTER).

Interior Renewal. Other effects of Baptism are the remission of original and actual sin and of the punishment due to them (Denz 1316) and regeneration in Christ or adopted sonship. In addition Baptism possesses sufficient power to suppress the anarchy of our tendencies. Victory over suffering and death and all of the physical consequences of sin, though due to Baptism, will be final only on the day of the resurrection. The "new man" of Rom 6.6 is not just individual man renewed by Baptism; it is humanity as a whole that has been reconciled by Christ. Christ is the New Adam (1 Cor 15.45). At present the regeneration is spiritual; the body does not yet participate in it but a day will come when the entire cosmos, affected by the sin of man, will also be renewed by the glory of the Spirit (Rom 8.19–23).

Minister of Baptism. While the ordinary minister of Baptism is the priest and it belongs to his office to baptize, in the case of necessity not only a priest or deacon but even a layman or laywoman, or pagan or heretic can baptize provided that they keep the form of the Church and intend to do what the Church does (CIC c.742.1).

An important development in the Church's understanding of Baptism and of the function of the minister occurred in the period of the heresy of *Donatism. The problem concerned the rebaptism of those Donatists who became Catholics. According to Cyprian there are no Sacraments outside the Church and rebaptism was necessary for them. Stephen I opposed this on the ground that the efficacy of Baptism comes from the rite and not the minister. If heretics or schismatics observe the rites, they baptize validly. Both parties died without resolving the debate. The Councils of Arles in 314 and

Fig. 2. *American Indian convert being baptized in a mission chapel, watercolor by Father Nicholas Point, a mission priest on the Western Plains of the United States during the first half of the 19th century.*

Nicaea in 325 pronounced against rebaptism (Denz 123, 127, 128). Finally the Council of Trent (Denz 1617) stated with regard to the reformers that, where the form is respected, Baptism by non-Catholics is valid. In 1570 Pius V recognized Calvinist Baptism, but there has been a less favorable view toward Protestant Baptism in the Church since that time. Except when one is absolutely certain, by knowing the minister, his doctrinal positions, and liturgical practice, that the Baptism is not doubtful, the practice today is to rebaptize conditionally. However, it is not permitted to give conditional Baptism just out of scrupulosity, or to avoid having to check into records for proof of a Baptism already administered. It seems that the differences among Christian groups are less grave regarding Baptism than those regarding the Eucharist. There is general accord on the meaning of the rite despite some outward differences and the disagreement on infant Baptism.

It is important that the minister record having given the Sacrament. The parish baptismal register must include the names of the person baptized, the minister, parents and sponsors, and the place and day on which Baptism was conferred. In the case of illegitimate children, the name of the mother is to be recorded, if the fact that she is the mother is publicly known with certainty, or if she voluntarily requests it in writing or in the presence of two witnesses. The same is true with regard to the father. Otherwise the baptized child should be recorded as the child of an unknown father or of unknown parents.

The record must be kept in the parish where the person is baptized. A hospital may have its own baptismal register to record emergency Baptisms, in which case copies of the record of a Baptism should be sent to the local parish and proper pastor of the person who has been baptized.

Recipient. In the Apostolic age there was no definite time for administration of Baptism. In the 2d century, to facilitate preparations for Baptism, in view of the growing number of Christians, joint preparation of adult candidates was restricted to certain times of the year and solemn Baptism was given only a few times, especially on Easter and Pentecost (Tertullian, *De baptismo* 19; CSEL 20:217). In the Eastern Church the Epiphany was a favorite time for the Sacrament. As Baptism of infants spread, the old fixed times became neglected and forgotten. According to the present ceremonial, Baptism can be given on any day, but, in the case of adults, the old times should be adhered to as far as possible (CIC c.772).

Who Can be Baptized? Every living human not yet baptized is capable of receiving the Sacrament. Because Baptism of water is necessary for salvation whenever it can be given, it is commonly held that in case of danger of death one should not wait to baptize until actual birth. A skilled person is permited to baptize in the womb, but if the child can be baptized when born also, Baptism should be conferred then conditionally (CIC c.746). For a valid Baptism the water must flow directly upon the fetus, which must be viable. Thus the membranes are ruptured and Baptism conferred through the use of a syringe or some other irrigating instrument.

Ecclesiastical law favors the view that the soul is present from the very moment of conception; this is at least a practical norm since Baptism is necessary for salvation. Any aborted fetus should be baptized, without condition if it is known to be alive, and otherwise conditionally. A monstrous form of the fetus should be baptized at least conditionally. If there is doubt whether there is more than one human being in the birth, one is to be baptized absolutely and the others are to be baptized conditionally.

Foundlings are to be baptized conditionally unless, after investigation, there is clear proof of Baptism. A tag on the child claiming that Baptism has been given is not sufficient without investigation.

An infant of non-Catholic parents can be baptized without consent of the parents if the infant is in danger of death. A child may be lawfully baptized if at least one of the parents consents even though there is no danger of death. In all cases the child would be validly baptized outside of danger of death, but for licit Baptism there must be hope of Catholic upbringing. If there is no guarantee that the child could fulfill his obligations, to give Baptism would be an injustice. That justification is already acquired for mankind as a whole does not mean that each man has a strict right to receive it personally. On the other hand, gratuity does not make it exceptional. Salvation comes to all men in different degrees with respect for liberty of spirit.

The question of infant Baptism is treated in more detail elsewhere (*see* BAPTISM OF INFANTS). In recent times it has been the writing of the Protestant theologian Karl Barth against the practice that has stirred up controversy [*The Teaching of the Church Regarding Baptism* (London 1948)]. According to Barth, Baptism is a matter of the cognition of salvation. Another Protestant theologian, O. Cullman [*Baptism in the New Testament* (London 1952)], has replied that the act of God as such possesses effective power; the grace of Baptism is not just in the declaration of this act and its reception by faith.

Catholic theologians grant the importance of personal faith together with the *ex opere operato* aspect of the Sacrament. Faith is not absent from the Baptism of infants; they are baptized in the faith of Christ and of the Church. Although in Baptism the virtue of faith is infused and exists in the infant as a "habit," as a personal act it will play its indispensable role only later. The gratuitous character of salvation and its community nature justify the Baptism of those who cannot yet have personal faith (cf. ST 3.68.9 ad 1 and ad 2; 3.68.10 ad 3). Schillebeeckx (134–135) holds that there is a difference in the manner in which each possesses grace. It is possessed in the full sense of the term only by an adult person.

Dispositions Required. For an adult to come to the Sacrament without believing would be of no avail for salvation. Since efficacy can be had also from the desire of Baptism the problem is raised of how the efficacy of Baptism and that of faith are to be coordinated. The question of justification without the symbol is not posed in the New Testament. There the faith of the Christian in Christ the Redeemer is determined in the symbol. There is an organic bond between Baptism and faith (Gal 3.26–27; 2.13). The answer rests in the fact that the Sacrament adds something to the word; the Sacrament confirms what the word has bestowed and produces a more permanent bond with Christ.

An adult should be baptized only when he desires it with an understanding of what he seeks. He must also be sorry for his sins. In danger of death, if he is not able to ask for Baptism but has given some sign of probable intention to receive it, he should be baptized conditionally. If the intention is certain, but there is some doubt as to faith and sorrow for sin and danger of death is imminent, Baptism is to be conferred ab-

solutely because these are conditions for licit reception only, not conditions for denial of absolute Baptism.

Obligations. By their incorporation into the Church through Baptism, all Christians receive a share in the function of the Church as a sign of Christ in the world. One who is baptized must integrate his involvement in the affairs of this world into his existence as a believer and member of the Church. The duty of the *lay apostolate flowing from Baptism and Confirmation was often spoken of by Pius XI and Pius XII. It is sufficient to say here that the active role of the layman in the Church has not only a juridical but also an ontological foundation through the characters of Baptism and Confirmation. The anointing in Baptism reminds the neophyte that he is now configured to Christ, the anointed High Priest, and must live his life as a continual sacrifice, acceptable to the Father through Jesus Christ (1 Pt 2.4). As he receives the lighted candle from the priest, he is admonished: "Receive this burning light and see that you guard the grace of your Baptism without blame; keep the commandments of God, so that when the Lord shall come to call you to the nuptials, you may meet Him with all the saints in the heavenly courts, there to live forever."

Sponsors. There are three distinct roots for the office of *sponsor: the system of witnesses or guarantors for the catechumen, the assistant at Baptism, and the spokesman (sponsor) at infant Baptism. The assistant helped in the ceremony and so was a "liturgical person," a deacon or deaconess. Since the rite for adults was used for infant Baptism in early times (because infant Baptism was not the rule), a spokesman who was also the guarantor was necessary. It is certain that in the Frankish Church the various functions were united in one person, commonly known from the 9th century at least as the *patrinus*, that is, sponsor or godfather.

In the present ceremony the sponsor must hold or touch the person being baptized, and immediately after Baptism he receives him from the hands of the minister. A spiritual relationship arises between him and the baptized. In the case of solemn Baptism (CIC c.764),

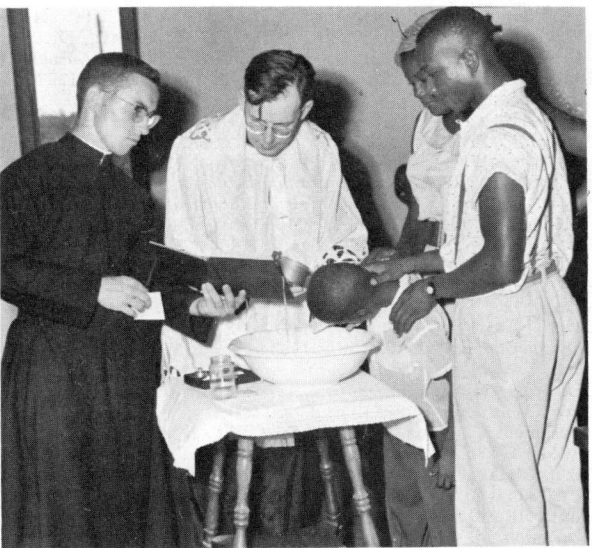

Fig. 3. Baptism in a mission church, South Carolina, 1956.

Fig. 4. Baptism during the Paschal Vigil. The taper symbolizes purity of soul and the white garb, newness of life.

there can be no more than two sponsors, a man and a woman, not closely related to the person baptized. For one to act *validly* as a sponsor, a person must have been baptized, have attained the age of reason and must intend to exercise the role of sponsor; he cannot be a heretic, schismatic, a declared excommunicate, deposed cleric, father, mother or spouse of the recipient; moreover, he must be designated as sponsor by the recipient, his parents or guardians, or the minister (CIC c.765). To act licitly as sponsor, a person must be at least 10 years old, a member in good standing in the Church, know the rudiments of the faith, not be a religious (unless he have the permission of his local superior in case of necessity), nor in major orders, unless he has the permission of his ordinary (CIC c.766).

See also, MARTYRDOM, THEOLOGY OF; WATER; LAY APOSTOLATE; CATHOLIC ACTION; BAPTISM (LITURGY OF); CATECHUMENATE.

Bibliography: General Works. J. BELLAMY ET AL., DTC 2:167–378. J. H. CREHAN, Davis CDT 1:228–237. E. DELAYE, DictSpir AscMyst 1:1218–1230. A. HULSBOSCH and L. HARTMAN, EncDict Bibl 198–206. G. JACQUEMET ET AL., *Catholicisme* 1:1207–27. Special Studies. A. BENOIT, *Le Baptême chrétien au second siècle* (Strasbourg 1953). R. E. BROWN, "The Eucharist and Baptism in St. John," ProcSocCathCollTeachSacrDoctr 8 (1961) 14–37. R. M. BROWN, *The Spirit of Protestantism* (New York 1961). L. CERFAUX, *Le Chrétien dans la théologie paulinienne* (Paris 1962). Church of Scotland, *Interim Report of the Special Commission on Baptism* (Edinburgh 1955). W. J. CONWAY, *The Time and Place of Baptism* (Washington 1954). J. DANIÉLOU, *From Shadows to Reality,* tr. W. HIBBERD (Westminster, Md. 1960). J. C. DIDIER, "À propos du caractère sacramentel," *Ami du Clergé* 72 (1962) 167–171. G. J. DYER, *Limbo: Unsettled Question* (New York 1964). N. HALLIGAN, *The Administration of the Sacraments* (New York 1963). C. JOURNET, *La Volonté divine salvifique sur les petits enfants* (Bruges 1958). R. J. KEARNEY, *Sponsors at Baptism According to the Code of Canon Law* (Washington 1925). E. J. KILMARTIN, "Patristic Views of Sacramental Sanctity," ProcSocCathCollTeachSacrDoctr 8 (1961) 59–85. K. RAHNER, *The Church and the Sacraments,* tr. W. J. O'HARA (New York 1963). W. F. RYAN, "The Teaching of St. Thomas in the *Summa* Concerning the Baptismal Character," AmEcclRev 149 (1963) 361–385. E. SCHILLEBEECKX, *Christ: The Sacrament of the Encounter with God* (New York 1963). V. WILKIN, *From Limbo to Heaven,* ed. M. BÉVENOT (New York 1961). L. VILLETTE, *Foi et sacrement* (Paris 1959). A. GEORGE et al., *Baptism in the New Testament,* tr. D. ASKEW (Baltimore 1964). **Illustration credits:** Fig. 1, Alinari-Art Reference Bureau. Fig. 2, Pius XII Memorial Library, St. Louis, Missouri. Fig. 3, Trinity Missions. Fig. 4, Clemens Kalischer.

[T. M. DE FERRARI]

BAPTISM FOR THE DEAD

A supposed ceremony in the Apostolic Church, the existence of which is deduced from 1 Cor 15.29: "Else what shall they do who receive Baptism for the dead? If the dead do not rise at all, why then do people receive Baptism for them?" (so in CCD). The Marcionites once believed, as the Mormons now do, that St. Paul clearly mentioned and approved such a ceremony. The Mormons, therefore, vicariously baptize a living person for someone who died without Baptism. This interpretation of 1 Cor 15.29 is irreconcilable with Christian tenets.

Until the 16th century, the exegesis of this text could be grouped into two schools. The Latin writers, repeating Ambrosiaster, taught that St. Paul referred to some Corinthians who, out of good faith, were vicariously baptized for their friends who had died without baptism. The Apostle, without approving it, used such a reference as an *argumentum ad hominem* against those Corinthians who denied the Resurrection. We cannot, however, conceive how a man like St. Paul could leave uncensured such a superstitious rite, had it existed. Moreover, this explanation is evidently wrong because it begs the question. First, it assumes the existence of vicarious baptism from the obscure words of St. Paul; then it uses this same assumed rite to explain the Pauline text.

The Greek Fathers followed Tertullian's and St. Chrysostom's view that St. Paul meant "baptism for our dead bodies," i.e., baptism received for the resurrection of our dying, or mortal, bodies. Thus St. Paul would use the purpose of baptism to expose the fallacy that "there is no resurrection of the dead." This opinion is based on the context and on Rom 6.4. However, it forces the text somewhat by taking the substantive νεκρῶν, "dead," as an adjective, i.e., dying or mortal.

From the 16th century on, scholars, especially Protestant ones, proposed many and new theories. Luther understood Paul's text as referring to baptism administered upon the sepulchers of martyrs. Calvin, echoing St. Epiphanius, explained it as baptism of dying people. Theodore Beza saw it as the washing of the dead. St. Robert Bellarmine took it metaphorically as "baptism of tears and penance" in suffrage of the dead.

It seems that an improved punctuation and a better understanding of ὑπέρ are necessary to solve this question. The punctuation can be changed because it is no part of the critical text. Many examples prove that, in Greek, ὑπέρ can be, and was often, used instead of εἰς. Therefore to be baptized ὑπέρ, "for," is the same as to be baptized εἰς "into, to." Accordingly, the Greek of 1 Cor 15.29 can be understood as: "Otherwise, what shall they do who are baptized? [Are they baptized] for the dead? If the dead do not rise at all, why are people baptized? For them [that are dead]?" And the meaning would be: Baptism leads us unto resurrection. But, if there is no resurrection, where then does Baptism lead us? To the kingdom of the dead? Then why are people baptized? To join those that are dead forever? This explanation seems grammatically possible, and best fits the text, context, and common doctrine of Christianity.

Bibliography: P. DÜRSELEN, "Die Taufe für die Toten I Kor. 15,29," *Theologische Studien u. Kritiken* 76 (1903) 291–308. H. NIBLEY, "Baptism for the Dead in Ancient Times," *Improvement Era* 51 (1948) 786–; 52 (1949) 24–, 90–, 146–, 212–. B. M. FOSCHINI, "Those Who Are Baptized for the Dead," *Cath BiblQuart* 12 (1950) 260–276, 379–388; 13 (1951) 46–78, 172–198, 276–283. A. CALMET, "Dissertatio de baptismate pro mortuis ad I Cor. 15,29," *Commentarius litteralis in S. Scripturam* (Venice 1797) 10:77–81. P. J. DELAZER, "De baptismo pro mortuis," *Antonianum* 6 (1931) 113–136.

[B. M. FOSCHINI]

BAPTISM OF CHRIST

The baptism of Christ in the *Jordan River by St. *John the Baptist is described by all four Evangelists (Mt 3.13–17; Mk 1.9–12; Lk 3.21–22; Jn 1.29–34). Its important place in the Gospel accounts is explained by the fact that it was a significant element in the *catechesis of the early Church.

Our Lord comes from Nazareth to associate Himself in baptism with those who because of the preaching of John are ready to share in the promises of the Messianic times. He is baptized by John in the waters of the Jordan, traditionally near its entrance into the *Dead Sea, where John is baptizing. The inversion of roles surprises John, who is assured by Christ that on this occasion it must be accepted since it is the divine will. Jesus accepts baptism from John in the same spirit as that in which he has submitted to other rites and duties proper to sinful men in order "to fulfull all justice" (Mt 3.16), that is, the will of the Father in His regard. Submission to this rite, an admission of sin in other men, is in Christ an act of humility dictated by His mission, which is to bring to perfect realization the OT virtue of justice, the acceptance of God's holy will.

Christ leaves the waters immediately after being baptized, since He has no need, as others have, to remain to confess His sins. This is followed by a theophany in which *God the Father publicly acknowledges Jesus of Nazareth as His Son and the *Holy Spirit descends in the form of a dove. The opening of the heavens and the descent of the Holy Spirit are reminiscent of the *spirit of God brooding over the primeval waters in Gn 1.2. This descent and resting of the Spirit upon Him is the solemn inauguration of the work of Jesus, His investiture for His Messianic destiny. It is also an announcement of *Pentecost, which will inaugurate the Baptism in water and the Spirit for the Church and for those who enter into it. The voice of the Father proclaims Jesus as His Son in words echoing those of the *Servant of the Lord Oracles (Is 42.1) and those describing the Messiah-King in Ps 2.9. The phrase *Son of God here does not designate divinity, but rather the favor shown by God to Jesus for Himself and for His special work. The Christian reader for whom the Gospels were written would see in the descent of the Spirit and the voice of the Father the second creation, the *rebirth through water and the Spirit in the Sacrament of Baptism. The recognition of Jesus as the beloved Son also indicates to the Christian reader the divine filiation of those who will believe in Jesus.

Jesus is baptized in view of His death, which later in the Gospels is itself called a baptism; baptism signifies the expiatory death He is to undergo for the sins of men. The people who are baptized in the Jordan bring to the waters their sins; when Jesus is baptized in the same waters He takes upon Himself their sins, for which He is to die (see Mk 10.38; Lk 12.50). In an allusion to the fourth Servant Song (Is 53.7) the Baptist (Jn 1.20) describes Christ as the *Lamb of God who takes away the sins of the world. The baptism of Jesus in the Jordan announces His baptism in death (Lk 12.50; Mk 10.38), which brings Jesus to His *Resurrection, when in receiving the plenitude of the Spirit His glorified humanity is constituted the vivifying principle of the communication of the Spirit to those who believe in Him. The public life of Christ is enclosed then between His two baptisms; an echo of this is found in Jn 19.34 when he mentions the blood and water coming forth from the pierced side of Jesus on the cross.

See also MYSTERIES OF THE LIFE OF JESUS.

Bibliography: H. HOUBAUT, DTC 8.1:646–656. A. MICHEL, DTC 8.1:1184–85. DTC, Tables générales 2:2626. "Taufe," "Taufe Christi," LexThK² v.9. J. LEBRETON, DBSuppl 4:987–990. EncDictBibl 199–201. X. LÉON-DUFOUR, ed., *Vocabulaire de théologie biblique* (Paris 1962) 83. H. CAZELLES, *Catholicisme* 1:1228–29.

[R. L. FOLEY]

BAPTISM OF INFANTS

From the very beginning the Church has administered the Sacrament of Baptism to infants. Not only was this practice considered lawful, but it was also taught to be absolutely necessary for salvation. This position results from the Church's teaching on the universality of original sin and on the Sacrament of Baptism as being the divinely instituted means to erase it. Thus the words of Christ, "Amen, amen, I say to thee, unless a man be born again of water and the Spirit, he cannot enter into the kingdom of God" (Jn 3.5), were understood as admitting no exception whatsoever. In her teaching the Church has admitted martyrdom as a substitute for actual Baptism in the case of infants, but this is the sole exception.

It makes little difference whether Scripture has any actual references to the practice of infant Baptism or not. Probably it can be conceded that no explicit references are to be found there. Moreover, the problem that results from a person's receiving the Sacrament of faith before the age of reason, when no personal acts or dispositions are present, did occur to the Fathers of the Church, though they did not consider this to be a great difficulty. After all, the infant was afflicted with original sin without its consent, and besides in the Old Testament God had already instituted a similar remedy for male infants in the rite of circumcision. The faith of the infant, which is obviously impossible, is supplied by the Church. This belief of the Church manifests itself in her disciplinary prescriptions, especially in the obligation placed on the parents to have newly born infants baptized as soon as possible.

Opposition to This Teaching. In the course of time objections arose to the practice of the Church. In broad outline, three periods can be distinguished: the period up to the Protestant Reformation, that of the Anabaptists at the time of the Reformation, and that of the present day.

Beginnings to Reformation. The first clash of any importance arose during the controversy over *Pelagianism in the early Church. Pelagius's denial of original sin logically made Baptism unnecessary for infants. But in the course of the conflict, in which St. Augustine (d. 430) played a great role, Pelagius attempted to defend the practice of infant Baptism and at the same time to deny original sin. He asserted the necessity of Baptism to enter the kingdom of heaven, but not to obtain eternal life. The full meaning of this distinction still puzzles us today. At any rate, on this occasion the Church reasserted her teaching at the Council of Carthage (418). Infants must be baptized so that the sin contracted in generation may be remitted through the Sacrament of regeneration.

Another denial appeared in the Middle Ages when certain sects such as the *Cathari rejected infant Baptism. Because of their dualist views on material things, all Sacraments were repulsive, but especially infant Baptism. In any other Sacrament the conscious assent of the recipient may mitigate the charge of materialism, but not in infant Baptism. Thus this case became an object of special contempt. In their view, visible creation came from an evil power, and thus it was impossible for material things to be considered as vehicles of grace.

Anabaptists. When Martin Luther (d. 1546) proclaimed the absolute supremacy of the Sacred Scriptures and tended to make the efficacy of the Sacraments depend on the faith of the recipient, tragic—though, it would appear, logical—conclusions were swiftly deduced. A faction arose at Zwickau in 1521. The leader was Thomas Münzer (d. 1525), the Lutheran pastor of that place. Two cloth weavers there, Nicholas Storch and Mark Stübner, claimed to have a direct call from God to preach. They attacked many doctrines of Luther but especially his teaching on infant Baptism. Hence they were called *Anabaptists. They denied the validity of infant Baptism and rebaptized adults who had been baptized in infancy. These fanatics took as their point of departure the reform ideas of Luther and by developing his ideas went beyond him. They were often referred to as the extreme left in the army of the reformers. Luther fought all his life to dissociate himself from these zealots. The hostility of the orthodox reformers to them cannot conceal the fact that the most peculiar doctrines of the Anabaptists were to them only corollaries—illegitimately drawn, as the orthodox reformers believed—from the fundamental principles common to both: the independence of the individual judgment and the supreme importance of the subjective element, personal faith, in religion. Besides there seems to be some evidence that the Anabaptists denied original sin as well. The annals of this movement lasted only about 15 years, though their principles continued to live on.

There is no doubt that Luther retained infant Baptism. The constant practice of the Church supplied him with a bulwark in support of his position. The Church, he says, could not have been permitted by God to remain in error for so long a time. He pointed out that the agreement of the entire Church about infant Baptism is a special miracle. To deny it is to deny the Church itself. This teaching of Luther about infant Baptism is clearly stated in the Confession of Augsburg, 1530. There the Anabaptists were condemned because they repudiated infant Baptism and asserted that children are saved without Baptism. The error of the Anabaptists was also clearly rejected by the Council of Trent.

Present-day Viewpoints. The tension born of the dilemma with the Anabaptists still persists in the Prot-estant communities and accounts for the diversity of practice in infant Baptism. Although lineally unrelated to the Anabaptists, those who do not practice infant Baptism—for example, the Seventh-day Adventists, Baptists, Mormons, Quakers, Disciples of Christ—show doctrinal affinity with them. The practice of infant Baptism is followed by the Lutherans, Episcopalians, Methodists, Presbyterians, and others. The Baptist position is that Baptism is a voluntary public profession of Christian faith and that only persons old enough to understand its significance and its symbolism should be accepted for Baptism. Moreover, Baptists give their children the right to decide for themselves whether or not they wish to be baptized as a public profession of faith.

Fate of Unbaptized Infants. From the Catholic teaching on the necessity of Baptism for salvation arises the difficult problem of the fate of infants who die without Baptism. Catholic doctrine clearly defends the loss of heaven and of the beatific vision as a penalty for original sin. Since infants dying without Baptism still have original sin on their souls, revealed data of faith forces us to conclude that they cannot enter heaven. At the same time it stands to reason that they should not be punished in hell as adult sinners. Thus a special state and place for them called *Limbo is postulated. Exclusion from heaven and absence of the torments of hell are the two pillars on which Limbo rests. This is the safe and widely held solution to the problem of unbaptized infants; at the same time it is clear that this is not official Catholic teaching. It seems that we are on very safe ground if we express the hope that God in His mercy and wisdom may have devised some way, unknown to us, to save all these infants. To reduce this pious hope to concrete explanation, however, is very risky, if not impossible. All the attempts to devise a means of salvation for them were labeled by the Holy Office on Feb. 18, 1958, as lacking solid foundation [ActApS 50 (1958) 114]. This shows that the problem is not an open question in the usual sense of the term.

This problem does not loom as large even among Protestant groups that practice infant Baptism, since they have mitigated their viewpoints considerably on the absolute necessity of Baptism. The doctrine of Limbo is dismissed as an effort to soften somewhat the cruel nature of the "erroneous" teaching that infants dying without Baptism are deprived of the beatific vision, but subject to no torment. Such is the Lutheran viewpoint. To clarify the fate of infants dying without Baptism, the Presbyterian Church in the U.S. stated that they believe that all who die in infancy are included in the election of grace and are regenerated and saved by Christ, through the Spirit, who works when and where and how He pleases. The assumption is made that death in infancy is an infallible sign of salvation, whether the infant is baptized or not.

Bibliography: J. BELLAMY et al., DTC 2:167–378. Enc. Brit. (1957) 1:857–858. J. A. HARDON, *The Protestant Churches of America* (Westminster, Md. 1956). P. J. HILL, *The Existence of a Children's Limbo According to Post-Tridentine Theologians* (Shelby, Ohio 1961). H. LENNERZ, *De sacramento baptismi* (Rome 1948). B. LEEMING, *Principles of Sacramental Theology* (new ed. Westminster, Md. 1956). L. ROSTEN, ed., *Religions in America* (New York 1963). J. P. WILLIAMS, *What Americans Believe and How They Worship* (New York 1952). P. DE PUNIET, DACL 2.1:251–346. C. V. HÉRIS, *Catholicisme* 4:151–157; "Le Salut des enfants morts sans baptême," *Maison-Dieu* 10 (1947) 86–105. M. LAURENCE, "Esquisse d'une étude sur le sort des enfants morts sans baptême," AnnThAug 12 (1952) 148–186. A. STENZEL, LexThK² 6:158–160. J. C. DIDIER, ed., *Le Baptême des enfants* (Paris 1959). K. ALAND, *Die Säuglingstaufe in Neuen Testament und in der alten Kirche* (Munich 1961).

[P. J. HILL]

BAPTISMAL FONT, container for baptismal water and the vessel over which the Sacrament of Baptism is conferred. Thus it is in a real sense the spiritual door of the church. The word font suggests flowing water, and this is what the early fonts often had, thus accomplishing the symbolism of living water. The font regularly took a central shape—round, octagonal, hexagonal, or cruciform. Early fonts, such as those of St. John Lateran, Rome (4th century), and Ravenna (5th century), were often quite large. In the Middle Ages the size gradually decreased, and the vessel itself was raised from the ground; it finally became hardly distinguishable from a holy-water stoup. In recent years there has been a notable move to make the font again a significant architectural element in the church (*see* BAPTISTERY). Church law concerning the font calls for a fitting place and form, watertight material, and a font appropriately designed and lockable. It also strongly recommends a representation of John baptizing Christ. For illustrations, see the two pages following.

Bibliography: C. H. MEINBERG, "The Baptistery and Other Spaces," *Worship* 35 (1960–61) 536–549. Miller FundLit. W. WEYRES and O. BARTNING, eds., *Kirchen: Handbuch für den Kirchenbau* (Munich 1959). Eisenhofer Lit. H. LECLERCQ, DACL 2.1:382–469. Righetti. **Illustration credits:** Fig. 1a, Dura-Europos Publications, Yale University. Fig. 1b, B. van Iersel, SMM. Fig. 1c, Hirmer Verlag München. Fig. 1d, A. C. L. Bruxelles. Fig. 2a, Anderson-Art Reference Bureau. Fig. 2b, Alinari-Art Reference Bureau. Fig. 2d, Lee A. Hanley.

[C. MEINBERG]

BAPTISMAL SYMBOL

The term baptismal symbol refers to the Creed recited during the baptismal ceremony. The Greek word σύμβολον generically means a sign or token of recognition. Its use in reference to the Creed has been explained in various ways. According to *Rufinus of Aquileia, the symbol is the token or password by which the preachers of authentic Apostolic doctrine can be distinguished from heretics pretending to be followers of Christ (*Com. in Symb. Apost.* 2).

St. *Augustine states that the creed is called *symbolum* in the sense of a pact contracted by businessmen (*Serm.* 212). Others have proposed a derivation of the Christian use of *symbolum* from the mystery cults, whose secret formulae (*symbola*) were employed in initiation rites. Some suspect that "*symbolum* initially denoted the triple baptismal interrogations; for St. Cyprian it may have covered the thrice-repeated dipping in the water as well" (Kelly, 58).

Apostolic Times. The New Testament attests that in Apostolic times there were inchoative statements of creed or conventional summaries of the faith; also indicated is an initial process of fixation in regard to creedal expression. These creedal forms are connected with various life situations in the early Church: preaching, catechesis, and liturgy. Perhaps the symbol originated in the liturgy, especially the baptismal liturgy, where the singular, "*I* believe," is appropriate and typical.

The earliest baptismal creed-prototypes are not so much doctrinal summaries, as personal acknowledgments and acceptances of Christ. This is seen in the account of the conversion of the Ethiopian courtier who, after instruction in the faith, exclaimed: "I believe that Jesus Christ is the Son of God" (*Acts* 8.37) and was then baptized by Philip.

New Testament creedal statements display considerable elasticity: sometimes there is only one element, for example, confession that Jesus is Lord (e.g., 1 Cor 12.3); other creedal types have two parts: parallel acknowledgments of God the Father and Jesus Christ (e.g., 1 Cor 8.6). Explicit Trinitarian confessions are rare; the best example is Christ's command to "make disciples of all nations, baptizing them in the name of the Father and of the Son and of the Holy Spirit" (Mt 28.19).

Efforts to reconstruct a unique and determined primitive creedal form (*Urtypus*) have proved unsatisfactory: variety seems the natural result of different kerygmatic and liturgical situations. Nor can it be proved that Christological creeds were prior to Trinitarian ones or that Christological creeds were used only in Jewish circles, while Trinitarian creeds were prepared for a Gentile milieu.

Confession of Christ. The Symbol, as a personal confession of Christ, forms a necessary part of the ceremonies of Baptism, the Sacrament of personal incorporation into Christ's Church. (1) After the initial stages of the *catechumenate in the early Church, the bishop delivered the creed (*traditio symboli*) to the more advanced catechumens (*competentes, phōtizomenoi* or enlightened), whose duty it was to learn it verbatim so that they could "render" it (*redditio symboli*) either at the end of their catechetical instructions or during the ceremonies preceding Baptism. Thus the recitation of a declaratory creed was connected with the catechumenate or with the baptismal liturgy. (2) As the person to be baptized stood by the water, he was asked successively whether he believed in the Father, the Son, and the Holy Spirit. At each affirmation (I believe), he was plunged into the water (Hippolytus, *Apostolic Tradition* 21). Here the creed assumed the form of a dialogue between the minister of Baptism and the one baptized (similar to the formalities requisite for legal contracts).

Creedal Structure. In the 2d and 3d centuries, along with the development of the catechumenate, there was a fusion of Christological and Trinitarian elements into stereotyped statements; earlier fluidity in expression was replaced with more theologically balanced phrases. The *Epistula Apostolorum* 5, exemplifies basic creedal structure in the 2d century in confessing belief "in the Father the ruler of the universe, and in Jesus Christ our Redeemer, and in the Holy Spirit the Paraclete, and in the Holy Church and in the forgiveness of sins."

Declarative creeds eventually predominated in the baptismal liturgy, and several factors help explain this. Ceremonies belonging to the catechumenate were apparently incorporated into the baptismal service in view of infant Baptism. Later, the discipline of the *Secret surrounded the *traditio symboli* with secrecy, and the assertion of Christological and Trinitarian heresies resulted in the reformulation of baptismal symbols.

In the East the interrogations eventually disappeared and were replaced by a declaratory creed and a declaratory baptismal form. In the West the interrogations, though sometimes omitted, never disappeared; the bap-

Baptismal font: (a) from the house church at Dura-Europos, c. 232–256, as restored in the Yale University Art Gallery; (b) in the Church of the Council at Ephesus, 4th century;

(c) in the Orthodox baptistery at Ravenna, 5th century, renovated in the later Middle Ages; (d) in the Church of St. Bartholomew, Liège, bronze, c. 1120.

Baptismal font: (a) in the cathedral at Siena, marble, work-shop of Federighi, c. 1485; (b) in the basilica of S. Maria Maggiore, Rome, designed by L. Valadier in 1825, with figures by Carlo Spagna; (c) in Sacré Coeur church, Mulhausen, France, 20th century; (d) in the abbey church, St. John's Abbey, Collegeville, Minn., 1961.

tismal form was declaratory, while the declaratory creed, previously included in the catechumenate, became part of the baptismal liturgy.

Creedal Development. At the Council of *Nicaea I (325), the bishops probably incorporated antiheretical statements (particularly the *homoousios*) into an already existing baptismal creed. The Nicene Symbol, and the symbols dependent upon it, influenced the baptismal creeds of other churches. By the 6th century the so-called Niceno-Constantinopolitan Creed, presumably the baptismal symbol of the "New Rome" in the 5th century, predominated throughout the East.

In the West, from the late 2d century to the 5th century, the old Roman Creed was the basic format for baptismal symbols. From the 6th to the 9th century, perhaps because of Arianism in the West, or because of Byzantine influence in Italy, the Niceno-Constantinopolitan Creed was used as a baptismal symbol.

Meanwhile, the Apostles' Creed, which despite Rufinus's legend of its Apostolic origin (*Com. in Symb. Apost.* 2), is an expanded version of the old Roman Creed, was accepted in southern Gaul as the baptismal symbol in the 7th century. In the wake of Carolingian liturgical reform, the Apostles' Creed replaced the Niceno-Constantinopolitan Creed, at first in France (9th century), and eventually in Rome and throughout the West.

Bibliography: J. N. D. KELLY, *Early Christian Creeds* (2d ed. London 1960). Quasten Patr 1:23–29. Ghellinck Patr v.1. P. FRANSEN and A. STENZEL, LexThK² 4:935–939.

[J. FORD]

BAPTIST OF MANTUA (SPAGNOLI), BL.,

Carmelite administrator and humanist; b. Mantua, Italy, April 17, 1447; d. Mantua, March 20, 1516 (feast, March 20). As a youth he studied at Mantua and the University of *Padua. He entered the *Carmelites at Ferrara in 1463 and completed his doctorate in theology at the University of *Bologna in 1475. Early entrusted with teaching and administration, he was vicar-general of the Congregation of Mantua for six 2-year terms from 1483 to 1513, and was prior general of the whole Carmelite order from 1513 till his death. *Leo XIII declared Baptist blessed in 1885, and his relics are preserved in the cathedral at Mantua. The friar was a zealous advocate of reform, and his *Fastorum libri duodecim,* dedicated to *Leo X, mentions the doom threatening the Church. Some of the Mantuan's strictures were so strong that *Luther simply borrowed them. A poet of Christian humanism, he enjoyed the reputation of "the Christian Vergil" even in his lifetime. He corresponded with and counseled other humanists; *Pico della Mirandola was his friend, and *Erasmus admired him as did John *Colet. His writings, all in Latin, had a phenomenal vogue in the 16th and 17th centuries; 179 incunabula have been catalogued, and there are more than 550 editions of his works printed after 1500. His poems include the famous *Eclogues,* written when he was 15 but later revised, and *Parthenice Mariana,* testimony to his tender devotion to the Blessed Virgin. His prose works include *De vita beata,* a Ciceronian dialogue with his father, first printed in 1474, and *De patientia.*

Bibliography: *Opera omnia,* 4 v. (Antwerp 1576); *The Eclogues of Baptista Mantuanus,* ed. W. P. MUSTARD (Baltimore 1911). E. COCCIA, *Le edizione delle opere del Mantovano* (Rome 1960). L. M. SAGGI, *La congregazione mantovana dei Carmelitani* (Rome 1954) 116–152. E. MEUTHEN, LexThK² 1:1228. P. A. DE SAINT-PAUL, DTC 9.2:1918–23; DHGE 5:525–527.

[E. R. CARROLL]

BAPTISTERY

The room or building in which Baptism is performed. The word *baptisterium* was used for the pool (also *frigidarium*) in the Roman *thermae* or baths. Among the early Christians it was referred to as the *fons* or *piscina* since it enclosed the fount or pool; and also as the *lavacrum* or *photisterion,* the place of spiritual washing or divine enlightenment.

While the early Christians baptized by immersion in rivers, fountains, and the sea (Justin, *1 Apol.* 61.3; Tertullian, *De Bapt.* 4), by the 3d century they used a pool or bath in a special room in the house of worship as is indicated by the square basin buttressed with two columns discovered at the foot of the chapel room in the Christian house at *Dura-Europos (c. 232). The basilica (possibly 3d century) at *Emmaus (modern 'Im-was?) also had a baptistery next to the apse.

Ancient Baptisteries. At *Rome, there is no trace of a baptistery before the 4th century. The claim that Baptism was performed in the catacombs is now generally abandoned. The ancient title churches of St. Pudentiana and St. Sabina were erected over foundations that served as private baths; but it is with the Constantinian epoch that evidence for a separate place for Baptism becomes certain.

In the still-standing Lateran baptistery next to the basilica of St. John, the foundations reveal two ancient pools that served as baptisteries. Beneath the octagonal wall that forms the present basin and goes back to the reconstruction under Pope *Sixtus III (d. 440), there is a round wall reinforced by eight pilasters; and before

Mid-5th-century baptistery of the Orthodox, Ravenna.

Baptistery in the narthex of St. Anthony's Church, Superior, Wis., erected 1960.

that, there was a still smaller round basin supported by pottery shafts.

Ancient baptisteries similar to that of the Lateran have been discovered in Italy, Gaul, Africa, and the Orient erected between the 4th and the 9th centuries, and ranging from the primitive to the magnificent in construction: circular, square, rectangular, cruciform, clover, hexagonal, and more frequently octagonal in form.

Later, ornamented baptisteries were modeled on the central room of the Roman baths with a cupola roof and frequently a baldachino over the pool. Some were separate buildings close to the episcopal residence or church as at the *Lateran; others were attached directly to the apse or a part of the church. Many were surrounded or preceded by a portico and frequently there were alcoves or rooms for the other ceremonies such as the exorcism and anointings as well as Confirmation (performed in the *consignatorium*) formed by columns on which drapes could be supported, particularly for undressing and to protect the nudity of the one being baptized from the audience. Steps on which the one baptizing stood led down into the pool itself.

At *Ostia a modest 4th-century baptistery has been discovered that was attached to the lateral nave on the left side of the church. A similar structure was built onto the early 5th-century church of St. Anastasia in Rome; and the 6th-century church of St. Chrysogonus had its baptistery on the left side of the apse. It is evident that by then public celebration of Baptism was performed by the parish priest as well as the bishop.

Ornamentation. The Liber pontificalis describes an ornamented baptistery probably of the mid-4th century with a circular pool of porphyry indented with inside

steps and fed by water flowing from the mouth of the golden head of a lamb and seven stags. Lifelike statues of Christ and St. John the Baptist stood by the side of the pool. At *Aquileia, Ravenna, *Salona, and Grado the baptisteries were covered with a cupola roof and richly ornamented with mosaics. At Albenga, Brescia, Fréjus, the baptisteries resemble the mausoleum of the Roman emperor *Diocletian at Spalato; and at Dura-Europos the walls were decorated with pictures of the *Good Shepherd and other Biblical scenes.

The development of baptismal theology is reflected in the decor with symbols of the fish and the living water, signifying the new life of Christ, the spiritual purification, and the death and resurrection with Christ, that is emphasized by the Epistle to the Romans (6:3–5).

With the prevalance of infant baptism, the need for large basinlike baptisteries diminished and they were replaced by fonts; frequently an ancient sarcophagus was turned to this usage as was done in the Roman church of St. Chrysogonus in the 10th century. In the 12th and 13th centuries in the West, Baptism by immersion for infants was replaced by infusion; but following tradition, large ornamented baptisteries separate from the church and dedicated to St. John the Baptist continued to be constructed. In recent times a simple chapel or room with a baptismal font in the church or cathedral has become the common practice.

Bibliography: N. MAURICE-DENIS and R. BOULET, *Catholicisme* 1:1234–36. J. H. EMMINGHAUS, LexThK² 1:1232. H. LECLERCQ, DACL 2.1:382–469. F. W. DEICHMANN, ReallexAnt Chr 1:1157–67. W. M. BEDARD, *Symbolism of the Baptismal Font* (Washington 1951). F. J. DÖLGER, "Zur Symbolik des altchristlichen Taufhauses," *Antike und Christentum* 4 (1934) 153–187. **Illustration credits:** Fig. 1, Anderson-Art Reference Bureau. Fig. 2, The Cerny Associates, Inc., Architects, Minneapolis.

[F. X. MURPHY]

BAPTISTS

A Protestant communion totaling about 25 million in more than 100 countries. Although derived from a common stock, they are organized in many separate bodies that, apart from a basic ideological core, exhibit great diversity.

Distinctive Emphases. It was their doctrine of the Church that originally impelled Baptists to form a distinct denomination. While they shared with other Christians a belief in "the holy, catholic church," they differed with most contemporaries regarding its visible manifestation. Most churches were territorial, indiscriminately embracing all believers within a given area regardless of spiritual qualifications. Baptists, to the contrary, held that membership in visible churches should be limited to those who were members of the true people of God. In their own terms, "Visible churches are made up of visible saints."

Although Baptists conceded the impossibility of ascertaining perfectly who belonged to God's elect people, they believed that there were signs that indicated whether a person were truly regenerate. Therefore, applicants for membership were required to relate their experience of God's grace before the entire congregation. When convinced of the authenticity of such a testimony, the church "by a judgment of charity" approved the person for baptism. Once admitted into the church, a member accepted covenant obligations and was subject to the discipline of the congregation. Baptists were not perfectionists, but they expected sincere commitment and an earnest attempt to be obedient to Christ.

Baptists also placed great importance upon each local congregation. Denying that the Universal Church is embodied in a single, concrete institution, they insisted that it is visible primarily in particular congregations. To every such "gathered church," they held, authority had been given to order its own affairs under the headship of Jesus Christ. All members were expected to participate in the worship and in the church meeting at which the will of Christ was sought on pertinent issues. The strong emphasis upon the local congregation was balanced by a recognition of the need for fellowship with other churches and for cooperation in common concerns. This sense of interdependence they acknowledged through forming associations.

In connection with their concept of the Church, Baptists had a strong conviction regarding religious liberty. Believing that congregations of disciplined Christians were a sensitive instrument for seeking the guidance of the Holy Spirit, they insisted that they should be free to obey the Lord's will. Therefore, they opposed interference from outside authorities, either civil or ecclesiastical.

Origin and Development in England. A late offshoot of the English Reformation, Baptists represented a variety of Puritanism. *See* REFORMATION, PROTESTANT (IN THE BRITISH ISLES); PURITANS. Although some have claimed for Baptists an unbroken succession from the 1st century, this view cannot be substantiated. Another theory relates Baptists to the Swiss Brethren of Zurich, via the Mennonite line; but if such a connection existed, it was very tenuous and had little significance for subsequent Baptist history (*see* ANABAPTISTS; MENNONITES). That Baptists emerged from English Congregationalism early in the 17th century is demonstrable, and there is no need to seek beyond this source to account for characteristic emphases of the Baptist faith (*see* CONGREGATIONALISTS).

At two distinct points, Baptist branches sprouted from the Congregationalist stalk. The first instance was

Worship service in a Baptist church. The choir usually faces the congregation over the pulpit and communion table.

that of an English refugee group of Congregationalists in Amsterdam, Holland, of whom John *Smyth was pastor. In about 1609 Smyth concluded that infant baptism was invalid, and he proceeded to baptize himself and the rest of his congregation, reconstituting the church on the basis of believer's baptism. Subsequently a part of that congregation returned to England to become the first Baptist church there. Two pastors of that church, Thomas Helwys and John Murton, published early pleas for religious freedom. Another separate emanation of Baptists occurred about 1638, when members of a Congregationalist church in London seceded to organize a new church that practiced believer's baptism. It appears that prior to 1641 Baptists practiced affusion, but after that date the rite was administered by the mode of immersion.

From these two churches the General and the Particular Baptists developed. In most respects they were alike, but they disagreed over the questions of predestination and human freedom. The General Baptists, stemming from Smyth's congregation, held that Christ's atoning death was *general*. This tinge of *Arminianism can be accounted for by their residence in the Netherlands when these issues were being fiercely debated. The Particular Baptists, arising from the London congregation of 1638, believed in a limited atonement. That is, since God had predestined those whom he would save, the atonement of Christ sufficed only for *particular* individuals who were of the elect.

Both General and Particular Baptists early declared their views in *Confessions of Faith. Although they are frequently referred to as belonging to the "left-wing" variety of Puritanism, along with Quakers, Baptists placed much more importance upon objective authority of Scriptures, confessional statements, and procedural regularity than did the latter group (*see* FRIENDS, RELIGIOUS SOCIETY OF). The most important document of the General Baptists was the Orthodox Creed of 1678. Explicitly affirming acceptance of the Apostles', Nicene, and Athanasian Creeds, this document set forth the theological views of the General Baptists in detail. The classic formulation of Particular Baptists was the Second London Confession of 1677. For more than a century and a half it was used as a standard in both England and America.

Both groups had a similar understanding of baptism and the Lord's Supper, which they referred to as sacraments or ordinances. Baptism was regarded as the sign of engrafting into the body of Christ, of remission of sins, and of fellowship with Christ in his death and resurrection. Baptists differed with regard to the degree of authority that belonged to their respective general assemblies, and there were some differences in their church officers. In relationship to other Christians, they felt particularly close to Congregationalists and Presbyterians, but they refused to join in observing the Lord's Supper with any paedobaptists.

During the Civil Wars and Cromwell's Protectorate (1641–60), Baptists flourished. Many were in positions of leadership in the army and navy. Even after the Restoration (1660) they survived, although many of their number, such as John *Bunyan, were persecuted. In 1689 the Act of Toleration brought religious freedom to all Protestants, but in the ensuing years both General and Particular Baptists lapsed into a period of stagnation.

Baptist minister performing the ordinance of Baptism. The minister and candidate stand in the water of the baptismal tank where the candidate will be baptized by a triple immersion.

Renewal came toward the end of the 18th century. A new theological development, led mainly by Andrew Fuller, brought a breath of fresh air into the atmosphere of hyper-Calvinism that had stifled the Particular Baptists. This Fullerism provided a platform for an aggressive evangelistic stand in England and for a new era in foreign missions, launched by William *Carey and the Baptist Mission Society. Throughout the 19th century, the Particular Baptists were vigorous, but the General Baptists faded into obscurity; nevertheless, a revitalized movement known as the New Connection General Baptists sprang from them in 1770. In 1891 the Particulars merged with the New Connection group. Out of the British Baptists have come great preachers, such as Robert Hall, Charles Haddon *Spurgeon, and John Clifford. They have also had renowned scholars, such as T. R. Glover, H. Wheeler Robinson, and H. H. Rowley. By mid-20th century British Baptists were diminishing in numbers, as they faced the secularism that has blighted both the Established Church and the Free Churches.

History in the U.S. In America, the first Baptist church was formed by Roger *Williams in Rhode Island. After his expulsion from Massachusetts Bay, he established a colony in which complete religious freedom was granted to all people. In 1638 he renounced infant baptism and formed a church of persons baptized upon a profession of faith. Soon thereafter, another Baptist church was organized at Newport by John Clarke. Before long both General and Particular Baptists were represented in Rhode Island, and at Newport in 1671 a Seventh Day Baptist church was constituted. Until about 1740 the General (Six-Principle) Baptists were predominant in New England, and in 1770 they organized an association. Their growth, however, was very slow.

Growth to 1800. The Particular Baptists were destined to become the mainstream of the denominational life in America as in Britain, and their earliest strength was in the Middle Colonies. In 1707 five churches in New Jersey and Pennsylvania organized the Philadelphia Baptist Association, which was to have great influence upon Baptist life in America. Delegates from churches met annually to discuss common interests, settle problems, and promote fellowship. Although each church retained its freedom of action, the association could eject churches that did not conform to the corporate will of the churches. By means of the association, doctrinal uniformity was long preserved, a ministry was provided, disputes were settled, and education was encouraged.

In keeping with the distinctive emphasis outlined earlier, each church was a close-knit fellowship. New churches were formed by means of a covenant that set forth the obligations of church members, and strict discipline was maintained by each congregation. Services of worship were simple, consisting of congregational songs, prayers, a Scripture lesson, and a lengthy sermon. Adornments and symbols such as candles, crosses, pictures, stained glass windows, and musical instruments were eschewed, and neither Christmas nor Easter was observed. Organization, too, was simple, vested in a pastor, deacons, clerk, and ruling elders. Ministers usually had little formal education, although a few attended colonial colleges and others were tutored by older ministers. The need of an educated ministry, however, was widely recognized, and many ministers achieved a surprising degree of learning by their own efforts. Ordination was kept in the power of each local church, but representatives from other churches were invited to help determine a candidate's fitness and to aid in the ordination service.

With the advent of the *Great Awakening, Baptists began to grow. In New England, Baptists benefited by the accession of hundreds of New Light, or Separate, Congregationalists. It was in the South that Baptists experienced the greatest increase, as Separates from New England moved into that region. Beginning with Shubael Stearns and William Marshall, who came from New England to Sandy Creek, N.C., a series of revivals produced numerous churches and pastors in a short time. From a handful of Baptists in the southern colonies in 1740, their number grew to more than 1,300 churches by 1800.

Baptists played an active role in the struggle for freedom. In the Revolutionary era they generally sided with the patriots, taking part in politics and serving as chaplains and soldiers. John Hart of New Jersey was a signer of the Declaration of Independence. In Massachusetts and Virginia, where they had suffered discrimination on religious grounds, Baptists carried on a vigorous campaign against the establishment. Isaac Backus, John Leland, and others made important contributions to the theory of religious liberty that became integral in American life.

Development after 1800. The early 19th century witnessed unprecedented activity in the churches, as interest in evangelism, missions, and education developed. In 1814 the Baptists organized a national society for foreign missions, when three Congregationalists became

Baptists. Adoniram *Judson, Ann Judson, and Luther *Rice had been sent to India by the Congregationalists, but when they decided that infant baptism was unwarranted by the Scriptures, they became Baptists. Learning that the Judsons and Rice were available to serve as their missionaries, Baptists in America organized the Triennial Convention. Within a few years, they had also organized a publishing society, a home mission society, and a Bible society. Simultaneously, state conventions and educational societies were being established. All of these agencies were composed of interested persons who paid annual dues. The adoption of this "society method" for supporting missions and education was of great significance, for it meant that denominational organization would for a long time be based upon single-purpose voluntary societies that had no direct relationship to the churches. No national Baptist convention was formed in the North until the 20th century. Accompanying the rising interest in missions were other signs of vitality. Sunday Schools were organized rapidly after 1820, and academies and colleges were established in nearly every state. Newton Theological Institution, Mass., was founded in 1825. Colgate, Rochester, and Southern Baptist seminaries also were founded prior to the Civil War. And Baptists were active in reform movements, particularly the temperance cause.

Divisions. With rapid growth, diverse cultural influences, and increasing individualism, Baptists began to form separate groups. Out of the Great Awakening had come the Free Will Baptists, when Benjamin Randall sought to maintain an Arminian theology. In the 1830s, on the other hand, an Old School (Primitive) Baptist movement arose in protest against abandonment of the traditional predestinarianism of the Baptists. About 1850, under the leadership of James R. Graves, the Landmark Baptist movement started. Insisting that Baptists comprised the only true church, the Landmarkists (now the American Baptist Association) refused to recognize other churches. They held that the term "church" in the New Testament always refers to a local church, and thus they further encouraged particularistic tendencies among Baptists.

No division was more important than that which resulted over slavery. For years the home and foreign mission societies maintained neutrality on this issue, but in 1845 an open break occurred. Consequently, the Southern Baptist Convention was founded at Augusta, Ga. Instead of adopting the "society method" of supporting missions, the Southern Baptists organized a convention with integral boards responsible for home and foreign missions.

After the Civil War, Negro Baptist churches flourished. Prior to that time Negroes and whites had belonged to the same churches, but after the war the freed men preferred their own churches. These were at first affiliated with the regular associations and state conventions, particularly in the North. In 1880 the National Baptist Convention was organized, and in 1916 it divided into two parts, the National Baptist Convention of America and the National Baptist Convention, U.S.A., Inc. These two bodies comprise the bulk of the Negro Baptist population.

Other Changes. Rapid industrialization, urban growth, and changing intellectual climate brought new challenges after 1865. Under the impact of new conditions, Baptists underwent further change. Social problems became more complex, as the gulf between rich and poor widened and city slums expanded. Among the Baptists who helped to awaken the social conscience of the churches were Walter *Rauschenbusch, Shailer *Mathews, Leighton Williams, and Samuel Zane Batten. Edward Judson developed a great institutional church in New York City, and Russell H. Conwell, in Philadelphia, Pa., developed institutions to help the working classes. At the same time new scientific theories and Biblical criticism posed a threat for traditional theological systems. Baptists shared in the theological ferment, producing such leaders as William Newton *Clarke and William Rainey Harper, who helped to popularize the new theological outlook.

As church memberships increased and organization became more complex, covenants fell into disuse and discipline declined. In the North, open communion (partaking the Lord's Supper with paedobaptists) became prevalent by World War I, and by mid-20th century open membership had become common (receiving paedobaptists without requiring that they be rebaptized). Worship services were tending toward greater formality, and there was much more use of symbolism in the sanctuaries. For the sake of efficiency, the Northern Baptist (now American Baptist) Convention was formed in 1907. Southern Baptists have been more reluctant to adopt open communion and open membership.

Many Baptists resisted the new social emphasis, the changing views of the Bible, and centralizing tendencies; but no party of protest was crystallized until about 1920. In the 1920s a "Fundamentalist" group within the Northern Baptist Convention sought to purge the schools and mission societies of unorthodox elements (*see* FUNDAMENTALISM). The flames were fed when Harry Emerson Fosdick, a Baptist minister, preached a sermon entitled "Shall the Fundamentalists Win?" By 1925 the Modernist-Fundamentalist controversy had reached a climax. Some of the more disaffected elements withdrew from the convention, and in 1932 the General Association of Regular Baptists was established. Dissatisfaction continued to smoulder within the convention, and in the 1940s the conflict was resumed, leading to a further exodus of churches to form the Conservative Baptist movement.

Southern Baptists were not as deeply affected by the *social gospel movement or theological *modernism in the 1920s. Evolution created a stir in some colleges, and a few professors were suspected of being unorthodox. In 1925 the Southern Baptist Convention voted to recommend the New Hampshire Confession of Faith to their churches, but the controversy did not reach major proportions as it had in the North. Four decades later, however, Southern Baptists were experiencing a tardy reaction to the changing views of Scripture that had penetrated at least some of their seminaries.

Membership and Organization. The growth rate of the various Baptist groups in the 20th century differed greatly. Negro Baptists experienced considerable growth, but the American Baptist Convention remained nearly static after 1930. The newer, fundamentalist bodies also increased rapidly. It has been the Southern Baptists, however, whose expansion has been phenomenal. Not only did their number become nearly double in 30 years, but they had expanded into every state of the Union by 1960 (*see* PROTESTANTISM IN THE U.S.).

Of the many Baptist groups in the U.S. in 1964, about 90 per cent of them belonged to the four largest: the Southern, American, and two National Baptist Conventions. In underlying principles and general structure, the larger bodies are similar, although there are important differences in operation. On various levels are the associations, state conventions, and national conventions, each of which is directly related to the local churches. At the national level are boards that shape policy and program for missions, education, evangelism, publications, and pensions. Each board has a permanent staff of professional workers, which is responsible to trustees elected by delegates (or messengers) to the annual meeting of the national body. To coordinate the work of various boards, there is a national executive officer and some type of executive committee. State conventions may develop their own programs, but much of the time of their staffs is devoted to implementing policies national in scope. Associations seldom have permanent staffs, and their functions are usually confined to fellowship gatherings and cooperation in local matters.

Within this system juridical power is weak, and the authority of connectional bodies is not clearly defined. The associational principle implies that some authority resides in the wider fellowship, but there is disagreement as to how much authority belongs to associations and conventions. Individual churches cannot be coerced into conformity with a convention policy with which they disagree, although the latter body can withdraw fellowship from an uncooperative church. In general, cooperation depends upon agreement in purposes, moral suasion, and Christian unity.

The lack of a strong central jurisdiction affects the process of ordination to the gospel ministry. Authority to ordain has traditionally been claimed by the local church, but in practice others have always shared in the process. Other churches are asked to send delegates to examine candidates and to take part in the act of ordination, and conventions may set standards for their recognition of an ordination. The American Baptist Convention, for example, has minimum educational standards for ordination, which include college and seminary degrees. Southern Baptists have not yet established official educational requirements, but they ordinarily expect a minister to have both college and seminary training. There is considerable diversity in ordination practices and in the educational level of ministers in all of the conventions.

Southern Baptists operate six seminaries, and American Baptists have nine. Both also have several colleges related to them, but these are liberal arts schools that have ministerial preparation as only one interest among many. Students preparing for the ministry often attend state universities or private colleges other than their denominational schools. There are also colleges and seminaries related to the National Baptist Conventions. Baptists have had outstanding scholars in many fields. Among those of the 19th and 20th centuries were E. Y. Mullins, A. T. Robertson, Augustus H. Strong, Edgar J. *Goodspeed, Shirley Jackson Case, E. D. Burton, Douglas Clyde *Macintosh, and Kenneth Scott Latourette.

In a congregational system, each church is responsible for securing a minister after a pulpit becomes vacant. Recommendations may come from seminaries, other ministers, or state secretaries; but a pastor is chosen by vote of the congregation. It should be noted that women may be ordained, but that there are very few of them in any of the conventions.

Missions. In 1964 there were nearly 3 million Baptists outside the U.S., but most of them were direct or indirect offspring of British or American missions (see MISSIONS, PROTESTANT). Even the European Baptists spring from the missionary outreach of Baptists in the U.S., many of them originating from the work of Gerhard Oncken, a German baptized by an American Baptist, Barnas Sears, in 1834. Other European Baptists stem from Southern Baptist missions. British Baptists have played a distinguished role in foreign missions, and they have extended their work to Australia, New Zealand, and India, as well as other former possessions. Canadian Baptists owe their beginnings to American itinerants, but much of their development has come about through influences from Great Britain.

Almost every Baptist group has home and foreign mission work. Baptists conduct missions in Japan, Southeast Asia, India, Pakistan, the Middle East, Africa, Europe, Latin America, and the Pacific Islands. Altogether, in 1964 there were 29 Baptist mission organizations, operating in more than 200 fields, with about 5,000 missionaries and approximately 15,000 national workers. They had 190 colleges and Bible schools and 346 hospitals. Home missions were extensive and included evangelism of various types, the establishment of new churches, town and country work, Christian centers and institutional churches, ministries to migrant workers, work with ethnic groups, and service to many others with special needs.

Ecumenical Relations. There is no organic relationship between the many Baptist bodies, except where a group is a mission of some sponsoring body. Many, but not all, Baptists are members of the Baptist World Alliance, which was organized in 1905 and meets about every 5 years. Its purpose is primarily to afford fellowship and encouragement, but it has given practical assistance to refugees and victims of natural disasters and has promoted and safeguarded religious liberty in some places. In the U.S. a Baptist Joint Committee on Public Affairs is located at Washington, D.C. For the most part, however, relationships between Baptist organizations are tenuous.

Although Baptists acknowledge the unity of the Body of Christ, they disagree about the extent to which this unity must be visibly manifested. The American (Northern) Baptist Convention helped to found the *National (originally called Federal) Council of Churches of Christ in the U.S.A., and has been active in it since 1908. Two of its number, Shailer Mathews and Edwin T. Dahlberg, have served as presidents of the council. The American Baptist Convention has also participated in the *World Council of Churches since its inception in 1948. The Southern Baptists have not affiliated with either National or World Council, but the two national conventions are members of both. Baptists of England are in the World Council, but those of Scotland are not. Thus there is no uniformity with respect to ecumenical relationships.

Bibliography: R. G. TORBET, *A History of the Baptists* (rev. ed. Valley Forge 1963). N. H. MARING and W. S. HUDSON, *A Baptist Manual of Polity and Practice* (Valley Forge 1963). W. L. LUMPKIN, *Baptist Confessions of Faith* (Chicago 1959); *Baptist Foundations in the South* (Nashville 1961). W. W. BARNES, *The Southern Baptist Convention, 1845–1953* (Nashville 1954). O. D. PELT and R. L. SMITH, *The Story of the Na-*

tional Baptists (New York 1960). W. S. HUDSON, ed., *Baptist Concepts of the Church* (Chicago 1959). C. C. GOEN, *Revivalism and Separatism in New England, 1740–1800* (New Haven 1962). P. M. HARRISON, *Authority and Power in the Free Church Tradition: A Social Case Study of the American Baptist Convention* (Princeton, N.J. 1959). *Baptist Advance: The Achievements of the Baptists of North America for a Century and a Half* (Nashville 1964). *The Chronicle* (Chester, Pa. 1938–57), a Baptist historical quarterly. Succeeded by *Foundations: A Baptist Journal of History and Theology* (New York 1958–), with important descriptive and interpretive articles. *The Review and Expositor* (Louisville, Ky. 1904–), a quarterly journal of the Southern Baptist Theological Seminary.

Recent works on Baptism. A. GILMORE, ed., *Christian Baptism* (Chicago 1959). R. E. O. WHITE, *The Biblical Doctrine of Initiation* (Grand Rapids 1960). G. R. BEASLEY-MURRAY, *Baptism in the New Testament* (New York 1962). **Illustration credits:** Fig. 1, Baptist Sunday School Board, Nashville—Photo, Bryce Finch. Fig. 2, Baptist Sunday School Board, Nashville, Tenn.

[N. H. MARING]

BAR, CATHÉRINE DE, foundress of the Benedictine Nuns of the Blessed Sacrament; b. Saint-Dié, Vosges, France, Dec. 31, 1614; d. Paris, April 6, 1698. At the age of 17 Catherine joined the convent of the Annonciades at Bruyère, and she was professed in 1633. A year later she became superior. Violent fighting during the Thirty Years' War forced her to flee her convent, and in 1639 she found shelter with the Benedictines of Rambervillers. Attracted to the Benedictine form of life, she requested a transfer from the Annonciades. On July 11, 1640, she took her vows as a Benedictine. War again forced her to move, this time to Montmartre. There she assumed the name Mother Mechtilde of the Blessed Sacrament. She founded the Benedictine Nuns of the Blessed Sacrament to make reparation for outrages committed against Our Savior in the Eucharist. She was in contact with such renowned religious figures of her day as St. John Eudes and Jean-Jacques Olier; she also wrote on spiritual topics.

Bibliography: I. HERVIN and M. DOURLENS, *Vie de la Très Révérende Mère Mechtilde du Saint-Sacrement* (Paris 1883). R. SÉJOURNÉ, DHGE 6:534–538.

[B. EGAN]

BAR, ARCHDIOCESE OF (ANTIBARENSIS)

Metropolitan see from 1032, archbishopric without suffragans and immediately subject to the Holy See since 1886; in Montenegro, south *Yugoslavia, at the Albanian border. In 1963 it had 18 parishes, 12 secular and 3 religious priests, and 21,050 Catholics in a population of 430,000; it is 6,564 square miles in area. The city of Bar, also called Antivari (opposite *Bari), near the Adriatic, fell to ruin after its capture by the Turks (1571). A new city, Novi Bar, is being built as a port on the Adriatic coast.

The See of Bar is the successor to that of ancient Doclea (Podgorica, now Titograd), the home of Diocletian, which had a Christian community c. 400 and a bishop at the Council of Chalcedon (451). From the early 7th century, Rome and Byzantium both sought supremacy among the Slavs, who had been granted the region to defend against Avars. In the 8th century, Byzantium attached Doclea and the See of Bar to *Durrës (*Dyrrhachium*), but Rome made the sees suffragan to the Latin Archdiocese of Dubrovnik (Ragusa). The Council of Delminium-Duvno (877) made Bar one of 12 suffragans of Doclea, which was destroyed by the

Bulgars (927), the archbishop fleeing to Dubrovnik. Bar and other sees, however, then looked to Split as their metropolitan.

In 1032 Bar became a metropolitanate with 8 or 10 suffragans; the prelates long held the title *Archiepiscopus Diocliensis et Antibarensis ecclesiae*. After the Serbian conquest of Dubrovnik, Bar was united with that archdiocese from 1078 until Bar was detached as a bishopric in 1172. In 1199 Bar again became a metropolitanate with six suffragans. But Venice, favored by the Latin conquest of Constantinople (1204), supported Dubrovnik. When Serbia inclined to Byzantine Orthodoxy (1221), Rome sent Franciscans and Dominicans, including *John da Pian del Carpine, Archbishop of Bar (1248–52). The Latin archbishops of Bar claimed to be the primates of the entire kingdom of Serbia. (In 1902 Rome recognized the title "primate of Serbia.") King Stephen V Duchan (1331–55), however, continued the trend toward Byzantine Orthodoxy and established a Patriarchate of Peć, independent of both Greeks and Latins; and Bar lost its ecclesiastical importance.

With absentee prelates, the neglected Catholics became Orthodox or Moslem. John Bruno of Ulcinj, Archbishop of Bar (1551–71), was captured by the Turks and died in irons. Under the Turks, Christians of the archdiocese were subject to the Greek Orthodox patriarch of Constantinople and to the patriarch of Peć, while Moslems and Orthodox took over the Latin churches. The Latin archbishops of Bar, who had to reside near Venetian Kotor to the north, succeeded in making visitations of their see from c. 1615 and combatted the trend to Orthodoxy with Tridentine reforms. In 1766 the Patriarchate of Peć was suppressed; and Montenegro and Serbia, accepting Russian protection, attached themselves to the patriarch of Constantinople. Austria, which replaced Venice as the defender of Latin Catholicism against Russian Orthodoxy, subsidized the archbishops of Bar. In 1867 the See of Bar was personally united with that of *Shkodër. After Montenegro established itself as a principality (1878), the Concordat of 1886 separated Bar from Shkodër and left Bar an archbishopric immediately subject to the Holy See, the only see in Montenegro. The Glagolitic, or Roman-Slavonic, liturgy, authorized by the concordat, was not introduced into the archdiocese in practice because half the Catholics spoke Albanian.

Bibliography: P. RICHARD, DHGE 3:717–724, with list of bishops. K. DRAGANOVIĆ, *Opći šematizam Katoličke Crkve u Jugoslaviji* (Sarajevo 1939) 357–362. G. VALENTINI, EncCatt 1: 1510–11. J. MATL, LexThK² 1:1233. AnnPont (1965) 53.

[M. LACKO]

BAR-CURSUS (JOANNES TELLENSIS), an exponent of the Monophysite Christology of Severus of Antioch; b. at Kallinikos, c. 483; d. Antioch, 538. He left the comfort of court life in order to enter monastic life. He became bishop of Tella in northern Mesopotamia in 519. In 533 he took part in the dogmatic discussions in Constantinople. He died a violent death in prison because of his convictions. He edited a collection of canons that is important for the history of liturgy and the Sacraments, especially for the Sacrament of the Holy Eucharist, e.g., the custom of giving Communion under one species.

Bibliography: T. J. LAMY, *Dissertatio de Syrorum fide et disciplina in re Eucharistia* (Louvain 1859). F. NAU, *Les Canons et les résolutions canoniques de Rabboula, Jean de Tella, . . .* (Paris 1906). PatrSyrO.

[L. R. KOZLOWSKI]

BAR-HEBRAEUS
(GREGORIUS IBN AL-IBRI)

Jacobite Syrian theologian and writer; b. Melitene (modern Malatya, Turkey), Armenia, 1226; d. Maragheh, Iranian Azerbaijan, July 30, 1286.

Called Bar-Hebraeus (son of a Hebrew father), Gregory Abou'l Faradj received the name John at baptism. He was educated in philosophy, theology, and medicine by his father, a converted Jewish physician, and a coterie of scholars. He emigrated to Antioch in Syria with his family before the Mongol invasions and spent several years in solitude as a hermit. He traveled to Tripoli and studied logic and medicine under James the Nestorian. He took the name of Gregory when he was consecrated bishop of Gouba by the Jacobite Patriarch Ignatius II (Sept. 14, 1246). The next year he changed to the See of Laqabin and was promoted to the metropolitan See of *Alep by Patriarch Denis of Antioch, whose candidacy he supported (1252) against the claims of John Bar Madani.

When the Mongols conquered Baghdad and took possession of Syria, Gregory approached their chief, Hulagu, to negotiate the proper treatment of Christians. He was taken prisoner, however, and Alep was sacked. Before the martyrdom of Denis, Bar-Hebraeus had made peace with Patriarch Bar Madani; and he played a part in the selection of Ignatius III as patriarch of Antioch in 1264. Bar-Hebraeus was consecrated Maphrian of Tagrit (the patriarchal vicar-general of the Jacobite Church, recognized by the Moslem governor) at Sis, Cilicia, in the presence of the Armenian King, Het'um; in 1273 he succeeded in healing a schism in the Jacobite Church caused by the influential physician Simon.

As Maphrian, Bar-Hebraeus visited the various communities of the Jacobite Church in western Armenia and in Baghdad; he used their libraries, encouraged their pastors, and entered into amicable relations with the Nestorian leaders. In 1277 he visited his see at Tagrit, which had been sacked by the Tartars. It was the first time in 60 years that a Maphrian had been able to visit the city. In 1282 he journeyed to Tabriz to give the new Mongol Prince Ahmed assurance of his loyalty and submission to the civil ruler.

In 1284 the partisans of the physician Simon elected him as the new patriarch without awaiting the arrival of Bar-Hebraeus; the latter accepted the *fait accompli* in the interest of ecclesiastical unity. He died at Maragheh while the Nestorian Patriarch Yabalaha was present in the city, and was interred in the monastery of Mar-Mattai at Mosul with Byzantine, Nestorian, and Jacobite prelates in attendance.

Of vast erudition, Bar-Hebraeus won the respect of the various Christian churches and of the Mohammedans by his learning and amiability. Among his principal writings was a synthesis or encyclopedia of philosophy called the *Cream* or *Science of Sciences,* in which he commented on every branch of human knowledge in the Aristotelian tradition, with compendia on logic, physics, metaphysics, and practical philosophy culled from Aristotle and the Syrian and Arabic authors. He wrote voluminous commentaries on the Old and New Testament published under the title, *Storehouse of Mysteries,* utilizing the works of both Nestorian and Jacobite exegetes. He controlled the *Peshitta version of the Scriptures with Greek, Hebrew, Septuagint, Ar-

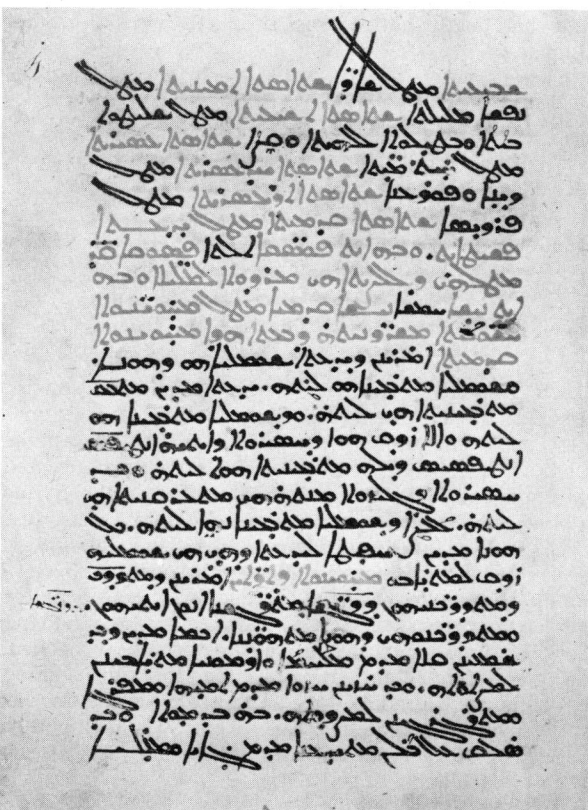

Page from a Syriac MS of Bar-Hebraeus, written at the convent of the Mother of God, Scete, in 1404.

menian, and Coptic versions; and he supplied materials for the recovery of the Hexapla of *Origen. In his *Lamp of the Sanctuary* he gave a systematic exposition of Jacobite doctrine; he wrote an *Ethics* whose moral philosophy was greatly influenced by Al Gazali. His ascetical treatise was called the *Book of the Dove,* a directory for monks, and he wrote a *Nomocanon* of ecclesiastical legislation that still plays a part in Oriental Canon Law.

As a historiographer, he produced a chronicle as a universal history whose first section, *Chronicon Syriacum,* dealt with secular events down to the Mongol invasions; and whose second section, *Chronicon Ecclesiasticum,* in its first subdivision gave a history of the Patriarchs of the Old Testament followed by those of the New Testament, namely the patriarchs of Antioch and the western Syrian Church. Its second subdivision covered the patriarchs of the Oriental Syrian Church down to 1285. His brother Barsauma continued this account to 1288, and an anonymous author carried it to 1496.

Bar-Hebraeus followed the history of *Michael I the Syrian for the earlier centuries, but in both method and originality he surpassed his model, supplying first class material for the later centuries. He made an Arabic synopsis of the work that he supplemented with information useful for a Moslem readership under the title *A History of the Dynasties.* He composed also a large grammar called the *Book of Splendors,* monographs on science and medicine, and liturgical, didactic, and polemical poetry that conformed to the artistic tastes of the Syrian culture. He wrote his own autobiography, and his death notice was supplied by his brother Barsauma.

Bibliography: E. HERMAN, DHGE 6:792–794. J. Assemani BiblOr 2:244, 468. J. GÖTTSBERGER, *Bar-Hebraeus und seine Scholien zur heiligen Schrift* (Freiburg 1900). P. BEDJAN, *Barhebraei Ethicon seu Moralia* (Paris 1878); *Barhebraei Chronicon syriacum* (Paris 1890); *Barhebraei nomocanon* (Paris 1898). G. CARDAHI, *BarHebraeus's Book of the Dove together with Some Chapters of His Ethicon,* tr. A. WENSINCK (Leiden 1919). J. B. ABBELOOS and T. J. LAMY, *Chronicon ecclesiasticum,* 3 v. (Louvain 1872–77). P. SBATH, *Traité sur l'âme par Barhébraeus* (Cairo 1928). W. WRIGHT, *A Short History of Syriac Literature* (London 1894) 265–281. A. BAUMSTARK, *Geschichte der syrischen Literatur* (Bonn 1922) 312–320. PatrSyrO 207–209. **Illustration credit:** Bibliothèque Nationale.

[F. X. MURPHY]

BAR-JESUS, Aramaic name (meaning "son of Jesus") of a Jewish magician, called also Elymas (Ἐλύμας), mentioned in Acts 13.4–12. The name Elymas may be of Semitic origin, possibly connected with the Arabic *'alîm* (wise, learned), or the Syriac *'ālūmā'* (malevolent), or the Aramaic *'alīmā'* (strong).

St. Paul evangelized *Cyprus on his first missionary journey. At Paphos, the Roman proconsul Sergius Paulus sought to hear the word of God and sent for Paul. However, Bar-Jesus, a magician attached to Sergius, opposed Paul and tried to turn the proconsul away from him. Paul, guided by the Holy Spirit, gazed upon him and predicted a temporary blindness for his sin, which immediately came to pass. Following this, Sergius Paulus "believed and was astonished at the Lord's teaching" (Acts 13.12).

The story of Bar-Jesus is significant for two reasons. First, it is a parallel to Peter's triumph over *Simon Magus (Acts 8.14–24); thus Paul is seen to have the powers of an Apostle, as does Peter. Secondly, Luke is interested in showing that Paul's missionary career, like that of Peter, begins with the conversion of a notable Roman official, despite the obstacles placed in his way by a notable sorcerer.

See also MAGIC (IN THE BIBLE).

Bibliography: EncDictBibl 209. A. WIKENHAUSER, LexThK² 1:1245. A. ROMEO, EncCatt 2:852–853. A. D. NOCK, "Paul and the Magus," Jackson-Lake 5:164–188. F. C. BURKITT, "The Interpretation of Bar-Jesus," JThSt 4 (1902–03) 127–129.

[J. A. GRASSI]

BAR KOKHBA, SIMON (BAR COCHEBA)

The political leader of the second Jewish revolt against Rome (A.D. 132–135). From autograph letters written by him to various officers under his command and found in 1951, 1960, and 1961 in caves of the wadies *Murabba'āt, Seiyâl, and Ḥabra in Jordan and Israel (*see* DEAD SEA SCROLLS), it is certain that his name was Simon ben Kosibah (*šm'wn bn kwsbh,* attested in a Greek letter as Σιμων Χωσιβα). In rabbinical writings (e.g., Babylonian Talmud, *Sanhedrin,* 11.1, 2, fol. 93b) his name is given as *bar* (or *ben) Koziba,* "son of the lie." This form is probably the result of a wordplay on his name (Hebrew *kzb,* "to lie"), which originated with the Jews who either did not approve of his uprising or ironically reflected later on its ill-fated outcome. Rabbi *Akiba ben Joseph, who approved of the revolt, regarded him as a messiah (Jerusalem Talmud, *Ta'anith* 4.68d) and applied to him the oracle of Balaam, "A star shall advance from Jacob" (Nm 24.17). He was thus responsible for another wordplay on his name, in which the patronymic *ben Kosibah* was changed to the Aramaic *bar Kokhba,* "the son of

the star" (Aramaic *kôkᵉbâ,* "star"). This name, which has clung to him in history, is found in a few Jewish writings. It is the only form used by Christian writers (Justin, *Apol.* 1.31; Eusebius, *Hist. Eccl.* 4.6.2).

Outbreak of the Revolt. Along with Rabbi Akiba, the intellectual leader of the time, and Eleazar the Priest, the spiritual leader, Bar Kokhba was the political and military commander of the Palestinian Jews in their second revolt against Rome. Coins minted during the 1st year of his uprising bear the title, "Simon, Prince of Israel" (*šm'wn nśy' yśr'l*), and the Murabbà'āt documents preserve the fuller form, "Simon ben Kosibah, Prince of Israel" [*šm'wn bn kwsb' nsy' yśr'l* (*Mur.* 24 B 2–3)]. The coins and the documents reveal that the revolt was dedicated to the "liberation of Jerusalem" and the "redemption of Israel."

The causes of the revolt are not certain. Dio Cassius (*Roman History* 69.12.1–2) states that it was due to Hadrian's attempt to build a Greco-Roman city (Aelia Capitolina) on the site of Jerusalem and to erect a shrine to Jupiter on the ruins of the Temple of Yahweh. This is usually recognized as a major factor. The *Vita Hadriani* (14.2) cites another cause, relating the revolt to an imperial edict forbidding circumcision (*quod vetabantur mutilare genitalia*). Hadrian, who renewed a former prohibition of castration, so understood it as to include circumcision. It was not directed against the Jews in particular, for a later decree of Antoninus Pius (A.D. 138) specifically permitted them to circumcise their children, while still forbidding circumcision to others. Both causes would have vexed the Jews and probably contributed to their revolt.

The Murabba'āt contracts preserve a synchronism that shows that the era of the "redemption of Israel" coincided with a cycle of *Sabbath Years (*Mur.* 24 B 1–10, E 1–10). From this synchronism the official date for the beginning of the era is calculated as 1 Tishri (October) A.D. 132. Another document (*Mur.* 30.8) is dated "21 Tishri, year 4," showing that the revolt at least began in its 4th year (end of A.D. 135).

Bar Kokhba's Activity. Besides acting as a military leader, Bar Kokhba administered the land politically from his headquarters, probably in Jerusalem. He preserved the elaborate administrative machinery and division of Judea into toparchies that the Romans had set up. After liberating Jerusalem, he never met the Romans in open field battles, but conducted a guerrilla-type warfare from many villages and outposts throughout the land. Chief among these were Herodium, Teqoa', 'En-gedi, Meṣad Ḥasidin (Khirbet Qumran?), Beth-Ter. His local deputies rented out in his name farm lands in the fertile foothills and in southern Judea to lessees who were obliged to pay an annual rent in kind to the "treasury of the Prince of Israel at Herodium" (*Mur.* 24 D 17–18), i.e., government granaries. His letters reveal his administrative concern for the observance of the *Sabbath, the celebration of the feast of *Booths (Tabernacles), the treatment of Galileans who had come to take part in the revolt, the arrest of certain individuals, and the seizure of the property of others.

At the beginning of the revolt the Roman governor of Judea, Tineius Rufus, although in command of Roman garrisons resident in the province (*Legio X Fretensis, Legio VI Ferrata*), was helpless. The governor of Syria, Publicius Marcellus, came to his aid with further troops. Finally, Hadrian had to send his best general, Sextus Julius Severus, recalling him from Britain.

Note found at Wadi Murabbaʿāt written by Bar Kokhba to Yešuaʿ ben Galgulah, dated in the 3d year of his revolt, A.D. *134. Its first words, "msʿwn bn kwsbh . . ." (From Simon ben Kosibah . . .), show his original name.*

He eventually put down the revolt after a slow process of starving out the Jews who had taken refuge in various strongholds and caves in the desert. Caves in the wadies Murabbaʿāt, Seiyâl, and Ḥabra were used by whole families, who fled there with a few household belongings, Biblical scrolls, and family archives. The officers from ʿEn-gedi fled to the Wadi Ḥabra cave, taking with them the letters of their commander-in-chief. The Romans set up camps in strategic positions about the caves to keep watch on them, lest the rebels escape.

End of the Revolt. After Jerusalem was once again taken by the Romans, Bar Kokhba withdrew and made his last stand at Beth-Ter (near modern *Bittîr*, about 6 miles west southwest of Jerusalem). The war reached its height there in Hadrian's 18th regnal year (A.D. 134–135). "The siege lasted a long time before the rebels were driven to final destruction by famine and thirst, and the instigator of their madness paid the penalty he deserved" (Eusebius, *Hist. Eccl.* 4.6.3). Subsequently Hadrian razed Jerusalem again to build Aelia Capitolina and decreed "that the whole [Jewish] nation should be absolutely prevented from that time on from entering even the district around Jerusalem, so that not even from a distance could it see its ancestral home" (*ibid.*). Ancient Christian writers were normally not sympathetic to Bar Kokhba, accusing him of persecuting and torturing the Christians, who would not join his uprising (Justin, *Apol.* 1.31; Eusebius, *Chronicon* 283; GCS 47.201).

Bibliography: M. NOTH, *The History of Israel,* tr. and rev. P. R. ACKROYD (2d ed. New York 1960). E. SCHÜRER, *A History of the Jewish People in the Time of Jesus Christ,* tr. J. MAC-PHERSON et al., 5 v. (Edinburgh 1897–98) div. 1, v.2; new and abr. ed. N. N. GLATZER (New York 1961). P. BENOIT et al., *Les Grottes de Murabbaʿât* (DiscJudDes 2; 1961). S. YEIVIN, *Milḥemet Bar Kôkᵉba* (Jerusalem 1952). J. A. FITZMYER, "The Bar Cochba Period," *The Bible in Current Catholic Thought,* ed. J. L. McKENZIE (New York 1962) 133–168. **Illustration credit:** Palestine Archeological Museum.

[J. A. FITZMYER]

BAR MITZVAH, the term for the religious rite by which a Jewish boy is formally initiated into the religious community and assumes the duties and responsibilities of a Jew. The words *bar mitzvah* (late Hebrew *bar miṣwâ*) literally mean, "son of precept." Though the expression is found in the Talmud (Baba Meẓiʿa 96a), it appears to have been used there simply to mean every adult Jew. The use of the word in the modern sense does not go back much beyond the 14th century. It was first so employed in the works of a German Jew, Mordecai ben Hillel.

Origin and Significance. Leopold Löw has established the fact that *bar mitzvah* was a fixed custom in Germany in the 14th century. Löw was of the opinion that the practice of *bar mitzvah* could not be traced beyond this point in time. There is, however, some probability that in a rudimentary form at least, *bar mitzvah* derives from an earlier period. With the solemnization of this rite, the Jewish boy is considered to have attained religious maturity. He may henceforth be called up to fill the *minyān*, i.e., the required number of 10 necessary for holding congregational worship. The *bar mitzvah* ceremony takes place on the Sabbath following a boy's 13th birthday (reckoned according to the Jewish calendar). As in Roman custom, the age of puberty is taken as the time for assuming responsibility.

Ceremony. There are three phases to the *bar mitzvah* ceremony. First, the boy must read in public from the Pentateuch and the Prophets. Meanwhile the boy's father prays in silence: "Blessed be he who has taken the responsibility of this child's doing from me." This disavowal of the father's further responsibility for his son's sins is omitted by the Sephardim (Spanish and Portuguese Jews). Next follows an address given by the *bar mitzvah* boy. As a general rule, this talk is prepared by the rabbi or teacher and is memorized by the boy. Lastly there is the Seʿudah or festive meal. It is customary at this celebration to give presents to the *bar mitzvah* boy. The *bar mitzvah* ceremony should be preceded by a period of training in which the boy is schooled in, among other things, the principal duties and observances of Jewish life.

Reform Judaism in the last century replaced *bar mitzvah* with Confirmation to which both boys and girls are admitted. This ceremony is held annually for all those of age at Shabuoth, the Feast of Weeks (Pentecost). In some Reform and Conservative congregations both Confirmation and *bar mitzvah* are held. In some synagogues too, *bath mitzvah* ("daughter of precept") is observed. This is a rite developed for girls that generally corresponds to *bar mitzvah*.

Bibliography: L. LÖW, *Die Lebensalter in der jüdischen Literatur* (Beiträge zur jüdischen Alterthumskunde 2; Szegedin 1875). National Association of Temple Educators, *Confirmation Practices* (Educational Research Survey 2; New York 1959). C. ROTH, "Bar-Mitzvah: Its History and Its Associations," *Bar-Mitzvah Illustrated,* ed. A. I. KATSH (New York 1955). I. LEVI-TATS, *Communal Regulation of Bar Mitzvah* (New York 1949). J. ARLOW, "A Psychoanalytic Study of a Religious Initiation Rite: Bar Mitzvah," *The Psychoanalytic Study of the Child* (New York 1945–   ) 6:353–374.

[J. C. TURRO]

BARABBAS, the criminal who was released instead of Jesus. Barabbas (Βαραββᾶς, for Aramaic *bar-ʾabbaʾ,* "son of Abba") was his surname; according to some Greek MSS in Mt 27.16–17 his first name was Jesus. He is described in Jn 18.40 as a λῃστής. Although this passage is commonly translated as, "Barabbas was a robber," here the word λῃστής does not mean a thief in the ordinary sense, but rather a bandit, a revolutionary, a meaning that the Greek word sometimes has also in the writings of Josephus. According to Mk 15.7 and Lk 23.19, Barabbas was an insurgent, a rebel against the Roman occupation forces. He was one of the rioters in an uprising in which someone was murdered, and he was arrested for the crime. In certain circles of the populace he was, no doubt, regarded as a local hero. Among such people he might even have aroused messianic expectations and hopes for the final unsheathing of the messianic sword.

According to Mt 27.20 and Lk 23.4 the Jewish authorities who accused Jesus before Pilate had with them a "crowd" or "crowds"; this has often been understood as a mob representative of the inimical attitude of the Jerusalem populace toward Jesus. Despite repeated assertions of popular support given Jesus in Jerusalem both before the Passion (Mk 11.18; 12.12, 37; 14.2) and even after it (Acts 2.41, 46–47; 3.11; 4.1–4, 21, 33; 5.13–14, 17, 26; 8.12; 9.31), this understanding has gone unquestioned for centuries. In Mk 15.7–8, however, the tight sequence of thought suggests that this "crowd" was actually composed of the followers or friends of Barabbas who came up to beg the paschal amnesty for their hero but had to fend off Pilate's attempts to release Jesus instead (see also Acts 3.14–15). After Barabbas had been released, the two λῃσταί between whom Jesus was crucified (Mk 15.27; Mt 27.38, 44) were presumably followers of the rebel leader.

Bibliography: J. J. TWOMEY, "Barabbas Was a Robber," *Scripture* 8 (1956) 115–119. D. M. CROSSAN, "Anti-Semitism and the Gospel," ThSt 26 (1965) 189–214. J. BLINZLER, LexThK² 1:1234. A. PENNA, EncCatt 2:794. J. MÜLLER-BARDORFF, RGG³ 1:869. EncDictBibl 206.

[D. M. CROSSAN]

BARADAI, JAMES, Monophysite bishop and founder of Jacobite Church; d. Romanos monastery of Kasion, Egypt, July 30, 578. James was Syrian by birth. He became a monk and priest at the Pesīltā monastery in the mountains of Izla, and *c.* 527 was sent to the Byzantine court in Constantinople, where he remained until 543 under the favor of the Empress *Theodora (1). Consecrated titular bishop of Edessa by the exiled Patriarch Theodosius of Alexandria, he was sent, at the request of the Arab prince Harith Ibn Gabala, to the eastern frontier of the Empire to convert the Arabs. He consecrated a large number of Syrian Monophysites as bishops and priests, thus founding a new hierarchy that was organized by the Monophysite Patriarch of Antioch, Sergius (d. *c.* 560). The Church thus established is still known as the Syrian Jacobite Church. Baradai left no authentic writings other than a few letters translated from Greek into Syriac.

Bibliography: E. HAMMERSCHMIDT, LexThK² 5:836. H. G. KLEYN, *Jacobus Baradaeus, de Stichter der syrische monophysitische Kerk* (Leiden 1882) 164–194. PatrSyrO 153–154. W. WRIGHT, *A Short History of Syriac Literature* (London 1894). Stein-Palanque HistBEmp 2:625–628, 684.

[I. ORTIZ DE URBINA]

BARAGA, FREDERIC

Pioneer missionary, first bishop of *Marquette (Mich.) diocese; b. Mala Vas castle, parish of Dobrinič, Carniola, a Slovene province later part of Yugoslavia, June 29, 1797; d. Marquette, Jan. 19, 1868. Baptized Irenaeus Frederic, he never used his first name. After receiving his preparatory education in Ljubljana, where his talent for languages was marked, he studied law at the University of Vienna, and during that period came

Bp. Frederic Baraga, Apostle of the Ottawas and Chippewas.

under the influence of the Redemptorist, Clement Mary *Hofbauer. Upon graduation in 1821 he broke his engagement to marry, renounced his inheritance, and entered Ljubljana's seminary. He was ordained Sept. 21, 1823, and sent first as curate to Šmartno, near Kranj, and in 1828 to Metlika, where he continued his pastoral zeal and literary activity. A prayer book, *Dušna Paša* (Spiritual Food), that ran to ten large editions, and two other devotional works are from this period.

Through the *Leopoldinen-Stiftung, founded in Vienna in 1829 to aid the American missions, Baraga volunteered for Cincinnati, thus realizing his ambition, inspired by Father Hofbauer, of laboring among the American Indians. Shortly after arriving there, Jan. 18, 1831, he was dispatched to the Ottawas of Arbre Croche (now Harbor Springs), Mich., where within 28 months he baptized 547 Indians and transformed a deteriorating mission into a model Christian community. Then followed his foundation of the Grand River (Grand Rapids) mission in September 1833, and in July 1835 his mission among the Lake Superior Chippewas at La Pointe, Madeline Island, where his church had to be twice rebuilt to accommodate his growing congregation. At L'Anse mission, which he established in 1843 on Keweenaw Bay, further success attended his efforts to convert hard-drinking, indolent pagans into sober, industrious Christians. Meanwhile, the development of copper mines on Keweenaw Peninsula attracted white pioneers and thus extended his labors and his territory, which he covered faithfully by foot and canoe.

In July 1853 Upper Peninsular Michigan became a vicariate apostolic, and on November 1 in Cincinnati Baraga was consecrated vicar apostolic with the title Bishop of Amyzonia *in partibus infidelium*. His first act, after issuing pastorals in English and Indian, the latter an innovation, was to travel throughout Europe in search of funds and priests. He was responsible for most of the territory bordering Lake Superior and the northern area of the peninsula, as well as Indian sections of other dioceses ceded to him by neighboring bishops because of his zeal and competence. With the expansion of copper and iron mining, the white population increased steadily and with it the need for more priests and churches; yet severe climatic and linguistic demands lessened the number of missionary candidates. During his 3 years as vicar apostolic, Baraga traveled constantly, preaching several times a day in various languages, building and maintaining churches and chapels. Though he lived frugally, his poverty was acute, especially during the Civil War when allotments from European societies, his chief source of income, shrank in purchasing power.

In 1857 his vicariate was raised to a diocese, and in 1866 Baraga transferred the see from Sault Ste. Marie to Marquette, joyfully reporting that it was now well provided with priests and churches. His Indian missions were also firmly established. During the fall of that year, however, he suffered a stroke while attending the Second Plenary Council of Baltimore. Though critically ill, he insisted upon returning to Marquette to await his coadjutor and to fulfill his vow to die among the Indians. Preliminary steps have been taken toward his beatification.

Baraga's writings include voluminous correspondence, records, diaries, and reports to European societies of great historical value. He also wrote: *Theoretical and Practical Grammar of the Otchipwe Language* (Detroit 1850); *Dictionary of the Ojibway Language* (Cincinnati 1853); *The History, Character, Life and Manners of the Indians* (in German and Slovene, Ljubljana 1837; in French, Paris 1837); *Animie-Misinaigan* (Ottawa prayerbook, later enl., rev., and tr., into Chippewa); *Jesus o Bimadisiwim* ("Life of Jesus" in Ottawa; Paris 1837); *Gagikwe-Masinaigan* (sermon book in Chippewa, containing abstracts from Old and New Testaments, and Epistles and Gospels of the year; 1839, 1859); *Kagige Debwewinan* ("Eternal Truths"); *Nana-gatawendamo-Masinaigan* (instructions on the Commandments and Sacraments); three devotional works for his friends and former parishioners in Slovenia, and many smaller items. His grammar and dictionary were the first published in the Chippewa and Ottawa languages and are still an aid to the study of Indian linguistics.

Bibliography: J. GREGORICH, *The Apostle of the Chippewas: the Life Story of the Most Rev. Frederick Baraga, D.D.* (Lemont, Ill. 1932). A. I. REZEK, *History of the Diocese of Sault Ste. Marie and Marquette,* 2 v. (Houghton, Mich. 1906–07). C. VERWYST, *Life and Labors of Rt. Rev. Frederic Baraga: First Bishop of Marquette, Mich.* (Milwaukee 1900). The Marquette diocesan library at Marquette contains holographs of the Journal (Diary) and of many letters, importantly those addressed to the Leopoldine Association, Vienna. Other materials are held by the Newberry Library (Ayer Collection), Chicago, the Notre Dame University archives, and private collectors.

[J. GREGORICH]

BARANAUSKAS, ANTANAS,

Lithuanian poet; b. near Anykščiai, Jan. 17, 1835; d. Seinai, Nov. 26, 1902. His parents were poor farmers, but they early decided that the boy was not adapted to such a life and sent him to the county clerks' school at Rumšiškés.

He entered the seminary of Varniai (1856), studied at the Theological Academy in St. Petersburg, and was ordained (1862). During his 1858–59 summer vacation he wrote his famous *Anykščių Šilelis* (The Forest of Anykščiai). He studied in western Europe (1863–64, Munich, Innsbruck, Rome, and Louvain). After a period as professor at the Theological Academy, he taught at the seminary of Kaunas (1867–84). In 1884 he was consecrated auxiliary bishop of the Kaunas (Samogitian) Diocese and in 1897, was appointed bishop of Seinai.

Baranauskas reached the peak of his creative powers during the short period of 1857–59, during which he wrote, in addition to *Anykščių Šilelis,* a group of songs that became very popular throughout the country. By 1863, however, his poetic fires had become dormant, to be rekindled only in his last years, when he wrote religious hymns. After his early poetic effort, Baranauskas plunged into the problems of the Lithuanian language, especially its dialects, leaving his mark on the terminology of Lithuanian grammar and becoming the first Lithuanian dialectologist. For several years he was absorbed in mathematics, but he was self-taught, and although he "discovered" some laws, he found out later that they had been long known; he did, however, leave some mathematical terms that are still in use in Lithuanian. After his appointment to Seinai, all his energy was channeled into translating the Bible; he devoted as much as 14 hours a day to this, but the project was unfinished at his death.

Baranauskas's masterpiece remains *Anykščių Šilelis,* a poem of 342 lines (Eng. tr. Los Angeles, Calif. 1956). Its deep emotion, colorful descriptions of nature, melodious language, and masterly orchestration place it second only to *Donelaitis's Metai* (The Seasons), in the earlier history of Lithuanian literature.

Bibliography: J. TUMAS, *Antanas Baranauskas* (Kaunas 1924). R. MIKŠYTĖ, *Antano Baranausko kūryba* (Vilnius 1964).

[A. VAIČIULAITIS]

BARAT, MADELEINE SOPHIE, ST.,

foundress of the *Sacred Heart Society; b. Joigny (Yonne), France, Dec. 12, 1779; d. Paris, May 25, 1865 (feast, May 25). She was the daughter of a Burgundy vinegrower and received her early education from her brother Louis, a priest. In 1800 he took her to Paris to continue her studies. There Joseph *Varin d'Ainville persuaded her to join a group of women living under religious rule. She followed this group to Amiens, where she became (1802) their superior general and head of their school for girls. In 1804 she founded the second house of the Society of the Sacred Heart in Grenoble, and there met Rose Philippine *Duchesne, who later introduced the congregation into the U.S. For the next 60 years Mother Barat labored to extend her institute, which numbered 86 houses by 1865. Although she never engaged in teaching after leaving Amiens, she retained an interest in the intellectual training of her nuns. She also shaped the society's constitutions to guard against the mores of the court circles from which many of the pupils came. This, and a desire to reeducate in Christian principles children reared in a postrevolutionary society, inspired her to resist successfully the efforts of a chaplain of the Amiens house to reshape the constitutions. A similar reaction occurred in 1839, when a group of members tried to make the congregation resemble more closely the *Jesuits. Although Mother Barat traveled much in order to establish and visit her foundations, her most fruitful years were spent at Grenoble with Philippine

St. Madeleine Sophie Barat.

Duchesne; at Poitiers, where the first noviceship was founded; at Montet in Switzerland, where the novices were sent after the 1830 revolution; at Rome; and at Conflans, outside Paris, where the general noviceship of the society was situated at the time of her death. Her body reposes incorrupt in Jette, Belgium. She was beatified in 1908 and canonized in 1925.

Bibliography: C. E. MAGUIRE, *Saint Madeleine Sophie Barat* (New York 1960). A. BROU, *Saint Madeleine Sophie Barat*, tr. J. W. SAUL (New York 1963). M. WILLIAMS, *St. Madeleine Sophie* (New York 1965).

[C. E. MAGUIRE]

BARAT COLLEGE OF THE SACRED HEART traces its origin to the first academy established by the Religious of the Sacred Heart in Chicago, Ill., in 1857. In 1904 the academy was transferred to Lake Forest, one of Chicago's north-shore suburbs, and in 1919 was chartered by the state of Illinois as a 4-year liberal arts college. It was named Barat College in honor of the foundress of the Society of the *Sacred Heart, St. Madeleine Sophie *Barat.

Barat College is accredited by the North Central Association and holds membership in the Association of American Colleges, the American Council on Education, the National Commission on Accrediting, and the American Association of University Women. It is governed by an executive council made up of religious of the Sacred Heart. The board of trustees includes in its membership the administrative officers of the College and 25 laymen, who through an effective committee structure advise the administration in matters of policy. They collaborate with the president and the director of development in securing financial support for the College. In 1964 the faculty included 30 laymen and 18 religious of the Sacred Heart. Twenty-three held doctorates and twenty-three had the master's degree. The College numbered 450 students of whom 50 were non-resident. The students represented 30 states and 7 foreign countries.

Barat College operates on an annual budget that exceeds $1 million, exclusive of expenses for capital expansion. Apart from the contributed services of the religious of the Sacred Heart, the College has an endowment of less than $200,000. Gifts from alumnae, parents, friends, business and industry, and foundations make up the difference between educational income and operating expense.

Barat is a liberal arts college offering majors in all departments included under the divisions of philosophy and theology, the humanities, and social and natural sciences. Barat is committed to depth in learning, the development of the capacity for independent study and research, and emphasis on the vital importance of skill and facility in modern languages. The lecture method of teaching, combined with discussion, and the seminar are most generally used. In every department there are independent study opportunities and honors programs. Barat offers the B.A. degree and by petition the B.S. degree.

In 1964 Barat's library had 45,000 volumes and received 326 periodicals. Included in the library holdings were more than 500 music recordings; a tape library of 190 plays, poetry, lectures, and music; and 2,000 35-mm art slides.

[M. BURKE]

BARBARA, ST., virgin and martyr (feast, Dec. 4). Data of her vita and *passio* are from a legend composed in the 7th century, perhaps of Egyptian origin. Her father Dioscorus is said to have kept her in a tower so that her beauty would not be contaminated by the world, but on learning that she was baptized a Christian, he had her condemned by the prefect Martinianus and himself beheaded her, whereupon he was consumed by lightning. There is an 8th-century fresco of Barbara in Rome. Her vita was taken from the *Menologion* of *Symeon Metaphrastes and introduced into European *martyrologies in the 9th century. She is one of the *Fourteen Holy Helpers and the patroness of those exposed to sudden death. She is portrayed with crown, palm and sword, and also with tower and peacock, and a chalice to symbolize a happy death; she was the subject of many Flemish and Italian artists in the 15th and 16th centuries (see illus., facing page).

Bibliography: V. SEMPELS, DHGE 6:627–628. A. P. FRUTAZ and K. RATHE, EncCatt 2:802–803. K. GROSS and H. BENDER, LexThK² 1:1235–36. G. D. GORDINI, BiblSanct 2:760–765. **Illustration credit:** The Metropolitan Museum of Art, The Cloisters Collection, Gift of Mrs. Solomon R. Guggenheim, 1950.

[M. J. COSTELLOE]

BARBARIAN NATIONS

The non-Italic, non-Greek peoples of Europe who inherited the Greco-Roman civilization and formed racially most of the present-day European nations. Like the Greeks and the Italic peoples, they were speakers of Indo-European dialects. The Ligurians, Illyrians, Thracians, and Balts were small or obscure groups; while the great migratory nations, Celts, Germans, and Slavs, played major historical roles.

The Celtic cradle was inner Europe from the Marne through the Middle Rhine where the La Tène culture flourished *c.* 500 B.C. Around 400 B.C. they began to migrate. Some crossed the Alps into Cisalpine Gaul, so-called from the Latin *Gallus,* "Celt." About 387 B.C. they captured Rome and long challenged its power in

Christianized and adopted Roman civilization. Modern historians generally accept Karl Müllenhoff's classification (1898) of the Germans into three branches on philological and historical grounds: (1) North Germans (i.e., Scandinavians) who remained isolated until they ventured forth in the 9th century as Vikings; (2) East Germans (embracing chiefly the Goths, Vandals, Burgundians, Heruli, Lombards, Rugians, and Scyrrians)—this branch migrated most widely but their own kingdoms on Roman soil perished quickly; (3) West Germans (including the Franks, Alamanni or Suevi, Angles, Saxons, Frisians, and Hessians)—they created the enduring states of early medieval Europe. E. Schwarz has suggested somewhat different categories, offering greater precision than Müllenhoff and calling closer attention to those who evolved into the modern Germans.

The primitive Slav homeland lay north of the Carpathians but did not reach the Baltic Sea; it stretched from the middle Dnieper westward to somewhere beyond the middle and upper Oder. East European scholars today tend to attribute to them the Bronze Age Lausitz culture of *c.* 700–500 B.C., but the evidence is uncertain. Late in impinging on classical civilization, the Slavs apparently did not attract the attention of Greek writers. Among the Romans, too, information is late. Pliny the Elder and Tacitus refer to Slavs under the name of Venedi, and place them east of the Germans on the Vistula. Ptolemy agrees. Then the sources fall silent until the 6th century A.D. when the Slavs reappear, moving toward the Balkans. Probably their migration began *c.* A.D. 200, influenced by East German movements and, after 560, the impact of the Avars, along with land hunger and expanding population. Politically backward and culturally weak, the Slavs were dominated by the stronger peoples who regularly swept over them. Some authorities identify the obscure Antes as Slavs; if so, these created the earliest but ephemeral Slav state *c.* 250–602. By *c.* 800 the Slav tribes began to coalesce into the modern groupings of Eastern Europe: (1) East Slavs, consisting of Great and White Russians and Ukrainians; (2) South Slavs, i.e., Slo-

St. Barbara with a tower representing the one in which she was imprisoned, stone sculpture, painted and gilded, French, 15th century.

north Italy. Others moved into what is now France, where they were conquered by Julius Caesar in the 1st century B.C. Eastwardly migrating Celts occupied Bohemia and approached Macedonia by 335 B.C. In the next decades they penetrated Illyria and Thrace and harassed Greece; in 279 B.C. they plundered Delphi. Crossing into Asia, they established the kingdom of Galatia in Asia Minor. Those Celts who colonized the British Isles came in two waves: the Goidels or Gaels (Irish) reached Ireland via Spain and southern Gaul, and they extended into Scotland during the early Christian era; the Cymri or Brythons reached Britain from northern Gaul, and survive today in Wales and Brittany.

Southern Scandinavia, Denmark, and its adjacent mainland was the original habitation of the Germans *c.* 1200–500 B.C. Expanding slowly northward and southward they found vacant land in inner Germany after the Celts migrated. By the time of Augustus (29 B.C.–A.D. 14) the Germanic area was clearly delimited, although the migrations continued for half a millennium longer. Tacitus wrote his detailed description of the primitive Germans in A.D. 95. Although helping to destroy the Roman state, the Germans were eventually

Barbarian Kingdoms
c. 511

venes, Croats, Serbs, and Bulgars, although the last three are Slavicized Sarmatians and Mongols; (3) West Slavs, consisting of Bohemians, Moravians, Poles, and the Polabian Slavs formerly of the Elbe-Oder area. Settled generally beyond the geographical limits of the Greco-Roman world, the Slavs were eventually converted to Christianity, the Western group receiving their Christianity from Rome, and the Eastern group from Constantinople.

Bibliography: C. S. Coon, *The Races of Europe* (New York 1954). E. Schwarz, *Germanische Stammeskunde* (Heidelberg 1956). F. Dvornik, *The Slavs: Their Early History and Civilization* (Boston 1956).

[R. H. SCHMANDT]

BARBARIGO, GREGORY, ST., bishop and cardinal; b. Venice, Sept. 16, 1625; d. Padua, June 18, 1697 (feast, June 18). Gregory, the son of Giovanni Francesco *Barbarigo, of illustrious family, was educated in Padua. In 1648, he accompanied the Venetian embassy to Münster for the Treaty of Westphalia and met the papal nuncio, later Alexander VII. Gregory took a degree in law and was ordained in 1655. At Alexander's request he organized the care of the plague-stricken Roman Trastevere in 1656. As bishop of Bergamo in 1657, he promoted the reforms of the Council of Trent, visiting parishes, organizing the teaching of Christian doctrine, and raising the standards of the seminary and the clergy. He was made a cardinal in 1660, and bishop of Padua in 1667. He adapted the curriculum of the seminary of Padua to contemporary needs, obtained books for its library throughout Europe, and wrote *Regulae Studiorum* (1690) for ecclesiastical studies. He set up a printing press with Latin, Greek, Hebrew, Syriac, Persian, and Slavonic types, preparing pamphlets for Christians under Moslem rule. His aid to Orthodox leaders was generous, and his death may have prevented negotiations for reunion with Rome. He took part in five papal conclaves and was a candidate in three, especially in 1691. His body is in the cathedral of Padua. He was beatified Sept. 20, 1761, and canonized May 25, 1960. John XXIII held him as a model during his seminary days. S. Serana has studied Gregory and his relations with mathematics, the Eastern Church, and his contemporaries (5 v., Padua 1932–40).

Bibliography: P. Paschini, EncCatt 2:817–819. John XIII, Act ApS 52 (1960) 437–462. Mercati-Pelzer DE 2:263. H. Raab, LexThK² 1:1236. C. Bellinati, *S. Gregorio Barbarigo* (Padua 1960); *Pensieri e massime di S. Gregorio* (Padua 1962).

[M. O'CALLAGHAN]

BARBARIGO, MARC' ANTONIO AND GIOVANNI FRANCESCO

Cardinals, members of a prominent Venetian family.

Marc' Antonio. Cardinal; b. Venice, March 6, 1640; d. Montefiascone, May 26, 1706. Barbarigo, a member of the Venetian Council at 25, left a promising political career for the priesthood and was ordained in 1671. When summoned to Padua by Gregory *Barbarigo, a distant relative, he became a canon in the cathedral and earned a degree *utroque jure* at the University of Padua. In 1676 he accompanied Cardinal Gregorio to the conclave that elected Innocent XI, and he remained in Rome at the new Pope's request. He was appointed to the vacant episcopal See of Corfù in 1678, and was installed on September 24 of the same year.

His peaceful and efficient administration lasted until 1685. On the first Sunday of Lent of that year, a controversy over a question of protocol arose between Barbarigo and Francesco Morosini, admiral of the Venetian fleet. Barbarigo fled to Venice to clear himself of charges brought against him. When denied a hearing and deprived of his possessions, he sought asylum in Rome. Having been cleared of the charges, he was made a cardinal by Innocent XI on Sept. 2, 1686. The following year he was appointed bishop of Montefiascone and Corneta, which he entered on Oct. 20, 1687. In this office, Barbarigo earned universal praise for his pastoral charity and his interest in education. Deeply concerned with the plight of underprivileged girls, he founded the institute of the Scuole e Maestre Pie for their care and education. In this work, he was assisted by Rose Venerini, foundress of similar schools in the diocese; one of the pupils, St. Lucy *Filippini, later became the superior of the Montefiascone institute. Barbarigo also promoted education and established a sound program of studies in the seminary "Barbarigo," which he generously endowed with a good library. He attended the conclaves that elected Alexander VIII, Innocent XII, and Clement XI. He is buried in the cathedral of Montefiascone. The process for his canonization is under way.

Giovanni Francesco. Cardinal, nephew of St. Gregory Barbarigo, cousin of Marc' Antonio; b. Venice, April 29, 1658; d. Padua, Jan. 26, 1730. Although ambassador of Venice at the court of Louis XIV, he renounced diplomacy for the priesthood. Bishop of Verona (1697) and of Brescia (1714), he was made cardinal by Clement XI in 1721, with the title of SS. Peter and Marcellinus. On Jan. 20, 1723, Innocent XIII named him bishop of Padua, where he distinguished himself for his piety and zeal, visiting hospitals, reorganizing ecclesiastical discipline, and promoting education. Barbarigo, munificent and learned scholar, published, at his own expense, the works of St. Zeno (1710) and of St. Gaudentius (1720). He is buried next to his uncle, Gregory.

Bibliography: M. A. Barbarigo. P. Bergamaschi, *Vita . . . del card. M. A. Barbarigo*, 2 v. (Rome 1919). G. Marangoni, *Vita del card. M. Barbarigo* (Montefiascone 1930). A. Zerbini, *Cultura e umanesimo nell'Alto Lazio* (Rome 1955). G. Loew, EncCatt 2:819. H. Raab, LexThK² 1:1237.
G. F. Barbarigo. H. Rabb, LexThK² 1:1236–37. Eubel Hier Cath 5:127, 309, 411. M. T. Disdier, DHGE 6:578–579.

[E. J. THOMSON]

BARBARO

Noted Venetian family of humanists, statesmen, and churchmen.

Francesco, statesman and humanist; b. Venice, *c.* 1398; d. Venice, January 1454. A student of Manuel *Chrysoloras, he was tutored in letters and Greek, and then studied at the University of Padua. He entered the Venetian senate in 1418 and was ambassador to Florence, Verona, Bologna, and other important Italian cities, as well as to the court of Pope *Martin V. In 1438 he led the defense of Brescia against Filippo Maria *Visconti, Duke of Milan, whose ambitions he considered the greatest danger to Venice. Francesco desired peace for all Italy. Active in negotiations for the Council of *Basel-Ferrara-*Florence, he tried to effect religious unity with the Greek Church and urged that steps be taken to prevent Constantinople from falling to the Turks. He wrote *De re uxorio libri II*

Ermolao Barbaro (the Elder?), by an unknown 15th-century artist, in the Uffizi Gallery at Florence.

in 1415 and was acquainted with most of the Italian humanists of his time (*see* HUMANISM). His letters, *Orationum ac epistolarum libri XV,* were edited by A. Quirini (Brescia 1743), whose edition was improved by R. Sabbadini (Salerno 1884) and L. Frati (Venice 1888).

Nicolo (dates uncertain), Venetian ambassador to *Constantinople, wrote a report of its siege and capture by the Turks in 1453; *Giornale dell'assedio di Constantinopoli,* which was published by both A. Sagredo (Venice 1856) and E. Cornet (Vienna 1856).

Ermolao the Elder, churchman and humanist, brother of Francesco; b. Venice, *c.* 1410; d. Venice, March 12, 1471. He became bishop of Treviso, Oct. 16, 1443, and of Verona, Nov. 16, 1453. In 1453 he wrote *Oratio contra poetas* objecting to excessive adulation of the ancient poets. His works are unpublished.

Ermolao the Younger, patriarch of *Aquileia, humanist, churchman, diplomat, nephew of Ermolao; b. Venice, May 21, 1454; d. Rome, June 14, 1493. At the age of 8, he was sent to Rome to study under *Pomponius Laetus; by 1477 he was professor of philosophy at the University of Padua. He served as Venetian ambassador to Milan in 1488 and to the court of Pope *Innocent VIII in 1491. Though he was named patriarch of Aquileia by Innocent on March 6, 1491, the Venetians prevented him from taking possession of his see because he had accepted it without consent of the senate. He remained in Rome and died of the plague. His principal work is *Castigationes,* against Pliny the Elder; he also translated some of the writings of Aristotle into Latin. His *Epistolae, orationes et carmina* are edited by V. Branca, 2 v. (Florence 1943).

Daniele, statesman, patriarch of Aquileia; b. Venice, Feb. 8, 1513; d. Venice, April 12, 1570. He was a student and professor at Padua, who in 1548 became ambassador to England. Though named patriarch of Aquileia (Dec. 17, 1550) by Pope Julius III, he never governed it; the patriarchate continued to be administered by Giovanni Grimani in order to prevent a non-Venetian from obtaining the position. In 1562 Daniele began active participation in the Council of Trent. His works can be found in J. Morelli, *Codices manuscripti latini bibliothecae Nanianae* (Venice 1776) 4, 31–32, 198.

Francesco, patriarch of Aquileia, reformer; b. Venice; d. Venice, April 27, 1616. On Oct. 7, 1585, he became archbishop of Tyre, then vicar-general and coadjutor with right of succession to Giovanni Grimani, whom he succeeded on Oct. 3, 1593. He combatted heresy and, in his attempts to effect the reforms of Trent, opened a seminary at Udine in 1601.

Ermolao, patriarch of Aquileia; d. Venice, Dec. 22, 1622. He had been archbishop of Tyre and coadjutor to his brother Francesco whom he succeeded as patriarch, but because of wars of the Uscocchi he could never take possession of his see.

Bibliography: Francesco, statesman. G. M. MAZZUCHELLI, *Gli scrittori d'Italia,* 2 v. (Brescia 1753–63) 2:264–269. P. GOTHEIN, *Francesco B.: Früh-Humanismus und Staatkunst in Venedig* (Berlin 1932). Ermolao the Elder. G. M. MAZZUCHELLI, *op. cit.* 2:253–256. Daniele. P. PASCHINI, "I scritti religiosi di Daniele Barbaro," RivStorChIt 5 (1951) 340–349. Francesco, patriarch. P. PASCHINI, "Riforma e contro-riforma al confine nord-orientale d'Italia," *L'Arcadia* 4 (1922) 72– . Ermolao, patriarch. E. A. CICOGNA, *Iscrizióni veneziane,* 6 v. in 7 (Venice 1825–53) v.4. P. PASCHINI and M. T. DISDIER, DHGE 6:582–590. P. PASCHINI, EncCatt 2:820–822. **Illustration credit:** Alinari-Art Reference Bureau.

[W. H. WALLAIK]

BARBASTRO, FRANCISCO ANTONIO, Franciscan prelate in northwest Mexico; b. Villa de Cariñena, Aragón, Spain, 1734; d. Aconchi, Sonora, Mexico, June 22, 1800. Barbastro took the habit at the Convento de Jesús in Zaragoza (1754), went to the Colegio of San Roque de Calamocha (1764), and from there to the Missionary College of Santa Cruz de Querétaro (1770). He was assigned to the missions of Sonora, of which he was made president. There he was the most outstanding of the missionaries because of his wisdom and his charity toward the Indians. He learned the languages of the various nations, particularly that of the Opatas, and preached in them. In 1783 he founded the school of Aconchi, the first in Sonora. On October 23 of that year the Custody of San Carlos was founded, and Barbastro governed it as vice custos until it was dissolved (1789) on his recommendation to Charles IV. Barbastro demonstrated that the custody was harmful to the missions. He wrote notes and reports for a history of the Province of Sonora as an *Apología* for the Franciscan provinces and colleges engaged in missions among the pagans.

[E. DEL HOYO]

BARBATIA, ANDREAS DE (ANDREAS SICULUS), lay canon lawyer; b. Messina, Sicily, *c.* 1400; d. Bologna, July 21, 1479. In 1425 he studied medicine at Bologna and then law. In 1438 he both taught and took his doctorate degree in Canon Law. From 1438 until 1442 he taught at Florence, then returned to Bologna and taught there until his retirement (1478). He was a renowned teacher and active practitioner of law. Among his students was Rodriquez Borgia, later Pope Innocent VI. His knowledge of both Canon and civil law caused pope, kings, and civil leaders to seek out his advice. His works include *Lecturae seu Repetitiones,* on the Decretals, *Tractatus de Praestantia Cardinalium* (Bologna 1487), *Tractatus de Cardinalibus a latere legatis* (Lyons 1518), *Tractatus de praetensionibus* (Bologna 1487).

Bibliography: A. AMANIEU, DDC 1:520–521. Schulte 2:306–311.

[T. F. DONOVAN]

BARBATUS, ST., bishop and patron of Benevento; b. Cerreto Sannita, Italy, early 7th century; d. Benevento, Italy, Feb. 19, 682 (feast, Feb. 19). Little is known of his life until he succeeded Hildebrand as bishop of Benevento in 663, but he devoted his attention both before and after his election to stamping out the remains of pagan superstitions in his diocese. It was reported that he won the support of his people by predicting both the calamities that would occur because of the invasion in 663 of the army of Emperor *Constans II and the later lifting of the siege. In 681 he attended the sixth general council, *Constantinople III; he died not long after he returned from this meeting. He is especially venerated in Benevento, where his body is buried under the main altar of the cathedral. There is a tendentious life of Barbatus dating from the 9th century (ed. G. Waitz, MGSrerLang 556–563).

Bibliography: BHL 973–975. A. P. FRUTAZ, LexThK² 1:1238. N. C. SCIPIONI, EncCatt 2:822–823. G. CANGIANO, *Origini della chiesa Beneventana* (Benevento 1923) 40–51; "Sulla leggenda della 'vipera longobarda' e delle 'streghe,'" *Atti della Società storica del Sannio* 5–7 (1927–29) 84–96. A. M. JANNACCHINO, *S. Barbato e il suo secolo* (Benevento 1902).

[R. E. GEIGER]

BARBEAUX, ABBEY OF, former French abbey, Diocese of Sens. Barbeaux was founded in 1146, by *Cistercians of Preuilly on the site of an early hermitage (*Sacer Portus*), but in 1156 it was transferred to Barbeaux, donated by King *Louis VII. The King continued to be a generous benefactor of the abbey and, according to his wishes, was buried there. In spite of royal patronage the monastery suffered during the Hundred Years' War and was deserted for 40 years. Reconstruction was hampered when Barbeaux came under commendatory abbots after 1498. When the 17 monks of the community embraced the Cistercian Strict Observance in 1643, there followed a period of financial and moral recovery. In 1768, there were 10 monks in the abbey, while revenues amounted to 18,500 livres. The abbey was suppressed by the French Revolution. While under private ownership, the church and cloister were demolished. Other buildings housed an orphanage in the Napoleonic era.

Bibliography: C. RABOURDIN, *L'Abbaye royale de Barbeaux* (Melun 1895). Chevalier TB 1:307. J. M. CANIVEZ, DHGE 6: 629–631. Cottineau 1:260–261.

[L. J. LEKAI]

BARBELIN, FELIX JOSEPH, pastor and educator; b. Lunéville, Lorraine, France, May 30, 1808; d. Philadelphia, Pa., June 8, 1869. After education in French schools and seminaries, he became a Jesuit in Maryland in 1831, was ordained Sept. 22, 1835, and taught at Georgetown University. He served as an assistant at St. Joseph's, Philadelphia, and became pastor there in 1844, remaining in that post until his death. He inaugurated the first parish sodality at St. Joseph's (1841) and established a St. Vincent de Paul conference and a free school for girls in Philadelphia. The Italian congregation he organized developed into the first Italian Catholic parish in Philadelphia. He gathered the first Negro congregation in Philadelphia and established a school for Negro children. He founded St. Joseph's Hospital and established St. Joseph's College, Philadelphia, serving as its first and third president. He also conducted a night school for adults.

Bibliography: J. M. DALEY, *St. Joseph's Church, Willing's Alley* (Philadelphia 1963). F. X. TALBOT, *Jesuit Education in Philadelphia* (Philadelphia 1927). RecAmCHSPhila. *Woodstock Letters.*

[H. J. NOLAN]

BARBER, a prominent New England family converted to Catholicism in the early 19th century. *Daniel* (b. Simsbury, Conn., Oct. 2, 1756; d. St. Inigoes, Md., March 24, 1834) was a soldier in the Continental Army and left the Congregational Church to become an Episcopal minister. In 1818 he terminated a 24-year career as resident Episcopal minister at Claremont, N.H., and entered the Catholic Church. He wrote *Catholic Worships and Piety Explained* (1821) and *The History of My Own Times* (1827). His son *Virgil Horace* (b. Simsbury, Conn., May 9, 1782; d. Georgetown, D.C., March 27, 1847) was educated at Dartmouth College, Hanover, N.H. He entered the Episcopal ministry and became the highly regarded resident pastor (1807–14) of St. John's Episcopal Church, Waterbury, Conn. On June 1, 1814, Virgil resigned his position at Waterbury to become principal of an Episcopal academy at Fairfield, N.Y. After his conversion to the Catholic Church in 1816 with his entire family, Virgil and his wife received permission to enter religious societies, and he was ordained in the Society of Jesus at Boston, Mass., Dec. 3, 1822. While assigned to Claremont, N.H. (1823–24), Barber opened the first Catholic church and school in that area. After a period of missionary work in Maine, he returned to varied assignments at and in the vicinity of Georgetown, D.C., until his death. His wife *Jerusha* (b. Booth, in Newtown, Conn., July 20, 1789; d. Mobile, Ala., Jan. 2, 1860) entered the Visitandines and made her vows at Georgetown, D.C., Feb. 2, 1820, selecting the name Sister Mary Austin (or Augustina). She served her community with distinction at Georgetown, Kaskaskia, Ill., St. Louis, Mo., and Mobile, Ala. It is fairly certain that the children of Virgil and Jerusha Barber, with the exception of the youngest, were born at Waterbury, Conn. All of them, four daughters and one son, eventually entered and achieved prominence in religious societies of the Church. *Mary* (b. Jan. 31, 1810; d. Quebec, Canada, May 9, 1848) entered the Ursulines, as did her two younger sisters, *Abigail, Sister St. Francis Xavier* (b. Feb. 5, 1811; d. Quebec, Canada, March 2, 1880) and *Susan, Sister Mary St. Joseph* (b. 1813; d. Three Rivers, Canada, Jan. 24, 1837). *Samuel Joseph,* the only son (b. March 19, 1814; d. St. Thomas Manor, Md., Feb. 23, 1864), was a priest in the Society of Jesus. *Josephine,* the youngest child (b. Fairfield, N.Y., Aug. 9, 1816; d. St. Louis, Mo., July 17, 1888) was a Visitandine nun.

Bibliography: L. DE GOESBRIAND, *Catholic Memoirs of Vermont and New Hampshire* (Burlington, Vt. 1886). H. MITCHELL,

"Virgil Horace Barber," *Woodstock Letters* 79 (1950) 297–334.
F. J. KINGSBURY, *A Narrative and Documentary History of St. John's Protestant Episcopal Church . . . of Waterbury, Connecticut* (New Haven 1907).

[J. W. SCULLY]

BARBERI, DOMINIC, BL., b. near Viterbo, Italy, June 22, 1792; d. Reading, England, Aug. 27, 1849 (feast, Aug. 27). He was the youngest child of Giuseppe, a tenant farmer, and Marie Antonia (Pacelli)

Dominic Barberi.

Barberi. Although without formal schooling, he entered the *Passionists (1814), made his profession (Nov. 15, 1815), and was ordained at Rome (March 1, 1818). From 1821 to 1831 he lectured on philosophy and theology to Passionist clerics. After serving as superior of the new monastery at Lucca, Italy (1831–33), he became provincial for southern Italy (1833). Moving to England (1841), he opened the first British Passionist monastery at Aston in Staffordshire (1842). Despite his ugly, ungainly appearance, ridicule by Catholics, and persecution by Protestants, he was responsible for many conversions because of his saintly life. His greatest consolation was to receive John Henry *Newman into the Church. Barberi was beatified on Oct. 27, 1963.

Bibliography: ActApS 55 (1963) 893–895, 996–1001, 1020–25. D. R. GWYNN, *Father Dominic Barberi* (London 1947). A. WILSON, *Blessed Dominic Barberi* (London 1966).

[D. MILBURN]

BARBERINI, surname of an aristocratic Italian family whose members played leading roles in the government of the Church and the beautifying of Rome in the 17th century. The family traced its descent from a family in Ancona named Tafani that, after becoming rich by trade, changed its name to that of the castle Barberini located in the region of Siena. In the 14th century there were Barberinis living in Florence. During the pontificate of Paul III, *Francesco* Barberini was in Rome, where he held the offices of prothonotary apostolic and referendary to both Segnaturas. His nephew *Maffeo* Barberini, from Florence, profited from his uncle's help and rose in the Church to a position from which he was able to be elected Pope on Aug. 6, 1623. He took the name *Urban VIII, and as Pope he saw to it that the other members of his family were

given important and lucrative positions in the Church and the government of the Papal States. One brother, *Carlo,* was named governor of the Borgo and a general of the Church. Two of Carlo's sons, *Francesco* (1597–1679) and *Antonio* (1607–71), were created cardinals at ages 25 and 20 respectively and appointed to high offices in the Church. Another son of Carlo, *Taddeo,* was married to Anne, the daughter of Filippo Colonna, by Urban VIII and became prince of Palestrina, castellan of S. Angelo, captain of the guard, and prefect of Rome. He succeeded his father as governor of the Borgo and a general of the Church. Another brother of Urban VIII, *Antonio* (1569–1646), was a Capuchin not very interested in possessions, but he too was made a cardinal in 1624 and became part of the governmental operations of the Church. Benefices were even assigned to two sisters of Urban VIII who were in the Carmelite convent of Florence.

The wealth amassed by Urban VIII's nephews during his pontificate was enormous. Like their uncle, however, they expended much of it in the service of art and literature. Francesco was the founder of the Barberini library, the richest library after that of the Vatican. Under Barberini patronage, Giovanni Lorenzo Bernini built the Palazzo Barberini on the slope of the Quirinal near the Quattro Fontane. Rome and its environs were beautified by the attention the Barberini paid to the rebuilding of churches, and the construction of fountains and piazzas; the three bees in their coat of arms could be found imprinted everywhere in Rome as a testimonial to their public spirit.

The coat of arms of the Barberini family, crowned with the papal crest, sculpture by Giovanni Lorenzo Bernini on the base of one of the columns of the baldachino in the Basilica of St. Peter, Rome.

When *Innocent X became Pope, the nephews fled to France, where they were protected by Cardinal Mazarin. They had feared that an investigation begun by the Pope into the way in which they had acquired their wealth might harm them, but eventually Innocent X pardoned them. As part of this reconciliation, Taddeo's son *Maffeo* married Olimpiuccia Giustiniani, Innocent X's niece. In 1690 *Francesco* Barberini, Urban VIII's great grandnephew, was made a cardinal; he died in 1738. The daughter and heiress of Maffeo's heir, *Urbano* (d. 1722), *Cornelia* Barberini, married Guilio Cesare Colonna di Sciarra in 1728.

Bibliography: P. PECCHIAI, *I Barberini* (Rome 1959). L. CÀLLARI, *I palazzi di Roma* (3d ed. Rome 1944). Pastor 29:439–447, 498–507. G. GRAGLIA, EncCatt 2:825–827. M. T. DISDIER and F. BONNARD, DHGE 6:640–645. **Illustration credit:** Alinari-Art Reference Bureau.

[V. PONKO, JR.]

BARBOSA, AGOSTINO, bishop and canonist; b. Guimarens, Portugal, 1589; d. Nov. 19, 1649. He studied Canon Law in Portugal and in Rome. He was noted for his sanctity, affability, and prodigious memory. In 1632 he went to Madrid and functioned as an ecclesiastical judge. In 1648 he was nominated as bishop of Ungento, in Otranto, by Philip IV. His many writings are noted for their erudition and familiarity with authors, sources, and controverted questions. His most important work is the *Historia iuris ecclesiastici universi libri tres* (Lyons 1633, 1645, 1718). He also published a commentary on the Council of Trent, which was later placed on the Index; a compendium of law; and a juridical lexicon. All his works were published at Lyons (1657–75) in 19 volumes, 16 volumes in folio, and again (1698–1716) 20 volumes, 18 volumes in folio.

Bibliography: J. RAFFALLI, DDC 2:203. Von Hove 1:388, 536, 555–556. Schulte 3:54, 746.

[J. M. BUCKLEY]

BARBOSA, JANUÁRIO DA CUNHA, Brazilian priest, journalist, and liberal politician; b. Rio de Janeiro, July 10, 1780; d. Rio de Janeiro, Feb. 22, 1846. Son of a Portuguese and a Brazilian woman, he lost both parents before he was 10. He was well educated by an uncle who, wanting a prominent place for his nephew in society, destined him to the priesthood. He studied in the Seminary São José in Rio. Ordained in 1803, he went to Europe to round out his studies. He returned to Brazil in 1805 and worked in a parish, where he gained a reputation as a preacher. In 1814 he was named professor of rational and moral philosophy in the seminary. He became one of the leaders of Brazilian independence and, with Joaquim Gonçalves Ledo, founded the *Revérbero Constitucional Fluminense.* Januário was a brilliant journalist, a terrible polemicist with a great sense of humor, and a preacher of amazing erudition. Frei Francisco do Monte Alverne, the greatest glory of the Brazilian pulpit, called him a "Giant of Oratory." His 400 sermons are in the panegyrist style of the epoch. After a year's exile because of his opposition to the Andrada brothers, who controlled the government, Januário enjoyed all the privileges of a royal courtier: canon and royal preacher of the imperial chapel, imperial chronicler, director of the national library, and editor of the governmental daily. He became a Mason during the independence movement, as did many other clergymen of the time, because of the political influence of the lodges. A man of strong liberal ideas in his early political battles, Januário was also a regalist and later on turned to conservativism. He was always a defender of the anti-Roman policy of the imperial government. In 1826 he was elected deputy to the General Assembly for the Province of Rio de Janeiro, but his real field was journalism: he became a satirist, composing plays and poems to ridicule his political adversaries, and even founded a witty newspaper, *Mutuca Picante* (big biting fly). Januário was cofounder of the *Revista do Instituto histórico e geográfico brasileiro,* a monthly journal that has contributed greatly to the improvement of arts and sciences in Brazil.

Bibliography: A. DA CUNHA BARBOZA, "Esboço biographico do conego Januário da Cunha Barboza," *Revista do Instituto histórico e geográphico brasileiro* 65.2 (1902) 197–284.

[T. BEAL]

BARBOSA, RUI

Brazilian statesman, jurist, and writer; b. Salvador, Bahia, Nov. 5, 1849; d. Petrópolis, March 1, 1923. He graduated in law in São Paulo. He worked as a journalist in his province until 1878 when, with the rise of the Liberal party, he was elected a deputy. He then drafted

Rui Barbosa.

famous legislative bills on public education, abolition of slavery, and electoral reform, revealing himself as a leading parliamentarian and receiving the title of councilor. After the Conservative victory in 1885, he did not return to the legislature, but he won great renown as a lawyer and jurist. Through the press he fought the last cabinets of the monarchy and supported the Republic, of whose provisional government he was vice president and minister of finance. He then undertook bold reform, trying to direct the country toward industrialism and away from the emphasis on agriculture. Inflation and market speculation, stimulated by easy credit, generated a crisis that was the favorite target of his critics.

He was the author of many basic laws of the regime, such as those that established the federation, the separation of Church and State, civil marriage, and the draft of the constitution submitted to the assembly in which he participated. From that time until his death he represented Bahia in the Senate and was twice a candidate for president of the Republic. He had two diplomatic appointments: delegate to the Second Hague Peace Conference (1907), in which he opposed, on the principle of the equality of states, the plan for a permanent court defended by the great powers; and special ambassador in Buenos Aires (1916), where he proposed the doctrine of vigilant neutrality, in accord with U.S. Pres. Woodrow Wilson. Later, he refused the post of representative to the Versailles Peace Conference. In 1921 he obtained the largest vote in the Assembly and Council of the League of Nations to be a member of the new Permanent Court of International Justice, but his death prevented him from serving. At the time of his centenary, his body was transferred from Rio de Janeiro to the capital of Bahia, where it lies in the crypt of the Palace of Justice. His house, acquired by the Brazilian government, was made a museum and a center for legal and philological research.

Rui Barbosa was considered an expert in language and was president of the Brazilian Academy of Letters. An exponent of liberalism, he defended the presidential system and an American type of judiciary. Toward the end of his life he made concessions to socialization, inclining toward Christian Democracy in the manner of Cardinal Mercier. Although a profound believer and a Christian, he gave up the practice of religion as a youth, receiving the Sacraments again only when he was dying. Yet he defended some interests of the Church, such as the indissolubility of marriage, religious education, the freedom of the religious orders, and representation at the Vatican. At the beginning of his career, because of his Masonic and secularistic attitudes, he was much opposed by the clergy. At the end, however, especially after his address of 1903 at the Jesuit College, he enjoyed the friendship of various prelates, including Cardinal *Arcoverde.

Bibliography: *Obras completas,* 32 v. in 66 (Rio de Janeiro 1942–63); *Escritos e discursos seletos* (Rio de Janeiro 1960). L. DELGADO, *Rui Barbosa, tentativa de compreensão e de síntese* (Rio de Janeiro 1945). **Illustration credit:** Pan American Union, Washington, D.C.

[A. J. LACOMBE]

BARCELONA

A major seaport on the Mediterranean in northeast Spain. The Diocese of Barcelona, the most populous see in Spain, became an archdiocese without suffragans in 1964. It had 369 parishes, 867 secular and 945 religious priests, 3,425 men in 148 religious houses, 8,305 women in 503 convents, and 2,459,000 Catholics. Its 1,161 square miles of territory, the smallest area of any Spanish see, cover half the civil province of Barcelona.

Barcelona's strategic position as a crossroads made it important during the Carthaginian, Roman, Visigothic, and Moslem periods. Caesar was grateful for its support against Pompey; Aetius fought the Roman Empire from there; the Visigoths Ataulf and Amalric made it their capital (414–418, 531); the Franks after reconquering it from the Moslems centered their *Marca hispanica* there (801); the counts of the 9th and 10th centuries built an independent principality upon it; and the far-flung holdings of the Crown of Aragon, from Languedoc to Greece, looked to it as the major royal center. The city's history thus often reflects the wider Arago-Catalan story.

As a medieval commune Barcelona evolved into a major maritime power, with a concomitant cultural and religious sophistication. Union with Castile in the 16th century coincided with a general decline of the city, followed by embroilment in revolt (1640), wars and troubles, and finally the Napoleonic occupation. The 19th and 20th centuries made Barcelona the principal industrial city of Spain but plunged her into Liberal, Carlist, anticlerical, and radical upheavals.

The diocese has kept roughly the same limits since the 4th century, though a sizable portion broke off (450–712) as the Visigothic Diocese of Egara (Tarrasa today). The traditional internal division (3 deaneries and a central officialate) yielded in the 1851 concordat to 12 archpresbyteries. Legend has obscured the early Church history, introducing apostolic preaching and a Bishop Severus, and moving St. Eulalia's martyrdom (304) from *Mérida to Barcelona. The earliest known bishops in the scanty episcopal lists are Praetextatus, who was with *Hosius at the Council of *Sardica (347), and the theological writer Pacianus (d. before 392). Visigothic councils took place in 540 and 599.

The liberated Church of the Franks was restored as a diocese before 858. Struggling for independence from its new metropolitan *Narbonne, Barcelona returned in the 11th century to the metropolitanate of reconquered *Tarragona, to which it was suffragan until 1964. Bishop Guislabert (1035–62), who replaced the damaged older cathedral, was succeeded by the famous St. *Oldegar. The vast new cathedral, begun in 1298 and finished in the 14th century, acquired a modern façade in 1887. Religious orders and monastic life flourished, especially at Sant Cugat del Vallès, a monastery for the nobility founded in Visigothic times and suppressed in 1835. Barcelona, which had 11 medieval hospitals, witnessed the rise of the *Mercedarians (*c.* 1220), who ransomed Christian slaves from the Moors. It also produced the greatest medieval lawyer, *Raymond of Peñafort (d. 1275). Under bishops such as Berengar de Palou (1212–41) and Arnold de Gurb (1252–84) the diocese developed excellent schools, crusaded valiantly, and welcomed the surge of mendicant orders. Barcelona allied with the Avignon antipopes (1378–1417) and gave refuge to Benedict XIII. Its municipal schools finally acquired a university charter in 1450; the present university was reconstructed in 1837 after an interim existence in Cervera.

During Barcelona's humiliating decline (16th–18th centuries) the Church identified itself closely with Catalan nationalism; Bp. Benito de Sala was exiled with 300 of his clergy (1714). In the Jansenist Bp. José *Climent (1766–75) the Church had an austere, effective leader, and in St. Joseph *Oriol (d. 1702) a holy

Souls in Paradise in the folds of the robe of an Old Testament patriarch, fragment of an 11th-century fresco from the Church of St. John, Boí, Spain, now in the Museo de Arte Cataluña, Barcelona.

Barcelona, Sagrada Familia Church, by Antonio Gaudí. Only the neo-Gothic choir, to the left, and the distinctive front of the east transept, seen here from the inside, have been built.

priest. Bloody anticlerical mob action occurred in 1835, 1909, and 1939.

The abbey *nullius* of *Montserrat, whose region has been attached to the diocese, and the Balmesiana Institute are centers of Catalan religious culture. Barcelona is notable for its Romanesque and even more for its Gothic monuments, some in the restored "Gothic Quarter" near the cathedral, the 12th-century frescoes in the Museo de Arte de Cataluña, the Tibidabo shrine overlooking the city, the protomodern façade by A. *Gaudí for the Sagrada Familia Church (1890–), and the ruins of Sant Cugat outside the city.

Bibliography: M. AIMERICH, *Nomina et acta episcoporum barcinonensium* (Barcelona 1760). C. BARRAQUES, *Los religiosos en Cataluña*, 4 v. (Barcelona 1906–17). J. MAS, *Notes històriques del bisbat de Barcelona*, 13 v. (Barcelona 1906–21). S. PUIG Y PUIG, *Episcopologio de la sede barcinonense* (Barcelona 1929). J. SANABRE, *El archivo diocesano de Barcelona* (Barcelona 1947); *El archivo de la catedral de Barcelona* (Barcelona 1949). A. LAMBERT, DHGE 6:671–747. F. SOLDEVILA, *Història de Catalunya*, 3 v. (Barcelona 1934–35; 2d ed. 1962). **Illustration credit:** Fig. 2, MAS, Barcelona.

[R. I. BURNS]

BARCELONA, NATIONAL UNIVERSITY OF

A state institution of medieval origin under the jurisdiction of the Ministry of Education.

History. Catalonia's first university, sponsored by James II, was founded Sept. 1, 1300, in Lérida, as Bar-

celona, already a center of learning, had refused to admit a *studium generale* with special constitutions. Classes were conducted by private teachers in the grammar school attached to the cathedral. In 1346 the city refused the University of Lérida permission to make a public announcement of its courses on the grounds that from time immemorial Barcelona had offered courses in the liberal arts, law, and medicine. In 1401, King Martin I, unable to found a university in Barcelona, established a School of Medicine near the School of Higher Studies operated by the city. For economic reasons, however, in 1450 the counselors petitioned the King for an annual fair and also for a *studium generale*. On Sept. 3, 1450, Alphonsus V authorized the establishment of the University of Barcelona, to be composed of the Faculties of Arts, Law, Philosophy, Theology, and Medicine; and on September 30 Pope Nicholas V approved the institution.

This concession did not become immediately effective as the city of Barcelona feared ceding its authority in education to the University. In 1507, however, the School of Higher Studies and the School of Medicine reached an accord and in 1533 the city agreed to erect a university building that was inaugurated in 1539. In 1701 the War of Succession cut short university activities. Barcelona was the last bulwark of resistance to the Bourbon dynasty. After its surrender in September 1714, the King ordered the transfer of the Faculties of Theology, Philosophy, and Canon Law to Cervera, province of Lérida. In August 1717 the University of Barcelona was suppressed and replaced by the University of Cervera established by Philip V. The schools of medicine, grammar, and rhetoric remained in Barcelona. The last two were entrusted to the Jesuits. Although the liberal senate and house of deputies reinstated the University in 1822, it was again suppressed in 1823 by the absolutist reactionaries. Toward the end of 1837 the University of Cervera was transferred to Barcelona, where it was formally reestablished in 1842.

Administration. The University of Barcelona was municipally controlled by the Moyano law of Sept. 9, 1857, until the Second Spanish Republic granted it autonomy on June 1, 1933. This ceased, however, in 1939 when the University was incorporated into the general legislation. It has since come under the law of July 29, 1943, governing universities. The University, which enjoys legal existence and relative financial autonomy, is under the jurisdiction of the Ministry of Education. It is governed by an administrative board composed of the rector, deans of the various Faculties, administrator, interventor, secretary general, and the local director of the Spanish university student syndicate. In 1964 the academic staff had 150 full-time and 880 part-time professors holding higher degrees. Enrollment numbered 7,882 national students, both men and women, and 313 representatives of foreign countries. The general library housed 400,000 volumes including 914 incunabula and 2,000 manuscripts. Faculty libraries numbered an additional 190,000 volumes in medicine, law, pharmacy, economics, and history.

Organization. The University comprises the five Faculties of Philosophy and Letters (including education); Law; Science; Medicine and Pharmacy; and Political, Economic and Commercial Sciences. There are also an Institute of Spanish Studies; the seven Schools of Modern Languages, Urology, Dermatology, Cardiology, Podology, Haematology, and Criminology; a Seminar in Mathematics; a Center of Animal and Human Genetics; and departments of organic chemistry, applied biology, and soil science. The licentiate is offered in all Faculties after completing 5 years, except in pharmacy and medicine, which require 7 years. The doctorate is granted by thesis. All Faculties require 4 years of religion. Religious services are held daily in the University chapel.

The offices of administration and the Faculty of Philosophy and Letters occupy the main building constructed in 1871. It also provides facilities for the School of Modern Languages, and the summer courses in Spanish language and culture for foreigners. The Faculty of Medicine and the hospital clinic were inaugurated in 1906. The remaining Faculties and Schools function in the University City (nucleus of the University of Pedrales). There are six University residences for men and five for women.

Bibliography: J. BALARI Y JOVANY, "Historia de la Universidad" *Annuario de la Universidad de Barcelona, 1896–97* (Barcelona 1897) 1–129. *Reseña histórica y guía de la Universidad* (Barcelona 1929). F. SOLDEVILA, *Barcelona sense Universitat i la restauració de la Universitat de Barcelona, 1714–1837* (Barcelona 1938).

[J. RUBIÓ BALAGUER]

BARCLAY, JOHN, cosmopolitan author, polemicist; b. Pont-à-Mousson, France, Jan. 28, 1582; d. Rome, Aug. 15, 1621. When Barclay was born, his Scottish father was a professor of civil law at the new college founded by the Duke of Lorraine; his mother was a French lady of distinguished family. Barclay, however, always considered himself a Scot and a subject of King *James I (VI).

He went to London probably shortly after James's accession in 1603 but soon returned to the Continent, first to Angers and then to Paris (1605), where he married Louise Debonnaire, an army paymaster's daughter, a Latin scholar, and a poetess. In 1606 they moved to London to seek James I's patronage. There in 1609, the year after his father's death, Barclay edited his father's *De potestate papae,* an attack on the usurpations of medieval popes, a work that provoked Robert *Bellarmine to reply. In 1616 Barclay left England, where his hopes of reward and advancement had been unrealized, and moved to Rome. Although his works were prohibited there, he was pensioned by Pope Paul V and was well received by his literary adversary, Bellarmine. He spent the rest of his life quietly, cultivating flowers and writing. Among Barclay's numerous works, four are perhaps most worthy of comment: the *Euphormionis Lusinini satyricon,* written when the author was only 21, a contribution to the picaresque novel, full of promise but rather disconnected, somewhat careless in plot and style, partly autobiographical, partly based on his father's life; the *Icon animorum* (1614), a study of the national characters of the principal European states; *Paraenesis ad sectarios* (1617), written in defense of his Catholicism; and *Argenis* (1621), his masterpiece, an ideal romance, more carefully constructed than his earlier works and stylistically superior to them. His Latin verse, much indebted to Petronius's works, is elegant and pleasing at its best and well adapted to its "modern" setting. His works have appealed to such diverse persons as Cardinal Richelieu (*Argenis* was dedicated to King Louis XIII), Leibniz, Cowper, and Coleridge. Barclay's works were frequently republished in the 17th century and were translated into many languages; the modern English-speaking world tends to neglect him, however.

Bibliography: R. GARNETT, DNB 1:1082–84. CambHistEngLit 4:290–299. Bateson CBEL 1:859–860. D. BUSH, *English Literature in the Earlier Seventeenth Century* (2d ed. Oxford 1962).

[H. S. REINMUTH, JR.]

BARCLAY, JOHN, founder of a religious sect known as Bereans or Barclayites; b. Muthill, Perthshire, Scotland, 1734; d. Edinburgh, July 29, 1798. He studied for the Presbyterian ministry at St. Andrews University, where he supported the heterodox views of his professor, Dr. Archibald Campbell, "that the knowledge of the existence of God was derived from revelation and not from nature." He was licensed as a preacher in the Church of Scotland in 1759, and held assistantships at Errol and Fettercairn; but while he gained a popular reputation as a preacher, his clerical brethren regarded his theological opinions as dangerous. Defying the censure of his theological opinions by the presbytery of Fordoun, he published his views in several books between 1766 and 1771. Since he was refused any appointment in the Church of Scotland, Barclay was ordained in 1773 at Newcastle, England, outside the jurisdiction of the Scottish church. Adherents of his views formed themselves into independent churches at Edinburgh, Fettercairn, and a few other places. These sectarians, while accepting the general Calvinist theology of the Church of Scotland, held that natural religion undermines the evidences of Christianity, that assurance is of the essence of faith, that unbelief is the unpardonable sin, and that the Psalms refer exclusively to Christ. Their constant appeal to Scripture in vindication of their views was regarded as similar to the attitude of the Bereans mentioned in Acts 17.10. Barclay was given charge of the Edinburgh congregation.

Bibliography: *The Works of John Barclay,* ed. J. THOMSON and D. MCMILLAN (Glasgow 1852). R. CHAMBERS, *A Biographical Dictionary of Eminent Scotsmen,* ed. T. THOMSON, 3 v. (3d rev. ed. London 1868–70).

[D. MC ROBERTS]

BARCLAY, ROBERT, Scottish Quaker theologian and apologist; b. Gordonstown (Elginshire), Dec. 23, 1648; d. Ury (Aberdeen), Oct. 3, 1690. His father, David (1610–86), had been a soldier in the army of Gustavus II Adolphus, and later served in the English parliament of Oliver *Cromwell (1654 and 1656). He joined the Society of *Friends in 1666, and Robert, who was educated at the Roman Catholic Scottish College at Paris, followed his example the next year. Robert was imprisoned several times for his Quaker beliefs, but in his travels through Germany and Holland he won the sympathy of Elizabeth, Princess Palatine, and on his return to England found favor with the Duke of York (later James II). This friendship was instrumental in obtaining a patent of the province of East New Jersey for William *Penn and 12 Quakers. Barclay was governor of this territory in 1683.

Barclay's learning is revealed in several publications: *A Catechism and Confession of Faith* (1673); *Theologiae verae christianae apologia* (Amsterdam 1676), translated into Dutch, French, Spanish, and entitled in English *An Apology for the True Christian Divinity: Being an Explanation and Vindication of the People Called Quakers* (1678); *The Anarchy of Ranters* (1676); *The Apology Vindicated* (1679); and *The Possibilty and Necessity of an Inward and Immediate Revelation*

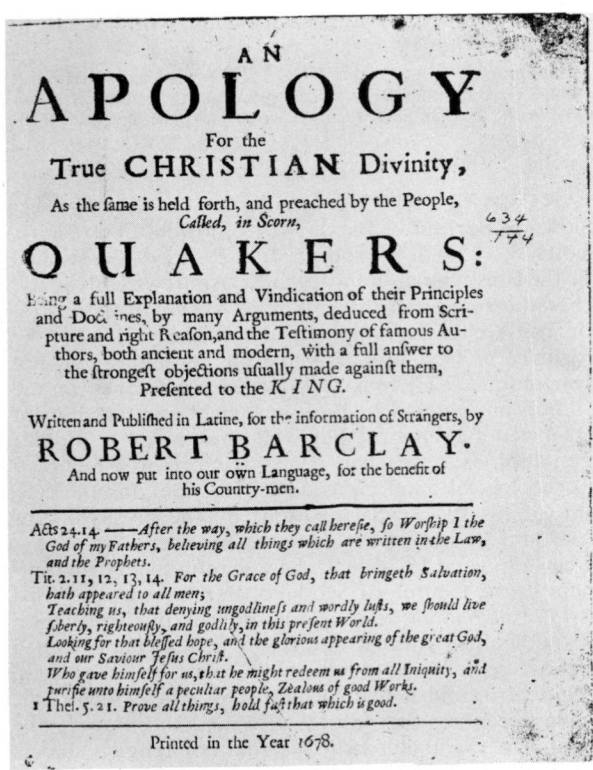

AN
APOLOGY
For the
True CHRISTIAN Divinity,

As the same is held forth, and preached by the People,
Called, in Scorn,

QUAKERS:

Being a full Explanation and Vindication of their Principles
and Doctrines, by many Arguments, deduced from Scripture and right Reason, and the Testimony of famous Authors, both ancient and modern, with a full answer to
the strongest objections usually made against them,
Presented to the KING.

Written and Published in Latine, for the information of Strangers, by

ROBERT BARCLAY.

And now put into our own Language, for the benefit of
his Country-men.

Acts 24.14. ——After the way, which they call heresie, so Worship I the
God of my Fathers, believing all things which are written in the Law,
and the Prophets.
Tit. 2.11, 12, 13, 14. For the Grace of God, that bringeth Salvation,
hath appeared to all men;
Teaching us, that denying ungodliness and wordly lusts, we should live
soberly, righteously, and godlily, in this present World.
Looking for that blessed hope, and the glorious appearing of the great God,
and our Saviour Jesus Christ.
Who gave himself for us, that he might redeem us from all Iniquity, and
purifie unto himself a peculiar people, Zealous of good Works.
1 Thes. 5. 21. Prove all things, hold fast that which is good.

Printed in the Year 1678.

Robert Barclay's "An Apology for the True Christian Divinity," title page of the first English edition of 1678.

(1680). His *Apology* is organized on the basis of 15 propositions: (1) The true knowledge of God is the most necessary knowledge. (2) Divine inward revelations are absolutely necessary for building true faith. (3) The Scripures give a faithful and historical account of God's acts, prophecies, and the principal doctrines of Christ. (4) All mankind fell with Adam. (5) Christ, the true Light, enlightens all (universal redemption). (6) This universal redemption must be placed in the evangelical principle of light and life. (7) Justification is "Jesus Christ formed within us," producing good works. (8) Perfection does not rule out the possibility of sinning. (9) The possibility of falling from grace exists. (10) Human commission is not needed for preaching. (11) The Spirit moves inwardly and immediately for a true and acceptable worship of God. (12) Infant baptism is a human tradition. (13) Participation of the body and blood of Christ is inward and spiritual. (14) The civil magistrate cannot force the conscience of others. (15) Customs and habits, such as removing the hat, bowing, and recreations (sports), are to be rejected and forsaken. Barclay's writings are still regarded as authoritative together with those of William Penn, and Barclay's humanitarian and pacifist views are followed by the Society of Friends.

Bibliography: W. ARMISTEAD, *Life of Robert Barclay* . . . (Manchester, Eng. 1850). M. C. CADBURY, *Robert Barclay* . . . (London 1912). M. SCHMIDT, RGG[3] 1:870. Cross ODCC 130. L. STEPHEN, DNB 1:1087–90. A. SCHMITT, LexThK[2] 1:1241–42.
Illustration credit: Library of Congress, Rare Book Division.

[C. S. MEYER]

BARCO CENTENERA, MARTÍN DEL,
politician and poet; b. Logrosán, Extremadura, Spain, 1535; d. Portugal, 1605. He went to La Plata in 1572 as archdeacon of the cathedral of the Assumption. He was very active in politics, neglecting his priestly duties somewhat. While he was at the cathedral of the Assumption, he put down an uprising against Juan de Garay. Later he went to Peru, where he remained for 9 years. In 1582 he was secretary of the Lima Council; soon afterward he became vicar of Charcas and commissary of the Inquisition in Cochabamba. As a result of his disorderly life, he was tried and punished by the Inquisition. He returned to Buenos Aires in 1590, and after governing the diocese *in sede vacante,* he left for Europe. In 1602 in Lisbon he published his *Argentina,* the first part of a poem in rhyme royal, a work of scant literary merit but of considerable historical value. It is a rhymed chronicle of the conquest and colonization of Rio de la Plata, republished in 1749, 1836, 1854, and 1912. The second part of the work was never published. Barco Centenera wrote also a volume entitled *El desengaño del mundo,* and in 1587, a long, interesting letter to the King describing the political and economic situation in La Plata; the last was published by Antonio Larrouy in 1910.

[G. FURLONG]

BARD, HENRY,
Baron Bromley and Viscount Bellamont, soldier, diplomat, and convert to Catholicism; b. Staines, Middlesex, 1604; d. Arabia, 1660. Bard, the son of an Anglican vicar, traveled extensively in Europe and the Middle East, becoming an accomplished linguist. A fervent supporter of Charles I, he served in the English Civil War and was rewarded with the Irish titles given above. In 1656 Charles II sent him as special ambassador to the Shah of Persia for financial aid; he failed in his mission, and returning through the Arabian desert, he was overtaken by a whirlwind and choked in the sand.

Bibliography: T. F. HENDERSON, DNB 1:1095. DictEngCath 1:128–129.

[G. ALBION]

BARDAS, CAESAR,
9th-century Byzantine statesman, brother of the Empress Theodora (2), uncle and regent (842–856) of the Emperor *Michael III; b. probably in Paphlagonia, date unknown; d. by assassination, Crete, April 21, 865. He was born of an Armenian family and educated probably in Constantinople. Bardas became director of state policy in the last years of the Byzantine Emperor Theophilus (829–842) and served as member of the council advising his sister, the Empress Theodora, during her regency for Michael III, until displaced by the logothete, or prime minister, Theoctistus, the favorite of Theodora [*see* THEODORA, BYZANTINE EMPRESS (2)].

Bardas made an alliance with Michael, who, envious of Theoctistus and chafing under his mother's tutelage, agreed to the murder of Theoctistus in 856. The Senate declared Michael an independent ruler and forced Theodora to retire. When, with the help of her intransigent supporters, she attempted to regain the throne, she was made to enter a monastery together with her daughters. The Patriarch *Ignatius refused to perform the ceremony of the tonsure, was interned, suspected of treason, and induced to resign. It is said that, previously, Ignatius had refused Holy Communion to Bardas because of incest with his daughter-in-law, an accusation that may have been invented by the enemies of Bardas. Only the separation from his wife, Theodosia, is firmly documented.

Bardas, first domestic of schools, then curopalates, and in 862 caesar, proved to be a very able regent who prepared the defeat of the Arabs in 863. Together with the Patriarch *Photius he was instrumental in sending SS. Constantine *Cyril and Methodius first to the Khazars (860), then to Moravia (863), and also in the conversion of the Bulgarians (864).

To Bardas belongs the credit of having reorganized the University of Constantinople under the direction of Leo the Mathematician, former iconoclastic archbishop of Thessalonica, and of supporting the revival of profane studies. Basil, the new favorite of Michael III, falsely accused Bardas of wanting to usurp the throne, and he was murdered in the presence of the Emperor, his nephew.

Bibliography: J. B. Bury, *A History of the Eastern Roman Empire . . . A.D. 802–867* (London 1912). F. Dvornik, *The Photian Schism: History and Legend* (Cambridge, Eng. 1948). Ostrogorsky 194–197, 201, 205–206.

[F. DVORNIK]

BARDENHEWER, OTTO,

patristic and exegetical scholar; b. München-Gladbach, Germany, March 16, 1851; d. Munich, March 23, 1935. He received a doctor's degree in classical philology at the University of Bonn in 1873, was ordained in 1875, and obtained a second doctorate (in theology) at the University of Würzburg in 1877. He taught Old Testament exegesis as a *Privatdocent* at the University of Munich in 1879. In 1884 he was appointed professor of Old Testament exegesis at the University of Münster in Westphalia and of New Testament exegesis at the University of Munich in 1886. He founded the *Biblische Studien* series (1896–1928), and the *Bibliothek der Kirchenväter*, for patristic translations, functioning as joint editor from 1911 until his death. Among his exegetical writings are *Des heiligen Hippolytus von Rom Kommentar zum Buche Daniel* (1877), *Polychronius, Bruder Theodors von Mopsuestia und Bischof von Apamea* (1879), *Der Name Maria: Geschichte der Deutung desselben* (1895), *Mariae Verkündigung: Ein Kommentar zu Lukas I 26–38* (1905), *Der Römerbrief des heiligen Paulus* (1926), and *Der Brief des heiligen Jakobus* (1928). His *Patrologie* (1894) was published in an English translation by Thomas Shahan in 1908. Bardenhewer's best-known work is the 5-volume *Geschichte der altkirchlichen Literatur* (1913–32), a standard work of reference valued by scholars for its comprehensiveness, lucidity, and soundness of judgment.

Bibliography: J. Sickenberger, *Erinnerungen an Otto Bardenhewer* (Freiburg i. Br. 1937) E. Peterson, EncCatt 2:839–840.

[J. QUASTEN]

BARDESANES (BAR-DAISĀN)

Christian astrologer and philosopher; b. Edessa, northwest Mesopotamia, 154; d. Edessa, 222. Bardesanes is often, though possibly erroneously, regarded as a leader of the Oriental school of *Gnosticism founded by the Egyptian *Valentinus. The many ancient and medieval accounts of the life and teachings of Bardesanes show little agreement about details. He was born of prominent pagan parents and educated by a pagan priest at Hierapolis (Mabog) in northern Syria. At 25 he was converted to Christianity and was ordained a deacon or priest. Bardesanes wrote many works in Syriac that were later translated into Greek by his disciples. His many metrical hymns earned him the title of the father of Syriac poetry. His works on astrology and on India and Armenia are lost. Eusebius (H.E. 4.30) credits him with dialogues written against the Marcionites (*see* MARCION) and the Valentinians (*see* VALENTINUS). Bardesanes' personal doctrine is given by Philip, one of his disciples, in the *Book of the Laws of the Countries* (PatrSyrG 1.2:490–658), the oldest extant original composition in Syriac.

Bardesanes ranks as a heretical figure largely because his astrological and philosophical speculations were mingled with his Christianity. He taught explicit errors concerning the human body and the body of Christ. His influence as a teacher was widespread, however, and the sect continued by his disciples was vigorously opposed by St. Ephrem as a form of Gnosticism.

See also GNOSTICISM; VALENTINUS.

Bibliography: *Spicilegium Syriacum*, ed. W. Cureton (London 1855). PatrSyrG 1.2:490–658. F. Nau, DTC 2.2:391–401. E. Beck, ed., *Des Heiligen Ephraem des Syrers Hymnen contra Haereses* CSCO v. 169 and 170. F. J. A. Hort, DCB 1:250–260. L. Cerfaux, ReallexAntChr 1:1180–86. Quasten Patr 1: 263–264.

[G. W. MAC RAE]

BARDO OF OPPERSHOFEN, ST.,

archbishop of Mainz; b. Oppershofen, Germany, c. 980; d. Dornloh, near Paderborn, June 10, 1051 (feast, June 10; at Mainz, June 15). Born of a prominent family, he was sent at an early age to the monastery of *Fulda, where he eventually became a monk and the director of the monastic school. In 1029 Bardo was made abbot of *Werden, and 2 years later he assumed the leadership of the important monastery of *Hersfeld. On June 29, 1031, he was consecrated archbishop of *Mainz and energetically undertook the task of completing the construction of the cathedral, which he consecrated in 1036 when the Emperor, *Conrad II, honored the occasion with his presence. The most important event during his episcopate was the synod held at Mainz in 1049 at which Pope *Leo IX presided. In addition to having a great reputation for piety and humility, Bardo was highly regarded as an eloquent preacher, and was frequently called another Chrysostom. If the sermon reported in his longer biography (MGS 11:330–35) can be taken as typical, the author was surprisingly familiar with Sacred Scripture. He was buried in the new cathedral at Mainz.

Bibliography: Sources. MGS 11:317–342. ActSS June 2:296–315. J. F. Bohmer and C. Will, eds., *Regesten zur Geschichte der Mainzer Erzbischöfe*, 2 v. (Innsbruck 1877–86) 1:165–176. Literature. G. Allemang, DHGE 6:775. P. Acht, NDB 1:586; LexThK² 1:1243. A. M. Zimmermann, BiblSanct 2:780–782. Zimmermann KalBen 2:297–299.

[H. DRESSLER]

BARDY, GUSTAVE,

patristic scholar, b. Belfort, France, Nov. 25, 1881; d. Dijon, Oct. 31, 1955. Educated at the Seminary of St. Sulpice (Issy), Bardy was ordained on June 30, 1906, attended the Institut Catholique of Paris until 1909, and lectured in theology at the University of Besançon. Called to military service in 1914, he was wounded and decorated for valor. In 1919, he joined the faculty of theology at Lille, remaining until 1927 when he transferred to the University of Dijon. He continued his patristic studies and edited the diocesan paper *Vie Diocésaine de Dijon* until his death.

His biography, *Didyme l'Aveugle*, appeared in 1910, and *S. Athanase* in 1914. He received doctorates in letters and in theology on the publication of his *Re-*

cherches sur . . . le texte . . . du De Principiis d'Origène and his magistral thesis, *Paul de Samosate*, in 1923. In the same year a study of the latter subject by the rationalist theologian Friedrich Loofs appeared. The two works demonstrated the difference in scholarly conclusions reached by men similar in competence and training, but divergent in belief and methods. Bardy's book was delated to the Holy Office, and in 1929 he brought out a thoroughly revised edition.

Bardy possessed a vast knowledge of the early Church and was abreast of diverse schools of investigation. He published more than 30 full-length books, edited several Greek texts, contributed major articles on patristic topics to the principal ecclesiastical encyclopedias, and wrote extensive articles on the theology of the early Church, monasticism, early Christian education, literary frauds, conversion, pagan survivals, Arianism, and the moral teaching of the Alexandrian Fathers. Encyclopedic in knowledge after the fashion of Louis Sébastien le Nain de *Tillemont, Bardy was long regarded as the dean of French patrologists. He spent his last days completing an introduction to his translation of the *Church History of Eusebius* (SourcesChr v.31, 41, 55, 73).

Bibliography: "Mémorial Gustave Bardy," RevÉtAug 2 (1956) 1–37. J. LEBON, RHE 51 (1956) 348–349.

[F. X. MURPHY]

BARI, ARCHDIOCESE OF (BARENSIS),

in south Italy, established in the 4th century, an archbishopric under the Byzantines in the 10th century, and recognized as a metropolitan see by Popes John XIX in 1025 and Alexander II in 1069 with 14 suffragan sees on both sides of the Adriatic. The first known bishop, Concordius, attended the Synod of Rome in 465. One of the oldest cities of Magna Graecia, founded near the cemetery of *Caeliae* (5th century B.C.), Bari went to the Ostrogoths after the fall of the Roman Empire. The Byzantine *Constans II sacked it in mid-7th century, and it then passed to the Lombards of *Benevento. Except for a Moslem occupation (831–870), Bari was held by Byzantium, despite German attacks and attempts at independence, until the Normans took it in 1071. Later it came under the Hohenstaufen and the house of Anjou before Aragon obtained it. Under Spain, the Hapsburgs, and the Bourbons, it declined in importance and population. A revival followed under Napoleon, and today Bari is the most important port of south Italy after Naples.

In 1089 Urban II made the archbishop, Elias, primate of Apulia. The relics of St. *Nicholas of Myra were brought to Bari from Lycia in 1087, and Elias built a basilica for them which was completed in 1108. Under a grand prior exempt of the archbishop (who today holds both titles), the Basilica of St. Nicholas is the foremost monument in Apulia. The cathedral of Bari, completed *c.* 1050 and damaged by the Normans in 1156, was rebuilt (1170–78) and has been restored since 1920. The castle, with a nucleus built by Frederick II (1233–40), is one of the most attractive in Apulia. Bari was a port of departure for many pilgrims and crusaders in the Middle Ages. In 1098 Urban II presided over a council of 185 prelates there seeking without success to unite the Greek and Latin Churches. The patrons of the diocese are the Mother of God of Hodegitria, St. Nicholas of Myra, and St. Sabinus of Canosa. Canosa, an ancient see, was incorporated into Bari in 844 and was the site of the See of Bari in the 10th and 11th centuries. In 1964 Bari had 77 parishes with 580,000 Catholics, 201 secular and 220 religious priests, 265 men in 32 religious houses, and 1,400 women in 110 convents; it is 473 square miles in area. Its two suffragan sees have 167,900 Catholics, 182 priests, and 370 sisters: Conversano (founded in the 7th century); and Ruvo (1025) and Bitonto (1089), united in 1818.

Bibliography: A. BEATILLO, *Historia di Bari* (Naples 1637). F. UGHELLI, *Italia sacra,* ed. N. COLETI, 10 v. (Venice 1717–22) v.7. F. BONNARD, DHGE 6:795–801, with list of bishops. P. F. PALUMBO and E. LAVIGNINO, EncCatt 2:847–852. V. Lagrasta, *Un raro opuscolo di P. Davino sulle chiese di Canosa e Bari* (Rome 1948). *Archivio storico pugliese* (Bari 1948–). Ann Pont (1964) 54, 1414.

[G. A. PAPA]

BARING, MAURICE

Novelist, poet, literary critic, and journalist; b. London, April 27, 1874; d. Beauly, Scotland, Dec. 14, 1945. He belonged to a well-known family of merchant bankers (his father became Lord Revelstoke); he was educated at Eton and Cambridge University, after which he spent several years (1898–1903) in the British diplomatic service and 1 year (1904) in the Foreign Office in London. From 1904 to 1907 he was in Russia as correspondent for the *Morning Post* during the Russo-Japanese War. These years explain his interest in Russian literature, of which he was an excellent translator and interpreter. During World War I he served with the Royal Flying Corps and after demobilization retained

James Gunn's portrait of Maurice Baring (standing), with his friends G. K. Chesterton and Hilaire Belloc.

his connection with the air force, becoming an honorary wing-commander in 1925.

In 1909 he was received into the Church at the London Oratory, remarking that it was "the only action of my life which I am quite certain I have never regretted." He became an intimate friend of *Belloc, *Chesterton, Ronald *Knox, and a number of the most distinguished Catholics of his time, although he was less well known to the general Catholic public than these figures. Yet his contribution, made chiefly through his novels, to a deeper appreciation of the fundamentals of the faith was important and lasting. The most significant of these novels were *Passing By* (1921), *C* (1924), *Cat's Cradle* (1925), and *Daphne Adeane* (1926), considered his best.

His output of poetry was not large (his *Collected Poems* were published in 1926), but some of his sonnets are examples of superb craftsmanship combined with deeply moving sentiment. His last published work, *Have You Anything to Declare?* (1936), shows his wide knowledge of literature and his fastidious taste.

Baring was a man of immense and delicate sensitivity, revealed in his literary work (his knowledge of ancient and modern European literature was remarkable) and still more in his personal relationships. He was completely modest and unassuming, content to deploy his unusual talents as much for the entertainment of a small circle of close friends as for gaining a wider reputation.

Bibliography: M. Baring, *Puppet Show of Memory* (Boston 1922). E. Smyth, *Maurice Baring* (Toronto 1938). L. Lovat, *Maurice Baring, a Postscript, with Some Letters and Verse* (New York 1948). **Illustration credit:** National Portrait Gallery, London.

[T. CORBISHLEY]

BARING-GOULD, SABINE, Anglican clergyman, hagiographer, novelist, antiquary, and hymn writer; b. Exeter, England, Jan. 28, 1834; d. New Trenchard, Devon, Jan. 2, 1924. After attending Clare College, Cambridge, he was ordained (1865), and became rector of East Mersea, Essex (1871) and of Lew Trenchard, Devon (1881–1924). He belonged to the *High Church, but was unsympathetic to Rome. His literary output was prodigious, but few of his 130 and more books are read nowadays. He enjoyed at one time a considerable reputation as a novelist, the best known of his 30 novels being *Broom Squire* (1896). He wrote also many volumes on folklore, mythology, folk songs, and ancient manners and customs; but later scholars did not approve of his emendations, made allegedly in the interests of decency. Baring-Gould published 20 volumes of sermons. His *Richard Hawker of Morwenstow* (1875), a biography of an eccentric Cornish clergyman, is among his better works. As hagiographer his most important works were the 15-volume *Lives of the Saints* (1872–77) and *Lives of British Saints* (1907). Baring-Gould's works suffered from being the products of an amateur scholar content to follow his enthusiasms. "Onward Christian Soldiers," "Now the Day is Over," "Through the Night of Doubt and Sorrow" (translated from Danish), and other hymns composed by Baring-Gould remain popular throughout the English-speaking world.

Bibliography: W. Purcell, *Onward Christian Soldier: A Life of Sabine Baring-Gould, Parson, Squire, Novelist, Antiquary* (London 1957). M. Coate, DNB (1922–30) 64–65.

[L. C. SHEPPARD]

BARKING ABBEY, Essex, England, a Benedictine nunnery dedicated to Our Lady and St. Ethelburga, was founded by St. *Erconwald, Bishop of London, *c.* 677; his sister *Ethelburga was its first abbess. It was burnt by the Danes in 870 and restored by King *Edgar. The abbey numbered among its abbesses St. *Hildelide (d. 717?), to whom *Aldhelm addressed his *De virginitate,* and Mary, the sister of Thomas *Becket. The shrine of St. Ethelburga was a center of pilgrimage in medieval England. Tradition says that *William the Conqueror resided at Barking after his coronation until the Tower of London was built. Dame Dorothy Barley surrendered the house to Henry VIII, Nov. 14, 1539. Of this once magnificent abbey, nothing now remains.

Bibliography: Dugdale MonAngl 1:435–446. J. B. L. Tolhurst, ed., *The Ordinale and Customary of the Benedictine Nuns of Barking Abbey,* 2 v. (HBradshSoc 65,66; London 1927–28). Cottineau 1:266. D. Knowles and R. N. Hadcock, *Medieval Religious Houses: England and Wales* (New York 1953) 210.

[F. CORRIGAN]

BARLAAM OF CALABRIA

Italo-Greek monk, theologian, and bishop, opponent of *Hesychasm; b. Seminara, Calabria, *c.* 1290; d. Gerace, Calabria, 1350. Born of schismatic parents and educated in the Byzantine monasteries of southern Italy, Barlaam appeared first as a teacher in the Holy Savior monastery and the Imperial University in Constantinople in 1326–27. After a public debate with *Nicephorus Gregoras on the physical sciences, he taught at Thessalonica, where he had Demetrius Cydones as a pupil. In 1334 he was chosen to dispute with two Dominican bishops, envoys of Pope John XXII, on the issues of papal primacy and the procession of the Holy Spirit. Pamphlets that he wrote for the occasion were criticized by Gregory *Palamas, and between 1334 and 1337 Barlaam engaged in a bitter dispute with the Hesychastic monks of Mt. Athos. He accused them of illuminism and a crude type of Messalianism and ridiculed their posture when engaged in contemplative prayer. He sarcastically called the monks *omphalopsychoi* (men-with-their-souls-in-their-navels) and ordered them to be delated to the patriarch John Calecas.

In 1339 the imperial court sent Barlaam to Pope Benedict XII at Avignon to solicit a crusade against the Turks and to discuss reunion. There he apparently taught Greek to *Petrarch, who persuaded him to reconsider the Catholic position. On his return to Constantinople (1341), a synod condemned his attack on the Hesychasts, and he had to make a public retraction. He was in Calabria in July 1341 and at Avignon again in 1342. Upon his full conversion to Roman Catholicism with the aid of Petrarch, he was consecrated bishop of Gerace in Calabria by Pope Clement VI at Avignon in 1342. He is said to have influenced the Italian Renaissance through his contact with the Italian humanists. In 1346 he was sent to Constantinople to discuss reunion, but the project proved fruitless since the Emperor was the Palamite, John Cantecuzenus. Barlaam returned to his diocese, where he died in 1350 (not 1348).

Barlaam seems to have denied the possibility of apodictic arguments in theology in his dispute with the Dominicans. He wanted to base reunion of the Churches on the fact that the disputes between East and West were really unresolvable and should not be cause for separation. In his disagreement with Palamas, he accused him of dividing God by teaching that while God's nature was invisible, his energies could be apprehended as in the white light that shone on Mt. Thabor at the Transfiguration. Most of Barlaam's writings are still unedited. He wrote 21 tracts against the Latins (18 on the Holy Spirit and 3 on the Roman primacy); a *Contra Messalianos;* 2 books on Stoic ethics; and a number of letters supporting the Catholic position after his conversion. He wrote also a *Reasoned Arithmetic* and a commentary on the second book of Euclid.

Bibliography: PG 151:1243–1364. Fabricius-Harles 11:462–470. M. Jugie, *Catholicisme* 1:1253–55; DHGE 6:817–834. J. Meyendorff, *A Study of Gregory Palamas,* tr. G. Lawrence (London 1964). K. M. Setton, ProcAmPhilS 100 (1956) 1–76. J. S. Romanides, *The Greek Orthodox Theological Review* 6 (1960–61) 186–205, Palamite controversy.

[H. D. Hunter]

BARLAAM AND JOASAPH, the title of a curious novel found among the works of St. John Damascene. The tale, which is an adaptation of a Buddhist legend, relates how the monk Barlaam converted the Indian prince Joasaph against his father's wishes. There is much discussion of the meaning of Christianity, monasticism, and the truths of faith. Joasaph, becoming king, converts his entire realm and then dies a hermit. The author attributes the rise of monastic fasting and penance to the desire of ascetics to imitate the sufferings of the primitive martyrs, that "becoming martyrs in intention they too might imitate the sufferings of Christ" (12.102).

Barlaam and Joasaph have been venerated in the Roman *Martyrology since 1583 on November 27 [see H. Delehaye et al., *Propylaeum ad Acta Sanctorum Decembris* (Brussels 1940) 551]. The cult became widely popular in the Middle Ages. P. Peeters [AnalBoll 49 (1931) 276] developed a strong case against the Damascene's authorship, suggesting that the novel was first translated into Greek from a Georgian source by Euthymius, abbot of Iviron, Mt. *Athos (d. 1028), to whom the work is attributed in some late MSS. But the case for Damascene's authorship was effectively renewed by F. Dölger in 1953. In addition to parallels in doctrine and style with the works of Damascene, several MSS possibly antedate Euthymius; four of the oldest MSS attribute the work to John, and none of the numerous Iviron MSS attribute it to Euthymius. Dölger accepts the idea of its transmission from a Buddhist original—to a Pehlevi version—thence to a possible Syriac version, from which came two branches, the Arabic version on the one side and the Greek version of John with the Georgian version on the other. The Damascene parallels in the area of Christology, the Trinity, and other points of doctrine are impressive, but Dölger's position is still controverted.

Bibliography: *Barlaam and Joasaph,* ed. and tr. G. R. Woodward and H. Mattlingly (LoebClLib; 1914). B. Studer, Lex ThK² 1:1246–47; *Die theologische Arbeitsweise des Johannes von Damaskus* (Ettal 1956). H. Bacht, ReallexAntChr 1:1193–1200. F. Dölger, *Der griechische Barlaam-Roman* (Ettal 1953). P. Devos, AnalBoll 75 (1957) 83–104. Altaner 639. G. Downey, *Speculum* 31 (1956) 165–168. **Illustration credit:** The Beinecke Rare Book and Manuscript Library, Yale University.

[H. Musurillo]

Folio from a 15th-century Greek manuscript of the novel "Barlaam and Joasaph" (MS Ziskind 13, fol. 37 v).

BARLACH, ERNST, German sculptor, graphic artist, and dramatist of the German expressionist movement; b. Wedel, Holstein, Feb. 2, 1870; d. Rostock, Oct. 24, 1938. He studied in Hamburg and later in Dresden under Robert Diez. Several trips to Paris (1895–96) introduced him to the work of Steinlen, *Millet, Meunier, and Van *Gogh. A trip to Russia in 1906 stimulated his mystical and humanitarian tendencies and led him to abandon the influence of the *Jugendstil* (*Art Nouveau*). In 1908 he settled in Gustrow, Mecklenburg.

Among his most important pieces are war memorials executed in the 1920s in Magdeburg, Hamburg, and Gustrow. The National Socialists (Nazis) destroyed the last-mentioned work, a powerful floating figure, and removed 381 of his pieces from public buildings. A replica of the Gustrow memorial has been placed in the Antoniterkirche in Cologne. The Minneapolis Institute of Arts has a second casting of the monument, "The Crusader." The original bronze is in the Nikolaikirche in Kiel.

Barlach, in common with some other German expressionists, was influenced by Gothic sculpture. He is credited with reviving on a major scale the practice of carving forms in wood, although he worked also in ceramics, bronze, and various metals. His sculpture is notable for its monumental simplicity, its religious and mystical feeling, and its expression of compassion for suffering mankind. Similar qualities are evident in his woodcuts and lithographs, some of which were pro-

Ernst Barlach, self-portrait, transfer lithograph made after the artist's death from a drawing of 1928.

duced to illustrate his own plays and works by Schiller, Goethe, and Von Kleist.

Bibliography: E. BARLACH, *Ein selbsterzähltes Leben* (Berlin 1928), autobiog. C. D. CARLS, *Ernst Barlach: Das plastische, graphische, und dichterische Werk* (7th ed. Berlin 1958). F. SCHULT, ed., *Ernst Barlach: Das plastische Werk* (Hamburg 1960). **Illustration credit:** Library of Congress.

[J. KAINEN]

BARLOW, AMBROSE (EDWARD), BL., English martyr; b. Barlow Hall, near Manchester, 1585; d. Lancaster, Sept. 10, 1641 (feast, Sept. 10). Although born a Catholic, he conformed to the Protestant church in his youth. When 22 he returned to the faith and entered the English seminary at Douai; in 1613, on a visit to England, Barlow was imprisoned for several months. After his release he joined the English Benedictine monks at St. Gregory's, Douai, where his brother was prior. He took the name Ambrose in place of his baptismal name Edward. He was professed in 1614 and ordained in 1617, and then returned to England. There is a detailed account of his apostolate in a short contemporary work, *The Apostolical Life of Ambrose Barlow* (Cheetham Society): for 24 years he labored in the Manchester and Liverpool districts. Resembling Thomas More in his wit and mildness, he was greatly loved by the poor, whom he entertained on the great feasts at his house. Barlow was partially paralyzed by a stroke in 1641, and on Easter day of that year he was captured at Leigh, Lancashire, while preaching to his congregation. Sitting on a horse with a man behind him to prevent his falling, he was taken to Lancaster Castle by an escort of 60 men. After 4 months in prison where he passed most of his time in prayer, he was brought to trial; he at once acknowledged his priest-

hood. When the judge offered to release him if he agreed "not to seduce any more people," he answered, "I am no seducer, but a reducer of the people to the true and ancient religion .... I am in the resolution to continue until death to render this good office to these strayed souls." On September 8 he was condemned. Five days before this a general chapter of the English Benedictine Congregation had accepted the resignation of his brother, Rudesind Barlow, as titular prior of Coventry and had elected Ambrose in his place. He was executed at Lancaster on September 10. Ambrose's skull is preserved at Wardley Hall, near Manchester, and his left hand at Stanbrook Abbey, Worcestershire. He was beatified by Pius XI on Dec. 15, 1929. (*See* MARTYRS OF ENGLAND AND WALES.)

Bibliography: B. CAMM, *Nine Martyr Monks* ... (London 1931). J. STONOR, *Ambrose Barlow* (Postulation pamphlet; London 1961). Butler Th Attw 3:535–537. R. CHALLONER, *Memoirs of Missionary Priests,* ed. and rev. J. H. POLLEN (rev. ed. London 1924). DictEngCath 1:134–135.

[G. FITZ HERBERT]

BARLOW, WILLIAM, Augustinian canon and successively bishop of St. Asaph, St. David's, Bath and Wells, and Chichester; said to have been born in Essex (date unknown); d. Aug. 13, 1568. He was a canon of St. Osyth's and became, successively, prior of several houses of Augustinian canons and, about 1524, prior of Bromehill, Norfolk. Its suppression in 1528 turned him into a violent enemy of Wolsey, and his enmity found expression in several pamphlets that were condemned as heretical in 1529. He recanted, but by 1535 he had become an ardent reformer. He was elected bishop of St. Asaph on Jan. 16, 1536, and soon afterward (April? 1536), was translated to St. David's where he quarreled frequently with his chapter, which denounced him as a heretic. In 1548 he was translated to Bath and Wells, but at the accession of Queen Mary he resigned his see and, after a short imprisonment, made his way to Germany. After Mary's death he returned to England and was nominated bishop of Chichester in 1559.

Bibliography: T. F. TOUT, DNB 1:1149–51. Hughes RE. C. JENKINS, "Bishop Barlow's Consecration and Archbishop Parker's Register," *Church Hist. Soc. Pub.* (London) NS 17 (1935).

[G. DE C. PARMITER]

BARLOW, WILLIAM RUDESIND, English Benedictine writer and administrator; b. Barlow Hall, Lancashire, 1584?; d. Douai, Sept. 19, 1656. He was the son of Sir Alexander Barlow and brother of Ambrose (Edward) *Barlow, the martyr. William entered Douai College in 1602, left to join the Benedictine Order in 1605, was professed in Spain in 1606, and was ordained in 1608. Barlow took doctorates in divinity at both Salamanca and Douai. From 1614 to 1620, and again from 1625 to 1629, he was prior of St. Gregory's, Douai. He served as president general of the English Benedictine Congregation (1621). He was for many years professor of theology at the College of St. Vedast, Douai. Equally renowned as a theologian and a canonist, he figured in two celebrated ecclesiastical quarrels: (1) with Richard *Smith, Bishop of Chalcedon, whose claim to possess ordinary jurisdiction over Catholics in England he vigorously opposed in his *Epistola ... ad RR. Provinciales et ad Definitores ...* (1627–28), commonly known from its opening word as "Mandatum," and (2) with Augustine Baker of his own order on the subject of conventual life. Baker drew an unflattering portrait of him in *An Introduction or Preparative to a Treatise on the English Mission* (1638).

Bibliography: T. B. SNOW, *Necrology of the English Congregation of the Order of Saint Benedict from 1600 to 1883* (London 1883). DictEngCath 1:136.

[A. F. ALLISON]

BARNABAS, ST.

A prominent member of the early Jerusalem Church and, with Paul, the first pioneer of the missionary apostolate outside of Palestine and Syria. Originally named Joseph, he received from the Apostles the Aramaic surname Barnabas (*bar-nᵉbû'â*, "Son of encouragement": Acts 4.36), probably because of his charismatic gift to speak words of "exhortation" (Acts 11.23; Rom 12.8).

His Background. A Levite, born in Cyprus (Acts 4.36), Joseph was a Hellenist from the *Diaspora. In Palestine he became a disciple of Christ, either during Jesus' public ministry or after Pentecost. Clement of Alexandria and Eusebius number him among the 72 Disciples mentioned in Lk 10.1. He first appears in Acts (4.36–37) as a fervent and well-to-do Christian who donated to the Church the proceeds from the sale of his property. He won the Apostles' acceptance of the newly converted Saul despite the doubts of others (Acts 9.27). Esteem for Barnabas and his Hellenist background prompted the leaders to send him as official visitor to the new, partly Gentile Church of Antioch in Syria (Acts 11.22). As this community grew, he brought Paul

St. Barnabas, detail of "Virgin and Child with Angels and Saints," by Botticelli, in the Uffizi at Florence.

to it, and they labored together there for a year (Acts 11.25–26). The order of the words in the phrase "Barnabas and Saul" of Acts 11.30 indicates that Barnabas headed the delegation that brought relief from Antioch to the famine-stricken Christians in Jerusalem (Acts 11.29–30).

Missionary Apostolate with Paul. On their return to Antioch the two friends were commissioned by the Holy Spirit for a wider apostolate in the Gentile world (Acts 13.2–3). Barnabas's controlling hand is evident here: Cyprus, his homeland, was the field of their ministry; John Mark, his cousin, was their assistant. Once they had evangelized Cyprus, Paul took the lead, as is indicated by the new phrasing, "Paul and Barnabas" (Acts 13.13, 46, 50). Leaving Cyprus, they went to southern Asia Minor (Acts 13.13–14.27). Here they converted many non-Jews but were persecuted by the synagogue. At Lystra, enthusiastic Gentiles hailed Barnabas as Zeus, chief of the gods, and Paul as Hermes, spokesman of the deity (Acts 14.11), because of the diverse impressions they created.

At the Council of Jerusalem. Once back in Antioch, "Paul and Barnabas" objected to the Judaeo-Christian claim that Gentile converts must be circumcised (Acts 15.1–2). To safeguard Christianity's distinctness from Judaism they went to Jerusalem for a meeting with the leaders of the Church (Acts 15.2–29). Because of his standing in Jerusalem, Barnabas moved to the fore in pleading for liberty from the bonds of Judaism (Acts 15.12, 25). Full support for their way of presenting the Christian message was obtained. Later, however, Barnabas, like Peter, failed to practice fully the principle of "liberty from the Law," so that Paul was forced to object (Gal 2.13–14).

Apostolate and Death in Cyprus. The success of the first mission and the approval of Jerusalem prompted Paul to urge another journey from Antioch to the Churches that he and Barnabas had founded. Barnabas asked again for John Mark as companion; but Paul refused because the young man had previously deserted them. The resultant "sharp contention" led to the separation of the two Apostles (Acts 15.36–39). Confident of Mark's loyalty, Barnabas "sailed for Cyprus." According to legend he met a martyr's death there; his body was later found with his own hand-written copy of Matthew's Gospel over his heart. Death apparently came to him after Paul wrote of him, as though still alive, in 1 Cor 9.6, and before Paul wrote to the Colossians that Mark was now his colaborer (Col 4.10). Tertullian has suggested that Barnabas authored the Epistle to the Hebrews; but there is no positive reason to support this opinion. The Epistle of Barnabas is certainly not to be attributed to him, since it was not written until A.D. 130.

Character. Luke's praise of Barnabas as "a good man and full of the Holy Spirit and of faith" (Acts 11.24) renders immortal his truly Christian spirit and the fullness of his charismatic gifts. As a Hellenist he had the vision necessary for his ministry in the Gentile world. His loyalty to the Jerusalem Church, however, made it difficult for him to break completely with its traditions (Gal 2.13). His greatness is manifest, above all, in his relations with Paul. Barnabas gave him to the Church by sponsoring him before the Apostles. He was one with Paul in those first labors that made the Church universal. When the time came he wisely stepped aside that Paul might become the unique "Apostle of the Gentiles."

Bibliography: EncDictBibl 209–210. A. KAPPELER, "St. Barnabas in vita S. Pauli," VerbDom 22 (1942) 129–135.

[B. M. AHERN]

BARNABAS, EPISTLE OF. As a source of theological instruction of the primitive Church, the Epistle of Barnabas was held in high esteem in antiquity. The precise motives and circumstances that led to its preservation and to its long favor remain obscure. Next to nothing is known of its author and place of origin. Barnabas is a mere name, for there can be no question of identifying the author of this Epistle with the Apostle Barnabas, companion of Paul, as *Clement of Alexandria and *Origen thought. Alexandria as a place of origin is no more than a learned guess, based on the questionable idea that everything allegorical in scriptural interpretation betrays some connection with the great intellectual metropolis of Egypt. With regard to literary form, the Epistle has not much of an epistolary character. Critics variously refer to it as a pamphlet, a homily, or a theological tract. But it is best classified as written "instructions" (*didakhai*), meant to be circulated in an otherwise unspecified community (18.1). In fact, it combines two instructions, loosely bound together and largely differing in tone as well as in subject matter. The first instruction deals, rather heavily, with the delicate question of the religious situation of Israel. According to the author, the Jews never properly understood the Law or the Prophets; in regard to sacrifice, circumcision, and food, they erred from beginning to end. They made the fatal mistake of a gross literal interpretation of what was meant to be lived spiritually and have been, therefore, justly rejected (ch. 2–17). The second instruction is based on the Two Ways already incorporated in the *Didache (ch. 18–20). Most scholars agree in placing the date of composition of the Epistle somewhere around the first quarter of the 2d century, under the reign of Emperor Hadrian. More recently, studies in early Christian symbolism and forms of Biblical quotations have revived interest in the Epistle of Barnabas.

Bibliography: K. BIHLMEYER and W. SCHNEEMELCHER, *Die apostolischen Väter* (2d ed. Tübingen 1956–) xx–xxiv, 1:10–34. J. A. KLEIST, *The Didache: The Epistle of Barnabas* (Westminster, Md. 1948). J. DANIÉLOU, *Les Symboles chrétiens primitifs* (Paris 1961). P. PRIGENT, *Les Testimonia dans le christianisme primitif: L'Épître de Barnabé 1–16 et ses sources* (Paris 1961).

[J. P. AUDET]

BARNABITES, the Clerics Regular of St. Paul (CRSP), or Barnabites, founded in 1530 in Milan, Italy, by St. Anthony *Zaccaria, Ven. James Morigia, and Ven. Bartholomew *Ferrari; the order was approved in 1533 by Clement VII. The founder's enthusiasm for St. Paul inspired the official name of the society and its Pauline spirit and tradition of studies; the popular name derives from the motherhouse built near the church of St. Barnabas in Milan.

The Barnabites' primary objective was to reform the corrupt morals of the time by the example of their own penitent life and by missions among the people. Their apostolate began in Lombardy and Venetia, amid hardships and persecutions; later they found in St. Charles Borromeo a staunch protector and second father. He promulgated the constitutions in the general chapter of 1579. In 1608 the order was divided into provinces. Suppressed by Napoleon in 1810, the order was later reestablished and many monasteries regained.

Since the 17th century, the Barnabites have been principally engaged in educating children in boarding schools and public schools. They also devote themselves to ministering in parishes and in missions. In 1964 the order had foundations in Italy, France, Belgium, the U.S., Brazil, Chile, and Argentina. The provost general, elected for a 6-year period, has his residence in Rome.

The Barnabites' missionary activity was extended in the 18th century to Burma, where the order distinguished itself for its scientific study of the flora and fauna and the native languages. In the 19th century Barnabites went to Scandinavia and also worked for the return of the Russian Orthodox Church. In 1964 they had missions in the Congo and served as chaplains for the Italian Embassy in Kabul, Afghanistan. Total membership in 1964 was 634 priests, of whom about 20 worked in the U.S.

Three canonized saints were members of the order: St. Anthony Zaccaria, the founder (d. 1539); St. Alexander *Sauli, Bishop of Aleria and Pavia (d. 1592); and St. Francis Xavier *Bianchi (d. 1815); a number of others are being considered for beatification. The order has had 7 cardinals, including the philosopher Hyacinthe S. Gerdil; Francesco L. Fontana, the companion of Pius VII during his French exile; and Luigi Lambruschini, the secretary of state of Gregory XVI; 63 bishops; and numerous scholars, particularly in historical, liturgical, literary, and physical-mathematical studies.

Bibliography: G. BOFFITO, *Scrittori Barnabiti*, 4 v. (Florence 1933–37). G. CHASTEL, *Saint Antoine-Marie Zaccaria barnabite* (Paris 1930). V. M. COLCIAGO, EncCatt 4:298–301.

[U. M. FASOLA]

BARNARD OF VIENNE, ST., archbishop; b. near Lyons, France, *c.* 778; d. Abbey of Saints-Severin-Exupère-et-Félicien, Valence, France, Jan. 22, 842 (feast, Jan. 23). He was one of the outstanding figures of the Frankish episcopate during the *Carolingian reform. He entered the army and, after 7 years of married life, decided to renounce the world. He founded the *Benedictine monastery of Ambronay, where he became a monk in 803 and where 4 years later he became abbot. He was elected archbishop of *Vienne in 810, and in this office he played an important role in the synodal movement that attempted to reestablish peace and order in both Church and State. By taking part in the consecration of *Agobard to the metropolitan See of *Lyons before the death of the reigning prelate *Leidradus, who had entered a monastery, he incurred the hostility of his colleagues and was accused of violating Canon Law. Barnard enjoyed the favor of *Louis I the Pious, for a time; but when he sided with his son Lothair against him, he was forced to escape to Italy after the victory of the Emperor. Louis forgave the luckless intervention, and the archbishop was able to return to his see and found the monastery of Saints-Severin-Exupère-et-

Félicien, where he retired to spend his last days and where he was buried. His cult was reconfirmed in 1903.

Bibliography: ActSS Jan. 3:157–161. Mansi 14:608, 734–740. P. É. GIRAUD, *Essai historique sur l'Abbaye de saint Barnard de Romans*, 5 v. (Lyons 1856–69). Zimmermann KalBen 1:118–120. A. M. ZIMMERMANN, LexThK² 1:1257. G. MARIÉ, DHGE 6: 858–859.

[T. C. CROWLEY]

BARNARD, HENRY

Pioneer in the U.S. public school movement; b. Hartford, Conn., Jan. 24, 1811; d. Hartford, Conn., July 5, 1900. He received his early education in the district schools of Hartford and in the Hopkins Grammar School in New Haven. In 1826 he entered Yale College where he distinguished himself scholastically and received academic honors. Upon graduation, he undertook the study of law, supporting himself by teaching for brief periods in an academy at Wellsboro, Pa. His admission as an attorney and counsel-at-law in Connecticut enabled him to finance a trip to Europe, where he made the acquaintance of Wordsworth and Carlyle. Shortly after his return, without his knowledge or consent, he was elected to a seat in the Connecticut Legislature.

For 3 successive years as a member of the house of representatives, he took an active interest in all educational enterprises. In 1838 he sponsored a bill that created the Board of Commissioners of Common Schools. The bill passed unanimously, and Barnard reluctantly accepted the post as secretary of the board. His duties included school visitations, public addresses to teachers and parents, and the publishing of the *Connecticut Common School Journal.* In all these endeavors, Barnard worked ceaselessly for a strong state-controlled educational program that would bring equal educational opportunities to all children of the state. But in 1842, a change in the political structure precipitated the abolition of the Board of Commissioners, and Barnard's efforts were brought to a close.

In December 1843, Barnard accepted the position as the first commissioner of schools in Rhode Island where for 5 years he struggled to bring about an educational awakening. By 1846 all Rhode Island towns were collecting taxes for school purposes, schools were built, and teachers were being trained and supervised.

Because of failing health, Barnard was forced to discontinue his services in 1849, but in 1851 he returned in triumph to his home state when he was named principal of the State Normal School and superintendent of the common schools of Connecticut. In this position, Barnard was able to resume many of the educational advances that he had begun 10 years earlier. His resumption of the *Journal* and his active encouragement for local taxation soon made the Connecticut common schools an example to the whole nation. Upon the advice of his physician, however, he retired in 1855, and began the publication of the *American Journal of Education.*

Barnard served as chancellor of the University of Wisconsin from 1858 to 1860 and, after the Civil War, was elected president of St. John's College, Annapolis. In March 1867, his long career in educational reform was rewarded by his appointment as the first U.S. commissioner of education, in which position he published many references for educational research and sponsored biographies of great teachers. He resigned in March 1870 to devote his time to the publication of the *American Journal of Education,* the crowning work of his career, a monumental cyclopedia of pedagogical literature, totaling 31 volumes, devoted to the encouragement of public education. He continued this work until his death in 1900.

Bibliography: B. C. STEINER, *Life of Henry Barnard* (Washington 1919). A. L. BLAIR, *Henry Barnard: School Administrator* (Minneapolis 1938).

[A. FLYNN]

BARON, VINCENT

Dominican theologian and preacher; b. Martres, Haute-Garonne, France, May 17, 1604; d. Paris, Jan. 21, 1674. He was born of a prominent family and from his earliest years showed clear signs of genius and integrity. At 17, he left the Jesuit college at Toulouse and entered the Dominican convent of St. Thomas in the same city. There he made his religious profession, May 16, 1622, and went on to complete his philosophical and theological studies. As early as 1634 he was first professor in his priory and conventual doctor at the University of Toulouse. In time he came to be considered one of the leading theologians of France. In addition to teaching he delivered courses of Lenten sermons in the principal churches of Toulouse, Avignon, Bordeaux, and other cities of southern France. At the invitation of the bishops of Languedoc he preached throughout their dioceses for 10 years, laboring to revive the faith of Catholics, to better their morals, and to combat the errors of the Calvinists, with whose ministers he frequently joined in open debate, sometimes in their public synods. He published an abridgment of these controversies under the title *L'Hérésie convaincue* (Paris 1668). Of his sermons to Catholic congregations we have only those preached at Paris in 1658 and 1659 (Paris 1660). They were doctrinal discourses and panegyrics of intellectual merit but composed in the forced style of his age. From 1630 to 1659 he filled the office of prior in the convents of Toulouse (twice), Rhodez, Castres, Albi, Avignon, and in the general novitiate in Paris. He strove to promote the reforms in study and religious observance inaugurated by Sebastian Michaelis in the first years of the century. Declining the office of provincial in Toulouse, he was sent by the master general in 1660 to make a canonical visitation of the Portuguese houses of the order. After his return to Paris he devoted the remaining 14 years of his life to the composition of theological works. His most important productions were written to satisfy the desire expressed by Alexander VII to the Dominicans assembled in a general chapter at Rome in 1656 that they should publish a course in moral theology conformable to the doctrine of St. Thomas, and thus correct the laxity of morals encouraged by certain casuists. These works were: *Theologiae Moralis adv. laxiores probabilistas pars prior* (Paris 1665); *Manuductionis ad moralem theologiam pars altera* (Paris 1665); *Theologiae moralis summa bipartita* (Paris 1667). In these writings, while condemning opinions that seemed too lax and censuring others that appeared too rigorous, he ably defended the system of probabiliorism. He engaged in an extended controversy with Jean de Launoy in regard to the authenticity of the *Summa Theologica* of St. Thomas Aquinas. Another valuable work is his

Libri V apologetici pro religione, utraque theologia, moribus ac juribus Ord. Praed. (Paris 1666). At the time of his death he was engaged in writing a complete course in theology to be entitled *D. Thomas sui intepres.* This work, only half completed and never published, is not to be confused with the one bearing the same title by Antonin Massoulié, OP.

Bibliography: P. MANDONNET, DTC 2.1:425–426. Quétif-Échard 2.2:655–656. A. TOURON, *Histoire des hommes illustres de l'ordre de Saint Dominique,* 6 v. (Paris 1743–49) v.5.

[R. J. RUST]

BARONIUS, CAESAR, VEN.

Cardinal and church historian; b. Sora, in the Campagna, Oct. 31, 1538; d. Rome, June 30, 1607. Though descendants of noble families, his parents were of ordinary means. Having completed his elementary education at Veroli, he studied philosophy, theology, and law at Naples until a French invasion in 1557 forced him to continue his studies at Rome; he gained a doctorate in law *in utroque,* May 30, 1561. In Rome he met Philip *Neri and placed himself under his spiritual guidance. Though Philip had not yet established the Congregation of the Oratory, he had begun the Oratory exercises. These meetings, open to the clergy and laity, aimed to draw souls closer to God through plain sermons and mental prayer.

The appearance of the *Centuriae Magdeburgenses,* a Lutheran polemical history of the Church, gave concern to Pius V and Gregory XIII (*see* CENTURIATORS OF MAGDEBURG). A refutation by a keen historian was needed, and Philip, detecting the germ of such scholarship in Baronius, directed him to deliver sermons on the history of the church. The 20-year-old Baronius began the research that served as the foundation for the 12-volume *Annales ecclesiastici* (Rome 1598–1607). This work had great success, being often reedited and translated into Italian, French, Polish, and German; it extended to the accession of Innocent III (1198) and was continued to 1565 by Odorico *Rinaldi (Raynaldus). After his ordination, May 27, 1564, Baronius lived at St. John of the Florentines with other priests who followed Philip. There he engaged in the ministry and continued his research. It was not until 1575 at the insistence of the Pope that the Oratory was formally established with Philip Neri as its reluctant superior. Baronius then lived under the same roof with the saint who began to test his spirit. Knowing that a scholar needs great patience in sifting minute details, must resist discouragement, narrate events truthfully, and not succumb to pride when praised, Philip drove Baronius relentlessly. In addition to the tedious research, he insisted that Baronius preach, hear confessions, visit the sick, and even cook. Baronius had hoped to publish one volume of the *Annales* a year, but he soon saw this to be impossible. The first volume appeared in 1588; the last, the year he died. Thus a 12-year plan became a 19-year program.

As a scholar Baronius was most exact. He read innumerable sources, investigated coins, inscriptions, or whatever else yielded information. In the interest of accuracy he became involved in an endless correspondence with other scholars. The manuscript and all the corrections were done in his own hand. He used secretaries only for his correspondence. He welcomed criticism even of trifles that proved time-consuming.

The life of Baronius was far from that of a tranquil scholar. In 1593 he succeeded Philip Neri as provost of the Oratory. He also displayed diplomatic skill in furthering the reconciliation of Henry IV of France with the Church (1593). Clement VIII made him his confessor and desired to confer honors on him. Baronius resisted, but on June 5, 1596, he was elevated to the cardinalate; he took as his motto "Obedience and Peace." For 2 years Baronius not only manifested sorrow at being torn away from the Oratory, but appeared resentful of his dignities. It was not until an enforced idleness while on a special mission to Ferrara that Baronius came to accept the honors as God's will.

In addition to his constant labors on the *Annales,* Baronius found himself the confidant of popes, served on various commissions, undertook the revision and correction of the Roman Martyrology at the request of Guglielmo *Sirleto, and held the post of Vatican librarian (1597). Constant study, lengthy correspondence, grave responsibilities, and adversities were ever present as the *Annales* were published. Over the years scholars have offered critiques of his work. Some believe Baronius was too intent on considering historical events from the point of view of papal primacy; they have also noted inaccuracies. However, they acknowledge that in such a pioneer work, the errors are far fewer than could have been expected. Baronius wrote also a life of St. Ambrose (Rome 1587) and the *Paraenensis ad rempublicam Venetam* (Rome 1606).

Caesar Baronius, engraving of the 17th century.

Of his numerous letters 451 were edited by R. Alberici, *Epistolae et opuscula inedita* (Rome 1759–70). Twice in 1605 Baronius narrowly escaped election to the papacy, due to his own pleading, the use of the *exclusiva* by Spain, and his opposition to the *Monarchia Sicula*. On Jan. 18, 1745, he was declared venerable by Benedict XV.

Bibliography: *A. Cesare Baronio: Scritti Vari* (Sora 1963), complete bibliog. of bks., MSS, articles on Baronius. A. KERR, *The Life of Cesare Cardinal Baronius of The Roman Oratory* (New York 1898). A. CAPECELATRO, *The Life of St. Philip Neri*, tr. T. A. POPE (2d ed. New York 1894; new ed. 1926). G. DE LIBERO, *Cesarae Baronio* (Rome 1939). Pastor v.19–25. A. G. RONCALLI (JOHN XXIII), "Il cardinale Cesare Baronio," ScCatt 13 (1908) 3–29. G. DE LIBERO, EncCatt 2:885–889. H. JEDIN, LexThK² 1:1270–72. A. MOLIEN, DHGE 6:871–882, bibliog.

[J. WAHL]

BARONTUS, ST., Merovingian monk of Lonray, Diocese of Bourges; d. *c.* 720 (feast, March 26 in the new Proper of Bourges). He has often been wrongly identified with a monk of the same name (commemorated in the Roman Martyrology on March 25) who was a hermit in Pistoia. The chief source for knowledge of Barontus is the *Visio Baronti monachi Longoretensis*, probably written by a contemporary. Barontus, after some years of married life, distributed his considerable possessions and entered the monastery of Saint-Pierre de Longoret in Lonray. On March 25, 678 (679), in the course of a violent fever, he had a vision which he later recounted. The fantastic journey through the otherworld recorded in the *Visio* witnesses to the eschatological curiosity of the time.

Bibliography: ActSS March 3:565–572. *Visio,* MGSrerMer 5:368–394. J. COIGNET, DHGE 6:882–885. G. RASPINI, BiblSanct 2:828–829.

[J. E. LYNCH]

BAROQUE, THE

The term is used loosely to designate a characteristic of a whole epoch of European culture, more specifically a style of art marked by complexity and tension. This article, after a brief history of the term, will include: (1) general trends and manifestations of baroque in architecture, sculpture, painting, music, poetry, prose and literary theory, drama and stagecraft; (2) further extensions of the general considerations on baroque language, motifs, symbols, devices, and conventions; (3) broader applications of baroque to styles of social living, to politics and political power, to science, to the psychology of the epoch, to philosophy, and to religion; and (4) the relation of baroque to humanism and classicism.

History Of The Term. The word was applied in the 16th century to pearls irregular in shape (*perolas barrocas*) as distinct from well-shaped ones in the Portuguese market at Goa. (This derivation has been challenged in recent scholarship in favor of an origin from "baroco," the name of a syllogism in scholastic philosophy; *see* ITALIAN LITERATURE, 2). The French were the first Europeans to transfer the adjective "baroque," meaning odd, to other objects. The French neoclassicists of the 18th century called baroque the art known as rococo because it was "odd," a striking departure from the forms of symmetric classical art (*see* ROCOCO ART). Authors in the 19th century, particularly in Switzerland and Germany, such as Franz Kugler (in 1832), Jakob *Burckhardt (1855), Jakob Falke (1866), and Cornelius Gurlitt (1888), extended the term to the late Renaissance, to designate the style of the age of the Whigs or to characterize the influence of the Jesuits of the 17th century (*see* RENAISSANCE ART). Such usage always connoted a lack of taste, even when coupled with names like *Bernini (1598–1680), *Borromini (1599–1667), or *Rubens (1577–1640).

A shift from a negative to a positive connotation of the term baroque gradually became noticeable, and can be traced to various causes. French impressionism, for instance, recalled similar techniques of * Velázquez and *Rembrandt. (*See* IMPRESSIONISM). Richard *Wagner's concept of the combination of the arts in the musical drama was reminiscent of attempts of the accepted opera and pageantry of the 17th century. The fantastic taste of the Bavarian King Ludwig II's sumptuous castles led to a favorable revaluation of the castles of the *grands seigneurs* of the 16th and 17th centuries, particularly of Versailles. Finally, relativists gradually refused to acknowledge objective criteria for the evaluation of art (*see* ART, 3). All these trends enabled Heinrich *Wölfflin (1888) to proclaim baroque art a different but no less beautiful art than that of the Renaissance.

General Trends. Whatever feature of the baroque one considers, one finds lines of descent despite the lapse of time between its last traces in one country and its first appearance in another. The German Balthasar *Neumann in the 18th century still holds the same architectural ideal as *Michelangelo held in 16th-century Italy. The same is true for the music of Johann Sebastian *Bach and of Claudio *Monteverdi.

The Renaissance forms running through various kinds of *mannerism (asymmetrical and generally crowded compositions that deliberately violate the classical "rules" of proportion) first developed into the Italian baroque. This, becoming congenial to the sensibility of the *Counter Reformation, spread first to Spain, where it was received enthusiastically, and then into the Catholic south of Germany and Austria, where it became popular with both courts and people. From Italy more than from Spain baroque spread to France where, although it became modified in its forms and somewhat secularized in spirit, it gained such vitality that it survived for a century in the forms of the rococo. From France and Austria baroque spread to the Protestant north, where it became thinner and rarer but nonetheless left unmistakable traces in Holland, the Scandinavian countries, and England.

Despite the fact that the origin of all strands of the baroque leads back to Italy, it is more properly associated with Spain. A serious religious spirit amenable to it, together with a propensity to paradox, exaggeration, and concrete representation as well as to coercion, was traditional in Spanish mentality. This is the reason why the Italian Renaissance never got a real foothold in Spain and why the art and literature of the Counter Reformation there met with such favor. As sponsor and propagandist, Spain became culturally important for its "eternal baroque," whose strong influences are visible in Central- and South-American churches.

SPECIFIC MANIFESTATIONS OF BAROQUE

Wölfflin in 1915 contrasted Renaissance art (which he characterized as flat, clear, loosely unified, linear, and closed) to the baroque, which was recessional, unclear, strongly unified, "painterly," and open.

Architecture. By 1900 baroque architecture was universally recognized as different, but, in beauty and value, comparable to Renaissance architecture. The Renaissance Rucellai Palace in Florence exemplified multiple, loosely unified structure, since the additive architectonic principle "two windows and one door and two windows" could be continued endlessly; but the baroque Palazzo Massimi alle Colonne in Rome showed a strongly unified order around a large, slightly curved entrance, decorated with columns.

Both styles are demonstrated by two great churches of the Society of Jesus in Rome: the interior of the Gesù is still almost a continuation of Renaissance style in its geometric and stereometric forms together with the linear arrangement of the walls and the straight continuation of the longitudinal nave into the apse, the whole covered by a mighty but simple dome whose baroque interior was painted much later. The Church of St. Ignatius, on the other hand, is fullest baroque in all the forms picturesquely segmented and merged into a dreamworld where the flowing lines of the solid walls, the painted curtains and balustrades, the real windows and their painted sills and columns cannot be distinguished.

The same distinctions can be found in Renaissance and baroque church façades, for instance, Santa Maria Novella in Florence and Borromini's S. Carlo alle Quattro Fontane in Rome. The former is seen as a plane, all décor arranged along the surface in a two-dimensional order, whereas the latter suggests a moving wave in its line of concave and convex forms, restless and recessional, and in its front with broad curves. A Renaissance church, as a building of "closed" form, fits into the house-front of a city, but a baroque church (like the Val de Grâce in Paris, the Stift Melk in Austria, or

Fig. 2. Borromini Church of S. Carlo alle Quattro Fontane, Rome.

the Santa Maria della Salute in Venice), as an "open" building, belongs to the landscape, where various foreshortenings offer to the viewer, as he shifts his point of observation, towers and cupola, frontal and lateral walls in ever new aspects (*see* BAROQUE ART).

Sculpture. Baroque, as applied to sculpture, suggests a restoration of the Gothic style refined under the influence of Renaissance figures while retaining the latter's heroic proportions. Baroque statues seem to leave their niches and to give the viewer an opportunity to see them from different angles; in this regard they are analogous to the "open" baroque of architecture. The revival of the spirit of the Council of *Trent, the introduction of new Spanish saints into the sanctuary of the whole Catholic world, the adulation of princes of Church and State, of generals and statesmen, all give statuary a different flowering on monuments and tombs. The church statues of Europe and Latin America follow the ideal of polychrome sculpture as exemplified by Juan Martínez Montañes (1568–1649), a tradition in Spain that reached its peak in Alonso Cano (1601–67). The plastic clouds surrounding the Blessed Virgin on Bavarian and Austrian Mary columns represent the same exuberance. In Italy Bernini's distorted and scantily draped marble statue of Mary Magdalene in the Cathedral of Siena permits the nude to intrude, so to speak, into the sanctuary. One senses Renaissance influence, but the picturesque grouping, the almost vibrat-

Fig. 1. Bernini sculpture group in the Church of S. Maria della Vittoria, Rome, depicting St. Teresa of Avila in ecstasy.

ing body of his St. Teresa, whose heart is being pierced by the arrow of the cherub, in Santa Maria della Vittoria in Rome, is baroque (*see* SCULPTURE).

Painting. If picturesqueness is a hallmark of baroque in architecture and sculpture, it is preeminently in painting that this quality emerges as the artistic expression of the baroque age. Renaissance painters such as *Raphael and *Leonardo da Vinci had stressed drawing almost too much to appear painterly. But with the first baroque generation, that of the so-called mannerists (such as Rosso and Parmigianino) Renaissance forms began to be replaced by the picturesque, in which contours were effaced and objects were fused with their surroundings. To this generation belong Michelangelo (1475–1564), with the gigantic figures of "The Last Judgment" in the Sistine Chapel: Pietro da *Cortona (1596–1669), famous for effectual foreshortening; Guido *Reni (1575–1642), known for the characteristic of the uplifted eyes of his figures; and finally the painters of elongated figures, beginning with *Parmigianino (1503–40) and his "La Madonna al collo lungo," or with *Primaticcio (1504–70) and his overelegant frescoes at Fontainebleau, and ending with El *Greco (1548?–1625?) in Spain.

The high baroque in Italy gradually yielded to the colorful Venetian Renaissance of *Veronese and *Titian, and culminated in the naturalism of *Caravaggio (1565–1609). Moreover, in accordance with the perspectivistic compositions of *Tintoretto (1518–94) and the Würzburg frescoes of *Tiepolo (1696–1770), Roman influences appear in the chiaroscuro murals of Federigo Barocci (1528–1612).

What had, however, become mere technique in Italy reached a new height under the Flemish influence of

Fig. 3. The Assumption of the Virgin, by Peter Paul Rubens.

*Brueghel with Peter Paul *Rubens; its powerful sensuality was expressed in theatrical groupings of nudes in grandiose environments. Spanish artists replaced colorfulness by the impressionistic brush strokes, color spots, and tonal gradations of the ingenious Diego *Velázquez (1599–1660), whose military and courtly subjects were to have technical parallels in the Madonnas of *Murillo (1617–82) and the monks of *Zurbarán (1598–1664?). Velázquez' subdued baroque had certain parallels also in the North. Closest in style to his interiors are those of Jan *Vermeer (1632–75); closest to the military display of his "Surrender of Breda" (1635) is the chiaroscuro "Night Watch" of Rembrandt (1641), with stress on golden chains, fur, and feathered hats. The same baroque impressionism present in Velázquez and Rembrandt characterizes also the Dutch landscapes of limitless aspect, such as those of Jacob Ruisdael (1628?–82) or Hobbema (1638–1709), and is found in the dream-light atmosphere of the French stage landscapes of *Claude Lorrain (1600–82). (*See* PAINTING, ARTICLES ON; BAROQUE ART.)

Music. Historians of music, such as Curt Sachs, Robert Haas, and Manfred Bukofzer, use the term baroque when discussing the invention of opera, the oratorio, the instrumental concert, the cantata, sonata, fugue, prelude, and organ music. These "novelties" account for a baroque era reaching from Claudio Monteverdi (1567–1643) to Henry *Purcell (1659–95), Johann Sebastian Bach (1685–1750), and Antonio *Vivaldi (1675?–1741). A line of Renaissance, exclusively vocal *a cappella* music culminating in *Palestrina (1526?–94) was extended into the baroque by the ecclesiastical *stile antico*.

Theoreticians, however, understand by baroque music a certain secular *stile moderno*. Unlike the *musica gravis* of the Renaissance, where a clear line and axis of polyphonic harmony stressed by the tenor voices oriented all the contrapuntal voices, the baroque *musica luxurians* had recourse to another leading principle. It was that of the general basso or *bassus continuus,* in which the leading upper voices were reflected according to movement, chords, cadences, and even dissonances, while the middle voices merely filled out the harmony without any contrapuntal significance. The basso and soprano furnished the skeleton of the composition. The consequence of this novelty was a monodic polarity between fundamental and ornamental instruments with the stress on the deep-toned cembalo, violoncello, viola da gamba, and viola da braccio.

Another baroque principle, comparable to the principle of openness in the graphic arts, was the combination of measured with free music as introduced by Giulio Caccini (1550?–1618) and Girolamo *Frescobaldi (1583–1643). (*See* MUSIC, SACRED, HISTORY OF, 5). According to this principle the polyphonic choir followed the traditional preestablished measurement while the two leading voices and the *bassus continuus* were free to hover (*senza battuta*) above the measured parts of the cantata or madrigal. This baroque novelty had a number of consequences: the recitative, or speech-song, as well as the strutting aria; the virtuosity of the coloratura and the dependence of minor and major keys on passions provided in the *libretti;* the hunting for *castrati* to combine in the voices boyish charm with virile decision; and the opportunity for mezzo-sopranos to match the new deep-toned instruments. The baroque combination of music and poetry in the opera is a parallel to the combination of baroque architecture and painting in church interiors.

Poetry. The baroque in poetry appeared as tension between a secularism entrenched since the Renaissance and new spiritual trends, which were evident in attitudes of escape from, revolt against, and interior consent to the ideals of the Catholic reform. As early as 1550 a spiritualization of the Renaissance love poetry of *Petrarch was leading to the praise of a spiritualized rather than a real lady. This is seen in the sonnets of the Portuguese poet, Luís de *Camões (1524–80). There is even the mystical shift to divine love, called in Italy *spirituale* and in Spain *a lo divino;* the new baroque tendency developed into the poetic works of St. *John of the Cross (1542–91). The further shift, that of the central motif from love to death, resulted in remarkable poems of disillusionment by *Góngora (1561–1627) and Francisco *Quevedo (1580–1645), as well as in the English *metaphysical poets, particularly John *Donne (1573–1631), Andrew Marvell (1621–78), and Richard *Crashaw (1613?–49).

Other poets escaped from this climate into a world of beauty, dreaming of perfect women in a perfect pastoral setting, and toying with riddle-metaphors and mythical allusions. From these stem the camouflages of *Gongorism, cultism, conceptism, and the *Schwulst,* typical of the German Andreas Gryphius (1616–64). Those who revolted, like the Italian Tommaso *Campanella (1568–1639), proclaimed their interior dissonance. But sometimes a deeper insight into the destructive effects of human passion, thanks to the new spirituality, inspired a baroque lyricism of repentance. This became evident in many poems of Lope de *Vega (1562–1635) and Torquato *Tasso (1544–95). Baroque poetry culminated in the Biblical and liturgical paraphrases and imitations by the Spaniard Fray Luis de *León (1527–91), and in the French poets *Corneille (1606–84) and *Racine (1639–99), as well as in the quasi-mystical alexandrines of the German convert *Angelus Silesius (1624–77).

Prose. The secular-spiritual tension apparent in baroque poetry occurred also in prose. Within the pastoral novel *Diana* by Jorge de Montemayor (1521?–61) in Spain, as in *Astrée* by Honoré d'Urfé (1568–1625) in France, appeared a love casuistry in which platonic friendship won out against sensuous relations. The type, taken up in France by Bishop Pierre Camus (1584–1652), led to the secularized but strictly moral-psychological novel, which reached its zenith in *La Princesse de Clêves* by Marie de La Fayette (1634–93). Baroque novels, in a certain parallelism to art, also exhibited formal innovations. The psychological questions discussed at length allowed a unified and open form with a larger extension of the plot than had the short, multiple stories of the Renaissance, closed within an artificial frame.

The frame ostensibly burst under the impact of the interlocked and inseparable episodes of the *Don Quixote* of Miguel de *Cervantes (1547–1616), imitated in Germany by Hans Jakob *Grimmelshausen (1620?–76) in his *Simplicius Simplicissimus.* Cervantes' novel also illustrated a tension suggestive of baroque, that between a self-willed idealism and an unrestrained materialism, neither of which can satisfy man, who is looking for something that transcends both, namely sanctity. Moreover, the baroque, particularly with Cervantes,

created a new prose style. Previously, an attempt to outdo Renaissance Ciceronianism, in the form of exaggerated pseudo-rhythms, was made by Fray Antonio de Guevara (1480?–1545) in Spain and John Lyly (1554?–1606) in England. On the other hand, a preference for directness and terseness, a kind of Tacitean style, was applied to the vernacular in the *Essais* of Michel de *Montaigne (1533–92). Both tendencies merge in Cervantes' rhythmic, Italianate but popular style. At the same time, an elaborate pulpit eloquence was revived by the *Ars praedicandi* of Lucas Baglioni (1562). Sacred oratory reached high peaks in the Spanish preacher Hortensio Félix Paravicino (1580–1633), in the Portuguese Jesuit Antônio *Vieira (1608–97), and most of all in the "Eagle of Meaux," the French court preacher *Bossuet (1627–1704), who departed from hackneyed themes in his famous funeral orations and sermons.

Literary Theory. A fundamental tension in literary theory was evident in a trend that, following too strictly the "rules" of Aristotle's *Rhetoric* and *Poetics,* at the same time prepared for a break from them. Not only was the question of unity of action, place, and time raised, but under the new religious trends the problems of verisimilitude and decency appeared, and especially the question whether literature ought primarily to instruct or to delight. The question was summarized by the *Poetics* of Antonio *Possevino, SJ (1595). After the commentaries of Julius Caesar *Scaliger and Castelvetro on Aristotle and the new "manneristic" poetic arts of Piccolomini, Rossi, Beni, La Mesnardière, and D'Aubignac, the answer was given in the fusing of instruction and delight within a profitable higher pleasure. On the question of how to achieve this fusion, the literary baroque theories differed in the different countries. In Spain Baltasar Gracián (1601–58), in his *Agudeza y arte de ingenio,* found the solution in a wholesale imagery that was required to reveal at the same time intelligence and wit. Nicolas *Boileau (1636–1711) in France, in his *Art poétique,* and Martin Opitz (1597–1639) in Germany, believed that by following the great literary patterns of the past, one would find a dignified and sublime circumlocution in which reason prevailed rather than a profusion of metaphors.

Drama. The epoch of the baroque, as has been stressed by Alejandro Cioranescu, was preeminently the age of drama, because of the tensions hitherto described. The contrasts between virtue and sin, will and passion were then foremost in the mind of theologians. Discussions concerning grace, free will, and their mysterious interrelationships attracted Lope de Vega, *Calderón (1600–81), *Shakespeare (1564–1616), Corneille, Racine, and the Dutchman, Joost van den *Vondel (1587–1679). In the variegated baroque drama, man is always shown within the limitations of his condition on the stage of the world while God is the unseen stage director. The motif of life as dream occurs in Calderón's *El gran teatro del mundo* but it is likewise discernible in Shakespeare's *Macbeth.* The dream-motif became famous through Calderón's *La Vida es Sueño,* but the convention is evident also in Shakespeare's *The Taming of the Shrew.* *Tirso de Molina's (1571?–1648) hero in *El condenado por desconfiado* came to realize that a proud hermit who tried to get to heaven by his own effort could be surpassed by a fundamentally charitable robber who, aware of his own weakness, ultimately relies on God. Racine's heroine in *Phèdre* (1677), worn out by an adulterous love and feebly resisting, let her will be so weakened that she caused murder and committed suicide out of jealousy and despair. Thus in the age of casuistry the passions were tracked down to their roots: the jealousy of suspicious husbands led to the killing of their innocent wives in Lope's and Calderón's versions of *El médico de su honra* as well as in Shakespeare's *Othello*. But the baroque drama had also a formal counterpoint. Progressive cutting of secondary actions from the plays of Lope to those of Calderón, from Shakespeare's to Racine's leads, as in art, from multiplicity to unity. Goethe saw that Calderón's secondary figures merely performed minuets between the protagonists. In France, dramatic unity culminated in a crisis-plot knit so tightly that it could actually burst into a catastrophe within the shortest imaginable time, a psychological time even less than the 24 hours then thought to have been prescribed by Aristotle.

Stagecraft. The gigantic baroque opera stage featured the supernatural, the miraculous, the unusual, the bizarre, the sumptuous, the limitless, and the grandiose. Here, the illusion of space verging on infinity was created by giving only half of a theatre building to the spectators who were enclosed in boxes, arranged in horizontal and vertical rows of great heights. The other half belonged to a deep platform where, with the help of mechanical devices, the same illusions of perspective could be produced as in the painted heavens of baroque churches. If a building could not house all the splendor of ballets and cavalcades, an open-air theater was created for such performances, and naval battles were enacted on artificial lakes. The baroque stage with its illusions and surprises was one of the most typical aspects of an age when ostentation played an enormous part, despite the fact that the dichotomy between outer show and inner worth was felt as a defect.

FURTHER EXTENSIONS OF BAROQUE

According to the pattern of baroque that has been explored thus far in the arts, language itself reflects the spirit of the age.

Language. Literary language centers around the paradox as the supreme figure of speech: life is death and death is life; love of God is hatred of the world; martyrdom is sweet and freedom is bitter; one is dying from not dying; one is victorious in defeat; chaste in one's nakedness; proud in one's humility; desperate in one's hope; one receives the brightest light from the darkest night. The paradox metaphor becomes a myth-creating force, striking, fresh, eloquent, grandiose though artificial. Metaphor and paradox join to create gigantic antitheses, suggestive of Michelangelo's Medici tombs in Florence. The whole epoch might be said to stand between light and shade, night and day, reason and faith. Epigrammatic condensation vies with lush description. Accordingly, playful, pleasant, and grotesque elements become counterparts of the grandiose, the majestic, and the magnificent. It is the time when the *précieuses* of the French salons speak of a drink as an interior bath, but also when Racine has Pyrrhus after the destruction of Troy declare his love in the image: "I am burning from more flames than I have lighted," and when Pascal declares man to be a thinking reed and a beast that tries to play the angel; Don Quixote is called the "wise fool" and Campanella, speculating in prison, considers himself free and fettered, in company and alone, crying in silence, mad to mortal eye, wise in God. The grandiose gesture of the baroque in language often carries metaphor to hyperbole.

Motifs. The clarity with which certain central motifs of the baroque are formulated in literature gives a lead to their recognition in painting. They stand out when they are contrasted to the motifs of the Renaissance, the *memento mori* to the *carpe diem*, the vanity of earthly pleasure to the enjoyment of life, instability to confidence in self, movement and change to a fixed untroubled attitude; dissimulation, disguise, confusion, madness and simulation of it to openly stressed doubt and passion. Cervantes' remark that hypocrisy is tolerable because it does no damage to anybody is a key to the ostentation of the baroque, which, however, carries with it laudable motifs, a certain modesty to cover a fundamental melancholy, interior solitude, and scruple. We see also the clash between Christian mores and those of certain levels of aristocratic society, as in the duel. Ostentatious honor, generosity, and detachment are pushed to heroism and virtue on the spiritual level. Here we find the exaltation of chastity, virginity, widowhood, suffering, martyrdom, sanctity—ideals little esteemed in the Renaissance with its feigned equanimity. The baroque motifs, however, are made concrete and presented within the sphere of the larger tension: duty versus passion, love versus renunciation, virtue versus intrigue, right versus might, hope versus despair, the finite versus the infinite, time versus eternity. The motif of fleeting life is appropriate in an epoch that marked the peak of the clockmaker's and watchmaker's art at the same time that it focused on eternity.

Symbols. Baroque symbols are often pushed to artificial extremes in emblems on coats of arms, in personified virtues surrounding the carriages of princes entering cities as victors or visitors, and in an endless series of representative but iconographically difficult paintings, such as Poussin's "Et in Arcadia ego." In literature they have a particular importance, and one is not surprised in that age of motion to encounter as its representative symbols the flame, the wave, the storm, the cloud, the reed, the foam, the fountain, the snowflake, the soap bubble, the labyrinth, the echo. There is particular stress on change, mainly with erotic overtones in the mythological figures of the Faun and Nymph, Circe, Proteus, Calypso, Alcina, Ariadne, and Hylas. But what has been stressed in both painting and literature are the symbols of the passing of life and of its nothingness compared to eternity: grave, graveyard, skeleton, ruins, prisons, and, as already mentioned, the theater whose figures "strut and fret their hour upon the stage and then are heard no more."

Devices and Conventions. Baroque motifs, in contradistinction to those of the Renaissance, appear combined with certain devices and conventions. The strongest device perhaps is the use of twilight, so much opposed to the clarity of the Renaissance. The French painter Georges de *La Tour (1593–1652), the Italian Michelangelo, and the Dutch Rembrandt (1606–69) prefer scenes of night or dark, and dimness illuminated by torches. Calderon symbolically underlines the atmosphere of dreamlike reality in the opening act of *La Vida es Sueño,* where Rosaura and Clarin at nightfall discover the tower where Segismundo is imprisoned and are guided by a beam of light from his cell.

Another device is the impressionistic blurring and successive clarification of an event. In Velázquez' "Las Lanzas," one moves from the blurred background of a military camp to a middleground of dim contours, and finally to the foreground of distinguishable soldiers and horses. In this way Cervantes and Góngora describe the meetings of people, revealing personality by progressively clearer bits of conversation until names and professions are clarified and such persons move to a goal, for instance, to a wedding feast first vaguely discussed; then apprehended from noises, illumination, and music; and finally confronted in detailed reality.

BROADER APPLICATIONS OF BAROQUE

Aspects of the baroque far removed from art and literature are to be detected in the culture of the times.

Social Life. The most typical feature of baroque luxury is the cult of the gardens. In the south they are characterized by cascades falling from rocky heights into sculptured basins, surrounded by grottos and porticoed stone pavilions. In the north they are turned into mazes and labyrinths of glades, clipped groves, shaded alleys with Greco-Roman statues, long latticed arbors, lakes, ponds, flower beds worked into different patterns, hedges, fountains with nereids and nymphs spouting jets of water. And, like all baroque art, this grandeur appealed to a seigneurial life, again of Roman origin, where the pontifical splendor called for *piazze* like Bernini's before St. Peter. In Rome as early as the end of the 16th century Cardinal Farnese built his garden palace on the Palatine Hill; Cardinal Riario, his in Trastevere; and the Villa Medici was erected on the Pincio; these were followed in the 17th century by the Villa Aldobrandini in Frascati. The secular princes of the north aggrandized this style. Versailles became the garden-palace par excellence; the endless park is so intricate that Louis XIV himself wrote a guide for it. England, generally aloof from baroque taste, changed the French park into a hilly lawn and woodland, like Mount Pleasant, yielding a panoramic view of Hampton Court, Wilton House, or Badminton.

Politics and Political Power. Political theories of the Renaissance culminated in a type of thinking and concrete application such as we find in *Machiavelli's *The Prince.* The practical problem was whether to use power not wantonly but only out of moral necessity and for the common good. The Christian humanism of *Erasmus had tried to establish a pure concept of justice and peace. Unfortunately this ideal, which coincided with the teaching of the Church, was made unrealistic by the Protestant *Reformation, which destroyed not only international but also national unity in Europe, with the result that princes in opposing camps tried to reconcile their concept of justice and peace with their own aspirations. This led to the compromises of modern diplomacy, expediency, "honest dissimulation," and "discretion." Such political tension between fundamentally Christian principles and opportunism actually may be called baroque, as proposed by Carl J. Friedrich. The Church at the moment of her highest prestige in history, restored by the Council of Trent and expanding to the countries of the New World, was, at the same time, a temporal power in Italy. It therefore fell into the pattern of using the same diplomacy as the national states. It should be noted, however, that a sound political doctrine was masterfully expounded and defended by

the Jesuit saint, Cardinal Robert *Bellarmine (1542–1621). He called for restriction of the might of princes. He proposed that international law bind sovereign states to moral principles and consolidate the human rights of the aborigines in the new colonies, and suggested an arbitration belonging by indirect power to the Roman pontiff. In practical politics, however, another Jesuit, G. Botero (1540–1617), through *Della Ragione di Stato* (1589), became the guide for modern states in the matter of admissible coercion. The problem of political coercion and opportunism finally became the tragedy of the baroque age. The Thirty Years' War (1618–48) and the shifting policies of its participants must be viewed in this context (*see* POLITICAL THOUGHT, HISTORY OF).

The inherited worldly and critical spirit of the Renaissance, strengthened in a way by the consolidation of the Protestant reform, blocked the permeation of culture in its totality by the renewed spirituality of the Church. The opposition to a spiritual renewal led to the stringencies of the Roman *Inquisition inaugurated by Pope *Paul III. The Inquisition controlled not only the faith but also the mores of writers and artists and led to the *Index of Forbidden Books under *Paul IV (1559). The Council of Trent with its emphasis on reform envisioned the suppression of all irregularities within the clergy and of all lax and nonconformist thought among the laity. St. *Pius V (1566–72) removed the last traces of Renaissance immorality from Rome, banishing all the prostitutes from the Holy City. *Sixtus V (1585–90) put the statues of SS. Peter and Paul on the top of the columns of the Roman emperors Trajan and Marcus Aurelius, and erected anew the Egyptian obelisk of the Emperor Caligula in St. Peter's square together with the cross inscribed *Christus vincit.* *Urban VIII (1623–44), under whose pontificate the ecclesiastical states reached their greatest geographical extension, reopened St. Peter's (1626), the restored majestic sanctuary of Christendom. With such triumphs ennobling the papacy, the Church left undisturbed to His Catholic Majesty, the King of Spain, and His Most Christian Majesty, the King of France, certain traditional powers in the political sphere. But the French and Spanish kings began competing, in their Escorial and Versailles, on a secular level with the baroque splendor of the pontiffs and developed a boundless state absolutism.

Science. It does not seem meaningful to speak about baroque science, and nothing would be gained by talking about baroque astronomy, physics, chemistry, anatomy, physiology, or biology, as Sir George Clark speaks about baroque mathematics, or by opposing baroque natural science to the humanistic Renaissance in the sense of Giuseppe Toffanin. In the 17th century, however, science did find itself in an atmosphere of tension. It found itself in conflict with superstition, traditional Aristotelianism, and ecclesiastical censorship—and this justifies a consideration of a baroque phase in the history of science. The principal aspect of this tension lies precisely in the fact that all those men who emphasized the inductive and deductive methods and their combination for valid scientific conclusions, as well as the analysis of the natural phenomena of movement and gravitation, were religious-minded people. Galileo *Galilei (1564–1642), *Kepler (1571–1630), and Isaac *Newton (1642–1727) lived in an environment wherein witchhunt, sorcery, astrology, and alchemy were still taken for granted while valid scientific discoveries were suspected. Francis *Bacon (1561–1626) had a hard time proving that the facts he discovered empirically could not be denied by philosophical speculation. Aristotle's theory of the four elements suffered when Robert *Boyle (1627–91) found the law of pressure in gases and William *Harvey (1578–1657) discovered the circulation of the blood. Galileo's observation of the movement of the earth came at a time when St. Ignatius had laid down his rules for "thinking with the Church." In this spiritual atmosphere Galileo appeared a quasi-heretic contradicting the Biblical passage that described how the sun stood still for Josue's victory. It was this particular constellation that made science of the 17th century "baroque" and maneuvered it into a unique historical tension that caused great interior tragedies for the scientists concerned.

Psychology. One of the attacks against the wide use of the term baroque is directed against its application to psychology. However, the existence of the baroque type of man between 1560 and 1690 cannot be denied; such a man tried desperately to come to an interior peace within the double tension of his time, which lay in the struggle between the critical intellect aroused by the natural sciences and submission to the tenets of the Christian faith, made more than ever mandatory by the strict decrees of the Council of Trent. This tension alone explains a Torquato Tasso who, still deeply entrenched in the chivalrous and amorous taste of the Renaissance epic of *Ariosto, accused himself before the Inquisition of not being able to write a Christian epic; he tried again and again to purify his *Gerusalemme Liberata* until it became the pious *Gerusalemme Conquistata.* Galileo recanted his discoveries out of fear that they might make him heretical, but during his very custody came back to his place of observation to perfect them. *Descartes, after elaborating his method, made a pilgrimage to Loretto to thank Our Lady, and after the condemnation of Galileo refrained from publishing his *Traité du Monde,* although living in Holland where he was not exposed to any exterior penalty.

The same tension occurred in the moral realm where the attractions of the world appeared diabolic in the new ascetic atmosphere. Symbolic of this situation was the figure of Don Juan, who covered under a mask of gentleness his unbridled voluptuosity, and ended in Hell. Lope de Vega, after a life of multiple adultery and public scandal, paid for by suffering and penance, became a priest but at an advanced age fell again when he met an actress performing in his comedies. Thus the "baroque man" did exist, a complex nature characterized by antithesis and paradox.

Philosophy. The term baroque was introduced into philosophy by the Spinoza specialist Carl Gebhart and by the Leibniz scholar Hans Barth. The impact of the discovery of an unshakable mechanism in the physical world and the general belief in liberty within the moral world led to a tension so difficult to bridge that it affected even the theological discussions on *free will and *predestination between Jesuits and Jansenists. In the domain of philosophy a tension arose between Descartes' (1596–1650) *res cogitans* and *res extensa,* a dilemma for the great metaphysician himself, who was idealistic in speculation and materialistic in observation. The Oratorian Nicolas de *Malebranche (1638–1715), laboring under the same dichotomy, tried to overcome it by a general principle of divine order that works differently in the material and the spiritual world, so that miracles follow a principle of order that the human mind is not able to discover. *Spinoza (1632–77) threw a desperate span from Descartes' thinking subject to Descartes' extension of matter by identifying in a pantheistic mood the traditional concepts of *natura naturans* and *natura naturata* with his monistic *Deus sive Natura.*

But the tension between matter and spirit offered itself in a quite different way to *Leibniz (1646–1716). He was not biased by Descartes' philosophical "first principle," *Cogito, ergo sum,* but started in the scholastic way from God as the immovable First Cause and Master of the material as well as of the moral-spiritual world. Both worlds are subject to His plan and purpose. There is a pre-established harmony between the macrocosm of creation and the microcosm of the human soul, which works out its destiny in liberty within the best imaginable of worlds, a world that pleads for the bounty of God (*Theodicy,* 1710). Pascal (1623–62), without achieving a philosophical system, had already rejected Descartes' approach as "useless" and satisfied his own interior tension by distinguishing not two but three "orders," the world of geometry, of "finesse" (art, life), and of charity (religion, the Church). (*See* PHILOSOPHY, HISTORY OF, 4.)

Religion. Renaissance mannerism was able to turn into a meaningful new art style called baroque only because the new forms were permeated by a new meaning that sprang from a new orientation of the mind. Thus, just as the term Renaissance was applied to an age of humanism, the term baroque was roughly applied to the era of the Counter Reformation. However, this is only half correct. Even before the Counter Reformation, a spontaneous growth of spirituality had resisted the paganism and worldly aspects of the Italian Renaissance and the romantic archaism and antiecclesiastical revolt of the German Reformation. The spiritual preparation for the Counter Reformation and the spiritual preparation for baroque art coincide, mainly in Spain. It is there that the great ascetics and mystics were at the same time founders or reformers of religious orders—saints such as *Peter of Alcántara (1499–1562), *Teresa of Avila (1515–82), and John of the Cross. Most important was *Ignatius of Loyola (1491–1556) with his motto: *Omnia ad maiorem Dei gloriam.* They all prepared that spirituality in which Christian feeling and thinking become radically theocentric, a concept that baroque ecclesiastical art translated into the centering of churches and whole cities around the tabernacle and the monstrance, symbolizing the spiritual heliocentricity of the baroque age.

The Spanish beginnings reached out to splendid theophoric processions by day and by night, and Calderón's *autos sacramentales* expanded into France where St. *Francis de Sales (1567–1622) was to concentrate Ignatian spirituality on the act of recalling as often as possible the presence of God, where Cardinal Pierre de *Bérulle (1575–1629) taught a more specific Christocentricity, and St. John *Eudes (1601–80), along with Bl. Marie de l'Incarnation (1599–1672) and St. Margaret Mary *Alacoque (1647–90), developed the cult of the Sacred Heart. St. Louis-Marie *Grignion de Montfort (1673–1716) stimulated the new baroque devotion to the Eucharist, and by following the Spanish devotion of the Purissima and the Eudist cult of the Immaculate Heart, strengthened the cult of Mary as mediatrix. *See* SPIRITUALITY (HISTORY OF).

RELATIONSHIP TO CHRISTIAN HUMANISM AND CLASSICISM

The well-known Ratio Studiorum of the Society of Jesus has actually been called baroque. The implication is that the pagan humanism of the Italian Renaissance, which tried to pattern life on the natural ideals of the ancients rather than on the morality taught by Christ and the Church, was unacceptable to the new age.

Relationship to Christian Humanism. Moreover, the so-called Christian humanism of Erasmus, who tried to compromise between pagan and Christian ideals by substituting an esthetically balanced life for asceticism, soon became so odious, particularly in Spain, that Pedro de *Ribadeneyra reports that St. Ignatius felt all spirituality evaporate whenever he read a page of Erasmus. The humanism of the Jesuits and its underlying baroque spirit is a "devout humanism," as Henri *Brémond says. Disinfected and sterilized, so to speak, it is selective and brought into harmony with Christianity on the basis of the principle: *Omnia ad maiorem Dei gloriam*. This baroque humanism became the principle of education of royalty and nobility throughout Europe. As a motive for practical life, it is the soundest but (like everything baroque) nonetheless somewhat artificial diet of exuberant freedom and restraint. In the most popular work patterned on this principle, the *Introduction to the Devout Life* by St. Francis de Sales, one can study the baroque in every detail, even in style. Here all concessions possible are made but always with the disillusioning, though convincing, restriction: Better not. (*See* HUMANISM; HUMANISM, CHRISTIAN.)

Relationship to Classicism. After the Italians had developed their Renaissance classicism on an almost national-natural basis by a close imitation of their Roman ancestors in art and literature, other Europeans tried to do the same, but, given the historical conditions, the result was somewhat artificial. France in the 17th century, England in the 18th, and Germany in the 19th created an artificial classicism. In other words, France marshaled her baroque, England her *neoclassicism, Germany her *enlightenment and her romantic forces toward a classical Greco-Roman ideal.

Pan-European Influence. It is a tragic misunderstanding of French art and literary historians to believe that their culturally directed classicism, restricted to certain genera, is a genuine epoch style and style epoch that filled the second half of the 17th century in contradistinction to the preclassicism or quasi-baroque of the first half. This view would bring France into a splendid isolation from the rest of Europe and would split her art and literature, both within themselves and from all the other domains of culture, costume, decoration, festivities, operas, funeral pomp, for all of which even Frenchmen admit the qualification "baroque." The view is fundamentally erroneous. The whole 17th century in France is baroque, and the second half still more than the first; it is this which logically develops into the rococo. It has to be admitted that French baroque is particularly refined in thought and form; it is also more secularized than in other countries, but it is a true and full baroque whose classical tendencies toward a more rational national taste also characterized other epochs

in France. Classicism does subdue, but does not change, the fundamentally baroque character of 17th-century France.

Baroque is the last pan-European style expressing the incipient tensions of modern man.

Bibliography: J. WEINGARTNER, LexThK² 1:1265–68. K. G. FELLERER, LexThK² 1:1268–69. W. FLEMMING, RGG³ 1:884–892. V. TAPIÉ, *Le Baroque* (Paris 1961). A. COUTINHO, *Aspectos da literatura barroca* (Rio de Janeiro 1950). G. R. HOCKE, *Die Welt als Labyrinth* (Hamburg 1957); *Manierismus in der Literatur* (Hamburg 1959). R. STAMM, ed., *Die Kunstformen des Barockzeitalters* (Bern 1956). W. SYPHER, *Four Stages of Renaissance Style: Transformations in Art and Literature, 1400–1700* (Garden City 1955). E. BATTISTI, *Rinascimento e barocco* (Turin 1961). H. WÖLFFLIN, *Principles of Art History: The Problem of the Development of Style in Later Art*, tr. M. D. HOTTINGER (London 1932; repr. New York 1950). W. WEISBACH, *Der Barock als Kunst der Gegenreformation* (Berlin 1921). M. F. BUKOFZER, *Music in the Baroque Era* (New York 1947). E. RAIMONDI, *Letteratura barocca: Studi sul Seicento italiano* (Florence 1961). O. DE MOURGUES, *Metaphysical Baroque and Précieux Poetry* (Oxford 1953). E. CASTELLI, ed., *Retorica e barocco* (Rome 1955). A. CIORANESCU, *El Barroco o el descubrimiento del drama* (Laguna 1957). J. ROUSSET, *La Littérature de l'âge baroque en France: Circé et le paon* (Paris 1953). C. J. FRIEDRICH and C. BLITZER, *The Age of Power* (Ithaca 1957). H. H. RHYS, ed., *Seventeenth Century Science and the Arts* (Princeton, N. J. 1961). A. PIGLER, *Barockthemen: Eine Auswahl von Verzeichnissen zur Ikonographie des 17. and 18. Jahrhunderts*, 2 v. (Budapest 1956). E. OROZCO DÍAZ, *Temas del barroco de poesía y pintura* (Granada 1947). G. CLARK, *The Seventeenth Century* (Oxford 1947). R. DE FÉLICE, *French Furniture under Louis XIV* (London 1923). I. A. LEONARD, *Baroque Times in Old Mexico: Seventeenth Century Persons, Places, and Practices* (Ann Arbor 1959). G. DÍAZ-PLAJA, *El espíritu del barroco* (Barcelona 1940). G. TOFFANIN, *History of Humanism*, tr. E. GIANTURCO (New York 1954). P. BUTLER, *Classicisme et baroque dans l'oeuvre de Racine* (Paris 1959). F. SIMONE et al., *Trois conférences sur le Baroque français* (Turin 1964). H. HATZFELD, *Estudios sobre barroco* (Madrid 1964). **Illustration credits:** Figs. 1, 2, Alinari. Fig. 3, National Gallery of Art, Washington D.C., Samuel H. Kress Collection.

[H. HATZFELD]

BAROQUE ART

The term baroque is ordinarily applied to the art of the 17th and early 18th centuries. It originally had a deprecatory meaning, with the connotation of something false, eccentric, or censurable. The close consistency existing between baroque art and the literature of the period has led critics of our time to disregard the preconceptions of neoclassical critics who denounced it and to judge baroque art in an objective light.

The formal content of 17th-century artistic expression is aptly characterized by a sense of the marvelous. Free imagination revolted against the domination of *mannerism and aimed at going beyond theoretical limits and traditional forms in every way possible. In architecture columns were twisted into huge spirals, ornamental façades were broken into sections and increased in number, and the desire for effects of light and shade took precedence over the limitations of constructive material. A wildness of movement was expressed in representations of the human figure, accentuated by the use of draperies that fantastically transfigured it. Because it was an expression of fundamental taste, baroque art cannot be assimilated to that of other periods and should be considered valid in itself and for itself and even admirable for the absolute triumph of fantasy, vitality, and exuberant liberty that constitutes its essence.

The word baroque was defined by Croce in his *Storia dell'età barocca in Italia* (1929). Calcaterra (1945) infers that in the 17th and 18th centuries the word baroque was associated with the scholastic syllogism "baroco" and meant a method of thought without any content of truth, by means of which it was easy to end in confounding the false with the true. In art it meant the contradiction of the classic rules. In addition to the interpretations of Croce and Calcaterra, attention must be called to the interpretations of writers outside of Italy (Rocisbach, 1925; Reymond, 1945), who claim it is derived from the Portuguese *barrueco,* a type of pearl that is irregular in shape.

In France the generic term was developed from the technical term and was applied to all that was unusual or strange and in art to all that was "degenerate." The term began to be used as a definition in art criticism of the 18th century, when it was linked with mannerism for the purpose of deprecation. Milizia, in the 1797 dictionary, wrote: "The century of correction was ended; it was the century of corruption . . .. Borromini in architecture, Bernini in sculpture, Pietro da Cortona in painting, Cavalier Marino in poetry, are plagues of taste, plagues that infected a great number of artists . . .." For Milizia, baroque was the superlative of the bizarre, the excess of the ridiculous.

The origin of modern discussions of the baroque must be sought in the reaction to 17th-century civilization and art. Specialized art criticism on the subject sprang up after the Romantic movement and led to a revision of viewpoint regarding the 17th century. It was actually in the climate of Wagnerian poetic that *Wölfflin published, in 1888, the first fundamental book on the subject, *Renaissance und Barock.* After Wölff-lin, an effort was made to arrive at a definition of the concept of baroque along three lines of thought: (1) baroque understood as nonstyle (Croce); (2) an artistic ideal that could stand as the perpetual antithesis to classicism; and (3) a cultural epoch, whose chronological limits extended from the end of the Renaissance to the beginning of the neoclassical period.

A relation was erroneously established not between the prevalent tendencies of the period and of the various artists but between a few of the tendencies and the abstraction of a "general style." The first steps in this direction were taken by those who strove to find a reason for baroque, individualizing it into the "distaste for existing forms" and the "search for a new approach." Finally such judgment was supported by referring to facts of history and of contemporary life as, for example, Jesuitism, the Counter Reformation, and the decadence of society, but without arriving at any really determining factors. A common spiritual and sociological root was sought in the period for the artistic as well as the political, historical, and cultural changes. The history of art had taken the field as a history of the human spirit. The history of baroque art that follows treats architecture first, then sculpture, and lastly painting.

See also CHURCH ARCHITECTURE, 7, BAROQUE; SCULPTURE, 2, RENAISSANCE TO MODERN; MANNERISM; ROCOCO ART; RENAISSANCE ART.

ARCHITECTURE

While baroque architecture was judged unfavorably during the neoclassical period, it is now considered as an evolution and not as a degenerate phase of the Renaissance. The contrast and accentuation of certain elements superseded the characteristic Renaissance harmony; exaggeration and eccentricity took the place of serenity and balance. Most of the churches built during the baroque period were colossal structures, in the interior of which the spatial harmony of the Renaissance was replaced by a play of light and shadow with intensely dramatic effects.

In the preceding period, a palace was an organic whole. In the baroque period, the architectural elements of the palace were broken up, dismembered, and given a purely scenographic value. Villas became popular and were used by architects as an outlet for the fullest expression of their delight in fantasy. Picturesque and unprecedented forms were employed to effect an atmosphere of mystery and to produce surprise.

Even the general appearance of the cities took on the character of the period. Large, grandiose fountains added an impression of scenographic richness to the public squares, around which imaginative buildings and statues were grouped.

Italy. The origins of Italian baroque architecture must be sought in the last phase of the Renaissance, especially in the architecture of Michelangelo, whose Medici Chapels, Laurenziana Library, and Campidoglio Piazza are creations in the baroque spirit. An even more decisive contribution was made by Giacomo da *Vignola. In his church of the Gesù in Rome he created the prototype of the baroque religious edifice. The dates that specify the beginning of baroque and its establishment are 1520 when the Medici Chapels were designed and 1568, the year of construction of the church of the Gesù.

Baroque architecture reached the peak of its expression in Rome. Carlo *Maderno (1556–1629) was among the first, Giovanni Lorenzo *Bernini (1598–1680) among the most famous of the architects. Bernini constructed the majestic colonnades of St. Peter's in Vatican City. Though a contemporary of Bernini, F. *Borromini (1559–1667) was of a different temperament, more elegant, more refined, less devoted to the extreme spirit of the period. Other baroque Roman architects were numerous: Martino Longhi the Younger (1602–60), Pietro da *Cortona (1596–1669), Carlo *Rainaldi (1611–91), Alessandro Algardi (1592–1654), and Nicola Salvi (1699–1751).

The Italian centers of baroque art, in addition to Rome, were Venice, Genoa, Turin, Naples, Milan, and Bologna. In Venice, imposing buildings were created, such as the Palazzo Correr by Vincenzo Scammozzi (1552–1661) and the Palazzo Pesaro by Baldassarre Longhena (1604–82). In Genoa, a competent baroque architect was Baccio di Bartolommeo Bianco (1604–56), who created one of the most sumptuous staircases of the period in the Jesuit College. In Turin, notable edifices were erected by Guarino Guarini (1624–83) and Filippo Juvara (1685–1735).

Although the principal characteristics of the period were still preserved, the cycle of Italian baroque ended in the first decades of the 18th century with a sharp reaction on the part of the architects Ferdinando Fuga (1699–1780) and Luigi Vanvitelli (1700–73). The persisting baroque elements and occasional rococo embellishments of their buildings do not cancel the restraint and classical purity that is fundamental to them.

Fig. 1. Baroque Art (Architecture): (a) Grand staircase, Palazzo Madama, Turin, F. Juvara, 1718. (b) Main portal of the Hospital of S. Fernando, Madrid, J. Churiguerra. (c) Palazzo Barberini, Rome, Carlo Maderno, c. 1625.

France. During the first half ot the 17th century, French architects turned to Italy for inspiration, particularly in the construction of ecclesiastical buildings. The church of the Gesù and St. Peter's in Vatican City were their chief sources. Jacques Le Mercier (1585–1654) designed the two great Parisian churches of St. Paul and St. Louis, and the city of Paris was transformed and enlarged (1676–90) by François Blondel (1618–86) and Pierre Bullet (1639–1716). Jules Hardouin *Mansart (1646–1708) built the church of the Invalides (1706) and St. Sulpice, both in Paris.

In France, the baroque was expressed in civil architecture, especially in the splendid palaces in which the French spirit of elegance, refinement, and love of splendor was embodied. The Louvre and Versailles are the exemplars of the period. Many master architects had a hand in building the Louvre, among whom were the Italians Bernini, Rainaldi, and Cortona. The most typical façade is the work of Claude Perrault (1613–88). Versailles, in a setting of spendid parks and gardens, was the product of the collaboration of numerous artists, among whom were Louis Le Vau (1612–70), André *Le Nôtre (1613–1700), and Jules Hardouin Mansart (1646–1708).

Spain. Baroque did not develop extensively in Spain and Portugal because of the prolonged influence of the Italian Renaissance and the subsequent advent of rococo and neoclassical art. Italian artists were principally responsible for the constructions of the period and exerted a strong influence. Francisco Herrera del Mozo took the Vatican Basilica as his model in building the church of Nostra Signora del Pilar at Saragossa.

The Spanish baroque is identified closely with the churrigueresque style, which derives its name from José Simon Churriguera (d. 1679). Admirable examples of his work are the portals of the hospice of San Fernando in Madrid, the palace of St. Elmo in Seville, and the cathedral of *Santiago de Compostela.

Belgium. The finest expression of baroque architecture is found in Belgium's religious edifices, particularly the church of the Jesuits in Antwerp (1614–21) and the Jesuit church in Louvain (1650–66), erected by Luc Faydherbe (c. 1617–97). The Italian influence was apparent in civil architecture, where the revived Palladian style determined Rubens' Maison du Jardin, Antwerp.

Austria. Baroque art had a short life in Vienna before it was replaced by the rococo. The Austrian architects drew their inspiration from the Roman churches. J. B. *Fischer von Erlach (1656–1723) constructed the church of St. Peter in Vienna after the style of Bernini, and built the church of St. Charles Borromeo, which recalls the Pantheon. The Belvedere in Vienna was the work of Johann Lukas von Hildebrandt (1668–1745). Italian architects who worked in Austria and neighboring countries included F. Bibbiena, Gabriele Gabrielli, and Carlo Lurago.

Germany. Baroque art flourished in Germany, particularly in Dresden and Berlin. The Zwinger in Dresden was built by Daniel Pöppelmann (1662–1736), with a sumptuous, heavy magnificence characteristic of the German baroque sensibility. In Berlin, A. Schlüter built the Royal Palace which suggests the Palazzo Barberini in Rome. In the Palace of the Electors in Würzburg, Balthasar *Neumann (1687–1753) designed a stupendous staircase that recalls those of Genoa but enriched it with Gothic elements. The procedure was standard for German architects during the baroque period.

England. Inigo *Jones (1573–1657), whose work shows the influence of Palladio, built the Queen's villa at Greenwich. St. Paul's Cathedral, whose façade and general plan were both inspired by St. Peter's in the Vatican, was the work of Christopher *Wren (1632–1723). J. *Gibbs and J. Vanbrugh continued, in the baroque tradition, the transfer of Roman influence to England.

Russia. Baroque art assumed creative forms in Russia through the aid of Italian architects. While the traditional churches with five cupolas continued to express the Byzantine spirit, Italian architects like Sebastiano Bracci, Dominico Trezzini (1670–1734), and Bartolomeo Francesco Rastrelli (1700–71) carried the influence of Bernini into many Russian cities. The same may be said for the neighboring countries, all of which were influenced by the work of Italian architects.

SCULPTURE

Baroque sculpture is characterized by interest in movement and dramatic, virtually theatrical, expression. The material with which the baroque sculptor worked was pushed to the limits of its capability as a medium. Colored marbles were employed for carving, and white stone was frequently colored in an apparent attempt to capture effects that were hitherto more commonly sought after in painting. In the vast array of work produced during the period, the influence of Italy was dominant.

Italy. Rome came to be considered the capital of baroque art in sculpture as well as architecture. In the Lateran, the Sistine Chapel, S. Maria Maggiore, and S. Andrea della Valle, sculptured groups were added to the architecture with exquisite taste and courtly refinement. The Lombards in particular produced sensitive portraits in marble.

Camillo Mariani (1556–1611) of Vicenza won fame in Rome for the decorative work he did for the interior of the church of St. Bernard, begun in 1600 in the remains of the Baths of Diocletian. Using pliant stucco, he was able to plan ambitiously; he placed figures of the saints between the niches and achieved a clear expression of epic motifs characteristic of the painting of *Tintoretto and *Veronese. Pietro Bernini (1562–1629), father of the great Giovanni Lorenzo, shared in the pulsing artistic life of the city that had caught the Venetian sense of color. He profited from the lessons of Mariani but applied them so literally that he fell into a rather arid mannerism and was saved only by his tactile sense of materials with which he created stirring effects.

Meanwhile Francesco Mochi (1580–1652) in the cathedral of Orvieto, the Pauline Chapel, and the Farnese equestrian monuments in Piacenza produced sculpture vividly alive and substantial from the viewpoint of form. The baroque here was wholesome and fine; he enriched his own creations with stylistic elements of *Donatello and *Verrocchio. Following a dispute with G. L. Bernini in 1635, Mochi's work began to show a change. The figure of St. Thaddeus in Orvieto and those in the "Baptism of Jesus" in the Braschi Palace are distorted into disconcerting abstractions, and the forms take on such paradoxical lines that they suggest romanticism.

Alessandro Algardi (1595–1654), a brilliant and perennially happy artist from Emilia, was working in Rome during the time the restless, tormented Mochi was active there. Algardi had been trained in Bologna with the Carracci, and then in Mantua and Venice he further developed the sense of color that makes all his work joyous and full of life. He also profited from his contacts with Guido *Reni, whose spirited yet delicate characteristics as a painter are seen in Algardi's work in the Magdalene and his St. John the Evangelist in the church of S. Silvestro al Quirinale.

Algardi's skill as a portraitist was equal to that of Bernini. He had a subtle and cultivated plastic sense. It is seen in the Laudivio Zacchia in Berlin and the Ulpiano Volpi of Poldi Pezzoli. His St. Phillip Neri with the Angel in the sacristy of S. Maria in Vallicella (1640) assured his renown as a sculptor, and thereafter he received very important commissions: the tomb of Leo XI, the "Beheading of St. Paul" in Bologna, and the altar of St. Nicholas of Tolentino. From then on Algardi showed increasing ability to communicate a sense of movement and to use chiaroscuro in the best Venetian-Umbrian tradition. His Innocent X in the Capitoline Museum challenges Bernini's work. The decoration of Villa Pamphili in very low stucco relief is the best illustration of the taste of the period and foreshadows the work of the 18th century. The Belgian artist François Duquesnoy (1594–1643), who made effective use of color, was in Rome during the period of Algardi and Bernini. Influenced by Poussin, Van Dyck, and Rubens, Duquesnoy achieved a fluid, coloristic sense worthy of the best Venetian tradition and was a formative influence on sculpture during the baroque period and after. His most noted works are the statue of St. Susanna in S. Maria di Loreto, the St. Andrew (1640) in St. Peter's, and the small scale angels with musical instruments in the church of the Holy Apostles in Naples. The last are typical of his style.

Of Bernini's many students Giuliano Finelli (c. 1601–57) was an early disciple, Antonio Raggi (1624–86) a product of Bernini's mature years. The work of Cosimo Fancelli (1620–88) shows the influence of Cortona in its vigor and subtlety. Pietro Tacca (1577–1640), a disciple of Giovanni da *Bologna, produced the characteristic fountain with the four moors at Livorno, the fountains of the Annunziata, and the bronzes of the chapel of the Principi. The sculptural decoration by Giovanni Battista Foggini (1652–1725) for the church of the Carmine constitutes the masterpiece of Florentine baroque.

In Bologna the Carracci influenced the sculptors Camillo Mazza (1602–72), Gabriello Brunelli (1615–82), and G. B. Barberini (d. 1666). In Venice, where colorism triumphed in sculpture, Alessandro *Vittoria (1525–1608) was the leader of Italian and foreign sculptors who gathered around him. In Sicily various tendencies of Italian baroque sculpture met in the Arcadian grace and youthful elegance of the works of Giacomo Serpotta (1656–1732).

France. French sculpture was dominated by Flemish and Italian influences and closely connected to the old mannerist tradition, but moderation and balance and the persistent return to classical inspiration still characterized the French art. François Girardon (1628–

1715), whose work was in accord with standards of the French Academy, achieved a remarkable refinement of execution in his elegant statuary for the gardens of Versailles and the courtly tomb of Richelieu in the church of the Sorbonne. Charles Antoine Coysevox (1640–1720), creator of the luxurious interior decoration of the Escalier des Ambassadeurs, the Galerie des Glaces, and the Salon de la Guerre, combined the incisive portraiture of Bernini with French naturalism.

Pierre *Puget (1620–94), a student of Cortona both in Rome and in Florence, was an isolated, morose artist who lived and worked far removed from the atmosphere of Versailles. There are glimpses of the work of Michelangelo in Puget's Palace of the Commune in Toulouse. His antiacademic and fiercely reactionary character is evident in his statues, "Milo of Crotona" and "Alexander and Diogenes."

The Low Countries. François Duquesnoy, who went from Brussels to Rome, where, by his own choice, he became an Italian citizen, left behind a younger brother, Jerome (1602–54), also a sculptor of very considerable merit. Artus Quellin the Elder (1609–68) produced the decorations of the Communal Palace of Amsterdam. In this period the art of the Low Countries was dominated by the robust personality of Rubens, who transmitted a measure of his powerful inspiration to all the work of the period.

Jean Delcour (1627–1707), who had been a student of Bernini in Rome, created the statues of the fountains in Liège and the tomb of the bishop of Allarmont in the church of St. Bavon in Ghent. Adriaen de Vries (c. 1560–1626) was from Holland but worked mainly in Germany. In Holland, members of the De Keyser family, led by Hendrik (c. 1560–1626), were successful sculptors.

England. English sculpture in the 17th century did not rise to the heights attained in the other European countries, though the nation had a few important artists: Nicholas Stone (1586–1647), who collaborated with Inigo Jones; Grinling Gibbons (1648–1721), who produced notable sculptures in wood; and Caius Gabriel Cibber (1630–1700), a sculptor and architect who was educated in Rome.

Germany. German sculpture of the baroque period was important. Some of the artists, such as Hans Reichle (c. 1570–1642) and Hans Krumpper (c. 1570–1634), received their training from Dutch artists. The characteristics of baroque art were developed on a substratum of Gothic motifs in the work of Hans Degler (d. 1637), Jörg Zürn (c. 1583–c. 1635), Matthias Rauchmiller (1645–86), and J. Meinrad Guggengichler (1645–86). The most notable artist of the early 18th century was Andreas Schlüter (c. 1660–1714), who had learned from Bernini, Tacca, Mochi, and Algardi. Balthasar Permoser (1651–1732), a sculptor of less talent than Schlüter, worked in Florence under Foggini's influence. His statues for the altar of the court church in Dresden suggest Bernini's influence and foreshadow the rococo.

Spain. Baroque sculpture in Spain developed without outside influences or sources, the pure product of local taste and inspiration. This seems rather strange, since Spain, in the preceding century, had been remarkably influenced by Italian artists. In accord with the typical Spanish taste, the statues were intensely mystical, and this effect was strengthened by the use of polychrome, which the painters of the period added to the work of the sculptors.

The sculpture of Gregorio Hernández (c. 1576–1636) is sensitive, impassioned, and intensely realistic. His best pieces are: the Pietà, St. Bruno, and the Baptism of Christ in the Valladolid Museum, and the Virgin of the Agony in the church of the Holy Cross. Hernández was the greatest artist of the Castilian school. Juan Martinez Montañés (1568–1649) was the best of the school of Seville and brought polychromed sculpture to a peak of perfection through the influence of Velázquez, who was his friend. Among his best known works are the crucifix in the cathedral of Seville and the statues of St. Dominic, of St. Bruno, and of the Infant Jesus in the church of Sagrario.

The work of Alonso Cano (1601–67), a pupil of Montañés, is characterized by greater delicacy, a more refined sense of color, and a more sensitive idealization. Examples of his work are the statues of St. Anthony in Murcia and of the Virgin in Belèn, and other works in Granada. His best student was Pedro de Mena (1628–88), with whom the baroque period of Spanish sculpture ended rather gloriously since De Mena was gifted with infinite richness of expression and a fine sense of the dramatic.

PAINTING

The conflicting traits of baroque art were fully exploited in the painting of the period. Though the compositions are organic, their unity is not that to be found in orderly disposition of elements. The world they picture is seen more often as an impassioned, fragmentary vision than as an idealized reproduction in microcosm of the universal order. The painting overflows the limitation of the frame, as in some of the great ceilings of the period, and is made to be deliberately indistinguishable from architectural ornament and accessory sculpture. Light and shade are used not, as had been prescribed in the Renaissance, to capture the external reality of the subject represented in all its visible nuances but rather to create an intense theatrical fullness or, as in the paintings of Rembrandt, to express the complexity of human character.

Italy. In Rome the process of rejecting 16th-century art principles was quickened by the presence of *Caravaggio, whose influence on foreign painters and in particular on the Italians who came to Rome from all parts of Italy reached its height in the first decades of the 17th century. Light became a new instrument in the hands of the artist, and innovations were made in iconographic programming and interpretation. Because of the support furnished by the Church and the increase in the number of collectors during this period, Rome was the most favorable center for this revolution.

The work of the Roman baroque artists was oriented in a classical direction by the *Carracci of Bologna. Their painting constituted an influence second in importance to that of Caravaggio. All three of the Carracci brothers embodied the ideas of the Renaissance in their work but transformed them into something entirely new by profiting from the advances made during the 16th century.

In 1595 Annibale Carracci (1560–1609) went to Rome, where he remained until his death. It was during this period that prime conditions existed for the formation of baroque art. Annibale's work in Rome was so impressive that it influenced even Caravaggio; Orazio Gentileschi (1563–1647) and Carlo Saraceni (c. 1585–1620) were influenced both by Caravaggio and the Carracci.

When Gentileschi reached Rome, he had already been so thoroughly educated in the Tuscan school that, though he assimilated characteristics from Caravaggio in his work, he nevertheless remained almost an independent artist. He became the standard bearer of the style he inaugurated, and he carried it even to Paris and to London, remaining in the latter city until his death. Like Gentileschi, Saraceni came to Rome with a local temperament and style but he swiftly adapted himself to the new currents in art.

Rome was a metropolis of painters: Orazio Borgianni (c. 1578–1616), whose work was influenced by his stay in Spain; Marcantonio Bassetti (1586–1630) and Alessandro Turchi (1578–1649) from Verona; Bartolomeo Cavarozzi (c. 1590–1625) from Viterbo; Francesco Rustici (d. 1626), Orazio Riminaldi (1586–1630), and Rutilio Manetti (1571–1639) from Tuscany; Domenico Fiasella (1589–1669) from Genoa; and Tanzio da Varallo (c. 1580–1635), Nicolò Musso (d. c. 1620), and Giuseppe Vermiglio (active 1604–35) from the Piedmont. The work of all these artists was influenced by Caravaggio, though each preserved characteristics he had brought from his local region. The last period of Roman baroque art was characterized by the Bamboccianti movement and the painting of Michelangelo Cerquozzi (1602–60) and Viviano Codazzi (1603–72).

The decorating of the Farnese Palace in Rome was a significant baroque project. The numerous artists from Emilia who came to Rome to do this work adopted the classical principles of the Carracci. They included Francesco Albani (1578–1660), Zampieri Domenichino (1581–1641), Guido Reni (1575–1642), and Giovanni Lanfranco (1582–1647). Reni was the most noted of them and for a long time was considered one of the major artists of the period. He had absorbed a delicacy in expressing ideas from *Raphael, emotional perception from Caravaggio, and the lyricism of Lodovico Carracci (1555–1619). His exquisite use of color and refinement of line and subject make Reni the best of the successors of the Carracci and also the source of inspiration of some of the forms characteristic of French art in the 18th century.

Roman baroque painting reached its peak in the polished rhetorical style of Pietro da Cortona. His use of the precedents set by Caravaggio and the Carracci, to which he added elements from the Venetian school, made him an exceptionally influential painter. His wide following included: Giovanni Battista Gaulli (1639–1709) of Genoa, Andrea Pozzo of Trentino, Giovanni Francesco Romanelli (1616–62) of Viterbo, Giacinto Gimignani (1611–81) of Pistoia, Francesco Allegrini of Gubbio (c. 1624–63), and Ciro Ferri (1634–89) of Rome.

Although Rome was the center at this time of Italian baroque painting, there were other Italian schools that, though basically influenced by Rome, displayed a variety of tastes and tendencies. Works of more than ordinary interest were produced in Naples by G. B. Caracciolo known as Battistello (c. 1570–1637), Carlo Sellito

(1581–1614), Paolo Finoglia (c. 1590–1656), and Massimo Stanzione (1586–1656). Baroque art was continued in Naples by the Calabrian artist Mattia Cuti, whose lyrical escapism provided a transition to the *rococo.

The principal painters of still life in southern Italy were Giovambattista and Giuseppe Ruoppolo, Giuseppe Recco (1634–95), and Paolo Porpora (1617–c. 1673). Flowers, fish, game, and objects of all kinds were vividly presented in their canvases mingling Flemish realism with the warmth of the Italian temperament. The type of still-life painting with rich chromatic tonalities that flourished in Naples was produced by Evaristo Baschenis (1617–77), whose paintings give evidence of the influence of Caravaggio interpreted in a provincial manner.

The baroque painting of Genoa shows the Flemish influence of Rubens in the richness of its colors and forms, as in the work of Assereto and Strozzi. Chromatic affectation and refinement are characteristic of this school, which ended with a whole generation of decorators. In Lombardy during this period mannerism held sway. G. B. Crespi called Cerano (c. 1575–1633), P. F. Mazzucchelli called Morazzone (1571–1626), and Giulio Cesare Procaccini (1570–1625) were its principal artists, together with Carlo Francesco Nuvoloni (1609–62), who was deeply influenced by the Spanish school. In Emilia, Giovanni Francesco *Guercino, (1591–1666) produced works of note.

In Venice the 17th century passed without the emergence of new characteristics. The splendor of the preceding century was preserved and presaged the grandeur that lay ahead. The artists of the period were not born there but came from other parts of Italy. For example, Domenico Fetti (1589–1624) was from Rome, Bernardo Strozzi (1581–1664) from Genoa, and Luca Giordano (1632–1705) was from Naples. Francesco Maffei (d. 1660) of Vicenza worked in a more typically Venetian style, initiating the manner that, with the work of Sebastiano Ricci (1659–1734), reveals the beginning of the taste of the following century.

France. As in other fields of artistic endeavor, French painting of the period drew its inspiration from Italian art. The French painters were influenced by Caravaggio and the Carracci, especially with regard to the use of light and volume.

Valentin de Boulogne (1594–1632) went to Rome in 1612, and shortly after his arrival one of his paintings was placed above an altar in St. Peter's. This artist, though he employed the techniques of Caravaggio in a sentimental and romantic manner, left his mark on the art of the period of France. Simon Vouet (1590–1649) and Jean Le Clerc (1587–1633) of Nancy also worked in Rome, the latter carrying back to France the influence of Saraceni.

In the French provinces, the artists who returned from Italy brought with them the influence of Caravaggio, with noticeable results. The canvases of Georges de *La Tour are obviously indebted to Caravaggio, along with artists of the Flemish school who had taught him the use of light. Simon Vouet experienced Italian baroque painting at the peak of its expressiveness. After his return from Rome, he reached the heights of success. He was a swift and fecund decorator who became a court painter to Louis XIII. He had a flourishing school of students, each of whom succeeded in developing his individual bent. This school of vigorous, enthusiastic painting was counterbalanced by the calmly classic, theorizing school of Nicolas *Poussin (1594–1665). The cultivation and lyricism of Poussin, based on mythological and classical sources, was popular in France for only a short time. The need for an artist with a less intellectual, more human appeal was met by *Claude Lorrain (1600–82), who satisfied the taste for more modern scenes filled with lyrical emotion.

In 1648 the Academy was founded, and Charles Le Brun (1619–90) eventually became its chancellor. He was admired by all the important political figures of France and supported by Louis XIV, who considered him the greatest painter of the period. Le Brun dominated French art for a long time but never freed himself completely from the influence of the court and the Academy. The painters of still life and genre subjects turned to the Flemish school for their inspiration.

Spain. The influence of Caravaggio was easily absorbed by the Spanish artistic temperament. Large collections of Italian paintings, and the presence of Italian artists like the Carducci brothers, Nardi, and Caxes resulted in the establishment of close artistic ties between Italy and Spain. Among the initiators of the new school of Spanish painting in the 17th century was Francisco Ribalta (c. 1555–1628), the master of Jusepe de *Ribera (1588–1652). Ribera's work was deeply influenced by the Roman school, though he profited from a stay also in Naples.

Spain produced three individualistic artists: *Velázquez, *Murillo, and *Zurbarán. The work of Francisco de Zurbarán (1598–1661), while it was characteristic of the spirit of the time, stands alone because of its mystical character. The figures in his paintings were the perfect expression of his religious sentiments. He used line and color in a completely individual manner. But after he went to Madrid, he painted in a softer style, symptomatic of the crisis of the school of Seville. Diego Rodríguez Velázquez (1599–1660), based his painting on the details of everyday life. His approach was formed by two visits to Rome, where he encountered the Bamboccianti movement, whose aims were in accord with his own search for naturalistic expression. His work left its mark on a whole period of Spanish painting; all the artists of his time gravitated around him, while retaining their special interests. In the work of Bartolomé Estéban Murillo (1617–82), plastic and dramatic accents were superseded by a great tenderness, a play of refined chiaroscuro, and a complete range of sentimental affections. His elegant, realistic, and detailed genre paintings were popular. The period of the greatest success of still-life painting was indebted to the work of these three masters.

Germany. There was no autonomous school of painting in Germany in the 17th century, probably because of the Thirty Years' War. But Johann Liss (1570–1629) must be mentioned; his painting showed the influence of Caravaggio and presaged the rococo of Giovanni Battista *Tiepolo (1696–1770) and Giambattista Piazzetta (1682–1754). Adam *Elsheimer (1578–1620) admirably combined in his painting Caravaggio's use of light and the ideas and principles of the Carracci.

Fig. 3. Giuseppe Recco, "Still-life with Fish," oil on canvas, Museo di San Martino, Naples.

Fig. 2. Pierre Puget, "St. Sebastian," in the church of S. Maria di Carignano, Genoa.

Fig. 5. Velázquez, "Adoration of the Magi," oil on canvas, in the Prado, Madrid.

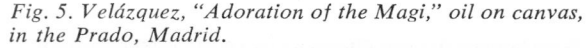

Fig. 4. Nicolas Poussin, "The Holy Family," oil on canvas, 28 by 21⅞ inches, 1641.

Fig. 6. Zurbarán, "The Miracle of St. Hugo," oil on canvas, Provincial Museum, Seville.

BAROQUE ART

Fig. 8. Peter Paul Rubens, "The Holy Family," oil on canvas, in the Pitti Palace, Florence.

Fig. 7. Rembrandt van Rijn, "Titus in a Monk's Habit," oil on canvas, 31¼ by 26½ inches.

Holland and Flanders. Dutch baroque painting is quite different from that of other countries. One reason for this difference is that the source of patronage had changed. Instead of kings and nobles, it was middle-class merchants. The large, austere canvases suitable for the ample rooms of royal palaces were replaced by small easel paintings that could easily be hung in the small rooms of more modest homes. Thus the tendency to illustration developed under the more active search for realism. Utrecht in Holland and Antwerp in Flanders were the most important centers for painting.

The two artists who were most influenced by Caravaggio were Hendrik *Terbrugghen and Dirk van Baburen (c. 1590–1624). Terbrugghen was a less dramatic painter than Baburen, but he produced genre paintings that portray Dutch life with the utmost sensitivity. Terbrugghen's color is luminous, his form highly refined. Another Dutch artist who lived in Rome a long time, Gerard van Honthorst (1590–1656), became known for candlelight effects. These three artists had numerous followers. Frans Hals (d. 1666) of Haarlem made portrait painting human and realistic; he had many followers.

Light and color in all their aspects and with all their attendant problems found their finest expression in the work of *Rembrandt van Rijn (1606–69). No regard for tradition could prevent this artist from throwing himself into a modernism without limits. All the emotions that swept through his soul were concretized in tormented, burning color employed in strong compositions. He is unequaled in his use of the portrait as a vehicle for setting forth the tragedy of the human condition. Rembrandt was also a master in painting landscapes, which he employed not merely as background but as an integral component of his paintings of figures. His engravings round out the work of this artist as an outlet for the torment of his soul. His work is in some respects the profoundest expression of the baroque age. So many artists followed him and continued his work that it is impossible to enumerate them.

Along with these international artists a flourishing school of provincial artists developed. They gave further expression to national tendencies that had appeared in the work of their predecessors. Hunting, battle, and animal scenes portrayed with extensive landscape backgrounds fill their canvases.

In Flanders the spirit of the Counter Reformation and the strong influence of *humanism combined to strengthen the restoration of the Church. Peter Paul *Rubens (1577–1640), the greatest painter of this period, is most noted for his great cycles of paintings like those of Marie de Médici for the Luxembourg Palace in Paris, the ceiling of White Hall in London, and the series, now lost, of paintings for the church of the Jesuits in Antwerp. He is noted also for his small paintings. In them Rubens was freed from the limitations of subject and dimensions imposed by the large canvases and painted in a manner that foreshadowed the romantic style.

Rubens's studio was crowded with students who carried on the tradition of the master without altering the spirit of his work. Two artists of completely different tendencies became noticeable, viz, Anthony *van Dyck (1599–1641), who did polished portraits of the aristocracy, and Jacob Jordaens (1593–1678), who painted rough, plebeian people. Van Dyck's work had an immediate and explosive success, and in Spain, Italy, and France his style of painting was universally adopted. In England, both he and Rubens were court painters during the region of Charles I.

As a result of the work done in the Lowlands, especially by Jacob Ruisdael (c. 1628–82), landscape painting became popular and spread all over Europe, and concomitant with it the taste for still-life painting spread as well.

Bibliography: For bibliography on baroque art, see C. CALCATERRA, *Il problema del Barocco* (Milan 1945). G. GETTO, *La polemica sul Barocco* (Milan 1954). EncWA 2:373–381. A. E. BRINCKMANN, *Barockskulptur*, 2 v. (Berlin 1919). W. WEISBACH, *Der Barock als Kunst der Gegenreformation* (Berlin 1921). M. J. FRIEDLÄNDER, *Die niederländischen Maler des 17. Jahrhunderts* (3d ed. Berlin 1923). S. SITWELL, *Southern Baroque Art* (London 1924); *Spanish Baroque Art* (London 1931); *German Baroque Sculpture* (London 1938). H. WÖLFFLIN, *Renaissance und Barock* (4th ed. Munich 1926), Eng. *Renaissance and Baroque*, tr. K. SIMON from the original Ger. ed. of 1888 (London 1964); *Principles of Art History*, tr. M. D. HOTTINGER (London 1932; repr. New York 1950). B. CROCE, *Storia della età barocca* (Scritti di storia letteraria e politica 23; Bari 1929). E. MÂLE, *L'Art religieux après le Concile de Trente* (Paris 1932; 2d ed. *L'Art religieux de la fin du XVIe siècle . . .*, Paris 1951). A. K. McCOMB, *The Baroque Painters of Italy* (Cambridge, Mass. 1934). E. K. WATERHOUSE, *Baroque Painting in Rome* (London 1937). Fokker RomBarArt. D. MAHON, *Studies in Seicento Art and Theory* (London 1947). A. BLUNT, *Art and Architecture in France 1500–1700* (PelHArt 24; 1953). W. F. FRIEDLÄNDER, *Caravaggio Studies* (Princeton 1955). H. P. LANDOLT, *Der barocke Raum in der Architektur: Die Kunstformen des Barockzeitalters* (Munich 1956). A. PIGLER, *Barockthemen: Eine Auswahl von Verzeichnissen zur Ikonographie des 17. und 18. Jahrhunderts*, 2 v. (Budapest 1956). R. WITTKOWER, *Art and Architecture in Italy, 1600–1750* (PelHArt Z16; 1958). G. KUBLER and M. SORIA, *Art and Architecture in Spain and Portugal and Their American Dominions, 1500–1800* (PelHArt Z17; 1959). **Illustration credits:** Figs. 1*a*, 1*c*, 2 and 8, Alinari-Art Reference Bureau. Fig. 1*b*, MAS, Barcelona. Fig. 4, Courtesy of the Detroit Institute of Arts. Figs. 5 and 6, Anderson-Art Reference Bureau. Fig. 7, Rijksmuseum, Amsterdam.

[S. GALIGANI]

BAROQUE THEOLOGY, the term describing the theology of the baroque age extending from 1550 to 1750 with its apex from 1590 to 1650. A new resurgence of Christian life springing from Tridentine renovations found expression in an elaborate, joyous, overawing art embodying not only a feeling of the freedom of faith, but a protest against Reformation variance and a revolt against Catholic absolute rulers and secular humanism. *Baroque art portrayed the exaltation of the Virgin, the supremacy of the papacy; it defended the Church's sacramental life and acclaimed the charity of the saints. Through symbol it fostered new devotions (Sacred Heart); through themes of ecstasy, it manifested the triumph of Christian mysticism.

Thus post-Tridentine theology is marked by Christian humanism. Under the leadership of the Jesuits, the humanity of God Incarnate was emphasized and man's sensitive, appetitive, and intellectual powers were fully enlisted. Influential were *The *Spiritual Exercises* of St. Ignatius and the "devout humanism" of St. Francis de Sales. In mystical theology, St. Teresa of Avila and St. John of the Cross predominate. Of singular importance in theological development were: the controversial theology of St. Robert Bellarmine, Thomas Stapleton, and Jakob Gretser; the new impetus given to patristic study,

Biblical science (introductions, textual criticisms), and Canon Law; and the revival of scholastic theology.

See also THEOLOGY, HISTORY OF.

Bibliography: A. BAER, Davis CDT 1:238–241. L. LENHART and F. STEGMÜLLER, LexThK² 1:1258–70. É. MÂLE, "Religious Art after the Council of Trent," *Religious Art from the Twelfth to the Eighteenth Century* (New York 1949) 167–199.

[M. A. HOTZE]

BARRANDE, JOACHIM, paleontologist and stratigrapher whose work in Bohemia made that area a classic ground of geology; b. Sangues (Haute-Loire), France, Aug. 11, 1799; d. Frohsdorf, Bohemia, Oct. 5, 1883. He graduated from the École Polytechnique (1821) and the École des Ponts et Chaussées (1824) with high honors. He studied under G. Cuvier, A. Brongniart, A. L. de *Jussieu, and Constant Prévost. Soon after graduation, he became tutor to the Comte de Chambord, the King's grandson, whom he served all his life. When the Bourbons went into exile in 1830, Barrande followed his master, serving him in later life as superintendent of finances. He was a deeply religious man, a royalist who believed in the divine right of kings, and an able and respected scientist. He had ample means, and his duties were light; he and the Count became interested in geology and collected intelligently from an area of 140 square miles in Bohemia. His industry and that of his many assistants resulted in the accumulation of enormous collections and the publication of his masterpiece, *Systême Silurien du Centre de la Bohême,* in more than 20 volumes, richly illustrated.

Bibliography: J. KOLIHA, "Joachim Barrande and His Paleontological Work," *Nature* 133 (1934) 437–438.

[A. LA ROCQUE]

BARRÉ, NICOLAS, pedagogue, founder of the Schools of Charity and of the Sisters of the Holy Infant Jesus; b. Amiens, France, Oct. 21, 1621; d. Paris, May 31, 1686. At 18 he entered the Order of the Minims and he was professed at Amiens in 1641. Even before his ordination he was given the chair of theology at Paris; he kept it with honor for 20 years. In Paris at the convent of the Royal Square, he had as confreres illustrious men of science, of wide knowledge, and profound spirituality. Although he trained many students in scholastic as well as spiritual matters, he spent the major part of his ministry in preaching, spiritual direction, and the great work of instituting free popular teaching. In Rouen first (1662) and later in Paris, he founded and directed those Schools of Charity of the Holy Infant Jesus that became models throughout France. To these schools he gave program, method, and teachers whose religious, cultural, and didactic preparation he scrupulously supervised. The Institute of the Sisters of the Holy Infant Jesus had two distinct branches: one in Rouen, also called the "Institute of Providence"; the other one in Paris, called the "Institute of the Dames of St. Maur," from the house of its foundation. Barré considered also a male branch of the Congregation: the "Teachers." This, however, was accomplished in the foundation of the Brothers of the Christian Schools by St. John de la Salle, whom Barré had directed, advised, and encouraged. He had a solid base of Thomistic theology and a sense of equilibrium that enabled him to avoid the excesses of rigorism and laxism. He fought both Jansenism and

quietism. Humility, faith, charity, mortification, and personal encounter with Jesus in the Eucharist are the pillars of his spiritual doctrine. He was an advocate of frequent Communion, and often affirmed that Holy Communion is the best disposition for Holy Communion. His extant spiritual works are: *Lettres spirituelles* (Rouen 1697; Tolouse 1876) and *Maximes spirituelles* (Paris 1694). His cause of beatification was introduced before the Sacred Congregation of Rites in 1931.

Bibliography: HENRI DE GRÈZES, *Vie du R. P. Barré . . .* (Bar-le-Duc 1892). G. MORETTI, *Un pedagogista santo* (Rome 1929); EncCatt 2:893–894. R. CHALUMEAU, *Catholicisme* 1:1263.

[A. BELLANTONIO]

BARREDA, IGNACIO MARÍA, Mexican painter; fl. 1775 to 1815. There is little information on his life. Like so many painters of the same period, he must have been a disciple of some of the earlier great masters, possibly of Miguel *Cabrera. After working as apprentices, artists went through various ranks before reaching that of masters, following the hierarchical scale that existed in all the guilds of New Spain, a survival of the medieval European guilds. Barreda painted

Dona María Manuela Romero, by Ignacio María Barreda in the Museum of Chapultepec. The attention to details of the period costume is typical of the artist's work.

mostly portraits. Rare during the 16th century and scarce during the 17th, portraits began to increase in the 18th century, and as time passed they were more and more common. Wealthy families had their portrait galleries; the universities, the schools, the guilds, and the monasteries made collections of portraits of their most outstanding members.

During this time, Barreda flourished, producing portraits through which he developed his uncommon gifts as an observer. His known paintings, whether of ladies (such as that of María Manuela Romero in the Museum of Chapultepec) or of gentlemen, give us, in addition to psychological studies of the subjects, a multitude of details on the way in which people dressed. Barreda's portraits are of two types, of the entire body or of the bust. He painted also some groups. Toussaint notes as a work of Barreda a large painting of Archbishop Haro y Peralta awarding prizes to the pupils of the seminary. No exhaustive study has yet been made of this painter, who may fairly be considered one of the best portrait painters of the end of the 18th century. Unfortunately, many of the series of portraits, both private and public, that were collected during the 18th century and to which Barreda contributed, were scattered during the period of Reform (1850–70). His known works are in the Museum of Chapultepec and in various private collections.

Bibliography: M. TOUSSAINT, *Arte colonial en México* (2d ed. Mexico City 1962). P. M. ROJAS RODRÍGUEZ, *Época colonial*, v.2 of *Historia general del arte mexicano* (Mexico City 1962–). **Illustration credit:** Archivo Fotográfico, Instituto Nacional de Antropología, Mexico.

[G. OBREGÓN]

BARRIENTOS, PEDRO NOLASCO, educator in Argentina; b. Paraguay, 1734; d. Buenos Aires, Oct. 15, 1810. He was the son of Juan Barrientos and Francisca Díaz Barbosa. In 1749 he entered the Franciscan Order in Buenos Aires where he did his ecclesiastical studies. In the competition for a professorship in philosophy, his presentation was considered outstanding. He became a lector, confessor, and preacher. In 1754 he was named master of students of the Franciscan convent, but left for Córdoba, where he was to do his principal work. On April 25, 1768, he was chosen rector of the University of Córdoba and he held this position until 1777. He also held the chair of sacred theology for many of those years. While he was rector he introduced many reforms in the modification of the constitution. He reorganized the program of studies of the university, thereby greatly increasing its prestige. His administration was memorable, earning the praise of the Church, the viceroys, and the governors. He was well versed in theology, philosophy, civil law, and Canon Law, as his writings show. He served for a time as counselor to the Viceroy Don Pedro Melo of Portugal. He was transferred to Buenos Aires, and died in the Convento de la Observancia, where he is buried.

Bibliography: L. R. ALTAMIRA, *El Seminario conciliar de Nuestra Señora de Loreto, colegio mayor de la Universidad de Córdoba* (Córdoba 1943).

[V. O. CUTOLO]

BARRIÈRE, JEAN DE LA, founder of the *Feuillants; b. Saint-Céré, France, April 29, 1544; d. Rome, April 25, 1600. His parents were nobles. After studying in Toulouse and Bordeaux, he was granted the Cistercian Abbey of Les Feuillans *in commendam* in 1565. He went to Paris to complete his studies and, influenced by Arnaud d'Ossat (a future cardinal), resolved to reform his abbey. In 1573 he became a Cistercian and was ordained. In 1577, after initial difficulties about the severity of his reforms, he became regular abbot with two novices and two professed clerics. Vocations multiplied until in 1587 there were 140 members. As an independent reform congregation, the Feuillants spread in France and Italy. Barrière became the first general superior but was deposed in 1592, unjustly accused for his part in the civil war raging in France. He bore the humiliation patiently, spending his last years in confinement in Rome. He was rehabilitated a few months before his death by the intervention of Cardinal Robert *Bellarmine. Pope Clement VIII, recalling the heroic nature of his asceticism, called him "blessed."

Bibliography: J. M. CANIVEZ, DHGE 6:924–926. Lenssen HagCist 1:173–176. E. G. KRENIG, LexThK² 2:2. M. STANDAERT, DictSpirAscMyst 5:274–287.

[L. J. LEKAI]

BARRIOS, GERARDO, president of El Salvador; b. 1813; d. San Salvador, Aug. 29, 1865. Barrios was a political liberal and a supporter of *Morazán. He too was an advocate of Central American federation. His military career included participation in 1857 in the defense against the invasion of Central America by William Walker. In 1858 he took over the government of El Salvador in a coup d'état and got legislative approval for the act as well as constitutional amendments to lengthen the presidential term. He required the clergy to take an oath of allegiance to the government. Most refused to do so and were expelled from the country. This was an excuse to introduce liberal and efficient government and to foster education. However, R. Carrera invaded the country from Guatemala and, on his second attempt, forced Barrios to surrender San Salvador. Barrios went to Panama, was captured by the Nicaraguans, and was taken to León. From there he was extradited to El Salvador, where he was court-martialed and shot.

[J. HERRICK]

BARRON, EDWARD, missionary bishop; b. Ballyneale, County Waterford, Ireland, June 28, 1801; d. Savannah, Ga., Sept. 12, 1854. As the youngest son of wealthy Pierse and Anna (Winston) Barron, Edward had exceptional educational advantages. He read successfully a law course at Trinity College, Dublin, to qualify for the Irish bar. In 1825 he began studies for the priesthood and in 1829 was ordained in Rome, returning to teach at St. John's College, Waterford, Ireland. Despite delicate health, he accepted Bp. Francis Kenrick's invitation to be rector of the Philadelphia, Pa., seminary. "Too easily imposed on," Barron was removed from the seminary. As pastor of St. Mary's, Philadelphia, and vicar-general, he volunteered for Liberia when Rome asked Kenrick (1840) to send priests to that difficult mission. Reluctantly, Kenrick released his talented vicar-general. While enroute Barron was named prefect apostolic of Upper Guinea; before his consecration in Rome on Nov. 1, 1842, his jurisdiction was extended to Sierra Leone and the whole western coast of Africa that was not under the care of other ecclesiastical authority.

In France the bishop procured seven priests of the Congregation of the Immaculate Heart and three young laymen. Difficulties arose at Cape Palmas, where the French missionaries were suspected of being instruments to extend the French West African empire. Barron consequently transferred all but one of his missionaries to French territory; however, the group, which had been joined by two from Ireland, was ravaged by disease, and only the bishop and one priest reached Senegal alive. Barron made a fresh start at Goree, planning a seminary. Again the climate caused the death of nearly all his priests, and in 1845 the sickly bishop resigned. He returned to the U.S. and assisted Bp. Peter Kenrick of St. Louis, Mo., especially with his Indian missions. Although both Kenricks wanted Barron as an auxiliary bishop, their requests were never honored.

Barron contracted advanced pulmonary tuberculosis and spent his final years as a missionary in Florida. In July 1854, for health reasons, he left Florida for Philadelphia, but hurried to Savannah when he heard of the yellow fever epidemic in Georgia. While administering to the sick, he succumbed to the fever.

Bibliography: M. J. Bane, *The Catholic Story of Liberia* (New York 1950); *Catholic Pioneers in West Africa* (Dublin 1956). R. K. MacMaster, "Bishop Barron and the West African Missions, 1841–1845," HistRecStud 50 (1964) 83–129.

[H. J. NOLAN]

BARROS, JOÃO DE, Portuguese historian and essayist, the greatest chronicler of the Portuguese conquests in the Orient; b. probably Viseu, Portugal, *c.* 1496; d. Ribeira de Litém, Oct. 20, 1570. As a boy he was appointed gentleman of the wardrobe of the future King, John III, thus beginning a career of government service that terminated on his retirement in 1567 as Factor of the Casa da Índia. He wrote one of the first romances of chivalry, *Crónica do Imperador Clarimundo* (1522), one episode of which may have been a source of *Camões' Os Lusíadas* (1570), as well as essays on morals and language, some of which are now lost. His *Ropicapnefma* (1532) is a philosophical dialogue tinged with Erasmian ideas and dealing with contemporary religious and social problems. He was the author of a Portuguese grammar, *Gramática da língua portuguesa* (1540) published with a defense of the national tongue, *Diálogo em louvor da nossa linguagem.* His *Panegíricos* on John III and the Infanta Maria (1655) are didactic essays on the moral qualities of their royal subjects and on the characteristics of the good prince.

From the time of *Clarimundo* Barros had been perfecting his style and gathering materials for the great work of his life, a panoramic study of Portuguese overseas expansion. It was to have included books on Asia, Africa, Brazil, and Europe and to have been arranged under the categories of conquest, navigation and commerce. The only part published (1552, 1553, 1563) during his lifetime comprised the first three sections or *Décadas* on the conquest of Asia; these carry the history up to 1526. The fourth *Década,* with additions and alterations by João Baptista Lavanha, appeared in 1615. Taking Livy as his inspiration, Barros attempted in his *Décadas* to erect a noble monument to Portuguese achievement. He was never in India, but he worked with documents that have since disappeared. The *Décadas* are of great interest historically, for the light they shed

upon Portuguese life in the Orient. They are marked by passages of unusual eloquence.

Bibliography: A. BAIÃO, *Documentos inéditos sôbre João de Barros* (Coimbra 1917). J. DE BARROS, *Ásia,* ed. H. A. CIDADE (6th ed. Lisbon 1945–) v.1. Primeira década.

[R. S. SAYERS]

BARROS ARANA, DIEGO

Chilean historian, educator, and public servant; b. Santiago, 1830; d. there, November 1907. He was educated at the Instituto Nacional of Chile. He early revealed intellectual leanings, and in 1853 he published a review, *El Museo,* which contained his first literary efforts. Noteworthy among his first works of research is his *Historia de la independencia de Chile* (4 v. 1856–58). Because of his political activities Barros Arana was obliged to leave the country during the final years of

Diego Barros Arana.

*Montt's administration (1851–61). His travels to Argentina, France, England, and Spain gave him the opportunity to visit the libraries and archives and to add to his collection of historical documents. When he returned to Chile, he was appointed rector of the Instituto Nacional. During his 10 years in that post he introduced reforms in secondary teaching, one of which was the introduction of scientific subjects into the curriculum. He also wrote several textbooks; some, e.g., his *Historia de América* (2 v. 1865) and his *Elementos de geografía física* (1870), were given wide distribution and have been used in schools in a number of Latin American countries. In 1876 he was sent to Buenos Aires on an important diplomatic mission that gave him the opportunity to study the border dispute between Chile and Argentina. When he returned to Chile, he began to write his *Historia general de Chile,* the first volume of which appeared in 1884. The work is a veritable encyclopedia of historical, geographical, and statistical information on the territory and the historical development of Chile. It begins with the discovery of the Strait of Magellan and the first geographical explorations of that part of America and ends with the promulgation of the Constitution of May 25, 1833, considered the cornerstone of Chile's political organization. The work is in 16 volumes, the last of which was published in 1902. This Chilean historian, with his special qualities and prejudices, is a characteristic American writer of the 19th century. He was a profound believer in the principles of economic liberalism and in the progress and unlimited perfectibility of society; his work is a clear reflection of the thought of liberal historians. In 1890 Barros Arana was appointed an adviser on the Argentina-Chile border question; the post had been created by the treaty of July 23, 1881. He spent almost 10 years in that post and published a book on this international problem, *La cuestión de límites entre Chile y la República Argentina* (1895). When the matter was submitted to the British government for arbitration, he wrote still another work to explain his geographical doctrine, *Exposición de los derechos de Chile* (1899). In 1893 Barros Arana was made rector of the University of Chile. He published a biography of Rodolfo A. Philippi and *Un decenio de la historia de Chile* (1841–1851; 2 v. 1906), the last of his important works.

Bibliography: *Obras completas,* 16 v. (Santiago de Chile 1908–14). R. DONOSO, *Barros Arana, educador, historiador, y hombre público* (Santiago de Chile 1931). **Illustration credit:** Library of Congress.

[R. DONOSO]

BARROW, ISAAC, English mathematician and theologian; b. London, October 1630; d. London, May 4, 1677. After attendance at Charterhouse and Felstead, Barrow completed his education at Trinity College, Cambridge, taking his degree in 1648. He accepted a fellowship in 1649. In 1655 he published his edition of Euclid's *Elements,* first in Latin and then in English (1660). In 1655 he began travels in eastern Europe, returning to England in 1659. He was ordained the next year and received an appointment to the chair of Greek at Cambridge, where he won a reputation as one of the best Greek scholars of his day. He was professor of geometry at Gresham College (1662–64), and in 1664 he was elected the first Lucasian professor at Cambridge. Six years later, however, he resigned in favor of his student, Isaac *Newton.

His most important work, *Lectiones Geometricae* (tr. J. M. Child, Chicago 1916), appeared in the same year as his resignation. In this publication he employed a near approach to the modern process of differentiation, utilizing the so-called differential triangle (*see* CALCULUS). Lectures delivered by him in 1664–66 were published as *Lectiones Mathematicae* (1683), as metaphysical bases for mathematical truths. His lectures on the analysis of Archimedes appeared in 1667.

After resignation from teaching, Barrow devoted the remainder of his life to the study of divinity. He did, however, publish an edition of the first four books of *Conics* by Apollonius, with numerous comments, and the extant works of Archimedes and Theodosius.

Bibliography: C. B. BOYER, *The Concepts of the Calculus* (New York 1949). H. EVES, *An Introduction to the History of Mathematics* (New York 1953).

[T. À K. KLOYDA]

BARRUEL, AUGUSTIN DE, Jesuit polemicist; b. Villeneuve de Berg (Ardèche), Oct. 2, 1741; d. Paris, Oct. 5, 1820. He entered the *Jesuits in 1756, was exiled (1762) with them, and returned to France on the occasion of their suppression (1774). In collaboration with Fréron on the *Année littéraire* from 1774, he attacked the *philosophes* in his *Helviennes ou Lettres provinciales philosophiques* (1781). He edited (1788–92) the *Journal ecclésiastique,* which he used to criticize the *French Revolution. He wrote pamphlets (1790–91) against the *Civil Constitution of the Clergy,

and then gathered into one *Collection ecclésiastique* (13 v. 1791–93) all documents on this subject. From England he published his *Histoire du clergé pendant la Revolution* (1784). His most provocative work, *Mémoires pour servir à l'histoire du Jacobinisme* (London 1787) underscored the role of Freemasonry and secret societies in the Revolution: his thesis, correct but too sweeping, precipitated a flood of refutations. Barruel returned to France at the fall of the Directory, and wrote in defense of the new political order. He upheld the *Concordat of 1801 and the right of the Pope to depose French bishops in *Du Pape et de ses droits religieux* (1803). He reentered the restored Society of Jesus (1815). His last years were spent preparing a refutation of Kant.

Bibliography: Sommervogel 1:930–945; 7:1767. J. J. DUSSAULT, *Notice sur la vie et les ouvrages d'Augustin de Barruel* (Paris 1825). R. DAESCHLER, DHGE 6:937.

[R. J. SEALY]

BARRY, SIR CHARLES, English architect, known primarily for his revival of high Renaissance building types and as architect of the Houses of Parliament; b. London, 1795; d. London, 1860. When Barry returned to England in 1820 from an architectural tour of the Continent, he found the Gothic revival firmly established in English architecture (*see* GOTHIC REVIVALISM). After designing several churches in this popular style for Manchester, Barry turned to the high relief style of Italian Renaissance architecture. Working against the neo-Gothic and Greek trends, he designed the Royal Institute of Fine Arts in Manchester and the Travellers' Club (1829) and the Reform Club (1837) in London, the London clubs being adaptations of the Italian *palazzo*. Builders of clubs and institutions found

Sir Charles Barry, by the English artist, J. P. Knight.

this "neo-Renaissance" style a satisfactory compromise between the extremes of the Greek and Gothic revivals, and Barry became a leading London architect for public buildings of this type. In 1836 Barry received the commission for the new Houses of Parliament. Despite the medieval decoration of the buildings by *Pugin, the buildings are laid out in neo-Palladian classicism by Barry; "Tudor details on a classic body," as Pugin himself put it. Barry also helped to establish the Victorian tradition of garden planning, i.e., elaborate formal gardens surrounding and subordinate to the house.

See also CHURCH ARCHITECTURE, 9.

Bibliography: H. R. HITCHCOCK, *Early Victorian Architecture in Britain*, 2 v. (New Haven 1954). J. N. SUMMERSON, *Architecture in Britain, 1530–1830* (4th ed. PelHArt Z3; 1963). **Illustration credit:** National Portrait Gallery, London.

[R. SWAIN]

BARRY, GERALD, MOTHER, educator, administrator; b. Inagh, Ennis, County Clare, Ireland, March 11, 1881; d. Adrian, Mich., Nov. 20, 1961. She was one of 18 children of Michael Barry, traveled scholar and prosperous farmer, and Catherine (Dixon) Barry, who had her christened Catherine Bridget. She immigrated to America as a young woman and engaged in business for several years before entering the Dominican Sisters of Adrian (Congregation of the Most Holy Rosary) Feb. 2, 1913. After making her vows (1914), she served as teacher and principal (1914–21), novice mistress (1921–33), and prioress general (1933–61). During her superiorship community membership increased from 930 to 2,480, and two senior colleges, four girls' high schools, and a sisters' house of studies (Washington, D.C.) were built. In addition, 70 parochial schools, a teachers' college (Nassau, Bahamas), and a businesswomen's residence were opened; an academy and two missions were established in Santo Domingo; and hundreds of sisters were assigned to study for baccalaureate and higher degrees. At the Holy See's request she acted as first executive chairman of the Sisters Committee for the National Congress of Religious in the U.S. (Notre Dame, Ind., August 1952); and she was appointed to preside at the Chicago, Ill., meeting of superiors (November 1956), from which developed the permanent Conference of Major Superiors of Women's Religious Institutes. She was the recipient of honorary degrees from the University of Santo Domingo (1949), Notre Dame (1952), and Loyola (1961) and was widely known as an energetic, humorous, and shrewd leader of her community.

Bibliography: M. GERALD BARRY, *The Charity of Christ Presses Us: Letters to Her Community*, ed. M. PHILIP RYAN (Milwaukee 1962). M. PAUL, "Mother Mary Gerald, O.P.," *Dominican Educational Bulletin* (Winter 1962).

[M. P. MC KEOUGH]

BARRY, JOHN, second bishop of Savannah, Ga.; b. Oylegate, County Wexford, Ireland, July 1799; d. Paris, France, Nov. 21, 1859. He studied under Bp. John England of Charleston, S.C., and was ordained there Sept. 24, 1825. He then served as assistant at the cathedral and secretary to the bishop until July 1828, when he was made pastor of St. Mary's Church, Charleston. Subsequently he was given charge of St. Peter's Church, Columbia, S.C. (1829), and later (1830) assigned to Holy Trinity Church, Augusta, Ga. At its Barnwell, S.C., mission he built St. Andrew's Church (dedicated 1833), the fourth Catholic church erected

in the state. When the Irish Volunteers of Charleston, a company of militia, joined the active forces in Florida at the outbreak of the Seminole War (1836), Barry was assigned as chaplain; he served with the unit throughout the campaign. During the yellow fever epidemic of 1839 in Augusta he turned his rectory into a hospital and obtained Sisters of Our Lady of Mercy from Charleston to attend the sick. He was highly commended by the city officials for his action. After the epidemic he conducted an orphanage in his rectory and opened a school.

He served as vicar-general under England and his successor, Bp. Ignatius Reynolds; attended the Fourth Provincial Council of Baltimore (1840) as England's theologian; and was named vicar-general of Savannah when that diocese was erected (1850). When Bp. Francis Gartland died in 1854, Barry was appointed administrator of Savannah and in that capacity attended the Eighth Provincial Council of Baltimore (1855). He was selected as bishop of Savannah and consecrated Aug. 2, 1857, in Baltimore, Md. However, he was already in poor health, and a year later, while traveling in Europe, he became seriously ill and died in the Paris hospital of the Brothers of St. John of God. Some years later his body was brought back to Georgia and buried in the crypt of St. Patrick's Church, Augusta.

Bibliography: J. J. O'CONNELL, *Catholicity in the Carolinas and Georgia 1820–1878* (New York 1879).

[R. C. MADDEN]

BARRY, JOHN, naval officer; b. Tacumshane, County Wexford, Ireland, 1745; d. Philadelphia, Pa., Sept. 13, 1803. He went to sea at the age of 10 and became master of a Philadelphia vessel about 1761. In the Revolutionary War he outfitted the first squadron of the Continental Navy and was placed in command of

John Barry, portrait by Gilbert Stuart.

the brig "Lexington." He captured the British tender "Edward" after a running fight off the Virginia Capes on April 7, 1776. Volunteering as an aide to Gen. John Cadwalader, he saw action in the Battles of Trenton and Princeton, N.J., 1776–77. He then served with Gen. Anthony Wayne on the Delaware River below Philadelphia in 1778. Barry commanded boats that assisted in procuring food for the Americans at Valley Forge, destroyed British forage, and captured three English supply vessels en route to Philadelphia. These harassments, which won a letter of commendation from George Washington, caused the British to concentrate an overwhelming naval force in Delaware Bay and the lower river. Given command of the frigate "Raleigh," Barry sailed from Boston in September 1778 and met a superior British force. He fought well against hopeless odds before running his vessel ashore to burn her. With the Continental Navy reduced to five frigates, Barry was assigned (September 1780) to command the "Alliance," which captured two British men-of-war on May 28, 1781. Following the victory at Yorktown, the "Alliance" took Lafayette to France, after which a long cruise in 1782 netted 10 British prizes. En route homeward via Martinique and Havana, Barry fought the last naval engagement of the Revolution on March 10, 1783, inflicting severe damage on one of three British frigates that attacked him. After the war he returned to merchant shipping, making a successful voyage from Philadelphia to Canton, China. When the U.S. Navy was established in 1794, he was appointed senior officer and given command of the frigate "United States." During the undeclared naval war with France, 1798 to 1801, he commanded the fleet in the West Indies, where he protected American commerce and took many French prizes. He also took to France the peace commissioners sent by Pres. John Adams. In 1803 Barry was ordered to the Mediterranean to protect commerce from the Barbary pirates, but he was too ill to sail and died shortly afterward.

Bibliography: W. B. CLARK, *Gallant John Barry* (New York 1938). **Illustration credit:** J. J. Ryan Collection, on loan to the White House.

[J. B. HEFFERNAN]

BARRY, PHILIP, playwright; b. Rochester, N.Y., June 18, 1896; d. Jupiter Island, Fla., Dec. 3, 1949. After graduating from Yale University in 1919, Barry studied playwriting under George P. Baker at Harvard until 1922, the year in which he married Ellen Semple. His first professionally produced play was *You and I,* which opened at the Belmont Theatre in New York Feb. 19, 1923. His early plays were a combination of whimsical comedy and mild social satire. *Paris Bound* (1927) was his first great success, but *Holiday* (1928) is a superior example of his early style. That he was not only a light comedian was evident when notes of social protest began to sound in his plays, presaging the drama of the 1930s. He broke clearly from his early work in *Hotel Universe* (1930), the first American play to make use of Freudian theories of personality, and in *Here Come the Clowns* (1930), a contemporary morality play. Among his other more important plays are *White Wings* (1926), *The Animal Kingdom* (1932), *The Philadelphia Story* (1939), and *Second Threshold* (1951). Two of his plays dealt with specifically Cath-

olic subject matter: *John,* about St. John the Baptist (1927), and *The Joyous Season* (1934), but neither of these works was successful. He shares with S. N. Behrman (1893–) the distinction of writing American comedy of manners. His plays attracted the talents of the leading actresses of his day, including Katharine Hepburn, Tallulah Bankhead, and Ethel Barrymore.

Bibliography: J. W. KRUTCH, *The American Drama since 1918* (rev. ed. New York 1957).

[L. C. BRADY]

BARRY COLLEGE

A liberal arts college for women in Miami, Fla., Barry College was founded in 1940 by three members of the same family: Bp. Patrick Barry of St. Augustine; Msgr. William Barry, his brother, of St. Patrick's Church, Miami Beach; and Mother Mary Gerald Barry, OP, their sister and mother general of the Adrian Dominican Sisters. John G. Thompson, a Baptist attorney and friend of the family, assisted in the foundation and, until his death in 1962, discharged the legal work of the College.

In June 1940 Bishop Barry blessed the first five buildings, and the following September the College opened with 47 students, 14 instructors, and a curriculum of 26 courses. By 1943 the students numbered 122 and the College had outgrown its residential facilities. Rented houses in the neighborhood sufficed for dormitories until 1946, when a 125-bed dormitory was opened. Science and library additions were completed in 1950 and the Fine Arts Quadrangle and auditorium were dedicated in 1955. In 1956 the College purchased more property to house approximately 70 students, and in December 1962 Monsignor Barry dedicated Thompson Hall union and 2 dormitories.

Bishop Barry died suddenly Aug. 13, 1940; Mother Mary Gerald died Nov. 20, 1961; and Thompson died suddenly April 12, 1962. Msgr. William Barry remains the only living founder of the College.

The College is governed by a board of trustees composed of the mother general, who serves as president of the board, and four elected councilors. A lay advisory board was formally installed on Founder's Day, November 1962. A resident president discharges the duties of the president on campus. College officers are the academic dean, registrar, treasurer, and dean of students. The faculty consists of 2 Dominican priests, 33 Dominican sisters, and 25 lay instructors. They hold 19 doctorates and 28 master's degrees.

Barry is accredited by state and national agencies as a liberal arts college with a teacher education program; it is affiliated with The Catholic University of America. A charter, authorizing the conferring of degrees, was granted by the state of Florida in January 1940. The curriculum encompasses five divisions: theology and philosophy, language and literature, natural sciences and social sciences, fine arts, and community service. The liberal arts are emphasized for all students regardless of the field of concentration. Undergraduate work leads to the B.S. and B.A. degrees; a Ph.B. degree was offered until 1947. The first B.S. in nursing was given in 1957. In 1954 the College opened a graduate division offering masters degrees in education and English. Since 1956, when 5 masters were given, 170 M.A. degrees have been conferred. Many of the administrators and counselors of the public schools of Dade and Broward Counties have been prepared in the graduate division of the College. In 1964 the library housed approximately 42,000 volumes, and received 330 periodicals.

Summer sessions have been held since the College was founded. The summer enrollments beginning with 48 students in 1941, had grown to 1,002 by 1964. Included in this number were representatives of 25 different religious orders of women, several orders of brothers and priests, and diocesan seminarians. About 30 per cent of the students were religious. Of the 70 per cent lay students, three-fifths were Protestants.

In 1960, in response to the national and community need, Barry started English classes for Cuban refugees, particularly doctors, dentists, and lawyers. The Dominican sisters and collegians also conduct English classes for Cuban children, undertake translations of foreign correspondence, give lectures, teach catechism, and place refugee children in schools and homes.

An endowment of approximately $300,000 in invested funds is augmented by an annual $15,000 subsidy from the motherhouse, Adrian, Mich. Until 1961–63, when the College received a government loan of approximately $2 million, all building was financed by the Dominican Sisters. Besides the dormitories mentioned, the housing loan made possible additional residential and recreational facilities.

[M. A. COLLINS]

BARRYMORE

The name of a family of famous actors in the U.S. during the first half of the 20th century.

Maurice; b. Fort Agra, India, 1847; d. Amityville, N.Y., March 26, 1905. After having changed his name from Herbert Blythe, he came to Boston in 1875 to play in John Augustin *Daly's *Under the Gaslight*. In 1876 he married Georgianna Drew. He performed with many great actresses, including Olga Nethersole, Lily Langtry, and Helena *Modjeska. In 1901, he suffered a mental collapse and spent his remaining years in a sanitarium.

Georgianna Emma Drew; b. Philadelphia, Pa., 1856; d. Santa Barbara, Calif., July 2, 1893. She made her stage debut in 1872 at her mother's Arch Street Theatre in Philadelphia. After her marriage, she joined Daly's company in New York where she played opposite Edwin Booth, Lawrence Barrett, and John McCullough. Late in 1892, she contracted tuberculosis and moved to California in the hope of arresting the disease. In 1884, influenced by admiration for the Catholic Helena Modjeska, she had had herself and her three children baptized Catholics.

Lionel; b. Philadelphia, Pa., April 28, 1878; d. Los Angeles, Calif., Nov. 15, 1954. He was educated at Episcopal Academy in Philadelphia, the public schools of that city, and at Seton Hall College (later University), South Orange, N.J. He first appeared on a stage at the Fourteenth Street Theatre, New York, on Dec. 25, 1893 as a footman in *The Road to Ruin*. He contributed notable portrayals as Milt Shanks in *The Copperhead* (1918) and as Macbeth (1921). His first motion picture was *The New York Hat* (1912), starring Mary Pickford. He won an Academy Award for his work in *A Free Soul* (1931). Among countless movies he made, perhaps the most widely known was the Dr. Kildare series in which he portrayed the gruff Dr. Gillespie.

Lionel (left), Ethel, and John Barrymore.

Beginning in 1934, his depiction of Scrooge in Dickens's *A Christmas Carol* became an annual radio event.

Ethel; b. Philadelphia, Pa., Aug. 15, 1879; d. Hollywood, Calif., June 18, 1959. She was educated in Philadelphia by the Sisters of Notre Dame de Namur, to whom her biography (*Memories,* 1955) expresses gratitude. After her starring success in Clyde Fitch's *Captain Jinks of the Horse Marines* (1901), she went on to one success after another, from *A Doll's House* (1905) to *The Second Mrs. Tanqueray* (1924). She made only a few films but won an Academy Award for her work in *None but the Lonely Heart* (1942). Her last great success was in *The Corn Is Green* (1940–42). She was married to Russell Griswold Colt and was the mother of three children.

John; b. Philadelphia, Pa., Feb. 14, 1882; d. Hollywood, Calif., May 20, 1942. He attended elementary school in Washington, D.C., and Seton Hall College in South Orange, N.J. A gripping performance in John Galsworthy's melodrama *Justice* in 1914 started him on the way to fame as a serious actor. Producer Arthur Hopkins starred John in a series of Shakespearian plays, notably *Richard III*. He played *Hamlet* in the fall of 1922 for 101 performances and was acclaimed the greatest Shakespearean actor of his day. Later he toured the play for 8 weeks; in 1925 he played it in London for 12 more. This performance was the peak of his career. In the 1920s he became a romantic idol with such motion pictures as *Beau Brummel* and *Don Juan*.

John and Lionel acted together in *Peter Ibbetson* (1917) and *The Jest* (1919), and the two of them joined their sister for a film, *Rasputin and the Empress* (1933). The trio once performed together in a bill of two plays: Ethel and John in *Alice-Sit-by-the-Fire,* and Lionel and John in *Pantaloon* (1906). In 1927, Edna Ferber and George Kaufman wrote a comedy, *The Royal Family,* which was a fictionalized treatment of the Barrymores.

See also AMERICAN LITERATURE, 2.

Bibliography: G. FOWLER, *Good Night, Sweet Prince* (New York 1944), biography of John Barrymore. E. BARRYMORE, *Memories: An Autobiography* (New York 1955). L. BARRYMORE, *We Barrymores* (New York 1951). H. ALPERY, *The Barrymores* (New York 1964). **Illustration credit:** New York Public Library Theatre Collection.

[L. C. BRADY]

BARTHIANISM

A theological system developed by Karl Barth (1886–), Swiss Protestant pastor, professor, and writer. Its influence on 20th-century thought has been enormous.

Career of Barth. Karl Barth was born during the heyday of Liberal Protestantism, but his father was a conservative theologian. The elder Barth was a pastor in the Swiss *Reformed Church, and his son has served in the same capacity. The father passed on to the son a penchant for history and politics. Karl attended various German universities and sympathized with the leaders of theological *liberalism. At Berlin he preferred the lectures in Church history delivered by *Harnack. Later, at Marburg, he was deeply affected by the teaching of Wilhelm Hermann, who affirmed that religion consists in the experience of free abandonment.

As a young ordained minister Barth met E. Thurneysen, a friend with whom he seems to have discovered the *eschatologism of Christianity. This orientation gradually sharpened during that decade of disillusion, especially by an exchange with Franz Overbeck. The writings of *Kierkegaard and *Dostoyevsky revealed to Barth more clearly the antinomy between Christianity and culture, and made him receptive to the rising tide of *existentialism.

Barth's initial conversion from liberalism did not result solely from the cumulative effect of these formative influences. Primary credit must go to Barth's personal reflection on his predicament every Sunday after 1911 when, as a preacher, he had to proclaim the Word of God in the Bible to men caught up in the opposing forces of life. All this bore fruit in the first edition of his commentary on St. Paul's Epistle to the Romans (1919). At this stage, however, Barth, with all liberals, still looked upon *Schleiermacher as his patriarch. The definitive break appeared in the second edition of the above work (1922). Here the liberal notion of Christ as author of a new type of religious experience (piety) was supplanted by the Barthian thesis that Christ is the author of a whole new existence.

Barth began in 1921 a professorial career that has included distinguished service in the universities of Göttingen, Münster, Bonn, and Basel. Gradually he conceived the idea of a systematic presentation of Christian doctrine. After one false start, he began publishing his *Kirchliche Dogmatik* (*Church Dogmatics*), whose first volume appeared in 1932. A last factor in his highly personal thought, which became a sort of principle in the *Dogmatics,* was the conscious rejection of philosophical existentialism as the basis for theological reflection. The norm that he set then, and that he has followed since with remarkable fidelity, despite his later development, was the Word of God revealed in Jesus Christ, witnessed to in the Holy Scriptures and preached by the Church.

Doctrine. Negatively, then, Barth's approach to theology opposes Schleiermacher's notion of religion. Therewith it rejects any attempt by man to initiate a relationship with God, even though it terminates in the "sentiment of total dependence." With this avenue closed, moreover, Barth has attempted to work out a theological system for which the name "coherent Christology" is quite apt. This system stands on the principle that theological understanding of any subject is totally dependent on the penetration of that subject's relation to Christ. Christology, then—or what Barth himself calls "the relation, Jesus Christ"—is the touchstone of theology.

The elaboration of this principle can be seen, at least germinally, in the schematization of the *Kirchliche Dogmatik.*

The Doctrine of the Word of God. In this part Barth works out a theory of the Word as divine activity present and revealed *solely* in Jesus Christ, to whom the Scriptures and the Church bear witness. It is also the occasion of his emphasizing the absolute gratuity of the Word's descent, to the degree that any attempt on man's part to prepare for this event (*Ereignis*) is impossible.

The Doctrine of God. Here Barth takes up the problem of man's knowledge of God, affirming that he is known *only* in Jesus Christ. Thus Barth denies the native power of reason to know even God's existence. Under this heading Barth also discusses the language men use in speaking of God, the mystery of predestination (Jesus Christ's being the *sole* object of God's free election), and the nature of God's command over men.

The Doctrine of Creation. The concern in this part is the understanding of Jesus Christ as the Word through whom the existence of all that is created is maintained and controlled.

The Doctrine of Reconciliation. This Barth believes to be the core of dogmatics, as well as of the preaching of the Church. In it he treats of the covenant between God and man, of grace and sin, of the atonement made by Jesus Christ, of the subjective appropriation effected by the presence of Jesus Christ working in the Church by the Holy Spirit (justification), and finally of the law of God, in so far as it punishes sin and heals and restores us with a view toward our eternal redemption.

Barth's reaction against liberalism must be judged as beneficial to Protestantism as a whole. His attempt to reinstate and systematically to defend the transcendence of God as a theological principle is altogether praiseworthy; for it puts man in his true position in relation to God, that of utter receptivity.

When, however, Barth's entire system is viewed in light of Catholic tradition, some sharp divergences appear. Most evident—but perhaps only symptomatic of a more radical difficulty—is the compromise of the consistency of creation, especially of rational creatures. To give Jesus Christ the primacy in all things is quite valid. *See* JESUS CHRIST, III, 12. St. Paul does this. Barth, however, in his "coherent Christology," seems to distort the true nature of things when he proposes this primacy as so sufficing as to make unnecessary and even impossible a true encounter between man and God. Scrutiny of his work evokes constantly the question of the reality of man's receptivity to God's word. Can man actually hear, believe, love, and obey?

Barth's effort to rehabilitate Protestant dogmatics, his partial success together with the evident exaggerations, points to a root difficulty indigenous to Protestantism itself, and in light of which its entire history may be better understood. The exaltation of God's transcendent majesty by Calvin and of His perfect freedom in the distribution of His grace by Luther are fully comprehended only when complemented by the truth of the immanent effect of the divine causality in creation as a whole and also in the world of grace. This balance Barth does not seem to have achieved in his *Dogmatics*.

See also PROTESTANT THEOLOGY, CONTEMPORARY TRENDS IN.

Bibliography: Works. *Church Dogmatics,* tr. G. T. THOMSON (New York 1955–   ); *Dogmatics in Outline,* tr. G. T. THOMSON (New York 1949); *Evangelical Theology: An Introduction,* tr. G. FOLEY (New York 1963). Complete list to 1955 in *Antwort: Karl Barth zum 70 Geburtstag* (Zurich 1956) 945–960. Catholic critique. H. U. VON BALTHASAR, *Karl Barth: Darstellung und Deutung seiner Theologie* (2d ed. Cologne 1962). H. BOUILLARD, LexThK² 2:5–8; *Karl Barth,* 2 v. in 3 (Paris 1957). H. F. DAVIS, "The Essence of Barthism," DownRev 68 (1950) 131–146. J. HAMER, *Karl Barth,* tr. D. M. MARUCA (Westminster, Md. 1962). H. KÜNG, *Rechtfertigung: Die Lehre Karl Barths und eine katholische Besinnung* (Einsiedeln 1957). G. GLOEGE, RGG³ 1:894–898.

[M. B. SCHEPERS]

BARTHOLOMAEUS ANGLICUS,

encyclopedist (known as Bartholomew the Englishman); b. late 12th century in Oldengland, England, possibly of the noble Norfolk family of Glanville. He studied at *Oxford before going to Paris (c. 1225–31), where he seems to have entered the French province of *Franciscans. He was a *baccalaureus biblicus* at the University of *Paris in 1231 when Franciscan Minister General *John Parenti sent him as lecturer to the Order's house of studies at Magdeburg (Salimbene, *Chronica, ad an. 1237*). Bartholomaeus' reputation as one of the

Folio from a manuscript of the "De proprietatibus rerum" of Batholomaeus Anglicus, French, c. 1400, in the collection of the Library of Congress, Washington, D.C.

great medieval encyclopedists rests on his *De proprietatibus rerum* (*On the Properties of Things*), a work devoted to the natural sciences, and intended as a tool for Biblical and theological students and preachers. It reflects the principles, methods, and scope of Oxford, where it was probably begun. Bartholomaeus, however, continued his work at Paris and finished it at Magdeburg (c. 1240–50). The encyclopedia is divided into 19 books: books 1–2, the spiritual substances, God and the angels; books 3–7, the mixed substance, man—the soul, the body, the members, his ages and infirmities; books 8–18, the corporeal substances; and book 19, the accidents—color, odor, taste, and liquidness. An appendix treats of numbers, weights, measures, and sounds. The books on medicine, geography, and ethnography are especially valuable. The encyclopedia has often been attributed to a mythical Bartholomaeus de Glanvilla of the 14th century.

Not always unoriginal but at times naive, the encyclopedia was largely a compilation of available scientific information, borrowed from the *Etymologies* of *Isidore of Seville, *Robert Grosseteste, *Alfred of Sareshel and others. The great diffusion of its manuscripts (Stegmüller RB n. 1564), early editions, and translations into French (e.g., by John Corbichon in 1372), into English (by John de *Trevisa, 1495), and into Dutch and Spanish testifies to its wide usage. It also circulated in several abridged versions. The best Latin text is the Frankfort edition of 1601. A critical edition is needed.

Other works attributed to Bartholomaeus are several scriptural writings (Stegmüller RB nn. 1561–63) and a *Sermonum liber.* He is not the author of *Tractatus septiformis de moralitate rerum.*

Bibliography: A. E. SCHÖNBACH, "Das Bartholomaeus Anglicus Beschreibung Deutschlands gegen 1240," MitteilIÖG 27 (1906) 54–90. A. SCHNEIDER, "Metaphysische Begriffe des Bartholomaeus Anglicus," BeitrGeschPhilMA Sup. 1 (1913) 139–179. T. B. PLASSMANN, "Bartholomaeus Anglicus," ArchFrancHist 12 (1919) 68–109. G. E. SE BOYAR, "Bartholomaeus Anglicus and His Encyclopaedia," JEngGermPhilol 19 (1920) 168–189. Thorndike 2:401–435. Sarton 2.2:586–588. Emden 2:771–772. T. GAYENS, DHGE 6:975–977.

[A. EMMEN]

BARTHOLOMEW, APOSTLE, ST.

Very little is known with certainty of Bartholomew (Βαρθολομαῖος). He is listed along with the other Apostles in Mk 3.18; Mt 10.3; Lk 6.14; Acts 1.13; but otherwise he is not mentioned in the NT, at least not by that name. However, it is quite probable that he should be identified with Nathanael (Ναθαναήλ), the disciple who figures prominently in Jn 1.45–51 and who is named, along with Peter, Thomas, James, and John, in Jn 21.2. The difference of names causes no problem, for Bartholomew is a patronymic or family name, bar-Talmai, meaning "son of Talmai"; it is at least possible that he had also a personal or first name, in this hypothesis Nathanael, to go with it. If the identification were not made, it would mean that the Nathanael named as one of the earliest disciples to be called would not be named at all in the Synoptic Gospels and that one of the twelve Apostles would find no mention in John; this is not impossible, but it is unlikely. A more positive argument can be drawn from the association of Bartholomew in the Synoptics and Nathanael in John with Philip. In Jn 1.45–46 it is Philip who brings Nathanael to Jesus,

St. Bartholomew, detail of a fragment of a silk embroidery of the last quarter of the 12th century.

and in the Synoptic lists likewise Bartholomew is paired with Philip.

Concerning Bartholomew's apostolic life, various traditions name Ethiopia, India, and Persia as his mission field; according to the Roman Breviary he also preached in Armenia, where he died a martyr's death, being flayed alive and then beheaded. August 24 is his feast day in the Latin Church. In Michelangelo's famous Last Judgment scene, St. Bartholomew is represented as flayed and holding his skin in his hands; more often, he is shown holding a knife as the instrument with which the flaying was done.

Bibliography: EncDictBibl 210, 1610–11. B. KRAFT, LexThK² 2:9–10. A. ROMEO, EncCatt 2:916–918. U. HOLZMEISTER, "Nathanael fuitne idem ac S. Bartholomaeus Apostolus?" *Biblica* 21 (1940) 28–39. Iconography. Réau IAC 3.1:180–184. Künstle Ikonog 2:116–120. K. RATHE, EncCatt 2:918–919. **Illustration credit:** Victoria and Albert Museum, Crown Copyright reserved.

[A. LE HOULLIER]

BARTHOLOMEW OF BRAGA, VEN., Dominican theologian and archbishop of Braga; b. Lisbon, May 3, 1514; d. Viana, July 16, 1590. Though his surname was Fernandez, he was called Bartholomeus de Martyribus after the church of his Baptism, S. Maria de Martyribus. He became a Dominican friar on Nov. 11, 1528; after the completion of his studies, he taught philosophy and then theology for 20 years. In 1558, against his inclination and at the wish of his provincial, Luis of Granada, he accepted the appointment to the archiepiscopal See of Braga. He was greatly influential in the reform activity of the Council of Trent in the sessions from 1562 to 1563. He promulgated the conciliar decrees and interpreted them strictly in his provincial council of 1566. He started a seminary in his palace, instituted chairs of moral theology in Braga and Viana do Castelo, composed a catechism, preached assiduously, and dedicated much time to the visitation of his nearly 1,300 parishes. Worn out from this pastoral activity, he resigned his bishopric in 1582 and retired to the Dominican priory of Viana do Castelo. Among his more than 30 works are the *Catecismo ou doutrina cristã* (1564), *Stimulus pastorum* (1565), and *Compendium spiritualis doctrinae* (1582).

Bibliography: P. DAMINO, *Il contributo teologico di Bartolomeo dé Martiri al Concilio di Trento* (Rome 1962). L. SOUSA, *Vida de D. Fr. Bartolomeu dos Mártires,* 3 v. (Lisbon 1946). A. WALZ, LexThK² 2:12–13. F. DE ALMEIDA, DHGE 6:983–984.

[R. DE ALMEIDA ROLO]

BARTHOLOMEW OF BRESCIA, canonist; b. second half of the 12th century; d. 1258. He studied Roman law and Canon Law in Bologna under Hugolinus de Presbyteris and Tancred, and taught Canon Law there from *c.* 1234. That he did not have a creative mind is best demonstrated by his works, which are all more or less a revision of the works of other authors. He is important as a transmitter of traditional material and as a learned popularizer.

His *Casus Decretorum* was a revision of the work of the same name by Benencasa Aretinus; Bartholomew composed this work while still a student. It was printed in 1505 with the *Glossa ordinaria* of the Decretum of Gratian. *Historiae super libro Decretorum* was an early revision of a collection of the description of Biblical events most frequently encountered in the glossaries on the Decretum. The author of the original is unknown. From 1505 the *Historiae* were printed also with the *Glossa ordinaria*. *Brocarda,* revision of a work of the same name by Damasus Ungarus undertaken shortly after 1234, has been printed frequently. *Ordo iudiciarius,* a revision of a work of the same name by Tancred, was finished after Tancred's death (1236). *Quaestiones veneriales* and *dominicales,* written between 1234 and 1241 are now considered to be a revision of sources already in extensive circulation and present in other collections. *Repertorium Decreti,* a *Summarium* of the Decretum, is attributed by many to Bartholomew, but it is not known for certain to be his work.

The *Glossa ordinaria Decreti,* Bartholomew's chief work, entitles him to a place in the history of Canon Law literature; it is a revision of the work of *Joannes Teutonicus and was published between 1240 and 1245. In the prologue he states in the words "Quoniam novis supervenientibus causis novis est remediis succurrendum . . ." the reason for and essence of the revision: a recasting of the citations from the *Compilationes antiquae* to harmonize them with the Decretals of *Gregory IX, an insertion of omitted citations and later decretals, expansions and corrections of the doctrines of Joannes. This version of the *Glossa ordinaria* was appended to most manuscripts of the Decretum. When printed editions began to be published, it was also often printed along with the text of the Decretum in the form of a marginal gloss.

Bibliography: Schulte 2:83–88. Kuttner, see index. S. KUTTNER, "Bernardus Compostellanus Antiquus," *Traditio* 1 (1943) 292. Van Hove v.1, see index. G. FRANSEN, "Tribunaux ecclésiastiques et langue vulgaire d'après les 'Quaestiones' des canonistes," EphemThLov 40 (1964) 409–412. G. LE BRAS, DDC 2:216–217. J. WENNER, DHGE 6:984–985. A. M. STICKLER, LexThK² 2:11.

[A. M. STICKLER]

BARTHOLOMEW OF EXETER, bishop of Exeter, English canonist; b. Diocese of Coutances (Normandy), *c.* 1110; d. Dec. 15, 1184. An eminent master at Paris in the years 1140–42, Bartholomew migrated to England, became a member of Archbishop *Theobald's *familia* at Canterbury for a while, and was archdeacon of Exeter by 1155. His rising influence was revealed at the London Synod of 1159, where he supported Pope *Alexander III against his schismatic rival. A friend of *John of Salisbury and later of *Roger of Worcester, as well as Theobald's intimate, Bartholomew was the archbishop's choice for the *Exeter See following the death of Robert Warelwast in March 1160. Bartholomew was finally elected bishop of Exeter between February and April 1161, after a protracted contest with a less worthy choice by the King, and he was consecrated, some short time after Theobald's death on April 18, 1161. A supporter in principle of Thomas *Becket in the archbishop's conflict with King *Henry II, Bartholomew nevertheless favored restraint and moderation in the crisis of 1164 (*see* CLARENDON, CONSTITUTIONS OF). Courted, and occasionally censured, by both sides, he moved decisively to Becket's cause during the latter's exile, remained in correspondence with the exiled party, withheld himself from hostile actions, and finally withdrew in 1169 from public involvement in the affair. He retained Becket's favor to the end and played a leading and conciliatory role in the settlement following

Becket's death in 1170 and after the agreement at *Avranches in 1172. Thereafter the central focus of Bartholomew's actions turned to pastoral and judicial functions. Highly esteemed by Alexander III, he received numerous commissions as papal judge-delegate, sometimes jointly with Roger of Worcester, these two being Alexander's *duo luminaria* of the English Church. Together with *Baldwin (later of Canterbury), Roger, and Abp. *Richard of Canterbury, he promoted the development of decretal law and codification, and of judge-delegate jurisdiction from the mid-1170s. He was present at Archbishop Richard's council at Westminster in 1175 but not at *Lateran Council III of 1179. A scholar of versatility and wide reputation, and a bishop of spirituality and high moral integrity, Bartholomew composed a *Penitentiale,* the *De libero arbitrio,* the *Dialogus contra Judaeos,* and various sermons.

Bibliography: A. MOREY, *Bartholomew of Exeter: Bishop and Canonist* (Cambridge, Eng. 1937). D. KNOWLES, *The Episcopal Colleagues of Archbishop Thomas Becket* (Cambridge, Eng. 1951) 27–28, 102–104. C. DUGGAN, *Twelfth-Century Decretal Collections and Their Importance in English History* (London 1963).

[C. DUGGAN]

BARTHOLOMEW OF LUCCA, called also Ptolomeo, Tolomeo, and de Fiadonibus, Dominican bishop of Torcello, historian and theologian; b. Lucca, Italy, *c.* 1236; d. Torcello (near Venice), 1327. He was born of a middle-class family and became a *Dominican in Lucca. A student and associate of *Thomas Aquinas from 1261 to 1268, Bartholomew traveled with him and lived with him in Naples during the last year of Thomas's life. In the 1280s and 1290s Bartholomew was prior of various houses in Tuscany and was occupied in teaching and preaching. From 1309 to 1319 he was almost continuously at the papal court in Avignon (*see* AVIGNON PAPACY), engaged in research and writing, and, some think, acting as papal librarian. Appointed bishop of Torcello in 1318, he came into conflict with the patriarch of *Grado, who imprisoned him. He was released on orders of Pope *John XXII. At Avignon, in March 1323, he was acquitted of all guilt; it is thought he was there for the canonization of Aquinas (July 1323). He died in Torcello, aged 91 years. His works include the following: *Determinatio compendiosa* (Turin 1924), written in 1280, a study on the limits of imperial jurisdiction in Italy; *Annales* (MGSrerGermNS 8), finished in 1307, a description of main events from 1061 to 1303; *Historia ecclesiastica* (Muratori RIS 11:740–1242), a work in 24 books on the history of the Church from the birth of Christ to 1314, books 22 and 23 being one of the most important sources for the life of St. Thomas [tr. K. Foster, *The Life of St. Thomas* (Baltimore 1959)]; *Exaemeron* [ed. P. Masetti (Siena 1880)], a work showing his wide acquaintance with the natural science of his day; *Tractatus de jurisdictione ecclesiae super regnum Siciliae et Apuliae* (Mansi, *Miscellanea* 1). The *Historia tripartita* to which Bartholomew often referred is not extant. The completion of St. Thomas's *De regimine principum,* with which he used to be credited, is now questioned [I. T. Eschmann, *On Kingship* (Toronto 1949) ix–xxv].

Bibliography: Quétif-Échard 1:541. I. TAURISANO, *I Domenicani in Lucca* (Lucca 1914) 44–77; ed., *S. Tommaso d'Aquino,*

O.P.: *Miscellanea storico-artistica* (Rome 1924) 163–170. Introduction, "Life and Works," in *Die Annalen des Tholomeus von Lucca*, ed. B. SCHMEIDLER (2d ed. MGSrerGermNS 8; Berlin 1955).

[P. F. MULHERN]

BARTHOLOMEW OF MARMOUTIER, ST.,

Benedictine priest and abbot of *Marmoutier near Tours from 1063 until his death on Feb. 24, 1084. He successfully resisted the claims of Geoffrey the Bearded, Count of Touraine and Anjou, to spiritual and temporal dominion over the monastery. He then so improved the discipline at Marmoutier that lay and ecclesiastical reformers sought monks from his abbey to reform old monasteries and to found new ones. When *William I, the Conqueror, founded *Battle Abbey in thanksgiving for his victory at Hastings, he sought and received monks from Bartholomew's house. Under Bartholomew's rule, Marmoutier thus acquired several churches and monasteries in France and in England. His name was included in many medieval Benedictine martyrologies but no cult in his honor has ever been approved.

Bibliography: PL 149:393–420. P. CALENDINI, DHGE 6:1014–15.

[J. C. MOORE]

BARTHOLOMEW OF ROME,

religious reformer, eminent preacher; b. Campo de' Fiori, Rome; d. monastery of San Benedetto Po, Mantua, 1430. He promoted religious reform in the territory of Venice and was among the principal members of the group reforming the monastery of Santa Maria di Fregionaia near Lucca. Out of this movement emerged the Congregation of Canons Regular of St. John Lateran (*see* CANONS REGULAR OF ST. AUGUSTINE). He was elected prior by his companions in 1403 and held the office again from August 1407 to 1408. He seems not to have held any office permanently, but rather to have continued to carry on his preaching career. At his death he had a reputation for sanctity. He was not, as some historians have believed, a member of the Colonna family, nor was he the founder of the Congregation of St. George in Alga near Venice, established later by Pope Clement IX in 1668.

Bibliography: N. WIDLOECHER, *La congregazione dei canonici regolari Lateranensi* (Gubbio 1929). K. EGGER, *Für Gottes Haus und Herde* (Bolzano 1952) 17–22.

[R. H. TRAME]

BARTHOLOMEW OF SAN CONCORDIO (OF PISA),

Dominican theologian; b. San Concordio near Pisa, 1262; d. June 11, 1347, Pisa, Italy. One of the most erudite men of his time, a great preacher and writer, he lectured at Lucca, Florence, and Pisa. Of his major works, *De documentis antiquorum* is a collection of opinions by classical and ecclesiastical authors; his own translation, *Ammaestramenti degli antichi,* is a Tuscan classic. His *Summa de Casibus Conscientiae* was very widely used during the 14th and 15th centuries. Besides a compendium of moral theology and a series of Lenten sermons, he also wrote treatises on the virtues and vices, on Latin pronunciation and orthography, and on the tragedies of Vergil and Seneca.

Bibliography: A. STEFANUCCI ALA, *Sulla vita e sulle opere di frate Bartolomeo da San Concordio* (Rome 1838). P. MANDONNET, DTC 2:435–436.

[J. R. COONEY]

BARTHOLOMEW OF SIMERI, ST.,

abbot and organizer of Basilian monasticism in southern Italy; b. Simeri, Calabria, Italy, mid-11th century; d. Rossano, Italy, Aug. 19, 1130 (feast, Aug. 19). In earliest youth, impelled by an urge to leave the world, Bartholomew became a disciple of the hermit Cyril. He built his first monastery in the mountains near *Rossano with the help of the distinguished Christodoulos, possibly a converted Saracen and later an emir of *Sicily, and also, through him, with the help of Count *Roger of Sicily, brother of *Robert Guiscard, and other Norman barons. This monastery of Santa Maria Odigitria (she who shows the way), built toward the close of the 11th century and before the death of Roger in 1101, was later called the Patirion to honor the saintly founder (Πατήρ); it became an important center of *Basilian monasticism in Calabria and Sicily. After 1104, having received a charter for his foundation from Count Roger II, Bartholomew was ordained by the bishop of Belcastro, and in 1105 he journeyed to Rome to obtain from Pope *Paschal II confirmation of immunity for his monastery. There is some evidence that Bartholomew visited Constantinople to obtain gifts of *icons, liturgical books, and sacred vessels from Emperor *Alexius I Comnenus and Empress Irene, as well as from Basil Kalimeris, a high official of the empire. The latter, as patron of the monastery of St. Basil the Great on Mount *Athos, charged Bartholomew with the task of reforming that institution. After his return to Italy, Bartholomew founded a second monastery, San Salvatore de Messina, with 12 monks sent from Santa Maria of Rossano. His cult seems to have spread through the Basilian monasteries of southern Italy soon after his death.

Bibliography: ActSS Sept. 8:792–826. L. BRÉHIER, DHGE 6:968–970. P. BATIFFOL, "L'Archive du Saint-Sauveur de Messine," RevQuestHist 42 (1887) 555–567; *L'Abbaye de Rossano* (Paris 1891) 1–10. M. SCADUTO, *Il monachismo basiliano nella Sicilia medievale* (Rome 1947). A. GALIETI, EncCatt 2:929–930.

[P. L. HUG]

BARTHOLOMEW OF TRENT,

Dominican hagiographer; b. Trent; d. Trent, *c.* 1251. He traveled widely in Italy (e.g., he was present at the first translation of St. Dominic's body, 1233) and visited France and Germany. Esteemed for piety and learning, he was also politically shrewd and was often at the papal and imperial courts. *Innocent IV entrusted him with at least one peace mission to *Frederick II. His chief work, the *Liber epilogorum* (1245–51), a series of concise, informative biographies of saints interlarded with ascetical and moral reflections, inaugurated a new type of hagiographic literature, intended not for liturgical use but to nourish the piety of the reader and to provide illustrative material for preachers. A *Summa theologica adversus sui temporis haereses* has also been ascribed to him.

Bibliography: Quétif-Échard 1:110. L. OLIGER, EncCatt 2:930. G. ABATE, "Il *Liber epilogorum* di fra Bartolomeo da Trento, O.P.," *Miscellanea Pio Paschini*, 2 v. (Rome 1948–49) 1:269–292.

[F. C. RYAN]

BARTHOLOMEW OF URBINO,

Augustinian bishop, compiler of patristic compendia; d. 1350. He served the last 3 years of his life as bishop of his native city of Urbino. In papal documents he is called Bartholomeus Hominis de Taiuti (Ditaiuti or Dio ti aiuti), of which the name given by certain Augustinian historians, Bartholomeus Simonis de Carusis, may be a corruption. He was a student at the Universities of *Bologna and *Paris and after 1321 was a teacher at Bologna, where no doubt he began his friendship with a fellow teacher, the canonist *Joannes Andreae, and where too he must have first met *Petrarch. From Petrarch's pen there is a letter to Bartholomew (*Fam.* 8.6), probably 1348 or 1349, forwarding two alternate sets of verses for the embellishment of the Augustinian's principal work. This opus, the widely used and still valuable *Milleloquium veritatis s. Augustini* (Lyons 1555), suggested by the *Hieronymianus* of Joannes Andreae, reveals in its compiler a knowledge of the writings of St. *Augustine probably unmatched in his time. Dedicated to *Clement VI, the work is an orderly assembly of perhaps 15,000 citations from Augustine's works, under about 1,000 subject headings (Abel-Zizania). A *Distinctio librorum,* in which Bartholomew lists and identifies the letters (about 190), the books, and more than 600 sermons from which he quotes, all apparently consulted directly *in originali,* places Bartholomew among the prehumanist discoverers of Latin manuscripts. Similarly arranged is a less widely dispersed *Milleloquium Sancti Ambrosii* (Lyons 1556). Little is certain about Bartholomew's other writings.

Bibliography: M. T. DISDIER, DHGE 6:1034–35. F. LANG, LexThK² 2:14–15. R. ARBESMANN, "Der Augustinereremitenorden und der Beginn der humanistischen Bewegung," first pt., in *Augustiniana* 14 (1964) 277–296; entire work to appear also as monograph. B. M. PEEBLES, "The Verse Embellishments of the *Milleloquium Sancti Augustini,*" *Traditio* 10 (1954) 555–566. G. POZZI, "Il Vat. Lat. 479 ed altri codici annotati da Roberto de' Bardi," *Miscellanea del Centro di studi medievali* 2 (1958) 142–145. Zumkeller 172–174; incomplete list of MSS of the two *Milleloquia,* also of a doubtful *De pugna spirituali.*

[B. M. PEEBLES]

BARTHOLOMEW OF VICENZA, BL.,

bishop, preacher, spiritual writer; b. *c.* 1200; d. 1270 at Vicenza (Breganze), Italy (feast, October 23). Bartholomew was an active Dominican preacher, a disputant with heretics, and a civil peacemaker. In 1233 he founded the Militia of Jesus Christ for knights. He served as regent of the theological faculty at the papal Curia before becoming bishop of Limassol, Cyprus, in 1252. He was transferred to Vicenza in 1255. While serving as papal envoy to England and France, he received from *Louis IX a thorn from the reputed *crown of thorns. "An Exposition of the Canticle of Canticles" and "The Search for Divine Love" are his principal works, though none of his writings are published. His theology is affective rather than speculative, having been derived from *Richard of St. Victor and *Pseudo-Dionysius. His cult was approved in 1793.

Bibliography: *Année Dominicaine* Oct. 2 (1902) 671–676. T. KÄPPELI, "Der literarische Nachlass des sel. Bartholomäus von Vicenza," *Mélanges Auguste Pelzer* (Louvain 1947) 275–301. L. OLIGER, EncCatt 2:931. Stegmüller RB 2:1576.

[J. F. HINNEBUSCH]

BARTHOLOMITES,

Armenian monks from Tarsus who sought refuge in Italy when their land was invaded by the Egyptian sultan in 1296. This first group landed in 1307 in Genoa, where the church of St. Bartholomew was built for them, hence the name Bartholomites. Others of these persecuted monks soon followed, establishing themselves in Parma, Siena, Florence, Bologna, and Milan. They observed the Rule of St. Basil and the *Armenian liturgy. Soon they aban-

doned their national traditions and adopted the Roman liturgy, the Rule of St. Augustine, and a habit similar to the Dominicans. Innocent VI approved this change in 1356 and confirmed the union of the monasteries, previously autonomous, into one congregation. Boniface IX granted the congregation the privileges of the Dominican Order but prohibited it from joining any other orders excepting that of the Carthusians. Superior generals, formerly elected for life, were ordered by Sixtus IV to have 3-year terms. For about 2 centuries this Armenian congregation flourished; then regular observance declined. Their membership decreased until many of their houses had to be closed. In the last half of the 17th century Innocent X authorized members either to enter another religious order or to become secularized, assuring the latter of a pension. In 1650 he suppressed the congregation, putting its houses and revenues to new uses. The congregation had several renowned preachers, such as Cherubini Cerebelloni of Genoa and Paul Costa of Milan. Among its celebrated writers was Gregori Bitio, who wrote the history of the order. In their church of St. Bartholomew in Genoa the celebrated portrait of Christ, "The Holy Face of Edessa," is still preserved. The Armenian Bartholomites are not to be confused with the religious community of the same name founded in Bavaria in the 17th century by Bartholomew Holzhauser.

Bibliography: P. HÉLYOT, *Histoire des ordres monastiques,* 8 v. (Paris 1714–19) 1:243–248. M. VAN DEN OUDENRIJN, "Les Constitutions des Frères arméniens de S. Basile en Italie," OrChrAnal 126 (1946) 7–117; LexThK² 2:16.

[C. LYNCH]

BARTMANN, BERNHARD,

theologian; b. Madfeld, Germany, May 26, 1860; d. Paderborn, Aug. 1, 1938. After teaching for a few years, he began his theological studies in 1884 at Münster and subsequently went to Würzburg, Eichstätt, and Paderborn. At Eichstätt, F. *Morgott and V. *Thalhofer greatly influenced him. He was ordained in 1888, received his doctorate in theology in 1896, and became professor of dogma on the Paderborn theological faculty in 1898. His chief work, *Lehrbuch der Dogmatik* (Freiburg 1905, 9th enl. ed. 1939), combining the teaching of St. Thomas with a Biblical, patristic, and historical approach, was the most widely used German text of his time.

Bibliography: R. BÄUMER, LexThK² 2:16.

[R. BÄUMER]

BARTÓK, BÉLA,

composer, pianist, and ethnomusicologist; b. Nagyszentmiklós (now Rumania), March 25, 1881; d. New York, N.Y., Sept. 26, 1945. After studying at the Royal Hungarian Academy of Music in Budapest, he became the principal piano teacher there (1907–34), simultaneously pursuing an international career as concert pianist. In 1905 he began collecting and systematizing Hungarian peasant music (of which little was then known) and subsequently published an important series of ethnomusicological studies of the music of Hungarians, Rumanians, Slovakians, Turks, and North African Arabs. His early compositions were strongly influenced by Brahms, Liszt, and Richard Strauss, but with the discovery of an authentic Magyar folk music he developed a highly personal style based upon its rhythmic and melodic elements, while not ignoring the influence of other folk music or that of Stravinsky, Schoenberg, and the French

Impressionists. His works include six remarkable string quartets; three piano concertos; two violin concertos; an opera, *Duke Bluebeard's Castle;* two ballets; several important works for orchestra (among them the *Dance Suite; Music for Strings, Percussion, and Celesta;* and *Concerto for Orchestra*); the *Cantata Profana* for chorus, soli, and orchestra; and *Mikrokosmos,* a set of 153 didactic piano pieces providing a comprehensive introduction to 20th-century styles. His influence upon younger composers in Hungary, western Europe, and America has been considerable.

Bartók was occupied at times with problems of philosophy and theology and in 1907 declared himself an atheist. In 1919, however, he and his family joined the First Unitarian Church in Budapest, where he was musical adviser, especially in compilation of the Hungarian Unitarian hymn book. In the U.S., where he had settled in 1940, he held an appointment for folk-song research and appeared frequently in concert. His autobiography, correspondence, and many writings on music (all edited by J. Demény) have been published in Budapest but are not yet translated.

Bibliography: *Hungarian Folk Music,* tr. M. D. Calvocoressi (London 1931). H. Stevens, *The Life and Music of Béla Bartók* (rev. ed. New York 1964), extensive bibliog. D. Bartha, MusGG 1:1345–50. Baker 93–94. B. Szabolcsi, *Bela Bartok: His Life in Pictures* (New York 1964).

[H. STEVENS]

BARTOLI, DANIELLO, Jesuit historian and literary author; b. Ferrara, Feb. 12, 1608; d. Rome, Jan. 13, 1685. He was admitted to the Jesuit novitiate at Novellara on Dec. 10, 1623, studied philosophy and theology at Parma, and was ordained (1636) at Bologna. After his entrance into the Society of Jesus he petitioned the Jesuit general, Mutius Vitelleschi, at least once each year to be sent to the missionary field, but he was kept in Italy, where he won praise as an orator in Genoa, Ferrara, Lucca, Florence, Rome, Naples, and Malta. Distressed by the harm done to youthful readers by popular romances, he wrote the *L'uomo di lettere* (Rome 1645), which in its first year went through nine editions and was translated into English, French, and German. A new general, Vincenzo Carafa, called him to Rome to use his talented pen in writing the history of the Society of Jesus in Italian. Except for the brief interruption as rector of the Roman College (1671–73), he was engaged in this and other histories of individual Jesuits until his death. Departing from the annalistic pattern of the official Latin history, composed by Niccolo Orlandini, Francesco *Sacchini, and Joseph de *Jouvancy, Bartoli arranged his history according to geographical divisions. After the introductory volume, *Della vita e dell' istituto di S. Ignazio* (Rome 1650), the history appeared in five volumes, *Dell' istoria della compagnia di Gesù* (Rome 1653–73). He wrote also biographies of several Jesuit saints, books on literature, and treatises on asceticism, natural science, and philology in a style that places him among classical Italian authors. The most nearly complete collection of his works appears in 38 volumes, *Opera del Padre Daniello Bartoli* (Turin 1825–56).

Bibliography: Sommervogel 1:965–985; 8:1771–72; 12:946. E. Lamalle, DHGE 6:1043–46. P. Tacchi-Venturi, EncCatt 2:906–908. P. P. Trompeo, EncIt 6:247–248, bibliog. B. Schneider, LexThK² 2:17.

[E. D. MC SHANE]

BARTOLO DI FREDI, Renaissance painter; b. Siena, *c.* 1335; d. Siena, 1410. Like his contemporary (St.) Catherine of Siena, Bartolo was closely associated with the Dominicans, though he was also employed by other groups. His Old Testament cycle on the south wall of the Collegiata, San Gimignano, signed and dated 1367, includes an unusually extensive group of scenes from Job. Among his important panels are a "Deposition" (1382), Montalcino; and a "Coronation of the Virgin" (1388), Siena. Various versions of his unique form of the "Adoration of the Magi" (see illus. below), datable between 1375 and 1380, show the early use of an extensive cavalcade. His use of small aedicules suggests an acquaintance with contemporary religious drama. Bartolo, in keeping with the seriousness engendered by repeated visitations of the plague and by Dominican preaching, developed an abstract and highly expressive style, which in its rejection of realistic detail, of spatial depth, and of exquisite courtliness, contrasts sharply with the style of the first half of the century. (*See* RENAISSANCE ART.)

Bibliography: S. L. Faison, Jr., "Barna and Bartolo di Fredi," ArtBull 14 (1932) 284–315; 15 (1933) 293–294. L. Rigatusa, "Bartolo di Fredi," *Diana* 9 (Siena 1934) 214–267. P. Schubring, Thieme-Becker 2:558–560. **Illustration credit:** Alinari-Art Reference Bureau.

[L. E. BUSH]

BARTOLO OF SASSOFERRATO, one of the most important jurists of the later Middle Ages; b. Sassoferrato, 1313; d. Perugia, 1357. He studied law under Cinus at Perugia and under James of Belvisio at Bologna where he received his doctorate of law in 1334. After further private study, he became professor of law at Pisa in 1339, and later at Perugia, where he remained until his death. He is most famous for developing a

Bartolo di Fredi, "Adoration of the Magi," tempera on panel, in the Accademia di Belle Arti at Siena.

method of applying Roman law to contemporary problems by use of the scholastic method. A group of jurists who followed his method were known as "Bartolists." He wrote many important works, the most famous being a commentary on the Code of Justinian.

Bibliography: C. N. WOOLF, *Bartolus of Sassoferrato: His Position in the History of Medieval Political Thought* (Cambridge, Eng. 1913). B. KURTSCHEID, "Bartoli de Saxoferrato, vita, opera, momentum, influxus," *Apollinaris* 11 (1938) 110–117. Van Hove 1:520–523.

[J. M. BUCKLEY]

BARTOLOCCI, GIULIO, eminent Hebraist; b. Celano, in the Abruzzi, April 1, 1613; d. Rome, Oct. 20, 1687. He made his profession as a Cistercian monk of the Italian congregation of the Feuillants (reformed Bernadines) at the monastery of St. Pudentiana in Rome. He studied theology at Mondovi and Turin, did extensive research in Jewish literature in the libraries of Italy, and taught Hebrew at Rome. He was named *Scriptor Hebraicus* at the Vatican Library, where he was assisted by the convert from Judaism Jehudah *Jonah ben Jiṣhaq. He was appointed a consulter to the Congregation of the Index, served as superior of Cistercian houses in Brisighella and Rome, presided at their general chapter, was visitor for the Roman province, and became titular abbot of San Sebastiano ad Catacumbas. His chief work was the *Bibliotheca magna rabbinica de scriptoribus et scriptis hebraicis,* which appeared in four volumes: in 1675, 1678 (dedicated to Pope Innocent XI), 1683, and 1694 (edited posthumously by his pupil Carlo Imbonati). Despite its shortcomings, this vast account of Jewish writers and literature was valued greatly by later compilers. Bartolocci's unpublished works include *Liber Tobiae,* a Hebrew version with interlinear Latin translation; *Defensio Christiana;* and *Collectanea de Trinitate, Messiae divinitate ac gentium vocatione.*

Bibliography: J. OLIVIERI, DB 1.2:1474–75. E. FLORIT, Enc Catt 2:914. K. SPAHR, LexThK² 2:17–18. J. M. CANIVEZ, DHGE 6:1050–51. EncJudaica 3:1102–03. C. J. MOROZZO, *Cistercii reflorescentis . . . chronologica historia* (Turin 1690) 123.

[C. BERNAS]

BARTOLOMMEO, FRA, Florentine painter who strongly influenced Raphael; b. Baccio della Porta, in Soffignano, 1475; d. Florence, 1517. He was a pupil of Cosimo Rosselli. While still very young, he and a fellow apprentice, Mariotto Albertinelli, left Cosimo's workshop and entered into partnership. He was among the defenders of Savonarola when the friar was besieged in S. Marco on April 8, 1498, and vowed, if he should be spared, to take the habit. Two years later he entered the Dominican Order, leaving his "Last Judgment" in S. Maria Nuova to be finished by Albertinelli. Assigned to the convent of S. Marco, Florence, he did not touch a brush until requested by his prior to do "The Vision of St. Bernard" (1504–07). Presumably about this time he met and exchanged ideas with *Raphael. After a trip to Venice in 1508, the partnership with Albertinelli was reestablished, but it was dissolved by the prior in 1512. Probably in that year Fra Bartolommeo went to Rome, but he left before completing his commissions there. Apparently he had contracted malaria, for the work of his last 5 years in Florence, Lucca, and elsewhere was punctuated by frequent visits to the Dominican hospice in Pian di Mugnone. His tender Madonnas and altarpieces with their subtly varied symmetry evoke

Fra Bartolommeo, "Madonna and Child," fresco, in the Galleria Antica e Moderna, Florence.

deep religious feeling. He was among the first to exploit the dramatic effect of three-dimensional movement in the human figure.

Bibliography: L. E. BAXTER (L. Scott, pseud.), *Fra Bartolommeo* (New York 1881), bibliog. R. E. FRY, *Transformations* (New York 1926) 82–94. **Illustration credit:** Alinari-Art Reference Bureau.

[H. V. NIEBLING]

BARTON, ELIZABETH, "the Nun of Kent"; b. c. 1506; d. London, April 20, 1534. In 1525 Elizabeth, a servant in the Aldington, Kent, household of Thomas Cobb, steward of William Warham, Archbishop of Canterbury, suffered an illness that gave rise to trances, religious ecstasies, and prophecies. A diocesan commission headed by Edward Bocking, OSB, examined her and pronounced her condition of divine origin. The "servant girl who spoke to angels" soon received much attention and renown. Removed to Saint Sepulchre Priory near Canterbury, Elizabeth became a nun and continued her warnings and prophecies, which found credence with high and low. Bocking and his fellow monks appear to have used her to revive pious devotions and to weaken heretical teachings. Miracles were attributed to her despite the skeptical attitudes of Thomas More and of the King himself. During the royal divorce proceedings, the Nun more plainly admonished the King and his sympathizers. Elizabeth seems to have convinced Warham, her patron, and to have swayed even Wolsey to oppose the King's insistence on marrying Anne Boleyn. John Fisher, Bishop of Rochester, the Marchioness of Exeter, the Countess of Salisbury, and other supporters of Queen Catherine, consulted Elizabeth from 1528 to 1532, and she became a champion of Henry's opposition. Catherine never consulted Elizabeth. Elizabeth announced that Henry would die if he remarried and that he had forfeited his throne before God. In 1533 Thomas Cranmer succeeded to the See of Canterbury, and with Thomas Cromwell, used the Nun to ensnare the enemies of Henrician reform. Cranmer skillfully extorted a confession in which Elizabeth admitted deceit and duplicity. Denounced as a fraud, Elizabeth, with a number of others, More and Fisher included, was eventually condemned by a bill of attainder. More's earlier skepticism won his exclusion from the action, but the Nun and six others were condemned to death. Fisher and five others were imprisoned and their goods confiscated. Elizabeth was executed at Tyburn, publicly confessing her guilt and pride. Cromwell's methods undoubtedly raise some question as to the validity of the charges made by him. On the other hand, it seems clear that Elizabeth was exploited by Bocking and others for religious and possibly political reasons.

Bibliography: S. LEE, DNB 1:1263–66. Hughes RE. G. MATTINGLY, *Catherine of Aragon* (Boston 1941).

[P. S. MC GARRY]

BARUCH, son of Neria, friend and secretary of the Prophet Jeremia. Jeremia dictated several of his oracles to Baruch (Heb. *bārûk,* blessed, probably a shortened form of *bᵉrûkyâ,* blessed of Yahweh), who wrote them on a scroll and then read them before the people in the Temple and later before the authorities; when King Joakim had heard the oracles, he burned the scroll, and Baruch wrote them down a second time at Jeremia's dictation (Jer 36.4–32). Because of Baruch's loyalty, special blessings were promised to him by Jeremia (Jer 45.1–5). After the fall of Jerusalem, the Jewish refugees took Jeremia and Baruch along with them to Egypt (Jer 43.6). According to a tradition recounted by St. Jerome, Baruch died there. He is important not only because he served Jeremia, but also because he is responsible for the biographical portions of that Prophet's book. Later generations credited him with the deuterocanonical Book of *Baruch and with two apocryphal books, the Syriac Apocalypse of Baruch and the Greek Apocalypse of Baruch. *See* BIBLE, III (CANON), 4.

Bibliography: EncDictBibl 210–211. V. HAMP, LexThK² 2:18–19. G. VON RAD, *Theologie des Alten Testaments,* 2 v. (Göttingen 1957–60) 2:218–220, Eng. tr. D. STALKER (New York 1962–). C. SCHEDL, *Geschichte des Alten Testament* (Innsbruck 1956–) 4:395–402.

[L. A. IRANYI]

BARUCH, BOOK OF

A deuterocanonical book of the OT whose title (Bar 1.1–2) attributes it to *Baruch, the erstwhile secretary of Jeremia (Jer 36.4), writing in Babylon during the Exile.

Authorship, Unity, and Contents. It seems established, on the basis of a number of indications, that Baruch was not the author of this book: (1) in spite of the authority that the name of Baruch would have given to it, the book was never taken into the Hebrew Canon (*see* CANON, BIBLICAL) or even preserved in Hebrew, if it ever existed in the language; (2) there are good grounds for believing that parts of it were composed in Hebrew, but other parts were probably composed in Greek (see below); (3) the book is not a unified prophetic composition, but a combination of different literary forms; (4) finally, many of the historical inaccuracies would be incomprehensible if they came from an author contemporary with the events, as Baruch was. For example, the introduction (1.1–14) supposes that the Temple was still standing and the liturgy was performed in it, while, in fact, the Temple

was in ruins; the incorrect supposition that *Belsassar (Bel-shar-usur) was the son of Nabuchodonosor is found (Bar 1.11–12), perhaps under the influence of Dn 5.2; and Jechonia is placed in the crowd of Jewish exiles (Bar 1.3), although at this time he was really in prison.

The book is, in fact, an artful combination of pieces of diverse origin. The first section (1.1–14) is an edifying unhistorical narrative intended to introduce the book as reading for the Feast of *Booths; then follows a penitential prayer placed in the mouths of the exiles (1.15–3.8), similar to the liturgy found in Neh 9.5–38 and based in part (1.15–2.19) on Dn 9.4–19; the third section (Bar 3.9–4.4), sapiential in character, is a Wisdom hymn; and the fourth section (4.5–5.9) is an anthology of poems in which Jerusalem speaks to her children (4.5–29), and her children speak to her (4.30–5.9). Note that 5.5–9 depends on Psalm of Solomon 11.2–7. *See* BIBLE, III (CANON), 4. For details on ch. 6, appended to Baruch in the Vulgate but separate in the Septuagint, *see* JEREMIA, LETTER OF.

Language and Time of Composition. While conservative opinion still retained Baruch as the author, it had to insist that the book was written in Hebrew and that its original was lost. Modern opinion (e.g., B. N. Wambacq), however, holds that the different parts of the book were written in different languages. It is suggested that 1.1–14 was written in Greek; 1.15–3.8, in Hebrew; 3.9–4.4, possibly in Hebrew but more likely in Greek; and 4.5–5.9, very probably in Greek.

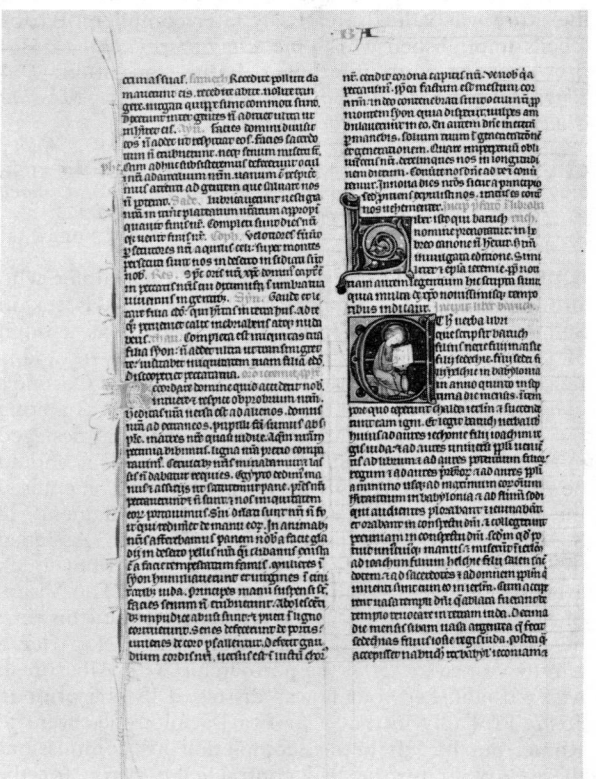

The beginning of the Book of Baruch in an illuminated 13th-century Bible from either France or England (Walter's MS 10.59, fol. 316 v.). The large capital "E" contains a figure of Baruch at his writing table.

It is most likely that the different parts of the book were written at different times. The following is the reconstruction suggested by Wambacq: 1.15–3.8 was written between 165 B.C. (about the time of the composition of Daniel) and A.D. 70, since it supposes that the Temple is still standing; 3.9–4.4 mirrors the doctrine of Sirach and presumably was written about the same time (160–130 B.C.); 4.5–5.9 depends on Psalm of Solomon 11 and therefore could not be earlier than 63 B.C. The final combination of these parts would have been *c.* 60 B.C., with 1.3–14 added at a later date. Extreme opinions hold that the book was written in Roman times and that Nabuchodonosor and Belsassar really stand for Vespasian and Titus. At the other extreme, A. Penna proposes that 1.1–3.8 was written by Baruch, but that 3.9–4.4 and 4.5–5.9 were written in the Persian and exilic era respectively. A. Gelin is of the opinion that 1.1–14 is from the Machabean period and that the rest is contemporary with Sir 24.1–31; 36.1–17.

Doctrinal Character. The book's central theme is collective sin and resulting suffering. There is no mention of a resurrection, but only of Sheol and no individual judgment is mentioned. Wisdom is identified with the Law or Torah (Bar 4.1–4; cf. Sir 24.23), which is the source of joy and happiness. God is referred to as eternal (Bar 4.14), as is the covenant (2.35) and the Law (4.1). The author's interest in eternity derives from Deutero-Isaia (*see* ISAIA, BOOK OF). The book reflects the mentality of the late Diaspora (*see* DIASPORA, JEWISH), as does Tobit. *See* TOBIT (TOBIAS), BOOK OF. It speaks of adaptation to the host country (cf. the prayer for the kings in Bar 1.11–12), although there is an occasional outburst of hatred against the oppressor (4.25).

The book emphasizes fidelity to Yahweh through the service of the synagogue and, above all, through observance of the Law. It is not surprising that it is on the Feast of Booths, the day on which the Law was read and the covenant renewed, that the author wishes his book to be read in the Lord's Temple (1.14).

Bibliography: EncDictBibl 210–212. A. GELIN, *Jérémie, Les Lamentations, Le Livre de Baruch* (BJ 23; 1951). V. HAMP, LexThK² 2:18–19. A. PENNA, *Geremia* (Turin 1954). B. N. WAMBACQ, "Les Prières de Baruch (1.15–2.19) et de Daniel (9.5–19)," *Biblica* 40 (1949) 463–475; "L'Unité littéraire de Bar. 1.1–3.8," *Sacra Pagina* 1 (1959) 455–460. **Illustration credit:** Courtesy of the Walters Art Gallery, Baltimore, Md.

[L. A. IRANYI]

BARZYŃSKI, VINCENT, missionary whose varied activities influenced Polish Catholic development in the U.S.; b. Sulislawice, Russian-held Poland, Sept. 20, 1838; d. Chicago, Ill., May 2, 1899. He was the son of Joseph and Mary (Sroczyńska) Barzyński and was baptized Michael. After studies at the diocesan seminary in Lublin, Poland, he was ordained there Oct. 27, 1861. He participated in the unsuccessful Polish uprising of January 1863 against Russia and then sought refuge in Austria and in France. At Paris he joined (1866) the recently founded Congregation of the Resurrection and was sent to the U.S. to work among Polish Catholics in the Diocese of Galveston, Tex. In 1874 he was appointed pastor of St. Stanislaus Kostka parish in Chicago, remaining there until his death. Besides administrating the largest Polish parish and grade school in America, he founded a publishing house that launched (1890) a Polish Catholic daily, *Dziennik Chicagoski,*

still in existence. He established (1891) St. Stanislaus Kostka High School for boys, which he unsuccessfully planned to expand into a college. He was active in the Polish Roman Catholic Union; in the organization of several Chicago parishes and parochial schools; in the formation of a new Polish-American sisterhood, the Franciscan Sisters of Bl. Kunegunda; and in the building of an orphanage and home for the aged. After serving as a superior of the Chicago Resurrectionists, he became the first provincial of the congregation's American province (1898–99); he has been described as one of the most effective executors of the Resurrectionist concept of the modern parish as a barrier against the radical socialist influences of the times in which he lived.

Bibliography: L. M. LONG, *The Resurrectionists* (Chicago 1947). S. SIATKA, *Krótkie Wspomnienie o Życiu i Działalności Ks. M. Wincentego Barzyńskiego CR* (Chicago 1901). W. KWIATKOWSKI, *Historia Zgromadzenia Zmartwychwstania Pańskiego na Stuletnią Rocznicę Jego Założenia 1842–1942* (Albano 1942).

[J. V. SWASTEK]

BASALENQUE, DIEGO, Augustinian chronicler and linguist of colonial Mexico; b. Salamanca, Spain, July 25, 1577; d. Charo, Mexico, Dec. 11, 1651. His parents, Alonso Serrano and Isabel Cardona, emigrated to New Spain (Mexico) when Diego was a child. He joined the Augustinians when he was 15, and made his religious profession in Mexico City, Feb. 4, 1594. Recognized as a man of unusual talents, he was assigned after ordination to teach the students of his order in the province of Michoacán (created in 1602). He was later awarded the degree of master of theology, and was chosen for various offices, including those of prior in the monasteries of San Luis Potosí and Valladolid (formerly Guayangareo, now Morelia), and provincial of Michoacán (1623). Though learned in many fields, Basalenque was probably best known for his skill in law, both civil and ecclesiastical, and in languages. He was proficient in Latin, Greek, and Hebrew, and in several Mexican tongues as well. He is reputed to be the author of numerous works on diverse subjects from theology to mathematics, but only three of his works are known to have been published. The most valuable for Augustinian history and biography is *Historia de la provincia de San Nicolás de Tolentino de Michoacán del orden de N. P. S. Agustín,* completed in three books in 1644 and published in Mexico City in 1673 (repr. Mexico City 1886). For the events of the 16th century, he copied much from the chronicle of Juan de *Grijalva. Basalenque's style, typical of his time, was excessively rhetorical. Of his two known studies on native tongues, only one was published—*Arte de la lengua Tarasca* (Mexico City 1714, 1805, and 1886). A treatise on the spiritual life, *Muerte en vida y vida en muerte,* was published in part in various numbers of *Archivo agustiniano* from volume 33 (1930) to volume 43 (1935). A life of Basalenque, who was regarded by his contemporaries as a man of holiness as well as learning, was published by one of his confreres, Pedro Salguero, in Mexico City in 1664 (repr. Rome 1761).

Bibliography: G. DE SANTIAGO VELA, *Ensayo de una biblioteca ibero-americana de la orden de San Agustín,* 7 v. in 8 (Madrid 1913–31) 1:331–337. I. MONASTERIO, *Archivo agustiniano* 29 (1928) 408–417. M. T. DISDIER, DHGE 6:1063–64.

[A. J. ENNIS]

BASAN (BASHAN), ancient Hebrew name *(bāšān),* meaning a "smooth, fertile land," used to refer to the plateau or tableland in Transjordan, north of *Galaad. It is an area of wide, fertile plains with an altitude of about 2,000 feet. Although not precisely designated, Basan is generally considered to be that region that extends southward from the foot of Mt. *Hermon, across the *Yarmuk River, to the mountains of Galaad, and westward from the Jebel Druze (Hauran) to the upper *Jordan. Since the Galilean hills to the west are relatively low, the wind and rains from the Mediterranean sweep into this region unobstructed; the resulting copious rainfall combines with the rich volcanic soil to produce excellent crops, especially grain. In antiquity Basan was famous for its fertility. Its forests were linked with those of Mt. *Carmel and *Lebanon in renown (Is 2.13; Ez 27.6; Za 11.2). Equally famous were its fat cattle (Dt 32.14; Ez 39.18; see also Am 4.1, where the Prophet likens the sybaritic women of Samaria to the fattened herds of Basan). The highest regions of Basan are to the north and east, the eastern area being notable for its tortuous and rugged ridges composed in the main of basalt produced in ages past by the flowing lava of now extinct volcanoes. The author of the difficult Psalm 67(68) poetically rebukes the majestic, many-peaked mount of Basan for looking down so disdainfully on tiny Mt. *Sion (v. 16–17). If the Jebel Druze can rightfully be regarded as being within the confines of Basan, it would perhaps better fulfill the description of the Psalmist than, as generally stated, Mt. Hermon. The chief towns of the Basan plateau were Carnaim (modern Shaykh Saʻad, Am 6.13), Astharoth (modern Tell ʻAshtara, Jos 9.10), Bosra (Buṣra-eski Shâm, 1 Mc 5.26), Edrai (modern Derʻā, Nm 21.33), Salecha (modern Salkhad), strictly in the Jebel Druze but numbered among the cities of the kingdom of Og in Basan (Dt 3.10), and Golan (Dt 4.43), which in the Hellenistic era gave its name to the region known as *Gaulanitis, somewhat as Basan itself became Batanaea, although the latter comprised only a part of the original Basan. The ancient history of Basan, as reconstructed from various Biblical references, was one of almost continual conflict. The earliest-mentioned inhabitants were the Raphaim, the pre-Israelite dwellers of the land, spoken of as "giants," whom Chodorlahomor and the kings subdued at Astharoth-Carnaim (Gn 14.5). Og, King of the Amorrites in Basan, thought to be the last of the Raphaim, was defeated by the advancing Israelites in a victory much celebrated in OT prose and poetry [Nm 21.33; Dt 3.1, 11; Jos 12.4; Ps 134(135).11; 135(136).20]. David held Basan for Israel, but later under Achab, Joram, and Jehu it was under control of Damascus, then regained by Jeroboam II, and lost again, this time to the Assyrians. The *Nabataeans held it briefly during the height of their power. In NT times it was subject in turn to *Herod the Great, *Philip the Tetrarch, and *Agrippa II.

Bibliography: N. GLUECK, *The Other Side of the Jordan* (New Haven 1940). D. BALY, *The Geography of the Bible* (New York 1957) 219–226. Abel GéogrPal 1:275–276, 2:155. EncDictBibl 212–213. H. HAAG, LexThK² 2:19–20. G. PRIERO, EncCatt 2: 940–941.

[C. F. DE VINE]

BASCIO, MATTEO SERAFINI DA, first vicar-general of the Friars Minor Capuchin; b. Bascio, near Pesaro, c. 1495; d. Venice, Aug. 6, 1552. He joined the Friars Minor Observants of the Province of Ancona c. 1511 and was ordained c. 1520. Restless for reform, Matteo left his friary at Montefalcone secretly in 1525, went to Rome, and there obtained from Clement VII verbal permission to observe the Rule of St. Francis to the letter, to wear a habit more in accordance with the type thought to be worn by Francis, and to preach wherever he wished without any fixed residence, provided that he presented himself to his provincial once each year. Once when obeying the last injunction, Matteo was confined in the friary at Forano as a fugitive, but was freed through the intervention of Caterina Cibo, Duchess of Camerino. The purely personal privilege that Matteo had obtained encouraged like-minded confreres to join him, and thus, unsuspectingly, he became the herald of a movement that resulted in the foundation of a new branch of the Franciscan family, the Friars Minor Capuchin. This new congregation received canonical approbation with the granting of the bull *Religionis Zelus,* July 3, 1528. The following year, Matteo, elected first vicar-general of the new order, accepted office with reluctance, resigning shortly afterward. He then continued his wandering apostolate first as a Capuchin, then from 1536, apparently, under the minister general of the Observants. Preaching with great success, he played a notable part in the Italian Catholic reformation. In 1546 he accompanied the papal troops that Paul III sent to Germany to assist Charles V against the members of the *Schmalkaldic League. At Mühlberg in April 1547, Matteo, crucifix held aloft, encouraged the Catholic soldiers to a decisive victory. He then continued his apostolate in Venice, where he was venerated for his holiness.

Bibliography: FATHER CUTHBERT, *The Capuchins,* 2 v. (London 1928). MELCHIOR A POBLADURA, ed., *Monumenta historica Ordinis Fratrum Minorum Capuccinorum,* (Assisi 1937–40; Rome 1950–). *Lexicon Capuccinum* (Rome 1951) 1075–76, gives general bibliog. F. SPRUCK, "Matteo da Bascio," *Round Table of Franciscan Research* 7 (1941–42) 123–146. D. DA PORTOGRUARO, "Il processo dei Miracoli del P. Matteo da Bascio," CollFran 15 (1945) 92–116. G. ABATE, "Fra' Matteo da Bascio e gli inizî dell'Ordine Cappuccino," *ibid.* 30 (1960) 31–77. F. CALLAEY, EncCatt 8:496–497.

[C. REEL]

BASEDOW, JOHANN BERNHARD, educator, theologian, and philosopher, whose writings and methods profoundly influenced educational principles and practices of the 18th century; b. Hamburg, Germany, Sept. 12, 1723; d. Magdeburg, July 24, 1790. The son of a struggling wigmaker of surly temperament and of a mother who suffered from melancholia, Basedow was unhappy in his early years. His unusual intelligence was recognized, however, and in 1774 he was enrolled in the Hamburg Johanneum, a classical high school. In 1744 Basedow entered the University of Leipzig where, while studying theology and philosophy, he discovered Rousseau's *Émile* and was impressed by his theory of naturalism in education. Upon leaving the University of Leipzig, he became tutor to the young son of the Danish privy councilor at Borghorst. In this capacity *Émile* was his guide, and the experiment met with success.

Basedow's naturalistic theories of education impressed persons of influence. Prince Leopold supported Basedow's theories and encouraged him to put them into practice. In December 1774 Basedow opened a school in Dessau called the *Philanthropinum, the first nonsectarian school established in Germany. Patronized by the children of gentlemen and nobles, the Philanthropinum inculcated play in all phases of learning. Basedow's work at the Dessau Philanthropinum greatly impressed his associates, J. H. Campé, who became known for his writings in the field of children's literature, and C. G. Salzmann, noted for his emphasis on practical education.

Although Basedow wrote about 100 books, only two received more than passing notice: *Elementarwerk* (Elementary Work), written as a dialogue on the instruction of children, and *Das Methodenbuch* (Methodical Instruction), a guide for teachers and parents of children who would use the *Elementarwerk*. It is in *Das Methodenbuch* that Basedow expounds his educational theories and principles.

Since Basedow believed that all practical instruction was moral, he did not favor formal moral training. His ideas on play-teaching prepared the way for J. H. Pestalozzi, F. W. *Fröbel, and others (*see* PESTALOZZIANISM). His insistence that teaching was a profession revolutionized the character of German education.

Bibliography: *Ausgewählte Schriften,* ed. H. GÖRING (Langensalza, Ger. 1880). O. H. LANG, *Basedow: His Educational Work and Principles* (New York 1891).

[C. A. SMITH]

BASEL, COUNCIL OF

An ecumenical council announced in Siena on Feb. 19, 1423, and convoked at Basel, Switzerland, by Martin V on Feb. 1, 1431, and after his death confirmed by Eugene IV. In 1437, it was transferred to Ferrara; in 1439, to Florence (*see* FLORENCE, COUNCIL OF). The *Western Schism of 1378 to 1417 had provoked the cardinals into summoning the Council of *Pisa (1409) independently of the papacy. This practical *conciliarism had been given theoretical expression in the Council of *Constance (1414–18), which declared that a general council was the highest authority in the Church with regard to heresy, peace, and reform of both head and members. The conciliarists focused on reform, especially reform of the head, i.e., the Pope and the Curia. The reform-minded conciliarists had been checked in the Council of Siena, but they asserted themselves at Basel. The events of the Basel Council fell into two periods: that of the council proper (1431–37) and the period of the *conciliabulum* (1437–49). The matters treated at the council proper can conveniently be described under the three headings of peace, reform, and heresy, which constituted the proper competence of a general council according to the conciliarists.

Peace or Unity. The council was inaugurated on July 23, 1431, but when its president, Cardinal Giuliano *Cesarini, arrived on September 9 he found very few people present. On December 18, because of the sparse attendance, war, and the prospect of a council with the Greeks in Italy, Pope Eugene prorogued the assembly at Basel with the plan to meet in Bologna after 18 months; this was despite Cesarini's expostulation. The council Fathers refused to disperse, and in the second session (Feb. 15, 1432) adopted the principle of the Council of Constance on conciliar superiority with an even more stringent interpretation. New members joined the council, which they thought stood for much-needed reform against a resisting Roman Curia. Thirty-eight prelates were present by the end of April and Eugene was told firmly to withdraw his dissolution and to come to the council in person or by proxy. The

cardinals began to desert him. The secular powers (except England, Venice, Florence, and *Sigismund after his coronation as emperor, May 31, 1433) supported the council. Eugene began to make concessions, but not quickly enough for the growing sense of power of the council. With its membership increasing and Eugene yielding, the council became more imperious and threatening still. It refused to accept the five presidents nominated by the Pope and imposed the text of a bull withdrawing the dissolution. Eugene, ill and very nearly without supporters, tried to evade the stringency of this proposed formula but finally promulgated the *Dudum sacrum* (Dec. 15, 1433) saying: "We decree and declare that the said general council from the time of its inception has been and is being legitimately carried on . . . that it ought to be carried on . . . for the aforesaid ends [heresy, peace of the Church, reform]." On Feb. 5, 1434 (16th session), 7 cardinals, 3 patriarchs (Latin), 50 bishops, 30 abbots, and 422 other members declared themselves satisfied. But they received the five papal presidents only after they had taken the conciliar oath with a special addition asserting conciliar supremacy (April 26, 1434). In July, three Greek envoys arrived with whom it was agreed to hold a unionistic council in one of certain specified towns (September 7). Eugene, who was at the time an exile in Florence from rebellious Rome, acquiesced even though he had earlier made different arrangements with the Greeks. The next year, June 9, 1435, the council forbade the payment of *annates and steadily refused any form of compensation to meet necessary papal expenses. On April 14, 1436, it published a plenary indulgence in favor of the Greek-Latin council, but afraid of the prestige that would accrue to the Pope if the council were held in Italy, it insisted on Basel or Avignon as the site, despite the repeated refusal of the Greeks and Eugene's opposition. The council's intransigent attitude on this issue, together with its fierce antagonism to the papacy, lost it its supporters. Cardinals returned to papal allegiance; secular governments, fearing a new schism, counseled moderation. The council itself split, for while the majority favored its being held at Basel or Avignon, a respectable minority voted for one of the towns named in the treaty. On May 7, 1437, both majority and minority parties promulgated decrees simultaneously. The minority, with the Greek delegates, took their decree to Eugene who was in Bologna and he agreed to implement it. Immediately hiring ships to transport the Greeks, Eugene transferred the Council of Basel to Ferrara by the bull *Doctoris gentium,* Sept. 18, 1437. This bull was confirmed December 30, whereupon the Council of Basel legally ceased to exist. The council, removed to Ferrara, lasted until 1439.

Reform. When the council met in 1431 the Church unquestionably needed reform, both in head and members. Members were plentifully represented at Basel but each section—bishops, princes, religious orders, cathedral chapters, universities—resisted reform of itself. Attention, therefore, was concentrated on the head. The reforms imposed, though few in number, were all theoretically good. Some, however, were impracticable, at least to the drastic degree envisaged by the council. On July 13, 1433, it limited papal *provisions to benefices; on Jan. 22, 1435, it forbade clerical concubinage and regulated excommunication; on June 9 it banished every form of payment except bare ad-

Woodcut of an ecumenical council; frontispiece to an edition of "Decreta et acta Concilii Basiliensis" published in 1511.

ministrative expenses upon the conferment of *benefices, including annates to the Pope and, of course, *simony; on March 24, 1436, it established new norms for papal elections, and for the conduct, number, and qualities of cardinals. Those reforms advantageous for France and Germany survived for a time, but the rest lapsed. During its 6 years the council's main occupations were opposition to the papacy and reform of and controversy with the *Hussites and the Greeks.

Extirpation of Heresy. The heresy of *Wyclif had been condemned both in England and in the Council of Constance where Hus and Jerome of Prague had died at the stake. But it was the basis of the Hussitism, intermingled with legitimate aspirations for reform, with which the Council of Basel was concerned. The Hussites insisted on four points: communion under both kinds, punishment of mortal sin by the secular power, unrestricted freedom to preach, and evangelical poverty for all clergy. Negotiations between the council and the Bohemians began with the "Accord of Eger" (May 18, 1432) making the Scriptures, councils, and doctors "the most reliable and impartial judge." Fifteen Hussite delegates with a suite of 300 came to Basel on Jan. 1, 1433. Council envoys went to Prague with the delegates, returning to Basel with three Hussites in August. Subsequently the Council of Basel sent its same long-suffering representatives to Prague (November 18), Regensburg (Aug. 21, 1434), Brünn (July 1,

1435), Stuhlweissenburg (Dec. 20), and Iglau. An agreement, the *Compacts,* had been reached in Prague in 1433 when the council conceded to the Bohemians the use of the chalice at Communion. Subsequent meetings were occupied with the interpretation of the four points, especially poverty. At Iglau (July 5, 1436), the *Compacts* were solemnly promulgated, largely because the Emperor Sigismund guaranteed their fulfillment. In spite of pressure the Czechs never joined the Council of Basel and did not loyally observe the *Compacts.* The agreement lapsed under Pius II in 1458.

Basel 1437–49—the Conciliabulum. With very reduced numbers, the "Council of Basel" defied Eugene's decree of translation to Ferrara. It sent its fleet to bring the Greeks from Constantinople, but they preferred the papal fleet. On Jan. 24, 1438, it declared Eugene suspended and deprived of all spiritual and temporal power. It sent strong delegations to the various French and German diets but resisted dissolution in favor of a third council. On May 16, 1439, it declared the principle of superiority of a council over the pope a truth of Catholic faith and on June 25 it deposed Eugene. On November 5 it elected an antipope, Felix V. Thereafter it wrote long answers to papal bulls, but passed no legislation. In February 1448 Frederick of Austria withdrew his safe-conducts and the council members joined Felix in Lausanne. Charles VII of France sponsored an arrangement whereby the "Council of Basel" would dissolve—Felix, who resigned, and its chief members being honorably treated. On April 19, 1449, the council elected the reigning *Nicholas V to succeed Felix and solemnly reenacted the principle of conciliar supremacy. Then, on April 25, it decreed its own dissolution.

Significance of the Council. The council at its height had some 500 members, divided into four deputations. There were, however, never more than about 100 bishops and abbots present and they alone, by tradition, had a deliberative vote. But in Basel every member had a vote. Several of the most important measures were passed by relatively few bishops plus a mass of others. Basel signified the height and defeat of conciliarism, which, despite the sincere motivation of several of the leading conciliarists, degenerated in the circumstances into antipapalism. The duplication at Basel of most departments of the Papal Curia, the refusal to compromise over annates and the site of the council with the Greeks, and the determination to abase the pope and his office, alienated princes, cardinals, and the moderate-minded, and led to the reconciliation of Eugene and such one-time conciliarists as Cesarini and Nicholas of Cusa. When the Council of Basel broke its pact with the Greeks rather than allow a council in Italy, it made possible the Council of Ferrara-Florence whose success and definition of papal supremacy were a grievous blow to Basel and conciliarism.

Bibliography: Sources. *Monumenta conciliorum generalium saeculi decimi quinti,* 4 v. (Vienna-Basel 1857–1935). J. HALLER et al., eds., *Concilium Basiliense,* 8 v. (Basel 1896–1936). Mansi v.19. ConOecDecr. Literature. A. BAUDRILLART, DTC 2.1:113–129. N. VALOIS, *Le Pape et le Concile, 1418–1450,* 2 v. (Paris 1909). Hefele-Leclercq v.7.2. A. M. JACQUIN, DHGE 6:356–362. B. TIERNEY, *Foundations of the Conciliar Theory* (Cambridge, Eng. 1955). J. B. VILLIGER, LexThK² 2:23–25. E. F. JACOB, "The Conciliar Movement . . . ," BullJRylLibr 41 (1958) 26–53. J. GILL, *Eugenius IV: Pope of Christian Union* (Westminster, Md. 1961).

[J. GILL]

BASHĪR II AL-SHIHĀBI, famous feudal lord of Lebanon from 1788 to 1840, restorer and reformer of greater Lebanon. Bashīr had to recover what *Fakhr-al-Dīn II al-Maʿnī's successors had lost. The Shihābi family, related to Mohammed's, had entered Lebanon in about 1170, intermarried with its Maʿnī emirs and succeeded them. Bashīr I (1697–1707) started the Shihābi line of emirs, of whom the first were Moslems.

Bashīr II's first acquisition was Baalbek (Baʿlabakk), with its fertile plain al-Biqaʿ (Bekaa), and Jabal ʿĀmil (southeast of Sidon). He centralized power in his hands at the expense of his Druze feudatories, launched a program of public works, including renovating or building of bridges and roads, and established security and administered justice on a scale hitherto unknown in the land. The sumptuous palace he built at Bayt al-Dīn is still a showplace and is used as a summer home for the president of the Lebanese Republic. Beirut played host to a growing number of French traders and boasted a bazaar of Greek and Italian shops. Maronites from the north expanded to south Lebanon. Christians from Syria migrated to the country. Bashīr, himself a Maronite, though professing Islam for political reasons, encouraged Roman Catholic, and admitted Protestant, missionary work. In 1823 the first American missionary settled in Beirut, which in 1834 became the seat of the first American mission school in the area. In that year the American Mission Press, still successfully operating, was established. The emir sent the first Lebanese students to study medicine in the earliest medical school of the Arab East, Qaṣr al-ʿAyni of Cairo, built by his ally Muḥammad ʿAlī, Egyptian Viceroy.

When in 1831 Muḥammad ʿAlī launched a military campaign against his suzerain Maḥmūd II, Bashīr collaborated in the conquest of Palestine and Syria. Ibrahīm Pasha, son of Muḥammad ʿAlī and commander in chief of his forces, penetrated the heart of Turkey, threatening the destruction of the entire Ottoman Empire. But in 1840 he was driven back and forced by Britain and France to relinquish all his conquests. Both nations considered it to their advantage to maintain a decadent Ottoman state between themselves and their growing empires in Africa and Asia.

Overtaxed and subjected to a decade of general military conscription, the Lebanese—under Turkish and British prodding—rose in rebellion against Bashīr. A British ship carried him to Malta, whence he later moved to Constantinople. There he died in 1850 to live in Lebanese saga as Bashīr al-Kabīr (the Great). His reign marked the end of feudal Lebanon and the acquisition by the tiny country of a new and enduring international dimension.

Bibliography: H. LAMMENS, *La Syrie: Précis historique,* 2 v. (Beirut 1921) v. 2. P. K. HITTI, *History of Syria, Including Lebanon and Palestine* (2d ed. New York 1957).

[P. K. HITTI]

BASIL, ST.

Bishop and Doctor of the Church, called Basil the Great of Caesarea; b. Pontus, Asia Minor, *c.* 329; d. Caesarea, Jan. 1, 379 (feast, June 14; Jan. 1, Jan. 30 in the East).

Life. Basil was the first Doctor of the Church to combine endowments that often recurred together in later Fathers: aristocracy of birth, refinement of culture, enthusiastic participation in the ascetical movement, and an episcopal ministry. His family were landowners of substance in Pontus, probably of the senatorial class, and had demonstrated heroic loyalty to Christianity during the persecutions; through *Gregory Thaumaturgus they became attached to Origenism. Basil's grandmother *Macrina, his parents Basil and Emilia, his sister Macrina, and his younger brothers *Gregory of Nyssa and Peter of Sebaste are all venerated as saints. Basil was trained in rhetoric at Constantinople and Athens and became a close friend of *Gregory of Nazianzus; he was baptized with him about

St. Basil, the oldest-known representation, fresco of the 8th century in the church of S. Maria Antiqua, Rome.

358 and gave up a brilliant administrative career to join his family in the life of ascetical retirement they were living at Annesi in Pontus, under the influence of *Eustathius of Sebaste.

Anyone belonging to the ascetical groups, which were then strongly deprecated by the ruling classes, could expect many difficulties; but Basil was admitted into the clergy of Caesarea, and divided his time between a retired ascetical life and priestly activity. He was ordained c. 365 and dedicated himself not only to the defense of Nicean orthodoxy but also to social work of Christian charity. After being elected bishop in the spring of 370, he relied heavily on the common people, who venerated his holiness and charity; his social standing gave him leverage for a vigorous opposition to the civil administration, which was protecting Arianism; but he was utilized by that administration to discipline the new forces and to develop mission activity in Armenia. He tried unsuccessfully to oppose the division of Cappadocia, which deprived him of some influence when a new ecclesiastical province was erected and centered in Tyana. His efforts to reunite all orthodox Christians divided by the schism of *Antioch extended to the whole of the East and were crowned with success, after his death, in the Synod of Antioch (379) and the Council of *Constantinople I (381). In 372 he failed in his efforts to win over his old mentor Eustathius of Sebaste, who had become a leading Pneumatomachian. Immediately after Basil's death, his friend Gregory of Nazianzus and his brother Gregory of Nyssa eulogized him in terms already redolent of hagiography; but none of his contemporaries wrote a detailed biography of Basil. Two ancient biographies, one in Syriac and the other in Greek, are wrongly ascribed to his disciple Amphilochius; they contain no useful information. There is evidence of local veneration shortly after Basil's death. The high regard in which Basil was held by *Athanasius, *Ambrose, and *Rufinus of Aquileia explains the rapid spread of this veneration to the other Churches, despite the scant sympathy of *Damasus I and *Jerome. Basil's doctrinal authority is evident in the writings of *Augustine and later of Pope *Leo I and in the *florilegia occasioned in such large quantities by the Council of *Chalcedon.

Works. With Gregory of Nazianzus Basil became from the beginning of his retreat in Annesi a disciple of *Origen and compiled an anthology of Origen's works, the *Philocalia*, apparently published posthumously. The *Moralia* is an anthology of 1,553 verses of the New Testament, with a preface, *On the Judgment of God;* a second preface, *On the Faith*, was added later by the author. The famous *Ad adolescentes, de legendis libris Gentilium*, on the reading of the pagan classics, must also be classed among the works of Basil's earlier years; it is an apology of asceticism addressed to a public with a highly developed Hellenistic culture. A final composition of his early maturity is the small treatise *On the Spirit*, probably authentic, inspired by *Plotinus, who was a source for Basil's later writings. The two most important dogmatic works can be dated with some precision: in 364 he wrote three books *Contra Eunomium* (books 4 and 5 in the preserved text are by Didymus of Alexandria) that refuted the *Apologia* of *Eunomius of Constantinople, the mouthpiece of the Anomoeans (361); the treatise *De*

Spiritu Sancto (375), addressed to *Amphilochius of Iconium, gives a report in its chapters 10 to 28 of a tense dialogue between Basil and Eustathius of Sebaste that took place in Sebaste in June 372.

The voluminous correspondence (366 letters) of Basil can often be dated with certainty and furnishes valuable documentation on the ecclesiastical politics of the age. The majority of the homilies are in all probability from the time of his sacerdotal ministry; but there are reasons for dating the nine homilies *On the Hexaemeron* at the end of Basil's career; these homilies contain a Christian explanation of the created universe, drawing heavily upon Greek science. The *Asceticon* consists of 55 Great Rules, or systematic regulations, for the cenobitic life and 313 Little Rules, or practical answers, to questions raised on the occasion of visitations to already established communities; they also contain elements from other occasions. The text translated into Latin by Rufinus of Aquileia (c. 400) contains only a rough draft of the first of the Great Rules and half of the Little Rules. This archaic version (Little Asceticon) enables us to grasp the institutions in their creative evolution (*Basilian monasticism).

Among the works of disputed authenticity should be listed the two books *De Baptismo*, written during the episcopate, and perhaps the *Commentary on Isaias*, the work of a 4th-century Cappadocian bishop, very well attested in the manuscript tradition. Basil probably did not put the finishing touches to these two works and is not entirely responsible for their style. The homily on Psalm 115 seems to be authentic, but not that on Psalm 37 (Eusebius of Caesarea) or on Psalm 132, or yet the second homily on Psalm 28 (the work of a disciple of Basil), or the homilies *On the Structure of Man* (probably by *Gregory of Nyssa) and *On Paradise*, which claim to be continuations of the *Hexaemeron*. Certainly spurious are the treatises *On Virginity* (probably by Basil of Ancyra), *Consolation to One Lying Sick* (perhaps by Proclus), *On the Incarnation* (also probably by Proclus), and *On Virginity* (of Syrian origin). The few homilies still not edited have scarcely any claim to authenticity.

Of the minor ascetical fragments, the Prologue (PG 31:1509) is authentic, as are the Prologue (PG 31:881) and a list of penances (1305, n. 1–11 and 1313, n. 1–19), at least in the sense that they come from a Basilian environment. Some discourses (PG 31:619, 647, and perhaps 869) are from the 4th or 5th century. The *Constitutions* (with the exception of ch. 1, which comes from a semi-Messalian environment) and the *Exhortation to Renunciation* (PG 31:1321, 625) are later works and come from environments influenced vaguely by Basil. The *Admonitio ad filium spiritualem* and the *De consolatione in adversis* are ancient but of Latin origin. The *De laude solitariae vitae* is by St. Peter Damien (*Opusc.* 11, ch. 19).

Spurious letters are Nos. 8 (*Evagrius Ponticus); 10, 16, and 38 (all three by Gregory of Nyssa); 39 to 45; 47 (Gregory of Nazianzus the Elder); 50, 166 to 167, and 169 to 171 (all five by Gregory of Nazianzus); 189 (Gregory of Nyssa), 197.2; 321 (Gregory of Nazianzus); 335 to 343 (though these may be authentic); 344 to 346 (likewise?); 347 to 356, 357, 359, 360, 365; 366 (taken from *Clement of Alexandria); 361 to 364 seem to be authentic.

Doctrine. The Cappadocians resumed the tradition of Origen; Basil did this in a critical and highly personal fashion, but it was precisely the sureness of touch with which he succeeded in integrating Origen into orthodoxy that made it possible for the two Gregorys, and later Evagrius Ponticus, to give Origen such importance. Basil drew on Stoic and Platonic philosophy, especially that of Plotinus; Dehnhard's researches show that Basil's assimilation of these philosophical currents was thorough, based on the tradition of the Church. Basil placed supreme reliance on the Bible and was conscientious in referring to it as touchstone for everything; at one point, however, his native sincerity in dialogue with Eustathius of Sebaste made him admit that the orthodoxy of his day had had to define more precisely certain Biblical formulas, and he thus for the first time took clear note of the nature and importance of unwritten *tradition (De Spiritu Sancto, c.27).

Trinity. Basil was far more aware than Athanasius and the Westerners of the danger, represented by *Marcellus of Ancyra, of not distinguishing sufficiently between the Divine Persons; that is why he adopted the formula "three hypostases." In his assertion of the perfect resemblance of the Son (and the Spirit) to the Father, he sometimes came close to Tritheism; if he escaped this danger, it was because of his entirely spiritualized conception of the Divine Being and his respect for the incomprehensibility of God. Basil's ascetical training convinced him that only the purified spirit could know things divine. He tried to avoid multiplication of formulas and to induce contemplation in an attitude of adoration: this is the essence of his monastic theology.

In refuting the subtleties of the heretics, however, he did not hesitate to introduce nonscriptural distinctions between what is common in the Trinity, the *ousia,* and what is typical of each of the hypostases. As Doctor of the Holy Spirit, he excommunicated those who asserted that the Spirit is a creature, but he did not demand any more positive confession of faith on this point of the divinity of the Third Person. His friends themselves were astonished at this *oeconomia.* It must be seen not as pure adaptation or "condescension" but as a profound respect for the mystery involved and a desire not to go beyond the terms of the Biblical revelation. In the face of the incipient difficulties of *Christology, Basil initially attempted to adopt the same prudential line, but he finally had to condemn *Apollinaris of Laodicea.

Ecclesiology. Basil's efforts to reconcile the various Churches were intimately connected with his specifically theological activity. *Caesarea was associated with *Antioch, where Bishop Meletius was in conflict not only with an Arian faction but with a small intransigent group headed by Paulinus of Antioch and supported by Athanasius and Pope *Damasus I.

Despite his attachment to the formula "one single hypostasis," Paulinus did not deviate from the orthodox faith, and the schism was primarily a matter of personality clashes. Full of nostalgia for the happy days when the Churches acted in unity as members of the same Body of Christ and aware of the harm being done to the faith of the ordinary laity by the clumsy intervention of the West, Basil made superhuman efforts. He tried not to persuade Meletius to bow out in favor of the man being supported by the Westerners but rather to enlighten those Westerners and if possible to persuade them to come and see on the spot who was in the right, to open their eyes to the actual state of affairs in the East.

Despite the misunderstanding of Basil's position by certain Westerners, he is a very important witness to Catholic unity; his action as mediator implies that he was in communion with Athanasius and Damasus as well as with Meletius. It cannot be denied, of course, that his conception of the local Church and episcopal collegiality, based on faith and charity, is already in line with later orthodox ecclesiology. He had a very clear conception of the freedom of the Church with regard to the imperial power.

Asceticism and Social Christianity. The specific mark of Basil's ecclesiology is its bond with asceticism. The disciples of Eustathius of Sebaste took so seriously the demands for evangelical renunciation that they were in danger of constituting a sect opposed to the official Church, as can be seen at the Council of *Gangra (c. 340). Basil criticized this enthusiasm from the inside, carefully checking its motives against the Gospel, conferring upon it wisdom and respectability and enlightening it with his humanistic culture. He took care not to mistake exterior manifestations, such as virginity or spectacular poverty, for the essential. His own status in the hierarchy facilitated contacts. In fact the discipline he imposed on his brothers made of them, little by little, distinct communities within the Church; but he himself took care not to regard them as such.

Basil based his entire doctrine of renunciation on perfect obedience to the two commandments of the gospel rather than on the evangelical counsels. He made the same demands in his preaching to the people, when he proposed a sort of Christian communism with communal use, if not ownership, of property and with charity serving as the incentive to labor. His preaching was so demanding upon the rich that it may be asked whether it did not express an exaggerated idealism that refused to see the economic realities. But the historical studies of economists on the fall of ancient civilization show that its essential defects were the disparity between the social classes and the increase in unproductive expenses, i.e., precisely the evils that Basil was combating in the name of Christian poverty.

Ecclesiastical Discipline. Three canonical letters of Basil to Amphilochius of Iconium have been received into the code of the Byzantine Church; they give operational directions on the duration and modalities of excommunication for various faults. Basil was there merely systematizing and correcting the severe usages that he found in force. He was not expressing his personal conception of Christianity as freely as he did in the *Asceticon* or in his preaching; rather he was giving proof of a remarkable capacity for adaptation.

Liturgy. Basil took into the Church the monastic tradition of the East and canonized psalm-singing, thus contributing to the molding of the ecclesiastical Office of the Hours. A witness as early as Gregory of Nazianzus bears witness to Basil's liturgical activity. Many prayers bear his name. It is difficult to say if all these are genuine; but the Eucharistic Liturgy attributed to him certainly has some connection with him. It survived in two forms, one called the Alexandrine, the other and longer version called the Byzantine. Some of the alterations typical of the second form bear an unmistakable personal mark of Basil. This does not mean, however, that this Liturgy today retains the form he gave it. As for the first, it is still difficult to say whether it represents an earlier Liturgy that Basil inherited or whether it has also been retouched by his hand. He was under no obligation to use one single and identical formula.

Bibliography: Biographical sources and editions of works. P. MARAN, ed., *Vita S. Basilii,* PG 29:v–clxxvii. M. M. FOX, *The Life and Times of St. Basil the Great* (CUA PatrSt 57; 1939). L. VISCHER, *Basilius der Grosse* (Basel 1953), ecclesiology. Annotated editions of ancient funeral orations. GREGORY OF NYSSA, *Discours funèbres,* ed. and tr. F. BOULENGER (Paris 1908); *Encomium of Saint Gregory, Bishop of Nyssa, on his Brother Saint Basil* ed. and tr. J. A. STEIN (CUA PatrSt 17; 1928); *Vita S. Macrinae,* ed. V. W. CALLAHAN in *Gregorii Nysseni opera,* ed. W. JAEGER, v.8.1 (Leiden 1952) 370–414. EPHREM THE SYRIAN, "Encomium in S. Basilium Magnum," in *Opera,* ed. S. G. MERCATI, v.1.1 (Rome 1915) 113–188. K. V. ZETTERSTÉEN, tr., "Eine Homilie des Amphilochius von Iconium über Basilius," OrChr, 3d ser., 9 (1934) 67–98. A. VÖÖBUS, "Das literarische Verhältnis zwischen der Biographie des Rabbūlā und dem Pseudo-Amphilochianischen Panegyrikus über Basilius," *ibid.* 44 (1960) 40–45. *Opera omnia,* PG v.29–32, reimpression with introd. and bibliog. by P. MARAN and J. GARNIER. The introd. by J. GRIBOMONT to the 1960 repr. gives a complete bibliog. of the eds. and studies on each of his works. F. E. BRIGHTMAN, *Liturgies Eastern and Western* (Oxford 1896), v.1 *Eastern Liturgies,* 309–344, 400–401. J. DORESSE et al., *Un Témoin archaïque de la liturgie copte de saint Basile* (Louvain 1960). Ancient Latin version of the Hexaemeron, E. AMAND DE MENDIETA and S. Y. RUDBERG, eds., *Eustathius* (TU 66; 1958). Homilies, M. HUGLO, RevBén 64 (1954) 129–132. *Asceticon,* PL 103:487–554. *De Spiritu Sancto,* ed. C. T. JOHNSTON (Oxford 1892); ed. B. PRUCHE (SourcesChr 17; 1947). *Letters,* ed. and tr. R. J. DEFERRARI, 4 v. (LoebClLib; 1926–34); (as an app., *Address to Young Men,* ed. with M. R. P. MCGUIRE, *ibid.* 4:363–435); tr. A. C. WAY, ed. R. J. DEFERRARI, 2 v. (FathCh 13, 28; 1951–55); ed. and Fr. tr. Y. COURTONNE, 2 v. (Paris 1957–61), v.3 still to appear, more critical text, insufficient annotation. *Exegetic Homilies,* tr. A. C. WAY (FathCh 46; 1963). *The Ascetic Works of Saint Basil,* ed. and tr. W. K. L. CLARKE (SPCK; 1925). *Selected Works,* ed. and tr. B. JACKSON in NicPNicChFath, 2d ser., 8 (1895).

Textual criticism. M. BESSIÈRES, *La Tradition manuscrite de la correspondance de s. Basile* (Oxford 1923). A. CAVALLIN, *Studien zu den Briefen des hl. Basilius* (Lund 1944). J. GRIBOMONT, *Histoire du texte des Ascétiques de saint Basile* (Louvain 1953). S. Y. RUDBERG, *Études sur la tradition manuscrite de saint Basile* (Upsala 1953); ed. and tr., *L'Homélie de Basile Césarée sur le mot "Observe-toi toi-même"* (Stockholm 1962).

History of doctrine. E. IVÁNKA, *Hellenisches und Christliches im frühbyzantinischen Geistesleben* (Vienna 1948) 28–67. H. DEHNHARD, *Das Problem der Abhängigkeit des Basilius von Plotin* (Patristische Texte und Studien 3; Berlin 1964). W. M. ROGGISCH, *Platons Spuren bei Basilius dem Grossen* (Diss. Bonn 1949). J. F. CALLAHAN, "Greek Philosophy and the Cappadocian Cosmology," *DumbOaksP* 12 (1958) 29–57. B. OTIS, "Cappadocian Thought as a Coherent System," *ibid.* 95–124. W. A. TIECK, *Basil of Caesarea and the Bible* (Doctoral diss. microfilm; Columbia U. 1953). J. GRIBOMONT, "Le Paulinisme de s. Basile," *Studiorum Paulinorum,* 2 v. (AnalBibl 17–18; 1963) 2: 481–490; "L'Origénisme de s. Basile" in *L'Homme devant Dieu: Mélanges Henri du Lubac,* 3 v. (Paris 1963–64) 1:281–294. T. SPIDLÍK, *La Sophiologie de S. Basile* (OrChrAnal 162; 1961).

Trinity. K. HOLL, *Amphilochius von Ikonium in seinem Verhältnis zu den grossen Kappadoziern* (Tübingen 1904), very incisive, but attributes to Basil letters 8 and 38. H. DÖRRIES, *De Spiritu Sancto: Der Beitrag des Basilius zum Abschluss des trinitarischen Dogmas* (Göttingen 1956). J. LEBON, "Le Sort du 'consubstantiel' nicéen," RHE 48 (1953) 632–682. B. PRUCHE, "Autour de traité sur le Saint-Esprit de s. Basile," RechScRel 52 (1964) 204–232. G. L. PRESTIGE, *St. Basil the Great and Apollinaris of Laodicea,* ed. H. CHADWICK (SPCK; 1956). H. DE RIEDMATTEN, "La Correspondance entre Basile de Césarée et Apollinaire de Laodicée," JThSt NS 7 (1956) 199–210; 8 (1957) 53–70.

Ecclesiology. P. BATIFFOL, "L'Ecclésiologie de s. Basile," ÉchosOr 21 (1922) 9–30. V. GRUMEL, "S. Basile et le Siège apostolique," *ibid.* 280–292. E. SCHWARTZ, "Zur Kirchengeschichte des vierten Jahrhunderts," in *Gesammelte Schriften,* 4 v. (Berlin 1960) 39–88. M. RICHARD, "S. Basile et la mission du diacre Sabinus," AnalBoll 67 (1949) 178–202, corrects the preceding work. E. AMAND DE MENDIETA, "Basile de Césarée et Damase de Rome," in *Biblical and Patristic Studies in Memory of R. P. Casey,* ed. J. N. BIRDSALL and R. W. THOMSON (Freiburg 1963) 122–166, exaggerates failure of negotiations. G. F. REILLY, *Imperium and Sacerdotium according to St. Basil* (Washington 1945). Ethics and sociology. S. GIET, *Les Idées et l'action sociales de s. Basile* (Paris 1941). B. TREUCKER, *Politische und sozialgeschichtliche Studien zu den Basilius-Briefen* (Munich 1961).

Liturgy. A. RAES, "Un Nouveau document de la liturgie de s. Basile," OrChrPer 26 (1960) 401–411. W. E. PITT, "The Origin of the Anaphora of the Liturgy of St. Basil," JEcclHist 12 (1961) 1–13. H. ENGBERDING, "Das anaphorische Fürbittgebet der Basiliusliturgie," OrChr 47 (1963) 16–52; 49 (1965) 18–32. J. MATEOS, "L'Office monastique à la fin du IVᵉ siècle: Antioche, Palestine, Cappadoce," OrChr 47 (1963) 53–88.

Culture. L. V. JACKS, *St. Basil and Greek Literature* (CUA PatrSt 1; 1922). A. C. WAY, *The Language and Style of the Letters of St. Basil (ibid.* 13; 1927). Y. COURTONNE, *Saint Basile et l'Hellénisme* (Paris 1934). W. HENGSBERG, *De ornatu rhetorico quem Basilius Magnus . . . adhibuit* (Diss. Bonn 1957). **Illustration credit:** Alinari-Art Reference Bureau.

[J. GRIBOMONT]

BASIL I, BYZANTINE EMPEROR, 867 to 886; b. near Adrianople, 812; d. 886.

Of a poor Armenian family settled in Macedonia, Basil began his career in Constantinople as a groom at the imperial court. Of great physical strength and intelligence he won the favor of the Emperor Michael III, married the latter's mistress, Eudocia Ingerina, murdered the Caesar Bardas and was crowned as coemperor (May 26, 866). After murdering his benefactor, Basil became the founder of the Macedonian dynasty (867–1056). To secure the support of Rome he favored the party hostile to the Patriarch *Photius; he deposed the latter and reinstated *Ignatius as Patriarch of Constantinople. At the council of *Constantinople III (869–870), convoked by Ignatius, the papal legates refused to reexamine the conflict between the two Byzantine patriarchs, and declined to leave the final decision to Basil, declaring that the affair had been definitively settled by Rome. Basil welcomed the decision taken at the Ignatian council by the Eastern patriarchs that placed the Church in Bulgaria under the jurisdiction of Constantinople, and the Emperor encouraged Ignatius to establish a hierarchy in that country that should enjoy a certain degree of autonomy. About 875 he recalled Photius, to whom the majority of the clergy had remained faithful, and entrusted him with the education of his sons. After the death of Ignatius (877) Basil reinstated Photius on the patriarchal throne, and the synod of 879–880 rehabilitated him as patriarch upon receiving assurance of acceptance from Pope *John VIII.

Basil supported the spread of Christianity among the Serbs and Slavic tribes of the southern coastal district (867–874). He had previously reestablished Byzantine authority in these parts by defeating the Arabs who were besieging Ragusa (Dubrovnik). By reorganizing the Byzantine navy, he reinforced Byzantine influence in Italy. In 872 he started his offensive wars against the *Paulicians in Asia Minor and advanced the Byzantine frontiers towards the east. On his initiative, a revision of the Justinian legislation was inaugurated that resulted in the publication of a new handbook of Byzantine law called the Procheiron (Πρόχειρος Νόμος); and another law book, the Συναγωγή, was compiled. They were to introduce a new version of law based on Justinian's Code. This work, initiated by Basil, was continued by Leo VI and finally published under the title

Βασιλικά. It was divided into 60 books and was a great achievement in the development of Byzantine law.

Bibliography: J. and P. Zepos, *Ius graecoromanum*, v.2 (Athens 1931) 109–228, Πρόχειρος Νόμος, 231–368, Epanagoge. K. G. E. Heimbach, ed., *Basilicorum libri LX*, 6 v. (Leipzig 1833–70), new ed. by H. J. Scheltema (Groningen 1953–). A. Vogt, *Basile Ier* (Paris 1908). A. Vogt and I. Hausherr, eds. and trs., "Oraison funèbre de Basile I," *Orientalia christiana* 26 (1932) 5–79. F. Dvornik, *The Photian Schism* (Cambridge, Eng. 1948). A. A. Vasiliev, *A History of the Byzantine Empire* (2d Eng. ed. Madison, Wis. 1952). Ostrogorsky 201–221.

[F. Dvornik]

BASIL II, BYZANTINE EMPEROR, 976 to 1025; b. Constantinople, 958; d. Dec. 15, 1025.

Perhaps the greatest of the Byzantine rulers, Basil (called also Bulgaroctonus or Slayer of Bulgars) was an outstanding general, administrator, and statesman. He attained actual power, however, only after ousting his great-uncle, the eunuch Basil (985). He survived two revolts, that of Bardas Sclerus (976–979), defeated during his minority by his great-uncle; and a second led by Bardas Phocas (987–989), whom he overcame with the aid of Vladimir, Prince of Kiev. He gave Vladimir as a reward the hand of his sister, Anna Porphyrogenita, and thus brought about the conversion of the Ukraine, and then of all Russia.

Basil first attacked the Empire's most dangerous enemy, Bulgaria, and after 20 years of warfare (991–994; 1001–18) he annexed the whole country but left its Church independent of the patriarch of Constantinople. In the decisive battle of 1014, Basil put out the eyes of 14,000 captives except for one out of every hundred, to whom he left one eye to lead home his fellow

Basil II, Byzantine Emperor, full-page miniature, Emperor's Psalter, Biblioteca Marciana, Venice (Codex Gr. 17).

countrymen. He had to interrupt his Balkan campaigns (995–999) to bring about peace in Syria with the Fatimids and arrange affairs in Armenia and the cis-Caucasus. To preserve the military system essential to the state he suppressed the landed aristocracy ruthlessly. It was under Basil II that Patriarch *Sergius II (1001–19) omitted the name of Pope Sergius IV (1009–12) from the commemoration in the liturgy, thus instituting the formal beginning of the schism between the Roman and Orthodox Churches.

Bibliography: CMedH² 4.1:175–195, 458–460, 517–518, 618–619, 723–726. Ostrogorsky 264–279, 283–286, 296, n.1. A. A. Vasiliev, *A History of the Byzantine Empire* (2d Eng. ed. Madison, Wis. 1952) 302, 311–315, 319–323, 336, 347–349, 366. B. Granić, *Byzantion* 12 (1937) 395–415. V. Grumel, ÉchosOr 29 (1930) 165–167; 30 (1931) 91–95. **Illustration credit:** Hirmer Verlag München.

[M. J. Higgins]

BASIL OF ANCYRA, 4th-century bishop and writer; d. in exile, c. 364.

A former physician, Basil became bishop of Ancyra (modern Ankara) when Marcellus was deposed for suspected Sabellianism in 336; and he soon became the leader of the moderate semi-Arian party at the Synod of Ancyra (358). In both his *Synodal Letter* and *Dogmatic Memoir* on the Trinity (preserved by Epiphanius, *Haer.* 73.2), Basil defended the homoiousian position, saying that "the Son is in all things like the Father, in will as well as hypostasis, in existence and in being."

Despite the efforts of Basil and his colleagues Eustathius of Sebaste and Eleusius of Cyzicus, the extreme Arian party, the Anomoeans, succeeded in winning over Emperor Constantius II, and both the Western synod held at Ariminum and the Eastern synod at Seleucia turned against the formula of Basil. He and his colleagues were sent to Constantius at Constantinople, where they signed the homoean formula of Ariminum in 359. As leadership of the group thus passed from Basil to Acacius of Caesarea, Arianism was at least temporarily in control. Acacius held a synod at Constantinople in 360, at which Basil and his friends were deposed and sent into exile. Basil was banished to Illyria; he apparently attempted to be reinstated under Emperor Jovianus, but died in exile c. 364 after recanting his consent to the formula of Ariminum.

Although *Epiphanius of Constantia is harsh on Basil, claiming he was merely an Arian in disguise, *Hilary of Poitiers and Athanasius are far more just; Athanasius (*De synodis* 41) suggests that his doctrine, apart from his rejection of the *homoousios, was nearly equivalent to the orthodox position, and such men "must not be treated as enemies." Athanasius' moderate view accords with Basil's actions during his last years and is surely right.

Jerome (*De vir. ill.* 89) mentions two other works, *Against Marcellus*, which has been lost, and a treatise *On Virginity*, which is almost certainly to be identified with the treatise *On the True Purity of Chastity*, dedicated to Letoius, recovered from the works of Basil the Great by F. Cavallera [RHE 6 (1905) 5–14]. The physiological and anatomical details found throughout this work suit the tradition that Basil had been a physician. The angelic life of virginity can be achieved only on the foundation of bodily harmony, which must be fostered by fasting, austerities, the avoidance of condiments and wine, and care in the use of foods that arouse the passions and lend a foothold to the devil. Moderation and balance are always to be observed: the reins of the chariot must be neither too tight nor too loose. Basil's doctrine here is Neoplatonic and Alexandrian. The Slavonic text of the treatise has been edited by A. Vaillant (Paris 1943), who disputes the thesis of Cavallera.

Bibliography: PG 30:669–810. F. CAVALLERA, DictSpirAsc Myst 1:1283. J. JANINI CUESTA, "Dieta y virginidad," *Miscelánea. Comillas* 14 (1950) 187–197. Quasten Patr 3:201–203.

[H. MUSURILLO]

BASILE OF SOISSONS, theologian; b. Soissons, date of birth unknown; d. Paris, March 3, 1698. He entered the Capuchins on April 20, 1635. His apostolic and literary activities were aimed chiefly at the defense of the faith. He contributed to this cause a fundamental work of four volumes, *Fondement inébranlable* (Paris 1680–82). Employing the only criterion admitted by his adversaries, Sacred Scripture, he treated successively the Creed, Decalogue, Sacraments, and prayer. The Eucharist holds a major place in his *Défense invincible* (Paris 1676). In *La Véritable décision* (Paris 1685) he shows that the only true judge in doctrinal and religious questions is the Catholic Church.

Bibliography: É. D'ALENÇON, DTC 2.1:464–465. I. DA MILANO, EncCatt 2:980–981. A. TEETAERT, DHGE 6:1157–58.

[M. DE POBLADURA]

BASILEIA (βασίλεια), the abstract term normally used in Greek versions of the Bible to designate God's reign, royalty, or realm in the sense of the prevalence of the divine will (rather than a territorial domain). Hence it is less appropriately translated as kingdom in most English editions. The notion of God's reigning first appears in the Canticle of Moses (Ex 15.18; cf. Dt 33.5). Under the monarchy, Yahweh is portrayed as king not only over Israel but over the universe [Psalm 46(47)]. After the division of the kingdom the two dynasties tended to eclipse Yahweh's kingship. In the postexilic era, when Juda was reduced to a worshipping community, the divine basileia assumed cosmic proportions in the apocalyptic literature and some of the Psalms [Daniel ch. 7; Ps 102(103).19; 144(145).13]. The preaching of both Jesus and John the Baptist reflects an eschatological dimension, although a purely otherworldly realm was equally foreign to Jewish and Christian tradition (*see* ESCHATOLOGISM). The Christ-event stands in the New Testament as Yahweh's decisive intervention, inaugurating the messianic basileia. Christ's *Resurrection constitutes Him *Lord and *Messiah; Christians have become the new *people of God. The universal, cosmic dimensions of the basileia will be realized at the Parousia (Mt 13.41, 43).

See also KINGDOM OF GOD; KINGDOM OF CHRIST; MESSIAHSHIP OF OUR LORD.

Bibliography: R. SCHNACKENBURG, LexThK² 2:25–31; *God's Rule and Kingdom,* tr. J. MURRAY (New York 1963). K. L. SCHMIDT et al., *Basileia* (Bible Key Words from Kittel ThW 7), ed. and tr. H. P. KINGDON (London 1957).

[M. K. HOPKINS]

BASILIAN MONASTICISM

The monastic development under *Basil of Caesarea is usually placed in the line of development after the anchoritism of St. *Anthony of Egypt and the *cenobitism of the large communities under St. *Pachomius, leading toward the establishment of Benedictine monasticism (*see* MONASTICISM, 2). This is an error in perspective. Basil was a successor in the tradition of the enthusiastic and sectarian asceticism of *Eustathius of Sebaste; he aimed not at constituting an isolated group but at reforming the Church according to the demands of the gospel, without clashing with the bulk of the faithful.

The Asceticon. The chronological development of Basil's thought can be followed through the two successive editions of his *Asceticon,* one in 202 questions (PL 103:487), the other in 55 great rules (which develop out of the 11 first questions of the first edition) and in 313 short rules (191 questions of the first edition with new ones added). When new brotherhoods began to develop, Basil in no way attempted to impose his own conceptions on them but, rather, sought to meditate with them on the New Testament, to put into practice the renunciation demanded by *Baptism.

*Obedience is understood in terms of the Biblical commandments, interpreted in the light of the need of one's neighbor. *Poverty is not a juridical convention but, rather, a generous devotion of the fruits of a conscientious toil to the service of the poor; and here Basil separates himself radically from Messalianism. Celibacy is taken for granted; in the second edition there is a requirement of a formal engagement in this matter, but it is never made a central point except when a virgin fails to honor her promises (*Epist.* 46).

Reference to the individual superior appears only in the latest texts; at the outset emphasis was placed on the group of those who had received the charisms of discernment of spirits; for each had his function and duties, expressing charity to the other members of the Body of Christ. Basil was a vigorous opponent of anchoritism. His stand must be understood in the light of the history of his day: he states that the tendency to isolation in one's environment is not healthy but, rather, is a self-willed anchoritism. Further, he shows little sympathy for the appeal of inwardness that so delighted his friend *Gregory of Nazianzus. Basil stressed the objective aspect of prayer; he thought of prayer as liturgical, and readily mingled prayer with work and apostolic responsibilities: prayer was for Basil more a song than a silence.

Basilians. Basil never promulgated any precise rule, nor did he found a centralized order; there is no justification for calling Basilian even those Oriental monks who recognize him as one of their fathers. The idea of a Basilian order is a Latin one, a product of the Roman Curia's extension of Western categories. Following the curial practice, the Uniate Oriental monks from the Middle Ages on can in a certain sense be considered Basilians, and the Curia officially made them such when it reformed them. The Italo-Greek monks, who also had a Spanish Latin-rite congregation; the Ukrainian Basilians of St. Josaphat, with a few Rumanian monks; and finally the Melchites of Lebanon should be mentioned.

Italo-Greek. The Greeks who had been so flourishing an ethnic group in south Italy in antiquity had not entirely disappeared there when *Justinian I in the 6th century reoccupied these provinces. Monasticism spread there despite the threat of Arab invasions. It prospered in *Sicily and especially in Calabria and Lucania, from the 9th to the 11th century, based on a Studite tradition but with direct contacts with Palestine

Christ and an abbot of the Basilian monastery at Grotta-ferrata, detail of a 13th-century mosaic at the monastery.

and Egypt. Numerous Italo-Greek manuscripts still witness to this culture. Although it was the first Byzantine province to be invaded by the Latins (Normans), south Italy did not, for all that, lose its characteristics; indeed the new dynasty relied on the monasteries for support and favored them in return. As many as 265 have been counted, most of them quite small. Confederations developed around S. Salvatore in Messina and St. Elias of Carbone. Leaders among the monks included St. Elias the Younger (d. 903), St. Elias Spelaiotes (d. 960), St. *Sabas the Younger (d. 990 or 991), St. *Nicodemus of Mammola (d. 990), St. Luke of Armento (d. 993), St. *Nilus of Rossano (d. 1005), St. *Simeon of Polirone (d. 1016), and St. Bartholomew of Rossano (d. 1020).

The influence of these spiritual centers on medieval spirituality (e.g., *Monte Cassino, St. *Romuald) and on the Greek culture in Rome itself should not be underestimated. Unfortunately the rule of the Angevins brought the beginning of a decline, and the Greek element disappeared little by little. When *Bessarion tried to reform the monasteries in 1446, the majority of the houses had passed to Latin religious or disappeared. Cardinal Santoro pursued Bessarion's efforts, and 1579 was to become the official date of the foundation of a congregation of 38 monasteries. With these were associated the Basilians of Spain. The emigrations from Albania revived the Greek-language groups. In 1866 the government suppressed the monasteries with the exception of *Grottaferrata (outside Rome), whose traditions of scholarship, liturgy, and music experienced a brilliant revival.

In Spain, two groups of Latin religious and hermits adopted almost simultaneously the Rule of St. Basil at Orviedo and Tardon (the so-called reformed province,

given more to manual labor) in 1561 and in 1568; in 1569 they were united to the Basilians of Italy. They were suppressed by the Spanish government in 1855.

Ruthenians, Rumanians, and Melchites. The Ruthenian Basilians of St. *Josaphat Kuncevyč were established shortly after the Union of Brest-Litovsk (1595), when St. Josaphat reformed about 30 Ukrainian monasteries, under the influence of the constitutions of St. *Ignatius of Loyola, and instituted an active congregation, which he called Basilian (1617). It played a crucial role in the Ruthenian Church, representing the cultural element and furnishing the bishops. It had provinces in Russia, Lithuania, Poland, and Austria. In the reform under Pope *Leo XIII, the personality of Metropolitan A. *Sheptyts'kyĭ gave the order a more Oriental character. In the wake of World War I the monks emigrated, especially to North and South America.

Rumanian Basilians consisted of a little congregation of monks around the monastery of Blaj, from 1750 to 1870; and another group, around Bixad from 1925 to 1945.

Among the Melchites, at the end of the 17th century, when a United Melchite Church was reconstituted, Euthymius Saifi organized the Congregation of Our Savior or Salvatorians (1684); and later, that of the Chouerites (1697), from which that of the Aleppans would branch off (1829). The three congregations are flourishing today in Lebanon.

Bibliography: D. AMAND, *L'Ascèse monastique de saint Basile* (Maredsous 1949). J. GRIBOMONT, in *Théologie de la vie monastique* (Maredsous 1961) 99–113. C. KOROLEVSKIJ, DHGE 6: 1180–1236; *Le Métropolite A. Szeptickyj* (Rome 1964). M. SCADUTO, *Il monachismo basiliano nella Sicilia medievale* (Rome 1947). B. CAPELLI, *Il monachismo basiliano ai confini calabro-lucani* (Naples 1963). A. GUILLOU, *Mélanges d'archéologie et d'histoire* 75 (1963) 79–110. R. DEVREESSE, *Les Manuscrits grecs de l'Italie méridionale* (StTest 183; 1955). B. HAMILTON, "The City of Rome and the Eastern Churches in the Xth Century," OrChrPer 27 (1961) 4–26. A. BENITO DURÁN, *Revista de la biblioteca* 20 (1951) 167–237. T. BORESKY, *Life of St. Josaphat* (New York 1955). *Analecta Ordinis S. Basilii Magni* (Zhovkua 1944) *passim.* J. GEORGESCO, DTC 14.1:66–67. R. JANIN, DTC 10.1:519–520. **Illustration credit:** Anderson-Art Reference Bureau.

[J. GRIBOMONT]

BASILIANS

A community of priests with simple vows who belong to the Roman rite and whose principal work is the Christian education of youth. The Congregation of Priests of St. Basil (CSB) engage also in parochial work and in missionary work among Latin Americans. The U.S. and Canada are the chief fields of their apostolate. Their total membership (1963) was about 450 priests (including 156 in the U.S.), 200 scholastics, and 50 novices.

Origin. The congregation had its origin in the Catholic movement for survival during the French Revolution. Abp. Charles d'Aviau (1736–1826) of Vienne appointed Joseph Bouvier Lapierre (1757–1838) pastor of the hamlet of Saint-Symphorien-de-Mahun in the Ardèche mountains and asked him to teach Latin to six aspirants to the priesthood. This rectory study group quickly grew into a school of 140 students which was transferred in 1802 to the city Annonay. Léorat Picansel (1741–1823), vicar-general of the Diocese of Viviers, drew up the first rule and guided the founders in the organization of a religious community. On Nov. 21, 1822, nine priest-teachers joined with Lapierre in forming a community of diocesan priests. Gregory XVI raised it to pontifical rank and bestowed on it the decree

Joseph Bouvier Lapierre.

of praise, Sept. 15, 1837. Papal approbations were given by Pius IX in 1863, Pius X in 1913, and Pius XI in 1938.

Growth was gradual, and the work limited to Annonay and a few neighboring towns, until 1850 when a graduate of the College of Annonay, Armand François, Comte de Charbonnel (1802–91), was named bishop of Toronto, Canada. Before leaving France for his diocese he obtained from his former teachers the services of a young Irish priest, Patrick Molony (1813–80). In 1852, the motherhouse of the Basilian Fathers in America, the University of St. Michael's College, was established at Toronto, with a staff of three priests and two seminarians. Under the direction of the first superior, Jean Soulerin (1807–79), a novitiate was opened, and soon vocations permitted expansion to other cities. The parish of St. Mary of the Assumption, Owen Sound, Canada, was taken over in 1863 with the mission field attached to it. In 1870, Denis O'Connor (1841–1911), later successively bishop of London and archbishop of Toronto, took charge of a school that later became Assumption University, Windsor. Attached to this institution is historic Assumption parish that began as a mission to the Indians in 1728.

The first permanent Basilian foundation in the U.S. was made at St. Anne's Church, Detroit, Mich., in 1886, when Pierre Grand (1845–1922) became pastor of the parish, which dates back to 1701. Other foundations included St. Louis College, opened at Louisville, Ohio, in 1867 and closed in 1873; and St. Basil's College, Waco, Tex., undertaken in 1899 and given up in 1915. The first successful school in the U.S. was St. Thomas High School, Houston, Tex., established in 1900 by Nicholas Roche (1866–1932).

Growth. Expansion in the U.S. and Canada during the second half of the 19th century was paralleled by a like growth in Europe that included the establishment of the College of Mary Immaculate at Beaconfield, England (1883), and three missions in Algeria. Unfortunately, this vitality did not last, partly because of a decrease in vocations after the Franco-Prussian War of 1870 and partly because of anticlericalism and the suppression of religious houses in France in 1902.

The canonical development of the Basilian fathers into a full religious community came about slowly. Founded as a community of diocesan priests, members first took the vows of obedience, chastity, and poverty on Oct. 1, 1852, although the constitutions retained the earlier practice of limited poverty. For several decades, modifications in the vow of poverty were a source of difficulty to those who wished to follow the religious life without reservation. On June 14, 1922, at the request of the French province, the Holy See erected the American and French provinces into distinct communities. The separation lasted until 1955 when a new decree united the two communities.

After separation, the Basilian fathers in America, under the leadership of Father Francis Forster (1873–1929), embraced the simple vow of poverty without any reservations. This step was followed by a notable increase in vocations, which made possible new foundations and the expansion of existing houses. In Canada, the congregation established houses in the Archdioceses of Ottawa, Toronto, and Vancouver; and in the Dioceses of Calgary, Hamilton, London, Saskatoon, and Sault Sainte Marie. Basilians conduct the Pontifical Institute of Mediaeval Studies, Toronto; the University of St. Michael's College, Toronto; Assumption University, Windsor; St. Thomas More College, Saskatoon; St. Mark's College, Vancouver; 9 high schools; and 8 parishes. They have developed a system of cooperation with state universities that has been copied by other Catholic colleges in Canada. John Read Teefy (1848–1911) was author of the first such affiliation, between the University of Toronto and St. Michael's College in 1881.

In the U.S., the congregation conducts the University of St. Thomas in Houston, Tex.; St. John Fisher College, Rochester, N.Y.; 4 high schools; 2 parishes; and 4 mission centers for Latin Americans in Texas. It has houses in the Archdiocese of Detroit and the Dioceses of Galveston-Houston, Tex.; Gary, Ind.; and Rochester. In 1961 the Basilians undertook the care of San Juan Crisóstomo parish in the suburbs of Mexico City, as an extension of their work with Latin Americans.

By the time of the union in 1955, the once flourishing Basilian houses in France were reduced to the motherhouse in Annonay, L'Institution Secondaire du Sacré-Coeur. All others had been closed or taken over by diocesan priests after the suppression of religious houses in 1902. In 1961 a house of studies for young members was opened in Paris.

Publications. Father Adolphe Vaschalde (1871–1942), for many years professor at The Catholic University of America, Washington, D.C., edited a number of Syriac texts. The works of Father Alexander Joseph Denomy (1904–57) in medieval literature included *The Heresy of Courtly Love* (New York 1947) and *Old French Lives of St. Agnes* (Cambridge, Mass. 1938). Father Michael Vincent Kelly (1863–1942), writer on pastoral problems, published the *Catechism of Christian Doctrine* (New York 1924) and *Catechism Teaching*

(Grand Rapids, Mich. 1923). In 1888, Father Laurence Brennan (1847–1904) published the first edition of the *St. Basil Hymnal,* which has sold more than 1 million copies and of which a completely revised edition was issued in 1958 (Cincinnati).

Bibliography: *Basilian Annals* (Toronto 1943–). *Basilian Teacher* (Toronto 1956–).

[R. J. SCOLLARD]

BASILIANS—NUNS

Officially entitled the Order of the Basilians of St. Macrina (OSBM), they trace their origin to St. *Basil the Great (329–379), who wrote his monastic rules for both religious men and women and with his sister St. *Macrina founded monasteries for religious women, which later developed parallel to those of religious men.

Early History. Between the 10th and the 14th century five of these monasteries for religious women were known to exist in Constantinople and others in Areia, later Boundse (Nauplia), and in Baionia (Crete). From the 6th century Byzantine monasteries were established also in Sicily and southern Italy. In the old Ukraine (Rus) the earliest known monastery for religious women was that of St. Irene in Kiev established in 1037; later other foundations were made in Kiev and in Polotsk, which flourished until the 13th century. Two 13th-century monasteries for religious women in Smilnytsia and Linyna (Galicia), founded under Byzantine law, fell under Polish rule and the law of *patronage in the 15th century. After the Ukrainian Church united with Rome (1596) the metropolitan of Kiev Joseph V. Rutskyj (1613–37) gave the nuns a rule. These constitutions, based on the ascetical writings of St. Basil, were published by the Basilian fathers in Vilnyus (1771) and later reprinted in Zovkva (1909).

In Kiev these monasteries for women were ruled according to the old Byzantine discipline. Unlike the Basilian order for men, where centralized government was introduced in 1617, each Basilian monastery for women was autonomous, under the jurisdiction of the local bishop. Although their main occupation was the Divine Office, the nuns concerned themselves also with some form of the apostolate, mainly the education of young girls. In 1720 the synod of Zamost introduced strict enclosure according to contemporary Latin discipline and regulated other aspects of religious life, such as the amount of dowry to be brought by candidates, the number of the nuns for each monastery, the common life, the age required for postulancy and novitiate, the forms of examination before profession and monastic profession, the election of the abbess, and the active life of nuns. Bishops were authorized to suppress small monasteries and transfer their goods to larger ones. As a consequence of the division of Poland (1772, 1793, 1795), the occupation by Russia, and the suppressing (1839) of the union of the Ukrainian Church with Rome, Basilian monasteries for women were almost completely destroyed.

In the division of Poland one part of the metropoly of Kiev, Galicia in West Ukraine, was annexed to Austria (1772). There, because of the "ecclesiastical reforms" of *Josephinism, the ten Basilian monasteries of nuns were reduced to two, one in Slovita (Archdiocese of Lvov) and one in Iavoriv (Diocese of Peremyshl). In 1821 Cardinal Michael Lewyckyj of Lvov (1816–58) obtained from the Austrian government permission to open a novitiate for the two monasteries on condition that the nuns would be occupied with education. The direction of the novitiate (in Slovita) was committed to the Basilian fathers, recently reformed (1882); it served as a common novitiate for the three monasteries, including the one founded in Lvov in 1881. The provincial synod of Lvov (1891) accepted, with slight modification, the regulations made by the synod of Zamost. In 1897, when Cardinal Silvester Sembratovych, Metropolitan of Lvov, sent the constitutions to Rome for approval, the Holy See authorized the metropolitan to ratify them. Chapters were held in 1902, 1909, 1923, and 1932. The chapter of 1909 made some revisions in the constitutions.

Expansion and Centralization. From the three monasteries mentioned above Basilian nuns made additional foundations: another in Lvov (1912), Pidmychajlivtsi (1930), and Stanyslaviv (1900), all in West Ukraine; Uzhgorod (1921), Mukachevo (1921), and Presov (1922) in Czechoslovakia; Kryzhevtsi (1917), Sid (1920), Osijek (1939), Myklucevci (1941), Zagreb (1936), and Novy Sad (1960) in Yugoslavia; Maria-Povcs (1935) and Nyiregyhaza (1939) in Hungary; Philadelphia, Pa. (1911), Chesapeake City, Md. (1912), Fox Chase, Pa. (1931), Elmhurst, Pa. (1921), Uniontown, Pa. (1931), and Astoria, N.Y. (1958) in the U.S.; Warsaw (1958), Lubomierz Slaski (1959), and Janowiec (1960) in Poland; and Apostoles-Misiones (1939), Berisso (1943), Buenos Aires (1952), and Mendoza (1963) in Argentina.

With the growth and diffusion of these monasteries in different countries the need for centralization arose. The first step in this direction was made when the Holy See committed the task of preparing new constitutions to one of the Basilian fathers, Theodosius Haluščynskyj (later Protoarchimandrite of the Basilian Order of St. Josaphat). In 1951 the Sacred Congregation for the Oriental Church granted temporary approval of the new constitutions, ordering the reunion of all monasteries in one pontifical order with minor pontifical enclosure and solemn profession in monasteries with enclosure (otherwise simple perpetual vows) under the government of one superior general. The first to hold this office was Mother Eusebia Bilas, appointed by the Holy See Nov. 14, 1951.

The order was divided into four provinces: two in the U.S. for two different groups (of Ukrainians with the provincial see in Philadelphia, Pa., and of Ruthenians in Uniontown, Pa.), one in Argentina (Berisso), and one in Europe (Osijek, Yugoslavia). The mother-house was located in Rome (from 1954).

Constitutions. In 1964, after accommodations had been made in accordance with the new Oriental Code, a revised text of the constitutions was approved by Rome *ad experimentum* for 7 years. Under the title of the Order of the Basilians of St. Macrina, the order is pontifical and nonexempt. Its general purpose is the Christian perfection of its members by observance of the three vows; the particular aim is the education of youth in schools, shelters, and orphanages; the care of the sick and aged; and the promotion of ecclesiastical arts. While the whole order is headed by one superior general and is divided into provinces, there are also special houses, which are called monasteries with strict enclosure of nuns (can. 146) and are directly dependent on the superior general. The superiors of these monasteries are elected by the nuns of their monasteries and confirmed by the superior general for 5 years. In 1965 only one monastery of this type existed—at Astoria, N.Y. (from 1958). Other houses are headed immediately by local superiors appointed for 3 years; provincials are appointed by the superior general for 5 years; and the superior general is elected by a general chapter for 8 years.

U.S. Foundations. In 1965 the two American provinces had 5 houses and about 50 residences. Basilian sisters directed more than 40 parochial schools, 2 academies for girls, and 1 college for girls. The novitiates were located in Fox Chase, Pa., and Uniontown, Pa.

Bibliography: M. S. CIOROCH, *Conspectus historiae et opera paedagogica monacarum Basilianarum* (2d ed. Rome 1964). OrientCatt 736–743.

[M. M. WOJNAR]

BASILIANS (BYZANTINE RITE)

There are, in several Oriental rites, five branches of the Order of St. Basil the Great (OSBM): Grottaferrata, in the Italo-Albanian rite; St. Josaphat, in the Ukrainian and Romanian rites; and St. Saviour, St. John Baptist, and Aleppo, in the Melkite rite. Each of these groups follows basically the Rule of St. *Basil the Great.

Basil, Archbishop of Caesarea in Cappadocia (modern Turkey), was the great legislator of Eastern monasticism. Beginning in 358, he composed a rule in two forms (a longer and a shorter series of articles) through which he became the founder of cenobitic monasticism. Although his teachings had their greater impact in the East, Basil exercised some influence also over the *Benedictine Rule in the West. Characteristic of Basil's rule (or rules) was *cenobitism (common life) in the strict sense, in contrast to the earlier eremitism of St. *Anthony of Egypt and the mitigated cenobitism of St. *Pachomius. Another characteristic was the addition of social activity to the customary monastic prayer and work. Specifically, Basil recommended the founding of schools for boys. Whether or not he intended also the centralization of monastic government has been disputed, but recent study indicates that he did. Basil's rule was further determined, in the late 8th century, by the *typikon* (constitutions) of (St.) *Theodore the Studite at *Studion, the famous monastery in Constantinople. In this later form the rule was adopted by the monasteries of the Byzantine Empire, including the great Laura on Mt. *Athos founded in the 10th century by (St.) *Athanasius the Athonite.

Basilian Order of Grottaferrata. In the 7th and 8th centuries monasteries following the Basilian rule were founded in southern Italy and Sicily by Greek monks who fled from their native countries during the persecutions arising out of *Iconoclasm. In the 10th century (St.) *Nilus of Rossano established the Greek monastery of *Grottaferrata outside Rome. Many other monasteries were erected in Italy in the 11th century under the Norman regime. The Rule of St. Basil was adopted also in Spain in the 16th century at a monastery in the Diocese of Jaén, upon the advice of Bp. Diego Tavera. The man designated to be the first superior, Bernardo de la Cruz, went to Grottaferrata where he made his profession. Pius IV then created (1561) the Spanish congregation, a Basilian group in the Latin rite. Not long afterward Gregory XIII first united all the Greek monasteries in Italy into one congregation and then, by the bull *Benedictus Dominus* (Nov. 1, 1579), erected the Italo-Spanish Basilian Congregation under one abbot general (archimandrite). Over the subsequent years the Italian branch tended to adopt the Latin rite, a move that was opposed by the Holy See. Both branches of the congregation later went out of existence, the Spanish in 1855, and the Italian in 1866. Grottaferrata, however, was restored in its Greek tradition in 1880 under the leadership of its abbot, Giuseppe Cozza-Luzi (d. 1905). New constitutions were approved in 1900, and in 1937 Pius XI elevated the monastery to the exarchal rank (*abbatia nullius*). Grottaferrata has several dependent foundations in southern Italy and Sicily, including the ancient monastery of Mezzoiusso (Calabria).

Basilian Order of St. Josaphat. In 1072 the Rule of St. Basil was introduced in the monastery Pecherska Lavra in Kiev, capital of the Ukraine, by (St.) Theodosius (d. 1074). Subsequently the rule became the model for other monasteries in the Ukraine, White Russia, and Russia. Following the union of the See of Kiev with Rome (1596) some monasteries of the Ukraine and White Russia formed in 1617 the Basilian Congregation of the Holy Trinity (also called the Lithuanian Congregation). Approval was given by Urban VIII in the brief *Exponi nobis,* Aug. 20, 1631. The initiators of this reorganization were the Archbishop of Kiev, Velamin Rutski (1574–1637), and (St.) *Josaphat Kuncevyč. Gradually other monasteries joined the congregation, but some remained independent until, by order of the synod of Zamosc (1720), the Congregation

SS. Anthony and Theodosius of Kiev, 20th-century mosaics in the Basilian Fathers' church at Rome.

of the Protection of the Holy Virgin (also called the Ruthenian Congregation) was formed in 1739. By decree of Benedict XIV (1742) both groups were joined in one Order of St. Basil the Great, and in the general chapter at Dubno in 1743 two provinces were created, Lithuanian and Ruthenian. In 1780 the order was divided into four provinces because of the partition of Poland (1772).

In the 17th and 18th centuries the Basilians were engaged in various missionary, pastoral, and educational activities, especially for the promotion of the union of the Ukrainian Church with Rome. In the beginning their novitiate was at Wilno (Lithuania) under the direction of Josaphat; later it was moved to Byten (White Russia) in the care first of the Jesuits, and later, of the Basilians themselves. The young clerical students, after their novitiate and religious profession, usually pursued their philosophical studies at the monastery of Zhytrovytsi, a renowned place of pilgrimage. For theology they went to western Europe where Urban VIII had established 22 scholarships for them in the pontifical schools of the following cities: 4 in Rome, 2 in Vienna, 2 in Prague, 2 in Olmütz (Moravia), 6 in Braunsberg (Prussia), and 6 in Graz (Austria). Basilians staffed the diocesan seminary at Minsk, capital of White Russia, and many colleges for boys, among which the most notable was that of Vladimir-Volynski, the birthplace of Josaphat.

All the metropolitans of Kiev in the 17th and 18th centuries were Basilians. Velamin Rutski and his four immediate successors in the metropolitan see were also the superiors general of the Order of St. Basil. Each of them held that office (protoarchimandrite) until death. After 1675 the two offices were separated and the protoarchimandrite (now simply a monk) was elected to a term of 4 years, later extended to 8 in 1751. He made his residence in one of the order's monasteries, while the procurator general resided in Rome. Provinces were ruled by *protohegumeni* (provincials); monasteries, by either archimandrites constituted for life, or by *hegumeni* (local superiors) in office for 4 years. By 1772 Basilian monasteries in the Ukraine and White Russia numbered 144 with 1,225 religious (944 priests, 190 clerical students, and 91 lay brothers).

The work of the Basilians for the union of the Eastern Churches with Rome was almost totally destroyed by the further partition of Poland, the hostility toward union in the Russian empire, and the suppression of Basilian monasteries. Toward the end of the 19th century only one province remained, that of Galicia in the Austrian empire. Here too the Basilians suffered, along with other religious orders, from *Josephinism. Leo XIII, in 1882, reorganized the remaining 14 monasteries of Galicia by placing them under the direction of the Jesuits in Dobromil. The members of the Dobromil reform gradually extended their activity among the following peoples: the Ukrainians in Galicia and, later, in the Carpathian Ukraine (Ruthenia); the Hungarians of Oriental rite; the Ukrainians, Croatians, and Macedonians in Yugoslavia; and the Romanians. The Basilians also followed the emigrants of these peoples to the U.S., Canada, Brazil, and Argentina. The reform begun at Dobromil was brought to completion when a general chapter was held there in 1931. The superior general elected at that chapter, Dionysius Tkachuk (1867–1944), took up residence in Rome for the first time. Pius XI, on Feb. 24, 1932, approved the present name of the order, the Basilian Order of St. Josaphat.

Before the Soviet occupation of eastern Europe the Basilians were organized in four provinces: Galicia, the Carpathian Ukraine, Hungary, and Romania. Their activity, as in the past, was diversified. They continued their traditional life, a combination of monastic prayer and active apostolate. In Galicia they conducted for a time three diocesan seminaries at Lvov, Peremyshl, and Stanislav; a boys' high school in Buchach; and a publications center in Zhovkva. In the Carpathian Ukraine there was a high school and publications' center at Uzhgorod. In Hungary the Basilians had charge of a pilgrimage church at Mariapocs, and in Romania they had a publications' center at Bixad. Two other seminaries were under their direction: a minor seminary at Zagreb, Yugoslavia, and the pontifical Ukrainian College of St. Josaphat in Rome. With the coming of the Communist governments many Basilians were arrested and sent to labor camps; some, however, have continued to work in secret. In Poland only one monastery has remained in Warsaw.

Outside of Europe the Order of St. Basil has carried on its apostolate among emigrant peoples of the Eastern rite. Since 1897 the Basilians have been in South America, where they have a province in Brazil and a vice province in Argentina, both erected in 1948. In 1902 they came to Canada where a province was created in 1932. The novitiate and house of studies were located in Mundare, Alberta, and a publications' center in Toronto, Ontario, where they conduct a school for boys. The U.S. branch began in 1926 and became a province separate from Canada in 1948. The novitiate, first founded at Dawson, Pa., was later moved to Glen Cove, N.Y. The Basilians have parishes in New York, N.Y., and Detroit, Mich., as well as several other cities.

The general curia, made up of the protoarchimandrite and his counselors, resides at Rome, where the *Analecta Ordinis S. Basilii Magni* (originally begun at Zhovkva, Galicia) is published. Many students of the order go to Rome for their theological studies. The constitutions of the order, revised according to the motu proprio, *Postquam apostolicis,* Feb. 9, 1952, were approved by Pius XII on June 14, 1954. The Basilian Order of St. Josaphat was declared to be an exempt, nonmonastic religious order. It retains its privilege of receiving candidates from any rite, without permission from the Holy See.

Basilian Orders of the Melkite Rite. The Basilian Order of St. Saviour was founded by the Archbishop of Tyre and Sidon (Lebanon), Euthymios Saifi, in 1684. Benedict XIV placed it under the rule of St. Basil in 1743. Before the occupation of Syria by the Egyptians in 1832, the Basilians were engaged in parochial ministry in Lebanon, Palestine, Egypt, and the city of Damascus. The constitutions and government of the order went through several changes before they were definitively determined by the Holy See in 1955. The revised constitutions were approved on Aug. 6, 1956. Basilian foundations are located in the Near Eastern Dioceses of Tyre, Sidon, Acre, Baniyas, Tripoli, and Damascus. In the U.S. there are seven parishes and a seminary at Methuen, Mass.

The Basilian Order of St. John Baptist, also known as the Order of Suwayr, or the Baladites, was begun in 1712 by two Syrian monks, Gerasim and Solomon, who had established themselves at the church of St. John Baptist in a valley near the village of Suwayr in Lebanon. The first superior of the group, Nicephore Karmi, prescribed four vows for the community in 1722. The vow of humility was added to the usual vows of poverty, chastity, and obedience. Efforts toward uniting this group with the Basilian Order of St. Saviour were not successful, and in 1743 Benedict XIV imposed the rule of St. Basil. The constitutions, approved by the same Pope in 1757, were developed from those of the Maronite monks of St. Anthony. As in the case of Order of St. Saviour, the canonical status of the Baladites was fixed by the Holy See in 1955. The motherhouse of the order is in Khonchara in Lebanon. These Basilians have six parishes in the U.S.

The Basilian Order of Aleppo is an offshoot of the preceding group; the separation took place in 1829 and was approved by the Holy See in 1832. Its canonical development was the same as that indicated for the aforementioned orders. The headquarters of the order is at the monastery of St. Saviour in Sarba, Djunieh, Lebanon. Acacius *Coussa, the Oriental canonist, was a member of this Basilian group.

Bibliography: C. KOROLEVSKIJ, DHGE 6:1180–1236. *Analecta Ordinis S. Basilii Magni,* Ser. 1 (Zhovkva 1924–1935) Ser. 2 (Rome 1949–). M. WOJNAR, *De regimine Basilianorum Ruthenorum a Metropolita J. V. Rutskyj instauratorum* (Rome 1949); *De capitulis Basilianorum* (Rome 1954); *De Protoarchimandrita Basilianorum* (Rome 1958). C. PUJOL, *De religiosis orientalibus ad normam vigentis iuris* (Rome 1957). M. KAROVETZ, *Velyka Revorma Chyna Sv. Vasyliia Velykoho,* 4 v. (Zhovkva 1933–38). A. SHEPTYCKYJ, *Pravyla dla monakhiv* (Zhovkva 1911); *Asketychni tvory Sv. O. N. Vasyliia V.* (Lvov 1929). **Illustration credit:** Giordani, Rome.

[M. M. WOJNAR]

BASILICA

A large rectangular, hall-like building, fully covered with a roof and usually supported by interior columns. At Athens the *Stoa Basilikē* (royal stoa) was a building on the Areopagus, where official and other business was transacted. In its Latinized form, basilica referred to a public building, hall-like in form, such as the Basilica Julia, erected by Julius Caesar and reconstructed by both Augustus and Diocletian (285–305). It was rectangular in shape and had a series of double colonnades that divided it into four aisles with a central hall, at one end of which was an apse or rounded court where the praetor sat. The other end contained the single entrance, and above the main aisle there was a second story. The basilica was used for the transaction of both public and private business, particularly in inclement weather. In the later Empire, every sizable city had one or more such buildings facing the forum.

CHRISTIAN HOUSE CHURCH

The primitive Christians, following the example of Christ, who presided at the Last Supper in a *coenaculum,* or upper room (Mk 14.15; Lk 22.12), and that of the Apostles and Disciples, who gathered in prayer while awaiting the coming of the Holy Spirit on the first Pentecost in an upper room (Acts 1.13–14), held their assemblies in private houses where they received instruction, broke bread in the Eucharistic celebration, and prayed (Acts 20.7–9). The Christians of Jerusalem were gathered in the home of Mary, the mother of John Mark, praying at night when Peter was delivered

from prison (Acts 12.12–17), and Paul refers several times to private homes in which he preached and prayed (1 Cor 16.19; Rom 16.3, 5; Col 4.15; Phlm 1.2–3).

At the end of the 1st century the *Didache describes the exhortation, the Eucharistic celebration, and preparation for Baptism in a private home (4.14; 14.1), and *Justin Martyr alludes (*c.* 160) to a place for the ablution or Baptism (Apol. 1.65–67), again clearly in a private home where the Christian mysteries were celebrated. *Minucius Felix uses the word *sacraria* to specify a special place where Christians gathered for worship (Octav. 9.1), but it was still in a private house (10.2).

Archeological Evidence. Archeological evidence from the 3d century confirms the fact that the so-called *domus ecclesia,* or house church, was the usual site of Christian liturgical gatherings. References to meetings in the cemeteries for the celebration of rites other than the commemoration of the dead before the middle of the 3d century are usually legendary, although SS. Chrysanthus and Daria, and Pope *Sixtus II and his companions, were surprised by the police in cemeteries and martyred respectively on the Via Salaria and the Via Appia outside Rome.

Evidence from the early 4th century presented by excavations beneath the Basilica of St. *Clement, Rome, which have revealed several levels of construction, are not conclusive as to the presence or place of Christian cult before the 4th-century construction of the original church; the same must be said of the excavations beneath the Basilica of St. *Anastasia and the title church of S. Martino ai Monti. However, those beneath the Basilica of SS. John and Paul do reveal a house church that existed during the late 3d or early 4th century, when its walls were decorated with Christian figures. At *Dura-Europos, the house church (*c.* 232) contained several rooms, only a few of which were devoted to Christian cult. At Qirq-Bezin, Syria, however, the early 4th-century house seems to have been a primitive model of the later Syrian type of basilica with a hall-like room for ceremonies preceded by an atrium; a room for relics; a bēma, or bishop's chair; and a martyrion.

Funerary monuments and crypts in the cemeteries display evidence of Christian usage early in the 3d century. The *tropaion,* or monument, erected over the grave of St. Peter at the *Vatican goes back to *c.* 180; but the *hypogeum,* or crypt, of the Flavii and that of Ampliatus in the *catacomb of Domitilla are later, as are the *cappella graeca* of the catacomb of *Priscilla and the crypt of Lucina on the Via Appia near the catacomb of *Callistus, in which many early popes were buried (*c.* 235). This evidence indicates Christian interest in construction that by the end of the 3d century had manifested itself in the erection of churches such as that close to the palace of the emperor in Nicomedia, which was destroyed at the outbreak of the persecution of *Diocletian.

Constantine I. Evidence for the existence of a Christian basilica (*c.* 306) has been discovered in Aquileia, but the first certain basilica-type construction must be credited to *Constantine I. In 313 he gave Pope Miltiades a palace at the Lateran for the papal residence and began the construction of a church called later the Basilica of St. John Lateran. He likewise transformed a hall of the Sessorian palace into a basilicalike

Fig. 1. Ruins of the three-aisled 4th-century basilica at Hippo Regius; it housed the cathedra of St. Augustine.

church where St. *Helena preserved a relic of the true cross (Santa Croce in Gerusalemme).

At the Vatican over the tomb of St. Peter, Constantine began construction of the ancient Basilica of St. Peter, and in Palestine he ordered the construction of the Basilicas of the Nativity at Bethlehem, the Annunciation at Nazareth, the Martyrion and Anastasis in Jerusalem, as well as basilicas at Capua, Antioch, Naples, Nicomedia, and Treves and the Church of the Apostles at *Constantinople. Constantine also authorized public funds for building churches in various parts of the Empire, and this work of construction provided all the large Christian centers with basilicas or greater churches in Africa and the Orient during the 4th century.

It was but normal that the Christian churches should have adopted the form of public buildings in the locale where they were constructed, and this was almost certainly the case of the basilicas that were built in Rome and Italy. From the beginning, however, the requirements of Christian cult dictated modifications.

THE CHRISTIAN BASILICA

The classical type of Christian basilica was a rectangular building supported by four walls and divided by two or more rows of columns into a central nave and two or more aisles on each side of the nave (ambulatories). The roof of the nave was raised higher than the roof above the aisles. The roofs were of timber, the one above the nave being an isosceles triangle of fairly low altitude crossing the span. The roof timbering was usually hidden by a flat ceiling. The walls supporting the roof above the nave constituted a clerestory whose windows, formed of pierced stone slabs, provided air and a mellow, diffuse light. The exterior was subdued and unadorned so that no architectural extravagance might detract from the spiritual purpose.

Furnishings and Adornment. The only departure from the simple rectangular design was the semicircular apse (concha, tribune), in which stood the throne (cathedra) of the bishop, flanked by seats for the clergy. At the opposite end was the main doorway leading into the nave and smaller doorways leading to the aisles or ambulatories. Beyond the entrance was a quadrangular court (atrium) in the center of which stood a fountain or cistern (*cantharus, pluviale*), in which the worshipers washed their hands and lips in preparation for receiving Holy Communion.

At times, the atrium was surrounded by a colonnaded cloister (S. Clemente in Rome, S. Ambrogio at Milan, old St. Peter's), but it was often reduced to a narrow portico or vestibule (narthex) as the entrance portico was called in the Eastern Empire. In some basilicas, a transept extended in front of the sanctuary to facilitate the procession of the people to and from the altar. At the juncture of the nave and the transept was a triumphal arch that served to direct and concentrate attention on the altar. The rounded apse was decorated with scenes from the Bible or portrayals of Our Lord in glory surrounded by martyrs.

To the front of the apse, faced by the cathedra, stood the table-shaped altar covered by a permanent canopy (*ciborium*) supported on marble columns. Mass was celebrated facing the people. Relics of the saint to whom the church was dedicated were often placed beneath the altar and were visible through a small window

Fig. 2. Basilica: (a) Hagios Dimitrios, Salonika, Greece, view of the exterior from the southwest. The building, which dates from the early 5th century, was restored in 629 and again after a fire in 1917. (b) West façade of the 6th-century basilica of Bishop Euphrasius at Poreč, Yugoslavia, as seen from the interior of the atrium.

Fig. 3. The interior of the Basilica of Hagios Dimitrios, Salonika, looking toward the sanctuary at the east end. This Byzantine basilica, founded about 412–413 by Leontius, Prefect of Illyricum, has a five-aisled cruciform plan, a narthex, a gallery, and an open timber roof. The atrium of the basilica has been destroyed.

(*fenestella confessionis*). In some cases, the relics were kept in a crypt opening under the apse and communicating with the altar. The altar was separated from the nave by low marble screens (*cancelli*) or by a chancel. The space reserved for the choir at the head of the nave was also railed off by *cancelli*. On each side of the nave screen were stone pulpits (*ambones*) for the reading of the Epistle and Gospel. The congregation occupied the aisles, the men on the south side and the women on the north. The rear of the nave was reserved for the catechumens, and the penitents were confined to the portico.

Although the basilica was austere in its exterior, it was richly adorned within. The wall spaces above the columns of the nave were covered with glass mosaics. The floor was decorated with marble mosaics in the fashion familiar to the Roman. The baptistery was usually a small domed structure erected near the church and connected with it by a covered passageway. A large basin or pool for immersion (*piscina, fons*) was sunk in the floor and provided with steps. When infant Baptism became general, the baptismal font replaced the basin and Baptism was administered in the church.

Liturgical Meeting. An early Christian document, the Syriac *Didascalia Apostolorum,* presents a description of a liturgical meeting and place of worship and at the same time suggests the problems facing the early Christian architect:

> In your assemblies in the holy churches . . . arrange the places of the brethren carefully with all sobriety. Let a place be reserved for the presbyters in the midst of the eastern part of the house, and let the throne of the bishop be placed amongst them; let the presbyters sit with him; but also at the other, eastern side of the house let the laymen sit; for thus it is required that the presbyters should sit at the eastern side of the house with the bishops, and afterwards the laymen, and next the women: that when you stand to pray the rulers may stand first, afterwards the laymen, and then the women . . . .
>
> As for the deacons, let one of them stand constantly over the gifts of the Eucharist, and let another stand outside the door and look at those who come in; and afterwards when you make offerings, let them serve together in the Church. And if a man be found sitting out of his place, let the deacon who is within reprove him, and make him get up and sit in the place that befits him. [Quasten Patr 2.148.]

The practice of "orienting" the basilica took cognizance of a symbolism that was older than Christianity. The *Apostolic Constitutions* required that the throne of the bishop be turned to face the east and that the liturgy should be celebrated facing that direction. The Jews and the pagans prayed facing the east, though for different reasons. The pagans, who adored the sun, greeted it at its rising and its setting. Their temples also were oriented. The Jews in their synagogues turned toward the east in their public prayer in order to be facing the Temple of Jerusalem. For the greater number of Jews of the Diaspora, the Temple of Jerusalem was in the east.

By the 5th century, the custom of orienting the basilica had become almost a rule. Socrates the Church historian protested when the altar of a certain church faced the west (*Hist. eccl.* 5.22). *Hagia Sophia at Constantinople and St. Apollinaris at Ravenna have their apses turned toward the east. At Rome there was resistance to this usage, which appeared to have become obligatory. Pope *Leo I (d. 461) rebuked Christians whom he observed turning toward the east and

inclining toward the sun before entering the Basilica of St. Peter (*Serm.* 27.4). The custom persisted in spite of papal disfavor, and as late as the 9th century Walafrid Strabo noted that orientation was general in the West but not rigorously practiced.

At Rome the so-called Constantinian basilicas gave no indication of orientation; but when they were. rebuilt, an effort was made to satisfy the wishes of the people, who had by now attached a mystic interpretation to the custom carried over from paganism. Nevertheless, there was no hesitation on the part of Christians to set orientation aside if there were sufficient reason for doing so. In the late 4th century, almost as many basilicas faced south and west as faced east.

LITURGICAL AND CANONICAL MEANING

The term basilica is applied today not only to large ecclesiastical structures at Rome or other places important in the history of Christianity; it is given also to structures of less importance than the Roman station churches. For a long time the term remained poorly defined, but in the 16th century the popes bestowed the title on churches that did not have the earlier qualifications of "antiquity, dimensions or fame." The actual legislation of the Church is defined in CIC c.1180: "No church can be honored with the title of basilica except by apostolic permission or immemorial custom; the privileges attached arise from one or the other reason." Canonical basilicas are either major or minor.

Major Basilicas. Among the major basilicas, a distinction must be made between those that are patriarchal and those that are not, but enjoy the title of major

Fig. 4. The double Basilica of San Lorenzo fuori le Mura, Rome, view from the later Basilica of Honorius III (1216–27) into the earlier one, built by Pelagius II (579–590).

basilica with certain privileges. Only four churches of Rome are called major primary, or patriarchal, in memory of the four patriarchal cathedrals: the Lateran, the Vatican, St. Paul on the Ostian Way, and the Liberian. The first, according to Macrius and other authors, in which the new pope is consecrated, places the See of Rome in relief; the second represents the See of Constantinople; the third, the See of Alexandria; the fourth, the See of Antioch. They all have accommodations adjoining the basilica in case councils or other business bring the patriarch to Rome.

Roman Basilicas. St. John Lateran was formerly the Basilica of the Holy Savior; it is the traditional residence of the pope as patriarch of the West, his cathedral church. It ranks before all other churches, even St. Peter's at the Vatican. After the return from *Avignon in the 15th century, the popes established themselves at St. Peter's because the Lateran was in ruins. The present basilica of St. Peter's is the largest in Christendom. Ceremonies formerly performed at the Lateran—the consecration of the new pope, beatifications and canonizations—now take place at St. Peter's.

St. Paul-Outside-the-Walls, or St. Paul on the Ostian Way, is the church of the patriarch of Alexandria. Since Rome was the see of Peter and Alexandria was allegedly the see of Mark, Pope Gregory I (590–604), writing to Eulogius, Bishop of Alexandria, spoke of the two cities as one see. The Liberian Basilica, called today St. Mary Major, is the largest church in the world in honor of the Blessed Virgin Mary. It was rebuilt in 434 and consecrated to Our Lady in memory of the definition of the Council of Ephesus (431), which declared Mary the Mother of God. It is the church of the patriarch of Antioch because the Blessed Mother was thought to have spent the greater part of her life within the limits of that patriarchate. The Patriarchate of Jerusalem was recognized when the major basilicas were already occupied by the other titulars. The question of Jerusalem's title to a patriarchate came up at the Council of Chalcedon (451). The Pope assigned St. Lawrence-outside-the-Walls, which thus became patriarchal without becoming major.

In order to establish seven as the number of basilicas to be visited on the pilgrimage called "the Roman basilicas," the Basilicas of the Holy Cross-at-Jerusalem and of St. Sebastian were added to the five patriarchal basilicas. Pius IX granted a plenary indulgence to be gained between first Vespers and sunset of the following day to those who visited these seven basilicas, provided the other conditions have been fulfilled. Outside Rome, the convent church of the Franciscans at Assisi was elevated to the rank of a patriarchal and papal basilica by Pope Benedict XIV because the body of St. Francis is there. The thrones in the upper and lower churches are reserved to the exclusive use of the pope, and no one but the pope may celebrate Mass at the principal altar (apostolic constitution *Fidelis Dominus,* April 4, 1754).

Penitentiaries and Jubilee. The major basilicas are in charge of a cardinal archpriest who represents the Holy Father. At St. Paul-outside-the-Walls, which is under the care of the Benedictines, the abbot fills this role. Besides a college of canons, major basilicas have a college of penitentiaries who hear confessions in different languages and have special powers for forgiving reserved sins. They can also grant an indulgence

Fig. 5. The pavilion, or conopoeum, of the Basilica of the Assumption at Covington, Ky.

by tapping a penitent on the shoulder with a thin pole that stands in front of their confessionals. Unlike the other churches of Rome, which are closed at certain hours of the day, the major basilicas are open all day long. They all have five naves and five doors, one of which is always closed; it is the Holy Door and is opened only during a jubilee year. The chapter of the major basilica has, as a body, all the privileges of *prothonotaries apostolic, and the canons wear the insignia. The pavilion is of cloth of gold and red velvet with gold fringes. Ordinarily only the pope may celebrate Mass at the principal altar. These basilicas enjoy spiritual favor, and their canons have a special Office with special lessons for the pope. The anniversary of the consecration of the four great basilicas is celebrated in the universal Church: the Lateran, November 9; those of SS. Peter and Paul, November 18; St. Mary Major, August 5.

Minor Basilicas. Minor basilicas are churches on which the Holy Father has conferred this title and to which he has granted many of the privileges of a major basilica. Rome has eleven basilicas with this title because of the part they played in the history of the papacy. They are the Holy Cross-in-Jerusalem (known also as Basilica Sessoriana), and in 433, the Basilica Heleniana; St. Sebastian *ad catacumbas,* where the memories of SS. Peter and Paul were honored during the persecution of Aurelian; St. Mary in Transtevere, formerly *titulus Julii* and *titulus Callixti;* St. Lawrence *in Damaso,* where Pope Damasus was elected; the

Twelve Apostles, dedicated at first to SS. Philip and James because the relics of the two Apostles are preserved there; St. Peter *in Vincoli,* in which are kept the chains that are alleged to have bound St. Peter at Rome; St. Mary *in Cosmedin;* St. Mary-in-Monte-Santo; St. Mary of the Angels; the Sacred Heart of the Praetorian Guard; and SS. Ambrose and Charles. Outside of Rome, numerous churches of all categories have received the title of minor basilica.

The characteristics of the minor basilica are a pavilion whose wooden frame is covered with bands of silk, alternately red and yellow; these are the colors of the papal government and of the Roman Senate in ancient times. Originally, this tent sheltered the patriarch. The pavilion is surmounted by a gilt copper cross. The second insignia is a *clochetta* composed of three parts: a baton, held against the bearer's chest with both hands; the small metal bell itself; and a wooden belfry with the titular of the basilica painted on one side and the escutcheon on the other. In procession, this insignia is carried close to the pavilion. The third insignia applies only where there is a chapter: the violet *cappa magna,* which the canons wear in choir. The clergy of a basilica precede all others in procession; but if the basilica is not a cathedral, the former yields and does not carry its insignia out of respect for the see.

The Christian basilica corresponded so closely to its sacred purposes that it has remained in essence the basis of church architecture. In it the Christian ceremonies attained a level of magnificence while the splendor of the interior satisfied the aesthetic needs of the Christian spirit. All the early basilicas, however, with the exception of St. Mary Major, St. Pudentiana, and St. Sabina, have undergone such extensive changes that their original disposition is difficult to determine.

Bibliography: V. CHIRONE, *The House of God through the Ages,* tr. K. NOTTRIDGE, 3 v. (Rome 1960–61) v.1. A. MOLIEN, DDC 2:224–249. G. DOWNEY, "The Architectural Significance of the Use of the Words *Stoa* and *Basilike* in Classical Literature," AmJArch 2d ser. 41 (1937) 194–211. V. MÜLLER, "The Roman Basilica," *ibid.* 250–261. Duchesne LP 170–304. R. C. DE LASTEYRIE DU SAILLANT, *L'Architecture religieuse en France à l'époque romane* (2d ed. Paris 1929). H. LECLERCQ, DACL 2.1: 525–602; 12.2:2618–45. R. LEMAIRE, *L'Origine de la basilique latine* (Brussels 1911). W. L. MACDONALD, *Early Christian and Byzantine Architecture* (New York 1962). O. MARUCCHI, *Basiliques et églises de Rome* (Paris 1902). A. P. SHEEHAN, *The New Temple of God as Reflected in the Early Church Edifices* (Master's diss. unpub. Catholic U. of America 1964). P. TESTINI, *Archeologia cristiana* (Rome 1958). A. C. A. ZESTERMANN, *De basilicis* (Brussels 1847). L. VOELKL and A. P. FRUTAZ, LexThK² 2:40–45. E. LANGLOTZ and F. W. DEICHMANN, ReallexAntChr 1:1225–29. T. F. MATHEWS, "An Early Roman Chancel Arrangement and Its Liturgical Functions," RivArchCrist 38 (1962) 73–95. R. KRAUTHEIMER, *Corpus basilicarum christianarum Romae* (Vatican City 1937–   ). **Illustration credits:** Figs. 2*a,* 3, and 4, Hirmer Verlag München. Fig. 2*b,* Marburg-Art Reference Bureau.

[M. C. HILFERTY]

BASILIDES, ST., martyr; d. Alexandria, 202–203 (feast, June 30). A soldier, he protected Potamiaena from the crowd as he led her, after tortures, to her martyrdom under boiling pitch. She promised to repay him for his kindness, and when Basilides was imprisoned as a Christian for refusing to take an oath, she appeared to him, wreathed his head with a crown, and promised soon to take him to herself. Basilides was baptized and the next day beheaded, the seventh catechumen of *Origen to suffer martyrdom. His story, which is preserved by Eusebius (*Hist. Eccl.* 6.5), is one of the earliest testimonies in the Church to belief in the intercession of saints. In the *martyrology of Jerome he is commemorated on June 28 with Potamiaena and Marcella, her martyred mother.

On June 12 the Roman martyrology commemorates a Basilides with Cyrinus, Nabor, and Nazarius. He was a Roman martyr buried at the 12th milestone of the Via Aurelia, where there was a shrine to him in the 7th century. The three accounts of him are late and without historical value, and there is no connection between him and Cyrinus (probably Quirinus, Bishop of Siscia) and Nabor and Nazarius (martyrs of Milan).

Bibliography: A. P. FRUTAZ and A. KREUZ, LexThK² 2:39–40. B. CIGNITTI and F. CARAFFA, BiblSanct 2:904–906.

[M. J. COSTELLOE]

BASILIDES

Gnostic teacher, 2d-century founder of a Gnostic school in Alexandria. Of the life of Basilides little is known with certainty. Epiphanius (*Haer.* 1.23) reports that he was a fellow pupil of Saturnilus under Menander in Antioch. Basilides taught at Alexandria, most probably under the reigns of Hadrian and Antoninus Pius (*c.* A.D. 120–145). The most distinguished disciple in his heretical sect, still in existence in the 4th century, was his son Isidore. Basilides composed his own version of the Gospels, a commentary on this work in 24 books called the *Exegetica* (fragments in *Hegemonius, *Acta Archelai* 67.4–12 and *Clement of Alexandria, Strom. 4.81–88), and some odes and psalms now lost.

It is difficult to determine precisely the doctrines of Basilides. According to *Irenaeus (*Adv. Haer.* 1.24) he began with a system of emanations starting with the Father, the Nous, the Logos, Phronesis, Sophia, and Dynamis, followed by 365 groups of angels and powers, each of which created a heaven, and the last of which created our world. Christ was the Nous who visited the world but was not really crucified. Salvation comes by knowledge of the Nous and the system, the acts of the body are a matter of indifference, magic and incantations have an important role. *Hippolytus of Rome (*Ref.* 7.20–27), however, describes a much more original doctrine involving a nonexistent God from whose seed arise a triple order of Sonship, a series of Archons, and upper and lower regions called the Ogdoad and the Hebdomad. A key feature of this presentation is the denial of the typically Gnostic doctrine of emanation. Despite the marked differences in their account of Basilides' teaching, it is possible that Irenaeus describes an earlier version of his doctrine and Hippolytus a later one. Hegemonius (*supra*) states that Basilides taught Persian dualism, though the other accounts present his system as monistic. Clement of Alexandria (*supra*) was chiefly concerned with ethical aspects of his teachings. Basilides seems to have been mainly a philosopher; his very subtlety may have impeded the spread of his sect beyond Egypt.

See also GNOSTICISM.

Bibliography: W. VÖLKER, *Quellen zur Geschichte der christlichen Gnosis* (Tübingen 1932) 38–57. F. J. A. HORT DCB 1:258–281. A. S. PEAKE, Hastings ERE 2:426–433. J. H. WASZINK, ReallexAntChr 1:1217–25. Quasten Patr 1:257–259. R. M. WILSON, *The Gnostic Problem* (London 1958). J. DORESSE, *The Secret Books of the Egyptian Gnostics,* tr. P. MAIRET (New York 1960). R. M. GRANT, *Gnosticism: A Sourcebook . . .* (New York 1961).

[G. W. MAC RAE]

BASILISCUS, BYZANTINE EMPEROR, 475 to 476; d. Cappadocia, 477.

As brother of the Empress Verina, wife of Leo I, Basiliscus rose rapidly at court, became consul in 465, and, although totally incompetent, led the expedition against the Vandals that was annihilated in 468. After the death of Leo and the coronation of Zeno (474), Verina organized a plot that led to the expulsion of Zeno and the proclamation of Basiliscus as emperor. Basiliscus soon alienated the court by his cupidity, incompetence, and unpopular religious policies. He favored the Monophysites, restored the exiled *Timothy Aelurus as patriarch of Constantinople and Peter the Fuller as patriarch of Antioch, and persecuted the Orthodox clergy, including Patriarch Acacius of Constantinople (see ACACIAN SCHISM). He published an encyclical condemning the decrees of the Council of *Chalcedon and the tome of Pope *Leo I. The sermons of the stylite Daniel and the public protests of Acacius roused the people of Constantinople, and the Emperor was deposed by a plot organized by Verina. On the return of Zeno, Basiliscus and his family were interred in a cistern in Cappadocia, where they died of starvation.

Bibliography: J. B. BURY, *History of the Later Roman Empire* (London 1923) 1:335–403. Fliche-Martin 4:284–285. Stein-Palanque HistBEmp 1:363–364. L. BRÉHIER, DHGE 6:1237–39. G. BARDY, *Catholicisme* 1:1301–02. Ostrogorsky 57–59.

[J. BRÜCKMANN]

BASQUE LITERATURE

The Basque language (*Euskera*) is spoken by some 100,000 inhabitants of the French Basses-Pyrénées and by perhaps 600,000 in northern Spain. The origins of the language are a linguistic mystery. It was first thought to be a descendent of Iberian, especially after the work of Wilhelm von Humboldt (1767–1835), but with the modern readings of Iberian inscriptions, scholars no longer consider Basque an Iberian language. In the first half of the 20th century, studies by linguists led to a belief in a possible relationship between the Basque and Caucasian languages; the strong criticism of other linguists, however, has clouded what seemed a promising hypothesis. At present it can only be said that Basque is the sole living language in western Europe that does not belong to the Indo-European family and that it probably represents one of the many languages that were spoken in Europe before the Indo-European invasions 3,000 years ago. It is divided into seven main dialects; this diversity, together with the ban on teaching Basque in state schools, greatly obstructs the language's preservation and development.

Early Oral and Written Literature. Oral literature is best represented in *bersolarism,* the improvisation of verses set to a tune. It was extremely popular and remained vigorous in mid-20th century. Among the vast number of adepts in the field, the prominent names carrying on the tradition were Etchahun (Pierre Topet, 1786–1862), Bilinch (Indalecio Bizcarrondo, 1831–76), Xenpelar (J. F. Petrierena, 1835–69); Basarri (I. Eizmendi, 1913–) and Xalbador (F. Aire). A popular drama, the obvious descendant of the medieval religious stage, remains widespread in the province of Soule (see DRAMA, MEDIEVAL, 1).

Despite the antiquity of the language, the most ancient texts, fragments of poetry, date from only the 14th century. Literature in any real sense began in the 16th century with Bernard Dechepare's *Lingua Vasconum*

Primitiae (1545); a collection of religious and love poems; a Calvinist catechism; and a translation of the New Testament, *Iesus Christ Gure Iaunaren Testamentu Berria* (1571) by Jean de Leizarraga. The 17th and 18th centuries mark a high point in Basque literature. Axular (1556–1644) showed great mastery of prose in his *Gvero* (1643), an eschatological tract. Other prominent prose writers were the Jesuits Manuel de Larramendi (1690–1766), Augustin de Cardaberaz (1703–70), and Sebastián de Mendiburu (1708–82); finally, there were M. Duhalde (1733–1804) and J. A. Moguel (1745–1804).

19th and 20th Centuries. Basque writers began to proliferate from the end of the 18th century, though the reading public was (and still is) small. In the French Basque area the eminent figure was J. B. Elissamburu (1828–91), with his novel *Piarres Adame* and his poems. Among the Spanish Basques, J. J. Moguel (1781–1849) and his sister Vicenta (1782–1854) were prominent; J. I. Iztueta (1767–1845) wrote a history of the memorable dances of Guipuzcoa, *Guipuzcoaco dantza gogoangarrien condaira edo historia* (1824); the Franciscan J. A. Uriarte (1812–69) and Jean Duvoisin (1810–91) respectively translated the Bible into the Guipuzcoan and Labourdin dialects. One very important publication was Felipe Arrese Beitia's *Ama Euskeriaren Liburu kantaria* (1900, The Song-Book of Our Mother Tongue).

The 20th century has been rich in the work of writers and philologists, despite much official opposition. The novels *Kresala* (1901, Sea-Water) and *Garoa* (1907, The Fern), by Father Domingo de Aguirre (1864–1920), are prominent. Orixe (Nicolas Ormaetxea, 1888–1961), an eminent translator and poet, is author of a long nationalistic poem, *Euskaldunak* (1935, The Basques). Father J. Zaitegi, translator of Plato and Sophocles, is also a poet and founder of the literary review *Euzko-Gogoa* (Basque Thought). The best among the poets are Lauaxeta (Esteban Urkiaga, 1905–37), Lizardi (J. M. Aguirre, 1896–1933), T. Monzon-Olaso (1904–), J. Mirande (1927–), Iratzeder (J. Diharce, 1920–), Father S. Mitxelena (1919–), and the Franciscan V. Gandiaga (1928–). J. Etchepare (1877–1935) was a remarkable essayist, e.g., *Buruchkak* (1910, Gleanings) and *Berebilez* (1931, In an Automobile). Prominent language experts were R. M. Azkue (1864–1951), A. Altube (1879–1963), and L. Michelena (1915–).

Mention should be made of literature written in Spanish by Basques. The list of authors is long and covers all aspects of Spanish literature from its beginnings to such modern authors as Miguel de *Unamuno—who also wrote in Basque, e.g., his salutation to the sacred tree of Guernica, *Agur, Arbola Bedeinkatuba* —Pio Baroja (1872–1956), J. A. Zunzunegui (1901–), and Ignacio Aldecoa (1925–). Literature in French by Basques is not so impressive; the Jesuit Pierre Lhande (1877–1957) and Pierre Apesteguy in the novel, Pierre d'Arcangues (1886–) in poetry, and M. Legasse (1918–) in the political essay should be mentioned.

The vast majority of literary figures have been Catholic priests. The ascetical and mystical element is accordingly strong in Basque literature, and its masterpieces are spiritual works. In recent years, however, literature has become increasingly secularized; even the reviews that are largely controlled and edited by the clergy devote ample space to secular literature, an element that has been strikingly lacking in Basque literature.

Bibliography: R. GALLOP, *A Book of the Basques* (London 1930). A. TOVAR, *The Basque Language,* tr. H. P. HOUGHTON (Philadelphia 1957). S. ONAINDIA, *Milla euskaloierti eder* (Amorebieta 1954). P. LAFITTE, *Le Basque et la littérature d'expression basque en Labourd, Basse-Navarre et Soule* (Bayonne 1941). L. MICHELENA, *Historia de la literatura vasca* (Madrid 1960). L. VILLASANTE CORTABITARTE, *Historia de la literatura vasca* (Bilbao 1961). G. L. REICHER, *Les Basques: Leur mystique, leur passé, leur littérature* (Paris 1939).

[I. BASTARRIKA; J. BILBAO]

BASRA, ARCHDIOCESE OF (BASRENSIS), archbishopric of the *Chaldean rite since 1953, without suffragans, in southeast *Iraq. In 1963 it had 7 parishes, 4 secular and 2 religious priests, 4 women in 1 convent, 425 pupils in 1 school, and 2,381 Catholics in a population of 1,139,000; it is 6,496 square miles in area. The city of Basra (population about 165,000), on the Shatt-al-Arab (confluence of the Tigris and Euphrates Rivers) 65 miles from the Persian Gulf, is the main port of Iraq. It dates from the 17th century and is 8 miles from the original Basra founded *c.* 636. Basra flourished under the *'Abbāsids but declined under the Turks (1534–1914) until taken by the British in World War I.

Perat of Maisan, an ancient town near the location of Basra, was the seat of a *Nestorian metropolitanate with a list of prelates obscurely known (410–893). The Carmelite mission in Basra was established in 1623. Joseph IV 'Aûdô, Chaldean *catholicos (1847–78), in 1860 made his emissary to the Malabar Coast titular metropolitan of Basra, and the title was used again in 1888. A patriarchal vicariate was established in 1892, and the archbishopric was created in 1953. A Franciscan, Roger, is reported to have been a Latin bishop of Basra *c.* 1360.

Bibliography: C. KOROLEVSKIJ, DHGE 6:1279–81. OrientCatt 359–377. AnnPont (1964) 57.

[J. A. DEVENNY]

BASSIANUS OF EPHESUS, 5th-century bishop; d. after 451. A popular and influential priest of Ephesus, Bassianus was forced by his bishop, Memnon, because of jealousy, to be consecrated bishop of Evaza (*c.* 431), but he refused to occupy his see. Memnon's successor, Basil, consecrated another bishop for Evaza and allowed Bassianus to return to Ephesus (*c.* 434). With the approval of Emperor *Theodosius II and Proclus, Patriarch of Constantinople, Bassianus was chosen to succeed Basil in Ephesus (444). Four years later, however, Bassianus was forcibly deposed, and Stephen was named his successor. Bassianus appealed to the Emperor, who referred the matter to the Council of *Chalcedon. The fathers heard the testimony of both sides at the 11th session (Oct. 29, 451). Although many sided with Bassianus, no decision was reached until the 12th session on the following day. The council then decided that both Stephen and Bassianus were to be deposed, and a new bishop to be chosen by the bishops of the province. Bassianus and Stephen, however, were each to receive 200 gold solidi a year from the See of Ephesus. Little is known of Bassianus after that.

Bibliography: Mansi 7:273–300. R. JANIN, DHGE 6:1274–75. Hefele-Leclercq 2.2:755–761. F. X. MURPHY, *Peter Speaks through Leo* (Washington, D.C. 1952) 87–89.

[R. K. POETZEL]

BASSVILLE, NICOLAS JEAN HUGOU DE, French diplomat; b. Abbeville (Somme), Feb. 7, 1753; d. Rome, Jan. 14, 1793. In his youth he was a tutor, professor, traveler, and author of historical and light works. A supporter of the *French Revolution from 1789, he published a brochure, *Le Cri de la nation à ses pairs, ou rendons les prêtres citoyens,* in which he demanded that the clergy be forced to renounce its "vow of obedience" and celibacy. He contributed to the short-lived *Mercure national ou Journal d'État et du citoyen,* soon called *Mercure national et Révolutions de l'Europe* (December 1789–March 1791). In 1790 he wrote four volumes of commentaries on the work of the National Assembly, *Mémoires historiques . . . de la Révolution.* In November 1792 while he was secretary to the embassy in Naples he was sent to Rome, after a recent incident, to attend to the rights of French citizens. His vehement attitude and proposals, his intention to affix the emblem of the Republic to the French consulate and French academy, and the tricolored cockade worn by his entourage made him the victim of a popular uprising on the Corso (Jan. 13, 1793), during which he was fatally stabbed in the abdomen. He died the next day after receiving the last rites. The assassination interrupted the initial steps toward reconciliation, then progressing, between the Holy See and France.

Bibliography: F. MASSON, *Les Diplomates de la révolution* (Paris 1882). G. BOURGIN, "L'Assassinat de Bassville et l'opinion romaine en 1793," *Mélanges d'archéologie et d'histoire* 33 (1914) 365–478. Pastor v.40. A. RASTOUL, DictBiogFranc 5: 769–770. J. COIGNET, DHGE 6:1286–87.

[C. LEDRÉ]

BASUTOLAND, mountainous country in *Africa, completely surrounded by the Republic of *South Africa; 11,716 square miles in area. Welded together from scattered Basuto tribes by the chief Moshesh (1820), it resisted European claims until 1871, when it was annexed to the Cape Town colony. Since 1884 it has been a British protectorate administered by a high commissioner, together with *Swaziland and *Bechuanaland; since 1959 it has enjoyed internal autonomy. In 1964 the population was estimated at 800,00, including 3,000 non-Africans. More than 60 per cent of the populace is Christian; the rest is pagan. Protestants in 1964 numbered 200,000 (59,000 being full members).

The first Catholic mission was established in 1862 by *Oblates of Mary Immaculate from the Vicariate Apostolic of Natal. Moshesh welcomed them and chose the site for the mission, later called Roma. The Prefecture Apostolic of Basutoland, created in 1894, became a vicariate apostolic in 1909. In 1924 the Oblates established at Roma a seminary, and in 1945, Pius XII University College. When the South African hierarchy was established (1951), the vicariate became the Diocese of *Maseru. In 1961 Maseru was made an archdiocese and metropolitan see for Basutoland, with Leribe and Quacha's Nek as suffragan sees. The first archbishop was the great-grandson of Moshesh. In 1963 there were 300,000 Catholics, 15,700 catechumens, 62 churches, 151 priests, 114 brothers, 681 sisters (489 Africans), and 910 catechists. In 1963 the University College became nondenominational, administered by the British government, but the Oblates remained in charge of Pius XII College. The 483 Catholic schools had more than 67,600 pupils.

Bibliography: W. E. BROWN, *The Catholic Church in South Africa,* ed. M. DERRICK (New York 1960) 207–223. AnnPont

(1965) 235, 266. *Bilan du Monde* 2:120–123. For additional bibliography, *see* AFRICA. For map, *see* SOUTH AFRICA, REPUBLIC OF.

[J. E. BRADY]

BATAILLON, PIERRE MARIE, pioneer Marist missioner in *Oceania; b. Saint-Cyr-les-Vignes (Loire), France, Jan. 6, 1810; d. Wallis Island, April 10, 1877. He joined the *Marist Fathers and was ordained. Leaving France with Bp. Jean *Pompallier (Dec. 24, 1836), he arrived at Wallis Island in the southwest Pacific (Nov. 1, 1837), where he and Brother Joseph Luzy began their apostolate in the face of privation and violent hostility. His courage, forcefulness, and charity so impressed the savage Polynesian chiefs that the entire population of about 2,700 was converted (1842). When Pompallier's Vicariate Apostolic of Western Oceania was divided (1842), Bataillon became the first vicar apostolic of Central Oceania, which included *New Caledonia, *New Hebrides, the *Fiji Islands, the *Tonga Islands, *Samoa, the Tokelau Islands, and *Wallis and Futuna Islands. Consecrated bishop (Dec. 3, 1843), Bataillon began with his slender forces an immediate evangelization of Fiji, Tonga, and Samoa, all three of which later became vicariates, and

Pierre Marie Bataillon.

also of Rotuma. To train a native clergy he opened on Wallis the first seminary in Oceania (1874). The vicar was an extremely apostolic man of vision and perseverance, but such an exacting taskmaster to his missionaries that Marist superiors became disturbed and promulgated new directives defining mission administration. As Fiji and Samoa became established missions, Bataillon's Central Oceania vicariate was restricted to Wallis, Futuna, and Tonga (1873).

Bibliography: A. M. MANGERET, *Mgr. Bataillon et les missions de l'Océanie Centrale,* 2 v. (2d ed. Lyon 1895); *La Croix dans les îles du Pacifique: Vie de Mgr. Bataillon* (Paris 1932). N. WEBER, *Brief Biographical Dictionary of the Marist Hierarchy* (Washington 1953).

[J. E. BELL]

BATALHA, former Dominican cloister of Santa Maria da Victoria, near Leiria, Portugal. On Aug. 14, 1385, at Aljubarrota, King John I of Portugal decisively vanquished the Spaniards who were attempting to incorporate Portugal into the Castilian kingdom. In fulfillment of a vow to the Virgin in return for the victory, John began the building of Santa Maria da Victoria at the nearby town of Batalha as a monument to Portuguese independence. The blind Portuguese architect Afonso Domingues was first entrusted with the con-

The abbey church of the former Dominican cloister of Santa Maria da Victoria near Leiria, Portugal.

struction; he was succeeded by Master Huguet, who was probably Flemish. The work progressed under successive monarchs. In April 1388 the Abbey was confided to the care of the *Dominicans. Built in Flamboyant *Gothic style with peninsular modifications, it is regarded as a prime example of Iberian art. The three imposing naves are 260 feet long and 120 feet high, and its slender ribs, graceful traceries, statues, mosaics, and bas-reliefs add to its reputation as one of the finest of all Gothic structures. Other features are a large chapter room and a number of burial annexes where King John, his family, including Prince *Henry the Navigator, and many other notables lie in magnificent tombs. It was closed in 1834 and made a national monument in 1840.

Bibliography: M. DE SOUSA COUTINHO, *Plans, Elevations, Sections and Views of the Church of Batalha in the Province of Estramadura in Portugal,* ed. and tr. J. MURPHY (London 1795). V. DE WILDE, DHGE 6:1310–11. P. DONY, *Batalha: Un Problème d'influences* (Lisbon 1957). **Illustration credit:** Casa de Portugal.

[A. O'MALLEY]

BATH, ABBEY OF, Anglo-Saxon Benedictine monastery in Bath, England (patron, St. Peter). The early history of Bath is obscure and involved in the complicated politics of the Mercian hegemony. It was founded probably by the underking of the Hwicce in the last quarter of the 7th century as a convent of nuns. Apparently the nunnery did not prosper, if indeed it was ever a real community at all, and it came into the possession of the local bishop of *Worcester. In the 8th century the great Mercian king *Offa took it from the bishop of Worcester and soon after some kind of genuine monastic community was found there. Bath did not prosper for long, and during the Viking wars it again became derelict. In the 10th century King Edmund gave the estates to a group of secular clerks who had been expelled from a monastery in Flanders by the reformer *Gerard of Brogne. The abbey was reformed again, probably by *Oswald of York, and turned into one of the greatest English abbeys in King Edgar's reign. Although it is said that the martyr *Alphege of Canterbury was abbot of St. Peter's in Bath, he was actually the abbot of a smaller, quite distinct community at Bath. After the Conquest St. Peter's was largely destroyed in the rebellion following the death of William the Conqueror in 1087. At the same time it was

Bath, abbey church with fan tracery of 17th century.

decided to move the local see from Wells to Bath, and St. Peter's was rebuilt and henceforth became the seat of the bishops of *Bath and Wells.

Bibliography: Dugdale MonAngl 2:256–273. Knowles-Hadcock 59, 253. Knowles MOE, *passim.* Knowles ROE, *passim.* **Illustration credit:** Reece Winstone, Bristol, England.

[E. JOHN]

BATH AND WELLS, ANCIENT SEE OF,

medieval Catholic diocese coterminous with the County of Somerset, England, in the ecclesiastical province of *Canterbury; it was formed by the union of the ancient Abbey of *Bath and the church of canons regular at Wells, Somerset, England. The original Diocese of Wells was founded in 909 with the appointment of Aethelhelm as bishop; Bishop Gisa (1060–88) made an important contribution to its establishment in the transitional period from the Old English State to the early Norman settlement. But the transfer of the episcopal seat to Bath by John de Villula (John of Tours) in 1090 interrupted this development. A dispute between the canons of Wells and the monks of Bath reached a crisis under Bp. Roger of Lewes (1136–66) and was temporarily settled by a papal ruling that both places should thenceforth be episcopal sees, both chapters sharing in the bishop's election; but that the prior of Bath should formally announce the election, and the bishop's enthronement should take place in both churches, but first in Bath. This precedence for Bath continued, and Bp. *Savaric of Bath (1192–1205) set up a see in *Glastonbury Abbey in 1197, and for a short time the diocese was subsequently known as Bath and Glastonbury, until the arrangement was dissolved by Pope *Honorius III in 1219. The death of Bp. *Jocelin of Wells in 1242 precipitated a final settlement, again by papal judgment, which re-

asserted the principle of joint election and established the title of Bath and Wells. This title survived the Reformation, though after the monastic dissolution the abbey church at Bath became a parish church and the Anglican episcopal seat was maintained at Wells alone. The last Catholic bishop was Gilbert *Bourne, who was deprived by Queen *Elizabeth I in 1559.

The abbey at Bath was rebuilt in the late Perpendicular style in the early 16th century. The Gothic cathedral at Wells evolved through several stages: the Norman cathedral of Robert of Lewes was replaced by Bp. Reginald Fitz Jocelin (1174–91), whose plans were brought to completion by Bp. Jocelin of Wells (1206–42); the tower with the famous inverted columns beneath it, the chapter house, and the lady chapel were added in the early 14th century.

Bibliography: LeNeve FastEcclAngli v.8. F. M. POWICKE and C. R. CHENEY, eds., *Councils and Synods* (Oxford 1964) 2.1: 44–46, 586–626. *The Victoria History of the County of Somerset,* ed. W. PAGE, v.2 (London 1911) 1–39. A. H. THOMPSON, *The Cathedral Churches of England* (London 1925). R. GRAHAM, DHGE 6:1317–18. I. J. CHURCHILL, *Canterbury Administration,* 2 v. (New York 1933). C. L. MARSON in *A Dictionary of English Church History,* ed. S. L. OLLARD et al. (3d ed. London 1948) 44–46. K. EDWARDS, *The English Secular Cathedrals in the Middle Ages* (Manchester 1949). Cross ODCC 141, 1444.

[C. DUGGAN]

BATHILDIS, ST., Queen of France; d. Chelles, Jan. 30, *c.* 680 (feast, Jan. 30; Jan. 26). A native of England, whence she had been kidnapped by pirates, she lived at the court of Neustria as a part of the household of Erchinoald, mayor of the palace, but refused to become his wife. She married Clovis II, King of Neustria and Burgundy, and bore him three sons: Chlotar, Childeric, and Theodoric. At the death of Clovis, she became Queen Regent under the nominal reign of her eldest son Chlotar, with such advisers as (St.) *Ouen and Chrodobert, Bishop of Paris. Before 673, the mayor of the palace Ebroinus deprived her of power and had her conducted to the abbey of *Chelles, France (Department Seine-et-Marne), where she lived in all simplicity. Bathildis founded the abbeys of *Corbie and Chelles and was lavish in endowing the churches and monasteries of her kingdom. Although not entirely vindicated for her part in the assassination of Bp. *Aunemund of Lyons (658), her memory is honored because of her struggle against slavery, simony, and abusive taxation. The *Vita prima s. Bathildis* is an excellent biography, written by a contemporary who used as a model the life of St. *Radegunda. A *Vita secunda* was composed at the end of the 8th century or at the beginning of the 9th. Her cult began before 822.

Bibliography: MGSrerMer 2:475–508. E. VACANDARD, *Vie de Saint Ouen* (Paris 1902). M. J. COUTURIER, *Sainte Bathilde, reine des Francs* (Paris 1909). L. VAN DER ESSEN, DHGE 6: 1321–22. Baudot-Chaussin 1:616–619. Fliche-Martin 5:350–352. R. AIGRAIN, *Catholicisme* 1:1194–95. E. EWIG, LexThK² 2:50. J. MARILIER, BiblSanct 2:971–972.

[É. BROUETTE]

BÁTHORY, Hungarian princely family stemming from the ancient Magyar clan of Gut-Keled.

Andrew (András), Bishop of Nagyvárad (1333), was the confidant of King Charles Robert of Hungary and builder of the famed Gothic cathedral of Nagyvárad, which was later destroyed by the Turks.

Ladislaus (László), Bl., a member of the Order of the Hermits of St. Paul, lived in the first half of the

Stephen (István) Báthory, Prince of Transylvania and King of Poland.

15th century. He translated the Bible into Hungarian.

Stephen (István) (1533–86), an outstanding soldier and diplomat, was unanimously elected to the vacant sovereignty of Transylvania in 1571. In 1575 he was elected king of Poland, thus ending the interregnum following the abdication of the Polish King Henry III (Valois). Stephen's marriage to the Polish Princess Anne of Jagello strengthened his position. He fought the Muscovites with skill, repeatedly defeating Ivan the Terrible. His other triumphs over the invading Turks and Tartars restored Poland to a leading position in northeastern Europe. He gave strong support to the Catholic reform movement, encouraged the Jesuits, and abolished the edict that gave equal rights to the Protestants. He also introduced the Gregorian calendar into Poland. Upon the death of Ivan the Terrible in 1584, Báthory prepared for a possible Polish-Muscovite union, but he died unexpectedly in 1586.

Sigismund (Zsigmond) (1572–1613) was elected sovereign of Transylvania in 1581, assuming power at the age of 16. He was a talented statesman and general, and scored a decisive victory over the Ottoman general, Sinan Pasha, in 1595. Four years later, upset at the desertion of his wife Maria Christina of Austria, and perhaps affected by an inherent eccentricity, he suddenly abdicated in favor of Emperor Rudolf II in exchange for the Duchy of Oppeln. His abdication was not approved by the Transylvanian estates; therefore in that year he offered the throne to his cousin Andrew, and it was accepted.

Andrew (András) (1566–99), cardinal bishop of Ermland. In 1599 he left his diocese to assume the sovereignty of Transylvania offered by his cousin Sigismund, but he died in battle.

Bibliography: S. Szilágyi, ed., *Monumenta comitialia regni Transylvaniae (1540–1699)*, 21 v. (Budapest 1875–98). I. Acsády, *A magyar birodalom története*, 2 v. (Budapest 1903–04) 2. I. Lukinich, *Erdély területi változásai a török hóditás korában, 1541–1711* (Budapest 1918). Polska Akademia Umiejętnósci, *Etienne Báthory, roi de Pologne, prince de Transylvanie* (Cracow 1935). B. Hóman and J. Szekfü, *Magyar történet*, 8 v. (Budapest 1928–34). L. Toth, DHGE 6:1323–25. N. del Re, EncCatt 2:996–997.

[G. C. Paikert]

BATHS

This article is concerned primarily with baths and bathing in Christian antiquity.

General Background. Baths and bathing were an important feature of Greek life from the age of Homer, but they played a much greater role among the Romans from the 3d century B.C. to the end of antiquity. The Romans developed elaborate heating arrangements for their baths and erected enormous bathing establishments (*thermae*), which included lounging rooms, lecture halls, and libraries, as well as the baths proper and their own complex of chambers, dressing rooms, etc. They corresponded in many respects to the modern social center. As early as 33 B.C., there were 170 public baths in Rome alone, and under the empire this number was greatly increased. The fee for admission was very small, thus making the baths accessible to the great majority of the population. All cities and towns throughout the empire had their public baths, and all men of wealth had elaborate private baths in their town houses and on their country estates. There were separate public bathing facilities for women as well as for men. Under the empire, however, the custom of mixed bathing was introduced and led to abuses that were severely condemned by pagan and later by Christian moralists. Physicians and moralists also denounced the tendency to spend long periods of time in the warm baths on the ground that this practice was enervating both physically and morally. On the other hand, they recommended bathing with moderation, especially in cold water, as beneficial for the mind as well as for the body.

Bathing and the baths were an essential part of everyday life and are referred to as such in casual terms by Christian writers such as Clement of Alexandria, Tertullian, and St. Augustine. The Christian Fathers, however, found it necessary to warn repeatedly against the dangers to morals in the public baths, and they were concerned in particular about the special moral dangers

Ruins of the Bath of Caracalla at Rome. Opened in 217, this bath remained in use well into the 6th century.

to which women bathers were exposed. As archeology has shown, rich Christians continued to erect and maintain elaborate baths in their own town houses and on their country estates to the very end of the empire in the West and in early Byzantine times.

In Christian Asceticism. The attitude of the early ascetical writers and founders of monasticism is entirely different. While the immorality connected with public baths was a cause of hostility, the chief reason for the stern prohibitions regarding baths and bathing came from the spirit of asceticism itself. The body was to be chastised severely for the good of the soul by fasting and was to be deprived of all else, along with food and drink, that could give it comfort and pleasure. Hence the ascetical opposition to the pleasure derived from scrupulous cleanliness and bathing. It is not difficult for moderns to understand how acutely painful was the loss of the bath and bathing to men and women for whom they were such a normal part of everyday life in its social as well as in its hygienic aspects. The Rule of St. *Pachomius (d. A.D. 346) permits complete bathing of the body only in case of sickness, but some ascetics even refused the comfort of bathing when seriously ill. St. Jerome, ardent champion of asceticism, makes practically no concessions. St. Augustine (*Letter* 211.13) permits a community of religious women to visit the baths only once a month, and then only on condition that they go at least three together. He permits more frequent bathing only on the advice of a physician. St. Caesarius of Arles (d. A.D. 542) in his rule for nuns (ch. 31) permits baths only to those who are ill. The Rule of St. Benedict (ch. 36) is relatively mild, but is couched in the same ascetical spirit. This monastic tradition passed on to the Middle Ages, sometimes in its most rigorous forms, and had its effects on general penitential discipline. A temporary prohibition from indulging in bathing was often given as a penance to laymen—in both East and West. Celtic monasticism in particular developed a special form of asceticism arising out of the idea of bathing, namely, the painful practice of standing for fairly long periods in water that was very cold or even icy.

It is hardly necessary to give more than passing mention to the legend that the years of the Middle Ages were bathless. The legend was undoubtedly based on the presumed application of the prohibitions of monastic rules and treatises, written for the guidance of ascetics, to all classes of society. In the later Middle Ages, even public baths were common in many cities and were very popular.

Bibliography: H. FLECKENSTEIN, LexThK² 1:1183–84. L. GOUGAUD, DictSpirAscMyst 1:1197–1200. J. JÜTHNER, ReallexAnt Chr 1:1134–43, with bibliog. J. ZELLINGER, *Bad und Bäder in der altchristlichen Kirche* (Munich 1928). P. GALLAND, *L'Église et l'hygiène en Moyen Âge* (Paris 1933). H. DUMAINE, DACL 2:72–117, with bibliog. E. JOSI and C. TESTORE, EncCatt 2:686–688. M. C. McCARTHY, *The Rule for Nuns of St. Caesarius of Arles* (CUA St. Med. Hist. NS 16; Washington 1960) esp. 122–123, 145–146. **Illustration credit:** Alinari-Art Reference Bureau.

[M. R. P. MC GUIRE]

BATIFFOL, PIERRE, theologian, Church historian; b. Toulouse, Jan. 27, 1861; d. Paris, Jan 13, 1929. He studied at the Seminary of St. Sulpice in Paris (1878–82), was ordained in 1884, and attended the Institut Catholique and the École des Hautes Études while serving as a curate in Paris. He was an early friend of the Biblical scholar M. J. *Lagrange, a protégé of the Church historian L. *Duchesne, and also came under the influence of the archeologist G. B. *Rossi in Rome. He was chaplain at L'École de Ste. Barbe in Paris from 1889 until he was named rector of the Institut Catholique of Toulouse in 1898. Here he devoted himself to the history of penance, the agape, and the *disciplina arcani,* publishing the results in his *Études d'histoire et de théologie positive* (1902). Though he opposed the Modernist movement (*see* MODERNISM) in his *L'Enseignement de Jésus* (1905), his *L'Eucharistie: la Présence réelle et la Transubstantiation* was put on the Index (1907). Thereupon he resigned his rectorship and returned to the chaplaincy in Paris, remaining there until his death. In 1913 he published a complete revision of the book on the Eucharist.

Batiffol's first important publications included *La Vaticane de Paul IV à Paul V* (1890), and *L'Abbaye de Rossano: Contribution à l'histoire de la Vaticane* (1891). His *Histoire du Bréviaire romain* (1893; Eng. tr. 1898) stimulated a revival of liturgical studies in France. Besides his *Studia Patristica* (1889–90) and editions of numerous texts, including the *Tractatus Origenis* (1900), he contributed studies on the Bible and on Byzantine historiography to leading German and French periodicals. His later works concerned with the early papacy include: *L'Église naissante et le catholicisme* (1909; Eng. tr., *Primitive Catholicism,* 1911), *La Paix constantinienne et le catholicisme* (1914), *Le Catholicisme de S. Augustin* (1920), *S. Léon le Grand* (DTC 9:218–301), and *S. Grégoire le Grand* (1928, Eng. tr. 1929). Batiffol advanced research in positive theology, and introduced his colleagues to non-Catholic and foreign scholarship in his fields of study.

Bibliography: J. RIVIÈRE, *Mgr. Pierre Batiffol* (Paris 1929) incl. bibliog.; DHGE 6:1327–30. G. BARDY, "L'Oeuvre de Mgr. Batiffol," RechSR 10 (1929) 393–400. DTC *Tables générales* (1960) 385–386.

[F. X. MURPHY]

BATISTA, CÍCERO ROMÃO, Brazilian priest, object of popular devotion; b. Ceará, Brazil, 1844; d. Rome, 1934. He was ordained in 1870, and had manifested mystic tendencies while still in the seminary. As pastor in Juazeiro, Ceará—a poor region, both geographically and culturally isolated, and of old messianic tradition—he worked to invigorate the religious faith of the inhabitants, preaching sermons in which he advised repentance and an ascetic life. The drought of 1877 to 1879 brought many more people to this parish and his reputation and authority increased. In 1889 there occurred "miracles" with hosts that were transformed into blood. Religious fervor increased and whole families migrated to Juazeiro. The diocesan bishop condemned the miracles (1891), prohibited the priest from preaching and confessing (1892), and from saying Mass (1896). Father Cícero traveled to Rome in 1898, where Leo XIII permitted him to say Mass only in a private oratory. Meanwhile, the popular devotion increased as did the population of Juazeiro. Little by little it became dominated by local politics, and clashes with the governors of the state of Ceará reached the point of armed conflict in which the priest's followers considered themselves supernaturally protected by their "padrinho," Father Cícero. The situation continued until his death. The city of Juazeiro even in 1963 continued to be one of the greatest centers of religious pilgrimage in Brazil because of the legends concerning this priest.

Bibliography: A. F. MONTENEGRO, *História do fanatismo religioso no Ceará* (Fortaleza, Brazil 1959).

[J. A. GONSALVES DE MELLO]

BATON ROUGE, DIOCESE OF (RUBRIBACULENSIS),

created Aug. 14, 1961, by John XXIII, who named as its first bishop Robert E. Tracy, formerly auxiliary of Lafayette, La. The see city is the capital of Louisiana and is the locale of Louisiana State University, where Tracy had been chaplain of the Catholic Student Center (1946–59). He was installed Nov. 8, 1961, in St. Joseph's Cathedral, the oldest (1792) parish. The diocese embraces 12 civil parishes (counties), which had formed part of the Archdiocese of *New Orleans. Of an estimated total population of 487,509, about 30 per cent are Catholic. The location of Baton Rouge on the Mississippi River, its oil refineries, and petrochemical and allied industries contribute to its economic importance. In 1964 the diocese had 57 parishes and 28 missions, 70 diocesan and 54 religious priests, 20 brothers, and 301 sisters. There were 9 high schools (2,435 students) and 35 elementary schools (13,145 students), 3 general hospitals, and an orphanage under Catholic auspices.

[H. C. BEZOU]

BATTHYÁNY,

Hungarian noble family stemming from the 16th-century Magyar conquering clan of Örs-Úr.

Joseph (József), b. Vienna, Jan. 30, 1727; d. Pozsony, Oct. 23, 1799; archbishop of Esztergom, prince-primate of Hungary, and cardinal. A brilliant orator,

statesman, diplomat, and influential advisor to Empress Maria Theresa, he was the choice of both Pope Pius VI and Emperor Joseph II to mediate in the disputes that arose from the latter's "enlightened" reforms.

Louis (Lajos), 1806 to 1849; Hungarian patriot and national martyr. He entered politics in 1840, after a brief military career, and became the close friend of Count Stephen Széchényi, the "Greatest of Magyars." In March 1848, he became prime minister to King Ferdinand V of Hungary, but his moderate and conscientious policies in this year of revolution forced his resignation. He was arrested by Prince Windischgrätz of the imperial forces and deported to an Austrian jail early in 1849, and on October 6 he fell before a firing squad.

Casimir (Kázmér), 1807 to 1854; opposition leader of the Hungarian upper chamber and champion of Hungary's secession from Austria during the revolutionary years 1848–49. He was foreign secretary in the cabinet of the revolutionary leader, Louis Kossuth. The failure of the revolution brought about the confiscation of Kázmér's fortunes and his death in exile.

Bibliography: J. BATTHYÁNY, *A Letter from Cardinal Bathiani . . . to the Emperor Joseph II* (London 1782). B. SZEMERE, *Graf L. Batthyány, A. Görgei, L. Kossuth,* 3 pts. in 1 v. (Hamburg 1853). W. J. WYATT, *Hungarian Celebrities* (London 1871). J. F. BRIGHT, *Maria Theresa* (New York 1897); *Joseph II* (New York 1897). B. HÓMAN and J. SZEKFÜ, *Magyar történet,* 5 v. (Budapest 1935–36). L. TOTH, DHGE 6:1340–41. T. V. BOGYAY, LexThK² 2:52.

[G. C. PAIKERT]

BATTLE, ABBEY OF,

former *Benedictine monastery near Hastings, Sussex, England, founded 1067. To commemorate the Battle of Hastings (1066) and his victory over Harold, *William I the Conqueror founded on the site of the battle an abbey dedicated to the Holy Trinity, St. Mary, and St. Martin and endowed it with all the lands within a radius of a mile and a half, as well as with several other manors in Kent and Sussex. The original community was drawn from the famous Abbey of *Marmoutier, near Tours, whose abbots also appointed the first two abbots of Battle, even though Battle was never a dependency of Marmoutier. Among the privileges of the abbey were the rights of sanctuary, of treasure trove, of free warren, of inquest, and of certain exemptions from episcopal jurisdiction. These exemptions led to a series of disputes with the bishop of *Chichester, settled finally by the *Compositio* of 1235. While the abbey was not exempt from the metropolitan visitations of the archbishop of *Canterbury, the episcopal visitation occurred only triennially and had to be carried out by two monks, of whom one was elected by the bishop and the other by the community itself. From 1295 to 1538 the abbots of Battle sat in the House of Lords. The abbey was suppressed in 1539; its annual income amounted then to £900, and the community consisted of the abbot and only 16 monks.

Bibliography: *Chronicon monasterii de Bello,* ed. J. S. BREWER (London 1846). *The Chronicle of Battle Abbey, 1066–1176,* tr. M. A. LOWER (London 1851). Dugdale MonAngl 3:233–259. *Custumals of Battle Abbey . . ., 1283–1312,* ed. S. R. SCARGILL-BIRD (Camden Soc., NS 41; London 1887). H. W. C. DAVIS, "The Chronicle of Battle Abbey," EngHistRev 29 (1914) 426–434. R. GRAHAM, "The Monastery of Battle," in *English Ecclesiastical Studies* 29 (1929). *The Victoria History of the County of Sussex,* ed. W. PAGE (London 1905–) v.2. *Descriptive Cata-*

St. Joseph's Cathedral, Baton Rouge, houses the oldest congregation in the state capital, dating from 1792.

logue of the Original Charters . . . (London 1835). *The Sussex Archaeological Collections* (Sussex Archaeological Society) v.3, 17.

[J. BRÜCKMANN]

BATTLE STANDARDS, CULT OF.

The early Roman army had a standard called the *signum* for each maniple, carried by the centurion who commanded the unit. When Marius established a professional army in Rome (about 100 B.C.), he reorganized the legion, making the cohorts the major tactical units, and giving it a standard, the eagle or *aquila*. This standard was regarded as the sacred emblem that personified the legion's existence. A chapel was built for it, and it was honored with a religious cult. The standard was made first of silver, later of gold. It was placed at the top of a long pole and variously ornamented. Its loss brought disgrace on the members of the legion and frequently led to the disbanding of the legion in question. In the period of the Roman Empire before Constantine, the image of the reigning emperor was carried also as a standard by various military units, and was likewise an object of worship. The cult of these standards created a formidable problem for Christian soldiers, and particularly for Christian officers.

Bibliography: M. MARÍN Y PEÑA, *Instituciones militares romanas* (Madrid 1956) 375–390. W. KUBITSCHEK, Pauly-Wiss RE 2.2:2335–44. H. LECLERCQ, DACL 11.1:1116–30.

[T. A. BRADY]

BAUCH, BRUNO,

German philosopher of the Neo-Kantian school; b. Gross-Nossen, Silesia, Jan. 19, 1877; d. Jena, Feb. 27, 1942. He was formed in the school of W. Windelband and H. Rickert, which concerned itself primarily with problems of value and took its point of departure from Kant's *Critique of Judgment.* Bauch, in turn, devoted himself to the two main interests of this branch of the Neo-Kantian movement: the theory of value and of culture and the history of philosophy. In the latter field, his greatest achievement is his *Immanuel Kant* (Berlin 1917), which ranks among the best monographs on that philosopher, exhibiting complete mastery of his writings and interpreting them in the perspective of the Windelband school. Important also are his studies on the theory of knowledge in Greek thought and on the moral philosophy of Martin Luther. In the theoretical area, he expounded his own conception of philosophy as the interpretation of the cultural consciousness in a mature work: *Die erzieherische Bedeutung der Kulturgüter* (Leipzig 1930).

Bauch's intense interest in the theory of value and of culture engendered some tension in his adherence to Kant. He defended the ethics of Kant from the charges of formalism, but accused Kant of misprizing cultural values, confusing them with hedonic values and thus bringing them within range of moral censure. The values of culture are understood by Bauch as the content of the hypothetical imperative; consequently, the duties of individuals depend not exclusively on the universal law of the *categorical imperative, but on the peculiar cultural circumstances of their action. In his most important theoretical work, *Grundzüge der Ethik* (Stuttgart 1935), he presented an extensive treatment of the general theory of value, relating value, on the one hand, to ethics, and, on the other, to a general theory of reality. Reality is not value, but it is the matrix for the perception and realization of value. Bauch served for an extended period as editor of the journal *Kantstudien.*

See also KANTIANISM; NEO-KANTIANISM; VALUE, PHILOSOPHY OF.

Bibliography: *Blätter für Deutsche Philosophie* (1937) 351–440, studies in tribute to B. Bauch. P. R. FÄH, *Begriff und Konkreszenz bei B. B.* (Diss. Sarnen 1940).

[A. R. CAPONIGRI]

BAUDELAIRE, CHARLES PIERRE

French poet; b. Paris, April 9, 1821; d. there, Aug. 31, 1867. His father died in 1827, and the following year his mother married Commander Aupick, later general, diplomat, and senator of the empire. His stepfather was stationed at Lyons in 1832, and there the boy received his early education. He went to the Lycée Louis-le-Grand in Paris (1836) and received his degree in 1839. His mother's second marriage seems to have occasioned psychological and spiritual disturbances for young Baudelaire, among them a conviction of having lost his mother's affections. This sense of estrangement seems to have aroused in him hatred of active society as symbolized in his stepfather and crystallized in the entire Second Empire French bourgeoisie. This nonactivist attitude in Baudelaire, as in *Flaubert, Théophile Gautier, and Charles Leconte De Lisle, leads to an aesthetics of art for the sake of art. Baudelaire's dedication to the cult of artistic form is partly explained, therefore, in terms of personal rejection, but at the same time it was the almost necessary pose of many idealistic young men unable to come to terms with an increasingly materialistic society.

Head of Baudelaire by Henri Matisse, etching illustrating "Le Tombeau de Charles Baudelaire" in the volume "Poésies de Stéphane Mallarmé" printed by Skira in 1932.

Early Bohemian Life. Immediately upon graduation, the young aesthete announced to a shocked family his intention of becoming a writer. To their consternation he lived a bohemian life for 3 years in the Latin Quarter, reading much, and becoming a disciple of the flamboyant Romantic, Gautier. In 1841 Colonel Aupick, alarmed at the independence of the young man, sought to regularize his life by paying his debts and sending him off on a trip to India, but Baudelaire was back in Paris 7 months later. Some critics regard this trip as a great influence on the exotic flavor of many of his poems. In 1842 he came into his patrimony and this enabled him to live for a time in the manner of a dandy.

These overly refined living habits, however, were cut short by a court order in 1844, which had been instigated by the family's concern over his reckless spending, and resulted in the strict administration of the remainder of his estate. For the rest of his life Baudelaire was either financially dependent on this dole or involved in schemes to sell the rights to some of his works. In the same period Baudelaire encountered the mulatto Jeanne Duval, called "Black Venus," who is generally credited with inspiring a great number of the more sensual poems in *Les Fleurs du Mal.* She is the first of three women whose influence can be discerned in that work. Some of its poems reveal the influence of the actress Marie Daubrun whom Baudelaire met in 1847; but the poems in honor of Madame Sabatier, the source of the idealistic love poetry, are more important, especially because of their contrast with the poems that were inspired by Jeanne Duval.

Burgeoning Talent. Baudelaire developed his multiple talents with great energy during the 1840s. He developed into a first-rate art critic, as his *Salons* (1845–46) and other essays in art criticism attest. In this decade he also discovered the works of *Poe, and spent a good part of his remaining years in translating them. The Revolution of 1848 strangely enough found this idealistic poet of aristocratic tendencies on the side of the revolutionaries. His stepfather died in 1857, and a reconciliation of mother and son followed.

Les Fleurs du Mal, the work on which his fame rests, was published in June 1857. The government quickly brought suit against the poet, using the same charge as that leveled at Flaubert earlier in the year for the publication of *Madame Bovary,* namely, that of corrupting public morals. Flaubert was acquitted; six of Baudelaire's poems were suppressed. It must be stated that if immorality was to be found, it was not in the poems but in their prurient critics. The charge of immorality was nothing more than a mask to hide the totalitarian procedures of the Second Empire, which, romantic in its sensibilities, must have found the modern character of the poems a daring innovation and definitely one to be suppressed.

The last years of Baudelaire's life were fruitful in continuous literary output, though he was progressively plagued by increasing debts and failing health. In March 1866 he collapsed while in the church of Saint-Loup at Namur. Paralyzed and unable to speak, but with his intellectual powers seemingly intact, he was returned to Paris by his mother in July of the same year. He died in her arms the following year. In addition to *Les Fleurs du Mal,* he was eminent for his translations, literary and art criticism, pioneering types of prose poems, as well as for his works on Gautier and Wagner, and his *Journaux intimes.*

Predominant Themes. Baudelaire's themes, as the title of *Les Fleurs du Mal* implies, drastically exploit the plight of fallen man, caught between his desire for the good and his inclination to evil. The volume was constructed in such a manner that, in addition to the aesthetic value of each poem as a unit, the entire collection would be considered as an allegory in individual but related poems of modern man caught up in the temporal but yearning for the absolute. The poet shows man as victim of his baser appetites, but at the same time as impelled to the highest artistic and spiritual idealism.

The variety of techniques introduced to illuminate his thought make Baudelaire a real innovator in French poetry. He created a daring new imagery heavily dependent not only on visual but on olfactory, kinesthetic, and tactile reactions. Baudelaire's poetic structure is nonetheless quite traditional as is his versification; allegory predominates, although certain poems reach a high degree of *symbolism. He leads the way to the symbolist poets because of his literary doctrine, expressed best in his *Correspondance* sonnet. This theory insists that there are hidden relationships between man and his surroundings, between the exterior and interior worlds, which are not apparent to the casual or nonpoetic observer. He suggests relationships that ultimately point to the harmony of all creation and existence, for reality is grasped in poetic knowing much as it is in mystical experience. The insistence in *Correspondance* that there is not just likeness between things, but a unity resulting from the intermingling of all life, and that life is not a mere biological phenomenon puts him squarely in opposition to the dominant *positivism of his epoch.

Catholic Aspects of His Work. Without doubt, Baudelaire as poet is eminently Christian, in spite of superficial contradictory evidence. This means he is basically a believer, although his life was far from devout. Baudelaire breaks with romantic religiosity and sentimentality, as well as with romantic agnosticism or indifference. The metaphysical question again becomes paramount, the quest for the absolute, the important act of life and art. Given the historical moment, and his background and temperament, a pure, uninhibited, and uncontaminated Catholicism seems to have been an impossibility for the poet, and throughout his work a mixture of pagan sensibility with Catholic yearnings is discernible. Nevertheless the Christian credo is reiterated throughout his work, typically in "Jésus des dieux le plus incontestable." Because of his recognition of and preoccupation with the problem of good and evil, and his eschatological vision of reality, he must be considered a major Catholic poet and forerunner of the *Catholic revival in France. *See* LITERARY REVIVAL, CATHOLIC.

Bibliography: *Oeuvres complètes,* ed. Y. G. Le Dantec and C. Pichois (Paris 1961); *One Hundred Poems from Les Fleurs du mal,* tr. C. F. MacIntyre (Berkeley 1947); *The Flowers of Evil,* ed. M. and J. Mathews (New York 1955). E. Starkie, *Baudelaire* (London 1933). R. Vivier, *L'Originalité de Baudelaire* (Brussels 1952). M. Turnell, *Baudelaire: A Study of His Poetry* (pa. Norfolk, Conn. 1954). L. J. Austin, *L'Univers poétique de Baudelaire* (Paris 1956). **Illustration credit:** Collection, Museum of Modern Art, New York. Abby Aldrich Rockefeller Fund.

[J. A. FREY]

BAUDISSIN, WOLF WILHELM, Protestant OT scholar; b. Sophienhof, near Kiel, Germany, Sept. 26, 1847; d. Berlin, Feb. 6, 1926. After his studies at Leipzig in theology and Semitics (Ph.D., 1870; S.T.L., 1876) he taught OT at Leipzig (1876–80), Strassburg (1880–81), Marburg (1881–1900), and Berlin (1900–26), where, notwithstanding his retirement allowance as emeritus in 1921, he taught until his death. Graf Baudissin's lifework was research in the religions of the Semitic peoples, particularly the Israel-Jewish religion. A comprehensive linguistical, historical, geographical, and archeological knowledge formed the basis of his studies, which were carried on in the conviction that in all religions there lies hidden a single religion that makes its appearance in the various historical religions on different levels of intensity. He rejected the assumption of a primitive revelation and primitive monotheism as well as every other speculative or anthropological violence done to history. In his *Studien zur semitischen Religionsgeschichte* (Leipzig 1876), in his treatise *Adonis und Esmun: Eine Untersuchung zur Geschichte des Glaubens an Auferstehungsgötter und an Heilsgötter* (Leipzig 1911), which has remained basic for the understanding of *Phoenician religion, and in his chief work *Kyrios als Gottesname im Judentum und seine Stelle in der Religionsgeschichte,* 4 v., O. Eissfeldt, ed., (Giessen 1926–29) he never tired in his endeavors to prove the bond between the religion of the Semites and that of the OT. The two last-named works mark the two poles around which all his studies revolved: faith in God as life and faith in Him as the Lord. The concept of God as the Lord, the leader and commander of the tribe and its members is characteristic of all Semitic religions, and this concept is the connecting point where the religion of the OT is bound to general Semitic religion. This basic idea is continued in the Christian expectation of the coming of the kingdom of God. The peculiar nature of Semitic religion enables it to develop from a national religion into a world religion, which finds its completion in Christianity as a religion of the spirit.

Among Baudissin's strictly OT works mention may be made of *Die Geschichte des alttestamentlichen Priestertums* (Leipzig 1889), the comprehensive *Einleitung in die Bücher des Alten Testaments* (Leipzig 1901) and the monograph " 'Gott schauen' in der alttestamentlichen Religion," *Archiv für Religionswissenschaft* 18 (1915) 173–239; reprint in preparation (Darmstadt).

Bibliography: O. Eissfeldt, ZDeutschMglGesell 80 (1926) 89–130; repr. in his *Kleine Schriften* 1 (Tübingen 1962) 115–142; RGG³ 1:919. F. Michels, NDB 1:632. H. J. Kraus, *Geschichte der historisch-kritischen Erforschung des Alten Testaments* (Neukirchen 1956) 296–297. L. Dürr, LexThK² 2:54.

[O. KAISER]

BAUDOUIN, FRANÇOIS (BALDWIN), French lawyer and humanist; b. Arras, Jan. 1, 1520; d. Paris, 1573 or 1574. He studied law and classical languages in Louvain and was acquainted with many of the leading French humanists, including Guillaume *Budé and Charles Dumoulin. Sympathetic to the *Reformation, he spent 3 years in Geneva and became one of Calvin's secretaries. From 1549 to 1555 he taught law at Bourges and later, at Strassburg (1556), Heidelberg (1556–62), and Angers (from 1562 until almost the end of his life). After returning to the practice of the Catholic faith *c.* 1560, he supported the group of humanists and *politiques* around Michel de *l'Hôpital, who tried to reconcile Catholics and Calvinists in France. He was present at the Colloquium of *Poissy in 1561, but was not permitted to participate. Baudouin has been attacked by both Catholics and Protestants, especially *Calvin and *Beza, for his apparent vacillation between the two religions. He should be understood as a humanist interested in Church reform, who remained a Catholic, but advocated toleration of Protestants by the French state, and believed in the possibility of reconciliation.

Bibliography: For a bibliography of his works, see J. Dedieu, DHGE 6:1426–28. J. Lecler, *Toleration and the Reformation,* tr. T. L. Westow, 2 v. (New York 1960) 2:55–56. D. R. Kelley, "*Historia integra:* François Baudouin and His Conception of History," JHistIdeas 25 (1964) 35–57.

[E. G. GLEASON]

BAUDOUIN, LOUIS MARIE, VEN., religious founder; b. Montaigu (Vendée), France, Aug. 2, 1765; d. Chavagnes-en-Paillers (Vendée), Feb. 12, 1835. Educated by the Vincentians at the seminary of Luçon, he was ordained in 1789 and appointed assistant to his brother, who was pastor in Luçon. When the *Civil Constitution of the Clergy was legislated during the *French Revolution, the Baudouin brothers refused to take the required oath and were barred from priestly ministrations in the village church. The two emigrated to Spain in 1792. When his brother died (1796) Louis returned to France, where he became a refugee at Sables d'Olonne. Since the persecution against priests had been renewed, he exercised a hidden apostolate. In 1802, he became a parish priest in Chavagnes. There he founded a religious congregation known as the Sons of Mary Immaculate of Luçon, more commonly as the Priests of Chavagnes which had 220 members in 1963. Together with Gabrielle Charlotte Ranfray de la Rochette, a former religious, he founded also a congregation of women devoted to the education of young girls, the Ursulines of Jesus, which had 1350 members in 9 countries in 1960. Named rector of the seminary of La Rochelle in 1812, he became vicar-general of the restored See of Luçon in 1822. He was proclaimed venerable in 1871.

Bibliography: P. Michaud, *Life of the Ven. Louis Marie Baudouin,* tr. W. A. Phillipson (London 1914). M. Prevost, Dict BiogFranc 5:881. J. Robin, DictSpirAscMyst 1:1286–87.

[L. P. MAHONEY]

BAUDRILLART, HENRI MARIE ALFRED, cardinal, scholar, educator, diplomat; b. Paris, Jan. 6, 1859; d. there, May 19, 1942. Trained in history, he received a doctor of letters degree in 1890. As a lay teacher he taught at schools in Laval, Caen, and Paris, and in 1883 became affiliated with the Institut Catholique. After joining the Oratory in 1890, he was ordained July 9, 1893, and 2 years later he received his doctorate in theology and returned to the Institut Catholique as professor (1894–1907). In 1907 he became rector of the Institut, which he built into a first class institution. He was made titular bishop of Himeria (1921), titular archbishop of Melitene (1928), and cardinal priest (1935). Baudrillart continued his scholarly researches and served as diplomatic representative of the Holy See. He was instrumental in the resumption of French diplomatic relations with the Vatican in 1921; in his diplomatic capacity he traveled in Europe, Africa, and North and South America, and twice visited the United States. He was made a member of the Académie Française in 1918, a chevalier of the Légion D'Honneur in 1920, and commander of the Légion in 1935. Among his publications were: *Philippe V et la cour de France* (5 v. Paris 1890–1901); *L'Église catholique, la Renaissance, le protestantisme* (Paris 1904), tr. into Eng. by Mrs. Philip Gibbs as *The Catholic Church, the Renaissance and Protestantism* (New York 1908); *Vie de Mgr. d'Hulst* (2 v. Paris 1912–14); *Lettres du duc de Bourgogne au roi d'Espagne* (2 v. Paris 1912–16); and *La France, les catholiques et le guerre* (Paris 1917). Perhaps his most important scholarly contribution was the initial organization and publication of the *Dictionnaire d'histoire et de géographie ecclésiastiques*.

Bibliography: V. CARRIERE, *Le Cardinal Baudrillart, 1859–1942* (Paris 1942). V. L. SAULNIER, DictBiogFranc 5:893–895. A. P. FRUTAZ, EncCatt 2:1063. A. GUNY, *Catholicisme* 1:1316–17.

[V. L. BULLOUGH]

BAUDRY OF BOURGUEIL, poet and bishop; b. Meung-sur-Loire, France, 1046; d. 1130. He studied at the cathedral school of *Angers but later entered the *Benedictine Order, and in 1089 he was made abbot of Bourgueil-en-Vallée. In 1107 he was consecrated archbishop of Dol in Brittany, but he often preferred the more pleasant life of Normandy. With poets such as *Hildebert of Lavardin and *Marbod of Rennes, Baudry revived the ideas of poetic friendship that had flourished in *Charlemagne's court. He often imitated *Ovid in his verse, and he had a deep appreciation of the past. Many of his works express also a love of nature; others are epitaphs or metrical letters to other friends, such as his great model, Godfrey of Reims (d. 1095). In the first decade of the 12th century he composed an account of the First *Crusade, probably using the *Gesta Francorum* as a basis for his study. Some of Baudry's works are somewhat frivolous for a bishop, and they indicate the growing secularization of the *cathedral and episcopal schools in this period.

Bibliography: PL 166:1057–1208. *Les Oeuvres poétiques de Baudri de Bourgueil*, ed. P. ABRAHAMS (Paris 1926). Raby SecLP 337–348. J. R. WILLIAMS, "Godfrey of Rheims, a Humanist of the Eleventh Century," *Speculum* 22 (1947) 29–45. P. F. PALUMBO, EncCatt 2:743. Manitius 3:883–898.

[E. J. KEALEY]

BAUER, BRUNO, Protestant Biblical critic and historian; b. Eisenberg, Germany, Sept. 6, 1809; d. Rixdorf, Germany, April 15, 1882. At Berlin he studied theology and philosophy, especially Hegel. He became an instructor at the University of Bonn in 1839, but was dismissed in 1842 when he abandoned his conservative *Hegelianism and published his *Kritik der evangelischen Geschichte des Johannes* (1840) and *Kritik der evangelischen Geschichte der Synoptiker* (2 v. 1841–42). Denying both the historicity of Jesus and traditional belief in God, Bauer held that the Gospels were derived neither from facts nor from the imagination of the Christian community, but from the Evangelists' own minds. He became increasingly radical in his criticism, portrayed Philo, Seneca, and the Gnostics as the real forces of Christianity, whose framework alone was Jewish and whose spirit was Western. In *Christus und die Cäsaren* (1877), he placed the first Gospel in the time of Hadrian (118–138) and the genesis of the Christian religion as late as Marcus Aurelius

(160–180). Friedrich *Nietzsche, Wilhelm Wrede, and Karl *Marx were among those influenced by Bauer's writings.

Bibliography: E. BARNIKOL, "Bruno Bauers Kampf gegen Religion und Christentum und die Spaltung der vormärzlichen preussischen Opposition," ZKirchgesch 46 (1928) 1–34; RGG³ 1:922–924. A. SCHWEITZER, *The Quest of the Historical Jesus*, tr. W. MONTGOMERY (New York 1956). K. LÖWITH, *Von Hegel zu Nietzsche* (Stuttgart 1958). W. BUFF, NDB 1:636–637.

[L. J. SWIDLER]

BAUER, WALTER, NT-Greek lexicographer; b. Königsberg, Prussia, Aug. 8, 1877; d. Göttingen, Germany, Nov. 17, 1960. After graduate studies at the universities of Marburg, Berlin, and Strassburg, Bauer taught NT exegesis at Marburg (1902–13), Breslau (1913–16), and Göttingen (1916–45). Among his outstanding publications are *Das Leben Jesu im Zeitalter der neutestamentlichen Apokryphen* (1909) and *Rechtgläubigkeit und Ketzerei im ältesten Christentum* (1934). His monumental work is, however, his revision of Erwin Preuschen's *Griechisch-Deutsches Handwörterbuch zu den Schriften des Neuen Testaments und der übrigen urchristlichen Literatur*, which, in the course of its five editions (1910, 1925–28, 1937, 1949–52, 1957–58), he so thoroughly revised and augmented that it should really be regarded as his own original work. Especially the 4th and 5th editions of this work include thousands of parallels to NT-Greek words taken from Greek literature of the 4th century B.C. to Byzantine times. The English translation and adaptation of the 4th edition made by W. F. Arndt and F. W. Gingrich, *A Greek-English Lexicon of the New Testament and Other Early Christian Literature* (Chicago 1957), is the best dictionary of NT Greek available in English.

Bibliography: F. W. GINRICH, NTSt 9 (1962) 1–2; "The Contributions of Professor Walter Bauer to New Testament Lexicography," *ibid.* 3–10. W. SCHNEEMELCHER, "Walter Bauer als Kirchenhistoriker," *ibid.* 11–22. E. FASCHER, "Walter Bauer als Kommentator," *ibid.* 23–38.

[L. F. HARTMAN]

BÄUERLE, HERMANN, priest, scholar, prominent in church music reform; b. Ebersberg (Württemberg), Germany, Oct. 24, 1869; d. Ulm, May 21, 1936. His parents were Christian, a schoolteacher, and Barbara (Frizle) Bäuerle. While preparing for the priesthood, the young man also studied ancient and modern philology at Tübingen. His first pastoral assignment following ordination in 1895 was at Ochsenhausen. Bäuerle attended the Kirchenmusikschule at Regensburg, center of the *Caecilian Movement, in 1898–99, and, after a brief court chaplaincy to the prince of Thurn and Taxis, returned to Regensburg to lecture on harmony and counterpoint for 7 years (1901–08). During that interval he took his doctoral degree at Leipzig (1906) with a musicophilological dissertation on the Seven Penitential Psalms of Orlando Lasso. After another period of parochial work he founded a music school in Ulm in 1921. Bäuerle composed a respectable body of sacred works—Masses, Requiems, settings of litanies and Vespers, and organ preludes—but he is far more important for his performance editions of Palestrina, Vittoria, Lasso, Fux, Bernabei, Galuppi, Lotti, and other polyphonic masters.

Bibliography: F. HABERL, MusGG 1:1074–75. Riemann. Baker 100–101.

[F. HABERL]

BAUHAUS

More properly, Das Staatliche Bauhaus, Weimar, a school of art founded in 1919 at Weimar, Germany, by the architect Walter Gropius for the dual purpose of delivering art and architecture from the historicism and aestheticism of the academies and of training commercial and industrial designers. It sought to integrate art and industry (artist and craftsman) to the mutual benefit of each. Like its predecessor, the *Deutscher Werkbund*, the Bauhaus derived some of its aims from the arts and crafts movement of England. Although Bauhaus philosophy stressed sound craftsmanship and overruled the conventional distinction of fine art from servile and applied art, it was essentially hostile to the spirit of romantic individualism associated with the earlier movement, favoring instead a rationalist approach in which the collaborative spirit was emphasized. Thus, with architecture as the master art governing and unifying all the others, all aesthetic considerations that depend on individual sensibilities were replaced by questions of logic and efficiency. Good design sense became a matter of sound engineering, and bad design sense was generally associated with an illogical use of materials (e.g., a Gothic façade on a steel-structured skyscraper). However, this rationalist (functionalist) conception of art, which subsequently came to identify in great part the *International Style in architecture, failed to provide a *raison d'être* for the painter until it was expanded to include the social and psychological requirements of modern life. Yet whatever may be its theoretical shortcomings, the Bauhaus program accomplished the sorely needed return from the mistakes of the opposite direction (i.e., aestheticism and historicism) and provided a revolutionary new curriculum for training the artist as creative designer.

The importance of and the enormous influence of the school, which moved in 1925 from the traditional Weimar to new quarters designed by Gropius in Dessau, are also partly accounted for by the abundance of talent on its faculty (e.g., Walter Gropius, Paul *Klee, Wassily *Kandinsky, Lyonel *Feininger, László *Moholy-Nagy, Marcel Breuer, Mies Van der Rohe, Josef Albers) and by their dispersion abroad in consequence of the Nazi suppression, which closed the school altogether in 1933. Many of these men emigrated to the U.S., where they continued to teach Bauhaus principles, notably at the New Bauhaus (now the Institute of Design), Chicago, and in established American schools of first rank (e.g., Gropius at Harvard, Albers at Yale, Kepes at M.I.T.).

Much of the achievement since the mid-1930s in the fields of graphic design, industrial design, architecture, and *art education is directly or indirectly related to the Bauhaus. A notable example of church art by a Bauhaus artist is the abbey church and monastery of St. John, Collegeville, Minn., by Marcel Breuer.

Bibliography: A. MEYER, ed., *Ein Versuchshaus des Bauhauses in Weimar* (Munich 1925). *Bauhaus: Zeitschrift für Gestaltung* (Dessau 1926–31). H. BAYER et al., eds. *Bauhaus 1919–1928* (New York 1938; 2d ed. Boston 1952), bibliog. W. GROPIUS, *The New Architecture and the Bauhaus,* tr. P. M. SHAND (Boston 1955); *Idee und Aufbau des Staatlichen Bauhauses Weimar* (Munich 1923); and L. MOHOLY-NAGY, *Bauhausbücher,* 14 v. (Munich 1925–28), monograph ser. L. MOHOLY-NAGY, *Vision in Motion* (Chicago 1956); *The New Vision and Abstract of an Artist* (3d rev. ed. New York 1946). L. GROTE, *Die Maler am Bauhaus* (Munich 1950), illus. catalogue of paintings at the Bauhaus until 1933. G. C. ARGAN, *Walter Gropius e la Bauhaus* (Turin 1951) 169–172, bibliog. on Gropius and Bauhaus. M. BILL, "The Bauhaus Idea from Weimar to Ulm," *Architectural Yearbook* 5 (1953) 29–32.

[G. M. MC CLANCY, JR.]

BÄUMER, SUITBERT, liturgist; b. Leuchtenburg, Rhineland, March 28, 1845; d. Freiburg im Breisgau, Aug. 12, 1894. He became a monk of Beuron in 1865, was ordained in 1869, and studied at Bonn and Tübingen. Sojourning in Belgium and England during the Kulturkampf (1875–90), he served as liturgical consultant to Desclée in Tournai for its editions of the Missal, monastic Breviary, the Vulgate, etc. He wrote numerous works on liturgy, patristics, and the history of monasticism. His most influential work was *Geschichte des Breviers* (Freiburg 1895), which was revised and enlarged in the French edition by R. Biron (2 v. Paris 1905).

Bibliography: P. SÉJOURNÉ, DHGE 6:1474–81. R. PROOST, DACL 2:623–626. S. MAYER, *Beuroner Bibliographie, 1863–1963* (Beuron 1963) 38–49.

[S. MAYER]

BAUMGARTNER, ALEXANDER, literary critic; b. Sankt Gallen, Switzerland, June 27, 1841; d. Luxembourg, Oct. 5, 1910. Alexander, son of Gallus Baumgartner, a prominent Swiss statesman, joined the *Jesuits in 1860. After ordination, he joined in 1875 the editorial staff of the recently founded *Stimmen aus Maria-Laach* (later called *Stimmen der Zeit*). Because of the expulsion of the Society of Jesus from Germany, the periodical repeatedly changed its place of publication during his 36 years of collaboration; it finally settled in Luxembourg. His contributions on literature greatly enhanced the periodical's renown. In the supplements published by *Stimmen* appeared his first important works: *Lessings religioser Entwicklungsgang* (1877), *Longfellow* (1877), and the first part of his reevaluation of Goethe, *Goethes Jugend* (1879). His Catholic interpretation, a reaction against the exaggerated cult of the poet, appeared in *Goethe, Sein Leben und Seine Werke* (3 v. 1885–86). His other principal work, *Geschichte der Weltliteratur* (6 v. 1897–1911), was not completed. The first two volumes discussed the writings of Asia, India, and Egypt. The third and fourth volumes (1900) treated the literatures of classical Greece and Rome, and the Greek and Latin writings of the Christian period. The fifth volume (1905), devoted to French literature, severely condemned the decadence of its latest evolution. The sixth volume, on Italy, was in press when the author died; it was published the following year (1911).

Bibliography: O. PFÜLF, StimZeit 79 (1910) 349–372. J. GRISAR, DHGE 6:1488–90. H. G. PETERS, *Die Ästhetik Alexander Gottlieb Baumgartners . . .* (Berlin 1934).

[R. J. SEALY]

BAUMSTARK, ANTON, liturgist and Orientalist; b. Constance, Aug. 4, 1872; d. Bonn, May 31, 1948. As inheritor of physical and spiritual gifts from his father, Reinhold Baumstark, Anton showed extraordinary versatility in an age of extreme specialization. He was a married layman and he devoted his rich energies to scholarship. He was knowledgeable in literature, philology, theology, and religious and art history, both classical and Oriental. One of the few arts he failed to master was that of German style; his style was difficult to follow as a result of this.

In 1901 at Rome he began, with Anton de *Waal, the journal, *Oriens Christianus*, and with but a short interruption edited it through 36 volumes. None of its issues appeared without a significant contribution from him. Into its pages he poured the results of his unique comprehensive grasp of the culture of the Mediterranean Basin. The journal stands as the most important monument of his life of scholarship. In the same field he published the *Geschichte der syrischen Literatur* (Bonn 1922).

With Odo *Casel, he began the *Jahrbuch für Liturgiewissenschaft;* to this he brought unusual qualifications. Since worship was the center of ancient culture, and Baumstark was by nature a very religious person, he made the study of the evolution of worship, especially the historical development of Christian liturgy, the object of his predilection. Although his ingenious hypotheses did not always prove to be correct, he nevertheless greatly stimulated research, and his own insights and discoveries have made irreplaceable contributions to liturgical scholarship. The results of the method of comparative liturgy, which Baumstark himself worked out, were published in *Liturgie Comparée* [Chevetogne 1940; *Comparative Liturgy* (London 1958)]. He traced the laws of all liturgical evolution in *Vom geschichtlichen Werden der Liturgie* (Freiburg 1923). In numerous articles (his published works number 546) he tried to determine the exact relations of the Christian liturgy to the Jewish and Hellenistic world.

In keeping with his broad and profound knowledge, he taught at several centers of learning: classical and Oriental philology at the University of Heidelberg (1898), early Christian Oriental civilization at the University of Bonn (1921–30), Semitic languages and comparative liturgy at the University of Nijmegen (1923), the science of Islam and Arabic languages at the University of Utrecht (1926), and Oriental studies at the University of Münster (1930–35).

During his last years, Baumstark led an increasingly isolated life because of his involvement in Nazism; he was, unfortunately, naive in political matters. He nevertheless remained constantly devoted to scholarship and, with a living piety, to the Church and her liturgy.

Bibliography: T. KLAUSER, EphemLiturg 63 (1949) 185–187. H. E. KILLY, EphemLiturg 63 (1949) 187–207, contains complete list of his works. G. GRAF, "Zum Geleit und zum Andenken an Anton Baumstark und Adolf Rücker," OrChr 37 (1953) 1–5. I. ORTIZ DE URBINA, EncCatt 2:1065–66.

[B. NEUNHEUSER]

BAUNARD, LOUIS PIERRE, French writer; b. Bellegarde (Loiret), Aug. 24, 1828; d. Gruson, near Lille, Nov. 9, 1919. His father was a wheelwright and innkeeper of moderate means. After studies at the seminary in Orléans Louis was ordained (1852) and then taught at the minor seminary there (1852–60). In 1860 he gained a doctorate in letters at the Sorbonne and in 1861 a doctorate in theology in Rome. He became professor (1877) and then rector (1888) at the Institut Catholique of Lille. From 1902 he dwelt at Gruson in retirement from academic pursuits. He is remembered now for his writings, particularly for his numerous biographies of religious personages including St. John the Apostle (1869), St. Ambrose (1871), St. Madeleine Sophie Barat (1876), Mme. Duchesne (1878), Car-

dinals Pie (1885) and Lavigerie (1896), St. Louise de Marillac (1897), and Frédéric Ozanam (1911). Baunard's biographical works, which utilized and incorporated correspondence, were psychological as well as historical studies, composed in an elegant, classical style. His best-known work in ecclesiastical history was *Un siècle de l'Église de France, 1800–1900* (1902).

Bibliography: L. MAHIEU, *Vie de Monsignor Baunard* (Paris 1924); DHGE 6:1496–97. G. MARSOT, *Catholicisme* 1:1319–20.

[C. E. MAGUIRE]

BAUNY, ÉTIENNE. Jesuit moral theologian; b. Mouzon (Ardennes), June 1, 1575; d. Saint-Pol-de-Léon, Dec. 12, 1649. He entered the Society of Jesus in 1593 and at first taught humanities and rhetoric. He then became professor of moral theology and casuistry at the college of Clermont in Paris, a position that he held for 16 years. He later became superior at Pontoise and then spent the last years of his life at Saint-Pol-de-Léon, where he enjoyed the friendship and confidence of the Bishop of Léon, René de Rieux.

Bauny enjoyed a reputation for great learning and holiness and was held in esteem by prominent prelates of his time. However, he came into difficulty with the publication of some of his works. His *Somme des péchés qui se commettent en tous états* (Paris 1640, many later eds.) was written to accommodate clerics whose knowledge of Latin was weak. It was followed by *Pratique du droit canonique au gouvernement de l'Église* (Paris 1633) and *De sacramentis ac personis sacris . . . Theologiae moralis* (*Pars prima* Paris 1640; *Pars altera* 1642). The first part of the latter work and the two publications in French were placed on the Index in 1640. His lenient interpretations had aroused the opposition of the Sorbonne and made him the target of Jansenist attack. This was in fact the beginning of the Jansenist campaign of accusing Jesuit theologians of laxism. Pascal was particularly severe in his attack on Bauny. Certain of the propositions advanced by Bauny were to find more precise and acceptable expression in the writings of St. Alphonsus; others were too vague, loose, or exaggerated. However, the personal orthodoxy of Bauny was never questioned. He later wrote *Tractatus de censuris ecclesiasticis* (Paris 1642) and *Libri tres quibus, quae in contractuum ac quasi contractuum materia videntur ardua ac difficilia, enucleantur* (Paris 1645).

Bibliography: Sommervogel 1:1058–60. Hurter Nomencl 1:494. R. BROULLIARD, DHGE 6:1497–98. H. FOUQUERAY, *Histoire de la compagnie de Jésus en France*, 5 v. (Paris 1910–25) 5:416–417. M. PETROCCHI, *Il problema del Lassismo* (Rome 1953).

[J. T. KELLEHER]

BAUR, FERDINAND CHRISTIAN, German Protestant ecclesiastical historian and founder of the new *Tübingen School; b. Schmiden, near Stuttgart, June 21, 1792; d. Tübingen, Dec. 2, 1860. After studying at Tübingen, he taught at Blaubeuren (1817–26) and then spent the remainder of his life at Tübingen as professor of historical theology (1826–60). At first Baur seems to have been a disciple of the more "orthodox" Tübingen school, but his convictions concerning its positions were shaken by his study of *Schleiermacher's *Glaubenslehre*. The radical change that came over his thought, however, depended much more on *Hegel's philosophy of religion. As a result Baur developed along Hegelian lines a theory of the history of the primitive Church. According to this theory there existed in apostolic times two sharply divided factions, personified in St. Peter and St. Paul. These two groups differed on the doctrine of justification and on the nature of the Church's polity. During the 2d and 3d centuries a "synthesis" evolved from these two factions, thereby producing Catholicism. This theory also led Baur to reject the apostolic origin of most of the New Testament canon. Thus he claimed to perceive this compromise, indicative of a later date of composition, in all the Pauline Epistles except Romans, 1 and 2 Corinthians, and Galatians, which alone Baur admitted as Pauline in origin. Baur participated later in the controversy surrounding the work of David *Strauss concerning the *synoptic problem. Among his numerous writings were: *Die christliche Lehre von der Versöhnung in ihrer geschichtliche Entwicklung* (1838); *Die christliche Lehre von der Dreieinigkeit und der Menschenwerdung Gottes* (3 v. 1841–43); *Lehrbuch der christliche Dogmengeschichte* (1847); *Paulus der Apostel Jesu Christi* (1845, Eng. tr. 1873–75); and *Geschichte der christlichen Kirche* (5 v. 1853–63). Only two volumes of the last work appeared during Baur's lifetime. The first volume was translated into English as *Church History of the First Three Centuries* (2 v. 1878).

Bibliography: Cross ODCC 142–143. M. TETZ, RGG³ 1:935–938. J. SCHMID, LexThK² 2:72–73. H. SCHMIDT and J. HAUSSLEITER, Herzog-Hauck PRE 2:467–483, with complete list of Baur's writings.

[M. B. SCHEPERS]

BAUTAIN, LOUIS EUGÉNE MARIE, philosopher and theologian; b. Paris, Feb. 17, 1796; d. Viroflay, Oct. 15, 1867. He went through stages of eclecticism and rationalism, but regained the faith of his childhood in 1819 under the influence of Louise Humann and began studies for the priesthood. He was ordained in 1828, and became dean of the faculty of letters at the University of Strasbourg in 1838. In the same year he went to Rome to disprove the accusation of *fideism brought against him by his bishop, Le Pappe de Trévern. From 1842 to 1846 he gave many conferences to the Cercle Philosophique de Paris. He became vicar-general for Monsignor Sibour, Archbishop of Paris in 1849, and was professor of moral theology at the Sorbonne from 1853 to 1863. He founded the Sisters of St. Louis, who have extended their teaching apostolate well beyond France (*see* ST. LOUIS, SISTERS OF).

His extreme reaction to rationalism made him one of the principal representatives of fideism. His bishop suspended him in 1834 because of his philosophical manifesto in 1833 that sustained the Augustinian thesis that "philosophy, which is the study of wisdom, is nothing else but religion." On April 26, 1834, however, he signed a profession of faith rejecting as erroneous these two propositions: reason alone cannot demonstrate the existence of God; reason alone cannot establish the credibility of the Christian religion. His principal works were *La Philosophie du Christianisme* (1835), *Philosophie, psychologie expérimentale* (1839), *Philosophie morale* (1842), and *L'Esprit humain et ses facultés* (1859).

Bibliography: E. DE RÉGNY, *L'Abbé Bautain* (Paris 1884). W. M. HORTON, *The Philosophy of the Abbé Bautain* (New York 1926). P. POUPARD, *Un Essai de philosophie chrétienne au XIX⁰ siècle: L'Abbé Louis Bautain* (Paris 1962). P. ARCHAMBAULT, *Catholicisme* 1:1322–23. G. MÜLLER, EncCatt 2:1069–70. M. A. MICHEL, LexThk² 2:73–74.

[P. POUPARD]

BAUZÁ, FRANCISCO, Uruguayan political and literary figure, orator, publicist, and historian; b. Montevideo, Oct. 7, 1851; d. there, Dec. 4, 1899. From a very early age he worked in journalism, and he entered public life as editor of the newspaper *Los Debates*. In 1875 he carried out a diplomatic mission to Buenos Aires. Soon afterward he entered the House of Representatives, and was successively reelected. In 1881 and 1890–92 he represented Uruguay in Brazil. He served as minister of government and as a senator. Bauzá was an outstanding statesman. His work as minister of government was valuable because of the reforms he introduced in the national administration and in the municipalities. But his greatest importance was as parliamentary orator, for he was one of the most eloquent in the history of the country. Author of the *Historia de la dominación española en el Uruguay* (3 v.), *Estudios constitucionales,* and *Estudios literarios,* he is considered the greatest historian his country has produced. His work was the basis for later research in the fields of history and literature. A stanch Catholic, militant and decisive in parliament, in journalism, in the university, in social centers, he, along with Mariano *Soler and Juan *Zorrilla de San Martín, opposed the liberal action of the Ateneo of Montevideo, and was one of the leaders of the Catholic cause in Uruguay. On the centenary of his birth, the Archbishop of Montevideo, Antonio María Barbieri, dedicated a pastoral letter to him, and the Historical and Geographical Institute of Uruguay honored him in a solemn public session.

Bibliography: J. M. FERNÁNDEZ SALDAÑA, *Diccionario uruguayo de biografías, 1810–1940* (Montevideo 1945). C. ROXLO, *Histoira crítica de la literatura uruguaya,* 7 v. (Montevideo 1912–16) 2:464–500.

[A. D. GONZÁLEZ]

BAVARIA

The largest of the nine states that compose the (West) German Federal Republic, it is 27,209 square miles in area, with a population of 9,731,200 (1963). *Munich, the capital, then had a population of 1,142,-600. Bavaria, an intermittently independent duchy until 794, when *Charlemagne incorporated it into his empire, was ruled by the Welf dynasty (1070–1180) and by the Wittelsbachs (1180–1918). Duke Maximilian I became one of the seven imperial electors (1623). As a result of Bavarian assistance to *Napoleon I, Maximilian I Joseph became king of Bavaria in 1805. Bavaria joined the German Empire (1870–1918) and the Weimar Republic (1919–34) after the beloved Ludwig III (1913–18) was deposed. It lost its independence under *National Socialism (1934–45) and was reestablished as a state in 1946. This article treats the ecclesiastical history of Bavaria.

Christian Origins and Medieval Period. The Bavarians belong to the great west Germanic tribe of the Suevi and are the descendants of the Marcomanni, whose name disappeared from historical records in the 4th century. Mixed with other Germanic national groups, they came into the region where they are settled today. As *Jordanis reports in his *History of the Goths* (551), they became eastern neighbors of the

Alemanni. Their name Baiawarioz, i.e., "people from Baia" (later Baiwari or Baiuwari), was probably given them by their Romano-Celtic neighbors. In the course of the great migrations, they occupied in the 6th century those parts of the Roman provinces of Rhaetia and Noricum that were situated between the Lech and Enns Rivers, the Northern Forest (Bavarian and Bohemian Forest), and the Alps. The presence of Christians in the region, within the period of Roman rule, evidenced by the martyrs' graves in *Regensburg (Sarmanina gravestone) and by the martyrdom of SS. *Florian, *Maximilian, and *Afra.

In the course of the 5th century, St. Valentius and St. Severinus worked in Rhaetia. In Eugippius's account of the life of St. Severinus, a well-established Christianity and an organized Church are presupposed (see MEDIEVAL LATIN LITERATURE). Churches with several priests existed in Juvavum, Joviacum, and Asturis, and there were monasteries in Favianis and Batava. Lorch Tiburnia, Aguntum, Virunum, Augsburg, and Säben were centers of Christian life and episcopal sees. The Romans who had remained spread Christianity among the Bavarians. After the Agilolfing House had attained domination in Bavaria under the suzerainty of the Franks (c. 550), the Irish and Frankish mission began. The missionaries *Eustace and Agilus, who came from *Luxeuil, had only limited success. The work of the missionary bishops *Emmeram, *Rupert, and *Corbinian (c. 700) was much more effective and lasting. They are considered the founders of Regensburg, *Salzburg, and Freising. Duke Theodo, as early as 700, strove to establish firm ecclesiastical organization. His conferences with Pope Gregory II were successful and led to the *Instructio* of May 16, 716.

The formal ecclesiastical organization of Bavaria was carried out by St. *Boniface and Duke Oatilo during Boniface's third sojourn in Bavaria, (738–739). Corresponding to the four duchies that had been created out of the original one, the country was divided into four bishoprics—Regensburg, Salzburg, Freising, and Passau—and thus the unity of the Bavarian Church was established. The efforts of Duke Oatilo to unite the Bavarian parts of the Diocese of *Augsburg into an independent bishopric were crowned with success by the foundation of the bishopric of Neuburg on the Danube (741). The foundation, however, did not last much beyond 800. The bishoprics of *Würzburg, *Eichstätt, and Augsburg, founded by Boniface, became the ecclesiastical province of Mainz, and Boniface became the first metropolitan (747). Under his stimulus, the two last Agilolfing dukes, Oatilo and Tassilo III, as well as the bishops and nobility of the country, erected many monasteries. The *Lex Baiuvariorum,* formulated at this time, accorded Christianity a favored position and guaranteed legal protection to ecclesiastical property, persons, ordinances, and institutions. Synods were held in Aschheim (750 and 756), Neuching (771), and Dingolfing (774). Through the deposition of Tassilo III (788), Bavaria lost its independence and was incorporated into France.

At the request of Charlemagne, Pope Leo III united Bavaria in 798 into an ecclesiastical province, with Salzburg as the metropolitan see for the suffragans Säben, Regensburg, Freising, Passau, and Neuburg, and for the southeastern Slavic lands. One of the reasons for the unification was the missionary activity in the adjacent regions, which came under the bishoprics of Salzburg, Passau, and Regensburg. Salzburg had already begun its missionary work in Carinthia and Pannonia under St. *Virgilius (Feirgil). Passau's missionaries carried on their work in Upper Pannonia between the Enns and Raab Rivers and in Bulgaria. Bohemia was under the ecclesiastical jurisdiction of Regensburg (see CZECHOSLOVAKIA). But ecclesiastical possession of these territories could not be maintained, despite missionary successes, and the appearance of SS. *Cyril and Methodius, the apostles to the Slavs, interrupted the German effort. In 972 St. *Wolfgang of Regensburg gave his assent to the establishment of an independent bishopric at *Prague. Under the Hungarian attacks of the 10th century and the secularization carried out by Duke Arnulf, the Bavarian Church suffered severely.

Under the dukes of the Ottonian and Salian Houses, the Church enjoyed a new flowering. Among the important churchmen of the time were the bishops *Ulric of Augsburg and St. Wolfgang of Regensburg. Wolfgang introduced the reform from the Abbey of *Gorze into many Bavarian monasteries, thus creating a broad basis for the renewal of the Church. The reforming efforts of the Canons Regular of St. Augustine and of *Hirsau had more important results. In 1007 *Henry II founded the bishopric of Bamberg. Under *Henry III, about the middle of the 11th century, three princes of the Church coming from the Bavarian territories ascended the papal throne: *Clement II, *Damasus II, and *Victor II. Furthermore, in the dukes of the House of Wittels-

Fig. 1. The Abbess Matilda and her brother Otto, Duke of Bavaria, detail of the "First Cross" of the Abbess, c. 973–1011, in the cathedral treasury at Essen, Germany.

bach (after 1180) the Church found magnanimous patrons, who gave much support.

During the *investiture struggle the lines were unmistakably sharp. Most of the bishops sided with the emperors; only *Gebhard of Salzburg and *Altman of Passau supported the *Gregorian Reform. In the struggles of the Hohenstaufen emperors and of Emperor *Louis IV the Bavarian with the popes, the sentiments of the bishops, clergy, and people generally favored the emperors. Through these conflicts, ecclesiastical life suffered severely, but the new mendicant orders brought about a renewal of ecclesiastical life and practice in the 13th century.

In the *Western Schism (1378–1417), the Bavarian Dukes of Landshut, Ingolstadt, and Munich were on the side of Popes *Urban VI, *Boniface IX, and *Innocent VII, the Roman line of claimants. Bavaria deserved especially well of the Council of *Basel, over which Duke William had assumed the protectorate. Bavarian efforts at reform manifested themselves at the Councils of *Pisa, *Constance, and Basel, and also in the founding of the monastic reform congregations of *Melk, *Kastl, and *Bursfeld.

16th to 18th Centuries. Many of these attempts at renewal were unsuccessful, and so the Reformation was able to gain numerous adherents in Bavaria. Duke William IV, on the advice of Johann and Leonhard von Eck, rejected Luther and the *Reformation in the declarations of 1521 and 1522. In 1524 Archduke Ferdinand of Austria, the Bavarian dukes, and 12 bishops of South Germany united to carry out the Edict of Worms. But even this action could not suppress the Reformation completely. While Old Bavaria (Altbayern) remained Catholic, the Reformation gained more ground in

Fig. 3. An altar of St. George in Kloster Weltenburg an der Donau, Bavaria, built during the 18th century.

Palatinate-Neuburg and in the Electoral Rhine Palatinate, and even triumphed in the imperial cities of Regensburg and Augsburg. The Interim Settlement was not promulgated by Duke William. Albert V signed the Peace of *Augsburg and continued the Catholic policy of his predecessor. In 1578 he added to the ducal law of succession the codicil that the sovereign must be a Catholic. He was an active promoter of the decrees of the Council of *Trent and brought to Bavaria the *Jesuits, notably St. Peter *Canisius. The transfer of the Rhenish and Westphalian bishoprics and later the electorate of Cologne to his son Ernst preserved these areas for the Catholic Church. In continuance of the policy of his father, William V regulated relationships between Church and State by concluding a concordat with the Pope and the Bavarian bishops (1585). This concordat remained in force until the 19th century.

During the Thirty Years' War, Elector *Maximilian I defended the Catholic cause. He favored the Jesuits and in 1608 founded the Catholic League to oppose the Protestant Union, which had been founded by the Wittelsbachs of the Palatinate. He bore the main burden of the war and strove unceasingly for peace.

Maximilian III Joseph (1747–77), influenced by his advisers J. A. von Ickstatt and P. von Osterwald, prepared the way for the *Enlightenment and State control over the Church. He attempted to subordinate the Church completely to the State. Against these encroachments of absolutism, the Bavarian bishops defended themselves at the Congress of Salzburg (1770–71). In 1777, following the death of Maximilian III Joseph, Bavaria fell to Charles Theodore of the Palatinate line of the Wittelsbachs. Under his rule a papal nunciature was established in Munich. Maximilian I (king after

Fig. 2. The nave of the church of St. Ulrich, Augsburg.

1806), together with his minister Maximilian *Montgelas, a strong advocate of Enlightenment ideas and policy, carried out in 1803 the general secularization of Church property. Besides the main foundations, 97 abbeys and 200 mendicant monasteries were confiscated in Upper and Lower Bavaria.

19th and 20th Centuries. Concordat negotiations undertaken between 1806 and 1807 failed initially, but renewed effort on both sides led to the conclusion of a concordat (June 5, 1817) between Bavaria and Cardinal *Consalvi, acting as representative of Pius VII. This regulated the distribution of bishoprics and the rights and obligations of the state. However, the concordat was published only on May 25, 1818, together with a constitutional charter and an edict on religion which partly contradicted the concordat through the oath on the constitution. The difficulties arising from this resulted in the King's Tegernsee declaration of 1821, legally almost meaningless. The distribution of dioceses established in the bull of circumscription (two archbishoprics and six bishoprics) still prevails even to this day.

In the 19th century a religious renewal was instituted by Bp. Johann Michael *Sailer. On his advice and that of Minister Abel, King Ludwig I appointed able men to the episcopate (*Reisach, Hofstätter, Riedel, Stahl, and Öttl) and restored a number of monasteries. Under him Bavaria became a center of ecclesiastical and religious life. The university, which in 1800 had been transferred from Dillingen to Landshut, was moved by him to Munich (1826). Under King Maximilian II, the Bavarian bishops at the Conferences of Würzburg (1848) and Freising (1850 and 1852) demanded freedom of the Church from the State. They won some concessions, but the State domination of the Church continued. Because of his disagreements with the government, Reisach, Archbishop of Munich and Freising, was transferred to Rome, where he was made a cardinal. Johannes Lutz, Minister of Public Worship and Education (1862–90) under Ludwig II, had a negative attitude toward *Vatican Council I, favored Döllinger and the *Old Catholics, and promoted the *Kulturkampf in the Reichstag. In Bavaria itself, in view of the strong Patriots' party (*Center party) founded in 1869, no direct measures in favor of the Kulturkampf were attempted. At *Vatican Council I, 11 Bavarian bishops sided with the minority but submitted after the proclamation of the doctrine of papal infallibility. Under the long rule of Prince Regent Luitpold (1886–1912) the Kulturkampf dwindled, and ecclesiastical life in Bavaria grew stronger. The abolition of the Bavarian monarchy at the end of World War I (1914–18) created completely different conditions; a new concordat became necessary and was signed on March 29, 1924.

From 1933 to 1945, the Catholic Church in Bavaria, as in all other German states, was in severe conflict with the National Socialist state, which aimed to destroy the Church. Church life suffered from measures like the closing of Catholic schools, dissolution and confiscation of monasteries, and restriction of ecclesiastical activity to the area of formal worship. The Catholic clergy and laity, led by Cardinal Michael von *Faulhaber, Archbishop of Munich and Freising, remained faithful to the Church.

World War II (1939–45) inflicted heavy losses in life and property on Bavaria. But the collapse of the Na-

Fig. 4. The interior of St. Joseph's Church, Hasloch-am-Main, Bavaria, designed by the architect Hans Schädel.

tional Socialist state in 1945 freed the Church. Catholic population increased substantially as refugees and expellees streamed into Bavaria. New parishes were created to care for their needs.

Besides the old Bavarian administrative districts of Upper Bavaria, Lower Bavaria, and the Upper Palatinate, Bavaria includes Upper, Middle, and Lower Franconia, and Swabia but not the Rhineland-Palatinate. Catholics in Bavaria constituted 71.7 per cent of the population (1963), distributed among the Archdiocese of Munich-Freising and its suffragans Augsburg, Passau, and Regensburg; and the Archdiocese of Bamberg and its suffragans Eichstätt, and Würzburg. Included in Bavaria are 258 deaneries and 3,736 parishes. The archbishop of Munich is traditionally a cardinal.

Lutheran Church. The Reformation was preceded in the late Middle Ages, especially in the northern parts of modern Bavaria, by popular religious movements of a Waldensian-Hussite type. The Reformation was welcomed in the episcopal cities of Augsburg, Bamberg, and Würzburg. Cities such as *Nuremberg, Memmingen, and Kempten had Lutheran religious services before 1525. Many Bavarian cathedral chapters sympathized with the Reformation, but the movement was checked by legislative measures after 1525. Many Protestant exiles from Austria and France entered Franconia (part of modern Bavaria) after the Thirty Years' War (1618–48).

Rationalism, especially promoted by the Brandenburg principalities, found a vehicle in the University of Erlangen (founded 1743). The reconstitution of the Bavarian state at the beginning of the 19th century produced a

Map of Bavaria showing sites important in the development of the Catholic Church in the area.

Bavarian Protestant Church under centralized administration. Groups favoring *pietism and a society for promoting Christianity in Nuremberg provided the stimulus to a revivalist movement, at first nondenominational in character. Hermann von Bezzel (1861–1917), a theologian, completed the process of imparting a distinctive character to the Bavarian Lutheran Church.

After 1918 reforming communities formed an independent Church. The Bavarian Lutheran Church and the Church of Coburg united and drew up a constitution that received state recognition (Nov. 15, 1924). Threatened by National Socialism, Bavarian Lutherans remained loyal to Bp. Hans Meiser and supported the *Bekennende Kirche.

In World War II Lutherans, like Catholics, suffered great losses in buildings, especially in the cities, and had to face likewise the almost insoluble task of caring for their refugee coreligionists by creating new parishes.

The Lutheran Church of Bavaria collaborated in the creation of the United Evangelical Lutheran Church of Germany and in the formation of the *Evangelical Church in Germany (EKD). The Evangelical Church, with 2,578,800 souls in 1963, constituted 26.5 per cent of the population. It comprised five administrative districts: Ansbach, Bayreuth, Munich, Nuremberg, and Regensburg. These administrative districts together include 73 deaneries and 1,150 parishes.

See also GERMANY.

Bibliography: R. BAUERREIS, *Kirchengeschichte Bayerns,* 5 v. (St. Ottilien 1949–55). Hauck. A. BIGELMAIR, DHGE 6:1524–1626; LexThK² 2:77–81. H. BRÜCK, *Geschichte der katholischen Kirche im neunzehnten Jahrhundert,* 4 v. (Mainz 1887–1908). G. GOYAU, *L'Allemagne religieuse* 9 v. (Paris 1898–1913). J. SCHLECHT, *Bayerns Kirchen-Provinzen* (Munich 1902). G. PFEILSCHIFTER-BAUMEISTER, *Der Salzburger Kongress und seine Auswirkung, 1770–1777: Der Kampf des bayerische Episkopats gegen die staatskirchenrechtliche Aufklärung* (Paderborn

1929). A. DOEBERL, *Die bayerische Konkordatsverhandlungen in den Jahren 1806 und 1807* (Munich 1924); *Entwicklingsgeschichte Bayerns*, 3 v. (3d ed. Munich 1916–30). M. BUCHBERGER, *Eineinhalb Jahrtausend kirchlicher Kulturarbeit in Bayern* (Munich 1950). K. BOSL and H. SCHREIBMÜLLER, *Geschichte Bayerns*, 2 v. (Munich 1952–55). B. HUBENSTEINER, *Bayerische Geschichte* (3d ed. Munich 1955). M. SIMON, *Evangelische Kirchengeschichte Bayerns* (Nürnberg 1952). Latourette Christ 19th–20th Cent v.1,2,4. *Zeitschrift für bayerische Kirchengeschichte* (Gunzenhausen 1926–). *Zeitschrift für bayerische Landesgeschichte* (Munich 1928–). *Veröffentlichungen der Kommission für bayerische Landesgeschichte bei der bayerische Akademie der Wissenschaften* (Munich 1949–). **Illustration credits:** Figs. 2 and 3, German Information Center, New York City. Fig. 4, Photo Archives, Das Münster, Munich.

[R. BRANDLMEIER]

BAVARIANS (BAVARII),

a Germanic people who settled in southeast Germany between the Lech and Enns rivers, and along the Danube, chiefly within the Roman province of Noricum. Their origin is obscure. Traditionally they have been considered remnants or descendants of the Marcomanni, long resident in Bohemia, the land of the Celtic *Boii*. Hence, supposedly, the origin of the names *Baioarii*, *Bajuvarii*, or *Bavarii*. Some recent scholarship rejects the Marcomannic theory, without supplying another generally acceptable. I. Zibermayr considers the Bavarians an independent East German people; E. Schwarz and H. Löwe believe their nucleus was West German, mainly *Suevi from Pannonia. Details of their migration are not known, but they seem to have occupied their new homeland between 489 and 539, and were a unified people under one ruler, a duke of the Agilolfing family. By the time of Garibald (560–590), the first known duke, the Bavarians had fallen under Frankish control, evidently without resistance. Frankish rule weakened after 639, but the Avar threat to the east inclined the Bavarians to remain under Frankish domination and protection. Duke Theodo (696–718) pursued a free, statesmanlike policy, but a dynastic dispute led to Frankish intervention in 743, when Pepin the Short again subjugated the Bavarii. When Charlemagne deposed Duke Tassilo III (748–788), the last Agilolfing, the first phase of Bavarian history ended. Meanwhile, the Bavarians colonized the Tirol, moved north across the Danube, and southeast into Austria and Carinthia. Their Latin law code, the *Lex baiowariorum*, received its final form in the middle of the 7th century, although many of its provisions are older. Borrowing in part from Visigothic sources, it devotes attention to wergelds and reveals a society consisting of the ducal family and five great noble houses, freemen, freedmen, and servile dependents.

Early traces of Christianity in such places as Lorch exerted little influence on the immigrant Bavarians. Between 620 and 639 Irish monks from *Luxeuil began evangelization; St. *Eustace, St. *Agil, and Agrestius, are their only known missionaries, and they worked without result. Frankish clergy later undertook a second evangelization, the initiative again probably coming from the Frankish court rather than from the pagan Duke Theodo. By 725 their conversion was virtually completed. St. *Emmeram (d. *c.* 716), apparently the first bishop for the Bavarians, preached in *Regensburg. St. *Rupert (d. *c.* 718) settled in Salzburg (*see* SALZBURG, ARCHDIOCESE OF). St. Corbinian (d. 725) became bishop of *Augsburg. St. Vivilo (d. *c.* 745) presided over a fourth bishopric at Passau. Freising, Staffelsee, and in part *Eichstätt and *Würzburg were also Ba-

varian sees. Monasticism took root quickly. In 715 Theodo visited Rome. The next year Gregory II attempted unsuccessfully to give an ecclesiastical organization to the duchy, a task accomplished by St. *Boniface in 739. Salzburg later became the metropolitan see.

Bibliography: I. ZIBERMAYR, *Noricum: Baiern und Oesterreich* (Horn 1956). R. BAUERREISS, *Kirchengeschichte Bayerns* (2d ed. St. Ottilien 1958–) v.1. A. BIGELMAIR, DHGE 6:1524–1626; LexThK² 2:77–81. H. LÖWE, RGG³ 1:947.

[R. H. SCHMANDT]

BAVO (ALLOWIN), ST.,

monastic founder and patron of Ghent; b. Hesbaye, Belgium, *c.* 600; d. at a hermitage near Ghent, Belgium, Oct. 1, 660 (feast, Oct. 1). The oldest vita of the saint was composed in the 9th century, some 200 years after his death; it records that Bavo was descended from a noble Belgian family and was married to the daughter of a certain Count Adilion. After his wife's death, he decided to devote himself to the religious life and sought out the missionary *Amandus, who was then at *Ghent. He sold all his possessions and founded in that city a *Benedictine monastery dedicated to St. Peter and later renamed Saint-Bavon. Bavo accompanied Amandus on a missionary journey through Flanders and on his return settled in a hermitage near the abbey he had endowed. He was buried at Ghent, and when the abbey church was destroyed in 1540, his relics were taken to the new cathedral. His name appears in the liturgy from the early 9th century.

Bibliography: ActSS Oct. 1:199–302. MGSrerMer 4:527–545. Mabillon AS 2:396–403. BHL 1049–60. L. VAN DER ESSEN, *Étude critique et littéraire sur les vitae des saints mérovingiens de l'ancienne Belgique* (Louvain 1907) 349–357. É. DE MOREAU, *Saint Amand* (Louvain 1927) 220–223. Zimmermann KalBen 3:122–124. R. PODEVIJN, *Bavo* (Bruges 1945). R. AIGRAIN, *Catholicisme* 1:1323–24.

[B. J. COMASKEY]

BAWDEN, WILLIAM (BALDWIN),

Jesuit priest; b. Cornwall, 1563; d. Saint-Omer, Flanders, Sept. 28, 1632. After 5 years' study at Oxford, he arrived at Douai on Dec. 31, 1582, and at Rome on Oct. 1, 1583. He took the college oath on May 31, 1584, and was ordained on April 16, 1588. After a year as penitentiary at St. Peter's, he entered the Society of Jesus in Flanders in 1590. He taught moral theology at Louvain, then set out for Spain disguised as a merchant in the winter of 1594–95. He was captured at sea and taken to England. The Privy Council failed to identify him and exchanged him for an English prisoner in Spain. Bawden ministered for 6 months in Hampshire and then functioned in Rome as minister at the English College. At Brussels, he was vice prefect of the English mission from about 1600–1610, being accused unjustly of complicity in the *Gunpowder Plot. An ineffective attempt was made for his extradition, but in 1610 he was recognized and taken while traveling incognito through the Palatinate; he was surrendered to the English government, which kept him in the Tower until June 15, 1618, when he was released at the insistence of Count Gondomar, the Spanish ambassador. In 1622, after a year as rector of Louvain, he became rector of Saint-Omer, governing the college successfully until his death.

Bibliography: H. MORE, *Historia Provinciae Anglicanae Societatis Jesu* (Saint-Omer 1660) lib. 8:374–378. H. FOLEY, ed., *Records of the English Province of the Society of Jesus*, 7 v. (London 1877–82) 3:501–520. H. CHADWICK, *St. Omers to*

Stonyhurst (London 1962). T. Cooper, DNB 1:959–960. Sommervogel 1:830. DictEngCath 1:156–157.

[F. EDWARDS]

BAXTER, RICHARD, Puritan divine; b. Rowton, Shropshire, England, Nov. 12, 1615; d. London, Dec. 8, 1691. His crude education under incompetent curates was compensated for by J. Owen at the Wroxeter free school and by a lifetime of private study. Baxter developed his theological views through a scrupulous introspection. He entered the ministry in 1638, accepting the establishment's tenets despite private tendencies toward moderate *Presbyterianism, which grew from his sympathy with *nonconformists. He favored latitudinarian views that might fuse Protestant sects into one national church based on fundamental doctrines in the Creed, Lord's Prayer, the Decalogue, and the Bible as revelation. He favored tolerance of Romanists if they worshiped privately. Baxter avoided political controversy in the civil war and supported the parliamentarians.

After 1653, he criticized Oliver *Cromwell and lamented the demise of legally constituted monarchy. Baxter cheered the Restoration but questioned the episcopacy. The Act of Uniformity of 1662 turned him from the state Church to the persecuted nonconformists with whom he suffered until the Toleration Act of 1690. Baxter spent most of his life, after 1653, in an extensive literary productivity, virtually unequaled then in quality or quantity. Prominent among his more than 200 works are: *Saints' Everlasting Rest* (1650), *The Reformed Pastor* (1656), and the autobiographical *Reliquiae Baxterianae* (1696).

Bibliography: R. Baxter, *The Practical Works of the Late Reverend and Pious Mr. Richard Baxter,* ed. W. Orme, 23 v. (London 1830); *The Autobiography of Richard Baxter,* ed. J. M. Lloyd Thomas (New York 1931); *Richard Baxter and Puritan Politics,* ed. R. Schlatter (New Brunswick, N.J. 1957). F. J. Powicke, *A Life of the Reverend Richard Baxter* (London 1924). A. B. Grosart, comp., *Annotated List of the Writings of Richard Baxter* (London 1868); DNB 1:1349–57.

[M. J. HAVRAN]

BAY PSALM BOOK, popular title of the first book produced by English-speaking American authors on a British-North American press; published by Stephen Day(e) in Cambridge, Mass., 1640, under the official title of *The Whole Booke of Psalmes Faithfully Translated into English Metre.* This psalter was a new translation begun in 1636 by a group of Puritan divines—Richard Mather, John Eliot, and Thomas Weld, with some additions by the English poet Francis Quarles—who had become dissatisfied with the Sternhold and Hopkins translation being used in Massachusetts Bay Colony. The new psalter was immediately adopted by the congregations, but around 1647 the ministers of the Bay Colony felt that a revision of their initial effort was needed. The result was the third, and definitive, edition of 1651, entitled *The Psalms Hymns and Spiritual Songs of the Old and New Testament, faithfully translated into English metre,* popularly known as the New England Psalm Book. The first known edition to contain examples of notated music was the ninth (1698). In its revised form the book was widely used for more than a century, not only in America but also among Puritan congregations in England and Scotland. It ranked among the most popular English psalters of its time.

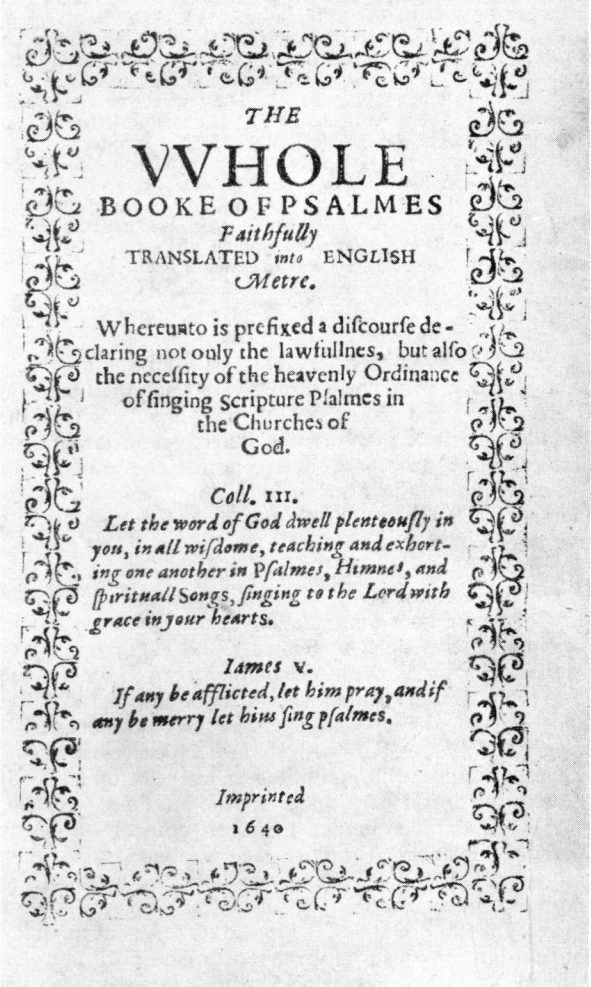

Title page of first edition (1640) of the Bay Psalm Book.

See also HYMNS AND HYMNALS; MUSIC, SACRED (U.S.); PSALTERS, METRICAL.

Bibliography: Z. Haraszti, *The Enigma of the Bay Psalm Book* (Chicago 1956). Chase AmMus 14, 19–21. **Illustration credit:** By courtesy of the Trustees of the Boston Public Library.

[A. M. GARRETT]

BAYBARS I, SULTAN, 1260 to 1277. Baybars (Rukn-ad-Dīn Baybards Bunduqdāri), Sultan of the *Mamelukes, ranks along with *Saladin as an opponent of the crusaders. As a Kipchak Turk in a slave market, Baybars attracted the attention of an emir, al-Bunduqdāri, who bought him. He rose rapidly from the ranks in the Sultan's guard and, upon the exile of his master, al-Bunduqdāri, became a part of the army of aṣ-Ṣāliḥ Aiyūb in 1247. In September 1260 the Sultan Kutuz with the aid of Baybars defeated Kitbogha and his Mongols at Ain Jālūt, a town near Nazareth. Baybars quickly exploited the victory by killing Kutuz and seizing the Sultan's throne. In the following 17 years he consolidated the Mameluke empire at the expense of Christians, Mongols, and the divisive Islamic states. His sudden death in 1277, purportedly from a cup of poisoned mare's milk, left the Mameluke Sultanate as the greatest power in the Near East and the *Crusaders' states as a weakened political force.

Bibliography: S. F. SADEQUE, ed., *Baybars I of Egypt* (Dacca 1956–). M. M. ZIADA, "The Mamluk Sultans to 1293," *The Later Crusades, 1189–1311,* ed. R. L. WOLFF and H. W. HAZARD, v.2 of *A History of the Crusades,* ed. K. M. SETTON (Philadelphia 1955–) 735–758.

[J. H. HILL]

BAYEUX

City and diocese (*Baiocensis*) in Calvados, Normandy, France. In 1802 it incorporated part of the Diocese of *Lisieux and in 1855 became the See of Bayeux-Lisieux. Its Christian origins are unknown. As the capitol of the *civitas Baiocassium,* it is first mentioned in the late 4th century, the time of its first three bishops—SS. Exuperius, Rufinianus, and Lupus. Bishop Vigor evangelized the pagans at the time of the Merovingian Childebert (511–558). Two nearby monasteries, Cerisy and Deux-Jumeaux, had early origins. The episcopal succession was disrupted by the invasion of the Normans, who slew Bishops Sulpicius (844) and Baltfrid (858). The disruption of the church lasted until Bishop Hugh (1015–49) began the religious restoration, building rural churches to combat paganism. The Norman barons began to donate to local churches their loot from elsewhere, and under William the Conqueror, Bishop *Odo, his half brother, and *Lanfranc began a reform of Normandy by holding councils and building abbeys. In the 12th century churches multiplied. After Philip II incorporated Normandy into France (1204), synods at *Rouen worked diligently to improve ecclesiastical discipline. When the English evacuated the area in 1450 at the end of the Hundred Years' War, it was in material and moral ruin and the clergy were at a very low status.

Lutheranism appeared by 1540 and Calvinist churches by 1555. Catholic worship was interrupted for months in 1562 when Huguenots sacked Bayeux, and Protestantism took a firm foothold in the area. The Holy *League again sacked the city in 1589. Bishops Édouard Molé (1647–52) and François Servien (1654–59) began the reform. St. John *Eudes undertook missions, and the *Compagnie du Saint-Sacrement took the offensive against Protestants. Bishop François de Nesmond (1662–1715) founded the seminary and restored discipline among secular and religious clergy. Bishop François de Lorraine-Armagnac (1719–28) was an ardent Jansenist. There was an influx of religious orders into the diocese in the 17th century, as there had been in the 13th. On the eve of the French Revolution there were 620 parish priests, 12 monasteries, and 2 convents. In 1963 the Diocese of Bayeux had 719 parishes with 457 secular and 69 religious priests for 450,000 Catholics in a population of 480,686. Enrollment in 30 Catholic schools at that time numbered 5,495 students.

The cathedral was rebuilt by Bishop Odo in 1046 after a fire, and again by Henry I of England after it was destroyed in 1105. In the 14th and 15th centuries it was enlarged and embellished. The seminary had 61 students in 1964, but the recruitment of clergy in Bayeux was difficult. St. Jean Brébeuf, the apostle of the Hurons, canonized in 1930, was born in Bayeux. The distinctive and conservative liturgy of Bayeux, to which *Durandus of Troarn contributed in the 11th century, is preserved in many MSS of the 13th, 14th, and 15th centuries. Since the 16th century the liturgy has been modified only slowly and gradually.

The Bayeux Tapestry is a linen roll of colored stitchwork, 231 feet long and 20 inches wide in its present state, representing in 72 scenes the events that led up to the battle of Hastings in 1066. It was made *c.* 1080, perhaps in England. Depicting 623 persons, 202 horses and mules, 55 dogs, 505 other animals, 37 buildings, 41 boats and ships, and 49 trees, it is of value for the study of arms and armor, warfare, architecture, dress, and the folklore of the period. The upper and lower

A detail of the 11th-century Bayeux Tapestry preserved in the Musée Tapisserie at Bayeux, France. At the left, the populace is terrified by the appearance of the comet; at the right, King Harold is told of the comet by a page.

borders are decorated with a series of animals, some of which are real, others, imaginary.

Bibliography: S. E. GLEASON, *An Ecclesiastical Barony of the Middle Ages: The Bishopric of Bayeux 1066–1204* (Cambridge, Mass. 1936). E. DE LAHEUDRIE, *Bayeux, capitale du Bessin, des origines à la fin de la monarchie,* 2 v. in 1 (Bayeux 1945). E. JARRY and J. HOURLIER, *Catholicisme* 1:1324–31. **Illustration credit:** From the *Bayeux Tapestry,* ed. SIR FRANK STENTON (Phaidon Press Ltd., London).

[J. GOURHAND]

BAYLE, PIERRE

French skeptic who had an enormous influence on 18th-century thought; b. Carla, southern France, Nov. 18, 1647; d. Rotterdam, Dec. 28, 1706. Bayle, son of a Calvinist minister, attended the Protestant school at Puylaurens, and then the Jesuit college at Toulouse, where he converted to Catholicism and shortly thereafter back to Calvinism. His second conversion made him a *relaps,* subject to severe penalties during the persecutions of the Huguenots. Bayle fled to Geneva and studied philosophy and theology at the university. He then secretly returned to France and lived in disguise, earning his living as a tutor in Paris and Rouen and later as professor of philosophy at the Calvinist academy at Sedan, as the protégé of the fanatic Calvinist leader, Pierre *Jurieu. In 1682, when the academy was closed by Louis XIV, Bayle and Jurieu became professors at the *École illustre* of Rotterdam. Here Bayle published his first work, his *Thoughts on the Comets of 1680,* a critical attack on superstition, intolerance, various philosophical and theological systems, historical inaccuracies, etc., followed by an answer to Father L. Maimbourg's *History of Calvinism* and a collection of defenses of *Cartesianism answering the attacks of the French Jesuits. From 1684 to 1687 he edited the *Nouvelles de la République des Lettres,* reviewing all of the important writings then appearing. His famous work on toleration, the *Philosophical Commentary* on the words of Jesus, "Constrain them to come in," appeared in 1686. Here Bayle offered a defense of toleration of all groups from Catholics to Moslems, Jews, Unitarians, and even atheists. His erstwhile supporter, Jurieu, then turned upon him and denounced Bayle as a secret atheist. Thereafter Bayle and Jurieu fought each other in a constant pamphlet warfare whose fruits included the termination of Bayle's academic career, which thus gave him time to write his most important and influential work, the *Historical and Critical Dictionary,* first published in 1697. Bayle's *Dictionary,* which grew to be between 7 and 8 million words long, consists of biographical articles on all sorts of people from the most obscure theologians to the most famous figures in the Old Testament, and the most notorious political figures. The "meat" of the *Dictionary* consists in the lengthy, digressive, erudite footnotes, and notes to the notes, attacking and dissecting every possible theory in philosophy, theology, and science, and retailing salacious tales about famous and infamous personages. Some of the articles (on David, the Manichaeans, Pyrrho, Rorarius, Spinoza, and Zeno) became major battlegrounds of the intellectual world for the next 50 years, eliciting replies from philosophers and theologians of every persuasion. Bayle spent his remaining years writing defenses and explanations of his views against attacks from conservative and liberal Protestants, from Catholics, and from philosophers such as G. W. Leibniz. Bayle died with pen in hand finishing off another rebuttal.

Throughout the *Dictionary* and his later works, Bayle argued that various theories in philosophy, theology, and science involve contradictions and absurdities that appear incapable of resolution. Over and over, Bayle contended that his massive skeptical barrage showed that rational endeavor in all areas is hopeless, and that man should abandon reason and turn to faith as the only source of true knowledge. He reinforced his *fideism by arguing that revealed truth was unintelligible, in conflict with reason, evidence, and morality. Heretical views such as Manichaeanism, he claimed, could be better defended rationally than could Christianity.

Many of Bayle's contemporaries assumed that his point was not the defense of religion, but its destruction. The *philosophes* saw the *Dictionary* as "the Arsenal of the Enlightenment," and used it to undermine traditional religion, theology, and philosophy. Leibniz, G. Berkeley, and D. Hume wrestled with Bayle's arguments and sought new solutions. But the 18th century ultimately found its resolution in replacing Bayle's skeptical treasury with scientific studies. As his learned biographies became outdated, his endless doubts came to be ignored and forgotten, and his fideism seen as a covert rationalistic critique of religion and philosophy, preparing the way for the Age of Reason. Recent studies, aimed at placing Bayle in the context of his time, have led to a reconsideration of his fideism, and suggest that he was, perhaps, a serious, though puzzled and puzzling believer, struggling with the various religious and scientific tensions of his day. His doubts and religious concern may have more lasting value than the scientific optimism that emerged from taking his texts as the death knell of the pre-Newtonian age.

See also SKEPTICISM; ENLIGHTENMENT, PHILOSOPHY OF.

Bibliography: *Oeuvres diverses,* comp. P. DES MAIZEAUX, 4 v. (The Hague 1727–31; repr. 1964); *A General Dictionary, Historical and Critical,* 10 v. (London 1734–41); *Selections from Bayle's Dictionary,* ed. R. H. POPKIN (New York 1965). P. DIBON et al., eds., *Pierre Bayle, le philosophe de Rotterdam* (Amsterdam 1959). E. LABROUSSE, *Pierre Bayle* (The Hague 1963–64).

[R. H. POPKIN]

BAYLEY, JAMES ROOSEVELT

Eighth archbishop of the Baltimore, Md., Archdiocese; b. New York, N.Y., Aug. 23, 1814; d. Newark, N.J., Oct. 3, 1877. A descendant of long-established families of English and Dutch ancestry, he was the son of Dr. Guy Carleton and Grace (Roosevelt) Bayley and the grandson of Richard Bayley, physician, and James Roosevelt, a prominent merchant. Elizabeth Bayley Seton, foundress of the Sisters of Charity in the U.S., was his aunt. He attended Mt. Pleasant Classical Institution and Amherst College in Amherst, Mass., and Trinity College, Hartford, Conn., from which he graduated in 1835. After a year in medicine, he studied for the Episcopal ministry under Dr. Samuel Farmar Jarvis, Middletown, Conn., and was ordained Feb. 14, 1840, while rector of St. Andrew's Church, Harlem, N.Y.

Worried by doubts concerning the claims of his church, he resigned the rectorship and late in 1841 sailed for Europe. At the Church of the Gesù in Rome he was received into the Catholic Church by Bartholomew Esmonde, SJ, April 28, 1842. Then, after a year at the Seminary of Saint-Sulpice in Paris, he finished his studies in New York and was ordained on March 2, 1844, in St. Patrick's Cathedral. After administrative

Archbishop James Roosevelt Bayley.

posts at St. John's College (Fordham University), New York City, and some pastoral experience, he served as secretary to Bp. John Hughes for 7 years. During this time he became interested in the history of the Church in the U.S.

In 1853 he was appointed the first bishop of the Diocese of Newark, covering the state of New Jersey. He was consecrated in St. Patrick's Cathedral, October 30, by Abp. Cajetan Bedini, Papal Nuncio to Brazil. The ensuing 19 years brought a great transformation in Newark as he organized and administered the growing diocese, founded a college, a seminary, and a community of Sisters of Charity, and brought in other religious communities of men and women. His attendance at Church councils, including Vatican Council I in 1869, journeys to Europe and the Holy Land, and his writing and lecturing indicated widening spheres of action.

Bayley's *Brief Sketch of the Early History of the Catholic Church on the Island of New York* (1853, 1870) and the *Memoirs of the Rt. Rev. Simon Wm. Gabriel Bruté, D.D., First Bishop of Vincennes* (1860) appeared when Catholic historical scholarship was just beginning in the U.S. Unfortunately, his duties left little time for his interest in Catholic history, literature, and bibliography. He was decided in his convictions and simple and direct in expressing them in the many pastoral letters he wrote and the many lectures he gave, especially in behalf of temperance. However, he believed in kindness and good example rather than controversy as the means of arousing interest in the Church. Against his wishes he was appointed on July 21, 1872, as successor to Martin J. Spalding, Archbishop of Baltimore. He was harassed by frequent illness and burdened by the demands of an extensive province and the conservatism of an old, established see. His last pastoral letter in 1876 pleaded for greater zeal and generosity in support of archdiocesan institutions.

In addition to his interest in the Indian missions and the American College in Rome, which he had helped from its founding, he was called upon by the Holy See for help in the school question and in the erection of new metropolitan sees. He conferred the biretta upon the first U.S. cardinal, Abp. John McCloskey of New York. He had the satisfaction of consecrating the Baltimore cathedral 55 years after its dedication. By 1876 chronic illness induced him to ask for a coadjutor with the right of succession in the person of Bp. James Gibbons of Richmond. The papal brief for this was received while Bayley was seeking relief from illness in Vichy, France. In August 1877, he returned to New Jersey critically ill and died in Newark. Following the Requiem in Baltimore, he was interred as he had requested at St. Joseph's Convent, Emmitsburg, Md., beside his aunt, (Bl.) Elizabeth Seton.

Bibliography: M. H. YEAGER, *Life of James Roosevelt Bayley, First Bishop of Newark and Eighth Archbishop of Baltimore 1814–1877* (CUA StAmChHist 36; Washington 1947). **Illustration credit:** The *Advocate,* Newark, N.J.

[M. H. YEAGER]

BAZ, JUAN JOSÉ, Mexican Liberal and virulent anticlerical; b. Guadalajara, 1820; d. Mexico City, 1887. After a youth spent among clergy, jurists, and military men, he studied law and graduated as a lawyer from the Conciliar Seminary of Mexico. He gained a reputation as a valiant soldier in the battalion Defensores de la Patria. Soon after completing his professional training, he showed himself an enemy of the clergy, the army, and the judicial institutions of the Spanish old regime. Between 1841 and 1854 he fought both Santa Anna, the military *caudillo,* and Paredes, the monarchist leader. He propagandized in favor of nationalization of ecclesiastical wealth and suppression of convents. After obtaining influential positions in government, he was exiled to Europe but returned when the Liberals took power. From 1855 on he led an extraordinarily diversified life. He wrote inflammatory articles for the revolutionary papers *Guillermo Tell* and *La Bandera Roja,* was a familiar figure in literary circles, and produced a political comedy. He fought in many battles during the War of Reform and the French intervention and took refuge in New York during Maximilian's reign. After his return he was three times governor of the Federal District and became well known for his efficiency in discovering and putting down anti-Liberal conspiracies and for his practice of opening new streets through former churches and convents. As a legislator in Lerdo's government, he was influential in promulgating laws forcing secularization of priests and nuns, of matrimony, and of cemeteries, and allowing freedom of worship.

Bibliography: J. J. BAZ, *Artículos diversos de la Bandera Roja de Morelia* (Mexico City 1861); *Discursos pronunciados en el Congreso* (Mexico City 1875). E. M. DE LOS RÍOS, ed., *Liberales ilustres mexicanos de la reforma y la intervención* (Mexico City 1890; repr. 1961). A. GARCÍA CUBAS, *El libro de mis recuerdos* (Mexico City 1945).

[L. GONZÁLEZ]

BAZIANUS. A 12th-century canonist whose *glossae* are variously designated by the sigla *B., Bar., Bac., Baç., Baça., Baz.* has been identified as Bazianus. He has frequently been confused with Joannes Bassianus, better known as a commentator on Roman law but also the author of some canonical literature. Bazianus has been called the first *doctor in utroque jure.* To which of the two does the distinction belong? Both seem to have worked in both fields. Further confusion has arisen from the use of the siglum *Bar.* and the later and better known *Bartholomew of Brescia. Bazianus belongs to the school of glossators and is certainly before *Joannes Teutonicus. If, as has been affirmed, he added glosses to the *Summa* of *Joannes Faventinus, then his period of activity falls in the last half or even the last quarter of the 12th century. It is perhaps safe to say that he was attached to the school of Bologna.

See also DECRETISTS.

Bibliography: Kuttner, index *s.v.* Bazianus. Schulte 1:154–156.

[T. P. MCLAUGHLIN]

BAZIN, JOHN STEPHEN, third bishop of Vincennes, Ind.; b. Duerne, France, Oct. 15, 1796; d. Vincennes, April 23, 1848. He was educated in Lyons, France, and ordained there on July 22, 1822. Eight years later Bazin, then a seminary professor, volunteered for the American missions in the diocese of Bp. Michael Portier of Mobile, Ala. He left France Oct. 8, 1830, and arrived 2 months later in Mobile, where he was assigned to the staff of Spring Hill College, a diocesan college-seminary founded by Portier in May 1830. During the 17 years Bazin was associated with the college, he served first as professor of philosophy and theology, as well as procurator and superior of the seminary, and then as president (1832–36, 1839, 1842–44, 1846). He is credited with establishing the college on a permanent basis in 1847, when he negotiated the transfer of the properties and administration of the institution to the Jesuits.

As vicar-general of the diocese and pastor of the cathedral (1836–47), Bazin promoted pioneer building programs and furthered the organizational work involved in parochial and institutional expansion. In his pastoral apostolate he gained recognition as a preacher and was known for his charity toward the sick and the orphans. He built a new cathedral, using his own personal wealth in an effort to meet some of the construction costs. On April 3, 1847, he was appointed third bishop of Vincennes and was consecrated there Oct. 24, 1847, in the Cathedral of St. Francis Xavier, the first bishop to be consecrated in the see city. During his 6-month episcopacy, Bazin restored peace and order in the diocese, where relations between his predecessor, Celestine de la Hailandière, and many of the clergy and religious communities had deteriorated. The new bishop initiated settlement of jurisdictional and property ownership issues where such lay at the root of the difficulties with religious communities. He tried to provide a stronger educational institution for the training of diocesan seminarians by merging the financially unsound St. Gabriel College with St. Charles diocesan seminary, assuming the financial debts of the college himself. Bazin also laid plans for the establishment of a diocesan orphanage. His Lenten pastoral letter (1848) exhorted the laity to be sensitive to the vocational needs of the diocese and outlined for them and for the clergy practical plans for the encouragement of vocations to the priesthood. He contracted pneumonia and died on Easter Sunday.

Bibliography: M. C. SCHROEDER, *The Catholic Church in the Diocese of Vincennes, 1847–1877* (CUA StAmChHist 35; Washington 1946). M. KENNY, *Catholic Culture in Alabama: Centenary Story of Spring Hill College* (New York 1931). M. B.

BROWN, *History of the Sisters of Providence of Saint-Mary-of-the-Woods,* v.1 (New York 1949).

[M. C. SCHROEDER]

BAZIOTES, WILLIAM, American abstract surrealist painter; b. Pittsburgh, Pa., June 11, 1912; d. New York, June 6, 1963. After high school (Reading, Pa.), he worked for a local newspaper and then in a

William Baziotes, "Flight," oil on canvas, 1950, 20½ by 24½ inches.

stained-glass factory, where his interest in art was awakened. He went to New York in 1933, studied at the National Academy of Design for 3 years, and in 1939 became a convert, as he said, to abstractionism. He began to turn out half-Cubist, half-surrealist paintings, which won him his first one-man show at Peggy Guggenheim's *avant-garde* Art of This Century gallery in 1944 and which linked his name to the new movement later known as abstract expressionism. But Baziotes always applied his muted colors according to a carefully throught-out aesthetic plan that, he said, "has to do with human personality and the mysteries of life, not simply colors or abstract balances." He was called a mystic, and though he spent his last years in relative comfort—commuting between New York, where he taught at Hunter College, and Reading, where he painted during the summers—he never attained the fame he deserved until after his death.

Bibliography: D. HARE, "William Baziotes, 1912–1963," *Location* 1 (1964) 82–90. *Baziotes,* introd. L. ALLOWAY (New York 1965), Guggenheim Museum catalogue. **Illustration credit:** The Solomon R. Guggenheim Museum, Collection of Mrs. William Baziotes, New York.

[J. GERASSI]

"BEAT" WRITING

In his novel *Go* (1952), John Clellan Holmes first used the tag "beat generation." It remained, however, for Jack Kerouac's frenetic novel of a cross-country search for thrills ("kicks"), *On the Road* (1955), to spread the mystique of the "new bohemia" to a larger audience. Perhaps nothing did more to focus national attention upon the North Beach (San Francisco) and Greenwich Village (New York City) colonies than the widely publicized censorship dispute over Allen Ginsberg's poem, *Howl* (1957). Save for Kerouac's work and a novel *Her* (1960) by Lawrence Ferlinghetti, most of the "beat" literary output has been poetry. The work of Robert Duncan, Robert Stock, David Meltzer, Philip Lamantia, John Richardson, Michael McClure, Philip Whalen, Gregory Corso, and Ferlinghetti is prominent.

Social Dissent. The roots of beat writing are fixed in the peculiar social, cultural, and spiritual bedrock of the U.S. in the fifties. Eschewing the "art for art's sake" cult and the social reform or proletarian involvements of earlier avant-garde groups, the new bohemians rejected outright the entire social system. The structure was so inherently corrupt, they felt, that even social reformers unwittingly supported and encouraged the system. The "beat generation" was not so much a literary movement as a movement of social disaffiliation that produced some literature almost as a by-product.

Their dissent was so sharp that it meant an almost total withdrawal from life as it was lived, or from what Kenneth Rexroth called "the Social Lie." *The Holy Barbarians,* by Lawrence Lipton (1959), who calls his book "an exploitation as well as an explanation of the beats by a longtime professional beat," is a handy guide to beat attitudes, but Paul Goodman's sociological study, *Growing Up Absurd* (1956), despite its flaws, is perhaps a more valuable tool for understanding the spiritual roots of this movement. Goodman unwraps the glittering technological bundle of modern existence and shows it to be empty of meaning for the young. Ferlinghetti's poem, *A Parade Tirade,* expresses the total rejection of all the symbols and slogans of the established order. But Brother Antoninus, OP (William Everson), the man Rexroth has called "the most profoundly moving and durable of the poets of the San Francisco Renaissance," has written:

> The beat generation is perhaps the most significant example of a universal trend: the reemergence in the 20th century of the Dionysian spirit. Its mood of positive repudiation, as summed up in the phrase "I don't know, I don't care; and it doesn't make any difference," is counterbalanced by an opposite mood of negative affirmation: "Beat means beatitude."

Gary Snyder (*Riprap,* 1959; *Myths and Texts,* 1960), and Brother Antoninus seem to be nearly alone in their progression from the repudiation of the social lie to a religiously based affirmation. For Snyder the movement has been into *Zen Buddhism (many beats talked about Zen, but few could accept its discipline), and his translations from the Japanese are considered among his best work. It is not without meaning that Brother Antoninus's entrance into the Church was marked by immediate involvement in the *Catholic Worker movement. His *Crooked Lines of God* (1962) and *Hazards of Holiness* (1963) reveal him as a powerfully sensual religious poet.

Nightmare and New Trend. If "beat means beatitude," not many beats seemed to reflect that state. Total rejection of the system, of "organized religion," of family and work, left many with a total concentration upon self; and they searched for self-liberation, self-fulfillment, and self-expression in a cult of experience for the sake of heightened self-awareness. Sexual promiscuity and alcoholic abandon exacted their toll. The use of marijuana and hallucinogenic drugs spawned less than beatific side effects. More often than not beat meant beaten down rather than beatific. William Burroughs's *Naked Lunch* (1959) bears tragic witness to a world of nightmarish depravity that was the not illogical extension of beat nihilism. In the spring of 1960, how-

ever, others moved from mere negation to positive reaction. Various social problems and crises in the U.S. led to beat demands for the abolishment of capital punishment, for civil rights, civil liberties, and world peace.

Journalists created a stereotype of sandaled, sweat-shirted, bearded "beatniks" easy to scorn. Despite this, and despite the general critical abuse heaped upon the

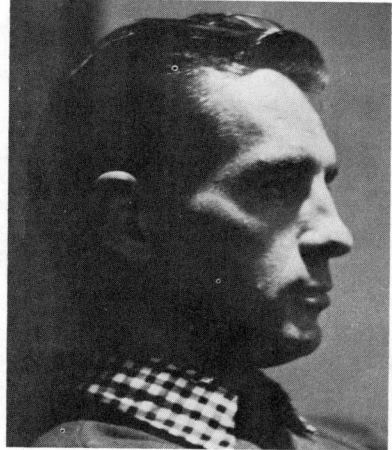

Jack Kerouac.

bulk of their literary efforts, the movement flourished. In a land where a book of poetry does well to sell 2,000 copies, *Howl* sold 70,000.

Reminder to Christians. In addition, the beats bore witness to transcendental values that many Christians neglect. By choosing poverty in the midst of a luxury-seeking society, they rebuked those who sold their souls for material gain. In a security-centered age, they elected material insecurity as they sought spiritual fulfillment. In a conformist age, they dared to dissent, accepting the scorn of society as part of the price of personal authenticity. They clung tenaciously to the primacy of love, even if they did not at all times distinguish eros from agape.

To criticize the beats for their errors would be easy, but their rejection of Christianity was a judgment passed upon the Christians they knew. If they sought fulfillment, love, joy, beatitude, in the wrong places and in the wrong ways, it might well have been because Christians had failed to show them the right.

Bibliography: D. ALLEN, ed., *The New American Poetry, 1945–1960* (New York 1960). G. FELDMAN and M. GARTENBERG, eds., *The Beat Generation and the Angry Young Men* (New York 1958). P. GOODMAN, *Growing up Absurd* (New York 1960). L. LIPTON, *The Holy Barbarians* (New York 1959). T. F. PARKINSON, ed., *A Casebook of the Beat* (New York 1961). **Illustration credit:** Keith W. Jennison.

[C. C. BARBEAU]

BEATA NOBIS GAUDIA, a hymn in iambic dimeter by an unknown author; attributed to *Hilary of Poitiers with very slight probability; and found quite generally throughout the Western liturgy since the 10th century. Sung at Lauds on the feast of Pentecost in the modern Roman Breviary, it relates poetically the two most important events of the feast, the descent of the Holy Spirit in tongues of fire, and the preaching of the Apostles with the gift of tongues to the community of Jerusalem, as described in Acts 2.2–4. A beautiful prayer follows, in which the Church requests that the gifts of the Holy Spirit be given to us also. Just as the time of the descent of the Holy Spirit upon the Apostles corresponded to the time of the Jewish jubilee, when debts were to be forgiven, so do we in this prayer beg forgiveness of our sins.

Bibliography: A. MIRRA, *Gl'inni del breviario romano* (Naples 1947). S. MATTEI, EncCatt 2:1090. AnalHymn 51:97–98. Szövérffy AnnLatHymn 1:348.

[J. J. GAVIGAN]

BEATIFIC VISION

The supernatural act of the created intellect by which the beatified angels and souls are united to God in a direct, intuitive, and clear knowledge of the Triune God as He is in Himself. This direct, intuitive, intellectual vision of God, with the perfection of charity necessarily accompanying it, is the consummation of the divine indwelling in the sanctified spirit or soul, for by this vision the blessed are brought to fruition in such a union with God in knowledge and love that they share forever in God's own happiness (*see* GOD, INTUITION OF).

Faith seeks understanding of the beatific vision in terms of its possibility, its existence, its nature, its characteristics, and its relation to the other mysteries of salvation revealed by God. This article approaches the mystery under each of these facets.

POSSIBILITY OF THE BEATIFIC VISION

When the question arises as to the possibility of the beatific vision, a distinction must be made between the natural possibility of an intuitive vision of God by intellectual creatures and the supernatural possibility of such a vision.

Impossibility on the Natural Level. No creature can by its own natural powers alone attain to the intuitive vision of God. Sacred Scripture shows that the only knowledge of God possible to the natural powers of man is that drawn from creatures and is indirect, analogous knowledge (Wis 13.1–9; Rom 1.18–21). Intuitive knowledge of God as He is in Himself is proper only to the Blessed Trinity (Jn 1.18; 6.46; Mt 11.27; 1 Cor 2.11), and God is essentially invisible (1 Tm 1.17), dwelling in light inaccessible to man (1 Tm 6.16; Jn 1.18). Moreover, the intuitive vision of God promised to man after death is expressly said to be linked to the order of grace (1 Jn 3.2; Jn 17.2–3; Rom 6.23).

The Church has insisted in its ordinary and in its solemn magisterium that the vision of God transcends the natural power of man. Eunomius, the leader of one of the Semi-Arian sects of the 4th century A.D., taught that man by his own natural intellectual power can come to a comprehension of the divine essence as it is in itself. In their refutation of Eunomius, St. Basil the Great [*Eun.* 1.4; 12.14 (PG 49:540, 544)] and St. Gregory of Nyssa (*Eun.* 12, PG 45:944; *Mort.*, PG 46:513; *V. Mos.*, PG 44:317) emphasized the eminently supernatural character of the intuitive vision of God and the incomprehensibility of God to any creature. The Council of *Vienne (A.D. 1311–12) condemned the teaching of the *Beguines and the Beghards that the soul does not need the light of glory to elevate it to the vision of God but is able to attain to this happiness by its own powers (Denz 894, 895). N. *Malebranche (1638–1715) and V. *Gioberti (1801–52) both eliminated the supernatural character of the

intuitive vision of God in their teaching that the first act of the intelligence is a natural intuition of being, which is so identified with God that the created intelligence knows God Himself intuitively and properly as object. Their philosophical-religious system, known as *ontologism, was condemned by a decree of the Holy Office in 1861 (Denz 2841–47). In their solemn definitions of the existence of the beatific vision, Pope Benedict XII and the Council of Florence both teach that only those who have been reborn supernaturally in grace see God after death (Denz 1000–02, 1304–06).

St. Thomas Aquinas points up the reason why the intuitive knowledge of God as He is in Himself is impossible on the natural level for any creature in the following argument. The knowledge of every knower is proportioned to the mode of being of the knower. Now God alone is self-subsistent being. Therefore to know self-subsistent being is natural only to the divine intellect. On the other hand, since neither angels nor men are self-subsistent beings, their created intellects cannot know God as He is in Himself by their natural powers (see ST 1a, 12.4; 1a, 64.1 ad 2; 1a2ae, 5.5; *In 2 sent.* 4.1.1; 23.2.1; *In 4 sent.* 49.2.6; *C. gent.* 3.49, 52; *De ver.* 8.3; *De anim.* 17 ad 10; *In epist. 1 ad Tim.* 6 lect. 3).

Possibility on the Supernatural Level. The beatific vision is strictly supernatural in every aspect. Therefore, the very concept of the beatific vision so transcends the natural cognitive power of any created intellect that it can be known only through divine revelation, and after the existence of such vision has been revealed, its nature still remains impenetrable by the mind of man in this life, even by the mind enlightened by faith. Further, the beatific vision is a wholly gratuitous gift from God in no way demanded by the natural requirements of a created nature. Once God has revealed the mystery of the beatific vision as man's ultimate end, however, reason illumined by faith can contemplate the fittingness of such a vision in terms of man's intellectual openness to truth in general and of the human desire to see God.

Obediential Potency. The supernatural elevation of the intellects of men to the intuitive vision of God involves no contradiction, for the proper object of the created intellect is the intelligible. A being is intelligible, however, insofar as it is in act. Therefore, God, who is *pure act, is in Himself infinitely intelligible. That God is unknowable as He is in Himself to created intellects that do not have the light of glory is because the very perfection of His intelligibility is blinding to the unaided intellectual faculty of angel or man. Because this same intellectual power is spiritual, however, and so able mentally to abstract the form from the concrete existent and to consider the concrete form and its existence in abstraction, this same created intellect is open to being elevated by divine grace to the contemplation of God, who is subsisting existence. This is often referred to as an obediential potency for the beatific vision. That such a potency be actuated, however, depends entirely upon the divine omnipotence and initiative, and is above the natural exigency or active potency of any creature (see St. Thomas Aquinas, ST 1a, 12.1; 12.4 ad 3; 85.1; 86.2; 87.3; 1a2ae, 3.8; 5.1; 2a2ae, 8.1; *In 4 sent.* 46.2.1; *C. gent.* 3.51, 54, 57; *De ver.* 8.1; *Comp. theol.* 104; *In Mt.* 5.2; *In Joann.* 1.2).

Nature and Grace. The fittingness of the beatific vision as evidenced by man's natural desire to see God is a very delicate question because it concerns the relation between the natural and the supernatural. Michel de Bay (*Baius) and the Jansenists claimed that in the state of original justice man's natural desire of the vision of God was efficacious in such a way that the beatific vision was due to human nature and natural for man (see JANSENISM). This erroneous position was condemned by Pope St. Pius V in 1567 (Denz 1903–05, 1921, 1923, 1926; see EX OMNIBUS AFFLICTIONIBUS) and Gregory XIII in 1580. Implicit in these papal condemnations is the affirmation of the Church's teaching that grace and its consummation in the beatific vision are always strictly supernatural and never due to the natural exigencies of any created nature.

St. Thomas Aquinas uses the argument of man's natural desire for the vision of God in support of the possibility of the beatific vision many times in his theological writings, but always in the context of the divine revelation that man is ordered to the beatific vision as his ultimate end, and that this end, which is supernatural to man in every way, is a matter of faith (see ST 1a, 12.1, 4–6; 38.1; 43.3–4, 6; 1a2ae, 5.5–6, 7 ad 3; 62.1–3; 63.3; 109.5; 110.1; 112.1–3; 114.2, 5; 2a2ae, 6.1; 24.2–3; *C. gent.* 3.50–54; *Comp. theol.* 104–106; *In Mt.* 5.2; *In epist. 1 ad Cor.* 13 lect. 4; *In epist. ad Rom.* 5 lect. 1; *In epist. ad Heb.* 13 lect. 3). St. Thomas analyzes the God-given ultimate end of man in ST 1a2ae, 1–5. In question 2, he approaches the problem of perfect happiness in terms of man's will, which necessarily desires happiness and seeks that which will perfect man and bring him happiness, although many err in regard to that in which their perfect happiness will be found. He shows that because the will is open to universal good, not all particular limited goods together will satisfy man's desires. Man can find perfect happiness only in God, who is infinite Goodness, for infinite goodness alone will so satisfy man's desire for good that nothing more can be desired. In question 3, St. Thomas considers happiness in terms of that human operation by which man can attain God. Although the good that alone can satisfy all man's desires will be the uncreated goodness of God, still man's attainment of that good must be an operation of man if it is to be his happiness. Since God is a spirit, however, this operation can only be that of one of man's two spiritual faculties—intellect or will. The will is a blind faculty that never takes possession of the good it desires directly, but does so through some other faculty and then rests in the enjoyment of the good attained. Therefore, the will takes possession of infinite Goodness through an act of the intellect, and it will be in this act of the intellect that happiness will be found essentially. If man is to be perfectly happy, this act of the intellect must be the contemplation of the divine essence itself, for only such contemplation will satisfy man's desire to come to the knowledge of the first cause of the created effects that cause wonder in him. God, the creator of man, would not put in man a natural desire that could in no way be fulfilled. Without the contemplation of the divine essence, however, man would be left with an unfulfilled desire. St. Thomas is always insistent, nevertheless, that this desire can be fulfilled only by a gratuitous, supernatural elevation of man to the order of grace and glory. According to St. Thomas, the very existence of the beatific vision as man's ultimate end can be known only through divine revelation and must be believed by divine faith. His argument from the natural desire to see God is not given as proof of the existence of the beatific vision, but as an argument from reason to indicate the harmony existing between nature and supernature in the providence of that God who is the author of both the natural and the supernatural orders. Man's created openness to the supernatural gift of the vision of God involves no contradiction.

The meaning of this natural desire for the vision of God has been much debated. Some (e.g., Ferrariensis, D. Báñez, John of St. Thomas, and many modern Thomists) speak of a conscious, elicited desire, which is conditional and ineffective without grace. Others (e.g., Domingo de Soto, John Duns Scotus, Durandus, Gregory of Valencia, H. Noris, G. Berti, and an increasing number of moderns among Thomists) consider this desire to be an innate, natural, but inefficacious desire that is reducible to the desire for happiness, but without a realization that happiness will be found only in the vision of God; hence, no conscious desire for such a vision. The second opinion would seem to be closer to the truth.

EXISTENCE OF THE BEATIFIC VISION

Only through divine supernatural revelation could man know that he is ordained to the intuitive vision of God in heaven.

Vision of God in the Old Testament. "To see" and "to know" in Biblical terminology often express a relation of nearness to someone in which there is an experience of the other person's presence. Because the eye is the principal instrument of knowing, the theme of vision is used to express the ineffable experience of the presence of the hidden God in a *theophany. In the Old Testament one reads that Jacob saw God (Gn 32.31) and Moses and the 70 elders beheld the God of Israel (Ex 24.10–11; Nm 12.8; Dt 34.10). Likewise it is asserted that Isaia "saw the Lord" (Is 6.1). In every instance, however, the context indicates that a theophany is meant, not an intuitive vision of the divine essence. To Moses' plea of "Do let me see your glory," Yahweh answered "I will make all my beauty pass before you . . . but my face you cannot see, for no man sees me and still lives" (Ex 33.18–20). Both the Old and the New Testaments teach that man cannot see God in this life (Ex 33.20; Jgs 6.22–23; 13.22; Is 6.5; Jn 1.18; 5.37; 6.46; 1 Jn 4.12; 2 Cor 5.7).

Although the theme of happiness goes through the whole of Biblical revelation, from paradise lost to paradise regained, nowhere in the Old Testament is there an explicit revelation that man's ultimate happiness will be found in an intuitive vision of God. Nevertheless, two positive aspects are to be noted in Israel's expectation of the happiness reserved for those who are faithful to Yahweh. In the first place, this happiness will be real, involving the whole man. Second, this happiness will be found not only in the possession of terrestrial goods in a transfigured earth, but most of all in a life lived in the divine presence [see Ps 15(16).7–11; 16(17).15; 35(36).9–10; 48(49).16; 72(73).23–28; Is 2.1–5; 25.1–9; 35.1–10; 40.1–11; 60.1–22; Jer 31.31–40; Ez 36.26–36; Os 2.20–25; Wis 4.4–17; 5.1–16].

In the measure that the messianic expectation develops, Israel desires to see the manifestation of God that brings salvation (see, e.g., Is 40.5; 52.10b; Mal 3.2), but in these texts one still has only the signs of

God's presence. Intimations were given, however, that man was destined for a union with God that would transcend the happiness the just Israelite found in the presence of God in His temple in Jerusalem. Psalms 15(16) and 72(73) especially pose the problem of the permanence of the joy with Yahweh and voice the hope of being always in the divine presence. Ps 15(16).11 would seem to indicate that one comes to the face of God in order to enjoy God alone. The faith of Israel in eternal life with God beyond the grave is expressed in Wis 4.7–17; 5.1–16; Dn 12.13; 2 Mc 7.9, 11, 14, 23, 36, and Psalms 15(16) and 72(73), but the revelation that the just man's happiness would be found in the intuitive vision of God was not given until the Word became incarnate.

Vision of God in the New Testament. When the Son of God, who is Himself the revelation of the Father (see Jn 1.18; 8.19; 10.30, 38; 12.45; 14.7, 9, 11; Col 1.15), became for men "God-given wisdom, and justice, and sanctification, and redemption" (1 Cor 1.30), He brought the good news that all who receive Him in faith and love become the sons of God (Jn 1.12–13; 3.5; Rom 8.15–17; Gal 4.3–7; 1 Jn 3.1–2; 4.15). The revelation of the mystery of the beatific vision is an intrinsic part of this fuller revelation of the meaning of divine adopted sonship; for all who participate in the divine nature will share in the divine inheritance, which is the eternal life of the beatific vision (2 Pt 1.4; Rom 8.15–17; Eph 1.3–14; 1 Cor 13.12; 1 Jn 3.2).

Christ summed up His mission as the giving of everlasting life to all whom the Father had given to Him (Jn 17.2) and then epitomized the meaning of everlasting life with: "Now this is everlasting life, that they know thee, the only true God, and him whom thou hast sent, Jesus Christ" (Jn 17.3). That this knowing is the intuitive vision of God as He is in Himself is clearly expressed by St. Paul in the climax of his hymn to charity: "We see now through a mirror in an obscure manner, but then face to face. Now I know in part, but then I shall know even as I have been known" (1 Cor 13.12). St. Paul distinguishes two phases in the Christian economy of salvation, marked by the antithesis between "now" and "then." During this life, which is likened to a time of childhood (1 Cor 13.11), the Christian knows God only in part, obscurely, as in a mirror. When the Christian attains to adulthood in adopted sonship, however, he will know God as God knows him; that is, he will know God in His very being albeit not so much as God is knowable. The Apostle further clarifies this knowledge of God by contrasting the obscure, indirect vision in the mirror of his time with the clear vision that comes when the knower is "face to face" with the known. This deliberate juxtaposition of a knowing in part with a knowing as God knows, and of an indirect vision of God through His created manifestations as in a mirror with a direct "face to face" vision through no created medium, emphasizes the difference between "face to face" vision in 1 Cor 13.12 and the intimacy of Moses with God in Ex 33.11; Nm 12.8, which was not the vision of God (Ex 33.20). In 1 Cor 13.12 St. Paul can mean only the clear intuitive vision of the divine essence [cf. St. Augustine, *In evang. Ioh.* 34.9; 101.5 (CorpChrist 36:315–316, 592–593); St. Ambrose, *De bono mortis* 11.49 (PL 14:562–563); St. Thomas

Aquinas, *In epist. 1 ad Cor.* 13 lect. 4; see also C. Spicq, *Agapè* . . . 2:94–107].

Charity, which leads to the vision of God, "never fails," so that in the end there will remain charity (v. 8) and the vision of God (v. 12). This bond between charity and the beatific vision is rooted in the mystery of divine adopted sonship, for the charity of God is poured forth into the hearts of His adopted sons by the Holy Spirit, who is given to them (Rom 5.5). Affective love for God becomes effective, however, only in the love of neighbor (cf. Mt 25.31–40; Jn 13.34–35; 1 Cor 13.4–7; 1 Jn 4.7–21). Through love of God in neighbor, the Christian is gradually assimilated to Christ (2 Cor 3.18; Eph 2.1–10; 5.1–2; Phil 2.5–11) and is prepared for the perfection of sonship in the union of vision (1 Jn 3.2).

Writing of the beatific vision, St. Augustine, St. Thomas Aquinas, and many modern exegetes intertwine Jn 17.3; 1 Cor 13.12; Mt 5.8; 1 Jn 3.2–3; Heb 12.14; Mt 18.10–11; and Ap 22.4 [see, e.g., St. Augustine, *In evang. Ioh.* 34.9; 53.12; 101.5; 111.3 (CorpChrist 36:315–316, 457–458, 593, 630–631); *Serm. de Vet. Test.* 38.3 (CorpChrist 41:478); *In psalm.* 84.9.39–85; 97.3 (CorpChrist 39:1168, 1373–74); St. Thomas Aquinas, *In Mt.* 5.2; *In Ioann.* 17.1.3; A. Gelin, " 'Voir Dieu' dans l'Ancien Testament," BiblVieChr 23 (1958) 11–12; A. George, "Heureux les coeurs purs! Ils verront Dieu!" *ibid.* 13 (1956) 78; L. Pirot, DBSuppl 1:937; C. Spicq, *Agapè* . . . 2:103; *La Sainte Bible,* see cross refs. for 1 Cor 13.12; 1 Jn 3.2; and Heb 12.14].

In His discourse at the Last Supper, Christ spoke of the mystery of the Trinity and of the divine indwelling in those who accept Him in faith and in love (John ch. 14–17). He promised that "he who loves me will be loved by my Father and I will love him and manifest myself to him" (Jn 14.21b). But the manifestation of the Son is also the manifestation of the Father, for to Philip's plea that He show them the Father, Christ replied: ". . . he who sees me sees also the Father" (Jn 14.8–9), for "I am in the Father and the Father in me" (Jn 14.10). The explicit revelation of the beatific vision in "Beloved, now we are the children of God, and it has not yet appeared what we shall be. We know that when he appears, we shall be like to him, for we shall see him just as he is" (1 Jn 3.2) is best understood in the context of this revelation of the mystery of the Trinity and of the divine indwelling in those who are made sons of God in and through the Son. Exegetes differ as to whether the Father or the Son is meant in "when he appears," but the revelation of the vision of God remains untouched by their difference. St. Augustine, who seems to consider this a reference to the appearance of the Father, insists that it also promises a vision of the Son in His divinity, because when "the one God is seen, the Trinity is seen—the Father and the Son and the Holy Spirit. . . . There is no difference between the vision of the Son and the vision of the Father" (cf. *In psalm.* 84.9.55–85, CorpChrist 39:1168–69; *Trin* 1.13.28, PL 42:840–841). Some modern exegetes are of the opinion that "when he appears" refers to the Son. Again, the revelation of the beatific vision remains the same, for the addition of the words "we shall be *like him, for* we shall see him *just as he is*" indicates that only those who are like him in divine sonship will see Him as He is. At least at the last judgment all the damned will see Christ in His glorious humanity. The

"The Beatific Vision," miniature in the 15th-century "Rohan Hours," preserved in the Biblio-thèque Nationale, Paris (MS lat. 9471, fol. 143v).

vision promised in 1 Jn 3.2, therefore, is that of His God-head, for it is reserved to those who are like Him in His divinity. Those who see Him in His divinity, however, see the Father and the Holy Spirit, too, for they see God.

Commenting on the sixth beatitude, "Blessed are the clean of heart, for they shall see God" (Mt 5.8), L. Pirot insists that this beatitude refers literally to the "face to face" vision of God. Christ beatifies interior purity. In Hebrew psychology the heart is the seat of thoughts, of emotions, of actions. This cleanness of heart, therefore, connotes a total submission to God in love and in obedience to His law (Pirot, 936). A. George refers to the sixth beatitude as "a summit of revelation" that goes further than all the other beati-tudes, for this one announces the Ineffable Presence, the Supreme *Good, as the reward of those who are faithful sons of God [78; cf. St. Aug., *Civ.* 20.21.44–50 (CorpChrist 48:737); *In psalm.* 84.9.74–85; 85.21.5–57 (CorpChrist 39:1168–69, 1193–94); St. Thomas Aquinas, *In Mt.* 5.2].

Teaching of the Church. The intuitive and beatifying vision of God already enjoyed by the Church triumphant is an essential part of the faith and of the eschatological hope of the Church militant [see Vatican Council II, *Dogmatic Constitution on the Church* 48–51; ActApS 57 (1965) 53–58]. In its ordinary and in its solemn magisterium, the Church proposes the mystery of the beatific vision as the revealed ultimate end of man, to be believed by supernatural faith.

Ordinary Magisterium. The best witnesses to the teaching of the ordinary magisterium of the Church in regard to the beatific vision will be found in the writings of the Fathers, who were themselves a part of the Apostolic hierarchy and so of the magisterium. For St. Ignatius of Antioch, the hope of the vision of Christ in His divinity was the incentive for a life given in martyrdom (Rom. 6.2; PG 5:692). St. Theophilus of Antioch wrote that "one day God will be contemplated face to face in glory" (*Autol.* 1.7; PG 5:1036). Although St. Irenaeus of Lyons erred in thinking the beatific vision is not given to the just until their resurrection, still he did teach that eternal life comes to each one from the act of seeing God (*Haer.* 4.20.4–7; PG 7:1035–37). St. Hilary of Poitiers affirms that by the gift of God all the clean of heart will see God (*In psalm.* 118.38; PL 9:555). St. Basil the Great speaks of a gradual perfecting and strengthening of the mind supernaturally so that the day will come when it will approach the unveiled divinity itself, and says "our mind will be elevated and quickened to the height of beatitude when it sees the oneness of the Word" (*Epist.* 8.7; PG 32:257–259). In his funeral oration for his sister Gorgonia, St. Gregory of Nazianzus rejoices that she sees the vision of glory and the splendor of the most Holy Trinity, which she contemplates and possesses—"the whole of it by the whole mind and shining on your soul with the whole light of divinity" (*Or.* 8.23; PG 35:816). In his funeral oration for St. Basil, St. Gregory looks forward to the day when "together we may behold in greater purity and fullness the holy and blessed Trinity," which he now knows incompletely through images (*Or.* 43.82; PG 36:604–605).

St. John Chrysostom in his first letter to Theodore writes that if Peter was so enraptured in the vision of Christ's glorious humanity, "what will happen when the full reality is presented . . . and it is permitted us to look upon the king Himself, no longer in an obscure manner, nor through a mirror, but face to face; no longer by faith, but by sight" (*Thdr.* 1.11; PG 47:292). St. Ambrose teaches that the just "have this as reward that they see the face of God and that Light which enlightens every man" (*De bono mortis* 2; PL 14:562–563). Pope St. Leo the Great preached that in the Transfiguration the Apostles saw the royal splendor that belongs in a special way to the nature of Christ's assumed manhood, but while they were in the flesh "they could not look upon and see the ineffable and inaccessible vision of the divinity itself, which is reserved for the eternal life of the clean of heart" (*Serm.* 51.2; PL 54:311). Pope St. Gregory the Great writes:

We ought to mention that there were some who have held that even in the region of blessedness God is beheld in His glory, but is not seen in His nature. These persons are deceived by the very lack of logic in their investigations, for in that simple and unchangeable essence, glory is not one thing and nature another. God's nature is itself His glory, and His glory is itself His nature. Because one day the Wisdom of God would show itself to those who love Him, He Himself promises the vision of His essence when He says: "He who loves me will be loved of my Father, and I will love him and will manifest myself to him" (Jn 14.21). It is as if He said clearly: "You who perceive me in your nature shall yet see me in my own." He says again: "Blessed are the clean of heart, for they shall see God" (Mt 5.8). Hence Paul says: "We see now through a mirror, but then face to face. Now I know in part, but then I shall know even as I have been known" (I Cor 13.12). [*Moralia* 18.54.90; PL 76:93–94.]

The book or sermon written by St. Augustine in which he did not mention the beatific vision is the exception, for the saint was absorbed in the mystery of the Trinity and on fire with the desire to contemplate God face to face. St. Augustine teaches that the reward of the just, after their purification, is the clear, intuitive, intellectual vision of the Triune God. By this vision they are made supremely happy forever. Although there are degrees in formal beatitude dependent upon the merits of the just, still all are filled with happiness and all see God as He is, even though none know Him as much as He is knowable [see, e.g., *In evang. Ioh.* 34.7–8; 53.12; 76.1–4 (CorpChrist 36:314–315, 457–458, 517–519); *Epist.* 92.4–6 (PL 33:319–320); *Epist.* 147.8.20; 9.21; 23.51 (PL 33:605, 606, 620); *Serm.* 4.4–6; 23.16–18; 38.3 (CorpChrist 41:21–23, 318–319, 477–478); *De videndo Deo* 15.37 (PL 33:612); *Trin.* 1.8.16–18; 1.13.28; 14.17–19.23–25 (PL 42:831–832, 840–841, 1054–56); *Civ.* 20.21.40–50; 21.24.125–152; 22.29.1–210; 22.30.99–152 (CorpChrist 48:737, 792, 856–862, 864–866); *In psalm.* 75.5.32–42; 78.8.52–80; 85.21.1–59; 97.3.15–35 (CorpChrist 39:1040–41, 1153–54, 1193–94, 1373–74); *In psalm.* 104.3.1–40; 109.12.20–78; 123.2.12–47; 139.18.1–44 (CorpChrist 40:1536–37, 1611–13, 1825–26, 2024–25)].

Solemn Magisterium. Implicitly the Council of Vienne taught the existence of the beatific vision in its insistence on the necessity of the light of glory for that vision (Denz 895). The first definition of the existence and nature of the beatific vision was occasioned by a dispute regarding the immediacy or the delay of the beatific vision for the souls of the just after death. Although the Church's faith in the existence of the beatific vision never wavered, an initial concentration upon the Parousia and the glorious resurrection of the elect tended for a time to obscure the realization of the glorification of the individual saint before the corporate triumph in Christ at the Last Judgment. The clear understanding that the vision of God is given at once to the soul that dies in grace and has been purified, matured only gradually. By the 14th century, however, the immediacy of the beatific vision for the just after death was the common teaching of the Church. Therefore, when in his advanced old age Pope John XXII espoused in several sermons St. Bernard's opinion that the souls of the just must wait until the final judgment to see God, a hot dispute ensued between certain Franciscans who supported the Pope's opinion and the Dominicans who defended the traditional position. In the conclusion of his second sermon, Pope John XXII clearly indicated he was speaking as a private theologian, however, and stated that he was open to correction in the matter. He himself earlier, in the bull of canonization of Louis d'Anjou (1317), had said that the soul of Louis had entered heaven to contemplate his God face to face. On his deathbed in 1334, the Pope declared it his opinion that the souls of the just when purified see God and the divine essence face to face so far as the state and condition of a separated soul allows this.

The arguments continued after his death, however, and so, for the peace of mind of the faithful, his successor, Pope Benedict XII, settled the question once for all in the constitution *Benedictus Deus,* issued on Jan. 29, 1336. In the *Benedictus Deus,* Pope Benedict XII "defines by apostolic authority and with a constitution that shall be valid forever" that the souls of all the saints who departed this world before the Passion of Our Lord Jesus Christ, and the souls of all the saints who die after they have received the sacred Baptism of Christ and have been purified, should they need such purification,

directly after their death and this purification in those needing such purification, even before the resumption of their bodies and the general judgment, after the Ascension of Our Lord and Savior Jesus Christ into heaven, have been, are, and will be in heaven, in the kingdom of heaven and the heavenly paradise, together with Christ . . . and that after the Passion and death of Our Lord Jesus Christ they have beheld and do behold the divine essence with intuitive and face-to-face vision, with no creature mediating in the manner of object seen, but the divine essence immediately showing itself to them without covering, clearly and openly; and that when they see in this way they have full enjoyment of that same divine essence. From this vision and enjoyment the souls of those who have already departed are truly blessed and have eternal life and rest; and the souls of those who will depart hereafter will also see that same divine essence and will have full enjoyment of it before the general judgment. This vision and this fruition of the divine essence do away with the acts of faith and hope in these souls insofar as faith and hope are theological virtues in the strict sense; and after this intuitive face-to-face vision and enjoyment has begun or begins to exist in these souls, the same vision and fruition exists continuously and will continue up to the last judgment and from then on through eternity. [Denz 1000, 1001.]

In its *Decree for the Greeks,* the bull *Laetentur coeli,* July 6, 1439, the Council of Florence added something to the clarity of the preceding definition in defining that

the souls of those who after the reception of Baptism have incurred no stain of sin at all, and also those souls which after the contraction of sin have been purged, whether in their bodies or when delivered of these same bodies . . . are immediately received into heaven and see clearly the one and Triune God, just as He is, yet one more perfectly than another, in proportion to the diversity of merits. [Denz 1305.]

NATURE OF THE BEATIFIC VISION

A fruitful doctrinal study of the beatific vision requires that the supernatural character of this vision be emphasized, for the object of the beatific vision is God, the holy and undivided Trinity. Nevertheless, elevated and strengthened by the light of faith, reason is able to penetrate the mystery to some extent from the analogy of sensible and intellectual vision and from the relationship of the beatific vision to the other mysteries of the faith that have been revealed.

The beatific vision is revealed to men as a kind of seeing that is at the same time a supernatural knowing (1 Cor 13.12; 1 Jn 3.2). From the analogy of natural vision, both sensible and intellectual, some light is thrown on the act of vision by which the blessed see God. The vision given by eyesight is an act that, by the activity of the seer and without transforming the seer into the colored object he sees, effects in the seer an actualizing of a color that has its real existence in an external object. A necessary condition for the production of this act is the presence of light and its common action upon the colored object and upon the sense of vision. In fact, light is required for the reception of visual sensation and for the unity of the image produced in the act of seeing. Now the act of intellectual perception of truth is called vision by an analogy with bodily vision. Intellectual perception of truth is an act that, by the activity of the knower and without transforming the knower into the being that he knows, effects in the knower an actualizing intentionally of an essence that has its real existence in an external object. As light is necessary in bodily vision, so also something analogous to light is required in intellectual vision, namely, the "light of truth," which must exist and act not only in the mind but also in the object that the mind knows. Therefore, intellectual vision has a threefold requirement: (1) the intelligibility of that which is known; (2) the power of knowing in the knower; and (3) a union between the knower and the known. How are these three requirements fulfilled in the beatific vision?

Intelligibility of That Which is Known. God, who is pure act, first truth in being, is most intelligible in Himself and so infinitely knowable. That God is unknowable as He is in Himself to created intellects on the natural level is because of the very excess of His intelligibility, which is blinding to the unaided intellectual power of angel or man.

Power of Knowing in the Knower. The intellectual power of the rational creature is a participated likeness of Him who is the first intellect (ST 1a, 12.2). The connatural object of this created power of intellectual vision, however, is not the divine essence, but created essences; hence, by its own unaided power neither the angelic nor the human intellect could ever see the divine essence. For the vision of God, the created intellect must be elevated and strengthened by a created supernatural gift, the light of glory. The light of glory, which is a new perfection of the intellect itself, replaces the light of faith and gives the created intellect a higher supernatural participation in the Divine Light. St. Thomas does not hesitate to say that by the light of glory the blessed are made deiform (ST 1a, 12.5). Not that the light of glory makes the essence of God intelligible, for He is always infinitely knowable, but rather this light perfects the created intellect for the act of vision in much the same way that a habit perfects a power for its most perfect act. Therefore, the light of glory is in no way a medium in which God is seen but rather one by which He is seen; and such a medium does not take away the immediate vision of God (cf. ST 1a, 12.5; *C. gent.* 3.53).

Union between the Knower and the Known. That God, who is the object known, be in the knower by His essence so that God becomes one with the knower is impossible, for even though God is present most intimately by His power, presence, and essence to all creatures, no creature can ever be so elevated as to be absorbed into the divine essence. Nor can God be known intuitively as He is in Himself by means of a created idea of God that is united with the mind of the beatified making it to know, for no created idea can be the uncreated as He is in Himself, or express Him as He is in Himself. Yet, God has revealed and the Church has defined that the just see God as He is in Himself. St. Thomas points out that there is a mode of union by way of likeness that makes possible a union between God and the created intellect, namely, that in which one and the same being is the principle of the power of knowing and is also the object known. This mode of union is uniquely possible in the vision of God, for God is the author of the intellectual power of man, and He is the object of vision present to the intellect in the beatific vision. In the beatific vision the divine essence is united with the created intellect in such a way that the act of vision terminates not in any created form, but in the divine essence itself. From this union of the divine essence and the supernaturalized intellect of the blessed one thing is understood, and that one thing is God as He is in Himself. St. Thomas explains the nature of this immediate union between God and the created intellect thus: "The divine essence is existence itself. Hence as other intelligible forms, which are not their own existence, are united to the intellect according to a kind of mental existence by which they inform the intellect and make it in act, so the divine essence is united to the created intellect as the object actually understood, by Itself making the intellect actually understanding" (ST 1a, 12.2 ad 3). This is what M. De la Taille, SJ, most aptly called created actuation by Uncreated Act (cf. M. De la Taille, *The Hypostatic Union and Created Actuation by Uncreated Act* 30–33). In the beatific vision God is the quasi form of the act of vision, not as the act informing the human intellect, but rather as the Act terminating the act of the intellect (cf. ST 1a, 12.5; *Comp. theol.* 105; *De ver.* 8.1; ST 3a, suppl., 92.1 ad 8; also De la Taille, *op. cit.*, and K. Rahner, "Some Implications of the Scholastic Concept of Uncreated Grace" 325–346). For this act of vision the creature must be assimilated supernaturally to the Triune God in essence and in operation. In His very gift of Himself to His creature God brings about that assimilation if there is no resistance to Him. In order that His rational creatures attain Him in the beatific vision, God perfects the essence of the soul through the entitative habit of habitual sanctifying *grace, which is a created participation in the divine nature that makes its possessor an adopted son of God and a member of the Divine Family. Likewise God elevates the spiritual faculties of intellect and will so that the rational creature may know and love God as He knows and loves Himself. The intellect is perfected by the light of glory, which is simultaneously the created effect of the Uncreated actuation of the intellect by the Object known and the disposition for the act of knowing the Uncreated. The will is perfected for the concomitant act of fruition by infused charity, which abides in heaven in one unending act of love of God. Although all the blessed know God as He is, not any know Him as much as He is knowable. The greater the love in the creature, the greater its participation in the light of glory; and the greater its participation in the light of glory, the greater the perfection of its act of

vision (Council of Florence, Denz 1305; St. Thomas Aquinas, ST 1a, 12.6, 1a2ae, 5.2).

In the vision of God the elect participate in a finite way in God's own knowledge. For example, the mysteries of the faith are now known not by faith but by vision, albeit this clear knowledge by vision is never exhaustive of the mystery. In the beatific vision each of the blessed also perceives the exact nature of the divine dispensation pertaining to his own salvation and perfection. The saints in heaven know their dear ones in God even more perfectly than they have or will know them in themselves, and in their vision of God the blessed continue to know and to interest themselves in all that concerns the Church and their dear ones on earth. The blessed also know in the vision of God all that He has created that is of interest to them. Everything other than God as He is in Himself, however, everything that involves the relationship of a creature to God is only secondarily the object of the beatific vision. Man's ultimate end consists primarily in God Himself, and man's beatitude will be in the immediate vision of God and the joy concomitant with the personal possession in vision and love of the Triune God, whose nature is identical with the intelligibility of Himself and with the intellection of Himself.

CHARACTERISTICS OF THE BEATIFIC VISION

Happiness is found not only in the act by which the soul takes possession of God in knowing Him as it is known by Him, but also in all the concomitant properties that are consequent upon that act of vision. (1) Comprehension is the first of these consequences of the act of vision—comprehension in the sense of attaining God, to repose in His presence, not in the sense of knowing Him as much as He is knowable, which is possible only to God Himself (ST 1a2ae, 4.3). (2) The beatific vision causes perfect joy to the soul, which now rests in the beloved in an unending act of perfect charity (ST 1a2ae, 4.1, 2; 2a2ae, 28.1, 3). (3) The beatific vision brings sinlessness as one of its effects, for since final happiness consists in an intellectual vision of Him who is infinite truth and beauty, and the will then reposes through that act in the possession of infinite goodness, it is psychologically impossible for the will to turn from its adequate object to a created good preferred to the uncreated good now possessed (ST 1a2ae, 4.4). (4) God has promised and the Church has defined that the beatific vision will last forever. Nothing less than eternal beatitude would be perfect beatitude (ST 1a2ae, 5.4). (5) The total person is beatified. Therefore, although it is the soul that alone can take possession of God, since God is a spirit, still the beatified soul will be substantially united to the body after the resurrection, and the joy of the soul will overflow into the body (ST 1a2ae, 4.6).

BEATIFIC VISION AND OTHER MYSTERIES OF FAITH

The mystery of the beatific vision is related to that of grace, for the intrinsic supernaturality of grace is pointed up by its term, the altogether supernatural act of knowing God as He is in Himself. But it is the Triune God who is known in this way; hence the mystery of the beatific vision is intrinsically related to the mystery of the Trinity and of the divine *indwelling in the rational creature. Light is thrown on the mystery of the beatific vision by the mystery of the *Incarnation and

*Redemption, for it is in and by the Son that men become sons of God; they are brought to the consummation of adopted sonship by sharing in the Son's inheritance. The beatific vision in turn casts light on the mystery of the Incarnation, for from the lesser created actuation by uncreated act in the vision of God the mind is helped, by analogy, to a deeper understanding of the grace of *hypostatic union, that created actuation of the sacred humanity of Christ by the uncreated Word of God. Since the beatific vision and the total beatitude of the human person is the goal of the sacramental life, the beatific vision gives a deeper understanding of that sacramental life (see SACRAMENTS, THEOLOGY OF). Likewise, the beatific vision gives some understanding of *purgatory, for only after the soul has been detached from all inordinate affections and unified in its being (Mt 5.8) is it capable of the total gift of self to God in the beatific vision. The glorifying vision is the key to a glorious *resurrection of the dead, for the qualities of the glorified body are due to its life principle, the beatified soul. The beatific vision is also a key to a better understanding of the *mediation of the Blessed Virgin Mary, for it is her total interiority in God through the beatific vision—the vision that is hers in terms of her fullness of grace and charity and of her total maternal vocation—that is the source of her mediation of grace now [see MARY, BLESSED VIRGIN, II (IN THEOLOGY)]. Her maternal desires are united to the very power and love of God. And last of all, the perfection of the *communion of saints will be found in their vision of God.

See also DEATH (THEOLOGY OF); DESIRE TO SEE GOD, NATURAL; DESTINY, SUPERNATURAL; ELEVATION OF MAN; ESCHATOLOGY, ARTICLES ON; GRACE, ARTICLES ON; HAPPINESS; HEAVEN (THEOLOGY OF); JESUS CHRIST, III (SPECIAL QUESTIONS), 1; LIGHT OF GLORY; MAN, 4; OBEDIENTIAL POTENCY; SUPERNATURAL; VOCATION TO SUPERNATURAL LIFE.

Bibliography: A. MICHEL, DTC 7.2:2351–94. R. SCHNACKENBURG and K. FORSTER, LexThK² 1:583–591. H. CAZELLES et al., *Catholicisme* 1:1342–54. A. PIOLANTI, EncCatt 12:1485–93. Cat Rom 132–140. F. CEUPPENS, *Theologia Biblica*, v.1, *De Deo uno* (rev. ed. Turin 1948) 103–125; *Quaestiones selectae ex epistulis s. Pauli* (Turin 1951). I. M. DALMAU, SacTheolSumma BAC 2.1:1–74. M. DE LA TAILLE, *The Hypostatic Union and Created Actuation by Uncreated Act*, tr. C. VOLLERT (West Baden, Ind. 1952). H. DE LUBAC, *Surnaturel: Études historiques* (Paris 1946). K. FORSTER, *Die Verteidigung der Lehre des heiligen Thomas von der Gottesschau durch Johannes Capreolus* (Munich 1955). R. GARRIGOU-LAGRANGE, *Beatitude*, tr. P. CUMMINS (St. Louis 1956) 33–129; *Life Everlasting*, tr. P. CUMMINS (St. Louis 1952) 205–255; *The One God*, tr. B. ROSE (St. Louis 1943) 306–381; "La Possibilité de la vision béatifique peut-elle se démontrer?" RevThom 38 (1933) 669–688. T. GILBY, in ST. THOMAS AQUINAS, *Summa theologiae*, v.3 (1a, 12–13), ed. H. MCCABE (McGraw-Hill; New York 1968) xix–xl. R. W. GLEASON, *The World to Come* (New York 1958) 129–169. G. HOFFMANN, *Der Streit über die selige Schau Gottes: 1331–1338* (Leipzig 1917). K. E. KIRK, *The Vision of God: The Christian Doctrine of the Summum Bonum* (London 1932; complete ed.). K. RAHNER, "Current Problems in Christology," *Theological Investigations*, v.1, tr. C. ERNST (Baltimore 1961) 149–200; "Concerning the Relationship between Nature and Grace," *ibid.* 297–317; "Some Implications of the Scholastic Concept of Uncreated Grace," *ibid.* 319–346. H. RONDET, *Do Dogmas Change?* tr. M. PONTIFEX (New York 1961) 22–35. M. J. SCHEEBEN, *The Mysteries of Christianity*, tr. C. VOLLERT (St. Louis 1946) 613–665; *Nature and Grace*, tr. C. VOLLERT (St. Louis 1954). C. SPICQ, *Agapè dans le Nouveau Testament: Analyse des textes*, 3 v. (Paris 1958–59) 2:94–120; 3:204–222, 285–299. J. STAUDINGER, *Life Hereafter*, tr. J. J. COYNE (Westminster, Md. 1964) 115–168. P. VAN IMSCHOOT, *Théologie de l'Ancien Testament*, 2 v. (Paris–Tournai 1954–56) 2:42–75. A. WINKLHOFER, *The Coming of His Kingdom*, tr. A. V. LITTLEDALE (New York 1963) 120–254. J. ALFARO, "Trascendencia e inmanencia de lo sobrenatural," Greg 38 (1957) 5–50. E. BRISBOIS, "Le Désir de voir Dieu et la métaphysique du vouloir selon saint Thomas," NouvRevTh 63 (1936) 1103–05. R. BRUCH, "Das Verhältnis von Natur und Übernatur nach der Auffassung der neueren Theologie," Th Glaube 46 (1956) 81–102. A. BRUNNER, "Gott schauen," ZKath Th 73 (1951) 214–223. P. DE LETTER, "Created Actuation by the Uncreated Act: Difficulties and Answers," ThSt 17 (1956) 60–92. P. J. DONNELLY, "The Supernatural: Father de Lubac's Book," RevPol 10 (1948) 226–232. A. GARDEIL, "Le Désir naturel de voir Dieu," RevThom 31 (1926) 381–410, 477–489, 523–527. F. M. GENUYT, "Voir Dieu," LumetVie 10 (April–May 1961) 89–114. A. GEORGE, "Le Bonheur promis par Jésus d'après le Nouveau Testament," *ibid.* 36–59. P. GRELOT, "La Révélation du bonheur dans l'Ancien Testament," *ibid.* 5–35. D. J. LEAHY, "St. Augustine and the Vision of God in Heaven," Am EcclRev 99 (1938) 128–142. L. MALEVEZ, "La Gratuité du surnaturel," NouvRevTh 75 (1953) 561–586, 673–689.

[M. J. REDLE]

BEATIFICATION

BEATIFICATION, the act by which the Church, through papal decree, permits a specified diocese, region, nation, or religious institute, to honor with public cult under the title of Blessed a person who has died with a reputation for holiness. The cult usually consists of a Mass and Office in the person's honor, and it may even be permitted for the universal Church. However, beatification is limited in its effects, e.g., a blessed may not be the titular patron of a church.

Formal beatification is a positive declaration, following a canonical process, that a person did practice heroic virtue, or suffered a true martyrdom, and after death worked authentic miracles upon being invoked in prayer. Besides witnesses' testimony to his virtues, evidence of two first-class miracles is required, though this requirement may be waived in the case of a martyr. Equivalent beatification is the silent consent of the Church, aware of, yet not opposing, the public cult given one of its children over a long period of time.

In proclaiming a person Blessed the Pope does not exercise his infallibility, for he does not declare definitively that the person is in glory. Beatification, then, does not demand faith yet gives moral certainty of its truth, and to deny it would be temerarious. It differs from canonization as permission to venerate differs from precept. (For illustration, see following page.)

See also SAINTS, INTERCESSION OF; CANONIZATION OF SAINTS (HISTORY AND PROCEDURE); CANONIZATION OF SAINTS (THEOLOGICAL ASPECT); VENERABLE.

Bibliography: T. ORTOLAN, DTC 2.1:493–497. **Illustration credit:** Felici, Rome.

[A. E. GREEN]

BEATITUDES (IN THE BIBLE)

The Beatitudes in the Bible may be treated under three headings: as a literary form; as they are found in the OT; as Our Lord used them in the *Sermon on the Mount.

The beatitude is a literary form. It begins by pronouncing someone happy (Gr. μακάριος; Heb. 'ašrê, literally, "the happiness of"). It then states the reason for his happiness and sometimes goes on to mention the reward he will receive.

The OT Beatitudes are found mainly in the sapiential literature. They usually praise the man who enjoys God's friendship. At times, they cite God's initiative, e.g., "Happy is he whose fault is taken away" [Ps 31(32).1]. At other times, they stress the response a man gives to God, e.g., "Happy are they who observe what is right" [Ps 105(106).3]. The rewards are usually in terms of a full life on earth, although the nearness of God is the source of such happiness. In Proverbs, wisdom as a source of beatitude is praised: "Happy the man who finds wisdom" (Prv 3.13). Sirach has the only extended list of beatitudes, 10 in number (Sir 25.7–11).

The most important Beatitudes in the NT are the two large collections in Mt 5.3–12 and Lk 6.20–26, where they introduce the Sermon on the Mount.

In Matthew, the first beatitude, "Blessed are the poor in spirit," sets the keynote for the whole group of nine. The OT helps us to identify the poor, the 'ănāwîm (Heb.). Since the poor, the materially destitute, were often unfortunate victims of the rich, the prophets taught that God would intervene in their favor. Especially in the Psalms the concept gradually became spiritualized to represent those who acknowledged their deep need and dependence on God. These "poor" looked only to Him as a savior and not to men or material things. Consequently, the later prophets looked to the messianic times for God's intervention to save His 'ănāwîm (So 3.12; Is 61.1, 2).

The first beatitude, then, announces that these last times have come: God has finally taken up the cause of His poor and will soon bring on the final stage of the messianic kingdom. "Blessed are the meek . . ." has the same sense as the first beatitude, but with emphasis on the patience of the poor. "For they shall possess the land . . ." [from Ps 36(37).11] is parallel to the possession of the kingdom in Mt 5.3, since the promised land is a symbol of messianic hopes. "Blessed are they who mourn for they shall be comforted" (the second and third beatitudes are in reverse order in most of the Greek texts) explains how those who are oppressed look for God Himself to be the consolation of the new Israel (cf. Lk 2.25). "Blessed are they who hunger and thirst . . ."—hunger and thirst are often figures of intense desire for God [e.g., Ps 41(42).2–4]; "for justice"—for God's coming regime of justice, a pure gift now anticipated in His grace and friendship; "for they shall be filled"—the figure is that of the coming joyful messianic banquet, which will completely satisfy all the elect (cf. Is 25.6).

The next three beatitudes concern the Christian's response to God's mercy. "Blessed are the merciful . . ." who reflect to others the generosity they themselves have received from God. "Blessed are the pure of heart for they shall see God"—Psalm 23(24) describes the single-hearted man in his relations to his neighbor; he alone can ascend to see Him, i.e., to experience the joy of His presence. "Blessed are the peacemakers . . ."—peace is the totality of blessings, including especially harmony among men, that results from the gift of God's friendship. It will be a great characteristic of the messianic age (Eph 2.14). The blessing is on those who spread the messianic kingdom not by violence but by love: "they shall be called children of God." In Os 2.1 it is said:

Morning ceremonies at the Altar of the Chair in St. Peter's Basilica at the beatification of Bl. John Neumann.

Christ pronouncing the Beatitudes before His Disciples. Ink impression made in the 19th century of one of the plates on the 12th-century lantern in the chapel of Charlemagne at Aachen. Because this is an impression, the wording is in mirror writing: BEATI QUI ESURIUNT ET SITIUNT JUSTITIAM Q[UIA] I[PSI] S[ATURABUNTUR].

"they shall be called children of the living God." This most intimate union with God, a loving Father, was to be the great privilege of the messianic era.

The last two beatitudes are addressed to the Church under persecution. They can rejoice and exult since they are undergoing the final sufferings of the last age that will precede the *Parousia, when their reward will be great.

In Luke, there are four beatitudes followed by four maledictions (6.20–26). While Matthew emphasizes the moral and eschatological viewpoint, Luke leans more to the present and social aspects: "Blessed are you poor . . . , but woe to you rich! for you are now having your comfort" (Lk 6.20, 24). The messianic community is composed of those who willingly share their goods with those in need, thus becoming poor in fact as well as in spirit.

Bibliography: J. DUPONT, *Les Beatitudes* (Bruges 1958), with extensive bibliography. EncDictBibl 215–217. **Illustration credit:** The Metropolitan Museum of Art, Dick Fund, 1923.

[J. A. GRASSI]

BEATITUDES (IN THE CHRISTIAN LIFE),

from the Latin *beatitudo,* meaning blessedness, because of the blessedness that Jesus Christ, in the Sermon on the Mount (Mt 5.3–10), ascribed to the doers of certain good works. Beatitude properly, the state of blessedness achieved in the beatific vision, is the full possession of the only truly perfect good. The activities of human life that most efficaciously lead to this beatitude, and so deserve to share its name, are those in which the Holy Spirit takes over the supernatural life of the soul. Hence St. Augustine, and St. Thomas Aquinas following him, saw in the beatitudes the description of a soul living under the direction of the Holy Spirit. Thus the beatitudes came to be known as the highest acts of virtue that can be performed in this life by one in whom the gifts of the Holy Spirit predominate.

The supernatural acts the Lord described in the first seven affirmations of blessedness represent the activities proper to the seven gifts. The application is confirmed by the terms Christ used. Poverty of spirit, evangelical meekness, hunger and thirst for justice, tears, compassion, detachment of heart, making of peace are effects that only absolute dependence upon God could achieve in the soul.

The beatitudes are the crowning achievement in the Christian's life on earth. They are acts of virtue that have been perfected to the highest possible degree by one who has become habitually docile to the Holy Spirit. So, while the beatitudes are acts of virtue, their activity is also the result of a life influenced by the gifts. They are the joint achievement of virtues and gifts. In reality they are the accomplishment of the greatest Gift, the Holy Spirit, who works in the soul, indirectly by way of the virtues, directly by way of the gifts.

According to St. Thomas, each beatitude corresponds to a gift. Poverty of spirit, for example, corresponds to fear. The virtue of temperance prompts a man to use what is delightful to the senses with moderation; the gift of fear goes further and inspires him with a certain contempt for such goods. Thus, he reaches poverty of spirit and in that act he is blessed or beatified. And so it is with the others: the beatitude of meekness corresponds to the gift of piety; tears, to that of knowledge; justice, to fortitude; mercy, to counsel; cleanness of heart, to understanding; the beatitude of peacemaking, to the gift of wisdom. The eighth beatitude, which is the suffering of persecution, or the acceptance of martyrdom, is a summary and a consummation of all the others. (For illus., see following page.)

See also HOLY SPIRIT, GIFTS OF.

Bibliography: L. M. MARTÍNEZ, *The Sanctifier,* tr. M. AQUINAS (Paterson, N.J. 1957). B. FROGET, *The Indwelling of the Holy Spirit in the Souls of the Just,* tr. S. A. RAEMERS (Westminster, Md. 1950). B. JARRETT, *The Abiding Presence of the Holy Ghost* (2d ed. London 1934). THOMAS AQUINAS, ST 1a2ae, 69–70. **Illustration credit:** The Metropolitan Museum of Art, Dick Fund, 1923.

[P. MULHERN]

BEATON, JAMES (BETHUNE)

Primate and archbishop of Glasgow (1509–22) and St. Andrews (1522–39), one of the regents during the minority of James V, Chancellor of Scotland (1513–26); b. *c.* 1473; d. St. Andrews, 1539. Eleven years after receiving his M.A. from St. Andrews in 1493, James Beaton was made abbot of Dunfermline. In the next year he was appointed by the King to succeed his brother Sir David on the staff of the high treasurer. His whole career was similarly divided between affairs of Church and State. Elected to the See of Galloway in 1508, Beaton was then consecrated archbishop of Glasgow, and in 1522 was appointed to the See of St. Andrews. In the struggles for the control of the young King James V, following the death of his father at the Battle of Flodden, Beaton was allied with the Duke of Albany. The regency had been transferred to Albany at the marriage of the Earl of Angus and Margaret Tudor, the Queen mother and former regent. Angus's policy was generally pro-English, while Albany's was dedicated to maintaining and strengthening the "auld

Second beatitude: "Blessed are they who mourn," impression of a plate from the 12th-century lantern at Aachen.

alliance" of the Scots with France. While in 1517 Albany began a 4-year stay in France for this purpose, Beaton entered into correspondence with Cardinal Thomas Wolsey in England. Beaton professed hopes at preserving peace between the two countries, although Wolsey's schemes for Scotland were bound to clash with Beaton's. During Albany's absence Beaton was included in the Council of Regency. A long-standing feud between Angus and the Earl of Arran for control of the King led to an outbreak in Edinburgh (1520), when Beaton was asked by Gawin Douglas, Bishop of Dunkeld, to mediate. In a famous encounter, while James Beaton struck his breast and announced that on his conscience he knew nothing of the intentions of the opposing faction, his own armor rattled beneath his vestments. Gawin Douglas remarked: "Faith, my lord, but yours is a poor conscience, for I heard it clatter."

By 1526 Angus had gained control, and Beaton was dismissed as chancellor. Angus proceeded to consolidate his power by defeating Beaton's faction and placing James V in confinement. In 1528 the King escaped, and Angus was forced to flee to England. Although the Scots negotiated a treaty with Henry VIII in 1534, Beaton's influence remained sufficiently strong to help bring about the marriage of James V to Madeleine de

Valois at Paris 3 years later. Madeleine died within a few months, and James married Marie de Guise-Lorraine the next year. Their daughter Mary, born December 1542, became *Mary, Queen of Scots (on the death of her father) when she was but 1 week old.

From his castle at St. Andrews on a rocky headland near the cathedral, Beaton opposed the heresies that were gaining strength throughout the nation. Several advocates of the new religious doctrines were sentenced to death during his administration. The most notable was probably Patrick *Hamilton, who was burned at the stake in 1528 and became a protomartyr as the first native born Scot to suffer death for the teachings that were to become those of the established church. Although Henry VIII's breach with Rome probably strengthened the Catholic sympathies of James V, the policies of James Beaton were nevertheless marked by a worldliness similar to that of many of his English ecclesiastical contemporaries. Despite the desperate need for radical reform within the Church of Scotland, Beaton too often acted as the astute politician guided by political expediency rather than as the churchman alert to the tragic ecclesiastical abuses within the realm. After his death he was succeeded in the archbishopric of St. Andrews by his nephew David Beaton, the first

Scottish cardinal. James Beaton was interred at the cathedral church of St. Andrews, where he had held the primacy of Scotland for 16 years.

Bibliography: M. MacArthur, DNB 2:18–19. D. McRoberts, ed., *Essays on the Scottish Reformation, 1513–1625* (Glasgow 1962). J. Herkless and R. K. Hannay, *The Archbishops of St. Andrews,* 5 v. (Edinburgh 1907–15). W. C. Dickinson, *Scotland from Earliest Times to 1603* (A New History of Scotland 1; New York 1961) 379–388, select bibliog. W. C. Dickinson et al., eds., *A Source Book of Scottish History,* 3 v. (2d ed. London 1958–61) v.2. R. K. Hannay, *The Letters of James IV,* ed. R. L. Mackie and A. Spilman (Edinburgh 1953); *The Letters of James V,* ed. D. Hay (Edinburgh 1954). D. Hay, ed., *The Anglica Historia of Polydore Vergil* (London 1950). J. Bain and C. Rogers, eds., *Liber protocollorum M. C. Simonis* (London 1875).

[J. G. DWYER]

BEATON, JAMES (BETHUNE), last pre-Reformation Roman Catholic archbishop of Glasgow, nephew of Cardinal David Beaton, and son of James Beaton of Balfarg; b. 1517; d. April 24, 1603. He received his early education chiefly at Paris. In 1552 he was consecrated archbishop of Glasgow at Rome. As adviser for Queen Mother Mary of Guise, he was a determined opponent of the new religious teachings. Provincial Councils of the Scottish Church in 1546, 1552, and 1559 had freely admitted the grave abuses in the Church. In April 1559 Archbishop Beaton promulgated decrees for the improvement of preaching, the repair of churches, the condemnation of pluralism and concubinage among the clergy, and other disciplinary and administrative reforms in ecclesiastical policy. The 1560 meeting of the Scottish Estates at Edinburgh brought about the establishment of the new reformed religious settlement. Several months earlier James Beaton had made good his escape to France. His departure at such a crucial moment has been questioned by many. However, his many years of loyal service to Mary Queen of Scots, as her ambassador in France and then to James VI, at least clear him of any suspicion of faintheartedness. When he fled to France he took with him many of the treasures and documents of his diocese. These records were later deposited in the Scots College. A considerable number of the documents were returned to Scotland after the French Revolution, to St. Mary's Catholic College at Blairs, Aberdeenshire. During his years in France he corresponded frequently with leading diplomats and churchmen, including Mary Queen of Scots, James VI, and the later Valois French Kings. James Beaton died while James VI of Scotland was on his way to London to become James I, King of England. In his will Beaton stated that he died "as a true and faithful Catholic." He asked that all his debts be paid and then stipulated that the remainder of his legacy should be used to endow a Scots College at Paris, where poor scholars from Scotland could pursue their studies of classical learning and theology. James Beaton established a reputation for faithfulness and loyalty. No scandal is known to have blemished his private life. He was interred in Paris at Saint-Jean de Lateran.

Bibliography: M. MacArthur, DNB 2:19–20. *Calendar of State Papers Relating to Scotland . . . 1547–1603,* ed. J. Bain et al. (Edinburgh 1898–). G. Donaldson, *The Scottish Reformation* (Cambridge, Eng. 1960). D. McRoberts, ed., *Essays on the Scottish Reformation, 1513–1625* (Glasgow 1962). F. W. Maitland, "The Anglican Settlement and the Scottish Reformation," in his *Selected Historical Essays* (Cambridge, Eng. 1962) 152–210. W. C. Dickinson et al., eds., *A Source Book of Scottish History,* 3 v. (2d ed. London 1958–61) v.2–3. J. B. Black, *The Reign of Elizabeth, 1558–1603* (2d ed. Oxford 1959) 507–509, good bibliog. on Anglo-Scottish relations.

[J. G. DWYER]

BEATRICE D'ESTE, BL., name of two members of the D'Este family.

Beatrice d'Este, Benedictine nun; b. c. 1191; d. Gemolo, Italy, May 10, 1226 (feast, May 10). Daughter of Azzo VI d'Este and Princess Leonara of Savoy, she entered the convent of St. Margaret at Solarola when 14 years old, but because of local political disturbances she and women companions who had joined her at St. Margaret's moved to the deserted monastery of St. John the Baptist near Gemolo. They adopted the Benedictine Rule and gained a reputation for their holiness. Her body was translated to the church of St. Sophia in Padua (1578). Her cult was approved in 1763.

Beatrice d'Este, Benedictine nun, niece of Bl. Beatrice; b. 1230; d. Jan. 18, 1262 (feast, Jan. 18; Feb. 28 in order). The daughter of Azzo VII d'Este and Joan of Apulia, she emulated her aunt, but her family planned her marriage to Galeazzo Manfredi, Duke of Vicenza and Veradino. When he died of wounds shortly before the projected marriage, she entered the convent at St. Lazarus. The D'Este family built a convent for her group at Ferrara that was called first St. Stephen, then St. Anthony's. She was professed in 1254 and died less than 10 years later. Clement XIV approved her cult in 1774.

Bibliography: ActSS May 2:597–602; Jan. 2:759. P. Balan, *Memorie della vita della b. Beatrice d'Este* (Venice 1878). G. Baruffaldi, *Vita della b. B. seconda d'E.* (New ed. Ferrara 1777). Zimmermann KalBen 2:166–169; 1:263–265.

[C. L. HOHL, JR.]

BEATRICE OF NAZARETH, Cistercian nun and spiritual writer; b. Tirlemont, c. 1200; d. Notre-Dame-de-Nazareth, near Lierre (Brabant), Aug. 29, 1268. Beatrice was only 7 when her father placed her with the Beguines at Léau. Later, he transferred her to Bloemendael, a Cistercian abbey he had just founded. When she was about 17, she was received into the religious life. A second foundation of the community was made at Maagdendael, and she was sent there. When a third house was opened at Notre-Dame-de-Nazareth, she was made its prioress and remained there until her death.

From an early age she kept notes on her ascetical and mystical experiences, and among these were included little treatises on spiritual topics. The autobiographical notes have been lost, but after her death they were abridged and translated into Latin by a Cistercian monk (perhaps Guillaume d'Affigham, Abbot of Saint-Trond) in the form of a biography. Data contained in the biography have made it possible to recognize as the work of Beatrice a treatise entitled *De divina charitate et septem ejus gradibus,* or *Van seven manieren van Heiligher Minnen,* which survived in a collection of sermons entitled *Limburgsche Sermoenen* that appeared in the early 14th century. This is the oldest known essay in Old Flemish and treats experimentally the ascent of the soul toward union with God in a manner that causes the reader to think of St. Teresa's seven castles of the soul.

Beatrice had a special devotion to the Sacred Heart and with this she associated the idea of reparation. Often ill, she was given to excessive penances, and her writings are not free of certain morbid, pathological characteristics. Her importance lies in her description in the vernacular of the speculative mysticism practiced by Beguines at the beginning of the great flowering of Flemish spirituality.

Bibliography: BEATRICE OF NAZARETH, *Seven Manieren van Minne*, ed. L. REYPENS and J. VAN MIERLO (Louvain 1926). J. VAN MIERLO, DictSpirAscMyst 1:1310–14.

[J. VERBILLON]

BEATRICE OF TUSCANY, noblewoman, identified with the *Gregorian Reform; b. Lorraine, c. 1015; d. Pisa, April 28, 1076. Her two marriages united the princely houses of Lorraine and Tuscany. She was the daughter of Frederick II, Duke of Upper Lorraine, and Matilda of Suabia, and the niece of Empress Gisela, wife of *Conrad II, at whose court she was educated. About 1036 she married Boniface III of Canossa, margrave of Tuscany, by whom she had three children. After Boniface was murdered in 1052, she ruled his former marches of Tuscany and Lombardy-Emilia in her son's name. In 1054, without the knowledge of Emperor *Henry III, she married her cousin, Godfrey the Bearded, then Duke of Upper Lorraine, who had twice rebelled against the Emperor. Henry took immediate action in Italy, imprisoning Beatrice and her only surviving child *Matilda, and transporting them to Germany (1055). Released by Empress Agnes after Henry's death, Beatrice yielded much of her power in Tuscany to Godfrey, devoting her energies to the education of her daughter and the service of ecclesiastical reform. After Godfrey's death in 1069, she ruled the Canossan dominions jointly with Matilda until her own death in 1076. She collaborated closely with *Gregory VII, whose letters bear testimony to a relationship of mutual trust. In the *investiture struggle her action was mediatorial, but her sympathies were clearly anti-imperial and pro-papal.

Bibliography: E. DUPRÉEL, *Histoire critique de Godefroid le Barbu, duc de Lotharingie, marquis de Toscane* (Ukkel 1904). A. FALCE, *Bonifacio di Canossa padre di Matilde*, 2 v. (Reggio-Emilia 1926–27). H. GLAESENER, "Un mariage fertile en conséquences (Godefroid le Barbu et B. de T.)," RHE 42 (1947) 379–416. E. SANTOVITO, EncCatt 2:1112–13.

[C. E. BOYD]

BEATUS, ST., apostle of Switzerland; d. 112 (feast, May 9). An unauthenticated 10th-century legend says that he was of Gallic origin, had been ordained by St. *Peter himself, and went to *Switzerland to convert the heathen Helvetiae in the area around Lake Thun. The legend further relates that he killed a dragon there, lived in its cave until he died at the age of 90, and was buried on the site. His cult did not become popular until the 13th century when the neighboring village of Beatenburg became the center of pilgrimage to him that lasted until the early 16th century. About 1300 an altar was dedicated to him in the Zurich Frauenmünster and a confraternity of St. Beatus was set up. In later medieval art he is portrayed as a hermit with staff and rosary in hand and with a dragon by his side. He was patron of central Switzerland and his assistance was invoked against plague, glandular diseases, and cancer. If he had a historical existence it was probably as an English or Irish missionary of the 6th century, or else he has been confused with the 9th century Beatus of Vendôme.

Bibliography: H. MORETUS, "La légende de s. Béat, apôtre de Suisse," AnalBoll 26 (1907) 423–453. W. STAMMLER, LexThK² 2:86. A. M. JACQUIN, DHGE 7:86–87. M. SCADUTO, EncCatt

2:1108. J. STAMMLER, *Der hl. Beatus, seine Höhle und sein Grab* (Bern 1904). O. SCHEIWILLER, "Beatus-Frage," *Zeitschrift für schweizerische Kirchengeschichte* 5 (1911) 21–52. Réau IAC 3:190.

[J. L. GRASSI]

BEATUS OF LIÉBANA, monk and writer; b. Liébana, near Santander, Spain; d. Feb. 19, 798. He combated *adoptionism and wrote a famous commentary on the Apocalypse in 12 books. *Alcuin mentioned him. In 784, he attacked the heretical proponents of adoptionism, Abp. *Elipandus of Toledo and Bp. Felix of Urgel in two letters, *Ad Elipandum epistulae duae* (PL 96:894–1030), composed jointly with Bp. Etherius of Osma. As teacher and adviser to Queen Adosinda of León, Beatus wrote the first redaction of the *Commentary* in 776, reediting it in 784 and 786. Since it was drawn from similar works of the Fathers from Irenaeus to Isidore of Seville, it was ascribed to various authors. Ambrosio de Morales and *Mabillon identified it as Beatus's work. *Flórez published it (Madrid 1770), as did H. A. Sanders (Rome 1930). But more important than the text are the illustrations in the 30 extant MSS (9th to 13th century), exemplifying the development of Spanish art. The geometric design and interlacing in the MSS are evidence of *Celtic (or *Coptic?) art influence; but the color, imagery, domed architecture, oriental flora and fauna are Mozarabic. The nimbus of red dots is Celtic, the "carpet-page" Coptic. The *Commentary* illustrations had an immense impact upon Romanesque sculptors at *Vézelay, *Saint-Benoît-sur-Loire, and especially at *Moissac where the tympanum shows 24 elders carrying, as viols, Spanish guitars identical with those in a Beatus MS of the same scene. Beatus probably wrote *O Dei verbum, Patris ore proditum,* a hymn for the feast of St. James. In Spain Beatus has a cult (feast, Feb. 19).

Bibliography: ActSS, Feb. 3:149–150. W. NEUSS, *Die Apokalypse . . . in . . . Bibel-Illustration* (Münster 1931). M. R. JAMES, *The Apocalypse in Art* (London 1931). É. MÂLE, *L'Art religieux du XIIᵉ siècle en France* (5th ed. Paris 1947). J. PÉREZ DE URBEL, DHGE 7:89–90. F. STEGMÜLLER, LexThK² 2:86–87.

[M. J. DALY]

BEATUS OF TRIER, ST., hermit; fl. 7th century (feast, Aug. 26; in Trier, July 31). According to a tradition not rich in detail, Beatus and his brother Bantus were priests who lived as hermits near *Trier when Modoald (d. between 647 and 649) was bishop of that city. The same local tradition reports that the brothers died with a great reputation for sanctity and that Beatus was buried in the church of St. Mary of the Martyrs. His relics were, after 1331, brought to Koblenz in the care of the *Carthusians at Beatusberg (*Mons S. Beati*). The beginnings of the cult are shrouded in obscurity, and the earliest document to refer to Beatus as a saint is the 10th-century *Psalter of Egbert,* where his name is listed in a *laetania universalis.* Still later documents from the 15th century report how Poppo, Archbishop of Trier (d. 1047), enclosed relics of the saint in the main altar of the abbey church of St. Mary, which he consecrated on Dec. 16, 1017 (MGS 15.2:1272).

Bibliography: MGS 8:159. ActSS July 7 (1868) 318–319. Cottineau 1:826; 2:3210–11. G. ALLEMANG, DHGE 6:518. Baudot-Chaussin 7:734. M. COENS, AnalBoll 59 (1941) 284–286. A. HEINTZ, LexThK² 2:87. G. FUSCONI, BiblSanct 2:747–748.

[H. DRESSLER]

BEAUCHAMP, RICHARD, bishop of Salisbury; d. Oct. 18, 1481. He was the son of Sir Walter Beauchamp, sometime speaker for the Commons in Parliament, and his second wife, Elizabeth, daughter and coheiress of Sir John Roche. Possibly resident in Exeter College, Oxford, in 1440, he was a doctor of Canon Law by 1442. Having served as canon lawyer, chancery clerk, and royal chaplain, he became bishop of *Hereford (1448), where he was the first to make good the episcopal claim to visit his cathedral officially. He was translated to *Salisbury (1450), where his predecessor, Aiscough, had been murdered by a mob during Jack Cade's rebellion. There Beauchamp was a capable administrator, vigorous in defending episcopal jurisdiction over the city, with whose inhabitants he disputed (1465–74). The result, with royal support, was a complete capitulation of the citizens and a half-century of comparative tranquility in episcopal-city relations. In 1456 the cathedral chapter secured the canonization of *Osmund, the 11th-century episcopal founder of Old Sarum cathedral, partly through Beauchamp's efforts. He served as an emissary in the contemporary Lancaster-York struggle in England and later as an envoy to France. He was allowed to hold the deanship of Windsor (1478) concurrently with his bishopric; this reflects his lengthy connection with the Order of the Garter, which he served as first chancellor in 1475. As master and surveyor of St. George's Chapel, Windsor, Beauchamp was deeply involved in the construction of one of the supreme glories of Perpendicular architecture. He was buried in his own chantry chapel in Salisbury cathedral, since destroyed.

Bibliography: *Registrum Ricardi Beauchamp, Episcopi Herefordensis . . .,* ed. A. T. BANNISTER (Canterbury and York Society; London 1919). Beauchamp's unprinted register in 2 v. is in the Diocesan Registry, Salisbury. *The Victoria History of Wiltshire,* v.3, ed. R. B. PUGH and E. CRITTALL (London 1956), v.6, ed. E. CRITTALL (1962). Emden 1:137–138.

[H. S. REINMUTH, JR.]

BEAUCHAMP, WILLIAM, English professional soldier; b. *c.* 1343; d. May 8, 1411. William was the fourth and youngest son of Thomas, Earl of Warwick, and Catherine, daughter of Roger Mortimer, Earl of March. He was originally intended for a clerical career and in his 14th year (1358) while studying at Oxford, was granted a papal dispensation to hold a benefice without cure of souls. While still at Oxford (1361) he was granted a further dispensation to hold a parish church and cathedral dignity. But probably in that year he gave up his intention of pursuing an ecclesiastical career. He served with John of Gaunt, Duke of Lancaster, on the Black Prince's Castilian expedition and fought at Nájera in 1367, by which year he had been knighted. Later he went with his brother Thomas to Prussia as a crusader with the *Teutonic Knights. With the continuation of the Hundred Years' War, his service with John of Gaunt continued in Gascony (1370) and France (1373). In 1375 he was made knight of the Garter. In 1381–82 he served with Edmund, Earl of Cambridge, as constable in an expedition to assist Ferdinand, King of Portugal. From 1383 until before 1390 he served as captain of Calais and occasionally as envoy; he engaged the French successfully on land and sea. Beauchamp's cousin John, Earl of Pembroke, entailed to him the castle and honor of Abergavenny, which entitled Beauchamp to be summoned to Parliament in 1392. He served as justice of South Wales from

1399 to 1401 and as King's lieutenant in South Wales and the Marches after 1405. His wife was Joan, sister and eventually coheiress of Thomas, Earl of Arundel.

Bibliography: Emden 1:138–139. P. E. RUSSELL, *The English Intervention in Spain and Portugal in the Time of Edward III and Richard II* (Oxford 1955).

[H. S. REINMUTH, JR.]

BEAUDENOM, LÉOPOLD, ascetical writer and spiritual director; b. Tulle, Nov. 23, 1840; d. Puteaux, France, Dec. 21, 1916. After seminary study in Servières and Tulle, he was ordained in 1863. Having long desired to be a missionary, Beaudenom joined the Marists in 1875, but poor health, thought to be the result of self-imposed mortifications in his seminary days, necessitated his returning to his former post of chaplain to the Ursulines of Beaulieu. He was also chaplain to other communities until 1896, when he retired to Puteaux. There he devoted the remaining 20 years of his life to writing, his works appearing anonymously.

Beaudenom's writings fall into two groups that together comprise his plan of instruction aimed toward the life of union with Christ. To the first group belong works about the very foundation of sanctity: *Formation à l'humilité* (Paris 1897); *Pratique de l'examen particulier* (Paris 1898); *Pratique progressive de la confession et de la direction* (2 v. Paris 1900); *Les Sources de la piété* (Paris 1908), conceived as the third volume of the preceding; and *Formation morale et religieuse de la jeune fille* (2 v. Paris 1906–11), which contains the application of his general method to a special category. In the second group are works that center in Christ: *Préparation et actions de grâces pour la sainte Communion* (Paris 1894); *Methods et formules pour bien entendre la messe* (Paris 1905); and *Méditations affectives et pratiques sur l'Évangile* (4 v. Paris 1912–18). Beaudenom acknowledged his special indebtedness to the method of St. Ignatius (thus the insistence on the importance of the particular examen) and to the spirit of St. Francis de Sales; the latter's ability to inspire confidence and courage seems to have been Beaudenom's outstanding characteristic as spiritual director.

Bibliography: A. BOUCHER, DictSpirAscMyst 1:1315–19.

[M. S. CONLAN]

BEAUDUIN, LAMBERT, liturgist; b. Rosouxlez-Waremme, Belgium, Aug. 5, 1873; d. Chevetogne, Jan. 11, 1960. He studied at the minor seminary of Saint-Trond, then at the seminary of Liège, where he came under the influence of Abbot Pottier, founder of the École Sociale de Liège. He was ordained in 1897 and, in 1899, rejoined the Aumôniers du Travail, a society of priests founded to care for workingmen. In 1906, he became a Benedictine at the Abbey of Mont-César, where he was initiated in the study of liturgy by Dom Columba *Marmion. Beauduin discovered the ecclesial importance of the liturgy while teaching a course in dogma after his religious profession. In 1909, he helped begin the Liturgical Weeks. In the same year, he began *La vie liturgique* (since 1911, *Les questions liturgiques*). He also wrote *La piété de l'Eglise* (Louvain 1914) as the manifesto of the liturgical movement.

In 1921, he was named professor of theology at S. Anselmo in Rome. There, he became interested in the Eastern liturgies. Pius XI wanted the Benedictine Order to mediate the work of reunion between East and West. As a result, in September 1925, Beauduin founded the monastery "de l'Union" in Amay (Liège) and the review *Irénikon*. At the same time, he joined Cardinal D. J. *Mercier in the *Malines Conversations. In a memoir of May 25, 1925, he originated the formula, "The Anglican Church united to Rome, not absorbed," which aroused lively reactions.

Lambert Beauduin.

The bold views of Beauduin in liturgy and ecclesiology shocked many people. In 1928 he had to leave Amay; in January 1931, when he returned from a visit in Bulgaria, he was brought before a Roman tribunal, condemned, and sent to the Abbey of En-Calcat. A retreat, preached by him in 1942, was the origin of the future Centre de Pastorale liturgique in Paris, and thus he became associated with the dominant figures of the Christian renewal in France. He visited numerous Protestants and members of the Orthodox Church for whom he had sympathy and understanding.

In 1950 he was able to return to the monastery he had founded, and in 1954, his spiritual sons celebrated his 80th birthday with the work, *L'Église et les Églises* (2 v., Chevetogne).

When Cardinal Angelo Roncalli, formerly nuncio to France, became Patriarch of Venice, he said: "The true method of working for the reunion of the churches is that of Dom Beauduin." The "condemned" of 1931 had one last joy: *John XXIII, the former Roncalli, announced in 1958, an ecumenical council for reunion.

Bibliography: O. ROUSSEAU, *Irénikon* 33 (1960) 3–28, 582. R. AUBERT, *Revue Nouvelle* 31 (1960) 225–249. T. BECQUET, *Revue Générale Belge* (April 1960) 109–117. A. G. MARTIMORT, "Dom Lambert Beauduin et le Centre de Pastorale Liturgique," *Maison-Dieu,* No. 62 (1960) 10–17. **Illustration credit:** *Questions Liturgiques et Paroissiales.*

[N. HUYGHEBAERT]

BEAUFORT, HENRY, cardinal and bishop of Winchester; b. Beaufort-en-Vallée, France, *c.* 1375; d. Winchester, England, April 11, 1447. He was the second of the illegitimate children of John of Gaunt (d. 1399) and Catherine Swynford (d. 1403), and therefore a half brother to King Henry IV (d. 1413) of England. He was eventually legitimated in 1396. Consecrated bishop of *Lincoln in 1398, he was transferred to *Winchester in 1405 by papal provision, and for the next 30 years he was one of Europe's leading ecclesiastical politicians. As a reward for the part he played at the Council of *Constance, Pope *Martin V made Beaufort a *cardinal without title in 1417, and then employed him in 1420 and again in 1427–28 to manage crusades against the *Hussites in Bohemia. For this purpose he was appointed legate to Germany, Hungary, and Bohemia and was made cardinal priest of Saint Eusebius. Beaufort's failure in Bohemia was due partly to the diversion of his troops to the service of

England in France, a move that marked the end of Beaufort's influence on the continent and his hopes of receiving the papal tiara. Conversely, his influence on English politics increased. He had already been chancellor of England (1403–04, 1413–17, and 1424–26), and then became the chief and successful rival to *Humphrey of Gloucester as the shaper of English policy during the reign of *Henry VI. Whereas his rival favored an aggressive foreign policy, Beaufort favored peace, an attitude determined by financial, not religious considerations, for he was the country's banker and the King's chief creditor, but an indifferent churchman. He was buried in Winchester Cathedral, whose construction he had seen completed.

Bibliography: L. B. RADFORD, *Henry Beaufort* (London 1908). K. B. MCFARLANE, "Henry V, Bishop Beaufort and the Red Hat, 1417–1421," EngHistRev 60 (1945) 316–348. Emden Cambr 46–49 or Emden 1:139–142.

[D. NICHOLL]

BEAUFORT, LADY MARGARET, Countess of Richmond and Derby, mother of King *Henry VII, and benefactress of *Cambridge University; b. May 31, 1443; d. 1509. She was the daughter and heiress of John Beaufort, Duke of Somerset (d. 1444). Her marriage as a child to the Duke of Suffolk's heir was later dissolved, and she became successively wife to Edmund Tudor, Earl of Richmond (d. 1456), by whom she bore Henry VII; to Sir Henry Stafford (d. 1471); and to Thomas Stanley, Earl of Derby (d. 1504). She was noted for piety and devotion, and took monastic vows in 1504, but never retired to a religious house. Under the influence of her confessor, John *Fisher, she became in later life an active and munificent patron of

Lady Margaret Beaufort, effigy in Westminster Abbey.

education. By 1503 she had established the two Lady Margaret professorships in divinity in *Oxford and Cambridge, and in 1504 founded the Lady Margaret preachership at Cambridge. She completed Henry VI's foundation of God's House, Cambridge, opened in 1505 as Christ's College, and in 1508 began the foundation of St. John's College, later completed by Fisher. She endowed also a school and chantry in the Beaufort seat of Wimborne Minster, Dorset.

Bibliography: JOHN FISHER, The Funeral Sermon of Margaret, Countess of Richmond and Derby, ed. J. HYMERS (Cambridge, Eng. 1840). C. H. COOPER, Memoir of Margaret, Countess of Richmond and Derby, ed. J. E. B. MAYOR (Cambridge, Eng. 1874). J. B. MULLINGER, The University of Cambridge, 3 v. (Cambridge, Eng. 1873–1911) 1:434–471. G. E. COKAYNE, The Complete Peerage . . ., ed. V. GIBBS et al. (London 1910–   ) v.10. Illustration credit: Warburg Institute, London.

[C. D. ROSS]

BEAULIEU, ABBEY OF (de Bello Loco Regis), former Cistercian monastery, daughterhouse of *Cîteaux, founded by King John (1203) near Southampton, England. Many of the conventual buildings remain. It was more splendidly endowed and constructed than any Cistercian house in south England, and its abbots were often sent on royal missions. The first abbot negotiated with the pope about the Interdict (1208); another went to the Lateran Council (1215). Beaulieu founded Netley (1239), Hailes (1246), Newenham (1247), and St. Mary Graces (1350). The order's general chapter frequently employed its abbots for visitations. Beaulieu was suppressed in 1538, the site being granted to Thomas Wriothesley. Of the 20 monks signing the surrender of the abbey, several had belonged to lesser monasteries until 1536. The monastic refectory now is used as the village church. (See illustration.)

Bibliography: J. K. FOWLER, History of Beaulieu Abbey (London 1911). Victoria County History, Hampshire. Knowles-Hadcock 105. Cottineau 1:303. Illustration credit: courtesy of Lord Montagu of Beaulieu.

[S. F. HOCKEY]

BEAUMONT, ÉLIE DE, geologist, teacher, and originator of the "Réseau pentagonal" theory for the origin of mountains; b. Canon, Calvados, France, Sept. 25, 1798; d. Canon, Sept. 21, 1874. De Beaumont, the son of a noble family of Normandy, studied at the Henri IV seminary and the École Polytechnique in Paris, then entered the École des Mines to study mineralogy (1819). One of his professors, Brochant de Villiers, was struck by his brilliance and took him and another student, A. Dufrénoy, with him when he went to Great Britain to study mines and methods of geological surveying.

On their return to France, the three embarked on an ambitious project: to make a detailed geological map of France. Brochant de Villiers soon dropped out, but his two students completed the work after 18 years. Publication of their map proved a powerful stimulus to the development of geology in France. In 1829 De Beaumont presented some of his ideas concerning mountains to the French Academy of Sciences. He suggested that the slow cooling of the earth resulted in deformation that caused furrows and fissures. His ideas were favorably received; among the few critics were Adam Sedgwick, Ami Boué, and Constant Prévost. De Beaumont was elected professor of geology at the École des Mines, but in 1835 he succeeded Brochant de Villiers as inspector general of mines.

He served as director of the Geological Survey of

Refectory (now parish church) of Beaulieu Abbey.

France until his death, but he found time, in spite of his administrative duties, to elaborate his ideas on the origin of mountains into a four-volume work On Mountain Systems (1852). Here, he proposed his "Réseau pentagonal"—a general geometrical law of orientation for the mountains of the earth. The theory met with wide acceptance in De Beaumont's day but is now considered of only historical interest. The book nevertheless contains much that has become accepted geologic theory, and it stimulated research by other geologists into the structure of mountains. His fame rests mainly on the prodigious amount of field work involved in preparing the geologic map of France and his great ability as an administrator and spokesman of geology in France.

Bibliography: M. P. FALLOT, "Élie de Beaumont et l'évolution des sciences géologiques au Collège de France," Annales des Mines: Mémoires 15 (1939) 75–107. S. MEUNIER, L'Évolution des théories géologiques (Paris 1911).

[A. LA ROCQUE]

BEAUNE, RENAUD DE, French prelate; b. Tours, Aug. 12, 1527; d. Paris, Sept. 17, 1606. His noble and influential family included several bishops. He held important juridical posts from 1555 (councilor of the Parlement of Paris) until he became councilor of state in 1573. He was bishop of Mende in 1568 and became archbishop of Bourges in 1581. Renaud was one of the first bishops to support *Henry IV, who made him grand chaplain in 1591 and commander of the Order of the Holy Spirit in 1592. He played a very important role in Henry's conversion in 1593, and in 1594 he was made archbishop of Sens. But the Pope disapproved of Henry's reconciliation as carried out by Beaune and refused the bulls of confirmation for the See of Sens. Beaune's attempt to have himself installed in the see met with opposition from the cathedral chapter, and it was only after investigations and the efforts of Cardinal d'*Ossat that he was accepted by Rome and the chapter in 1602. He was succeeded in the see by J. *Duperron.

Bibliography: E. CHARTRAIRE, DHGE 7:223–225. R. D'AMAT, DictBiogFranc 5:1156–58.

[D. R. PENN]

BEAUREGARD, PIERRE GUSTAVE TOUTANT, general; b. near New Orleans, La., May 28, 1818; d. there, Feb. 20, 1893. After graduating second in his class from the U.S. Military Academy, West

Point, N.Y. (1838), he served in the War with Mexico on the staff of Gen. Winfield Scott. He took part in the siege of Veracruz and in the Battles of Cerro Gordo, Contreras, and Chapultepec, and in the capture of the City of Mexico, where he was twice wounded. Brevetted a major, he became a regular captain of engineers March 3, 1853. Throughout the next 8 years, Beauregard engaged in fortification construction on the Gulf Coast. Appointed to the superintendency of West Point, he served only 5 days, Jan. 23 to 28, 1861, when he was removed because of his secessionist sympathies. He resigned from the U.S. Army on Feb. 20, 1861, became a Confederate brigadier general, and was given command of the defenses of Charleston, S.C. There, acting under orders from the Confederate capital, he initiated the Civil War by directing the bombardment of Ft. Sumter. Beauregard was then given command of forces in Manassas, Va., and vicinity, and drew the preliminary plans for the battle of Bull Run on July 21, 1861. Following that victory he was promoted to full general and was transferred to the West, where he served under Gen. Albert Sidney Johnston at Shiloh, Tenn. Ill health handicapped Beauregard's later service, although he defended Petersburg, Va., in 1864 in a crucial situation, and surrendered with J. E. Johnston on April 25, 1865. Declining military posts offered him in Rumania and Egypt, he devoted his later years to the work of railway executive in Louisiana.

Bibliography: U.S. War Dept., *The War of the Rebellion: A Compilation of the Official Records of the Union and Confederate Armies*, 70 v. in 128 (Washington 1880–1901). D. S. FREEMAN, *Lee's Lieutenants: A Study in Command*, 3 v. (New York 1942–44). A. ROMAN, *The Military Operations of General Beauregard in the War between the States* (New York 1884). T. H. WILLIAMS, *P. G. T. Beauregard: Napoleon in Gray* (Baton Rouge 1955). P. G. T. BEAUREGARD, *With Beauregard in Mexico: The Mexican War Reminiscences*, ed. T. H. WILLIAMS (Baton Rouge 1956).

[J. W. COLEMAN]

BEAUTY

Viewed as a perfection of being, beauty is said to be ontological or metaphysical, and as such is frequently enumerated among the *transcendentals; viewed as a quality delighting the senses and otherwise giving pleasure to the person perceiving it, enjoyed for its own sake, beauty is said to be aesthetic, and as such is the object of study in *aesthetics. This article first surveys the historical development of the concept of beauty in general, then discusses the status of beauty as a transcendental, and concludes with an analysis of beauty from the viewpoint of aesthetics.

HISTORICAL DEVELOPMENT OF THE CONCEPT

Philosophical views on the nature of beauty may conveniently be traced from their origins in Greek philosophy, through their development in the patristic and medieval periods, to the various teachings that have been proposed from the Renaissance to the 20th century.

Greek Philosophy. Most Western concepts of beauty, whether ontological or aesthetic, stem from the Greeks, with Plato and Aristotle standing at the headwaters of streams that have since flowed through the various philosophies of beauty. Almost at the outset, however, a distinction appeared between a metaphysics of beauty and the role of beauty in a metaphysical system. A meta-

physics of beauty gave to beauty a central place. Certain philosophers (Plato among the ancients; Schopenhauer, Bergson, Santayana, and Camus in more recent times) viewed existence as a structure in an aesthetico-ethical mode in which the Greek ideal of καλοκἀγαθία, the beautiful and good, dominated.

*Plato proposed in the dialectic of the *Symposium* (201C–211B) that whoever has been initiated into the mysteries of Eros comes to the vision of beauty that he has longed for by indeliberate inspiration; he finds beauty a self-subsisting idea shining through bodies, laws, and knowledge itself. Every beautiful thing partakes of this eternal oneness of beauty. Beauty and goodness are found together (*Philebus* 64E) and are measured by the same standard (*Rep.* 452E); in fact, they are identical (*Tim.* 87C). All beautiful things, even material copies of the Ideas, are beautiful by the power of the Idea of Beauty, the first and most easily grasped of the Ideas (*Phaedrus* 250D). Proportion and measure constitute it (*Philebus* 64E, 66B; *Tim.* 87C).

*Aristotle, however, developed no metaphysical concept about manifestations of beauty. It is clear that beauty is assigned importance in his theory of tragedy. The beauty that he claims should be a requisite of tragedy is characterized by order (τάξις) and size (μέγεθος; see *Poet.* 1450b 34–1451a 6; cf. *Eth. Nic.* 1123b). Things are found beautiful (καλῶς ἔχειν) when they are in the condition in which they ought to be (I. Bywater, comment on 1447a 10). Aristotle considers beauty free of meanness (*Rhet.* 1404b) and likely to vary in accord with different purposes and occasions (1361b). In the *Metaphysics*, where his treatment is more general, beauty is noted to have order, symmetry (συμμετρία), and boundary (ὡρισμένον); and these are said to be demonstrable by mathematics (1078a 36). He sometimes mentions it in connection with the moral good (1013a 22, 1091a 30–37, 1093b 13), but he makes a distinction between them: whereas goodness is always in actions (ἐν πράξει), beauty is also in "motionless things" (ἐν τοῖς ἀκινήτοις; see 1078a 31–33). Moreover, the passages that associate the two are in books held to be of earlier date and, therefore, more Platonic than those that made the distinction [W. Jaeger, *Aristotle,* tr. R. Robinson (Oxford 1934) 171, 178–179].

It was in the mystical teaching of *Neoplatonism that the theory of beauty came to be concerned with the metaphysical. According to *Plotinus, the beautiful and the good are to be looked for together, for beauty is being in the same manner that goodness is being. As the first principle (τὸ πρῶτον) is the good (τἀγαθόν), so likewise is it beauty itself (καλλονή, see *Enn.* 1.6.6). The soul is beautiful through Mind (νοῦς, τὸ καλόν), and everything else is beautiful through the soul. Plotinus meditated on the procreation from beauty indicated in the *Symposium*. He said the soul is carried past discursive thought to conscious union with Mind, but it reaches beyond intelligence to mystical union with the One itself, of which Mind is the first emanation. Thus the degrees of beauty correspond with degrees of emancipation from matter (*Enn.* 5.8.4).

As to the characteristic of beauty, whether in the sense world, the world of intelligence, or the sphere of the One, Plotinus reacted against the emphasis laid by the Stoics on material proportions. He argued that beauty cannot depend wholly on external ordering even in material things (*Enn.* 1.6.2–3). Still less does it depend on such ordering in the realm of mind and morality (*Enn.* 1.6.5–8). As true beauty is spiritual, the true quality of beauty must be that of radiance. In an echo of the *Phaedrus,* Plotinus describes the world beyond as a place where "everything is clear for all: Light for light." Even here below, it is the luminous character of things, rather than their order and proportion, that compels one to call them beautiful (*Enn.* 5.8.4, 10).

Patristic Teaching. Chiefly through Gregory of Nyssa, Augustine, and Pseudo-Dionysius, Greek teaching about beauty passed into Christian literature. *Gregory of Nyssa applied Platonic theories to his description of divine beauty, which draws to itself all that turns to it (*De anim. et resur.;* PG 46:89A-B). Not only is God beautiful, but He is the essence and archetype of beauty (*De virg.;* ed. Cavarnos, 295–297); and the human soul in contemplating its own beauty grasps the image of the divine nature, for the soul is that image (*De beat.;* PG 44:1269C–1271A, 1197C–D).

*Augustine brought not only the Platonic and Neoplatonic concepts to bear on his teaching, but also the Pythagorean interest in number. The laws of number, weight, and measure that govern beauty, he claimed, come before all sensible manifestations of them (*Lib. arb.* 2.8.22–23). Number, as a constituent of all things, is the touchstone of beauty, for from number flow the ratios that make proportion satisfying; from due proportion comes the form, as it dwells both in the thing and in the mind of God (*ibid.* 2.16.40–43; *Ordine* 2.15.42). Whereas with the Stoics Augustine defined corporeal beauty as a "congruence (*congruentia*) of parts with a certain delightfulness (*suavitate*) of color" (*Civ.* 22.19.2, 11.22; *Epist.* 3), he aimed chiefly at leading man by means of action progressively to the "beauty ever ancient, ever new" that is God Himself (*Conf.* 10.27.38). The Neoplatonic character of Augustine's aesthetic is visible in many of its aspects. He sees the order of creation as steps of a ladder from the visible to the invisible, from the mortal to the immortal, a gradation that he calls beauty (*pulchritudo*); this is noted to be continuous but tempered with variety (*In psalm.* 144; PL 37:1878). Moreover, he holds that when an image corresponds perfectly with that of which it is an image, it realizes its form perfectly and thus engenders beauty (*Trin.* 10.11; PL 42:931). And he manifests the Neoplatonic tendency to identify values, considering wisdom the truest "beauty" (*C. acad.* 2.3).

Even more influential on medieval interpretations of beauty was a treatise, *De divinis nominibus,* with its chapter on God as the good and the beautiful. It was written probably early in the 6th century by a monk who, passing for Denis the Areopagite, is known as *Pseudo-Dionysius. The work hands on a metaphysics grounded in *Platonism. All things, it says, even the least of material beings, are beautiful by participating in the beauty of God. They do so by analogy (ἀναλογία), that is, in their own way, up to their own capacities and according to their merits (4.22, 724B; 11.6, 956B). The divine beauty is essentially an efficient cause, an exemplar, and a final cause; but it is most properly a final cause. The features of the beautiful that stem from the causal power of God are: (1) the selfhood, identity (ταὐτότης), or perfection that comes from participating, according to one's capacity, in the beauty of God; (2) the harmony that orders the universe in a hierarchy; and (3) radiance, fundamentally a spiritual qual-

ity, an enlightening of the mind, of which visible clarity is but an image.

Medieval Doctrine. Meanwhile, St. Augustine's ideas profoundly influenced the school of Saint-Victor; Alexander of Hales; and, through Alexander, St. Bonaventure. *Alexander of Hales, in emphasizing the beautiful among values, started a new direction; he claimed that insofar as a form is comfortable to the wisdom of God, who created it, it is in its fullness, a fullness that radiates from the object in its sensible aspect. The good and the beautiful differ logically, for the beautiful is the good considered as satisfying the apprehension, whereas the good itself, properly speaking, satisfies desire. The beautiful is related to the formal cause (*Summa* 1.1.3.3.1.-1.2). That *Bonaventure had read St. Augustine is clear from his observations on the ladder of beauty (*Itinerarium mentis ad Deum* 1.2; in *Tria opuscula . . .,* 5th ed. Quaracchi 1938). Commenting on the *Sentences* of Peter Lombard, however, Bonaventure invokes four transcendentals and links them to the causes: unity to the efficient cause, truth to the formal cause, goodness to the final cause, and beauty to all the causes. Thus, the relating of beauty to the formal cause is lost sight of. For Bonaventure, beauty presupposes the other transcendentals; and as a consequence, the causes associated with each of them [Assisi Bibl. Com. MS 186, fol. 51va; see Pouillon, Arch Hist Doct Lit 15 (1946) 281].

*Albert the Great offered the beginning of several philosophies of beauty. He alternated between associating beauty with goodness in a Platonic or moral sense and connecting it with truth or wisdom as the source of light and form. In the early treatise *De bono* he discusses the relationship of the true, the good, and the beautiful to the faculties, deciding that the true is the object of the speculative intelligence and the good that of the affections; the beautiful, for him, is then the commensuration of the true and the good (*bonum honestum*). Here he describes too the effect of contemplation of beauty on the faculties. It is that of illumination, brought about by light and beauty and resulting in beauty and goodness in the being (*De bono* 1.2.1–2; ed. Kühle, 22–27). Beauty, he says later in his *Summa theologica* (1.6.26.2.3; ed. Borgnet 36:240–242), pertains to the perfection of a being as related to divine wisdom, whereas goodness in a creature relates to the divine goodness. In his commentary on the *De divinis nominibus* (4.5–6, unedited MS), Albert presents the classic medieval definition of beauty as "the splendor of substantial or accidental form shining upon the well defined and proportioned parts of matter or upon different faculties and actions." Thus, the metaphysical basis for beauty, in this later presentation, as in *De bono,* is light or form.

*Ulric of Strassburg, a student of Albert, inherited much of his Neoplatonic doctrine from his master. Ulric teaches that the beautiful and the good differ only logically: the good is form as perfection, whereas beauty is form as intelligible light (*lumen intellectualis*). In his metaphysics, intelligible light is the formal cause of the beauty of all forms, even those that dwell in matter. Moreover, evil, as physical or spiritual defect, may possess relative beauty. The more the intelligible light suffuses a thing, the higher it ranks and the more beautiful it is. The divine beauty contains virtually every form and, therefore, all that is caused (*Summa de bono* 4.2.5). God is not only the *dator formarum;* He is also the *mundus archetypus,* or model, of all created forms. Yet the divine beauty is not diverse and manifold. Whatever distinctions exist in reality must arise from creatures themselves. Their different potentialities make the form they receive more or less distant from the first intellectual light, for the form is the principle of likeness whereby things are images of the divine beauty. Ulric goes even further to say that, through the Incarnation, every creature shares in the essence of the divine beauty in a natural and personal union; before the Incarnation, the creature shared in the divine beauty only by similitude.

*Thomas Aquinas, commenting on the *De divinis nominibus,* indicates the requirement of fit proportion conducing to clarity (*propria ratio . . . ad claritatem—In Dion. de div. nom.* 4.6). Wherever there is beauty, there is proportion or order (ST 2a2ae, 145.2). In fact, three elements are necessary: integrity, suitable (*debita*) proportion, and clarity (ST 1a, 39.8). Although beauty and goodness are fundamentally identical in a thing because both are based on form, they differ logically. Whereas goodness relates to the appetite and has the aspect of end, beauty relates to a cognitive power; this is so because a thing is said to be beautiful if it pleases when sensed. Beauty consists in due proportion, delighting the senses. It has the nature of a formal cause. The sense to which beauty makes its primary appeal is sight, and the appeal is made both by proportion of parts in size and in position, giving clarity, and by what Aquinas terms *nitidum colorem.* For the object that appeals to the sense of hearing he uses the term *gratiosum* (ST 1a, 39.8; 1a2ae, 27.1 ad 3); *In Psalm.* 44; *In Dion. de div. nom.* 4.5).

Renaissance to 19th Century. The humanists of the Renaissance recovered the dialogues of Plato and the writings of Plotinus, and yet their notion of beauty descended more often than not to the level of rules of composition. L. B. *Alberti distinguished degrees of beauty in nature and claimed the existence of innate ideas, at least for the judgment of beauty. The chief characteristic of beauty, in his opinion, is harmony, i.e., concord of part with whole and that of the whole with itself. Marsilio *Ficino, in his *Theologica Platonica,* fused the classical with the Christian and spoke of God as absolute beauty and absolute goodness. *Pico della Mirandola combined Aristotelian and Platonic doctrine while teaching that lesser beauties are a reflection of absolute beauty. G. *Vico, rather than A. G. Baumgarten (1714–62), is the precursor of philosophies of the beautiful that offer no apologies to the other sciences. Baumgarten presented beauty as the perfection of sensibility. J. Addison (1672–1719) found the sublime as significant as beauty, and F. Hutcheson (1694–1746), in distinguishing between absolute and relative beauty, decided that neither lies in the object unless there is a mind to perceive it. Absolute beauty "we perceive in objects without comparison to anything external," whereas relative beauty "is founded on a conformity or a kind of unity between the original and the copy" (*An Inquiry into the Original of Our Ideas of Beauty and Virtue,* London 1725). Lord Kames (Henry Home, 1696–1782) agreed that beauty is not an inherent property, yet that it is the result of relations among parts (*Elements of Criticism,* 2 v. Edinburgh 1762). E. *Burke, in his *Philosophical Enquiry into the Origin of Our Ideas of the Sublime and the Beautiful*

(London 1757), found the notions of sublimity and beauty mutually exclusive, and relegated beauty to the level of the slight, the delicate, and the pretty on the material plane and to the inconsequential in the spiritual order.

I. *Kant, who drew on English sources, lifted the discussion of beauty back into the realm of philosophy. Looking for the link between the world of natural necessity presented in scientific knowledge and the world of freedom apprehended in moral experience, he finds it in the judgment, i.e., in "the power of thinking the particular as being contained under the universal" [*The Critique of Judgement,* tr. J. C. Meredith (repr. Oxford 1957) 18]. The judgment of taste, carefully distinguished from teleological judgment, is subjective in the sense that it decides about a form, whether of a natural object or of a work of art, with reference to the feeling it sets up, and nevertheless pronounces that the thing itself is beautiful. The analysis frees beauty from utilitarian interest, purely private taste, representation of outside purpose, and dependence on a concept. The beautiful pleases in the very act of being judged so. For Kant, beauty is not synonymous with perfection or final good; this is embodied in the sublime rather than in the beautiful. Beauty itself is subjective, but for reasons of convenience it may be treated as if it were objective. If it belongs to the noumenal order or if it is identified with the "supersensible substrate," it is unknowable; if not, it is purely ephemeral. Even were one to say with some Kantian scholars that certain elements of beauty reside in the object, one would still be in the subjective domain, since an object for Kant is only the appearance of the thing known.

G. W. F. *Hegel more ambitiously attempted to show how phenomenal experience and ultimate reality come together in Absolute Mind. Beauty fuses the abstract concept with the material given in sense. Truth Hegel calls "Idea as Idea"; beauty, "the physical appearance of the Idea" (*The Philosophy of Fine Art* 1.1). Yet he goes on to say that "it is impossible for understanding alone to lay hold on beauty. The understanding remains rooted in the finite, that is, in incomplete abstraction. Beauty is, on the contrary, essentially infinite and free" (*ibid.*). However, since the struggle between idea and image is resolved with less necessity than the emergence of pure reason in philosophy, aesthetics is less perfect than metaphysics, although beauty itself lies between the two.

A purely objective contemplation was considered by A. *Schopenhauer to be the only release. He saw the world as an objectification of a Will that devours man. Science is at its service, and disinterested knowledge offers intervals of respite. Beings in the world are ordered in a Platonic hierarchy of ideas. Life is a succession of anguished desires and empty attainments. There are only two ways of escape: the imperfect freedom of the aesthetic experience and the total abandonment of sanctity. In both cases the tyranny of the Will is eluded; in the one, for a time; in the other, permanently in a Nirvana of self-forgetfulness. In the contemplation of beauty, itself an eternal idea manifest in things, the "particular thing becomes at once the Idea of its species, and the perceiving individual becomes pure subject of knowledge" [*The World as Will and Idea,* tr. R. B. Haldane and J. Kemp (3 v. London 1833–86) 1:232]. Art is the only really good thing in life.

20th Century. H. L. *Bergson, in his *Évolution créatrice* (Paris 1907), stresses the aspect of change and progression in reality, and emphasizes the role of intuition and the function of the artist as a man who remains close to the sources of being. B. *Croce, in a synthesis of positivism and idealism, unfolds the implications of the Hegelian dialectic and condemns idolatry paid to abstractions (*Breviario di estetica*, Bari 1920). For him, beauty always belongs to the individual and is inaccessible to deduction. It may be reached only by an intuition quickened by feeling and will. Accordingly, at a time when the problems of beauty and creativity were being treated by methods of empirical research, he held that the best writing on the subject came from literary critics rather than from philosophers and scientists.

In the naturalism of G. *Santayana, beauty belongs in the realm of what can be perceived. The experience of beauty is the standard of all values, testifying to the possibility of perfection and revealing it [*The Sense of Beauty* (New York 1896) 7–8]. For S. *Alexander, behaviorism and a theory of values combine in an evolutionary interpretation of reality. The propositions and things esteemed for their own sakes are so because they have beauty, truth, and goodness. The beauty of natural objects becomes recognized by the beholder's power of selectivity, composing the scene as the artist does [*Beauty and Other Forms of Value* (London 1933) 33].

A. N. Whitehead characterized beauty as harmony and found it in the "mutual adaptation of the several factors in an occasion of experience" [*Adventures of Ideas* (New York 1933) 324]. Beauty and evil may be found together because actualization is finite and the finite excludes alternatives. Thus beauty reaches further than truth, which relates appearance and reality. Whitehead concludes that the universe tends toward the making of beauty since it is realized in "completely real things" (*ibid.* 328, 341).

Hundreds of books and articles in the third quarter of the century were devoted to the nature of the work of art and what constitutes genuine art. Since the latter half of the 18th century, however, many factors had combined to produce the idea that artistic works, for centuries the expression of the beautiful, should now be the expression of the artist's interior responses to himself and to the world. Hence, the tendency is to consider art as a clue to some ultimate meaning. The consideration of the beautiful is not as relevant to art so conceived, and it is entertained principally by isolated individuals or is investigated in the realm of the history of ideas.

See also ART (PHILOSOPHY).

Bibliography: General. J. AUMANN, *De pulchritudine: Inquisitio philosophico theologica* (Valencia 1951), patristic and Thomistic doctrine. E. F. CARRITT, *What Is Beauty? A First Introduction to the Subject and Modern Theories* (Oxford 1932), equates beauty with expression; ed., *Philosophies of Beauty: From Socrates to Robert Bridges* (Oxford 1931), an anthology. MENÉNDEZ Y PELAYO, *Espasa* 22:910–937, good, if dated, summary. E. PANOFSKY, *Idea: Ein Beitrag zur Begriffsgeschichte der älteren Kunsttheorie* (2d ed. Berlin 1960), Greek and Renaissance theory, but cosmopolitan in sweep. Ancient. F. BOURBON DI PETRELLA, *Il problema dell' arte e della bellezza in Plotino* (Florence 1956). E. GRASSI, *Die Theorie des Schönen in der Antike* (Cologne 1962). R. LODGE, *Plato's Theory of Art* (New York 1953). J. G. WARRY, *Greek Aesthetic Theory* (New York 1962). Patristic and Medieval. E. DE BRUYNE, *Études d'esthétique médiévale*, 3 v. (Bruges 1946), a classic study. E. CHAPMAN, *St. Augustine's Philosophy of Beauty* (New York 1939). J. L. CALLAHAN, *A Theory of Esthetic according to the Principles of St. Thomas Aquinas* (Washington 1947). G. B. PHELAN, "The Concept of Beauty in St. Thomas Aquinas," *Aspects of the New Scholastic Philosophy*, ed. C. A. HART (New York 1932). C. C. PUTNAM, *Beauty in the Pseudo-Denis* (Washington 1960). J. STAUDINGER, *Das Schöne als Weltanschauung im Lichte der Platonisch-Augustinischen Geisteshaltung* (Vienna 1948). Renaissance to 19th century. A. BLUNT, *Artistic Theory in Italy, 1450–1600* (Oxford 1940; pa. 1950). A. CHASTEL, "Marsilio Ficino et l'art" in T. W. ADERNO et al., *Filosofia dell'arte* (Archivo di filosofia I; Rome 1953). I. GALANTIC, *A Late Renaissance Theory of Imitation* (Doctoral diss. unpub. Harvard U. 1964). J. STOLNITZ, "Beauty: Some Stages in the History of an Idea," *JHist Ideas* 22 (1961) 185–204, attitudes of the English moralists. I. KNOX, *The Aesthetic Theories of Kant, Hegel, and Schopenhauer* (New York 1936). F. T. VON VISCHER, *Asthetik, oder Wissenschaft des Schönen*, 6 v. (Munich 1922–23), Hegelian classic. F. WILL, *Intelligible Beauty in Aesthetic Thought from Winckelmann to Victor Cousin* (Tübingen 1958), contains also perceptive appraisal of Platonic and Neoplatonic theories. 20th century. V. M. AMES, *Introduction to Beauty* (New York 1931). S. BEHN, *Schönheit und Magie, ein Versuch* (Munich 1932), relationship to ritual and demonism. T. GILBY, *The Poetic Experience* (New York 1934). É. H. GILSON, "Art et métaphysique," *Revue de métaphysique et de morale* 23 (1916) 243–267; *Painting and Reality* (Bollingen Ser 35; 4; New York 1957). Gilson Arts. T. M. GREENE, "Beauty and the Cognitive Significance of Art," *Journal of Philosophy* 35 (1938) 365–381. T. HAECKER, *Schönheit: Ein Versuch* (3d ed. Munich 1953), a realistic view. C. E. M. JOAD, *Matter, Life and Value* (London 1929) 266–283. G. VAN DER LEEUW, *Sacred and Profane Beauty: The Holy in Art*, tr. D. E. GREEN (New York 1963). A. MARC, "Métaphysique du Beau, I," *RevThom* 51 (1951) 112–233. J. MARITAIN, *Art and Scholasticism and the Frontiers of Poetry*, tr. J. W. EVANS (New York 1962); *Creative Intuition in Art and Poetry* (Bollingen Ser. 35; New York 1953). B. MORRIS, "Metaphysics of Beauty," *Journal of Philosophy* 32 (1935) 596–604, behaviorist view. G. MUELLER, "Value and Evaluation of Beauty," *Monist* 41 (1931) 52–66. H. MUNSTERBURG, "The Problem of Beauty," *Philosophical Review* 18 (1909) 121–146.

[C. PUTNAM]

BEAUTY AS A TRANSCENDENTAL

The theory of the transcendental properties of being was formally expounded by Aristotle. Yet even before him thinkers had indicated the transcendentality of beauty, and later philosophers through the centuries have held the same view.

Ancient and Early Medieval Views. At least three pre-Aristotelian thinkers speak, more or less clearly, of the transcendentality of beauty, viz, Heraclitus, Socrates, and Plato. Of the three, *Heraclitus (Diels FrgVorsokr 22 B 102, 1:173) and *Socrates (Xenophon., *Mem.* 3.8.5, 7) assert that everything is both good and beautiful. *Plato teaches the same doctrine in two ways: indirectly, by teaching that whatever is good is beautiful (*Lysis* 216D, *Tim.* 87C) and that everything participates in the good (*Rep.* 517C); and directly, by holding that everything is made both good and beautiful (*Tim.* 53B).

Expounding his theory, *Aristotle lists unity (*Meta.* 1003b 22–23, 1054a 13–19), truth (*ibid.* 993b 31), and goodness (*Eth. Nic.* 1096a 23–24) as transcendental properties, but not beauty—a feature that has become just as characteristic of the Aristotelian tradition as the inclusion of beauty among the transcendentals is characteristic of the Platonic tradition. Among the Platonists, *Plotinus (*Enn.* 5.8.9, 6.6.18, 6.7.31–32) adds beauty to the Aristotelian list of transcendentals, as do St. *Augustine (*Civ.* 11.4.2; *Ver. relig.* 20.40) and Pseudo-Dionysius, all of them maintaining that every being is both good and beautiful. In contrast, the more Aristotelian thinkers, such as *Boethius and the medieval Arabian philosophers, give lists of transcendentals that do not contain beauty. This procedure is the more conspicuous because Avicenna adds two new transcendentals (*res* and *aliquid*) to those mentioned by Aristotle.

In two typically Platonic ways, *Pseudo-Dionysius is an enduring model for medieval thought on transcendental beauty: indirectly, by stressing the real identity of beauty and goodness (*De div. nom.* 4.10, 7; PG 3:705C-D, 704A-B) together with the goodness of God and all creatures; and directly, by teaching that God is beautiful by essence and every creature by participation (*ibid.* 4.7, 701C–704B; 4.10, 708A; *De cael. hier.* 2.3, 141C). See also *John Scotus Erigena, *De div. nat.*, 4.16 and *Hier. coel.* 1.2 (PL 122:827D, 828C; 134), and *Hugh of Saint-Victor, *In hier. coel.* 2.1, and *Didasc.* 7.4 (PL 175:943–944, 176:960–61, 815A).

High and Late Scholastic Theories. The influence of Pseudo-Dionysius continued long after the turn of the 13th century. For instance, the *De bono et malo* (1228) of *William of Auvergne stresses the identity of beauty and goodness at the level of both the divine and the creature, whereas *Thomas Gallus of Vercelli, in his commentary on *De divinis nominibus* (1242), teaches both this identity and the participation of all creatures in God's beauty. On the other hand, one finds St. *Anselm of Canterbury considering truth and goodness as fundamental notions (*De ver.* 7, 10, 13; PL 158:475B-C, 479A, 486B-C) and *Dominic Gundisalvi, a late 12th-century thinker strongly influenced by Boethius and by Arabian Aristotelianism, writing a treatise on unity, the third of Aristotle's transcendentals (*De unitate et uno*). Even *Philip the Chancellor omits beauty from his *Summa de bono* (c. 1230), which lists all three Aristotelian transcendentals.

Compromise Solution. There existed in this period, then, an age-old Neoplatonic and a revived Aristotelian line of thought on the transcendentals. The meeting of the two by way of a genial compromise is to be found in the so-called *Summa fratris Alexandri*—a joint effort of *Alexander of Hales, *John of La Rochelle, and other Franciscans. Their compromise consists of two seemingly clashing doctrines: an initial list of transcendentals containing only unity, truth, and goodness (*Summa* 1.1.2) and the proposal of a real identity and a merely conceptual difference between beauty and goodness (*ibid.* 1.1.3.3.1.1.2 sol.). The latter part of this Franciscan compromise clearly conformed to and continued the old Neoplatonic (i.e., Augustinian and Dionysian) position, whereas the omission of beauty from the list of transcendentals and its treatment only as related to goodness were a concession to the ever-growing Aristotelianism of the times. And, as if to symbolize the relative strength of Neoplatonism over the Aristotelianism then current, the compromise itself was made in the spirit of Plato's *Philebus,* where the idea of beauty is treated as a mere component of the idea of goodness (65A).

This compromise was eventually adopted by Alexander's contemporaries, such as *Robert Grosseteste (unpub. commentary on *De div. nom.*; see Pouillon, 287–288), as well as by the leading thinkers within high scholasticism. Thus, both St. *Albert the Great (*Opusc. de pulchro et bono* 11; ST 1.6.26.1.2.3; 2.11.62.1 sol.; *Summa de bono* 1.2.2 *sol.* 8, 9) and St. *Thomas Aquinas (*In Dion. de div. nom.* 4.5; ST 1a, 5.4 ad 1; 1a2ae, 27.1 ad 3) hold the real identity and virtual dis-

tinction of beauty and goodness, and imply thereby the transcendental coextension of beauty with being, although both (St. Albert in ST 1.6 and St. Thomas in *De ver.* 1.1) omit beauty from their formal list of transcendental properties. St. Albert's disciple *Ulric of Strassburg holds a similar position (*Summa de bono* 2.3.4).

Only a small group of Franciscans rejected the compromise formula. *Thomas of York (unpub. *Sapientiale, c.* 1260) and St. *Bonaventure unhesitatingly list beauty together with the other transcendentals (unpub. comm.; see Pouillon, 281), while also using traditional expressions for transcendental beauty (*In 2 sent.* 34.2.3.6a; *Itin.* 2.10). Thus their philosophies represent the culmination of high scholasticism's concern with transcendental beauty; they were to find an isolated follower a century later in *Denis the Carthusian (*Tr. de venustate mundi et pulchritudine Dei* 1, 3).

Status as a Transcendental. In this light no one can contest that Thomas of York and St. Bonaventure held the transcendentality of beauty. But whether the users of the above-described compromise, i.e., Alexander of Hales, St. Albert, and even St. Thomas, really regarded beauty as a transcendental has been both denied (G. Sanseverino, J. J. Urráburu, D. J. Mercier, P. M. de Munninck, C. Boyer, etc.) and defended (J. Jungmann, J. Maritain, É. H. Gilson, G. B. Phelan, T. C. Donlan, C. A. Hart, J. Owens, etc.). What, then, is the truth?

The Aristotelian and high scholastic criteria for a transcendental property are three: predicability of every being; logical posteriority to being, i.e., by the addition of a logical note, or general mode, to being; and coextension and convertibility. Now, the *Summa fratris Alexandri* (1.2.1.3.6 and 3; 1.2.1.1.2.1.2.3), St. Albert (ST 2.10.39.1.1.2.2 ad 8; 2.11.62.1 sol.), and St. Thomas (*In Dion. de div. nom.* 4.5; ST 1a, 36.2) agree that both God and creatures are beautiful. They all hold also that the beautiful is cognitively delightful and, as such, directly subsequent to the good (*Summa* 1.2.1.2.3; 1.1.3.3.1.1.2 sol.; St. Albert, ST 1.6.26.1.-2.3.8a and sol.; St. Thomas, ST 1a2ae, 27.1 ad 3; 1a, 5.4 ad 1; *De ver.* 21.3). Finally, they hold coextension and convertibility either implicitly, through the real identity and virtual distinction of beauty and goodness, or explicitly (St. Thomas, *In Dion. de div. nom.* 4.22; *De ver.* 22.1 ad 12; ST 1a, 5.4 ad 1). Therefore, the only difference between them and Bonaventure is that they do not, whereas Bonaventure does, explicitly list beauty among the transcendentals. Some hold that this reasoning establishes that these thinkers held beauty to be a transcendental notion only and not a transcendental property of being (*see* THING). Yet any such distinction is of much later origin and is doctrinally difficult to maintain, since nothing but being itself can be the sufficient reason for any transcendental predicability.

John *Duns Scotus does not adopt St. Thomas's compromise treatment of transcendental beauty, nor does he share St. Bonaventure's deep concern with the same. Instead, he stands closest to St. Albert, for both of them add new transcendentals to the traditional list (St. Albert, *honestum* and *decorum*; Scotus, the disjunctive transcendentals), and both reject at least one of the Avicennian additions on St. Thomas's list. They differ, however, in their treatment of beauty: St. Albert often and clearly speaks of beauty as a transcendental, whereas Scotus never goes beyond some cryptic remarks (e.g., *Quodlib.* 18.1 schol.; *De prim. princ.* 3.19) that are difficult to evaluate.

This antitranscendentalist tendency concerning beauty is further strengthened by the interpretation proposed by Tommaso de Vio *Cajetan of a crucial text in St. Thomas's philosophy of beauty (ST 1a2ae, 27.1 ad 3) as meaning that beauty is a species of goodness. Since the *species is less universal than its *genus, the implication is clear: St. Thomas did not hold beauty to be a transcendental. Owing to Cajetan's great authority, this view became widely accepted, although it ignored such Thomistic texts as "truth is the good of the intellect" (*De ver.* 1.10 ad 4 in contr.; ST 1a2ae, 57.2 ad 3) and "truth is a kind of goodness; and goodness, a kind of truth" (*De ver.* 3.3 ad 9; *De mal.* 6.1). Thus, F. de *Toledo, commenting on a parallel text (ST 1a, 5.4 ad 1), does not mention transcendental beauty as an obvious fourth conclusion of the text, and *John of St. Thomas treats only of the three Aristotelian transcendental properties of being. In the meantime, F. *Suárez, himself an antitranscendentalist, introduced the distinction between transcendental notions and transcendental properties of being (*Disp. meta.* 3.2.1)—a doctrine that eventually became an additional basis for antitranscendentalist positions concerning beauty.

These, then, were the factors leading to the virtually universal rejection of transcendental beauty among the schoolmen of the Renaissance and modern times down to the rebirth of scholasticism after the encyclical *Aeterni Patris* (1879).

Neoscholastic Positions. Following the example of some isolated textbook authors (Sanseverino, D. Palmieri, T. Zigliara, etc.), the author of the first elaborate neoscholastic aesthetics, Josef *Jungmann, declared beauty to be a transcendental property [*Ästhetik* (Freiburg im Breisgau 1884) 161]. Although his position was moderate on the question, it elicited a strong negative reaction lead by Urráburu [*Ontologia* (Vallisoleti 1891) 535–541]. Thus began the neoscholastic controversy over the transcendentality of beauty that divided contemporary schoolmen into the transcendentalists, the antitranscendentalists, and the undecided.

The antitranscendentalists are represented by at least three currents of thought. One version consists in explicitly rejecting transcendental beauty on historical (Urráburu, De Munninck), practical (S. Reinstadler, M. de Wulf, E. de Bruyne, C. Frick), or speculative grounds (T. Pesch, F. van Steenberghen, C. N. Bittle). A less immoderate version asserts that a list of transcendentals not including beauty is complete, without explicitly denying, however, the transcendentality of beauty (T. Harper, Mercier, J. Gredt). The most moderate version does not assert the completeness of the list of transcendentals not containing beauty, nor does it raise the question of transcendental beauty at all when treating other transcendentals or beauty itself (S. Tongiorgi, M. Liberatore, K. Gutberlet).

The second main group of modern schoolmen appreciate the arguments of both sides and, consequently, are undecided. Some of them raise the question of transcendental beauty but leave it unanswered or otherwise manifest express their uncertainty over the true answer (J. Donat, A. G. Sertillanges, H. Carpenter, R. J. Kreyche). Others show their indecision by making statements some of which endorse, others reject, transcendental beauty (F. Egger, J. Rickaby). Others again

resort to a compromise formula, referring to beauty as a quasitranscendental or something similar (E. R. Baschab, A. Dupeyrat).

The transcendentalists, who seem presently to constitute the majority, express their position either implicitly (J. S. Hickey, R. Spiazzi) or explicitly, and in the latter case, either with or without qualification. Those who qualify the transcendentality of beauty distinguish between fundamental and formal transcendentality (P. Coffey), transcendentality in the broad and strict sense (A. Rother), transcendental notion and transcendental property of being (H. Grenier, F. X. Maquart), transcendental properties not to be listed and those to be listed separately (Jungmann, H. J. Koren, Boyer, M. Vaske), essential or specific and accidental or individual (A. Stöckl, E. Hugon, L. Callahan), and metaphysical and sensible transcendentality (J. B. Lotz, R. E. McCall, Owens), and concede beauty to be a transcendental in the former but not in the latter senses. Another and much larger group of transcendentalists assert without further qualification that beauty is a transcendental property of being with a unique relation to the intellect and to the will (M. de Maria, V. Remer, L. Baur, P. J. Wébert, Maritain, Phelan, L. de Raeymaeker, E. Chapmann, J. F. McCormick, H. Renard, J. Aumann, G. Esser, G. P. Klubertanz, D. J. Sullivan, Hart, Gilson, J. A. Peter, etc.).

See also TRANSCENDENTALS.

Bibliography: L. DE RAEYMAEKER, *Metaphysica generalis*, 2 v. (new ed. Louvain 1935). H. POUILLON, "La Beauté, proprieté transcendentale chez la scholastique (1220–1270)," ArchHist DoctLitMA 15 (1946) 263–314. F. J. KOVACH, "The Transcendentality of Beauty in Thomas A.," *Die Metaphysik im Mittelalter*, ed. P. WILPERT (Miscellanea mediaevalia 2; Berlin 1963); *Die Ästhetik des Thomas v. A.* (Berlin 1961) 5–10, 20–24, 182–214.

[F. J. KOVACH]

BEAUTY IN AESTHETICS

Beauty is a *quality constituting the nonutilitarian value of a *form, inhering in it as a subtle and hazardous union of the quantitative and qualitative elements, and discovered with increasing interest and adherence of the mind. Although the subtlety of its nature, the complexity and persistence of disputes regarding it, and the radical vicissitudes of the arts have led many of even the best aestheticians to abandon the word beauty, efforts to distinguish the phenomenon it denotes continue undiminished.

Distinctness from Other Values. Because beauty inheres in the organization of the elements of a beautiful object, many consider its value that of substantial rather than of accidental being. However, beauty is not the object organized, but a quality of its organization. Thus an object is not beautiful if its parts lack variety, if their interrelationships lack subtlety, etc. As value, beauty is desirable; but unlike the value that makes things useful or exchangeable, that of beauty is value as end and desirable for contemplation. Such value is said to be aesthetic. Values in the individuated object are suffused and qualify one another, but they can be abstracted by the mind and simplified for the sake of clear distinctions.

Beauty's distinctness from the *good appears in the fact that whereas a thing is beautiful through the internal ordering of its parts, it is good through their external ordering. Hence the good inclines the natural appetite, the sensitive appetite, or the will toward possessing it, whereas the desirability of beauty leads not to possession but only to contemplation. Beauty differs from *truth, for it depends on internal fitness of parts, whereas truth depends on conformity between what is in the mind and what exists in reality independently of the mind. Moreover, unlike beauty, truth qualifies the intellect, not the object known. Only metaphorically and hypothetically can beauty be said to be a "sensuous manifestation of the Absolute." Taken literally, this assertion would make the condition of beauty a fitness between the beautiful object and the ultimate metaphysical reality "behind" appearances, instead of a fitness of part to part within the boundaries of the object itself. By implication it would make beauty a phenomenon of the supernatural rather than of the natural order.

Although the term beauty is sometimes loosely used as a synonym for all aesthetic value, more rigorous usage discriminates between aesthetic qualities. For example, although the sublime or the graceful or both may qualify an object characterized also by beauty, these two aesthetic values are distinguishable from beauty: they both tend, though in opposite ways, toward dynamic disequilibrium, whereas beauty imposes equilibrium. Disequilibrium is inequality between actual formal expression and the intuitive expectation of it in a receiver (viewer, listener, reader). If the sublime characterizes a structure (of meaning), the unexpressed potential seems, by the natural movement of the mind, to be multiplied, while the actual (expression) seems to advance toward relative annihilation. A new potentiality accrues to the scope of meaning. On the other hand, if grace qualifies the form, the actual expression—casually and without strain—exceeds the expectation of already superior expression, and inference is drawn of potential still unactualized. This potential accrues to the agent, who is suspected of an exciting superiority. By contrast with the sublime and the graceful, the beautiful reveals equality between the actual (interrelationship discovered) and the potential. Its potential is perceived as the threat to unity provided by delicate hazards, namely, qualitative and quantitative lures so subtle and various that they are, practically speaking, inexhaustible; thus, as relation is discovered, interest mounts increasingly. Its unactualized potential accrues to the perfection of the structure.

Nature of Beauty. Beauty qualifies both *nature and art, and originates ultimately in the "mind" of God. More immediately, the beauty of an art object originates by the human agency of the artist. The concept of artistic agency is contradicted by the idea that an object is invested with beauty when "touched by a ray of transcendent light." Taken metaphorically, as the familiar image of sunlight illuminating the surfaces of things and so making the world beautiful, it has validity; but this image is rather one of enormous complexity unified by a common reflection. Beauty qualifies structure, whether this organizes the relations among physical elements or among relations simply as such (incorporeal form). However, inquiry inclines usually toward the beauty of what is perceptible by the senses, particularly sight and hearing. Beauty is not imposed on matter as form is, but qualifies form itself. Multiple categorical dissimilarities naturally tend to confusion or to waste. But if in complex aspects of material and formal elements some native similarity is discoverable, the similar parts are perceived as unified, and in the recognition of

this unity the mind is suffused with pleasure. The interest it awakens stimulates apprehension of further relationship, and thus heightens awareness and affectivity. The more profound and hazardous the relationships, the greater the excitement experienced. Relevancies seem privileged and original.

In a beautiful form relationships themselves are found related (proportion), by discoveries that occasion at each instant a pleasurable sense of their inevitability. Hence proportion is apprehended as "due." The affective impulse of the mind as it finds subtle proportions drives it to enjoy relationship, and creates the illusion that unity is inviolable (organic). In the totality of arrangement, as complexity is constantly explored, the surprising new appearances of fitness announce that nothing due is missing (integrity); no incompatibility remains. The unique mode of the relation that unifies relationships specifies the hierarchies in the posture of elements.

Although related surfaces, sounds, aspects, etc., are perceived through the senses, their interrelationships are actualized by the mind. The more delicate these are, the more engaged is the mind—not analytically, but in immediate, primary perception of the whole. Subtlety effects a multiple beguiling of the notice that alternates between synoptic distribution over fields of relatedness and the savoring of individual parts of rare insistence. Beauty is both objective and subjective. It inheres in objects and, being distinguishable, can also provide an objective criterion; yet beauty depends for its appearance on the mind, since it is the mind that renders relation actual.

See also AESTHETICS.

Bibliography: ARISTOTLE, *Poetics,* ed. I. BYWATER (Oxford 1909). R. BAYER, *L'Esthétique de la grâce,* 2 v. (Paris 1933). M. BEARDSLEY, "Beauty and Aesthetic Value," *Journal of Philosophy* 59 (1962) 617–628. W. A. HAMMOND, ed., *A Bibliography of Aesthetics and of the Philosophy of Fine Arts from 1900 to 1932* (rev. ed. New York 1934). T. E. JESSOP, "The Definition of Beauty," *Proceedings of the Aristotelian Society,* NS 33 (1932–33) 159–172. JAesthArtCrit, index to v.1–20. J. LAIRD, *The Idea of Value* (Cambridge, Eng. 1929). H. OSBORNE, *The Theory of Beauty* (New York 1953); *Aesthetics and Criticism* (New York 1955) 325–334, bibliog. on aesthetics. *Proceedings of the 4th International Congress on Aesthetics,* ed. P. A. MICHELIS (Athens 1960) 29–36, 206–209, 458–464, 525–537. P. VALÉRY, *Aesthetics,* tr. R. MANHEIM, v.13 of *Collected Works* (Bollingen Series 45; New York 1964). W. WEIDLÉ, "Biology of Art," *Diogenes* 17 (Spring 1957) 1–5.

[M. F. SLATTERY]

BEAUVAIS

French town at the confluence of the Thérain and Avelon Rivers, 49 miles north of Paris. It is the seat of a diocese (*Bellovacensis*) suffragan to *Reims. The Roman *Caesaromagus,* capital of the Gallic *Bellovaci* tribe, was part of *Belgica II* and no earlier than the 4th century came to be called *Bellovacum* (Beauvais). The introduction of Christianity in the 3d century is traditionally attributed to the martyr Lucian, a Roman, whose 8th-century vita has little historical value. The process of Christianization was set back in the early 5th century by barbarian invasions. The 13th bishop, Maurinus (632), is the first who can be dated. The relics of St. Angadrisma, who entered a nearby monastery (*c.* 660), were translated to Beauvais (851), of which she and Lucian are patron saints.

Merovingian monasteries seem to have been abandoned during the Norman invasions (852–940). *Hincmar was elected archbishop of Reims in a council of Beauvais (845). By 900 the bishops were temporal lords; the last lay count appeared in 1035. In the 12th century the bishops were feudal lords; in 1789 they held 450 fiefs. The commune, which was full grown in 1099, probably received its rights from Bishop Guy (1063–85). *Louis IX used an uprising of the commune as an excuse to violate the episcopal rights of Bp. Milo of Nanteuil (1217–34), who had been a crusader in the East (1218–19) and was with *Louis VIII in southern France (1226). Although a council of *Noyon condemned Louis (1233) and a compromise was achieved (1248), royal authority was entrenched in Beauvais. *Bourgeoisie* uprisings continued, however. During the Hundred Years' War, which devastated the diocese, Bp. Pierre Cauchon (1420–32) helped condemn Joan of Arc. In 1472 Beauvais valiantly withstood a siege of Charles the Bold of Burgundy. In the wars clerical morals declined, buildings were destroyed, and there was no attempt to rebuild. Abbeys were held in *commendation. Beauvais's bishop Cardinal Odet de Châtillon abjured Catholicism for Calvinism (1562), married, and took the title Count of Beauvais (1564); it took until 1569 to depose him.

Claude Gouine, vicar-general of Bp. Nicholas Fumée (1575–92), administered the see until his death (1607), rebuilding churches, reforming religious houses, bringing in Capuchins (1603), and applying some of the decrees of the Council of Trent. The founders of the seminary, which opened in 1648, and Bp. Nicholas Choart de Buzanval (1650–79) were Jansenist, but Toussaint de Forbin-Janson (1679–1713) purged the see of Jansenists, including the erudite hagiographer Adrien Baillet (1649–1706). Bishop F. J. de *La Rochefoucauld died a martyr in Paris (1792), as did the Carmelites in *Compiègne; but most of the clergy accepted the *Civil Constitution of the Clergy. The diocese, which is rural, was suppressed and incorporated into the See of *Amiens (1801) but was restored (1817–22).

The unfinished Gothic cathedral of St-Pierre, begun c. 1240, has collapsed several times. It has a choir, transept, and seven chapels, and a vault 158 feet high; the 13th- to 16th-century stained glass of the windows is famous, as are the tapestries depicting the lives of SS. Peter and Paul. Beauvais's tapestry industry was stimulated by the royal establishment there in 1664.

Bibliography: E. JARRY, *Catholicisme* 1:1361–64. J. BÉREUX, DHGE 7:255–302.

[E. P. COLBERT]

BEBEL, HEINRICH, German humanist; b. Ingstetten, near Justingen, Germany, 1472; d. Tübingen, Germany, 1518. He studied law at the University of *Cracow and belles-lettres at Basel. In 1496 he began teaching rhetoric and poetry at the University of *Tübingen, and he continued in that post for 22 years until his death. He was crowned poet laureate in 1501 by Emperor *Maximilian I, before whom he delivered the *Oratio de laudibus Germaniae* (Pforzheim 1504), a memorable oration on the significance of the *Germania* of *Tacitus. Bebel was in contact with some of the most noted and erudite men of his time, such as *Erasmus, *Reuchlin, *Peutinger, *Wimpfeling, and *Nauclerus. He was considered one of the most celebrated Latinists of his age and authored works on the

methodology of Latin study, such as the *Ars versificandi* (Pforzheim 1506) and the *Commentaria epistolarum conficiendarum* (Strasbourg 1503). Bebel also produced historical and political writings and works on German folklore, publishing in Latin the *Proverbia germanica* (Strasbourg 1508) and, following the example of *Poggio Bracciolini, the *Facetiae* (Strasbourg 1508), popular jokes and anecdotes of a satirical nature directed especially against the clergy. An equally famous work of Bebel is the *Triumphus Veneris* (Pforzheim 1509), a satirical hexameter poem condemning the general moral decadence. Closely linked to the German peasant world, Bebel was the interpreter of its basic traits and expressed its spirit in his writings.

Bibliography: G. W. ZAPF, *Heinrich Bebel nach seinem Leben und Schriften* (Augsburg 1802). F. GELDNER, LexThK² 2:88–89. G. BEBERMEYER, *Tübingen Dichterhumanisten* (Tübingen 1927). H. GRIMM, NDB 1:685–686. Chevalier BB 1:490. L. GEIGER, ADB 2:195–199. J. HALLER, *Die Anfänge der Universität Tübingen 1477–1537*, 2 v. (Stuttgart 1927–29) 1:212–235; 2:76–78; "Heinrich Bebel als deutscher Dichter," ZAlterLit 66 (1929) 51–54. H. HERMELINK, "Die Anfänge des Humanismus in Tübingen," *Württembergische Vierteljahrschefte für Landesgeschichte* 15 (1906) 319–336.

[M. MONACO]

BEC (LE BEC-HELLOUIN), ABBEY OF

Benedictine foundation in Normandy, Diocese of Évreux, north France. It was founded by *Herluin (1034) and eventually established by the stream Bec. After the arrival of *Lanfranc (1041), a brilliant professor of law and grammar at *Pavia and Avranches, the community developed with a cloister school for monks and an outside school for clerics and sons of Norman nobles. As prior, Lanfranc got Pope Nicholas II to grant a dispensation to Duke William of Normandy to marry his cousin Matilda of Flanders (1063); the Duke named Lanfranc abbot of the new monastery of Saint-Étienne in *Caen, built in thanksgiving. After his conquest of England, *William made Lanfranc archbishop of *Canterbury (1070) to reorganize the Church there and be his private counselor, as were later abbots of Bec. *Anselm (of Canterbury), prior of Bec after Lanfranc (1059), was elected abbot after Herluin's death (1078) and, despite the opposition of the community, had to accept the See of Canterbury after Lanfranc's death (1093).

History. At first a poor monastery, Bec soon received many donations from Norman lords and Anglo-Norman kings, especially Henry I and Matilda: liturgical furnishings and relics (1134), many priories in Normandy and England (St. Walburga in *Chester), churches, domains, and fiefs. In 1704 Bec had 87 possessions in the Diocese of *Rouen, 32 in *Évreux, 32 in *Lisieux, 17 in *Paris, and 15 in *Chartres. After Lanfranc and Anselm, *Theobald became archbishop of Canterbury, Gondulf and Arnulf bishops of *Rochester, Hugh and *Gilbert Crispin abbots of *Saint Augustine (Canterbury) and *Westminster.

Bec was a ducal, then a royal abbey, the abbots being confirmed by the dukes, then by the kings of England. The archbishop of Rouen, who blessed the abbot and received the oath of obedience, made 13 canonical visitations; *Odo Rigaldus, who made 13 visitations (1248–69), called Bec the best ruled monastery in Normandy. The kings of France intervened in the 13th century and, from the time of Louis XI, designated commendatory abbots; the first, Jean Boucart, was royal confessor and bishop of Avranches (1471–84); some were generous, some greedy.

In the 14th century there were frequent differences with nobles over tithes and the patronage of churches. Commendatory abbots disputed with the monks over revenue; Roger de la Rochefoucauld (1708–13) demanded an additional 13,000 livres but finally ceded all his holdings for an annual revenue of 48,000 livres. There were frequent and heavy levies by the popes (Syrian Crusade, 1307–12; rebuilding of *Monte Cassino, 1369) and by the kings for war (Charles VI, 1412; Louis XI, 1471) and for levies on the clergy in 1567, 1588, and in 1710 for a final redemption of the head tax.

After an occupation by Anglo-Navarrese troops (1356), Bec was fortified with a French garrison (1358); the cloister and part of the dormitory were torn down and the church used to house refugees and their possessions. Geoffrey Harenc (1388–99) rebuilt the cloister, restored the chapter, and reclaimed the farmland; William of Auvillars (1399–1418) completed an immense wall on the order of the French King (1405–15). Bec sheltered a garrison and refugees when Henry V devastated Normandy. After a 3-week siege it surrendered to the English (May 1418), who pillaged it and kept a large garrison there. Abbot Robert (1418–30) took an oath of fidelity to Henry V (1419). When a French coup almost regained the abbey (June 1421), the monks were expelled and the abbot imprisoned; but Henry V did not hold the monks responsible and restored the temporal goods, ordering the fortress demolished. After his death (1422) anarchy and pillaging ensued. In 1563 Huguenots pillaged Bec, and two monks were slain.

Architecture. The first church burned down in 1158 and was rebuilt and consecrated by the archbishop of Rouen in the presence of the King of England and his sons (1178). After a partial collapse (1197) it was rebuilt under Richard of St. Leger with towers and a spire (1215–17); burned again (1263), it was rebuilt with the aid of a bull of Urban IV and taxes imposed on priories. The lantern tower collapsed, bringing with it the choir and transept (1274); transept and choir with apsidal chapels were rebuilt in grandiose style at a different height than the nave (1275–1327). Painted glass and 16 large statues of Apostles, Evangelists, and Latin Doctors of the Church that were painted and gilded in the 15th century gave added beauty. A square belfrey tower for large bells was completed in 1468. The nave collapsed (1591) and was rebuilt (1639–43), reduced from nine to two bays. The main portal was replaced with a classical façade, bells were recast, and liturgical furnishings renewed (1644–74). The monk architect-sculptor Guillaume de la Tremblaye did the main altar and side altars, the pulpit, a large jube, and a new tomb of Matilda (1684), which was transferred to Rouen (1847). The organs were of English make (1671). Nave vaulting was restored (1699), and choir and sanctuary pavement was done in black and white marble dalles (1710).

The first cloister buildings (1073) were enlarged by Roger I Bailleul (1159–79) with a large hostel, an infirmary and dormitory, and an aqueduct to a covered reservoir. Reconstruction took place under Geoffrey Harenc after 1392, Robert Valée from 1428, Geoffrey

d'Epaigne (1452–76), Louis de Bourbon-Condé (1742–58), and recently under Abbot Grammont (1948).

Culture. Lanfranc (1042–63) was a lucid teacher, subtle, learned, and a skillful dialectician who disputed with *Berengarius. Anselm turned more to the soul, silence, and composure, and fixed the use of philosophy in theology. They had many famous disciples in the school of Bec: Abp. William Good Soul of Rouen, *Ivo of Chartres, Bp. Fulk of Beauvais, Hervé, dean of Canterbury, Gilbert and Miles Crispin (biographers of Herluin and Lanfranc), the prolific writer *Robert of Torigny, Stephen of Rouen (*Draco Normannicus*, a chronicle of Normandy), and Peter of Dives (*Gesta septem abbatum Beccensium*, PL 181:1709–18).

Monastic laxity accompanied wars. The *Maurist reform was introduced (1626) by Abbot Dominic de Vic, Archbishop of *Auch. Peace and order brought prosperity and an increase in revenue; the monks' revenue increased from 30,000 livres (1654) to 48,000 (1685), but the riches benefited the nobility. A theological school was installed (1651) with famous professors: René Massuet (1665–1716), editor of the works of St. Irenaeus, and Guillaume Bessin. A chronicle of Bec to 1331 by Thibaut and a collection by Jouvelin (both in MSS) are valuable historical works.

Lanfranc's library of 160 volumes, primarily on Holy Scripture and the Fathers, increased with bequests by Bp. Philip d'Harcourt of Bayeux (d. 1164; 113 volumes) and the priest and medical doctor Jean de Bessay (14th century). But Estout d'Estouteville took away beautiful MSS in 1391. In 1421 there were 700 volumes besides liturgical books. Some 5,000 volumes were rearranged by the Maurists in 1677. A general inventory of 1671 divided charters into two charter rooms and three chartularies (13th–14th centuries). In 1789 there were 5,000 printed books besides pamphlets, and 220 MSS, of which 19 are extant (12 in Paris Bibliothèque Nationale).

The tradition of generosity to the poor and strangers goes back to St. Anselm. In the 13th century 200 loaves of bread a week were distributed to the poor. Many refugees were cared for in crises (1358, 1417, 1418), and in 1693 some 10,000 were fed in time of need. The people were kindly disposed toward the abbey.

In 1792 the eight remaining monks had to leave. Ten bells and much silver work were sent to Rouen (1789) and *Bernay (1792) to be melted down. The furniture was sold for almost nothing. The lead roof of the church was pillaged. The church itself, fallen to ruin, was condemned and demolished (1810–24); the main altar, jube, statues, and the dalles of the sanctuary were obtained by the pastor of Sainte-Croix in Bernay. The chapter hall was demolished (1816–17). The buildings became a stud farm.

Olivetan Benedictines from Mesnil-Saint-Loup (Champagne) reoccupied Bec (1948), which with 20 monks and many visitors is expanding under Abbot Grammont. The old refectory has been made into a church.

Bibliography: GILBERT CRISPIN, *Vita Herluini*, PL 150:695–714; Eng. ed. in J. A. ROBINSON, *Gilbert Crispin* (Cambridge, Eng. 1911) 87–110. *Chronicon Beccense* (1034–1467), in PL 150:639–695. *Chronique du Bec . . .* (1149–1476), ed. A. PORÉE (Rouen 1883). J. BOURGET, *The History of the Royal Abbey of Bec, near Rouen in Normandy,* tr. from Fr. by A. C. DUCAREL (London 1779), "Philosophe," admirer of Voltaire who ignores early authors because of miracles; brief. A. PORÉE, "L'Abbaye du

Bec au XVIIIᵉ siècle," *Congrès archéologique de France* (Paris 1881) 372–455; *L'Abbaye du Bec et ses écoles, 1045–1790* (Évreux 1892); *Histoire de l'abbaye du Bec*, 2 v. (Évreux 1901). E. VEUCLIN, *Fin de la célèbre abbaye du Bec-Hellouin* (Brionne 1885). B. HEURTEBIZE, DHGE 7:325–335. G. NORTIER, "La Bibliothèque de l'abbaye du Bec," *Revue Mabillon* (Paris 1957) 57–83. M. DE BOUARD and J. MERCET, "La Remise en état de l'abbaye du Bec," *Monuments historiques de la France* 5 (Paris 1959) 149–173. M. P. DICKSON, "Introduction à l'édition critique du Coutumier du Bec," *Spicilegium Beccense* 1 (Paris 1959) 599–632. M. M. MORGAN, *The English Lands of the Abbey of Bec* (New York 1946) J. TAIT, ed., *The Chartulary or Register of the Abbey of Saint Werburgh, Chester*, 2 v. (Manchester 1920–23). Cottineau 1:316–319.

[P. COUSIN]

BECANUS, MARTIN, Jesuit theologian and controversialist; b. Hilvarenbeek (northern Brabant), Holland, Jan. 6, 1563; d. Vienna, Jan. 24, 1624. He received his degree in philosophy at the Jesuit college in Cologne, and in 1583 he entered the Society of Jesus. After teaching philosophy at Cologne, he taught theology for many years at Würzburg, Mainz, and Vienna. During these years he enjoyed great respect for his teaching and produced most of his important writing. In 1620 he became royal confessor to Ferdinand II and he spent his remaining years in Vienna. There he advised the Emperor on the difficult problems concerning relations with the Holy See and toleration of Protestants within the realm.

Becanus was one of the most highly esteemed theologians in Germany in his time and was a prolific writer. He devoted large part of his work to refuting Calvinist teachings and to presenting Catholic doctrine in clear, logical fashion. In this respect his writing was unsurpassed, and the bitterness that characterized so much polemical writing of the day was singularly lacking in his work. His chief theological study, the *Summa theologiae scholasticae* (4 v. Mainz 1612), is for the most part a compendium of the commentary of Suárez on St. Thomas Aquinas. The *Controversia anglicana de potestate regis et pontificis* (Mainz 1612) was placed on the Index in 1613, apparently not because it contained any gross error, but rather to prevent the faculty of the University of Paris from condemning it and at the same time adding their own declarations against papal authority. A short time later the *Controversia* was published again in a corrected edition with a dedication to Paul V. Another important work of Becanus was the *Manuale controversiarum* (Mainz 1623), which went through many editions and was translated into several languages.

Bibliography: Sommervogel 1:1091–1111; 8:1789–90. Hurter Nomencl 1:293–294. E. LAMALLE, DHGE 7:341–344. J. BRUCKER, DTC 2.1:521–523.

[J. T. KELLEHER]

BECCARIA, CESARE BONESANA, political economist credited with ushering in modern criminal law and penal practice; b. Milan, March 15, 1738; d. Milan, Nov. 28, 1794. He was of a noble family, attended the Jesuit college at Parma, and graduated in jurisprudence from the University of Pavia in 1758. Although diffident about his formal education, he was prompted by his association with the intellectual circle of Pietro and Alessandro Verri to write his *Tratto dei Delitti e delle Pene* (1764), first published anonymously, and translated into English as *Essay on Crimes and Punishments*. It was received so enthusiastically throughout the Continent that by 1770 it had appeared in three Italian editions, had been translated into French and English with prefaces attributed to Voltaire, and had received approbation from Catherine the Great as well as from the monarchs of Naples and Austria. Beccaria acknowledged his debt to Jean Jacques *Rousseau, Charles de *Montesquieu, and the *Encyclopedists, for he was in the mainstream of rationalist thought; his influence on Jeremy *Bentham is clear and they are linked as the founders of the classical school of *criminology. Although others had rebelled at the barbarity of prevailing penal practices, it was Beccaria who systematically set forth the principles that punishment should be proportionate to the crime and serve the sole purpose of societal protection.

Bibliography: E. MONACHESI, "Pioneers in Criminology: Cesare Beccaria," *The Journal of Criminal Law, Criminology and Police Science* 46 (1955) 439–449.

[R. LANE]

BECERRA TANCO, LUIS, Mexican scholar whose writings are an important source of information about the apparitions of Our Lady of *Guadalupe; b. Taxco, 1602; d. Mexico City, 1672. He received the baccalaureate in liberal arts and Canon Law from the University of Mexico, where he was appointed to the chair of mathematics. He also distinguished himself in physics and chemistry. Becerra Tanco was regarded by his contemporaries as a marvel in the field of linguistics, for he mastered Hebrew, Greek, Latin, Italian, French, Portuguese, and English, and taught the native Indian tongues of Nahuatl and Otomi. He was renowned also as poet, preacher, philosopher, historian, and scientist. He was ordained under benefice in 1631, and he served in various curacies of the Archdiocese of Mexico. As a historian of the Church in Mexico, he is noted principally for his research on the apparitions of the Blessed Virgin at Tepeyac. His book *Origen milagroso del Santuario de Nuestra Señora de Guadalupe* (Mexico City 1666) was reissued in an enlarged posthumous edition in 1675 under the title *Felicidad de Mexico en la admirable aparición de la Vírgen María Nuestra Señora de Guadalupe* and has been reprinted many times.

Bibliography: BERISTAIN, *Diccionario universal de historia y de geografía*, 10 v. (Mexico City 1853–56) 1:520.

[J. A. MAGNER]

BECHE, JOHN, BL., abbot executed by Henry VIII, also known as Thomas Beche or Marshall; b. 1500?; d. Dec. 1, 1539 (feast, Dec. 1). He received a B.D. at Oxford (1509). He was first a Benedictine monk at the Abbey of Chester. In 1533 he was elected abbot of St. John's Colchester, and he took the Oath of Supremacy in the following year. In 1538, however, he refused to surrender his abbey to the Crown, which in 1539 sought evidence of Beche's treason in order to secure his domain. He was indicted for denying the royal supremacy and sent to the Tower. He made a complete retraction of this denial, but was tried for treason on Dec. 1, 1539, found guilty, and condemned. There is no evidence that he ever reasserted belief in the papal primacy, not even after condemnation.

See also MARTYRS OF ENGLAND AND WALES.

Bibliography: Knowles ROE 3:376, 491. J. E. PAUL, "The Last Abbots of Reading and Colchester," *Bulletin of the Institute of Historical Research* 33 (1960) 115–121.

[J. E. PAUL]

BECHUANALAND, arid, mostly agricultural country, 225,000 square miles in area, in the interior of *Africa, bordered by the Republic of *South Africa, *Southwest Africa, and *Rhodesia. Since 1884 it has been a British protectorate. Together with *Swaziland and *Basutoland it is administered by a high commissioner. The estimated population in 1964 was 350,000, including about 3,000 Europeans and 1,100 Asians. About three-fourths of the inhabitants were pagans. Protestants numbered about 75,000; and Catholics, 7,800. The Holy Ghost Fathers established the first Catholic missions *c.* 1880; but in 1889 the territory was confided to the Oblates of Mary Immaculate. German Oblates labored in the southern section after 1923. In 1930 Mariannhill Missionaries began to labor in the northern parts. The Prefecture Apostolic of Bechuanaland, created in 1959 and entrusted to the Passionists, includes the entire country. In 1964 it had 17 Passionist priests, 2 seminarians, 2 brothers, and 21 sisters.

Bibliography: W. E. BROWN, *The Catholic Church in South Africa* (New York 1960). *Bilan du Monde* 2:123–124. AnnPont (1964) 775. For additional bibliography, *see* AFRICA.

[J. E. BRADY]

BECKER, CHRISTOPHER EDMUND, Salvatorian founder of the Medical Mission Institute of Würzburg; b. Elsoff, near Frankfort am Main, Oct. 22, 1875; d. Würzburg, March 30, 1937. He entered the Society of the Divine Savior in Rome in 1889 and obtained doctorates in philosophy and theology before his ordination in 1898. He was professor and then rector of the Salvatorian house in Merano until in 1905 he was made first prefect apostolic of the Salvatorian mission field in Assam, India. He labored there until World War I interrupted mission activities. With his missionaries, Becker was first interned and then expelled from India. Since it was impossible to return, Becker resigned his position of prefect apostolic after the war. In 1922 he founded the Medical Mission Institute of Würzburg, the first of its kind to train qualified physicians for work in the foreign missions (*see* MEDICAL MISSIONS). He remained director of the institute until his death, and also served as professor of missiology at the University of Würzburg. His writings include: *Im Stromtal des Brahmaputra* (Munich 1927); *Indisches Kastenwesen und christliche Mission* (Aachen 1921); and *Missionsärztliche Kulturarbeit* (Würzburg 1928).

Bibliography: G. WUNDERLE, "Professor C. E. Becker: Gründer des Missionsärztlichen Instituts," *Katholische Missionsärztliche Fürsorge: Jahresbericht* 14 (1937) 3–14. G. SCHREIBER, *Deutsches Reich und deutsche Medizin* (Leipzig 1926) 292– . G. B. TRAGELLA, EncCatt 2:1129.

[W. HERBST]

BECKER, THOMAS ANDREW

Theologian, writer, first bishop of *Wilmington, Del., sixth bishop of *Savannah, Ga.; b. Pittsburgh Dec. 20, 1832; d. Washington, Ga., July 29, 1899. The son of John and Susannah Becker, German Protestants, he attended Allegheny Institute and Western University, Pittsburgh, Pa. While studying at the University of Virginia, he became a friend of Joseph H. Plunkett, pastor of St. Joseph's Church, Martinsburg, W.Va., who probably interested him in Catholicism.

He was received into the Church May 22, 1853, was accepted for the priesthood by Bp. John McGill of Richmond, Va., and in June 1855 entered the College

of the Propaganda in Rome, where he distinguished himself as a student and earned the degree of S.T.D. Following ordination at the basilica of St. John Lateran on June 18, 1859, he was temporarily assigned to St. Peter's Cathedral, Richmond, and in January 1860, succeeded Father Plunkett as pastor at Martinsburg. There, his secessionist position resulted in his arrest for refusing to recite certain public prayers ordered by the provost-marshal for the Union cause. Archbishop Kenrick of Baltimore obtained his release and appointed him to Mt. St. Mary's College, Emmitsburg, Md., to teach dogma, Scripture, and Church history. *See* MT. ST. MARY'S COLLEGE AND SEMINARY. A year later he became secretary to Kenrick's successor, M. J. *Spalding of Baltimore, with whom he collaborated on the *Catholic Miscellany,* and for whom he worked with other theologians on the agenda for the second Council of Baltimore (1866). At the Council's close he returned to the cathedral staff in Richmond, and there organized and directed a boys' school and prepared a prayerbook, *Vade Mecum.* When the see of Wilmington was erected March 3, 1868, Becker was named its bishop and was consecrated (along with the future Cardinal Gibbons) at Baltimore that August 16. Despite the record of his accomplishments as founding bishop, he became discouraged at what he felt was lack of progress, and in September 1879 submitted his resignation, which was not accepted. Meanwhile he worked with Gibbons on preparations for the Third Plenary Council (1884), produced the important chapter on clerical education, and delivered before the Council a sermon on the Church and the promotion of learning. In May 1886, he was transferred to the older see of Savannah, Ga. Eleven years later, incapacitated by malaria, he told Cardinal Gibbons of his intention of retiring. He died at Washington, Ga., while substituting for one of his priests.

Though naturally reticent, Becker was a vigorous and original thinker. He was among the first to advocate establishment of a national Catholic university, in two articles in *American Catholic Quarterly Review* in 1876: "Shall We Have a University?" and "A Plan for a Proposed Catholic University." In discussing secret societies in the same review (1878), he confronted the then controversial topic of labor unions, upholding the right of labor to organize and pronouncing clearly upon the morality of labor practices.

Bibliography: J. G. D. SHEA, *The Hierarchy of the Catholic Church in the United States* (New York 1887). J. T. ELLIS, *The Life of James Cardinal Gibbons,* 2 v. (Milwaukee 1952). Archives of the Archdiocese of Baltimore, of the Diocese of Wilmington, of the Diocese of Richmond, of Mt. St. Mary's College, Emmitsburg, Md.

[E. B. CARLEY]

BECKET, THOMAS, ST.

Archbishop and martyr; b. London, 1117–18; d. *Canterbury, Dec. 29, 1170 (feast, Dec. 29). He was educated at Merton Priory (Surrey) and at Paris. Thomas, of Norman bourgeois parents, became a merchant's clerk in London, but soon joined the household of Abp. *Theobald of Canterbury, and may subsequently have studied at *Bologna. Tall, handsome, vigorous, extroverted, intelligent but not intellectual, Thomas of London, as he was called, lived the life of an ambitious young cleric, ingratiating himself to the old archbishop, who made him archdeacon of Canterbury, and to other prospective patrons.

Chancellor. In 1154, on Theobald's recommendation, the young King *Henry II (b. 1132), to whom Thomas was bound by strong mutual affection, appointed him chancellor. His gifts of administration and initiative and his taste for magnificence together with his charm, his energy, and his efficiency were displayed to the full. He amassed wealth and spent lavishly and generously; he even appeared, while archdeacon, in full armor at the siege of Toulouse. Yet he remained pure and even devout.

Archbishop. Theobald's death (1161) was followed by a long vacancy of the See of Canterbury. The King had begun his lifelong endeavor to gain complete control of his kingdom, with a program that included a submissive Church, and saw in his chancellor the perfect agent and ally. Passing over the respectable Gilbert *Foliot, he pressed Thomas upon the unwilling monks and bishops (1162). The chancellor resisted sincerely, knowing both the King and his own conscience. Once elected, he changed utterly his style of life into one of regularity, piety, and austerity, while retaining his magnificence, his generosity, and his commanding personality. He resisted with audacity all royal encroachments on ecclesiastical liberty, as well as attacks on the possessions and prerogatives of his see.

Conflict with Henry. Discord between King and Archbishop came to a head in the matter of "criminous clerks," the King asserting his traditional right of judgment, the archbishop maintaining the strictest canonical position of complete jurisdiction for the courts Christian. At a council at Westminster (1163) the King demanded from the bishops acceptance of all the "ancient customs" of the realm. They refused, but Thomas later submitted in private. The King repeated his demands at *Clarendon (Wiltshire) in January 1164, finally producing in writing the 16 celebrated Constitutions to which he demanded assent. The bishops submitted, but Thomas immediately repented.

Meanwhile Pope *Alexander III condemned some of the constitutions. In October 1164 the King, in a council at Northampton, demanded the condemnation of the Archbishop for feudal insubordination. His colleagues demurred, but in the end yielded. Henry then pressed a series of frivolous and punitive demands, and there were threats of imprisonment and even of death. The bishops, forbidden by Thomas to judge him, appealed against him to the Pope while the lay barons passed judgment. Anticipating his sentence, the Archbishop fled and escaped to France, taking refuge in the Cistercian Abbey of *Pontigny and devoting himself to penitential exercises and the study of Canon Law. His exile lasted till 1170; the King of France welcomed him, and the Pope, then in France, proclaimed the justice of his cause. But Alexander III was himself in grave difficulties with the Emperor and his antipope, and was unwilling to go to extremes with Henry, and the months and years passed while the King harassed and exiled the Archbishop's relatives and allies, and the Archbishop excommunicated and suspended his opponents. Negotiations, and even a meeting of the two in 1169, broke down.

At last Henry and some bishops made the grave error of crowning (June 14, 1170) "the young king," Henry's son, in defiance of Canterbury's rights, which had been reaffirmed by the Pope. The bishops were excommunicated, and the King felt it necessary to yield. A recon-

Murder of St. Thomas Becket, miniature in the Carrow Psalter (Walters MS 34, fol. 15 v.), English, c. 1250. This is one of the earliest representations of the act.

ciliation, satisfactory to Thomas, took place at Fréteval (Orléanais) on July 22. Once more the King broke faith, supported by some bishops; once more Thomas excommunicated his enemies. His return to England was a triumph. But the injured prelates had inflamed the King's mind; he called for a riddance from his enemy and four knights crossed at once to Canterbury where, after a stormy interview, they murdered the Archbishop in his cathedral (December 29). The atrocity shocked all Europe. Miracles were reported at the tomb; the Pope excommunicated the King, who later did penance and abated his principal claims and was reconciled at Avranches (1172). In 1173 Thomas was canonized, and his tomb rapidly became a resort of pilgrims; churches were dedicated to him from Iceland to Spain.

Estimate of Becket's Career. The issue between King and Archbishop was confused by clashes of temperament and emotion and embittered by the King's insincerity and the Archbishop's pugnacity. Henry aimed at a complete control of the Church at a time when Europe had accepted the papal claims of *Gregory VII (see GREGORIAN REFORM). Thomas stood for those claims in their entirety. Had he not resisted, England might have become for a time a separated unit in Christendom. By his death he won for his cause an immediate victory, which gave place in time to a compromise in practice. His biographers all wrote to celebrate a saint, but there will always be disputes about his character and his cause. Worldly and ambitious for long, and retaining even as archbishop traits of impetuosity and harshness,

Gold pendant reliquary of St. Thomas Becket, Norman or Sicilian, made before 1183 for Queen Margaret of Sicily, who is shown receiving episcopal blessing. If the figure of the bishop represents Becket, it is the earliest known effigy of the saint.

he nevertheless showed in adversity a steadfast courage and devotion to principle that gained him a death he and others regarded with justice as a sacrifice for the freedom of the Church in England.

Bibliography: Sources. *Materials for the History of Thomas Becket,* ed. J. C. ROBERTSON, 7 v. (RollsS 67; 1875–85); for criticism, E. WALBERG, *La Tradition hagiographique de Saint Thomas* (Paris 1929). Literature. D. KNOWLES, *The Episcopal Colleagues of Archbishop Thomas Becket* (Cambridge, Eng. 1951); *The Historian and Character* (New York 1963). There is no adequate modern life. R. FOREVILLE, *L'Église et la royauté en Angleterre . . . 1154–1189* (Paris 1943), is full and scholarly, but biased. **Illustration credits:** Fig. 1, Courtesy of Walters Art Gallery, Baltimore. Fig. 2, The Metropolitan Museum of Art, Purchase, 1963, Joseph Pulitzer, Bequest.

[M. D. KNOWLES]

BECOMING, a philosophical term (Gr. γίγνεσθαι; Lat. *fieri*) that is not strictly definable but is understood by contrast with permanent *being. Man's senses show him all things as coming-to-be and passing away. *Heraclitus made this process essential to physical bodies to the exclusion of any permanent being. The Heraclitean position was revived with some modification in modern philosophy by G. W. F. *Hegel and H. *Bergson. *Parmenides declared becoming illusory and emphasized the absolute and unchangeable character of being, as conceived by the intellect. *Plato tempered this opposition with the distinction that becoming is perceived by opinion with the help of sensation, while being is perceived

by reason (*Rep.* 508D). The reconciliation of becoming with being thus became the central problem of Greek philosophy. *Aristotle distinguished the kinds of being—potential and actual, substantial and accidental—and thus was able to show that there is becoming with respect to each class of being (*Phys.* 201a 8, 225a 12–19). The term becoming in an unqualified sense came to be reserved for the coming-into-being of substances. The coming-into-being of accidents is called "becoming with qualification." When an accident is changed from a less to a more perfect state, the process is called motion. Contemporary psychology, under the stimulus of existentialism, uses the term becoming to signify the development of *personality.

See also CHANGE; MOTION; GENERATION-CORRUPTION.

[M. A. GLUTZ]

BÉCQUER, GUSTAVO ADOLFO, Spanish poet; b. Seville, Feb. 17, 1836; d. Madrid, Dec. 22, 1870. Orphaned at an early age, Bécquer went to Madrid at 18 and devoted himself to journalism. The many privations he suffered there ruined his already fragile health, and he was just winning a literary name at the time of his early death. His collaborative work with Juan de la Puerta, *Historia de los templos de España,* appeared in 1857, but Bécquer's independent work was published only posthumously under the title *Rimas* (1871). Bécquer produced his lyrics when the anti-Romantic reaction appeared to be triumphant. He remained faithful to the old poetic movement; yet at the same time he transcended *Romanticism and approached a very modern concept of the poetic phenomenon. His lyrics—intimate, delicate, and very simple—contrast strongly with the high-sounding, heavily ac-

Gustavo Adolfo Bécquer.

cented poetry of José Zorrilla, *Espronceda, or the Duke de Rivas. Some critics have explained Bécquer's uniqueness by exaggerating the evident influence of H. Heine. Undoubtedly Bécquer's preference for amorous themes concisely expressed in a minor key does liken him to the German poet, especially if one considers Heine's "Intermezzo," which Bécquer certainly knew. However, other critics have shown not only that Bécquer and Heine were quite different personalities, but that Bécquer's best contribution to the Spanish lyric is found precisely in the poems that owe the least to Heine.

In his prose Bécquer reflects more clearly the spirit of the preceding generation, both in his language and in his choice of subject matter, which embraces folklore, medievalism, mystery, magic, old monasteries or palaces, and ruins. But the fundamental intimacy of *Rimas* also infuses his prose works; indeed, the simple title of *cartas* used for two of his works (*Cartas literarias a una mujer* and *Cartas desde mi celda*) suggests the idea of "confidences." His *Leyendas* always begin with the narration of a personal experience that justifies the remembrance or invention of the story. The key theme of *Rimas,* the conflict of the poet's somber and somewhat disillusioned imagination with reality, also informs these stories.

Bibliography: *Obras completas* (repr. Buenos Aires 1944). L. CERNUDA, "Bécquer y el romanticismo español," *Cruz y Raya* 26 (May 1935) 45–73. J. CASALDUERO, "Las *Rimas* de B.," *ibid.* 32 (Nov. 1935) 91–112. B. JARNÉS, *Doble agonía de Bécquer* (Madrid 1936). J. GUILLÉN, *La poética de Bécquer* (New York 1943). E. L. KING, *G. A. Bécquer: From Painter to Poet* (Mexico 1953). J. P. DÍAZ, *G. A. Bécquer: Vida y poesía* (Montevideo 1953). **Illustration credit:** Embassy of Spain, Washington, D.C.

[A. RISCO]

BECQUEREL, ANTOINE CÉSAR, French physicist; b. Châtillon-sur-Loing (Loiret), March 8, 1788; d. Paris, Jan. 18, 1878. He is credited with the development of batteries and early studies of thermoelectric phenomena. After entering l'École Polytechnique at 18, he fought in Spain with the Napoleonic armies. He was a captain at 24, married Aimée-Cecile Darlui at 25, and retired from the army at 27 because of poor health. His most important scientific achievements were in electricity, but he was interested in all aspects of physics as evidenced by over 500 studies written by him. After demonstrating that electric energy in a battery is due to chemical activity rather than to physical contact between substances, he developed a constant output battery free from polarization. His studies in piezoelectric and thermoelectric phenomena led him to invent the electric thermometer, the differential galvanometer, and the electromagnetic balance.

Bibliography: J. A. BARRAL, *Éloge biographique de M. Antoine-César Becquerel* (Paris 1879). G. BARRAL, *Le Panthéon scientifique de la Tour Eiffel* (Paris 1892). E. LE GAL and L. KLOTZ, *Nos grandes savants* (Paris 1926).

[E. T. SPAIN]

BECQUEREL, ANTOINE HENRI, French physicist, discoverer of *radioactivity; b. Paris, Dec. 15, 1852; d. Croisic, in Brittany, Aug. 25, 1908. He was the son of Alexandre Edmond and the grandson of Antoine César; he entered l'École Polytechnique at 19 and taught there later, as well as at the Museum of Natural History, like his father and grandfather. He was a member of the most important scientific societies, obtained the Rumford prize (London 1900), the Helmholtz

medal (Berlin 1901), the Nobel prize with Pierre and Marie *Curie (1903), and the Barnard medal (U.S. 1905). After the discovery by Röntgen of cathode rays, Becquerel started experimenting with phosphorescent

Antoine Henri Becquerel.

substances. One cloudy day he noted that some uranium salts, unactivated by sunlight, exposed photographic plates. Becquerel concluded the radiation came from the uranium itself, not from the action of light on it. The radiation was the result of the splitting of uranium or radium atoms and was independent of pressure, temperature, or chemical composition. It was complex, being magnetically separable into α, β, and γ components. Becquerel also discovered and studied properties about the magnetic polarization of light, showing the influence of the earth's magnetic field on the plane of polarization of sunlight. Other studies include those on absorption spectra in crystals. His writings appeared mainly in *Comptes Rendues, Annales de Chimie et de Physique,* and *Journal de Physique.*

Bibliography: A. BROCA, *Revue générale des sciences* (Oct. 30, 1908). G. LE BON, *L'Évolution de la matière* (Paris 1905) 18–42. J. BECQUEREL, *La Radioactivité et les transformations des éléments* (Paris 1924). **Illustration credit:** French Embassy Press and Information Division, New York City.

[E. T. SPAIN]

BEDA COLLEGE

In 1852 Pius IX, supported by Cardinal Nicolas P. Wiseman, founded the Collegio Ecclesiastico in Rome to provide a house of studies for a number of distinguished Anglicans who had joined the Church as the result of the *Oxford Movement and wished to become priests. Later, this College became better known as the Collegio Pio and moved from the Piazza Scossa Cavalli to the English College in the Via Monserrato, though preserving its distinct character. In 1897 Cardinal Herbert Vaughan interested Leo XIII in the development of the College, and Msgr. Rafael Merry del Val (later Cardinal) was deputed to study the question. In 1898 a *motu proprio* was issued whereby the constitution and rules (drafted by Merry del Val and Msgr. John Prior) were sanctioned. The College was thereby founded anew and called after the Venerable Bede. In 1917, after an Apostolic Visitation under Benedict XV, the Congre-

Beda College for late vocations, with the Basilica of St. Paul's, Rome, in the background.

gation of Studies decided upon the total separation of the Beda from the Venerable English College, thereby giving to Beda its own corporate life and its own premises. As a result it moved to the Via San Nicolo da Tolentino in 1922. Thirty-eight years later, the generosity of Pius XII made possible the erection of a much larger college opposite the Basilica of St. Paul's. This was completed in 1960 and was formally opened by John XXIII on October 20. In the constitutions appended to Leo XIII's motu proprio the object of the Beda is spoken of as threefold: to train and form English converts for the priesthood, to train candidates of mature age, and to enable English priests to pursue further studies in Rome.

The College is governed by a rector and vice rector, with a staff of professors. The Beda Association, a group of former students and friends of the College, provides financial help toward the cost of training late vocations to the priesthood. The Beda differs from ordinary seminaries and has a character all its own. No one under 24 is eligible, and no one is admitted unless he is first adopted and sent by a bishop. If a student is able to attend one of the universities in Rome, he does so; otherwise he takes the Beda course, in which philosophy is concentrated into 1 year, and theology into a cycle of 3 years. Although explanations are given in English, studies are made from the ordinary Latin textbooks. In this way the student becomes familiar with the complete scholastic system.

Apart from the main library, which is noted for a fine collection of the works of Cardinal Henry Newman, there is also the Charles Duchemin library, a memorial to Msgr. C. L. H. Duchemin, for 33 years rector of the College (1928–61). In this latter is housed the bequest of Msgr. H. K. Pierce, a former student, who left a collection of rare Anglican works on theology and history for the benefit of research students.

In 1964 there were 75 resident students besides 8 members of religious orders who lived in their own communities. Many distinguished men have passed through the Beda, either as postgraduate priests or as regular students. Some have been raised to the episcopate in England, the U.S., and other parts of the world. Among outstanding names is that of Msgr. Horace K. Mann, the writer of the volumes on the *Lives of the Popes of the Middle Ages* (rector 1917–28).

Almost every calling and profession is represented at the College. The non-Catholic ministry, soldiers, sailors, doctors, lawyers, schoolmasters, businessmen, craftsmen, musicians, artists—all meet on the common ground of service in the priesthood. Another important element is composed of the priests recently ordained who are doing postgraduate studies in Rome and whose bishops find the Beda a convenient place for them to work. Under Beda's freer discipline the students can enjoy the wider cultural advantages of Rome without foregoing the benefits of a religious institution. They also gain by association with men whose experiences are extensive and varied. On the other hand, for converts and late vocations it is of the greatest importance to be associated with Catholic priests trained in the normal seminary from boyhood.

Bibliography: LEO XIII, "Partem multo maximam" (Motu Proprio, December 29, 1898) *Leonis XIII Acta* 18 (1898) 204–210. "Constitutiones Collegii Bedani de Urbe," ActApS 10 (1918) 203–206. *Regulae Collegii Bedani* (Vatican City 1918). *The Beda Book* (London 1957).

[J. J. CURTIN]

BÉDARD, PIERRE STANISLAS, statesman and judge; b. Charlesbourg, near Quebec, Canada, Nov. 13, 1762; d. Trois-Rivières, Canada, April 26, 1829. He was the son of Pierre Stanislas and Marie Josephte (Thibault) Bédard. After studies at Quebec College, he took up law and was one of the first Canadians to be admitted to the bar of Lower Canada. In 1792 he was elected representative of Northumberland County to the Legislative Assembly of Lower Canada, a position he held until 1812, at which time he was appointed to the magistracy. As one of the founders and editors of the newspaper *Le Canadien* (1806), he was imprisoned without trial by Gov. James Craig (1810). In 1812 the new governor, Sir George Prévost, released him and, as compensation for his unlawful imprisonment, Bédard was appointed judge in Trois-Rivières, a post he held until his death. He married Jeanne Louise Luce Françoise Fremiot de Chantal, daughter of François Lajus, and they had four sons.

Bibliography: N. E. DIONNE, *Pierre Bédard et ses fils,* v.1 of *Galerie historique,* 8 v. (Quebec 1909–13). F. J. AUDET, "L'Honorable Pierre-Stanislas Bédard," in *Proceedings of the Royal Society of Canada* (Ottawa 1926).

[G. CARRIÈRE]

BEDE, ST.

Monk, priest, theologian, and Doctor of the Church; b. in the English kingdom of Northumbria in the region south of the River Tyne, probably 672 or 673; d. in his monastery in the same region, probably 735. Knowledge of the main facts of his life and work is solidly based on his own account at the end of his *Historia Ecclesiastica gentis Anglorum* (completed 731). Born on land that shortly afterward came to belong to the dual monastery of SS. Peter and Paul, with houses at Wearmouth and Jarrow, Bede was entrusted by relatives to that monastery. He spent the rest of his life there, being ordained deacon at the unusually early age of 19 and priest at 30. The "Venerable" by which he is commonly known was probably the title given to priests then (*see* JARROW, ABBEY OF; WEARMOUTH, ABBEY OF).

Scope of His Work. In the course of an outwardly quiet life, Bede used the considerable monastic library assembled by the founder and abbot, Benedict Biscop (*c.* 628–690), to become one of the great polymaths of the medieval Church. His works cover secular areas, such as grammar, metrics, and chronology; the latter a speciality of his, related both to his historical interests and to his concern with the controversy, still alive in his day, against those Celts who had not yet accepted Roman practice in computing the date of Easter (*see* EASTER CONTROVERSY). The *Ecclesiastical History* is commonly and rightly regarded as a decisive moment in the development of the art and science of historiography. Bede's voluminous commentaries on Scripture were highly valued by his contemporaries and throughout the Middle Ages. Here Bede seems to have aimed primarily at presenting clearly the opinions of the great Latin Fathers, mainly (but not exclusively) Augustine, Jerome, Ambrose, and Gregory; but he certainly knew Greek and probably some Hebrew. Some of Bede's letters, particularly one to his former student *Egbert (d. 766), Archbishop of York, are also of importance. Other of his historical works are the *History of the Abbots* (of his monastery) and a life of Cuthbert in verse and prose.

More specifically literary works include Latin poems, homilies, and a poem on death in five alliterative lines in Northumbrian English. In general, present literary taste finds Bede at his best in the great sections of the *Ecclesiastical History* and in passages of a more personal character, such as prayers, scattered throughout his works.

The general image of Bede suggested by these passages is borne out by an account of his death written by a pupil who was present. Bede was a monk radiant with a holy joy in teaching and learning. All who come to know him in his work will understand why Plummer wrote in 1896: "We have not, it seems to me, amid all our discoveries, invented as yet anything better than the Christian life which Bede lived, and the Christian death which he died." Regard for the beauty of Bede's character, however, should not obscure appreciation of his intellectual acuity and of the originality of his contribution to the development of practice and thought in the Western Church. Bede had a sense for contemporary fact. His exegetical works show, in their precision and clarity, his feeling for the needs of the monastic students of non-Latin background who would use them. The letter to Egbert is full of sane practical suggestions, including use of the vernacular in prayers, for improving the religious life of the Northumbrian laity.

Significance of the Work. Bede's own sense for the exigencies of time and situation sharpened his awareness of the same quality in others and hence contributed to the value of the *Ecclesiastical History*. The notable portrait of St. *Aidan (of Lindisfarne, d. 651) is a case in point. Almost everything known about Aidan is from Bede, and what Bede tells of the specific working of the Irish mission makes it possible to say that Aidan was one of the great missionary geniuses of all time. Knowledge of another practical genius, the Easterner Theodore of Tarsus (602–90), who came to England well advanced in age, and, as Archbishop of Canterbury, inaugurated a golden era of early English Christianity, is likewise derived mainly from Bede's pages. That golden age was coming to an end by the time of Bede's death, but it had fulfilled its purpose; it had brought to completion the long and demanding task, begun 300 years earlier by British and Irish Celts, of preparing Western Christianity to assimilate the un-Romanized and barbarous North.

With almost prophetic genius Bede saw and judged clearly the importance of what had been going on in the England of his own and the preceding generation. His *Ecclesiastical History* images forth great events in a way that reveals their significance. Therein lies its value as history; but more than historical insight is involved. It may well be that Bede's scriptural commentary is derivative and presents little in the way of theological development. The *Ecclesiastical History*, however, does represent a significant advance in theological insight. Here an opening to a new day in the life of the Church was recognized, even as it took place, and was preserved in a form that taught posterity to sense the theological significance of the contemporary.

See also ENGLISH LITERATURE, 1; HISTORIOGRAPHY, ECCLESIASTICAL.

Bibliography: *The Complete Works*, ed. J. A. GILES, 12 v. (London 1843–44), latest complete ed. A new ed. meeting modern philological requirements is now appearing in CorpChrist; v.119 (1962) and v.120 (1960), *Opera exegetica*, ed. D. HURST, and v.122 (1955), *Opera homiletica*, ed. D. HURST, and *Opera rhythmica*, ed. J. FRAIPOINT, have appeared. *Eccl. Hist.*, ed. C. PLUMMER, 2 v. (Oxford 1896; repr. 1956), indispensable notes and best general account and appreciation of Bede. Trs. of *Eccl. Hist.* T. STAPLETON (1565), rev. J. E. KING (LoebClLib; New York 1930), bilingual. EngHistDoc, v.1, *c.* 500–1042, ed. D. WHITELOCK, select bibliog. Laistner ThLett. *Bedae Venerabilis opera de temporibus*, ed. C. W. JONES (Studies in Medieval History NS 9; Cambridge, Mass. 1943). T. A. CARROLL, *The Venerable Bede: His Spiritual Teachings* (Washington 1946). **Illustration credit:** Through the courtesy of the director of the Biblioteca Sanctorum, Vatican City.

[C. J. DONAHUE]

BEDFORD, GUNNING SAMUEL,

physician; b. Baltimore, 1806; d. New York, Sept. 5, 1870. In 1825 he graduated from Mt. St. Mary's College, Emmitsburg, Md., and in 1829 received his medical degree from Rutgers Medical College. The next 3 years he spent in special studies in Europe. In 1833 he became professor of obstetrics in Charleston (S.C.) Medical College; in 1840 he and Dr. Valentine Mott established the University Medical College in New York, where he held the chair of obstetrics until 1862. Dr. Bedford founded the first obstetrical clinic in the U.S. for the gratuitous care of

Last page of a manuscript of the "Historica Ecclesiastica" preserved in the public library at Leningrad (fondo MS Lat. Q.v.I.18, fol. 161) with the autograph(?) of Bede ("Beda Famulus Christi indignus") at the lower right.

indigent women. Two of his works, *Diseases of Women and Children* (1855) and *Principles and Practice of Obstetrics* (1861), were adopted as textbooks in both the U.S. and Europe. Dr. Bedford had an important place in the teaching and development of obstetrics, and he influenced both physicians and the general public.

Bibliography: *The National Cyclopedia of American Biography* 35 v. (New York 1892–1949) 9:361. *Catholic Builders of the Nation,* ed. C. E. McGuire, 5 v. (Boston 1923) 4:55–56.

[M. A. STRATMAN]

BEDINGFELD, FRANCES, English religious and educator during penal times; b. Redlingfield, Norfolk, 1616; d. Munich, Germany, 1704. Frances, a member of a devout Catholic family of Norfolk, from which 12 daughters entered religion, joined the English Institute of Mary, known also as the Institute of English Virgins, at Munich and was professed in 1633. This society had been founded in 1603 for the Catholic education of young Englishwomen. Mother Bedingfeld succeeded her sister as superior of the motherhouse in 1666 and 3 years later was invited by Catherine of Braganza, Catholic consort of Charles II, to open a school in London. With several English companions she founded an academy at Hammersmith; 7 years later another school was established at Mickelgate Bar, York. Mother Bedingfeld's years in England coincided with the intensification of harassment of Catholics by the authorities. She was forced to adopt the alias of Mrs. Long and to wear secular dress, and she was repeatedly haled before the local magistrates. During the hysteria of the "Popish Plot," she was briefly committed to Ousebridge jail in York in 1679. In 1699 she returned to the convent at Munich, where she enjoyed a wide reputation for sanctity. She lived to see the rule of her order approved by Clement IX in 1703.

Bibliography: DictEngCath 1:166–168. H. Foley, ed., *Records of the English Province of the Society of Jesus,* 7 v. (London 1877–82) 5.1:579–582.

[H. F. GRETSCH]

BEDINI, GAETANO, cardinal, priest, diplomat, administrator; b. Sinigaglia, Italy, May 15, 1806; d. Viterbo, Sept. 6, 1864. After his ordination at Sinigaglia on Dec. 20, 1828, by Cardinal Fabrizio Sceberas-Testaferrata, Bedini held a variety of posts. He was appointed secretary to Cardinal Ludovico Altieri, Papal Nuncio to Vienna (1838); then became apostolic internuncio to the Imperial Court of Brazil (1846); substitute secretary of state of the Vatican (1848); prolegate to Bologna (1849), and later extraordinary pontifical commissioner of the four legations of Bologna, Ferrara, Forti, and Ravenna. Raised to the rank of titular archbishop of Thebes and apostolic nuncio to Brazil (March 15, 1852), he was consecrated in Rome, May 1852, by Cardinal Altieri. Supposedly on his way to Brazil, Bedini visited the U.S. (June 30, 1853–Feb. 4, 1854). In June 1856 Pius IX named him secretary of the Congregation of Propaganda Fide. On March 18, 1861, he was elevated to the See of Viterbo-Toscanella and in the consistory of Sept. 27, 1861, he was created cardinal priest with the title church of Santa Maria Sopra Minerva.

Bedini's trip to the U.S. secured his place in the history of the American Church. He came to investigate the Church in the U.S. and the possibility of establishing an apostolic nunciature in Washington. Rome needed more information about the missionary Church in the U.S. Astounded at the continued increase in the number of Catholics and the resulting pressing need for more bishops, dioceses, priests, churches, and charitable institutions, the Holy See desired a firsthand report. The need for this knowledge was made sharply evident by Rome's failure to assess the rampaging anti-Catholicism in the U.S. at that time.

Almost as soon as he landed in New York, Bedini felt the sting of this anti-Catholicism, which was instigated by German and Italian revolutionaries and American nativists and encouraged by some of the press during his visit to more than 20 cities in the U.S. and Canada. In Philadelphia, Pa., and Buffalo, N.Y., he was unsuccessful in solving the trustee problems. There were disturbances in Pittsburgh, Pa., and a riot in Cincinnati, Ohio, while he was present, and he was constrained to sail secretly from New York.

When he returned to Rome, without going to Brazil, he inspired the foundation of the North American College. The first part of the report he submitted to the Vatican secretary of state gave a detailed description of the Church in the U.S.; the second part stressed the necessity, but also inopportuneness of establishing an apostolic nunciature in Washington. The Bedini mission having failed, Rome waited until 1893 to act in this matter, and then erected an apostolic delegation.

Bibliography: J. F. Connelly, *The Visit of Archbishop Bedini to the United States of America* (Rome 1960).

[J. F. CONNELLY]

BEDJAN, PAUL, missionary and orientalist; b. Khusrawi, Iran, Nov. 27, 1838; d. Cologne-Nippes, Germany, June 9, 1920. He studied at the minor seminary of the French Vincentians in Khusrawi (1850–56), changed from the *Chaldean to the Latin rite, and entered the Vincentian novitiate in Paris in 1856. He was ordained May 25, 1861, and returning to northwest Persia did missionary work in Khusrawi and Rizaiyeh until 1880. It distressed him that only Protestants were printing books in Neo-Syriac, the vernacular of his people, and he returned to Europe to devote himself thereafter to the publication of texts in Syriac (36 v., Paris 1885–1912). Some of these were popular works of religious devotion, his own compositions or translations into Neo-Syriac, but most were carefully prepared editions of ancient Syriac texts based on MSS of libraries and museums in Europe and the Near East. With the approval of the Holy See, which made him a consultor on the Congregation of the Propaganda in 1886, he printed a new edition of the Breviary for priests of the Chaldean rite (3 v., 1886–87), but the Chaldean patriarch of Mosul, Abp. Elias Abolionan, rejected the Missal he had likewise prepared because of its innovations. Noteworthy are Bedjan's editions of the Acts of Martyrs and Saints of the East (7 v., 1890–97), the Sermons of Jacob of Sarûg (5 v., 1905–10), and the Book of Heraclides of Damascus (1910), an authentic but then unknown writing by *Nestorius.

Bibliography: A. Rüker, *Kulture* 31 (1912) 200–208. F. Combaluzier, DHGE 7:410–413. J. M. Vosté, "Paul Bedjan, le lazariste persan," OrChrPer 11 (1945) 45–102.

[L. F. HARTMAN]

BEDÓN, PEDRO, Ecuadorian Dominican painter and social worker; b. Quito, c. 1555; d. there, Feb. 27, 1621. Bedón was the son of the Asturian Pedro Bedón and Juana Díaz de Pineda of Quito, daughter of the conquistador and scribe, Gonzalo Díaz de Pineda. Bedón studied philosophy in Quito under professors who had come from the University of San Gregorio in Valladolid. He studied theology at the University of Lima, where he learned the art of painting under the Jesuit brother Bernardo *Bitti. Returning to Quito in 1587, he taught philosophy and theology at the Dominican school. He devoted his free time to social service, through the Confraternity of the Rosary, which he organized with Spanish, Indian, and Negro members. In addition, he founded a school of painting for the Indians, whom he put to work making copies of choral books with beautiful initial letters. He raised the question of the legality of the sales taxes and as a result was forced to go to Bogotá and soon afterward to Tunja. In both cities he left examples of his artistic skill. At Bogotá he held the chair of theology. In 1596 he returned to Quito, where he resumed his scholarly career and his social apostolate. He founded the convent of Riobamba and of La Recoleta in Quito, and one in Ibarra. Elected provincial, he traveled about the cities of the *audiencia,* examining not only the religious establishments but also the situation of the Indians. On behalf of the Indians, he negotiated with the authorities with a zeal worthy of *Las Casas. Bedón is one of the most important representatives of Ecuadorian culture and of the social apostolate. He is considered the father of painting in Quito.

Bibliography: J. M. VARGAS, "El venerable padre maestro fray Pedro Bedón, O.P.: Su vida, sus escritos," *El Oriente Dominicano* 8 (1935) 115–117.

[J. M. VARGAS]

BEDOS DE CELLES, FRANÇOIS, mathematician, authority on organ building; b. Caux (near Beziers), France, Jan. 24, 1709; d. Abbey of Saint-Denis, Nov. 25, 1779. Dom Bedos entered the Benedictine monastery of La Daurade, Toulouse, in 1726(?), and was professed in 1746(?). By virtue of his high competence in mechanical and mathematical sciences, he was named a corresponding member of the Académie royale des sciences de Paris in 1758 and of that of Bordeaux in 1759. His treatise *La Gnomique pratique ou l'art de tracer les cadrans solaires* (sun dials) appeared in 1774. For many years he was called upon from every corner of Europe to lend his assistance in designing, building, or renovating great organ installations of his time, including those at Tours, Narbonne, Carcassonne, Bordeaux, and Mans, as well as the clock chimes at Saint-Denis. His monumental work, *L'Art du facteur d'orgues* (4 v. 1766–78), has become a basic sourcebook for the theory and practice of both organ construction and organ registration.

See also ORGAN.

Bibliography: *L'Art du facteur d'orgues,* ed. C. MAHRENHOLZ, 4 v. (Kassel 1935–36). B. HEURTEBIZE, DHGE 7:414. C. MAHRENHOLZ, MusGG 1:1494–99. F. GEHRING, Grove DMM 1:527–528. F. RAUGEL, *Recherches sur quelques maîtres de l'ancienne facture d'orgues françaises* (Paris 1925). W. L. SUMNER, *The Organ: Its Evolution, Principles of Construction and Use* (3d ed. London 1962). W. H. BARNES, *The Contemporary American Organ* (7th ed. Glen Rock, N.J. 1959).

[C. BERNIER]

BEDYLL, THOMAS, clerk of Privy Council; b. unknown; d. London?, September 1537. He received his education at New College, Oxford, and became secretary to William Warham, Archbishop of Canterbury, remaining in his service until the archbishop's death in August 1532. He was then appointed clerk of the Privy Council. As such, he was engaged in securing the support of Oxford University for Henry VIII's proposed divorce from Catherine of Aragon. When, in May 1533, Archbishop Cranmer declared the marriage invalid, Bedyll, who was present, wrote Thomas Cromwell expressing his approval of the decision and assuring him that it would "please the King's Grace very well." Throughout the next 2 years he was occupied in administering the oath supporting the royal supremacy, in various religious communities. In 1536, after the trials of John Fisher and Thomas More, in which he had participated, Bedyll made a series of visits to confiscated monastery lands and was then appointed to a committee considering the validity of certain Papal bulls. Bedyll's only surviving works are his letters that, despite his later change of allegiance, show him to have been on moderately friendly terms with More and Erasmus in his youth.

Bibliography: C. T. MARTIN, DNB 2:120–121. Hughes RE. *The Epistles of Erasmus,* ed. F. M. NICHOLS, 3 v. (New York 1962).

[J. G. DWYER]

BEECHER, a prominent New England family headed by Lyman Beecher, whose 13 children included the well-known Harriet Beecher Stowe and Charles, Edward, Thomas, Catherine, and Henry Ward Beecher.

Lyman, Congregational preacher and first president of Lane Theological Seminary in Cincinnati, Ohio; b. New Haven, Conn., Oct. 12, 1775; d. Brooklyn, N.Y., Jan. 10, 1863. He was born just a year before the Declaration of Independence and he died just after Lincoln's Emancipation Proclamation. During his undergraduate days at Yale University, New Haven, Conn., he was strongly influenced by its Pres. Timothy *Dwight and became an ardent exponent of revivals, especially during his third pastorate (1826) at the newly organized Hanover Street Church in Boston, Mass. His earlier pastoral experience had been obtained at the Presbyterian Church at Easthampton, N.Y. (1799), and the Congregational Church at Litchfield, Conn. (1810). Beecher, a colorful personality, became famous for his sermons against dueling, intemperance, infidelity, disestablishmentarianism, and slavery. His *Six Sermons on Temperance* (1825) underwent several editions and translations. In 1832, with Dr. Leonard Bacon, Beecher formed an American Anti-Slavery Society, which focused the interest of churches on the antislavery movement. Although prosecuted for "heresy, slander, and hypocrisy," he was eventually cleared by his Synod, most of whom had "Old School" sympathies. His seven sons entered the ministry, and his two daughters became famous authors. In 1871 Yale University inaugurated the annual Lyman Beecher Lectures on Preaching in his memory.

Henry Ward, Congregational preacher, journalist; b. Litchfield, Conn., June 24, 1813; d. Brooklyn, N.Y., March 8, 1887. In 1834 he graduated from Amherst College, Mass., and entered Lane Theological Seminary, Cincinnati, Ohio. After pastorates near Cincinnati and in Indianapolis, Ind., he was called (1847) to the Plymouth Congregational Church of Brooklyn, N.Y., and preached there with unremitting zeal for 40 years. Accused of dallying with the affections of Elizabeth Til-

The Beecher family, photograph by Matthew Brady. Lyman is seated at the center, Henry Ward stands at the extreme right, Harriet is seated second from the right.

ton, wife of his good friend Theodore Tilton, who had succeeded him as editor of the *Independent,* he successfully weathered "the great scandal" of the 1870s and retained his position and influence. He was intensely opposed to slavery, favored woman suffrage, and supported the theory of evolution. In 1870 he became editor of the *Christian Union.* As the most eloquent preacher of his day, he attracted thousands by his dramatic, warm, and Christocentric Gospel message. His published works include *The Life of Jesus the Christ* (1871) and *Evolution and Religion* (1885).

Bibliography: L. BEECHER, *Autobiography, Correspondence, etc.,* ed. C. BEECHER, 2 v. (New York 1864). L. ABBOTT et al., *Henry Ward Beecher* (new ed. Hartford 1887). R. SHAPLEN, *Free Love and Heavenly Sinners* (New York 1954). **Illustration credit:** Library of Congress, Brady-Handy Collection.

[J. R. WILLIS]

BEELEN, JAN THEODOOR, exegete and Orientalist; b. Amsterdam, Holland, Jan. 12, 1807; d. Louvain, Belgium, March 31, 1884. He made higher studies in Rome, where he received the doctorate in theology, and in 1836 he was appointed professor of Sacred Scripture and Oriental languages at the Catholic University of Louvain. In 1876 he relinquished his position to his pupil, T. J. *Lamy. He was the author of many Biblical works; his commentary on the Epistle to the Romans (Louvain 1854) was held in high regard. He published also works in the field of Oriental scholarship, including a useful *Chrestomathia rabbinica et Chaldaica* (3 v. Louvain 1841–43). He revived Oriental studies in Belgium, where he established an Oriental printing plant, for which he purchased complete fonts of Hebrew, Syriac, Arabic, and Ethiopic type. He was made domestic prelate of the pope, consultor of the Congregation of the Index, honorary canon of Liège, and Knight of the Order of Leopold.

Bibliography: O. REY, DB 1.2:1542–43. A. KLEINHANS, Enc Catt 2:1140. F. BECHTEL, CE 2:388.

[M. C. MC GARRAGHY]

BEELZEBUB, a name used in the NT for "the prince of *demons" (Mt 12.24; Lk 11.15). The enemies of Jesus said that He was possessed by Beelzebub (Mk 3.24), that He was Beelzebub in person (Mt 10.25),

and that it was by the power of Beelzebub that He cast out demons (Mt 12.24–26;. Lk 11.15, 18–19). However, the form of this name as Beelzebub is found only in the Latin and the Syriac versions; almost all the Greek MSS have Βεελζεβούλ (Beelzebul), while a few very old MSS (Vaticanus and Sinaiticus) have Βεεζεβούλ (Beezebul). A comparison of Mt 12.24 with Mt 12.26 shows that this name, whatever its correct form may have been, was used interchangeably with that of *Satan or the *devil. Since both Satan in Hebrew (*śāṭān*) and devil in Greek (διάβολος) have the meaning of adversary, accuser, and slanderer, the peculiar Gospel name for the same evil spirit may rightly be surmised to have the same meaning. The form Beelzebub cannot be disconnected from the Aramaic word *bʿʿel-dᵉbābā,* which has precisely the same meaning as the above-mentioned Hebrew and Greek words (i.e., adversary, accuser, Satan) and is itself a loanword from the Akkadian term *bêl dabābi* (literally "master of speech," but in usage, "litigant, adversary in a lawsuit"). There can be hardly any doubt, therefore, that the original Gospel form was Beelzebub, and not Beelzebul or Beezebul. The latter forms (of the Greek MSS) may represent dialectal pronunciations or may have been caused by confusion with the name of the pagan god of Accaron (Ekron), who is mentioned in 4 Kgs 1.2–16.

However, the original form and meaning of the name of this god of Accaron are doubtful. In the Masoretic Text it is given as *baʿal zᵉbûl,* which is commonly explained as meaning "the lord of flies." Perhaps the Israelites, too, attached this meaning to the term. But it is hard to believe that the people of Accaron so understood it. More likely *zᵉbûl* in this term meant "dwelling, temple" (cf. Is 63.15; 3 Kgs 8.13), or it is to be connected with the Ugaritic word *zbl,* meaning prince, ruler. The rendering of *baʿal zᵉbûl* as Βεελζεβούβ (Beelzebub) by the Septuagint and Symmachus was probably due to its phonetic resemblance with the Aramaic word for Satan.

Bibliography: J. SCHNACKENBURG, LexThK² 2:97. A. PENNA, EncCatt 2:1140–41. EncDictBibl 218. W. FOERSTER, Kittel ThW 1:605–606.

[M. R. RYAN]

BEETHOVEN, LUDWIG VAN

German composer; b. Bonn, Jan. 15 or 16, 1770; d. Vienna, March 26, 1827. The composer's grandfather, Louis van Beethoven, had been Kapellmeister in the chapel of the archbishop elector of Bonn (1761); his father, Johann, a member of the electoral chapel choir until 1789, was a teacher of clavier and violin. In 1767 Johann had married Maria Magdalena Laym; three children of this marriage survived infancy: Ludwig, Caspar Anton Karl (b. 1774), and Nikolaus Johann (b. 1776). In 1787 Maria Magdalena died; 2 years later Johann van Beethoven, for whom life had never been very smooth, was dismissed from his position. Thus at the age of 19 his son Ludwig was in fact the head of a family, with two younger brothers to support and guide.

Early Years. He had given early evidence of his musical talent, and, although his first music teachers were not particularly distinguished, Beethoven did have the opportunity sometime about 1781 to study under a competent composer, Christian Gottlob Neefe, who was organist at the electoral court. Under his tutelage Beethoven studied Bach and other composers so well that

Ludwig van Beethoven, crayon drawing by August Karl Friedrich von Klöber, c. 1818.

at the age of 12 he was permitted, in Neefe's absence, to supervise orchestra rehearsals for the court theater. At 14 he was appointed assistant court organist. In 1788 while still serving as organist, Beethoven was also playing viola in the orchestra for operatic performances at the court; this position helped him become familiar with operas by the leading composers of the day—Mozart, Cimarosa, Paisiello, Gluck, and others.

It is possible that Beethoven may have met Mozart in 1787, and had a few lessons in composition from him. He may have met Haydn in 1790; at any rate, Haydn, impressed by an original composition Beethoven had written, brought the young man to Vienna (1792) to continue his study of composition under him. These lessons ended sometime before early 1794. Among others with whom Beethoven studied were Albrechtsberger, known for his sacred music and his theoretical work on counterpoint; Johann Schenk, a composer of Singspiele; and Antonio Salieri, Kapellmeister at the Viennese court and a composer of Italian operas. The association with Salieri continued until 1802.

In 1798 and 1799 Beethoven became aware of increasing difficulty in hearing. Doctors and treatments could not help him, and the inexorable progress of his deafness caused that great spiritual crisis that is reflected in the "Heiligenstadt Testament," a letter Beethoven wrote to his brothers in 1802.

Personal Traits. Beethoven seems to have been extremely careless about his physical appearance; he certainly was absentminded. As his hearing grew worse, he became more and more moody and irritable. He

appears never seriously to have lacked money; his compositions, however much they may have been misunderstood by his contemporaries, were evidently very much appreciated. Beethoven's income had been derived from playing the piano before his deafness cut off this source of revenue; he also taught, and derived further income from dedicating works for a fee, and from the sale of rights to his compositions. In these negotiations he seems often to have been deplorably unscrupulous, selling the same rights to different persons at the same time. From 1809 on he received an annuity provided by the Archduke Rudolph, Prince Lobkowitz, and Prince Kinsky. Freed in these ways from economic and patronal pressure, Beethoven was able to compose his music to please no demands but those of his own genius.

In Bonn he was in the service of the archbishop, and among the dedications of his compositions there are several to the Archduke Rudolph, Beethoven's patron and former pupil who became archbishop of Olmütz in 1820. He was generous with his services for charity and more than once permitted his music to be used at a concert for the benefit of an Ursuline convent school at Graz.

Beethoven's relationships with his family were unhappy. He never married, and the two younger brothers, whose guardian he had become at 19, both made marriages of which he disapproved. His brother Caspar died in 1815, and Beethoven was declared sole legal guardian of Caspar's son, Karl (1819). The youth, who did not respond well to Beethoven's well-intentioned but often misplaced efforts, attempted suicide in 1826. Beethoven's relations with his youngest brother, Nikolaus Johann, were complicated by the composer's dislike for Nikolaus's wife. It was after a visit to their home with Karl in 1826, that, on the trip back to Vienna, he fell ill, and died several months later, after receiving the last rites of the Church.

His Music. Among his compositions are nine symphonies, 11 overtures, various concerti (including five for piano and one for violin), 16 string quartets and much other chamber music, 30 piano sonatas and numerous sets of variations for piano, the oratorio *Christus am Ölberg* (1802), the opera *Fidelio* (1804), and two Masses. The earlier of these, the Mass in C, Op. 86, was composed in the honor of Princess Esterhazy and was first performed on the Sunday after her name day, Sept. 13, 1807, in Eisenstadt—the same occasion and place for which in other years some of Haydn's Masses were composed. The other, the Mass in D, usually known as the *Missa solemnis,* Op. 123, was begun in 1819, and was to have been performed at the installation of the Archduke Rudolph as archbishop. The *Missa solemnis,* however, was not completed until 1823.

Beethoven's Masses, traditional in many respects, are scored for solo quartet, chorus in four parts, and orchestra. They feature word painting (rising lines on "ascendit in caelos," for example), dramatic contrast (sharp difference in scoring, dynamics, and rhythm between the phrases "Gloria in excelsis Deo" and "et in terra pax"), standard devices for setting certain words (rests between repetitions of the word "non"), and the use of instrumental forms in some movements. These characteristics of Beethoven's Masses are similar to those to be found in the works of numerous other composers of the late 18th and early 19th centuries.

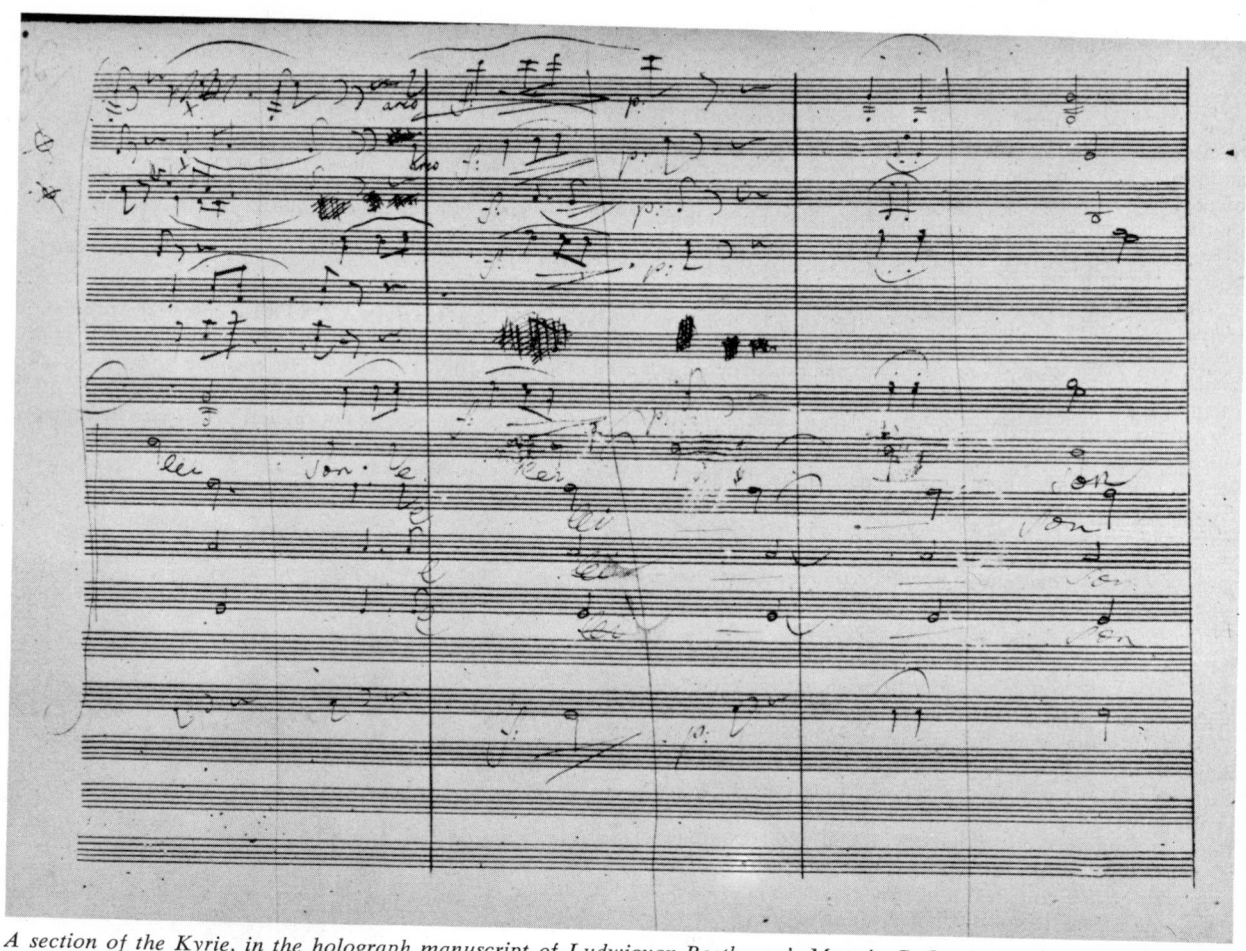

A section of the Kyrie, in the holograph manuscript of Ludwigvan Beethoven's Mass in C, Op. 86.

At times, however, the scoring in Beethoven's Masses differs from that of other Masses of the classic period. Orchestral introductions and interludes are more prominent. Great attention is paid to orchestration: there are monumental, brilliantly written *tutti* passages (e.g., "Gloria in excelsis Deo" in the *Missa solemnis*). There are also passages where the use of sharply reduced orchestral forces produces very impressive effects (e.g., the beginning of the Benedictus in the same Mass, where there are only two flutes and a solo violin; the middle of the Agnus Dei, with only two trumpets and tympani). The solo singers often have highly dramatic and individual lines, which would be artistically impossible for a chorus to perform. A particularly striking example of this is in the Agnus Dei of the *Missa solemnis* where each of the soloists sings "Agnus Dei, qui tollis peccata mundi" in the style of operatic accompanied recitative to an ominous background of trumpets, drums, and strings *tremolo*. On the other hand, Beethoven sometimes has the solo quartet sing together unaccompanied in a homophonic style, similiar to that of the chorale; this happens, for example, in the Benedictus of the Mass in C.

A composer of Masses who wishes, as Beethoven did, to compose music reflective of the rhythm and the meaning of the words, has a particular problem with the long texts. If each new idea in the text is given its own theme, the work becomes too diffuse; if each of these themes is developed, the movement can become too long. The use of some sort of refrain is one way of solving this problem. In the Gloria of the *Missa solemnis,* Beethoven creats a vigorous rising figure for the opening line which he brings back on the phrases "laudamus te" and "Domine Deus," as well as at the end, after the fugue, with its original text.

Missa Solemnis. However, if the movements with short texts are not to be dwarfed by the others, their texts must be repeated to expand the length of the movement. For example, in Masses of the classic period, the Benedictus is often a slow lyrical movement, with many repetitions of text, in binary form. It is preceded by a Sanctus set briefly and in homophonic style, a Pleni in a terse but brilliant style—sometimes polyphonic—and an Osanna similarly set. It is followed by a second Osanna section (sometimes a literal repeat of the first) and, in some cases, by a phrase of the Benedictus and a final Osanna. This basic form is found in the Sanctus of the *Missa solemnis* and also in that of the Coronation Mass (k. 317) of Mozart. The *Missa solemnis* Sanctus differs from the earlier work most conspicuously in its length. In such late works as the *Missa solemnis,* Beethoven writes very long lines, avoiding cadences through a variety of devices, and expanding the length of movements proportionately.

The *Missa solemnis* is gigantic in length, style, and emotional range. It is true that in Bach's Mass in B minor, for example, changes in scoring, range, rhythm, and texture dramatize the text: the "Crucifixus" sounds tragic, the "Et resurrexit" jubilant. But Beethoven explores the possibilities of text expression even further; he uses the changing emotions inspired by the Mass text as impulses toward the creation of a musical expression of the text. Further, he works and reworks his ideas so that in each movement there is a strong and compelling drive from one idea to the next, and an ending that is both overwhelming and inevitable.

The *Missa solemnis* contains two ponderous and extremely complex fugues that end the Gloria and the Credo; but it also has passages of serene lyricism, such as the Benedictus. This Mass is not an objective statement of the text, but an emotional expression of it resulting from a serious and highly personal reflection on the words. Its inappropriateness for the liturgy has not prevented it from affecting many listeners quite deeply.

Bibliography: W. M. McNAUGHT, Grove DMM 1:530–595. D. F. TOVEY, *Essays in Musical Analysis,* v.1 (London 1935) 21–67. *Thayer's Life of Beethoven,* rev. and ed. E. FORBES, 2 v. (Princeton 1964). **Illustration credit:** Beethoven House, Bonn.

[R. STEINER]

BEGA (BEE), ST., Irish saint, 6th–7th century (feast, Sept. 6 or Oct. 31). Although nothing certain is known of her life, legend says that she was a daughter of an Irish king, and that, having vowed virginity, she fled Ireland rather than marry a son of the king of Norway. Her name was early corrupted to Bee. She is thought to have been the founder (*c.* 650) of St. Bees in Cumberland, England, a cell later belonging to St. Mary's York. This and other indications of the presence of her cult in the northwest of England (e.g., the name of the town and headland, St. Bees) are evidence of early Irish influence in that area. Through the centuries her life became confused with that of Heiu of Hartlepool, the first Northumbrian woman to take the veil, receiving it from *Aidan of Lindisfarne (d. 651). Heiu founded the monastery of Hartlepool, which was later taken over by *Hilda of Whitby. Both Bee and Heiu must be distinguished from St. Begu (*Begga), an Anglo-Saxon nun who died Oct. 31, 681, and whose feast is September 6 or October 10. Begu was a nun at Hackness in Northumbria, one of the houses under Hilda, and, according to *Bede (*Eccl. Hist.* 3, 4), it was Begu who had the vision of the soul of St. Hilda being received into heaven.

Bibliography: ActSS Sept. 2:694–700. C. COTTON, DHGE 7:423–424, 449–450. Zimmermann KalBen 3:19–21. Baudot-Chaussin 10:1012–13. Butler Th Attw 3:498.

[E. JOHN]

BEGGA, ST., widow, patron of Beguines; d. Andenne, Dec. 17, 693 (feast, Dec. 17). She was the daughter of Pepin of Landen and St. *Iduberga, and the older sister of St. *Gertrude of Nivelles. Begga married the nobleman Ansegis and was the mother of *Pepin the Short. After becoming a widow she founded (in 691–692) a convent at Andenne, near Namur, Belgium. The first nuns came from Nivelles and introduced Irish monastic customs. Begga's remains are preserved at Andenne; her vita was written in the late 11th century. She is invoked for the cure of hernias and of infants' diseases. Although she has been the patroness of

the Beguines [*see* BEGUINES AND BEGHARDS] since the 14th century, she was not their foundress.

Bibliography: Sources. J. G. DE RYCKEL, *Vita S. Beggae* (Louvain 1631). P. SMET, *Acta Sanctorum Belgii selecta,* ed. J. GHESQUIÈRE et al., 6 v. (Brussels 1783–94) 5:70–125. Literature. L. VAN DER ESSEN, *Étude critique et littéraire sur les Vitae des saints mérovingiens* (Louvain 1907) 182–186. F. BAIX, DHGE 7:441–448. Butler Th Attw 4:579. Baudot-Chaussin 12:504–505. É. BROUETTE, "Le Plus ancien MS de la *Vita Beggae,*" *Scriptorium* 16 (1962) 81–84. H. PLATELLE, BiblSanct 2:1077–78.

[É. BROUETTE]

BÉGIN, LOUIS NAZAIRE, cardinal archbishop of Quebec, Canada; b. Lévis, Canada, Jan. 10, 1840; d. Quebec, July 18, 1925. He was the son of Charles and Luce (Paradis) Bégin. After attending the minor seminary of Quebec, he completed his studies in Europe, was ordained in Rome (1865), and received a doctorate

Louis Nazaire Bégin.

in theology. Back in Quebec, he taught theology, held various offices at the seminary, and published several works that merited him entrance into the Royal Society of Canada. In 1888 he was appointed second bishop of Chicoutimi, where he built a bishop's palace. He was transferred to Quebec as coadjutor (1891) and became, successively, administrator (1894), archbishop (1898), and cardinal (1914). He founded 70 parishes, welcomed several religious communities to the archdiocese, and sanctioned ecclesiastical and charitable institutions, as well as the work of the newspaper *L'Action Catholique* and a famous diocesan temperance campaign. He reestablished the cathedral chapter of canons in 1915. The First Plenary Council of Canada took place (1909) during his reign.

Bibliography: L. A. PAQUET in *The Royal Society of Canada. Proceedings* (Ottawa 1926), eulogy. **Illustration credit:** Public Archives of Canada.

[H. PROVOST]

BEGUINES AND BEGHARDS

The feminine religious movement known as the Beguines and the masculine counterpart, the Beghards, belong to the blossoming and multiplicity of the religious life that, with the *vita apostolica* as the premise for reform, accompanied urbanization and the increasing articulation of laymen in spiritual matters during the high Middle Ages. The terms Beguine and Beghard occur persistently in contemporary literature, but they are often used loosely: sometimes as abusive epithets by opponents, through confusion with doctrinal aberrations, sometimes as synonyms for kindred lay movements. Possibly originating with a Catharist tinge (*see* *CATHARI), *beghini* continued to denote, in Provence, the *Apostolici, *Fraticelli and Franciscan *Spirituals. In the Rhineland they were identified with the heretical *Brothers and Sisters of the Free Spirit. However, if their way of life had much in common with that of the penitential associations, hospital orders, and the *Humiliati of Lombardy, as well as the *third orders, it also looked back to recluses, *Cistercians, and *Premonstratensians and forward to the *Devotio Moderna. Although Beguinal convents were common in German towns, it was above all in the Low Countries that they prospered. Beghards never achieved the same prominence (*see* SPIRITUALITY OF THE LOW COUNTRIES; SPIRITUALITY, RHENISH).

Way of Life. Beguines can best be described as extra-regulars, since they occupied a position midway between monastic and lay status. Although not bound by irrevocable vows, orthodox Beguines, particularly in Flanders, Brabant, and the Diocese of Liège, partook of the instruction and examples of older monachism, chiefly Cîteaux (J. Greven), the canons regular, and eventually the friars. As *congregationes beguinarum disciplinatarum*, they exemplified popular mysticism, guided by hierarchy and sacrament. They put a premium on geographical stability as long as they owed obedience to local statutes, the superior of the Beguinage, and ecclesiastical authority. In their espousal of the common life they dwelt either in small convents, as in Germany, or in a large, walled enclosure, known as a Beguinage (e.g., in Burges, Ghent). Beguines promised to observe chastity during their sojourn in the community, but they could freely leave to marry or to engage in ordinary lay pursuits. In place of a formal vow of poverty they retained possession of house and property; they emphasized manual work, whether caritative (education, nursing) or industrial (cloth-and lace-making). Whether in temporary or permanent retreat, they sought to leaven their daily life with religious practices.

History. To underscore their quasi-religious character the women were at first called *mulieres religiosae* or *sanctae, virgines continentes,* or *dilectae Deo filiae.* The fact that the term *beguina* in its earliest appearance in the north (*Caesarius of Heisterbach in *c.* 1199 and the *Chronica regia of Cologne* in 1209) is prejorative suggests that it may be a corruption of "Albigeois" (J. Van Mierlo). Derivation from St. *Begga may be dismissed as a tradition rooted in regeneration in the 17th century. Although place and date of origin cannot be determined with certainty, Lambert le Bègue (d. 1177), a reforming priest in Liège, organized what might be called proto-Beguines. The Beguinage was one answer to socioeconomic problems—the *Frauenfrage*—relating to widows and unmarried women, but to associate the inmates only with the dispossessed, at least in the beginning of the movement, begs oversimplification (Grundmann). Their infirmary not only served as a hospital, but, as a foundation for the indigent, it supplemented the Holy Ghost Table. However, the Beg-

hards or Bogards, who were often fullers, dyers, and weavers in the Flemish cloth industry, reflect wider recruitment from the lower classes. This is even more true of the vagrants in the Rhineland who, dependent on mendicancy, were wont to shout *Brod durch Gott* ("Bread for the love of God"). That the feminine religious movement continued to be the object of disparagement is evident from *Jacques de Vitry's vita of *Mary of Oignies (ActSS June 4:630–684), written shortly after her death (1213). His is an eloquent description of the spirituality of the coteries at Nivelles and Oignies. In spite of attempts of *Lateran Council IV to curb the proliferation of new orders and to exact submission to an approved rule (c.13), Jacques obtained from Pope *Honorius III in 1216 oral approbation for the *mulieres religiosae* in France and the Empire (*tam in regno quam in imperio*), as well as in the Diocese of Liège, to live together under one roof and to exhort each other to perform good works [*Ep.* 1, ed. R. B. C. Huygens, *Lettres* (Leiden 1960) 74]. The crusade preacher saw in these women an antidote to the *Albigenses. Pope Gregory IX's bull *Gloriam virginalem* (1233) hastened the maturing of the Beguinages. If Jacques was their patron at the papal Curia, closer to home the *beguinae clausae* could expect protection from the episcopate as well as from the counts of Flanders and the dukes of Brabant. While they enjoyed in Paris the all-encompassing endowment for which King Louis IX was renowned, Rutebeuf included them in his vast indictment of "pseudo-religious."

Beguines continued to be suspected of heretical inclinations, and the brief career of Margaret Porete (d. 1310) or Bloemardinne of Brussels (d. 1336) seemed to substantiate the charges. But it was the Beguines and Beghards in Cologne and Strasbourg who gave the gravest concern. After many tentative steps at discipline, Henry II of Virnebourg, Archbishop of Cologne (1306–32), took action against the Beghards in 1307. But it remained for the two Clementine decrees, *Cum de quibusdam mulieribus* and *Ad nostrum qui desideranter*, promulgated at the Council of *Vienne in 1311, together with reenactments by *John XXII, to focus attention on the Beguine-Beghard issue and to enlist papal support in the efforts of the episcopate to crush heretical confraternities. Yet *Clement V had added a saving clause when he exempted the orthodox communities in the West from persecution. In his bull *Racio recta non patitur* (1318) John XXII acknowledged that many Beguines led a life in obedience beyond reproach and therefore should be tolerated. This statement was supplemented the following year by the bull *Sacrosancta romana*, which put the *beguinae clausae* of Brabant, together with their property, under papal protection. The sporadic prosecution of the extraregulars in the Rhineland during the 14th century was thus paralleled by the rehabilitation of those in Belgium and their incorporation into the ecclesiastical fabric through closer identification with approved religious orders, adoption of the Rule of St. *Augustine, and parochial organization.

Modern Era. After a period of decay the 17th century witnessed a reform that assured the Beguinages fresh vitality. Although hard pressed during the French Revolution, Belgian Beguinages have continued to the present day to maintain something of the rich heritage of medieval spirituality. Beguine literary figures included the Flemish *Beatrice of Nazareth and the poetess *Hadewijch (fl. 1240), and the German *Mechtild of Magdeburg. To the Beguines and Beghards in Strasbourg Meister *Eckhart delivered sermons.

Bibliography: J. GREVEN, *Die Anfänge der Beginen: Ein Beitrag zur Geschichte der Volksfrömmigkeit und des Ordenswesens im Hochmittelalter* (Münster 1912); "Der Ursprung des Beginenwesens," HistJb 35 (1914) 26–58, 291–318. L. J. M. PHILIPPEN, *De Begijnhoven: Oorsprong, Geschiedenis, Inrichting* (Antwerp 1918). J. VAN MIERLO, DHGE 7:426–441, 457–473; DictSpir AscMyst 1:1341–52. F. VERNET, *ibid.* 1329–41. D. PHILLIPS, *Beguines in Medieval Strasburg: A Study of the Social Aspect of Beguine Life* (Stanford 1941). A. MENS, *Oorsprong en betekenis van de Nederlandse Begijnen en Begardenbeweging, Vergelijkende Studie: XIIde–XIIIde Studie* (Louvain 1947). E. W. MCDONNELL, *Beguines and Beghards in Medieval Culture, with Special Emphasis on the Belgian Scene* (New Brunswick, N.J. 1954). R. MANSELLI, *Spirituali e Beghini in Provenza* (Istituto Storico Italiano per il Medio Evo. Studi Storici 31–34; Rome 1959). E. G. NEUMANN, *Rheinisches Beginen- und Begardenwesen* (Meisenheim am Glan 1960). H. GRUNDMANN, *Religiöse Bewegungen im Mittelalter* (2d ed. Hildesheim 1961). G. KOCH, *Frauenfrage und Ketzertum im Mittelalter* (Berlin 1962).

[E. W. MC DONNELL]

BEHAIM, MARTIN (BÖHEIM), cartographer, constructor of the first globe; b. Nuremberg, Germany, 1459? (some traditions say as early as 1436); d. Lisbon, Portugal, Aug. 8?, 1507. Much of what was written of Behaim is now subject to serious doubt. He went to Portugal in connection with Flemish trade and gained some scientific reputation by claiming to be a pupil of *Regiomontanus. He was appointed to the commission (the "junta dos mathematicos") that advised John II on navigation. The claims that he introduced the cross-staff into Portugal, that he improved the astrolabe, and that he accompanied Diogo Cam on his second African expedition are all highly questionable, the last being no longer held at all. In 1490 Behaim returned to Nuremberg, where he constructed a globe, the earliest extant. It is about 21 inches in diameter, and its geography is mainly Ptolemaic. Despite his associations in Portugal, he did not even represent the Portuguese discoveries correctly. The globe is of great historical interest, but it is doubtful that it has any connection with Columbus, as has sometimes been claimed.

Bibliography: C. G. VON MURR, *Diplomatische Geschichte des portugiesischen berühmten Ritters Martin Behaim* (Nuremberg 1778). F. W. GHILLANY, *Geschichte des Seefahrers Ritter Martin Behaim* (Nuremberg 1853). E. G. RAVENSTEIN, *Martin de Bohemia* (Lisbon 1900); *Martin Behaim: His Life and Globe* (London 1908). Germanisches National Museum, *Martin Behaim und die Nürnberger Kosmographen*, ed. L. GRATE (Nuremberg 1957).

[N. SCHEEL]

BEHAN, BRENDAN

Playwright and novelist; b. Dublin, 1923; d. there, March 20, 1964. He was born of working-class parents, Stephen and Kathleen Behan, and inherited from both sides of the family a strong rebel tradition—his uncle, Peadar Kearney, wrote Ireland's national anthem, "The Soldier's Song." Behan joined the illegal Irish Republican Army (IRA) in the 1930s and was arrested (1939) at the age of 16, in Liverpool, for possession of explosives. He was sentenced to 3 years in Borstal prison, an experience recounted in his incomparable autobiographical *Borstal Boy* (1958). Beneath its profane, ribald surface, the book is a unique document of

Brendan Behan.

youthful innocence confronting a sinful world. Back in Ireland, Behan was soon in prison again—first in the Curragh, then Mountjoy—for IRA activities. Released in 1946, he went to England, served another short sentence, and went on to Paris, where he had some poems and stories published in the magazine *Points*. His first play (1954), *The Quare Fella*, produced in Dublin's tiny Pike Theatre, was an immediate success. In it he drew on his prison experiences to compose one of the most powerful indictments of capital punishment to appear on a modern stage. The action takes place during the night before an execution—a night of terrific tension, made bearable only by the superb ironic humor, the human insight and compassion with which the atmosphere of the prison is rendered. The play moved to London's West End in May 1956, where it had a tremendous success, coinciding with a vigorous newspaper campaign being waged for the abolition of the death sentence in Britain.

In 1955 Behan married Beatrice ffrench Salkeld, daughter of a distinguished Dublin artistic family. It was an enduring marriage that supported him throughout the ill health, depressions, and excesses (largely alcoholic) that accompanied his increasing celebrity. His greatest success came with his next play, *The Hostage*, an adaptation of his Gaelic play, *An Giall*, which had been staged at Dublin's Damer Hall in 1957. After its first production by Joan Littlewood at her Theatre Workshop on Oct. 14, 1958, *The Hostage* moved to the West End on Dec. 4, 1958, for a long run. It had subsequent successful presentations in New York, Paris, Berlin, and Dublin. *The Hostage* reaffirmed Behan's concern with death and modern man. In it a young British soldier is held by the IRA in a Dublin brothel against the possible execution of one of their men by the British authorities. A daring blend of satire, pathos, and black farce, it presents a harrowing vision of modern society and its indifference to human anguish: its readiness to inflict death, its refusal to face the challenge of understanding that inflicted death demands. Before he had completed his last play, *Richard's Cork Leg*, Behan died at the Meath Hospital, Dublin, in a diabetic coma, having received the Last Rites of the Church. In his last years he published some popular but unimportant sketch books: *Brendan Behan's Island*, with illustrations by Paul Hogarth (1962); *Hold Your Hour and Have Another*, with illustrations by his wife (1963);

Brendan Behan's New York (1964); and one novel, *The Scarperer* (1964).

Bibliography: D. Nores, "Reconnaissance de Brendan Behan," *Lettres Nouvelles* (Oct. 1962) 132–137. A. Simpson, *Beckett and Behan and a Theatre in Dublin* (London 1962). **Illustration credit:** Dennis Hughes-Gilbey.

[A. Martin]

BEHAVIORISM

A system, theory, or school of psychology based on objective study of behavior, human and animal, in terms of stimulus-response bonds, habit formation; and conditioning. It can also be regarded as a methodological orientation toward a psychology elaborated without reference to mind or consciousness. Behaviorism as a school of psychology originated in the U.S. about 1913 in vigorous opposition to traditional psychology. It rejected mind and consciousness as the subject matter of psychology, and introspection as its method. The school gained a wide following among American psychologists, because it embodied the tendencies of American psychology to become more scientific, objective, and quantitative. But behaviorism also found strong opponents and met with bitter criticism, particularly from the hormic and Gestalt schools. The influence of behaviorism on European psychological thought has been minimal. Even though its reflexology and Pavlov's work were sources of inspiration for American behaviorists, Soviet psychology is negatively disposed toward behaviorism.

History. The founder of behaviorism was John Broadus *Watson (1878–1958), the first public declaration of whose views was entitled "Psychology as the Behaviorist Views It" [PsychRev 20 (1913) 158–177]. From the beginning, his system was explicitly intended to be a revolt against all existing psychology. Studies in animal psychology, with which Watson was engaged for over 20 years, were a strong factor in the formation of his views. His doctoral dissertation and his research prior to 1913 were exclusively in the field of animal psychology. Later Watson also conducted experiments with infants and young children.

A systematic presentation of Watson's behaviorism is found in *Behavior: An Introduction to Comparative Psychology* (New York 1914) and *Psychology from the Standpoint of a Behaviorist* (Philadelphia 1919). The latter, particularly in the 3d edition of 1929, represents the most complete exposition of Watson's system. In 1925 he published *Behaviorism* (rev. eds. New York 1930, 1958), written in a popular vein. The general recognition of Watson's contributions was reflected in his election to the presidency of the American Psychological Association in 1915, when he was only 37 years old. From 1908 on Watson was professor of psychology at the Johns Hopkins University; he left this post in 1920, however, and gradually withdrew from research and active participation in psychology. In 1957 the American Psychological Association honored Watson, citing his work as "one of the vital determinants of the form and substance of modern psychology" and his writings as "the point of departure for continuing lines of fruitful research."

Among prominent American psychologists who followed the behavioristic tradition were Albert P. Weiss (1879–1931), Edwin B. Holt (1873–1946), Walter S. Hunter (1889–1954), Karl S. Lashley (1890–1958),

Clark L. Hull (1884–1952), and Edward C. Tolman (1886–1959). Lashley made notable contributions to physiological psychology, Hull developed a behavioristic theory of learning, and Tolman studied purposiveness in behavior. Among younger representatives of behavioristic psychology are B. F. Skinner (1904–) and a Canadian, D. O. Hebb (1904–). In Europe a supporter of behavioristic psychology is Henri Piéron (1881–), a leading French psychologist who developed a system similar in many respects to behaviorism.

Basic Concepts. Watson defined psychology as the science of behavior. In his understanding, behavior consisted of responses, reactions, or adjustments of an organism as a whole to antecedent stimuli or stimulus situations. Defined in this way, behavior was studied over a full range, from its simplest manifestation in the amoeba to its most complex form in man. The a priori supposition was made that the behavior of men and the behavior of animals do not differ essentially, but only in the level or degree of complexity. "The behaviorist," Watson said, "in his efforts to get a unitary scheme of animal response, recognizes no dividing line between man and brute." Behavior, being the response of an organism, is explained in terms of neurophysiological events: stimulation of receptors (sense organs), processes in the nervous system, and responses carried out by effectors (muscles and glands). Mental processes, states of consciousness, and subjective experience are not matter for behavioristic psychology. Only responses that are observable and measurable in some objective way constitute the subject of its study.

Responses. A response may be simple, e.g., a reflex jerk of the knee stimulated by tapping on the knee cap, or complex, e.g., eating, unlocking a door, or building a house. More and more complex behavior is built from simple reflexes or simple stimulus-response units.

Responses or behavior may be overt or explicit, such as a knee jerk or eating, or covert or implicit, such as thinking, which is not directly observable. In Watson's view, thought is simply subvocal speech, i.e., motor responses normally present in vocal speech but suppressed through learning. Although these responses are not easily observed, their existence can be demonstrated by sensitive devices that record movements of the tongue, lips, larynx, and other parts of the body involved in speaking. The expectation of the behaviorist is that such implicit responses will be better ascertained as measuring instruments are improved. Just as with thinking, other forms of implicit behavior are thought to be reducible to muscular and glandular responses, viz: perception, to discriminatory responses; imagery, to kinesthetic reactions; feelings and emotions, to glandular and visceral responses; and memory and learning, to conditioned reflexes and habits. Personality is explained as a constellation of habits developed mostly in early childhood in response to environmental conditions. Thus behaviorism attempts to explain psychological events in terms of an organism's response without reference to mind or consciousness. It regards *introspection, the principal method of the older psychology, as worthless and categorically bans it as a methodological device.

Are all the responses of the organism learned, or are some inborn or instinctive? Watson continually modified his answer to this question, but in the end held that only a few behavior patterns are innate, most being learned. The concept of the conditioned reflex, developed by I. P. *Pavlov, helped Watson explain how an organism can acquire various responses and habits.

Conditioning. The conditioned reflex is a response that originally occurs in a natural way only to a definite stimulus (the unconditioned stimulus) but which eventually, through training, can be elicited by an inappropriate stimulus or stimuli (the conditioned stimulus). When food is placed before a dog, the animal's salivary glands secrete saliva—the natural response or unconditioned reflex. If a bell is sounded before the placing of the food, and this is done a number of times, the dog's glands will secrete saliva at the sound of the bell before, or even without sight of, the food—the conditioned reflex. Watson's experiments, conducted on a 1-year-old boy, illustrated the acquisition of emotional reactions through conditioning. The child was presented with a rabbit, which he handled without showing any fear. After a few trials a loud noise was suddenly made each time the child reached for the rabbit. On subsequent presentations of the rabbit, the child began to show signs of fear even when the loud noise was discontinued. Fear reactions also extended to anything that resembled the rabbit, such as furry objects. Watson called this latter phenomenon transfer or spread of conditioned reflex, and believed this process accounted for many emotional reactions. Watson extended the principle of conditioning to all forms of *learning.

Stimulus-Response Bond. The essential concept in Watson's psychology was the stimulus-response association. He considered the bond between stimulus and response so definite and absolute that he could say: "Given the stimulus, psychology can predict what the response will be; or, on the other hand, given the response, it can specify the nature of the effective stimulus." Because of this emphasis on stimulus-response bonds as the key to understanding behavior, Watsonian psychology was called S-R psychology and was attacked by those who saw in this paradigm a gross oversimplification of behavior. Later behaviorists tried to correct and improve the concept.

Considering Watson's notions about stimulus-response bonds and conditioning, one is not surprised to find him adopting an environmentalistic position with regard to the development of behavior. His later thesis was that there are no innate capabilities, tendencies, or traits in man, and therefore an individual's development is shaped solely by his environment. "Give me a dozen healthy infants, well-formed, and my own specified world to bring them up in" he said, "and I'll guarantee to take any one at random and train him to become any type of specialist I might select—doctor, lawyer, artist, merchant-chief and yes, even beggar-man and thief, regardless of his talents, penchants, tendencies, abilities, vocations, and race of his ancestors."

Later Developments. Although American psychology was greatly transformed by behaviorism and accepted the concept of psychology as a science of behavior, pure Watsonian behaviorism found few adherents. Watson's notion of behavior was thought naïve, and many of his theses were either abandoned or modified. Several variants of behaviorism were formulated and identified by such names as neobehaviorism, molar behaviorism, and purposive behaviorism. The majority of American psychologists, however, while subscribing to behavior-

istic methodology, refused to be enslaved by dogmatic "isms." Thus after 1930 the division of psychological schools began to disappear, and behaviorism, particularly the Watsonian brand, was no longer identified as a distinctive school. Nevertheless, the behavioristic orientation of American psychology remained strong.

Theoretical formulations of behavioristic psychology showed considerable fluctuation between 1930 and 1960. One of the early influences during the period was *logical positivism and a movement associated with this, *operationalism. The latter was based on the principle that the validity of a scientific finding or theory is dependent upon observable events and the procedures employed in verifying these. Operational definitions thus became popular in psychology. They related abstract concepts, which created semantic difficulties for many, to concrete elements, and encouraged psychologists to seek a type of *verification modeled after that of the physical sciences. Behavioristic theory continued to be further modified and "liberalized" between 1940 and 1960. The gamut of theoretical positions in the 1960s with respect to psychology as a science, and specifically to such varied psychological processes as perception, learning, emotions, and motivation, attests to the extensive revision of behaviorist thought since its inception in 1913.

Evaluation. In evaluating behaviorism one must distinguish its historical role in the development of psychology from its theoretical aspects. Historically behaviorism was of great importance. Its effects actually transcended the field of psychology proper and reached into sociology, education, literature, and philosophy. Under its impact, psychology, traditionally a study of the soul, mind, consciousness, or mental activities, became for most practitioners the science of behavior. Consequently psychology was thought to have a clearly defined subject matter that could be studied with objective scientific methods. Questions concerning the nature of the mind and consciousness were relegated to philosophy, thus terminating the impasse psychologists had encountered in the study of consciousness and their frustrating controversies over this subject.

From the methodological viewpoint behaviorism brought high standards of scientific rigor to psychological research. It curbed the exaggerations of introspectionism and introduced empirical methods and procedures. It stimulated experimentation and encouraged quantification of psychological data and the use of mathematics and statistics. In this way behaviorism won greater prestige for psychology among scientists.

As a theory or school, behaviorism, despite a disavowal of philosophical affiliation or influences, implicitly contained suppositions that can only be identified as philosophical. Indeed some critics considered behaviorism essentially a metaphysical doctrine, charging that it construed its own metaphysics to destroy other metaphysics. The metaphysical premises of behaviorism were in essence, if not formally, materialistic and positivistic. Behaviorism's declaration that no dividing line exists between man and brute, its rejection of mind and consciousness from psychological study, its reduction of behavior to stimulus-response bonds or organismic processes, were not merely convenient methodological postulates. They presupposed the existence of only one realm of reality—that of matter—and on the basis of this assumption accepted or rejected data for scientific study. The tenor of the behavioristic school, particularly Watson's, was that mind and consciousness were not simply beyond the scope of psychological inquiry, but that they actually did not exist, or were reducible to mere physio-chemical events.

In summary, then, behaviorism as a method and movement had a salutary effect on psychology by diverting it from mentalism and by strengthening its scientific character. But its ambition and promise to make psychology a science in the same sense as physics and chemistry were not, and could not be, fulfilled. As a doctrine, behaviorism tended to restrict the scope of psychology, to narrow its view, and to push it in one direction to the neglect of, and at the expense of, others. American psychology in the 1960s, however, shows signs of maturing beyond the point of being confined or straightjacketed by behaviorist doctrine.

See also PSYCHOLOGY; PSYCHOLOGY, HISTORY OF; POSITIVISM.

Bibliography: T. W. WANN, ed., *Behaviorism and Phenomenology* (Chicago 1964). L. O. KATTSOFF, *The Design of Human Behavior* (St. Louis 1953). B. F. SKINNER, *Science and Human Behavior* (New York 1953). J. B. WATSON and W. McDOUGALL, *The Battle of Behaviorism* (New York 1929). E. C. TOLMAN, *Purposive Behavior in Animals and Man* (New York 1932); "Operational Behaviorism and Current Trends in Psychology," *Proceedings, Twenty-Fifth Anniversary Celebration of the Inauguration of Graduate Studies, The University of Southern California,* ed. H. W. HILL (Los Angeles 1936) 89–103. A. P. WEISS, *A Theoretical Basis of Human Behavior* (2d ed. Columbus, Ohio 1929). A. A. ROBACK, *Behaviorism and Psychology* (Cambridge, Mass. 1923). M. MEYER, *The Psychology of the Other-one* (Columbia, Mo. 1921).

[H. MISIAK]

BEHEIM, LORENZ, humanist; b. Nürnberg, Germany, *c.* 1457; d. Bamberg, Germany, April 11, 1521. He studied theology, first in Ingolstadt and then at the University of *Leipzig, where he obtained the degree of *magister artium.* He moved to Italy in 1480, where he obtained a doctorate in Canon Law. For 22 years he was in the service of Cardinal Rodrigo Borgia, the future Pope *Alexander VI, and had contact also with his son Cesare *Borgia. He held various posts in the Curia, and in 1505 joined the chapter of St. Stephan in *Bamberg. During his stay in Rome he transcribed, in a collection of Roman epigraphs, the inscriptions under the frescoes of Pinturicchio (d. 1513) celebrating the main events of the pontificate of Alexander VI, thus preserving descriptions of masterpieces that have since been destroyed.

Bibliography: K. PILZ, NDB 1:794. H. ROSENFELD, LexThK² 2:124. E. REICKE, "Der Bamberger Kanonikus L. Behaim, Pirckheimers Freund," in *Forschungen zur Geschichte Bayerns* 14 (1906) 1–40. F. GREGOROVIUS, *History of the City of Rome in the Middle Ages,* tr. A. HAMILTON, 8 v. in 13 (London 1894–1902). ADB 2:276.

[M. MONACO]

BEHEMOTH, a herbivorous animal, in fact the hippopotamus, described in Job (40.15–24; Vulg. 40.10–19) as a chief marvel of God's handiwork. The name is a plural, indicating an altogether exceptional individual, of the Hebrew word, *b⁰hēmâ,* a term for four-footed, most often domestic, beasts. A supposed Egyptian antecedent, which would mean "the water ox," is found in no ancient source. No legendary background, such as that for *Leviathan (Jb 40.25–41.26), is known for behemoth. It is, rather, a unique literary legacy from the author of Job, by whom it is portrayed as a powerful and tranquil beast, unafraid of flooding waters. Certain of its traits are described by conventional imagery (cf. Ct 5.14–15); but the Biblical writer had real knowledge of the hippopotamus, whether from a visit to Egypt or from its attested presence in the coastal swamps of Palestine until about the 4th century B.C. Later Christian and Jewish sources identify behemoth with Satan or with the elephant.

Bibliography: G. HAAS, BullAmSchOrRes 132 (1953) 30–34.

[P. W. SKEHAN]

BEHISTUN INSCRIPTION, a large trilingual inscription in Old Persian, Elamite, and Akkadian, with accompanying bas-reliefs, carved on the face of a steep cliff overlooking the main caravan route from Baghdad to Teheran, about 65 miles southwest of Hamadan (Ecbatana) near the modern village of Bīsitūn (Behistun). The inscription and pictorial reliefs were commissioned by *Darius I, King of Persia (521–486 B.C.), to commemorate his victories over Gaumata, the Magian, and nine rebel chieftains. In the early and middle 19th century this inscription drew the attention of many Western European scholars, who eventually managed to decipher all three of these previously unknown languages largely as a result of studies made from this text.

The sculptured panel portrays at the left a standing life-size figure of Darius, with two attendants behind him. His right foot is placed on the chest of the prostrate Gaumata. To the right of Gaumata the nine rebel chiefs stand in line, with their hands tied behind their backs and a rope around their necks linking them together. The figure of the god *Ahura Mazda hovers over the scene. Each figure in the panel is identified by a label, but the main inscription is placed on separate sections below and to both sides of the panel. The text records the name, titles, and ancestry of Darius, the favors received by him from Ahura Mazda, and the history of his exploits against the various rebels.

The key to the decipherment of the ancient text was discovered by the young German, G. F. Grotefend, who,

Behistun inscription, which provided the key to the decipherment of cuneiform writing.

as early as 1802, had identified some of the royal names and titulary at the beginning of the Old Persian inscription on the basis of similar phrases occurring in later Pahlavi documents. The first reasonably accurate, complete translation of the Old Persian was published by H. C. Rawlinson from 1846 to 1849, and the decipherment of the Akkadian and Elamite versions followed shortly thereafter with the help of further documents which had been unearthed in these languages.

Bibliography: L. W. KING and R. C. THOMPSON, *The Sculptures and Inscription of Darius the Great on the Rock of Behistûn in Persia* (London 1907). R. G. KENT, *Old Persian: Grammar, Texts, Lexicon* (2d rev. ed.; New Haven 1953) 107–108, 116–134. **Illustration credit:** Courtesy of the Oriental Institute, University of Chicago.

[J. A. BRINKMAN]

BEHRENS, PETER, German industrial designer and architect; b. Hamburg, 1868; d. Berlin, 1940. Behrens began his career as a painter and designer in the *Art Nouveau arts and crafts movement in Munich. Soon, however, he took up architecture in Darmstadt, rejecting his early training in favor of a style of severe symmetrical composition in cubical masses, flat surfaces, and free-flowing interior spaces under the influence of Olbrich and Mackintosh. In 1903 Behrens became director of the arts and crafts school in Düsseldorf, but it was in 1907 that he received his most important appointment as artistic director of the Allgemeine Elektrizitäts-Gesellschaft, an important electrical manufacturing concern in Berlin. Behrens introduced art into industry by designing everything, from the company's trademark to its products and its factory buildings. The latter, built between 1909 and 1912, established a new conception of industrial building design with its severely elegant steel framing, glass curtain wall, and poured concrete. Behrens' later buildings include other industrial complexes for the Mannesman Werke in Düsseldorf (1913) and the Farbwerke at Hochst (1924). During his early years in Berlin Behrens included among his assistants Walter Gropius, Ludwig Mies van der Rohe, and Le Corbusier.

Bibliography: F. HOEBER, *Peter Behrens* (Munich 1913). H. R. HITCHCOCK, *Architecture: 19th and 20th Centuries* (2d ed. PelHArt Z15; 1963).

[R. SWAIN]

BEING

Being (Lat. *ens, esse;* Gr. τὸ ὄν, εἶναι) may be defined as what is; that which exists; *reality. The term being signifies a *concept that has the widest extension and the least comprehension. Being is the first thing grasped by the human *intellect, but it is also the principal interest of the philosopher in his capacity as metaphysician. It is necessary, therefore, to distinguish being as what everybody first knows from being as the subject of *metaphysics. Generally speaking, the transition from the former to the latter is made in virtue of the recognition that not every being is sensible and material. No attempt can be made here to trace the history of philosophical doctrines concerning being (*see* EXISTENCE; PARMENIDES; PLATO; ARISTOTLE; PLOTINUS; PROCLUS; HEGEL, GEORG WILHELM FRIEDRICH; BERKELEY, GEORGE; and KANT, IMMANUEL). The emphasis here is on the teaching of St. *Thomas Aquinas.

Being as What Is First Known. Being is the first concept the human mind forms; that is, if one knows anything at all he knows being. The concept of being is not simply chronologically prior to all others; it is also analytically prior, insofar as every subsequent concept is some modification of this first concept. This does not mean, of course, that "being" is the first word uttered by a child. Man's first concept formed on the basis of sense experience of the things of this world is of something there, what is, being; it is involved in every other concept and is a latent content of the meaning of the first word he employs. Intellectual life begins in dependence on sense experience, since the mind comes into play in an effort to understand what has been seen, heard, tasted, smelled, or felt. The recognition of the "thereness" of what is so sensed underlies the formation of the concept of what exists, what is there, what is present to the senses. This does not mean that to be is to be perceived (*esse est percipi*), as was proposed by *Berkeley, but that what is first called being is what is sensed. Things do not exist because they are sensed; rather they can be sensed because they exist.

The concept of what is, of what is there, thus enables the mind to embrace in a confused and universal manner whatever can be grasped by the senses. We can see from this why the concept of being is said to tell us the least about anything, but something of everything. As the first concept and the commencement of the intellectual life, it could hardly be otherwise. Man attains a more exact and precise knowledge the more he recognizes how one being differs from another. Being as first conceived is not the knowledge of the sensible singular as such, nor is it the knowledge of something apart from sensible singulars. The universality of the concept is in consequence of the way in which sensible things are grasped intellectually.

Being as the Subject of Metaphysics. Being as being is the subject of metaphysics. As the very name of this science indicates, it is after or beyond (μετά) the *philosophy of nature (φυσικά), which is concerned with material and changeable being. If there were no immaterial beings, there would be no need for a science beyond natural philosophy. But if immaterial beings exist and if this is known, it becomes of interest to investigate the properties or characteristics and causes of being, not as material and mobile, but precisely as being. For reasons indicated below, this cannot mean that metaphysics is concerned with immaterial beings as a realm of entities other than physical entities; it particularly does not mean that *God is the subject of metaphysics. Before these assertions can be justified, however, we must inquire into the various meanings of being.

Meanings of Being. An investigation of the ways in which being is employed in philosophy will clarify the content of the first concept of the intellect as well as the subject of metaphysics.

Being and Essence. The term being sometimes designates positive being, sometimes propositional being (*ens ut verum*) and logical being. Consider the following statements: (1) Peter is; (2) Uncle Sam needs you; (3) Definitions abound. Only the subject of (1) can be said to be without qualification; it signifies positive or extramental being. Uncle Sam exists in the sense that he can figure in statements like (2), for if we asked where he could be found the reply would be that he does not "really" exist. So too logical entities like *definition— as in (3)—*species, etc., do not enjoy extramental existence. Thus, if there is a sense in which mythical or fictional as well as logical entities exist, in the full sense of the term they do not exist and are not beings. Only what enjoys positive or extramental existence has an *essence, meaning by essence that whereby something can exist in the real order (*see* ESSENCE AND EXISTENCE). Since the concern of the metaphysician is with positive being, with what enjoys existence independently of man's knowing, he is concerned with whatever has essence.

Substance and Accident. All real or positive beings, however, do not have essence in the same sense. Although essence is that whereby real being has existence, men, *motion, colors, and sizes do not exist in the same manner. Motion, color, and size exist as modifications of a more basic type of existent; their mode of being is one of inherence, of being in a subject. A man, on the other hand, does not exist in a subject. Rather he is a subject in which motion, color, and size inhere in order to enjoy the mode of existence that is theirs. In short, the kind of being that has essence, positive or real being, is subdivided into two types, substantial and accidental being, and essence means either that whereby a *substance exists or that whereby an *accident exists. The doctrine of the *categories of being is founded on this distinction.

Primary and Secondary Senses. If both substance and accident are instances of real being, the term being is not predicated of them equally. Substance is what is chiefly and obviously meant by "what has essence" and "what exists extramentally"; accident is rather *in* what exists—it is a modification of what *is* in a more fundamental sense. The meaning of being as applied to accident therefore incorporates the meaning that is predicated directly of substance. In a precise sense, when predicated of accident, being takes on a secondary meaning. Thus Socrates, a dog, and a tree are said to be and to have essence in a primary and direct sense, while the activities of such beings, their colors and sizes, are said to "be" in the secondary sense that they exist in such beings as Socrates, a dog, and a tree.

Analogy of Being. That being is predicated unequally of substance and accident is emphasized in the traditional tenet that being is not a *genus. A simple way of stating the grounds for this tenet follows: If being were a genus, substance and accident would have to differ in something other than being; but only *nonbeing is other than being, and for substance and accident to differ in nonbeing is no difference at all (cf. Thomas Aquinas, *In 3 meta.* 8.433). Since being is not a genus, it cannot be predicated univocally of substance and accident. (A term is predicated univocally when said of several things with exactly the same meaning; it is predicated equivocally when said of several things with wholly different meanings; and it is predicated analogically when said of several things with meanings that are neither exactly the same nor wholly different.) Being is predicated analogically of substance and accident because its meaning as said of accident includes its meaning as said of substance, but not conversely. (*See* ANALOGY.)

Transcendental Attributes of Being. The division of being into substance and accident gives rise to words whose scope is less than that of being itself. For example, while every substance is a being, not every being is a substance. There are other terms, however, whose range and scope are equal to those of being itself. Since what they mean transcends the division into categories, they are called transcendental attributes of being. Their predicable community equalling that of being, these transcendental terms are common in just the way being itself is,

namely, analogically. That is, their meaning may vary as they are predicated of different categories, but there is a controlling or focal meaning which gives proportional unity to their diversity of signification. (*See* TRANSCENDENTALS.)

One, true, and good are examples of such transcendental attributes. Whatever *is* is undivided in itself; that is, it is one. To say of something that it is one "does not add something real to being but only the negation of division, since 'one' means only a being which is undivided. From this it is clear that one is convertible with being, since every being is either simple or composed and what is simple is neither actually nor potentially divided. What is composed does not have being so long as its parts are divided but only when they constitute the composite. Thus it is clear that for a thing to be involves indivision" (ST 1a, 11.1). The primacy of substance is strikingly clear in this analysis of St. Thomas. So too, whatever *is* is said to be true insofar as essence is a principle of *intelligibility as well as of existence. Whatever *is* is good insofar as its existence is perfective of it. This is first and most obviously seen in the case of composed beings that result from change, for the product is the goal, term, or good aimed at by the process. (*See* UNITY; TRUTH; GOOD.)

Abstraction and Separation. It was mentioned earlier that if all beings were material and changeable there would be no need for a science beyond physics. Yet God, who is the immaterial and unchangeable substance *par excellence,* is not part of the subject of metaphysics. To understand this, one must compare the subject of metaphysics with those of other theoretical sciences. Two criteria for the object of a theoretical science enter into the distinction of such sciences. Given the mode of operation of the mind, the object of knowledge must be immaterial; given the demands of *science, it must be necessary, that is, unchangeable. If, then, there are formally different references to *matter and *change in the definitions of objects, we can speak of different theoretical sciences. The objects of natural science include sensible matter in their definitions, but since such science studies mobile things in terms of common characteristics, there is a certain departure from the material singular. *Mathematics, in this context, is said to consider things in a way in which they do not exist extramentally. The geometrician's definitions of line, plane, etc., while doubtless suggested by the sensible world, do not refer to, nor are they verified of, physical things. (*See* SCIENCES, CLASSIFICATION OF.)

Metaphysics is possible to the degree that scientific objects can be defined without sensible matter and that such definitions can be verified extramentally. The objects of natural science and mathematics can be attained by *abstraction; they leave aside, simply do not consider, certain aspects of physical things (singularity and sensible matter, respectively), while in no way implying that things exist without the aspects left aside. The objects of metaphysics are not simply more general characterizations of physical things; rather the implication is that things exist that verify metaphysical definitions because they exist independently of matter and motion. For this reason metaphysics presupposes what are called judgments of separation; for example, the truth of such statements as "Not all being is material and mobile" and "Not every substance is physical." Since neither of these propositions is self-evident, they must be reached, if at all, by *demonstration. When we know that some beings are immaterial, we have a warrant for a science beyond physics but unlike mathematics.

Being as Being. Metaphysics takes its rise from the recognition that there is a realm of beings, of substances, beyond the physical. Does this mean that metaphysics has God and the angels for its subject? The whole thrust of philosophy, in the traditional sense, is in the direction of natural knowledge of the divine, and yet simple substance cannot be the subject of any human science. If metaphysics is to be *theology, this can only be indirectly. The only kind of being directly accessible to man is physical being, and it is to this that he turns when he sets out to do metaphysics. "There are some objects of theoretical science," St. Thomas writes, "which do not depend upon matter in order to exist because they can exist without matter whether because they are never in matter, like God and the angels, or because they are sometimes in matter and sometimes not, like substance, *quality, being, *potency, *act, the one and many, and so forth . . ." (*In Boeth. de Trin.* 5.1). The second class of names enumerated by Aquinas indicates the bridge the metaphysician builds between physical substance and immaterial substance, qualities of material things and those of immaterial things, and so forth.

This effort accents what has been called the grandeur and misery of metaphysics. From the point of view of physical things, the concept of substance that the metaphysician forms seems inadequate and abstract, for he constructs a definition free of matter, and physical substance is material. From the point of view of separate substance, immaterial substance, such a concept is also representationally poor. In discussing the view of *Avempace, who held that in order to get concepts appropriate to immaterial things all one has to do is abstract from, or drop the material notes found in concepts of physical things, St. Thomas observes, "This would be cogent if immaterial substances were the forms and species of material ones. . . . If this is not granted and it is assumed that immaterial substances are of a quite different definition from the *quiddity of material things, no matter how much our mind abstracts the quiddity of the material thing from matter, it will never arrive at something similar to immaterial substance" (ST 1a, 88.2). He concludes that any approach to immaterial substance from material substance falls short of perfect knowledge of the former. The difficulty is that no other approach is open to man. The metaphysician has no alternative to his attempt to "purify concepts" so that they provide him with an indirect, analogical, and always inadequate knowledge of immaterial substance.

God and Metaphysics. Metaphysics is often called theology because its principal concern is God. Psychological reasoning shows that God cannot be the subject of metaphysics. The proportionate object of the mind is the nature of sensible being; since man has no direct knowledge of God, God can enter into human science only as related to the subject of that science. A logical argument can also be given against immaterial substance's being the subject of a science. "Given that in any question we ask something about something, for example, we seek the cause of matter, which is the formal cause, or the cause of form being in matter, namely the end and efficient cause, it is clear that with respect to simple substances, which are not composed of matter and form, no questions are relevant. For in

every question, as has been shown, something must be known and something must be sought. Such substances, however, are either wholly known or wholly unknown. . . . Hence no question can be asked concerning them and because of this there is no doctrine like that of theoretical sciences concerning them" (*In 7 Meta.* 17.1669–70).

Being and Participation. Being is what has existence: "Being is that which finitely participates existence" (*In lib. de caus.* 6). From a logical point of view, one speaks of a common being (*esse commune*) that is shared by substance and accident analogically. But God, too, is spoken of as *esse commune,* not as predicably common to created beings but rather as something numerically one whose *causality extends to all creatures. God as common being is conceived of as the totality of perfections only partially reflected in each creature and indeed in the sum of creatures. By means of a subtle dialectical procedure, the metaphysician compares the real hierarchy to the logical one, but whereas in the latter the highest terms express the least, in the former God is conceived as a kind of limit, comprising all perfection (*see* PERFECTION, ONTOLOGICAL). Creatures are then seen as forming a hierarchy of being that reaches from the highest angel to the least material thing. This *via descensus,* which is considered the Platonic component of the Thomistic synthesis, is currently being explored and providing a deepening understanding of the achievement of Aquinas. In his metaphysics Thomas is seen as the heir not only of *Aristotelianism, but also of Proclus, *Pseudo-Dionysius, and *John Scotus Erigena. (*See* PARTICIPATION.)

See also METAPHYSICS; ESSENCE; EXISTENCE; CATEGORIES OF BEING.

Bibliography: R. M. McINERNY, *The Logic of Analogy* (The Hague 1961). J. BOBIK, "Some Disputable Points Apropos of St. Thomas and Metaphysics," NewSchol 37 (1963) 411–430. E. H. GILSON, *Being and Some Philosophers* (2d ed., Toronto 1952). J. MARITAIN, *A Preface to Metaphysics: Seven Lectures on Being* (New York 1945). T. C. O'BRIEN, *Metaphysics and the Existence of God* (Washington 1960). C. FABRO, *Partecipazione e causalita secondo S. Tommaso d'Aquino* (Turin 1960). B. MONTAGNES, *La Doctrine de l'analogie de l'être d'après saint Thomas d'Aquin* (Louvain 1963).

[R. M. MC INERNY]

BEIRUT

The ancient Berytus, French Beyrouth, situated on a coastal promontory of the Eastern Mediterranean with the Lebanon mountains in the background, has been the capital city of the Republic of Lebanon since 1926.

As early as the 15th century B.C. Beirut was a Phoenician seaport mentioned in the *Amarna Letters. It was destroyed during the post-Alexandrian wars, but later rebuilt by the Romans. SS. *Gregory Thaumaturgus and *Gregory of Nazianzus studied at its famous school of Roman law in the 4th century A.D., as did also the Byzantine jurist Trebonius. Earthquakes ruined the city in A.D. 555 and Emperor *Justinian I had it rebuilt.

It was a bishopric in the 4th century, the fatherland of Panfilus, later bishop of Caesarea. In 448 a synod at Beirut judged the case of Ibas of Edessa in preparation for the council at Tyre. *Theodosius II made Beirut a metropolitan see in 449; but this status was not accepted by the Council of *Chalcedon (451).

Engulfed by the Arabian expansion in 635, Beirut was under Moslem control, except during the Crusades (1110 to 1291), until the end of the Ottoman Empire in 1918. It had been under French influence since 1840, was captured by French troops in 1918, and became the capital of the French Protectorate of Lebanon in 1926. In 1946 Lebanon gained its autonomy, retaining Beirut as its capital. With the influx of thousands of Arab refugees from the Palestine area, the population of Beirut increased rapidly, approaching the 500,-000 mark (1964). An important highway link between Damascus and Baghdad, Beirut is the seat of four universities: the French, the American, the Lebanese, and an Academy of Arts.

Modern Beirut is an important episcopal see for five Christian rites. (1) The Maronite rite established a bishopric at Beirut in 1577, and has had an uninterrupted hierarchical succession since 1691. It has a seminary at Gazir and 112 parishes, 166 priests, and 157,000 Catholics. (2) The Melchite rite has maintained a metropolitan in Beirut since 1701 and has 52 parishes, 58 priests, and 50,000 Catholics (1963). (3) The Syrian (or Jacobite) rite, which is the least numerous, being comprised of the descendants of converts from Jacobite Monophysitism, has had its see of Beirut since 1817, but only since World War I has the residence of the Syrian Catholic patriarch of Antioch been transferred to Beirut. Under the patriarch's jurisdiction are vicariates in Lebanon, Turkey, Egypt, and Jerusalem. The rite counts some 21,000 Catholics with 22 priests and 14 parishes (1960). (4) The Armenian rite, for which Beirut has been the seat of the patriarch of Cilicia since 1928, cares for Armenian Catholics who immigrated into Lebanon from Turkey after World War I. It has 35 priests, 11 parishes, and some 18,500 Catholics (1963). (5) The Chaldean rite has a bishop, 2 parishes, 6 priests, and 3,000 Catholics (1962).

The University of St. Joseph in Beirut has been a cultural center for the whole area, under the direction of the Jesuit fathers, who founded it as an interritual seminary with the cooperation of Armenian, Maronite, Greek, and Syrian patriarchs, and the approval of Pope *Gregory XVI in 1843. The seminary was housed at nearby Gazir until 1875 when the support of American Catholics provided more suitable quarters in Beirut itself. In 1881 Pope *Leo XIII granted to this Oriental seminary the faculty of conferring degrees in philosophy and theology, elevating it to the rank of a pontifical university. In 1950 the Faculties of Medicine, Law, Oriental Literature, and Engineering were added with the power to grant degrees recognized by the local government. The University's press publishes the scholarly publications *Mélanges* in French and *al-Masriq* in Arabic, and began publication of the daily Arabic newspaper *al-Basir* in 1947.

Bibliography: I. ORTIZ DE URBINA and G. DE VRIES, EncCatt 2:1150–51. C. KOROLEVSKIJ, DHGE 8:1300–40. *Les Jésuites en Syrie 1831–1931,* 12 fasc. (Paris 1931). *Université Saint-Joseph de Beyrouth* (Beirut 1948). AnnPont (1964) 4, 6, 49.

[A. H. SKEABECK]

BEIRUT, ARCHDIOCESE OF (BERYTENSIS)

Beirut, the episcopal see of the Patriarchate of *Cilicia in the *Armenian rite since 1928, as well as the residence of the patriarch of *Antioch and the seat of the patriarchal Vicariate of Lebanon in the *Syrian rite. It is also the seat of an archbishopric of the *Maronite rite and is 309 square miles in area. In 1962 it had 143 secular and 22 religious priests, 102 men in 21 religious houses, 188 women in 26 convents, 12,887 pupils in 100 schools, and 157,000 Catholics in a population of 500,000. A Latin vicariate apostolic was established in Beirut in 1953, as was a *Chaldean rite bishopric in 1957.

Like *Alep, the other Maronite archdiocese, Beirut has no suffragans, the bishoprics being under the Maronite patriarch of Antioch, who resides in Bkerké, near Beirut, and whose see is Jubayl (*Byblos) and Batrun in Lebanon. There are five other Maronite bishoprics in Lebanon: Baalbek (established in the 17th century), Sarba (1959), near Beirut, *Sidon (1838), Tarabulus esh Sham or Tripoli (17th century), and *Tyre (1838). The date Beirut became a Maronite archbishopric has been a matter of debate, as has its right to the archiepiscopal title.

Beirut, of which *Eusebius of Nicomedia was bishop before 318, did not have a Monophysite bishop afterward. Maronites settled in the mountains of Lebanon in the 8th or 9th century but were not numerous in Beirut until the Crusades. A Latin bishop of Beirut appears in 1136, the see moving to Nicosia in Cyprus in 1291 and thereafter becoming titular. Under the Ottomans, Maronites allied with Druses to maintain a political autonomy. In 1577 a Maronite bishop of Beirut appears, and with the next mentioned bishop in 1691 the episcopal list becomes regular.

Maronite prelates of Beirut include Abdulla Qarā' āli (1716–46), a noted jurist and founder of the Antonine monks of Alep; Peter Karam (1819–44), who moved the seat of the see from the monastery of St. John of Qatâleh to Beirut; Tobias 'Aūn (1844–71), a good administrator; Joseph Debs (1872–1907), restorer of the cathedral of St. George, founder of a minor seminary and the College de la Sagesse (1875), publisher of liturgical books, and compiler of a seven-volume history of Syria; and Peter Chebli (1908–17), educated in France, who died in exile at Adana. Before World War II a Maronite central seminary was founded at nearby Ghazir.

The uninterrupted series of patriarchs of the Syrian rite (from 1781) fled *Mardin for Lebanon before they moved to Alep (1831). Patriarch Mar Ephraim II Rahmani (1898–1929) resided in Beirut, as have his successors after World War I. The present patriarch, Cardinal Ignatius Gabriel Tappouni (1929–   ), has brought many *Jacobites back to Catholicism, especially those in Lebanon. In 1960 the patriarchate, which also includes the patriarchal Vicariate of Egypt, had 14 parishes, 22 secular priests, 2,885 pupils in 16 schools, and 20,500 Catholics.

Protestant activity in Beirut began in 1833. Large scale Maronite emigration occurred (1864–1914), and since 1949 many Moslems have emigrated from Palestine. In Beirut there are also non-Catholic sees for Greek Orthodox, Jacobites, and Armenians.

See also LEBANON.

Bibliography: G. LEVENQ, DHGE 5:688–689. C. KOROLEVSKIJ, *ibid.* 8:1319–22. G. DE VRIES, LexThK² 2:134–135. I. ORTIZ and G. DE VRIES, EncCatt 2:1150–51. OrientCatt 393–413. Ann Pont (1964) 49, 742.

[J. A. DEVENNY]

BEIRUT AND JUBAYL, ARCHDIOCESE OF (BERYTENSIS ET GIBAILENSIS), archbishopric of the *Melchite rite in *Lebanon. In 1963 it had 52 parishes, 30 secular and 27 religious priests, 4,414 pupils in 31 schools, and 50,000 Catholics in a population of 600,000. Jubayl, ancient *Byblos, was one of the six sees taken from *Tyre and made suffragan to Beirut (449–451), which remained an autocephalous metropolitanate after the suffragans were withdrawn.

Little is known of the Christian history of Beirut from the late 5th to the 15th century. The Melchite bishopric that appears at the time of the Council of Florence (1439) was Catholic, and it seems that prelates were on good terms with Rome after the Ottoman conquest (1516). *Alep became a Catholic center c. 1585, and by the late 17th century Catholic influence was strong in Beirut, whose bishop declared for Catholicism in 1701. Basilian Chouerite monks provided the first unequivocally Catholic bishop of Beirut (1736), but dissidents forced him to live outside the city until 1754. After 1736 most bishops came from the Chouerite monks, who cared for the see and laid claim to the cathedral until 1934. Byblos, a Latin bishopric in the 12th and 13th centuries and titular see since the 14th century, was detached from Beirut, against the wishes of the bishop, by Patriarch *Maximos III Mazlūm (1833–55), the first patriarch since 1724 who could return to Damascus from Lebanon. In 1881 Rome confirmed Meletius Fakkâk (1879–1904) as metropolitan of Beirut and Jubayl, a title the see has held since. The Chouerite Athanasius Sawâyâ (1905–19) was in France during World War I and died in Marseilles. Elections to the See of Beirut have brought to the fore differences between Lebanese and Syrians and between the secular clergy and the religious.

Bibliography: G. DE VRIES, EncCatt 2:1150–51. C. KOROLEVSKIJ, DHGE 8:1304–17. OrientCatt 247–272. AnnPont (1964) 49.

[J. A. DEVENNY]

BEK, ANTHONY, bishop of Durham and titular patriarch of Jerusalem; b. c. 1240; d. Eltham, Kent, England, March 3, 1311. He and his brother Thomas (d. 1293), later bishop of *Saint Davids, were sons of a Lincolnshire baron and were students at the University of *Oxford by 1267. Even before that time, however, Anthony had begun his career in the royal service, which was to bring him from lowly messenger under *Henry III to chancellor of the realm briefly in 1274 under *Edward I. He was one of the three principal councilors of Edward I and was frequently used by Edward on diplomatic missions. Although he fell into disfavor in 1297, Bek was again shown signs of royal favor by *Edward II upon his accession in 1307. The suggestion of Edward I to the monks of *Durham Cathedral in 1283 that they elect Bek to the vacant bishopric was taken up readily by a chapter deep in dispute with the archbishop of *York, their *metropolitan. Ironically enough, by asserting his right of *visitation of the priory in 1300, Bek occasioned a dispute that lasted more than 5 years and saw appeals and counterappeals to the court of Rome. As temporal ruler of the palatinate of Durham, Bek urged its rights with vigor and ambition, but as a bishop he enjoyed a reputation for magnanimity and chastity among his contemporaries. Pope *Clement V named him *patriarch of Jerusalem in 1305, but he was never able to assume the administration of the see, for the Latins had been expelled more than a century before. His body was buried in the east end of Durham Cathedral near the tomb of St. *Cuthbert of Lindisfarne.

Bibliography: *Records of Antony Bek, Bishop and Patriarch, 1283–1311,* ed. C. M. FRASER (London 1953). R. BRENTANO, *York Metropolitan Jurisdiction and Papal Judges Delegate, 1279–1296* (Berkeley 1959). M. CREIGHTON, DNB 2:134–136. C. M. FRASER, *A History of Antony Bek, Bishop of Durham, 1283–1311* (Oxford 1957). R. K. RICHARDSON, "The Bishopric of Durham under Anthony Bek, 1283–1311," *Archaeologia Aeliana,* 3d ser., 9 (1913) 89–229. A. H. THOMPSON, DHGE 7:485–489. Emden 1:151–152.

[F. D. LOGAN]

BEKENNENDE KIRCHE, or Confessing Church (BK), an organization within the German Evangelical Church (DEK) that actively opposed the *German Christians (DC) during the period of the Third Reich. The DEK included almost all German Protestants. At a BK conference in Ulm (April 22, 1934) attended by many bishops, pastors, and delegates from free synods and from many congregations, the BK claimed to be the genuine representative of the DEK and upheld as unchanging a set of Christian beliefs that the DC sought to subordinate to the views of the Nazi government and its racist policies. The first confessional synod of the BK, held at Barmen (May 29 to 31, 1934), approved a "Theological Declaration," composed mainly by Karl Barth, that restated those basic Reformation beliefs that the members held in common against the DC. The Barmen declaration was revolutionary in that it was a joint confession of Reformed and Lutheran Christians, but it was not a "union confession." The second confessing synod, held at Berlin-Dahlem (October 1934), protested effectively against the arrests of bishops and pastors; it marked the peak of BK resistance. After the synod DC influence declined rapidly. Within the BK some groups had a much stronger sense of confessional identity than others. The rift between these two outlooks widened and subsequently split the movement, which disappeared soon after World War II. The Nazi government also tried to weaken the BK by depriving confessing clergymen of financial support, expelling them from their pastorates, imprisoning them, and even putting them to death. Thus Pastor Martin Niemöller, the most influential BK spokesman, was incarcerated from 1939 to 1945. In addition to opposing the DC, the BK acted as a leaven in German Protestantism by its advocacy of liturgical renewal, ecumenism, and interest in social problems and international affairs.

Bibliography: H. BUCHHEIM, *Glaubenskrise im Dritten Reich* (Stuttgart 1953). W. NIEMÖLLER, *Die evangelische Kirche im Dritten Reich* (Bielefeld 1956). J. P. MICHAEL, *Christen suchen eine Kirche* (Freiburg 1958); LexThK² 2:138–142. A. COCHRANE, *The Church's Confession under Hitler* (Philadelphia 1962). Cross ODCC 325–326. E. WOLF, RGG³ 1:984–988.

[L. J. SWIDLER]

BEKHTEREV, VLADIMIR MIKHAILOVICH, Russian neurologist, psychiatrist, physiologist, and experimental psychologist; b. village of Sorali, Vyatka Gubernia, Jan. 20, 1857; d. Leningrad, Dec. 24, 1927. Travels in western Europe (1884–85) brought him into contact with the neuroanatomist Flechsig, the neuropsychiatrist J. *Charcot, and the psychologist W. *Wundt. Bekhterev became professor of psychiatry at Kazan University (1885), professor of neurology and psychiatry at the Military Medical Academy, St. Petersburg, and professor at the Women's Medical Institute (1897). He organized the Psychoneurological Institute (1907) and later became director of the new State Institute for Brain Research (1918).

He was the author of some 600 publications, among them a dozen major works containing significant contributions to the morphology of the nervous system and to neurological diagnosis. Bekhterev studied problems of cortical localization and phenomena of reciprocal innervation. As a psychiatrist, he used occupational therapy and hypnosis. He is best known in the West for his views on psychology as an objective study of the reactions of the organisms (behavior), in contrast with subjective, introspective psychology. Subsequently, the term "objective psychology" was to Bekhterev not objective enough and "psychoreflexology" became "reflexology." Its cornerstone is the concept of "associative reflexes" acquired individually by animals and men as a result of the coincidence of external stimuli with inborn responses of the organism. His most important work in English translation is *General Principles of Human Reflexology* (New York 1932).

Bibliography: G. RAZRAN, "Russian Psychologists' Psychology and American Experimental Psychology," PsychBull 63 (1965) 42–64. P. I. YAKOVLEV in *The Founders of Neurology*, ed. W. HAYMAKER (Springfield, Ill. 1953) 244–247. V. N. MIASISCHEV and T. IA KHVILITSKIĬ, eds., *V. M. Bekhterev and Contemporary Problems of Normal and Pathological Structure and Function of the Brain* (Leningrad 1959), in Russian.

[J. BROŽEK]

BEKYNTON, THOMAS (BECKINGTON),

reforming bishop, royal official, English humanist; b. Beckington, near Frome, Somerset, England; d. Wells, Jan. 14, 1465. Nothing is known of his parentage. He was admitted to Winchester College (1404) and to New College, Oxford (June 24, 1406), where he was a fellow (1408–20). He incepted as doctor of civil law (1418) and was subwarden (1419). There he probably attracted the notice of *Humphrey, Duke of Gloucester, whom he served (1420–c. 1438), principally as chancellor. As Gloucester's protégé, he quickly became an ecclesiastical pluralist. About 1438 he was appointed King *Henry VI's secretary, beginning 4 years of continuous royal service. He was one of the diplomats with Cardinal Henry *Beaufort at Calais (1439), and led the abortive but lengthy Armagnac marriage negotiations at Bordeaux (1442–43). He was a valuable supporter of Henry's educational foundations, Eton College and King's College, Cambridge. While still in the royal service, as keeper of the privy seal (1443–44), he was appointed bishop of *Bath and Wells, being consecrated Oct. 13, 1443. Soon out of the royal service, he resided at Wells, where he proved an able and energetic administrator, making episcopal *visitations of *Bath Abbey in 1449 and 1454 and of *Glastonbury Abbey in 1445 over the protestations of the aged abbot, Nicolas Frome, whose objections he treated with consummate contempt. His ordinances for the vicars choral of Wells (1450) are still largely in effect today. He was a munificent benefactor to Wells, where he spent some 6,000 marks on buildings, both in the cathedral precincts and in the city, where a fountain and conduit bear his name. The vicar's close that he built has been considered a splendid example of 15th-century domestic architecture.

Bekynton was a friend and correspondent of many contemporary Italian humanists such as Flavio *Biondo, who presented him with a copy of his *Decades*. In addition he encouraged younger English scholars such as Thomas *Chaundler, who dedicated his Latin works to Bekynton. He changed the Latin style of diplomatic correspondence from the prolixities of previous medieval practice to the more restrained and direct Latin of the Italian humanists and so commenced a trend of humanistic Latin studies among later royal servants. What remains of his library bears eloquent testimony to his interest in theology and Canon Law and in contemporary Latin poetry and prose.

Bibliography: *Memorials of the Reign of King Henry VI. Official Correspondence of Thomas Bekynton, Secretary to King Henry VI, and Bishop of Bath and Wells*, ed. G. WILLIAMS, 2 v. (RollsS 56; 1872), biog. in 1:xv–lviii. *The Register of T. B., Bishop . . .*, ed. H. C. M. LYTE and M. C. B. DAWES, 2 v. (Somerset Record Society 49–50; London 1934–35). *The Victoria History of The County of Somerset*, v.2, ed. W. Page (London 1911). Emden 1:157–159. R. WEISS, *Humanism in England during the Fifteenth Century* (2d ed. Oxford 1957) 71–83, valuable refs. to works and articles on Bekynton. A. JUDD, *Life of Thomas Bekynton* (Chichester 1961).

[H. S. REINMUTH, JR.]

BEL, title of the chief god of Mesopotamia. The word (Akkadian *bêl*) is a contraction of the older Semitic form *ba'al* (lord), which in West Semitic (Canaanite, etc.) retained its original form as *Baal, the Canaanite god of rain and fertility. In Babylonia the word Bel was first used as the Akkadian equivalent of Sumerian *e n* (lord) and in particular as the Akkadian name for Sumerian Enlil, the god of *Nippur, the most sacred city of ancient Mesopotamia, where he had his main temple, the É-kur (house of the mountain). Associated with Enlil (lord of the air) were the other members of the supreme triad of the Sumerian pantheon, An or Anu (the sky) and En-ki (lord of the ground, i.e., the nether world and the subterranean waters). According to Sumerian mythology, Anu, the father of all the gods, bestowed on Enlil kingship over all the land. When *Hammurabi made Babylon the leading city of Mesopotamia, its local god *Marduk received Enlil's title of Bel, and as such took over Enlil's function as divine king of all the land; see Pritchard ANET 164.

In the Bible, Deutero-Isaia (Is 46.1) speaks of the downfall of Bel and the god *Nebo (Nabu); Jeremia, too, announces the punishment inflicted on Bel by Yahweh (Jer 51.44); and Baruch ridicules Bel as a deaf and dumb idol (Bar 6.40). But the most devastating OT polemic against Bel is in Dn 14.1–22—the story of how Daniel showed that Bel's priests ate the food given to the god.

See also MESOPOTAMIA, ANCIENT, 3.

Bibliography: ReallexAssyr 2:282–390. EncDictBibl 220–221.

[H. MUELLER]

BEL AND THE DRAGON. Two stories, now united as one, that constitute a deuterocanonical addition ending the Book of Daniel (Dn 14.1–42) in the Catholic canon [*see* BIBLE, III (CANON), 2]. The story of Bel (v. 1–22) tells how Daniel, Cyrus's court favorite, proved that the statue of *Bel, i.e., *Marduk, was no true god and that the food offered it was consumed, not by the idol, as Cyrus believed, but by the priests. Through Daniel's clever detective work Cyrus was convinced, the priests were put to death, and the idol was handed over to Daniel, who destroyed it—Theodotion's text [see BIBLE, IV (TEXTS AND VERSIONS), 8] adds: "and its temple," i.e., the renowned Esagila. The story of the *dragon (v. 23–42) tells how Daniel destroyed a living dragon (serpent?) worshiped at Babylon by feeding it cakes made from a mixture of pitch, fat, and hair, which caused it to burst asunder. The irate populace obliged the King to condemn Daniel to be thrown into a den of lions (a doublet of the story in Dn 6.2–25), where he was fed by Habacuc (Theodotion adds "the prophet"), who was brought through the air from Palestine, and where he was kept unharmed by God until his release. The King then put his accusers to death.

Both stories, in the manner of Wis 13.1–14.31, the Letter of *Jeremia (Bar 6.1–72), and other OT texts, ridicule idol worship. They were probably intended to strengthen Jewish faith against idolatry, particularly of the Babylonian type that experienced a reflorescence in the 3d century B.C. Their popular, burlesque character explains the presence of such improbable elements as Cyrus's credulity and Habacuc's journey. Since there is no evidence of a cult of living serpents in Babylon, the dragon story may be another attack on Marduk, who was accompanied or symbolized by a dragon in the Babylonian art, and it may contain a remote reference to the myth of Marduk's victory over Tiamat (i.e., *chaos represented as a sea monster) at creation. Preserved only in Greek, the stories were probably composed in Hebrew or Aramaic between the 3d and 1st centuries B.C.

Bibliography: R. H. PFEIFFER, History of N.T. Times (New York 1949) 436–438, 455–456. F. ZIMMERMANN, "Bel and the Dragon," VetTest 8 (1958) 438–440. E. D. VAN BUREN, "The Dragon in Ancient Mesopotamia," Orientalia 15 (1946) 1–45.

[M. MC NAMARA]

BELASYSE, JOHN, soldier and English Catholic politician; b. Newburgh Priory, North Riding, Yorkshire, c. 1614; d. London, Sept. 10, 1689. It seems clear that John, second son of an ambitious country landowner of covert Catholic sympathies, conformed to Anglicanism at home, at Peterhouse, Cambridge, and while serving as Member of Parliament for Thirsk, 1640–42. During the first Civil War he emerged as a capable royalist general; he was present at the Edgehill, Newbury, Naseby, Selby, and Newark actions. He was created Baron Belasyse of Worlaby, Lincolnshire, by Charles I in 1645. His father, the first Viscount Fauconberg, eventually became a Catholic on his death-bed, but John's nephew, the second Viscount Fauconberg, was resolutely Protestant and was married to Oliver Cromwell's daughter, Mary. After the Restoration of the monarchy in 1660, John became Governor of Tangier and Lord-Lieutenant of the East Riding. By 1664 his refusal to take the anti-Catholic oaths of office for Tangier revealed a definite shift in his religious views, and in 1673 the House of Lords accounted him a papist. In 1678 he and four other Catholic peers were imprisoned in the Tower during the Popish Plot scare, and he was not released until the accession of James II in 1685. He was then aged and very lame.

Though elevated by James to the Privy Council and made first Lord Commissioner of the Treasury, he was politically moderate and it seems played no major part in the politics of the reign.

Bibliography: V. GIBBS, ed., The Complete Peerage (London 1910–   ). F. C. TURNER, James II (New York 1948). DictEng Cath 1:178–179.

[H. AVELING]

BELAUNZARÁN, JOSÉ MARÍA DE JESÚS, Mexican bishop; b. Mexico City, Jan. 31, 1772; d. La Profesa, Mexico, Sept. 11, 1857. He received the Franciscan habit in 1789 in the monastery of Recollects of the Apostolic College of Pachuca. In 1796 he became a priest. Because he was so esteemed as a preacher, he was considered the apostle of Mexico City. Gregory XVI appointed him bishop of Linares, Monterey, on Feb. 28, 1831. Bishop Vázquez of Puebla consecrated him November 28 in the church of San Diego in Mexico City; after that Belaunzarán undertook the visitation of his immense diocese. His active involvement in the struggle against the laws of Gómez Farías persecuting the Church resulted in his exile from the country in 1834. Still later he made further petitions to General Santa Anna, asking for repeal of Farías's laws, but without success. As a result of these difficulties and his failing health, he offered his resignation from the bishopric on various occasions. The third time (1839) it was accepted by Gregory XVI. Belaunzarán then withdrew to the monastery of San Francisco in Mexico City. Santa Anna bestowed on him the cross of Knight of the Order of Guadalupe and made him his honorary councilor. Among the bishops that he consecrated was Francisco García Diego, Bishop of the Californias.

Bibliography: M. CUEVAS, Historia de la Iglesia en México, 5 v. (5th ed. Mexico City 1946–47) 5:207. E. VALVERDE TÉLLEZ, Bio-bibliografía eclesiástica mexicana (1821–1943), 3 v. (Mexico City 1949) 1:159–164.

[L. MEDINA-ASCENSIO]

BELCOURT, GEORGE ANTHONY, missionary; b. Quebec, Canada, April 22, 1803; d. Magdalen Islands, May 31, 1874. He was born of French parents. After attending the Petit Seminaire of Nicolet, Canada, he was ordained on March 10, 1827, and assigned to parish work in the District of Montreal. Four years later he accompanied Bp. Joseph Provencher to the Winnipeg–St. Boniface area, where they labored together for 17 years. Learning the Indian language, Belcourt compiled an Indian dictionary and endeavored to make settled agriculturists out of the nomadic Indian hunters. There were frequent misunderstandings with Provencher, who could not agree that a priest should teach farming along with Christianity. When Hudson's Bay Company officials also expressed their disapproval, Belcourt was recalled to Quebec in 1848. The following year he was sent by Bp. Mathias Loras to Pembina in North Dakota. There among the Indians he taught catechism, started schools, erected buildings, encouraged agriculture, and even accompanied them on buffalo hunts. But Belcourt again found himself unable to work successfully with other priests, and he was forced to leave the diocese in 1859. The sisters he had founded were disbanded, his buildings were neglected, and his settlement at St. Joseph (Walhalla) failed to prosper. He spent his remaining years in parishes on Prince Edward

Island and the Magdalen Islands, where he lived in retirement until his death.

Bibliography: J. M. REARDON, *George Anthony Belcourt: Pioneer Catholic Missionary of the Northwest* (St. Paul 1955).

[P. ZYLLA]

BELÉM, ARCHDIOCESE OF (BELEMENSIS)

Located in the state of Pará in northern Brazil; created a diocese in 1719; raised to an archdiocese in 1906. In 1964 it included 10 prelatures *nullius*: Santarém (1903), Santíssima Conceição do Araguaia (1911), Guamá (1928), Marajó (1928), Xingu (1934), Macapá (1949), Cametá (1952), Óbidos (1957), Abaeté dos Tocantins (1961), and Ponta de Pedras (1963).

1964 STATISTICS

Area	Population	Parishes	Clergy Sec.	Clergy Reg.
Belém	*602,062	35	38	51
Santarém	*180,000	11	3	11
Santíssima Conceição do Araguaia	222,000	2	0	4
Guamá	*187,000	7	0	16
Marajó	*95,693	9	0	8
Xingu	*28,300	4	0	8
Macapá	79,420	4	0	17
Cametá	*117,373	7	0	14
Óbidos	87,566	5	0	11
Abaeté dos Tocantins	115,000	7	0	0
Ponta de Pedras	60,000	5	0	5

*This figure includes Catholics only.

The city was founded by the Portuguese in 1616 and the first parish was created in the next year or two. The Franciscans founded a house in 1617 and shortly thereafter were followed by the Carmelites, Mercedarians, and Jesuits. The Jesuit house founded in 1653 later developed into a college. The ecclesiastical and missionary history of this early period is inextricably linked with that of São Luís do Maranhão, the capital of the state (*see* SÃO LUÍS, ARCHDIOCESE OF). When the diocese was created, it included the whole Amazon basin and was suffragan to Lisbon, as was the parent diocese of São Luís. The white population is still very small and the secular clergy are few. In Belém as in Maranhão, there was a continuous struggle between the colonists and the missionaries over the liberty of the Indian. The first bishop, Bartolomeu do Pilar (1724–33), was involved in a controversy with the Jesuits over the right to visit their Indian missions. During the administration of the Dominican Bishop Miguel de Bulhões (1749–60) restrictive laws were applied to the missionaries. The bishop was a confidant of Pombal and carried out faithfully all the decrees from the home government against the Jesuits and other missionaries. At the time there were 63 *aldeias,* 19 run by the Jesuits, 26 by the Franciscans, 15 by Carmelites, and 3 by Mercedarians, caring for about 50,000 Indians. In 1755 missionaries were removed from the temporal administration, and all these missions were made parishes. In 1760 the Jesuits were expelled along with some Franciscans. Lay directors were substituted for the missionaries as administrators;

the spiritual jurisdiction was sometimes continued by the religious, sometimes turned over to the secular clergy. Most of the Indians retired into the forests. This period of confusion and decline persisted. Bishop José de São José Queiroz (1760–63) had so many conflicts with his own clergy and the Carmelites that he was recalled by the court in Lisbon.

The first Brazilian bishop was Romualdo de Souza Coelho (1821–41). During the independence period he used his influence to calm the people and to reconcile the Brazilian and Portuguese factions. As a result of independence, in 1828 the diocese was made suffragan to Bahia. This era marked the beginning of the struggle against Masonry. In 1842 the Italian Capuchins arrived in Pará and under the direction of Frei Gregório de Bene took up mission work and the catechizing of the Indians who had been almost completely abandoned. They replaced the old orders: the last Franciscan died in 1878, and the last Carmelite in 1893.

Antônio de *Macedo Costa (1860–90) was one of the outstanding figures of the Brazilian hierarchy in the 19th century. An energetic and enlightened prelate, he reformed the clergy, reorganized the seminary, and fought against the interventions of the regalist government. Along with Dom Vital, Bishop of Olinda, he was one of the heroes of the "Religious Question" (*see* BRAZIL). In the 20th century the bishops have brought more religious orders into the province, reformed and rebuilt the seminary, initiated workingmen's organizations and Catholic Action, and held a Eucharistic congress. In 1954 an important meeting of all the prelates *nullius* of northern Brazil was held in Belém, at which the problems of the missions were discussed. In 1963 the first Biblical Congress of Amazônia was held on the occasion of the inauguration of part of the new seminary building.

In 1964 the prelacies were under the care of Franciscans, French Dominicans, Barnabites, Augustinian Recollets, Precious Blood priests, the Institute of Foreign Missionaries of Milan, Vincentians, Missionaries

Baroque cathedral of the Archdiocese of Belém, Brazil.

of St. Francis Xavier, and Jesuits. Also serving in the province were Salesians, Redemptorists, Capuchins, Marist Brothers, and almost 600 sisters of various congregations.

Bibliography: M. C. KIEMEN, *The Indian Policy of Portugal in the Amazon Region, 1614–1693* (Washington 1954). A. C. FERREIRA REIS, *A conquista espiritual da Amazônia* (São Paulo 1942). A. G. RAMOS, *Cronologia eclesiástica da Amazônia* (Manaus 1952). A. PRAT, *Notas históricas sôbre as Missões Carmelitanas no extremo norte do Brasil* (Recife 1941). METÓDIO DA NEMBRO, *Storia dell'attività missionária dei Minori Cappuccini nel Brasile* (Rome 1958). **Illustration credit:** Pan American Union, Washington, D.C.

[O. VAN DER VAT]

BELFORD, JOHN LOUIS, educator, editor; b. Brooklyn, N.Y., Oct. 15, 1861; d. Brooklyn, Dec. 12, 1951. He was the son of Matthew and Rose (Donnelly) Belford. He attended St. Mary Star of the Sea parochial school in Brooklyn, N.Y., and St. Charles College and St. Mary's Seminary in Baltimore, Md. After ordination May 13, 1888, he was assigned to a curacy in St. Augustine's parish, Brooklyn. In 1893 Bp. Charles E. McDonnell appointed him first superintendent of schools in the Diocese of Brooklyn. In 1895 he was assigned to found the parish of St. Dominic in Oyster Bay, Long Island, and to build a church there. Theodore Roosevelt, a resident of Oyster Bay at that time, sought Belford's assistance in starting a town library. In 1899 Belford succeeded Sylvester *Malone as pastor of SS. Peter and Paul parish in the Williamsburgh section of Brooklyn. While there he established Epiphany parish. In 1905 he was transferred to Nativity parish, Brooklyn, where he built a new church and convent.

He was created a papal chamberlain in 1924 and a domestic prelate 2 years later. Belford became widely known as a Catholic spokesman on public issues. A parish monthly, the *Mentor,* was in existence when he arrived at Nativity parish, and he soon made it an organ for the expression of his opinions. He opposed Mayor John Purroy Mitchel and Gov. Charles S. Whitman in a bitter controversy concerning Catholic charitable institutions, attacked Tammany Hall on charges of graft, denounced the Ku Klux Klan, and opposed Prohibition. In demand as a preacher to adult audiences, he also wrote a prayerbook for children, which sold more than 3 million copies.

Bibliography: J. K. SHARP, *History of the Diocese of Brooklyn, 1853–1953,* 2 v. (New York 1954).

[F. E. FITZPATRICK]

BELGIAN LITERATURE

Belgium is a bilingual country, French being the language of the South and Flemish of the North. It may be concluded that there is, strictly speaking, no Belgian literature, since there is no Belgian language. This article, accordingly, surveys the literature of Belgium written in French; for literature in Flemish, *see* NETHERLANDIC LITERATURE.

French-language literature in Belgium began to be properly self-conscious near the close of the 19th century. Under the slogan *Soyons-nous* (Let's be ourselves), the La Jeune Belgique movement (1881) and the review of the same name undertook to foster a truly original, national literature that would nevertheless be unfettered by rigid geographical boundaries. This literature quickly proved its brilliance throughout Europe, reaching its apogee between 1890 and 1915 in

the works of Maurice *Maeterlinck and Émile *Verhaeren. Since that time, the French literature of Belgium has faithfully reflected the literary climate of Paris.

Prose Writing. Charles de *Coster was the precursor in prose with his *Légende d'Ulenspiegel* (1869), in which, by means of archaic language and a truculent, Rabelaisian style, he drew an irreverent picture of 16th-century Flanders. Camille Lemonnier (1844–1913), called "the field-marshal of Belgian literature," showed himself a fervent disciple of the realism of *Zola in exuberant novels marked by their irresistible attraction to a life of vigor, instinct, and violence (e.g., *L'Hystérique,* 1885). In contrast to this extrovert appeared melancholy Georges *Rodenbach; his *Bruges la morte* (1892) depicts a city whose rather gloomy atmosphere corresponded so well to his own disposition.

The succeeding generations saw the lyrical realism of Lemonnier inherited by Charles *Plisnier, whose *Faux Passeports* (1937), *Marriages* (1937), and *Meurtres* (1939–41) adopted the techniques of psychoanalysis; by Franz Hellens (1881–1920), who joined sensualism to an exquisite poetic fantasy to such an extent that it is difficult to distinguish fact from fantasy, as for example in his masterpiece, *Fraicheur de la mer* (1933); and by Jean Tousseul (1890–1944), whose work recalls on a minor scale the cycle of Romain Rolland's *Jean Christophe.*

Finally, in the mid-20th century, appeared the astonishing novelist Georges Simenon (1903–), whose prolific work has already been translated into some 20 languages; he "discovered" the novel of atmosphere (*roman d'atmosphère*) and created the famous Inspector Maigret, said to be influenced by his reading of *Bergson. Simenon's detective stories owe their fascination to the fact that the author deems it less important to discover who is guilty than to ascertain

Georges Simenon.

why he has become guilty. In this period Françoise Mallet-Joris found an international audience for her psychological novels, *Les Personnages* and *L'Empire celeste;* Alexis Curvers, the poet-novelist, produced an exquisite work, *Tempo di Roma;* and Felicien Marceau gave promise in *Les Elans du coeur* of a highly refined sensibility that later works have not fulfilled.

Poetic Achievement. A large cluster of names, some of them particularly prominent in the Symbolist movement, can be found in poetry (*see* SYMBOLISM, LITER-

ARY). Émile Verhaeren offers several literary scenic transformations in the manner of *Rubens, Jacob Jordaens, and D. Teniers the elder in *Les Flamandes* (1883), details of morbid introspection in *Les Débâcles* (1888), a paean to technical and modern science in *Les Villes tentaculaires* (1895), and, finally, his enthusiastic belief in human brotherhood in *La Multiple splendeur* (1906), a work that won him the name of the Belgian Walt Whitman. Maeterlinck caught the attention of the literary world with *Serres chaudes* (1889) and *Douze chansons* (1896). Charles van Lerberghe (1861–1907) has lately won a growing reputation. His *La Chanson d'Eve* (1904) is without doubt one of the great moments in French Symbolism and is ranked by some with the *Charmes* of *Válery, who admired Van Lerberghe's work. In the shade of these three stand Fernand Severin (1867–1931), alone, apart from the quarrels of any school, and dwelling in a land of dreams and mystery (e.g., *Un Chant dans l'ombre,* 1895); Georges Rodenbach, whose *Les Vies encloses* (1896) and *Le Miroir du ciel natal* communicate the solitude of deserted neighborhoods and the silence that reigns within the old dwellings; and Max Elskamp (1862–1931), reserved and fearful, singing in elliptical phrases *La Louange de la vie* (1898), a humble vision of the world and men that had no little influence on *Peguy and *Claudel.

In the wake of the Symbolists came: Gregoire Le Roy (1862–1941) with *Les Chemins dans l'ombre;* pure poetry bearing the mark of *Mallarmé in Georges Marlow's *Hélène* (1927); and a Verlaine-like charm in Thomas Braun's *Le Livre des Bénédictions* (1900). And finally, apart from the others, there is Henri Michaux (1899–), stridently satiric, tormenting his readers with an inventive and percussive use of language in the manner of *Rimbaud, as, for example, in *Epreuves exorcismes*.

Drama. In the world of the drama, Maeterlinck, who was quickly recognized as the theoretician of European Symbolism, must receive first mention. The publication of *La Princesse Maleine* (1889) marks an important event in the history of the Symbolist theater. *Palléas et Mélisande* (1892), enhanced by the haunting strains of Debussy, introduced into the theater the reign of a fate without pathos. Lastly, his *L'Oiseau bleu* (1909), whose symbolism is somewhat more accessible, presents an allegorical treatment of happiness after the manner of *Ibsens's *Peer Gynt*.

Unfortunately, this first brilliant phase did not continue, apparently because Belgium lacked a theatrical tradition. Only during the period following World War I did two great names make their appearance. The first is that of Fernand Crommelynck (1886–). After some rather affected beginnings that bore the marks of Symbolism, he produced his masterpiece, *Le Cocu magnifique,* in 1920. The deliberate discord of its expressionism set beside the lulling, soothing imagery of its poetry make this play worthy of the attention it attracts. The visionary Michel de Ghelderode (1878–1962), fascinated by the Flemish 16th century, created a world in which God and Satan became entangled, together with dwarfs and buffoons, in scenes that seem to have been inspired by Pieter Brueghel and *Bosch. Among his many works, *Images de la vie de Saint François d'Assise, Barrabas, Magie rouge,* and *Pantagleize* are especially worthy of mention, all of them displaying the author's penchant for an unwholesome brand of burlesque and vulgar pathos.

Bibliography: H. LIEBRECHT and G. RENCY, *Histoire illustrée de la littérature belge de langue française* (2d ed. Brussels 1931). G. DOUTREPONT, *Histoire illustrée de la littérature française en Belgique* (Brussels 1939). C. HANLET, *Les Écrivains belges contemporains de langue française, 1800–1946,* 2 v. (Liège 1946). G. CHARLIER and J. HANSE, *Histoire illustrée des lettres françaises de Belgique* (Brussels 1958). S. LILAR, *The Beglian Theatre since 1890* (New York 1950); *Soixante ans de théâtre belge* (Brussels 1952). R. GUIETTE, *Poètes français de Belgique: De Verhaeren au surréalisme* (Brussels 1948). J. M. CULOT, *Bibliographie des écrivains français de Belgique, 1881–1950* (Brussels 1958–).

[J. DAX]

BELGIUM

A country, 11,775 square miles in area, with a population of 9,328,000 in 1963, situated between *France, *Luxembourg, the *Netherlands, and the North Sea. In antiquity it was a part of the Roman Empire; in the Middle Ages, together with the bordering countries, it was called the Low Countries. After passing under different dynasties, the country gradually began its unification in the 15th century. Its present frontiers date mostly from the 17th century. It was not until 1830 that Belgium became an autonomous state.

Origin of Christianity. Before the 4th century there was little sign of Christian life in these regions almost without towns because Christianity was primarily a Mediterranean and urban religion. Christianity probably owes its origins to merchants and soldiers who followed the Roman roads or descended the Rhine. To the east, Tongeren (Tongres) formed a *civitas* whose first bishop was Servatius or Sarbatios. At the Council of Sardica (343) he vigorously defended St. Athanasius, who was acquitted and restored to his see in Alexandria. At the Council of Rimini (359), Servatius, together with Phebadius of Agen, resisted for 7 months the entreaties of Emperor Constantius II before consenting to sign an equivocal formula on Arianism. It has been claimed that if Servatius had resisted to the end, he would today occupy a place in the history of the Church alongside Athanasius of Alexandria and Hilary of Poitiers. The Diocese of Tongeren comprised the entire eastern part of the country, and Christianity seems to have been the dominant religion in the vicinity of the city of Tongeren and in some towns or *vici*.

In the western part of the country mention is made of Superior, Bishop of Bavai or *Cambrai (c. 350), and of the martyrs Piat, Fuscien, and Victoric, and the two laymen Amabilis and Aluvefa. These few traces of Christianity in this region seem to have been effaced during the German invasions, whereas the Church continued to exist to the east. *Clovis (481–511), the first great king of the *Merovingians, was baptized in 506. This led to the conversion of all his people, the *Franks. Both Arras and Tournai had a bishop at the beginning of the 6th century, but for want of Christians, Arras was soon united with the See of Cambrai and Tournai with that of Noyon.

Widespread Evangelization and Consolidation (625 to 9th century). St. *Amandus, a native of southern France, was responsible for the enduring conversion of this region. He settled at Elnone, not far from Tournai, c. 625 and there founded an abbey. He then descended the Schelde River, converted the inhabitants of Ghent, became bishop of Tongeren and Maastricht for 3 years, and labored also for the conversion of the people of

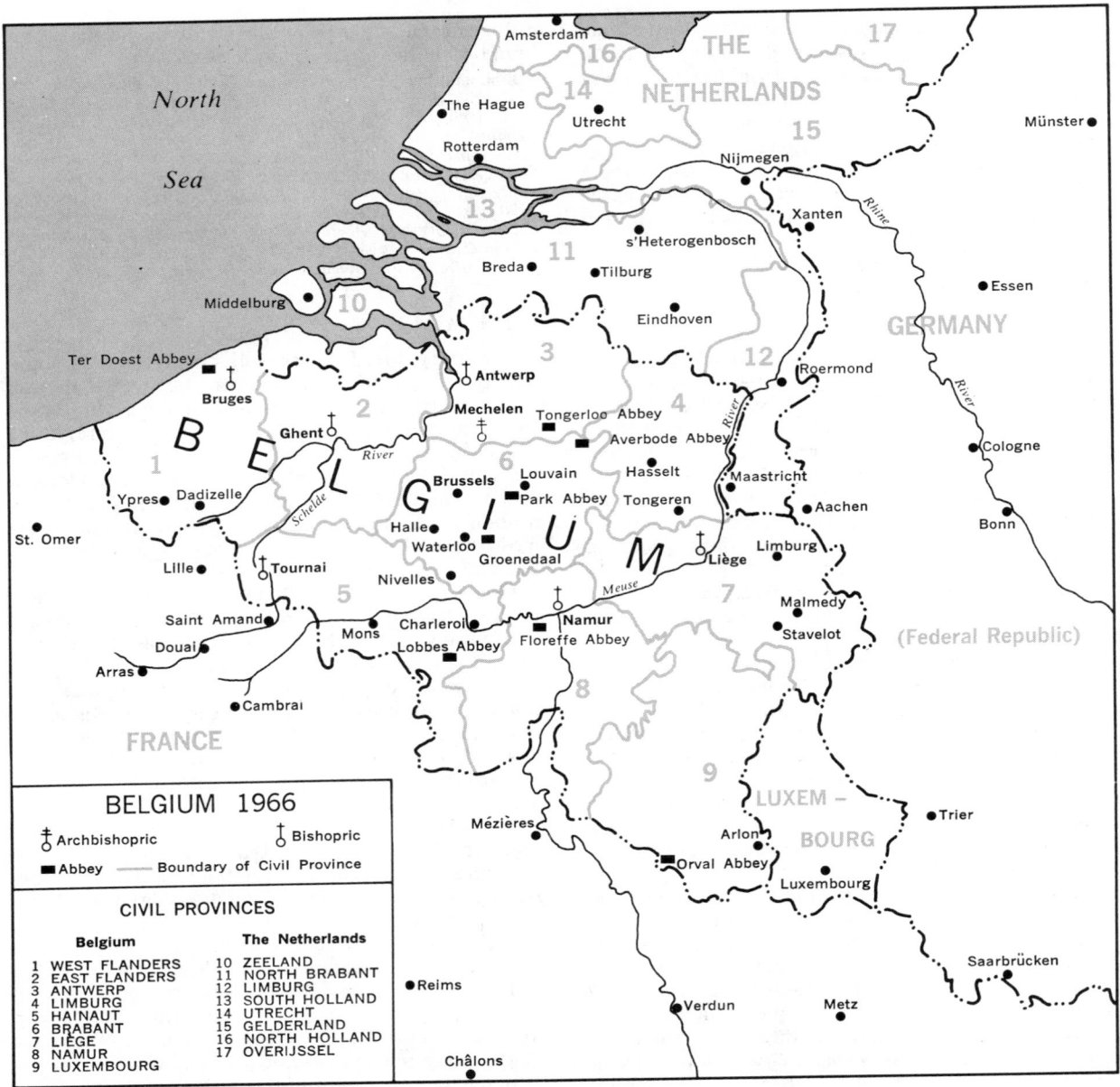

Fig. 1. Belgium, showing points of ecclesiastical interest.

Antwerp. Besides founding several abbeys, among them St. Pierre and St. Bavon at Ghent, he gave Christianity its start in this section. His title, Apostle of Belgium, is well deserved. The region to the west was evangelized also by St. *Eligius, Bishop of Noyon, and St. *Willibrord, Bishop of Utrecht. In the eastern section St. *Lambert and St. *Hubert, Bishops of Maastricht and *Liège, converted the last pagans. After a century of continuous efforts, the present area of Belgium was completely converted c. 730.

Between 625 and 730, 48 abbeys were founded in the Low Countries, 25 of which are in present-day Belgium. These abbeys played an important role in the propagation and consolidation of the faith. Monks and nuns exemplified for the people the good example of a life truly Christian and consecrated to prayer and penance. Missionaries were trained in the monasteries and could

return to them to revitalize their forces. So many were the saints in this period that it is called the century of saints.

From the 8th to the 10th century many rural parishes were founded. The earliest ones were *proprietary churches (*Eigenkirchen*) built on the estate of the founder, who continued to be their proprietor and who could dispose of them as he saw fit. Thus he could sell them, cede them as a benefice, appoint the pastor, and take for himself the revenues. This system was open to grave abuses, which did not fail to manifest themselves.

The union of the Church and the State during the Middle Ages favored the penetration of the spirit of Christianity into all elements of Western civilization. At the same time, this union permitted some rulers to engage in *caesaropapism. Thus *Charlemagne demanded that the bishops hold synods and visit their dioceses; he supervised clerical training and reminded clerics of their obligation to preach and visit the sick; he favored the multiplication of parishes and prescribed the payment of the tithe for the support of the pastors. He was instrumental in the cultural revival called the *Carolingian Renaissance. During it Charlemagne established an academy at his court, and certain abbeys, notably *Lobbes, *Stavelot, and *Saint-Amand, produced literary works. It was at this time that the church of St. Trond and the palace chapel at *Aachen (Aix-la-Chapelle) were built. All abbeys *c.* 800 were obliged to follow the *Benedictine Rule. In the second half of the 9th century the Norman invasions partially depopulated the country and devastated the episcopal towns and almost all the abbeys, which had been the centers of faith and of civilization.

The Feudal Church (10th to 12th centuries). Since the eastern part of the country belonged to the German empire, the German emperors established an imperial church at *Liège, and made the bishop a prince-bishop, a title held until the French Revolution. In the *investiture struggle Bp. *Wazo of Liège (1042–48) was one of the principal supporters of the reformer Pope Gregory VII, but Wazo's successors sided with the emperors in their conflicts with the popes.

In the 10th century the monastic and cathedral schools enjoyed great renown. Lobbes possessed the most celebrated monastic school. Liège was called the Athens of the North because of its cathedral school, which attracted Germans, French, English, and Slavs. Bishop *Notker (972–1008) was the one principally responsible for this progress, while Wazo of Liège was an outstanding theologian. Monastic life fell into decadence, partly because of the Norman invasions, but it was restored by reformers such as St. *Gerard of Brogne, who founded a reformed abbey near Namur and who was appointed by the Count of Flanders to reform several other abbeys, including those of St. Pierre and St. Bavon in Ghent. In the 11th century Richard of St. Vannes created a new reform current, with the chief representative St. *Poppo, abbot of Stavelot-Malmédy. The *Premonstratensians, founded by St. *Norbert, a native of the Low Countries, established in the 12th century numerous abbeys, such as those at *Floreffe, *Park, *Tongerloo, and Averbode. In their apostolate the Premonstratensians were especially noted for their work in rural parishes. The *Cistercians, who increased rapidly during the lifetime of St. Bernard, founded the abbeys of *Villers, *Orval, Ter Duinen, and *Ter Doest. They also cleared the uncultivated lands, drained swamps, and recovered part of the coastal lands from the sea.

In the 11th century the Church persuaded warlike lords and knights to abide by the *Peace of God, which protected women, religious, peasants, and pilgrims; and also by the Truce of God, which forbade wars during Lent, Advent, and other periods. The knights of the Low Countries were prominent in the *Crusades. *Godfrey of Bouillon, a mediator between the French and Germans because of his character and knowledge of the two languages, was the first ruler of Jerusalem, but he would accept only the title Advocate of the Holy Sepulcher. Thierry of Alsace, Count of Flanders, later traveled four times to the Holy Land and brought back the relic of the Precious Blood that is still venerated in *Bruges. Baldwin I, Count of Flanders,

was the first emperor of the *Latin Empire of Constantinople. This period saw the erection of masterpieces in the Romanesque style, including the churches of St. Servais at Maastricht, St. Gertrude at Nivelles, and particularly the nave and the transept of the cathedral at Tournai. Renier de Huy cast some admirable brass baptismal fonts at St. Barthélémy in Liège (*c.* 1100).

The Church During the Period of the Communes and the Dukes of Burgundy (13th–15th centuries). Towns developed in the Low Countries in the 11th and 12th centuries. In these flourishing centers Franciscans and Dominicans settled in the 13th century and soon acquired profound influence through their preaching and their sympathy for the common people. The *Beguines, a creation peculiar to the Low Countries and the Rhineland, were not nuns; but they observed the vow of chastity during their residence in the Beguine houses; they devoted themselves to prayer, manual works, care of the sick, and also to teaching. Houses of Beguines can still be visited in Ghent and Bruges. The Cistercian St. *Lutgardis was one of the first to venerate the Sacred Heart. St. Juliana of Liège, an Augustinian canoness of the Monastery of *Mont-Cornillon, collaborated in the institution of the Feast of Corpus Christi. This feast was celebrated for the first time at Liège (1251); it was prescribed for the whole Church in 1264 by Pope Urban IV. The poetess Bl. *Hadewijch extolled mystic love in her Flemish strophic poems. By far the most renowned mystic of the Low Countries was Bl. Jan van *Ruysbroeck (1293–1381), the devout prior of the convent of Groenendaal. In several treatises in Flemish, the best known of which is *Die Chierheit der gheesteleker Brulocht* (the beauty of mystic marriage), he revealed how the soul is elevated to contemplative and joyous participation in the divine life of the Holy Trinity. Ruysbroeck was also one of the promoters of the *Devotio Moderna, which insisted on the interior life and methodical meditation, and which produced a spiritual classic in the *Imitation of Christ* by *Thomas à Kempis. In the 14th and 15th centuries the Carthusians established several charterhouses in the Low Countries. *Denis the Carthusian (1402–1471), *doctor exstaticus,* was a celebrated mystical writer. Since the country had as yet no university, *Henry of Ghent, *doctor sollemnis,* and *Siger of Brabant went abroad to teach and became renowned professors at the University of Paris. Then in 1425, John IV, Duke of Brabant, erected the University of *Louvain, after obtaining a papal document of approval (*see* SPIRITUALITY OF THE LOW COUNTRIES).

The ecclesiastical division of the Low Countries at this time was as follows. In the western part were the Dioceses of Cambrai, Tournai (reestablished in 1146), Arras (reestablished in 1094), and Thérouanne (erected *c.* 639). All four sees were part of the ecclesiastical province of *Reims in France. In the eastern part was the See of Liège (which had replaced Maastricht since 717 or 718) and in the north the See of *Utrecht, founded in 696. Both sees were part of the ecclesiastical province of *Cologne. During the Middle Ages the Dukes of Brabant, the Counts of Flanders and the Dukes of Burgundy made several vain attempts to have new dioceses erected in the most important principalities, especially in Flanders and Bra-

Fig. 2. View of Tournai, Belgium. Just to the left of center are the five towers of the cathedral.

bant. During the *Western Schism (1378–1417) the inhabitants of the Low Countries remained faithful to the Roman line of claimants, but they were at times obliged by their bishops and by Duke Philip the Bold (1384–1404) to change their obedience. The Dukes of Burgundy installed several members of their family in episcopal sees.

Gothic architecture was represented. Flemish Gothic showed a marked preference for massive structures, such as the church at Pamel-Oudenaarde, the choir in the cathedral at Tournai, and in the church of St. Nicholas in Ghent. Brabançon Gothic, on the other hand, preferred majestic churches with soaring spires, such as the cathedrals of St. Rombaut in *Mechelen (Malines), St. Michael in *Brussels, and Notre Dame in Antwerp, and the collegiate church of St. Peter in Louvain. The tableaux of the Flemish primitives combined profound piety and recollection with charm and attractive coloring. The brothers Jan and Hubert van *Eyck, renowned for their "Mystical Lamb," Roger van der *Weyden, Dirk *Bouts, Hugo van der *Goes, Hans *Memling, Gérard David, Hieronymus *Bosch, and many other artists attest to the profound faith of the Flemings in this period. Guillaume *Dufay, Gilles *Binchois, Jakob *Obrecht, and others were among the outstanding composers of religious music.

1500 to 1640. At the beginning of the 16th century the traditionally strong faith of the inhabitants of the Low Countries remained deeply rooted in their souls, but their piety was too external. Many priests were ignorant and gave scandal by their disordered private lives and lack of zeal. The *Renaissance and *humanism fostered religious indifference. *Erasmus, the leading humanist, was a native of the Low Countries.

*Lutheranism penetrated the Low Countries through the great port of Antwerp, where the convent of the Augustinians provided the first Lutheran center. *Charles V himself organized the *Inquisition and

published some very severe edicts (*placards*) against the Lutherans. From 1530 on Anabaptism began to spread, especially in Holland and in Antwerp. After the experience at *Münster, however, the *Anabaptists were regarded by all other Christians, Catholics and Protestants alike, as disturbers of the social order. In putting into effect the *placards* during the 16th century, the civil authorities put to death nearly 2,000 heretics, mostly Anabaptists.

The peace of Cateau-Cambrésis with France (1559) opened the southern frontier of the Low Countries to *Calvinism. The Calvinists were well organized and won many followers in Tournai, Cambrai, *Lille, and in the textile centers of French Flanders; later they advanced toward Antwerp. *Philip II, who succeeded his father Charles V in 1555, was eager to apply the *placards* rigorously, but the situation had meanwhile changed completely. The Spanish King, who had resided in Spain since 1559, was not well informed of the rapid developments of the distant Low Countries, nor could he comprehend them. The Compromise of the Nobles (1566), which demanded the cessation of the Inquisition and abolition of the *placards,* and especially the iconoclasm in the summer of 1566, made evident the failure of a purely negative repression. When the Catholic restoration occurred, it succeeded through positive measures. At the request of Philip II, Pope Paul IV completely reorganized the ecclesiastical hierarchy of the Low Countries by erecting 14 new sees and grouping the 18 bishoprics into three ecclesiastical provinces that were independent of the archiepiscopal Sees of Reims and Cologne. The new sees created in 1559 within the limits of modern Bel-

Fig. 3. View of a transept of the cathedral at Tournai.

Fig. 4. Louvain, the town hall (left) and the apse of the church of St. Peter. The town hall, built between 1448 and 1463, is the most renowned civil building in Belgium. The church of St. Peter was begun in the 11th century and was reconstructed as a Gothic structure in the early 15th century after having been ravaged by fire.

gium were the Archdiocese of Mechelen and the Dioceses of Ypres, Bruges, Ghent, Antwerp, and Namur. The decrees of the Council of *Trent were finally promulgated in the Low Countries (1565–66), the dogmatic constitutions being promulgated in their entirety, but the disciplinary decrees with important omissions. The bishops established seminaries, which soon trained priests who were well educated and morally exemplary.

Unfortunately the revolution of the Low Countries erupted for reasons partly political and partly religious. The resulting 80 years of war (1568–1648) ended with the permanent separation of the northern and southern section of the Low Countries. By 1600 the north had won its independence and was persecuting Catholics. Since then Catholics have remained a minority in the Netherlands. They constituted in 1965 about 40 per cent of the population and dwelt mostly in northern Brabant and Dutch Limburg, areas that were not conquered by the northern rebels until the 17th century. The southern section of the Low Countries, comprising for the most part present-day Belgium, remained subject to Spain but preserved its Catholic faith.

Under Archduke Albert and Archduchess Isabella (1598–1633) the Catholic restoration made the latter region one of the most Catholic in the world. Many fervent bishops, aided by the nuncios at Brussels,

trained an enlightened clergy and attacked abuses. The *Jesuits, who had 1,704 members there in 1630, opened about 40 colleges in whose sodalities they oriented the laity toward a more profound piety and toward apostolic works. The Jesuits also taught the catechism to thousands of children. Henri *Pirenne, the great Belgian historian, wrote of the Jesuits: "In no country were they more numerous; nowhere else did they influence a nation so profoundly." The Capuchins (*see* FRANCISCANS, CAPUCHIN), who founded 41 convents between 1585 and 1629, were highly esteemed by the populace for their simplicity of life, joyous abnegation, and simple, apostolic manner of preaching.

The baroque style created in the 17th century the basilica of Montaigu and several churches designed by Jesuit architects, such as St. Charles in Antwerp, St. Michel in Louvain, and St. Loup in Namur. Among the leading composers of religious music were Adrian *Willaert, Philippe de *Monte, and above all Orlando di *Lasso, whose 2,000 Masses, motets, and madrigals made him the rival of Palestrina. Peter Paul *Rubens and Anthony *Van Dyck, were outstanding among the many painters whose skill in composition and coloring was more impressive than their depth of religious sense. Among the most famous sculptors were Artus Quellien, Jerôme Duquesnoy, and Frans Duquesnoy, whose statue of St. Andrew is in the basilica of St. Peter in Rome (*see* BAROQUE ART).

Fig. 5. Antwerp, the church of St. Charles Borromeo.

1640 to 1830. In 1640 appeared *Augustinus,* the posthumous work of Cornelius *Jansen, who for 19 years had been a professor at Louvain and for 2 years bishop of Ypres. Despite the book's condemnation (1643), Jacques *Boonen of Mechelen and Antoine *Triest, Bishop of Ghent, supported the Jansenists. Both bishops were suspended and did not submit until 1653. During the second half of the 17th century, *Jansenism numbered fervent adherents among Louvain professors, bishops, clergy, and educated laymen. Thanks to several succeeding archbishops of Mechelen, the Jesuits, and some professors at Louvain Jansenism was subdued in the 18th century. Meanwhile it had considerably chilled the fervor of the Catholic restoration.

In 1643 Jean Bolland, SJ, began to publish the *Acta Sanctorum,* a critical publication of the lives of the saints. This remarkable scholarly enterprise still continues under the direction of the *Bollandists, all of whom are Belgian Jesuits. By 1965 the 68 volumes of the *Acta Sanctorum* included the saints listed in the calendar up to November 10. Since the 16th century many missionaries have departed the Low Countries for the missions overseas. The most celebrated one is Ferdinand *Verbiest, SJ, whose influence as head of the astronomical observatory in Peking enabled him to safeguard the free expansion of Christianity in China in the second half of the 17th century.

In 1715 the Catholic Low Countries came under the control of Austria. During the 18th century, the *Enlightenment made slight headway in Belgium except in the principality of Liège. *Freemasonry, whose first grand lodge was started in London in 1717, was not in the 18th century noted for the *anticlericalism characteristic of Belgian lodges in the 20th century. Among its members were many Belgian nobles, some priests, and even one bishop (Von Velbruck of Liège).

Johann Nikolaus von *Hontheim, coadjutor bishop of Trier and a pupil of Zeger van *Espen, professor of Canon Law at Louvain, published under the pseudonym Febronius the treatise *De statu Ecclesiae* (1763), which conceded to the state great power over the Church while reducing the papal primacy to a mere primacy of honor (*see* FEBRONIANISM). In the Hapsburg territories in the Low Countries the ministers of *Maria Theresa (1740–70) manifested their anticlericalism. Thus, when the Society of Jesus was suppressed by Clement XIV (1773), they formed a Jesuit committee that treated the Jesuits with special severity.

Emperor *Joseph II (1780–90), an enlightened despot, believed he had a vocation to reform thoroughly the Church in the Catholic Low Countries. In 1781 he published an edict of tolerance for the small groups of Protestants, but withdrew from foreign religious superiors their jurisdiction over monastic orders. In 1782 he suppressed contemplative orders and confiscated the property of the 2,600 contemplative religious. He also reorganized parishes and liturgical worship. In 1786 he required that seminarians study at the college of philosophy that he instituted at Louvain and staffed with professors imbued with his own ideas (*see* JOSEPHINISM). These religious changes, together with administrative and judiciary reforms, incited a revolution that drove out the Austrians in 1789. After a progressive revolution in Liège, also in 1789, the prince-bishop fled and the inhabitants proclaimed the equality of all citizens. However, the troops of the new emperor, Leopold II, reinstated the prince-bishop and reconquered the Catholic Low Countries.

Soon after the French Revolution began (1789), the French conquered Belgium (1792–94). Religious persecution started in Belgium in 1796, but it was especially after the coup d'état of Fructidor 18 (Sept. 4, 1797) that antireligious hate was given free rein. When the oath of hatred for royalty and of submission to the laws of the republic was put into effect, the great majority of the Belgian clergy refused to subscribe to it. As a result 8,565 priests were condemned to deportation, although only 865 were actually apprehended. Since the civil authorities closed the churches, religious services could be celebrated only in secret. Ecclesiastical properties were sold, the University of Louvain was closed, and all religious orders and congregations of religious were suppressed. The Flemish population became so exasperated by this persecution and by compulsory military conscription that in 1798 it began the wars of the peasants (*Boerenkrijg*). But lack of organization and failure to receive help from the English caused the quick defeat of the uprising. Bonaparte gained the good will of Belgian Catholics by the French *Concordat of 1801. Henceforth Catholic worship was free. Belgium had the archbishopric of Mechelen and Dioceses of Ghent, Tournai, Namur, and Liège. But when *Napoleon I imposed the Imperial *Catechism (1806), arrested and imprisoned Pope *Pius VII (1809–14), interfered in religious matters, and closed the seminaries in Ghent and

Tournai, he aroused a silent opposition. His downfall at Waterloo was hailed in Belgium with great joy.

From 1815 to 1830 William I was king of both Belgium and Holland. The Fundamental Law, which suppressed all the privileges enjoyed by the clergy during the *ancien régime* while proclaiming religious liberty, displeased many Catholics. Still more disquieting to them was the King's determination to rule the Church as an enlightened despot. He subjected private education to severe restrictions, banished the Jesuits and *Christian Brothers, and in 1825 imitated Joseph II by compelling seminarians to attend the college of philosophy at Louvain. Previous to 1825 Catholic opposition aimed only to restore the privileges of the *ancien régime,* but from 1825 to 1830 it sought also to win religious freedom. When negotiations for a concordat between the King and the Holy See failed (1827), Catholics joined forces with the Liberals to demand both civil and religious liberties. This union created a climate favorable for the successful revolution of 1830 (*see* LIBERALISM).

Since 1830. The Belgian constitution of 1831 accorded liberty of association, of reunion, of education, of the press, and of worship. It deprived the government of all right to interfere in clerical appointments or to prevent clerics from corresponding with their superiors. It provided also that the state would assume the obligation of giving an annual financial compensation to clergymen, as agreed in the Concordat of 1801. In regard to marriage the constitution provided that the civil ceremony precede the religious one. The cults recognized by the constitution were the Catholic, Protestant, and Jewish. Rome was very suspicious of this liberal constitution. The encyclical of *Gregory XVI *Mirari vos* (1832) was aimed directly against Hugues Félicité de *Lamennais, the pioneer leader of Catholic Liberalism who enjoyed great influence in Belgium, but it seemed to be aimed indirectly against the Belgian constitution.

From 1830 to 1847 the unionist spirit brought together political figures of the right and the left for the purpose of consolidating the foundations of the new Belgian state. This period witnessed also a Catholic restoration. From 1835 on a papal nuncio resided in Brussels. In 1834 the Diocese of Bruges was reestablished and the six Belgian bishops reorganized their seminaries, which were soon provided a plenitude of priests to replace a thinly scattered and aged clergy. The number of religious men and women increased from 4,791 in 1829 to 11,968 in 1846. Missions preached by Redemptorists, Jesuits, and secular priests were the chief means of effecting the religious revival among the populace. Soon the country was covered with a network of Catholic primary and secondary schools. The bishops reopened the Catholic University of Louvain in 1834.

The Liberal party, organized in the liberal congress in 1846, obtained a majority in the Chambers from 1847 to 1870 and from 1878 to 1884. One of the crushing arguments of the Liberals was that Catholic approval of the constitution was feigned. To be sure, one group of Catholics, those who were promoting *ultramontanism, was suspicious of this liberal constitution. Fortunately Cardinal *Sterckx, Archbishop of Mechelen (1832–67), was always a vigorous defender of it. *Montalembert upheld the Belgian Catholic lib-

erals at the Catholic congress in Mechelen (1863), but the *Syllabus of Errors (1864) came as a hard blow for them. It was *Leo XIII who put an end to this dispute among Catholics by stating (March 1879): "The Belgian constitution consecrates some principles that I, as Pope, could not approve of; but the situation of Catholicism in Belgium, after the experience of half a century, demonstrates that in the present state of modern society, the system of liberty established in this country is most favorable to the Church. Belgian Catholics should not only abstain from attacking the constitution, they should also defend it."

As early as 1850 the Liberals passed a law on secondary education that displeased Catholics. But it was not until 1879 that they opened a 5-year war over the school question. Laws were passed obliging each commune to erect an official school and permitting the teaching of the Catholic religion only outside class hours. Catholic opinion reacted vigorously. Out of the total of 2,515 communes, 1,936 were soon endowed with private schools (*écoles libres*). These schools, which enrolled only 13.1 per cent of the total school population in 1878, accounted for 63.5 per cent of it by Dec. 15, 1880, when they had 580,380 pupils, compared with 333,500 in the public schools. In 1880 the Liberals caused Belgium to sever diplomatic relations with the Holy See because of the latter's refusal to disapprove the Belgian bishops. The Catholic governments that came into power after 1884 restored educational freedom. In 1909 private secondary schools (*collèges*) reported a student population of 16,538, whereas the state schools had only 6,000.

The Belgians have traditionally been loyal to the pope. During the attacks on the *States of the Church

Fig. 6. Furness; in the background, the abbey church.

(1859–70), they founded the Denier de Saint Pierre to provide for the pope's financial needs. Within 3 months Flanders counted 400,000 members. Later they sent volunteers to fight in the ranks of the papal *zouaves. At the Battle of Mentana (1867) there were 543 Belgian soldiers and 9 Belgian officers. At *Vatican Council I Victor *Dechamps, Archbishop of Mechelen, was a leader of the majority group and played an important part in the drafting of the doctrinal constitution on papal primacy and infallibility. By 1910 the number of religious had risen to 38,140. Besides engaging in educational work, caring for the sick, and devoting themselves to other social and charitable works, Belgian religious were second only to the French in the numbers who served in mission territories. In 1927 there were 1,656 Belgian priests and brothers and 976 sisters in the missions. Best known among these missionaries are Pierre Jean *de Smet, SJ, who labored among the Indian tribes in the U.S. and whose statue is in the capitol in Washington, D.C.; Joseph *Damien, a Picpus priest and apostle of the lepers in Molokai; and Konstant Lievens, SJ, the defender of the aborigines in Chota-Nagpur, India. The conversion of nearly half the Africans in the *Congo has been due almost exclusively to the labors of Belgian missionaries.

Catholic leaders in the 19th century unfortunately tried to remedy the social ills of the proletariat almost exclusively in a paternalistic spirit. The Catholic Congresses of Liège (1886, 1887, 1890), under the direction of Bishop Doutreloux of Liège, were deeply concerned with the social question. It was the encyclical *Rerum novarum* (1891) that finally set in motion a soundly conceived Catholic social movement. Not until c. 1900, however, were *Christian trade unions established. Meanwhile the masses of workers, especially in Wallonia, had lost the faith.

Among the leading Catholic scholars was Cardinal Dechamps, the author of several works in apologetics and theology. At Louvain Désiré Joseph *Mercier, later archbishop of Mechelen and cardinal, established the philosophical institute that became a center in the revival of Thomism. Outstanding in the field of ecclesiastical history were Godefroid *Kurth and, above all, the Bollandists. Alfred *Cauchie started the celebrated historical school of Louvain.

The Catholic party became a confessional party because of the activities of the anticlerical liberal government (1878–84). Between 1884 and 1914 the Catholic party had an absolute majority in the legislature. It lost this majority after the introduction of universal suffrage (1919) and was then obliged to form coalition governments.

Three movements founded by Flemish priests are worthy of special note. The first was the foundation made by P. Meeus of the Leagues of the Sacred Heart, which has led hundreds of thousands of men and women to monthly Confession and Communion. The second was the establishment by Edward Poppe of the Eucharistic Crusade, which promoted the reception of Communion by the very young. In 1925 the Jeunesse ouvrière chretienne (JOC), a movement that has since spread throughout the world to the immense benefit of millions of young, was organized by the parish priest Jozef Cardijn, created cardinal by Paul VI in 1965 (see YOUTH ORGANIZATIONS, CATHOLIC).

During World War I, Cardinal Mercier was a symbol of Belgian patriotism. During World War II the Belgian bishops were firm in their opposition to the doctrines of *National Socialism and in their protest against the deportation of workers. Between 1940 and 1945 there were 85 Belgian priests and religious who were put to death by the Germans or who perished in concentration camps.

Current Status of Catholicism. In a total population of 9,328,000 in 1963, there were 5,160,000 in the Flemish section of Belgium, 3,069,000 in the Walloon area, 59,000 in the German sector, and 1,040,000 in Brussels, the capital. Flemish (Netherlandish), the same language as that used in the Netherlands, is the official language in four provinces and French in four others (along with German in the eastern cantons). Brabant in central Belgium has a mixture of tongues; its population in 1963 included 800,000 Flemings, 200,000 French-speaking Walloons, and more than 1 million in Brussels, which is officially bilingual.

The Walloon section was the one most highly industrialized in the 19th century. The majority of the working class there quit the Church, although in Flanders, which was industrialized later and which imbibed much less influence from French anticlericalism because of language differences, the faith was much better safeguarded.

In 1963 the birthrate for Belgium as a whole was 16.96 per thousand; for the Flemish section, 18.50; for the Walloon part, 15.36; and for Brussels, 13.78. There were 62,449 marriages and 4,894 divorces, compared with 71,624 marriages and 2,491 divorces in 1930 when the population was 8,092,000 and the birthrate 18.97 per thousand.

Ecclesiastical Divisions. From 1834 to 1961 Belgium had six dioceses united in one ecclesiastical province whose metropolitan see was Mechelen (Mechelen-Brussels since 1961). The Diocese of Antwerp was added to this province when it was restored in 1961. These seven sees averaged 1,310,000 Catholics, whereas the average for Europe is 310,000. Belgium would have 30 sees if it had the same average number of faithful as dioceses in the U.S. In the seven dioceses there were 243 deaneries and 3,890 parishes.

Priests and Religious. Belgium had in 1965 two cardinals, Abp. Leo Suenens of Mechelen-Brussels and Jozef Cardijn, created in 1965. There were also 12 bishops (6 auxiliary) and 19 vicars-general. In 1963 there were 10,375 diocesan and 4,830 religious priests, 1,150 seminarians, and 195 newly ordained priests. There were six seminaries, with another in preparation at Antwerp. There was an average of one priest in parish work for every 1,470 Catholics, but the proportion varied widely, especially between rural and large city parishes.

In 1965 there were 57 institutes of religious men in 573 houses with 14,925 members (9,987 priests or seminarians, 4,938 brothers) and nearly 400 institutes of religious women in 3,523 convents with about 42,600 members (29,315 in Flanders, 12,279 in the French sections). The institute for men with the largest membership was that of the Jesuits, followed by the Scheut Fathers, Christian Brothers, Brothers of Charity, Franciscans, Benedictines, White Fathers, Capuchins, Salesians, and Dominicans. To study problems of common interest and to coordinate activities, there has existed for some years an assembly of major superiors, grouping all male institutes, and another grouping all female ones.

Catholic Education. The position of Catholic education is very strong. In 1964 Catholic schools for children between the ages of 3 to 6 enrolled 269,683, or 64 per cent of all children (80 per cent in Flanders). Catholic primary schools (for ages 6 to 12) had 498,-522 students, 53 per cent of all students (62.5 per cent in Flanders); also many communal schools might be classified as Catholic. Catholic secondary schools (ages 12 to 18) had 408,377 students, 64 per cent of the total. The eight Catholic institutes of higher education had 18,800 students, of whom 15,750 were attending Louvain University; this number represented 49 per cent of the total for the country.

The government pays the annual salaries of the teaching personnel in Catholic primary and secondary schools and supplies a fixed sum also for each student, but it does not defray the expenses for buildings and equipment. The state also bears the greater part of the expenses of Catholic higher education. Diplomas from Catholic schools have the same legal status as those from state institutes.

In the state, primary and secondary school children can choose between a course in morals and one in religion. The latter type of course is conducted by persons belonging to the belief in question, who are appointed and paid by the state. In 1960 there were 84,273 students (88.7 per cent of the total) in the state primary schools (ages 6 to 12) taking the course in the Catholic religion, 1,430 in the Protestant faith, and 219 in the Jewish; another 9,066 chose the course in morals. In the state secondary schools (ages 12 to 18), 65,231 students (68.5 per cent) studied the Catholic religion, 1,604 the Protestant, and 410 the Jewish, and 28,072 the course in morals.

Catholic Charitable Institutions. Since 1938 the various Catholic charitable institutions have been grouped in the Caritas Catholica, which comprises four large sections. The Fédération des Institutions Hospitalièreres is concerned with hospitals, clinics, psychiatric institutions, and homes for the aged. In 1963 there were 382 hospitals in Belgium, with 40,925 beds. Of these, religious communities possessed 144, with 15,-200 beds. Another 120 clinics were confided to them. Thus in Flanders 92 per cent of all clinics were confided to religious, 65 per cent in Wallonia, and 48.5 per cent in Brabant. Of the 48 psychiatric institutes in Belgium, with 27,900 patients, 34 belonged to religious and 5 others were confided to them. Thus 80 per cent of all mental patients in Belgium were tended by religious congregations, all of which had their motherhouses in Flanders, a situation unique in the world. Of the 799 homes with 42,000 beds for the aged, 345 belonged to religious and 264 more were confided to their care.

The Fédération des Services Médico-sociaux, the second section, is concerned with various home services and institutions for preventive medicine and small children. The Fédération des Institutions de l'Enfance Inadaptée supervises the care of retarded children. Caritas-Secours gives aid in unusual situations, such as catastrophes in Belgium or elsewhere. Outside of the Caritas Catholica there exists also a large number of charitable groups of various kinds.

Catholic Scholarly, Cultural, and Literary Activities. Catholic scholars as a rule affiliate with neutral groups instead of forming separate societies. Specifically Catholic scholarly periodicals are rare, except in theology and allied sciences. Thus the University of Louvain publishes *Ephemerides theologicae Lovanienses* and *Revue d'Histoire ecclésiastique,* and the Jesuits edit *La Nouvelle Revue Théologique* and *Bijdragen. Tijdschrift voor Filosofie en Theologie.*

The situation is different in regard to general culture and literary life. The Dominicans publish a periodical of general interest called *Kultuurleven;* the Jesuits, *Streven;* and Catholic laymen, *De Maand, La Revue Générale, La Revue Nouvelle,* and the monthly literary review, *Dietsche Warande en Belfort.* Davidsfond, the most important Catholic cultural association in Flanders, has distributed more than 15 million books since its foundation in 1875. In 1963 it had 63,000 members in 658 local sections, distributed 275,000 books and arranged 1,250 conferences, 360 theatrical and 200 musical performances, and 500 cinema performances. Among the 47 daily newspapers in Belgium, with a combined circulation of 3 million, 23 are Catholic with a total circulation of 1.3 million (*see* CATHOLIC PRESS, WORLD SURVEY, 5).

Catholic Political Parties. The three largest political parties are the Catholic, the Liberal (a rather conservative party), and the Socialist. For decades the Catholic party was confessional, and the two others patently anticlerical. Since World War II the tendency has been to disassociate politics from religion. An increasing number in the Socialist party have sought to turn it into a workers' party. The Catholic party removed its confessional character in 1946 and changed its name to the Parti Social Chrétien (PSC). The Liberal party became in 1961 the Parti de la Liberté et du Progrès (PLP) in order to reassemble all the conservative forces. The Flemish national party, De Vlaamse Volksunie, seeks to end the actual if unofficial minority status of the Flemings. Voters tend to remain loyal to one party in election after election. In 1961 the two Marxist parties received 39.8 per cent of the votes; the Liberals 12.3, and the two Catholic parties 44.9. The Liberals, although a small minority, have been able to swing the balance of power. Thus they allied with the Socialists (1954–58) to unleash a "school war," which the voters clearly disavowed in 1958 when a "school pact" was concluded.

Another characteristic of Belgian elections is that between 1919 and 1961 the Catholic party obtained in Flanders between 56 and 60 per cent of the votes, in Wallonia between 27 and 34 per cent, in Brussels between 30 and 35 per cent. The percentages for the leftist parties were 39 to 43 in Flanders, 63 to 70 in Wallonia, and 56 to 68 in Brussels. These percentages approximated those for practicing Catholics in these three areas.

Catholic Social Activities. More than 80 per cent of Belgian youths who are affiliated with organizations belong to Catholic ones. There were in 1963 about 30,-000 young men in the Jeunesse ouvrière chrétienne (JOC) or the Katholieke Arbeidsjeugd (KAJ) and another 32,000 young women in the affiliated societies. All were founded by Jozef Cardijn in 1925 to engage young workers in Catholic Action and to protect their professional and economic interests. Diverse Catholic youth organizations are designed to attract farmers, rural dwellers, students, or other groups. Similar organizations exist for adult Catholics and have larger memberships. Of the Catholic associations dealing with social problems the Boerenbond plays a particularly important role in Belgian social and economic life and watches over the interests of its 225,000 agricultural members. The Confédération des Syndicats Chrétiens (CSC), which fosters the interests of workers in the light of Christian social principles, had 812,257 members (661,288 Flemish) in 1963, whereas the Socialist syndicates had about 100,000 less. The Alliance Nationale des Mutualités Chrétiennes, which insures members against a wide variety of risks, had some 1,235,-000 members in 1962, compared with 825,000 in the similar Socialist alliance. The Fédération des Patrons Catholiques de Belgique enrolled about 25 per cent of the business leaders in Flanders, but a much smaller percentage in Wallonia.

Church-State Relations. Separation of Church and State was incorporated in the liberal constitution of 1831. Belgian governments since then have not wanted a concordat with the Holy See, although they have cooperated with Rome at various times. Thus Belgium has maintained diplomatic relations with Rome constantly since 1835 (except 1880–84 during the quarrel over education). In the state schools students who so desire may take a course in the Catholic religion 2 hours a week conducted by a priest or person designated by the bishops but paid by the state. The government paid an annual salary to 6,889 Catholic priests engaged in parish work and also to 34 Protestant pastors, 9 Anglican chaplains, and 19 rabbis (in 1963). In 1920 the bishops, with the assent of Rome, agreed to renounce the exemption from military service provided by Canon Law, as long as secular seminarians and religious fulfilled their obligation by caring for the ill or wounded. The Belgian army contains about 100 Catholic chaplains, paid by the state and named by the vicar for the armed forces, who is always the archbishop of Mechelen-Brussels. Another 45 Catholic chaplains work in prisons or in rehabilitation schools. The pact concluded in 1958 between the three leading political parties and already described above regulates Church-State relations in educational matters.

Vitality of Catholic Life. About 97 per cent of Belgian infants are baptized in the Catholic Church. Between 24 and 30 per cent of the Catholics in Antwerp, Ghent, Liège, and other large cities regularly attend Sunday Mass. In Flanders the percentage is about 60, in Wallonia 40, and in Brussels 35. In some places, however, the percentage is almost 100, in others 25. Purely civil marriages are rare in country districts, but more and more frequent in cities, partly because of remarriages after divorce. In 1950 Limburg had only 47 purely civil marriages out of 4,309, and Eastern Flanders only 705 out of 19,614. In the city of Ghent 26 per cent were purely civil, but in the diocese as a whole 3.6. In Brussels 68 per cent of the marriages were religious, and in the section around Antwerp 70. In rural areas almost all burials are religious, in Liège 80 per cent, in Brussels 89.

Devotion to the Blessed Virgin is deep rooted among the Flemings, less so among the Walloons. The most celebrated centers of *pilgrimages in Flanders are Oostakker-Lourdes, Dadizelle, Halle, and Scherpenheuvel (Montaigu); in Wallonia, since the 1930s, Banneux and Beauraing (*see* SHRINES). Of the 51 retreat houses, 33 are accessible to men, 23 to women.

Ordinations of seminarians totalled 1,113 (1951–55) and 974 in the next 5 years. Flanders supplied the highest percentage of these 2,087 new priests, 2.84 per 10,000 inhabitants; Wallonia, 2.10, and Brabant 1.53. In 1963 there were 195 seminarians ordained (105 in the three Flemish dioceses, 41 in the Diocese of Liège, 49 in the other three dioceses). The trend, therefore, has been toward a constantly decreasing number of secular priests, especially among the French population.

Religious orders and congregations of priests received 1,557 candidates between 1948 and 1953; 1,615 between 1953 and 1958; and 1,364 between 1958 and 1963. The decline in recruitments has been particularly noticeable in mission congregations. In 1940, 25 to 30 per cent of those who entered seminaries departed before ordination, while 35 to 40 per cent departed in 1965.

Brothers totalled 4,938 in 1965. Congregations of brothers had 3,369 members but only 57 novices. The number of brothers in other orders and congregations was 1,398, 57 of whom were novices. Since 1930 the numbers entering the brotherhood have declined and the number leaving it has increased. Religious institutes of priests totalled, together with their brothers, 11,556 members in 1965 (7,400 in Flanders, with 214 novices; 4,154 in French sections, with 184 novices).

The 400 or so orders and congregations of religious women had about 42,600 sisters in 1965. Since World War II vocations have declined considerably. Vocations to *secular institutes have compensated for only a small part of this change.

Both in absolute and relative figures Belgium ranks second in the world in the number of its missionaries. Of the 10,070 Belgian missionaries in 1960 in territories subject to the Congregation for the Propagation of the Faith, 75 per cent were Flemish. Of these 4,317 were priests or scholastics, 926 brothers, 4,611 sisters, and 216 laymen.

Non-Catholics. Belgium had in 1964 about 75,000 Protestants belonging to 15 denominations and 15,000 to 20,000 Jews. The Protestant faculty of theology in Brussels had 40 students, of whom Belgians accounted for 19 men and 10 women.

Bibliography: Bibliography. H. PIRENNE, *Bibliographie de l'histoire de Belgique,* rev. H. NOWÉ and H. OBREEN (3d ed. Brussels 1931). General. É. DE MOREAU, DHGE 7:520–756; *Histoire de l'Église en Belgique,* 5 v. (Brussels 1945–52), 2 Suppl; *L'Église en Belgique* (Paris 1944). Special studies. A. CAUCHIE, *La Querelle des investitures dans les diocèses de Liège et de Cambrai,* 2 v. (Louvain 1890). U. BERLIÈRE, *Monasticon belge,* 3 v. (Maredsous-Liège 1890–1960). G. KURTH, *Notger de Liège et la civilisation au Xe siècle,* 2 v. (Brussels 1905). C. TERLINDEN, *Guillaume Ier, roi des Pays-Bas et l'Église catholique en Belgique, 1814–30,* 2 v. (Brussels 1906). A. PASTURE, *La Restauration religieuse aux Pays-Bas catholiques sous les archiducs Albert et Isabelle* (Louvain 1925). A. PONCELET, *Histoire de la Compagnie de Jésus dans les anciens Pays-Bas,* 2 v. (Brussels 1927–28). F. WILLCOX, *L'Introduction des décrets du Concile de Trente dans les Pays-Bas et dans la principauté de Liège* (Louvain 1929). L. J. VAN DER ESSEN, *De gulden eeuw onzer christianisatie VIIe–VIIIe eeuw* (Diest 1943). M. LOBET, *L'Épopée belge des Croisades* (Liège 1944). J. SCHEERDER, *De Inquisitie in de Nederlanden in de XVIe eeuw* (Antwerp 1944). A. MENS, *Oorsprong en betekenis van de Nederlandse Begijnen- en Begar-*

denbeweging (Louvain 1947). S. AXTERS, *The Spirituality of the Old Low Countries*, tr. D. ATTWATER (London 1954); *Geschiedenis van de vroomheid in de Nederlanden*, 4 v. (Antwerp 1950–60). L. WILLAERT, *Les Origines du jansénisme dans les Pays-Bas catholiques* (Brussels 1948). M. DIERICKX, *De oprichting der nieuwe bisdommen in de Nederlanden onder Filips II, 1559–1570* (Antwerp 1950). A. SIMON, *Le Cardinal Sterckx et son temps, 1792–1867*, 2 v. (Wetteren 1950); *Le Parti catholique belge, 1830–1945* (Brussels 1958). H. HAAG, *Les Origines du catholicisme libéral en Belgique, 1789–1839* (Louvain 1950); "The Catholic Movement in Belgium," in *Church and Society*, ed. J. N. MOODY (New York 1953) 279–324. É. DE MOREAU, *Les Abbayes de Belgique, VIIe–XIIe siècles* (Brussels 1952). M. BECQUÉ, *Le Cardinal Dechamps*, 2 v. (Louvain 1956). P. HILDEBRAND, *Les Capucins en Belgique et au nord de la France* (Antwerp 1957). K. VAN ISACKER, *Het daensisme* (Antwerp 1959). V. MALLINSON, *Power and Politics in Belgian Education, 1815–1961* (London 1963).

Contemporary Church. J. KERKHOFS and J. VAN HOUTTE, *De Kerk in Vlaanderen* (Tielt 1962). *Rapport annuaire de la Fondation Universitaire* (Brussels 1964). *Annuaire statistique de l'enseignement catholique, 1960–1961* (Brussels 1963). *Caritas, 1938–1963* (Brussels 1963). *Het Verbond der Verplegingsinstellingen van Caritas Catholica* (Brussels). E. DE SMET et al., *Atlas des élections belges, 1919–1954*, 2 v. (Brussels 1958), with app. for the elections of 1958. *Each One for All. All for Each: The Belgian Boerenbond* (Louvain 1958). *Mouvement ouvrier chrétien: Rapport d'activité, 21e congrès, Bruxelles 17–19 avril 1964* (Brussels). A. BRYS, *Comment est conçu et organisé le Mouvement ouvrier chrétien en Belgique* (Brussels 1960). *Bilan du Monde* 2:124–142. *Annuaire catholique de Belgique, 1963–64* (Brussels 1964). AnnPont has annual data on all dioceses. **Illustration credits:** Figs. 2, 3, and 5, Official Belgian Tourist Bureau, New York City. Figs. 4 and 6, Arthur O'Leary.

[M. DIERICKX]

BELGRADE, ARCHDIOCESE OF (BELOGRADENSIS)

Latin archbishopric without suffragans since 1924, immediately subject to the Holy See; in Serbia, east *Yugoslavia. In 1963 it had 7 secular and 20 religious priests, 429 sisters in 22 houses, and 50,000 Catholics in a population of 3,500,000; its 18,919 square miles comprise the Serbia of 1912. The city of Belgrade, at the confluence of the Danube and Sava Rivers, was a Celtic (3d century B.C.) and a Roman fort called *Singidunum* until it was destroyed by Avars and Slavs in the early 7th century. Strategically located between the upper and lower Danube and between Hungary and Serbia, it was rebuilt in the early 9th century by the Bulgars, who renamed it the White City (Belgrade). It was contested repeatedly by many powers (including Byzantium) and in 1427 was ceded by Serbia to Hungary. The Turks, defeated at Belgrade by the Hungarians under John *Hunyadi and St. *John Capistran (1456), held the city from 1521 until they withdrew in 1867; Austria held it occasionally (1688–90, 1717–39, and 1789–92), as did Serbian rebels (1807–13). As the capital of Serbia (1878) and of Yugoslavia (1918), Belgrade was heavily damaged in World Wars I and II. The university (1905) derives from a school at Kragujevac (1838).

Christianity was introduced into Belgrade early. There were martyrs there (*c*. 310), and *Constans II protected its Arian Bishop Ursacius (335–370). The See of Belgrade, as well as those of *Naissus* (Niš), *Horreum Margi* (Ćuprija), and *Viminacium* (Kostolac), all within the area of the present archdiocese, was destroyed by the Avars and Slavs early in the 7th century. During the 8th and 9th centuries, missionary efforts continued. From the 10th century there was a Byzantine-Slavonic rite See of Belgrade,

which became suffragan to Ohrid in 1020. But the Serbian Church aligned itself with the Byzantine schism against Rome. In 1830 Belgrade became the metropolitan see of the Serbian autonomous Church (autocephalous in 1879), and in 1920 it became the see of the Serbian Orthodox patriarch.

Attempts to restore a Latin See of Belgrade succeeded by 1334, from which time the episcopal list is almost continuous, although little is known of the early bishops. Under the Turks, the episcopal administration was nominal; the title of Belgrade was held by certain Hungarian titular bishops, while the few Latin Catholics were cared for by neighboring bishops (Prizren and Djakovo) and by missionaries, especially Franciscan. In 1723 the See of Belgrade was united with that of Smederevo, which had a Latin bishop (1544–1624). Bishop J. J. *Strossmayer of Djakovo was apostolic administrator of Belgrade (1851–97). From 1898 to 1924 the see was under the Congregation for the *Propagation of the Faith, the provision of the concordat of 1914 that Belgrade should be an archdiocese being postponed by World War I. Skoplje, intended as a suffragan see in 1914, became a bishopric immediately subject to the Holy See in 1924. Since 1925 the archbishop has been also apostolic administrator for the Yugoslavian Banat, formed of the Yugoslavian part of the former See of Csanád (Hungary).

Bibliography: M. PREMROU, "Serie dei vescovi romano-cattolici di Beograd," ArchFrancHist 17 (1924) 489–508; 18 (1925) 33–62; 19 (1926) 29–45. V. WAGNER, "History of the Catholic Church in Serbia in the 19th Century," *Bogoslovska Smotra* 21 (1933); 22 (1934), in Croatian. K. DRAGANOVIĆ, *General Directory of the Catholic Church in Yugoslavia* (Sarajevo 1939), in Croatian; EncCatt 2:1176–77. F. BULIĆ and A. DE MEYER, DHGE 7:756–758, with list of bishops. J. MATL, LexThK² 2:159. AnnPont (1964) 62, 734.

[M. LACKO]

BELIAL, a term derived from the Hebrew word *beliya'al*, a compound of *beli* (without) and *ya'al* (usefulness), often used in the OT to designate an evil or worthless person or thing. It usually occurs as a genitive rendered in English as if it were a personal name. Thus a scoundrel is a "man of Belial" (2 Kgs 20.1; 3 Kgs 21.13) or a "son of Belial" (Jgs 19.22; 1 Kgs 1.16). A malignant disease is a "disease of Belial" [Ps 40(41).9]. Destroying floods are "torrents of Belial" [2 Kgs 22.5; Ps 17(18).5]. Belial occurs as a substantive only in Jb 34.18 and Na 2.1; both in the sense of the "scoundrel, the worthless man."

In rabbinic literature from the 2d century B.C. Belial was identified with *Satan, the personification of evil. By NT times Belial (Βελιάλ) or the variant form, Beliar (Βελιάρ), was used as the name for the antagonist of God, Antichrist. With this meaning St. Paul uses it in 2 Cor 6.15: "What harmony is there between Christ and Belial [Beliar]?"

In later apocryphal books (*Sibylline Oracles* 2.167; *Ascension of Isaias* 1.8–9) Beliar is mentioned as the great evil power in the world. In the *Testaments of the Twelve Patriarchs* (Reuben 2.4.6) he is the source of impurity, who sends evil spirits against men but cannot overcome the chaste man.

Bibliography: EncDictBibl 221. W. FOERSTER, Kittel ThW 1:606. A. ROMEO, EncCatt 2:1177–79. K. GALLING, RGG³ 1:1025–26. O. SCHILLING, LexThK² 2:159.

[M. R. RYAN]

BELISARIUS, 6th-century Byzantine general; b. Illyricum, *c.* 500; d. March 565. Belisarius had the historian *Procopius as his juridical and administrative adviser from 527 to 540, while he was the faithful and efficacious instrument of the politics of *Justinian I in the recovery of Italy from the Goths. He was implicated in the troubled events marking the passage of the pontificate from *Silverius (536–537) to *Vigilius (537–555). According to the Liber pontificalis, the *Anecdota,* and the *Breviarium* of the Carthaginian deacon *Liberatus, he acted as an unwilling executor of the intrigues of the Empress Theodora, who hoped that with Vigilius's accession she could recover the See of Constantinople for her protégé *Anthimus of Trebizond. Belisarius campaigned successfully against the Persians (541–542), bringing them to submission after they dealt a surprise attack near Nisibis occasioned by Belisarius's pacificatory attitude. He served as the Emperor's official representative in the negotiations with Pope Vigilius before and during the Council of *Constantinople III (553). He fell into disfavor in 562 when unjustly accused of conspiracy against the Emperor, but returned to favor before his death. Procopius described him at the height of his glory; and although he may have given him too much credit, Belisarius's campaigns were wholly successful. A gold cross, his gift for the tomb of St. Peter, is preserved in Rome, as is a hospice that he founded on the Via Lata. Legends about Belisarius can be traced to the Middle Ages.

Bibliography: L. Bréhier, DHGE 7:776–787. Stein-Palanque HistBEmp 284–286, 312–324, 386, 494–498, 665–666, 719–720, 779.

[P. ROCHE]

BELL, BERNARD IDDINGS, educator, author; b. Dayton, Ohio, Oct. 13, 1886; d. Chicago, Ill., Sept. 5, 1958. He was the son of Charles and Vienna (Iddings) Bell. After receiving his B.A. degree from the University of Chicago, Ill., he continued his studies at Western

Bernard Iddings Bell, by H. Hanatschek, 1929.

Theological Seminary, Chicago, where he was awarded his S.T.B. in 1912 and his D.D. in 1921. He received his S.T.D. from the University of the South, Sewanee, Tenn., in 1923. After his ordination in the Episcopal Church in 1910 and his marriage to Elizabeth Wood Lee, Bell served at St. Christopher's Church, Oak Park, Ill.; St. Paul's Cathedral Church, Fond du Lac, Wis.; and St. John's Cathedral, Providence, R.I. He served also as professor of religion at Columbia University, New York City, having earlier taught at the University of Chicago; Lafayette College, Easton, Pa.; and Ohio Wesleyan University, Delaware, Ohio. His many religious and educational works include *Common Sense in Education* (1928), *The Altar and the World* (1944), *God Is Not Dead* (1945), *Man Can Live* (1946), and *Crisis in Education* (1949), which is concerned with the problems facing education in the 20th century.

Illustration credit: Columbia University News Office.

[J. L. MORRISON]

BELLAMY, JEAN JULIEN, theologian; b. Moustoir-ac, France, 1857; d. Vannes, May 22, 1903. At the major seminary of Vannes he taught philosophy from 1881 to 1887, and Scripture and Church history from 1887 to 1895. He contributed articles to the *Dictionnaire de théologie catholique* and to Vigouroux's *Dictionnaire de la Bible.* After he became a chaplain at the civil hospital in Vannes, he wrote three books: *La Vie surnaturelle considérée dans son principe* (Paris 1895); *Les Effets de la communion considérés au triple point de vue théologique, historique et social* (Paris 1900); and *La Théologie catholique au 19e siècle* (Paris 1904).

Bibliography: E. MANGENOT, DTC 2.1:559.

[G. MOLLAT]

BELLARMINE, ROBERT, ST.

Cardinal and Doctor of the Church; b. Montepulciano, Tuscany, Oct. 4, 1542; d. Rome, Sept. 17, 1621 (feast, May 13). His parents were Vincent Bellarmine and Cinthia Cervini, a sister of Marcellus II (d. 1555). In 1560 Bellarmine entered the Jesuits' Roman College, made his first vows as a Jesuit, and began a study of Aristotelian philosophy.

Career as Teacher. After a brief study of Thomistic theology at Padua, Bellarmine was sent in 1569 to Louvain, Belgium, where he became the first Jesuit professor at the University of Louvain. He was ordained in 1570. Bellarmine taught theology from the *Summa Theologiae* of St. Thomas Aquinas in the Jesuit house of studies, and began the groundwork for his major work, the *Controversies.* The University of Louvain was part of the Church's front-line defense against the Reformers. The atmosphere was one of practical defensive scholarship rather than of calm speculation or the reasoned development of dogmas securely held. Catholic Church history and patristic studies were in a sad state of neglect. As if in answer to the needs of the time, Bellarmine devoted his energy to the study of Scripture, Church history, and patristics in order to systematize Church doctrine against the attacks of the Reformers. He wrote a Hebrew grammar and compiled a patristic work, *De Scriptoribus ecclesiasticis.*

In 1576 Gregory XIII requested him to teach theology to English and German missionary students in the Roman College, and Bellarmine continued teaching until 1588. The vast synthesis of Protestant and Catholic theology resulting from these lectures appeared in three volumes, *Disputationes de Controversiis Chris-*

St. Robert Bellarmine. Antique engraving after the portrait from life by Passerotti which now hangs in the Jesuit College at Madrid.

tianae Fidei adversus hujus temporis haereticos (Igolstadt 1586–88–93). It is Bellarmine's largest and most important work, containing most of the ideas he developed later. Particularly noteworthy are the sections on the temporal power of the pope and the role of the laity. Along with the *De translatione Imperii Romani* (Antwerp 1584), these constitute Bellarmine's earliest major writings on papal power. The *Controversies* are monumental because they put order into the chaotic argumentation of attack and defense waged between Reformers and Catholics. His criticism of reform theology was remarkably fair and just in that he pointed out its strength as well as its weakness. This was in direct contrast to much of the polemic writing of the times. The *Controversies* were small enough to be carried by missionaries, yet afforded more than the excellent but sketchy catechism of St. Peter Canisius for warding off the attacks of scholarly adult disputants. They were so effective a weapon against reform theology that special chairs of learning were erected just to combat their influence, and they seem to have occasioned the return of many to the Church.

In 1588 Bellarmine became spiritual director of the Roman College. From his catechetical lessons to lay brothers and students resulted the small catechism for children, *Dottrina cristiana breve* (Rome 1597), and the catechism for teachers, *Dichiarazione più copiosa della dottrina cristiana* (Rome 1598). Clement VIII (d. 1605) solemnly approved both manuals. They were often translated and widely used, and they remained popular until Vatican Council I.

In 1590 Bellarmine experienced his first major difficulty over his theory of indirect papal power. Only the sudden death of Sixtus V prevented the Pope from putting the first volume of the *Controversies*, which contained this theory, on the Index.

Career as Churchman. After serving as rector of the Roman College (1592), provincial of the Jesuits' Neapolitan province (1594), and theologian to Clement VIII (1597), in 1599 he was made a cardinal by the same Pope. From that time on, Bellarmine served as a member of all the Roman Congregations and of many commissions. One of Bellarmine's continual concerns was the discipline of bishops, e.g., their appointment, residency, and transfer.

At the turn of the century Bellarmine became involved in the controversy over efficacious grace. He defended his disciple Leonard *Lessius; wrote a report, *De Controversia Lovaniensi*, for the president of the *Congregatio de Auxiliis;* and debated on paper with Domingo Bañez. *See* BÁÑEZ AND BAÑEZIANISM; GRACE, CONTROVERSIES ON.

In 1602 Clement VIII personally consecrated Bellarmine archbishop and sent him to Capua, where he lived a pastoral life of charity, preaching, and reform. In 1605 Paul V recalled him to Rome to serve the Church at large.

Bellarmine spent the next few years in controversies involving papal power: against the Republic of Venice over clerical immunities, 1606–07; against King James I of England over the *divine right of kings and the English oath of allegiance, 1607 to 1609; against the *Gallicanism of William Barclay and Roger Widdrington, 1610, which occasioned Bellarmine's famous *Tractatus de potestate Summi Pontificis in rebus temporalibus adversus Gulielmum Barclaeum.*

Bellarmine is famous, not because he invented the theory of the indirect power of the pope in temporal affairs, but because he used it so effectively in the history of *Church and State relations, clearly distinguishing between the temporal and the purely spiritual power of the pope. By applying Thomistic political philosophy to the confusions and exaggerations of his age, he emphasized the purely spiritual power of the Church, yet showed that because the spiritual power of the Church is primary and the temporal secondary, the pope may act regarding those temporal things affecting the spiritual. While Bellarmine is famous for defending the distinction and subordination of powers as part of Catholic doctrine, his practical applications of these principles manifest a confusion of what is permanent with what was contingent in the Church's actual use of her power. Perhaps this stems from the fact that he looked upon the state not as having an existence independent of the Church but as making up one society with the Church. Bellarmine seems further to have failed to note that the Church intervenes in temporal affairs for two basically different reasons: either she has a divine right to act, or she fills a vacuum left by political society's failure to act. No doubt Bellarmine's understanding of history was greatly influenced by the sources available to him.

The last major controversy of Bellarmine's life came in 1616 when he had to admonish *Galileo, whom he admired; he gave the admonition on behalf of the Holy Office, which had decided the the heliocentric theory of N. *Copernicus was contrary to Scripture. Although Bellarmine had served on commissions for the revision of the Vulgate and the Greek New Testament, there is some question whether he understood the Council of Trent's teaching on the interpretation of Scripture as well as Galileo did. Bellarmine also hesitated on the question of how to reconcile Scripture and science.

Bellarmine's ascetical works, such as *In omnes Psalmos dilucida esposito* (Rome 1611), *De gemitu columbae* (Rome 1615), and *De arte bene moriendi* (Rome 1620), appeared near the end of his life.

Bellarmine practiced self-sacrifice, poverty, disinterestedness, and devotion to duty. He fostered a special devotion to St. Francis of Assisi. The process for his canonization, begun in 1627, was delayed for political reasons until 1930. In 1931 Pius XI declared him a Doctor of the Church. Bellarmine's body lies in the Church of St. Ignatius in Rome.

Bibliography: Collected Works. *Opera omnia,* ed. J. Fèvre, 12 v. (Paris 1870–74); *Epistolae familiares,* ed. J. Fuligatti (Rome 1650); *Opera oratoria postuma,* ed. S. Tromp, 9 v. (Rome 1942–50). Sommervogel 1:1151–1254. X. M. LeBachelet, *Bellarmin avant son cardinalat: Correspondance et documents* (Paris 1911); DTC 2.2:560–599. R. Bellarmine, *Auctarium Bellarminianum,* ed. X. M. LeBachelet (Paris 1913). J. Brodrick, *The Life and Work of Blessed Robert Francis Cardinal Bellarmine,* 2 v. (London 1928). P. Dudon, DHGE 7:798–824. J. Lebreton, *Catholicisme* 1:1379–84. A. Piolanti, EncCatt 10:1043–49. S. Tromp. LexThK² 2:160–162. S. Merkle, "Grundsätzliche und methodologische Erörterungen zur Bellarminforschung," ZKirchgesch 45 (1927) 26–73. F. Z. Arnold, *Die Staatslehre des Kardinals Bellarmin* (Munich 1934). E. A. Ryan, *The Historical Scholarship of Saint Bellarmin* (New York 1936). J. C. Murray, "St. Robert Bellarmine on the Indirect Power," ThSt 9 (1948) 491–535. N. Hens, *Die Augustinusinterpretation des hl. Robert Bellarmin bezüglich der wirksamen Gnade und der Vorherbestimmung nach der Kontroverse* (Rome 1949). J. Hardon, *A Comparative Study of Bellarmine's Doctrine on the Relation of Sincere Non-Catholics to the Catholic Church* (Rome 1951). J. Beumer, "Die Frage nach Schrift und Tradition bein Robert Bellarmin," *Scholastik* 34 (1959) 1–22.

[J. FRISKE]

BELLARMINE COLLEGE

A Catholic college of arts and sciences for men in Louisville, Ky., conducted by the Archdiocese of Louisville. Its establishment was announced Nov. 18, 1949, by the Most Rev. John A. Floersh, Archbishop of Louisville, who appointed as administrative officers to organize the new institution: Rev. Alfred F. Horrigan, president and academic dean; Rev. Raymond J. Treece, vice president and business manager; and John T. Loftus, OFMConv., registrar and dean of students. Construction of the first building, Pasteur Hall, was begun Dec. 31, 1949, and the College received its first freshman class on Oct. 3, 1950. On June 21, 1954, 42 members of the first graduating class received their B.A. degrees.

Bellarmine College began its work in affiliation with The Catholic University of America, Washington, D.C. Accredited by the Southern Association of Colleges and Secondary Schools (Dec. 1956), it holds membership in the Association of American Colleges, the National Commission on Accrediting, the Association of University Evening Colleges, and the National Catholic Adult Education Commission. During its first 7 years, the College was an operation of the corporate entity, the "Roman Catholic Bishop of Louisville." On July 1, 1957,

it was incorporated independently under the laws of the Commonwealth of Kentucky, and a board of control, designated as the Board of Visitors, was established. From the foundation of the College in 1950, the responsibility of providing the priests charged with its administration and much of its teaching has been shared with the Archdiocese of Louisville, by the Franciscan Fathers, Friars Minor Conventual, of the Province of Our Lady of Consolation.

The College opened in 1950 with an enrollment of 210 students. In the fall semester of 1963–64, 2,126 students were engaged in the College's various programs of study. This total included 1,034 students in the day division, 492 in the evening division, and 600 persons enrolled in the adult education program. The 90-member administrative and teaching staff was composed of 29 priests and 61 laymen. They held 24 doctorates and 49 master's degrees.

Work on the $1 million administration-library building was begun in 1953. In 1959 a student dormitory with accommodations for 120 students was built; and in December 1960 an $800,000 auditorium-gymnasium, with a seating capacity of 3,500, was completed. The 1960–61 academic year also saw the construction of two faculty houses, Lenihan and Bonaventure Halls. In the summer of 1963 ground was broken for a new residence hall to house 160 students.

The patron saint of the College is the 16th-century Jesuit, cardinal, educator, and doctor of the Church, St. Robert Bellarmine. Its motto, *In veritatis amore,* is taken from the Collect of the Mass for his feast day. The College derives its educational philosophy and purpose from this motto and seeks to "instill in its students a deep love of truth not only as a guide for their college work, but also as an abiding philosophy of life."

In its curricular organization, Bellarmine follows a program of concentration that stresses seminar work and independent study. Fields of concentration include the humanities, sciences, business, psychology, and sociology. Preprofessional training is offered in medicine, law, dentistry, pharmacy, and veterinary medicine. The College also provides a double-degree program in engineering in collaboration with the University of Louisville and the University of Detroit. In 1964 the College library housed 32,184 volumes and received 372 periodicals.

Men only are accepted as full-time students. Women may register on a part-time basis for classes in the evening and summer divisions.

[A. F. HORRIGAN]

BELLESHEIM, ALFONS, ecclesiastical historian; b. Monschau, near Aachen, Germany, Dec. 16, 1839; d. Aachen, Feb. 5, 1912. He studied theology at Cologne and then at Tübingen, where Carl von *Hefele introduced him to the study of ecclesiastical history. After ordination (1862), he continued his studies in Canon Law and ecclesiastical history in Rome. In 1865 he became vicar to the cathedral chapter and secretary in the office of the vicar-general of Cologne. In 1886 he was named canon, and in 1902 provost, in the cathedral chapter at Aachen. Bellesheim wrote extensively in various German periodicals on history, theology, and current controversy; but his most important work concerned the history of the Catholic Church in the British Isles. His *Geschichte der katholischen Kirche* *in Schottland* (2 v. 1883; Eng. tr. 4 v. 1887–90) and *Geschichte der katholischen Kirche in Irland* (3 v. 1890–91) were important as the first serious studies of these topics by a Catholic. He published also biographies of Cardinals Giuseppe Mezzofanti (1880), William Allen (1885), and Henry Manning (1892). Much of the material in these works came from archival research in Rome, Paris, and London (1881–84); but the author seems to have mastered his sources insufficiently at times and to have been lacking in critical sense. Although the books frequently cite primary and secondary sources, Bellesheim did not build his own narrative on them. Instead, he tended to utilize documents to illustrate his own views and to further his apologetic aims. He was perceptive in grasping the significance of ecclesiastical developments, but he supplied little of the Continental background of events in Great Britain and Ireland. In dealing with early Irish history, his account was not up-to-date, and for the period of Rinuccini the narrative relied mostly on this nuncio's report. Bellesheim appears to have envisioned as his readers the German Catholics of the Kulturkampf period and to have emphasized topics especially interesting to them.

Bibliography: J. GRISAR, DHGE 7:877. G. SCHREIBER, *Irland im deutschen und abendländischen Sakralraum* (Cologne 1956).

[R. D. EDWARDS]

BELLESINI, STEFANO, BL., priest; b. Trent, Italy, Nov. 25, 1774; d. Genazzano, Italy, Feb. 2, 1840 (feast, Feb. 3). Aloisio Giuseppe Bellesini was the son of Giuseppe and Maria Ursula (Meichembeck) Bellesini. After joining the *Augustinians in 1790, he took the name Stefano. During his theological studies at Bologna, the forces of the French Revolution forced him home to Trent, where, as a deacon, he did much preaching. He was ordained in 1797. During the suppression of the religious orders, he lived as a secular priest and established free schools for the Christian education of youth. His success led to his appointment by the Austrian government as inspector of all schools in Trent. In 1817, when the Augustinians were reestablished in the States of the Church, Stefano went there, and became master of novices successively in Rome, in Città della Pieve, and in Genazzano at the basilica of Our Mother of Good Counsel, where he was appointed pastor in 1830. His zeal in caring for the sick during a typhoid epidemic led to his fatal contraction of the disease. He was beatified Dec. 27, 1904.

Bibliography: F. BALZOFIORE, *Della vita . . . Stefano Bellesini . . .* (Rome 1868). P. BILLERI, *Vita del Beato Stefano Bellesini* (Rome 1904).

[M. J. HALPHEN]

BELLEVILLE, DIOCESE OF (BELLEVILLENSIS), suffragan of the metropolitan See of Chicago, comprising that part of southern Illinois below the northern borders of the counties of St. Clair, Clinton, Marion, Clay, Richland, and Lawrence, an area of 11,678 square miles. At Holy Family Mission in Cahokia (1699) the Jesuit missionary Jacques *Marquette introduced Christianity, and from there missionaries evangelized the Mississippi Valley. Kaskaskia (1703), which became Illinois's first capital, and Fort Chartres (1718) were important foundations. Farms, coal mines, and railroads led to rapid immigration and the consequent establishment of mission stations that have since grown into thriving communities and parishes. In southeastern Illinois a number of isolated Catholic settlements sprang up along the Ohio and Wabash Rivers as early as 1820. They were served by Rev. Elisha Durbin, of Kentucky, until the parish of Shawneetown was established in 1859.

The Diocese of Alton, created in 1857 (transferred to *Springfield, Ill., in 1923), had grown to such proportions that on Jan. 7, 1887, the new Diocese of Belleville was formed with John Janssen as its first bishop and a Catholic body of about 50,000. Under his administration new parishes were formed, a diocesan orphanage established, and two new high schools added to the already existing academy in Belleville (1857) and the Precious Blood Sisters' school and motherhouse at Ruma (1876). The diocese developed further under Henry Althoff, who was consecrated Feb. 24, 1914, after Janssen's death the previous spring. Althoff's episcopacy was particularly noteworthy for the establishment of St. Henry Minor Seminary at Belleville in 1926. The school system was modernized and schools standardized under the direction of a superintendent's office, created before Althoff's death on July 3, 1947.

On Nov. 29, 1947, Albert R. Zuroweste was named third bishop, and he was consecrated Jan. 29, 1948. Under his leadership progress continued with more than 100 major programs of new construction and expansion. The renovation of the cathedral and the Cahokia log church; the building of six new hospitals, new schools, churches, and halls; St. John's Orphanage; and King's

St. Peter's Cathedral, Belleville, Ill.

House of Retreats were among the projects completed. Many diocesan organizations were reactivated and new spiritual programs were adopted. A diocesan weekly, the *Messenger,* was established in 1907 and has continued uninterruptedly to serve the diocese; Zuroweste was editor from 1934 to 1948. In 1963 Catholics numbered more than 118,000 in a total population of about 790,300. There were 133 parishes and 15 missions; 230 priests, including 45 religious (Precious Blood, Oblates of Mary Immaculate, Sons of Divine Providence, Trinitarians, and Jesuits); and 28 brothers (Diocesan Brothers of Christ the King and Brothers of Mary). A total of 831 sisters helped to staff the institutions of the diocese, which included 7 high and 86 elementary schools, 8 general hospitals, 4 homes for the aged, and an orphanage. At Cahokia, the Jesuits operated Parks College of Aeronautical Technology of *St. Louis University.

Bibliography: F. BEUCKMAN, *History of the Diocese of Belleville, 1700–1914* (Belleville 1914).

[M. VANDELOO]

BELLINGS, RICHARD, Irish historian, b. Dublin, 1600?; d. Dublin, 1677. Richard, son of Sir Henry Bellings, a substantial landholder of Leinster, was educated at Lincoln's Inn, London, where he wrote a sixth book of the *Arcadia* of Sir Philip Sidney. On his return to Ireland, Bellings served as a member of parliament. He was elected to the newly formed Irish Confederation in 1642, serving as secretary of the supreme council while Viscount Mountgarrett, his father-in-law, assumed the presidency. In 1644 Bellings was sent to Rome to secure papal recognition and a papal nuncio who would have sufficient religious powers to consolidate into one homogeneous body all the contending Roman Catholic factions in Ireland. The mission of Giovanni *Rinuccini was a direct result of Bellings's mission. From 1645 to 1649, during his stay in Ireland, Bellings supported the royalist cause. When Charles I was executed, Bellings left for France and did not return to Ireland until 1660–61. His loyalty to the Stuarts was rewarded by Charles II, who restored a good portion of Bellings's estates that had been confiscated during his exile. Bellings's reputation is based chiefly on his *History of the Irish Confederation and the War in Ireland 1641–1648* (J. T. Gilbert, ed., 7 v. Dublin 1882–91). This collection of narrative history, letters, and documents constitutes a contemporary picture of Confederation Ireland. Though not without shortcomings, it is still a valuable source for the era with which it is concerned. Lost for many years, the original manuscript was not completely printed until 1882.

Bibliography: J. T. GILBERT, DNB 2:194–195. M. J. HYNES, *The Mission of Rinuccini* (Dublin 1932). E. W. HAMILTON, *The Irish Rebellion of 1641* (London 1920).

[P. S. MC GARRY]

BELLINI

Surname of a father and his two sons, painters who worked principally in Venice. Their works exemplify the main currents of north Italian painting in the 15th century.

Jacopo; b. Venice, early 15th century; d. there, 1470 or 1471. He was probably trained in Florence by *Gentile da Fabriano, and his few autograph Madonnas (Venice, Accademia; Florence, Uffizi) show the influ-

Giovanni Bellini, "Madonna and Child in a Landscape," oil on wood, 29½ by 23 inches.

ence of the international style (*see* INTERNATIONAL GOTHIC) in their soft modeling and delicate colors. The quiet poses, impassive faces, and bulky forms give them monumental dignity. Interesting aspects of Jacopo's work are revealed in two large volumes of his drawings (London, British Museum; Paris, Louvre). These contain studies of animals and costumes, compositional sketches, copies of antique monuments and inscriptions, and highly finished narrative compositions set in elaborate architectural perspectives. The books combine humanist preoccupations with the medieval tradition of model books.

Gentile; b. Venice, 1429; d. there, 1507. His early works (organ doors, Venice, San Marco) reveal his contact with Paduan art. The low vanishing point, elaborate "antique" architecture, and harsh plasticity are typical also of his brother-in-law Andrea *Mantegna. In 1479 Gentile traveled to Constantinople, where he portrayed Sultan Mohammed II (London, National Gallery). In this and in portraits of Venetian nobility he suggests character with precise lines and minute detail. Gentile is perhaps best remembered for a series of huge canvases depicting miracles that take place in panoramic Venetian cityscapes crowded with colorful processions (Venice, Accademia; Milan, Brera).

Giovanni; b. Venice, *c.* 1430; d. there, Nov. 20, 1516. Although also influenced by Paduan art ("Transfiguration," Venice, Correr), he early demonstrated his extraordinary gift for unifying a composition through rich and subtle use of color. By the 1470s Giovanni was painting on a monumental scale works that explore the possibilities of delicate oil glazes while retaining the crystal clarity of earlier works ("Coronation of the Virgin," Pesaro; "St. Francis," New York, Frick). From the 1480s Giovanni's gradual loosening and softening of the color achieves greater effects of atmospheric luminosity, and the figures develop breadth and monumentality. He left a notable series of half-length Madonnas (Bergamo; Venice, Accademia) and altarpieces of the Madonna and saints (Venice, Accademia; Frari, 1488; and San Zaccaria, 1505). In these altarpieces the Madonnas are enthroned under hemispherical church apses. The architecture defines and unifies the space in which the figures are harmoniously arranged. Giovanni's work thus spans the era from mid-15th-century experimentation to the classic phase of the High Renaissance. His paintings are among the most beautiful and profound of the Venetian Renaissance. (*See* RENAISSANCE ART.)

Bibliography: G. GRONAU, *Die Künstlerfamilie Bellini* (Leipzig 1909). V. GOLOUBEW, *Les Dessins de Jacopo Bellini au Louvre et au British Museum,* 2 v. (Brussels 1908–12). L. PLANISCIG, "Jacopo und Gentile Bellini," *Jahrbuch der Kunsthistorischen Sammlungen in Wien* NS 2 (1928) 41–62. P. HENDY and L. GOLDSCHEIDER, *Giovanni Bellini* (New York 1945). L. DUSSLER, *Giovanni Bellini* (Vienna 1949). R. PALLUCCHINI, *Catologo illustrato della mostra di G.B.* (Venice 1949); *Giovanni Bellini* (Milan 1959). M. RÖTHLISBERGER, "Studi su Jacopo Bellini," *Saggi e memorie di storia dell'arte* 2 (1958–59) 41–89. G. ROBERTSON, "The Earlier Work of Giovanni Bellini," *Journal of the Warburg and Courtauld Institutes* 23 (1960) 45–59. F. HEINEMANN, *Giovanni Bellini e i Belliniani,* 2 v. (Venice 1962). M. MEISS, *Giovanni Bellini's St. Francis in the Frick Collection* (Princeton 1964). **Illustration credit:** National Gallery of Art, Washington, D.C., Samuel H. Kress Collection.

[L. A. ANDERSON]

BELLINI, VINCENZO, renowned opera composer; b. Catania, Sicily, Nov. 3, 1801; d. Puteaux (near Paris), Sept. 23, 1835. He was the namesake of his grandfather, *maestro* at the Catania cathedral, who saw to his musical training. Bellini's first opera, *Adelson e Salvini* (1825), was produced while he was still a pupil of *Zingarelli at the Naples Conservatory. He was soon composing with increasing popularity for the leading opera houses of Italy. His most celebrated works are

Vincenzo Bellini, c. 1825.

Montecchi e Capuletti (*Romeo and Juliet;* Venice 1830); *La Sonnambula* and *Norma,* both produced in Milan in 1831; and his last opera, *I Puritani,* first performed in 1835 in Paris, where he had been residing

since 1833. Although Bellini was gifted neither in comedy as was Donizetti nor in the grand manner as was Rossini, he, like Donizetti, continued and refined the *bel canto* vocal tradition associated with Rossini, and strongly influenced the singing style of Chopin's piano. Despite the threadbare sentiments and poor literary value of his libretti, coupled with the conventional harmony and thin orchestral accompaniments of the music, the above-mentioned operas are often revived because of their graceful, elegiac melodies and because they serve admirably as vehicles for virtuoso singing. In his younger years Bellini composed some Masses and psalms that are now forgotten.

Bibliography: A. POUGIN, *Bellini* (Paris 1868). Grout HistOp. A. EINSTEIN, *Music in the Romantic Era* (New York 1947). *La Revue musicale* 66 (May 1935), special issue on Bellini. F. BONAVIA, Grove DMM 1:608–610. G. BARBLAN, MusGG 1:1611–16. Baker 123. **Illustration credit:** Museo Teatrale alla Scala.

[R. W. LOWE]

BELLINTANI, MATTIA DA SALÒ, Capuchin preacher and spiritual writer; b. Gazzane (Italy), June 28, 1534; d. Brescia, July 20, 1611. After his primary education in Salò he entered the newly founded Capuchin Order in Bergamo, Oct. 7, 1552, and was ordained Dec. 24, 1560. He taught philosophy and theology in various towns of Italy and repeatedly held the office of minister provincial. In 1575 he was appointed commissary general and visited France, Switzerland, and Bohemia in the interests of his order. A renowned preacher, he established the Confraternity of the Blessed Sacrament and promoted the Forty Hours devotion in many places. Among his many publications were: *Corone spirituali* (meditations on the life and death of Christ), which appeared in Bologna in 1570 and was recommended by St. Francis de Sales; *Prattica dell'orazione mentale* (Brescia 1573); *Trattato della Santa Oratione delle 40 Hore* (Brescia 1583); *Historia Capuccina* (ed. Melchior a Pobladura, *Monumenta Historica Ordinis Minorum Capuccinorum,* v.5–7, Rome 1946–50); and several volumes of sermons.

Bibliography: Sbaralea 3:234–235. *Lexicon Capuccinum* (Rome 1951) 1078–80. V. MULLEN, "Matthias of Salò, His Life," *Round Table of Franciscan Research* 12 (1947) 134–144. D. MANOUSOS, "M. of Salò, His Works," *ibid.* 145–161. P. UMILE DE GENOVA, DictSpirAscMyst 1:1355–57.

[G. GÁL]

BELLINZAGA, ISABELLA CRISTINA (LOMAZZI), author of a controversial book on the spiritual life; b. Milan, 1551; d. there, Jan. 26, 1624. Lomazzi was her family name; Bellinzaga, the name of the maternal uncle who adopted her. In 1584 she made a private vow to follow the spiritual direction of the Jesuits. Under the guidance of Achille *Gagliardi, and perhaps with his collaboration, she wrote between 1584 and 1594 her little book, *Breve compendio intorno alla perfezione cristiana* (Brescia 1611), better known in its French translation as *Abrégé de la perfection* (Paris 1596). Its central thesis is that perfection consists principally in contempt of all created things, especially self, and in determination to die rather than offend God. That she makes three stages of perfection correspond to increasing passivity of the will caused the book to be suspected of *quietism; it was placed on the Index from 1703 until 1900. Going through numerous editions and translated also in German, Dutch, and Spanish, the

Breve compendio exercised considerable influence on subsequent spiritual writers, including: in France, Pierre de *Bérulle, the Capuchin Laurent de Paris, the Dominican Antoine du Saint-Sacrement, and the Jesuits Jean Joseph *Surin and Jean Rigoleuc; in Italy, the Basilian Giuseppe de Camillis and Miguel de *Molinos.

Bibliography: M. VILLER, DictSpirAscMyst 1:1940–42. U. BONZI DA GENOVA, EncCatt 2:1197–98. Brémond 11:3–16.

[M. S. CONLAN]

BELLMAN, CARL MICHAEL, Swedish poet; b. Stockholm, Feb. 4, 1740; d. there, Feb. 12, 1795. Bellman was born into a pious middle-class family and received a good, if not very complete, education at home. In 1757 he was appointed a trainee of the National Bank of Sweden, and the following year he entered the University of Uppsala. His principal interest in his youth, however, centered on the gay life of the well-to-do young people of Stockholm, and he was gradually entangled in ever-growing debts, from which the only escape was an admission of failure and an ensuing flight from the country in 1763. He returned the next year, however, and took various posts in the public service. A temporary alleviation of his financial difficulties occurred when his fame as a charming and gifted social entertainer and poet reached the court of King Gustav III. The King allowed him a small pension (1775) and appointed him a court secretary and secretary of the State Lottery (1776). In 1777 he married Lovisa Fredrika Grönlund. Bellman's inept business sense, however, and his total inability to manage his own affairs kept him in constant economic straits. He had to file a petition in bankruptcy (1788); he was distrained for rent (1790); and finally he was imprisoned for debt for a few weeks (1794).

Bellman's literary work may be considered under two categories. His "earnest," i.e., religious and didactic, poems do not rise above most of 18th-century Swedish poetry of that kind, although they are of the utmost importance for an understanding of the poet's personality. His fame as one of the greatest Swedish poets rests solely on his parodies and Anacreontica, written over a long period of years and presented by the author himself at private parties. His principal work is the cycle of poems *Fredmans epistlar* (1790) and *Fredmans sånger* (1791), in which he celebrated the life and excesses of the lower classes of Stockholm, personified in a circle of seedy persons grouped around the title figure Fredman, "a famous watchmaker of Stockholm, without watches, workshop, and working capital." The peculiar charm of these songs springs, at least to some extent, from the fact that the poet identifies himself with one of the figures of the slum milieu that is described with a frequently biting realism, and at the same time retains the manners of the 18th-century rococo poet, depicting the orgies of the Stockholm drunkards and whores in terms of bucolic poetry. With the Fredman poems, the tunes of which were sometimes composed by Bellman himself, perhaps more often silently borrowed from other composers, Bellman stands out as the founder of the special Swedish ditty tradition that was an essential part of Swedish literature even into recent times, as may be seen in the works of Birger Sjöberg (1885–1929), Nils Ferlin (1898–   ), and Evert Taube (1890–   ).

Bibliography: C. M. BELLMAN, *The Last of the Troubadors,* tr. and biog. by H. W. VAN LOON and music arranged by G. CASTAGNETTA (New York 1939). *Ny illustrerad svensk litteraturhistoria,* ed. E. N. TIGERSTEDT, 5 v. (Stockholm 1955–58) 2:249–292, extensive bibliog. 606–610. N. AFZELIUS, *Myt och bild: Studier i Bellmans dikt* (Stockholm 1945); *Bellmans melodier: Anteckningar* (Stockholm 1947). **Illustration credit:** Swedish Information Service, New York.

[T. D. OLSEN]

BELLO, ANDRÉS

Spanish American humanist; b. Caracas, Venezuela, Nov. 29, 1781; d. Santiago, Chile, Oct. 15, 1865. He was the son of Bartolomé Bello, a jurist and musician, and of Ana Antonia López, daughter of Juan Pedro López, a noted painter of the colonial period in Venezuela. Bello's life was spent in Caracas until 1810. At a very early age he began the study of Latin at the Convent of Las Mercedes. He studied at the Santa Rosa Seminary (University of Caracas) and obtained the degree of bachelor of arts, June 14, 1800. He began the study of law and medicine, but was unable to continue for economic reasons. During his youth he gave private lessons to a number of individuals, including Simón *Bolívar. After 1802, he was an official in the secretariat of the captaincy general of Venezuela. While still very young, Bello distinguished himself as a writer of verse and prose. He translated and adapted poetry from Latin and French, and wrote poems of his own that were clearly influenced by Latin and Spanish classical writers. He also began his research on the Spanish language.

In 1810 he went to London as secretary of the diplomatic mission headed by Bolívar. He remained there until 1829. These were years of maturation: he worked on political subjects; he did research in the British

Carl Michael Bellman, by Johan Tobias Sergel.

Andrés Bello, Spanish American humanist.

Museum; he rounded out his linguistic and philosophical knowledge and his study of literary history; he was a private tutor; he directed publications (the journals *Biblioteca americana* and *El repertorio americano*); he wrote his great original poem (*Silva: A la agricultura de la zona tórrida*); and he expanded his critical studies and his studies on literary and philological history (e.g., Sismondi, Spanish pronunciation, the reform of Spanish orthography, studies on the ballad rhyme). In 1829 he went to Chile, where he published the greater part of his work, accomplishing the magnificent and complex cultural undertaking that has given him universal renown. He worked in many fields: grammar, legislation, education, journalism, literary criticism and research, law, historiography, philosophy, etc. He was a humanist and a versatile writer who established the groundwork of civilization for a politically independent country and assisted in the creation of its administrative institutions. His principal works are his poetry, the *Gramática de la lengua castellana*, the *Código civil chileno*, and the *Derecho internacional*. He made important contributions to Hispanic-American culture during his presidency of the University of Chile, which he refounded in 1843.

A man of deep Catholic convictions, he demonstrated them in his conduct, in his poetry ("La oración por todos," "Miserere"), in his ideas (except for some irresolution during his London days), and in his basic documents for the orientation of education: ". . . proper religious and moral education is the primary and most important purpose of the University" (inaugural address at the University of Chile, 1843).

Bibliography: *Obras completas,* 22 v. (Caracas 1951–62). M. L. AMUNÁTEGUI ALDUNATE, *Vida de don Andrés Bello* (2d ed. Santiago de Chile 1962). R. CALDERA RODRÍGUEZ, *Andrés Bello* (3d ed. Caracas 1953). **Illustration credit:** Pan American Union, Washington, D.C.

[P. GRASES]

BELLOC, JOSEPH HILAIRE PIERRE

Historian, biographer, essayist, poet; b. La Celle-Saint-Cloud, France, July 27, 1870; d. Guildford, England, July 16, 1953. Hilaire (as he always called himself) and Marie, herself later a writer, were the only children of Louis and Elizabeth Belloc. The family moved to England in 1870, but Belloc spent much of his childhood in France. He served his term (1891) in the French army, not becoming an English citizen until 1902. He attended the Edgbaston Oratory School (1880–87), and matriculated at Oxford in 1892. At the Oratory he was grounded in classics; at Balliol he read history, was awarded the Brackenbury scholarship, and gained a first class in the History Honours School. Having been unsuccessful in an attempt to secure an expected fellowship, he left Oxford in 1896 for a public career. In the same year he married Elodie Hogan, a Californian whom he had met in England in 1889. Her death in 1914 left him with the responsibility of rearing their five children.

Belloc's first publication was *Verses and Sonnets* (1895). This was followed by biographies—*Danton* (1899), *Robespierre* (1901), *Marie Antoinette* (1909); and by a short work on the French Revolution (1911). His travel and critical essays, *The Path to Rome* (1902), and *Averil* (1904) aroused considerable interest in his ideas and style. He was a Liberal Member of Parliament (1906–10) and wrote forcefully on political subjects in such works as *The Party System* (1911, with Cecil Chesterton), and *The Servile State* (1912). During World War I Belloc wrote weekly military comments for the journal *Land and Water*. His son Louis was killed in action just before the armistice.

From 1920 to 1942, Belloc wrote voluminously and lectured in the U.S. and Europe, arousing as much controversy as admiration. His deep personal convictions led to dogmatism and to a myopic view of Germany

Joseph Hilaire Pierre Belloc.

and of Protestantism; no spark of ecumenism exists in his flaming apology for the Faith. In his handling of moot questions his expository prose was not always as convincing as his earlier writings. Equally dubious in *Europe and the Faith* (1920) are the style and the thesis that "the Church is Europe: and Europe is the Church."

Likewise in *The Jews* (1922), the manner in which he proposed Jewish segregation was as offensive to many of his readers as was the longstanding suspicion that he was anti-Semitic. There is more foundation for the annoyance of readers of *The Jews* who try to discover whether Belloc means what he literally says.

Scholars received with coolness Belloc's 4-volume *History of England* (1925–31). Understandably they expected documentation of this reinterpretation of history; his personal statement scarcely convinced serious readers that "religion is the determining force of society," and that English institutions have not Anglo-Saxon origins but stem "from known and recorded civilization." The *History,* some commentators declared, was a good story written with force and lucidity, but it was not genuine history.

Belloc himself doubted that he was a historian. He never doubted he was a writer and a good one. He produced more than 150 books: history, essays, fiction, light verse, and poetry. He will be best remembered, it seems, for his poetry. The author of *Tarantella* and of rousing songs and ballads was a charming troubadour.

After 1942, he continued to write articles, but produced no new books. The death of his son Peter in 1941 was a shock from which he never recovered. After a stroke in 1942, his mind was frequently clouded. On July 12, 1953, he fell near an open fireplace and was fatally burned. His simple funeral was held at West Grinstead; a more elaborate memorial service took place later at Westminster Cathedral.

Bibliography: R. SPEAIGHT, *The Life of Hilaire Belloc* (New York 1957), contains the best bibliographical data on primary and secondary sources. M. A. LOWNDES, *I, Too, Have Lived in Arcadia* (New York 1942); *Young Hilaire Belloc* (New York 1956). E. and R. JEBB, *Testimony to Hilaire Belloc* (London 1956). J. B. MORTON, *Hilaire Belloc* (New York 1955).

[M. A. HART]

BELLOT, PAUL, Benedictine architect active in the modern renewal of church architecture; b. Paris, June 7, 1876; d. St.-Benoit-du-Lac, Canada, July 5, 1944. The son of an architect, he entered the École des Beaux-Arts in 1894 and received his architect's diploma in 1900. After he entered the novitiate at *Solesmes (1902), the monks were exiled from France (as all religious were) under the new law of 1903. The Solesmes monks moved to the Isle of Wight (England), where between 1907 and 1912 Dom Bellot built the abbatial church of *Quarr Abbey, which established his reputation. His earlier designs of 1906 for the Abbey of Oosterhout, Holland (where the monks of the Abbey of Wisque took refuge), had initiated his architectural career. In his monastic life he was professed on May 29, 1904, and ordained June 10, 1911.

Having moved to Holland after World War I, he designed a number of brick churches both there and in Belgium; when the French monks returned to the Abbey of Wisque, he went with them and designed several new buildings there. Besides brick he began to employ cement and stone in churches he designed from 1930 to 1937; among those in France are: the priory convent of Sainte-Bathilde, Vanves (1930–35); Nôtre-Dame des Trévoix, Troyes (1933); Saint-Joseph at Annecy (1936); and the Dominican convent at Montpellier. He also furnished plans for the church of Our Lady of the Conception at Porto, Portugal (1936).

Paul Bellot, cloister of the Abbey of Saint-Benoit-du-Lac, Austin, Brone County, Quebec, Canada.

After being called to Canada (1937) to work on the Oratory of Saint-Joseph, Montreal, he was invited in 1938 to lay plans for a definitive monastic structure at the Abbey of Saint-Benoit-du-Lac. With the collaboration of two Canadian architects, M. Félix Racicot and Dom Claude Côté, he made a master plan; construction began in 1939, and the first two new buildings were dedicated on July 11, 1941. His death followed a year of suffering with cancer.

Although his churches are clean and show a sensitive use of materials, in his efforts to create a religious architecture in the 20th century he was unable to break with a strong sentiment for the Middle Ages. Yet his considered use of light and shadow along with studied proportions and rhythms in arches, stairways, and fenestration have created works with a dignity superior to the popular work of his time.

See also CHURCH ARCHITECTURE, 10.

Bibliography: J. PICHARD, *Les Églises nouvelles à travers le monde* (Paris 1962); Eng. *Modern Church Architecture,* tr. E. CALLMANN (New York 1960). *Abbaye Saint-Benoit-du-Lac* (Saint-Léger-Vauban 1962), 50th anniversary brochure. R. GAZEAU, *Catholicisme* 1:1391.

[J. PICHARD]

BELLOY, JEAN BAPTISTE DE, cardinal archbishop of Paris; b. Moragles (Oise), Oct. 19, 1709; d. Paris, June 10, 1808. He studied in Paris, receiving his doctorate in theology in 1737. He was consecrated bishop of Glandèves in 1752. The famous Assembly of 1755 split the French clergy into moderates and zealots, the latter denying the Last Sacraments to all nonsubscribers to Clement XI's *Unigenitus* (1713). Henri *Belsunce de Castelmoran, Bishop of Marseilles, died during the Assembly, and Belloy, a supporter of the moderate party, was at once named to replace him. Belsunce's misguided zeal for *Unigenitus* had created the danger of schism. Belloy's conciliatory spirit won both sides and restored peace. In July 1790 the National Assembly suppressed the Marseilles diocese. Belloy protested, quietly withdrew to Chambly, and remained there during the Revolution. In 1801, to help his concordat with Napoleon, Pius VII asked the French bishops to resign. Belloy quickly complied. In 1802 Napoleon named him archbishop of Paris. Belloy accepted the new order with its freedom of conscience and worship and urged Catholics to do the same. Despite his admiration for Napoleon he avoided politics.

Bibliography: A. LESORT, DHGE 7:929–31. R. DE CHAUVIGNY, *Le Card. de Belloy e l'Église de Marseille de 1789 à 1802* (Avignon 1930). J. F. MICHAUD, *Biographie universelle ancienne et moderne*, 45 v. (Paris 1854–65) 3:593–594.

[W. E. LANGLEY]

BELLS

This article is a survey of the background and development of the bell and carillon as a musical instrument familiarly associated with Catholic liturgical tradition.

Origin. A medieval legend held that the bell was "invented" in Nola, in the Campania, Italy, and that St. *Paulinus of Nola was responsible for its adoption into the Church. Actually it was the fruit of primitive man's discovery that striking one hard object with another produced a sound that could mark the rhythm of his dances. Dried peas in a pod, forerunner of the rattle and the Egyptian sistra, induced man to form rattles of shell, wood, and later hammered metal (the crotal),

enclosing hard pellets to produce the sound. When the rattle was opened on the bottom, a finger loop attached to the head, and a pellet hung on the inside to form a clapper, the bell came into being. With the progress of civilization, men became intrigued by bronze vessels, whose resonant tone was not long left unexplored. The deep cup was an ancestor of the Western bell and the Oriental barrel-formed bell, while the shallower dish developed into the cymbal. Small bells of one form or another (*tintinnabula* to the Romans) evolved several centuries before Christ. When the Church adopted the bell as a signal in its liturgy, the tinkling cymbal was gradually transformed into the campaniform object that the West knows today.

Early Use. The early Church first used a small bell at the Sanctus, and later to mark other solemn parts of the Mass. Another bell hanging in a turret announced the Elevation to those within earshot outside the sanctuary. As communities grew larger and more people sought protection within monastery or town walls, greater and louder bells were needed. Larger bells meant larger housing—in belfry or campanile, the interesting new architectural form of the 10th and 11th centuries. As the use of bells spread, more and different-sounding bells were required to distinguish one announcement from another. Church and community often shared the bells of the same belfry, as they do in the Low Countries today. There were bells to announce high and low Mass, the *Angelus, birth and death, wedding and feast, fire and flood, to warn of enemies or pestilence, to appease the storm, to call to work, and to cover the fires for the night (Fr. *couvre feu,* curfew). In the 14th century the great tower clocks evolved, marking the quarters on the smaller bells, the hours on the deepest bourdon.

The Musical Bell. As the number of bells hung from a given belfry increased, it became customary, early in the 15th century in the Low Countries and to some extent in the section of England just across the North Sea, to ring the bells together. Until that time it had been enough that the bell function as a signal; it did not have to be pleasing to the ear as well. Since, however, musi-

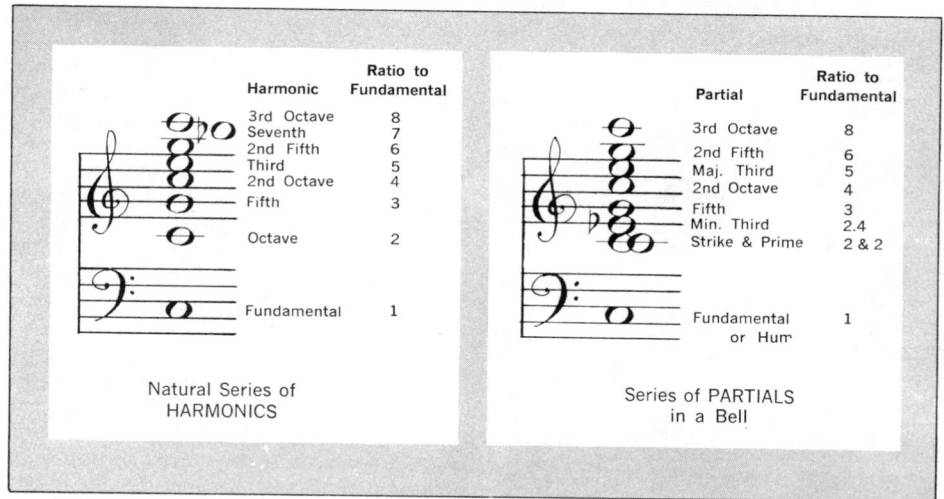

Fig. 1. The series of overtones in the man-developed bell compared with overtones in nature's string and pipe.

cians of that same region were on the threshold of evolving the science of harmony, this new development meant searching for forms that would allow the bell to sound euphonic not only when ringing alone but also when pealed with others. The bell then took on its characteristic campaniform aspect. The more experienced and musically educated bellfounders discovered that the bell produced not just one note but a whole series of tones, the pitches of which played a determining part in the purity of the bell. They then developed a form that would embrace the most musical series and learned how to tune each of these partials to desired pitch. It was found that it was possible to give the bell almost the same series of overtones as that produced by nature in the taut string and the pipe—with one exception: the bell has a minor third, quite contrary to nature. It is this tone that gives the bell its distinctive characteristic, its plaintiveness and appeal. If a bell does not possess this tonal series or if any of the partials are not on pitch, the bell sounds false in direct measure to the deviation from the norms. Since the 15th century one criterion of a good founder has been the success with which he tunes his bells. The string and the pipe are nature's instruments; man developed and perfected the bell.

Thereafter in the Low Countries, in adjoining northern France and western Germany, and in parts of Switzerland, peals of three or more bells produced music more pleasing than even the purest single bell. In Flanders and Holland particularly the number of bells was augmented to cover a range of two octaves. After the Reformation the English, on the contrary, abandoned this practice, in whose development they had participated with the Continent, and now demanded only that their bells occupy positions in the scale. From this time dates "change ringing"—i.e., pealing rings of from 5 to 12 bells in ever changing sequences sometimes for hours at a time—which has become the traditional practice of the Anglican Church. Little by little the entire Occident adopted the general form of the musical bell; in Spain, most of Italy, Scandinavia, the Balkans, and Russia, however, no thought has been given to

purity of bell tone, and any definite pitch is purely accidental. The Orient has never modified its barrel-formed bells, a form incapable of pitch or harmony.

Sounding the Bell. Bells are sounded either by ringing or by tolling. Just as early bells were shaken by hand, their clappers striking the sides of the bell, so larger bells were made to ring in much the same way. The bell hangs from a "yoke," the "crown" bound to it by thongs at first, then by iron straps as bells became larger, and now by steel bolts and cleats. The yoke is mounted on axles that revolve in bearings on the frame, allowing the bell to rotate. The classic manner of ringing is to pull on a rope over a wheel attached to the yoke, causing the bell to swing and its clapper to strike it each time it changes its direction. The ringing bell produces a tone full of life, color, warmth, and resonance. Bells weighing several tons were rung by two teams of ringers alternately putting their weight to treadles mounted on the yoke. Now electricity has largely supplanted the ringers. When a bell is tolled, either its clapper is pulled to the stationary bell or a hammer strikes the bell on the outside. The "de profundis" bell, all clock bells, chime bells, and carillons are sounded in this way.

Fabrication. Bells are fashioned in several ways. Some of the oldest extant are small, cast, elongated cups, only an inch or so in diameter, with or without a clapper, and sounded by jangling them together. The Roman *tintinnabula,* a few inches in diameter, was cast by the same process as was used for bronze vessels. Where bronze was not available, bells were fashioned by hammering iron into a sheet, cutting it to the shape of a Maltese cross, folding the sides together and riveting them. The addition of a loop at the top and a clapper within completed the bell. The bells of the early Irish Church were made in this manner, and from there the style spread to the Continent.

Bells are cast in a mold consisting of a "core" to form the inner surface and a "cope" to give the bell its outer surface. In one method of fabrication the molds are prepared separately, with the inscriptions and ornamentation pressed into the cope before baking. The two parts are then assembled, and molten bronze is poured into the space between them. After the metal has cooled, the mold is broken away, and the bell revealed. Or, the core may first be built, coated with wax, and a "false bell" of clay formed upon it, reproducing exactly the bell to be. The false bell is then coated with wax, and upon it are placed the inscriptions, bas-reliefs, and other ornamentation, all made of wax. Thin coats of clay are now carefully painted onto this "waxen bell," then heavier coats of the material are wiped upon it to form the cope. Heat is applied to the mold, baking the clay and entirely melting the wax so that the cope may be removed. The false bell is broken away, and the cope placed over the core for casting.

The metal producing the finest tone is a bronze of 78 per cent copper and 22 per cent tin. Bronze bells seem to have been the rule in southern Europe from the first; even though some made of bronze were seen in the north, the iron bell persisted there until the 10th century, when southern craftsmanship and a more ready supply of tin and copper finally fixed bronze as the official metal of the Church's bells. Legends exist in which gold, or especially silver, has been used to produce a richer tone; but, if these soft metals are present

Fig. 2. David playing a set of small bells, miniature in a Psalter illuminated in the north of France, c. 1290.

Fig. 3. The consecration of bells: (a) The bells of the carillon of the Shrine of the Immaculate Conception, Washington, *D.C., dressed for their consecration. (b) The incensing of the bells of the Shrine carillon.*

in any sizable proportion, the alloy will be robbed of its elasticity and therefore its resonance. There are founders today who still experiment with other less expensive metals, ostensibly to reduce the cost of their product, but copper and tin remain "noble metals" in the vocabulary of bellfounding.

Liturgical Use. Bells used in the liturgy are consecrated according to a fixed ritual. In a ceremony popularly called "baptism," the bell, dressed in white and decorated with flowers, is anointed, incensed, and given a name, to the accompaniment of psalms, prayers, liturgical music. Present are the donors as godfather and godmother. When there is more than one bell in the tower, the instrument becomes a "peal" or a "ring" of bells. Three or more form a liturgical peal, each having a well-defined place in the program of the church or cloister. A smaller bell rings for early low Mass, Vespers, or Compline; two bells rung together announce a later Mass or other important event; three signify a high Mass. Four and five bells, depending on the number, ring on the vigil of the more solemn feasts and at solemn Mass on Christmas and Easter. As there is a difference in the pendulosity of bells of different sizes, the larger ones swinging more slowly than the smaller ones, their tones will weave many patterns during the time they are pealing. From five bells sounding *sol-la-do-re-mi*, combinations of two, three, or four bells may be used to produce peals of major or minor character.

The Bell in the New World. Developed first in the abbeys of Europe, bells were almost simultaneously adopted by parish churches. Catholic churches in the New World, however, have been slow to accept them. One bell, for the Angelus, was considered essential, but two or more were considered unnecessary luxuries. Moreover, in a pluralistic society some of the "unchurched" regard even such vestigial calls to prayer as threats to the separation of Church and State, or at least a disturbance of the peace.

Contrary to popular belief, bells are not expensive. Their first cost is their last; they endure for centuries and require very little maintenance. Not even a high and imposing tower is needed to house them. In the interest of bringing the sound of bells to the church at a minimum investment, the "electronic" bell was developed during the last 2 decades. No tower is needed, and a brace of loudspeakers may be installed on a cornice of the structure. Despite this apparent simplicity, electronic bells are not at all in the economic interest of the institution. The first cost here is by no means the last. Maintenance is reckoned in hundreds of dollars per year, depending upon the installation; additions and new models are forever being introduced; and the bell has joined the rank of product rather than work of art. Concerned with improper installations inadequately serving the dignity of the Church and her liturgy, Pius XII in his 1955 encyclical *Musicae Sacrae Disciplina* advises that none but true bronze bells are acceptable. Manufacturers of electronic equipment have sought to counter this by hanging a facsimile of a bell somewhere in their apparatus, but serving the liturgy no better. In the sound of bronze bells there is a fullness, a realness of tone, and the effect of the vibrating presence of the true bell that cannot be duplicated by a substitute.

Great Bells. Some of the greatest bells in Christendom, installed either singly or as the bourdons (bass bells) of peals or carillons, are the 18,000-pound bell in

Fig. 4. The bells of the carillon at St. Joseph's Oratory, Montreal, Canada, at the foundry for testing.

the Basilica of St. Peter, in Rome; the 55,000-pound bourdon of the peal of five bells in Cologne cathedral; St. Stephen's 4,000-pound bell in Vienna; the 40,000-pound bourdon of the carillon in the Riverside Church, New York; and the 38,000-pound bourdon of the carillon at the University of Chicago chapel; the University of Notre Dame's 28,700-pound bell; Sacre Coeur de Montmartre's 44,000-pound bell in Paris; St. Paul's 11,500-pound bell in London; and Lincoln cathedral's 12,000-pound bourdon. In Moscow three bells (none of which is hung to swing) top all of these: one weighing 60,800 pounds; another at 120,000 pounds; and the Tsar Kolokol, the "King of Bells," which has never been used, at 443,772 pounds.

The Carillon. The carillon (Latin, *quadrilionem*, signifying four bells) is a percussive instrument consisting of a minimum of two octaves of fixed, cup-shaped bells tuned in chromatic order and played from a keyboard. By means of the keyboard (also the pedal board) the bells may be sounded chordally or in sequence to reproduce musical compositions designed for the instrument or adapted from works for other instruments. Expression and dynamics are controlled by the keyboard through variation of touch.

The carillon originated in the 16th century in the Low Countries, where the early development of keyboard instruments and the science of harmony, the existence of great towers and belfries, and a favorable economic situation all contributed to the evolution of musical bells, the *sine qua non* of the new instrument. The earliest carillons were limited in resources, containing principally the bells serving church and town, to which a few more had been added to form a series. Medieval MS illuminations show us that music had been attempted on series of much smaller bells, by tapping them with a hammer. Only a keyboard connected to the clappers made it possible for the musician to control the larger and more numerous bells of the carillon. Paralleling the development of organ keyboards, primitive carillon keyboards had pedals to control the lower notes while the hands struck keys to sound the mediums and trebles. The same system is used today. "Mechanical music" developed with the carillon; great peg-studded drums similar to the Swiss music box were installed to play clock tunes every quarter hour and strike the hours on the bourdon, or largest bell. These musical tower clocks were and are a mark of civic pride.

With refinements of keyboard and mechanical action, it was possible in the 18th century for bell masters to perform the often complicated baroque music of the period. More notes meant greater range, and in the 19th century, if the bell tower contained deeper pealing bells or other bells used for signals, these were connected to the pedalboard, extending the range still further. Carillons of from 30 to 40 bells, completely chromatic and finely tuned, were by no means uncommon. Today many instruments greatly exceed this number, providing the musician with a medium through which he can realize all shades of musical expression in an extensive repertory.

The love of this singular music spread early to other lands beyond the Low Countries and France. Carillons of Dutch and Flemish manufacture are found in Germany, Austria, and even as far away as Russia and Portugal. The French Revolution ended the so-called heyday of the instrument, during which time the "Stradivarii" of carillons were cast. Those in Amsterdam, Mechlin, Antwerp, Gent, Utrecht, Bruges, and Louvain are famous. During the 20th century, however, the craft has revived, and most contemporary carillons outdistance in tuning and performance those of earlier times. The instruments of New York City, Chicago, Princeton (N.J.), Ottawa (Ontario), Ann Arbor (Mich.), Sewanee (Tenn.), Lake Wales (Fla.), and Washington, D.C. (with four distinguished instruments), are among the larger and better-known installations in North America. A guild of carillonneurs also thrives in the Northern Hemisphere. When played by a master who understands his bells and the tones to be found in them, the carillon is capable of a music of unearthly beauty and very special appeal. It is man's latest and most sophisticated addition to the percussion family, a triumph of tonal research and technique.

Bibliography: A. L. BIGELOW, *Carillon* (Princeton, N.J. 1948), with specifications of U.S. and Canadian carillons; *The Acoustically Balanced Carillon* (Princeton, N.J. 1961). S. N. COLEMAN, *Bells* (New York 1928). F. P. PRICE, *The Carillon* (New York 1933). W. G. RICE, *Carillon Music and Singing Towers of the Old World and the New* (rev. ed. New York 1931). C. MAHRENHOLZ, "Glocken," MusGG 5:267–291. P. VISSER, "Glockenspiel," *ibid.* 5:291–296. W. W. STARMER and H. M. HOWARD, Grove DMM 2:68–70. J. S. VAN WAESBERGHE, ed., *Cymbala: Bells in the Middle Ages* (Amer. Inst. of Musicology. Studies and Documents 1; Rome 1951). H. THURSTON, CE 2:418–424. **Illustration credits:** Fig. 2, The Walters Art Gallery. Fig. 3, The National Shrine of the Immaculate Conception, Washington, D.C., Reni Photos. Fig. 4, Courtesy, St. Joseph's Oratory, Montreal, Canada.

[A. L. BIGELOW]

BELMONT, FRANÇOIS VACHON DE,

Sulpician missionary; b. Grenoble, France, April 2, 1645; d. Montreal, Canada, May 22, 1732. He came from a family of judges and scholars and possessed both fortune and talents. In 1680 he was sent to Canada, where he worked as missionary among the Indians, rebuilding at his own expense the "Mountain Mission" burned down in 1694. In 1701 he was appointed superior of Saint-Sulpice in Montreal and played an important part in the affairs of the French colony, including the digging of the Lachine Canal, begun by Dollier de Casson, and the erection of the Jesuit Chapel and the façade of Notre Dame Church. He was the author of a history of Canada from 1608 to 1700, published (1840) by the Literary and Historical Society of Quebec in its first series of *Historical Documents*.

Bibliography: O. MAURAULT, *Le Fort des Messieurs* (Montreal 1925). H. GAUTHIER, *Sulpitiana* (Montreal 1926).

[J. LANGIS]

BELMONT, ABBATIA NULLIUS OF,

an independent ecclesiastical territory, immediately subject to the Holy See and governed by the Benedictine abbot of Belmont, who is also the ordinary. Since March 26, 1960, it has comprised only the monastic property of the abbey in Gaston County, N.C. There is one parish, that of the abbey cathedral of Mary Help of Christians, serving a total Catholic population of 445 (1964).

The *abbatia nullius* owes its origin to Maryhelp Priory, formerly a dependency of *St. Vincent Archabbey, Latrobe, Pa., and founded near Garibaldi (later Belmont), N.C., on April 21, 1876. A school, later *Belmont Abbey College, was opened in 1878. The priory became an abbey on Dec. 19, 1884; and on July 14, 1885, Leo M. *Haid, OSB, was elected abbot. Under his jurisdiction were missions in Richmond, Va., and Savannah, Ga. On Dec. 7, 1887, he was named vicar apostolic of North Carolina, and the following year he was consecrated bishop. Despite the already heavy burden, he took charge (1889) of the Florida Benedictine missions, which became autonomous in 1894, and he founded (1893) St. Joseph's Institute, Bristow, Va. (closed in 1927). The Savannah and Richmond mis-

Belmont Abbey cathedral, Belmont, N.C., the only abbey cathedral in the U.S.

sions became dependent priories in 1902 and 1911 respectively. On June 8, 1910, the Holy See withdrew eight counties from the vicariate apostolic to form the *abbatia nullius* of Belmont. After Haid's death, July 24, 1924, the two jurisdictions were separated. Vincent G. Taylor, elected Aug. 20, 1924, and blessed as abbot at Belmont March 19, 1925, governed only the *abbatia nullius*. He was occupied with the development of Belmont Abbey seminary, junior college, and preparatory school and the military high schools in Savannah and Richmond. Belmont Abbey College became a senior college in 1952, and its rapid growth led to the closing of the preparatory school in 1956. On Jan. 8, 1944, the territory was restricted to Gaston County because of the abbey's heavy commitments. On April 10, 1956, Walter A. Coggin became monastic superior as the vicar of the ailing Abbot Taylor, who died Nov. 5, 1959. The former vicar was chosen his successor and was blessed as abbot at Belmont June 18, 1960. A building program, inaugurated in 1957, was speeded up, and in 1961 the Savannah priory became autonomous. In 1964 the total number of religious attached to the abbey was 71. Of this number, 48 were priests, 26 of whom were serving the parish and schools of the *abbatia nullius*.

[A. G. BIGGS]

BELMONT, ABBEY OF, founded Nov. 21, 1859, and dedicated to St. Michael, in Hereford, Archdiocese of *Cardiff; it belongs to the English Congregation of Benedictines. Land and church were the gift of F. R. Wegg-Prosser in thanksgiving for his conversion. It was the common novitiate and house of studies for English Benedictines, and the church was the cathedral for the Diocese of Newport and Menevia, the senior monks comprising the bishop's chapter. Modeled after cathedral priories in England before the Reformation, it was the only such priory in existence, its prior ranking as a prelate with the right to use pontificals. The monastic chapter and cathedral made it unique in the English-speaking world. Moreover, until Westminster Cathedral was opened in 1903 it was the only cathedral in England where the canons chanted the entire Divine Office daily. In 1901 it accepted its own novices and in 1917 became an independent priory, ceasing to be a common novitiate and house of studies. In 1920, on the request of the monks, the cathedral church were abolished, and the priory became an abbey. In 1964 the boys school, founded in 1926, numbered 200 students. Five parishes were served by the abbey, with its 57 monks.

Bibliography: B. WHELAN, *The History of Belmont Abbey, England* (London 1959). *SS. patriarchae Benedicti familiae confoederatae* (Rome 1961) 44–46.

[B. WHELAN]

BELMONT ABBEY COLLEGE

A liberal arts degree–granting institution near Belmont, Gaston County, N.C., Belmont Abbey is the only Catholic college in the state. Benedictine monks of St. Vincent Abbey, Latrobe, Pa., founded the Priory of Mary Help of Christians on land donated by Jeremiah J. O'Connell in 1876. In 1878 they began the education of boys in what was then called St. Mary's College. The monastery became an abbey in December 1884, and on July 14, 1885, Leo Haid, OSB, was elected abbot. Ex officio he became first president of the College, which

on April 1, 1886, obtained a charter from North Carolina. The school was renamed Belmont Abbey College in 1913. Classes were first offered on the elementary, secondary, and college levels, but the elementary school ceased operation in 1929. In 1928 the junior and senior years of college were restricted to seminarians, and the freshman and sophomore years were reorganized as an accredited junior college. In 1952 the junior and senior years of college were restored to laymen, and the institution grew so rapidly that in 1956 the high school was closed. Accreditation by the Southern Association as a senior college followed in 1957.

When Haid died in 1924, he was succeeded as president by Vincent Taylor, OSB, who in 1956 relinquished the post to Walter Coggin, OSB. On July 18, 1956, Coggin became chancellor, and Cuthbert Allen, OSB, succeeded as president. The fifth president, John Oetgen, OSB, took office in 1960. The board of trustees consists of the chancellor and five monks, three of whom are ex officio members and two are elected annually by the Belmont Abbey College corporation. They are assisted by a board of advisors, consisting of laymen prominent in business and the professions. In 1964 the faculty of 69 was composed of 39 members of the monastic community, 3 sisters from the nearby Sacred Heart College of the Sisters of Mercy, and 27 laymen. The staff held 8 doctorates, 5 professional degrees, and 24 master's degrees. Total enrollment numbered 623. The College, unendowed except for the contributed services of the monks and sisters, depends upon tuition, fees, and gifts. Belmont Abbey College is a men's school, although a few qualified women, living within commuting distance, may enter the junior year.

Liberal arts and science curricula are offered. All students must satisfy the core curriculum, which includes English, philosophy, modern language, mathematics, laboratory science, survey of civilization, and physical education. Catholics add theology. The B.A. and the B.S. degrees are offered. The college also provides a preengineering program, and in cooperation with the Engineering Schools of Notre Dame University and North Carolina State College, a double-degree program in liberal arts–engineering. In the fall and spring terms, a few evening classes are available to part-time and special students and to local teachers seeking to gain or renew certification. Chief among a number of lectures are the Abbot Vincent Taylor Lectures. Outstanding seniors are nominated to *Who's Who among Students in American Universities and Colleges,* and academically superior upperclassmen are accepted into the Gamma Iota Chapter of Delta Epsilon Sigma. Social fraternities are represented by chapters of Phi Kappa Theta, Tau Kappa Epsilon, and Sigma Phi Epsilon.

The Abbot Vincent Taylor Library, which in 1964 housed 60,000 volumes and received 293 periodicals, was the first structure (1958) in an expansion program that has also contributed two new residence halls and a dining hall.

[A. G. BIGGS]

BELO HORIZONTE, ARCHDIOCESE OF (BELLOHORIZONTINUS), located in the state of Minas Gerais, Brazil; created a diocese in 1921; raised to an archdiocese in 1924. In 1964 it had four suffragan sees: Luz (1918), Oliveira (1941), Sete Lagoas (1955), and Divinópolis (1958).

1964 STATISTICS

Area	Population	Parishes	Clergy	
			Sec.	Reg.
Belo Horizonte	*960,000	96	122	168
Luz	387,000	35	25	21
Oliveira	*212,789	23	31	9
Sete Lagoas	*153,328	21	20	8
Divinópolis	*298,000	32	22	32

*This figure includes Catholics only.

The first church in the area dates from 1712, and it became a parish in 1748. This was little more than a village named Curral del-Rei until 1893, when it was chosen as the capital of the state and given the name Belo Horizonte. At that time it belonged to the Archdiocese of Mariana. The first bishop and archbishop, Antônio dos Santos Cabral, organized his bishopric materially and spiritually until it gained the reputation of the Catholic capital of Brazil. He created 37 new parishes and brought in a number of religious orders to care for them. He founded Catholic Action, Obra das Vocações Sacerdotais, Perpetual Adoration, and the Círculo Operário. He promoted the catechetical and social apostolate. He provided a house for ill and old priests and built the bishop's residence, a diocesan high school, a minor and a major seminary. He founded the Catholic paper O Diário, which has reached a circulation of 45,000. In 1944 he presided over the first archdiocesan synod. He also established a Catholic university, which has 10 faculties and about 2,000 students. His successors carried on his work of founding parishes and schools. Among the recent social actions of the archdiocese is the founding of the Banco da Providência for the poor. Belo Horizonte has been plagued with a serious lack of vocations.

Until 1961 the Diocese of Luz was called the Diocese of Aterrado. The other three suffragans were all carved out of the archdiocese. In 1964 religious orders working in the province included Redemptorists, Fathers of the Divine Word, Salesians, Franciscans, Marists, Sacramentines, Sacred Heart Fathers, Crosiers, Holy Ghost Fathers, and more than 2,400 sisters of various congregations.

Bibliography: *Dom Cabral e suas obras* (Belo Horizonte 1943). A. NÓBREGA, *Dioceses e bispos do Brasil* (Rio de Janeiro 1954). **Illustration credit:** Pan American Union, Washington, D.C.

[O. VAN DER VAT]

The provisional cathedral of the Archdiocese of Belo Horizonte, Brazil.

BELSASSAR (BEL-SHAR-USUR), KING OF BABYLON, according to the Book of Daniel. In Daniel ch. 5 King Belsassar (Aramaic and Hebrew *bēlš'aṣṣar* or *bēl'šaṣṣar;* hence the variant form in English, Belshazzar) is introduced as the son and successor of King *Nabuchodonosor (Nebuchadrezzar), the King mentioned in Daniel ch. 1—4: at a feast, when Belsassar made sacrilegious use of the sacred vessels that had been taken from the Temple of Jerusalem, he saw the handwriting *Mene-Tekel-Peres on the wall of his banquet hall, and the same night Babylon was taken by "Darius the Mede" and Belsassar was slain. Certain visions received by *Daniel the seer are dated in the 1st (Dn 7.1) and the 3d year (Dn 8.1) of the reign of this King. In the Vulgate (and versions that follow its spelling of proper nouns, e.g., the Douay) the name of this King is given as Baltassar, in obvious confusion with the Babylonian name given to Daniel (Dn 1.7; 2.26; 4.5).

Before A.D. 1887 a king of Babylon by any such name was unknown outside the Book of Daniel and writings dependent on this book (e.g., Bar 1.11—12). But in Babylonian cuneiform texts published in 1887 and thereafter, the name Bel-shar-usur (Babylonian *Bel-šarra-uṣur,* "O *Bel, protect the King") occurs as that of the oldest son of *Nabu-na'id (Nabonidus), the last king of the Neo-Babylonian Kingdom (555–539 B.C.), who was captured, dethroned, and exiled by *Cyrus, King of Persia. Neither Nabu-na'id nor Bel-shar-ushur was a direct descendant of Nabuchodonosor. Bel-shar-usur, though crown prince, was never officially king. During his father's 10-year sojourn at the oasis of Tema in the Arabian Desert, he ruled Babylon as viceregent (see Pritchard ANET² 313b), and his name is coupled with his father's in some incantation texts (*ibid.* 309, footnote 5); therefore, he may have been popularly considered King of Babylon during his father's absence.

The Belsassar of the Book of Daniel is evidently the Bel-shar-usur of the cuneiform texts, and his father "Nabuchodonosor" is a composite figure made up partly of the historical Nabuchodonosor and partly of the historical Nabu-na'id; for such historical inaccuracies in this book, *see* DANIEL, BOOK OF.

Bibliography: EncDictBibl 194–195. F. GÖSSMANN, LexThK² 2:166–167. E. FLORIT, EncCatt 2:756–758. R. P. DOUGHERTY, *Nabonidus and Belshazzar* (New Haven, Conn. 1929). B. ALFRINK, "Der letzte König von Babylon," *Biblica* 9 (1928) 187–205. For additional bibliog., *see* DANIEL, BOOK OF.

[M. MC NAMARA]

BELSUNCE DE CASTELMORAN, HENRI FRANÇOIS XAVIER DE, Bishop of Marseilles, foe of Jansenism; b. Chateau de la Force, Périgord, 1671; d. Marseilles, 1755. He was the son of the Marquis de Castelmoran and Ann de Caumont de Lausun. After classical studies at the Collège de Clermont (Louis-le-

Grand), he entered the Society of Jesus, but left to become vicar-general of Agen in 1699, and bishop of Marseilles in 1709. By his heroic care of plague victims in 1720–21, he earned the title of "Good Bishop" and mention in Pope's *Essay on Man*. Louis XV offered him the See of Laon, with first ecclesiastical peerage in France, and the office of metropolitan of Bordeaux. Both rewards Belsunce refused. As bishop, he fought Jansenism by participating in the synod of Embrun (1727), by ordering his priests to refuse absolution to appellants against *Unigenitus,* and by pastoral letters (although these may have been the work of the Jesuit Lemoire). His writings include a biography of his aunt, *Vie de Suzanne-Henriette de Foix* (Agen 1702); *Antiquités de l'Église de Marseille et la sucession de ses évêques* (Marseilles 1747–51); and translations of St. Augustine's *De agone christiano* and St. Robert Bellarmine's *De arte bene moriendi.*

Bibliography: *Oeuvres choisies,* ed. A. JAUFFRET, 2 v. (Metz 1822). T. BÉRENGIER, *Vie de Mgr. Henry de Belsunce, évêque de Marseille,* 2 v. (Lyon 1886–87). P. BARBET-MASSIN, *Éloge de Belzunce* (Paris 1821). P. CALENDINI, DHGE 7:951–53.

[V. HEALY]

BELTRÁN, LUIS, Franciscan friar, collaborator of José de *San Martín and *Bolívar; b. Mendoza, Argentina, Sept. 8, 1784; d. Buenos Aires, Dec. 8, 1827. In the course of his studies as a Franciscan he became interested in mathematics, physics, and mechanics. He was at the motherhouse of the order in Santiago, Chile, when the revolution against Spain broke out. He volunteered in the Chilean army and served as chaplain under General Carrera. His interest in ordnance stood him in good stead, and when the Chilean army had to flee to Argentina in 1814, he was asked by San Martín to take charge of assembling cannon and munitions for the march across the Andes. An indefatigable worker, Beltrán worked near miracles with practically no resources. After the victory of the Army of the Andes over the Spaniards at Maipú in 1818, O'Higgins and San Martín gave Beltrán carte blanche to create the largest and best ordnance establishment in America and to assemble *matériel* for an army of 4,000 men. Beltrán accompanied the Argentine-Chilean expedition to Peru in 1820, supervising the loading of all military supplies on the ships. He served as arms director of the entire artillery in the Peruvian campaign, 1820 to 1824, gaining the rank of lieutenant colonel. After San Martín's withdrawal from Peru, Beltrán served under Bolívar for 2 years. He returned to Argentina in 1824, but soon left for the front along the Uruguay River, serving in the war against Brazil as chief of munitions under Gen. Martín Rodríguez. His rank of lieutenant colonel was recognized by the government of Buenos Aires in 1826, and to this honor was soon added the rank of sergeant major. He also supervised the provisioning of Admiral Brown's navy. With the victory over Brazil at Ituzaingó, in which Beltrán participated, he retired from the army for reasons of health and returned to Buenos Aires. He was buried in his friar's habit. Beltrán's services to his country can hardly be overestimated. An Argentine historian has said that "he knew how to convert into forge and anvil the very bosom of the Cordillera itself to assure the independence and liberty of the Continent . . . [making] possible, with Franciscan

self-abnegation, the liberating movement of San Martín."

Bibliography: L. CÓRDOBA, *Fray Luis Beltrán: Reivindicación histórica del prócer* (Mendoza 1938). F. L. HOFFMANN, "A Franciscan Fighter for South American Independence," *Americas* 10 (1954) 289–300.

[F. L. HOFFMANN]

BELVISIO, JACOBO, jurist; b. Bologna, *c.* 1270; d. Bologna, January 1335. He studied law in Bologna under *Dinus Mugellanus and Franciscus Accursius. Unable to obtain the doctorate in Bologna because he was a Ghibelline, he went to the court of Charles II in Aix-en-Provence, where he received his doctorate of law in 1297. His degree was confirmed the following year by the University of Naples, where he was teaching law and serving as counselor to the King. He was permitted to return to Bologna in 1304, and was granted the doctorate after a new examination. In 1306 he left the University of Bologna, then under interdict, to teach at Padua. He taught in Perugia from 1308 until 1321, except for a brief period in Bologna (1310–11) and perhaps in Naples (1313–16). In 1321 he returned definitively to Bologna and joined the Guelfs. A great jurist, he helped introduce the ideas and methods of French jurisprudence to Italy. His works consist of a commentary on the *Libri feudorum* (before 1310); a commentary on the *Authenticum* (after 1325); and a canonical work, *Tractatus de excommunicatione* (*c.* 1300), in which he defended the juridic capacity of an excommunicated person to make a will.

Bibliography: Savigny 6:60–67. Schulte 2:233. J. WEYGANT and H. WAGNON, DDC 6:79–80. G. ERMINI, *Storia della Università di Perugia* (Bologna 1947) 104–107. E. M. MEIJERS, *Études d'histoire du droit,* ed. R. FEENSTRA and H. F. FISCHER, v.3 (Leiden 1959) 162–165.

[C. ROSEN]

BEMBO, PIETRO, humanist, master of Italian letters, and cardinal; b. Venice, May 20, 1470; d. Rome, Jan. 19, 1547. He belonged to a patrician family of Venice, and through his father, Bernardo, senator and vice doge, Pietro was early acquainted with the humanist courts of Italy. At Padua he studied philosophy under Pietro Pomponazzi; at Ferrara he was friendly with Alfonso d'Este and his wife, Lucrezia Borgia; at Messina he widened his knowledge of Greek by contact with Constantin Lascaris; at Urbino (1513–21) he shone within a brilliant circle of humanists. From 1513 to 1521 he joined Jacopo Sadoleto as secretary to Leo X. During this period Morosina (Ambrogia della Torre), by whom Bembo had two sons and a daughter, became his mistress. He left Rome for Padua in 1521 because of illness and fatigue to reside in his villa, called Noniano. There, surrounded by his literary friends, collections of valuable MSS, and antiquities, he devoted his time to writing and experimenting in his botanical gardens. In 1530 he was appointed historiographer of the Venetian Republic and librarian of St. Mark's. Upon the death of Morosina (1535) Bembo underwent a personal reform that led him to austerities, and he turned his interests from the classics to Scripture and patristic literature. He was created a cardinal by Paul III in 1538, at which time (aged 68) he received Major Orders. He was bishop of Gubbio (1541) and Bergamo (1544). Among his writings are: (Latin) *Rerum Venetarum historiae libri XII* (1551), a history of Venice from 1487

Pietro Bembo, portrait by Titian, oil on canvas, 37⅛ by 30⅛ inches.

to 1513, later translated into Italian; *De Guido-Ubaldo liber* (1530); *Epistolarum Leonis X nomine scriptarum libri XVI* (1535); *De culice Vergilii et Terentii fabulis* (1530); *De imitatione* (1513); *Epistolarum familiarium libri VII* (1552); *Carmina* (1533); (Italian) *Lettere* (1548); *Gli Asolani* (1505, Eng. tr. 1954), a dialogue on Platonic love dedicated to Lucrezia Borgia; *Rime* (1530), poems in imitation of Petrarch; *Prose della volgar lingua* (1525), the first example of Italian philology.

Bibliography: *Opere,* 12 v. (Milan 1808–10). V. CIAN, *Un decennio della vita di M. Pietro Bembo, 1521–1531* (Turin 1885). M. SANTORO, *Pietro Bembo* (Naples 1937) bibliog. P. PASCHINI and G. TOFFANIN, EncCatt 2:1208–10. A. ROERSCH, DHGE 7:979–982, bibliog. **Illustration credit:** National Gallery of Art, Washington, D.C., Samuel H. Kress Collection.

[E. D. MC SHANE]

BEN-ADAD (BEN-HADAD) I, II, III OF DAMASCUS

The Hebrew name *Benhădad* (Aramaic *bar-hadad,* "son of Hadad," the storm god of the Aramaeans) is apparently given in the OT to three different kings of Damascus who ruled this Aramaean city-state in the 9th century B.C. The relatively little that is known of them is gathered from the annals of the Assyrian kings, the Bible, and a few inscriptions.

Ben-Adad I, the son of Tabremon and grandson of Hezion (3 Kgs 15.18), began his reign *c.* 880 B.C. He was sent a lavish gift from the royal Temple treasuries by *Asa, King of Juda (*c.* 913–873), to persuade him to break his alliance with Baasa of Israel (*c.* 900–877) and to aid Juda in war against the Northern Kingdom (3 Kgs 15.16–21; 2 Chr 16.1–5). Ben-Adad sent his forces against Israel, invaded the upper valley of the Jordan, and conquered the Israelite cities of Ijon, Dan, and Abel-beth-maacah, and the western section of Galilee. This same Ben-Adad erected a votive stele, written in ancient Aramaic, to the Tyrian god Melcarth. The stele was found a few miles from Aleppo. W. F. Albright, basing his argument in part on the paleography of this inscription, which he dates about the middle of the 9th century B.C., maintains that Ben-Adad I had a long reign, extending down as far as 843 B.C., thus eliminating the commonly accepted reign of Ben-Adad II.

Ben-Adad II, however, is usually identified with a certain Adad-idri (the form used in Assyrian inscriptions, equivalent to the Hebrew Hadadezer), who, according to the more common opinion, succeeded Ben-Adad I. Thus besides his personal name of Hadadezer (Adad-idri), this King also had the throne name of Ben-Adad. Accordingly it was Ben-Adad II who besieged Samaria during the rule of *Achab, King of Israel (*c.* 869–850), but was repelled (3 Kgs 20.1–21). A second invasion was disastrous for the Aramaeans and Ben-Adad himself was captured at Aphec, only to be released after making a peace treaty with Achab (3 Kgs 20.21–34). Sharing the threat posed by Assyria, Ben-Adad and Achab were allies in the battle of Karkar (853 B.C.). This battle seems to have checked the Assyrians, for it was not until 848 that they attempted another attack against Damascus and its allies. Meanwhile (*c.* 850), Achab joined with Josaphat of Juda (*c.* 873–849) in an attempt to regain Ramoth-Galaad from Ben-Adad's control; Achab himself was killed in the battle (3 Kgs 22.1–40; 2 Chr 18.1–34). During the reign of Joram (*c.* 849–842), Ben-Adad again came to Israel and laid siege to Samaria; the siege was suddenly lifted when the Aramaeans fled, mistakenly fearing that the Hittites and Egyptians were coming to relieve the city (4 Kgs 6.24–7.16). About 843 an ailing Ben-Adad was murdered in Damascus by his successor, Hazael (4 Kgs 8.15).

Ben-Adad III, Hazael's son, succeeded after Hazael died (*c.* 805). About this time Adad-nirari III of Assyria (811–784) had resumed an aggressive policy against Damascus and by 802 the Aramaean kingdom was broken and under ruinous tribute. Nevertheless, sometime during this period Ben-Adad apparently managed to humble Israel (4 Kgs 13.3). However, Joas, after his ascent to the throne of Israel (*c.* 801), was able to take advantage of the prostrate condition of the kingdom of Damascus and to defeat Ben-Adad three times, recovering the Israelite cities lost to Hazael (4 Kgs 13.25; see also Am 1.4; Jer 49.27). Further details of this Ben-Adad's life are unknown.

Bibliography: W. F. ALBRIGHT, "A Votive Stele Erected by Ben-Hadad I of Damascus to the God Melcarth," BullAm SchOrRes 87 (1942) 23–29. R. DE VAUX, "La Chronologie de Hazael et de Benhadad III, Rois de Damas," RevBibl 43 (1934) 512–518. EncDictBibl 224–225.

[J. J. CUNNINGHAM]

BEN ASHER, name of a prominent family of Masoretes that flourished in *Tiberias, Palestine, during the 9th and 10th centuries, of whom the most famous were Moses and his son Aaron. Little is known of their lives, but it is believed that they were Karaites (*see* KARAISM), i.e., believers in the literal sense of Scripture rather than its Talmudical interpretation, and therefore concerned especially with the accurate transmission of its text. They sought to fix, in detail, the vocalization and accentuation of the consonantal text of the Hebrew Bible and therefore provided it with the *Masora, the compendium of variants and reference data intended to stamp their recension with the authority of tradition. Aaron authorized several editions of a manual of Masoretic principles entitled *Diqduqe Ha-Te'amim* (accent rules).

The Ben Asher texts are rightly regarded as more authentic than the Hebrew text of the 16th-century edition by Jocob ben Chayyim in Bomberg's second *Rabbinical Bible, which until recently was the quasi-official text. But a comparison between the Ben Asher texts and the work of the rival Tiberian family of *Ben Naphtali indicates that the Ben Ashers were not the only representatives of the Palestinian Masoretes.

Among the identified Ben Asher MSS are: the Codex of the Prophets in the Karaite synagogue in Cairo, written and vocalized by Moses in A.D. 895; the Aleppo Codex of the entire Hebrew Bible (now in truncated form in Israel), pointed and provided with the Masora by Aaron *c.* 930 and endorsed for its accuracy by *Maimonides; and the Leningrad Codex B 19a of A.D. 1008, copied from a text of Aaron and now the basis of Kittel's third edition of the *Biblia Hebraica* that has supplanted the Ben Chayyim text of Kittel's earlier editions.

See also BIBLE, IV (TEXTS AND VERSIONS), 2.

Bibliography: B. J. ROBERTS, *The Old Testament Text and Versions* (Cardiff 1951) 67–83, bibliog. 286–299. P. E. KAHLE, *The Cairo Geniza* (2d ed. New York 1960) 75–188; *Masoreten des Westens*, 2 v. (Stuttgart 1927). M. ZOBEL, EncJudaica 1:70–72.

[R. KRINSKY]

BEN NAPHTALI, name of a family of Masoretes that flourished during the 9th and 10th centuries in *Tiberias, Palestine, of whom the most famous was Moses ben David. Nothing is known of his life and very little of his work, which paralleled that of the *Ben Asher family, his contemporaries and rivals. Both families were concerned with standardizing the Hebrew Bible by fixing the vocalization and accentuation of the consonantal text. Most of the variations between the two are vocalic, although there is some evidence to suggest slight differences in the consonantal text as well. A list of more than 800 such variations was compiled sometime in the 10th century by Mishael ben 'Uzziel. Manuscript material of Ben Naphtali's work is scanty, but fragments from the Cairo Geniza and the Codex Reuchlinianus at Karlsruhe written in 1105 have been identified as Ben Naphtali texts. Some Ben Asher MSS contain marginal readings of the Ben Naphtali school, and there are many MSS that contain a composite text, seemingly derived from both traditions. There are also traces of Ben Naphtali in Jacob ben Chayyim's edition of the Hebrew text in Bomberg's second *Rabbinical Bible.

See also BIBLE, IV (TEXTS AND VERSIONS), 2.

Bibliography: B. J. ROBERTS, *The Old Testament Text and Versions* (Cardiff 1951) 64–66, bibliog. 286–299. P. E. KAHLE, *The Cairo Geniza* (2d ed. New York 1960) 115–118. C. LEVIAS, JewishEnc 2:677–678. M. ZOBEL, EncJudaica 4:67–71.

[R. KRINSKY]

BENARD, EDMOND DARVIL, theologian, author, preacher; b. Boston, Mass., Aug. 9, 1914; d. Washington, D.C., Sept. 4, 1961. He was ordained for the Diocese of Springfield, Mass., June 7, 1941. After graduating from Cathedral High School, Springfield (valedictorian 1932), he studied at Holy Cross College, Worcester, Mass. (A.B. 1936), and the University of Montreal, Canada (S.T.D. 1942). In 1943 he joined the faculty of the School of Sacred Theology at The Catholic University of America, Washington, D.C., and was appointed associate editor (1944) of the *American Ecclesiastical Review*. His area of theological competence was apologetics and related sciences. In 1951 he was elected president of the Catholic Theological Society of America, and he was awarded the Pro Ecclesia et Pontifice medal. He received the Ph.D. degree in philosophy from Catholic University in 1952, the same year he was appointed associate professor of theology. Benard received (1955) the Cardinal Spellman award for outstanding work in theology; he was named dean of the faculty of theology at the university, as well as field editor (1959) for *The New Catholic Encyclopedia*. His writings include *A Preface to Newman's Theology* (St. Louis 1945); *The Appeal to the Emotions in Preaching* (Westminster, Md. 1945); and articles in the *American Ecclesiastical Review* (1944–46), the CUA *Bulletin* (1944), and the *Proceedings* of the Catholic Theological Society of America (1951). Benard died at the height of his productive capacity in a fire in his rooms at the university.

[J. P. WHALEN]

BÉNARD, LAURENT, Benedictine reformer and founder of the Congregation of Saint Maur; b. Nevers, France, 1573; d. Paris, April 20, 1620. Laurent entered the Monastery of St. Stephen, Nevers, then a dependency of Cluny. He studied at Bourges and Paris, becoming a doctor of the Sorbonne. After his ordination he devoted himself to preaching. As prior of the College of Cluny at Paris, he reintroduced cloister and other necessary reforms. He was associated with the founder of the Congregation of St. Vanne, Dom Didier de la Cour, in reforming French monasteries. Laurent was visitor for the Abbey of Fontevrault and helped to reestablish observance at the Abbey of Montmartre. In May 1618, a general chapter of reformed Benedictines commissioned him to form a congregation independent of Lorraine. Six months later, the newly founded Congregation of Saint Maur held its first chapter at the Monastery of Blancs-Manteaux. Laurent had applied to Rome for a bull of erection, but he died before it was promulgated. His writings deal mainly with religious topics, especially with the Benedictine rule and life.

Bibliography: B. HEURTEBIZE, DHGE 7:1028–30. R. P. TASSIN, *Histoire littéraire de la congrégation de Saint-Maur* (Brussels 1770). J. FRANÇOIS, *Bibliothèque générale des écrivains de l'Ordre de Saint Benoît*, 4 v. (Bouillon 1777–78; reprint Louvain 1961) 1:106–107.

[B. EGAN]

BENAVENTE Y MARTÍNEZ, JACINTO, Spanish dramatist; b. Madrid, Aug. 12, 1866; d. there, July 14, 1954.

He is one of Spain's two greatest modern dramatists; his work has scarcely been equaled since the *Siglo de Oro*. In his own time he was perhaps surpassed only by

*García Lorca. Benavente freed drama from the moral bombast of the tradition of José Echegaray (1832–1916) and adapted the Spanish language to the modern world. He was a contemporary of many of the authors

Jacinto Benavente y Martínez.

of "the generation of '98," and reflects their tendencies in his desire for literary renovation, in a touch of ivory-tower *modernismo* in his earlier work, and in the barbs directed at the complacency of a society he held responsible for the decadence of the nation. Apparently he was not buffeted by the religious anguish or anticlerical controversies of '98. His approach tended to be cosmopolitan, and he frequently confronted problems of universal significance as well as those of typically Spanish concern.

Benavente's large production is usually divided into three necessarily overlapping categories: realistic village scenes depicting rural customs; stark tragedies, such as the famous *La Malquerida* (1913); and satiric salon pieces which were urbane revelations of human shortcomings. To the last category belong the noted *Los Intereses Creados* (1907) and *La Ciudad Alegre y Confiada* (1916), companion pieces, in which artificial values are examined in the light of permanent ones.

Despite the strident anguish of *La Malquerida,* the salon tone tends to dominate the bulk of his work, the best part of which was produced up to the time of his Nobel Prize (1922). His view is ironic, humorous, and occasionally acid. At the same time a certain gentleness is evident. He is discriminating, aristocratic, sober in manipulating his material, and more interested in character than in plot. An excellent craftsman, Benavente has been called a dramatist's dramatist. His work embodies the frequent Spanish synthesis of realism and idealism: he accepted the world for what it is, but believed in the possibility of a better world. This tendency appears, for example, in the social preoccupations in *Los Malhechores del Bien* (1905). Although he is a leading dramatist of a Catholic country, his work reflects little concern for any religious evaluation.

Bibliography: *Obras completas,* 11 v. (Madrid 1940–58). F. DE ONIS Y SÁNCHEZ, *Jacinto Benavente* (New York 1923). A. LAZÁRO, *Jacinto Benavente: De su vida y de su obra* (Madrid 1925). J. DE ENTRAMBASAGUAS, "Don Jacinto Benavente en el teatro de su tiempo," *Cuadernos de Literatura Contemporanea* 3 (1944) 219–222. J. CALVO-SOTELO, *El tiempo y su mudanza en el teatro de Benavente* (Madrid 1955). **Illustration credit:** Embassy of Spain, Washington, D.C.

[J. DEVLIN]

BENAVIDES, ALONSO DE, Franciscan missionary in New Mexico; b. San Miguel, Azores, *c.* 1580; d. 1636. He joined the Franciscan Order in Mexico City, making his religious profession on Aug. 12, 1603. He worked in various parts of Mexico, carrying out functions of the Holy Office on several occasions. On Oct. 19, 1623, he was chosen as *custos,* or regional superior, of the Franciscan missions of New Mexico. He did not arrive there until the end of 1625, taking formal possession of his office on Jan. 24–25, 1626. He governed the activities of the Church in New Mexico until early 1629. In 1630 he was sent to Spain to give an account of the mission work in New Mexico to the King and the Franciscan minister general. In that year he presented to the royal court a report that gained the attention of both King and Pope. Remaining in Spain, he publicized the work of the Franciscans in New Mexico and sought the appointment of a bishop for the area. On Feb. 12, 1634, he presented a revised Memorial on the missions of New Mexico to Pope Urban VIII. In late 1634 royal provision was made for his return to Mexico, but he stayed on in Spain until February 1636. He then went to Lisbon and soon afterward was appointed auxiliary bishop of the Diocese of Goa in India. He sailed for his new post in April 1636 but died before reaching it.

Bibliography: *Fray Alonso de Benavides' Revised Memorial of 1634,* ed. and tr. F. W. HODGE et al. (Albuquerque 1945); *Memorial of 1630,* tr. P. J. FORRESTAL and ed. C. J. LYNCH (Washington 1954).

[F. B. WARREN]

BENAVIDES, MIGUEL DE, Dominican missionary and archbishop of Manila; b. Carrión de los Condes (Palencia), Spain, 1552; d. Manila, June 26, 1605, or July 26, 1607. Benavides studied under D. Bañez and taught at Valladolid. In 1586 he sailed for Manila, where he and his companions established the Dominican province of the Most Holy Rosary. He was the first of the missionaries to learn the Chinese language in order to instruct the Chinese living in Manila. In 1589 he went to China but was imprisoned there and later expelled. He was sent to Madrid in 1590 to act as procurator for the Dominican province of the Philippines and to carry on important negotiations with the Royal Council for the Indies. In 1595 he was named bishop of New Segovia in the Philippines and in 1597 became archbishop of Manila. Zealous for learning, he founded the Colegio de Santo Tomás in Manila, which later became a university.

Bibliography: Quétif-Échard 2:363–364. Streit-Dindinger 4:358–359. J. FERRANDO and J. FONSECA, eds., *Historia de los PP. Domenicos en las islas Filipinas* (Madrid 1870–72). EncRelCat 1:1402. A. WALZ, EncCatt 2:1212–13.

[P. K. MEAGHER]

BENEDEN, ÉDOUARD VAN, cytologist; b. Belgium, March 5, 1845; d. there, April 28, 1910. Édouard was the son of Pierre Joseph (1809–94), a parasitologist of considerable ability and fame. While a professor at Liège, Édouard showed (1887) that the number of chromosomes is the same for each cell of a given body and that this number was probably characteristic of the species. He showed further that the number of chromosomes was reduced during maturation and restored during the sexual process. For this work he used *Ascaris megolacephala,* the intestinal round-worm of the horse, which has but four large chromosomes in the diploid phase, and two in the haploid. He published the journal *Archives de biologie* and the book *Recherches sur la maturation de l'oeuf* (Paris 1883).

Bibliography: H. DE WINIWARTER, *Biographie nationale de Belgique* 26:174–184. M. ARNIM, *Internationale Personalbibliographie, 1800–1943,* v.1 (Leipzig 1944) 86.

[N. SCHEEL]

BENEDICAMUS DOMINO

The concluding formula in the Latin rite for the Divine Office, and later an alternate concluding formula for the Mass (*see* DIVINE OFFICE, ROMAN, CHANTS OF; MASS, ROMAN; MASS, ROMAN MUSIC OF). To the deacon's *Benedicamus Domino* (Let us bless the Lord) the assembly responds *Deo gratias* (Thanks be to God). The earliest traces of the *Benedicamus* as a concluding formula at Mass are to be found in the Gallican liturgy *c.* 800 (Bishop, *Liturgica historica* 323; Theodulf of Orleans, *Capitulare* 2; *see* GALLICAN RITES, CHANTS OF).

As a replacement for the *Ite, missa est* in the Roman rite it appears, under Gallican influence, for the first time in the 11th century (*Bernold of Constance, Micrologus* 19, PL 151:990). The criterion for its use to replace the *Ite* appears to have been twofold. First, it was used on days when the Mass did not have a *Gloria.* Thus, the idea developed that the *Ite* was an expression of joy to be used only on festive days, while the *Benedicamus* was substituted on days of a more penitential character. Similarly, the *Requiescant in pace* began to

A page from the 12th-century "Codex Calixtinus" (fol. 185r) at Compostela. The lower half of the page carries the "Benedicamus" trope "Congaudeant catholici."

replace the *Ite* in Requiem Masses from about the 12th century. Second, it was used when the divine service continued, as at the midnight Mass of Christmas when Lauds followed, or on Holy Thursday when the procession with the Blessed Sacrament followed the evening Mass. The present use of the *Benedicamus Domino* as a concluding formula at Mass is restricted to the evening Mass on Holy Thursday, which is followed by the solemn reposition of the Blessed Sacrament, and to any other Mass that is followed by some procession (decree of the S.R.C., May 27, 1961).

The medieval melodies for the *Benedicamus Domino* may be grouped in three basic categories: (1) those composed for the Divine Office (e.g., Lauds and Vespers); (2) those adapted from the *Ite, missa est* melodies for use at Mass; and (3) those composed especially for the Mass. The melodies composed for use at the Divine Office show the greatest sensitivity toward the characteristics of the Latin language: the adapted melodies for use at Mass are decidedly inferior in this regard. The *Benedicamus* *tropes, as found in early 12th-century MSS of the school of St. Martial in Limoges (Paris B.N. lat. 1120, 903, 887, nouv. acq. 1871), show the development of one of the most important structural devices in all medieval music: the *tenor.* Furthermore, the *Benedicamus* trope *Humane prolis,* also of the St. Martial school, has two simultaneously sung texts (the chief feature of the early motet). The *Benedicamus* trope *Congaudeant catholici* found in the Codex Calixtinus (*c.* 1140) of Santiago de Compostela is often cited as the oldest three-part composition known.

Bibliography: *Antiphonale monasticum* (Paris 1934). *Gradual Romanum* (New York 1961). J. HANDSCHIN, "Trope, Sequence and Conductus," NewOxHMus 2:128–174. J. A. JUNGMANN, *The Mass of the Roman Rite,* tr. F. A. BRUNNER, 2 v. (New York 1951–55) 2:434–437. Reese MusMA. Apel GregCh. **Illustration credit:** MAS, Barcelona.

[C. KELLY]

BENEDICITE DOMINUM (CANTICLE)

A deuterocanonical hymn (Dn 3.52–90), composed probably in Hebrew or Aramaic sometime before the 1st century B.C., but extant only in the Greek Septuagint (LXX) and Theodotion [*see* BIBLE, IV (TEXTS AND VERSIONS), 5, 7]. Since it is not in the Hebrew text (MT) and the Aramaic Qumran fragment of 3.22–28 (1QDan, *c.* 50–1 B.C.), it probably never formed part of the original Book of *Daniel but was an independent hymn inserted along with 3.24–51 to fill a seeming lacuna between MT 3.23 and 3.24. The original hymn probably comprised only 3.52–66 and 3.69–87; v. 88 is an editorial note linking the canticle to its context; v. 89–90 form a liturgical antiphon [cf. 2 Chr 7.3, 6; Ps 135 (136).1]. The texts of the LXX and Theodotion are practically identical, but their versification is different in places. The verse sequence of the LXX is followed by the Vulgate (though Jerome rendered Theodotion), the Latin liturgy, and the CCD translation (RSV follows Theodotion's verses). Theodotion places v. 59 before LXX's 58, and for LXX's verses 69–72, has 71, 72, 69, 70. The LXX text is extant only in an 11th-century MS (Chisianus) and in late 2d- to early 3d-century fragments (3.72–78, 81–89) in the Chester Beatty papyri, which differ slightly from Codex Chisianus.

Verses 52–87 have the form of a litany, like Psalm 135(136). The hymn has two parts, differing in content

The illuminated initial to the canticle "Benedicite Dominum" in the 12th-century "St. Alban Psalter" preserved in the treasury of the cathedral at Hildesheim.

and in the form of the responsories. The first part (3.52–56) extols the God of Israel, who resides in His holy temple in heaven [Ps 28(29).10] and contemplates all creation from His throne above the *cherubim. With the addition of v. 57, this part of the canticle is now recited at Second Lauds on Sundays. The second part (3.57–88a), called the *Benedicite* from its opening Latin word, is an invitation to all creation to praise God. With v. 56 added after v. 88a but without the responsories and without 3.88b–90, it is now recited at First Lauds on Sundays and is recommended to priests as a thanksgiving prayer after Mass. The responsories may have been liturgical additions to the original hymn.

The *Benedicite* invites all creatures to praise God, in general in the opening verse (57) and in detail in the rest of the hymn. First come the heavenly beings (3.58–63), including angels, the firmament, the waters massed above the firmament [according to ancient cosmography, *see* COSMOGONY (IN THE BIBLE)], and the "hosts of the Lord," i.e., the stars and heavenly bodies. The second class comprises natural phenomena (3.64–66, 69–73; v. 67–68 are absent from the MS Vaticanus of Theodotion, repeat v. 64 and 69, and are probably to be deleted as not original). Lastly come earthly creatures (3.74–88), inanimate and then animate in the order of their creation (see Gn 1.20–27). The "servants of the Lord" (3.85) are *Levites, i.e., liturgical ministers lower in rank than the priests. The "spirits and souls of the just" (3.86) are not departed souls but the just on earth, who should praise God with their entire being. In v. 88 the invitation is addressed to the very men who were supposed to be singing the hymn in the fiery furnace. Also, their Hebrew rather than their Babylonian names are used—and in different order (cf. Dn 3.12). These

factors indicate the redactional and liturgical provenance of the canticle.

Bibliography: C. KUHL, *Die drei Männer in Feuer* (*Daniel Kapitel 3 und seine Zusätze*) BeihZATWiss 55 (1930). F. CABROL, DACL 2.1:660–664. J. BAUR, LexThK² 2:170. **Illustration credit:** Warburg Institute, London.

[M. MC NAMARA]

BENEDICT, ST.

Monastic founder, inaugurator of the Abbeys of *Subiaco and *Monte Cassino, and author of the most celebrated monastic rule, which bears his name and has made of him a saint and confessor among the most honored of the Latin Church; b. Norcia, Italy, 480; d. Monte Cassino, after 546 (feast days, March 21 and July 11).

The life of St. Benedict is contained in St. *Gregory the Great's *Dialogues,* written in 593 and 594. Book II is entirely consecrated to Benedict, and Gregory's informers are Benedict's disciples, many of them eyewitnesses. Despite the particular literary genre of the *Dialogues,* the details they furnish are in conformity with the general history of central Italy in the 6th century, thus giving a guarantee for the biographical elements that accompany them. On the other hand, the *Benedictine Rule, whose archetype is anonymous, cannot be used for this purpose, since the text itself does not give biographical details and only hints at the intellectual and moral attitudes of its author.

Life. Of a distinguished family from Norcia, central Italy, Benedict made his literary studies in Rome and was influenced by the Byzantine monastic centers, which

St. Benedict, 8th-century, Catacomb of Hermes, Rome.

were receiving the favor of the Roman Curia. He began his "conversion" at Affile and, having put on a monastic habit, became a hermit in a grotto that is now thought to have been in the neighborhood of Subiaco (Sacro Speco) near the artificial lake on Nero's ancient villa. Among the many disciples who came to him were Maurus and Placidus of senatorial family, who turned his thought to *cenobitism, and he began the construction of 12 lauras, among them those of the present Abbey of St. Scholastica and of SS. Cosmas and Damian, whose ruins have been recently excavated.

St. Gregory the Great credits Benedict with a thaumaturgic (miraculous) activity that he compares with that of the saints in Scripture. The enmity of a local cleric, as well as the evolution of his own thought, made Benedict unhappy with the primitive monastic manner of life and prompted him to found a Grand Monastery, such as those at Lérins and Agaunum, and closer, the Vivarium of *Cassiodorus and the Lucullanum of Eugippius. He transported his group to Monte Cassino, a fortified hill where there were a sacred woods and two groves that have been uncovered in recent excavations beneath the monastery. Having destroyed the sacred wood, Benedict transformed the groves into oratories, which he consecrated to St. John the Baptist and to St. Martin. Cassino has always been considered Benedict's principal foundation, and the redaction of the Rule that St. Gregory says he wrote should be put there. The community developed in such fashion that another monastery was founded in the Diocese of Terracina (St. Stephen's). Benedict was likewise in contact with the monastic foundations in the *Campagna* made by the patrician Liberius, protector of Lérins, friend of *Caesarius of Arles, who presided at the Council of *Orange (529). The *Dialogues* portray Benedict in his relations with such personalities as Constans of Aquino, Sabinus of Canosa, Germanus of Capua, and the Gothic King Totila. He had a sister, Scholastica, who became a nun and was buried at Cassino. The relation between this account and the taking of Rome by Totila (Dec. 546), suggested by Gregory, seems to indicate that Benedict's death took place after that date. He was buried with his sister in the Oratory of St. John the Baptist at Cassino.

Cult and Patronage. There is no indication of a cult to St. Benedict before the destruction of Monte Cassino by the Lombards about 577. After its restoration under *Petronax (c. 720) a poem attributed to a certain Mark testifies to the cult surrounding his tomb. The Cassinese martyrologies and calendars, the earliest of which goes back to the 8th century, mention a solemnity on March 21, which seems to have been celebrated in concurrence with a feast on July 11. Later March 21 was attached to the *transitus* (death), while July 11 marked the translation of the relics to Fleury near Orléans in the monastery of *Saint-Benoît-sur-Loire. In modern times that date is celebrated as the Patronage of St. Benedict. The translation is celebrated in the French Benedictine congregation with a branch at Subiaco, the rest of the order knows only of the patronage.

Relics at Fleury. The cult of St. Benedict is difficult to study because of its universal diffusion and the controversies that surround the translation of his relics. An 8th-century liturgical document affirms that at the end of the 7th century, when Cassino was deserted, the tomb was violated and the relics of Benedict were transported to Fleury. A literature was occasioned by the presence of the bones in this new monastery; it includes a letter of Pope *Zachary calling for the restitution of the relics and a mention by *Paul the Deacon in his History of the Lombards. The construction of a sanctuary at Fleury, visited in the Middle Ages by monks from all over western Europe, particularly England, and a feast of the translation on July 11, which was celebrated at Cassino itself and in the Christian West until at least the 9th century, permit a detailed history of the deposit of these relics at Fleury. An official process of recognition has shown that the bones are actually those that were transported there at the end of the 7th century.

Cassinese Relics. In the restoration of Cassino Petronax had naturally instituted a cult around the tomb, and Cassino has always been, along with Fleury, a place of pilgrimage in honor of St. Benedict. In the 11th century (c. 1068) the Abbot Desiderius, the future Pope *Victor III, believed that he had discovered an undisturbed tomb. A literature has likewise developed around this event and includes two liturgical studies by Dom Paul Meyvaert, which indicate the historical evidence but leave open the question of the authenticity of the discovered bones.

Since Monte Cassino considers itself in possession of the true relics, July 11 is celebrated there and in the dioceses of Italy as the feast of the patronage. The excavations made after the bombardment of 1944 have brought to light important vestiges of the Lombard epoch: a necropolis and in one of the tombs near the high altar a coffin in which in 1659 Angelo della Noce, after a process of recognition, had placed the bones discovered by Desiderius. They had been rediscovered by John of Aragon (1484), then by Jerome of Piacenza (1545). Historians who have studied the cult of St. Benedict find it difficult to pronounce on the authenticity of the relics in either Monte Cassino or Fleury.

Religious Family. In the course of the Middle Ages all of occidental monasticism had been gradually subjected to the Rule of St. Benedict. Before the Carolingian epoch, one could distinguish in Europe (outside of Southern Italy and Rome) four Benedictine regions: Anglo-Saxon England (Theodore, Bede); certain monasteries of Southern Gaul (Venerandus); the Columbanus-Benedictine monasteries of north and central Gaul (Luxeuil); and finally the great mission in Germany of St. Boniface. With *Benedict of Aniane and *Louis the Pious in the Council of Aix-la-Chapelle (816–817) it was decided that all monks of the Empire had to follow the Benedictine Rule. But it was actually at the beginning of the 11th century that this decision was enforced. In modern times the Benedictine family is represented by two large branches, the Black Monks of the Benedictine Confederation and the two Cistercian branches (White Monks).

Ancient iconography of Benedict includes frescoes in the 8th-century subterranean basilica of Hermes at Rome, the 9th-century monastery of Monte Civate, and the 10th-century lower church of St. Chrysogonus in Trastevere; minatures in 10th- and 11th-century manuscripts; the antependium of the 11th-century cathedral of Basel; capitals on the 12th-century basilica at Fleury; and frescoes on the 13th-century church at Subiaco.

The cult of St. Benedict has been popularized by a medal that originated at Metten in Bavaria and can be traced to Bavarian and Austrian devotions in the 14th century. Modern numismatics include a jubilee medal from Monte Cassino in 1880. On Oct. 24, 1964, Benedict was declared patron saint of Europe in a brief of Pope Paul VI.

Bibliography: Kapsner BenBibl. T. F. LINDSAY, *St. Benedict: His Life and Work* (London 1949). I. SCHUSTER, *Storia di san Benedetto e dei suoi tempi* (3d ed. Viboldone 1953); Eng. tr. G. J. ROETTGER, *Saint Benedict and His Times* (St. Louis 1951). P. CAROSI, *Il primo monastero benedettino* (StAnselm 39; 1956). A. PANTONI, "L'identificazione della basilica di S. Martino a Montecassino," *Benedictina* 7 (1953) 347–356. A. MUNDÓ, RevBén 59 (1949) 203–206, Totila. S. HILPISCH, *Studien und Mitteilungen zur Geschichte des Benediktiner-Ordens und seiner Zweige* 61 (1947–48) 114–125. H. FRANK, "Die ältesten Zeugnisse für das Fest des hl. Benedikt am 21. März," *Vir Dei Benedictus,* ed. R. MOLITOR (Münster 1947) 333–339. A. VIDIER and A. and J. PICARD, *L'historiographie à St. Benoît-sur-Loire et les "Miracles de St. Benoît"* (Paris 1964). *Il Sepolcro di S. Benedetto* (Miscellanea Cassinese 27; Montecassino 1951). P. VISENTIN, RevBén 67 (1957) 34–48, Bede and the translation. P. MEYVAERT, *ibid.* 65 (1955) 3–70; 69 (1959) 287–336, Cassinese tradition and relics. E. DUDLER, *Das Bild des hl. Benedikt bis zum Ausgang des Mittelalters* (St. Ottilien 1953). **Illustration credit:** Leonard Von Matt.

[J. MALLET]

BENEDICT I, POPE, June 3, 575, to July 30, 579. The successor of Pope *John III was very likely elected soon after his death but could not be consecrated until a year later, apparently awaiting imperial confirmation. The Lombards reached Rome and besieged the city (579). Help had been requested of the Emperor *Justin II in the name of the Pope and the Roman Senate, but the troops the Emperor sent were inadequate, and the grain ships from Egypt provided only temporary relief for the city. It seems to be to Benedict that the Emperor and his wife Sophia gave the precious reliquary in the form of a jeweled cross containing a piece of the true cross, which is still preserved in the treasury of the Vatican basilica, a masterpiece of Byzantine workmanship. Pope Benedict I was buried in St. Peter's.

Bibliography: Duchesne LP 1:308; 3:92. Caspar 2:348, 350, 777. H. LECLERCQ, DACL 13.1:1222. O. BERTOLINI, *Roma di fronte a Bisanzio e ai Longobardi* (Bologna 1941). I. DANIELE, EncCatt 2:1267–68. R. U. MONTINI, *Le tombe dei papi* (Rome 1957) 112.

[J. CHAPIN]

BENEDICT II, POPE, ST., June 26, 684, to May 8, 685 (feast, May 7). He was elected soon after the death of Pope *Leo II (July 3, 683), but because of delay in obtaining imperial confirmation, he was not consecrated until June 684. A Roman, he was trained in the urban *schola cantorum* and ordained to its priesthood. Two letters antedating his consecration designate him *electus.* Good relations between Emperor *Constantine IV Pogonatus and Benedict are reflected in the former's sending the Pope locks of his son's hair and in his remitting the mandate that papal elections be imperially ratified, though the exarch at *Ravenna still had to be notified. (The new procedures for installing a pope are recorded in the Roman *Liber diurnus,* form. 82–85). Benedict's directive of 683–684 that *Wilfrid of York be restored to the See of *York, of which he had been deprived in 677, was partially honored in 686. Benedict's support of the acts of the Third Council of *Constantinople was manifest in his futile effort to secure the recantation of *Monotheletism by Macarius, the deposed (since March 681) patriarch of Antioch and in his dispatching the notary,

Peter, to Spain to secure its hierarchy's adherence to the acts of the Council. In November 684 the Council of *Toledo XIV endorsed the anti-Monothelite decrees of Constantinople III, but the Pope objected to two expressions in the *Apologia* forwarded by Abp. *Julian of Toledo.

Bibliography: Duchesne LP 1:363–365; 3:96. Jaffé E 1:241–242; 2:699. Dölger Reg 252. Mansi 11:1086–92; 12:10–12, 1035. Mann 1.2:54–63. F. BAIX, DHGE 8:9–14. O. BERTOLINI, *Roma di fronte a Bisanzio e ai Longobardi* (Bologna 1941). Caspar 2:614–619, 673–676, 782–785.

[H. G. J. BECK]

BENEDICT III, POPE, Sept. 29, 855, to April 17, 858. He was cardinal-priest of St. Calixtus when elected to the papacy. The party of the Emperor, *Louis II, however, supported the anti-pope, *Anastasius the Librarian, even though *Leo IV had excommunicated him in 853. But Benedict won recognition because the clergy and people of Rome remained loyal. According to a 13th-century legend the popess *Joan governed the Church during this pontificate. In attempting to curb the licentiousness of the nobility, Benedict threatened to excommunicate Hubert, the brother of Queen Theutberga of Lorraine, for plundering monasteries; and insisted that Ingeltrude leave the court of *Lothair II of Lorraine and return to her husband, Count Boso. Benedict protested against the English who had deposed their bishops without trial, and condemned the inaction of the French hierarchy in not removing clerical abuses. He refused to sanction the deposition of Gregory, the Archbishop of Syracuse, by *Ignatius, the Patriarch of Constantinople, until he had examined the evidence. At the request of *Hincmar of Reims, Benedict approved the acts of the Council of Soissons (853), which upheld Hincmar's claim to the See of *Reims, provided that the rights of the Holy See were preserved.

Bibliography: Jaffé L 1:235–236. Duchesne LP 2:140–150. F. BAIX, DHGE 8:14–27. Haller v.2. Mann 2:308—329.

[S. MC KENNA]

BENEDICT IV, POPE, May or June 900 to July or August 903. A Roman, ordained by Pope *Formosus, Benedict summoned a Lateran synod (900), which validated the consecrations and ordinations of Formosus. His generosity toward those in distress was praised by Frodoard the historian. This is evident in his support of Stephen, unjustly deprived of his see at Sorrento, Italy, and of an eastern prelate, Malacenus, who had been driven into exile by the Saracens. He formally excommunicated the murderer of Fulk, the Archbishop of Reims, and ordered the French bishops to promulgate this decree throughout the country. In February 901 he crowned Louis III, the Blind, King of Provence and Emperor of Italy. But Louis was defeated by *Berengar I in 902 and forced to take an oath to leave Italy forever. At Benedict's death, the papacy became the object of party strife.

Bibliography: Jaffé L 1:306. Duchesne LP 2:233. Mann 4:103–110. F. BAIX, DHGE 8:27–31. W. KÖLMEL, *Rom und der Kirchenstaat im 10. und 11. Jahrhundert* (Berlin 1935). Haller 2:193, 546.

[S. MC KENNA]

BENEDICT V, POPE, May 22? to June 23, 964; d. Hamburg, Germany, July 4, 966?. He was a deacon of Rome, noted for virtue and learning. His election infuriated the Emperor *Otto I, who regarded *Leo

VIII as lawful pope. The Romans tried to prevent the Emperor's army from entering their city, but hunger forced their surrender. In a Lateran synod, convened by Otto and Leo VIII (June 23, 964), Benedict admitted, according to Liutprand, that he was an intruder. He was publicly degraded, reduced to deacon, and sent to Hamburg, where he was placed in the charge of Archbishop *Adaldag until death. In 988, *Otto III transferred his remains to Rome.

Bibliography: Sources. MGS ser. 4, 3:626–627. Jaffé L 1:325. Duchesne LP 2:251. Literature. Mann 4:273–281. F. Baix, DHGE 8:31–38. P. Brezzi, *Roma e l'Imperio medioevale* (Bologne 1947). Haller 2:213. H. Zimmermann, "Die Deposition der Päpste . . . Benedikt V," MitteilIÖG 68 (1960) 209–225.

[S. MC KENNA]

BENEDICT VI, POPE, Jan. 19, 973, to July 974. A Roman by birth and a member of the clergy, he was chosen as pope by *Otto I. When Otto died, May 7, 973, and while his son *Otto II was fully occupied with

Pope Benedict VI, on a 10th-century silver denarius.

German affairs, the nobility of Rome rose against Benedict. Under the leadership of Crescentius I (*see* CRESCENTII) they made Benedict a prisoner (June 974) and chose as antipope a deacon named Franco, who called himself Boniface VII. All the evidence indicates that it was he who ordered Benedict to be strangled in prison, July 974. Surviving documents of Benedict's pontificate concerning the dispute between Archbishop Frederick of Salzburg and Bishop *Pilgrim of Passau over the jurisdiction in Noricum and Pannonia (Hungary) are forgeries.

Bibliography: Jaffé L 1:331, 2:707. Duchesne LP 2:255–256, 568. Mann 4:305–314. F. Baix DHGE 8:38–43. Haller 2:217–255. **Illustration credit:** Leonard Von Matt.

[S. MC KENNA]

BENEDICT VII, POPE, October 974 to July 10, 983. Benedict was a Roman and former bishop of Sutri. He was chosen as pope by the Emperor *Otto II. At his election, the antipope, Boniface VII (Franco), fled

to Constantinople. Working in harmony with the Emperor, Benedict granted many privileges to the churches and monasteries of Germany and concerned himself with the conversion of the *Slavs. But his decision to suppress the German See of Merseburg (981) was a setback in the conversion of Central Europe. Benedict published a strongly worded condemnation of simony (981). He allowed St. *Majolus of *Cluny to place his monastery under the special protection of the Holy See and granted the same privilege to the Abbey of *Saint-Valéry, recently founded by Hugh Capet. This practice later became more common and prepared the way for the reform movement of the 11th century.

See also CLUNIAC REFORM; GREGORIAN REFORM.

Bibliography: Jaffé L 1:402–443, 2:707. Duchesne LP 2:258. Mann 4:315–329. F. Baix, DHGE 8:43–61. G. Schwaiger, LexThK² 2:174–175.

[S. MC KENNA]

BENEDICT VIII, POPE, May 18, 1012, to April 9, 1024; b. Theophylactus. He was a brother both to that Alberic who became *consul et dux* of Rome and to the future Pope *John XIX, and was the first pope of the *Tusculani. Benedict, and not the candidate of the *Crescentii, the antipope Gregory VI, obtained the approval of *Henry II, whom he crowned emperor in Rome in 1014. Benedict was a statesman of stature. In 1016 the alliance of the Pope, Genoa, and Pisa successfully liberated *Sardinia from the Spanish Saracens and freed the mainland from their incursions. Byzantine pressure in southern Italy was, however, too strong for the local forces to contain, and in 1020, Benedict journeyed to *Bamberg to solicit imperial support. While in Bamberg he consecrated St. Stephen's church, and Henry renewed the *Ottonianum* (*see* PAPACY, 2), at the same time granting the bishopric of Bamberg as a fief to the Roman Church. The campaign of the Emperor, accompanied by the Pope, in southern Italy (1021–22), could do no more than restore the status quo. The most pressing problem of the age was *reform in the Church. Benedict followed the leadership of Henry II. The Roman synod of 1014 had issued decrees concerning irregular ordinations (*see* SIMONY) and the alienation of *church property. The great synod of Pavia, August 1020, which opened with the Pope's address, decreed degradation for uncelibate clerics in higher orders and the reduction of their offspring to the status of slavery (*see* CELIBACY, HISTORY OF). The Emperor approved these decrees and enacted them as the law of the empire.

Bibliography: Jaffé L 1:506–514. Duchesne LP 2:61–92. Kehr ItalPont. Kehr GermPont. Mann 5. F. Baix, DHGE 8:61–92. W. Kölmel, *Rom und der Kirchenstaat im 10. und 11. Jahrhundert* (Berlin 1935). Fliche-Martin 7. Haller 2:229–234. H. Schmidinger, "Die Palliumverleihung Benedikts VIII. für Ragusa," MitteilIÖG 58 (1950) 31–49. Seppelt 2:402–408.

[V. GELLHAUS]

BENEDICT IX, POPE, Aug. 8 or Sept. 3?, 1032, to May 1, 1045; b. Theophylactus; d. Grottaferrata, 1055?. He was a son of Alberic III, leader of the *Tusculani, and he simoniacally succeeded his uncles, *Benedict VIII and *John XIX. Though young (perhaps 30), Theophylactus was certainly not a boy of 12 when he became pope. His personal conduct was often not edifying. The first 12 years of Benedict's pontificate were peaceful, and he was free to meet

*Conrad II at Cremona and Spello and to journey to Marseilles. There was no controversy with the Emperor; and when Conrad uncanonically deposed Abp. Heribert of Milan, Benedict compliantly excommunicated him. In 1044 a revolt drove Benedict from Rome and installed Bishop John of Sabina as antipope Sylvester III. In March 1045 Benedict in turn drove out Sylvester. Then on May 1 Benedict sold his papal office to his baptismal sponsor, the reforming archpriest John Gratian, Pope *Gregory VI. In the fall of 1045 the reform-minded Emperor *Henry III entered the fray. Reform synods held at Pavia, Sutri, and Rome deposed Gregory, and Suidger of Bamberg was acclaimed Pope *Clement II. After Clement's untimely death in 1047, Benedict again controlled Rome, Nov. 8, 1047, to July 16, 1048, until Boniface of Tuscany, acting on Henry's orders, drove him out for good and installed the new pope, *Damasus II. Benedict died probably at the end of 1055.

Bibliography: Jaffé L 1:519–523. Kehr ItalPont 6.2. Duchesne LP 2:270–272. G. B. BORINO, "L'elezione e la deposizione di Gregorio VI," *Archivio della Società Romana di Storia Patria* 39 (1916) 142–252, 295–410; "Invitus ultra montes cum domno Papa Gregorio abii," StGreg 1 (1947) 3–46. R. L. POOLE, "Benedict IX and Gregory VI," *Proceedings of the British Academy* 8 (1917–18) 199–235. Mann v.6. F. BAIX and L. JADIN, DHGE 8:93–105. Fliche-Martin v.7. T. SCHIEFFER, "Heinrich II und Konrad II," DeutschArch 8 (1951) 384–437. Seppelt v.2–3.

[V. GELLHAUS]

BENEDICT XI, POPE, BL.,

Oct. 22, 1303, to July 7, 1304; b. Niccolo Boccasini, at Treviso, Italy, 1240; d. Perugia (feast, July 7). The son of a notary, he entered the *Dominicans in 1254 and studied at Venice and Milan, becoming lector for his fellow re-

The tomb of Pope Benedict XI, with sculpture by Giovanni Pisano, in the church of San Domenico at Perugia.

ligious in 1268. He was distinguished both as a scholar, having written commentaries on the Psalms, Job, Matthew, and Apocalypse, and as a religious superior. After serving as subprior, prior, and provincial of Lombardy (1282–96), he was elected master general of the order in May 1296. He kept the Dominicans loyal to Pope *Boniface VIII in the crisis of 1297; served on Boniface's peace embassy to England and France; and as cardinal (1300), acted as legate to Hungary in the mission in favor of Carobert of *Anjou. He was one of two faithful cardinals with Boniface VIII at Anagni. The major reason for his first-ballot election as pope was the universal esteem for his sanctity and prudential administrative talents. Benedict proved to be a peace-seeking pontiff. Anxious to end the discord of Boniface's pontificate without sacrificing principle, he modified *Clericis laicos* and reconciled *Philip IV of France to the papacy. Benedict's acts should be interpreted as pastoral not appeasive. Furthermore, he did not absolve *Nogaret and Sciarra *Colonna, the principal perpetrators of Anagni. While processing their case, Benedict died suddenly at Perugia, where his cult developed immediately. He was beatified by Clement XII, April 24, 1736.

Bibliography: C. A. GRANDJEAN, ed., *Le Registre de Benôit XI* (Paris 1905). B. GUIDO, Muratori RIS 3.1:672–673. L. JADIN, DHGE 8:106–116. **Illustration credit:** Anderson-Art Reference Bureau.

[E. J. SMYTH]

BENEDICT XII, POPE

Pontificate, Dec. 20, 1334, to April 25, 1342; b. Jacques Fournier, at Saverdun (Ariège) France; d. Avignon. The talent of this *Cistercian for inquisitorial matters was used by *John XXII, who sought his advice concerning cases of heresy being appealed to the papal court. As bishop of Pamiers (1317) and of Mirepoix (1326), he freed the dioceses of any *Waldenses, *Cathari, and *Albigenses still infesting them. He was a zealous inquisitor, masterfully wresting confessions from the accused and never faltering in his integrity. A harsh man on occasion, he showed clemency to heretics who confessed their guilt: only four Waldenses and one relapsed Catharist died at the stake (*see* INQUISITION). He was made cardinal priest in 1327. A doctor of theology from Paris, he took part in the great controversies of the age centering on the *poverty controversy and the *beatific vision; he wrote a treatise against the *Fraticelli; a refutation of the errors of *Joachim of Fiore and Meister *Eckhart; a dissertation on the doctrines propagated by *Michael of Cesena, *William of Ockham, and *Peter John Olivi; an explanation of the state of the holy souls before the last judgment and of questions concerning the theories of *Durandus of Saint-Pourçain.

Succeeding John XXII during the *Avignon papacy, Benedict was crowned pope on Jan. 8, 1335. He quickly ended the discussion on the beatific vision, imprudently begun by his predecessor in 1331. John had stated that before the resurrection of the body the souls of the just would not enjoy the intuitive vision of God, but only after the Last Judgment, and that they would remain until then *sub altare Dei,* diverted by the view of the humanity of Christ. Benedict's bull *Benedictus Deus* of Jan. 29, 1336, held that just souls immediately see the divine essence with an intuitive and even facial

diplomatic domain the rigid character of the Pope hardly predisposed him for compromise, and almost nothing but defeats are recorded. Instead of maintaining an armed force in Italy, he allowed himself to be duped by minor local tyrants; the temporal authority of the Church in the Romagna, the March of Ancona, and even in Bologna, practically ceased to exist. Such events made him little anxious to return to Rome, and he began building the papal palace at *Avignon. Negotiations to reconcile Emperor *Louis IV the Bavarian with the papacy were fruitless. On the one hand, Benedict was influenced by King Philip VI of France and the King of Naples, who, for private political reasons, were hostile to all compromise, while, on the other hand, Louis promulgated the edict *Licet juris* (1338), which sanctioned the decision of the electors at Rense to free the imperial dignity from the customary approval and sanction of the Holy See (*see* HOLY ROMAN EMPIRE). He was unable to curb Edward III and the nascent Hundred Years' War.

Bibliography: Sources. BENEDICT XII, *Lettres communes,* comment. J. M. VIDAL, 3 v. (Paris 1902–11); *Lettres . . . intéressant les pays autres que la France,* comment. J. M. VIDAL, 6 fasc. (Paris 1913–50); *Lettres . . . à la France,* comment. G. DAUMET, 3 v. (Paris 1899–1920). J. M. VIDAL, "Notice sur les oeuvres . . . ," RHE 6 (1905) 557–565, 785–810. É BALUZE, *Vitae paparum Avenionensium,* ed. G. MOLLAT, 4 v. (Paris 1914–27). Literature. U. BERLIÈRE, "Les Chapitres généraux . . . ," *Mélanges d'histoire bénédictine,* ed. U. BERLIÈRE, 4 v. (Maredsous, Bel. 1897–1902) 4:52–171; *Notes supplémentaires* (Bruges 1905), for Benedictine reform. J. B. MAHN, *Le Pape Benoît XII et les cisterciens* (Paris 1949). C. SCHMITT, *Un pape réformateur . . .* (Quaracchi-Florence 1959), for Franciscan reform. Pastor 1:83–86. H. JENKINS, *Papal Efforts for Peace under Benedict XII* (Philadelphia 1933). H. OTTO, "Zur politischen Einstellung Papstes Benedikts XII," ZKirchgesch 62 (1943–44) 103–126. G. MOLLAT, *The Popes at Avignon,* tr. J. LOVE (New York 1963). B. GUILLEMAIN, *La Politique bénéficiale du Pape Benoît XII* (Paris 1952). F. WETTER, *Die Lehre Benedikts XII vom intensiven Wachstum der Gottesschau* (Anal Greg 92; 1958). **Illustration credit:** Alinari-Art Reference Bureau.

[G. MOLLAT]

Pope Benedict XII. Bust by Paolo da Siena (1342) in the grotto of the Vatican, Rome.

vision. As a reformer, Benedict set up an inquest that confirmed the existence of many abuses in the papal court. He then decreed salutary regulations for his Curia.

As a former abbot of *Fontfroide, Benedict was aware of the contemporary defects of discipline in the religious orders: the *Cistercians, the *Benedictines, and the *Franciscans were compelled to observe new severe constitutions, which regulated the question of the orders' temporal power, prescribed the regular holding of *chapters and visitation of monasteries (*see* VISITATION, CANONICAL, HISTORY OF), demanded that young religious attend the universities, and repressed luxury and vagrancy. As for the secular clergy, Benedict's revocation of *commendation, restriction of *expectancies, insistence on *residence, tailoring on *annates, and encouragement toward sacred studies assured its proper behavior. In the *States of the Church, scrupulous inspections were a prelude to reforms. In the

BENEDICT XIII, POPE

Pontificate, May 29, 1724, to Feb. 21, 1730; b. Pietro Francesco Orsini, Gravina, Feb. 2, 1649; d. Rome. He was the son and heir of the Duke of Gravina. The Orsini family, prominent in Rome for many centuries, had already seen two of its members become popes—Celestine III (1191–98) and Nicholas III (1277–80). Against great family opposition, Pietro abandoned his splendid inheritance to become Fra Vincenzo Maria of the Order of Preachers. Like Aloysius Gonzaga, whom he later canonized, he gave all his rights of inheritance to his younger brother. Fra Vincenzo Maria proved to be an excellent religious and a dedicated student. He studied philosophy and theology at Naples, Bologna, and Venice. After these studies he taught philosophy at Brescia. But even if he had fled from his family's secular honors, his family saw to it that he received ecclesiastical honors. Clement X made him a cardinal at the age of 23. Three years later he became archbishop of Manfredonia, then of Cesena (1680), and then of Benevento (1686). Here he remained for 38 years. In all his dioceses he strove to promote good discipline and morals in his flock. He loved Benevento and was extremely paternalistic and charitable to the people. Living like a Dominican friar, he summoned two provincial councils

Pope Benedict XIII, tomb designed by Carlo Marchionni, in the church of S. Maria sopra Minerva, Rome.

and wrote three volumes of scholarly and spiritual works.

When elected pope after a conclave of more than 2 months, he accepted only with the greatest reluctance. Benedict XIII was religiously well qualified for his lofty task, but he proved to have serious deficiencies in practical administration and diplomacy. While he fulminated against the use of wigs by the clergy and devoted himself to liturgical functions, a group of Beneventans made a good thing out of the Pope's imprudent favors. The leader of these grafters was Niccolò Coscia, who had been Benedict's chancellor and secretary at Benevento. Coscia, later made a cardinal, had a great appetite for graft, a fact lost on the unworldly Pontiff. Benedict XIII was none too successful in his dealings with the powers. Although a great defender of Church rights in theory, he compromised on the *monarchia sicula* question and gave extensive privileges in ecclesiastical matters to the Court of Turin.

In matters more completely spiritual, Benedict XIII was eminent. He took a firm stand against the Jansenists; fostered the progress of religious orders, approving, among others, the Institute of the Brothers of the Christian Schools; held a provincial council in Rome in 1725; and canonized many saints, including the Latin Americans Turibius and Francis Solano, and the youths Stanislaus and Aloysius.

Bibliography: Pastor 34:98–299. A. F. ARTAUD DE MONTOR, *The Lives and Times of the Popes,* 10 v. (New York 1910–11) 6:230–245. BullRom v.22. C. CASTIGLIONI, EncCatt 2:1279–81. P. MIKAT, LexThK² 2:177. H. HEMMER, DTC 2.1:704–705. J. CARREYRE, DHGE 8:163–164. **Illustration credit:** Alinari-Art Reference Bureau.

[J. S. BRUSHER]

BENEDICT XIII, ANTIPOPE

Pontificate in Avignon, Sept. 28, 1394, to July 26, 1417; b. Pedro de Luna, Illueca, Aragon, *c.* 1328; d. Peñiscola, Valencia, between May 23 and Nov. 29, 1423. After having taught Canon Law in France, he was made a cardinal in 1375. With the beginning of the *Western Schism, he chose to follow the antipope *Clement VII in *Avignon. He served as Clement's legate to Aragon, Castile, Navarre, and Portugal. In 1393 he was legate to France, Flanders, and Scotland. At the conclave in Avignon after the death of Clement VII in 1394, he and his colleagues swore to work with all their strength toward the reunion of Rome and Avignon, and even to open the way for abdication if the majority of the cardinals approved. He was elected pope because of his canonical knowledge and his successful legations in Spain, and was crowned Oct. 11, 1394. When Benedict proved lax in working for the end of the Schism, the French King, Charles VI, Benedict's most important supporter, sent a French deputation in May 1395 to compel him to make some effectual decisions. The Pope hedged. According to him abdication was anticanonical; he had committed himself only to the path of compromise. In July 1398 Charles tried to force him to act by taking away his right of provision to major offices and that of advowson to minor benefices. On August 8 a new decree annulled all the expectancies distributed by him. France, along with Navarre, Castile, and several other areas, officially withdrew obedience to Benedict. These radical measures deprived the Pontiff of both his influence and his revenue. His court was abandoned by most of the cardinals, and he was a prisoner in his Avignon palace. During the night of March 11, 1403, Benedict made his escape and sought refuge in Provence. The cardinals submitted to him and in May France and Castile restored their obedience. Benedict's plans for compromise with *Boniface IX in Rome and afterward with *Innocent VII and then *Gregory XII never bore fruit. Finally, weary of Benedict's vacillations, France changed her support to neutrality (1408). Then the Council of *Pisa declared both Gregory and Benedict to have forfeited their pontifical rank (June 5, 1409). With continuing support from Aragon, Benedict fought this decision. He likewise opposed his deposition pronounced by the Council of *Constance, July 26, 1417, and still confident of his rightful claim, named four cardinals as late as November 1422.

Bibliography: É. BALUZE, *Vitae paparum Avenionensium,* ed. G. MOLLAT, 4 v. (Paris 1914–27) v.2, 4. H. DENIFLE, ed., *Chartularium Universitatis Parisiensis,* 4 v. (Paris 1880–97) 4:1–164. MARTIN DE ALPARTIL, *Chronica . . . ,* ed. F. EHRLE (Paderborn 1906–). S. PUIG Y PUIG, *Episcopologio Barcinonense: Pedro de Luna, último Papa de Aviñón, 1387–1430* (Barcelona 1920). Pastor 1:174–177. G. BARRACLOUGH, "Un Document inédit sur la soustraction d'obédience en 1398," RHE 30 (1934) 101–115. F. BAIX and L. JADIN, DHGE 8:135–163. J. ZUNZUNEGUI, *Miscellanea Historiae Pontificiae* 7 (1943) 83–137. H. LAPEYRE, "Un Sermon de Pedro de Luna," *Bulletin Hispanique* 50 (1948) 129–146. G. MOLLAT, *Annales de Saint-Louis des Français* 6 (1909) 445–470; RHE 23 (1927) 489–501; RevMALat 1 (1945) 149–163; RHE 43 (1948) 90–147. G. PILLEMENT, *P. de Luna* (Paris 1955). M. DIJOL, *Le Procès de B. XIII . . . devant l'histoire et le droit* (Paris 1959). A. M. RODRIGUEZ, "B. XIII y el reino de Aragon," *Hispania* 19 (1959) 163–191.

[G. MOLLAT]

BENEDICT XIV, POPE

Pontificate, Aug. 17, 1740, to May 3, 1758; b. Prospero Lorenzo Lambertini, Bologna, March 31, 1675. He came of a noble Bolognese family. After an early education from tutors, he was sent to the Collegium Clementinum in Rome, where he studied for 4 years. In 1694 he received the doctorate in theology and law from the University of Rome.

He began his public career as an assistant lawyer in Rome during the pontificate of *Innocent XII. Among the 11 offices he held under *Clement XI and *Innocent XIII, the first two were of special significance. In 1701 Clement appointed him consistorial advocate for two canonizations and in 1708, Promoter of the Faith. In the latter office he had charge of all canonizations until 1727. Seeing the need for a record of such work, he wrote *De servorum Dei beatificatione et beatorum canonizatione,* which is still an important book.

In 1728 Benedict XIII created him a cardinal, having appointed him archbishop of Ancona in 1727. Four years later Clement XII transferred him to Bologna as archbishop. In both archdioceses he showed the zeal and devotion that were characteristic of him. He sought to improve the spiritual state of his people, for example, by visiting even remote villages and later checking to see that the proposed changes had been made. He held synods and from that experience published another important book, *De synodo diocesana.*

When elected pope he faced the aggressive monarchs who sent armies through the Papal States in the War of Austrian Succession, but he could only protest this violation of neutrality and distribute alms to his suffering people. During preceding pontificates rulers had also

Marble figure of Benedict XIV by Antonio Bracci, detail of the Pope's monument in St. Peter's Basilica.

sought to gain supremacy over the Church in their kingdoms, but Benedict acted quickly regarding this problem. Before 1740 ended he had begun new negotiations with the kings of Savoy, Naples, and Spain. Because of his willingness to make concessions concordats were signed with Savoy and Naples in 1741. The negotiations with Spain were much more difficult. Finally the concordat was signed in 1753, with Benedict making concessions for which he has been criticized. However, a complete rupture, which he feared, would have hampered the spiritual work of the Church. Ranke praised Benedict's ability to understand how much he must concede and how much he must retain without weakening the papacy. This was particularly clear in his diplomatic handling of the crisis between the French bishops and the parliaments over the refusal of Sacraments to persons suspected of *Jansenism. When the government asked him to send instructions to the bishops in an encyclical rather than a bull, he complied in 1756.

In the Papal States he improved living conditions by having granaries built in all villages and towns, roads repaired, and necessary commodities exported without fees. A great deal was done to preserve historic objects and buildings: statues were purchased for the Capitoline Museum and a picture gallery added; a Museum of Christian Antiquities was established in the Vatican Palace; and both major and minor churches in Rome and other cities were restored. According to Montesquieu he was the "scholars' pope." He founded four academies where papers were read about the Church and Roman history, purchased manuscripts and books for the Vatican Library, and improved the University of Rome. At his suggestion new editions and books were published.

Above all he was a good pastor. By instructions and by example he showed his great interest in the spiritual life. Two months after his election he established a congregation to select worthy bishops and a month later, another congregation to answer bishops' questions. His briefs to bishops emphasized their duties: the training of priests, visiting of parishes, and promoting of missions and other religious exercises. The bulls of 1742 and 1744 suppressed the pagan *Chinese and *Malabar rites used by natives who had been converted to Christianity; thus a long controversy was ended. A bull in 1745 answered arguments about usury; one in 1746 pertained to the residence of bishops in their dioceses; another in 1748, to mixed marriages. He set an example for spiritual growth by his simple living, humility, and charitable attitude toward the faults of others.

No pope before him left so full a written record about himself. There are extant 760 personal letters to Cardinal Tencin in France and many others to Italian friends. The letters show his sarcasm and humor, about which so much has been written, but the letters also show his good characteristics. There is no discrepancy between his own statements about his duties and the judgments of men who had seen his work, such as Charles de Brosses of France and Francesco Venier, the Venetian ambassador.

Bibliography: *Opera,* ed. J. SILVESTER, 17 v. (Prato, Italy 1839–47). Pastor 35–36, with a long bibliography to 1931. L. VON RANKE, *The History of the Popes During the Last Four Centuries,* tr. MRS. FOSTER, ed. G. R. DENNIS, 3 v. (London 1912) v.2–3. Cross ODCC 154. P. MIKAT, LexThK² 2:177–178. J. CARREYRE, DHGE 8:164–167. **Illustration credit:** Alinari-Art Reference Bureau.

[M. L. SHAY]

BENEDICT XV, POPE

Pontificate, Sept. 3, 1914, to Jan. 22, 1922; b. Giacomo Della Chiesa, Pegli (Genoa), Italy, Nov. 21, 1854. His parents, Marchese Giuseppe Della Chiesa and Giovanna Migliorati, belonged to the patrician class of Genoa.

Prepapal Career. Giacomo's delicate health prevented his participation in children's games, but promoted his early acquired studious habits and his tendency to solitude and introspection. His elementary education came from private tutors, his secondary schooling from diocesan priests at the Istituto Donavaro e Giusso. His father, fearing the current anticlericalism, caused him to defer his priestly ambition. Instead he attended the Royal University of Genoa, where he received a doctorate in civil law (1875) after writing a thesis entitled "The Interpretation of Laws." Thereupon the father acquiesced to his son's persistent request to study for the priesthood. In Rome Giacomo resided at the Capranica College, attended classes at the Gregorian University, and was ordained (Dec. 21, 1878). He received a doctorate in theology (1879) and one in Canon Law (1880).

Papal Diplomat. Archbishop *Rampolla, representative of Leo XIII at seminars held in the Accademia dei Nobili Ecclesiastici, invited the young priest to join the staff of the papal secretariat of state as *apprendista.* When Rampolla became apostolic nuncio to Spain (1882), he took Della Chiesa as secretary. In Spain an extraordinarily violent cholera epidemic broke out. The nuncio and his secretary organized primitive relief agencies and worked as male nurses. This experience proved helpful later, when Benedict XV demonstrated a practical grasp of the needs in World War I by directing personally the organization of Vatican relief agencies. In 1887 Rampolla was named papal secretary of state and cardinal. After serving as his *minutante* or secretary, Della Chiesa was appointed *sostituto* or undersecretary (1901). His natural sense of gracious diplomacy often won Leo XIII's approval of projects that the somewhat choleric Rampolla was unable to achieve.

With the accession of Pius X (1903), Rafael *Merry del Val replaced Rampolla as secretary of state, but Della Chiesa remained as undersecretary. Although he enjoyed favor with Pius X, the years from 1903 to 1907 were increasingly difficult for him. The crisis over *Modernism had given rise to an extreme rightist movement called *Integralism. Della Chiesa discreetly but repeatedly cautioned against unwarranted condemnations of well-meaning scholars. So far was Della Chiesa from espousing Modernists, however, that Pius X once referred to him as his "right arm in fighting Modernism."

Archbishop of Bologna. When the position of nuncio to Spain fell vacant (1907), Della Chiesa seemed destined for the post. Merry del Val, however, felt that his policies could be better executed if Della Chiesa were removed from the diplomatic service. With some embarrassment Pius X summoned Della Chiesa and asked him to accept the See of *Bologna. The Pontiff himself consecrated him bishop in the Sistine Chapel (Dec. 22, 1907).

Although disappointed in not realizing his desire of returning to Spain, Della Chiesa went to Bologna, a see bristling with difficulties. The city was then in turmoil because of socialist agitators. The preceding archbishop,

Pope Benedict XV, oil portrait by August Benziger.

Cardinal Svampa, had governed the see with a relaxed hand. Della Chiesa, trained in Roman legalistic precision, meant to institute system and order. Svampa had been impressive in external appearance and his successor was not; the Bolognese did not conceal their disappointment. However, the new archbishop's instinctive kindness, his pastoral solicitude, and his generosity soon canceled their first impression. He made a thorough episcopal visitation of every church, institution, and chapel in his see, often traveling on horseback to the most remote mountain villages. This project occupied his first 4 years and elicited from Pius X a very laudatory autograph. Bologna had long been a cardinalitial see, but Pius X waited 7 years before conferring on Della Chiesa the red hat (1914).

Pontificate. Within 3 months of this elevation, Pius X died (August 20). At this time, the qualities demanded in his successor included a diplomatic skill in coping with World War I, which had erupted on June 28, and a combination of strength and prudence in dealing with Integralism. The conclave was brief. Della Chiesa was not regarded at its opening as one of the leading *papabili*, but he was elected on the 10th ballot (September 3). He took the name Benedict principally to honor the last pope elected from the See of Bologna, Prospero Lambertini, Benedict XIV, who also had been an expert in jurisprudence. The coronation took place September 6, in the Sistine Chapel, on a very modest scale because of the widespread misery caused by World War I.

Curial Appointments. Benedict XV made extensive changes in the personnel of the Roman Curia. Cardinal

*Ferrata was named secretary of state, but died within 2 weeks; P. *Gasparri succeeded him. Merry del Val became secretary of the Holy Office.

Charities. Charity, especially in the alleviation of human misery, became the leitmotiv of the pontificate. For example, the Holy Father instituted an international missing persons bureau in the Vatican to reestablish contact between prisoners of war and their families. He prevailed upon Switzerland to accept ailing soldiers who had fallen prey to tuberculosis, then very prevalent. He personally selected ecclesiastics to visit the sick and the wounded and to extend to them his sympathy and blessing.

Peace. His seven-point peace note was sent to the heads of the Central and the Allied Powers (Aug. 1, 1917). It called for (1) substitution of the "moral force of right" for the law of material force, (2) simultaneous and reciprocal decrease of armaments, (3) international arbitration, (4) true freedom and community of the seas, (5) reciprocal renunciation of war indemnities, (6) evacuation and restoration of all occupied territories, and (7) examination "in a conciliatory spirit" of rival territorial claims. Most of the belligerents returned polite but equivocal replies. Austria was willing to accept the terms, Great Britain showed good will, but France expressed reservations. Foreign secretary Richard von Kühlmann in Germany did not favor a Vatican-motivated peace. Robert Lansing, U.S. Secretary of State, issued a somewhat didactic refusal. The debacle of this peace effort was perhaps the greatest disappointment that Benedict XV suffered during his pontificate. He had to close his missing persons bureau because of calumnies that it was a façade for espionage. In his introduction to the peace note, the Pope revealed that, immediately after his election to the papacy, he had resolved to observe absolute impartiality but not disinterested neutrality. But calumnies did not cease. The Central Powers referred to him as "der französische Papst"; the Allied Powers called him "le pape boche." He did not raise his voice again until after the close of the war, when his encyclical *Pacem Dei munus* (May 23, 1920) pleaded for a restoration of brotherly love.

Diplomatic Relations. The Pope worked assiduously to restore diplomatic relations with the Holy See that had been ruptured by the war. He was especially anxious to heal the breach with France. His allocution at the canonization of *Joan of Arc did much to accomplish this. When he was elected, 14 countries were represented at the Vatican; when he died the number had risen to 26.

Roman Question. The *Roman question remained important. Repeatedly the Holy Father protested against the Law of *Guarantees. Owing to his careful planning, a secret meeting took place between Benito *Mussolini and Cardinal Gasparri in the home of Count Carlo Santucci, an old friend of the Pope. Here the first decisive steps were taken that culminated in the *Lateran Pacts (1929).

Canon Law. The codification of Church law, inaugurated by Pius X and placed under the direction of Cardinal Gasparri, was completed much earlier than at first envisioned. The success of the project rose largely from Benedict XV's special interest and close supervision. The *Code of Canon Law was published on June 28, 1917.

Oriental Church. Benedict XV paved the way for a better understanding between the Oriental and the Latin Churches. On May 1, 1917, he announced the establishment of the Sacred Congregation for the *Oriental Church, with the Pope as prefect. A motu proprio, *Orientis catholici* (Oct. 15, 1917), established the *Pontifical Oriental Institute in Rome.

Pronouncements. Benedict XV wrote 12 encyclicals. His inaugural one, *Ad beatissimi Apostolorum* (Nov. 1, 1914), was a blueprint of what he hoped his pontificate would accomplish. It dealt with peace between nations, among social classes, and within the Church. He dealt with the Integralists without using the name, stating merely that of late an adjective had been affixed to the word Catholic, but that there was no need to qualify it by "fresh epithets." *Spiritus Paraclitus* (Sept. 15, 1920), marking the 15th centenary of the death of St. Jerome, pleaded for a return to the study of Holy Writ. It built on the principles laid down by Leo XIII, explaining them or contracting the latitude of their application. *Maximum illud,* an apostolic letter (Nov. 30, 1919), called for a better spiritual and intellectual preparation of missionaries and also for the formation of native clergies.

Characteristics. As the result of a birth injury, one eye, one ear, and one shoulder of Benedict XV were noticeably higher than the other. He was short, extremely thin, stoop-shouldered, somewhat bluish in complexion, and limped perceptibly. His temperament was kind and sympathetic. He was invariably approachable and frequently asserted: "Everyone has the right to see the pope." He was generous almost to a fault. The Holy See had to borrow money to bury him, so much had he depleted the treasury with his almsgiving. At times his native nervousness showed itself in eruptions of temper, against which he admitted he had had to fight all his life. When he failed, he made reparation by profuse apologies and acts of kindness. He was incapable of sustaining rancor or of harboring grudges. His humor took the form of a gentle, kindly irony.

His final illness lasted only a few days and was caused by influenza that developed into pneumonia.

Bibliography: M. C. CARLEN, *Dictionary of Papal Pronouncements: Leo XIII to Pius XII, 1878–1957* (New York 1958). W. H. PETERS, *The Life of Benedict XV* (Milwaukee 1959). H. E. G. ROPE, *Benedict XV: The Pope of Peace* (London 1940). J. SCHMIDLIN, *Papstgeschichte der neusten Zeit,* 4 v. (Munich 1933–39) v.3. A. DE WAAL, *Der neue Papst: Unser heiliger Vater Benedikt XV* (Hamm 1915). F. VISTALLI, *Benedetto XV* (Rome 1928). F. HAYWARD, *Un Pape méconnu: Benoît XV* (Tournai 1955). F. PIFFL, "The Conclaves of Benedict XV and Pius XI," *Tablet* 217 (London 1963) 1004–06, 1028–29, 1059–61. E. DEUERLEIN, "Zur Friedensaktion Papst Benedikts XV (1917)," StimZeit 155 (1955) 241–256. **Illustration credit:** Courtesy of Marieli Benziger.

[W. H. PETERS]

BENEDICT OF ANIANE, ST.

Benedictine reformer; b. Witiza, Lat. Euticius, *c.* 750; d. at the monastery of Kornelimünster near Aachen, Feb. 11, 821 (feast, Feb. 11 for *Benedictines and the Dioceses of Cologne, Aachen, and Nîmes). He came from a Visigothic noble family of Aquitaine and entered court service under *Pepin III, but left it to become a monk in 773 at the monastery of Saint-Seine near Dijon. In 779 he founded a monastery on his parental inheritance at *Aniane (Diocese of Montpellier) and became its abbot. At first inspired by the ideals of

Page from an early MS of the "Epitome" of St. Benedict of Aniane in the British Museum (Cotton MS Tiberius III, fol. 164).

Benedict has been adversely criticized for his prohibition against educating externs in the monastic schools. He aimed thereby to strengthen the contemplative character of the monasteries thus paving the way for Cluniac emphasis (overemphasis?) on the recitation of the Divine Office. Benedict is certainly responsible for the addition of 15 Psalms before the night Office and probably also for the daily recitation of the Office of the Dead. Benedict was a highly educated man and collected ancient monastic rules, which he harmonized in his *Concordia regularum.* He is possibly the author of a collection of homilies and of several works on doctrine. Some of his letters also are extant.

Bibliography: Sources. PL 103:393–664, 703–1420, works. MGEp 4:561–563, letters. J. LECLERCQ, "Les *Munimenta fidei* de S. Benoît d'Aniane," *Analecta monastica* 1 (1948) 21–74. Conclusions from Abbots' conference of 817, ed. J. SEMMLER in K. HALLINGER, ed., *Corpus consuetudinum monasticarum* 1 (Siegburg 1963) 453–481; also the so-called *Regula Benedicti Aniani,* 503–536 and *Modus poenitentiarum,* 565–582. J. SEMMLER, "Zur Überlieferung der monastischen Gesetzgebung Ludwigs des Frommen," DeutschArch 16 (1960) 309–388. *Vita,* MGS 15.1:200–220.
Literature: Hauck 2:588–614. Zimmermann KalBen 1:199–202. L. BERRA, Mercati-Pelzer DE 1:338–339. J. SEMMLER, LexThK² 2:179–180. E. BISHOP, *Liturgica historica* (Oxford 1918; repr. 1962) 211–218. S. DULCY, *La Règle de saint Benoît d'Aniane et la réforme monastique à l'époque carolingienne* (Nîmes 1935). P. SCHMITZ, *Histoire de l'ordre de Saint Benoît,* 7 v. (Maredsous 1942–56) v.1; DHGE 8:177–188; "L'Influence de S. Benoît d'Aniane dans l'histoire de l'ordre de St-Benoît," *Il monachesimo nell' alto medioevo* (Spoleto 1957) 401–415. K. HALLINGER, *Gorze-Kluny,* 2 v. (Rome 1950–51) v.2. J. WINANDY, "L'Oeuvre monastique de Saint Benoît d'Aniane," *Mélanges bénédictins* (Saint-Wandrille 1947) 235–258. **Illustration credit:** Courtesy of the Trustees of the British Museum.

[S. HILPISCH]

ancient monasticism, he led a severe penitential life but gradually he changed and began to fight for a new interpretation of the *Benedictine Rule. Numerous monasteries in western France joined with him in observing the new rule that he introduced at Aniane. Benedict enjoyed the confidence of *Louis the Pious and became his advisor on monastic affairs. In 814, at the Emperor's behest, Benedict became abbot of *Marmoutier in Alsace, then at Inden (Kornelimünster), established in the vicinity of Aachen. He strove for recognition of a uniform rule for all monasteries and for a close federation of monasteries united under a superimposed jurisdiction. Louis made him superior over all the monasteries of his kingdom, which he likewise wished to observe the same customs (*una consuetudo*) as well as the same (Benedictine) rule.

Toward that end the Emperor convoked a meeting of abbots at Aachen in July 817, which was primarily the work of Benedict and issued in the *Capitulare institutum,* the first general code for all the monasteries of one area. Louis supported the capitulary by appointing royal *missi* as inspectors of monastic observance, a provision that guaranteed the ultimate unification in rule and custom observed by the monasteries of France.

Louis the Pious was generous in assessing the obligations of the monks but extremely cautious about according them any rights. Benedict secured—for some monasteries only—the right of free election of an abbot from within the monastic community. Even so, for each abbatial election permission had to be secured—and could, of course, be withheld.

BENEDICT OF BENEVENTO, ST.,

missionary and martyr; b. Benevento, Italy; d. near Miedzyrzec, Poland, Nov. 11, 1003 (feast, Nov. 12). He was the leader of the Five Brothers—himself, John, Isaac, Matthew, and Christian—a group of Christians massacred in Poland in 1003. Benedict had been a monk of San Salvatore in Calabria, and he later took up the life of a hermit. In 1001 he was persuaded by *Bruno of Querfurt, who was eventually his biographer, to become a missionary in Poland. He and his companion John were well received by the Duke, Boleslav I (d. 1025), who built a hermitage for them. Their work prospered, and they were joined by people of the district, among them Isaac, Matthew, and Christian. On a rumor that the Duke had given them a great treasure, they were murdered one night by a former servant and his accomplices. They were buried in their hermitage, and the site soon became a center of pilgrimage. Their cult was popular in the Polish Church from an early date and was confirmed by Pope Julius II in 1508.

Bibliography: BRUNO OF QUERFURT, *Vita quinque fratrum,* ed. R. KALE in MGS 15.2:709–738. M. BARONIUS, *Vitae gesta et miracula sanctorum quinque fratrum* (Cracow 1610). J. DAVID, DHGE 8:3–5. Zimmermann KalBen 3:291–294.

[J. L. GRASSI]

BENEDICT BISCOP, ST.,

Benedictine abbot, known also as Baducing, founder of the joint monasteries of SS. Peter and Paul at *Wearmouth and *Jarrow; b. c. 628; d. Jan. 12, 690 (feast, Jan. 12). He was of noble birth, a thane of King Oswiu of Northumbria. In 653 he renounced the world, traveling to Rome to learn more about the Church's teaching and institutions.

*Wilfrid of York was his companion as far as Lyons, and thence he traveled alone, returning after some months filled with enthusiasm for Roman institutions, art, and learning. He revisited Rome in 665, later becoming a monk at *Lérins; after 2 years he went back to Rome, just in time to conduct the newly consecrated Abp. *Theodore of Canterbury to England. After acting temporarily as abbot of SS. Peter and Paul, Canterbury (*see* SAINT AUGUSTINE, ABBEY OF), he again visited Rome in 671, returning laden with books. Soon afterward he established a monastery at Wearmouth on land given by King Ecgfrith, building a stone church with the assistance of glaziers and masons from Gaul. At the new monastery he introduced the *Benedictine Rule, but with certain modifications. He was back in Rome in 678 with his kinsman Ceolfrith. This time he brought back John, precentor of St. Peter's, to instruct the English in Church music. In 682 he founded the monastery at Jarrow, returning to Rome in 687 to bring back more books and church furnishings. Back in Jarrow, he fell ill and died after a short illness. He did much to bring England into contact with western European civilization, while the magnificent library he gathered together made *Bede's work possible.

Bibliography: BEDE, *Hist. eccl.* 4.18; 5.19, 24, and *Historia abbatum,* ed. C. PLUMMER, 2 v. (Oxford 1896). W. R. W. STEPHENS, DNB 2:214–216. Zimmermann KalBen 1:71–75. W. LEVISON, *England and the Continent in the Eighth Century* (Oxford 1946). E. S. DUCKETT, *Anglo-Saxon Saints and Scholars* (New York 1947).

[B. COLGRAVE]

BENEDICT II OF CLUSE, VEN.,

Benedictine reformer; b. Toulouse, c. 1030; d. Cluse, May 31, 1091. When he was very young his father confided him to the Abbey of Saint-Hilaire at Carcassone, France. Later, seeking a more perfect religious observance, he retired to the monastery of San Michele della Chiusa (Cluse) in Piedmont, Italy. He succeeded as abbot in 1066 and was consecrated by Pope Alexander II himself. He then began the reform of his abbey, insisting on humility, asceticism, and manual labor. When *Gregory VII became Pope, Benedict's bishop, Cunibert of Turin, a partisan of Emperor *Henry IV, devastated the properties of Cluse and put the abbey under interdict. Because he was faithful to Gregory, Benedict had to flee. The rest of his life was disturbed by strife with William, successor to Cunibert, and Bp. Gregory of Vercelli. Benedict's life, written by William, one of his disciples, attributes visions and miracles to him.

Bibliography: Mabillon AS 9:696–715. PL 150:1447–50, 1459–88. MGS 12:196–208. G. SCHWARTZ and E. ABEGG, "Das Kloster San Michele della Chiusa," NeuesArch 45 (1924) 235–255. F. BAIX, DHGE 8:200–203.

[É. BROUETTE]

BENEDICT THE LEVITE,

or Deacon Benedict, the name of the unknown author of a collection of forged capitularies (1,319 specimens) belonging to the group of the *False Decretals (Pseudo-Isidorian forgeries). The collection is appended as bks. 5 to 7 to the four books of the genuine collection of Ansegis. The last of the additions may have been written at the time of the Pseudo-Isidorian Decretals, but all the rest must be dated earlier, about 850, and come probably from Le Mans. About one-fourth of them are genuine, as such, but forged in this text. The majority reproduce genuine, notably ecclesiastical, sources falsified into Frankish imperial laws and in the process subjected to repeated interpolations. Benedict sought to give the impression that the laws were the product of a collaboration between state and ecclesiastical authorities. The collection embraces almost all areas of Canon Law. It was calculated to remedy the sad state of the Frankish Church. Dominant principles are freedom of the Church and independence of its hierarchy.

Bibliography: Editions. F. H. KNUST, MGL 2.2:17–139. PL 97:698–912. Literature. E. SECKEL, "Studien zu B. L.," pts. 1–8.3 NeuesArch 26 (1900) 37–72; 29 (1904) 275–331; 31 (1905) 59–139, 238–239; 34 (1909) 319–381; 35 (1910) 105–191, 433–539; 39 (1914) 327–431; 40 (1915) 15–130; 41 (1916) 157–263; pts. 8.4–5, ed. J. JUNCKER, ZSavRGKan 23 (1934) 269–377; 24 (1935) 1–112; "B. L. decurtatus et excerptus" in *Festschrift für Heinrich Brunner* (Munich 1914) 377–464. Fournier-LeBras 1: 145–171, 190–192, 202–209. F. BAIX, DDC 2:400–406. S. WILLIAMS, "The Pseudo-Isidorian Problem Today," *Speculum* 29 (1954) 702–707. R. GRAND, "Nouvelles remarques sur l'origine du Pseudo-Isidore source du Décret de Gratien," *Studia Gratiana* 3 (1955) 1–16. R. BUCHNER, RGG³ 1:1032–33. G. MAY, "Die Infamie bei B. L.," *Österreichisches Archiv für Kirchenrecht* 11 (1960) 16–36. H. FUHRMANN, "Die Fälschungen im Mittelalter," HistZ 197 (1963) 529–554.

[G. MAY]

BENEDICT THE MOOR, ST.,

Franciscan lay brother, patron of the Negroes of North America; b. San Fratello, near Messina, Italy, 1526; d. Palermo, Italy, April 4, 1589 (feast, April 4). He was the son of Christopher and Diana Manasseri, Negro slaves converted to Christianity after they had been brought to Sicily from Africa. As a field hand, he was given his liberty when he attained the age of 18, and thereafter he earned his living as a day laborer. He generously shared his small wages with the poor and spent much of his leisure time caring for the sick. Among the beneficiaries of his charity he became known as "The Holy Negro." But there is also evidence that he was often the object of ridicule because of his race and his servile origin. While still a young man he joined a company of hermits who lived in the hills near San Fratello under the direction of Jerome Lanza, a nobleman who had forsaken the world for the solitary life. When Jerome died his followers chose Benedict as their new superior, and under his leadership the group prospered. When in 1562 Pope Pius IV ordered independent groups of hermits incorporated into the established religious orders, Benedict chose to enter the Order of Friars Minor of the Observance as a lay brother. For some years after his reception into the order he was employed as cook at the Friary of St. Mary of Jesus in Palermo. Although he could neither read nor write, he was chosen in 1578 as guardian of the Palermo friary. After serving one term in this office, he was appointed master of novices. An austere man, he was granted extraordinary gifts of prayer; his counsel was sought by persons of every class; and the fame of his sanctity spread throughout Sicily. Toward the end of his life he asked to be relieved of all offices in the order and he resumed his duties as cook. At the age of 63 he contracted a severe illness, and after receiving the Last Rites with intense fervor, he died at the exact hour he had predicted. He was buried in the friary church in Palermo. In 1611 King Philip III of Spain provided in the same church a new shrine to which the saint's incorrupt remains were transferred and where they are still venerated by the faithful. Immediately upon Benedict's death a vigorous cult developed. His veneration became especially popular in Italy, Spain,

St. Benedict the Moor, 16th-century polychromed wood statue in the museum at Valladolid, Spain.

and Latin America; and the city of Palermo chose him as its heavenly protector. He was beatified by Pope Benedict XIV in 1743 and canonized by Pope Pius VII in 1807. Within the Franciscan Order his feast is celebrated on April 3.

Bibliography: "Bulla canonizationis beati Benedicti a S. Philadelphio laici professi Ord. minorum," *Acta Ordinis Fratrum Minorum* 26 (1907) 214–222. M. ALLIBERT, *Life of St. Benedict the Moor* (London 1895). LEON DE CLARY, *Lives of the Saints and Blessed of the Three Orders of St. Francis,* 4 v. (Taunton, Eng. 1885–87) 2:14–31. B. NICOLOSI, *Vita di San Benedetto di San Fratello* (Palermo 1907). **Illustration credit:** MAS, Barcelona.

[C. LYNCH]

BENEDICT OF PETERBOROUGH, abbot, chronicler of Thomas Becket; d. Peterborough Abbey, England, 1193. He was very probably a *Benedictine at Christ Church, *Canterbury; hence his writings on Thomas *Becket are most likely eyewitness accounts. In 1174 he became chancellor to Becket's successor, Abp. *Richard of Canterbury, and in 1175, prior of Christ Church. In 1177 he was elected abbot at *Peterborough Abbey, a post vacant since Abbot Waterville was deposed, 2 years earlier. Though he found the abbey heavily in debt, Benedict was able during his 15 years as abbot to restore solvency. A notable builder, he completed a portion of the nave of the abbey church and built certain chapels as well as the great abbey gate. He was a friend of King *Richard I, the Lion Heart, and, like most of the leading abbots of his day, was called on to play an active part in government service. In a somewhat enthusiastic biography (ed. J. Sparke, *Historiae Anglicanae scriptores varii,* 1723), Robert Swafham, a monk of the abbey, describes Benedict's efforts to build up the Peterborough library by having the monks copy a number of manuscripts. Undoubtedly one of these was the valuable *Gesta Henrici II* (London B.M., Cotton MS Julius A.xi), a chronicle of the reigns of Kings *Henry II and Richard I long ascribed to Benedict's pen but now generally recognized as the first draft of *Roger of Hoveden's *Chronica* (ed. W. Stubbs, 2 v., RollsS 49). Benedict wrote a *passio* of the martyrdom of Becket; and although the complete work is lost, substantial portions of it were incorporated by the compiler of the *Quadrilogus* (*Materials . . . T. Becket* 4:386–408 or 2:1–20). As the second section of the *passio,* Benedict composed an account of the *Miracula* of Becket, but this has survived as a separate work (*ibid.* 2:21–281).

Bibliography: *Materials for the History of Thomas Becket,* ed. J. C. ROBERTSON and J. B. SHEPPARD, 7 v. (RollsS 67; 1875–85) 2:xix–xxi. BHL 8170–75. E. M. THOMPSON, DNB 2:213–214. D. M. STENTON, "Roger of Howden and 'Benedict,'" EngHistRev 68 (1953) 574–582.

[M. J. HAMILTON]

BENEDICT THE POLE, *Franciscan missionary and interpreter, fl. 1245–47. In March 1245 Pope Innocent IV sent *John da Pian del Carpine to the Great Khan of the *Mongols. Leaving Lyons in mid-April, he went to Prague, where he was joined by Stephen of Bohemia, and then to Wrocław (Breslau), Poland, where Benedict became his companion and interpreter. Stephen became ill and went only to Cumania, but Benedict and John reached the camp of Batu Khan in February 1246, and the camp of Kuyuk on July 26. They saw Kuyuk proclaimed Great Khan August 24, and departed November 13. They reached Batu Khan May 9, 1247, then returned to Lyons via Cologne. It was in Cologne that Benedict gave an account of their journey to a prelate and to a scholastic, who wrote it down. Thus John of St. Anthony included Benedict among the Franciscan authors.

See also MISSIONS, HISTORY OF (MEDIEVAL).

Bibliography: Annales S. Pantaleonis Coloniensis, MGS 22:542. Critical ed. of B.'s account in *Sinica franciscana,* ed. A. VAN DEN WYNGAERT, 5 v. (Quaracchi-Florence 1929–54) 1:131–143. Good list of works in Jean de Plancarpin, *Histoire des Mongols,* ed. and tr. C. SCHMITT (Paris 1961). A. VAN DEN WYNGAERT, DHGE 8:250.

[J. CAMBELL]

BENEDICTINE RULE

The Rule composed *c.* 530 to 540 by St. *Benedict of Nursia when he was abbot of *Monte Cassino. It is a relatively short document, comprising a prologue and 73 chapters, of which ch. 67 to 73 may be an afterthought. Its directions for the formation, government, and administration of a *monastery and for the spiritual and daily life of its monks have been found valid and practical for more than 14 centuries. It gives advice to the abbot and other officials and outlines the principal monastic virtues such as obedience (ch. 5), silence (6), and humility (7). The Rule provides for an autonomous, self-contained community (66) and gives instructions for the election of an abbot (64); for the reception, training, and profession of novices (58–60); and for the appointment and duties of prior (65), cellarer (31), novice-master (58), guestmaster (53), and councillors (3). Psalmody and prayers at the Divine Office (*opus Dei*) are regulated in detail (8–19). Food (39–41, 56), sleep (22), clothing (55), and daily work (48) have their chapters. The monastery of the Rule is a microcosm containing inmates of every age and condition, from children and boys to old men (37), oblates (59), converted adults (58), former serfs (2), clerics (60, 62), monks from other houses (61), and sons of men of means and position (58–9). The waking hours are divided almost equally between three occupations: prayer in common, religious reading (*lectio divina,* 48), and manual work of domestic, craft (57), and horticultural (48) character.

A unique feature of the Rule is the space given to practical and spiritual advice. The prologue and chapters on humility and obedience and the chapters outlining the abbot's duties (2, 27, 64) are recognized masterpieces of wisdom. Though strictly impersonal, the Rule has impressed readers from the time of *Gregory the Great as the reflection of a wise, holy, firm, and paternal character in an author who can combine strict principles with moderation and humanity. His use of

Folio from the St. Gallen manuscript of the Benedictine Rule (MS 914, fol. 103) thought to be a copy of the autograph sent to Charlemagne from Monte Cassino.

common feeling and natural inclination as criteria of moral goodness is notable in an age influenced by the rigorist teaching of St. *Augustine. St. Benedict indeed deprecates extreme severity more than once, and in the course of centuries, his authority has been invoked, not always validly, on the side of condescension to human weakness. Among the virtues, humility, obedience, and stability stand out; the monk's life is a return from disobedience in sin to obedience in the service of God under an abbot who teaches and follows the Rule. No works, pursuits or ends outside the monastery are considered; there is no connection with any other establishment or superior save the local bishop. This lack of disciplinary sanctions and constitutional machinery, inevitable in a document of the 6th century, has sometimes been seen as a weakness in the Rule. Yet it has served to maintain abbatial authority and the autonomy of the individual monastery throughout the ages. It has been well said that the Rule presupposes and needs for its viability an abbot of unassailable virtue. No provision is made for new foundations, but varied climatic conditions are envisaged (55). The regulations for recruitment and profession, and the integration of Prime and Compline into the Office, have passed from the Rule into universal practice. St. Benedict used Eastern rules, patristic maxims, the work of *Cassian, and contemporary codes. He is recognized as having given to the West the wisdom of the desert adapted to a fully cenobitical life and to the capabilities of normal Western men.

Authorship. This was unquestioned until 1938, when Dom A. Génestout argued that the Rule was closely based on the anonymous *Regula Magistri* (PL 88:943–1052), of which the prologue and ch. 1 to 10 are almost identical with the prologue and ch. 1 to 7 of the Rule, with frequent further resemblances. In the long discussion that followed, doubt was cast also upon the very existence of the Rule in the 6th century, and of any Rule composed by St. Benedict. These extremes of skepticism have been abandoned, but it is now widely granted that the Rule of the Master preceded, and was in part adopted by, St. Benedict. In any case, the firm outline of the liturgical, administrative, and spiritual life, together with the characteristics noted above, are the achievement of Benedict alone. The Rule as we know it, and not the Rule of the Master, is the document that gave form to European monachism and has been found valuable by every generation of monks (*see* MONASTICISM; BENEDICTINE SPIRITUALITY).

Text. The Rule is written in the vernacular Latin of the 6th century, and is preserved in countless medieval MSS of which Oxford Bodley Hatton 48 (*c.* 700, from Worcester) is the earliest. For the last 7 centuries a vulgate text has been current in which classical orthography and grammar have been adopted. Modern critical study has followed Ludwig *Traube (d. 1907), who showed that MS 914 of *Sankt Gallen is a careful copy of the reputed autograph from Monte Cassino sent to Charlemagne; but another early tradition represented by Oxford Hatton 48 still presents a problem. These modern editions may be noted: Abbot E. C. *Butler (Freiburg im Breisgau 1912; 2d ed. 1935), the first to display the literary sources; P. Linderbauer (Metten 1922; Bonn 1928) with valuable philological notes; and P. Schmitz (2d ed. Maredsous 1955), with a linguistic essay by C. Mohrmann. The fully critical (though crit-

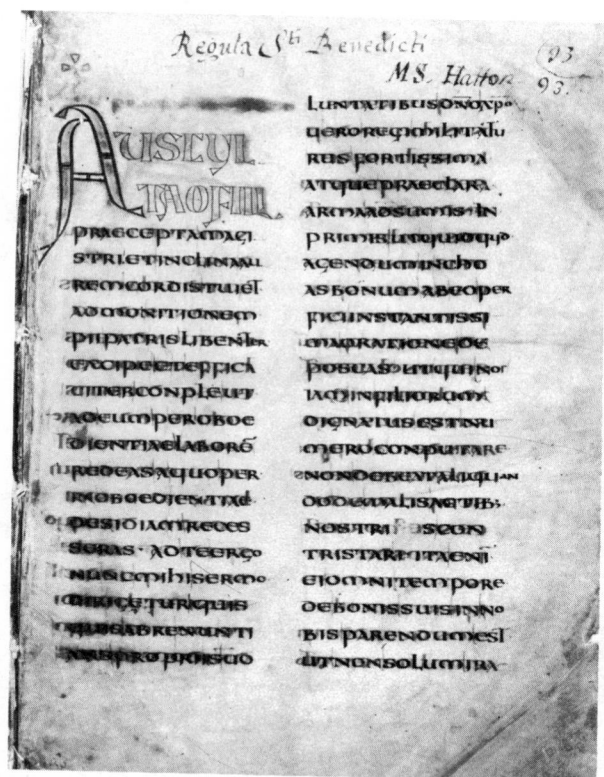

First folio in the manuscript of the Benedictine Rule (MS Bod. Hatton 48), c. 700, from Worcester.

icized) edition by R. Hanslik, CSEL 74 (1960), has a full discussion of MSS, a verbal concordance, and valuable indexes. The best English translation, with notes, is by J. McCann (London 1952).

Commentaries. These are numerous whether learned or devotional. The commentary of *Paul the Deacon (778–780) is an invaluable witness to early tradition; that of Dom Augustin *Calmet (1732) is excellent, and sums up the learning of the *Maurists and others. Of modern works that of Abbot P. Delatte of Solesmes is standard (Paris 1913; Eng. tr. J. McCann, London, 2d ed. 1950).

Bibliography: The best general work on the Rule in all its aspects is E. C. BUTLER, *Benedictine Monachism* (2d ed. London 1924; reprinted Cambridge, Eng. 1961). For the *Regula Magistri* controversy, see AmBenRev 1 (1950) 11–36. D. KNOWLES, *Great Historical Enterprises* (Edinburgh 1963). **Illustration credit:** Fig. 1. Leonard Von Matt. Fig. 2. Reproduced by permission of the Bodleian Library, Oxford.

[M. D. KNOWLES]

BENEDICTINE SPIRITUALITY

The word "Benedictine" is relatively modern; it scarcely existed before the 17th century. It evokes the name of St. Benedict, who lived in the 6th century, together with all those who have been inspired by the Benedictine Rule and belong to the Benedictine spiritual tradition. Giovanni *Bona, who had been abbot general of the Cistercian Order (d. 1674), wrote: "St. Anselm and St. Bernard were both Benedictines" ["Anselmus et Bernardus, ambo benedictini," *Epistolae Selectae*, ed. R. Sala (Turin 1755) 152]. On the other hand, St. Benedict himself is only the representative of monastic spirituality in its ensemble.

Monastic Spirituality. The thing that distinguishes monks from other religious in the Catholic Church is not a matter of monastic institutions or observances, because all of these are found in other forms or religious life. It is rather the fact that monastic existence is a form of religious life having no secondary end. It is specified solely by consecration to God and sanctioned by public vows. Tradition assigns no other end to the life of a monk than to "seek God" or "to live for God alone," an ideal that can be attained only by a life of penance and prayer. The first and fundamental manifestation of such a vocation is a real separation from the world. All monks are by definition "solitaries," and this is the original meaning of their name, which comes from the Greek word *monachos*, derived from *monos*, to which corresponds the Latin *solus* (alone). The second characteristic of the monastic vocation is that it demands a life of which a privileged part is given to prayer. Private prayer is traditionally exercised under the form of meditative reading of Holy Scripture and of authors who explain it, according to the three phases designated by the words reading, meditation, and prayer. In monastic life public prayer is only one observance among those which help the soul to go to God. It is not one of the distinguishing characteristics of the monastic life. Only in recent times and especially since the 19th century has it occupied a more important place in monastic life than in the observance of the majority of nonmonastic religious congregations, with the consequence that it is now considered a special feature of monastic spirituality.

The ascetic and contemplative orientation of the monastic life was accompanied historically by such cultural activities and manifestations as were compatible with separation from the world, mortification, and a life of contemplative prayer.

St. Benedict and Monachism. The textual sources of our knowledge of St. Benedict go back to the 6th century. At this period monachism had been in existence for a very long time. In the East it dates to the 3rd century with St. Anthony, and in the West to the 4th century with St. Martin and other founders of monasteries. It was not founded by a particular saint. It appeared little by little wherever the Church took root, a spontaneous manifestation of the Holy Spirit urging Christians to become monks in response to the counsel given by Jesus in the Gospel: "If you wish to be perfect, go, sell your possessions . . . , follow me . . ." (Mt 19.21). Thus when St. Benedict appeared monachism was already solidly implanted in Egypt, Syria, Palestine—the whole East—and in Ireland, Gaul, Italy, Spain, and Africa in the West. The term was applied to two principal types: the hermits who lived alone or in small unorganized groups, and the cenobites who lived in community. There were also other forms of monastic life, but they were more or less eccentric in comparison with the two main types and sometimes led to abuse.

The name of St. Benedict is connected with two texts: Book 2 of the *Dialogues* of St. Gregory the Great, and the Benedictine Rule. The "Life" of St. Benedict that St. Gregory narrates includes some nonhistorical elements that, however, suppose the existence of a person called Benedict, whose historicity is confirmed by the fact that his cult goes back to very ancient times. We know little about his life. The only certain date is that

The word "Ausculta" cut from a German manuscript of the second half of the 13th century. In the lower half of the capital "A" St. Benedict reads his Rule to a group of monks; in the upper portion is enthroned the Madonna.

of his conversation with Sabinus, Bishop of Canosa, in December 546, probably a short time before his own death. He had founded monasteries at Subiaco, then at Monte Cassino and elsewhere in Italy. In treating of him, St. Gregory illustrates the ideal "man of God," the spiritual father who is entirely under the guidance of the Holy Spirit and who teaches monks to practice detachment from the world and from themselves and to seek God in a community life marked by obedience, mortification, and prayer.

St. Gregory says that he wrote a rule. Less than a century after the death of St. Benedict there is a rule attributed to him, and it is the same as the one we call today the Benedictine Rule. Its attribution to Benedict has been subjected to discussion by scholars of our time. When the researches now in progress have reached their conclusion, it seems very probable that the traditional attribution will be confirmed. The principal question is whether the Benedictine Rule depends on another rule of the same period called the *Regula Magistri*. Many scholars today think that it does. It depends also on Cassian and some other patristic sources. Be that as it may, its author gave proof of a very great unity of concept and expression. He realized a very personal work that shows him to have been a genius and a saint.

What gives this rule its exceptional quality has commonly been called its "discretion," in the double sense of the word: discernment and moderation. It sets up a framework of life, an institution, of which the essential and constitutive elements are firmly determined: life in common under the government of a superior called an abbot, who has the help of a prior and other officials and takes counsel of the whole assembly of brethren. As for details, the legislator left something to the discernment and initiative of the superior. Furthermore, he avoids anything that would be excessive or beyond the capacity of the average monk. By his attention to discretion and moderation, he merely followed the practice already established in the Eastern and Western monachism that preceded him. He neither innovated nor broke with tradition. He simply organized a form of cenobitic life in complete conformity with the demands of the monastic vocation, which is but integral Christian life. Thus the text of the Rule refers frequently to the "divine commandments" and often cites the Bible, particularly the Gospel. Its principal source is the Word of God.

Evolution of the Rule. The diffusion of the Benedictine Rule in the West was slow. The Rule acted and penetrated not as a legislative text imposed from without by authority but rather as a leaven by virtue of its intrinsic power. Other rules were drawn up in the 6th century. In the 7th and 8th centuries the Benedictine Rule was often combined with others, especially that of St. Columban (d. 615). Little by little, however, the Benedictine became the principal rule, particularly in the Anglo-Saxon countries and in Italy. Yet even for the 10th century we have no proof that any of the numerous monasteries in Rome lived according to this rule. And where it was adopted, it was looked upon as a venerable text but not necessarily requiring observance in all its prescriptions. It was considered as proposing a spiritual program, while daily life was regulated by "Customaries," to which succeeded, from the beginning of the 16th century, "Declarations" and "Constitutions" as well as the "Ceremonial." Even the Cistercians, who in the 12th century had intended to return to the observance of the Rule, added numerous statutes to it from the very beginning. This does not mean that the Rule had become a text of the past and a dead document. It continued to live and to vivify, but its very fecundity, its inexhaustible youth—fruits of its discretion—explain how it was able to inspire different realizations. More than a founder in the juridical sense of the word, its author had been an educator, or better, a spiritual father, and he aimed at forming consciences capable of spiritual liberty. He did not intend to impose uniformity; he foresaw and intended diversity and reserved to each monastery the possibility of adapting its prescriptions to various circumstances, provided the essential values of a monachism were safeguarded.

The principles of evolution just recalled enable us to understand how within one and the same Benedictine spiritual tradition there could appear and subsist different tendencies, the two principal of which we can characterize as follows. On the one hand the monastic life, because it is separated from the tumult of the world, demands and favors a certain stability. We speak of monastic "foundations." This continuity is also a principle of material prosperity and expansion, which can become a danger for the ascetical and contemplative character of monachism. On the other hand, to safeguard separation from the world there are monks who insist on the prophetic character, so to speak, of their life. Protesting against the dangers that prosperity represents for spiritual enterprises, they insist on the need of poverty, austerity, and the contemplative life, and devote themselves to humble labors. This sort of dialectic causing monks to oscillate between the different forms that the realization of their vocation can take has marked the whole history of Benedictine spirituality.

Evidences of the Evolution. In order to recall briefly the stages of this history, we can cite the men and monasteries associated with its principal dates. The writings of St. Gregory the Great have exercised a constant influence on the monastic spirituality of the West. In the 7th century the Venerable Bede knew the Benedictine Rule. It was known by St. Boniface and the monks and nuns who came from insular Britain to live the monastic life on the Continent, especially in the Germanic countries. A certain number among them, being motivated either by desire of ascetical peregrination—that is, of voluntary exile—or by force of circumstances, or in answer to a call from Church authority, or again by reason of a personal and exceptional vocation to apostolic action, were led into the work of evangelization. Some became bishops. But the idea that this work was part of the monastic vocation never obtruded itself. The principal means by which the influence of the monks radiated outward was the *monastic schools.

At the beginning of the 9th century St. Benedict of Aniane (d. 821) sought to impose observance of the Benedictine Rule throughout the Carolingian Empire. A little later two important commentaries on the Rule were composed: that of Smaragdus, Abbot of St. Mihiel, composed about 817, and that of Hildemar, written shortly after 845, of which some scattered recensions exist in France, Germany, and Italy. In the 10th century the Rule plays a certain role in reforms attached to the names of the abbeys of Fleury in Gaul, St. Gerard of Brogne in Lorraine, and St. Dunstan and St. Ethelwold in England. Not long after, two of the principal centers of reform will be the abbeys of Gorze in Lorraine (reformed 933) and Cluny in Burgundy (founded 909). Cluny, thanks to a line of holy abbots, to an exceptional literary and artistic production, and to an extensive influence in Gaul, Italy, England, and Spain, as well as some relations with monasteries of the Empire, spread and illustrated a form of monastic life that apart from certain variations was almost the same everywhere.

In the course of the 11th century and particularly in the great community of Cluny itself, choral prayer became highly developed, but without excluding reading, private prayer, or the work of copyists together with the diffusion of its cultural and spiritual influence.

Prosperity and ties with temporal society gradually led many monasteries, especially the larger, to depart more or less from certain fundamental observances required by the Rule, notably separation from the world, real poverty, and manual labor. Certain movements of reform arose at the beginning of the 11th century in favor of these observances. Such was the case in Italy with the movement flowing from the influence of St. Romuald (d. 1027) at Camaldoli and elsewhere, and illustrated by St. Peter Damian (d. 1072), who gave to his action an orientation clearly and constantly eremetical. The same is true of the reform of St. John Gualbert at Vallombrosa; also of the Cistercian movement, which spread throughout Europe in the 12th century and was illustrated above all by St. Bernard of Clairvaux (d. 1153). Between the spiritual masters of this new or renewed monachism and those of traditional monachism—such as John of Fécamp (d. 1078), Rupert of Deutz (d. 1129), Peter the Venerable, Abbot of Cluny (d. 1156), Geoffrey of Admont (d. 1165), and Peter of Celle (d. 1183)—there was a unity in the conception of the monastic ideal. Observances vary, but monastic spirituality remains the same and is essentially contemplative. Moreover the Benedictine tradition has frequently presented examples of spiritual men, many of them venerated as saints, who in the line of this vocation have sought to unite themselves to God by the eremetical or solitary life, normally in dependence on their abbot and in the neighborhood of their monastery. The Cistercian Order reinforced the eremetical character of the cenobitical life itself. For all, the ideal remained "solitude of heart" with God, guaranteed by the "order of charity" in the communitary institution.

From the 13th century, monasteries felt the influence of spiritual movements coming from nonmonastic sources. The *devotio moderna is an example. In this, affective piety and the contemplative study of the mysteries of God were no longer so strictly united as in the preceding centuries, in which the patristic spirit had been preserved. The authors of the 15th and 16th centuries, Jean of Kastl (d. after 1410), Louis Barbo (d. 1443), Garcia of Cisneros (d. 1510), and Louis of Blois (d. 1566), appealed to methods of prayer and ascesis that were foreign to monastic tradition. Yet all maintained the contemplative character of the monastic life. To promote reform, certain congregations were formed, such as those of St. Justine of Padua in Italy, Bursfeld in Germany, Valladolid in Spain, Chezal-Benoît and Saint-Vanne and Saint-Maur in France. In England Dom Augustine Baker (d. 1641) published his great work *Holy Wisdom*.

By this time clericalization of monasteries had become accentuated, giving rise in the 17th century to a controversy between Mabillon, defending a program of clerical studies, and Rancé, adhering more nearly to the traditional concept. Rancé in 1683 published his great work *De la Sainteté et des devoirs de la vie monastique*, which, in spite of certain extremes, sounds a clearly traditional note.

In the 19th century monachism continued to develop in various countries, especially in Central Europe, according to orientations inherited from the baroque period. In countries where it had been suppressed, it was restored mainly along lines of inspiration inherited from the end of the Middle Ages. Such is the case particularly at Solesmes with Dom Guéranger, at Beuron with Dom Maurus Wolter, and at Pierre-qui-Vire with Père Muard. Dom P. Delatte published in 1913 his *Commentary on the Rule*, which was full of balanced spiritual doctrine. Dom C. Butler in his work *Benedictine Monachism*, which appeared in 1919, proposes a concept founded in part on ideas not justified by the sources, such as that the monastery should be a family, or that St. Benedict had wished to break with ancient tradition. Dom I. Herwegen (d. 1946) wrote two books

in which reconstructions of the same kind were found, particularly that of the abbatial authority as inspired by the Roman notion of the *paterfamilias*.

From the middle of the 20th century there appeared in Europe, America, Africa, and elsewhere foundations that, drawing their inspiration from more ancient sources, tended to return to forms of monastic life that are simpler, more contemplative, and put more stress on poverty. The solid book of Dom A. de Vogüe on *The Community and the Abbot in the Rule of St. Benedict* (1961) reestablished exact perspectives on several important points. In the U.S., Thomas Merton helped to throw light upon certain authentic values of monachism, and Dom Wilfrid Tunink, in his work *Vision of Peace: The Wisdom of St. Benedict and His Rule* (New York 1962), proposed an interpretation of the Rule founded on its actual text and it principal source, Cassian.

Conclusion: Influence. If the influence of the Benedictine Rule was slow in spreading during the early Middle Ages, the influence of monachism nevertheless has been constant, universal, and important. In great part it fashioned Western Christian culture until the end of the 12th century. Thereafter, monastic writings did not cease to be read by the religious of the new orders, Franciscans, Dominicans, and others, and later by the Jesuits. Nevertheless, monastic influence was on the decline. In the 19th century and the first half of the 20th it made itself felt especially in the liturgical revival. Today it contributes to the renaissance of a Catholic culture of a patristic type.

Bibliography: J. WINANDY, "Benedictine Spirituality," *Some Schools of Catholic Spirituality*, ed. J. G. GAUTIER, tr. K. SULLIVAN (New York 1959), the best overall picture. J. LECLERCQ, *Aux Sources de la spiritualité occidentale* (Paris 1964), 6th to 12th centuries. J. LECLERCQ et al., *La Spiritualité du moyen âge* (Paris 1961), overall view of the Middle Ages. M. WOLTER, *The Principles of Monasticism*, tr. B. A. SAUSE (St. Louis 1962), rich collection of sources. **Illustration credit:** National Gallery of Art, Washington, D.C., Rosenwald Collection.

[J. LECLERCQ]

BENEDICTINES

The Order of St. Benedict (OSB) signifies not a centralized institute but the confederated congregations of monks and nuns following the Rule of St. Benedict (*see* BENEDICTINE RULE). Each monastery is an autonomous family, bound by only weak links to other monasteries of the same congregation and by no juridical ties to the rest of the confederation.

St. *Benedict of Nursia, in his 6th-century rule, legislated for the fully cenobitic community, which should constitute a family under its abbot, elected for life by the monks. The vow of stability bound the monk to the monastery of his profession; that of *conversatio morum* obliged him to the practice of the evangelical counsels as a cenobite. The daily activity consisted of the public worship of God, serious reading, and manual labor. Everything, including asceticism, was subject to the abbot's discretion. The spiritual program, grounded on obedience, recollection, and humility, and flexible enough to satisfy all degrees of generosity, was essentially the total living of the Gospel. Benedict is known to have founded only *Subiaco, *Monte Cassino, and Terracina, but his fame may have induced other Italian monasteries to adopt his rule. Whether or not *Cassiodorus introduced it at Vivarium, his program of

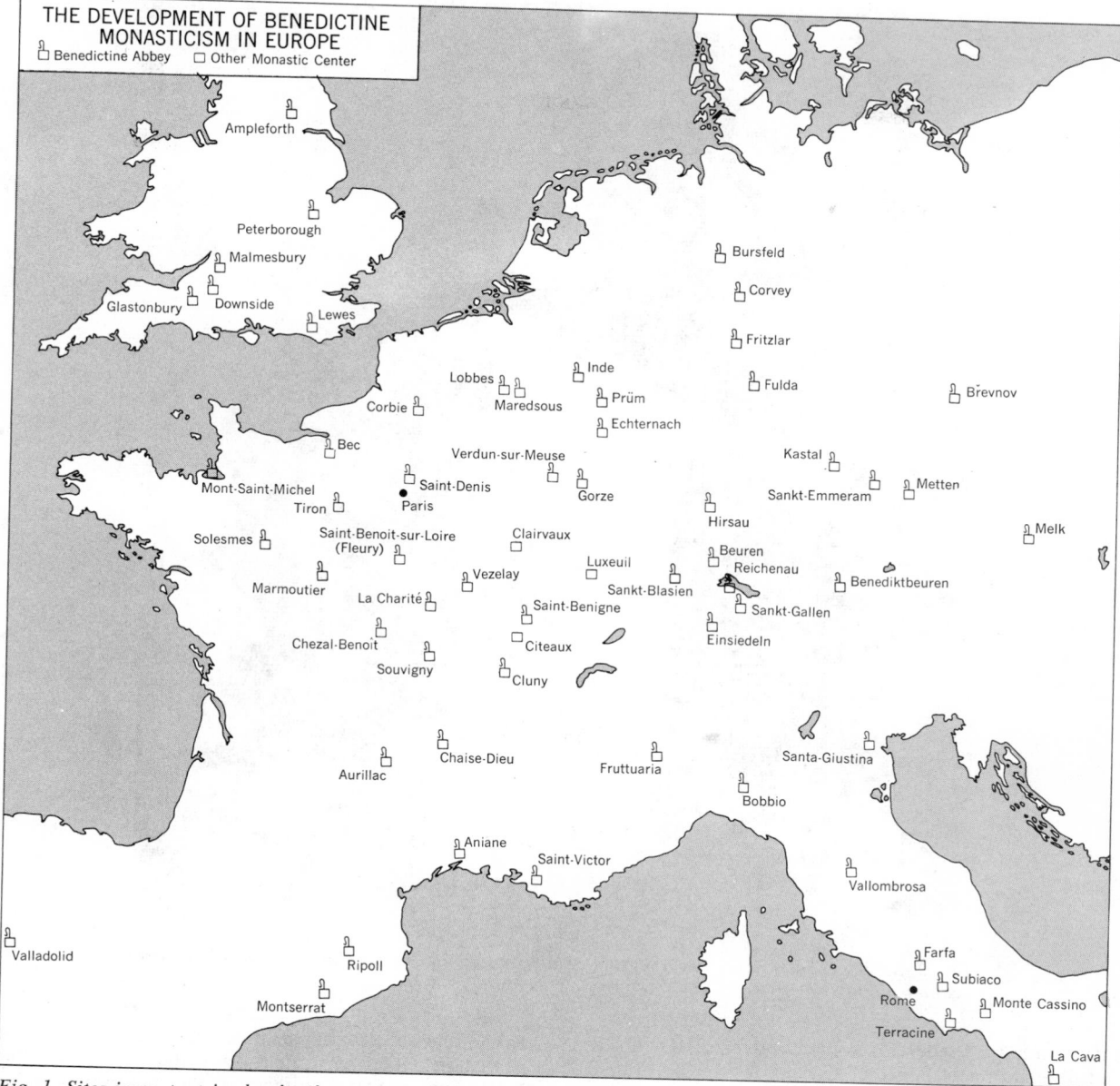

Fig. 1. Sites important in the development of the Benedictine Order in Europe.

intellectual activity quickly grafted itself onto Benedictinism throughout Europe.

The Lombard invasion of 568 virtually destroyed every sort of monachism in Italy. Monte Cassino fell about 577, but the community escaped to Rome, thereby enabling the future Pope Gregory the Great, recently become a monk, to make the acquaintance of the Benedictine Rule, which he then adopted for the monasteries he had founded. Through his *Dialogues* Gregory advanced Benedict's fame in the West and prepared the spread of the rule. The wisdom and moderation of the rule itself, as well as the missionary zeal of the monks and the papal patronage, were the chief factors contributing to the preeminence so quickly acquired by the Benedictine Rule in Latin Christendom. By 800 it had supplanted most other observances. By the same date most monks were priests and many of them had become bishops. Intellectual work came more and more into

favor, and manual labor was left to illiterate lay monks. The very numerous monasteries were centers for the civilizing of the neighborhood as well as houses of worship; hence they were sources of the Western Christian culture that was coming to birth.

Earliest Expansion, 596–814. In 596 Gregory launched the rule on its career when he sent some 40 monks to convert the Anglo-Saxons. Their superior, *Augustine, became the first archbishop of *Canterbury. Despite numerous setbacks, the work progressed, and sees and monasteries were founded. Penetrating northward, the Benedictines met Irish monks from *Iona, who had arrived in Northumbria in 634. The tension produced by the different disciplinary usages was resolved in 663 with the triumph of the Roman Benedictine tradition. By 686 all the Anglo-Saxon kingdoms had accepted the faith. Flourishing schools became the sources of a brilliant culture, which reached

Fig. 2. St. Benedict receives the monastic habit from St. Romanus, illumination in an 11th-century manuscript from Monte Cassino (Vat. Cod. lat. 1202).

its zenith in *Bede. En route to Britain, the mission of 596 had made Benedictinism known in the Frankish kingdom, where the predominant monastic influence was that of the Irish monk *Columban. But his harsh observance lost its prestige after his death in 615, and from 629 it was supplemented and eventually supplanted by Benedict's monasticism. The transfer of Benedict's relics from the desolate site of Monte Cassino to *Saint-Benoît-sur-Loire (*c.* 672) gave to the latter an unrivaled renown among the increasingly numerous Frankish monasteries.

Anglo-Saxon Benedictinism was marked by a powerful attraction toward missionary work. The evangelization of Frisia, undertaken by *Wilfrid, Bishop of York, in 678, was resumed in 690 by *Willibrord, who in 696 established the See of Utrecht as his base. His plans for Denmark were premature, but in southern Frisia he was highly successful. Beyond the Rhine, Benedictinism was first planted at *Reichenau, founded by a Frankish monk, *Pirmin, in 724. At least eight other houses quickly arose in Alamannia, all under his jurisdiction. Farther north, Kaiserswerth, established by the Anglo-

Saxon *Swithbert, became a center of the apostolate in its region. Central Germany was the field of another Anglo-Saxon, St. *Boniface, whose methods of evangelization became a model for subsequent missionaries. He assisted Willibrord in southern Frisia from 719 to 722, when he was consecrated bishop by Gregory II and commissioned to evangelize Hesse and Thuringia. Careful to keep in close contact with Rome, he planted monasteries, the most important being *Fulda (744), organized the Church in the newly won lands, reinvigorated and reorganized the Bavarian Church, persuaded the Bavarian monasteries to adopt the Benedictine Rule, and inaugurated the urgent reform of the Frankish Church. In 753 he proceeded to still pagan northern Frisia, where he was martyred the next year.

The gradual conversion of the Lombards permitted the revival of Benedictinism in Lombard Italy. The first agents of the restoration were Franks and Lombards, who founded *Farfa in 705 and St.-Vincent-on-the-Volturno about 710. *Petronax of Brescia gathered about himself some hermits living at Monte Cassino; from 729 they were instructed in the Benedictine Rule by the Anglo-Saxon *Willibald (later Bishop of Eichstätt). South of the Pyrenees the rule was followed only in the March of Spain, erected by *Charlemagne in 795.

Reform and Centralization, 814–1125. The Carolingian period witnessed serious abuses because kings and magnates, with no concern for the true purpose of monastic life, had delivered many monasteries to lay abbots who were often crude soldiers. Reform was instituted by *Benedict of Aniane, who in his own foundation at *Aniane (c. 780) insisted on the literal observance of the rule. His ideas, more austere than the letter of the rule, spread to other houses in Aquitaine, thanks to the support of *Louis the Pious. When in 814 Louis succeded Charlemagne as emperor, he installed Benedict at Inden as superior general of all monasteries of the Empire. At Aachen in 817 the Frankish abbots adopted a uniform discipline, and inspectors were appointed to guard it. In an effort to protect the community against abusive lay abbots, the property of each house was divided into the *abbatia* and the *mensa conventualis;* the abbot had no control over the latter. In addition, the reform gave to public worship a predominance not envisaged by the rule; thereafter the liturgy became more elaborate and more solemn, while manual labor ceased to be performed.

The absolute uniformity insisted on by Benedict of Aniane was foreign to the spirit of the rule and too dependent upon imperial patronage. Only the Italian abbeys maintained the purer tradition. Nevertheless, the first half of the 9th century was characterized by regularity of discipline in the Frankish houses and by a brilliant scholarship, nourished in numerous schools. The fruits of serious intellectual work are seen in such writers as *Smaragdus, *Paschasius Radbertus, *Ratramnus, *Lupus of Ferrières, *Rabanus Maurus, and *Walafrid Strabo. Missionary zeal was exemplified in *Ansgar, monk of *Corbie, who in 826 undertook the evangelization of Denmark and Sweden. His successor, *Rembert, continued his work until death brought the enterprise to a close.

The dismemberment of the Empire in 843 and the succeeding fratricidal wars, in which kings distributed monastic property to their allies as guarantees of fidelity, the forcible assimilation of monasteries to benefices, and the attacks of Vikings, Muslims, and Magyars all but engulfed Benedictinism in total ruin. The monks who survived were constrained to beg their livelihood, and discipline collapsed. When they were once again able to recover their houses, they had to place themselves under the protection of the local magnate, who arrogated to himself the abbatial election or even the abbacy itself. Thus, for sheer suvival, monasteries took their place in nascent *feudalism. Abbots became the vassals of the territorial prince, from whom they held in fief the monastic lands and often a more extensive domain. They were also lords, exercising public authority over their fiefs. Functions not proper to ecclesiastics were performed within each fief by the abbot's advocate, a layman who was commissioned to protect the monastery's property, but who often became its pillager, especially when king, duke, or count assumed the office. Such a situation in no way promoted the monastic life, and by 900 it was extremely difficult to discover a house where the rule was observed even reasonably well.

The violent 10th century, however, witnessed a brilliant revival of Benedictine life almost simultaneously in Burgundy and Lotharingia. The recovery, not dependent upon royal favor or enforced by any general legislation, was more lasting than the reform of the preceding century. It began by delivering monasteries from every external influence, freeing them to live the rule. The earliest and most influential reform center was *Cluny, founded in 910 by *William of Aquitaine, who placed it exclusively under papal authority. Three long-lived and extremely capable abbots directed Cluny's destinies during 154 years with remarkable consistency of policy—*Majolus (954–994), *Odilo (994–1048), and *Hugh (1049–1109). They organized the new foundations and the reformed houses into an "order," which in the 12th century included some 1,450 monasteries; most of them were ruled by priors, and all were subject to the abbot of Cluny. The "order" did not embrace the entire Benedictine family, but many nonCluniac abbeys adopted its observance. The abbot of Cluny was, in the 11th and 12th centuries, one of the most important and influential personages in the Church, ruling monasteries in France, Germany, Spain, Italy, England, and elsewhere. For 2 centuries Cluny's fervor was maintained at white heat. Stern centralization was foreign to the Benedictine idea, but in the 10th and 11th centuries it was the only solution to the problem of freedom. More pernicious was the gradually increasing overemphasis on an ever more elaborate worship, which left neither time nor energy for labor, study, or even personal prayer, and prompted a fatal lowering of admission standards. Eventually everything became pure formalism, but Cluny had, meanwhile, reinvigorated monasticism and freed it from external control.

Saint-Benoît-sur-Loire, reformed by Cluny in 930, retained its autonomy, and became a secondary reform center for France, Lotharingia, and England. Entirely independent of the Cluniac influence were *Brogne in Lower Lotharingia, founded in about 919 by *Gerard of Brogne, and *Gorze in Upper Lotharingia, restored in 933. The Brogne observance extended into Flanders, Normandy, and the German Empire; that of Gorze covered Lotharingia. These movements did not long survive their authors, but they were reactivated later by Richard of Saint-Vanne (d. 1046) and *Poppo of Stavelot. The Cluniac observance penetrated very early into Italy. In 936 *Odo of Cluny was made superior of all abbeys in the Papal State; he and his successors reformed old houses and established new ones. In the 9th century the Danes had totally ruined the once numerous Anglo-Saxon monasteries. From 943 monasticism was restored in England by *Dunstan, *Ethelwold, and *Oswald of York, the chief influences being those of Fleury and Brogne. The Benedictine Rule entered the slowly expanding Spanish principalities from 895, and Sancho III of Navarre introduced the Cluniac observance in 1022. Most Spanish abbeys were in some degree dependent on a celebrated French or Italian house.

The Benedictine recovery of the 10th century was accompanied by a new zeal for evangelization, whereby the rule, too, was spread. The work of Ansgar in Denmark and Sweden was resumed in 934 by *Unni, monk of *Corvey. Anglo-Saxon monks were soon active throughout Scandinavia. In the 11th century Denmark, Sweden, Norway, and Iceland had Benedictine abbeys. In 933 Bohemia obtained its first monastery at Brevnov, built by *Adalbert of Prague; the 11th century saw numerous foundations. The conversion of Poland, begun

Fig. 3. Palm Sunday procession in the cloister of the Collegio Sant'Anselmo at Rome, the international college of the Benedictine Order.

in about 967, was largely the work of Benedictines from Fulda; Adalbert of Prague also gave Poland its first monastery, Meseritz (*c.* 996). The apostles of the Wends were monks from German houses. Adalbert of Prague in 997 and *Bruno of Querfurt in 1009 were martyred while seeking to convert the Prussians. Hungary owes its faith in large measure to Benedictines; the first missionary was *Wolfgang of Regensberg. The first monastery, *Pannonhalma, was founded in 996. Dalmatia's attachment to the Latin Church was the work of Benedictines, first sent there from Monte Cassino in 986. In the 12th century the rule acquired a new home also in the Crusader Kingdom of Jerusalem.

The monastic reform of the 10th century deeply stirred the conscience of Europe and contributed powerfully to the general reform of Christian society after 1049. The popes fostered the monastic revival by granting numerous houses exemption from episcopal control. In turn, monasticism cooperated actively in the reform by supplying ideas and leaders, notably Popes Stephen IX, Gregory VII, Victor III, Urban II, Paschal II, and Gelasius II. Cluny's vast family and the other reform groups incessantly reminded clergy and laity of the claims of the moral law and in most cases actively seconded the papal program. Among the most influential centers were: *Saint-Victor in Marseilles, Saint-Bénigne de Dijon, *Tiron, *Chaise-Dieu, *Bec, and Sauve-Majeur, in France; Saint-Vanne (*Verdun-sur-Meuse), in Lotharingia; *Sankt Blasien, *Reichenau, *Einsiedeln, *Sankt Emmeram, *Fulda, and *Hirsau, in Germany; and *Monte Cassino, *Farfa, *Fruttuaria, and *La Cava, in Italy.

The foremost German center was Hirsau. About 150 monasteries, new and old, followed its observance in a union that left them their autonomy. The institute of lay brothers, sketched by *John Gualbert at *Vallombrosa, was organized in the 11th century by *William of Hirsau, who prescribed a special mode of life for religious assigned to menial tasks and to the management of distant estates. The Norman Conquest of 1066 meant the internal strengthening of Benedictinism in England and its brilliant flowering. French abbeys, including Cluny, founded priories in England. Queen *Margaret, wife of Malcolm III, introduced the rule in Scotland. The first Benedictine houses in Ireland were established in the 12th century.

The existence of so many varying interpretations shows that the Middle Ages knew no unified Order of Saint Benedict. Each group was a sort of "order," more or less firmly compacted. Most of them lacked a stable organism or depended too much on the personality of an abbot. Excess of organization and overemphasis on one element in the life eventually stifled the spirit, but from the 9th to the 12th century the Benedictine family virtually monopolized religious life in the West. The great age of Benedictine predominance ended around 1125; the houses continued to be powerful and wealthy, but were more respectable than vigorous. The history of the main trunk was to be one of decadence, sterility, and false starts for the next 3 centuries.

The 11th century, which witnessed Cluny's splendor, witnessed also a strong reaction against Cluny's one-sidedness through return to the letter of the rule, manual labor, corporate poverty, and even the eremitical and penitential ideal of primitive monachism. Thus several shoots from the main trunk grew into new institutes. The *Camaldolese, the *Vallombrosans, and the monks of *Grandmont, in the 11th century, provided for the eremitical life in a greater or lesser degree. Similarly, there developed in the 13th century the *Celestines and Sylvestrines, and in the 14th, the Olivetans (*see* BENE-DICTINES, OLIVETAN; BENEDICTINES, SYLVESTRINE). The Cistercians (1098) retained the cenobitic life and aimed to restore the rule's wise balance and complete withdrawal from the world.

Decadence, 1125–1408. The feudal system had undermined not only the rule but the vows themselves, since not only the abbacy but the several claustral offices became fiefs, belonging to their holders. Before long the individual monk had his own pecuniary benefice, and monasteries came to be regarded as suitable places for locating persons undesirable elsewhere. Some monasteries reserved admission to nobles, who continued their former way of life. Hence the Benedictine houses were avoided by persons seriously in search of perfection. Few abbeys escaped this moral decay, and the failure to gain recruits had disastrous effects on the liturgy, intellectual life, and external influence.

Those seeking to effect a reform had recourse especially to a Cistercian institution, the general chapter. Popes Innocent III, Honorius III, and Gregory IX took vigorous steps, but not always with consideration for the essential nature of Benedictinism, and hence their success was not great. Innocent III prescribed general chapters, restored free abbatial election, and insisted on poverty and control of finances. The Fourth Lateran Council in 1215 established triennial provincial chap-

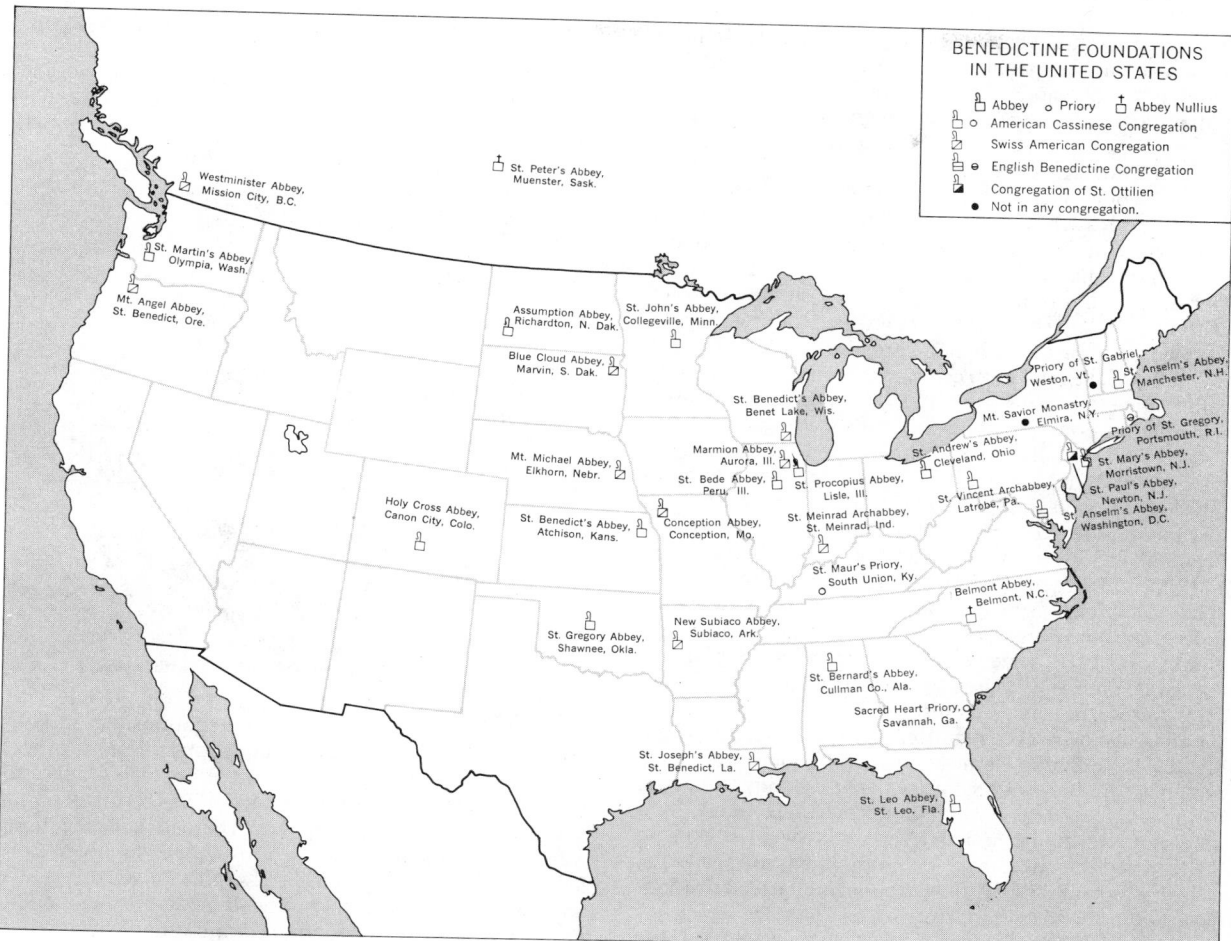

Fig. 4. Map showing the Benedictine foundations in the United States.

ters, which were to elect visitors to supervise the carrying out of legislated reforms. Honorius III required annual chapters, and Gregory IX extended the powers of visitors. Councils, papal legates, and bishops also sought to elevate the moral tone, but only in England, and to some extent in Scotland and Aragon, was the papal program really carried out. Elsewhere the chapters rarely met or their regulations were not obeyed, and after 1243 the Holy See often granted dispensation from the legislation of Gregory IX. Decline set in again, and several communities had themselves secularized as canons.

In 1336 Benedict XII undertook a more suitable program of reform. He gathered all monasteries into 32 provinces, prescribed a triennial chapter and visitation in each, and demanded the raising of the intellectual level. In 1338 he ordered an inquiry by special agents into the condition of every monastery. This legislation remained in force for 2 centuries, but there was no effective organ of enforcement. Princes, fearing the loss of their claims, hindered the holding of chapters, popes mitigated the regulations, and the system of papal reservations too often meant the naming of unfit abbots. The notorious *commenda,* whereby the abbacy of a monastery was given to a secular ecclesiastic as his benefice, grew rapidly. The commendatory abbot reserved for himself the lion's share of the income, frequently leaving the monks an insufficient portion. In

France the community continued to control the *mensa conventualis,* but elsewhere the commendatory abbot took what he wanted; to increase his income he often hindered recruitment. Only England and Germany escaped this evil. The Hundred Years' War (1337–1453), the Black Death (1348), and the Western Schism (1378–1417) brought about the depopulation and demoralization of religious houses. Not all monasteries, however, fell into complete decline; a good abbot was often able to preserve discipline or restore fervor, and many monasteries were exemplary. But, in general, too many monks forgot their ideals and became worldly.

Reform Congregations, 1408–1815. The 15th century saw the rise of a new institution, the congregation, which more efficaciously guaranteed a lasting regular life. Luigi Barbo (d. 1443), becoming abbot of Santa Giustina at Padua in 1408, instituted regular discipline in the decayed house. Recruits were so numerous that he was able to found new monasteries and reform existing ones, all of which were united in a congregation in 1419. To avoid the *commenda,* the office of local superior was made temporary, and all authority was concentrated in the annual general chapter. All monks made their profession for the congregation, and the chapter could move them about. All the monasteries of Italy and Sicily eventually joined the congregation, which, with the accession of Monte Cassino in 1504, called itself the Cassinese Congregation. A high intellectual level was maintained and the religious exerted a salutary influence on the people. The reform movement was adopted in the monasteries of Catalonia, Poland, and Dalmatia; it also inspired the congregations of Chezal-Benoît, Sainte-Vanne, Saint-Maur, and Valladolid.

The Council of Constance (1414–18) influenced the spread throughout south Germany of the reforms introduced at *Kastl and at *Melk, but weak organization made these unions too dependent on individual abbots. More enduring, because better organized, was the Congregation of Bursfeld, approved in 1446 by the Council of Basel. Under Abbot John Dederoth *Bursfeld Abbey adopted an observance which spread so rapidly in north Germany that in the 16th century the congregation numbered some 200 houses. In 1514 the Hungarian abbeys united in a congregation, with the statutes of Monte Cassino and Melk. The Congregation of Valladolid (1489), with temporary abbots, embraced the monasteries of Castile and some in Catalonia, and eventually spread to Mexico and Peru. The Congregation of Portugal (1566) united all the houses of the kingdom and those of Brazil. In France the reform efforts of the abbot of Cluny were obstructed by the political disorders, the *commenda*, and the resistance of many monks. In 1481 renewed efforts were successful. At the same time the houses of the Tiron observance accepted reform, as did also *Chezal-Benoît, which founded its own congregation. The vigorous new life in the Benedictine family was confronted by Protestantism in the 16th century. In England, Scotland, Denmark, Sweden, Norway, Iceland, Holland, and much of Germany monasticism was swept away. In Switzerland, France, and Belgium it endured a cruel ordeal. Of some 3,000 Benedictine monasteries, about 800 ceased to exist.

The Council of Trent (1545–63) legislated for the restoration and maintenance of discipline, defined the conditions of admission and profession, the choosing of superiors, and the administration of property, and ordered all monasteries to unite in congregations, with triennial general chapters and visitations. Thereby the congregational system became ecclesiastical law, enforced by the Holy See, and exempt from episcopal authority. The exempt Congregation of Flanders (1564) and that of the Presentation (1629) were organized in the Belgian Netherlands. In France the earliest was that called the Exempt (1580). The Congregations of Brittany (1604), Saint-Denis (1607), and Allobroges (1622) were short lived. In 1604 Didier de la Cour (d. 1623) founded the Congregation of Saint-Vanne de Verdun. At its head was a president, annually appointed by the general chapter, which exercised sovereign authority. It was outstanding for the spiritual and intellectual formation of its members, and included houses in Lorraine and Franche-Comté. In 1621 the Congregation of Saint-Maur was constituted of those French monasteries that had adopted the Saint-Vanne reform. It absorbed the Breton Congregation in 1628, that of Chezal-Benoît in 1636, and eventually all French monasteries except the Cluniac. Grégoire Tarisse (d. 1648) reorganized the congregation in 1645, giving it an effective government. The *Maurists were celebrated for scholarship, and at the same time they were exemplary religious. Cardinal Armand Richelieu in 1629 decided to unite the Cluniac Congregation to Saint-Maur, but the Holy See disapproved. Many of the Cluniacs had

been won to a strict observance and in 1646 became a distinct congregation.

English Benedictines lived in various monasteries on the Continent or in residences at Douai and Dieulouart in France, and elsewhere. Some English monks joined

Fig. 5. Abbot Boniface Wimmer, founder of the American Cassinese Congregation of the Benedictines (1846).

the Valladolid and Cassinese Congregations, but in 1619 Paul V united all of them in an English Congregation. In 1592 Clement VIII reformed the Spanish Congregation of Claustrales, founded in 1336. In Germany about a dozen weakly organized and isolated congregations were eventually formed, the most important being the Swiss (1622), the Alsatian (1624), the Austrian (1630), and the Bavarian (1684). The Benedictine University of Salzburg (1617) brightened an otherwise gloomy situation.

Around 1700 the Benedictine family was, in general, in a healthy state, thanks to the new congregations. The 18th century, however, witnessed a new decline and virtual extinction under the attacks of the *Enlightenment, the French Revolution, and wholesale secularization. Of 410 French Benedictine houses, 122 were thus suppressed by 1768. The Revolution completed the task by 1792 and extended it to Belgium (1796), Switzerland (1798), the left bank of the Rhine (1802), and Central Italy (1810). Monasteries under Hapsburg rule had been subjected to annoyance since 1754 and *Joseph II suppressed many of them. Between 1803 and 1807 all monasteries of Baden, Bavaria, Württemberg, and Prussia—141 of them—disappeared. By 1815 only about 30 monasteries were still in existence. Those of Portugal and Spain were swept away in 1834 and 1835.

Recovery and Expansion, 1815 to the Present. Despite the Prussian *Kulturkampf, the suppressions in Portugal, Spain, France, Italy, and Switzerland, and the Brazilian prohibition of receiving novices, the 19th century was an age of vigorous renewal and worldwide expansion. Hungary led the way in 1802, reopening monasteries for the sake of education; Austria quickly followed suit, and in Spain and Italy monks were able to recover some of their houses. English monks, refugees from revolutionary France, were welcomed in England, where *Ampleforth (1802) and *Downside (1814) were established (*see* BENEDICTINES, ENGLISH). English and Spanish monks transplanted Benedictinism to Australia, where *New Norcia was founded in 1846.

In France the Benedictine life was restored at *Solesmes by Prosper *Guéranger in 1833, and the French Congregation came into existence 4 years later. Ludwig I of Bavaria reopened *Metten in 1830, and then other houses, and the Bavarian Congregation was approved in 1858. From Metten the rule was brought to the U.S. in 1846 by Boniface *Wimmer, founder of the American Cassinese Congregation (see BENEDICTINES, AMERICAN CASSINESE). The Swiss-American Congregation (1881) originated with Saint Meinrad, Ind., and Conception, Mo. (see BENEDICTINES, SWISS-AMERICAN). Placidus and Maurus *Wolter established themselves at *Beuron, Germany, in 1863; the Beuronese Congregation (1868) modeled itself on that of Solesmes except in regard to its more active life. In 1872 Beuron founded *Maredsous in Belgium; in 1920 four Belgian abbeys were separated from Beuron to constitute the Belgian Congregation. The Brazilian Congregation, erected in 1827 and nearly wiped out by hostile laws in 1853, revived with the help of Maredsous. In 1904 the Congregation of Sankt Ottilien was founded for work in the foreign missions. The reform of Subiaco, Italy, in 1851 was to give birth in 1872 to the Congregation of the Primitive Observance, which is divided into six provinces. Two Austrian Congregations, both established in 1889, were united in 1930. In 1945 six Slavonic houses were organized to form the Congregation of Saint Adalbert. In 1888 Leo XIII revived the Collegio Sant' Anselmo in Rome, originally founded in 1687 by Innocent XI, as an international college for young monks of all congregations. In 1893 he created the office of abbot primate, who, elected every 12 years by all the abbots, is the head of the confederated families and Abbot of Sant' Anselmo. Gradually the unwelcomed office grew in prestige and influence. On March 21, 1952, Pius XII approved the codification of the *Lex Propria* governing the confederation.

In addition to the pursuits proper to contemplation, most Benedictines today are engaged in the traditional activities—education, scholarship, and parochial and missionary work. Many are prominent in the *Liturgical Movement. The oblate institution, whereby both clerical and lay persons are affiliated to a particular monastery, is very popular. Although Benedictine life in recent times has suffered at the hands of hostile governments, especially during the Spanish Civil War and in Communist countries, the Confederated Benedictine families had increased to more than 12,000 members by 1964.

Bibliography: P. SCHMITZ, DHGE 7:1060–1206, esp. the section "Oeuvre littéraire," 1137–55; *Histoire de l'Ordre de Saint-Benoît*, 7 v. (Maredsous, Bel. 1942–56). Kapsner BenBibl. T. LECCISOTTI, EncCatt 2:1233–46, esp. bibliog. S. HILPISCH, Lex ThK² 2:184–192, esp. bibliog.; *Geschichte des benediktinischen Mönchtums* (Freiburg im Breisgau 1929); *Benedictinism Through Changing Centuries*, tr. L. J. DOYLE (Collegeville 1958). H. VAN ZELLER, *The Benedictine Idea* (Springfield, Ill. 1960). E. C. BUTLER, *Benedictine Monachism* (2d ed. 1924; reprint New York 1961). **Illustration credits:** Fig. 2, Biblioteca Apostolica Vaticana. Fig. 3, Photo von Matt.

[A. G. BIGGS]

BENEDICTINES—SISTERS

The women's branch of the Order of St. Benedict (OSB) embraces numerous convents spread over the world, but united in their observance of the *Benedictine rule. Benedictine nuns and sisters trace their origin to the 6th century, when (St.) *Benedict of Nursia drew up his famous rule for monks, which was later adapted for the use of women. Although probably not a religious herself, since it appears unlikely that any Benedictine convent existed in 6th-century Italy, St. *Scholastica was a consecrated virgin and undoubtedly followed the spiritual teaching of her brother Benedict. Her example, therefore, has traditionally been another source of inspiration to Benedictine nuns. Under the influence of Pope Gregory the Great, the Benedictine rule began to be widely diffused in Europe. Nevertheless, most nuns of that time followed rules given to them by their local bishops, who devised them in eclectic fashion from existing rules. The result was that in Italy, Spain, and France, there were as many rules as there were convents. With its introduction into convents early in the 7th century, the Rule of St. Benedict gradually supplanted other rules, remaining the standard guide for most convents until the 12th century.

Early Growth. It seems likely that the Benedictine rule was first accepted in the convents of England, where Benedictine monachism experienced its first great expansion. The earliest foundations were in Kent at *Folkstone (630) and Thanet (670). Under the influence of the monks of Canterbury, these convents probably observed the Rule of St. Benedict from their beginning. Other important convents were founded at *Ely (673), *Barking (675), *Wilton (800), and Ramsey (967). *Whitby, founded by St. *Hilda in 657, was the scene of the famous synod of 664, which adopted the Roman rite in preference to the Celtic observance. Coldingham (673), ruled by St. *Cuthburga, was another important convent in Northumbria. Contemporary writings reveal the interest of these early English nuns in theological, scriptural, and patristic studies, and their skill in the arts of illumination, gold lettering, and needlework. Although practically all these convents, with the exception of Barking, were destroyed during the Danish invasions of the 9th and 10th centuries, some were subsequently restored and many others were founded in England after the Norman Conquest (1066).

In Germany the first convent to adopt, at least basically, the Rule of St. Benedict, was probably *Nonnberg in Salzburg, founded about the year 700 by St. *Rupert; this monastery is still in existence. Among other early convents were four founded by St. *Boniface: Tauberbischofsheim, Kitzingen, Ochsenfurt, and Schornsheim, all under the direction of St. *Lioba, cousin of Boniface, who came from *Wimborne Abbey to bring the Anglo-Saxon tradition to the convents of Germany. Lioba, St. *Thecla, St. *Walburga, and other Anglo-Saxon nuns succeeded in imparting to Teutonic women not only the faith and the Christian heritage, but also a tradition of learning that continued through the Middle Ages and was a marked characteristic of St. *Hildegarde's convent at Rupertsberg and of the convent of *Helfta, the home of St. *Gertrude the Great and other 13th-century mystics. At Rupertsberg another type of work was undertaken by the nuns. While prayer, psalmody, and the intellectual life flourished in St. Hildegarde's abbey, the nuns devoted themselves also to the care of the sick and the needy. The abbess herself set up a drug dispensary and a center for therapy.

In France during the 7th and 8th centuries the rules most widely used in convents were those of SS. Caesarius and Columban. About 629 Luxeuil, the center of Celtic

Fig. 1. Nonnberg Abbey, Salzburg, founded around 700.

monasticism, adopted a rule combining those of SS. Benedict and Columban. When convents followed suit, Remiremont became for the nuns what Luxeuil had been for the monks. Among the more important convents that followed a mixed observance were Sainte-Marie in Soissons, Rebais, Saint-Martial in Paris, *Faremoutiers, *Jouarre-en-Brie, and Chelles. The Council of Aix-la-Chapelle in 817 made the Rule of St. Benedict obligatory for all monasteries. One of the most famous convents during the Middle Ages was the Abbey of Notre-Dame at Angers (1028), which had under its jurisdiction a large number of priories.

Benedictine convents were similarly founded in Italy in the 7th and 8th centuries and became so numerous during the Middle Ages that practically every city had its convent. Since the nuns in Italy were purely contemplative, their cultural activities were more restricted. By the early 11th century, Benedictine convents were established also in Spain, Portugal, and in the Scandinavian countries.

Reform Congregations. When the various tribal invasions threatened European monastic life, convents were reduced in number and greatly impoverished. During the *Cluniac reform movement, St. Hugh, sixth abbot of Cluny, founded a convent for the nobility of France at Marcigny. According to tradition, the monastery, although built for 100 nuns, at no time had more than 99; Our Lady, under the title of "Notre Dame Abbesse," completed the number. The number of Cluniac convents never exceeded 12, and the number of nuns in each convent, with the exception of Marcigny, was rarely more than 50. Under the centralized government of Cluny, affiliated convents were directly under the control of its abbot and were obliged to observe its constitutions. But many convents not belonging to the congregation were influenced by its spirit and adopted some of its customs. However, Cluny's one-sided emphasis on the liturgy tended to weaken both the letter and the spirit of the Benedictine rule, which prescribed a harmonious arrangement of prayer, work, and meditative reading. Thus the 11th century witnesses a strong reaction favoring a return to the ideals of the rule.

In contrast to the elaborate ritual and ceremonial that characterized life at Cluny, the ideal at *Cîteaux was simplicity in worship and the restoration of a more balanced ordering of life. By directing attention to mental prayer, the *Cistercians effected a deepening of the interior life. This affective form of prayer, with its mystic tendencies, had a special attraction for women and was actually an intensification of the liturgical piety manifested in the life and writings of St. Gertrude the Great, St. *Mechtild of Hackeborn, and *Mechtild of Magdeburg. Women also participated in the new congregations within the Benedictine family, such as the *Camaldolese, the *Vallombrosans, and, somewhat later, the Olivetans. Other reform movements of the 14th and 15th centuries, such as that later known as the Cassinese Congregation, as well as the Bursfeld Congregation in Germany, and the congregation of Claustrales in Spain, likewise had branches for women.

Post-Reformation Development. The Protestant Reformation of the 16th century practically obliterated convent life in northwest Europe. Convents were suppressed in England, Germany, Denmark, and the Scandinavian countries. The practice of *commendation, a form of secular control of monasteries, and the religious wars in France weakened convent life there. Eventually, however, as the legislation of the Council of Trent (1545–63) became effective, monastic life began to flourish again all over Europe.

France. France was one of the first countries to respond to this renewal. Although two of the most influential foundations of men, Saint-Vanne and Saint-Maur, refused to admit nuns into their congregations, old convents were revived and new ones established with the help of such prominent figures as St. *Francis de Sales and Cardinal Pierre de *Bérulle. In the general renewal of this period, the convents at Montmartre, Beauvais, Val-de-Grâce, and Douai played an important part. The new spirituality also influenced the foundation of the Benedictine nuns of Calvary and the Benedictine nuns of the Blessed Sacrament and Perpetual Adoration. Both congregations stressed the interior motive of reparation and enjoined severe penitential observances. The French Revolution and subsequent secularization decrees resulted in a new decline in Benedictine life. However, later 19th-century developments included a resurgence of monasticism, marked by a renewal of the contemplative aspect of the Benedictine vocation and a remarkable expansion of missionary activity.

Germany. German participation in the post-Reformation renascence of Catholic life was evidenced in the new statutes drawn up for the convents at Hohenwart, Fulda, Nonnberg, Chiemsee, and St. Walburga, Eichstätt. In them emphasis was placed on the Divine Office; the nuns at Eichstätt were also enjoined to participate annually in a retreat under the direction of a Jesuit.

England. England benefited from the French Revolution, which brought a return of English nuns to their native land. From Brussels, where the first post-Reformation English convent was organized in 1597, the nuns escaped to Colchester, England. The community of Cambrai (1623) returned to England to establish what became *Stanbrook Abbey in Worcester. A member of the Cambrai community, Dame Gertrude More, great-great granddaughter of Thomas More, reached a high degree of contemplation under the direction of Dom Augustine *Baker. Her writings included the *Spiritual Exercises and Practices in Divine Love.* Dame Laurentia McLachlan, abbess of Stanbrook, became well known for her research in Gregorian manuscripts.

The renascence of Benedictine life in Europe was

Fig. 2. The refectory at Stanbrook Abbey, Worcester.

effected largely through the efforts of Abbot Prosper *Guéranger of Solesmes and Archabbot Maurus *Wolter of Beuron. Both were convinced that nuns, unhampered by priestly duties, were in a better position to live the Benedictine life than were the monks. For Guéranger and Wolter, the exemplar of Benedictine life was not to be found in the early Middle Ages or in a congregation like that of Saint-Vanne; Cluny was the ideal to which they aspired. Thus Solesmes and Beuron fostered the liturgy among the nuns, and Guéranger founded the convent of Sainte-Cécile, near Solesmes, while the Beuronese Congregation erected a convent in Prague. Beuron's solicitude for the nuns was characteristic also of its daughterhouses, especially those in Germany and in Belgium. To Maria Laach in Germany, the convents of Eibingen, Herstelle, and Fulda have been indebted for a flourishing liturgical life. Maredsous in Belgium had a formative influence on the convent of Maredret. Strictly contemplative, the nuns in all these convents devote themselves to the recitation of Divine Office in accordance with the practice of Solesmes and Beuron; they do not teach or engage in other forms of the external apostolate. The writings of Jenny H. Cécile *Bruyère, Abbess of Sainte-Cécile, clearly reflect the spirit of Guéranger. Missionary activity brought about the establishment of new congregations, such as the Sisters for Foreign Missions, founded in Tutzing, Bavaria, and the Missionary Benedictine Nuns, founded in France. In the mid-19th century there began also the establishment of convents in Australia, North America, and South America.

U.S. Foundations. The first Benedictine foundation in the U.S. was made at Latrobe, Pa., in 1846 by Boniface *Wimmer, monk of *Metten Abbey in Bavaria (*see* BENEDICTINES, AMERICAN CASSINESE). At his invitation the first three sisters from Eichstätt arrived in the U.S. in 1852 and, with Mother Benedicta Riepp as foundress, opened St. Joseph's Convent and School at St. Marys, Elk County, Pa. During the next 15 years, 9 independent houses were founded from the original community. Five of these convents remain in existence at Erie, Pa.; Ridgely, Md.; St. Joseph, Minn.; Bristow, Va.; and Pittsburgh, Pa. In 1964 a total of 31 independent houses traced their origin, directly or indirectly, to St. Marys, Pa., and 6 other motherhouses to 3 convents in Switzerland: Maria Rickenbach, Sarnen, and Melchthal. Maria Rickenbach founded convents in Clyde, Mo.; Yankton, S.Dak.; Mount Angel, Ore.; and Jonesboro, Ark. Sarnen established the convent in Cottonwood, Idaho; from Melchthal came the motherhouse in Sturgis, S.Dak. The convent in Yankton established houses in Waunakee, Wis. (1897), and in Pierre, S.Dak. (1961). French convents also sponsored U.S. foundations, including the convent in Ramsay, La., from the Basses-Pyrénées section, while Bethlehem, Conn., was founded from Jouarre. Unsettled conditions in Germany led the Eichstätt nuns of St. Walburga convent to open dependent houses at Latrobe, Pa. (1930), and Boulder, Colo. (1934). Earlier, the Benedictine sisters from Tutzing had set up a dependent priory at Norfolk, Nebr.

Benedictine Sisters of Pontifical Jurisdiction. In 1964 about 80 per cent of the Benedictine sisters in the U.S. were under pontifical jurisdiction, in contrast to the 4 per cent in Europe, where the majority of convents remained subject to the local ordinary.

Fig. 3. Dame Gertrude More.

Major U.S. Congregations. Among the American congregations of pontifical status, that of St. Scholastica is the oldest and largest. Under the guidance of Louis Mary Fink, OSB, Bishop of Leavenworth, later the

Fig. 4. St. Joseph's Convent and School at St. Marys, Elk County, Pa., the first American foundation of the Benedictine Sisters. This early photograph shows (center to right) the first monastery, church, and school.

Diocese of Kansas City, Kans., Mt. St. Scholastica Convent, Atchison, Kans., took the initiative in 1881 and drew up plans for the Congregation of St. Scholastica. Because of difficulties over the question of whether to classify the American Benedictine as a *nun (*monialis*) or as a religious *sister (*soror*), final approval of the congregation was delayed until 1930. Subsequently the path was clear for the formation of other congregations; the Congregation of St. Gertrude the Great was approved in 1937, and the Congregation of St. Benedict in 1956. The Congregation of St. Scholastica and St. Benedict are based on the American Cassinese Congregation. In 1964 the Congregation of St. Scholastica had about 2,600 sisters in 16 motherhouses in the U.S. and 1 in Mexico. That of St. Benedict had more than 2,175 sisters in 7 U.S. motherhouses. Since most of the charter convents of the Congregation of St. Gertrude the Great were of Swiss origin, this congregation is associated with the Swiss American Congregation (*see* BENEDICTINES, SWISS-AMERICAN). In 1964 St. Gertrude's had approximately 1,700 sisters in 10 motherhouses in the U.S. and 1 in Canada. Individual convents under pontifical jurisdiction included Regina Laudis (1944) in Bethlehem, Conn.; St. Gertrude (1906) in Ramsay, La.; and Immaculata (1923) in Norfolk, Nebr., whose motherhouse was in Tutzing.

Most of the sisters in the Congregation of St. Scholastica engage in educational work. They conduct schools ranging from kindergarten through college. In addition to educational work, the Congregations of St. Gertrude the Great and St. Benedict direct hospitals, orphanages, and homes for the aged. All three congregations are active in home mission work among the Latin Americans, Negroes, and Indians. The Convent of St. Benedict, St. Joseph, Minn., engages also in foreign mission work in Puerto Rico, China, Japan, and Formosa. The fourth pontifical congregation, Benedictine Sisters of Perpetual Adoration, are a contemplative group, with constitutions approved by Rome in 1925.

[T. A. DOYLE]

Benedictine Sisters of Perpetual Adoration. This congregation was founded in 1875 at Conception, Mo., by three sisters from the Convent of Maria Rickenbach in Switzerland. It includes the motherhouse of St. Louis, Mo., and five dependent priories: Our Lady of the Blessed Sacrament (1928), Mundelein, Ill.; Christ the King (1935), Tucson, Ariz.; Holy Spirit (1945), Kansas City, Mo.; and St. Pius X (1954), San Diego, Calif., all subject to the authority of the prioress general. With four general councilors, she resides at Clyde, where postulants and novices are trained at a central novitiate. The primary apostolate of the congregation is perpetual adoration of the Blessed Sacrament; the members engage only in such active works as accord with their semicloistered life, such as the publication of a monthly magazine, *Spirit and Life,* and other religious booklets and leaflets. They also do translating; make altar breads, liturgical vestments, and linens; and operate an art shop. The successors of Mother Anselma Felber, foundress and first superior, included Mothers John Schrader, Dolorosa Mergen, and Carmelita Quinn. Also important in the development of the congregation were Benedictines from *Conception Abbey, including Abbots Frowine Conrad, Philip Ruggle, and Stephen Schappler, as well as Dom Lukas Etlin, who was spiritual director of the Clyde convent (1891–1927).

[M. C. QUINN]

Missionary Benedictine Sisters. This congregation of pontifical jurisdiction originated in 1885, in Bavaria, Germany, with Mother M. Birgitta Korff as first prioress general. Three years later the first group of missionaries was sent to assist the Benedictine fathers working in Africa, where four priories have since been established. In 1964 the congregation had about 1,300 members scattered throughout the world. The prioress general's residence was at Grottaferrata, Rome, Italy; in Germany the general motherhouse was at Tutzing, Bavaria; and missions were operating in Brazil; the Philippine Islands; East, South, and Southwest Africa; Korea; and Japan. In 1923, at the invitation of Bp. Jeremiah J. Harty of Omaha, Nebr., the congregation arrived in the U.S., where their work includes teaching, nursing, lay retreats, and social work among the Indians. In 1964 the 80 U.S. members served in parts of Nebraska and Minnesota, where they staffed three elementary schools and one high school, three hospitals, and one Indian mission. Headquarters in the U.S. were located at Norfolk, Nebr.

[M. I. KOCH]

Benedictine Sisters of Diocesan Jurisdiction. Although most Benedictine convents in Europe are under diocesan jurisdiction (96 per cent), the percentage is much smaller in the U.S. (21 per cent). Of the other Benedictine convents throughout the world, about 6 per cent are subject to the local ordinary.

Olivetan Benedictine Sisters. This diocesan community at Holy Angels Convent, Jonesboro, Ark., was founded by sisters from the Convent of Maria Rickenbach, Switzerland, who had established a foundation in Clyde, Mo. (1875). Answering an appeal of the bishop of Little Rock, Ark., four Sisters arrived in Pocahontas, Ark., on Dec. 13, 1887. The new convent was named Maria Stein and the distinctive title Olivetan Benedictine was obtained by affiliation with the Benedictines of Mount Olivet in Rome, Italy (1893). In 1897 the motherhouse was transferred to Jonesboro, Ark., and renamed Holy Angels Convent. Numbering about 175 members in 1964, the community staffed elementary and high schools in Arkansas, Texas, and Louisiana, and were in charge of the culinary departments of St. John's Seminary, Little Rock, Ark., and St. John's Hospice, Hot Springs, Ark. Hospitals staffed by the sisters included St. Bernard's, Jonesboro; Carroll County Hospital, Eureka Springs, Ark.; and Iberia Parish Hospital, New Iberia, La.

[M. L. FRANKENBERGER]

Others. From the motherhouse in Eichstätt, a number of U.S. establishments under diocesan jurisdiction were made, including St. Emma (1931) at Latrobe, Pa., which in 1964 had about 40 members; St. Therese (1935) at Canon City, Colo., 9 members; and St. Walburga (1934) at Boulder, Colo., 17 members. Benedictine convents of diocesan rank were established also at Holy Name (1889), San Antonio, Fla.; and St. Scholastica (1878), Fort Smith, Ark.; in 1964 their membership totaled 60 and 315 respectively.

Summary. The Rule of St. Benedict adapts itself and makes its appeal to each succeeding century. Its fruitfulness stems from its simplicity. A vocation, according to the prologue of Benedict to his rule, is an invitation to follow Christ. To prepare those who accept such an invitation, Benedict set up a school of the Lord's service, organized on a simple plan. It is a family whose head is the abbot or superior; he is responsible for the temporal and the spiritual welfare of the community. While the abbot is the center of unity for the whole house, he consults the entire community when important matters concerning the common interests are involved. The family life envisioned by Benedict is the fruit of that spiritual orientation which comes through contact and understanding of the liturgy, whereby the natural is spiritualized and the spiritual, so to speak, becomes natural. Although the object of the religious is to seek God, he cannot pray all day. Nor does God's honor demand it. Therefore, work is an integral part of the school of the Lord's service, and through the centuries Benedictines have engaged in various types of work. In 1964 the total number of Benedictine nuns and sisters was more than 22,600, of whom about 57 per cent were in the U.S. They conducted approximately 800 schools throughout the world. More than 600 of these were located in the U.S. (about 500 grade schools and 100 high schools), as well as 10 colleges. Of the 96 hospitals operated by Benedictines, 57 were in North America, 32 in Africa, 3 in the Far East, and 4 in Europe. Statistics in the 1960s showed that Benedictine communities were flourishing in the U.S., but on the decline in Europe. Following the lead of Leo XIII, Pius XII endeavored to strengthen conventual life by stressing the advantages of organization whereby individual convents could be strengthened by membership in a congregation or union, without loss of autonomy. His *Lex propria* set down the laws and regulations governing the Confederation of Monastic Congregations of the Order of St. Benedict.

Bibliography: M. R. BASKA, *The Benedictine Congregation of Saint Scholastica: Its Foundation and Development* (CUA StAmChHist 20; Washington 1935). H. BREMOND, *Literary History of Religious Thought in France from the Wars of Religion down to Our Own Times,* tr. K. L. MONTGOMERY, 3 v. (New York 1928–37). E. C. BUTLER, *Benedictine Monachism* (2d ed. 1924; repr. New York 1961). B. A. SAUSE, *The School of the Lord's Service,* 3 v. (St. Meinrad, Ind. 1948–51). *Catalogus Familiarum Confoederatarum, OSB* (Rome 1961). G. ENGELHART, ed., *Spring and Harvest: St. Walburg's Shrine,* tr. from Ger. (St. Meinrad, Ind. 1954). *The Life and Revelations of Saint Gertrude,* tr. M. F. C. CUSACK (Westminster, Md. 1949). S. HILPISCH, *History of Benedictine Nuns,* tr. M. J. MUGGLE (Collegeville, Minn. 1958). D. KNOWLES, *The Benedictines* (New York 1930). M. G. MCDONALD, *With Lamps Burning* (St. Joseph, Minn. 1957). M. A. SCHROLL, *Benedictine Monasticism as Reflected in the Warnefrid-Hildemar Commentaries on the Rule* (New York 1941). P. SCHMITZ, *Histoire de l'Ordre de Saint-Benoît,* 7 v. (Maredsous, Bel. 1942–56). Stanbrook Abbey, *In a Great Tradition: Tribute to Dame Laurentia McLachlan, Abbess of Stanbrook* (New York 1956). **Illustration credit:** Fig. 1, Austrian Information Service.

[T. A. DOYLE]

BENEDICTINES, AMERICAN CASSINESE

The American Cassinese Congregation of the Order of St. *Benedict (OSB) is the oldest and largest Benedictine group in the U.S. The name Cassinese derives from the ancient monastery of *Monte Cassino, although there is no direct relationship between that monastery and the American group (*see* BENEDICTINES). The American foundation sprang from the Bavarian monastery of *Metten, when a few monks, led by Boniface *Wimmer, came to the U.S. in 1846 to attend to the needs of German immigrants. In that same year Wimmer and his companions established at Latrobe, Pa., a monastery, which subsequently became *St. Vincent Archabbey. St. Vincent became a priory in 1852 and was raised to abbatial status 3 years later. The creation of the American Cassinese Congregation was approved by Pius IX on Aug. 24, 1855. Wimmer was chosen first president of the congregation. When the first general chapter of the congregation met in Latrobe in 1858, Abbot Wimmer was reelected to the office of president and then confirmed for life by the Holy See. The congregation at that time comprised one abbey and two independent priories, St. Louis (now *St. John's Abbey) in Collegeville, Minn., and St. Benedict in Atchison, Kans. By 1900 abbeys and priories had been established in 15 states.

Sanctuary of the basilica at St. Vincent Archabbey, Latrobe, Pa., motherhouse of the American Cassinese Benedictine Congregation.

In 1964 the congregation was presided over by Rt. Rev. Denis Strittmatter, Archabbot of St. Vincent, and consisted of 16 abbeys and 2 independent priories. Besides Latrobe, the member abbeys are as follows: St. John's (1856), Collegeville, Minn.; *St. Benedict's (1857), Atchison, Kans.; St. Mary's (1858), Morristown, N.J.; *Belmont (1876), Belmont, N.C.; *St. Gregory's (1876), Shawnee, Okla.; *St. Procopius (1885), Lisle, Ill.; Holy Cross (1886), Canon City, Colo.; *St. Leo (1889), Pasco Co., Fla.; *St. Anselm's (1889), Manchester, N.H.; *St. Bernard (1891), Cullman Co., Ala.; Assumption (1893), Richardton, N. Dak.; *St. Martin's (1895), Olympia, Wash.; *St. Bede (1910), Peru, Ill.; and St. Andrew's (1922), Cleveland, Ohio. Belmont became an *abbatia nullius* in 1910. In Canada the Abbey of St. Peter at Muenster, Saskatchewan, also belongs to the congregation. Established originally at Wetaug, Ill., in 1892, this foundation was moved to Canada in 1903 and raised to the status of *abbatia nullius* in 1921.

Governed in the beginning by the constitutions of the Bavarian congregation, the American Cassinese Congregation adopted its own constitutions when the latter were approved by the Holy See in 1908. They have since been twice revised in 1925 and 1947. The chief organ of government is the general chapter, which meets every 3 years and has the right to legislate for the entire congregation. Presiding over the congregation is the abbot president, assisted by a council made up of two abbot visitors. Although subject to visitation, each abbey in the congregation enjoys, according to the Benedictine concept of monastic organization, considerable autonomy under the rule of its abbot. Besides the traditional Benedictine dedication to prayer, study, and the devout performance of the liturgy, the monks are engaged in many works of the apostolate: education, preaching, publishing, and parish work. The congregation has both home and foreign missions; overseas missions are located in Japan, Nationalist China, Puerto Rico, the Bahamas, Mexico, Panama, Colombia, and Argentina. Total membership in 1964 was more than 2,000.

Bibliography: Kapsner BenBibl. C. J. BARRY, *Worship and Work: St. John's Abbey and University, 1856–1956* (Collegeville, Minn. 1956). P. BECKMAN, *Kansas Monks: A History of St. Benedict's Abbey* (Atchison, Kans. 1957).

[M. BENKO]

BENEDICTINES, ENGLISH

The English Congregation of the Order of St. *Benedict (OSB) traces its origin back to the early Middle Ages. Monasticism was brought to England in 597 by the monk, (St.) *Augustine of Canterbury, sent from Rome to convert the Anglo-Saxons. The first monastery was established at *Canterbury in Kent. Monastic communities gradually took root in other parts of the Heptarchy, and a brilliant period of missionary and cultural activity followed. Outstanding figures of this period were the saints, *Benedict Biscop, *Wilfred of York, *Bede, and *Boniface, and the scholar *Alcuin. The Danish invasions arrested this initial development, and by the time of the reign of *Alfred the Great (871–899), monasticism was practically extinct. In the 10th century (St.) *Dunstan, with royal assistance initiated a restoration that was so successful that Benedictine monasticism from that time until its extinction in the 16th

century enjoyed uninterrupted development and expansion. The Norman Conquest brought only new vigor to this growth, drawing the greater houses into the feudal pattern. Abbots sat with the bishops, as barons, in the councils of the realm. As landlords the monks enjoyed a reputation for benevolence.

In 1215 a decree of the Fourth Lateran Council initiated the gradual association of the autonomous monastic communities into congregations by means of general chapters with defined rights of legislation and visitation. In 1218 the first Benedictine general chapter convened at Oxford, but not all the English monasteries were united to the congregation until the 4th century. Monasteries following the Benedictine Rule continued to spread throughout the kingdom. Central to the life and activities of the Benedictine monk is the *Opus Dei*, the daily and reverent performance of the sacred liturgy. Work in the beginning was largely manual, but in time intellectual activities came to predominate, and the monks provided a substantial cultural contribution through scholarship, instruction of the young, and the practice of the fine arts.

In the 16th century the monastic communities were dissolved by *Henry VIII, and their property was confiscated. During the years of persecution that followed, English Catholics who wished to be monks had to make their profession in communities abroad. English monks had established themselves in Lorraine and the Netherlands. Later the French Revolution compelled these monks in exile to seek refuge in their native England, and from these returning communities has developed the present English Benedictine Congregation, which now consists of 13 monasteries, 8 of which are of abbatial status. In 1919 a property was acquired at Portsmouth, R.I., for the purpose of bringing English Benedictinism to America. St. Gregory's Priory, Portsmouth, is now a flourishing community. Five years later St.

St. Anselm's Abbey, Washington, D.C.

Anselm's Priory was established in Washington, D.C.; it became an abbey in 1961. A third American foundation, St. Louis' Priory, was made at Creve Coeur, Mo., in 1955. Each of these monasteries conducts a school for boys. The total membership of the congregation in 1964 was 603.

Bibliography: Knowles MOE. BEDE, *A History of the English Church and People*, tr. L. SHERLEY-PRICE (Penguin Bks. Baltimore 1955). B. WELDON, *Chronological Notes Containing the Rise, Growth and Present State of the English Congregation of the Order of St. Benedict* (London 1881). J. McCANN, "The English Benedictine Revival 1588–1619," AmBenRev 2 (1951) 261–286. W. W. BAYNE, "Thirty-Three Years of Portsmouth History," *ibid.* 3 (1952) 315–339.

[W. W. BAYNE]

BENEDICTINES, OLIVETAN

A monastic order, whose Latin title is *Congregatio Sanctae Mariae Montis Oliveti Ordinis Sancti Benedicti* (OSBOliv). The Olivetan Benedictine monks, who have belonged to the Benedictine Confederation since 1959, were established in the 14th century when Bl. *Bernard Tolomei and his followers withdrew (1313) to a place of solitude called Accona (about 12 miles from Siena, Italy), where Bernard later founded the Abbey of Mount Olivet. The congregation was approved by Clement VI (Jan. 21, 1344); its constitutions, based on the *Benedictine Rule, were revised in 1932. The monks, most of whom are priests, profess solemn vows, wear a white habit, and pursue a semicontemplative, monastic life, giving special attention to liturgical solemnities. They engage also in the active ministry, particularly in teaching and retreat work. The monasteries of the congregation, each ruled by an elected abbot or a prior, are independent of one another, but are subject to the abbot general, who is also the abbot of the motherhouse, the Abbey of Mount Olivet. He is elected by the general chapter for a term of 12 years; his councilors, similarly elected, serve for 6 years.

The Olivetans came into existence during a period of decline in Benedictine monasticism, adopted a form of government suitable for the correction of abuses, and restored a rigorous observance of the rule. The reform spread rapidly, first in Tuscany, then in all of Italy, where, by the end of the 14th century, some 50 Olivetan monasteries were flourishing under the protection of popes and bishops. While the growth of the congregation continued into the 17th century, when there were nearly 2,000 monks in about 100 monasteries, monastic discipline deteriorated, especially because noblemen entered the monasteries without true vocations. The political disturbances and suppressions of the 18th and 19th centuries brought grave harm to the order, but from these misfortunes there emerged some outstanding monks who worked for a restoration of the congregation in Italy. Foundations, never before successful, were established outside of Italy, first in France (late 19th century), then in Austria, Brazil, and Lebanon (early 20th century). In more recent years houses were founded in Belgium, England, and Mexico. A beginning was made also in the U.S., where the Olivetans are represented in the Dioceses of Albany, N.Y., and Lafayette, La.

Among the monks noteworthy for holiness of life, in addition to the founder, are Bl. Bernard of Vercelli (fl. *c.* 1450), Bl. Jerome of Corsica (d. 1479), Ven. Nicola Roverella of Ferrara (abbot general 1472–76),

and Ildebrando Polliuti (abbot general, d. 1917). Since the days of the Renaissance the Olivetans have made numerous contributions to the fields of art (especially in miniature and marquetry), literature, music, and other studies. The most prominent artist was John of Verona (d. 1525). Abbot Placido Lugano (1876–1947) was a noted historian and founder of the *Rivista storica benedettina* (1906). Among Olivetans raised to the hierarchy was the abbot general, later cardinal, Placido Schiaffino (1829–89).

In 1965 the Olivetan Benedictines numbered 265 (185 priests, 52 clerics, and 28 brothers). There were 20 monasteries: 12 in Italy, 2 in France, 2 in Brazil, and 1 each in Belgium, England, Lebanon, and Mexico. Several communities of sisters are aggregated to the congregation (*see* BENEDICTINES—SISTERS).

Bibliography: M. SCARPINI, *I monaci benedettini di Monte Oliveto* (Alessandria 1952). G. PICASSO, "Aspetti e problemi della storia della Congr. Benedettina di Monte Oliveto," *Studia Monastica* 3 (1961) 383–408. V. CATTANA, "La preghiera alle origini della tradizione olivetana," *La preghiera nella Bibbia e nella tradizione patristica e monastica* (Rome 1964) 703–731. Heimbucher 1:214–217. R. CAPRA, EncCatt 2:1248–49.

[G. PICASSO]

BENEDICTINES, SWISS-AMERICAN

The Swiss-American Congregation of Benedictines was established by Pope Leo XIII on April 5, 1881, with St. Meinrad Abbey, St. Meinrad, Ind., and Conception Abbey, Conception, Mo., as charter members. Both monasteries had been founded by Swiss abbeys: St. Meinrad by Maria Einsiedeln in 1854 and Conception (then known as New Engelberg) by Engelberg in 1873. In 1965 the Swiss-American Congregation of Benedictines numbered 1 archabbey, 10 abbeys, 1 independent priory, and 4 dependent priories, with approximately 1,000 members. The abbeys of New Subiaco (Subiaco, Ark., 1878), St. Joseph (St. Benedict, La., 1890), Marmion (Aurora, Ill., 1933), Blue Cloud (Marvin, S.Dak., 1952), St. Charles Priory (Oceanside, Calif., 1958), and Priorato de San Benito (Huarez, Peru, 1964) were founded by St. Meinrad Abbey, which was declared an archabbey in 1954. Mt. Angel Abbey (St. Benedict, Ore., 1882), St. Benedict Abbey (Benet Lake, Wis., 1945), St. Pius X Priory (Pevely, Mo., 1951), Mt. Michael Abbey (Elkhorn, Nebr., 1956), and Skt. Knud Kloster (Trorod pr. Vedbaek, Denmark, 1963) were established by Conception Abbey. Westminster Abbey (Mission City, B.C., Canada, 1939) owes its origin to Mt. Angel; Corpus Christi Abbey (Corpus Christi, Tex., 1927), to New Subiaco; and the independent Our Lady of Glastonbury Priory (Hingham, Mass., 1954), to St. Benedict Abbey.

The monasteries of this congregation are governed both by the Rule of St. Benedict and the Declarations and Constitutions of the Swiss-American Congregation. The constitutions, approved in 1901 and revised in 1924, provide for a general chapter, consisting of all the governing abbots of the congregation; an abbot *praeses*, elected every 6 years by the general chapter; and two abbot assistants. Although the abbot *praeses*, or his delegate, conducts a visitation of each abbey once every 3 years, the autonomy of each monastery and the paternal authority of its abbot, who is elected for life, are safeguarded by the constitutions.

The chief religious characteristic of the Benedictine monasteries of the Swiss-American Congregation is the

Conventional Mass, St. Meinrad Archabbey, Indiana.

carrying out of the liturgy of the Church through choral recitation and singing of the Divine Office and the daily conventual High Mass. In the active apostolate, their work consists primarily of education; parochial, missionary, and retreat work; and the apostolate of the press. Diocesan students are trained in four major seminaries (St. Meinrad, Conception, Mt. Angel, Westminster) and five minor seminaries (St. Meinrad, St. Joseph, Mt. Angel, Westminster, and Mt. Michael). Subiaco, Mt. Angel, Marmion, and Corpus Christi conduct a high school for lay students. Swiss-American Benedictines staff 67 parishes and missions and provide extensive weekend assistance; 42 priests are institutional chaplains and 6 others are military chaplains. In the missionary field, Blue Cloud conducts missions among the Sioux Indians; St. Benedict staffs both home and foreign missions (Morelia, Mexico, and Quesada, Costa Rica), and St. Joseph cares for the Shrine of El Señor de Esquipulas in Guatemala. Other missions in Guatemala are staffed by Blue Cloud and by Marmion. Retreats for married couples are conducted by Conception, Mt. Angel, St. Meinrad, and St. Pius X. Magazines published by St. Meinrad (*Marriage*), Conception (*Altar and Home*), and Mt. Angel (*St. Joseph Magazine*) have a national circulation.

Bibliography: *Declarations on the Holy Rule and Constitutions of the Swiss-American Congregation, OSB* (Conception, Mo. 1938). A. KLEBER, *History of St. Meinrad Archabbey, 1854–1954* (American Benedictine Academy [Latrobe, Pa.] Historical Studies: Monasteries and Convents 1; St. Meinrad, Ind. 1954).

C. GEDERT, *The Swiss-American Congregation of Benedictines and Its Contributions to the American Catholic Church* (Cincinnati 1956). O. L. KAPSNER, *A Benedictine Bibliography*, 2 v. (Collegeville, Minn. 1962). T. J. ALLEN, *The Benedictine Fathers of the Swiss-American Congregation as a Factor in the Educational Life of the United States* (thesis, U. of Notre Dame 1935). S. HILPISCH, *Benedictinism Through Changing Centuries*, tr. L. J. DOYLE (Collegeville, Minn. 1958) 149, 154.

[A. FUERST]

BENEDICTINES, SYLVESTRINE

A monastic congregation, originally named *Ordo Sancti Benedicti de Monte Fano,* and now designated *Congregatio Silvestrina Ordinis Sancti Benedicti* (OSB Silv). The Sylvestrines, as they are commonly called, were founded by St. *Silvester Guzzolini (1177–1267) in 1231 at Montefano, near Fabriano (Ancona), Italy. Silvester led a reform movement at a time when the *Benedictines were in decline, and when the *mendicant orders appeared to be supplanting the monastic orders. The followers of Silvester lived in caves, in huts, and in poor, cramped monasteries. They restored the primitive spirit of the *Benedictine Rule by alternating prayer with manual labor and apostolic work among the simple and uncultured people of the countryside. Innocent IV issued a bull of approval (June 27, 1227), despite the decrees of the Fourth Lateran Council (1215), which aimed to consolidate the various monastic institutes, and to prevent the birth of new ones. Papal approval was more easily granted because of the Sylvestrines' organized juridical structure with its centralization of authority under a prior or abbot general.

In the 14th century the order counted more than 1,000 monks and dozens of monasteries, among which was the celebrated San Marco in Florence, which later passed to the Dominicans. Meanwhile the original eremitical ideal gave way to a cenobitic form of monastic life. In time much of the vitality of the movement was sapped by poverty, by the evils of the system of *commendation, and by the sizable contribution of 300,000 *scudi* requested by Alexander VII in 1664 for the support of Christian armies. After the Holy See had suppressed about 15 of the smaller monasteries, the Sylvestrines were ordered (1662) to unite with the *Vallombrosans in one congregation. Five years later, however, the union was ended, and in 1690 Alexander VIII approved the constitutions of the Sylvestrine congregation. These critical circumstances rendered ineffective the attempts to expand into Portugal, Brazil, and Cochin China. Not until 1845 was a mission opened in Ceylon, where, by 1964, there were 60 monks, most of them natives.

In the 19th century the suppression by Napoleon I, and later, by the Piedmontese government, reduced the order to a few dozen members. In the middle of the 20th century a recovery was under way. By 1964 the monks had 11 monasteries in Italy. They administered five parishes, including one in Rome, and they established schools and health camps for poor children. There were single foundations in India, Australia, and Canada. In the U.S., where they arrived in 1910, there were 36 professed members located in three monasteries and caring for three parishes in Michigan and New Jersey. Total membership, under the abbot general in Rome, was more than 200.

In art and culture Sylvestrines won renown with their papermill in Fabriano (1276), one of the oldest in Eu-

"Madonna and Child with SS. Benedict and Sylvester," by the Sienese painter Segna di Buonaventura (fl. 1305).

rope. Fra Bevignate, sculptor and architect, designed the great fountain (*fontana grande*) in Perugia (1278), and developed the first plan for the cathedral in Orvieto (1290). Varino Favorino, Bishop of Nocera (1514) and humanist (d. 1538), composed the *Magnum et perutile dictionarium,* the first printed Greek lexicon. Numerous Sylvestrines were noted for sanctity. Besides the founder Silvester (feast, Nov. 26), the most venerated are Bl. Ugo degli Atti (d. 1250), Bl. Giovanni dal Bastone (d. 1290), and Bl. Paolino Bigazzini.

Bibliography: A. M. Cancellieri, *S. Silvestro Abate e l'opera sua* (Milan 1942). G. Pagnani, *I codici dell'Archivio di Montefano* (Picena 1958). G. Penco, *Storia del monachesimo in Italia* (Rome 1961). M. Papi, *La voce della selva* (Rome 1962); *Il poema figurativo di Fra' Bevignate* (Casamari 1965). Heimbucher 1:211–212. S. Pedica, EncCatt 2:1249–50. **Illustration credit:** The Metropolitan Museum of Art, Dick Fund, 1924.

[M. PAPI]

BENEDICTION OF THE BLESSED SACRAMENT,

a devotion consisting in the exposition of the Sacred Host on the altar, and after the singing of appropriate hymns, a blessing with the Sacred Host.

In all probability it developed from the showing of the Host at the various stations of the Corpus Christi procession. The first known example of Benediction similar to that common today was at Hildesheim in the 15th century. It was a response to the growing desire on the part of the faithful to look upon the Host, a desire enhanced by the earlier theological disputes over transubstantiation and the exact moment of consecration.

Concurrent with the strengthening of this desire was the gradual introduction of an evening service for the faithful, a kind of Vespers that would in general correspond to the Rosary instead of the Psalter, to the Way of the Cross instead of a pilgrimage to the Holy Land, and to the scapular instead of the religious habit. This evening devotion centered around the *Salve Regina,* which had been composed in the 11th century. By 1221 it had been joined to Compline in the Dominican monastery in Bologna. As early as 1250 it was part of a popular evening devotion in France. During the next 2 or 3 centuries the two devotions, one to the Blessed Mother, the other to the Blessed Sacrament, were combined, whence Benediction is still known in France as *Le Salut.*

The emphasis upon Benediction, as we know the devotion today, is not without certain dangers. The Church has always been hesitant to give free rein to it, as is evident from the restrictions, gradually lessened, of its use. The *Instruction on Sacred Music and Liturgy* of Sept. 3, 1958, was the first Roman document to declare Benediction of the Blessed Sacrament to be a true liturgical action. Some of the excesses that have to be guarded against are tendencies to substitute Benediction for Holy Mass, to celebrate it with more solemnity than the Mass, or to allow it to replace Vespers. The customary hymns during the exposition are *O Salutaris* and *Tantum Ergo,* though only the latter with the oration is prescribed. Any Eucharistic hymns, in Latin or the vernacular, may be sung before the *Tantum Ergo.* Two incensations of the Sacred Host before the blessing are prescribed.

Related to Benediction is the private exposition of a closed and veiled ciborium containing the Sacred Host. Unless the participants in the devotion are to be blessed with the ciborium, it is not removed from the tabernacle, though the door of the tabernacle is opened.

Bibliography: E. DUMOUTET, *Le Désir de voir l'hostie* (Paris 1926). V. L. KENNEDY, "The Moment of Consecration and Elevation of the Host," MedSt 6 (1944) 121–150.

[M. BURBACH]

The angel of the Lord seals the lips of Zachary, illuminated capital "B" of the Benedictus in the "St. Alban Psalter," an English manuscript of the 12th century preserved in the Treasury of the cathedral at Hildesheim.

BENEDICTUS (CANTICLE OF ZACHARY)

A lyric passage (Lk 1.68–79) attributed to *Zachary, the father of St. John the Baptist. It is usually called the Benedictus from the first word of its text in the Latin Vulgate. The context of Lk 1.59–67 suggests that the canticle was spoken extemporaneously on the occasion of the circumcision of the Baptist, but it may in fact have been composed at some later date, perhaps occasioned by v. 64: "And immediately his tongue was loosed, and he began to speak, blessing God."

Composition. The canticle is clearly divided into two sections: v. 68–75 and v. 76–79. Any further division into stanzas is purely conjectural. The first part is closely related to the theme of the *Magnificat, because Zachary praises and gives thanks to God, who through the Incarnation has already begun to fulfill the promises of messianic salvation made to the Patriarchs and Prophets (*see* MESSIANISM). In the second part he addresses his son as the Messiah's prophet and precursor whose mission is to make clearly known the spiritual character of the messianic kingdom (this has already been indicated in v. 74–75, and thus the two parts of the canticle end on the same note). The Greek text of v. 78b is very difficult; "the Orient" is perhaps the rising sun rather than a star (cf. Mal 3.20), for in the OT, light often signifies messianic benefits (Is 9.1; 60.1–3); a reading to be preferred to "has visited" is "will visit," and this phrase taken with v. 68 is also a weak example of inclusion. The Benedictus, like the Magnificat, contains many allusions to the OT (see E. Klostermann, 25), but the tone is strongly messianic and the specifically Christian content is in opposition to the rabbinical atmosphere of that period (v. 76–79).

Provenance. The origin of the Benedictus is much disputed. Did Zachary compose it? Or Luke? Is it a composition of John the Baptist's followers? A hymn taken from the early Christian liturgy? Does it have a specifically Jewish origin? The problem arises because the Benedictus, like the Magnificat and the Canticle of *Anna (1 Sm 2.1–10), seems to be an insertion into the text. Even though Luke attributes the canticle to Zachary, the answer to the problem is intimately bound up with the literary genre of the infancy narrative (*see* INFANCY GOSPEL). The antiquity of its composition seems assured, because if it were composed after the Resurrection and the worldwide spread of Christianity, there would have been a greater insistence on the messianic character of Jesus, His divinity, etc. (cf. the sermons of Peter in Acts and the Epistles of Paul).

There are various hypotheses to explain the Semitic character of the Greek; it has been suggested that the canticle is an original composition that imitates the style of the Septuagint or that the author used a Greek source influenced by Semitic idioms, an Aramaic source, or a Hebrew source. Most exegetes agree that the language points to a Hebrew original but that Luke used a Greek version as his source. P. Winter claims that v. 68–75 came from a Machabean paean sung before a battle (cf. 1 Mc 4.30–33). M. Gertner maintains that v. 76–79 represent a midrash based on Nm 6.24–25. Nevertheless, the perspective of the Benedictus is not narrowly nationalistic, but of the "new" era.

See also CANTICLES, BIBLICAL.

Bibliography: L. PIROT, DBSuppl 1:956–962. M. J. LAGRANGE, *L'Évangile selon Saint Luc* (ÉtBibl; 7th ed. Paris 1948). S. M. GILMOUR, InterBibl 8:45–48. E. KLOSTERMANN, *Das Lukasevangelium* (2d ed. Tübingen 1929). M. GERTNER, "Midrashim in the N.T.," JSemitSt 7 (1962) 267–292. P. WINTER, "Magnificat and Benedictus: Maccabaean Psalms?" BullJRylLibr 37 (1954) 328–347. **Illustration credit:** Warburg Institute, London.

[S. D. RUEGG]

BENEDICTUS DEUS, title of a constitution of Benedict XII issued Jan. 29, 1336. It was occasioned by the activity of his predecessor, John XXII, who had preached that it is only at the resurrection of the body on the last day that the just will begin to enjoy the beatific vision and sinners suffer the pains of hell; however, the day before he died John retracted these views in the bull *Ne super his.* Benedict had as a cardinal written a full account of the condition of the disembodied souls prior to the general judgment; he had this book thoroughly inspected by theologians and then made the infallible pronouncement contained in *Benedictus Deus.* This document states that in the ordinary plan of God all who after death have undergone whatever purgation is necessary immediately (i.e., prior to the recovery of their bodies at the general judgment) enjoy the beatific vision and do so continuously. It further states that in God's ordinary plan all who die in actual mortal sin immediately suffer the pains of hell (i.e., prior to their appearance at the general judgment).

See also ESCHATOLOGY, ARTICLES ON.

Bibliography: Mansi 25:985–987. Denz 1000–02.

[B. FORSHAW]

BENEDIKTBEUERN, ABBEY OF, Benedictine abbey founded in the Bavarian Alps by Count Huosi, 739–740, and consecrated by St. Boniface on Oct. 22, 742. Although pillaged by invading Magyars (955), Benediktbeuern (Buron, Beweren, Benedictoburum) was restored by the priest Wolford and staffed with a community of canons regular by St. *Ulric of Augsburg (969). Benedictine rule was reinstated in 1031 by Abbot Ellinger and 11 monks from the neighboring Abbey of *Tegernsee. During the long term of Ellinger's successor, Abbot Gothelm (1032–62), the abbey was fully repaired, and its library was reorganized. In spite of fires (1248, 1377, 1378, 1490), it prospered and became a center of learning and also of pilgrimage, since it possessed a relic of St. Benedict given by Charlemagne, as well as a relic of St. Anastasia brought there by St. *Gottschalk in 1053. It received privileges from popes and kings and acquired princely status from Rudolph of Hapsburg; with Abbot Ortholph II (1271–84) begins the list of prince-abbots. The abbey was depleted by the plague of 1611 and ransacked by the Swedes who invaded Germany under Gustavus Adolphus in 1632. At this time the monk Simon Speer was tortured and slain for refusing to surrender the goods of the monastery. Much of Benediktbeuern's fame rests with its impressive library. When catalogued

The baroque abbey church of the Abbey of Benediktbeuern.

(1736) by M. *Ziegelbauer (d. 1750), it numbered 338 MSS and 30,000 volumes; 40,000 at the time of its suppression. It is here that the scholarly historian of the Bavarian Benedictines, C. Meichelbeck, worked. The church, rebuilt by Abbot Placidus (1672–90), is an example of Bavarian high baroque style and has frescoes by H. G. Asams (1649–1711). Benediktbeuern was suppressed by the government in 1803 and became successively a barracks and a military hospital; it is now a theological seminary for Salesian students.

Bibliography: Kapsner BenBibl 2:190. P. VOLK, DHGE 7: 1235–36, list of abbots. K. MINDERA, LexThK² 2:183–184. Cottineau 1:340–341. **Illustration credit:** German Information Center.

[E. D. MC SHANE]

BENEFICES

A benefice is defined (DDC 2:407) as "a sacred or spiritual office to which the authority of the Church has attached the perpetual right to gather revenues from the goods of the Church" [Wernz, *Jus decretalium* (Rome 1906) 2.2:3].

Origin. Even as early as apostolic times the Church was interested in freeing the clergy from the need to work at manual tasks for their own support (Lk 10.7). The care of souls should not be hindered (Acts 6.2) by engaging in trade or business. It was the duty of the Christian community to provide livelihood for the clergy. A self-supporting clergy was the exception, not the rule. It cannot be imagined that St. Paul financed by his own work his long travels and his enormous ministerial work in the Mediterranean area. Consequently, the obligation of the Christian community to support the clergy is the primary root of the benefice. *John Chrysostom in the 4th century urged rich landlords to provide for all the needs of the clergy. Actually the ability to guarantee the necessary income of the clergy became an indispensable condition for the foundation of new churches. Consequently, ordination, particularly to the priesthood, was dependent on assurances that housing and living (title of *ordination) would be available.

The term benefice has its origin in similar institutions in the feudal state. In the 8th century *secularizations of church property, the intermingling of secular and ecclesiastical properties, the use of such property by clergy and laity, and the trend of certain economic patterns hastened the development of benefices. The system of the *proprietary church was likewise influential. Various councils urged the owner of a proprietary church to provide necessary income to his priest, who was wholly dependent on the lord—in fact, had often been his serf before ordination. Many abuses, such as the dismissal of clergy by the owner without recourse to the local bishop, necessitated new legislation. In the 9th century the Church obtained greater security for the clergy (*Capitularies of Aachen, 818, 819). The owners of proprietary churches were henceforth obliged to set aside the necessary land for the use and adequate income of the appointed clergy. Here the benefice, not yet in name but in its legal structure, began shaping a new ecclesiastical institution. The next step was the combination of office and income. With the bestowing of office and income *uno actu* in the 11th century, the ecclesiastical benefice was patterned along feudal lines. The benefice had gained its definite place among the institutions of the Church. The *res spirituales* (office) and *res temporales* (estate providing income) were legally united into one institution: the benefice. Certain regional and temporary variations are noticeable, but the fundamentals remain the same.

Prebends. Another root of the benefice was the prebend, i.e., a living of stipend. After the dissolution of the *vita communis* (9th century) in the chapters and the partitioning of the chapters' income and real estate, the prebend, as a rule, became the possession of each member of the chapter (canon). In the decretals the last differentiation between prebend and benefice gradually disappeared, as the fundamental difference between these two institutions, i.e., that the office had originally been combined only with the benefice, no longer held. Beginning with the *Decretum* of *Gratian, the benefice became the normal institution and the most important type of office and income. The law as well as the canonists' theory from then on developed a great variety of benefices and enlarged the legal provisions for them. During the late Middle Ages gifts and foundations bestowed on the Church and made available to individual clergymen (e.g., *beneficium manuale, beneficium altaris,* annual Mass *stipends, etc.) broke down the line between ecclesiastical benefices and secular foundations. The practice of accumulating benefices and offices because of economic devaluation or avarice caused the decline of this institution. Reforms by the Council of *Trent, by the *Reformation, and through expropriation by the various state governments, as well as concurrent economic changes reduced the value or caused the total loss of many benefices. As a result of the *Enlightenment, the state converted benefice-supporting properties or similar foundations to social purposes such as providing small pensions to invalids or to the poor. The French kings made use of this property to enrich their favorites (who became lay abbots). In Austria the *Religionsfonds* (funds for religious purposes) of *Joseph II were derived from seizure of benefices or other church properties. These funds were then used to establish new benefices, especially parochial ones aimed at securing an equal income for the parochial clergy. In other regions the introduction of church taxes or the particular circumstances of mission territories or of a *diaspora* (e.g., in the U.S.) caused the abandonment of the benefice as a regular institution in wide areas of the Church. In modern times the old benefice to which special property is attached is becoming a rarity, and financial support ensuring housing and living of the office-holding clergy has been taking its place.

Bibliography: G. PEISER, *Der deutsche Investiturstreit unter König Heinrich V. bis zum päpstlichen Privileg vom 13. April 1111* (Berlin 1883); U. STUTZ, *Die Eigenkirche als Element des mittelalterlich-germanischen Kirchenrechtes* (Berlin 1895). R. BIDAGOR, *La Iglesia propria en España* (AnalGreg 4; 1933). W. M. PLÖCHL, *Geschichte des Kirchenrechts,* v.2 (2d ed. Vienna 1962). D. E. HEINTSCHEL, *The Mediaeval Concept of an Ecclesiastical Office* (CUA CLS 363; Washington 1956).

[W. M. PLÖCHL]

BENEFICES, CANON LAW OF

The *Code of Canon Law defines an ecclesiastical benefice as a perpetual juridical institute established by competent ecclesiastical authority and consisting of a sacred office and of the right of receiving the income from the endowment attached to the office (CIC c.1409). Thereafter, the Code treats of the funds of the endowment of a benefice together with their union and conversion, the ways in which benefices are conferred, and, finally, the loss of the benefice.

A benefice is a creation of law, namely, a moral, noncollegiate person subject to rights in law. The formal decree of the competent ecclesiastical authority brings this juridic or moral personality into being by erecting it as a legal entity consisting of a sacred office and the right of receiving the income attached to the benefice. These last two elements are considered the constitutive elements, combining as they do the spiritual factor of ecclesiastical office with the right to receive an income, which is the temporal aspect of the benefice. The necessary conditions for the existence of a benefice are the establishment by ecclesiastical authority and the notion of perpetuity. This perpetuity is described as objective, that is, permanent from the point of view of the benefice, not of the beneficiary. Its character of being perpetual flows from the benefice's moral personality in law.

The right to the income of a benefice must be attached to a sacred office. Offices in the Church are reserved to clerics and involve some sharing of ordinary power together with the obligation of rendering specific services on the part of the incumbent. The ecclesiastical office and the spiritual function it serves is the sole reason for establishing the beneficial income.

Constituent Funds of Endowment. The endowment of a benefice is constituted either by the property owned by the juridical person itself; by regular, pledged payments made by some family or moral person; by regular, voluntary offerings of the faithful that belong to the administrator of the benefice; by so-called stole fees as determined by the diocesan schedule or legitimate custom; or by choir allotments, exclusive of the third part of them if the entire income of the benefice consists of them. The endowment of a benefice clearly consists not only of funded capital or pledged payments, but also other alternate means in law of fulfilling the obligation of providing the incumbent of a benefice with his adequate support. Voluntary offerings on the part of the faithful that furnish an established salary to the beneficiary is a fully recognized source of beneficial income. This practice, which is followed almost exclusively in the U.S. in providing the income for pastors, has been looked upon by some as a deviation from the law regarding beneficial incomes.

Classification of Benefices. Ecclesiastical benefices are called: (1) consistorial, if they are customarily conferred in consistory—others are called nonconsistorial benefices; (2) secular or religious, according as they are restricted respectively to the secular clergy or the religious clergy; (3) double or residential, simple or nonresidential, depending on the existence of the obligation of residence attached to the office of the benefice; (4) manual, temporary or removable, or perpetual or irremovable, according as they are conferred revocably or perpetually; (5) those having the care of souls attached or those not so obligated. In doubt, all benefices are presumed to be secular if they are established outside the churches of the houses of religious. A residential bishop or local ordinary holds a consistorial benefice. A pastor holds a residential benefice to which the care of souls is attached. His is a manual benefice, unless he is of irremovable status.

Institutes That Are Not Benefices. Although they have some likeness to benefices, the following positions are not juridically considered benefices: (1) parochial vicarages that are not perpetually established; (2) lay chaplaincies, namely, those that have not been established by competent ecclesiastical authority; (3) the post of coadjutor with or without the right of succession, because both perpetuity and moral personality are lacking; (4) personal pensions; (5) a temporary allotment (*commenda*), i.e., the grant of the income of a church or a monastery to a given person with the provision that when he ceases to have a claim to it, it shall revert to the church or monastery.

Procedure for Election, Alteration, or Conferral. The establishment of consistorial benefices, together with the founding of dignities in cathedral chapters (CIC c.3942) is reserved to the Apostolic See. Ordinaries, but not the vicar-general without a special mandate, in their respective territories share the authority in law to establish nonconsistorial benefices.

Benefices shall not be established unless it is certain that a stable and adequate endowment producing an adequate income in perpetuity is available. The investment of money for this purpose is the responsibility of the ordinary in consultation with the diocesan council of administration (CIC c.1520). Parishes, as has been noted, can be established without this type of endowment provided the ordinary foresees that the needs of the parish will be met. Before a benefice is established, interested persons should be heard. The founder of a benefice can, with the consent of the ordinary, impose certain conditions that must be respected in the conferring of the benefice. The actual establishment of the benefice should be accomplished by a legal instrument wherein shall be fully defined the place in which the benefice is established, the endowment, and the rights and duties of the incumbent of the benefice. Since a parish is always a benefice, once the law regarding the erection of a parish is fulfilled, a benefice is established. Once established, a benefice is presumed to endure. It can, for a justifying reason, be united to another benefice by either extinctive, equal, or subordinating union. The transfer of a benefice occurs when the site of the benefice is moved; its division, when two or more benefices are made out of one; its dismembering, when a portion of its territory or its property is taken from it and given to another benefice, pious cause, or ecclesiastical institute; its conversion, when it is changed into a benefice of a different kind; its suppression, when it is entirely dissolved. Most of these acts, especially that of extinctive union or the suppression of a benefice, are reserved to the Holy See. For a just reason the ordinary can divide a parish, take away a portion of the territory or the people of one parish and assign them to another parish, or establish a new parish. He must hear the comments of the interested persons, but does not need their consent. Reasons justifying such actions would be: great difficulty in reaching the parish church, a population too large to be served by the appointment of additional parochial assistants, or, generally, the good of souls. In dividing or establishing a new parish, the bishop has the obligation to see to it that an adequate income is available. A union, transfer, division, or dismembering of a benefice is effected by an authentic written document issued by the ordinary after hearing the board of diocesan consultors.

The Church has exclusive rights in making appointments to benefices since this pertains radically to its spiritual work. The pope, because of his primacy, has the right of conferring benefices throughout the universal Church. Besides all consistorial benefices and all dignities in cathedral and collegiate churches, the conferring of the following benefices are by law reserved to the Apostolic See: (1) those vacated by the death, promotion, resignation, or transfer of cardinals, legates, major officials of the Roman Curia, and honorary members of the papal household; (2) benefices established outside the Roman Curia if they become vacant through the death of the incumbent in Rome; (3) benefices invalidly conferred because of simony; (4) any benefice in which the pope or his delegate has intervened. The valid conferment of a benefice requires the expressed acceptance of the appointee. No cleric can hold two incompatible benefices. Incompatibility exists when the one incumbent cannot fulfill the obligation of both benefices or when either one of the two benefices is sufficient for his adequate support. The formalities of installation must be observed in the taking possession of a benefice unless the ordinary, for cause, expressly and in writing, dispenses from this obligation.

Other Noncollegiate Institutes. Besides benefices, the Church recognizes other noncollegiate institutes established with an adequate fund to defray the expenses of a religious or charitable undertaking. Hospitals, orphan asylums, and other similar institutions dedicated to works of religion or spiritual or corporal charity can be established by the local ordinary and constituted as a juridical person in the Church. The Society of St. Vincent de Paul is an example of such a lay institute. The directors of these institutes have the care and administrative responsibility for the welfare of the institution in accordance with the articles of foundation, which should describe the purpose, function, endowment, use of income, and distribution of its property, should it be dissolved. The local ordinary has the obligation of supervising the work of the institute and assuring himself that the articles of foundation are being faithfully observed. Unless it is permitted in the articles of foundation, permission of the Apostolic See is needed to suppress or unite these institutes or to divert them to purposes other than those that are specified in the foundation.

Bibliography: Vermeersch-Creusen EpitCanIur 2:741–811. M. CONTE A CORONATA, *Institutiones iuris canonici,* v.2 (4th ed. Turin 1951) 971–1032. W. F. ALLEN, "Parish-Benefice Revenue," *Jurist* 8 (1948) 323–332.

[W. B. CLANCY]

BENEFICIARIES (CANON LAW)

A beneficiary in ecclesiastical law is one who holds a Church office to which is attached the right of receiving a stable income from an endowment permanently established for that purpose by competent authority. Every beneficiary enjoys all the temporal and spiritual rights attached to his benefice from the moment of taking legitimate possession of it. The spiritual rights of the beneficiary flow from his holding an office in the Church. This includes in every instance some participation in ecclesiastical power, whether of orders or jurisdiction (CIC c.145). More specific spiritual rights flow from the nature of the office held by the beneficiary, e.g., the office of pastor.

The temporal rights of the beneficiary center on the title to the income attached to the benefice. He is entitled freely to use the income of the benefice to the extent that it is necessary for his proper support. All income in excess of that amount he is bound to give to the poor or to a pious cause. Cardinals are not bound by this rule (CIC c.239.1–19).

In calculating superfluous income, the beneficiary is not obliged to include revenues derived from sources entirely outside the benefice. This is referred to as patrimonial income. Authors designate two other sources of income that fall in this same category: quasi-patrimonial and parsimonial income. The former includes all revenues that come through the benefice but not specifically from the endowment, e.g., such sources of income as stole fees or collections taken up at Christmas and Easter, unless they are constituted specifically as a part of the beneficial income. Parsimonial income accrues when the beneficiary lives more frugally than necessary. The beneficiary is under no obligation to distribute this type of income as superfluous. Canonists generally concede, e.g., that what a pastor in the U.S. saves from his salary is parsimonial income.

If the reception of a certain order is required for obtaining a benefice, the beneficiary must have received that order before the benefice is conferred on him. The conferring of any benefice on one who has not received tonsure is invalid. This is true also of the appointment of a person without priestly orders to a parochial benefice (CIC c.453.1).

The beneficiary is obliged to fulfill faithfully the special duties attached to his benefice, and he has the obligation of daily reciting the canonical hours. If, without legitimate excuse, he fails to satisfy this obligation, he forfeits a portion of the income in proportion to the extent of his neglect, and he is bound to give that portion of the income to the church fund, to the diocesan seminary, or to the poor.

Administration of Goods. The beneficiary must administer the goods and property of his benefice according to the rules of Canon Law; and if through neglect he causes loss to the benefice, he is bound to repair the damage and is to be forced by the local ordinary to do so. If he is a pastor, he may be removed from the parish in the manner prescribed by CIC cc.2147–62.

The expenses connected ordinarily with the administration of the goods of the benefice and the collecting of the revenue must be borne by the beneficiary. Expenditures for extraordinary repairs of the residence belonging to the benefice must be borne by those who have the obligation to repair the church of the benefice, unless the charter of the foundation or legitimate agreements or customs rule otherwise. Minor repairs incumbent upon the beneficiary must be made as soon as possible to avert the necessity of greater repair.

Local Ordinary's Supervision. The local ordinary is bound to supervise the preservation and the proper administration of the property of the benefice, but he may discharge this duty through the deans.

The local ordinary also is charged with the responsibility of imposing adequate guaranties to prevent any lease from resulting in loss to the pious place or to the successors of the incumbent in the benefice. Any lease of beneficial property involving payments in advance of more than 6 months requires the permission of the local ordinary. He is charged also with the responsibility

of determining a just distribution of the annual income between an incumbent and his predecessor, if that is necessary and not adequately provided for in the duly approved particular statutes of the benefice or by legitimate custom. When the benefice is vacant, half of the income of the vacant benefice accrues to the endowment of the capital of the benefice, the other half to the church or the chapel, unless legitimate custom provides that the entire income accrue to the common good of the diocese. This distribution of the income of a vacant benefice is to be made only of funds remaining after the normal expenses of the benefice, including the adequate support of the vicar administrator, have been deducted. The Code of Canon Law also mentions the tax (*media annata*), amounting to half the first year's income of the benefice, for the repair of the cathedral. Where such an institution of law is in existence, the special statutes and laudable customs governing it in the respective regions must be observed. This tax was never introduced into the U.S.

The administration of the episcopal benefice (*mensa episcopalis*) is the responsibility also of the bishop. The episcopal residence must be kept in good repair from the revenues of the benefices in every case in which this responsibility does not fall to others by law. The law requires that an exact inventory of all the furnishings or other movable property connected with the episcopal benefice be kept. The Third Plenary Council of Baltimore required also that a bishop keep an inventory of his own personal property so as to distinguish his own goods from those of the Church.

In the U.S., only two kinds of benefice seem to exist: episcopal and parochial benefices. Both the bishops and the pastors are supported by free-will offerings on the part of the faithful in the form of a salary. Thus, the greater majority of the laws governing the beneficiary would not have application in ths U.S.

See also BENEFICES, CANON LAW OF.

Bibliography: Vermeersch-Creusen EpitCanIur 2:797–806. M. CONTE A CORONATA, *Institutiones iuris canonici,* v.2 (4th ed. Turin 1951) 1016–19. K. R. O'BRIEN, *The Nature of Support of Diocesan Priests in the United States* (CUA CLS 286; Washington 1949). T. H. KAY, "The Rights of the Parochial Beneficiary in the United States," *Jurist* 15 (1955) 318–336.

[W. B. CLANCY]

BENEVENTO, ARCHDIOCESE OF (BENEVENTANUS)

Metropolitan see since 969, founded as a bishopric in the first century, in south Italy. In 1963 it had 333,-500 Catholics in 163 parishes, 198 secular and 156 religious priests, 101 men in 27 religious houses, and 84 women in 28 convents; it is 579 square miles in area. Its 12 suffragans, which had 866,171 Catholics, 774 priests, and 1,553 sisters, were: Alife (founded *c.* 499), Ariano (969), Ascoli Satriano (1058) and Cerignola (1818, when united), Avellino (5th century), Boiano-Campobasso (1058, moved to Campobasso in 1927), Bovino (10th century), Larino (*c.* 493), Lucera (*c.* 500), San Severo (1057), Sant' Agata de' Goti (970), Telese (5th century), and Termoli (10th century).

The patrons of the diocese are the Apostle St. Bartholomew and St. Photinus, who according to a 17th-century legend was its first bishop, in Apostolic days. The first bishop known with certainty, however, is the 12th after Photinus, St. *Januarius, a martyr under Diocletian in 305. The list of bishops from Theophilus,

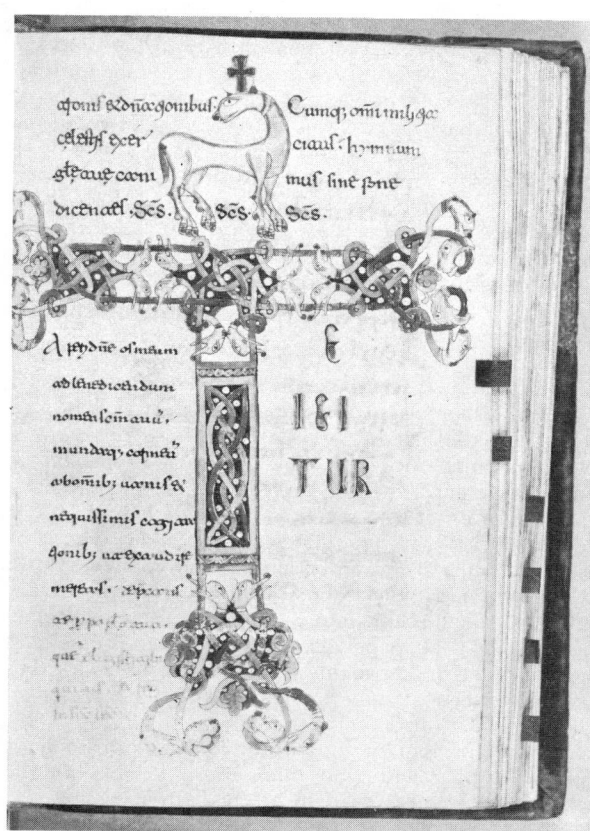

Benevento. Folio of a Beneventan 11th-century Missal at the "Sanctus" and "Te Igitur" of the Mass, showing the Beneventan script and an interlaced illuminated capital (Wal. MS 112, fol. 63 r).

who attended a council in Rome in 313, is fairly complete.

Ravaged by Vandals and Goths, favored by *Theodoric the Great, and sacked in 545 by Totila, the city was restored by the Byzantine *Narses, whose niece Artella was venerated from the time of her early death in 567. Benevento was the capital of the Lombard duke, Zoto, who ruled most of south Italy with 24 counts under him. In 589 Zoto destroyed *Monte Cassino. Duke Arechi and the Lombards became Christian *c.* 600, and thereafter Benevento, separated from the Lombard north by the Exarchate of *Ravenna, maintained independence of Byzantium, Saracens, Franks, and papal suzerainty. The diocese of Siponto (*Manfredonia), with the famous shrine of St. Michael of Monte Gargano, was united to Benevento under St. *Barbatus for 4 centuries, beginning in 663. All traces of the Basilica of St. Sofia, modeled after that in Constantinople and consecrated in 760, have disappeared; it was attached to a convent and cloister that depended on Monte Cassino. The Byzantine liturgy was used in Benevento for some time. In the late 9th century *Salerno and *Capua separated from the duchy of Benevento, but in the 11th century the metropolitanate had 25 suffragans. The beautiful Beneventan script, used in Dalmatia and south Italy from the late 8th to the 13th century, developed in the duchy of Benevento. In 1053 Pope Leo IX exchanged papal claims to *Bamberg for Henry III's claims to Benevento; but Normans con-

quered the duchy and became nominal vassals of the popes, who thereafter paid many visits to Benevento and held numerous councils there. After Frederick II destroyed the city it declined. Taken by the French (1799) and given to Talleyrand (1806), it was restored to the papacy by the Congress of Vienna in 1815. In 1860 Garibaldi annexed it to Italy.

From 1059 to 1927, 25 provincial councils were held. Since 1680 almost all Benevento's prelates have been cardinals. The 7th-century cathedral was expanded to three naves in the 11th century and to five naves by Archbishop Roger (1179–1221), Benevento's first cardinal; in 1943 it was destroyed by bombing. Cardinal V. M. Orsini (later Pope Benedict XIII) repaired the damage of earthquakes (1688, 1702) that destroyed most of the monuments of old. Popes Felix IV (526–30), Victor III (1086–87), and Gregory VIII (1187) were Beneventans.

Bibliography: Gams. Eubel HierCath. P. F. PALUMBO et al., EncCatt 2:1321–29. F. BONNARD, DHGE 7:1280–89, with list of bishops. J. SYDOW, LexThK² 2:201. AnnPont (1964) 61, 1412. **Illustration credit:** Courtesy of the Walters Art Gallery, Baltimore, Md.

[G. A. PAPA]

BENEVENTO, RITE OF. A Benedictine archbishop, B. Bonazzi (d. 1915), was the first to recognize that Benevento once had a rite of its own. Of this, no more is known than a series of texts and chants retained in 12 Roman manuscripts, not earlier than the 10th century or later than the 12th. The rite would have been practiced in an area coterminous with the orbit Terracina-Chieti, Salerno-Bari. It probably ceased under Prince Arechis II (d. 787), a ruler preoccupied with Church affairs. When the relics of St. Bartholomew arrived in Benevento (808), the rite was Roman, and there was no Mass of the saint in the old repertory. The sanctoral had included St. Michael, SS. Simon and Jude, Twelve Brothers (Apulian martyrs), and All Saints. All Saints was the last Beneventan entry. From the end of the 8th century to the close of the 13th, Benevento had a distinctive script, which lingered in the monasteries of Monte Cassino and Cava.

The chants of the rite do not accord with the Roman genius; many of them are similar to those of Milan, but the term "Ambrosian" in the chant books merely implied "non-Roman." There were also local variations. The frequent bilingual chants (Latin and Greek) were a legacy of the Byzantine occupation. An undoubted rapport, but no more than that, existed between the Beneventan and *Milanese rites. The more ancient texts are discernible in the Holy Week liturgy, producing at one time a series of double formularies at Benevento. The responsories for Palm Sunday were similar to those of the Gregorian repertory but independent of it. *Ante sex dies Paschae* with the verse *Magister* is unknown elsewhere. Good Friday had a truly hybrid liturgy. The first antiphon at the Adoration of the Cross, *O quando in cruce,* was a Greco-Latin trope found only in south Italian manuscripts. It appeared in a 7th-century Georgian Kanonarion and is sung today in the Byzantine rite. As at Milan, the solemn prayers were recited after the adoration. Despite the disappearance of Beneventan vestiges from the chant books in the 12th century, the Good Friday Vespers appear in a Roman setting in a Salerno Breviary printed at Naples in 1542. On Holy Saturday, fire and the paschal candle were blessed after the 11th lesson. *Omnes sitientes* was sung on the way to the font; a similar chant was found in the Mozarabic rite. The *Gloria in excelsis* was bilingual. The Communion chant, *Ymnum canite,* is the transitorium for Easter Thursday in the Milanese rite.

Bibliography: D. Andoyer, "Ancienne Liturgie de Bénévent," *Revue du chant grégorien* 20–24 (1911–14, 1919–21). R. J. Hesbert, "La Tradition bénéventaine dans la tradition manuscrite," PalMus 14 (1931). A. A. King, *Liturgies of the Past* (Milwaukee 1959). E. A. Loew, *The Beneventan Script* (Oxford 1914). G. Dix, *The Shape of the Liturgy* (2d ed. London 1945).

[A. A. KING]

BENEVOLI, ORAZIO, Italian composer of the early baroque period; b. Rome, April 19, 1605; d. there, June 17, 1672. He was a choirboy under V. *Ugolini at the church of San Luigi de'Francesi from 1617 to 1623, then served as *maestro di cappella* at S. Maria in Travestere (1624–30) and San Luigi (1638–44). An appointment to the Austrian court at Vienna followed (1644–46), during which time he first published a collection of motets. Upon his return to Rome he became *maestro di cappella* at St. Mary Major (Feb. 1646), then at St. Peter's (Nov. 1646), which post he held until his death. His works, most of which were written after his return to Rome, consisted chiefly of Masses and motets for 12 to 48 voices in 4 to 12 choirs, and represent an attempted synthesis of the Venetian polychoral technique and the conservative style of the Roman school after *Palestrina. In practice this consisted of expanding limited musical ideas through the use of several choirs in technical display rather than true musical development. His famous Mass in 52 parts plus continuo, written for the consecration of the Salzburg cathedral in 1628, is scored for 2 choirs of 8 voices each, 3 instrumental choirs, plus 2 separately placed choirs of brass and timpani. The vocal sections include some solo parts. It is printed in DenkTonÖst 10 together with a similarly orchestrated hymn, *Plaudite tympana,* in 56 parts.

Bibliography: H. F. Redlich, MusGG 1:1658–61. Eitner QuellLex 1:445. E. Wodehouse, Grove DMM 1:620–621. Buk MusB 68–69. Baker 127.

[A. DOHERTY]

BÉNÉZET, ST., patron of bridgebuilders, initiator and promoter of the bridge across the Rhone at *Avignon; b. perhaps at Hermillion-en-Maurienne (Savoie), c. 1165; d. Avignon, c. 1184 (feast, April 14). Arriving as a young man in Avignon in 1177, Bénézet (Benedictus) convinced the Avignonais that God willed them to build the first bridge across the turbulent Rhone. For 7 years he collected funds and organized a group of laymen (*donati*) as the *fratres pontis* to carry on his work. The bridge was completed in 1188 (*see* BRIDGEBUILDING). Documents in 1202 refer to him as blessed, in 1237 as saint. His relics are in St. Didier in Avignon.

Bibliography: ActSS April 2:254–263. F. Lefort, "Histoire d'un manuscrit du 13e siècle relatif à la construction des premiers ponts sur le Rhône," *Travaux de l'Académie Nationale de Reims* 86 (1884–85) 206–227; "La Légende de saint Bénézet," Rev QuestHist 23 (1878) 555–570. P. Pansier, "Histoire de l'ordre des frères du pont d'Avignon (1181–1410)," *Annales d'Avignon et du Comtat Venaissin* 7 (1920–21) 5–74. J. Garin, DHGE 7:1292–93.

[M. N. BOYER]

BENIGNI, UMBERTO, Italian ecclesiastical historian, journalist, integralist; b. Perugia, March 30, 1862; d. Rome, Feb. 26, 1934. After ordination (1884)

he became secretary to the archbishop of Perugia and then professor of ecclesiastical history in the diocesan seminary. As a result of his interest in Catholic journalism and in social problems, he acted also as editor of a local journal until he founded (1892) *La Rassegna Sociale,* the pioneer Catholic periodical of this type in Italy. He went to Genoa in 1893 to edit *L'Eco d'Italia* and later to Rome as a collaborator in *La Voce della verità.* One fruit of a stay in Germany to study the language and the social situation was a polemical book on papal grain policies, *Die Getreide politik der Päpste* (1898). While holding the chair of ecclesiastical history at the Apollinaris in Rome (1901–04), he was noted for his lectures, delivered in Italian rather than in the traditional Latin, which were vivacious but lacking in order, precision, and depth. For the use of his students he published *Historiae ecclesiasticae repertorium* (1902), which incorporated his earlier *Propedeutica.* In 1904 he entered the Congregation for the Propagation of the Faith as a secretary (*minutante*). He transferred in 1906 to the secretariat of state, where he worked until 1911 as an undersecretary connected with the press office in the section dealing with extraordinary affairs. There he came into contact with Cardinal Rafael *Merry del Val, papal secretary of state. From 1911 he taught at the Academy of Noble Ecclesiastics. His useful *Manuale di stilo diplomatico* (1920) represented the content of his lectures there.

Monsignor Benigni's opposition to *Modernism made him a leading figure in *Integralism. Because of the clandestine nature of many of his activities, his role in the anti-Modernist movement, though central, remains shrouded in considerable mystery and controversy. Until the necessary documents are brought to light, this situation is likely to continue. When *Correspondenza di Roma,* which he founded in 1907, changed its title to *Correspondance de Rome* in 1908, it served as a kind of international news agency, particularly for the dissemination of information concerning Modernism. In this publication appeared many denunciations of scholars and others who were thought to bear a Modernist taint. After leaving the secretariat of state in 1911, Benigni devoted himself to the *Sodalitium Pianum, which he founded in 1909 and in which he remained the key figure until its dissolution by order of Benedict XV (1921). From this date until his death as a poor man, he continued to favor *Action Française.

The most important of Benigni's several books was *Storia sociale della Chiesa* (5 v. in 7, 1906–33). This study, which was carried to the 14th century, contains considerable source material of a heterogeneous kind, but suffers from a defective critical sense and an imprecise notion of the proper scope of this subject. He contributed numerous articles to the *Catholic Encyclopedia.*

Bibliography: N. Fontaine (pseud. for L. Canet), *Saint-Siège: Action française et catholiques intégraux* (Paris 1928). Schmidlin v.3. DizBiogItal, s.v. "Benigni, U."

[T. P. JOYCE]

BENIGNUS OF DIJON, ST., early martyr (feast, Nov. 1). According to the unhistorical legend from the 6th century, he came from Asia Minor as a disciple of St. *Polycarp and a missionary to Burgundy. He is supposed to have suffered martyrdom at the order of the Roman Emperor *Marcus Aurelius. He was venerated as a saint even before the 6th century and was recognized as the patron of *Dijon. The basilica and the Abbey of Saint-Bénigne were built over his tomb in Dijon.

Bibliography: ActSS Nov. 1:134–194. E. EWIG, LexThK² 2:203–204. G. BARDY, DHGE 7:1314–15. Butler Th Attw 4:236.

[P. VOLK]

BÉNILDE, BL., educator; b. Thuret, near Clermont-Ferrand (Puy-de-Dôme), France, June 14, 1805; d. Saugues (Haute-Loire), France, Aug. 13, 1862 (feast, April 4). Bénilde was the name in religion of Pierre Romançon. From 1817 to 1820 he attended the school in Riom conducted by the *Christian Brothers, and then entered the novitiate of this congregation after being refused admission in 1819 because of his short stature. He taught at Aurillac, Limoges, and Clermont-Ferrand until 1842 when he was assigned to a school newly opened in Saugues. There he spent the remainder of his life as head of the school and superior of the religious community. Under his direction the school became noted for its large number of vocations to the priesthood and brotherhood. Despite his unprepossessing appearance Bénilde had little difficulty in exercising authority over boys. During his externally uneventful life his reputation for sanctity became widespread. His sanctification came through the perfect accomplishment of everyday duties, as Pius XII pointed out on the occasion of Bénilde's beatification, April 1, 1948.

Bibliography: G. RIGAULT, *Un Instituteur sur les autels: Le bienheureux Bénilde* (Paris 1947). A. J. LIDDY, *Chalk-Dust Halo: Life of Blessed Benildus* (London 1956).

[W. J. BATTERSBY]

BENINCASA, URSULA, VEN., foundress of the Theatine Sisters; b. Naples, Oct. 20, 1547; d. St. Elmo's Mount, Naples, Oct. 20, 1618. At the age of 10 she received mystical gifts. In 1579, when refused admission to the Capuchinesses, she retired as a solitary to the nearby St. Elmo's Mount. There she built a church in honor of the Immaculate Conception. After a vision on March 12, 1582, Ursula went to Rome to interest Gregory XIII in her plans for assisting in Church reform. Again in Naples in 1583, she founded the Oblates of the Immaculate Conception, whose members consecrate themselves to God in the education of youth. In 1617 Ursula founded the Contemplative Hermit Sisters, an order with solemn vows and strict enclosure. Gregory XV approved its rules on June 23, 1623, and put this institute and the Oblates under the direction of the Theatine Fathers. To Ursula's vision of Feb. 2, 1617, is attributed the origin of the Blue Scapular of the Immaculate Conception. Pius VI proclaimed the heroicity of her virtues on Aug. 7, 1793.

Bibliography: Heimbucher 2:104–106. N. DEL RE, EncCatt 2:1349. F. M. MAGGI, *Compendium vitae venerabilis matris Ursulae de Benincasa* (Brussels 1658).

[A. SAGRERA]

BENJAMIN, youngest son of *Jacob and a full brother of Joseph; his mother, Rachel, died at his birth (Gn 35.16–19, 24). The Joseph narratives depict Benjamin (Heb. *binyāmîn,* "son of the right hand," i.e., southerner) as the instrument of the estranged Joseph in reuniting and reconciling Jacob's family in Egypt (Genesis 39–50). Little more is known of him than that he had 10 sons (Gn 46.21). According to the census

Thirteenth-century mosaic on a lunette in the vestibule of St. Mark's Basilica, Venice. At right: Joseph's brothers bring Benjamin to Joseph in Egypt (Gn 43). In center: below, Joseph's brothers depart with full sacks; above, Joseph's cup is found in Benjamin's sack. At left: Joseph welcomes his father and brothers to Egypt.

recorded by the *priestly writers, the tribe of Benjamin had 35,400 males of military age at the beginning of the 40 years of wandering in the desert, and 45,000 at its end; on the value of these figures, *see* CENSUS (IN THE BIBLE). At the Israelite conquest of Canaan, the Benjaminites received as a possession a narrow tract of central hill country bounded by Ephraim, Dan, Juda, and the Jordan, containing some of the principal cities of Israelite history (Jos 18.11–28). A barren territory, naturally defensible and strategically located at the heart of the chief routes of communication in Canaan, it determined the warlike character of the tribe and its role in Israelite history as reflected in the blessings of Jacob (Gn 49.27). During the period of the Judges, Aod, a Benjaminite, overthrew a Moabite oppressor, Eglon (Jgs 3.12–30), and under the leadership of Debora and Barac, Benjamin joined the tribal coalition that defeated Sisera (Jgs 5.14). Because of an attempt to protect fellow Benjaminites guilty of a heinous crime, the tribe was nearly exterminated by the reprisal of all Israel. The remnant abducted wives to restore their decimated ranks (Jgs 19–21). Benjaminite martial glory reached its zenith against the Philistine aggression of the 11th century B.C., a crisis that precipitated the establishment of the monarchy and Israelite unification. *Saul, a Benjaminite warrior, rallied Israel and was anointed its first king (1 Sm 9.1–12.25). At his death (*c.* 1000 B.C.) a power struggle ensued between Saul's son *Is-Baal, supported by Abner, general of the army, and David, the newly elected king in Juda (2 Sm 2.1–11). Most Benjaminites remained faithful to Saul's house against Juda until Abner's break with Is-Baal and his pact with David (2 Sm 2.12–3.21). Upon Is-Baal's death David was acknowledged as king by all Israel and shifted his capital from Hebron in Juda to Jerusalem in Benjaminite territory, a neutral location (2 Sm 4.1–5.10). Benjaminite dissatisfaction with David manifested itself in the two abortive rebellions of Absalom and Seba (2 Sm 15–18; 20). Benjamin seems initially to have joined the Northern Kingdom under Jeroboam I at Solomon's death (*c.* 922 B.C.; 3 Kgs 12.20), only to become and remain annexed to Juda when Roboam occupied its territory in order to keep Jerusalem as his capital (3 Kgs 11.29–36; 2 Chr 11.1, 5–12, 23; 14.8). Subsequently, Benjamin became a buffer state in the internal wars for supremacy between the Northern and Southern kingdoms (3 Kgs 15.17–22; 2 Chr 13.19; 15.8). With the destruction of the North in 721 B.C., Benjaminite fortunes became linked with those of Juda. Elements of the tribe are mentioned in the post-Exilic tribal lists of Nehemia's time (1 Chr 8.1–40). The most famous of the later Benjaminites was Saul of Tarsus, the NT Apostle of the Gentiles (Phil 3.5).

Bibliography: EncDictBibl 225–226. J. BRIGHT, *A History of Israel* (Philadelphia 1959). **Illustration credit:** Alinari-Art Reference Bureau.

[R. BARRETT]

BENJAMIN BEN JONAH OF TUDELA

Famous Spanish-Jewish traveler whose Hebrew chronicle *Massa'oth shel Rabbi Benjamin* (Travels of Rabbi Benjamin) is probably the foremost source for the knowledge of Jewish life in Europe, Asia, and North Africa during the 12th century; his birth and death dates are unknown.

From the preface, which was written by another hand anonymously, one learns that Benjamin was the son of Jonah, that he was a scholar, a man of wisdom and understanding, that he came from Tudela, a small community on the river Ebro in the kingdom of Navarre, and that the work was compiled from recordings that he had made—based on his own keen observations and on what had been told him by men of integrity—as he traveled from place to place. Except for these facts, nothing further is known about his background.

Benjamin departed Saragossa in 1160, and for the next 13 years, until his return in 1173, he traversed approximately 300 localities. His itinerary took him through southern France, Italy, Greece, Cilicia, Syria, Palestine, Mesopotamia, Persia, and India, until he penetrated the frontiers of Tibet and China. From China his route homeward lay across Khuzistan, the Indian Ocean, Aden, Yemen, Egypt, and Sicily. He meticulously preserved valuable statistical information on the Jews, recording their populations in the areas he visited and reporting on their manner of living, their communal and educational institutions, their religious life, and their principal vocations. From Benjamin one learns that the Jews of Palestine and Antioch excelled in the arts of dyeing and glassmaking, respectively, and that the large congregation of Thebes in Greece was engaged in the production of silk. He states that in 1168, at the time when Benjamin arrived in *Baghdad, there were 40,000 Jews and 28 synagogues there, that the institution of the exilarchate was still in existence, that Daniel the *exilarch was held in high esteem by the *caliph and the entire city, and that his rule over the Jews extended from Persia to Arabia and Anatolia.

Fortunately, Benjamin did not limit his accounts to Jewish affairs but incorporated into his diary numerous significant details concerning the internal development (political as well as commercial) and geographical location of many of the countries he mentions. At times he appears to have been quite credulous and accepted impossible tales as historical truth; he explains in detail, for example, why the glass coffin that was supposed to contain the body of the Prophet Daniel was suspended by heavy chains from the middle of a bridge at *Susa. On the whole, however, his work is marked by sobriety,

and the geographical information that he presents agrees substantially with the records of contemporary Arabian geographers. With the exception of Abraham ibn Daud's *Sefer ha-Kabbalah,* which was written in 1161, no other source of Jewish statistics of the 12th century is available; thus, Benjamin's *Travels* must be considered a work of prime importance.

Bibliography: M. N. ADLER, tr., *The Itinerary of Benjamin of Tudela* (London 1907), critical text, tr., and comment. M. KOMROFF, ed., *Contemporaries of Marco Polo* (New York 1928). W. BACHER, JewishEnc 3:34–35. A. KAMINKA, UnivJewishEnc 2:180. P. BORCHARDT, EncJudaica 4:130–136, with map of Benjamin's travels.

[N. J. COHEN]

BENJAMIN, JUDAH PHILIP, lawyer and statesman; b. St. Thomas Island, British West Indies, Aug. 6, 1811; d. Paris, France, May 6, 1884. Of Portuguese Jewish descent, Benjamin went as a youth to Charleston, S.C. In 1825 he entered Yale but left after 2 years to go to New Orleans, La., where he married (1833) Natalie St. Martin. After preparing for the legal profession by clerking for a notary in New Orleans, he was admitted to the bar in 1832; 2 years later he and Thomas Slidell published a digest of Louisiana court decisions that remained for many years the standard work on Louisiana law. Benjamin joined the Whig party and was elected (1842) to the Louisiana state legislature. Ten years later he was elected to the U.S. Senate, where he sponsored a Southern Pacific railroad and, ultimately, a canal across the Isthmus of Tehuantepec to link Southern trade with that of the Orient.

Accepting the idea that a Southern party was necessary to repair the sectional balance destroyed by the Compromise of 1850, Benjamin joined the Democratic party in 1856 and announced his support of James Buchanan. In 1858 he was reelected to the Senate. Two years later, he announced his support of secession, defending the right of secession in the Senate. In February 1861 Jefferson Davis named Benjamin attorney general of the Confederate States of America; 7 months later he was transferred to the war department (1861–62), where he was beset by troubles arising from the Confederacy's lack of money and munitions. After the defeat at Roanoke Island, Benjamin's enemies accused him of failing to supply the troops adequately. A congressional investigation followed, during the course of which Davis named Benjamin secretary of state (1862–65). As a Southern leader, he viewed the problems of his government with objectivity and detachment. In 1864 he advocated the enlistment of slaves into the Army, a plan that further embittered his enemies.

In 1865 Benjamin escaped to the West Indies and then to England, where he was admitted (1866) to the British bar and published his *Treatise on the Law of Sale of Personal Property* (1868). He was named queen's counsel (1872) and appeared 136 times (1872–82) in appeal cases before the House of Lords and the privy council's judicial committee. In 1883 he retired to his home in Paris, where he died.

Bibliography: P. BUTLER, *Judah P. Benjamin* (Philadelphia 1907). R. D. MEADE, *Judah P. Benjamin: Confederate Statesman* (New York 1944).

[J. Q. FELLER]

BENNETT, JAMES GORDON, editor; b. Keith, Scotland, Sept. 1, 1795; d. Brooklyn, N.Y., June 1, 1872. After studying for the priesthood in Scotland, he took up teaching at Halifax, Nova Scotia, Canada, in

1819. Immigrating to the U.S., he settled in New York City, where he became (1827) associate editor and Washington correspondent of the *New York Enquirer.* Combining the *Enquirer* with the Charleston, S.C., *Courier* in 1829, Bennett made the paper a leading spokesman for Jacksonian democracy until 1832, when he resigned to establish a newspaper of his own. After several failures, he founded (1835) the *New York Herald,* one of the first penny newspapers. By the time of his retirement (1867), he had built the *Herald's* daily circulation to 90,000 and created an unrivaled staff of American and European correspondents. Bennett's journalistic methods brought charges of sensationalism and vulgarity, but the *Herald's* coverage of financial news, the European scene, and the Civil War was outstanding. The paper was generally Democratic in its political views. Bennett's personal controversies with such figures as Daniel O'Connell of Ireland, Pres. Martin Van Buren, and Bp. John Hughes of New York enlivened the *Herald's* pages. His son James Gordon (1841–1918) succeeded him, establishing (1887) a Paris edition of the *Herald.*

Bibliography: D. C. SEITZ, *The James Gordon Bennetts: Father and Son* (Indianapolis 1928). A. NEVINS, DAB 2:195–199.

[J. L. MORRISON]

BENNO OF MEISSEN, ST., bishop; b. according to legend, Hildesheim, Germany, 1010; d. *c.* 1106 (feast, June 16). Benno, son of a noble Saxon family, became a canon attached to the imperial collegiate church in Goslar and then bishop of Meissen (1066). He was imprisoned by Emperor *Henry IV in 1075–76, apparently for not supporting the Emperor during the revolt of the Saxon nobles, but was later released. In 1077, when Henry IV was excommunicated and deposed by Pope *Gregory VII during the *investiture struggle, Benno took part in the election of Rudolph of Swabia as German king in Henry's stead. He was removed from his see by the prelates of the imperial party at the synod of Mainz in 1085, but restored in 1088 on the recommendation of the antipope *Guibert of Ravenna (Clement III), to whom he had appealed on a trip to Italy (1085–86). After 1097 he recognized *Urban II as legitimate pope. He seems to have earned the title "Apostle of the Wends" by preaching to the Slavonic tribes in his diocese. His cult was established in 1285, when his relics were honored in the reconstructed cathedral of Meissen. Contemporary chronicles record many miracles at his tomb. His canonization in 1523 and the solemn exposition of his relics in 1524 evoked much protest, including a brochure by Martin Luther entitled "Wider den neuen Abgott und alten Teufel, der zu Meissen soll erhoben werden" (Against the New Idol and the Old Devil about to be set up at Meissen). To prevent desecration, his relics were transferred to Bavaria in 1576. Since 1580 they have been in the cathedral of Munich. Benno is patron of Munich, of the bishopric of Meissen, and of old Bavaria. In iconography he is represented with a fish holding in its mouth the keys of the cathedral of Meissen. He is patron of fishermen and drapers, and is invoked for rain.

Bibliography: ActSS June 4:121–186. For more reliable information see articles by O. LANGER in *Mitteilungen des Vereins für Geschichte der Stadt Meissen* 1.3 (1884) 70–95; 1.5 (1886) 1–38; 2.2 (1888) 99–144; 7.1 (1906) 122–125. Hauck 3:841–850. A. BIGELMAIR, DHGE 7:1363–65, good bibliog. Zimmermann KalBen 2:320. H. SCHIECKEL, NDB 2:52–53.

[M. F. MC CARTHY]

BENNO OF METZ, bishop; d. Aug. 3, 940. Benno came from a noble Swabian family. While still a young man he was made a canon at Strassburg. In 906, he retired to the hermitage that had formerly housed St. Meinrad. He rebuilt the chapel and the dwelling and soon gathered a group of disciples. Benno was named bishop of Metz in 927 by King Henry I, who opposed the locally elected candidate; but in 929 Benno was attacked by his enemies and blinded. Although the attackers were excommunicated and banished at the Synod of Duisburg (929), Benno renounced his episcopal office and returned to his former hermitage. In 934 he was joined by Eberhard, provost of Strassburg Cathedral, who developed the hermitage into the celebrated monastery of *Einsiedeln. Benno's cult has never been formally recognized, and he should properly be titled venerable.

Bibliography: A. BIGELMAIR, DHGE 7:1361–62. A. M. BURG, LexThK² 2:206.

[F. BEHRENDS]

BENNO II OF OSNABRÜCK, BL., bishop; b. Böhningen, Swabia, *c.* 1020; d. Iburg, Germany, July 27, 1088 (feast, July 22, Nov. 20). Benno was the student of *Hermannus Contractus, and headed the cathedral school of *Hildesheim, which he revitalized. He was cathedral provost, served in the imperial administration at Goslar and was coadjutor of Abp. *Anno of Cologne before being elected bishop of Osnabrück as the candidate of Emperor *Henry IV (1068). In the investiture struggle, he was excommunicated by Pope *Gregory VII for participating in the Synod of *Worms (1076). He thereafter attempted mediation, interceding for Henry IV at Canossa (1077), at Rome (1078–79), and during Henry's siege of Rome (1082–84). He skillfully retained the trust of both parties. Benno was a noted architect and worked on the imperial residence at Goslar, Speyer Cathedral, the imperial fortifications in Saxony, Hildesheim Cathedral, and his own foundation, the Abbey of Iburg.

See also INVESTITURE STRUGGLE.

Bibliography: *Vita,* MGS 12:58–84. L. THYEN, *Benno II: Bischof von O.* (Osnabrück 1869). G. MEYER VON KNONAU, *Jahrbücher des deutschen Reiches unter Heinrich IV. und Heinrich V.,* 7 v. (Leipzig 1890–1909) v.1 and 4. I. HINDENBERG, *B. II. . . . als Architekt* (Strasbourg 1921). A. FLICHE, *La Réforme grégorienne,* 3 v. (Louvain 1924–37) v.3. Butler Th Attw 3:165–166. G. BÖING, LexThK² 2:206–207. E. N. JOHNSON, "Bishop Benno II of Osnabrück," *Speculum* 16 (1941) 389–403.

[D. ANDREINI]

BENOÎT, MICHEL, astronomer; b. Autun or Dijon, Oct. 8, 1715; d. Peking, Oct. 23, 1774. He entered the Society of Jesus at 22 at Nancy and was sent to the China missions at 25. For this he studied astronomy in Paris under Delisle, Lacaille, and Le Monnier. Upon his arrival in Peking he was assigned to a group of missionary mathematicians of the court. For all his astronomical preparation, Emperor Kien Lung asked him to landscape his gardens. He built in them European houses and a monumental water clock. He prepared a 12.5 by 6.5 foot map of the world, incorporating astronomical as well as geographical data. He also engraved in copper a map of the Chinese empire, creating for this task a group of native specialists in copper engraving. He wrote many of the letters in *Lettres édifiantes* and translated the *Imitation of Christ* into Chinese. From 1762 to 1772 Benoît was superior of the Jesuit mission in

Peking. He died of a stroke a few days after being notified of the suppression of the Society of Jesus.

Bibliography: Streit-Dindinger.

[E. T. SPAIN]

BENSON, WILLIAM SHEPHERD, first chief of naval operations; b. Bibb County, Ga., Sept. 25, 1855; d. Washington, D.C., May 20, 1932. He was the son of Richard Aaron and Catherine Elizabeth (Brewer) Benson. After graduating from the U.S. Naval Academy (1877) he married Mary Augusta Wyse in 1879. In 1907–08, he served as commandant of midshipmen at the Naval Academy. He was promoted to captain in 1909, and he commanded the battleship Utah from 1910 to 1913. When Congress established the office of naval operations, Benson became its chief, May 11, 1915, with the rank of rear admiral; the rank of admiral was authorized for the post in 1916. After serving through World War I, he retired on Sept. 25, 1919. In recognition of their wartime services, bills were proposed (1919) in Congress to award the permanent rank of admiral to Benson; Adm. Henry T. Mayo, commander of the Atlantic Fleet; and Adm. William S. Sims, commander of naval forces in European waters. However, a public controversy between Sims and Secretary of the Navy Josephus Daniels caused the failure of the bills. In 1920, Benson was named chairman of the U.S. Shipping Board, and he continued as a board member until June 1928. He was the author of *The Merchant Marine* (1923), and earlier published a revised edition of Luce's *Seamanship* (1898). Benson, a convert to the Catholic faith, became an active layman in later life. The destroyer *Benson* (DD-421) was named for him.

[J. B. HEFFERNAN]

BENTHAM, JEREMY. Philosopher, legal theorist whose writings stimulated the rise of *utilitarianism in England; b. London, Feb. 15, 1748; d. London, June 6, 1832. Bentham, the son of a wealthy attorney, studied, but never practiced, law and devoted his life to legal reform. Faced with a prevailing interpretation of English common law so closely related to natural law that "law as it is" was almost indistinguishable from "law as it ought to be," he sought a way to put legal and social criticism on a scientific basis. In certain views of T. Hobbes, J. Locke, D. Hume, J. Priestley, W. Paley, C. A. Helvétius, and C. B. Beccaria he found hints of a solution, and these he developed into a form of *hedonism known as utilitarianism.

Adam *Smith argued that the wealth and prosperity of a nation could be best promoted by permitting maximum individual freedom of action, limited only by government as a referee. Bentham agreed, but believed that the referee often followed rules that could be justified only as ancient practice or as what was "natural," with the result that the wrong people were rewarded or punished. We judge machines only on the basis of their utility, why not laws? The effect of Bentham's critique was to show how—in the spheres of civil, penal, and constitutional law—government could so lay down rules that the prospect of painful consequences would lead individuals (acting freely out of self-interest) to act for the public good, equivalent for Bentham with the greatest happiness of the greatest number.

Bentham's ethical theory, found in his *Introduction to the Principles of Morals and Legislation* (1789) and his *Deontology* (1834), was developed for the purpose of finding the springs of human conduct that could be tapped by the legislator. It is open to objection on a number of grounds: as a form of *egoism, as a form of psychological and ethical hedonism, and also on the ground that Bentham failed to show why one morally ought to seek the happiness of everybody. Further, Bentham vastly overrated the practicality of his balance-of-pleasure-over-pain criterion for judging individual acts and laws. Again, although Bentham's influence on modern legal reform in England is perhaps second to none, the lack of a notion of *good more ultimate than quantity of "pleasure," together with an inadequate notion of justice, permits his philosophy to justify any of a broad range of socioeconomic systems from laissez-faire *liberalism to egalitarian *socialism.

See also UTILITARIANISM.

Bibliography: *Works,* ed. J. BOWRING, 11 v. (Edinburgh 1843). C. M. ATKINSON, *Jeremy Bentham: His Life and Work* (London 1905). G. KEETON and G. SCHWARZENBERGER, eds., *Jeremy Bentham and the Law: A Symposium* (London 1948). D. BAUMGARDT, *Bentham and the Ethics of Today* (Princeton 1952).

[R. L. CUNNINGHAM]

BENTIVOGLIO, a Bolognese family that originated from the castle of that name near Bologna. It claimed descent from Enzio (1224?–72), King of Sardinia. The family belonged to a guild of workingmen at Bologna during the 14th century and became powerful in the 15th. It contracted alliances with Aragon, Milan, and later, Ferrara. The following members are prominent:

Guido, cardinal; b. Ferrara, Oct. 4, 1579; d. Rome, Sept. 7, 1644. He studied law at Padua, where he was also taught by Galileo Galilei. He was named private chamberlain by Clement VII in 1587. Paul V sent him as nuncio to Flanders (1607) and to France (1617)

Cardinal Guido Bentivoglio, detail of a portrait by Anthony Van Dyck in the Galleria Pitti at Florence.

and appointed him cardinal in 1621. Louis XIII of France made him protector of French interests in Rome. Guido also served in the Curia as the head of the Inquisition. A very trusted friend of Urban VIII, he would perhaps have succeeded him, had he not died in the conclave. He served at various times as bishop of Bologna, Rhodes, and Palestrina, to which he was appointed in 1641. His writings were a chronicle of the curial life of his time and were published at Venice in 1688. Among the more noted are *Della guerra di Flandria* and *Lettere diplomatiche di Guido Bentivoglio*. His portrait by Van Dyck hangs in the Pitti Palace in Florence.

Annibale, archbishop; date of birth unknown; d. April 21, 1663. Of the poetry in his native tongue that he produced, only *Applausi poetici in lode di Lionara Barroni* remains. He was nominated titular archbishop of Tebe in 1644.

Marco Cornelio, cardinal; b. Ferrara, March 27, 1688; d. Rome, Dec. 30, 1732. After holding various offices in the Roman Curia he was sent as nuncio to France on Oct. 21, 1711, by Clement XI. There his dealings with the Jansenists were unsuccessful because of his insistence upon the propositions of the bull *Unigenitus* (Sept. 8, 1713). He was recalled at the death of Louis XIV, calumniated, it is said, by the regime. He was created a cardinal (Nov. 29, 1719) and Spanish minister plenipotentiary at Rome (July 1726), which post he held until his death.

Domenico, soldier; b. Bologna, July 3, 1781; d. Rome, Dec. 26, 1851. He was admitted to the guard of honor of Eugene Beauharnais in 1805 as a lieutenant, and then as captain he took part in the Napoleonic campaigns from 1800 to 1814. He entered pontifical service after the fall of the Empire and was made a colonel for the gallant defense of Rieti against Sercognani.

Bibliography: J. WODKA, LexThK² 2:208. Pastor v.23, *passim.* R. D. TUCCI, *Il Cardinale Guido Bentivoglio e i suoi Rapporti con la Repubblica di Genova* (Genoa 1934). R. BELVEDERI, *Guido Bentivoglio e la politica Europea del suo tempo, 1607–1621* (Padua 1964). **Illustration credit:** Alinari-Art Reference Bureau.

[R. L. FOLEY]

BENTLEY, RICHARD, distinguished English classical scholar and Christian apologist; b. Oulton, Yorkshire, Jan. 27, 1662; d., Cambridge, July 7, 1742. After taking his B.A. at Cambridge at 18, he served as tutor to the son of E. Stillingfleet, Dean of St. Paul's, and later Bishop of Worcester (1689–99). In Stillingfleet's house he had access to one of the best private libraries of the time, and when he accompanied his pupil to Oxford, he was able to make full use of the Bodleian. In 1690, he was ordained to the Anglican ministry and was appointed chaplain to Stillingfleet. In 1694, he was made Keeper of Royal Libraries, and in 1700 he became Master of Trinity College, Cambridge. Despite bitter feuds occasioned in part by his efforts at reform and in part by his own personality, he retained his mastership until his death, 42 years later.

His *Letter to Mill* (London 1691), published as an appendix to John Mill's edition of the chronicle of the Byzantine historian, John Malalas, revealed his profound knowledge and his brilliant critical powers. It was the first of a series of epoch-making contributions to Greek and Latin textual criticism, metrics, literary history, and historical criticism. Bentley's involvement in a controversy with Sir William Temple over Temple's claim that the *Epistles of Phalaris* was an authentic work led to the writing of his *Dissertation on the Epistles of Phalaris* (London 1697; rev. and enl. ed., 1699). By a critical use of chronological, historical, literary, and linguistic evidence, he proved that the work did not date from the 6th century B.C., but was a forgery of the Hellenistic age. In this work, his masterpiece, he founded higher literary and historical criticism.

Bentley's activity in religious controversy and in Biblical studies is important also and deserves more attention than it usually receives. As the first preacher appointed under the Boyle foundation at Cambridge, he delivered eight sermons on the *Folly of Atheism* (London 1692), making full use of the latest discoveries of Isaac Newton in his apologetic. In 1713, under the pseudonymn, Phileleutherus Lipsiensis, he published his *Remarks,* a strongly worded refutation of the *Discourse of Free-Thinking* by the deist Anthony Collins (1676–1729). His *Proposals for the Edition of the Greek Testament* (London, 1720) is a pioneer work that anticipates in many respects the method of Biblical textual criticism developed by Lachmann and other 19th-century Biblical scholars. Through his own achievements and through his influence, Bentley is universally recognized as one of the greatest representatives of classical scholarship.

Bibliography: J. E. SANDYS, *History of Classical Scholarship,* 3 v. (Cambridge, Eng. 1903–08) 2:401–410. M. L. W. LAISTNER, "Richard Bentley, 1742–1942," *The Intellectual Heritage of the Early Middle Ages: Selected Essays by M. L. W. Laistner,* ed. C. G. STARR (Ithaca, N.Y. 1957) 239–254. R. C. JEBB, DNB 2:306–314. A. T. BARTHOLOMEW, *Richard Bentley, D.D.: A Bibliography of His Works* (Cambridge, Eng. 1908).

[M. R. P. MC GUIRE]

BENUSSI, VITTORIO, Italian experimental psychologist of the Austrian school at Graz; b. Trieste, 1878; d. Padua, 1927. The school at Graz is the "early" Gestalt school, as distinguished from the better-known group led by M. *Wertheimer, K. *Koffka, and W. Kohler (1887–) in Germany in the first 2 decades of the 20th century (*see* GESTALT PSYCHOLOGY).

Benussi was interested in problems of visual and somesthetic perception; he worked also on the perception of time, publishing his results in *Psychologie der Zeitauffassung* (Heidelberg 1913). The perception of weight and solidity, optical illusions, and visual and tactual movement claimed his attention as subjects for experimentation. He emphasized variability, as opposed to apparent constancy, of sensational or qualitative aspects of perception, insisting that configurational phenomena are subject to distortion as compared with the objective situation. He held that for spatial, temporal, and tactual Gestalt, there was dependence upon the inner conditions of attitude and volition of the subject. He also maintained that the sense organ was independent insofar as the same Gestalt can be comprehended through different senses; thus he established a striking similarity between touch and vision. Successive stimulation of two points of the skin, he proved, provokes the impression that the object is moving from one place to another.

Between 1902 and World War I, Benussi did most of his experimental work at Graz, publishing a long list of articles in *Zeitschrift für Psychologie* and in *Archiv für die gesamte Psychologie*. During a period of controversy between the psychologies of act and of content, he demonstrated that most of the data of perception could be interpreted in terms of act.

Bibliography: Boring HistExpPsych. H. HELSON, "Psychology of *Gestalt*," AmJPsych 36 (1925) 342–370, 494–526; 37 (1926) 25–62, 189–223.

[M. G. KECKEISSEN]

BENVENUTUS SCOTIVOLI, ST., bishop; d. Ancona, March 22, 1283 (feast, March 22). Having studied law at Bologna, he returned to his Diocese of Ancona, was ordained, and became archdeacon there. In 1263 he was appointed administrator, and in 1264 bishop, of the Diocese of Osimo, vacant since 1239. He was also made governor of the March of Ancona. Buried in the cathedral of Osimo, he became the city's patron saint in 1755. An earlier inspection of his tomb had revealed a gray capuche sewn to a lambskin, and this led the popular biographer Jean Baldi (1620) to assert that this bishop had been a Franciscan. L. *Wadding accepted the evidence and F. Diaz obtained the concession of a Mass and Office (1697) for the new edition of the Franciscan Breviary. In 1765, D. Pannelli, a priest of Osimo, contended that Benvenutus had not been a Franciscan, opening a lively controversy with Flaminio da Latera. Although da Latera could not establish his position the feast of St. Benvenutus was nevertheless retained in the Franciscan calendar.

Bibliography: A. DU MONSTIER, *Martyrologium franciscanum* (2d ed. Paris 1753). ActSS March 3:390–393. Wadding Ann 4:246; 5:4–5. D. PANNELLI, *Memorie istoriche de'santi Vitaliano e Benvenuto, vescovi d'Osimo,* 2 v. (Osimo 1763). D. FILLARETI, *Lettere . . . a un Padre Minorita* (2d ed. Osimo 1765). L. OLIGER, "Discussiones della vita e degli scritti del P. Flaminio Annibali da Latera, O.F.M.," ArchFranctHist 7 (1914) 577–620, esp. 596–598; DHGE 3:393–394. L. JADIN, *ibid.* 8:292–293. LÉON DE CLARY, *Lives of the Saints and Blessed of the Three Orders of St. Francis,* 4 v. (Taunton, Eng. 1885–87) 1:517–519. Baudot-Chaussin 3:497–498.

[J. CAMBELL]

BENZIGER, a family associated with the publication of Catholic books in Europe and the United States. The founder of the publishing house was Joseph Charles Benziger (1762–1841), who had started a small business in religious articles in Einsiedeln, Switzerland in 1793. When the French invaded Switzerland during the Revolution, he and his family were forced to abandon the enterprise and flee the country. On returning home, he set up as a bookseller. In 1833, when Charles and Nicholas Benziger succeeded their father, they began printing and publishing books. In 1853 a sales branch of the firm was opened in New York, and it became a publishing house in 1860, under the direction of J. N. Adelrich Benziger (d. 1878) and Louis Benziger (d. 1896). In 1897, the American branch separated from the Swiss firm.

When Louis Benziger retired, he was followed by Louis G. Benziger and Nicholas C. Benziger. In 1912, 1919, and 1923, respectively, Xavier N., Bernard A., and Alfred F. Benziger were admitted to membership in the firm, their father, Nicholas, having retired. In 1964, Bernard C. Benziger, a member of the family's sixth generation, was president of Benziger Brothers, Inc., with headquarters in New York City. The publishing house also maintained branch stores in Cincinnati (1860), Chicago (1887), San Francisco (1929), and Boston (1937). A press room, bindery, and warehouse, originally established in Brooklyn in 1894, have been maintained in Totowa, N.J. since 1962.

In addition to general publications and the publishing of textbooks for Catholic schools and colleges, the firm also specializes in the publication of missals for the laity. It is the only publishing house in the U.S.

Nicholas Benziger.

permitted by the Holy See to print and publish official liturgical texts, which are under the control of the Holy See. The firm has been granted recognition as printers of the Holy Apostolic See (1867) and as printers to the Congregation of Rites (1944). Since its beginning in the U.S., the house has published more than 2,500 titles.

Bibliography: K. J. BENZIGER, *Geschichte der Familie Benziger von Einsiedeln, Schweiz* (New York 1923).

[W. C. SMITH]

BENZIGER, AUGUST, portrait painter; b. Einsiedeln, Switzerland, Jan. 2, 1867; d. New York, N.Y., April 13, 1955. His parents were Adelrich and Marie (Koch) Benziger, of the well-known Catholic publishing families. After attending Downside College, England, he studied at the Royal Academy, Vienna, and the Académie Julian, Paris, where he worked under the academic artist, A. W. Bouguereau. In Paris and in the U.S. Benziger specialized in portraiture of great technical finish and gratifying idealization of his subjects, among whom were Presidents William McKinley and Theodore Roosevelt; Charles Schwab and J. Pierpont Morgan; Cardinals James Gibbons of Baltimore, William O'Connell of Boston, and John Farley of New York; and Popes Leo XIII, Benedict XV, and Pius XI. His unposed portrait of Pope Leo catches the lively spirit behind the aged face, whereas in most of his portraits the subjects seem stuffy and pompous by later standards.

Bibliography: R. BRAUNGART, *August Benziger: His Life and Work* (Munich 1922). M. G. and R. BENZIGER, *August Benziger: Portrait Painter* (Glendale, Calif. 1958).

[F. GETLEIN]

BENZO OF ALBA, bishop, Gregorian polemist; b. northern Italy, early 11th century; d. 1086–89. There is little certain knowledge about Benzo. He first appears at a Roman council (1059) where he signed himself as bishop of Alba. An extreme imperial partisan and bitter papal enemy, he vigorously supported Cadalus, the imperial antipope Honorius II, against Pope *Alexander II (1061). After Cadalus's deposition (May 1064), Benzo continued to attack the papacy in his writings until the *Patarines drove him from his see (1076). About 1086 he collected all his writings into a single volume, which he dedicated to Emperor *Henry IV under the title *Libri VII ad Heinricum IV*. At this point he disappears from history. His verse and prose prove Benzo well grounded in the classics and a skillful parodist.

See also INVESTITURE STRUGGLE.

Bibliography: K. PERTZ, MGS 11:591–597. Hauck 3:707 and *passim*. C. MIRBT, Herzog-Hauck PRE 2:605–606. Mann 6:242 and *passim*. Manitius 3:454–457. T. SCHIEFFER, LexThK² 2:210–211. A. FLICHE, *Catholicisme* 1:1456.

[S. WILLIAMS]

BENZONI, GIROLAMO DE, Italian chronicler of the New World; b. Milan, 1517; d. 1570. In 1541 he went to the New World and traveled with the Spaniards, particularly in the provinces of Central America, for 15 years. In 1556 he returned to Italy and published the account of his experiences in the Americas. *La Historia del Mondo Nuovo* (Venice 1565) was translated into Latin, French, Dutch, and English. It was not translated into Spanish, for Benzoni had little good to say of the Spaniards or their colonial empire. His work is full of gossip and atrocity stories, which made the book very popular and gave Theodore de Bry subject material for his engravings. Benzoni was thus a contributor to the development of the Black Legend.

[J. HERRICK]

BEOWULF

The greatest surviving Old English poem, an epic that recounts two main events in the life of the legendary hero, Beowulf, with some digressions on apparently historical matters. In the first episode, Beowulf slays Grendel and Grendel's mother, demons who, in human form, are terrorizing the court of the Danish king; in the second, he kills a marauding dragon with the help of his kinsman Wiglaf, but is himself mortally wounded.

The poem exists in only one manuscript, the Cotton MS Vitellius A XV, 129a–198b, in the British Museum, London. This text dates from *c.* 1000, but scholars now generally date the poem's composition in the late 8th century. Some German critics (e.g., Ettmüller, Möller, Boer) in the 19th century insisted that it was the work of several authors. Further, such scholars held that it was substantially a pagan poem into which Christian interpolations had been introduced much later. Both these notions have been almost universally discounted. The author is, of course, anonymous. He was, however, familiar not only with the rich pagan Scandinavian and Germanic heroic legends but also, as F. Klaeber, R. W. Chambers, and C. W. Kennedy have shown (see bibliography), well instructed in the Christian virtues that permeate the poem. Its language is predominantly West Saxon with an admixture of other, particularly Anglian, elements. This combination of language and the poem's substantially Christian spirit would suggest that it was written either by a monk of West Mercia (known today as the West Midlands) or by a court poet.

Saga Elements. Much of the old Nordic tradition is unquestionably evident in the epic. The loyalty of thane to lord, the chief bond of early Germanic society, is prominent. Emphasis on gift giving, the lord's way of recognizing and rewarding the loyalty of his thane, is also important. The old element of fate or Wyrd that so permeated the old Nordic tales is still present but far less pervasively. The blood feuds that disrupted families and kingdoms in primitive northern society have a place as well, but it is significant that they are alluded to in the historical episodes or asides rather than made prominent in the main action of the poem. The character of Beowulf himself, with his fabulous handgrip, owes something to the bear-man motif that runs through many of the old Norse sagas, and, in general, a great deal of the physical detail of the story comes from the same source. The struggles with man-monsters, with water trolls in mysterious caves at the bottom of the sea, and with fire-breathing dragons all had a history in older Nordic legend, and practically all the details of the burial ceremonies for Beowulf are derived from pagan Nordic custom.

Distinctive Features. Despite these many similarities, *Beowulf* is remarkably and fundamentally different from the pagan sagas. In the first place, the character of Beowulf himself has undergone a substantial transformation. He is no longer the ruthless, self-centered pagan hero in pursuit merely of his own glory. He is eager for fame, as he frequently tells us, but performs all his exploits in a spirit of Christian humility and charity: he frequently acknowledges his dependence upon God for his prowess and in each episode dedicates his powers to help others.

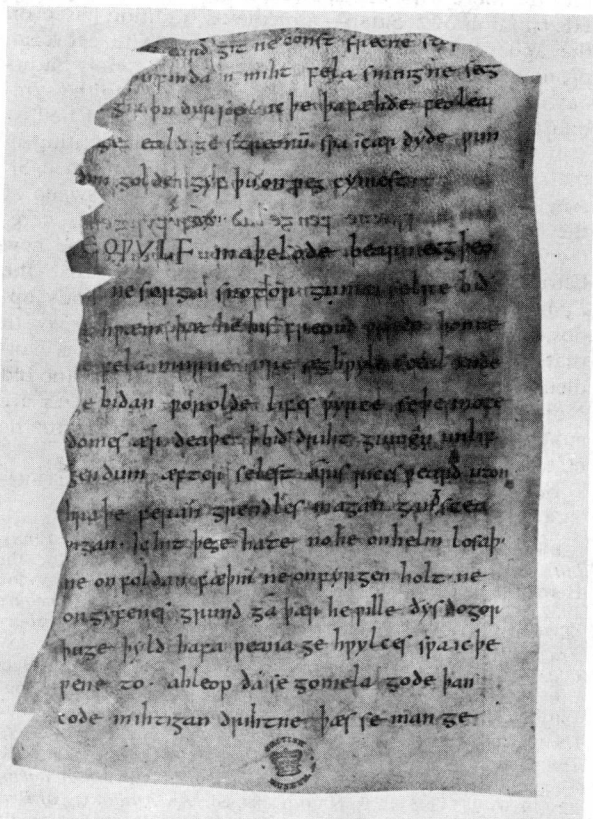

The unique manuscript of "Beowulf," written in England c. 1000 in Anglo-Saxon (Cotton MS Vitellius A XV).

Christian Allegory. Moreover, a deeper transformation has taken place. It extends to the whole substance and movement of the poem, to such an extent that it may be considered an allegory of the Christian story of salvation. In the story of Beowulf saving the kingdom of Hrothgar from the depradations of Grendel and his dam, and his own people from the ravages of the dragon, the Beowulf poet, it seems clear, was adapting the familiar legends of the North to allegorize for a Christian audience man's fall from a state of innocent happiness into the power of Satan and his absolute need of a savior who came to him through the Incarnation. Sufficient clue for such an audience to identify Beowulf with the Savior would be the clear identification of Grendel and his dam in the first episodes with the powers of darkness or the forces to be overcome by the Savior, and, in the last episode, the parallel, which Klaeber has pointed out, between the circumstances that precede the deaths of Christ and Beowulf.

Relationship to the Harrowing of Hell. Particularly striking is the parallel between the second episode and Christ's harrowing of hell that had become a literary tradition before the time of the *Beowulf* poet. Beowulf descends into a mere to a burning cave, slays Grendel's dam, cuts off the head of the dead man-monster Grendel, and then ascends through the waters triumphantly bearing the magic sword and the severed head. It was an Anglo-Saxon tradition (as Anglo-Saxon illuminated manuscripts reveal) to represent hell as a lake infested by man-monsters and serpents. Hence the *Beowulf* audience would readily have associated Beowulf's descent into the mere with Christ's descent into hell to signalize His triumph over Satan—a medieval tradition based on the apocryphal Gospel of Nicodemus. The exorcism pronounced over the baptismal water in the Holy Saturday liturgy would also have lent significance to the symbolism of demon-infested waters as a symbol of hell.

It would seem that the *Beowulf* poet was writing in the spirit of Pope St. Gregory, who had cautioned St. Augustine of Canterbury not to make a clean sweep of the old, native Anglo-Saxon customs, myths, ceremonies, and traditions but to adapt them to the new Christian message. It would seem further that the *Beowulf* poet was proceeding in a manner exactly opposite to that of the authors of poems like *Andreas*. In that work an explicitly Christian subject matter is handled in the language and literary conventions of the old Norse sagas, whereas in *Beowulf* the pagan sagas are subtly reshaped and reorganized to shadow forth the essential facts of the new story of salvation.

See also ENGLISH LITERATURE, 1; OLD NORSE LITERATURE; ICELANDIC LITERATURE; SAGA.

Bibliography: R. W. CHAMBERS, ed., *Beowulf: With the Finnsburg Fragment* (2d ed. New York 1932); "Beowulf and the Heroic Age in England," *Man's Unconquerable Mind* (London 1952). F. KLAEBER, ed., *Beowulf and the Fight at Finnsburg* (Boston 1950). C. L. WRENN, ed., *Beowulf: With the Finnesburg Fragment* (London 1953). C. W. KENNEDY, tr., *Beowulf: The Oldest English Epic* (New York 1940). M. B. McNAMEE, "Beowulf: An Allegory of Salvation," JEngGermPhilol 59 (1960) 190–207; "Beowulf: Christian Hero," *Honor and the Epic Hero* (New York 1960). A. CABANISS, "Beowulf and the Liturgy," JEngGerm Philol 54 (1955) 195–201. J. R. R. TOLKIEN, "Beowulf: The Monsters and Critics," *Proceedings of the British Academy* 22 (1936) 245–295. L. E. NICHOLSON, ed., *An Anthology of Beowulf Criticism* (pa. Notre Dame, Ind. 1963). **Illustration credit:** Courtesy of the Trustees of the British Museum.

[M. B. MC NAMEE]

BERAKHOT

The first tractate of the first order of the *Mishnah. The Mishnah contains the oral law transmitted together with the written Law at Mt. Sinai and passed down through the generations until Rabbi *Judah ha-Nasi compiled it into a set written text comprising six orders. The order Zeraim (Seeds) contains laws pertaining to the cultivation of the land and the produce of the soil. Its opening tractate, Berakhot (Blessings), specifies the benedictions for various foods and also discusses two sources of spiritual nourishment—the Shema [Hear (O Israel)], with its strong declaration of faith, and the Tephillah (Prayer), with its focal point in man's reliance on divine assistance.

The 64 folios (double pages) of the tractate are divided into nine chapters, each named after the opening words. The first three chapters deal with the Shema, consisting of the three passages of the Pentateuch (Dt 6.4–9; 11.13–21 and Nm 15.37–41) that are recited twice daily, morning and evening. Chapter 1 opens with the question: "From what time may the Shema be read?" and then designates the time for its recitation in the evening and the morning, and the proper manner of recitation.

Chapter 2 discusses the dedicated intention to fulfill a divine command. Valid and invalid recitations are listed, and reasons are given for the sequence in which the sections of the Shema are recited. Special occasions are enumerated when an individual may be excused from reciting the Shema.

Chapter 3 provides for further exemptions from the recitation of the Shema and also from the duty of reciting the Tephillah and putting on the *phylacteries.

Chapters 4 and 5 deal with the Tephillah. The first of these prescribes the three periods during the day when the Tephillah has to be recited, as well as the time for the recitation of the Musaph (the additional prayer) on the Sabbath, New Moon, Festivals, and Holydays. Chapter 5 discusses preparation for prayer to ensure devoted concentration and to guard against error or deviation from the set prayer. It also outlines prayers for special purposes, e.g., for rain or for the termination of the Sabbath.

The last four chapters deal with blessings. Chapter 6 contains blessings for enjoyment of food, drink, and scent, since "if one enjoys aught of this world without reciting a benediction over it, it is as if he robbed the Almighty" (*Ber.* 35b). The question is raised whether one benediction may serve for a number of foods. The closing portion of the chapter begins the subject of grace after meals. Chapter 7 outlines the procedure for grace when three or more persons are present and one leads in the recitation of grace. Chapter 8 discusses laws and ceremonies regarding Kiddush (sanctification) and Havdalah ("distinction," a ceremony marking the end of the Sabbath), as well as additional laws regarding the saying of grace.

Chapter 9 contains a variety of blessings giving praise and thanksgiving for unusual occasions, as on beholding a place where miracles have been wrought; on seeing lightning or mountains or hearing thunder; on entering and leaving a strange town. The last Mishnah of this chapter enjoins a benediction over evil tidings as well as over what are considered good tidings; the outcome of events is hidden from mortals by a veil, so that they are not in a position to pass an accurate final judgment. The closing words of advice are that the spiritual influence of faith should govern daily human relations.

*Halakah (law) and *Haggadah (related legends) are intertwined throughout. Haggadic material is abundant in Berakhot, proportionately more so than in any other of the 63 tractates of the Mishnah.

Bibliography: I. EPSTEIN, ed. and tr., *Hebrew-English Edition of the Babylonian Talmud,* 4 v. (London 1960). J. D. HERZOG, ed. and tr., *The Mishnah: Berakoth, Peah, Demai* (New York 1946). A. COHEN, tr., *The Babylonian Talmud: Tractate Berakot* (Cambridge, Eng., 1921). M. FRIEDLANDER, JewishEnc 3:47–50. H. REVEL, UnivJewishEnc 2:190–191. A. MARMORSTEIN, Enc Judaica 4:167–171.

[E. SUBAR]

BERARD OF CARBIO AND COMPANIONS, SS.,

Franciscan protomartyrs; d. Morocco, Jan. 16, 1220 (feast, Jan. 16). At the Franciscan General Chapter of 1219, *Francis of Assisi decided to send friars to the missions and six were chosen for Morocco: Vitalis, Berard, Peter, Adjutus, Accursio, and Odo. Vitalis, who became ill, remained in Aragon. The others went to Coimbra, then to Alenquer, and thence to Seville. To free himself from their proselytizing, the Moorish governor Aboul Ala banished them to Morocco in charge of the Christian, Pedro Fernandez. In Marrakech, the missionaries stayed at the home of Dom Pedro, exiled brother of Alfonso II of Portugal. Berard, who alone knew Arabic, insisted on preaching. Sultan Aboidile (Abou Yacoub) in vain ordered the friars to leave the country; he then imprisoned them for 20 days without food. But as soon as they were free, they resumed their apostolate in the city. During an expedition led by Dom Pedro against bandits, Berard, who was serving as a chaplain for the Prince, gained the good will of the Prince's Moorish troops. Upon returning to the capital, Berard persisted in preaching, until the Sultan himself encountered the friars on the road. During the interrogation—in which Prince Abou Said tried to save them—Odo drew attention by his fearless answers, and the Sultan, exasperated, ordered their execution. Dom Pedro collected the relics of the martyrs in two silver reliquaries and, upon his return to Portugal, brought them to Ceuta, to Seville, and then to Coimbra, where they were deposited at *Santa Cruz. The career of these martyrs and the presence of their relics in the church of the *Canons Regular of St. Augustine in Coimbra determined the Franciscan vocation of *Anthony of Padua. The cult of Berard and his companions was approved by Sixtus IV, Aug. 4, 1481.

Bibliography: *Chronica XXIV Generalium Ordinis Minorum,* AnalFranc 3 (1897) 579–596. JORDAN OF GIANO, *Chronica fratris Jordani,* ed. H. BOEHMER (Paris 1908) 7, n.1. GILES OF ASSISI, *Dicta* (Quarracchi-Florence 1905). LÉON DE CLARY, *Lives of the Saints and Blessed of the Three Orders of St. Francis,* 4 v. (Taunton, Eng. 1885–87) 1:99–111. H. KOEHLER, *L'Église chrétienne du Maroc . . .* (Paris 1935). E. LONGPRÉ, *Catholicisme* 1:1457–58. BiblSanct 2:1271–72.

[J. CAMBELL]

BERARDI, CARLO SEBASTIANO,

priest, canonist; b. Oneglia, Italy, Aug. 26, 1719; d. Turin, 1768. His theological training was directed by the Piarists at Savona. After his ordination he studied law at Turin, particularly the jurisprudence of ecclesiastical law. His appointment to the law faculty of the royal University of Turin came in 1749, and in 1754 he was given the chair of Canon Law at the same place. He devoted the remainder of his life to the teaching and research work of Canon Law. His principal works are: *Commentaria in ius ecclesiasticum universum* (4 v. Taurini, 1776), *De rebus ad canonum scientiam pertinentibus* (2 v. Milan 1846), and *Gratiani canones genuini ab apocriphis discreti, suivis de De variis ss. canonum collectionibus ante Gratianum* (4 v. Taurini 1752–66). Although great effort was expanded in preparing this work, a number of erroneous impressions are interjected necessitating caution in its use.

Bibliography: L. CARRET, DDC 2:766. Hurter Nomencl 5.1: 206–208. Schulte 3.1:524.

[T. F. DONOVAN]

BÉRAULT-BERCASTEL, ANTOINE HENRI JEAN FRANÇOIS DE,

Church historian; b. Briey (Meurthe-et-Moselle), France, Nov. 21, 1720; d. Noyon, 1794. He was accepted into the Society of Jesus on Sept. 28, 1736, but left it in 1753 to become a parish priest at Omerville (Seine-et-Oise), and later a canon of Noyon. After writing poetry and fiction of no great merit, he began his famed *Histoire de l'église* (Paris 1778–90), which was to reach 24 volumes. It had a wide circulation, since it was written for the general educated reader rather than the scholarly specialist, and it passed through several editions (Maastricht 1780–91, Toulouse 1811) and translations into Italian (Venice 1793), and German (Vienna 1784). M. R. A. Henrion has published the finest French edition, with a continuation to 1844, in 13 volumes (Paris 1844). It exists in a condensation extending to 1857 made by P. B. Gams in 3 volumes and a supplement (Innsbruck 1854–60).

Bibliography: Sommervogel 1:1322. Hurter Nomencl 3:347. L. BERRA, EncCatt 2:1369. R. Metz, LexThK² 2:211.

[E. D. MC SHANE]

BERCHARIUS, ST.,

b. Aquitaine; d. 685 or 696 (feast, Oct. 16). Bercharius was educated perhaps at Reims and then entered the Benedictine Abbey of *Luxueil, possibly during the abbacy of Waldebert (629–670). Nivard, Bishop of Reims, asked his help for the foundation of Hautvillers, making him its first abbot. He built churches in honor of St. Peter and of the Virgin Mary and founded two monasteries in the forest of Der, one for women, Puellemontier, and one for men, the more famous Montier-en-Der, where he was buried. The *Vita* states that Bercharius died of wounds inflicted by a monk, Daguinus, whom he had been moved to correct. His cult began soon after his death and is well attested in the 9th and 10th centuries.

Bibliography: W. LEVISON, "Die Merowingerdiplome für Montier-en-Der," NeuesArch 33 (1908) 757. *Vita Bercharii,* Mabillon AS 2:797–826, late-10th-cent. life by ADSO, Abbot of Montier-en-Der. *Vita Nivardi,* MGSrerMer 5:164–168, foundation of Hautvillers. Manitius 2:432–442. E. DE MOREAU, DHGE 8:343–344. J. VAN HECKE, Preface to *Vita* in ActSS Oct. 7.2: 986–1010. Butler Th Attw 4:128–129.

[V. I. J. FLINT]

BERDÎAEV, NIKOLAÏ ALEKSANDROVICH,

apocalyptic and existential-personalist philosopher; b. Kiev, March 6, 1874; d. Clamart, France, March 24, 1948. He was the second child of a military family dating to Louis VI of France. He entered Kiev university (1894) where he met L. Chestov and engaged in Marxist activities, was arrested, and finally exiled (1898) to Vologda. With S. Bulgakov he edited (1904) a social-religious periodical, *Novy Put'* (The

New Way). After serving 2 years as professor of philosophy at Moscow, he was deported by the Leninists (1922) and established the Religious Philosophical Society in Berlin but transferred its activities (1924) to Paris; there, as leading Russian *emigré* spokesman and critic of communism, he edited the religious-philosophical review *Put'* (1925–40). He also organized interconfessional meetings of Orthodox, Protestant, and Catholic figures, but he himself tended to the "left" of Orthodox positions. Cambridge awarded him an honorary doctorate in divinity (1947).

Berdíaev's mature philosophy, combining Alexandrine-Cappadocian *Gnosticism, medieval *exemplarism, Rineland *mysticism, German*idealism, and Russian religious thought, is designated "eschatological metaphysics," a term that represents "the maximum experience of human existence" as revealed by the Christian promise of an ultimate transfiguration of creation. Discontent with the given world and hope for its renewal prompted Berdíaev to forswear logic for a prophetic and mystical language. He held that man's destiny is to create his personality as a unique and universal theandric image, despite the objectivizations of legalist ethics, culture, and society. Creativity is realized in "existential time" that ultimately prepares the human community (*Sobornost*) for the coming of God's Kingdom. As the Philo of his age, Berdíaev speaks a "profoundly Christian" language employing many Catholic elements, but he has been inaccurately described as a Manichaean and, possibly because of an anti-Thomistic bent, an opponent of Christian philosophy. *See* EXISTENTIALISM.

Bibliography: Works. *Dream and Reality: An Essay in Autobiography,* tr. K. LAMPERT (New York 1951); *The Divine and the Human,* tr. R. M. FRENCH (London 1949); *The Beginning and the End,* id. (London 1952); *The Destiny of Man,* tr. N. DUDDINGTON (New York 1960). Literature. B. SCHULTZE, Lex ThK² 2:213. L. MÜLLER, RGG³ 1:1041–42. D. A. LOWRIE, *Rebellious Prophet* (New York 1960). M. SPINKA, *Nicolas Berdyaev: Captive of Freedom* (Philadelphia 1950). E. PORRET, *Berdiaeff: Prophète des temps nouveaux* (Neuchâtel 1951).

[D. A. DRENNEN]

BERENGAR I, KING OF ITALY, king from 888 and emperor from 915; b. *c.* 850; d. Verona, Italy, April 7, 924. He was the Marquis of Friuli and a grandson of *Louis I the Pious through his mother, Gisela. On the deposition of *Charles III the Fat as emperor (887), he accepted election by the Italian magnates to the iron crown of Lombardy, ignoring the claims of *Arnulf, an illegitimate member of the *Carolingian dynasty, who had been elected emperor in Germany. He was crowned king of Italy at Pavia on Jan. 6, 888. Thereafter a series of rivals forced him to defend his position. The Lombard duke, *Guido III of Spoleto, inflicted a serious defeat on Berengar and had himself crowned king of Italy in 889 and then emperor at Rome in 891. After Guido's death, Pope *Stephen V supported the claims of Arnulf of Carinthia, but *Lambert, Guido's son, was able to gain the backing of Pope *Formosus, from whom he received the imperial crown in 892. To add to his troubles, Berengar suffered a defeat at the hands of the Magyars, who invaded the peninsula in 899, and he found himself faced with yet another rival when Louis III (d. 928), King of Provence, a grandson of *Louis II, had himself crowned emperor in 901 by *Benedict IV. Berengar was, however, able to drive his various opponents from the field. He captured and blinded Louis in 904, and after a successful campaign against the Saracens in alliance with the papacy, he at last received imperial coronation in Rome at the hands of Pope *John X (December 915). By 922 he had fallen out with the Pope, who meanwhile had crowned Rudolf II of Burgundy (d. 937) as king. Although Berengar was able to defeat the pretender's forces in the field, he soon fell victim to an assassination plot worked out by his rival.

Bibliography: E. L. DÜMMLER, ed., *Gesta Berengarii imperatoris* (Halle 1871). L. SCHIAPARELLI, ed., *I diplomi di Berengarie I* (Fonti per la storia d'Italia 35; Rome 1903). P. HIRSCH, *Die Erhebung Berengars I von Friaul, König in Italien* (Strassburg 1910). O. PÀSTINE, *Il regno di Berengario I* (Longo 1912). G. FASOLI, *I re d'Italia, 888–962* (Florence 1949) 1–95. C. G. MOR, *L'età feudale,* 2 v. (Milan 1952–53) 1:1–83. S. GENESTET, DHGE 8:360.

[B. J. COMASKEY]

BERENGARIUS OF TOURS

Author of Eucharistic heresy; b. Tours, *c.* 1000; d. Saint-Cosmas Island, near Tours, 1088. His writings initiated the first clear-cut heresy in the history of Eucharistic theology; they gave occasion to the Berengarian controversy, in which a series of opposing monographs clarified and substantially developed the Eucharistic doctrine (*see* EUCHARISTIC CONTROVERSIES).

Life and Work. Berengarius studied under *Fulbert at Chartres. He became *scholasticus* at St. Martin's school at Tours in 1031, and was appointed archdeacon of Angers in 1041. His Eucharistic teachings first came under ecclesiastical notice at a Council held in Rome in 1050. There his doctrine was condemned along with that of a 9th-century monk, *Ratramnus of Corbie, though the Council wrongly attributed the work of Ratramnus to *John Scotus Erigena. Further condemnations took place at Vercelli (1050), Paris (1051), Rome (1059), and again at Rome (1079), where Berengarius signed a formula in which the words *substantialiter converti* appear for the first time in an ecclesiastical document (DB 355). He retired from public life and died at peace with the Church. Berengarius seems to have been a chaste and upright man, charitable to the poor; but the evidence of his writings points to intellectual pride.

Direct knowledge of the teachings of Berengarius is derived from four sources: some early correspondence; extracts surviving from a lost *opusculum,* written shortly after the Roman Council of 1059 and cited by *Lanfranc of Bec in his own treatise, which is a reply to this lost *opusculum;* the lengthy *De sacra coena,* a polemic against Lanfranc; and finally a brief memorial of the events of 1078–79, written by Berengarius shortly after the Roman Council of 1079. Berengarius's major work, the *De sacra coena,* is an extremely rare work discovered in 1770 in a single extant MS. Considered entirely apart from the doctrine it presents, the *De sacra coena* is extremely lengthy and prolix, written in bad Latin without any semblance of order or consecutive development, lacking chapter headings and even paragraphs, and worst of all, made entirely tedious by the repetition of its themes.

Controversy. The three great works of anti-Berengarian controversy are the treatises of Lanfranc, *Guitmund of Aversa, and *Alger of Liège. Other writers contributed, but these three are traditionally cited. The controversy had its roots in the *Paschasius Radbertus–Ratramnus controversy of the 9th century. There is no doubt that Berengarius based his Eucharistic theology on that of Ratramnus, although he thought Ratramnus's work to be that of John Scotus, while the adversaries of Berengarius followed Paschasius Radbertus. This is not to say that the views of Berengarius would necessarily have been accepted by Ratramnus. However, it is generally held that Berengarius and Ratramnus can be reconciled in substance, if not on every point.

Berengarius approached the Eucharistic mystery as a rationalist and dialectician, not as a believer. He had only contempt for the common belief, which he called the opinion of the mob. He cited the Fathers where it suited him in support of his views, but emphatically proclaimed the "incomparable superiority" of reason over traditional authority. He rejected scornfully ("council of vanities, a hub-bub") the authority of the Church when it was brought to bear upon his teachings. Yet the "reason" upon which he built was an immature philosophical system, the dialectics of the prescholastic schools. Berengarius did not know metaphysics; yet his basic Eucharistic error was in the metaphysical order. He believed that the senses grasp not only the appearances of an object but also its essence, in a direct and immediate manner. Thus the distinction between substance and accident was lost on him, and he regarded as absurd a doctrine that held for a change of substance while the accidents remained.

Berengarius's inability to understand the traditional teaching of a Real Presence of the Body and Blood of Christ *in specie aliena* led him to adopt a crude and materialistic interpretation of the doctrine of substantial conversion. Finally, he criticized the realist formulas with arguments that amounted to mere logic-chopping and playing with words. "If bread is called the Body of Christ," he said, "then bread must remain." But Berengarius had to take account of the realistic language of the Fathers, and thus built up a positive theory of the Eucharist as mere sign and symbol. He held that through the Consecration a conversion occurs, not of the Eucharistic elements themselves, but of the sentiment of the believer with respect to them. The elements remain what they had been before, but they become the Body and Blood of Christ in the contemplation of the recipient, and are endowed for him with the value of Christ's passion and death. Thus the conversion is purely in the moral order, and the Eucharistic activity begins and ends within the consciousness of the believer himself.

The opponents of Berengarius clarified and organized the revealed teaching, and carried it to a point of development considerably in advance of the Fathers and postpatristic writers. Most importantly, they brought to an end the series of prescholastic discussions of the *veritas* and the *figura,* by saying that there is in this Sacrament both the reality and the symbol: the reality, because Christ's Body is actually present; the symbol, because He is present under the sign of bread and wine. Thus the Holy Eucharist is the true Body and Blood of Christ; but as a Sacrament, under the sacramental symbols, it is the sign of many things: of the Lord's Passion, of the union of the faithful with Christ, and of the unity of the Mystical Body, of the bond of love which should unite all who partake of the one spiritual bread.

Bibliography: Sources. *Berengarii Turonensis de sacra coena adversus Lanfrancum liber posterior* (Berlin 1834), ed. W. H. BEEKENKAMP (The Hague 1941). Martène-Durand 4:103–109. LANFRANC, *De corpore et sanguine Domini,* PL 150:407–442. GUITMUND, *De corporis et sanguinis Christi veritate,* PL 149:

1427–94. ALGER, *De sacramentis corporis et sanguinis dominici,* PL 180:739–854. Literature. F. VERNET, DTC 2.1:722–742. R. HEURTEVENT, *Durand de Troarn et les origines de l'hérésie bérengarienne* (Paris 1912). J. GEISELMANN, *Die Eucharistielehre der Vorscholastik* (Paderborn 1926). A. J. MACDONALD, *Berengar and the Reform of Sacramental Doctrine* (New York 1930). M. CAPPUYNS, DHGE 8:385–407. C. E. SHEEDY, *The Eucharistic Controversy of the Eleventh Century* (Washington 1947).

[C. E. SHEEDY]

BERENSON, BERNARD, father of art connoisseurship; b. Butremanz, Lithuania, 1865; d. Settignano, Italy, Oct. 7, 1959. Berenson's parents were immigrants from Lithuania to Boston, where he attended school, eventually receiving his degree from Harvard (1887) in Near Eastern languages. After a few years of European

Bernard Berenson.

travel, financed by professors and friends, he became deeply interested in art and manifested an overwhelming desire to attribute every work of Italian Renaissance painting to its proper master. Aware that documentation is often falsified, Berenson developed a purely visual method of identification based on the tenets of Giovanni *Morelli. In 1899 he married Mary Costelloe and settled in Italy at his famous Villa I Tatti, near Settignano. His first publication, *Venetian Painters of the Renaissance* (1894), created a stir among collectors. It included dates and teachers for each artist as well as a listing of paintings, their location, and known dates of execution; this essay was followed by three others (*Florentine Painters,* 1876; *Central Italian Painters,* 1897; *North Italian Painters,* 1907). Revised, including more artists and pictures, the four volumes were published as *Italian Painters of the Renaissance* (1932), a classic in Renaissance studies. Besides works on aesthetics and criticism he wrote monographs on Piero della Francesca, Sassetta, Caravaggio, and Lotto; did pioneer work in the study of drawings; and amassed a 50,000 volume library of art history and the humanities that, with his estate, he bequeathed to Harvard to be a "lay monastery for leisurely culture." He was also an important liaison and impetus for the flow of Renaissance paintings into U.S. collections.

Bibliography: B. BERENSON, *Sketch for a Self Portrait* (New York 1949); *Sunset and Twilight: From the Diaries of 1947–*

1958 (New York 1963); *Bernard Berenson Treasury,* ed. H. KIEL (New York 1962). K. M. CLARK, *Burlington Magazine* 102 (1960) 381–386. **Illustration credit:** Italian Information Center, New York City.

[S. L. HENRY]

BERGAMO

Episcopal see on the Lombard Plain of Northern Italy, at mouth of Brembana and Seriana valleys. The city is divided in two parts: the medieval town on the height, containing its principal ancient monuments still enclosed in Venetian walls (1561–88), and the modern town on the lower plain.

A city of Cisalpine Gaul on the Imperial Road between Milan and Pavia, Bergamo was first inhabited by Ligurians, Etruscans, and Gauls. After being sacked by Attila (452), it was successively the seat of a Lombard duchy and of Frankish counts. In the 10th and 11th centuries its bishops exercised both civil and ecclesiastical jurisdiction and in the 12th, it had a communal government. But internal wars prepared for the progressive penetration of the Visconti, who held Bergamo from 1329 to 1427, when the Carmagnola took possession in the name of Venice.

In 1430 with final aggregation to Venice, Bergamo began a period of peace and prosperity, favored by administrative autonomy. Venetian domination ceased in 1797, and the city was added to the Cisalpine Republic by Napoleon I, then made part of the Kingdom of Italy (1805). It became part of the Lombard-Venetian Realm in 1815 under Austrian control, and was one of the nine provincial capitals. In the Risorgimento it was the fatherland of many great patriots, and was united to the Kingdom of Sardinia (June 8, 1859), then to the Kingdom of Italy in 1861.

Christianity penetrated into Bergamo at the end of the 3d century. On the tomb of the Bergamask martyr Alexander, patron of the city, a basilica was erected in the 4th century. St. Filastrius (d. before 397) was consecrated by St. *Ambrose, but a St. Narnus seems to have been the first bishop (*c.* 340). Bishop Prestantius assisted at the Council of Milan against Eutyches in 451, and Laurentius assisted at the Council of Rome in 501.

During the struggles over investiture, Bishop Arnulf (1077–96) was on the Emperor's side. Bergamo

Bergamo, left to right, the Torre del Comune, the Palazzo della Ragione, the Baptistery, the Cathedral, the Colleoni Chapel and the church of S. Maria Maggiore.

saw a flowering of the clerical reform with monasteries at Fontanella (Saint Giles) and Pontida (St. James), the Cassinese monastery of St. Paul of Argon, the Vallombrosan monastery of the Holy Sepulcher in Astino, and the Cistercian monastery in Vallalta begun by St. *Bernard of Clairvaux.

During the Venetian regime Bergamo had several great bishops: Peter Lippomani (1517–44), a precursor of the reform of the Council of Trent; Frederick Cornero (1561–77), founder of the seminary; and St. Gregory *Barbarigo (1657–64), who restored the cultural level of the seminary and clergy and published a *Regulae Studiorum.* The government of Bps. Camillus Guindani (1879–1904) and Radini-Tedeschi (1904–14) saw a renaissance of the social activity of the clergy and Catholic laity, and the beginnings of many initiatives that, since 1885, have encouraged the Catholic movement among the workers. From 1910 to 1932 a School for Social Studies flourished and attracted students from within and outside Italy. In 1949 a seminary was opened with the intention of furnishing vocations for the dioceses of Italy lacking priests (Missionary Seminary of the Paradiso).

Bergamo has a 12th-century Romanesque cathedral and ancient walls. In 1964, a suffragan of Milan, it had 661,186 inhabitants in 418 parishes, of which 43 follow the Ambrosian rite; 1,060 diocesan and 186 religious priests; and 19 monasteries with 251 professed and 443 convents with 9,220 nuns. In 1955 it had 3 Waldesian Churches with 417 members.

Angelo Giuseppe Roncalli, who became Pope John XXIII (1958–63), was born in the Diocese of Bergamo at Sotto il Monte, Brusico, Nov. 25, 1881.

Bibliography: A. GIULIANI and F. BORRONI, EncCatt 2:1378–82. F. SAVIO, *Gli antichi vescovi d'Italia dalle origini al 1300,* 4 v. (1898–1932) v.3. A. G. RONCALLI and P. FORNO, eds., *Gli atti della visita apostolica di S. Carlo Borromeo a Bergamo,* 2 v. in 5 (Florence 1936–46). EncWA 8:543–544, with bibliog. **Illustration credit:** Alinari-Art Reference Bureau.

[G. ORLANDI]

BERGENGRUEN, WERNER

German novelist and poet; b. Riga, Latvia, Sept. 16, 1892; d. Baden-Baden, Germany, Sept. 2, 1964. Riga was under Russian control during his youth, but Bergengruen always maintained that his conservative, aristocratic manner of thinking had been formed by the aristocratic German circles of the Baltic area among which he grew up. His father, a doctor, sent him to Germany to study law, history, and literature at the universities in Marburg, Munich, and Berlin. Typical of his social class, he immediately entered the war in 1914 as an officer in the German army and then fought in the Baltic militia against the Red army. In 1920 he began work as a journalist, editing the *Ost-Informationen* and in 1925 he became the chief editor of the *Baltische Blätter.* While traveling a great deal, he gradually devoted himself to imaginative writing. Through a Renaissance love of form and restraint acquired in sojourns in Italy, he learned to control his tendency toward the bizarre, crass, and mysterious, a tendency characteristic of the influence of his Baltic birthplace. His stories, usually historical, are in the main centered either in the Italian Renaissance or the past of the Baltic states. He showed little interest in portraying the normal and everyday but felt that every story or novel should be built around a unique, startling event. He was awarded (1958) an honorary doctorate by the University of Munich, and in the same year, the medal Pour le Mérite for distinctive work in literature.

Some of the most read and discussed of his works are

Werner Bergengruen.

Rosen am Galgenholz (1923, stories), *Das Kaiserreich in Trümmern* (1927, novel), *Capri* (1930, poetry), *Die Feuerprobe* (1933, a story together with a valuable autobiographical sketch), *Der Grosstyrann und das Gericht* (1935, novel), *Die Rose von Jericho* (1936, poetry), *Die drei Falken* (1936, story), *Der ewige Kaiser* (1937, poetry, published anonymously), *E. T. A. Hoffmann* (1939, essay), *Der Tod von Reval* (1939, stories), *Am Himmel wie auf Erden* (1940, novel), *Der spanische Rosenstock* (1940, story), *Das Hornunger Heimweh* (1942, story), *Dies Irae* (1946, poetry), *Das Feuerzeichen* (1949, novel), *Die heile Welt* (1950, poetry), *Der letzte Rittmeister* (1952, stories), *Die Rittmeisterin* (1954, novel), *Die Heiraten von Parma* (1955, story), *Mit tausend Ranken* (1956, poetry), and *Hubertusnacht* (1957, story).

His most successful work is the novel *Der Grosstyrann und das Gericht* (Eng. ed. *A Matter of Conscience*, 1952), in which, against an Italian Renaissance background, he analyzes and condemns the philosophy of *national socialism. In 1936 he became a Catholic, and in 1939 he was censored by the Nazis as "unfit to help build up German culture by means of literary works." Thereafter he concealed his true thought until the end of the war, when he moved to Zurich (1946). *Der letzte Rittmeister* (Eng. ed. *The Last Captain of Horse*, 1954) is considered by critics to be in many ways a self-portrait. Bergengruen's characters approach life affirmatively, finding their strength in Christian thought and action. They give the impression that he himself had found a special inner peace.

Bibliography: G. KLEMM, *Werner Bergengruen* (Wuppertal-Barmen 1949). H. BÄNZIGER, *Werner Bergengruen: Weg und Werk* (Thal 1950). E. SOBOTA, *Das Menschenbild bei Bergengruen: Einführung in das Werk des Dichters* (Zurich 1962), with bibliog. P. SCHIFFERLI, ed., *Dank an Werner Bergengruen* (Zurich 1962). **Illustration credit:** German Information Center.

[T. A. RILEY]

BERGER, SAMUEL, Protestant exegete who made valuable contributions to the history of the text of the Bible; b. Beaucourt, in Alsace, March 5, 1843; d. Sèvres, near Paris, July 13, 1900. Ordained a Protestant minister, Berger had a leading part in the founding (1877) and development of the faculty of Protestant theology at the University of Paris, of which he was secretary and librarian and where he taught church history and

archeology from its foundation. His lifework was the study of the Latin Vulgate and the versions of the Bible in the Romance languages. His principal works are *De glossariis et compendiis exegeticis quibusdam medii aevi* (Paris 1879), *F. C. Baur: Les origines de l'École de Tubingue et ses principes* (Paris 1876), *La Bible au seizième siècle* (Paris 1879), *La Bible française au Moyen-Âge* (Paris 1884), and *Histoire de la Vulgate pendant les premiers siècles du Moyen-Âge* (Paris 1893; repr. New York 1958).

Bibliography: Herzog-Hauck PRE 23:187–189. A. LAMBERT, DHGE 8:451.

[J. SCHMID]

BERGIER, NICOLAS SYLVESTRE, theologian, the best apologist the Church in France produced during the second half of the 18th century to oppose the *rationalism of *Voltaire, J. J. *Rosseau, P. H. D. *Holbach, and their disciples; b. Darnay, Dec. 31, 1718; d. Versailles, April 9, 1790. From Besançon, he was called to Paris by Abp. Christophe de Beaumont as defender of the faith. His *Le Déisme réfuté par lui-même* (1765) is a serious attempt to expose the errors of Rousseau, particularly in his *Emile.* Indefatigably, often intemperately, Bergier reduced Rousseau's theology to its main tenets and denounced the contradictions in the profession of faith of the celebrated vicar. A modern theologian might use more finesse but would reach identical conclusions. In 1782 a second edition of Diderot's *Encyclopédie* appeared, entitled *Encyclopédie méthodique.* Bergier had agreed to contribute some 700 articles on theology, provided he was allowed to revise the 1,800 appearing in the original edition. Although criticized for lending his name to this rationalistic enterprise, he was nonetheless supported by his superiors, who saw the apologetic value of his contribution. These articles were published separately in his *Dictionnaire théologique* (3 v., 1788). He also wrote *Certitude des preuves du Christianisme* (1767), *Examen du matérialisme* (2 v., 1771), and *Traité de la vraie religion* (2 v., 1780). The apologetic nature of his works led him to emphasize the polemic aspect of theology—hence a certain haziness in his treatment of grace, the supernatural, and revelation, where at times he himself betrays the influence of rationalism. Yet this same influence led him to abandon the contemporary exegesis of the *compelle intrare* in favor of one completely acceptable to modern theologians.

See also ENCYCLOPEDISTS.

Bibliography: E. DUBLANCHY, DTC 2.1:742–745. L. CROCKER, *An Age of Crisis: Man and World in Eighteenth Century French Thought* (Baltimore 1959). R. R. PALMER, *Catholics and Unbelievers in Eighteenth Century France* (Princeton 1939).

[A. R. DESAUTELS]

BERGSON, HENRI LOUIS

French philosopher who overthrew the exaggerated scientism and mechanistic evolutionism of the 19th century and advanced a new theory of evolution acknowledging the spiritual dimension of man; b. Paris, Oct. 18, 1859; d. Paris, Jan. 4, 1941. Educated at the Lycée Condorcet and the École Normale Supérieure, where he distinguished himself in mathematics and physics, Bergson turned to philosophy, receiving the *agrégé* in 1881. After teaching at Angers and Clermont-Ferrand, he returned to Paris in 1888 to teach at the Lycée Henri Quatre and the École Normale Supérieure. At the Collège de France he held the chair of the history of philosophy from 1900 to 1921, attracting huge crowds to his lectures by the beauty and eloquence of his language and by the extraordinary appeal of his message. He be-

Henri Bergson.

came a member of the Académie Française in 1918, was elected president of the International Commission for Intellectual Cooperation after World War I, and received the Nobel prize for literature in 1927. Although born of Jewish parents, Bergson grew up without religion and began his philosophical career as an enthusiastic follower of Herbert *Spencer. However, his attempts to give a full and accurate account of reality led him to abandon Spencer's evolutionary theory, and the subsequent development of his thought brought him closer and closer to Catholicism. In his will he confessed his moral adhesion to the Catholic Church and revealed that he would have become a convert had he not felt obliged to remain with his Jewish brethren, then being persecuted under Hitler. Shortly before his death he arose from his sickbed to appear for the registration of Jews in Paris. A Catholic priest said the prayers at his funeral, as he had requested.

Philosophy. Although deeply influenced by *evolutionism and *empiricism, Bergson rejected the narrow conception of man and of the world characteristic of scientific *positivism, and sought to continue the metaphysicospiritualist tradition of *Maine de Biran and Félix Ravaisson (1813–1900). His philosophy constitues a defense of spirit against *materialism, intuition against *rationalism, freedom against *determinism (both physical and biological), creativity against *mechanism, and philosophy against *scientism. Setting out from the "intuition of duration," which is the dominant idea in his philosophy, Bergson offered a renovated empiricism and a new and profoundly original doctrine of evolution.

In a thoroughgoing critique of science Bergson showed why, in his opinion, science does not and cannot give a true picture of life or of reality as a whole. Science is the product of intelligence, which evolved solely to assure man's physical survival and to make possible his dominion over nature. Intelligence views all reality as solid, timeless, and spatial. Since its function is the manipulation of matter for practical purposes, it seeks exact formulas for things and expresses them in ready-made concepts that serve as substitutes for the real. A

mechanistic explanation of the universe results. All reality is described as static, homogeneous, discontinuous, and predictable; nothing vital, dynamic, novel, or unforeseeable is admitted. The very structure of intelligence renders it incapable of comprehending *life, *becoming, *spirit, and *freedom. The refusal to admit the existence of *God, the human *soul, or *free will is the consequence of recognizing as real only what can be grasped by intelligence.

Although Bergson held that intelligence is man's natural mode of knowing, he believed that the human mind is also capable of *intuition—a direct contact or coincidence with things. To think intuitively is to think in duration, thereby experiencing the inner dynamism of being. Bergson regarded intuition as the kind of knowledge proper to philosophy, and attributed the failures of most philosophers to their having ignored intuition and based their metaphysics on abstraction, generalization, and reasoning. The true philosophy dispenses with all ready-made concepts in order to achieve an inner view of being. To communicate his intuition the philosopher must invent new words and employ those images best suited to suggest the inexpressible. According to Bergson, philosophy must be both empirical and intuitive. Although he rejected the prevailing empiricism, it was not because it placed too high a value on *experience. Bergson believed that all philosophical problems must be solved according to the experimental method, since it is only experience that can give one certitude. An integral empiricism, however, must admit not only the knowledge of matter, but also all that man knows through *introspection, all the vague suggestions of *consciousness, all that is revealed in the intuition of duration.

To start with the intellect's view of reality meant for Bergson to attempt a reconstruction of life and movement out of concepts appropriate only to inert matter. He sought to reverse the order and to start with life and movement grasped in intuition. Life (or consciousness) is then seen to be the primordial reality, and matter but its degradation or descending motion. From this fresh perspective reality appears to be ever moving and growing, a ceaseless flux. It is essentially dynamic, qualitative, creative, and unpredictable. To know existing things as they really are is to grasp them intuitively, that is, *sub specie durationis*. The implications of this approach to reality so impressed William *James that he hailed it as a new Copernican revolution comparable in its significance for philosophy to that of G. *Berkeley or I. *Kant.

Principal Works. Bergson's leading ideas are encompassed in four principal works. In *Time and Free Will* he showed that free will is the most evident of facts and that its denial follows upon the confusion of succession with simultaneity, duration with intensity, and quality with quantity. In *Matter and Memory* he proved that spirit as well as matter exists. By demonstrating that consciousness is not identical with cerebral activity, he paved the way for a proof of the survival of the soul after death. In *Creative Evolution,* his most famous work, he showed that the mechanistic interpretation of evolution is not justified by the facts. Viewing the data of evolution in the light of his intuition of duration, he described the evolutionary process as the forward thrust of a great spiritual force, the life impulse (*élan vital*), rushing through time, insinuating itself into matter, and producing the various living forms culminating in man. Its movement is not predetermined but creative, ever generating novel and unpredictable forms. *The Two Sources of Morality and Religion* represents the full flowering of Bergson's thought. Morality and religion are traced back to their double source in the evolutionary process. Bergson distinguished two separate moralities and religions—the open and closed moralities, the static and dynamic religions. Closed morality pertains to social cohesion. It is static and rooted in social pressure, the morality of a group enclosed upon itself. It represents a halt in the evolutionary process. Open morality transcends the group to unite all mankind in a common brotherhood. It is progressive and creative, a forward thrust of the *élan vital*. Whereas closed morality and static religion originate in the instinct for survival, open morality and dynamic religion are inspired by the moral heroes, saints and mystics, those superior representatives of the human race who, like a new species, foreshadow the future condition of man. They draw man upward to a higher spiritual level by their vision of human destiny and of God, the source of all love. It is in the experience of the mystics that Bergson found the most convincing evidence for the existence of God.

Influence and Critique. Bergson's manner of philosophizing—his repugnance for definition and for a technical vocabulary and his method of attacking each problem separately—did not lend itself to the formation of a Bergsonian school. Yet his influence on 20th-century thought has been profound. Among the philosophers whose works reflect a strong Bergsonism are Édouard *LeRoy, Maurice *Blondel, Max *Scheler, and Maurice Pradines. Many Catholic scholars, notably Jacques Maritain, Étienne Gilson, and Gabriel Marcel, though voicing disagreement on certain points of doctrine, have acknowledged with gratitude his great inspiration. Bergson's influence is also discernible in the thought of numerous scientists, including Alexis *Carrel, Pierre *Lecomte du Noüy, and Pierre *Teilhard de Chardin; in many literary works, including those of Marcel *Proust and Charles *Péguy; and in some schools of painting and music. From the start his books gained unprecedented fame. Appealing to a wide reading public, they were translated into many languages and have been reprinted again and again.

Acclaimed by many of his contemporaries as the long-awaited liberator from the tyranny of materialism, mechanism, and determinism, Bergson was criticized by some for stopping short of the Christian conception of God, creation, the human soul, and free choice. From the viewpoint of Christian doctrine, Bergson's philosophy remains at best—and in spite of his intentions perhaps—ambiguous and incomplete. For the primacy of *being as a reality accessible to intellect, he substituted the primacy of becoming as a reality accessible only to intuition. His depreciation of reason necessitated the denial that the existence of God can be rationally demonstrated. Man's approach to God can be only through the intuitive experience of the mystic, he said. God is described as Love and Creative Energy; but since the relationship between Creative Energy and the *élan vital* is never clearly defined, the distinction between God and creatures remains blurred. The depreciation of rational knowledge also led Bergson to base morality on the infrarational faculty of instinct and the suprara-

tional faculty of intuition. He allowed to reason no essential role in moral obligation; its function is merely to formulate and coordinate moral rules and to assure their logical consistency.

Furthermore, having identified being with becoming, Bergson was forced to deny the substantiality of the soul and to define soul as a duration or participation in the *élan vital*. While upholding the distinction between soul and body, he was unable to avoid a dualistic position in fixing their mutual relationship. A champion of free will, Bergson rejected all forms of determinism; yet he regarded freedom not as the rational determination of a human act but as the spontaneous bursting forth of vital energy from the depths of the self, a creative but nonrational act expressive of the total personality. To the Catholic philosopher or theologian such points of criticism, together with a misunderstanding of the supernatural character of Christian mysticism, represent important deficiencies in Bergson's thought. Yet no evaluation of his philosophy that is limited to pointing out its metaphysical inadequacies will render it full justice. It must also be seen as the sincere and arduous endeavor of a great soul to discover the truth, a spiritual itinerary from materialistic mechanism to the God known and loved by the Christian mystics.

See also TIME; LIFE PHILOSOPHIES.

Bibliography: Works. *Oeuvres*, ed. H. GOUHIER and A. ROBINET (Paris 1959), critical ed. of Bergson's major works; *Time and Free Will (Essais sur les Données Immédiates de la Conscience* 1889) tr. F. L. POGSON (New York 1910; repr. 1950); *Matter and Memory (Matière et Mémoire* 1896), tr. N. M. PAUL and W. S. PALMER (New York 1911); *Creative Evolution (L'Évolution créatrice* 1907) tr. A. MITCHELL (New York 1911); *Mind-Energy: Lectures and Essays (L'Énergie Spirituelle* 1920), tr. H. W. CARR (New York 1920); *The Two Sources of Morality and Religion (Les Deux Sources de la morale et de la religion,* Paris 1932), tr. R. A. AUDRA and C. BRERETON (New York 1935); *The Creative Mind (La Pensée et le Mouvant* 1934), tr. M. L. ANDISON (New York 1946), collected essays. Studies. I. W. ALEXANDER, *Bergson: Philosopher of Reflection* (New York 1957). J. CHEVALIER, *Henri Bergson,* tr. L. A. CLARE (New York 1928). É. LE ROY, *The New Philosophy of Henri Bergson,* tr. V. BENSON (New York 1913). L. ADOLPHE, *La Philosophe religieuse de Bergson* (Paris 1946). L. HUSSON, *L'Intellectualisme de Bergson* (Paris 1947). R. M. MOSSÉ-BASTIDE, *Bergson éducateur* (Thèse; Paris 1955), contains 90 pages of bibliog. M. T. L. PENIDO, *La Méthode intuitive de M. Bergson* (Paris 1918). B. A. SCHARFSTEIN, *Roots of Bergson's Philosophy* (New York 1943). For evaluation of Bergson's thought from the Catholic viewpoint, see esp. J. MARITAIN, *Bergsonian Philosophy and Thomism,* tr. M. L. and J. G. ANDISON (New York 1955) and É. H. GILSON, *The Philosopher and Theology,* tr. C. GILSON (New York 1962). **Illustration credit:** French Embassy, Press and Information Division, New York City.

[I. J. GALLAGHER]

BERINGTON, CHARLES, vicar apostolic of the English Midland district (1795–98) and controversialist; b. Stock Hall, Essex, 1748; d. Longbirch, Staffordshire, June 8, 1798. He was the third son of Thomas Berington of Moat Hall, Salop, and Anne Bates, heiress of Stock Hall, Essex. Educated at Douay College from 1761 to 1765 and St. Gregory's College, Paris, from 1765 to 1776, he was ordained in 1775, and won his doctorate at the Sorbonne the following year. He worked in the English mission at Ingatestone, Essex, and later became the tutor to the son and heir of Peter Giffard of Chillington, Staffordshire. On Aug. 1, 1786 he was consecrated titular bishop of Hierocaesarea at Longbirch, and appointed coadjutor to Bp. Thomas Talbot, Vicar Apostolic of the Midland district. At Talbot's death, he succeeded to the vicariate. His membership in the "Gallican" Catholic Committee (founded in 1783), whose sympathies were nationalistic and antipapal, placed him strongly at variance with the other vicars apostolic and with the policy of the Holy See toward England. This brought him the dislike of most of the clergy, though personally he was amiable, learned, and kindly. On his accession to the vicariate, Rome refused him faculties unless he recanted his views. After 3 years of difficult negotiations he gave way under protest, but died as the result of an accident before his faculties could reach him.

Bibliography: W. M. BRADY, *The Episcopal Succession in England, Scotland, and Ireland,* A.D. *1400 to 1875,* 3 v. (Rome 1876–77) v.3 *passim.* DNB 2:337. B. N. WARD, *The Dawn of Catholic Revival in England, 1781–1803,* 2 v. (London 1909) 1:123, 2:131. C. BUTLER, *Historical Memoirs Respecting the English, Irish and Scottish Catholics from the Reformation to the Present Time,* 4 v. (London 1819–21) v.4.

[B. WHELAN]

BERISFORD, HUMPHREY, gentleman lawyer, student at Douai; b. Derby, England; d. there, *c.* 1588. After his preliminary education in England, Berisford, son of an Anglican Derbyshire squire, traveled to the Continent and spent 2 years at Douai. On his return to England he adopted the legal profession and undertook the prosecution of a case for his father. In the course of the proceedings he was accused by his opponent of being a recusant and was interrogated by the judge. During the examination Berisford openly admitted his profession of the Catholic faith. The judge made every effort to have him retract his opinion and offered him a favorable decision and complete liberty, on the sole condition that Berisford would attend the services of the Church of England. Upon his adamant refusal, Berisford was thrown into prison for 7 years; he died in Derby jail *c.* 1588. Apparently few details concerning this man are extant. The main source for the sparse material available is Christopher Grene's manuscript, historical notes and collections copied from originals in the English College at Rome, and printed in Foley's *Records.*

Bibliography: DictEngCath 1:200. H. FOLEY, ed., *Records of the English Province of the Society of Jesus,* 7 v. (London 1877–82) v.3. CathRecSoc v.10–11.

[J. G. DWYER]

BERISTÁIN Y SOUZA, JOSÉ MARIANO, Mexican bibliographer; b. Puebla, May 22, 1756; d. Mexico City, March 23, 1817. He was the son of Juan Antonio Beristáin y Souza and Lorenza María Ana Romero. He received a bachelor's degree in philosophy at the University of Mexico in 1772 and a doctorate in theology at the University of Valencia, Spain, in 1776. In Spain he gained a permanent professorship in Valladolid and through competition won the canonries of Toledo and Victoria. In 1790 he returned to New Spain, where the next year he failed to win a competition for a canonry in Puebla. He decided to return to Spain but was shipwrecked and endured 11 months of hardship before he landed at Coruña. At sea he lost the bibliographical data he had been collecting. In Madrid he received the Cross of Charles III and the grant of a canonry in Mexico City. Therefore he returned again to Mexico to take possession of his benefice. By 1813 he had become dean of the cathedral. He was also director of the Hospicio de Huérfanos, and in his capacity as school visitor he supervised more than 3,000 children. He was a member of many scientific and literary societies in Spain and Italy. During the independence movement of 1810 Beristáin vehemently defended the Spanish Crown in the pulpit and in the press. His sermons were heard with respect, but his writings were rudely challenged by the insurgents. Many of his sermons, discourses, apologies, and funeral orations were published, and he listed them in his bibliography.

The main work of Beristáin was his *Biblioteca Hispano Americana Setentrional,* a monumental bibliographic summary that resulted from 20 years of examining the libraries of the University of Mexico, of the archdiocese, and of almost all the monasteries in Mexico City and neighboring towns. It lists the works of more than 3,600 writers who were born or flourished in Spanish North America and includes biographical sketches of most of the authors. At times he changed, shortened, or rephrased the titles of works. Certainly he did not personally handle all the books, for he assumed some were printed when they were only manuscripts. But these defects do not destroy the greatness of the bibliography. Beristáin did not have time to correct his work. He became paralytic in 1815 and saw only part of volume 1 in print the next year. His nephew Rafaél Enríquez Trespalacios Beristáin finished the work of publication (3 v., 1816, 1819, 1821). In 1883 Fortino Hipólito Vera, pastor in Amecameca, republished the three volumes. A fourth was published by José Toribio *Medina in Santiago de Chile in 1897; it contains works of anonymous authors that Beristáin had reviewed but that his nephew did not publish because of the expense; it contains also lists of authors after 1817 and some biographical data of Beristáin himself.

[E. GÓMEZ TAGLE]

BERKELEY, GEORGE

Anglican bishop of Cloyne, divine, and philosopher; b. Kilcrene, near Kilkenny, Ireland, March 12, 1685; d. Oxford, Jan. 14, 1753.

Life. Berkeley was educated at Kilkenny College and at Trinity College, Dublin, which he entered as a "pensioner" in 1700. He studied mathematics, languages (Latin, Greek, French, and Hebrew), and philosophy, taking his B.A. degree in 1704. In 1707 he was elected to a junior fellowship and graduated as M.A. Earlier in the same year he published (anonymously) two short works, *Arithmetica* and *Miscellanea Mathematica.* In 1709 he was ordained deacon, and in 1710, a priest of the Anglican Church. From 1709 to 1713 he was a tutor at the College and held various academic posts, including that of junior Greek lecturer.

It was during these early years at Trinity that Berkeley's philosophy was born and grew rapidly to its final shape. Between 1704 and 1707 he read J. Locke, S. Clarke, I. Newton, and N. Malebranche, and sought a remedy against skepticism, materialism, atheism, and the waning influence of religion. Between 1707 and 1708 he made a collection of private notes—jottings of ideas as they occurred to him. There one can follow the progress of his discovery of the principle, *esse est percipi et percipere,* with which he launched his attack on hidden, nonsensible substance existing "absolutely," or independently of mind. Out of these notes Berkeley

George Berkeley, oil portrait by J. Smibert, 1725.

prepared his two first philosophical works: *An Essay towards a New Theory of Vision* (Dublin 1709), and *The Principles of Human Knowledge* (Dublin 1710). In 1713 he went to London where in 1714 he published the *Three Dialogues between Hylas and Philonous.*

During the next 8 years Berkeley traveled in France and Italy. In 1720 he wrote a short treatise *De motu* on his immaterialism and the principles of mechanics for the Royal Academy of Sciences at Paris, which offered a prize for an essay on the causes of motion. Berkeley did not receive the prize, but he published his treatise in London in 1721. He returned to Dublin in the same year and resumed his work as a tutor at Trinity. He had been co-opted senior fellow in his absence in 1717, took his B.D. and D.D. in 1721, and was thereupon appointed divinity lecturer and preacher. In 1724 he was appointed dean of Derry, and resigned his fellowship at Trinity.

Berkeley's thoughts then turned to the foundation of a College in Bermuda for the training of clergy for missionary work in America. He obtained a charter for the foundation of St. Paul's College and set sail for Rhode Island in 1728, settling at Newport early in the following year. As he realized that his scheme would fail, he devoted several months of enforced leisure to writing *Alciphron, or the Minute Philosopher*, which he published in London in 1732 on his return. Because he designed it as a vindication of the Christian revelation against current disbelief rather than as a purely philosophical work, he refrained from making use of his principle of immaterialism.

In 1734 Berkeley was appointed bishop of Cloyne, and wrote *The Analyst, or Discourse addressed to an Infidel Mathematician*, in which he attacked Newton's theory of fluxions. Two years later he replied to an attack on this work by a Dr. Jurin in *A Defence of Free-Thinking in Mathematics*. Berkeley then devoted much time to spreading his ideas on the virtues of tar water in curing diseases. He set them forth, with his views on metaphysics and theology, in *Siris* (London 1744), in its day the most celebrated of all his works. Its publication provoked some controversy about the medicinal properties of tar water, which Berkeley defended with energy to the end. His last work, *Farther Thoughts on Tar-Water*, formed the opening paper of his *Miscellany*, published in 1752.

In 1752 Berkeley left Ireland to settle with his family in Oxford, where he died in his house in Holywell Street in January 1753. He was buried in the chapel of Christ Church, the Anglican cathedral of Oxford.

Teaching. Berkeley has suffered both from the seemingly incurable habit of historians of seeing him as little more than one of the leading empiricists, linking Locke with Hume, and from the misjudgment of Kant, who regarded him as a subjective idealist. He was unquestionably an empiricist of a kind; he was certainly not a thoroughgoing subjective idealist.

To appreciate his work as a philosopher one must understand his intentions, and to understand his intentions one must, as Ardley has shown (10–11) regard him primarily as "one of the company of Anglican divines and reformers" that includes such men as Stillingfleet and Butler, and recognize that "his excursion into philosophy was ancillary to the proper business of his calling." His constant aim in all his work was to revivify Christian *theism, to meet the challenge of the contemporary rationalist *deism, and to check the rising tide of the new empirical philosophy toward skepticism. At the roots of all the evils he fought, Berkeley saw the currently accepted philosophy of physics—a philosophy that had shaped the metaphysics of Descartes and the *empiricism of Locke. He set himself the task of making a critique of the metaphysical assumptions of the new philosophy of ideas. The "new physics" assumed, for the purpose of safeguarding its own method of work, that the universe is a vast mechanical system of purely extended particles that move without purpose in space and time; and that both the particles and their movements are purely quantitative, so that the physical order of things can be expressed adequately by mathematical laws. Berkeley realized that if this postulate of the total mathematicization of nature came to be accepted as more than a rule of method for correlating mathematical abstractions, and as constituting a metaphysics of nature, the world of ordinary human experience would have to be set aside. This would become one vast illusion concealing from man's mind an unknowable, but supposedly real, world of matter or hidden substances. Such a universe could never be known as the work of God. Berkeley claimed to show that the world of the "new physics" is not a real, existent world of things but an artificial construction fabricated out of unreal abstractions, and that the world of common sense, the world of particular things rich in their individual qualities, is the one and only real world that man ought to designate when talking of material things.

Abstraction. The capital error of the 17th-century philosophers lay in their unwarrantable assumption that unthinking, inert matter exists on its own, "absolutely," or independently of mind. They fell into this error because they thought in a world of bogus abstractions, which their fanciful theories of abstraction led them to regard as the sole realities. Berkeley rejected the theory expounded by Locke—that the mind can form a positive, universal idea of the nature of a thing, or of a triangle, for example, which is no particular triangle but which enables man to think of all particular triangles. The abstract nature of a sensory object is not anything, and what is not cannot help one think of concrete particulars. But though he rejected abstract universal ideas, Berkeley realized that man cannot think without general ideas, for generality is involved in meaning. Man has, he held, general ideas that are not abstract. Such ideas are formed, not by abstracting or separating, but by the mind's considering a particular aspect or "idea" of a thing and relating it to like particular aspects of other things. Man can, he argued, fix the attention on one aspect of a thing, e.g., its squareness, and then use this "idea" that he sensibly perceives in one object as the sign or symbol of all other square shapes in other objects. Generality is, in other words, not a denial of the singularity of things, but a purely functional relation of a particular idea—the result of regarding it as the representative sign of other like ideas.

Esse est percipi et percipere. Matter, pure extension, and passive substances are unreal abstractions. What, then, is a material thing? It is a purely sensible thing. A tree, for example, is just what it is perceived to be; it is that, all that (not merely its primary mathematical qualities), and nothing other than that (not something concealed by its qualities and serving as their support). It is the individual thing a person perceives sensibly to be of a certain size, mass, solidity, shape, volume, of various colors, degrees of hardness, softness, etc. The real apple is the thing one eats, tastes, handles, and smells, and not some insensible substrate of these qualities. As a natural thing is wholly sensible, a material substance is nothing but the assemblage of its sensible properties. But since sensible qualities can exist only in being perceived, or dependently on mind, it follows that the whole being of a sensible thing consists in its being perceived. The primary qualities of extension and motion, being inseparable from the secondary qualities, must be as mind-dependent as the secondary. Sensible qualities need a "support"; however, this must be found not in inert, passive substances (which could neither support anything nor produce any impressions on one's senses), but in active mind, the very nature of which is to perceive sensible qualities and thereby maintain them in existence. Berkeley did not say that material things are modes of mind, as an idealist would say; he denied this categorically: "These qualities are in the mind only as they are perceived by it, not by way of *mode,* or *attribute,* but only by way of *idea*" (*Principles* 1.49; also 34).

Matter and Mind. Berkeley's universe comprises the world of sensible things that are neither substances nor material but "ideas of sense," and the world of men who are finite spirits or minds, active substances that think, will, and perceive, and thereby exist. God is infinite spirit or mind, whose creative activity of mind and will set before men's minds the world of sensible things in law and order.

Critique. Berkeley's most enduring contribution to philosophy lies in a field overlooked by historians, namely, his philosophy of science. His critique of the philosophy of the new mathematico-physics, which he likened to a grammar of nature (*Principles* 1.108), anticipated many of the findings of P. *Duhem and A. N. *Whitehead. Berkeley's metaphysics has often been presented and criticized out of its historical setting, and the justifiable criticisms that have been made against his principle of immaterialism and his theory of nonabstract, general ideas have made all too familiar the weaker aspects of his system. Furthermore, the conventional associations of Berkeley with Locke and Hume, as well as with subjective *idealism, have hidden from view the import of Berkeley's constructive efforts to remedy the very ills empiricism and idealism brought about. He saw the need to restore man to his central place in the universe; to restore man's esteem for the order of nature, which he considered to have been dismissed as illusory by Descartes and Locke; and to display the universe in its dependence on God, making known His being and providence. In setting man at the heart of his metaphysics, and in highlighting the particularity of existent things, Berkeley is closer in his empiricism to the Christian existentialist philosophers of the 1960s than to the classical empiricists of his day. His pioneering efforts to harmonize the work of the sciences, philosophy, and theology should have won for him a place among the foremost divines and Christian humanists of the 18th century.

Bibliography: *The Works of George Berkeley, Bishop of Cloyne,* ed. A. A. LUCE and T. E. JESSOP, 9 v. (London 1948–57). A. A. LUCE, *The Life of George Berkeley, Bishop of Cloyne* (London 1949); *Berkeley's Immaterialism* (London 1945); *Berkeley and Malebranche* (London 1934). G. W. R. ARDLEY, *Berkeley's Philosophy of Nature* (Auckland 1962). J. WILD, *George Berkeley: A Study of His Life and Philosophy* (Cambridge, Mass. 1936). A. L. LEROY, *George Berkeley* (Paris 1959). N. BALADI, *La Pensée réligieuse de Berkeley et l'unité de sa philosophie* (Cairo 1945). E. A. SILLEM, *George Berkeley and the Proofs for the Existence of God* (New York 1957). C. D. BROAD, *Berkeley's Argument About Material Substance* (London 1942). *British Journal for the Philosophy of Science* 4 (1953–54) 13–87, George Berkeley bicentenary issue. *Revue Internationale de Philosophie* 7 (1953) 3–156, George Berkeley issue. G. STAMMLER, *Berkeleys Philosophie der mathematik* (Berlin 1921). **Illustration credit:** National Portrait Gallery, London.

[E. A. SILLEM]

BERLAGE, ANTON, theologian; b. Münster, Dec. 21, 1805; d. Münster, Dec. 6, 1881. After studying philosophy and theology in Münster and Bonn, he received his doctorate in theology from the University of Munich in 1830 and was ordained in 1832. At first attracted by G. *Hermes, he turned away from his teaching under the influence of J. A. *Möhler. In 1835 he became professor of dogma in Münster. His chief works are *Apologetik der Kirche* (Münster 1834) and *Katholische Dogmatik* (7 v. Münster 1839–64).

Bibliography: R. BÄUMER, LexThK² 2:231. E. HEGEL, *Die Katholisch-theologische Fakultät Münster in ihrer geschichtlichen Entwicklung, 1773–1961* (Münster 1961). A. HEUSER, *Die Erlösungslehre in der katholischen deutschen Dogmatik* (Essen 1963) 108–116.

[R. BÄUMER]

BERLIÈRE, URSMER, Benedictine medievalist and editor; b. Gosselies, Hainaut, Belgium, Sept. 3, 1861; d. Maredsous Abbey, Aug. 27, 1932. Berlière, who was baptized Alfred, was educated by the Jesuits at Charleroi and entered the minor seminary at Tournai. He was professed a *Benedictine in 1881 at the Abbey of *Maredsous, where he later (1885–92) taught after 2 years of study at *Seckau (1883–85). He was ordained in 1886. From 1894 to 1912 he directed the *Revue bénédictine.* He wrote the monumental *Monasticon belge* (1890–1929), which treated the history of monasticism in the Low Countries; a perceptive history, *L'Ordre monastique des origines au XIIe siècle* (Maredsous 1912); and also *L'Ascèse bénédictine des origines à la fin du XIIe siècle* (Paris 1927). Berlière held the posts of president of the Royal Historical Commission of Belgium and curator of the Royal Belgian Library (1912–14). He organized (1902) the Institut Historique Belge de Rome and launched the collection (1906) of Belgian-Vatican correspondence, *Analecta vaticano-belgica.* In 1930 he was named consultor for the historical section of the Congregation of Rites.

Bibliography: P. H. PIRENNE et al., *L'Hommage à dom U. B.* (Brussels 1931). H. DE MOREAU, "Dom U. B.," *Studien und Mitteilungen zur Geschichte des Benediktinerordens und seiner Zweige* 50 (1932) 31–32. J. CUVELIER, "Dom U. B.," *Annuaire de l'Académie Royale de Belgique* 105 (1939) 111–171, with Berlière's bibliog. R. GAZEAU, *Catholicisme* 1:1470–71.

[B. F. SCHERER]

BERLIN

City in north central Germany, the center of a network of canals, with access to the North Sea and the Baltic Sea. Since the end of World War II the former capital of the German Reich has been a divided city. West Berlin, the larger part (1962 population 2,147,000), with certain restrictions necessary because of garrison rights of the Western control powers, is part of the German Federal Republic. East Berlin (1962 population 1,061,200) in 1949 was declared the capital of the "German Democratic Republic." In 1958 the Diocese of Berlin, suffragan to Breslau (*Wrocław) since its creation in 1930, had some 560 secular and 250 religious priests, 230 men in 25 religious houses, 2,350 women in 150 convents, and 1,286,000 Catholics in a population of 7,325,000. Comprising 23,166 square miles in both parts of the city and the surrounding area, it was once part of the Prussian Provinces of Brandenburg and Pomerania.

Berlin and Köln were founded *c.* 1200, probably located on earlier Slav settlements in the Spree valley, and they soon became a single town. From its favorable location on the Spree-Havel link with the Elbe River, Berlin shipped grain to Hamburg and early joined the *Hanseatic League. It became the residence of the Elector of Brandenburg *c.* 1470 and so an important city for the future. In the Middle Ages Berlin was part of the See of Brandenburg. The oldest parish church, Nikolaikirche (*c.* 1200), was destroyed in World War II. After Elector *Joachim II became Protestant (1539), Catholic life died out. The adoption of Calvinism by Elector Johann Sigismund (1613) started conflict among Protestants; court and dynasty became Calvinist, city and countryside remained Lutheran. Under the Great Elector (1640–88) and his successor Frederick III (1688–1713, King Frederick I of Prussia from 1701), Calvinists increased in Berlin with the immigration of *Huguenots expelled from France after the revocation of the Edict of *Nantes in 1685. The parity gradually achieved between Protestants did not favor

Catholicism. Berlin was under the jurisdiction of the Apostolic Vicariate of Upper and Lower Saxony (1699–1821). Catholic services could be held only in the embassies of Catholic powers.

A change came under the Soldier King, Frederick William I (1713–40), a fourth of whose army stationed in Berlin was Catholic (recruited outside Prussia). Two Dominicans were made military chaplains, and in 1719 the king allowed Catholics to use a chapel in Berlin for services. Under *Frederick II the Great (1740–86) Berlin was a ranking European capital, the commercial and industrial center of the Prussian monarchy, and, through the systematic support of wool, cotton, and silk manufacture, the main textile city of Germany. The increase in population from 81,000 (1740) to 150,000 (1786) brought a like increase in Catholics, who came to Berlin from abroad and from Catholic areas of the kingdom (Silesia). St. Hedwig was built for them (1747–73), a circular church with a pillared hall after the Pantheon in Rome; destroyed in World War II, it was rebuilt by 1963. With full parish rights, it was put under a provost. Although the General Prussian Civil Code (1794) gave Catholics the same rights as Protestants, the legal position of Catholic parishes in Berlin, Brandenburg, and Pomerania was obscure until the papal bull of 1821 placed them together as an apostolic delegation under the *Prince-bishop of Breslau. The provost of St. Hedwig, as the Prince-bishop's delegate, administered the area. After Berlin became the capital of the Reich (1871), the delegate faced great tasks. Catholics increased with the population (110,000 in 1887; 200,000 in 1897); new suburbs required new parishes. Catholic schools, religious houses, and charitable institutions were built under difficult conditions in a city with a growing industrial proletariat.

The delegation became a bishopric (suffragan to Breslau) in the Weimar Republic after the papal nunciature under Eugenio Pacelli (later Piux XII) moved to Berlin. The Concordat between Tunisia and the Holy See (1929) made St. Hedwig the cathedral, and the first bishop was named in 1930. Under National So-

The interior of the Maria Regina Martyrium, Berlin-Charlottenburg, built to commemorate those who died under Nazi oppression during World War II.

The Kaiser Wilhelm Memorial Church on Breitscheidplatz, Berlin. The new steel, concrete, and glass Evangelical church by the architect Egon Eiermann flanks the bomb-shattered ruins of the older edifice.

cialism (1933–45) both Catholic and Protestant clergy were persecuted. The cathedral provost B. Lichtenberg died a martyr (1943). Despite the difficulties posed for the Church by the present division of the city (blockade in 1948, uprising in 1953, wall in 1961) and the separation of West Berlin from the Communist-ruled areas of the diocese, the unity of the Church in Greater Berlin has survived World War II. In the city live 406,000 Catholics (12 to 13 per cent of the population) in 83 parishes with 215 churches and public chapels; there are 129 religious houses and 2,076 priests and religious. Archbishop A. Bengsch (1961–) resides in East Berlin, while West Berlin has a vicar-general.

Humboldt University in East Berlin is the successor to the old University of Berlin (Friedrich Wilhelm University to 1945), which opened in 1810 as the successor to the University of Halle (suppressed by Napoleon) and initiated the reorganization of German universities. It was closely associated with the reorganized Academy of Sciences from 1812. The first elected rector was J. G. *Fichte; noteworthy professors included the philosophers G. W. *Hegel and F. W. *Schelling and the historians B. G. *Niebuhr and L. von *Ranke. The theological faculty, which existed from the beginning, included W. *De Wette, J. A. *Neander, A. von *Harnack, A. *Schlatter, R. *Seeberg, H. *Gunkel, H. *Gressmann, K. *Holl, and H. *Lietzmann. In 1948 the Free University of Berlin was founded in West Berlin.

Bibliography: M. ARENDT et al., *Geschichte der Stadt Berlin* (Berlin 1937). W. WENDLAND, *700 Jahre Kirchengeschichte Berlins* (Berlin 1930); *Die Entwicklung der katholischen Kirche in Gross-Berlin bis 1932* (Jahrbuch für brandenburgische Kirchengeschichte 30; 1935). B. STASIEWSKI, *Die katholische Kirche im Bereich des Bistums Berlin* (Berlin 1938). L. JABLONSKI, *Geschichte der fürstbischöflichen Delegatur*, 2 v. (Berlin 1929). H. HERZFELD, *Berlin als Kaiserstadt und Reichshauptstadt, 1871–1945: Ausgewählte Aufsätze* (Berlin 1962) 281–313; *Die Entscheidungsjahre der Berliner Nachkriegsgeschichte, 1946–48: Ausgewählte Aufsätze* (Berlin 1962) 356–416. *Schematismus für das Bistum Berlin* (1963). J. GRISAR, DHGE 8:510–523. K. KUPISCH, RGG³ 1:1056–60. J. ALLENDORF, LexThK² 2:232–233. AnnPont (1965) 63. H. ZOPF and G. HEINRICH, *Berlin-Bibliographie* (Berlin 1965), to 1960. **Illustration credit:** Fig. 1, G. E. Kidder Smith. Fig. 2, German Information Center, New York City.

[S. SKALWEIT]

BERLIOZ, LOUIS HECTOR

Romanticist composer whose works and ideas were decisive in the evolution of modern music; b. La Côte Saint-André (near Grenoble), France, Dec. 11, 1803; d. Paris, March 8, 1869. His father was a dedicated physician with Voltairian ideas and, like his wife, of high social rank in the region. The child's musical gifts were soon evident, and long before his formal training he was setting songs from which he later rescued some of his most haunting melodies. His nonmusical studies were supervised by his father, who hoped he would become a doctor. To that end Berlioz went to Paris in 1821 to master the basic sciences. When he began studying with *LeSueur (Napoleon's favorite composer) with a view to enrolling at the Paris Conservatory, Hector's allowance was cut off, and he survived by doing hackwork for music publishers and by singing in comic-opera choruses. He studied at the conservatory and, more importantly, at the Opera (then still dominated by the *Gluck and *Spontini repertory), but his teachers were slow to grasp his genius. Four times he was denied the Prix de Rome; when the prize was finally his, on the eve of the 1830 revolution, he had already performed his first masterpiece, *Symphonie Fantastique.*

In 1833 began what he called his "Thirty Years' War against the pundits, the routineers, and the tone-deaf." This crusade consisted of (1) "campaigns" of conducting in Europe's great cities, which set a new standard of orchestral musicianship; (2) tireless exposition, through brilliant writings in journals of opinion, of his beliefs on the current music-drama question—in essence, that music should be inherently expressive, not the handmaiden of text or program, but relying for dramatic effect on deployment of musical means (melody, rhythm, harmony, orchestration) within musical forms; and (3) composition of large- and small-scale works, which gave form to his ideals. Chief among these are the early dramatic symphonies: the *Fantastique* (1830), *Harold in Italy* (1834), *Romeo and Juliet* (1839), and *Symphonie Funèbre et Triomphale* (1840); the dramas *per musica: Benvenuto Cellini* (1838), *Damnation of Faust* (1846), *The Trojans* (1858), *Beatrice and Benedict* (1862); and the religious "dramas": *Requiem* (1837), *Te Deum* (1852), and *L'Enfance du Christ* (1854).

Although never a church composer, Berlioz was repeatedly drawn to religious subjects, and his intimate knowledge of the religious experience is reflected in his contemplative, ecstatic passages. His First Communion, which took place at an Ursuline convent to the accompaniment of the nuns' choir, became for him an ineffaceable experience of the ancient Catholic music

Louis Hector Berlioz, by Gustave Courbet.

tradition. Later, when he could no longer accept the Church's dogma, he never lost his aesthetic sympathy and respect for its forms or his humility before its wisdom. All his works, sacred and secular, are character-ized by dazzling variety in atmosphere, structure, and orchestral texture. His method of development and his harmonic progressions bewildered most of his contemporaries, and it is only since World War II that a more perceptive scholarly outlook has combined with the advantage of long-playing recordings to set Berlioz in proper perspective; the figure of an extraordinary artist and theorist is emerging.

Bibliography: L. H. BERLIOZ, *Memoirs,* ed. E. NEWMAN, tr. R. and E. HOLMES (rev. ed. New York 1935); *New Letters,* ed. and tr. J. BARZUN (New York 1954); *Grand traité d'instrumentation et d'orchestration* (Paris 1844). R. ROLLAND, *Musicians of Today,* tr. M. BLAIKLOCK (New York 1915). T. S. WOTTON, *Hector Berlioz* (London 1935). W. J. TURNER, *Berlioz: The Man and His Work* (London 1934). B. VAN DIEREN in *Down Among the Dead Men* (New York 1935). J. BARZUN, *Berlioz and the Romantic Century,* 2 v. (Boston 1950); *Berlioz and His Century* (New York 1956), contains complete list of literary pubs. A complete edition of his works is in preparation. **Illustration credit:** Museo teatrale alla Scala.

[J. BARZUN]

BERMUDA, a group of small islands in the Atlantic Ocean approximately 700 miles east and south of New York, the same distance south of Halifax, and 1000 miles north of Nassau. The climate is semitropical. In 1964 the population was about 45,000, of whom two-thirds were Negroes. Catholic population was about 5,000, of whom 700 were Negroes. Universal franchise for all Bermudians and British subjects, men and women, 25 years of age and over, was introduced in 1963. In recent years general integration of the races has been introduced with a good measure of success.

Up to 1800, Catholics (designated Papists) and non-Conformists (to the Church of England) were not allowed on the Islands. By decision of the Colonial Office, London, such restrictions fell into disuse. The first priest came to the Islands in 1832. Thereafter, until about the beginning of the 20th century, priests came periodically from the Archdiocese of Halifax to take care of the few Catholics. Early in the 20th century, several priests from Halifax took up residence on the Islands, and it was generally accepted that Bermuda was a part of the Archdiocese of Halifax. Monsignor Isaac D. Comeau had St. Theresa's Church built. Since 1956 it has been the bishop's cathedral. In 1953 Bermuda was detached from the Archdiocese of Halifax by the Holy See and made a prefecture apostolic. In 1956 it became a vicariate apostolic and was assigned to the Fathers of the Congregation of the Resurrection. Robert S. Dehler, CR, became the first bishop vicar-apostolic, March 19, 1956.

In 1964 there were seven churches on the Islands with five residences, served by eight Resurrection priests and one other priest, on loan from Portugal, who took care of the Portuguese people. Mount St. Agnes Academy, conducted by the Sisters of Charity of Halifax since 1890, is the only Catholic school on the Islands. It is a large school for Bermuda with an enrollment of nearly 600. In 1961 this school accepted Negro children, becoming the first school in Bermuda to begin integration.

[R. S. DEHLER]

BERMUDEZ, JOÃO, pseudo-patriarch of Ethiopia, adventurer; d. S. Sabastião de Pedreira, Lisbon, 1570. Bermudez was a barber or surgeon in the Portuguese embassy, under Rodrigo de Lima, from Goa to the

Ethiopian port of Massawa in 1520. He was in the suite of the Negus of Ethiopia, David Lebna Dengel, for 5 years. When the Portuguese left the country in 1527, he remained behind. In 1535 when the Negus was attacked by Moslems of Somalia and Galla under Ahmed Granye, Bermudez was sent to Portugal for help. In Rome in 1538–39, he claimed that he had been ordained as his successor by the schismatic Ethiopian patriarch, Marcos. When Bermudez returned to Ethiopia in 1541 with a Portuguese force under Cristovão, the son of Vasco da *Gama, he claimed he had been confirmed by the Pope. Although suspect in Rome and in Ethiopia, Bermudez succeeded in occupying the Ethiopian patriarchate until 1555, when he was expelled by the Negus Galawdewos and replaced by a Jesuit from Portugal. He was back in Portugal in 1559 and later (Lisbon 1565) published an account of his embassy to Portugal.

Bibliography: I. ORTIZ DE URBINA, DHGE 8:542–543. E. CERULLI, LexThK² 2:233–234. S. EURINGER, "Der Pseudopatriarch Johannes Bermudes," ThGlaube 17 (1925) 226–256.

[C. VERLINDEN]

BERMUDO, JUAN,

Franciscan Observant, whose music treatises and organ pieces were signally influential in Renaissance Spain; b. Écija (Seville), *c.* 1510; d. in a friary of the Andalusian province, after 1560. Although his family was well to do, he became a novice vowed to poverty in 1525. First assigned to Seville, he later studied mathematics at the University of Alcalá de Henares. During convalescence after a long illness he grappled for the first time with the mathematical bases of music theory. These investigations culminated in his highly informative and critically invaluable *Libro primero de la declaración ·de instrumentos* (1549), *El arte Tripharia* (1550), and *Declaración de instrumentos musicales* (1555), all issued at Osuna. After publishing his magnum opus, Bermudo gave himself solely to the religious life. On June 24, 1560, he was elected one of the four *definidores* of the Andalusian province.

Bibliography: F. PEDRELL, *Salterio sacro-hispano* (n.p. 1883), 13 organ pieces. J. BERMUDO, *Declaración de instrumentos musicales (1555)* (fac. Kassel 1957). R. STEVENSON, *Juan Bermudo* (The Hague 1960). H. ANGLÈS, MusGG 1:1764–65. F. PEDRELL, *Diccionario biográfico y bibliográfico de músicos españoles* (Barcelona 1894–97) 1:179–190. O. KINKELDEY, *Orgel und Klavier in der Musik des 16. Jahrhunderts* (Leipzig 1910). Reese MusR.

[R. STEVENSON]

BERNABEI, GIUSEPPE ERCOLE,

church musician of the "colossal" baroque; b. Caprarola (Papal States), 1620 or 1622; d. Munich, 1687 (buried Dec. 6). After studying with *Benevoli, he became organist in 1653 at S. Luigi dei Francesci in Rome and from 1655 to 1667 was chapel-master at the Lateran. In 1672 he transferred to the Vatican, where his compositions are still performed, but in 1674 he left to become court conductor in Munich. Although two librettos are all that remain of his five operas, many of his sacred compositions (Masses, psalms, etc.) are preserved in MS. They reveal such mastery of the strict polyphonic style that he is regarded as one of the foremost 17th-century imitators of *Palestrina. Ercole's son, Giuseppe Antonio (b. Rome, 1649; d. Munich, March 9, 1732), was his father's assistant and successor in Munich. In addition to sacred works, Giuseppe Antonio wrote 14 operas, several of which are in the National-bibliothek, Vienna.

A second son, Vincenzo, was organist at Munich in 1685, and likewise a composer of church music.

See also MUSIC, SACRED, HISTORY OF, 5.

Bibliography: R. C. CASIMIRI, *Ercole Bernabei* (Rome 1920). W. BOLLERT, MusGG 1:1772–75. A. LOEWENBERG, Grove DMM 1:674. Eitner QuellLex 1:464–466.

[R. STEINER]

BERNADOT, MARIE VINCENT,

author, editor, and publisher; b. Escatalens, June 14, 1883; d. Labastide Lévêque, June 25, 1941. He was of peasant stock from southern France; he studied at the Grand Seminary at Montauban, and was ordained in 1906. After serving as a parish priest, he entered the Order of Preachers (the Dominicans) in 1912, made his noviceship at Fiesole, Italy, and studied at Rome. He

Marie Vincent Bernadot.

returned to France during World War I, where he resided at the priory of Saint-Maximin. He wrote several books on the spiritual life, of which *De l'Eucharistie à la Trinité* was most influential. His *L'Ordre des Frères Prêcheurs* (1917–18) remains an authentic interpretation of the ideals and achievements of the Dominicans. In 1919 Bernadot founded the journal *La Vie spirituelle*, which helped enormously in the spiritual rebirth of France. Within a year its circulation had reached 3,300, and the revenues enabled the editor to launch *La Vie intellectuelle* in 1928. His purpose was to enrich the interior life by this monthly commentary on current events—political, religious, social, and artistic—and to this end he attracted the talent of such authors as Jacques Maritain, François Mauriac, Paul Claudel, Étienne Gilson, Henri Daniel-Rops, and Pierre Henri Simon. In 1928 Bernadot moved to a new priory at Juvisy, near Paris, and founded the publishing house L'Editions du Cerf, later moved to Paris. He inaugurated a weekly, *Sept* (1934), which soon had a circulation of 50,000. His editiorial policy became increasingly involved in current political events (e.g., he advocated collaboration with the Socialists and declared that the Spanish Civil War was not a "holy crusade") and occasioned some shock and scandal. In August 1937, when he had to give up his work on the weekly he had created, lay friends, among them Mauriac and Maritain, continued its publication under the name *Temps présent,* with the approbation of the hierarchy. Bernadot returned to his religious studies and wrote *Notre Dame dans ma vie* (1937). He also started the journal *La Vie chrétienne avec Notre Dame,* which developed after the war into *Fêtes et saisons* and *La Vie catholique illustrée.*

See also CATHOLIC PRESS, WORLD SURVEY, 10.

Bibliography: VieSpirit (Aug. 1941, Nov. 1944). M. V. BERNADOT, *Lettres de direction* (Paris 1946).

[G. HOURDIN]

BERNANOS, GEORGES

French novelist, playwright, and essayist; b. Paris, Feb. 20, 1888; d. Neuilly, July 5, 1948. A family legend, doubtless based on the sound of the name, ascribed to Bernanos a Spanish ancestry. It told of ancestors who had lived in Santo Domingo until 1787, and hinted that one of these could have been a corsair during the time of Jean Bart. This picturesqueness, fitting as it may have been to the writer's temperament—his haughty air, love of the sun, and pugnacious vitality—is pure fiction. As far back as one can trace, Bernanos's roots are entirely French: Lorrainese on the side of his father Émile, from the vicinity of Metz; natives of Berry on the side of his mother, Hermance Moreau, a daughter of countryfolk of Pellevoisin, where the writer is buried near his parents. Bernanos's true native soil, however, is Artois. His home was in this province at Fressin (Pas de Calais). Since the meetings of the clergy of the deanery took place there, the child met many priests. After attending several colleges and minor seminaries at Paris and Bourges, he received his decisive character molding at the College of Saint Mary at Aire-sur-la-Lys. Finally, he chose Artois as the site of all his novels.

As a student at the Sorbonne (where he took degrees in the arts and in law), he was in the thick of the political struggle in which Catholics were opposing the monarchists of the *Action Française under Charles *Maurras and Léon Daudet, and the democrats of the Sillon organization, led by Marc *Sangnier. On the eve of World War I, for which he volunteered as a *poilu,* he was a journalist at Rouen. On May 11, 1917, he married Jeanne Talbert d'Arc, a direct descendant of a brother of Jeanne d'Arc (*see* JOAN OF ARC, ST.). She bore him six children. The necessity to support this large family without giving up his independence as a writer was not the least of the reasons for his nomadic existence. He never knew material security, though he sought it in various parts of France and then in Majorca, where the Spanish Civil War overtook him. On July 20, 1938, he embarked with his family for Paraguay, but he had to settle in Brazil. He stayed there until July 1945, when he returned to France at the call of General de Gaulle. He resumed his nomadic habits and while in Tunisia (1947–48) he became ill, at a time when he had vowed to write nothing more except *La Vie de Jesus.*

Literary Career. Bernanos came into literary prominence rather late. His first book, the novelette *Madame Dargent,* was published in 1922. He was an insurance inspector when his novel *Sous le soleil de Satan* (1925) brought him immediate fame. The novel of Catholic inspiration owes its revitalization in France to this book —those that followed could only plumb somewhat deeper, and the influence of Bernanos's priest character on the agnostic writers of the period was profound. The hero of *Sous le soleil de Satan* was indeed a priest, the Abbé Donissan, another Curé of Ars (*see* VIANNEY,

JEAN BAPTISTE MARIE, ST.). A priest is the principal character in nearly all the Bernanos novels, and the significant factor of Bernanos's portrayal is that it is not a matter, as it so often is in other fiction, of depicting a social specimen (however edifying) of the same category as a doctor or a lawyer, but of creating a being consecrated to and engaged body and soul in the spiritual drama. Bernanos tried to present these priests from an internal viewpoint, as if he and they were kindred spirits of the same calling; he succeeded so well that the critic Albert Béguin could style him "the priestly novelist."

Novelist of Holiness. Of course the Bernanos priest does not conform to plain reality. He represents a special "case" each time. Abbé Donissan, devoid, one might say, of armor, struggles with the demon and suffers the "temptation of despair" in ransoming those souls he saves. Abbé Cénabre (*L'Imposture,* 1927), who has lost his faith but keeps up outward appearances, is taken in charge by Abbé Chevance, who on his deathbed passes the burden on to a young woman, Chantal de Clergerie (*La Joie,* 1929), herself subject to some rather ecstatic phenomena. The parish priest of Ambricourt (*Le Journal d'un curé de campagne,* 1938, a novel of most classic construction, which won the Grand Prix of the Académie Française) is a hereditary alcoholic suffering from cancer, a condition that common sense would accept as an explanation of his apostolic "imprudences." But it is necessary, in dealing with the tumultuous and tormented genius of Bernanos to renounce what one ordinarily calls common sense. What animates this writer is a "supernatural sense." François Mauriac has written that Bernanos was very close to being "the novelist of holiness"; at the very least he suggests the mystery of holiness, and those contemporaries furthest removed from the faith were fascinated by the all-pervading presence of the supernatural in a literary work.

The Supernatural in Bernanos. Bernanos believed that "the supernatural cannot be set apart," meaning that human life is not lived in two compartments, one profane, the other sacred. The characters of his novels are at the extremes in their choices between good and

Georges Bernanos.

evil, or perhaps it would be better to say that they play to the hilt the game of God or devil, and at all hazards. Bernanos disdained the middle ground, the "average man," of whom he did not think except, in a polemical vein, as an imbecile or a coward (*La Grande peur des bien pensants,* 1931). More important, he portrayed in his novels the unhealthy unrest, even the crime and decay, that surrounds those who claim the supernatural does not affect them one way or the other, whose position is neither a clear "Yes" nor "No" (*M. Ouine*, 1943) and thus make of a town—drawn as an image of a great part of the contemporary world—a "dead parish." In thus embracing the absolute, the romance of Bernanos enhances the tragedy of life, but in it destiny bears the name of vocation. The calamity is never such, nor is the obvious Manicheism such, that love cannot prevail over it. The confrontation of good and evil is made concrete in the struggle of "a soul for a soul" as expressed by the little parish priest of Ambricourt (*Le Journal d'un curé de campagne*), whose last words, borrowed from St. Thérèse de Lisieux, are well-known: "What matter? All is grace."

In Bernanos's novels the champions of God never stop until they have snatched away the devil's prey; the strong pick up the burdens of the weak, as in the drama *Dialogues des Carmélites* (1948), where the ignoble death of a prioress, during the French Revolution, ensures the glorious martyrdom of a young religious overtaken by morbid cowardice. There is a constant illumination of the dogma of the *Communion of Saints "whose majesty fills us with wonder," in the author's own words; no less constant is the illustration of what Bernanos called "the eternal youthfulness of the Beatitudes." These stances explain, in their somewhat extreme evangelical viewpoints, a certain reversal of some current values: the characters for whom Bernanos showed the greatest affection, to begin with the priests (just as in Dostoievskiĭ), are the most humble, indeed the most disinherited, humanly speaking. He showed deep compassion and a veritable tenderness toward the young woman in *La Nouvelle histoire de Mouchette* (1937), where it is evident that the heroine's suicide is an appeal from the deceit of this world to the justice of the kingdom of heaven. In this supernatural vision of the human soul, "psychology," in the usual sense of the word, plays no part. Bernanos, who in more than one novel (notably in *La Joie*) evidenced his detestation of psychiatrists and psychoanalysts, excelled at "confessing" the essential reality of the soul. For him, this reality is demonstrated by the faithfulness of the young, and by that "spirit of youth" that is candor, honor, generosity, and courage. He associated it strongly with "the spirit of Christianity," which sustains all his polemical works.

Polemical Works. Considered apart from the situations that occasioned them and from their contemporary French relevance, and making allowance for the vehemence and extremism of his writing, his polemical works manifest in general the same uncompromising spirituality as his novels. Bernanos possessed a sort of "gift of prophecy"; a number of his statements concerning the lot of peoples during and after World War II are now seen to have been amazingly correct. But the most interesting and most fundamental of these essays, some of them single self-contained pieces (*Les Grands cimitières sous la lune*, 1938; *Scandale de la vérité*, 1939; *Lettre aux Anglais*, 1942), others in the form of diaries or journalistic contributions (*Les Enfants humiliés*, 1949; *Le Chemin de la Croix des âmes*, 1942), concern the demands of the Christian for his rights. The essayist, like the novelist, refused to accept a radical separation between the supernatural and the temporal; he grew indignant if the former came to terms with the latter, or if the latter guarded itself unduly against the requirements of the former; an obedient son of the Church, he

did not hesitate to belabor ecclesiastical diplomacy when he judged that it had bargained with the "honor of Christianity"; he wanted to "reconcile morals with politics"; he believed that countries—but not "nations" —are individuals, that each has its proper calling, and that they, too, run the risk of losing their souls.

In short, Bernanos dreamt of the Sermon on the Mount as the master plan for that "kingdom of the meek on earth." This role of the "great objector" is inseparable from the personality of Bernanos himself, although it is the novelist who will best evidence this to posterity. Isolated, dragged this way and that by opposing camps, the author on various occasions made himself heard as the voice of the Catholic conscience; in a sense, he was a living apologetic.

Bernanos's other works are: novels—*Un crime* (1935), *Un mauvais rêve* (posthumous, 1950); essays —*Saint Dominique* (1926), *Jeanne relapse et sainte* (1934), *Noël à la maison de France* (1931), *Nous autres Français* (1942), *La France contre les robots* (1944); novelettes—*Une Nuit* (1928), *Dialogues d'ombres* (1928); articles—*Ecrit de combat* (1944), *La liberté pour quoi faire?* (collected 1953).

Bibliography: G. BERNANOS, *Bernanos par lui-même*, ed. A. BÉGUIN (Paris 1954). H. U. VON BALTHASAR, *Le Chrétien Bernanos*, tr. M. DE GANDILLAC (Paris 1956). L. ESTANG, *Présence de Bernanos* (Paris 1947). P. MACCHI, *Bernanos e il problema del male* (Varese 1959). G. PICON, *Georges Bernanos* (Paris 1948). T. MOLNAR, *Bernanos, His Political Thought and Prophecy* (New York 1960). W. M. FROHOCK, "Georges Bernanos and his Priest-hero," *Yale French Studies* 12 (1953) 54–61; "The Vocation of Georges Bernanos," *Catholic World* 168 (March 1949) 448–452. H. HATZFELD, "Georges Bernanos, 1888–1948, A Bibliography," *Thought* 23 (1948) 405–424; "Georges Bernanos and Henri Bremond," *Renascence* 3 (1951) 120–127. **Illustration credit:** French Embassy, Press and Information Division, New York City.

[L. ESTANG]

BERNARD OF AOSTA, ST., known also as Bernard of Menthon, of Mont-Joux, restorer and patron of two famous Alpine hospices in the passes that bear his name; b. probably Italy (not Savoy); d. Novara, June 15, 1081? (feast, May 28, June 15). Archdeacon of Aosta for 40 years, his renown for holiness was consequent on the long years spent as a tireless, itinerant preacher through much of Piedmont, where his cult has always been popular. But his worldwide reputation today is chiefly linked with the hospices he reestablished and placed under the care of clerics and laymen who later became *Canons Regular of St. Augustine. The same order still conducts the hospices. According to a 15th-century document, Bernard was canonized by Richard, Bishop of Novara (1115–21). In 1923, *Pius XI proclaimed him patron of mountain climbers.

Bibliography: ActSS June 3:547–564. ActApS 15 (1923) 437–442. A. P. FRUTAZ, EncCatt 2:1417–21. A. DONNET, *Saint Bernard et les origines de l'Hospice du Mont-Joux* (Saint-Maurice 1942), critical. A. LÜTOLF, ThQschr 61 (1879) 179–207. A. PONCELET, AnalBoll 26 (1907) 135–136. B. DE GAIFFIER, ibid. 63 (1945) 269–270. Butler Th Attw 2:411–413.

[N. M. RIEHLE]

BERNARD OF AUVERGNE (ALVERNIA), French Dominican theologian; fl. 1294 to 1307. Originally from Gannat, he entered the Dominican Order at Clermont in the province of Auvergne. Known as *Malleus* (hammer) to his contemporaries, he taught at Paris as a bachelor of theology (1294–97) and commented on the *Sentences* (ed. Lyons 1519). Although direct evidence is lacking, it is probable that he became a master in theology, for five *Quaestiones disputatae* of his are extant and some MSS attribute that title to him. He was prior of Saint-Jacques in 1303, when he and the entire priory signed the appeal against *Boniface VIII. Four sermons that he preached between 1301 and 1305 are extant. As an ardent defender of the doctrines of St. *Thomas Aquinas, he vigorously opposed the views of *Henry of Ghent, *Godfrey of Fontaines and *James of Viterbo. Thus Bernard was one of the earliest theologians who contributed to the spread and development of *Thomism. Although the bulk of his extant writings is polemical in nature, he did not reply to the *Correctorium* of *William de la Mare (*see* CORRECTORIA). After the death of *Peter of Auvergne toward the end of 1304, Bernard was elected bishop of Clermont by the cathedral chapter, but *Clement V annulled this election in 1307. It is certain that Bernard never took possession of the see.

Bibliography: M. GRABMANN, "Bernhard von Alvergne, O.P., ein Interpret und Verteidiger der Lehre des hl. Thomas von Aquin aus alter Zeit," DivThomF 10 (1932) 23–35. F. J. ROENSCH, *Early Thomistic School* (Dubuque 1964). E. FILTHAUT, LexThK² 2:242. G. BRUNI, EncCatt 2:1417. A. D'AMATO, EncFil 1:660.

[P. GLORIEUX]

BERNARD OF BESSE,

early Franciscan chronicler; fl. in France c. 1283. Little is known of his life beyond the fact that he was a member of the Franciscan custody of Cahors in the Province of Aquitaine and was a secretary of the Minister General, *Bonaventure. In January 1250 he was probably residing at the convent of Limoges. His writings include a lost *Life of Brother Christopher of Romagna,* who died at Cahors in 1272, inserted in the *Chronicle of the 24 Generals* [AnalFranc 3 (1897) 161–173]; the *Speculum disciplinae,* called also *Libellus de proposito regulae,* intended for the formation of novices (Quaracchi, *S. Bonaventurae opera omnia* 8:583–622); a letter, *Ad quendam novitium insolentem et instabilem* (*ibid.* 663–666); *De laudibus b. Francisci* [AnalFranc 3 (1897) 666–679, 687–692]; *De triplici statu religionis b. Francisci* (ibid. 679–687); and a *Catalogus generalium ministrorum OFM* (*ibid.* 693–707; MGS 32:657–674), ending with Bonagratia Tielci (1283). Moderation and zeal characterize all his writings; the ascetical works—intended for the young—contain practical advice useful even for non-Franciscans. The prologue of the *De laudibus* discusses the biographers of St. *Francis (not mentioning Brother *Leo of Assisi, however); the first chapter is the oldest Franciscan hagiographic catalogue. It should be noted that in certain chapters Bernard drew inspiration not only from *Thomas of Celano but also from the *Anonymus Perusinus.*

Bibliography: *Chronica XXIV generalium O.F.M.,* AnalFranc 3 (1897) 161; 225, 228, 241, 262, 349, 361, 377. MARIAN DE FLORENCE, *Compendium chronicarum Fratrum Minorum,* Arch FranchHist 2 (1909) 463; 4 (1911) 569. J. DE DIEU, DictSpirAsc Myst 1:1504–05. A. VAN DEN WYNGAERT, DHGE 8:594–595.

[J. CAMBELL]

BERNARD OF CHARTRES,

humanist master of Chartres; b. Brittany, end of 11th century; d. between 1124 and 1130. The elder brother of *Thierry of Chartres, he taught logic and speculative grammar at the cathedral school of Chartres (1114–19) and was chancellor of the school from 1119 until at least 1124.

Although none of his writings has survived, *John of Salisbury has preserved not only three fragments of his verse and the title of one work, *De expositione Porphyrii* (*Metal.* 4.35; *Polycrat.* 7.13), but also typical doctrines of Bernard. He cultivated faith and morals in his students as carefully as memory and talent (*Metal.* 1.24). Echoing the Platonism of *John Scotus Erigena and *Pseudo-Dionysius, he held that divine ideas are eternal, but not coeternal with God; mutable individuals are unworthy to be designated by substantive terms, and still less worthy to establish genera and species (*ibid.* 2.17, 4.35). Substantive terms designate pure, ideal forms, while all derivatives designate degrees of defilement of form by matter (*formae nativae*). This doctrine was developed by his most eminent disciple, *Gilbert de la Porrée. Although Bernard tried to subsume Platonism and Aristotelianism within his humanism, John termed him "the most thorough-going Platonist of our age" (*ibid.* 4.35).

See also SCHOLASTICISM, 1.

Bibliography: R. L. POOLE, *Illustrations of the History of Medieval Thought and Learning* (2d ed. rev. Gloucester, Mass. 1961). G. BONAFEDE, EncFil 1:660–661. A. CLERVAL, *Les Écoles de Chartres au moyen-âge (du Vᵉ au XVIᵉ siècle)* (Chartres 1895). É. H. GILSON, "Le Platonisme de Bernard de Chartres," RevNéoscPhil 25 (1923) 5–19.

[E. A. SYNAN]

BERNARD OF CLAIRVAUX, ST.

Abbot, monastic theologian, and Doctor of the Church; b. Fontaines-les-Dijon, a village near Dijon, 1090; d. Clairvaux, Aug. 20, 1153.

Life. Bernard's family was of noble lineage, both on the side of his father, Tescelin, and on that of his mother, Aleth or Aletta, but his ancestry cannot be clearly traced beyond his proximate forebears. The third of seven children, six of whom were sons, Bernard as

"St. Bernard of Clairvaux Worshiping Christ," woodcut by the 16th-century German artist Lucas Cranach.

a boy attended the school of the secular canons of Saint-Vorles, where it is probable that he studied the subjects included in the medieval trivium. In 1107 the early death of his mother, to whom he was bound by a strong affective tie, began a critical period in his life. Of the 4 years that followed little is known but what can be inferred from their issue. In 1111 Bernard left the world and withdrew to the locality of Châtillon, where he was soon joined by all his brothers and a number of other relatives. He so distinguished himself in following the rule of the Cistercians, the strictest rule of the time, that after only 3 years he was chosen as abbot for a new foundation. For it, he with his 12 companions chose a solitary valley not far from the Aube, which they called Clara Vallis or Clairvaux. He was ordained by William of Champeaux, Bishop of Châlons-sur-Marne. In 1115, at 25 years of age, he was already at the juridical summit of his career, but he was to go on growing in the esteem of his contemporaries and in the effectiveness of his activity until he became the center of unity and the forward impetus for the ecclesiastical life of his time.

The first years of his abbacy were spent dealing with problems of monastic life—the organization and strengthening of the community at Clairvaux and the making of new foundations, the number of which was to reach 68 by the time of Bernard's death.

Controversy with Cluny. But if Clairvaux was to become a model of strict observance, Cluny, which was still a greater power in the Benedictine world, followed an adaptation of the Rule of St. Benedict. The beginning of Bernard's polemic against the disciplinary decadence of the Cluniacs occurred in 1119. [See Bernard's letter of 1119 or 1120 to his cousin Robert and the famous *Apologia ad Guillelmum S. Theodorici abbatem* of 1124 or 1125, *S. Bernardi opera, ed. Leclercq-Rochais* (Rome 1963) 3.81–108; hereafter, *Opera.*] In these writings the zeal of the saint expressed itself hotly at times and with some asperity, but in the warmth of debate a good fruit ripened, namely, the friendship between Bernard and *Peter the Venerable, Abbot of Cluny. Because of the contrast of temperament between the two, they were not by nature inclined to look upon each other sympathetically, but the vicissitudes of their relationship made each respect the holiness of the other, and they overcame the difficulty of temperament by their charity and mutual esteem.

Bernard was troubled about the relationship of his to other forms of the monastic life, and he had views of his own with regard to *transitus* or the transfer of a monk or a canon regular from one observance to another. Bernard was guided by his conviction of the superiority of the Cistercian life to every other manner of pursuing evangelical perfection and thought that when a soul sought a higher way of life, it was moved *duce spiritu libertatis,* and such being the case, the matter transcended the disposition of the Rule of St. Benedict (ch. 61), or the agreements existing between orders, or papal privileges, and it even escaped the line of reasoning Bernard himself took in his *Liber de precepto et dispensatione* (*Opera* 3.283–288).

Schism. But the ardent charity of the saint went beyond the horizons of the world of monks and canons and reached out to all the members of the Church. His qualities as a man of action were brought to light in the schism that took place in the Church in consequence of the election of two popes in 1130, Innocent II and Anacletus II, representatives of opposing factions, whose rivalry was reflected in the division of the College of Cardinals into two parties. Those who supported the Curia and were traditionalist in their conception of ecclesiastical life and methods of reform espoused the cause of Anacletus. The monastic party, of more recent formation, supported Innocent. Throughout the schism Bernard devoted himself strenuously to the task of securing the recognition of Innocent, on whose side he had stood from the beginning.

Abelard, Gilbert de la Porrée, and Arnold of Brescia. Successful in this battle, Bernard did not retire to the peace of the cloister for long. In 1140 he conducted the delicate operation that led to the condemnation of Abelard. Bernard's part in this was not unlike the part he played in the attempted condemnation of *Gilbert de la Porrée in 1148 at the Council of Reims. Many have been puzzled by his passionate involvement in these affairs. His polemical vehemence is impressive, even when due allowance is made for the peculiarities of that kind of literary genre (see *Tractatus ad Innocentium II pontificem contra quaedam capitula errorum Abaelardi* PL 182.1053–57; *Epistolae 188–189, 191–193, 331–338*). There is no doubt that he was sincerely convinced that the teaching of Abelard constituted a grave danger for the faith, and his reaction was harsh and precipitate and showed little concern for literal exactitude or for distinguishing between the written and the spoken word or between the teaching of the master and the interpretation of his disciples. The same can be said of his reaction to Gilbert [see John of Salisbury, *Historia pontificalis,* ed. M. Chibnall (Edinburgh 1956) ch. 8–12; Otto of Freisingen, *Gesta Friderici imperatoris,* MG SrerGerm, ed. G. Waitz-von Simson, 48, 61].

Between 1144 and 1145 Bernard opposed himself to Arnold of Brescia, whose preaching against the wealth and luxury of the Church favored a movement of rebellion among the Roman people whom Bernard strove to win to the obedience of Lucius II and later of Eugene III. The election of the latter, a disciple of Bernard at Clairvaux, to the pontificate in 1145 further increased Bernard's influence upon ecclesiastical life at the center of Christendom, which reached its zenith in the first years of Eugene's pontificate.

The Crusades. In 1146 and 1147 Bernard was officially in charge of the preaching of the Second Crusade. Although the crusade itself ended in failure—a fact that saddened Bernard's last years—his success in winning support for it stood as evidence of the profound resonance evoked in the Christian West by the words and the personal charm of the saint. The war against the infidels was not Bernard's only cause in his popular preaching. Certain heresies then flourishing at home evoked his eloquence. Against the heretics he depended chiefly upon persuasion, but without neglecting, in cases of pertinacity, recourse to the secular arm.

At the hour of Tierce, Aug. 20, 1153, Bernard died, consumed by sickness and austerity. He was canonized by Alexander III, Jan. 18, 1174, and proclaimed a Doctor of the Church by Pius VIII in 1830. The most recent act of the Holy See with regard to St. Bernard was the encyclical *Doctor mellifluus* of Pius XII on the occasion of the 8th centenary of his death.

Personality. Those of his contemporaries who spoke of Bernard agreed in attesting to the spiritual charm that emanated from him; the more analytical sought to trace it to his fascinating eloquence, fed by a rare combination of natural gifts and by a continuous and skillful use of the Scriptures, sustained by a life in conformity with his words, and strengthened by charismatic graces. Nevertheless Bernard's behavior could be looked upon from different points of view, and it provoked discordant judgments.

Otto of Freisingen, in the most penetrating appraisal of the personality of Bernard made by a contemporary (*Gesta* 1.49), singled out certain traits that help to clarify attitudes indicated above: the ardent zeal that made him quick to intervene when he perceived a danger to the integrity of the faith and the facility, peculiar to impulsive temperaments, in accepting evidence without properly evaluating it. Nevertheless, a historically accurate reconstruction of the saint's personality does not lessen but puts into clearer relief the essential greatness of the man. He was perhaps the most authentic and complete representative of the monastic tradition in the current of medieval civilization. The life of Bernard remains an example of the Christian ideal, realized with total service and self-sacrifice, without egoism or personalism. The difficulty of the struggle he had to face because of his temperament, and the humility with which he recognized his own defects should not be undervalued. [See *Epist.* 70 and its appraisal by Dimier, RHE 50 (1955) 550–551.]

Theology. St. Bernard was a typical exponent of what has been called monastic theology by certain modern scholars. It is a theology that aims at a clear, orderly, warm exposition of truth, such as will serve to dispose the soul to prayer and contemplation. Bernardine theology was not distinguished by the discovery of new modes of thought or the achievement of new conclusions but by its continual permeation with a rich interior experience. Bernard's sources were principally the Scriptures, then the Fathers of the Church, works concerned with the regulation of monastic life (especially the Rule of St. Benedict), and finally the liturgy. The whole design of his theology can be reduced to a few lines: God, that is charity, created man by love and by love redeemed him. The supreme proof of that love is the Incarnation of the Word and the Redemption. Another exquisite proof of that love is the presence of a Mother, who is also the Mother of God, in the great picture of the Redemption.

It would be erroneous to attribute the detailed attention Bernard gave to the Blessed Virgin to reasons of pure sentiment. If the influence of his delicately sensitive spirit, sharpened by the sad loss of his own mother, cannot be denied, it must nevertheless be noted that Bernard exhibited a profound theological understanding of the function of Mary in Catholic dogma and particularly in the work of the Redemption.

Three points in his Mariology have been much commented upon. (1) With regard to the Immaculate Conception, there is his famous letter (n. 174), from which it can be certainly deduced that he did not admit that truth. (2) As to the dogma of the Assumption, clear texts are wanting, although a passage from the sermon recently published by J. Leclercq ["Études sur St. Bernard et le texte de ses écrits," in *Analecta S. Ordinis Cisterciensis* 9 (1953)] seems to point in the direction of that truth. (3) The mediation of Mary is one of the themes upon which Bernard insisted with great effectiveness, for example, in his well-known *Sermo de aquaeductu* (PL 183.437–448).

Apologetic and polemic considerations led Bernard to certain points in sacramental theology in his *Tractatus de baptismo*. He maintained, for example, that Baptism of water was not absolutely necessary, and it could be substituted for by that of blood or desire. He also held the justification of unbaptized infants in virtue of the faith of their parents.

Ascetical Doctrine. The theology of Bernard was so closely bound to personal experience of ascent to God that it is impossible to draw a clear dividing line between his dogmatic and his ascetical teaching. His fundamental ascetical treatises were three. (1) *De gratia et libero arbitrio* (*Opera* 3.165–203) is important because it provides the dogmatic and historical premises of Christian *ascesis* and describes the state of fallen but repaired human nature. Bernard insisted upon the primacy of the will, whose freedom from sin is actuated in Christ and through Christ. He strongly affirmed the necessity of grace, taking the strictly antipelagian position of St. Augustine. (2) The *De gradibus humilitatis et superbiae* (*Opera* 3.13–59) shows the fundamental importance that humility had for Bernard as the indispensable premise of charity. For him, humility was truth and was based in men on the humility-truth that is Christ, which takes possession of men and fills them with the gifts of His love. In the first part of the treatise are described the 3 degrees of humility; in the second, the 12 degrees of pride. This work, strongly marked by St. Bernard's personal experience, reveals his singular capacity for penetrating the human soul. (3) His brief *Liber de diligendo Deo* (*Opera* 3.119–154) is important for an understanding of his ascetical doctrine, but it is useful also for his mystical teaching, because it is centered upon the love of God and explains its motives. The first motive for loving God is the gifts He has given to mankind in general (ch. 2) and more especially those given to the Christian (ch. 3–4); the second is the good of man, who in God alone can satisfy his thirst for happiness. In the development of this meditation one encounters the central and vital function that the mysteries of the humanity of the Word have in Bernardine ascetical doctrine and piety. In a well-known passage of *Sermo 43 super cantica* (*Opera* 2.43) Bernard returns to the mysteries of the life and Passion of Jesus as the only wisdom and salvation and presents the Crucified as "mea subtilior, interior philosophia"—a statement that reveals the Christocentric nature of his theology as well as the strongly affective character of his piety.

There is also ascetical doctrine of importance in the *De consideratione libri quinque ad Eugenium III* (*Opera* 3.393–493). The "consideration" in question is, at least in part, mental prayer, and the whole treatise, although divided into points strictly connected with the high office of the one to whom the work was addressed, still contains a development of the theme capable of broader application. Book 1 brings out the necessity of meditation as an essential element of piety (ch. 7–8). In book 2 Bernard proposes four series of themes for meditation: *te, quae sub te, quae circa te, quae supra te sunt* (ch. 3). Books 3 and 4 are concerned with the duties of the pontiff. In book 5, after having declared that meditation finds its fullness and high point in mystical contemplation (ch. 2), Bernard suggests many motives for meditation.

Mystical Doctrine. Bernard left no systematic exposition of mystical theology, but the *Sermones in cantica* and numerous passages in his other works contain the fruit of a genuine mystical experience, and in them, in spite of the lack of a systematic exposition, certain fundamental lines can be discerned. The ultimate and culminating development of theology for Bernard consisted in mystical experience. It represents the apex of all the works of God. Love wants to unite the soul to itself by charity even to the extent of mystical nuptials or spiritual marriage. In the stage of mystical union Bernard always presented the Word as the spouse of the soul, according to the characteristic Christocentricity of his thought.

His mystical teaching reveals another striking characteristic of the saint, his need to communicate his religious experience to others. In dispensing the riches of his interior life, he uncovered the whole grandeur of his mystical life. Few indeed even of the great mystics have had the ability to describe the mystical states so effectively. His truly great talent as an artist and a stylist was helpful to him in this, as can be seen in the descriptions of the visit of the Word to the soul in ch. 5 and 6 of *Sermo 74 in cantica*. To be noted are the limpid simplicity with which Bernard succeeds in expressing the ineffable; the paratactic construction permitting the period to proceed more rapidly and brokenly, thus giving more effective expression to the sighing of the soul; the exquisite use of rhythm extending to groups of phrases and giving rise to strophes and hymnic passages [see C. Mohrmann, "Le Stile de St. Bernard" in *S. Bernardo* (Milan 1954) 170–184].

St. Bernard must be ranked among the saints who have had a most profound influence by their doctrine and spirituality upon the life of the Church. The Franciscan school received some of its Christocentric orientation from St. Bernard. The author of the *Imitation of Christ* shows signs of having been abundantly nourished by the reading of the works of Bernard, and the French school of the 17th century manifests a notable affinity with certain fundamental lines of Bernardine theology (see Le Bail, 1.1492–98).

Culture and Art. Bernard was one of the most notable exponents of the monastic culture of the Middle Ages. He achieved a mastery of prose, despite his lack of direct acquaintance with the classics. Recent investigations by J. Leclercq of the MSS tradition appear to show that although Bernard dictated with facility and without much fussiness, he nevertheless took some care with the revision and polishing of his works.

His style, besides its well-known use of rhythm, was characterized by parallelism, antithesis, alliteration, and assonance, all of which are evidence of the influence of St. Augustine. One of his most admirable qualities as a stylist was his brilliant and fascinating ability to adapt the sacred text to the exigencies of artistic expression and to weave the passages of Scripture, which he had assimilated so well, into ever new designs (see John of Salisbury, *Historia pontificalis* 12).

Bernard was hostile to the scholastic culture of his time, which was characterized by a growing sense of the function and autonomy of reason in the sphere of its competence. Nor did he look with favor upon the related demand for a theology that, although deduced from revealed premises and with all the reverence due to mystery, nevertheless built itself up with the exercise of reason and assumed the dignity of a science. Bernard could not see the need for such a theology. For him the search for truth simply out of a desire for truth was not a positive value, nor did he clearly recognize a field reserved to reason, although the beginning of such recognition can be found in certain passages of his writings.

In general, however, it can be affirmed that he had an awareness of the part study and knowledge can play in the ascent of the soul to God. But he valued knowledge only in that context. He was acutely conscious of the dangers involved in intellectual investigation, and he distrusted all that could give nourishment to pride. This attitude is to be explained in large part by his own inner experience that enabled him to draw supreme certitude from the joys of contemplation and from his own experience of the fecundity of grace. He felt no need for much reasoning and subtlety. He was inclined rather to be bored with it, and he viewed it as an obstacle. Nevertheless, within the limits he would set, Bernard valued study. At Clairvaux he laid the foundations of one of the best monastic libraries of the Middle Ages and maintained relations with William of Champeaux, Hugh of Saint-Victor, John of Salisbury, and Peter Lombard.

Bibliography: The four ancient lives of St. Bernard are in PL 185:225–368. Biog. sources. E. VACANDARD, *Vie de Saint Bernard* (5th ed. Paris 1920). J. M. CANIVEZ, DHGE 8:610–611. Bernardine bibliog. L. JANAUSCHEK, *Bibliographia bernardina* (Vienna 1891). J. BOUTON, *Bibliographie bernardine* (Paris 1958). J. LECLERCQ, "Les Études bernardines en 1963," *Bulletin de la société internationale pour l'étude de la philosophie médiévale* 5 (1963) 121–138.

Bernardine apocrypha and disputed writings. F. CAVALLERA, DictSpirAscMyst 1:1499–1502. Information on the critical ed. of the text. J. LECLERCQ, "L'Édition de St. B.," RHE 45 (1950) 715–727. H. M. ROCHAIS, "L'Édition critique des oeuvres de St. B.," StMed 1 (1960) 701–719.

Biog. studies. The biog. by Vacandard, mentioned above, was the first attempt at a truly hist. reconstruction of the personality of St. B. Hist. Commission of the Order of Citeaux, *Bernard de Clairvaux* (Paris 1953). W. W. WILLIAMS, *Saint Bernard of Clairvaux* (Westminster, Md. 1952). J. CALMETTE and H. DAVID, *Saint Bernard* (Paris 1953). B. SCOTT-JAMES, *Saint Bernard of Clairvaux* (London 1957).

Special studies. E. GILSON, *Mystical Theology of St. Bernard* (2d ed. New York 1955). *St. Bernard théologien: Actes du Congrès de Dijon* (Rome 1953). J. LECLERCQ, "Un Guide de la lecture pour St. B.," VieSpirit 102 (1960) 440–447; *Saint Bernard mystique* (Paris 1948). *Festschrift zum 800 Jahrgedächtnis des Todes Bernhards von Clairvaux* (Vienna 1953). *Mélanges St. Bernard*, 24e Congrès de l'Assoc. bourguignonne des sociétés savantes (Dijon 1954).

Encyclopedia articles. E. VACANDARD, DTC 2.1:746–785. A. LE BAIL, DictSpirAscMyst 1:1454–99. P. OPPENHEIM and K. RATHE, EncCatt 2:1423–36. B. OPFERMANN, LexThK² 2:239–242. H. WOLTER, *ibid.* 2:253–255. **Illustration credit:** National Gallery of Art, Washington, D.C., Rosenwald Collection.

[P. ZERBI]

BERNARD OF CLUNY, Benedictine monk and poet; fl. mid-12th century, known also as Bernard of Morlas. Nothing is known for certain about his early years, although later unsubstantiated tradition describes him as a native of England or Brittany who entered religious life at the Abbey of Saint-Sauveur d'Aniane, transferring to the great *Benedictine foundation at *Cluny in the time of Abbot Pons de Melgueil (d. 1126). It is certain, however, that he was a monk at Cluny under *Peter the Venerable (1122–57), for he dedicates his major work to that abbot. Bernard is best known for his *De contemptu mundi,* a Latin poem of about 3,000 lines in dactylic hexameter, written c. 1140. It is a bitter satire against the moral disorders of his time, and the author did not flinch from protesting the vices of the leading churchmen of the day and the abuses that he saw in Rome itself. In his somewhat discursive fashion he enlarged upon the transitory nature of all material things and the permanence of spiritual values. His vivid descriptions of heaven and hell might be compared with those of *Dante, and the whole work ends on an apocalyptic note. Bernard also produced a number of sermons and is usually credited with the authorship of the *Mariale,* a poem in praise of the Blessed Virgin, as well as the *Constitutiones cluniacenses,* a compilation of the early monastic customs that had been the basis of the *Cluniac Reform.

See also OMNI DIE DIC MARIAE.

Bibliography: Works. *De contemptu mundi by Bernard of Morval,* ed. H. C. HOSKIER (London 1929); *Constitutiones cluniacenses,* ed. B. ALBERS in *Constitutiones cluniacenses antiquiores* (Monte Cassino 1905). *Mariale,* AnalHymn 50:423–483. Literature. HistLittFranc 12:236–246. *The Rhythm of Bernard of Morlaix,* ed. and tr. J. M. NEALE (5th ed. London 1864). Manitius 3:780–783. A. WILMART, "Grands poèmes inédits de Bernard le Clunisien," RevBén 45 (1933) 249–253. M. DISDIER, DHGE 8:699–700. L. BERGERON, DictSpirAscMyst 1:1506–07. R. C. PETRY, "Medieval Eschatology and Social Responsibility in Bernard of Morval's *De contemptu mundi,*" Speculum 24 (1949) 207–217. Raby ChrLP 315–319. Szövérffy AnnLatHymn 2:86–89. G. J. ENGELHARDT, "The *De contemptu mundi* of Bernardus Morvalensis: A Study in Commonplace," MedSt 22 (1960) 108–135.

[B. J. COMASKEY]

BERNARD OF COMPOSTELLA, THE ELDER,

Spanish canonist at Bologna in the early 13th century, dates and places of birth and death unknown. He held the dignity of archdeacon of Compostella, and some time before 1210 he was perhaps employed in a judicial or consulting capacity by the papal Curia. He may at some time have been also a member of the short-lived (1204–09) law school of Vicenza. At Bologna, where many Spaniards were active in the schools at that period, he apparently associated in particular with his fellow countrymen Melendus (later bishop of Osma, d. 1225), Pelagius (later cardinal-bishop of Albano, d. 1232), and Petrus Hispanus. After c. 1217, no further traces of his academic activities have been found. Bernard (Bernardus Compostellanus Antiquus) was particularly remembered at Bologna as the *decretalist who put together the so-called *Compilatio Romana* (1208), a compilation of decretals from the first 10 years of Innocent III; but the work was criticized by the Curia because it included papal letters not meant to be used as binding precedents. It was soon replaced by an official collection (known as Compilatio III antiqua), which the Pope sent to the schools. The failure of Bernard's *Compilatio Romana* probably explains why his achievements as a glossator received little recognition by the leading masters of his time in both the decretist and decretalist fields at Bologna.

Modern manuscript research has established that, apart from the decretal compilation, he wrote: (1) an apparatus of glosses on the *Decretum* of *Gratian (c. 1206), until recently known only from citations in other commentaries; (2) additions to and annotations on the *glossa ordinaria* of Joannes Teutonicus (c. 1217); (3) glosses on the *Compilatio I* of decretals (c. 1205–06; but no evidence has been found for his glosses on the *Compilatio II,* which were still known in the 14th century); and (4) *Quaestiones disputatae* (c. 1204–09, at Vicenza?).

Bibliography: S. KUTTNER, "Bernardus Compostellanus Antiquus," *Traditio* 1 (1943) 277–340, with full bibliog. Edition of the *Compilatio Romana* (in the form of a calendar, except for the texts not elsewhere transmitted), ed. H. SINGER in SBWien, Philos.-hist. Klasse 171.2 (1914). R. WEIGAND, in *Bulletin of the Institute of Research and Study in Medieval Canon Law* in *Traditio* 21 (1965) 482–485, on a MS of the *apparatus decretorum.*

[S. KUTTNER]

BERNARD OF COMPOSTELLA, THE YOUNGER,

bishop, canonist; d. Rome, 1267. He was dean of Lisbon in 1252. He is called "the Younger" to distinguish him from Bernard of Compostella "the Elder" (early 13th century), with whom, as Joannes Andreae testifies, he was being confused as early as the first part of the 14th century.

In a very busy lifetime he found time for only three works: (1) a *Margarita* or analytical table to Innocent IV's *Apparatus in quinque libros decretalium,* (2) a commentary on Innocent's own decretals—both of these were minor works written about 1250—and (3) a *Lectura* or commentary on the decretals of Gregory IX (which was begun about 1260 and had reached only as far as bk. 1, tit. 6 by 1267). For all its lack of originality the fragmentary *Lectura* is of value, chiefly because it is the product of a writer who not only endorsed but also was perfectly familiar in practice with Innocent IV's ideas on centralization. Thus, drawing at one point on his own experience as an auditor, Bernard adds *Notabilia* to CorpIurCan X 1.3.30 (*De rescriptis*), which provide a fascinating glimpse of the century-old system of provisions at the very moment when the canonist-pope was giving it a juridical framework that would endure for centuries.

Bibliography: BERNARD of COMPOSTELLA, *Lectura aurea,* in *Perillustrium tam veterum quam recentiorum in libros decretalium aurei commentarii,* v.1 (Venice 1588). G. DURANTIS, *Speculum iuris,* glossed by JOANNES ANDREAE et al., 4 pts. in 3 (Venice 1576) pt. 3, lib. 3, p. 28, "De inquisitione," gloss k. Schulte 2: 118–120. F. GILLMANN, *Zur Lehre der Scholastik vom Spender der Firmung und des Weihesakraments* (Paderborn 1920) 88–90, 226–227. G. BARRACLOUGH, "Bernard of Compostella," Eng HistRev 49 (1934) 487–494; DDC 2:777–779. Kuttner 318. S. KUTTNER, "Bernardus Compostellanus antiquus," *Traditio* 1 (1943) 277–278. P. G. KESSLER, "Untersuchungen über die Novellen-Gesetzgebung Papst Innozenz' IV," ZSavRGKan 32 (1943) 316–354. Van Hove 1:477–478, 480–481.

[L. E. BOYLE]

BERNARD OF CONSTANCE,

writer, teacher; b. Saxony; d. probably *Corvey, c. 1088. After being educated by Adalbert of Constance and Meinhard of Bamberg, he taught at the cathedral schools of Constance and (after 1072) *Hildesheim. His many letters to his student *Bernold of Constance and to Adalbert of Constance are proof of his competence in the classics and in Canon Law. After 1085 he became a monk, probably at Corvey. He called himself Bernard the

Saxon. As a faithful adherent of *Gregory VII, he wrote the so-called "Saxon Report" of 1085 (MGS 6:721), the *Liber canonum contra Heinricum IV* (MGLibLit 1:471–), and the *De damnatione schismaticorum* (MGLibLit 2:29–). He is also the author of the Hildesheim collection of letters (MG Briefe der deutschen Kaiserzeit 5; 1951).

Bibliography: F. THANER, "Zu zwei Streitschriften des 11. Jh.," NeuesArch 16 (1891) 529–543. P. J. G. LEHMANN, *Corveyer Studien* (Munich 1919). C. ERDMANN, *Studien zur Briefliteratur Deutschlands im 11. Jh.* (Leipzig 1938) 203–224. F. J. SCHMALE, LexThK² 2:244.

[V. H. REDLICH]

BERNARD OF CORLEONE, BL.,

Capuchin lay brother; b. Corleone, Sicily, Feb. 6, 1605; d. Palermo, Sicily, Jan. 12, 1667 (feast, Jan. 12). Bernard (baptized Philip) was the third of six children born to Leonard and Frances (Xaxa) Latini, who owned a small vineyard. Bernard supported his widowed mother as a cobbler. He received no formal schooling but, in a town garrisoned by mercenaries employed by Spain, he learned swordsmanship so well that his name became a legend throughout Sicily. He wielded the sword, however, only in what he called "Christian" causes, especially the defense of women and poor peasants oppressed by the town's soldiers. His conversion to the religious life was occasioned when at the age of 27, he gravely wounded an adversary who had repeatedly provoked him to a duel. He entered the novitiate of the Capuchin Order at Caltanissetta, Dec. 13, 1632, as a lay brother. Although endowed with gifts of contemplation and miracles, Bernard is best remembered for heroic penance. His fasts and macerations recall the desert fathers. He is frequently pictured burning his mouth with a brand snatched from the kitchen fire, a penalty inflicted on himself for an unkind word to a confrere. Bernard was beatified by Clement XIII, April 29, 1768.

Bibliography: D. DA GANGI, *Dalla spada al cilicio: Profilo del beato Bernardo da Corleone* (Tivoli 1934). B. VON MEHR, Lex ThK² 2:243. A. TEETAERT, DHGE 8:647–648. Butler Th Attw 1:124. G. SANITÁ, EncCatt 2:1436. *Lexicon Capuccinum* (Rome 1951).

[T. MAC VICAR]

BERNARD OF FONTCAUDE,

*Premonstratensian theologian; d. *c.* 1192. He seems to have been first abbot of Fontcaude in the former Diocese of Saint-Pons-de-Thomières, which he governed in 1172 and which Pope *Lucius III in 1184 placed under the jurisdiction of the archbishop of *Narbonne. In 1182 Bernard signed a charter in favor of the Abbey of *Aniane, and in 1188, a document concerning the monastery of Combelongue. He wrote polemical tracts against the *Waldenses, published by Gretzer, together with two similar works in *Tria scriptorum adversus Valdensium sectam: Ebruardus Bethunensis, Bernardus abbas Fontis Calidi, Ermengaudus* (Ingolstadt 1614; PL 204:793–840). Bernard had been present at a disputation between Waldenses and Catholics and afterward undertook to edit and summarize the various points presented by both sides. His work is therefore considered to be an important source on the origins of the sect and the basis of their doctrinal position.

Bibliography: J. B. BOSSUET, *The History of the Variations of the Protestant Churches*, 2 v. (New York 1836) bk. 9, ch. 75–79. GallChrist 6:267. HistLittFranc 15:35. C. DE VIC and J. VAISSETE,

Histoire générale de Languedoc, 16 v. in 17 (rev. ed. Toulouse 1872–1904) 6:218. L. E. DUPIN, *Histoire des controverses et des matières ecclésiastiques*, 9 v. (Paris 1694–98) 5:599. J. A. FABRICIUS, *Bibliotheca latina mediae et infimae aetatis*, 6 v. in 3 (Florence 1858–59) 1:213. L. VERREES, AnalPraem 31:5–35. A. BORST, LexThK² 2:243.

[J. DAOUST]

BERNARD GUI,

or Bernardus Guidonis, historian, inquisitor, bishop; b. Royère, Roche l'Abeille (Limousin), *c.* 1261; d. Lodève, Hérault, France, Dec. 30, 1331. Bernard became a *Dominican and was professed at Limoges on Sept. 16, 1280. A student of philosophy (1283), he lectured on logic at Brives (1284). He studied theology at Limoges (1285–88) and at Montpellier (1289–90). He was appointed sublector at Limoges (1291); lector at Albi (1292–93) and at Castres (1294); then prior at *Albi (1294–97), at Carcassone (1297–1301), and at Castres (1301–05); and then lector at Carcassone (1305). By August he was prior at Limoges (1305–07) and then inquisitor at *Toulouse from Jan. 16, 1307, to 1323 or 1324, at the same time serving as procurator general (1317–21) under the Master General Hervé de Nedellec. Bernard served on a peace embassy to Lombardy and Tuscany in 1317–18 and to Flanders in 1318. He was later made bishop of Túy in Galicia (Spain) on Aug. 26, 1323. On July 20, 1324, he was transferred to Lodève and died at the castle of Lauroux and was buried by his own wish in the Dominican church at Limoges.

As a historian and compiler Gui showed love for research, exceptional precision, and a sound and selective appreciation of the sources. The lack of any literary elegance in his writings is compensated by his preservation of numerous documents and much information, whose original sources have since been lost. His most important work is the *Flores chronicorum* (no crit. ed.), a universal chronicle. His numerous other works include *Reges Francorum* and *Priores Artigiae*, the *De quatuor in quibus Deus Praed. Ord. insignivit* [ed. T. Kaeppeli, MonOPraed 22 (1949)], the *De fundatione et prioribus conv. prov. Tolos. et Provinciae O.P.* [ed. P. A. Amargier, MonOPraed 24 (1961)], his hagiographical work called *Sanctorale*, and the *De actibus fidei* and *De peccato originali*. His writings on heresy and the *Inquisition include *Practica officii inquisitionis* [ed. C. Douais (Paris 1886)] and the *Liber sententiarum inquisitionis Tolosanae* [ed. P. a Limborch (Amsterdam 1692)].

See also INQUISITION.

Bibliography: Quétif-Échard 1:576–580. L. DELISLE, "Notice sur les manuscrits de Bernard Gui," *Notices et extraits des manuscrits de la B. N. et autres bibliothèques* 27.2 (1879) 169–455. HistLittFranc 35 139–232, list of works. G. MOLLAT, DHGE 8:677–681; DDC 2:779–781. J. BREQUET, "Aux origines du prieuré de l'Artige . . .," *Bulletin de la Société archéologique et historique du Limousin* 90 (1963) 85–100.

[S. L. FORTE]

BERNARD OF KRAIBURG,

bishop and humanist; b. Kraiburg on the Inn River, Austria, 1415; d. Lake Chiem, Bavaria, Oct. 17, 1477. Having been professor of Canon Law (1442) and chancellor (1450) at the University of Vienna, and then ambassador to Rome (1460), he became bishop of Lake Chiem (1467), and auxiliary and vicar-general of Salzburg. He was a friend of Aeneas Sylvius Piccolomini (*Pius II) and of *Nicholas of Cusa, whom he addressed at the Synod of Salzburg (1451) in a manner typically humanistic (HistJb 632–   ). Among his works, mostly in the form of letters and sermons, are the *Deploratio miseriarum sui saeculi* (on the fall of Constantinople, 1453) and two important letters on the Battle of Belgrade (1456). About 100 MSS from his library are extant in Vienna, Salzburg, and Munich.

Bibliography: P. Joachimsohn, *Programm des Realgymnasiums Nürnberg* (Nuremberg 1901). V. Redlich, *Tegernsee und die deutsche Geistesgeschichte im 15. Jh.* (Munich 1931). P. Ruf, "Eine altbayerische Gelehrtenbibliographie," *Festschrift für Eugen Stollreither* (Erlangen 1950) 219–239. A. Bigelmair, NDB 2:116; LexThK² 2:244. F. C. H. Babinger, *Der Quellenwert der Berichte über den Entsatz von Belgrad am 21./22. Juli 1456* (Munich 1957). R. Bauerreiss, *Kirchengeschichte Bayerns* (St. Ottilien 1949–55; 2d ed. 1958–   ) v.5.

[V. H. REDLICH]

BERNARD LOMBARDI, French Dominican theologian; fl. 1323 to 1333. He entered the order at Perpignan in southern France. In 1323, when he was prior of the house in Avignon and vicar provincial, he was elected seventh provincial of Provence. At the general chapter of the order in 1326, he was assigned to read the *Sentences* at Paris the following year, but he was not relieved of his administrative office. At the request of certain brethren, *John XXII absolved him from administrative duties during his academic term at Paris. He lectured on the *Sentences* in 1327–28, becoming master during the academic year 1331–32. He was regent for at least 1 year; one of his *quodlibets* is still extant. Avignon MS 320 contains a number of his sermons (*collationes*). His unpublished commentary on the *Sentences* gives full details of the three commentaries on the *Sentences* composed by *Durandus of Saint-Pourçain. In it he expresses clearly his own views on the Thomistic doctrines questioned by Durandus. This stand was prompted by the strong legislation of the general chapter of the order in 1329 regarding adherence to the teaching of St. *Thomas Aquinas.

See also THOMISM.

Bibliography: Quétif-Échard 1.2:560–561. Glorieux L 2:64–65. J. Koch, *Durandus de Sancto Porciano, O.P.*, BeitrGeschPhilMA 25 (1927) 314–340. Stegmüller RS 1:52, 103. E. Filthaut, Lex ThK² 2:245.

[P. GLORIEUX]

BERNARD OF MONTMIRAT, abbot and canonist; b. Montmirat (southern France), c. 1225; d. Monte Cassino, 1296. It is not known whether he was already a Benedictine monk when he studied in Bologna under *Peter of Sampson, whom he followed to Avignon. Subsequently he taught Canon Law at Béziers, and it is now known that he was a professor also at Toulouse. Appointed abbot of Montmajour in 1266 and rector of the March of Ancona in 1277–78, he continued as abbot until 1286, when Pope Honorius IV appointed him bishop of Tripoli in Syria. Unable to take possession of his see because of political circumstances, he was employed on various missions, notably on legations to England and Sweden (1291–92) in connection with the projected crusade of Nicholas IV. In 1295 he was appointed administrator of the abbey of Monte Cassino. His canonical works were very successful: his *Lectura* (1259–66; printed Strasbourg 1510, Venice 1588) on the Decretals of *Gregory IX and his commentary (unprinted) on the *Novellae* of Innocent IV are famous; parts of his *Distinctiones* have survived also. These

writings display a remarkable knowledge of classical Canon Law and are on a level with the works of other great doctors of the 13th century. Bernard was known at first as Abbas, and later called Abbas antiquus to distinguish him from the great abbot-canonist of the 15th century, Nicolaus de *Tudeschis (Abbas modernus).

Bibliography: Schulte 2:130–132. A. Villien, DDC 1:1–2. S. Kuttner, "Wer war der Dekretalist 'Abbas Antiquus'?" ZSav RGKan 26 (1937) 471–489. Van Hove 1:456. P. Ciprotti, Enc Catt 1:24–25.

[P. LEGENDRE]

BERNARD OF OFFIDA, BL., Capuchin lay brother famed for his sanctity and charity (real name Domenico Peroni; b. Lama, Italy, Nov. 7, 1604; d. Offida, Aug. 22, 1694; feast, Aug. 23). He was born of peasant folk and received little education. He entered the Capuchin Order at Corinaldo on Feb. 16, 1626, and made rapid progress in the spiritual life. When sent to Fermo, he served as cook and infirmarian. Transferred to Offida at the age of 65, he became porter and questor. A plague in that area gave him occasion to devote his energies to the sick and poor, and this became his apostolate for the rest of his life. He worked many miraculous cures and brought many into the Church. His reputation for holiness spread throughout that region. In the bull of his beatification on May 25, 1795, Pope Pius VI cited his charity to the poor and needy and his profound humility. His cause for canonization is no longer active.

Bibliography: *Lexicon Capuccinum* (Rome 1951) 212. A. Teetaert, DHGE 8:709. *Bullarium O.F.M. Cap.*, v.1–7 (Rome 1740–52), v.8–10 (Innsbruck 1883–84) 10:771. Pellegrino da Forli, *Annali del'Ordine dei FF. Minori Cappuccini*, 4 v. (Milan 1882–85) 3:505–516.

[B. SMITS]

BERNARD OLIVER, Catalan bishop, theologian, diplomat; b. Valencia, late 13th century; d. Tortosa, July 14, 1348. He was regarded as among the most learned men of his time. Bernard entered the Augustinians in Valencia before 1310, and studied theology at Paris. He returned to the University of Valencia in 1320 to lecture on *Peter Lombard's *Sentences* and there became prior of his convent. He became provincial in 1329 and in 1334 preached at the papal court. Appointed bishop of Osca on Oct. 1, 1337, he held a synod there, reformed the cathedral chapter of Jaca in 1340, and attended the council of Zaragosa in 1342. Translated to the See of Barcelona (Jan. 12, 1345), he held a synod in August concerning the life of ecclesiastics and promulgated two sets of cathedral statutes before becoming bishop of Tortosa (June 26, 1346). There he drew up two constitutions with his clergy. He was ambassador of Peter IV of Aragon (1341), persuading France and Majorca not to fight for Montpellier. In 1344 he accompanied the papal envoy, Bernard of Albi, to Barcelona in a vain attempt to make peace between Aragon and Majorca, and in 1347 he represented the Catalans before Peter IV. Before becoming bishop, he wrote an *Excitatorium mentis ad Deum* (ed. Madrid 1911), which was translated into Catalan and Castilian; a treatise against the Jews [ed. *Sefarad* 5 (1945) 311–336, 7 (1947) 49–62]; and other works in MSS.

Bibliography: S. Puig y Puig, *Episcopologio de la sede barcinonense* (Barcelona 1929). A. Lambert, DHGE 8:756–759.

[D. W. LOMAX]

BERNARD OF PARMA, ST.

BERNARD OF PARMA, ST., Vallombrosan, cardinal, bishop of Parma, Italy; b. Florence c. 1055; d. Cavanna Abbey, near Parma, Dec. 4, 1133 (feast, Dec. 4). According to tradition he was born of the noble Uberti family. He entered the newly founded *Vallombrosan Order at San Salvi (c. 1075), where he became abbot (c. 1093) and then abbot general of the order (1098). Because of his unceasing zeal for the order's welfare he is considered its second founder. Shortly after becoming abbot general he was called to Rome and created cardinal by Pope *Urban II. The *investiture struggle was then at its height: Bernard was sent to Lombardy by Pope *Paschal II with powers of legate and with the mission of liberating the Lombard cities from the dominion of Emperor *Henry IV; Bernard won the friendship of Countess *Matilda of Tuscany; he was at Canossa in 1102. Insulted and imprisoned by schismatics in Parma, he was liberated after 3 days through Matilda's intervention. Before 1106 he was elected bishop of Parma where he proved a zealous pastor. He founded several monasteries, including that of Cavanna. He assisted Matilda on her death bed. At the Council of Piacenza, held under Pope Innocent II, he met *Bernard of Clairvaux. He was frequently the subject of Renaissance painters, e.g., of *Correggio (the cupola of Parma's cathedral), of Perugino, and of Andrea *del Sarto, whose Episode from the Life of St. Bernard of Parma is shown below.

Bibliography: ActSS Dec. (Propylaeum) 566. MGS 30.2:1314–27, vita. F. BONNARD, DHGE 8:718–721. N. PELICELLI, *I vescovi della chiesa parmense,* v.1 (Parma 1936) 137–154. **Illustration credit:** Alinari-Art Reference Bureau.

[T. C. CROWLEY]

BERNARD OF PARMA, important canonist and glossator; b. Parma, c. 1200; d. Bologna, c. 1264. He studied under *Tancred at Bologna, where he later taught. While at Bologna he received an ecclesiastical benefice (*canonicatus*) and became a chaplain to the Pope. He wrote several works that are important in the history of decretal law. His *glossa* (c. 1245) on the Decretals of *Gregory IX became the standard commentary (*glossa ordinaria*) on that collection of decretals. Bernard's *glossa* was the result of his life's work. His glosses are noted for their clarity and juridic precision; their understanding of Roman law in addition to Canon Law; and their comprehension of the ideas of the earlier glossators (especially those of the *Quinque compilationes antiquae*). Bernard produced also a compilation of juridic cases (known as the *Casus longi*) contained in papal decretals; several MSS and editions of this work still exist. His *Summa super titulis decretalium* is a short study on the material contained in each chapter of the Decretals of Gregory IX; it follows closely the works of Tancred and Bernard of Pavia. The *Summa* was used extensively by later jurists.

Bibliography: P. OURLIAC, DDC 2:781–782. Van Hove 1:473 and *passim*. Kuttner. Schulte.

[J. M. BUCKLEY]

BERNARD OF SAISSET, first bishop of Pamiers, France; b. 1232; d. 1311. As abbot of the Canons Regular of Saint-Antonin in Pamiers, he disagreed with the Count of Foix regarding the rights of the monastery. *Boniface VIII supported Bernard, and asked *Philip IV the Fair to intervene; he created the Diocese of Pamiers, and, without Philip's consent, made Bernard its first bishop. Bernard, accused of sympathy for the cause of Aragon, of enmity to the King, and of heresy and simony as well, was arrested (July 12, 1301), placed at Senlis under the surveillance of the bishop of Senlis, and dispossessed of his patrimony. Boniface VIII responded by the bulls *Ausculta fili (March 5, 1301) and *Salvator mundi* (Dec. 4, 1301). In 1302, how-

Episode from the Life of St. Bernard of Parma, painting by Andrea del Sarto, 1528, in the Uffizi at Florence.

ever, Bernard participated, with royal permission, in the synod held at Rome. He returned to France in 1304 and was pardoned in 1308.

Bibliography: J. M. VIDAL, *Histoire des évêques de Pamiers,* v.1 *Bernard Saisset (1232–1311)* (Paris 1926). R. FAWTIER, *L'Europe occidentale de 1270 à 1380* (Paris 1940). Haller 5:162–164. Seppelt 4:26–29. H. TÜCHLE, LexThK² 2:248.

[É. BROUETTE]

BERNARD SILVESTRIS (OF TOURS),

philosopher and poet; fl. *c.* 1150. His main work, dedicated to *Thierry of Chartres, is his cosmography, the *De mundi universitate*. In bk. 1, the *Megacosmus*, Nature complains to Noys about the confusion of primary matter (hyle). Out of chaos, Noys divides the four elements, establishes the hierarchies of angels, sets the stars in the firmament, and arranges the constellations and planets. Earth with its created life is put in the center. In bk. 2 Noys glories in the beauty of the universe and decides to complete it with the creation of man, which is described in detail. The commentary on six books of the *Aeneid* is allegorical. It is chiefly a treatise on wisdom, the seven liberal arts, and moral philosophy, and had great influence on the early Italian humanists. The *Experimentarius* is a work of geomancy with discussions about the zodiac. Its extensive use of Arabic, rather than classical, sources gives rise to doubts about its authenticity. Bernard of Tours was a humanist who did not hesitate to identify Biblical Sapientia and Minerva or to use Horace and Ovid to describe creation. For this reason he has been called a cryptopagan. The contrary is true, however, for in his mind pagan literature and mythology were no longer a threat to the Christian faith.

Bibliography: C. S. BARACH and J. WROBEL, *De Mundi Universitate libri duo, sive megacosmus et microcosmus* (Innsbruck 1876). W. RIEDEL, *Commentum Bernardi Silvestris super sex libros Eneidos Virgilii* (Greifswald 1924). M. DE MARCO, "Un nuovo codice del commento di Bernardo Silvestre all' Eneide," *Aevum* 28 (1954) 178–183. M. BRINI SAVORELLI, "Un manuale di geomanzia presentato da Bernardo Silvestre de Tours: L'Experimentarius," *Revista critica di storia della filosofia* 14 (1959) 283–342. B. BERULFSEN, "Et Blad av en Summa dictaminis," *Avhandlungen utgitt av det Norsk Videnskaps—Akademi in Oslo II Historisk—filosofisk Klasse* 3 (1953). Two best works on Bernard of Tours are unpub. dissertations: A. VERNET, *Position de thèses de l'école nationale des Chartes* (Paris; Jan. 1937), to be pub. presently with new ed.; and M. McCRIMMON, *The Classical Philosophical Sources of Bernard Silvestris* (Doctoral diss. Yale 1952–53). T. SILVERSTEIN, "The Fabulous Cosmogony of Bernardus Silvestris," ModPhilol 46 (1948) 92–116, good bibliog. É. H. GILSON, "La Cosmogonie de Bernardus Silvestris," ArchHistDoctLitMA 3 (1928) 5–24. G. PADOAN, "Tradizione e fortuna del Commento all' Eneide di Bernardo Silvestre," *Italia Medioevale e Umanistica* 3 (1960) 227–240. J. R. O'DONNELL, "The Sources and Meaning of Bernard Silvester's Commentary on the Aeneid," MedSt 24 (1962) 233–249. P. CALENDINI, DHGE 7:746–748.

[J. R. O'DONNELL]

BERNARD OF TIRON, ST.,

Benedictine reformer; b. Abbeville (Somme), France, *c.* 1046; d. April 14 or 25, 1117 (feast, April 14). He studied grammar and dialectics until he was 20 years old and then entered the Benedictine Abbey of Saint-Cyprien in Poitiers, soon transferring to *Saint-Savin-sur-Gartempe, where he was prior for 20 years. When Abbot Gervais died, Bernard fled the abbey to avoid succeeding as abbot and became a hermit. However, a

little later (1100) he was made abbot of Saint-Cyprien; but when he, like *Robert of Arbrissel, fell into disagreement with *Cluny's claims on the abbey, he again retired to the forest. Forced to return as abbot, he undertook a trip to Rome. Upon his return he reformed the lax discipline of his own abbey with the full approval of the Pope, and with the help of *Ivo of Chartres and of King *Louis VI he founded (1114) the Abbey of *Tiron (Eure-et-Loir), France, which enjoyed great prosperity (500 monks). From France and elsewhere came requests for these religious living the strict *Benedictine Rule. The new congregation soon numbered 10 abbeys and 40 priories in France alone. Bernard's life was written by his disciple, Geoffrey the Fat, between 1131 and 1148.

Bibliography: ActSS April 2:220–254. PL 172:1363–1446. C. CLAIREAUX, *Saint Bernard de Thiron* (Bellême, Fr. 1913). P. CALENDINI, DHGE 8:754–755. Zimmermann KalBen 2:54–57. J. B. MAHN, *L'Ordre Cistercien et son gouvernement, des origines au milieu du XIIIᵉ siècle (1098–1265)* (new ed. Paris 1951) 29–34. R. AIGRAIN, *Catholicisme* 1:1482–83.

[É. BROUETTE]

BERNARD TOLOMEI, BL,

founder of the Olivetan Benedictines; b. Siena, May 10, 1272; d. Siena, Aug. 20, 1348 (feast, Aug. 21). As a youth, Bernard wanted to become a religious but could not obtain his father's consent. He served in the armies of King Rudolph I, studied law, and became *podestà* (magistrate) of Siena. In 1313, with two companions, he withdrew into solitude at Accona, and in 1319 Bishop Guido of Arezzo gave the little community a white habit and the Benedictine Rule. At Accona, Bernard founded the monastery of Our Lady of Monte Oliveto, from which developed the strongly centralized Olivetan Benedictine Congregation (*see* BENEDICTINES, OLIVETAN). The primitive penitential observance exercised a strong appeal and for a while the institute grew rapidly. Bernard died caring for victims of the *Black Death.

Bibliography: P. LUGANO, "La causa . . . B. Bernardo . . . ," *Rivista Storica Benedettina* 17 (1926) 204–289. B. HEURTEBIZE, DHGE 8:728–730. P. SCHMITZ, *Histoire de l'ordre de Saint-Benoît,* 7 v. (Maredsous 1942–56) 3:22–23. C. TESTORE, EncCatt 6:611. Butler Th Attw 3:379–380.

[A. G. BIGGS]

BERNARD OF TRILLE,

of Trilia, or de la Treille, Dominican Thomistic philosopher and theologian; b. Nîmes, southern France, *c.* 1240; d. Avignon, Aug. 4, 1292. After lecturing in various Dominican houses in Provence between 1266 and 1276, he was sent to the University of Paris in 1279 to lecture on the *Sentences*. He taught as master in Paris (1284–87). His unfinished *quodlibets,* as well as the greater part of his writings, date from the period of his mastership. Active in the internal affairs of the order, he was elected provincial of Provence in 1291, but was removed in 1292 because of his defense of the Master General, F. Munio, who had been deposed by *Nicholas IV. He then retired to Avignon. Highly esteemed as a teacher and writer, he applied strictly Thomistic doctrines to problems of his day. Among his works are a commentary on the *Sentences, Quaestiones 18 de cognitione animae coniunctae, Quaestiones de differentia esse et essentiae, Quaestiones de spiritualibus creaturis et de potentia Dei,* three *Quodlibets,* postils on several books of the Bible, two sermons, and questions on the *De sphera* of

*John de Sacrobosco. Only a few of his works are printed and many are incomplete or lost.

Bibliography: M. GRABMANN, "Bernhard von Trilia, O.P.," DivThomF 13 (1935) 385–399; Glorieux R 1:155–157; DTC 15.1:1543–44. Quétif-Échard 1.1:432–434. Stegmüller RB 2: 1739–45. E. FILTHAUT, LexThK² 2:249. F. J. ROENSCH, *Early Thomistic School* (Dubuque 1964).

[J. F. HINNEBUSCH]

BERNARD, CLAUDE

Outstanding physiologist; b. Saint-Julien, near Villefranche, July 12, 1813; d. Paris, Feb. 10, 1878. He studied in the local Jesuit school and briefly at the college of Lyons but left there to become an apothecary's apprentice. He began a literary career with some local

Claude Bernard.

success as the author of a short comedy, but in 1854 when he took a five-act play to the critic Saint-Marc Girardin, he was advised to study medicine for a more substantial living.

His internship at Hôtel-Dieu in Paris brought him under F. Magendie, the great experimental physiologist, who was physician to the hospital. Magendie left his imprint on the young physician's outlook and methodology. Bernard impressed the master with his dexterity of hand and mind; he became Magendie's deputy at the hospital (1849) and eventually, his successor (1855). When a chair of physiology was established at the Sorbonne in 1854, Bernard was summoned to fill it. After a meeting with Louis Napoléon (1864) a physiology laboratory was provided for him at the Sorbonne. The Emperor built another laboratory at the Natural History Museum of the Jardin des Plantes, and Bernard went there in 1868. In the same year he was elected to the French Academy. The following year he became a senator of the empire. His funeral, from Notre Dame cathedral, was arranged and financed by the government —the first time a French scientist was so honored.

Immediately upon completing his doctoral dissertation on gastric juices in 1843, he began a 7-year period of great productivity. He determined that not only bile but glycogen is formed by the liver; he established the nature of diabetes by his experiments with the pancreas; his investigations of animal heat disclosed the vasomotor system, which dilates and constricts vessel walls to effect thermal variations; and he introduced the study of poisons into physiology, noting especially the effects of carbon monoxide and curare on living systems. His researches led to a more generalized approach to physiology by showing that a community of principles is involved in both animals and plants and in both large and microscopic organisms; he probed the chemical and

physical processes of living organs and their cells. This led to his celebrated concept, "internal environment." It in turn pointed to the intriguing principle, homeostasis: that there is a dynamic scheme of adjustments inherent in organisms, with every deviation from the norm producing an opposite and rectifying reaction. This experimental and speculative activity placed him in the then-current dialectics of vitalism and mechanism. He rejected both and usually labeled his position as determinism. Actually, according to his private notes, his published writings, and his teachings, he wandered into and out of the peripheries of both schools of thought, but he was most understandable and at ease in his direct questioning of nature via experiment. He called himself a secretary of nature and declared that he could "observe without preconceived ideas." Bernard is Aristotelian when he recognizes entelechy: "the physiologist is led to admit a pre-established and harmonic finality in the organism, for its partial activities are interdependent, one activity engendering another"; and again, "It is no chance encounter . . . which constructs each being according to a pre-existing plan . . . and produces . . . the harmonious concert of organic activities." Although his thought was basically Cartesian, it was tempered by Aristotle and a restraining skepticism. His philosophical credo is contained in his foremost work, *An Introduction to the Study of Experimental Medicine* (1865), a classic in self-analysis; the substance of his experiments is in his collected lectures.

Bibliography: C. BERNARD, *An Introduction to the Study of Experimental Medicine*, tr. H. C. GREENE (New York 1949). R. VIRTANEN, *Claude Bernard and His Place in the History of Ideas* (Lincoln, Nebr. 1960). **Illustration credit:** Library of Congress.

[L. P. COONEN]

BERNARD, ÉMILE

BERNARD, ÉMILE, Postimpressionist artist and critic; b. Lille, 1868; d. Paris, 1941. He studied in Cormon's studio, Paris, where he was a precocious painter, absorbing much of past art as well as philosophy and aesthetic theory by the time he was 16. There he began the significant friendships that were eventually immortalized by his publication of letters from Van *Gogh, *Redon, *Cézanne, and *Gauguin; he also wrote enthusiastic articles about these artists. His own painting was initially academic, then became pointillist (1884–86) until the age of 18, when he moved to Pont-Aven to work closely with Gauguin. He produced paintings, woodcuts, sculpture, and some furniture. With Louis Anquetin he evolved his theory of cloissonism, based on the simplification of nature into decorative pattern and pure color, reminiscent of stained glass. Through this theory Bernard claimed to have been the father of Symbolism in a bitter controversy in 1891 with friends of Gauguin. His artistic philosophy is considered close to Gauguin's but not its direct source. In 1887 Bernard met and exchanged paintings with Van Gogh, and in 1890 and 1891 he published articles on this artist and Cézanne. In 1894 he traveled to Italy and then to Egypt, where he lived for 10 years. After his return to Paris, his painting style became more and more derivative, losing the simplified, religious quality of his Pont-Aven work. However, he secured his reputation by subsequent articles and lectures and by his work as cofounder and editor of the review *La Rénovation Esthétique.*

Bibliography: V. VAN GOGH, *Letters to Émile Bernard*, tr. D. LORD (New York 1938). *Dictionary of Modern Painting*, ed.

C. LAKE and R. MAILLARD, tr. A. BIRD (New York 1955). Reward Post-Impr.

[S. L. HENRY]

BERNARDES, MANOEL, Oratorian writer and scholar; b. Lisbon, Aug. 20, 1644; d. there, Aug. 17, 1710. After studying Canon Law and philosophy at the University of Coimbra, he entered the Oratorians at Lisbon and dedicated himself to a life of study and preaching. He is remembered principally for his numerous writings, which rank among the classics of Portuguese literature, and as a foremost representative of Oratorian mysticism. Written with a simplicity of language, an elegance of style, and a vivid imagination, his spiritual treatises reveal a breadth of knowledge and deep religious inspiration. Among his works are: *Exercicios espirituaes e meditaçôes* (2 v. Lisbon 1686); *Luz e calor* (Lisbon 1696); *Nova floresta* (5 v. 1706–28); and *Os últimos fins do homem* (Lisbon 1728).

Bibliography: A. F. DO CASTILLO, *Manoel Bernardes* (Rio de Janeiro 1865). L. A. REBELO DA SILVA, "O Padre Manoel Bernardes," *Bosquejos historico-literaros* 2 (1909) 93–139. J. S. RUGGIERI, EncCatt 2:1403–04. P. AUVRAY, DictSpirAscMyst 1:1514.

[J. C. WILLKE]

BERNARDINE OF ASTI, Capuchin vicar-general whose influence formed and stabilized the Capuchin reform; b. Asti, Italy, 1484; d. Rome, May 12, 1554. Bernardine, son of wealthy Count Boniface Palli, studied in Rome and joined the Franciscan Observants in 1499. Several times provincial of the Roman province of the Observants, he actively promoted the reform movement within that order. Because of opposition to the movement, he joined the Capuchins in 1534. The next year he was elected vicar-general for 3 years. At the chapter he directed the revision of the Constitutions, giving the order a more stable form of government. He represented the Capuchin Order at the Council of Trent in 1546. While there he was reelected vicar-general, and in 1549 he was reconfirmed in office. A man of poverty, deep personal prayer, and brotherly love, he guided the reform through its first crises, saved it from extinction, and gave it its authentically Franciscan spirit and form of life.

Bibliography: *Lexicon Capuccinum* (Rome 1951) 200–201. C. REPOLE, "Bernardine of Asti," *Round Table of Franciscan Research* 9 (1943–44) 63–75; repr. ed. (1949) 22–32. FATHER CUTHBERT, *The Capuchins,* 2 v. (London 1928) v.1. MELCHIOR A POBLADURA, *Historia generalis Ordinis Fratrum Minorum Capuccinorum,* 3 v. in 4 (Rome 1947–51) 1:44–48.

[N. CROSBY]

BERNARDINE OF FELTRE, BL., Franciscan preacher; b. Feltre, in Venezia, Italy, 1439; d. Pavia, Sept. 28, 1494 (feast, Sept. 28). He was born Martin Tomitano. After proving himself an excellent student in his early years, he was sent to the University of *Padua. Impressed by the preaching of *James of the Marches, he joined the Franciscan Observants in May 1456, taking his religious name after *Bernardine of Siena who had just been canonized. Ordained in 1463, he began his public preaching some 6 years later. He soon became immensely popular, and crowds flocked to hear his sermons (*Sermoni del beato Bernardino da Feltre,* ed. Carlo da Milano, Milan 1940) as he journeyed through the towns of northern Italy. Like his contemporary *Savonarola he denounced the numerous abuses of the day and often ended his preaching with the burning of various vanities on a bonfire. Bernardine has become almost equally well known through his connection with Barnabas of Terni (d. 1472) and the establishment of the *montes pietatis, a scheme whereby the poor could borrow money at low interest rates on the pledge of various goods, thus avoiding the clutches of usurious bankers, who were the contemporary scandal of Italy. Although he met much opposition from the bankers, as well as from those who objected to his charging even a reasonable rate of interest (*see* USURY) to make the operation self-supporting, Bernardine helped to establish some 30 montes pietatis during the last years of his apostolate. He was buried at S. Maria del Carmine in Pavia, and his cult was recognized in 1654. He is honored by the *Franciscans and is the patron of pawnbrokers.

Bibliography: L. DE BESSE, *Le Bx. Bernardin de Feltre et son oeuvre,* 2 v. (Tours 1902). H. HOLZAPFEL, *Die Anfänge der Montes Pietatis, 1462–1515* (Munich 1903). A. VAN DEN WYNGAERT, DHGE 8:790–791. A. PELLIN, *Beato Bernardino da Feltre* (Lecco 1938). F. CASOLINI, *Bernardino da Feltre: Il martello degli usurai* (Milan 1939). E. LAZZARESCHI, *Il beato Bernardino da Feltre gli Ebrei ed il Monte di Pietà in Lucca* (Lucca 1941). É. LONGPRE, *Catholicisme* 1:1486.

[B. J. COMASKEY]

BERNARDINE OF SIENA, ST.

Franciscan preacher and propagator of devotion to the Holy Name; b. Massa Marittima, in the territory of Siena, Sept. 8, 1380; d. Aquila, May 20, 1444 (feast, May 20).

Life. When Bernardine was 3 years of age his mother (Nera degli Avveduti) died, and 3 years later the death of his father (Tollo degli Albizzeschi) left him a complete orphan. He was confided to the care of a maternal aunt, but at the age of 11 he was taken by paternal relatives to Siena, where he attended school and studied the humanities and philosophy (1391–97), and for another 3 years he studied Canon Law at the university in that city. Bernardine was devoted to the Latin classics, but he gave himself with no less enthusiasm to the study of Scripture and theology and to practices of piety. During the pestilence of the jubilee year 1400 he spent 4 months ministering to the plague-stricken in the hospital of Santa Maria della Scala until he himself became ill. He entered the Friars Minor when he was 22, was professed in 1403, and was ordained the following year. In 1405 he was commissioned to preach, and he continued in that work until his death.

Little is known of the first 15 years of his religious life. No doubt he spent them gathering his abundant knowledge of scholastic writings. During this period he transcribed or caused to be transcribed various books, two of which, entirely in his own hand, were discovered in 1962–63 (Codex 102 in the library of the University of Budapest and Codex VI. A. 19 of the National Library of Naples). He also began to attract attention as a preacher. For 3 years (1414–17) he held the office of vicar provincial of the Observants of Tuscany, at the completion of which he gave himself completely to the evangelization of Lombardy. The years 1417–29 were the most important period of his preaching. During this time he was engaged without remission in preaching throughout central and northern Italy. In the last 15 years of his life Bernardine continued his apostolic journeys, but these became more

Placard painted with the monogram of the Holy Name of Jesus used by St. Bernardine of Siena when preaching.

slowly paced because of the infirmities of age and his administrative responsibilities (he was vicar general of the Observants of Italy from 1438 to 1442) and because of his repeated and increasingly prolonged stays in the Sienese convent of Capriola, his ordinary place of residence, for the purpose of writing down and revising his treatises and sermons. In 1444, after completing his Lenten preaching in his native city of Massa, and in spite of his age and infirmity, Bernardine set out to evangelize the Kingdom of Naples. Some miles from Aquila in the Abruzzi he was stricken with a fever and could not go on. He was taken to Aquila and received in the convent of St. Francis, where he died peacefully on the vigil of the Feast of the Ascension. The city gave him the honor of a funeral of unprecedented splendor, and he was buried in the church of St. Francis. There were many miracles after his death, and he was canonized by Nicholas V, May 24, 1450. His body was transferred May 17, 1471, to the nearby basilica erected in his honor and put in a magnificent shrine, where it is still preserved in an incorrupt state.

Preaching. The apostolate of Bernardine was singularly fruitful. He was the greatest preacher of his time. Cities everywhere invited him to come and preach, and when he did appear, churches were too small to contain the throngs that gathered to hear him, so that he was obliged to preach in the open. It is said that his audience sometimes numbered as many as 30,000. The reason for his success was, above all else, his holiness of life. St. Francis was his model of virtue, and he was like the holy patriarch also in his zealous concern to maintain a high standard of religious observance in the Franciscan community and to labor tirelessly for the moral reformation of the people. He was Franciscan—persuasive, fervent, joyous, and sometimes even merry. Other factors contributing to his success were: his acute intelligence, coupled with an intuitive understanding of the needs of his time and the mental and spiritual condition of his hearers; his superb gift of eloquence; the clarity and vivacity of his language; his use of a kind of dialogue form in the development of his argument; and his practicality in confining himself to themes of general interest. He disapproved of the practice, common at the time among preachers, of inveighing against the vices of ecclesiastics, for he considered it better to inspire the people with reverence for the priestly state, and it was his wont to speak to the clergy separately at the conclusion of his "missions." He was temperate when touching upon political matters and strove to rise above factionalism and differences of government.

Devotion to the Holy Name. St. Bernardine is especially remembered for his zeal in promoting devotion to the Holy Name. This devotion was not a new thing in the Church, but he contributed greatly to its spread, and he devised a symbol to help people appreciate its profound theological basis. This was the trigrammatic abbreviation "yhs," in minuscule Gothic letters, of the name of Jesus. The trigram was set in the midst of a blazing sun, to whose spreading rays he attributed a mystical significance. He desired that this emblem should displace superstitious symbols and the insignia of factions. Through the apostolate of Bernardine and his disciples the cult of the Holy Name spread rapidly, and its symbol began to appear in churches, homes, and public buildings. Certain humanists and theologians of the time viewed this with distrust and considered the devotion a dangerous innovation. Three attempts were made to induce ecclesiastical authority to take action against Bernardine (in 1426 under Martin V, and in 1431 under Eugene IV, and in 1438 an appeal was made to the Council of Basel). St. Bernardine's vindication was such that no shadow of suspicion remained upon his orthodoxy, the rightness of his intentions, or the holiness of his life. Perhaps by way of amends and reward he was offered, successively, the bishoprics of Siena (to which he was elected), Ferrara, and Urbino, but he declined these honors.

Writings. Bernardine's literary work is almost entirely homiletic. A distinction should be made between the sermons, etc., edited by himself for the use of preachers, and true theological treatises, compiled with acumen and discernment from the writings of the great scholastic doctors, from the *Expositio super Apocalypsim* of Matthias of Sweden (of Linköping), from the *Arbor vitae crucifixae* of *Ubertino of Casale, and from the writings of *Peter John Olivi. Of notable importance are the sermons and treatises on the name of Jesus, the Passion, and St. Joseph. Of special value, also, are the 11 sermons on the Madonna, which, taken together, constitute a complete Mariology. For their novelty and originality of method the sermons met with great success, which explains the considerable number of codices (about 300), all transcribed within the span of about 40 years, until they were all printed in various incunabula editions (1470–1501) or reprinted in sequence in *S. Bernardini Sen. Ord. Min. opera quae ex-*

tant omnia (4 v. Venice 1591; Paris 1635; Lyons 1650; Venice 1745). These editions, however, contain certain works now known to be spurious. The Franciscan Fathers of Quaracchi have been preparing a critical edition of St. Bernardine's works, eight volumes of which had been published by 1964: *S. Bernardini Sen. O.F.M., Opera omnia, studio et cura PP. Collegii S. Bonaventurae ad fidem codicum edita* (Quaracchi-Florence 1950–1963).

Bernardine's sermons taken down by others do not have the same authority as those the saint edited himself, because it is improbable that his words were always put down in shorthand with absolute fidelity. Nevertheless, they are of considerable interest, especially those preached in Siena in 1427 (whose word-for-word accuracy is better authenticated), because of the biographical and historical data they provide and because of the light they throw upon the real personality of Bernardine and upon his abilities as a popular preacher.

Bibliography: Modern biographies. P. THUREAU-DANGIN, *Un Prédicateur populaire dans l'Italie de la Renaissance: S. Bernardin de Sienne* (Paris 1896). A. G. F. HOWEL, *St. Bernardino of Siena* (London 1913). V. FACCHINETTI, *San Bernardino da Siena, mistico sole del secolo XV* (Milan 1933). Studies. V. FACCHINETTI, "Bollettino bibliografico: San Bernardino da Siena," *Aevum* 4 (1930) 319–381. H. SCHMIDT, "Bernhardin-Literatur, 1939–1949," FranzStud 32 (1950) 308–418. A. GHINATO, *Saggio di bibliografia bernardiniana* (Rome 1960). Catholic University of San Cuore, *San Bernardino da Siena Saggi e ricerche pubblicati nel V centenario della morte, 1444–1944* (Milan 1945). "St. Bernardine of Siena," special No. of FrancStudies 4 (1944) 309–405. "S. B. da S. nel V centenario della morte," special No. of *Studi Francescani* 42 (1945). D. PACETTI, EncCatt 2:1411–16; *L'Expositio super Apocalypsim di Mattia di Svezia, 1281–1350: Precipua fonte dottrinale di S. Bernardino da Siena,* ArchFranc Hist 54 (1961) 274–302; "Le postille autografe sopra l'Apocalisse di S. B. da S. recentemente scoperte nella Biblioteca Nazionale di Napoli," *ibid.* 56 (1963) 40–70; "Le fonti dottrinali di S. B. a servizio del suo fecondo apostolato," *Studi Francescani* 60 (1963) 3–19. M. BERTAGNA, "Vita e apostolato senese di S. B.," *ibid.* 20–99. **Illustration credit:** Fig. 2, Alinari-Art Reference Bureau.

[D. PACETTI]

BERNARDINO OF LAREDO

Physician, Franciscan laybrother, ascetical and mystical writer whose works influenced St. Teresa; b. Laredo, Spain, 1482; d. 1540, near Seville. Bernardino came from a distinguished family, probably originating at the small fishing port of Laredo on the Cantabrian coast. As a boy he was placed as a page in the household of a Portuguese nobleman, the Conde de Gelves. Before he was 12 he had a desire to join the Franciscan order and thought of applying to the Capuchin province of Los Ángeles in southern Spain. However, he was dissuaded from giving effect to this desire by the majordomo of the Gelves household. Continuing to cherish his longing for perfection, Bernardino then devoted himself to study, following an arts course and afterwards reading medicine, possibly at the University of Seville. He graduated and later obtained a doctor's degree. When Bernardino found that one of his friends, a doctor in law, had become a Franciscan laybrother, he determined to follow his example. He asked for the laybrother's habit at the Convento de San Francisco del Monte, a house of Franciscans of Regular Observance near Seville. There he lived a life of great austerity, fasting on bread and water on Mondays, Wednesdays, and Fridays, and on other days of the week eating the friars' leavings. He was eventually made infirmarian, and his medical knowledge was much sought after. Among the many patients he treated successfully was John II, King of Portugal, who, when the illness from which he was suffering took a dangerous turn, sent for the Franciscan laybrother.

Laredo found time and opportunity for writing, however. Besides two medical treatises, he wrote a work on asceticism and contemplation, the *Subida del Monte Sion.* Contemplation, Laredo says, can be achieved only through the Cross. Contemplative prayer is for all who are prepared to pay the price, for layfolk and married people as well as for friars and priests. He attaches considerable importance to fasts and vigils; it would seem that his own health was robust. At the same time he stresses the need for discretion. In a second edition of his book, Laredo's teaching on contemplation shows modification. He there emphasizes that contemplation is the work of the will rather than of the mind and puts forward the theory of love without knowledge, later taken up in Spain by John of the Angels and Jerónimo Gracián.

Bibliography: Works. BERNARDINO DE LAREDO, *Metaphora medicinae* (Seville 1522 and 1546); *Modus faciendi cum ordine medicandi* (Seville 1527, 1534, 1542, 1627); *Subida del Monte Sion* (Seville 1535). Studies. BERNARDINO DE LAREDO, *The Ascent of Mount Sion,* tr. and ed. E. A. PEERS (New York 1952) book 3 only of the treatise. FIDÈLE DE ROS, *Le Frère Bernardin de Laredo: Un inspirateur de sainte Thérèse* (Paris 1948). Espasa 29:824.

[K. E. POND]

St. Bernardine of Siena, detail of a tempera on panel by the Sienese artist Pietro di Giovanni.

BERNAY, ABBEY OF, Benedictine monastery in Lower Normandy, France, formerly in the Diocese of *Lisieux (today *Évreux). It was founded by Judith, wife of Duke Richard II of Normandy (1010–15), with the counsel of Abbot William of Dijon, who sent the first monks from *Fécamp. On Judith's death (1017) her husband confirmed the donations in a charter signed also by their three sons and by bishops and lords of Normandy (1025). Thierry and Ralph were guardian priors who administered the abbey after 1028. The first abbot, Vital of Fécamp, was promoted to abbot of *Westminster (1075). Begon of Murat was rector of the Cluniac college of St. Martial in Avignon, procurator general, vicar of Abbot John of Cluny, and visitor for the reform of Cluniac monasteries (1384–95). François Bohier, dean of Tours and provost of Normandy, was the delegate of the Regent Louise of Savoy to the comitia of Normandy (1525–26) and became bishop of Saint-Malo (1535–69). Drogon Hennequin de Villenoce, canon of Paris and commendatory abbot (1598–1651), rebuilt church and buildings and introduced the *Maurist reform (1628). Léon Potier de Gesvres (d. 1744) was abbot of Bernay (1666) and *Aurillac (1679), archbishop of *Bourges (1693), cardinal (1719), and abbot of *Saint-Amand-lès-Eaux (1720) and *Saint-Remi (1729). Bernay was pillaged by both sides in the Hundred Years' War. In the Wars of Religion, Calvinists took it, killed the priests, burned the charter room and treasury, and left it in ruins (1562–63). Rebuilt, it was burned by the *League (1590–96).

The abbey church (220 feet by 64 feet by 54 feet) was built in three stages (1020–55), determined by the style of the capitals. The nave had seven bays with aisles and a prominent transept topped by a massive tower; the transept had cross aisles terminated by apsidal chapels. In the 16th century the oven-shaped apse was replaced by a five-sided chevet; and its apsidal chapels, by straight walls pierced by windows with flamboyant tracery. The Maurists replaced two bays with a monumental façade and redid the vaulting. Chevet and tower were destroyed in the French Revolution; the church, an interesting Romanesque monument of Normandy, noteworthy for capitals influenced by those of the Burgundian Saint-Benigné in Dijon, continues to be secularized.

Bibliography: GallChrist 11:830–834. J. BILSON, "La Date et la construction de l'église abbatiale de Bernay," *Bulletin Monumental* 75 (1909) 403–422. A. A. PORÉE, "L'Église abbatiale de Bernay," *Congrès archéologique de France* 75 (1910) 588–614. G. BONNENFANT, *Histoire générale du diocèse d'Evreux,* 2 v. (Paris 1933), *passim.* L. GRODECKI, "Les Débuts de la sculpture romane en Normandie: Bernay," *Bulletin Monumental* 108 (1950) 7–67. P. CALENDINI, DHGE 8:812–815.

[P. COUSIN]

BERNETTI, TOMMASO, cardinal, papal secretary of state; b. Fermo, Italy, Dec. 29, 1779; d. there, March 21, 1852. After studying philosophy and law at the University of Fermo, he went to Rome (1800) and soon became secretary to the Rota. He accompanied the papal court to France (1808), and joined Cardinal Brancadoro, his uncle, in Reims, where Napoleon I exiled him (1810). There he acted as intermediary between the captive Pius VII, the cardinals, and the Belgian Catholics. Following Bernetti's return to Rome (1814), Pius VII sent him to persuade Austria to evacuate the *Legations (1815). After serving as papal legate to Ferrara, governor and head of the police of Rome (1820–26), and papal representative at the coronation of Czar Nicholas I in Moscow (1826), he became a cardinal (1827), but was not ordained priest until 1832. He succeeded *Della Somaglia as secretary of state from June 17, 1828, until the death of *Leo XII on Feb. 10, 1829, after which Cardinal Giuseppe *Albani assumed the office under Pius VIII (1829–30), who sent Bernetti as legate to Bologna. *Gregory XVI appointed Bernetti as prosecretary of state (Feb. 10, 1831) and secretary from Aug. 10, 1831, to Jan. 20, 1836. Revolution in the *States of the Church (1831), followed by intervention of the great powers who submitted a memorandum (May 21, 1831) demanding civil reforms, taxed Bernetti's abilities. He upheld papal independence, sternly repressed continuing disorders, organized a voluntary local militia, obtained Austrian military aid, and thereby preserved the state. When the French occupied Ancona (1832), Bernetti procured their evacuation by his diplomatic skill and patience. His unwillingness to become dependent on Austria, while seeking its military help, led Metternich to have *Lambruschini named secretary of state. Pius IX named Bernetti, together with Cardinal Gizzi and Lambruschini, a member of a consultative commission to help govern the States of the Church (1846). During the Roman uprising in 1848 Bernetti suffered a brief arrest, then joined the Pope at Gaeta. Ill health caused his retirement to Fermo (1850). He was an active, cultured, and good man, although the revolutionaries considered him intransigent and reactionary.

Bibliography: L. JADIN, DHGE 8:828–830. A. M. GHISALBERTI, EncCatt 2:1443–44. E. MORELLI, *La politica estera di Tommaso Bernetti* (Rome 1953). L. PÁSZTOR, "I Cardinali Albani e Bernetti e l'intervento austraico nel 1831," RivStorChIt 8 (1954) 95–128.

[A. RANDALL]

BERNGER, BL., abbot; d. Oct. 29, 1108 (feast, Oct. 29). He was the first abbot of the *Benedictine monastery of Formbach near Passau in Bavaria, having been brought there in 1094 by Bp. Ulric of Passau (d. 1121) from the reforming monastery of Schwarzach am Main. He was succeeded as abbot by his friend *Wirnt in 1108. He was known for his personal sanctity, his capable rule, and his generosity to widows, orphans, and the poor. At his order, the first collection of the customs of Formbach was begun.

Bibliography: *Vita Wirntonis,* ch. 1, MGS 15.2:1127–28; PL 194:1427–28. Zimmermann KalBen 3:231, 233. K. HALLINGER, *Gorze-Kluny,* 2 v. (StAnselm fasc. Rome 1950–51) v.1. J. OSWALD, LexThK² 2:237.

[J. C. MOORE]

BERNIER, ÉTIENNE ALEXANDRE

Bishop of Orléans, prominent in politicoecclesiastical affairs; b. Daon (Mayenne), France, Oct. 31, 1762; d. Paris, Oct. 1, 1806. After ordination (1786) he became a doctor of theology (1787), professor at the University of Angers, and pastor of St. Laud's parish in that city. During the French Revolution he refused to take the oath (1790) in support of the *Civil Constitution of the Clergy. For this he was replaced by the constitutional pastor Yves Besnard, but Bernier's opposition made the intruder's position unbearable. After the taking of Saumur, Bernier joined the army in the Vendée. By his ability, valor, and intrigues, he became one of the leaders of the insurrection, although lacking official title. He sided with Stofflet against Charette, and negotiated the peace of Saint-Florent with the generals of the Republic. After the deaths of Stofflet and Charette, Louis XVIII named him *agent général* of the Catholic and royal armies. But Bernier, realizing that the Vendée was incapable of continuing the battle, remained aloof from the final uprising in 1799.

Unable to deal with the Directory, he bided his time in order to begin a new career as a negotiator. The Coup d'État of Brumaire (Nov. 9, 1799) supplied a favorable opportunity, which he hastened to seize by offering his services to *Napoleon. He duped the last Vendean leaders, and concluded (Jan. 19, 1800) with General Hédouville the Peace of Montfaucon, which granted religious liberty to the Vendeans. Crowned with this success, he went to Paris, where Bonaparte frequently received him and listened to his counsels. The First Consul also chose him to negotiate a concordat with *Spina, the papal representative, promising to reward him with the see of Paris and a cardinal's hat. Bernier, a very capable but somewhat unscrupulous diplomat, revealed his skill by defending to the best of his ability the interests of the Holy See. Once the *Concordat of 1801 was concluded, Bernier helped put it into effect, and also acted as an intermediary between *Portalis and the papal legate *Caprara. His double role resulted in his composing both the notes of the French government and Cardinal Caprara's replies to them, in order to make more certain their agreement. This, plus his doubtful attitude at the time of the pretended retractation of the constitutional bishops promoted to new sees under the Concordat, led to his disgrace. Instead of obtaining the archdiocese of Paris, he had to content himself with the bishopric of Orléans (1802). If Pius VII named him cardinal, it was merely *in petto*.

*Talleyrand had further recourse to his tact, having him negotiate the Italian and German Concordats and the imperial coronation of Napoleon. Bernier was the one who drafted the famous note that decided the Pope to come to Paris for the imperial consecration. He also regulated the entire ceremonial of this event in conjunction with Pius VII, who agreed to let Napoleon crown himself. In vain did he try to reestablish his personal position by having himself appointed nuncio to Germany. Confined to his diocese, Bernier proved a remarkably good administrator and an exemplary bishop. Ambitious, crafty, but exceptionally intelligent, he performed great services in his own fashion without succeeding in raising himself to the highest level, or in dissipating the very mixed impression created by his enigmatic character and his over-clever manner.

Bibliography: J. LEFLON, *Étienne-Alexandre Bernier, évêque d'Orléans*, 2 v. (Paris 1938); *Étienne Bernier: Lettres, notes diplomatiques, mémoires, rapports inédits* (Reims 1938).

[J. LEFLON]

BERNIÈRES-LOUVIGNY, JEAN DE, mystic;

b. Caen, France, 1602; d. Caen, May 3, 1659. Son of Baron Pierre de Louvigny and Marguerite de Lion-Roger, Bernières-Louvigny came of one of the most distinguished houses of Normandy. Little is known of his early life or education. He did not become a priest or religious but lived devoutly as a layman. He had part in the establishment of a center of the celebrated *Compagnie du Saint-Sacrement, through which he engaged in many charitable works. He assisted, financially and otherwise, in the foundation of many religious houses, hospitals, and seminaries. One of his charitable works was the erection of the Ursuline convent at Caen, where his sister, Jourdaine, was foundress and superior. He placed himself under the direction of a well-known Franciscan, Père Jean-Chrysostome, and following his advice built a hermitage in the outer courtyard of the Ursuline convent, to which he retired with a few companions.

In 1647 he made a private vow of poverty, giving his possessions to his nephews and charity. He led a life of celibacy, and as a layman was noted for austerities commonly associated with the most strict religious life. He acquired a singular reputation as a spiritual director, and after the death of Jean-Chrysostome took over the direction of a number of souls who had been dependent on the friar. He entered into correspondence and was associated with many other contemporary ascetics, particularly St. John Eudes, Marie des Valles, and Mère *Marie de l'Incarnation. Bernières-Louvigny was associated with Mère Marie and a Madame de la Peltrie in the foundation of the Ursuline community at Quebec. He seems to have attended to much of the financial and business negotiations connected with the support of the foundation.

Bernières-Louvigny published nothing himself; but he left notes he had dictated on spiritual topics, and a number of his letters were preserved. Some of his notes were published the year of his death under the title *L'Intérieur Chrétien*, and others soon after under the title *Le Chrétien Intérieur*. Both editions were very popular, and there were at least a dozen other publications, all anonymous and some rather dubious. In 1670 his sister brought out *Les oeuvres spirituelles de M. de Bernières-Louvigny*, which also became popular. *Le Chrétien intérieur* was placed on the Index in 1689 and *Les oeuvres* in 1692, both cited for *quietism. There is some doubt that he was really responsible for the objectionable doctrine, because the MSS may have been tampered with. Corrected editions have since been issued.

Bibliography: P. POURRAT, *Catholicisme* 1:1491–92. R. HEURTEVENT, *L'Oeuvre spirituelle de Jean de Bernières* (Paris 1938); DictSpirAscMyst 1:1522–27.

[A. J. CLARK]

BERNINI, GIOVANNI LORENZO

The greatest sculptor and architect of the Italian baroque; b. Naples, 1598; d. Rome, Nov. 28, 1680. A child prodigy, Bernini learned the rudiments of his art from his father, Pietro, a Florentine late mannerist sculptor. In 1605 the family moved to Rome, where Bernini remained, except for a 6-month sojourn (1665) at the court of Louis XIV in Paris. He was named architect to St. Peter's, where for more than 50 years he directed vast enterprises in the area of the Vatican (*see* ST. PETER'S BASILICA). Throughout the city he renovated and designed churches, squares, chapels, tombs, palaces, and fountains; he invented the full baroque portrait bust; he officiated in a gamut of civic undertakings from the planning of illuminations, carnival floats, fireworks,

Fig. 1. Giovanni Lorenzo Bernini: (a) "Apollo and Daphne," marble, Galleria Borghese. (b) Interior of the church of S. Andrea al Quirinale, Rome, 1658–67. (c) "Blessed Lodovica Albertoni," marble, 1671–74, over life size.

Fig. 2. Giovanni Lorenzo Bernini, detail of the "Cathedra Petri" in the apse of St. Peter's Basilica, Rome. Executed between 1657 and 1666, it enshrines a chair traditionally said to have been used by St. Peter himself.

Fig. 3. Giovanni Lorenzo Bernini, self-portrait in the Galleria Borghese, Rome.

and catafalques to the presentation of operas and comedies for which he created the costumes and stage machinery. Bernini was one of the last of the "universal men." He gave Rome its baroque character and Europe a new sculptural style that reigned for several centuries.

Bernini's early reputation was made with three lifesize marble groups (1618–24): "Aeneas and Anchises," "Pluto and Proserpina," and "Apollo and Daphne," as well as with "David," executed for Cardinal Scipione Borghese. He divided his attention equally between antique sculpture and contemporary painting; his astonishing craftsmanship delighted in technical feats of realism until then considered outside the realm of sculpture. The Roman Curia, notably Popes *Urban VIII, *Innocent X, and *Alexander VII were Bernini's principal patrons. Among his achievements in St. Peter's are some of the most opulent expressions of the *Ecclesia triumphans*: the "Baldacchino" (1624–33); the decoration of chapels and nave; the "Scala Regia" (1663–66); the "Cathedra Petri" in the apse (1657–66); and the design for St. Peter's Square (1656–67). As in all Bernini's churches, S. Andrea al Quirinale (1658–67) combines architecture, sculpture, and ornamentation to form an indivisible unity whose purpose is to illumine the mystery of St. Andrew's salvation. So, too, in the Cornaro Chapel (1645–52, S. Maria della Vittoria), with the altar of St. Teresa in ecstasy (for illustration, *see* TERESA OF AVILA, ST.), and in the Altieri Chapel, with Bl. Lodovica Albertoni (1671–74, S. Francesco a Ripa), a theatrical setting is used to transport the faithful to the realm of exultant mystical reality. A fervent practitioner of the spiritual exercises of St. Ignatius of Loyola, Bernini summoned every resource of his stupendous baroque rhetoric to deny the barrier between the real and imagined, the better to celebrate the spirit of 17th-century Catholicism.

See also BAROQUE ART; CHURCH ARCHITECTURE, 7.

Bibliography: Sources. F. BALDINUCCI, *Vita di Bernini* (Florence 1682), ed. S. S. LUDOVICI (Milan 1948). P. F. DE CHANTELOU, *Journal du voyage en France du chevalier Bernin,* ed. L. LALANNE (Paris 1930). See also the *Vitae* of G. BAGLIONE (1642), L. PASCOLI, 2 v. (1730–36), and G. B. PASSERI (1772).
Literature. M. REYMOND, *Le Bernin* (Paris 1911). M. VON BOEHN, *Lorenzo Bernini, seine Zeit, sein Leben, sein Werk* (2d ed. Bielefeld 1927). V. MARTINELLI, ed., *Bernini* (Milan 1953). E. BENKARD, *G. L. Bernini* (Frankfurt a.M. 1926). A. MUÑOZ, *G. L. Bernini: Architetto e decoratore* (Rome 1925). L. GRASSI, *Disegni del Bernini* (Bergamo 1944); *Bernini pittore* (Rome 1945). R. PANE, *Bernini architetto* (Venice 1953). R. WITTKOWER, *G. L. Bernini, the Sculptor of the Roman Baroque* (New York 1955). **Illustration credits:** Fig. 1*a, b,* and *c,* Alinari-Art Reference Bureau. Fig. 2, Leonard von Matt. Fig. 3, Anderson-Art Reference Bureau.

[R. M. ARB]

BERNIS, FRANÇOIS JOACHIM DE PIERRE DE, French cardinal and statesman; b. Saint-Marcel de l'Ardèche, Diocese of Viviers, May 22, 1715; d. Rome, Nov. 2, 1794. François, descendant of a noble but impoverished family, was educated in the humanities by the Jesuits and then studied theology at Saint-Sulpice. Through his cousin, the Baron de Montmorency, he was introduced to the Parisian court, where his charm and gallantry became well known. In 1744 in recognition of his poetical writings he was admitted to the French Academy, and under the patronage of Mme. de Pompadour he received a pension of 1,500 livres and apartments in the Tuileries. Louis XV appointed him ambassador to Venice in 1751. There he learned much of diplomacy and intrigue and earned the gratitude of Pope Benedict XIV for his intervention in papal differences with the Venetian government. In 1755 he returned to Paris, where he was ordained to the priesthood, and the next year he was sent to Vienna to secure an Austrian alliance with *Maria Theresa against England and Prussia in the maneuvers that later led to the

François Joachim de Pierre de Bernis preaching in the house of Mme. Geoffrin, painting by Gabriel Lemonnier, 1755, in the Musée des Beaux Arts in Rouen.

Seven Years' War (1756–63). On his return (June 27, 1757) he replaced Pierre Rouillé as minister of foreign affairs, but the adverse course of the war lost him popular favor and the support of Mme. de Pompadour. His office was given to Étienne François, Duke de *Choiseul, in November 1758, and Bernis retired in disgrace to his abbey of Saint-Médard near Soissons. He had received the cardinal's hat from Clement XIII on October 2 of that year, and after regaining the friendship of Louis XV·in 1764, he was made archbishop of Albi and 5 years later, ambassador to Rome. He was a powerful influence in selecting a candidate sympathetic to the French crown in the conclaves of 1769, which elected G. Vincenzo Ganganelli as Clement XIV, and 1775, which chose Angelo Braschi as Pius VI. He represented Louis XV in the negotiations for the suppression of the Jesuits, and though he seems to have found the mission distasteful, he terminated it successfully through the pressure of the Bourbons of France, Spain, and Naples. When he refused to take the constitutional oath demanded by the Revolutionary government on March 3, 1790, he lost his rich incomes. He spent his last years taking care of French exiles in Rome. He was buried in the French church of St. Louis in Rome.

Bibliography: *Memoirs and Letters of Cardinal de Bernis,* tr. K. P. WORMSLEY, 2 v. (Boston 1902). R. CHALUMEAU, *Catholicisme* 1:1492–93. M. DES OMBIAUX, *Éloge du Card. de Bernis* (Paris 1944). P. CALENDINI, DHGE 8:847–849. E. SANTOVITO, EncCatt 2:1454–55. S. SKALWEIT, LexThK² 2:257–258. M. CHEKE, *The Cardinal de Bernis* (New York 1959). **Illustration credit:** Archives Photographiques, Paris.

[E. D. MC SHANE]

BERNO, BL., first abbot of *Cluny; b. Burgundy, *c.* 850; d. Jan. 13, 927 (feast, Jan. 13). He entered the *Benedictines at St. Martin of Autun. Later he was sent to reform the Abbey of Baume-Les-Messieurs. About 890 he founded Gigny and remained its superior. On Sept. 2, 909, the Duke of Aquitaine, William the Pious, officially handed over to him the territory of Cluny, where he established a new monastery dedicated to SS. Peter and Paul. It was placed under the immediate authority of the Holy See (*see* CLUNIAC REFORM). Several houses were placed under Berno's care, notably Déols and *Souvigny. Before his death, he had provided for the election of (St.) *Odo of Cluny as his successor.

Bibliography: ActSS 2:106–112. Mabillon AS 7:66–88. M. MARRIER and A. DUCHESNE, eds., *Bibliotheca cluniacensis* (Paris 1614 repr. Mâcon 1915) 1–12 (PL 133:843–858). A. BRUEL, ed., *Recueil des chartes de l'abbaye de Cluny,* 6 v. (Paris 1876–1903) 1:124–129. E. SACKUR, *Die Cluniacenser,* 2 v. (Halle 1892–94) 1:36–69. Butler Th Attw 1:75. R. AIGRAIN, *Catholicisme* 1:1493–94.

[R. GRÉGOIRE]

BERNO OF REICHENAU, orator, hymn writer, musician, and liturgist; b. Prüm, near Trier, Germany; d. *Reichenau, June 7, 1048. He was educated at *Sankt Gallen. From the Benedictine monastery of *Prüm, where he was a monk, Berno was named abbot of Reichenau (1008–48) by *Henry II to replace Abbot Immo, whose zeal for the *Cluniac reform had caused defections among his monks. A strong adherent of the reform, Berno, by adapting its spirit to the Reichenau tradition, was able to renew religious fervor in the monastery. He twice accompanied Henry II to Rome, once for Henry's coronation in 1014. After the latter's death, Berno supported Conrad the Young for emperor. When the rival candidate took the throne as *Conrad II, Berno gave him unswerving loyalty, despite the losses sustained by Reichenau during Conrad's struggle against the feudal princes, notably Duke Ernest of Swabia. When Conrad died in 1038, Berno gave his allegience to the Emperor, *Henry III. In 1043 he took an active part in the Synod of Constance. He was buried in the St. Mark's choir, which he had built in the church of Reichenau. His grave was rediscovered in 1929. As abbot, Berno maintained cordial relations with persons and monasteries on both sides of the Alps. His writings (some of which are preserved, though with many interpolations, in PL 142:1055–1210) include liturgical works: *Liber qualiter adventus celebretur, quando nativitas Domini feria secunda advenerit; Dialogus qualiter quattuor temporum jejunia per sua sabbata sint observanda; De quibusdam rebus ad officium missae pertinentibus;* and musical works: *De consona et tonorum varietate,* and *Tonarius.* A collection of letters, sermons, and the *Vita Udalrici* by Berno are also extant.

Bibliography: R. MOLITOR, "Die Musik der Reichenau," *Die Kultur der Abtei Reichenau,* ed. K. BEYERLE, 2 v. (Munich 1925) 2:802–820. H. ENGEL, Stammler 1:204–208 with critical bibliog. H. OESCH, *Berno und Hermann von Reichenau als Musiktheoretiker* (Bern 1961).

[M. F. MC CARTHY]

BERNOLD OF CONSTANCE, noted chronicler (known also as Bernold of St. Blaise); b. *c.* 1050; d. Schaffhausen, Sept. 16, 1100. He was educated in the cathedral school of *Constance, attended the 1079 Lenten synod in Rome, and was ordained in Constance in 1084 by the Cardinal Legate Otto of Ostia. As an opponent of Emperor *Henry IV in the *investiture struggle, he presumably took part in 1085 in the Quedlinburg Synod of the anti-Emperor Hermann of Salm and certainly was at the battle of Pleichfeld in 1086. After 1085 Bernold called himself *ultimus fratrum* of *Sankt Blasien, and from about 1091 he lived in All Saints monastery in Schaffhausen.

In his first treatise, written in 1074, Bernold came out strongly against the married clergy (*see* CELIBACY, HISTORY OF), and he later composed a number of polemical tracts as a partisan of *Gregory VII. In the *Apologeticus* he defended the authority of the papal decrees against all other sources of Canon Law. Bernold's chief work was his chronicle (MS Munich, Clm 432), accepted as his own work. After extracts from older chroniclers, this work presents Bernold's own account of historical events beginning from 1075 and extending to Aug. 3, 1100. It is strongly slanted against Henry IV. Bernold wrote also a liturgical work called the *Micrologus* and compiled a treatise on the Eucharist from texts used in the condemnations of *Berengarius of Tours.

Bibliography: MGS 5:385–467, chronicle. MGLibLit 2:1–168; 3:601–602. PL 151:978–1022, *Micrologus.* J. R. GEISELMANN, *Bernold von St. Blasien: Sein neuentdecktes Werk über die Eucharistie* (Munich 1936). H. WEISWEILER, StGreg 4:129–147. Wattenbach-Holtzmann 1:521–528. J. AUTENRIETH, NDB 2:127–128; *Die Domschule von Konstanz zur Zeit des Investiturstreits* (Stuttgart 1956); LexThK² 2:259.

[L. KURRAS]

BERNOLD OF OTTOBEUREN, BL., priest, monk, and ascetic; fl. probably 11th century (commemoration, Nov. 25). A *Benedictine monk of the Abbey of *Ottobeuren, he was especially noted in life for his dedicated spirit of mortification and heroic practice of penance. The annals of his abbey report that after Bernold's death miracles were performed through his intercession. On Dec. 25, 1189, Bl. Udalschalk solemnly translated his remains to the choir of the chapel of St. Michael; a second translation occurred in 1553. Since 1772 his body has rested in the chapel of St. John Nepomuc in the basilica of Ottobeuren.

Bibliography: M. FEYERABEND, *Des ehem. Reichsstiftes Ottenbeuren . . . sämtliche Jahrbücher,* 4 v. (Ottenbeuren 1813–16) 2:218–219; 4:400. Zimmermann KalBen 3:354, 356. F. ZOEPFL, LexThK² 2:259.

[O. J. BLUM]

BERNULF, ST., known also as Bernhold, Bennon, bishop of Utrecht; d. July 13, 1054 (feast, July 19). The opinion that Bernulf's appointment to his see was the result of strife over electing a successor to Adelboldus and of an accidental meeting with *Conrad II is probably groundless. Conrad always appointed the bishops, choosing imperial officials who continued to work for him even after consecration. Bernulf's friendship with *Henry III resulted in notable gifts of land to his diocese (e.g., March 1040; September 1042; May 22 and Aug. 23, 1046). He devoted himself energetically to the work of reform, participating in synods, building churches, and renewing monastic vigor even at the expense of reducing the privileges of his see over the monastery of Hohorst. His body lies in St. Peter's church in Utrecht. He is patron of the Netherlands' guild for Christian art (estab. 1870).

Bibliography: ActSS June 4:654–656. S. MULLER and A. C. BOUMAN, *Oorkondenboek van het sticht Utrecht tot 1301,* v.1 (Utrecht 1921) 173–193, 231, 302. G. J. LIEFTINCK, "De herkomst van Bischofs van Utrecht," *Jaarboeke van "Oud-Utrecht"* (Utrecht 1949) 23–40. G. BÖING, LexThK² 2:260. P. POLMAN, DHGE 8:856–857.

[R. BALCH]

BERNWARD OF HILDESHEIM, ST., bishop and art patron; b. *c.* 960; d. Nov. 20, 1022 (feast, Nov. 20). Bernward was the scion of a noble Saxon family; his maternal grandfather, Adalbero, was count palatine in Saxony. His uncle Volkmar, Bishop of Utrecht (d. 990), brought Bernward to the cathedral school of Hildesheim, where he studied under *Thangmar sometime before 975. In Mainz Archbishop *Willigis (d. 1011) ordained him and later introduced him at court. In 978 Empress Theophano (d. 991) made him tutor of her son, *Otto III, who later arranged his election to the Diocese of *Hildesheim in January 993. Once there Bernward built castles against the invading Danes and Slavs, introduced the system of archdeaneries, and established an annual diocesan synod. In 996 he called monks from Sankt-Pantaleon in Cologne under Abbot Goderamnus to form the first monastery of men in the diocese at the Abbey of Sankt-Michael, and he endowed their chapel with a relic of the true cross. In his struggle with Willigis over the Abbey of *Gandersheim he went to Rome (1000–01), where his rights over the abbey were confirmed, and in 1007 the archbishop finally abandoned his claims. Shortly before his death Bernward consecrated the unfinished church of Sankt-Michael (Sept. 29, 1022) and accepted the habit of the *Benedictine Order (Nov. 11, 1022). He was buried in the crypt of Sankt-Michael's, and Pope *Celestine III canonized him (Dec. 21, 1192). His biography was begun by Thangmar (MGS 4:757–786). Bernward played an outstanding role in the spiritual and political life of his period. His intellectual clarity and power of abstraction as well as his artistic sensitivity are reflected in the rich production of his workshop. He is the patron of goldsmiths and an important figure in his own right in the development of 11th-century art. Today his name is most commonly associated with the bronze doors cast for Sankt-Michael *c.* 1008 to 1015 and the bronze column from *c.* 1018 to 1020. The unity of the door reliefs, which develop the theme of man's fall and Redemption, lies not in the narrative sequence, but in the symbolic structure. Geometric clarity and harmony of proportions, already visible in the true cross reliquary, a *crux gemmata,* reach their perfection in Sankt-Michael itself. In this greatest of Ottonian churches the classical tradition for the first time is translated completely into the medieval language of symbolic order.

Bibliography: F. J. TSCHAN, *St. Bernward of Hildesheim,* 3 v. (Notre Dame 1942–52). H. BESELER and H. ROGGENKAMP, *Die Michaeliskirche in Hildesheim* (Berlin 1954). R. WESENBERG, *Bernwardinische Plastik* (Berlin 1955). W. VON DEN STEINEN, "Bernward von Hildesheim über sich selbst," *DeutschArch* 12 (1956) 331–362. R. DRÖGEREIT, LexThK² 2:260–261. H. JANTZEN, *Ottonische Kunst* (2d ed. Hamburg 1959). K. ALGERMISSEN, *Bernward und Godehard von Hildesheim* (Hildesheim 1960). Zimmermann KalBen 3:335–338.

[A. A. SCHACHER]

BEROSSUS

Author of a three-volume history of Babylonia in Greek called Βαβυλωνιακά (in Latin, *Babyloniaca*); b. Babylon, *c.* 340 B.C.; d. Cos (island off the southwestern coast of Asia Minor), *c.* 270 B.C. His name Βηρωσός probably represents the Akkadian name *Bēl-rē'ušu* (Bel is his shepherd). He was a priest of the god *Bel (*Marduk) in Babylon. At an advanced age he wrote his book and dedicated it to the *Seleucid King Antiochus I Soter (281–261 B.C.). There seems to be no reason to doubt the statement of *Vitruvius (1st century B.C.) that Berossus, some time after the completion of his work, went to the island of Cos, where he established a school of astrology. This move from the Seleucid to the Ptolemaic sphere of influence may have been due to a loss of Antiochus's favor. Probably the purpose of Berossus' history of Babylonia (then a part of the Seleucid kingdom) had been the glorification of the Seleucid dynasty, just as his contemporary *Manetho had written a history of Egypt in Greek for the purpose of glorifying the *Ptolemies.

Berossus' work is not extant, but fragments of it have been preserved in citations of later Greek historians, principally Flavius *Josephus, *Clement of Alexandria, *Eusebius of Caesarea, and *George Syncellus. None of these, however, was directly conversant with Berossus' work; they knew it only through other writers, of whom the most important was Alexander Polyhistor (1st century B.C.). In the course of such citation and re-citation, even those fragments of the original work that remain have inevitably been subject to corruption; nonetheless, they are of great importance in the study of Babylonian mythology and history.

The first book recounts in mythic form the origins of man and of human civilization. Beginning with the latter, Berossus tells of the emergence of the monster

Oannes, half fish and half man, from the Red Sea, and of his arrival in Babylonia, where he taught men, as yet living like beasts, the elements of civilized life—"literature and mathematics and all kinds of arts," including the construction of cities and temples, the use of legal institutions, and the practice of geometry and agriculture.

The story of the creation of world order and of mankind that follows was evidently placed in the mouth of Oannes. In the beginning the world was a chaos peopled by monstrous beings uniting the characteristics of men and animals, and ruled by a woman named "Sea." Into this chaos the god Bel introduced order, overcoming "Sea" and cleaving her body into two parts, from which he formed heaven and earth. He then created the first men, fashioning them from earth and the blood of the gods. As related by Berossus, this story is clearly derived from the Babylonian creation epic *Enuma Elish. Elements of the myth, such as the use of the sea to represent a primeval chaos that was reduced to order by divine intervention, were a common possession of the ancient Near East.

The second book contains the history of Mesopotamia from the first kings to the period of Nabonassar (747–728 B.C.). Its form, according to Eusebius, was essentially a mere listing of kings' names with the duration of their reigns. Similar documents are well known from Babylonian cuneiform archives, and it was undoubtedly from cuneiform records that Berossus derived his material. Noteworthy is the list of 10 antediluvian kings. Comparing this list to the corresponding section of the Sumerian King List [see Pritchard ANET² 265–266; T. Jacobsen, *The Sumerian King List* (Chicago 1937)] of the early 2d millennium B.C., one finds that Berossus' list, though it has grown from 8 to 10 names, is similar to that of the earlier document. The mythical regnal periods assigned by the King List, averaging some 30,000 years for each king, have been further increased to an average 43,200 years. Berossus' list has often been compared to Genesis' list of 10 antediluvian Patriarchs, and it is possible that there is some historical connection between them; the life spans assigned to the Biblical Patriarchs, though exaggerated, are modest by comparison with the Babylonian tradition.

The Babylonian story of the Flood was evidently used in Berossus' second book. Berossus' account differs only in detail from the 11th Tablet of the *Gilgamesh Epic;* both compositions show a striking similarity to the parallel narrative in Genesis.

It is only in the third book of Berossus' work that one enters the realm of true history, with a detailed discussion of events and a realistic and generally accurate chronology. For this section of the work, Berossus evidently had access to a cuneiform chronicle source or sources reaching back to 747 B.C.; the information given agrees with Babylonian chronicles known from the cuneiform inscriptions and supplements them in several particulars.

Several fragments concerned with astrological lore have been attributed by Greek writers to Berossus. Though some modern scholars have been inclined to postulate a professedly astrological work as the source of these, there is no evidence of such a work, and it seems most probable that they were culled from the *Babyloniaca.* Interest in the subject was natural for a Babylonian scholar of Berossus' day, and undoubtedly his comments were welcomed by the Hellenistic readers for whom his book was intended.

Bibliography: C. MÜLLER, ed., *Fragmenta historicorum graecorum*, 5 v. (Paris 1878–85) 2:495–510. E. SCHWARTZ, *Griechische Geschichtschreiber* (Leipzig 1957) 189–197. C. F. LEHMANN-HAUPT, ReallexAssyr 2:1–17. A. ROMEO, EncCatt 2:1459. F. M. T. DE LIAGRE BÖHL, LexThK² 2:261–262. W. VON SODEN, RGG³ 1:1069.

[R. I. CAPLICE]

BERQUIN, LOUIS DE,
French royal counselor and humanist; b. Passy, 1490; d. Paris, April 17, 1529. He was a member of the circle of Margaret of Valois in the 1520s, and he translated Erasmus' *Enchiridion* and other works, and treatises of Hutten, Luther, and Melanchthon. He wrote a defense of Luther and a treatise, *De Sacerdotio.* Arrested, he was rescued in 1523, 1525, and 1526 from the wrath of Parlement and the Sorbonne by Francis I's intervention. It is uncertain whether he adhered to Luther's doctrines, but he was attracted by Luther's early boldness. At the end of the decade, Berquin was arraigned again during the French alliance with Rome and outbreaks of iconoclasm in Paris. He was condemned and burned as a heretic on the same day. Efforts were redoubled to unmask "secret Lutherans," and the "Meaux Group" under Margaret's protection dispersed.

Bibliography: N. WEISS, *Bull. Soc. Hist. Prot. Français* 67 (1918) 162–183, 209–211. W. G. MOORE, *La Réforme allemande et la littérature française* (Strasbourg 1930). A. BAILLY, *La Réforme en France* (Paris 1960). J. CADIER, "Luther et les débuts de la réforme française," *Positions Lutheriennes* 6 (1958). J. VIÉNOT, *Histoire de la réforme française* 2 v. (Paris 1926–34). R. NÜRNBERGER, RGG³ 1:1069. J. RATH, LexThK² 2:262.

[R. H. FISCHER]

BERRUGUETE, ALONSO,
Renaissance artist and architect, best known for his bold contribution to Spanish sculpture; b. Paredes de Nava, Spain, 1486–90s; d. Toledo, end of September 1561. He probably studied with Pedro, court painter to Ferdinand and Isabella (fl. 1483–1503 or 1504), before working with *Michelangelo and other famous sculptors in Italy (c. 1504–17). Returning to Spain, he fulfilled commissions in Zaragoza, Valladolid, Toledo, and elsewhere and became Charles V's painter and sculptor. Michelangelo awakened in him "the conscience of his personality," and he transformed his master's qualities into his own expression, reflecting a hypersensitive and impetuous temperament. The spiritual rather than the harmonious dominated in his work, which anticipated an exalted Christian baroque; yet there remained a pictorial sense in his sculpture. Cossío called him a "modern in his time," likening him in sculpture to Góngora in poetry, *Calderón in the theater, and El *Greco (Domenico Theotocopuli) in painting. (For illustration see following page.)

See also RENAISSANCE ART.

Bibliography: M. BARTOLOMÉ COSSÍO, *Alonso Berruguete* (Valladolid 1948). J. M. AZCÁRATE, *Escultura del siglo XVI,* v. 13 of *Ars Hispaniae,* 18 v. (Madrid 1946–62) 143–152 *passim.* F. JIMÉNEZ PLACER, *Historia del arte español* (Barcelona 1955) v.2. G. KUBLER and M. SORIA, *Art and Architecture in Spain and Portugal and Their American Dominions, 1500–1800* (PelHArt Z17; 1959). O. F. L. HAGEN, *Patterns and Principles of Spanish Art* (Madison 1943). EncWA 2:482–483. **Illustration credit:** MAS, Barcelona.

[A. L. MARTIN]

Alonso Berruguete, "St. John the Baptist," c. 1540, wood, 31½ by 19¼ inches, Toledo Cathedral, Spain.

BERRUYER, ISAAC JOSEPH, Jesuit exegete; b. Rouen, France, Nov. 7, 1681; d. Paris, Feb. 18, 1758. Berruyer's most noteworthy exegetical work was the ill-fated "History of the People of God." The first part, entitled *Histoire du peuple de Dieu depuis son origine jusqu'à la venue du Messie*, appeared in 7 volumes in 1728; by 1736 seven editions and four translations of the work had been published. The second part, *Histoire du peuple de Dieu depuis la naissance du Messie jusqu'à la fin de la Synagogue*, followed in 1753; a revised edition was published at Antwerp in 1754. Berruyer's name appears on few copies of the second part, which was published without the knowledge and against the will of his Jesuit superiors in Paris, and, possibly, of Berruyer himself. The third part, *Histoire du peuple de Dieu, ou paraphrase des épîtres des apôtres*, was printed at Lyons in 1757.

As the various parts of the work appeared, controversy grew increasingly bitter. Berruyer was denounced for cavalier treatment of the sacred texts, and some critics felt that his attitudes were dangerously Nestorian; but the chief complaint seems to have been that he was influenced by the eccentricities of Father Jean Har-douin. The *Histoire* was condemned by many French bishops, the superiors of the Society of Jesus, the Sorbonne, and the Parlement of Paris. The three divisions of the work were consigned to the Index in 1732, 1754, and 1758, but an approved revision of Part I was issued at Besançon in 1828.

Bibliography: Sommervogel 1:1357–70. L. Bopp, LexThK² 2:262. J. Brucker, DB 1.2:1627–29. E. Lamalle, DHGE 8: 890–891. P. Delattre, *Catholicisme* 1:1495–96.

[J. B. DONNELLY]

BERSABEE (BEERSHEBA), modern Tell es-Seba' near Bir es-Seba'; the southernmost city of Juda during the monarchy, midway on an east-west line between the Dead Sea and the Mediterranean. Bersabee [Heb. $b^e\bar{e}r$ $\check{s}eba'$, seven wells(?), well of the seven(?), well of the oath(?)] defines the southern boundary of Palestine in the stereotyped phrase "from Dan to Bersabee" frequently employed in the OT (e.g., Jgs 20.1; 1 Sm 3.20). This expression and its converse "from Bersabee to Dan" (1 Chr 21.2; 2 Chr 30.5) are frequently employed to designate the entire Israelite nation or territory. Bersabee was an important station as one headed along the route from Juda to Sinai. Elia fled from Jezabel along this route (3 Kgs 19.3). It served as a stopping place for caravans going from Hebron to Egypt. There was an important sanctuary at Bersabee from early times. A sacred tamarisk tree was said to have been planted there by Abraham (Gn 21.33). Isaac built an altar there after the Lord appeared to him at this sacred site (Gn 26.23–25). There Jacob sacrificed on his way to Egypt, and there the Lord spoke to him in a vision (Gn 46.1). Amos referred to Bersabee as a city to which the Israelite went on pilgrimage (Am 5.5). Two sons of Samuel were judges there (1 Sm 8.2), which indicates its importance as a populous center. Bersabee was one of the cities resettled by the Jews after the Babylonian Exile (Neh 11.27).

Bibliography: EncDictBibl 227–228. A. Barrois, DBSuppl 1:963–968. H. Haag, LexThK² 2:98. Abel GéogrPal 1:307; 2: 263. W. Zimmerli, *Geschichte und Tradition von Beersheba im AT* (Giessen 1932).

[F. F. BERGEWISCH]

BERSE, GASPAR (BARZEO), Jesuit missionary in India and associate of St. Francis Xavier; b. Goes, Netherlands, 1515; d. Goa, Oct. 18, 1553. In his youth he studied philosophy at Louvain and, among other things, served for a time in the army of Charles V. He entered the Society of Jesus at Coimbra and was ordained shortly thereafter. The following year he left Lisbon for the missions in India, arriving in Goa in 1548. After teaching philosophy and Sacred Scripture for a short time at the college in Goa, he was deputed by Francis Xavier to evangelize Ormuz in Persia. For 2½ years (May 1549 to November 1551) Berse worked among the Moslems and Jews of the coastal city, earning their respect and achieving notable results. He was called back to Goa by Xavier, who appointed Berse rector of the college there and vice provincial of the entire foundation. Xavier left Berse with detailed directives for the discharge of his duties while Xavier was in China; but without a prudent superior to moderate his activities, Berse expended himself with more zeal than caution. A year later he was dead. Throughout his brief career on the mission, Berse took the spirit and methods of Xavier as his ideal. Like his master,

Berse was able to move souls by his preaching and to inspire them by his zeal and holiness.

Bibliography: MonHistSJ, *passim.* G. SCHURHAMMER and J. WICKI, *Epistolae s. Francisci Xaverii,* 2 v. (Rome 1945–46), *passim.* Streit-Didinger 4:155–156. Sommervogel 1:906–937; 7:1772. E. LAMALLE, DHGE 6:1059–61, with extensive bibliog.

[J. C. WILLKE]

BERTHA OF BLANGY, ST.,

Benedictine abbess; b. Arras, France, second half of 7th century; d. *c.* 725 (feast, July 4). She appears to have been married to a certain Sigfrid and to have had five daughters; her biography, written about 2 centuries after her death, is somewhat unreliable. It is certain, however, that she founded the monastery of Blangy *c.* 686 and retired there with two of her daughters, Gertrude and Deotila. Her body was transferred from Blangy *c.* 895 to the monastery of Erstein in Alsace, but it was returned after 1032, by which date *Benedictine monks again occupied Blangy.

Bibliography: ActSS July 2:47–60. BHL 1:1266–70. L. VAN DER ESSEN, *Étude critique et littéraire sur les vitae des saints mérovingiens de l'ancienne Belgique* (Louvain 1907); DHGE 8:944–945. A. M. ZIMMERMANN, LexThK² 2:263. R. AIGRAIN, *Catholicisme* 1:1499. Zimmermann KalBen 2:399–401.

[P. BLECKER]

BERTHA OF VAL D'OR, ST.,

foundress and abbess of Avenay, France (near Reims); d. *c.* 690 (feast, May 1). By mutual consent she lived in a state of virginity with the saintly Gombert, the founder of the convent of St. Peter at Reims. When he was murdered on a missionary journey, Bertha founded a convent at Avenay in a place once called Val d'Or, and was made its first abbess. She is said to have been murdered by two nephews of her husband. The chief sources for her life are the chronicler *Flodoard of Reims (d. *c.* 966), and a later and largely worthless vita, which may contain, however, some material from the earlier vita used by Flodoard, but subsequently lost. Bertha and Gombert are honored together as saints and martyrs in the Proper of Reims for May 1.

Bibliography: Zimmermann KalBen 2:132–133. ActSS May 1 (1866) 115–120. Flodoard, MGS 13:416–548, 595–596. F. BAIX, DHGE 8:943–944. P. SÉJOURNÉ, *ibid.* 5:1016–18.

[M. R. P. MC GUIRE]

BERTHARIUS, ST.,

abbot and martyr; b. Lombardy, Italy, early 9th century; d. Teano, Campania, Italy, Oct. 22, 884 (feast, Oct. 22). He was received into the *Benedictine Order at *Monte Cassino by Bassacio, whom he succeeded as abbot in 848. He enriched the abbey church with precious vessels and Gospel Books, and when he entertained Emperor *Louis II in 866, he obtained many privileges for his monastery. From Pope *John VIII he secured the exemption of Monte Cassino from episcopal jurisdiction. Bertharius encouraged the development of sacred studies and saw many of his students raised to the episcopate. Although he was in his own time a well-known author and medical writer, most of his writings have not survived; but a homily on St. Scholastica (d. 543) and a poem on the life, death, and miracles of St. *Benedict (PL 126:975–990) do exist. When the Saracens overran southern Italy, Bertharius and a group of monks were martyred in the abbey church at Teano, where they had sought refuge. In 1514, after several transfers, his remains were placed under the altar of a chapel constructed in his honor at Monte Cassino. Pope *Benedict XIII approved his cult on Aug. 26, 1727.

Bibliography: ActSS Oct. 9:663–682. BHL 1107–09, 1271. *Biblioteca Casinensis,* 5 v. (Monte Cassino 1873–94). Manitius 1:608–609. E. CARUSI, "Il Memoratorium dell'abate Bertario," *Casinensia* 1 (1929) 457–548. G. PENCO, *Storia del monachesimo in Italia* (Rome 1961).

[B. D. HILL]

BERTHIER, GUILLAUME FRANÇOIS,

Jesuit spiritual writer and teacher; b. Issoudun, France, April 7, 1704; d. Bourges, Dec. 15, 1782. He entered the Society of Jesus in 1722 and taught philosophy at Rennes and Rouen and theology at Paris. From 1745 to 1749 he published volumes 13 to 18 of the *Histoire de l'Église gallicane* begun by J. Longueval. As editor of *Mémoires de Trévoux* from 1745 to 1762, he maintained a spirited defense against the caustic attacks of Voltaire and the Encyclopedists. Upon the suppression of the Jesuits in France in 1762, he became court librarian and tutor to the sons of the Dauphin (the future Louis XVI and Louis XVIII), but after 18 months he was forced to join other Jesuits in exile in Germany. While there he refused an invitation from Maria Theresa to take up residence in Vienna, for he preferred to devote himself to study and meditation. After the accession of Louis XVI in 1774 he returned to France and spent his remaining years in retirement at Bourges. His works were published posthumously by Y. M. Querbeuf. They include: *Les Psaumes traduits en français avec des notes et des réflexions,* with a biographical notice by Querbeuf (8 v., Paris 1785), which was frequently reprinted; *Isaïe traduit en français avec des notes et réflexions* (5 v., Paris 1788–89); and *Reflexions spirituelles* (5 v., Paris 1790).

Bibliography: Sommervogel 1:1377–86. E. LAMALLE, DHGE 8:954–955. M. VILLER, DictSpirAscMyst 1:1528–30. Hurter Nomencl 4.1:411–413.

[J. C. WILLKE]

BERTHIER, JEAN BAPTISTE,

missionary of Our Lady of la Salette, founder of the Institute of the Holy Family (Missionaries of the Holy Family) for late priestly vocations, and ascetical writer; b. Chatonnay, Isère (France), Feb. 24, 1840; d. Grave, Holland, Oct. 16, 1908. Berthier made his great impact through his 36 ascetical and theological works, the dominating theme of which is that sanctity is possible in any walk of life through imitation of the Holy Family and constant fidelity to the duties of one's state. Among his greatest works are *La Mère selon le coeur de Dieu* (Lyon 1866), which has been translated into five languages; *Le Prêtre dans le ministère* (Paris 1883); *Breve compendium theol.* (Grenoble 1887); *Le Sacerdoce* (Paris 1894); and *Des États de vie chrétienne et de la Vocation* (Rome 1875). He considered infused contemplation as "ordinary" and not to be ranked with ecstasies and visions and taught his followers how to dispose themselves to contemplation, "the short-cut to sanctity." Few writers have sought to influence so wide a range of people.

Bibliography: P. J. RAMERS, *Bonus miles Christi Jesu* (Betzdorf 1931); *Le R. P. J. Berthier, missionaire de la Salette* (Fribourg 1925). J. M. DE LOMBAERDE, *La vie et l'esprit du Tr. R. P. Jean Berthier* (Grave 1910). A. BATTANDIER, *Annuaire pontifical catholique* (Paris 1909). M. COLPO, EncCatt 2:1467. P. J. RAMERS, DictSpirAscMyst 1:1530–32. M. T. DISDIER, DHGE 8:955–956.

[M. J. BARRY]

BERTHOLD OF CHIEMSEE (BERTHOLD PÜRSTINGER)

BERTHOLD OF CHIEMSEE (BERTHOLD PÜRSTINGER), bishop and theologian; b. Salzburg, 1465; d. Saalfelden, July 16, 1543. Berthold, a fine sensitive person of high character and a skilled writer, was a late medieval ecclesiastical reformer. He studied Canon Law in Perugia, became a priest at Schnaitsee and Stellung, and was made prince-bishop of Chiemsee (1508) and suffragan bishop of Salzburg. He mediated between the burghers of Salzburg and the archbishop in 1511, and between the rebellious peasants and Cardinal Matthäus Lang, the Archbishop (1524–26). Depressed by the outrages of the revolutionaries, he resigned on May 11, 1526, and withdrew to the Cistercian monastery at Raitenhaslach and then to a hostel and chapel in Saalfelden, which he had built (completed 1541) for a brotherhood of retired priests and for poor laymen. He wrote a *Tewtsche Theologey* (Munich 1528), the first German dogmatics based on Scripture and St. Thomas Aquinas, for the education of priests and laymen. His *Tewtsche Rational über das Ambt heiliger Mess* and his *Keligpuechl* (both 1535) defended the Mass and Communion under one species against the Protestant reformers.

Bibliography: R. BAUERREISS, LexThK² 2:265–266. K. EDER, NDB 2:162, with good bibliog. ADB 2:519.

[L. W. SPITZ]

BERTHOLD OF GARSTEN, ST.

BERTHOLD OF GARSTEN, ST., Benedictine, first abbot of Garsten; d. July 27, 1142 (feast, July 27). He was descended from a family of *ministeriales,* probably Swabian. He became a monk at *Sankt Blasien and rose to position of subprior. He was prior at *Göttweig (1107) and abbot of Garsten (1111–42); the abbey flourished as a center of reform under his guidance. He was a strict but loving master in enforcing monastic observances. Humble, much given to prayer and the ascetical life, he was noted for charity to the poor and much sought as a wise and helpful confessor. Miracles at his grave in the monastery church made it a place of pilgrimage; a decree of canonization was issued by the bishop of Passau, July 16, 1236. Hearings on the recognition of his cult began in Rome in 1951.

Bibliography: ActSS July 6:469–494. F. X. PRITZ, *Kurzgefasste Lebensgeschichte des heiligen Berthold* (Linz 1842). W. NEUMÜLLER, "Berthold von Garsten: Ein Kremsmünster Beitrag zur Geschichte seiner Verehrung," *Kremsmünster Ober-Gymnasium Jahresbericht* 94 (Wels 1951). J. LENZENWEGER, *Berthold: Abt von Garsten* (Linz 1958), includes vita and rich bibliog.

[D. ANDREINI]

BERTHOLD OF REGENSBURG

Greatest popular preacher of the German Middle Ages; b. Regensburg, Germany, c. 1210; d. Regensburg, Dec. 14, 1272. He received a good education, probably at the Magdeburg Studienanstalt, and possibly under the learned Bartholomaeus Anglicus, with whose *De Proprietatibus rerum* he was unquestionably familiar. He subsequently became lector (c. 1230–34), then preacher (1240), in the Franciscan monastery in Regensburg. In 1246, with David of Augsburg (probably his companion and not, as was formerly thought, his teacher), Berthold was a member of a commission that inspected Niedermünster convent for women. The report of this commission is preserved in the Reichsarchiv in Munich. From 1240 on, his activities as a popular preacher took him throughout his native Bavaria, to other parts of Germany, then to Switzerland, Czechoslovakia, and, in 1262–63, Hungary. In Hungary, if one can believe the legend, he preached so effectively that the people later honored him as a saint and made yearly pilgrimages to his grave in Regensburg. In 1263, directed by Pope Urban IV to preach against heresy, he again traversed much of Germany and Switzerland, and even reached Paris, where he met King Louis IX.

Berthold was well acquainted with the Bible; the legends of the saints; the patristic writings of Augustine, Gregory the Great, and Bernard of Clairvaux; and he had a considerable knowledge of the natural sciences. Yet his sermons to the people, preached mostly in the open, and sometimes, according to contemporary accounts, to audiences numbering tens of thousands, are marked by simplicity. Primarily didactic, they stress moral practice, often in its negative aspect (the seven capital sins and violations of the Ten Commandments), rather than dogma. The style of Berthold's sermons is graphic, the diction pictorial. By invective, warning, pathos, humor, exhortation, and imagery, they strive to move the people to repentance and moral betterment.

Stylistic studies of Berthold's German sermons are based chiefly on the Pfeiffer-Strobl edition (*Berthold von Regensburg: Vollständige Ausgabe seiner Predigten,* 2 v., Vienna 1862, 1880). Remo Iannucci, *The Treatment of the Capital Sins and the Decalogue in the German Sermons of Berthold von Regensburg* (Washington 1942) contains a bibliography to 1942. Unfortunately, though it is certain that Berthold preached in German, no extant sermons in the vernacular have been positively ascribed to him. It is clear, however, from his own preface to the *Rusticani de Dominicis* that some of his sermons were taken down in Latin by clerics and religious present at their delivery and later edited by Berthold himself. These Latin sermons, with others not certainly Berthold's, have been published under five headings: *Sermones [rusticani] de Dominicis, de Sanctis, de Communi, ad Religiosos et quosdam alios, speciales et extravagantes.*

Bibliography: The most comprehensive study of Berthold's life and work to date is A. E. SCHÖNBACH, "Studien zur Geschichte der altdeutschen Predigt," *K. Akademie der Wissenschaften, Vienna: Philosophisch-historische Klasse, Sitzungsberichte* (1900–07) v.142.7; v.147.5; v.151.2; v.152.7; v.153.4; v.154.1; v.155.5.

[M. F. MC CARTHY]

BERTHOLD OF REICHENAU

BERTHOLD OF REICHENAU, chronicler; b. c. 1030; d. probably March 12, 1088. He was the pupil of *Hermannus Contractus and his successor as chronicler. Berthold made his reputation by his continuation of the Chronicle of Hermannus, which, before he died in 1054, Hermannus had asked Berthold to do. There are two extant versions, both bearing Berthold's name, but not the product of the same author. The *Vita Herimanni* at the beginning of both versions is certainly Berthold's work. As to the Chronicle itself, most probably Berthold was the author of the shorter, simpler and pro-imperial version, entitled *Chronici Herimanni continuatio, auctore ut dicitur Bertholdo* (MGS 13:730–732), which stops in mid-1066. The longer version, which extends to 1080 (MGS 5:264–326) and contains an account of the years 1075 to 1080, is pro-*Gregorian Reform and anti-*Henry IV and is apparently not the work of Berthold but instead that of an anonymous Swabian annalist.

Bibliography: Manitius 3:403–404. A. FLICHE, *La Réforme grégorienne,* 3 v. (Paris 1924–37) 2:39–44; DHGE 8:987. Wattenbach-Holtzmann 1.3:514–524. T. SCHIEFFER, LexThK² 2:268.

[V. GELLHAUS]

BERTHOLET, ALFRED, Protestant OT scholar and historian of religion who contributed to the movement of Biblical criticism in the early 20th century; b. Basel, Nov. 9, 1868; d. Münsterlingen (Bodensee), Aug. 24, 1951. He published *Die Stellung der Israeliten und der Juden zu den Fremden* (1896); wrote OT commentaries, especially on Ezechiel (1896 and 1922, and in Eissfeldt's *Handbuch,* 1936); and contributed *Die jüdische Religion von der Zeit Esras bis zum Zeitalter Christi* (1911) as v.2 to B. Stade's *Biblische Theologie des Alten Testaments.* Moreover, he contributed to K. Budde's *Geschichte der althebräischen Literatur* the section on apocrypha and pseudepigrapha (1906). He also edited E. Kautzsch's *Die Heilige Schrift des Alten Testaments* (4th ed. 1922–33).

Bertholet tended increasingly to the approach of the *religionsgeschichtliche Schule* (school of comparative religion), e.g., in his *Kulturgeschichte Israels* (1919). He edited the *Religionsgeschichtliches Lesebuch* (1926–32); with E. Lehmann, he edited the *Lehrbuch der Religionsgeschichte* of Chantepie de la Saussaye (4th ed. 1925); and, with others, *Die Religion in Geschichte und Gegenwart* (2d ed. 1927–33). Professor Bertholet was attached to the OT faculty at the Universities of Basel, Tübingen, Göttingen, and Berlin.

Bibliography: O. EISSFELDT et al., eds., *Festschrift für Alfred Bertholet* (Tübingen 1950) 564–578. E. KUTSCH, RGG³ 1:1071. T. SCHWEGLER, LexThK² 2:268–269.

[T. W. BUCKLEY]

BERTI, GIOVANNI LORENZO, theologian; b. Sarravezza, Tuscany, May 28, 1696; d. Florence, March 26, 1766. A Hermit of St. Augustine, he taught philosophy and theology and held high offices in his order. His superior general, A. Schiaffinati, directed him to write an exposition of the doctrine of St. Augustine. This eight-volume work, entitled *De theologicis disciplinis* (Rome 1739–45), was accused of Jansenism. In defense of his doctrine, Berti wrote several works, chief of which was *Augustinianum systema de gratia vindicatum* (Rome 1747). His writings were examined in Rome under Benedict XIV and declared orthodox. He wrote also a widely used work on Church history, which was entitled *Ecclesiasticae historiae breviarium* (Pisa 1760).

Bibliography: Hurter Nomencl³ 5.1:1–4. E. PORTALIÉ, DTC 1.2:2485–2501. B. HEURTEBIZE, DTC 2.1:795–796. M. T. DISDIER, DHGE 8:997–998. A. TRAPÉ, EncCatt 2:1469–70.

[A. ROCK]

BERTIERI, GIUSEPPE, theologian; b. Ceva, in Piedmont, Nov. 9, 1734; d. Pavia, July 5, 1806. He was a professor of theology at the University of Vienna. He published *De rebus theologicis* (3 v. Vienna 1774) and *Theologia dogmatica in systema reducta* (Vienna 1778). Though useful in their time his writings are of little value today. He was considered sympathetic to Josephinism and was named bishop of Como in 1789. Though criticized as excessively submissive to the Emperor, he was named bishop of Pavia (1792), where he courageously defended the Church's rights during the French invasion. He was elected a deputy to the assembly at Bologna in 1802.

Bibliography: L. JADIN, DHGE 8:1003–04. D. FALCIONI, Enc Catt 2:1470.

[A. ROCK]

BERTILLA OF CHELLES, ST., Benedictine abbess; b. near Soissons, first half of the 7th century; d. Chelles, Nov. 5, 705–713 (feast, Nov. 5). Following the advice of St. *Ouen of Rouen, she became a nun at *Jouarre-en-Brie, *c.* 659. Bertilla distinguished herself by her virtues, especially obedience. At the request of Queen *Bathildis, she left Jouarre to become the first abbess of *Chelles, where Bathildis later lived in her enforced retreat. There, too, Bertilla was a model of religious life. Her relics are preserved at Chelles-Saint-André, except for her head which is at Jouarre. May 26 is the anniversary of the elevation and translation of her relics in 1185.

Bibliography: MGSrerMer 6:95–109. ActSS Nov. 3: 83–94. Zimmermann KalBen 3:262–263. L. VAN DER ESSEN, DHGE 8:1004–05. Baudot-Chaussin 11:175–177. Butler Th Attw 4:268–269. R. AIGRAIN, *Catholicisme* 1:1503.

[É. BROUETTE]

BERTINUS, ST., Benedictine abbot; b. Orval near Coutances, France, *c.* 615; d. Sithiu, France, Sept. 5, *c.* 709 (feast, Sept. 5). Like his mentor, St. *Omer of Thérouanne, Bertinus came from Normandy and was trained at *Luxeuil. Omer called him to Morinia (modern Pas-de-Calais), which was still only semiconverted. There he succeeded Momelin as abbot of SS. Peter and Paul on the island of Sithiu, when Momelin was elevated to the episcopal see of Noyon-Tournai in 660. At that time the abbey on Sithiu (later called *Saint-Bertin) and the church of Sainte-Marie on the hill were under the same abbot. Bertinus wisely administered the tem-

St. Bertinus and two companions, miniature (Bibl. Mun. Boulogne MS 107, fol. 6ᵛ) attributed to Odbert, abbot of Saint-Bertin near Saint-Omer, France (986–1007).

poral domain of the monastery, and an exchange of property with Momelin is recorded. During his tenure four men came from Armorica (Brittany), asking to be received as monks: Quadanoc, Ingenoc, Madoc, and St. *Winnoc. Bertinus accepted them and built for them a *cella,* or small monastery, at Wormhout, on property he had received from a Flemish noble, Heremarus. When Bertinus began to fail, he called upon Rigobert to help him, and the latter built the church of Saint-Martin on Sithiu. Five years later Bertinus retired and was succeeded by Erlefrid. Almost 100 years old at the time of his death, Bertinus was buried at Saint-Bertin.

Bibliography: ActSS Sept. 2:549–630. MGSrerMer 5:729–769. BHL 1:763, 1290–98. O. BLED, "Les Reliques de saint Bertin . . .," *Mémoires de la Société des Antiquaires de la Morinie* 32 (1914–20) 1–112. L. VAN DER ESSEN, DHGE 8:1006–07. Butler Th Attw 3:493–494. V. REDLICH, LexThK² 2:269–270. **Illustration credit:** Bibliothèque Municipale, Boulogne.

[G. COOLEN]

BERTONIO, LUDOVICO, Jesuit missionary and linguist; b. Rocca Contrada, Ancona, Italy, 1557; d. Lima, Peru, Aug. 3, 1625. He entered the Jesuit province of Rome on Oct. 29, 1575. Assigned to Peru, he arrived in Lima in 1581 and taught humanities there. He was sent to the mission of Juli in the department of Puno, Peru, in 1585 "because he much desired to concern himself with the Indians and he is an angel and has much aptitude for helping them." He made his profession on Nov. 1, 1593. For 40 years he served as a missionary in that Aymara parish. Then, ill of arthritis, he was transferred to Arequipa and then to Lima. In addition to his extraordinary virtues, he was distinguished for his specialization in the Aymara language and for his devotion to the principle of adaptation, even when it ran counter to certain directives of the civil power. He composed two dictionaries, one Spanish-Aymara and one Aymara-Spanish, plus a grammar "with a forest of phrases," a treatise for confession in both languages, and a life of Christ published in Peru and Chile in 1613. His work as a linguist is an indispensable source for the history of linguistic evolution that occurred in Upper Peru.

Bibliography: A. DE EGAÑA, *Monumenta Peruana* (Rome 1954–). J. E. DE URIARTE and M. LECINA, *Biblioteca de escritores de la Compañía de Jesús . . . ,* 2 v. (Madrid 1925–30) 1:477–479.

[A. DE EGAÑA]

BERTRAM OF LE MANS, ST., bishop; b. near Rouen, France, *c.* 550; d. June 30, *c.* 626 (feast of June 30 changed to July 3). The son of a rich land owner, he received the *tonsure at Tours and major orders from *Germain, Bishop of Paris, who appointed him archdeacon. In 586 Bertram became bishop of *Le Mans and, as a loyal supporter of Chlotar II (d. 629), courageously bore imprisonment and harassments during the regime of Theodebert II (d. 612). Upon Chlotar's return to power, Bertram was restored to his see. In 614 he attended the Synod of Paris, and his name appears 16th in the list of prelates who signed the acts of the council (MGConc 1:191). His last will and testament, dated March 26, 616, bears eloquent testimony to his lifelong fatherly concern for the poor and afflicted of his diocese; its churches, especially that dedicated to SS. Peter and Paul which he erected; and also his own

serfs and slaves, whom he manumitted at his death. He was buried in the basilica of SS. Peter and Paul.

Bibliography: Sources. ActSS June 1:699–714. Literature. AnalBoll 26 (1907) 467–468. H. LECLERCQ, DACL 10.2:1490–1520. Gams 562. L. CALENDINI, DHGE 8:930–932. Baudot-Chaussin 6:523–524. E. EWIG, LexThK² 2:270. J. VANDAMME, BiblSanct 3:136–137.

[H. DRESSLER]

BERTRAND OF AQUILEIA, BL., patriarch of Aquileia; b. probably at Château de Saint-Géniès near Montcuq, France, *c.* 1260; d. near Spilimbergo, Italy, June 6, 1350 (feast, June 6). By 1314 Bertrand was licensed in both Civil and Canon Law, having studied at the University of Toulouse. There he was for a time professor while also holding many *benefices. In 1318 he became a pontifical chaplain and heard pleas at the Roman *Rota under *John XXII. He was employed also on diplomatic missions and was rewarded by nomination as patriarch of *Aquileia on July 4, 1334. Bertrand immediately set about reconquering the lands and reestablishing the privileges of his patriarchate. He recaptured the town of Sacile and certain fortresses from the Count of Goritz and then successfully waged war with *Venice. His increasing strength alarmed the city of *Florence, which turned *Benedict XII against him, and the Pope brought about an alliance between the Florentines and Venetians causing Bertrand to lose the ground he had gained. In another attempt to stop the encroachment of the nobles on Church property and their intimidation of its officials, a provincial synod at Aquileia, meeting on April 25, 1339, decreed that grave punishments be meted out to those who threatened the life and liberty of prelates. Bertrand wanted the proscription renewed at the Synod of Padua in 1350, but the cardinal-legate, Guy of Boulogne (d. 1373), preferred to reconcile the patriarch with his enemies. He failed, however, and as Bertrand left the synod, his escort was attacked by the retainers of the Count of Goritz, and he was mortally wounded. Many miracles were attributed to his intercession, and his cult was officially recognized by Pope *Clement VIII on April 27, 1599.

Bibliography: BHL 1:1301–03. G. MOLLAT, DHGE 8:1075–78. C. TOURNIER, *Le Bx. Bertrand de Saint-Géniès* (Paris 1929). P. PASCHINI, EncCatt 2:1482–83. C. SCHMITT, *Un Pape réformateur et un défenseur de l'unité de l'eglise: Benoît XII et l'Ordre des frères mineurs, 1334–1342* (Florence 1959) 241–243, 301–302. Baudot-Chaussin 6:121–124. P. ALBERS, LexThK² 2:271.

[C. R. BYERLY]

BERTRAND OF COMMINGES, ST., bishop; b. Isle-Jourdain (then in the Diocese of Toulouse), *c.* 1050; d. Oct. 16, 1123 (feast, Oct. 16). He was born of a noble family, educated in the Abbey of La Chaise-Dieu, and chosen canon and archdeacon of Toulouse. In 1073 he was elected bishop of Comminges, and energetically served his see for 50 years. He reorganized his ravaged diocese, visiting every section of it. Several times he faced opposition to his preaching, but after one such incident the penitent men of Azon offered to his see in perpetuity all their butter produced during the week before Whitsunday. Apparently this pledge was paid annually until the French Revolution. The story called the "Great Pardon of Comminges," which relates Bertrand's deliverance of a certain thieving lord from Moorish exile and the apparition of the bishop to this prisoner who once vigorously opposed him, is commemorated locally every May 2.

Bibliography: ActSS Oct. 7.2:1140–84. P. BEDIN, *Saint Bertrand, évêque de Comminges, 1040–1123* (Toulouse 1912). L. MÉDAN, DHGE 8:1050–51.

[E. J. KEALEY]

BERTRAND DE GARRIGA, BL.,

early Dominican; b. southern France, *c.* 1172; d. Toulouse, after 1230 (feast, Sept. 6). An early follower and friend of St. *Dominic, he joined the *Dominicans at Toulouse in 1215. On Dominic's frequent journeys, Bertrand, if not taken as a companion, was left in charge of the brethren. He was an eyewitness to many of Dominic's miracles, which he kept secret in obedience to the saint's wishes, and revealed only at the insistence of *Jordan of Saxony. In 1217, Bertrand was sent to Paris; he returned to Toulouse in the following year as prior of St. Romanus, where he remained until his death. He became provincial of Provence, 1221. He was described as prayerful, humble, and austere. Many miracles were performed at his tomb, and 23 years after death his body was reported to be intact. Leo XIII approved his cult in 1881.

Bibliography: Taurisano Cat 9. B. ALTANER, *Der hl. Dominikus* (Breslau 1922). A. TOURON, *The First Disciples of Saint Dominic,* ed. and tr. V. F. O'DANIEL (Washington 1928). V. DE WILDE, DHGE 8:1060–61. G. GIERATHS, LexThK² 2:272.

[L. M. SCHIER]

BERTRAND, LOUIS, ST.,

Dominican preacher and missionary; b. Valencia, Spain, Jan. 1, 1526; d. there, Oct. 9, 1581. He entered the Dominican Order at the convent in Valencia on Aug. 26, 1544, and was

St. Louis Bertrand, portrait attributed to Ribalta, in the possession of Corpus Christi College, Valencia, Spain.

ordained in October 1547. More distinguished for his extraordinary sanctity than for his scholarship, he spent much of his life as master of novices, first serving in that position in Valencia from 1553 to 1555. During the plague of 1557 he went into the city to care for the sick and help bury the dead. His preaching became so famous that the cathedral could not accommodate the crowds and he began preaching in the public squares. In 1562 he went to America as a missionary, working first in the kingdom of New Granada in the Turbará, Palauto, and Turbaco missions. Later he worked in the Diocese of Santa Marta in the area of Tenerife and Tamàlameque, and he also visited several of the West Indian islands. His love and concern for the Indian and Negro brought remarkable results to his missionary work wherever he went. After 7 years in the mission area, just as he was named prior of Santa Fe, he was recalled to Spain. There he became prior of the convent of San Onofre, then master general, and he eventually went back to the convent in Valencia as master of novices and prior. Louis Bertrand was distinguished by his edifying penitential spirit and by the remarkable wonders that accompanied his preaching. Everywhere he was admired for his prudence and his religious spirit. He received extraordinary graces, including the gift of prophecy. He was beatified by Pope Paul V and canonized by Clement X in 1671. He was named patron of the New Kingdom of Granada (now Colombia) in 1690.

Bibliography: V. GALDUF BLASCO, *Luis Bertrán: El santo de los contrastes* (Barcelona 1961). A. DE ZAMORA, *Historia de la provincia de San Antonio,* ed. C. PARRA and A. MESANZA (Caracas 1930). **Illustration credit:** MAS, Barcelona.

[J. RESTREPO POSADA]

BERTRAND, PIERRE,

cardinal and canonist; b. Annonay (southern France), 1280; d. 1349. He was a canon of Notre-Dame du Puy in 1296 and dean in 1314; he taught Canon Law in Avignon, Montpellier (1307), and Paris (after 1312); and in 1312 he was also professor of Roman law in Orléans. From 1314 he was immersed in juridical or political activities, both at the Parlement of Paris (1315) and as a member of King Philip V's Council of State (1318); in 1320 he became chancellor of Queen Joan of Burgundy. When appointed bishop of Nevers in January 1320, he refused the see, accepting instead that of Autun some 4 months later. In 1329 in the famous memorandum *Super jurisdictione ecclesiastica et temporali,* which is his only work to be printed (Paris 1495), he upheld the Church's jurisdiction at a royal consultative assembly at Vincennes. He was subsequently named archbishop of Bourges (1330). In 1331, at the request of the King and Queen, he was made a cardinal. He was entrusted with various papal diplomatic missions. Although a fervent polemicist, he had a taste for erudite works, and compiled in the manner of the period a *Tabula super Decretum* and a *Scrinium iuris.* As a canonist, he has left two important works: an *Apparatus* on the *Liber Sextus* and one on the *Clementinae.* He also added a fourth part to the *De origine jurisdictionum* of *Durandus of Saint-Pourçain, OP. His teaching is very informative on the Church's constitutional problems in the 14th century.

Bibliography: F. DU CHESNE, *Histoire de tous les cardinaux français,* 2 v. (Paris 1660). O. MARTIN, *L'Assemblée de Vincennes de 1329 et ses conséquences* (Paris 1909). M. DÉRUELLE,

DDC 2:789–792. P. Fournier, HistLittFranc 37 (1938) 85–120. Van Hove 1:458, 462. A. M. Stickler, LexThK² 8:351.

[P. LEGENDRE]

BERTULF OF BOBBIO, ST.,

Benedictine abbot; d. Aug. 19, 640 (feast, Aug. 19). A member of a prominent pagan Frankish family, Bertulf was converted to Christianity by *Arnulf of Metz, a near relative, and became a monk at *Luxeuil under Abbot *Eustace (620). A few years later he accompanied Abbot Attala to *Bobbio and succeeded him as abbot there (627). In 628 a conflict with the bishop of Tortona over jurisdiction took him to Rome to discuss the matter with *Honorius I, who, in the first known instance of this procedure, granted Bobbio complete *exemption from episcopal jurisdiction. The account of this mission is found in the life of Bertulf written (642) by *Jonas of Bobbio, who accompanied Bertulf to Rome.

Bibliography: E. de Moreau, DHGE 8:1111. Butler Th Attw 3:356–357. E. Ewig, LexThK² 2:273. BHL 1:1311–15. ActSS Aug 3:750–754. Mabillon AS 2:150–157. MGSrerMer 4:143–152. Jaffé E 1:224. C. Cipolla and G. Buzzi, eds., *Codice diplomatico del monastèro di S. Colombano di Bobbio,* 3 v. (Fonti per la storia d'Italia 52–54; 1918).

[C. P. LOUGHRAN]

BERTULF OF RENTY, ST.,

abbot; b. Germany, mid-7th century; d. Renty, France, Feb. 5, c. 705 (feast, Feb. 5). It is fairly certain that he founded the Abbey of Renty near Saint-Omer, but little else is known of his life, since his biography dates from the late 11th century and appears to depend on material that can be traced no farther back than the 10th century. According to this account he was born a pagan in Germany, went to Gaul, was baptized, and became the *economus* of a count whose properties at Renty he inherited. He later entered the monastic foundation he had made, became abbot, and died there. His relics were transferred from Renty to Boulogne, then to Harlebeke, Belgium (after 935), and finally (955) to Saint-Pierre-de-Gand. They disappeared during the course of the religious wars of the 16th century.

Bibliography: ActSS Feb. 1:681–694. J. Ferrant, *Esquisse historique sur le culte et les reliques de saint Bertulphe de Renty en l'église d'Harlebeke* (Bruges 1898). AnalBoll 17 (1898) 373–374. L. Van der Essen, *Étude critique et littéraire sur les vitae des saints mérovingiens de l'ancienne Belgique* (Louvain 1907) 422–423. E. de Moreau, DHGE 8:1112–13. Zimmermann Kal Ben 1:170–172. R. Aigrain, *Catholicisme* 1:1511.

[P. BLECKER]

BÉRULLE, PIERRE DE

Cardinal, diplomat, theologian, mystic, spiritual writer, founder of the French Oratory, leading figure in the French school of spirituality; b. Chateau de Sérilly, between Sens and Troyes, France, Feb. 4, 1575; d. Paris, Oct. 2, 1629. Born of an old and distinguished family, Bérulle was brought up from infancy in a deeply religious environment in which he developed with such remarkable precocity that at the age of 17 he was considered a master of the spiritual life. He was educated by the Jesuits and at the Sorbonne and was ordained June 5, 1599. That same year he was named honorary almoner of King Henry IV. In 1607 the King proposed to make him tutor to the Dauphin, but Bérulle declined. He also refused repeated and pressing offers of commendatory prelacies and bishoprics, preferring to devote himself entirely to spiritual direction, contro-

versy with Protestants, and the promotion of reform among religious communities. The Augustinians, Benedictines, and Feuillants were among the beneficiaries of his efforts in this last sphere. In his zeal for a spiritual

Pierre de Bérulle.

restoration, Bérulle undertook long and difficult negotiations to introduce the Carmelite nuns of the Teresian reform into France. He, together with André Duval and Jacques Gallemant, was put in charge of these religious by Paul V, but in spite of his spiritual influence upon them he encountered difficulties and resistance with regard to disciplinary matters and the vow of servitude.

After 1605 Bérulle took an interest in the decrees of the Council of Trent concerning the education of the clergy. This led him to found at Paris the Oratory of Jesus, usually known as the French Oratory, modeled after the Oratory of St. Philip Neri. This undertaking was a great success, and the Oratory quickly spread to other places. By the time of Bérulle's death he had established 17 colleges, and his engagement in this work brought him into much disagreeable conflict with the university and the Jesuits.

As confidant and counselor of Queen Marie de Médicis and as friend of Louis XIII, he was a powerful influence for good at court. Besides his work as peacemaker (he effected a reconciliation between the Queen and her son, Louis XIII, in 1620), he engaged in political activity of importance and conducted a number of diplomatic missions for the King. In this he was motivated chiefly by religious rather than nationalistic considerations. He desired to reunite Christians in an effective struggle against Protestantism. Hoping for the conversion of England, Bérulle supported the marriage of Henriette, sister of Louis XIII, to the Prince of Wales, the future Charles I of England, conducted the negotiations with Rome for the dispensation for the marriage, and accompanied the Queen to Great Britain. He refused in 1629 to sign the treaty of alliance with England and the Low Countries because he could not abide the thought of France entering into a compact with Protestants against Catholic Spain. Nevertheless the policy of alliance with the Protestants prevailed, and this put an end to Bérulle's political activity. He fell in disgrace, and Cardinal Richelieu wanted to have him sent from France.

Although he was deeply involved in political affairs, Bérulle remained essentially a contemplative, as is apparent in the many spiritual works that he composed. For the most part these were composed for the occasion, were hastily written, and have the appearance of being unfinished drafts. They are discourses and effusions that express the ardor of his faith rather than treatises in the strict sense. He was eminently a man whose orientation was spiritual; his speculation was joined with prayer in an indistinguishable act of adoration (see M. Dupuy, *Bérulle, une spiritualité d'adoration,* Tournai 1964). His principal works were: *Discours de l'état et des grandeurs de Jésus* (1623, 2° partie 1629); *Élevations à Jésus-Christ sur sa conduite . . . vers S. Madeleine* (1625); *Bref discours de l'abnégation intérieure* (1597); and *Oeuvres de piété* (184 opuscula, ed. G. Rotureau, Paris 1944).

Bérulle was created cardinal in 1627 and died with a reputation for holiness. To his intercession 45 miracles were attributed. At the petition of François Bourgoing, superior general of the French Oratory, Innocent X introduced the process for Bérulle's beatification, but this was interrupted in consequence of Jansenist intrigues.

See also SPIRITUALITY, FRENCH SCHOOLS OF.

Bibliography: *Oeuvres complètes,* ed. J. P. MIGNE (Paris 1856); *Correspondance,* ed. J. DAGENS, 3 v. (Paris 1937–39). J. DAGENS, *Bérulle et les origines de la restauration catholique* (Bruges 1952) 383–387, a complete list of Bérulle's works and MSS; 379–383, of his biographies. J. F. NOURRISSON, *Le Cardinal de Bérulle: Sa vie, ses écrits, son temps* (Paris 1856). M. HOUSSAYE, *M. de Bérulle et les carmélites de France* (Paris 1872); *Le Père de Bérulle et l'Oratoire de Jésus* (Paris 1874); *Le Cardinal de Bérulle et le cardinal de Richelieu* (Paris 1875). A. MOLIEN, *Le Cardinal de Bérulle,* 2 v. (Paris 1947); DictSpirAscMyst 1: 1539–81; DHGE 8:1115–35. A. GEORGE, *L'Oratoire* (Paris 1928). C. TAVEAU, *Le Cardinal de Bérulle, maître de la vie spirituelle* (Paris 1933). B. KIESLER, *Die Struktur des Theozentrismus bei Bérulle und de Condren* (Berlin 1934). R. BELLEMARE, *Le Sens de la créature dans la doctrine de Bérulle* (Ottawa 1959). P. COCHOIS, *Bérulle et l'École française* (Paris 1963). J. MOIOLI, *Teologia della devozione B. al Verbo Incarnato* (Varese 1964). J. H. CREHAN, Davis CDT 1:263–266. J. ORCIBAL, *Le Cardinal de Bérulle: Évolution d'une spiritualité* (Paris 1965).

[A. LIUIMA]

BERYLLUS OF BOSTRA; d. after 244. As an intellectual and the bishop of Bostra in Arabia, Beryllus was the most important person in the Arabia of his day. He was a Monarchian who believed that after the Incarnation the divine nature of the Father entered Jesus Christ. Eusebius tells us that *c.* 244 *Origen disputed with Beryllus and converted him to orthodoxy (*Hist. Eccl.* 6.33.1–4). According to Eusebius (*ibid.* 6.20.2) and Jerome (*De vir. ill.* 60), Beryllus wrote several letters concerning this episode; however, they are no longer extant.

Bibliography: P. GODET, DTC 2.1:799–800. H. RAHNER, LexThK² 2:286. Quasten Patr 2:40, 62. Bihlmeyer-Tüchle 1:162.

[R. K. POETZEL]

BERZELIUS, JÖNS JAKOB, Swedish physician, whose experiments, theories, and books made him the leading chemist of his time; b. Wäfversunda (Linköping), Aug. 20, 1779; d. Stockholm, Aug. 7, 1848. His father, a school principal, died in 1783. In 1785, his mother, née Elisabet Dorotea Sjösteen, married Anders Ekmark, who interested the children in natural history. He died in 1788. Jöns and his sister lived in poverty with an uncle. At 15, after a year at the gymnasium, he became a private teacher, then returned to the gymnasium. He went to the University of Uppsala, where he passed the medico-philosophical examination. In 1801, practicing medicine at Medevi, he cured the hand of an invalid by galvanic currents. With W. Hisinger, a mine owner, he discovered a new earth, cerite, in which C. G. Mosander also found lanthanum (1839). The Karoline Medico-Chirurgical Institute, founded in 1809, elected Berzelius professor of chemistry and pharmacy. His textbook of chemistry was expanded from one volume in 1808 to three in 1816 and to eight volumes in the third edition and its translations.

Impressed by J. B. Richter's work on equivalents and Dalton's atomic theory, Berzelius carried out many analyses with improved methods. In 1814, he published a list of new symbols for 47 elements with atomic weights for 41. He had already begun his dualistic theory, based on his studies of galvanism: each atom has a positive and a negative pole, of which one predominates to make the atom electropositive or electronegative. He regarded the theory as "little more than a play of the imagination," yet its advantage, "that every compound . . . can be divided into two parts, one being positively electric, the other negatively," brought it success. He began an annual review of chemistry and physics in 1821 and continued it through 27 volumes. In this review, *Jahresberichte,* he suggested the new terms isomer, metamer, and polymer (1832), and catalysis (1836). In 1818 he discovered the element he named selenium, and 10 years later the new earth thoria. He was the first to isolate the elements silicon, zirconium, and tantalum.

Bibliography: *Autobiographical Notes,* ed. H. G. SÖDERBAUM, tr. O. LARSELL (Baltimore 1934); *Bref,* ed. H. G. SÖDERBAUM, 6 v. (Uppsala 1912–32). H. G. SÖDERBAUM, *Berzelius' Werden und Wachsen,* ed. G. W. A. KAHLBAUM (Leipzig 1899). A. J. IHDE, "Berzelius," *Great Chemists,* ed. E. FARBER (New York 1962).

[E. FARBER]

BESANÇON, ARCHDIOCESE OF (BISUNTINUS)

Metropolitan see in east France, comprising the departments of Doubs (of which the city of Besançon is the capital) and Haute-Saone and the territory of Belfort; 4,324 square miles in area. In 1964 it had 899 parishes, 1,040 secular and 92 religious priests, 166 men in 21 religious houses, 2,040 women in 242 convents, and 603,000 Catholics in a population of 636,000. Its four suffragans, which had 2,051 parishes, 1,871 secular and 156 religious priests, 3,092 sisters, and 1,403,038 Catholics, were: *Nancy (created in 1777), Saint-Claude (1742) known in early times for St. *Eugendus and for Condat Abbey, Saint-Dié (1777) from a chapter of Augustinians dating from St. Deodatus in 669, and Verdun (4th century). The city of Besançon, with 73,445 people, on both banks of a bend in the Doubs River, was the center of Franche-Comté.

Besançon, capital of the Gallic *Sequani,* was taken by Caesar and became in 238 the center of a province (*Maxima Sequanorum,* named after Emperor Pupienus Maximus). Pancharius, the first known bishop, attended the pseudocouncil of Cologne (346). Ruined by invasions of Alamanni (4th century) and Hungarians (10th century), Besançon was restored by the energetic Bp. Hugh of Salins (1031–67), who founded the temporal power of the bishops, imposing himself as suzerain on neighboring feudal lords. A commune and an imperial

The city of Besançon on the Doubs River.

free city under the nominal suzerainty of the Emperor, Besançon was a little republic from 1290 to 1674. Wars in the 14th century brought spiritual and material ruin. Besançon was held by the dukes of Burgundy and the Spanish Hapsburgs (1567) before Louis XIV conquered it (1674) and fortified it as the capital of the County of Burgundy, replacing Dôle as an administrative and intellectual center. Its bishops include St. *Donatus (d. *c.* 660); Cardinal Antoine de *Granvelle (1585–86), chancellor of Charles V; the Tridentine reformer Antoine-Pierre I de Grammont (1662–98), who founded the seminary; and Cardinal Adrien-Jacques Marie Mathieu (1834–75). The two saints mentioned by Gregory of Tours (d. 593) as apostles of Besançon, Ferreolus (d. *c.* 212) and Ferrucius, connected with the legend of St. *Benignus, have a poor historical base. St. *Helena (d. *c.* 330), Constantine's mother, stayed in Besançon. Nicholas, father of Cardinal Granvelle, and Pope Callistus II, born at Quingey in the family of the counts of Burgundy, are also noteworthy citizens. The 12th-century cathedral has apses at both ends. Councils (444, 1123–24) and the imperial diet (1157) where Frederick I Barbarossa threatened papal legates are famous. There have been many diocesan synods in Besançon.

The diocese originally corresponded to the Gallo-Roman *civitas*, with suffragan bishops of *Equestres* (Nyons, later Belley), of *Helvetes* (with the see in Ehl, Windisch, Avenches, and Lausanne in turn), and of Basel. Invasion and divisions between Merovingian kings disrupted the province, and Besançon lost its title of metropolitan and became suffragan to *Lyons. Frankish conquests returned the title and four suffragans until the French Revolution. In 1742 the Abbey of *Saint-Claude was made a see, taking parishes from Besançon. The *Concordat of 1801 gave Besançon the territory of Doubs, Haute-Saone, and Jura with *Autun, *Metz, *Strasbourg, Nancy, and *Dijon as suffragans. The changes of 1817–22 restored Saint-Claude (Jura) and gave to Besançon as suffragans Strasbourg, Metz, Verdun, Belley, Saint-Dié, and Nancy. After the Franco-Prussian War, Metz and Strasbourg became immediately subject to the Holy See (1870), and the Alsatian territory of Belfort (formerly under Strasbourg) was attached to Besançon. Before the Revolution there were many religious establishments in the

diocese: 21 collegiate chapters, 21 men's abbeys (Faverney, with the Eucharistic miracle of 1608; *Luxeuil, founded by St. *Columban in the 6th century), and 12 women's abbeys. The university founded in Dôle (1422) was moved to Besançon (1671); its faculties of theology and canon law were suppressed in the 19th century. The diocese has several pilgrimages; a chapel at *Ronchamp was built by Le Corbusier.

Bibliography: J. GAUTHIER, *L'Université de Bescançon* (Besançon 1900). A. MONNOT, *Le Vieux Besanéon religieux* (Besançon 1956). P. BROUTIN, *La Réforme pastorale en France au XVIIe siècle*, 2 v. (Tournai 1956) 1:309–329; 2:301–310. M. PERROD, DHGE 8:1144–62. E. JARRY, *Catholicisme* 1:1516–20. AnnPont (1965) 64. **Illustration credit:** French Embassy, Press and Information Division, New York City.

[E. JARRY]

BESCHI, COSTANZO GIUSEPPE, Italian Jesuit missionary in South India and the foremost Christian poet in the Tamil language; b. Castiglione, Italy, Nov. 8, 1680; d. Manapar, India, Feb. 4, 1747. During studies at Rome he mastered Greek, Latin, French, Portuguese, and other European languages. He joined the Society of Jesus in 1698, left for India; after some time in Goa he reached Tirunelveli in the extreme south (1711) and later proceeded to Madura (1716). He became expert in Tamil under the guidance of a noted scholar, Supradīpa Kavirāyar, and learned Sanskrit, Telugu, and other South Indian languages, as well as Persian and Urdu. He composed poems, dictionaries, grammars, and manuals on religious, didactic, and medical themes, and wrote Tamil grammars in Latin; he also translated the *Kural* into Latin verse.

Like another Italian Catholic missionary in the South, Robert de *Nobili, Beschi adopted the customs of the Tamils in diet and dress and won their affection and trust. During his long ministry of about 35 years, he built many churches, and he spread the gospel through his Tamil writings. It is said that he won the confidence of the Moslem ruler of Trichinopoly (1736) and indeed served as his *diwan* (prime minister); but when the Marathas took over (1741), Beschi went to Ramnad and Tirunelveli and retired a few years before his death.

Beschi is more popularly known in southern India as Vīramāmunivar (The Heroic Sage) and Dhairyanāthar (Lord of Courage). As the author of the first Tamil dictionary, *Chaturaharāthi,* he is called the father of Tamil lexicography; as the author of the Tamil grammar, *Tonnūl Vilakkam,* he seems to have advocated certain innovations in Tamil orthography; his Tamil prose writings—religious as well as secular—like those of De Nobili, have helped to lay the foundations of modern Tamil prose. Among his poems are the hagiological *Kiṭṭēriammāl Charitram* (On the Martyr St. Quiterea) and *Tēmbāvani* (1726, Unfading Garland), his magnum opus. This epic is divided into 3 parts, 36 cantos, and 3,615 stanzas. The reference in the opening verse to "three worlds" and the fusion of philosophy and theology with a drama that is both human and divine have led critics to hail Beschi as the Tamil Dante. Beschi was obviously steeped in the ancient Tamil classics—for example, the *Jīvakachintāmani* and the *Rāmāyana* of Kamban—and he naturally followed the Tamil epic tradition when he composed this work on the life of Joseph and Mary, set in the background of the Old and New Testament world. *Tēmbāvani* has been described as "the noblest poem in honor of St. Joseph written in any literature East or West."

Bibliography: C. G. BESCHI, *Tembavani* (Madras 1849). Sommervogel 1:1402–09. Streit-Dindinger 6:30–41, 53, 55, 64, 83, 84, 88, 92, 106. M. LEDRUS, DHGE 8:1167–70. E. LAMALLE, EncCatt 2:1490–91. M. S. VENKATASĀMI, *Christianity and Tamil* (Madras 1948), in Tamil. L. BESSE, *Father Beschi of the Society of Jesus: His Times and His Writings* (Trichinopoly 1918).

[K. R. SRINIVASA IYENGAR]

BESOLD, CHRISTOPH,

German jurist, writer, and political scientist; b. Tübingen, Sept. 22, 1577; d. Ingolstadt, Sept. 15, 1638. In his legal studies he formed a close friendship with Johann *Kepler. He was much esteemed as professor of law at *Tübingen (1610–35), and consultant for the civil administration. He read nine languages, and studied Scripture, the Fathers, and mystics, thus fostering an inclination toward Catholicism. His public conversion took place at Heilbronn in 1635 (not 1630, cf. Hurter Nomencl 3.347). In 1636 he became professor of Roman law at Ingolstadt, and had received an invitation from Urban VIII to teach at Bologna when he died. Besold is generally recognized for nobility of character as well as for his learning, though his conversion is sometimes ascribed to self-interest. He published documents from the Stuttgart archives to prove that the dependency of the Wurtemberg monasteries on the empire (*Reichsunmittelbarkeit*) required the dukes to restore confiscated religious property. He is the author of 92 publications, noted for vast erudition, clarity, and juridical precision, and important for the history of the Thirty Years' War.

Bibliography: H. GÜNTER, *Das Restitutionsedikt von 1629* (Stuttgart 1901) 294–306. J. GRISAR, DHGE 8:1178–80. E. NIETHAMMER, NDB 2:178–179. H. TÜCHLE, LexThK² 2:300.

[G. J. DONNELLY]

BESSARION, CARDINAL

Fifteenth-century Greek bishop, theologian, and humanist; b. Trebizond, Jan. 2, 1403; d. Ravenna, Italy, Nov. 18, 1472. Originally of a modest family, Bessarion was apparently adopted by the Metropolitan Dositheus of Trebizond and educated in rhetoric, philosophy, and asceticism at Constantinople, where he had Manuel Chrysococcus for a master and *Filelfo and George Scholarius (*Gennadius II Scholarius) as fellow students. Under the guidance of the archbishop of Selymbria, he took the monastic habit (Jan. 30, 1423), changed his name from Basil (not John) to Bessarion, and wrote an encomium in honor of the 5th-century saint thus chosen as his patron. He became a deacon in 1426. Ordained in 1431, he traveled to Mistra in the Peloponnesus, studied with George Gemistos, *Plethon, and wrote a series of *monodia,* or panegyrics, for the court. He settled a dispute between the Emperor and his brother, the despot Theodore II of Morea (1436), and was recalled to Constantinople and made hegumen, or abbot, of the monastery of St. Basil.

In preparation for the Council of *Florence, he was created archbishop of Nicaea (1437), and he sailed with the Emperor and Greek delegation to Venice. At the Council, both in Ferrara and Florence, he served with Mark *Eugenicus of Ephesus as spokesman for the Greeks; eventually he accepted the Roman position on the *filioque and procession of the Holy Spirit and helped win over most of the other Byzantine delegates.

Cardinal Bessarion, 18th-century engraving after a contemporary portrait in Santa Maria Caritatis, Venice.

He signed the decree of union (June 6, 1439) and, despite an offer to remain in the Roman Curia, returned to Constantinople (Feb. 1, 1440), where he wrote three public letters of consolation to the Emperor on the death of his wife, and took part in the election of the new patriarch of Constantinople, Metrophanes II (March 1, 1440).

When created a cardinal by Pope *Eugene IV, Bessarion returned to Florence (Dec. 10, 1440); signed the decree of union with the Jacobites (Feb. 5, 1442); and consecrated the Franciscan church of the Holy Cross. He returned to Rome with the Curia (Sept. 28, 1443) and took up residence close to his title church of the 12 Apostles. Bessarion quickly achieved a perfect knowledge of Latin and Italian. He was charged with the beatification process for St. Bernardine of Siena (1449), and he served as papal legate to settle a peace between Venice and Milan (September 1449). He was made papal governor of Bologna (1450–55) and went on embassies to Naples (1457), Germany (1460–61), Venice (1463), and France (1472), in the vain hope of stirring the rulers of these lands to join a crusade against the Turks. On his return from an unsuccessful mission to King Louis XI of France he died at Ravenna; his body was returned to his title church in Rome, and Nicholas Capranica delivered his panegyric.

Bessarion's early writings were mainly court elegies, panegyrics, and letters. Before the Council of Florence, influenced by the doctrine of Thomas Aquinas concerning essence and existence in God, he had rejected the doctrine of Gregory *Palamas in a defense of the writings of *John XI Beccus. At the council he delivered a *Dogmatic Oration* in favor of union, helped compose most of the Greek speeches, and wrote the treatises on the Eucharist and the epiclesis. After the council he published a refutation of the Syllogisms of Mark Eugenicus against the council; a "Justification of the Union" addressed to Alexis Lascaris Philanthropinus (c. 1444); and a *Letter to the Despot Constantine* on the defense of Greece. Appointed protector of the Greek monks in Italy, he wrote an epitome of the rule of St. Basil, reorganized their government, held a general chapter for the Basilians (1446) and supervised visitations. He was endowed with numerous benefices and used the revenue in aiding the Italian humanists and Greek émigrés, both princes and scholars. After the fall of Constantinople (1453) he determined to collect all the extant Greek literature, both classic and patristic, and before his death he bequeathed a library of over 30 cases of MSS to St. Mark's in Venice (1468).

He had secured the patronage of Popes Nicholas V, Paul II, and Pius II for having both the classic and patristic Greek literature translated into Latin. He aided and protected such humanists as *Poggio Bracciolini, Laurenzo *Valla, and *Platina, who also wrote a panegyric in his honor. Bessarion had translated some of Aristotle's works, and he wrote a *De natura et arte* and turned most of his own Greek writings into Latin. With his *In calumniatorem Platonis* Bessarion defended the Greek philosopher's reputation and provided the West with a good knowledge of Plato's philosophy, demonstrating its reconcilability with both Aristotle and Christianity. On the death of *Isidore of Kiev he was made patriarch of Constantinople (1463) and sent an encyclical to the Greeks living under Turkish rule. In 1470 he wrote an *Oration to Princes* calling them to a crusade; it was spread in northern Europe by William Fichet of Paris. Bessarion had encouraged L. Valla in his application of philological principles to textual criticism of the Bible, and composed a tract on the pericope in the Gospel of John (21.22). A man of deep piety and universal scholarly interests, he played a crucial part in the development of the Italian *Renaissance.

Bibliography: PG 161:137–746. Mansi 31:893–966. L. Mohler, *Kardinal Bessarion,* 3 v. (Paderborn 1923–42), ed., v.2 *In Platonis calumniatorem,* v.3 circle of scholars, v.1, chronology of life and works; to be corrected according to R. Loernertz, OrChrPer 10 (1944) 116–149, and EncCatt 2:1492–98. E. Candal, OrChrPer 4 (1938) 329–371, Thomas Aquinas; *ibid.* 6 (1940) 417–466, council; ed., *Oratio dogmatica* (Rome 1958). G. Hofmann, OrChrPer 15 (1949) 277–290, letters. H. Vast, *Le Cardinal Bessarion* (Paris 1878). P. Joannou, AnalBoll 65 (1947) 107–138, St. Bessarion. L. Bréhier, DHGE 8:1181–99. A. Palmieri, DTC 2.1:801–807. Beck KTLBR 767–769. A. G. Keller, CambHistJ 11 (1955) 343–348. J. Gill, *The Council of Florence* (Cambridge, Eng. 1959), index 435. B. Kotter, LexThK² 2:301.

[F. X. Murphy]

BESSARION OF EGYPT, ST., 5th-century Egyptian monk (feast, June 17). He is known as a miracle worker and founder of a pilgrim shelter in Jerusalem and of a monastery on Mt. Sion. Bessarion, or Passarion, is to be distinguished from a number of similarly named saints in the synaxarions and menologies. He is mentioned in the vita of St. Euthymius by *Cyril of Scythopolis and is said to have accompanied Bishop Juvenal of Jerusalem when he consecrated the laura of Euthymius in 429. He is also thought to have presented the Emperor Theodosius II (425–450) with the hand of St. Stephen the protomartyr as a relic. An encomium on him was written by Cardinal *Bessarion.

Bibliography: ActSS June 4:240–243. F. Delmas, ÉchosOr 3 (1899–1900) 162–163. E. Schwartz, ed., *Kyrillos von Skythopolis* (TU 49.2; 1939) 26–27, 90. P. Joannou, AnalBoll 65 (1947) 107–138, encomium and details of life. O. Volk, LexThK² 2:301–302.

[F. X. Murphy]

BESSEL, GOTTFRIED VON, Benedictine statesman and historian; b. Buchen, Baden, Sept. 5, 1672; d. Göttweig, Austria, Jan. 22, 1749. He made his religious profession at Göttweig, and was ordained in 1696. In 1703 he was appointed vicar-general and supreme judge of the Archdiocese of Mainz. He was employed on various diplomatic missions, three to Rome to settle differences between the Pope and the Emperor. In 1710 he returned to Göttweig and in 1714 was elected abbot, an office he held for 35 years, twice meanwhile serving as honorary rector of the University of Vienna. In rebuilding his abbey after it was destroyed by fire in 1718, he undertook to make it a center of art and learning, collecting treasures of archeology and art and enriching the library with thousands of volumes, chiefly on historical topics, as well as incunabula and MSS. His *Chronicon Gottwicense* is a monumental work in diplomatics.

Bibliography: P. Volk, DHGE 8:1207–08. A. Pratesi, EncCatt 2:1499. L. Koller, *Abtei Göttweig* (Göttweig 1953). J. Wodka, LexThK² 2:302.

[O. L. Kapsner]

BEST SELLERS, a term applied almost exclusively to books of wide popular appeal, which seems to have originated in 1895 when the monthly magazine, the *Bookman* (since defunct), began to print a list of "Books in Demand" in bookstores of several of the larger cities of the U.S. By 1903, this monthly listing was limited to six titles and was widely noted in newspapers. Since then, a weekly listing of best-selling fiction and nonfiction is a feature in many newspapers and journals, notably in the New York *Times'* and the New York *Herald-Tribune's* Sunday book-review sections, and in *Publishers' Weekly.*

What makes a best seller is difficult to define, since sales are affected by a variety of influences. Political and economic conditions of a particular period, the amount of money budgeted by the publisher for the advertising or promotion of a particular book, its choice by one or another of the more popular book clubs are among the reasons for increased sales. It is even more difficult to analyze best sellers on a basis of subject matter. A study of best-seller titles over 50 years indicates that religion, in some form or other, is the most consistent best-seller material in both fiction and nonfiction. The promise of success in personal, social, or business relations, and instructions on "how to do it" (e.g., cookbooks) provide a second important ingredient. Historical novels, detective stories, books about animals, adventure stories, and biographies follow in popularity. The treatment of sex, whether in good or more lurid taste, is also a consistent element in the making of these popular books. It seems, therefore, that a combination of religion, sex, and adventure provides the most successful formula for a best seller. In most instances, serious critical esteem has little to do with determining whether or not a book will reach the best-seller lists.

The cultural effect of the best sellers is debatable. The more popular books are not necessarily the best books, either morally or artistically, but excellent books not infrequently appear on lists. A reader who reads only best sellers will not grow culturally or intellectually, but a dicriminating use of some of the books that "everybody is reading and talking about" can help a reader to keep abreast of worthwhile contemporary issues, problems, and movements.

See also PAPERBACKS; LITERATURE, POPULARIZATION OF; BOOK CLUBS, CATHOLIC.

Bibliography: A. P. HACKETT, *Sixty Years of Best Sellers, 1895–1955* (New York 1956). F. L. MOTT, *Golden Multitudes* (New York 1947). J. D. HART, *The Popular Book* (New York 1950).

[R. F. GRADY]

BESTIARY

A type of short medieval beast allegory of didactic purpose, written in verse or prose. One may trace the bestiary to the *Physiologus* (4th century) and treat rather as natural history those traditions that derive from Aristotle. During the Middle Ages, the bestiaries fused myth and legend with characteristics of certain regions; with religious symbols; or later, with practical problems of the training, breeding, and medical care of domesticated animals. The genre varied with the dominant preoccupations of given periods, and its golden age extended through the 13th and 14th centuries. Importance is attached to bestiaries by the fact that literatures of many countries derived a vast amount of beast lore and legendary material from their sources.

Early Types. Until about 1230, progress of a scientific kind was not widespread, and variations in natural science resulted from arbitrary rearrangements of animal lore to fit certain projects. If we consider Pliny's *Historia naturalis* an objective survey of the field, Solinus's *Collectanea rerum memorabilium* appears to have been a reaction against rationalism and objective science, and St. Isidore's *Etymologiae* a return to the encyclopedic type of objectivity. Running concurrently with these works, the *Physiologus* maintained an immutable form and scope, with strong Christian symbolism; the characteristics of these works mingled in the vast compilations of Bartholomeus Anglicus and Vincent of Beauvais.

Pliny had given a vast repertory of mammals (Book 8), fishes (Book 9), and birds (Book 10), either briefly described as a catalogue, or developed in some detail. He classified fish according to shape and other traits (9.36, 43–44), and as polyps (9.46–48) or crustaceans (9.50–52); but classifications were implicit in the groupings of domestic animals (8.69–77); birds were categorized as having claws or webbed feet, or as being able to speak or transmit omens (10.13). Pliny was interested particularly in animals that have some immediate relationship to man; and he noted anecdotes relative to customs and to the faithful services of dogs, horses (8.61, 64–69), and dolphins (9.7–10) and wrote of animals that had been seen in Rome. His most ex-

tensive information came from Africa and Asia; northern animals, such as the Scythian elk (8.15–16), were rare; the detailed chapter on the bear (8.54) is noteworthy. Of the few fabulous creatures that he treated, the basilisk and mantichora—a man-headed lion—(8.33, 45), the Indian whale and the phoenix (9.2, 10.2) reappeared in bestiaries.

Exotic Developments. The Plinian formula yielded to the irrational and exotic presentation of the *Collectanea rerum memorabilium* of Solinus, who introduced details basic in the later bestiaries and whose colorful accounts appealed strongly to medieval compilers. Insofar as the *Collectanea* was a survey of geography, it was based in part on Mela's *De Situ orbis*. Solinus, however, reduced the classical and archeological content of his model and developed the treatment of animals and stones as the principal noteworthy exotic curiosities in specific countries—Greek partridges and Numidian bears; and beavers, dolphins, cranes, and such fabulous monsters of Africa and India as the mantichora and the monoceros; he boldly passed from legend to generalities and included a multiplicity of sphinxes and gorgons.

The picturesque and the exotic were counteracted by St. Isidore's *Etymologiae* (PL 82). This book, tending strongly to offer objective fact, was one of the principal prototypes of the later encyclopedias. Isidore made extensive use of Solinus without in any way reducing the esteem held for this source. His Book 12 gathered the animals by categories, domestic and familiar (ch. 1), beasts of prey (ch. 2), *De minutis animantibus* (ch. 3), *De serpentibus* (ch. 4), *De vermibus* (ch. 5), *De piscibus* (ch. 6), and *De avibus* (ch. 7–8). The *Etymologiae* was popular among the revisers of the *Physiologus* as well as the encyclopedists for its verisimilitude and its incisive presentations.

Among Isidore's sources was the *Hexaemeron* of St. Ambrose (PL 14), constructed according to the "days" of Creation. The presentation of fishes and birds is exactly that of the *Physiologus,* with mention of a few physical or moral traits, and a Christian moralization for each. In Book 5 of the *Etymologiae* the birds (ch. 12–23) correspond well with those in the *Physiologus,* with the noteworthy terminal addition of the "gallus." Book 6, hastily compiled, treats the animals pell-mell and without formal moralizations, and quite inappropriately, after the fox, includes the partridge as equally "fraudulent," with some 50 words copied verbatim from the Latin *Physiologus.*

Influence of the Physiologus. The *Physiologus* was in fact the other major formative tradition of the bestiaries. This 4th-century Latin text, preserved intact in very few copies, was enriched in several steps by the use of Solinus and of Isidore, and had finally become the massive *De Bestiis et aliis rebus,* in turn expanded to four books (PL 177). Transpositions and eliminations in Books 2 and 3 hide the origins. Book 3, which should open with a prologue ("*Bestiarum vocabulum . . .*") and the chapter on the lion, is an amplification of *versio L* (in 27 chapters) attributed to Chrysostom; it is extant in more than 20 MSS, and was published by M. R. James as *The Bestiary* (Oxford 1928), in 112 chapters, but 13 more should be added, e.g., from MS Harley 3244, etc. The innovations included the tiger, bear, and bee; dogs were presented as in Pliny. The compiler copied verbatim from the *Etymologiae* the

Ciuitas syrie que nunc tyrus dicit. olim
serra uocabat a pisce quodam qui illic
abundabat. quem sua lingua sar apellat
ex quo diruatu est hui similitudinis pis
ciculos sardas. sardinas _____ q̃ uocari.

The Serra or Saw Fish, illumination in an English bestiary, possibly from Lincoln, c. 1185 (Morgan MS 81, fol. 69). The sea symbolizes the world, the sailors represent those who pass safely through its dangers, and the Serra is the symbol of those who exercised themselves in good works but fell into the waves through various sins.

orous, nocturnal, domestic, and more or less intelligent; he discussed physiological traits, explaining all such variations in the light of moral and religious criteria. The immense *Speculum naturale* of Vincent of Beauvais consisted of notes.

Falconry. Books on hunting birds and their care and training suddenly appeared early in the 13th century and seem to have been derived from technical manuals of Persian origin. The visit of the Emperor Frederick II to the East in 1230 sets a probable date. The many tracts were interrelated and appeared both in Sicily and in Provence. Their source is sometimes identified as one "Moamin," who used an Arabic model; some scholars consider Theodorus, named in 1239, the source; another person frequently credited was an anonymous author involved in the *Libro del Gandolfo Persiano*, a book devoted primarily to medical treatment and training. By the mid-century, a tract attributed to a King Dancus, and Daude de Pradas's *Dels auzels cassadors* appeared. These treatises were not, strictly speaking, bestiaries, but were so closely related as to deserve mention.

The most significant medieval book on falconry was the *Tractatus de arte venandi cum avibus* of Frederick II, revised by his son Manfred, and translated into French late in the 13th century. Frederick presumably composed this book himself shortly before 1250, after a decade of research and observation, and he may have

Illuminated page from "Manafi al-Hayawan" or "Advantages Derived from Animals," by Ibn Bakhtishu, Persian, end of the 13th century (Morgan MS 500, fol. 36 v). This famous volume, the earliest surviving manuscript of the Persian Mongol school, was written at Maragha near Tabriz and gives less fanciful information than the better-known European bestiaries.

treatment (ch. 43–54) of snakes and worms (*Etym.* 12.4–5), fish, precious stones, and trees (*Etym.* 17.7); the last mentioned is traceable ultimately to Dioscorides or Vitruvius. Book 1 dwells at great length on a few birds, especially doves, geese, chickens, and peacocks (ch. 1–55), and the domestic Accipiter (ch. 13–16). Book 2 deals with 36 creatures, of which the *crocodilus, ibex, canis, lupus,* and *draco* alone are not derived from the *Physiologus;* they are developed by the addition of moralizations. Book 4 is a convenient dictionary covering the names found in the preceding sections; of the 400 or more names, 300 appear in Book 3.

Flowering of the Genre. The 13th century brought the flowering of the bestiaries, either in the older pattern used by Solinus, according to regions and as a function of geography, or in massive forms convenient for reference. *L'Image du monde,* composed in French about 1250, and attributed to Gossouin or Gautier of Metz, is a *mappe-monde* or survey of the world, more realistic than that of Solinus; it was translated into English and published several times before 1500; it included dragons, elephants, the mantichora, and several magic stones. *De Proprietatibus rerum,* by Bartholomeus Anglicus, was translated into Italian in 1309 and into French in 1372, and printed more than 15 times from 1482. In Book 12, Bartholomeus presented the birds mentioned in the Bible, and cited Isidore, Ambrose, and Aristotle's *De Animalibus;* Book 18, dealing with 115 animals, proposed such classifications as carniv-

directed the preparation of the fine illustrations. He used Aristotle as a point of departure, noting many of his errors and questionable hypotheses, and undoubtedly he knew other books of Eastern origin, such as the *De scientia venandi per aves* of Moamin, which he had translated around 1240. His principal source, however, beyond the practical knowledge from the falconers he brought to Italy in about 1230, was his own experience. After *De arte venandi,* the principal medieval treatises on falconry were the *Deduiz de la chasse* of Gaston Phébus, composed by 1370 and often printed, and the *Livre de la chasse du roi Modus.*

Later Developments. One may illustrate the status of the bestiaries in about 1260 by the contents of Brunetto Latini's *Li Livres dou Tresor.* Latini compiled and translated from a wide range of Latin sources. Intending his encyclopedia as a manual for the well-informed ruler, he selected rather than accumulated and used a well-organized plan. In his first book he surveyed general knowledge, including history (according to St. Isidore); geography (according to Solinus); and natural science, with a short tract on farming (based on that by Palladius) and a bestiary dealing with 70 animals, each developed in some detail and in symmetrical form.

Latini's basic source was the expanded *Physiologus* as found in Book 3 of *De Bestiis et aliis rebus,* further enriched from the *Etymologiae,* the *Collectanea,* and St. Ambrose. The moralizations disappeared along with almost all of the fabulous creatures and mystic stones. The animals were fairly well grouped as fish, birds, and mammals, each in its own alphabetical series. From *De Bestiis* Latini borrowed the mole and the peacock; from Solinus, the parrot, dog, and bear; and from Palladius, in part as an aspect of husbandry, a group of chapters on domestic animals, chickens, geese, cattle, horses, and sheep. Latini's chapters on hunting birds alone were gathered in a special group out of alphabetical order, and reflected the same kind of interest that one finds in *Dels auzels cassadors* and in the *Libro del Gandolfo Persiano.* Latini added no new information, but his selective method reflected a rational didactic purpose and a tendency to avoid sheer accumulation of detail.

Use of Semitic Lore. As a last step in compilation of intriguing and exotic creatures, we may mention the introduction of medieval Semitic lore through Bochart's *Hierozoicon,* about 1660. In methodical fashion, Bochart enriched a broad classical bibliography on the whale (Aelian, Aristotle, Homer, Nearchus, Philostratus), not only with the full Old Testament documentation on large fish (including the Leviathan), but also with that of the Hebrew *Porta caeli* and of the 12th-century *Miracula rerum creaturarum,* by Alkazuinus. He included also a work of Muhammad ad-Damir, which was his main source for *De dubiis vel fabulosis* (tragelaphus, myrmecoleon, gryphes) and *Aves fabulosae apud Arabes;* in it we find an echo of the *Zend-Avesta* in the Simorgh-Anka, a kind of "coq d'or."

See also ANIMALS, SYMBOLISM OF; ART, EARLY CHRISTIAN; SYMBOLISM, EARLY CHRISTIAN; SYMBOLISM, RELIGIOUS.

Bibliography: F. CARMODY, "De Bestiis et aliis rebus and the Latin Physiologus," *Speculum* 13 (1938) 153–159. B. LATINI, *Li livres dou Tresor,* ed. F. J. CARMODY (Berkeley 1948). FRIEDRICH II, *The Art of Falconry,* tr. and ed. C. A. WOOD and F. M. FYRE (Stanford 1943), critical translation of Friedrick's *De arte venandi* with bibliographies for Daude de Pradas, Dancus, etc. S. BOCHART, *Opera omnia,* 3 v. (4th ed. Utrecht 1712), sources listed in 2:62–63. F. T. McCULLOCH, *Medieval Latin and French Bestiaries* (Chapel Hill, N.C. 1960). **Illustration credit:** The Pierpont Morgan Library.

[F. CARMODY]

BETANCUR, PEDRO DE SAN JOSÉ, VEN.

Founder of hospital, school, and homes for the poor; b. Chasna, Tenerife Island, March 1626; d. Guatemala City, Guatemala, April 25, 1667. Brother Pedro Betancur (or Bethancourt) was a descendant of Juan de Bethancourt, one of the Norman conquerors (1404) of the Canary Islands. His immediate family, however, was very poor and his first employment was shepherd of the small family flock. In 1650 he left for Guatemala,

Pedro de San José Betancur, 18th-century engraving.

V.P.FR. PETRUS A S. IOSEPH DE BETANCUR
Fund. Ord Hospital Fratrum Bethlemitarum cuius virtutes in gradu heroico approbavit.   Clem.XIV.P.M.25 Iulii 1771

where a relative had preceded him as secretary of the governor general. His funds ran out in Havana and Pedro had to pay for his passage from that point by working on a ship. He landed in Honduras and walked to Guatemala City, arriving there on Feb. 18, 1651. So poor was he that he had to join the daily bread line at the Franciscan friary. In this way he met Fray Fernando Espino, a famous missionary, who befriended him and remained his lifelong counselor. Through Fray Fernando Pedro was given work at a local textile factory, which also employed culprits condemned by the court. At least, he could support himself. In 1653 he entered the local Jesuit college of San Borja in the hopes of fulfilling his main purpose in coming to America—that of becoming a priest. His complete incapacity in school soon forced him to give this up. However, he had met in the college Manuel Lobo, SJ, who was his confessor throughout his life.

Fray Fernando invited him to join the Franciscan Order as a lay brother, but Pedro felt that God called him to remain in the world. Hence, in 1655 he joined the Third Order of St. Francis and took the tertiary habit as his garb. By this time his virtues were widely recognized in the city. In 1658 María de Esquivel's hut was given to him and Pedro, remembering the experiences of his first desperate days in Guatemala, immediately began a hospital (Nuestra Señora de Belén) for the convalescent poor, a hostel for the homeless, a school, and an oratory. From then on all his time was spent in alleviating the sufferings of the less fortunate. He begged alms with which to endow Masses to be celebrated by poor priests; he also endowed Masses that were to be celebrated at unusually early hours so that the poor might not have occasion to miss Mass because of their dress. He also had small chapels erected in the poorer sections where instruction was also given to the children. On August 18 he would gather the children and have them sing the Seven Joys of the Franciscan Rosary in honor of the Blessed Mother, a custom that passed to Spain but today remains only in Guatemala. On Christmas Eve he inaugurated the custom of imitating St. Joseph in search of lodgings for the Blessed Mother. Many historians see in this practice the origin of the famous *posadas* now so characteristic of Christmas in Central America and Mexico.

The gentle and kind Pedro died in his hospital, hoping that his companions would carry on the many works he had begun for the poor, the sick, and the less fortunate. In 1709 his cause for beatification was presented to Rome. In 1739 he was declared a servant of God; on July 25, 1771, his virtues were declared heroic by Clement XIV. Recent years have brought new interest in the life and virtues of the man who has been called the "St. Francis of the Americas." The cause of beatification has profited greatly from this interest.

Bibliography: F. VÁZQUEZ, *Vida y virtudes del venerable Hermano Pedro de San José Betancur*, ed. L. LAMADRID (Guatemala City 1962), containing the narrative by M. LOBO. D. VELA, *El Hermano Pedro en la vida y en las Letras* (Guatemala City 1935). **Illustration credit:** Library of Congress.

[L. LAMADRID]

BETANZOS, DOMINGO DE, Dominican missionary in Española and Mexico, inquisitor in Mexico, founder and first provincial of the province of Santiago de Mexico; b. León, Spain, *c.* 1480; d. Valladolid, Spain, September 1549. He earned a licentiate in civil law at the University of Salamanca, and then was a hermit for 5 years on the island of Ponza. According to Cuervo, Betanzos was professed at the Convent of San Esteban, Salamanca, May 30, 1511, and he was ordained in Seville on his way to America. According to Biermann, Betanzos and seven other Dominicans, on Oct. 8, 1513, were registered as passengers on Capt. Juan de Medina's vessel. Betanzos arrived at Española about the beginning of 1514 and was one of 12 Dominicans who went to Mexico in 1526. Within a year five died, and four returned to Spain. Betanzos, a priest, Gonzalo Lucero, a deacon, and Vicente de las Casas, a novice, were the only Dominicans left in Mexico. Twenty-four more Dominicans arrived in 1528, and Betanzos went with his companions to Santiago, Guatemala, in 1529. About January 1531 he was recalled to Mexico. The same year he made a trip to Naples, Italy, hoping to discuss with the ailing general the matter of the formation of an independent Mexican province. The general died in October 1531, and at Rome in 1532 Betanzos saw the new general. By the authority of Pope Clement VII, on July 11, 1532, the province of Santiago de Mexico was instituted independent of the Dominicans of Española. By July of 1534 Betanzos had obtained all the necessary documents and by the end of 1534 he reached Mexico, with the title of vicar-general. On Aug. 24, 1535,

Domingo de Betanzos, fresco at Tepetloaxtoc, Mexico, dating probably from the first half of the 16th century.

Betanzos was elected provincial, and he served from 1535 to 1538.

Bibliography: J. CUERVO, *Historiadores del convento de San Esteban de Salamanca,* 3 v. (Salamanca 1914–15). F. R. DE LOS RÍOS ARCE, *Puebla de los Angeles y la Orden dominicana,* 2 v. (Puebla 1910–11). A. M. CARREÑO, *Fray Domingo de Betanzos* (Mexico City 1924). B. BIERMANN, "Die Anfänge der Dominikanertätigkeit in Neu-Spanien und Peru," ArchFrPraed 13 (1943) 5–58. J. J. DE LA CRUZ Y MOYA, *Historia de la santa y apostólica Provincia de Santiago de Predicadores de Mexico en la Nueva España,* 2 v. (Mexico City 1954–55). **Illustration credit:** Archivo Fotografico, Instituto Nacional de Antropología, Mexico.

[A. B. NIESER]

BETANZOS, JUAN DE, chronicler and linguist; b. Spain, 1510; d. Peru, March 1, 1576. Little is known of his early life. He apparently took no part in the major events of early Peruvian history, for his name is not on any of the early lists. The date he went to Peru is not known. Certainly he was not there before the civil wars. In those wars he sided with Gonzalo Pizarro and was with Carbajal on the expedition to Charcas. Later he supported La Gasca against Gonzalo and received an encomienda as a reward. Married to a daughter of Hayna Cápac, he became one of the first Quechuists of Peru. While living in Cuzco, he wrote one of the early catechisms in Quechua. He served as an intermediary between the viceroys and the Incas and seems to have arranged the renunciation of royal power by Sayri Tupac. Viceroy Antonio de Mendoza ordered him to write down the Inca traditions, and so he produced his famous work, *Suma y narración de los Incas*. It is a chronicle from the legends of origin to the reign of Pachacutec. Apparently only part of it is extant; that part is primarily a biography of Inca Yupanqui (Pachacutec), who was an empire builder and a great reformer. This work first presents the idea that the Inca empire was late in being established. The style is generally poor and difficult to read; the work resembles an epic tale in prose, written in a mediocre fashion. Some scholars have suggested that it is the translation of a Quechua epic. However, there is important information in it on Inca ceremonies and architecture.

Bibliography: R. PORRAS BARRENECHEA, *Cronistas del Perú 1528–1650* (Lima 1962).

[J. HERRICK]

BETANZOS, PEDRO DE, Franciscan missionary;

b. place and date unknown; d. near Chómez, Costa Rica, c. 1570. He came to New Spain in 1542. After a few months in Mexico, he mastered the Mexican language. In 1543 Toribio *Motolinía took Betanzos to Guatemala, where he quickly learned the three native languages, Kiche, Tzutuhil, and Cakchiquel, so perfectly that the Indians said he knew them as well as they did. He composed a grammar of Cakchiquel in cooperation with Francisco de Parra, who introduced several symbols for sounds not found in Spanish. He translated a group of prayers, which became the basic prayer formula for the Indians, and with Juan de Torres he prepared a catechism in the Indian language. His work was criticized by the Dominicans because he insisted on retaining the Spanish word *Dios* for God rather than using the Indian word, which he considered tainted with idolatry. His usages were eventually accepted. In the 1550s he moved on with the conquerors into Honduras-Costa Rica, where with four other friars he laid the foundations for the province of Honduras.

Bibliography: F. VÁZQUEZ, *Crónica de la provincia del Santísimo nombre de Jesús de Guatemala*, ed. L. LAMADRID, 4 v. (Guatemala 1937–44) 1:119–128; 2:171–178.

[F. B. WARREN]

BETH-SAMES (BETH-SHEMESH), ancient

Canaanite city on the site of modern Tell er-Rumeileh, near Ain Shems, 15 miles west of Jerusalem, on the lowlands between the hill country and the coastal plain of Palestine. Although designated as a Levitical city (Jos 21.16) and located on Juda's northern boundary (Jos 15.10), Beth-Sames (Heb. *bêt šemeš*, house of the sun) was probably identical with Ir-Sames (*'ir šemeš*, city of the sun) in Dan (Jos 19.41) and Har-Hares (*har-heres*, mountain of the sun) that remained in Canaanite possession for some time after the Israelite invasion (Jgs 1.35). During Samuel's lifetime, it was in Israelite hands, since the ark was received by the Bethsamites with great joy and with sacrifices to *Yahweh (1 Sm 6.9–15). It was listed in Solomon's second

administrative district (3 Kgs 4.9). Joas of Israel defeated *Amasia, King of Juda, at Beth-Sames c. 798 B.C. (4 Kgs 14.8–14). In the reign of *Achaz, the *Philistines occupied the city for some time (2 Chr 28.18).

Excavations on the site by D. Mackenzie (1911–12) and by Elihu Grant (1929–33) uncovered a very reduced habitation in the Hellenistic period and five successive cities dating from c. 2200 to 586 B.C. City VI (2200–1700), recognized only by pottery and stone utensils, was probably destroyed by the *Hyksos. City V (1700–1500), in which ruins of buildings were found, was probably a victim of Egyptian campaigns under Thutmose I. City IV (1500–1200) reveals signs of great prosperity along with evidence of two devastating destructions. The first was caused shortly before 1350, possibly by *Habiru; the second c. 1200, perhaps by the Israelites (but see Jgs 1.35). City III (1200–1000), much less prosperous, was burned down probably by the Philistines. City II shows three stages (1000–950; 950–825; 825–586). Storehouses indicate that it was the center of a rich farming district. After *Nabuchodonosor destroyed Beth-Sames in 586, it remained uninhabited for several centuries. The last stage, dating from the Hellenistic period, includes traces of a Byzantine monastery. Among the important finds are a clay tablet inscribed in the script of *Ugarit and reading from right to left (c. 1400); an *ostracon with writing from the Late Bronze Age identified as hieratic Egyptian [L. H. Vincent, RevBibl 41 (1932) 281–284], and some examples of early Hebrew writing, including three jar handles stamped with the words "belonging to Eliakim, steward of Yaukim" (Joachim).

Bibliography: E. GRANT, *Beth-Shemesh (Palestine)* (Haverford, Pa. 1929); *Ain Shems: Excavations I–III* (Haverford 1931–34); *Ain Shems: Excavations IV–V* (Haverford 1938–39). E. POWER, DBSuppl 1:975–981. L. HENNEQUIN, *ibid.* 3:331–335. Abel GéogrPal 2:282. EncDictBibl 234–235. H. HAAG, LexThK² 2:315–316. B. MARIANI, EncCatt 2:1511–13.

[T. C. SCHAUB]

BETH-SAN (BETH-SHAN), ancient Canaanite

fortress city strategically located at the eastern end of the Valley of *Jezrael, where it meets the Jordan Valley. The imposing mound of ruins on the site (Tell el-Huṣn), near the modern village of Beisān, was first excavated by C. S. Fisher of the University of Pennsylvania Museum in 1921. The work, which continued until 1933 under the successive leadership of Alan Rowe and G. M. Fitzgerald, uncovered some 17 levels of occupation in the 70 feet of debris forming the mound. The earliest settlement is ascribed to the late Chalcolithic Age (c. 3300 B.C.). The wealth of architectural and inscriptional material unearthed clearly shows that the city was under Egyptian influence throughout the 3d and much of the 2d millennium. *Thutmose III, who reoccupied Beth-San after his victory at *Mageddo (c. 1468), recognized its value as a garrison point to control the important east-west trade route from Transjordan to the Mediterranean Sea. Although Beth-San was originally within the territory of *Issachar, it was assigned to *Manasse (Jos 17.11). But even this warlike tribe was unable to conquer the city (Jgs 1.27); besides the fact that the Israelites were unable to penetrate the massive double wall fortifications, the defenders employed iron chariots, which seem to have frightened the invaders

(Jos 17.16). Thus Beth-San long maintained its independence as a Canaanite enclave. The Philistines, however, succeeded where the Israelites had failed, for they had occupied the place before their victory over Saul; the Philistines' mutilation of the slain King and his three sons took place in Beth-San (1 Sm 31.8–13). The city finally succumbed to Israelite pressure in the reign of David. Solomon established the city as a headquarters of one of his tax districts (3 Kgs 4.12). The Egyptian King *Sesac probably included Beth-San in his devastating raid in the time of King Roboam of Juda (3 Kgs 14.25–26). The city remained an important place through Hellenistic times (during which it was known as Scythopolis; see Jdt 3.10; 2 Mc 12.29–31). It was later recognized by Pompey as one of the free cities of the Roman *Decapolis. Beth-San has proved exceptionally rich in cultic remains. The foundations of four Canaanite temples have been delineated (two were rededicated by the Egyptians to Mekal/Resheph and *Astarte). The many religious statuettes and cult appurtenances recovered there have aided toward filling out the picture of external influences on Israelite worship.

Bibliography: EncDictBibl 235–236. L. HENNEQUIN, DBSuppl 3:421–426. H. HAAG, LexThK² 2:315. T. ANTOLÍN, EncCatt 2:1513–14.

[T. KARDONG]

BETHANY, name of two places mentioned in the NT. The first is near Jerusalem, east of the Mount of Olives, and is probably to be identified with the Anania settled by Benjaminites returning from the Exile (Neh 11.32). The name (Βηθανία) is possibly derived from Hebrew bêt-'ănānyâ, house of Anania. In later times the name changed to Lazarium because the tomb of Lazarus was located there. The shrine there became a much venerated pilgrim spot. Today the Arabs call it el-Azariyeh. Here were the homes of Lazarus, Martha, and Mary (Jn 11.1) and of Simon the leper (Mt 26.6; Mk 14.3). Jesus passed through Bethany on Palm Sunday (Mk 11.1; Lk 19.29) and spent the following nights there (Mt 21.17; Mk 11.11). He went out toward Bethany before He ascended into heaven (Lk 24.50). S. Saller excavated the site from 1949 to 1953, and found evidence of at least five churches, two chapels, an abbey, other buildings, and a cemetery. Findings in a nearby olive grove show that the area began to be inhabited in the 6th century B.C.

The location of the other Bethany on the east side of the Jordan, whose existence is attested in Jn 1.28 (according to most manuscripts), is uncertain. The name of this Bethany may be derived from Hebrew bêt-'ênôn "place of springs" (cf. Jn 3.23).

Bibliography: EncDictBibl 228–229. A. BARROIS, DBSuppl 1:968–970. D. TRISOGLIO, EncCatt 2:1506–07. W. VAN WINKEL, LexThK² 2:305–307. Abel GéogrPal 2:243, 255. S. J. SALLER, *Excavations at Bethany (1949–1953)* (Studium biblicum franciscanum 12; Jerusalem 1957). C. KOPP, *The Holy Places of the Gospels,* tr. R. WALLS (New York 1963). **Illustration credit:** Mr. and Mrs. Ross W. Sloniker Collection of 20th Century Biblical and Religious Prints, Cincinnati Art Museum.

[S. MUSHOLT]

"The Anointing at Bethany," woodcut by the American artist Mario Pitocco (1933–   ).

BETHARRAM FATHERS

Popular name for the Congregation of the Priests of the Sacred Heart of Jesus of Betharram (PSCJ), founded in 1832 at Bétharram in the Department of Basses Pyrénées in southwestern France, near Lourdes, by St. Michael *Garicoïts. Its chief ministries are preaching domestic and foreign missions, conducting retreats, parish work, spiritual direction of religious women, and educational work in schools, colleges, and seminaries.

Members are clerics or brothers, who follow the rule of St. Augustine, but possess their own constitutions. They take three simple vows, temporary at first, then perpetual. For many years the community consisted of priests alone, owing to the will of the local bishop who opposed the founder's ideas. The Holy See approved the institute with the *decretum laudis* (July 30, 1875); and the *decretum approbationis* (Sept. 5, 1877), obtained by Father Auguste Etchécopar (1830–97), third Superior General and the most eminent disciple of the founder. Etchécopar's cause of beatification was introduced in 1945.

At the head of the congregation is a superior general and four counselors, elected for 12 years by the general chapter. These appoint the provincial and local superiors and provincial counselors. The superior general's curia was at Bétharram, but was expected to move to Rome soon after 1964.

Members aim to develop the dispositions of the Heart of Jesus, especially those of love and obedience to the will of His Father for the salvation of the world. The principal mottoes are: *Ecce venio* (Behold I come); and *Fiat voluntas Dei,* or F.V.D. (God's will be done).

During the founder's lifetime the congregation spread into South America, to Buenos Aires (1856) and Montevideo (1861). Until the 20th century, growth was slow. The persecutions of 1903, which forced religious from France, favored expansion. In 1964 members numbered 503, of whom 368 were priests, living in 50 houses in 14 countries: France, Italy, Spain, England, Algeria, Morocco, Ivory Coast, Jordan, Israel, Thailand, Brazil, Argentina, Uruguay, and Paraguay. Its 19 schools in 1962 had 12,037 students.

Bibliography: F. VEUILLOT, *Les Prêtres du Sacré-Coeur de Bétharram* (Paris 1942).

[P. DUVIGNAU]

BETHEL, ancient city and sanctuary on the site of the modern town of Beitîn, 12 miles north of Jerusalem. Archeology has determined that Luza, as the city was originally called (Gn 28.19), was first occupied *c.* 2200 B.C. When Abraham visited its vicinity about 4 centuries later (Gn 12.8), it was a flourishing Middle Bronze Age city with heavy fortifications and elaborate buildings. Though it was probably the site of an ancient Canaanite sanctuary, its continuance as an Israelite one was connected with a tradition that both Abraham and Jacob (Gn 35.1–7) had set up altars there to Yahweh. Jacob was credited (Gn 28.19) with renaming the place (Heb. *bêt'ēl*, house of God; but originally, house of the god El). After a silence of several centuries, the quiet and prosperity of Bethel were shattered by the invading Israelites (Jgs 1.22–25). Clear archeological evidence of a devastation of the Canaanite town toward the end of the 13th century B.C., overlaid by a much less developed occupation, proves the substantial historicity of the account of the Israelite capture of the place as given in Jgs 1.22–25. Modern research has relegated the parallel account of the destruction of *Hai as given in Jos 8.1–29 to an etiologic explanation of the extensive but much more ancient ruins near Bethel. Samuel's annual tour of towns included Bethel (1 Sm 7.16). Bethel's location, so close to Juda's expansion into Benjamin's territory (Jos 16.1–2; 18.12–13; 3 Kgs 14.30), made it a constant object of strife in the divided kingdom (2 Chr 13.19). Added to this was the fact that *Jeroboam I of Israel chose Bethel as the chief northern sanctuary and the rival of Jerusalem. The temple and golden calf that he established there (3 Kgs 12.26–13.32) were the object of severe censure by Osee (Os 4.15–19; 10.5). Amos had already accused this sanctuary of luxurious and hypocritical worship (Am 4.4–5; 5.21–25) and had been expelled from it (Am 7.12). The people of Juda often referred to Bethel as Bethaven (*bêt 'āwen*), "house of wickedness" (Os 5.8; Jos 7.2; 18.12; etc.). During the Assyrian occupation (after 721 B.C.), Bethel escaped destruction. The conquerors even dispatched one of the exiled priests to care for its sanctuary (4 Kgs 17.28). When *Josia controlled Bethel, its altar and *high place were included in the general destruction of all sanctuaries except the Temple in Jerusalem (4 Kgs 23.14). Bethel escaped the common destruction in 587, when the Babylonians ravaged all of Juda. During the exilic period, however, the town experienced rapid decline, and only a few Benjaminites were mentioned as peopling it in the reconstruction period (Ezr 2.28). It regained its former prosperity in Hellenistic (1 Mc 9.50) and Roman times and flourished until late in the Byzantine period. The excavations carried out at Bethel in 1934 by W. F. Albright and J. L. Kelso, and again in the 1950s by the latter, were very successful and fruitful in illuminating the problems and background of the OT.

Bibliography: Abel GéogrPal 2:270–271. EncDictBibl 229–230. H. HAAG, LexThK² 2:307–309. D. TRISOGLIO, EncCatt 2:1507–08. L. HENNEQUIN, DBSuppl 3:375–377. BullAmSchOrRes 29 (1928) 9–11; 55–58 (1934–35); 74 (1939) 17–18; 137 (1955) 5–10; 151 (1958) 3–8; 164 (1961) 5–19. J. L. KELSO, "Excavations at Bethel," BiblArchaeol 19 (1956) 36–43.

[T. KARDONG]

BETHESDA, name of a pool near the Sheepgate in Jerusalem where Jesus cured a man infirm for 38 years (Jn 5.2–9). Excavations have revealed the outlines of a large oblong pool in the location; this pool was provided with five porches (as in St. John's description—see 5.2), four lateral and a fifth central to divide the pool into two parts. A Hebrew graffito found there proves that the building existed before the time of Hadrian (A.D. 118), and it has been concluded that the complex was the work of Herod the Great (37–4 B.C.). At the site may now be seen a reconstructed pool and the foundations of a 5th-century Byzantine church.

The reading and derivation of the name of the pool are disputed. Bethesda (Βηθεσδά) is usually derived from the Aramaic *bêt ḥesdā'*, "house of mercy." Many, however, prefer the MS reading Bethzatha [Βηθζαθά, from Aramaic *bêt zētā'*, "house of olives" (?)]. J. T. Milik, however, believes that both readings and their derivation can be explained with the aid of a topographical reference in the Copper Scroll (11.12) found among the *Dead Sea Scrolls. The reading *byt 'šdtyn* he understands to mean a rectangular double (note the dual ending) reservoir; Bethesda, then, would transliterate the singular form of the word, Bethzatha the emphatic plural.

It is to be noted that the reference to the angel who regularly "went down into [or, according to some MSS, "washed himself in"] the pool" to stir up the water is probably not part of the original Gospel text. Textual evidence suggests that these words were originally a marginal gloss containing the popular explanation of the movement of the water referred to in Jn 5.7 (probably caused by an intermittent underground stream) and the healing properties attributed to it, which was later incorporated into the text by a copyist.

Bibliography: EncDictBibl 231. L. HEIDET, DB 1.2:1723–32. C. KOPP, LexThK² 2:332. L. H. VINCENT and F. M. ABEL, *Jérusalem nouvelle,* 2 v. in 4 (Paris 1912–26) 2:669–684. J. JEREMIAS, *Die Wiederentdeckung von Bethesda, Johannes 5, 2* (Göttingen 1949). J. T. MILIK, RevBibl 66 (1959) 347–348.

[J. E. WRIGLEY]

BETHLEHEM

Modern Bethlehem is a small town (population about 15,000) in the Hashemite Kingdom of Jordan, 6 miles south of Jerusalem. It is situated on a limestone ridge of the Judean highland, running east-northeast, overlooking to the west the main highway from Jerusalem to Hebron. The ridge is about 2,500 feet in elevation and forms a sort of semicircle with two little elevations at the ends. The Basilica of the Nativity is located on the southern end (*see* PALESTINE, 9). Originally the spot was more isolated from the village proper. Many of the streets are narrow and lined with substantially built, cubical, flat-roofed stone houses revealing how the city may have looked at the time of Our Lord.

Several Canaanite cities bore the name Bethlehem, which is thought by some scholars to have meant "Sanctuary of Lahm (god of grain)," although it has almost certainly no connection with the god Laḥmu or the goddess Laḥamu of the Sumerians. Others prefer not to go

Southern section of modern Bethlehem, seen from the east, from above the traditional "Shepherds' Field." In the center, the Basilica of the Nativity, partly hidden by surrounding monasteries, over the cave that since the early Christian centuries has been regarded as Christ's birthplace. To the right, site of the OT town.

further than the obvious meaning of the Hebrew form of the name *bêt-leḥem*, "house of bread." The modern Arab name for the town is Beit Laḥm, "house of meat." *Ephrata, another name of the place, means "fruitful." All these names seem to be a reflection on the natural fertility of the environs.

Bethlehem is already mentioned before the Israelite conquest in the *Amarna Letters (14th century B.C.) as belonging to the district of Urusalim (Jerusalem). After the conquest, the Calebite (1 Chr 2.19, 24, 50) clan of Ephrata settled in the vicinity of Bethlehem (1 Sm 17.12; Ru 1.2). Later the name Ephrata was applied to Bethlehem itself (Jos 15.59; Ru 4.11; Mi 5.1). Bethlehem was the native town of the Levite who became Micha's officiating priest (Jgs 17.7–13) and of the unfortunate wife of the Levite from Ephraim (Jgs 19). It was also the setting for the love idyll of Ruth, the Moabite, and Booz, David's ancestor, as told in the book of *Ruth. Other famous Bethlehemites were Jesse, David's father, and the sons of Sarvia (Zeruiah), David's sister (2 Sm 17.25). These nephews of David were Joab, Abisai, and Asael (2 Sm 2.18; 1 Chr 2.16). Loyal but ruthlessly cruel, they became at once a protection and a menace to their royal relative. Young David roamed the hills and fields around Bethlehem as a shepherd boy (1 Sm 17.15) and later was anointed king of a new dynasty there by Samuel (1 Sm 16.1–13). In the early years of David's reign Bethlehem fell for some time to the Philistines. This was the occasion for the courageous errand to a Bethlehem well, narrated in 2 Sm 23.13–17; 1 Chr 11.16–19. Roboam, son and successor of King Solomon, fortified Bethlehem to guard the approach to Jerusalem (2 Chr 11.6). After the fall of Samaria (721 B.C.) and the consequent end of the kingdom of Israel, the prophet Michea (5.1–3) announced the future birth of the Messiah, the new David, at Bethlehem. The village was repeopled after the Exile (Ezr 2.21; Neh 7.26), but it remained in obscurity until the birth of Our Lord (Mt 2.1, 5–8, 16; Lk 2.4, 15; Jn 7.42).

Bibliography: Abel GéogrPal 2:276. R. LECONTE, "Bethlehem aux jours du roi Herode," *Bible et Terre Sainte* 15 (1958) 4–9; *ibid.* 42 (1961) a whole number on Bethlehem with excellent photos. C. KOPP, *The Holy Places of the Gospels,* tr. R. WALLS (New York 1963) 1–48. **Illustration credit:** Wolfe Worldwide Films.

[E. LUSSIER]

BETHLEHEM FATHERS. The Foreign Mission Society of Bethlehem (SMB) is one of 14 pontifical communities under the direct jurisdiction of the Congregation for the Propagation of the Faith. The society, founded in Immensee, Switzerland, in 1921 by Pietro *Bondolfi, the first superior general, consists of 408 members (1964) whose exclusive purpose is missionary work and the education of native clergy. In Switzerland there are: a motherhouse, a major and a minor seminary, and two preparatory seminaries. The society is governed by the superior general, who is elected by the general chapter for a 10-year term, and four assistants general. Regional superiors guide the activities in their respective territories.

The Bethlehem Fathers are engaged in missionary work in Southern Rhodesia, Japan, Formosa, and Colombia. They have made some notable contributions in Japan, where George Sturm is the leading Catholic musician and Charles Freuler has been influential in religious architecture. The society's missions in Manchuria, established in 1926, and in Peking (1946) ceased because of Communist pressure in 1954. Missionary refugees from China, arriving in Colorado in December 1948, established a mission 2 years later at Cheyenne Wells. The rapid extension of the enterprise prompted Urban J. Vehr, Archbishop of Denver, to sanction the transfer of the establishment to his see city in 1955. Land was purchased for the development of the existing foundation into a future regional residence with adequate school facilities.

The spirit of the Bethlehem Fathers is that taught by Christ from the crib in Bethlehem, a spirit of simplicity that accepts everything from God in a childlike manner. Members of the society make a solemn promise in which the three customary vows are included in a modified way.

Bibliography: A. RUST, *Die Bethlehem-Missionare, Immensee* (Fribourg 1961).

[A. J. BORER]

BETHLEHEMITES, a former hospital order of men and women under the Rule of St. *Augustine. Its presence in England is attested by *Matthew Paris in 1257, but his account is vague and probably confused. The order's only well-known foundation was the hospital of St. Mary of Bethlehem in London, established in 1247; St. Mary's housed mental patients well before the Dissolution under *Henry VIII. In 1547 it became a royal establishment for the care of lunatics, and its unenviable reputation gave the word bedlam to the language. A few other hospitals and churches are known (there was one in Scotland, one in Pavia, Italy, and one in Clamécy, in the Diocese of Auxerre). All were under the direction of the bishop of Bethlehem, whose see was transferred to Clamécy in the 14th century, where he built on a site previously given (like the site of the London hospital) to the bishop and chapter of Bethlehem; the Clamécy house survived to the French Revolution. The habits worn by the brothers and sisters attached to the order's hospitals featured a red star, and this design has led to unfortunate confusion with a quite distinct, but equally obscure, Bohemian hospital order, the *Cruciferi cum stella,* established in Prague in the 13th century.

See also HOSPITALS, HISTORY OF, 1.

Bibliography: GallChrist 12:686–699. *The Register of John Le Romeyn, Lord Archbishop of York,* part 1 (*Publications of the Surtees Society* 123; Durham 1913) xviii, 1–2. D. E. EASSON, *Medieval Religious Houses: Scotland* (London 1957). For several other groups, see M. T. DISDIER, DHGE 8:1253–54.

[R. W. EMERY]

BETHPHAGE, the hamlet mentioned in Mt 21.1; Mk 11.1; and Lk 19.29 as the place where Jesus began His triumphal entry into Jerusalem. The name (Βηθφαγή) is of Semitic origin and means "house of green figs." The location has not been identified with certainty, but most probably it was on the eastern slope of the Mount of Olives. Here, in 1876, a stone block, dating from the period of the Crusades, was found; a carving on it shows Jesus sitting on an ass, the people with palm branches, and the resurrection of Lazarus. Archeological evidence points to a rather intense occupation of the area from the 2d century B.C. until the 8th century A.D.

Bibliography: EncDictBibl 232–233. C. KOPP, LexThK² 2:314. Abel GéogrPal 2:279. B. BAGATTI, "Le pitture medievali della Pietra di Betfage," *Studii biblici franciscani liber annuus* 1 (1950–51) 227–246. S. J. SALLER, "The Archeological Setting of the Shrine of Bethfage," *ibid.* 11 (1960–61) 172–250. C. KOPP, *The Holy Places of the Gospels,* tr. R. WALLS (New York 1963) 267–268.

[S. MUSHOLT]

BETHSABEE (BATHSHEBA), daughter of Eliam, partner in *David's adultery, later his wife, and mother of King *Solomon (2 Sm 11.2–27; 12.24); she may have been the granddaughter of Achitophel (2 Sm 23.34). Bethsabee (Heb. *bat-šeba'*, daughter of abundance) had been the wife of Uria the Hittite before David's sin with her; when David was unable to make Uria appear responsible for Bethsabee's pregnancy, he arranged for Uria's death in battle and was rebuked for his double crime by the Prophet *Nathan. The adulterine child died, but later Bethsabee, now married to David, gave birth to Solomon, Sammua, Sobab, and Nathan (2 Sm 12.24; 1 Chr 3.5). Bethsabee, acting in concert with Nathan, induced David to proclaim Solomon king in place of Adonia, David's oldest living son (3 Kgs 1.5–40). When she later acceded to Adonia's request and asked Solomon to permit Adonia to marry Abisag, David's erstwhile concubine, the request, since it could be interpreted as an attempt by Adonia to establish a claim to the throne (see 2 Sm 16.20–22), resulted in his death (3 Kgs 2.13–25). Bethsabee is referred to, though not named, in the genealogy of Jesus (Mt 1.6).

Bibliography: EncDictBibl 233. A. PENNA, EncCatt 2:1510.

[F. BUCK]

BETHULIA, strategically located city guarding the plain of *Esdraelon (Jdt 4.6 in the Septuagint), which becomes the focal point of activity in the narrative of the book of *Judith. No city by this name has ever been discovered outside the book in which it figures so largely. A town called Bathuel or Bethuel existed far to the south, in the area of the Negeb (1 Chr 4.30) and was in the possession of the tribe of Simeon, to which both Judith and Ozia (the civic leader of Bethulia) belonged (Jdt 6.11; 8.1); but although Bethulia might be a corrupted form of this name, the location makes any identification impossible. The same must be said for the town of Betylion in the Gaza strip that is mentioned in a decree of Ptolemy IV (221–203 B.C.) and was identified with Bethulia as early as the 6th Christian century. Abandoning the attempt to discover the city by name, geographers and exegetes have concentrated on sites in the area in which Bethulia is said to have existed. No small number of identifications, most of them in the neighborhood of Tell Dothan, have been proposed, but there is no more agreement in the matter today than there was 75 years ago. Of those suggested, however, modern Sheikh esh-Shibel and Sanûr have received long-standing support. Given the character of the Book of Judith, it seems best to suppose that the author has deliberately veiled the scene of his plot in order to emphasize the symbolic values in which he is primarily interested. In this respect the opinion of those who regard Bethulia as being merely a transliteration of the Hebrew *beṭûlâ* (virgin) is probably correct. In this event, of course, the "virgin city" could stand for "virgin daughter Jerusalem" or for any other place the reader might choose.

Bibliography: Abel GéorgPal 2:283. F. STUMMER, *Geographie des Buches Judith* (Stuttgart 1947). EncDictBibl 237. F. DINGERMANN, LexThK² 2:316–317.

[J. E. BRUNS]

BETROTHAL (CANON LAW)

The notion of betrothal (from Old English *bi,* to a greater degree, and *trouthe,* truth), the promise to marry or give in marriage, gains in clarity by the consideration of kindred terms and their etymologies. The ancient Germans called their betrothal practice *beweddung;* the root *wed* is Anglo-Saxon and means a pledge or a surety. Thus, the English word "wedding" is derived from this term because betrothal, originally preceding actual marriage, became in the course of time part of the nuptial ceremony itself.

Among the early Latins betrothals were called *sponsalia,* from the verb *spondere,* to promise or stipulate. The ancient Greeks used the word σπονδαί, which originally signified libations offered to the gods in the espousal ceremony. Early Hebrew practice called for solemnities prior to marriage. These were *thenaim* or *schidduchim,* which properly meant the promise of the parents or guardians to give the girl in marriage.

Although canon 1017 of the Code of Canon Law and canons 6 and 7 of the Codification of Oriental Canon Law (CrebAllat) do not directly define betrothal, they refer to it as a bilateral and as a unilateral contract. When both parties agree to take each other as future spouses, the agreement is regarded as a bilateral betrothal contract. When one party promises to marry and the other party accepts this promise of future marriage, the agreement is regarded as a unilateral espousal or engagement contract.

Earlier ecclesiastical law followed the definition of Pope Nicholas I (858–867): Espousals (betrothals) are pacts of promise of future marriage. Hence canonical betrothal may be defined as a contract of promise to marry in the future. This is practically the same wording found in Justinian's Code.

Validity. To meet canonical requirements and to be legally acknowledged by the Church, the promise of marriage must be internal, that is, true; literal; and specific, that is, determinate as to time of fulfillment. Furthermore, in the bilateral type it must be mutually and freely exchanged; in the unilateral form the promise must be freely proposed by one party and freely accepted by the other party.

For validity of the contract it is required that the promise be: written, witnessed by the bishop or pastor or two lay witnesses, and signed by the contractants. The Church invalidates in both the internal forum of conscience and the external forum of its ecclesiastical courts an espousal agreement in which any of the foregoing conditions is lacking. The bishop or the priest alone will suffice as sole legal witness, but in his absence two lay witnesses are mandatory. The priest must be the pastor of at least one of the contractants in order to qualify as the sole legal witness. Delegation of another priest to act as sole witness is not permitted in the Western Church.

On the part of the principals, the pair must possess physical, mental, and juridic capacity to enter into the betrothal pact. Canon Law does not lay down any minimal age, as it does for marriage, but since contractual obligation to marry is involved, the couple must enjoy the knowledge and freedom necessary for so serious a step. Child betrothals of the past did not bind until the above-mentioned conditions were ratified on the occasion when the couple attained sufficient knowledge and freedom to become affianced of their own volition.

Binding Force. Once the betrothal contract has been duly signed by all concerned, six obligations flow from the action: (1) The parties must wed within the time specified in the contract or within a reasonable waiting period (3 months to 1 year). (2) The betrothed parties must associate with each other in a manner conformable to custom, circumstance, and moral considerations. (3) Each must avoid undue familiarity with others and mutually bestow the usual signs of affection without falling into sins of incontinence. (4) Neither may validly enter into a new engagement with another party until the first betrothal is lawfully dissolved. (5) Neither may licitly contract marriage except with the other, unless the pact ceases to bind—as will be explained below. (6) On the unjustifiable breach of the promise to marry, the guilty party is bound to recompense the innocent party for any resultant damages sustained by the unprovoked infidelity, short of enforcing the marriage itself. Marriage may never be enforced in virtue of the betrothal contract, as marriage is valid only when freely contracted.

Rescinding the Contract. Sufficient grounds to rescind the betrothal contract are: mutual consent; failure to fulfill the conditions stipulated in the contract, e.g., marriage within a specified period; entry into the seminary or religious life; appearance of any diriment impediments to the contemplated conjugal union; violation of espousal fidelity, e.g., desertion, incontinence with another; serious change in circumstances that would militate against a happy marriage, e.g., loss of income, employment, physical health, mental health, moral health, or emotional health; prudent foreknowledge of an unhappy union gained subsequent to the engagement; parental dissent, when this is reasonable and justified, e.g., when proffered because of the youthfulness, incompetence, or immaturity of the boy and girl and the foreseeable failure to maintain a stable marital life; papal dispensation for just and reasonable causes. Authorities below the Roman pontiff cannot dispense but may declare any of the above factors present and prejudicial to a successful marriage.

Bibliography: R. NAZ, DDC 5:838–846. Abbo 2:1017. Woywod-Smith 1:982–989. W. SMITH, *Dictionary of Christian Antiquities*, 2 v. (Hartford 1880) 1:202–204. *Roman Ritual*, tr. and ed. P. T. WELLER, 3 v. (Milwaukee 1946–52) 1:588–594. Cappello Sac 5:82–138. C. WRZASZCZAK, *The Betrothal Contract in the Code of Canon Law* (CUA CLS 326; Washington 1954). G. JOYCE, *Christian Marriage* (2d rev. ed. London 1948) 50.

[C. WRZASZCZAK]

BETTI, UGO

Italian poet and dramatist; b. Camerino (Marche), Feb. 4, 1892; d. Rome, June 9, 1953. He began writing poetry as a prisoner during World War I (*Re pensieroso*, 1922). After completing studies in law he became a magistrate at Parma, and then transferred to Rome in 1931. His first work for the theater, *La Padrona*, won a prize in 1927. Thereafter, without entirely abandoning poetry, Betti wrote 25 plays. Unlike the theater of *Pirandello, Betti's plays, in themes and characters, are developed and receive their meaning within an unmistakable Judaeo-Christian tradition. Whereas Pirandello's characters are doomed to suffer misunderstanding and isolation in a world where truth, the person, evil, and good are hopelessly relative, the people of Betti's world are painfully aware of an obscure but absolute quality attached to these same things; they suffer not only a social but a metaphysical anguish and operate within view of a superior judgment seat, however much some of them may seek to hide from or defy

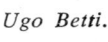
Ugo Betti.

it or remain perplexed in seeking it out. The constant and dominating motif of Betti's dramas is the anguished enquiry into the mysterious but terribly real and corrosive presence of evil in the world, the mystery of iniquity. Betti thus has affinities with authors such as *Dostoevskiĭ and *Kafka; the struggle between evil and good that he portrays is accompanied by the urgent need to fix responsibility. For this reason his dramas take on the quality of a judicial inquest, but, even though his wide experience as a magistrate is drawn upon and suggests the structure of some of his plots, the true drama—the moral life of man—easily transcends any such immediacy. In a world shot through with the results of original sin, who is guilty? Is it any one individual, or do all share the responsibility for any evil act (*Frana allo Scalo Nord,* 1932; *Ispezione,* 1942; *L'aiuola bruciata,* 1951–52)? Where *Ibsen found only society to be guilty, Betti saw the roots of guilt as inherent to the human condition itself (*Ispezione*). As in Kafka's world, so in Betti's, mankind is continually on trial, and even among those who may escape the judgment of the human assize (for indeed, human justice is relative and imperfect), there are some who will be tormented by their conscience. If some become defiant or sneering champions of evil, there are others who will ultimately respond to the voice of conscience and find liberation in confession and expiation. For in the midst of evil, the human soul still retains a dim remembrance of original innocence, which, if not allowed to wither, may work for the soul's redemption. Suffering and the capacity for remorse are the saving features of man's existence; they may elevate him and help him to find his human dignity, they may lead him to compassion and pity, and, ultimately, to God.

If, in most of his plays, Christ's presence is not clearly discernible, Betti nevertheless seems to suggest that atonement necessitates the immolation of an innocent victim; or perhaps it is rather that atonement becomes possible when there is awareness that the very innocence men have trampled upon and wounded unto death is their truer heritage and their secret desire. These various motifs are found to a greater or lesser degree in most of Betti's plays, but perhaps nowhere so compactly and compellingly as in *Corruzione al palazzo di giustizia* (1949). Betti's last plays, while continuing to inquire into man's desolate condition, recognize more overtly the presence of God in the universe and the possibility of man's rehabilitation by Christian faith (*La Fuggitiva,* 1952–53; *L'aiuola bruciata*).

Betti had an unusual capacity for creating an atmosphere of high tension in which his characters and their world take on symbolical or even allegorical dimensions and universal significance. And yet within this framework psychological and moral veracity are not sacrificed but enhanced.

Bibliography: U. BETTI, *Teatro completo* (Rocca San Casciano 1957); *Poesie* (Rocca San Casciano 1957). A. FIOCCO, *Ugo Betti* (Rome 1954). C. APOLLONIO, "Ugo Betti," in *Letteratura italiana: I contemporanei,* 2 v. (Milan 1963) 2:1021–36. J. A. SCOTT, "The Message of Ugo Betti," *Italica* 37 (1960) 44–57. **Illustration credit:** Italian Information Center, New York.

[N. J. PERELLA]

BEURON, ABBEY OF

Benedictine archabbey on the Danube River, 20 miles west of Sigmaringen, Diocese of *Freiburg im Breisgau, southwest Germany; dedicated to St. Martin. An earlier foundation of Augustinian canons (1077), confirmed by Urban II (1097), had few canons and little property, and became an abbey only in 1687; in 1802 it was suppressed and became part of the Hohenzollern-Sigmaringen estate.

Beuron was restored as a Benedictine cloister in 1863 from *St. Paul-Outside-the-Walls by Maurus and Placidus *Wolter, its first abbots, thanks to the widowed Princess Catherine von Hohenzollern (d. 1893). An abbey in 1868 and an archabbey in 1884, Beuron became the head of the Beuron Congregation (approved by the Holy See in 1884), with daughterhouses in Belgium, England, Austria, and Germany. The Prussian *Kulturkampf drove the community to Volders in the Tirol

(1875–87) but could not stop the growth of the Congregation, which included monks in Emmaus (Prague), *Seckau, *Maria Laach, St. Joseph (Gerleve), *Neresheim, *Weingarten, Grüssau, Neuburg (Heidelberg), and Las Condes (Santiago, Chile); and nuns in Bertholdstein, Eibingen, Herstelle, and Kellenried. Belgian and English abbeys left the Congregation (1920) as did Mount Sion in Jerusalem and Emmaus in Prague (1945). In 1895 Beuron undertook the restoration of Brazilian Benedictines at the request of the Holy See.

Under the Wolters, Beuron became the center of a liturgical monastic revival in Germany (Anselm *Schott, Suitbert Bäumer). Gregorian chant was studied and used. Hildebrand *Höpfl was a noted exegete. The school of theology is devoted to scholarship and offers monks of the Congregation a 4-year course. Alban *Dold (d. 1960) founded the series *Texte und Arbeiten,* 57 v. (1917–64) for texts and studies of the liturgy. Studies of the Old Latin Bible are pursued under Bonifatius Fischer at the Vetus Latina Institute, to which is attached the Palimpsest Institute. Since 1919 Beuron's press has published *Benediktinische Monatschrift.* Pastoral care of the many pilgrims to Beuron's miraculous image (a 15th-century Pietà), retreats, excursions, the training of lay catechists, and youth work are in the hands of the monks. Clergy and laity work closely together in Beuron's Secular Oblate Institute.

The 17th- and 18th-century buildings have had additions for the school of theology, the library (235,000 volumes), and the Vetus Latina; the church is baroque (1732–38). Beuron's school of art which began in 1894 with Desiderius *Lenz was opposed to naturalism; it gained followers, including Willibrord *Verkade, but declined after 1913 (*see* BEURONESE ART).

Bibliography: *Konstitutionen der Beuroner Kongregation von 1884* (ArchKathKRecht 54; 1885). K. T. ZINGELER, *Geschichte des Klosters Beuron* (Sigmaringen 1890). H. S. MAYER, *Benediktinisches Ordensrecht in der Beuroner Kongregation,* 4 v. (Beuron 1929–36). U. ENGELMANN, *Beuron* (Munich-Zurich 1957); LexThK² 2:324–325. *Beuron, 1863–1963: Festschrift zum hundertjährigen Bestehen der Erzabtei St. Martin* (Beuron 1963). P. VOLK, DHGE 8:1279–82. R. GAZEAU, *Catholicisme* 2:5–7. Cottineau 1:370–371. Kapsner BenBibl 2:190–191. S. MAYER, *Beuroner Bibliographie, 1863–1963* (Beuron 1963).

[U. ENGELMANN]

BEURONESE ART

BEURONESE ART, a school founded in the Benedictine archabbey of *Beuron by Desiderius *Lenz, sculptor and architect. Beginning in 1864, Lenz developed his concepts in actual art projects and still more in sketches and theoretical treatises. Work was carried on from 1894 by the Beuron school, after G. Wüger and L. Steiner had associated themselves with it. Lenz aimed at an integral, liturgically inspired ecclesiastical art. Rejecting the dominant tendency of the period toward naturalism, he reverted to primitive Christian, early Greek, and especially Egyptian art. A more immediate influence was that of the German *Nazarene school. He developed an aesthetic geometry in order to discover the primordial dimensions in nature and those of the human body. In looking to ancient sources as a starting point for modern religious art and architecture, the monastic artists of the Beuron school envisioned a religious art that was to be ordered and serene, hieratic in conception and style. The principal Beuronese monument is the St. Maur Chapel near Beuron (1868–71). In the last quarter of the 19th century, extensive projects of decoration were carried out in

"The Virgin and Child with Saints Scholastica and Benedict," Beuronese fresco altarpiece at Monte Cassino.

Monte Cassino and in churches in Prague. After the decoration of the Monte Cassino crypt church in 1913, Beuronese art suffered a steady decline that terminated in extinction. Despite its fate, however, the Beuronese school may be considered one of the forerunners in the movement for renewal of art and architecture in the Church.

Bibliography: Benedictine Abbey of Maredsous, Bel., *S. Benedictus* (Ghent 1880), pls. Benedictine Abbey of Emmaus, Prague, *Leben und Regel des heiligen Vaters Benedictus* (Prague 1901), illus. A. Pöllmann, *Vom Wesen der hieratischen Kunst* (Beuron 1905). G. Prezzolini, *La teoria e l'arte di Beuron* (Siena 1908). S. M. Vismara, *La nuova arte di Beuron* (Rome 1913). J. Kreitmaier, *Beuroner Kunst: Eine Audrucksform der christlichen Mystik* (5th ed. Freiburg 1923). D. Lenz, *Zur Aesthetik der Beuroner Schule* (Vienna 1927). C. Kniel, *Leben und Regel des heiligen Vaters Benediktus* (Beuron 1929), pls. G. Mercier, *L'Art abstrait dans l'art sacré* (Paris 1964) 30–32. **Illustration credit:** Alinari-Art Reference Bureau.

[U. ENGELMANN]

BEWERUNGE, HENRY, music educator and historian; b. Letmathe (Westphalia), Germany, Dec. 7, 1862; d. Maynooth, Ireland, Dec. 2, 1923. After finishing Gymnasium at Düsseldorf and musical studies at Würzburg university, Bewerunge entered the diocesan seminary at Eichstätt and was ordained in 1885. After further music studies at Regensburg and a year's service as chanter in the Cologne cathedral, he became professor of church music at St. Patrick's Seminary in May-

nooth (1888), remaining until 1914, when he transferred to the University College of Dublin. He left Ireland for Cologne in 1916, but returned after World War I. Between 1891 and 1897 he edited *Lyra Ecclesiastica,* bulletin of the Irish Society of St. Cecilia. *Die vatikanische Choralausgabe* (Düsseldorf 1906–07), later translated into English and French, is his chief work. For the *Catholic Encyclopedia* he wrote essays on Gregorian chant, neum, and organ which were excellent summaries of the state of scholarship in his day and showed a keen and balanced judgment on controverted subjects.

Bibliography: Riemann v.1. *The Catholic Encyclopedia and Its Makers* (New York 1917) 14. Baker 149.

[R. G. WEAKLAND]

BEYERLINCK, LAURENT, Belgian historian, theologian, and bibliophile; b. Antwerp, April 12, 1578; d. there, June 7, 1627. After humanistic studies at the Jesuit college, he received a licentiate in theology from the University of Louvain and was ordained sometime before 1602. He was a professor at Louvain until called by Jean Miraeus (Le Mire), Bishop of Antwerp, to assume the duties of president of the seminary at Antwerp, where he remained until his death. During those years he collected a valuable library, which he left to the University of Louvain, and edited books over a wide range of historical and theological subjects. Among them are: *Apophthegmata christianorum* (Antwerp 1608); *Promptuarium morale super evangelia festorum anni totius* (Cologne 1616); *Biblia sacra variarum translationum,* 3 v. (Antwerp 1616); *Tractatus synopticus ad synodum Dordracense* (Antwerp 1619). An eight-volume compendium of poetry, philosophy, and theology, *Magnum theatrum vitae humanae* (Cologne 1631), was published posthumously.

Bibliography: J. F. FOPPENS, *Bibliotheca belgica,* 2 v. (Brussels 1739). V. SEMPELS, DHGE 8:1299–1300. F. STEGMÜLLER, Lex ThK² 2:330–331.

[E. D. MC SHANE]

BEZA, THEODORE, John Calvin's chief assistant and successor as leader of Reformed Protestantism; b. Vézelay, France, June 25, 1519; d. Geneva, Oct. 13, 1605. Beza was born of a minor Burgundian noble family, and received an excellent education in classical literature and law at Orléans, Bourges, and Paris; he was awarded several benefices while a student. In 1548 he moved to Geneva, announced his conversion to Protestantism, and married. Beza served the Reformed Church as professor of Greek at the Lausanne Academy (1549–58), professor of theology (1559–99) and first rector (1559–63) of the Geneva Academy, and pastor of the Geneva church (1559–1605) and moderator of its company of pastors (1564–80). He served his church also in a number of diplomatic missions to Protestant Germany, Protestant Switzerland, and France. He headed the Protestant delegation at the Colloquy of Poissy (1561), an attempt to reconcile Catholics and Protestants under royal auspices, and saw it founder over disagreements on Eucharistic theology. He was an adviser to the princes who led the Huguenot armies in the French wars of religion. He fought successfully for tighter ecclesiastical discipline at several national synods of the French Reformed Church, over one of which he presided (La Rochelle, 1571). Beza probably served his church most effectively, however, with his voluminous and varied publications, many of them distinguished by substantial erudition and an elegant Latin style. His writings include: (1) several editions of an annotated New Testament, based on an important manuscript Greek text (the Codex Bezae), rather freely translated into Latin, with extensive notes providing a Calvinist interpretation of the text; (2) translations into French verse of the Psalms, prepared jointly with Clément Marot, widely used in Reformed liturgies then and since; (3) polemical tracts, vehemently defending key Calvinist doctrines on such issues as double predestination, the Eucharist, and the necessity of persecuting heretics, against adversaries of Catholic, Lutheran, and Sacramentarian persuasions; (4) popular works, including anti-Catholic satirical pieces and short biographies, such as one of Calvin; (5) political tracts, notably *Du droit des magistrats,* a defense of the right to resist and even overthrow governments for religious reasons; (6) collections of Latin poems, some of them quite secular in tone; and (7) manuals for the study of Greek and French. Many of these works were published in both Latin and French, and a good number were also translated into other vernacular languages. They provide further evidence of Beza's great contemporary influence not only in his native France and in Switzerland, but also in England, the Protestant Netherlands, parts of Rhenish Germany, and parts of central Europe. Altogether he made the Reformed movement more tightly organized, more active in politics, more intellectual, and more rigid.

Bibliography: T. BEZA, *Correspondance,* ed. F. AUBERT et al (Geneva 1960–). M. H. VICAIRE, LexThK² 2:331–332. O. E. STRÄSSER, RGG³ 1:1117. C. CRIVELLI, EncCatt 2:1531–34. H. M. BAIRD, *Theodore Beza* (New York 1899). P. F. GEISENDORF, *Théodore de Bèze* (Geneva 1949). F. GARDY and A. DUFOUR, *Bibliographie des oeuvres . . . de Théodore de Bèze* (Geneva 1960). **Illustration credit:** Giraudon.

[R. M. KINGDON]

Theodore Beza, portrait owned by the Société d'histoire du Protestantisme français at Paris.

BHARATI, SUBRAMANIA, Indian poet and patriot whose writings heralded the Tamil renaissance in the 20th century; b. Ettayapuram (Tirunelveli District), Dec. 11, 1882; d. Sept. 12, 1921. He was of an orthodox Brahman family; he served for a time as a teacher of Tamil, and became assistant editor of the Tamil paper *Swadesamitran* (1904). He entered politics and edited the revolutionary weekly *India* (1906). This activity led to his exile in Pondicherry (French India) in 1908 for 10 years. On his return to India, he rejoined *Swadesamitran.* His death resulted from injuries sustained in an accident with a temple elephant.

Bharati is undoubtedly the greatest modern Tamil poet. He released Tamil from the fetters of dead convention and, by his use of the speaker's voice and the living language, gave vigor and flexibility to his verse. His considerable poetic output comprised patriotic songs, devotional hymns, prose poems, autobiographical fragments, an epic (*Pānchāli Sapatam*), and a poetic fantasy on the phases of love. If his stirring patriotic poems showed no rancor, his religious poems were not narrowly sectarian. He could, for example, seize the central symbolism of the Resurrection:

> If Sense is bound to the Cross of Truth
> And crucified on the thorn, Austerity,
> Jesus of the sanctified Soul
> Will loom as the limitless Sky.

Kannan Songs (1917) is a lyric garland offered to Lord Krishna. *Pānchāli Sapatam* (1912, Panchali's Vow), while rendering dramatically the key episode of the dishonoring of Droupadi in the *Mahābhārata,* takes on allegorical significance in the context of India's subjection to British rule. *Kuyil's Song* (1923) is fantasy and fable, romance and philosophy, and ranks supreme in the Bharati canon. Bharati's prose poems on power, wind, ocean, and freedom are in a class apart, and have clear affiliations with the poetry of Walt *Whitman. Bharati wrote also a great deal of sensitive and vigorous prose: political journalism, philosophy, and fiction. His English writings have been posthumously collected in *Agni and Other Poems and Translations* and *Essays and Other Prose Fragments* (Madras 1937). Although Bharati died young, he had already achieved mastery and maturity, and he had nobly lighted the path for later writers to follow with ease and confidence. His songs have now become incorporated as a part of popular Tamil culture.

Bibliography: *Mahākavi Bhāratiyār kavitaikal* (Madras 1962), collected poems of Bharati. *Bharati in English Verse,* tr. S. PREMA (Madras 1958). P. NANDAKUMAR, *Subramania Bharati* (Mysore 1964).

[K. R. SRINIVASA IYENGAR]

BHOPAL, ARCHDIOCESE OF (BHOPAL-ENSIS), metropolitan see since 1963, in Madhya Pradesh state, central *India; it was carved from the Dioceses of Indore, Jabalpur, and Ajmer-Jaipur. In 1963 its three suffragans, which had 102 priests, 310 sisters, and 66,000 Catholics in a population of 23 million, were: Indore (created in 1952), Jabalpur (1954), and Raigarh-Ambikapur (1957). Bhopal was once the largest Moslem principality in India after *Hyderabad. Founded in 1723 by an Afghan adventurer and bound to the British by treaty from 1817, it was ruled by women through the female line of royal descent (1844–1926).

Bibliography: AnnPont (1964) 64.

[E. P. COLBERT]

BHUTAN, independent kingdom in the Himalayas northeast of India and south of Tibet, 16,000 square miles in area. The population, estimated at 700,000 in 1964, adheres almost in its entirety to Lamaist *Buddhism (*see* LAMAISM). Numerous Buddhist monasteries exist. Christianity made its appearance when two Jesuit missionaries on their way from Bengal to Tibet entered the country in 1626. Detained by the nation's religious leader, the Dharma-Raja, at Paro for several weeks, they studied Tibetan with a Tsaparang lama. No other Catholic missionaries seem to have succeeded them, and Catholicism has never gained a following. Because of its relations with the Catholic schools in Darjeeling, India, the Bhutan government invited two Canadian Jesuits in 1963 to establish an educational system in Bhutan, beginning with primary grades. Ecclesiastically,

Bhutan is subject to the bishop of Shillong in Assam, India.

Bibliography: C. A. BELL, *Tibet, Past and Present* (Oxford 1924). C. WESSELS, *Early Jesuit Travellers in Central Asia, 1603–1721* (The Hague 1924).

[E. R. HAMBYE]

BIALIK, CHAIM NACHMAN (BYALIK), modern Hebrew poet; b. Radi (Volhynia), Russia, Jan. 9, 1873; d. Vienna, Austria, July 3, 1934. His early life, marked by poverty and orphanage, intensive study of rabbinical literature, and tasting of the fruits of modern creativity, was a time of searching and learning that left a considerable impress on his poetry. After some false starts following his studies at the Volozhin Yeshiva and a period of service in his in-laws' lumber business, he settled in Odessa, where he collaborated in the establishment of a publishing house (1905). Leaving the Soviet Union (1921), he continued his activities briefly in Germany and finally made his home in Palestine (1924).

Considered the poet laureate of the Jewish renaissance, Bialik was many-sided in his offerings. His poems commented on the tragedy of Jewish life, protested the people's martyrdom, expressed hope for the despairing, observed the phenomena of nature, and reflected on the poet's personal sense of inner sorrow. In whatever vein he spoke, the Jewish experience, whether of the past or the present, was at the root of his expression, and he captured the soul of the people in his verse. He was also a novelist, anthologist, translator of classics into Hebrew, editor of critical editions of medieval Hebrew poetry, Yiddishist, and popularizer of rabbinic lore.

Bibliography: I. EFROS, ed., *Complete Poetic Works of H. N. Bialik, Tr. from the Hebrew* (New York 1948). M. WAXMAN, *A History of Jewish Literature,* 5 v. in 6 (New York 1960) 4:219–259. S. SPIEGEL, *Hebrew Reborn* (Philadelphia 1930; Meridian Bks. 1962) 296–312; UnivJewishEnc 2:276–278. EncJudaica 4:465–470.

[R. KRINSKY]

BIANCHI, FRANCESCO SAVERIO MARIA, ST., b. Arpino (Frosinone), Dec. 2, 1743; d. Naples, Jan. 31, 1815 (feast, Jan. 31). Because of parental opposition to his religious vocation, he studied law at the University of Naples before joining the *Barnabites (1762). Almost all his priestly life was spent in Naples, where he was superior in the College of Portanova (1773–85) and from 1778 professor of theology at the university. He was a member of several academies and soon gained a reputation as a learned man, but his writings have not been published, except for a few sermons. Charitable and pastoral labors, aid to the poor, and contemplation kept gaining more ascendancy over his studious activities, especially after his mysterious ecstasy on Pentecost, 1800. A strange and terrible disease afflicted his legs and immobilized him from 1804 until death. Bianchi was the spiritual guide of St. Maria Francesca *Gallo and many other elect souls. His fame for performing miracles was widespread, especially because of his prophecies and his arrest of the lava flow from Vesuvius in 1804 and 1805. Characteristic of his spirituality was a mystic ardor joined to a joyous serenity and a lively devotion to the Mass. His remains are in the church of S. Giuseppe a Pontecorvo in Naples.

The Virgin and Child with Saints Felix and Adauctus, fresco, A.D. 528, in the Catacomb of Commodilla at Rome. The figure in black at the left is the donatrix of the painting. Better preserved than many frescoes found above ground, this work exhibits the high quality of the art of the period.

He was beatified Jan. 22, 1893, by Leo XIII, and canonized Oct. 21, 1951, by Pius XII.

Bibliography: A. BARAVELLI, *Vita del b. F. S. M. Bianchi* (2d ed. Rome 1893). F. T. MOLTEDO, *Vita del b. F. S. M. B.* (Florence 1893). F. M. SALA, *L'Apostolo di Napoli* (Rome 1951). G. BOFFITO, *Scrittori Barnabiti,* 1 (Florence 1933) 212–217.

[U. M. FASOLA]

BIANCHINI, FRANCESCO, historian, astronomer, antiquary; b. Verona, Dec. 13, 1662; d. Rome, March 2, 1729. After study in Bologna and Padua, he settled at Rome, remaining a deacon all his life. He was highly regarded all over Europe for his learning in history, chronology, mathematics, and astronomy (he drew the meridian, or *gnomon Clementinus,* still visible in the church of St. Mary of the Angels, Rome). He was librarian for Cardinal Peter Ottoboni (later Pope *Alexander VIII), a member of the commission for *calendar reform under Pope *Clement XI, historian for the Council of Rome in 1725 under *Benedict XIII, and an associate of many European academies. He had a reputation for moral integrity and modesty. His principal works include *Istoria universale* (5 v. Rome 1697), *De kalendario et cyclo Caesaris ac de pascali canone s. Hippolyti* (Rome 1703), *Solutio problematis paschalis* (Rome 1703), *Liber pontificalis* (4 v. Rome 1718, 1723, 1728, 1735; PL v.127, 128).

Bibliography: L. M. O. DUCHESNE, *Étude sur le Liber pontificalis* (Paris 1877) 118–119. M. T. DISDIER, DHGE 8:1381–82. G. BOVINI, EncCatt 2:1542–43.

[A. CONDIT]

BIBER, HEINRICH JOHANN FRANZ VON, baroque church composer influential in the development of violin technique; b. Wartenberg, Bohemia, Aug. 12, 1644; d. Salzburg, Austria, May 3, 1704. Biber was raised to the nobility by Emperor Leopold I, and spent many years with the archbishop of Salzburg, in whose service he composed Masses, Requiems, litanies, and Vespers in the *concertato* style prevalent in the late baroque era. His *Missa Sti. Henrici* (1701), e.g., is scored for five-part chorus and orchestra of strings, brass, timpani, and organ. The text is set with care, though there are many textual repetitions. The voice parts contain florid operatic sections, but only to dramatize specific words. Biber revolutionized violin playing in Germany through his virtuoso violin writing, which employs such innovations as double stops, wide skips, and *scordatura* (the tuning of the strings to other than usual pitches for special effects), as exemplified in his sonata cycle honoring the "15 Mysteries of the Life of Mary" (1674).

Bibliography: *Selected Works* in DenkmTonkÖst v.11, 25, 49, 59, 92, 97, see introd. to each vol. P. NETTL, *H. F. von Biber* (Reichenberg 1926). T. RUSSELL, "The Violin *Scordatura,*" MusQ 24 (1938) 84–96. A. LEISS, MusGG 1:1827–31.

[W. C. HOLMES]

BIBLE, I

The term Bible is derived, through the Latin *Biblia* (originally a neuter plural, but treated since the early Middle Ages as a feminine singular), from the Greek τὰ βιβλία, literally "the books," with the word ἱερά (sacred) expressed or understood. The singular of this Greek word, βιβλίον (a diminutive in form, but with the diminutive force lost), occurs in Lk 4.17 in reference to the "*scroll" of Isaia from which Jesus read in the synagogue at Nazareth. The earlier form ἡ βίβλος (the book, i.e., the Bible), which occurs in 2 Mc 8.23, as does its plural, αἱ βίβλοι, in the Septuagint of Dn 9.2, comes from an original form, ἡ βύβλος, designating Egyptian papyrus, first known to the Greeks as writing material imported from the Phoenician city of *Byblos. Synonymous terms for the sacred book(s) are αἱ γραφαί (the writings, the Scriptures) and ἡ γραφή (the writing, Scripture, the Bible as a whole), which are used in Mt 21.42; 22.29; 26.54; etc. and Acts 8.32; Rom 4.3; 9.17; etc., respectively.

The use of the singular number in these terms to designate the many writings that constitute the Bible comes from the regarding of the collection as a single unit that, despite its many human authors, has God as its chief author. Therefore, all who regard the Bible as a sacred book consider it, in some way, as written under divine inspiration and as establishing a norm of religious faith, whether alone or, as Catholics do, together with divine tradition [*see* TRADITION (IN THEOLOGY)].

The whole Bible possesses both its sacredness and its unity also by reason of its subject matter, which is *salvation history (*Heilsgeschichte*). From beginning to end the Bible is concerned primarily with the acts of God for man's salvation, wrought through His covenants with man, particularly His covenant with Israel, through the mediatorship of Moses, whereby He assured Israel of ultimate salvation; and His covenant with the new people of God, the Christian Church, through the mediatorship of Jesus Christ, whereby He achieved this definitive salvation. Those who do not accept this New Covenant, i.e., the Jews, have a Bible consisting only of the books of the Old Covenant or Old Testament, whereas Christians have a Bible made up of the books of both the Old and the New Testament. *See* COVENANT (IN THE BIBLE); TESTAMENT (IN THE BIBLE).

All matters concerning the Bible as a whole are treated here under the general heading of BIBLE. After this first article on the concept and nature of the Bible, the following articles, some with many subdivisions, are presented.

II. Inspiration
III. Canon
IV. Texts and Versions
V. Textual Criticism
VI. Exegesis
VII. Papal Teaching

Bibliography: B. HESSLER, LexThK² 2:335–336. G. RICCIOTTI, EncCatt 2:1545–47. EncDictBibl 238–241. Robert-Tricot 3–6. G. SCHRENK, Kittel ThW 1:613–617. H. HÖPFL, DBSuppl 2:457–465.

[L. F. HARTMAN]

BIBLE, II (INSPIRATION)

By inspiration of the Bible is meant a unique divine influence in virtue of which the men responsible for the OT and NT were so moved and enlightened by God that their work may truly be called the Word of God. The present article discusses the existence of inspiration, the nature and extent of it, the effects of inspiration in the Bible and the Church, and Protestant thought concerning inspiration.

Existence of Inspiration. It has been the constant belief of the people of God both before and after the time of Christ that their Sacred Scriptures have been divinely inspired. Testimony to this fact, together with information concerning the nature of the inspired character of the Scriptures, is found in the OT, in Jewish writers, in the NT, as well as in the tradition of the Church.

Evidence in the Old Testament and in Jewish writers. Toward the end of the 2d century B.C., the translator of Sirach recognized the normative character of the Law, the Prophets, and other writings for the Jewish people (*Foreword to Sirach;* see also 1 Mc 1.59–60; 7.16–17; 12.9; 2 Mc 2.13; Dn 9.2). The prophetic origin of this literature accounted for its authority. Moses and the great Prophets of Israel were themselves conscious of speaking to the people in the name of God Himself (e.g., Ex 4.15–16; 19.7–8; Jer 1.9; 20.7–9; Ez 38.1). The phenomenon of prophecy was attributed to the spirit of God that filled the prophet (Nm 11.25–26; 1 Sm 10.6; Os 9.7). Occasional mention is made of the same spirit of God at work in the priest (2 Chr 24.20) and the psalmist (2 Sm 23.2).

The Prophets of Israel were primarily moved by God to speak the word of God to their contemporaries. Others recorded their words at a later date. Some prophetic oracles, however, were originally given in writing (Hab 2.2; Is 30.8); Jeremiah was instructed to record all his oracles for posterity (Jer 30.1–3; 36.1–3). At the time of Christ the Jews sought the word of the Lord in this threefold collection of the Law, the Prophets, and the Writings (cf. Jn 5.39; 10.35). The rabbis so venerated the letter of the text that they saw a divine meaning in the very flourishes of the script (cf. Mt 5.18).

In the Diaspora the Jewish philosopher Philo wrote of the inspired character of the Hebrew Scriptures in their Greek translation. He explained the phenomenon of inspiration in terms of Greek religious ecstasy: the Prophet was deprived of personal consciousness and possessed by God whenever he spoke or wrote (ἐνθουσιασμός; *Quis rerum divinarum heres* 53.265; LoebClLib 4.418). According to the Jewish historian Flavius Josephus, the Prophets wrote by inspiration received from God (κατὰ τὴν ἐπίπνοιαν τὴν ἀπὸ τοῦ θεοῦ: *Contra Apionem* 1.7.37; LoebClLib 1.179). The Jews were more concerned with the divine character and authority of their sacred writings than with their human origins.

Evidence in the New Testament. The countless NT references and allusions to the Jewish Scriptures testify to the veneration that Christ and the Apostles had for the Law, the Prophets, and the other writings (Lk 24.27, 44; Acts 3.22; 4.25; 28.25; Gal 3.8; Mk 7.10, 13; 12.36). In fact, the person, work, and teaching of Christ are presented in the NT as the supreme fulfillment of all that is written in the OT (Heb 1.1–2; Mt 5.17–19; 1 Cor 15.3–4; Rom 3.21, 31).

In 2 Pt 1.19–21 the OT prophetic texts are clearly attributed to the special influence of the Holy Spirit. To confirm the confidence that may be placed in OT prophecy, the author says that "no prophecy of Scripture is made by private interpretation. For not by will of man was prophecy brought at any time; but holy men of God spoke as they were moved [φερόμενοι] by the Holy Spirit." The permanent value of the OT is insisted on in 2 Tm 3.15–16 by explaining that "all Scripture is inspired by God [θεόπνευστος] and useful for teaching, for reproving, for correcting, for instructing in justice; that the man of God may be perfect, equipped for every good

work." For these reasons the OT was retained as authoritative and useful in the Church (1 Cor 10.11).

Among the NT writings the Apocalypse testifies to its own divine origin (1.1–3), and in 2 Pt 3.16 the epistles of St. Paul are treated as Scripture. Moreover, the Apostles claim for themselves and their teaching an authority superior to their predecessors (2 Cor 3.7–8; Eph 3.5; Col 1.26; 1 Thes 2.13; 2 Thes 2.15).

Evidence in the Tradition of the Church. By the middle of the 2d Christian century there is evidence that the NT writings were being treated on a par with the OT (Justin Martyr, *Apol.* 1.66, 67; *Dial. c. Trypho* 119; Irenaeus, *Adv. Haer.* 3.1.1–2; Theophilus of Antioch, *Ad Autolycum* 3.12; Hippolytus, *In Cant.* 2.8 (XI); Muratorian Fragment, EnchBibl 1–7).

Christian antiquity, in its prayer, preaching, and theological writing, universally recognized that the writings of the OT and NT were the work of the Holy Spirit and were all equally the word of God. It was the unanimous teaching of the Fathers that the Sacred Scriptures were free from error and from all contradiction. Even though other ecclesiastical writers were considered to be inspired by God (Clement of Rome says this of himself, 1 Clem 63.2; Gregory Nazianzus, of Basil, *In Hex. Proem.*, PG 44:61; Augustine, of Jerome, *Epist.* 82.2; Gregory the Great, of himself, *In I Reg. Proem.* 5, PL 79:21), the canonical Scriptures were always considered to be in a class apart. Athenagoras (*c.* 177) spoke of the Prophets as the *organa* or instruments of God, writing in ecstasy as the flutes of the Holy Spirit (*Legatio pro Christianis* 7, 9). About A.D. 250 the *Cohortatio ad Graecos* (8) called them the harps or lyres of the Holy Spirit (see also Theophilus of Antioch, *Ad Autolycum* 2.9; Hippolytus, *De Antichristo* 2). The metaphor of the musical instrument is common among the Fathers but tends to minimize the role of the human author. Nevertheless, at the time of the Montanist heresy, Catholic writers rejected the notion that the sacred writers wrote in ecstasy, deprived of their senses and intellectual awareness (see Epiphanius, *Adv. Haer.* 48; Jerome, *In Is. Prol.*, CorpChrist 73.2–3; *In Nah. et Hab. Prol.*, PL 25:1232, 1274).

The Fathers inherited from the rabbis the notion of divine dictation (ὑπαγορεύειν, *dictare*; see John Chrysostom, *In illud: Salutate Priscillam et Aquilam*, PG 51:187; Augustine, *Cons. Evang.* 1.35, 54), but it must be remembered that, when used by the magisterium, this Latin word has a wider sense than mechanical and verbal dictation. It expresses origin, causality, and responsibility; the Council of Trent used it of oral traditions (EnchBibl 57). It remains true, however, that the Fathers investigated primarily the divine meaning of the Scriptures in the full light of Christian faith, and little attention was actually paid to a historical investigation of the human writer's work (see Gregory the Great, *Moralia in Job Praef.* 1.2, PL 75:517). Indeed, the tools for such a study were lacking to the Fathers. At the same time, however, men such as the Antiochenes, Jerome, and Augustine, recognized the importance of investigating the character, style, and work of the human writers (Jerome, *In Am. Prol.*, PL 25:990; Augustine, *In evang. Ioh.* 1.1; *Civ.* 17.6.2; *Cons. Evang.* 2.12.27–29). St. Augustine (*Doctr. christ.* 2.5) wrote: "In reading it [i.e., Sacred Scripture], men are desirous only of discovering the thoughts and intentions of those by whom it was written. Through these in turn they discover the will of God, according to which we believe such men spoke" (FathCh 4.64). Again in *Epist.* 82. 1.3: "If I do find anything in these books which seems contrary to truth, I decide that either the text is corrupt, or the translator did not follow what was really said, or that I failed to understand it" (FathCh 9.392).

Although the Fathers treated the Scriptures as letters addressed by God to his people (John Chrysostom, *In Gn. Hom.* 2.2, PG 53:28; Augustine, *In psalm.* 90 *serm.* 2.1), the term *auctor* (author) is not explicitly applied to God until the time of St. Gregory the Great (*Moralia in Job Praef.* 1.2, PL 75:517). In defending the faith against Marcion, the Gnostics, and the Manichees, Catholic writers and the magisterium insisted that one and the same God was at the origin of both the OT and the NT. In this context the Latin word *auctor* may simply mean principle or originator of both dispensations, although literary authorship cannot be excluded [see A. Bea, "Deus auctor sacrae scripturae: Herkunft und Bedeutung der Formel," *Angelicum* 20 (1943) 16–31]. The *Statuta Ecclesiae Antiqua* (*c.* 600) refer to God as "the author [*auctor*] of the OT and the NT, i.e., of the Law and the Prophets and [the writings of] the Apostles" (EnchBibl 30). The Decree for the Jacobites issued at the Council of Florence (1441) suggests literary authorship more explicitly: "The holy Roman Church acknowledges [*profitetur*] one and the same God as author of the OT and the NT, i.e., of the Law and the Prophets and the Gospel, because the holy men of both Testaments, whose books it receives and venerates, spoke under the inspiration of the same Holy Spirit" (EnchBibl 47). The same formula appears in the teaching of the Council of Trent (1546), although the Council itself was concerned primarily with maintaining equal reverence and authority (*pari pietatis affectu ac reverentia*) for oral traditions, in view of Protestant insistence on Scripture alone (EnchBibl 57). *See* TRADITION (IN THEOLOGY).

In the 18th and 19th centuries, with the rise of rationalism and positivism, the inspiration and divine authority of Sacred Scripture were seriously questioned. Textual, literary, and historical criticism discovered many imperfections, apparent errors, and seeming contradictions in the sacred texts. The human origins of the Bible appeared to be irreconcilable with divine inspiration. Outside the Church the notion of inspiration was reduced to religious and poetic genius. Within the Church some Catholics taught that the Church made certain books into Sacred Scripture by giving her approval to outstanding human works (D. Haneberg). Others taught that God merely protected the human authors from error in matters of faith and morals (M. Jahn). The Vatican Council I (1870) defended the traditional teaching against contemporary errors by a solemn and infallible expression of Catholic faith: "The Church holds them [the books of the OT and the NT] as sacred and canonical, not because, having been composed by human industry alone, they were afterwards approved by her authority; nor only because they contain revelation without error; but because, having been written under the inspiration of the Holy Spirit, they have God as their author and, as such, have been handed over to the Church" (EnchBibl 77).

In view of new attempts to restrict unduly Biblical inspiration and inerrancy, Leo XIII, in his encyclical *Providentissimus Deus* (1893), repeated the teaching of Trent and Vatican Council I, and further explained the Catholic doctrine of inspiration: "Hence, because the Holy Spirit employed men as His instruments, we cannot therefore say that it was these inspired instruments who, perchance, have fallen into error, and not the primary Author. For, by supernatural power, He so moved and impelled them to write—He was so present to them—that the things that He ordered, and those only, they, first, rightly understood, then willed faithfully to write down, and finally expressed in apt words and with infallible truth. Otherwise it could not be said that He was the author of the entire Scripture" (EnchBibl 125). It is therefore of divine and Catholic faith that the entire extent of Scripture is inspired by God in such a way that He may be truly called its author.

Nature and Extent of Inspiration. Leo XIII, reflecting Christian tradition, spoke of the sacred writers as instruments of the Holy Spirit. It is necessary to conceive this divine and human cooperation in such a way as to preserve the free and responsible character of the human author, for modern study has made us acutely aware of the complex historical process that produced the literature of the Bible. The inspiration of the Bible must, however, be seen as one aspect of that divine providence which is leading men to salvation through Jesus Christ. God's supernatural revelation took place in the history of Israel and in the life of Christ before it was recorded in the pages of Scripture. The Bible then is the record of a progressive revelation, written according to the modes of writing prevalent in the ancient Near East at the time. Consequently, it is the fruit of a long oral and written tradition in which early texts were reinterpreted, glossed, and reorganized before reaching the state in which we read them today. Many have played a role in this process, but the work of all had a common social character; it was ordered to the service of a religious community. The Prophets and the Apostles were the spiritual guides of Israel and the early Church, but they did not always write. Others recorded their teaching for posterity or sought to inculcate it by a literary presentation peculiar to themselves (see Lk 1.1–4; 2 Mc 2.27–32; 15.39). By His special providence God guided this entire process, whether it involved action, speech, or writing. Such divine guidance may fittingly be called inspiration, since inspiration is simply any impulse brought to bear upon an intelligent creature from without (see ST 1a2ae, 68.1).

Human Authors as God's Instruments. The inspiration by which God moves his free creatures is distinguished according to the various effects produced. Biblical inspiration produces a book of which God is the author. In order to provide the Church with Sacred Scripture, the Holy Spirit elevated all the human activity required for its production in such a way that the books produced were entirely the work of God, the principal cause, and entirely the work of the human authors as instrumental causes (*C. gent.* 3.70). The notion of an instrumental cause is a fruitful one, provided it is not applied too rigidly to the inspired authors. St. Thomas developed the notion in treating the Sacraments (ST 3a, 62.1 ad 2). An instrument, such as a saw or a trumpet, cannot produce any effect unless it is used by a carpenter or a musician. When so used, it produces an effect proper to its own nature; a saw is designed to cut wood, a trumpet to make music. The effect, however, surpasses the proper causality of the instrument even though the latter receives and conditions the action of the principal agent.

On occasion St. Thomas spoke of the prophet or sacred writer as an instrument (e.g., ST 2a2ae, 173.4; 172.4 ad 1; *In Heb.* 11.1.7; *Quodl.* 7.6.1 ad 5). These, however, were free instruments and responsible agents. They understood what they had to speak or write and went about their work as conscious and free authors, working according to the methods proper to their own culture. Their work surpasses their human powers only insofar as it has divine authority and efficacy, and insofar as they may not have fully understood all that God intended in the events of which they treated and in the words they used. They are at the same time true authors in their own right, even though they act only when moved by the Holy Spirit. Only in this wider sense (see *De ver.* 24.1 ad 5) may we speak of the sacred writers as instruments of the Holy Spirit. It is not necessary that they be conscious of this divine activity, but it seems fitting that they be consciously aware of undertaking a work of religious significance for the people of God. The manner in which God efficaciously moves a free agent, respecting his liberty and proper mode of action, is treated in the theology of *grace.

Human Intellect under Inspiration. The intellect plays a central role in any truly human work. St. Thomas's study of prophetic revelation (ST 2a2ae, 171–174) contains valuable principles for Biblical inspiration when wisely and prudently applied. By the natural light of the human intellect a man judges the ideas or species that have been received through the channels of the senses, the imagination, and the agent intellect. In prophetic revelation God may disclose new ideas or species to the mind of the prophet by direct action upon the senses or the imagination, or by reordering existing ideas or species in an original way, or by direct action upon the intellect. When such action is accompanied by an infusion of the divine light, thereby ensuring the truth of the human judgment, one may speak of revelation in the strict sense; for God has disclosed to men truths that surpass their natural powers of reason or which they are naturally unable to attain in their peculiar circumstances. But God may also be satisfied to fortify the judgment of the prophet concerning truths that he has acquired in a normal human manner from tradition, instruction, experience, or investigation. St. Thomas considered this case as an imperfect mode of prophetic revelation (ST 2a2ae, 173.2; 175.2 ad 4); some writers prefer to call it inspiration without revelation. The important consequence of this distinction is the realization that everything in Sacred Scripture need not be directly revealed by God, but everything in Scripture is inspired inasmuch as the judgment of the sacred writers is always fortified with the divine light. *See* REVELATION, CONCEPT OF (IN THE BIBLE).

St. Thomas was interested primarily in the communication of divine truth to the prophet's intellect and in the action of God upon his speculative judgments. To communicate this truth to others in speech or writing necessitates many practical judgments if the message is to be suitably presented and to achieve the desired result in the audience for which it is intended. A speaker or writer does not merely instruct the intellect; he may also want to act upon the emotions and move the will to conviction, repentance, enthusiasm, or action (see 2 Tm 3.15–16). These practical judgments also benefit from the charism of inspiration, but now the proper effect of inspiration is to assure the most suitable execution of the desired purpose in view of the peculiar circumstances of both the author and his audience. Formal truth and error are no longer at stake, for these are the concern only of the speculative judgment. Hence, in order to evaluate the truth of Scripture, one must consider the purpose of the whole work, the specific intention of the author concerned, and his method of composition. One must allow for the total psychology of human authors in the ancient Near East. If God has chosen to speak to us through such instruments, His intention can be discovered only by the investigating of the intentions of these human authors. In his encyclical *Divino afflante Spiritu* (1943) Pius XII invited Catholic exegetes to this study (EnchBibl 557–560).

Analogous Notion of Inspiration. Biblical inspiration, however, is not restricted to the illumination of the intellect; it elevates all the faculties of the sacred authors for the limited work they have to perform. Such an analogous notion of inspiration is supple enough to embrace all those who contributed in any way to giving the Bible in its present form to the Church. It may also be extended to the Septuagint translators, if it can be established that their work positively contributed to the progress of revelation [see P. Auvray, "Comment se pose le problème de l'inspiration des Septante," RevBibl 59 (1952) 321–336]. The suppleness of this concept may also resolve the problem of verbal inspiration. No one today would hold that God dictated the words of Scripture in an audible manner to the ear of the sacred writer. Cardinal Franzelin taught that God could be the author of Sacred Scripture provided He inspired all the ideas, but the choice of words could be left to the human authors. This theory applied a human notion of authorship univocally to God and violated the psychological integrity of the human instrument; for in man ideas are inseparable from the words in which they are expressed. A proper application of the notion of an instrument to a free agent and the analogous notion of inspiration suffice to explain how God may be considered responsible even for the words without violating the personal integrity and human freedom of the instruments He uses. In this way God may truly, though analogously, be called the author of the entire Bible.

Effects of Inspiration. If God is the author of Sacred Scripture, the truth of Scripture follows as a necessary consequence. Since all the judgments of the sacred writers are fortified by the divine light, they must necessarily be clothed with divine truth.

Inerrancy of Scripture. Negatively, this quality of Scripture is known as inerrancy. The inerrancy of Scripture has been the constant teaching of the Fathers, theologians, and recent Popes in their encyclicals on Biblical studies (Leo XIII, EnchBibl 124–131; Benedict XV, EnchBibl 453–461; Pius XII, EnchBibl 560). It is nonetheless obvious that many Biblical statements are simply not true when judged according to modern knowledge of science and history. The earth is not stationary (cf. Eccl 1.4); Darius the Mede did not succeed Belsassar (cf. Dn 5.30–6.1). Even in religious matters, the OT testifies to an imperfect knowledge of morality and life after death (cf. Dt 24.1; Ps 6.6). Leo XIII, appealing to St. Augustine, explained that it was not the purpose of the Biblical writers to teach us the intimate nature of the physical universe, for this knowledge was in no way profitable for salvation. Consequently, they spoke of the physical universe as it appeared to their senses, according to the custom of their day (EnchBibl 120–121). The Pope asserted also that similar principles might be applied to matters of history (EnchBibl 123).

Following the directive of Leo XIII, some exegetes hastily sought to resolve particular difficulties by proposing theories that postulated implicit citations not approved by the author, history according to appearances, and a relative character for Biblical truth. These solutions failed to go to the root of the problem of Biblical inerrancy and hence occasioned new interventions of the magisterium. The truths of history are more intimately associated with our salvation than are the truths of science. The historical truth of Israel's history and of the life of Christ are an integral part of God's supernatural revelation. There is no doubt that the sacred writers have used sources without citing them, but it must be presumed that they have made this material their own, unless the contrary is quite clearly demonstrated (decree of the Pontifical Biblical Commission, Feb. 13, 1905; EnchBibl 160; on the force of such decrees, see PONTIFICAL BIBLICAL COMMISSION). Similarly, all narrative is not necessarily historical, but if a historical event is an integral part of the author's argument, it must correspond in substance to the facts; nonetheless, it may be presented according to those forms in which ancient peoples remembered their past (decree of the Pontifical Biblical Commission, June 23, 1905; EnchBibl 161; Benedict XV, *Spiritus Paraclitus* Ench Bibl 456; Pius XII, *Divino afflante Spiritu* EnchBibl 559). Moreover, profane matters are certainly treated in the Bible in the light of their religious significance, but positive affirmations in their regard cannot be excluded from the privilege of Biblical inerrancy. Nor is Biblical truth simply relative to its time and culture; its expression is conditioned by the culture of the time, but whatever is affirmed is thereby clothed with the truth of God (see *Spiritus Paraclitus* EnchBibl 454–455).

The total truth of the Scriptures can be appreciated only by trying to recapture the mind of the Biblical writers and to see the relationship of each part of Scripture to the whole. We must know the intention of the sacred author and the literary form that he is using if we are to determine what he intended to teach and what role he assigned to the various elements in his writing. This basic principle of all literary criticism is valid also for Sacred Scripture, once we recognize that God in His condescension deigned to entrust His revelation to the frail vessel of human language. When Pius XII encouraged Catholic scholars to investigate Biblical literary genres or forms, he assured us that no ancient mode of expression need be excluded from the Scriptures, provided it does not contradict the holiness and truth of God (EnchBibl 559). These literary forms may be determined only by a careful and comparative study of ancient Near Eastern literature.

The investigation of literary forms has already provided a solution for many difficulties of the past, e.g., those connected with the *primeval age in the Bible and with the books of *Judith and *Jona, but such studies alone will not remove all obscurities from the message of Scripture. For besides being far removed from us in time and culture, the sacred writers are trying to express in human language the fruit of their own personal en-

counter with God and the mystery of His saving plan, or to record what others have taught them of this ineffable mystery. Their affirmations are true insofar as they affirm; but they may also hesitate, grope, doubt, opine, or suspend judgment entirely (decree of the Pontifical Biblical Commission, June 18, 1915; EnchBibl 415). They may reflect the common opinions of their day without making them the object of their teaching. The exegete must, as a consequence, be sensitive to these varying degrees of human assertion and to the common psychology of human communication, if he is to evaluate correctly the teaching purpose of the sacred writers and to avoid taxing them with error in matters that are not the object of their teaching. *See* FORM CRITICISM, BIBLICAL; LITERARY GENRES, BIBLICAL; MIDRASH.

Role of Scripture in the Church. Inerrancy, however, is not the only consequence of Biblical inspiration. Preoccupation with the so-called "Biblical question" has led to the neglect of other aspects of the Bible's role in the life of the Church. Theologians are now beginning to look more closely at these other effects of Biblical inspiration. In the first place, the Bible provides the Church with a written record of God's self-manifestation to men, which is itself a history of divine pedagogy. God did not reveal Himself completely in the beginning; He adapted His revelation to the cultural and religious condition of the men He visited; He tolerated their moral imperfections until such a time as He was able to educate their consciences; He led men by historical and moral experience to realize their need of His saving grace, which was fully revealed in Jesus Christ. The Apostles in turn used this record of OT revelation to explain the full significance of the mystery of Christ. The knowledge of this divine pedagogy is itself a revelation of the mercy and gentleness of God from which the Church may profit.

Secondly, the Bible contains so manifold an expression of the word of God that all Christians may find in its pages spiritual nourishment adapted to their needs. In the Bible the chosen mediators of God's revelation teach us little by little what they have learned of the mystery of God. The written word of God thus mediates to us the personal experience of the Prophets and Apostles. Through them we may come in contact with God Himself. A privileged place of this mediation is the Church's liturgy of the word.

Finally, the Church is committed to continuing the work of Christ in the world. She must, therefore, preserve, explain, and safeguard the faith of the Apostles, for they were the privileged witnesses of the mystery of Christ. In the NT the Church finds the written record of Apostolic faith to which she always refers in fulfilling her divine mission. These other finalities of Sacred Scripture are the object of modern Biblical study. The Scriptures are not simply a code of dogmatic truths, but an integral part of God's self-communication to men. This self-communication was complete in the living person of Jesus Christ; it will be complete for the individual only in the beatific vision.

Protestant Thought Concerning Inspiration. The Reformers taught the self-sufficient and self-explanatory character of the divinely inspired Scriptures and rejected the teaching authority of the Church. Luther and Calvin did not profess a consistent doctrine of inspiration; Luther received the Scriptures insofar as they bore witness to Christ; Calvin appealed to the interior witness of the Holy Spirit in the individual Christian. From the 16th to the 18th century Protestant theologians taught an excessively rigid doctrine of inspiration, based on the theory of mechanical dictation. In the 19th century, liberal Protestantism abandoned all faith in the divine inspiration of Scripture; the Bible was merely an outstanding expression of man's religious aspirations. Conservative Protestantism still held the Bible to be the sole channel of divine revelation to men, but only the Biblical authors themselves were inspired; their writing was not inspired, since human error was to be found in the Bible. The religious truth of the Bible was judged by the common assent of Christians and the practical testimony of experience.

In the 20th century, apart from some fundamentalist sects (*see* FUNDAMENTALISM, BIBLICAL), the doctrine of Biblical inerrancy is generally abandoned because of modern Biblical criticism. Where inspiration is still mentioned, no attempt is made to explain its nature or its effects. The modern believer may disagree with the Biblical authors even in religious matters if he feels that modern times demand it. The existentialist theologians view the Scriptures as the unique place in which the believer encounters the Word of God. Christ alone is the Word of God, and the Bible is a fallible, human witness to Christ. The Bible becomes the word of God only because God uses this fallible, human word to reveal Himself to the believer. This revelatory event takes place whenever the Scriptures are preached or heard in faith.

The Catholic receives the Scriptures from the infallible teaching authority of the Church, but he believes them to be the word of God through the Holy Spirit who gives him the gift of faith. The Catholic doctrine of inspiration and inerrancy presupposes that God has given His revelation once and for all to chosen individuals and has so illumined their intellects that they may communicate it to others with infallible truth.

See also BIBLE, III (CANON); OLD TESTAMENT LITERATURE.

Bibliography: G. COURTADE, DBSuppl 4:482–559, with bibliog. Historical. C. PESCH, *De inspiratione Sacrae Scripturae* (Freiburg 1906; repr. 1925). G. M. PERRELLA, "La nozione dell'ispirazione scritturale secondo i primitivi documenti cristiani," *Angelicum* 20 (1943) 32–52. N. I. WEYNS, "De notione inspirationis biblicae iuxta Concilium Vaticanum," *ibid.* 30 (1953) 315–336. Theological. J. M. VOSTÉ, *De divina inspiratione et veritate Sacrae Scripturae* (2d ed. Rome 1932). P. SYNAVE and P. BENOIT, *Prophecy and Inspiration,* tr. A. DULLES and T. L. SHERIDAN (New York 1961). Robert-Tricot 1:9–59. P. BENOIT, "Les Analogies de l'inspiration," *Sacra Pagina,* ed. J. COPPENS et al., 2 v. (Gembleux 1959) 1:86–99; "Révélation et inspiration," RevBibl 70 (1963) 321–370. A. DESROCHES, *Jugement pratique et jugement spéculatif chez l'écrivain inspiré* (Ottawa 1958). J. T. FORESTELL, "The Limitation of Inerrancy," CathBibl Quart 20 (1958) 9–18. R. A. F. MACKENZIE, "Some Problems in the Field of Inspiration," *ibid.* 1–8. J. L. MCKENZIE, "The Social Character of Inspiration," *ibid.* 24 (1962) 115–124. K. RAHNER, *Inspiration in the Bible,* tr. C. H. HENKEY (Quaestiones disputatae 1; New York 1961). D. M. STANLEY, "The Concept of Biblical Inspiration," CathThSoc 13 (1958) 65–95. P. GRELOT, "Études sur la théologie du Livre Saint," NouvRevTh 85 (1963) 785–806, 897–925; "L'inspiration scripturaire," RechScRel 51 (1963) 337–382. Protestant. D. M. BEEGLE, *The Inspiration of Scripture* (Philadelphia 1963). H. D. MCDONALD, *Ideas of Revelation: An Historical Study, A.D. 1700 to A.D. 1860* (New York 1959); *Theories of Revelation: An Historical Study, 1860–1960* (New York 1963). K. RUNIA, *Karl Barth's Doctrine of Holy Scripture* (Grand Rapids 1962).

[J. T. FORESTELL]

BIBLE, III (CANON)

Canonicity, the history of the canon, and the history of the religious books rejected from the official canon of the Bible are concepts that are quite distinct from the concept of the inspiration of the Bible. After an introductory section on the canon of Scripture in general, this article treats of the history of the OT canon, the history of the NT canon, the apocryphal (or rejected) books of the OT, and the apocrypha of the NT.

1. INTRODUCTORY

Understanding of the canon of Sacred Scripture in general requires clarification of the terminology used in this matter, the relationship between inspiration and canonicity, the criterion of the canon for the Catholic Church, and the criteria used in other Christian Churches.

Terminology. The Greek word κανών, from which the English word canon is a direct borrowing, signifies (1) a cane, a straight rod; (2) a measuring rod; and (3) a norm, a law. In the last sense the term is used for a law, or canon, of *Canon Law. In regard to the Bible the term was first used to designate the idea of the Sacred Scripture as the norm of true religion, but it was soon employed also in the sense of norm or list defining what books constitute the Sacred Scriptures. It is in the last sense that the term is used throughout this article. The Catholic canon of the Bible is the list of books that the Catholic Church officially declares to be inspired by God and presents as such to the faithful (*see* CANON, BIBLICAL).

Disagreement on which books are inspired already existed among the early Jews; the Palestinian Jews accepted a shorter list than did the Alexandrian Jews. In the first Christian centuries those books that were recognized by all were called ὁμολογούμενοι, the books "agreed upon"; those not accepted by all were called ἀντιλεγόμενοι, "contradicted" or ἀμφιβαλλόμενοι, "doubtful." Since the 16th century the terms introduced by *Sixtus of Siena have superseded the old terms, so that the ὁμολογούμενοι are now called protocanonical, and the ἀντιλεγόμενοι are called deuterocanonical. Catholics today accept both protocanonical and deuterocanonical books as inspired and part of the canon. Protestants generally reject the deuterocanonical books and call them apocryphal. Catholics reserve the term apocryphal for books other than the deuterocanonical books, e.g., the Gospel of James. This latter category of books, which Catholics call apocryphal, are called pseudepigraphical ("falsely titled") by Protestants. *See* BIBLE, III (CANON), 4, 5.

Inspiration and Canonicity. All the books in the canon are inspired, but it is debated whether or not there is or could be any inspired book that, because of its loss, is not in the canon. The Church has not settled the question. The more general opinion is that some inspired books probably have been lost. In 1 Cor 5.9, St. Paul refers to a previous letter of his, and in 2 Cor 2.3–9; 7.8–12 he refers to an earlier letter different from 1 Corinthians. However, not all agree on these conclusions. In Col 4.16 Paul speaks of a letter that he wrote to the Laodiceans, which as such is not extant, although it may possibly be our Ephesians. The OT, too, mentions lost books, which may have been inspired (1 Chr 29.29; 2 Chr 9.29; 12.15).

Catholic Criterion of Canonicity. The problem of the criterion of the canon remains only partially solved. Catholics hold that the proximate and ultimate criterion is the infallible decision of the Church in listing its sacred and canonical books. St. Augustine says (*C. epist. fund.* 5.5; CSEL 25:197): "I would not believe the Gospel, if the authority of the Catholic Church did not move me."

But the question remains: By what means did the Church determine the matter? The testimony of Christ and the Apostles, who cite the OT as a sacred work, is indicative of the inspiration of the books they cite. Their testimony may suffice for the entire OT, inasmuch as they often quote from the Septuagint (LXX), which contained both protocanonical and deuterocanonical books. Once the inspiration of 2 Peter is established, the fact that 2 Pt 3.16 refers to certain Pauline Epistles in conjunction with other Scriptures (i.e., the OT) suffices to show the inspiration of genuinely Pauline writings. Some hold that the Church in determining the canon preserves a revelation left by the Apostles on this matter. It is difficult to suppose, however, that the Apostles left behind an explicit tradition about the canon. The history of the canon shows too many doubts and fluctuations for this theory to be plausible.

M. J. Lagrange and S. Zarb hold that apostolic authorship suffices to establish inspiration for the NT, and prophetic authorship for the OT. In this case, although Mark and Luke were not Apostles, they wrote down the gospel as preached respectively by Peter and Paul, who thus became the ultimate authors of the second and third Gospels. Christ gave the Apostles a special understanding of the kingdom (Mk 4.11) and promised special guidance (Jn 14.16; 16.13) so that their word was received as the word of God (Lk 10.16; 1 Thes 2.13). Thus, although apostolicity and inspiration are not the same, yet, when the Apostles wrote, they were inspired. Tradition supports this theory. The *Muratorian Canon excludes the Shepherd of *Hermas as not apostolic. St. Justin (*Apol.* 1.67; PG 6.429) says the Gospels are "memoirs" of the Apostles. Origen (*Peri archon* 1.4; PG 11:118) says: "It is manifestly preached in the churches . . . that that Spirit inspired each of the holy prophets and Apostles." St. Irenaeus (*Adv. haer.* 3.1.1; PG 7:844) says of the Apostles: "They then preached it, but afterwards, by the will of God, handed it down to us in the Scriptures." Tertullian (*Adv. Marc.* 4.2.1; CorpChrist 1:547) says: "The evangelical instrument has the Apostles as authors, on whom this duty of promulgating the gospel was imposed by God Himself." St. Augustine (*C. adv. leg.* 1.20.39; PL 42:626) says that if the apocrypha attributed to Andrew and John "were really theirs, they would have been accepted by the Church."

Opponents of this view note that not all books of the OT are by prophets and say the patristic texts merely show that these books were traditionally accepted, but they do not make apostolicity a criterion. K. Rahner suggests that the NT is willed by God as a constituent element of the Church and is inspired in that sense and that the Church is able to recognize its own constituent elements. Although Y. M. J. Congar accepts this view in general, he objects that it minimizes the role of Apostles and prophets. He admits that inspiration was a grace of the primitive Church, but he holds that it was primarily a personal grace of the Apostles.

Protestant Criteria of Canonicity. Early Protestant attempts to solve the problem made the criteria subjective: Luther made the criterion consist in the intensity with which Christ is preached according to the principle of justification by faith alone, and therefore he excluded James from the canon. Others, especially Calvin, appealed to the interior testimony of God given to each reader, or to the edifying nature of the matter, or to its sublimity and simplicity.

More recent Protestant attempts have sought a more objective criterion. T. Zahn tried to explain the origin of the canon by saying that the early Christians used the present canonical books in public worship and eventually came to revere them as sacred. The liturgical reading of the words and acts of Jesus strengthened the religious life of the Assembly. To this one may object: why was canonical acceptance not given to works like the Shepherd of Hermas, or to the first Epistle of Clement (which also was read at public worship)? A. von Harnack suggested that all the men of the first generation had charisms, and so all that they wrote was considered inspired. The Roman Church, to defend itself against Montanists and other dissidents, in A.D. 180 drew up a closed list of inspired works. Against von Harnack's view is the objection that the Church never put charismatic utterances on the same plane as apostolic teaching. R. H. Grützmacher tries to find a middle way between the historical and authoritative approach. According to him, historical criticism chooses a number of books, as early as possible in origin, from which each Christian by an inner light chooses those on which to found his faith. The Church aids this choice, having worked on the canon for centuries and having settled on those books that experience shows useful for salvation. Another Protestant, G. B. Smith, concludes that only when one admits a divine authority in the Church can there be an infallible canon. Liberal Protestants, because of a loose concept of inspiration, show little concern with the problem of the criterion of the canon.

Bibliography: H. OPPEL, KANΩN: *Zur Bedeutungsgeschichte des Wortes und seiner lateinischen Entsprechungen (regula-norma)* (Leipzig 1937). L. WENGER, "Canon in den römischen Rechtsquellen und in den Papyri: Eine Wortstudie" SBWien (PhilosHist) 220.2 (1942). H. HÖPFL, DBSuppl 1:1022–45. S. ZARB, *De historia canonis utriusque testamenti* (2d ed. Rome 1934). K. RAHNER, *Inspiration in the Bible*, tr. C. H. HENKEY (New York 1961). Y. M. J. CONGAR, "Inspiration des écritures canoniques et apostolicité de l'Église," RevScPhilTh 45 (1961) 32–42. G. B. SMITH, "Can the Distinction between Canonical and Non-canonical Writings be Maintained?" *Biblical World*, NS 37 (1911) 19–29. J. VAN DODEWAARD, EncDictBibl 308–314. T. VON ZAHN, *Geschichte des neutestamentlichen Kanons*, 2 v. (Erlangen 1888–92) 1:83; *Einige Bemerkungen zu A. Harnacks Prüfung der Geschichte des neutestamentlichen Kanons* (Leipzig 1889). A. VON HARNACK, *Die Entstehung des Neuen Testaments und die wichtigsten Folgen der neuen Schöpfung (Beiträge zur Einleitung in das N.T.* 6; Leipzig 1914). R. H. GRÜTZMACHER, *Die Haltbarkeit des Kanonbegriffes: Theologische Studien Th. Zahn dargebracht* (Leipzig 1900).

[W. G. MOST]

2. HISTORY OF OLD TESTAMENT CANON

The broad phases of this topic can best be treated by a consideration of the history of the development of the OT canon among the Jews and then treating of the history of this canon in the Christian Church. The particular treatment of each of these is noted below.

CANON OF THE OLD TESTAMENT AMONG THE JEWS

In the development of the OT canon among the Jews, note should be taken of the early stages in the formation of the three parts of the Hebrew canon, of the motives for the canonization of the sacred books, of the formal closing of the canon, and of the collections of the sacred books among the Jews of the Diaspora and among the Jewish sectaries at Qumran.

Early Formation. The formation of the OT books themselves is a matter distinct from the formation of the OT canon. The former was the material growth of the OT, book by book; the latter was the origin and development of the special attitudes toward these books that saw in them works inspired by God. These two aspects of the story of the OT are so closely akin that they tend to fuse with one another in any discussion of the development of the OT. There is, nevertheless, a true distinction between them, and it is useful to take note of it at the very outset.

The first clear harbinger of Jewish convictions toward the canon of Scripture is met with in Josephus (*Contra Apion* 1.38–42). He held the hallmarks of the canonical books to be: that their number is fixed, that they are sacred and as such are to be distinguished from all other books, that they are of divine origin and therefore enjoy supreme authority, and that they were written in the span of time between Moses and Artaxerxes I. On this last point Josephus was obviously mistaken, because several of the OT books were demonstrably written after the time of Artaxerxes I (d. 423 B.C.).

The Hebrew collection of sacred books evolved over several centuries. Of this historical process there is not very much definite information at hand. Some have supposed that the threefold division of the Hebrew canon into the Law, the Prophets, and the Writings really marks three stages in the development of the collection. According to this view, the first canon was the Law, the second the Prophets, and the third the Writings. There is another point of view favored by Hölscher that sees the Law, the Prophets, and the Writings growing more or less concurrently, with no fixation of the three sections being effected separately at different times. The determination would have been made for the tripartite whole at one time.

The Law. In 4 Kgs 22.8 it is reported that the high priest Helcia (*c.* 621 B.C.) discovered the book of the Law in the Temple. This was probably the nucleus of Deuteronomy as it is now known (Deuteronomy ch. 12–26). It was recognized as divinely authoritative, for it was taken as the foundation of a fresh dedication of the people to God (4 Kgs 23.1–14). The growth of the Torah entered upon a new stage with the arrival of Ezra in Jerusalem *c.* 397 B.C. He promulgated a book of law that is identified by some with the Priestly Code. It agrees with the latter in requiring that the Feast of Booths (Tabernacles) be celebrated for 8 days, rather than 7 as prescribed by Deuteronomy (Dt 16.13).

Frequently the Samaritan schism is introduced as a help in fixing the dates of the *Pentateuch. The argument runs thus: The *Samaritans have a Pentateuch that agrees in substance with that of the Hebrews. The Pentateuch must have achieved its final form and have been acknowledged as inspired at some time before the Samaritan break with the Jews, since it is unlikely that the Samaritans would have taken anything from the

Jewish community after they separated from it. The difficulty comes, however, in ascertaining the dates of the Samaritan breach from the available data. The probable conclusion is that the Pentateuch was a complete collection received as inspired at least by the middle of the 4th century B.C., when it is estimated the Samaritan schism took place.

The Prophets. Around the Law as center there soon began to cluster other books that were held in veneration by the people. The Former Prophets, as the Hebrews referred to the books of Josue, Judges, Samuel, and Kings, are known to have been grouped together with the five books of the Law from as early as the mid-4th century B.C. The fact that they were associated in this fashion with the Torah seems to indicate that in the minds of the people these books too were sacred.

As to the Latter Prophets, Isaia, Jeremia, Ezechiel, and the Twelve (Minor Prophets), these books were being produced since the 8th century B.C. Eventually they were brought together in a collection. A letter reproduced in 2 Mc 1.10–2.18 speaks of the formation of a library containing, among others, prophetical books (2 Mc 2.13). Nehemia (*c.* 425 B.C.; Neh 13.6–7) is credited with founding this library. Some understand its establishment as marking an early stage in the collection of prophetical books that were accepted as inspired. Even if all credit is denied to this letter, it is justifiable to conclude that, at the time when 2 Machabees was written, the Prophets were known as a collection of sacred books. In Sirach (Ecclesiasticus) Ben Sirach (*c.* 180 B.C.) alludes to the books of the Twelve Prophets besides the three great Prophets (Sir 48.22; 49.7–10). He appears to know the Prophets as a collection. Daniel (167–164 B.C.) makes mention of "the books" and then cites from Jeremia (Dn 9.2). This can be taken as an oblique testimony to the author's acceptance of Jeremia's work as inspired. It seems, therefore, safe to conclude that, at least by the beginning of the 2d century B.C., the Prophets were received as an inspired collection.

The Writings. In the preface, which is usually not considered canonical, to the Greek translation of Sirach there are allusions that imply the existence of the Writings as a collection. These references date from the time when Sirach was translated into Greek (*c.* 132 B.C.). The translator speaks of "the Law and the Prophets and the later authors," and of "the Law itself, the Prophets and the rest of the books." It appears from this that the third division of the canon was only falling into place at the time, since it had not yet been named. From these words in the preface to Sirach it is obviously not possible to establish the precise number of books or which ones were contained in the collection.

By the beginning of the Christian Era the third group was definitely recognized as inspired, since certain passages in the NT presuppose the Writings as part of the OT by that time. In Lk 24.44, for example, Christ speaks of what is written in "the Law of Moses, the Prophets and the Psalms" as having to come true. The sacred character of these books is obviously assumed. Though some are dubious about understanding the term in this way, it is very probable that the whole collection of the Writings is referred to under the name of the first book in it, the Psalms.

Josephus, writing at the end of the 1st Christian century, alludes to an OT canon that included the Writings

(*Contra Apion* 1.38–42). Philo too is familiar with the tripartite division of Scripture (*De Vita Contempl.* 25). There is an explicit reference to the Writings in the Talmud (*Baba Bathra* 14b–15a). Though this would have been written down only after A.D. 200, it probably stems from an earlier tradition.

The Writings do not seem to have been accepted as readily as the Law or the Prophets. Perhaps this is to be explained in terms of the liturgical usage noted below. Though gradually both the Prophets and the Writings found a place in the Hebrew canon, neither of these two was considered to enjoy the same importance as the Law.

Motive for Canonization. The formation of the OT as sketched above marks the stages along the way to final canonization. Canonization in the strict sense came later and involved not only the acceptance of some books but also the exclusion of others. There is no general agreement among scholars about the motives that impelled the Jewish community to accept the OT books as canonical. Some have supposed that certain books were received as canonical because of their legal character; they contain "the canons," the Law. Others maintain that it is an inspired quality of this literature that led to its canonization. These books were regarded as sacred because they contained the Word of God. Östborn's theory proposes that a book was held to be canonical if it had a specific motif, i.e., if in some way it celebrated or at least reported Yahweh's activity. This underlying idea endowed the book with a cultic value, so that it could be employed in the *Jewish liturgy of the synagogue. A book in which Yahweh's activity was memorialized was held to be canonical, i.e., religiously right and suitable for worship. Östborn's hypothesis has not convinced many, because his endeavor to discover a fundamental theme throughout the whole OT is forced and open to question at several points.

Closing of Old Testament Canon. From the earliest times the people of Israel held certain writings in the highest regard as having originated from God. In Dt 31.26, for example, the Levites are enjoined to reserve the book of the Law beside the ark of the covenant. Although there are frequent references to the early collecting of books [Dt 31.9–13, 24–26; Jos 24.26; 1 Sm 10.25; 2 Chr 29.30; Ps 71(72).20; Prv 25.1], there is no explicit evidence of an official closing of the OT canon in pre-Christian times. The absence of such information has encouraged speculation. It was believed for a time that the collection of OT books was fixed conclusively by Ezra. The proponents of this theory relied largely on the apocryphal 4 Ezra 14.19–48, written *c.* A.D. 90, about 500 years after Ezra lived. But when carefully examined this passage does little more than ascribe to Ezra some role in the preservation of the OT texts. It does not unequivocally affirm that he was the final arbiter of the OT canon.

At another time it was believed that the OT canon was determined by Ezra together with his associates, "the men of the Great Synagogue." Elias Levita first suggested this in *Massoreth ha-Massoreth* (1538). The view was approved by Johannes *Buxtorf the Elder in *Tiberias sive Commentarius Masorethicus* (Basel 1620). Buxtorf's endorsement helped the theory gain wide acceptance for a time. Brian *Walton also wrote concerning the men of the Great Synagogue: "Their work of establishing the Canon possessed truly divine authority . . ." (*Polyglott. Proleg.* 4.2, London 1657).

The very existence of the Great Synagogue, to say nothing of its alleged canonizing function, is open to question. One grave objection to its existence is the complete silence about it in the OT itself, as well as in Josephus, Philo, and the Apocrypha. The earliest reference to such a group is in the Mishnaic treatise, *Pirke Avoth* (c.1), which dates only from the 2d or 3d Christian century.

The canon of the OT was not formally and authoritatively defined during the pre-Christian era. It was the threat of the Christian "heresy" with its wide diffusion of Christian writings that led Judaism to make certain decisions about its sacred canon. The books of the Law and the Prophets were exactly known, having been established as sacred by fairly long liturgical use. At least by the beginning of the Christian Era, lessons from the Law and the Prophets were read in the synagogue (Lk 4.16–19; Acts 13.15, 27). The Writings were credited also with a sacred quality. They were not, however, in general use in the synagogue, except for the Psalms. Thus the people could not have accepted from liturgical practice the books that were in the third part of the canon.

Other factors in the final settlement of the Jewish canon may have been the developing rivalry between Greek and Jewish culture and the rise and spread of apocalyptic literature. The influence both of Greek philosophy and of the proliferating Jewish apocalypses was viewed with alarm by Jewish religious leaders. They moved to neutralize this threat to the faith by establishing a collection of books that Jews could accept as authoritative. The decision taken at Jamnia (Jabneel) *c.* A.D. 100 by a Jewish synod was the issue of a longstanding discussion about which books, particularly among the Writings, belonged to the canon. Though the action of the synod was given as final and decisive, the canonicity of Esther, the Song of Songs, and Ecclesiastes continued to be doubted after Jamnia.

Alexandrian Canon. It is problematical whether one may speak of a LXX canon in the sense of a formally authorized list of books. There appears to be little warrant, direct or implied, for concluding that in the Jewish *Diaspora any authorized group ever independently took a stand on the canon. All too commonly it is assumed that great differences of opinion divided Palestinian Jews from those of the Dispersion and that the differences sprang from divergent theories of inspiration prevalent in Alexandria and Jerusalem. This is a purely gratuitous inference [see Peter Katz, ZNTWiss 47 (1956) 209]. The Hellenistic Jews before the fall of the theocracy in Palestine looked reverently toward Jerusalem and favored religious currents coming from it. Doubts were referred there for solution (Josephus, *Contra Apion* 1.30–36). They turned to Jerusalem for their Scriptures (2 Mc 2.13–15) and for its translation [Est 11.1 (Vulg); 10.31 (LXX)]. If they used the deuterocanonical books in the Diaspora, it was because they had received them from Palestine. Moreover it is not patent that these books gained anything in transit, as though they came to enjoy a canonical status in Alexandria that they had never possessed in Palestine. Canonicity could not have been a problem at that time, for a rigid concept of it had not yet emerged. Palestine, then, was the source of the esteem for the deuterocanonical works. The OT, as it is found in the LXX, reflects, therefore, a tradition older than the present Hebrew Bible in regard to its list of sacred books.

Canon of the Qumran Community. The bearing of the writings of the *Qumran Community upon the question of the OT canon remains a matter for discussion. Although fragments of some of the deuterocanonical books (Tobit and Sirach) have been found among the *Dead Sea Scrolls, not everyone thinks that this is sufficient evidence to establish their acceptance as canonical by the Qumran community. The Qumran scribes apparently adhered to a particular script and format in copying unquestioned canonical works; the deuterocanonical books did not receive this special treatment. This treatment of Biblical texts, however, was not invariable; and therefore hard and fast conclusions cannot be drawn from it.

One must keep in mind that the notion of a strict canon was not fully developed at this time. That the deuterocanonical books were copied at all at Qumran would indicate that the sectarians saw them as works of some special religious value. That they were not copied in the precise way as were the Law and the Prophets may merely point to the lesser degree of veneration in which they were held. The Qumran collection, then, was similar to the Greek collection. Neither was absolutely fixed, and both displayed considerable variation regarding their number and arrangement. Both reflected a tradition antedating the Masoretic canon and one less restrictive in recognizing books as sacred.

CANON OF THE OLD TESTAMENT AMONG CHRISTIANS

In the history of the OT canon among Christians, note should be taken of the use of the OT in the NT, of the attitude of the Fathers and writers in the Western Church until the Council of Trent, of the OT canon in the Eastern Churches, and of the divergences between the Catholic and the Protestant canons of the OT.

In the New Testament. An examination of the NT use of the OT shows that the NT writers had the same broad view of the sacred books as the Hellenist and Qumran Jews had of them. The NT writers knew and used a fuller collection that included the so-called deuterocanonical books. The OT of the early Church was not the Masoretic Text (MT), but the Septuagint (LXX), which contained the deuterocanonical as well as the protocanonical books. In the LXX the former were not, as in some later versions, relegated to a limbo of doubt by being grouped together in a place apart. Rather, they were interspersed throughout the whole OT and assigned to places where they seemed best to fit. For example, historical books such as 1 Esdras, Tobit, and Judith found their place following Chronicles and Nehemia. Books of a poetical character such as Wisdom and Sirach followed Job, Canticles, Ecclesiastes, and Proverbs. This led to the acceptance of these books as an integral part of the OT used by the early Church in the West.

Canon of the Western Church. The consensus of the Church through the 2d and 3d centuries was favorable to the full OT catalogue. It is supported by Pope St. *Clement I, St. *Polycarp, the Shepherd of *Hermas, St. *Irenaeus, and *Tertullian, all of whom employ the deuterocanonical writings as Scripture.

Doubts began to develop in the East in the 4th century. These doubts seem to have emerged as an aftermath of the Christian polemic with the Jews. Since the Jews from the time of the Synod of Jamnia no longer recognized the deuterocanonical literature, it would have been futile for Christian apologists to make use of them. *Justin Martyr says this expressly (*Dial. Tryphon*). These hesitations gradually evolved into misgivings about the canonicity itself of the books. Attitudes toward the canon through the next several centuries were marked by a curious discrepancy between statement and practice. Several writers express themselves in favor of the restricted Hebrew canon; yet, in practice, they freely employ the deuterocanonical books as Scripture. The people who lapsed into this ambiguity, again, did not have a clearly thought out concept of canonicity and consequently did not express themselves with precision. Though they seem to imply that the deuterocanonical works were of lesser authority than the protocanonical books, they nonetheless admit that they were received by the Church, and thus they implicitly attest to their authoritative status.

St. *Jerome (A.D. 340–420) distinguished between "canonical books" and "ecclesiastical books." The latter, he judged, were circulated by the Church as good "spiritual reading," but were not recognized as authoritative Scripture. St. *Augustine, however, did not recognize this distinction. He accepted all the books in the LXX as of equal value, noting that those designated as apocryphal by Jerome were of either unknown or obscure origin. Augustine's point of view prevailed and the deuterocanonical books remained in the Vulgate, the Latin version that received official standing at the Council of Trent.

The situation remained unclear in the ensuing centuries, although the tendency to accept the disputed books was becoming all the time more general. In spite of this trend some, e.g., John Damascene, Gregory the Great, Walafrid, Nicholas of Lyra and Tostado, continued to doubt the canonicity of the deuterocanonical books. St. *Thomas Aquinas has for a long time been listed as a dissenter because of his supposed doubts about Wisdom and Sirach, but P. Synave has argued convincingly to clear him of this imputation [RevBibl 21 (1924) 522–533]. The Council of Trent definitively settled the matter of the OT Canon. That this had not been done previously is apparent from the uncertainty that persisted up to the time of Trent.

Canon of the Oriental Church. The Syrian Church employed only the Hebrew canon in the Peshitta translation. Subsequently, under the influence of the LXX, it used a canon substantially the same as the LXX. The Nestorians, however, refrained from this adjustment.

M. Jugie has shown conclusively that from the earliest times through the Middle Ages there was general agreement in the Byzantine Church that the disputed books were canonical. The disputations between Latins and Greeks in the years following the breach show no disagreement centering on the OT canon. In presenting to the Greeks theological arguments that they should find relevant and decisive, the Council of Florence did not hesitate to make free use of texts from the deuterocanonical books to bolster the doctrines on purgatory and the *filioque.

Only in the 17th century, because of Protestant influence, was the canonicity of the deuterocanonical books first seriously questioned in the Oriental Churches. Zachary Gerganos (1627), a Greek who had studied at Wittenberg, was the first to dissent from the traditional Byzantine teaching. Such views, aired by others in the East, drew the fire of significant persons both in the Slavic and Greek churches. In Russia, throughout the 18th century, opinion was fluid regarding the deuterocanonical works. Finally in the 19th century Russian Orthodox theologians universally excluded them from the canon.

The misgivings about the traditional Greek canon in Russian Orthodoxy gradually filtered into the Greek Church, and traditional canonicity became an open question.

Divergences between Catholic and Protestant Canon. Differences between Catholic and Protestant views on the OT canon are the result of differing attitudes toward the deuterocanonical books. The Wyclif Bible (1382), under Jerome's influence, reproduced only the books found in the Hebrew canon. The Coverdale Bible (1535) included the deuterocanonical works. Luther's translation (1534) grouped them together at the end of the OT under the caption: "Apocrypha: these are books which are not held equal to the sacred Scriptures and yet are useful and good for reading." The Thirty-Nine Articles of Religion (1563) of the Church of England asserted that they were to be read "for example of life and instruction of manners," though they ought not to be employed "to establish any doctrine." The King James Bible of 1611 printed the books between the OT and the NT. John Lightfoot (1643) spoke out against this arrangement because he feared that "the wretched Apocrypha," so placed between the OT and NT, might give the mistaken impression that they form a link between the two Testaments. The Westminster Confession (1647) decreed that the books, "not being of divine inspiration, are no part of the canon of Scripture, and therefore are of no authority in the Church of God; nor to be in any otherwise approved, or made use of than other human writings." The British and Foreign Bible Society decided (1827) to omit the controverted books in future publications, except for some pulpit Bibles, with this statement: "The Principles of the Society exclude the circulation of those Books or parts of Books which are usually termed Apocryphal." On the Continent the Protestant position does not seem to have changed essentially from what it was shortly after the Reformation.

Edmond Jacob expressed a current of thought in modern Protestantism when he describes the Apocrypha as a "bridge" between the OT and NT and a "link" in the chain of the unity of revelation. He adds that, though their witness is secondary, they should be inserted at the end of the OT as was done at the time of the Reformation [E. Jacob, "Considerations sur l'Autorité canonique de l'Ancien Testament," *Le Problème Biblique dans le Protestantisme*, ed. J. Boisset (Paris 1955) 81–82].

Bibliography: EncDictBibl 308–313. E. Mangenot, DTC 2.2: 1569–82. H. Höpfl DBSuppl 1:1022–45. Hastings DB (1963) 121–123. W. R. Smith, *The Old Testament in the Jewish Church* (London 1902). M. Jugie, *Histoire du canon de l'Ancien Testament dans l'église grecque et l'église russe* (Paris 1909). M. L. Margolis, *The Hebrew Scriptures in the Making* (Philadelphia 1922). S. Zeitlin, *An Historical Study of the Canonization of the Hebrew Scriptures* (Philadelphia 1933). G. Östborn, *Cult and Canon: A Study of the Canonization of the OT* (Uppsala 1950). H. H. Rowley, *The Growth of the Old Testament* (New York 1950). F. V. Filson, *Which Books Belong in the Bible? A Study of the Canon* (Philadelphia 1957). W. Barclay, *The Making of the Bible* (New York 1961). B. J. Roberts, "The Dead Sea Scrolls and the Old Testament Scriptures," BullJRylLib 36 (1953) 75–96. A. C. Sundberg, "The Old Testament of the Early Church," HarvThRev 51 (1958) 205–226. P. Katz, "The Old Testament Canon in Palestine and Alexandria," ZNTWiss 47 (1956) 191–217.

[J. C. Turro]

3. HISTORY OF NEW TESTAMENT CANON

The complete list of NT books was recognized as sacred and canonical only after a protracted history. The nature of this history and its theological implications will be discussed first. Then consideration will be given to the actual formation of the collection of NT books, the final fixation of the canon, and the criteria of NT canonicity.

Problem of the New Testament Canon

The development of the NT canon is an example of the development of dogma. Its history was locally vague and varied and not definitively completed until the Council of Trent.

Historical Summary. Before the middle of the 2d century the question had never been raised as to what books were sacred or how many sacred books there were. The canon, already implicitly present in the apostolic age, gradually became explicit through a concatenation of providential factors forming and fixing it. God works slowly through men's minds and historical events to produce His ultimate purpose.

The Church in the early postapostolic age was aware of but three authorities: the OT, the spoken word of Christ, and the oral testimony of the Apostles. Only gradually and obscurely did the words of Christ as recorded by His disciples assume the authority of Scripture. Then, as people's memory of the Apostles dimmed, their writings along with the letters of St. Paul, came into prominence as sacred.

To give a summary glance, the 27 NT books may be divided into two categories. (1) The protocanonical books, or books of the "first list": the 4 Gospels, the 13 Pauline Epistles (excluding Hebrews), 1 John, and 1 Peter. These books were universally accepted from the middle of the 2d century with practically no doubts or hesitations. (2) The deuterocanonical books, or books of the "second list": Hebrews, Apocalypse, 2 Peter, 2 John, 3 John, James, and Jude. These suffered awkward moments, both locally and universally. The last five had an obscure and fluctuating history of acceptance, especially among the Latins and the Syrians. The Latins doubted the Pauline authorship of Hebrews and therefore also its canonicity. The Greeks and the Syrians, after the 2d century, doubted the Johannine authorship of Apocalypse and thus also its canonicity. Besides the protocanonical and deuterocanonical books, there were many rival books for which canonicity was claimed, particularly among the Greeks.

In the East the canon was fluid and extended to many books not now recognized as canonical. Justin's εὐαγγέλιον, for instance, was any proclaiming of the good news, and many writings could have fulfilled this definition. In the West the canon was more juridical and normative, tending to exclude rather than include sacred books. Only in the 5th century did the Church come to a universal stabilization of the canon, and not until the Council of Trent did the canon receive its dogmatic definition.

Church's Relationship to Canon and Inspiration. Befor the history of the canon is traced from its apostolic formation to its fixation among the Latins, Greeks, and Syrians, it must be placed into proper relationship to both inspiration and the Church [see BIBLE, II (INSPIRATION)]. The history of the canon was a dramatic recognition by the Church that the living Word of God (God's activity as a revealer of divine truth) is intrinsically joined to the inspired written word of God. NT Scripture is the original self-representation in written concretization of what the early Church lived and believed. Sacred writings developed and formed as its very life processes, the distilled essence of itself. Whether Gospel, letter, or sermon, these writings were the intrinsic expression of its life—in a unique way.

God definitively and eschatologically formed the Church in a historical process, "the Christ Event." The mysteries of Christ, His life, death and Resurrection (with His Ascension and gift of the Spirit) were God's revelation of Himself to man, His Word in the Christ Event. These mysteries have been continued in the *Mystical Body of Christ, the Church. Scripture was thus a constitutive element of the early Church, and through it the living Word of God became objectivized in the written word of God wherein His saving activity is contained and expressed. Scripture, therefore, came into existence, not only on the occasion of the founding of the early Church, but also as an inner moment of its formation under God's direction. In the process of the canonization of the NT canon the Church, the prolongation of the Christ Event, rediscovered itself in the written concretization of its very essence.

Yet, it seems, the fact of the inspiration of Scripture could have become known only by a revelation given by God in the apostolic age. Otherwise it would be impossible to ensure the historical plausibility of this revelation in view of the uncertainties and doubts involved in the proclamation of the canon.

Two things must be considered: first, the original revelation contained in the inspired writings, which was initially and essentially the self-knowledge of the Church; second, the reflex knowledge and expression of this revelation wherein the Church claimed and proclaimed what had always belonged to it. The first revelation, the inspired content of the NT Scriptures, was complete with the death of the last Apostle. The reflex knowledge, however, involved a subsequent, divinely guided historical process.

FORMATION OF THE COLLECTION OF
NEW TESTAMENT BOOKS

Through the ages the Church connaturally recognized within its sacred writings something consonant with its nature. It recognized itself. The historical process of this recognition began with the Church of the first postapostolic age, which held three authoritative sources of revelation: the OT, Christ, and the Apostles.

Authoritative Sources in the Early Church. From its very beginning and as a part of its essence the Church possessed a canon of inspired writings: the OT. Humanly and psychologically speaking, Jesus "discovered" Himself in the OT by uniting in Himself all the OT paradoxical themes of *salvation history. He found His coming, His work, and His death foretold there (see

Lk 4.16–22; 24.24–27, 44–46; Jn 5.39). Further, He used the OT as the incontestably authoritative word of God to prove, for instance, the indissolubility of marriage (Gn 1.27; 2.24; see Mk 10.6–9), the resurrection of the dead (Ex 3.6; see Mk 12.26–27), the superiority of the Messiah over David [Ps 109(110).1; see Mk 12.35–37]. As eschatological fulfillment, He transformed what was temporary and changeable into the eternal and unchangeable. This is exemplified by His position on divorce (Mk 10.2–12) and by the so-called antitheses of the *Sermon on the Mount: "You have heard that it was said to the ancients. . . . But I say to you . . ." (Mt 5.21–46). He had not come to destroy, but to complete the Law and the Prophets (Mt 5.17).

The apostolic Church, following its Master, held the OT as absolute authority in demonstrating the Christ Event. This conviction stemmed fundamentally from the fact that the OT was revered as the inspired word of God (2 Pt 1.19–21; 2 Tm 3.14–17). NT writings are full of "proof texts" from the OT; especially Romans, Galatians, Hebrews, and the Petrine sermons in Acts.

The Fathers of the postapostolic age likewise considered the OT as authoritative, but with notable variations. The letters of *Ignatius of Antioch, for instance, contain only two explicit OT quotations, both from Proverbs (Ad Ephes. 5.2; Ad Magn. 12). The Gospels, which he significantly calls "the flesh of Christ," dominate his letters. The Prophets are important because "they foretold the gospel of Christ, hoped in Him, and awaited His coming" (Ad Philad. 5.2). The Shepherd of *Hermas, on the other hand, indicates no acquaintance at all with the OT. Yet 1 Clement, composed about 40 years earlier in Rome, gives more than 100 citations from the OT and only 2 from the Gospels. For Clement, God speaks to Christians through the OT. This Father continuously reinforces his teaching by citations from the OT, but with an unquestionably Christian interpretation. According to the Epistle of *Barnabas the Christians were the first to understand the OT correctly.

The very fact that a Christian interpretation was given to the OT accredits supreme authority not primarily to the OT Scriptures but to Christ whose person, in word and work, was glimpsed shining through these Scriptures. The Apostles preached not so much the OT as Christ and His work of redemption. The Gospels give witness to Him in whom alone are hid all the treasures of wisdom and knowledge. St. Paul considers Christ's word the supreme norm that decides matters without further discussion (1 Cor 7.10; 9.41; Acts 20.35).

Authorized by Jesus and endowed with the power of the Holy Spirit to preach the gospel and establish the Christian community, the Apostles were regarded, not only as "the eyewitnesses and ministers of the word" (Lk 1.2), but also as the final authority on the traditions in which the authentic words of Christ and their interpretation were found. To resist false teachers was the duty of the Apostles (Jude 17–19; 2 Pt 3.1–2).

In the early postapostolic age the authority of the Apostles was further enhanced. Ignatius exhorts the Magnesians to hold fast to the teachings of the Lord and His Apostles (13.1), and Polycarp sets before the Philippians the example of "Paul . . . and the other Apostles" (9.1; 3.2; 11.2–4). The letter known as 2 Clement put "the Apostles" (i.e., the writings of the Apostles) on the same level as "the sacred books" of the Prophets (14.2). However, the authority of the Apostles was not equated with that of Christ, and they were quoted much less often. Yet, as early as 200, Serapion of Antioch said, "We accept Peter and the other Apostles as we accept Christ" (Eusebius, *Hist. Eccl.* 6.12.3).

A canon of Christian inspired writings was inevitable. At first the remembered words of the Lord were preached. But very early they began to be committed to writing. As missionary territory expanded, the Apostles sent letters to individual churches as a substitute for preaching. These were regarded not merely as private letters but as official communications. Yet a considerable time had to elapse before these were gathered together and acknowledged as a second canon of incontestable authority along with the OT.

Development of a Canon of Christian Writings. There was a substantial continuity and development of the Christian Church from its birth until the time when its emergence into full relief in the latter part of the 2d century was witnessed to by profane history. Although from a historical viewpoint the early moments of the Church and its inspired books are shrouded in obscurity, Luke (1.1–2) nevertheless indicates that there was much careful investigation and that many undertook to write of Christ. These endeavors, which produced the collection of the four Gospels and the collection of the 13 Epistles of St. Paul, formed the basis for the eventual full canon of 27 NT books.

The Gospels. Probably each of the four canonical Gospels was primarily composed for liturgical reading. From the part of the world where each of these was originally written in the 2d half of the 1st century, copies were soon circulated to other parts of the Christian world, and to some extent the earlier writings seem to have affected the later ones (*see* SYNOPTIC PROBLEM). The four Gospels, however, did not have the canonical authority of the OT before the middle of the 2d century. In the writings of the *Apostolic Fathers there are only three places where the words of Christ as found in the Gospels are introduced by the phrase that is used for the introduction of quotations from the OT, "it is written": Barnabas 4.14 (quoting Mt 22.14), 2 Clement 2.4 (quoting Mt 9.13) and 14.1 (quoting Mk 11.17). Generally the words of Christ, though known from the canonical Gospels, are introduced by the phrase, "the Lord says" or "the Lord has said." Therefore, they are cited, not so much under the authority of Scripture as under that of Our Lord. Further, in the *Didache 8.3 and 2 Clement 8.5 we find the expression, "the Lord directed in His gospel," where the last word refers to the "good news" as preached by Christ rather than to a written Gospel. This can be seen in the fact that the quotations are often not in the precise form as they occur in the canonical Gospels (see, e.g., 1 Clement 13.1–2; 46.7; Polycarp 2.3). Moreover, the Apostolic Fathers cite a few sayings of Christ that are not contained in the canonical Gospels but stem apparently from oral tradition or from apocryphal books (see, e.g., Ignatius, *Ad Smyrn.* 3.2; 2 Clement 4.5; 5.2–4; 8.5; 12.2). These citations, however, are not numerous, and although Justin Martyr uses traditions about Christ that are not in the canonical Gospels, he never introduces them with the formula, "Scripture says." Probably he had a noncanonical Gospel, possibly the so-called Gos-

pel of the Hebrews, from which he quotes the words of Christ (see 5. Apocrypha of the NT). He also mentions the custom of reading "the Memoirs of the Apostles" or "the Prophets" in the liturgy (*1 Apol.* 67.3–5).

Although the Apostolic Fathers speak of the Gospel in the singular only, Justin almost always speaks of the Gospels in the plural, the only exception being in *Dial.* 100.1. This indicates that in his time written accounts of the Gospel were assuming importance. However, he still uses the formula, "the Lord says," which shows that the written Gospels were not yet given an authority in their own right as the word of God.

*Tatian, a disciple of Justin, composed *c.* 170 his *Diatessaron or "harmony" of the four Gospels (see Eusebius, *Hist. Eccl.* 4.29.6). Although he incorporated some apocryphal material, his work is based substantially on the four canonical Gospels and is thus a witness to the special authority that these had now acquired.

Pauline Epistles. Collections of the writings of St. Paul, at first of varying size, were made at a very early period, long before the four Gospels were gathered together. Probably by the end of the 1st or the beginning of the 2d century, the full corpus of the 13 Pauline Epistles (not including Hebrews) was known in most of the Christian communities. In 2 Pt 3.15–16, reference is made to the "epistles" of Paul as already well-known to the faithful to whom 2 Peter is sent, but there is no way of knowing which of Paul's Epistles were included in this collection. Ignatius of Antioch (*c.* 110) used 1 Corinthians, Romans, Ephesians, and Galatians, and probably also Colossians, 1 Timothy, and 1 Thessalonians.

The letter of *Polycarp to the Christians of Philippi is important in determining the time in which the Epistles of St. Paul were known and recognized as having special authority. This letter, which is usually dated between 107 and 117, although ch. 1 through 12 have been recently dated as late as the 4th or 5th century, makes use of almost all the 13 Pauline Epistles, the only ones (perhaps accidentally) not referred to being 1 Thessalonians, Titus, and Philemon. Polycarp often introduces the words of Paul with the phrase, "You already know," thus indicating the acknowledged authority of Paul's letters. Justin uses Romans, 1 and 2 Corinthians, Galatians, Ephesians, Philippians, Colossians, 2 Thessalonians, 1 Timothy, and also Hebrews, although he does not name Paul as the author of these writings.

Full NT Canon. *Melito of Sardes (*c.* 170–180) speaks of the "books of the OT," thereby implying that there were also "books of the NT" that were recognized as inspired Scripture. Justin introduces his numerous quotations from the Gospels with the technical formula for introducing Sacred Scripture, "It is written," as also does Tatian in citing Jn 1.5. When *Marcion broke with the orthodox Church in 140, he drew up his own list of sacred books, in which he rejected the whole OT and accepted only a mutilated version of Luke and 10 of the Pauline Epistles (excluding the three Pastoral Epistles). According to D. de Bruyne and A. von Harnack, it was in reaction to Marcion that the Church established and fixed its NT canon between 160 and 180. For the NT canon of the Roman church at this time *see* MURATORIAN CANON. In 180 the Christian martyrs at Scillium in Numidia, when asked what they had in their satchel, replied: *"Libri et epistolae Pauli,"* the *libri* no doubt including the Gospels, if they also had the Pauline Epistles. During this period also the Apocalypse, 1 John, and 1 Peter reached full canonical stature.

FIXATION OF NEW TESTAMENT CANON

At the beginning of the 3d century the NT canon had passed the first major step toward fixation. Further doubts would center on other than the Gospels and the main Pauline corpus. Since the history of the NT canon at this time differed somewhat from place to place, the process of final fixation will be treated here as this took place separately among the Greeks, the Latins, and the Syrians.

Among the Greeks. The two main centers of the Greek Church at this time were at Alexandria in Egypt and at Caesarea in Palestine. Disputes about the doubtfully authoritative books took different forms at these two places.

In Egypt. Before *Clement of Alexandria (d. after 217) the history of the NT canon in Egypt is obscure. Clement apparently knew all the 27 books of the later-defined NT canon, with the possible exception of James, 2 Peter, and 3 John. But he also attributed a high degree of authority to several other books. Some of these he considered even divinely inspired, such as the Didache, Shepherd of Hermas, Kerygma of Peter, and probably 1 Clement.

*Origen (185–255) largely reflects the view of the Egyptian Church as given by Clement, but he is also aware of controversies regarding the canonical status of 2 Peter, James, Hebrews, 2 and 3 John. He likewise speaks of Jude with reservations.

The Egyptian Codex D contains a canon, known as the *Canon Claramontanus*, probably drawn up in the 3d century, that lists OT and NT books. It has the complete NT canon, including all seven of the *Catholic Epistles as well as the Epistle of Barnabas, Shepherd of Hermas, Acts of Paul, and Apocalypse of Peter. However, the last four (noncanonical) books are marked with a horizontal stroke indicating that they were not accepted as Scripture either by the copyist of the manuscript or in the practice of his community. On the other hand, the Egyptian collection of the Chester Beatty Papyri, dating from the 3d century, does not have the seven Catholic Epistles included in its otherwise correct canon.

*Athanasius lists, in his well-known *Paschal Epistle* of 367, the present complete NT canon of 27 books, concerning which he says: "These are the sources of salvation, for the thirsty may drink deeply of the words to be found here. In these alone is the doctrine of piety recorded. Let no one add to them or take anything away from them." Egypt was thus the first province of the Church to have a fixed and definite canon of 27 NT books.

In Palestine. *Eusebius of Caesarea (d. 340), who is important as a witness to the Palestinian canon, but even more so for his abundant information on the state of the canon in various other Christian communities, gives the following classifications. (1) *Homologoumena*, "agreed on," i.e., books accepted everywhere. These are the four Gospels, Acts, the 14 Pauline Epistles, 1 John, 1 Peter, and, "if it seems right," Apocalypse (*Hist. Eccl.* 3.25). In regard to the Pauline Epistles he says: "Definitely and certainly the 14 Epistles are by Paul, but it must

be noted that some have opposed the Epistle to the Hebrews, appealing to the Roman Church, which does not acknowledge it as Pauline" (3.3, 5). (2) *Antilegomena*, "disputed," i.e., books whose canonicity is challenged. Some of these are books that are revered by a majority, but rejected by a minority: "the so-called Epistle of James, the Epistle of Jude, the Second Epistle of Peter, and the so-called Second and Third Epistles of John that were written either by the Evangelist or by another John." Therefore, Eusebius puts in this group five of the seven so-called Catholic Epistles. Of the Epistles of James and Jude he says that, even though they are not well-attested in antiquity, "they have been publicly read in most churches" (2.23, 24–26). In connection with the *antilegomena* Eusebius lists the *notha*, "spurious" works: Acts of Paul, Shepherd of Hermas, Apocalypse of Peter, Epistle of Barnabas, Didache, and "if it seems right," the Apocalypse of John. Because of the influence of St. *Dionysius of Alexandria, who judged the Apocalypse of John as unauthentic on literary grounds, Eusebius is personally inclined to include it with the *notha*. He also mentions that "the Gospel of the Hebrews" could be listed with the *notha* because it is held by some as sacred. (3) Heretical writings, mostly apocryphal gospels, to be completely rejected; no ecclesiastical writer of recognized authority deemed these writings worthy of the slightest notice (3.25).

Among the Latins. Consideration of the canon among the Latins can be well divided into two periods, because there is a distinct change of attitude after the middle of the 4th century.

Before the Middle of the 4th Century. In Gaul St. *Irenaeus (d. 202), who was familiar with the traditions of the churches not only in Gaul but also in Italy and Asia Minor and was closely connected through his teachers with the apostolic age, explicitly names and accepts at least 21 NT books as canonical. He uses the four canonical Gospels in about 625 quotations, and he rejects the apocryphal gospels; he quotes the Acts (54 times), 12 of the Pauline Epistles (280 times), accepts the Apocalypse as Johannine (quoted 29 times) and quotes the Catholic Epistles of 1 Peter and 1 and 2 John (15 times); but he never quotes James. References are uncertain about the others. He does not refer to Philemon and, though he knows Hebrews, he does not admit its Pauline origin. He introduces the Shepherd of Hermas with the formula "Scripture says." He does not use the name New Testament for the Christian canonical writings but describes them as the "evangelical and apostolic writings."

In Italy the canon of the Muratorian Fragment, probably composed *c.* 180 to 190 (possibly by Hippolytus), is our earliest ecclesiastical list of the NT canon (if we except the anti-Marcionite prologues to the Gospels). It lists 22 (or 23) NT books; for details *see* MURATORIAN CANON.

St. *Hippolytus of Rome (d. 235), a disciple of Irenaeus, calls the Scriptures of the two Testaments "the two breasts of Christ," indicating the intimacy of nourishment in the inspired word. His NT includes at least 21 books. Hebrews he regards as not Pauline, and therefore, to him uncanonical. He does not use Philemon, 2 or 3 John, James, or Jude.

The Edict of Diocletian (303) that the Sacred Books should be sought out and burned must have led the various churches to determine more sharply which books constituted Sacred Scripture.

In Africa, Tertullian used all of the NT books except 2 Peter and 2 and 3 John. He ascribes Hebrews to Barnabas and excludes it from Scripture, although he admits it is widely used by the various churches. Difficulties persisted with Hebrews and the Catholic Epistles. Even St. *Cyprian of Carthage (d. 253) never used Hebrews; of the Catholic Epistles, he quoted only from 1 Peter and 1 John. In the North-African Monsen Canon, written around 360, Hebrews, James, and Jude were still missing.

After the Middle of the 4th Century. The middle of the 4th century is a turning point in the history of the canon for the Latin Church. Intensive exchange of ideas and closer contact with the East, caused principally by the Arian struggle, had a far-reaching effect in bringing the Western canon up to the level of the Eastern. Then, too, translating the Greek Fathers into Latin and Jerome's Vulgate (containing all 27 NT books) helped to unify and stabilize a universal canon. The so-called Decree of Gelasius, reputedly written in 382, contains a list of all 27 NT books. Its authenticity, however, is disputed. Under Augustine's influence three African synods, one at Hippo (393) and two at Carthage (397 and 419), accepted all 27 books as canonical. In the first two synods, Hebrews is not listed as Pauline, even though it is regarded as canonical, but the last of the three councils considers it to be Paul's. The letter of Pope St. *Innocent I to Exuperius in 405 officially lists all 27 NT books.

Among the Syrians and in Asia Minor. In the Greek-speaking part of Syria St. *Lucian of Antioch (d. 312), founder of the Antiochian School [see BIBLE, VI (EXEGESIS), 2] rejected Apocalypse, 2 Peter, 2 and 3 John, and Jude. With minor variations, this represents the attitude of the Syrian Church from *Theophilus of Antioch (d. 186), who, however, accepted the Apocalypse, to the time of St. *John Chrysostom (d. 407). During the 5th century all 27 books except the Apocalypse were accepted, but the Catholic Epistles were considered second-rank authorities. In the Syriac-speaking parts, prior to the publication of the *Peshitta, all the Catholic Epistles and the Apocalypse are missing from the canon, but a third (apocryphal) Epistle of Paul to the Corinthians is accepted, St. *Ephrem even censuring those who question its canonicity. [This apocryphal Epistle is not listed in the Syrian Catalogue (c. 400) discovered by A. S. Lewis in St. Catherine's Monastery, Mt. Sinai.] With the publication of the Peshitta, James, 1 Peter, and 1 John were accepted. The Syrian Jacobite canon is practically limited to the 22 books of the Peshitta; the Apocalypse, 2 Peter, 2 and 3 John, and Jude are omitted. In the 2d half of the 4th century, the Council of Laodicea in Asia Minor and St. *Gregory of Nazianzus list the full canon except the Apocalypse, although this is included in the canon of St. *Basil, St. *Gregory of Nyssa, and *Epiphanius of Constantia.

Final Stabilization. Since the 5th century, the NT canon of 27 books has been universally accepted by the Greek and the Latin Church alike. Yet during the Middle Ages, Hebrews, Apocalypse, and the Catholic Epistles except 1 Peter and 1 John were still the subject of some controversy. The Shepherd of Hermas and the third Epistle to the Corinthians are also found in some

medieval MSS. *Cajetan (Tommaso de Vio; d. 1534) doubted the authenticity of Hebrews, James, Jude and 2 and 3 John, and considered them less authoritative. Luther was bolder. His interpretation of Paul was the criterion for all the NT books. On this basis he formed three groups: Romans, Galatians, and John; the other NT books, including the Synoptics, he relegated to second place; he severely censured Hebrews, Jude, 2 Peter, and Apocalypse, while he called James "a straw epistle." Despite this, all Protestants have the same NT canon as Catholics.

In the 16th century both literary and dogmatic criticism of the traditional canon became so intense that the Council of Trent dogmatically defined the canon on April 8, 1564. This dogmatic decree, *De Canonicis Scripturis,* lists by name the sacred and canonical books of both Testaments: 45 for the OT, 27 for the NT. According to the minutes of the Council, it was merely repeating, after a month of heated debate, the list given at the Council of Florence (1442) in the decree for the Jacobites. The decree of Trent, repeated by Vatican I on April 24, 1870, is the infallible decision of the magisterium. In the decree, certain doubtfully authentic deuterocanonical sections are also included with the books (*cum omnibus suis partibus*): Mk 16.9–20; Lk 22.19b–20, 43–44; and Jn 7.53–8.11.

CRITERIA OF CANONICITY

Distinction must be made between the internal criterion and external criteria.

Internal Criterion. The internal criterion lies in the mysterious nature of the Church, which recognizes in Scripture something intrinsic to its nature and canonizes it as a normative constitutive element of its existence. Inspiration, which links the personal Word of God to His written word, is a supernatural charism. It thus lies beyond human deduction. The Church, as supernatural, simply recognizes itself in Scripture. Time and history become dramatic elements in this sublime perception.

External Criteria. These helped articulate its act of recognition, especially apostolicity and liturgy. Every book of the NT was either written or guaranteed by an Apostle. This, then, was the reason why each was accepted as sacred and normative, for doctrinal apostolic authority is the foundation of the Church: "You are built upon the foundation of the apostles and prophets" (Eph 2.20; see Mt 28.18–20). In practice the Church also showed its reverence for the NT as holy and canonical by sanctioning its use in public worship. The liturgy made the community participate in the Mystery of Christ, proclaiming it through the word. Thus, in various regions the apostolic Church guided the faithful to acceptance of the apostolic, inspired word. In this process other nonapostolic traditions were added, which accounted for the doubts and disputes of the early years. But the Church needed only to apply the principle of apostolic approbation to solve the doubts. When called upon to do so at Trent, through its infallible, apostolic magisterium, it decisively recognized what God had given it through the Apostles—the 27 NT books, the written embodiment of its existence.

Bibliography: H. HÖPFL DBSuppl 1:1022–45. EncDictBibl 312–313. E. MANGENOT, DTC 2:1550–69, 1582–1605. G. RICCIOTTI, EncCatt 2.2:1550–51. J. MICHL and K. RAHNER, LexThK² 5:1280–84. E. JACQUIER, *Le Nouveau Testament dans l'église chrétienne* (Paris 1911) v.1. M. J. LAGRANGE, *Histoire ancienne du canon du Nouveau Testament,* v.1 of *Introduction à l'étude* *du N.T.* (EtBibl; Paris 1933–   ). G. M. Perrella, *Introducción general a la Sagrada Escritura* (Turin 1954). A. Wikenhauser, *New Testament Introduction* (New York 1958). Robert-Tricot 1:87–103. C. F. D. Moule, *Birth of the New Testament* (New York 1962). H. Riesenfeld, *The Gospel Tradition and Its Beginning* (London 1957).

[F. SCHROEDER]

4. APOCRYPHA OF THE OLD TESTAMENT

Under this term are included those books that were written by Jews for the purpose of continuing their sacred tradition. Many of the compositions contain several Christian additions, and a few of them, according to some scholars, may even be completely Christian in their extant form (e.g., the Odes of Solomon and the Testament of the Twelve Patriarchs). The style, however, is closely modeled upon that of the OT, and the thought represents the religious currents circulating among the Jews during the intertestamental period, the 2 or 3 centuries before the NT writings appeared. The apocrypha can be conveniently arranged according to the threefold Septuagint (LXX) division of the OT: historical books, prophetic books, and didactic or sapiential books. From ancient catalogues of books and from quotations in early Church Fathers it is certain that many more apocrypha existed than are now extant.

The pseudohistorical apocrypha are Jubilees, 3 Esdras, 3 Machabees, Life of Adam and Eve, Ascension of Isaia, and Lives of the Prophets. (*See* ARISTEAS, LETTER OF.)

The prophetic-apocalyptic apocrypha are the Books of Henoch, or Enoch (i.e., the 1 or Ethiopic, 2 or Greek, and 3 or Hebrew), Assumption of Moses, 4 Esdras, Baruch (Syriac), Baruch (Greek), and Sibylline Oracles (Jewish).

The moral-didactic apocrypha are the Testament of the Twelve Patriarchs, Psalms of Solomon, Odes of Solomon, Prayer of Manasses, and 4 Machabees. (*See* DEAD SEA SCROLLS.)

THE PSEUDOHISTORICAL APOCRYPHA

Works patterned after the historical books of the OT but only in a very loose way have been so designated. They try to recapture and relive the glorious stages in the history of salvation.

The Book of Jubilees. Other names for the Book of Jubilees are Little Genesis, because it retells the stories and laws of Gn 1.1–Ex 12.36, and The Apocalypse of Moses, because it claims that God revealed its contents during Moses' 40 days and 40 nights on Mt. Sinai. The name Jubilees is the most appropriate, not only because the book divides history into 49 jubilee periods of 49 years each (Lv 25.8–22), beginning with creation and concluding with the revelation of the Mosaic Law, but also because it places great importance upon the sacred, solar calendar (*see* CALENDARS OF THE ANCIENT NEAR EAST), the fixation of feast days, and the certainty with which history is striding forward to the messianic millennium or jubilee. The author had still other purposes in writing his book: to expand and clarify the Law, which he claims was kept before Moses' time by every great personage; to defend Judaism against the corroding influence of pagan Hellenism; and to exalt the privileged place of the Levitical priests. Also worth noting in the content of the book are these details: silence about

any personal, royal Messiah; well-developed angelology and demonology; and expectation of a messianic period of 1,000 years, after which the just will enjoy immortality in the spirit world.

The style is best described as that of an enlarged Targum (R. H. Charles), like the *Haggadah in the narratives and the *Halakah in the legal sections. It was most probably written first in Hebrew, but until the discovery of the Dead Sea Scrolls there existed only an Ethiopic text, some Syriac and Latin fragments, and a few Greek citations in the Fathers. There is sufficient manuscript evidence, however, testifying to the popularity of Jubilees in ancient Jewish and Christian circles.

The author seems to have been a Palestinian Jew, scrupulously observant of the Law, devoted to the Machabees and the priestly tribe of Levi, cool toward any messianic aspirations in the tribe of Juda, and hostile toward Hellenistic influences. These facts help to locate him in the Machabean period, before the Pharisaic rupture with King John Hyrcanus (135–104 B.C.) and possibly even before Jonathan assumed the high priestly office in 152 B.C. The author's determined views on the calendar associate him with a Jewish sect like the *Essenes. His book was very popular in the *Qumran community.

Third Esdras. Four books are attributed to Esdras (Ezra in the Hebrew spelling). The distinction between these books is confusing because of manuscript and denominational differences:

Vulgate (Catholic)	Septuagint	Hebrew text	Protestant & Jewish
1 Esdras † (Ezra)		Ezra †	Ezra †
2 Esdras † (Neh)	2 Esdras †	Nehemia †	Nehemia †
3 Esdras	1 Esdras	missing	1 Esdras
4 Esdras	3 Esdras	missing	2 Esdras

(†) = canonical books.

Third Esdras (in Vulgate) chronicles events from the time of King *Josia (640–609 B.C.) through the Exile and into the postexilic period up to and including the ministry of Ezra. For the most part it simply repeats, with some minor revision and transposition, what already exists in the canonical books of Chronicles, Nehemia, and especially Ezra. Third Esdras, however, expunges any mention of Nehemia, and in 3.1–5.6 it adds a legend of Hebrew or Aramaic origin about a battle of wits among Darius's bodyguard, who contended the relative strength of wine, women, kings, and truth. Zorobabel, who championed truth, won the contest and as a reward was allowed to rebuild the Temple of Jerusalem [*see* TEMPLES (IN THE BIBLE)]. Most scholars have noticed that 3 Esdras ends very abruptly, in the middle of a sentence quoted from Neh 8.13, but O. Eissfeldt claims that 3 Esdras has a normal conclusion since the second part of Neh 8.13 and the succeeding verses are secondary to the latter text.

The origin of 3 Esdras cannot be adequately explained. Third Esdras could actually be the original LXX version of the canonical books, while the current Greek translation of Chronicles, Ezra, and Nehemia could represent the work of Theodotion. [*See* BIBLE, IV (TEXTS AND VERSIONS), 5, 8.] The case of 3 Esdras would then be very similar to that of Jeremia. Or it is possible, but not generally held, that 3 Esdras is a compilation taken from the present Greek translation. Finally, it may trace its independent way to a Hebrew text or tradition noticeably different from the Masoretic reading.

The book was certainly compiled before A.D. 90, for the Jewish historian Josephus quoted from it (*Ant.* 11); but its exclusive concern with Jewish interests puts its composition before the Christian era, closer to 100 B.C. Until the 5th century, Christians very frequently ranked 3 Esdras with the canonical books; it is found in many LXX MSS and in the Latin Vulgate (Vulg) of St. Jerome. Protestants therefore include 3 Esdras with other apocrypha (deuterocanonical) books such as Tobit or Judith. The Council of Trent definitively removed it from the canon.

Third Machabees. This is a fantastic novel about a persecution of Jews in Alexandria, Egypt. It can make very little claim to literature, and it has nothing whatever to do with the Machabees, except that many LXX MSS, including A and V, place it immediately after 2 Machabees. The story is a succession of quick reversals. Ptolemy IV Philopator, Pharao of Egypt (221–204 B.C.), is victorious in a battle fought in northern Palestine. In thanksgiving he sacrifices at the Jerusalem Temple, but when he attempts to enter the *Holy of Holies, God strikes him dumb (cf. Heliodorus in 2 Mc 3.8–40). Returning to Egypt, Philopator determines upon a pogrom, to have drunken elephants trample the Jews to death in the hippodrome. When heavenly visitors appear, the elephants turn upon the soldiers; the Jews are then granted many favors. These events are reminiscent of the Book of Esther and the origin of the feast of *Purim. It is possible that some major misfortune may have been the cause for the writing of the book, perhaps the persecution by Ptolemy VII Physkon (146–117 B.C.) or the revoking of Jewish civil rights in 25–24 B.C. Josephus, in *Contra Apionem* 2.5.53–55, recorded a plan to drive a herd of elephants against a mass of Jews during Physkon's reign. The author may have combined facts drawn from the lost memoirs of Philopator with other events spun out of his own imagination.

The style of 3 Machabees is mouthy and declamatory; the plot, artificial and forced. In this regard there are many points of similarity with 2 Machabees and especially with the letter of Aristeas.

The book was written in Alexandria, Egypt, *c.* 100 B.C.; the latest date would be A.D. 70, when the Jerusalem Temple was destroyed by Titus. Third Machabees presumes that Jerusalem and its Temple are still in the possession of the Jews.

Life of Adam and Eve (Apocalypse of Moses). A large group of legends about man's first parents that once circulated among the Jews and the early Christians was collected and entitled The Life of Adam and Eve. It is extant only in Latin, although a Greek version often appears beneath the surface. The Apocalypse of Moses, wrongly so named by its discoverer K. von Tischendorf, exists in a Greek text. Scholars generally agree, however, that both forms were originally written in Hebrew or Aramaic, somewhere between 20 B.C. and A.D. 70, because of references to the Herodian Temple (cf. Jn 2.20). The two books frequently run parallel to one another, as each tells the story of the first parents: their fall and repentance; new temptations and sorrows; dreams and predictions about the Jewish race up to the last judgment; the death, and finally the burial of Adam and Eve by angels. There seem to be Christian interpolations, especially in the prophecies. The story is told with pathos, often with literary finesse; at times it emphasizes penance and ascetical practices.

Ascension of Isaia. This is a compilation, according to most scholars, of three separate works, put together between the 3d and the 5th Christian centuries, when it became very popular among heretical Christians. The first section, "The Martyrdom of Isaia" (ch. 1–5), expands upon a brief reference in 4 Kgs 21.1–8 and recounts the events, including the intrigues of the apostate King Manasse, a Samaritan, and a false prophet Belchira, that led up to Isaia's martyrdom. The prophet is said to have been cut in two by a wood saw. The story, reflected in Heb 11.37 and in the Jewish *Talmud and Targums [see BIBLE, IV (TEXTS AND VERSIONS), 11] has its literary origins in Palestinian Judaism of the 1st century B.C. The second section (3.13b–4.18) is a "Christian apocalypse," originating around A.D. 100 and only later placed within the martyrdom story as a reason for Isaia's violent death. It proposes to be the Prophet's "predictions" of Jesus' life and work, the mission of the 12 Apostles, the faults of the early Church, the Antichrist and Beliar (identified with Nero), and the Second Coming (*Parousia). Such details probably account for the work's appeal to heretical and splinter groups of Christians. The final section (ch. 6–11) of the 2d Christian century recounts the "Vision [or Ascension] of Isaia" in the seventh heaven and his discovery of celestial secrets. This revelation of Christian *Gnosis, or mysterious knowledge, also fitted appropriately into the religious system of the early heretics. The complete book has survived only in an Ethiopian version; scattered fragments exist in Greek, Latin, Coptic, and Old Slavonic.

Lives of the Prophets. Biographies were written, not only of the 4 Major and the 12 Minor Prophets, but also of other prophetic figures such as *Elia (Elijah), *Elisae (Eliseus, Elisha), Nathan (David's adviser), Ahia (3 Kgs 14.1–18), Joed (Neh 11.7, said to be the same as Addo the seer in 2 Chr 9.29 and the anonymous prophet in 3 Kings ch. 13), Azaria (2 Chr 15.1–8), and Zacharia (2 Chr 24.20–24, mentioned in Mt 23.35 and Lk 11.51). The author draws upon legendary stories and popular traditions in order to supplement the Biblical account. The work was composed in Hebrew by a Palestinian Jew during the 1st Christian century. There is a large Christian addition to the life of Jeremia, referring to Jesus' virginal birth and the flight into Egypt. For the most part, however, Christian interpolations are scarce. Little historical value is attached to the events narrated in the work. [See C. C. Torrey, *The Lives of the Prophets* (JBiblLit Monograph Series 1; Philadelphia 1946).]

THE PROPHETIC-APOCALYPTIC APOCRYPHA

The apocryphal books classified under this heading imitate the *prophetic books of the OT and the apocalyptic literature of late *Judaism (see APOCALYPSE, BOOK OF).

The Books of Henoch (Enoch). These represent the remnants of an extensive Henoch literature, circulating between 200 B.C. and A.D. 300. There are three rather divergent books, which are usually distinguished by the language in which they were transmitted: 1 or Ethiopic Henoch; 2 or Slavonic Henoch (called also The Secrets of Henoch); and 3 Henoch, preserved in the original Hebrew.

Ethiopic Henoch. The longest and certainly the most important Book of Henoch was the Ethiopic, used by the authors of Jubilees, Testament of the Twelve Patriarchs, and the Apocalypse of Baruch. It is quoted in Jude 14 and cited as a divine authority by Pseudo-Barnabas and Tertullian. Except for a few Latin fragments the book was known only in the Ethiopic version that was brought to Europe in 1773 by James Bruce; but recently there have turned up in cave 4 along the Dead Sea 10 Aramaic MSS of ch. 1–36 and ch. 83–90, besides 4 additional Aramaic MSS of ch. 72–82 (following R. H. Charles's chapter division). These discoveries not only establish the original language to be Aramaic rather than Hebrew and supply a very early text, but they also reveal the popularity of the Henoch literature among the Palestinian Jews (see Gn 5.21–24; Sir 44.16; 49.14; Heb 11.5).

The earliest collection of 1 Henoch found among the Dead Sea Scrolls consists of ch. 1–36 and ch. 83–90. The first section describes Henoch's journey through the celestial spheres and discusses the origin and spread of sin through the fall of the angels, the punishment of sinners, the eschatological blessedness of the just, and the bodily resurrection. The second part comprises apocalyptic stories, similar to those in Daniel ch. 7–12, in which there is presented a history of Israel from the Deluge to the messianic reign. Since the last historical reference is to Judas Machabee, who died in 160 B.C., the book was probably composed sometime between the period 167 to 164, the date for the great persecution and the Book of Daniel, and the year 160. From the Qumran evidence it is apparent that ch. 72–82 circulated as a separate piece; it reflects the astronomical and meteorological beliefs of the Palestinian Jews, and, among other important details, it agrees with the Book of Jubilees in favoring the solar year calendar.

Another major division is ch. 91–105 (plus the conclusion, ch. 106–108), which consists principally of "Admonitions" and the "Apocalypse of Weeks." The author is preoccupied with the doom awaiting the unjust and the final glorification of the elect. The "Admoni-

Fig. 1. Fragment of the Book of Henoch in Aramaic from Qumran Cave 4.

tions" was composed *c.* 160 B.C., i.e., very soon after the death of Judas Machabee, while the "Apocalypse of Weeks" appeared sometime before the Roman conquest of Palestine in 63 B.C.

The fifth major portion of 1 Henoch is the very important series of "Similitudes," or "Parables," pronouncing judgment upon men and angels (ch. 37–71). In these chapters occur the repeated references to the "*Son of Man," who seems to be some kind of suprahuman person, combining in himself all the hopes and triumphs of Israel. If these chapters are pre-Christian, then the concept of "Son of Man" represents a stage of development, slightly beyond the symbolic usage in Dn 7.13 and closer to the personal messianic meaning on the lips of Jesus (Mk 14.62). The absence of these chapters at Qumran does not disprove but only throws doubt upon their pre-Christian origin; in any case, the absence of definitely Christian ideas certainly indicates a Jewish author.

When the five major sections were gathered into one book—possibly in imitation of the five books of Moses in the Torah and the five books of Davidic Psalms—a few other minor selections, such as the Book of Noe, were interspersed among the chapters. The author of the final, edited book seems to have belonged to an eschatological circle, similar to the Pharisees or the Qumran covenanters; he accepted the final triumph of the just, the complete damnation of the wicked, the resurrection of the body, and the belief in angels. The messianic joys are frequently described in terms quite earthly and sensuous (10.17; 25.4); the solar religious calendar is preferred to the lunar.

Second or Slavonic Henoch. This book, also called the "Secrets of Henoch," presents a fanciful apocalypse of Henoch's assumption to the 10th heaven, his visions, and admonitions. As he journeys through the heavens, he views the rewards and punishments of the future life and the various movements of the sun, moon, and stars (ch. 1–21), in the 10th heaven he sees the appearance of the Lord (ch. 22) and is told many secrets, especially an elaborate account of how the universe was created in 6 days (ch. 23–30). The last part of the book consists mostly of a long series of admonitions by Henoch to his sons (ch. 31–68).

The book now exists in two Slavonic recensions of very unequal length. It is very difficult to account for the relationship of these two versions to one another, but there is no doubt that both go back to an original Greek text, now lost. An acrostic explanation of Adam's name in 30.13 is intelligible only in Greek. This Greek composition is usually attributed to a Jewish author, living in Egypt, before the destruction of the Temple of Jerusalem (A.D. 70). This last detail is based upon his references to sacrifice (51.4; 59.1–2; 61.4; 62.1). His work was very influential and seems to be responsible for statements in other apocryphal literature such as the Books of Adam and Eve, the Apocalypses of Moses and Paul, and the Ascension of Isaia. A few scholars, however, e.g., F. C. Burkitt and J. K. Fotheringham, argue for a much later authorship, the 7th century A.D. at the earliest.

Third Henoch. This is an amalgam of disparate Hebrew parts, treating of angels, the divine chariot or throne (Ez 1.14), and the destinies of a rather illusive figure called Metatron (perhaps the Son of Man or the Elect One of 1 Henoch). The title ascribes the work "to

Rabbi Ishmael ben Elisha, high priest" and dates it at the beginning of the 2d Christian century; but Hugo Odeberg, who first edited the Hebrew manuscripts in 1928, traces individual parts to a period immediately after the revolt of Bar Kokhba (A.D. 132–135). Before the book reached its present form in the 3d century, it had felt the impact of Gnosticism and various religious movements within Judaism.

Fourth Esdras. What is sometimes called 2 Esdras by non-Catholics is called 4 Esdras in the Vulgate. It was one of the most popular and most frequently translated books of all the apocrypha. Although written originally in Hebrew and subsequently translated into Greek, both of which texts are lost, the book has survived in Christian editions in Latin, Syriac, Ethiopic, Arabic, Armenian, Sahidic, and Georgian. It has supplied several liturgical passages: the reproaches (*improperia*) of Good Friday (ch. 1.13, 14–24); the Easter antiphon for martyrs (ch. 2.35); and the *requiem aeternam* in the prayer for the deceased (ch. 2.34–35). In their attachment to this book, Christians not only made slight modifications in the text [ch. 7.28–35(?); 8.3; 13.29–32(?)], but they also wrote a new introduction and conclusion (ch. 1–2, sometimes called "5 Esdras," and ch. 15–16, sometimes called "6 Esdras"). The newer chapters (1–2 and 15–16) are missing in the Syriac, Ethiopic, Arabic, and Armenian versions.

The Jewish original can be dated *c.* A.D. 100, i.e., "thirty years after the downfall of the city [Jerusalem, in A.D. 70]" (ch. 3.1) and a few years after A.D. 96, the end of the reign of "the three heads," i.e., the Flavian Roman emperors, Vespatian, Titus, and Domitian (11.1). The author drew his material from preexisting sources and put together a mosaic of ideas. Composing in an apocalyptic style, he assumed an ancient name, Ezra, and pretended to be writing from Babylon. He was, however, a devout Jew, perhaps a Pharisee, living in Rome (see 1 Pt 5.13). He was crushed by the destruction of the Holy City and was continually obsessed with the mystery of sin, human misery, the trials of the just, the prosperity of the wicked, and the large number of the reprobate. Pessimistic is the evaluation usually attached to his character. He firmly expected a divine judgment upon Israel's enemies, once the number of the elect was complete, and he hoped for a general resurrection and a new creation.

Chapters 3–14 present an account of seven visions. The third vision (6.35–9.25) describes the death of the Messiah, but in the succeeding judgment scene the Messiah does not appear—in opposition to the Gospel story about Jesus. In the sixth vision (ch. 13) there are many parallels to the Son of Man image in Daniel ch. 7. The last vision (ch. 14) is important for the study of the formation of the canon. Ezra is said to have dictated the sacred books to five secretaries who wrote "in letters they did not know"; Ezra spoke around the clock, and at the end of 40 days, 94 books had been transcribed: 24 open to the worthy and the unworthy; 70 reserved for the initiated. The number 24 accorded with one of the more common Jewish ways of combining and numbering the canonical books (5 in the Torah, 8 in the earlier and later Prophets, and 11 in the Writings).

Syriac or Second Baruch. Several works were attributed to Jeremia's secretary, Baruch. First Baruch belongs to the list of deuterocanonical books received into the LXX, the Vulgate, and the canon as formulated at

Fig. 2. Baruch reading his account of the future of Jerusalem, wood engraving by Wladislaw Skoczylas for "The Apocrypha" of the Cresset Press.

the Council of Trent, but rejected by Jews and Protestants from their canonical list. Second Baruch has survived in a single Syriac copy. Third Baruch, the least important, was written originally in Greek.

Second Baruch is an apocalyptic work that reveals a marked dependency upon 4 Esdras. A pious Jew, drawing upon the latter and other disparate sources, describes a vision that, he pretended, was granted to Jeremia's secretary about Israel's future after the destruction of Jerusalem in 587 B.C. Not only did some of the facts in the vision disagree with Biblical history, but the author was actually writing about another devastation of the Holy City, that by Titus in A.D. 70, and the concomitant frustrating condition of his people. The author is ignorant of the revolt of Simon *Bar Kokhba (Bar Cocheba) in A.D. 132–135, nor does he know anything of the events that followed the revolt and the expulsion of all Jews from the Jersualem area of Palestine. He must have written, therefore, before A.D. 130.

A summation of 2 Baruch follows. The opening 12 chapters present Baruch's announcement of the destruction of Jerusalem, its collapse before the power of four angels, and the Babylonian possession of the city. Contrary to the Bible, Jeremia withdraws to Babylon, there to comfort the exiles (see Jer 40.1–6 and the LXX and Vulgate introduction to Lamentations), while Baruch remains to chant a lamentation over the ruins of Jerusalem. After his 7-day fast, divine revelation comes to Baruch's tortured mind, assuring him that the godless will eventually be punished and that *Sion (Zion) was ravaged in order to hasten the day of judgment and the dawn of a new age for the righteous. Baruch is then told to "seal it [the message] in the recesses of your mind" and "sanctify [another] seven days" of fast. In ch. 21–34 God consoles Baruch by allowing him to peer into the heavens and see that everything must be judged in the light of the appointed end of all creation. Twelve woes must first scourge the earth, and only then will the Messiah appear, the manna drop down from heaven, and the dead arise from their sleep. In an important section (ch. 35–46) Baruch uses an image from Daniel, the four world empires of wickedness; the Messiah will be revealed to capture and execute the last world leader and to establish a kingdom that will endure as long as the world. Baruch then announces his own death and encourages the people to maintain their hope in God. Chapters 47–52 repeat familiar themes—fasting, revelation of the future, the resurrection of the just and the damned to the identical bodies that they once possessed on earth, and the final judgment. After a mysterious vision of black and clear water rained upon the earth, Baruch receives an explanation that spans world history from Adam to the appearance of the Messiah in the form of lightning (ch. 53–76). A golden age follows. Finally, in ch. 77–87, two letters are introduced, but only the first is preserved. It announces the catastrophe of Jerusalem (that of A.D. 70) and future happiness, and it provides suitable advice.

The book, written in apocalyptic style, is full of visions and symbols that attempt to make vivid sacred history, Israel's great calamities, the resurrection, and the final victory. The work would have been lost except for a single Syriac manuscript, translated from a no longer extant Greek version, and a few Greek fragments (ch. 12–14). The original language was Aramaic.

Greek or Third Baruch. This is a Jewish work, highly apocalyptic in style with a free blending of visions, symbols, astronomical details, and eschatological facts. In places, e.g., ch. 6–8, the book attains an extremely poetical style. The author was dependent upon 2 Baruch and, therefore, wrote sometime after A.D. 130. Origen (d. 254) seems to have had this composition in mind when he referred to a book of the Prophet Baruch and the latter's evidence of seven worlds or heavens. A Greek text, speaking of but five heavens, was discovered only in 1896. Until then there existed only a Slavonic version, much shorter and envisaging only two heavens. Upon investigation the Greek text of 3 Baruch was found colored with heretical Gnostic ideas adapted to Christian truths. In ch. 4, for instance, Baruch sees the tree or vine that Adam was forbidden even to touch (Gn 3.3); but after the Deluge the angel Sarasael instructs Noe to plant a twig of this vine for "its bitterness shall be changed into sweetness and . . . it shall become the blood of God" (4.15).

The book opens with Baruch's weeping over the ruins of Jerusalem. An angel approaches to calm his questioning and anxious mind (ch. 1). Baruch is led through five successive heavens and is initiated into many mysteries of sacred history. (A similar idea of seven heavens occurs in the Testament of the Twelve Patriarchs and the Ascension of Isaia, while the notion of many heavens is reflected in Dt 10.14; 3 Kgs 8.27; 2 Cor 12.2.) Baruch sees the builder and designer of the *Tower of Babel in the first and second heavens, the serpent, the forbidden tree, Hades (the huge belly of the serpent), the bird

Phoenix, who is the guardian of the earth and who feeds on the manna, in the third heaven, the souls of the just in the stately form of beautifully singing birds in the fourth heaven, and the angel Michael, who alone can open the fifth heaven and who holds an immense vessel that other angels fill with the good works of the righteous, in the fifth heaven (see Ap 5.8). Baruch is then "restored . . . to the place where I was in the beginning" (17.2).

Jewish Sibylline Oracles. This is a Jewish-Christian adaptation of the Greco-Roman oracles; it was composed between 160 B.C. and A.D. 240. The collection consists of 12 books (bks. 1–8, 11–14; bks. 9, 10, and 15 are lost) and scattered fragments among other writers. Sibylla, or Sibyl (Counsel of God), was the name of a Greek prophetess, very advanced in years, who lived at least before the 5th century B.C. and therefore before the great classical period. She uttered prophecies, mostly of doom and tragedy, in Greek hexameter; tradition even claims that Homer copied his style from her. The Sibyl's prophecies consisted of past history written in the future tense (*vaticinia ex eventu*). When the oracles became increasingly popular, other Sibyls appeared and the birthplace of the original one became a center of controversy. The popularity of the Sibyl appears in the reverential way in which Aristophanes and Plato speak of her.

*Sibylline oracles were preserved at Rome until the great fire of 82 B.C. destroyed them. Rome sent agents through the empire to recopy the sayings; the demand created such a proliferation of false oracles that Augustus ordered 2,000 volumes of them to be destroyed. The oracles were frequently consulted by the Roman government.

In order to gain a hearing and to win respect with their non-Hebrew neighbors, Hellenistic Jews of Alexandria, Egypt, proceeded to adapt some of the Sibylline oracles to Israelite history and to compose some new ones of their own. They boldly pretended that the Sibyl was the daughter-in-law of Noe. What they produced, however, amounted to a weak parroting of the prophetic oracles against the nations (Isaia ch. 13–23; Jeremia ch. 46–51; Ezechiel ch. 25–32). Themes of doom and terror are continually repeated, even to the point of monotony, as in one way or another cataclysmic forces of water, fire, earthquake, pestilence, and war sweep through the universe. Idols are overturned, and Israel alone survives to enjoy the messianic prosperity.

These Jewish Sibylline oracles became very popular among the Christians down to the 5th century, especially among Gnostic sects, who may have been responsible for books 6–7. They were edited in their present form in the 6th Christian century. An echo of them is still heard in the *Dies Irae,* the Sequence in Masses for the dead, where doomsday is spoken of as *teste David cum Sibylla.*

The rambling, repetitious style is apparent from a survey of book 3. This tells of Beliar, from the stock of Sebaste in Palestine (i.e., Simon Magus; see Acts 8.9–24), and of a lawless widow, both of whom manage to lead even the Jews astray, till God rains destruction upon everything (ll. 63–92). A short Christian interlude prays for the return of the Savior (ll. 93–96). Other lines describe the prosperity of the Jews, which incites the envious Gentiles to attack (see Ps 2.1–3; Ezechiel ch. 38–39). God destroys the enemy in a wondrous way and grants great favors to His people. The Gentiles consequently seek conversion, study the Law, and embrace Judaism. The Messiah has an important part in the war of deliverance but disappears from the scene in the victory celebration. No word is heard of a bodily resurrection. The kingdom is described in very earthly tones. In the midst of book 3 occur indirect references to Alexander the Great, Ptolemy VII Physkon, and other notables; the historical sequence is rather chaotic.

MORAL-DIDACTIC APOCRYPHA

These works imitate the style and content of the didactic books of the OT, i.e., the Wisdom Books and the Psalms.

Testament of the Twelve Patriarchs. One such work purports to give the farewell discourses spoken by the 12 sons of Jacob at their deathbeds. It follows a literary pattern fairly common during the century before and the century after the birth of Christ. The origin can be traced to such Biblical passages as Jacob's final words in Genesis ch. 49 and Moses' last message in Deuteronomy ch. 33 and is found also in intertestamental literature, such as Ethiopic Henoch (i.e., the book of admonition in 92.1–5; 91.1–11, 18–19), Jubilees (discourse by Isaia in 31.4–22 and by Jacob in 45.14–16), and the Assumption of Moses. Jesus' parting discourse in John ch. 13–17 may have been composed according to this literary style.

Each of the 12 testaments follows a tripartite division: first, a pseudohistorical narrative of the Patriarch's life with particular attention to some major fault of his; then, the moral lessons to be learned from his experience; finally, a messianic-apocalyptic view of each tribe's future. The first part especially is embellished with legendary and popular traditions, while the third section reflects a tense messianic expectation. The suggestion has been made, not without good reason, that these 12 testaments constitute an anthology of liturgical sermons in which the preacher applied scriptural readings to contemporary problems and needs.

The testaments do not always follow the order of births in Genesis ch. 29–30, but the four eldest sons of Jacob speak first. *Ruben (Reuben), of course, shamefully remembers his act of incest with his father's wife Bala (Gn 35.22; 49.4) and repeatedly warns his own sons against fornication. Great caution is necessary, because of the seven evil spirits, the hostile Beliar, and the fickleness of all women. The author shares the *Sapiential Books' suspicion of womankind. The messianic section is practically nonexistent in this, the first testament. *Simeon, because of his part in the betrayal and selling of Joseph (see JOSEPH, SON OF JACOB) into slavery, speaks against jealousy and envy. The messianic lines are again very few, and, like Ruben, Simeon expresses loyalty to the priestly tribe of *Levi and the kingly tribe of Juda. The testament of Levi is one of the longer and more developed pieces; it reveals a strongly apocalyptic style of visions and heavenly secrets, of past history recounted in the future tense, and of keen eschatological concern. The slaughtering of the Sichemites is justified as an order placed upon Levi and Simeon by an angel, when Levi stood in the divine throne room. Although an eternal right to the priesthood is granted to Levi, he is told nonetheless that a new priest shall arise from the tribe of Juda, who will assist Gentiles as well as Jews, remove sin forever, bind

Beliar, open the gates of Paradise, and show the way to the tree of life. Apocalypticism dominates over moralism in the testament of Levi. Because the royalty became Juda's prerogative, his testament begins with a grandiose account of his extraordinary feats of valor and strength. The incident of Juda's relations with his daughter-in-law Thamor provides the preacher with an opportunity to speak forcefully against the dangers of wine and women. After a quick summary of the destruction of Jerusalem in 587 B.C. and the return from the Exile, Juda foresees the Messiah to arise from his offspring, a man who will be meek, without sin, filled with the Spirit, a life–giving fountain, a judge, and a savior of all who call upon the Lord. The eight other testaments, of *Issachar, *Zabulon, *Dan, *Nephthali, *Gad, *Aser, Joseph, and *Benjamin, proceed more or less in this same style.

Doctrinal teaching and moral ideals reach a very high quality in this apocryphon. Its authors preferred honest morality to liturgical ceremonies; they kept apocalyptic interests under control, so that hopes in any imminent, divine breakthrough never confused immediate moral demands. Sin is resolutely condemned, but the sinner is always offered the possibility of repentance. Fasting is seen as a mighty weapon against the evil spirits. Besides the seven principal spirits of depravity, the testaments refer also to the leader, Beliar (the word is derived from the Biblical *Belial; see Dt 13.13; Jgs 19. 22; 1 Sm 1.6). Beliar is an individual person (testaments of Joseph 20.2; of Simeon 5.3; of Nephthali 2.6). The resurrection of the body is clearly taught (testament of Benjamin 10.6–8), and, in fact, the future age is filled with all kinds of earthly delights. The place of the messiahs and their special qualities have already been mentioned. The testaments expect two messiahs, the one a religious leader, a priestly messiah from the tribe of Levi, by far the more important, and the other a royal messiah of the tribe of Juda. A few scholars (e.g., M. J. Lagrange) deny that the references add up to a belief in any personal messiahs; the authors, instead, look forward to messianic, redemptive movements in which the tribes of Levi and Juda will take the lead. Most scholars, however, especially with the evidence of the Dead Sea Scrolls at hand, recognize the expectation of individual messiahs.

Until research was made on the Dead Sea Scrolls, questions about the authorship of the testaments were generally settled in favor of a Jewish origin, with later Christian interpolations. The bulk of the 12 testaments were said to have been composed by a Jew, who may have belonged to the Essene sect, sometime after 200 B.C., perhaps during the reign of the worldly Hasmonaean King Alexander Janneus (102–76 B.C.). This age accounts for the antagonism to the royalty (testaments of Juda 21.6–23.5; of Levi 14.5–16.5). Christian additions were inserted into the text c. A.D. 100 in order to sharpen the messianic references in favor of Jesus Christ (testaments of Joseph 19.11; of Benjamin 3.8; 9.3–5). Representative scholars (e.g., O. Eissfeldt) still prefer this explanation; but others (e.g., J. T. Milik) hold a different opinion on this question. The sections of the testaments found at Qumran (an Aramaic fragment of Levi; a Hebrew fragment of Nephthali) are longer, and, especially in the case of Nephthali, they are considerably different. They represent the source from which a Jewish Christian of the 1st or 2d Christian century prepared a set of testaments for all 12 Patriarchs. The original Hebrew or Aramaic texts no longer exist, except for the Dead Sea Scrolls and a Hebrew fragment of Nephthali that was found in the Cairo Geniza at the end of the 19th century. There are extant 10 Greek MSS, of two basic forms, besides two translations from the Greek, one in Slavonic and a more important one in Armenian.

Psalms of Solomon. These are 18 hymns, composed originally in Hebrew but existing now only in Greek and in a Syriac version derived from the Greek. These psalms (hereafter *Ps. Sol.*) must be kept distinct, not only from the Book of Psalms in the Bible, but also from another collection, *The Odes of Solomon,* 42 hymns by a 2d-century Christian (see next section).

Because of cryptic historical references in *Ps. Sol.,* it is usually stated that the author(s) wrote a little after the violent death of Pompey, who, in 48 B.C., was slain, left unburied, and finally cremated on an improvised pyre in Egypt. The second psalm seems to refer to the manner in which the Jewish leaders, Aristobulus II and John Hyrcanus II, first welcomed the approaching army of Pompey; then, when Aristobulus's group resisted, Pompey fought back, razed the walls around the Temple enclosure, and sacrilegiously entered the Holy of Holies (*Ps. Sol.* 2.2, 29–31; 8.15–20). At least the second and eighth psalms can be traced back to the middle of the 1st century B.C.; but a further question is still not completely solved, whether the same poet composed all the psalms or whether the collection grew over a long period of time. Because the psalms breathe a certain peace, at least in not expecting any violent changes, their composition must have been completed before the great unrest of the 1st Christian century.

Another open question is the identity or character of the author(s). The name Solomon was adopted because this King was the model of a glorious, wise, and peaceful monarch; in *Ps. Sol.* faith is expressed in a new king of the line of Juda who will receive wisdom from God and will conquer the world not by the sword but "with the word of his mouth forever" (*Ps. Sol.* 17.39). It was the customary style, ever since the emergence of apocalyptic literature in the postexilic age, for authors to use pseudonyms (as in Daniel, Jona, Wisdom, and Ecclesiastes). Not only because of the messianic interests of the writer but also because *Ps. Sol.* ch. 17 argues very vigorously against the Hasmonaean kings, it is often presumed that the poet belonged to the sect of the Pharisees. Toward the end of his reign the Hasmonaean King Alexander Janneus (103–176 B.C.) ordered a large number of Pharisees to be impaled before his very eyes. But this evidence does not suffice to establish the author as a Pharisee; many of the common people hated the Hasmonaeans. Nor were messianic interests in a king of the line of Juda confined to the Pharisees. Such a key Pharisaic doctrine as the resurrection of the body is found in *Ps. Sol.* 3.16 but not in the important *Ps. Sol.* 17–18. Finally, *Ps. Sol.* 4, according to M. J. Lagrange, seems directed against Pharisaic hypocrisy. It is better to conclude, with O. Eissfeldt, that the author of *Ps. Sol.* was not necessarily a Pharisee; he may have belonged to the Essenes. He was a layman, very devoted to his religion, feeling deeply its abuses, and firmly confident in God's deliverance.

The principal purpose of the poet(s) was to sustain hope in divine promises by assuring the people that God would replace the depraved Hasmonaeans with a worthy king of the house of David. The Messiah of the tribe of Levi is passed over in silence, and here one notes quite a change from the Testament of the Twelve Patriarchs and the Qumran Scrolls. (No copy of *Ps. Sol* has yet turned up among the Dead Sea Scrolls.) The Davidic Messiah will not be a suffering redeemer or a priest or a warrior. He will cleanse Jerusalem and make the Holy City a world capital "with the word of his mouth." All members will become "*sons of God." The messianic picture, it will be noted, is peaceful but very nationalistic. An exalted moral ideal is constantly to the fore, including personal freedom and responsibility, the righteous fear of God, patience and long-suffering, and the expectation of a reward after death.

The style is what one would expect in songs that arose within the Israelite liturgy. Compared to the Biblical Book of Psalms, *Ps. Sol.* sometimes has similar titles (for the leader in *Ps. Sol.* 8.1) and identical liturgical rubrics (the *selâ* in 17.31; 18.10). The same general types are found in both cases: hymns (*Ps. Sol.* 2.20, 33–37; 3.1–2); collective or individual plaints (2.19–25; 7; 8.22–34; 16.6–15); thanksgiving songs (13.1–4; 15.1–6; 16.1–5); didactic songs (3.3–12; 6). These various kinds of songs, however, now freely intermingle, so that a single psalm, like canonical Psalm 2, shifts from one type to another. *Ps. Sol.* also manifest a greater precision in historical references than one is accustomed to meet in the Biblical Psalms. One last feature about *Ps. Sol.* is noteworthy: the apocalyptic imagery is held in restraint. One senses no imminent cataclysm to break up the present age and suddenly inaugurate the new. The Messiah will conquer, but peacefully and mysteriously.

Odes of Solomon. These are 42 hymns, known principally through a Syriac translation discovered in 1908 by J. Rendel Harris, but written originally in Greek in the early 2d Christian century for liturgical usage in the Eastern Church. These songs are not to be confused with the previously mentioned apocryphon, the *Psalms of Solomon.* The odes reveal a strong Jewish influence: the parallelism of the Biblical Psalms, references to Christ in the form of prophecy rather than of history, and a strong monotheism. Christian references, however, are almost everywhere present, and they are too intimate a part of the text to be considered additions to an earlier Jewish work. The author never quotes any single word of Jesus from the Gospels; in fact, he never uses the proper name Jesus, but he prefers the common Jewish form Christ (i.e., the Messiah, the Anointed One). An exalted mysticism, derived from the writings of St. John and especially of St. Paul, spreads a contemplative spirit throughout the hymns.

The poet is particularly interested in the illumination that proceeds from the resurrected Christ (ode 42 is one of the oldest Christian poems on the Resurrection). He shies away from the humiliating details of Jesus' earthly life. Baptism, the Sacrament of initiation and enlightenment, is the only rite of the Christian Church to receive special attention. The author's Christology is not heretical, but it could become very compatible with Docetist Gnosticism, especially in odes 19 and 35. It is not surprising that five of the odes were included in the Gnostic book *Pistis Sophia.* [See J. Labourt and P. Batiffol, *Les Odes de Salomon* (Paris 1911); J. R. Harris and A. Mingana, *The Odes and Psalms of Solomon* (2 v.

Manchester 1916–20); J. Quasten, *Patrology* (v. 1 Westminster, Md. 1950) 160–168.]

Prayer of Manasses. This is a penitential psalm of Jewish origin, consisting of only 15 verses (from 37 to 42 lines in the Greek text), composed around the beginning of the Christian era. The Greek style is very impressive, with its flowing rhythm and rich vocabulary. Most scholars, therefore, deny the possibility of a translation from the Hebrew. R. H. Pfeiffer and R. H. Charles consider that at least in verse 7 one can detect traces of an original Hebrew text beneath the surface of the Greek language. They have found only a limited number of supporters for this position.

The prayer pretends to express the contrite spirit of Manasses (687–642 B.C.). This King of Juda had reversed the fervent religious policy of his father, King *Ezechia (716–687), introduced pagan rites into the Temple compound (idols, child sacrifice, and fertility cult), and violently removed all opposition among the Prophets and people (4 Kgs 21.1–18). Manasses' apostasy may have been forced on him by a resurgent Assyria, who expected vassal countries to worship its gods. It is not clear whether or not Manasses finally decided to resist Assyrian pressure, but it is stated in 2 Chr 33.11–12 that the Assyrians took Manasses in chains to Babylon, where the Judean King humbled himself and did penance before the God of his fathers. According to 2 Chr 33.18 a prayer uttered by Manasses on this occasion was preserved in the "Chronicle of the Kings of Israel" and the "Chronicle of the Seers," records that are no longer extant. This apocryphon fills in the

Fig. 3. "The Prayer of Manasses," wood engraving by Hester Sainsbury for the edition of "The Apocrypha" published by the Cresset Press, 1929.

lacuna and in doing so makes the ancient past meaningful for a later age.

The Prayer of Manasses was rejected by St. Jerome along with all deuterocanonical and apocryphal works, and the Council of Trent did not include it in the Church's official list of inspired books. Its presence, however, among 14 canticles or odes in the 5th-century MS Alexandrinus and in many other Greek, Latin, Syriac, Ethiopic, Arabic, Armenian, and Coptic MSS indicates that it was a popular liturgical piece in the Eastern Church. The religious doctrine of the prayer is very encouraging: God is infinitely compassionate, and sincere repentance obtains forgiveness for the worst sins.

Fourth Machabees. This is a philosophical sermon or disquisition demonstrating the Mosaic Law as the supreme example of reason's triumph over the passions (1.1). Its present title dates back to LXX MSS Sinaiticus (4th century) and Alexandrinus (5th century), in which the book follows immediately upon the other three Books of Machabees. It has, however, very little in common with any of them. Unlike 1 and 2 Machabees, it does not feature the Machabean wars of independence, and it is unlike 3 Machabees in that it does not follow a narrative style. The book is found also among the collected works of Flavius Josephus, where it is entitled more appropriately, "On the Supremacy of Reason."

The 18 chapters of 4 Machabees can be divided into four principal sections. (1) The introduction (1.1–12) states the theme and gives a general plan of development. Here it is plainly admitted that "inspired reason is supreme ruler over the passions, and . . . the greatest virtue . . . [is] self-control" (1.1–2). (2) In the philosophical exposition (1.13–3.18) an attempt is made to "define what the reason is and what passion is." Wisdom is "the knowledge of things, divine and human, and of their causes, . . . the culture acquired under the [Mosaic] Law" (1.14–17). (3) The third section (3.19–17.24) establishes and illustrates these statements, especially the one on the importance of the Law, by drawing upon the events narrated in 2 Machabees ch. 3; 6.18–7.42, namely, Heliodorus's futile attempt to rob the Temple treasury, the martyrdom of Eleazar, and the agonizing death of a mother and her seven sons (called the Machabean martyrs in the Christian liturgy). The gruesome and graphic account of their tortures are frequently interrupted with speeches in praise of the Law and its wisdom. (4) The final section (ch. 18) presents a peroration on obedience to the Law, addressed like the entire book to "Israelites, children born of the seed of Abraham."

The style and vocabulary of the book is thoroughly Greek, following the literary form of the diatribe as known among the Cynics and Stoics, i.e., a popular discourse on philosophical or religious matters. The author shows himself superior to the epitomizer of 2 Machabees and far more capable than the composer of 3 Machabees. The subject matter, however, is Jewish through and through, so that some scholars think that the book may have originated as a synagogal sermon.

Four Machabees drew freely upon Jewish tradition. The author mentions the paradise in which he claims that Eve was beguiled into a sexual sin by the serpent; Cain, Abel, and the sacrifice of Isaac; David the psalmist; the Prophet Ezechiel; and the deuterocanonical stories of Daniel. The expiatory suffering of the innocent for the sinful is clearly taught, a rare example of the influence of the Suffering Servant of the *Servant of the Lord Oracles (Is 52.13–53.12) on later Jewish thought (4 Machabees 1.11; 6.28–29; 17.21–22). Retribution after the death of the just and the wicked is presumed throughout the work, but, contrary to 2 Mc 7.11, 14, 19, 22–23, the resurrection of the body is not taught. Immortality is presented in a more Platonic fashion (4 Machabees 5.37; 9.8; 10.11; 12.13).

Eusebius of Caesarea (A.D. 270–340) and St. Jerome (A.D. 342–420) identified the author with the Jewish historian Flavius Josephus (A.D. 37–100), but this opinion is not accepted today. The author's name, therefore, remains unknown, but from his book one can deduce that he was a fervent Jew, well versed in the Hebrew Scriptures and in later traditions. He shows himself very favorable to Greek philosophical influences, the Platonic, the Cynic, and particularly the Stoic. For these reasons he must have lived in the Jewish *Diaspora, either in Syria, birthplace of the Stoic philosopher Zeno and possibly the home of the Jewish author of 2 Machabees, or Alexandria, Egypt, where the LXX originated and where the MSS Sinaiticus and Alexandrinus were written. He composed his work sometime after 2 Machabees but before the spread of Christianity—therefore, in the 2 or 3 decades before or after the beginning of the Christian Era.

Bibliography: R. H. CHARLES et al., eds., *The Apocrypha and Pseudepigrapha of the O.T. in English,* 2 v. (Oxford 1913), the standard book for Eng. tr. and the longest commentaries. O. EISSFELDT, *Einleitung in das A.T.* (3d ed. Tübingen 1964) 777–864, the most incisive and up-to-date introd. R. H. PFEIFFER, Inter Bibl 1:391–436. H. H. ROWLEY, *The Relevance of Apocalyptic* (2d ed. London 1952). A. BENTZEN, *Introduction to the O.T.,* 2 v. in 1 (2d ed. Copenhagen 1952) 2:218–252. J. B. FREY, DBSuppl 1:354–460. I. M. PRICE et al., Hastings DB (1963) 39–41, 820–823. R. J. FOSTER, "The Apocrypha of the O.T. and N.T.," CathCommHS 92–94. D. S. RUSSELL, *The Method and Message of Jewish Apocalyptic* (Philadelphia 1964). **Illustration credits:** Fig. 1, Palestine Archaeological Museum, Jerusalem, Jordan. Figs. 2 and 3, Mr. and Mrs. Ross W. Sloniker Collection of Twentieth Century Biblical and Religious Prints, The Cincinnati Art Museum.

[C. STUHLMUELLER]

5. APOCRYPHA OF THE NEW TESTAMENT

The NT Apocrypha, as the term is used here, are the early Christian writings that more or less resemble the books of the NT but have not been received as canonical Scriptures by the Church. The beginnings of the NT apocryphal literature coincide with the slow crystallization of the NT canon. Most of the Apocryphal books are known only by title because their existence was mentioned by the Fathers of the Church in their struggle against heresy. Origen, Irenaeus, Jerome, Eusebius, and especially Epiphanius in his comprehensive *Panarion,* or Refutation, of all heresies (PG v.41) are the main sources of information on the NT Apocrypha; some information is found also in the Stichometry of Nicephor (PG 100:1060) and the Pseudo-Gelasian Decree (PL 59:162–164; TU 3.8.4).

The main characteristics of the NT Apocrypha are not only their pseudonymous use of the names of the Apostles or other personages who were supposed to know something of the life and teachings of Our Lord, but also their general imitation of the four kinds of NT canonical writings—the Gospels, Acts, Epistles, and Apocalypse. They differ, however, from the canonical writings by the excess of the miraculous element in their stories and by the esoteric aspect of their teachings. In regard to their doctrinal contents one can distinguish those that are heretical (mostly Gnostic, but later at times purged by orthodox editors) from those that are merely fictitious and can be considered as the beginnings of Christian devotional literature or even as the first attempts at dogmatic development (e.g., in regard to the Assumption of Mary). They had a great influence on the liturgy (e.g., the Feasts of the Presentation, of St. Joachim, and of St. Anne), the iconography, and Christian symbolism. Their greatest value consists in the witness they offer in proof on the one hand, of the first daring movements of Christian thinking and imagination, and on the other, of the sure discriminatory power of the Church in distinguishing them from the canonical writings.

Bibliography: J. A. FABRICIUS, *Codex Apocryphus Novi Testamenti,* 3 v. (Hamburg 1719–43). J. C. THILO, *Codex Apocryphus Novi Testamenti* (Leipzig 1832). S. SZÉKELY, *Bibliotheca Apocrypha* (Freiburg 1913). J. BOUSQUET and É. AMANN, *Les Apocryphes du Nouveau Testament* (Paris 1910; 3d ed. 1922). E. KLOSTERMANN and A. HARNACK, *Apokrypha,* 4 v. (Kleine Texte 3, 8, 11, 12; v.1, 3d ed. Bonn 1921; v.2–4, 2d ed. 1910–12). Altaner 51–73. Quasten Patr 1:106–157. Bardenhewer. E. HENNECKE, *Neutestamentliche Apokryphen,* 2 v. (3d ed. Tübingen 1959–64), Eng. tr. of v.1 (London 1963); references below to v.1 are to the Eng. ed. James ApocNT. A. WALKER and B. P. PATTERN, AnteNicChLibr 8:349–644, 657–665. W. MICHAELIS, *Die apokryphen Schriften zum Neuen Testament* (Bremen 1956). R. H. PFEIFFER, *History of NT Times with an Introduction to the Apocrypha* (New York 1949). C. C. TORREY, *The Apocryphal Literature* (New Haven 1945). É. AMANN, DBSuppl 1:1217–33. A. PENNA, EncCatt 1:1629–33. L. VAGANEY, *Catholicisme* 1:699–704. J. MICHL, LexThK² 1:698–704, 712–713, 747–754; 2:688–693; 3:1217–33. B. M. METZGER, RGG³ 1:473–474.

APOCRYPHAL GOSPELS

The term Apocryphal Gospels is applied to those NT Apocrypha that claim to contain supplementary information in regard to the earthly life, deeds, and sayings of Jesus or even of persons associated with His life, such as Joseph and Mary. A systematic listing of aspects to be considered would include: (1) the nature of the pretended authors, mostly Apostles but also other Gospel personages and even heresiarchs; (2) the historical contents, e.g., infancy Gospels and Passion Gospels; (3) the doctrinal tendencies, e.g., of Nazareans, Gnostics, and Ebionites; (4) the state of preservation, since many are merely mentioned, of some there are only fragments, of some the original text has been preserved, and of some others only later, variant translations are available. No treatment is attempted here of those that are known or are preserved only in fragment or of the *Agrapha (for all these, see De Santos Otero, 81–130; James ApocNT 25–37; Michl, 1218–19). The other Apocryphal Gospels are treated here under the following headings: Infancy Gospels, Apostolic Gospels, Jewish-Christian Gospels, Writings on or by Gospel Personages, and Heretical Gospels.

Bibliography: C. TISCHENDORF, *Evangelia apocrypha* (2d ed. Leipzig 1876). C. MICHEL and P. PEETERS, *Évangiles apocryphes,* 2 v. (2d ed. Paris 1924). G. BUONACCORSI, *I vangeli apocrifi* (Florence 1948). A. DE SANTOS OTERO, *Los Evangelios apocrifos* (Madrid 1956). F. AMIOT, *Évangiles apocryphes* (Paris 1952). H. J. SCHOENFIELD, *Readings from the Apocryphal Gospels* (London 1940). J. MICHL, LexThK² 3:1217–33. James ApocNT 38–227.

Infancy Gospels. Apocryphal writings on the immediate prehistory, Nativity, and childhood of Jesus are numerous. In some way or other they are all derived either from the *Protoevangelium Jacobi* or from the *Thomas Gospel of the Infancy.* According to P. Peeters all are rooted in a common Syriac source written sometime before A.D. 400 that contained tales even of Buddhistic origin. J. Michl supposes that possibly there was a collection of infancy legends as early as the 2d century.

Protoevangelium Jacobi. The title comes from the Latin translation of G. Postel (1552). It was formerly known also as the *Gospel of James.* It must have been written c. A.D. 150, since its existence is witnessed to by Justin (*Dial.* 78.5), Origen (*In Mt.* 10.17), and Clement of Alexandria (*Strom.* 7.93.7). It was rejected as noncanonical by the *Gelasian Decree. The author (who was ignorant of the customs and geography of Palestine) must have been a *Judaeo-Christian of the *Diaspora. He pretended to be St. *James the Less (son of Alphaeus), Bishop of Jerusalem and brother of the Lord, who could have been a witness of all the events in the fantastic stories in this Apocryphal Gospel. It contains the oldest account on the early life of the Blessed Virgin (whose parents are called Joachim and Anne), her presentation in the Temple (hence the feast of November 21), her espousal with Joseph (an aged widower with children, perhaps in order to explain the "brothers and sisters" of the Lord), and her virginal birth of Jesus (on the testimony of the midwife). It ends with the slaughter of the Holy Innocents, the murder of Zachary, and the death of Herod. The text is preserved in the original Greek (30 MSS) and in Syriac, Armenian, Coptic, and Old Slavic translations with many redactional variations.

Bibliography: C. TISCHENDORF, *op. cit.* 1–50. É. AMANN, *Le Protoévangile de Jacques* (Paris 1910). M. R. JAMES, *Latin Infancy Gospels* (Cambridge, Eng. 1922). A. E. W. BUDGE, *Legends of Our Lady . . .* (Oxford 1933); *One Hundred and Ten Miracles of Our Lady* (Oxford 1933). P. VANUTELLI, *Protoevangelium Jacobi synoptice* (Rome 1940). J. ROBSON, "Stories of Jesus and Mary," *The Muslim World* 40 (Hartford, Conn. 1950) 236–243. M. TESTUZ, ed., *Papyrus Bodmer V: Nativité de Marie* (Cologne 1958). E. DE STRYCKER, *La Forme plus ancienne du Protoévangile de Jacques* (Brussels 1961). Quasten Patr 1:118–122. Altaner 67–68. James ApocNT 38–49. A. DE SANTOS OTERO, *op. cit.* 135–188, 293–294. E. HENNECKE, *op. cit.* 1:370–388. J. MICHL, LexThK² 3:1221–22.

Thomas Gospel of the Infancy. It is called *The Infancy of the Lord Jesus* in Syriac MSS; a Greek MS adds, "by Thomas, the philosopher of Israel." No reason has yet been found why Thomas could be considered an authentic witness to the childhood of Jesus. This Apocryphal Gospel has nothing in common with the Gnostic *Gospel of Thomas* (see below). It is a collection of legendary stories—full of manifestations of a miraculous knowledge and power and told at times rather tastelessly—about the life of Jesus in Nazareth up to His 12th year. It is preserved in two Greek MSS (one much longer than the other) and in many Latin, Syriac, and other versions. The Greek original, from the East, might date from the 2d century.

Bibliography: C. TISCHENDORF, *op. cit.* 140–157 (longer Gr. text), 158–163 (shorter Gr. text), 164–180 (Latin version). W. HAYS, *The Gospel according to Thomas* (London 1921). M. R. JAMES, *op. cit.* 49–70; JThSt 30 (1928) 51–54. Quasten Patr 1:123–125. Altaner 69. A. DE SANTOS OTERO, *op. cit.* 299–324. E. HENNECKE, *op. cit.* 1:388–404. J. MICHL, LexThK² 3:1222.

Arabic Gospel of the Infancy. This Gospel is probably not older than the 6th century. The first part (ch. 1–11) is based on the *Protoevangelium Jacobi,* and the last part (ch. 41–55) on the *Gospel of Thomas;* the middle section contains some strange new incidents from Oriental legends.

Bibliography: J. C. THILO, *op. cit.* 6–131 (Lat. and Arab. texts). C. TISCHENDORF, *op. cit.* 181–209. C. MICHEL and P. PEETERS, *op. cit.* 2:1–65, i–xixx. P. PEETERS, AnalBoll 41:132–134. Graf GeschChArabLit 225–227. James ApocNT 80–82. A. DE SANTOS OTERO, *op. cit.* 325–357. J. MICHL, LexThK² 3:1223.

Armenian Gospel of the Infancy. Probably in the 6th century monotonous compilation from the previous three Infancy Gospels was made. In the 10th century it was translated into Armenian from a Syriac original. It is now divided into 28 chapters.

Bibliography: I. DAIËTSI, *Ankanon girkh nor ketakar anatz, Noncanonical books of the NT* (Venice 1898) 1–235. C. MICHEL and P. PEETERS, *op. cit.* 2:69–128. James ApocNT 83–89. A. DE SANTOS OTERO, *op. cit.* 379–386. J. MICHL, LexThK² 3:1223.

Pseudo-Matthew. The *Liber de Ortu Beatae Mariae et Infantia Salvatoris* is commonly known as *Pseudo-*

Fig. 4. The meeting of the Holy Family with Affradosius, detail of the mosaic of the apsidal arch of the basilica of Santa Maria Maggiore, Rome, executed c. 432–440; based upon the 24th chapter of Pseudo-Matthew.

Matthew, but in some MSS it is attributed to St. James. It is, in fact, a Western 6th-century compilation from the canonical infancy stories and from Apocryphal Gospels of James and Thomas. Jerome's introductory letter accrediting the stories is a fabrication invented simply *ad hoc.*

Bibliography: J. C. THILO, *op. cit.* 339–400. C. TISCHENDORF, *op. cit.* 50–105. James ApocNT 70–79. A. DE SANTOS OTERO, *op. cit.* 189–257. J. MICHL, LexThK² 3:1223.

Historia de Conceptione Beatae Mariae. Two Latin MSS of the 13th and 14th century have preserved this apocryphal account of the events preceding the birth of Mary. The first, Codex Arundel (British Museum), follows *Pseudo-Matthew;* the second, Codex Hereford, is similar to the *Protoevangelium Jacobi.* Both were discovered and published by M. R. James.

Bibliography: JAMES ApocNT 80–94. M. J. LAGRANGE RevBibl 37 (1928) 544–557. J. A. ROBINSON, JthSt 29 (1928) 205–207. A. DE SANTOS OTERO, *op. cit.* 275–292 (the Arundel text). J. MICHL, LexThK² 3:1224.

Gospels of the Apostles. Some Apocryphal writings that more or less imitate the canonical Gospels pretend to have been written by an Apostle. Since apostolic authorship lent great authority to a book, the authors of these pseudepigrapha attributed their works to one of the Twelve.

Gospel of Peter. This Gospel was written in Syria (between 150–200), but not necessarily by sectarians. Fragments of the work were discovered by U. Bouriant in the tomb of a monk at Akhmîm in Upper Egypt (1886–87). Until then it was known only from references to it made by Origen (*In Mt.* 10.17) and Eusebius (*Hist. eccl.* 3.3.2; 6.12.4–6). The latter stated that the *Gospel of Peter* had been rejected as heretical by Bp. Serapion of Antioch as early as *c.* 190.

Bibliography: U. BOURIANT, *Fragments du text grec du livre d'Enoch et de quelques écrits attribués à saint Pierre* (Paris 1892) 93–147. P. GARDNER and M. R. SMITH, JThSt 27 (1926) 255–271, 401–407. E. FASCHER, Pauly-Wiss RE 19:1373–81. L. VAGANEY, *L'Évangile de Pierre* (2d ed. Paris 1930). G. BUONACCORSI, *op. cit.* 16–28. A. DE SANTOS OTERO, *op. cit.* 398–417. Quasten Patr 1:114–115. Altaner 67. E. HENNECKE, *op. cit.* 1:179–187. J. MICHL, LexThK² 3:1228–29. James ApocNT 90–94.

Gospel of St. Thomas. The lost original text of this work was probably Greek, written *c.* 140, if not earlier. A Coptic (Sahidic) adaptation was found in Nag' Hammâdi (1945), written probably in the 4th or 5th century. It contains 113 sayings attributed to Jesus. The doctrinal tendency is Gnostic-Manichaean. According to Hippolytus (*Ref.* 5.7.20) it was used by the Naassene Gnostics. Origen (*In Lc. hom.* 7) and Ambrose (*In Lc.* 1.2) referred to it. The introduction and the first 17 sayings in Greek are contained in Oxyrhynchus Papyrus 1.654, 655. Also, Cyril of Jerusalem (*Cath.* 4.36; 6.31) mentioned a *Gospel of Thomas* that was a fabrication by a disciple of Mani; it is not sure, however, that he was referring to the same document that is now known as the *Gospel of Thomas.*

Bibliography: G. Quispel, VigChr 11 (1957) 189–207. J. LEIPOLDT, ThLitZ 83 (1958) 481–493. J. DORESSE, *Les Livres secrets des Gnostiques d'Égypte* (Paris 1959) 245–251; Eng. tr. P. MAIRET (New York 1960). A. GUILLAUMONT et al., *The Gospel according to Thomas* (New York 1959). J. MICHL, LexThK² 3:1229. E. HENNECKE, *op. cit.* 1:278–307, 511–522. B. GAERTNER, *The Theology of the Gospel according to Thomas* (New York 1960). R. M. GRANT and D. N. FREEDMAN, *The Secret Sayings of Jesus* (Garden City, N.Y. 1960). R. M. WILSON, *Studies in the Gospel of Thomas* (London 1960). J. JEREMIAS, *Unbekannte Jesusworte* (3d rev. ed. Gütersloh, 1963).

Gospel of Matthias. Three Apocryphal writings are attributed to St. Matthias. Origen (*In Lc. hom.* 1) mentions a *Gospel of Matthias,* which is apparently the same as the one rejected by the Gelasian Decree as heretical. M. R. James and O. Bardenhewer think, contrary to O. Stählin and J. Tixeront, that the Gospel of Matthias is identical with the *Traditions of Matthias* quoted by Clement of Alexandria (*Strom.* 2.9.45; 3.4.26; 7.13.82, etc.) as a heretical book of secret doctrines written *c.* 150 in Egypt (probably at Alexandria). According to Hippolytus (*Ref.* 7.20.1) the Gnostic *Basilides and his disciple Isidor spoke of secret doctrines obtained from Christ by Matthias. The Nag' Hammâdi findings revealed the *Book of Thomas the Athlete That He Wrote for the Perfect;* it purports to contain secret words of Jesus addressed to Thomas and written down by Matthias.

Bibliography: James ApocNT 12–13. A. DE SANTOS OTERO, *op. cit.* 62–64. J. DORESSE, *op. cit.* 243–245. J. MICHL, LexThK² 3:1229–30. E. HENNECKE, *op. cit.* 1:307–313.

Gospel of Philip. Epiphanius (*Haer.* 26.13) cites a passage of the *Gospel of Philip* used by the Gnostics of Egypt. The Coptic *Pistis Sophia* (42.44) refers to some secret doctrines given by Jesus to Philip after His Resurrection. The writings found in Nag' Hammâdi also have a set of Gnostic utterances entitled as the *Gospel of Philip* (but without the passage quoted by Epiphanius), written probably in the 3d century.

Bibliography: P. LABIB, *Coptic Gnostic Papyri in the Coptic Museum of Old Cairo,* v.1 (Cairo 1950) 99–134. J. DORESSE, *op. cit.* 239–243, 251. H. M. SCHENKE, ThLitZ 84 (1959) 1–26. J. MICHL, LexThK² 3:1230. E. HENNECKE, *op. cit.* 1:271–278. R. M. WILSON, ed. and tr., *The Gospel of Philip: Translated from the Coptic Text . . .* (New York 1963).

Gospel of Barnabas. The Gelasian Decree rejected a *Gospel of Barnabas* as Apocryphal. It was certainly not identical with the Italian *Gospel of Barnabas* that is contained in a 16th-century MS in Vienna. The latter was written by a 14th-century Christian converted to Islam who tried to argue that Mohammed was the Messiah and Islam the true religion.

Bibliography: L. and L. RAGG, eds. and trs., *The Gospel of Barnabas* (Oxford 1907). J. SCHMID, ReallexAntChr 1:1209–12. Quasten Patr 1:127. Altaner 71. J. MICHL, LexThK² 3:1233.

Gospel of Bartholomew. Jerome (*Prol. in Mt.*) and the Gelasian Decree refer to a *Gospel of Bartholomew.* It was probably identical with the *Questions of Bartholomew* composed originally in Greek by Gnostics in Egypt in the 3d or 4th century. It is preserved in a Greek MS in Vienna and in another in Jerusalem, and there are also some fragments in Coptic, Latin, and Slavonic versions of it. It narrates that the risen Lord answered some questions of Bartholomew concerning His descent into hell; Mary tells Bartholomew about the Annunciation; and even Satan is interrogated on the sin and downfall of the angels.

Bibliography: E. A. W. BUDGE, *Coptic Apocrypha in the Dialect of Upper Egypt* (London 1913) 1–48 (Coptic text), 179–230 (Eng. tr.). Quasten Patr 1:127. Altaner 69–70. James ApocNT 166–181. A. DE SANTOS OTERO, *op. cit.* 570–608. J. MICHL, LexThK² 3:1227. E. HENNECKE, *op. cit.* 1:484–508.

Gospel of Judas Iscariot. Irenaeus (*Haer.* 1.28.9), Epiphanius (*Haer.* 1.38), and Theodoretus of Cyrrhus (*Haer. fab. comp.* 1.15) refer to the *Gospel of Judas Iscariot.* This 2d-century Gnostic writing has not been preserved, but according to Irenaeus it taught that only

Judas knew the truth and by his betrayal achieved the desired separation of the heavenly from the earthly.

Bibliography: A. DE SANTOS OTERO, *op. cit.* 75–76. E. HENNECKE, *op. cit.* 1:313–314. J. MICHL, LexThK² 3:1230.

Gospel of Andrew. The Gelasian Decree rejected a *Gospel of Andrew* as heretical. Perhaps it is identical with the *Acts of Andrew* (see below).

Bibliography: Altaner 71. Bardenhewer 1:538. J. MICHL, LexThK² 3:1227.

Gospels of John. There is a 14th-century Arabic MS in the Ambrosian Library, Milan, that purports to contain revelations given to John by the risen Lord; it was derived probably from a Syriac original of about the 6th century. There are also a Coptic *Apocryphon of John* (preserved in four MSS) and some fragments of a *Dialogue between John and Jesus.*

Bibliography: J. MICHL, LexThK² 1:1227. E. HENNECKE, *op. cit.* 1:314–333.

Judaeo-Christian Gospels. In this class of Apocrypha earlier scholars distinguished only the *Gospel of the Hebrews* and the *Gospel of the Ebionites,* but most modern scholars agree that the fragments that are known must be divided into three distinct Judaeo-Christian Gospels.

Gospel of the Hebrews. The most frequently mentioned is the *Gospel of the Hebrews.* It was perhaps used by Papias; it was known to Eusebius and quoted by Clement of Alexandria and Origen. The fragments that have been preserved do not show any special relationship to the canonical Gospels; their doctrine contains Gnostic and syncretistic elements. The *Gospel of the Hebrews* was probably written originally in Greek, perhaps in Egypt (2d century); it was used especially in Judaeo-Christian circles of the Transjordan.

Gospel of the Nazarenes. The Nazarenes (or Nazaraeans) were a Syrian Judaeo-Christian sect. Their Apocryphal Gospel was written in a Semitic language (Aramaic or Syriac). It is mentioned by Hegesippus, Eusebius, Epiphanius, and Jerome. Formerly it was wrongly regarded as the original Aramaic Gospel of St. Matthew, with which it has certain similarities. It was composed probably between 110 and 150.

Gospel of the Ebionites. Epiphanius quoted several passages from the *Gospel of the Ebionites.* The Ebionites (literally "poor men") were an early Judaeo-Christian sect in Transjordan. The Apocryphal Gospel was a revision of Matthew adapted to their tenets (of opposition to sacrifice). Probably it was written originally in Greek in the 2d century. According to many scholars it is the same as the *Gospel of the Twelve* referred to by Origen.

Bibliography: James ApocNT 1–10. Quasten Patr 1:111–114. Altaner 66–67. A. DE SANTOS OTERO, *op. cit.* 32–57. E. HENNECKE, *op. cit.* 1:117–165. J. MICHL, LexThK² 3:1219–21. J. T. DODD, *The Gospel according to the Hebrews* (London 1933).

Heretical Gospels. Although most of the NT Apocrypha contain certain heretical elements, the writings listed under this heading are essentially heretical, and most of them are products of Christian *Gnosticism.

Pistis Sophia. The original Greek text of the work inaccurately called by its first editors *Pistis Sophia* (Faith Wisdom) is now lost. But from the Coptic version of it preserved in a 4th-century MS (Codex Askewianus of the British Museum) it seems that the original work was written by Barbeliote Gnostics in Egypt in the 3d century. It is divided into four books. According to the first three, which form a unit, Jesus returned from the world of aeons to the earth 12 years after His Ascension and taught His disciples, especially John and Mary Magdalene, about the fall and redemption of a female aeon, the Sophia who was called Pistis. The fourth part, originally an older, independent work, contains Jesus' teachings on the punishment for sin, the mysteries of Baptism, and the remission of sin.

Bibliography: G. HORNER, *Pistis Sophia* (London 1924). C. SCHMID, *Pistis Sophia* (Leipzig 1925). E. HENNECKE, *op. cit.* 1:250–259. J. SCHMID, LexThK² 8:524. G. QUISPEL, RGG³ 5:386–388. Pauly-Wiss RE 19.2:1813–21.

Gospel of Truth. The original Greek text of *Gospel of Truth,* written by Valentinian Gnostics *c.* 150, is now lost. But a Coptic version of it was discovered at Chenoboskion (near Nag' Hammâdi; *see* CHENOBOSKION, GNOSTIC TEXTS OF). It is a pious meditation on Jesus' revelation of that knowledge by which man comes to know God and thereby finds salvation.

Bibliography: M. MALININE et al., *Evangelium veritatis* (Zurich 1956); suppl. (1961). F. L. CROSS, ed. and tr., *The Codex Jung* (London 1935). L. CERFAUX, NTSt 5 (1958–59) 103–112. E. HENNECKE, *op. cit.* 1:233–241, 523–531. J. MICHL, LexThK² 3:1232. K. GROBEL, *The Gospel of Truth: A Valentinian Meditation on the Gospel* (New York 1960). S. ARAI, *Die Christologie des Evangelium Veritatis* (Leiden 1964).

Sophia Jesu Christi. A Coptic version of *Sophia Jesu Christi* is preserved in two MSS (Pap. Berolin. 1896 and Nag' Hammâdi Cod. I, 1945). The original, of which some fragments are preserved in Oxyrhynchus Pap. 1081, was written in Greek, probably in the 3d century in Egypt. According to this Apocryphon the risen Christ appeared to the 12 Apostles and 7 women and answered their questions about the invisible world.

Bibliography: A. DE SANTOS OTERO, *op. cit.* 87–89. E. HENNECKE, *op. cit.* 1:243–248. J. MICHL, LexThK² 3:1232.

Dialogus Salvatoris. The Coptic version of the *Dialogus Salvatoris* was found among the Gnostic texts of Chenoboskion (Cod. I, after the *Sophia Jesu Christi*). The original was composed probably in the 3d century. It is a dialogue of Jesus with His disciples on cosmological questions and is apparently related to the first three sections of the *Pistis Sophia.*

Bibliography: H. C. PUECH and J. DORESSE, *Les Nouveaux écrits gnostiques découverts en Haute-Égypte: Académie des inscriptions et belles lettres 1948* (Paris 1949) 87–95. E. HENNECKE, *op. cit.* 1:248–250. J. MICHL, LexThK² 3:1233.

Other Heretical Gospels. Known only by title or from fragments are (1) the *Evangelium vivum,* mentioned by Timotheus of Jerusalem (PG 86.1:21c) as used by the Manichaeans; (2) the *Evangelium consummationis,* a Nicolaite Gnostic Apocryphon, probably of the 2d century, mentioned by Epiphanius (*Haer.* 26.2.5) and Philastrius (d. *c.* 397; *De haer.* 33.7); (3) the *Gospel of the Four Heavenly Regions,* referred to by Irenaeus (*Adv. haer.* 3.11.11); (4) *Gospel of Cerinthus,* mentioned by Epiphanius (*Haer.* 28.5.1), probably a truncated version of Matthew; (5) the *Gospel of Basilides,* mentioned by Origen (*In Lc. hom.* 1), Ambrose, and Jerome; (6) the *Gospel of Marcion,* a tendentious redaction of Luke, omitting Luke ch. 1–2 completely and changing other parts, which was cited by Irenaeus (*Adv. haer.* 1.27.2; 3.14.4), Tertullian (*Adv. Marc.* 4.4.3–5), and Epiphanius (*Haer.* 42.9.1–2); (7) the *Gospel of Apelles,* mentioned by Jerome (*Com. in Mt.,*

Prol.), merely another form of the *Gospel of Marcion;* (8) the *Gospel of Mani,* known from the so-called Turfan fragments, Coptic-Manichaean writings discovered in 1930, perhaps the same as the *Evangelium vivum;* (9) the *Gospel of the Egyptians,* written originally in Greek some time after 150 and accepted as canonical in Egypt, partially known from citations from it by Clement of Alexandria, Hippolytus, and Epiphanius (see Hennecke, 1:166–170), a work showing encratistic (forbidding marriage), Naasite (with strange view on body and soul), and Sabellian (modalistic) tendencies; (10) the *Gospel of Eve,* known only from a passage quoted by Epiphanius (*Haer.* 26.2–3); (11) the 2d-century Gnostic *Gospel of Mary Magdalen,* known from a Greek fragment (Oxyrhynchus Pap.) of the 3d century in J. Ryland Library, Manchester, and from a fragmentary 5th-century Coptic version (Pap. Berolin. 8502), in which Jesus, after His Resurrection, teaches first His Apostles, and then Mary Magdalene, who had His special confidence and who conveys to them further sayings of Jesus; and (12) the (greater and lesser) *Questions of Mary* (Magdalene), really two different Gnostic works, from which Epiphanius (*Haer.* 26.8) quotes certain rather obscene and blasphemous passages.

Bibliography: (1) A. DE SANTOS OTERO, *op. cit.* 78. J. MICHL, LexThK² 3:1232. (2) A. DE SANTOS OTERO, *op. cit.* 79. E. HENNECKE, *op. cit.* 1:232–233. J. MICHL, LexThK² 3:1232. (3) A. DE SANTOS OTERO, *op. cit.* 74. E. HENNECKE, *op. cit.* 1:231. (4) A. BARDY, RevBibl 20 (1921) 373. E. HENNECKE, *op. cit.* 1:345–346. J. MICHL, LexThK² 3:1231. (5) E. HENNECKE, *op. cit.* 1:346–348. J. MICHL, LexThK² 3:1231–32. (6) James ApocNT 20. E. HENNECKE, *op. cit.* 1:348–349. J. MICHL, LexThK² 3:1231. (7) A. DE SANTOS OTERO, *op. cit.* 74–75. E. HENNECKE, *op. cit.* 1:349–350. J. MICHL, LexThK² 3:1231. (8) E. HENNECKE, *op. cit.* 1:350–361. (9) James ApocNT 10–12. A. DE SANTOS OTERO, *op. cit.* 57–61. E. HENNECKE, *op. cit.* 1:166–178. Quasten Patr 1:113. Altaner 67. J. MICHL, LexThK² 3:1228. (10) A. DE SANTOS OTERO, *op. cit.* 76–77. E. HENNECKE, *op. cit.* 1:241–243. J. MICHL, LexThK² 3:1230. (11) A. DE SANTOS OTERO, *op. cit.* 106–108. E. HENNECKE, *op. cit.* 1:340–344. J. MICHL, LexThK² 3:1230–31. (12) E. HENNECKE, *op. cit.* 1:338–340. J. MICHL, LexThK² 3:1231.

Apocrypha about or by Gospel Personages. Piety rather than heresy led Christians during the early centuries of the Church to compose imaginary stories about Mary and Joseph and John the Baptist for the sake of supplementing the meager information that the canonical Gospels offer on these beloved saints. A similar need for more information on the Passion and Resurrection of Christ produced Apocryphal documents connected with these events.

De Transitu Beatae Mariae Virginis. A Pseudo-Johannine fictitious narration about the last days, death, and assumption of Mary, this work is known also as the *Dormitio* [κοίμησις] *Mariae.* According to this Apocryphon, all the Apostles are transported miraculously on clouds to her house. After Christ Himself comes for her soul, her body is laid into the tomb, but it is assumed from it into heaven. A 5th-century Latin form of the text attributes it to *Melito of Sardes, but the work is not earlier than the 4th century. The work, which became extremely popular, was written originally in Greek. The present Greek form of the text, however, has suffered extensive revisions. The purest form is in the Syriac version. Other versions are in Coptic, Armenian, and Arabic.

Bibliography: C. TISCHENDORF, *Apocalypses apocryphae* (Leipzig 1866) 95–112. A. DE SANTOS OTERO, *op. cit.* 611–700. M. JUGIE, *La Mort et l'Assomption de la sainte Vierge: Étude*

historico-doctrinale (StTest 114; 1944) 103–171; ÉchosOr 29 (1930) 265–295. C. DONAHUE, ed., *The Testament of Mary: The Gaelic Version of the Dormitio Mariae together with an Irish Latin Version* (New York 1942). A. C. RUSH, AmEcclRev 116 (1947) 5–31; 123 (1950) 93–110; CathBiblQuart 12 (1950) 367–378. Quasten Patr 1:247–248. J. MICHL, LexThK² 3:1224.

Evangelium de Nativitate Mariae. Under this title a fictitious account is given of Mary's birth, infancy, girlhood, marriage to Joseph, and miraculous pregnancy. In the Middle Ages it was generally thought to have been written by St. Jerome. It was first mentioned formally by *Fulbert of Chartres (d. 1028) as written by St. Matthew and translated by Jerome. Actually it was written *c.* 800 and used Pseudo-Matthew as one of its sources. It was the main source for the Marian contents of the *Legenda aurea* of Bl. *James of Voragine.

Bibliography: PL 30:297–305. C. TISCHENDORF, *Evangelia apocrypha,* op. cit. 113–121. James ApocNT 79–80. J. BOUSQUET and É. AMANN, *op. cit.* 340–365. A. DE SANTOS OTERO, *op. cit.* 258–274. J. MICHL, LexThK² 3:1223–24.

Lament of the Virgin. This is an account of Mary's mourning after the death of her Son and His apparition to her after His Resurrection. It was written probably in Egypt, not before the 5th century. It is preserved in an Arabic version and in a Coptic fragment.

Bibliography: R. HARRIS, BullJRylLibr 12 (1928) 411–425. A. MINGANA, *ibid.* 427–488. Graf GeschChArabLit 1:247–248.

History of the Blessed Virgin Mary. This legendary life of Mary was written probably in Syria about the 5th century. It was compiled from the infancy Gospels and other Marian Apocrypha and is preserved in Syriac, Armenian, and Arabic MSS.

Bibliography: E. A. W. BUDGE, *History of the Blessed Virgin Mary,* 2 v. (London 1899) 1:3–153; 2:3–168. A. BAUMSTARK, *Geschichte der syrischen Literatur mit Ausschluss der christlichpalästinensischen Texte* (Bonn 1922) 70, 99. Graf GeschCh ArabLit 1:246–247.

History of Joseph the Carpenter. This imaginary Life of St. Joseph, as narrated by Jesus to His disciples, was originally written in Greek, probably in Egypt toward the end of the 4th century. It is preserved in a Coptic version and in an Arabic translation from the Coptic with various additions. The Latin version appeared first in the 14th century. According to this Apocryphon Jesus told His disciples on the Mount of Olives about the preparations for His birth, about His nativity and early childhood (ch. 1–11), and about Joseph's sickness, death, and burial (ch. 12–32). The last part of the narrative is strongly influenced by the usages of the cult of Osiris. (*See* ISIS AND OSIRIS.) The book is one of the earliest signs of the veneration of St. Joseph.

Bibliography: S. MORENZ, *Die Geschichte von Joseph dem Zimmermann* (TU 56; 1951). James ApocNT 84–86. A. DE SANTOS OTERO, *op. cit.* 356–378. Graf GeschChArabLit 1:234–236. Quasten Patr 1:125. Altaner 68–69. J. MICHL, LexThK² 3:1225.

Life of St. John the Baptist. This work recounts the Baptist's childhood, life in the desert, and death—all adorned with fantastic details. The original was a Greek homily given at Alexandria by Bishop Serapion toward the end of the 4th century. It is preserved in two MSS of a Arabic version, which contains some later additions.

Bibliography: R. HARRIS, BullJRylLibr 11 (1927) 342–349. A. MINGANA, *ibid.* 439–489. J. MICHL, LexThK² 3:1225. E. HENNECKE, *op. cit.* 1:414–417.

Fig. 5. An angel announces the death of the Virgin Mary, and the Virgin tells the Apostles of her approaching death, full-page miniature, based upon passages in the "De Transitu Beatae Mariae Virginis," in the York Psalter, written in England in the 12th century and preserved in the library of the Hunterian Museum at Glasgow (MS U. 3. 2.).

Narratio de Praeciso Joannis Baptistae Capite. The narrative of the beheading of the Baptist is preceded by an account of the flight of Elizabeth with John into the mountains, the murder of Zachary, and John's activity, arrest, and imprisonment. The work is preserved in an 11th-century Greek MS at Monte Cassino. Although the MS attributes it to a certain disciple of John called Eurippos, the work is actually not older than the 5th century.

Bibliography: J. MICHL, LexThK² 3:1225. H. WALL, "A Coptic Fragment concerning the Childhood of John the Baptist," RevÉgypt 8 (1951) 207–214.

Gospel of Nicodemus. This 5th-century composition from earlier writings is preserved in both the original Greek and in Syriac, Armenian, Coptic, Arabic, and Latin versions. It was intended as a defense against the accusations propagated by the Roman government under Emperor Maximinus Daza (311–312). According to the book, a certain Christian called Ananias found an account, written in Hebrew by Nicodemus, of Pilate's trial of Jesus, and he translated it into Greek in 425. The account continues with Jesus' death and burial (ch. 1–11), a discussion in the Sanhedrin of Jesus' Resurrection (ch. 12–16), and finally a narration of Jesus' descent into hell by two witnesses who rose at Christ's Resurrection, Leucius and Karinus, sons of Simeon. Justin (*Apol.* 1.35.9; 48.3) and Tertullian (*Apol.* 21.24) were acquainted with a certain work called *The Acts of Pilate* concerning the Roman trial of Jesus. It is possible the work they refer to forms the basis of the first part of the *Gospel of Nicodemus.* Other Acts of Pilate, such as the *Anaphora Pilati* and *Paradosis Pilati,* are medieval productions.

Bibliography: S. J. CRAWFORD, *The Gospel of Nicodemus* (Edinburgh 1927). James ApocNT 94–161. Quasten Patr 1:115–118. Altaner 70–71. A. DE SANTOS OTERO, *op. cit.* 418–569. J. MICHL, LexThK² 3:1226. E. HENNECKE, *op. cit.* 1:444–484.

Gospel of Gamaliel. The full text is contained in a 14th-century Ethiopic translation from the Arabic. There are also some Coptic fragments and several Arabic redactions. Besides, it is found in a fragment of an Ethiopic version of a Coptic homily by Bishop Kyriakos of Oxyrhynchus, who refers to it as the Laments of Mary. According to this Apocryphon *Gamaliel the Elder relates an investigation ordered by Pilate about the empty tomb. Pilate is convinced, believes in the Resurrection of Jesus, and exchanges letters with Herod on this matter. The original work was composed by a Coptic Christian in the 5th or 6th century.

Bibliography: M. A. VAN DEN OUDENRIJN, *Gamaliel: Äthiopische Texte zur Pilatusliteratur* (Freiburg 1959). E. HENNECKE, *op. cit.* 2:508–510. James ApocNT 151–152. J. MICHL, LexThK² 3:1226–27.

APOCRYPHAL ACTS OF THE APOSTLES

Following the pattern of the canonical Acts, popular legendary writings began, mostly in the 2d and 3d centuries, to celebrate the heroic adventures of the Apostles and of their companions. The stories are basically fictitious, although they may contain some historical elements. Information deriving from these Acts has been used in the readings of the Roman Breviary. Although most of the Apocryphal Acts were first written by heretics in order to propagate their doctrines, they were purged in later versions and used for devout reading. They contain much valuable information on early Christian life, prayer, and moral views.

Bibliography: R. A. LIPSIUS, *Die apokryphen Apostelgeschichten und Apostellegenden,* 3 v. (Braunschweig 1883–90). R. A. LIPSIUS and M. BONNET, *Acta Apostolorum apocrypha,* 3 v. (Leipzig 1891–1903). W. WRIGHT, *Apocryphal Acts of the Apostles,* 2 v. (London 1871). B. PICK, *The Apocryphal Acts of Paul, Peter, John, Andrew and Thomas* (Chicago 1909). A. WALKER, AnteNicChLibr 8:354–358, 477–564. B. P. PATTERN, *ibid.* 657–665. R. SÖDER, *Die apokryphen Apostelgeschichten und die romanhafte Literatur der Antike* (Stuttgart 1932). M. BLUMENTHAL, *Formen und Motive in den apokryphen Apostelgeschichten* (TU 48.1; Leipzig 1933). James ApocNT 228–475. Quasten Patr 1:128–143. Altaner 72–79. J. MICHL, LexThK² 1:747–754. E. HENNECKE, *op. cit.* 2:111–404.

Acts of Peter. Eusebius (*Hist. eccl.* 3.3.2), Jerome (*Vir. illus.* 1), and the Gelasian Decree were acquainted with this work. It was written apparently toward the end of the 2d century, probably in Asia Minor, Syria, or Palestine; the author did not know Rome. It has been preserved in three redactions: (1) fragments of the story of the daughter of Peter (Coptic MS), the story of the gardener's daughter, and some lines of a sermon; (2) the Vercelli Acts, preserved in a 7th-century Latin MS, which tells of Peter's apostolate in Rome and especially of his contention with *Simon Magus; and (3) Peter's martyrdom, in two Greek MSS, including the *Quo vadis* legend and Peter's last sermon (with a strongly Gnostic flavor), which is not to be confused with the late Latin legend known as the *Martyrium beati Petri apostoli a Lino conscriptum.*

Bibliography: R. A. LIPSIUS and M. BONNET, *op. cit.* 1:1–22, 45–103. C. SCHMIDT, *Die alten Petrusakten* (TU 9.1; Leipzig 1903); *Studien zu den Pseudo-Clementinen* (TU 46.1; Leipzig 1929); "Studien zu den alten Petrusakten," ZKirchgesch 47 (1926) 481–513; "Zur Datierung der alten Petrusakten," ZNT Wiss 29 (1930) 150–155. L. VOUAUX, *Les Actes de Pierre* (Paris 1922). J. N. REAGAN, *The Preaching of Peter* (Chicago 1923). J. T. SHOTWELL and L. R. LOOMIS, *The See of Peter* (New York 1927) 133–153. C. H. TURNER, "The Latin Acts of St. Peter," JThSt 32 (1930–31) 119–133. G. BOTTOMLEY, *The Acts of Peter* (London 1933). E. FASCHER, Pauly-Wiss RE 19:1377–81. James ApocNT 330–336. Quasten Patr 1:133–135. Altaner 74–75. J. MICHL, LexThK² 1:748–749. E. HENNECKE, *op. cit.* 2:177–221.

Acts of Paul. According to Tertullian (*De bapt.* 17) this fictitious account of St. Paul's apostolate and death was written by a priest in Asia Minor. Its composition must therefore antedate Tertullian's *De baptismo* (between 198 and 200). The nature of the Apocryphon as a whole was not known until C. Schmidt found fragments of it in a Coptic (Leipzig 1904) and a Greek version (Hamburg 1936). Until then three parts of the work were known as individual writings: (1) the *Acta Pauli et Theclae,* preserved in the original Greek and in many versions, a romantic story of Thecla, a noble virgin from Iconium, who was converted by Paul, preached as a missionary, was miraculously saved from many deaths, and finally baptized herself in the arena; (2) *Letter of Paul to the Corinthians,* the same as the Apocryphal *Third Epistle to the Corinthians* (see below); and (3) the *Martyrium Pauli,* of which a later Latin amplification was attributed to Pope Linus.

Bibliography: R. A. LIPSIUS and M. BONNET, *op. cit.* 1:235–272. E. J. GOODSPEED, "The Book of Thekla," AmJSemLang 17 (1901) 65–95. W. WRIGHT, *op. cit.* 1:128–169; 2:116–145. James ApocNT 270–299. A. WALKER, AnteNicChLibr 8:487–492. E. HENNECKE, *op. cit.* 2:221–268. Quasten Patr 1:130–133. Altaner 73–74. J. MICHL, LexThK² 1:749–750.

Acts of Peter and Paul. The author of this Apocryphon, perhaps of the 3d century, combined the *Acts of Peter* and the *Acts of Paul* into a new work, which is purged of the heresies contained in the earlier separate works. It is preserved in Greek and Latin.

Bibliography: R. A. LIPSIUS and M. BONNET, op. cit. 1:118–222. Bardenhewer 1:564–568. A. VAN LANTSCHOOT, "Contribution aux 'Actes de S. Pierre et S. Paul,'" Muséon 68 (1955) 17–46, 219–233. Quasten Patr 135. J. MICHL, LexThK² 1:750–751.

Acts of Andrew.

Eusebius (Hist. eccl. 3.25.6) and the Gelasian Decree mention this 3d-century Apocryphon. It is the latest and the longest of the Apocryphal Acts, and it is the only one that is not completely anonymous, since it is attributed to a certain Leucius Charinus, who was accused of composing several other Apocrypha. It is known mostly from the summary of Gregory of Tours (see M. Bonnet, MGSrerMer 1.2:826–846; AnalBoll 13:309–378) and from certain parts of the work that circulated separately, such as Andrew and Matthias among the Cannibals, the Story of Peter and Andrew, and Andrew's Martyrdom in Patrai (Achaia). There is also a Greek fragment giving an account of Andrew's sufferings in Achaia and his preaching in prison.

Bibliography: R. A. LIPSIUS and M. BONNET, op. cit. 2.1:1–127. James ApocNT 337–363. E. HENNECKE, op. cit. 2:270–297. Quasten Patr 1:137–138. Altaner 75–76. J. MICHL, LexThK² 1:751–752. J. FLAMION, Les Actes apocryphes de l'Apôtre André (Louvain 1911). F. BLATT, Die lateinischen Bearbeitungen der Acta Andreae et Matthiae apud anthropophagos (Giessen 1930). F. DVORNIK, The Idea of Apostolicity in Byzantium and the Legend of the Apostle Andrew (Cambridge, Mass. 1958).

Acts of Thaddeus.

The text of this work is conserved in two widely different forms: (1) in a document from the archives of Edessa [translated from Syriac into Greek and mentioned by Eusebius (Hist. eccl. 1.13)], purporting to contain an exchange of letters between King Abgar V Ukkama (4 B.C.–A.D. 50) of Edessa and Jesus, on the basis of which the Apostle Thomas sends Thaddeus (Addai), one of the 72 Disciples, to heal the King and preach in his country (see ABGAR, LEGENDS OF); and (2) in the Doctrina Addai in Syriac, in which there is a message (not a letter) from Jesus and an account of the royal messenger's taking home of a picture of Jesus painted by Himself.

Bibliography: R. A. LIPSIUS and M. BONNET, op. cit. 1:273–283. G. PHILIPS, The Doctrine of Addai, the Apostle (London 1876). E. HENNECKE, op. cit. 1:437–444. Quasten Patr 1:140–143. Altaner 77–78. J. MICHL, LexThK² 1:753.

Acts of John.

This is the earliest of the known Apocryphal Acts. It was composed in Greek about the middle of the 2d century, probably in Asia Minor. From the 5th century on it was attributed to a certain Leucius Charinus, a real or fictitious companion of John (such as Luke was of Paul) in his missionary travels. The work was rejected as heretical by Eusebius (Hist. eccl. 3.25.6). It is preserved only in fragments (see Altaner 76). According to the Apocryphon, John visits Ephesus twice, performs many miracles, and destroys the temple of Artemis. Docetic views (see DOCETISM) are manifested in the account of John's relations with Jesus (e.g., in ch. 93); even Christ's death is declared illusionary (ch. 99–102). Of much importance, however, is the description of the celebration of the Eucharist for the dead in the 2d century (ch. 72 and 85).

Bibliography: R. A. LIPSIUS and M. BONNET, op. cit. 2.1:151–216. James ApocNT 228–270. E. HENNECKE, op. cit. 2:125–176. Quasten Patr 1:135–137. Altaner 76–77. J. MICHL, LexThK² 1:751. A. C. RUSH, Death and Burial in Christian Antiquity (Washington 1941) 262–264.

Acts of Thomas.

The work gives an account of St. Thomas's missionary travels, teachings, miracles, and death—all in India. It was composed in the first half of the 3d century in Gnostic-Manichaean circles with encratistic tendencies. However, the 4th-century Syriac copy of it (the only ancient Apocryphal Acts completely preserved) was partially revised according to more orthodox teachings. There are two partial Latin variant versions: the De miraculis sancti Thomae apostoli, attributed to St. Gregory of Tours, and the Passio sancti Thomae apostoli. A more recent Greek version is closely related to the Ethiopic Legend of Thomas in the collection edited by E. A. W. Budge, The Contendings of the Apostles (London 1899).

Bibliography: R. A. LIPSIUS and M. BONNET, op. cit. 2.2:99–291. W. WRIGHT, op. cit. 1:171–333; 2:146–298. James ApocNT 364–438. E. HENNECKE, op. cit. 2:297–372. Quasten Patr 1:139–140. Altaner 77. J. MICHL, LexThK² 1:752. A. F. J. KLIJN, The Acts of Thomas (NovTest Supp. 5; 1962).

APOCRYPHAL EPISTLES

In contrast to the canonical Epistles, the Apocryphal Epistles represent the least frequently occurring type of Apocryphal literature. The reason may be that a letter calls for a concrete historical situation, and both writer and addressee must be indicated. It is scarcely conceivable that a community that received a genuine apostolic letter would not have been proudly conscious of the fact.

Bibliography: L. VOUAUX, Les Actes de Paul et ses lettres apocryphes (Paris 1913). James ApocNT 476–503. Quasten Patr 1:150–157. Altaner 79–83. W. MICHAELIS, op. cit. 440–446. J. MICHL, LexThK² 2:688–693. E. HENNECKE, op. cit. 2:53–109.

Epistle of St. Paul to the Laodiceans.

In Col 4.16 Paul tells the Colossians that they should read the letter that he wrote to the Christians at *Laodicea. Either the authentic Epistle to the Laodiceans has been lost, or it is to be identified with the canonical Epistle to the *Ephesians, which, according to Tertullian (Adv. Marc. 5.11, 17), was called the Epistle to the Laodiceans in Marcion's canon. In any case, the Latin Epistle to the Laodiceans that is included in many Vulgate MSS (of which the Codex Fuldensis of 546 is the oldest) is merely a compilation of 20 verses from the canonical Pauline Epistles (mostly from Philippians) and certainly not the original Epistle to the Laodiceans. It was compiled, perhaps first in Greek, not later than the 4th century. It is doubtful whether this compilation is the same as the Epistle to the Laodiceans that was rejected by the *Muratorian Canon, *Theodore of Mopsuestia, *Theodoret of Cyr, and the Council of *Nicaea II as a Marcionite forgery.

Bibliography: J. B. LIGHTFOOT, St. Paul's Epistles to the Colossians and to Philemon (8th ed. New York 1897) 287–289. A. VON HARNACK, Die apokryphen Briefe des Paulus an die Laodicener und Korinther (Kleine Texte; 2d ed. Berlin 1931); Marcion (2d ed. Leipzig 1924) 139–149. James ApocNT 478–480. Quasten Patr 1:154–155. Altaner 79. Bardenhewer 1:598–600. W. C. McKNIGHT, "The Letter to the Laodiceans," Biblical Review 16 (1932) 519–535. J. KNOX, Marcion and the NT (Chicago 1942). J. SCHMID, LexThK² 6:792–793. E. HENNECKE, op. cit. 2:80–84.

Correspondence of Paul and Seneca.

A spurious collection of 14 letters (8 by Seneca and 6 by Paul), written in Latin probably c. 380, was known to Jerome (Vir. ill. 12) and Augustine (Ep. 153.14), and it became very popular (preserved in more than 300 MSS). Probably it originated as a student's composition in a

Roman school of rhetorics; the letters are poor both in style and in thought. Seneca likes Paul's doctrine, but he scolds him for his literary shortcomings and sends him a book from which he can learn a better style. He reads Paul's letters to the Emperor and deplores the persecution of the Christians blamed for the burning of Rome. Paul asks Seneca to preach Christianity at the court.

Bibliography: C. W. BARLOW, ed., *Epistolae Senecae ad Paulum et Pauli ad Senecam quae vocantur* (Rome 1938). L. VOUAUX, *op. cit.* 332–369. Bardenhewer 1:606–609. Quasten Patr 1:155–156. Altaner 80. P. BENOIT, "Sénèque et saint Paul," RevBibl 53 (1946) 7–35. J. MICHL, LexThK² 2:691–692. E. HENNECKE, *op. cit.* 2:84–89. J. N. SEVENSTER, *Paul and Seneca* (Leiden 1961).

Third Epistle of St. Paul to the Corinthians. According to this Apocryphon Paul answers a letter from the Corinthians denouncing Simon and Kleobius, who rejected the Prophets and denied God's creation of the world and of man (it was done by angels), the resurrection of the flesh, and the Incarnation. The doctrinal content of the letter, therefore, is an important anti-Gnostic statement. Both the letter sent by the Corinthians and Paul's answer to it were accepted into a Syriac collection of the Pauline Epistles before the time of the *Peshitta and were regarded as authentic (for a commentary on them was written by St. Ephrem) in the early Syriac Church; from there they passed into the Armenian canon. The Greek original in a 3d-century papyrus was first published by M. Testuz, *Papyrus Bodmer X–XII* (Cologny-Geneva 1959) 7–45. There are also a Coptic and two Latin versions. Besides, it forms part of the Apocryphal Acts of Paul (see above).

Bibliography: A. VON HARNACK, *op. cit.* Bardenhewer 1:601–606. Quasten Patr 1:155. Altaner 79. L. VOUAUX, *op. cit.* 135–140. J. SCHMID, LexThK² 6:556. M. TESTUZ, *La Correspondance apocryphe de saint Paul et des Corinthiens* (Recherches bibliques 5; Bruges 1960). E. HENNECKE, *op. cit.* 2:234–238. A. F. J. KLIJN, "The Apocryphal Correspondence between Paul and the Corinthians," VigChr 17 (1963) 2–23.

Epistle of the Apostles. Another name for this spurious letter is the *Testament of Our Lord in Galilee*. It was written probably between 140 and 150 in Asia Minor (C. Schmidt), Egypt (H. Lietzmann), or Syria (J. Delazer). The original text (in Greek or Syriac) is entirely lost, but 15 leaves of a Coptic version, a single leaf of a Latin version, and the whole of an Ethiopic version have been preserved. It is the most important of the Apocryphal Epistles, purporting to be an encyclical letter of the 11 Apostles to all churches. It contains a short life of Jesus and an account of the revelations that He gave between His Resurrection and His Ascension. It was strongly influenced by John's Gospel, and it used also the *Apocalypse of Peter*, the *Epistle of Barnabas*, and the *Shepherd of *Hermas*. The doctrine is clearly anti-Gnostic, emphatic about the two natures of Christ (ch. 21), the Incarnation of the Logos (ch. 3), and His identical divinity with the Father (ch. 17). Gabriel is considered the personification of the Logos at the Annunciation (ch. 14).

Bibliography: L. GUERRIER and S. GRÉBAUT, "Le Testament en Galilée de Notre-Seigneur Jésus-Christ," PatrOr 9.3 (1913) 12–62. C. SCHMIDT and J. WAYNBERG, eds. and trs., *Gespräche Jesu mit seinen Jüngern nach der Auferstehung* (TU 43; Leipzig 1919). H. DÜNSING, *Epistula Apostolorum* (Kleine Texte 152; Bonn 1925). H. LIETZMANN, "Die Epistula Apostolorum," ZNTWiss 20 (1921) 173–176. J. DELAZER, "De tempore compositionis Epistolae Apostolorum," *Antonianum* 4 (1929) 257–292, 387–430.

James ApocNT 485–503. Quasten Patr 1:150–153. Altaner 82. J. MICHL, LexThK² 2:690–691. E. HENNECKE, *op. cit.* 1:189–227.

Epistle of Barnabas. This Apocryphon, which was written between 115 and 140, was regarded as authentic by Clement of Alexandria (*Stromata* 2.6–20; 5.8–10) and Origen (*Con. Celsum* 1.63) but rejected as spurious by Eusebius (*Hist. eccl.* 3.25.4) and Jerome (*De. vir. ill.* 6). The first complete Greek text was discovered by C. Tischendorf (1859) in the Codex Sinaiticus. The content is radically anti-Jewish: the people of the OT were misled by a bad angel and falsely interpreted the OT prescriptions in a literal "carnal" sense. The second part (ch. 18–21) describes, like the Didache (ch. 1–6), the two ways of the light and of the darkness. The author was probably a Christian teacher of Gentile origin from Alexandria, for he seems to have been strongly influenced by Philo's allegorical exegesis. Most scholars list the Epistle with the Apostolic Fathers. For details and bibliography, *see* BARNABAS, EPISTLE OF.

Epistle of Titus, Disciple of Paul. The full title adds *de dispositione sanctimonii* (on the arrangements for a holy life). The work was discovered in 1896 by Dom G. Morin among the homilies of St. *Caesarius of Arles in an 8th-century MS and edited by Dom D. *de Bruyne. It is not a letter but a sermon addressed to certain ascetic groups of men and women. It is written in barbarous Latin and makes copious use of Apocryphal Acts and Apocalypses. Its ascetic teachings are similar to those of Pseudo-Cyprian and Pseudo-Jerome writings. It lauds virginity and combats the abuse of the so-called spiritual marriage (*see* VIRGINES SUBINTRODUCTAE), which was practiced mainly by the Priscillians in Spain, where the bishops condemned it. Hence it seems that the Apocryphon was written most likely in Spain about the 5th century.

Bibliography: D. DE BRUYNE, RevBén 37 (1925) 47–72. E. HENNECKE, *op. cit.* 2:91–109. A. VON HARNACK, SBBerlin 17 (1925) 180–213. H. KOCH, ZNTWiss 32 (1933) 131–144. E. HENNECKE, *op. cit.* 2:90–91; ZKirchgesch 74 (1963) 1–14. J. MICHL, LexThK² 2:693.

APOCRYPHAL APOCALYPSES

The NT Apocryphal Apocalypses are writings that, following the basic pattern of the canonical Apocalypse, purport to contain revelations from heaven received by NT personages concerning the end of the world and the future life in heaven or hell. Several scholars list with the NT Apocrypha also those apocalyptic writings of which the contents have been influenced by the NT, even though their pretended writers belonged to the OT period (e.g., the *Ascension of Isaia, Fourth Esdras* in its Christian recension, and the *Sibylline Oracles*). However, since not only the authors but also the literary patterns are of the OT type, they are treated here with the OT Apocryphal literature (see above, section 4). On the origin and nature of this type of literature, *see* APOCALYPTIC.

Bibliography: H. WEINEL, "Die spätere christliche Apokalyptik," *Eucharisterion: Festgabe für Hermann Gunkel*, 2 v. (Göttingen 1923) 2:141–173. M. GOGUEL, "Eschatologie et apocalyptique dans le christianisme primitiv," RevHistRel 106 (1932) 381–434, 490–524. H. H. ROWLEY, *The Relevance of Apocalyptic* (3d ed. New York 1964). E. HENNECKE, *op. cit.* 2:405–625. R. SCHÜTZ, RGG³ 1:467–469. J. MICHL, LexThK² 1:696–704.

Apocalypse of Peter. A Greek work written in the second quarter of the 2d century. It was listed as canonical by Clement of Alexandria and the Muratorian

Canon (with some doubts). *Sozomen (*Hist. eccl.* 7.19) reports that in the 5th century it was still read on Good Friday in some churches of Palestine. It was rejected by Eusebius (*Hist. eccl.* 3.3.2) and Jerome (*Vir. ill.* 1). Thereafter it was almost completely lost, until large fragments of the Greek text were found by U. Bouriant in Akhmîm (1886–87) and a reworked form (from the Arabic) was discovered in a complete Ethiopic version by S. Grébaut (1910). It is the most important of the Apocryphal Apocalypses. According to this Apocryphon Jesus, after His Resurrection, reveals to His Apostles on the Mount of Olives many things concerning not only the end of the world and His Second Coming (based on Matthew ch. 24) but also the *Antichrist, who will come from among the Jews and be opposed by Henoch and Elia. Then Jesus shows them the joys of the blessed in heaven and the gruesome punishments of the wicked in hell. The Apocalypse ends with Christ's Ascension into heaven in the company of Moses and Elia.

Bibliography: U. BOURIANT, *Mémoires publiés par les membres de la mission archéologique française au Caire* 9 (1892) 142–146. S. GRÉBAUT, "Littérature éthiopienne pseudo-clementine," *Revue de l'Orient chrétien* 15 (1910) 198–214, 307–323, 425–439. E. KLOSTERMANN, *Kleine Texte* 3 (Bonn 1910) 8–12. A. MINGANA, ed. and tr., *Woodbrooke Studies* 3.2 (Cambridge Eng. 1931). M. R. JAMES, JThSt 32 (1931) 270–279. Bardenhewer 1:610–615. Quasten Patr 1:144–146. Altaner 83–84. James ApocNT 505–520. W. MICHAELIS, *op. cit.* 469–481. E. HENNECKE, *op. cit.* 2:468–483. J. MICHL, LexThK² 1:699–700. É. AMANN, DBSuppl 1:525–527.

Apocalypse of Paul. This Apocryphon, which is not the same as the *Ascent of Paul,* a lost Gnostic writing from the 2d or 3d century referred to by Epiphanius (*Haer.* 38.2), is mentioned by Augustine (*In Joh.* 98.8) and the Gelasian Decree. It is preserved in a revised Greek MS of the late 4th century that is based on a lost Greek text from Egypt (2d or 3d century) that was known to Origen. There are also Syraic, Coptic, Ethiopic, and Latin versions of it extant. The Latin version, *Visio Pauli,* is the closest to the lost original. The passage in 2 Cor 12.2 (Paul caught up to the third heaven) gives the author, who is a gifted writer, the opportunity to portray Paul's vision. He is shown the guardian angels of individuals and of the nations reporting to God every evening and morning. An angel takes Paul to the place of the just in heaven and then to the golden city of Christ in the lake Acherusa. Later he is shown the river of fire where the damned are in torments. There he sees the different punishments for the various ranks of the fallen clergy and special tortures for those who denied the humanity of Christ and His real presence in the Eucharist. At the intercession of St. Paul, of St. Michael, and of all the Christians, Christ grants the damned partial rest from their sufferings on Sunday. Angels, especially St. Michael, are the guides and the guardians of souls as they leave the earth for heaven, whereas the counterpart of Michael as Psychopompos (the "soul guide") is Tartarus, who drags the damned to hell. The Apocryphon was very popular in the Middle Ages and had great influence on Christian art and literature. *Dante Alighieri was much indebted to it.

Bibliography: C. TISCHENDORF, *op. cit.* 34–60. M. R. JAMES, *Apocrypha anecdota* (Cambridge, Eng. 1893) 11–42. T. SILVERSTEIN, *Visio sancti Pauli: The History of the Apocalypse* (London 1935). G. RICCIOTTI, *L'Apocalisse di Paolo siriaca* (Brescia 1932); *Orientalia* 2 (1933) 1–32. James ApocNT 525–555. A. RUTHERFORD, AnteNicChLibr 9:149–166. E. HENNECKE, *op. cit.* 2:536–597. Bardenhewer 1:615–620. Quasten Patr 1:146–149. Altaner 88–89. J. MICHL, LexThK² 1:700–701.

Apocalypses of John. Since John was the author of the canonical Apocalypse, it was natural that several Apocryphal ones also should have been attributed to him. (1) The *Apocalypse of St. John the Apostle* written in Greek some time after 400 was first mentioned in the 9th century. According to this Apocryphon Jesus, after His Ascension, reveals to John on Mt. Thabor many things about the Parousia, the antichrist, the resurrection of the dead, the destruction and renovation of the world, the Last Judgment, and the state of the blessed in heaven and of the wicked in hell. (2) A shorter *Apocalypse of John,* also in Greek, was published by F. Nau in 1914. Apparently it originated in Cyprus some time between the 6th and the 8th century. It purports to give Christ's answers to John on certain moral, disciplinary, and liturgical questions. (3) The work called *Mysteries of the Virgin Apostle St. John* is preserved in a Coptic MS of the 11th century, but the original was probably in Greek. It tells how John ascended into heaven on the wings of a cherub, where he had visions of the earthly paradise, of Adam before and after the fall, of the arrangement of the universe, and of its mysterious angelic powers. (4) The 2d-century Gnostic *Apocalypse of John* that was known to Irenaeus (*Adv. haer.* 1.29) is preserved in a Coptic version of the Greek original. According to this Apocryphon the risen and glorified Christ gives John a negative description of God, from whom emanate many divine light-spirits who, all together, make up the *pleroma* (the fullness of all that is). The Jews, says the Apocryphon, had for their God the monster Jaldabroth, the counterpart of the light-substance Sophia.

Bibliography: (1) C. TISCHENDORF, *op. cit.* 70–94. Graf Gesch ChArabLit 1:273. J. MICHL, LexThK² 1:702. (2) F. NAU, "Une Deuxième Apocalypse apocryphe grecque de St. Jean," RevBibl 23 (1914) 209–221. J. MICHL, LexThK² 1:702. (3) E. A. W. BUDGE, *Coptic Apocrypha in the Dialect of Upper Egypt* (London 1913) 59–74, 241–257. E. HENNECKE, *op. cit.* 2:535. J. MICHL, LexThK² 1:702. (4) W. C. TILL, JEcclHist 3 (1952) 14–22.

Apocalypse of Thomas. The Gelasian Decree rejected this Apocryphon. It was used by the Priscillianists (*see* PRISCILLIANISM), and it was known in England in the 9th century. Thereafter it was completely lost until 1907, when fragments of it were rediscovered by P. Bihlmeyer in a Latin MS in Munich. Later some fragments of Anglo-Saxon versions were discovered in Vercelli, and some Latin fragments, in Vienna. It claims to contain revelations given by Jesus to Thomas concerning the end of the world; the signs are distributed over 7 days, and the 8th day brings the end.

Bibliography: P. BIHLMEYER, "Un Text non interpolé de l'Apocalypse de Thomas," RevBén 28 (1911) 270–282. M. FORSTER, "Der Vercelli Codex CXVII," *Studien zur englischen Philologie: Festgabe für Lorenz Morsbach* (Halle 1913) 20–179. E. HAULER, "Zu den neuen lateinischen Bruchstücken der Thomasapokalypse und eines apostolischen Sendschreibens im Cod. Vindob. Nr. 16.," *Wiener Studien* 30 (1908) 308–340. James ApocNT 555–562. E. HENNECKE, *op. cit.* 2:568–572. Bardenhewer 1:620–621. Quasten Patr 1:149–150. Altaner 89. J. MICHL, LexThK² 1:701.

Apocalypsis Beatae Mariae Virginis de poenis. The text of this 9th-century Apocryphon is preserved in the original Greek and in Armenian, Ethiopic, and Old

Slavic versions. Mary prays God to reveal to her through Gabriel the pains of the damned. Michael comes instead and shows her the torments of those who refused to believe in the Holy Trinity or to accept Mary as the Mother of God or who committed other sins. On Mary's request that Michael should intercede for Christians in hell, Michael refuses it and says that he tried it already without any success. So Mary herself is lifted up to heaven and, together with Moses, St. John, St. Paul, and the Holy Angels, prays for the damned that they may have a respite on Pentecost Sunday. God through Jesus grants their petition.

Bibliography: M. R. James, *Apocrypha, op. cit.* 115–126. A. Rutherford, AnteNicChLibr 9:167–174. E. Hennecke, *op. cit.* 2:535. J. Michl, LexThK² 1:702.

Visio Mariae Virginis. This work is preserved only in an Ethiopic version, and the original language is uncertain. Since it contains a reference to the Moslems, it cannot have been written before the 7th century. John writes down the revelation received by Mary when praying at noon on Golgotha. She is rapt to the third heaven and sees the rewards bestowed on the blessed and the punishments meted out to the damned, especially to wicked clerics and monks. Because of her prayers the damned are granted a respite from their sufferings every weekend from Friday evening to Monday morning.

Bibliography: A. Delatte, *Anecdota Atheniensia* 1 (1927) 272–288. M. Chaine, ed. and tr., *Apokrypha de Beata Maria Virgine* (CSCO, Scriptores aethiopici, ser. 1.7; 1909) 43–68. J. Michl, LexThK² 1:702–703. **Illustration credits:** Fig. 4, Anderson-Art Reference Bureau. Fig. 5, The University of Glasgow.

[C. H. HENKEY]

BIBLE, IV (TEXTS AND VERSIONS)

Under this heading a series of articles treats the text of the books of the OT and the NT in the original languages in which they were written and the various ancient and modern versions in which the Bible has appeared.

1. INTRODUCTORY

The sequence of the series of articles is as follows:

1. Introductory	22. Catholic English
2. Text of the OT	Versions
3. Text of the NT	23. Protestant and Jewish
4. Greek Versions	English Versions
5. Septuagint	24. German Versions
6. Aquila	25. Dutch-Flemish Versions
7. Symmachus	26. French Versions
8. Theodotion	27. Italian Versions
9. Hexapla	28. Spanish Versions
10. Aramaic Versions	29. Portuguese Versions
11. Targums	30. Catalan Versions
12. Syriac Versions	31. Polish Versions
13. Latin Versions	32. Czech-Slovak Versions
14. Coptic Versions	33. Ukrainian Versions
15. Ethiopic Versions	34. Russian Versions
16. Armenian Versions	35. Hungarian Versions
17. Georgian Versions	36. Maltese Versions
18. Arabic Versions	37. Japanese Versions
19. Gothic Versions	38. Irish Versions
20. Slavonic Versions	39. Welsh Versions
21. Pre-Reformation English	40. Other Vernacular
Versions	Versions

Most of the OT was written originally in Hebrew; but parts of it were composed in Aramaic or in Greek, and some of its books that were originally written in Hebrew or Aramaic have been preserved wholly or partially in early translations, particularly Greek ones. All of the NT was composed in Greek. At the time of Christ the vast majority of the Jews were either Aramaic-speaking (in the Near East) or Greek-speaking (in the rest of the Roman Empire); relatively few of them could understand Hebrew. Translations, therefore, of the Scriptures into Aramaic (including Syriac) and Greek were necessary, especially of the parts of the Bible that were used in the liturgy. Likewise, when Christianity spread among people who did not understand Greek, it became necessary to translate the Bible into the languages spoken by these people, first into Latin (in the West) and Syriac (in the East) and later into the other languages spoken by the newly converted nations. The history of the Bible is thus part of the history of the spread of Christianity.

The ancient versions made directly from the original languages of the Bible are of prime importance for the textual criticism of the Bible [*see* BIBLE, V (TEXTUAL CRITICISM)]; they are often witnesses of readings that are not well preserved in the original texts. This is true particularly of the Septuagint (LXX), the ancient Greek translation of the Hebrew and Aramaic Scriptures, and to a lesser degree of the Syriac and Latin versions of the original OT and NT texts. Secondary versions, i.e., translations of translations, are seldom of much value for textual criticism, although the Old Latin version of the OT can be of considerable value at times for restoring original readings in the LXX from which it was made. All versions, modern as well as ancient, are of interest for Biblical exegesis [*see* BIBLE, VI (EXEGESIS)], since every version is at the same time an interpretation; the translator, unless he produces a slavishly literal rendering of the text he is translating, necessarily presents the meaning that he thinks the author wished to convey.

Bibliography: Robert-Tricot 1:587–677. EncDictBibl 2416–22, 2528–44. J. Ziegler et al., LexThK² 2:375–411. G. D. Kilpatrick, RGG³ 1:1166–74, 1193–1219. G. Ricciotti, EncCatt 2:1551–78.

[L. F. HARTMAN]

2. TEXT OF THE OLD TESTAMENT

The received Hebrew text of the OT as it appears in modern printed Bibles includes a basic consonantal text in "square-letter" Aramaic characters that was stabilized with entirely minimal variations by about A.D. 100. This basic text was already provided with its own verse and paragraph divisions, indicated exclusively by intervals of varying width within the text itself. No other markings, headings, colophons, or numberings of any kind are a part of this text. Though a spacing arrangement was known that would set off visually the hemistichs (half-line units) of Hebrew verse, most OT poetry is transmitted in the same format as that used for prose; exceptions are made always for Ex 15.1–18 and Dt 32.1–43 and often for Job, Psalms, and Proverbs.

This basic text is accompanied in modern Bibles by a traditional apparatus for its pronunciation and public reading, which reached its standard form in the days of Aaron ben Moses *ben Asher of Tiberias in Palestine, c. A.D. 930. (*See* MASORA.) Other Masoretic systems were developed both in Palestine and in Babylonia between the 8th and 10th centuries, but these are now mainly of historical interest. The few parts of the OT transmitted in Aramaic (in Gn 31.47; Jer 10.11; Ezr

4.8–6.18; 7.12–26; Dn 2.4–7.28) share in all respects the textual history of the Hebrew books. The OT books composed in Greek (Wisdom and 2 Machabees) or preserved complete primarily in that language (Sirach, Tobit, Judith, Baruch, 1 Machabees, and parts of Esther and Daniel), share in the distinctive history of the Septuagint [see BIBLE, IV (TEXTS AND VERSIONS), 5]. The Semitic evidence for Sirach and Tobit will be mentioned below; see also the articles on the books named, individually. What follows traces back the Hebrew text through the various stages of transmission for which evidence is available, namely (1) printed editions of the OT; (2) collations of manuscript materials; (3) medieval manuscripts and Origen's second column; (4) Sirach and Tobit; (5) the Samaritan Pentateuch; (6) the oldest MSS, from the 3d century B.C. to the 2d Christian century.

(1) Printed Editions of the Old Testament. The first Hebrew Biblical book to be printed was the Psalms, with D. *Ḳimchi's commentary (Bologna 1477); the first complete printed OT in Hebrew was that from Soncino (1488). The text of the Alcalá Polyglot of 1521 (see POLYGLOT BIBLES), somewhat marred by typographical errors, was nevertheless based in part on two excellent 13th-century Spanish MSS and on another MS now lost that seems (so P. E. *Kahle) to have had Babylonian connections. The prototype for most editions of the Hebrew Masoretic text (MT) is the second *rabbinical Bible published by Daniel *Bomberg in Venice (1524–25); its editor was the Jewish scholar Jacob ben Chayyim. Separated by 6 centuries from the fixing of the Ben Asher tradition, he dealt in eclectic fashion with the Masoretic data available to him, accepting, from Ashkenazi manuscript sources, a number of overrefinements and inconsistencies in details. Fine control of the Ben Asher system is reflected in the critical apparatus *minḥat šay* of Shlomo Yedidiah de Norzi (d. 1626) printed in an OT from Mantua (1742). The later undertakings of S. Baer, sponsored by Franz *Delitzsch, between 1869 and 1895, and of C. D. Ginsburg in OT editions (1894, 1908–26) failed to provide a sounder basic MT than the Ben Chayyim form of it.

Two current editions deserve notice: the *Biblia hebraica,* third and later editions (Stuttgart 1929–37 and later dates) with the text prepared under the supervision of Kahle and a critical apparatus by various scholars under the leadership of R. *Kittel; and the 1958 edition by N. H. Snaith for the British and Foreign Bible Society of London (see BIBLICAL SOCIETIES). The critical apparatus of the Kittel-Kahle edition has been roundly criticized, with a good deal of reason, for its treatment of Septuagint (LXX) evidence in particular; its actual Hebrew text, based on a Leningrad MS [see (3) (i) (c) below] is quite successful in recovering the Ben Asher Masoretic tradition in a consistent form close to the source. A fully revised edition is actively being prepared. In its disposition of the text on the printed page, the Stuttgart OT abandons the traditional prose arrangement for the modern editors' judgment of poetic structure; this can be, and often is, a valuable aid, but it is also sometimes quite misleading. The Snaith edition, taking its start from Norzi's results, follows a carefully selected but much later MS [see (3) (i) (f) below] and presents, on its editor's testimony, a text very close to the Kahle text, in the standard prose arrangement with Psalms, Proverbs, and Job printed as verse. An undertaking now in progress at the Hebrew University in Israeli Jerusalem proposes to issue an OT text based on the Aleppo Codex [see (3) (i) (a) below] and other good MSS, with an apparatus of variants from all pertinent sources. An earlier Israeli edition bearing the name of M. D. Cassuto was issued by others after that scholar's death and has little to recommend it.

(2) Collations of Manuscript Materials. Three systematic compilations of some size for variants within the MT tradition exist, besides narrower collations from smaller MS groups (e.g., by J. H. Michaelis, 1720). The earliest, *Vetus Testamentum hebraicum cum variis lectionibus,* ed. B. *Kennicott (2 v., Oxford 1776–80) concerns the consonantal text only. Its collating base is derived through E. van der Hooght's 1705 OT from the Ben Chayyim text of 1524–25; it provides variants from more than 600 MSS and 50 editions of the OT or its parts. In the Pentateuch it supplies also the Samaritan text [see (5) below] from the London Polyglot, with a collation of 16 Samaritan MSS. The next, *Variae lectiones Veteris Testamenti . . .,* ed. Giovanni Bernardo de Rossi (4 v. Parma 1784–88), with a supplement, *Scholia critica in V.T. libros . . .* (Parma 1798), presumes, but does not print, the same collating base as Kennicott. De Rossi controlled a collection of some 800 MSS not included in the Kennicott collation. He presented not an exhaustive, but a selective listing of variants. For those that he did take into account he repeated Kennicott's evidence, added his own, and supplemented the Hebrew collation with data from the versions both supporting and differing from the received MT. Variants bearing not on the consonants, but on the vowel pointing, are also selectively cited. Though the versional evidence always needs rechecking in the light of later critical study, this is the most instructive compilation of variants antedating the discovery of the *Dead Sea Scrolls [see (6) below]. Ginsburg's collation of more than 70 MSS, largely from the British Museum's collection, and of 19 early printed editions of the MT, in *The Old Testament . . . Diligently Revised* (3 v. in 4 London 1908–26) goes over some of the same ground as the earlier compilations and is generally disappointing in its presentation and in its results.

(3) Medieval Manuscripts and Origen's Second Column. Here are included (i) the basic witnesses to the Ben Asher tradition; (ii) MSS with divergent vocalization from the Tiberian; and (iii) Origen's transcription of the OT Hebrew text into Greek letters.

(i) Basic Witnesses to the Ben Asher Tradition. Noteworthy MSS that contain the MT with the standard Ben Asher Tiberian vocalization are the following:

(a) The Aleppo Codex (known as A), originally a complete OT furnished with its vowel pointing and accents by Aaron ben Moses *ben Asher (c. A.D. 930). It was donated to the Karaite Jewish community in Jerusalem (see KARAISM) and subsequently endorsed for its accuracy by *Maimonides; it is known to have been in Aleppo at least as early as 1478. During the Arab-Jewish hostilities in 1947 it disappeared for a time and was thought destroyed; the recovery of the MS in a badly truncated state was announced in Israel in 1958. It now lacks all of the Pentateuch to Dt 28.17; 4 Kgs 14.21–18.13; Jer 29.9–31.33; 32.2–4, 9–11, 21–24; Am 8.12–Mi 5.1; So 3.20–Za 9.17; 2 Chr 26.19–35.7; Ps 15.1–25.2 (MT enumeration); Ct 3.11 to the end, and all of Ecclesiastes, Lamentations, Esther, Daniel, and Ezra-Nehemia. Never before available for systematic collation, it is under intensive study as part of the *Textus* project of the Hebrew University in Jerusalem and is to be employed, when possible, as the foundation for a new critical edition of the MT, as stated above [see (1)].

(b) The Cairo Prophets (known as C), the oldest dated Hebrew MS, written and pointed by Moses ben Asher in 895. Originally, like A, the property of the Karaite community in Jerusalem, it was seized during the First Crusade, then restored by King Baldwin at the instance of the Karaites of Cairo, among whom it is still preserved. It contains the prophetic portion of the Jewish canon, hence the so-called Earlier Prophets (Josue, Judges, 1 and 2 Samuel, 3 and 4 Kings) in addition to the so-called Later Prophets (Isaia, Jeremia, Ezechiel, and the 12 *Minor Prophets; *see* PROPHETIC BOOKS OF THE OLD TESTAMENT). This MS was collated for the Kittel-Kahle OT apparatus and also by Cassuto. It is now alleged to conform rather to *Ben Naphtali readings than to those of Aaron ben Moses ben Asher in the subsequent generation.

(c) The Leningrad Codex (known as L), dated 1008, MS B 19a of the Russian Public Library in Leningrad, brought originally from the Crimea by A. Firkowitsh in 1839. A colophon to this MS affirms that it was equipped with vowels and Masora from books corrected and annotated by Aaron ben Moses ben Asher. The pointing shows evidence of some reworking in the direction of conformity with what is otherwise known of Ben Asher practice. It was chosen as the best available base for the Kittel-Kahle edition, and its claim to transmit Ben Asher readings was cross-checked with the 10th- or 11th-century treatise of Mishael ben Uzziel on the differences between the Ben Asher and Ben Naphtali traditions; by this criterion it is trustworthy, but Mishael's list is of uncertain date.

(d) British Museum or. 4445, in London, a Pentateuch of which Gn 39.20–Dt 1.33 survives with brief lacunae in Nm 7.47–73 and 9.12–10.18; from the first half of the 10th century, referring in its margin to the scholar (Aaron) ben Asher in a manner that supposes he was still alive. This codex was used by Ginsburg, who dated its consonantal text a century earlier than the pointing; according to Kahle, text and pointing are contemporaneous.

(e) An OT in Parma, copied in Toledo in 1277, used by de Norzi for his critical work and later collated by De Rossi (his number 782).

(f) British Museum or. 2626–28, a complete and richly illuminated OT copied in Lisbon in 1483; the foundation, along with De Norzi's treatise and some supplementary MSS, for Snaith's edition. Like most good Sephardic MSS, it has been subsequently reworked to bring its pointing into agreement with the Ben Chayyim text; it is the unrevised readings of the first punctator that Snaith has followed.

(g) The second Firkowitsh collection, in Leningrad, contains 10th-century MT materials, notably a Pentateuch from the year 930.

(*ii*) *Manuscripts with Divergent Vocalization from the Tiberian.* Not all, but a large part of what is known about medieval Hebrew MSS outside the Ben Asher tradition is derived from the contents of the *geniza (repository for disused religious texts) of the Ezra synagogue in Old Cairo (which before A.D. 969 was the

Melchite church of St. Michael). The Biblical MSS from this source, scattered among libraries at Cambridge, Oxford, Paris, New York, and elsewhere, were studied especially by Kahle and his pupils, and more recently by A. Díez Macho. They include:

(a) Fragments with a Palestinian vowel–pointing older than that of the competing schools of Tiberias; the MSS that contain it often provide consonantal variations also.

(b) Manuscripts ascribed by Kahle to the Ben Naphtali school, rivals of the Ben Asher family. A number of these MSS are now seen by Díez Macho and others as transitional between the Palestinian and the full-fledged Tiberian systems. To this category seem to belong, in addition to various geniza fragments, the *Codex Reuchlinianus* of 1105, now in Karlsruhe; also a Pentateuch and a complete OT in Parma (De Rossi's codices 668 and 2, respectively). Díez Macho distinguishes three stages: a tentative proto-Tiberian form, the elaborated divergent form in the codices mentioned, and a later accommodation to the victorious Tiberian system in most features of the text. The difference between the Ben Asher and Ben Naphtali schools is narrowed according to this interpretation to some 900 small details, largely in the use of a single accent mark (the *meteg*).

(c) Manuscripts with a Babylonian vowel–apparatus written above the consonants of the text, hence called supralinear. The Cairo geniza yielded texts of this class in some profusion: the introduction to the Kittel-Kahle edition enumerates more than 120 such MSS, and Díez Macho has since enlarged the count. These fall into two classes, one with an early, simpler, and the other with a later, more developed, vowel system; the range in time is from about the 8th to the 10th century. Parallel to the geniza materials in this class is the firsthand vocalization in MS Berlin or. qu. 680, from the Yemen, of which (including 7 leaves in New York) some 101 leaves are wholly or partially preserved. The St. Petersburg codex of the Later Prophets (known as P), dating from 916, already shows the use of the Babylonian symbols to record what is in fact an accommodation to the Tiberian Masoretic system.

(*iii*) *Origen's Second Column.* The principal current interest in the divergent vowel systems so far described lies in the opportunity they give for testing the Ben Asher vocalization, late and in many respects artificial, against other traditions and tendencies reaching back closer to the period of spoken Hebrew. The endeavor has also been made to exploit for this purpose the traditional Hebrew pronunciation among the Samaritans [see (5) below]; and the fuller consonantal orthography of some Qumran texts [see (6) below] is pertinent evidence on certain points. Transliterations of Biblical proper names into Greek or Latin letters are of interest in the same regard; and in the so-called Theodotionic recension of the LXX, for reasons not fully understood, there is a sprinkling of transcriptions into Greek letters of ordinary Hebrew words. The most notable single source of this kind is, however, the preserved evidence, mainly from the Ambrosian Library's palimpsest Psalter published by Cardinal G. *Mercati, for the second column of *Origen's Hexapla [see BIBLE, IV (TEXTS AND VERSIONS), 9]. This systematic transposition of the Hebrew text into Greek letters presents, within the limitations of the Greek alphabet, a sampling of the way the text was pronounced in the first half of the 3d century at the latest. On the basis of the uniformity of this transcription and its variance from proper name forms in the LXX, Mercati sees it as contemporary with Origen; Kahle would make it Jewish in origin, like everything else in the Hexapla, and therefore, presumably, earlier. In any case it reflects the standardized Hebrew (consonantal) text subsequent to *c.* A.D. 100.

The materials listed up to this point pertain strictly to the Jewish canon of the OT and to the consonantal text as stabilized for the future by about the end of the 1st Christian century. Although that text has authentic roots in pre-Christian Judaism, the evidence of the LXX, the NT, Josephus, the Samaritan Pentateuch, and the Qumran and other discoveries combine to indicate that both the scope and the form of OT literature as it circulated among the Jews was somewhat more fluid and varied before that time. The textual evidence for this is discussed in what follows.

(4) Sirach and Tobit. The Cairo geniza contained not only MSS of the OT books received in the Jewish canon, but also five fragmentary Hebrew MSS of Sirach, dating from the 10th to the 12th century. Of these, four were published between 1897 and 1901, the first direct evidence for the original text of the book apart from dubious and undependable scattered citations in rabbinic literature. The fifth MS was brought to light in 1931, and again in 1958 and 1960 additional leaves of two of the known MSS appeared in print. Controversy over the authenticity of these materials sprang up with their initial publication, and skepticism on the part of Jewish scholars in particular has been somewhat widespread in recent years. There can, however, be no doubt, either of the basic authenticity of the text or of the fact that a certain amount of retroversion from the Syriac, done in the period when these copies were made, has been introduced. An added anomaly in the history of this book is that, although the citations of the earlier rabbis are nearly all vague and inaccurate, Gaon *Sa'adia ben Joseph al-Fayyumi (d. 942) quotes Sirach in Hebrew quite exactly in 25 cases out of 26. A clue to this situation seems to be afforded by the Qumran discoveries and related research. From cave 2 at Qumran come late 1st-century B.C. fragments of Sir 6.20–31 (2Q18), published by M. Baillet, which are just large enough to show a coincidence of wording and a similarity of stichometric arrangement with the geniza copies (though the wording relates to geniza MSS A and C, while it is MS B, not extant for this portion, that is stichometric in the Cairo group). Also in 11QPsᵃ cols. 21–22, edited by J. A. Sanders, copied in the 1st Christian century, stand the first half and the last two words of the acrostic poem in Sir 51.13–30, this time in an authentic text where the geniza form has long been recognized as secondary to the Syriac. The 1963–64 excavations at Masada (near the southwest end of the Dead Sea) yielded fragments of 13 columns of a scroll of Sirach in a Hebrew script of the first half of the 1st century B.C. They contain portions of Sir 39.27–44.17 written stichometrically, two hemistichs to a line. It is reported by Y. Yadin [*Yediot* 29 (1965) 120–122, in Hebrew] to be in general agreement with the text of MS B from the Cairo geniza and to put the authenticity of the medieval copies beyond dispute. When one combines these facts with the indications from Christian, Jewish, and Moslem sources that MSS from a "cave" sect turned up near Jericho shortly before A.D. 800, it seems possible to identify both the

occasion for recovery of an incomplete text of Sirach before Sa'adia and a part of the impetus to textual study among the Karaites that accompanied the activity of the several schools of Masoretes—the more so as the *Damascus Document* of the Qumran group also first came to light in the Cairo geniza.

In this connection may be mentioned the Qumran cave 4 fragments of Tobit, from four MSS in Aramaic, the original language, and one in Hebrew. J. T. Milik, who is publishing these, affirms that they support in all cases the longest available form of the book, usually represented by the Greek Codex Sinaiticus and by the Old Latin Version. The medieval Aramaic and Hebrew texts of this book, however, are all entirely secondary; none has appeared from the geniza. Of Baruch ch. 6 (the "Letter of Jeremia"), which was certainly composed in Hebrew, only a Greek fragment (7Q2, published by Baillet) is known from Qumran.

(5) The Samaritan Pentateuch. This is a pre-Christian Palestinian Hebrew recension of the Mosaic books, transcribed in an archaic script derived from the paleo-Hebrew form of the Canaanite alphabet. The earliest copy of it to reach western Europe was secured in Damascus by Pietro della Valle in 1616. It was published in the Paris and London polyglots, and its critical significance became the focal point of controversy. It is an expanded, repetitious form of the text, with a limited number of specifically sectarian details. The fact that in a large number of individual readings it coincides with the LXX against the MT has made it a continuing stimulus to text-critical study of the OT. It is now represented in European libraries, notably the John Rylands Library in Manchester, England, and the Russian Public Library in Leningrad, by a large number of copies, some dating from the 12th and 13th centuries. The famous "scroll of Abisha," kept by the Samaritans at Nablus and ascribed by them to the 13th year after the conquest of Canaan by Josue, is in its oldest part a MS of the 11th Christian century. Having been twice photographed and its oldest part having been published by F. Perez Castro, it has proved to be a factitious piecing together of materials of varying ages. Kennicott was able to collate 16 MSS of the Samaritan text; a hand edition with variants was published by B. Blayney in 1790. A. von Gall issued (1914–18) from Berlin an edition with ambitions to be critical; it describes and collates a number of significant MSS; but since others of equal or greater importance were not available to the editor, a definitive edition (now promised by Perez Castro) remains to be produced.

In the light of the new evidences from Qumran [see (6) below], it is clear that the point of departure of the specifically Samaritan text from the earlier Palestinian recension on which it depends is to be sought in about the days of John Hyrcanus (134–104 B.C.). The Samaritan text and script, as well as history, converge on this result. Critical evaluation of this text will now be in a new setting, since it is henceforth only one of several witnesses to the state of the text in Palestine at the end of the 2d century B.C. Transmission of this consonantal text in its older copies has, however, been remarkably faithful, as is proved by comparison with 4QpaleoExᵐ [see (6) below]. In general, the expanded, transposed, and reworked features of this text are of no great moment from the standpoint of the textual critic, though the Palestinian recension represented is of historical importance; but its witness to specific ancient Palestinian

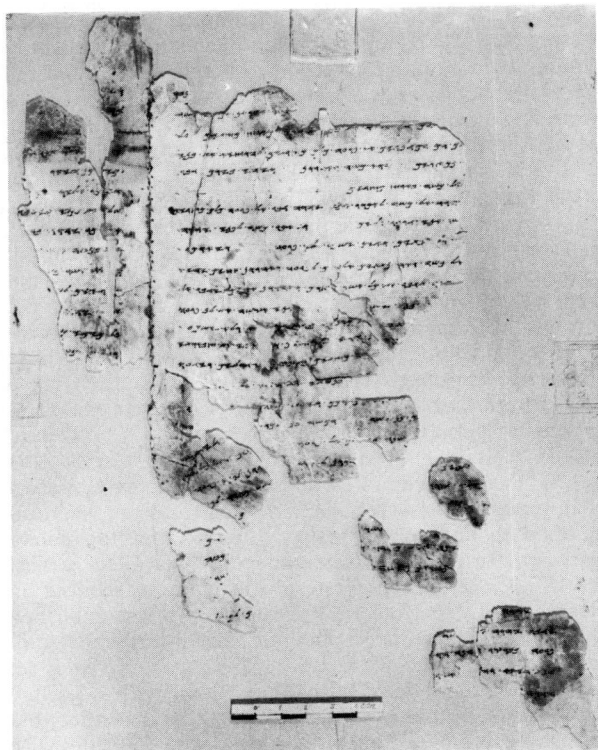

Fig. 1. Parts of adjoining columns of old Palestinian text of Exodus from Qumran (4QpaleoEx^m) in paleo-Hebrew script, 2d century B.C.; the text is of the expanded recension from which the Samaritan Pentateuch derives.

readings divergent from those of the MT continues to be instructive and significant.

Study of the Samaritan pronunciation of Hebrew has been carried forward by several scholars from a variety of sources: oral dictation by Samaritans of portions of the Pentateuch transcribed into a Western phonetic orthography by Europeans; a vocalization contained in four Samaritan Pentateuch MSS; and grammatical and lexical treatises of Samaritan authors published in Hebrew and Arabic. Whether the evidence from these sources can be integrated with other (Qumran, Hexaplaric) materials to furnish a coherent impression of earlier pronunciation of Biblical Hebrew remains to be seen.

There is a Samaritan Aramaic Targum to the Pentateuch [see BIBLE, IV (TEXTS AND VERSIONS), 11], not to be confused with the Hebrew text just described. This Targum has origins going back to the 4th Christian century and varies greatly from one MS to the next. Published editions of it are inadequate; but when fully known, it seems likely to be of much greater interest for the history of Palestinian Aramaic than for Biblical studies as such. On the other hand, the survival, mostly from the Hexapla, of a number of passages out of the Samaritikon, or Greek translation of the Samaritan Pentateuch, forms a useful link between the earliest Samaritan MSS and the older Palestinian recension from which they were ultimately derived.

(6) The Earliest Manuscripts. These come from the 3d century B.C. to the 2d Christian century. For the period before Origen, direct evidence of the Hebrew OT text was almost nonexistent up to 1947; the unique exception was the Nash papyrus, c. 150 B.C., from Egypt, containing Dt 6.4–6 and the Ten Commandments. Since that time, distinct discoveries of 2d-Christian-century materials from the Wadi *Murabba'āt and of still earlier texts from Khirbet Qumran and other, thus far less productive sites (the wadies west of Engeddi, and Masada) have yielded copies of some OT books (Ecclesiastes and Daniel) scarcely more than a century later than the composition of the books themselves. By the end of 1964 the number of separate OT MSS of which at least some fragments are extant from these various sources stood at about 180; 10 are from 2d-Christian-century contexts (Wadi Murabba'āt, Wadi Khabra) and the rest all antedate A.D. 68 (Qumran) or A.D. 73 (Masada) at the latest.

All these MSS, on leather or papyrus, were written in columns on one side only of the material; no Hebrew text of the 2d century or earlier in codex (book) form is known. The complete scroll of Isaia (1QIs^a) from Qumran is made up of 17 strips of carefully prepared leather sewn end to end to a length of 24½ feet, 10½ inches high, meant to be kept rolled up when not in use. In it the text is disposed in 54 vertical columns, with an intentional main division after col. 27, the end of the present ch. 33 (of 66 ch.). This arrangement is suggestive for the format of any large Biblical book at this period; nevertheless, from Qumran there are MSS with as few as 9 lines of text to the column, and others with more than 60, whereas 1QIs^a averages 30 lines to the column.

To take first the 10 MSS left by refugees after the Second Jewish Revolt (A.D. 132–135), the evidence includes fragments of Genesis, Exodus, and Numbers by one same scribe; of Genesis in a different hand; of three other MSS of Numbers, two of Deuteronomy, and one each of Psalms, Isaia, and the Minor Prophets. Only the MS of Psalms from the Wadi Khabra (fragments in Jordan, some few in Israel) is actually of 1st century date and exhibits some variation from the MT. The rest show the fixity of script, format, orthography, and content that constitutes the basic MT text. This might be expected for the Pentateuch and Isaia. The Minor Prophets (Mur 88), however, is preserved in very substantial portions representing 10 of the 12 books; there are only 3 meaningful variants in it from the MT consonants, and only one of these is notable, though not an improvement.

Quite different are about 170 MSS from the 1st century and before. They include some archaic texts (4QEx^f, Sam^b, Jer^a) dated from c. 250 to 200 B.C. by F. M. Cross on paleographical grounds. A somewhat larger number of 2d-century B.C. texts is followed by the bulk of the MSS, dating from the 1st century B.C., with texts of the 1st Christian century also present in quantity. All books of the full Catholic OT canon are somehow represented (although 1 and 2 Chronicles by one isolated fragment with about nine incomplete lines of text), except Esther, Judith, Wisdom, 1 and 2 Machabees, Baruch ch. 1–5, and the LXX additions to Daniel. A limited number of these early MSS are in the paleo-Hebrew script descended from preexilic forms; besides Pentateuch MSS, surprisingly, there is one of Job. The orthography is not so consistent as in the MT. Although some of the oldest MSS have narrowly consonantal spelling, perhaps a third of the Biblical MSS show in varying degrees a much fuller orthography with lavish use of the weak consonants *h, w, y* and ' (*aleph*) to mark the place of vowels in the word. This usage, common also in extra-Biblical texts from Qumran, parallels that of Syriac and differs from medieval Hebrew practice, in that all "o" and "u" vowels are represented by *w*, regardless of their length, whereas only long "î" or "ê" vowels are indicated by *y*.

Unknown individual readings that are not mere vagaries of the particular copyist are on the whole somewhat rare. But textual tendencies in Palestine that could be envisaged only doubtfully and obscurely from the LXX and Samaritan evidence can now be studied directly in these texts. Far from proving the overall superiority of the LXX, these Hebrew MSS help to endow that version with a continuous history of development that makes the jumbled evidence in extant Greek MSS more adequately subject to control.

At the present stage of investigation, the incidence of fuller Palestinian readings coinciding with the LXX or the Samaritan, and the identifiable Palestinian tendency to an expansionist technique in copying and editing Biblical texts, from an early postexilic date until the reaction that is represented by the MT, have led Cross to posit for the Pentateuch (at least Exodus through Deuteronomy) and Samuel in the received text a Babylonian origin that would have kept them apart from the development in Palestine. For Samuel in particular, where the MT represents a surprisingly truncated and defective recension, some such explanation is surely called for.

The MT of the Pentateuch is a sound, tightly organized, unexpanded text of a quite different character; but again, it is doubtful that such a text can be directly filiated to the fuller and less stabilized forms evidenced for Palestine from the proto-Lucianic LXX, the Samaritan, and now the Qumran sources.

Of individual MSS thus far published, only brief mention can be made. The complete Isaia scroll (1QIs^a) dates from *c.* 100 to 75 B.C. It is a reworked text of Isaia, disclosing—beneath the very full orthography of its second half especially and beneath its harmonizations of related passages, simplified readings, and borrowings from other OT books—a basic text quite close to the MT tradition, with which all other (at least 14) Qumran MSS of Isaia coincide more closely still; however, the degree of nearness of 1QIs^b, a later and more fragmentary MS, to the MT has in fact been overstated in the literature. An early 2d-century B.C. copy of Exodus in the old script (4QpaleoEx^m) contains all the expansions known previously from the Samaritan Pentateuch [see (5) above], except that about the unhewn altar on Mt. Garizim after Ex 20.17. It proves the Samaritan recension quite faithful to a pre-Christian Palestinian form of text; but there are now a number of Qumran MSS that evidence, in varying degrees, these same Palestinian tendencies to expansion in Exodus through Deuteronomy, of which the Samaritan text is no longer the prime witness. In general, Qumran MSS of the historical books tend to coincide with the LXX evidence, especially that of a proto-Lucianic type; very remarkable in

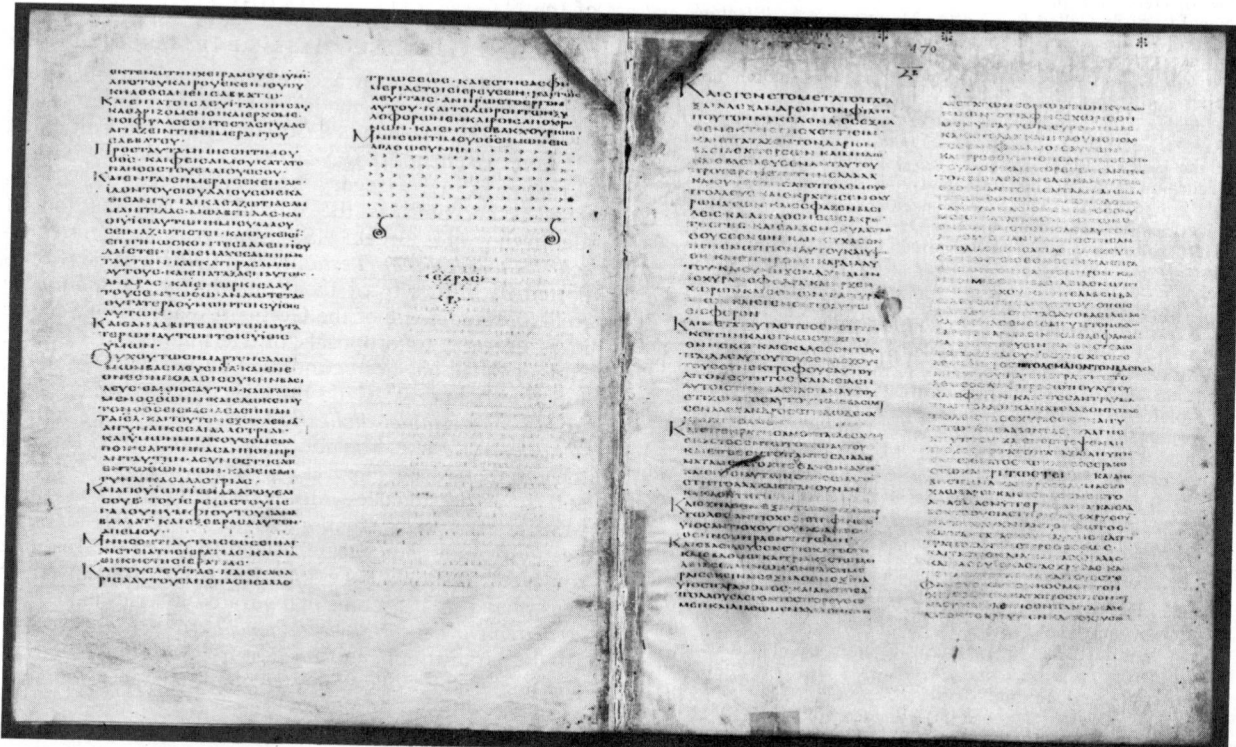

Fig. 2. Pages of the Codex Alexandrinus (Royal MS 1 D. viii, fols. 469b and 470), middle of the 5th century. Formerly in the patriarchal library at Alexandria, it was presented in 1627 to King Charles I of England by Cyril Lucar, Patriarch of Constantinople. Containing originally the whole Bible in Greek (parts of which are now lost in this MS), it is one of the three most important MSS for the Septuagint and the Greek NT. Shown here are the end of the Book of Nehemia (Neh 13.21–31) and the beginning of 1 Machabees (1 Mc 1.1–23). This is not the usual order of the books in the Septuagint, in which Nehemia is ordinarily followed by Esther.

this regard is 4QSamᵃ (1st century B.C.), in which a notable amount of the text of 1 and 2 Samuel is preserved. The short recension of Jeremia hitherto known only from the LXX is present in 4QJerᵇ, one of four MSS of that Prophet at Qumran. The compilation in 11QPsᵃ (1st Christian century), which combines 35 canonical Psalms in an irregular order with 8 other compositions, seems to show special interest in David as a person and as author; various considerations suggest that the standard canonical order of the Psalms is presupposed by this unique collection.

In addition to the strictly Biblical MSS, the several hundred extra-Biblical texts from the same sources will have to be studied extensively for Biblical *lemmata* (formal citations of Biblical verses as a basis for commentary in the *pesharim*), incidental quotations and allusions, before the full contribution of the discoveries since 1947 to an understanding of the history of the OT text can be assessed.

Bibliography: O. EISSFELDT, *The Old Testament: An Introduction,* tr. P. ACKROYD (New York 1965) sections 115–118, 126. P. E. KAHLE, *The Cairo Geniza* (2d ed. New York 1960); *Der masoretische Text des A. T. nach der Überlieferung der babylonischen Juden* (Leipzig 1902); *Masoreten des Ostens* (Leipzig 1913); *Masoreten des Westens,* 2 v. (Stuttgart 1927–30). M. GREENBERG, "The Stabilization of the Text of the Hebrew Bible, Reviewed in the Light of the Biblical Materials from the Judean Desert," JAmOrSoc 76 (1956) 157–167. G. E. WEIL, "La Nouvelle édition de la Massorah (BHK iv) et l'histoire de la Massorah," (VetTest Suppl 9; 1963) 266–284. *Textus: Annual of the Hebrew University Bible Project,* ed. C. RABIN (1960–63), v.1–3. A. I. KATSH, *Ginze Russiyah* (New York 1958), fac. of Heb. MSS preserved in the U.S.S.R. A. DÍEZ MACHO, "A New List of So-Called *Ben Naftali* Manuscripts . . .," *Hebrew and Semitic Studies presented to G. R. Driver . . .,* ed. D. W. THOMAS and W. D. MCHARDY (Oxford 1963). G. MERCATI, *Psalterii hexapli reliquiae* (Vatican City 1958); "Il problema della colonna II dell' Esapla," *Biblica* 28 (1947) 1–30, 173–215. F. PEREZ CASTRO, *Séfer Abiša'* (Madrid 1959), see the important review by E. ROBERTSON, VetTest 12 (1962) 228–235. N. H. SNAITH, "New Edition of the Hebrew Bible," *ibid.* 7 (1957) 207–208. M. BAILLET, "La Récitation de la Loi chez les Samaritains d'après Z. Ben-Hayyim," RevBibl 69 (1962) 570–587. B. J. ROBERTS, "The Hebrew Bible since 1937," JThSt 15 (1964) 253–264. D. BARTHÉLEMY and J. T. MILIK, *Qumrân Cave I* (DiscJudDes 1; 1955). P. BENOIT et al., *Les Grottes de Murabba'ât (ibid.* 2; 1961). M. BAILLET et al., *Les "Petites Grottes" de Qumran (ibid.* 3; 1962). J. A. SANDERS, ed., *11Q Psᵃ (ibid.* 4; 1965). M. BURROWS, *The Dead Sea Scrolls of St. Mark's Monastery,* 2 v. (New Haven 1950–51). E. L. SUKENIK, *The Dead Sea Scrolls of the Hebrew University* (Jerusalem 1955), in Heb. Y. YADIN, "The Expedition to the Judaean Desert, 1960: Expedition D," IsrExplorJ 11 (1961), 40 and plate 20D, a MS of Psalms. J. T. MILIK, *Ten Years of Discovery in the Wilderness of Judaea,* tr. J. STRUGNELL (Studies in Biblical Theology 26; Naperville, Ill. 1959). A. A. DI LELLA, *The Hebrew Text of Sirach: A Text-Critical and Historical Study* (The Hague 1965). F. M. CROSS, JR., *The Ancient Library of Qumran and Modern Biblical Studies* (rev. ed. Anchor Bks. 1961); "The Development of the Jewish Scripts," *The Bible and the Ancient Near East,* ed. G. E. WRIGHT (Garden City 1961); "The History of the Biblical Text in the Light of Discoveries in the Judaean Desert," HarvThRev 57 (1964) 281–299. P. W. SKEHAN, "Qumran and the Present State of O.T. Studies: The Masoretic Text," JBiblLit 78 (1959) 21–25; "Exodus in the Samaritan Recension from Qumran," *ibid.* 74 (1955) 182–187; "The Qumran Manuscripts and Textual Criticism," (VetTest Suppl 4; 1957) 148–160; "A Psalm Manuscript from Qumran (4Q Psᵇ)," Cath BiblQuart 26 (1964) 313–322; "The Biblical Scrolls from Qumran and the Text of the Old Testament," BiblArchaeol 28 (1965) 87–100. Y. YADIN, *The Ben Sira Scroll from Masada* (Jerusalem 1965). **Illustration credit:** Fig. 1, Palestine Archaeological Museum; Fig. 2, Courtesy of the Trustees of the British Museum.

[P. W. SKEHAN]

3. TEXT OF THE NEW TESTAMENT

This article will treat in chronological order the forms in which the Greek text of the NT has appeared from the earliest extant manuscripts (MSS), discussing printed editions and indicating projects in progress to reproduce the text more adequately.

The autographs of the 27 canonical books of the NT, written or dictated by several inspired authors over a period of two generations, were lost before almost any extant manuscript (MS) was penned. After having been produced on papyrus scrolls, the autographs had been copied by hand, and these MSS had circulated among individual Christian communities until they in turn were replaced. In the course of transmission both scribal errors and conscious alterations modified the form of the original text. Short clarifications, modification of unfamiliar words, omissions, and harmonizations appeared in MSS. Those in ancient languages into which the NT was translated for Christians who did not speak Greek indicate some modifications not found in any extant Greek MS (see 4. Greek Versions, 10. Aramaic Versions, and 13. Latin Versions in the following sections). In addition, homilies and commentaries of early ecclesiastical writers at times present other textual variations. The Greek text of the NT, as it appears in modern printed editions, is reconstructed on the basis of study and evaluation of all such witnesses, which are only a fraction of its many forms in history. This article deals with the Greek witnesses and modern critical presentations; for the use of these in restoring the original text of the NT, *see* BIBLE, V (TEXTUAL CRITICISM), 3.

EXTANT GREEK NEW TESTAMENT MANUSCRIPTS

The first attempt at a complete listing of all extant Greek NT MSS was made by C. R. Gregory (1847–1917) in the *Prolegomena* of the great 8th edition of C. von Tischendorf's *Novum Testamentum Graece* (Leipzig 1894). Gregory later completed this list in what is accepted as the official list and method of identifying NT Greek MSS (*Die griechischen Handschriften des Neuen Testaments.* (Leipzig 1908). Supported by authority of the *Kommission für spätantike Religionsgeschichte* of the German Academy of Science in preference to proposals of Hermann von *Soden, Gregory's list has been continued by E. von Dobschütz, J. Schmidt, and K. Aland through notices in *Zeitschrift für die neutestamentliche Wissenschaft und die Kunde der älteren Kirche.* The notice by Aland in 1957 brought the number to 67 papyri, 241 uncials, 2,533 cursives, and 1,838 lectionaries, although many of these 4,689 MSS contain only small parts of the Greek text. To keep information accurate, Aland founded the Institute for New Testament Textual Research at Münster in Westphalia in 1959 and inaugurated a series called the *Arbeiten zur neutestamentlichen Textforschung* in 1963. Of the large number of MSS, Gregory could list only one uncial, the Codex Sinaiticus, and about 35 cursives as having the entire NT.

With regard to the material on which the text is written, NT manuscripts are of papyrus, vellum or parchment, and paper. Since paper MSS are late and relatively unimportant, the official list divides the MSS into papyri, uncial vellum, and cursive vellum MSS. The use of vellum became common only from the time of Constantine, who ordered 50 copies on vellum for the churches of his empire. Since it was expensive and limited in quantity, usable parts of worn vellum codices were salvaged to be used again. Thus parts of the NT have been preserved in later writing on such *palimpsest MSS. The following is a brief description of the most important NT MSS in each of the three groups. Since the dates proposed depend upon paleographic evidence, they are at times only tentative (see PALEOGRAPHY, GREEK).

Principal NT Papyri. Significant progress has been made in knowledge of early forms of the NT text because of discoveries of papyri, some of which were written as early as 150 years before the oldest vellum MS (see PAPYROLOGY). In the official list they are designated by a capital P followed by the Arabic numeral indicating the order in which their discovery was reported. By 1964 some 77 papyri containing parts of the Greek text had been announced, dating from the 2d to the 8th century. Although most of these are fragmentary, about half of the Greek NT is now extant on papyrus, parts of every book except 1 and 2 Timothy. Four of these fragments are from *scrolls, the rest from codices (MS books). The oldest (P 52, John Rylands Library Gr. 457) contains parts of Jn 18.31–34, 37–38, written during the first half of the 2d century in a text type like that of the Codex Vaticanus.

The most complete descriptive list of Greek NT papyri appears in the article "Papyrus Biblique" by B. Botte [DBSuppl 6 (1960): 1109–20]. It gives content, date, location, publication, and text type of each papyrus to P 72, except for P 38, erroneously omitted. P 38 (University of Michigan C. 1571) is a 3d-century fragment of a popular, i.e., unrevised, text of Acts 18.27–19.6 and 19.12–16. Botte's article fails to give information on photographic facsimiles. The papyri most important for NT study have been found in this century and form part of the Chester Beatty and Bodmer collections.

Chester Beatty Papyri. In 1930 an Irish businessman, A. Chester Beatty, purchased in Egypt a collection of 11 Biblical papyri, including 3 of the NT. All these were edited by Sir Frederic George *Kenyon with photographic facsimiles as *The Chester Beatty Biblical Papyri* (7 v. and pl. London 1933–37). From the NT are: (1) P 45 (Chester Beatty I). This consists of 30 mutilated leaves of a 3d-century codex about 10 by 8 inches. Extant are fragments of all the Gospels and Acts in a popular text with no particular Western characteristics. This papyrus revolutionized understanding of the NT text by showing so-called Caesarean readings at a date much earlier than had previously been suspected. (2) P 46 (Chester Beatty II plus University of Michigan Inv. 6238). This early 3d-century single-quire codex measures about 9 by 5½ inches. The 86 extant leaves of the original 104 contain parts of almost all the Pauline Epistles and the Epistles to the Hebrews, which follows immediately after Romans. About half of Romans, most of 1 Thessalonians, and all of 2 Thessalonians are missing, and Ephesians precedes Galatians. G. Kuntz has shown that this is an extremely valuable witness of the proto-Alexandrian text type, despite its many scribal errors. The University of Michigan owns 40 leaves but permitted Kenyon to edit them with the rest of the codex. Independently H. A. Sanders also studied the Michigan leaves in *A

Third-Century Papyrus Codex of the Epistles of Paul (Ann Arbor 1935). (3) P 47 (Chester Beatty III). This 3d-century codex, consisting of 10 leaves of Ap 9.10–17.2 with lacunae, is the earliest MS of this book and presents a text similar to that of the Codex Sinaiticus.

Bodmer NT Greek Papyri. These form part of the collection of classical, Biblical, and apocryphal texts in Greek and Coptic acquired by the Swiss industrialist whose name they bear, for his private library in Cologny near Geneva. Of the 19 published, the following 6 are Greek NT texts: (1) P 66 (Bodmer II). This is the extant 108 pages in a codex of 5 quires about 6½ by 5½ inches containing most of Jn 1.1–14.26, except for a lacuna of 6.11–35, and fragments of the remainder of John. V. Martin edited the first 14 chapters in 1956 and part of the fragments in 1958. Shortcomings of this edition and the lack of photographic reproductions were remedied in a second edition of the fragments, which includes a facsimile of the entire papyrus [V. Martin and J. W. B. Barnes, *Papyrus Bodmer II. Supplément. Evangile de Jean XIV–XXI* (Bibliothèque Bodmer, Cologny-Geneva 1962), 54pp and 154 plates]. The first editor dated this codex earlier than A.D. 200, and H. Hunger says that it is no later than A.D. 150. However, J. Duplacy refers to two unnamed papyrologists who place it in the 4th century [RechScRel 50 (1962) 251]. It omits the pericope of the woman taken in adultery (Jn 7.53–8.11) and of the moving of the waters at the pool of Bethesda (Jn 5.4). Carelessly written, it is often corrected by the original and by later scribes. The text, which fluctuates in its agreements with classical text-types, shows clear resemblances to the Old Latin. (2) P 72 (Bodmer VII and VIII). This 3d-century codex contains the Epistles of Jude and 1 and 2 Peter. M. Testuz, curator of the Bodmer library, edited these in 1959 and found the text much like that of Codex B and the Bohairic version, especially for 2 Peter. A complete collation of 1 Peter by E. Massaux indicates that it bears greatest similarity to the cursives 104, 424, 326, and 81 and reveals one of the many popular texts of the 2d and 3d centuries [EphemThLov 39 (1963) 616–71]. (3) P 74 (Bodmer XVII). This is a 6th- or 7th-century codex containing all of Acts and fragments of all the Catholic Epistles. Since the back part of the codex was severely damaged, the fragments decrease rapidly in size. R. Kassar edited this papyrus for the Bodmer library in 1961. (4) P 75 (Bodmer XIV and XV). This is the extant part of a 144-page codex from about A.D. 300 originally containing Luke and John. Extant are 25 full pages, 26 pages almost complete, and fragments of others. These were edited for the Bodmer library in two volumes with 98 plates by V. Martin and R. Kassar in 1961. Bodmer XIV contains Luke 3–17 and 22–24 in a text similar to Codex B. It contains the long text in Lk 22.19–20; 24.12, 40, 51b and omits the bloody sweat of Christ (Lk 22.43–44), also omitted by the Vaticanus and the first hand of Sinaiticus. Bodmer XV is the text of John 1–15, similar to that of Codex B. (5) P 73 is a fragment of Mt 24.43 and 26.2–3 that was found between leaves of P 74 and is unedited.

Principal NT Uncials. Most NT vellum MSS copied between the 4th and 10th centuries were without separation of words, had little punctuation, and were written in large, unconnected letters called uncials, a Latin word meaning "one-twelfth," i.e., of a line of letters. In general these are the most highly esteemed witnesses of the text because of their careful composition. They are identified by a capital letter or by 0 plus an Arabic number, known as a siglum. Uncials fundamental for the study of the NT text are listed below.

Codex Vaticanus. The Vatican codex Gr. 1209, siglum B or 03, is a 4th-century MS originally containing the entire Bible in Greek, but Gn 1.1–46.27, Ps 106 (107)–138(139) and Heb 9.14 to the end of the NT are now missing. Since the Catholic Epistles are before Paul, they are extant, but the Pastoral Letters and the Apocalypse are lost. Although this codex was in the Vatican Library when it was first catalogued in 1475, it was published completely only in 1857. The splendid photographic edition of the Vatican Library appeared in 1889–90 in seven volumes. Although the entire NT seems to have been copied by one scribe, this is uncertain because the letters were inked over by a monk in the 12th century. Codex B offers the best example of the refined text existing in Egypt in the early 3d century and, except in Paul, is free from the readings of the widely diffused popular 2d-century texts. Codex B is the chief witness for the text type called "neutral" by Hort, "Hesychian recension" by von Soden, "text B" by Lagrange, "proto-Alexandrian" by Zuntz, and "Beta" by many recent critics. Westcott and Hort used it as the fundamental text for their edition, and through them it has played the decisive role in many manual editions. Its chief defects are mechanical, such as doubling or omission of letters, syllables, or lines.

Codex Sinaiticus. This is the Codex Frederico-Augustanus plus British Museum Add. MS 43725, siglum S or Hebrew aleph. K. von Tischendorf found this MS

Fig. 3. A page of Codex Vaticanus (Vat. cod. gr. 1209), a 4th-century manuscript which originally contained the entire text of the New Testament. The page shown here carries the text of 2 Thess 3.11–18 and Heb 1.1–2.2. In this manuscript the order of the books is not that which is familiar to us today. Consequently, Hebrews follows directly after 2 Thessalonians without the Pastoral Letters being interspersed between.

on two of his expeditions to the monastery of St. Catherine at Mt. Sinai, part of the OT in 1844 and the NT plus the Letter of Barnabas and the Shepherd of *Hermas in 1859. His second find of 199 leaves was sold by the Soviet government to the British Museum in 1933. In their study, *Scribes and Correctors of the Codex Sinaiticus* (London 1938), H. J. M. Milne and T. C. Skeat date the codex from the 2d half of the 4th century and attribute it to three scribes writing from dictation. It has many mistakes, especially in the part executed by the third scribe and was corrected in different ages by nine hands. Its place of origin seems to have been Caesarea. Kirsopp Lake and Helen Lake edited a photographic facsimile (Oxford 1911).

Codex Alexandrianus. This is an early 5th-century MS (British Museum, Royal MS 1 D V–VIII; siglum A or 02) that once contained the entire Bible. Now the NT begins with Mt 25.7 and lacks Jn 6.50–8.22 and 2 Cor 4.13–12.6. A photographic edition begun for the museum by K. Lake in 1909 was completed only in 1957 by T. C. Skeat in five volumes. This codex, noteworthy for its frequent substitution of synonyms, presents a text of unequal quality. The Gospels belong to the inferior Byzantine type, Acts and the Epistles to the Alexandrian type.

Codex Ephraemi Rescriptus. This is in the Paris National Library, Codex Gr. 9; siglum C or 04. The extant 209 leaves of this 5th-century palimpsest were employed in the 12th century for a Greek translation of the sermons of Ephraim. The 145 leaves from the NT preserve passages from all books except 2 Thessalonians and 2 John. In 1845 Tischendorf published as much as he could read of it. Fundamentally the text is Alexandrian, but it contains mixed readings. After Codex C the list of Gregory uses the same letter for more than one uncial because the rest contain only limited parts of the NT. Four of these demand mention here.

Codex Bezae. A MS of only Gospels and Acts; siglum D or 05. It is commonly known by the name of its 16th-century owner, Theodore *Beza, and is now preserved at Cambridge University. This 5th- or 6th-century uncial is the oldest extant Greek and Latin codex. The order of the Gospels is that of most Latin MSS, Matthew, John, Luke, and Mark. Its text, which is complex, is the leading witness of the Western text and the oldest MS with the pericope of the woman taken in adultery.

Codex Claromontanus. This 6th-century Greek and Latin Codex (siglum D or 06) of the National Library, Paris, contains 533 leaves written in sense lines of unequal length. The text type is also Western.

Codex Washingtonianus. This MS (siglum W or 032) of 187 leaves, now in the Freer Gallery, Washington, D.C., presents a modified uncial script of the 5th century except for the quire containing Jn 1.1–5.11, written by another scribe and offering an early Egyptian form of text. Mark often agrees with P 45, but other parts exhibit a variety of types. After Mk 16.14 is found the so-called Freer logion, a 16-line addition partly quoted by St. Jerome as being found in many MSS.

Codex Koridethi. This codex (siglum Θ or 038), found in a monastery on the Black Sea, was published by Gregory and Beerman in 1913. It cannot be dated exactly because its writing is unique, but it is placed between the 7th and the 9th centuries. It is related to families 1 and 13 mentioned below, and is a witness of the Caesarean text of the Gospels.

Principal NT Cursives. During the 9th century a cursive or miniscule book-hand began to replace the uncial style of writing, and this prevailed until the introduction of printing. Cursive MSS are generally of lesser value as witnesses, but some of them preserve early readings otherwise lost. They are identified simply by an Arabic number. The "queen of the cursives" is 33, a 9th-century codex containing most of the NT except Apocalypse in an Alexandrian text. The large number of cursives has enabled critics to trace relationships between "families," that is, groups of MSS originating from the same archetype. Two of these are described below.

Family 13. The collection is known also as the Ferrar family, after an Irish clergyman, W. H. Ferrar, who first established a relationship between four cursives in 1868. After his death a collation of these, 13, 69, 124, 346, was published by his collaborator, T. K. Abbot, in 1877. Further research, especially by Von Soden and K. Lake, enlarged this family to 13 medieval codices including one lectionary, all containing only the Gospels except 69, which includes the entire NT. The most striking feature of this family is the position of the pericope of the woman taken in adultery (Jn 7.53–8.11) after Lk 21.38. They preserve the Caesarean text-type and were copied in monasteries in southern Italy. J. Geerlings has continued research on this family in the series *Texts and Studies*. In v. 19–21 he published the hypothetical archetype of the Ferrar family text for Matthew, Luke and John.

Family 1. This is a designation for a group known also as the Lake family. Kirsopp *Lake, in *Codex 1 and its Allies* (Cambridge 1902), identified four cursives, 1, 118, 131, and 209, as members of the same family. After relationship had been established between these, the Ferrar family, and the Codex Koridethi, B. H. Streeter, in *The Four Gospels* (London 1924; rev. 1930; repr. 1953), postulated the existence of a local, so-called Caesarean text of the Gospels. K. Lake, R. P. Blake, and S. New made a brilliant corporate effort to recover this text in "The Caesarean Text of the Gospel of Mark" [HarvThRev 21 (1928) 207–404], in which they published a reconstruction of Mark ch. 1, 6, and 11 in this form. However, the discovery of P 45 showed that the "Caesarean" text had roots in Egypt. In projected studies on Family II, Geerlings hoped to shed more light on this intricate phase of the history of the NT text.

Greek NT Lectionaries. For the convenience of monks and clerics, volumes of liturgical readings from the Gospels and Epistles, called lectionaries, were compiled as early as the 6th century. Of the 1,838 of these in Gregory's list, fewer than 200 are uncials, and more than 1,200 contain readings from the Gospels only. Since most of them have not been investigated critically, their value as witnesses to the NT text is still unknown. To remedy this neglect, E. C. Colwell and D. W. Riddle inaugurated the series *Studies in the Lectionary Text of the New Testament* with their *Prolegomena to the Study of the Lectionary Text of the Gospels* (Chicago 1933). This series reached its fifth study with the monograph of William D. Bray, *The Weekday Lessons from Luke in the Greek Gospel Lectionary* (Chicago 1959). Since these researches have reached only the preliminary stages, results are not conclusive. Indi-

cations are that the lectionaries may belong predominantly to the Byzantine text-type but may at times support ancient readings.

Patristic Citations. Additional information about the text of the NT can be gleaned also from citations of ecclesiastical writers and Fathers of the Church, especially those who wrote before the widely diffused Byzantine text began to prevail in the 7th century. Gathering and evaluating this information is extremely difficult because of the lack of reliable critical editions and uncertainty about the accuracy of citations. Up to the 1960s, evidence had often been inconclusive. In his introduction to the pioneering study of P. M. Barnard, *The Biblical Text of Clement of Alexandria in the Four Gospels* (*Texts and Studies* 5; Cambridge 1899), F. C. Burkitt weakened Hort's theory of a neutral text by concluding that Clement was a witness for the Western text-type, related to the Sinaitic Syriac version of the Gospels. In the Pauline Epistles G. Zuntz cites Clement as having made use of a proto-Alexandrian text.

In three articles in the *Journal of Theological Studies* from 1935 to 1937, R. V. G. Tasker presented evidence to show that the text of *Origen (d. c. 254) usually follows the Alexandrian type but offers Caesarean readings in parts of Matthew and John. Although no critical edition of St. John Chrysostom is available, those who have investigated NT citations in his writings are agreed that he is not the father of the Byzantine text and that his text differed from that of any extant MS. He evidently combined readings from more than one source for greater clarity. In his study *The Gospel Text of Cyril of Jerusalem* (Copenhagen 1955) J. G. Greenlee indicated that Cyril's text was "pre-Caesarean" with similarities to Sinaiticus for the synoptics but a popular type for John. Among contemporary critics, M. E. Boismard places great stress upon the testimony of early ecclesiastical writers, and in his work on John he has shown that at times they witness to readings that may be original, although not found in any extant Greek MS.

PRINTED EDITIONS OF THE NEW TESTAMENT

The use of printing gradually brought to an end the multiplication of textual variants of the NT.

Early Editions. Desiderius *Erasmus published the first printed edition of the NT in a hurried and faulty Greek and Latin edition at Basel in 1516. The Greek text had already been printed in 1514 in the text of D. L. Stunica for the Complutensis *Polyglot Bible of Cardinal Ximenes, but this edition did not actually appear until 1520. Erasmus used it to improve his 4th edition of 1527.

Critical notations of alternate readings were first added in the margins of the text published by R. *Estienne, who edited the text four times from 1546 to 1551. His final edition, which introduced the present division of the text into verses, was often reprinted. Another edition destined to have marked influence upon the diffusion of the NT text for 200 years was produced by the brothers B. and A. Elzevir (Leiden 1624). They introduced their second edition of 1633 as the *textus receptus,* "the text received" by all. Although this represents the official text of the Greek Church and is based on the largest number of uncials, e.g., N, Y, V, K, II, Ω for the NT as a whole and A, E, F, G, H for the

Gospels, and the vast majority of cursive manuscripts, this text type is of an inferior critical quality.

Preliminary research to improve the quality of printed editions was made by Richard *Simon, who pointed out the insufficiency of the *textus receptus* in his *Critical History of the NT Text* (London 1689), translated from the French edition of the same year. In 1734 J. A. Bengel made a positive contribution toward an improvement of printed editions by dividing MSS into "families, tribes and nations," thus facilitating a more accurate critical evaluation of their text [*Novum Testamentum graecum* (Tubingen 1734)]. A major improvement in the presentation of MSS in the critical apparatus was introduced by J. J. Wettstein, whose edition was based on 330 MSS. He was the first to designate uncials by capital letters and cursives by Arabic numerals in his sigla, anticipating the system of Gregory [*Novum Testamentum graecum,* 2 v. (Amsterdam 1751–52; photographic reproduction Graz, Austria 1961)]. For his edition of the received MSS, J. J. *Griesbach divided the Gospel MSS into the three classes that were to be commonly accepted, to which he gave the misleading names Western, Alexandrian, and Constantinopolitan recensions (Halle 1777; 2d ed., Leipzig 1796–1806).

Later Improved Editions. Only in 1830 did a NT editor depart from the custom of editing the received text. This was the distinction of the small but revolutionary edition of Karl Lachmann, who published also a larger edition (Berlin 1842–50). His goal was to reproduce the text current in the 4th century, and he limited his edition to a small number of witnesses. The English editor S. P. Tregelles, whose edition was completed after his death by Hort in 1879, likewise concentrated on a limited number of older witnesses. Most famous of all NT editors was Konstantin von *Tischendorf, who collated and published more than 40 Biblical MSS and produced 8 critical editions of the NT with 4 widely divergent texts. His final text, the 8th *editio critica major* (Leipzig 1865–72), was marred by his excessive preference for the readings of Codex Sinaiticus, which he had recently discovered. The lengthy introductory volume, which his pupil C. R. Gregory worked 22 years to write, is still a fundamental source of information about NT MSS, although surpassed and antiquated in many ways.

The 19th-century text that proved most decisive for NT studies was the result of 28 years of collaboration between Brooke Foss *Westcott, later an Anglican bishop, and Fenton John Anthony *Hort [*The New Testament in Greek,* 2 v. (London 1881; 2d ed. 1898)]. In contrast to Tischendorf, who refused to rely on the classification of MSS, this edition insisted that the history of the text must be considered in order to arrange the MSS according to their exact critical value. Hort's introductory volume, which is a treatise on NT textual criticism, explains that their text is based on "the best documentary evidence." To find this, MSS were divided into four classes, neutral, Western, Alexandrian and Syrian. Internal criticism was to remain supplementary (see paras. 76 and 82). Critics found fault with the narrow basis for choosing the text, and the editor of the second edition, Francis Crawford *Burkitt, acknowledged this fault (additional note to para. 170), because the discovery of the Old Syrian

palimpsest of the Gospels by Mrs. Agnes Lewis in 1892 had emphasized the possibility that other combinations of witnesses, such as agreement of versions, could command more critical reliability than the primary Greek witnesses. As early as 1904, K. Lake called the edition by Westcott and Hort "a failure, though a splendid one." A generation later, comparing the work of Westcott-Hort with that of Marie Joseph *Lagrange, he commented that perhaps no thesis more subjective than that of Hort ever existed [RevBibl 48 (1939) 498]. The edition was attacked also because of its hypothesis of a neutral or uncontaminated text in Codex B and because the editors used internal criticism in a way incompatible with their stated principles. An effort to make greater use of all MS witnesses including the ancient versions appears in the edition of Bernard Weiss (Leipzig 1894–1900; 2d ed. 1905), but it also depends chiefly upon Codex B.

The fruits of the critical researches on the NT text by Tischendorf, Westcott-Hort, and Weiss have been widely diffused chiefly through the frequently edited manual edition of Eberhard *Nestle [*Novum Testamentum graece* (Stuttgart 1898)]. Its fourth edition was used also as the text of the first edition of the NT by the British and Foreign Bible Society. During its 24 editions the Nestle publication has incorporated new information on the text as far as possible in its present format. K. Aland, who along with Erwin Nestle is the current editor, is preparing an entirely new edition in a new format that will represent a major revision.

The last complete critical edition was prepared by a staff of 40 under the direction of H. von Soden [*Die Schriften des neuen Testaments in ihren ältesten erreichbaren Textgestalt,* 2 v. (Berlin-Göttingen 1902–13)]. After a thorough examination of the Greek MSS, he divided them into three recensions: H (Eta) by Hesychius in Egypt; I (Iota or Jerusalem) by Pamphilius of Caesarea, and K (Kappa) by Lucian of Antioch. Although Von Soden's text and new system of sigla were severely criticized, his introductory studies on the MSS contain information of great value. His critical researches influenced the manual editions of three Catholic editors. These were Heinrich Joseph Vogels, *Novum Testamentum graece* (Düsseldorf 1920; 3d ed. Herder, Freiburg 1950); J. M. Bover, *Novi Testamenti Biblia* (Madrid 1943; 3d ed. 1953), and Augustin *Merk, *Novum Testamentum graece et latine* (Rome 1933; 8th ed. by J. P. Smith 1957). A revised edition of the last mentioned has been announced.

In an attempt to provide an edition of the NT with a more complete and accurate critical apparatus than was available, a committee of English scholars undertook the project and entrusted editorship to S. C. E. Legg. Severe criticism of the two volumes that appeared, Mark in 1935 and Matthew in 1940 (Oxford), caused a modification of plans. To prepare this complete critical apparatus an international committee was set up with M. M. Parvis as American secretary; the British secretary, G. D. Kilpatrick, was also editor of the second edition of the Greek NT of the British and Foreign Bible Society (London 1958). Another smaller international NT project was begun in 1956 under the direction of the American Bible Society and similar groups in other countries. The editorial committee undertook to prepare a new critical text with a limited apparatus of variants having theological and exegetical importance, and an accompanying supplement to explain the choice of readings adopted. The publication date was set for 1966.

Bibliography: V. TAYLOR, *The Text of the NT: A Short Introduction* (New York 1961). F. G. KENYON and A. W. ADAMS, *Our Bible and the Ancient Manuscripts* (5th ed. rev. New York 1958). B. BOTTE, "Manuscrits grecs du NT," DBSuppl 5:819–835. G. ZUNTZ, *The Text of the Epistles* (New York 1953). W. H. P. HATCH, *The Principal Uncial Manuscripts of the NT*, with 76 plates (Chicago 1939). K. and S. LAKE, eds., *Dated Greek Minuscule MSS to the Year 1200*, with 150 tables (Boston 1934–38). M. M. PARVIS and A. P. WIKGREN, eds., *NT Manuscript Studies* (Chicago 1950). B. M. METZGER, *The Text of the New Testament* (New York 1964). L. VAGANAY, *An Introduction to the Textual Criticism of the NT*, tr. B. V. MILLER (St. Louis 1937). EncDictBibl 2419–22. **Illustration credit:** Fig. 3, Biblioteca Apostolica Vaticana.

[J. M. REESE]

4. GREEK VERSIONS

As early as the 3d century B.C. the need was felt by the Greek-speaking Jews of the Hellenistic Diaspora for a translation of the Hebrew Scriptures in their own language (*see* DIASPORA, JEWISH). This need was gradually met in the course of the next few centuries by the Greek version known as the Septuagint. During the early Christian centuries the Septuagint was subjected to several recensions, such as those of Aquila and the so-called Theodotion; and a new Greek version, at least for some of the books of the Hebrew Bible, was made by Symmachus. On the basis of these and other recensions of the Septuagint, Origen endeavored in the 3d century to establish a critical text of the Greek Bible in his work known as the Hexapla. The Septuagint, in somewhat altered form because of these various recensions, has remained throughout the centuries the official Bible of the Greek Church. For versions of the Bible in modern Greek, see section 40, below. The ancient Greek versions are discussed in the next five articles as follows: (5) Septuagint, (6) Aquila, (7) Symmachus, (8) Theodotion, (9) Hexapla.

Bibliography: J. ZIEGLER, LexThK² 2:375–380. E. VOGT, Enc Catt 6:1056–58. G. GERLEMAN, RGG³ 1:1193–95. EncDictBibl 2165–71, 2529.

[L. F. HARTMAN]

5. SEPTUAGINT

The accepted name for the earliest translation of the OT into Greek. Based on Latin *septuaginta*, 70, it reflects the legend that the 5 Mosaic books were rendered into Greek by a group of 72 translators sent from Jerusalem to Alexandria during the reign of Ptolemy II Philadelphus, 285–246 B.C. (*see* ARISTEAS, LETTER OF). The time and place thus given for the compilation of the Greek Pentateuch are in keeping with what is otherwise known of Hellenistic Judaism (*see* DIASPORA, JEWISH) and its literature, and can be taken as fact. The extension of the name Septuagint or "Seventy," abbreviated LXX, to the Greek OT as a whole became established usage among Christian writers by the 4th century; and the name is applied today to the printed text of the OT in Greek and to its manuscript witnesses, even for those books either composed in Greek, or based on a Semitic original now wholly or partly lost, and excluding only the identifiable work of revisers and translators subse-

quent to the 1st Christian century, such as Aquila, Symmachus, and (though the case is confused) Theodotion. (See parts 6, Aquila; 7, Symmachus; and 8, Theodotion of this article.)

Formative Period. The assembling of this corpus of OT texts was the work of fully 400 years, from the early 3d century B.C. to the early 2d Christian century (Ecclesiastes). The prologue to Sirach (Ecclesiasticus), written about 116 B.C. by its Greek translator, grandson of the author, admits of the inference that the Jews of Alexandria had, by that date, translations of the Law and of substantial portions of the historical books and the writing Prophets, as well as at least some of the "other books," i.e., the wisdom literature and the Psalms. An occasional note, such as the vague one attached to the end of the Greek Esther, points in the same direction; see 2 Mc 1.9. Also, internal evidence of the type of Hebrew text actually translated, of the time of origin in Greek of the deuterocanonical books and of the *Letter of Aristeas,* and of the use in Wisdom and 1 Machabees especially of existing LXX materials helps to establish that by the end of the 2d century B.C. the repertory of OT materials in Greek was nearing completion in substantially the form in which it is now known.

Question of Unity of the LXX. In the period 1941 to 1960, vigorous controversy was waged, especially in England, on the subject of LXX origins. P. E. *Kahle was the protagonist for a theory that denied that the materials transmitted as the one "Septuagint" for most OT books actually represent one single, pre-Christian, accepted Jewish rendering. He proposed instead that the earliest Greek renderings were oral and fluid, like the Palestinian targums, and that in the midst of a number of fluctuating partial translations no standardized Greek OT came into being until the early 4th Christian century, when the Greek Biblical text became fixed by the authoritative decision of the hierarchy of the Christian Church. This position is historically untenable; but it was based on real difficulties in the actual texts and early citations (in Philo, the NT, Josephus, Justin, etc.). The difficulties could not be resolved as long as it was presumed that the first serious critical work on the LXX text dated from the days of *Origen (d. A.D. 254) and his Hexapla. (See 9, Hexapla.) The opposite standpoint to that of Kahle, maintained by P. Katz in England and H. Orlinsky in America, harked back to the 100-year-old enterprise of P. A. de *Lagarde, directed toward identifying in the extant MSS recognizable families that can be used as avenues of approach to the single underlying rendering posited for pre-Christian times. This view governed the comprehensive editorial projects (see below) centered in Cambridge and in Göttingen. The latter, in the Prophets especially, through the efforts of Msgr. Joseph Ziegler, yielded very satisfactory results during the same period in which the theoretical discussions were being carried on.

New Evidence of Continuity. Evidence in the form of actual text fragments in Greek of pre-Christian and 1st-Christian-century date has been accumulating in recent years both from Egyptian sources and as a result of the *Dead Sea Scrolls discoveries at Khirbet Qumran and in the Wadi Khabra in Palestine. From Egypt have come two fragmentary MSS of Deuteronomy: P. Rylands Gr. 458 of the mid-2d century B.C., and P. Fuad inv. 266 of a slightly later date. From Qumran are an Exodus fragment (7Q1), bits of Leviticus on leather (4QLXX Lev[a]) and on papyrus (4QLXX Lev[b]), of Numbers on parchment (4 QLXX Num), and of the "Letter of Jeremia" on papyrus (7Q2); the oldest of these is 4Q LXX Lev[a], about 100 B.C., the youngest 4Q LXX Num, about the turn of the era. From the Wadi Khabra comes a fragmentary scroll of the Minor Prophets of the 1st Christian century, which has been studied by D. Barthélemy, OP. None of these gives any warrant for the hypothesis of a lack of continuity between the pre-Christian Jewish texts and the medieval MSS; quite the contrary. Later witnesses, but illustrating the character of the text before Origen, are the papyrus codices and fragments of many OT books from the 2d and 3d Christian centuries (see below). Between these and the witness of the early Coptic and Old Latin secondary versions, the evidence for a continuity of transmission of one same written LXX text for most of the books of the OT is overwhelming.

Expansions, Recensions, and Supplements. To the unity of the LXX certain qualifications are necessary, however; and these are of major importance. Added to the collection were not only certain books that had been composed wholly in Greek (Wisdom, 2 Machabees), but also others that were translated from Semitic texts now no longer extant, in whole or in part (Tobit, Judith, Sirach, Baruch, 1 Machabees). Still other LXX texts show a recension of a Semitic book differing from that in the Masoretic Text and including some purely Greek additions (Daniel, Esther). For some books the LXX offers an expanded text in all MSS (Proverbs) or in some (Sirach) that is based on copious reworkings and double renderings with an eye to the original. Finally there are books that show in the LXX MSS two strikingly different recensions (Judges) or even three (Tobit); in which an existing Alexandrian rendering is generally ignored (Daniel, 3 Esdras) in favor of a later, more labored but less erratic translation; or in which a primitively short LXX text, whether bad (Job) or good (Jeremiah), has been filled out at a different time in a different style by another hand.

Proto-Theodotion. Barthélemy's study of the Wadi Khabra fragments of the Minor Prophets has disclosed that they represent a recension made in the 1st Christian century of the earlier LXX on the basis of a Hebrew text; that it is this same recension that supplied the seventh column, or *quinta editio*, of Origen's Hexapla for these books; that it also accounts for approximations to the Hebrew text in the Sahidic Coptic and in the Freer codex in Greek; that it is the recension that Justin Martyr quoted in the mid-2d century; that it is identical in technique with the valid evidence at hand for the so-called Theodotion, and that it forms the actual substratum for the work of Aquila. Extending his study to other putative work of Theodotion, he is able to establish that the recension in question is Palestinian in origin and that its witnesses include the supplements to Job and Jeremia in the LXX, the "Septuagint" renderings of Lamentations and (probably) Ruth, the so-called Theodotion text of Daniel, the *quinta* form of the Psalms, and the text of 2 Sm 11.2 to 3 Kgs 2.11 in the LXX column of the Hexapla. The same recension again stands as "Septuagint" for Origen in 3 Kgs 22.1–54 with all of 4 Kings. As a corollary to all this, Barthélemy reaffirms what has long been suspected, that the

"Septuagint" of Ecclesiastes is in fact the work of Aquila (see section 6 of this article).

Other Recensional Activities. In the perspectives thus opened up, it becomes possible to find other evidences of early recensional activity in the LXX. Since the secondary recension of Sir 12.1 is quoted in the Didache 1.6, the expanded form of Sirach in codex 248 and the Old Latin dates back to at least the 1st Christian century. Since the variant form of Prv 2.21 is quoted in Clement of Rome (*1 Clem.* 14.4), the reworking of the first nine chapters of the LXX of that book may be dated in the same 1st century at the latest. In Ezechiel, Ziegler has shown that pap. 967 (the Beatty-Scheide MS) displays a pre-Origen, 1st-century recensional treatment of the text. The reworked and harmonizing character of Deuteronomy and Isaia in the Greek tradition reflects, not only tendencies of that sort in Greek translators or revisers in pre-Christian times, but, in Isaia at least, a harmonizing, expansionist technique in the Hebrew text from which the Greek was prepared.

Proto-Lucian. For the Pentateuch and Samuel a further step has been made possible to F. M. Cross by the evidence of Hebrew MSS from Qumran cave 4. The recension of the LXX associated with the name of St. *Lucian of Antioch (d. 312) has long presented problems equally thorny with those in the "Theodotion" material: typified most strikingly by the fact that Josephus Flavius at the end of the 1st Christian century employed a characteristically "Lucianic" text. For Exodus through Deuteronomy it has been possible to establish that a "proto-Lucianic" form of the LXX was the type of text circulating from pre-Christian times in Palestine and Syria and cited by the Fathers of the "School of Antioch"; it was this and a similar text in Samuel and Kings that were available to Josephus. The MS 4Q LXX Num is of this type, though it seems already to have "Theodotionic" features also. A "Lucianic" text is identified by Barthélemy as having been displaced from the LXX column of the Hexapla for 1 Sm 11.2—3 Kgs 2.11 and for 3 Kings ch. 22 plus 4 Kings by a later, "Theodotionic" reworking (see above); the displaced text found room in the adjoining 6th column of the Hexapla, where it appears related to the "Lucianic" material of the minuscule MSS *b, o, c[2], e[2]*. On the basis of three Hebrew MSS of Samuel, i.e., 4Q Sam[a,b,c], Cross is able to affirm that this "proto-Lucianic" text is not the primitive LXX subject to incidental corruption, but it is part of a deliberate recension carried out in the 2d or 1st century B.C. to bring the Greek rendering from Egypt into better harmony with the Hebrew MSS then current in Palestine. He applies the same interpretation to the Pentateuch evidence, where he sees again a deliberate harmonizing of the older LXX text from Egypt with the evolved Palestinian Hebrew MSS of the 2d or 1st century B.C. For the portions of Samuel and Kings where the "Theodotionic" recension has made inroads into the main stream of LXX transmission, the proto-Lucianic stage is the first one available because, according to Cross, a primitive LXX from Egypt is not extant in these sections.

From this it can be seen that the forthcoming period of LXX criticism will be aided by a chronology, both relative and absolute, for the known text types, such as will clear up many existing anomalies in their evaluation. This will be accompanied by a fuller appreciation of the nature and extent of the recensions described above; and it will be backed up by a generous sampling of Hebrew texts of pre-Christian date and varied text types from Qumran, which will illustrate the prototypes available for consultation at different stages of the evolution of the LXX. The realization that Aquila (c. A.D. 130) builds on "Theodotion," and that "Theodotion" builds on "Lucian," which in turn revises the primitive LXX, and that Symmachus late in the 2d century and Origen before 245 stand rather toward the end than toward the beginning of an intensive reworking of the LXX text lays the foundation for a much more effective use of the successive Greek recensions to penetrate to the underlying Hebrew originals in the period before the definitive fixing of the Hebrew consonantal text c. A.D. 100.

Manuscripts of the LXX. Apart from the eight fragmentary witnesses described above (fragments of early *scrolls), the MSS of the LXX are almost all in codex (book) form: either on papyrus, or on vellum in uncial (rounded capital) script, or on vellum or paper in a cursive minuscule hand.

Papyri of the LXX. These provide our oldest extensive texts. In the Chester Beatty collection, now in London, there are portions of Numbers, Deuteronomy, and Jeremia of the 2d Christian century; of similar date are fragments of the Psalms in London and Oxford. In the same group of MSS from the Egyptian Fayyûm, purchased in part by C. Beatty and in part by J. H. Scheide, there are 3d-century texts of portions of varying size of Genesis, Isaia, Ezechiel, Daniel, and Esther. Of a 3d-century MS of the Minor Prophets, 33 leaves are in the Freer collection in Washington, and further fragments of 3d-century date representing Genesis, Psalms, Proverbs, Wisdom, and Sirach are in Oxford, Geneva, and London. With the 4th century, papyrus witnesses begin to multiply; some 200 may be counted through the 7th century.

Uncial Codices. The great uncial codices on vellum of the 4th to the 10th century were, until the 1900s, not only the most careful and the most complete, but also the oldest available witnesses to the LXX. They are usually pandects, or complete Bibles, including also the NT. The most significant for the LXX are the following.

The *Codex Vaticanus* (known as B), Vat. Gr. 1209, of the mid-4th century, lacking only Gn 1.1–46.8 at the beginning, some verses of 2 Samuel ch. 2, and about 30 Psalms; 1 and 2 Machabees were never contained in it. For a number of OT books this codex is in a class by itself as the best single witness to the earliest form of the LXX text.

The *Codex Sinaiticus* (S or *Aleph*), also of the 4th century, is presently in the British Museum except for 43 leaves in Leipzig and some sizable lacunae. Careless though it is in its orthography, it is witness to a very early text tradition often related to that of B. In Tobit it is the unique Greek witness to the longer and more nearly original form of the text. With 1 Machabees is joined 4 Machabees; 2 and 3 Machabees were never in the MS.

The *Codex Alexandrinus* (A), also in the British Museum, 5th century, with slight OT lacunae in Genesis and 1 Samuel, and again missing about 30 Psalms. It is often at variance with B, strikingly so in Judges; in general, it shows proto-Lucianic and also hexaplaric tend-

encies. It includes 3 and 4 Machabees in addition to the canonical books.

The *Codex Marchalianus* (Q), Vat. Gr. 2125, 6th century, containing Prophets only. It is notable for the copious citations of Aquila, Symmachus, and Theodotion in its margins.

Minuscule Codices. Of cursive MSS between the 9th century and the spread of printing in the 16th, some 1,500 contain the LXX text. Nearly 300 were collated, with varying degrees of accuracy, early in the 19th century for the edition of R. Holmes and J. Parsons. [*Vetus Testamentum Graecum cum variis lectionibus,* 5 v. (Oxford 1798–1827)].

Printed Editions. The LXX of the Complutensian Polyglot, published in 1521 (*see* POLYGLOT BIBLES) offers, from the minuscule MS *b* (Holmes and Parsons, 108), a text of "Lucianic" type, mingled with portions and eclectic readings from other minuscules, notably cod. 248. The Aldine Greek Bible of 1518 based its LXX text on minuscule MSS in Venice. The Sixtine edition of 1587, an outgrowth of the Council of Trent, had great influence on subsequent editions; as it was based largely on codex B, it offered a good foundation for critical study. J. E. Grabe's edition based on codex A (Oxford 1707–20) is noteworthy. The extensive collations undertaken by Holmes and Parsons drew on 20 uncials, nearly 300 minuscules, and evidence from several daughter versions of the LXX and from patristic citations. K. von *Tischendorf produced a good manual edition of the LXX, several times revised from 1850; the 1887 edition overseen and supplemented by E. *Nestle attained a high degree of accuracy; it offered a revised Sixtine text with an apparatus from the great uncials. Manual editions in current use are those of H. B. Swete, *The Old Testament in Greek* (3 v. Cambridge, England; several editions since 1894), and A. Rahlfs, *Septuaginta* (Stuttgart 1935, 6th ed. 1959). Both offer a collation from the great uncials, Rahlfs under an eclectic text, Swete under that of B where it is extant (in Genesis, that of A; the Psalms lacuna from S); useful for ready reference though they are, neither is now an adequate critical instrument. Of a projected Lucianic edition by P. de Lagarde, v.1 appeared in 1883; though Lagarde was a great scholar, this edition was not really successful, and it is now antiquated. The full-scale undertaking, to include all pertinent evidence for text, secondary versions, and citations of LXX, directed by A. E. Brooke, N. McLean, and H. St. John Thackeray at Cambridge has yielded editions of all the historical books from Genesis (1906) to 1 and 2 Chronicles; Esther, Judith, and Tobit are included (1940). The continuous text reproduces an uncial (B when available); the user is left largely to his own devices in disentangling from the apparatus the jumble of recensions described above. The Göttingen Academy of Sciences sponsors a parallel endeavor that has so far published in full the LXX Prophets (Isaia, Jeremia with Lamentations and Baruch, Ezechiel, Daniel, and the Twelve, ed. J. Ziegler, between 1939 and 1954); 1, 2, and 3 Machabees (W. Kappler and R. Hanhart, 1936, 1959–60); Psalms (Rahlfs, 1931); Wisdom (Ziegler, 1962); Sirach (also Ziegler, *Sapientia Jesu filii Sirach,* 1965). In this series, the editor establishes the running text, and presents his collations, by family groups when possible, against that base. Outside these series, M. Margolis pub-

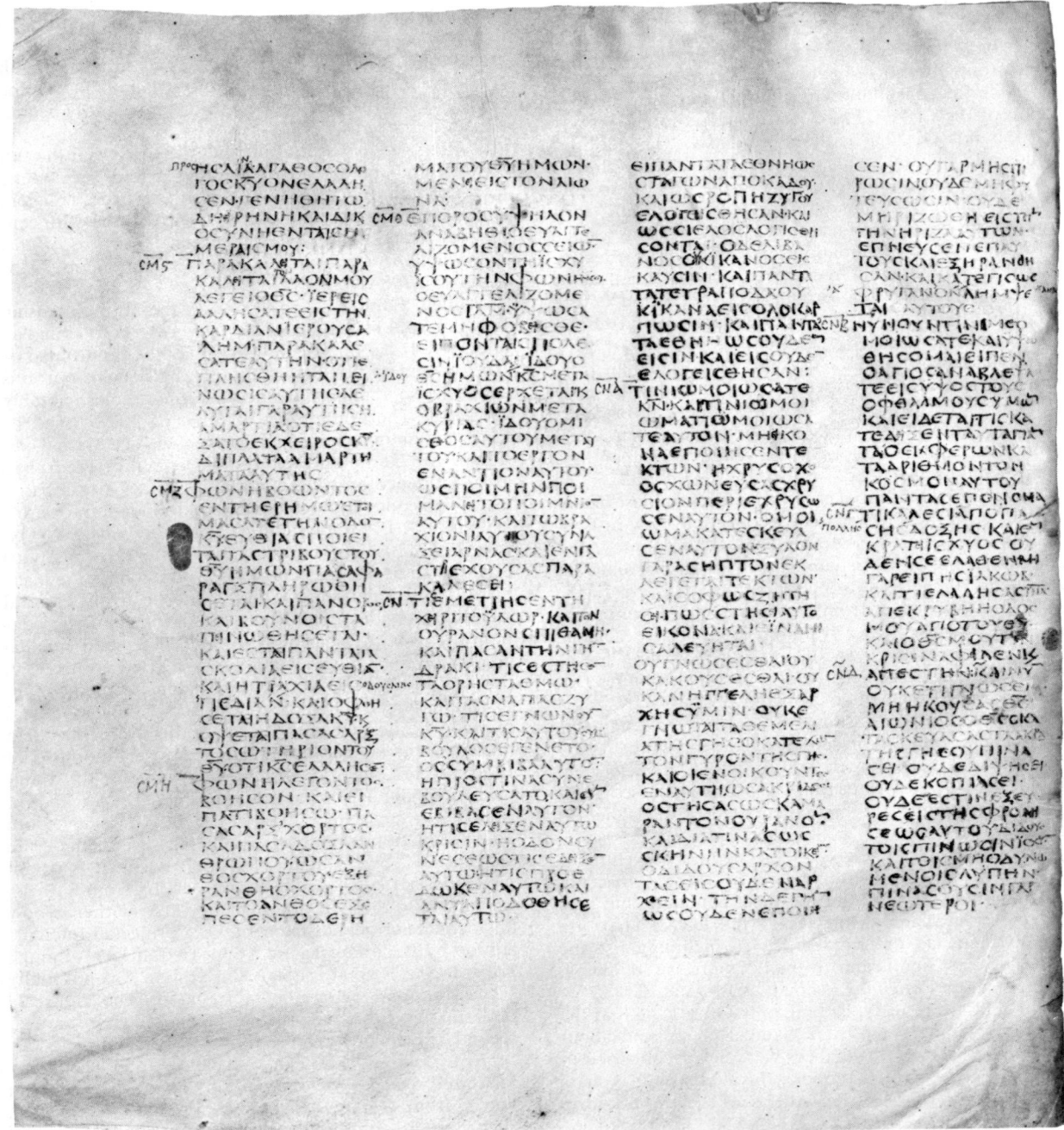

Fig. 4. Folio of the Codex Sinaiticus (Add. MS 43725), with text of Is 39.8–40.30 according to the Septuagint Version. The codex, which originally contained the whole Bible in Greek, dates from the mid-4th century.

lished (Paris 1931–38) a separate edition of most of Josue, and the Göttingen undertaking offered sample editions of Genesis (1926) and Ruth (1922).

Significance of the LXX; Its Use in Textual Criticism. The LXX is especially noteworthy as having provided a cultural milieu and a literary vehicle for the preaching of earliest Christianity. This providential role for it, combined with its not infrequent shortcomings and liberties in dealing with the Hebrew, and its notable divergence from the more narrowly based and rigid standard of the Hebrew consonantal text of about A.D. 100, made it increasingly distasteful to the Jews, who replaced it with Aquila for the most part.

For the use of the LXX in textual criticism, the primary rule is that each book of the OT in Greek had its own history and must be studied on its own terms: competence and idiosyncrasies of its translator(s), possible recensions, time of its original rendering and its successive modifications, and only then at last the force of its individual readings in their relation to a presumed He-

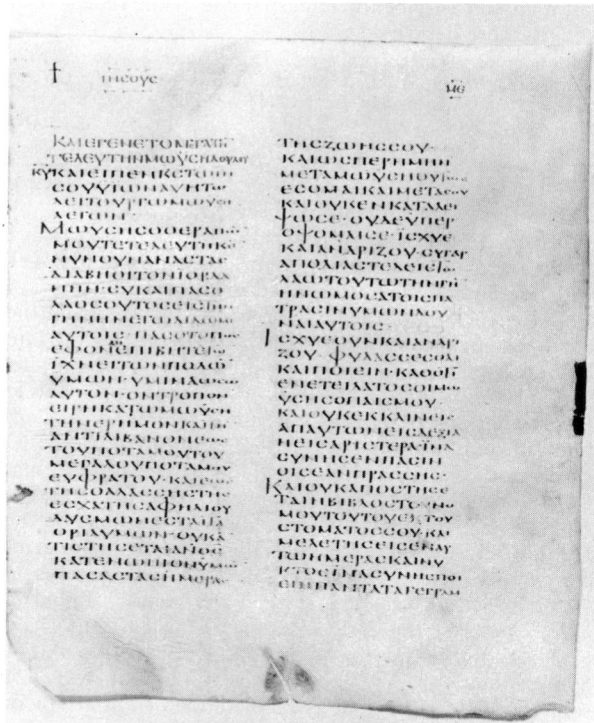

Fig. 5. Folio of the Codex Washingtoniensis I, with text of Jos 1.1–8. The codex, which dates from the 4th or the 5th century, contains the Septuagint version of the Books of Deuteronomy and Josue (Joshua).

brew prototype that may or may not coincide with the received Hebrew text or with variants on it known from elsewhere. It is often our earliest witness, and is sometimes the best; but any sweeping general statement about the value of the LXX as a whole, whether for praise or for blame, is the fruit of ignorance.

Bibliography: Hatch-Redpath. H. B. SWETE, *An Introduction to the O.T. in Greek* (rev. ed. Cambridge, Eng. 1914). A. RAHLFS, *Verzeichnis der griechischen Handschriften des A.T.* (Berlin 1914). F. G. KENYON, *Our Bible and the Ancient Manuscripts,* rev. A. W. ADAMS (5th ed. New York 1958) 97–134. R. DEVREESSE, *Introduction à l'étude des manuscrits grecs* (Paris 1954). P. E. KAHLE, *The Cairo Geniza* (2d ed. New York 1960). P. KATZ, "Septuagint Studies in the Mid-Century," *The Background of the N.T. and Its Eschatology,* ed. W. D. DAVIES and D. DAUBE (Cambridge, Eng. 1956) 176–208. J. ZIEGLER, *Die Septuaginta: Erbe und Auftrag* (Würzburg 1962); LexThK² 2:375–380. H. M. ORLINSKY, "The Textual Criticism of the O.T.," *The Bible and the Ancient Near East,* ed. G. E. WRIGHT (New York 1961) 113–132. D. BARTHÉLEMY, *Les Devanciers d'Aquila* (VetTest Suppl. 10; 1963). F. M. CROSS, "The History of the Biblical Text in the Light of Discoveries in the Judaean Desert," HarvThRev 57 (1964) 281–299. O. EISSFELDT, *Einleitung in das Alte Testament* (3d ed. Tübingen 1964) 951–973, 1031. E. VOGT, EncCatt 6: 1056–58. G. GERLEMANN, RGG³ 1:1193–95. EncDictBibl 2165–71. **Illustration credit:** Fig. 4, Courtesy of the Trustees of the British Museum. Fig. 5, Courtesy of the Smithsonian Institution, Freer Gallery of Art, Washington, D.C.

[P. W. SKEHAN]

6. AQUILA

A Jewish proselyte from Pontus, reviser of the Septuagint Greek Old Testament, said to have flourished under the Emperor Hadrian and to have worked under the guidance of Rabbi *Akiba ben Joseph. Aquila's

work would thus have reached its final form in the years preceding the second Jewish revolt against Rome (A.D. 132–135); internal evidence supports such a dating. Aquila is known to Talmudic tradition as Onkelos, under which name was later placed the Aramaic Targum to the Pentateuch standardized among the Jews in Babylonia some 3 centuries later than Aquila. Further biographical details reflected by St. Epiphanius (*De mens. et pond.* 14–15) and others, such as Aquila's relationship to Hadrian, his conversion to Christianity in Jerusalem at the time of the founding of Aelia Capitolina, through the influence of Christians from Pella, his subsequent excommunication, and his explicit anti-Christian purpose in undertaking his elaborate recension of the OT text, may be viewed with cumulating skepticism. Aquila's activity seems to have extended to all parts of the Jewish canon of the OT. The Book of Ecclesiastes in the Greek version transmitted with the Septuagint is rendered with his techniques and peculiarities of treatment, though not fully developed; it may be an early stage of his undertaking. Other materials from his pen are preserved from 3 and 4 Kings and Psalms especially; along with snatches and isolated words in what survives by way of quotation or extract from the Aquila column of Origen's Hexapla. His method of rendering is rigidly mechanical; where the untranslatable Hebrew particle *'et* occurs, and can be represented in no other way, Aquila introduces σύν followed by the accusative case, against Greek usage, to reflect its presence. Specific Hebrew roots in all their noun and verb derivatives are reflected by variants, sometimes coined for the purpose, on one same Greek stem. Although it is a useful critical tool because of this rigidity with which it matches its underlying Hebrew text, the version of Aquila has no special merits of intelligibility and is hopeless for continuous reading as Greek. The text from which this contorted version is derived seems often to have been the less systematic early Palestinian recension known to us as Theodotion.

Bibliography: H. B. SWETE, *An Introduction to the O. T. in Greek* (rev. ed. Cambridge, Eng. 1914) 31–42. G. MERCATI, ed., *Psalterii hexapli reliquiae* (Vatican City 1958–) v.1.

[P. W. SKEHAN]

7. SYMMACHUS

Translator of the Hebrew OT into Greek, apparently in the last decades of the 2d Christian century. Eusebius of Caesarea (*Hist. Eccl.* 6.17) notes that Origen received copies of Symmachus's work from a certain Juliana, who had them from the author. The connection between this datum and an alleged Ebionite commentary on St. Matthew by Symmachus may be attributable to Eusebius himself and seems to have little more to recommend it than the allegation of St. Epiphanius (*De mens. et pond.* 15) that Symmachus was a Samaritan convert to Judaism. At least for some books (see D. Barthélemy), Symmachus as translator seems to have depended on an existing Palestinian recension of the Septuagint, that which is ascribed in a misleading manner to Theodotion. Though subsequent to Aquila, Symmachus goes his own way on different principles. He is known for the respect he shows for the Greek idiom into which he is rendering the text; though faithful to the Hebrew, he varies sentence structure, particles, and diction somewhat freely. The result was agreeable to St.

Jerome, whose Vulgate draws on Symmachus for aid in matters of both interpretation and style. Like the other late Greek translators, Symmachus, who seems to have rendered all parts of the Hebrew OT, is known only through fragments, chiefly from the remains of Origen's Hexapla. The readings from Ecclesiastes ascribed to Aquila out of this source belong rather to Symmachus.

Bibliography: H. B. SWETE, *An Introduction to the O. T. in Greek* (rev. ed. Cambridge, Eng. 1914) 49–53. D. BARTHÉLEMY, *Les Devanciers d'Aquila* (VetTest Suppl 10; 1963) 27–30, 261–263.

[P. W. SKEHAN]

8. THEODOTION

It is no longer possible, with St. Epiphanius, to ascribe the revision of the Greek OT known now under the name of Theodotion to a Jewish convert of the late 2d Christian century. St. Irenaeus, who speaks of Theodotion as having lived before Aquila (*Adv. Haer.* 3.21.1), is surely correct in this, though whether a person named Theodotion came from Ephesus, as he also affirms, is not verifiable elsewhere. The name Theodotion is associated with a text that was an accommodation of the existing pre-Christian Greek version loosely known as the Septuagint to the more thoroughly edited Hebrew manuscripts circulating in Palestine in the 1st century B.C. and the early 1st Christian century. This work was done with a measure of mechanical matching of more or less insignificant Hebrew particles (e.g., *gām*) with fixed Greek equivalents (in the case cited, $\kappa\alpha\acute{\iota}\gamma\epsilon$); with sporadic transliterations of Hebrew words, sometimes well-known and fairly frequent ones, into Hebrew letters; and with a tendency toward verbal consistency (even rigidity) in a rendering that paves the way for the virtuoso performance of Aquila. The work was done in Palestine, with some heed to the developing hermeneutical techniques and principles (*middōt*) of the rabbis; the unrevised basis for such work is often preserved in Antiochene sources, not uncommonly labeled Lucianic; this tends to be another misnomer (see 5, Septuagint). Certain parts of the Greek Bible now preserved integrally with the so-called Septuagint in our MSS and printed texts that are in the Palestinian recension of so-called Theodotion are, very probably, the translations of Lamentations; Canticles; Ruth; 2 Sm 11.2 to 3 Kgs 2.11; 3 Kgs 22.1 to 4 Kgs 25.30; Judges in the B recension (more exactly the minuscules *i, r, u, a₂*); the so-called Theodotion text of Daniel, and the additions to the short Greek texts of Job and Jeremia. To these must be added the Quinta version of the Psalms, and most of the material cited for the so-called Theodotion column of Origen's Hexapla (but not 2 Sm 11.2 to 3 Kgs 2.11 or the Minor Prophets). Some texts of this kind, notably from Daniel, are already cited in the NT and by Clement of Rome in the 1st Christian century. Clarification of these problems is progressing; the converging evidence of a "Theodotionic" recension of the Minor Prophets known to St. Justin Martyr in the mid-2d century A.D. and recovered in 1952 from a cave in the Wâdī Khabra in the Judean Desert, plus the Hebrew texts from Khirbet Qumran (*see* DEAD SEA SCROLLS) have led D. Barthélemy to important advances, largely repeated here. Barthélemy identifies Theodotion with the Jonathan ben Uzziel to whom Jewish tradition (wrongly) attributes certain Aramaic targums (see 11, Targums); he dates the work *c.* A.D. 30–50. This dating is none too early,

but it could easily be too late for some of the recensional activity here described.

Bibliography: D. BARTHÉLEMY, *Les Devanciers d'Aquila* (Vet Test Suppl. 10; 1963). H. B. SWETE, *Introduction to the O.T. in Greek* (2d ed. Cambridge, Eng. 1914) 42–49.

[P. W. SKEHAN]

9. HEXAPLA

The body of manuscript evidence compiled by *Origen at *Caesarea in Palestine before A.D. 245 for comparison of the existing Greek versions of the OT with the Hebrew text current in his day. The name ($\tau\grave{\alpha}$ $\acute{\epsilon}\xi\alpha\pi\lambda\hat{\alpha}$, i.e., $\beta\iota\beta\lambda\acute{\iota}\alpha$, the sixfold books) derives from the arrangement given to the pages of this work by Origen. For most of the OT books, he presented in six parallel vertical columns (1) the Hebrew consonantal text in Hebrew letters; (2) a spelling out of the Hebrew as actually pronounced, insofar as that could be represented with the Greek alphabet; (3) the rendering of Aquila; (4) the rendering of Symmachus; (5) the ancient Septuagint (LXX) rendering, modified in the light of the Hebrew and the Greek of the other columns, with critical symbols (see below) to call attention to ways in which the older Greek form and the Hebrew failed to agree; and (6) the early revision of the LXX ascribed to Theodotion. (See parts 5, Septuagint; 6, Aquila; 7, Symmachus; and 8, Theodotion of this article.) For some books, Origen had available added translations or recensions, so that in the Psalms, for instance, mention is made of a *Quinta* (fifth), a *Sexta* (sixth), and even a *Septima* (seventh) Greek rendering by unknown hands; the number of columns would correspondingly increase from six to at least eight. (The *Septima*, however, may never have been more than marginal notes.) The Hexapla was thus a complex and bulky work; it remained available for consultation at Caesarea till about A.D. 600 and was used by St. Jerome among others. Copies of it were mainly by way of extracts. Origen himself is said to have prepared an abridged edition (*Tetrapla*, fourfold) omitting the two Hebrew columns. The final fate of the complete work is unknown; today it survives to us only in fragments from the Books of Kingdoms (Samuel and Kings) and the Psalms, along with excerpts in the margins of Greek LXX MSS, citations in the patristic literature in several languages, and extensive portions of the fifth column especially in Syriac and Arabic translations. The recompiling and critical evaluation of these materials is one of the continuing tasks of students of the LXX; attribution of a particular reading to one or another of the original columns is often either lacking or incorrectly given in the sources.

The Hebrew in Origen's first column was, like all other Hebrew OT texts from the early 2d Christian century onward, extremely close to the consonantal text as printed in the Hebrew Bibles of today. The second column transliteration is sufficiently consistent in its orthography (see G. Mercati, "Il problema . . .") so that one must suppose that in this form it was contemporary with Origen. It has been shrewdly conjectured, however, (T. W. Manson, cited by Kahle), that this kind of transcription is at least the heir to a Jewish practice of providing a reader's guide in Greek letters to the liturgical sections to be proclaimed from Hebrew scrolls in the synagogues of the *Diaspora. That the LXX translation was originally made from transliterations of this sort rather than from a Hebrew consonantal text is a quite fanciful theory; the true interest of the second column for modern scholars is its pre-Masoretic evidence for the historical pronunciation of Biblical Hebrew. In editing the fifth or LXX column, Origen inserted, marked with an asterisk (✱), usually from "Theodotion," the Greek equivalent of those passages in the Hebrew text not to be found in the older translation. Passages in the LXX for which the Hebrew showed no equivalent were retained, but signaled at the beginning with an obelus (÷). The limits of either type of variant text were marked at the end by a metobelus (✔). There is some question whether this apparatus was employed in the Hexapla itself (the Mercati Psalm fragments do not show it), or whether it was used in a resultant text drawn from the fifth column for separate circulation.

That the Hebrew text of his own day should have served as Origen's exclusive norm leaves something to be desired from the point of view of modern textual criticism; but the invaluable collection of materials is none the less precious on that account. It is simply not true, however, that this was the first critical work done on the OT in Greek; rather Origen was the heir of a continuing process of revision carried on in Jewish circles in Palestine both in Hebrew and in Greek during the 1st century B.C. and the 1st and early 2d Christian centuries. Sometimes the basis for the fifth column was not an unrevised LXX, but the product of "Theodotion," or even, for Ecclesiastes, of Aquila. Nor was the arrangement of the columns invariable throughout the OT; in the case of Ecclesiastes, when the "LXX" column was occupied by Aquila's work, the third column apparently contained Symmachus, and this has led to faulty attributions by later writers. In the Psalms, the *Quinta* seems to have occupied the customary place of "Theodotion." From 2 Sm 11.2 to 3 Kgs 2.11, "Theodotion" stands in the fifth column and a "Lucianic" text in the sixth. Abridged transcriptions of the Hexapla after the time of Origen have led to further inconsistencies in the evidence for the content of the various columns.

Bibliography: F. FIELD, *Origenis Hexaplorum quae supersunt*, 2 v. (Oxford 1875). G. MERCATI, *Psalterii hexapli reliquiae* (Vatican City 1958–) v.1; "Il problema della seconda colonna dell' Esaplo," *Biblica* 28 (1947) 1–30, 173–215. D. BARTHÉLEMY, *Les Devanciers d'Aquila* (VetTest Suppl.10; 1963). P. KAHLE, "Die von Origenes verwendeten griechischen Bibelhandschriften," *Studia patristica* 4 (TU 79; 1961) 107–117. H. B. SWETE, *An Introduction to the O.T. in Greek* (rev. ed. Cambridge, Eng. 1914) 59–86.

[P. W. SKEHAN]

10. ARAMAIC VERSIONS

From about the middle of the 1st millennium B.C. to the time of the Moslem conquest (7th Christian century) the *Aramaic language was widely spoken throughout the Near East. It was the common language both of the postexilic Jews and of the Christians who lived in that part of the world. For the sake of these people the Bible was translated from the original languages into Aramaic. The Aramaic versions of the Jews are known as the Targums, from a post-Biblical Hebrew word meaning translation. The Aramaic versions of the Christians are called the Syriac versions because the more important of them are written in a northern dialect of Aramaic that, on account of the large amount of Christian literature written in it, ranks as a distinct language known as Syriac (*see* SYRIAC LANGUAGE AND LIT-

ERATURE). The Targums and the Syriac versions, respectively, are discussed in the next two sections of this article.

Bibliography: V. HAMP and A. VÖÖBUS, LexThK² 2:384–392. P. NOBER, EncCatt 11:741–745. A. PENNA, *ibid.* 11:1761–62. B. J. ROBERTS, RGG³ 1:1197–1201. EncDictBibl 2393–94; 2530–32.

[L. F. HARTMAN]

11. TARGUMS

Jewish Aramaic versions of the OT. After explaining the origin and character of the Targums and their place in ancient *Jewish liturgy, this article will treat of the various Targums to the three main sections of the Hebrew Bible—the Pentateuch, the Prophets, and the Writings. (A Targum is regarded as "related to" the book or books of the Bible of which it is a translation; hence the technical term, a Targum "to" the Pentateuch, etc.)

Origin and Character. The term "Targum" (plural, Targums or Targumim) comes from the Aramaic and post-Biblical Hebrew word *targûm,* meaning translation; in a limited sense used here it denotes specifically an Aramaic translation made by Jews of a book or books of the Hebrew OT. At some uncertain date after the Exile, but well before the Christian era, the majority of the Jews no longer understood Hebrew, since their vernacular in Babylonia and Palestine had become Aramaic. Because of the desire of having the people understand the doctrinal message of the Bible, particularly of the Pentateuch (Torah, Law), the custom was introduced of having the portions of the Law and the Prophets that were read in Hebrew in the *synagogues rendered into Aramaic in Aramaic-speaking communities. While the Jewish tradition (*Meg.* 3a) that traces the origin of Targums to the time of Ezra (based on Neh 8.8) is scarcely creditable, written Targums to some books (e.g., the Targum to Job; see below), as well as oral translations of the Hebrew pericopes from the Law and the Prophets that were read in the synagogues, must have existed in NT times. Very probably there was also a Targum to the Psalms (cf. Mt 27.46; Mk 15.34).

Although the extant Targums differ greatly among themselves in language, nature, and date of composition, they have certain common characteristics; thus, the anthropomorphisms and anthropopathisms of the Masoretic Text (MT) are generally avoided: God is said to act *ad extra* through his *memrā'* (word), a term used in this way only in Targumic literature; He guides Israel through [the *Shekinah (Presence) of] His Glory; Israel sees not the Lord Himself but His Glory (*Tos. Meg.* 4.41; *Kidd.* 49a; cf. Jn 12.41; 1.14; etc.).

The Targums and the Synagogue Liturgy. In the Synagogue service before the time of Christ certain passages from the Pentateuch (Acts 15.21; 14.15) and the Prophets (Lk 4.16–21; Acts 13.14–15, 27) were read and, at least in Palestine, rendered into Aramaic [for details see G. F. Moore, *Judaism in the First Centuries of the Christian Era* (Cambridge, Mass. 1927–32) 1: 296–307]. The rendering had to be given extempore, without the aid of written translations. Certain passages (e.g., Gn 35.22; Ex 32.21–24; Nm 6.24–26) were read but not translated. Some current Aramaic translations (e.g., of Lv 18.21; 22.28) were censured by the rabbis. It is probable that in early, even NT, times the OT was not read consecutively from service to service. The liturgical Targum may then have arisen only gradually, over a lengthy period. The Targum used for the common people would tend to be paraphrastic rather than literal, as is the case of the extant Palestinian Targum to the Pentateuch.

Targums to the Pentateuch. There are several Targums to the Pentateuch, the most important being the Babylonian, the Palestinian, and the Samaritan Targums.

Babylonian Targum. This is the official Jewish Targum to the Books of Moses. It is customarily called the Onkelos Targum, although it is really an anonymous composition. The name of Onkelos, to whom it is ascribed in *bMeg.* 3a, is now generally considered to be merely a dialectic form of Ἀκύλας, i.e., Aquila, who is mentioned in the parallel passage of *jMeg.* 71c. Some scholars believe that Aquila's Greek version of the Hebrew OT was meant in both passages. (See part 6 of this article.) Onkelos is generally a literal translation that gives the correct halakic (*see* HALAKAH) understanding of nearly all the pertinent passages of the Pentateuch (not, however, of Lv 24.20). It is written in an Aramaic that imitates the Aramaic of the Bible. Although it was edited in Babylonia, probably between the 2d and the 5th centuries, to bring it into conformity with the Biblical text, the Mishnah, and the Babylonian Talmud, Onkelos apparently originated in Palestine around the 1st Christian century. A comparison of certain passages of Onkelos with those of the Palestinian Targum indicates a relation between them (see W. Bacher, 60). Onkelos may actually be an early form of the Palestinian Targum later revised in Babylonia. Before its introduction from Babylonia c. A.D. 800, Onkelos was unknown to Palestinian Judaism, but it later replaced the older Palestinian Targum in Western Jewry. It was first printed at Bologna in 1482 and often later, e.g., at Sabbioneta in 1557, and by A. Berliner with an excellent introduction (Leipzig 1882–84). A. Sperber published a new edition based on Yemenite MSS [*The Bible in Aramaic I* (Leiden 1959)]. In the West Onkelos was pointed with Tiberian (Western) vowels; the Yemenite MSS have a mixture of Eastern and Western vowel points. A. Díez Macho is to publish Onkelos from MSS with Eastern vowel points for the Madrid *Polyglot Bible [see VetTest 8 (1958) 113–133]. A Latin version of Onkelos is given in B. Walton's Polyglot Bible. An English translation (not always faithful) was published by J. W. Etheridge [*The Targums* . . . (2 v., London 1862–65)].

The Palestinian Targum. This is a paraphrastic translation of the Pentateuch that was current in Palestine and among Jews of Palestinian origin before it was replaced by the Onkelos Targum. Unlike Onkelos, the Palestinian Targum was never issued in an official edition, so that it is now known in several different forms. It has been preserved in the Codex Neofiti 1, in portions of Pseudo-Jonathan, in fragments from the Cairo Geniza, in the so-called Fragment Targum, in glosses (Tosefta) on Targum MSS, and in rabbinic citations from the 2d to the 16th century.

The Codex Neofiti 1 of the Vatican Library, written at the beginning of the 15th century, was identified as a MS of the Palestinian Targum by A. Díez Macho between 1949 and 1956 [see VetTest 7 (1959) 222–245; *Christian News from Israel* (July 1962) 19–25]. It is a translation of the entire Pentateuch into good and relatively old Palestinian Aramaic. While the geographical data [see VetTest 7 (1959) 229] may point to the 2d

Christian century as the date of composition, Codex Neofiti 1 itself appears to bear traces of later recension and to be in its present form a copy of a text that was made no earlier than the 5th century. The following passages show how the Mishnah with its Talmudic halakah compares with its Targumic renderings: cf. *Meg.* 4.9 with Lv 18.21; *Meg.* 4.10 with Gn 35.22; Exodus ch. 32; Nm 6.24–26; *jMeg.* 4.9.75c (*c.* A.D. 350) with Lv 22.28. Its translation of Gn 6.2, 4 reproduces verbally the exegesis of R. Simeon ben Yohai (*c.* A.D. 150); cf. *Genesis Rabba* on Gn 6.2, 4.

In the 14th century mention was made of a translation (*targûm*) of the Torah of which the author ·was said to be a certain Jonathan (ben Uzziel), a title due probably to a wrong solution of the abbreviation TJ as Targum of Jonathan instead of Targum of Jerusalem; hence the modern name of Pseudo-Jonathan. It is a translation that essentially represents the Palestinian Targum, but its text has been made to conform in many passages to that of Onkelos. It has some late references [e.g., in Gn 21.21 (7th century); Ex 26.9; Nm 24.24] and many paraphrases found in no other text of the Palestinian Targum. It has at least 12 antihalakic passages that are similar to the halakah of *Philo Judaeus and the Karaites (see KARAISM). In many passages of halakah [see A. Marmorstein, ZATWiss 49 (1931) 234–235] and midrashic paraphrase, Pseudo-Jonathan is very old and probably pre-Christian. Some scholars, e.g., P. E. Kahle [*Cairo Geniza* (2d ed. Oxford 1959) 203–204], would date its translation of Dt 33.11 to *c.* 130 B.C. The origin of Pseudo-Jonathan's composite text and the earlier history of its transmission are important, but unsolved, problems. It was published first at Venice in 1591; it was later uncritically edited from a MS of the British Museum by M. Ginsburger [*Pseudo-Jonathan* . . . (Berlin 1903)]; a new edition of the same MS is being prepared for the Madrid Polyglot.

The fragments of the Palestinian Targum from the Cairo *Geniza were published mainly by Kahle [*Masoreten des Westens* (Stuttgart 1930) 2:1–62; for other fragments see *Christian News* . . . 64], who dates the earliest MSS to the 7th and 8th centuries; J. L. Teicher, however, claims none is earlier than the mid-9th century [VetTest 1 (1951) 125–129; see also A. Díez Macho, VetTest 8 (1958) 116].

The so-called Fragment Targum, of which four MSS are known, translates only certain portions of the Pentateuch and is probably a collection of glosses on the Palestinian Targum taken from MSS of Onkelos. It was published first at Venice in 1517; and later, in the Walton Polyglot (1654–57). A somewhat different type of text was published by M. Ginsburger [*Das Fragmententhargum* (Berlin 1899)] on the basis of Paris MS 110.

The Samaritan Targum. This is a literal translation of the Samaritan Pentateuch into the Aramaic dialect of the *Samaritans. (See part 2 of this article.) Like the Palestinian Targum, its texts vary greatly among themselves. It was published first in the Paris Polyglot (1645), then in corrected form in the Walton Polyglot. It was edited by A. Brüll (1875) and from various MSS by H. Petermann and C. Vollers (1872–91). A new edition from recently discovered MSS [on which see Est Bibl 18 (1959) 183–197] is in preparation. The *Peshitta of the Pentateuch is in some yet undetermined way related to the Palestinian Targum, on which it may be based to a certain extent.

Knowledge of the Palestinian Targum can be useful in NT exegesis. Despite some later editing, the extant texts of the Palestinian Targum appear to represent, in great part, the liturgical Targum of the NT period. It can have a bearing on NT exegesis because: (1) its Aramaic language is very close to that spoken in Palestine in Christ's day; (2) its free paraphrase represents many theological concepts then current among the ordinary Jews; (3) since it was connected with the synagogue, it would have been familiar to more people than would other Jewish writings of the period. Its value for NT exegesis is now becoming ever more appreciated; for a full list of examples and a view of earlier work, see A. Díez Macho, "Targum y Nuevo Testamento," *Mélange E. Tisserant,* v.1 (*Studi e Testi* 231; Vatican City 1964); M. McNamara, *The Palestinian Targum to the Pentateuch and the N.T.* (Rome 1966). Among the various forms of this Targum, that of Pseudo-Jonathan shows the closest relationship with the NT, particularly with the Apocalypse. For textual criticism all the Targums must be used with great caution (Eissfeldt, 945; Roberts, 211).

Targum to the Prophets. The Targum to the Former and the Latter Prophets (*see* PROPHETIC BOOKS OF THE OLD TESTAMENT) is written in Aramaic similar to that of Onkelos but with more extensive haggadah. It was edited in its present form in Babylonia, some time later than Onkelos, which it quotes; but it is of Palestinian origin and may contain some early, even pre-Christian paraphrase; cf. its Is 65.5 with Ap 20.14. The author of the Targum is unknown; the Jonathan (ben Uzziel) to whom it is ascribed in *Meg.* 3a is now taken to be a mere Hebraization of the name of Theodotion who translated the Bible into Greek; cf. the equation of Onkelos and Aquila above. (See part 8 of this article.) Some scholars believe that Theodotion's Greek translation is intended in *Meg.* 3a. In the Babylonian Talmud the Targum to Prophets is associated with the name of R. Jose of Pumbeditha (d. A.D. 333), although he is not its author. It was first printed in the *Rabbinical Bible of 1517, and often later, e.g., by P. de Lagarde, *Prophetae Chaldaice* (Leipzig 1872), and A. Sperber, *The Bible in Aramaic,* v.2–3 (Leiden 1959–62). A new edition based on "Eastern" MSS will be published in the Madrid Polyglot. A Latin translation of it is given in the Walton Polyglot. Of a Palestinian Targum to the Prophets, which probably once existed, little is known.

Targums to the Writings. All these are written in Palestinian Aramaic and vary from one another in style and age. A written Targum to Job existed in the 1st Christian century (*Shabb.* 115a) and may be identical with that used at Qumran, extensive fragments of which (from *c.* 100 B.C.) have been found [see J. van der Ploeg, *Le Targum de Job de la grotte 11 de Qumran . . .* (Amsterdam 1962)]. The Qumran fragments differ from the traditionally known Targum to Job, which, with the Targum to the Psalms, forms a class apart, both in language and in the nature of its paraphrase. The Targum to the Psalms often agrees with Septuagint (LXX) against the MT, and at times it has conflated readings from both the LXX and the MT. It is probably an old work with later additions. From the paraphrase to Ps 107(108).12 some (e.g., Bacher) date it before A.D. 476, but its language seems to be more recent (S. Bialoblocki). The Targum to Chronicles is similar in language to the Targum to Psalms and Job. Although

it received its present form in the 8th or 9th century, it probably originated in the 4th century. The Targum to Proverbs, an extremely literal translation, is closely related to the Peshitta of the same book. Both were probably made from an old Jewish Syriac translation. The Targums to the Five *Scrolls (i.e., Canticles, Ruth, Lamentations, Ecclesiastes, and Esther) are, with the exception of the first Targum to Esther, very paraphrastic and recent compositions (from the 8th and 9th centuries) and possibly contain occasional older traditions (cf. the Targum to Lam 2.20 with Mt 23.35). A Targum to Esther existed as early as Tannaitic times (*Meg.* 2.1). There are three Targums to this book. The first is a literal translation; the second (*targûm šēnî*) and the third are similar to each other, and are both paraphrastic. There is no known Targum to Daniel or to Ezra and Nehemia. The Targum to the Writings (except to Chronicles) was first printed in 1517, and often later, e.g., by P. de Lagarde, *Hagiographa Chaldaice* (Leipzig 1873). The Targum to Chronicles was first published by M. F. Beck (Augsburg 1680–83), and later from more complete MSS by D. Wilkins (Amsterdam 1715).

Bibliography: E. MANGENOT, DB 5.2:1995–2008. V. HAMP, LexThK² 2:384–386. A. PENNA, EncCatt 11:1761–62. EncDict Bibl 2393–94. T. WALKER, Hastings DB 4:678–683. S. BIALOBLOCKI, EncJudaica 4:570–581. W. BACHER, JewishEnc 12:57–63. F. SCHÜHLEIN, CE 14:454–457. B. J. ROBERTS, *The Old Testament Text and Versions* (Cardiff 1951) 197–213. O. EISSFELDT, *Einleitung in das AT* (3d ed. Tübingen 1964) 944–947. P. E. KAHLE, *The Cairo Geniza* (2d ed. New York 1960) 191–208. P. CHURGIN, *Targum Jonathan to the Prophets* (Yale Oriental Series, Researches 14; New Haven 1907). R. H. MELAMED, "The Targum to Canticles according to Six Yemen MSS . . .," Jewish QuartRev 10 (1919–20) 377–410; 11 (1920–21) 1–20; 12 (1921–23) 57–117; repr. Philadelphia 1921.

[M. McNAMARA]

12. SYRIAC VERSIONS

The history of Bible versions in Syriac is best treated by considering the OT and the NT separately. In each case, however, the developments are roughly parallel: an archaic version, or "Old Syriac" form, now preserved only in part; the standard "Peshitta" version comparable to the Latin Vulgate; two increasingly labored and somewhat artificial versions based on the Greek (even for the OT); and a Western, "Palestinian Syriac" form in a dialect of Aramaic divergent from the Eastern Aramaic (standard literary Syriac) of the other versions.

Old Testament. Jewish influence in the region of Adiabene, east of the Tigris, was quite pronounced in the 1st century A.D., and there were other notable Jewish centers in Mesopotamia. It may be presumed that the first endeavors, oral or written, at putting Biblical texts into an Eastern Aramaic form originated in these circles.

Old Syriac OT. That the Peshitta contains a stratum of Targumic tradition was noticed long ago. More systematic analysis by A. Baumstark and C. Peters made the extent of this underlying material tangible. Manuscript research in the patristic and liturgical materials (A. Vööbus, *Peschitta*) has opened new avenues, as have the Qumran documents (*Genesis Apocryphon*) and the Palestinian Targum recension in the Vatican MS *Cod. Neofiti 1.* It can now be seen that not only in the Pentateuch, but also in the Prophets and Psalms, an archaic pre-Peshitta form stems from the ancient

Palestinian Targumic traditions. The character of this text, if it was Christian at all, points to Jewish Christian origin.

Peshitta OT. The text of the Peshitta OT has in part been preserved and transmitted with remarkable fidelity. Some codices are very ancient; MS Br. Mus. Add. 14,-425 containing Genesis, Exodus, Numbers, and Deuteronomy is of the year 464, and there are other MSS not much younger. Yet the literary and historical problems of this version are extremely intricate. Its date and the identity of the translators are unknown. In its various parts the Peshitta reveals divergent characteristics: some sections are more literal (e.g., the Pentateuch and Job); others show more freedom (e.g., Psalms); still others (e.g., Chronicles and Ruth) are quite paraphrastic. Disparate elements appear even in the fabric of the same books. All these are marks of a very complicated history. It is obvious that different parts of the Peshitta go back to different bases, and their origins must belong to different periods. The influence of the Septuagint on the later transmission of its text is also obvious. As to whether the Peshitta is of Jewish or Christian provenance, opinions are divided. The negligence in rendering Levitical laws seems to point to Christian origin.

Philoxenian Version of OT. References to readings in Isaia found in a Syro-Hexaplar MS testify that Philoxenus's activity (see New Testament, below) covered also the OT. The fragment of Isaia in MS Br. Mus. Add. 17,106 most probably belongs to this version. The same type of text appears in the quotations of Isaia in the Syriac translation of Cyril's *Glaphyra* prepared by Moses of Aghel not long after Philoxenus. The base used for this version was not the Peshitta but a more archaic form of the text, and the Greek text used for its revision was not the Alexandrian Septuagint but the Lucianic text.

Syro-Hexaplar Version. A second volume of this translation has been preserved in MS Ambr. C 313 of the 9th century, containing Job, the Wisdom literature, the Prophets, etc. Of the lost first volume we possess only a number of individual books, mostly with gaps; and of other books, only fragments. A secondary Arabic version of it, made from a 7th-century codex, preserves only the Pentateuch, Job, and Wisdom. The Syro-Hexaplar version was prepared by order of Athanasius I, Patriarch of Antioch; according to *Bar-Hebraeus, its author was Paul, Bishop of Tella. A colophon in MS Par. syr. 27 testifies that Paul was the translator of Kings, which he finished in February 616. Nevertheless, there are reasons to reckon with a team of coworkers. According to a note appended to the text, the work of translation was completed between 615 and 617 in a monastery at the ninth milestone near Alexandria. The importance of this version is very great. It is based on the fifth column of the *Hexapla* of Origen. Since the translation was produced with meticulous accuracy in reflecting the least details of the Greek, it is very valuable as a witness to the text of the Hexapla that is otherwise lost except for fragments. Besides this, the translation is furnished with the asterisks and obeli of *Origen, which help to establish the provenience of the Greek materials and their place in the broader history of the Septuagint. Also the marginal notes preserve for us readings of Aquila, Theodotion, and Symmachus. Among the Syrians themselves, this version was em-

ployed even by such East-Syrian writers as *Īshō'dād of Merv, and it found its way also into the liturgical domain.

Revision by James of Edessa. During the last years of his life, James (Ja'qob) of Edessa (d. 708), one of the greatest Syriac scholars, produced in the monastery of Telada a new recension of the OT with an elaborate apparatus. According to the MS evidence in MS Par. syr. 26, 1 Samuel and Daniel were completed in the year 705. Other parts originated before and after this date. The version has survived only in part, namely, the Pentateuch in MS Par. syr. 26; 1 and 2 Samuel and the beginning of Kings, in MS Br. Mus. 14,429, copied in 719; Daniel in MS Par. syr. 27 and Ezechiel in MS Vat. syr. 5, all with some gaps. There are also fragments and citations of other parts. James's version is a revision of the Peshitta and the Syro-Hexaplar, remolding the latter according to more normal Syriac idiom. It provides also the first systematic work in the Syriac Masora, furnished with marginal glosses regarding the pronunciation and variants. And it introduces chapter divisions and summaries of their content.

The Palestinian Syriac Version of OT. This has survived mainly in lectionaries, the most important being one with the text of the Pentateuch, Job, and Proverbs. The best represented book is the Psalter with 42 Psalms complete, in addition to fragments. There is no reason to doubt that the lectionary texts rest on a more ample Syro-Palestinian Bible. The dialect differs slightly from Syriac and belongs rather to Western "Palestinian" Aramaic; its script is also distinctive, a rigid and archaic form of the early "Estrangelo" script. There have been Targumic influences in its text. The origin of the version is obscure. Manuscript evidence in palimpsests leads to the 9th century, and there is external evidence in Ibn Isḥāq that the version existed about the year 700. A hint in St. Jerome's reference to the burial of St. Paula (d. 404) in Bethlehem, *Graeco Latino Syroque sermone psalmos in ordine personabant* (*Ep.* 108. 29), may be the earliest echo of the existence of this version. As to whether its home was Antioch (F. C. Burkitt), Egypt (T. Marshall), or Palestine (M. J. Lagrange), the discovery of a Palestinian inscription of the 6th or 7th century (Milik) and of a letter argue for the last supposition.

New Testament. The question of the earliest form of NT text in Syriac, its date and its relationship to the standard Peshitta, is a question primarily of the relationship between Tatian's *Diatessaron and the oldest separate texts of the Four Gospels.

Old Syriac Gospels. Evidence for an early Syriac form of the Four Gospels was provided by the MS Br. Mus. Add. 14,451, from the Syrian Monastery of Mary, Mother of God, in Egypt; its text was published in 1842 by W. Cureton (Syr-Cur). A distinct, though related, recension was discovered 50 years later by Mrs. A. S. Lewis and Mrs. M. D. Gibson in MS Sin. syr. 30, a palimpsest in the monastery of St. Catherine at Sinai (Syr-Sin). Both MSS are from the first part of the 5th century. Burkitt alleged that this text type was a library copy that had no part in the history of the Gospel text in Syriac; but systematic research has disclosed completely new vistas for its role. Materials have emerged in the patristic sources (Vööbus, *History*), and scrutiny of the entire Gospel MS tradition and the liturgical codices has given access to further evidence (Vööbus,

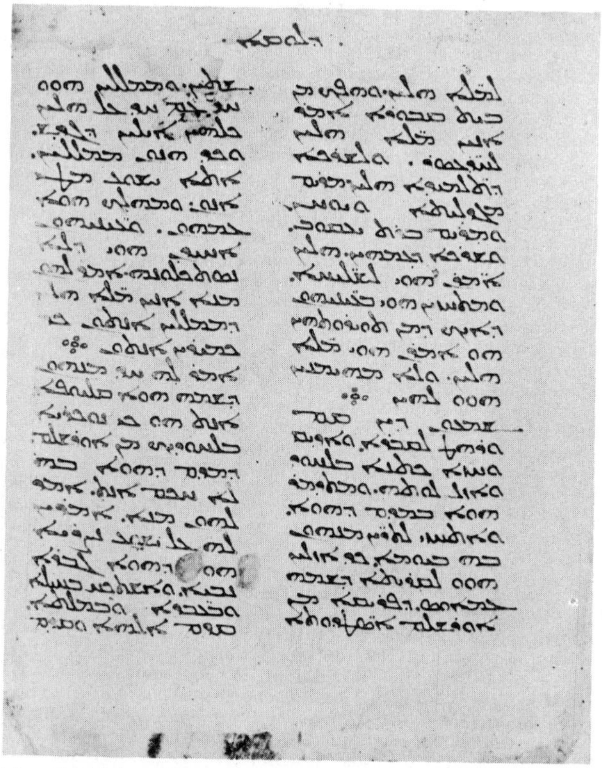

Fig. 6. Codex Syrus-Curetorianus (Add. MS 14451, fol. 85 v.), a Syriac MS of the first half of the 5th century. The page reproduced shows Luke 23.41–52.

New Materials). The Syriac name of the version, *Euangelion da-Mepharrešē*, "the Gospel of the Separated Ones," (i.e., fourfold Gospel), indicates that this text-type rests on the harmonistic work of Tatian's Diatessaron. That this is the relation and not vice versa, is definitively settled by the newly discovered sources. The text in this version belongs in general to the "Western" text and is marked by linguistic features of archaic provenance. Although the origin of the version is shrouded in darkness, some facts (Vööbus, *Neue Angaben*) justify the assumption that it probably belongs to the 3d century. New textual materials reveal its very important role in the history of the Gospel text, even centuries after the Peshitta text was prepared. It did not escape revision at later times and came to be circulated in hybrid forms. Its historical significance is enhanced by the fact that this Old Syriac version became the basis for a number of other Oriental versions of the Gospels.

Peshitta NT. The transmission of the standard version, the *Peshitta, is excellent. Manuscripts reach back to the 5th century, the earliest being MS Par. syr 296 with Luke, written probably in 463–464. Several other codices belong to the same century, a considerable number to the 6th century, and there are many later MSS. The Gospels in this version rest on the Old Syriac, revised according to a Greek text of Byzantine type. But revision has not erased all the contours of the archaic prototype. Linguistically the Peshitta is smooth and flexible, faithful to the genius of Syriac. Syntactic constructions of the older language have been retained, but room is made for the later development of the idiom. The generally accepted axiom that *Rabbula, Bishop

of Edessa (411–435), is its author is refuted by the discovery of remnants of the text that Rabbula himself employed near the end of his life (Vööbus, *Investigations*). A detailed analysis of the text shows that the revision is uneven. For instance, in Acts, the Peshitta retains a larger proportion of "Western" readings. Nor is its vocabulary consistent. These are instructive signs, pointing to a gradual building up of the version by the work of many hands. The centers of Greco-Syriac exegetical studies (Edessa, Nisibis) would be the most likely places for the creation of this revision. The Syrians themselves have no firm tradition as to who produced it. Its origins can be placed in the last decades of the 4th century, and early remnants of its text are discernible in a codex written in 411 in Edessa (Vööbus, *Oldest Traces*). Its limited NT canon is an evidence of antiquity. It took centuries before the Peshitta gained the unchallenged supremacy that is now accorded it by all Syrian Christians.

Philoxenian Revision. This was carried out under the auspices of *Philoxenus, or Aksenāiā, Bishop of Mabbugh, in 507–508. Moshe of Aghel, who was almost his contemporary, testifies that the man who did the work was the Chorepiscopus Polycarp. What Polycarp actually produced, and how his work related to the later text known as the Harklean (see below), has been debated for the last 2 centuries. The question can be solved with the help of newly discovered materials (Vööbus, *New Data*). Remnants of the undertaking appear in MS Br. Mus. Add 14,534, in the commentary of Philoxenus, who used the recently prepared version for this purpose. As these excerpts clearly show, the purpose was to achieve a greater conformity between the Peshitta and the Greek original. No Philoxenian MS of the Gospels, Acts, or those Epistles contained in the Peshitta canon, has survived. It has been assumed that extant texts of the minor Catholic Epistles, 2 Peter, 2 and 3 John, and Jude, and that of the Apocalypse, originally not included in the Peshitta, actually stem from this version. Printed editions of the Peshitta NT frequently contain these books.

Harklean Version. The colophon that the author, Thomas of Harkel, Bishop of Mabbugh, added to his MS furnishes information about the genesis of this text. It is a revision carried out by Thomas and his coworkers in 616 at the Enaton, a monastic community 9 miles distant from Alexandria. The MS tradition of the version is rich. The earliest codex, MS Vat. syr. 268, once regarded as the autograph, probably belongs to the 7th century. Some MSS belong to the 7th or 8th century, others are of later date. The colophon further states that the text of Philoxenus was revised on the basis of two (some MSS read "three") Greek MSS, representing the Byzantine text type. The result was a scholarly version in which many words and phrases are equipped with obelus, asterisk, and metobelus in the text, and the margin is reserved for a great number of variant readings and notes. This critical apparatus, which does not appear in all the codices, begins with the most ancient MS and is of special value. Particularly in Acts, the apparatus is one of the most important witnesses to the "Western" form of the text, second in importance only to that of the Codex Bezae itself. With this revision the process of Hellenization reaches its climax. Syriac idiom is sacrificed to extreme literalness and a slavish adaptation to the Greek. Surprisingly, the Harklean MSS are furnished with liturgical rubrics, and there are also lectionaries evidencing liturgical usage of this labored text among the Western Syrians. In consequence of its intrusion into the exclusive area of liturgy and rite, the Harklean text underwent alterations based on the influence of the previous and better-known versions. This is clear from the text of the MSS; and the information provided by MS Chester Beatty syr. 3 may be added. A colophon to this MS states that about 2 centuries after Thomas of Harkel the copies in circulation had undergone modifications. Furthermore, we learn that the need was felt to restore the text to its original purity and that this particular codex was the product of such a revision according to a good codex.

Palestinian Syriac. This version of the NT has survived only in lectionaries, containing the lessons from the Gospels, Acts, and the Pauline corpus and in smaller fragments. The most ancient lectionary preserved is MS Vat. syr. 29, written in 1029. Its dialect is Western Aramaic, as is also the case in the Palestinian Syriac version of the OT. Of the several Syriac NT versions, this one is closest to the standard Byzantine text. Yet it does not go all the way with this text but shows a polymorphic character, having affinities also with the text of Origen, and reaching back into the Old Syriac version. The question of its time and place of origin is still open, as it is also for the OT text that parallels it.

Bibliography: Old Syriac O.T. A. Baumstark, ZDeutschMgl Gesell NS 14 (1935) 89–118. C. Peters, *Muséon* 46 (1933) 1–54; 52 (1939) 275–296. A. Vööbus, *ibid.* 68 (1955) 215–218; *Peschitta und Targumim des Pentateuchs* (Stockholm 1958). Peshitta O.T. Editions. S. Lee, *Vetus Testamentum syriace* (London 1823–26); ed. American Protestant Missionary Society (Urmia 1852); ed. Dominicans (Mosul 1887–91), fac. repr. (Beirut 1951). There is as yet no critical ed.; a project for one is centered in Leiden. Studies. A. Rahlfs, ZATWiss 9 (1889) 161–210. L. Haefeli, *Die Peschitta des A.T.* (Münster 1927). J. van der Ploeg, "Recente Pešiṭta-studies (sinds 1927)," *Jaarbericht Ex Oriente Lux* 10 (1948) 392–399. B. J. Roberts, *The Old Testament Text and Versions* (Cardiff 1951) 214–227. A. Vogel, *Biblica* 32 (1951) 32–56, 198–231, 336–363, 481–502. A. Vööbus, *Peschitta und Targumim, op. cit.* 37–112. M. H. Gottstein, *Text and Language in Bible and Qumran* (Jerusalem 1960) 65–85, 163–204. Philoxenian Version of O.T. Editions. A. M. Ceriani, ed., *Monumenta sacra et profana*, 5 v. (Milan 1866–74) 5. 1:1–40, only v.1, 2, 3, 5, 7 pub. Studies. A. Baumstark, *Geschichte der syrischen Literatur* (Bonn 1922) 144–145. L. Delekat, ZATWiss 69 (1957) 21–54. PatrSyrO 150–151. Syro-Hexaplar Version. Editions. A. M. Ceriani, *op. cit.* v.7. P. de Lagarde, *Veteris Testamenti ab Origine recensiti fragmenta* (Göttingen 1880); *Bibliothecae Syriacae* (Göttingen 1892). Studies. A. Baumstark, *Geschichte, op. cit.* 186–188. J. M. Vosté, *Biblica* 26 (1945) 12–36. C. T. Fritsch, JBiblLit 72 (1953) 169–181. M. H. Gottstein, *Muséon* 67 (1954) 291–296; *Biblica* 37 (1956) 162–183. Revision by James of Edessa. Editions. G. Bugati, ed., *Daniel secundum editionem LXX. interpretum* (Milan 1788). A. M. Ceriani, *op. cit.* v.2. M. Ugolini, OrChr 12 (1902) 409–420. Studies. A. Baumstark, *Geschichte, op. cit.* 248–256. PatrSyrO 166–171. Palestinian Syriac Version of O.T. Editions. J. P. N. Land, *Anecdota syriaca*, 4 v. (Leiden 1862–75) 4:103–224. A. S. Lewis, *A Palestinian Syriac Lectionary* (London 1897), *Suppl.* (Cambridge, Eng. 1907); *Codex Climaci Rescriptus* (Cambridge, Eng. 1909). Studies. A. Baumstark, OrChr 32 (1935) 201–224. F. Rosenthal, *Die aramäistische Forschung seit Th. Nöldekes Veröffentlichungen* (Leiden 1939) 144–159. J. T. Milik, Rev Bibl 60 (1953) 526–539. L. Delekat, ZATWiss 71 (1959) 165–201. Old Syriac Gospels. Editions. F. C. Burkitt, *Evangelion da-Mepharreshe*, 2 v. (Cambridge, Eng. 1904) v.1. A. S. Lewis, ed., *The Old Syriac Gospels* (London 1910). A. Hjelt, *Syrus Sinaiticus* (Helsinki 1930). A. Vööbus, *New Materials for the History of the Vetus Syra*, 2 v. (in preparation). Studies. F. C. Burkitt, *op. cit.* v.2. M. J. Lagrange, *Critique textuelle*, v.2 of *Introduction à l'étude du N.T.* 2 v. (2d ed. Paris 1935–37) 202–218. C. Peters, *Das Diatessaron Tatians* (Rome 1939) 29–48. A. Vööbus, *Neue Angaben über die textgeschichtlichen Zustände in Edessa* (Stockholm 1951); *Studies in the History of the Gospel Text in Syriac* (CSCO Subs. 3; Louvain 1951) 25–45; *Early Versions of the N.T.* (Stockholm 1954) 73–88. Peshitta N.T. Editions. P. E. Pusey and G. H. Gwilliam, *Tetraevangelium syriacum* (Oxford 1901). *The N.T. in Syriac* (British and Foreign Bible Society; London 1905–1920, repr. 1950). See also Peshitta O.T. Editions. Studies. F. C. Burkitt, *Evangelion, op. cit.* 2:160–165. A. Baumstark, *Geschichte, op. cit.* 73–74. M. J. Lagrange, *Critique textuelle, op. cit.* 218–223. A. Vööbus, *Investigations into the Text of the N.T. Used by Rabbula* (Pinneberg 1947); *Muséon* 63 (1950) 191–204; *Early Versions, op. cit.* 88–103. Philoxenian Revision. Editions. J. Gwynn, ed., *Remnants of the Later Syriac Versions* (London 1909); *The Apocalypse of St. John* (Dublin 1897). Studies. G. Zuntz, *The Ancestry of the Harklean N.T.* (London 1945). A. Vööbus, "New Data concerning the Philoxenian Version," *Festschrift K. Kundzinš* (Eutin 1953) 169–186; *Early Versions, op. cit.* 103–121. Harklean Version. Editions. J. White, *Sacrorum evangeliorum versio syriaca philoxeniana* (Oxford 1778); *Acta et epistulae* (Oxford 1799–1803). R. L. Bensly, *The Harklean Version of the Epistle to the Hebrews Chap. XI, 28 to XIII, 25* (Cambridge, Eng. 1889). Studies. S. New, HarvThRev 21 (1928) 376–395. M. J. Lagrange, *Critique textuelle, op. cit.* 223–233, 445–448, 517–518. W. H. P. Hatch, HarvThRev 30 (1937) 141–155. W. D. McHardy, JThSt 49 (1948) 175–178. G. Zuntz, *The Ancestry, op. cit.;* RevBibl 57 (1950) 550–582. A. Vööbus, "New Data . . . ," *op. cit.* 169–186; *Early Versions, op. cit.* 103–121. Palestinian Syriac N.T. Editions. A. S. Lewis and M. D. Gibson, *The Palestinian Syriac Lectionary of the Gospels* (rev. ed. London 1899). A. S. Lewis, *A Palestinian, op. cit.;* Suppl., *op. cit.; Codex, op. cit.* Studies. F. C. Burkitt, JThSt 2 (1901) 174–183. M. J. Lagrange, RevBibl 34 (1925) 481–504. M. Black, OrChr 36 (1939) 101–111. F. Rosenthal, *Die aramäistische, op. cit.* 144–159. A. Vööbus, *Early Versions, op. cit.* 121–131. L. Delekat, NTSt 3 (1957) 223–233. C. van Puyvelde, "Orientales de la Bible (Versions) VI. Versions Syriaques," DBSuppl 6:834–884. L. Leloir, ed. and tr., *Saint Éphrem, Commentaire de l'Évangile Concordant* (Dublin 1963). **Illustration credit:** Fig. 6, Courtesy of the Trustees of the British Museum.

[A. Vööbus]

13. LATIN VERSIONS

Because of the immense importance of the Latin Vulgate among the various Latin versions of the Bible, these are most naturally divided into (1) the Old Latin versions made before the Vulgate, (2) the Vulgate itself, and (3) the later versions.

Old Latin Versions

The material dealt with in this section comprises the Latin texts of the Bible that precede those revisions and fresh translations, largely produced by St. Jerome, that form the complete Latin Bible known for centuries as the Vulgate. In broad terms, then, the Old Latin Bible is the pre-Hieronymian Latin Bible—the body of the Latin Scripture that first came into being when the Church spread among people who were not at home in Greek. (No use will be made here of the term Itala as a general equivalent for Old Latin; the word derives solely from a passage in St. Augustine, *Doctr. christ.* 2.22, where both the text and the meaning are doubtful.) In the NT the Old Latin presents translations from the Greek original; in the OT, retranslations of Greek versions of Semitic originals.

Origin. The following statement made in 1963 by the scholar perhaps best qualified to speak, Pater Bonifatius Fischer of Beuron, summarizes modern knowledge on certain essential points: "The Old Latin translation of the Bible came into being little by little during the 2d century, perhaps in Africa, perhaps in Rome or Gaul, probably in different places, in any event not in one effort and not as the work of one single translator. It underwent rapid and extensive development and differentiation." A few comments may be in order.

In Africa. As the cradle of Latin renderings of Scripture, Africa has much to be said for it. The use in proconsular Numidia of books containing a Latin translation of the NT is established for A.D. 180, when one of the Christians of Scillium revealed upon examination before his martyrdom that he was carrying "books and epistles of Paul, a just man." Books used by such provincials as these Scillitans can hardly have been in Greek, so that these Pauline Epistles must have been written in Latin; moreover, where there was a Latin version of St. Paul's writings there must have been Latin Gospels also. In Carthage, at the same period, *Tertullian, though he sometimes translated directly from the NT Greek, made extensive and fruitful use of preexisting Latin renderings of both Testaments. The most important among the early witnesses of the Old Latin Bible is Tertullian's younger Carthaginian contemporary St. *Cyprian, who cites nearly one-ninth of the entire NT.

In Rome. Meantime, however, at Rome, where Christian Latin was used much earlier than has until recently been generally believed, Pope *Cornelius wrote seven letters in Latin to Cyprian; and well before the persecution in which Cyprian fell, *Novatian, in his *On the Trinity,* quoted from a Latin version of the Bible. Evidence for what may indeed be the earliest translation of the Bible into Latin comes from the Scripture quotations in a Latin version of Clement I's *Epistle to the Corinthians* made most likely in the first half of the 2d century. Finally, if it be true that the Latin translation of the Gospels began with a rendering of the synopsis contained in Tatian's *Diatessaron, it is most reasonably at Rome that this took place. This polarity existing between Africa and Rome (mainly) as place of origin of the Latin Bible text has led, especially in the study of the NT, to the positing of two large varieties of text, the so-called African and the so-called European. But it should be remembered that the two types were interdependent and that contamination occurred both between the two types and also with the Vulgate when, later on (in the 5th and 6th centuries), this revision entered the field.

Several Translators and Revisers. For any given book of Scripture (or for any group of books) Fischer's conclusion is consistent with the initial existence either of a single translation that, through development and diversification, generated widely dissimilar texts or of two or more independent translations at the outset, whose copies maintained or even extended the points of difference. Both possibilities have been verified through the minute study of various scholars. Thus, for example, for the Heptateuch (the first 7 books of the OT), for 1 and 2 Machabees and Wisdom, and, in the NT, for the 13 letters of St. Paul (Hebrews excluded), there was a single basic translation (A. V. Billen, D. *De Bruyne, H. J. Frede); for 2 Chronicles, possibly two or more (R. Weber); for the Apocalypse, at least three (H. J. Vogels). De Bruyne found three translators at work in a single book, the Old Latin Ecclesiasticus (Sirach): an African translator supplying ch. 1 to 43 and 51; a European, ch. 44 to 50; and a third translator, the pref-

ace. In determining whether a single or a multiple Old Latin text underlies the much-studied Gospels, one must face the fact that a new translation may be indistinguishable from a vigorously conducted revision or recension of a preexisting translation.

Characteristics. A number of characteristic features stand out in the Old Latin texts, with their abundant richness of forms, generated by a freedom of approach to the Scriptures that readily permitted adaptations, modifications, or changes. The language itself is peculiar, reflecting Greek syntax, and expecially the Latin coinages produced to represent in neo-Latin form the Greek words that the translator saw before him (thus, e.g., *salvator, sanctifico, glorifico*), coupled with the transliterations from the Greek (e.g., *apostolus, baptizo, parabolor*). The vulgar and colloquial flavor in the Old Latin versions makes clear that they were prepared not for a cultured elite but for the ill-educated. The widespread influence of this Old Latin Biblical text has naturally been felt in subsequent writings, the effect being sometimes direct, sometimes through the absorption of Old Latin readings into the Vulgate, and quite regularly through quotations in patristic texts. The *Thesaurus linguae latinae* (like the lexicons of A. Souter and A. Blaise) cites rare Old Latin words from the editions of texts available at the time, but it will not be for many years that the whole linguistic material will be in the hands of scholars. The indices that accompany editions and studies of Old Latin texts are meanwhile most useful.

Preservation. No complete Old Latin Bible, or anything approximating one, has been preserved. The text of the nine-volume Bible that Cassiodorus (see below) provided for normal use in his monastery appears certainly to have been Old Latin; but no part of this, much less the whole, is known to have been preserved. In the direct tradition of the Old Latin text scholars are well provided if they have single books complete, or, at best, considerable remains of a Pentateuch or a Heptateuch, or, as often, a complete (or nearly complete) set of the Gospels, or the Gospels and Acts in combination. More frequently they are reduced to the selections found in lectionaries or in collections of the Biblical *canticles, to fragments preserved by chance in the underscript of *palimpsest leaves or in leaves once employed in bindings and subsequently removed, to patches of the Old Latin text appearing within a Vulgate context, to the Old Latin readings noted on the margins of MS (or even printed) copies of the Vulgate, or to the printed record of readings of MSS now lost. But oftentimes, especially in the OT, the Old Latin text is known only from quotations found in ecclesiastical writers of every kind, from Tertullian on. This indirect tradition is very rich and, for many parts of the Bible, quite extensive.

Printed Editions. As is evident, then, a special problem of collection and presentation is involved in editing the Old Latin Bible text. Such work stems from an early stage of Latin patristic, if one considers the scattered instances in which a Jerome, an Augustine, or a Cassiodorus opposes one Biblical reading to another.

Sabatier's Edition. The systematic assembly of Old Latin text goes back at least to a Latin rendering of the Septuagint published at Rome in 1588 (under the editorship of Flaminio de Nobili), which was in part made up of Biblical quotations drawn from the Latin Fathers. The Blessed Giuseppe *Tommasi concerned himself with the task in the 17th century, but it is not until the 18th that it was performed by the Maurist Benedictine Pierre *Sabatier (1682–1742), who made it his life's work. His well-ordered collection had its first printing (in part posthumously) in Reims in 1739–49 (repr. Paris 1751). The title of the three volumes (v.1–2 present the OT; v.3, the NT) reveals their ample scope: *Bibliorum sacrorum latinae versiones antiquae seu vetus italica et ceterae quaecunque in codicibus manuscriptis et antiquorum libris reperiri potuerunt.* On a typical page the wider, outer column supplies the Old Latin text (*Versio antiqua*); and the narrower, inner column, the Vulgate. Marginal notes indicate, from passage to passage, the source of the text chosen by Sabatier for his *Versio antiqua,* and extensive notes at the bottom of the page supply variant readings of this older Latin version along with the Greek. Although Sabatier's materials—among them a few MSS that have since perished—were far from complete, his work did notable service before gradually becoming antiquated through the availability of new materials and the advances of textual criticism. Having in mind a "new Sabatier" and working alone, Josef Denk (1848–1927), parish priest of Freising, Germany, produced vast collections of citations. These, along with his project itself, went at Denk's death to the Abbey of *Beuron, where, after new planning and yet more extensive collecting, the "new Sabatier" has begun to become a reality under the direction of Pater Bonifatius Fischer and with the support of a broadly based foundation created for the purpose.

Beuron Edition. In 1949 there was published at Beuron an index of the sigla assigned both to the Biblical MSS to be collated and to the ecclesiastical writings to be drawn upon. This index has already received revision. Volume 1.1 (1963) is an updating of the list of the printed ecclesiastical writers; its leaves are presented in a loose-leaf binder so as to permit gradual leaf-by-leaf revision as new texts are discovered or found relevant or new editions appear of the already known writings. A similar updating of the list of MSS will appear as v.1.2. From 1951 to 1954 Genesis appeared, in 600 large-quarto pages, the first of a planned series of 26 volumes (exclusive of the sigla). Work then shifted to the end of the series, and from 1956 to 1960 James and 1 and 2 Peter were published as the beginning of v.26. Since then (from 1962 to 1964) the complete Ephesians, under the editorship of H. J. Frede, has been published, which brings to completion the first half of v.24. It is projected next to complete the *Catholic Epistles in v.26 and to furnish, in v.11, the text of Wisdom and Ecclesiasticus.

The broad coverage and inner intricacy of the edition itself is mirrored in the typographical complexity seen in a typical page of the *Vetus Latina,* which shows a horizontal division in three levels. At the top is the *Schema;* below it is the *Kritischer Apparat;* at the bottom (in two columns), the *Zeugenapparat.* The *Schema* presents the text proper and is made up of one or more line systems, each of which will rarely contain less than three lines. At the top is the Greek, and at the bottom is either H (Jerome's new rendering from the Hebrew or Aramaic) or V (the revision that became adopted in the Vulgate). Between the Greek and H or

V, in as many lines as there are types (or subtypes) of text, lies the Old Latin. Variants strike the eye at once, being set out, in smaller type, without indication of source, directly below the text selected as typical, word under word or phrase under phrase; much of this is after a pattern of presentation used by Jülicher (see below) in his edition of the Old Latin Gospels. The *Kritischer Apparat* presents a positive attestation of all the variants presented in the *Schema.* The *Zeugenapparat* gives a complete report, for every phrase or clause in question, of all the citations found in the many hundreds of works of ancient Christian Latin writers from which the Beuron editors, following Sabatier and Denk, have culled. When any verse of Scripture has never been cited in any extant writings prior, say, to those of St. Bede (the approximate *terminus ad quem* of the citation coverage), the *Zeugenapparat* is silent. Usually, however, at least half the page is given to this report of citations, and sometimes the yield is enormous. Not less than 25 large two-column pages are required for the *Zeugenapparat* on three verses of Ephesians (6.11–13); the count of citations for verse 12 alone is about 545, and for the entire letter, about 14,000.

Jülicher's Edition. Such report of *testimonia* forms no part of the edition (1938–63) of the four Gospels begun by A. *Jülicher and continued after his death by A. Matzkow, and after the death of Matzkow, by K. Aland. This edition confines itself to the directly transmitted text, which for the Gospels is quite abundant; it was projected to embrace the whole of the NT, but in fact it has terminated with the Gospels. It is from Jülicher that the Beuron *Vetus Latina* adopted its arrangement of text in bracketed line systems (two or more lines in each, representing the two or more text types in question), with the variants of each text type set out directly under the word or phrase it relates to.

Ayuso's Edition. Another projected edition of Old Latin text, centered in Spanish material but designed to cover the entire Bible, may not survive the death (1962) of its Spanish founder, Msgr. T. Ayuso Marazuela. Of his project, besides the monumental collection of Psalters mentioned in the next paragraph, there has appeared the *Prolegómenos* (Madrid 1953), which formed the first of eight projected volumes. The 600 folio pages of this introductory volume will remain valuable for the bibliography and lists of MSS and Spanish ecclesiastical writers. Also, in a related framework, that of the ambitious *Biblia polyglotta Matritensia,* Ayuso published an elaborate edition of the Old Latin *Psalterium Visigothicum-Mozarabicum* (Madrid 1957).

Editions of Old Latin Psalters. The Visigothic Psalter is an important element in the *Salterio* that forms v.5 of Ayuso's *Vetus Latina Hispana* (see preceding paragraph), which appeared in three parts (Madrid 1962). In six parallel columns Ayuso sets out as many texts, as follows: the Gallican, Mozarabic, and Roman Psalters, a *Salterio Patristico* (presenting Latin Psalter quotations from early Spanish writers), St. Jerome's Psalter *Iuxta Hebraeos,* and finally the Greek Septuagint. (Nearly one third of the 1167 folio pages that make up the total volume present an elaborate "Introduction.") The Visigothic Psalter is also one of the 14 Old Latin Psalters whose texts are reported, through their variants from that of the *Psalterium Romanum,* in a critical edition of the latter issued in 1953 by Dom Robert Weber, as v.10 in the *Collectanea Biblica Latina*. In the same series an edition is planned of an additional Old Latin Psalter (incomplete; cited as Cod. Slav. 5) discovered in the library of St. Catherine's Monastery, Mt. Sinai, too late to find place in Weber's assembly. E. A. Lowe [*Scriptorium* 9 (1955) 177–199, with plates] argued from the paleography of this exotic MS that it was produced in the East at some time in the late 9th or early 10th century. The text is related to Weber's *Veronensis* Capit. I(1) (α) and the palimpsest *Sangallensis* 912 (β), both known for their agreement with the Psalter used by St. Augustine for his *Enarrationes*. Pending the separate edition in the *Collectanea*, the principal readings of the Sinai Psalter may be found in the Dekkers-Fraipont edition of the *Enarrationes*, CorpChrist v.38–40 [on 38, xxiv add the siglum (κ)]. In the MS, fols. 82r–105v contain a new series of 18 numbered Biblical canticles.

An accessory element in the Sinai Psalter has already received separate publication, viz, the titles that stand before each of the Psalms to help make their singing or recitation an act of Christian prayer. [Thus at Psalm 10(11) this Psalter shows *De passione Christi*.] Such headings, distributed in six series, have been published by Abbot Pierre Salmon [*Collectanea Biblica Latina* 12 (Rome 1959)]. The Sinai titles form part of Series II, whose text has come down in a mixed tradition. The purpose envisaged by these Psalm titles is seen further developed in the Psalter Collects that likewise are found in many Old Latin MSS. These, collected by Dom André *Wilmart and distributed into three series, were published after his death by Dom Louis Brou (1949).

Manuscripts of Old Latin Versions. A provisional enumeration of MSS containing Old Latin text of any part of Scripture was given in 1949 by Fischer in v.1 (*Verzeichnis der Sigel*) of the *Vetus Latina* already mentioned. The sigla assigned are numerical; the exceedingly large number of items involved precluded any convenient use of letters as sigla and therefore reduced to a subordinate position the system that had assigned the lower-case letters of the Latin alphabet to the leading MSS of the Old Latin NT. Some 350 MSS are listed, with the sigla numbers ranging from 1 to 453. The items are grouped by batches (e.g., 1 to 49, Gospel Books; 300– , Psalter texts), with gaps left for later additions. A separate table arranges the MSS according to the portions of Scripture contained in each. Leading here are the Psalms (161 MSS); next are the Gospels (41); thereafter, the Biblical canticles (24, exclusive of the many Psalters that also include them); 1 and 2 Machabees (22); Heptateuch (18); Judith and Acts (17 each); Epistles, both Pauline and Catholic (16 each); Prophets (15); 1 and 2 Chronicles, Tobit (Tobias), Esther, and Job (14 each). No other book (or group of books) shows more than 10. The least represented is the Old Latin Ruth, found only at Madrid, accompanied in the same MS (*Complutensis* I) by the Vulgate version.

Composite Manuscripts. The Madrid Ruth is one example among many in which a single MS presents both Old Latin and Vulgate texts, not necessarily of the same Biblical book. That such combinations should have appeared is a natural consequence of the fact that the Latin versions, both Old Latin and Vulgate, were prepared and published book by book, or group by

group, and only afterward brought into larger assemblages or even into complete Bibles. The bilingual MS is of rarer appearance. Wolfenbüttel Weissenb. 64 [late 5th century; Lowe CodLatAntiq (hereafter simply Lowe) 9:1388] contains four leaves in which Gothic and Latin stand in parallel columns. Among Greco-Latin MSS (see Berger, 113–116; *Vet. Lat.* 1, e.g., Nos. 5, 27, 75–78) the most famous is surely the Codex Bezae (Cambridge Univ. Nn. II.41, 5th century; Lowe 2:140), containing Gospels, Acts, and 3 John, with Greek and Latin on confronting pages.

It is not within the range of this article to enumerate the more than 350 Old Latin MSS controlled in the Beuron *Vetus Latina* project or even the 27 codices employed by Jülicher and his successors for the Gospels alone (one of these a parchment scrap of John from Egypt—Aberdeen Univ. Pap. 2a, 5th century; Lowe 2: 118). An annotated inventory of much of the more recent material is furnished by B. Botte, DBSuppl 5:335–344; and the already mentioned Beuron list of sigla is the ultimate guide.

Classification. The long-established division of Old Latin text into two major classes, African and European, has been maintained, though greatly refined, in the editions thus far produced at Beuron. A text form K (Karthago) reflects primarily the readings of Cyprian (and Pseudo-Cyprian); C stands for a related later African text. The editions of Genesis, James, and 1 and 2 Peter all show a theoretical E (European text), which is represented in practice, however, by several subclasses, including S (Spanish). In Genesis and Ephesians an I class includes the readings of the North-Italian (or Gallic) writers Rufinus, Ambrose, Hilary, and also Augustine (Ambrose and Augustine forming, or leading, where it is deemed necessary, subclasses M and A, respectively). In the canonical Epistles, V (Vulgate) is a type parallel to S; in Ephesians, V is on a parity with I (S here representing the Spanish readings in Peregrinus's edition of the Vulgate). It should be emphasized that the text history and consequently the editor's classification vary in detail from book to book.

In the Jülicher-Matzkow-Aland Gospels the text (represented here by MSS alone) shows a simple two-fold classification: *Itala* (*versio*) and *Afra*, the former text found in the majority of the MSS, the latter, in two alone, now in one, now in the other, now in both. These two MSS are *k* (*Vet. Lat.* "1")—the *Bobiensis*: Turin Bibl. Naz. G. VII. 15, 4th–5th century (Lowe 4:465); and *e* (*Vet. Lat.* "2")—the *Palatinus*: Trent Museo Naz. (with fragments in Dublin and London), 5th century (Lowe 4:437, see also 2 p. 17).

The mention just made of the Vulgate as entering into the Old Latin tradition of certain of the Epistles is a reminder that some pre-Hieronymian material will be treated in the following section.

THE VULGATE

Typically, the production of the Old Latin text of the Bible is the work of unknown writers (even though certain of the Fathers produced their own renderings as occasion demanded and Augustine in particular came to revise a large portion of the Latin Scriptures).

Work of St. Jerome. The production of the body of renderings that are called the Vulgate, however, is dominated by one individual, St. *Jerome (d. 420), Father and Doctor of the Church, acting as reviser,

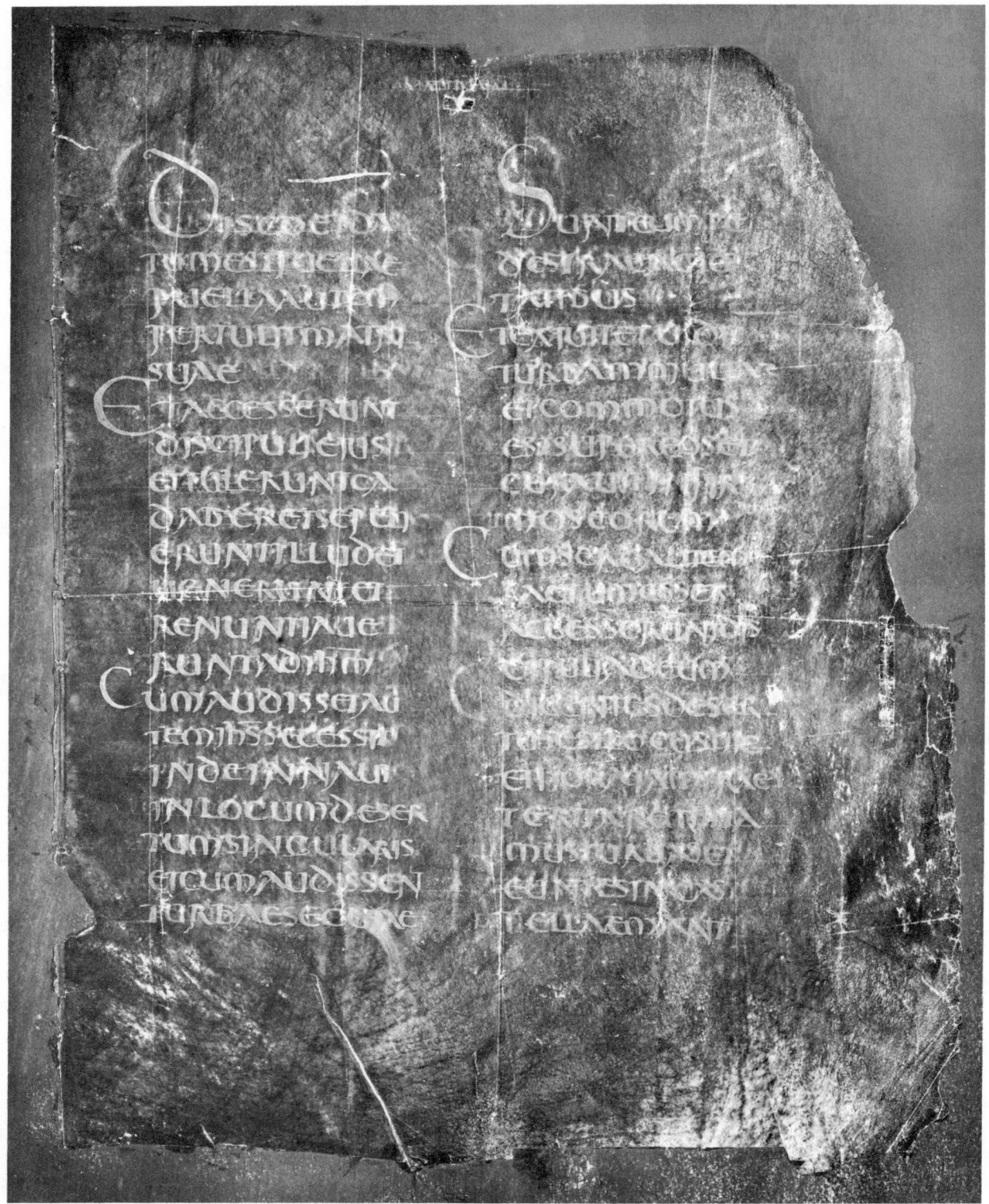

Fig. 7. *Page from the 5th-century Codex Palatinus, having the Afra form of the Old Latin Gospels (here Mt 14.11–15).*

acting as translator, and in some instances refusing to act at all. If these distinctions are made one may with reasonable accuracy call the Vulgate his work. It is providential that what was to become the standard Bible of the Latin Church reflects in so large a measure the religious conviction, the critical acumen, the learning and scholarship, and the writing skill of such a man.

Revision of Old Latin Gospels. Jerome's production of the Latin Bible text extends over a period of some 22 of his middle years, from 383 to 405. Most of it took place in the first 2 decades of his long, final residence in Bethlehem; but it began during the nearly 3 years that he spent in Rome in his late 30s, largely occupied as secretary to Pope St. Damasus. According to Jerome, it was the Pope himself who directed him to the most impressive of these Roman achievements, the correction of an Old Latin text of the Gospels against the Greek in order to erect a standard of correctness among a welter of widely divergent and often faulty copies. In acceding to the Pope's invitation—official commission it hardly can have been—Jerome produced what is now known as the Vulgate Gospels, the four texts that in due course became and still remain official in the Latin Church. They are best read today in the edition produced (1889–95) by the Anglican Bishop of Salisbury, John Wordsworth (d. 1911), and his colleague Henry Julian White (d. 1938), who presented the text as Jerome did to Damasus, with the dedicatory letter *Novum opus* prefixed. One learns from Jerome's preface to the first of the two Psalter texts that he produced at Bethlehem, that he similarly corrected at Rome an Old Latin text of the Psalms. What may have been the fate of that work and whether Jerome passed from his correction of the Gospels to a similar correction of any or all of the remaining NT books will be dealt with shortly.

Partial Revision of Old Latin Old Testament. Settled in Bethlehem, Jerome found in the library of nearby *Caesarea in Palestine the stupendous work of Biblical erudition that Origen achieved in his *Hexapla.* (See section 9 above.) The fifth of the six columns in this massive assemblage contained Origen's own edition of the Septuagint (LXX), with its spits (*obeli*) and asterisks to mark redundancies or deficiencies in the LXX. It would seem that Jerome felt impelled to translate the whole of this into Latin or at least to revise existing Latin in the light of it, continuing his Roman procedures but now using an authoritative and critical Greek text. Some modern scholars hold that he fully achieved this exacting task, even if little now remains of it; others, that his Hexaplaric recension was applied only to 1 and 2 Chronicles, the so-called books of Solomon (Proverbs, Ecclesiastes, and the Canticle of Canticles), Job, and the Psalms. In these four cases the evidence is compelling. The text of the Hexaplaric 1 and 2 Chronicles is lost, but the preface that Jerome prefixed to it is preserved. [Jerome's Biblical prefaces are found in PL v.28–29 at the head of the books they refer to; the present preface is in PL 29:401 (423); they are also assembled conveniently in F. Stummer's *Einführung in die lateinische Bibel* 222–262 (241 for Chronicles); and they are best consulted in the critical editions now being produced in the Vatican Vulgate (*Vat. Vulg.*) by the monks of S. Girolamo, Rome (Chronicles is in 7:7).] For the three books of Solomon there is again Jerome's preface (*Vat. Vulg.* 11:6); moreover, extracts

from the text itself are found in a St. Gall miscellany (Cod. 11, 8th century; Lowe 7:896) and are presented under the siglum *Sang.* in *Vat. Vulg.* 11; other extracts have been culled from other sources by A. Vaccari (*Scritti* 2:83–146), who also had the good fortune in the 1950s to discover the full text of Jerome's Hexaplaric Canticle of Canticles in MS *Vat. lat.* 5704 (6th century; Lowe 1:25) as forming the base text (*lemmata*) used by Epiphanius Scholasticus, a friend of Cassiodorus, in translating the commentary on the Canticle of Canticles by Philo Carpasinus (text in Vaccari, *Scritti* 2:129–140). Of the Hexaplaric Job there are both text and preface: PL 29:61–114 (63–118); variants are noted in *Vat. Vulg.* (sigla *Sang., Ox., Tur.*).

Gallican Psalter. The most fruitful result of Jerome's concern with Origen's *Hexapla* was the Psalter that he based on it—Jerome's second (*Vat. Vulg.*). This was the Psalter that gradually achieved an ascendancy even over Jerome's own direct translation from the Hebrew. It was probably introduced in the liturgy in Gaul before Alcuin, who was led by this fact to adopt it for his recension of the Bible. It thus won its place in the typical Bible of the Middle Ages, and was absorbed into the Roman Breviary, where it reigned supreme until the coming of the New Latin Psalter in 1945 (see below). (The term Gallican applied to it came from the popularity the Psalter received in Gaul in the early Middle Ages and does not refer, as sometimes asserted, to the Abbey of St. Gall in Switzerland.) As the Vulgate Psalter par excellence, this Hexaplaric Psalter was retained by the Benedictines of S. Girolamo to form part of the Vatican Vulgate, where it appeared in 1953 as v.10, furnished with Origenic critical signs such as Jerome had noted down in Caesarea. For all its popularity the Gallican Psalter contains a large number of verses that trouble readers. Some of these readings resist comprehension because they are faulty translations; others are hard to understand either because they are slavish translations or because of difficulties inherent in the original Hebrew or because of the reader's lack of familiarity with Biblical locutions or Christian Latin vocabulary. Pius XII's new Psalter of 1945 came into being partly for the purpose that those who recite the Psalter might have an intelligible text in every verse. There were many who thought that its editors had gone much too far, showing little tendency to conserve the excellencies of Jerome's work. Consequently, in 1961, at Clervaux, Dom Robert Weber, OSB, brought out *pro manuscripto* a "new recension" of the Gallican Psalter (*Psalterii secundum Vulgatam Bibliorum Versionem nova recensio*) in which only those verses are reworded that required it for intelligibility. How far this recension or anything similar will gain favor with Benedictines generally or with others who chant or recite the Psalms remains to be seen, but its very preparation is proof of the continued vitality of one of Jerome's most influential writings.

New Version of OT Protocanonical Books. While he was still occupied with his revisions according to the *Hexapla,* Jerome had entered upon the most important phase in his provision of Latin Bible text, the translation from the Hebrew itself. His awareness of the apologetic value of presenting the *Hebraica veritas* directly, bypassing even Origen's Septuagint, is found in a letter (*Ep.* 32.1) written before he left Rome,

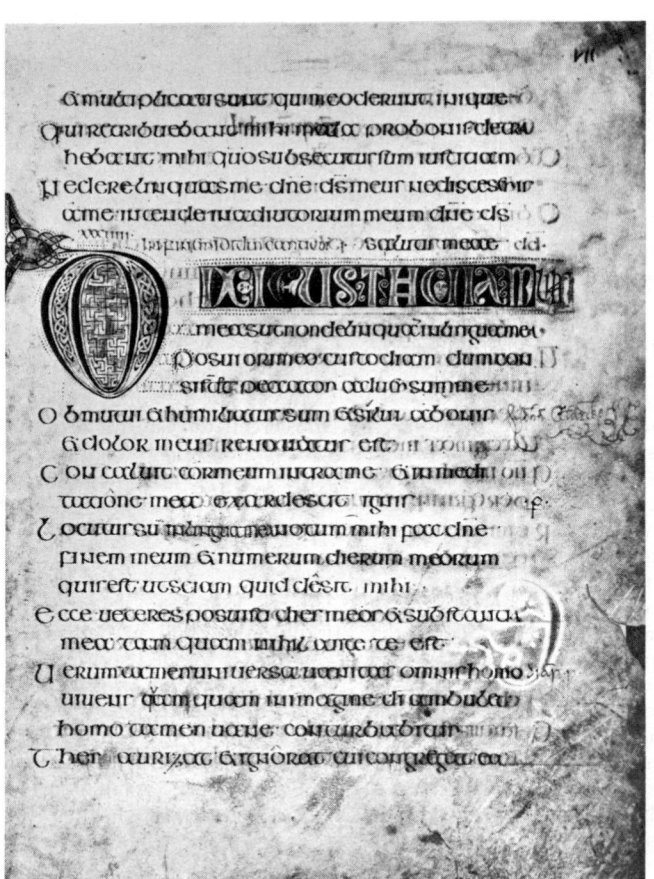

Fig. 8. Page from a MS (Morgan MS 776, folio 7r) of the so-called Roman Psalter, written in England in the second half of the 8th century. Shown here is Ps 37.20–38.7. The first words of 38.1 are illuminated.

LATIN VERSIONS
OF THE BIBLE

Fig. 9. Detail of Morgan MS 776 (see Fig. 8), folio 40r, showing Ps 79.19–80.6. In light letters over the illuminated beginning of Psalm 80 is its superscription. Small Anglo-Saxon glosses are over some Latin words.

where he seems to have had at his disposal at least the greater part of the Hebrew text of the Bible, and it is elsewhere explicit [see *Praef. in Isa.,* PL 28:774 (828); *Adv. Rufin.* 3.25, PL 23:476 (498)]. At Bethlehem he provided himself with Hebrew teachers, especially a certain Baranina (*Ep.* 84.3).

The basic chronology of Jerome's activity is reasonably clear. If ch. 134 of the *De viris illustribus* of 392–393 is a later addition of the author and hence does not prove that Jerome had already by then completed the Psalms and the Prophets (less Baruch), it at least groups these books together as occupying the translator in the first stages. What prompted the order in which Jerome proceded was less the scheme of any Biblical canon than the promptings of friends eager to have one or another book translated. If one adopts the chronology determined by F. Cavallera, 1 and 2 Samuel, 3 and 4 Kings, and Job were grouped with the Psalter and the Prophets in the early period from 389 to 392. Ezra and Nehemia followed in 394; 1 and 2 Chronicles, 2 years later. In 398 the three books of Solomon were rendered in 8 days, but Jerome was busy also at the Octateuch, which was completed by 405. The prefaces and dedicatory letters that accompanied Jerome's translations show that most frequently the unit of publication was the single book (the four Major Prophets separately, the Psalms, Job, Ezra and Nehemia, 1 and 2 Chronicles, Tobit, Judith, and Esther), but in some cases the books were published in groups, as had been the Gospels at Rome (1 and 2 Samuel with 3 and 4 Kings, the Minor Prophets, the books of Solomon, the Pentateuch, Josue with Judges and Ruth).

New Version of Some of the OT Deuterocanonical Books. Having done so much, Jerome regarded his work on the OT text as complete, for he declined to issue translations of five books that had a place in the canon of the Greek-speaking Jews but were lacking in the Palestinian—Wisdom, Ecclesiasticus (Sirach), Baruch, and 1 and 2 Machabees. These books, consequently, came into the Latin Bible only in Old Latin texts that had received not even revisory attention from Jerome. To Tobias (Tobit) and Judith, which were in the same position, he was more receptive, for he produced Latin versions from Aramaic sources available to him. If Jerome is to be taken literally in what he says in his preface to Tobias, he had the Aramaic text of that book translated to him orally by a person who knew both Aramaic and Hebrew, and both prefaces stress the rapidity with which he worked at these two versions. Jerome was similarly receptive toward certain sections of Daniel and Esther that were not to be found in the Hebrew. For the well-known passages in Daniel—the Song of the Three Youths in the fiery furnace and the stories of Susanna and of Bel and the Dragon (Dn 3.24–90; 13.1–14.42)—Jerome drew upon the Greek of the so-called Theodotion recension (presumably as found in the sixth column of Origen's *Hexapla*), as he himself tells us in notes before 3.24, after 3.90, and after 12.13. The parts of Esther that Jerome found present in the LXX Greek but wanting in the Latin he set out after 10.3 with full notes accompanying the several excerpts to indicate the places from which they had been assembled. In *Vulg. Vat.* every line in this entire supplementary passage has a spit (÷) prefixed in conformity with Jerome's note after 10.3. These critical notes in Daniel and in Esther bring one face to

face with the scholar-translator at work. Omitted in the edition of Sixtus V, they were, happily, restored 2 years later.

Books of the NT after the Gospels. To the evolving complete Latin Bible that was eventually to become known as the Vulgate, all three periods of Jerome's application to the sacred text contributed. From the triennium at Rome came the Gospels; from the earlier years at Bethlehem, with their special dedication to Origen's *Hexapla,* came the Psalms (the Gallican Psalter); from Jerome's continued residence there, centered in rendering the *Hebraica veritas,* came all the OT except the five deuterocanonical books, which he declined to translate or revise. The Vulgate was thus complete except for the second half of the NT—the Acts, the Epistles, and the Apocalypse. What is the origin of the Vulgate text of these books? There is no consensus on this question. The common opinion has been that these books, showing in any event a correction of Old Latin text from the Greek, received this treatment from Jerome himself, who would have continued in their case the process he began with the Gospels. This position is consistent with, but not proved by, Jerome's twice uttered declaration that he had indeed revised the NT after the Greek (*De vir. ill.* 135; *Ep.* 71.5; see also *Ep.* 112.20 near end). A strong denial to Jerome of the Vulgate Pauline Epistles made by D. De Bruyne in the early decades of the 20th century still has its effect and tends moreover to involve the other Epistles and the Acts and Apocalypse as well. At Beuron, while H (Hieronymus) is the siglum used to identify the Vulgate Genesis, a circumspect V represents the Vulgate James, 1 and 2 Peter, and Ephesians; and the Vulgate James is described simply as "an old text that, beginning with Augustine's early writings, is adduced by most witnesses." Yet greater skepticism can be found at Rome, where J. Gribomont, a leading figure in the official revision of the Vulgate, declared that it "can be held as certain" [*Maison-Dieu* 62 (1960) 48, n.27] that Jerome's zeal for the *Hebraica veritas* led him to abandon, after the Gospels, his project to revise the entire NT; and as to whether Jerome did continue, a *non constat* was the conclusion reached by the Roman Biblicist S. Garofolo in presenting to the public in 1959 an important edition of the Vulgate. De Bruyne held that the Vulgate text of St. Paul goes back to Pelagius. However, the current editor of Ephesians in the *Vetus Latina,* H. J. Frede, has shown that, although Pelagius was the first to use the Vulgate St. Paul, he did not compose it—and neither did Jerome. Among Frede's positive conclusions are these (*Vet. Lat.* 24.36*): "The Vulgate text of St. Paul's letters came into being in the last years of the 4th century at the latest. . . . Its author is unknown, although he is identical with the man who gave to the Vulgate at least the Catholic Epistles and perhaps the whole of the NT outside of the Gospels."

Psalterium Romanum. It remains here to return briefly to the Psalter that Jerome produced at Rome *c.* 384. The common opinion is an attractive one: that this Psalter is the *Psalterium Romanum,* whose use, once widely extended, is now virtually limited to the canons of St. Peter's Basilica in Rome, but which was the source of many of the older chants (Introits, etc.) of the Roman Missal. Once again it was Dom De Bruyne who in recent times (1930) most effectively contested the tradition. Studies made or reported by Vaccari (*Scritti* 1:211–221) have modified De Bruyne's conclusions and give reason to believe that the *Romanum*, while indeed not Jerome's work, was used and studied by him and ought to be regarded as the text on which he based his now long lost, first rapid correction and revision of the Psalms.

Transmission of the Vulgate Text. The universal use that St. Jerome's new versions and revisions would ultimately receive could hardly have been predicted from the person-to-person basis in which he issued his works one by one as he executed them or from the reactions of influential contemporaries. In one quarter were the objections collected by *Rufinus and answered by Jerome in his *Contra Rufinum* [2.24–35, PL 23:447 (468)]; and in another was St. Augustine, with his loyalty to the LXX, who first showed himself disturbed by the new venture (*Epist.* 71.4–5; 82.35; CSEL 34.2: 252, 386) and only gradually changed his position (*Doctr. christ.* 4.15, PL 34:96; *Civ.* 18.43, CorpChrist 47:638). In one of his letters (*Epist.* 71.5) Augustine tells Jerome of the tumult aroused at Oea (present-day Tripoli in North Africa) when passages from the new version were used in public worship.

Gradual Acceptance. Enthusiasts, however, were not lacking; one of them, Jerome's friend Sophronius of Bethlehem (d. after 392), rendered part of the new translation into Greek. Possibly the staunchest supporters of Jerome's versions in the 5th century were the disciples of Pelagius (notably, *Julian of Eclanum); it is in works of Pelagians that the earliest witness to the Vulgate text of certain of the NT Epistles is to be had. In the Gaul of the 5th and 6th centuries a selective use of the Vulgate was made by John *Cassian, St. *Eucherius of Lyons, Salonius (d. after 451), St. *Avitus of Vienne, and St. *Gregory of Tours. In an early 6th-century Lectionary of Wolfenbüttel (Dekkers, *Clavis* 1947), which may go back to 5th-century use at Clermont-Ferrand, the Vulgate is extensively employed.

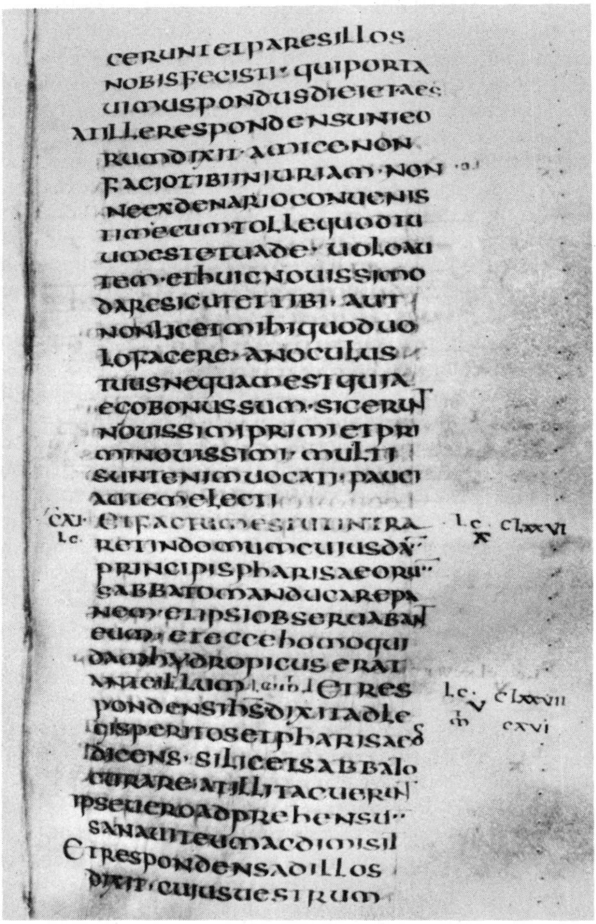

Early Pandects. As an effective agent in the dissemination of Vulgate text, Gaul was surpassed in the 5th, 6th, and 7th centuries by Italy. The ecclesiastical writers, in their quotations from Scripture, furnish important evidence, but not a little is based on what has been shown—especially by B. Fischer—of the origins of early editions of the Bible, whether these present single books (or groups of books) or the whole Bible in one volume (pandect). Fifth-century Italy was probably the source of an edition of the Vulgate 1 and 2 Samuel that carried in its margins 114 Old Latin readings. No portion of the original still exists, but few subsequent Vulgate MSS of these books are free of its influence. The Spanish Bishop Peregrinus produced in the 5th century an edition of the letters of Paul that was based in part on a Vulgate text of Italian origin. To northern Italy of the 7th century probably belongs the source of the two-volume 9th-century Bible known complete to Robert *Estienne at St. Germain-des-Prés in Paris in the early 16th century but now reduced to its second volume (B.N. lat. 11553). Among all Bibles this *Sangermanensis* has been found by Fischer to give a "reasonably accurate reproduction of an ancient pandect." From *Cassiodorus (d. *c.* 580) comes the earliest-known evidence of such Latin pandects; but as will at once be clear, his copies have not themselves survived or, in their text, been reproduced in later codices. Important as being preserved in its original form is a NT produced under the direction of Bp. Victor of Capua (d. 554) in Campania and completed in 547, a volume that has been at Fulda since St. *Boniface owned it there. In this book the Gospels are represented only in a harmony, based, it seems, on an Old Latin form of Tatian's Diatessaron. Victor put this into Vulgate form through the use of a contemporary Gospel Book whose good text stands back also of the *Amiatinus* and the Gospels of Lindesfarne. Only in the Gospel harmony did Victor's NT exercise discernible influence, becoming in time the model for the first Biblical translations into Old High German and Italian. The various streams of transmission that united to form the remainder of the Capua NT appear to have stopped there.

Cassiodorus. In his library at Vivarium Cassiodorus had codices, now lost, covering a broad range of Latin Bible text. There was a nine-volume Old Latin Bible set for normal study. A relatively small codex contained the whole Bible (less the deuterocanonical books of the OT) in the Vulgate version. Finally there was a larger pandect, the *codex grandior*, the OT text of which followed St. Jerome's revision according to the Hexapla. The last-named codex, the only one of the 11

Fig. 10. Page from the NT of Victor of Capua, Landesbibliothek (Codex Bonif. 1, p. 103), Fulda, Germany, one of the earliest MSS of the Vulgate NT. Its Gospel text (here Mt 20.12–16; Lk 14.1–5) has the form of a harmony.

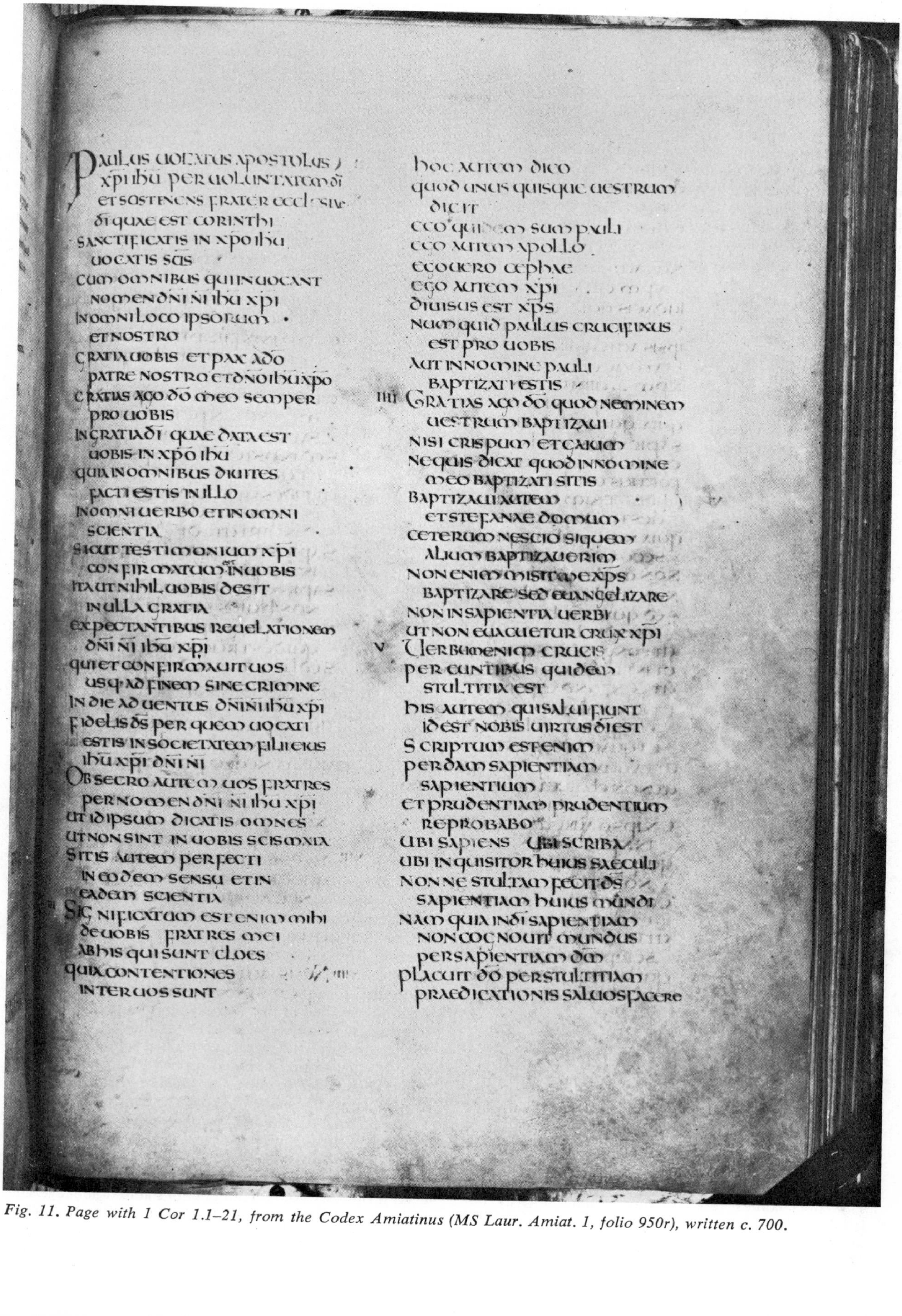

PAULUS UOCATUS APOSTOLUS
XPI IHU PER UOLUNTATEM DI
ET SOSTENENS FRATER ECCLESIAE
DI QUAE EST CORINTHI
SANCTIFICATIS IN XPO IHU
UOCATIS SCS
CUM OMNIBUS QUI INUOCANT
NOMEN DNI NI IHU XPI
IN OMNI LOCO IPSORUM ·
ET NOSTRO
GRATIA UOBIS ET PAX A DO
PATRE NOSTRO ET DNO IHU XPO
GRATIAS AGO DO MEO SEMPER
PRO UOBIS
IN GRATIA DI QUAE DATA EST
UOBIS IN XPO IHU
QUIA IN OMNIBUS DIUITES
FACTI ESTIS IN ILLO
IN OMNI UERBO ET IN OMNI
SCIENTIA
SICUT TESTIMONIUM XPI
CONFIRMATUM EST IN UOBIS
ITA UT NIHIL UOBIS DESIT
IN ULLA GRATIA
EXPECTANTIBUS REUELATIONEM
DNI NI IHU XPI
QUI ET CONFIRMAUIT UOS
USQ AD FINEM SINE CRIMINE
IN DIE ADUENTUS DNI NI IHU XPI
FIDELIS DS PER QUEM UOCATI
ESTIS IN SOCIETATEM FILII EIUS
IHU XPI DNI NI
OBSECRO AUTEM UOS FRATRES
PER NOMEN DNI NI IHU XPI
UT IDIPSUM DICATIS OMNES
UT NON SINT IN UOBIS SCISMATA
SITIS AUTEM PERFECTI
IN EODEM SENSU ET IN
EADEM SCIENTIA
SIGNIFICATUM EST ENIM MIHI
DE UOBIS FRATRES MEI
AB HIS QUI SUNT CLOES
QUIA CONTENTIONES
INTER UOS SUNT

HOC AUTEM DICO
QUOD UNUS QUISQUE UESTRUM
DICIT
EGO QUIDEM SUM PAULI
EGO AUTEM XPOLLO ·
EGO UERO CEPHAE
EGO AUTEM XPI ·
DIUISUS EST XPS
NUM QUID PAULUS CRUCIFIXUS
EST PRO UOBIS
AUT IN NOMINE PAULI
BAPTIZATI ESTIS
IIII GRATIAS AGO DO QUOD NEMINEM
UESTRUM BAPTIZAUI
NISI CRISPUM ET CAIUM
NE QUIS DICAT QUOD IN NOMINE
MEO BAPTIZATI SITIS
BAPTIZAUI AUTEM ·
ET STEFANAE DOMUM
CETERUM NESCIO SI QUEM
ALIUM BAPTIZAUERIM
NON ENIM MISIT ME XPS
BAPTIZARE SED EUANGELIZARE
NON IN SAPIENTIA UERBI
UT NON EUACUETUR CRUX XPI
V UERBUM ENIM CRUCIS
PEREUNTIBUS QUIDEM
STULTITIA EST
HIS AUTEM QUI SALUI FIUNT
ID EST NOBIS UIRTUS DI EST
SCRIPTUM EST ENIM
PERDAM SAPIENTIAM
SAPIENTIUM
ET PRUDENTIAM PRUDENTIUM
REPROBABO
UBI SAPIENS UBI SCRIBA
UBI INQUISITOR HUIUS SAECULI
NONNE STULTAM FECIT DS
SAPIENTIAM HUIUS MUNDI
NAM QUIA IN DI SAPIENTIAM
NON COGNOUIT MUNDUS
PER SAPIENTIAM DM
PLACUIT DO PER STULTITIAM
PRAEDICATIONIS SALUOS FACERE

Fig. 11. Page with 1 Cor 1.1–21, from the Codex Amiatinus (MS Laur. Amiat. 1, folio 950r), written c. 700.

to have any known effect upon the tradition of the Latin Bible, served Abbot *Ceolfrid (d. 716) in *Wearmouth-*Jarrow in Northumbria as the model for the external layout of the most famous of Vulgate Bible MSS, the single-volume *Amiatinus* (see below). Except for the first eight leaves, which in text and illustration were copied from the Cassiodorian codex, the text of this Northumbrian pandect was drawn from a variety of locally available Vulgate sources, including the good Campanian 6th-century Gospel already mentioned. As a whole, the *Amiatinus,* like Victor of Capua's NT, cannot be found to have exercised any unitary influence, until, that is, it began, already in the 16th century, to have a conspicuous place in the modern revision of the Vulgate.

Italy, north and south, was not unique in this early period in owning pandects of the Vulgate. Spain also had them, but only one has thus far been identified—in the underscript of 82 leaves of a MS (15) of the León Cathedral chapter (Lowe 11:1636), these forming less than one-eighth of the 7th-century original. Certain later Spanish Bibles of the 9th and 10th centuries may well reflect more or less faithfully models close in date to the León fragments.

Supplanting of the Old Latin. While none of these Spanish Bibles has been satisfactorily linked with St. *Isidore of Seville, this influential bishop (600–636) handed down more than one strong commendation of the Vulgate. He declared Jerome's translation "justly preferred to all others" (*Etym.* 6.4.5), stating his reasons in the very language—as Dom Gribomont has noted—used by St. Augustine (*Doctr. christ.* 2.22, PL 34:46) in praise of the "Itala." The tone Isidore employed elsewhere (*De ecclesiasticis officiis* 1.12.8, PL 83:748C) in commending Jerome's version for liturgical use suggests approbation of the *status quo* rather than a newly proposed position. And, indeed, a generation earlier St. *Gregory I at Rome had given strong support to the Vulgate OT through his prevailing use of it in his commentaries. (His Psalter, however, is pre-Hieronymian.) Again, insofar as the Roman Lectionary of the period may be judged from the *Comes* of Würzburg (Dekkers, *Clavis* 1985), the OT at least was overwhelmingly represented there in the Vulgate version. A Gallican Lectionary (that of the Abbey of *Luxeuil: Dekkers, *Clavis* 1948), continuing the early tendency already noted in a Wolfenbüttel book, indicates an established preference for the Vulgate. Farther to the north—in Ireland and England—the Vulgate had long before penetrated, in some cases in the best texts of southern Italy. The liturgical agreements reached in the synod of Clovesho (747) tended to terminate local Celtic usages in favor of the Roman—the beginning of a reform that would, in turn, through the missionaries, affect both Germany and Gaul. The insular shift in Bible text may be seen in the writings, on the one hand, of SS. *Patrick and *Columban, who still used the Old Latin, and on the other, in the *De excidio,* attributed to St. *Gildas, where a mixed Biblical text shows strong Vulgate infusion. Wax tablets of *c.* 600 found in an Irish bog and reported on by D. H. Wright in 1962 show Psalms 30–32 in a basically Gallican text.

Such diversity in the Biblical text found in ecclesiastical writers comes about in more than one way but partly reflects the Bible MSS themselves, to which the crosscurrents of transmission often brought a pattern of mixture. Thus, in a single volume a set of the Prophets may show Jeremia in St. Jerome's translation along with the others in the Old Latin; or the canticles that are scattered through the books of the Bible may appear as Old Latin set in a Vulgate context. The resulting difficulty of categorizing as either Old Latin or Vulgate a codex that contains text of both kinds must be borne in mind as affecting the close interpretation of the statistics that follow, though hardly as vitiating their conclusions. Dom Gribomont has recently analyzed by date and text-variety (Old Latin or Vulgate) the 280 Biblical MSS treated by E. A. Lowe in the first 9 volumes of his *Codices latini antiquiores,* which are fairly representative of what will be covered in the complete set of 11 volumes. (Where Lowe wavers between an earlier and a later dating, the earlier has been chosen; and where the text in a single volume is mixed, it has been treated as Vulgate.) Dom Gribomont's report follows.

> Three codices may go back to the 4th century, and these give an Old Latin text. In the 5th century, there is a count of 26 Old Latin witnesses against 7 that represent the Vulgate. In the 6th century, there are 15 Old Latin codices against 24 Vulgate; in the 7th, 11 against 37; in the 8th, 15 against 142. The late Old Latin witnesses are mainly Psalters. Down through the 6th century the witnesses are nearly all Italian; in the 7th, the Italian codices still form the majority (7 of the 11 Old Latin examples, 16 of the 37 of the Vulgate; moreover 7 English Vulgate witnesses depend on Italian models); in the 8th century, England and the Anglo-Saxons missions in Germany make a very important contribution, respectively 41 and 22 [Vulgate] MSS over against 14 Italian. [*Maison-Dieu* 62:58.]

The supremacy of the Vulgate, which had begun to be quite clear in the 6th and 7th centuries, was by the 8th established beyond question, and Italian books had played the major part in it.

Alcuin. The reign of *Charlemagne was eventful and, in at least one point, decisive for the editing and copying of the Vulgate Bible. Attention commonly focuses here upon *Alcuin of York, who migrated to France in 793 and died there in 804; he was abbot of St. Martin's, Tours, from 796 on and for more than 20 years was a close associate of Charlemagne. In a letter for Easter 800 Alcuin declared himself occupied in the "emendation of the Old and New Testaments" at the "king's instruction [*praeceptum*]" (MGEp 4.322–323), but the Biblical MSS associated with him carry no foreword or title page to mark them as officially sponsored.

Alcuin was not the only one or the first of Charlemagne's subjects to show serious concern for Bible production. There had been the impressive Bible of Corbie (*see* CORBIE, ABBEY OF) in some 12 volumes (5 survive at Amiens; see below) copied under Abbot Maurdramn, who died in the year Alcuin met the King; also, the earliest members in a series of Gospel Books and Psalters that issued from the "Court School"—the so-called "Ada group"—copied probably at Aachen; and, finally, the oldest-known Carolingian pandect, copied at Metz, possibly under Bishop *Angilramnus (d. 791; Lowe 6:786). But Tours displayed a productivity of Biblical codices unrivaled for the time, and about 30 of these Tours MSS older than *c.* 850 are extant. These jointly yield the image of the "Alcuin Bible," even if only six come from Alcuin's actual abbacy. The pictures and decoration of the finest of the 30 mark a

Fig. 12. The beginning of the Prologue to the Gospel according to St. Luke in a Gospel Book (Morgan MS 728, folio 95r) written at Reims at the time of Archbishop Hincmar (845–882), a chief example of Carolingian art.

high point in *Carolingian art, as their text marks an epoch in the history of the Latin Bible—the MS on which Gutenberg was to draw some 650 years later was little more than a somewhat debased descendant of the Alcuin Bible. The Alcuin text, Vulgate throughout, was not formed with very great care. In correctness and orthography, the books from Alcuin's own time in particular are deficient and lag behind the Bibles of Maurdramn and Angilramnus; but some improvement appeared under Alcuin's successors at St. Martin's.

The Alcuin Bible was not based upon a preexisting pandect. Like the *Amiatinus,* it was a composite of different texts assembled into one. A distinctive component was its Psalter—Jerome's revision after Origen's Hexapla, not his translation from the Hebrew. The latter would logically have accompanied Jerome's other versions from that language and did accompany them in the *Amiatinus,* as also in the *Cavensis* and other Spanish Bibles. The preference in Charlemagne's realm for the Psalter that thereafter was to be called "Gallican" may have been initially independent of Alcuin. The choice had been made in the home (Aachen?) of the "Ada group," where the Dagulf Psalter of Vienna (Lowe 10:1504) was produced in time to be a present to Pope Hadrian I (d. 795). However, the Alcuin Bible put the seal upon the choice and, in the Latin rite, determined the near universality of the Gallican Psalter for a millennium.

Theodulf. One subject and adviser of Charlemagne who withstood the preference for the Gallican Psalter—choosing rather Jerome's rendering from the Hebrew—was *Theodulf, Bishop of Orléans (d. 821) and Abbot of the nearby monasteries of Fleury and Micy. From him have come down a series of six or eight Bibles, small in format and written in small script, two of which have been described by Lowe in the CodLatAntiq: Paris B.N. lat. 9380 (5:576) and the copy in the Le Puy Cathedral (6:768). Equipped with additional texts to assist the interpretation of the Scripture and beautifully transcribed, these Bibles are at once works of art and truly scientific editions of the sacred text. Characteristic are the variants set in the margin with indication of source. With the help of a baptized Jew, Theodulf went back to the Hebrew and dared to improve upon Jerome. This truly remarkable work of his stands somewhat apart from the main stream of the tradition yet did not altogether fail to affect it. Thus at St. Gall in the later 9th century both the Alcuin text and that of Theodulf were used by the correctors.

The 10th to the 15th Century. The long period that falls between the reign of Charlemagne and the stabilization of the Vulgate text through the use of printing has its very special importance for the prescholastic and scholastic interpretation (*see* EXEGESIS, MEDIEVAL) but is less significant for the study of the text, since recension leading to the recovery of the archetype can draw but little from these 6½ centuries. Only certain salient matters from this period will be touched on here.

First in a succession of revisers is St. *Peter Damian, who in his *De ordine eremitarum* (*Opusc.* 14, PL 145: 334) said that he had corrected the entire Bible, although, he added, cursorily and therefore with insufficient precision. Since the actual copy in which his corrections were entered has not been preserved, the nature of Damian's work must remain uncertain. There

is better evidence for the revisions of *Lanfranc, who, in a remarkable statement (in the *Life* by Milo Crispinus of Bec, PL 150:55), is declared to have taken pains to correct both Testaments and also the "writings of the Holy Fathers . . . in accordance with the orthodox faith" (see E. Mangenot, DB 5:2478). Glunz reports traces of Lanfranc's work in two English Gospel MSS (*Vulgate in England,* 159), and Miss Smalley makes frequent reference to his glosses. With St. *Stephen Harding one is on still more solid ground (see DB 5:2479–80). The four folio volumes that make up MS 9*bis* of the Bibl. Municipale of Dijon present a Bible prepared by him at Cîteaux as a model for Cistercian use; v.2 (completed in 1109) contains a statement on the principles employed in preparing the text. Like another Theodulf, St. Stephen had recourse here and there to "certain Jews skilled in their own Scriptures." Not long afterward similar Jewish aid was used also by another Cistercian, Nicholas Maniacoria (d. *c.* 1145), of the Abbey of Tre Fontane, near Rome. Recent researches by Dom André Wilmart and Dom Robert Weber have begun to show how thoroughly and with what enterprise Nicholas worked at the text of all three principal Latin Psalters. Here also should be mentioned the striking results that are being secured from studies by B. Smalley and R. Loewe on Hebrew scholarship in 12th- and 13th-century England.

In the central stream of the tradition lay the study of Scripture in the schools and universities and especially that study as practiced in the University of Paris. It was here around 1225 that the present usual system of chapter division in the Bible, introduced by *Stephen Langton, came into being. The normal University text, against which *Roger Bacon voiced strong criticism, has been shown by Quentin (*Mémoire,* 388) to derive mainly from the Alcuinian recension, with subordinate derivation from the Theodulfian and from a group of medieval Italian codices that includes the giant atlas-sized Bibles, whose art has recently been studied with much profit by E. B. Garrison. Three MSS representing the Paris University text are mainly being used by the current editors of the Vulgate. One of these is a 13th-century Bible in four volumes once owned in Paris by the Dominicans of St. Jacques (the "Jacobins"), now Paris B.N. lat. 16719–22.

In the margins of the Bible of the Jacobins, against the standard University text, stands an extensive array of variant readings representing the critical conclusions of the Dominicans. These marginalia represent one form of the *correctorium biblicum* current at this time as a means of eliminating an accumulation of errors. A second type of *correctorium* appears by itself apart from the Bible text and simply presents, often with appropriate notes, the readings that are to be rejected or retained. The current Benedictine editors of the Vulgate use both the Jacobin *correctorium* and two examples of the second type, one the work of *Hugh of Saint-Cher, OP (d. 1263), the other of the Oxford Franciscan *William de la Mare (d. 1298), both now the property of the Vatican Library (respectively, Ottob. lat. 293 and Vat. lat. 3466).

If from the *exemplar Parisiense* this article passes all but directly to the printed Bible of Mainz, it should not be supposed that immediately after the discovery of printing scribes and illuminators ceased to produce handmade Bibles. It was a post-Gutenberg Evangeliary of *c.* 1480, penned and painted for Federico da Montefeltro, Duke of Urbino (MS Vat. Urb. lat. 10), that was used by the Fathers of *Vatican Council II as the Gospel Book of the council.

Vulgate Manuscripts. In listing here the principal MSS of the Vulgate—a few out of the thousands that exist—those will be selected that have been found by recent editors to be the most important for establishing the text.

Genesis through Esther. For the OT the report will be confined largely to the well-advanced but still unfinished Benedictine revision (*Vat. Vulg.*) of the Vulgate (see below). Here an average of 30 MSS are reported for each Biblical book, but generally the text chosen depends on a very small number—in the typical case, and especially in the Octateuch (Genesis through Ruth), the three that represent as many families (Quentin, *Mémoire*, 453–456). Since the listing of the MSS that belong to the various families of the text may not interest the general reader, smaller type is used below for such technical matters.

For the greater part of the Octateuch the heads of family are exactly three (the second and third families are named respectively after the two scholars, Alcuin and Theodulf, under whom characteristic 9th-century copies were produced): (1) the *Turonensis S. Gatiani* (G: Paris B.N. nouv. acq. lat. 2334, 7th–8th century; Lowe 5:693a-b), heading a Spanish family; (2) the *Amiatinus*, justly the most renowned of all the MSS of the Vulgate (A: Florence Bibl. Laur. Amiat. 1, *c.* A.D. 700; Lowe 3:299), heading the Alcuinian family; and (3) *Ottobonianus* (O: Vat. Ottob. lat. 66, 6th–7th century; Lowe 1:66), heading the Theodulfian family. After G gives out in Nm 36.6, headship of the Spanish family passes first to the *Cavensis* [C: Cava Abbaz. 14, 9th century; E. A. Lowe in *Quantulacumque: Studies Presented to K. Lake* (London 1937) 325–331], then (in Judith and Ruth) to Vat. lat. 5763 plus Wolfenbüttel Weiss. 64 (V: palimpsest, end of 5th century; Lowe 1:40; see also 9 p. 43). Support within the family is sometimes gained from the agreement (Λ) of two MSS still in Spain, one at León of the year 960, the other at Madrid of the 12th century; and also from the agreement (Π) of certain MSS at Monte Cassino of the 10th or 11th century. Called in sometimes in support of the *Amiatinus* is the multi-volumed *Bible of Maurdramn* of Corbie (M: Amiens 6, 7, 9, 11, 12 plus Paris B.N. lat. 13174, 8th century, before 781; Lowe 6:707). In 1 and 2 Samuel and 3 and 4 Kings the place of primacy is taken (A and C leading the other groups) by *Verona Capit.* II (2) (R: early 7th century; Lowe 4:477). In 1 and 2 Chronicles and Ezra the leading codices are the familiar A and C, matched often with the aforementioned MS of León (Λᴸ) and *Lyons Bibl. de la Ville 401 (327)* (D: late 8th century; Lowe 6:769); in Ezra, M also plays a leading role. For Tobit and Judith, C and A are joined at the top by an old MS of Lorsch, the *Laureshamensis* (L: Vat. Palat. lat. 24, *c.* A.D. 600; Lowe 1:68a-b), and weight is also given to a *Coloniensis* (K: Cologne Capit. 43, late 8th century; Lowe 8:1148). For Esther L, C, and A remain the leading MSS, and these are joined in Job by the early Vatican-Wolfenbüttel palimpsest (V).

Psalter and Protocanonical Wisdom Books. With the Psalter (the Gallican), the MSS in the top rank are entirely new, partly because a number of the familiar manuscript Bibles, notably the *Amiatinus*, show as Psalter not the Gallican but Jerome's *Iuxta Hebraeos.*

The three leading MSS are, in fact, not manuscript Bibles but simply Psalters. A famous *Reginensis* heads the list (R: Vat. Regin. lat. 11, second half of the 8th century; Lowe 1:101). Next comes a *Corbeiensis* (F: Leningrad Bibl. Publ. F. v. I. n° 5, middle or late 8th century; Lowe 11:1601), and then the *Cathach of St. Columba* (C: Dublin Royal Irish Acad., second half of the 6th century; Lowe 2:266). With the three books of Solomon, the *Amiatinus*

and the *Cavensis* return, joined in Proverbs, in a position of high authority, by *Paris B.N. lat. 11553* [G (N in 1 and 2 Chronicles and Ezra), 9th century]; in Ecclesiastes and the Canticle of Canticles by *Metz Bibl. Munic. 7* (Z: 8th–9th century; destroyed in 1944; photographs in San Girolamo, Rome; Lowe 6:786).

Deuterocanonical Books. With the deuterocanonical books Wisdom and Sirach, the Vulgate offers its first non-Hieronymian elements.

In addition to paying close attention to the underlying Greek, *Vat. Vulg.* assigns special authority to seven MSS, two of them the very familiar C and A, a third the G of Proverbs; S is *St. Gall Stiftsbibl. 28* [early 9th century; A. Bruckner, *Scriptoria medii aevi Helvetica*, v.2 (Geneva 1936) 56]; T, a surrogate for G, is *Salzburg St. Peter a. IX. 16* (late 8th century; Lowe 10:1462); Σᶜ is *Madrid Univ. Centr. 32* (9th–10th century; T. Ayuso Marazuela, *La Vetus Latina Hispana* 1:353); Σᵀ, *Madrid Bibl. Nacion., Tol. 2.1* (10th century; T. Ayuso Marazuela, *op.cit.* 1:352, the T of the NT and Acts below).

Still to appear in *Vat. Vulg.* is the text of 1 and 2 Machabees, but a provisional critical edition (based mainly on well-known Vulgate MSS, A and C among them) was published in 1932 by Dom De Bruyne and Dom B. Sodar. Basic among the several varieties of early Latin text that accompany this edition of the Vulgate is that presented from *Lyons Bibl. de la Ville 356 (430)* of the 9th century.

Gospels. The 30 MSS used by Wordsworth and White (WW) in their critical edition of the Gospels are divided into three classes: (1) the old, uninterpolated MSS (with texts written in Italy or traceable thereto); (2) those whose text shows clear local characteristics (three groups: Celtic, Irish-Gallic, and Spanish); (3) those that supply the recensions (Theodulfian, Alcuinian), plus a Salisbury Bible of 1254 (W) as an example of a scholastic text.

Among these witnesses WW distinguish four levels of worth. (1) First come the *Amiatinus* (A: see above, OT), the *Stonyhurst St. John* (S: 7th–8th century; Lowe 2: 260), the *Gospels of Lindisfarne* (Y: London B.M. Cott. Nero D. IV, early 8th century; Lowe 2:187), *Durham Cath. A. II. 16* (Δ: 8th century; Lowe 2:148a-b), the *Hubertianus* (H: London B.M. Add. 24142, 9th century—the original readings are here meant); then (2) the *Gospels of St. Augustine* (O: Oxford Bodl. Auct. D. II. 14, 7th century; Lowe 2:230) and Cambridge Corp. Chr. Coll. 286 (X: 6th century; Lowe 2:126); next (3) the *Foroiuliensis* (J: Cividale Mus. Arch.; parts also at Prague and Venice, early 6th century; Lowe 3:285), *Milan Bibl. Ambr. C. 39 inf.* (M: second half of 6th century; Lowe 3:313), *Perugia Capit. 1* (P: same date; Lowe 4:407); and finally (4) the *Fuldensis* (F: Fulda Landesbibl. Bonif. 1, A.D. 546–547 or before; Lowe 8:1196), the *Epternacensis* (Ept.: Paris B.N. lat. 9389, 7th–8th century; Lowe 5:578), *London B.M. Harl. 1775* (Z: end of 6th century; Lowe 2:197). Also important are: the *Bigotianus* (B: Paris B.N. lat. 281 and 298, end of 8th century; Lowe 5:526), the *Beneventanus* (Benev.: London B.M. Add. 5463, middle of the 8th century; Lowe 2:162), the *Sangermanensis* (G: Paris B.N. lat. 11553, early 9th century). The most important families are the one represented by A, (F, H, M), and Y and the one represented by B (Benev., F., G, J, O, W, X) and Z.

Among the MSS of the Gospels that were unknown to WW or passed over by them [see B. Fischer, in ZNTWiss 46 (1955) 191; the whole article, 178–196, is a valuable critique of the Oxford Vulgate NT], three may be noted here: the *Claromontanus* (Vat. lat. 7223, fols. 67–283, 7th century; Lowe 1:54), *St. Gall Stiftsbibl. 1395* (Σ: fragments, some in other libraries, 5th century; Lowe 7:984), and *Autun 21* (S. 24) plus *Paris B.N. nouv. acq. lat. 1628* (palimpsest, 5th century; Lowe 6:722). The last two appear to be the oldest MSS of the Vulgate Gospels.

Acts. In the Acts WW used 17 MSS (aside from the 10 with Old Latin text), of which 10 were used for the

Gospels and 7 were new. In respect of their textual value, four classes are indicated: the principal witnesses, the derivative witnesses, the recensions, and again W, the medieval MS from Salisbury.

In terms of kinship, three families emerge. The first shows, among the principal witnesses, A and G (named above as Gospel MSS) and the *Book of Armagh* (D: Dublin Trinity Coll. 52, *c.* A.D. 807; Lowe 2:270); among the derivative, *Rome Bibl. Vallicell. B. 25II* (I: 8th–9th century; Lowe 4:430), *Munich lat. 6230* (M: 9th century), and *Oxford Bodl. Selden Supra 30 (3418)* (O: first half of the 8th century; Lowe 2:257). The second family is led by the above-mentioned *Fuldensis*, a principal witness, followed by two derivative ones: *St. Gall Stiftsbibl.* 2 p. 301–303 (S: second half of the 8th century; Lowe 7:894) and *Ulmensis* (U: London B.M. Add. 11852, end of the 9th century); sometimes also by the *Theodulfianus* (θ: Paris B.N. lat. 9380, 9th century), but especially by the Alcuinian MSS—the *Karolinus* [K: London B.M. Add. 10546, 9th century; E. K. Rand, *Survey of the Manuscripts of Tours* (Cambridge, Mass. 1929) No. 77], the *Bambergensis* (B: Bamberg A. I. 5, 9th century; Rand, *Survey* No. 47), *Vallicellanus* (V: Rome Bibl. Vallicell. B. 6, 9th century; Rand, *Survey* No. 147), the Bible of Rosas (R: Paris B.N. lat. 6, 10th century), and the medieval W. Old Latin admixture characterizes the third class (Spanish). Here the purest text is seen in the *Cavensis*, named above among the MSS of the Vulgate OT; accompanying it are the Toletanus (T; ΣT in *Vat. Vulg.*), and occasionally also θ and the Irish text (D and O).

Epistles and Apocalypse. The MSS used by WW for the Epistles (Pauline and Canonical) and the Apocalypse were mainly those already drawn on in editing the Gospel and the Acts.

Among early MSS still to be used for the Vulgate Pauline Epistles, Fischer (*loc. cit.*) cites: *Orleans 19 (16)*, fols. 26–30, plus *Paris B.N. lat. 2389*, fols. 41–48 (second half of the 6th century; Lowe 6:800), and *León Cath. 15* (3 leaves, palimpsest, 7th century—the palimpsest text of 1 and 2 Machabees, Acts, and Catholic Epistles is Old Latin; Lowe 11:1636).

Printed Editions. The first book of importance to be produced with movable type, the 42-line Bible printed at Mainz between the years 1452 and 1455 by Johann *Gutenberg, had as its model a typical Bible of the University of Paris; no MS closer to this presumably lost model has been found than *Mainz Stadtbibl. II 67* (14th century). The editions that appeared up to 1511 all derived from this Gutenberg Bible except one printed at Vicenza in 1476. The latter is, however, derived from a type of text well known in certain Italian MSS of the 11th and 12th centuries currently used in the Benedictine revision of the Vulgate. From this period, therefore, the printed Bibles may be reduced, in terms of text recension, to the 42-line Bible of Mainz.

Early Attempts at Critical Editions. The first attempts at criticism in the printed Bibles begin in 1511; that year, under the editorship of Albert Castellano, OP, there appeared at Venice a Bible with a system of marginal variants, reminiscent in the last analysis of the work of Theodulf of Orleans. Some corrections from the Hebrew were introduced by the Protestants Andreas *Osiander and Johannes Petreius in Nuremberg editions of the years 1522 and 1527, respectively. Up to this point corrections brought into the text were not assigned to their source, and frequently none had been used. A new period, however, began with the scholar-printer of Paris and Geneva Robert *Estienne (Étienne), whose Bibles run from 1528 to 1556–57. Some of these show a variety of critical signs, and that of 1540 shows

in the margin readings from 20 identifiable MSS and editions. Fortunately there is only one case in which modern scholars do not themselves have direct access to Estienne's sources; Paris B.N. lat. 11553 (N and G in *Vat. Vulg.*) is the imperfectly preserved second volume of a two-volume Bible of the 9th century that Estienne knew complete. One of Estienne's Bibles, printed by Badius in Geneva in 1555, is celebrated as being the first to carry the numbered division of verses within the chapters (those of *Stephen Langton) that is still in use. The Bible prepared by Gobelinus Laridius, Cologne 1530, presents a superior and independent text; unfortunately, its sources are not stated.

Having in mind criticisms of the Vulgate voiced as early as Lorenzo *Valla, then by *Erasmus, and in turn by the Reformers, the Council of Trent in 1546 issued a decree (see below) that assigned to that Bible the character of "authenticity" and called for the printing of a carefully corrected text. What was printed at Rome in 1590 was scarcely that. Before 1590 there had appeared at Louvain and Antwerp a series of Bibles prepared in the spirit of the council, the work especially of Joannes Hentenius, OP (notably, the Bible of 1547, in which the readings of 28 MSS and 2 incunabula are set out in comparison with the text of Estienne), and of Franciscus Lucas of Bruges (Plantin Bibles of 1574 and 1583), later to be known also for his Concordance (1617) of the Sisto-Clementine Bible.

Sistine Edition. The work of revision called for by the fathers of Trent—introduced by extensive and minute collations made under now unknown auspices by the Benedictines of Monte Cassino in the period 1550–69—was carried out through three pontifical commissions, appointed, in turn, by Pius IV, Pius V, and Sixtus V. The first of these was not specialized to the Vulgate and left nothing of importance for it. The commission of *Pius V, which had the revision of the Vulgate as its sole objective, began its work April 28, 1569. It was an industrious and able group, but unanimity was lacking; its work, which lasted into December 1569, came to little. Under Gregory XIII, who succeeded to Pius V, more was done for the Septuagint than for the Vulgate; there was, indeed, a Septuagint commission, which, as has been noted, had interesting incidental results for the assembly of the Old Latin Bible text. The leader of the Septuagint project, Cardinal Antonio *Carafa, was named by Gregory's successor, *Sixtus V, as president of the third commission concerned with the Vulgate. This held its first session on Nov. 28, 1586. Of materials available at Rome, it made use of two fine Carolingian Bibles and of the *Ottobonianus*, which came in *Vat. Vulg.* to play a leading role. Even the *Amiatinus* was brought from Tuscany for the commission's use, while from Spain came collations of two great Bibles of León (ΛL) and Toledo (ΣT). Although the minutes of the meetings of the commission are not preserved, most of its findings are recorded in the cancellations and marginal variants added by hand to a copy of the Plantin Bible of 1583 that, known as the *Codex Carafianus*, is MS Vat. lat. 12959–60 (the present-day Benedictine editors use a small black-letter *v* for readings left intact by the consultors and a small black-letter *w* for the revisions proposed, whether changes, omissions, or additions).

By November 1588 Pope Sixtus had become impatient with what he regarded as the slow progress of the commission, and, having himself practiced the critical art earlier on the works of St. Ambrose, he took personal charge of the edition, thus beginning a sorrowful chapter in the history of the Vulgate text. In his quite energetic, personal, and often arbitrary corrections, Sixtus only rarely followed the recommendations of his own commission. After hardly more than 6 months of work the near septuaginarian had completed his almost single-handed work of correction. With less than 6 months consumed at the presses, the printing was complete on Nov. 25, 1589.

Clementine Edition. The bull *Aeternus ille caelestium* that introduced the folio volume is dated March 1, 1590. On August 27 came the sudden death of the Pope, occurring when only the first copies had been distributed. In view of the criticism that had been raised against the edition even in Sixtus's lifetime and that was to become more intense thereafter, the cardinals, hardly a week after the Pope's death, suspended the sale of the new Bible, and copies already purchased or received as gifts were later recovered by the publishing authority. What drew the criticism was not, however, the Pope's refusal to adopt more of the good readings recommended by the Carafa Commission but rather the changes that he did make, many of them in opposition to the MSS. Hence the edition was considered likely to have a disturbing effect among Catholics and to have propaganda value for the heretics. Sixtus's successor, Gregory XIV, taking counsel from St. Robert *Bellarmine, decided, therefore, to have a new revision made in which the faulty changes of the Sistine text might be removed and the Bible republished, still under Sixtus's name. A group of 11 experts, Bellarmine among them, along with a few survivors from the Carafa Commission, withdrew to Cardinal Colonna's villa at Zagarolo near Rome and in 19 days (March and April 1591) almost finished what they set themselves to do. After Gregory's death in the next October and the 2-month pontificate of Innocent IX it was upon *Clement VIII, elected Jan. 30, 1592, that the task of publishing the revised Bible fell. As his agents, Clement used the very two men who had witnessed and to some extent assisted the personal editorial efforts of Sixtus—the Jesuit Francesco de *Toledo and the Augustinian Angelo *Rocca. In the mid-autumn of 1592 the new Bible appeared, made in frontispiece, title, and disposition of the text on the pages to resemble as closely as possible the volume it was replacing. The name of Sixtus V alone appeared on the frontispiece, and it was not until 1604 that the now regular form *Biblia Sacra Vulgatae Editionis Sixti V Pont. Max. iussu recognita et Clementis VIII auctoritate edita* is found, and even then it did not at once displace the original shorter title. But there were in fact some 4,900 differences between the two editions, many, of course, all but negligible yet forming a mass of divergence large enough to arouse among Protestant controversialists such a work as the satirically entitled *Bellum Papale* of Thomas James (London 1600). Relatively few of the differences represented substantive improvements, and possibilities for improvement were passed by; for example, of the 150 largely excellent proposals made by the Carafa Commission in the last eight chapters of Genesis, only 16 were adopted in the Clementine text (Quentin, *Mémoire* 197). Official printings of 1593 and 1598 brought in numerous largely mechanical improvements, to produce what has remained, in its successive reappearances, the official Vulgate of the Church. The yield of the three editions is most scrupulously given in the Vulgate produced by the Capuchin Michael *Hetzenauer (Innsbruck 1906; repr. 1922); and that prepared by L. Gramatica (*nova ed.* Vatican Press 1929) is especially valuable for the indications of the Biblical texts that have been turned to liturgical use.

Critical Studies. The Vulgate of the 1590s was not, then, the carefully amended recension prescribed by the Council of Trent. One saint among the Popes, Pius V, had seen promising but ineffectual work go forward toward the production of the edition that the Church required. It remained for another, *Pius X, in 1907, to impose the task that would in fact bring this edition into being—the yet incomplete Vatican Vulgate. Much in the intervening 3 centuries had taken place in the world of scholarship that would help the 20th-century project toward its success. Only a few of these events can be mentioned here.

As early as 1618 there were the *Romanae correctiones* of the aforementioned Lucas of Bruges. The Maurists A. Pouget and J. Martianay, in editing (1693) the works of St. Jerome, produced a new text of the Vulgate, largely based on the Theodulfian recension. Lacking a certain balance, therefore, this edition was not worthy to replace the Clementine and, fortunately, did not do so (in D. Vallarsi's reediting it occupies PL v.28, 29). Of the monumental work on the Old Latin text done in the early 18th century by another Maurist, Pierre Sabatier, mention has already been made. In England Richard *Bentley and J. Walker projected a New Testament (Greek and Latin). The plan did not mature, but their extensive collections were preserved at Cambridge and proved useful to later scholars. At Rome in 1830 the Barnabite Aloysius M. Ungarelli (d. 1845) discovered the already mentioned *Codex Carafianus,* a document, as has been shown, of prime importance for following the work of revision under Sixtus V. Ungarelli's work on this document passed to his confrere Carlo *Vercellone, whose *Variae lectiones Vulgatae latinae* . . . (2 v. Rome 1860–64) proved a valuable assembly of readings. Meantime, at Leipzig in 1850, Konstantin von *Tischendorf, known also in Latin Biblical scholarship for editions of more than one Old Latin text, printed that of the *Amiatinus.* In 1873 he produced also an OT begun by T. Heyse, in which the Clementine text was divided according to the *cola et commata* of the *Amiatinus* (also, the *capitula* of that MS were printed here). In 1893 Samuel Berger, a young Protestant pastor, encouraged to studies in the Latin Bible by Léopold V. *Delisle (d. 1910), produced his invaluable *Histoire de la Vulgate pendant les premiers siècles du moyen âge* (Paris 1893). Near at hand was the professorship at Munich of Ludwig *Traube (d. 1907), pregnant with blessing for those paleographical and historical studies in "the age of photography" that brought about and made fruitful the vast collections of facsimiles of MSS on which so much of 20th-century Biblical scholarship depends.

New Testament of Wordsworth and White. This rapid survey may serve to introduce a brief account of the two projects in the critical editing of Latin Vulgate text that are here called for—the Oxford edition of the NT of Wordsworth-White-Sparks (WWS) and the Benedictine work at Rome on the whole of the Vulgate

Fig. 13. Title page of the first edition of the Sisto–Clementine Vulgate Bible, Rome, 1592.

Latin Bible (*Vat. Vulg.*). Some suggestion of the fine qualities of the former project may have been gained from the account given earlier of the MSS of the Vulgate NT, based as that was on the reports contained in the edition itself and in the article by B. Fischer there cited. Three scholars, helped indeed by many friends and assistants (among them Baron Von *Hügel), were the makers of this edition. Its first leader, John Wordsworth, when made Anglican bishop of Salisbury, found an able collaborator in another Oxford scholar, Henry J. White, at whose death (1934) yet a third Oxonian, H. F. D. Sparks, brought to completion in 1954 what had been started in 1889 and dedicated then to Queen Victoria. As the three-volume work progressed, the attention given by the editors to the Old Latin sources became greater, so much so that in the second and third volumes WWS goes far toward replacing Sabatier. Valuable supplements to the edition itself are the seven volumes (1883–1923) of *Old-Latin Biblical Texts.* In his assessment of WWS, Fischer (*op. cit.*) pointed out various ways in which advances must still be made in editing the Vulgate NT.

Benedictine Edition. The stimulus to the current Benedictine revision of the Vulgate came with a letter addressed by Pope Pius X on April 30, 1907, to the abbot primate asking the united efforts of the Benedictines of the Confederated Congregations toward realizing the truly adequate edition of the Vulgate that the Council of Trent had entrusted to the Holy See. When the abbots presidents accepted the invitation, a commission was set up under the direction of Dom Aidan (Francis Neil) *Gasquet (d. 1929), the well-known historian and a somewhat younger contemporary of his fellow countryman John Wordsworth. Among the members of the commission were Dom De Bruyne and Dom Henri *Quentin (d. 1935), both often mentioned in this article. In the recruitment of the funds required for the material needs of the commission—and especially for the all important photographs of MSS—citizens of the U.S., both Protestant and Catholic, were especially generous. Publication began in 1913 with a series of *Collectanea Biblica Latina,* now in its 13th volume. The sixth in this series is of outstanding importance, Dom Quentin's *Mémoire sur l'établissement du texte de la Vulgate,* providing conclusions and directives valid for all the future work of revision, and describing a method for classifying the MSS that, though not without its partisans, embroiled scholars on both sides of the Atlantic and has for the most part been rejected. In 1926 came the first volume of the new revision, presenting the text of Genesis. The form of presentation there adopted has continued throughout the dozen volumes that have to date appeared. Horizontally the page is divided into four parts: at the top is the text in double columns, underneath is a triple apparatus. The first part of the latter presents the reading of the key MSS, whose relations generally determine the choice of reading; next, below, comes the full apparatus of variants, in double columns; the apparatus at the bottom presents from selected MSS the evidence for the *cola et commata* divisions of the text. Edited with no less diligence than the Scripture itself are the prologues or prefaces (especially those of St. Jerome) found in the MSS reported and the various sets of chapter headings or summaries (10 series in the case of the Book Genesis, which are subdivisible into 18 types).

In 1933 Pius XI gave a new structure to the group of monks who would work on the Vulgate. The commission was suppressed, and in its place, with Dom Quentin its first abbot, was set up the Abbey of S. Girolamo, occupying in the suburbs near the Vatican a new building designed for the use of this specialized community. Abbot Quentin survived his promotion less than a year; he was succeeded in the abbacy by Dom Pierre Salmon, under whom the 10 volumes beginning with the 3d have been published. With the Sapiential books completed in v.12 (1964), there remains of the OT, besides Machabees [of which Dom De Bruyne, while yet a member of the Vulgate Commission, published a separate edition (Maredsous 1932)], the challenging array of the Prophets, approximately equal in length to the Octateuch, whose publication occupied the first four volumes in the series. Beyond that, with its own problems, some solved in the Oxford edition, others in fact raised by that edition, lies the NT. Earlier, however, will probably come, in relation to the OT, other indices to match the painstaking index of *Orthographica totius Octateuchi* appended to v.4. When will the edition be completed? Confronted with that question, a monk of S. Girolamo recently replied: "Nous n'avons jamais songé à donner une date pour terme à nos travaux. Dieu y pourvoira!"

New Editions of the Vulgate. In 1959, from the publishing house of Marietti in Rome, appeared a new Vulgate, noteworthy on several counts. One novelty is the generous provision of Psalter texts. The customary Gallicanum is joined in parallel columns not only by the New Psalter of Pius XII (1945; see below) but also by St. Jerome's *Iuxta Hebraeos* in the text of Dom H. de Sainte-Marie [*Coll. Bibl. Lat.* 11 (Vatican City 1954)]. More remarkable, the Marietti edition presents, in a critical apparatus attributed to the monks of S. Girolamo, the significant differences between the Clementine text and that of the Oxford NT, that of the *Vat. Vulg.* (through v.11: Proverbs, Ecclesiastes, and the Canticle of Canticles), and Dom De Bruyne's edition of the Machabees (Vulgate column). The appearance of such an assembly of variants in an official edition of the Vulgate is noted by S. Garofalo in his preface as a first occurrence, permitted under a declaration of the Pontifical Biblical Commission of Nov. 17, 1921. The ecumenical flavor imparted by the variant readings taken from the edition founded by the future Anglican bishop of Salisbury will be sensed more strongly in a yet more novel Vulgate now for some years in preparation and scheduled to appear in 1966 from the Württembergische Bibelanstalt of Stuttgart. Three distinguished Benedictines [Dom Weber (head), Dom Fischer, and Dom Gribomont] are joined on the board of editors by Prof. H. F. D. Sparks of Oxford and Dr. W. Thiele, a German Lutheran associated with the Beuron *Vetus Latina* project. The edition will offer not the Clementine text with variants but—after the fashion of *Vat. Vulg.* and WWS—a new text critically arrived at and solidly presented on the basis of some dozen MSS per book yet forming a manageable single volume (*Handausgabe*). This genuine unity of approach, which cuts across national and confessional lines, well befits a Bible that for a millennium and a half has served prayer, meditation, and scholarship the world over.

Council of Trent and the Vulgate. On April 8, 1546, after more than a month of deliberation, the Fathers of the Council of *Trent issued two decrees on Sacred Scripture. The second of them, called *Insuper* from its opening word and inspired in no small part by a work published in 1533 by the Louvain theologian J. Driedo [d. 1535; see R. Draguet, "Le maître louvaniste Driedo inspirateur du décret de Trent sur la Vulgate," *Miscellanea historica in honorem Alberti De Meyer* (Louvain and Brussels 1946) 836–854], declares that of the then circulating Latin editions of the sacred books, "precisely the ancient and widely current [*vulgata*] edition that had been approved by long use within the Church for so many centuries . . . should be held as authentic"; it also determined that that edition "should be printed in as correct a form as possible" (Denz 1506, 1508; EnchBibl 61, 63). If effective action toward the production of a correct edition of the Vulgate came only slowly—with the Sisto-Clementine Bible of 1592 and, definitively, with the still-continuing Benedictine revision—there was an immediate critical response toward the declaration of authenticity, as there already had been toward reports of the council's preliminary deliberations on the point. The criticisms introduced from the Roman Curia and reflected and enlarged in controversies that flourished in the 16th and 17th centuries, especially in Catholic Spain but in Protestant circles as well (a treatise from *Melanchthon appeared in the very year of the decree), embraced many elements, some of them grounded in misconceptions—e.g., did not the decree debase the scriptural originals and ignore the manifest faults of the Vulgate? [See B. Emmi, "Il Decreto Tridentino sulla Volgata nei commenti della prima (seconda) polemica protestanticocattolica," *Angelicum* 30 (1953) 107–130, 228–272.] A dissertation by St. Robert Bellarmine published posthumously in 1749 largely anticipated the now clear, official interpretation but could not check the continuing· criticism of the council's action.

As recently as 1941 a long letter had to be addressed by the *Pontifical Biblical Commission to the archbishops and bishops of Italy to put them on their guard against an anonymous attack, made earlier in the year, upon the scientific study of Scripture, that claimed justification in the Tridentine decree *Insuper* (Denz 3794; EnchBibl 526). This letter, issued under the authority of Pope Pius XII, and especially two paragraphs of the same Pontiff's encyclical of September 1943, *Divino afflante Spiritu* (par. 21–22; Denz 3825; EnchBibl 549), state plainly the meaning of the council's use of the term "authentic": that the decree applied only to the Latin Church and to its public use of the Scriptures; that it diminished in no way the authority and value of the original texts, Hebrew or Greek; that the decree in effect affirmed that the Vulgate was free from any error whatever in matters of faith and morals and so could be quoted with complete authority in disputations, lectures, and preaching—that, in short, the term had been used primarily in a juridical rather than a critical sense; and that there had been no intention to prohibit the making of vernacular versions from the original texts rather than from the Vulgate.

LATER VERSIONS

The report to be given here will be confined to printed Bible text dating from the early 16th century on. In preamble, however, some mention should be made of a few characteristic medieval versions, especially of the Psalms, that remained in MS form at least until the 20th century and show marked variance from standard versions.

A Psalter in a 12th-century Monte Cassino Bible (MS A. 557), published by A. Amelli in 1912 and basically reflecting the Psalter of Tertullian and Cyprian, contains peculiar elements to such an extent as to cause Dom Weber to exclude its variants from his edition (1953) of Old Latin Psalters. Two further Monte Cassino Psalters are among several noted by Dom De Sainte-Marie as showing a somewhat radical conformation to the Hebrew original. The case of Nicholas Maniacoria (see above) is clear evidence of a 12th-century scholar working in or near Rome with a rabbi to secure a Psalter more faithful to the original Hebrew (De Sainte-Marie, ed., *S. Hieron. Psalt. sec. Heb.* xxxiv–xxxv). From the Italian Renaissance has come a most notable example of this same fresh approach to the originals. From the Florentine Giannozzo *Manetti there is in MS a translation of the NT from the Greek and, as the beginning of what was to have been an entire OT freshly translated from the Hebrew, a Psalter from which S. Garofalo has recently provided the text of Psalms 72(73)–82(83).

It need hardly be added that Latin verse renderings or adaptations of Scripture are not included here—whether so early a specimen as the Gospel poem of *Sedulius or such late productions as the Latin metrical psalms of George Buchanan (1506–82) and Theodore *Beza (1519–1605), both found in a Paris printing of the time (1566; No. 6149 in the Darlow-Moule *Historical Catalogue,* cited as DM).

Of the printed material, from the 16th to the 20th century, that presents new non-Vulgate Latin Bible renderings, only a selection may be noted here. These renderings arose mainly from a desire to gain new understanding of Scripture through a fresh, direct study of the Hebrew and Greek originals; and both Catholics and Protestants had a part in them.

Early 16th-century Versions. In the earliest edition of his Greek NT (Basel 1516; DM 6096), Desiderius Erasmus included his own Latin version; this was repeatedly revised and frequently reprinted, often accompanying vernacular versions. In a 1522 Nuremberg Vulgate (DM, note after 6102) the editor, Andreas *Osiander, in addition to revising the current text, added in the OT notes on the Hebrew original. A somewhat similar and often reprinted production came from Andreas's son Lucas, first printed in Tübingen 1573–86 (DM, note after 6175). From the years 1514–17 came the first of the great *polyglot Bibles, the Complutensian of Francisco *Ximénes de Cisneros (DM 1412), the work of a group of scholars and published at Alcalá de Henares (Complutum). Here the Septuagint is accompanied by an interlinear Latin version (in the Psalms the version is the well-known *Psalterium Romanum*); an Aramaic version (Targum) of the Pentateuch is flanked by its Latin translation. A Dominican, Santes *Pagnini, native of Lucca, is responsible for the first Latin translation in modern times of the whole Bible, the OT from the Hebrew, the NT from the Greek. First published in Lyons in 1528 (DM 6108), this version fared first well, then badly with the critics and experienced a number of revisions and reeditions, the first being that of the unfortunate Michael *Servetus (Lyons 1542; DM 6120). In the course of his various commentaries on the Bible another Dominican, Cardinal *Cajetan (Tommaso de Vio), frequently presents, in both the OT and the NT, texts rendered by himself from the originals, with the help, respectively, of a Jew and a Greek.

The first important Protestant Latin version came from the Hebraist Sebastian *Münster, whose Hebrew Bible (Basel 1534–35; DM 6115) includes the editor's own Latin version. Revising and completing a 14th-century Jewish version of St. Matthew into Hebrew, Münster added his own Latin rendering of this version and published the two versions together at Basel in 1537 (DM 5088; dedication to Henry VIII of England). In later printings (first in 1557) a similar Hebrew-Latin presentation of the Epistle to the Hebrews was added (see DM 5105). Some of Münster's notes accompany the somewhat injudicious revision of the Vulgate made by the Benedictine Isidorus Clarius and published first at Venice 1542 (DM 6121; in the preceding year a NT alone), a Bible that, like the others of Clarius, was placed on the *Index Expurgatorius*.

Mid-16th-century Versions. The four translations next to be named all came from Protestants. A partisan of Zwingli, Leo *Jud died (1542) without having finished a rendering of the Hebrew OT into Latin; the task was completed by Theodor Bibliander (Buchmann, d. 1564), and the Apocrypha were rendered from Greek by Petrus Cholinus. This composite Latin OT, accompanied by a signed revision of Erasmus's Latin NT, was printed in 1543 to form the first edition of the "Zurich Latin Bible" (DM 6124). Elegance and classical flavor were dominant objectives in the translation from Hebrew and Greek carried out by a professor of Greek at Basel, Sebastian *Castellio (Châteillon), first printed at Basel in 1551 (DM 6131) and dedicated to Edward VI of England. Among the remarkable features of Castellio's Latinity was the use of *respublica* for *ecclesia*. The fifth folio edition of Robert Estienne's complete Bible (Geneva 1557; DM 6140) contains, along with the Vulgate, a revision of Pagnini's OT and a fresh translation of the NT by Theodore Beza. Beza's often reprinted Latin NT appeared also, along with the Vulgate, in the first major edition of his Greek NT (Geneva 1565; DM 6147, 4629).

Next in this selection of 16th-century Latin renderings comes the work of the Benedictine Arias *Montanus and his helpers as found in the second great polyglot Bible, that published at Antwerp by Christophe *Plantin in eight volumes (1569–72; DM 1422, 6156). A number of non-Vulgate Latin versions appear here: in v.1–4, translations of the Septuagint and of the Aramaic Targum; in v.5, a Latin translation of the Syriac NT; in v.7, a translation of the Hebrew OT revised from that of Pagnini.

Late 16th- and 17th-century Versions. Yet another fresh approach to the Hebrew and, for the deuterocanonical books, to the Greek appeared in an OT first published at Frankfurt am Main in 1575–79 (DM 6165) by the Protestants Immanuel Tremellius (d. 1580) and his son-in-law Franciscus Junius (d. 1602). The translation from the Hebrew is a joint effort, whereas that of the deuterocanonical books from the Greek is the work of Junius alone. In a London printing of 1580 (DM 6166) the Frankfurt OT was rounded out with Tremellius's rendering of the Syriac NT to form England's first complete Latin Bible. From 1602 to 1610 there appeared, in parts, from the hand of a well-known Protestant commentator of the 17th century, Johannes Piscator (Fischer, d. 1625), still another Latin version, accompanying that of Tremellius-Junius (DM, note after 6203). Versions from both Catholic and Protestant sources are found in the London polyglot of 1655–57 (DM 1446, 6227): a revised Pagnini OT (from the Antwerp Polyglot), a Latin rendering of the Sistine Septuagint next to be mentioned, and the Latin renderings of the various Aramaic, Syriac, Arabic, Samaritan, Ethiopic, and Persian texts presented in this fourth and last of the great polyglots [the third—Paris 1629–45 (DM 1442)—adhered closely to that of Antwerp].

To the 19th Century. Four Catholic productions carry the present account down to the middle of the 18th century. The first of these, already described in connection with the Old Latin Bible, is the Latin version of the Septuagint (Rome 1588; DM 6179) that forms a supplement to the Sistine edition of the Greek issued in the preceding year (DM 4647). Where available, existing renderings found as quotations in the various Latin Fathers were used, and these were pieced together into a whole by direct translation from the Greek, all under the direction of Flaminio de Nobili. A translation from the Hebrew, based in part on older versions, accompanies the *Commentaria* of Tomás *Malvenda, published posthumously (Lyons 1650) under the direction of Thomas Turcus. In an attempt to remain faithful to the Hebrew, Malvenda coins strange, new Latin words. From Jean de *la Haye we have two impressive productions, the *Biblia magna* (5 v. Paris 1643; DM, note after 6218) and the *Biblia maxima* (19 v. Paris 1660; DM, note after 6230). Here appear a wide variety of Latin translations—in the *Maxima*, as many as 20 or 30 offered, in confusing abundance, for a single passage. An Oratorian, C. F. *Houbigant (1686–1783), produced (Paris 1753) in 4 volumes a *Biblia Hebraica* (DM 5154) with an accompanying new Latin translation that embodies the emendations adopted by the editor from a variety of sources. The Greek of the deuterocanonical books is provided also with a Latin version.

In the later 18th and in the 19th century very little in the way of significant new Latin translations of the Bible appeared. Latin was still used as a quasi vernacular in presenting Bible text in an uncommon language [e.g., in E. Benzl's *Gothic Gospels* (Oxford 1750); DM 4560] or in a new recension [thus H. A. Schott's Latin version of J. J. *Griesbach's Greek NT (Leipzig 1805); DM 6275, 4780]. Emanuel *Swedenborg, writing in Latin, included in some of his writings, e.g., the *Arcana caelestia* (London 1749), original Latin renderings of various parts of the Bible.

20th-century Versions. It remains to record an event of the mid-20th century that in a certain way is without parallel in the Church's history—the official procurement by the Holy See of a new Latin rendering of a book of the Bible—in this case, the Psalms—and its prompt authorization for use in private and choral prayer. The official authorization given the Gallican Psalter in the Roman Breviary by Pope St. Pius V in 1570 is in part parallel, but that Psalter text was then already more than 1,000 years old. The new translation of the Psalms, the work of professors of the *Pontifical Biblical Institute at Rome, was commissioned by Pius XII in 1941. Authorized by a motu proprio of March 24,

1945, it was promptly published as a *Liber psalmorum,* with prolegomena and both critical and explanatory notes (a second edition of the same year carries a preface dated August 15); accompanying the Psalms were new renderings of the OT and NT canticles used in the weekly *cursus* of the Roman Office. The same year saw the new Psalter published by the Vatican Press for Office recitation as a *Psalterium Breviarii Romani,* and many subsequent Latin and vernacular Breviaries the world over have adopted the *Psalterium Pianum.* In the judgment of some the manifest virtues of the *Pianum*—its faithful presentation of the thought of the original and the clarity of its Latin—are offset by a neglect to take adequate account, for style and diction, of the *Gallicanum* and other ancient versions. Actually, Vatican Council II (Constitution on the Liturgy, § 91) has called for a new version of the Latin Psalter more faithful to Christian Latin and the liturgy.

As if following in the train of the Psalter of 1945, there appeared 5 years later, again from the Pontifical Biblical Institute, a rendering of *Ecclesiastes,* translated from the original by Agostino Bea (later Cardinal), who issued in 1953 a similar *Canticle of Canticles).* Moreover, the utility of maintaining Latin within the Church as the basic and universal language of Biblical translation was expressed early in December 1963 by the bishop of Purwokerto (Java) when he called on Vatican Council II to direct that, for ultimate official adoption as a replacement of the Old Vulgate, there be prepared by the most competent scholars available, Catholic or other, and from the original sources, a new and complete Latin Bible. What will become of this proposal remains to be seen, but the Council was not yet over when another came into the first stages of being. A notice in the *Osservatore Romano* of December 1, 1965, listed the persons appointed by the Pope to a Commission charged, under Cardinal Bea's presidency, with the "revision of the Vulgate"—that is, of the Vulgate as now being restored to its primitive form in the current Benedictine edition. What was intended was not a thoroughly new Latin Bible but a sort of "neo-Vulgata" that would bring correctness or clarity to such passages in the Vulgate text as may be found to be unfaithful to the original or not adequately comprehensible. The style of the rewritten passages was to follow the norms of traditional Christian Latinity.

Bibliography: New work on the Latin Bible annually reported in the *Année philologique* (s.v. "Testamenta, -um") and in *Biblica* (in the "Elenchus bibliographicus biblicus," III, 5 and 6). Critical reports on the yield of successive periods of years in the "Bulletin d'ancienne littérature latine chrétienne" (suppl. to RevBén), in the section "Bulletin de la Bible Latine"; latest installment (M. BOGAERT's report on 298 items) pub. with Rev Bén 74 (1964) and 75 (1965). See also B. M. METZGER, *Annotated Bibliography of the Textual Criticism of the NT 1914–1939* (Copenhagen 1955) 30–45 (nos. 352–527); *cf.* NTSt 2 (1955–56) 3–5; "Latin Versions," *New Testament Manuscript Studies,* ed. M. M. PARVIS and A. P. WIKREN (Chicago 1950) 51–61.

Latin Bible in general. A. PENNA, EncCatt 7:941–943. K. T. SCHÄFER, LexThK² 2:380–384. W. THIELE, RGG³ 1:1196–97. A. TRICOT, Robert-Tricot 1:637–664, 674–676 (includes refs. on Biblical Latinity). A. ALLGEIER, "Haec vetus et vulgata editio," *Biblica* 29 (1948) 353–390. "Prooemium," *Biblia Polyglotta Matritensia* (Madrid 1957). L. BIELER, *The Grammarian's Craft: An Introduction to Textual Criticism* (Worcester, Mass. 1964) 21–27 (on Quentin's method), repr. from *(Classical) Folia* 10.2 (1958) 13–19. L. BROU, ed., *The Psalter Collects from V–VIth Century Sources . . . from the Papers of the Late Dom André Wilmart* (HBradshSoc 83; 1949). D. DE BRUYNE and B. SODAR,

eds., *Les Anciennes traductions latines des Machabées* (Anecdota Maredsolana 4; Maredsous 1932). Dekkers CPL, Nos. 1947–94 (on Lectionaries), with Elenchus codicum, 462–467. O. EISSFELDT, *Einleitung in das Alte Testament* (3d ed. Tübingen 1964) 973–977. B. FISCHER, "Die Bibel im Abendland," *Vetus Latina: Arbeitsbericht* 4 (1955) 12–23; "Bibelausgaben des frühen Mittelalters," *La Bibbia nell'alto medioevo* (Settimane di studio del Centro di studi sull'alto medioevo 10; Spoleto 1963) 519–600, 685–704; abr. in *Vetus Latina: Arbeitsbericht* 12 (1963) 10–38; "Codex Amiatinus und Cassiodor," BiblZ 6 (1962) 57–79. H. J. FREDE, *Die lateinischen Texte des 1. Petrusbriefes* (Vetus Latina: Aus der Geschichte der lateinischen Bibel 5; Freiburg 1965); *Pelagius, der irische Paulustext, Sedulius Scottus* (ibid. 3; 1961). J. GRIBOMONT, "Conscience philologique chez les scribes du haut moyen âge," *La Bibbia nell'alto medioevo, op. cit.* 601–630, 705–714; "L'Église et les versions bibliques," *Maison-Dieu* 62 (1960) 41–68. F. G. KENYON, *Our Bible and the Ancient Manuscripts,* 5th ed. rev. A. W. ADAMS (New York 1958) 138–144, 238–264. M. J. LAGRANGE, *Introduction à l'étude du N.T.,* pt. 2: *Critique textuelle* 2: *La Critique rationelle* (2d ed. ÉtBibl; 1935) 240–312, 421–441, 488–515, 539–568, 598–616. Lowe CodLatAntiq. E. A. LOWE, *English Uncial* (Oxford 1960); "Codices rescripti," *Mélanges E. Tisserant* (St Test 5; 1964) 67–113, with 6 plates. P. McGURK, *Latin Gospel Books from A.D. 400 to A.D. 800* (Les Publications de Scriptorium 5; Paris 1961). A. MERK, ed., *Novum Testamentum Graece et Latinum* (9th ed. Rome 1964). B. M. METZGER, *The Text of the New Testament* (New York 1964) 72–79 and (on Quentin's method) 163–165. *Richesses et déficiences des anciens psautiers latins* (Collectanea Biblica Latina 13; Vatican City 1959). P. SALMON, *Les "Tituli Psalmorum" des manuscrits latins* (ibid. 12; 1959). H. RÖNSCH, *Itala und Vulgata* (2d ed. Marburg 1875). H. ROST, *Die Bibel im Mittelalter: Beiträge zur Geschichte und Bibliographie der Bibel* (Augsburg 1939); *Die Bibel in den ersten Jahrhunderten* (Westheim bei Augsburg 1946). K. T. SCHÄFER, "Pelagius und die Vulgata," NTSt 9 (1962–63) 361–366. B. SMALLEY, *The Study of the Bible in the Middle Ages* (2d ed. New York 1952; repr. Notre Dame, Ind. 1964). Stegmüller RB, esp. v.1. O. STEGMÜLLER, in *Geschichte der Textüberlieferung der antiken und mittelalterlichen Literatur,* ed. H. HUNGER et al., 2 v. (Zurich 1961–64) 1:190–194. F. STUMMER, *Einführung in die lateinische Bibel* (Paderborn 1928). E. F. SUTCLIFFE, "The Name *Vulgate," Biblica* 29 (1948) 345–352. W. THIELE, *Wortschatzuntersuchungen zu den lateinischen Texten der Johannesbriefe* (Vetus Latina: Aus der Geschichte der lateinischen Bibel 2; 1958). A. VACCARI, *Scritti di erudizione e filologia,* 2 v. (Rome 1952–58). H. J. VOGELS, ed., *Codicum Novi Testamenti specimina* (Bonn 1929), plates 19–41, 50, 52–54; *Handbuch der Textkritik des NT* (2d ed. Bonn 1955) 78–110. A. VÖÖBUS, *Early Versions of the NT: Manuscript Studies* (Stockholm 1954) 33–65. Wikenhauser NTIntro 93–108.

Old Latin. B. BOTTE, DBSuppl 5:334–347. L. MÉCHINEAU, DB 4:97–123. *Vetus Latina: Die Reste der altlateinischen Bibel nach Petrus Sabatier neu gesammelt und herausgegeben von der Erzabtei Beuron,* ed. B. FISCHER et al. (Freiburg 1949–) v.1, Verzeichnis der Sigel; v.1.1 (2d ed. 1963, with suppls.); v.2, Genesis; v.24.1–5, Ephesians; v.26.1–3, James, 1 and 2 Peter. *Vetus Latina: Arbeitsbericht* 1 (1951–52) and annually thereafter. A. JÜLICHER et al, eds., *Itala: Das Neue Testament in altlateinischer Überlieferung,* 4 v. (Berlin 1938–63). T. AYUSO MARAZUELA, ed., *Psalterium Visigothicum-Mozarabicum* (Biblia Polyglotta Matritensia 7, L.21; Madrid 1957); *La Vetus Latina Hispana: Prolegómenos* (Madrid 1953); v.5 in three parts, *El Salterio* (Madrid 1962). D. DE BRUYNE, "Le Problème du psautier romain," RevBén 42 (1930) 101–126; "Saint Augustin reviseur de la Bible," *Miscellanea Agostiniana* 2 (Rome 1931) 521–606; RevBén 45 (1933) 20–28. H. J. FREDE, *Altlateinische Paulus-Handschriften* (Vetus Latina: Aus der Geschichte der lateinischen Bibel 4; 1964). J. GRIBOMONT, "Le Calendrier en latin du Sinaï," AnalBoll 75 (1957) 110, with nn. 1 and 2. J. SCHILDENBERGER, "Die Itala des hl. Augustinus," *Colligere fragmenta: Festschrift A. Dold* (Beuron 1952) 84–102. A. VACCARI, "St. Augustin, St. Ambroise and Aquila," *Augustinus Magister* 3 (Paris 1955) 471–482. R. WEBER, *Les Anciennes versions latines du deuxième livre des Paralipomènes* (Collectanea Biblica Latina 8; Vatican City 1945); ed., *Le Psautier romain et les autres psautiers latins* (ibid. 10; 1953).

Vulgate. E. MANGENOT, DB 5:2456–2500. A. PENNA, EncCatt 12:1584–90. *Biblia sacra iuxta Latinam vulgatam versionem ad codicum fidem . . . cura et studio monachorum (Sancti Benedicti) edita . . .* (Rome 1926–) v.1–12 embrace Genesis through Sirach. J. WORDSWORTH et al., eds., *Novum Testamentum Domini*

Nostri Iesu Christi Latine secundum editionem Sancti Hieronymi, 3 v. (Oxford 1889–1954); see review by B. FISCHER, ZNTWiss 46 (1955) 178–196. *L'attività della Santa Sede,* v.12– (1950–), annual reports on the work of the S. Girolamo Vulgate. T. AYUSO MARAZUELA, ed., *Psalterium S. Hieronymi de Hebraica veritate interpretatum* (Biblia Polyglotta Matritensia 8, L.21; Madrid 1960). S. BERGER, *Histoire de la Vulgate pendant les premiers siècles du moyen âge* (Paris 1893; repr. New York 1958); see review by P. CORSSEN, GöttGelAnz (1894) 855–875. T. J. BROWN and R. L. S. BRUCE-MITFORD, *The Lindisfarne Gospels: A Complete Facsimile . . . ,* 2 v. (Olten-Lausanne 1956–60) 2:3–104, 281–295. F. CAVALLERA, *Saint Jérôme: Sa vie et son oeuvre,* 2 v. (SpicSacLov 1, 2; 1922). L. COTTINEAU, "Chronologie des versions bibliques de Saint Jérôme," *Miscellanea Geronimiana* (Rome 1920) 43–68. D. DE BRUYNE, "Étude sur les origines de notre texte latin de Saint Paul," RevBibl 12 (1915) 358–392; "La Reconstitution du psautier hexaplaire latin," RevBén 41 (1929) 297–324, esp. 299 on the name "Gallican." H. DE SAINTE-MARIE, ed., *Sancti Hieronymi Psalterium iuxta Hebraeos* (Collectanea Biblica Latina 11; Vatican City 1954). B. FISCHER, *Die Alkuin-Bibel* (Vetus Latina: Aus der Geschichte der lateinischen Bibel 1; 1957); "Bibeltext und Bibelreform unter Karl dem Grossen," in *Karl der Grosse: Werk und Wirkung,* ed. W. BRAUNFELS, v.1, *Das geistige Leben,* ed. B. BISCHOFF (Düsseldorf 1965) 156–216. E. B. GARRISON, "Notes on the History of Certain Twelfth-Century Central Italian MSS of Importance for the History of Printing," *La Bibliofilia* 54 (1952) 1–34; *Studies in the History of Mediaeval Italian Painting,* 4 v. (Florence 1953–60). H. H. GLUNZ, *History of the Vulgate in England from Alcuin to Roger Bacon* (Cambridge, Eng. 1933). J. GRIBOMONT, "Les Éditions critiques de la Vulgate," StMed, 3d ser., 2 (1961) 363–377. *Libri Iudicum capitula selecta* [10.1–12.15] *iuxta Latinam Vulgatam versionem ad codicum fidem* (Vatican City 1939), useful guide to the new Vatican Vulgate, with valuable *adnotationes* on the text and apparatus. R. LOEWE, "The Mediaeval Christian Hebraists of England," HebUCAnn 28 (1957) 205–252. G. MORIN, "Saint Jérôme et ses maîtres hébreux," RevBén 46 (1934) 145–164. M. B. OGLE, "The Way of All Flesh," Harv ThRev 31 (1938) 41–51; "Bible Text or Liturgy," *ibid.* 33 (1940) 191–224. W. E. PLATER and H. J. WHITE, *A Grammar of the Vulgate* (Oxford 1926). H. QUENTIN, *Essais de critique textuelle* (Paris 1926); *Mémoire sur l'établissement du texte de la Vulgate* (Collectanea Biblica Latina 6; Rome-Paris 1922). F. ROSENTHAL, *Christian Hebraists of Western Europe: The Hebrew Scriptures in Christian Learning from the Time of the Vulgate of Jerome to the "Opus Grammaticum" of Münster* (U. of Pittsburgh Bulletin 42.1; 1946). J. O. SMIT, *De Vulgaat . . .* (Roermond 1948), rich in illus. esp. of MSS and the working materials of the Benedictine Vulgate project. D. H. WRIGHT, AmJArch 67 (1963) 219, on the Springmont Bog Psalter tablets.

Later versions. H. LESÈTRE, DB 4:123–125. A. BEA, ed. and tr., *Liber Ecclesiastae . . . nova e textu primigenio interpretatio* (Rome 1950). T. H. DARLOW and H. F. MOULE, comps. *Historical Catalogue of the Printed Editions of Holy Scripture in the Library of the British and Foreign Bible Society,* 2 v. in 4 (London 1903–11; repr. New York 1963). S. GAROFALO, "Gli umanisti italiani del secolo XV e la Bibbia," *Biblica* 27 (1946) 338–375; "Il Salterio di Asaf in una traduzione umanistica inedita dall'ebraico," *Miscellanea Biblica B. Ubach,* ed. R. M. DÍAZ (Montserrat 1953) 227–242. A. KLEINHAUS, "Correttori biblici," EncCatt 4:648–649. *Liber Psalmorum cum canticis Breviarii romani: Nova . . . interpretatio Latina . . . cura professorum Pontificii Instituti Biblici edita* (Rome 1945). C. MOHRMANN, tr. J. McCANN, "The New Latin Psalter: Its Diction and Style," AmBenRev 4 (1953) 7–33; repr. in her *Études sur le latin des chrétiens* 2 (Rome 1961) 109–131. R. WEBER, "Deux préfaces au psautier dues à Nicolas Maniacoria," RevBén 63 (1953) 1–17. **Illustration credits:** Fig. 7, Courtesy of the Trustees of the British Museum. Figs. 8, 9, 12, and 13, The Pierpont Morgan Library, New York City. Fig. 11, Biblioteca Mediceo-Laurenziana, Florence.

[B. M. PEEBLES]

14. COPTIC VERSIONS

Translations of the Bible or parts of the Bible that were used by the Copts, the Christians of the Coptic Church in Egypt who spoke Coptic (see COPTIC LANGUAGE AND LITERATURE). In the various parts of Egypt the Bible was read in the Coptic dialect that was proper to each particular part.

Date and Origin. There are no historical testimonies on the origin of the Coptic versions; in this matter one is limited to paleographical criteria, to Biblical citations made by writers who composed works in Coptic, and to certain well-established historical facts. On the basis of such evidence, it is possible to set the end of the 2d century or the beginning of the 3d as the date of the earliest Coptic version, which seems to have been the Sahidic, the most important of the Coptic versions for its literary and critical value. From the *Life of St. *Anthony of Egypt* written by St. *Athanasius, it is known that Anthony, who was born *c.* 250, felt the call to the monastic life when in his youth he heard the reading of the Sacred Scriptures in church. Since he was completely ignorant of Greek, he must have heard the Scriptures read in Coptic. A little after the time of St. Anthony, St. *Pachomius and his disciples constantly cited the Bible in their (Coptic) writings, and their citations agree with the readings of the Coptic Biblical text as it came down in its direct line of transmission.

Moreover, certain parts of the OT were translated into Coptic apparently before *Origen made his Hexapla, which he began *c.* 218 (see above, section 9). The Coptic version of Job, for instance, is based on a pre-Hexaplar Greek text. Also, many readings of the Coptic version of the Prophets agree with the pre-Hexaplar Greek MSS, even though the Coptic text was later corrected according to the Hexaplar tradition. The same can be said also of the Coptic version of the Books of Kings. All this would seem to indicate that the end of the 2d century or the beginning of the 3d was the time of the first phase of the Coptic versions.

Paleography corroborates this opinion. Faiyumic glosses on a Greek MS of Isaia in Papyrus VII of the Chester Beatty Collection, Sahidic glosses on a Washington MS of the Minor Prophets, an Akhmimic fragment of a certain Psalm, and a bilingual Greek-Coptic glossary to Osee and Amos can all be dated paleographically in the 3d century. A few strictly Biblical MSS date from the end of the 3d century, and Coptic MSS of the Bible become more numerous in the 4th century.

Various Versions. At least five different versions are known in the various dialects. The earliest version was probably in the Sahidic dialect; the other versions derive from it, and at least in many of the Biblical books they are merely transpositions of the Sahidic version. The Bohairic, however, is in general an independent version, and its origin is much discussed. Whereas some scholars think that this version was made toward the end of the 3d century, some others are of the opinion that it does not antedate the Arab invasion of Egypt (A.D. 640). However, there seems to be documentary proof that there was a primitive form of a Bohairic version (MS f 7 of Deir el-Bala'izah), different from the later standard Bohairic version, and that even the Faiyumic version depended on the primitive Bohairic form, of which there is a MS datable to the 4th or 5th century.

Nothing is known of the authors of these translations, but it can be established by internal criteria that there were several different translators. The Gospel of St. Mark, for instance, which is never cited by the disciples of St. Pachomius, was probably translated after the Gospels of St. Matthew and St. Luke, and apparently it depends on them in its choice of words.

Nature. Coptic Biblical MSS are very fragmentary. Those that contain a complete book of the Bible are very few, and there are none that contains the whole Bible or even the whole NT. However, from the fragments that have been preserved, it seems that there was once a more or less complete Bible in each of the Coptic dialects, even though nothing is yet known of a Sub-Akhmimic OT.

The Coptic version of the OT was made from the Greek Septuagint, in part independently of Origen's Hexapla; but it was later revised according to a text that resembled the so-called Hesychian recension of the Septuagint (see section 5, above). The Coptic versions, therefore, are of considerable value as textual witnesses for the reconstruction of the different forms of the Greek text. The NT is completely preserved in both Sahidic and Bohairic, and since it is a more faithful translation than the Coptic OT, it is more valuable for textual criticism. The Sahidic version in particular was made by translators who knew both Greek and Coptic perfectly, and it is the outstanding classical monument of the Coptic language. Its usefulness for the reconstruction of the Greek is supreme. The Sahidic and the Bohairic versions are of almost equal value in the help they offer for the reconstruction of the best form of the Greek NT text, which is represented by the Codex Vaticanus and the Codex Sinaiticus; but this is somewhat more pronounced in the Bohairic, for the Sahidic has a fair number of readings of the so-called Western type of text.

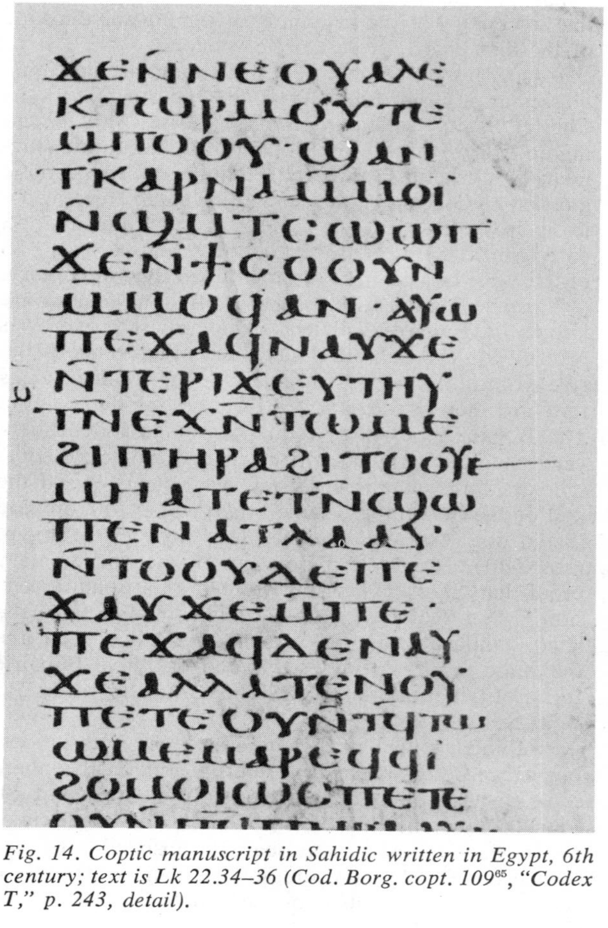

The versions in the other dialects of Coptic—Faiyumic, Akhmimic, and Sub-Akhmimic—are in general merely transpositions of the Sahidic in its primitive form, before it was subjected to a revision undertaken primarily for the sake of improving its grammar.

Bibliography: Publications of Coptic Biblical texts. A. VASCHALDE, RevBibl 16, 29–31 (1919–22), *passim,* see Index, for Sahidic texts; *Muséon* 43 (1930) 409–431; 45 (1932) 117–156, for Bohairic texts; *ibid.* 46 (1933) 299–313, Faiyumic and Akhmimic texts. W. C. TILL, "Coptic Biblical Texts Published after Vaschalde's Lists," BullJRylLibr 42 (1959–60) 220–240. J. SIMON, "Note sur le dossier des textes fayoumiques," ZNTWiss 37 (1938) 205–211; "Note sur le dossier des textes akhmimiques," *Memorial Lagrange* (Paris 1940) 197–201; "Note sur le dossier des textes subakhmimiques," *Muséon* 59 (1946) 497–509. G. W. HORNER, *The Coptic Version of the N.T. in the Northern Dialect* (Bohairic), 4 v. (Oxford 1898–1905); *The Coptic Versions in the Southern Dialect* (Sahidic), 7 v. (Oxford 1911–24), with lists of MSS. H. THOMPSON, *The Coptic Versions of the Acts of the Apostles and the Pauline Epistles in the Sahidic Dialect* (Cambridge, Eng. 1932); *The Gospel of St. John according to the Earliest Coptic Manuscript* (London 1924), Sub-Akhmimic.

Studies. H. HYVERNAT, "Étude sur les versions coptes de la Bible," RevBibl 5–6 (1896–97), *passim,* see Index. P. E. KAHLE, ed., *Bala'izah in Upper Egypt,* 2 v. (London 1954). M. J. LAGRANGE, *La Critique textuelle, II: Critique rationnelle* (ÉtBibl; 1935). E. M. HUSSELMAN, ed., *The Gospel of John in Fayumic Coptic* (Ann Arbor, Mich. 1962). T. C. PETERSEN, "An Early Coptic Manuscript of Acts: An Unrevised Version of the Ancient So-called Western-Text," CathBiblQuart 26 (1964) 225–241. F. KENYON, *Our Bible and the Ancient Manuscripts,* rev. A. W. ADAMS (5th ed. New York 1958). A. BÖHLIG, LexThK² 2:392–394. F. P. RIDOLFINI, EncCatt 4:511–514.

NT concordances. L. T. LEFORT, *Les Mots d'origine grecque* (CSCO; 1950). M. WILMET, *Les Mots autochtones,* 3 v. (CSCO; 1957–59). R. DRAGUET, *Index copte et grec-copte de la concordance du N.T. sahidique* (CSCO; 1960). **Illustration credit:** Fig. 14, Biblioteca Apostolica Vaticana.

[P. BELLET]

Fig. 14. Coptic manuscript in Sahidic written in Egypt, 6th century; text is Lk 22.34–36 (Cod. Borg. copt. 109⁹⁵, "Codex T," p. 243, detail).

15. ETHIOPIC VERSIONS

The Bible is usually quoted in the Ethiopian theological schools as "the 81 volumes." But as early as 1859 the French scholar A. D'Abbadie noted that "there is (in Ethiopia) a general agreement about the number of the Sacred Books, which they fix unanimously as 81; but everybody fills that number according to his own choice."

Canon of the Bible in Ethiopia. Though the above may be something of an overstatement, the lists of the Books of the Bible accepted in the Canon of the Ethiopian Church are divergent in the MSS (e.g., British Museum Add. 16, 188; British Museum Add. 16, 205; and D'Abbadie 96), while the list in Vaticanus Borgianus 10 is a late Catholic addition to that manuscript. A full MS of the Bible, now in the Vatican Library, was prepared lately under the direction of Abuna Abrehām, Bishop of Gondar and subsequently Metropolitan of Ethiopia, a distinguished follower of the traditional school; this is the best witness of the text now accepted in the Ethiopian schools. The differences between the Ethiopian Canon and that of the Catholic Church appear to be as follows: the Book of Jubilees ("the Little Genesis") and Enoch are considered by the Ethiopians as canonical [see BIBLE, III (CANON), 4.]; they count three Books of Machabees (see below); and in the ancient lists some other books are added to the NT: the Qalemēntos (the so-called *Pseudo-Clementine literature) and the Senodos (by which name the *Canones Apostolorum* are probably meant; see APOSTOLIC CONSTITUTIONS). But these works are not included in the MS of Abuna Abrehām, which, therefore, contains only 76 books.

Translation of the Bible into Ethiopic. The books of the Bible were not translated into Ethiopic at one time or by one author but according to the needs of the schools and the liturgy, as Greek, which had been the cultural language of the first Christian communities in the region, was supplanted by Ethiopic. The OT was based on the Greek text of the Septuagint; but neither the method nor the quality of the translation is uniform in the various books. It is remarkable that in two passages of Sirach (31.11 and 37.24), the name of God was rendered as "Astar," which is the name of the ancient Semitic pagan deity, corresponding to the planet Venus. This is proof that when Sirach was translated, the ancient paganism of the South Arabian immigrants to Ethiopia was not wholly extinguished. It has often been repeated that this translation of Sirach was made in A.D. 678; but this is a false interpretation of the colophon of MS 7 of the Stadt-Bibliothek in Frankfurt, which, in any case, was copied in A.D. 1755. The NT also was translated into Ethiopic from the Greek and from an Antiochene text type. But the original translations of both OT and NT were revised, probably more than once, during the long history of the Ethiopian Church. In the 13th and 14th centuries, when the links with Egypt and its Coptic culture were intensified by the Metropolitan Salāmā and his successors, a revision took place on the basis of the Arabic text then current in the Patriarchate of Alexandria. It is possible also that further variants were introduced during the short revival of theological studies in the second half of the 17th century. Western scholars (E. Ullendorff, A. Vööbus) have recently advanced the hypothesis that the Ethiopic of some Biblical books might have been at least influenced by the Aramaic version.

Apocryphal and Pseudepigraphic Literature in Ethiopic. The Ethiopians' fondness for literature with a Biblical flavor has led them to preserve numerous books from Christian and Jewish sources that have not been accepted elsewhere in the East. We must enumerate at least the following OT apocrypha: (1) A *Book of the Machabees,* which differs entirely from the *Machabees* of the other Churches, and tells the legend of a king named Ṭiruṣāydān (a curious deformation of "Tyre and Sidon"), and the martyrdom of three Jews. (2) The *Reliqua Prophetae Baroc,* with the legend of the dream of Abimelech and the stoning of Jeremia in Babylon. (3) The *Ascensio Isaiae,* containing a vision of Heaven attributed to the Prophet. This book, now fully extant only in Ethiopic, had been considered as sacred by the *Bogomils of Bulgaria and later on by the *Cathari of Southern France. (4) The Shepherd of *Hermas, which was identified and edited by D'Abbadie from a unique Ethiopian manuscript in the convent of Gundagunde in Northern Ethiopia. A second MS of this work from the same monastery has recently been brought to Europe by A. Mordini and described by A. Van Lantschoot. (5) The *Apocalypse of Ezra,* which is the *IV Esdras* kept as an appendix to the Latin Vulgate. (6) The *Wisdom of the Sibyl* (Ṭebaba Sabēlā), describing 10 ages of human history from the Golden Age until the final Judgment. (7) The *Explanation of Jesus (Fekkārē Iyāsūs),* said to be revealed by Jesus to His Disciples during the Last Supper, regarding the future of humanity until the advent of a King Theodore

who will again bring peace to the world. (8) The *Book of the Letter of Athanasius (Maṣḥafa Ṭomara Atnātēwos*), allegedly sent down from heaven in Rome, under a legendary Pope Athanasius, and containing various precepts for Christian life. (9) The *History of Adam and Eve,* a composition of the Middle Ages. (10) The *Book of the Passing of Abraham, Isaac and Jacob,* who are all brought finally to heaven by the Archangel Michael, after different vicissitudes and discussions with the Angel of Death. For the NT should be added: (11) An apocryphal *Acts of the Apostles,* a collection of tales on the miracles and martyrdoms of the 12 Apostles. (12) The *Proto-Evangelium Jacobi.* (13) The *Book of the Passing of Our Lady* (translation of the Λόγος εἰς τὴν κοίμησιν τῆς ἁγίας θεοτόκου). (14) The *Apocalypse of Mary.* (15) The letters exchanged between Our Lord Jesus and King Abgar of Edessa (*see* ABGAR, LEGENDS OF). (16) *The Miracles of Jesus,* an apocryphal Gospel of John.

The profusion of such works, which is by no means exhausted in the above list, is another clear evidence of the significance of Ethiopic literature for the history of the Christian East. It is, as has been said, "the end of the corridor," where ancient materials that have been lost elsewhere may be recovered and studied.

See also ETHIOPIC LANGUAGES AND LITERATURE.

Bibliography: A. DILLMANN, ed., *Biblia Veteris Testamenti Aethiopica,* 5 v. (Leipzig 1853–94). R. M. J. BASSET, tr., *Les Apocryphes Éthiopiens,* 10 v. (Paris 1893–1900). I. GUIDI, "La traduzione degli Evangeli in arabo ed in etiopico," *Reale Accademia dei Lincei Memorie* (Rome 1888). L. HACKSPILL, "Die Äthiopische Evangelienübersetzungen (*Math IX*)," ZAssyr 11 (1896) 117–196, 367–388. B. COTTE, DBSuppl 6:825–829.

[E. CERULLI]

16. ARMENIAN VERSIONS

Armenian historical sources attribute the Armenian translation of the Bible to St. Maschtotz (Mastotz, *Mesrop, Mesrob; c. 361–440), priest and inventor of the Armenian alphabet, and to the Patriarch Sahak I (*Isaac the Great; c. 350–439); both men were, in fact, involved in the work. The first book of Holy Scripture translated into Armenian was Proverbs. By 414 the Bible, practically in its entirety, seems to have been translated into Armenian. This first hastily made translation (*Arm. 1*) was later improved, so that it became at once more faithful and more literary. Several books, such as 1 and 2 Chronicles, 1 and 2 Machabees, Canticle of Canticles, and Sirach, have been preserved both in the original translation and in its improved edition. Some parts of the earlier version of the Psalms have been kept in the Armenian Breviary. After 436 the second translation was itself revised by Eznik and Sahak on the basis of new copies brought from Constantinople.

The first Armenian version of the Gospels and Acts appears to be based on a Syriac model and, at least in regard to the Gospels, the Old-Syriac Version. (See part 12 of this article.) Moreover, it seems probable that the earliest version of the Gospels was a translation of Tatian's *Diatessaron. The first versions of most of the other books of the Bible seem to be based on the Syriac also. One exception must be made for Canticle of Canticles, the first version of which, according to P. Zarbhanélian, was begun with the Syriac as a model and continued with the Greek. Besides, the first version of Sirach presents special problems both in regard to the order of the chapters (the rejection, after Sir 30.24,

Fig. 15. Gospels in Armenian, written in Armenia A.D. 966, the oldest dated copy of the Armenian Gospels, now in Baltimore (Walters 573, fol. 1v–2r). On the left is the end of canon 10 of the Eusebian Canons.

of the transposition of the Greek MSS) and their number (the omission of the praise of the Fathers) and in its text. The latter, ordinarily based on the Greek, is sometimes founded on the *Peshitta, while at other times it differs from both these sources. The second version, although based on the Greek, has retained some elements of *Arm. 1*. The Gospels of this version are of the Caesarean type of text.

In spite of several unavoidable contaminations, the Armenian version displays remarkable literary qualities, combining intelligent and flexible accuracy with a respect for the genius of the language and the shades of meaning that modify words in context. It has rightfully been called "the queen of versions."

The first edition of the Armenian Bible was that of Bishop Oskan (Amsterdam 1669; new ed. Constantinople 1705). Although its text was established in a rather arbitrary and eclectic fashion, it has preserved some early readings. The edition of Abbot *Mechitar (Venice 1733) and especially that of J. Zohrab (Venice 1805) are decidedly superior, although they do not present a definitive critical text. Later editions, e.g., that of A. Bagratuni (Venice 1860) and the Constantinople edition of 1895, depend on Zohrab's.

Bibliography: L. LELOIR, DBSuppl 6:810–818, with extensive bibliog. J. MOLITOR, LexThK² 2:397–398. A. VÖÖBUS, *Early Versions of the New Testament* (Stockholm 1954) 133–171. **Illustration credit:** Fig. 15, Courtesy of the Walters Art Gallery, Baltimore.

[L. LELOIR]

17. GEORGIAN VERSIONS

It was apparently in the first half of the 5th century that the Gospels, the Pauline Epistles, and the Psalms were translated into Georgian, the most important of the distinct family of the Caucasian languages (*see* GEORGIA, CHURCH IN ANCIENT). The Gospels were probably the first Biblical books translated; the oldest extant translation is from the MS of Adiš, transcribed in 897. In the earliest manuscripts the Epistles of St. Paul appear in the following order: Romans, 1 and 2 Corinthians, Hebrews, 2 Timothy, Philemon, 1 Timothy, Galatians, Ephesians, Philippians, Colossians, and 1 and 2 Thessalonians. The first version of the Acts of the Apostles dates probably from the 6th century. The Prophets, together with Nehemia and Ezra, were translated gradually during the following centuries. The translation of 1 and 2 Machabees, however, was done only in the 18th century.

The first Georgian version of the Scriptures was based on the Armenian version. See part 16 of this article. Following the schism of 608–609, however, Georgia wished to free itself from the controlling influence of Armenia. Consequently, a new Biblical translation, based on the Greek, made its appearance, still bearing some traces of the Armenian version. The versions of Aquila, Theodotion, and Symmachus, rather than the Septuagint, were sometimes preferred as the bases for the translation of the OT. See parts 5–8 of this article. The translation of 1 and 2 Machabees was based on the

Slavonic version. See part 20 of this article. The text of the Gospels seems to follow the Caesarean type of text.

Bibliography: L. LELOIR, DBSuppl 6:829–834, with extensive bibliog. J. MOLITOR, LexThK² 2:398. A. VÖÖBUS, *Early Versions of the New Testament* (Stockholm 1954) 173–209.

[L. LELOIR]

18. ARABIC VERSIONS

When Christianity penetrated into the territories of Arab speech (*see* ARABIA, 5), the Biblical resources that accompanied it were in Syriac and, later, in Greek. Though a pre-Islamic origin for the Arabic versions now extant in MSS or citations has sometimes been claimed, e.g., by A. Baumstark [*Islamica* 4 (1929–31) 562–575], no fixed Biblical text in Arabic is demonstrably of such antiquity. The Arabic versions are of most varied origin, since they were based on texts in Syriac, Hebrew, Greek, Coptic, and Latin; the medieval Bible of the Melchites in Egypt (*see* MELCHITE RITE) included elements of all but the last, which was proper to Spain and North Africa. Although they are sometimes interesting for questions of history and exegesis, the Arabic versions are in general too late and secondary to be of any special advantage for textual criticism.

Earliest Texts. The earliest extant fragment of the Bible in Arabic is a Greco-Arabic Psalm 77(78) of the late 8th century, discovered in the Umayyad mosque of Damascus in 1901 and published by B. Violet [*Ein zweisprachiges Psalmfragment aus Damascus* (Berlin 1902)]. The Vatican MSS Vat. Ar 13 and Vat. Borgia 95 were said to be of the 8th century by I. Guidi [*Le traduzioni degli evangeli in arabo e in etiopico* (Rome 1888)]; but G. Graf attributes these copies to the 9th century and argues for a post-Islamic origin of the rendering, at the Monastery of St. Catherine on Mt. Sinai. K. Peters claims to have discovered traces of early Arabic versions in writers of the 8th to 9th centuries ["Die arabische Psalmenzitate bei Abu Nu'aim," *Biblica* 20 (1940) 1–6; "Psalm 149 in Zitaten islamischer Autoren," *ibid*. 138–151]. The first full-scale Arabic Bible would be that alleged by the Moslem writer Mas'ūdī to have been prepared by *Johannitius (Ḥunayn ibn Isḥāq, d. 873 or 877) from the Septuagint (LXX). No traces of this translation have as yet been found.

Complete Bibles. Much later MSS containing all the books of both the OT and the NT are the MS Or. D. 226 of the Asiatic Museum in Leningrad and its allied Vat. MS Ar. 468. The latter was written in 1578–79 in Syria, contains a mixed text, and is reproduced in the Roman edition of 1671. The Leningrad MS is seemingly also of the 16th century, though before 1539 (Graf, 92); after having changed hands many times, it reached St. Petersburg (Leningrad) in 1913 [A. Vaccari, "Una Bibbia Araba per il primo Gesuita venuto al Libano," *Mélanges de l'Université de Saint Joseph* 10 (1925) 79–104; "La storia di una Bibbia Araba," *Biblica* 11 (1930) 350–355]. Another complete Bible is Paris Ar. 1, copied in Cairo in 1584–85, containing a different mixed text, which underlies the Paris and London Polyglots (*see* POLYGLOT BIBLES).

Versions from the Hebrew. The most notable is that of Gaon *Sa'adia ben Joseph (b. 882; d. 942). His rendering of the Pentateuch, filled with exegetical details and of interest for traditional Jewish interpretation, was taken over by Egyptian Christians and ap-

pears (in Arabic script) in Paris Ar. 1 and in Arabic type in the Paris and London polyglots. Transmitted in Hebrew letters, it appears in the Constantinople polyglot Pentateuch of 1546 and in the edition of Sa'adia's works by J. Derenbourg (v. 1 Paris 1886). Sa'adia's renderings of Psalms (in part), Job, and Isaia have also been published in modern times. The Arabic Pentateuch published by T. Erpenius in 1622 (from Leiden, cod. Ar. 33) is a rendering by a North-African Jew of the 13th century. Yefet ibn 'Alī, a 10th-century Karaite (*see* KARAISM), in Jerusalem, translated the OT in its entirety, and his work, which includes also commentary, is preserved extensively in MS. The 13th-century Samaritan Arabic recension of the Pentateuch attributed to one Abū Sa'īd is apparently a reworking of the translation of Sa'adia [thus P. Kahle, *Cairo Geniza* (2d ed. Oxford 1959) 53–56].

Other Old Testament Translations. Of the Pentateuch, there are in the MSS separate renderings from the Greek, from Bohairic Coptic (based ultimately on the LXX), and perhaps a half dozen from Syriac. Worthy of special note is the 10th-century rendering from the Syro-Hexaplar by al-Ḥārit ibn Sinān ibn Sinbāt, which preserves evidence of the compilation by Origen no longer extant either in Greek or Syriac. Of similarly mixed origin (but mainly from the Syriac) are the rest of the OT historical books in Arabic; Tobit is known

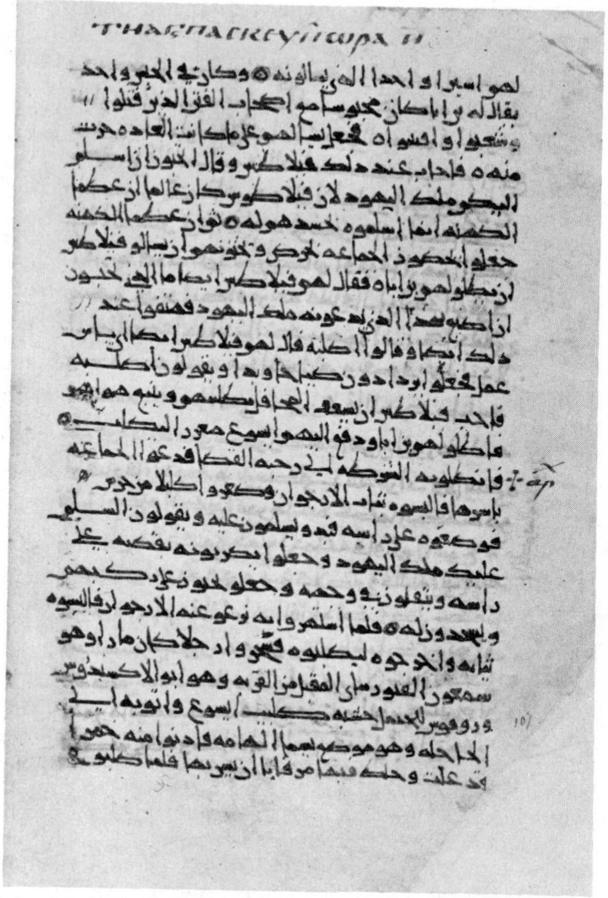

Fig. 16. Folio from a fragment of a Bible in Arabic, 8th or 9th century (Cod. Vat. Arabic 13, fol. 73 v).

only from the Latin, since the Crusades; 1 Machabees was not included in the Syrian tradition, and 2 Machabees (from the Greek) is sometimes accompanied by *Josippon or a reworked compendium of this, labeled 5 Machabees (see Graf, 221–223).

The same al-Ḥāriṭ is credited with the translations of the Wisdom books from the Syriac; the text in the Polyglots is derived rather from the LXX. Job in the Polyglots is from the Syriac; a distinct rendering of it from the same source into an Arabic, using by preference phraseology familiar to Moslems, was done in the 9th century by Pethion ibn 'Ayyūb al-Sahhār, who also translated Isaia, Jeremia, Ezechiel, and Sirach.

Needs of the liturgy have called forth multiple versions of the Psalms. A revision in the 11th century of the Psalter from the LXX by Abū 'l-Fatḥ 'Abdallāh ibn al-Faḍl of Antioch circulates widely for such purposes (also among the Copts), and was itself revised again in 1735 by *'Abdallāh Zāhir. A Mozarabic Psalter goes back to Latin sources. The texts in the Polyglots and most printed editions, including A. *Giustinani's polyglot Psalter (Genoa 1516) are based mainly on the Greek. Sirach also exists in an early rendering from the Greek uncial tradition, preserved in a Sinai MS.

The Prophets in the Polyglots are basically the rendering from the LXX attributed to a 10th-century Alexandrian priest named al-'Alam (as in Paris Ar. 1), which in Daniel at least has been retouched from Coptic sources. Since, however, lacunae were filled in from any MS at hand, there are elements also of Syriac origin. The Arabic Bible of Rome (1671) on the other hand, has a text of the Prophets based on the Syriac, except for Daniel (from the Greek, retouched), and shows a strong Latin Vulgate influence.

New Testament. In addition to the Gospel rendering connected with the Mt. Sinai monastery (see above, Earliest Texts), there is a partial collection of the Pauline Epistles from the same source, in a 10th-century MS. Besides a variety of disparate renderings from the Greek, a number of versions from the Syriac also circulated; and some influence of the Old Syriac as well as the Peshitta has been supposed for a part of this tradition. The Arabic *Diatessaron, in two recensions, is an important witness to that Gospel harmony. The text in the Polyglots is from the Greek (an "Egyptian vulgate" recension of the Gospels), with Syriac influence on Apocalypse.

Modern Arabic Bibles. During the 19th and 20th centuries, the Bible and the NT in Arabic have been repeatedly reprinted by both Catholic and Protestant organizations, chiefly in Beirut, Mosul, and London. The texts were often the earlier versions, retouched on the basis of the Greek and Hebrew originals, sometimes with new influences from Syriac or Latin, and usually with an eye to smoothing out the literary quality of this translation Arabic. Three more serious undertakings deserve special mention. The American Protestant mission in Beirut enlisted native Arabic speakers in contact with the mid-19th-century Arabic literary renaissance to collaborate in the production from the original languages of a NT rendering (1860) and a complete Bible (1864). From the Dominican press in Mosul, the Eastern rite prelate C. J. David produced a noteworthy revision of the existing texts (4 v., 1875–78). The

Jesuits in Beirut enlisted the aid of a well-known literary figure, Ibrāhīm al-Yāzijī, for a fresh rendering from the Hebrew and the Greek, first issued in three volumes (1876–80). These last three form the source for most Arabic Bible texts in current circulation and use.

Bibliography: G. GRAF, *Geschichte der christlichen arabischen Literatur* (StTest 118; 1944–) 1:85–297. B. BOTTE, DBSuppl 6:807–810. H. HYVERNAT, DB 1.1:845–856. E. NESTLE, Herzog-Hauck PRE 3:90–95. P. P. SAYDON, "The Origin of the 'Polyglot' Arabic Psalms," *Biblica* 31 (1950) 226–236. J. F. RHODE, *The Arabic Versions of the Pentateuch in the Church of Egypt* (Leipzig 1921). P. KAHLE, *Die arabischen Bibelübersetzungen* (Leipzig 1904). R. M. FRANK, "The Jeremias of Pethion ibn 'Ayyūb al-Sahhār," CathBiblQuart 21 (1959) 136–170. On the question of pre-Islamic Arabic versions. A. M. MAQDISI, al-Machriq 31 (1933) 1–12, in Arabic. G. GRAF, *op. cit.* 41–52, 142–146. **Illustration credit:** Fig. 16, Biblioteca Apostolica Vaticana.

[P. P. SAYDON]

.19. GOTHIC VERSIONS

Ulfilas (Gothic Wulfila; 311–383), Bishop of the Goths, according to Socrates (*Hist. Eccl.* 4.33–34), invented the Gothic characters, based on the Greek, and translated the Gospels. He succeeded Theophilus who had been present at the First Council of Nicaea, but he later subscribed to the Arian Creed (*ibid.* 2.41; Sozomen, *Hist. Eccl.* 6.37), possibly under political pressure. The Gothic version of the Gospels is best represented in the *Codex Argenteus* in the University library of Uppsala. Only about one-half of the original manuscript is still extant, preserving considerable fragments in the order Matthew, John, Luke, and Mark. A fragment of

Fig. 17. Folio with Gothic text of Luke 1.6–14, 6th-century "Codex Argenteus" of the University Library at Uppsala, Sweden (Cod. DG I, fol. 118 v.). This manuscript is written with silver letters on purple parchment and is reproduced here in negative for greater clarity.

two leaves at the Ambrosian Library, Milan contains part of ch. 25 to 27 of Matthew.

The translation shows uniform stylistic characteristics and must have been the work of Ulfilas himself. It is the work of a man who knew both languages well, and he may have on occasion compared his work with the Old Latin Version. However, it is generally agreed that the syntax of the Greek original influenced the Gothic. The underlying Greek text, which formed the basis of the Gothic translation, was a Constantinople text. There also exist fragments of the Epistles of St. Paul in Gothic and two pieces from the Old Testament, from the books of Ezra and Nehemia, but the OT fragments are certainly not the work of Ulfilas. A commentary on the Gospel of St. John in eight fragments known as the *Skeireins* is probably not the work of Ulfilas. It may be a translation of a Greek or Latin commentary on St. John.

Bibliography: E. BERNHARDT, ed., *Vulfila oder die Gotische Bibel* (Halle 1875). W. STREITBERG, ed., *Die Gotische Bibel*, 2 v. in 1 (3d ed. Heidelberg 1950). G. FRIEDRICHSEN, *The Gothic Version of the Gospels: A Study of Its Style and Textual History* (London 1926). W. BENNETT, ed. & tr., *The Gothic Commentary on the Gospel of St. John* (New York 1960).

[R. T. MEYER]

20. SLAVONIC VERSIONS

The Old Slavonic version of the Bible was made from the Septuagint under SS. Cyril and Methodius. In order to record the new version, St. Cyril devised the Glagolitic alphabet, which seems to derive from Greek cryptographic writing. During the lifetime of these holy brothers, essential liturgical books, lectionaries of Gospels and Epistles, and parts of the OT (Psalms, Prophets) were rendered into Old Bulgarian. No original copy survives, but we have the MSS written by their disciples; through the efforts of modern scholars, the original text has been in great part restored, and we can form an idea of the language used by the translators. This was an old form of the Macedonian dialect, which incorporated a certain number of Greek loanwords. Textual investigation has proved that the earliest version was made by one person; it is a new, accurate, and independent version of the Greek text. The Antiochene text was long thought to be the basis of the Slavonic version; in recent years, however, a difference between earlier (10th–11th century) and later MSS has been established. Most scholars now concede that the earliest copies contain a certain number of Caesarean and Hesychian readings. There are conjectures about the location and source of the MSS used by the translators; it is not improbable that they used the MSS of the Polychron monastery located near the city of Sigriane.

After the death of St. Methodius, the Cyrillic alphabet was created by his disciples in Bulgaria. The older version was revised, and additional books were translated from the current Byzantine text. The Slavonic Bible reached its completed form in the 15th century in Novgorod; the last missing books (including 1 and 2 Chronicles, Ezra, Tobit, Judith) were translated from the Vulgate. Old Slavonic MSS are extant in two alphabets: Glagolitic and Cyrillic.

Glagolitic (10th–11th century): (1) Seven leaves of a Roman Missal, composed in Moravia, now in Kiev (ed. P. C. Mohlberg, 1928). (2) *Codex Zographensis*, Gospels, in Leningrad (ed. V. Jagic, 1879). (3) *Psalterium*

Fig. 18. The beginning of St. Luke's Gospel in Slavonic, from a 16th-century Russian manuscript in Cyrillic script.

Sinaiticum (ed. S. Severianov, 1922). (4) *Euchologium Sinaiticum* (ed. R. Nachtigal, 1942–43). (5) *Codex Marianus*, Gospels, in Moscow (ed. V. Jagic, 1883). (6) *Codex Assemianus*, Gospels, in the Vatican (ed. J. Vajs and J. Kurz, 1929–48). (7) *Glagolita Closianus* (ed. A. Dostál, 1959). Besides these, a few fragmentary MSS exist.

Cyrillic (11th–12th century): (1) Burial inscription of Czar Samuel, from 933. (2) The Sava Gospels (ed. V. Sčepkin, 1903). (3) The Ostromir Gospels (ed. A. Vostokov, 1843). (4) *Codex Supraslensis* (ed. S. Severianov, 1904). Complete Old Slavonic Bibles were published in Ostrog (1581) and Moscow (1663 and 1751). Single books were published by: F. Miklosich (Matthew); E. Kaluzniacki (Acts, Epistles); I. E. Jevšejev (Isaia, Daniel); V. Jagič (Psalterium Bononiense); J. Vajs (Psalterium Palaeoslovenicum croatico-glagoliticum) and Gospels (Matthew, Mark, John).

Bibliography: M. LACKO, *Saints Cyril and Methodius* (Rome 1963). H. HÖPFL and L. LELOIR, *Introductio generalis in Sacram Scripturam* (6th ed. Naples 1958). G. BONFANTE and B. M. METZGER, "The Old Slavic Version of the Gospel according to St. Luke," JBiblLit 73 (1954) 217–236. **Illustration credit:** Fig. 18, The Rare Book Department, Free Library of Philadelphia.

[S. S. SHAWEL]

21. PRE-REFORMATION ENGLISH VERSIONS

The Bible in English has followed the development of the language itself; the pre-Reformation forms of it belong to the Anglo-Saxon and Middle English periods, with an interruption between, owing to the temporary predominance of Norman French literary purposes.

Anglo-Saxon. About 670 *Caedmon wrote a verse paraphrase of Genesis and other parts of the Bible in Anglo-Saxon, the ancient form of English from A.D. 500 to 1150. St. *Aldhelm (d. 709) translated the Psalms from Latin into Anglo-Saxon. About this time, St. *Guthlac made another Psalter translation. St. Bede (d. 735) translated at least the Gospel of St. John. King Alfred the Great (d. 901) prefixed a translation of the Ten Commandments and parts of the Law of Moses to his own code of laws. Aelfric, Abbot of Eynsham in Oxfordshire (d. c. 1020), paraphrased the first seven books of the Bible, which became known as Aelfric's Heptateuch. He also translated several OT books. The earliest continuous translations of the four

Fig. 19. Latin Vulgate text of Mt 1.18 in the Lindisfarne Gospels, c. 700, with Aldred's Anglo-Saxon gloss of c. 950 (Cotton MS Nero D. iv, fol. 93b).

anxious for a Bible in English, which language had by now achieved a common form. Through his influence this result was achieved. To what extent he actually made the translation we cannot be sure. The part from Gn 1.1 to Bar 3.20 was translated by one of his associates, Nicholas of Hereford, and it is thought by some that Wyclif may have translated the rest. Shortly after Wyclif's death in 1384 this translation was revised and a preface added, probably by his friend John Purvey. This revised version supplanted the original and became the usual form of the Bible during the 15th century. Of the 170 MSS of this version now extant, about 140 contain the revised edition and about 30 the original.

Was there a pre-Wyclifite English version? It is impossible to give a definite answer. St. Thomas More in his *Dialogue concerning Tyndale*, 3.14 (1528), says that the whole Bible was translated into English before Wyclif, and that he had seen such Bibles in the hands of lay people. It is probable that he was mistaken, and the Bibles he thought pre-Wyclifite were the earlier version of the Wyclif Bible. The latter had no preface to identify it with Wyclif's views, which might explain the misunderstanding. The absence of manuscript evidence of pre-Wyclifite Catholic Bibles, in view of the many Wyclifite MSS, would seem to support this evaluation. Cardinal Gasquet put forward a view that the known 170 MSS were in fact not Wyclifite but pre-Wyclif Catholic Bibles. This view cannot be upheld

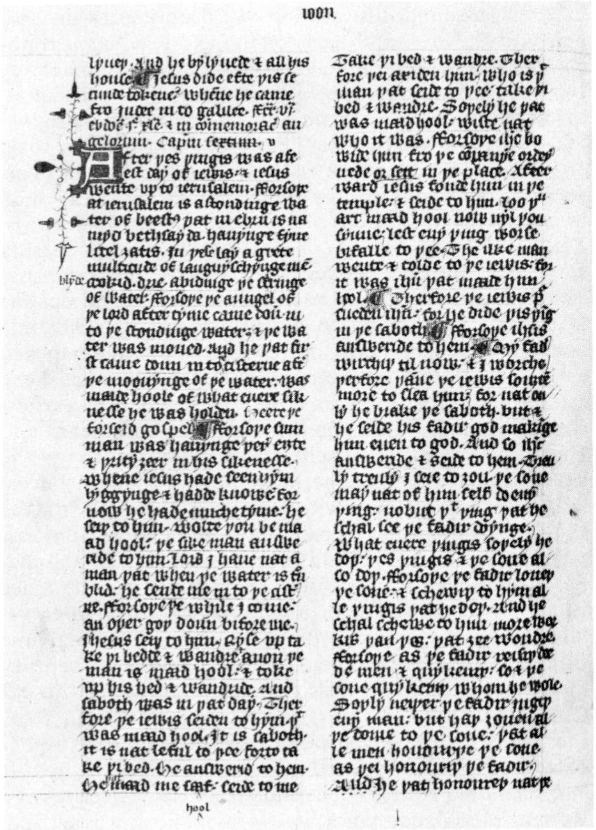

Gospels were interlinear glosses, i.e., word-for-word translations written between the lines of the Latin text. The oldest existing copy is the Lindisfarne Gospels, a magnificent illuminated volume written in Latin around 700 and glossed in Anglo-Saxon in about 950 by Aldred. A later gloss is known as the Rushworth Gospels. Toward the end of the 10th century a full vernacular version of the Gospels was needed and translations were made from the Latin text. Six copies are extant, one printed in London in 1571 by John Daye.

Middle English. After the Norman Conquest of 1066 the new rulers sought to impose their language on the English, and the Bible was eventually translated into Anglo-Norman. The Conquest retarded the literary development of English, but toward the close of the 12th century, when English as distinct from Anglo-Saxon was beginning to take shape, an Augustinian canon named Orm produced a series of metrical homilies in Middle English on the Gospels read at Mass. This was called the *Ormulum* after his name. One manuscript, about one-eighth of the whole, written probably by Orm himself, is in the Bodleian Library, Oxford. In the first half of the 14th century two prose versions of the Psalms were made, one attributed to William of Shoreham, the other made by Richard *Rolle de Hampole. Rolle added a verse-by-verse devotional commentary and translated other parts of the Bible. William *Caxton, in the 15th century, stated that John of Trevisa (1326–1414), a priest well known as a translator, rendered the Bible into the vernacular, but there is no manuscript evidence for this.

John Wyclif, a priest born about 1330, who was critical of the conditions prevailing in the Church, was

Fig. 20. Folio from a manuscript of the earlier Wyclif English version of the Bible, before 1397 (Egerton MS 618, fol. 60v).

and there is no doubt that these MSS are Wyclifite (Kenyon, 278–281).

Bibliography: H. POPE, *English Versions of the Bible*, rev. and enl. S. BULLOUGH (St. Louis 1952). F. G. KENYON, *Our Bible and the Ancient Manuscripts*, rev. A. W. ADAMS (5th ed. New York 1958). F. F. BRUCE, *The English Bible: A History of Translations* (New York 1961). **Illustration credit:** Figs. 19 and 20, Trustees of the British Museum.

[R. J. FOSTER]

22. CATHOLIC ENGLISH VERSIONS

English was almost the only important European language that did not have a printed Bible before the Reformation. From the Reformation to the middle of the 20th century there was little contact between Catholic and non-Catholic versions in English. This article, therefore, treats only of the Catholic English versions published in Reformation and post-Reformation times. The Protestant and Jewish versions in English are discussed in section 23, below.

GREAT BRITAIN AND IRELAND

The post-Reformation history of the Catholic versions of the Bible in English begins with the original Rheims and Douay texts (1582, 1609–10); a turning point comes with the revisions by Bishop Challoner (from 1749), which held the field almost exclusively until the appearance of recent versions. The present treatment will therefore be in four parts: the Rheims and Douay version before Challoner; Challoner's revisions and after; recent versions in Great Britain and Ireland; Catholic versions by Americans.

Rheims and Douay Version before Challoner. The English College at *Douai (Douay) was temporarily housed at Rheims from 1578 to 1593, and it was during this period that the decision was made to provide a text translated from the Vulgate into English. It is known from the *Douay Diaries* that Dr. Gregory *Martin began the task in 1578 and finished the whole Bible shortly before his death in 1582. The NT was "printed at Rhemes by Iohn Fogny 1582" in quarto. The publication of the OT was delayed until the college had returned to Douai, and it was then produced in two volumes "printed at Doway by Laurence Kellam . . . MDCIX [1609; and 1610]" also in quarto. The correct names are therefore the Rheims NT and the Douay OT, often together referred to as the Douay Bible. These spellings have become standard, but the old English pronunciations of "Rhemes" and "Doway" have remained traditional among English Catholics. Both NT and OT were provided with lengthy prefaces, defending (1) the need of a Catholic version, (2) the value of translating the Vulgate, whose text was much surer than the Greek at that time, and (3) the deliberately literal translation, even including the coining of Latin-English words for theological technical terms. In fact, the peculiar latinizing vocabulary of Rheims-Douay enriched the English language; it also influenced the Protestant Authorized Version of 1611, as the preface to the Revised Version recognizes.

Editions of Original Rheims Text. The Rheims NT was republished in 1600 by Vervliet of Antwerp (quarto), and in 1621 by Seldenslach, also of Antwerp (a very small duodecimo volume). Hugh *Pope (*Eng. Vers.*, 271) reported a rare reprint (1630) of this edition. What is called the "4th edition" was printed by Cousturier of Rouen in 1633 (octavo). The fifth and sixth editions of 1738 and 1788 (the latter reproduced in a Bible of 1816–18) were published in England (folio) with the erratic spelling of 1582 modernized. Later editions were made for historical interest, in 1834 (Leavitt, New York), 1841 (Bagster, in the *English Hexapla*, with the original spelling), 1872 (Bagster), and finally as a modern book in 1926 (Burns, Oates and Washbourne). The only subsequent edition of the Douay OT was that of Cousturier in 1635 (quarto). All other editions of the NT or OT are revised texts.

Nary's New Testament. Independent of Rheims ("the language whereof is so old") is the NT of Cornelius *Nary, a parish priest of Dublin, who in 1718 "endeavoured to make this New Testament speak the English tongue now used," while also taking "all the care imaginable to keep as close to the letter as the English will permit" (preface). Nary also translated from the Vulgate, and his preface is remarkable as evolving, perhaps for the first time, a reasoned theory of Biblical translation into English—literal, but in current idiom.

Witham's Revision of Rheims NT. In 1730 Robert Witham, then president of Douay, published his *Annotations of the New Testament* in two volumes, under the initials R. W. This is in fact the first attempt to revise Rheims, and it is likely that Challoner, who was under Witham at Douay and gave the *nihil obstat* to Witham's work, was influenced by it in his own revisions. Witham provided entirely new notes throughout, and also a long and interesting preface, in the course of which he states the principle that passages that are "obscure and hard to be understood . . . must be obscure in a literal translation, as they are in the original." He also defends the use of "thou," but sets out to adapt the diction of 1582 to English "as it is now chang'd and refin'd."

Challoner and After. In 1730 Richard *Challoner (1691–1781) left Douay for the English mission, and he was made a bishop in 1741. He immediately became aware of the needs of the English Catholics, and in 1749 he brought out his first revision of the Rheims NT. In 1750 he produced his revision of the OT in four pleasant little duodecimo volumes and in a fifth volume a further revision of the NT, with (on Cotton's reckoning) 124 new changes. The OT he hardly touched again, but these two revisions of the NT, 1749 and 1750, constitute what we may call the "Early Challoner," as distinct from the "Late Challoner," beginning with his third revision of the NT in 1752, which involved (again on Cotton's reckoning) over 2,000 new alterations and much modernization of style and syntax. The fourth revision of 1763–64 (which included the OT as in 1750) and the fifth of 1772 involved hardly any further changes. Unlike Nary and Witham, Challoner left no indication of his principles, methods, or collaborators, if any; and no printer is named until 1772, when the name of Coghlan of London appears. His object seems to have been purely practical: to provide the faithful with plentiful and cheap editions of the Scripture that were also accurate, readable, portable, and pleasantly printed.

Editions Stemming from Challoner. After Challoner's death in 1781, all Catholic editions of the NT or the whole Bible until modern times (except for the handful reproducing 1582) are dependent upon one or other of his revisions; and many further variations were introduced. These factors account for the considerable variety to be found among Catholic Bibles to this day. At first all were based upon the "Late Challoner" text of 1752, the most notable editions being those of Bernard MacMahon in Ireland from 1783 (reappearing in the large Haydock Bibles from 1811 in Manchester); the Philadelphia Bible of 1790; an edition of 1792, printed probably in Edinburgh; and George *Hay's Bibles in Scotland from 1796. Then came a sudden return to the "Early Challoner" of 1749–50, especially in the edition of Syers in Manchester of 1811, the "Catholic Board" edition of 1813, and above all, Daniel *Murray's "Stereotype Edition" of 1825 in Ireland. It was Murray's text, especially in the many editions issued by Denvir in Ireland from 1836, that became current throughout England in the 19th century. In view of the difficulties and small resources of the Irish publishers of that time, the output is astonishing and the occurrence of variant readings and misprints is hardly surprising. In the U.S. the same text came to be followed, but a number of 1752 elements found their way into the text, derived from the MacMahon or the Philadelphia editions, and influenced the classical American text of Challoner, Cardinal Gibbons' Baltimore Bible·of 1899.

Geddes, Lingard, and Newman. We should notice here the work of a wayward genius, Alexander *Geddes (1737–1802). Under the patronage of Lord Petre he produced his two handsome volumes of scholarly translation from the Hebrew of Genesis to Chronicles, with copious notes, in 1792 and 1797. When we read his "mythological" interpretation of Genesis and that "the authority of Scripture is by no means weakened by this interpretation" (preface, xi), we are on familiar ground. But in the 18th century it was otherwise, and Geddes, a man before his time, but also most indiscreet and arrogant, was frequently in trouble, and is said to have died under ecclesiastical censure.

In 1836 John *Lingard brought out the first Catholic translation of the Gospels made from the Greek text, published as "by a Catholic." Mention should be made also of the invitation sent in 1857 by Cardinal Wiseman to John Henry *Newman to become the editor of a new English version of the Bible. Newman began at once to plan his work and to select his collaborators. But the next 3 years were a period of misunderstandings, and after an alternative suggestion in 1860 that Newman should collaborate with Abp. Francis Patrick *Kenrick of Philadelphia in his revision of Douay (by then nearly finished and published in 1860–61), the whole scheme lapsed, to Newman's distress [details in W. P. Ward's *Life*, 3d ed., 1927, 1:419–429; cf. Meriol Trevor, *Newman* 2 (Light in Winter) 169–173].

Recent Douay-Challoner Editions. Current editions of Rheims-Douay in Great Britain and Ireland show a kind of *textus receptus* of Challoner, based mainly upon his revision of 1749–50 as edited by D. Murray. There are, however, two distinct streams: Irish publishers, followed by Burns and Oates, favored a pure "Irish text" from Murray, while Washbourne's Bible of 1900 and their NT adopted an "American text" with some 1752 elements, based on the Baltimore Bible of 1899; when the two firms merged, they were producing texts of both types in different editions. At the same time, various publishers issued NTs and Bibles printed for

them by Brepols in Belgium, and these almost invariably show an "American text," or even for the NT a revision of Challoner made by J. A. Carey in America in 1935. Again, other Bibles on sale in England exhibit the Confraternity NT text of 1941. In 1947 Sheed and Ward produced a NT which shows a good "Irish text" with few "American" features. The Catholic Truth Society published separate Gospels from 1900 on in a pure "Irish text," though their 1920 reprint showed an unusual return to original Challoner in Jn 2.4 "What is to me . . .?" Finally in 1956 the same society produced their pocket-size Bible, which is based on an "American text" from Washbourne of 1900, but introduces a few "Irish" elements as better readings, and a handful of new alterations, marked as such. (The article in Cath CommHS lists some keywords distinguishing the "Irish" and the "American" traditions.)

Recent Versions. The Westminster Version, initiated by Cuthbert *Lattey, is translated from the original languages into "Biblical English," individuals being responsible for particular books. The NT appeared in fascicles between 1913 and 1935, with a fine four-volume edition between 1921 and 1936, and a small one-volume edition, with abridged notes, in 1948. A few volumes of the OT began to appear between 1934 and 1939, and again in 1949 and 1953; since then no further issues have been projected.

Ronald A. *Knox was requested in 1939 by the hierarchy of England and Wales to undertake a completely new translation of the NT. This he produced, single-handed, in draft form in 1944 and after a few alterations, in final form (which was granted an official status by Cardinal Griffin of Westminster in his preface) in 1945. A draft edition of the OT appeared in 1949, and the final edition of the whole Bible, with considerable alterations in the OT, but with no further changes in the NT, in 1955. The translation is from the Vulgate "in the light of" the originals and with many textual notes. The Knox Bible has a style all of its own, perhaps more discussed than any other modern version. The translator explained his principles in a book, *Trials of a Translator,* a collection of essays published in 1949.

New translations of individual books appeared with the commentaries of P. Boylan on the Psalms (Dublin 1920), of T. E. Bird on the Psalms (London 1927), and of Edward *Kissane on Job (Dublin 1939) and Isaiah (Dublin 1943–44). A translation of all the Psalms, devised for singing to the melodies of P. Gelineau, sponsored by the Grail and edited by Father Hubert Richards, was published in 1963.

An English translation of the French *Bible de Jerusalem* with its notes, by a large team of translators, was near completion in 1964, under the editorship of Alexander Jones, who is responsible also for the accuracy of the translation according to the original texts. Two non-Catholic bodies engaged in the production of English texts have invited Catholic scholars in England to prepare Catholic editions of their texts, with variants noted; such an edition of the (American) *Revised Standard Version* NT appeared in 1965, with an edition of the OT to follow.

Bibliography: "The History of the Rheims-Douay Version," CathCommHS 29–34, under the name of H. Pope, but entirely rewritten by S. Bullough, comprehensive sketch, full bibliog., references to other Catholic versions. H. Cotton, *Rhemes and Doway* (Oxford 1855) main bibliog. source for all Catholic versions to 1854, written from a hostile standpoint but for the most part accurately. H. POPE, *English Versions of the Bible*, rev. and enl. S. BULLOUGH (St. Louis 1952) a complete but inadequately revised account to be used with caution. Two older sources are N. P. WISEMAN, "Catholic Versions of the Scriptures," *Dublin R* 2 (1837) 475–492. J. H. NEWMAN, "History of the Text of the Rheims and Douay Version of the Holy Scripture," *Rambler* 12 (July 1859) reprinted in *Tracts: Theological and Ecclesiastical* (London 1895) 403–445. Most histories of the English Bible include brief sections on Catholic texts. [For additional bibliography *see* BIBLE, IV (TEXTS AND VERSIONS), 23.]

[S. BULLOUGH]

THE UNITED STATES

The first Catholic Bible in English to be printed in the U.S. was published in Philadelphia in 1790. Until 1937 all subsequent editions of the Bible, except the Kenrick version, were Douay-Rheims or Douay-Rheims-Challoner texts, often varied, edited in England or Ireland and reprinted in the U.S.

The English Catholic versions of the Bible made in the U.S. are: (1) Kenrick (K); (2) Spencer (S); (3) Kleist-Lilly (KL); (4) Confraternity of Christian Doctrine Revision (CR); and (5) Confraternity of Christian Doctrine Version (CV).

Kenrick Version. In 1829 the Provincial Council of Baltimore ordered a new and emended edition of the Bible to be made, supplemented by suitable notes (*see* BALTIMORE, COUNCILS OF). Accordingly Dr. Francis Patrick *Kenrick, Coadjutor Bishop of Philadelphia and later archbishop of Baltimore, undertook the work. His translation from the Latin Vulgate, compared with the original languages, was published in New York City between 1849 and 1860 in five volumes, as follows: the four Gospels (1849); Acts, Epistles, and Apocalypse (1851); Psalms, Wisdom, and Canticle of Canticles (1857); Job and the Prophets (1859); Historical Books and Pentateuch (1860).

Kenrick's NT, in which he freely availed himself of J. *Lingard's version of the Greek, resulted in a revision of the Rheims text. A second, revised edition was published in 1862 in Baltimore. Kenrick's simple and practical notes show his familiarity with the work on the Greek text by J. M. *Scholz, J. J. *Griesbach, and S. T. Bloomfield. His version was based for the most part on R. *Challoner's third revision (1752), without being a direct reworking of it. He also manifests considerable independent judgment. In his introduction to Proverbs (265–266) he considers verses or parts of sentences of the Septuagint (LXX) not found in the Hebrew text to be either second translations or marginal notes introduced into the text.

The prefaces to the various volumes of Kenrick's version reveal the guidelines he followed in his work. In his preface to the Historical Books (9) he says, "I have read the Hebrew text with a disposition to prefer its readings, unless critical reasons weighed in favor of the Vulgate." Yet he seems by the references in his notes to wish to defend the Vulgate's integrity in its relation to the original language. For his English expression in the Gospels (Preface 29) Kenrick shows dependence on the Rheims, Challoner, and Lingard versions; in the rest of the NT he shows dependence on Rheims. He also accepts help from the King James version.

Kenrick's text was better and more readable than the existing English editions, yet it was not accepted as an official text. For that matter, Kenrick himself did not intend to replace what was in use.

Spencer Version. In 1901 Francis Aloysius *Spencer, son of an Episcopalian minister, convert to the Catholic faith, and priest of the Dominican Order, published *The Four Gospels* in New York City. The translation was made directly from the Greek, with reference to the Vulgate and Syriac versions. An annual edition was printed thereafter for 4 years. Spencer completed the rest of the NT just before his death in 1913. At the suggestion of the American hierarchy (1935) the Dominican Fathers Charles J. *Callan and John A. *McHugh prepared the Spencer MSS for the press, with introductions to the various books and additional notes. The entire NT was published in New York City in 1937.

Spencer divides his text into parts, rather than chapter headings, then into paragraphs with separate subject headings. There are references to parallel passages and verse numbers in the margins. The words of Christ are printed in italics. Quotations from the OT are in small capital letters. Hebrew spellings are used for OT Hebrew names, e.g., Elijah, Elisha, Isaiah. He uses Bible English, careful, however, to avoid archaic forms except "thou," "thee," etc. "Indeed, indeed" is used for "Amen, amen."

The translation is readable, clear, and in substantial agreement with the original Greek. The book is furnished with a chronology of the Gospels and Acts, an index of subjects for meditation, indexes of names and subjects, and maps. The following are examples of the Spencer version. " 'Take care not to perform your religious duties before men in order to be observed by them; for if you do, you will have no reward with your Father, who is in heaven. When therefore thou givest alms, do not have a trumpet blown before thee as the hypocrites do in the synagogues and in the streets, that they may be honored by men. Indeed, I tell you, they have received their reward!' " (Mt 6.1–2). " 'My flesh is real food, and My blood is real drink. . . . It is the Spirit that imparts life; the flesh can give no help whatever' " (Jn 6.55, 63).

The Kleist-Lilly Version. Among modern English translations of the Bible from the original languages *The New Testament* by James *Kleist, SJ, and Joseph *Lilly, CM, deserves a prominent place. It was published in 1952 in Milwaukee after the deaths of both authors. Kleist translated the Gospels; and Lilly, the Acts, Epistles, and Apocalypse. The translators availed themselves of the findings of Biblical scholarship and sought to render the Greek original into modern English in a manner appealing to American Catholics. Kleist explains that he changed the word order and sentence structure of the original when he considered it necessary for expressing proper English usage. He succeeded in producing an accurate, popular, and intelligible rendering of the Gospels from the original Greek. The notes are largely the work of H. Wilmering, SJ.

In Lilly's Acts and Epistles the work is less uniform. Large sections of Acts contain the text of the CR version with slight modification. In the Epistles, too, there are at times shifts from genuine originality to the lack of it.

The character of the KL version is seen in these sample readings. " 'I tell you the plain truth,' he said, 'this widow, the beggar woman that she is, has put in more than all the others, for all the others took from their superfluities what they put in as offerings to God; but this woman, in her extreme want, put in all that she had to live on'" (Lk 21.13). "'Love is long-suffering; love is kind, is not envious; love does not brag; it is not conceited; it is not ill-mannered; it is not self-seeking; it is not irritable; it takes no note of injury; it is not glad when injury triumphs; it is glad when the truth prevails. Always it is ready to make allowances; always to trust; always to hope; always to be patient'" (1 Cor 13.4–7).

In a comparison of versions KL, despite defects, has a claim to excellence. It is a modern version in the common speech of the 20th century, as the Greek NT also was written in the common speech of its time.

The Confraternity Revisions. Catholics were becoming increasingly aware of the need of revising the Douay-Rheims-Challoner Bible. There were discrepancies in its numerous editions introduced by private typographers and publishers; there were instances of lack of identification of the ecclesiastical authority approving the editions. The need of revision was intensified by the Confraternity of Christian Doctrine's (CCD) promotion of Bible instructions and study clubs throughout the U.S. Accordingly on Jan. 18, 1936, the chairman of the Bishops Committee of the CCD, Edwin V. O'Hara, proposed to Biblical scholars meeting at the Sulpician Seminary in Washington a revision of the Douay-Rheims-Challoner Bible. The meeting resulted in a twofold decision: to undertake the revision of the Catholic English Bible in use and to form an association of Catholic Biblical scholars that would promote scientific and popular Scripture studies and publications. The Bishops Committee of the CCD offered its patronage to the association and its work. October 3, 1936, was the founding date.

New Testament. At this time the principles of revision for the NT were drawn up. It was agreed to adhere to the Latin Clementine Vulgate and to render its sense exactly and in clear and simple English. Recourse to the Greek was made for the sense of the Latin but not for deviation from the Vulgate. Variants between Latin and Greek were treated in footnotes. Diction, style, and rhythm of the current text were retained as far as possible; mistakes were corrected; obsolete words, modernized; and words introduced for sense, italicized. Thee's and thou's were retained; first words of sentences, rather than of verses, were capitalized; long and involved sentences were broken up without detriment to sense. The text was arranged in paragraph form; chapter and verse numbers were indicated in the margin. Cross references were placed between the text and footnotes; poetic passage were printed in verse form. Divisions, subdivisions, and boxed paragraph headings enhanced the format and readability of the text. The names of the revisers and editors appeared on the final page.

The NT revision was completed in 1941. It was published by the St. Anthony Guild Press of Paterson, N.J. The Holy Name Society undertook the task of distribution. More than 1 million copies were sold in the first year. Though the work had been planned as a revision, the amount of independent translation was such that it was aptly regarded as a new translation.

Old Testament. The revision of the OT Vulgate presented its own special problems. Not all the books were translated by St. Jerome from the original languages into a uniform Latin version. The Psalter of the Vulgate is Jerome's revision of the Old Latin version from the LXX. Sirach, Baruch, Wisdom, and 1 and 2 Machabees are from the revised Old Latin. The principles govern-

ing the revision of the OT [see CathBiblQuart 1 (1939) 267–269] followed those for the revision of the NT as far as they could be applied. Proper names translated by St. Jerome were restored.

Sample portions of the OT revision were printed, not published; e.g., the minor Prophets and the first 40 Psalms. Though the OT revision was well under way by 1944, the project was abruptly terminated in favor of a complete change of plan, as explained in the following section.

Confraternity Version. A response of the *Pontifical Biblical Commission (Aug. 22, 1943) favored translation of the Bible from the original into modern languages [ActApS 35 (1943) 270]. The encyclical of Pius XII *Divino afflante Spiritu* (1943) urged the study of Oriental languages and literatures and recourse to the original texts. These directives caused the committees for the OT and NT translations to choose the original texts of Hebrew, Aramaic, and Greek as the basis of an entirely new translation called the Confraternity Version. The Bishops Committee of the CCD was in agreement with this. Edward Arbez, SS, notified the Catholic hierarchy of the change in a letter dated April 22, 1944.

Old Testament. The new principles of translation of the OT [see CathBiblQuart 6 (1944) 363–364] prescribed the use of the Kittel-Kahle edition of the Hebrew and Aramaic texts for translating the protocanonical books and the Swete edition of the OT in Greek for the deuterocanonical books except for the parts of Sirach that have been preserved in Hebrew. Textual corrections were made on the basis of the ancient versions. Conjectural emendations were kept to the minimum. St. Anthony Guild was the publisher. The final board of editors consisted of Louis F. Hartman, CSSR, Msgr. Patrick W. Skehan, and Stephen J. Hartdegen, OFM, all members of the Catholic Biblical Association. These were authorized to pass final judgment on all the OT books. A list of translators and editors was printed in the back of each volume. After Genesis (1948) and Psalms (1950) were published as samples, the OT volumes appeared in this order: v.1, *Genesis to Ruth* (1952); v.3, *The Sapiential Books: Job to Sirach* (1955); and v.4, *The Prophetic Books: Isaia to Malachia* (1961). Volume 2, *The Historical Books: Samuel to Maccabees,* was scheduled for publication in 1967.

In harmony with the ecumenical spirit of *Vatican Council II, some outstanding non-Catholic scholars were engaged to edit 1 and 2 Samuel (F. M. Cross) and 4 Kings (J. A. Sanders) and to revise Genesis (D. N. Freedman). In the interest of uniform Bible usage, the completed OT adopted the Hebrew name forms instead of the Vulgate forms previously used.

The critical textual notes appended to each volume are a valuable feature of the CV, especially for study. They indicate every correction of the Hebrew, Aramaic, or Greek texts. The sense paragraphs, the indented and boxed side-headings, the clear divisions, the verse form of poetic compositions, the footnotes and cross references enhance the usefulness of the work. The CV OT is now used in all the liturgical books, missal, breviary, and ritual.

New Testament. The CV NT, translated from the original Greek, was entrusted to a separate committee headed by Msgr. Myles M. Bourke, assisted by R. E. Brown, SS; D. Stanley, SJ; J. A. Fitzmyer, SJ; R. Kugelman, CP; T. Halton; E. F. Siegman, CPPS; B. Vawter,

CM, J. Quinn, and the Protestant scholars W. D. Davies and John Knox. The first portions appeared in the form of scriptural readings in the Roman Missal. Completion of the work was scheduled for 1967. The OT translation principles also guided the NT translation as far as applicable. The same applied to its external form. Confronted with the variety of style of the various books, the translators strove to reflect this variety and to render the text faithfully, even in its informal, conversational, and derogatory nuances. Before publication of the entire NT, the work was submitted to the critical examination and judgment of a literary editor.

The aim of the CV was to produce a new and modern translation, up-to-date and more accurate through its use of the latest historical, textual, and linguistic findings, popular in its living and modern expression, devoid of the sense of strangeness and remoteness through its sense of reality, simple, and understandable to learned and unlearned. Time will test and judge the success of these aims. The 22 years it took to accomplish it were dedicated by love for the Incarnate Word expressed through painstaking labor to reclothe in modern English God's inspired word.

Comparison of Texts. A few samples of the same passages from different versions, cited side by side, will illustrate the characteristics of the respective versions.

Douay Version of Jb 42.1–3, 5–6.

Then Job answered the Lord, and said: I know that thou canst do all things, and no thought is hid from thee. Therefore I have spoken unwisely, and things that above measure exceeded my knowledge . . .. With the hearing of the ear I have heard thee, I have heard thee but now my eye seeth thee. Therefore I reprehend myself, and do penance in dust and ashes.

Confraternity Version of Jb 42.1–3, 5–6.

Then Job answered the LORD and said:
I know that you can do all things,
and that no purpose of yours can be hindered.
I have dealt with great things that I do not understand;
things too wonderful for me, which I cannot know.
I have heard of you by word of mouth,
but now my eye has seen you.
Therefore I disown what I have said,
and repent in dust and ashes.

Douay Version of Is 61.1–3.

The spirit of the Lord is upon me, because the Lord hath anointed me: he hath sent me to preach to the meek, to heal the contrite of heart, and to preach a release to the captives, and deliverance to them that are shut up; to proclaim the acceptable year of the Lord, and the day of vengeance of our God; to comfort all that mourn.

Confraternity Version of Is 61.1–3.

The spirit of the Lord is upon me,
because the LORD has anointed me;
He has sent me to bring glad tidings to the lowly,
to heal the brokenhearted,
To proclaim liberty to the captives
and release to the prisoners,
To announce a year of favor from the LORD
and a day of vindication by our God,
to comfort all who mourn.

Rheims-Challoner Version of Mt 11.28–30.

Come to me all you that labour, and are burdened, and I will refresh you. Take up my yoke upon you, and learn of me, because I am meek, and humble of heart: and you shall find rest to your souls. For my yoke is sweet and my burden light.

Confraternity Version of Mt 11.28–30.

Come to me all of you who are wearied from toil and heavily burdened; and I will refresh you. Take my yoke upon your shoulders and receive my instruction, because I am gentle and humble of heart. Thus will you find refreshment for your souls. For this yoke of mine lies easy; this burden of mine is light.

Rheims-Challoner Version of Gal 4.14–18.

God forbid that I should glory, save in the cross of our Lord Jesus Christ; by whom the world is crucified to me, and I to the world. For in Christ Jesus neither circumcision availeth anything, nor uncircumcision, but a new creature. And whosoever shall follow this rule, peace on them, and mercy, and upon the Israel of God. From henceforth let no man be troublesome to me; for I bear the marks of the Lord Jesus in my body. The grace of our Lord Jesus Christ be with your spirit.

Confraternity Version of Gal 4.14–18.

Brethren: May I never boast except in the cross of our Lord Jesus Christ! Through it the world has been crucified to me, and I to the world. Really, it means nothing whether one is circumcised or not; what does count is that one be created anew. Peace and mercy upon all who follow this principle, and upon the Israel of God. Henceforth, let no man make difficulties for me! See, I bear on my body the brand-marks of Jesus! Brothers, may the favor of our Lord Jesus Christ be with your spirit.

These samples show how the CV has gained in clarity by being made in modern English directly from the original Hebrew and Greek texts. The first two samples demonstrate also the advantage of printing the translation of poetic passages in lines corresponding to those of the original Hebrew poetry.

Bibliography: J. WRIGHT, *Early Bibles of America* (3d ed. New York 1894). H. POPE, *English Versions of the Bible*, rev. S. BULLOUGH (St. Louis 1952) 458–463, 491–493, 497–499, 505–506. J. E. STEINMUELLER, "American Catholic Versions of the Bible," HomPastRev 36 (1936) 1268–74. F. F. BRUCE, *The English Bible: A History of Translations* (New York 1961). C. H. PICKAR, "Principles Governing the Revision of the O.T.," CathBiblQuart 1 (1939) 267–269. J. A. KLEIST, "An Important Principle in Rendering the Gospels into Modern English," AmEcclRev 110 (1943) 435–443. P. W. SKEHAN, "The O.T. Revision Project," CathBiblQuart 5 (1943) 214–219. M. J. GRUENTHANER, "*Divino afflante Spiritu:* The New Encyclical on Biblical Studies," AmEcclRev 110 (1943) 330–337; "Principles for the Translation of the O.T. from the Original," CathBiblQuart 6 (1944) 363–364. J. L. MCKENZIE, *ibid.* 16 (1954) 491–500, review of Kleist-Lilly N.T. E. P. ARBEZ, "The New Catholic Translation of the O.T.," *ibid.* 14 (1957) 237–254.

[S. J. HARTDEGEN]

23. PROTESTANT AND JEWISH ENGLISH VERSIONS

Although the history of the English versions of the Bible that were produced in England by Protestants and Jews is intertwined since the 18th century with the history of the non-Catholic versions that were made in the U.S., for the sake of clearer presentation the two groups of versions are here treated separately.

GREAT BRITAIN AND IRELAND

The history of the English printed Bible begins with William Tyndale, whose work from 1525 forms the basis of the Authorized Version (AV), known also as the King James Version (KJV), of 1611, which remained the only official text in the Church of England for the next 2½ centuries. In 1870 a revision was proposed by authority, and the Revised Version (RV) appeared in 1881–85; a corresponding American Standard Version (ASV) came out in 1901. An entirely fresh revision, the Revised Standard Version (RSV) was produced by the Protestants of America between 1946 and 1952, and this has had an important influence in England as well. Meanwhile, since 1611, a large number of "Private Versions" appeared, continuing to today. Finally the Protestant Churches in Great Britain produced in 1961 the NT of the New English Bible (NEB), a text that holds a quasi-official position in England, while in 1963 there appeared the important Revised (Prayer Book) Psalter. This study will therefore have six sections, treating (1) the period from Tyndale to the AV, (2) the AV of 1611 itself, (3) its official revisions, the RV (and ASV) and the RSV, (4) the "Private Versions," (5) the NEB, and (6) the Revised Psalter. An appendix will deal with Jewish versions produced in England.

(1) Tyndale to the Authorized Version. The period before the AV is a tangled piece of history, mainly because all the Biblical texts, except Tyndale's and part of Coverdale's, are revisions of preceding versions. It is probably easiest, therefore, to present the history in tabular form and then to comment on each version in turn.

*(a) William *Tyndale* (c. 1480–1536).* After his studies at Oxford, Tyndale was ordained and then lived in Cambridge, where no doubt he saw Erasmus's new

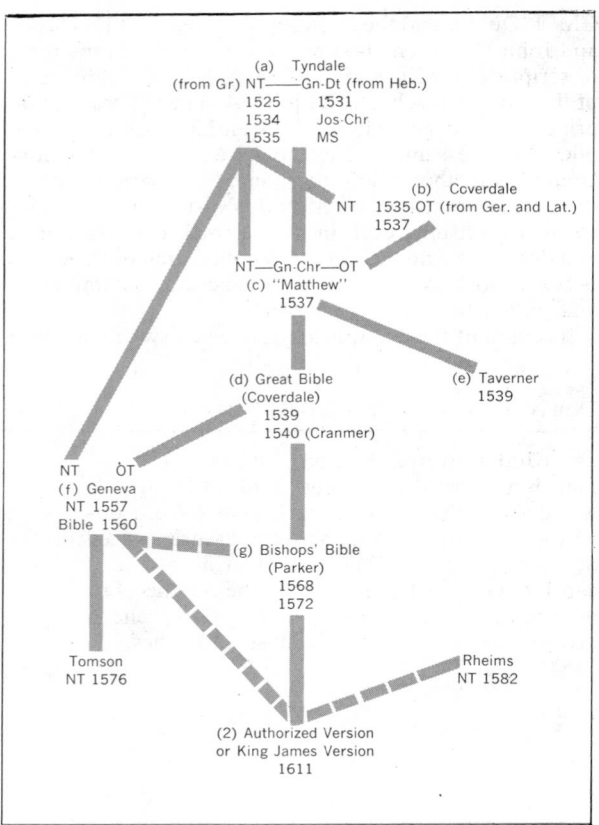

Fig. 21. Chart showing how the successive English versions of the Bible, from Tyndale's to the Authorized, are essentially revisions of earlier versions. The unbroken lines denote direct descent, the broken lines indirect influence. The letters in parentheses refer to the subdivisions in section (1) of the article.

Greek NT of 1516. In 1520, as a private tutor in Gloucestershire, he began to translate the NT from the Greek. In 1523 he sought support for his venture in London, but it was received with much disfavor, and in 1524 he went abroad, first to Hamburg and then to Wittenberg and to Cologne, where the printing of his NT began early in 1525, until the work was stopped by the city authorities on the grounds of its Lutheran associations. Tyndale fled to Worms, taking the printed sheets with him. Whether this printing was continued at Worms is uncertain, but two complete editions were printed there in 1525 or early in 1526. They found their way to England in 1526 and were at once proscribed as Lutheran. Although Tyndale did draw upon Luther for his notes, his translation was independent and had been begun before the appearance of Luther's version in 1521–22. By 1534 there had been at least three reprints of Tyndale's NT, and a number of variations had crept in. This was the ostensible reason for the unauthorized revision by George Joye in 1534, which aroused Tyndale's indignation but also hastened his own revision, published in the same year. A final revision appeared in 1535.

In January 1531 (N.S.; 1530, O.S.) Tyndale published his translation from the Hebrew of the Pentateuch, which was printed by Hans Luft of "Marlborow," which J. I. Mombert (107–115) argues to be, not Mar-

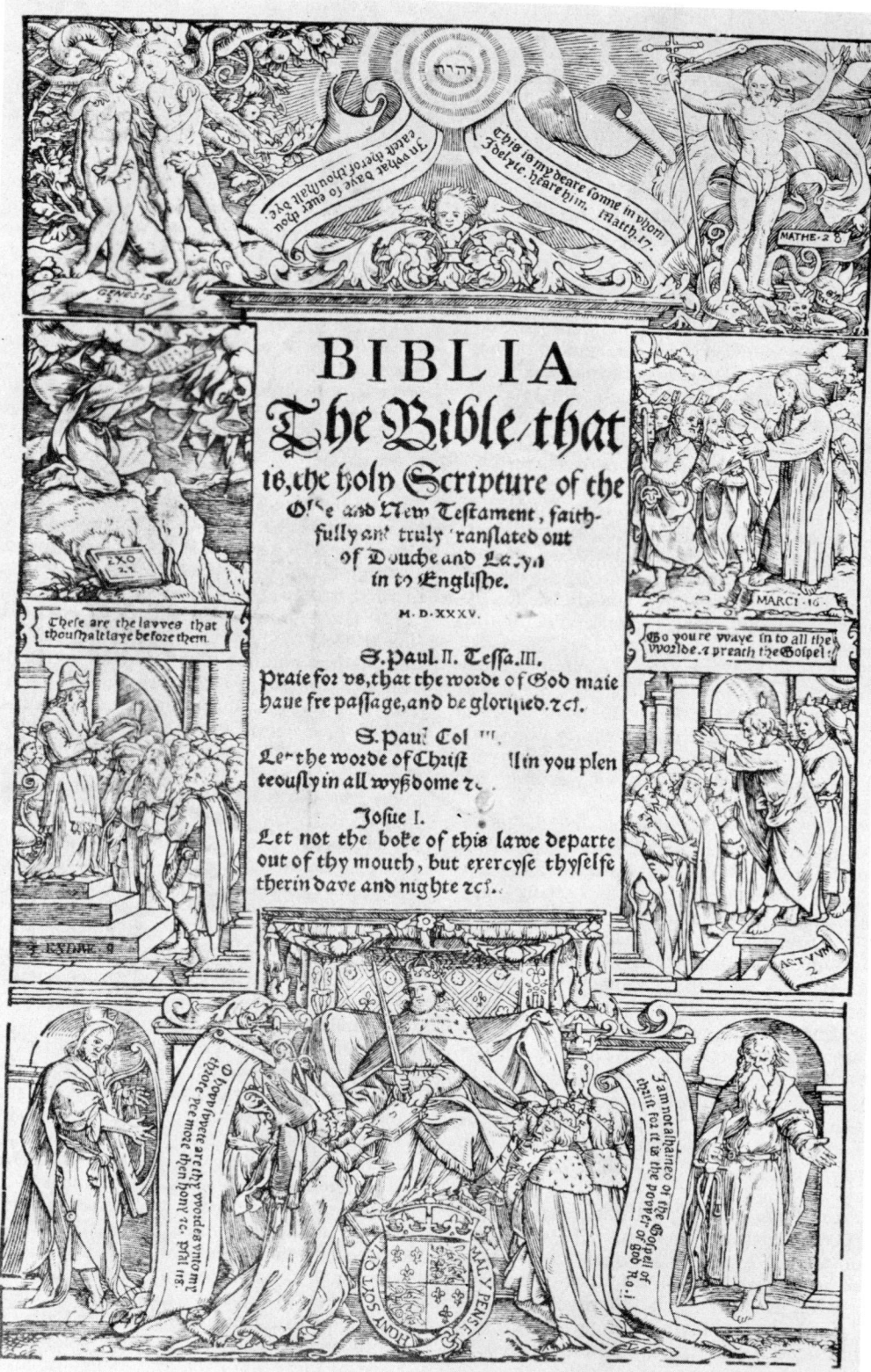

Fig. 22. Woodcut decorated title page of the Coverdale Bible of 1535, the first edition of the Bible in English, probably printed at Zurich. The bottom vignette shows the King (Henry VIII) handing a Bible to a bishop.

burg (as often stated), but a pseudonym for Wittenberg, the residence of the printer Luft. There is also evidence (Mombert, 115–117, 139) for Tyndale's association with Luther at this time, and for his having learned Hebrew. Also in 1531 he published his translation of Jona. He revised his Pentateuch in 1534 and left a translation of Josue-Chronicles in manuscript. In 1536 he was put to death by the imperial officers at Vilvorde in Brabant (of the Low Countries).

The debt of subsequent versions to Tyndale is very great; indeed, much of the vocabulary of "Biblical English" and the general pattern of its style is traceable to him.

(b) Miles *Coverdale (c. 1488–1569). He was at first an Augustinian in Cambridge, where he became a friend of Thomas *Cromwell. About 1528 he went to Germany, where, with Cromwell's encouragement if not commission, he began work on his translation of the Bible. Whether at this time he was in touch with Tyndale is uncertain. In 1534 King *Henry VIII, who had hitherto opposed the vernacular translations, chiefly on the grounds of suspected Lutheranism, was persuaded to decree that a translation should be made by "honest and learned men, to be nominated by the King." Things had been well planned, and Coverdale's Bible was ready and published in 1535 as "faithfully translated out of the Douche [i.e., German] and Latyn," printed probably at Zurich and dedicated to the King. The translation is eclectic: the NT is mainly from Tyndale, and for the OT he used the new current German and Latin versions. He revised his Bible in 1537, and the NT again in 1538 according to the Vulgate.

Coverdale's influence on English Biblical style is second only to Tyndale's, and it was his Psalter that became incorporated into the Book of Common Prayer, not to be ousted when the text of the AV was imposed on all other readings in 1662.

(c) "Matthew's" Bible. This appeared in 1537, like Coverdale's of that year "with the King's most gracious license." The identity of "Thomas Matthew" has been the subject of much speculation, but it now seems fairly certain that this was a pseudonym used by John Rogers (c. 1500–55), a friend of Tyndale and the first of the Protestant martyrs under Queen *Mary Tudor. The text is composite: the NT and the Pentateuch are Tyndale's, and Josue-Chronicles were apparently taken from his unpublished manuscript, while the rest of the OT is from Coverdale. Its importance, however, lies in the fact that it is the text basically underlying the AV, to which it transmitted the work of Tyndale and Coverdale.

Neither Coverdale's nor "Matthew's" (with its strongly Lutheran notes) were entirely acceptable texts, so that Thomas *Cranmer and Cromwell decided upon a new revision.

(d) The Great Bible. So called from its large folio size, this Bible was finished in London in 1539, printed by R. Grafton and E. Whitchurch (whence it is sometimes referred to as "Whitchurch's"), though printing had begun in Paris. It is the text of "Matthew's" Bible, revised by Coverdale probably according to the latest German and Latin versions. It was at once ordered by Cromwell to be placed in every church. The edition of 1540 has a lengthy preface by Cranmer, whence it is sometimes known as "Cranmer's Bible."

(e) Richard Taverner (c. 1505–77). As a lawyer with a good knowledge of Greek, Taverner was encouraged by Cromwell to revise "Matthew's" Bible. His NT has contributed some phrases to the AV, but his OT was revised according to the Vulgate and has small importance.

(f) Geneva Bible. The Protestant (Calvinist) exiles at Geneva during Queen Mary's reign (1553–58) produced their NT in 1557, on the basis of Tyndale revised according to the latest Greek texts of Robert *Estienne (1550–51). The chief translator was William Whittingham. In 1560 they produced the whole Bible; the OT was based on the Great Bible but with many corrections, and the NT was revised. The Geneva Bible at once became popular; it was the most accurate translation so far, and many turns of phrase came from it into the AV. It is said that at least 140 editions were printed before 1644, and it was by far the most widespread text until the AV. The important revision of the NT by Laurence Tomson in 1576 was based upon the new Latin translation of Beza, of 1565.

(g) The Bishops' Bible. The 1568 Bishops' Bible was a revision of the Great Bible, proposed by Archbishop Parker, especially in view of the embarrassing popularity of the strongly Protestant Geneva version. The work was parcelled out to various bishops: they were to follow the Great Bible except "where it varieth manifestly from the Hebrew or Greek original," and they were to make "no bitter notes." The result is a scholarly, moderate work, profiting by most of what had gone before; and it was the first text issued by episcopal authority in England.

(2) The Authorized Version (AV) or King James Version (KJV), 1611. Accepting the proposal of the Puritans at the Hampton Court conference in 1604, King *James I ordered a new translation to be undertaken. The reason was the Puritans' discontent over the imposition of the Bishops' Bible. The King at once appointed the translators at Westminster, Cambridge, and Oxford. The basic text was to be the Bishops' Bible, "as little altered as the truth of the original will permit," and they were to consult Tyndale, Coverdale, "Matthew," "Whitchurch" (the Great Bible), and Geneva. In fact they also consulted Rheims of 1582, as is recognized in the preface to the RV. The text was to be a revision rather than a new version, and scholarship, especially with regard to Hebrew, had developed greatly during the previous half-century. For its time the KJV was the most accurate, but its dependence on earlier versions rendered the diction a little archaic for its date. The great work was published in 1611, as "Newly Translated out of the Originall Tongues and with the former Translations diligently compared and reuised by his Maiesties speciall Commandment." It soon eclipsed all the previous versions and remained the single official text within the Church of England until the RV, and it also became generally accepted among the Free Churches.

(3) The Revised Version (RV), 1881–85. In 1870 an official decision was made within the Church of England to set about the revision of the AV. The revisers included members of the Free Churches and a Unitarian; J. H. Newman had been invited, but felt unable to accept. They were "to introduce as few alterations as possible into the text of the AV consistently with faithfulness," and to limit themselves, as far as possible, "to the language of the Authorized and earlier English Versions" (Preface). Moreover, no change was to be made except by vote of two thirds, though alterations approved by a simple majority found a place in the margin. The NT appeared in 1881, the OT in 1885, after which a smaller committee revised the Apocrypha (appeared 1895).

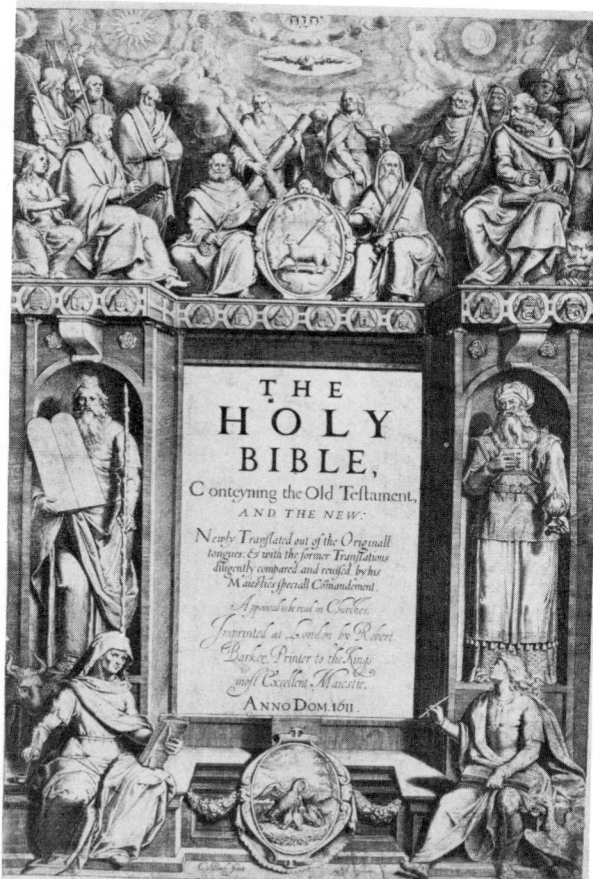

Fig. 23. Title page of the first edition (1611) of the King James Version of the Bible.

The parallel work of the American revisers (ASV, 1901), whose preferences are listed at the back of the English RV, is treated below, together with the further revision of the RSV of 1946–52; but it should be noted here that the RSV has achieved a wider popularity in England than any other recent text, both for study and for worship.

The RV had, in a sense, the misfortune of being born just before the modern discoveries in archeology and paleography came to throw so much light on Biblical problems, and also in an atmosphere of conservatism that inhibited the use of critical findings. Hence although the RV was a dutiful rendering, in worship it never replaced the AV, and in study it has been largely eclipsed by the RSV. But for its period it remains a dignified and noble effort.

(4) "Private Versions" since 1611. It is less well known that a number of versions of the Bible, or the NT, or notable parts of them, were made independently of the official or "public" versions (RV, RSV, NEB). The following account includes all such versions made in the British Isles, to the number of 81. (Translations of single books are not included.)

The editor's or translator's name is given, followed by his denomination unless it was Church of England, the extent of his work, the date of first issue, and the place unless it was London. Occasionally a note is added and quotation marks used if the words are from the title page or preface of the work itself.

(a) Paraphrases of the AV. These print the words of the AV, with explanatory sections, either italicized and interwoven, or adjacent to the text; there are usually accompanying "Annotations."

Henry Hammond, *NT* 1653

Abraham Woodhead, Richard Allestrey and Obadiah Walker, *Epp.*, Oxford 1675 (Woodhead and Walker were crypto-Catholics, and their exegesis is Catholic)

Richard Baxter (Indep.), *NT* 1685

Daniel Whitby, *NT* 1703

Samuel Clarke, *Gosp.* 1701–02

Thomas Pyle, *Hist. Books OT* 1717–25, *Acts and Epp.* 1725 ("in the manner of Dr. Clarke"), *Rev.* 1735 (Clarke and Pyle were leaders of the Arian movement in the C. of E. at the time)

John Guyse (Indep.), *NT* 1739–52 (anti-Arian)

Edward Barlee, *Epp.* 1837 (a sudden and last appearance of this style)

(b) Revisions or Corrections of the AV. All these are stated by their writers to be revisions of the AV, or corrections according to a new edition of the Greek NT.

Edward Wells, *Bible* 1711–28 (6 large v., with corrected text and paraphrase: the first attempt at correction)

William Whiston, *NT* 1745 ("Primitive NT" based on Codex D; Whiston was an Arian and later became a Baptist)

John Wesley (Meth.), *NT* 1755 ("as near as possible to the original")

Abp. William Newcome (Primate of Ireland), *NT,* Dublin 1796 (an important scholarly work; first advocacy of a revision of AV by authority; first based on Griesbach's Greek text of 1774–75)

Anon. [Thomas Belsham (Unitarian)], *NT* 1808 ("Improved Version" for Unitarians; based on Newcome's)

William Alexander (Friend?), *OT* (v. 1 only), York 1828

Anon. [Granville Penn], *NT* 1836 ("most ancient manuscripts")

Samuel Sharpe (Unitarian), *NT* 1840, *OT* 1865

Anon. [Edgar Taylor (Dissenter)], *NT* 1840 (from Griesbach)

Anon. [John T. Conquest], *Bible* 1841 ("with 20,000 Emendations")

T. J. Hussey, *Bible* 1844 (prints AV parallel)

Charles Wellbeloved, George V. Smith, John S. Porter, *OT* 1859–62

H. Highton, *NT* 1862

Henry Alford, *NT* 1869 (from his own critical Greek text; he became a reviser of the RV)

Robert Ainslie, *NT* 1869 (from Tischendorf's text)

F. C. Cook, *Bible* 1871–81 ("The Speaker's Commentary" including revised text; an opponent of the RV)

John Brown McClellan, *Gosp.* 1875

F. W. Gotch, B. Davies, G. A. Jacob, S. G. Green, *Bible* 1877 ("not such a complete revision" as RV is to be, but to correct "indisputable errors")

(c) Further revisions after the RV. Attempts at deliberate improvement on the RV, or a different approach.

Samuel Lloyd, *NT* 1905 (from Nestle's text)

Sir Edward G. Clarke, *NT* 1913 ("more current than the AV and more acceptable than the RV")

E. E. Cunnington, *NT* 1914, revised 1935

R. Mercer Wilson, *NT* 1938 ("The Book of Books")

T. F. and R. E. Ford, *NT* 1948 (the "Letchworth Version" is the AV with archaic words modernized)

(d) New Translations until the "Modern Speech" Versions. An imprecise but practical division. Some of these in fact follow the AV closely, but claim to be more original than a simple revision.

Henry Ainsworth (Brownist), *Pent., Ct, Ps,* Amsterdam 1616–27

Anon. [Daniel Mace (not, as often, William)], *NT* 1729 (one of first critical Greek texts from manuscripts, with a "new version")

Philip Doddridge (Indep.), *NT* 1739 ("new version interwoven with the paraphrase")

John Heylin, *NT* 1749–61 ("An Interpretation"; in reality a new version)

Richard Wynne, *NT* 1764 ("a just medium between a servile literal translation and a paraphrastic loose version"—the first time such a principle is enunciated)

Anthony Purver (Friend), *Bible* 1764 ("a new and literal translation")

Edward Harwood (Presb.), *NT* 1768 (the most well-known of all these: "A Liberal Translation" made with "Freedom, Spirit and Elegance")

John Worsley, *NT* 1770 (in "the Present Idiom of the English Tongue"—a "modern speech" version of the time)

George Campbell (Presb.), *Gosp.* 1789

Gilbert Wakefield (Dissenter), *NT* 1791 ("completely vernacular without vulgarity")

James Macknight (Presb.), *Epp.* 1795 ("literal," with Greek text; this, with Campbell's Gospels and Doddridge's Acts and Revelation was published in a Presbyterian Version in 1818)

Thomas Haweis, *NT* 1795

Nathaniel Scarlett (Baptist), *NT* 1798 ("nearer to the English idiom at this day," with "personification" of speakers)

J. M. Ray, *Bible,* Glasgow 1799 (using evidence of recent discoveries in the East)

Anon. [William Williams], *NT* 1812 ("modern, correct and close")

William Thomson, *NT,* Kilmarnock 1816

Benjamin Boothroyd, *Bible,* Pontefract 1817 (at his own press, where in 1810 he had printed a Hebrew Bible)

John Bellamy, *OT* (*Gn–Ct*) 1818

Thomas Belsham (Unitarian), *Paul* 1822

Philip N. Shuttleworth, *Epp.,* Oxford 1829 ("periphrastic")

Charles Eyre (Unitarian), *Paul,* Ipswich 1832 (free paraphrase)

Anon. [W. Heberden], *Epp., Rev.* 1839 ("literal")

Sir Lancelot Brenton, Bt, *OT* (*LXX*) 1844 (the only translation of the Septuagint, apart from Thompson in the U.S. in 1808)

W. J. Conybeare and J. W. Howson, *Paul* 1852 (in "Life and Epistles")

Herman Heinfetter [pseud. of F. Parker], *NT* 1854–62 (literal translation, and then a new version made from this)

Joseph Turnbull, *Paul* 1854, with *Rev.* 1858

Robert Young, *Bible* 1863 (the most literal of all)

G. W. Brameld, *Gosp.* 1863 (from five critical Greek texts)

John Bowes (Indep.), *NT,* Dundee 1870

J. B. Rotherham, *NT* 1872 (from Tregelles), *Bible* 1897–1902 ("emphatic texts" with rhetorical markings)

Samuel Davidson (Presb.), *NT* 1875 (from Tischendorf)

W. B. Crickmer, *NT* 1881

J. N. Darby (Brethren), *Bible* 1884

Mrs. Helen Spurrell, *OT* 1885

James Moffatt (Presb.), *NT* 1901 ("Historical NT," not to be confused with his "modern speech" version of 1913)

(e) The "Modern Speech" Versions. Preceded by Norton (1855) and Sawyer (1858) in America. For NEB see section (5) below.

Ferrar Fenton, *Bible* 1883–1903 ("in Modern English"; the work of an English businessman)

Ernest Bilton, *Gosp.* 1888 ("language of everyday life")

Anon., "The Twentieth Century NT" 1898–1901, revised 1904 (a text that has remained in circulation)

Henry Hayman, *Epp.* 1900 ("current and popular idiom")

A. S. Way, *Paul* 1901 ("Letters to Seven Churches and Three Friends")

Richard Francis Weymouth, *NT* 1903 ("everyday English," based on his own critical Greek text)

James Moffatt (Presb.), *NT* 1913, *OT* 1924 ("Moffatt Bible" 1926; the most popular of all these)

G. W. Wade, *NT* 1934 ("Documents of the NT" in chronological order)

S. H. Hooke, *NT* 1941, *Bible* 1949 (in "Basic English" using only 1000 words)

Bp. J. W. C. Wand, *Epp.* 1943 (Australia), revised 1946 (England) ("paraphrased," but in fact often a fine close translation)

J. B. Phillips, *Epp.* 1947, then other parts, *NT* 1958 ("in Modern English"; the furthest experiment in modern diction)

E. V. Rieu, *Gosp.* 1952 (Penguin Classics)

C. Kingsley Williams (Meth.), *NT* 1952 ("in plain English")

C. H. Rieu (son of E. V.), *Acts* 1957 (Penguin Classics)

British and Foreign Bible Society, *NT* begun 1958—in parts (a "Greek-English Diglot" with modern literal translation, as a guide to translators, printed "for private circulation only")

(5) The New English Bible (NEB), NT 1961. In 1946 a suggestion was made by the Church of Scotland that the Christian Churches in the British Isles should consider a completely new translation "into the current speech of our own time" (intro. to NEB). As a result, a Joint Committee was set up, composed of members of the Church of England, of the Church of Scotland, and of other Protestant Churches, and of the Society of Friends. The general director is Prof. C. H. Dodd, and an important feature is the panel of literary advisers. The NT appeared in 1961, and the OT and Apocrypha are in preparation. The NEB NT was well received, and 2½ million copies were sold in the first 4 months. It should be stressed that the NEB is in no sense a revision, but an entirely fresh attempt, using all the resources of scholarship and setting out to lift the meaning of the words from their original pattern into a completely English form. This may lose certain overtones, but readability and intelligibility are gained.

(6) The Revised Psalter, 1963. The importance of Coverdale's Psalter in English Protestant worship is such that it would be incorrect not to notice the new Psalter of 1963, the first revision of Coverdale's ever officially made. It was undertaken by a commission headed by Archbishop Coggan, the principal Hebraist being Prof. D. W. Thomas of Cambridge. "It has not been our duty to make a new translation, but to mend an old one" and "to bring our renderings into the closest accord . . . with Coverdale's vocabulary, syntax, and rhythm; our aim has been 'invisible mending'" (Preface). In this attitude the Revised Psalter is somewhat unique, and at the time of its publication represented a last word in the translating of the Psalms. A trial edition of Book I appeared in 1961, and the final text was submitted to the Convocations in 1963.

Appendix: Anglo-Jewish Versions. It was not until the 18th century that the Jews in England began to feel the need for an English text of the Bible, and then they adopted the AV. The first Jewish editions, with English alongside the Hebrew, reproduced the AV: these were A. Alexander's Pentateuch and Five Rolls of 1785, and David Levi's Pentateuch and Haftorahs of 1787. In 1789 Isaac Delgado produced an English Pentateuch with the AV and a "thorough correction" printed in parallel, except where he felt none was necessary, and then no text was printed.

In 1851–61 A. Benisch made a new translation "free from all un-Jewish preconceptions" for his *Jewish School and Family Bible;* and in 1881 M. Friedländer revised the AV for his massive *Jewish Family Bible.* Meanwhile the translation of Isaac Leeser, made in America in 1854, gained currency in England, and the so-called "Jewish American" text of 1917 won even wider circulation there; but these are described below, as well as the "New Jewish Version" begun in 1962.

More recently in England, from 1929 to 1936, appeared Rabbi J. H. Hertz's edition of the Pentateuch and Haftorahs, which uses the RV text or margin, whichever is "most in accordance with Jewish tradition"; and in 1958–62 I. Levi issued a translation of S. R. Hirsch's translation and commentary on the Pentateuch. In general, however, English Jews have used the AV, or more recently the RV or RSV.

Finally, two Jewish translations of the NT should be noticed. In 1827 appeared "The Gospel of God's Anointed, the Glory of Israel," whose translator, Alexander Greaves, declared himself in the 1828 edition; the text is basically the AV, but with many alterations, and the work is offered "to my Gentile brethren." In 1955 Hugh J. Schonfield published "The Authentic NT," designed to bring into proper relief the Jewish background of the NT.

Bibliography: The classical histories. J. I. MOMBERT, *Handbook of the English Versions of the Bible* (New York 1883). B. F. WESTCOTT, *A General View of the History of the English Bible*, ed. W. A. WRIGHT (3d ed. New York 1905). F. F. BRUCE, *The English Bible: A History of Translations* (New York 1961). Less detailed are *The Cambridge History of the Bible: The West from the Reformation to the Present Day*, ed. S. L. GREENSLADE (Cambridge, Eng. 1963) ch. 4, 10. L. A. WEIGLE, *The English N.T. from Tyndale to the Revised Standard Version* (Nashville 1949). F. C. GRANT, *Translating the Bible* (Greenwich, Conn. 1961). Special areas. C. C. BUTTERWORTH, *The Literary Lineage of the King James Bible, 1340–1611* (Philadelphia 1941). Articles in *The Bible Today* (London 1955), J. F. MOZLEY, 127–131, before AV; anonymous, 132–139, Geneva; N. SYKES, 140–148, AV; G. R. DRIVER, 149–161, RV; S. BULLOUGH, 162–168, other versions. E. H. ROBERTSON, *The New Translations of the Bible* (Naperville, Ill. 1959). S. YEWIN, EncJudaica 4:606–608. For the "Private Versions" there is no complete account, but the writer has handled every v. listed here except one, and also all the Jewish texts. Bibliographies. H. COTTON, *Editions of the Bible and Parts Thereof in English* (2d ed. Oxford 1852). T. H. DARLOW and H. T. MOULE, comps., *Historical Catalogue of the Printed Editions of Holy Scripture in the Library of the British and Foreign Bible Society*, 2 v. (London 1903–11). **Illustration credits:** Fig. 22, The Pierpont Morgan Library, New York City. Fig. 23, From the copy in the Folger Shakespeare Library.

[S. BULLOUGH]

THE UNITED STATES

The first book printed and published in the English colonies in America was the Bay Psalm Book (1640), a literal translation of the Book of Psalms into English meter, by John Cotton and other ministers of Massachusetts Bay. Intended to be sung by the congregation in public worship, it contains some inversions of word order that roughen the path of the reader. An expanded and revised edition published in 1651, commonly called the New England Psalm Book, was used by the churches of the Puritan heritage for a period of more than 100 years.

Protestant Versions. The English Bibles used in the colonies were imported from England until the Revolution; then Robert Aitken published a first edition of the NT in 1777 and a first edition of the whole Bible, King James or Authorized Version (AV), without the Apocrypha, in 1782 at Philadelphia. Thereafter the number of editions and publishers of the AV multiplied rapidly.

The first English translation of the Bible to be made in America was by Charles Thomson, secretary of the Continental Congress from 1774 to 1789. A good Greek scholar, he translated the OT from the Greek Septuagint, excluding the Apocrypha, and the NT from the textus receptus. The work was published in four volumes (Philadelphia 1808).

Most of the English translations of the Bible made in America have been related more or less directly to the AV; have been translations of the NT only rather than of the entire Bible; and have been made by individuals acting on their own initiative rather than by a committee of scholars appointed by the Churches. Some are in certain respects eccentric, as Rodolphus Dickinson's

NT (1833) and Julia Smith's literal translation of the Bible (1876); and some are obviously directed to the propagation of the belief of a sect, as the New World Translation (1950–60).

Alexander Campbell's version of the NT (1826) was based upon the critical Greek text of Griesbach. He continued to revise it until the 6th edition, 1839, and it has often been reprinted. Other translations based upon the textual studies of J. J. Griesbach, K. Lachmann, and K. von Tischendorf were by John G. Palfrey (1828), Andrews Norton (1855), Leicester A. Sawyer (1858), George R. Noyes (1869), and Nathaniel S. Folsom (1869).

A sustained effort to secure an English version that would substitute "immerse" for "baptize" and "immersion" for "baptism" was made by the American Bible Union, organized by Baptists in 1850. After much publication and repeated revision, the movement ended in a translation of the Bible with the subtitle *An Improved Edition (Based in part on the Bible Union Version)*, 1912. In this volume "immerse" and "immersion" appear in parentheses, as available alternatives to "baptize" and "baptism."

Modern-speech Versions. Noah Webster, the American lexicographer, held that the need was not for a new English translation of the Bible but simply for a few "amendments of the language." He cited about 150 terms in the "Common Version" which have so changed in meaning as to be misleading. He published an edition with the required amendments in 1833 and a second in 1841; then it passed from the current scene. His amendments were too few to challenge attention, and he failed to take into account the problems that were emerging with respect to the Greek text of the NT. Yet he pointed the way for future revisers to deal with changes in English usage.

American translations of the NT into "modern speech" include those by Frank S. Ballentine (1897), William G. Ballantine (1923), Edgar J. Goodspeed (1923), Gerrit Verkuyl (1945), and Charles B. Williams (1937). J. M. P. Smith with three other scholars published *The Old Testament: An American Translation* (1927), and this was combined with Goodspeed's translations of the Apocrypha and the NT under the title *The Complete Bible: An American Translation* (1939). Verkuyl's translation was combined with a translation of the OT made by a staff for which he was editor in chief, as *The Berkeley Version in Modern English*, 1959.

Revised and Revised Standard Versions. In 1870 the Church of England decided to undertake "a revision of the Authorized Version of the Holy Scriptures" and appointed two companies of scholars to do the work. It also invited the cooperation of a committee of American scholars brought together under the leadership of Philip Schaff, Union Theological Seminary. The Revised Version (RV) of the NT was published in 1881, that of the OT in 1885, and that of the Apocrypha in 1895.

The American Standard Version of the Bible, published in 1901, is a variant of the RV (1881–85), "newly edited by the American Revision Committee." It embodies the full list of recommendations by the American committee, many of which had not been accepted by the British committee.

In 1928 the copyright of the American Standard Version was acquired by the International Council of

Religious Education, and it thus passed into the ownership of the Churches of the United States and Canada that were associated in the Council through their boards of education and publication. In 1937 the Council authorized a thorough revision of the version of 1901 and directed that the resulting version should "embody the best results of modern scholarship as to the meaning of the Scriptures, and express this meaning in English diction which is designed for use in public and private worship and preserves those qualities which have given to the King James Version a supreme place in English literature."

The Revised Standard Version (RSV) of the NT was published in 1946, of the OT in 1952, and of the Apocrypha in 1957. Since 1950 the publication of the RSV has been authorized by the National Council of Churches, into which the International Council of Religious Education has merged as the major factor in its Division of Christian Education. Thirty-two scholars served on the committee making the revision. Luther A. Weigle, Yale University, served as chairman of the committee and of each of its sections. The Standard Bible Committee continues as a standing committee of the Division of Christian Education, responsible for the text of the RSV.

Jewish Versions. Translations of the OT into English did not seem necessary to the earlier Jewish immigrants. Judah Monis, instructor in Hebrew at Harvard College from 1722 to 1760, published "A Grammar of the Hebrew Tongue" intended especially for the use of the students, and printed by the Harvard press in 1735. In the first half of the 19th century no less than six Hebrew grammars were published in Philadelphia, Andover, or New York, by as many Jewish scholars.

In 1845 Isaac Leeser published an English version of the Torah in five volumes, containing the Hebrew text and the parallel English translation on facing pages. In 1853 he published an English translation of *The Twenty-Four Books of the Holy Scriptures* in one volume, without the Hebrew text. This was often reprinted and became a standard Bible for English-speaking Jews. In 1912 an edition appeared in four volumes, giving the Hebrew and English texts on facing pages for easy reference.

Steps toward the cooperation of scholars in the preparation of a new English translation were taken by the Jewish Publication Society as early as 1892. Efforts to accomplish this by correspondence proved to be futile. In 1908 the society and the Central Conference of American Rabbis joined in appointing an editorial board of seven members, with Max L. Margolis as editor in chief and secretary. The translation made by this board was published in 1917, with a preface describing the procedure that had been followed and stating the aim of the work as follows: "The present translation is the first for which a group of men representative of Jewish learning among English-speaking Jews assume joint responsibility, all previous efforts in the English language having been the work of individual translators. It has a character of its own. It aims to combine the spirit of Jewish tradition with the results of biblical scholarship, ancient, mediaeval, and modern. It gives to the Jewish world a translation of the Scriptures done by men imbued with the Jewish consciousness, while the non-Jewish world, it is hoped, will welcome a translation that presents many passages from the Jewish traditional point of view." Among other English translations, this Jewish translation most closely resembles that used in the RV of the OT which was published in 1885.

In 1955 the Jewish Publication Society appointed an advisory editorial committee of seven scholars, with Harry M. Orlinsky as editor in chief, to make a new translation. As a member of the Standard Bible Committee since 1945, Professor Orlinsky had contributed effectively to the preparation of the RSV of the OT; and he brought to this new task the experience gained in that work. In 1962 the first section of the new translation was published, entitled *The Torah: The Five Books of Moses.* It is an excellent, straightforward translation, based upon modern scholarship and using modern diction without falling into the paraphrastic vagaries of many "modern speech" versions. It is based strictly upon the Masoretic Text without emendations and with only an occasional footnote recognizing a reading from the ancient versions, as at Gn 4.8 or Ex 19.18. It uses "You" rather than "thou" in the language of prayer addressed to God. The philosophy of Bible translation underlying this work is described by Orlinsky in the *Journal of Biblical Literature* 82 (1963) 249–264.

Bibliography: International Council of Religious Education, *An Introduction to the Revised Standard Version of the N.T.* (Chicago 1946); *An Introduction to the Revised Standard Version of the O.T.* (New York 1952). L. A. WEIGLE, *The English N.T. from Tyndale to the Revised Standard Version* (New York 1949). H. G. MAY, *Our English Bible in the Making* (Philadelphia 1952). E. C. COLWELL, *What Is the Best N.T.?* (Chicago 1952).

[L. A. WEIGLE]

24. GERMAN VERSIONS

This article treats, in order, the pre-Reformation, the Reformation, and the post-Reformation renderings of the Bible into the German vernacular. The discussion of the Reformation and the post-Reformation periods takes into account the Protestant as well as the Catholic versions. There is also a brief notice of the German translations of the OT prepared under Jewish auspices.

Pre-Reformation Versions. There was no want of early German translations of Scripture. Among the significant specimens the following may be noted.

The Gothic versions of the Biblical books are the oldest surviving translations of Scripture in a Germanic language. The Gothic version of the Gospels dates from the middle of the 4th century and is from the hand of Ulfilas, the apostle to the Goths. (See section 19, Gothic Versions.)

The so-called German Tatian is preserved in a 9th-century MS that shows an East-Frankish rendering of *Tatian's *Diatessaron (harmony of the Gospels). It originated in Fulda. The quality of the translation is smooth and clear.

Some 18 German editions of the whole Bible were printed prior to Luther. Four of these were in Low German. The first of these 18 editions was printed at Strassburg in 1466. All 14 of the High German editions exhibit the same version, the precise origin of which remains in doubt. It is thought to have been in existence for a full century before it was first printed.

Reformation Versions. Any consideration of German translations made during the Reformation period must necessarily center on Martin *Luther. Luther was firmly committed to the principle that a vernacular transla-

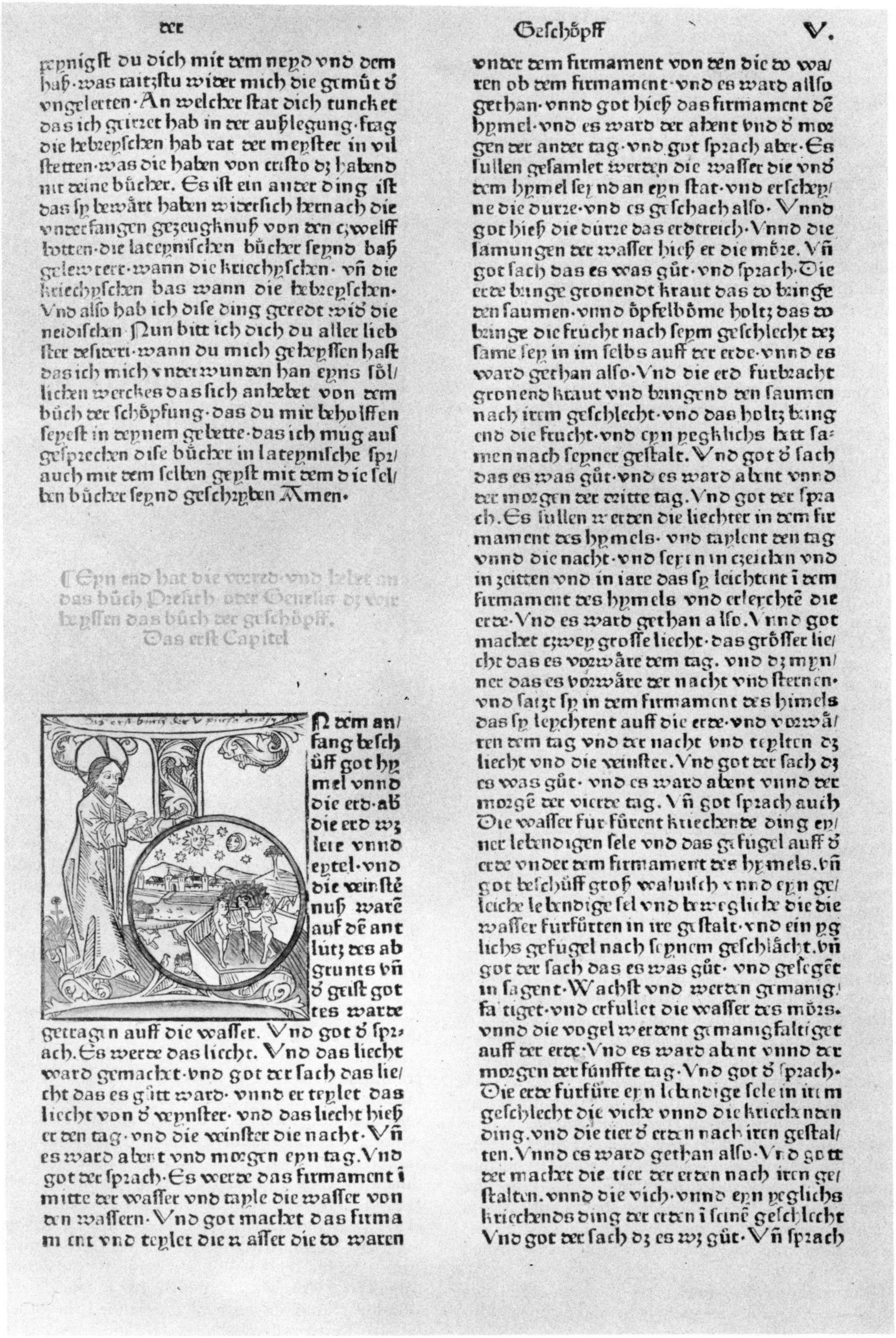

ccc Geschöpff V.

reynigst du dich mit dem neyd vnd dem haß·was raitzstu wider mich die gemût d vngelerten·An welcher stat dich tuncket das ich geirret hab in der außlegung·frag die hebreyschen hab rat der meyster in vil stetten·was die haben von cristo dz habend nit deine bücher. Es ist ein ander ding ist das sy bewärt haben widersich hernach die vnderfangen gezeugknuß von den zwelff botten·die lateynischen bücher seynd baß gelewtert·wann die kriechyschen·vñ die kriechyschen bas wann die hebreyschen·Vnd also hab ich dise ding geredt wid die neidischen Nun bitt ich dich du aller liebster desideri·wann du mich geheyssen hast das ich mich vnderwunden han eyns söl/lichen werckes das sich anhebet von dem büch der schöpfung·das du mir behollffen seyest in deynem gebette·das ich müg auß gesprechen dise bücher in lateynische spr/auch mit dem selben geyst mit dem die sel/ben bücher seynd geschriben Amen·

Eyn end hat die vorred·vnd hebet an das büch Bresith oder Genesis dz wir heyssen das büch der geschöpff.
Das erst Capitel

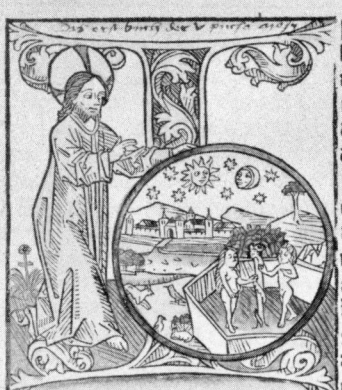

In dem an/fang beschüff got hymel vnnd die erd·aber die erd wz lere vnnd eytel·vnd die veinstenuß wärē auf dē antlütz des abgrunts vñ d geist gottes warde getragen auff die wasser. Vnd got d sprach. Es werde das liecht. Vnd das liecht ward gemachet·vnd got der sach das lie/cht das es gütt ward· vnnd er teylet das liecht von d veynster· vnd das liecht hieß er den tag·vnd die veinster die nacht·Vñ es ward abent vnd morgen eyn tag.Vnd got der sprach·Es werde das firmament i mitte der wasser vnd tayle die wasser von den wassern·Vnd got machet das firmament vnd teylet die wasser die do waren vnder dem firmament von den die do wa/ren ob dem firmament·vnd es ward allso gethan·vnnd got hieß das firmament dē hymel·vnd es ward der abent vnd d morgen der ander tag·vnd got sprach aber·Es sullen gesamlet werden die wasser die vnd dem hymel seynd an eyn stat·vnd erschey/ne die dürre·vnd es geschach allso· Vnnd got hieß die dürre das erdtreich·Vnnd die samungen der wasser hieß er die möre. Vñ got sach das es was güt·vnd sprach·Die erde bringe gronendt kraut das do bringe den saumen·vnnd öpfelböme holtz das do bringe die frücht nach seym geschlecht dez same sey in im selbs auff der erde·vnnd es ward gethan allso·Vnd die erd fürbracht gronend kraut vnd bringend den saumen nach irem geschlecht·vnd das holtz bringend die frucht·vnd eyn yegklichs hett sa=men nach seyner gestalt. Vnd got d sach das es was güt·vnd es ward abent vnnd der morgen der dritte tag. Vnd got der sprach. Es sullen werden die liechter in dem firmament des hymels· vnd taylent den tag vnnd die nacht·vnd seyen in zeichen vnd in zeitten vnd in iare das sy leichtent i dem firmament des hymels vnd erleüchtē die erde·Vnd es ward gethan allso. Vnnd got machet zwey grosse liecht·das grösser lie/cht das es vorwäre dem tag. vnd dz myn/ner das es vorwäre der nacht vnd sternen·vnd satzt sy in dem firmament des himels das sy leychtent auff die erde·vnd vorwä/ren dem tag vnd der nacht vnd teylten dz liecht vnd die veinster. Vnd got der sach dz es was güt· vnd es ward abent vnnd der morgē der vierde tag. Vñ got sprach auch Die wasser für fürent kriechende ding ey/ner lebendigen sele vnd das gefügel auff d erde vnder dem firmament des hymels. Vñ got beschüff groß walvisch vnnd eyn ge/leiche lebendige sel vnd beweglicke die die wasser furfürten in ire gestalt·vnd ein yglichs gefugel nach seynem geschlächt. Vñ got der sach das es was güt· vnd gesegēt in sagent·Wachst vnd werden gemanig/faltiget·vnd erfullet die wasser des mörs·vnnd die vogel werdent gemanigfaltiget auff der erde·Vnd es ward abent vnnd der morgen der fünffte tag·Vnd got d sprach·Die erde furfüre eyn lebendige sele in irem geschlecht die viche vnnd die kriechenden ding·vnd die tier d erden nach iren gestal/ten. Vnnd es ward gethan allso·Vnd got der machet die tier der erden nach iren ge/stalten·vnnd die vich·vnnd eyn yeglichs kriechends ding der erden i seinē geschlecht Vnd got der sach dz es wz güt·Vñ sprach

Fig. 24. The beginning of Genesis in the German Bible printed by Günther Zainer at Augsburg in 1475 or 1476, the first illustrated printed Bible. The woodcuts incorporated into the initials were hand-colored.

tion must be made from the original languages and must be done in a vernacular idiom easily understood by all.

Protestant Versions. At the suggestion and urging of Philipp *Melanchthon, professor of Greek at Wittenberg, Luther undertook to render the NT into German. The first edition of any of Luther's Bible translations was one of the NT made from the Greek; it appeared under the title *Das Neue Testament Deutzsch* in September 1522. It came to be known popularly as the September Testament. While the NT was still in the press, Luther began his translation of the OT from the Hebrew. It was published in parts. The Pentateuch was issued in the summer of 1523. The series of books from Josue to the Canticle of Canticles, including the Psalter, appeared in the course of the following year, 1524. Because of illness and various pressing commitments, Luther was able to devote himself only sporadically to the translation of the Prophets, which was published only in March 1532. With the help of friends Luther prepared the apocrypha, and by the autumn of 1534 the first complete edition of Luther's translation of the Bible into High German appeared at Wittenberg. (See Fig. 25.) During the several printings that followed in the ensuing years, Luther was tireless in making emendations. Luther's version is not characterized by a slavish adherence to the style and syntax of the original. It ranks as a masterpiece of German prose. As a factor in the development of modern German it cannot be overestimated.

Luther's was, of course, not the only German translation to see the light of day during this period. A reprint of an earlier German Bible appeared at Augsburg in 1518. This version was dismissed by both Protestants and Catholics alike as being un-German, overliteral, and in part incomprehensible. A translation of the Prophets prepared in 1527 by two Anabaptists, Ludwig Hätzer and Hans Denck, was regarded as a notable linguistic achievement. Though critical of some aspects of this translation, Luther resorted to it in making his own version of the Prophets.

Catholic Versions. Hieronymus Emser, secretary to the Duke of Saxony, undertook a Catholic vernacular translation that, it was hoped, might prove an effective antidote to Luther's work. It was an ill-starred endeavor. Finding himself unable to match Luther's facility with German prose, Emser ended by correcting Luther's September Testament in accordance with the Vulgate text. This work was published in 1527 at Dresden. A Dominican, Johann Dietenberger, pieced together a complete German Catholic Bible by taking over Emser's NT translation and joining it to a translation of the OT that was based partly on Luther's version and partly on that of Hätzer and Denck (for the Prophets). These latter versions Dietenberger revised, as Emser before him had done with the September Testament, to harmonize them with the Vulgate. Dietenberger's Bible was printed at Mainz in 1534. The least successful attempt at a Catholic version was made by Johann Eck. It was a translation into the Swabian dialect and was published in Ingolstadt in June 1537.

Post-Reformation Versions. The literary excellence of Luther's translation was such as to make superfluous any further translation for some time to come. Some of the translations that were ventured proved wanting in one way or another.

Fig. 25. Title page of the OT, from the first edition of Luther's complete Bible, which was printed by Hans Luft at Wittenberg in 1534.

Protestant Versions. The version of Johannes Piscator (1602–03), for example, was uneven in quality. The translation of the NT made by Count Zinzendorf was free and slanted to favor the theology of the Moravian Brethren. There were exceptions, however. Wilhelm *de Wette produced (1809–14) a sober and scholarly translation of both the OT and the NT.

In time, however, a need was felt for a revision of Luther's translation; by the middle of the 19th century there were no less than 10 different forms of that version in circulation. The Church Conference at Eisenach commissioned such a revision in 1861. This and the later revisions of the Lutheran version betray a certain sense of obligation to a translation made once for all. Among the subsequent translations produced, mention should be made of the scholarly version of the OT produced by Emil Friedrich *Kautzsch and his colleagues (1894). The NT translation by Carl von Weizsäcker (1875) saw several editions. The whole Bible was translated by Herman Menge (1929 onward) and also by Adolf *Schlatter (1931). A modern translation, published in 1939, was provided by Friedrich Pfäfflein. Whatever qualities have recommended the other translations, Luther's has surmounted and survived them all and is today, as it was when first issued, the most influential form of the Bible among German Protestants.

Catholic Versions. Dietenberger's translation was revised in 1630 by Caspar Ulenberg and was subsequently revised a second time at Mainz in 1662. It then became the standard Catholic Bible for a time and went through some 50 editions. In the first quarter of the 19th century Karl and Leander van Ess, working from the original languages, produced a translation that was made to agree with the Vulgate. J. von *Allioli's translation (1830–37) achieved considerable popularity among German Catholics. It was based on the Vulgate, but in footnotes it noted variants in the original languages. Some notable modern Catholic translations are the Grünewald Bible (1924–26), Pius Parsch's complete Bible (1952), Riessler's OT, the NT of the *Kepplerbibel* (1915), and the translations of the NT by K. Rösch (1921), F. Tillmann (1925–27), R. Storr (1926), J. Perk (1947), and O. Karrer (1950).

Jewish Versions. The OT has from time to time been rendered into German by Jewish scholars. Noteworthy examples are the translations by L. Zunz (1837), S. Bernfeld (1902), H. Torczyner (1935–37), and the OT German paraphrase by M. Buber and F. Rosenzweig (1926).

Bibliography: J. Kürzinger, LexThK² 2:401–404. H. Volz et al., RGG³ 1:1201–10. EncDictBibl 2540–42. G. Ricciotti, EncCatt 2:1566–68. H. Volz and B. Dammermann in *The Cambridge History of the Bible,* ed. S. L. Greenslade (Cambridge, Eng. 1963) 94–109, 339–347. H. Rost, *Die Bible im Mittelalter* (Augsburg 1939). W. J. Kooiman, *Luther and the Bible,* tr. J Schmidt (Philadelphia 1961). E. P. Arbez, "Modern Translations of the O.T.," CathBiblQuart 16 (1954) 343–347. **Illustration credits:** Fig. 24, Library of Congress, Rosenwald Collection. Fig. 25, New York Public Library, Print Division.

[J. C. TURRO]

25. DUTCH-FLEMISH VERSIONS

These are in the language spoken in the present Kingdom of the Netherlands, the northern part of Belgium, and the adjacent region of the French Département du Nord. The history of the Bible translations in this language may be divided into three periods.

Manuscript and Early Printed Bibles. Beginning about the 10th century many partial versions (Gospels, Psalms) in old-Netherlandish dialects circulated in the Middle Ages, but only fragments of these are still preserved. Among the 13th-century versions the Liège "Leven van Jesus," based on a Latin form of Tatian's *Diatessaron (*c.* 1280), is noteworthy. About the same time, Van Mearlant composed the "Rijmbijbel," an adaptation in verse form of the "Historia Ecclesiastica" by Peter Comestor, a widely read work that inspired, from *c.* 1360 on, several "history Bibles," i.e., translations of the historical books of the OT with additions from other sources plus explanations. In the northern Netherlands the **devotio moderna* of the school of Gerard *Groote gave rise to many translations, especially of the NT and Psalms. The first printed Bible (Delft 1477), containing the OT without Psalms, was soon followed by many other Biblical texts, e.g., the liturgical pericopes (Gouda 1477, Utrecht 1478, etc.), the printers being eager to satisfy the growing demands of individual piety.

16th through 18th Century. A period of much confusion began with the edition of the NT translated from M. Luther's text (Amsterdam 1523), followed by the NT according to D. *Erasmus (Delft 1524). The complete Luther Bible was printed at Antwerp (1526) by J. van Liesveldt, who in subsequent editions added more and more Lutheran marginal notes, which cost him his head after the 1542 edition. W. Vosterman tried in vain to avoid censorship by "purging" Liesveldt's edition. His Bible (Antwerp 1528), an odd mosaic of Lutheran, Erasmian, and Catholic elements, reflects the reigning confusion. At Louvain, Van Grave, confident in his closeness to the theological faculty, published a translation from the Vulgate, by N. van Winghe (1548). This "Louvain Bible," later printed at Antwerp by C. Plantijn and revised after the Sixto-Clementine by his son-in-law J. Moerentorf (1599) remained the Bible of the Catholics until the 19th century. Of the "Reformed" Bibles, printed secretly or abroad and often omitting or camouflaging their place of origin, may be mentioned that of Biestkens (1560), based on Liesveldt and circulating for some time among the Baptists, and the Deux-Aes Bible (Embden 1562), so called after a marginal note on Neh 3.5 borrowed from Luther. After 1580, when the crisis had passed, there was an increasing demand for replacing the many hybrid secondary translations by one made directly from the original languages. The Synod of Dordrecht installed a commission of scholars, whose achievement, sponsored by the States General, was first published at Leiden ("Statenbijbel," 1537) and remained the official Bible of the Reformed Churches.

Modern Times. The 19th century saw several new translations, both Protestant ones, made from the orig-

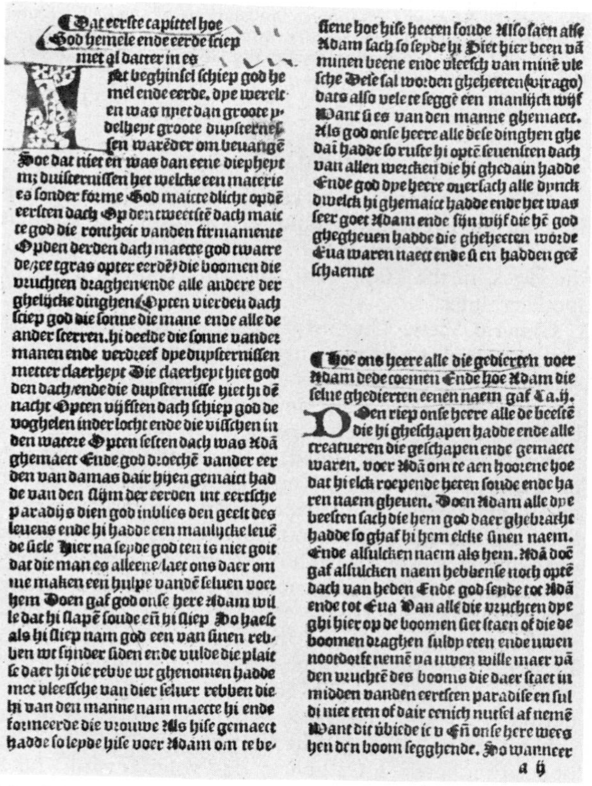
Dat eerste capittel hoe
God hemele ende eerde sciep
met al datter in es
In het beghinsel schiep god he
mel ende eerde. dye werelt
en was nyet dan groote y-
delheyt groote duysternes-
sen wareder om beuangẽ
Hoe dat niet en was dan eene diepheyt
m; duisternissen het welcke een materie
es sonder forme God maicte dlicht opdẽ
eersten dach Op den tweetstẽ dach maic
te god die rontheit vanden firmamente
Opden derden dach maecte god twatre
de/zee tgras opter eerdẽ/die boomen die
vruchten draghen ende alle andere der
ghelijcke dinghen Opten vierden dach
sciep god die sonne die mane ende alle de
ander sterren. hi deelde die sonne vander
manen ende verdreef dye duysternissen
metter claerheyt Die claerheyt hiet god
den dach/ende die duysternisse hiet hi dẽ
nacht Opten vijfsten dach schiep god de
voghelen inder locht ende die visschen in
den watere Opten sesten dach was Adã
ghemaect Ende god droechẽ vander eer
den van damas dair hijen gemaict had
de van den slijm der eerden int eertsche
paradijs dien god inblies den geest des
leuens ende hi hadde een manlijcke leuẽ
de siele Hier na seyde god ten is niet goit
dat die man es alleene/laet ons daer om
me maken een hulpe vandẽ seluen voer
hem Doen gaf god onse here Adam wil
le dat hi slapẽ soude eñ hi sliep So haest
als hi sliep nam god een van sinen rebben wt synder siden ende vulde die plaet
se daer hi die rebbe wt ghenomen hadde
met vleessche van dier seluer rebben die
hi van den manne nam maecte hi ende
formeerde die vrouwe Als hise gemaect
hadde so leyde hise voer Adam om te be-
siene hoe hise heeten soude Also saen alse
Adam sach so seyde hi Siet hier been vã
minen beene ende vleesch van minẽ vle
sche Dese sal worden gheheeten (virago)
dats also vele te seggẽ een manlijck wijf
Want si es van den manne ghemaect.
Als god onse heere alle dese dinghen ghe
daĩ hadde so ruste hi optẽ seuensten dach
van allen wercken die hi ghedain hadde
Ende god dye heere oversach alle dynck
dwelck hi ghemaict hadde ende het was
seer goet Adam ende syn wijf die hẽ god
ghegheuen hadde die gheheeten worde
Eua waren naect ende si en hadden geẽ
schaemte
Hoe ons heere alle die gedierten voer
Adam dede coemen Ende hoe Adam die
selue ghedierten eenen naem gaf Ca.ij.
Doen riep onse heere alle de beestẽ
die hi gheschapen hadde ende alle
creatueren die geschapen ende gemaect
waren. voer Adã om te aen hooren hoe
dat hi elck roepende heten soude ende ha
ren naem gheuen. Doen Adam alle dye
beesten sach die hem god daer ghebracht
hadde so ghaf hi hem elcke sinen naem.
Ende alsulcken naem als hem. Adã doẽ
gaf alsulcken naem hebben se noch optẽ
dach van heden Ende god seyde tot Adã
ende tot Eua Van alle die vruchten dye
ghi hier op de boomen siet staen of die de
boomen draghen suldy eten ende uwen
nootdorst nemẽ na uwen wille maer vã
den vruchtẽ des booms die daer staet in
midden vanden eertsten paradise en sul
di niet eten of dair eenich nutsel af nemẽ
Want dit verbiede ic u Eñ onse here wees
hen den boom segghende. So wanneer
a ij

Fig. 26. First page of a book containing portions of the Old Testament in Dutch, published at Antwerp by Claes de Graue in 1516. The selections in this book, printed just before the Reformation, are very free paraphrases greatly abridging the full text, rather than translations of the Latin Vulgate, on which they are based.

inal languages and published in Holland (e.g., J. H. van der Palm, Leiden 1818–30, renowned for its polished Dutch; and the "Leidsche Vertaling," OT 1899–1901, NT 1912, with supercritical introductions), and Catholic ones, based on the Vulgate, mostly published in Belgium (e.g., J. T. *Beelen's NT Louvain 1859–66; OT Bruges 1894–96).

The place of the "Statenbijbel" has now been assumed by the "Nieuwe Vertaling van het Nederlansch Bijbelgenootschap," completed 1951, recommended for its accurate rendering in fairly modern Dutch and accepted by all the Protestant Churches. The only complete Catholic Bible available is still that published by the "Petrus Canisius Society" (NT 1929, OT 1936–39, 1 v. Utrecht 1948). Though its Dutch is still highly regarded, it reflects exegesis before World War II (e.g., less confidence in the Masoretic text and many conjectures in the OT and notes and introductions too brief and very apologetic). The new "Katholieke Bijbelstichting Sint Willibrord" published a fresh translation of the NT (1961) in current Dutch, with up-to-date introductions and notes, in the manner of the *Bible de Jérusalem* (see 26. French Versions). The OT is in preparation. Only the Book of Psalms has appeared, translated by J. van der Ploeg (1963).

Bibliography: J. Van Kasteren, DB 4:1549–57. J. Schmid, LexThK² 2:408–410. C. C. de Bruin, *Middelnederlandse vertalingen van het Nieuwe Testament* (Groningen 1935); *De Statenbijbel en zijn voorgangers* (Leiden 1937). S. L. Greenslade, ed., *The Cambridge History of the Bible: The West from the Reformation to the Present Day* (Cambridge, Eng. 1963) 122–125. E. P. Arbez, "Modern Translations of the O.T.: Dutch and Scandinavian Language Translations," CathBiblQuart 16 (1954) 201–209. **Illustration credit:** Fig. 26, Library of Congress, Rosenwald Collection.

[L. H. Grollenberg]

26. FRENCH VERSIONS

After a general view of certain distinctive characteristics of the French translations of the Bible, this article offers a brief history of the French versions in the Middle Ages, in the 16th, 17th, and 18th centuries, and in modern times.

General View. The history of the French Bible presents a complex picture. There have probably been considerably more translations of the Bible in French than in any other European language. The multiplicity of translations was caused especially by the absence of a normative version accepted by all or the vast majority of the people, as certain versions were received in England and Germany. Conversely and again contrary to the situation in England and Germany, because the text of the Bible was never fixed in France, Biblical language had relatively little influence on the language of that country.

The principal reason for the absence of a standardized French Bible was the unfavorable situation for such a version in France of the 16th and 17th centuries, the period when the first great vernacular versions of the Bible were in full swing in western Europe. The bitter opposition between Catholics and Protestants in France hardened into mutual intolerance, which exploded into endless religious wars. The government, which was ordinarily associated with the Catholic cause, automatically regarded the publishing of Bibles as a heretical enterprise. Consequently, the principal French versions of that period, the Bibles of Antwerp, Louvain, Geneva,

and Sacy, were printed outside France. Moreover, the constant changes that the French language was then undergoing did not allow a permanent translation. In this respect, the Bible of Sacy was the first version that had a chance of being widely received, since its language reflected French classicism. Unfortunately, however, this Bible, which came from a Jansenistic group, was looked upon as suspect, and the notes that accompanied the text were not of a nature to lessen the suspicion. About the same time, the Catholic hierarchy of France entertained the notion of issuing an official Bible in French; but the project came to nought, because it was not regarded as a major concern.

In the Middle Ages. The history of the French versions of the Bible began c. 1100, when the Psalter was translated into the Norman dialect. The first French Bible was completed c. 1226. The first printed edition appeared at Lyons c. 1477. For more than 4 centuries the most popular presentation of the Bible was the *Bible historiale*. This consisted in a paraphrase of the *Historia Scholastica* of *Peter Comestor, to which was added the French Biblical text. It was drawn up by Guyard des Moulins c. 1200 and was subsequently revised many times. The edition of J. M. Rely, which was printed c. 1487, influenced the Bible version of Jacques Lefèvre d'Étaples and thus formed a bond between the medieval and the modern period.

In the 16th, 17th, and 18th Centuries. An anonymous NT that was published at Paris in 1523 inaugurated the

Fig. 27. Page with part of the story of Isaac, from a MS in Latin and French of extracts from the Old and New Testaments, a "Bible Historiée et Vies des Saints," written in the north of France c. 1300 (Spenser Coll., MS 22).

period of the modern French Bible. The translator was almost certainly Jacques Lefèvre d'Étaples. The OT appeared at Antwerp in 1528 with his name attached as that of the author. The complete Bible was finally published there in 1530. This edition alarmed the Catholics, especially because of its glosses, and in 1546 it was put on the Index. Meanwhile, in the Vaudois Synod of 1532 the Swiss Protestants decided to publish a French Bible. Therefore, in 1535 P. R. *Olivétan produced the *Bible de Serrières,* which closely followed Lefèvre's version in the deuterocanonical books of the OT and in the NT. After being frequently revised by the Protestant leaders at Geneva, this version became the *Bible de Genève* (the revision of 1588, edited by Theodore *Beza), which remained almost unchanged until 1693.

In order to counterbalance the influence of the Protestant Bibles, the faculty of Louvain authorized the publication of a Catholic Bible (1550). It reproduced Lefèvre's version, but without his glosses and with some borrowings from Olivétan's version. The edition of 1578 was reprinted at least 200 times.

At the beginning of the 17th century there were, therefore, two authorized French Bibles: the Louvain Bible of the Catholics and the Geneva Bible of the Protestants. Both were derived, in large part, from Lefèvre's version. In France's classical period, the need was felt for new versions that would be more in harmony with the pure language of the time. Among the Protestants, however, the high regard in which the Geneva Bible was held restrained the undertaking of new Bible translations. The Catholics, in the favorable circumstances of a religious revival, showed themselves more active; yet none of their attempts at a new version succeeded. Even the decision of the General Assembly of the Clergy (1655) to publish an official Bible proved largely ineffective; only the NT appeared (Paris 1666–70). The only project that did succeed was the version produced by the Jansenist group of *Port-Royal; its principal author was Isaac le Maistre de Sacy. Its NT was finished in 1657, but was not published until 1667 (probably at Amsterdam). The OT appeared piecemeal (Paris 1672–96). Despite adverse criticism and ecclesiastical condemnation (by the archbishop of Paris in 1667, by Clement IX in 1668, and by Innocent IX in 1679), this Bible remained one of the most popular until the beginning of the 20th century.

The 18th century was hardly a time favorable for new versions. The Bible was attacked and ridiculed by the philosophers. Besides, the Catholic Church in France had lost its vitality. The activity of the Protestants, though more intense, was confined to groups of expatriates. Their most noteworthy efforts at new versions were those of D. Martin (Amsterdam 1696–1707) and J. F. Ostervald (Neuchâtel 1744), but both these versions were only revisions of the Geneva Bible.

Modern Times. After the 18th century, Protestant and Catholic versions became more numerous. The work of the Protestants was stimulated by the establishment of a branch of the British and Foreign Bible Society at Paris in 1820 (*see* BIBLICAL SOCIETIES). The most widely circulated Protestant Bible toward the end of the 19th century was that of L. Segond (1874–80); it was based on a revision of the versions of Martin and Ostervald and was basically, therefore, a continuation of the Geneva Bible and the Olivétan version. The imposing edition of E. G. E. *Reuss, with commentary

(16 v. Paris 1874–81), showed vast erudition but could not win a wide reading public. In 1884 the Reformed Synod of France decided to revise Ostervald's version; this version appeared in 1910 under the title *Version Synodale.* The most recent Protestant version is the *Bible du Centenaire* (4 v. Paris 1916–46).

The French Jews published the *Bible du rabbinat français* under the editorship of Z. Kahn (2 v. Paris 1899–1906, 2d ed. 1926–30).

The most popular Catholic Bible in the first half of the 20th century was that of J. T. *Crampon (Tournai 1894–1904, most recent ed. 1960). After World War II there appeared the *Bible de Maredsous* (Brussels 1949) and the *Bible du Card. Liénart* (Paris 1951). However, the most original version and one of the best in any language is *La Sainte Bible traduite en français sous la direction de l'École Biblique de Jérusalem,* commonly called the *Bible de Jérusalem* (43 fascicles, Paris 1948–54, in 1 v. 1956, new editions of the fascicles in the course of publication).

A contribution of high quality, the *Bible de la Pléiade,* under the editorship of E. Dhorme, is (1965) in the course of publication (the first 2 v. Paris 1956–59).

Bibliography: S. L. GREENSLADE, ed., *The Cambridge History of the Bible* (Cambridge, Eng. 1963) 113–122, 347–352, 540. D. LORTSCH, *Histoire de la Bible en France* (Paris 1910), at times unreliable. E. MANGENOT, DB 2.2:2346–73, with extensive bibliog. up to 1895. E. BEAUCAMP and J. SCHMID, LexThK² 2:406–408. EncDictBibl 2538–39. **Illustration credit:** Fig. 27, Spenser Collection, New York Public Library.

[J. L. D'ARAGON]

27. ITALIAN VERSIONS

The history of the Italian versions of the Bible can be divided into four periods, covering about 8 centuries: (1) the early period of the manuscripts and incunabula—13th to 15th century; (2) the period of the Council of Trent—16th and 17th centuries; (3) the recent period—18th and 19th centuries; (4) the present period—20th century. For the sake of brevity, the treatment here will be limited almost exclusively to complete versions. A dagger [†] will indicate non-Catholic versions or versions condemned by the Church.

Early Period—13th to 15th Century. The earliest traces of Biblical translations in Italian (Tuscan or Venetian dialect), all of them anonymous, go back to the beginning of the 13th century. These vernacular renderings of parts of the Bible were the result of the widespread religious movement among the ordinary people that was fostered by the Dominicans and Franciscans, while the clergy and learned laity continued to use the Latin Vulgate. The oldest of these translations in Italian were Biblical paraphrases, Gospel harmonies, and liturgical pericopes, which were soon followed by versions of whole Biblical books, especially the Psalms, the Gospels, and the Apocalypse. The earliest manuscripts of the whole Bible in Italian date from the 14th century. They are rather rare. Their text, which is of varying exegetical and literary value, can be reduced to two or three main types. Only the celebrated literary version of the Acts of the Apostles attributed to D. Cavalca (d. 1342) is based on good manuscript tradition.

Shortly after the introduction of printing in the middle of the 15th century a uniform text made its appearance. In 1471 Italy received two different editions of the vernacular Bible, both printed in Venice. One of

Fig. 28. The beginning of Genesis from the 1494 edition of the Italian Bible of Nicolò Malerbi, printed in Venice by Joannes Rubeus Vercellensis; a compilation of 14th-century Tuscan texts adapted to the Venetian dialect.

these, that of Nicolò Malerbi (not Malermi or Manerbi, as it is often spelled even in some of the oldest incunabula), should be regarded as a compilation of 14th-century Tuscan texts adjusted to the Venetian dialect, rather than a new translation. It practically became the typical vernacular Bible, and was continually reprinted for about a century. The other version, the text of which although less polished was more valuable because unreworked, did not succeed in competing with Malerbi's version. Between 1882 and 1887 it was reappraised for literary purposes in a second edition by C. Negroni.

Period of Trent—16th and 17th Centuries. The new Latin versions by the humanists, the acquaintance made with the original texts in their first complete editions, and the proliferation of vernacular versions in Germany and Switzerland sharpened the desire for new translations of the Bible in Italy also. The first complete version of the Bible in Italian made by a single translator was that of A. Brucioli†, printed at Venice (NT 1530, OT 1532). Although it was only of mediocre value, it was frequently reprinted by Catholics and even more frequently by Protestants, until in 1559 it was put on the Index because of the heretical tone of its exegetical notes; thereafter it disappeared from circulation, at least in Italy. More orthodox in spirit, though of less literary value, was the version of S. Marmochini (Venice 1538), which adopted the NT of F. Zaccaria (Venice 1536); the whole was reprinted in 1546.

The severe restrictions that the Church, following the Council of Trent, imposed on vernacular Bibles for the sake of stemming the tide of Protestant abuses (*see* BIBLE READING) kept Catholics from undertaking new versions and even from reprinting those already in existence. The Italian Reformers were provided by the Calvinist G. Diodati with the first Italian Bible made directly from the original texts. This version, which was of considerable value, was printed first at Geneva in 1607, and for 3 centuries it remained the standard version† for Italian Protestants. But because of its origin and tendentious tone it was never accepted by the Catholic Church.

Recent Period—18th and 19th Centuries. The mitigation of the discipline of the Index in 1757 opened the way for new vernacular versions. Under the pretext of modernizing Malerbi's version, A. Guerra published a version (Venice 1773) that was neither very original nor entirely independent of Diodati's version. The Italian translation from the French of the commentary on the Bible of Port Royal by L. J. Le Maistre de Sacy contains its own Italian version of the Bible based on the Latin Vulgate (Venice 1775–85). However, the most important Italian version of this period was that of Antonio Martini, first published at Turin (NT 1769–71, OT 1776–81); the definitive edition appeared at Florence between 1782 and 1792, while Martini was archbishop of this city. Based on the Vulgate, but with regard for the original texts, it became, both because of the circumstances of its composition and because of its literary merits, the classical Bible of Italian Catholics, was reprinted innumerable times and is still being reprinted.

Of the many partial Italian versions of the Bible produced in the 19th century, mention should be made, because of their scientific and literary value, of those of G. B. de *Rossi (Parma 1808–23), G. Ugdulena (Palermo 1859–   ), and N. Tommaseo (Milan 1869). The Jews also produced their own version† of the OT in this century; it was the work of D. S. Luzzatto and others (Rovigo 1872–75).

Present Period—20th Century. Characteristic of the 20th century are the numerous editions of various Italian versions of the Bible, including those of the original texts, following the encouragement of the encyclical *Divino afflante Spiritu*. A revision of Martini's version was used in the older part of the commentary by M. Sales and G. Girotti (Turin 1911–42) and served as the basis for two new translations of the Latin Vulgate, one by G. Castoldi and collaborators (Florence 1929), later reedited by G. Ricciotti (Florence 1939–41), and the other by E. Tintori in his complete Bible (Alba 1931).

On a higher level are the Italian versions that are based on the original texts and that make use of the recent advances in Biblical studies. In this class is, first, the translation made by the Waldensian G. Luzzi†, intended to be the common Bible of all Italian-speaking Christians (complete ed. Florence 1921–30); but as it is distributed by the Protestant Bible Society without the deuterocanonical books of the OT, it is rightly rejected by Catholics. Next, there is the *Sacra Bibbia* of the Pontifical Biblical Institute, under the general editorship of A. Vaccari, the first Bible of its kind on the part of Catholics in Italy (Milan 1923-Florence 1958). In the wake of this excellent version there followed the edition of the Edizioni Paoline (Rome 1958), the *Editio Minor* of S. Garofalo (Turin 1960), the pocket edition of F. Nardoni (Florence 1960), and the edition prepared by E. Galbiati, A. Penna, and P. Rossano (Turin 1963). The latest to appear was the Franciscan Bible edited under the general editorship of B. Mariani (Milan 1964). The Italian Jews also are publishing a new version of the OT†, of which the Pentateuch and the books of the Earlier Prophets have been issued (Turin 1960–62).

Among the partial versions worthy of mention are those of S. Minocchi, G. Ricciotti, G. Re, P. Vannutelli, A. Rizzato, and especially the translation of John by S. Quasimodo (Milan 1950).

Bibliography: S. MINOCCHI, "Italiennes (versions) de la Bible," DB 3:1012–38, the most complete for the period up to 1903. A. VACCARI, "Bibbia," EncIt 6:899–903. **Illustration credit:** Fig. 28, Rosenwald Collection, Library of Congress, Washington, D.C.

[E. RAVAROTTO]

28. SPANISH VERSIONS

Despite the Spanish contribution to Biblical studies made by the *Polyglot Bibles of Alcalá (Complutensis, 1514–17) and Antwerp (1569–73), it can be said that vernacular versions of the Bible were neither as numerous nor as important in Spain as in the other countries of Europe. The Spanish *Inquisition always acted as a check, at times extremely tight, on the spread of the Bible in the vernacular, although it did allow the popular diffusion of Biblical themes in the classical Spanish theater of the 16th and 17th centuries. The medieval Spanish versions, most of which were made by Jews, were followed by a few Protestant translations and editions of the Bible in Spanish. It was not until the 18th century that Catholic versions began to circulate.

Medieval Versions. One of the oldest Spanish versions is known as the Alphonsian because it was the translation of the OT that King *Alfonso X of Castile (1252–84) incorporated in his *Grande e General Estoria*. This version was based in part on two older (pre-Alphonsian) versions made by Christian scholars from the Latin Vulgate and in part on the Hebrew text. (In one of the two older Christian versions the Psalms were translated by Hermann el Alemán.) In the 14th and 15th centuries Spanish versions were made especially for the needs of the synagogues. Of the eight known medieval Spanish versions of Jewish origin, five are preserved in the rich library of the *Escorial.

These projects of the Spanish Jews—mention is made also of a version by David *Kimchi (c. 1232)—culminated during the 15th century in the famous translation made by Rabbi Moses Arragel of Guadalajara at the instance of Don Luis de Guzmán, Grand Master of Calatrava. It was begun in 1422 and finished in 1433. A copy of it in a beautiful codex, which is highly and magnificently illuminated, is in the possession of the Alba family, and this version is therefore commonly known as *La Biblia de la casa de Alba*. Among the Spanish versions made by Jews in the 16th century mention should be made of the *Pentateuco de Constantinople* (1547) and particularly of the so-called *Biblia de Ferrara* (1533), which was produced by Tobias

Athias and Abraham Usque for the Spanish-Jewish community that had taken refuge in Italy after the expulsion of the Jews from Spain (1492); one edition of it, a word-for-word translation, was intended for Jews; another edition, with some slight changes and signed by Jeronimo de Vargas and Duarte Pinel (perhaps pseudonyms for Athias and Usque), was intended for Christians.

Protestant Versions. The work of the Spanish Jews was continued by Spanish Protestants who had taken refuge in England, Germany, and Switzerland. As early as 1543 Francisco de Enzinas (1520–70) published a Spanish version of the NT at Antwerp, which became popular among Protestants and of which Juan Pérez de Pineda made generous use in his Spanish version of the NT (Geneva 1556). The latter scholar published also a Spanish version of the Psalms (marked as of Venice, but really printed at Geneva, 1557), for which he made use of an older version by Juan de Valdés (d. 1541) that remained unpublished until 1880. However, the first complete Bible in Spanish was the work of the Lutheran Casiodoro de Reina (Basil 1567–69), who was very dependent on the Ferrara Bible and the Latin version of Santes *Pagnini. Copies of the original edition of the version of Casiodoro de Reina, known as the *Biblio del Oso* because of the device on the title page that shows a bear looking for honey in a tree, are extremely rare. This version as later revised by the Calvinist Cipriano de Valera (Amsterdam 1602) became the commonly received Bible of Spanish Protestants and went through numerous editions.

Catholic Versions. The first Biblical versions in Spanish prepared by Catholics suffered from the Inquisition. In 1512, at the request of King *Ferdinand V of Castile (d. 1516), Fray Ambrosio de Montesinos prepared a revision of an older version of the liturgical Epistles and Gospels; but it was withdrawn by the Inquisition and first published in 1586 by Fray Román de Vallecillo. About 1561 Fray Luis de *León made a literal prose translation of the Canticle of Canticles, the circulation of which in MS form (it was first published at Salamanca in 1798) was one of the charges brought up in the well-known trial of the illustrious poet. Only when ecclesiastical censorship and the power of the Inquisition were mitigated in the 18th century could vernacular versions of the Bible be published in Spain. The Piarist Felipe Scio de San Miguel, who became bishop of Segovia in 1795, published a complete Bible in Spanish (Valencia 1790–93) on the basis of the Latin Vulgate. More in accord with the original Hebrew and Greek was the version (Madrid 1823–25) made by Canon [later (1833) Bishop] Félix Torres Amat (1772–1847), who apparently made use of an unpublished version of the Jesuit José Miguel Petisco.

In the 20th century, with the rebirth of Biblical studies in Spain and South America, several Spanish versions of the Scriptures based on the original texts were published. The very literal version of the NT by Guillermo Juenemann (Concepción, Chile 1928) was based on the most ancient Greek MSS. Canon E. Nácar Fuster and the Dominican Alberto Colunga published their *Sagrada Biblia* (Madrid 1944, 9th ed. 1959) under the auspices of the Pontifical University of Salamanca. The version of the NT by Msgr. Juan Straubinger (Buenos Aires, Argentina 1944) was based on the Greek texts of A. *Merk and E. *Nestle. Finally, the

Sagrada Biblia of the Jesuit José M. Bover and the professor of Hebrew Francisco Cantera Burgos (Madrid 1947, 5th ed. 1957) is considered the most exact and faithful of the Spanish versions.

Bibliography: A. PAZ Y MELIA, "La Biblia de la casa de Alba," *Homenaje a Menéndez y Pelayo,* 2 v. (Madrid 1899) 2:5–93. S. BERGER, *Les Bibles castillanes* (Paris 1899). C. RICCI, *La Biblia de Ferrara* (Buenos Aires 1926). M. MENÉNDEZ Y PELAYO, *Historia de los heterodoxos españoles,* 7 v. (2d ed. Madrid 1911–32); ed. E. SÁNCHEZ REYES, 8 v. (*Edición nacional* 35–42; Santander 1946–48) 4:123–208. F. PÉREZ, "La Biblia en España," *Verbum Dei,* ed. B. ORCHARD (Barcelona 1956–   ) 1:83–97. J. LLAMAS, ed., *Biblia medieval romanceada judío-cristiana,* 2 v. (Madrid 1950–55). L. ARNALDICH, *Los estudios bíblicos en España (1900–1955)* (Madrid 1957). E. M. WILSON, "Spanish Versions," *The Cambridge History of the Bible: The West from the Reformation to the Present Day,* ed. S. L. GREENSLADE (Cambridge, Eng. 1963) 125–129, 354, 540–541. F. PLAINE, DB 2.2:1952–65.

[J. M. SOLA-SOLE]

29. PORTUGUESE VERSIONS

The earliest versions were the work of the Cistercian Monks of Alcobaça: *Actos dos Apóstolos* and "excerpts of the OT" of the 13th or 14th to the 15th century. The first printed Biblical version was that of *Vita Christi,* the popular Gospel harmony of *Ludolph of Saxony (Lisbon 1495). In 1497 the *Evangelhos e Epístolas* were published at Oporto: a French text with Portuguese rendering by the publisher himself, Rodrigues Alves. In 1505 the *Autos dos Apóstolos* and *Epístolas Católicas,* translated by Bernardo d'Alcobaça, were printed at Lisbon. All these renderings were based on the Latin Vulgate (Vulg).

The first complete Portuguese version was done by J. Ferreira d'Almeida, a Calvinist missionary in the Orient: NT published at Amsterdam in 1681; OT posthumous (2 v., Batavia 1748–53; from Ez 48.21, completed by J. op den Akker, after Almeida's death). This version from the original texts was often reprinted. Afterward came the translation of A. Pereira de Figueiredo, made from Vulg; of a much better literary quality than Almeida's work, its first edition (23 v. Lisbon 1778–90) was reprinted several times. In 19th-century Brazil two versions, at least, of the NT were made: one from Vulg by Dom Friar Joaquim de Na. Sa. da Nazaré (S. Luís do Maranhão 1845–47), afterward published by C. Ballester (2 v. Lisbon 1916–17); the other from the Greek by the American Protestant missionary A. Blackford (Rio de Janeiro 1879).

In the 20th century in Portugal, Father M. Santana published *Evangelho de S. Mateus* (Lisbon 1909; tr. from Vulg, with excellent notes). Msgr. Matos Sooares published a version of the whole Bible (Oporto 1927–30, from Vulg), several times reprinted. Finally, there is the NT translated from the Greek with introductions and notes by J. Falcão (Lisbon 1956–65). A *Bíblia Ilustrada* is being published with the collaboration of the late G. da Fonseca of the Biblical Institute in Rome and others, in large format with versions from the original languages: NT (2 v. Oporto 1957); OT in progress. There are also the NT of the Capuchin Fathers (tr. from the Greek, 2d ed. Lisbon 1963), a *Sinopse dos 4 Evangelhos* of A. Cardoso (Coimbra 1952), and the Gospel harmonies of F. Wakkers (2d ed. Lisbon 1941) and I. Viegas and A. Neves (4th ed. Lisbon 1953). In Brazil versions of the NT have been published by the following authors: H. Rohden (Petrópolis 1934), J. J. Pedreira de Castro (4th ed. Rio

de Janeiro 1950), M. Hoepers (2d ed. Rio de Janeiro 1958), and L. Ramos (2 v. Rio de Janeiro 1956–58; the best), the last two from the Greek. In 1955 the "Liga de Estudos Bíblicos" began to issue its *Santa Bíblia* in fascicles (like the *Bible de Jérusalem*), a version from the original languages, in progress. Finally there are the NT by Monsignor Negromonte (Rio de Janeiro 1961) and the *Bíblia Sagrada* based on the "Bible de Maredsous" (4th ed. S. Paulo 1962).

Bibliography: A. RIBEIRO DOS SANTOS, "Memória sobre algumas traducções bíblicas," *Memórias da Litteratura Portugueza* 7 (Lisbon 1806) 23–57. J. PEREIRA, "Versions Portugaises de la Bible," DB 5.1:562–565. G. L. SANTOS FERREIRA, *A Bíblia em Portugal: Apontamentos para uma monographia, 1495–1850* (Lisbon 1906). E. MOREIRA, *Versões Bíblicas* (Lisbon 1957). H. WENDT, *Die portugiesische Bibelübersetzung: Ihre Geschichte und ihre Aufgaben mit besonderer Berücksichtigung des A. T.* (Diss. Heidelberg 1962).

[J. FALCÃO]

30. CATALAN VERSIONS

Early Catalan translations of the Bible met the same difficulties that other vernacular versions encountered. In 1233 King James I of Aragon (1213–76) prohibited the making of versions of the Bible in the vernacular. However, in 1287 Alfonso III of Aragon (1285–91) ordered a translation of the Bible to be made from a French version into Catalan. Other Catalan Bibles are known from royal documents of 1382 and 1398 to have existed in the 14th century. Probably these versions influenced the Catalan Bibles that are preserved in 15th-century MSS: the three-volume one in Paris (Bib. Nat., Esp. 2–4), the one of the year 1465 in the British Museum (Egerton 1526), and the one of the year 1461 in Paris (Bib. Nat., Esp. 5), which contains the books from Genesis through Psalms. All of these versions were made from the Latin Vulgate.

The most important Catalan version, however, was that of the Valencian friar Bonifacio Ferrer (1355–1417), the brother of St. *Vincent Ferrer. It was made probably between 1396 and 1402 and was printed at Valencia in 1478—one of the earliest printed vernacular Bibles. Shortly after it was printed, every copy of it was destroyed by order of the Spanish Inquisition. Only one remnant of it has been preserved—the last page of the Apocalypse of St. John—now in the possession of the Hispanic Society of America, New York (see illustration). The Book of Psalms of the Ferrer Bible was printed separately (Barcelona 1480); a single copy of it is preserved in the Mazarine Library (No. 1228). Moreover, parts of the Ferrer Bible are known from 15th-century MSS that contain sections of the Gospels, Daniel, 1 and 2 Machabees, and Acts. Another important Psalter was that of Roiç de Corella (Venice 1490). The only other Catalan version before the 20th century worthy of note was the Protestant NT of J. M. Prat published by the British and Foreign Bible Society (London 1832).

In the 20th century, besides certain translations of particular books of the Bible, three Catholic versions of the whole Bible in Catalan should be mentioned: (1) the version of the Foment de Pietat (1924–   ), made from the Latin Vulgate and of a popular character; (2) the one of the Catalan Biblical Foundation (1928–48), made from the original texts and having the Greek text at the side of the Catalan text of the NT books; and (3) the Bible of Montserrat (1926–   ), translated from the original texts and accompanied by a scientific commen-

45

·Apocalypsis·

363

E yo ioan qui oi e viu aquestes coses . E puix
que les hagui oices e vistes :caygui perque avo
ras vauant los peus vel angel :qui mostraua a
mi aquestes coses·E vix ami:guarda nou faces
Seruent so ensemps ab tu e ab los frares teus
prophetes :e ab aquells qui seruen les paraules
vela prophecia ve aquest libre . Al veu avora . E
vix ami :no sagelles les paraules vela prophe /
cia ve aquest libre ·Car lo temps es prop .Qui
nou noga encara:e qui en les sutzures es ensut
zeeixca ccara :e qui iust es sia iustificat encara
e lo sant sia santificat encara.Veus que vinch
tost :e lo guardo meu es ab mi: retre a cascu se
gons les obres sues · yo so alpha e o : primer e
varrer :principi e fi . Benauenturats son los
qui lauen les stoles sues en la sanch vel anyell:
perque sia la potestat ve ells en lo fust ve vida:
e per portes entren en la ciutat . Defora los
cans e fents veri e los luxuriosos e los homici

ves e losseruints ales icoles : e tot aque...
ama e fa mentira .yo iesus he trames lo angel
meu a testificar aquestes coses a vosaltres en
les esglesies .yo so rael e linatge ve vauid: stela
resplandent e matutina .E lo spos e la sposa vi
en :vine . E lo qui ou:viga vine . E qui ha ser
vinga . E qui vol prenga vegrat aygua ve vi /
va . Car fac testimoni a tot oint les paraules
vela prophecia ve aquest libre . Si algu hauza a
iustat a aqstes :aiustara veu sobre aqll les pla /
gues que son scrites en aquest libre : e si algu
haura viminuit veles paraules vela prophecia
ve aquest libre :tolra veu la part ve ell vel libre
ve vida e vela ciutat sancta: e ve aquestes coses
que son scrites en aquest libre . Diu ho lo qui
testimoni vona ve aqstes coses .Encara. Vinch
tost :amen . Vine senyor iesus . La gracia vel
senyor nostre iesu crist sia ab tots vosaltres
Amen .

Gracies infinides sien fetes al / omnipotēt deu/e senyor nostre/

Iesu crist : e ala humil/e sacratissima verge maria mare sua . Acaba la
biblia molt vera/e catholica : treta ve vna biblia vel noble mossen berē /
guer viues ve boil cauuller: la qual fon trellavava ve aquella propria que
fon arromançava en lo monestir ve portaceli ve lengua latina en la no /
stra valenciana per lo molt reuerend micer bonifaci ferrer voctor en ca
scun vret /e en facultat ve sacra theologia : e von ve tota la Cartoxa :gez
ma vel benauenturat sanct vicent ferrer vel orve ve pricavors :en la qual
translacio forē /e altres singulars homēs ve sciencia . E ara verreramēt
aquesta es stava diligentment corregiva/vista/e regoneguva per lo reue
rēd mestre iaume borrell mestre en sacra theologia vel orve ve pricavors :
e inquisivor en regne ve valēcia . Es stava empremtava en la ciutat ve
valencia a vespeses vel magnifich en philip vizlant mercaver vela vila ve
isne v alta Alamāya: per mestre Alfonso fernāvez ve Corvoua vel Reg /
ve Castella/e per mestre lambert palomar alamāy mestre en arts: comē
çava en lo mes ve febrer vel any mil quatrecents setāta set : e acabava
en lo mes ve Maz vel any Mil . CCCCLXXVIII.

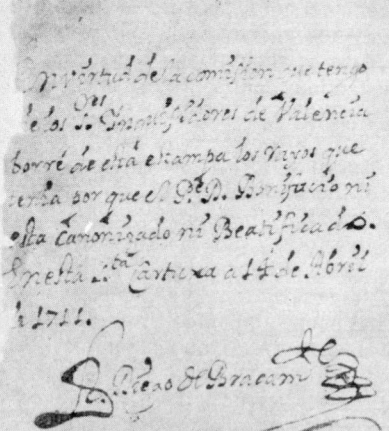

Fig. 29. Last page, with colophon, of a Catalan version of
the Bible printed at Valencia in 1478. The translation had
been made between 1396 and 1402 by Friar Boniface
Ferrer, superior general of the Carthusians and head of
the Monastery of the Gate of Heaven near Valencia.
In 1490 the Spanish Inquisition ordered all copies of the
printed edition to be destroyed. This one page is the
only known fragment of the entire edition.

tary. The monks of Montserrat publish also an illustrated commentary on the Bible and other books on the Bible of a popular nature.

Bibliography: M. MORREALE, "Apuntes bibliográficos para la iniciación al estudio de las traducciones bíblicas medievales en catalán," AnalSacTarracon 31 (1958) 271–290. P. BOHIGAS, "Dos fragments catalans del Evangelis restes de la traducció de la Bíblia de Bonifaci Ferrer," *Saggi e ricerche in memoria di Ettore Li Gotti,* 3 v. (Palermo 1962) v.1. L. ARNALDICH, *Los estudios bíblicos en España desde el año 1900 al año 1955* (Madrid 1957). R. M. DÍAZ CARBONELL, *Dom Bonaventura Ubach, l'home, el monjo, el biblista* (Barcelona 1962). **Illustration credit:** Fig. 29, The Hispanic Society of America.

[P. BELLET]

31. POLISH VERSIONS

The earliest indication of a Polish version of the Bible dates from the 13th century; a life of Bl. *Kunigunde or Kinga (d. 1292) states that she recited the Psalms in the vernacular. Two such translations have survived in manuscript form: the 14th-century Florian Psalter and the 15th-century Pulawy Psalter. A third manuscript text is the 15th-century Queen Sophia, or the Szaros Patak Bible.

The oldest printed Biblical text dates from 1516; it contains the beginning of St. John's Gospel. In 1526 J. Landecki edited fragments of OT and Gospel texts. Also in the 16th century the Psalters of Wróbel, Rej, and Kochanowski were published, the last a poetic work of lasting literary value. In 1556 appeared the Scharffenberger NT, and the entire Bible of Leopolita came out in 1561.

The Polish equivalent of the English Douay version is the Bible of J. Wujek, a great Jesuit scholar. His revision is faithful, clear, and beautiful. Wujek translated the Vulgate but based his renderings also on the original texts. His NT appeared in 1593 and his Psalter in 1594; his OT was issued posthumously in 1599. The Wujek Bible went through more than 20 editions. Recognizing its value, the Protestants also reprinted it many times. In 1900 the American Bible Society edited Wujek's NT in New York. In the 19th century the Wujek Bible underwent modernization. A. Szlagowski edited the NT in 1900, and J. Kruszyński edited the Gospels, Acts, and Psalms, in 1908–09. The Poznań Bible, a collective work, appeared between 1926 and 1932; the Kraków Bible, edited by S. Styś and J. Rostworowski, came out in 1935.

Translations from the original languages include A. Symon's Epistles of St. Paul in 1906, the Gospels and Acts done by W. Szczepański in 1917, and J. Kruszyński's Prophetical and Historical Books of the OT issued between 1926 and 1939. The New Latin Psalter of 1945 was translated almost simultaneously but independently in 1947 by S. Wójcik, F. Mirek, and A. Tymczak. In the same year F. Gryglewicz translated the Gospels and the Acts. An important event was the translation of the NT from the Vulgate by E. Dąbrowski in 1947. It is considered the best since Wujek's time. In 1960 Dąbrowski translated the NT from the original. So did S. Kowalski in 1957. There is (1965) in preparation a new version of the entire Bible from the original, a collective work by a group of Polish Biblical scholars. It is to be called the Tyniec Bible.

Of the Protestant versions, there is the Evangelical NT of L. Murzynowski, edited by J. Seklucyan in 1552. The Calvinists produced the Brest Bible in 1562; it is

known also as the Radziwill Bible and possesses literary value. The Nieświez Bible of S. Budny in 1572 and the NT of M. Czechowic in 1577 were Unitarian versions. In 1632 appeared the Reformed Augsburg version, called the Danzig Bible. Valued highly by the Protestants, it went through many editions, the more recent being a New York imprint in 1916 and one in Geneva in 1944.

Polish-Jewish versions of the OT include the translations by I. Cylkow (1883–1914), F. Aszkenazy (1927–30), J. Mieses (1931), and S. Spitzer (1937).

Bibliography: T. H. DARLOW and H. F. MOULE, comp., *Historical Catalogue of the Printed Editions of Holy Scripture . . .,* 2 v. (London 1903–11). E. DĄBROWSKI, ed., *Podręczna encyklopedia biblijna,* 2 v. (Poznan 1959). L. STEFANIAK, "Die polnischen Bibelübersetzungen," NTSt 5 (1958–59) 328–333.

[J. RYBINSKI]

32. CZECH-SLOVAK VERSIONS

As distinct from the much older Old Slavic versions, Czech renderings originated in the 14th century. The "Bible of Olomouc," finished in 1417, is regarded as the best of these early Czech translations, whose authors usually relied on Old Slavic texts. A new group of translations appeared in the 16th century, this time in printed form. Even the best of them, however, the "Melantrich Bible," translated by Zikmund of Púchov, and the "Kralice Bible" (of which the NT was translated by Jan Blahoslav) suffered from a Renaissance tendency to imitate the ornate style of Ciceronian Latin. This was only partially corrected in the "St. Wenceslas Bible," published between 1677 and 1715 by the Jesuits, which was then generally adhered to by numerous 18th- and 19th-century publishers. Among the modern translations, that of Sýkora, revised by Hejčl, and most recently (1947) by Col, is the most popular. Josef Heger, a Czech Orientalist, published between 1925 and 1948 his own translations of the majority of the OT books from their Hebrew or Greek texts. While of a rather independent character and disregarding many of the usages fixed by the received rendering from the Vulgate, Heger's versions, because of their attempt to render faithfully the ancient style and ways of expression and because of their poetic qualities, are regarded as an outstanding contribution to Czech literature.

Slovak Biblical texts are of more recent origin. During World War II a manuscript was found containing a Slovak version of the whole Bible that had been made by a Camaldolese monk in the late 15th century; it has been shown that this formed the basis of various parts of later Slovak versions. The earliest printed Slovak Bible, made from the Vulgate, is that of J. Palkovič (Gran 1829–32). This has been supplanted by another rendering from the Vulgate by J. Donoval et al. (Trnava 1926). A translation of the NT from the Greek by Š. Zlatoš and A. Šurjanský (Trnava 1946) has been well received. Another 20th-century version of the NT is that of K. Strmen (Scranton, Pa. 1954). All these are Catholic versions. Under Protestant auspices a Slovak version of the NT (Budapest 1913) and a complete Bible (Prague 1926) were made by J. Rohaček. In 1942 a new Lutheran version of the NT was made in Slovak to replace the Czech version previously used by Lutherans in Slovakia.

[B. CHUDOBA]

33. UKRAINIAN VERSIONS

A Ukrainian recension of the Old-Bulgarian text is represented by the following printed editions: the Ostrog Bible of 1581 and the Catholic Bibles published in Pochayev (1798) and Peremyshl (1859). The Ostrog Bible, the first complete Slavonic Bible printed in eastern Europe, was published under the auspices of Constantine, Prince of Ostrog, by a group of Orthodox scholars under the direction of Herasym Smotrytsky. They had at their disposal the MSS of the Gennadius Bible and printed Bibles in Greek and Latin. The complete NT and some OT books of the Gennadius Bible (see 34. Russian Versions) were incorporated in the new version; other OT books were translated from the Greek; and Tobit, Judith, and 1 and 2 Machabees were from the Vulgate. The distinctive feature of this version was its replacing of the books translated in earlier centuries from the Vulgate and transmitted in the manuscripts with a more recent version made from the Greek. The scholars thus endeavored to produce a standard Slavonic version. Although its textual value is not great, partly because the text is disparate, partly because of inaccuracies in certain parts, the influence of the Ostrog version on subsequent printed Slavonic editions was enormous. The Catholic Bibles printed in Pochayev and Peremyschl were based on the Russian Synodal Bible of 1751. They have, however, much in common with the Ostrog Bible as to language and style and with the Vulgate as to textual variants. Extant versions are:

Catholic. A. Bachynsky made a version of the NT and Psalms from the Old-Slavonic (Lvov 1903). J. Levytsky rendered the NT from the text of H. von Soden (Zovkva 1921), the Pentateuch and Psalms from the Greek. T. T. Haluscynskyj translated the Gospels from A. Merk's Greek NT (Rome 1946). For the first time a new, direct, and independent version of the whole Bible, including the OT deuterocanonical books, was produced from the original languages by John Khomenko and published, with introduction and notes, by the Basilian Fathers (Rome 1963).

Non-Catholic. F. Skorina published 23 books of the OT (Prague 1517–19), also an Epistularium and the Psalms (Vilnyus 1526); the version was made from the Vulgate. Popular and widely spread was the version of the Gospels made in 1561 from the Old-Slavonic by Gregory, a Basilian monk of Peresopnycia in Volhynia. P. Morachevsky translated the Gospels from Greek in 1861. A complete version of the Bible from the original languages was done by P. Kulish, I. S. Levytsky, and J. Puluj (Vienna 1903). In an attempt to supersede the preceding version, Metropolitan Ilarion (John Ohienko) made a new version of the Bible from the original languages (London 1962). The last two versions were published by the British and Foreign Biblical Society without the deuterocanonical books of the OT.

Bibliography: D. CIZEVSKY, *Istoriya Ukrainskoyi literatury* (New York 1956). N. KOROLIWA, "Notes sur la traduction des Écritures en langue ukrainienne," ÉchosOr 24 (1925) 212–220. T. T. HALUSCYNSKYJ, "De Ucrainis S. Scripturae versionibus," *Bohoslovia* 3 (1925) 218–225, 309–319.

[S. S. SHAWEL]

34. RUSSIAN VERSIONS

SS. Cyril and Methodius did not translate the whole Bible into Old Bulgarian, but only those portions used in divine services. The Slavs still did not have a translation of the whole Bible in the time of Gennadius, Archbishop of Novgorod (1485–1504). To fill the gaps, Benjamin, a Croatian Dominican, translated the following books from the Vulgate: 1 and 2 Chronicles, Ezra, Nehemia, Tobit, Judith, Wisdom, Jeremia, 1 and 2 Machabees, and Esther ch. 11 to 16. The Catholic character of this Bible is certain. The first printed Bibles in the Cyrillic alphabet present a Ukrainian recension of the Old-Bulgarian text. Such was the first complete Bible printed at Ostrog in 1581 by Ukrainian scholars (see 33. Ukrainian Versions). The first Russian recension of the Old-Bulgarian text was printed in Moscow in 1663. A new critical edition of the Bible was published in 1751 after a long and careful examination of different texts by six successive commissions (1712–51). The OT was translated from Grabe's Oxford edition of the Septuagint. The Holy Synod published, despite opposition, a NT in colloquial Russian in 1821 and the OT in 1876. Both proto- and deuterocanonical books were printed. A Protestant version of the OT was published in London 1875, but banned from Russia. The same version was later published in Russia itself. A new, revised version of Psalms was published in Rome (1950); and a complete Bible, in Washington (1952).

Bibliography: M. SPINKA, "Slavic Translations of the Scriptures," JRelig 13 (1933) 415–432. A. OSROFF, "Publication of Russian Bible," *Bible Translator* 7 (1956) 56–65, 98–101. J. SCHWEIGL, "La Biblia slava del 1751 (1756)," *Biblica* 18 (1937) 51–73. J. SCHMID, ed., *Moderne Bibelübersetzungen* (Vienna 1960).

[S. S. SHAWEL]

35. HUNGARIAN VERSIONS

The oldest Hungarian version of the Gospels and of the OT (1416–35) is conserved in three manuscripts: MS Révai (Uj Nyelvemléktár I, Budapest 1916), MS Jászay (Nyelvemléktár I, Budapest 1874), MS Apor (Nyelvemléktár VIII, Budapest 1879). Further partial versions are in MSS from the first quarter of the 16th century. The first printed editions are Epistles of St. Paul translated by Benedek Komjáti (Kraków 1533); Gospels by Gábor Pesti (Vienna 1536); NT by János Sylvester (Ujsziget 1541); Psalter by István Benczédi Székely (Kraków 1548); Bible (OT incomplete) by Gáspár Heltai et al. (Kolozsvár 1551–65); 1–4 Kings and Job by Péter Méliusz Juhász (1565); NT by Tamás Félegyházi (1586). The first complete Protestant version was made by Gáspár Károlyi (Vizsoly 1590), who used the Vulgate but also referred to available original texts. This became the classical Protestant version. The first complete Catholic version was made by the Jesuit György Káldi (Vienna 1626). After 3 centuries of different revised editions, the Society "Szent István" made a completely revised edition with up-to-date notes and references to the original texts (Budapest 1927–34). The NT was reedited with more detailed doctrinal notes (1954–57). A new version of the NT from the Greek original into modern Hungarian was made by G. J. Békés and P. Dalos with short notes (Rome 1951, 3d ed. 1957, 4th ed. 1964). The Hungarian Protestant Bible Council, concerned with the Károlyi version, is preparing (1965) a new version of the original; already issued are the NT (1956) and, of the OT, Genesis to Job (1951–   ). A. Raffay's version of the NT (1929) was edited by the British and Foreign Bible Society. The Hungarian Jewish Literary Society edited a conscientious version of the OT (Budapest 1898–1907); most of it was reedited in a new version in 1925; the same society later issued a completely new version of the Pentateuch and the synagogue readings from the Prophets, with commentaries of J. H. Hertz (Budapest 1939–42).

Bibliography: R. SZENTIVÁNYI, *A szentírástudomány tankönyve* (5th ed. Budapest 1946). I. HARSÁNYI, *A magyar Biblia* (Budapest 1927). L. M. PÁKOŻDY, "The New Revision of the Hungarian Bible," *Bulletin of the United Bible Societies* (1951) v.2.

[G. J. BÉKÉS]

36. MALTESE VERSIONS

Maltese is basically a Semitic language written in Roman script and enriched with Romance vocabulary and syntactical forms. It asserted itself as a literary language at the close of the 18th century.

The first Maltese versions of the Bible were published by the Church Missionary Society of London: the Gospel of St. John by J. Cannolo (London 1822); Gospels and Acts by M. A. Vassalli (London 1829); complete NT, *Il Ghaqda il-Gdida ta' Sidna Gesu' Kristu* (Malta 1847). This consisted of the 1829 Gospel edition and of the Epistles and Apocalypse from a MS of Vassalli, both revised by M. A. Camilleri to conform to the English Authorized Version. The Society for Promoting Christian Knowledge published in Malta in 1845 a Maltese version of the *Book of Common Prayer* and the Psalms (from the Hebrew) prepared by the same Camilleri. The British and Foreign Bible Society has since published a number of revised pocket editions of these versions. Cannolo and Vassalli adhered to the Vulgate; Camilleri worked on the English Authorized Version. Only Vassalli made any serious effort for accuracy and literary refinement.

R. Taylor published a poetical rendering of the Psalms and Canticles (Malta 1847) and a version of the Holy Week Office (Malta 1849), adapting the Protestant versions for Catholic use. G. Muscat Azzopardi translated the four Gospels (Malta 1895–1917) and Acts (Malta 1924). Partial translations were published by P. P. Grima (NT) and A. M. Galea (OT) between 1924 and 1932. M. G. Paris edited the four Gospels separately (Malta 1939–50) and in a single volume (1963). All these versions are based on the Vulgate with no literary or scientific pretensions. A Maltese version of Ruth direct from the Hebrew was published by C. Cortis (Malta 1924). The first complete translation of the whole Bible direct from the original languages is that prepared by P. P. Saydon of the Royal University of Malta: *Il-Kotba Mqaddsa bil-Malti* (Malta 1929–59). This one-man undertaking is scientifically produced, accurate in its vocabulary, and vigorous in expression.

Bibliography: P. P. SAYDON, "History of the Maltese Bible," *Melita Theologica* 10 (1957) 1–15; "Philological and Textual Notes to the Maltese Translation of the Old Testament," Cath BiblQuart 23 (1961) 249–257. C. SANT, "Merits of the Maltese Translation of the Bible by Prof. P. P. Saydon," *Melita Theologica* 13 (1961) 13–18. J. SCHMID, "Moderne Bibelübersetzungen," *ZKathTh* 82 (1960) 325. E. P. ARBEZ, notices in JNEastSt 12 (1953) 135–138; CathBiblQuart 16 (1954) 450–457; JBiblLit 78 (1959) 254.

[C. SANT]

37. JAPANESE VERSIONS

The first parts of the Bible to be translated into Japanese were the Gospels of the Mass. This was done by the early missionaries (c. 1560). But only one manuscript survived the cruel end of the old Japan Mission

(1549–1614); it was written by M. Barreto, SJ, in 1591, and is kept in the Vatican Library (Reg. Lat. 459). It was edited in facsimile and in Japanese script in 1962 [*Kirishitan Kenkyū*, nr. 7 (2 v. Tokyo)]. Though the fact is often denied and no copy is extant, there is no reason to distrust the testimony of two reliable sources (Cieslik, 40) that in 1613 a printed version of the whole NT existed in Miyako (present Kyoto).

After the reopening of Japan (1859), the first to produce a complete (teamwork) translation of the Bible were the Protestants (NT, 1879; OT, 1887). Although Catholics had minor portions earlier (e.g., the four Gospels in 1895), they had to wait until 1910 for the whole NT in Japanese, which was published by E. Raguet, MEP. Though written in the literary style of that time, called *bungo* (the colloquial Japanese of the 13th century, and now hardly understood), it became very popular and is still used.

One of the first to use modern colloquial (*kōgo*) in extensive Bible translation was B. Totsuka (Gospel Harmony, 1930). After World War II, the general development of the written language toward *kōgo* called for new translations. In 1953 four *kōgo* versions of the NT were published, one of them Catholic (by F. Barbaro, SDB, now the most diffused among Catholics: 150,000 copies by 1964).

Of the OT, Catholics had no complete version until 1959, when the Hokkaido Franciscans finished a (*bungo*) version of the Vulgate OT (4 v.). A learned translation of the OT from Hebrew, started by O. Shibutani (Genesis, 1940; Psalms 1 to 50, 1945), has been discontinued. To meet the demand, Msgr. A. Ogihara,

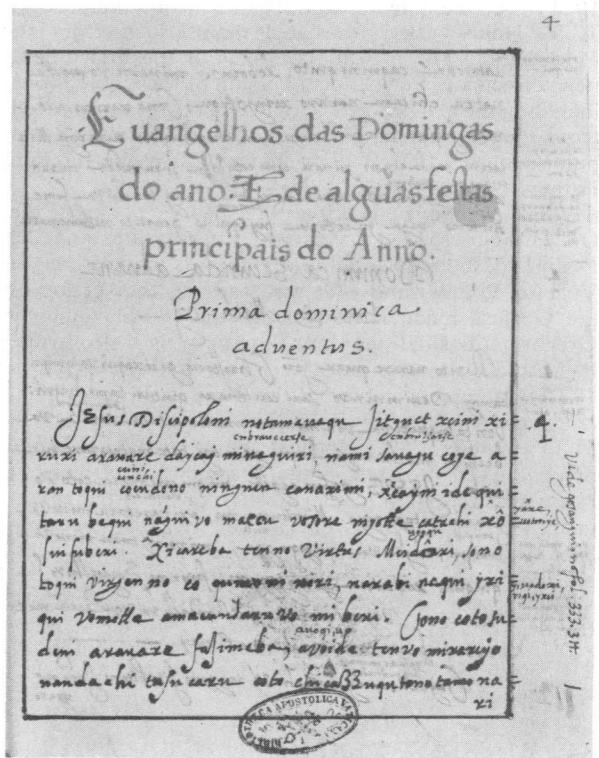

Fig. 30. Father Barreto's MS of Gospels in Japanese, written in 1591 (Vat. Cod. Reg. Lat. 459, fol. 4 r.). The text is not written in Japanese characters, but has been transliterated into Latin script.

マテオ 5. 16—23   19

Fig. 31. Page from a New Testament (Mt 5.16–23) in modern Japanese (tr. F. Barbaro), with additional notes.

SJ, published a (*bungo*) OT selection from modern language sources (1947). At present, a learned translation (in *kōgo*) from the original texts by Studium Biblicum Franciscanum (ed. B. Schneider, eight Biblical books in 1964) is in preparation. An unpretentious one, made from modern languages, was issued by the Salesians, ed. F. Barbaro (Tokyo 1964), the first complete Catholic Bible in modern Japanese.

Protestant Bible diffusion exceeds the Catholic by far. Their most important translation is the *kōgo* version of the Japan Bible Society, made by a committee of eight Protestant Japanese, who finished the whole Bible (Protestant canon) in 1955 (by 1964, 800,000 copies; NT 3,800,000 copies). Worth noting also is the private effort of M. Sekine (four OT books by 1964). Considering that only 700,000 Japanese are Christians (1964), the interest in the Bible is remarkable.

Bibliography: H. Cieslik, "Die Heilige Schrift in der alten Japanmission," NZMissw 11 (1955) 30–41. J. L. VAN HECKEN, "Les Publications bibliques catholiques en langue japonaise (1859–1959)," *ibid.* 16 (1960) 81–94, 193–205. B. SCHNEIDER, "Catholic Japanese Bible Translations in Modern Times, 1895–1964," *The Japan Christian Quarterly* 31.2 (1965) 79–86. **Illustration credit:** Fig. 30, Biblioteca Apostolica Vaticana.

[H. KRUSE]

38. IRISH VERSIONS

That Irish scholars busied themselves with Biblical translation from very early times can be deduced from the many Latin MSS of Holy Scripture that are glossed with Irish words. Homilies contain many fragments of translation from both the OT and NT, but there is no complete translation of the Bible in Old or Middle Irish.

Protestant. In 1571 Queen Elizabeth I sent a font of type and a press to Dublin for the printing of the Bible in Irish, with the prayerful hope "that God in His mercy would raise up some one to translate the New Testament in Irish." In 1573 the translation was begun, and William O'Donnell, a Fellow of Trinity College, Dublin, signed the preface to the complete work in 1602. However, the sheets were not folded for the binder before the Queen died, and a dedication to King James was prefixed to the work. In 1629 William Bedell was consecrated bishop of Kilmore, and at 58 he began to study Irish with a view of producing a complete Irish Bible. He engaged Murtagh O'Conga, an excellent Irish scholar, to help him translate the NT. This Irish Bible was translated from the English version, and there were some misunderstandings of the original at times. Robert Boyle, the physicist, was greatly interested in the Irish Scriptures and paid for the printing in 1685. Fifty copies of the OT were sent to Scotland for the use of the Gaelic-speaking Highlanders, and eventually, by 1767, a translation into Scotch-Gaelic was published, based on the Irish translation. Whitley Stokes, a Trinity College professor of physics and grandfather of the great Celtic scholar of the same name, published a new translation of the Gospel of Luke and the Acts of the Apostles in 1799, and the four Gospels and the Acts in both Irish and English in 1806. In 1817 the British and Foreign Bible Society published the complete Irish Bible.

Catholic. In 1858 Abp. John MacHale of Tuam began a translation of the Vulgate Bible into Irish, but it did not go beyond the Pentateuch, although the title page called for the translation as far as Josue. It was published in 1861 with an English version from the Douay and some notes. Father Peter O'Leary, one of the founders of the Society for the Preservation of the Irish Language, published a translation of the Gospels in 1904. The late Msgr. Padraig de Brun, Rector of University College, Galway, published a new translation of the NT from the Greek in 1929.

Bibliography: *Bibliography of Irish Philology and of Printed Irish Literature* (Dublin 1913) 243–244. R. I. BEST, *Bibliography of Irish Philology and Manuscript Literature: 1913–1941* (Dublin 1942) 2047–48. T. K. ABBOTT, "On the History of the Irish Bible," *Hermathena* 17 (1912) 29–50. E. R. M. DIX, "The First Printing of the N.T. at Dublin," *Proceedings of the Royal Irish Academy*, sec. C. no. 6, 29 (1911) 180–185; "The N.T. in Erse," *Acts of Privy Council of England (sub anno 1587)* in *Printing in Dublin prior to 1601* (2d ed. Dublin 1932) 32.

[R. T. MEYER]

39. WELSH VERSIONS

In medieval times there were some translations of Biblical extracts, as in the so-called *Y Bibyl Ynghymraec* (Bible in Welsh) and the *Llyfr ancr Llandewibrefi* (Book of the Anchorite of Llandewibrefi) of 1346, but full Biblical translation in Welsh came only with the Reformation. In 1551 William Salesbury (*c.* 1520–*c.* 1584) produced the liturgical Epistles and Gospels in Welsh; and in 1567 the first Welsh NT appeared, translated from Greek by Richard Davies (1501–81), Thomas Huet (d. 1591), and again William Salesbury. In 1588 the whole Bible was printed, the work of William Morgan (*c.* 1541–1604), later bishop of Llandaff, assisted by the poet Edmwnd Prys (1544–1623). This text appeared in 1620, slightly revised, chiefly in orthography and certain grammatical forms, under the name of Richard Parry (1560–1623), but apparently the work of the grammarian John Davies (1567–1644).

The most striking thing about the history of the Welsh Bible is its homogeneity: every edition presents the text of 1588–1620 with very small variations (and a Catholic prayer book of 1837 uses the same text almost unchanged). In 1955 the traditional text was issued with revised modern orthography.

From 1926, under the auspices of the University of Wales, a new translation began to appear in pamphlets, and most of the NT was done by 1945. At present, however, an entirely new modern version is being prepared by scholars from all denominations, including Catholics. The publication in 1941 of *Y Llithau Sul* (the Sunday Lessons) for Catholics, in a new translation by Canon J. Barrett Davies, should be noticed.

Bibliography: S. L. GREENSLADE, ed., *The Cambridge History of the Bible: The West from the Reformation to the Present Day* (Cambridge, Eng. 1963) ch. 4, app. 2. T. PARRY, *Hanes Llenyddiaeth Gymraeg* (Caerdydd 1953); Eng. *A History of Welsh Literature*, tr. H. I. BELL (Oxford 1955). J. BALLINGER, *The Bible in Wales* (London 1906). J. LLOYD-JONES, *Y Beibl Cymraeg* (Caerdydd 1938).

[S. BULLOUGH]

40. OTHER VERNACULAR VERSIONS

With the spread of Christian missionary activity since the 16th century, the Bible (in whole or in part) has been translated into all the more important modern languages and even into numerous dialects of primitive peoples. Such versions are at times the only printed books in these languages or dialects and are thus of considerable linguistic value. They are usually not made from the original texts, but from the official version of the missionary group, e.g., from the King James Version by English-speaking Protestants or from the Latin Vulgate by Catholics. Most of these versions were produced under the auspices of Protestant Bible societies (*see* BIBLICAL SOCIETIES), but Catholic missionaries were by no means inactive in this field. Biblical versions are now distributed in more than 1,200 languages, although in most of these languages the version consists in only the NT or even only one book, e.g., a Gospel. Here only a few of the more interesting modern versions that have not been mentioned in the preceding articles will be listed alphabetically.

Albanian. The NT in the Tosk (southern) dialect of Albanian was published in 1827 and in the Geg (northern) dialect in 1869. The NT and parts of the OT in the orthography of standard Albanian appeared in 1913. (*See* ALBANIA; ALBANIAN LITERATURE.)

Basque. The version of the NT in Basque by the Protestant J. de Leizarraga (Rochelle 1571) was one of the first works printed in the Basque language (*see* BASQUE LITERATURE). A Catholic NT in Basque by J. Harender appeared at Bayonne, France, in 1855. The whole Bible, translated into Basque from the Latin Vulgate, was published in London (1859–65).

Breton. As early as the 15th century there was a version of the NT in Breton (or Armoric), a Cymric-Celtic language similar to Welsh. A Catholic version of the whole Bible in the Léon dialect of Breton was published by Le Gonidec at Saint-Brieuc in 1866; a Protestant one, in the dialect of Tréguier by Le Coat at London in 1889–90.

Bulgarian. At least parts of the Bible were translated into Old Bulgarian by the disciples of SS. *Cyril and Methodius in the 9th and 10th centuries (see part 20 of this article). In modern Bulgarian the NT was published by N. Rilski in 1840; the whole Bible, by P. R. Slaveykov at Constantinople (1860–64). In 1925 the Synod of the Bulgarian Orthodox Church issued a new, official version of the Bible. (*See* BULGARIAN LITERATURE.)

Danish. The "Oldest Danish Bible Version" is a MS of *c.* 1470 containing Genesis through Kings; its first part, including Ruth, was edited by C. Molbech, *Den ældste danske Bibel-Oversættelse* (Copenhagen 1828). Another pre-Reformation translation of parts of the Bible into Danish was by canon Christiern Pedersen (*c.* 1480–1554); it was published in Paris (1514–15). Pedersen, who later became a Protestant, published a whole NT in 1529 and a whole Bible in 1543. The latter version, as revised according to Martin Luther's and other translations, was probably the basis for the Danish Reformation Bible or so-called Christian III Bible (Copenhagen 1550). It was only gradually supplanted by the "learned" Bible that was translated from the original texts by H. P. Resen (1605–07) and revised by H. Savne (1647). The Resen-Savne Bible, which was revised several times, remained until recently the most popular Bible in Denmark. In the 20th century a fresh translation from the original texts was made the new authorized version (OT 1931; NT 1948). See *Bidrag til den danske Bibels Historie* (ed. Aarhus University; Copenhagen 1950).

Finnish and Estonian. Michael Agricola (*c.* 1510–57), a disciple of Luther and one of the leaders of the Reformation in *Finland, made a Finnish translation of the NT from the Greek with the aid of Luther's version (1548). A Finnish version of the whole Bible was published in 1642 and thereafter frequently revised, most recently in 1933 (the OT) and 1938 (the NT).

In the 17th and 18th centuries Biblical versions appeared also in Estonian, a language related to Finnish. In the Dorpat dialect of Estonian the NT was published in 1686 and revised in 1727. In the Reval dialect, the literary language of *Estonia, the NT was published in 1715 and the whole Bible in 1739. Subsequently the versions in both dialects were frequently revised.

Greek, Modern. A Protestant version of the NT in modern Greek by Maximos of Gallipoli was published (at Geneva or Leyden?) in 1638; a Catholic one, by Colletus at Venice in 1708. In 1828 Abbot Hilarion issued a new version of the NT in modern Greek. The British and Foreign Bible Society published the whole Bible in modern Greek (OT, London 1840; NT, Athens 1848). A fresh translation of the Bible in modern Greek is being prepared by the theological faculty of the University of Athens. However, according to a recent decree of the government, the Septuagint for the OT and the original Greek text for the NT must still be used for Bible instruction in Greek schools.

Lithuanian. The earliest versions of the Bible in Lithuanian were made by Protestants. The first Lithuanian NT appeared at Königsberg in 1727; the whole Bible, there in 1735. This edition was frequently revised, most recently in 1897. A fresh version of the Gospels was published in 1934. A Catholic version of the NT in Lithuanian made from the Latin Vulgate by Bp. Giedraitis of Samogitia was published in 1816 and often reprinted. New Catholic versions of the whole Bible appeared in 1922 and 1936. (*See* LITHUANIA; LITHUANIAN LITERATURE.)

Norwegian. Fragments of a 13th-century version of Genesis through Kings in Old Norwegian have been preserved [ed. C. R. Unger, (Christiania 1862)]. Until the political separation of *Norway from Denmark (1814) the Danish Bible was used in Norway. A revision of this Bible that brought it closer to the language of Norway was published in 1819 and with further revisions in 1830 and 1873. Several new versions appeared in "Danish-Norwegian" or Riksmål, the official and literary language: by the Norwegian Bible Society (OT, 1842, rev. ed. 1891; NT, 1870–1904; whole Bible, rev. ed. 1930), by S. Mowinckel et al. (Genesis through Proverbs, 1929–55), and by L. Brun (NT, 1945). A Catholic version of the whole Bible in Riksmål from the Latin Vulgate was published in 1902 and a revised form (corrected according to the original texts) in 1938. The Bible (Protestant version) appeared also in Landsmål, pure Norwegian unaffected by Danish (NT, 1889; whole Bible, 1921, and in revised form, 1938).

Rumanian. The second book printed in Rumanian was a version of the Gospels by Deacon Coresi (Kronstadt 1516; *see* RUMANIAN LITERATURE). The whole NT was published at Belgrad in 1648; and the complete Bible, at Bucharest in 1688 (in revised form in 1795). There was a new version that had been prepared by various scholars (1865–69), and in revised form by W. Mayer (1873). The Rumanian Orthodox Church sponsored a NT by Galaction in 1927 and a whole Bible in 1936. Catholics of the Rumanian rite use a NT by Bălan.

Serbo-Croatian. Serbian is the same language as Croatian (a branch of the South-Slavic tongues); but in Serbia, where most of the population is Orthodox, the Cyrillic script is used, whereas in Croatia, where the majority of the people are Roman Catholics, the language is written in Roman characters. In Croatian a version of the NT liturgical pericopes appeared in Venice as early as 1495. A Croatian Bible based on Luther's version was published by A. Dalmata and S. Consul (Tübingen 1562–63). In Serbian a Catholic Bible, with the Latin text in parallel columns, was printed in 1831. The Orthodox version containing the NT by Vuk Stefanović Karadžić (1847) and the OT by his disciple G. Daničić was revised in 1932. A fresh version appeared in 1933. (*See* CROATIAN LITERATURE; SERBIAN LITERATURE.)

Slovenian. Primus Trubar (1508–86), a leader of the Protestant Reformation in Carniola (then part of Austria), published the first NT in Slovenian (Tübingen 1555–77). The whole Bible for Slovenian Protestants was prepared by G. Dalmatin (Wittenberg 1584). The Slovenian Bible of the British and Foreign Bible Society was revised as recently as 1946. Slovenian Catholics had the NT liturgical pericopes in their language as early as 1612, a whole Bible from the Vulgate (1784–1802), and another from J. von *Allioli's German version (1856–59). A fresh version of the NT was issued by the bishop of Laibach (1925–29).

Swedish. Some fragments have been preserved of a Swedish Bible that appeared *c.* 1420, based on earlier partial versions that went back to the time of St. *Bridget of Sweden (d. 1373). The Lutheran NT was published in 1526; the whole Bible ("the Gustaf Vasa Bible"), in 1541. A thoroughly revised edition of this authorized version appeared in 1917. A Catholic version of the NT in Swedish was printed in 1895.

Bibliography: P. H. VOGEL, RGG³ 1:1210–19. J. SCHMID, Lex ThK² 2:410–411. T. H. DARLOW and H. T. MOULE, eds., *Historical Catalogue of the Printed Editions of Holy Scripture in the Library of the British and Foreign Bible Society,* 2 v. in 4 (London 1903–11). R. KILGOUR, *The Gospel in Many Years* (2d ed. London 1930). E. NORTH, ed., *The Book of a Thousand Tongues* (New York 1938). E. H. ROBERTSON, *The New Translations of the Bible* (Naperville, Ill. 1959). B. NOACK, *The Cambridge History of the Bible: The West from the Reformation to the Present Day,* ed., S. L. GREENSLADE (Cambridge, Eng. 1963) 135–140, 355–358, 541, for Scandinavian versions.

[L. F. HARTMAN]

BIBLE, V (TEXTUAL CRITICISM)

Biblical textual criticism is the art of applying philological principles to extant manuscripts and indirect textual traditions in order to restore the lost autographs of the canonical books of the Bible. An introductory section setting the general principles of textual criticism is followed here by two sections in which these principles are applied to the textual criticism of the OT and the NT respectively.

1. INTRODUCTORY

The art of textual criticism demands skill in paleography (*see* PALEOGRAPHY, GREEK; PALEOGRAPHY, LATIN) and *papyrology and a knowledge of the *Biblical languages. F. J. A. *Hort called it "negative" in the sense that it comes into question only when witnesses disagree and a choice must be made about the original. Yet variants in Biblical manuscripts are so numerous that textual criticism is needed in every chapter.

Methods of Biblical Textual Criticism. Critical disciplines were developed in pre-Christian times in Alexandria to insure accurate preservation of classical texts. Early Christians applied them first to the Greek text of the Bible. Modern Biblical criticism coined the term "lower criticism" for textual criticism in contrast to the "higher," which investigates sources, style, authenticity, and aims. Currently the terminology historical, literary, and textual criticism is preferred. As adapted to the Bible, where the large amount of material and complicated transmission create unique problems, the method of textual criticism involves the following steps.

Recovery of the Oldest Forms of Extant Witnesses. Manuscripts must be grouped according to their place in the history of the text and evaluated for their trustworthiness. Characteristic errors usually serve as the chief guide in making the stemmata (family trees).

Examination of the Variant Forms of the Text. By external and internal criticism the entire textual tradition is studied to determine the sources, nature, and reasons for all the modifications. Internal criticism investigates individual variants in order to ascertain which readings have intrinsic and transcriptional probability. The former is established from context and style of the author; the latter results from application of principles for detecting mechanical or involuntary errors of copyists. These errors include confusion of letters, repetition, transposition or omission of letters, words, or lines, misinterpretation of abbreviations, false word division, and misunderstandings when the scribe copies from dictation. Internal criticism seeks also to determine deliberate modifications, such as glosses, omissions, simplifications, harmonizations, and stylistic alterations. Its most difficult task is to deal with contamination arising from oral traditions, revisions, and recensions, which are ancient critical editions produced by the use of more than one manuscript. When internal criticism fails to eliminate doubt about the choice of the original reading, external criticism, by using the knowledge of the history of the text gained in the first step, guides the critic in choosing the more probable reading.

Emendation. This is a critical correction of the text when none of the extant readings are satisfactory. Skillful use of emendation is especially necessary in the OT, where extant witnesses fail to provide meaningful readings in many cases. Here the indirect tradition as found in ancient versions and in rabbinical and early ecclesiastical writers may be helpful. When these offer no satisfactory basis for emendation, editors must either indicate a corruption or have recourse to conjectural reconstruction. The need of conjectural emendation is much less for the NT.

Contribution of Textual Criticism to Biblical Studies. Origen's great work on the Greek OT, the Hexapla, is well known. *See* BIBLE, IV (TEXTS AND VERSIONS), 9. St. Augustine urged the use of corrected texts, and St. Jerome used his knowledge of criticism to improve the Latin version of the Bible. Pope Leo XIII, in his encyclical on Biblical studies, *Providentissimus Deus,* encouraged the use of sane textual criticism (EnchBibl⁴ 106). Pope Pius XII, in his *Divino afflante Spiritu,* strongly affirmed the duty of Catholic exegetes to use textual criticism as well as other scientific tools in recovering and explaining the inspired texts (EnchBibl⁴ 548). Application of this art is often more difficult for the Hebrew Bible, where the Masoretic text eliminated other forms almost entirely. Better knowledge of languages of the ancient Near East and the Ugaritic tablets discovered since 1928 are being exploited to clarify obscure OT passages.

In the NT, progress in textual criticism has made possible control and integration of new materials coming principally from papyri discoveries, and this leads to improved editions. Because of the large number of witnesses, the "multiple reading method" is being used to fit newly discovered manuscripts into the complicated textual tradition. Simplification of methodology since Gerhard von Maastricht formulated 43 rules for NT textual criticism in 1711 has been made possible by a deeper understanding of the history of the text. Today most critics use a flexible form of what M. J. Lagrange called "rational criticism," which tries to find the reason for the variant and then apply the appropriate correction without prejudice to preconceived rules or solutions.

Bibliography: P. MAAS, *Textual Criticism,* tr. B. FLOWER (New York 1958). L. DENNEFELD, DBSuppl 2:240–256. H. J. VOGELS and L. PIROT, *ibid.* 256–274. E. C. COLWELL, "Method in Locating a Newly-Discovered Manuscript within the Manuscript Tradition of the Greek N.T.," *Studia Evangelica,* ed. K. ALAND et al. (TU 73; 1959) 757–777. M. DAHOOD, "The Value of Ugaritic for Textual Criticism," *Biblica* 40 (1959) 160–170. See also the "Elenchus bibliographicus" of *Biblica* each year for emendations. R. DEVREESSE, *Introduction à l'étude des manuscrits grecs* (Paris 1954).

[J. M. REESE]

2. TEXTUAL CRITICISM OF THE OLD TESTAMENT

Textual criticism of the OT is not simply the endeavor to identify or to reestablish, by all practicable means, the exact original text of the individual sacred books as they came from the hand of an inspired author or editor at a fixed point in time. From this, the customary goal of text-critical study of literary works, OT textual criticism shows several variations.

Peculiar Nature. In the numerous cases in which an OT book represents a collection or an adaptation of earlier materials, it is not the function of the OT text critic to present his results on the basis of the presumed prehistory of the collected or edited pieces. Rather, he identifies the form of text that has been transmitted and received as canonical. For example, Ps 13(14).5–6 and Ps 52(53).6 almost certainly derive from a single original wording within an otherwise identical Psalm. Unless, however, it can be shown that this original wording was known to the compiler of the canonical Psalter and that it was this that he proposed to transmit, the task of the OT text critic is not to emend the one passage by the other, or both by a hypothetical original, but to accept the two divergent passages as having canonical standing, each in its own place.

Meaningful glosses that are attested as having been transmitted integrally with an OT book as it was received by the Church in the beginning can be identified as glosses (though this is rather a function of literary than of textual criticism); but they cannot be excised as having no relevance. Thus Jgs 1.8 is not directly in accord with Jgs 1.21; but both are necessary to the integrity of the canonical book.

Where varying recensions of an OT book have come down in the Church from earliest Christian times, the establishment of which text is the more fully authentic embodiment of the canonical work is in part a matter of literary and of historical criticism, but in the last analysis it is subject to definition by the Church. For books such as Tobit and Sirach a univocal response to the question may not be available at present. In such cases and also in cases, such as Daniel and Esther, in which a book produced in one tradition includes in its canonical form expansions that originated in another milieu, the Christian textual critic is perhaps obliged to define his scope as the identification of those forms of text that have exercised an influence in the Church, thus going beyond any strict criterion of originality. In addition, he is bound to take a particular interest in all forms and constructions of the OT text, however arrived at, that have exercised an influence on the NT.

Resources for Establishing the Original Hebrew Consonantal Text. Once these qualifications have been made, however, it remains the normal function of the OT textual critic in the great majority of cases to establish scientifically the one correct consonantal reading of a Hebrew word or phrase as it was originally set down by the inspired writer and to derive from the Masoretic tradition (*see* MASORA), from the ancient versions [*see* BIBLE, IV (TEXTS AND VERSIONS)], or from Biblical or non-Biblical parallels, linguistic or literary, how that writer meant it to be read and understood.

Witnesses of the Standardized Hebrew Text. For this purpose his resources, though they will not solve all problems, are yet very considerable. The vocalization of the text by the Tiberian Masoretes gives, for the entire Hebrew OT, an understanding of the consonantal text that the textual critic has a duty to appreciate at its full value, not only when he accepts it, but above all when he feels obliged to set it aside. Other resources for the purpose preserved by continuous tradition within the

Jewish community include citations, adaptations, and renderings of the text in *Talmud, *Midrash, and Targum [see BIBLE, IV (TEXTS AND VERSIONS), 11], particularly for the earlier period; from these a basic reading may be inferred. To them should be added the formal testimony of medieval Jewish exegetes such as David *Kimchi, *Rashi (Rabbi Shelomoh Yiṣḥaq), and Abraham *Ibn Ezra as to how the text should be read; also the work of translators such as Gaon *Sa'adia ben Joseph, and the various medieval Jewish Biblical texts, largely from the Cairo *Geniza, that fall outside the Tiberian Masoretic tradition.

Witnesses almost always to the same consonantal text as that supposed in the foregoing, namely, that stabilized c. A.D. 100, are the Latin Vulgate and the Syriac *Peshitta versions (when these have not been influenced by the Septuagint), as well as the Hebrew second column of Origen's Hexapla, and the late Greek translators Aquila and Symmachus. See BIBLE, IV (TEXTS AND VERSIONS) 5, 6, 7, 8, 9, 12, 13. The evidence of Theodotion needs now to be reassessed; but though it may frequently include materials from the 1st Christian century, these too tend to correspond with the received text in many cases. The great value that these witnesses possess is therefore most often in the realm of interpretation and rarely enough as independent witnesses to a distinctive text. The Hebrew scroll materials of the 2d Christian century from the Wadi *Murabba'āt represent the same fixed text.

Evidence from the Septuagint and Samaritan Pentateuch. To obtain a critique of the standardized text through materials of a comparable age, and to form an idea of how it came to be established, there are available principally the Septuagint (LXX), the Samaritan Pentateuch, and the Hebrew texts and fragments of Targum from Khirbet Qumran and Masada (see DEAD SEA SCROLLS). They are occasionally supported by surviving traces of early readings in the other witnesses already mentioned, especially the Palestinian forms of Targum and the Peshitta. Within this earlier period, ranging from the 1st Christian century back to the beginning of the 3d century B.C. (for parts of the LXX), witnesses must still be evaluated, not merely counted. Thus, it is methodologically quite wrong to presume that, because the Samaritan Pentateuch and the LXX together witness to a reading different from the received Hebrew text, the reading in question must be preferred. The Samaritan Pentateuch is representative of an expanded, reworked, Palestinian type now known also from the Qumran scrolls. In itself the Samaritan form of this text scarcely antedates 100 B.C., and many of its fuller readings are rather scribal interpretations of the same basic text as the received one than survivals of earlier readings not otherwise attainable. In view of the complicated history of the transmission of the LXX, with the many recensions it has undergone, and the initial difficulty of rendering a Hebrew sentence exactly into readable Greek, the Greek version has to be scrutinized most carefully before its evidence is applied. The reinforced credit that it receives from the Qumran Hebrew evidence, in the Pentateuch and Samuel particularly, does not make it an equally good witness in Isaia or Job. In these books there is much to be learned from it, but since their translators never set themselves the goal of reflecting in Greek the full wording of the original, reconstructions based on it can easily be truncated or misleading. The only safe procedure in use of LXX evidence is to move from a general understanding of the techniques and the competence of the translator(s) in a specific book, and of the nature of the Hebrew text presupposed by the rendering, to a consideration of the testimony it offers in a specific passage. Use of the LXX is additionally complicated by the fact that the earliest form of it sometimes survives scarcely, or not at all, in the Greek manuscript tradition but has to be reconstructed from secondary translations of it, especially the Old Latin, Coptic, or Ethiopic. Important evidence for the state of the OT text in the period before A.D. 100 is obtainable also from *Philo Judaeus (the running discourse, not the *lemmata* or formal opening citations), Flavius *Josephus, and the NT.

Evidence from Qumran Texts. The Qumran scrolls, now the oldest Hebrew witnesses for the considerable part of the OT they preserve, have the limitation that they were prepared on private initiative and circulated apart from any standardizing authority. If this means that their individual readings cannot be accepted without some reserve, they are nevertheless very instructive for the technique of OT text transmission and study; they open up a whole new period in this regard, and when they are more widely and fully known they will place the Masoretic, the LXX, and the Samaritan texts in a new perspective that will make greater discrimination possible in the evaluation of the evidence previously at hand. One point that they do suggest is that the repair of a damaged text in one OT passage by calling on a separate place of similar import is an ancient technique; the LXX form of Ps 71(72).17 is probably to be viewed as a conscious use of Gn 12.3 in this way. Similar accommodations of the text occur in the LXX of Isaia and in the large Qumran scroll (1Q Isᵃ) of the Hebrew text of that Prophet.

Means for Resolving Textual Difficulties. When all available explicit evidence for the text has been canvassed, including citations or allusions in the non-Biblical "Dead Sea Scrolls" and from apocryphal and pseudepigraphical works bearing on the OT, there still remains a task for the textual critic. The substantial preservation of the OT books as a witness to the progress of divine revelation is a fact; and over the centuries the text shows a remarkable degree of integrity and of faithful transmission. Yet it is also a fact that in matters of detail and in the transmission of some books and passages [e.g., Osee ch. 4–6; 3 Kings ch. 7; Job ch. 24–27; Ps 140(141).6–7] there are difficulties that cannot be resolved on the basis of the known text or any interpretation of it that has been preserved. There then remain several possibilities.

Recourse to Other Semitic Languages. The first and in many cases the most prudent and the most fruitful expedient is to presume the consonantal text correct, and to explain it by lexical or grammatical features known from other parts of the OT (as was done even in ancient times) or from non-Biblical texts in the languages akin to Hebrew. This latter alternative is modern, and at present the appeal to Ugaritic, Phoenician, Akkadian, Aramaic, Arabic, and later Hebrew literature may be proposed as significant in a decreasing order of relative importance (the list is not exhaustive). Respect for the Biblical context, which seldom admits of wholesale reinterpretation in the interest of a newly identified form or meaning, and respect for the structure of Hebrew poetry are necessary for the successful employment of this method. It cannot be used to the exclusion of other methods of textual study, and like any other, it often has claims made for it in particular cases which go beyond its actual merits.

Detection of Scribal Errors. Use of evidence from the versions will already have provided the textual critic with an insight into various kinds of indeliberate error to which the copyist of a Hebrew text may be especially liable; as well as to the manner in which such copyists have tended to preserve, in whole or in part, duplicate or alternative wordings of a passage and to absorb the additional material into the continuous text. Common scribal errors are the transposition of letters, words, or phrases; the confusion of letters or words of very similar appearance (in either the square-letter or the earlier paleo-Hebrew script); faulty division of sentences or of words. Changing orthographic practice in Hebrew within the OT period, from sparse and strictly consonantal at first to a fairly copious use of certain consonants in a part of the textual tradition in the Hellenistic period as reading signs for purely vocalic sounds, and then to a restrained but somewhat inconsistent use of the same signs in all of the received text tradition, yielded particular occasions for misreadings and misinterpretations at each of the three stages. While these features are helpful in accounting for the state of the received text when evidence from other ancient sources offers a more intelligible and appropriate reading, they must also be considered when the evidence is all for one same reading, yet the reading in question conveys no suitable sense. The element of conjecture that is present in textual criticism at this point is not always greater in positing indeliberate error of a familiar kind than it would be in positing, on the basis of non-Biblical literature, forgotten meanings or associations, or grammatical forms or usages unknown to the later stages of the Hebrew language.

In either of the two cases mentioned, therefore, the principles should obtain, that the textual critic advocates, because of his method, no turn of thought out of harmony with the known mentality of the particular book or writer; and that the emendation proposed for the sake of the intelligibility of the text is not to be made the basis for a historical, or above all for a doctrinal, construct not witnessed to by other and unambiguous testimony.

Textual Emendation. Careful study of the context and of related passages will help to confirm the likelihood, perhaps even the necessity, of emendations arrived at in either of the above ways if it can be shown that the general context or the book as a whole gains in intelligibility in a direction in keeping with its established thought patterns, from the adoption of the proposed reading. This will be true with especial force in poetic passages, if it can be shown that the normal processes of composition involving parallelism within the line and a calculated climactic effect are violated by the received reading, but apparently reconstituted by the proposed emendation. In general the ease with which a reading based partly on conjecture both fulfils the requirements of the particular context and at the same time helps to account for the actual form or forms historically transmitted, will be an argument in its favor.

See also BIBLE, IV (TEXTS AND VERSIONS), 2.

Bibliography: W. L. MORAN, "The Biblical Language in Its Northwest Semitic Background" in G. E. WRIGHT, ed., *The Bible and the Ancient Near East* (Garden City, N.Y. 1961) 54–72. H. M. ORLINSKY, "The Textual Criticism of the O.T.," *ibid.* 113–132. A. JEPSEN, "Von den Aufgaben der Alttestamentlichen Textkritik," VetTest Suppl 9 (1963) 332–341. P. W. SKEHAN, "Qumran and the Present State of O.T. Text Studies: The Masoretic Text," JBiblLit 78 (1959) 21–25. R. MARCUS, "On the Textual Criticism of the Hebrew Bible," *ibid.* 68 (1949) 29–34. J. COPPENS, "La Critique du texte hébreu de l'A.T.," *Biblica* 25 (1944) 9–49. S. TALMON, "Double Readings in the Massoretic Text," *Textus* 1 (1960) 144–184; "Aspects of the Textual Transmission of the Bible in the Light of Qumran Manuscripts," *ibid.* 4 (1964) 95–132. F. DELITZSCH, *Die Lese- und Schreibfehler im A.T.* (Berlin 1920). A. BERTSCH, LexThK² 2:371–372. L. DENNEFELD, DBSuppl 2:240–256. R. RENDTORFF, RGG³ 1:1166–71.

[P. W. SKEHAN]

3. TEXTUAL CRITICISM OF THE NEW TESTAMENT

Ecclesiastical writers as early as St. Irenaeus were conscious of variations in existing MSS of the NT, but not until the era of the printed text was an effort made to organize variant readings in a methodical way in order to recover the original. Thus began scientific NT textual criticism. This article explains causes for early textual variations, critical efforts to improve the NT texts, the characteristics of the NT text types, and finally the present position of NT textual criticism.

Early Textual Variations. For more than 200 years after the composition of its individual books, the NT was diffused, not by professional scribes working under careful supervision but by devout Christians seeking copies of their Holy Scripture for liturgical and devotional use, for instruction, and apologetics. These copies circulated widely with little control; they were carried to most of the civilized world by Christian teachers eager to communicate their new faith. To Christians these writings were not dead texts but the embodiment of living tradition handed down from the Apostles. Early Christian scribes were heirs to a variety of oral traditions and had no single text that was universally accepted as final authority; consciously and unconsciously they modified NT MSS by harmonizing parallel passages, inserting local recollections, clarifying obscure passages, or deleting details. Earliest textual modifications existed even before the inspired books, written originally on papyrus scrolls and transferred to the convenient codex form in the 2d century, were collected into a single NT corpus.

Study of variations in the Greek MSS and in the versions show that most changes resulted not from scribal errors but from deliberate editorial modifications, which were at work in two directions. The first tendency was to adapt and harmonize, especially in the Gospels. This produced the widely diffused popular or "wild" 2d- and 3d-century texts, which have become better known from modern papyrus discoveries (*see* PAPYROLOGY). A second trend, striving to counteract these, was the effort of trained editors to eliminate such adaptations and to transmit the original text. Such efforts can be traced first to the great center of Hellenistic textual criticism, Alexandria. They soon spread to Caesarea in Palestine where the martyr Pamphilius (d. 310) established an important Christian library. Another significant influence upon the Gospels during the latter half of the 2d century was a synopsis made by Tatian. Although composed probably in Syriac, this *Diatessaron was soon translated into other languages, including Greek, and helped to diffuse a short form of the text.

As a result of such influences the more than 4,900 extant Greek NT MSS, a small fraction of the total once existing, contain more variant readings than there are words in the original texts. In the Pauline letters most of these are of a stylistic nature; in the Gospels numerous glosses appear. Many of them are characteristic of the ecclesiastical text that developed around Constantinople for use in the Greek Church. This polished but critically inferior text was the form most widely prevalent during the Middle Ages, and the first printed texts were based on such MSS. Under the name "received text," coined by the Elzevir brothers in 1633, it continued to prevail for 2 more centuries.

Critical Efforts to Improve NT Text. The French Oratorian Richard *Simon not only was one of the first to point out the inferior quality of the received text, but he also showed a way to improve editions by establishing a relationship between the Codex Bezae, the Latin, and the Syriac texts in 1690. His work stimulated research to evaluate and group witnesses to the NT text with a view of recovering the original. In a letter of 1720 containing his "Proposals for Printing" the NT, Richard *Bentley formulated valid principles for editing the Greek text prevailing in the 4th century through a comparison of the oldest Greek MSS with the Vulgate. The first NT editor to group witnesses systematically in his critical apparatus according to the type of variants was John A. Bengel in 1734. He arranged MSS according to families, tribes, and ultimately into two nations, the older of which he called African and the more recent Asian. J. S. *Semler, in his introduction to an improved edition of J. J. Wettstein's text in 1764, attributed the division into text types to three recensions, which he called Alexandrian, Eastern, and Western. Making use of these studies in his edition of 1777, J. J. *Griesbach divided the Gospel MSS into three groups: (1) the Western family, headed by Codex Bezae; (2) a small Alexandrian family led by Codex L; (3) the family of Constantinople, the ecclesiastical text to which most of the witnesses belonged.

Although these editors of the received text were amassing information needed to improve future editions, at the same time, because of a lack of early witnesses, they created misconceptions still common in introductions to the NT. Semler's use of the term recension conveyed the impression that the text types were products of the critical revision of a single scholar, such as Hesychius in Egypt or Lucian at Antioch, instead of a long process as is now commonly recognized. The misleading term "Western" given to popular texts still creates confusion. A more accurate term was that of "common edition" by J. L. *Hug, German Catholic critic, who also was first to show the great importance of Codex Vaticanus (B) in 1808.

The many assaults upon the received text produced a reaction at the other extreme when Karl Lachmann edited a text based solely upon ancient MSS in 1830. By ignoring other witnesses, he renounced the possibility of going back further than the 4th-century text found in the Greek Fathers at the time of the Council of Nicaea and in the Latin Vulgate. Vast new resources for NT textual criticism were opened by Konstantin von *Tischendorf (1815–74), "the man with an apparatus," as E. von Dobschütz styled him. He made available an unparalleled amount of material by his discovery, collation, and publication of MSS. The critic who undertook to synthesize all available information was Fenton J. A. *Hort, author of the masterful introductory volume for the edition of the Greek text that he published with

Brooke F. *Westcott in 1881. Basing his conclusions on the principle that the value of a MS as a witness depends on its relationship to the author's autograph, Hort sought to recover the original by the use of the genealogical method. Thus, despite the great age of Western witnesses, he considered their popular origin as impugning their critical value. He concluded that the original text had been preserved free of contamination in a small number of ancient uncials, especially B, which he called the "neutral" text. Herman Hoskier called this the "Hortian heresy," and other critics have presented evidence to show that Codex B also was the product of critical editorial work. This evidence has mounted with the discovery of the Chester Beatty and the Bodmer papyri, which are key factors in the revolution taking place in NT textual criticism. Until the new discoveries are integrated into comprehensive critical editions, however, the Westcott-Hort text will continue to exercise a fundamental influence.

New Testament Text Types. The outstanding accomplishment of NT textual criticism to date (1965) has been to group extant witnesses into text types according to their outstanding characteristics. Critics are continuing to investigate their origin and development, and terminology still fluctuates, but tested results may be summarized as follows.

Popular Text. This is not a stable or unified type but rather the extant evidence from MSS, ecclesiastical writers, and ancient versions of the numerous popular texts of the 2d and 3d centuries. Unfortunately it was called "Western" because the Old Latin Version preserved many characteristic readings. *See* BIBLE, IV (TEXTS AND VERSIONS), 13. H. von *Soden rejected this term only to substitute the heterogeneous Iota or Jerusalem text, which he divided into twelve groups for the Gospels and four for Paul. M. J. *Lagrange called it the D text, but F. G. *Kenyon and most contemporary critics refer to it as the Delta text. Gunther Zuntz has demonstrated that, until true "Western" readings are isolated from the wide range of popular readings, research on this type will not make significant progress. Fundamental marks of such popular texts are their great freedom, tendency to harmonize in the Gospels, and the presence of additions, especially in the last part of Luke and in Acts. At times its witnesses exhibit a shorter text. Where Hort felt that these were original, he designated them as "Western non-interpolations." Of Hort's 27 examples, Lagrange accepted the short reading as certainly correct only in Mt 21.44; 27.49b; Jn 3.31. In Paul popular readings are less sharply defined and less frequent. Principal witnesses are the Codex Bezae, although this uncial has other features also, the Old Latin, the Sinaitic Syriac Gospel *palimpsest, *Marcion, and most Fathers before the Council of Nicaea and for Paul the Greek and Latin Codices D, E, F, G, and 565.

Alexandrian Text. This is the most appropriate name for the type used as the basis of the Westcott-Hort edition, although Hort called it "neutral." Following J. L. Hug, Von Soden attributed it to a recension by the Egyptian bishop and martyr Hesychius (d. 310). His theory has recently been advocated by Sidney Jellicoe [JBiblLit 82 (1963) 409–418]. However, the time of Hesychius is much too late, because this form of the text derives from the critical use of excellent early MSS now lost but available to skillful Alexandrian editors anxious to recover the original. Its rare witnesses are the best single form of the NT text, but they are not without defects and show a progressive corruption from popular influence. Hence, critics, such as H. V. G. Tasker, W. H. P. Hatch, B. M. Metzger, and G. Zuntz, favor the designation of "proto-Alexandrian" for better witnesses, chiefly Codex B, P46 for Paul, cursive 1739, Clement of Alexandria, Origen, and both Coptic versions. Remaining witnesses are called simply Alexandrian and include uncials Sinaiticus ('aleph or S), Alexandrinus (except for the Gospels), CKLΨΔ, cursives 33 and (for the Gospels) 579 and 892.

Byzantine Text. Hort called the Byzantine text Syrian because of its relation to the Syriac *Peshitta and traced its origin to *Lucian of Antioch, martyred in 312 A.D. It is clear, however, that this form of the NT developed its distinctive characteristics only gradually by the persistent efforts of churchmen to produce a clear, complete, and polished text. These late and secondary qualities are seen most clearly in the Gospels: difficulties are removed, narratives harmonized, and interpolations admitted. From Constantinople this type spread throughout the Greek Church and became the official ecclesiastical text from about the 8th century. Von Soden, who called it the Kappa text, isolated various stages until it reached its final form in about the 12th century. It is found in more than 200 cursive codices and in the early printed editions. Although its critical value is inferior, this type, which many critics now prefer to call the Alpha text, cannot be ignored, because at times it preserves ancient readings lost from other extant witnesses.

Caesarean Text of the Gospels. This elusive type, whose origin Lagrange put at the "nerve center of all NT criticism" (*Critique Rationelle,* 164), was isolated chiefly by the research of K. *Lake, Von Soden, and R. P. Blake, but it did not receive this name until 1924 when B. H. Streeter concluded that it was the local form of the Gospel text found at Caesarea. Discovery of the Chester Beatty fragment (P45) proved Lagrange's contention that its place of origin was Egypt, although distinct from the Alexandrian text. This form, which is more often described as a recensional process, was carefully studied by Msgr. Teófilo Ayuso. He proved that it must be divided into a "pre-Caesarean" type, older than Origen, whose witnesses are P45, the Freer Codex (W), families 1 and 13, and the later, properly called "Caesarean" type, headed by the Koridethi Codex (Θ), cursives 565 and 700, with some support from Eusebius. Corresponding to this critical work on the Gospels at Caesarea is an edition of Acts and Paul, referred to as the Euthalian edition, but not adequately investigated.

Present Position of NT Textual Criticism. Difficulties in this study come not from lack of materials but from an abundance so great that no man can control all of it. The NT is better attested than any ancient book, and current critical editions show remarkable agreement. Studies by K. Aland showed that, among editors of manual editions for the text of Mark, substantial agreement approaches 99 per cent. G. Zuntz optimistically holds that 99 per cent of the original text of the Pauline Epistles is or could be recovered. Yet, much work remains to be done. Lagrange made the last great synthesis of materials in 1935. His plea at that time for a flexible "rational criticism" is becoming more popular. The most pressing need, pointed out as early as 1933 by Kenyon, is for a complete critical apparatus of the NT. Such an apparatus, however, must be supplemented by studies on the versions and the Fathers and by funda-

mental research on specific problems, such as that of Josef Schmid on Apocalypse and M. E. Boismard on John.

See also BIBLE, IV (TEXTS AND VERSIONS), 3.

Bibliography: L. VAGANAY, *An Introduction to the Textual Criticism of the N.T.,* tr. B. V. MILLER (St. Louis 1937). M. J. LAGRANGE, *Critique textuelle,* v.2 of *Introduction à l'étude du Nouveau Testament,* 2 v. (2d ed. Paris 1935–37). H. J. VOGELS, *Handbuch der Textkritik des N.T.* (2d ed. Bonn 1955). J. DUPLACY, *Où en est la critique textuelle du N.T.?* (Paris 1959), repr. from RechScRel 45 (1957) 419–441; 46 (1958) 270–313, 431–462; additional material in the *Bulletin* of RechScRel 50 (1962) 242–263, 564–598; 51 (1963) 432–462. B. M. METZGER, *Chapters in the History of N.T. Textual Criticism* (Leiden 1963). K. ALAND, "The Present Position of N.T. Textual Criticism," in *Studia Evangelica,* ed. K. ALAND et al. (TU 73; 1959) 717–731. H. H. OLIVER, "Present Trends in the Textual Criticism of the N.T.," *Journal of Bible and Religion* 30 (1962) 308–320. E. C. COLWELL, "The Origin of Texttypes of N.T. Manuscripts," in *Early Christian Origins,* ed. A. P. WIKGREN (Chicago 1961) 128–138. A. F. J. KLIJN, *A Survey of the Researches into the Western Text of the Gospels and Acts* (Utrecht 1949); NovTest 3 (1959) 1–27, 161–173. G. ZUNTZ, "Réflexions sur l'histoire du texte paulinien," RevBibl 59 (1952) 5–22. H. J. VOGELS and J. SCHMID, LexThK² 2:372–375. H. J. VOGELS and L. PIROT, DB Suppl 2:256–274. G. D. KILPATRICK, RGG³ 1:1171–74. EncDict Bibl 2419–22.

[J. M. REESE]

BIBLE, VI (EXEGESIS)

By Biblical exegesis is meant the exposition of a passage or a book of the Sacred Scriptures. After an introductory section treating of the nature and forms of Biblical exegesis, this article first offers an account of its history, to show how the Bible was interpreted throughout the centuries, and then sets forth the rules of Biblical *hermeneutics that govern the correct interpretation of the Scriptures.

1. INTRODUCTORY

Since the Bible as a divinely inspired book is a unique work of literature, its exegesis differs in many respects from the interpretation of other ancient documents.

Nature. On the one hand, the Sacred Scriptures are the products of many human authors who lived at various times over at least a millennium and wrote in several different literary genres; on the other hand, all the Scriptures were written under divine inspiration and so have God as their principal author. Therefore, Biblical exegesis employs, not only the sciences that are used in the study of other ancient documents that come from a culture differing considerably from the modern, such as philology, history, archeology, and so forth, but also the theological disciplines that enable the exegete to obtain a deeper understanding of God's word and revelation as contained in the Scriptures. A synthesis of the theological exegesis of the Bible forms the basis of *Biblical theology. Sciences that are auxiliary to Biblical exegesis are the rules of interpretation or Biblical hermeneutics (see section 3, below) and the study of each book as a whole, which is the subject of *Biblical introductions.

Forms. Even a translation of the Scriptures is, to a certain extent, a form of exegesis; for unless a version is extremely literal, it involves a considerable amount of interpretation in the sense of explanation. The more free or paraphrastic a translation is, the more exegetical it is. Short exegetical notes, usually written on the margin of the page of a Bible, are known as Biblical *glosses. In former times an exegetical note, especially if rather long, was known as a *scholium. A collection of exegetical notes excerpted from the writings of the Church Fathers form so-called Biblical *catenae.

The fullest form, however, of Biblical exegesis is that of *Biblical commentaries. The scope of a strictly scientific commentary is to set forth as faithfully as possible the thought of the author by using all available scientific means in so far as they apply, such as textual criticism [to establish the original text; see BIBLE, IV (TEXTS AND VERSIONS), 1, 2, 3], literary criticism (to ascertain the specific type of literary genre in which the book is written; see LITERARY GENRES, BIBLICAL; FORM CRITICISM, BIBLICAL), philology (see BIBLICAL LANGUAGES), geography (see PALESTINE), history, and so forth. But since every book of the Bible is not only a human document but also a record of God's revelation, a genuine commentary should set forth also the religious message or *kerygma of the book. Moralizing conclusions, however, that do not flow directly from the Biblical text belong to *homiletics rather than to exegesis. In the Middle Ages such moralizing notes were often called postils or in Latin postillae, from the full phrase post illa verba textus (after the words of the text).

Bibliography: R. SCHNACKENBURG and K. H. SCHELKE, Lex ThK² 3:1273–74. EncDictBibl 1069–71.

[L. F. HARTMAN]

2. HISTORY OF EXEGESIS

In the various periods of history, ever since the Bible was accepted as the inspired word of God, men have endeavored to explain and interpret its meaning through what is known as Biblical *exegesis. But every age has had its own characteristic exegesis. This article treats of the following types of exegesis principally according to historical sequence: (1) the exegesis of the OT made in the NT, (2) Jewish exegesis, (3) patristic exegesis, (4) medieval, Renaissance, and 18th-century exegesis, (5) exegesis of the OT in the 19th and 20th centuries, and (6) exegesis of the NT in the 19th and 20th centuries.

EXEGESIS OF THE OLD TESTAMENT IN THE NEW TESTAMENT

Modern stress on the essential unity of the Bible has drawn attention to the necessity of understanding how and to what extent the OT is used in the NT. The reader of any Bible edited with copious marginal references to OT texts knows how extensively NT writers cite the OT directly or indirectly.

Quotations from the Old Testament. In the NT there are more than 200 direct quotations from the OT, more than half of which, 118, are found in the Pauline Epistles (see L. Venard, Robert-Tricot 1:679). If references of all kinds are counted, the total number is about 350, of which about 300 are cited according to the Septuagint (LXX) version. Matthew's manner of quoting the OT is noteworthy; when he is using Greek sources (i.e., when he depends on Mark) he retains their Greek wording; when working independently, he generally quotes an OT text according to the Hebrew, though on occasion the influence of the LXX can be traced. For example, in Mt 21.16 Psalm 8.3 is cited according to the LXX for apologetic reasons; see A. Wikenhauser, New Testament Introduction, tr. J. Cunningham (New York 1958) 195. Except for the author of the Epistle to the Hebrews, who always quotes the LXX exactly,

most NT authors show little concern for exactness in their quotations. Their practice of free rendering of OT texts must not be ascribed to memory lapses, but rather to common literary custom or, as in many Pauline texts, to an exegetical purpose; see E. Ellis, Paul's Use of the OT (London 1957) 14–15. Some NT writers use interesting combinations in their OT quotations. Paul, for instance, uses three types of combined texts: (1) OT texts strung together to form a single quotation [e.g., Rom 3.10–18 is composed of Ps 13(14).1–3; 5.10; 139(140).4; 9B(10).7; Is 59.7–8; Ps 35(36).2]; (2) chain quotations or ḥāraz (e.g., Rom 9.25–29); (3) looser midrashic commentary (e.g., Romans ch. 9–11; Galatians ch. 3). See Ellis, op. cit., 11, 186 for charts of Pauline combinations.

Interpretations of Old Testament Passages. The NT interpretation of the OT reveals the following characteristics: (1) the allegorical method, so venerated by interpreters of ancient literature and so extensively used by the Alexandrian Jew, Philo, is employed only infrequently by NT writers. Paul expressly says that his interpretation of the story of *Agar and *Ismael (Gn 21.9–21) is by way of allegory (Gal 4.21–31). The story of Melchisedec (Gn 14.18–20) receives similar treatment in Heb 7.1–10. Such examples, however, are rare. The allegorical method is not characteristic of NT interpretation of OT texts. (2) Though their interpretations were generally literal in the wide sense of being based on the literal meaning of the OT text, NT writers exercised a great deal of freedom with respect to the original historical sense of the OT text quoted. Nevertheless, these writers were always conscious of the OT as history, and it is not likely that they would ever be unmindful of the historical setting of the OT texts they used; see C. H. Dodd, The Old Testament In The New (Philadelphia 1963) 8. (3) Literary allusions to OT words, phraseology, and imagery abound, reflecting the NT writer's familiarity with the OT. (4) OT texts are sometimes cited by way of illustration or analogy, as Dt 21.23 in Gal 3.13. (5) OT texts, especially from the Prophets, are sometimes cited as direct proof of a NT writer's argument. Such is the use of the *Servant of the Lord Oracles from Is 42.1–4; 49.1–7; 50.4–11; 52.13–53.12.

For St. Paul's exegetical method and relation to rabbinic exegesis, see especially: W. D. Davies, Paul and Rabbinic Judaism (London 1948, rev. ed. 1955, repr. 1964) and J. Bonsirven, Exégèse rabbinique et exégèse paulinienne (Paris 1939). From his study of the NT writers use of the OT, C. H. Dodd [According to the Scriptures (London 1952)] concludes that individual passages cited are often only pointers to the OT total context, which is really the basis of the argument.

JEWISH EXEGESIS

A natural division of the Jewish exegesis of the OT is between that of the Talmudic period (from the beginning of the 1st to the end of the 8th Christian century) and that of the Middle Ages (from c. 800 to c. 1300).

Talmudic Period. The object of the rabbinical exegesis from the 1st century B.C. to the end of the 8th Christian century was twofold: (1) to determine precisely the true meaning of the text, and (2) to establish the Biblical basis for the *halakah or system of jurisprudence composed of traditional legal decisions, commandments of the ancient Fathers, and prescriptions of the Scribes, and to support the *haggadah or nonjuridical interpretations and traditions forming an immense literature that was historical, folkloristic, and homiletic in character (see A. Vincent, 42–69; J. Bonsirven, DBSuppl 4:561–569; and Robert-Tricot, 684–693, especially the translator's notes). To achieve the first object required a literal exegesis, and in fact this became characteristic of Jewish juridical commentaries of the 2d century of the Christian Era. However, the use of texts as proofs sometimes led to an abuse of the literal sense.

Jewish exegesis is found in a great body of rabbinical literature, which is composed of the following: (1) the *Mishnah and its additions in the *Tosephta (explanatory notes on oral traditions not included in the Mishnah); (2) the *Gemarah, written in Aramaic, which commented on, applied, and widely extended the teaching of the Mishnah, as well as incorporating non-Mishnah material; and (3) the midrashim (see MIDRASHIC LITERATURE), which were rabbinical commentaries on either the legal texts of the Bible (halakah) or on the historical or moral texts (haggadah). The Mishnah and its commentary, the Gemarah, comprise the *Talmud. See Vincent, 54; and Robert-Tricot 1:685–687, footnotes.

The Torah (Mosaic Law) was always considered to be the basis of all prescriptions applied to new circumstances of Jewish life, no matter how far removed from the Law these appeared to be. They were linked to the Law by certain logical rules. Hillel (see HILLEL AND SHAMMAI) had these seven: (1) from the less to the greater and from the simple to the difficult, (2) from like to like by analogy, (3) according to one passage in the Law, (4) according to two passages in the Law, (5) from the general to the particular and from the particular to the general, (6) explanation of one text by another, and (7) explanation of a text by the context. Rabbi Ishmael ben Elisha (d. c. 135) increased these 7 to 13; to Rabbi Eliezer ben Yose (d. c. 150) 32 are attributed. See Vincent, 46. In spite of its well-known defects, Talmudic exegesis contains much that is of permanent value to Biblical scholarship, as some of the early Fathers, as well as the scholastic and Reformation exegetes, were well aware. Historians of exegesis are not unmindful of the contribution of early rabbinical exegesis to the treasury of Christian interpretation.

Middle Ages. Biblical exegesis in the strict sense, as distinct from the use that the Talmudic rabbis made of the Bible, began among the Jews in the 9th century primarily as a reaction against the Karaites (see KARAISM), a Jewish sect that arose toward the end of the 8th century. The Karaites rejected the traditional teachings of the Talmud and demanded a return to the Bible understood in the literal sense. The orthodox rabbis were therefore forced, in defense of traditional Judaism, to study the Hebrew Scriptures and explain their literal sense ($p^e\check{s}\bar{a}t$) in conformity with orthodox Judaism. A contributing factor was the contact that the rabbis of the time made with Arabic scholars, particularly in Spain, whose grammatical and lexicographical studies in connection with the study of the *Koran led the Jewish scholars to make similar studies of the Hebrew Bible. An additional reason for the improvement in Jewish exegesis in the Middle Ages was the growing interest among Jews as well as among Moslems and Christians in Aristotelian philosophy, which led to a more rational method in the study of the Sacred Scriptures.

The pioneer of the new Jewish exegesis was the arch-opponent of the Karaites, Gaon *Sa'adia ben Joseph (822–942). The study of the Scriptures was only one of his many fields of interest, but here, besides his Arabic translation of the Bible, he produced the first Hebrew dictionary and the first Hebrew grammar. In the East, however, where he lived, he had no scholarly successors. His influence was felt, instead, in Spain and later in France. Spanish Jewry of the Middle Ages had several important Hebrew philologists, such as Menachem ben Saruk (c. 910–c. 970), Dunash ben Labrat (c. 920–c. 990), Judah ben David Ḥayyuj (c. 940–c. 1010), and especially *Jonah Marinus (Abū'l Walīd Merwān ibn-Janaḥ; c. 990–c. 1050), the greatest Hebrew grammarian of the Middle Ages.

The medieval Jewish exegetes built on the work of these philologists. The most important of the commentators in Spain was Abraham ben Meïr *ibn Ezra (c. 1092–1167). On the whole, his Biblical commentaries are based on the literal sense, often arrived at by philological or grammatical arguments. A product of the Spanish school, though he spent most of his life in Egypt, was the renowned Jewish scholar *Maimonides (Moses ben Maimon; 1135–1204). Although he wrote no commentary, in his works, particularly his *Guide to the Perplexed,* he explained many Biblical passages according to philosophical or even rationalistic principles. The influence of the Jewish exegetes of Spain soon reached France. At Troyes in northern France the renowned Talmudist, *Rashi (Rabbi Shelomoh ben Yiṣḥaq; 1041–1105), produced popular commentaries on almost all the books of the Hebrew Bible. The commentaries of his grandson, Samuel ben Meïr, known also as Rashbam (c. 1085–c. 1160), though more diffused, are of greater scientific value. At Narbonne in southern France the *Kimchi (Kimḥi) family, Joseph (c. 1105–c. 1170) and his sons Moses (d. 1190) and particularly David (c. 1160–1235), wrote Biblical commentaries that are still valuable for their philological and grammatical observations. The commentaries of the Spanish Jewish scholar, *Naḥmanides (Moses ben Naḥman, known also as Ramban; c. 1195–c. 1270), though containing much valuable material, indulge too often in mystical, cabalistic speculations. After the 13th century medieval Jewish exegesis fell almost completely under the spell of the *Cabala, and the works of this period are thus practically worthless from an exegetical viewpoint. But the writings of the earlier Jewish lexicographers, grammarians, and exegetes proved extremely useful to the Christian Hebraists of the later Middle Ages and the Renaissance [see HEBREW STUDIES (IN THE CHRISTIAN CHURCH)], and they still merit study by modern Biblical scholars.

PATRISTIC EXEGESIS

The history of exegesis in the patristic period (extending to the beginning of the 7th century) can best be treated by considering separately the Fathers before Origen, Origen, the school of Alexandria, the school of Antioch, and the Latin Fathers (see PATROLOGY).

Before Origen. The Apostolic Fathers left no Biblical exegesis in the strict sense. They used the Biblical text either to support their exhortations to lead a fruitful Christian life or, as in the case of Pope St. *Clement

I in his *First Epistle to the Corinthians* (c. A.D. 98), to form a spiritual mosaic of scriptural texts. Generally, the Apostolic Fathers did not attempt to prove their teaching from Biblical texts. A notable exception, however, was the author of the *Epistle of *Barnabas,* who had recourse to an allegorical and typical interpretation of the OT to prove that the Jews failed to understand properly God's will and the Mosaic Law, even its clearest precepts; for example, God's inspired precept regarding abstinence from certain meats really commanded the Jews to flee from the particular vices signified by impure animals (see G. Bardy, Robert-Tricot 1:695). The Christians, said the author, were the first to understand the OT properly.

The Apologists of the 2d century, in addressing unbelievers, could hardly appeal to the OT as proofs of their teaching but had to be content to urge the antiquity of the OT over pagan works. Although it was not characteristic of the Apologists, St. *Justin Martyr (d. c. 165) used arguments from the Prophets effectively in both his first *Apology* and his *Dialogue Against Trypho.* Second-century heretics attacked this type of proof by trying to underscore the apparent contradictions between the teaching of the OT and that of Jesus; hence the origin of Marcion's *Antithesis* and Apelles's *Syllogisms.* St. *Irenaeus (c. 140–c. 202) in his *Adversus Haereses* and *Tertullian (c. 160–c. 230) in his *Contra Marcionem* and in other works defended the OT against the heretics. Heracleon (2d century), a Gnostic, wrote the oldest commentary on St. John, using principally the allegorical method. Ptolemy, another Gnostic, in a *Letter to Flora,* was probably the first one to attempt to place exegesis on a firm, scientific foundation. (For the light shed on Gnosticism by the discovery of numerous Coptic texts near Nag' Hammâdi in Egypt, see CHENOBOSKION, GNOSTIC TEXTS OF.)

Origen. The first Biblical scholar to study critically the LXX was Origen (c. 185–c. 254), one of the most important figures in the early history of exegesis (*see* ORIGEN AND ORIGENISM). His many exegetical writings appear in scholia (simple notes on difficult or obscure passages; *see* SCHOLIUM), commentaries, and homilies. He wrote scholia on the first four books of the Pentateuch, on Isaia, Ecclesiastes, the Psalms, Matthew, John, Galatians, and the Apocalypse. He commented on Genesis ch. 1–4, on several Psalms, twice on the Canticle of Canticles, and on Matthew, Luke, John, and the Pauline Epistles except 1 and 2 Corinthians and Timothy. In 1941 at Tura, a few miles south of Cairo, a papyrus containing fragments of the original Greek of Origen's commentary on Romans was discovered. His homilies, about 200 of which have been preserved, were delivered at Caesarea in Palestine.

Unlike his predecessors, Origen set down his ideas on hermeneutics, especially in the fourth book of his *De principiis.* Applying Plato's threefold distinction of body, soul, and spirit to the senses of Scripture, Origen taught that Holy Scripture contained (1) a corporeal or historical sense, which seems to be simply the ordinary proper literal and historical sense that the Biblical text directly conveys; (2) the psychic or moral sense, generally ignored by Origen in practice, which seems to be concerned with moral correction and is often indistinguishable from (3) the spiritual sense, which embraces all other senses that can be derived from the Biblical text. Origen never claimed that all Scripture contained this threefold sense. He believed that it was possible for the sacred author to err, on rare occasions, regarding the corporeal sense, which would then have to be rejected. Again, allegory was not present in every text. Origen thought that the corporeal sense was sufficient for the needs of the simple faithful, but that the perfect sought a deeper meaning hidden beneath the words. At times his allegory is exaggerated, but he made a permanent contribution to textual criticism, typology, and the allegorical method which was to characterize the exegetical school of Alexandria.

School of Alexandria. The foundation of this first Christian theological school (*see* ALEXANDRIA, SCHOOL OF) is commonly attributed to St. *Pantaenus, of whom very little is known. He was born in Sicily and became a convert to Christianity from Stoicism and taught at the exegetical school of Alexandria toward the end of the 2d century (c. 180).

Clement, Dionysius, and Eusebius. Pantaenus was succeeded by his pupil *Clement of Alexandria (c. 150–c. 215), a scholar of vast erudition, who was strongly influenced in his exegetical method by the allegorical one of Philo. Clement believed that it was of the very nature of higher truths that they should be communicated only through symbols. He acknowledged three senses of Scripture: the literal, the moral, and the prophetical or allegorical. He believed that all Scripture must be interpreted allegorically. His major works, *Stromata, Paedagogus,* and *Protrepticus* are remarkable for their wealth of Biblical erudition.

St. *Dionysius (c. 190–265), Bishop of Alexandria from 247 to 265, stated his exegetical principles in a work entitled *On the Promises,* written in response to an attack on the allegorists by a certain Bishop Nepos. St. Dionysius confessed that much in the Apocalypse was beyond his comprehension, but he did not doubt that it contained many profound and hidden senses. It seems that Dionysius wrote commentaries also on Ecclesiastes and Luke.

*Eusebius of Caesarea (c. 260–c. 339) as a historian was inclined to the literal sense in his exegesis, but he had received training in the allegorical method from *Pamphilus (d. 310), a pupil of Origen. In his commentaries on Isaia, the Psalms, and Luke, Eusebius was generally free from allegorical exaggerations.

Athanasius and Didymus. Of the works of St. *Athanasius (c. 295–373), who was more a defender of orthodoxy and a shepherd of souls than a professional exegete, we have only fragments, a commentary on the Psalms, and a little work entitled *Interpretation of the Psalms,* which reveals his ideas on how to profit best from a prayerful study of the Psalter.

*Didymus the Blind (c. 313–c. 398), for many years the head of the school of Alexandria, wrote commentaries on a large number of the books of the OT and the NT, which were highly praised by St. Jerome. The fraction of these commentaries that has been preserved reveals these characteristics: there are two senses of Scripture, the literal and the spiritual; the OT must be interpreted allegorically and, whenever possible, messianically, if it is to be fully understood; his interpretation of the NT is generally according to the literal sense. As a true disciple of Origen, Didymus had learned from experience to control prudently all allegorical applications. G. Bardy (Robert-Tricot 1:700) suggests that the commentaries of Didymus on Genesis, Job, and Zacharia have apparently been recovered through the discovery of the papyri at Tura (see above).

Cappadocian Fathers. Among the great Cappadocians who were strongly influenced by Origen and the Alexandrians were St. *Basil (*c.* 329–379), St. *Gregory of Nazianzus (*c.* 330–*c.* 390), and St. *Gregory of Nyssa (*c.* 335–394), the younger brother of Basil. St. Basil used Scripture primarily for the instruction and edification of the faithful. His homilies *On the Hexameron* as well as those on various Psalms reflect his intention to use the Bible to nourish the spiritual life of his hearers. St. Gregory of Nazianzus used Scripture in much the same fashion. He was above all else a theologian, and he treated the Scriptures primarily as a *locus theologicus* in his conflicts with the Arians and Apollinarists. The finest exegete of all the Cappadocians was the highly gifted St. Gregory of Nyssa. Although he was an allegorist to the core, he nevertheless knew how to use effectively the literal sense when necessary, e.g., in his *De hominis opificio* and *Explicatio Apologetica in Hexaemeron.* His other works include homilies on Ecclesiastes, the Canticle of Canticles, the Lord's Prayer, and the Beatitudes, as well as a homily on the titles of the Psalms, in which he observes that Holy Scripture does not narrate historical facts for their own sakes but in order to teach man how to live virtuously.

Cyril. St. Cyril of Alexandria (d. 444), the great opponent of the Nestorians, was a thoroughgoing allegorist in both his *Adoration and Worship in Spirit and Truth* and *Glaphyra.* The former was written to prove the complete harmony between the OT and the NT, whereas the latter interpreted typically (especially with regard to the person of Christ) passages selected from the Pentateuch. In his commentaries on Isaia and the Minor Prophets, Cyril leans more toward the historical literal sense, but not always with complete success. His commentary on St. John's Gospel is concerned mainly with doctrinal content and the refutation of heresy.

School of Antioch. The foundation of the Antiochian school (*see* ANTIOCH, SCHOOL OF) at the end of the 3d century is generally attributed to St. *Lucian of Antioch (*c.* 240–317), famous for his role in establishing the Greek *textus receptus.* We know nothing of the exegesis of Lucian. The school's history may be divided into three periods: (1) From Lucian to the coming of Diodore of Tarsus (i.e., from *c.* 280 to 360), (2) From Diodore to Theodore of Mopsuestia (i.e., from 360 to 428), and (3) the period of decline (i.e., from 428 to 500). The exegetical principles of Antioch were directly opposed to those of its rival, Alexandria. Antioch insisted upon expounding the literal and historical meaning of the text. The typical sense (*theoria*) was acknowledged and carefully determined. The allegorical method of Alexandria found little welcome at Antioch.

The following are the more important Antiochians: St. *Eustathius of Antioch (d. *c.* 335), in his *On the Witch of Endor,* attacked the allegorical method of Origen. *Diodore of Tarsus (*c.* 330–*c.* 392), the teacher of St. John Chrysostom and Theodore of Mopsuestia and one of the most illustrious of the Antiochians, wrote many exegetical works on the books of the OT and the NT. His exegesis is strictly literal, though he accepts the typical when it is well founded upon the literal and historical sense. The exegesis of St. *John Chrysostom (*c.* 349–407) is found chiefly in this great preacher's homilies. He never formulated any rules of interpretation, but he accepted the literal sense, both proper and improper (i.e., allegorical) and the typical. He was concerned primarily with what he could draw from the sacred text for the good of souls.

*Theodore of Mopsuestia (d. 428) is the best-known Biblical pupil of Diodore. The Council of *Constantinople II (553) condemned some of Theodore's opinions on the nature of inspiration and the books to be excluded from the Canon and his restriction of the number of messianic Psalms to four [i.e., Psalm 2; 8; 44(45); 109(110)]. Even today it is difficult to evaluate properly his exegetical works. He is well-known for his boldness and strict adherence to the literal and historical sense. He explained his exegetical principles in two works now lost: *De allegoria et historia* and *De perfectione operum contra allegoricos.* (But on these works see the translator's note 3 in Robert-Tricot 1:702.) On the exegetical method of Theodore of Mopsuestia see especially the two works of R. Devreese: "La Méthode exégètique de Theodore de Mopsueste," RevBibl 53 (1946) 207–241, and *Essai sur Theodore de Mopsueste,* StTest 141 (1948).

*Theodoret of Cyr (d. before 466) deserves special mention for his solid interpretation of the Scriptures, which had enduring popularity. He claimed no originality but composed his commentaries only after assiduously studying the best of patristic exegesis. But he was, in fact, far more than a mere copyist and compiler. His many works were often cited in the Biblical *catenae as authoritative. Faithful to the Antiochian school, he was principally concerned with the literal sense; yet a good deal of solid typology is often expounded in his works. He wrote commentaries on the Psalms, on the Canticle of Canticles, and on all the Prophets, and he considered special questions on the Octateuch and the books of Samuel, Kings, and Chronicles. His exposition of the Pauline Epistles is considered by some to be second only to that made by St. John Chrysostom. Theodoret was the last of the great Antiochians.

Others associated with the School of Antioch were: St. *Ephrem the Syrian (*c.* 306–373), who wrote commentaries in Syriac on all the books of the Bible; *Apollinaris of Laodicea (d. *c.* 390); *Severian of Gabala (d. after 408); and Polychronius of Apamea (d. *c.* 430), the brother of Theodore of Mopsuestia. *Adrianus (fl. 1st half of the 5th century) composed an *Introduction to Holy Scripture* that set forth the principles of the Antiochians. The insistence of the Antiochians on the historical literal sense proved to be the correct position for sound exegesis according to the mind of the inspired author.

Latin Fathers. The exegetical principles of both Antioch and Alexandria found adherents among commentators of the West. Since no exegetical schools existed there during the patristic period, the following order of authors is simply chronological. *Tertullian (d. after 220), who gave the West its theological Latin, wrote no commentaries on Sacred Scripture, but he frequently interpreted Biblical texts in his writings, generally in the literal sense. St. *Hippolytus of Rome (d. *c.* 236) wrote many works in Greek that exhibit Alexandrian influence. One would expect allegory in his commentary on the Canticle of Canticles, but it appears also in his work on Daniel. St. *Victorinus of Pettau (d. *c.* 303) commented on many books of the OT and the NT. However, only his work on the Apocalypse has survived. The influence of Origen is reflected also in the works of St. *Hilary of Poitiers (d. 367), whose exegesis is strongly allegorical. A commentary of his on Matthew and another on the Psalms (partly preserved) are extant. A part of his *Tractatus mysteriorum,* a work on OT prophecies, was recovered in 1887. St. *Ambrose (d. 397) composed no commentaries in the strict sense on the books of the Bible. His exegesis, found chiefly in his many homilies on various books of the OT and NT, is allegorical and well-balanced, and it reflects the preacher's concern for the formation and salvation of souls.

St. *Jerome (d. 419 or 420) is the patron of Biblical studies. His Latin translation of the Bible, his many commentaries on the OT and NT books, especially on the prophetical books, and his knowledge of the principal Biblical languages and of the country and customs of the Holy Land itself have merited for him a special place in the history of Biblical studies. His exegesis, at first strongly allegorical, became more and more literal. We have his commentaries on Ecclesiastes and the Prophets in the OT and on Matthew, Galatians, Ephesians, Titus, and Philippians in the NT. An unknown author referred to as *Ambrosiaster or Pseudo-Ambrose composed an excellent literal commentary on the Pauline Epistles c. A.D. 380, probably at Rome. Tyconius the Donatist wrote the first Latin treatise on Biblical *hermeneutics, *Liber Regularum, c.* A.D. 370.

St. *Augustine (d. 430) used allegorical and mystical interpretations in his preaching, but he preferred literal exegesis in his theological writings. Though he himself was not well-equipped for scientific exegesis, he insisted upon the necessity of learning, and especially of philological training, for the proper study of the written word of God. He interpreted the first few chapters of Genesis four times: *De Genesi contra Manichaeos libri 2* (c. 389); *De Genesi ad litteram imperfectus liber* (c. 393), more literal than the previous work; the story of creation, allegorically interpreted, in the last three books of his *Confessions* (c. 400); and *De Genesi ad litteram libri 12* (c. 401), his major work on Genesis. Other important exegetical works of Augustine include: several books of *Quaestiones* and *Locutiones* on the Heptateuch; *Enarrationes in Psalmos,* probably his best exegetical work; *De consensu Evangeliorum,* a study of parallel passages in the Gospels; *Quaestiones* on the Gospels and on certain texts in Romans; and (in treatises or homilies) the Sermon on the Mount, the Gospel of St. John, Galatians, and the beginning of Romans. In his *De doctrina christiana* he set forth his ideas on the nature of exegesis and on the relation of Scripture to theology.

Worthy of mention are also St. *Peter Chrysologus (d. c. 450), who expounded allegorically many NT passages in 176 homilies; Cassiodorus (d. c. 580), who interpreted the Psalms and the NT literally; and the long influential St. *Gregory the Great (d. 604), who interpreted allegorically Job (*Moralia*), Ezechiel, and the Gospels and whose primary interest in exegesis was pastoral.

MEDIEVAL, RENAISSANCE, AND 18TH-CENTURY EXEGESIS

Little in medieval exegesis was really new. The influence of the traditional patristic approach was strong. Yet commentators, such as Venerable Bede, Peter Lombard, St. Albert the Great, St. Bonaventure, St. Thomas

Aquinas, and Nicholas of Lyra, added valuable contributions to the treasury of the Fathers. The exegesis of the Middle Ages is usually divided into two periods: (1) monastic exegesis, from c. 650 to c. 1200, and (2) scholastic exegesis, from c. 1200 to c. 1500. The writers of the first period were concerned principally with producing works of edification. Their lack of adequate knowledge of the original Biblical languages made scientific exegesis impossible. C. Spicq (*Esquisse . . .,* 16) characterizes the period as one that "was essentially and universally allegorical." For a detailed study of this period, *see* EXEGESIS, MEDIEVAL.

In the second period there was a rise, flowering, and decadence of what was best in medieval exegesis. Toward the end of the 12th century exegesis emerged as a separate discipline and theology developed into an independent science. As in the past, theology still consisted chiefly in the study of the Bible but with this significant difference: *sacra doctrina* no longer meant the simple reading of the Scriptures with the help of patristic commentaries; the *quaestio de divina pagina,* a theological explanation of the sacred text derived from grouping into logical order scriptural texts referring to the same subject, succeeded the *lectio* and gradually developed into an independent theological treatise. In the 13th century these *quaestiones* became completely separated from the text and were grouped together to constitute theology as an independent science; see Spicq, 66–69.

Medieval Biblical Science. At the threshold of this period of evolution in exegetical methods stands the *Glossa ordinaria* of *Anselm of Laon (d. 1117), a mine of patristic exegesis and theology (*see* GLOSSES, BIBLICAL). The authority which the *Glossa* enjoyed from the 12th to the 16th century has been compared to that of the works of Aristotle in philosophy, the *Sentences* of Peter Lombard in theology, and the decrees of Gratian in Canon Law. Its composition and wide diffusion mark a decisive stage in the history of exegesis (see Spicq, 113). Other 12th-century works worthy of special mention are: the *Major glossatura* of *Peter Lombard (d. 1160), an enlargement of the *Glossa ordinaria;* the *Historia scholastica* of *Peter Comestor (d. 1179), which won an honored place at the universities alongside the Bible and the *Sentences;* and finally the works of *Richard of Saint-Victor (d. 1173), the most able Biblical scholar of the 12th century. In the 13th century, at the newly founded university centers of Oxford, Paris, and Bologna especially, two ranks of professors shared the teaching of sacred doctrine: (1) the *biblicus ordinarius* who guided the students through the entire Biblical *cursorie,* hence his title of *cursor;* and (2) the *magister,* who made more detailed studies of individual books of the Bible, selected passages, and the like, all according to the *Glossa* or the *Sentences* of Peter Lombard. Gradually, however, the office of both the ordinary Biblicist or *cursor* and the *magister* underwent a significant change. The ordinary Biblicist came to confine himself exclusively to expounding the Biblical text. His role was inferior to that of the master in sacred theology, as the *magister* came to be called, whose basic text in theology soon became the *Sentences* of Peter Lombard, or, as at Oxford, the *Historia scholastica* of Peter Comestor. As a result of this change, the study of speculative theology in the second half of the 13th century became more clearly distinct from the study of the Biblical text itself. Other important contributions to Biblical studies in the 13th century were: a clearer concept of the criterion of canonicity, due principally to the ideas of St. *Thomas Aquinas (d. 1274); the division of the Bible into books suitably arranged among themselves, and the division of the books into chapters, introduced by *Stephen Langton (d. 1228); the first *correctoria* and verbal concordances, both under the direction of *Hugh of Saint-Cher (d. 1263); the renewed interest in the study of ancient languages, in order to understand better the sacred text, promoted especially by *Robert Grosseteste (d. 1253), *Roger Bacon (d. 1294), and *Raymond Martini (d. 1282); and the clear distinction made between the spiritual and literal senses of Scripture, as well as the care exercised by the great scholastics to determine the literal sense intended by the sacred author. Finally, mention should also be made of the appearance of the *postillae* (*post illa verba*), the continuous and orderly commentary that replaced the glosses. The first and classic example is the *Postillae* of Hugh of Saint-Cher, a work that covered the whole Bible and was often reprinted from the 15th to the 17th century.

Thirteenth-century Exegetes. The more important exegetes of the 13th century include Stephen Langton, Raymond of Cremona, St. Bonaventure, St. Albert the Great, and St. Thomas Aquinas.

Stephen Langton (d. 1228) composed a long series of glosses on the books of the OT and the NT. He belongs with Peter Comestor and *Peter Cantor (d. 1197), all three of whom made original contributions to Biblical studies; see B. Smalley, 156–218. Langton formed a bridge between the work of Peter Lombard and that of St. Thomas Aquinas.

*Roland of Cremona (d. 1259) wrote the first commentary on Job according to the literal or historical sense. In view of the long-standing influence of St. Gregory's *Moralia* this literal commentary is a landmark in the history of medieval exegesis; see A. Dondaine, "Un Commentaire scriptuaire de Roland de Crémone 'Le Livre de Job,'" ArchFrPraed 11 (1941) 109–137.

St. *Bonaventure (d. 1274) wrote a few exegetical works (commentaries on Wisdom, Ecclesiastes, John, and Luke) in the scholastic tradition of his time. These are characterized by the familiar innumerable divisions and subdivisions of the text.

The exegetical works of St. *Albert the Great (d. 1280) are very numerous; see J. M. Vosté, *Angelicum* 9 (1932) 238–335. The oldest catalogues state that Albert commented on every book of the Bible; see Spicq, 293, especially note 7. However many authorities question the authenticity of the commentary on the Psalms attributed to him, and the commentaries on the four Gospels are the only NT writings of which the Albertine authorship is certain; see Spicq, 296. The commentaries on the four Gospels, written toward the end of his life, are Albert's best exegetical works. His interpretations are strictly literal. For example, in their exposition of the temptation of Jesus to turn stones into bread, commentators were fond of comparing the hard stone with the Law or with the hardness of a sinner's heart, but Albert rejected this as absurd and contrary to the mind of the writer. Again, he withstood the temptation to moralize the story of Peter's denials: "All this can be expounded morally, but it does not seem profitable to me to distract my readers' minds from the piety of faith; so we pass over such expositions" (B. Smalley,

233). Other exegetical works of St. Albert include the literal and historical commentaries on the often neglected books of Lamentations and Baruch, as well as on Daniel, the 12 Minor Prophets, Job, Isaia, Jeremia, Ezechiel, and the Canticle of Canticles. St. Albert's exegesis stands between that of Hugh of Saint-Cher and that of St. Thomas Aquinas, though closer to that of the latter.

St. Thomas Aquinas, the greatest of all scholastic exegetes, composed commentaries on Job, the first 50 Psalms, chapters 1 to 42 of Jeremia, Matthew, John, the Pauline Epistles, and the *Catena aurea*, a continuous exposition of the four Gospels drawn from 54 Greek and Latin commentators. Some doubt has been expressed on the authenticity of the commentaries on Matthew and the Canticle of Canticles. The exegetical works of St. Thomas are the high water mark of medieval exegesis. They are the fruit of his teaching duties as *magister sacrae paginae*. Both the sacred books chosen for study and the manner of exposition reveal that St. Thomas aimed at a clear, literal, and theological exegesis. For a complete evaluation of his contribution to the history of exegesis, see Spicq, 298–316; and Smalley, 300–308.

Attention should be called also to the exegetical works of the Dominicans *Peter of Tarentaise (d. 1276) and *Nicholas of Gorran (d. 1295).

Renaissance Exegesis. The 14th century produced almost no exegetical works of permanent value. Three outstanding writers of the period were: the Dominicans Meister *Eckhart (d. 1327) and *Nicholas Trevet (d. c. 1330) and the Franciscan *Nicholas of Lyra (d. 1349). Eckhart wrote two commentaries on Genesis, one literal and the other allegorical, as well as expositions of Exodus, Wisdom, Sirach, and 1 Corinthians and a very long commentary on John. More philosophical and theological than exegetical, these works are heavily indebted to the theology of St. Thomas Aquinas. Nicholas Trevet revealed his good knowledge of Hebrew in his strictly literal commentaries on Genesis, Exodus, Leviticus, Chronicles, and the Psalms.

Nicholas of Lyra's exegesis reflected the beginnings of a new scientific approach to exegesis which, after many vicissitudes in succeeding centuries, would eventually prevail. His best known work, *Postillae perpetuae in Vetus et Novum Testamentum*, exercised wide influence. The *Postillae,* which completed and renewed the *Glossa Ordinaria* of Anselm of Laon, was almost exclusively literal in its interpretations; see Spicq, 336. Lyra refused to accept the interpretations of the Fathers unless, in his judgment, they conformed to the literal sense of the text. During the course of the Middle Ages, Biblical exegesis had made great progress over previous centuries. It had become more and more theological and more than ever before concerned with the literal sense intended by the sacred author. The future would remedy the period's two chief defects: an imperfect knowledge of philology and an inadequate sense of the Bible as the record of God's intervention in history.

The decline in the 15th century of scholastic exegesis and the return to allegory and moralizing is reflected in the works of Jean *Gerson (d. 1429) and *Denis the Carthusian (d. 1471).

In the 16th century profound changes in Biblical studies took place, caused by the new emphasis on the study of Greek and Hebrew, the improvement in basic scriptural tools, and the exegetical principles of the Reformers, which were partially followed and partially controverted by 16th- and 17th-century Catholic exegetes.

Biblical Philology. Through the efforts of Johann *Reuchlin (d. 1522), the two Johannes *Buxtorfs (father d. 1629; son d. 1664), and the Anglican John Lightfoot (d. 1675), Biblical scholars were provided with better Hebrew grammars, dictionaries, Hebrew and Aramaic concordances, and a better knowledge of rabbinical literature. The works of such scholars as Desiderius *Erasmus (d. 1536), Santes *Pagnini (d. 1541), and Robert *Estienne (d. 1559) enriched the field of textual criticism. The publication of the first *polyglot Bibles (at Alcalá, 1514–17; Antwerp; 1569–72; Paris, 1628–45; and London, 1653–57) made easier the comparison of different Biblical texts. The principles to be followed in the restoration of the Hebrew text were set forth by the Protestants Jacques Cappel (d. 1624) and his brother Louis (d. 1658) in their *Critica Sacra* (1634).

Reformation Exegesis. The translation of the Bible into German by Martin *Luther (d. 1546) is an admitted literary masterpiece. However, neither his OT commentaries nor those of Huldrych *Zwingli (d. 1531), Philipp *Melanchthon (d. 1560), or John *Calvin (d. 1564) made any advance over similar works of their predecessors. The Reformers' polemical aims rendered objective, scientific exegesis difficult. They admitted the inspiration of the Bible but claimed that one's private judgment was sufficient to arrive at its evident sense. Rationalistic exegesis, the logical consequence of this principle, was soon evident in the writings of Hugo *Grotius (d. 1645) in his *Annotationes in Vetus Testamentum* and in those of Jean *Le Clerc (d. 1736) in his *Moysis libri quinque.*

Catholic OT commentaries of the period include: Tommaso de Vio *Cajetan (d. 1534), who commentated on all the OT except the Canticle of Canticles, the deuterocanonical books, and the Prophets, and whose exegetical principles involved him in a celebrated 16th-century controversy [see T. A. Collins, "Cajetan's Fundamental Biblical Principles," CathBiblQuart 17 (1955) 363–378]; Johannes *Maldonatus (d. 1583), whose OT exegesis was not equal to that of his famous Gospel commentaries; St. Robert *Bellarmine (d. 1621), who wrote an excellent commentary on the Psalms; Cornelius a *Lapide (d. 1637), whose voluminous commentaries on all the OT books except Job and the Psalms enshrine what is best in patristic exegesis and provide useful homiletic material; Jacques Bonfrère (d. 1642), who wrote commentaries on the Pentateuch, Josue, Judges, Ruth, and Chronicles; and, last but not least, Simon de Muis (d. 1644), whose *Commentarius litteralis et historicus in omnes Psalmos et selecta Veteris Testamenti cantica cum versione nova ex Hebraico* is surprisingly modern.

For the history of exegesis, however, the most significant 17th-century Catholic Biblical scholar was Richard *Simon (1638–1712), called the founder of Biblical historical criticism. In his *Histoire critique du Vieux Testament* Simon showed his keen awareness of the problems raised by the careful study of the Pentateuch, and he was the first to perceive the organic development of the OT books. His views were bitterly opposed by some as scandalous and a danger to the faith.

Despite some serious defects, Simon's work won for its author a permanent place in the history of exegesis.

Eighteenth-Century Exegesis. The 18th century made little positive contribution to the history of exegesis. The works of Augustin *Calmet (1672–1757) reached a new peak in Catholic exegesis, but they lacked originality. His literal commentaries on the books of the OT and the NT were solid works of great erudition and exercised great influence especially in France. Textual criticism received contributions from Charles F. *Houbigant (d. 1784), Bernard de *Montfaucon (d. 1741), Pierre *Sabatier (d. 1742), Benjamin *Kennicott (d. 1783), Robert Holmes (d. 1805), and Giovanni Battista de *Rossi (d. 1831).

OLD TESTAMENT EXEGESIS IN 19TH AND 20TH CENTURIES

A new era began with Jean *Astruc's (d. 1766) *Conjectures sur les mémoires originaux dont il parait que Moise s'est servi pour composer le livre de la Genese* (1753). The 19th century would see this literary dissection (of the Pentateuch especially) carried to extremes. Only the principal authors and their proposals can be noted here.

Literary Criticism of Pentateuch. Johann Gottfried Eichhorn (d. 1827) offered the documentary hypothesis, which added other sources to the Yahwistic and Elohistic ones. Alexander *Geddes (d. 1802) proposed the fragment hypothesis in 1792. G. H. A. *Ewald (d. 1875) countered with the supplement hypothesis, according to which a fundamental historical document (*Grundschrift*) was supplemented by several other sources. Hermann Hupfeld (d. 1866) further extended the documentary hypothesis in 1853 by distinguishing three basic documents: a basic source called First Elohist, a Yahwistic source, and a Second Elohistic one. In 1854 Eduard Karl August Riehm (d. 1888) proposed Deuteronomy (D) as a fourth source, and in 1869 Theodor Noeldeke (d. 1930) extended the Documentary Hypothesis to the whole Hexateuch. He proposed three sources from the 10th and 9th century B.C. according to the following chronological order: (P) Priestly Code or First Elohist; (E) Second Elohist; (J) Yahwist, and a fourth source (D), dating from just prior to the reform of Josia (621 B.C.). Noeldeke suggested that the Pentateuch attained its final form under Ezra, who successfully promulgated it.

Wellhausen School. The brilliant Julius *Wellhausen (d. 1918) championed the ideas of E. G. E. *Reuss (d. 1891) and Karl Heinrich Graf (d. 1869) in proposing his own widely accepted hypothesis. The classic Wellhausen thesis of the literary sources of the *Pentateuch reads as follows: a 9th-century B.C. Yahwistic and an 8th-century B.C. Elohistic source (the latter reflecting the religious traditions of the Northern Kingdom), a fusion of J and E by the Prophets, Deuteronomy, and the Priestly code. S. R. *Driver (d. 1914) in England, Léon Gautier (d. 1897) in France, and many leading scholars in Germany promoted the Wellhausen thesis. A pivotal point in the Wellhausen school was the conclusion that the principal codes of Law were composed after, not before, the period of the Prophets, who were the real founders of Israelite monotheism, fraudulently attributed to Moses. The solemn promulgation of the Law was deferred until after the Babylonian Exile. For a fuller history and elaborate bibliography of the history of OT criticism, see J. Coppens, *The Old Testament and the Critics,* tr. E. A. Ryan and E. W. Tribbe (Paterson, N.J. 1942).

In applying their theories to the whole of the Bible members of the Wellhausen school distinguished the literary history of the Israelites into three periods: (1) that of the ancient Prophets, (2) that of the composition of the various codes of the Torah (admitting that some parts of these codes, e.g., the Book of the Covenant, may well have been contemporaneous with the work of the Prophets), and (3) that of the didactic and apocalyptic literature; see Coppens, *op. cit.* 35–36. Wellhausen himself as well as others, notably, Abraham Kuenen (d. 1891) in 1869, Bernhard Duhm (d. 1928) in 1873, and B. Stade in 1905 and 1911, added to the documentary theory a reconstruction of Israel's religious history founded upon the philosophy of G. W. F. *Hegel (d. 1831) as applied to Israel's religion by certain scholars of the school of W. M. L. *De Wette (d. 1849), especially J. K. Wilhelm Vatke (d. 1882). According to this school, the history of Israel's religion ought to conform to an evolutionary pattern alleged to be observable in all human history. It was claimed that the religious experience of Israel began with an animism or polydaemonism, evolved into a national henotheism, and finally, under the impetus of the great prophetical movement, as mentioned above, it developed into the ethical monotheism of the exilic and postexilic periods; see G. E. Wright, ed., *The Bible and the Ancient Near East* (New York 1965) 3–5.

Post-Wellhausen research has considerably altered many positions originally assumed concerning the dates assigned to the four classic sources (J, E, D, P), the unity of these documents and their relative chronology, and the late date assigned by Wellhausen for the origins of all the Deuteronomic or sacerdotal laws. These researches were carried on especially by K. F. R. *Budde (1890 and 1902), Immanuel Benzinger (1921), Rudolf Smend (1921), Gustav Holscher (1923), and Otto Eissfeldt (1925), among others. More recently, Gerhard von Rad, R. H. Pfeiffer, P. Romanoff, and Sigmund Mowinckel have sought for other special sources for certain parts of the Torah.

Study of Predocumentary Traditions. At the turn of the century a new phase of critical scholarship began with the work of Hermann *Gunkel (d. 1932) and H. *Gressmann (d. 1927), who turned their attention to the study of the individual units of tradition contained within the various documents (*see* LITERARY GENRES, BIBLICAL). It became quickly apparent that the dating of a given document by no means dated the material or traditions contained therein. The modern study of the Patriarchs clearly demonstrates this; see R. de Vaux, RevBibl 53 (1946) 321–348; 55 (1948) 321–347; 56 (1949) 5–36. The new attention being paid to the Biblical traditions in their preliterary form makes it abundantly clear that, whereas documents containing these traditions may be arranged chronologically, the material they contain cannot be as easily arranged chronologically, and as a consequence they cannot be confidently used to support an evolutionary theory of the development of Israel's religion.

As John Bright has noted (G. E. Wright, ed., *op.cit.* 7–8), all this has led scholars to abandon classical Wellhausenism without abandoning the documentary hypothesis, which stands or falls independently of Well-

hausen's views; "and, so far at least, it seems in general to have stood." Opposition to Wellhausen, in whole or in part, came from several outstanding scholars, including E. *König (d. 1936) and R. *Kittel (d. 1929). The search for the oral and written sources of the OT books continues.

Catholic Reaction. Catholic scholarship showed little interest in these literary problems until the end of the 19th century. M. J. *Lagrange (d. 1938) faced the problem squarely in 1898 with his "Les Sources du Pentateuque" [RevBibl 7 (1898) 10–32]. In his last published article, "L'Authenticité mosaïque de la Genèse et la théorie des documents" [RevBibl 47 (1938) 163–183], he acknowledged the existence of documents and proposed that E was used by Moses who sketched the outline for J, which was written by an associate. P was a sort of *Summa* containing only essentials. Many Catholic OT scholars now agree that the documentary hypothesis is valid in principle as at least a partial answer to the problem of the origin of the OT books.

Rationalistic Criticism. In the 19th century another strong current, which came from the 18th century, was rationalistic criticism. Among its principal exponents were: G. E. *Lessing (d. 1781), who divorced religion from the Bible; J. S. *Semler (d. 1791), who taught that Scripture accommodated itself to contemporary prevailing beliefs; I. *Kant (d. 1804), for whom exegesis meant extracting from the Bible ethical truths only; and G. W. F. Hegel, who held that each religion, with its own legends, images, and myths, reflects a stage in a religious evolutionary process; consequently, OT narratives should be interpreted merely as the myths of Israel's religion. The theory of Israel's religious evolution from lesser forms was strengthened by the works of E. B. Tylor (d. 1917) in 1871, H. *Spencer (d. 1903), J. Lippert (d. 1909) in 1881, B. Stade in 1884, and F. Schwally in 1892. Monotheism, the last stage in Israel's religious evolution, was attributed to the work of the Prophets. The panbabylonian school of Hugo Winckler (d. 1913), Friedrich *Delitzsch (d. 1922), and others (*see* PANBABYLONIANISM) attributed it to a hidden monotheism in Mesopotamia; see Robert-Tricot 1:713–722.

Twentieth-Century Exegesis. At the turn of the century, despite variety concerning details, there was substantial agreement on most OT problems among all leading scholars; see H. H. Rowley, "Trends in OT Study," *The Old Testament and Modern Study* (London 1961) xv–xxxi. After World War I, however, a greater variety of positions on fundamental points emerged. Scholars now recognize a far greater unity in the Bible than heretofore. This has led to a renewed interest in the *Biblical theology of the OT; see R. C. Dentan. During the mid-20th-century there has arisen new knowledge, new approaches to old problems, new applications of older principles, and new tests of conclusions long since held sacred. A host of new OT scholars have already won a permanent place in the history of exegesis (W. F. Albright, J. Bright, M. Burrows, W. Eichrodt, F. V. Filson, A. Gelin, H. W. Hertzberg, R. A. F. MacKenzie, J. L. McKenzie, S. Mowinckel, J. Lindblom, M. Noth, G. von Rad, H. H. Rowley, P. W. Skehan, R. de Vaux, A. Vincent, to name but a few). There has been a gradual tendency among 20th-century exegetes to adopt a more conservative opinion on many OT problems.

During this period Catholic Biblical scholarship has come of age. Inspired by the directives of the Church, Catholic scholars in both Europe and America have won for themselves honored places in Biblical studies. New Catholic Biblical societies have been formed, new scientific journals founded, scholarly Biblical faculties erected, and many praiseworthy Catholic OT works continue to appear.

Among the tendencies evident in present OT studies, the following may be noted: in Pentateuchal criticism new stress is being placed on the oral traditions behind the main sources, new sources have been discovered, and reconsideration is being given to the dates assigned to the old sources; there is a widespread tendency to interpret as rituals many historical and prophetical texts as well as many Psalms; there is a strong proposal from the Scandinavian school that the traditio-historical method of investigation is more fruitful than literary criticism in solving various OT problems. For fuller details, see H. H. Rowley.

NEW TESTAMENT EXEGESIS IN 19TH AND 20TH CENTURIES

The exegesis of the principal reformers, M. Luther, J. Calvin, and P. Melanchthon, had ignored the interpretation of the Church and was subjective and mystical in character and far removed from traditional historical enquiry.

Rationalistic Exegesis. The rationalists, in the name of the "*enlightenment," sought to emancipate themselves from the "darkness" of Christian revelation. Their fundamental principles denied the existence of the supernatural and affirmed that only what is rational is real. In France, England, and Germany charges of fraud and deception were hurled against Christ and His Apostles. H. S. *Reimarus (d. 1768) attributed the beginnings of Christianity to the Apostles, who had idealized the person and teachings of Christ. Heinrich E. G. Paulus (d. 1851) claimed that the Gospels narrated the testimony of witnesses more or less subject to hallucinations. In his *Life of Jesus* (1835) D. F. *Strauss (d. 1874) held that the Gospel texts, which the rationalists found so difficult, were really mythical in origin. F. C. *Baur (d. 1860) tried to reconstruct the history of the early Church before the appearance of the Gospel myths. Bruno *Bauer (d. 1882) maintained that Christ's very existence was a myth. All these writers used Hegelian philosophy as a foundation for their rationalistic exegesis (*see* HEGELIANISM AND NEO-HEGELIANISM).

Reaction to these extreme positions came from J. Ernest *Renan (d. 1892) and especially such liberal Protestants as Bernhard Weiss (d. 1918), Karl Theodor Keim (d. 1878), E. G. E. Reuss (d. 1891), Albert Reville (d. 1906), H. J. *Holtzmann (d. 1910), and A. von *Harnack (d. 1930). The liberals themselves, however, were opposed by those who wished to free the study of Christ and the Gospels from all philosophies, e.g., Johannes Weiss (d. 1914) and William Wrede (d. 1906). Another strong current at the turn of the 20th century was syncretism, which sought to trace Christian teachings back to various elements in Near Eastern religious speculations, especially those derived from Hellenism. For good summaries of NT trends in the 20th century, see A. Hunter; R. H. Fuller. Only the highlights can be noted here.

Quest for the Historical Jesus. Most influential was the eschatological approach of Albert Schweitzer (d. 1965), in his *Von Reimarus zu Wrede* [1906; *The Quest of the Historical Jesus,* tr. W. Montgomery (New York 1961)], which forced NT scholars to face the problem of eschatology in the Gospels. In his detailed story of the quest of the historical Jesus in the 19th century Schweitzer had revealed the aim of the search: to discover the original teachings of Jesus and through these teachings to test the authenticity of the Church's version of Christianity. The historico-critical method that was used promised objective and scientific results, but unfortunately the method (as it had been used especially by Wrede and Wellhausen) demonstrated quite clearly that the liberals had not reconstructed a very scientific portrait of the historical Jesus after all; see Fuller, 26–27.

Form Criticism. A new and somewhat original approach to the study of the Gospels strongly supported this conclusion. Biblical *form criticism focused its attention upon the several literary forms or types found in the Gospel narratives. Through an analytical and comparative study of these various literary forms the form critic hopes to be able to retrace the preliterary history of the Gospel traditions. The studies of M. Dibelius, *Die Formgeschichte des Evangeliums* (Tübingen 1919), Eng. tr. by B. L. Woolf, *From Tradition to Gospel* (London and New York 1934); K. L. Schmidt, *Der Rahmen der Geschichte Jesu* (Berlin 1919); R. Bultmann, *Die Geschichte der synoptischen Tradition* (Göttingen 1921), Eng. tr. of 3d ed., 1957, by John Marsh, *History of the Synoptic Tradition* (New York 1963); and M. Albertz, *Die synoptischen Streitgesprache* (Berlin 1921) showed that the Synoptic Gospels were not written as biographies of Jesus but rather to enshrine the faith of the early Church. The critics claimed that the Gospels could not be used as a source for the reconstruction of the portrait of the historical Jesus because they had been written on a theological rather than a historical basis. These critics claimed further that any quest of the historical Jesus, taking that word historical in its usual modern sense, would prove to be in vain. Dialectical theologians, such as Karl Barth and Martin Kähler, maintained it was unnecessary, since the object of our faith is not the Jesus of history but the Jesus of faith, whose saving action is proclaimed in the *kerygma. For a balanced judgment and bibliography of form criticism, see A. Wikenhauser, *New Testament Introduction* (New York 1958), Eng. tr. by J. Cunningham, 253–277.

Demythologizing. In 1941 Rudolf Bultmann delivered his now famous lecture, *Neues Testament und Mythologie,* in which he offered an outline of a program to demythologize the NT (*see* DEMYTHOLOGIZING). Much scholarly literature has been published in the course of the debate concerning NT myths; see H. W. Bartsch, ed., *Kerygma and Myth* I (London 1960), Eng. tr. by R. H. Fuller, for "New Testament and Mythology" (1–44) and bibliography (224–228). For a dozen years (1941–53) a most heated debate raged over Bultmann's aims and methods.

The New Quest. The debate is hardly finished, but it has occasioned a return to the quest of the historical Jesus. This began in 1953 when Ernst Käsemann, one of Bultmann's outstanding pupils, delivered a lecture in which he turned his attention to the old problem of the Jesus of history. The story of this new quest, as well as an evaluation of contributions by Käsemann, G. Bornkamm, H. G. Conzelmann, and others has been well told by J. M. Robinson in *A New Quest of the Historical Jesus* (London and Naperville 1959); see also Fuller, 25–53.

Synoptic Studies. Present-day studies in the Synoptic Gospels exhibit a significant shift of emphasis in many areas (*see* SYNOPTIC PROBLEM). Formerly little attention was paid to the Evangelists' personal contributions to their Gospels. As Fuller (71) remarks, the Synoptic Evangelists were considered more as simply collectors of oral traditions, as men standing at the end of a pipeline collecting in a bucket what came through, arranging it a little, perhaps, but making little personal contribution to NT theology. Nowadays more attention is paid to the distinctive interpretation each Evangelist applies to the traditions at his disposal and the principles that guide him in the arrangement of these traditions for his own kerygmatic purposes. The problem of distinguishing the main strata or layers of Synoptic material remains only partially solved and continues to invite new and improved solutions. The Synoptic problem intrigues the new generation of NT scholars as it always did in the past. The scholars in the forefront of modern studies in the Synoptic Gospels are G. Bornkamm, R. Brown, J. M. Robinson, H. G. Conzelmann, and W. Marxsen, among many others. For further details, especially concerning the Lucan writings, see Fuller, 70–100.

Johannine Studies. In Johannine studies, too, a remarkable change has taken place during the 20th century. No longer are commentators concerned primarily with the questions of authorship, date, and provenance. The earlier critics were intent upon studies of vivisection, partition, and rearrangements of the original order of the Fourth Gospel. Nowadays many agree with C. H. Dodd that it is "the duty of an interpreter at least to see what can be done with the document as it has come down to us before attempting to improve upon it."

Other present positions on principal Johannine problems may be stated briefly. (1) Regarding authorship, most scholars are content to attribute the Fourth Gospel to an unknown disciple of the Apostle (so, more or less, C. H. Dodd, C. K. Barrett, and R. Bultmann), although R. H. Lightfoot notes that no one has shown it is impossible that the Apostle John was the author. (2) Regarding the date, the general tendency has been toward A.D. 100 or even earlier. (3) On the question of John's relation to the Synoptics there has been a shift from the older position that claimed John knew and used at least Mark and Luke to the total rejection of any dependence (so Dodd and Bultmann but not Barrett). B. Noack in *Zur Johanneischen Tradition* (Copenhagen 1954) and S. Schulz in *Untersuchungen zur Menschensohn-Christologie im Johannes Evangelium* (Göttingen 1957) have made important contributions to the study of pre-Johannine material imbedded in the Johannine discourses; see Fuller, 112–115. (4) Whereas the older view of an Aramaic origin for the Fourth Gospel was received indifferently, few scholars today would reject entirely M. Black's contention that there are Aramaic logia enshrined in the Fourth Gospel's discourses; see M. Black, *An Aramaic Approach to the Gospels and Acts* (Oxford, 2d ed. 1954). (5) Various proposals have been offered in the important study of the sources of Johannine theology. The more important sources suggested are: the OT and rabbinic literature (the conservative view), Greek philosophy and Greek religion (the older liberal view), the OT plus Greek influences by way of Hellenistic mysticism (so Dodd, Barrett, and others), and *Gnosticism (so Bultmann and his school with variations in details); see Fuller, 118–125.

The discovery of the *Dead Sea Scrolls has opened up new avenues of approach to many Johannine problems. More recent studies arising from the material of the *Qumran community seem to tend, at least in some measure, toward conservative positions in the questions of authorship, date, and provenance.

Pauline Studies. At the beginning of the 20th century the great problem concerning the Pauline Epistles was their authenticity. Today only the Ephesians and the Pastorals are considered by some to be doubtfully authentic. The old question of the meaning of the term *Galatia is still being debated, though the weight of critical scholarship seems to be on the side of the defenders of the South-Galatian theory, who claim Paul used the term politically (*see* GALATIANS, EPISTLE TO THE). The provenance of the *Captivity Epistles, the destination of the 16th chapter of Romans, and the literary unity of 2 Corinthians still exercise present-day NT scholars.

Especially in the mid-20th century new and significant studies have been published, including R. Bultmann, *Theology of the New Testament*, tr. K. Grobel (2 v. London 1955–56), which devotes more than 300 pages in v.1 to an anthropological treatment of Pauline thought; J. Munck, *Paul and the Salvation of Mankind*, tr. F. Clarke (London and Richmond 1959), which stresses the concept of *salvation history in Paul's writings [see C. K. Barrett, *From First Adam to Last* (New York 1962) for a similar treatment and R. H. Fuller, 54–68 for an appraisal of both Bultmann and Munck]; and R. Schnackenburg, *New Testament Theology Today*, which should be consulted for all modern aspects of NT theology.

Catholic Exegesis. In the period following the Council of Trent Catholic exegesis was understandably characterized by a strong apologetic spirit, prompted by the polemical writings of the Protestants. Until about the middle of the 19th century Catholic exegetical works were, for the most part, little more than excellent compilations of Patristic citations fashioned into a strong defense of the chief doctrines of the Church and providing a treasury of homilectic source material. There were, of course, notable exceptions. J. *Maldonatus (d. 1583) composed excellent commentaries on the Gospels, which supplanted all previous Gospel commentaries; see J. M. Bover, "El P. Juan Maldonado, Theologo y escriturario," *Razón y Fe* 34 (1934) 481–504. G. *Estius (d. 1613) wrote outstanding expositions of the Pauline and Catholic Epistles, which became classics. The NT commentaries of Cornelius a Lapide (d. 1637) were, like his OT works mentioned above, mosaics of Patristic quotations and references; see R. Galdos, "De scripturisticis meritis Patris Cornelii a Lapide," VerbDom 17 (1937) 39–44, 88–96.

From the middle of the 19th century Catholic Biblical works of a more learned and scientific nature began to appear. Many now famous collections had their beginnings after the mid-19th century: *Cursus Sacrae Scripturae, Étude Bibliques, Exegetisches Handbuch zum A.T., Die Hl. Schrift des N.T., Die Hl. Schrift des A.T., Verbum Salutis, Herders Bibel Kommentar: Die Hl. Schrift fur das Leben erklart, La Sainte Bible* (Pirot-Clamer), *Regensburger Neues Testament,* and *Die Echter-Bibel.* Also many *Biblical periodicals under Catholic auspices made their appearance at this time: *Revue Biblique, Biblische Studien, Biblische Zeitschrift, Biblische Zeitfragen, Alttestamentliche Abhandlungen, Biblica, Verbum Domini, The Catholic Biblical Quarterly, Revista Biblica, Estudios Biblicos, Cultura Biblica, Biblische Warte, Lumière et Vie, Bible et Vie Chrétienne,* and *The Bible Today.* Evidence of the vitality of Catholic Biblical studies in the 20th century may be found in Catholic scholars' active participation in both national and international Congresses, whether sponsored by Catholic organizations or others.

Credit for the new impetus given to Catholic Biblical studies must be accorded first to the Roman Pontiffs, Leo XIII for his encyclical *Providentissimus Deus,* Benedict XV for his encyclical *Spiritus Paraclitus,* and especially Pius XII for his encyclical *Divino afflante Spiritu* [see BIBLE, VII (PAPAL TEACHING)]. With full support and encouragement from the Church a new generation of highly equipped NT scholars has emerged from such centers of Biblical studies as Rome, Jerusalem, Louvain, Paris, and Washington, D.C. Among the more familiar names of Catholic NT scholars of the mid-20th century are those of B. M. Ahern, P. Benoit, M. E. Boismard, R. Brown, S. Lyonnet, B. Rigaux, K. H. Schelkle, R. Schnackenburg, C. Spicq, D. M. Stanley, B. Vawter, and A. Voegtle, to mention but a few. These and other outstanding scholars have faced the more difficult problems of NT exegesis and made significant contributions to such questions as the historicity of the Gospels, the nature of the Evangelical parables, the unfolding and development of Pauline thought, and many thorny questions concerning the interpretation of the Fourth Gospel, as well as such problems as the relation between the Bible and tradition as sources of revelation and the nature of Biblical inspiration.

Special mention should be made of the rise of Biblical scholarship among American Catholics, who, after slow beginnings, have made great progress. The Catholic Biblical Association of America (1936–   ), especially under its executive secretary L. F. Hartman (1948–   ), and *The Catholic Biblical Quarterly* (1939–   ) under a series of capable editors (W. *Reilly, M. *Gruenthaner, E. F. Siegman, R. E. Murphy, and B. Vawter) have won deserved praise for their efforts in behalf of the study of the Bible in America.

Bibliography: J. BONSIRVEN et al., DBSuppl 4:561–646, with detailed bibliographies after the various sections. L. VENARD et al., Robert-Tricot 1:679–780. R. M. GRANT et al., InterDictBibl 1:106–141. J. SCHMID et al., LexThK² 3:1273–93. C. KÜHL and W. G. KÜMMEL, RGG³ 1:1227–51. F. HESSE et al., RGG³ 5: 1513–37. R. M. GRANT, *A Short History of the Interpretation of the Bible* (rev. ed. New York 1963). A. VINCENT, *Judaism,* tr. J. D. SCANLAN (London 1934). W. BACHER, *Die exegetische Terminologie der jüdischen Traditionsliteratur* (Leipzig 1899). W. BACHER, JewishEnc 3:164–174. M. MIELZINER, *Introduction to the Talmud* (New York 1925) 115–187. S. ROSENBLATT, *The Interpretation of the Bible in the Mishnah* (Baltimore 1935). B. SMALLEY, *The Study of the Bible in the Middle Ages* (2d ed. New York 1952; repr. Notre Dame 1964). C. SPICQ, *Esquisse*

d'une histoire de l'exégèse latine au moyen âge (Paris 1944). R. C. DENTAN, *Preface to Old Testament Theology* (rev. ed. New York 1963). H. H. ROWLEY, ed., *The Old Testament and Modern Study* (Oxford 1951). R. H. FULLER, *The New Testament in Current Study* (New York 1962). A. M. HUNTER, *Interpreting the New Testament, 1900–1950* (Philadelphia 1951). E. KÄSEMANN, *Essays on New Testament Themes,* tr. W. J. MONTAGUE (London 1964). W. KLASSEN and G. F. SNYDER, eds., *Current Issues in New Testament Interpretation* (New York 1962). R. SCHNACKENBURG, *New Testament Theology Today,* tr. D. ASKEW (New York 1963).

[T. A. COLLINS]

3. HERMENEUTICS

The science of scriptural interpretation and explanation. The term hermeneutics is derived from the Greek noun ἑρμηνεύς (of non-Indo-European origin) meaning an interpreter both in the sense of a translator and in that of an explainer. Etymologically it is not connected with the name of the god Hermes (Ἑρμῆς), who was the messenger, but not the interpreter, of the gods. The denominative verb ἑρμηνεύω means both to translate (e.g., in Jn 1.42; 9.7; Heb 7.2) and to explain (e.g., in Lk 24.27, where the better MSS, however, have διερμηνεύω—said of Jesus explaining the OT prophecies about Him). From the verb are derived the nouns ἑρμηνευτής (e.g., in 1 Cor 14.28, with the variant διερμηνευτής), interpreter, translator, and ἑρμηνεία (e.g., in 1 Cor 12.10; 14.26), interpretation, translation—both words in 1 Corinthians in regard to the need of explaining the meaning of the unintelligible words spoken by those who had the *gift of tongues.

The term hermeneutics was coined during the 17th century, after the Renaissance and Reformation had focused new interest upon the classics of Greece and Rome and upon the Bible in their original languages and sense. Scientific rules of interpretation were established and the art or science of hermeneutics became distinguishable among the manifold arts and sciences of modern times. J. C. Dannhauer, *Hermeneutica Sacra, sive methodus exponendarum Sacrarum Litterarum* (Strassburg 1654) seems to have been the first to use the term.

Natural Principles. One cannot simply pick up the Bible and hope to have a completely satisfying understanding of its message. The work is very ancient and emanates from a culture alien to Western man and modern man in general. A person must first of all determine whether he has in his hands an unadulterated copy of the ancient book, for many things can happen to a text as it passes from generation to generation over 2,000 or more years. Ordinarily he must have the work translated accurately into his own tongue. But even then there will be much obscurity, for the modern reader will be unfamiliar with the literary forms, the stylistic modes and stresses of the ancient composers; he will be unfamiliar with the times, persons, places, and the political and religious milieu to which there are so many references. Thus, before the Bible can be read intelligently, its text must be cleared of distracting and distorting scribal accretions or omissions, it must be faithfully translated, its forms determined by comparison with other contemporary literatures, its historical and cultural background probed and clarified, which brings into play the expensive physical as well as intellectual labor of the archeologist. Careful, disciplined study by specialists in the various fields of linguistics, textual and literary criticism, ancient history, geography, and archeology contributes to and may be said to fall under the title of hermeneutics in a broad sense.

Principles of Faith. One who has no belief in the divine origin and authority of the Scriptures can, of course, apply all these arts and sciences to the text and come to a clearer understanding of the books. The believer will add another ingredient to his hermeneutical effort, the normative force of certain tenets within his ecclesial tradition. For instance, the Catholic believes that Jesus is divine. He bases his belief in the divinity of Jesus upon the Scriptures, where Jesus is frequently given divine description or makes divine claims. The Catholic cannot suddenly say without qualification, therefore, that all these Scriptural descriptions of Jesus as divine are literary exaggerations or ways of saying that Jesus was an extraordinary man and no more. He will always opt to take the divinity of Jesus in the NT writings at face value. The tenet of Jesus' divinity will be hermeneutically normative for him as much as accurate linguistics, knowledge of forms, history, etc., are hermeneutically imperative. The Catholic believes in the historicity of salvation. Salvation itself is a pleasant concept, but it remains unreal until events, datable in time, definable in space, identifiable in a people, begin to happen. Then one has *salvation history, historical or actual salvation. The finger of God touches earth, and the event is recordable. The Catholic believes in salvation history, which really includes more than belief in salvation. Holding to this belief and deriving it, in fact, from Biblical testimony to salvific events, the Catholic cannot interpret passages descriptive or declarative of the Resurrection of Jesus as simply metaphorical ways of saying that the spirit of Jesus lives on beyond the grave. He will take such passages as basically descriptive or declarative of historical fact and not consider them totally metaphorical. Thus the general tenet of the historicity of salvation is normative in Catholic interpretation of scriptural passages.

This may appear nonscientific. It seems to allow faith and fixed principles of faith to interfere with candid, untrammeled human investigation and interpretation of the Bible. But it seems at least scientifically probable that the NT writers did mean to say that Jesus is divine and that He did rise from the dead. It would be most unscientific, then, to read back into their writings a metaphorical intent simply because a divine man and bodily resurrection are scientifically unpalatable. This would mean moving from a set principle or rigid dogma of the impossibility of an incarnate God or a resurrection to an interpretation compatible with that principle, a principle that stands just as normative for the nonbeliever as a tenet of faith for the believer. Ultimately, if scientific hermeneutics leads to the conclusion that the writers do literally declare Jesus divine and His Resurrection a fact, science must stop there; the scientifically disciplined interpreter must then either move into personal acceptance of the content, of possibilities and actualities beyond his experience, or remain uncommitted. In either case he is faithful to scientific investigation as far as it goes.

The interpreter, be he believer or nonbeliever, becomes unscientific only when he starts, not from the text, but from himself as subject and reads into the intention of the sacred writer a purpose or statement more in accord with the interpreter's estimate of what is true and possible. Thus the believing fundamentalist may insist that there were really walls of water at the Israelites' crossing of the "Reed Sea," when the sacred author merely wished to embellish his account of the Exodus; and the rationalist may insist that Resurrection or Transfiguration narratives are obvious idealizations of Jesus, when in fact the sacred author wished to bear witness to definite events and experiences.

In summary, hermeneutics, or interpretation of the Bible, involves scientific activity by which the true sense of the ancient author is determined. The interpreter utilizes the skills of the linguist, textual critic, literary critic, historian, and archeologist. He takes into account ancient interpretations by rabbis and Church Fathers. And if he is a believer, he submits his scientific understanding of a text to the judgment of his basic faith, a faith based on a genuinely traditional understanding of Scripture. The phrase, genuinely traditional, is used intentionally because there is much so-called tradition that scientific investigation exposes as untrue and not properly normative, e.g., the historicity of the *Tower of Babel story or of Jona's sojourn in the belly of a whale (see JONA, BOOK OF).

Textual Criticism. It is to be expected that the interpreter of a book or passage should have that book or passage before him. But when a manuscript is hundreds of years old and is itself a copy of the original work written hundreds of years earlier, one may legitimately wonder whether he has the original book before him after all. The fact is that the original works of Mark, Luke, Matthew, John, and Paul, as well as the original works of Isaia and Ezechiel as they came from their own or their disciples' pens, are gone. Even the copies closest to them in time have vanished through age, fire, and loss. The copies or fragments that are extant, though numerous enough, are centuries removed from the originals. The textual critic here steps in to make his invaluable contribution to correct Biblical interpretation. He painstakingly compares the hundreds of early and late copies, translations, and commentaries; he checks the isolated quotations of Scripture found in the sermons, letters, and expositions of the Church Fathers; he gleans from the few words on fragile Biblical fragments a continuity of thought, reconstructs a word or phrase, exercises paleographic skill to eliminate the accumulated scribal errors of centuries; he distinguishes a copyist's gloss from the true text of the author; and he discovers and completes omissions. In a word, from the mass of Biblical manuscripts, codices, and fragments available he attempts to reconstruct the Biblical text and to present the interpreter with a text that resembles the original documents as closely as is scientifically possible. *See* BIBLE, V (TEXTUAL CRITICISM).

Literary Criticism. To understand accurately any piece of literature, an interpreter must appreciate its literary form. Men communicate through a variety of forms suited to their purposes. This is true of oral communication. When a man wishes to convey light, intimate matter he chats. When the same man wishes to expound upon some serious matter, his tone becomes formal and sophisticated, and his vocabulary technical and more complex; he lectures. In the pulpit a man is also serious but edifying and moralizing in intent; he preaches. A person desirous solely of communicating his feelings about some person, experience, or object will move into rhythm and rhyme; he speaks poetry and may even break out into song.

Modern Literary Genres. Experience shows that when a man expresses himself he does so in one of a variety of modes suitable to his particular subject matter, his circumstances, and his purpose. These modes are to a great degree impersonal, for while the speaker's content may be new, he does not entirely fashion the forms he uses. These he accepts as established by society and provided in great variety to suit all conditions and purposes of communication. It is evident, too, that the individual must adhere to fixed modes of expression if he is to be understood, if he is to communicate effectively with society, for only to these supraindividual modes can society react sympathetically, with full comprehension of his message and true perception of his purpose. Just as man's oral expression must fulfill certain exigencies of society, so must his literature, his written self-expression. Literature is merely a more formal dialogue with society. And here, too, if true communication of one's purpose, ideas, sentiment, etc., is to be had, there must be some respectful recognition of society's literary habits, some dependence on those forms to which society can intelligently react. Depending on whether he wishes to report an event or comment on it, a newspaper writer will compose either an impersonal, brief, factual story or an editorial with its more intimate and persuasive touch. Whatever form he uses will receive sympathetic response from the contemporary reader.

Question of the appreciation of literary forms in modern literature may be purely academic, for in general a person will react correctly to current forms. Deliberate attention becoms imperative, however, when one treats writings of a bygone age, literature that had its origin centuries, even millennia earlier. In this case appreciation of the form is not quite so spontaneous, for in the course of time forms change, evolve, perhaps pass out of current use along with the people who used and understood them. A man finds himself faced with relics of that literature and yet completely out of contact with the milieu that shaped it, the society that sanctioned it, and the mentality that fully and fruitfully understood it; he is incapable of reacting intelligently to that literature or of perceiving the purpose for which the form was fashioned. He runs the risk of some rash attempt to interpret the literature in the light of his more recent forms. Some sense may thus be made of the work, but the more likely possibility is that one will arrive at a very inaccurate interpretation of the work's temper and message.

Ancient Literary Genres. The Bible is an ancient work. It is, moreover, the product of a region, culture, and mentality far removed from the modern world. Its forms, therefore, can strike a modern man as very unfamiliar and create difficulties of interpretation unless he can recapture the mentality of the authors and audience, revive the forms, and understand once again their particular intent. For centuries, however, men have read the story of *Noe (Noah) and responded to it as to some strictly historical report, the details of which correspond to those of some ancient event. Convinced of its historical form, men in time past have gone to great mental and even archeological exertion to prove the occurrence of a universal flood, to find the ark, etc. It is generally agreed now that the episode of Noe and the ark is not a piece of historical reporting but an imaginative literary creation of another form entirely, having not history so much as sublime religious truth

to convey. To read it as history upon the presumption that the author's intention was the detailed description of an ancient happening leads only to confusion, to intellectual difficulties, and thence to difficulties of faith. The form of the Noe story, instead of being considered strictly historical, must be understood as a primitive literary form that always attempted in a symbolic way to make sense out of reality, penetrate sense-perceptible reality for some answer to the whys and wherefores of it all. It was a form that, by means of symbolic events and beings, intended a concrete yet profound explanation of the origin of the surrounding world, the origin of the unique creature man, the problem of evil, etc. For want of a better term the equivocal title "myth" is generally given to this form but always with the above definition. What discursive thought was to the Greek, the mythical art was to the Semite—an attempt to explain reality. *See* MYTH AND MYTHOLOGY (IN THE BIBLE). Such were the pagan myths of antiquity—a rough philosophy. The story of Noe is an example of such a form. The story of Jona was read for centuries as a historical narrative. As such it creates many problems. But if it is read as a didactic tale of postexilic times dramatizing the point that Juda (Jona) must not run from its responsibilities toward the unenlightened Gentiles, it takes on perennial value.

Great progress has been made in this most vital task of properly appreciating the literary forms of the Bible. Through the archeological discoveries of the 19th century the civilizations of the ancient Near East have been more clearly revealed; the literatures of Egypt, Mesopotamia, Canaan, and the Hittite world have been brought to light and have revived the history and customs of those times and the mentality of the Biblical world. New insight has been gained into forms once alien. Modern man finds it easier now to attune himself to their mood, their purpose, and their particular truth.

Biblical Literary Genres. Hermann *Gunkel in particular directed the attention of Biblical scholars to serious appreciation of literary forms in Scripture. Scholars such as Martin Dibelius and Rudolf Bultmann have carried Gunkel's concern and method over into Gospel study and interpretation. Roman Catholic authority cautiously directed its scholars to the value of literary criticism in decrees promulgated by the *Pontifical Biblical Commission, e.g., those of June 23, 1905, and June 30, 1909. But Catholic authority and scholarship really backed into the area of *form criticism while waging a somewhat discouraging battle in defense of the inspiration and inerrancy of the Bible. During the 19th century, advances in archeology, ancient history, geology, and anthropology brought sometimes serious, sometimes sophomoric attacks upon the traditional data of the Bible in these areas. Critics saw cosmographical, anthropological, astronomical, and historical error on almost every page—statements and data that did not square with newly attained and valid scientific positions in these areas. After efforts to meet these challenges upon the authority of the Bible, which in retrospect smack of desperation, the Church saw the apologetical value of form appreciation and turned to literary criticism with greater dedication.

For example, the Book of Judith describes *Nabuchodonosor (Nebuchadrezzar), the neo-Babylonian empire builder, as a king of Assyria. This would be a gross historical error if the author of Judith really intended to write history. But if his intention were to write drama, a symbolic narrative offering consolation to its Jewish reader—if Nabuchodonosor and his Persian General Holofernes and the Assyrian host were deliberately chosen as symbols of Gentile oppression and Judith as a symbol of weak yet ultimately victorious Jewry, the charge of formal historical error could hardly be pressed. By giving more than superficial attention to the form of his literature the Catholic scholar can come to perceive as an allegory, a transformed myth, or didactic history what both he and his adversary once presupposed to be strict history or science. This settled, all conclusions drawn from erroneous presuppositions find themselves deprived of foundation. The problem of historical or scientific error vanishes. *See* LITERARY GENRES, BIBLICAL.

Importance of Literary Criticism. From its apologetical value Catholic authority came to see the positive, exegetical value of literary criticism. The encyclical of Pius XII, *Divino afflante Spiritu,* gave expression of this recognition:

> What the literal sense of a passage is, is not always as obvious in the speeches and writings of the ancient authors of the East as it is in the works of our own time. For what they wished to express is not to be determined by the rules of grammar and philology alone nor solely by the context; the interpreter must, as it were, go back wholly in spirit to those remote centuries of the East and with the aid of history, archeology, ethnology, and other sciences accurately determine what modes of writing, so to speak, the authors of that ancient period would be likely to use and in fact did use . . . . In explaining the Sacred Scripture and in demonstrating and proving its immunity from all error [the Catholic commentator] should make a prudent use of this means, determine to what extent the manner of expression or the literary mode adopted by the sacred writer may lead to a correct and genuine interpretation; and let him be convinced that this part of his office cannot be neglected without serious detriment to Catholic exegesis. [EnchBibl 558–560.]

This statement was supplemented by the response of the Pontifical Biblical Commission to Cardinal Suhard (Jan. 16, 1948) and by the Commission's "Instruction on the Historical Truth of the Gospels" (April 21, 1964).

Literal Sense. When the interpreter of the Bible is equipped with a Biblical text that approximates the long-lost original, when he is capable of probing the literary form of the text by comparison with the ancient literature unearthed by modern archeology and by application of critical ingenuity, when he is aware of the historical and cultural milieu within which the text was composed, and when he is guided by certain tenets of his faith, he is then in a position to discover more accurately the message intended by the sacred author. The sense he is primarily interested in is the literal sense—a term used to define the one sense the author himself wished to convey. It seems superfluous to say that an interpreter of any man's writings should, out of respect for that author and out of a sense of honesty and justice, try to read out of the work what the author meant to say. This becomes imperative, however, when his work has been accepted by generations as a norm of life, a revelation from God, who is considered the Author behind the human author. The Bible is universally and perpetually relevant, but too often in the course of time its word has been forced to fit the individual or the situation; in reality the individual or the situation ought to conform to the word, which is often a more painful process. A variety of forced, spurious interpretations may in the course of time come about and the meaning of the original inspired author become obscured. This experience has sharpened the concern of exegetes since the 18th century that the sense of the original author be of absolutely primary interest to the serious interpreter and that every scientific tool be used to assure objectivity in the search.

This interest in the literal sense is not to be confused with gross literalism. The literal sense of a passage is not to be identified with the sense that immediately and superficially strikes the modern reader. The first chapter of Genesis describes the origin of the world: in 7 days an earth-centered sphere is formed within a primeval sea. Some may conclude: the author wished to give an accurate description of the world's formation. But that would be naïve literalism. The true sense, the literal sense can be reached only when the author's times, purposes, and poetic inclinations are appreciated, and these can be appreciated only through difficult scientific critique of the text.

Typical and Fuller Senses. The NT itself interprets OT passages and applies many of them to Christ and the Christian event. For instance, in Ex 12.46 it is stated: "It [the Passover lamb] must be eaten in one and the same house; you may not take any of its flesh outside the house. You shall not break any of its bones." In Jn 19.32–34 it is said that the soldiers on Golgotha hastened the death of the thieves crucified with Jesus by breaking their legs, but that they had no need to do this to Jesus because he was already dead. The Evangelist then adds: "These things came to pass that the Scripture might be fulfilled, 'Not a bone of him shall you break'" (19.36). The author of the Exodus passage certainly spoke only of the *Passover lamb; he had no thought of Jesus or of this incident on the cross. John the Evangelist obviously given the words new meaning and added a sense that is other than the literal or primary sense of the original author. Catholic exegetes, respecting the inspiration of John, accept his interpretation of the Exodus passage; they admit that Ex 12.46 refers to Jesus in some way, even though the first inspired author had and could have had no such intention.

Typical Sense. Christians believe that Israel's long history culminated in Jesus and His new exodus from death to life. Since He drew those many persons and events to fulfillment in Himself and His activity, it should not be too much to expect that reflections, vague or clear anticipations of Jesus and the Christ event should be present in the events or persons that led up to Him. The Exodus under Moses prefigured the Exodus under Jesus; for that matter, Moses prefigured Jesus, as did Josue, David, and Elia. The Passover lamb, whose blood protected Israelites from the avenging angel, prefigured Jesus, whose blood saved all humanity. Since all these persons, events, and items set up a pattern that Jesus filled most amply, anything said of them in Scripture might be carried over and applied to Jesus by some later inspired writer who saw the fulfillment Jesus brought them.

The original OT author, it is true, may not have seen all this or intended to say more than he did about immediate events, persons, and items. But if these events, persons, and items have some typical relationship to Jesus, then the statements made about them are legitimately transferable to Jesus. This new Christian sense read into many OT passages has traditionally been called the spiritual or typical sense to distinguish it from the literal or primitive and primary sense of the original author. (*See* TYPE AND ANTITYPE.)

It is obvious that some control must be placed upon reading typical senses out of passages of the OT. Christians do indeed believe that Christ and Christianity are prefigured by the OT as a whole, but to look for Christ and Christianity in every figure or event or item of the OT would lead only to distasteful and arbitrary allegorizing and to confusion rather than edification. Pius XII in his encyclical *Divino afflante Spiritu* stated the traditional guide lines for typology: "The exegete, just as he must search out and expound the literal meaning of the words intended and expressed by the sacred writer, must also seek the spiritual sense, provided it is clearly intended by God . . .. Now our divine Savior Himself points out to us and teaches us this same sense in the holy Gospel; the Apostles also . . . profess it in their spoken and written words; the unchanging tradition of the Church approves it; and finally the most ancient usage of the liturgy proclaims it . . .." In effect, wherever the typical sense of an OT passage is explicitly or implicitly cited in the inspired NT, such an OT passage has typical value. It is applicable to Christ. Later ecclesiastical or patristic or liturgical citations may also determine OT passages with typical value, but there is little inclination today to give too definitive a force to these criteria.

Fuller Sense. Many Catholic exegetes, in treating the Christian sense of OT passages, dislike the term typical because there seems an implication that the OT words themselves do not refer to Christ and that the OT writers themselves refer, not to Christ, but only to those extra-Biblical realities to which the words are primarily directed. One could imagine that the actual words of the OT refer not directly to the NT, but only obliquely through their description of persons, events, and things that prefigured Christ regardless of the Bible. These exegetes prefer to get the Christian reference back into the words themselves and not leave the OT authors and their compositions so myopic that they lose all future thrust and all focus on Christ. This is called the *sensus plenior* or fuller sense of Scripture.

The upholder of the fuller sense of an OT passage may admit that the sacred author did not see Christ on the cross when he legislated that no bone of the Passover lamb should be broken. But the Bible is not only a human work; it is also God's work, inspired by a divine author, with a vantage point beyond that of the human author. From that vantage point God may intend more to be read from a particular OT passage than the human author and his contemporaries could hope to or need understand. But a NT writer, having attained through the fulfillment that Christ brought to the OT something of the divine Author's own vantage point, would be able to see the deeper, fuller sense of that Exodus passage and declare it openly.

Persons partial to the fuller sense would not rule out all openness to this fuller sense on the part of the OT author. If Isaia, in predicting the birth of a great king and the commencement of a new era of peace and prosperity—the arrival of messianic fulfillment in the future —fell short and expected all this in the near future (Is 7.14), within the reign of King Ezechia, he nevertheless did speak of messianic fulfillment and his words are

therefore legitimately applicable to the coming of Jesus. No radical violence seems to be done to Isaia and his intended sense in the process.

But since the theory of the fuller sense to Scripture arises from the NT and ecclesiastical readings of OT passages, one would not look for a fuller sense except in those OT passages (or NT passages in the case of later ecclesiastical developments of NT passages) where the NT (or strictly official ecclesiastical authority) sees a fuller sense. This places the search for the fuller sense of Scripture under the same definite control that bridles typology.

Consequent and Accommodated Senses. Interpretation of the Scripture need not cease with arrival at the genuine sense of the sacred author. Speculation upon his meaning and application of his words to newer situations follows. This may mean a lengthy development of the man's thought and the re-presentation or application of his thought by means of newer and more understandable thought and speech patterns. In other words, men theologize and preach the Biblical word and give it precision and further extension beyond the limited realm and forms of the author himself. There is or should be no real void between the genuine sense of the sacred writer and the elucidations and applications of the later theologians; the statements of theologians, whether scholastically or existentially couched, may be considered legitimate "interpretations" of Scripture. The term consequent sense has been current in Catholic circles until recently to describe the issue of this process.

The popular usage of Biblical passages, picked at random to fit random human situations, has little to do with serious interpretation of the Bible. One may say of the political fortunes of public servants, "Many are called, but few are chosen" (Mt 22.14). Certainly the sacred author did not have these individuals or this area of life in mind when he wrote those words. Only the most naïve would take such accommodation of scriptural passages as clear and valuable interpretations of the mind and interest of the Biblical writer.

Modern Tensions within Hermeneutics. There is a continual tension experienced by Biblical interpreters, a tension between two poles of scientific and religious interpretation that are really complementary. Scientific exegesis was emphasized throughout the 18th and 19th centuries and established itself firmly above confessional differences and other influences during the 20th. It has been emphasized in Catholic circles since the turn of the century and has received increasing vindication and official support since the 1943 encyclical of Pius XII; its approbation in the NT area was markedly evident in the *Instruction on the Historical Truth of the Gospels* of 1964.

Scripture and Theology. Scientific exegesis, utilizing the tools of textual criticism, historical and literary criticism, etc., helps the interpreter pin down the meaning of Scripture. By scientific discipline he is freed to arrive as near as possible to the truth offered by the sacred writer. His science serves and expresses his reverence for the sacred text. Too often nonessential yet rigid theological positions, apologetic stances, and pastoral or historical needs have led to pious manipulation of the Scriptures to fit the stance or need. Scripture became an argument in support of some thesis. The dignity of Scripture was recognized by placing it first among patristic, scholastic, and magisterial arguments in favor of the thesis. Yet the taking of Scripture passages out of context and reading a thesis no longer out of the passage but into it betrays only a superficial reverence for God's word. Scientific exegesis reacted to that tendency, freed the text and the author from obscuration, and allowed the Biblical word to receive something of its complete impact.

The scientific approach has not been without profound ecumenical effect. While exegetes do not leave their norms of faith behind to work only with their exegetical disciplines, they do first use their disciplines honestly, seeking whatever truth the disciplines offer, and then (if it is possible to speak of a temporal breakdown of the process) they bring their authentic faith to judge the result and add the penetration that touches the heart of the matter. The area of scientific discipline is shared by all respectable exegetes regardless of religious confession, and this makes for much unanimity and cooperation. The American Catholic exegete John L. McKenzie has written this on the subject:

> For all exegetes the problems are the same in fixing the text and establishing the historical background of the OT and NT. Indeed, if all scholars were perfectly objective, entire unanimity should be theoretically possible in exegesis itself; for the meaning of the Bible has been determined by its authors, not by its interpreters. Even in the theology of the Bible agreement should be possible, if we mean by biblical theology a synthesis formed by induction. But we are not entirely objective, and it is doubtful if we ever shall be before the Second Coming. As long as confessional differences persist, the best each of us can do is to know his own biases and to see that his scholarly work is affected by them as little as possible. [JBiblLit 79 (1960) 199.]

Danger of Overspecialization. The work of scientific or historical exegesis is by no means over. It has hardly begun. But emphasis in this direction has brought some reaction by Biblical theologians who would like to bring the sacred word into the present day and allow it to take deep effect. There is a feeling that concentration on the text itself, a very disciplined discovery of the precise meaning of Isaia in the 8th century B.C. or of a Psalm verse, may put the interpreter back into the book and out of his own times. There is anxiety over the specialization and isolation that the scientific approach actually leads to, so that textual criticism, historical criticism, study and evaluation of forms, archeology, and linguistics maintain only a tenuous relationship among themselves and stand even more tenuously related to kerygmatic needs, i.e., the need to make the Biblical word a powerful challenge to modern man and a meaningful address to his needs.

Kerygmatic Application of Scripture. The theologically and kerygmatically inclined school stresses the need of faith as well as of scientific discipline in interpreting the Scriptures. It sees Sacred Scripture not so much the object to be studied in a sterilized laboratory, as the subject speaking to the reader and interpreter, who is the object of the inspired word. It does not repudiate the scientific approach, by any means—indeed, it embraces the security that disciplined study provides. But it insists that Scripture has to be read with commitment if it is to be read with any value; it insists that the exegete must not only discover correctly the content of Scripture but must somehow, through utilization of modern forms, translate its challenge to the hearer and reader. Relevant *Biblical theology and *Kerygmatic theology are desiderata in this regard.

Charismatic Interpretation. But the new hermeneutic actually goes deeper than that, for relevant theology has always been desirable and sometimes even attained. The new hermeneutical thrust, influenced by *existentialism, sees in exegesis and theology no mere interpretation or detached evaluation of the book. Exegesis and Biblical theology must extend the inspired word itself and convey it with all its creativity right into the present. Hermeneutic activity, which would embrace exegesis, theologizing, kerygmatic preaching, and catechizing, is simply the vital prolongation of the inspired word itself to modern man. It seems that the very charism of the sacred writer must carry through and stimulate the interpreter, theologian, preacher, and teacher to speak the sacred word as his very own, to be a vehicle of it even as the prophet and sacred author were vehicles of it, for ultimately it is God's word uttered to all men out of time and space and into all times and places.

Conclusion. This trend is understandable. The need for relevance in a totally new human era has promoted the trend. But it causes understandable anxieties among those who feel that a scientific attitude to Scripture may suffer under the pressure for relevance to the here and now. The pull in both directions is legitimate; the hermeneutical problem is to reach the harmony that will respect both poles and prove beneficial to men in general. James Muilenberg has summed up the situation well:

> I should like to make clear what really should be taken for granted, that in our endeavor to interpret the OT we assume the twofold role of both *spectator* and *auditor.* As spectator we must inquire into the original text with all the instruments available to us for such an undertaking: textual criticism; philology (grammar, syntax, lexical study); literary form, style and rhetoric; historical criticism including historical setting and situation; and psychological analysis. These gains we may not forfeit. The tendency in various quarters to reject historical criticism is a fatal *Irrweg* of contemporary scholarship. . . . But the interpreter is also the *hearer.* He must appropriate the word to himself, the ancient words must somehow become his, he must participate in the live dialogue of the *I* with the *Thou.* This interior relation of subject and object, speaker and hearer, is more than a psychological state of empathy or *Einfühlung.* It is determined rather by his belonging to the community, his sharing in its life and faith, by his understanding of the singularity of his own historical life revealed to him in Scripture. He does not stand aloof as a spectator; he himself participates in the *narrative* life of Israel; he appropriates its symbols and images. Unless some such relationship is established, he will be standing on the outside looking for ideas, conceptions, principles, etc., and other values which it is not the purpose of Scripture in the first instance to offer him. [JBiblLit 77 (1958) 22.]

Bibliography: P. CRUVEILHIER, DBSuppl 3:1482–1524. A. BEA, LexThK² 2:435–439. A. METZINGER and A. PENNA, EncCatt 7:100–108. R. TAMISIER, *Catholicisme* 5:670–673. G. EBELING, RGG³ 3:242–262. L. VAGANAY, Robert-Tricot 1:731–780. P. SYNAVE and P. BENOIT, *Prophecy and Inspiration,* tr. A. DULLES and T. L. SHERIDAN (New York 1961). J. LEVIE, *The Bible: Word of God in Words of Men,* tr. S. H. TREMAN (New York 1962). J. M. ROBINSON and J. B. COBB, eds., *The New Hermeneutic* (New York 1964). J. MUILENBERG et al., "Problems in Biblical Hermeneutics," JBiblLit 77 (1958) 18–38. J. L. MCKENZIE, "Problems in Hermeneutics in Roman Catholic Exegesis," *ibid.* 197–204. L. ALONSO SCHÖKEL, "Hermeneutics in the Light of Language and Literature," CathBiblQuart 25 (1963) 371–386. C. WESTERMANN, ed., *Essays on O.T. Hermeneutics* (Richmond, Va. 1963). R. E. BROWN, *The Sensus Plenior of Sacred Scripture* (Baltimore 1955); "The Sensus Plenior in the Last Ten Years," CathBiblQuart 25 (1963) 262–285. B. VAWTER, "The Fuller Sense: Some Considerations," *ibid.* 26 (1964) 85–96. R. NORTH, "Scripture Trends in 1964," AmEcclRev 152 (1965) 361–397.

[G. WOOD]

BIBLE, VII (PAPAL TEACHING)

Official Catholic teaching concerning the Bible is to be found in various classes of documents: decrees of the general ecumenical councils, letters and encyclicals of popes, decrees of Curia Congregations, and decrees of particular councils. These documents do not have identical authority or binding force. Decrees of ecumenical councils, being infallible, are essential to Catholic belief. The other sources, not infallible and of lesser authority, present nevertheless official Catholic teaching concerning the Bible (Denz introd. pp. 7–9).

Papal teachings described in this article refer to: the existence of a collection of inspired books, inspiration of the Bible, inerrancy of the Bible, interpretation of the Bible, study of the Bible, texts and translations of the Bible, and reading the Bible. *See* VATICAN COUNCIL II for its *Constitution on Divine Revelation,* which treats of the relation of Scripture and Tradition as forming one sacred deposit of revelation, Biblical inspiration, literary genres, salvation history, use of the Bible, etc.

Papal Teaching on the Canon of Sacred Scripture. Catholic teaching holds that there exists a collection of sacred Christian books known as the Bible. The exact contents of the Biblical canon are determined by the infallible Church alone. *See* BIBLE, III (CANON). The fundamental reason for canonicity is the divine inspiration of a book. Because of inspiration, the books of the Bible have God as their author.

As the Jews had their sacred books, so the Christian Church possessed its own collection of sacred writings. The author of 2 Pt 3.16 places the writings of Paul on a level with "Scripture."

The definitive listing of the NT books was accomplished neither swiftly nor easily. The early popes repeatedly found it necessary to condemn apocryphal works (Denz 202, 213, 354). During the 3d and 4th centuries, doubts were expressed concerning the canonicity of several particular books—those books now called deuterocanonical by Catholics and apocryphal by non-Catholics.

Early Canons. In effect, the canon was established by A.D. 393, when the Council of Hippo recorded it (EnchBibl 16–19). Occasional doubts concerning the canonicity of deuterocanonical books were voiced until the 15th century. There was no pressing need for an authoritative statement by the Church concerning the canon, however, until a century before the Protestant Reformation; consequently the canon was given authoritative and clear determinations only in the 15th and 16th centuries. *See* TEACHING AUTHORITY OF THE CHURCH (MAGISTERIUM).

The Council of Paris (1527–28) taught in its fourth decree that the authority of the Church is necessary to determine which books are in the Bible. The Council stated: "When disagreements arise concerning the faith, Scripture often is consulted in vain—unless the certain and infallible authority of the Church, which separates the canonical book from the apocryphal, . . . settles the question" (EnchBibl 53). Catholic teaching, therefore, maintains that only the certain authority of the Church is sufficient to determine which books are in the Bible. Catholics find only in the infallible witness of the Church a theologically satisfactory basis for accepting the canon of Scripture.

The same Council, appealing to the divine guidance of the Holy Spirit, affirmed the traditional canon of the Scriptures as taught by the third Council of Carthage in 397, by the decree of Innocent I in 405, and by the *Gelasian Decree (EnchBibl 53, 54, 19, 21, 26).

Definitive Canon. The traditional canon had already been formally set down by the Ecumenical Council of Florence in its "Decree for the Jacobites," on Feb. 4, 1442 (EnchBibl 47). The books were again listed by the Ecumenical Council of Trent in *Sacrosancta* of April 8, 1546. Trent added: "If anyone, however, does not accept, as sacred and canonical, the same books entire with all their parts, as they are accustomed to be read in the Catholic Church and as they are contained in the old Vulgate Latin edition . . . let him be anathema" (Denz 1504). This decree made it clear that the deuterocanonical sections of Esther and Daniel are canonical. Since the Council of Trent, then, the question of canonicity has been settled. The number of books of the Bible is 72, with 45 in the OT and 27 in the NT.

The internal reason for canonicity was described by the first Vatican Ecumenical Council. Referring to the decree of Trent mentioned above, Vatican I stated: "But the Church accepts them as sacred and canonical, not because, composed by human industry alone, they were then approved by its authority, nor only because they contain revelation without error, but because, having been written under the inspiration of the Holy Spirit, they have God as author, and as such have been handed down to the Church" (Denz 3006).

One must note, however, that no action of the Church causes a book to be inspired. The Church exercises its infallible judgment to certify *post factum* that a particular book was inspired when it was written. The fact that God is its Author makes a book to be inspired. The Holy Spirit merely prevents the Church from erring in judging which books are inspired and included in the Bible.

Papal Teaching on Inspiration. Catholic teaching describes inspiration as a supernatural action by which the Holy Spirit influences the will, intellect, and faculties of the human author, without, however, impairing his freedom or erasing his human imprint on the inspired book. Because of inspiration, the primary Author of Sacred Scripture is God Himself; the secondary author, the human writer [*see* BIBLE, II (INSPIRATION)].

The attribution of inspiration to the Holy Spirit is constant in Catholic teaching. It is found in formulas of profession of faith as early as the 4th century (Denz 41, 46, 48); it is expressly used by the Councils of Florence (Denz 1334) and of Trent (Denz 1501). The same attribution is expressed by the opening and identifying words of the Biblical encyclicals of Benedict XV (*Spiritus Paraclitus* or "The Paraclete Spirit") and of Pius XII (*Divino afflante Spiritu* or "Under the Inspiration of the Divine Spirit").

Definition of Leo XIII. In the first papal encyclical devoted to the Bible (*Providentissimus Deus,* "The Most Provident God") Leo XIII described the manner in which inspiration took place. Referring to the influence of God on the human authors of these books, the Pontiff wrote: "For by supernatural power He so moved and impelled them to write—He so assisted them when writing—that the things which He ordered, and those only, they first rightly understood, then willed faithfully to write down, and finally expressed in apt words and with infallible truth." (Denz 3293).

Explanation of Benedict XV. Benedict XV added that inspiration did not impair the freedom of the human author nor subtract from the imprint of his labors. The Pontiff stated that the individual authors worked in complete freedom under the divine influence of inspiration, and that each of them wrote in accordance with his individual nature and character. The result of this freedom, wrote Benedict, was that in composition, in language, and in style and mode of expression, each human author used his own gifts and powers (EnchBibl 448). Consequently, Catholic teaching holds that the single or plural authors of books of the Bible were intelligent, free, and active authors.

Since 1893 the popes have repeatedly rejected any interpretation of inspiration that denied or reduced its essential supernatural nature. Thus Leo XIII opposed the denial of inspiration by the Rationalists (EnchBibl 100); Pius X in 1907 warned against a similar Modernist understanding of inspiration (Denz 3491); and in 1943 Pius XII complained about inspiration's being restricted to faith and morals or to a hidden divine meaning (Denz 3887).

According to papal teaching, then, inspiration is a supernatural action by which God influenced the human author in such fashion that the written message is the word of God—attributed primarily to God as its Author. At the same time, the written word is, mysteriously, also the product of the talents and free labors of the secondary human author.

Papal Teaching on Inerrancy. Catholic doctrine maintains that, because the books of the Bible have God as Author, they are free from error. Any theory that detracts from Biblical inerrancy is reprobated. Sacred Scripture was not, however, written to teach physical sciences and should not be interpreted as a scientific work.

Vatican I alluded to the Bible's inerrancy. The Council stated that the specific reason for canonicity is inspiration and not other reasons, not even "because they [the canonical books] contain revelation without error" (Denz 3006).

As Presented in Providentissimus Deus. The clearest statement of Catholic doctrine on Biblical inerrancy is found in *Providentissimus Deus.* Leo XIII states that inerrancy is an inescapable corollary of divine inspiration. "For all the books . . . are written wholly and entirely, with all their parts, at the dictation of the Holy Spirit; and so far is it from being possible that any error can coexist with inspiration, that inspiration not only is essentially incompatible with error, but excludes and rejects it as it is impossible that God Himself, the supreme Truth, can utter that which is not true" (Denz 3292). The Pontiff adds that those who maintain that error is possible in any genuine passage of the sacred writings must either pervert the Catholic notion of inspiration or must make God the author of such error (EnchBibl 126).

The popes have emphasized, however, that the original texts, only, were inspired and free from error and that copies and translations are inerrant insofar as they conform to the original texts. But no original texts are extant, and copies and translations contain additions, omissions, and other textual faults. It is the task of textual criticism to correct these mistakes. Pius XII wrote of textual criticism: "Its very purpose is to ensure that the sacred text be restored as perfectly as possible, be purified from the corruptions due to the carelessness of copyists and be freed, as far as may be done, from glosses and omissions, from the interchange and repetition of words and from all other kinds of mistakes . . ." (EnchBibl 548).

The popes have insisted that any theory that diminishes inerrancy cannot be tolerated. In 1893 Leo XIII wrote: "It is absolutely wrong . . . to admit that the sacred writer has erred" (Denz 3291). In similar fashion interpretations making the Bible a purely mythical story have been condemned: by Pius IX in 1864 (Denz 2907) and by Vatican I (Denz 3034).

In 1920, Benedict XV in *Spiritus Paraclitus* denounced theories that attempted to exclude from inerrancy nonreligious or profane elements, that regarded historical sections to be without foundation in reality, that discovered in the Bible noninspired "tacit" or hidden quotations, or that undermined in any way Scripture's authority and credibility (Denz 3652–54). In 1950, Pius XII in *Humani generis* repudiated the opinion that inerrancy pertains only to religious sections in the Bible (Denz 3887).

No Conflict between Bible and Science. Referring to apparent conflicts between the Bible and the physical sciences, Leo XIII made it clear that the purpose of the Bible is not to teach scientific data and that it is therefore unjust to judge the Bible as if it were a book of science. The Bible expresses scientific data according to external appearances, with the same concepts and words that the comparatively uneducated people of antiquity used in writing of natural phenomena. The sacred writers did not seek to penetrate nature's secrets, but described things in figurative language, or in terms commonly used at the time, "and which in many instances are daily used at this day, even by the most eminent men of science" (Denz 3288).

Hence the Holy Father ruled out any true discrepancy between the theologian and the scientist, as long as each confines himself to his own field (Denz 3287). The Church does not dictate to scientists doctrines about the age of the universe, the world, or the human race, or about evolution. The Church tells all people to search for religious, not scientific, data in the salvation history of the Bible. It asks scientists to recognize theories as theories and not to ridicule the Bible for something it was never intended to teach.

The recent popes were confident that objections against Biblical inerrancy would in time be satisfactorily answered. The statement of Leo XIII is noteworthy: "There have been objections without number perseveringly directed against Scripture for many a long year, which have been proved to be futile and are now never heard of" (Denz 3294). A half century later Pius XII, looking back on the crisis of rationalism, wrote: "Thus it has come about that confidence in the authority and historical value of the Bible, somewhat shaken in the case of some by so many attacks, today among Catholics is completely restored" (EnchBibl 562). He also stated that progress made in the past offered hope for the future resolution of difficult Biblical problems (EnchBibl 563).

Papal Teaching on Biblical Interpretation. Catholic teaching holds that the interpreter must follow the teaching authority of the Church. Interpretation that neglects the supernatural character of the Bible or that insists upon independent and purely individual interpretation is rejected. True Biblical interpretation is founded upon the literal sense of the text.

The words of 2 Pt 3.16–17 have set the tone for subsequent papal teaching concerning interpretation of the Scriptures. In reference to Paul's epistles, the text states: "In these epistles there are certain things difficult to understand, which the unlearned and the unstable distort, just as they do the rest of the Scriptures also, to their own destruction. You, therefore, brethren, since you know this beforehand, be on your guard lest, carried away by the error of the foolish, you fall away from your own steadfastness." The successors of Peter have similarly insisted on the care to be used in interpreting the Scriptures. On April 23, 451, Leo I wrote that "it is not permitted . . . to think concerning the divine scriptures otherwise than the blessed Apostles and Fathers declared and taught" (EnchBibl 25).

Authentic Interpretation of the Church. This fundamental rule is based upon the guidance of the Holy Spirit promised to the Church in Jn 14.26. After having been repeated by councils and popes, it was formally stated by Trent: ". . . the Council declares that no one, relying on his own ingenuity, in matters of faith and morals pertaining to the development of Christian doctrine, should distort Sacred Scripture to suit himself, contrary to that sense which the holy Mother Church has held and continues to hold, whose place it is to judge concerning the true sense and interpretation of Holy Scriptures" (Denz 1507). The same doctrine was later affirmed by Vatican I (Denz 3007).

The doctrine is based upon the divine character of the Bible and of the Church and the transmission of the Bible to the Church. In the words of Leo XIII: "God has delivered the Holy Scripture to the Church, and . . . in reading and making use of His Word, (men) must follow the Church as their guide and teacher. St. Irenaeus long ago taught that where the *charismata* of God were, there the truth was to be learned, and the Holy Scripture was safely interpreted by those who had the apostolic succession" (EnchBibl 108). The same doctrine was repeated by Benedict XV when he quoted Jerome's statement, "Any man who is joined to Peter's Chair is my man," and stated that Jerome had a "rule of faith" that enabled him to refute false interpretations, namely, "Yes, but the Church of God does not admit that" (EnchBibl 471–472). Pius XII confirmed the same doctrine in his *Divino afflante Spiritu* (Denz 3826).

An analysis of the *analogy of faith as a guide to correct interpretation was given by Leo XIII. After stating that the same God was the Author both of the sacred books and of the doctrine committed to the Church, he wrote that it is impossible for any legitimate interpretation to be extracted from the Bible that is at variance with the doctrine of the Church. Any interpretation is therefore false that makes the sacred writers disagree or that is opposed to Church doctrine (EnchBibl 109).

Unanimous Interpretation of the Fathers. An additional source of Catholic interpretation is the writings of the Church Fathers. Their unanimous agreement on an interpretation is considered binding. Thus the 9th-century Council of Meldense (EnchBibl 37), the 16th-century Council of Florence (EnchBibl 50–51), Trent (EnchBibl 62), and Vatican I (EnchBibl 78) all obliged Catholics to follow the Fathers in interpreting the Bible. The last two councils mentioned, both of them ecumenical, specifically obligated Catholics not to interpret

the Bible contrary to the unanimous agreement of the Fathers. Leo XIII stated: "The Holy Fathers, we say, are of supreme authority, whenever they all interpret in one and the same manner any text of the Bible, as pertaining to the doctrine of faith or morals; for their unanimity clearly evinces that such interpretation has come down from the Apostles as a matter of Catholic faith" (Denz 3284). This principle, however, is not easily applied to an individual text of Scripture. Only a few texts can be demonstrated to have been interpreted unanimously by the Fathers.

The obligation of Catholics to follow the Fathers is certainly not a deterrent against further study of Biblical passages. Leo XIII explicitly stated that "the unshrinking defense of the Holy Scripture . . . does not require that we should equally uphold all the opinions which each of the Fathers or the more recent interpreters have put forth . . .." The authority of the Fathers obtains in areas of faith. In other areas, especially in that of natural science, they enjoy no special authority (EnchBibl 122).

False Systems of Interpretation. The popes frequently warned against false systems of interpreting the Bible. Each of these repeated injunctions reflected the difficulties that the Church was then facing. Innocent III in 1299 warned the people of Metz that, though the desire to study the Scriptures was commendable, it was wrong to study them apart from the Church's teaching authority and to presume themselves superior to the priests in Scriptural studies (Denz 770–771).

Shortly after the Protestant Reformation, Trent forbade private interpretation of the Scriptures contrary to the Church's doctrine (Denz 1507). This fundamental issue of the Reformation was the reason for the reluctance of the Church in some countries (notably England) to permit vernacular translations without notes to express the guidance of the Church. Indiscriminate reading of the Bible with independent interpretation was forbidden by Pius IV in 1564 (Denz 1853). For the same reasons, non-Catholic Bible societies, established to spread Bible translations to be interpreted without the Church's guidance, were reproved by Pius VII in 1816 (Denz 2710–12), by Gregory XVI in 1844 (Denz 2771), and by Pius IX in 1846 (Denz 2784).

The rationalistic attitude toward interpretation of Scripture—an attitude equivalent to a denial of the supernatural in the Bible—was the occasion for Leo XIII's vigorous *Providentissimus Deus*. Referring to the adversaries of the Bible, the Pontiff wrote: "Now we have to meet the rationalists, true children and inheritors of the older heretics who, trusting in their turn to their own way of thinking, have rejected even the scraps and remnants of Christian belief which have been handed down to them" (EnchBibl 100). Fourteen years later Pius X condemned the modernist approach to the Bible that attempted to emancipate interpretation from the Church's teaching authority (Denz 3401, 3546).

Importance of Literal Sense. A further papal concern has been to combat a type of interpretation that is founded only on a "spiritual" or mystical understanding of the Scriptures. The pontiffs insisted upon interpreting Scripture according to the literal sense, as intended by the human author, rather than according to a mystical interpretation that neglected the literal sense. Thus in the 5th century a prospective bishop was to be examined on, "Whether he is careful in the senses of the Scriptures" (Denz 325). The question of the Biblical senses is treated in detail by Benedict XV: "In the first place, then, we must study the literal or historical meaning. . . . Jerome then goes on to say that all interpretation rests on the literal sense. . . . Consequently he repudiates many mystical interpretations alleged by ancient writers; for he feels that they are not sufficiently based upon the literal meaning" (EnchBibl 485–486).

In 1940 the booklet of Dain Cohenel, an anonymous priest, was placed on the Index because of its excessive reliance on mystical interpretation while neglecting the literal sense. The Biblical Commission in 1941 again stressed the fundamental importance of the literal sense (Denz 3792–93). The same teaching was expressed by Pius XII in 1943 (Denz 3826–28).

The literal sense is the sense intended by the human author and expressed by the words in their context. It includes metaphors and other figures of speech intended by the author. Pius XII wrote that interpreters must consider their foremost task to be the discerning and defining of the literal sense of Scripture (Denz 3826). He admits, however, the existence of the "spiritual" sense. The spiritual sense is found in OT passages where God intended to prefigure something to come in the NT. It is a true sense of Scripture (because intended by God) and can be known only through a divine revelation—expressed by Christ, the Apostles, or the Church. The Pope concluded: "Let Catholic exegetes then disclose and expound this spiritual significance, intended and ordained by God, with that care which the dignity of the divine Word demands; but let them scrupulously refrain from proposing as the genuine meaning of Sacred Scripture other figurative senses" (Denz 3828). The neglect of the literal sense and excessive reliance on a hidden spiritual meaning was again repudiated in 1950 by Pius XII in *Humani generis* (Denz 3888).

Directives of Biblical Commission. As a help to Catholics in understanding Biblical questions, Leo XIII established in 1902 the *Pontifical Biblical Commission. Its duty was "to effect that in every possible manner the divine text will find here and from every quarter the most thorough interpretation which is demanded by our times, and be shielded not only from every breath of error, but also from every temerarious opinion" (EnchBibl 139). The Commission issued a series of responses that gave authoritative guidance to Catholics in difficult areas of Scripture studies. The responses were not unchangeable decrees, but answers to "what is demanded by our times," (Denz 3862–64, "Letter to Cardinal Suhard"). See also A. Kleinhans, LexThK² 2:359–360; E. F. Siegman, CathBiblQuart (1956) 23–39, 144–146.

Specific directives on the interpretation of certain passages were given by Benedict XII in 1341 (EnchBibl 45), by Pius VI in 1779 (EnchBibl 74), by Leo XIII in 1897 (EnchBibl 135). All the responses of the Biblical Commission are collected in *Rome and the Study of Scripture* (St. Meinrad, Ind. 1958) 115–136. The Commission published in 1941 its "Letter to the Archbishops and Bishops of Italy" (Denz 3792–96) on literal and spiritual senses and on the meaning of Trent's decree on the authority of the Vulgate. Its "Letter to Cardinal Suhard" (1948) gave new directives on the Pentateuchal sources and the literary form of the first 11 chapters of Genesis (Denz 3862–64). Its *Instruction*

on the Historical Truth of the Gospels (1964) gave new directives on the sources and understanding of the Gospels.

Study of the Bible. The history of the Church shows persistent efforts to encourage Bible study. In the 4th century, shortly after the official recognition of Christianity in Rome, Pope Damasus directed Jerome to prepare an improved Latin translation of the Bible. The efforts of Damasus are described in *Spiritus Paraclitus* (EnchBibl 445). In 798 the local Council of Riesbach obligated priests to "read and understand the Sacred Scriptures" (EnchBibl 35). The Council of *Vienne in 1311 passed legislation making scientific Biblical study possible. It endowed chairs of Hebrew, Greek, Arabic, and Aramaic languages at the universities of Rome, Paris, Oxford, Bologna, and Salamanca (EnchBibl 41–43). Trent, while making Scripture reading obligatory in churches and monasteries, recommended the establishment of free schools "for clerics and other poor scholars" so that they might learn to read the Scriptures and gave privileges to those who taught and studied the Bible (EnchBibl 65–72).

Seminary Study. Since the end of the 19th century, papal directives on Scripture study have been more voluminous. Leo XIII outlined the seminary Scripture course and recommended the study of Oriental languages and of natural sciences for a better understanding of the Bible (EnchBibl 100–119). In 1906 Pius X set down a revised curriculum for seminary Biblical studies (EnchBibl 162–180). A decade later the *Code of Canon Law made Scripture a mandatory course in major seminaries and recommended that Scripture professors teach no other subjects (EnchBibl 433–434). In 1924 Pius XI insisted that seminary Scripture professors have the requisite Roman academic Biblical degree (EnchBibl 508); in 1950 the Biblical Commission issued a lengthy instruction on the duties of a Scripture professor and further recommendations on the curriculum of studies and the manner of teaching (EnchBibl 582–610).

Graduate Study. To assure that Scripture teachers would be properly trained, Pius X in 1909 founded in Rome the *Pontifical Biblical Institute (EnchBibl 282–298). The institute, entrusted to the Jesuits, has trained Scripture professors to teach in seminaries throughout the world. Revised rules for its operation were issued by Benedict XV in 1916 (EnchBibl 417–432).

The popes also established the degrees of bachelor, licentiate, and doctor of Sacred Scripture. They can be granted by either the Biblical Commission or the Biblical Institute. Requirements for them were set down in 1904 (EnchBibl 149–157), revised in 1910 (EnchBibl 344–382), in 1939 (EnchBibl 521), and revised again in 1942 (EnchBibl 534). Hence the popes have endeavored to keep the requirements for the degrees in pace with Biblical developments.

Scholarly Research. To Catholics generally the popes have given considerable latitude in Bible studies. Recent popes have stated that few Biblical texts have been authoritatively interpreted by the Church and that a vast area is available for free investigation. Leo XIII, after instructing Scripture students to follow the teachings of the Church in matters of faith and morals, wrote: "A wide field is still left open to the private student, in which his hermeneutical skill may display itself with signal effect and to the advantage of the Church" (Denz 3282). He approved St. Thomas Aquinas's statement: "For 'in those things which do not come under the obligation of faith, the saints were at liberty to hold divergent opinions, just as we ourselves are,' " (Denz 3289; *In 2 sent.* 2.1.3). He also noted that, except in questions of faith and morals, an improvement and a correction of interpretation should be expected (Denz 3294). Pius XII specifically mentioned the liberty of Scriptural scientific investigation enjoyed by Catholics: "In the immense matter contained in the sacred Books— legislative, historical, sapiential, and prophetical—there are but few texts whose sense has been defined by the authority of the Church, nor are those more numerous about which the teaching of the Holy Fathers is unanimous" (Denz 3831).

In promoting a scientific study of the Bible the popes have commended to scholars several auxiliary sciences. Leo XIII stressed the study of Oriental languages, true literary criticism, natural science, and history (Denz 3286–90). Pius XII called for a greater facility in Biblical and other Oriental languages, in textual criticism, and in archeology (EnchBibl 561); with unusual force that has greatly influenced Catholic Bible studies, he directed Scripture students to study carefully ancient literary forms in order to interpret the Bible more correctly (EnchBibl 560).

Texts and Translations of the Scriptures. Catholic teaching upholds the supreme importance of the original texts in studying and interpreting the Bible. In the Latin rite the authoritative liturgical and theological text is the Vulgate version. Other translations are recommended, provided they are published with notes and with ecclesiastical approval.

Importance of Original Text. Pius XII stated clearly the obligation of Biblicists to study the original texts of the Bible: "In like manner therefore ought we to explain the original text which, having been written by the inspired author himself, has more authority and greater weight than any, even the best translation, whether ancient or modern" (EnchBibl 547). This was in accord with earlier papal emphasis on the study of Hebrew, Aramaic, and Greek.

Pius XII also stressed the importance of scientific textual criticism of the original texts. He described textual criticism as a most valuable aid to the scholar in obtaining a more accurate reading. He further called for Catholic scholars to publish critical editions "which . . . unite the greatest reverence for the sacred text with an exact observance of all the rules of criticism" (EnchBibl 548).

Value of Latin Vulgate. The Catholic Church developed an official Latin version only near the end of the 4th century, when Pope Damasus commissioned St. Jerome to produce a Latin version of the OT from the original Hebrew. The work of Jerome became the Latin translation known as the Vulgate. [See BIBLE, IV (TEXTS AND VERSIONS) 13.] It won acceptance after many centuries as the standard Catholic Bible for classroom and pulpit. Its selection as an official Latin text was due to its merits as an accurate translation from the original languages. During the Middle Ages the knowledge of even the Greek language had declined in the West. Consequently medieval Biblicists had recourse only rarely to the Greek original of the NT and scarcely at all to the original Hebrew of the OT. The Council

of Trent in 1546 decreed that the Vulgate should be held as official: "Besides, the same sacred Council . . . hereby declares and enacts that that well-known Old Latin Vulgate edition, which has been approved by the long use of so many centuries in the Church, is to be held as authentic in public readings, disputations, preachings, and explanations, and that no one shall dare or presume to reject it under any pretense whatever" (Denz 1506).

Later, with the development of textual criticism, the word "authentic" in the decree led to misunderstanding. Pius XII explained that the authenticity of the Vulgate should be understood in a juridic and not in a textual sense. Moreover, he said that the decree of Trent refers only to the Latin Church and to the public use of Scriptures, and in no way diminishes the authority or preeminence of the original texts. The decree was issued "so that, as the Church herself testifies and affirms, it [the Vulgate] may be quoted safely and without fear of error in disputations, in lectures and in preaching; and so its authenticity is not specified primarily as critical, but rather as juridical" (Denz 3825).

Use of Vernacular Versions. The production and use of other Bible translations have been highly commended to Catholic readers. Until 1943 the translations were to be based on the Vulgate, but since 1943 this dependence of translations on a translation has been abrogated: "Nor is it forbidden by the Council of Trent to make translations into the vulgar tongue, even directly from the original texts themselves, for the use and benefit of the faithful" (Denz 3825).

A further departure from the Vulgate tradition came in 1945, when a new Latin version of the Psalter made directly from Hebrew was approved for optional use in public and private recitation of the Roman Breviary (EnchBibl 571). On the whole the Vulgate remains, however, the official liturgical Bible of the Latin Church, and translations of liturgical sections are to be made from it (EnchBibl 535–537).

Canon 1391 of the Canon Law of the Church rules that, for the use of the faithful, vernacular versions must have ecclesiastical approval and "annotations taken especially from the holy Fathers of the Church and from learned Catholic writers" (EnchBibl 436). Canon 1399 forbids Catholics the use of editions of the Bible published by non-Catholics. Canon 1400 permits Catholics who "in any way whatsoever" are students of theological and Biblical sciences the use of such Bibles so long as the translations are faithful and complete and the annotations do not attack Catholic faith (EnchBibl 437–438). These laws recall the unfortunate days when the Bible was edited and used by Christian sects to further their doctrines and when the Catholic Church was faced with the complex problem of the proliferation of tendentious Bible translations into popular languages.

Latin was the language of the literate well into the Middle Ages. As the various vernacular languages developed, Bibles with glosses of the Latin and with partial translations came into existence in various European countries as a normal development. At the end of the 12th century, tendentious vernacular translations were used by heretical *Albigenses in Metz. On July 12, 1199, Innocent III forbade clandestine meetings, preaching by the laity, and the studying of scriptural sections translated by the laity into French. In his letter the Pope commended the study of the Bible, but forbade the neglect of the Church's teaching authority and the study of the profundities of Scripture without guidance (Denz 770–771).

Abuse of Vernacular Versions. The appearance of authorized Catholic translations in France, Spain, Italy, and Germany during the 14th and 15th centuries shows that the Church was not opposed to vernacular translations in themselves. Its objection was to versions published independently of its authority and to further erroneous interpretations of Christian doctrine. In certain regions the vernacular Bible was a symbol of the belief that Scripture contained all revelation without relation to the Church. Some early Protestant translations (e.g., Tyndale's NT, the Geneva Bible) frequently included introductions or notes destructive of Catholic faith. [*See* BIBLE, IV (TEXTS AND VERSIONS) 23.] The Catholic Church prohibited translations in these instances because they were not faithful to the original texts, because they excluded parts of the Bible, or because their explanatory notes were false or insufficient.

At times the Church's disciplinary measures were severely and rigidly applied. However, when the danger to the faithful diminished, the Church encouraged the production of vernacular translations. Pius XII explicitly stated that attachment to the Vulgate does not exclude other translations from the original texts "for the use and benefit of the faithful and for the better understanding of the Divine Word, as We know to have already been done in a laudable manner in many countries with the approval of the ecclesiastical authority" (Denz 3825). This encouragement stimulated even more Catholic translations. In the major languages, there is presently a variety of Catholic vernacular translations of the Bible.

Reading of the Bible. *Bible reading, private and liturgical, is strongly encouraged as a means to spiritual perfection, although it is not necessary for salvation. The popes in the last 100 years have issued numerous instructions on the Bible, have founded various chairs of Scripture as well as the Biblical Institute, and have established academic degrees for Bible teaching. Their ultimate purpose has been to make the Bible known and read, so that the faithful may learn the truths of revelation contained in the Scriptures and be influenced spiritually by the Word of God.

Older Practice. In this the modern popes were following long-standing tradition. Gregory the Great in 595 strongly commended Scripture reading to Theodore: "The Ruler of heaven, the Lord of men and angels has transmitted to you his letters for your life, and yet, glorious son, you neglect to read ardently those very letters" (EnchBibl 31). During the 8th century, a day of widespread illiteracy, the local council of Riesbach ordered priests to read the Scriptures to the people (EnchBibl 35). In the following century the local Council of Chalon directed that bishops study and teach Scripture (EnchBibl 36). In similar fashion the Council of Trent, after forbidding jocose use of Scripture, ruled in detail that ecclesiastics responsible for religious instruction must explain and interpret Sacred Scripture to the people, under penalty of deprivation of benefice, "lest that heavenly treasure of sacred books, which the Holy Spirit with greatest liberality gave to men, should lie neglected" (EnchBibl 64–65).

Modern Practice. Leo XIII in *Providentissimus Deus* stated: "The solicitude of the apostolic office naturally urges and even compels us . . . to desire that this grand source of Catholic revelation should be made safely and abundantly accessible to the flock of Jesus Christ" (EnchBibl 82). And on Dec. 13, 1898, he granted specific indulgences for reading the Scriptures. A notice concerning these indulgences is ordinarily printed in the first pages of Bibles published for Catholics.

Benedict XV described at length the knowledge and love of St. Jerome for the Bible and held up Jerome as an example to Catholic clergy and laity. He praised the Society of St. Jerome and similar Catholic Bible societies that were established to give to inexpensive copies of the Bible the widest possible distribution (EnchBibl 478).

Pius XII in *Divino afflante Spiritu* expressed most clearly his concern for Bible reading: "The sacred books were not given by God to men to satisfy their curiosity or to provide them with material for study and research, but, as the Apostle notes, in order that these Divine Oracles might 'instruct us to salvation, by the faith which is in Christ Jesus' and 'that the man of God may be perfect, furnished to every good work' " (EnchBibl 566; 2 Tm 3.15–17).

In its *Constitution on the Liturgy,* Vatican II gave impetus to the use of Sacred Scripture in liturgical worship: "Sacred Scripture is of the greatest importance in the celebration of the liturgy." The Council stated that its projected restoration and the adaptation of the liturgy must be based upon "that warm and living love for Scripture to which the venerable tradition of both eastern and western rites gives testimony." It encouraged Bible services and directed that a wider cycle of Bible readings be included in the Mass: "The treasures of the Bible are to be opened up more lavishly, so that richer fare may be provided for the faithful at the table of God's Word" (*Constitution on the Sacred Liturgy* 24, 35, 52).

Because of the teaching of *Jansenism that Bible reading is necessary for salvation, in 1713 Clement XI declared that Bible reading is not obligatory for all (Denz 2479–85). Pius VI made a similar declaration in 1794 (Denz 2667). These declarations, however, in no way lessen the importance of Bible reading; for, as our modern popes have so often emphasized in quoting St. Jerome, "to be ignorant of the Bible is to be ignorant of Christ."

Bibliography: EncDictBibl 577–580. P. CRUVEILHIER, DBSuppl 3:1512–24.

[J. F. WHEALON]

BIBLE AND LITURGY

This article will treat the influence of the liturgy upon the formation of the Scriptures, the role of the Word of God in divine worship, and the use of the Bible in the Mass, in the Divine Office, and in other ceremonies.

Influence of Liturgy on Formation of Scriptures. Modern scholarship recognizes a liturgical origin for a still undetermined number of Biblical passages. Many of the Biblical books were not studied literary productions of authors working singly, but literature that proceeded from the religious life of the Israelite and Christian people, gradually formed through the efforts of many collaborators. The Pentateuchal narratives, before being put into their present form by editors, were handed down by oral traditions. These traditions seem to have originated in the sanctuaries under the form of recital of the great events of the sacred history of Israel. Something similar is true of the laws, which originated as oracular pronouncements by the priests who served the sanctuaries. The Psalms are religious poems, the majority of which were either originally composed for, or later adapted to, use in the temple liturgy and which came to enjoy a similar use in the synagogal and Christian liturgies. Modern scholars believe that a certain number of passages in the prophetic literature and other OT books also had a liturgical origin.

In the NT the influence of the primitive Christian liturgy can be discerned in the Gospels. Since the liturgy existed before the NT writings, it helped to preserve, transmit, and formulate the Gospel tradition. Passages such as the baptismal formula in Mt 28.19 and the Eucharistic formula of Mk 14.22–25 are believed to be the actual liturgical formulas that were used in the early Church. Liturgical elements also appear in other NT books: hymns (Phil 2.6–11; Eph 5.14; 1 Tm 3.16; Ap 5.13); acclamations (1 Cor 14.6; 2 Cor 1.20; 1 Cor 16.22; Ap 22.20); and credal formulas (Rom 10.9; 1 Cor 12.3; Rom 1.3–4).

Role of the Word of God in Divine Worship. The liturgy is the place of the encounter between God and man, in which the Church offers worship to God and is in turn sanctified by Him, under the veil of sacramental signs. Consequently the liturgy re-presents and continues the history of salvation that is narrated in the Bible. This sacred history is a record of the successive self-revelations that God made to mankind. Since the definitive revelation has been given in Christ, it is now incumbent upon the Church to listen attentively to the Word of God as it has been revealed, be filled with its power, proclaim it to its members, and respond to it through worship and self-consecration.

The liturgy accordingly includes two movements, a descending movement in which the Church receives and absorbs the divine Word, and an ascending movement in which it responds to the Word by prayer. The first of these is a continuation of the process of revelation initiated in the OT. The Word of God was spoken to the people by priest and prophet before it was committed to writing. This Word, now contained in the Bible, the Church continues to proclaim. The liturgy of the Word occurs principally in the fore-Mass and in the Scriptural readings of the Divine Office and prepares the people for their response of worship.

The ascending movement of the worshippers to God is also inspired by the Bible. For its prayer the Church uses principally the words of Scripture itself, especially the Psalms. This phase of the liturgical action, found principally in the psalmody of the Divine Office, the sacrificial liturgy of the Mass, and in the other sacramental rites, is the Church's response to the divine Word, in which it humbly submits itself to the vivifying action of the Word.

Use of the Bible in the Mass. The Mass liturgy is filled with Biblical texts and allusions. The principal part of the fore-Mass consists of readings, which are always taken from the Bible. The number and provenance of the readings varies considerably in the different rites, but always culminates in the proclamation of the Gos-

pel. At present the Roman liturgy has only two readings as a rule, but some of the older Mass formularies have three, of which the first two are from the OT. The chants of the Mass also are derived almost exclusively from the Bible. The Introit, Gradual, Tract, Alleluia verse, Offertory, and Communion chants employ Biblical texts, usually derived from the Psalms, though sometimes taken from other books. While today these chants are often reduced to one verse, originally the entire Psalm was sung, usually together with a refrain in which all the people joined. Although the prayers of the Mass are not taken directly from the Bible, they show a profoundly Biblical inspiration. This is especially true of the anaphora or canon, which in all the liturgies reviews the entire panorama of sacred history. In the Roman liturgy this is accomplished by the variation of the Preface and the Communicantes.

Use of the Bible in the Divine Office. The principle that guides the Roman liturgy is that the entire Bible should be read in the Office in the course of the year. However, the readings of the vigil Office have been reduced to only a section of each Biblical book, which is considered to stand for the whole. The readings of the vigil Office thus represent the *lectio continua* of the Scriptures that was traditional in the ancient Church. In the other hours only brief passages occur, which are called *capitula*. The other liturgies have longer readings at the other hours also and thus give greater prominence to the liturgical presentation of sacred history.

The ancient principle that the entire Psalter should be recited every week is still maintained in the present Roman Breviary. Thus the Church follows the Jewish and early Christian tradition of expressing its prayer in the words of the inspired singers of Israel. The other parts of the Divine Office, especially the antiphons, versicles, and responsories, are also usually derived from Biblical texts. Many of the orations are filled with Biblical reminiscences, though the Roman liturgy no longer retains the Psalter Collects, which provided a prayer for the end of each Psalm, in order to sum up its sentiments and interpret them in a Christian sense.

Use of the Bible in other Ceremonies. Although the richness of its ancient formularies has been considerably reduced, the Roman liturgy still makes an extensive use of the Bible in its sacramental rites. While many Biblical texts are employed in these ceremonies, the chief role of the Bible consists in the typology that it supplies. Baptism is the richest in Biblical allusions, especially when taken together with the Paschal vigil ceremony. The entire baptismal liturgy constitutes a synthesis of Biblical theology, with its references to the deliverance from Egypt, the crossing of the Red Sea, and the entry into the Promised Land, types of the experience of Christian initiation. The marriage ceremony likewise develops the continuity of sacred history, with its reference to the love of God for His people under the prophetic symbolism of marital love, to Adam and Eve, to the holy women of the OT, and to the Pauline teaching that Christian marriage is a symbol of the bond of love between Christ and the Church. The rites of the other Sacraments and the principal sacramentals, contained in the *Ritual* and the *Pontifical*, also make extensive use of the Psalms and other Biblical texts and are filled with references to events of Biblical history. Thus, by means of the Scripture readings in the liturgy,

Christians relive in a sacramental way the main events of sacred history and thereby cooperate in the development of God's total plan for the salvation of all men.

Vatican Council II. The *Constitution on the Sacred Liturgy* of Vatican Council II defines the importance of the Bible in the liturgy (24) and the relationship of the liturgy of the Word to the Eucharistic liturgy (56; cf. 48), urges promotion of love for the Bible among the faithful (24), prescribes that teachers of Sacred Scripture should point out the relationship of the liturgy to their subject (16), decrees a more abundant use of Scripture in the liturgy (35.1), both in the Mass (51) and in the Divine Office (92a), and officially approves and encourages Bible services (35.4).

Bibliography: J. A. Jungmann, LexThK² 2:337. L. Bouyer, "La Bible et la liturgie," *Initiation Biblique,* ed. A. Robert and A. Tricot (3rd ed. Paris 1954) 1011–20. A. G. Martimort et al., *The Liturgy and the Word of God* (Collegeville 1959). C. Breen, "The Bible and the Liturgy," *The Word of Life* (Westminster, Md. 1960) 95–102. D. Stanley, "Liturgical Influences on the Formation of the Four Gospels," CathBiblQuart 21 (1959) 24–38. A. Bea, "The Pastoral Value of the Word of God in the Sacred Liturgy," *The Assisi Papers* (Collegeville 1957) 74–90. C. Vagaggini, *Il senso teologico della liturgia* (Rome 1957). J. Daniélou, *The Bible and the Liturgy* (Notre Dame, Ind. 1956). C. Burgard, *The Scripture in the Liturgy,* tr. J. H. Smith (Westminster, Md. 1960).

[C. J. Peifer]

BIBLE AND PIETY

The relationship between the written Word of God and Christian spirituality.

Bible and Life. The Bible, since it contains the living Word of God, is the principal source of Christian spirituality and a guide for Christian living, as was already recognized by the Biblical writers themselves (2 Tm 3.14–17). The men of the patristic period were particularly conscious of the role of the Word of God in Christian formation. After a period of neglect since the Counter Reformation, the Bible is again assuming its normative function in the lives of the faithful due to the 20th-century Biblical revival. The Bible is not a collection of abstract propositions regarding religion and morality, but a sacred history that approaches the relationship between God and man in a concrete, dynamic, and existential manner (Heb 4.12). It is the record of God's revealing Himself in action to His people and summoning them to share in His own happiness. Its precepts and counsels, which are presented in a variety of interlocking themes, must be understood within the framework of this historical context. Despite the variety of materials of which it is composed, the Bible has a unity that confers a Christian meaning upon the entire revelation and supplies a concrete norm for Christian life.

Bible and Prayer. Since prayer is the principal activity of the spiritual life, the influence of the Bible is felt principally in this sphere. The Church makes extensive use of the Bible in her liturgical prayer, which is the model for private prayer (*see* BIBLE AND LITURGY). Prayer, the fundamental attitude toward God, is exemplified in the lives of the great figures of the Bible; and it is by steeping himself in the mentality of the Bible that the Christian can best dispose himself for prayer. This requires a meditative reading of the Scriptures, through which man assimilates the living Word of God and thus prepares himself to respond actively to it in personal prayer (*see* BIBLE READING). Through contact with the Bible, the Christian takes his place in the development of sacred history by passing through the same stages recounted in the Scriptural narrative.

Bibliography: A. Lefèvre et al., DictSpirAscMyst 4.1:128–278. G. Brillet, Robert-Tricot 2:533–546. N. Peters and J. Décarreaux, *Notre Bible: Source de vie* (Bruges 1950). C. Charlier, *The Christian Approach to the Bible,* tr. H. J. Richards and B. Peters (Westminster, Md. 1958). L. Leloir, *La Bibbia, scuola di preghiera* (Quaderni della rivista "Bibbia e Oriente" 1; Milan 1959). K. Condon, *Word of Life* (Westminster Md. 1960) 112–123. "Bible, Life and Worship," *Proceedings of the 22nd Annual North American Liturgical Week* (Washington 1961). Paul Marie of the Cross, *Spirituality of the Old Testament,* tr. E. McCabe, 3 v. (St. Louis 1961–63).

[C. J. Peifer]

BIBLE AND THEOLOGY

The word of God is the first and fundamental reality upon which the whole Christian mystery depends. It is the manifestation of the "mystery which has been hidden from eternity in God . . . which he accomplished in Christ Jesus our Lord" (Eph 3.9–11; see also Col 1.26; 2.2). Revelation therefore is the primordial mystery of God manifesting Himself to man. This mystery communicates in itself all other divine mysteries. Fulfilled in Jesus Christ, revelation in human history is the means by which the gifts of salvation descend to man. It is the entrance which opens to man the knowledge of the will and goodness of God (Jn 14.6; 10.9; Eph 1.9). It is above all the word by which God reveals Himself in His saving act, communicating it to the object of that act—man, who thereby becomes existentially involved in the salvific process. This redemptive message of revelation is transmitted by the Church, which is the mystical continuation of the unique principle of the redemptive mystery, Jesus Christ, the revealing word, and it is recorded in the writing of the sacred texts.

The Bible as such teaches no philosophy or theology, using these words in their technical sense. By definition philosophy and theology are sciences that use a specialized literary form understood by their initiates. The sole aim of the Bible is to teach the ordinary man living even in a milieu in which philosophy or theology is not known the notion of the divine and freely bestowed salvation realized by an envoy sent from God. It is true that philosophy and theology are professedly concerned with and closely allied to the truths revealed in the Bible. Hence, they offer a greater opportunity for integration with Biblical reflection than the natural sciences. Philosophy deals with the rational principles that underlie revelation at its point of contact with the human mind, whereas theology denotes the intellectual ordering of the truths that are still in a rough-hewn state in the Bible. Nevertheless it is true to say that as sciences, philosophy and theology move on a level quite different from that of the Bible.

Yet philosophy and theology are indispensable guides to interpretation, even in their technical and rational sense. On the deeper level of living, religious wisdom and knowledge, the Bible and theology are practically one. Every experience of faith that is intensely felt must be a repetition of that of the first believers. In this sense and at this level one can say that the Bible in the Church is the sum total of theology (the study of God) and philosophy (the love of wisdom), since it is the word of God given to man as the divine wisdom by which he is to live. But on the scientific level philosophy and theology are distinct from the Bible, and in this sense it is misleading to speak of a *Biblical theology. Technical theology is a scientific elaboration of the truths of faith. The Bible is a transmission of the truths of faith in a living tradition. Technique, as such, comes into Biblical study only in scientific exegesis aimed at determining as precisely as possible the objective Biblical truth. The purpose of scientific theology, on the other hand, is to rationalize this truth. Therefore it lies in a different sphere.

Mutual Relationship. Since the Biblical scholar may be capable of intellectual synthesis, he can direct his analytical investigations into the area of theological exegesis. From this one derives an authentic Biblical theology. After the exegete has achieved an adequate literary and textual criticism with its investigations into documentary and source analysis, he can conclude it with an exhaustive examination of the literal sense, which arrives at the precise doctrinal criticism of the author's thought. He then proceeds to explore the implications of the divine word that extend further than the meanings realized by the writer. He determines the writer's exact position in the development of revelation, seeing his thought in relation to those who went before and those who followed, in order to develop the ideas to which he gave birth. In the exegete's analysis of themes and their transposition and in his recognition of the cycles in the evolution of *salvation history he discerns the converging trends in their relation to the focal point of the divine word become incarnate. In this way he is able to project the original thought in the light of its fulfillment by a typological or recapitulative study. Such an anagogical synthesis can be said to be the determinative point of theological exegesis. It then remains for the Biblical theologian only to identify himself with the word so that he achieves a sapiential or contemplative union.

However, the propensity of human intelligence is not satisfied with this. It seeks the universalization of the concrete expressions of Biblical revelation, not for reasons of pure rationalism, but to offer the simple homage of the entire human intelligence by humbly placing itself in the service of the evangelical word that it may arrive at an achievement of systematic or doctrinal theology. Basically this is nothing more than a rigorous reflection of divine faith that brings into play all of the resources of reason to arrive at a better understanding of its object, which is the word of God. By introducing the natural conceptual power of the human intellect into the process of divine revelation human wisdom attempts to integrate the historical phenomena of salvific action with its transcendental understanding of the necessary principles of being and existence. Through the instrumental use of logic and metaphysics theology strives toward a systematization of the many scriptural nuances and an elaboration of the relationships that have been established by God and are intrinsic to the essential significance distinguishing Biblical themes. Theology thereby illuminates the multiple synoptic analyses of revelation as well as the propriety of the divine redemptive scheme relative to the anthropological structure of cosmic reality. Moreover, by the perceiving of the fundamental sense of contingent realities many insights into the transcending significance of Biblical expression with their correlative values can be acquired.

Yet doctrinal theology not only employs a suitable metaphysics but even aids in the erection of an adequate philosophy of being that can function as a universalizing agent regarding the unique experiences in Scripture.

Accordingly systematic theology is capable of satisfying the following demands. (1) It can mark out clearly the limits between the natural and the supernatural. (2) It can distinguish what is of necessity and is imposed by the divine wisdom from what is contingent and realized only through the free choice of God. Thus one can perceive, for the vital nourishment of one's faith, the distinction between salvation history and the essential structure of the cosmic universe. A concrete example of this may be given: the elevation of the created order of man into a supernatural existence with the destiny of divine beatitude. Only by acute precision of intellectual insight can the parallel distinctions of the natural order and that of the free reconstitution of the divine plan be illuminated. (3) It can, if based upon the understanding of the essential structure of reality, envisage the divine economy in the most profound and open perspectives. A synthesis can thus be achieved that both unifies the entire structure of Biblical themes and integrates philosophical data by attending to the knowledge of causes that one can perceive in the panoramic view of God's gratuitous act of salvation.

Bible and Theology in the Church's Doctrinal Development. Catholic theology has scarcely treated or developed all the variations of a theology of the word. Revelation seems to have played the role of one of those fundamental truths that, without being expressed, runs through the entire structure of what is being said and lived, similar to the role of creation in the philosophy of St. Thomas. As for the development of theology throughout the Christian Era, it appears that in the early centuries, after a period in which there was a keen understanding of the illuminative role of the word of God, Christian thought subsequently turned more readily first to a theology of the Word of God Himself, then to an examination of the relations between Scripture and tradition, and finally to an analysis of the ultimate motive for faith.

The "Christ Who Reveals" in the Writings of the Apostolic Fathers. The Apostolic Fathers make all Christian doctrine depend directly on the word of God. They explicitly relate the prophetical activity of the OT and the mission of the Apostles to the revelation of Christ Himself. The Didache (10.2) gives thanks for the "knowledge and faith of immortality that You have made known to us through Jesus, Your servant." For Ignatius of Antioch, Christ was the "Gnosis of God." In this sense Ignatius established the perspective of doctrinal history for the first 3 centuries inasmuch as he delineated the functions of Christ as "He who reveals." This prompted the variety of titles given to Christ in this period, such as "the Messenger [ἄγγελος] of God," "the Face [πρόσωπον] of God," "the Voice [φωνή] and Word of God," "the One Sent [ἀπόστολος] by God," and "the Master [διδάσκαλος] who teaches." In short, the postapostolic age designated Christ principally as "He who makes God known." This element of the evolution of Christian doctrine throughout the 2d and 3d centuries, in which the function of Christ was illuminated as the revelatory power of the divine Word, should currently demand the greatest attention.

Theologians of the Postapostolic Age and Apologists of 2d Century. These clearly understood that the ultimate source of the word of God lay in the person, words, and works of Jesus Christ in the context of the revelation of which He was the climax. However, they could not help but pass on to more complex problems, such as the question of the media by which the original revelation was preserved and handed down in the Church. Herein was laid the foundation for the perennial and authentic theology of the Church, which, though not disputing the value of the role of Scripture and tradition in revelation, nevertheless kept in mind that any justification for the communication of revelation through human intermediaries always had to make appeal to a direct encounter with the Word of God Himself or Christ or the Holy Spirit. Tradition is faithful to the principal word only inasmuch as it is, first of all, the "tradition of the Lord" in the double sense that the Lord is both its content and its author. It was in this atmosphere that the first liturgical texts were composed. This principle underlay the patristic writings. The Fathers of the Church, especially in their homilies, commentaries, and sermons, primarily manifested composites of Scripture passages. From St. Ambrose to St. Bernard their preaching was woven from Scripture.

The supreme importance of patristic theology is that the revealing and teaching function of Christ was never considered abstractly but always remained situated in the ensemble of His manifestation and His mystery. The mission of Christ appears in His Incarnation and presence; in His life, Passion, and Resurrection; and in His dignity as prophet, priest, and king to achieve His glory as head of the Church. Thus Augustine indicated the primary significance of the Word assuming flesh to be that faith is made more certain by believing God Himself who speaks. It was this identity of faith in the persons of God that already enabled Augustine to trace the correlationship between the act of the intellect and the self-commitment of faith, between philosophy and theology. Subsequent thought does not seem to have added much to what Augustine wrote on the matter. Moreover, he initiated insight into a more profound relationship between theology and the Word by relating intellectual activity with the processions of the mystery of the Holy Trinity, founding the latter upon the concept of an "intellectual word." That which Augustine proposed as an image, Aquinas would extend to an analogy of proper proportionality by relating the divine filiation with the production of the intellectual species.

Medieval Theological Syntheses. Scholastic speculation advanced doctrinal development into problematic theological conclusions. St. *Thomas Aquinas (1225–74) showed himself distinct from many of his contemporaries by envisioning revelation as not being limited to the transmission of a document or to the recalling of an event. The visible mission of Christ in His Incarnation and in His message remains linked to His "invisible mission." Man's understanding and experience of the Word of God in the present is not simply the recounting of an event or of a teaching of a body of religious truths but rather a participation in the mystery of Christ. Accordingly revelation is neither mere history nor mere teaching but a transformation of the person to whom that revelation is directed. It is the coming of the new order of existence, a new creation that is grace in its basic reality; it is the entry of the person in the mystery of Christ.

Patristic theology paved the way for the consequent scholastic synthesis that reached its culmination in Aquinas. He observes that the intellectual enlightenment that is derived from divine revelation through the Word, which is one of the effects of the new existence, is simultaneously grace, wisdom, and love. The Word who gives this life is the Word who breathes and who brings out love; that is to say, it is linked to the mission of the Holy Spirit who creates and increases ἀγάπη (love, charity). As long as Catholic theology emphasizes that revelation is the act of God communicating the mystery of salvation, then it is an authentic theology of the Word, Scripture, and tradition, indeed, a genuine analysis of faith. St. Thomas seems to have come to the crux of the matter in the first question of his *Summa theologiae,* where he taught that revelation is the first principle, the decisive event, the fundamental category from which is derived the sacred teaching that surpasses all philosophy. Although he did not present an integral explanation of the inner structure of the act of God who reveals in the person of Jesus Christ, nevertheless he asserted that the personal actions, words, and deeds of Christ are all individual aspects of the unity of the total manifestation that expresses the supreme revelation of God. This revelation not only addresses itself to the intellectual comprehension of human faith but also calls for the liberation, redemption, and transfiguration of man's being (see ST 3a, 36.1 ad 3).

The early medieval theology of the schools based its enquiring reflections upon a valid principle: the plan of God reveals itself in events, persons, symbolic actions, visions, ecstatic states, symbols, images, and dreams, but it reveals itself also in intellectual intuition. A method of explanation that is too strict, whether it be intellectualist, historicist, or symbolist, does not take into account the complexity of the facts and the different modes by which God employs His Word. It appears from the history of scholasticism that, through an intrinsic force, intellectual speculation in theology is too prone to transfer contingent analogy into necessary concept. Even the best theology of the Middle Ages, though it had well understood that faith was the fundamental reality and the beginning of salvation, was still occupied principally with proving the objective efficacy of the Sacraments. There is no similar preoccupation whatever for a systematic explanation of the essence and efficacy of the message of faith. Neither *Hugh of Saint-Victor, *Alexander of Hales, *Duns Scotus, nor St. Thomas studied the problem of the theology of the Word in its depth and coordinated synthesis. Moreover, in pastoral care the accent was more on the Sacraments than on the faith or the Word of God that makes them sacred. This is a characteristic attitude of post-Tridentine theology.

Consequently the renewal of theology needs to rediscover the profound link between the Word and the Sacrament. Just as the mystery of the Incarnation was accomplished in the union of the Word of God with visible flesh, so also the Sacrament depends on the revealed Word. The words not only supply the determining element that makes clear the meaning and sense of the Sacrament, but they also give efficacy to the Sacrament because it is a word that refers to and addresses the faith. The Word is the means through which man has faith in the Sacraments. The union between doctrine and event, between concept and person, has been at least implicit throughout Catholic theology, even if the idea of the Christian message has not been dominant in this body of thought. Before the emergence of the most recent *kerygmatic theology it has not seemed to have aroused much interest in the minds of theologians. It would seem that this stems from a conviction that the message should never be considered apart from the messenger. If Catholic theology has never composed a treatise dealing specifically with the concepts of the *gospel, the good news or the word of God, it would seem that this is because the Christian is attached by a mysterious link to the person of the living Christ, the Savior. Hence Christ is both the teacher of faith (Heb 2.3) and the revelatory Word (see ST 3a, 7.7; 42). Thus one is able to perceive in the writings of Aquinas the truth that in much of Christian experience, a certain intuitive element has been present in the acceptance of doctrine and the commitment to faith; there is an unexpressed realization that it is the person of God who is speaking and who intimately encounters the human heart. Such theology would counter any inclination toward naïve anthropomorphism or the theology of so-called dictated theses, which arose in certain segments of scholastic tradition.

The authority of Scripture is stressed by Gerard of Bologna in his *Summa* (A.D. 1317). He could not understand any separation of Scripture from tradition, since faith in the Scripture depends totally on God and one does not believe in the authority of men except in the measure that they are inspired and informed by God (*op. cit.* 4.1). Later, Melchior *Cano (1509–60) emphasized the vital aspect of tradition that linked it to an evangelical law, which is the law of the spirit, not of the letter. The ultimate foundation of faith is neither the authenticity of the Church nor that of the Scripture but that of the testimony of God Himself revealing. Herein one finds an authentic experience of revelation that is again an encounter with the divine missions and persons (*De locis,* 2.8). Although Robert *Bellarmine (1542–1621), as well as an array of Counter Reformation theologians, insisted more on the conceptual experience of revelation, *John of St. Thomas (1589–1644) still reflected pristine Thomistic tradition when he considered the assent of faith as a personal awareness of the divine testimony. In his *Cursus Theologicus* [v.1 (Alcalá 1637)] he commented that the assent of faith is achieved by a light in which the object that is itself believed is contemplated [Solesmes ed. (Paris 1931) 1:316].

However, Catholic theologians who later were alienated from the authentic scholastic notions pursued an apologetic Counter Reformation line that engaged in vain logical subtleties. This reached its nadir in the writings of Juan de *Lugo and Honoré de *Tournely. Eventually they asserted that revelation in its strict sense is a divinely produced declaration or manifestation of a thing previously unknown [Tournely, *Praelectiones theologicae* (Paris 1725) 1:108]. Herein rationalism predominated over personal contact with Jesus Christ.

Growth of a Catholic Apologetic for Revelation in the 18th and 19th Centuries. Because the supremacy of the intellect was emphasized by Baruch *Spinoza, John *Locke, and David *Hume, the German school of the *Enlightenment (*Aufklärung*) headed by G. E. *Lessing (1729–81) had concluded to a radical immanence and subjectivism of all religion: revelation is nothing but a subjective consciousness that appears to itself in the form of an exterior revelation.

On the Catholic side the necessities of a polemical response caused a negative and apologetic reaction. It was formulated in a treatise, entitled *De Revelatione,* that basically followed the format of the Dutch Protestant Hugo *Grotius (1583–1645), whose tract was published in Amsterdam in 1627. The method and structure chosen by this writer, who was less a theologian than a jurist and diplomat, attempted to show, by rational and historical arguments, the possibility and the necessity of the revelation of God, the fact that revelation has shown the divinity of Christ, its proof and confirmation by the prophecies of the OT, and its ultimate demonstration by the miracles and resurrection of the Messiah. Accordingly, instead of a profound consideration of the notion and fact of the Word of God as it should be contemplated in God, Catholic apologetics emphasized its exterior manifestation as miracle. Such a reaction placed Christ, the messenger of God, as detached from the content of His message, which is the mystery of His person and His πλήρωμα (fullness). The apologetics of revelation can never replace a theology of revelation.

Challenge to Modern Theology. The task of theological reform today, then, is to give adequate attention to the fundamental concepts of revelation and faith. The Word of God is first of all a revelation as manifested in Scripture. But the latter can not be envisaged as the sole and unique aspect of the Word of God; rather it is a testimony that allows man to go back into the primitive tradition, the *kerygma, the proclamation of the glad tidings. This is the announcement of the events accomplished in Christ, which were foreseen in the OT prophecies (Acts 3.18; 13.32–33). These events, in the final analysis, were based upon and willed by the fixed purpose and intention of God (Acts 2.23). Thus an authentic Biblical theology will turn man's gaze toward the eternal mystery of the will of God, toward the preexistent Word, toward the Word incarnate in the Son, and toward the testimonies gathered in tradition. The Church as the continuous proclamation of the Word derived from apostolic preaching is inseparable from other aspects of the Christian mystery: this kerygma stirs up faith and keeps it alive. It is fulfilled in the Sacraments, and it assembles the community in the mystery of worship. The characteristic trait of Christian revelation then is both history and eschatology. The Word of God is realized in a series of events but it is governed by the eternal plan of God and directed toward the end and accomplishment of history, toward the *day of the Lord. Finally, a theology of the Word cannot, by definition, remain foreign to the world of today. By examining the philosophy of language, Protestant research, and even the traces found in the history of religions, this theology is fulfilling its mission: to bring to light the mystery revealed in Christ and preached in the Church.

Bibliography: V. Hamp et al., LexThK² 2:439–451. K. Rahner et al., *ibid.* 3:439–454. C. Spicq, "Nouvelles réflexions sur la théologie biblique," RevScPhilTh 42 (1958) 209–219. H. Schlier, *Kerygma und Sophia: Zur neutestamentlichen Grundlegung des Dogmas* (Freiburg 1956) 206–232. H. Cazelles, "La Place de la théologie dans l'enseignement de l'Écriture," NouvRevTh 89 (1956) 1029–41. R. Schnackenburg, "Der Weg der katholischen Exegese," BiblZ 2 (1958) 161–176. O. Kuss, "Exegese als theologische Aufgabe," *ibid.* 5 (1961) 161–183. A. Descamps, "Réflexiones sur la méthode en théologie biblique," *Sacra Pagina* 1 (1959) 132–151. L. Alonso-Schökel, "Argument d'Écriture et théologie biblique dans l'enseignement théologique," NouvRevTh 81 (1957) 337–354. R. A. F. MacKenzie, "The Concept of Biblical Theology," CathThSoc 10 (1955) 48–73. F. J. Cwiekowski, "Biblical Theology as Historical Theology," CathBiblQuart 24 (1962) 404–411. H. U. von Balthasar, "Parole et histoire," *La Parole de Dieu en Jésus-Christ* (Paris 1961) 227–240. A. Leonard, "La Parole de Dieu: Mystère et événement, vérité et presence," *ibid.* 307–310. R. Latourelle, "L'Idée de révélation chez les Pères de l'Église," *Sciences ecclésiastiques* 11 (1959) 297–344; *Théologie de la révélation* (Bruges 1963). A. Marc, "L'Idée de revelation," Greg 34 (1953) 390–420. P. Fransen, *Divine Grace and Man,* tr. G. Dupont (rev. ed. New York 1965). Y. M. J. Congar, *La Tradition et les traditions,* 2 v. (Paris 1960–63), v.1 *Essai historique;* "Sainte Écriture et Sainte Église," RevScPhilTh 44 (1960) 81–88; "Traditio und *Sacra Doctrina* bei Thomas von Aquin," in *Kirche und Überlieferung,* ed. J. Betz and H. Fries (Freiburg 1960) 170–210. R. Geiselmann, "Un Malentendu éclairci: La Relation 'Écriture-tradition' dans la théologie catholique," *Istina* 5 (1958) 197–214, tr. of "Das Missverständnis über das Verhältnis von Schrift und Tradition und seine Überwindung in der katholischen Theologie," *Una Sancta* 11 (Sept. 1956) 131–150. E. Schillebeeckx, *Révélation et Theologie* (Brussels 1965). P. Lengsfeld, *Tradition und Schrift* (Paderborn 1960). K. Rahner and J. Ratzinger, *Offenbarung Überlieferung* (Freiburg 1965).

[A. H. AMADIO]

BIBLE CYCLES IN ART

By Bible cycle is meant an organic complex of visual representations intended to illustrate either various phases or aspects of one Biblical subject, or many Biblical subjects bound together by a single "thematic" idea.

EARLY CHRISTIAN

The decorations found in the catacombs and on the earliest Christian tombs are the first examples of Bible cycles in art. These date from the 2d and 3d centuries A.D. and are based upon themes of a symbolical nature. A few isolated exceptions, such as the 2d-century frescoes in the cemetery of Priscilla (Rome) of the "Virgin, the Child and Isaia" and the "Breaking of the Bread," are of a more concrete narrative character. The cycles of symbolical reference are interpreted according to the taste and style of composition characteristic of contemporary late Imperial painting. With only a few strokes of striking visual concreteness, the figures are depicted either alone or in groups on a white background, skillfully arranged in the allotted spaces and unified by the symmetry of the composition. The pictorial cycle of this "impressionistic" type succeeds, despite its sketchlike quality, in evoking with immediacy people and events from the Bible stories. Presented, as they are, in a single organic unit, the figures are gradually transformed into "symbols," sensible images of transcendent values.

Sepulchral Art. Early Christian catacomb and tomb art, especially in Rome, provides typical examples of the Bible cycles. The frescoes in a cubicle of the Roman catacomb of SS. Peter and Marcellinus have figures of Lazarus, Moses, Noe praying, and the three Magi on the walls; on the ceiling, in the center, is the Good Shepherd between four scenes where the stories of Jona alternate with *orans figures. These Biblical representations are clearly symbolic of faith in the divinity of the Redeemer risen from the dead. Also typical are the representations of Daniel in the lions' den in the catacomb of Lucina, or those of Noe in the ark in the catacomb of Domitilla, both symbolizing the mystery of the Resurrection. This kind of cycle was created to present the Biblical incidents to viewers with an adequate spiritual preparation. The depicted events recall facts or ideas that were well known and whose transcendent meaning could be evoked from the images presented.

A similar aim is seen in the early Christian tombs. Here, the plastic figuration tends to acquire a conscious artistic autonomy, and in addition there is greater interest in the narrative as such, over and above the idea that it symbolizes (sarcophagus of Jona, no. 119, Lateran Museum, Rome). The general theme of the Resurrection of Christ, recalled in a series of episodes from the Old and New Testaments, is overshadowed by the capricious ornament, laden with Hellenistic accents. Analogous in spirit but more typically Roman in style and dating from the height of the 4th century, is the sarcophagus of Junius Bassius (Grottoes of the Vatican). Lastly, of decidedly narrative character and showing a conscious intent to celebrate the mystery, is the sarcophagus of the Passion (no. 171; Lateran, Rome). Here the emphasis is on the cross in the central panel, surmounted by the monogram of Christ within a triumphal crown. There are many other contemporary examples similar in spirit and emphasis in which, however, the youthful and triumphant figure of Christ usually appears on a throne in place of the cross.

4th and 5th Centuries. Bible cycles found in the bas-reliefs of sarcophagi of the 4th and 5th centuries are clearly narrative in character and have a strong dramatic unity (nos. 135, 125, 155, and 183, Lateran Museum, Rome; sarcophagus of Adelfia, Syracuse Museum). They have a figurative quality that is free of the mannerisms of late classical art, and is founded on a previously unknown historical understanding of religious truths. Later, this conception became a strong determining force in neo-Latin art and civilization.

Among the earliest exemplifications of this tendency are the mosaics of the nave of St. Mary Major in Rome, depicting stories from the Old Testament, and those of the triumphal arch, with the glorification of Mary and stories of the childhood of Christ. The cycle was executed during the pontificate of Sixtus III (432–440). The mosaics of the nave are clearly in the Western tradition; they are constructed with a dramatic power and a solid sense of volumes, as if they had been produced by "tachist" brush strokes. In the triumphal arch, on the other hand, the symmetrical rows of flat-frontal figures produce an effect of hieratic solemnity.

Only a few decades later, the mosaics of the triumphal arch of the Roman basilica of St. Paul-Outside-the-Walls, created by order of Galla Placidia in the last years of her reign, show the fulfillment of the early Western style. The 24 Elders of the Apocalypse are represented in a rhythmic procession in two parallel lines. Clad in white robes, they stand out majestically against a gold background, which emphasizes the strikingly tragic and severe face of Christ the Judge in the center.

The face of Christ is placed in even stronger relief by a radiant halo of sharply contrasting color.

Art of this period suggested intimate and profound sensitivity that was to strengthen the historical consciousness of the neo-Latin world. Foreshadowings of the coming changes of values can be seen in fundamental works of the 5th century: the wooden doors of St. Sabina in Rome, with events from the life of Christ and of Moses, and those of St. Ambrose in Milan, with episodes from the life of David; also (though in the 6th century) the Evangeliary of St. Augustine at Cambridge (Corpus Christi College, MS 286), and the mosaics of the chapel of S. Vittore in Ciel d'Oro in Milan.

Ravenna. In Italy the passing of the early style tradition is evident in the mosaics of Ravenna, especially in the New Testament series of the nave of S. Apollinare Nuovo, which dates from the period of Theodoric. A highly refined culture is evident in the pictures filled with Christological scenes, on the upper parts of the walls, where the serene balance of the composition and the softly blended colors give the story depicted an unreal and dreamlike distance. The dramatic austerity of the mosaics of St. Paul is exhibited through silent, linear figures of far greater rhythmic rigor—in the series of the Prophets, on a golden background between the windows; as in the two "Theophanies" around Mary and Christ below. In the mosaics of S. Apollinare in Classe, the most subtle harmonies of color and composition envelop in an immobile silence scenes depicted with a striking descriptive power. There is in them an almost surrealistic clarity.

The same values are continued with more consistency in the mosaic cycles of the presbytery and the apse of S. Vitale at Ravenna (6th century), which celebrate the prefiguration of the Eucharistic Sacrifice in the deeds of Moses, Abraham, and Melchisedec.

EARLY MEDIEVAL

A complicated theological program guided the development of the Biblical cycles in mosaic work, which superseded the earlier abstract type of decoration, in the basilicas of the Holy Apostles and of Hagia Sophia in Constantinople, of the Dormition of the Virgin in Nicaea (destroyed 1921–22), and of St. Demetrius at Salonika. The mosaics of the latter closely resemble contemporary work in S. Vitale.

Byzantine. The initial golden period of Byzantine civilization, from the beginning of the 6th century to the iconoclastic crisis, presents the triumph of the Biblical cycle, especially in the field of illumination work, of which authentic masterpieces are still extant: the Vienna Genesis and the Paris Gospel of St. Matthew from Sinope (Bibliothèque Nationale); the so-called Purple Codex of Rossano (Treasury of the Cathedral), whole pages of which are decorated with miniatures in which the almost complete disappearance of landscape elements and nervous proportions accompany the abstract theological theme of the typological relation between the prophecies of the Old Testament and the events of the New Testament; the 6th-century Syrian Codexes of Paris (Bibliothèque Nationale) and the Gospel Book of Rabbula (Laurentian Library, Florence).

In Rome the principal monumental cycles of the 7th and 8th centuries are characterized by fidelity to the classical tradition (frescoes of S. Maria Antiqua and those in the catacomb of Commodilla; mosaics in the oratory of John VII) and by the presence of a Greek stylistic manner analagous, for example, to that of the mosaic cycle of St. Catherine at Sinai (7th century). Thus Christian art, both Eastern and Western, reflected the consequences of the iconoclastic crisis whose effects persisted even after its official end in 843. Only in this period did Biblical cycles of great importance reappear, in general, in European painting, sculpture, and illumination work, and not only in art of Byzantine inspiration. More ancient examples of cycles had appeared in Rome or within its sphere of influence, for instance in the mosaics of the triumphal arch, of the apse, and of the chapel of St. Zeno in S. Prassede in Rome (early 9th century), and the frescoes of the church of S. Vincenzo of Volturno (826–843).

In the Byzantine world during the middle decades of the 9th century, after more than a century there was, on the whole, a resumption of the forms and artistic preferences of the period immediately preceding the iconoclastic crisis. Important examples are the Vatican copy (MS gr. 699) of the *Cosmographia Cristiana* of Cosma Indicopleuste, dating from the second half of the century, and the collection of the *Sermons* of St. Gregory of Paris (Bibliothèque Nationale, gr. 510) executed in Constantinople around 880 for Basilius I, founder of the Macedonian dynasty.

Several great Italian mosaic cycles of a later date also belong to the sphere of Byzantine artistic culture; these include the cycles of Martorana and of the Cappella Palatina in Palermo (c. 1150); New Testament mosaics in the cathedral of Cefalù (c. 1150); mosaics of the cathedral of Monreale (c. 1776–89); those of the nave (c. 1150) and the porch (early 13th century) in St. Mark's, Venice; and mosaics of the cathedral of Torcello (c. 1210–20).

Carolingian. In Western Europe, the artistic renaissance under *Charlemagne (emperor 800–814) was accompanied by a revival of interest in history that was manifested in the triumphal return of cycles of religious, and especially Biblical, subjects regarded as histories valid in themselves over and above any symbolism. The admirable frescoes of S. Maria Foras Portas at Castelseprio belong to the Carolingian period, even though their style springs from an Oriental culture, and they were probably executed by Greek artists. The frescoes depict the story of Mary and the childhood of Jesus according to the apocryphal gospels of the Oriental tradition. Local artists were responsible for the almost contemporary frescoes of St. John at Münster (in a high valley of the Grisons), which narrate with stiff forms in the Byzantine style, but with expressionistic vigor, the stories of David and of Christ along the walls of the nave. The exaltation of the Redeemer is depicted in the three apses, with the Last Judgment on the inner façade. Such an arrangement became common in western Europe during the Middle Ages.

Manuscript Illumination. From this period on, there was an immense flowering of Biblical cycles in the illuminated manuscripts of the Gospels, of the Psalters, and, in general, of religious books. There was a resurgence of classic influences in the sphere of Byzantine art, beginning before the 9th century and continuing into the succeeding centuries (Paris *Psalter*, Bibliothèque Nationale, gr. 139; the Vatican Bible, Reg. Svev. gr. I; the *Joshua Roll*, Vatican Library, Palat. graeco. gr. 431), characterized by very conservative

Fig. 1. "Epiphany," fresco of the 3d century in the Catacomb of SS. Peter and Marcellinus, Rome.

Fig. 2. "Job on the Dungheap," detail of the 4th-century sarcophagus of Junius Bassus in the Grottoes of the Vatican.

Fig. 3. "The Separation of Abraham and Lot," 5th-century mosaic in the basilica of St. Mary Major, Rome.

BIBLE

CYCLES

IN ART

Fig. 4. "Christ and Barabbas before Pilate," folio 8 of the "Purple Codex" in the cathedral at Rossano, Italy.

Fig. 5. Scenes from the Book of Joshua, detail of the "Joshua Roll," Vatican Library (Vat. Palat. gr. 431).

tendencies both in style and in iconography. Only in the 11th century, for example, does a *Book of the Gospels* of Paris (Bibliothèque Nationale, gr. 74) offer one of the first examples of the insertion of the Gospel parables into an iconographic setting of strictly Byzantine origin. Analogous conservative characteristics and tendencies appear also in 11th-century monumental cycles such as that of the church of St. Luke in Phocis, the mosaics in Hagia Sophia in Constantinople, and the mosaic cycles of the church of Nea Moni of Chios and the church at Daphni. In these last two, however, the New Testament iconography is relatively renewed by themes from the apocryphal gospels and above all by themes freed from their traditional liturgical references.

Biblical illumination of German manuscripts by the school of Ada (9th century) limits figurative art almost entirely to the frontispieces, full-page illuminations, and small scenes contained within the capital letters. Several characteristic cycles of the Passion done in ivory can be attributed to the influence of the school of Ada; scenes are carved in a closely fitted series of squares surrounding the central figure of Christ Crucified, as in the ivory cover of the Codex at Munich (*c.* 870; Clm. 4452) and the ivory of Narbonne (9th-10th century; Cathedral Museum). Throughout the 10th and 11th centuries, under the influence of the Ottonian civilization, the German illumination work of the school of Reichenau, fresco cycles of St. George at Oberzell, St. Sylvester at Goldbach and of Echternach display a taste for narrative that displays complete stylistic freedom; its fundamental roots are classical and early Christian in origin, but to it have been added the influences of the Carolingian renaissance. Among the best examples are: *Codex Egberti,* of Trier; the Evangelistary of Otto III, at Munich (Clm. 4453); the Golden Evangelistary of Henry III, at the Escorial; *Codex aureus Epternacensis* at Nuremberg; Book of the Pericopes of Henry II, at Munich (Clm. 4452); and the Evangelistary of Otto at Aquisgrana.

English illumination work is related also to the school of Reichenau. The principal centers in England, Winchester and Canterbury, produced the Benedictional of St. Aethelwold by Godeman, School of Winchester, 975–980, British Museum); the Evangelistary of Grimbald (British Museum, Add. 34890, London); Caedmon's *Poem* (Bodleian Library, Oxford). The same influence is apparent in other sectors of the figurative arts: the Biblical cycles of the Milanese and Spanish ivories; the ciborium of St. Ambrose and the Arca Santa of Orvieto; the bronze doors of Bernward in the cathedral of Hildesheim; and the cathedrals of Augusta and of Novgorod.

HIGH MEDIEVAL

The Bible cycles of the Romanesque and Gothic periods manifest an increased complexity in their arrangement and give evidence of new artistic and spiritual values.

Romanesque. From the 11th century to the beginning of the 12th, Romanesque sculpture was almost entirely devoted to Biblical figures, arranged in true, organic cycles. French sculpture was the guiding source of European taste. The leading schools were those of Aquitaine (St. Saturnin in Toulouse and the abbey church of Moissac); of Burgundy (the abbey church of Cluny, the priory of Anzy-le-Duc, and St.

Lazare at Autun); of Provence (St. Gilles at Saint-Gilles-du-Gard and St. Trophîme at Arles); and of Auvergne (Saint-Foy at Conques). In Italian sculpture, in addition to schools such as the Lombardian and Emilian, there are individual artists of primary importance. Among them was *Wiligelmo, who created (*c.* 1099–1106) one of the noblest Biblical bas-reliefs of Genesis in the cathedral of Modena. In the intimate dialogue between our first parents and a very human God, as in the tragedy of Cain, Wiligelmo exalts human energy, for the first time in medieval Europe, with a force equal to the dolorous physical appearance of the bodies, which seem almost to burst forth from the confines of the limited space.

Gothic. The cycles of the Old and New Testament by Benedetto *Antelami in the baptistery of Parma, at Borgo S. Donnino, and S. Andrea at Vercelli (*c.* 1196–1225) display a dynamism of genuinely Gothic inspiration. Parallels to the work of Antelami may be found in the oldest examples of the French *Bible moralisé* and the German *Biblia pauperum*. The sculpture of the Gothic Biblical cycles of France and northern Europe in the 13th and 14th centuries is dramatic and moving. The important masterworks include the reliefs of the Old Testament of the north portal of the cathedral of Chartres; the sculptures of the "Master of Nuremberg" at Magonza and Nuremberg; the Biblical reliefs of the choir of Nôtre-Dame of Paris; and the portals with New Testament cycles around the "Crucifixion" of St. Gilles, Strasbourg, and Reims.

Stained-glass windows presented Bible cycles in the 13th, 14th, and 15th centuries, reaching extraordinary mastery in the New Testament windows of the south nave of the cathedral of Chartres and those of Saint Remi at Reims. The tradition of the Bible cycle in manuscript illumination was continued by the celebrated miniaturist Jean de Berry, and by Bohemian miniaturists, especially those of the court of Charles IV of Prague.

The 13th-century Italian artist Niccolò *Pisano created the Biblical cycles of the pulpits of the baptistery of Pisa and of the cathedral of Siena, and collaborated with his son Giovanni on the sculptures of the fountains of Perugia. He combined the unity characteristic of classic Latin art with lively action and sensitivity of style. The Nativity and the Crucifixion at Pisa and the Massacre of the Innocents and the Last Judgment at Siena are revivals of classical sculpture.

The work of *Arnolfo di Cambio, and of Giovanni *Pisano, and their collaborators was inspired by the art of Niccolò Pisano. In the cycles from the Old and New Testament in the pulpits of the cathedral of Pisa and in S. Andrea at Pistoia, as well as on the façade of the cathedral of Siena, Giovanni Pisano expressed power in clear Gothic style.

Influence of St. Francis. The effect upon 13th-century Italian art of Franciscan spirituality, in particular with reference to the iconography of the New Testament, was visible in a new interpretation of the humanity of Christ. A new version of the "suffering Christ" replacing the medieval conception of the Crucified Christ as the Judge, or King, is exemplified by the "Crucifixion" of Giunta Pisano in S. Domenico, Bologna.

The New Testament cycles in mosaic of the life of the Virgin by Pietro *Cavallini in S. Maria in Trastevere (*c.* 1291) and the frescoes of St. Cecilia in Rome, though in

Fig. 6. Five scenes from the Passion, full-page miniature from the late 10th-century "Codex aureus Epternacensis."

a certain sense parallel to the classical revival of Niccolò Pisano, reflect also the new iconography of Franciscan origin. The same may be said for the work of Torriti and the so-called "Master of Isacco," who produced the frescoes in the church of St. Francis in Assisi, and, above all, for the Old and New Testament cycles created by *Cimabue in the upper church of St. Francis in Assisi. In paintings of the "Assumption" and the "Crucifixion" the Florentine artist combined ancient iconography with a fresh human concreteness.

New Testament iconography was given a new expression in the same period in the cycle of stories of Mary and Christ painted by the Sienese artist *Duccio in a series of paintings for the front and back of the altar, comprising his famous "Majesty" (Museum of the Cathedral, Siena). Duccio's pictorial invention is equal to that of Cimabue in exquisiteness of style.

Early Renaissance

At the beginning of the 14th century, *Giotto painted the life of Christ and of Mary in fresco (1303–05) in the chapel of the Scrovegni in Padua. Giotto's psychological insight underlines in the divine history the essential motives of the soul and of human action, presenting them with an almost violent clarity and showing a masterly disposition of the figures in space. A revolution in the relations between man and his natural surroundings foreshadowed the humanistic arrangement achieved in the 15th century in the Florentine Renaissance.

Representative of the continuing transition in Bible cycles are the bas-reliefs of Andrea *Pisano on the doors of the baptistery and the bell tower of Florence; Ghiberti's doors for the same baptistery; the sculptures of the baptismal font of the cathedral of Siena; and the Biblical bas-reliefs of Jacopo della *Quercia in the portal of St. Petronius at Bologna.

Masaccio and Donatello. The frescoes of *Masaccio in the Brancacci chapel of the Carmine of Florence, including the "Banishment of Adam and Eve" and the "Stories of St. Peter" (1424–27), emphasize in principal figures like Christ and St. Peter an emotion that binds the landscape and the men into a "perspective" unity at once both physical and spiritual, and of striking epic power.

In the cycle of the Passion sculptured by *Donatello in the pulpits of S. Lorenzo in Florence, moral suffering is rendered in a tormented style. In the "Deposition" the important figures and all three crosses are in dramatic high relief; moreover, the center perspective toward which all the architectural and construction lines lead, is placed outside the limits of the composition. In this way the artist represented the tragic human events of the scene centered on Mary and the dead body of Christ as a "fragment" of a much greater picture whose limits cannot be measured by human means.

But formal balance was retained in the cycles of frescoes of Fra *Angelico portraying scenes from the life of Mary and Christ in the convent of San Marco in Florence and the stories of SS. Stephen and Lawrence from the Acts of the Apostles in the chapel of Nicholas V in the Vatican. The interpretation from a humanistic viewpoint given by the Florentine Renaissance to Biblical subjects virtually dominated European art until the beginning of the 17th century. Thereafter, new interpretations affected the form of the Bible cycles.

Northern Symbolism and Italian Rationalism. One case, however, of striking independence stands out in painting in the "Mystical Lamb" of Ghent, painted in 1439 by Van *Eyck. This is a huge complex of the greatest themes of the Old and New Testament, skillfully bound together by light and by symbolical elements, the whole center of interest being the Lamb. In effect the densely populated background is flooded with the sunlight of a bright morning hour.

Flemish art continued through the 15th and 16th centuries to express religious themes in a symbolic manner. The use of symbols was sometimes almost obsessive and in strong contrast to the clear, analytical, concrete use of pictorial material. Works of this kind include the "Seven Capital Sins," the "Parables," the "Garden of Delights," and the many aspects of the Passion by Hieronymus *Bosch; and the "Triumph of Death" and the "Parables" of Pieter *Brueghel.

Italian Renaissance painting, on the other hand, was marked by a rational interpretation of Biblical themes. The emotional content was not diminished, but there was clearer harmony in the forms and more concrete employment of human elements. Among the most important Italian cycles around the turn of the 15th century were the frescoes with parallel scenes of the Old and New Testaments executed by *Perugino, Pinturicchio, *Signorelli, *Ghirlandaio, *Botticelli, C. Rosselli, and Piero di Cosimo on the lower part of the walls of the *Sistine Chapel in the Vatican; the fresco cycle of the "Novissima" by Signorelli in the cathedral of Orvieto (c. 1499); the New Testament ceramics of the *Della Robbias in the sanctuary of Alvernia; and the frescoes of Fra Lippo *Lippi in the cathedral of Prato and of *Gozzoli in the chapel of the Medici. The subject of *Piero della Francesca's fresco cycle of the "Legend of the Cross" in the church of St. Francis in Arezzo was a derivation from the sacred history recorded in the New Testament. Piero's cycle, as well as the frescoes executed in the 16th century by *Raphael in the Vatican stanze, synthesize the artistic and religious culture both of the artists and of the civilization in which they lived. The "Last Supper" of *Leonardo da Vinci was the culmination of the synthesis.

High Renaissance to Modern

From the late 15th century to the 17th century the Bible cycles in European painting occurred in various and rich succession under the inspiration of earlier art.

Michelangelo. The cyclical works of *Michelangelo include "Genesis" on the ceiling (1508–12), the "Last Judgment" behind the altar (1536–41) of the Sistine Chapel, and the frescoes of the Pauline Chapel in the Vatican (1546). They are the greatest works of their kind. The artist penetrates the depths of religious mysteries. The ceiling seems so molded by the painting that the cornices around the gigantic scenes appear real and firmly constructed. They bind the composition together and repeat the vibrant movement in the groups of Prophets, Sibyls, and naked figures that animate the interior of the structures. By contrast, in the Last Judgment no linear frames obstruct the whirling movement of the bodies, either tossed down or upraised as if by the power in the arm of Christ, who is at the center of a composition marked by continuous vertical ascending and descending movement. The frescoes of the Pauline Chapel show a new contrast. A silent landscape spreads

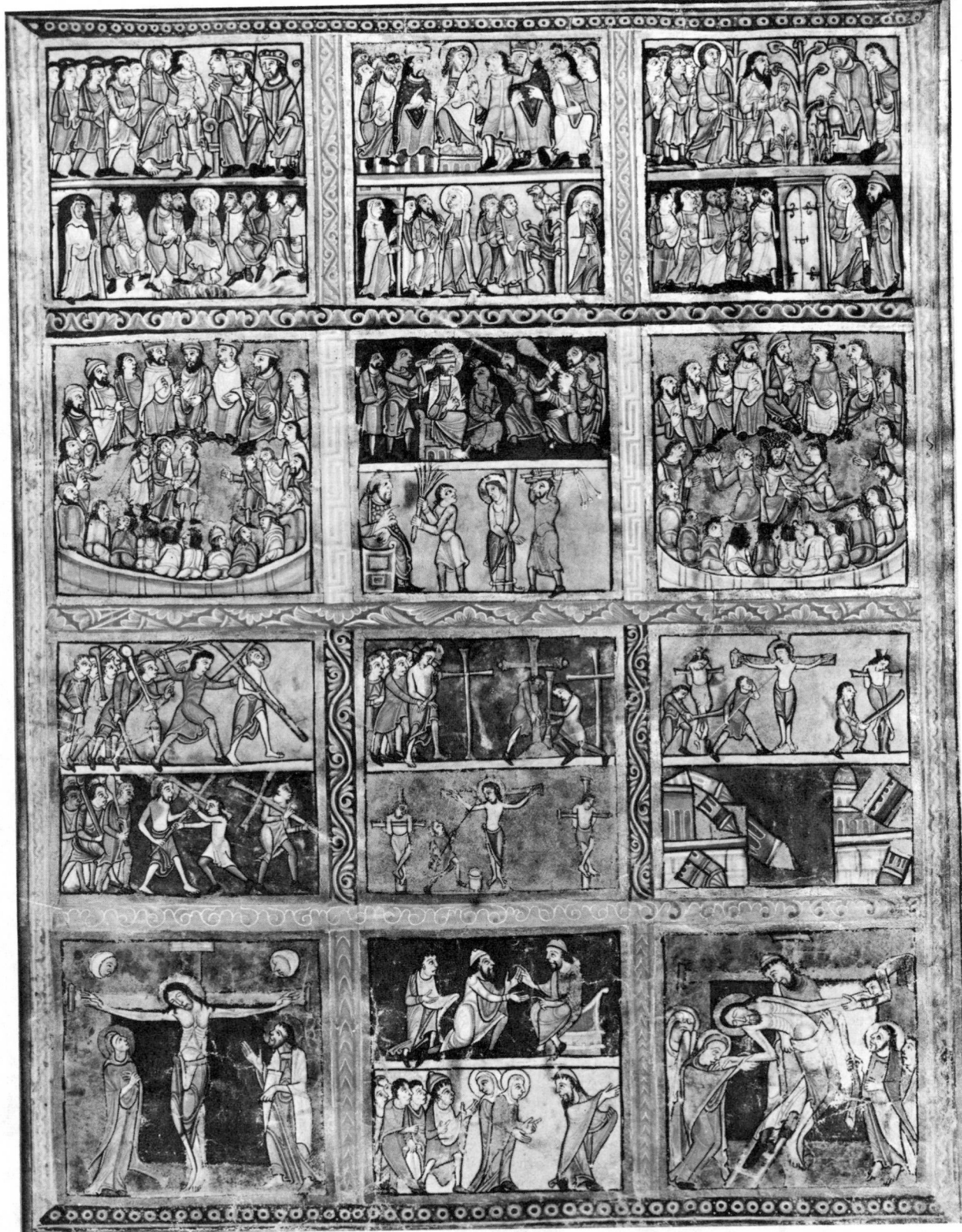

Fig. 7. Twenty scenes from the Passion, leaf of a 12th-century manuscript from Bury-St.-Edmunds or Canterbury.

Fig. 8. John the Baptist with a priest and a Levite, relief by Benedetto Antelami in the baptistery at Parma.

Fig. 9. "The Presentation in the Temple," relief by Niccolò Pisano, 1260, on the pulpit in the baptistery, Pisa.

Fig. 10. "The Last Supper," 15th-century fresco by Fra Angelico in the Convent of San Marco, Florence.

out beyond the tightly knit human group surrounding Peter's inverted cross. The Apostle's figure, with eyes glaring at the viewer, produces a dramatic complement to the rearing, isolated horse in the center of the "Conversion of St. Paul" that serves to measure the distance from the deserted horizon.

Tintoretto and Others. The artistic productions that appeared in the wake of Michelangelo's supreme effort exhibit the widest ranging imagination; they include the colossal and intensely moving cycle of huge canvases of the Old and New Testaments painted by *Tintoretto for the Scuola of S. Rocco in Venice (1564–87) and the numerous Biblical paintings of *Titian, *Veronese, *Lotto, and Jacopo Bassano. The spectacular Bible cycles by the "Sacri Monti" of the 16th, 17th, and 18th centuries, especially the work of Varallo, are in every sense of the word sacred representations from the plastic, pictorial, and architectural viewpoint.

New Trends. The work of *Caravaggio is symptomatic of the progressive decline of interest in the creation of organic Biblical cycles after the Renaissance. Although Caravaggio was a brilliant painter his attention was centered on brief fragments of reality, and then concentrated in compositions of extreme formal purity, with light audaciously used against solidly dark backgrounds. It was the beginning of a new age in European art, which—with an intensification of impassioned, personal research, and the vivid awareness of the value of the individual—lost contact with the sense of history as a series of universal events in which the individual had a part.

Two fundamental lines of development can be discerned in the 17th and 18th centuries. First, there was a tendency to paint sumptuous, superficial canvases on sacred themes, sometimes for their scenic effects, as in the work of *Carracci, Gaulli, *Pozzo, Piazzetta, Ricci, and *Tiepolo; sometimes for their episodic value, as in the elaborate, affected type of sacred painting produced by Flemish, Dutch, and German artists, as well as those of Brescia and Bologna, which gave rise to genre painting; and sometimes for purely decorative effect, as in Tiepolo's cycle in the cathedral of Udine or that of *Guardi in St. Raphael in Venice.

The second line of development tended to render the Biblical theme subjective, either by a tormented, personal search or by a fragmentary view of reality from which the specific sense of the sacred was banished, even though generalized spiritual values remained. The highest point in the art of personal search was reached in the throbbing luminosity of *Rembrandt's paintings, which shifted the focus to the human and immeasurable vastness of dark spaces. In the art of generalized spiritual values, while *Velázquez made decisive advances, the greatest developments were made in the 18th, 19th, and 20th centuries in the social interpretations of *Goya and *Millet, the chromatic transfigurations of Van *Gogh, *Gauguin, and *Matisse, and the torturous personal testimonies of Emil *Nolde and the German *expressionists. In his cycle of the "Passion," *Rouault attempted to constitute an organic cycle in the precise sense.

After World War II numerous works of art in cycles appeared, though rarely of purely Biblical subjects. Illustrations for the Bible by Marc Chagall (1956) have a quality of dreamlike, pictorial lightness. The "Door of Death" was created by Manzù for St. Peter's, Rome (1963). In it eight stupendous bas-reliefs suggest by broken rhythms the relation between Biblical and present-day events. It is a vertically oriented composition of utmost purity, crowned by the soaring movement of the "Death of the Virgin" and of the "Crucifixion."

Bibliography: E. STEINMANN, *Die Tituli und die kirchliche Wandmalerei* (Leipzig 1892). J. TIKKANEN, *Die Psalterillustrationen im Mittelalter* (Helsingfors 1895). J. REIL, *Die altchristlichen Bildzyklen des Lebens Jesu* (Leipzig 1910). A. DE LABORDE, *La Bible moralisée,* 4 v. (Paris 1911–21). G. MILLET, *Recherches sur l'iconographie de l'Évangile* (Paris 1916). E. B. SMITH, *Early Christian Iconography* (Princeton 1918). H. CORNELL, *Biblia pauperum* (Stockholm 1925). Künstle Ikonog. E. PANOFSKY, "Imago pietatis," in *Festschrift M. J. Friedländer* (Leipzig 1927). H. SCHRADE, *Zur Ikonographie der Himmelfahrt Christi* (Vorträge der Bibliothek Warburg 1928–29). H. VON CAMPENHAUSEN, *Die Passionssarkophage* (Marburg 1929). E. SANDBERG VAVALÀ, *La Croce dipinta italiana* (Verona 1929). H. SCHRADE, *Ikonographie der christlichen Kunst* (Berlin 1932). É. MÂLE, *L'Art religieux de la fin du XVIᵉ siècle, du XVIIᵉ siècle et du XVIIIᵉ siècle: Étude sur l'iconographie après le concile de Trente* (2d ed. Paris 1951). A. WALZER, *Das Bildprogramm an den mittelalterlichen Kirchenportalen Frankreichs und Deutschlands* (Leipzig 1938). F. GERKE, *Christus in der spätantiken Plastik* (3d ed. Mainz 1948). K. WEITZMANN, *Die Illustration der Septuaginta* (Munich 1952). *Lukasbücherei zur christlichen Ikonographie* (Düsseldorf 1949–). J. KOLLWITZ, *Das Christusbild des 3. Jahrhunderts* (Münster 1953). Réau IAC. 3. PIGLER, *Barockthemen,* 2 v. (Budapest 1956), v.1. A. KATZENELLENBOGEN, *The Sculptural Programs of Chartres Cathedral* (Baltimore 1958). E. FRANCESCHINI, "La Bibbia nell'alto Medioevo," in *Nel Bibbia nell'Alto Medioevo* (Spoleto 1963) 13–38. A. GRABAR, "Les Sujets bibliques au service de l'iconographie chrétienne," *ibid.* 387–411. K. HOLTER, "Das Alte und Neue Testament in der Buchmalerei," *ibid.* 413–471. **Illustration credits:** Fig. 1, Pontificia Commissione di Archeologia Sacra. Figs. 2 and 8, Leonard Von Matt. Figs. 3, 9, and 10, Alinari-Art Reference Bureau. Fig. 4, Hirmer Verlag München. Fig. 5, Biblioteca Apostolica Vaticana. Fig. 6, Germanisches Nationalmuseum Nürnberg. Fig. 7, Victoria and Albert Museum. Crown Copyright.

[A. M. ROMANINI]

BIBLE DEVOTIONS

Pious exercises drawn from the Bible and structured according to the traditional principles of liturgical worship. Basically these exercises consist of a Service of the Word to which is added an Action.

Background. It has been pointed out that the basic pattern in prayer services is a reading-hymn-prayer sequence. This structure is evident in the synagogue services, in the aliturgical instruction of the catechumens in the ancient Lenten practices, in the Vigil service of Holy Saturday, and the opening rite of Good Friday. It is found also in the Divine Office, and in a somewhat obscured manner is evident in the present form of the Roman Mass: Epistle, Gradual, Gospel, homily, Eucharistic liturgy.

The modern form of Bible devotions is a result of pastoral endeavors in postwar France. Because of the difficulty of Latin and the obscurity of liturgical symbolism, the pastors involved in the "mission" situation acted out the liturgical services in the vernacular with copious commentaries, sometimes in a spectacular manner. Many bishops and theologians feared that this was leading away from the liturgy; but in 1954 these paraliturgies, as they were called, were approved by the French hierarchy with certain reservations.

Owing to more profound study of ancient liturgies of East and West, the basic pattern of prayer became clearer, and with the new translations of the Scriptures and better congregational music, these paraliturgies began to mold themselves into the truer form of liturgical practice. The results of experimentation in this field were published in the various European liturgical periodicals. Paraliturgies as spectacles faded in favor of Biblical vigils. The confusion caused by the word "vigil" has led to the adoption of the term "Bible devotion."

Format. The advantage of this type of service is elasticity of its form and the freedom of choice of vernacular readings from Scripture and liturgical prayer. In the carrying out of the devotion, the ceremony is divided into four major parts: (1) entrance rite, (2) readings, (3) prayers, and (4) closing rite or "action."

The entrance rite consists of a procession. While the congregation is singing a hymn, the ministers enter the sanctuary carrying the Bible. The celebrant then greets the community with a blessing that expresses the theme of the service.

This blessing leads into the readings. The ideal is to have three readings in the following order: Old Testament, New Testament (Acts, Epistles, Apocalypse), and Gospel. Each is ordinarily introduced by a few words from a commentator and followed by a homily and hymn of meditation (preferably from the Psalms). Ordinarily no hymn follows the Gospel. At times only one homily, uniting all the reading, may be preferred. The order would then be: Old Testament, hymn, New Testament, hymn, Gospel, homily. Other practitioners prefer to repeat three times the basic pattern of reading, homily, hymn, prayer by the celebrant.

After the readings, the assembly prays in common in response to the Word of God. The best form is the litany prayer, followed by a period of silent prayer and concluded by a gathering of all intentions into a "collect" by the celebrant.

For the final action there is an abundance of possibilities. The celebrant may simply bless the congregation with a longer formula. But often the service leads into an action involving the community: veneration of a relic or of the Sacred Scriptures, a renewal of Baptism, a form of absolution, etc. Sometimes it ends with Benediction of the Blessed Sacrament. Whatever action is chosen, the service always ends with a recessional hymn of faith and thanksgiving.

The personnel may be many or few, depending on the size of the community and the occasion. The celebrant may be assisted by a deacon; readings may be done by one or several lectors; in the procession the Bible may be accompanied by thurifer and acolytes. At the least, there ought to be a priest-celebrant, lector, and a chanter. But it is still possible to celebrate a Bible devotion without a priest. The role of the leader is then taken by the leader in the community, or the father of the family. The homily is replaced by a reading from the Fathers or some spiritual book. This has been suggested as a form of service for Sundays in mission districts where the priest is not always available for Sunday Mass. This service can be set within any time limit.

Roman Encouragement. The pastoral possibilities of the Bible devotions have been recognized by many bishops and pastors. Such celebrations were encouraged by the Vatican Council II (*Constitution on the Sacred Liturgy*, 35.4). The Synod of Rome (1960) listed some of the reasons for the use of these services: to revive evening devotions, to restore the age-old need for reading the Word of God, and to contribute to a greater knowledge and love of the liturgy and the Church seasons.

Bibliography: J. GÉLINEAU, *Montons à Jérusalem* (Paris 1954); "The Vigil as an Evening Service for the Parish," *Unto the Altar*, ed. A. KIRCHGAESSNER (New York 1963) 107–118. J. CONNOLLY, "Bible Devotions: Principles and Sample," *Worship* 36 (1962) 115–120.

[T. KELLY]

BIBLE MORALISÉE, the most complete and systematic commentary of the Bible, both visual and literary; it appeared in the 13th century. The original consists of 5,000 scenes, inscribed in roundels and featuring some 30,000 characters. It is believed to have been dedicated to King Louis IX (1226–70). The manuscript is scattered among the Bodleian Library, Oxford (270b), the Bibliothèque Nationale, Paris (lat. 11560), and the British Museum (Harl. 1526–27). A copy, kept in the library of Vienna, was presented to King Louis IX, and another one is exhibited in the treasure room of the cathedral of Toledo, Spain. There exist various French translations of the Latin original. The scenes are disposed in medallions assembled by pairs in two columns of four, with grounds of alternating color. The chromatic pattern of the ground also alternates between two consecutive folios. The disposition, which is reminiscent of certain stained-glass windows in the Ste-Chapelle of Paris (1248), was used also in the *Psalter of Saint Louis* (The Pierpont Morgan Library). The arrangement was adopted in the 12th century for illustrating the Souvigny Bible, and it was repeated toward the end of the 13th century in the *Albenga Psalter*. The formal connection of the layout of the illustrations in the *Bible Moralisée* with that used in a Psalter from Artois (Bibliothèque Nationale, lat. 10425) suggests that the main artist responsible for planning the decoration of the *Bible Moralisée* may have come from northern France. The illustrations are accompanied by iconographical comments, stressing the parallelism between the "figures," or events, of the Old Testament and the "mysteries" of the New Testament: the life of Christ and the Sacraments. According to an allegorizing exegesis, four meanings are distinguished in the Holy Scripture: *sensus litteralis, sensus allegoricus, sensus tropologicus, sensus anagogicus. See* BIBLE, VI (EXEGESIS), 3. The scenes illustrate, in preference to the three other meanings, the *sensus tropologicus;* that is, the symbolic imagery of the Old Testament (type) is explained *verbatim*, word

Folio with the beginning of the Book of Genesis in the "Bible Moralisée" presented to King Louis IX (Cod. 1179, fol. 3v). The third and fourth medallions in the left column show the creation of Eve from the side of Adam (Old Testament type) and the creation of the Church from the side of Christ (New Testament antitype).

for word and image for image, by the revelations of the New Dispensation (antitype). The method is in line with typological art of the 12th century, which originated in the Meuse Valley and was adopted in the abbey church of Saint-Denis by Abbot Suger. On the other hand, the *Bible Moralisée* follows strictly the *Concordantiae* of the Bible by *Hugh of Saint-Cher and the Dominicans (second quarter of the 13th century). Like Hugh's *Postilla*, the written comments of the medallions in the *Bible Moralisée* expatiate particularly on the moral and disciplinary implications to be derived from the verses of the Bible.

See also MANUSCRIPT ILLUMINATION.

Bibliography: A. DE LABORDE, *La Bible Moralisée*, 4 v. (Paris 1911–21). **Illustration credit:** Austrian National Library, Vienna.

[P. VERDIER]

BIBLE READING

Private reading of the Scriptures is an extension of the public proclamation of the Word of God in the liturgy. The Church reads the Bible to her children, and their private reading is performed in the context of the Church's life (*see* BIBLE AND LITURGY). The history of Bible reading in the Church falls into three periods: from NT times to the Reformation, the Counter Reformation, and the modern Biblical revival.

From NT Times to the Reformation. Like their Jewish ancestors, the early Christians valued the reading of the Sacred Books. Following the example of Jesus (Mt 4.4; 5.18; Lk 24.44; Jn 5.39), the Apostles enjoyed a familiarity with the OT that supposes prolonged and careful reading and study, and urged this upon their disciples (Rom 15.4; 2 Tm 3.15–17). In the early Church, the Bible was considered to belong to the Christian people, who knew it through contact with a living liturgy and in their own vernacular languages. The Fathers, whose works betray a vast Biblical knowledge, enjoined the reading of the Bible upon their flocks, as can be seen from the homilies of John Chrysostom and the letters of Jerome. The Bible remained the basic source of the religious instruction and spirituality of the people down through the early Middle Ages, and was quickly translated into the new vernacular languages of Europe. More than 100 printed vernacular editions were in circulation before the Reformation.

In the course of the Middle Ages, however, the people gradually became estranged from the Bible, due to widespread ignorance, the decay of the liturgy, and lack of contact between clergy and laity. Consequently, movements such as the Waldenses, Albigenses, and Wycliffites arose, clamoring for a return to the Bible. This justifiable demand was unfortunately mixed with less orthodox tenets that culminated in the Reformation, with its principle of private interpretation.

The Counter Reformation. Certain restrictions upon Bible reading had already been issued during the Middle Ages in opposition to heretical sects (at the Councils of Toulouse in 1229, Tarragona in 1234, and Oxford in 1408), but these restrictions were only for particular cases and were conditional. The Medieval Church showed no opposition to vernacular versions as such. But since the Bible became the rallying point of the Reformation, the Council of Trent felt obliged to regulate Bible reading. The Index drawn up by a conciliar commission and published by Pius IV in 1564 required the permission of the bishop or inquisitor for the reading of vernacular versions (CIC Fontes 2:415). This defensive measure, which remained in force until it was somewhat relaxed by Benedict XIV in 1757, had the unfortunate effect of separating the laity further from the Bible. In 1897 Leo XIII permitted the use of vernacular versions approved by the Holy See or published with doctrinal notes under the supervision of the bishops (CIC Fontes 3:506–507). This legislation was adopted by the Code of 1918 and is still the law today (CIC cc.1391, 1400).

Modern Biblical Revival. The reversal of the neglect of the Bible that resulted from the Counter Reformation began with the encyclical *Providentissimus Deus* of Leo XIII in 1893, which provided encouragement and guidance for Biblical studies within the Church. The same Pontiff in 1898 encouraged the reading of the Gospels by granting indulgences [AmEcclRev 20 (1899) 418]. Further impetus was provided by Pius X [ActSSed 40 (1907) 134–136] and by Benedict XV (EnchBibl 495). The real charter of the modern Biblical movement, however, is the encyclical *Divino Afflante Spiritu* of Pius XII (1943), in which he approved of the application of modern critical methods to the study of the Bible and exhorted the bishops to foster a greater knowledge of the Bible among the faithful (EnchBibl 566).

The popular Biblical movement has progressed rapidly because of the impulse provided by this encyclical, first in Europe and more recently in America. The Catholic Biblical Association of America, established in 1936, publishes the *Catholic Biblical Quarterly* (1939) and the Confraternity of Christian Doctrine translation of the NT (1941) and the OT (1952, 1955, 1961). The remainder of the OT and a translation of the NT from the Greek are in preparation. The Association has contributed in various other ways to furthering the use of the Bible by the faithful. Since World War II an increasing volume of popular Biblical literature has appeared, including the periodical *The Bible Today* (1962), the purpose of which is to promote popular appreciation of the Scriptures.

Bibliography: A. STONNER, LexThK² 2:366–367. W. LEONARD, "The Place of the Bible in the Church," CathCommHS 1–12. A. VON HARNACK, *Bible Reading in the Early Church,* tr. J. WILKINSON (New York 1912). F. CAVALLERA, "La Bible en langue vulgaire au concile de Trent," *Mélanges E. Podechard* (Lyons 1945). A. VACCARI, "La lettura della Bibbia alla vigilia della Riforma protestante," *Scritti di erudizione e di filologia,* 2 v. (Rome 1952–58) 2:367–390. S. DE DIÉTRICH, *Le Renouveau biblique* (Neuchâtel 1945). P. AUVRAY et al., *L'Ancien Testament et les chrétiens* (Paris 1951). C. CHARLIER, "La Lecture sapientielle de la Bible," *Maison-Dieu* 12 (1947) 14–52; *The Christian Approach to the Bible,* tr. H. J. RICHARDS and B. PETERS (Westminster, Md. 1958). R. POELMAN, *How to Read the Bible,* tr. a nun of Regina Laudis (New York 1953). B. VAWTER, *The Bible in the Church* (New York 1959). D. LUPTON, *A Guide to Reading the Bible* (Chicago 1960). L. DANNEMILLER, *Reading the Word of God* (Baltimore 1960).

[C. J. PEIFER]

BIBLIA PAUPERUM, Bible of the illiterate, one of the small, late-medieval picture books (*biblia picta*) for religious instruction of the poor in spirit (*pauperes spiritu*); used also by clerics who could not afford a complete Bible or expensive handbooks, such as historiated and moralized Bibles for preaching and catechism. The layout of the material differs according to the quality of the book. In principle, a central roundel or rectangular, picturing one of the most important events of the New Testament (the Annunciation, the

Page from a Biblia pauperum printed in the Netherlands in 1465. The central vignettes illustrate the crossing of the Red Sea, the Baptism of Our Lord, and the return of the spies from Canaan. The final development of the Biblia pauperum was in the printed editions such as this.

Assumption of the Virgin, or the Last Judgment), is surrounded by four half-length figures of Prophets and flanked, on either side, by a roundel or rectangular with typological incidents from the Old Testament. Textual instruction is given in a general title, in an explanation of each of the Old Testament scenes and, on scrolls, in prophetic sayings. The name *Biblia pauperum* occurs only in late MSS, but the content of the work is derived from an ancient Christian method of teaching by means of typological picture cycles. It was prepared by an unknown late-13th-century theologian; the oldest MSS suggest Bavarian origin. It was particularly popular in Germany, France, and the Low Countries. More than 70 MSS (from *c.* 1300), blockbooks (*c.* 1450–80), and *incunabula (1st ed. Albert Pfister, Bamberg 1462–63) exist. Together they give about 65 New Testament scenes; texts are in Latin or German. Illustrations differ widely; the usual pen-drawings with washes hardly ever have artistic value.

Bibliography: GesamtkW 4:4325–27. *Reallexikon zur deutschen Kunstgeschichte,* ed. O. SCHMITT (Stuttgart 1937–) 1:1072–84. P. HEITZ and W. L. SCHREIBER, *Die Entstehung . . . der Biblia pauperum* (Strasbourg 1903). P. KRISTELLER, *Biblia pauperum* (Berlin 1906). H. CORNELL, *Biblia pauperum* (Stockholm 1925). H. ROST, *Die Bibel im Mittelalter* (Augsburg 1939). G. SCHMIDT, *Die Armenbibeln des 14. Jahrhunderts* (Graz-Cologne 1959). **Illustration credit:** National Gallery of Art, Washington, D.C., Rosenwald Collection.

[S. J. P. VAN DIJK]

BIBLICAL ATLASES, bound collections of maps of the Holy Land. This definition, however, applies, strictly speaking, only to the older Biblical atlases, which consist essentially of nothing but maps, with or without indexes. In modern so-called Biblical atlases the maps are usually but a secondary feature, while much more space is given to the text, which treats of the geography of Palestine, especially from an archeological and historical viewpoint.

Of the Biblical atlases that are strictly cartographic, worthy of special mention are: C. R. Conder and R. C. Kitchener, *Survey of Western Palestine* (London 1880); H. Fischer et al., *Handkarte von Palästina;* and particularly the maps prepared by British surveyers, such as the 16 sheets, 1:100,000, and the 3 sheets, 1:250,000. Other older atlases containing only maps are by M. Hagen (Paris 1907), R. von Riess (3d ed. Freiburg 1924), H. Guthe (2d ed. Leipzig 1926), and R. Koeppel (Tübingen).

Of Biblical atlases in the recent style, in which much more space is given to the accompanying text than to the maps, the best are: G. E. Wright and F. V. Filson, *The Westminster Historical Atlas of the Bible* (Philadelphia 1946, 2d rev. ed. 1956); L. H. Grollenberg, *Atlas of the Bible,* tr. J. M. H. Reid and H. H. Rowley (London 1956), profusely illustrated; and P. Lemaire and D. Baldi, *Atlante storico della Bibbia* (Turin 1955). Other similar works worthy of note are: H. G. May, *Oxford Bible Atlas* (Oxford and New York 1962); E. G. Kraeling, *Rand McNally Bible Atlas* (Chicago 1956); and C. F. Pfeiffer, *Baker's Bible Atlas* (Grand Rapids, Mich. 1961).

Other studies that contain maps of Palestine but are essentially treatises on Palestinian geography are: F. M. Abel, *Géographie de la Palestine* (2 v., Paris 1933–38); M. Buit, *Géographie de la Terre Sainte* (2 v., Paris 1958); and D. Baly, *The Geography of the Bible* (New York 1957). The last-mentioned book is good particularly for the geology of Palestine. The atlas that was published in connection with the 1915 reprint of the 4th edition (London 1896) of *Historical Geography of the Holy Land* by G. A. Smith, is, like that venerable classic, entirely outmoded.

Bibliography: A. STROBEL, "Biblische Geographie," LexThK² 2:433–434. G. S. GLANZMAN and J. A. FITZMYER, *An Introductory Bibliography for the Study of Scripture* (Westminster, Md. 1961) 93–95.

[F. J. MARCOLONGO]

BIBLICAL COMMENTARIES

Systematic presentations of the Biblical *exegesis (verse-by-verse explanation) of the text of the Sacred Scriptures, usually preceded by a discussion of the individual Biblical book. Such a discussion, however, is, strictly speaking, the proper function of *Biblical introductions. A Biblical commentary may sometimes treat of all or of several books of the Bible, but more often modern commentaries are limited to an individual book. Series, however, of separate volumes on the individual books, either by the same commentator or (more frequently) by different commentators are common. At times the exegesis is printed together with the Biblical text, either in a standard version or in a new translation made by the commentator; at other times the reader must have recourse to a separate volume of a standard text while using the commentary. The number of Biblical commentaries is very large. Only a select list can be given here. For the older commentators, *see* BIBLE, VI (EXEGESIS), 2.

Catholic Commentaries. Modern Catholic commentaries in English are still limited to popular works and pamphlet series; a series of detailed commentaries written in English by Catholic scholars remains a desideratum. The large one-volume work, *A Catholic Commentary on Holy Scripture* (London 1953), by various authors (mostly British and Irish) under the editorship of E. F. Sutcliffe and B. Orchard, contains some articles on the more general topics that are still valuable; but as a whole the work is outmoded, both because of its extremely conservative tone and because of its use of the antiquated Douay-Rheims Version (not printed in the volume) as the text commented on. Based on the best modern scholarship, but limited in scope, are two pamphlet series: the Paulist *Pamphlet Bible Series* (New York 1960–) and *New Testament Reading Guide* (Collegeville, Minn. 1963–); they are based on the Confraternity Version.

In French, a strictly scientific series of commentaries was begun by M. J. *Lagrange under the title *Études bibliques* (Paris 1903–); it is still incomplete. The 12-volume *La Sainte Bible* (Paris 1935–), containing the Vulgate text and a French translation made from the original languages, together with a commentary under the editorship first of L. Pirot and then of A. Clamer, is complete except for the Minor Prophets. Although not a commentary in the strict sense, *La Sainte Bible traduit en français sous la direction de l'École Biblique de Jerusalem* (Paris 1948–54) contains excellent introductions to the individual books of the Bible and fairly copious exegetical footnotes. This work, commonly called the Jerusalem Bible, presents one of the best translations of the Scriptures made from the original texts. The *Verbum Salutis* series by the French Jesuits (Paris 1924–) offers short but solid commentaries on all the Biblical books.

German Catholics have several excellent series of Biblical commentaries, such as the so-called *Bonner Altes Testament* (Bonn 1923–), ed. F. *Feldmann and H. *Herkenne; the so-called *Bonner Neues Testament* (Bonn, 4th ed. 1931–), ed. F. Tillmann; the so-called *Echter Bibel* (Würzburg 1947–), ed. F. Nötscher and K. Staab; the *Regensburger Neues Testament* (Regensburg 1938–), ed. A. *Wikenhauser and O. Kuss; and the strictly scientific series of 14 planned volumes, the *Theologischer Kommentar zum Neuen Testament,* of which only one volume, by R. Schnackenburg, *Die Johannesbriefe* (Freiburg 1953), has so far appeared.

The Italian series, *La Sacra Bibbia* (Turin 1947–), ed. S. Garofalo, is similar in spirit and scope to *La Sainte Bible* of Pirot and Clamer. In Catalan, *La Biblia: Versio dels textos originals i commentari pels monjos de Monserrat* (Monserrat 1928–) is an elaborate and scientific series, of which 15 of the 22 projected volumes have appeared.

Protestant Commentaries. In keeping with the great stress that Protestant theology lays on the Bible, Biblical commentaries by Protestants are more numerous than those by Catholics. J. Perowne and A. F. Kirkpatrick, eds., *The Cambridge Bible for Schools and Colleges,* which was begun in 1800, has frequently been reedited and brought up to date; though intended for popular use, it contains some excellent commentaries; it is complete for the OT. Of a more scientific scope is C. A. Briggs et al., eds., *The International Critical Commen-*

tary (Edinburgh 1895–). More recent works are G. A. Buttrick, ed., *The Interpreter's Bible* (New York 1951–57); H. Chadwick, ed., *Harper's New Testament Commentaries* (New York 1957–); and C. F. D. Moule, ed., *Cambridge Greek Testament Commentary* (Cambridge, Eng., 1957–). Of exceptional promise is the new interdenominational series, W. F. Albright and D. N. Freedman, eds., *The Anchor Bible* (Garden City, N.Y. 1964–); of the planned 38 volumes of new translations and commentaries the first 5 to appear are: E. A. Speiser, *Genesis* (1964); B. I. Reicke, *James, 1 and 2 Peter, Jude* (1964); M. H. Pope, *Job* (1965); J. Bright, *Jeremiah* (1965); R. B. Y. Scott, *Proverbs, Ecclesiastes* (1965).

Some of the best modern commentaries are in German, such as: V. Herntrich and A. Weiser, eds., *Das Alte Testament Deutsch* (Göttingen 1949–); M. Noth, ed., *Biblischer Kommentar: Altes Testament* (Neukirchen 1955–); O. Eissfeldt, ed., *Handbuch zum Alten Testament* (Tübingen 1934–); H. A. W. Meyer, *Kritisch-exegetischer Kommentar über das Neue Testament* (Göttingen 1832– ; often reedited and still being revised); and P. Althaus and J. Behm, *Das Neue Testament Deutsch* (Göttingen, 5th ed. 1949–50).

Of French Protestant commentaries, worthy of special mention are E. Dhorme, ed., *La Bible: L'Ancien Testament* (2 v. Paris 1956–59), and P. Bonnard et al., eds., *Commentaire du Nouveau Testament* (Neuchatel and Paris 1941–).

Bibliography: G. S. GLANZMAN and J. A. FITZMYER, *An Introductory Bibliography for the Study of Scripture* (Westminster, Md. 1961) 63–72. J. SCHMID, LexThK² 2:356–359.

[F. J. MARCOLONGO]

BIBLICAL CONCORDANCES, DICTIONARIES, AND ENCYCLOPEDIAS

A Biblical concordance is an alphabetical listing of the words in the Bible with citations of the book, chapter, and verse of each occurrence, usually accompanied by a sense quotation in which it is used. The earliest work to bear the name concordance, although not properly a verbal concordance as just defined, was the anonymous 13th-century *Concordantiae Morales.* It was made from the Latin Vulgate for the apologetic purpose of demonstrating that passages of the Bible dealing with the same matter were consistent or in concord with each other. The name was aptly chosen, since it derives from the late Latin *concordantia,* meaning harmony, agreement. It is regularly used in the plural, each group of parallel passages forming a *concordantia.* The principle of classification subsequently came to be individual words rather than subject matter, but the name *concordantiae* was retained.

Concordances. The first strictly verbal concordance was prepared c. 1230 from the Latin Vulgate under the direction of *Hugh of Saint-Cher; it is known as the *Concordantiae Sancti Jacobi,* from the name of the Paris monastery where it was composed to help the monks with their work on various commentaries. This work is the first of all verbal concordances, and as modified by its two immediate successors, it served as the model for every similar work down to the present day. It fell short of giving full satisfaction, chiefly because it failed to quote a phrase containing the word cited. To remedy this defect three English Dominicans prepared the *Concordantiae Anglicanae* (c. 1250; first printed at Nuremberg in 1485), but the passages they quoted are frequently irrelevant and invariably too lengthy. Conrad of Halberstadt in his *Concordantiae bibliorum* (*c.* 1290, first printed at Strasbourg, 1470—the earliest printed concordance) struck a happy mean, quoting only essential sense phrases. Over the centuries many other Biblical concordances followed these pioneer efforts, and today they are available for both the original text and its principal ancient and modern versions. There are also many non-Biblical concordances.

The usefulness of Biblical concordances to the exegete, the textual critic, the apologist, the preacher, and anyone interested in systematic work on the Bible is self–evident. No concordance is better than the manuscripts on which it is based, so that reference to more recent critical editions of the text may be necessary. This article treats only Latin, Hebrew, Greek, and English concordances.

Latin Concordances. In addition to the three mentioned above, there are several concordances of the Latin Vulgate prior to the official 1592 Clementine edition. Among these, perhaps the outstanding one is that of Robert *Estienne, *Concordantiae bibliorum utriusque Testamenti Veteris et Novi, novae et integrae, quas revera majores appellare possis* (Paris 1555). Among the numerous post-Clementine Vulgate concordances are the following: (1) *Concordantiae Bibliorum juxta recognitionem Clementinam* (Antwerp 1599); this is the first such. (2) F. F. Dutripon, *Vulgatae editionis bibliorum sacrorum concordantiae* (Paris 1838); held by many as the best; often reprinted. (3) C. Legrand, *Concordantiae librorum Novi Testamenti D. N. J. C. juxta Vulgatam editionem* (Bruges 1889). (4) V. Coornaert, *Concordantiae librorum Veteris et Novi Testamenti juxta Vulgatam editionem ad usum praedicatorum* (Paris and Bruges 1892, Amsterdam 1909). (5) E. Peultier, L. Etienne, and L. Gantois, *Concordantiarum universae sacrae Scripturae thesaurus* (Paris 1897, 2d rev. ed. Paris 1939).

Hebrew Concordances. (1) The earliest Hebrew concordance of the OT, that of Rabbi Isaac Nathan, entitled *Mĕ'îr nātîb* (Light of the Way), with the word concordance transcribed on the title page (Venice 1523, Basel 1556); several times reprinted, but now completely superseded by more recent works, it is arranged alphabetically by roots and omits proper names. (2) Marius de Calasio, OFM, *Concordantiae sacrorum bibliorum hebraicorum, in quibus chaldaicae etiam librorum Esdrae et Danielis suo loco inseruntur* (Rome 1621, 1622); it corrected and enlarged that of Isaac Nathan. (3) Conrad Kircher, *Concordantiae V. T. graecae* (Frankfort 1607); because of its title, it is often listed as a concordance of the Septuagint; the Hebrew words are in their alphabetical order with the Greek words under them. (4) John *Buxtorf and son, *Concordantiae bibliorum hebraicae, nova et artificiosa methodo dispositae* (Basel 1632); still useful, although references are by Hebrew letters and relate to rabbinical divisions of the text. (5) Julius Fuerst, *Hebräischen und chaldäischen Concordanz zu den Heiligen Schriften des Alten Testaments* (Leipzig 1840; Eng. tr., London 1867); a revision of Buxtorf, but greatly superior textually. (6) Solomon Mandelkern, *Vetris Testamenti Concordantiae hebraicae atque chaldaicae* (Leipzig 1896; other editions, Berlin 1925, Jerusalem and Tel Aviv 1956 and 1959); it supersedes all its predecessors.

Concordances of the Septuagint. (1) A. Trommius, *Concordantiae graecae versionis vulgo dictae LXX interpretum, cujus voces secundum ordinem elementorum sermonis graeci digestae recensentur, contra atque in opere Kircheriano factum fuerat* (Amsterdam and Utrech 1718); a monumental work, indispensable until Hatch and Redpath, but still useful. (2) E. Hatch and H. A. Redpath, *A concordance of the Septuagint and the other Greek versions of the Old Testament including the Apocryphal Books* (Oxford 1892–97, supplement Oxford 1906); indispensable, but it has its limitations because it is based on only four uncials, viz, A, B, S, and R, and therefore it must be checked for variant readings.

Concordances of the Greek New Testament. (1) S. Betulius, *Novi Testamenti Concordantiae Graecae* (Basel 1546); the earliest concordance of the Greek NT. (2) Robert Estienne, *Concordantiae Testamenti Novi graeco-latinae* (Paris 1594). (3) E. Schmid, *Novi Testamenti Jesu Christi graeci, hoc est, originalis linguae tamieion* (Wittenberg 1638). (4) G. V. Wigram, *Englishman's Greek Concordance of the New Testament* (London 1839). (5) C. H. Bruder, *Concordantiae omnium vocum Novi Testamenti Graeci* (Leipzig 1842 and 1888, Göttingen 1913); originally based on the *textus receptus,* but improved in later editions from more critical texts. (6) W. F. Moulton and A. S. Geden, *A Concordance to the Greek Testament according to the Texts of Westcott and Hort, Tischendorf and the English Revisers* (New York and Edinburgh 1926); textual improvement over Bruder. (7) J. B. Smith, *Greek-English Concordance to the New Testament: A Tabular and Statistical Greek-English Concordance, based on the King James Version with an English to Greek Index* (Scottdale, Pa. 1955); strictly statistical, no quotations, useful for limited purposes.

Concordances of the English Bible. The first English concordance was of the Authorized Version of the NT, compiled by Thomas Gybson and quaintly titled, *The concordance of the New Testament most necessary to be had in the handes of all soche as delight in the communicacion of any place contayned in ye new Testament* (London 1535). The first English concordance of the entire Authorized Version, compiled by John Marbeck bore an equally quaint title, *A Concordance, that is to saie, a worke wherein, by the ordre of the letters of the A.B.C., ye may redely finde any word conteigned in the whole Bible* (London 1550). Among later concordances of the several English versions are: (1) S. Newman, *A Large and complete concordance to the Bible in English according to the last Translation,* i.e., Authorized Version (London 1643). (2) A. Cruden, *Complete Concordance to the Old and New Testaments, to which is added a concordance to the books called Apocrypha* (London 1737); based on the Authorized Version; complete and accurate, this work became a minor classic, was often reprinted, and is still available. (3) R. Young, *Analytical Concordance to the Bible* (Edinburgh 1873); it includes Hebrew and Greek equivalents of the English words. (4) J. Strong, *The Exhaustive Concordance of the Bible together with a Comparative Concordance of the Authorized and Revised Versions* (New York and London 1894). (5) M. C. Hazard, *Complete Concordance to the American Standard Version of the Holy Bible* (New York 1932). (6) N. W. Thompson, *Verbal Concordance to the New Testament,* Rheims version (Baltimore 1928); good quotations of passages, but with many lacunae. (7) N. W. Thompson and R. Stock, *Complete Concordance to the Bible,* Douay-Rheims version (St. Louis 1942, 1945). (8) W. J. Grant, *The Moffatt Bible Concordance* (New York 1950). (9) *Complete Concordance of the Revised Standard Version of the Bible* (New York 1957); done by computer within 5 years of the completion of the Bible text itself.

Dictionaries and Encyclopedias. The words dictionary and encyclopedia (var., cyclopedia) are used more or less interchangeably to denominate a work containing relatively exhaustive information on the Bible. Some of these confine themselves to the words, including proper names, of the Bible; others treat of related subjects, sometimes including biographies of commentators and Biblical scholars. The earliest examples of this type of work are the *Onomasticon* of Eusebius and Jerome's *Liber interpretationis hebraicorum nominum* and the *De situ et nominibus locorum hebraicorum liber.* The present list, however, begins with scientific works of the 17th century. (1) J. H. Alstedt, *Triumphus bibliorum sacrorum seu encyclopaedia biblica* (Hanover 1625); long a popular pioneer work in this field. (2) A. *Calmet, *Dictionnaire historique, critique, geographique et litteral de la Bible* (Paris 1720); Eng. tr., *Calmet's Dictionary of the Bible* (5 v. London 1800, 9th ed. New York 1847). (3) G. B. Winer, *Biblisches Realwörterbuch* (Leipzig 1820, 1847). (4) J. Kitto, *A cyclopaedia of Biblical Literature* (London 1835–38); reprinted several times; it is outdated, but contains many articles scholarly for their time; long very popular. (5) J. von Allioli, *Wörterbuch der hl. Schrift* (Regensburg 1837, 1845). (6) W. Smith, *A Dictionary of the Bible* (Boston 1863); articles of solid scholarship, especially in subjects touching on the classical field, but outdated. (7) J. Hastings, *Dictionary of the Bible, Dealing with its Language, Literature and Contents, Including Biblical Theology* (5 v. Edinburg and New York 1898–1904); conservative, thoroughly scholarly, but for the general reader also. (8) T. K. Cheyne and J. S. Black, *Encyclopaedia Biblica, a Critical Dictionary of the Literary, Political and Religious History, the Archaeology, Geography and Natural History of the Bible* (4 v. New York 1899–1903); scholarly, representing the views of advanced higher criticism of its day. (9) J. Hastings, *Dictionary of the Bible* (New York 1909); an independent work, not a condensation of (7); frequently reprinted. (10) F. Vigouroux et al., *Dictionnaire de la Bible, contenant tous les noms de personnes, de lieux, de plantes, d'animaux mentionnés dans les Saintes Écritures, les questions théologiques, archéologiques, scientifiques relatives a l'Ancien et le Nouveau Testaments et des notices sur les commentateurs anciens at modernes* (Paris 1895–1912); the *Supplément* volumes, from A to Paul (1929–61), have brought this work largely up to date. (11) J. Davis, *The Westminster Dictionary of the Bible* (5th ed. Philadelphia 1944); scholarly, conservative in viewpoint. (12) J. E. Steinmueller and K. Sullivan, *Catholic Biblical Encyclopedia* (New York, NT 1950, OT 1956). (13) G. A. Buttrick, ed., *The Interpreter's Dictionary of the Bible* (4 v. New York 1962). (14) A. van den Born, *Bibels Woordenboek* (Roermond 1941, 2d ed. 1954); Eng. tr. and adaptation, L. F. Hartman, *Encyclopedic Dictionary of the Bible* (New York 1963). (15) J. L. McKenzie, *Dictionary of the Bible* (Milwaukee 1965).

Many encyclopedias that cover a more extensive field than Scripture studies contain important scholarly articles on Bible subjects; *see* ENCYCLOPEDIAS AND DICTIONARIES, CATHOLIC.

Dictionaries of the Biblical Languages. The term Biblical dictionary (or lexicon) may be applied also to an alphabetical listing of the Hebrew or Greek words that occur in original texts, with their vernacular equivalents.

Old Testament Lexicons. (1) H. F. Wilhelm Gesenius, *Hebräisches und aramäisches Handwörterbuch über die Schriften des Alten Testaments* (Leipzig 1810); an excellent work, revised several times. (2) F. Brown, S. R. *Driver, and C. A. Briggs, *Hebrew and English Lexicon of the OT* (Oxford 1906, 1929, rev. ed. 1953); based on (1). (3) F. *Zorell and L. Semkowski, *Lexicon hebraicum et aramaicum Veteris Testamenti,* (Rome 1940–54); the Aramaic section is not yet published. (4) L. Koehler and W. Baumgartner, *Lexicon in Veteris Testamenti Libros* (Leiden 1953, 2d ed. and supplement Leiden 1958).

New Testament Lexicons. (1) C. L. W. Grimm, *Lexicon graeco-latinum in libros N.T.* (Leipzig 1862–68, 4th ed. 1903); Eng. tr. and revision, J. H. Thayer, *Greek-English Lexicon of the NT* (Edinburgh and New York 1886, 4th ed. 1908). (2) F. Zorell, *Lexicon graecum N.T.* (Paris 1911, 2d ed. 1931); the first to make use of Greek papyri. (3) J. H. Moulton and G. Milligan, *The Vocabulary of the Greek NT Illustrated from the Papyri and Other Non-literary Sources* (London 1914–29, 2d ed. 1949); not a complete lexicon, it contains only words found in the papyri and other nonliterary sources. (4) W. Bauer, *Griechisch-Deutches Wörterbuch zu den Schriften den N.T. and der übrigen urchristlichen Literatur* (Giessen 1910, 1928, Berlin 1937); its 4th ed. (Berlin 1952) was translated and adapted into English by W. F. Arndt and F. W. Gingrich, *A Greek-English Lexicon of the NT and Other Early Christian Literature* (Chicago 1957). (5) G. *Kittel et al., *Theologisches Wörterbuch zum N.T.* (Stuttgart 1933–); the fifth of the seven planned volumes was published in 1958; many of its articles are long philological-historical-theological monographs.

Bibliography: J. SCHMID, LexThK² 2:360–363, 367–370. E. MANGENOT, DB 2:892–905. C. R. GREGORY, Herzog-Hauck PRE 10:695–703.

[C. O'C. SLOANE]

BIBLICAL INTRODUCTIONS

Books that serve as guides to the historical and literary background and nature of the Bible as a whole and to its individual books. Many of these works were written primarily as classroom manuals for the course known as Biblical introduction, which is usually divided into general introduction, treating of matters that pertain to the Bible as a whole (Biblical inspiration, hermeneutics, textual criticism, etc.); and special introduction, treating of the individual books of the OT and the NT. The corresponding manuals are therefore often called by the same terms. Some of these works include all these aspects of Biblical introduction.

General Introductions. An excellent Catholic introduction, covering the whole field, is A. Robert and A. Feuillet, ed., *Introduction à la Bible,* 2 v. (2d rev. ed. Tournai, Belgium 1959). The articles on the historical background are well done, but the bibliographies are often insufficient. Another very good Catholic work of both general and special introduction is A. Robert and A. Tricot, ed., *Initiation biblique* (1st ed. Tournai 1939, 2d rev. ed. 1948, 3d rev. and augmented ed. 1954). The English translation by E. P. Arbez and M. R. P. McGuire, *Guide to the Bible*, 2 v. (New York 1955) is based on the 2d French edition, but a new edition of v.1 (New York 1960) is based on the 3d French edition. Besides the usual materials in Biblical introductions, there are special articles on Biblical geography, history, archeology, theology, and languages. The bibliographies are extensive, especially in the English editions.

Old Testament Introductions. Of the special introductions to the OT, the best available is O. Eissfeldt, *Einleitung in das Alte Testament* (3d ed. Tübingen 1964), translated by P. Ackroyd as *The Old Testament: An Introduction* (New York 1965). The detailed introduction to each book of the Bible, including the deuterocanonical ones, and also to the pseudepigraphical books and the Qumran documents, shows formidable erudition. Another introduction, this one written by a non-Catholic, highly recommended to seminarians and college students is B. W. Anderson, *Understanding the Old Testament* (Englewood Cliffs, N.J. 1957). It sets the Biblical writings in their historical context and is well supplied with chronological charts, maps, and illustrations. A quite original work, which treats OT literary problems very well and highlights the importance of oral tradition (according to the Scandinavian school) is A. Bentzen, *Introduction to the Old Testament* (2d rev. ed. Copenhagen 1952). A useful introduction of great scholarship and well-organized content, though much shorter than Eissfeldt's, is A. Weiser, *Einleitung in das Alte Testament* (4th rev. ed. Göttingen 1957). A work that despite its age still retains its value is S. R. Driver, *An Introduction to the Literature of the Old Testament* (9th ed. Edinburgh 1913). Worthy of special mention are also: R. H. Pfeiffer, *Introduction to the Old Testament* (New York 1941); N. K. Gottwald, *A Light to the Nations* (New York 1959); A. Lods, *Histoire de la littérature hebraïque et juive*, ed. A. Parrot (Paris 1950); H. J. Kraus, *Geschichte der historisch-kritischen Erforschung des A.T. von der Reformation bis zur Gegenwart* (Neukirchen 1956); and J. Hempel, *Althebräische Literatur und ihr hellenistisch-jüdisches Nachleben* (Wildpark-Potsdam 1930–34).

New Testament Introductions. For the NT, the best product of Catholic scholarship is A. Wikenhauser, *New Testament Introduction*, tr. J. Cunningham (New York 1956) from the 2d German edition, *Einleitung in das N.T.* (Freiburg 1958); this work is valuable particularly for its treatment of Biblical *form criticism. A more conservative and less detailed presentation is M. Meinertz, *Einleitung in das N.T.* (Paderborn 1950). Other good Catholic works are A. Moraldi, *Introduzione alla Bibbia*, v.1 *I Vangeli* (Turin 1959); and P. Gaechter, *Summa introductionis in N.T.* (Innsbruck and Leipzig 1938), now somewhat outmoded. Among Protestant NT introductions, one of the best is P. Feine et al., *Einleitung in das N.T.* (13th rev. ed. Heidelberg 1964). More popular and less comprehensive is W. Marxen, *Einleitung in das N.T.* (Gütersloh 1963). The conservative Protestant view is well represented by W. Michaelis, *Einleitung in das N.T.* (3d ed. Bern 1961). Somewhat outdated but still useful is K. and S. Lake, *An Introduction to the N.T.* (New York 1937). Writ-

ten primarily for seminarians and college students are A. H. McNeile, *An Introduction to the Study of the N.T.* (Oxford 1953); and T. Henshaw, *The New Testament Literature in the Light of Modern Scholarship* (London 1952). The history of NT introductions is presented in G. Kümmel, *Das N.T.: Geschichte der Erforschung seiner Probleme* (Freiburg 1958).

Bibliography: G. S. GLANZMAN and J. A. FITZMYER, *An Introductory Bibliography for the Study of Scripture* (Westminster, Md. 1961) 53–61. History of Biblical introd. and Biblical criticism. P. DE AMBROGGI, EncCatt 7:116–119. J. SCHMID, LexThK² 2:363–366. F. BAUMGÄRTEL and E. DINKLER, RGG³ 1:1184–90.

[F. J. MARCOLONGO]

BIBLICAL LANGUAGES, the tongues used by the inspired authors in writing the Sacred Scriptures. All the protocanonical books of the OT (*see* CANON, BIBLICAL) were written in Hebrew, except about one-half of Daniel (Dn 2.4b–7.28) and two sections of Ezra (Ez 4.8–6.18; 7.12–26), which were composed in Aramaic. Of the deuterocanonical books of the OT, two (2 Machabees and Wisdom) were composed in Greek; the others were written originally in Hebrew or Aramaic, but have been preserved only in ancient translations (especially Greek), except that about two-thirds of Sirach has been preserved in its original Hebrew. All the books of the NT were composed in Greek. On the nature of these tongues as used in the composition of the Sacred Scriptures, *see* HEBREW LANGUAGE; ARAMAIC LANGUAGE, 2; GREEK LANGUAGE, BIBLICAL; SEMITIC LANGUAGES.

[L. F. HARTMAN]

BIBLICAL PERIODICALS

The development of Biblical periodicals, primarily by non-Catholics, in the last decades of the 19th century and their multiplication by Catholic as well as non-Catholic organizations in the first half of the 20th century witness to a phenomenal growth in scriptural studies. These journals encourage creative research and dialogue and anticipate trends and insights that only later appear in book form. The publication of these periodicals has made an important contribution to the ecumenical movement, since Catholics now frequently write for non-Catholic periodicals, while Catholic Biblical journals are in turn widely read in non-Catholic academic circles.

This article first enumerates major current scriptural journals, beginning with the oldest; it then mentions some recent Catholic periodicals in the field of Biblical popularization. Brief reference is made to some Biblical-archeology journals. Next follows a discussion of bibliographical and abstracting periodicals for the Bible. Finally, some general remarks about the history of Biblical journals, especially in America, are appended.

Obviously important scriptural articles will occasionally appear in theological journals of broader scope (e.g., *Journal of Theological Studies, Nouvelle Revue Théologique, Theologische Literaturzeitung,* and *Theological Studies*). Increased interest in the relationship of systematic theology to Biblical theology, the hermeneutical problem, and the use of "proof texts" has led theological journals to feature scriptural articles. Journals devoted principally to systematic or dogmatic theology are not listed here. No reference is made to publications concerned with devotional and homiletic treatments of Scripture.

Major Current Journals. The oldest American scriptural journal still being published is the *Journal of Biblical Literature,* begun in 1881. The Society of Biblical Literature and Exegesis sponsors this quarterly, which is now published in Philadelphia. Its contributions, representing various nondenominational viewpoints, treat both Testaments and the intertestamental period with scholarship and competence.

In the same year, 1881, the German Protestant publication *Zeitschrift für die alttestamentliche Wissenschaft* appeared. This leading scientific journal, now published three times a year in Berlin, accepts manuscripts pertaining to the OT and written in the major European languages. Besides heavily documented, full-length articles and shorter notes, brief abstracts from OT periodical literature are included.

The *Expository Times,* a less technical but scholarly monthly treating Biblical questions, has appeared at Edinburgh since 1889. Uniformly excellent articles discuss hermeneutics, various phases of exegesis, Biblical theology, etc. Besides a survey of new books a homiletic section attends to pastoral needs.

The oldest continuing Catholic Biblical publication is the *Revue Biblique,* a quarterly started in 1892 by M. J. *Lagrange and other Dominicans of the École Pratique d'Études Bibliques in Jerusalem (*see* ÉCOLE BIBLIQUE). This scholarly and influential journal contains lengthy articles on the OT and NT. Archeology receives heavy emphasis. Penetrating long reviews and shorter notices of new books are regular features.

Designed as a NT companion publication to its OT equivalent, the *Zeitschrift für die neutestamentliche Wissenschaft und die Kunde der Älteren Kirche* has been published in Berlin since 1900. Although originally a quarterly, it now appears annually in two double issues, with full-length articles, shorter comments, and a useful bibliographical analysis of periodical literature on the NT. No book reviews are included. G. Bornkamm, E. Käsemann, and J. Jeremias shared in 1964 the editorial duties of this German Protestant publication.

The foremost German Catholic Scripture journal covering OT and NT is the *Biblische Zeitschrift.* The early series of the journal covered the years 1903 to 1939. Bibliographical notices of books and periodical articles about the Bible were featured from 1903. Ninety-four periodicals were regularly covered by 1939. Revived in 1957, the new series, published at Paderborn, has two issues a year. V. Hamp for the OT and R. Schnackenburg for the NT were editors in 1964; the articles are consistently of high caliber. The book reviews are thorough: related books are frequently compared and contrasted.

In 1920 the Jesuits at the *Pontifical Biblical Institute in Rome began publication of *Biblica,* a quarterly containing technical contributions in the major European languages. Both Testaments are treated and attention is given to Biblical archeology, studies on the canon, linguistic research, etc. Apart from feature reviews, its book reviews tend to be short. One notable feature of the journal is the "Elenchus Bibliographicus Biblicus," an exhaustive index of periodical articles and of new books together with a list of critical reviews of these books.

The following year, 1921, the same institution inaugurated *Verbum Domini,* published in Latin and designed especially for the clergy. The periodical appears six times a year and often contains among its articles résumés of significant dissertations presented at the Biblical Institute. A survey of periodicals and *Festschriften* is included in the bibliographical supplement to the *Biblica* "Elenchus." The supplement began in 1960.

The Association to Foster Biblical Studies in Spain published its quarterly *Estudios Bíblicos* in Madrid from 1929 to 1936. A new series began in 1941. Of all the Spanish Biblical journals this is the most technical; in recent years some of the detailed manuscript studies have been outstanding.

The *Journal of Bible and Religion* first appeared in 1933. This quarterly from Philadelphia is sponsored by the American Academy of Religion, until 1964 known as the National Association of Biblical Instructors. It aims at a wide audience but includes informative articles on the OT and NT.

Since 1936 the University of Uppsala, Sweden, has issued the annual *Svensk Exegetisk Årsbok,* containing contributions of the Scandinavian school in Swedish and the principal European languages.

The *Catholic Biblical Quarterly,* published in Washington, D.C., since 1939, reflects the growth and scope of the Biblical movement in the American Catholic Church. Its 25th anniversary issues (1963) contained contributions from distinguished Catholic and non-Catholic scholars in America and Europe. This organ of the Catholic Biblical Association of America publishes articles on the OT and NT, shorter notes, and many reviews. The previous practice of including surveys or chronicles has been abandoned now that there are specialized bibliographical and abstracting services.

Technical and popular journals of Sacred Scripture notably increased after World War II. After the publication of *Divino afflante Spiritu* (1943), the Catholic Biblical Association in Great Britain began in 1946 its quarterly *Scripture,* published in Edinburgh. Its pages are few, its format similar to a small brochure. Although intentionally nontechnical, its articles are well written and informative. Very few book reviews are offered.

In 1947 the Protestant Union Theological Seminary in Richmond, Va., issued its first number of *Interpretation: A Journal of Bible and Theology.* Four issues yearly contain consistently good popular expositions of exegetical and hermeneutical questions with an occasional homiletic treatment as well.

The *Bible Translator* has been published quarterly in London since 1950 by the United Bible Societies. Its purpose is to solve the problems of translating the Bible into difficult modern tongues, especially those of Africa and Asia. Two other Biblical journals appeared that year. *Biblical Theology* originates in Belfast, North Ireland, appearing three times a year with two or three articles and a book review in each issue. In the same year the Franciscans in Jerusalem sponsored the annual *Studii Biblici Liber Annuus,* which contains long contributions in the major European languages on both the Old and the New Testament as well as on Biblical archeology.

In 1951, under the direction of the International Organization for the Study of the OT, there appeared the important publication *Vetus Testamentum,* printed in Leiden, The Netherlands. Contributions in English, French, and German discuss various aspects of the OT and Judaism. Besides full-length articles, there are short contributions and some book reviews.

Also in 1951 there appeared at Melbourne, first in modest mimeographed form, the *Australian Biblical Review,* an interdenominational journal. Now issued in regular printed form, it is the leading journal for Biblical research in Australia.

The Italian Biblical Association inaugurated in 1953 the *Rivista Biblica,* printed originally in Florence, now in Brescia. This Catholic quarterly treating both Testaments has attained a high level of scholarship in its articles and reviews.

In 1954 *New Testament Studies,* perhaps the most important English NT publication, became the regular quarterly of the esteemed Studiorum Novi Testamenti Societas. From 1950 to 1952 three *Bulletins* of the Society had been issued (reprinted in one volume as *Bulletin of the Studiorum Novi Testamenti Societas Nos. I—III*). Out of this bulletin grew the journal, which is published in Cambridge, England, and includes contributions from all faiths. The quality of its articles, sometimes written in French or German, is consistently high. Very few book reviews are included.

The publishing house of E. J. Brill of Leiden, The Netherlands, inaugurated in 1956 the publication of *Novum Testamentum* (An International Quarterly for New Testament and Related Studies Based on International Cooperation). The format is similar to that of *Vetus Testamentum;* its articles in English, French, or German treat a wide range of NT questions. Book reviews are not a regular feature.

Biblical Research, Papers of the Chicago Society of Biblical Research, is a yearly publication begun in 1956.

The expert will consult the *Revue de Qumrân* (Paris 1958–   ) for light on the *Dead Sea Scrolls as background for the Bible. Some of the articles are written in English. A bibliographical survey of the periodical literature on Qumran is regularly provided.

Finally, several other publications should be mentioned apart from chronological sequence of appearance, because they often treat the OT and Jewish Biblical history: *Jewish Quarterly Review* (Philadelphia 1888–   ), published by Dropsie College for Hebrew and Cognate Learning; *Hebrew Union College Annual* (Cincinnati 1914–   ); *Journal of Near Eastern Studies* (Chicago 1942–   ), published quarterly at the University of Chicago; *Journal of Jewish Studies* (London 1948–   ), published quarterly by the Institute of Jewish Studies; *Journal of Semitic Studies* (Manchester 1956–   ), published twice a year by the Department of Near Eastern Studies, University of Manchester, England.

Popularizations. The appearance in 1962 of the first issue of the *Bible Today,* published six times a year at Collegeville, Minn., marked a late entry by American Catholics into the field of Biblical *haute vulgarisation.* Whereas Europe had several of these popularizations with pastoral and liturgical preoccupations, Americans had relied chiefly on the Biblical articles in *Worship* (formerly *Orate Fratres*). The *Bible Today* filled that lacuna with solid presentations written by experts for those with little or no background in the Bible. The format is small; occasionally, surveys and news of the field will be included.

This sort of journal had several European predecessors sponsored by various Bible societies: *Bibel und Kirche* (Stuttgart 1946–   ), published quarterly by the Katholische Bibelbewegung; *Évangile: Cahiers bibliques trimestriels* (Paris 1951–   ), published by the Ligue Catholique de l'Évangile; *Bible et Vie Chrétienne* (Paris 1953–   ), published by the Belgian Abbey of Maredsous; *Bible et Terre Sainte* (Paris 1957–   ), a popular illustrated Biblical archeological and geographical publication; *Bibbia e Oriente* (Milan 1959–   ), published six times a year; *Bibel und Leben* (Düsseldorf 1960–   ), a quarterly. The *Way,* although primarily a journal of spirituality, founded by the English Jesuits (London 1960–   ), includes numerous articles on Biblical theology and themes.

Biblical Archeology. Although it is beyond the scope of this article to include detailed listings of archeological journals, mention should be made of the *Biblical Archaeologist,* published quarterly in New Haven since 1938 by the American Schools of Oriental Research. It discusses in a scholarly yet uncomplicated way archeological discoveries pertinent to Biblical data.

More technical reports on expeditions, etc., can be found, e.g., in the *Journal of the American Oriental Society* (New Haven 1843–   ), a quarterly; *Bulletin of the American Schools of Oriental Research* (New Haven 1919–   ), a quarterly; *Palestine Exploration Quarterly* (London 1937–   ), published by the Palestine Exploration Fund; *Israel Exploration Journal* (Jerusalem 1951–   ), a quarterly published by a joint editorial board of the Israel Exploration Society, the Department of Archaeology of the Hebrew University, and the Department of Antiquities of the Ministry of Education and Culture.

Journals of Bibliographies and Abstracts. The above list makes no pretense at completeness but attempts to indicate the more significant publications. Because five or more major articles may appear in one issue of a Biblical journal or even one in a journal of systematic theology, the need for accurate bibliographical surveys and, more importantly, for abstracting services have become imperative. Such aids unite in a synthetic fashion the principal contributions to Biblical research.

Bibliographies. Chief in the area of bibliographical aids for the Biblical student are the listings in *Biblica* and *Verbum Domini* mentioned above. The *Ephemerides theologicae Lovanienses* (Louvain 1924–   ) contains a rather full theological bibliographical service with sections for the Bible. Less complete but useful is the listing in the *Theologische Revue* (Münster 1902–   ).

The British Society for Old Testament Study provides a yearly *Book List* giving new titles along with a brief evaluation. This service was begun in 1946 by H. H. Rowley and continued by him until 1956. These were later published in book form: *Eleven Years of Bible Bibliography. The Book Lists of the Society for Old Testament Study 1946–56.* The *Book List* has continued to appear yearly under the direction of G. W. Anderson.

A nonevaluative selective listing is the *Quarterly Checklist of Biblical Studies,* an international index of current books, monographs, brochures, etc., published by the American Bibliographic Service, Darien, Conn., since 1958.

Abstracts. In 1952, under the editorship of F. Stier of Tübingen, there appeared the first issue of the *Internationale Zeitschriftenschau für Bibelwissenschaft und*

Grenzgebiete (*International Review of Biblical Studies*), published in Düsseldorf. This annual gives brief summaries, mostly in German, of the periodical literature on Biblical and cognate sciences. Especially valuable and unique are its résumés of *Festschriften* contributions. Its nearly 2,000 entries are arranged thematically according to text, interpretation, milieu, history of Israel, etc.

A fuller coverage for the NT is provided by *New Testament Abstracts,* a record of current periodical literature on the NT, published three times a year under the editorship of John J. Collins, SJ, of Weston College, Weston, Mass., in collaboration with an international group of abstractors of different denominations. After two experimental issues in 1956, the first regular issue appeared in the autumn of 1956. New Testament articles are abstracted from more than 250 journals. Important contributions are ordinarily given résumés of some 300 words arranged in the categories of introduction, Gospel–Acts, Epistles–Apocalypse, Biblical theology, early Church, and Dead Sea Scrolls. Abstracts also of book reviews of significant new works are included in each issue. A regular feature is the "Book Notice Section," which lists, with brief descriptions, the latest books on the NT in all the major languages. Biographical notes on four or five scholars are provided in each issue.

Religious and Theological Abstracts has been published quarterly by Theological Publications, Inc., Youngstown, Ohio, since 1958. The abstracts are very brief, and the Biblical coverage is considerably less complete than the other two abstracting publications just mentioned.

Although not strictly a periodical, the *Index to Religious Periodical Literature* indexes 76 journals, many of which are predominantly scriptural in their interests. It first appeared in 1953 and is distributed by Princeton Theological Seminary, although published in Chicago by the American Theological Library Association. Its lists of book reviews appearing in Biblical periodicals are a useful tool.

History of Biblical Journals. The parent of Biblical periodicals was a publication begun in 1777 in Leipzig reporting the Biblical and Near Eastern research current in Europe at the time: the *Repertorium für biblische und morgenländische Litteratur* (Part 1–10, 1777–86, ed. J. G. Eichhorn). This was succeeded under the same editorship by the *Allgemeine Bibliothek der biblischen Litteratur* (v. 1–10, 1787–1801).

The U.S. had an interesting succession of short-lived Biblical journals that, if carefully studied, would indicate the preoccupations of the American Protestant Biblical movement in the 19th century. The following were especially noteworthy. The *Christian Examiner* (Boston and New York 1824–69) featured a bimonthly section called "Notes upon the Bible." The *Biblical Repertory* (Princeton 1825–88), under changing titles, remained the strong fortress of old-school Presbyterianism, reflecting the conservative views of the Princeton school. The *Biblical Repository and Classical Review* (New York 1831–50) published three series of volumes on numerous aspects of Biblical investigation. The *Biblical Journal* (Boston 1842–43) came to a premature end. The *Biblical World* (Chicago 1882–1920) was also known under the titles *Hebrew Student* (1882), *Old Testament Student* (1883–88), *Old and New Testa-*

ment Student (1889–93), and *Biblical World* (1893–1920). The *Biblical World,* a significant landmark in the history of American Biblical periodicals, contained valuable information on the history of American exegesis inasmuch as it provided bibliographical references to the leading periodicals of its day. Also its "Synopses of Important Articles," with frank evaluation, was the first abstracting service of its kind.

Two British publications that also circulated in America during this period were the *Journal of Sacred Literature and Biblical Record* (London 1848–68), founded "not . . . as the organ of any one religious denomination, or of any one country, but [as] . . . the means of enabling different denominations and different countries . . . to advance the general interests of Biblical literature" (1:1); and the *Expositor* (London 1875–1925), which included nine series of varying length and a wide spectrum of Biblical topics.

The history of all these and other Biblical periodicals in Europe and America is yet to be written, and is much needed. The above account is limited to the principal journals and periodicals, and for the most part to the 20th century. But understanding of these and of the development of knowledge would be deepened if they were seen in the framework of the broader historical movement reflected in the journals, major and minor, of the preceding centuries.

See also BIBLICAL SOCIETIES.

Bibliography: J. SCHMID, LexThK² 2:413–416. *Biblica* current v. gives list of pertinent periodicals. K. G. STECK et al., RGG³ 6:1885–91. G. S. GLANZMAN and J. A. FITZMYER, *An Introductory Bibliography for the Study of Scripture* (Westminster, Md. 1961) 3–10, 125–129. J. LEVIE, "Trends in Catholic Exegesis 1880–1914," *The Bible: Word of God in Words of Men,* tr. S. H. TREMAN (New York 1962) 40–60. E. V. ALDRICH and T. E. CAMP, *Using Theological Books and Libraries* (Englewood Cliffs, N.J. 1963).

[M. A. FAHEY]

BIBLICAL SOCIETIES

A Bible society may be defined as any organization for the distribution and study of the Bible. Such organizations range from small study clubs to international learned associations.

PROTESTANT SOCIETIES

The term "Bible society" has in a special way been associated with Protestantism. Following the principle that the Bible is the sole rule of faith and preaching, Protestants have placed notable emphasis on the distribution of partial or complete Bibles and various Bible aids, at home and in foreign missions. There is a close connection between the diffusion of Bibles all over the world and Protestant missionary effort. Special groups, such as the Sunday School Society, the London Tract Society, and the Church Missionary Society, existed in the 16th and 17th centuries. But the special distribution centers that resulted in Bible societies were founded in Germany and in England at the end of the 18th and the beginning of the 19th centuries. From their example and financial support, similar organizations have spread throughout all Christian states and pagan territories.

Nature. These societies set out to provide people with copies of the Bible in their own language, on a local, national, and international level. This was done "without note or comment." Bibles have always been distributed below the cost of production; but it has been felt that at least a nominal charge should be made for these copies. The Bible was translated into as many languages and dialects as were needed. Translators were provided with all necessary help, but the Bibles and their translations were frankly confessional in character. However, since the beginning of the 20th century translators have been supplied with the Hebrew Masoretic Text of R. *Kittel, the Septuagint of A. *Rahlfs (in a completed short edition, and a continuing full critical edition), and the Greek New Testament of E. *Nestle, published by the Privilegierte Würtembergische Bibelanstalt of Stuttgart, Germany. And there now exists a Hebrew Old Testament by N. H. Snaith (London 1958) and a Greek New Testament (London 1958). The *Bible Translator* (London 1941–   ) gives scholarly assistance.

British Bible Society. The most influential of these organizations is the British and Foreign Bible Society (BFBS), founded in London on March 7, 1804. Originally planned by nonconformists, the BFBS soon won the support of the Established Church and other British sects. It is composed of a governing board of clergy and laity. Its growth and influence over the world has been phenomenal. In the course of its history it has provided assistance for the foundation of similar societies in Europe (Sweden in 1812, Holland in 1814, etc.), the U.S. (in 1817), and in mission lands all over the world, particularly those of the British Empire. For a long time it retained supremacy because of its wealth and the extent of its operations.

American Bible Society. Even before the needed assistance was received from the BFBS, interest in the spread of the Bible in the American colonies was manifested. There were local Bible societies in the original 13 colonies. In 1777 the Continental Congress recommended the publication of 20,000 copies of the Bible to fulfill the demand, but this recommendation was never carried out because of a lack of funds. Not until 1816 were local groups united to form the American Bible Society (ABS). It spread rapidly throughout the U.S., and its influence on the rest of the world has been surpassed only by the BFBS. Agencies were established in foreign countries (e.g., Turkey in 1836). An agreement was made between the BFBS and the ABS whereby either one or the other society or both societies jointly distributed Bibles in certain countries, e.g., the ABS in the Philippines, the BFBS in Iran, and both in China. There are now five foreign distribution centers of the ABS.

Since its foundation, the BFBS has distributed more than half a billion copies of complete Bibles, entire Testaments, separate books, or their parts; the ABS is rapidly approaching that amount. Translations of the whole or of parts of the Bible have been made into 1,202 languages: 228 for the whole Bible, 285 of complete Testaments, 689 of a complete Gospel, or other book. New languages are being added each year. The 1962 figures for the ABS are 17,932,714 Bibles distributed outside the U.S., an increase of 48.3 per cent over the previous record year (for the use of American and other missionaries), and 14,705,461 in the U.S. It has representatives in 107 countries. In 1962 it sponsored 65 entirely new editions in 50 languages and launched a vigorous promotional program.

International Organization. With the continued growth and financial stability of national societies, and their independent work all over the world, a tendency toward union of effort and a pooling of resources of all the societies began in 1939. The first consolidation took place in May 1946, in London, where a constitution for a central society was drafted and conditions for the addition of other members were established. Annual meetings are held in various countries, at which plans for future expansion and present problems are discussed. The United Bible Societies is an international confederation of partly independent national Bible societies. Present members are the Austrian Bible Committee, ABS, Belgian Bible Society, Bible Society of India and Ceylon, Bible Society of Brazil, BFBS, BFBS in Australia, BFBS in New Zealand, Canadian Bible Society, Danish Bible Society, Finnish Bible Society, Indonesian Bible Society, Japan Bible Society, Korean Bible Society, National Bible Society of Scotland, Netherlands Bible Society, Norwegian Bible Society, Swedish Bible Society, Swiss Bible Society, and the Union of Evangelical Bible Societies in Germany. Ninety countries are served by twenty-three of these and other national Bible societies and their agencies. The following list of Bibles distributed does not include circulation by commercial publishers: 35,512,381 (1960), 40,076,664 (1961), and 51,089,209 (1962). For the service of its members the United Bible Societies publishes the *Bulletin* and the *Bible Translator*.

There always have been other societies that distributed many Bibles, such as the Gideon Society, for the use of commercial travelers. An important one is the Watchtower Bible and Tract Society. By the end of 1963 the society printed 10,899,733 Bibles; of this, more than 8,000,000 copies were new translations into Italian, Dutch, French, German, Portuguese, and Spanish.

Learned Societies. Bible societies in a wider sense are interdenominational in character. Members and contributors to their learned journals are Protestants, Jews, and today even Catholics. Of particular note for its age and high standards is the American Society for Biblical Literature and Exegesis (1880), with its *Journal of Biblical Literature* and monographs. The American National Association of Biblical Instructors (1909) publishes *The Journal of Bible and Religion*. The International Organization for the Study of the Old Testament and the similar International Organization for the Study of the New Testament publish respectively *Vetus Testamentum* (1951–   ) and *Novum Testamentum* (1956–   ). The Society for Old Testament Study in England (1917) publishes booklists and holds annual conferences. And the Studiorum Novi Testamenti Societas of Cambridge presents *New Testament Studies* (1954–   ).

CATHOLIC SOCIETIES

The position of the Catholic Church toward the work of Bible societies has long been one of disapproval. Poor editions and the spread of sectarian translations often met with open hostility. There had been attempts by some Catholics to form similar societies in reaction to the success of Protestant efforts. But all such attempts soon died out or were expressly forbidden by Church authorities. Cooperation in the spread of the Bible, like that of Leander van Ess and the BFBS (1815), was prohibited. There were papal pronouncements about the dangers of indiscriminate distribution of the Bible (Pius VII, Denz 1602–06, Leo XII, Denz 1607ff., Gregory XVI, Denz 1630ff., Pius IX, Denz 1718); these warnings have been crystallized in the prescriptions of canons 1399 and 1400, on the publication and use of religious books, particularly Bibles, by non-Catholic publishers. However, with the foundation of the Society of St. Jerome in Italy (1902) for the spread and study of the gospels, and the influence of the Bible Movement, together with the present Protestant position toward critically accurate copies, there has been a greater tendency toward cooperation. American Catholic and Protestant Biblical scholars are now collaborating on a series of volumes containing a new translation, with commentary, of the individual books of the Bible.

Spread of Bible Reading. Special forms of Biblical associations (societies in the broader sense) have been formed through the marvelous growth of the Catholic Biblical Movement. The roots of this movement can be found in the encouragement and initiative of the popes for the past 100 years. The milestones in this history are the *Providentissimus Deus* of Leo XIII (1893), the foundation of the Pontifical Biblical Institute in Rome by St. Pius X (1910), the *Spiritus Paraclitus* of Benedict XV (1920), and especially the direction given by the *Divino Afflante Spiritu* of Pius XII (1943). The purpose of these societies is to use every available means for the study and spread of the Bible. Through encouragement of personal reading and study, participation in institutes and conferences (regional and national), the institution of national Bible weeks, it is hoped that the spiritual life of Catholics will be deepened. This movement follows the earnest recommendation of St. Pius X that not only a deeper knowledge but also the religious meaning of the Bible for the entire spiritual life should be fostered. It is thus closely joined with religious renewal through Catholic action and the understanding of the liturgy. The latter has been the especial recommendation of the first session of the Vatican Council II (1962). Periodicals for general patronage, such as the *Bible Today* (U.S., 1962–   ), *Bible et la Vie Chrétienne* (France), and books and pamphlets for the average Catholic layman, have contributed greatly to the success of this movement.

Learned Societies. Even more than in Protestant circles, there has been a remarkable growth in Catholic learned societies. These are national in character, with membership restricted to qualified Catholic scholars. But attendance at their conventions by lay people is not unknown, and non-Catholics sometimes contribute articles to their periodicals. Even though France does not have any such association, it has contributed notably to the movement of the superior quality of its scholarly publications in the Biblical field. Germany has a Katholisches Bibelwerk, which goes back to World War I, but its publication *Bibel und Kirche* began only in 1933. The American Catholic Biblical Association (founded in 1936) sponsors the *Catholic Biblical Quarterly* (1939–   ) and the *Confraternity Bible* (1941–   ). The Sociedad Argentina de Profesores de Sagrada Escritura publishes the *Revista Biblica* with a "Secion Liturgica," and is sponsoring a Spanish Bible for all of South America. The Asociación para el Fomento de los Estudios Biblicos en España (AFEBE, 1922) used to publish the *Cultura Biblica*. The *Estudios Biblicos* is today the organ of the Biblical Association of Spain (1929–   ). The Liga de Estudos Biblicos of Brazil (1947) offers the *Revista de Cultura Biblica* (1957–   ). The Catholic Biblical Association of England (1940) has as its organ *Scripture* (1949–   ). The Catholic

Biblical Association of Canada was also founded in 1940. And the Associazione Biblica Italiana (1953) publishes the *Revista Biblica Italiana* and *Parole di Vita*.

Bibliography: L. BOUYER, "Où en est le mouvement biblique," BiblVieChr 13 (1956) 7–21. J. M. GILLIS, CE 2:544–546. J. KÜRZINGER, LexThK² 2:344–346. J. SCHMID, LexThK² 2:346–349.

[L. A. BUSHINSKI]

BIBLICAL THEOLOGY

All theology, if it is true to itself, is Biblical, for it is defined as a discourse about God. This God, who "dwells in light inaccessible" (2 Tm 6.16), has revealed Himself; and the Bible is the record of this revelation. In the sense that any true theology's point of departure and primary datum is the Bible, it is of necessity Biblical. But, if all theology is Biblical, not every theology is Biblical theology. This term, which might have sounded tautological to the Fathers and surprising to the scholastics, is of relatively recent coinage even as the sacred discipline it designates is still in quest of sharper definition. It is the purpose of this article to study the meaning of the term Biblical theology mainly by tracing the general lines of its development and by considering its formulations in recent theologies of the OT and the NT. This, at the present stage in the progress of Biblical theology, is as near a definition of the science as one can come; for no satisfactory definition has yet been formulated. There is, however, nothing surprising in this. Often in the history of the Church a reality is lived for centuries before its definition is formulated; and the newness of a term to designate such a reality is no argument against either its verity or its validity (an example from the mid-20th century is the term collegiality).

EARLY PERIOD

Sacred Scripture is God's word to man; theology is man's word about God. This word of man about God, in its prophetic, sapiential, priestly, evangelical, or apostolic formulation, was and remains a theology. To understand God's word—to expound its meaning, elucidate its content, and interpret its message—has been the task of the Church from its very inception. This task has ever been conditioned by the needs and circumstances of successive generations.

Patristic Age. In the first centuries of the Christian Era, patristic exegesis was determined by the vital needs of a nascent Church. Early controversies and scripturally founded apologetics, whether with Trypho the Jew or with the pagan *Celsus, paved the way for a progressive elaboration of orthodox expressions of dogma and the attempt to synthesize in a systematic theology the datum of revelation with human knowledge. This was not simply the preference of a so-called Greek bent of mind, but the response to a conscious need to grow in the understanding of the faith. The world in which the Church was born and the very circumstances of its early growth conditioned the formulation of its message and oriented its theological speculation for centuries.

The Fathers put the rational speculations of their culture at the service of the faith. In their orthodox expressions of dogma and their systematic formulation of a theology they used Sacred Scripture, not merely as a support for their tenets, but also as a norm for their formulas and as a source for their theological vocabulary. But the expanding needs of their culture exerted pressures that caused their exegetical methods to multiply into an ever-increasing number of so-called senses. In their interpretation of the OT they followed, and greatly enlarged upon, the method already discernible in the NT: the quest for the "spirit" behind the "letter," projection of the mystery of Christ, and recourse to typology as a foundation for allegory. In exploring the action of the mystery of Christ upon the Christian soul and in reflecting upon its eschatological consummation, the Fathers sought to see what the facts of Christ's life symbolized. As, in principle, their exegetical interpretation of the OT was justified by the NT, so their understanding of the NT received its general guidelines from the Fourth Gospel. Thus the cultural milieu of *Hellenism favored a systematic development of Pauline allegory and Johannine symbolism. While the mystery of Christ was and remained the unique object of Biblical revelation, its elucidation was conditioned by the day-to-day needs of the Church. Pastoral care and the liturgy required a preponderance of allegory and symbolism; apologetics and controversies necessitated a stress on the historic and literal sense of the Scriptures.

Medieval Age. In the Middle Ages, as long as the pastoral care of souls predominated, the patristic method was followed both by compilers, such as St. *Bede, the Venerable, and by creators, such as St. Bernard of Clairvaux. But from the 13th century on, a double trend, systematic (starting with the *lectio* of the *pagina sacra* and terminating in the *summae*) and apologetic (refuting the claims of the Jews and the Moslems) became evident. In both trends a strongly rational reflection was discernible, for Aristotelian dialectic had furnished theology with an instrument that was then judged to be adequate. Consequently, whereas in the early Middle Ages, in the use of Sacred Scripture, the principles of St. *Augustine were adhered to and the practice of St. *Gregory the Great was followed, in the later Middle Ages it was St. *Jerome's authority that was in the ascendancy. Jerome's attention to the original text, care to translate well, effort at literary analysis, and regard for the historical references of the Biblical narrative made his work most valuable for the theologizing of men, such as *Hugh of Saint-Victor and St. *Albert the Great. But it was left to the great genius of St. *Thomas Aquinas to achieve a new synthesis between Biblical revelation and rational speculation. He stressed the literal sense of Scripture as that alone on which a theologian can base his work. His exegetical method still remained faithful to the principles found in the NT and followed by the Fathers. His theology, like that of the scholastics and the Fathers, drew its inspiration from the Bible, rested its arguments upon it, and attempted to interpret and systematize its message. In that sense it was Biblical. (See EXEGESIS, MEDIEVAL.)

Thus, from its earliest days, confronted by the need both of apologetics and controversies with the enemies without and of the pastoral care for its members within, the Church's use of the Bible followed lines of development that increasingly came to regard it as an arsenal for its polemics, a storehouse of premises for its dogmatic syntheses, and a rich mine of wisdom for its pastoral ministry. The drift away from the Bible as an integral entity that merited study by itself and for itself was accentuated in post-Tridentine times, whether by the instinctive reaction against the Reformers' *sola scriptura* or by the very educational system of the clergy. It was to culminate in the reduction of the Bible to ciphers cited as proof texts that had priority of place over patristic references and Denzinger numbers. The Biblical message thus underwent the myriad procrustean coercions to which minds sharply honed in Aristotle's *Organon* chose to subject it in the defense of the faith (e.g., justification, predestination, Redemption) and the codification of Christian morals (e.g., divorce, the Sabbath rest, mental reservation).

17th to 19th Centuries. The term Biblical theology was not always used with the same technical connotations and nuances that it possesses today. One of the first to use it, Abraham *Calov (1612–86) in his *Systema locorum theologicorum* (12 v. Wittenberg 1655–77), employed it to describe the whole field of Biblical and exegetical studies. But it was Johannes Cocceius (1603–69) who first attempted to "theologize in a purely Biblical manner," to formulate a theology drawn from the Bible alone. His *Summa doctrinae de foedere et testamentis Dei* (Leipzig 1648) belongs to a school that came to be known as "Federal theology." This school was a reaction against the aridities of scholasticism not unlike the reaction evident in the *Pietism of that age, which was exemplified in the work of Philipp Jakob *Spener (1635–1705). Toward the end of the 18th century Gottlieb Christian Storr (1746–1805) published his *Doctrinae christianae e solis sacris libris repetitae pars theoretica* (1793), in which he too attempted to develop a system of theology drawn solely from the Bible. Though these theologies foreshadowed future trends, they exerted no direct influence on the development of the discipline of Biblical theology.

This discipline, ironically enough, owes its beginnings much more to the *collegia biblica*, the collections of Scriptural proof texts that were then used in dogmatic theology. Although the texts were accompanied by exegesis and appropriate comment to facilitate their use, there was very often no attempt to distinguish the OT from the NT, or to differentiate various authors and modes of composition. The traditional order of subjects was followed in such *collegia* as Sebastian Schmid(ius)'s *Collegium biblicum . . . iuxta seriem locorum communium theologicorum* (1671). But the Biblical theology of that era, which most approximated what modern usage understands by the term, was Carl Haymann's *Biblische Theologie* (1768).

New Hermeneutics. There was, however, no real possibility for the rise of Biblical theology in the modern sense until a revolution in hermeneutics took place allowing a less rigid understanding of the principles of *analogia fidei* and *analogia scripturae*. Two 18th-century scholars, Johann Salomo *Semler (1725–91) and Johann August Ernesti (1707–81), did much to bring this revolution about by stressing the need to interpret the Sacred Scriptures in a purely grammatical and historical way. From that time on books began to appear that used the classical proof texts with greater independence of dogmatic tracts and their structure. It was Anton Friedrich Büsching (1724–93) who gave, in his *dissertatio inauguralis* at Tübingen in 1755, what has been considered a first sketch of pure Biblical theology. He followed it in 1757 with his work *Epitome theologiae e solis literis sacris concinnatae*. In 1785 and 1789 Wilhelm Hofnagel published the two volumes of his *Handbuch der biblischen Theologie* that sought to discover the meaning intended by the original author through an examination of the classical proof texts arranged in a theology-anthropology-soteriology pattern. But the man whose work "seems to stand at the point of transition between the old dogmatic interest in the proof texts and the science of Biblical theology which was shortly to be born" (Dentan, 21) was Gotthilf Traugott Zachariae (d. 1772). His *Biblische Theologie* (1772–75) attempted the study of the Bible as a whole according to a plan derived from the Bible itself and not limited simply to the study of isolated *dicta probantia.*

Biblical Distinguished from Dogmatic Theology. Opinion is almost unanimous in crediting Johann Philipp Gabler's *Oratio de justo discrimine theologiae biblicae et theologiae dogmaticae regundisque recte utriusque finibus,* which was his inaugural lecture at the University of Altdorf, March 30, 1787, with being the starting point of the modern discipline of Biblical theology. Gabler (1753–1826) set up a distinction between dogmatic theology and Biblical theology: whereas dogmatic theology is a philosophizing on divine things ["theologia dogmatica e genere didactico, docens, quid theologus quisque pro ingenii modulo, vel temporis, aetatis, loci, sectae, scholae similiumque id genus aliorum, ratione super rebus divinis philosophetur," *Opuscula Academica,* ed. T. A. and I. G. Gabler 2 v. (Ulm 1831) 2:183–184], Biblical theology is basically historical, setting forth the thoughts of the inspired writers on divine things ["e genere historico tradens quid scriptores sacri de rebus divinis senserint" (*ibid.* 183)]. The method advocated by Gabler for the study of Biblical theology consisted of (1) the interpretation of the scriptural passage on purely grammatical and historical grounds; (2) comparison of passages with each other to note both similarities and differences; and (3) the formulation of *notiones universae,* but without distorting them.

The Biblical theologians who followed in Gabler's wake were, like Gabler himself, rationalists. This is perhaps why they could make such a break with dogmatic traditions and traditional modes of theologizing. Among them was Georg Lorenz Bauer (1755–1806), who was the first really to follow Gabler's distinction and write a Biblical theology that broke away from the proof texts and was independent of dogmatic theology. His *Theologie des A.T. oder Abriss der religiösen Begriffe der alten Hebräer* (1796) not only separated the OT from the NT, but clearly distinguished persons, periods, and books of the former. It comprised two parts—theology (God's relation to man) and anthropology (man's relation to God)—and was intended as a preparatory step toward the study of NT theology. What had hitherto been a study of the literary, exegetical, and historical questions raised by the Scriptures would henceforth also be a study of the religion of the Bible, of its "religious ideas." Shortly after Bauer's work there appeared the three volumes of G. P. C. Kaiser's *Die biblische Theologie* (1813–21), which was the first work to apply systematically the *Religionsgeschichtlich* method to Biblical interpretation. This work was followed by D. G. C. von Cölln's *Biblische Theologie* (1836), which insisted on the need of treating the Biblical ideas "genetically" and conceived Biblical theology as but the first chapter in the history of dogma.

Adoption by Conservatives. Rationalism and *Religionsgeschichte* (history of religion or comparative religion), however, were not the only factors operative in the formative years of Biblical theology. Hegelian dialectic in the philosophy of religions was bound to be applied to the study of the religion of the Bible. Care to present the matter chronologically was, of course, quite characteristic here as is seen, for example, in *Die biblische Theologie* (1835) of J. K. Wilhelm Vatke (1806–62). To this triple threat to Biblical orthodoxy the conservative reaction furnished a necessary and needed counterweight. As often happens initially, the opposition to the methods and the principles behind them led to a rejection of the discipline; but as happens no less often, the initial opposition yielded to a moderated tolerance and ended in the adoption of Biblical theology by the conservative circles, which were by no means slow to recognize that it was not incompatible with devoted acceptance and orthodox interpretation of Sacred Scripture.

A representative work of the conservative circles was the *Vorlesungen über die Theologie des A.T.* (1840) of J. C. F. Steudel (1779–1837), which, using a strictly grammatical-historical method, attempted to show the content of the OT in such a way as to make it possible to understand the religious notions of a particular period in history. Steudel's student G. F. Oehler published a work that dealt exclusively with the theory and method of OT theology. His *Prolegomena zur Theologie des A.T.* (1845) stated that the function of OT theology was to discover the "idea" that formed the basis of OT religion, viz, "the divine Spirit." "Old Testament religion," Oehler wrote, "is rather mediated through a series of divine acts and commands and through the institution of a divine state" (quoted by Dentan, 45).

Methodological Refinement. In the latter half of the 19th century there was another clash of opinions that proved both illuminating and fruitful. In 1878 Julius *Wellhausen published his *Prolegomena zur Geschichte Israels,* which for a while at least seemed to have dealt the death blow to all OT theology. By insisting that Israel's religion was but another instance in the field of *Religionsgeschichte,* it reduced OT theology to an erudite history of the religion of Israel, to one more instance of a general pattern of religious development discernible in any of the religions of the ancient Near East. But reaction to this trend was not slow in coming. The *Handbuch der alttestamentlichen Theologie* of August Dillmann (1823–94; posthumously edited and published by Rudolf *Kittel in 1895) pointed out the inadequacy of Wellhausen's approach by underlining the uniqueness of Israel among its neighbors as well as the uniqueness and incompleteness of the OT "religion of holiness." It was, however, Hermann Schultz who produced the greatest work on OT theology in the 19th century. His *Alttestamentliche Theologie: Die Offenbarungs-religion auf ihrer vorchristlichen Entwicklungsstufe* went through five editions between 1869 and 1896 and was translated into English [*OT Theology* (Edinburgh 1892)]. Schultz pointed out that the method of Biblical theology is historical; its function, to supply material needed by systematic theology and furnish a rule against which to measure later development; and its unifying principle, the kingdom of God on earth. Consequently, as the subtitle of his work indicates, OT theology without its NT counterpart is one-sided and incomplete; while NT theology without an OT theology remains unintelligible. Fortunately the great work of Schultz on

OT theology was paralleled by the *Lehrbuch der Neutestamentlichen Theologie* (1896–97) of Heinrich Julius Holtzmann (1832–1910) and the *Über Aufgabe und Methode der sogennanten neutestamentlichen Theologie* (1897) of William Wrede (1859–1906).

Incomplete Success. From the early beginnings of Biblical theology the theology of the OT and that of the NT were closely linked together. The successes and failures, the merits and shortcomings of the various Biblical theologies inevitably influenced later theologies of both Testaments. Throughout the various periods, the Augustinian principle of *Novum in Vetere latet, Vetus in Novo patet* was never very far from the minds of those who attempted to write a Biblical theology. Many of the authors saw in their theologies of the OT but a first step toward the formulation of a NT theology. In the study of the NT, no less than in that of the OT, the influence of the *Enlightenment and the effects of rationalism, *Religionsgeschichte,* and Hegelianism were in evidence (*see* HEGELIANISM AND NEO-HEGELIANISM). Both the literary-critical and the historical methods, in OT and NT theologies alike, were greatly enriched by the improved understanding of Biblical languages and the extensive contributions of archeology to the history of the Biblical period. Both methods shed light on the progress of Biblical revelation and its successive steps. As G. L. Bauer had divided his Biblical theology into a study of the religion of the Jews before Christ, the religion of Jesus, and the religion of the Apostles, so similarly, Wilhelm M. L. *De Wette, *Biblische Dogmatik des A. und N.T.* (1813), distinguished two steps in the OT, the religion of Moses and the religion of the Jews, and two levels in the NT, the religion of Jesus and its interpretation in the message of the Apostles.

In both OT and NT theologies the influence of Wellhausen was greatly felt, and with the triumph of his school, theological interest declined in favor of the historical. The contributions of *Religionsgeschichte* were numerous, but its failure to evaluate the matter of both Testaments theologically was serious and damaging. The influence of G. W. F. *Hegel was greatly felt in both Testaments also, and here too a serious failure threatened to bring Biblical theology to a halt. Hegelian dialectic might have succeeded in analyzing phenomena, but it failed to comprehend the living experience underlying them. There were not wanting those who carried Hegelian dialectic to absurd extremes, e.g., Eduard Zeller (1814–1908) and Albert Schwegler (1819–57) in the NT and Wilhelm Vatke and Bruno *Bauer in the OT. Thus they did great disservice both to the method they employed and the science in which they employed it.

MODERN PERIOD

Varied though the attempts were, both in method and in achievement in the Biblical theology of the 18th and 19th centuries, the discipline began its growth into maturity only in the period that preceded and followed World War II. Apart from the many trends in thought and the reactions to them, solid scientific contribution in a variety of fields contributed a great deal toward the maturation process of Biblical theology. The work of Sir James George *Frazer and W. Oesterly in anthropology; of Max Weber in sociology; of Gustav Dalman (1855–1941) in geography; of A. Alt, W. F. Albright, and M. Noth in history and archeology; of E. *Schürer, W.

*Bousset, and Richard Reitzenstein (1861–1931) in the background of Christianity—all were contributions that made the study of Biblical theology not only possible but necessary. That Biblical theology is a modern discipline owes as much to these various contributions as to the fact that the orientation of thought and interest in theology before the 18th century lay elsewhere.

Old Testament Theologies. In the period between the two world wars Biblical theology received a fresh and new start along a path that has proved most rewarding and rich in possibilities. The number of works on the theology of either Testament has been so great since the 1920s as to preclude anything resembling even a quick survey of the field. The most that can be hoped for in this brief space is to mention some indicative works in a field that has produced much of lasting worth and interest. The aggregate of Biblical and allied sciences continues to widen scholars' knowledge of, and increase their acquaintance with, the Biblical world. The school of *Formgeschichte,* or Biblical *form criticism, and its application to the literature of the OT, the better understanding of Israel's cult and worship as well as the various influences operative therein, and the growing appreciation of the Prophets and their function in the life of Israel all made, and continue to make, the study of OT theology more fruitful and rewarding.

Eissfeldt and Sellin. Otto Eissfeldt's article "Israelitisch-jüdische Religionsgeschichte und alttestamentliche Theologie" [ZATWiss 44 (1926) 1–12] could well be taken as a starting point of the most recent and the richest period in the development of OT theology. Eissfeldt insisted that OT theology has religious faith as its only organ of knowledge and divine revelation as its subject. Accordingly, after a historical investigation of Israelite religion, OT theology must undertake a systematic presentation of the timeless truths of OT revelation. It was Ernst *Sellin who first elaborated an OT theology according to Eissfeldt's conception. His *Alttestamentliche Theologie auf religionsgeschichtlicher Grundlage* (2 v. Leipzig 1933) was divided into two parts: the first treated of the religion of Israel; the second presented OT theology according to the categories of God, man, and eschatology. The "holiness of God" was seen as the central and ruling idea throughout.

Eichrodt. Though Walther Eichrodt's "Hat die alttestamentliche Theologie noch selbständige Bedeutung innherhalb des alt. Wissenschaft?" [ZATWiss 47 (1929) 83–91] challenged Eissfeldt's conception of OT theology 3 years after its publication, it was not until 1933 that the first volume of Eichrodt's monumental *Theologie des A.T.* (3 v. Leipzig 1933–39; Eng. tr. of v.1, London 1961) appeared. The work was completed in three parts: God and People, God and the World, and God and Man—a plan that Eichrodt derived from his teacher, Otto Procksch, whose own *Theologie des A.T.* did not appear until 1949 (Gütersloh). Eichrodt was consciously engaged in describing a living process. He described his work as "taking a cross section [*Querschnitt*] of the realm of OT thought"; hence it had to maintain throughout a constant interplay between a historical survey and a theological synthesis. Eichrodt sought to delineate the religion of the OT as a "self-contained entity" that, despite the mutability of historic conditions, manifests "a constant basic tendency and character." The operative principle of this constancy is covenant theology, which, as T. C. Vriezen pointed out later, underscored the communion aspect rather than the contract aspect of the relation between Yahweh and His people. Moreover, even though the Prophets often seem to have avoided the term covenant, it must be realized that for them "election" was but the beginning of a permanent intercourse between Yahweh and His people. Thus they too could make their valuable contribution to covenant theology. The work of Eichrodt, which has gone through several editions, will always remain a major milestone in the development of OT theology.

Vriezen. T. C. Vriezen's *Hoofdlijnen der Theologie van het Oude Testament* (Wageninen, Holland 1950), Eng. tr., S. Neuijen, *An Outline of OT Theology* (Oxford 1958), stresses, more than Eichrodt did, the OT as an integral part of the Christian Scriptures. For Vriezen Biblical theology is not a purely descriptive and historical science, nor is it sufficient to present it systematically by taking a cross section through the history of the religion of Israel. The OT, first and foremost, is a book bearing witness to a divine revelation. This witness is not systematic, nor can it be forced into a system. To present it efficiently and faithfully, a thematic exposition of the most representative themes of Israel's faith and their interrelations would be required. Accordingly, Vriezen presents his *Theology* in themes of God; man; intercourse between God and man, between man and man; and God, man, and the world present and to come. This loose thematic pattern allows Vriezen to include Israel's cult and piety into his OT theology, two basic elements of OT life and thought that many another OT theology has not succeeded in including.

Von Rad. Since Eichrodt's, several other OT theologies have appeared (by the Protestant scholars Otto J. Baab, Edmond Jacob, George A. F. Knight, and G. Ernest Wright; and by the Catholic scholars, Paul *Heinisch, Albert Gelin, Jacques Guillet, and P. van Imschoot); but one of the most important among them is Gerhard von Rad's *Theologie des A.T.* (2 v. Munich 1957–60; Eng. tr., Edinburgh 1962–65). It is important, not simply because of the respect commanded by its author in the field of OT studies, but because it embodies an approach and a point of view that are bound to leave their mark on the evolution of Biblical theology. Von Rad objects to Eichrodt's approach to the OT because of the fact that Israel's witness is primarily to what Yahweh has done in history. This witness is not a structured pattern of religious concepts; and consequently, Biblical theology cannot be limited to a *Begriffsuntersuchung* (investigation of concepts) that, of its nature, tends to abstraction and generalization. *Salvation history (*Heilsgeschichte*) dominates the OT, and Biblical theology must elaborate this sacred history within a theological framework. OT theology must assume a historical form; it must be a retelling of the narrative (*Nacherzählung*) of Yahweh's redemptive acts. See G. E. Wright, *God Who Acts: Biblical Theology as Recital* (Chicago 1952).

New Testament Theologies. Theologies of the NT have kept pace with those of the OT. Here, however, apart from the theologies as such, one major phenomenon stands as a unique accomplishment in the field: Gerhard *Kittel's *Theologisches Wörterbuch zum N.T.* (Stuttgart 1935– ; abbreviated Kittel ThW or TWNT), which has as yet no comparable counterpart for the OT. Of course, Kittel's dictionary itself gives due

attention to the vocabulary of the OT, and several recent Biblical dictionaries (by J. J. von Allmen, X. Léon-Dufour, and A. Richardson) that treat of OT concepts are available; but none treats the OT vocabulary with the thoroughness with which Kittel's monumental opus treats the NT. Whatever may be said in criticism of the method used in Kittel ThW, it will long remain an indispensable tool of far-reaching consequences in NT theologies, however diverse their approaches and their points of view.

Moreover, there are two opposing points of view that have been expounded in the realm of NT interpretation. Their protagonists are the Swiss theologian Karl Barth and Marburg's Prof. Rudolph Bultmann. Their main concern, and it is a crucial one, is the role of reason vis-à-vis the divine message: whether a philosophy is necessary to make the categories of this message meaningful, and, if so, which philosophy? Bultmann responds affirmatively and opts unequivocally for Heideggerian existentialism as the philosophy best suited to achieve self-understanding by encounter with the message.

Special Problems. Still another factor in contemporary NT theology is the result of the method of *Redaktionsgeschichte* (investigation of the editorial work done by Biblical authors on earlier material). After the recent work of W. Marxsen on Mark and H. Conzelmann on Luke, not only has the Synoptic question changed radically, but the individual theological genius of each Synoptist has come to the fore. If previously there were Pauline and Johannine theologies, henceforth there should be Marcan, Matthean, and Lucan theologies as well. Another factor operative in the NT and one of far greater complexity here than in the OT is the passage from the doctrine of the NT to the dogmatic formulations of the Council of *Chalcedon. The intertestamental period has, in recent times, been brought into sharper focus both through a better knowledge of later Judaism and rabbinic literature and through the epoch-making discoveries at Qumran. (*See* DEAD SEA SCROLLS.) But the period immediately following NT times is far more complex and problematic both because of the controversies that are discernible even in the evangelical and apostolic formulations of the NT itself and because of the introduction of categories other than the Semitic into the formulation of the message in post-Apostolic times. All these factors must be taken into account in NT theology; but beyond all this, it must be remembered that, even more than for the OT, NT theology is theology within the Church, of the Church, and for the Church. With this in mind, not the least important of the problems that must be confronted in NT theology is that of the canon. (See Stendahl, 428–430.)

Modern Studies. To see what has been done concretely in NT theology, only a few examples can be given here. R. Bultmann's *Theology of the N.T.*, tr. K. Grobel (2 v. London 1952–55) for all the shortcomings noted even by its favorable critics (such as extreme critical positions, failure to take the Synoptists as serious theologians, a somewhat too rigid adherence to lexicographic method, and insufficient attention to the influence of the OT on the NT) is an important landmark in the evolution of NT theology. Of two possibilities of presenting NT writings, "as a systematically ordered unity" or in their variety in which they can then "be understood as members of an historical continuity" (2:237), Bultmann chooses the latter. His rejection of the first alternative raises the question of the possibility of presenting NT theology as a single system composed of the ideas of the different writers, a NT "system of dogmatics."

Ethelbert Stauffer's *N.T. Theology,* tr. J. Marsh (London 1955) first appeared in Germany in 1941 and antedates Bultmann's by more than 10 years. In it Stauffer follows precisely the alternative rejected by Bultmann. Accordingly, he divides his *Theology* into three parts: the development of primitive Christian theology, the Christocentric theology of history in the NT, and the creeds of the primitive Church. The dominant theme of the theology is well summed up by the title of the second part: the NT presents a theology of history, a redemptive history of God's redemptive acts centered in Christ. Bultmann objects that this method "transforms theology into a religious philosophy of history."

The differences between the two approaches are as yet not resolved. NT theologies have appeared using one or the other alternative in their elaboration: A. Richardson and Oscar Cullmann, for example, favor the "synthetic" approach, whereas the two major Catholic contributions to the field, J. *Bonsirven's and M. Meinertz's, opt for the other. The differences between the two are crucial, not because either approach would deny the evident Christocentricity of the NT or its historical element, but because ultimately they differ on what precisely NT theology in particular, and Biblical theology in general, is all about.

Complexity and Unity of Biblical Revelation. Differences in method and in object both in the theology of the NT and of the OT are due ultimately to the complexity of the subject of Biblical theology itself. It is not sufficient to classify it either as the first chapter in the history of dogma or an intermediary step between exegesis and dogmatic theology; nor is it enough to say its task is merely descriptive or merely systematic; nor is it accurate to characterize it either as a historic science or a theological discipline. Biblical revelation is in history, and thus historical; it is the revelation of a personal God, and thus theological; and it is addressed to man in a community, and thus anthropological and sociological. This revelation inexorably moves toward its climax and plenitude in the revelation of Christ; hence it is both Christological and Christocentric. But in revealing Christ to man God revealed man to himself; therefore, in this profounder sense it is anthropological. Moreover, through all the periods of *Heilsgeschichte,* through the endless succession of events, civilizations, cultures, and languages, there is both a community of spirit and of expression among the sacred authors and a unity of purpose and direction in the sacred books. The unity of the Bible, an essential datum of faith, is verified at the concrete level of language at the same time that it is, in essence, theological.

Because of this unity of the Bible it is possible to have a Biblical theology that strives to be a direct echo of the immediate content of the inspired message in it. Such a theology can assume any of the various points of view that mark the principal moments in the development of revelation: Yahwist or Deuteronomic history, priestly or sapiential tradition, the Synoptic Gospels, Pauline doctrine, apocalyptic frescoes, or Johannine mystique. But beyond all this, a Biblical theology can assume a broader point of view, seek to comprehend the unity of the Bible as an integral whole, and attempt to grasp the organic continuity and intelligible coherence that guarantees the profound unity of all the moments of the history of salvation. Then, and perhaps only then, can one hope to formulate a strict definition of Biblical theology, its function, and its purpose.

Bibliography: V. HAMP et al., LexThK² 2:439–451. J. HEMPEL and H. RIESENFELD, RGG³ 1:1256–62. K. STENDAHL, InterDict Bibl 1:418–432. O. BETZ, *ibid.* 1:432–437. X. LÉON-DUFOUR, ed., *Vocabulaire de théologie biblique* (Paris 1962) xiii–xix. J. ALONSO, "La Teología Bíblica a través de la historia: Consideración de algunas tendencias," *Miscelanea Comillas* 29 (1958) 9–27. F. M. BRAUN, "La Théologie biblique," RevThom 53 (1953) 221–253. S. LYONNET, "De notione et momento Theologiae Biblicae," VerbDom 34 (1956) 142–153. R. A. F. MAC-KENZIE, "The Concept of Biblical Theology," CathThSoc 10 (1955) 48–73. C. SPICQ, "L'Avènement de la théologie biblique," RevScPhilTh 35 (1951) 561–574; "Nouvelles réflexions sur la théologie biblique," *ibid.* 42 (1958) 209–219. P. S. WATSON, "The Nature and Function of Biblical Theology," ExposTimes 73 (1961–62) 195–200. J. GRAY, "Towards a Theology of the O.T.: The Contribution of Archaeology," *ibid.* 74 (1962–63) 347–351. N. W. PORTEOUS, "The Present State of O.T. Theology," *ibid.* 75 (1963–64) 70–74. C. K. BARRETT, "Ethelbert Stauffer's Theology of the N.T.," *ibid.* 72 (1960–61) 356–360. J. C. FENTON, "Rudolph Bultmann's Theology of the N.T.," *ibid.* 73 (1961–62) 8–11. K. GRAYSTON, "Alan Richardson's Theology of the N.T.," *ibid.* 73 (1961–62) 45–50. C. L. MITTON, "A. M. Hunter's Theology of the N.T.," *ibid.* 73 (1961–62) 77–80. A. RICHARDSON, "Present Issues in N.T. Theology," *ibid.* 75 (1963–64) 109–113. R. C. DENTAN, *Preface to O.T. Theology* (rev. ed. New York 1963), with bibliographies: before A.D. 1787 (127–128); 1787–1949 (128–135), and 1949–63 (135–144). R. SCHNACKENBURG, *N.T. Theology Today,* tr. D. ASKEW (New York 1963), with copious bibliog. H. VORGRIMLER, ed., *Dogmatic vs. Biblical Theology* (Baltimore 1965). G. S. GLANZMAN and J. A. FITZMYER, *An Introductory Bibliography for the Study of Scripture* (Westminster, Md. 1961) 79–86.

[S. B. MARROW]

BICHAT, MARIE FRANÇOIS XAVIER, physiologist and pioneer histologist; b. Thoirette, France, Nov. 14, 1771; d. Paris, July 21, 1802. His father, a physician, personally instructed him in anatomy and dissection, and after studying philosophy at St. Irenée's Seminary at Lyon, Bichat took up medicine under M. A. Petit in 1791. Two years later, he went to Paris and studied under the direction of the renowned surgeon, P. *Desault. When the master died in 1795, Bichat published his works in the *Journal de chirurgie* (1798–99). He had mastered Desault's ideas and set them forth in clear and orderly arrangement; this was the first printed manifestation of his own genius. In 1800, the appointment of Bichat as physician at the Hôtel-Dieu of Paris marked the beginning of a period of intensive laboratory research and prolific publications, of which his last, the five-volume *Anatomie descriptive,* was completed posthumously by his disciples, Buisson and P. J. Roux (1801–03).

Bichat approached anatomy and pathology primarily through the study of tissues, rather than organs or systems. This was a break with tradition, and an important contribution to the growth of the science. He held that since the body is fundamentally a structural and functional assemblage of tissues, these basic units, above all, must be considered for an understanding of anatomy and pathology. His new idea of tissues as units of structure and function brought him face to face with the doctrines of mechanism, as maintained by H. Boerhaave, and vitalism, supported by G. Stahl and G. Leibniz. He opposed both as extremes, in favor of a vitalism that he saw manifested within tissues and that he resolved philosophically into animal life (pure intelligence) and organic life (transformations and passions). The essential phenomenon of life, as he saw it, was the continuous and successful rejection of imminent and threatening disintegration of the organism. Bichat's most important

Marie François Xavier Bichat.

works were: *Traité des Membranes* (Paris 1800); and *Anatomie générale* (Paris 1801, 2 v.).

Bibliography: M. F. X. BICHAT, *Traité des Membranes,* ed. M. HUSSON (Paris 1816). E. NORDENSKIOLD, *The History of Biology,* tr. L. B. EYRE (New York 1935). **Illustration credit:** Library of Congress.

[L. P. COONEN]

BICHIER DES AGES, JEANNE ÉLISABETH, ST., cofoundress of the Daughters of the Holy Cross of *St. Andrew; b. Le Blanc, near Poitiers, France, July 5, 1773; d. Paris, Aug. 26, 1838 (feast, Aug. 26). She was the daughter of a public official and was educated at Poitiers. Her early spiritual formation was influenced by an uncle, Abbé de Moussac. After her father's death (1792), she successfully conducted a protracted lawsuit with the revolutionary government to save the family property from confiscation. With her mother she settled at La Guimetière, near BethinesPoitou, and followed a regular routine of prayer and good works.

Jeanne became the center of the local resistance to the Constitutional clergy. In 1797 she met St. André *Fournet, a priest of nearby Maillé, who had continued his pastoral labors despite his refusal to take the oath supporting the *Civil Constitution of the Clergy. Fournet became her spiritual director and advised against her emigration to join the Trappistines. After her mother's death (1804), Jeanne wore peasant clothing and gathered others to aid in her works. When Fournet presented her with a plan to establish a religious congregation to care for the sick and to educate the poor of the district, Jeanne entered the novitiate of the Carmelites at Poitiers to prepare for her superiorship. In 1805 Jeanne and five companions began the first community at La Guimetière. It moved closer to Maillé in 1806, and in 1811 to Rochefort. Jeanne made her religious profession in 1807. The bishop of Poitiers approved the community in 1816 as the Daughters of the Holy Cross of St. Andrew. "La Bonne Soeur," as she was popularly known, guided the new community through a rapid growth, despite some misunderstanding with Fournet. By 1820 there were 13 convents, and by 1830 more

than 30. When a convent was opened in the Basque country at Ignon, Jeanne came to know St. Michael *Garicoïts, who became spiritual director of the congregation after Fournet's death in 1834. Jeanne traveled frequently to establish new houses and to carry out her tasks as superior general, but ill health forced her to curtail her activity and to retire to Paris after 1834. She was beatified May 13, 1934, and canonized with Michael Garicoïts July 6, 1947.

Bibliography: J. SAUBAT, *Élisabeth Bichier des Ages* (Paris 1942). PIUS XII, "Plus d'une fois" (Allocution, July 7, 1947), ActApS 39 (1947) 401–408. Butler Th Attw 3:410–413.

[T. P. JOYCE]

BICKELL, GUSTAV, Orientalist best known for his studies in Syriac literature and Hebrew metrics; b. Kassel, Germany, July 7, 1838; d. Vienna, Austria, Jan. 15, 1906. His father was the well-known German Protestant canonist Johann Wilhelm Bickell (1799–1848). Gustav, after his studies at Marburg and Halle, became an instructor in Semitics and Indo-European philology at Marburg (1862) and Giessen (1863). In 1865 he was converted to Catholicism, and in 1867 he became a priest. He was appointed professor of Semitics at Münster (1871) and of Christian archeology at Innsbruck (1874) and Vienna (1891). His knowledge of Syriac poetry led him to propose a theory according to which the Hebrew *poetry of the OT would be scanned like Syriac poetry, in which the verse is determined by a fixed number of syllables, without regard to vowel quantity or grammatical accent; but his theory found few followers. Especially noteworthy among his numerous scholarly articles and books are his *Grundriss der hebräischen Grammatik* (2 v. Leipzig 1869–70), of which English (1877) and French (1884) translations were published; his translations of Syriac works, especially the poetry of St. Ephrem (Leipzig 1866) and the story of Kalilag and Damna together with its Syriac text (Leipzig 1876); and his studies of Hebrew metrics, such as *Metrices biblicae regulae exempli illustratae* (Innsbruck 1879) and *Carmina Veteris Testamenti metrice* (Innsbruck 1882).

Bibliography: A. GUBERNATIS, *Dictionnaire international des écrivains du jour,* 3 v. (Florence 1890–91) 1:300. R. KUKULA, ed., *Bibliographisches Jahrbuch der deutschen Hochschulen,* 2 v. (Innsbruck 1892–93) 1:53–54; 2:19. O. KAISER, LexThK² 2:453. A. KLEINHANS, EncCatt 2:1622–23.

[J. M. SOLA-SOLE]

BICKELL, JOHANN WILHELM, statesman, canonist; b. Marburg, Germany, Nov. 2, 1799; d. Kassel, Germany Jan. 23, 1848. He studied law at Marburg and taught Canon Law there from 1820. In 1832 he went into legal practice. In 1846 he was a legal consultant of the Ministry of Justice. His chief interest was the study of the sources of Canon Law. His principle works are *Ueber die Entstehung der beiden extravaganten Sammlungen des Corpus iuris canonici* (Marburg 1825); *De paleis quae in Gratiani decreto occurunt disquisitio* (Marburg 1827); *Geschichte des Kirchenrechts,* (v.1 Giessen 1843; the second volume was printed posthumously from Bickell's notes in 1849). He wrote also *Ueber die Reform der protestantischen Kirchenverfassung* (Marburg 1841) and *Beitrage zur Civilprocess* (Kassel 1836).

Bibliography: R. NAZ, DDC 2:825–826. Schulte 3.2:199.

[T. D. DOUHERTY]

BIDDLE, JOHN, polemicist, pamphleteer; b. Wotton, Gloucestershire, 1615; d. London, 1662. As a grammar school boy, he "outran his instructors and became tutor to himself," translating Vergil and Juvenal. Upon graduating from Magdalen Hall, Oxford (1638), he became master of the Free School, Gloucester, where he wrote "Twelve Arguments against the Deity of the Holy Ghost." For this he was imprisoned and his manuscript seized. It was published in 1647 and ordered to be burnt publicly as blasphemous. Despite a penalty of death (1648) on all who denied the Trinity, he published two tracts against the doctrine. He was saved by friends in Parliament, and withdrew to Staffordshire in extreme poverty, preaching and editing the Septuagent. Cromwell's Act of Oblivion (1652) enabled Biddle to gather his followers for public Sunday worship but, on publishing two scriptural catechisms, he was indicted before Parliament (1654). After periods in several prisons, he was banished to close custody in the Scilly Isles. He wrote with pathos and power for release, and was brought for trial to Westminster and discharged by Lord Chief Justice Glynn. Biddle at once restarted his Bible classes. Again he was tried, fined, and put in prison; he died of disease contracted in the foulness of conditions there.

Bibliography: J. TOULMIN, *A Review of the Life, Character and Writings of the Rev. John Biddle, M.A.* (London 1791). A. B. GROSART, DNB 2:475–478.

[G. ALBION]

BIEL, GABRIEL

Scholastic theologian and principal representative of late medieval *nominalism, sometimes referred to as *Doctor profundissimus;* b. Speyer, Germany, *c.* 1410; d. Einsiedel, Tübingen, Dec. 7, 1495. About 1460, after several years of study at the Universities of Heidelberg, Erfurt, and Cologne, he became principal preacher and vicar at Mainz. Having entered the Brothers of the Common Life *c.* 1468, he became Propst of the brotherhouse in Butzbach (Hessen) in 1470 and in Urach (Württemberg) in 1479. In 1484 he took over the chair of theology to teach the *via moderna* at the University of Tübingen (founded in 1477); he was invested as its rector in 1485 and again in 1489. In theology and philosophy, Biel professed to follow the teachings of *William of Ockham, but he also adopted certain views of St. *Bonaventure, of St. *Thomas Aquinas, of *Richard of Middleton, and, above all, of *Duns Scotus. Characteristic of his thought are his logic of suppositions, his interpretation and evaluation of intuitive knowledge, and his strong emphasis on the simplicity, omnipotence, and freedom of God. Particular notice should be paid to his development of an ethics covering social and economic questions: property, commerce, a just price (he favored authorized price control, since the formation of a monopoly could endanger the maintaining of a just price), fair taxation, interest rates, monetary operations, currency fluctuation, and the like. His commentary on the *Sentences* serves as the classical handbook of nominalism; it reveals a thorough, systematic, practically serviceable, and Church-orientated attitude, which sets him above any other theological spokesman of his time. Luther received his scholastic orientation through Biel and reflects his influence in both a positive and a negative manner.

Bibliography: Works. Systematic Writings. (1) *Collectorium super IV libros Sententiarum* (Tübingen 1501 and later), bk.4 is incomplete (to d. 23). Extracts. *De potestate et utilitate mone-* *tarum* (bk.4, *Sent.* d.15, q.9; Offenbach 1516), Eng. tr. R. B. BURKE (Philadelphia 1930); *Quaestiones de iustificatione,* ed. C. FECKES (Münster 1929); *In primam Quaestionem Prologi,* ed. P. BÖHNER (Paterson, N.J. 1939). (2) *Sacri canonis missae expositio* (Reutlingen 1488 and later); a critical ed. (Weisbaden 1963–), 2 v. pub. to 1965. Extracts. *Epitoma expositionis sacri canonis missae* (Tübingen 1499 and later); *Expositio brevis et interlinearis sacri canonis missae* (Tübingen *c.* 1500).

Preaching. *Sermones I–IV: De festivitatibus Christi, B.V. Mariae, de sanctis, de tempore* (Tübingen 1499–1500 and later). *Sermo historialis passionis dominicae* (Tübingen 1489 and later). *Sermones medicinales contra pestilentiam,* ed. with *Sermones I–IV.*

Shorter writings. *Regula puerorum* (Urach 1483). *Ars grammatica* (Urach *c.* 1483 and later). *Dictata varia de dialectica* (MS; Giessen, Cod. 1250, B.G. 16:86–199. *Defensorium obedientiae apostolicae ad Pium papam II,* ed. in *Sermones III.* *De communi vita clericorum,* ed. W. M. LANDEEN, in *Research Studies* 28 (1960) 79–95. Three academic addresses (MS; Giessen) Cod. 853, fol. 285–288.

Literature. C. FECKES, *Die Rechtfertigungslehre des Gabriel Biel* (Münster 1925). J. HALLER, *Die Anfänge der Universität Tübingen,* 2 v. (Stuttgart 1927–29) 1:153–172; 2:54–64. W. M. LANDEEN, "Gabriel Biel and the Brethren of the Common Life in Germany," ChHist 20 (1951) 23–36; "Gabriel Biel and the *Devotio Moderna* in Germany," *Research Studies* 27 (1959) 135–214; 28 (1960) 21–45, 61–79. L. GRANE, *Contra Gabrielem. Luthers Auseinandersetzung mit Gabriel Biel* in *Disputatio contra scholasticam theologiam, 1517* (Gyldenal 1962). H. A. OBERMAN, *The Harvest of Medieval Theology: Gabriel Biel and Late Medieval Nominalism* (Cambridge, Mass. 1963).

[V. HEYNCK]

BIELSKI, MARCIN, chronicler and poet; b. Biala, province of Sieradz, Poland, 1495; d. probably Biala, 1575. Few details of his life are known: he was born of a knightly family and was probably self-educated while serving at the courts of Polish princes. Contrary to the opinions of some, he remained a Catholic throughout his life, though his writings evidence a strong, even anti-Catholic, criticism of abuses within the Church and an equally strong sympathy for the Protestant sects. He fought against the Tartars and Wallachians, chiefly between 1524 and 1534. During these military activities he began his literary career, principally at Cracow, where he came under the influence of the humanists and religious reformers. *Zywoty filozofów* (1535, Lives of the Philosophers) was his first work, largely a translation from the Czech. In 1551 he published the *Kronika wszystkiego świata* (Chronicle of the Whole World), the first important history in the vernacular, which contains, moreover, the first reference in a Polish work to America. His *Komedyja Justyna i Konstancyjej* (The Comedy of Justinian and Constantia) appeared in 1557, the first morality play written in Polish. In 1569 he published *Sprawa rycerska* (Knightly Affair), a didactic, historical work designed to awaken his countrymen to the Turkish threat. About this time he wrote also three political satires, published posthumously by his son Joachim: *Sen majowy* (May Dream), *Rozmowy baranów* (Lambs' Conversations), and *Sejm niewieści* (Woman's Parliament). The satires are a unique source of information on the life of the Polish and Hungarian nobility and, more important, on the life of the Polish townsfolk.

Bielski belongs to that group of Polish writers who began writing in the vernacular before Mikolaj Rej, to whom he was inferior in the quality of his works. Nevertheless, he remains one of the leading contributors to the development of prose in the Polish language during the 16th century.

Bibliography: I. CHRZANOWSKI, *Marcin Bielski, Studium historyczno-literackie* (2d ed. Lvov 1926), in Polish.

[E. KUSIELEWICZ]

BIENER, FRIEDRICH AUGUST, Protestant jurist; b. Leipzig, Feb. 5, 1787; d. Dresden, May 2, 1861. He was a professor of law at the University of Berlin from 1810. He was appointed councilor of justice in 1832, and retired in 1834. All his life's work was dedicated to the field of law. He wrote and edited particularly in the field of the history of law. The following are a few of his more important works: *Historia authenticarum* (Leipzig 1807), *Geschichte der Novellen Justinians* (Berlin 1824–49), *De collectionibus canonum Ecclesiae graecae* (Berlin 1827), *Beiträge zur Geschichte der Inquisitions-Prozesses und der Geschwornengerichte* (Leipzig 1827).

Bibliography: R. NAZ, DDC 2:835–836. Schulte 3.2:194–195.

[J. M. BUCKLEY]

BIENVILLE, JEAN BAPTISTE LE MOYNE DE, governor of Louisiana; b. Montreal, Canada, Feb. 24, 1680; d. Paris, March 7, 1768. He was the son of Charles, Sieur de Longueuil, and Catherine (Thierry) *Le Moyne; his brother Pierre, Sieur d'*Iberville, established the Louisiana colony and was its first governor. Bienville entered the navy and accompanied his brother Iberville on the expedition to Hudson Bay (1697), taking part in the capture of Fort Nelson. In 1698 he was a member of the group that explored the mouth of the Mississippi and founded Biloxi; he became its commandant (1700) and acted as governor of Louisiana from 1706 to 1740, with the exception of the years 1712 to 1715, 1717, and 1726 to 1734. He founded New Orleans, which became the seat of government of the colony in 1722. His long career in Louisiana included successful expeditions against the Natchez (1716) and Chickasaw Indians (1739) and the Spanish in Florida. During his governorship, immigration to the colony increased, Negro slave labor from Guiana was introduced, and the economy flourished. In 1740 Bienville retired to France, closing his military and official career in the colony.

Bibliography: G. E. KING, *Jean Baptiste Le Moyne: Sieur de Bienville* (New York 1892).

[M. P. CARTHY]

BIFFI, EUGENIO, member of the Milan Institute of Foreign Missions and bishop of Cartagena, Colombia; b. Milan, Dec. 22, 1829; d. Barranquilla, Colombia, Nov. 8, 1896. He studied at the seminary of Monza and was ordained in Milan, May 21, 1853. He entered the seminary of Foreign Missions of Milan that same year. He was sent to Cartagena (1856), but was expelled in the persecution of Tomas C. de Mosquera. He worked with the Jesuits in the mission of Belize, British Honduras. In 1867 he was named apostolic prefect of Eastern Birmania with residence in Toungoo, where he organized the mission. In 1882 Leo XIII named him bishop of Cartagena at the request of the city, and he was consecrated in Milan on Feb. 19, 1882. In Cartagena he reorganized the seminary and entrusted it to Eudist fathers from France. He founded schools and social welfare agencies, and restored the church of St. Peter *Claver and spread the veneration of this saint. He frequently visited his vast diocese and through his kindness gained the love of his people.

Bibliography: P. A. BRIOSCHI, *Un apóstol de dos continentes: Vida del excelentísimo Sr. Eugenio Biffi, de las misiones extranjeras de Milán* (Cartagena 1940).

[J. M. PACHECO]

BIGAMY (CANON LAW)

The term bigamy is given two distinct meanings in the Code of Canon Law. In CIC c.984n4 it characterizes a man who has contracted two or more valid marriages. This is successive bigamy and is one of the irregularities impeding reception of *Holy Orders including first tonsure (CIC cc.984n4, 949, 950). Secondly, bigamy characterizes persons already validly married who attempt to contract another marriage, even a so-called civil marriage. This constitutes adulterous or simultaneous bigamy. It is contrary to both the unity and the indissolubility of marriage (CIC c.1013.2) and involves the penalty of legal infamy (CIC c.2356).

Historical Background. In the Roman law the praetor attached the stigma of legal infamy to a second marriage even after the death of a spouse (CorpIurCivDig 3.21). Justinian decreed that lectors, the only members of the clergy who were permitted to marry, could never attain a higher rank if they married a second time (CorpIur CivNov 6.5).

The scriptural basis for considering bigamy an irregularity impeding orders is found in St. Paul (1 Tm 3.2; 12; Ti 1.6). The *Canons of the Apostles* (cc.17, 18) declared that a man who married twice after baptism or who married a widow could not enter the ranks of the clergy. The Council of Trullo (c.3) renewed this strong expression of Eastern feeling against more than one marriage after baptism. The Fathers of the Eastern Church held that baptism wiped out the consequence of a marriage that had taken place before baptism (CorpIurCan D26 c.1; C.28 q.3 c.1), a consequence productive of an irregularity to orders. They ascribed the suspicion of incontinence as the reason for the irregularity (CorpIurCan X 2; 3.1.21). On the other hand, the Fathers of the Latin Church, including St. Augustine, laid greater emphasis on the symbolism of marriage reflecting the mystical union of Christ and His Church (Eph 5.32) as the basis for the irregularity (CorpIurCan D.26 cc.2–5). Accordingly, they held that baptism did not remove the irregularity. This latter doctrine received the approbation of Pope Innocent I (CorpIurCan D.34 c.13; C.28 q.3 c.2). It was received into the decretal Collections of Gregory IX (CorpIur Can X 1.21.4) and Boniface VIII (CorpIurCan VI° 17.1.12). The Council of Trent forbade to bigamists the exercise of any office or function of minor orders even such as were allowed, by permission, to married laymen (sess. 23 de ref. matr. c.17).

The bigamy of canon 984n4 is the *bigamia vera* of the pre-Code law. There were, however, other categories of bigamy introduced as extensions or fictions of *bigamia vera*. In all cases it was necessary that carnal knowledge intervened (CorpIurCan D.34 c.14; VI° 17.1.12). There was the *bigamia interpretiva* that constituted an irregularity in the case of a man who contracted marriage either with a widow who had been a party to a consummated marriage or with any nonvirgin (CorpIurCan D.34 c.9). There was also the *bigamia similitudinaria*, nowhere enacted into law but constantly and universally represented as bigamy by canonists and theologians; it applied to those who, after they had received major orders or taken a solemn vow of chastity, attempted marriage and those who dared to marry virgins dedicated to God. The irregularity that arose from *bigamia similitudinaria* is included in the Latin Code under irregularities arising from delict (CIC c.985n3).

The Code of Canon Law. Bigamy, as an institute of Canon Law, has not yet been included in those sections of the Oriental Canon Law recently codified. Our commentary on the present law will, therefore, be confined to the Code of Canon Law. Furthermore, our comments on simultaneous bigamy, as set forth in CIC c.2356, will be very brief. The canon states penalties that are incurred or are to be applied only for the violation of divine law (Mt 5.32; Conc. Trent, sess. 24 de ref. Matrim., c.2). Simultaneous bigamy is more specifically described as polygamy or polyandry. All authorities agree that polyandry is opposed to the natural law. According to most present day authorities polygamy, though permitted by God in the Old Law (Dt 24.1), is contrary to at least the secondary precepts of natural law. Several popes, including Leo XIII in his encyclical *Arcanum* (1880) and Pius XI in his encyclical *Magnum Illud* (1930), favor this doctrine.

Canon Law follows the tradition of Roman law and pre-Code law (CorpIurCan X 4.1.21) in attaching the penalty of legal infamy, with all its consequences, to the crime of simultaneous bigamy (CIC cc.2356, 2294.1). Canon 2356 of CIC states also that if, after admonition by the ordinary, the parties persist in their unlawful union, they become liable to the penalties of excommunication or personal interdict. They may also be held suspect of heresy (CIC cc.1325.2, 2315); they are irregular *ex delicto* (CIC c.985.3); they are to be debarred from the reception of the Eucharist (CIC c.855), as well as from ecclesiastical burial (CIC 1240.1n6). Simultaneous bigamists moreover incur that diriment impediment to marriage which is constituted by *crime (CIC c.1075.1). The penalty of excommunication, reserved to the ordinary, decreed by the Third Plenary Council of Baltimore against Catholics who, after they have obtained a civil divorce, attempt to contract another marriage, still obtains.

To incur the penalties leveled against bigamists in CIC c.2356, it is not necessary that the previous valid marriage or the subsequent bigamous union be consummated.

The irregularity arising from successive bigamy (CIC c.984n4) carries with it no implication of physical or moral stigma. It was introduced *propter defectum sacramenti* (CorpIurCan D.34 c.13; ST Suppl. 3ae, 66.3 ad 3). Its significance is mystical. Successive marriage does not adequately reflect the union of Christ and His Church which involves both unity and indissolubility. In the Code law, the only requirement for the irregularity to arise is successive valid marriage. A putative marriage does not give rise to the irregularity nor is consummation of either marriage necessary. Whether the successive valid marriages were contracted before or after baptism makes no difference. Although the irregularity has apostolic sanction, it can be dispensed by the supreme authority in the Church. The irregularity is of its nature permanent and ceases only with dispensation.

Bibliography: Wernz-Vidal 4.1:241. G. H. JOYCE, *Christian Marriage: An Historical and Doctrinal Study* (2d ed. London 1948). Abbo 2:984, 2356.

[J. F. GALLAGHER]

BIGAMY, U.S. LAW OF

Bigamy is the crime of marrying while a former marriage is in force and the spouse by it is still alive. Both types of polygamy (plural marriage)—polyandry (plurality of husbands) and polygyny (plurality of wives)—can be bigamy. The criminal act is the undertaking to contract the second marriage by having the ceremony performed. In some states cohabitation as man and wife after a bigamous marriage constitutes the crime of bigamous cohabitation. This offense usually extends to such cohabitation whether the second ceremony was performed within the jurisdiction or elsewhere.

A second marriage attempted during the time a valid prior marriage is undissolved by the death of one of the parties or by legal action is absolutely void. No judicial decree is needed to terminate it, and it is subject to collateral attack in court at any time. In the absence of a saving statute, children born of such a union are illegitimate. Although void, a bigamous marriage is a matrimonial offense against the first spouse, and as such constitutes grounds for divorce of the bigamist.

A valid first marriage, or a voidable one that was not annulled by judicial decision before the second marriage, must be established as a foundation for a bigamy case. A prosecution will fail if the first marriage was void; in such case there was no spouse living when the second ceremony was performed. But a bigamy prosecution is not defeated by some defect in the second marriage other than the existence of an earlier marriage. Because of the prior valid marriage the subsequent one is bigamous.

Dissolution of Bond. When the bonds of matrimony are severed by death, remarriage by the survivor is legally proper. A problem arises, however, when a party to a marriage takes a subsequent spouse on the erroneous assumption that the first one is dead. The unexplained absence of a marital partner for a specified period of time, varying in different states, is a defense to bigamy, even though the first mate is later found to be alive. The Model Penal Code proposed by the American Law Institute provides that remarriage is not bigamous, if "at the time of the subsequent marriage: (a) the actor believes that the prior spouse is dead; or (b) the actor and the prior spouse have been living apart for five consecutive years throughout which the prior spouse was not know by the actor to be alive."

When a marriage union is terminated by a final judicial decree of divorce or annulment, subsequent marriage by either of the parties is not bigamy. It is possible, though, for a person to believe mistakenly that an earlier relationship has been legally dissolved. In *People v. Vogel,* 46 Calif. 2d 798, 299 P.2d 850 (1956), after his first wife had testified that she had not divorced him, the defendant in a bigamy prosecution sought to establish his good-faith belief that she had divorced him and married another man. The state supreme court held that his testimony was material because the defendant would not be guilty of bigamy, "if he had a bona fide and reasonable belief that facts existed that left him free to remarry." The Model Penal Code adopts this position. In many states, however, even a reasonable error as to whether the first mate had sought and obtained a divorce is not a defense in a bigamy case.

Migratory Divorce. The law of bigamy is complicated in the U.S. by "migratory divorces"—cases in which persons leave a state to obtain a divorce elsewhere and then return to live with another husband or wife. Generally, states will recognize a divorce decree from a sister state and do not consider a party to such a proceeding who has remarried guilty of bigamy or bigamous cohabitation. But in some cases extrastate divorce decrees are not recognized. Most unrecognized decrees come from states granting "quickie" divorces, states that assume jurisdiction after a short residence period by one spouse. In *Williams v. North Carolina*, 317 U.S. 287 (1942) and 325 U.S. 226 (1945), North Carolina decided that an ex parte Nevada decree was invalid and that the party who had obtained it, remarried in Nevada, and returned to North Carolina to live with a second spouse was guilty of bigamous cohabitation. The Supreme Court upheld the conviction on the ground that Nevada did not have power to grant the divorce, since neither party to the action was really domiciled there.

In 1948 the National Conference of Commissioners on Uniform State Laws adopted the Uniform Divorce Recognition Act; this attempts to discourage migration in pursuit of divorce by denying the validity of decrees in any state adopting the Uniform Divorce Recognition Act if both parties to the union are domiciled therein, and by establishing legislative presumptions as to place of domicile. This statute has been adopted by 10 states.

Religious Polygamy. A belief that religious commandment compels plural marriage does not defeat a bigamy prosecution. In *Reynolds v. United States*, 98 U.S. 145 (1878), it was held that, even though his religion required Reynolds to take a second wife, he could be punished under a Federal law making bigamy a crime in territories of the U.S. The Supreme Court determined that the First Amendment guarantee of religious freedom deprived Congress of "all legislative power over mere opinion," but left the legislators "free to reach actions which were in violation of social duties or subversive of good order." Plural marriage was characterized as an evil against which Congress could legislate.

See also POLYGAMY, U.S. LAW OF; DIVORCE (U.S. LAW OF).

Bibliography: R. M. PERKINS, *Criminal Law* (New York 1957) 331, 835–840. J. W. MADDEN, *Handbook of the Law of Persons and Domestic Relations* (St. Paul 1931) 39–46. American Law Institute, *Model Penal Code: Tentative Draft[s]* (Philadelphia 1954–) no. 4 (1959) 86–87, 220–230. G. W. STUMBERG, *Principles of Conflict of Laws* (3d ed. New York 1963) 291–312. National Conference of Commissioners on Uniform State Laws, 56th, *Handbook* (Baltimore 1947). R. J. DAVIS, "The Polygamous Prelude," *American Journal of Legal History* 6 (1962) 1–27.

[R. J. DAVIS]

BIGOTRY, an intolerant, obstinate, and usually unthinking attachment to one's views, party, or religion. Regrettably, it can and does occur even among doctrinally orthodox Catholics. It must be regarded as an evil, and that on several counts. It offends against the virtues of wisdom and prudence, for bigotry is heedless of truth, even when the cause in favor of which the bigot is prejudiced is basically sound. Moreover, it flouts the obligation to treat one's fellow man with sympathy, respect, and love, and it is grievously disruptive of social unity.

Some forms of bigotry tend to become virulent because they center on basic values or vital needs, and hence involve powerful emotions. Religious bigotry has always been common. Political bigotry exists most conspicuously under totalitarian regimes, but it is found also under other forms of government, especially among those persons who represent extremist positions. Racial bigotry underlies most antimiscegenation and segregation efforts. Class bigotry is often discernible in labor-

management conflicts, in the attitude of one national group to another, etc.

Bigotry may arise from a variety of causes. It can result from an individual's education: racial bigotry, for example, is often begun at home, developed at school, maintained by the communications media, and institutionalized in laws and customs. Bigotry may be the effect of the pressures of popular opinion or of propagandists, as in the attitudes developed during a time of war. It may be considered necessary to an individual's economic, social, or political status, as in the case of the South African apartheid mentality and its American analogues. It may also be a neurotic defense mechanism, as in the case of many extremists.

Since bigotry is partly an intellectual defect and partly a character defect, its extirpation must proceed on various fronts by eliminating its causes. Discriminatory laws must be replaced by others that satisfactorily ensure the rights of all. Civic leaders must initiate or support action that leads to mutual understanding and cooperation and denounce bigots as they appear. The policies, curricula, and teaching of the schools should aim at eliminating budding bigotry. More necessary and basic than anything else, however, is the witness of the churches to the brotherhood of man.

Bibliography: G. MYERS, *History of Bigotry in the United States* (New York 1943). G. W. ALLPORT, *The Nature of Prejudice* (Cambridge, Mass. 1954).

[G. J. DALCOURT]

BIHL, MICHAEL, Franciscan historian; b. Filsdorf (Lorraine), May 10, 1875; d. Metz, April 24, 1950. He entered the order in 1896 and was ordained in 1902. From 1907 (excepting the period 1915–20) until shortly before his death, he was active at the Collegio di S. Bonaventura in *Quaracchi as head of its historical section and as historian of the Franciscan Order. He was cofounder and for more than 30 years editor of the *Archivum Franciscanum Historicum.* Through his editing of the *Analecta Franciscana* (esp. v.10) and his many other publications he became recognized as a leader in the research on the sources of the life of St. *Francis and of Franciscan history in the Middle Ages. In his numerous critical reviews (about 350) he passed important judgments on current Franciscan historical literature.

Bibliography: ArchFrancHist 37 (1944) 355–402, biog. and bibliog. L. OLIGER, *Acta Ordinis Fratrum Minorum* 69 (1950) 180–182; RivStorChIt 4 (1950) 296–297.

[L. HARDICK]

BIHLMEYER, KARL, Catholic theologian and church historian; b. Aulendorf, Germany, July 7, 1874; d. Tübingen, March 27, 1942. Bihlmeyer studied theology at the University of Tübingen and was ordained in 1897. After a period of pastoral work he became an instructor at Wilhelmstift, Tübingen, and later succeeded his master, F. X. Funk, as professor of church history at Tübingen University, where he lectured from 1907 to 1940. He revised the sixth edition of Funk's *Kirchengeschichte,* or Manual of Church History, expanding it to three volumes and bringing out five successive editions based on new historical research and discoveries between 1911 and 1940. The most recent revised editions have been prepared by H. Tüchle [1951–64; Eng. tr., *Church History*, 3 v. (Westminster, Md. 1958–65)]. Bihlmeyer's early interest centered on the ancient Church, and he produced *Die syrischen*

Kaiser in Rom und das Christum (Tübingen 1916); "Das Erste Allgemein Konzil zu Nizäa," AnalSac Tarracon 2 (1926) 199–218; and an edition of Funk's *Die Apostolischen Väter* (Tübingen 1924). His interest extended also to medieval German mysticism, and he published *Heinrich Seuse, Deutsche Schriften* (Stuttgart 1907). He wrote articles for the *Tübinger Theol. Quartalschrift.* In his teaching and writing, Bihlmeyer exhibited a strictly scientific spirit, unconditional adherence to the truth combined with a discriminatory critical sense, and deep loyalty to the Church.

Bibliography: F. X. SEPPELT, HistJb 62–69 (1942–49) 906–908. J. R. GEISELMANN, ThQschr 123 (1942) 73–78. H. TÜCHLE, LexThK² 2:457; NDB 2:234–235. I. DANIELE, EncCatt 2:1635.

[F. DE SA]

BIJNS, ANNA, Flemish poet and Catholic apologist; b. Antwerp, 1493; d. there, 1575. There is little biographical material available. She was a teacher and remained unmarried. Her first collection of poetry was published in 1528; the following year Eligius Eucharius of Ghent translated that work into Latin and published it at Antwerp. Two other published collections of her poems appeared, in 1548 and in 1567. Many of her other poems were preserved in 16th and 17th century MSS, the two most important of which were published in 1886 and in 1902. Some historians believe she was the author of many popular tales and even of the miracle play *Mariken van Nieumeghen* (Mary of Nimmegen), but this ascription is doubtful. Bijns' lyrics are cast as "Refereinen," a form roughly similar to the French *ballade* of the *rhétoriquers;* their verse technique resembles that of the *Meistersinger* genre in German literature.

Her poems, striking in imagery and stirring in rhythm, are concerned chiefly with religion, education, friendship, and love. Much of Bijns' religious poetry had a controversial temper: she began writing shortly after Luther's original attacks on the Catholic Church, and her passionate defenses, while often partisan, were eloquent, and were convincing at least to the popular mind. Her noncontroversial verse, even when occasionally marred by overt moralizing, reflects both her deep love of Christ and Mary, and a moving filial attachment to the Church. Other lyrics reveal her trust in God, especially in the face of death, a theme she handled with delicacy and power. Her love poems, also somewhat moralistic, are to an extent in the medieval tradition of *courtly love; they are alive with deep feeling, but are less carefully and sensitively wrought than the best of her religious poems.

She was one of the first writers in Low Country literature to describe the beauty of nature, but she rejected the worldly spirit of the Renaissance. Notwithstanding her fervent interest in the religious events that announced the modern age, she might well be considered one of the last representatives of the Middle Ages.

Bibliography: A. BIJNS, *Refereinen,* ed. W. L. VAN HELTEN (Rotterdam 1875); *Nieuwe refereinen* (Ghent 1886); "Onuitgegeven gedichten van Anna Bijns," ed. E. SOENS, *Leuvensche Bijdragen* 4 (1902) 199–368. L. ROOSE, *Anna Bijns: Een rederijkster uit de Hervormingstijd* (Vlaamse Academie voor Taal- en Letterkunde, 6th ser. Bekroonde Werken 93; Ghent 1963), with full bibliog.

[L. ROOSE]

BILBAO, FRANCISCO, Chilean radical liberal writer; b. Santiago, Chile, 1823; d. Buenos Aires, 1865. After spending some years in Peru as a youth when his father was exiled there, Bilbao returned to Chile in 1839 and became a part of the young liberal intellectual group around Vicente Fidel López and José Victorino Lastarria. He was a disciple and friend of Andrés Bello, and later of Lamennais, Quinet, and Michelet. At 21 Bilbao wrote *Sociabilidad chilena,* which was so virulent an anti-Catholic and anti-Spanish attack that he was excommunicated and exiled to Europe. Returning to Chile in 1850, he founded a Society of Equality but soon found it expedient to leave for Peru. There his writings were equally unwelcome, and he was exiled in 1854. From 1857 to his death, Bilbao lived in Buenos Aires, where he became an active Mason. Bilbao termed himself a radical rationalist. His dogma was God and Liberty. He equated lack of liberty with Catholicism and saw the only hope for Spanish America in complete control by reasonable men, not hampered by the Church. Only in that way, he felt, could America achieve its destiny as the "altar of human brotherhood" and bring about the Bolivarian ideal of an American union of federal republics. Many Chileans proclaimed him an apostle of liberty in an era in which he was the most vociferous, but hardly the most profound, spokesman for Spanish American liberalism.

Bibliography: *Obras completas,* 2 v. (Buenos Aires 1866). A. DONOSO, ed., *El pensamiento vivo de Francisco Bilbao* (6th ed. Santiago 1940).

[J. HERRICK]

BILHILD, ST., abbess, foundress of Altmünster near Mainz; fl. early 8th century (feast, Nov. 27). She is listed in a Fulda calendar of the 9th century, but details of her life are known only through legends written down in the 12th century. These have her born of noble parents at Veitshöchheim near Würzburg (probably confused with Hocheim near Mainz) and married at 17 to Hetan I, Duke of Thuringia. During a war in which he died, she fled to her uncle, Bp. Rigibert of Mainz, became a nun, and founded the cloister, which in the 12th century possessed property at Veitshöchheim and Hettstadt.

Bibliography: J. MABILLON, *Annales ordinis s. Benedicti,* 6 v. (2d ed. Lucca 1739–45) 2:90. G. KARCH, *Die Legende der hl. Bilhildis* (Würzburg 1869). M. STIMMING, "Die heilige B.," MitteilIÖG 37 (1917) 234–255, with text of a falsified foundation charter from the 12th century. A. BIGELMAIR, DHGE 8: 1471–72. J. BRAUN, *Tracht und Attribute der Heiligen in der deutschen Kunst* (Stuttgart 1943). T. FREUDENBERGER, LexThK² 2:475–476.

[W. E. WILKIE]

BILIO, LUIGI, Italian cardinal; b. Alessandria (Piedmont), March 25, 1826; d. Rome, Jan. 1, 1884. He came from a poor family and entered the *Barnabites in Genoa. After ordination he taught philosophy for some years in various Barnabite colleges. In 1857 he went to Rome to teach theology in the Barnabite house of studies. He became a consultor of the Holy Office (1864) and of the Congregation of the Index (1865). In 1866 he was named cardinal. He served as bishop of the suburbicarian Diocese of Sabina, as prefect of the Congregations of Rites and of the Index, and as *Penitenziere Maggiore* in the Sacred Penitentiary. At the conclave in 1878 he was *papabile* but declined election. Bilio participated in the definitive drafting of the *Syllabus of Errors, whose composition was accelerated and completed after his appointment as consultor of the Holy Office, and as head of the commission that prepared the document. His courteous and conciliating character would indicate that he exercised a moderating influence on the contents of the Syllabus. He was one of the presidents at *Vatican Council I, where his action was always moderate and considerate toward the arguments of the minority group in the discussion concerning papal infallibility, and in the preparation of the constitution *Pastor aeternus*. Bilio's very valuable diary of Vatican Council I has been preserved but not published.

Bibliography: G. Boffito, *Biblioteca barnabitica*, 4 v. (Florence 1933–37) 1:220–227. C. Butler, *The Vatican Council*, 2 v. (New York 1930). G. Martina, "Osservazioni sulle varie redazioni del *Sillabo*," in *Chiesa e stato nell'Ottocento: Miscellanea in onore di P. Pirri*, ed. R. Aubert et al., 2 v. (Padua 1962) 2:419–523. U. Betti, *La costituzione dommatica "Pastor aeternus" del Concilio Vaticano* (Rome 1961) 554, *passim*.

[A. MARTINI]

BILLERBECK, PAUL, specialist in the theology of Judaism; b. Bad Schönfliess, Neumark, Province of Brandenburg, April 4, 1853; d. Frankfurt an der Oder, Dec. 23, 1932. After serving as pastor of the Evangelical Church successively in Zielensieg and Heinersdorf, Billerbeck lived in retirement at Frankfurt an der Oder from 1914 to 1932. His lifework, composed entirely by himself, is his *Kommentar zum NT aus Talmud und Midrasch* (4 v. Munich 1922–28; 2d ed. 1956 with 2 index v. by K. Adolph, 1956–61), a collection made, with a comprehensive grasp of all the material, of everything that Jewish, particularly rabbinical, literature has to offer for an understanding of the NT. With this contribution Billerbeck influenced lastingly and gave a new direction to NT studies throughout the world.

Bibliography: J. Jeremias, *Theologische Blätter* 12 (1933) 33–36.

[J. SCHMID]

BILLIART, MARIE ROSE JULIE, BL., religious foundress; b. Cuvilly, France, July 12, 1751; d. Namur, Belgium, April 8, 1816. Daughter of a small shopkeeper, Julie resided in what is now the French department of the Oise. After hardships occasioned by the failure of her family's small business and the shock of witnessing the attempted murder of her father, Julie

Bl. Marie Rose Julie Billiart.

became a complete cripple unable to walk for 22 years. During her illness she developed her contemplative and apostolic interests by counseling and teaching those who visited her. During the *French Revolution she

gained a reputation for harboring nonjuring clergymen and refusing the services of constitutional priests. Her life imperiled, she was forced to take refuge in Amiens. There she met Françoise Blin de Bourdon, later Mother St. Joseph. The two, under the direction of Joseph *Varin d'Ainville, undertook the foundation of a religious community that developed into the *Notre Dame de Namur Sisters. In 1809 the motherhouse was transferred to Namur, Belgium, where Mother Julie, as superior general, established sound ascetical and educational traditions. She also started seven other houses. The Sisters of Notre Dame of Amersfoort, Netherlands, whose first postulants were trained by Mother St. Joseph, regard Mother Julie as their foundress. So also do the Sisters of Notre Dame of Coesfield, Germany. Mother Julie was beatified May 13, 1906.

Bibliography: J. Clare, ed., *The Life of Blessed Julie Billiart* (2d ed. St. Louis 1909). M. G. Carroll, *The Charred Wood: The Story of Blessed Julie Billiart* (London 1952). M. F. McManama, *As Gold In the Furnace: The Life of Blessed Julie Billiart* (Milwaukee 1957). M. Halcant, *Educational Ideals of Blessed Julie Billiart* (New York 1922).

[J. BLAND]

BILLICK, EBERHARD, theologian of the Catholic Reformation; b. *c.* 1499; d. Cologne, Jan. 12, 1557. Having entered the Carmelite Order at Cologne in 1513, he received the doctorate in theology and was professor (1540–52) and dean (1545–46) of the theology faculty of Cologne. A zealous defender of the Catholic faith, he was deeply concerned with the internal reform of the Church and his Order, as well as with the urgent questions raised by the Reformation. Hermann von Wied, the Archbishop of Cologne, used him as theological consultant for the question of reform and sent him as his representative to the religious discussions held at Hagenau (1540) and at Worms and Regensburg (1540–41). However, when Hermann himself joined the Reformation forces (1542–43) and took the reformer Martin Bucer into his archdiocese, Billick at once sharply opposed him. During the struggle for the preservation of the Catholic faith in the Archdiocese of Cologne he became, with J. Gropper (d. 1559), the center of resistance to Protestantism. His importance as a theologian shows in his polemical and controversial writings: *Judicium deputatorum universitatis et secundarii cleri Coloniensis de doctrina et vocatione M. Buceri ad Bonnam* (Cologne 1543); *Judicii universitatis et cleri Coloniensis defensio* (Cologne 1545), *De ratione summovendi praesentis temporis dissidia* (Cologne 1557), and *De dissidiis Ecclesiae componendis* (Cologne 1559); in his participation as the Emperor's representative at the negotiations for reconciliation at Regensburg (1546) and Augsburg (1548); and in his appointment (1551–52) as the theologian of Adolf von Schaumburg, Archbishop of Cologne, at the Council of Trent.

Bibliography: A. Postina, *Der Karmelit Eberhard Billick* (1901), v.2.2–3 of *Erläuterungen und Ergänzungen zu Janssens Geschichte des deutschen Volkes*, 4 v. (Freiburg im Br. 1899–1902). P. Ferdinand, DHGE 8:1480–81. H. Jedin, "Die deutschen Teilnehmer am Trienter Konzil," ThQschr 122 (1941) 252–253. NDB 2:238–239.

[A. FRANZEN]

BILLOT, LOUIS

Theologian; b. Sierck (Moselle, France), Jan. 12, 1846; d. Galloro (near Rome), Dec. 18, 1931. He studied at Metz and Bordeaux and at the major seminary in Blois, where he was ordained in 1869. In the same year, he entered the Society of Jesus. He then preached in Paris (1875–78) and at Laval (1878–79). He began to teach dogmatic theology first at the Catholic University of Angers (1879–82), then at the Jesuit scholasticate on the Isle of Jersey (1882–85), and finally at the Gregorian (1885–1910), with a brief stay in Paris (1886). Leo XIII, most eager to promote a return to Thomistic doctrine, had him called to Rome. In 1910 he was named consultor to the Holy Office, and in 1911 he was created a cardinal by Pius X. Because of his sympathies for the movement Action Française, which was condemned by Pius XI in 1927, he was persuaded to renounce his cardinalitial dignity. His obedience was irreproachable, and he prevailed upon the members of the movement to sacrifice their ideas and conform to the orders of the Pope. He then left for the novitiate of the Jesuit Roman province at Galloro and remained there until his death.

His works consist chiefly in theological treatises: *De Verbo Incarnato* (Rome 1892); *De Ecclesiae sacramentis* (2 v. Rome 1894–95); *Disquisitio de natura et ratione peccati personalis* (Rome 1894); *De peccato originali* (Rome 1912); *De Deo uno et trino* (Rome 1895); *De Ecclesia Christi* (2 v. Rome 1898–1910); *De virtutibus infusis* (Rome 1901); *Quaestiones de novissimis* (Rome 1902); *De Inspiratione Sacrae Scripturae* (Rome 1903); *De Sacra Traditione* (Rome 1904); *De gratia Christi* (Rome 1912). Added to these, besides several articles in the review *Gregorianum*, are two series of 10 articles each: "La Parousie," *Etudes* 54–56 (1917–19), edited in one volume (Paris 1920); and "La Providence de Dieu et le nombre infini d'hommes en dehors de la voie normale du salut," *Etudes* 56–60 (1919–23).

Following the directives of Leo XIII, Billot gave primary importance in his teachings to the fundamental theses of St. Thomas's metaphysics, especially the analogy of being, the distinction between act and potency, and the real distinction between essence and existence. He viewed the last distinction as one of greatest importance: *essentia* and *esse* are really distinct in creatures, and one and the same in God. Here is what the whole of metaphysics hinges upon, the very root of the assertion that nothing univocal can be ascribed to God and creatures. Billot used this distinction in the treatise on the Incarnation to explain the distinction between person and nature; having recourse to and renewing Capreolus's opinion, he defined the person of Christ as *Esse Verbi*.

His treatise on the Trinity is of special merit because of his subtle analysis of the concept of relation; it exemplifies a theological treatise, the rational explanations of which are systematically constructed with admirable logic upon a metaphysical notion. In his treatise on the infused virtues, he stressed the rational basis of the judgment of credibility. In the treatise on the Eucharist, he insisted on the notion of conversion as characterizing transubstantiation. He also developed a theory of the Mass according to which the sacrifice is to be understood as essentially a mystical immolation.

His thesis on the salvation of infidels was somewhat less acceptable. He held that a very great number of adults remain children from a moral point of view and, therefore, upon death go to Limbo. This was a solution that was generally rejected by theologians.

Among the doctrines or movements that he fought against especially were *Modernism and Liberalism. He denounced Modernism with vigor, and in the encyclical *Pascendi* his ideas, his formulas, and even excerpts from his works can be recognized. In Liberalism he saw a heresy that had issued from the ideas of the French Revolution and that was founded on an atheistic philosophy; he strove to refute the error that consists in claiming that individual liberty is man's supreme good. He did not conceal his hostility toward democratic ideas and he vividly criticized the *Sillon* movement (*see* SANGNIER, MARC). Billot is justly praised for possessing a remarkable ability to speculate dogmatically and for his concern in giving a vigorous philosophical structure to theology. On the other hand, it must be admitted that he showed almost no interest at all in positive theology, and that at times he even mistrusted it.

Bibliography: H. LE FLOCH, *Le Cardinal Billot* (Paris 1947). J. LEBRETON, *Catholicisme* 2:61–63. A. MICHEL, DTC, Tables générales 1:444–446. Hocedez HThéol v.3. F. COPLESTON, Davis CDT 1:268–270.

[J. GALOT]

BILLUART, CHARLES RENÉ. Dominican theologian and controversialist; b. Revin, Belgium, Jan. 28, 1685; d. there, Jan. 20, 1757. He received his early education from the Jesuits at Charleville. At the age of 16, he took the Dominican habit at the priory in Revin, and was ordained in 1708. After 2 years of graduate study at Liège, he became professor of philosophy at Douai. At various times he held positions of responsibility in his province, of which he was three times provincial, but his chief interests were theological and academic. He engaged in much controversy on matters of contemporary interest, especially Jansenism and quietism, and the Thomistic position with respect to both. His major work, however, was his *Summa S. Thomae hodiernis academiarum moribus accomodata* (Liège 1746–51), in which he attempted to present the ideas and even the order and letter of St. Thomas Aquinas together with certain questions from ecclesiastical history. The provincial chapter of the Belgian province had requested such a work in 1733, and the master general had entrusted its composition to Billuart. Its success is indicated by its reaching 13 editions. Billuart later abridged this work in his *Summa Summae Sancti Thomae sive compendium theologiae* (Liège 1754), of which seven editions were made.

Billuart stated that his primary sources would be St. Thomas and his principal disciples. His references to Cajetan, John of St. Thomas, and the Salmanticenses are relatively infrequent. He depended chiefly upon Francis *Sylvius, also a native Belgian and a professor at Douai, but not a Dominican. Billuart borrowed from *Gonet's *Clypeus theologiae thomisticae* for his method and proofs from Scripture and tradition. For historical materials he turned to Alexander *Natalis. Billuart was no eclectic, however, for in making use of many authors he was selective and accepted only those conclusions that corresponded with his own thought. His writings have exerted a considerable influence upon subsequent Thomism, an influence clearly discernible in the works of many contemporary Thomists.

Bibliography: P. MANDONNET, DTC 2.2:890–892. C. R. BILLUART, *Supplementum Cursus Theologiae,* ed. D. LABYE, 20 v. (new ed. Paris 1827–31), "Vita auctoris." L. FLYNN, *Billuart and His Summa Sancti Thomae* (London, Canada 1938).

[R. P. STENGER]

BILLY, JACQUES DE, Benedictine monk and patrologist; b. Guise (Aisne), 1535; d. Paris, Dec. 25, 1581. Educated in the humanities at Paris, Billy studied law at Orléans and Poitiers, and after the death of his parents, devoted himself to Greek and Hebrew letters at Lyon and Avignon. He succeeded his brother as abbot of St-Michel-en-l'Herm (Vendée) and of Notre-Dame des Châtelliers (île de Ré). Driven from his abbey by religious wars, he lived at Nantes, Laon, and Paris, and studied, edited, commented on, and translated (into Latin or French) the Greek Church Fathers. His interest centered on Gregory of Nazianzus, John Damascene, Isidore of Pelusium, Epiphanius, and John Chrysostom; but he contributed also studies on Augustine, Gregory I, Irenaeus, Basil, Nicetas, Serronius, Psellos, Nonnus, and Elias of Crete. His Greek dictionary, *Locutiones graecae,* achieved a quick success. He published also books of sermons and spiritual verses; his letters are still in MSS at Sens and Troyes.

Bibliography: R. METZ, LexThK² 2:478. P. SCHMITZ, DHGE 8:1488–90. R. GAZEAU, *Catholicisme* 2:63–64. GallChrist 2:1296, 1421–22. B. HEURTEBIZE, DTC 2.1:888–889.

[P. ROCHE]

BILOCATION. The location of one body in two places at the same time. This presents a special difficulty in scholasticism, where the Aristotelian notions of *location (ubi)* and *place are applied to events of the supernatural order. The difficulty is usually resolved by distinguishing between true bilocation, or simultaneous location in two places commensurately, and apparent bilocation, where the second supposed location is noncommensurate.

*Suárez and his followers maintain that, because of the Catholic doctrine of the Eucharist, true bilocation is both possible and necessary to hold. The argument for this rests ultimately on Suárez' understanding of location as absolute and independent of external place. St. Thomas Aquinas and scholastics in general hold the contrary. If location means that a body is completely surrounded by its place, then to admit a second location at the same time is to say the body is both surrounded and not surrounded—a contradiction. These authors explain the Eucharist as a noncommensurate presence in place. Similarly, they answer difficulties raised by reputed bilocations of the saints by maintaining that these also are only apparent bilocations—the second apparent location being explained miraculously.

See also BILOCATION, MYSTICAL; EUCHARIST; MIRACLES (THEOLOGY OF).

Bibliography: R. MASI, *Cosmologia* (Rome 1961). P. H. J. HOENEN, *Cosmologia* (5th ed. Rome 1956).

[P. R. DURBIN]

BILOCATION, MYSTICAL. An extraordinary mystical phenomenon in which the material body seems to be simultaneously present in two distinct places at the same time. Since it is physically impossible that a physical body completely surrounded by its place be present in another place at the same time, this could not occur even by a miracle. Therefore, bilocation is always an apparent or seeming bilocation. The most noteworthy cases among the saints are those of Clement, Francis of Assisi, Anthony of Padua, Francis Xavier, Joseph Cupertino, Martin de Porres, and Alphonsus Liguori. When bilocation occurs, the true and physical body is present in one place and is only apparently present in the other by means of a representation of some kind. This representation could be caused supernaturally, diabolically, or by means of a natural power or energy as yet unknown. If the apparent bilocation is caused supernaturally, the body is physically present in one place and represented in the other place in the form of a vision, i.e., through the instrumentality of angels or through an intellectual, imaginative, or sensible vision caused by God in the witnesses. Another possible explanation is that the body of the mystic was transported instantaneously, through the gift of *agility, from one place to another and was returned in the same manner. In this case the apparent bilocation would be reduced to the phenomenon of agility.

Bibliography: R. OMEZ, *Psychical Phenomena,* tr. R. HAYNES (New York 1958). A. ROYO, *The Theology of Christian Perfection,* tr. and ed. J. AUMANN (Dubuque 1962). J. G. ARINTERO, *The Mystical Evolution in the Development and Vitality of the Church,* tr. J. AUMANN, 2 v. (St. Louis 1949–51). A. TANQUEREY, *The Spiritual Life,* tr. H. BRANDERIS (2d ed. Tournai 1930; reprint Westminster, Md. 1945). A. WIESINGER, *Occult Phenomena in the Light of Theology,* tr. B. BATTERSHAW (Westminster, Md. 1957).

[J. AUMANN]

BINCHOIS, GILLES, polyphonic composer of the Burgundian school; b. Mons (Hainaut), Belgium, c. 1400; d. Soignies (near Mons), Sept. 20, 1460. After a military service in his youth, Binchois served from c. 1430 as chaplain at the Burgundian court. He composed motets, hymns, Magnificats, and Mass sections that employ with distinction the technical devices of his day. One motet is isorhythmic; another, in honor of the Holy Cross, uses *"fermata-*marked block chords" to emphasize the important words; and several call for added voices in faux bourdon. The Magnificats are often characterized by faux bourdon–like writing (perhaps an effect of English influence). Plainsong melodies are paraphrased in some Masses, and one *Agnus Dei* is noteworthy for its use of the lower range of the bass voice. Despite his excellent sacred music, he was known chiefly for his chansons. Many of these became the basis of later compositions, notably *De plus en plus* and *Comme femme desconfortée,* used, respectively, by *Okeghem in a Mass and by *Desprez in a *Stabat Mater.* Binchois is mentioned by *Tinctoris and others as among the most distinguished musicians of his era, and Okeghem wrote a *Déploration* on his death.

See also MUSIC, SACRED, HISTORY OF, 4.

Bibliography: J. MARIX, ed., *Les Musiciens de la cour de Bourgogne au XVe siècle, 1420–1467* . . . (Paris 1937), 10 Mass parts, 4 Magnificats, 17 sacred and 36 secular works. Modern reprs. in *Trienter Codices,* ed. G. ADLER and O. KOLLER, DenkmTonk Öst 14, 15, 22, 53. J. SCHMIDT-GÖRG, MusGG 1:1853–57. C. VAN DEN BORREN, *Études sur le XVe siècle musical* (The Hague 1941). Reese MusR. Roland-Manuel, v.1.

[C. V. BROOKS]

BINDING AND LOOSING. This couplet occurs in the NT only in Matthew, where Christ promises to *Peter (16.19) and to the *Disciples (18.18) that whatever they bind or loose on earth will also be bound or loosed in heaven. In most of the examples of the rabbinic usage given by Strack-Billerbeck (1:738–741) 'āsar and šᵉrā' mean to declare something forbidden or allowed by the Law; there are a few examples of their meaning to exclude someone from the community or to readmit him. According to J. Jeremias (Kittel ThW 3:751), the technical meanings that the couplet had in the rabbinic schools are particular applications of the original sense, which was to pass judgment, whether of condemnation or of pardon. While Peter and the Disciples are to exercise this power "on earth," their acts will be ratified "in heaven," that is, by the divine judgment. The exegesis of this phrase has been much influenced by the immediately preceding context (Mt 18.15–17), where is given the rule of fraternal correction, leading up to the excommunication of the obdurate offender. In the light of this context, v.18 has been taken to refer to the power to excommunicate or to absolve from *excommunication, and hence to the power to retain or forgive sin. It is now generally agreed, however, that the connection between these verses is not original, and that from the context one can only conclude that the Evangelist, along with the community for which he wrote, saw the power to excommunicate as an application of the power to bind and loose. Most modern Catholic exegetes understand the terms in a broader sense: of the authority to pass judgments, both doctrinal and disciplinary, which are binding in conscience on the members of the Church. Vatican Council II clearly took the terms in this broad sense when, in reference to the supreme and universal power of the whole episcopate, it declared [*Dogmatic Constitution on the Church* 22; ActApS 57 (1965) 26]: "It is certain that that office of binding and loosing which was given to Peter (*Matth.* 16, 19) was also granted to the college of the Apostles, joined with its head (*Matth.* 18, 18; 28, 16–20)."

See also KEYS, POWER OF; PETRINE TEXTS; AUTHORITY, ECCLESIASTICAL; DISCIPLINE, ECCLESIASTICAL; HIERARCHY; JURISDICTION, POWER OF; OFFICE, ECCLESIASTICAL.

Bibliography: F. BÜCHSEL, Kittel ThW 2:59–60. O. MICHEL, ReallexAntChr 2:374–380. H. THYEN and J. HEUBACH, RGG³ 5:1449–53. A. VÖGTLE, LexThK² 2:480–482.

[F. A. SULLIVAN]

BINET, ALFRED, French psychologist, "the father of mental testing"; b. Nice, July 8, 1857; d. Paris, Oct. 18, 1911. Though originally trained for the law, he earned degrees in natural science at the Sorbonne for his work on the nervous system of insects (licentiate, 1890; doctorate, 1895). With H. E. Beaunis, he founded in 1895 the first psychological laboratory in France and, in the same year, the journal *L'Année psychologique.*

Binet's first publication, *La Psychologie du raisonnement* (Paris 1886), foreshadowed his later interest in intelligence testing. In 1904 he was commissioned by the minister of education of Paris to discover, if he could, the mental level of school children. This occasioned an experimental attempt universally recognized as the origin of the first individual intelligence test. With Theodore Simon, Binet set up a series of 30 tasks; by questioning children individually, he succeeded in distinguishing the subnormal from the normal. In 1908 and again in 1911, the authors revised and refined this instrument, applying suggestions and criticisms from both sides of the Atlantic. Though simple in construction, the Binet scales involve many complex activities, among them, knowledge of common objects, memory of many kinds, language comprehension, imagery, reasoning, and vocabulary. To Binet, the world of testing owes a great debt not only for a very useful instru-

ment for measuring intelligence, but also for precise and methodical standardization procedures that provided a model for subsequent work in testing.

See also INTELLIGENCE; PSYCHOLOGICAL TESTING.

Bibliography: F. L. BERTRAND, *Alfred Binet et son oeuvre* (Paris 1930), complete bibliog. A. BINET and T. SIMON, "The Development of Intelligence in Children," *Classics in Psychology,* ed. T. SHIPLEY (New York 1961) 872–919.

[M. G. KECKEISSEN]

BINET, ÉTIENNE, Jesuit preacher and spiritual writer; b. Dijon, 1569; d. Paris, July 4, 1639. He entered the Society of Jesus at Novellara, Italy. After Henry IV had authorized in 1603 the reestablishment of the society within his realm, Binet returned to France, where he played an important part in Jesuit affairs. He was rector of the Jesuit colleges at Rouen and Paris and provincial of the provinces of Paris, Champagne, and Lyons successively. He had a widespread reputation as a preacher, and his finest writing from a literary point of view, *Essay des merveilles de la nature* (Rouen 1621), was written as an aid for preachers.

He is remembered chiefly as an important figure in the renewal of religious life in France in the 17th century. A close friend of St. Francis de Sales and St. Jane Frances de Chantal, Binet had a cheerful sort of piety closely resembling that of the Salesian school. He was the author of many popular spiritual works that went through countless editions in various languages. One of the most striking is *La Grand chef-d'oeuvre de Dieu et les souveraines perfections de la sainte Vierge* (Paris 1634). He also wrote the lives of various saints, including SS. Ignatius Loyola, Francis Xavier, and Louis Gonzaga. Binet's testament as an eminent religious superior was contained in *Quel est le meilleur gouvernement, le rigoureux ou le doux?* (Paris 1636). He was one of the outstanding religious figures of his day, one who contributed notably to the popularization of the devout life among the people.

Bibliography: Sommervogel 1:1487–1506. Bremond, v.1, *passim.* M. OLPHE-GALLIARD, DictSpirAscMyst 1:1620–23. R. DAESCHLER, DHGE 8:1504–05.

[J. T. KELLEHER]

BINGHAM, JOSEPH, English clergyman and scholar whose dedication to ecclesiastical antiquities enriched the literature of the English Church; b. Wakefield, September 1668; d. Havant, Hampshire, Aug. 17, 1723. He won renown as a student at University College, Oxford, receiving his B.A. in 1688 and a fellowship in 1689. Two years later he was made a college tutor. In 1695, when the Trinitarian controversy was at its height, Bingham was accused of preaching unsound doctrines and was forced to withdraw from the university. Assigned immediately to the rectory of Headbourn-Worthy, he began his scholarly work *Origines ecclesiasticae,* or *The Antiquities of the Christian Church* (10 v. 1708–22), which remains a valuable treatment on the customs and exercises of the Church during the first 500 years. He was the father of 10 children by Dorothy Pocock, daughter of R. Pocock, Bishop of Winchester. Pocock assigned Bingham (1712) to the rectory at Havant, near Portsmouth, where, less impoverished, he was enabled to complete his monumental *Antiquities.* Among his lesser works were *The French Church's*

Apology for the Church of England (1706) and *The Scholastical History of Lay Baptism* (1712–14).

Bibliography: *Works*, ed. R. Bingham, 10 v. (new ed. Oxford 1855), with biography. J. H. Overton, DNB 2:510–512. D. Carter, RGG² 1:1294. Cross ODCC 173. N. Sykes, DHGE 8:1506–08. H. Armbruster, LexThK² 2:483.

[M. A. FRAWLEY]

BINIUS, SEVERIN, editor of conciliar texts; b. Randerath, near Aachen, Germany, 1573; d. Cologne, Feb. 14, 1641. His career was centered in Cologne, where he was rector of the university from 1627 to 1629, and vicar-general of the diocese from 1631 to 1641. He published the histories of *Socrates, *Theodoret, *Sozomen, and *Evagrius Scholasticus (Cologne 1612). In his main work *Concilia generalia et provincialia* (4 v., Cologne 1606), he made use of the work of L. *Surius, A. *Carafa, and Gracia de Loaisa's 1593 edition of Spanish councils, but he printed no Greek texts. The second edition (9 v., 1618) included Greek texts and made use of the Roman edition of Paul V (1608–12). But Binius abandoned the typographical distinction, observed in the Roman edition, for 17th-century Latin versions of ancient Greek and Latin texts, and the resulting confusion persists to the present. A third edition in 11 volumes appeared in Paris in 1636.

Bibliography: J. B. Martin, DTC 2.1:900–901. A. Franzen, LexThK² 2:483–484.

[B. L. MARTHALER]

BIOCHEMISTRY

The science that studies the chemical composition and nature of living matter and the chemical changes occurring in it. It is an interdisciplinary science since it is inextricably related to the content and methodology of the biological sciences on the one hand, and to chemistry on the other. Accordingly, in the history of its development biochemistry has been variously referred to as chemical physiology, biological chemistry, and physiological chemistry. It is possible to subclassify biochemistry from the biological viewpoint into such divisions as pathological, immunological, pharmacological, cytological, microbiological, agricultural, and clinical biochemistry; and from the chemical viewpoint into physical, molecular, and analytical biochemistry.

History. Food fermentation associated with yeast or leaven cannot be dated with accuracy. Man's skill in bread- and wine-making using fermentative processes is evident in Biblical times.

The notion that chemical changes accompany and underlie the functions and behavior of the human organism may be traced to Plato in the *Timaeus* and to Aristotle in the fourth book of his *Meteorologica*. However, the rudiments of biochemistry as a science emerged during the period of "iatrochemistry" (16th century) when *Paracelsus (1493–1541) applied the new science of chemistry to the solution of medical problems. It was he who first emphasized the importance of chemical interpretation of vital processes and the use of chemicals against disease. Johannes Hartmann (1563–1631), established at Marburg, Prussia, the first university chemistry laboratory that was used primarily for research in medicinal chemistry. Medieval and early modern chemists were mainly physicians, and many of them pursued the study of the more conspicuous body fluids.

Toward the close of the 18th century, concomitant with the organization of chemical knowledge as a whole, what can be conceived of as modern biochemistry originated from the basic investigations of photosynthesis by J. *Priestley (1733–1804), J. Ingenhousz (1730–99), and J. Senebier (1742–1809) and studies of the chemistry of animal respiration by A. *Lavoisier (1743–94), P. *Laplace (1749–1827), and A. Séguin (1767–1835).

The 19th century fostered a rapid burgeoning of research in experimental physiology, and organic and physical chemistry, which provided the conceptual and methodological substrata upon which contemporary biochemistry has built so extensively. However, it was not until the beginning of the 20th century that the thin margin between chemistry and physiology vanished, and biochemistry became a science in its own right.

The fundamentals of protoplasmic composition and nutritional biochemistry had their roots in the works of M. *Chevreul (1786–1889), who first characterized the fats or lipids in plant and animal tissues, and F. Magendie (1783–1855) indicated the importance of nitrogen in the diet of animals and the composition of living matter. The nitrogenous compounds were later investigated and named proteins by G. Mulder (1802–80). A third group of substances, the carbohydrates, comprising the sugars and starches, were characterized, and their physiological role elucidated, by the pioneering studies of the physiologist Claude *Bernard (1813–78) and the chemist Emil Fischer (1852–1919). Justus von Liebig (1802–73) improved the methods of organic chemical analysis, thereby advancing chemical definition of vital processes. The possibility of the synthesis of organic compounds and therefore biochemicals from inorganic materials became a reality with the synthesis of urea by F. Wöhler in 1828.

Great strides have been made during the 20th century in the explanation of biological processes and architecture in molecular terms. Diverse areas such as *cytology, *genetics, pharmacology, and *medicine are being drawn together and unified by an evolving knowledge of the relationship between molecular structure and visible vital activity. From the early part of the 20th century until 1960 work has centered about the fruitful physical-organic chemistry approach to the problems of chemical transformation occurring in such diverse forms as viruses and man.

Nomenclature. Since many chemical compounds have been discovered in protoplasm before their molecular structure could be determined, such substances have been named either in reference to their source, e.g., *nucleic acids from the nuclei of cells, or from the biological activity they elicit, e.g., secretin, a hormone that stimulates the secretion of digestive juice in the pancreas. As the structures of such biochemicals become accurately known, they take their place in the general system for the nomenclature of organic compounds.

Composition of Living Matter. *Protoplasm, the living substance, differs from nonliving material in its capacity for growth, self-repair, nutrition, and reproduction. It is organized in the living creature in the form of basic structural units, called cells, which serve as the repositories for the biochemical apparatus. Its functions depend upon the continuous production of energy, which is provided by chemical-bond energy stored in food molecules. The chemical reactions that release this energy for use are called exergonic reactions. These are coupled to energy-consuming reactions called endergonic reactions. Thus, the two types of reactions cannot be sharply separated since exergonic reactions are driven by endergonic reactions, which in turn must be driven by other exergonic reactions. The total of all these processes constitutes what is called *metabolism. This concept implies that compounds carrying or storing energy must be replaced constantly in order that the chemical sequences of cellular metabolism can continue.

Protoplasm is chemically composed of a multiplicity of various carbon-containing substances called organic compounds as well as mineral substances, metals, and water, which are classed as inorganic compounds. The latter are common also to the nonliving world. Its chief organic constituents are carbohydrates, fats or lipids, proteins, nucleic acids, vitamins, and combinations of these. These compounds break down into their constituent parts during combustion. All these contain carbon; most of them also contain hydrogen and oxygen as well; and, in many, nitrogen is an added constituent; while sulfur, phosphorus, or iodine may be present in a few.

The carbohydrates, an extensive group of biochemicals, include the familiar starches and their simpler components, the sugars. They function primarily as the chief fuel source of cellular energy, and secondarily as a structural component of many tissues, such as mucoproteins in animals and cellulose in plants. In nature, carbohydrates are formed by photosynthesis in the green plants. Animals cannot synthesize their own carbohydrates in this manner, and ultimately must depend upon plant life for this essential fuel. The starches serve as the chief form of stored carbohydrate in plants, and glycogen represents their animal counterpart.

The fats or lipids are a heterogeneous group of compounds. They are classified as: (1) simple, including the true fats, oils, and waxes; (2) compound, such as the phospholipids or phosphatides, exemplified by the lecithin in egg yolk; and (3) derived, such as fatty acids, e.g., palmitic acid, and the sterols, e.g., cholesterol, vitamin D, and the sex hormones. Fats, like carbohydrates, can be stored by the living organism and utilized as a source of energy. They also enter into the composition of tissue and blood as lipoprotein. The selectively permeable membrane surrounding cells is largely composed of lipoprotein.

Proteins are the most abundant group of organic compounds in the cell. They constitute the primary structural material of the living organism. All simple proteins contain nitrogen in addition to carbon, hydrogen, and oxygen. Unlike carbohydrates and fats, protein cannot be stored in the body and consequently represents an indispensable food for animals. Plants must obtain nitrogen from the soil for the synthesis of protein even though photosynthesis provides the principal source of their carbohydrate and fat material.

Protein molecules are highly complex. They are composed of long links of characteristic building-blocks known as amino acids. There are about 20 different amino acids but their possible different arrangements in a protein molecule are practically infinite, a fact attested by the observation that every species possesses its own peculiar type of protein. Thus, from 20 amino acids, living cells can synthesize all the diverse proteins they require by varying the amino acids used, their positions in the molecule, and their ratio to each other. The particular proteins synthesized by a cell are controlled by the genetic material within the cell.

Perhaps the most important proteins manufactured by a cell are the *enzymes. The vast majority of chemical reactions that occur within the living organism would occur so slowly as to be virtually unnoticeable if it were not for the presence of catalytic agents capable of enormously accelerating biochemical reactions. These biocatalysts or enzymes are present in all living organisms although no given cell or tissue will contain all of the more than 900 such agents that have been discovered. Despite the multiplicity of enzymes, they catalyze a comparatively small number of reactions, since many of them effect the same type of reaction in different molecules. Enzymes are capable of acting independently of the cells that manufactured them. For this reason they have been employed by industry to catalyze a large number of commercially valuable reactions from tenderizing meat to the preparation of leather.

Although all known enzymes have been found to be proteins, many of them, particularly those associated with intracellular metabolism, associate with a nonprotein component known as a coenzyme. Coenzymes are organic compounds that play an essential role in an enzyme-catalyzed reaction or some enzyme system without being used up in the process. All the coenzymes characterized thus far have been found to contain vitamins, particularly members of the water-soluble B-complex group. Coenzymes I, II, and III contain the vitamin niacin, and associate with various enzymes that effect the oxidation of foodstuffs by the removal of hydrogen (dehydrogenases). Coenzyme A contains the vitamin pantothenic acid and plays multiple roles with the enzymes that degrade fats and carbohydrates in the body. Many organisms are unable to synthesize coenzymes, and thus have to be supplied with the essential vitamins for such syntheses. With the exception of vitamin D, a coenzyme function has been assigned to all other vitamins.

Perhaps the greatest objects of biochemical scrutiny today are the nucleoproteins possessed by all living cells and simple acellular systems such as the viruses. Even more significant is the presence of nucleoprotein in the cellular hereditary apparatus. Any abnormality in the cell's mechanism of nucleoprotein formation is followed by alterations in the growth and reproduction of the cell.

Nucleoproteins were first isolated from the nuclei of living cells by Miescher in 1870. They consist of proteins (protamines and histones) conjugated to nonprotein materials known as nucleic acids. Two main groups of nucleic acids are recognized depending upon whether they contain the pentose sugars ribose or deoxyribose. These are deoxyribonucleic acid (DNA) and ribonucleic acid (RNA). With the discovery by J. Watson and F. Crick (1953) of the structure of DNA and the subsequent realization of the importance of the nucleic acids in the transmission of hereditary characteristics, this area of investigation became one of the most important and most rapidly developing in the whole field of biochemistry.

Viruses. These represent a large group of submicroscopic infective agents that have been isolated from animal, plant, and microbial materials. Biochemical studies have revealed that they are self-reproducing (autocatalytic), crystallizable, protein molecules containing nucleic acids. They are capable of growth and reproduction only in living cells and are small enough to pass through filters that retain bacteria (*see* VIRUS).

Many investigators liken viruses to genes because of certain similarities in their chemistry and behavior. Both have a basically similar chemistry, since all are composed of DNA or RNA and protein. Both are of submicroscopic dimensions. Both manifest autocatalysis, i.e., the capacity to organize the cellular environment to replicate themselves. Viruses contain either DNA or RNA, never both. This property distinguishes them from all living cells. The polio and tobacco mosaic viruses are of the RNA type. Certain viruses that attack bacteria, called bacteriophages, are of the DNA type. It has been found that the RNA and DNA extracted from such viruses and applied to healthy living cells are capable of initiating infection by employing the cell's enzyme and protein-synthesizing machinery to replicate itself.

Viruses have been implicated in the causation of cancer in chickens, mice, rabbits, and plants. Whether these observations are specifically applicable to the human cancer problem is the subject currently under active research.

Hormones. *Hormones are organic compounds exhibiting the following properties: (1) they are produced by a specific type of cell or tissue; (2) they are secreted into an internal medium of the organism, such as blood, body fluids, or plant sap, and conveyed to all parts of the body; (3) they provoke a specific activity or metabolic effect in distant organs or tissues that are susceptible to their influence; and (4) they are active in minute quantites without contributing energy or matter in significant amounts.

Since their discovery by Bayliss and Starling in 1903, many hormones have been isolated and some specific structural formulas have been determined. According to their chemical structure, hormones can be classified into three main groups: (1) phenol derivatives or amines, e.g., adrenalin and 5-hydroxytryptamine, both of which influence neural and cardiovascular activity in animals; (2) proteins or constituents of proteins called polypeptides, e.g., the hormones of the pituitary gland and insulin from the pancreas; and (3) steroids, e.g., the sexual hormones, such as testosterone in the male and estrogen in the female, and the adrenocortical hormones, such as cortisone. Each chemical class of hormone is produced by endocrine tissue of different embryonic origin.

Modern biochemistry has produced revolutionary concepts in the treatment of disease and in the methods of chemical technology, such as the utilization of waste products as animal fodder, the clearing of wine, and the modification of textiles. Many new ideas have emerged that bear upon philosophy and, less directly, upon theology, e.g., viruses that possess properties both of life and nonlife and neovitalistic concepts concerning what constitutes "life" and "nonlife."

Bibliography: E. S. WEST and W. R. TODD, *Textbook of Biochemistry* (3d ed. New York 1961). H. A. HARPER, *Review of Physiological Chemistry* (9th ed. Los Altos, Calif. 1963). A. WHITE, *Principles of Biochemistry* (2d ed. New York 1959). *Annual Review of Biochemistry*, ed. J. M. LUCK (Palo Alto, Calif. 1932–).

[D. J. ROSS]

BIOGENESIS

The process by which life has its origin. More specifically, in the sense coined by T. H. *Huxley (1870), it means that living things always arise through the agency of preexisting organisms. Abiogenesis is the opposite hypothesis—living things arise from inanimate sources. Spontaneous generation, an abiogenetic theory, postulates the origin of lower plants and animals from the slime of the earth and microorganisms from nutrient broth. A more sophisticated modern version of spontaneous generation is neobiogenesis, a theory that viruses are still being produced *de novo* from organic materials by spontaneous extraorganismal chemical syntheses. Biopoesis, the most popular abiogenetic theory of the mid-20th century, holds that only the first living form or forms arose in the remote past from inorganic matter by spontaneous generation.

In this article biogenesis is taken in its widest meaning to include a discussion of the different ways life may have arisen on earth and to consider some philosophical problems associated with biogenetic theories.

TYPES OF BIOGENESIS

The different processes through which life may have had its origin on earth include spontaneous generation, neobiogenesis, cosmozoic processes, creation, and biopoesis.

Spontaneous Generation. Until the mid-17th century it was generally held that living things could arise spontaneously, as well as by sexual or nonsexual reproduction. In 1668 Francesco *Redi provided experimental evidence that maggots thought to be spontaneously generated had actually been produced from the eggs of adult flies. Redi put a snake, eels, a slice of veal, and some fish into two sets of four large, wide-mouthed flasks, covered one set of jars with fine gauze, and left the other set open. Flies entered and left the open jars, and worms soon appeared in them. No worms were discovered in the covered jars, although a few fly deposits and maggots appeared on the gauze cover. Redi noticed that the adult flies that finally emerged were like those crawling on the meat before the appearance of the maggots. Redi's experiments discouraged belief not only in the spontaneous generation of maggots, but in that of macroscopic animals and plants in general.

In the 18th century, Anton von Leeuwenhoek's invention of the microscope and his important subsequent disclosures about microorganisms reopened the controversy over spontaneous generation. An Italian abbot, L. *Spallanzani, performed hundreds of experiments to show that no animalcules appeared when nutrient broth was heated in phials and sealed off from the air. The English Jesuit, John Turberville, countered that Spallanzani had heated his liquids too vigorously and had in this way destroyed the "vital force" of the infusions and of the air in the sealed container.

In the 1860s Louis *Pasteur ended the debate over whether or not microorganisms developed *de novo* without parents in nutrient solutions. After heating flasks of nutrient materials to the boiling point, he either sealed off the neck of the flask or drew it out into an S-shaped curve and left it open to the air. In the cases where he sealed the portals of entry no microorganisms appeared, whereas in the open flasks the microorganisms were trapped in the moisture in the S-shaped necks.

As a result of Pasteur's experiments, many biologists ruled out spontaneous generation as a theory of the origin of life. *Omne vivum e vivo* became the accepted dictum; yet this did not preclude the possibility of life's having arisen spontaneously in the remote past.

Neobiogenesis. In 1960 John Keosian proposed another form of spontaneous generation, neobiogenesis. The term refers to the generation of organisms *de novo* from some organic source present in the environment. Whereas biopoesis refers to the origination of organisms in the remote past, neobiogenesis refers to an evolution from the nonliving to the living throughout time up to and including the present. Keosian rejected the idea commonly held that conditions favoring the spontaneous generation of organisms no longer obtain. He proposed to account for present-day variations in organisms by prebiotic changes in the organic compounds from which they arose. In his view, it is more plausible to accept present-day viruses as recently generated units than as primitive forms that have descended relatively unchanged over 2 or 3 billion years. A serious difficulty with this theory is that viruses cannot reproduce outside a living cell. Until someone succeeds in cultivating a virus in vitro, many scientists will not accept them as the missing link between the living and the nonliving (*see* ORGANISM).

Cosmozoic Processes. H. von *Helmholtz and Lord *Kelvin were among the scientists who speculated that viable spores floating through interstellar space may have accidentally seeded life on earth when conditions were favorable. Adherents of this theory held that life, like matter, is eternal. Therefore, it was not the origin of life that needed explanation, but the passage of the seeds of life from one planet to another. Helmholtz postulated that live germs were brought to earth in meteorites. In 1908 S. A. Arrhenius published a similar theory, known as panspermia, which included careful calculations of the pressure of the sun's rays acting on live germs to bring them to earth.

The cosmozoic theory has not awakened enthusiasm among scientists. While some biologically significant material has been found in meteorites, those examined have all been on earth long enough to have been contaminated. The extreme cold, the absence of moisture and oxygen, the intense ultraviolet radiation, and the vast interstellar and interplanetary distances to be traveled make the passage of highly organized living things through space virtually impossible. Such a theory, moreover, does not solve the problem of the origin of life; it merely locates the origin on another planet or in space, and leaves the question basically unsolved.

Creation. The author of the book of Genesis states that God created the heavens and the earth and that God then said, "Let the earth bring forth vegetation: seed-bearing plants and all kinds of fruit trees that bear fruit containing their seed" (Gn 1.11–12). St. *Augustine (*Gen. ad litt.* 5.4–5, PL 34:323–372) interprets Genesis to mean that God created animals and plants only virtually, in the sense that the earth was given the power to bring forth living things in time. Although this idea lends support to modern evolutionary theories, Biblical exegetes insist that the Scriptures neither affirm nor deny scientific theories of the universe. The sacred writer teaches only that a transcendent God called the cosmos into being and set man, made in His own image and likeness, over visible creation. (*See* CREATION.)

Biopoesis. This theory, holding that the first living things evolved naturally from inorganic matter, lends itself to verification by experimental investigation. In 1924 A. I. Oparin theorized that the complex properties of living things arose in the natural process of the evolution of matter. In his view, large amounts of complex organic compounds in the oceans of the primitive earth reacted to form yet more complex molecules until one or more evolved that could be designated as alive. Oparin later showed that by mixing solutions of different proteins and other substances of high molecular weight he could produce coacervate droplets that readily adsorb organic substances from the surrounding medium. He proposed that the first primitive cells may have been much like these coacervate droplets. J. B. S. Haldane (1926) speculated that ultraviolet light acting on a mixture of water, carbon dioxide, and ammonia could produce a wide variety of organic compounds in the primitive oceans. If the first living things were formed in such a medium, the nutrient material there would sustain them. J. D. Bernal proposed that fine clay deposits in pools and lagoons might have served as adsorbents to concentrate selectively large organic molecules and to promote their reaction in forming the first living being.

In the 1950s, experimental work to establish the possibility of a prebiological formation of "building blocks" for living things originated in the laboratories of Melvin Calvin of the University of California and of Harold Urey at the University of Chicago. Calvin and his associates treated carbon dioxide and water in a cyclotron and produced formaldehyde and formic acid. S. L. Miller, a student of Urey, then exposed a mixture of water vapor, methane, ammonia, and hydrogen—gases believed to have been present on the primitive earth—to a silent electric discharge for a few days. Analysis of the results by the method of paper chromatography revealed a mixture of amino acids, several of which are essential components of proteins.

By heating concentrated solutions of hydrogen cyanide in aqueous ammonia for several days, J. Oró was able to produce adenine, an essential building block of nucleic acids. C. Ponnamperuma exposed to ultraviolet light a dilute solution of hydrogen cyanide—not more than was probably present in the atmosphere of the primitive earth—and produced guanine as well as adenine, the only purines found in RNA (ribonucleic acid) and DNA (deoxyribonucleic acid). In another contribution, P. Abelson isolated amino acids from fossil material many millions of years old. The steps from amino acids to proteins are very complex, but Sidney Fox has had some success in forming protein-like polypeptides under anhydrous conditions in vitro. With carefully controlled conditions of temperature and hydration he produced proteinlike polymers with structures suggestive of cellular systems, which he called microspheres.

These experiments lend support to Oparin's and Urey's hypothesis of the reducing character of the atmosphere of the primitive earth. In an oxidizing atmosphere it is doubtful that delicate organic molecules could have remained stable long enough for complex organic systems to have been formed. Except for Calvin's experiments with carbon dioxide and water, attempts to synthesize organic substances in an oxidizing atmosphere have been relatively unsuccessful. If the substance of the earth came from the same source as the sun, however, it is likely that the primitive earth had no free oxygen but an excess of free hydrogen. Some of this hydrogen is assumed to have been combined with other elements in such simple compounds as methane, water, and ammonia—compounds used in Miller's classical experiments, where the electrical, thermal, and solar energy sources employed approximate those available on the primitive earth. If life arose 2 billion years ago, sufficient time was available for the present atmosphere to have been evolved by such mechanisms. Most of the oxygen was doubtless produced by living organisms. In a reducing atmosphere the first organisms would have been heterotrophic, i.e., receiving their energy-rich carbon compounds from the environment. N. H. Horowitz (1945) proposed a theory of successive mutations by which heterotrophic organisms could acquire various synthetic abilities and gradually evolve into autotrophic organisms, such as present-day chlorophyll-bearing plants.

Yet the theory of biopoesis is still highly conjectural. Indirect evidence of the kind just adduced in no way demands complete assent. But as more and more evidence is advanced, biopoesis becomes more firmly established as a reasonable hypothesis.

Was biopoesis a unique event or a phenomenon that took place time and again on the primitive earth? The fundamental similarities in living things suggest that they came from one source. All known living things are made up of protein, and only a-amino acids, that is, amino acids in which the amine and the acid group are attached to the same carbon, are found in proteins. Except for glycine, these amino acids exist in two forms that are mirror images of each other. They are referred to as "right-handed" and "left-handed" because of their ability to turn a beam of polarized light to the right or to the left. The fact that proteins of almost all living things are left-handed is strong evidence that biopoesis was a unique event. The similarity in the metabolic pathways and biosynthetic reactions by which anabolism and catabolism are accomplished in plants and animals also points to their common origin.

PHILOSOPHICAL PROBLEMS

Philosophical problems associated with the origin of life are closely related to the definition one adopts for life itself (see LIFE). The lower forms of life have manifest affinities with the nonliving as well as with the higher forms of the living, and depending on which affinities one emphasizes, less or greater difficulty is encountered in explaining the production of life from inorganic matter. What follows will be a discussion of the possibility of biopoesis in the context of Thomistic teaching on life and its need for an adequate cause, and the possible role of chance in the biopoesic process.

Possibility. From his writings one may surmise that St. *Thomas Aquinas would admit the possibility of biopoesis. He wrote that "the completeness of the universe requires that there be no gaps in its order, that in nature there should be everywhere a gradual development from the less to the more perfect" (*In 2 anim.* 5.288). He did not reject St. Augustine's teaching that the earth produced plants and trees in their causes, that is, that it received the power to produce them (ST 1a, 69.2). In fact, explaining Gn 1.11–12 he states that since plants "are firmly fixed in the earth

their production is treated as part of the earth's formation" (ST 1a, 69.2 ad 1).

Yet St. Thomas was aware that plants are alive, since they have the power of growth and nourishment (*In 2 anim.* 3.258), and thus he would be presented with the philosophical difficulty of explaining how the higher (the living) can come to be from the lower (the nonliving) in biopoesis. In the context of medieval teaching on spontaneous generation—which extended to frogs, mice, and other vertebrates as well as to plants and invertebrates—St. Thomas proposed such an explanation in terms of the causal influence of living substantial beings. He attributed this causality to the agency of the angels who, because they have greater knowledge of the operations of living things than man, exercise a superior, but natural (not supernatural), control (see SPONTANEOUS GENERATION).

Were St. Thomas living in the 1960s, he might not have resorted to angels for this causality, but would possibly regard human knowledge and control of cosmic forces as adequate to the task. He did allow that the potentiality for such living forms could be present in primary matter, and thus would be concerned only with identifying an efficient cause of sufficient power to educe such forms from matter (see MATTER AND FORM). That plants have properties not found in the inanimate is only to be expected: water has different properties from the hydrogen and oxygen of which it is constituted, and even a watch has properties not found in its parts. Thus there seems to be no repugnance to biopoesis on the part of the organism's intrinsic causes; granted a sufficiently powerful and knowledgeable agent, biopoesis could take place in the order of nature.

Role of Chance. Can *chance account for the origin of life? Charles Darwin wrote in a letter to Asa Gray that the problem of the origin of living things is too profound for the human intellect. Nevertheless he concluded: "I am inclined to look at everything as resulting from designed laws, with the details, whether good or bad, left to the working out of what we may call chance."

Popular science books and textbooks of the mid-20th century explain the origin of life as a fortuitous event. Yet many scientists exhibit concern over the attribution of the ability to synthesize proteins and other cellular constituents—a unique property of cells and organisms —to the primitive earth. At the present time only organisms or parts of organisms can synthesize proteins. Since the process by which they do this is regular, few would claim that biosynthetic reactions are completely random or chance events. The strong uphill thrust that organisms exhibit, in opposition to the second law of *thermodynamics, can hardly be explained by chance.

Two forces would thus seem to be at work in the world, both needed to account for the origin of life. One is a certain randomness in particular causes that operates in special events, such as that by which a left-handed protein may have been incorporated into a proto-organism; the other a kind of fundamental determinism, such as that causing all subsequent living things to be made of left-handed proteins. Those who emphasize the operation of particular chance events at work in the universe take a kind of opportunistic view. Since statistical data reveal that the improbable does occur, they feel that a series of such events could account for the origin of life. Typical of the deterministic view, on the other hand, is the statement of Oparin: "The origin of life is not a 'fortunate,' extremely improbable event, but quite a regular phenomenon subject to a deep scientific analysis." Those who favor this view of the workings of nature hold that, where conditions were favorable, life had to originate.

Aquinas held that spontaneously produced animals and plants were generated by chance (*In 7 meta.* 6.1398). In agreement with 20th-century scientists, he also held that a concatenation of material elements determines the species of things spontaneously generated (ST 1a2ae, 60.1). Thus he might have held that the exact time life originated on the earth resulted from a combination of circumstances that can be considered a chance event. Yet Thomas was also convinced that higher causes determined such an event to come to pass: "A naturally contingent cause," he wrote, "must be determined to the effect by some external power" (ST 1a, 19.3 ad 5). Again: "Things are said to be fortuitous as regards some particular cause from the order of which they escape. But as to the order of divine providence, 'nothing in the world happens by chance,' as Augustine declares" (ST 1a, 103.7 ad 2). Thus he would also assert a divine determinism, over and above that of the order of nature, in the appearance of the first living thing.

See also EVOLUTION, ORGANIC; SOUL, HUMAN, ORIGIN OF; UNIVERSE, ORDER OF; CAUSALITY, DIVINE.

Bibliography: J. D. BERNAL, *The Physical Basis of Life* (London 1951). A. I. OPARIN, *The Origin of Life,* tr. and ed. S. MORGULIS (2d ed. New York 1953). International Symposium on the Origin of Life on Earth, Moscow, 1957, *Proceedings,* ed. A. I. OPARIN et al. (New York 1959). H. F. BLUM, *Time's Arrow and Evolution* (2d ed. New York 1962). R. J. NOGAR, *The Wisdom of Evolution* (Garden City, N.Y. 1963). C. HAURET, *Beginnings: Genesis and Modern Science,* tr. and ed. E. P. EMMANS (Dubuque 1955). N. H. HOROWITZ, "On the Evolution of Biochemical Synthesis," *Proceedings, National Academy of Sciences* 31 (1945) 153–157. S. L. MILLER, "A Production of Amino Acids under Possible Primitive Earth Conditions," *Science* 117 (1953) 528–529. G. WALD, "The Origin of Life," *Scientific American* 191 (Aug. 1954) 44–53. S. L. MILLER and H. C. UREY, "Organic Compound Synthesis on the Primitive Earth," *Science* 130 (1959) 245–251. H. GAFFRON, "The Origin of Life," *Perspectives in Biology and Medicine* 3 (1960) 163–212. J. KEOSIAN, "On the Origin of Life," *Science* 131 (1960) 479–482. M. and G. J. CALVIN, "Atom to Adam," *American Scientist* 52 (1964) 163–186. G. G. SIMPSON, "The Nonprevalence of Humanoids," *Science* 143 (1964) 769–775. W. J. SCHMITT, "Spontaneous Generation and Creation," *Thought* 37 (1962) 269–287.

[A. M. HOFSTETTER]

BIOLOGY, I (HISTORY OF)

Biology is a systematic body of knowledge concerned with organisms and their vital processes. It had its primary roots in man's activities in acquiring food, clothing, shelter, and protection.

Greek Period. Between the 7th and 6th centuries B.C. the Greeks laid the foundation for the superstructure of modern medicine. They alone among the peoples of antiquity, through the observation and classification of diseases, made a truly scientific endeavor to explain the origin of disease on rational grounds. From carefully collected data they proceeded to generalize. The spirit and achievement of such research were embodied in the works of the father of medicine, *Hippocrates (fl. 400 B.C.). However, most of the 60 or 70 separate treatises attributed to him were written over a period of several centuries and are obviously by different authors. Precisely which ones were written by Hippocrates cannot

be ascertained, but from these works and the comments of others about him, Hippocrates emerged as the type of the perfect physician.

From Ionia to Sicily there appeared in the ancient Greek cities a number of philosophers who were unhampered by popular mythological concepts of nature. Their endeavors in the realm of pure reasoning enriched physics, astronomy, mathematics, and biology. But in biology particularly, all are overshadowed by *Aristotle (c. 384 B.C.), founder of biology as a school and the foremost biologist of antiquity.

The works in natural science attributed to Aristotle fall into three groups: physics, biology, and psychology. Although they have had a lasting influence, they show little trace of direct and original observation, and this same weakness is betrayed in his works dealing with human physiology (body functions). They present a striking contrast to his writing on natural history, where he faithfully extended the Hippocratic tradition of making generalizations from collected observations. In his use of the inductive method and his careful observations of living nature Aristotle made his finest scientific contributions. He wrote a fascinating account of the development of the octopus and sepia, or cuttlefish. Acquainted with the characteristic features of mammals, he was able to recognize whales, dolphins, and porpoises as properly belonging to this group and not to the fishes. He knew that some fish bring forth their young alive, and that one in particular approaches the mammals even more closely in that its young develop within the uterus of the female and are attached to a type of placenta. The existence of the placental dogfish and other facts unearthed by Aristotle were not substantiated until the 19th century. In an incubating hen's egg, Aristotle followed the day-by-day development of parts from a relatively homogeneous mass. In comparative anatomy he made noteworthy observations; for example, he gave a clear and correct account of the four-compartmented stomach of ruminants. None of Aristotle's botanical treatises have survived, but a few works by Theophrastus, his pupil, successor, and the father of botany, have come down to us. In his description of the parts of plants (plant anatomy), Theophrastus sought to devise a technical terminology. He valued developmental study (embryology) and distinguished various modes of plant reproduction.

Greek science reached its zenith at Alexandria in the period from about 300 to 150 B.C. In the field of medicine, anatomy and physiology were placed on a sound basis. The points of human anatomy and physiology discovered by Herophilus and Erasistratus are still remembered.

Roman Period. About the middle of the 2d century B.C., Greece succumbed to the Roman legions. The Romans made contributions in politics—codification of laws and formulation of governmental procedure—but their interest in science was primarily in its application. Thus, in biology, both medicine and agriculture were encouraged because of their importance to the welfare of the army and the empire. Three Romans deserve special mention, Pliny, Dioscorides, and Galen.

Pliny the Elder (A.D. 23) put together a natural history of 37 volumes, which throughout the Middle Ages influenced the development of biology and natural history. This encyclopedia of nature, mixing fact and fancy, embodied all the knowledge of nature possessed by

Fig. 1. *Imaginary portrait of Galen with St. Luke by Hans Weiditz, from a 16-century handbook of medicine.*

ancient Rome together with its application to medicine, technology, and economy. It contained little original observation, being for the most part a compilation gleaned from the hundreds of sources Pliny had read.

Dioscorides (*c.* A.D. 64) was an army surgeon under Nero. He originated the pharmacopoeia, tersely describing plants of value to medicine and frequently including their habits and habitats. Annotated copies of this *materia medica* formed the chief source of botanical knowledge for the next 1,500 years.

The 2d century A.D. saw the last great biologist of antiquity, *Galen of Pergamum, who standardized anatomy and physiology for the next 15 centuries. Court physician to Marcus Aurelius, he composed voluminous works containing the ideas of his predecessors as well as his own contributions. He described from dissections, and performed experiments on living animals. By severing the spinal cord of living animals at different levels he gained knowledge of nerve functions. Galen also distinguished between motor and sensory nerves. He seems never to have dissected a human body, relying chiefly on his dissections of the Barbary ape. Most of his errors in human anatomy and physiology stem from the fact that he frequently attributed to the human body structures found in some other animal.

Middle Ages. From many and varied causes that had been piling up for centuries, the Western Empire crumbled in the 6th century. With the barbarians invading from the north, Christianity busied itself primarily with conversion efforts, and scientific progress came to a standstill. The few important links with the learning of the past were the hand-copied manuscripts carefully guarded in the monasteries of Britain and Italy. Although this period of the Middle Ages was not a time of scientific progress and experiment, men were trained to think. The habit of definite, exact thought was implanted in the European mind by theologians and philosophers of the late Middle Ages. With the spread of Is-

lamism after the death of Mohammed, the almost forgotten culture of the Greeks and the Near East was reintroduced into Western Europe. From the 9th to the 11th century this transmission vivified medieval thought with Arabic translations of Plato, Aristotle, Theophrastus, and others. In this same period the founding of the great universities aided the dissemination of learning.

Renaissance. A period characterized by a revival of classical learning and a rebirth of science, the Renaissance is generally said to have run from the 14th to the 16th century. Rather than being a marked break with the Middle Ages, the Renaissance was a natural flowering of medieval culture. The restlessness, probing curiosity, and many-sided learning of the Renaissance are epitomized in such a man as *Leonardo da Vinci (1452–1519). Known primarily as an artist, he was also a talented engineer, inventor, observer of nature, and anatomist. Had his notes and drawings in human anatomy been published when made, anatomy might have been advanced by a century. He made scientific studies of the action of the eye, the mechanisms of various joints, and of the flight of birds. Embryological and comparative anatomical studies alike came within the compass of his work.

Biology in the 16th century is represented in the herbals, encyclopedias of nature, and monographs of the period. The German fathers of botany produced herbals that ranged from annotated texts of Dioscorides, like that of Otto Brunfels (1489–1534), to the beautifully illustrated manual of Leonard Fuchs (1501–66), which was intended as a guide for the collection of medicinal plants in Western Europe. The encyclopedias attempted to gather together in one work all of the available knowledge about living things. The most influential of these was the *History of Animals* by Konrad Gesner (1516–65) of Switzerland, probably the most learned zoologist of the period. Some of Gesner's less ambitious contemporaries confined their efforts to treatises or monographs on special groups of organisms.

Human anatomy in the Renaissance was studied through a slavish interpretation of Galen by the teacher, while an attending barber's assistant crudely made the actual dissections. However, by his own skilled and careful dissections, Andreas *Vesalius (1514–64) of Belgium showed his anatomy students at Padua that Galen, great as he was, could be wrong. In 1543 he published his wonderfully illustrated book, *On the Structure of the Human Body,* which marked the end of the servile adherence to the authority of the past.

Until the functioning of the heart and blood was understood it was impossible to grasp the natural ordering of the bodies of the higher animals. The publication in 1628 of William *Harvey's (1578–1657) treatise *On the Motion of the Heart and Blood in Animals* was a giant step in the advancement of biological science. Numerous observations, carefully planned and executed experiments, and quantitative calculations led Harvey inductively to the conclusion that the heart is a muscular pump that propels the blood in a closed circuit throughout the vertebrate body.

The study and description of the parts composing a plant or an animal are referred to as morphology. When this work is done with the unaided eye, the result is gross anatomy. In the 17th century, however, the compound microscope was added to the apparatus of the biologist. As used by such men as Grew (1641–1712) in England

Fig. 2. Etching of William Harvey by Wenzel Hollar, 17th-century Bohemian artist.

and *Malpighi (1628–94) in Italy to study the fine structure of living things, it led to the development of a new branch of biology called histology. The world of microbes was first seen by Leeuwenhoek (1632–1723) through his homemade lenses. As a result two new disciplines, bacteriology (*see* BACTERIA) and protozoology, were added to biology.

The 18th Century. In the 18th century new impetus was given to biology by the comparative method applied to anatomy and *embryology. The classification (*taxonomy) of living things as well as a system of naming them (nomenclature) were standardized. Georges Cuvier (1769–1832), the founder of modern comparative anatomy and paleontology, was able with his knowledge of animal structures and by the application of the theory of the "correlation of parts" to place many fossil forms in their correct systematic positions in the animal kingdom. He surmised that each species was specially created and that the existence of dissimilar fossils in series of rock strata could be explained by catastrophism. According to this theory, wide expanses of the earth were from time to time subjected to great cataclysms (floods, quakes, etc.), which obliterated all life in those areas. Later, such territory would be populated by different animal species, which migrated into the denuded areas from distant parts. These would eventually leave some descendants in the fossil record that would contrast with the fossils in the lower strata of sedimentary rocks.

The most important figure in 18th-century biology was Carolus *Linnaeus (1707–78) of Sweden. From his youth, he had displayed a passion for classification

and an extraordinary genius for accurate and detailed observation. He visited and collected plant specimens in Lapland, Norway, France, Germany, Holland, and England. As an outcome of these travels and studies he wrote his famous *Systema naturae*, published in Holland in 1735, in which he attempted to describe and classify every known animal and plant. In so doing he set standards for describing animals and plants with accuracy and succinctness.

During most of his life, Linnaeus firmly adhered to the idea that all of the present-day species of plants and animals were the unchanged linear descendants of original species individually created. However, having observed in 1742 one of the first recorded mutations of species, Linnaeus was led to revise his initial conceptions. In his *Fundamenta fructificationes* (1762) he conceded that perhaps there was a common stock for all of the species of a single genus, or even perhaps of a single order. The direct work of the Creator was confined then to the genera, or to the orders, the diversification of which was accomplished as a result of crossing or hybridization.

The 19th Century. Advances far-reaching in their effects were made in biology in the 19th century. The enunciation of the theory of evolution colored the thought of the period in many fields extraneous to biology. The germ theory of disease affected our entire civilization, as did the discovery of the basic laws of inheritance. Slightly less notable were the formulation of the cell theory and the forward steps taken in embryology and physiology.

Fig. 3. Carolus Linnaeus, Swedish botanist, in the costume of Lapland, where he did extensive research.

The term "cell" in its biological sense comes down from the 17th-century work of Robert Hooke, who thus described the tiny divisions that he saw in thin slices of cork under the microscope. The formulation of the cell theory was, however, a gradual development of the early 19th century. In brief, the cell theory states that all organisms are composed of cells (or a single cell) that are essentially alike in their composition and formed in the same fundamental manner by division of a preexisting cell. The basic points of the cell theory were stated and confirmed with clear-cut observations by Schleiden (1804–81) and *Schwann (1810–82), in 1838 and 1839 respectively. The study of cells, *cytology, became a distinct branch of biology in the 20th century. *See also* CELL PHYSIOLOGY; CELL THEORY OF LIFE; CELL DIVISION.

Although crude ideas of evolution can be found among the Greek philosophers, it was not until the 19th century that a definite theory of evolution was presented. J. B. *Lamarck (1744–1829) believed that a felt need on the part of an organism might give rise to new organs and suggested that the use of an organ or part strengthens and develops it, while a lack of its use leads to a gradual atrophy, diminution, and eventual disappearance. The heart of the theory, as Lamarck proposed it, was that these changes were passed on through heredity; in other words he claimed there is an inheritance of acquired characteristics.

Evolution, however, has become almost synonymous with the name of Charles *Darwin (1809–82). No other publication has exerted so profound an influence on biology as his book *The Origin of Species by Means of Natural Selection* (1859). Darwin had spent 20 years gathering facts to substantiate his theory. Although the same theory was arrived at independently by Alfred Wallace at the same time, Wallace had not the same wealth of observational data to support it as had Darwin. Each had published a short presentation of his views in the same issue of the *Proceedings of the Linnean Society* the previous year. The first edition of *The Origin of Species* was sold out on the first day of its publication, and it brought forth a storm of controversy in the fields of religion and sociology, which has only lately subsided. (*See* EVOLUTION, ORGANIC; EVOLUTION, HUMAN.)

In the 16th century, the Italian physician Fracastoro (1483–1553) had contended that infection of all kinds, including fermentation, was the work of minute "seeds" or germs. This was proven by *Pasteur (1822–95) on experimental grounds. Though Pasteur was a chemist, his great discoveries were in microbiology and preventive medicine. He showed that diseases like hydrophobia and anthrax could be prevented by inoculation with the attenuated or even dead germs causing the disease.

*Genetics is that branch of biology concerned with the phenomena of inheritance and the origin of heritable variations. Although genetics did not emerge as a full-fledged science until well into the 20th century, the basic laws of inheritance upon which it is founded were discovered by an Augustinian monk, Gregor *Mendel (1822–84); his work marks the beginning of precise knowledge of genetics. Working principally with garden peas, he combined the experimental breeding of pedigreed strains of plants and the statistical treatment of the data secured in regard to the inheritance of sharply contrasting characteristics, such as short and tall plants, or white and red flowers. His work, published (1866) in an obscure journal, remained almost wholly unnoticed until 1900. (*See* HEREDITY.)

August Weismann (1834–1914), who opposed the theory of the inheritance of acquired characteristics, published (1892) a volume entitled *The Germ Plasm.* He identified the chromosomes found in every cell nucleus as the bearers of hereditary traits and emphasized a sharp distinction between germ cells and somatic cells.

Ecology is another biological discipline that developed in this era; it deals with the relationships between living things and their environment, which consists not only of the physical but also the biotic elements and their complex interactions.

The 20th Century. The 20th century has witnessed the breakdown of biology into numerous specialized branches as well as the synthesis of paleontology, genetics, ecology, systematics, and related fields, which resulted in a reaffirmation of organic evolution along Darwinian lines. One of the three men who had independently discovered Mendel's work in 1900 was a Dutch botanist, Hugo De Vries (1848–1935). His work in plant breeding had convinced him of the significance of the distinction between heritable and nonheritable variations. Among his plants he found variations in some individuals that marked them distinctly from the parent generation, and he discovered further that these bred true. In his book *The Mutation Theory,* he proposed that evolution proceeded by means of rather large mutations or saltations. This contrasted with Darwin's concept that natural selection had acted upon small, continuous, heritable variations. T. H. Morgan (1866–1945) showed that mutations occur constantly and range from minute, barely perceptible changes in structure and function to the large, discontinuous variations of the type considered by De Vries, but most were in the category of minute changes.

Morgan actually followed up the work of another American experimental zoologist, E. B. Wilson (1856–1939), who had opened the way with his studies in cellular biology—particularly those dealing with the chromosomes and their relation to heredity. H. J. Muller (1890–   ), who received the Nobel prize for his investigations in genetics, showed that the frequency of gene mutations is affected by temperature, age, and the stocks used. He discovered that ionizing radiations would speed up the mutations that normally occur at a relatively slow rate.

The electron microscope has revealed the ultrastructures within the physical basis of life called protoplasm. The biologist has borrowed tools and techniques from the physicist and the chemist and is exploring the activities within protoplasm on the molecular level as well as on the submolecular level. Almost certainly the heritable characteristics of living things are passed from one generation to the next encoded in the structure of DNA (deoxyribonucleic acid) molecules. How does this encoded message bring about the development of a bird, or a reptile, or a man from a single fertilized egg cell?

The space age has brought new problems and new questions. How can man be supplied with the necessary food, water, and oxygen during sustained flights into outer space beyond the reaches of gravity? Machine and industrial wastes threaten life with air and water pollution.

Paul Weiss has written: "This is the century of the biological sciences. In the life sciences analytical understanding is little more than rudimentary, unifying concepts are still scarce, and many fundamental principles remain to be discovered."

See also MEDICINE.

Bibliography: G. A. SARTON, *A Guide to the History of Science* (Waltham, Mass. 1952); Sarton v.1. A. N. WHITEHEAD, *Science and the Modern World* (New York 1925). L. THORNDIKE, *Science and Thought in the Fifteenth Century* (New York 1929); Thorndike. E. NORDENSKIÖLD, *The History of Biology* (new ed. New York 1935). ARISTOTLE, *Works*, tr. W. D. ROSS, 12 v. (Oxford 1908–52) v.4 *Biological Treatises*. E. RÁDL, *History of Biological Theories*, tr. E. J. HATFIELD (London 1930). C. J. SINGER, *Greek Biology and Greek Medicine* (Oxford 1922); *History of Biology to about the Year 1900* (3d ed. rev. New York 1959). F. J. COLE, *History of Comparative Anatomy* (London 1944). **Illustration credits:** Philadelphia Museum of Art.

[P. STOKELY]

BIOLOGY, II (CURRENT STATUS)

The biological sciences from their beginnings were considered to be areas of investigation quite distinct and separate from the other natural sciences, notably chemistry and physics. Two only incompletely separate classes of reasons can be cited for this distinction. Before the natural sciences became separated from natural philosophy, the conviction that the living was essentially different in the philosophical sense from the nonliving supported the separation of biology from its kindred growing sciences. Even apart from philosophical considerations, the empirical data accumulated by observation of living things, whether this observation was systematic or casual, also supported the distinction between living and nonliving. It is not difficult to summarize what must have been, on the basis of observation, the main reasons for separating the living from the nonliving as objects of systematic study. Living things are markedly unstable and variable—they move, they grow, they change—whereas the nonliving are relatively immutable and stable. Living things further undergo such changes in a cyclic, orderly pattern within a time span short enough to be readily observed by man. The cycle of growth, the cycle of reproduction, the cycle of birth to death, the cycle of stimulus and its orderly response in durations less than, or roughly equal to, the life span of man makes of the living thing something unique. These changes are different from the apparently spontaneous changes occurring in the rest of nature and are distinctly different from the slow, drawn-out changes one associates with other natural phenomena. Finally, the similarity of the cycles in other living things to the cycles of man's own experience has always brought living things into a real or at least a postulated kinship to man. Since man so obviously is different from the nonliving, other living things must be too.

Development of Theory. This inherent notion that the living, even simply on empirical, nonphilosophic terms, is significantly different from the nonliving has been responsible from the beginning of biological investigation for a framework of theory that has distinguished biology from the other natural sciences, and which still continues, on a reduced scale, to persist today.

It is erroneous to assume that the natural sciences, among them biology, are distinguished from other disciplines by the greater objectivity of the former. This is not so today, nor has it been so in the past. Although the natural sciences deal more than other disciplines with objects that can be delineated with some precision, and although the gathering of data and the making of observations does have logical primacy over interpretation, i.e., the fashioning of an explanation from the accumulated observations, the biologist has never really separated the two. There is no such thing in biology, at any time in its history, as an observation without a concurrent interpretation. The interpretation, furthermore, may be as much colored by the biologist's general (including nonbiological) background as by the biological facts with which he is immediately concerned. Thus *Aristotle, who did so extensive an amount of fundamental biological investigation on the development of a number of animals, notably the chick, cast his remarkably sound observations in terms of his philosophical system. He saw in the egg the material cause for the new organism, while for him the sperm was the "form." This extension of philosophical ideas to the physical entities involved in reproduction persisted for a remarkably long time, and overtones of it can be found even in modern biology. Immediate consequences of this mode of thinking were notions such as the immutable stability of biological species, which constituted in biology the main conceptual barrier to theories of *evolution.

It was Aristotle too who gave force to a postulate of *Empedocles that in development the heart is the first organ formed; but for Aristotle it was also first in conceptual importance, from which followed a variety of ideas on the heart as the seat of the soul and the blood as the carrier of its vital spirits. Notions such as these served not only to keep the study of living things distinct from studies of the nonliving but eventually led to a variety of theories on the cycle of change in living systems. These theories reflected differing philosophical positions as applied to biological data and can, without too much violence, be reduced to two classes: those dealing with *preformation as opposed to *epigenesis and those dealing with one or another form of *vitalism as fundamental to the living thing. The casting of empirical data in a philosophical framework was not limited to the early stages in the development of biology; the history of astronomy bears witness to the struggle to preserve circular motion of heavenly bodies on the basis of just such a philosophical presupposition.

It would appear that Aristotle and, some 20 centuries later, W. *Harvey were the most prominent of the relatively few students of the living who in that span spoke strongly for epigenesis. Aristotle, with his insistence on knowledge through a hierarchy of causes, necessarily maintained that the changes observed during development in living things were indeed cyclic, that is, they consisted of a series of events related to each other as cause and effect and resulted eventually in the new organism. This is the fundamental tenet of epigenesis—the formation in every reproductive cycle of the organism *de novo.* Harvey defended very much the same position: "All . . . parts are not constituted at once, but successively and in order" (1651, *Exercitatione de generatione animalium*). The interesting contrast, however, between Harvey and Aristotle is that for Aristotle the concept of epigenesis was in effect a universal one, applicable a priori without question to all embryological development; for Harvey it was a generalization, applicable in some instances but not extensible to others without observational evidence to support such extension. Thus for some forms he suggests a "making entire at once." Harvey was not inclined to consider the microscope as more than a curiosity, and his ambivalent position may be attributed to a lack of refined microscopic evidence to support epigenesis in all cases. But the more important point here is the clear-cut indication of a changing attitude in patterns of thought among biologists. The idea that a biologist, a scientist, deals with generalizations, that is, with symbols into which are compressed multitudes of concrete observations, rather than universals, arrived at by stripping away the concrete, is one that is fundamental to science, including biology, today.

Preformation. The opposed position of preformation seems to have antedated Aristotle and to have held sway until the middle of the 18th century. Preformation would seem to be in biology a reflection of the difficulty the early philosophies encountered in reconciling change and stability. Preformation is really an escape from the necessity of explaining how from a multitude of diverse, sequential events a single, whole organism could arise and how this transition from diversity to a single whole could be repeated with such rigor innumerable times. Preformation simply asserted that all the diverse parts of the adult existed preformed in the egg or sperm and that development therefore was an expansion, a rendering visible of what was already there in miniature, without any really significant series of steplike transformations. Preformation logically would seem to lead to absurd conclusions and indeed was extended into the ridiculous by many biologists of the 17th and 18th centuries. Thus A. Vallisnieri (1661–1730) speculated that not only the whole human race but all human parasites must have existed preformed in the ovaries of Eve. Despite its logical inconsistency, preformation survived for a surprisingly long time, due in part to what seemed to be sound observations in support of it and due also to its apparent conceptual necessity.

M. *Malpighi in 1673, using the microscope, examined what he thought to be an unincubated egg and described the existence, in miniature, of what seemed to be preformed parts of the adult fowl. Although Malpighi himself did not use the term preformation in his explanation of his observations, his work, plus the fact that it was done with a new, marvelous tool, overrode any reservations he might have had and constituted scientific support for the preformationist point of view. G. *Leibniz seems to have adhered to preformation both philosophically and biologically, since it appeared on both counts more consistent with the idea of immutability of species. One can also find a number of attempts purporting to reconcile preformation with Cartesian mechanism, since the living machine, if it is that, must be the machine from its beginning. On the biological level Malpighi's observations made it easier for other early microscopists to interpret what they saw along preformationist lines. Thus N. Hartsoeker (1694) and others were able to provide the biologists of this period with drawings of a complete "homunculus" (miniature man) they claimed to have seen in the human sperm with the aid of the microscope.

The controversy involving epigenesis and preformation provides at this point another example of the manner in which observations made scientifically can be fitted into existing preconceptions about what they should tell us.

Charles Bonnet (1720–93), an eminent biologist of his time, was aware that the evidence of the microscope did not support the part-to-part correspondence in miniature of the early embryo to the adult. He nevertheless felt constrained to support preformation. He therefore proposed that the rudiments of the organs, instead of being preformed in their adult positions and relations to each other, were distributed in the egg as organic points that had to undergo a great deal of spatial rearrangement and recombination to assume their final adult form. Preformation therefore was saved, and at the same time the lack of structural resemblance between the embryo and the adult was explained away. The fact that there was no way, observational or experimental, to demonstrate the actual existence of such organic points or seeds of the actual adult structures in the egg seems not to have caused Bonnet himself or his fellow preformationists any difficulty. Indeed, Bonnet considered his formulation to be a happy one precisely for this reason, and he describes it as "a most striking victory of reason over the senses." This fundamentally alogical position of Bonnet has had its recent counterpart in Lysenko's formulations in genetics. Russian genetics fitted observations into Michurin's concepts of the transmission of acquired characteristics and, like Bonnet's ideas, suffered from a basically alogical pattern of reasoning.

Epigenesis. Caspar Friedrich Wolff (1733–94) is generally credited with providing both the conceptual and the observational basis for the overthrow of preformation in biology. Wolff adduced as evidence the fact that the primordia of leaves are basically like the primordia of flower parts and that both come from plant cells that are alike in their lack of any visible specialization. He extended the same reasoning, on the basis of evidence, to animal development, maintaining that the egg cell, like the early cells in plants, is unspecialized and homogeneous. For him any explanation of development had to be in terms of an ordered origin of diversity from nondiversity rather than in terms of enlargement or relocation of already existing adult structures. The latter preformationist explanation was for Wolff no explanation at all but rather a denial of development. It would be too much to say that Wolff singlehandedly overthrew preformation. His contributions came at a time when the general outlook in the biological sciences, as well as in philosophy, was undergoing a transformation. The accumulated evidence by this time, as a result of extensive applications of the microscope, that change was real in the cycle of living things made the notion of development by means of change, or epigenesis, more palatable. This concern with change, with instability, was beginning to be reflected also in philosophical systems. The atmosphere generated by I. *Kant, with the limitations it set on knowledge and with its questioning of absolutes, made it possible for Wolff's ideas to grow. Kant had great impact in this period in fostering a distrust of reason. For the scientist, Kant's position became, by an interesting kind of inversion, a defense of reason. For if one could not really come to know anything about living things in the sense that the knowing corresponded to the outside reality, then one dealing more and more with the concrete, observable aspects of the living, as biologists were beginning to do, need not concern himself with philosophical justification for his deductions and theoretical constructs but could be content with a solely logical justification. If the patterns of relations into which the observations were cast were consistent and if the observations and experimental results could be duplicated, this was beginning to be, and in large measure still is, enough. Thus the growing sciences were slowly but surely separating themselves from any formal reliance on specific philosophical systems. The ascendancy of epigenetic rather than preformationist approaches in biology therefore was as much a product of the intellectual environment of the time as it was Wolff's creation.

One last point is worth making concerning Wolff's contribution to the ideas on epigenesis and preformation. Wolff found no difficulty in claiming that in terms of epigenetic development there was no difference between plants and animals. One as well as the other began from an unspecialized cell from which the organism developed progressively. Indeed, Wolff often extended findings in plant forms to animals and vice versa. This is an overt example of the application of a principle that has served as the underpinning of much, indeed most, of the biological investigation and interpretation from the time of Wolff to the present, and which was almost a necessary prelude to theories of evolution. But even this idea, which has been so effective in binding together most of the information biology has uncovered over the years, was in a sense a substitution. With the change in the intellectual atmosphere mentioned above, one of the pillars by which the growing science of biology supported itself distinct from the other natural sciences, namely, the existence of and immutability of species in the living world, began to crumble. The idea that species were mutable and that species itself was a category useful in breaking up a continuous spectrum of living things into a series of workable units had begun to be defended. Consequently the "all life is one" principle had among its other benefits the virtue of at least binding the living world into a whole, distinct from the nonliving, even if such a separation could not much longer be maintained biologically on the basis of the Aristotelian specific form for specific species.

Two more points need to be made concerning the preformationist-epigenesis controversy. The first is that the prevalence of the preformationist point of view was the reason for the form of the early ideas in genetics. For example, C. Darwin's notion of pangenes, particles contributed from every part of the parent to the fertilized egg, is a direct descendant of preformationism. The second point is that preformation was really not demonstrated as biologically impossible until the work of E. Geoffroy St. Hilaire (1772–1844), who under experimental conditions succeeded in producing abnormal forms out of chick embryos and pointed out that such monsters could not have been the consequence of preformation. The same, he suggested, must apply to normal developmental patterns. Better known for supplying equally damning evidence against preformation is Hans Driesch (1892), who demonstrated in many forms that the first few cells produced at the beginning of development could be separated and could, in some instances, give rise to perfectly normal organisms. Preformation obviously was helpless before such a finding.

Vitalism. The mention of Driesch serves as a convenient transition to a second aspect of the early formulation of theory in biology that was mentioned earlier: the postulation in biological explanations of vitalism in one form or another, for Driesch was one of the leading advocates of a vitalistic position. He was, in his own way, following Aristotle, whose ideas on epigenesis finally came to hold the field over preformation, since Aristotle was himself a vitalist.

Although Aristotle explained development in terms of linked causes, this was not yet enough. He postulated for the "soul" an active role in controlling the mechanical forces and processes of development. This idea persisted until after Driesch, until the rise of experimental embryology, and until the erection of biology as a discipline quite distinct from philosophy was achieved. The crux of the difficulty, and the reason for the persistence of vitalistic theories in biology, would seem to be a failure to distinguish between philosophical vitalism and biological vitalism. There arose, both among philosophers and biologists, either the notion that the essence and the vital principle or "soul" of living things were distinct (the one the philosophical principle of being, the other a supraphysical entity directly, mechanically responsible for the activities of living things) or the notion that, even though essence and vital principle were one, the same kind of immediate, mechanical control over the chemical processes of living things was exercised by the vital principle.

Vitalistic explanations took a variety of forms. Two are perhaps worthy of brief consideration. K. E. von Baer (1792–1876), who was an eminent embryologist, is often spoken of as the father of the science. He further developed Wolff's idea of development in all animal forms from three generalized germ layers that appeared to have specificity, i.e., the same germ layer gave rise by serial specialization to the same structures and organ systems in all animals. Despite this rather elegant evidence for epigenesis, which, with minor modifications, holds sway generally in embryology today, von Baer did not consider development to be a succession of cause-effect events but a set of conditions, controlled and regulated by the essential nature of the developing embryo. Thus some vital force is the agency by which the developing embryo is made physically to do what it must to reach maturity.

Driesch much more patently embraced biological vitalism. His experiments with embryos, alluded to earlier, in which some forms were able to develop complete individuals from every one of the early few cells artificially separated one from the other while other forms produced monsters or nothing at all, seemed to Driesch to defy any explanations along rigorously physical lines. There must be "entelechies," supraphysical entities, responsible for the physical events taking place in development, entities that are fundamentally fickle, sometimes acting one way, sometimes another. It has since been shown that the apparently haphazard behavior of developing organisms that Driesch was able to induce can be explained as the result of physical causes of which Driesch was not aware.

The overthrow of biological vitalism came about more perhaps through the rapid crystallization of methodology in biology than through anything else. Biologists by the time of Driesch had accepted as their position very much the same point of view as that already established in physics and chemistry. The description of the physical, concrete properties of the organism by measurement, observation, and experiment became the established method. On the one hand, the phenomena the biologist was interested in were more and more found to follow consistently the laws already discovered for the nonliving world; on the other, the admission of an "entelechy," or a vital principle operating specifically at the level of the physical and mechanical to which biology was restricting itself, carried with it the assumption that the laws of physics and chemistry were not laws in living systems, for they could presumably be contravened by the entelechy. The latter position was distasteful both because no evidence could be adduced to support it and because it made the construction of coherent systems of explanations in terms of chemistry and physics impossible in biology. Echoes of biological vitalism can still occasionally be heard. It is sometimes alleged, for example, that even if biology succeeds in explaining every last molecule and process in the living systems along physical and chemical lines there will be a residue that biology will not be able to reach. The fallacy here is that the question is contradictory. Biology has set as its goal specifically the study of the physics and chemistry of living systems. For the biologist as a biologist, not necessarily as a person, anything beyond these limits is moot. Quite clearly, if biology restricts itself to the elucidation of the physical phenomena of living systems, it is not concerned formally with more.

Theory in Modern Biology. It might be well, in the transition to a consideration of modern biology, to summarize the main characteristics of early biology from which modern biology has departed. The early integral association of biology with specific philosophical systems no longer exists, for biology has chosen to concern itself formally solely with the physical, sensible properties of living things. The assumption in the older biology that its aim was the understanding of nature as it really is, is largely by-passed in modern biology, for the assumption carries with it epistemological implications with which modern biology is not explicitly concerned. The gradual rise, conceptually as well as on the basis of experiment, of epigenesis served to foster the two departures mentioned, for epigenesis in its full development eliminated biological vitalism and contributed to the limited approach modern biology has made its own.

It remains but to transfer the ideas that have so far been mentioned to the modern science of biology. Perhaps the most fundamental of these is the elimination from modern biology of any explicit concern with fundamental epistemological questions. One need only cite James B. Conant's definition of modern science in *Modern Science and Modern Man* to make the point: "I venture to define science as a series of interconnected concepts and conceptual schemes arising from experiment and observation and fruitful of further experiment and observation." The ideas expressed in the definition are repeated, in one form or another, by a wide variety of modern scientists and biologists and serve accurately to emphasize a number of facets characteristic of modern biology. Examination of the position announced in the definition makes the following conclusions possible concerning modern biology: (1) The criterion for the validity of its findings rests not on any philosophical concept of what is true, least of all on any realist notions of conformity between knowledge and the known outside reality; it rests rather on the duplicability, via experiment and observation, of the data arrived at from sense impressions, without questioning the source of these impressions. (2) Modern biology therefore uses as the raw material for its activities repeatable, observable, and measurable characteristics of the living thing. It ignores all other characteristics. It can do nothing, for example, with an absolutely unique bit of sense data about a living thing, for, as indicated earlier, modern biology is concerned with the construction of generalizations into which are compressed multitudes of repeated observations about the concrete aspects of the living thing. For such operations duplicability is the *sine qua non*. (3) Modern biology is well aware that it is less concerned with the correspondence of its findings to existing living things (this question it simply bypasses as impertinent) than it is with the congruity of its concepts among themselves. Since this is so, it follows that the modern biologist is aware also that his concepts concerning the living will be colored by his own subjective approach to his field. An example may serve to illustrate the point. Modern biology seeks a coherent system of concepts by which currently even the highly complex molecular populations of living systems can be reduced to coherent conceptual formulations. Two approaches are possible: one, extensively favored until quite recently and still the majority point of view, seeks some hierarchy, some primacy among the many chemical reactions everlastingly occurring in living systems. It seeks explanations in terms of controlling mechanisms. It interprets, for example, the recent knowledge on the DNA molecule and its transfer of information to the rest of the organism as the very foundation, the determiner, of the kinds of processes specific to different kinds of living things (*see* NUCLEIC ACIDS). A more recent approach would maintain that all conceptual systems built around control and coordination are largely the result of hindsight and are analogical. This second approach would maintain that what have been interpreted up to now as coordinated, self-regulating activities can just as readily be conceived of as basically random reactions occurring in a huge population of molecules of given kinds and numbers and therefore resulting in a statistically predictable pattern of events that can analogously be interpreted as "controlled," "orderly," or "directed." The processes occurring in living things today would be, in other words, as random as the processes by which life first appeared on earth, arising simply from the exigencies of specific kinds of matter at a given time and place. It is not the object here to argue the merits of either position but simply to stress that since the construction of theory in modern biology is guided more by congruity of concepts than by conformity to objects either position can be and is defended and that the formulation of theory in modern biology encompasses more than simply the collected information itself.

Despite the close relation to physics and chemistry that has been stressed for modern biology, modern biologists are not inclined to view biology as simply an extension of physics and chemistry. Rather, the position is that the living world exhibits a unique organization of physical and chemical properties and that biology can legitimately be maintained as the discipline dealing specifically with the unique organizational aspects of physical and chemical systems as these are exhibited in living things.

It must finally be pointed out that although modern biology, by its rigorous, self-imposed limitations to the quantifiable and observable of living things, has had remarkable success in building an imposing conceptual structure of the living world, some dissatisfaction with its modern approaches is from time to time expressed. The main point of most of the objections is simply that even if science is limited to operations upon sense data, its limitation to the quantifiable of such data obviously overlooks the qualitative aspects. A feeling therefore persists that the boundaries of sciences must somehow be enlarged if science is not to become an arcane and esoteric discipline. Perhaps the best-known of modern scientists suggesting such a fundamental change in the methodology of modern science is P. *Teilhard de Chardin, with his plea for the incorporation of all phenomonological experience in the raw material of the sciences. Although such an extension of the limits of biology has intrigued and fascinated many, there is at present much skepticism concerning the feasibility of such a change.

Bibliography: L. VON BERTALANFFY, *Modern Theories of Development,* tr. and ed. J. H. WOODGER (New York 1962); *Problems of Life* (New York 1952). J. B. CONANT, *Modern Science and Modern Man* (New York 1952). E. NAGEL, *The Structure of Science* (New York 1961). E. NORDENSKIÖLD, *The History of Biology,* tr. L. B. EYRE (new ed. New York 1935). K. R. POPPER, *The Logic of Scientific Discovery,* tr. J. and L. FREED (New York 1959). P. P. WIENER and A. NOLAND, eds., *Roots of Scientific Thought* (New York 1957). W. P. D. WIGHTMAN, *The Growth of Scientific Ideas* (New Haven 1951). B. H. WILLIER et al., eds., *Analysis of Development* (Philadelphia 1955).

[H. E. WACHOWSKI]

BIONDO, FLAVIO, humanist, historian of Roman antiquity, and secretary at the papal Curia; b. Forlì, Italy, November or December 1392; d. Rome, June 4, 1463. He usually signed himself Blondus. His literary education seems to have included little Greek, for he relied on translations of Greek literature. He was secretary for divers people in many places in north Italy (1420–32), entered the papal service by early 1433, and, despite the fact that he was not trained in Canon Law, served as scriptor of apostolic letters under Popes Eugene IV, Nicholas V (except 1449–53), Callistus III, and Pius II from 1436 to his death. In 1423 he married, and by 1440 he was the father of 10 children, one of whom, Gaspar (d. 1493), succeeded him as scriptor. Biondo lived and died poor, seeking no riches. His scholarly, methodical work contributed more to knowledge of the Middle Ages than that of his Renaissance colleagues, who disparaged his unrhetorical style. His *Historiarum ab inclinatione Romanorum imperii decades,* which imitates Livy, was intended as the contemporary history (1401–40) of Decades III and IV and was completed in 1453; this was supplemented with Decades I and II (410–1400), the whole being published in Venice in 1483. Both his *Roma instaurata,*

a descriptive catalogue of ruins and monuments of Rome, completed in 1446 and published in 1471, and his *Italia illustrata,* an archeological and historical account of Italy from the Alps to Salerno, completed in 1453 and published in Rome in 1474, offer valuable data on monuments extant in 15th-century Italy. *Romae triumphantis libri X* (1460), a manual of Roman antiquities, sacerdotal and private rather than public, is the basis for much subsequent antiquarian interest. Biondo is important in the development of the idea of a "Middle" Age inasmuch as he thought the barbarian invasions ushered in a new period. He held that the Rome of the popes was at least the equal of that of the emperors and that Christians should unite against the new barbarians, the Turks, who took Constantinople in 1453. Biondo wrote other lesser works; many of his letters are lost.

Bibliography: *Opera omnia* (Basel 1531); *Scritti inediti e rari di Biondo Flavio,* ed. B. NOGARA (StTest 48; 1927). A. MASIUS, *Flavio Biondo, sein Leben und seine Werke* (Leipzig 1897). B. NOGARA, EncIt 7:56. L. MOHLER, LexThK[1] 2:363–364. F. BAIX, DHGE 8:1513–19.

[E. P. COLBERT]

BIRETTA, a square cap with three peaks or ridges on top. A pompon in the center usually ornaments it. Most diocesan clergy wear it today. By the Middle Ages, the hood of the cope was rarely worn because it had

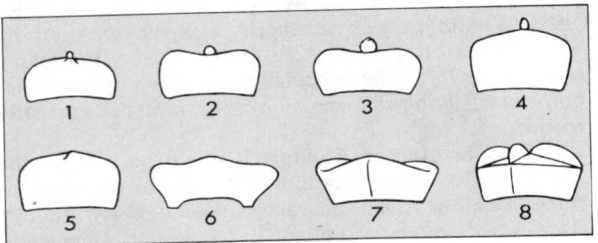

Evolution of the biretta.

become tight-fitting and richly ornamented. Some other protection from the cold was necessary for the head of the tonsured cleric. A skullcap was used, but more often a cap of soft material was worn with a tuft on top by which it could be removed easily. This cap was known as a pileus or *birettum.* By the 16th century, the *birettum* was reinforced with an interlining of stiff canvas to give it a neat appearance. The mortarboard used in academic dress seems to be a flattened *birettum* and skullcap combined.

Bibliography: A. A. KING, *Liturgy of the Roman Church* (Milwaukee 1957). H. NORRIS, *Church Vestments: Their Origin and Development* (New York 1950).

[M. MC CANCE]

BIRINUS, ST., bishop, apostle of the West Saxons; d. between 648 and 650 (feast, Dec. 3 or Dec. 5). He was commissioned by Pope *Honorius I as a missionary to England and consecrated by Asterius, Archbishop of Milan (not Genoa as is commonly said). A contemporary of *Aidan of Lindisfarne, Birinus arrived in Wessex c. 634. He originally intended to work in the remoter parts of England, but finding the West Saxons still heathen he stayed there. He baptized the West Saxon King Cynegils in the presence of King *Oswald, the Christian overlord of Britain, and was given Dorchester for his see (635). His patron King Cynegils died in 643, and his successor Cenwalh lapsed into paganism but was soon sent into exile. Cenwalh was finally converted and restored c. 648, and when Birinus died about a year later, the Church was securely established in Wessex.

Bibliography: Bede, *Eccl. hist.* 3, ed. C. PLUMMER (Oxford 1956). J. E. FIELD, *St. Berin: The Apostle of Wessex* (London 1902). T. VARLEY, *St. Birinus and Wessex* (Winchester, Eng. 1934). F. M. STENTON, *Anglo-Saxon England* (2d ed. Oxford 1947) 102, 117–118. R. GRAHAM, DHGE 8:1530–31.

[E. JOHN]

BIRMINGHAM, ARCHDIOCESE OF (BIRMINGHAMIENSIS),

a diocese since 1850 and a metropolitanate since 1911, in Warwickshire, central England. In 1964 it had 208 parishes, 393 secular and 275 religious priests, 476 men in 28 religious houses, 1,517 women in 101 convents, and 309,500 Catholics in a population of 4,635,500; it is 3,373 square miles in area. Its two suffragans, which had 308 secular and 239 religious priests, 1,150 sisters, and 278,000 Catholics in a population of 3,422,000, were Clifton and Shrewsbury, both created in 1850. In 1965 the suffragan Plymouth became suffragan to *Southwark. The city of Birmingham is second to London in population in the United Kingdom. Mentioned in Domesday Book (1086) and a market in 1166, it became industrial in the 16th century and grew quickly after 1700; it was incorporated as a town in 1838 and as a city in 1889. The university was chartered in 1900.

Birmingham was the seat of the Vicariate of the Midland District (1688–1850), whose most notable vicar was Bp. John *Milner (d. 1826), until it became a see with the restoration of the Catholic hierarchy. The first bishop was the distinguished W. B. *Ullathorne (1850–88). John Henry *Newman, who lived at the Oratory of St. Philip Neri in Birmingham, preached the sermon on the Second Spring in the diocesan seminary at Oscott at the first provincial synod of *Westminster (1852). In 1916 *Cardiff and Menevia were withdrawn from the province of Birmingham to constitute a province for *Wales. In 1962 the archdiocese registered 13,118 baptisms, 4,470 marriages, and 1,166 conversions; it had 252 schools with 59,582 pupils. St. Chad Cathedral, built after plans by A. W. *Pugin and consecrated in 1841, was the first Catholic cathedral built in England after the Reformation. The extensive archdiocese comprises the Counties of Warwick, Stafford, Worcester, and Oxford.

Bibliography: D. MATHEW, DHGE 8:1356–57. *Catholic Directory* (London 1838–), annual. *Catholic Directory of the Archdiocese of Birmingham* (London 1937–).

[G. CULKIN]

BIRTH CONTROL, U.S. LAW OF

Both Federal and state legislation against contraception was enacted in the second half of the 19th century. Militant reformers under the leadership of Anthony Comstock and the Society for the Suppression of Vice were the main force behind these enactments.

Federal Legislation. The Federal government prohibits the use of the mails or interstate carriers for the transportation of contraceptive articles or information on where to buy or how to use them (18 U.S.C.A. 1461–62). Federal law also forbids the importation of contraceptives from abroad (19 U.S.C.A. 1305). When read literally, these restrictions appear quite extensive, and many attempts were made in Congress to modify them. But where legislative action failed, judicial interpretation succeeded. The Federal courts in the 1930s ruled that information on contraception need not be considered "obscene" [*U.S. v. One Book Entitled "Contraception,"* 51 F. 2d 525 (1931)]. More significantly, the Federal courts determined that the statutes proscribe an intent to use contraceptive articles for illegal or immoral purposes but do not forbid an intent to use them for the health or welfare of married couples [*Davis v. U.S.,* 62 F. 2d 473 (1933) and *U.S. v. One Package,* 86 F. 2d 737 (1936)]. In the latter case, Judge Augustus Hand argued that Congress did not intend to prohibit the distribution of contraceptives "which might intelligently be employed by conscientious and competent physicians for the purpose of saving life or promoting the welfare of their patients" (p. 739). As judicially interpreted, therefore, Federal law today effects no practical restraint on the distribution of contraceptives to married couples.

State Legislation. State laws vary from total freedom to total prohibition of contraceptive practices. Twenty states (Alabama, Alaska, Florida, Georgia, Illinois, Maryland, New Hampshire, New Mexico, North Carolina, North Dakota, Oklahoma, Rhode Island, South Carolina, South Dakota, Tennessee, Texas, Utah, Vermont, Virginia, and West Virginia) and the District of Columbia have no legislation at all.

Sixteen states (Arkansas, Colorado, Delaware, Idaho, Indiana, Iowa, Kentucky, Minnesota, Missouri, Montana, Nevada, New Jersey ["without just cause"], New York, Ohio, Oregon, and Wyoming) prohibit the sale and advertisement of contraceptives but exempt doctors, pharmacists, or special licensees. Wisconsin bans the sale of contraceptives to minors, sale from slot machines, and all advertisement of contraceptives.

Five states (Connecticut, Kansas, Massachusetts, Mississippi, and Nebraska) prohibit absolutely the sale and advertisement of contraceptives. Eight states (Arizona, California, Hawaii, Louisiana, Maine, Michigan, Pennsylvania, and Washington) restrict or prohibit only the advertisement of contraceptives. However, fifteen states with restrictive legislation (Arkansas, Colorado, Idaho, Indiana, Iowa, Kansas, Kentucky, Missouri, Montana, Nebraska, New York, Ohio, Oklahoma, Pennsylvania, and Wyoming) allow advertisements in medical journals and textbooks. One state, Connecticut, prohibited the use of contraceptives till 1965.

Of the five states whose statutes on their face prohibit absolutely the sale and advertisement of contraceptives, only in Massachusetts and Connecticut do the laws have practical effect. Contraceptives, however, are accessible outside the latter two states, and even within their boundaries the prescription, sale, and use of contraceptives are permitted for prophylactic purposes. Moreover, the authorities have made no attempt to enforce the laws except with respect to birth-control clinics. The only practical effect of existing legislation against contraception, therefore, is to prevent the operation of birth-control clinics in Massachusetts and Connecticut. Repeated efforts in the state legislatures to modify these laws have all failed. Two referendums in Massachusetts (1942 and 1948) also failed to change the law of that state.

Constitutional Objection. Only the application of the Massachusetts and Connecticut statutes to married couples has been challenged as violating the U.S. Constitution. Opponents claim that the 14th Amendment protects the right of married couples to sexual relations at the time and manner of their choosing. In 1938 a Massachusetts physician appealed to the U.S. Supreme Court from a decision of the state supreme court that rejected his claim to a privilege to counsel married patients on contraception. The Court dismissed the appeal in a *per curiam* opinion "for want of a substantial federal question" [*Gardner v. Massachusetts,* 305 U.S. 559 (1938)]. In 1961 a Connecticut doctor and his patients appealed in vain against a decision of the state supreme court sustaining the statute prohibiting use of contraceptives by married couples and their prescription by physicians. In 1965 the Court declared the statute unconstitutional (*Griswold et al. v. Connecticut,* 85 S.C.R. 1678).

Bibliography: R. J. REGAN, *American Pluralism and the Catholic Conscience* (New York 1963). N. ST. JOHN-STEVAS, *Life, Death and the Law* (Bloomington, Ind. 1961).

[R. J. REGAN]

BIRTH CONTROL MOVEMENT

The term birth control is somewhat ambiguous. Essentially it denotes voluntary control of the reproductive effect of sexual intercourse. Popular usage, however, usually refers not only to the intentional limitation of family size or the spacing of births through any of the several possible means, including *continence or periodic abstinence (*rhythm), but tends to restrict the meaning to the practice of *contraception to achieve desired results. Margaret Sanger (1883–) claims to have coined the expression "birth control" in 1914 when she and several friends were selecting a name for a national organization to promote family limitation in the U.S. Subsequently the term "planned parenthood" came to be preferred, and in 1942 the Birth Control Federation of America was renamed the Planned Parenthood Federation of America in order to emphasize the avowed positive objective of proponents of birth control. This is defined as the utilization of medical knowledge for the procreation of the number of children desired by a couple at the intervals desired. In this way attention to the treatment of infertility is also included.

In a much broader sense, reference may be made to limits upon the growth of *population in a given society that may or may not involve intentional curbs upon fertility. In some primitive societies, for example, fertility was reduced unintentionally by taboos forbidding sexual intercourse at certain times. During the Middle Ages, the large number of celibates in holy orders or religious life undoubtedly had some limiting effect upon European birth rates. Late marriages have similar consequences in contemporary Ireland. On the other hand, deliberate control of family size has a long history. It was attempted among primitives and among ancient peoples mainly by the practices of *coitus interruptus,* *abortion, and *infanticide; however, the Egyptians and the Greeks and Romans also attempted to prevent conception by the use of potions or, more effectively, by concoctions made from herbs, honey, gum, and oils that were inserted into the vagina. Islamic medicine developed a variety of contraceptive techniques, partly on the basis of knowledge received from Greek sources. There was little investigation of the subject in Christian Europe, however, until after Gabriel *Fallopius (1523–62) provided the first published account of a linen condom in his treatise on venereal disease, *De Morbico Gallico* (1564). Sheaths of various sorts had been used for protective purposes even among some primitive peoples, and by the 18th century they were used to prevent conception; but contraception was still associated exclusively with immorality and vice. In general, therefore, it can be said that "prior to late modern times, say 1800 in western civilizations, much later in eastern civilizations, the numbers of a people on a given territory have been determined by various factors affecting natality and mortality, independently of attempts artificially to control conception" [N. E. Himes, *Medical History of Contraception* (Baltimore 1936) 168].

Origin and Growth of the Movement. The earliest phase of the modern birth control movement is too obscure to be traced in any detail. An unorganized but strong tendency to limit family size seems to have begun in France during the 18th century. The decline in fertility that ensued became evident throughout western Europe after 1875. Except in Ireland, the critical factor in this development was probably the invention of effective contraceptive devices, especially a condom made of animal membranes (until the vulcanization of rubber in 1843–44), and later the diaphragm. The decline in birth rates began among the upper classes and in urban centers where knowledge of these devices spread most rapidly. The evidence points also, however, to continuing recourse to abortion and to an increase in the practice of *coitus interruptus* (which continues to be used by millions of couples in Europe and the U.S. in the 20th century).

Among the intellectual progenitors of the organized movement for birth control were the Marquis de *Condorcet (1743–94), the influential champion of the perfectibility of humanity; the utilitarian Jeremy *Bentham (1748–1832), who in 1797 advocated the use of the sponge as a means of lowering English poor rates; the philosophical radical James *Mill (1773–1836), who also stressed family limitation as a means of reducing poverty; and the anarchistic William Godwin (1756–1836), like Condorcet a believer in extreme notions of social progress. Godwin, perceiving a threat to his views in the pessimistic conclusions of the English clergyman and economist Thomas Robert *Malthus (1766–1834), attempted ineffectually to refute the latter's *Essay on the Principle of Population as It Affects the Future Improvement of Society* (1798), especially in defense of social reform. Others, however, found in the book an intellectual argument for birth control that Malthus himself did not intend and explicitly rejected. Malthus asserted that, when unchecked, population increases in a geometric ratio, while subsistence increases only in an arithmetic ratio. War, famine, pestilence, misery, and vice were, according to his analysis, the natural checks upon uncontrolled fertility. To these he added in a revised edition (1803) the proposal that "moral restraint," by which he meant postponement of marriage and strict continence before marriage, would offer an additional check. He rejected as immoral any destructive interference with the product of conception and all methods of birth control now popularly designated as artificial contraception.

Neo-Malthusian, Utopian, and Eugenicist Influences. It was Francis Place (1771–1854), a London tailor and labor leader and the father of 15 children, who was the real founder of the birth control movement in England. In his *Illustrations and Proofs of the Principle of Population* (1822) and in handbills distributed among workers (1823–26), he termed moral restraint an absurdity and defined a position in favor of contraceptive means of population control that came to be called neo-Malthusian. The English neo-Malthusians gained much of their knowledge of birth control techniques from French sources. Among the most resolute of Place's converts was the freethinker Richard Carlile (1790–1843), whose article "What is Love?" (1825), reprinted as *Every Woman's Book* (1826), dealt frankly —in fact, coarsely—with the social, economic, and medical aspects of birth control.

His introduction to this book led Robert Dale Owen (1801–77), who had accompanied his father in the establishment of New Harmony, Ind., to publish his *Moral Physiology* (1830), the first American treatise on birth control. Owen's associate in the publication of the New Harmony *Gazette* and its successor, the *Free Enquirer,* was Frances Wright (1795–1852), reputed as the first woman agitator for birth control. Charles Knowlton (1800–50) of Boston, who attempted to influence medical opinion in favor of the practice, was fined and jailed for his publication, at first anonymous, of *The Fruits of Philosophy* (1832). Apart from the efforts of these propagandists but also arousing popular interest was the utopian experiment of John Humphrey Noyes (1811–86), who instituted a combination of eugenic mating and free love, with conception control by *coitus reservatus;* his communal settlement was first established at Putney, Vt. (1842–47), and then moved to Oneida, N.Y. (1847–80) before mounting opposition to his activities prompted him to flee to Canada.

Views that attained considerable notoriety in England and elsewhere were advanced in a book, *Elements of Social Science* (1854), by George Drysdale, a physician, who maintained that only by contraception could society escape the "three primary social evils: poverty, prostitution, and celibacy." In 1861 Drysdale joined with Charles Bradlaugh (1833–91) in an abortive attempt to found a Malthusian League. Bradlaugh edited the *National Reformer* (London 1860–93), the most influential neo-Malthusian periodical of its time. Meanwhile, the neo-Malthusian thesis gained increasing, if more cautious, support in intellectual circles. Thus John Stuart *Mill (1806–73), who at 17 years of age had been involved in the distribution of Place's handbills, considered the morality of contraception to be a private matter and remarked in his *Principles of Political Economy* (1848) that the emancipation of women and "the increase of intelligence, of education, and of the love of independence among the working classes, must be attended with a corresponding growth of the good sense which manifests itself in prudent habits of conduct, and that population, therefore, will bear a gradually diminishing ratio to capital and employment" (4.7.3).

After 1865, neo-Malthusianism was supplemented by increasing attention to the alleged dysgenic effects of moral restraint when exercised by the "prudent" and "desirable" elements in society but not by the "swarms" of "sensual" lower-class people who continued to breed. This was emphasized by Sir Francis *Galton (1822–1911), the founder of *eugenics, and by William R. Greg (1809–81), from whose works Charles Darwin drew extensively in writing the chapter on "Natural Selection as Affecting Civilized Nations" in *The Descent of Man* (1871).

Early Growth and Organization. Between 1876 and 1878 there occurred in the U.S. and England legal proceedings in two cases that had far-reaching effects. In June 1876 the physician Edward Bliss Foote (1829–1906) was indicted in the U.S. District Court of New York for mailing a copy of his pamphlet *Words in Pearl* (*c.* 1860) to a Chicago decoy in violation of the Comstock law of 1873, which had closed the U.S. mails to contraceptive literature and devices and prohibited their importation from abroad and their transportation by common carriers in interstate commerce. Foote was convicted and fined. The following year in England, Bradlaugh and Annie Besant (1847–1933) set up a test case by organizing the Freethought Publishing Company to republish Knowlton's early pamphlets, already widely circulated in the country. Their conviction in a lower court was set aside by the High Court of Justice [*Bradlaugh v. R* (1878) 3 QBD 607], but the notoriety attending the trial increased enormously the circulation of the pamphlet, led to a renewed and successful effort to found the Malthusian League (1878), and diffused interest in contraceptive information in both England and the U.S. A decline in the British birth rate followed as an apparent result.

Charles R. Drysdale (1829–1907), a brother of George Drysdale, served as president of the Malthusian League from 1878 until his death. Annie Besant was the first secretary. The neo-Malthusian thesis was propagated through lectures, pamphlets, and a journal, *The Malthusian* (London 1879–1921). A medical branch of the League was established in the late 1870s, and in 1881 it used the occasion of the International Medical Congress held in London to call a meeting of British and foreign physicians for discussion of its interests. The League's first publicly distributed leaflet on birth control techniques appeared in 1913. By 1927 the League considered its work completed and it disbanded. Meanwhile, in 1921, Marie Stopes (1880–1958) organized the Society for Constructive Birth Control and Racial Progress to stress the medical and eugenic arguments for birth control rather than those based on classical economics, and set up the first birth control clinic in London. Later, the Family Planning Association, founded in 1930, became the principal birth control organization of England.

The international extension of the movement resulted in the opening of offices or clinics specializing in contraception—the first in Amsterdam about 1878—and in the organization of counterparts of the Malthusian League in Holland (1885), Germany (1889), France (1895), Bohemia (1901), Spain (1904), Brazil (1905), Belgium (1906), Cuba (1907), Switzerland (1908), Sweden (1911), Italy (1913), and Mexico (1918).

Development in the U.S. During the last quarter of the 19th century, American freethinkers such as Ezra Heywood (1829–93), Robert G. Ingersoll (1833–99), Emma Goldman (1869–1940), and Ben Reitman (1879–1942)—like Fanny Wright before them—advocated contraception in association with a variety of other reforms for which they pressed, e.g., woman suffrage, temperance, relaxed divorce laws, free love, and anarchism. Their significance, and that of their precursors, lay in preparing the way for the acceptance of utilitarian arguments emphasized by the birth control movement after the beginning of the 20th century.

Margaret Sanger. The name associated more than any other with the American movement is that of Margaret Sanger, who began a career of intense activity and publication in 1912 as a result of her experience in public health nursing on New York's lower East Side. She was little impressed by the neo-Malthusian approach of the English movement, but she was prompted to action in July 1912 by the death, following a second abortion, of a patient whose physician would not give her contraceptive advice. During the fall of 1913 she spent several months in Europe studying birth control techniques. Upon her return to the U.S. she inaugurated *The Woman Rebel,* a magazine that the Post Office Department declared unmailable after the appearance of the first issue. She was indicted for sending birth control propaganda through the mails but left for Europe on the eve of her trial, having first published surreptitiously a pamphlet, *Family Limitation* (1914), that has since been reprinted many times in several languages. Her indictment was quashed in 1916, before trial, allegedly at the instance of Pres. Woodrow Wilson, who was subjected to pressure from friends of the movement.

With Mary Ware Dennett (1872–1947) and others, Mrs. Sanger founded in 1914 the National Birth Control League, the first organization to promote the birth control movement in the U.S. It was reorganized during 1915 while she was abroad and she remained outside it thereafter. Under the leadership of Mrs. Dennett it was renamed the Voluntary Parenthood League in 1918 before its demise in 1925. Mrs. Sanger preferred direct action to the League's legislative approach in attacking state and federal obscenity statutes that restricted the progress of the movement. Thus in 1916 she opened the first birth control clinic in the U.S. in the Brownsville section of Brooklyn, N.Y., for which she was arrested, convicted, and sentenced to jail for 30 days. The movement not only gained greatly in publicity but, in sustaining her conviction, an appellate judge interpreted the state law in such a way as to exempt physicians from legal restrictions upon the dissemination of birth control information to married persons "for the cure or prevention of disease" [*People v. Sanger,* 222 N.Y. 192, 194–195 (1918), 118 N.E. 637 (1918)]. While Mrs. Sanger was in jail, in February 1917, an associate in the New York Birth Control League, Dr. Frederick Blossom, successfully launched her *Birth Control Review,* the movement's principal voice for more than 2 decades.

Organizational Growth. Mrs. Sanger organized and presided over the first major birth control conference in the U.S., held in New York City, Nov. 10–13, 1921. At the instigation of Abp. Patrick *Hayes, the police disbanded the closing session and jailed Mrs. Sanger for the night. The American Birth Control League was founded as the conference convened and, as its president, Mrs. Sanger embarked on a world tour in 1922, holding many meetings in Japan, China, and Hawaii. She organized international birth control conferences

at New York City in 1925 and Geneva, Switzerland, in 1927. She resigned as president and as editor of the *Review* in 1928 in order to form the National Committee on Federal Legislation for Birth Control and to give more time to the New York Birth Control Clinical Research Bureau that she had organized in 1923 with Dorothy Bocker. The Bureau was intended to perfect contraceptive techniques and to encourage medical support of the movement; it was directed by Hannah M. Stone (1894–1941) and, after her death, by her husband, Abraham Stone (1890–1959), until his death. In 1940 it became the Margaret Sanger Research Bureau, following the merger the previous year of its education department with the American Birth Control League to form the Birth Control Federation of America. The name of the latter was changed in 1942 to the Planned Parenthood Federation of America, and Mrs. Sanger was made honorary chairman. As the name suggests, it is a federation of organizations and their affiliated local committees. For example, the National Medical Council on Birth Control, founded in 1936, is integrated with the Federation.

In 1961 the Federation joined with the World Population Emergency Campaign, organized the previous year, to emphasize the interest of both groups in population problems both at home and abroad. Planned Parenthood—World Population, with headquarters in New York City, encourages and helps to finance research in contraceptive techniques and in the social, economic, and biological implications of human reproduction. It disseminates information about planned parenthood through conferences and the mass media as well as through its own publications and films. During 1964, according to its annual report, its 275 family planning centers in 138 major U.S. cities provided medical birth control services for 281,960 women (22 per cent more than in 1963); these centers offer contraceptive information and care, treatment of infertility, and marriage counseling.

International Organization. Mrs. Sanger emphasized the international expansion of the birth control movement throughout her career. During the winter of 1935–36 she visited China, Hawaii, and India, launching the movement in the last country with the establishment of 50 teaching centers. In 1948 she organized the Cheltenham Congress on World Population and World Resources in Relation to the Family, and in 1952, when the International Planned Parenthood Federation was founded at Bombay, she and Lady Rama Rau (1893–   ) were elected honorary presidents. By 1965 this Federation had 38 national affiliates in 28 countries and territories; in addition to its London headquarters it had regional offices at Bombay, Singapore, Tokyo, and New York and was planning to establish others at Cairo and Nairobi; and it had consultative status with the United Nations Economic and Social Council.

This expansion of the movement reflected the increasing attention given to population problems throughout the world. In the so-called underdeveloped areas—Africa, Asia, Latin America, and Oceania—the reduction of mortality after World War II, without corresponding reduction of the traditional high fertility, produced what popular writers termed a "population explosion," with dimensions foreshadowed by threats of further declines in already low standards of living, the extension of Communism, and even war. There began a search for measures to combat illiteracy and ancient traditions and taboos retarding capital formation and the scientific and technological development prerequisite to full utilization of natural resources, industrialization, and mechanization of agriculture. In attempting to formulate effective population policies, an increasing number of governments began to finance or support family planning services through public health and other medical facilities. By 1965 strong policies intended to restrict population growth had been adopted in Japan, India, Pakistan, Singapore, Egypt, Korea, and Taiwan. Partial support was initiated in Ceylon, Hong Kong, and Malaya. The International Planned Parenthood Federation undertook to support family planning programs in countries where governments were not participating officially. In general, except in Japan, the national impact of governmental or private programs was hardly discernible. The degree of motivation necessary for the success of the programs was slow to manifest itself within the diverse cultural and social patterns of the so-called developing countries.

Decline of Legal Restrictions on Birth Control in the U.S. In the U.S. the momentum that produced the Comstock law of 1873 led to its use as a model for similar legislation in every state except New Mexico and North Carolina. Proponents of birth control first attacked these Federal and state laws on the ground that they interfered with individual liberties, but greater prominence was soon given to the argument that they were in conflict with sound medical considerations. Modification began to be achieved at least as early as 1918 with the previously cited exemption of New York physicians from restrictions on advice to married persons. Mrs. Sanger's National Committee on Federal Legislation for Birth Control, organized in 1929, sought the repeal of the Comstock law but proved more successful in obtaining its lenient interpretation by Federal courts. The committee was able to disband in 1937 following a series of decisions by a circuit court of appeals that excluded contraceptive practice by married couples from the definition of immoral and illegal acts intended to be covered by Federal law and, in the case of *U.S. v. One Package*, 86 F. 2d. 737 (1936), removed virtually all restrictions from physicians. Meanwhile, state legislation was also amended or ignored. *See* BIRTH CONTROL, U.S. LAW OF.

By the mid-20th century only Connecticut and Massachusetts continued to recognize as potentially enforceable state laws preventing the prescription, distribution, and—in Connecticut—even the use of contraceptives. Attempts to repeal these laws in the legislature or by popular referendum were unsuccessful. Such attempts were usually opposed by Roman Catholic authorities on the ground that, since contraception is intrinsically evil, Catholics could not cooperate in the repeal of legislation intended to prohibit it. Most Catholic spokesmen recognized that the legal prohibitions were virtually unenforceable and pointed out that they had not been enacted as a result of Catholic influence and that there was no Catholic pressure for the enactment of similar laws elsewhere. By the 1950s some Catholic publicists, and eventually even Cardinal Richard Cushing of Boston, questioned the necessity or wisdom of continued opposition to the amendment or repeal of the laws, noting traditional Catholic teaching that not all immoral acts are proper objects of legislation, that

laws that are unenforceable do not meet the tests of good law, and that insofar as Catholic teaching on birth control had become a unique moral position it should not be imposed upon others in a pluralistic society. Legally, at least, the issue was settled by the U.S. Supreme Court, which, after having twice refused jurisdiction in similar cases, ruled in *Griswold v. Connecticut* 381 U.S. 479 (1965) that the Connecticut law invaded the constitutionally protected rights of privacy of married couples. This argument had been supported in briefs submitted to the Court by, among others, the *Catholic Council on Civil Liberties.

Medical Policies. Organized medicine in the U.S. was slow to accept birth control as within its province. Arguments for the practice appeared sporadically in medical journals, beginning with one in the *Michigan Medical News* in 1882. It was advocated before the American Medical Association (AMA) as early as 1912, in the presidential address of Abraham Jacobi (1830–1919), the father of American pediatrics. Beginning in 1922, the AMA was asked repeatedly to interest itself in securing changes in legislation to permit physicians to give contraceptive advice when they considered it to be medically indicated. Its gynecological section passed a motion to this effect in 1925. As late as 1932, however, a past president of the AMA assured the Committee on Ways and Means of the House of Representatives that the medical profession as a whole did not sponsor or favor the passage of a so-called birth control bill "because it requires no aid in this direction and because it realizes the dangers inherent in such legislation"; he prefaced his remarks by asserting, "Whenever man departs ever so little from the natural laws of the universe, destructive influences to a greater or lesser extent creep in; and in the laws of nature there is no provision for birth control through contraceptic devices" [William Gerry Morgan, in *Hearings . . . on H.R. 11082* (Washington, D.C. 1932), 74–75].

By 1935 so much medical discussion was devoted to the topic that an AMA committee was appointed to study the problem. In 1937 the AMA House of Delegates passed recommendations that (a) action should be taken by the Bureau of Legal Medicine and Legislation to make clear to physicians their legal rights to prescribe contraceptives, (b) the Council on Pharmacy and Chemistry and the Council of Physical Therapy should investigate the various contraceptive methods and publish their findings for the profession, (c) the Council on Medical Education and Hospitals should promote thorough instruction on fertility and sterility in medical schools, and (d) contraceptive advice should be given only in properly licensed agencies under medical control. The House of Delegates went further in 1938 and urged the amendment of all remaining legislation interfering with the prescription of contraceptives by physicians. Until late 1964, however, the AMA insisted that its resolutions and its published lists of approved contraceptives should not be construed as endorsement of contraception *per se*; it disapproved "propaganda" on the subject from nonmedical agencies. In 1963 it established a Committee on Human Reproduction to consider a wide range of problems related to family planning. The next year, following similar previous action by a growing number of state and county medical societies, it abandoned its official neutrality, expressing its readiness to cooperate with nonprofessional groups and urging that the "prescription of child-spacing measures should be made available to all patients who require them, consistent with their creed and mores, whether they obtain their medical care through private physicians or tax- or community-supported health services."

Previously, in 1959, the American Public Health Association had formally endorsed family planning as an integral part of preventive medicine, and in 1963 it established a program area committee on population and public health. In the same year the American College of Obstetricians and Gynecologists approved for the first time a resolution urging that birth control information should be made available to all persons in accordance with their religious convictions and that research on all aspects of human fertility should be expanded. Also in 1963, government-sponsored birth control programs for indigent families were strongly endorsed by the president of the National Medical Association, the organization of Negro physicians. Officials of Planned Parenthood were associated with most of these developments.

Religious Teachings. Until about 1930 the official teachings of religious bodies were virtually unanimous in opposition to artifical birth control. The story of *Onan (Gn 38.7–10), a common inheritance of Jews and Christians, was interpreted as a strict scriptural condemnation of the practice. The first religious proponents of birth control in the U.S. were Universalists, Unitarians, or adherents of Reformed Judaism. The first official Protestant acceptance of contraception was announced in 1930, in a statement of the Lambeth Conference of the bishops of the Church of England recognizing abstinence from sexual intercourse as the ordinary means of family limitation but allowing contraceptive means in cases in which abstinence was deemed impossible. "Careful and restrained" use of contraceptives was approved in 1931 by the Committee on Marriage and the Home of the Federal Council of Churches in the U.S. This established a precedent that was gradually followed by all major Protestant denominations. In 1961 the general board of the National Council of Churches declared that "couples are free to use the gifts of science for conscientious family limitation, provided the means are mutually acceptable, non-injurious to health and appropriate to the degree of effectiveness required in the situation." Delegates of the Orthodox churches to the Council abstained from voting on this pronouncement in order to dissociate themselves from it, abstinence being the only method of family limitation approved by Orthodoxy and by most fundamentalist Protestant groups not belonging to the Council. Meanwhile, the Central Conference of American Rabbis (Reform) in 1930 and the Rabbinical Assembly of America (Conservative) in 1935 approved contraception for social and economic as well as health reasons; in 1958 the Rabbinical Alliance of America (Orthodox), while still condemning contraceptive practices on the part of males, indicated approval of such practices by married women for reasons of health and after consultation between medical and rabbinical authorities.

Pius XI summarized the traditional Roman Catholic position on birth control in the encyclical *Casti connubii (1930): "Any use whatsoever of matrimony exercised in such a way that the act is deliberately frustrated in its natural power to generate life is an offense against the law of God and of nature, and those who indulge in such are branded with the guilt of a grave sin" [ActApS 22 (1930) 560]. At the same time he upheld the legitimacy of periodic abstinence under certain circumstances as a means of child spacing and family limitation: "Nor are those considered as acting against nature who in the married state use their right in the proper manner, although on account of natural reasons either of time or of certain defects new life cannot be brought forth" (*ibid.* 561). Pius XII, reaffirming this teaching in 1951, indicated that serious reasons of medical, eugenic, social, or economic character might justify the temporary and even permanent use of periodic abstinence, and he expressed hope that scientific research would make this method increasingly effective [*Vegliari con sollecitudine,* ActApS 43 (1951) 846; *Nell'ordine della, ibid.* 859].

The subsequent introduction of *anovulant pills opened widespread discussion of their legitimacy and even a reexamination of the bases of the Church's teaching on birth control. Pius XII applied the traditional norms in commenting on the anovulants in 1958: "A direct and, therefore, illicit sterilization is provoked when ovulation is arrested to protect the uterus and the organism from the consequence of pregnancy" [*Le VIIe Congrès International,* ActApS 50 (1958) 735]. This teaching was reiterated as a norm in 1964, in the wake of continued controversy, when Paul VI remarked, "Let us say in all frankness that so far We do not have sufficient reason to regard the norms laid down by Pius XII on this matter as superseded and therefore no longer binding. So these norms must be considered valid, at least until We may feel obliged in conscience to alter them. In a matter of such importance it seems right that Catholics desire to follow one single law propounded authoritatively by the Church. So it seems advisable to recommend that for the present no one should arrogate to himself the right to take a stand differing from the norm now in force" [*L'intenzione che qui,* ActApS 56 (1964) 588–589]. Both scholarly and popular discussion increased, however, in view of the form of the Pope's statement and the knowledge that a commission initially constituted by John XXIII was studying the entire question of birth control in relation to problems of population growth, on the one hand, and family morality, on the other.

Current Practices and Issues. With knowledge of the means of birth control almost universally available in developed countries, with every major religious denomination tolerating at least qualifiedly some form of family limitation, and with information about the practices of others easily obtainable through social contacts in urban areas and through the mass media, it is not suprising that there have been revolutionary changes in popular attitudes. In 1958 the contraceptive trade in the U.S. was estimated at $200 million a year. The most comprehensive data available on the actual extent of family limitation in the U.S. are provided in a 1955 study of a carefully drawn national sample of white married women aged 18 to 39, inclusive (R. Freedman, P. K. Whelpton, and A. A. Campbell, *Family Planning, Sterility, and Population Growth,* New York 1959). The investigators found that 83 per cent of fecund couples in the sample had used some means of family limitation prior to the time of interview, and that only 4 per cent did not intend to use any measure to limit family size at any time. Among fecund couples married 10 years or longer, 92 per cent had attempted family limitation. In the opinion of the authors of the study, all classes of the American population are coming to share common values concerning family size.

This study revealed expected economic and educational differentials, e.g., among fecund couples with wives 35 to 39 years of age, 78 per cent of the wives who had not gone beyond elementary school but 91 to 97 per cent of those who had more than a grade-school education reported use of some method of family limitation. Religious differences, however, appeared to be more important than any other with respect to both the decision to limit family size and the means adopted. Among fecund Catholic wives, 70 per cent had practiced family limitation before the time of the study and an additional 10 per cent expressed an intention to do so in the future. Among all Catholic couples, 70 per cent had either made no effort to control family size or had used only methods acceptable to the Church, but among fecund Catholic couples married at least 10 years, 50 per cent had used a method other than rhythm. Among all couples reporting attempts to limit family size, 47 per cent of Catholics, 89 per cent of Protestants, and 96 per cent of Jews had used chemical or mechanical means.

It may be noted that the fertility of Catholic populations varies greatly throughout the world. Birth rates in some Catholic countries of Europe (Belgium, France, Italy, Portugal, and Spain) are lower than in the U.S.; in Latin America, on the other hand, the rates are higher than in any other major region of the world. In the U.S., the fact that Catholic birth rates continue to be somewhat higher than non-Catholic birth rates suggests not only that Catholics recognize and observe Catholic moral teaching to the degree indicated, but also that their values include preferences for larger families. This conclusion is supported by studies of comparative fertility and family-size preferences (e.g., C. F. Westoff et al., *Family Growth in Metropolitan America*, Princeton 1961). In any case, by the 1960s Catholic authorities acknowledged more readily than formerly the good faith of those whom they considered to be in moral error because of their approval of contraception, even while there remained at both local and national levels sharp divisions between Catholics and others concerning issues of community welfare and public policy.

Policies of Catholic Hospitals. There have been controversies in some communities because non-Catholic physicians on the staffs of Catholic hospitals have been affiliated with birth control organizations. The hospitals, of course, must draw on the medical talent available in the community, not only on Catholic physicians. It is understood that advice at variance with Catholic moral teaching may not be given in Catholic hospitals. In a few instances, however, hospitals have attempted to restrict staff physicians from giving contraceptive advice even in private practice or, more often, have requested them to withdraw from membership in birth control agencies. The hospitals have thus been subject to the criticism that attempts to control physicians' activities beyond the limits of the contract relationship

infringe individual liberties, coerce consciences, and unnecessarily embitter professional and community relations.

Admission of Birth Control Agencies to Community Organizations. More frequently, local controversies have resulted from the application of planned parenthood agencies for admission to councils or fund-raising campaigns of community-wide private welfare groups. Especially where Catholics are numerous, threats of Catholic withdrawal from participation in Community Chest or United Fund campaigns have usually resulted in the exclusion of birth control agencies from these community efforts. For example, in 1953 Catholic agencies resigned from the Health and Welfare Council of New York City because, reversing a former policy, the Council admitted what the Catholic agencies termed "an organization whose principal activity, in our judgement, is gravely immoral." These agencies considered that their continued membership in the Council would constitute cooperation with evil. Some Catholics have questioned this view, since approval of the policies of all member organizations is not usually implied in adherence to groups of the type in question, and withdrawal or the threat of withdrawal from such community-wide endeavors tends to handicap them and to arouse hostility. Among the numerous questions that arise are the following: Can planned parenthood services be classified properly as health and welfare services? If they are so classified within a local community, does their admission to welfare councils or centralized fund-raising campaigns compromise the position of those participating groups that consider their activities to be immoral? Are any measures of accommodation possible? What means of opposition are prudent?

Birth Control Services in Public Agencies. By the 1960s these issues were subordinated to others involving the participation of the state in the extension of birth control. Within the U.S. such participation began in North Carolina, in 1937, when birth prevention services were made available through public health facilities. Six other southeastern states soon established similar programs. Subsequently, Planned Parenthood conducted an increasingly vigorous campaign for the provision of contraceptive advice or assistance in tax-supported hospitals or public health and welfare clinics. At the end of 1964 birth control services were included to some extent in publicly-financed health and welfare programs in 34 states and the District of Columbia—in 14 states the programs were new—and it was estimated that 200,000 women had utilized such services during the year. The American Public Welfare Association, a national association of public welfare agencies, added its voice to those of others urging that advice or assistance compatible with a client's religious and ethical beliefs should be given on request.

Catholic resistance to these developments was prominent in many communities, especially during 1958 in a highly publicized controversy in the city of New York and during the early 1960s in the state of Illinois. The provision of contraceptive services to unmarried women on relief was often a subject of special concern. Proponents of publicly financed birth control services often seemed most concerned about the reduction of costs resulting from births—large numbers of them illegitimate—to public welfare clients who came to be mainly Negroes or, in a few cities, Puerto Ricans culturally deprived of conventional marital and family patterns (*see* ILLEGITIMACY). In some localities, at least, Catholics accepted birth control programs preserving individual freedom of choice with respect to family limitation and the means employed. Objection was raised, however, to the tendency to promotion of contraception by the state.

Noting the deep division of the citizenry concerning the morality of the various means of family limitation, Catholic spokesmen either maintained that any promotion of birth control by government was an invasion of privacy or held that the state should confine itself to seeking practical accommodations preserving the right of conscience. The issues were sharpened by proposals in various localities to utilize funds from the Federal antipoverty legislation of 1964 to support birth control programs, and by the introduction in the U.S. Senate of a bill involving the Federal government directly in the support and conduct of such programs. In testifying on this proposed legislation during August 1965, a group of Catholics presented a statement acknowledging the legitimacy of governmental birth control assistance "so long as human life and personal rights are safeguarded and no coercion or pressure is exerted against individual moral choice." At the same hearing, however, the endorsement of the administrative committee of the National Catholic Welfare Conference was given to a statement opposing the bill as a violation of marital privacy, particularly in the relationship of government to recipients of public welfare assistance. The problems presented by the intervention of the state are complex and divide people along various social and political, as well as religious, lines, even when most prominence is given to the position of the Church on the morality of contraception.

Birth Control and Foreign Policy. The international expansion of the birth control movement was given added impetus after World War II. Official and popular attention to population problems was accompanied by pressure for the inclusion of birth control information or services in foreign aid programs of the U.S. and in programs of the United Nations and its specialized agencies. Thus, in 1959 a presidentially-appointed committee to study the U.S. military assistance program, in a report known by the name of its chairman William H. Draper, Jr., recommended that the U.S. foreign aid program should include the supply of birth control information to countries requesting it. The Catholic bishops of the U.S. expressed their flat opposition to the proposal, and the public officials concerned assumed a defensive posture, Pres. Dwight D. Eisenhower himself declaring, "I cannot imagine anything more emphatically a subject that is not a proper political or governmental activity or function or responsibility" (*New York Times,* Dec. 3, 1959). Senator John F. *Kennedy, then a presidential aspirant, asserted that it would be a "mistake" for the U.S. to advocate birth control in other countries, but that if the subject should arise during his administration he would be obligated by his oath to do whatever appeared to be in the best interest of the U.S. In 1962, as president, he authorized a U.S. statement in the UN General Assembly's Committee on Economic and Financial Affairs offering to provide information and technical assistance concerning population problems upon request from a country.

Changes in public opinion could be measured by the fact that in 1964 both of the nation's living former presidents, Eisenhower and Harry S. Truman, agreed to serve as co-chairmen of the honorary sponsors of Planned Parenthood-World Population, the former remarking that perhaps he had carried "too far" his previous feeling that inclusion of birth control information in foreign aid programs "would violate the deepest religious convictions of large groups of taxpayers" (*Saturday Evening Post,* Oct. 26, 1963). In his state of the union message of Jan. 14, 1965, Pres. Lyndon B. Johnson gave renewed encouragement to proponents of population control at home and abroad by declaring, "I will seek new ways to use our knowledge to help deal with the explosion in world population and the growing scarcity in world resources."

Population Policy in the United Nations. Although specialized agencies of the UN have manifested an interest in world population problems from their foundation, the official policy of the international organization is described as one of neutrality. At a UN World Population Conference in Rome during 1954 it was agreed that cooperative action required respect for different ethical and religious values and the promotion of mutual understanding. Proposals for the encouragement of family planning have been opposed by delegates from Roman Catholic and Communist countries. In 1952, for example, Catholic delegates opposed a Norwegian proposal for a World Health Organization study of contraception, which was then abandoned. Since only the rhythm method is acceptable to all major world religions, a UN project teaching this method was undertaken in India between 1952 and 1954, but with little success. In December 1963 delegates from France, Argentina, Lebanon, Liberia, and Peru pressed for the deletion from a General Assembly resolution of a clause authorizing UN technical assistance "for national projects and programs dealing with problems of population"; the serious division on the question was shown by the tally of 34 votes for and 34 votes against retention of the clause, while 32 states (including the U.S.) abstained from voting. At the UN World Population Conference in Belgrade in 1965 the undersecretary for economic and social affairs reiterated the UN policy of neutrality out of its "respect for all beliefs" and its realization that "in the present state of our knowledge there could be no question of attempting to define a United Nations doctrine on the subject of birth control." At the same time he noted the organization's readiness "to respond to all requests for assistance from any country which, on the basis of its own assessment of the situation, had decided to embark on such a policy or to explore its possibilities." The first such technical assistance mission was sent to India early in 1965. Hence in the UN, as in local communities and state and Federal agencies in the U.S., there was increasing recognition of certain principles of accommodation, e.g., respect for individual conscience or for cultural values, in spite of the difficult practical problems involved in such accommodation.

See also CONTRACEPTION; POPULATION.

Bibliography: R. M. FAGLEY, *The Population Explosion and Christian Responsibility* (New York 1960). N. E. HIMES, *Medical History of Contraception* (Baltimore 1936). A. F. GUTT-

MACHER et al., *Planning Your Family* (New York 1964). G. A. KELLY, *Birth Control and Catholics* (Garden City, N.Y. 1963). J. C. ROCK, *The Time Has Come* (New York 1963). N. ST. JOHN-STEVAS, *Birth Control and Public Policy* (pa. Santa Barbara, Calif. 1960). M. SANGER, *My Fight for Birth Control* (New York 1931); *Autobiography* (New York 1938). M. G. SHIMM, ed., *Population Control: The Imminent World Crisis* (New York 1961).

[M. J. HUTH]

BIRTH CUSTOMS IN THE BIBLE.

In Biblical thought the birth of a child was considered a gift of God and the sign of His good pleasure [Ps 126(127). 3–5; 127(128).3; Prv 17.6]. The joy that resulted made the mother forget the pains of labor (Jn 16.21). The pains of childbirth so impressed the Israelites that all manner of danger and suffering came to be compared to the pangs of a woman in labor [Ps 47(48).7; Jer 22.23]. But successful childbirth was naturally depicted as a time of rejoicing at which the parents were congratulated by their friends and neighbors (Ru 4.14; Lk 1.58). Midwives practiced in Israel, as elsewhere (Ex 1.15). Their care of the newborn child is detailed in Ez 16.4. According to this passage, it was customary for the child to be washed, rubbed with salt, anointed with oil, and wrapped in swaddling clothes.

The woman who bore a child incurred ritual uncleanness by reason of the birth. At the time of *purification (40 days after the birth of a boy, 80 days after the birth of a girl) it was necessary to make a sin offering and to offer a holocaust (Lv 12.1–8). A *firstborn son was to be dedicated to the Lord and then redeemed by the sacrifice of an animal (Ex 13.1–16; 22.29–30; 34.19–20). On the 8th day after birth a male child was circumcised (Gn 17.9–14). This was also a time for rejoicing among the friends and neighbors of the new parents. Either at birth or at the time of *circumcision, a name was given to the child. At times the name of the child was suggested by some particular circumstance of his birth, or it expressed the hopes and desire of the parents for their child (see Gn 29.31–30.24). Since the only Biblical reference to the observance of the anniversary of one's birth is in connection with the birthday party of King Herod Antipas (Mk 6.21), it would seem that such an observance was a Greek, rather than an Israelite custom.

Bibliography: EncDictBibl 248–249. De Vaux AncIsr 41–48. J. SCHARBERT, LexThK² 4:562.

[S. M. POLAN]

BĪRŪNĪ, ABŪ-AL-RAYḤĀN MUḤAMMAD, AL-,

generally considered the most original and profound scholar in *Islam; b. Bīrūn, modern Uzbek S.S.R., 973; d. Chazni, Afghanistan, c. 1050. To his people he was known as al-Ustādh, the master, and a master he was: in history and chronology, geography, mathematics, astronomy, natural science, and philosophy. He spoke Persian, wrote in Arabic, translated from Sanskrit, and knew some Hebrew and Syriac. In intellectual honesty, devotion to truth, and critical approach he stands almost alone in medieval Islam.

Al-Bīrūnī was born in Bīrūn, a suburb of Kath, capital of Khwarizm (Khiva), of Persian parentage. He professed Shī'ism but displayed skeptic tendencies. He studied at home, journeyed in neighboring lands, and when the powerful Sultan Maḥmūd al-Ghaznawi in 1017 overran his country, he was taken among other learned prisoners to Ghazna in Afghanistan. He accompanied the Sultan, possibly as an official astrologer, on his military campaigns to northwest India. There he settled for a time, teaching Greek science and philosophy and studying Sanskrit and Hindu philosophy, which fascinated him. More than that, he acquired a wealth of information about the Hindu way of life that served him well in his future writings.

Al-Bīrūnī is credited with 180 works, many of which are treatises. His major work is *Al-Āthār al-Bāqiyah 'an al-Qurūn al-Khāliyah,* which was edited (Leipzig 1878) and translated by Edward Sachau as *The Chronology of Ancient Nations* (London 1879). His account of India, *Taḥqīq Mā li-al-Hind* (Hyderabad, Deccan 1958), was translated also by Sachau as *History of India* (2 v. London 1888; reproduced London 1910). In it he offers material that can be found nowhere else. His third major production was dedicated to his patron Sultan Mas'ūd, son of Maḥmūd, as indicated by the title *Al-Qānūn al-Mas'ūdī fi al-Hay'ah w-al-Nujūm* ("the Mas'ūdi canon on astronomy and the stars," 3 v. Hyderabad, Deccan 1954–56). Closely related was his *Kitāb al-Tafhīm li-Awā'il Ṣinā'at al-Tanjīm,* reproduced and translated by R. Ramsey Wright as *The Book of Instruction in the Elements of Astrology* (London 1934). An important treatise, *Kitāb al-Jamāhir fi Ma'rifat al-Jawāhir* (Hyderabad, Deccan 1936) deals with precious stones and jewels.

Al-Bīrūnī's other scholarly contributions include: a clear account of Hindu mathematics, accurate determination of latitudes and longitudes, geodetic measurements, and a remarkably accurate determination of the specific gravity of 18 precious stones and metals. Al-Bīrūnī recognized that the speed of light was far in excess of the speed of sound. He suggested that the Indus Valley might have been an ancient sea basin filled up with alluvium.

Bibliography: Iran Society, *Al-Bīrūnī, Commemoration Volume, A. H. 362–A. H. 1362* (Calcutta 1951). D. J. BOILOT, Enc Islam² 1:1236–38. Sarton 1:707–709.

[P. K. HITTI]

BISCAYNE COLLEGE.

The first Catholic liberal arts college for men in Florida, Biscayne College was founded by the Augustinians in Miami in 1961 on the invitation of Bp. Coleman F. Carroll. The 50-acre campus was deeded to the Augustinians by the bishop, who also made available a gift of $500,000 from an anonymous benefactor. Chartered in 1961 by the state of Florida, the College began construction in April 1962; and the first all-purpose building, Mary Kennedy Hall, was ready for occupancy in November of the same year. Until then, classroom facilities were provided by Barry College. Affiliated with The Catholic University of America in 1963, the College is sponsored by the Augustinian Educational Association and is a member of the Florida Association of Colleges and Universities.

The board of trustees is composed of five religious and two laymen. The administrative officers are the president, vice president, dean of studies, treasurer, librarian, and chaplain. In 1964 there were 51 full-time students and 13 faculty members—11 religious and 2 laymen—of whom 3 held doctorates and 5 held masters' degrees. Auxiliary personnel numbered 4. Besides an endowment fund of $40,000, the College is financed by tuition, fees, and the contributed services of the non-salaried religious community.

The threefold curriculum comprises the humanities, business, and natural science, basic to which are courses in theology and philosophy. Methods used are the standard lecture, recitation, and laboratory work. Courses lead to the B.A., B.A. in Business Administration, and B.S. degrees. In 1964 the library had 6,102 bound volumes and subscribed to 49 periodicals. The average annual increase in library holdings is 3,000 volumes, toward a total capacity of 20,000. Building plans include facilities for library expansion and the accommodation of 2,000 students.

[R. M. SULLIVAN]

BISHOP, EDMUND, historian, liturgist; b. Totnes, Devon, England, May 17, 1846; d. Barnstaple, Devon, Feb. 19, 1917. The youngest child of a country innkeeper, he went to school at Ashburton, Exeter, and Vilvorde (Belgium). He served Thomas Carlyle as amanuensis (1863) and joined the British civil service as a clerk in the Education Department in 1864. He spent all his spare time in historical research, working initially from documents in the British Museum. He was received into the Catholic Church on Aug. 16, 1867, and through his friendship with Dom (later Cardinal) Gasquet and his associates he was attracted by the attempted revival of monastic ideals at Downside Priory. Retiring from the Civil Service in 1885, he went to Downside as a postulant in 1886, but was disappointed by the initial failure of efforts to revitalize the English Benedictine congregation. Although he left the Benedictines in 1889, he never wavered in his affection for Downside, where he spent a substantial part of the last 15 years of his life and was buried with the monks. His earliest learned work, and especially his discovery in 1877 of the *Collectio Britannica* (an important document in the history of Canon Law) had by 1880 earned Bishop a high reputation as a medieval historian. In collaboration with Dom Bäumer of Beuron Abbey (d. 1894), he began about 1891 to publish brilliantly original work on the history of the Missal and Breviary, sharply at variance with the positions adopted and popularized by P. *Batiffol and L *Duchesne, but nonetheless commanding respect. Bishop showed unequaled knowledge of the printed and manuscript literature in the libraries of Western Europe and used profoundly scholarly judgment. He collaborated with Gasquet in more polemical work on the history and position of the Catholic Church in England, particularly of the Black Monks.

From about 1900 Bishop lived in increasing retirement, intellectually in sympathy with many of the ideas associated with the Modernist movement (*see* MODERNISM). Nevertheless, his occasional publications, and still more his generous contributions to other scholars' work, continued to advance the frontiers of knowledge of the origins and early development of Western liturgies. Much of his most significant work was collected and revised by him in his *Liturgica Historica,* published posthumously in 1918. Apart from these specialized studies, his lifelong interest, by example, exhortation, and encouragement, was to stimulate English Catholics to greater intellectual activity and a more scientific approach to history. This was reflected in many of his articles in Catholic periodicals, and in a voluminous private correspondence. Bishop was the foremost English-speaking liturgist of the late 19th and the early 20th century.

Bibliography: E. C. BUTLER, DNB (1912–21) 47–48. H. LECLERCQ, DACL 9.2:1735–36. N. ABERCROMBIE, *Life and Work of Edmund Bishop* (London 1959).

[N. ABERCROMBIE]

BISHOP, WILLIAM, Bishop of Chalcedon; b. Warwickshire, England, *c.* 1554; d. on the English mission, April 13, 1624. Brought up a Catholic, he apparently went to Oxford but did not take a degree. He trained for the priesthood at Reims and Rome, was ordained in 1583, and came back to England. He spent part of the next few years on the mission and part in Paris, where he took his doctorate in divinity. Bishop was a prominent member of the Appellant party among the English secular clergy and one of the 13 priests who in 1603 signed a declaration of allegiance to Queen Elizabeth repudiating the Pope's power to depose her. He refused, however, after 1606, to sign the oath of allegiance that Paul V had condemned. He was imprisoned but was released in 1611 and went to join the little community of Catholic controversial writers at Arras College, Paris. When in 1623 Gregory XV decided to restore a measure of local episcopal rule to the Catholics in England, he appointed William Bishop as bishop for the whole country, with the titular See of Chalcedon in Asia Minor. Bishop proceeded to act on the assumption that he possessed the full rights and privileges of an ordinary. He created a dean and chapter (*see* OLD CHAPTER) and a number of other canonical offices and embarked on a major reorganization of the Roman Church in England. He died before the full effects of his radical changes were felt. His successor was Richard *Smith.

Bibliography: T. COOPER, DNB 2:558–559. CathRecSoc v.10. DictEngCath 1:218–223. P. HUGHES, *Rome and the Counter-Reformation in England* (London 1942). A. F. ALLISON, "Richard Smith, Richelieu and the French Marriage," *Recusant History* 7.4 (1963–64). A. F. ALLISON and D. M. ROGERS, *A Catalogue of Catholic Books in English . . . 1558–1640,* 2 v. (London 1956).

[A. F. ALLISON]

BISHOP, WILLIAM HOWARD

Founder of the Glenmary Home Missioners; b. Washington, D.C., Dec. 19, 1885; d. Glendale, Ohio, June 11, 1953. His mother, Ellen Teresa Knowles, was a Catholic; his father, Francis Besant Bishop, a rural doctor, was received into the Church by Cardinal Gibbons. Bishop was educated in Washington public schools, attended Harvard College from 1907 to 1908, and St. Mary's Seminary, Baltimore. He was ordained for the Archdiocese of Baltimore on March 27, 1915, and was sent to study at The Catholic University of America in Washington, D.C. In 1917 he became pastor of St. Louis parish, Clarksville, Md. With the approval of Abp. Michael J. Curley he founded the Archdiocesan League of the Little Flower to aid needy rural pastors. In 1925 he organized the Archdiocesan Rural Life Conference of Baltimore, the first of its kind in the U.S. He became president of the National Rural Life Conference in 1928 and served in that capacity until 1933.

In the 1930's, when the unemployed were looking to the national government for relief, Bishop took courses

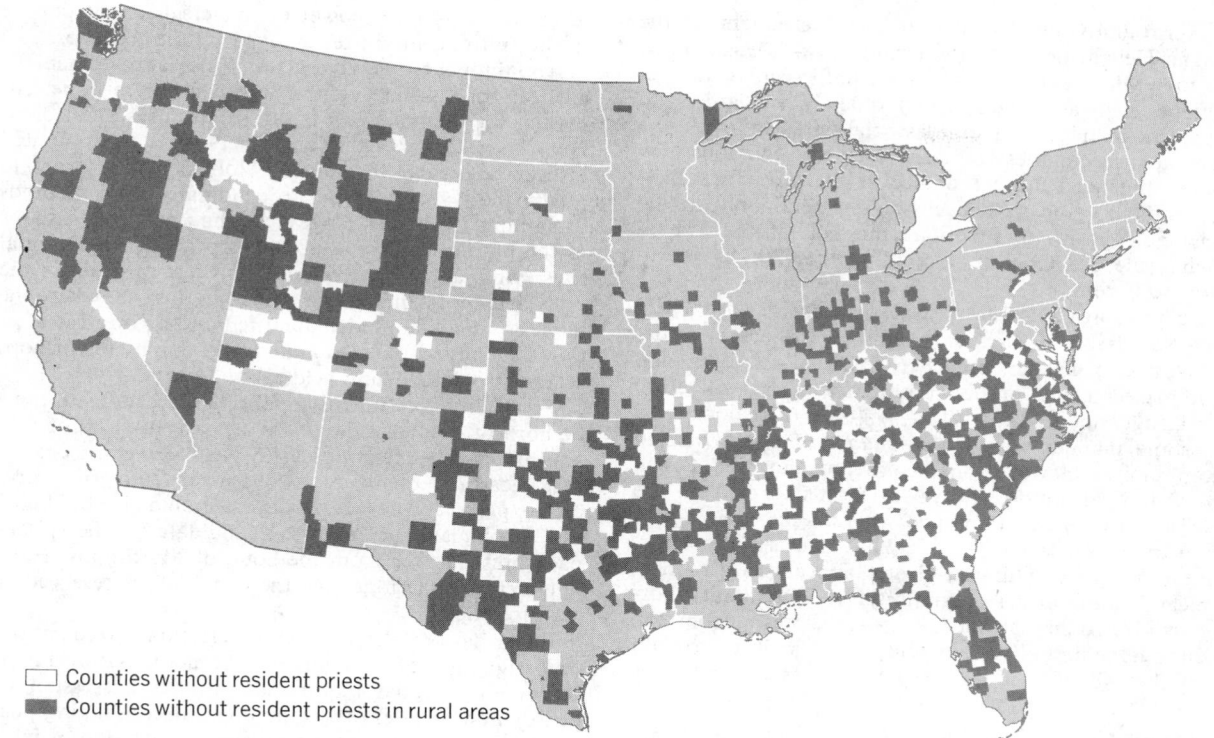

☐ Counties without resident priests
■ Counties without resident priests in rural areas

1961 version of the "No-Priest Land" map.

in agriculture and studied the complex economic problems associated with it. Concern for the spiritual malaise of the country led him to compile statistics that he set forth on his "No-Priest Land" map; they showed that nearly half the counties of the U.S. were without resident priests.

In March 1936 Bishop published a plan for a society of Catholic home missions to operate in rural sections where Catholics numbered as few as one-tenth of 1 per cent of the population (*see* GLENMARY HOME MISSIONERS). The following year he was invited to the Archdiocese of Cincinnati by Abp. John T. McNicholas to found such a society. Within 2 years he had acquired six students and a priest; by 1949 he had started a theological seminary at Glendale, Ohio. The Glenmary Lay Brothers Society and the Glenmary Home Mission Sisters were also organized by Bishop and received approval from the Holy See before his death.

Bibliography: H. W. SANTEN, *Father Bishop, Founder of the Glenmary Home Missioners* (Milwaukee 1961).

[C. F. BORCHERS]

BISHOP (IN THE BIBLE)

A title applied in the NT to the higher officers in the early Christian communities. The Greek word ἐπίσκοπος, from which the English word bishop is derived (through the Latin *episcopus*), means etymologically inspector, overseer, superintendent.

New Testament Usage. The word ἐπίσκοπος occurs five times in the NT. It is used once of Christ, in 2 Pt 2.25, where, like the Good Shepherd of Jn 10.11–16, Christ is called "the shepherd and guardian (ἐπίσκοπος) of your souls"; cf. Wis 1.6, where God is called the inspector (ἐπίσκοπος) of man's heart. In Phil 1.1, Paul

greets the Christians at Philippi "with their bishops and deacons"; since there were several such "overseers" in this single community, the term here cannot have the later technical meaning attached to the monarchical episcopate. In Acts 20.28 Paul says to the πρεσβύτεροι (*presbyters, *elders) of Ephesus who had assembled at Miletus (20.17–18), "Take heed to yourselves and to the whole flock in which the Holy Spirit has placed you as bishops to rule the Church of God"; here again, the fact that there were several bishops in one community excludes the monarchical concept of the term, and the fact that the term is here synonymous with presbyters shows that at this time no clear distinction was made between bishops and priests—a term derived from πρεσβύτεροι.

In the *Pastoral Epistles the term occurs twice: in 1 Tm 3.2 and Ti 1.7. After stating in 1 Tm 31 that the ἐπισκοπή (office of bishop—the only NT occurrence of this word in such a technical sense) is a noble occupation, the passage (3.2–7) goes on to describe the qualities that should be found in a good bishop; but nothing is said here of his functions. Similarly, in Ti 1.7–9 there is a description of qualities to be found in one who is to be appointed bishop, with no mention of his functions; moreover, this passage follows immediately after an order to appoint presbyters, again showing that no distinction is made here between the two terms.

Therefore, since there is no clear evidence in the NT for a monarchical episcopate, this office, which was firmly established by the early decades of the 2d century, must have been based on oral apostolic tradition going back ultimately to Christ. *See* BISHOP (IN THE CHURCH).

Term and Office Outside the New Testament. In the pagan Hellenistic world the term ἐπίσκοποι was applied to men who held various offices, both secular and religious, such as state and city officials, stewards, and business managers of cult associations. Although the term as used of these officials in cult associations may have influenced the NT choice of the term for Christian officials, the influence would extend only to the terminology; in its functions the NT office of men "who rule the Church of God" (Acts 20.28) is entirely different.

In the so-called Damascus Document of the *Dead Sea Scrolls the *meba*qqēr* (examiner, inspector) is described as a teacher, preacher, financial manager, and authorized leader of his community. It has therefore been suggested that the NT ἐπίσκοπος is to be connected in some manner with the *meba*qqēr* of the *Qumran community. However, in the Septuagint this Greek word is used almost always for words formed on the Hebrew root *pqd* (to visit), whereas the root *bqr* is rare in the Hebrew OT. But what is more important, the *meba*qqēr* of Qumran clearly appears as a monarchical leader of his community; if Christianity borrowed the office of the ἐπίσκοπος directly from the Qumran community, it would be difficult to explain why the NT office of the episcopacy does not appear as monarchical from the beginning.

Bibliography: L. MARCHAL, DBSuppl 2:1297–1333. J. LÉCUYER, DictSpirAscMyst 4.1:879–884. J. GEWIESS, LexThK² 2:491–492. InterDictBibl 1:441–443. EncDictBibl 249–250. J. COLSON, *L'Évêque dans les communautés primitives* (Paris 1951); *Les Fonctions ecclésiales aux deux premiers siècles* (Bruges 1956). E. SCHWEIZER, *Church Order in the New Testament*, tr. F. CLARKE (Naperville, Ill. 1961). K. G. GOETZ, "Ist der *meba*qqēr* der Genizafragmente wirklich das Vorbild des Christlichen Episkopats?" ZNTWiss 30 (1931) 89–93. J. DANIÉLOU, "La Communauté de Qumrân et l'organization de l'Église ancienne," RevHistPhilRel 35 (1955) 104–116. R. MARCUS, "*Meba*qqēr* and *Rabbim* in the Manual of Discipline 6.11–13," JBiblLit 75 (1956) 298–302.

[J. J. O'ROURKE]

BISHOP (CANON LAW)

The ecclesiastical law that delineates the office, duties, and rights of bishops who are ordinaries is found throughout the *Code of Canon Law and in the motu proprio *Cleri Sanctitati* of the *Oriental Codes, but CIC cc.329–349 and ClerSanc cc.392–416 have particular reference to them. Auxiliary *bishops and coadjutor *bishops are treated in separate articles. *See* BISHOP (IN THE CHURCH) and BISHOP (SACRAMENTAL THEOLOGY OF).

Nature of the Episcopal Office. Bishops are successors of the Apostles, and, by divine institution, are placed over particular churches, which they rule with ordinary power under the authority of the pope (CIC c.329.1; ClerSanc c.392.1). These canons refer specifically to the residential bishop, who is appointed to govern a diocese or territory in the Church. Since the power with which they rule is inherent in their office, it is termed ordinary. This jurisdictional power is exercised under the authority of the Holy Father, who may limit its exercise or territorial extent, but may not suppress or change its essential character. Bishops succeed the Apostles as a college, not as individual Apostles. They share the same collegiate ordinary power possessed by the Apostles. They do not, however, succeed

to the extraordinary power of universal jurisdiction or to the spiritual privileges enjoyed by the Apostles.

Appointment and Conferral. Final appointment of all bishops is subject to the approval of the pope. Although the common law of the Church reserves to the Holy Father the designation of persons to be appointed bishop, particular law of the Holy See may grant to others the right to designate candidates. The methods of naming candidates range from the election of bishops in the patriarchates and archbishoprics of the Oriental rites, with antecedent or subsequent approval by the Holy See, to the method employed in the U.S. where the names of candidates are submitted to the Holy See after they have been discussed and voted upon by the bishops at a provincial meeting held every 2 years.

To qualify for the episcopal office a candidate must be born of lawful wedlock, be at least 30 years of age, and ordained a priest at least 5 years. He must possess the necessary qualities of character: integrity, prudence, piety, and zeal for souls; he should also be skilled as a theologian or canonist. A candidate for the episcopacy must be free from the bond of Matrimony. Final judgment on the fitness of the candidate is reserved to the Holy See.

Regardless of the manner of election, presentation, or designation of a candidate, the actual conferral of office, an essential requirement to the possession of jurisdiction, is reserved to the pope. Before taking possession of his office, he must make a profession of faith and take an oath of fidelity to the Holy See.

Under ordinary circumstances, the candidate must receive episcopal consecration within 3 months of the day on which he receives the apostolic letters of appointment, and within 4 months he must take possession of his diocese. The bishop takes canonical possession of his diocese by showing his apostolic letters of appointment to the diocesan chapter or to the board of diocesan *consultors, whose secretary or chancellor should be present to record the proceedings. However, no particular ceremony of taking possession is required by the law.

Power of the Bishop. Once he has taken possession of his diocese, the residential bishop may exercise ordinary and immediate jurisdiction as pastor of the diocese. His jurisdiction is called ordinary because it is vested in him by reason of his office and not by delegation. It is immediate because he may exercise it without need of an intermediary. In addition to his ordinary jurisdiction, the bishop possesses further power that is delegated to him by the Holy See. *See* JURISDICTION (CANON LAW).

Canon 335.1 specifies the pastoral jurisdiction of the bishop. He has the right and duty to govern the diocese in both spiritual and temporal affairs. To this end he possesses legislative, judicial, and coercive power that must be exercised according to the precepts of Canon Law.

The bishop is the official legislator of his diocese and may make laws either in synod or out of synod, provided these do not conflict with the common or particular laws of the Church or the laws of a plenary or provincial council. The laws of the bishop oblige all his subjects unless the general law of the Church or the bishop himself makes specific exemption.

The bishop has the right to exercise his judicial power by acting as judge in any ecclesiastical cause not reserved to a higher judge. Ordinarily this power is exercised by the *officialis of the diocese, a judge appointed by the bishop and acting in his name and with his authority.

The coercive power of the bishop entitles him to administer the spiritual and temporal affairs of the diocese and to require the observance of ecclesiastical laws, especially those concerning the immediate spiritual welfare of his people. Among others, the canons specifically enumerate the following laws as of special importance: the worship of God, preaching the Word of God, the administration of the Sacraments and sacramentals of the Church, safeguarding the faith and morals of the faithful, and the religious instruction of the faithful, especially the young. The bishop has both the right and duty to enforce observance of these laws and to apply fitting punishment when they are violated. However, he must bear in mind that he is the father as well as the judge of his people, thus tempering judicial severity with paternal mercy.

By reason of his office, the bishop is the official and principal preacher in his diocese. It is his personal responsibility to preach the Word of God to his people. The priests of his diocese share in this important work of the priesthood to the extent determined by the bishop.

Through episcopal consecration the bishop receives the fullness of the priesthood with its consequent power of administering all of the Sacraments. In his own diocese the bishop is the ordinary minister of the Sacraments of Confirmation and Holy Orders.

As a consequence of his power of jurisdiction, the bishop has the right to perform in his own diocese the sacred functions reserved to him and for which the liturgical laws require the insignia of his office, i.e., the crosier and miter. He may also occupy the bishop's throne in any church within his diocese. Outside his own diocese, the bishop may use these insignia of office only with the express or reasonably presumed consent of the local ordinary or religious superior.

Obligations. The bishop of a diocese must personally reside within his diocese for the major part of the year, even though he may have an auxiliary or coadjutor bishop. He may absent himself from his diocese continuously or intermittently no more than 2 or 3 months each year, always making adequate provision that no harm will result from his absence from the diocese. Absence for a longer period of time is justified only in the case of attendance at councils or the *Ad limina* visit to the Holy See. The bishop has a particularly serious duty to be present at his cathedral church during the seasons of Advent and Lent and on the greater feasts of the Church: Easter, Pentecost, Christmas, and Corpus Christi. Only a serious or urgent cause justifies absence at these times.

As pastor of the diocese, the bishop assumes the grave responsibility of prayer and sacrifice for his people. He is obliged by CIC c.339 to offer the Sacrifice of the Mass for all the faithful of his diocese on all Sundays and major feast days of the year. The obligation is personal, requiring that the bishop himself celebrate Mass on the appointed days, if this is possible. When the bishop is lawfully prevented from celebrating the Mass, however, he may appoint another priest to do so.

Every 5 years each residential bishop must submit to the Holy See a report concerning the state of his diocese. The report, termed quinquennial, is drawn up according to a formula provided by the Holy See, written in Latin, and dated and signed by the bishop. It is sent to the *Consistorial Congregation at Rome in the case of the Latin Rite bishop and to the Congregation for the *Oriental Church in the case of an Oriental-rite bishop. The dioceses of the world have been divided into five groups, based principally on geographic location and language. Each group has been assigned a year within a 5-year period in such a way that each bishop submits his report during a specified year, completing the cycle each 5 years. The bishops of the U.S., for example, submit their reports during the years 1964, 1969, 1974, etc.

In conjunction with the quinquennial report the residential bishop must journey to Rome during the same year to venerate the tombs of the Apostles Peter and Paul and to visit the Holy Father. A concession granted to the bishops who reside outside of Europe permits them to make this *Ad limina* visit once each 10 years. The visit to Rome is to be made by the residential bishop himself or by his coadjutor bishop if he has one. However, with permission of the Holy See, the bishop may delegate a qualified priest of his diocese to make the visit in his name.

Among the primary duties of the bishop is the visitation of his diocese. Pastoral concern and vigilance dictate that the bishop visit each part of his diocese frequently. The common law of the Church obliges a bishop to arrange his visitation in such a way that he covers the entire diocese every 5 years. The Third Plenary Council of Baltimore prescribed that American bishops visit all parts of their dioceses within 3 years. The bishop is to make this visit personally under ordinary circumstances, usually accompanied by two clerics of his own choice. In many cases, the bishop conducts his visitation in conjunction with the administration of the Sacrament of Confirmation in the various parishes of the diocese.

The purpose of the bishop's visit is to preserve sound doctrine; protect good morals; correct abuses; promote peace, innocence, piety, and discipline among the clergy and faithful; and provide for the welfare of religion in other suitable ways. All persons, pious places and things are subject to the episcopal visitation unless they have been exempted by the Holy See. The visitation of the houses of exempt religious in the diocese is regulated by special provision of canon and particular law.

The bishop is instructed to conduct this visit in a fatherly rather than a judicial manner. If correction is necessary, any penalties imposed should be moderate and not vindictive. A bishop may make precepts and decrees during his visitation; and although his subjects may have recourse, they must obey the decrees while the decision is pending. The visit is to be carried out diligently but without any undue delay that may cause unnecessary hardship or expense on the part of the subjects. No gifts may be offered or accepted in consideration of the visit, but local customs may be observed with regard to the expenses of food, lodging, and travel.

Privileges. As members of the divinely instituted hierarchy of the Church, all bishops enjoy personal privileges bestowed upon them because of their rank in the Church. They also enjoy certain privileges attached to the office of diocesan ordinary. Thus each bishop in his own diocese enjoys the right of precedence over all other bishops and archbishops, with the exception of cardinals, papal legates, and his own metropolitan.

From the time they receive authentic notification of their promotion to the episcopacy, bishops enjoy certain privileges of the cardinals. These privileges are concerned chiefly with the celebration of Mass, preaching, choice of a confessor, and blessings. Bishops also enjoy the right to wear the episcopal insignia according to the norms of liturgical law.

Bibliography: Abbo 1:329–349. Bousc-Ellis 329–349. Bousc-O'Connor. Woywod-Smith 1:329–349. Beste 329–349. Vermeersch-Creusen EpitCanIur 1:443–463. C. A. BACHOFEN, *Rights and Duties of Ordinaries* (St. Louis 1924). I. SIPOS, *Enchiridion iuris canonici,* ed. L. GALOS (6th ed. Rome 1954) 202–216.

[T. A. FAULKNER]

BISHOP (IN THE CHURCH)

If one centers his attention on the diocesan bishop (or *ordinarius loci*) as distinct from auxiliary bishop or coadjutor bishop, he may define a bishop as one who in unity with and with due dependence on the supreme pontiff possesses in a local Church, or diocese, proper and complete power, priestly, doctrinal, and pastoral (cf. CIC c.329, 335). His power is said to be proper because, though it is exercised in the name of Christ, it is not exercised in the name of, or as vicar of, the Roman pontiff. And, while subordinate to the supreme power in the Church, it is complete in the sense that ordinarily without the consent of other persons or groups it is adequate and valid for all ecclesiastical acts. The bishop is, then, the high priest, the teacher, the shepherd of the faithful within the diocese.

For centuries in theological and historical writing the episcopate so described has been spoken of as the monarchical episcopate. The term monarchical is used not to deny the superior authority of the pope but to differentiate this form of episcopate from any collegiate episcopate, in which the direction of local communities would rest in the hands of a group of clerics. This Catholic view of the episcopate—individual pastors as successors of the *Apostles ruling in individual Christian communities—has, especially during the past 400 years, been disputed and denied by many non-Catholic theologians and ecclesiastical historians on the grounds that the apostolic function at no time involved any real power to direct Christian communities (so with variations F. C. Baur, J. B. Lightfoot, E. Hatch, A. Harnack, R. Sohm, K. Barth, E. Brunner, H. von Campenhausen), or it was in any case intransmissible (so O. Cullmann), or, granting the existence in the Apostles of some real transmissible power, it did not vest during the first postapostolic generations in any one single man but rather in a number of elders or functionaries grouped more or less closely in a college. For nearly all these writers the monarchical episcopate is the result of a long natural evolution that owed much to the doctrinal and disciplinary differences that plagued the communities, threatening their unity and pointing the need for concentration of leadership. Many of them fix the term of such transition at the beginning of the 3d century.

This is not the place to list the reasons why Catholic theologians hold that the Apostles as plenipotentiaries of Christ had real pastoral authority in His Church or the reasons to which they appeal in maintaining that, along with some intransmissible prerogatives, the Apostles possessed by divine institution transmissible powers

A bishop ordaining (a) acolytes, (b) subdeacons, and (c) a deacon, miniatures from the "Pontifical of Arles," written and illuminated in the second half of the 14th century (MS lat. 9479, fols. 29r, 31r, 33r, details).

for the conservation of the Church. It will be sufficient to outline the reasons for holding that monarchical bishops legitimately and from the first postapostolic generations continued the apostolic functions. At the outset one may note that while it is a common opinion of theologians that it is by divine will (*jure divino*) that the apostolic succession took the form of the monarchical episcopate, this view has never been canonized by the Church, and one may hold that while Our Lord established a perennial apostolic function, He may have left it to the Apostles themselves to decide just how and in whom their perennial powers should vest. If one prescinds from a divine mandate, it is hard to believe that the monarchical episcopate could have arisen as promptly, as universally, as peacefully as it did, unless the Apostles themselves had by word and deed, example and arrangement, implanted in the Church a *nisus* or tendency to this form of control within individual communities.

The remains of the earliest Christian literature nowhere gives positive indication that after the disappearance of the Apostles the Churches were administered collegiately by a group of *presbyters. It is true that the Epistle of Clement to the Corinthian Church, *c.* A.D. 96—at a moment when that community was in sad disarray—is silent about any single ecclesiastic at the head of the community there, and that the letter of Polycarp to the Church at Philippi makes no mention of a single bishop there, but neither document envisages or speaks of collegiate control as an institutional arrangement. Further, it is to be noted that Polycarp's letter is of the very same period (the opening years of the 2d century) as the epistles of St. Ignatius of Antioch, who repeatedly and unmistakably witnesses to the monarchical episcopate and in his letter to the Trallians (ch. 3) speaks of that arrangement—one single bishop assisted by priests and deacons—as a feature "without which the name Church is not applied." The testimony of Ignatius from the first decade of the 2d century, along with the evidence of the writers from the second half of that century and the earliest catalogs of bishops in the principal Churches—all of which trace a line of succession of individual bishops back to the apostolic age—satisfies most Catholic theologians that this form of Church government was the only one ever recognized as normal and regular. A few writers (e.g., Abbé Jean Colson, following the Anglican scholar Gregory Dix) think that there may have been a brief transitional period during which the "successors of the Apostles" were distinguished from the head or heads of the local Churches, but it is hard to square this theory even in the case of Clement of Rome (whom they cite as the clearest instance of such a successor) with the tone of the epistle attributed to him and addressed to the Church at Corinth. Were Clement writing as personal successor of the Apostles Peter and Paul—and that quite apart from any connection with the Roman Church—it is difficult to see why that letter should have been written in the name of the Roman Church and why the figure of Clement is all but lost in the shadow of the Roman Church.

Role of Bishops. From the time of Ignatius, the bishop has been the living and visible symbol, the center and effective principle of unity, the unity of communal charity. ". . . there is really one only flesh of Our Lord, one only cup to unite us in His blood, one only altar, as there is one only bishop . . ." (Ignatius, *Philad.* 4). There is indeed a spiritual union of souls to Christ, but this necessarily expresses itself in a visible union with the one who for a given community is the image of what Christ is for the Church and whose role it is to make concrete the mystical union with Christ. Ignatius time and again insists that to maintain such union no liturgical celebrations are to be held, no communal actions taken, no doctrine received except in union with and submission to the bishop, who as surrogate of Christ is the pole of unity around which Christian life centers (*Magn.* 3, 7, 13; *Philad.* 3; *Trall.* 2; *Eph.* 1, 5–6; *Smyr.* 8). From the dawn of the 2d century, when men and women were alive who had seen and heard the Apostles, the Catholic concept of what a bishop should be has

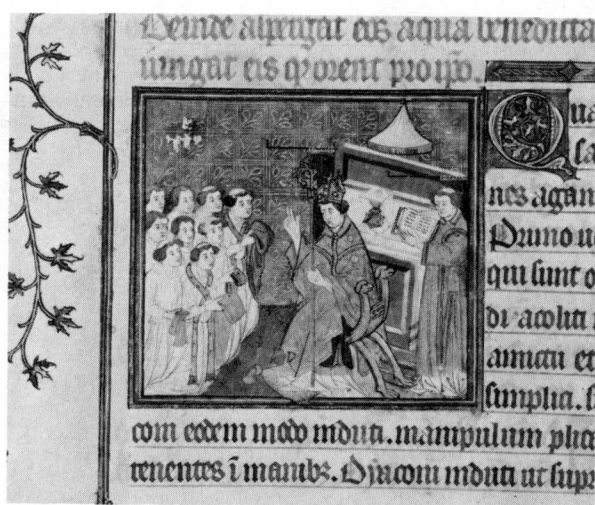

A bishop with various ordinands, miniature from the 14th-century "Pontifical of Sens" (MS lat. 962, fol. 126v).

remained the one sketched by the martyr bishop of Antioch.

Present Problems and Theories. Much of the theological treatment of the episcopal office has developed over the centuries in the context of the relationship of the individual bishop to his flock and of his individual relationship to the bishop of Rome as successor of St. Peter and pastor of the whole flock of Christ. The declarations of Vatican Council I stemming from its primary concern with the papal office stress more the relationship of the bishop to his own diocese and his subordination to the universal pastorate of the pope. In recent years —and in the sessions of Vatican Council II—the focus has changed, and the discussion has turned to the significance of the episcopate viewed under its collegiate aspect. Bishops are not merely so many individual heads of local Churches, they are also members of an episcopal body that in union with the pope corporately shares a charge and mission for the universal Church.

If it has long been clear that the bishop secures unity within his community, it is now being asked how he provides the catholicity of his community. Is it simply by his subordination to the center of unity or also through his membership in an episcopal college that succeeds to the apostolic college? Again, to what extent is his mission within his own diocese a concrete and specialized application of his mission (as member of the episcopal body) within the whole Church? Is there some discernible priority between two distinguishable functions: is he to be looked on first as local pastor and only then as having place in a body charged with direction of the whole Church, or is it more conformable to Christ's intention to see him first as a member of a body with worldwide mission and solicitude, and only then as one assigned to actuate that concern in a special way through the fullness of his priesthood in a part of the Church—a part with the capacity or potentiality so to represent the totality that the whole can in some mysterious way realize itself as "event" in this part? (Cf. K. Rahner.)

Though it would seem that the concept of episcopal collegiality (and, even more, that of the "virtuality" of the local Church) needs reflection and refinement, it may at least be said that the discussion of it has stressed a dimension of the episcopal office that has too often been overlooked: the role of the bishop for the good of the Church everywhere and for its worldwide mission of evangelization. The discussion has, besides, aroused on the part of the episcopate a desire, frequently expressed in the sessions of Vatican Council II, to participate more actively under the Roman pontiff in the direction of the Church universal.

See also BISHOP (IN THE BIBLE); BISHOP (SACRAMENTAL THEOLOGY OF); BISHOP (CANON LAW); APOSTOLIC SUCCESSION; AUTHORITY, ECCLESIASTICAL; BISHOP, AUXILIARY; BISHOP, COADJUTOR; DISCIPLINE, ECCLESIASTICAL; EPISCOPAL CONFERENCES; EPISCOPALISM; HIERARCHY; OFFICE, ECCLESIASTICAL; PRIMACY OF THE POPE.

Bibliography: F. PRAT and E. VALTON, DTC 5.2:1656–1725. DTC, Tables générales 1:1193–1204. M. SCHMAUS, LexThK² 2:492–497. H. W. BEYER, Kittel ThW 2:604–619. A. ADAM et al., RGG³ 1:1301–11. E. M. KREDEL and A. KOLPING, Fries HbTh Grdbgr 1:169–184. F. HOLBÖCK, Holböck-Sartory 1:201–346. K. RAHNER and J. RATZINGER, *The Episcopate and the Primacy,* tr. K. BARKER et al. (New York 1962). J. COLSON, *L'Évêque dans les communautés primitives* (Paris 1951); *Les Fonctions ecclésiales aux deux premiers siècles* (Bruges 1956); *L'Épiscopat catholique: Collégialité et primauté dans les trois premiers siècles de l'église* (Unam Sanctam 43; Paris 1963). É. M. GUERRY, *L'Évêque* (Paris 1954). K. E. KIRK, ed., *The Apostolic Ministry* (London 1946, repr. 1957). J. M. URTASUM, *What is a Bishop?* tr. P. J. HEPBURNE-SCOTT (New York 1962). **Illustration credit:** Bibliothèque Nationale, Paris.

[S. E. DONLON]

BISHOP (SACRAMENTAL THEOLOGY OF)

Vatican Council II, in its *Constitution on the Church,* declared that "one is constituted a member of the body of bishops by the power of sacramental consecration together with hierarchical communion with the head and members of this body" (22). Episcopal consecration and its effects have long been subjects of theological debate, but although many problems remain open in this area, substantial advance has been made. Little has been defined on this precise point, but the magisterium has determined closely relevant matters, and history has shed some light on the question.

Episcopal Consecration. This order has always been administered by a bishop and, whenever possible, by more than one bishop. Since the 3d century it has been fairly clear that schism, heresy, or sinfulness does not necessarily invalidate a Sacrament but that, if the minister has the required order and intention and employs the correct sign, the Sacrament is valid. Yet there is some question as to whether the proper intention exists, or even can exist, on the part of a bishop attempting to consecrate against the will of the episcopal college. This question is considered by B. Leeming ["Are They Really Bishops?" *Heythrop Journal* 5 (1964) 259–267] and is certainly raised by the wording of the constitution cited above. K. Rahner claims that sacramental theology is not certain about the Church's power to deprive the act of ordination of its validity ["Über den Episkopat," *Stimmen der Zeit* 173 (1963) 187].

An apostolic constitution of Pius XII (Nov. 30, 1947) determines the matter and form of episcopal consecration but expressly avoids determining whether the matter has always been the same [ActApS 40 (1948) 6]. It indicates that the specific matter and form of each

of the various degrees of the Sacrament of Orders does not belong to the *substance* of the Sacrament (that which Christ Himself specifically determined) and is therefore open to determination by the Church. Whatever it may have been in the past, the matter and form now necessary for valid episcopal consecration is the imposition of hands and the words of the Preface, "Give your priest the plenitude of your ministry and by heavenly anointing sanctify him upon whom you have conferred supreme honor."

It seems from these words that the subject of episcopal consecration must be a priest, and perhaps that is now the case. However, it was not always so. There is no doubt that on many occasions episcopal consecration was conferred on deacons and even laymen and was accepted as valid [see H. Lennerz, *De Sacramento Ordinis* (Rome 1947) 84–85]. From this historical fact implications can be drawn concerning the nature of the episcopate and the effects of episcopal consecration.

Effects of Episcopal Consecration. The *Constitution on the Church* of Vatican II asserts that the special outpouring of the Holy Spirit given to the Apostles is passed on to the bishops by episcopal consecration. It is obvious from the rest of the document that the fathers of Vatican II had no intention of departing from the traditional teaching that the bishops are successors of the Apostles as bishops, not as apostles. This special outpouring produces the fullness of the Sacrament of Orders that is called "the high priesthood" (21). At the Council of Trent A. Salmerón quoted texts that indicate that in the early 3d century many considered episcopal consecration to have been conferred on the Apostles at the time of the Ascension. The rite of consecration fits this idea well, since it indicates that the principal office of the bishop is the proclamation of sacred truth to which the Apostles were especially charged at the Ascension (Mk 16.15–20; Acts 1.8).

That bishops are superior to priests is defined by the Council of Trent (Denz 1777). This was clearly affirmed in the early 2d century (St. Ignatius, *Ad Phil.* 4; *Ad Smyrn.* 8), but to counter an attempt by deacons to be accepted as superior to priests, some early writers (e.g., Ambrosiaster, St. John Chrysostom, St. Jerome) overemphasized the elements of equality between priests and bishops (see F. Prat, DTC 5.2:1661–63).

The Council of Trent defined that ecclesiastical hierarchy is of divine institution (Denz 1776) and that *de facto* it is composed of bishops, priests, and other ministers. That the *de facto* composition is of divine institution is not defined, but its divine institution is theologically certain. This is confirmed by Vatican Council II (27).

The Council of Trent asserted moreover that episcopal consecration conveys a power over the Sacraments of Confirmation and Holy Orders that does not belong in the same way to a priest. Yet this cannot be the radical power over these Sacraments, since, without episcopal consecration, priests have been commissioned to confer the priesthood, and it is common for them to be commissioned to confirm (see C. Journet 1:98–120). Since the historical evidence is, for all practical purposes, unquestionable that priests share with bishops the radical power to confirm and ordain, the special manner in which bishops possess these powers must be found in the line of jurisdiction. An excessive distinction between the power of Orders and jurisdiction has retarded the development of the theology of the episcopate. It has led theologians either to deny that episcopal consecration is a true Order or to attempt to brush aside the historical evidence of priests being empowered to ordain even to the priesthood (though there is no clear evidence of a priest ever conferring episcopal consecration).

K. Rahner suggests the possibility that history testifies only that priests *have* shared the radical power to ordain, that perhaps the Church determines the powers granted by priestly ordination according to the needs of the times (see *Bishops: Their Status and Function* 75, 9). Although this idea can be entertained only in the context of Rahner's general ecclesiological-sacramental teaching, it well illustrates the extensive area for development that remains in the theology of the episcopate.

St. Thomas Aquinas, for example, in his *Commentary on the Sentences* (repeated in ST Suppl 40.5) denied that consecration confers a character since it is directly concerned with imparting power over the Mystical Body (jurisdiction) rather than power over the Eucharistic Body (Orders), which is the pinnacle of the sacramental Order. Yet this theory did not accord well with valid sacramental principles. He recognized this in his later writings and opened the way to the acceptance of the episcopate as a true Order. This teaching is theologically certain today [see Journet, *op. cit.;* E. Seiterich, "Ist der Episkopat ein Sakrament?," *Scholastik* 18 (1943) 200–219].

Keeping in mind the less essential distinction between the line of orders and the line of jurisdiction, one may consider the effects of episcopal consecration from the point of view of the powers conferred and of the grace imparted. Vatican Council II has spoken of the sacred character impressed by episcopal consecration and of the bishops as those who admit new members to their ranks "by means of the Sacrament of Orders" (21). Certainly, then, consecration either imparts a character or in some manner transforms the sacerdotal character. As Robert Bellarmine notes, it makes little difference which is the case (*De Sac. Ord.* 1.5). There is one power of ordination and of jurisdiction that makes up the supreme power of the Church. The power of jurisdiction is included "substantially" in the episcopal character, though it requires the canonical mission to be actualized [see W. Bertrams, "La collegialità episcopale," CivCatt 115 (March 7, 1964) 443].

That the episcopate is a true Sacrament impressing a character (or perfecting the sacerdotal character already impressed) and conferring grace is now theologically certain. It seems even to be *de fide* from the ordinary magisterium, which includes direct statements to this effect on the part of John XXIII on the occasion of consecrating bishops [ActApS 52 (1960) 466] and of Paul VI on a similar occasion (*L'Osservatore Romano,* July 1, 1964), as well as the *Constitution on the Church* of Vatican Council II.

Paul VI said that "[consecration] is a source of grace, a gift of God, a spiritual treasure, a higher sanctification. It is not just a transmission of liturgical, teaching, and juridical power, but a perfection conferred upon the one consecrated, who before sanctifying others is himself sanctified" (*loc. cit.*). Thus, like any social Sacrament, it provides the grace necessary to fulfill the role conferred. In the case of the episcopate this role is of the highest order in the sanctification of the Church and the salvation of men. It requires a high degree of charity (Thomas Aquinas, ST 2a2ae, 135.1).

Bibliography: J. H. CREHAN, Davis CDT 1:273–283. K. RAHNER, *Bishops: Their Status and Function,* tr. E. QUINN (London 1964). F. AMIOT et al., *Catholicisme* 4:781–820. C. JOURNET, *The Church of the Word Incarnate,* tr. A. H. C. DOWNES, 4 v. (London 1955) 1:98–120. J. LÉCUYER, "Aux origines de la théologie thomiste de l'épiscopat," Greg 35 (1954) 56–89; "La Grâce de la consécration épiscopale," RevScPhilTh 36 (1952) 389–417. J. B. BROSNAN, "Episcopacy and Priesthood in St. Thomas," AmEcclRev 121 (1949) 125–135.

[A. ROCK]

BISHOP, AUXILIARY

According to CIC c.350.3, an auxiliary bishop is a coadjutor bishop without right of succession given by the Holy See to the person of a residential bishop. Hence, if a bishop is assigned with right of succession or if he be given to the see rather than to the person of the residential bishop, he is not in the strict sense an auxiliary.

His rights (CIC c.351.1) are gathered from the document of the Holy See by which he is appointed. If he is assigned to help a residential bishop who is altogether incapacitated, the auxiliary has all the rights and offices of the residential bishop. Otherwise, the auxiliary's duties are in general those assigned by the residential bishop (CIC c.351.2). What the auxiliary is able and willing to undertake the ordinary should not habitually delegate to someone else (CIC c.351.3); on the other hand, so long as he is not legitimately impeded, the auxiliary at the request of the ordinary ought to exercise pontifical functions to which the ordinary himself is bound (CIC c.351.4). In the matter of residence within the diocese the auxiliary is held by the same obligations as the ordinary (CIC c.354). The function of an auxiliary, unless the letters of appointment provide otherwise, ceases with the death or transfer of the one whom he has been assigned to assist (CIC c.355.2).

The general role then of the auxiliary is clear: he is to assume such duties and functions within the diocese as the ordinary because of his health or the size of the diocese cannot fulfill, especially functions that require the sacramental power of a bishop. In very large dioceses several auxiliaries may be assigned.

At the time of his consecration the auxiliary is given a titular diocese; generally the title will be that of some ancient Christian center in the Near or Middle East in which the Church once flourished but in which for centuries it has almost completely disappeared. The auxiliary has no power in his titular diocese (CIC c.348).

Under the present legislation embodied in the Code (c.223.2), auxiliaries when called to a general council have a deliberative vote, unless it is expressly stated otherwise in the decree of convocation. This legislation follows a decision reached by the Central Committee in preparation for Vatican Council I and was endorsed by Pope Pius IX. The decision recommended the admission of merely titular bishops as a privilege, not a right, and that if admitted, they should have voice and vote in the proceedings. A change of viewpoint in this regard is discussed more fully in the article on coadjutor bishops.

See also BISHOP, COADJUTOR; BISHOP (IN THE BIBLE); BISHOP (IN THE CHURCH); BISHOP (SACRAMENTAL THEOLOGY OF); DIOCESE (EPARCHY); COUNCILS, GENERAL (ECUMENICAL), HISTORY OF; COUNCILS, GENERAL (ECUMENICAL), THEOLOGY OF.

Bibliography: E. VALTON, DTC 5.2:1705–06. "Weihbischof," LexThK² v.10. G. JACQUEMET, *Catholicisme* 4:820–824. G. E. LYNCH, *Coadjutors and Auxiliaries of Bishops* (CUA CLS 238; Washington 1947).

[S. E. DONLON]

BISHOP, COADJUTOR

A coadjutor bishop is assigned by the Holy See to assist the principal bishop of a diocese. Canon Law (CIC cc.350–355; ClerSanc cc.417–421) refers to three types of coadjutor bishop. Two of these are said to be "given to the person of the bishop" since their office of coadjutor expires with that of the principal bishop of the diocese. Such coadjutor bishops may be appointed by the Holy See with or without the right of succession to the diocesan see. The coadjutor without the right of succession is called an auxiliary *bishop. The third type is said to be "given to the see" (*coadiutor sedi datus*) inasmuch as his office continues even during the vacancy of the diocese. Coadjutors to the see itself are appointed only in certain dioceses of Europe where a special privilege or immemorial custom has been sanctioned by the Holy See. This type of coadjutor is unknown in Oriental Canon Law.

Reason for Appointment. The circumstances in a diocese that require the Holy See to make such an appointment vary. Where it is customary to appoint a coadjutor "given to the see," the diocese is so large, either in territory or in the number of the faithful, that a coadjutor is necessary to relieve the principal bishop, completely or in part, of the duties requiring the power of episcopal Orders. For the appointment of a coadjutor "given to the person of the bishop" the same reasons may apply, whether or not the coadjutor is to have the right of succession. A common reason for the appointment of either type is the chronic ill health or old age of the principal bishop. Other reasons are the stature of the one to whom a coadjutor is assigned, e.g., a cardinal or archbishop, or the large population or area of the diocese. The designation of a coadjutor with right of succession is occasioned by weightier reasons than those for an auxiliary bishop. Traditional aversion to appointing a successor to an office before it is vacant was overcome only gradually as the need for such coadjutor bishops became more evident.

Functions. It is a matter of dispute whether coadjutor bishops hold an ecclesiastical office in the strict sense. They do not receive ordinary power of jurisdiction by reason of their appointment. However, the Code (CIC cc.351.2, 353.1, 355.2, 3; ClerSanc cc.418.2, 419.1) uses the term office in reference to them. The powers, rights, and duties of coadjutor bishops are indicated only in a general manner in the canons pertaining to them. In determining what these powers are in individual instances, the apostolic letter of appointment must be considered and given preference over other considerations even when it may appear to run counter to general legal norms. If the apostolic letter indicates that the principal bishop is to be regarded as entirely incapacitated, the coadjutor "given to the person of the bishop," whether or not he has the right of succession, has all the rights and duties of the principal bishop. Moreover, even if the apostolic letter says nothing of the matter, the coadjutor automatically has these rights and duties if the principal bishop becomes entirely incapacitated, even temporarily. Otherwise the coadjutor has only the duties assigned by the residential bishop. The principal bishop can delegate to the coadjutor powers, rights, and duties besides those specified in the letter of appointment. Coadjutorship in itself does not include any ordinary power of jurisdiction, and only the coadjutor "given to the see" may exercise the full power of orders exclusive of the power to ordain. If the residential bishop becomes incapacitated, the coadjutor "given to the see" does not assume the disabled bishop's powers and duties.

Assumption of Office. Coadjutor bishops assume office with the presentation of the apostolic letter of appointment to the proper authority. Ordinarily, all coadjutors must show the apostolic letter to the residential bishop. The auxiliary bishop need present the letter to no one else. The coadjutor "given to the see" and the coadjutor with the right of succession must present it to the cathedral chapter as well as to the residential bishop (*see* CANONS, CHAPTER OF; CONSULTORS, DIOCESAN). In the U.S. and in all dioceses not having a cathedral chapter, the diocesan consultors take the place of the chapter and the apostolic letter must be presented to them. If the principal bishop is dying or has died, the auxiliary bishop may not proceed to the canonical possession of his office unless the letter of appointment states that his office is to continue during the vacancy of the see. Other coadjutors may in such circumstances assume their office.

Cessation of Office. Ordinarily the office of coadjutor "given to the person of the bishop" (with or without the right of succession) ceases with that of the principal bishop; not so, however, the office of the coadjutor "given to the see," since this continues during the vacancy of the see. The coadjutor with right of succession immediately becomes the principal bishop, provided he has taken canonical possession of his office as coadjutor bishop in the prescribed manner. The office of the auxiliary bishop ceases with that of the bishop to whom he was assigned unless the letter of appointment stated otherwise. The auxiliary bishop's appointment, therefore, would ordinarily have to be reconfirmed by the Holy See.

See also CHORBISHOP.

Bibliography: F. PRAT, DTC 5.2:1656–1701. G. E. LYNCH, *Coadjutors and Auxiliaries of Bishops* (CUA CLS 238; Washington 1947). G. CHELODI, *Ius canonicum de personis praemissis notionibus de iure publico ecclesiastico de principiis et fontibus iuris canonici* (3d ed. Trent 1942). Wernz-Vidal 2:612–620.

[G. E. LYNCH]

Relationship to College of Bishops. The role of the coadjutor bishop within the diocese in which he has been assigned to assist the ordinary has been explained by what has preceded; this part discusses his relationship to the episcopal college as such and hence his right to a place in general (ecumenical) *councils. Though one cannot at the moment (1965) rule out further developments in the understanding of this relationship of coadjutor bishops (and other bishops who are not ordinaries) to the episcopal college, one can say that the teaching of the third chapter of the *Dogmatic Constitution on the Church* [ActAps 57 (1965) 5–71] issued by Vatican II at the end of its third session substantially advances one's understanding.

The advance made by Vatican II will be better appreciated if the view prevalent at the time of Vatican Council I is recalled, a view that is enshrined in the present Code of Canon Law (c.223). This canon clearly implies that *titular bishops need not be called to an ecumenical council. Their admission is rather a privilege than a right, and if called they need not be granted a deliberative vote. They would seem therefore to stand outside that *corpus episcopale* that by divine right must be summoned if the council is to be truly ecumenical. The coadjutor bishop (and other titulars) would be a successor of the Apostles insofar as he possesses by consecration and the sacramental character the power of Orders enjoyed by the Apostles; he would not succeed to their doctrinal and pastoral powers either within a local community or (except by way of privilege at the time of a council) within the Church universal. *See* APOSTLES.

In the years prior to Vatican II, however, theologians suggested that episcopal consecration within the unity of the Catholic Church carries with it membership in the college that corporately succeeds the apostolic college and consequently entails participation in its power over the whole Church. If such be the meaning of consecration, every bishop (residential or not) would possess a right to be seated in an ecumenical council. The fact that this pastoral power had not been actuated at the local level would not derogate from the bishop's fundamental right as member of the episcopal corps. For K. Rahner (see bibliog.) and others it is not necessary to think that bestowing episcopal power means nothing else than giving territorially limited authority or that membership in the college is a secondary consequence of installation as ruler of a diocese. For these theologians it would not be in principle impossible to belong to the college without any role other than that of the college itself, and so one could belong to the supreme governing body of the Church without holding jurisdiction (as local pastor) over any particular territory.

This newer viewpoint appears to have won the approval of Vatican Council II, for it teaches in the *Dogmatic Constitution on the Church* (21.2) that "besides the office [*munus*] of sanctifying, episcopal consecration confers the offices [*munera*] of teaching and ruling, though these offices are of their nature such that they cannot be discharged except in hierarchical communion with the head and members of the college," and again (22.1) that "one is constituted a member of the episcopal college by reason of [*vi*] sacramental consecration and hierarchical communion with the head and the members of the college." Since the conditions for membership in the college are fulfilled in every titular bishop, it would appear that they enjoy the right to place and vote in an ecumenical council, even though the constitution makes no explicit mention of it.

It may be noted, however, that this pastoral power of nonresidential bishops remains a power in relationship to the whole Church and is not exercised in a special way in regard to any local group (as is the pastoral function of a residential bishop). In other words, the pastoral power as it exists in titular bishops who are coadjutors or auxiliaries of a residential bishop in no way of itself limits or conditions the full pastoral power

or right of the residential bishop in regard to the faithful of his diocese.

See also BISHOP (CANON LAW); BISHOP (IN THE CHURCH); BISHOP (SACRAMENTAL THEOLOGY OF); HIERARCHY; PONTIFF.

Bibliography: E. VALTON, DTC 5.2:1705–06. R. STRIGL, Lex ThK² 6:362–363. K. RAHNER and J. RATZINGER, *The Episcopate and the Primacy,* tr. K. BARKER et al. (New York 1962). J. BRINKTRINE, "Quomodo se habeat collegium episcoporum ad summum pontificem," FreibZPhilTh 10 (1963) 86–94. J. HAMER, "Note sur la collégialité épiscopale," RevScPhilTh 44 (1960) 40–50.

[S. E. DONLON]

BISHOP, MONASTIC

According to *Bede, speaking of Iona (*Eccl. Hist.* 3.14), "This isle is wont always to have an abbot who is a priest as ruler, to whom the whole province and the bishops themselves by an unusual arrangement, are expected to be subject, a situation that goes back to the first teacher (St. *Columba) who was not a bishop but a priest and a monk." Iona was so much part of the Irish Church that Bede's statement has been given universal application. It has also been rigidly interpreted to mean that in the Irish Church all jurisdiction was in the hands of the abbots of the great monasteries.

The situation in Ireland was in fact much more complex. Priest-abbots were the ultimate in authority within their monasteries, and it is probable that they were the highest authority in the *paruchia,* the lands, often scattered, which each monastery held by gift as private property. The very possession of great holdings would give the abbot a position comparable to that of a noble or prince and would account for such titles as "Abbot of Rome" for the pope and "Abbot of the Blessed" for Christ himself.

In Ireland the title came to connote high ecclesiastical authority. Nevertheless, the abbot in Ireland was always inferior to the bishop in dignity. This is evident not merely in ecclesiastical documents, e.g., the *Collection of Canons* and the *Lives of the Saints,* but also from native secular law. Every Irish noble had his "honor-price," and the honor-price of a bishop was equivalent to that of a king, while the abbot's was on a lower level, depending on his personal prestige and not on his professional status. In the *Old Irish Litanies* bishops had a place of special honor; they were invoked in groups of seven and even in greater numbers.

According to the *Rigail Pátraic,* the so-called rule of St. *Patrick (*c.* 8th century), every *tuath,* or state, should have a chief-bishop (prím-epscop) to ordain clergy and act as confessor and spiritual father to princes and nobles. It was the duty of the bishop to see that the *tuath* had worthy priests to celebrate Mass, to administer the Sacraments, and to bury the dead. The care of all priests rested with the bishop, whose duty it was to supervise priests in giving due and conscientious service to the laity. Obviously, the bishop was by far the most important ecclesiastic in the state. He might live in a monastery, but he was certainly not subject to its abbot. It may be taken as certain that a monk, once raised to the episcopate, ceased to owe obedience to any abbot. The nearest parallel to the Irish monastic bishop is the modern mission bishop of regular orders. All his clergy belong to the same order and have as their immediate head a superior nominated by the order. Thus the bishop would appear to depend utterly on the order, yet he is not subject to its superior general. Similarly, the Irish bishop might depend on the monastery in various ways, but as a bishop he would not be subject to its abbot. It is noteworthy that, when the Synod of Rathbresail (1111) divided Ireland into dioceses on the continental model, more than 50 bishops were present.

In Britain, after the destruction of towns by the Anglo-Saxon invaders, bishops had their sees in monasteries, which at the same time they ruled as abbots. On the Continent bishops might be found living in exempt monasteries, but that did not conflict with a diocesan system already well established.

Bibliography: BEDE, *Eccl. hist.,* 3.4, with note by C. PLUMMER, in *Opera Historica,* 2 v. (Oxford 1896) 2:133–134. ADAMNAN, *Life of Saint Columba,* ed. W. REEVES (Edinburgh 1874), with note 198f. C. PLUMMER, comp., *Vitae sanctorum Hiberniae,* 2 v. (Oxford 1910), introd. xxxi, n.3; ed. and tr., *Irish Litanies* (HBradshSoc 62; 1925). *Ancient Laws of Ireland,* ed. W. N. HANCOCK et al. 6 v. (Dublin 1865–1901) 1:16, 40, 202; 3:408; 5:22, 234, 412. J. G. O'KEEFFE, "The Rule of Patrick," Ériu 1 (1904) 216–224. E. MACNEILL, "Ancient Irish Law. The Law of Status or Franchise," *Proceedings of the Irish Academy, Section C* 36 (1923) 265–316. H. FRANK, LexThK² 6:346–347.

[J. RYAN]

BISMARCK, OTTO VON

German statesman; b. Schönhausen, Brandenburg, April 1, 1815; d. Friedrichsruh, near Hamburg, July 30, 1898. He came from the Pomeranian landed gentry, and studied law at the Universities of Göttingen and Berlin (1832–36). After working as a government law clerk (1836–39) and devoting 1 year to army service, he returned to Pomerania to manage successfully the family estates, and also read and traveled extensively. In 1847 he entered a very happy marriage with Johanna von Puttkamer, by whom he had three children. His political career began in 1847 at the United Diet, where he was a spirited and articulate defender of extreme conservatism and royalism. Bismarck was elected to the

Otto von Bismarck, portrait by Franz von Lenbach, 1880.

lower chamber of the Prussian Diet in 1849, and acted as diplomatic representative of *Prussia at the federal diet in Frankfort. After serving as ambassador to Russia (1859–62) and to France (1862), he was appointed Prussian prime minister and foreign minister by King William I (1862). His repressive measures maintained the government's authority in the face of bitter opposition to army reform by the liberal majority in the lower chamber. By his masterful use of *Realpolitik,* unencumbered by moral considerations, Bismarck became the one mainly responsible for achieving the unification of *Germany and the formation of the German Empire under Prussian leadership with Catholic Austria excluded (1871), after engineering the military defeat of Denmark (1864), Austria (1866), and France (1871). Bismarck was named the first imperial chancellor (and also a prince) in 1871 and remained in office until his dismissal in 1890, after conflicts with the young Emperor William II, chiefly over domestic issues. As chancellor, Bismarck aimed primarily to maintain peace with other countries and stability at home. His domestic policies brought him into violent conflict, however, with Catholics and, after 1878, with the Social Democrats. His social legislation greatly improved the lot of the workers, but left this class dissatisfied.

Bismarck remains a controversial figure in recent historical studies. Much of the hostile criticism has flowed from religious, nationalistic, and patriotic prejudices. As a power politician, the Iron Chancellor displayed many Machiavellian traits; but it would be an oversimplification to characterize him as a precursor of Hitler and the Third Reich. Without exaggeration Bismarck described his political ideal in the phrase "with blood and iron." Basically he was one of the last great European cabinet politicians, who promoted the idea of a conservative federal state.

It is difficult to discern the content of Bismarck's Christian beliefs and their influence on his policies. Recent research indicates that he believed in God and even in Christ, but it does not supply conclusive evidence concerning the detailed contents of his religious convictions. His family was Lutheran, but he tended toward Deism and pantheism in his student days. In 1843 he participated in a Pomeranian revival movement; it failed to win him over to *Pietism, but did lead thereafter to his regular reading of the Bible. Belief in the Trinity and other basic Christian teachings made little impression on him. He lacked understanding of the life of a Christian community and generally kept aloof from attendance at church services or reception of the Eucharist. His piety was minimal and very individualistic; yet it bore the typical marks of Lutheran subjectivism. The frequent mentions of God or of Divine Providence in his letters and speeches were introduced to embellish his successes and impulses, or merely to provide rhetorical flourishes. Bismarck had a sense of responsibility toward service of the state that was priestly, but he kept at a distance from clergymen and organized forms of religion.

Bismarck lacked any religious grasp of Roman Catholicism. He shared the liberal outlook on the Church (*see* LIBERALISM); this led him to repel and despise what seemed to him a cult disfigured by magic and priestcraft. After the publication of the *Syllabus of Errors (1864) and the definition of papal infallibility by *Vatican Council I (1870), which was completely misunderstood by the liberal mentality, Bismarck became more than ever opposed to the Church and prepared to engage it in a power struggle. He started the *Kulturkampf mainly to put into effect the liberal concept of the state. In this struggle the chancellor gained a few victories, such as the introduction of civil marriages and state control of education; but in the long run he emerged as loser in this great conflict. Determined opposition by convinced Catholics forced Bismarck to back down. Like a wise statesman, he admitted his gigantic blunder and tried to make amends for his political error.

Bibliography: E. C. MARCKS, *Bismarck: Eine Biographie, 1815–51,* 2 v. (Stuttgart 1909–39; 2d ed. in 1 v. 1954). C. G. ROBERTSON, *Bismarck* (London 1918). E. EYCK, *Bismarck: Leben und Werk,* 3 v. (Erlenbach-Zurich 1941–44); *Bismarck and the German Empire* (London 1950). A. O. MEYER, *Bismarck* (Leipzig 1949). A. J. P. TAYLOR, *Bismarck, the Man and the Statesman* (New York 1955); EncBrit (1965) 3:714–722.
A. O. MEYER, *Bismarcks Glaube* (2d ed. Munich 1933). H. BORNKAMM, "Die Staatsidee im Kulturkampf," HistZ 170 (1950) 41–72, 273–306. R. MORSEY, "Bismarck und der Kulturkampf," *Archiv für Kulturgeschichte* 39 (1957) 232–270. O. VOSSLER, "Bismarks Ethos," HistZ 171 (1951) 263–292. K. KUPISCH, "Der Staatsmann und die Kirche," *Theologia viatorum* 4 (1952) 274–303; RGG³ 1:1312–15. L. VON MURALT, "Über Bismarcks Glauben," HistZ 176 (1953) 45–91; *Bismarcks Verantwortlichkeit* (Göttingen 1955). A. DORPALEN, "The German Historians and Bismarck," *Review of Politics* 15 (1953) 53–67. F. PAHLMANN, "Der Stand des Gesprächs über Bismarcks Glauben," *Geschichte in Wissenschaft und Unterricht* 7 (1956) 207–222. H. HEFFTER, NDB 2:268–277. K. KLUXEN, STL⁶ 2:53–60. H. SACHER, Lex ThK² 2:510–511. **Illustration credit:** Nationalgalerie, Berlin.

[V. CONZEMIUS]

BISMARCK, DIOCESE OF (BISMARCK-IENSIS),

suffragan of the metropolitan See of St. Paul, Minn., embracing 34,268 square miles in the western half of North Dakota. Established on March 21, 1910, the diocese earlier formed part of the Vicariate Apostolic of Dakota (1879–89) and the Diocese of *Fargo (1889–1910). The first bishop, Vincent Wehrle, OSB (1910–39), as founder of the mission centers of St. Gall's monastery at Devil's Lake (1894) and St. Mary's Abbey at Richardton (1899), had done much to preserve the faith of the German-speaking immigrants from Russia and Austria-Hungary, who formed part of his flock of 25,000 Catholics. Wehrle's episcopate was characterized by missionary conditions, but prosperity and great building activity coincided with the episcopacy of his successor, Vincent J. Ryan (1940–51). When the third bishop, Lambert A. Hoch (1952–57), was transferred to Sioux Falls, S.Dak., Dec. 5, 1956, he was succeeded by Hilary B. Hacker (1957–   ).

In 1963 Catholics in the diocese numbered 73,300 in a total population of about 245,700. There were 92 parishes and 45 missions, cared for by 156 priests, including diocesan, Benedictine, and Precious Blood fathers. Twenty-one brothers and 449 sisters helped to staff the institutions of the diocese, including 28 elementary and 11 high schools, 2 colleges (*Mary College for women, Bismarck, and *Assumption College for men, Richardton), 2 homes for the aged, 7 hospitals, 2 schools of nursing, and Home on the Range for Boys at Sentinel Butte, a protective institution. Besides the Benedictine nuns from Minot, Bismarck, Crookston, and Pierre, other sisters teaching and nursing in the diocese included the Sisters of Notre Dame, of the Precious Blood, Mercy of the Union, Mercy of the Holy Cross, St. Francis, St. Francis of Penance and Christian Charity, Holy Family, and the Domini-cans, Felicians, and Ursulines. Of the 2,000 Catholic Indians in the diocese, those on Standing Rock and Fort Berthold reservations were cared for by Benedictine priests and sisters.

[L. PFALLER]

BISTICCI, VESPASIANO DA,

bookseller and author; b. Florence, 1421; d. Antella, Italy, 1498. His family had moved to Florence from Bisticci, a nearby village. Vespasiano did not have a thorough education that prepared him for one of the professions, but he joined the guild of stationers as a young man and eventually became the most famous of *Renaissance booksellers, *il re dei cartolari* (see BOOK, THE MEDIEVAL). In the 15th century, before the advent of printing, codices written by hand and frequently beautifully illuminated were much sought after by private collectors. Italian *humanism stressed the need for returning to the original texts of the classical authors, the sources for the study of language, literature, and philosophy. Princes, kings, popes, and wealthy men began assembling libraries. It was fashionable to possess a collection of fine manuscripts, often in exquisitely executed buildings. Vespasiano opened a shop in Florence that supplied copies of well-known works and of recently discovered manuscripts to many famous men. His bookshop became a meeting place for humanists, scholars, artists, and prelates. Among his patrons were Cosimo de' *Medici, for whose library at the Badia of Fiesole Vespasiano's scribes copied numerous books; Duke Federico Montefeltre of Urbino; Popes *Eugene IV and *Nicholas V; the *Este; and *Matthias Corvinus, King of Hungary. Rather than deal in printed *books, which were gradually displacing manuscripts, Vespasiano retired in 1480 to the village of Antella, where he devoted the last years of his life to writing. His best-known work is the *Vite di Uomini Illustri del secolo XV,* or *Lives of Illustrious Men,* in which he vividly described many of his great contemporaries whom he knew through his trade. Other works by Vespasiano include *Libro delle lodi delle donne* (ed. L. Sorrento, Milan 1910), *Lamento per la presa di Otranto* (1481), and *Trattato e conservazione dei Christiani* (1495).

Bibliography: The most recent English version of the *Lives* is *The Vespasiano Memoirs: Lives of Illustrious Men of the XVth Century,* tr. W. G. and E. WATERS (London 1926; Torchbks., New York 1963), with bibliog.

[E. G. GLEASON]

BISTRITA, ABBEY OF,

name of two abbeys in Rumania.

The one in Moldavia, district of Neamt, was founded in 1420 by Prince Alexander the Good and richly endowed with land and privileges by him and his wife, both of whom are buried there. The bell tower was built by Stephen the Great in 1498; it contains a small chapel, where beautiful 16th-century frescoes of pure Moldavian art were discovered in 1924. The principal church was completely reconstructed by Alexander Lapusneanu in 1554, with the help of Venetian architects and painters. Traces of ancient frescoes may still be seen in its cupola and vestibule.

The Abbey of Bistria in Wallachia, district of Vîlcea, was built in 1487 in a Serbo-Byzantine style by the brothers Craiovescu (Barbu, Pârvu, Danciu, Radu, Preda, and Mircea), sons of a boyar from Craiova.

Radu purchased and transferred there the relics of St. Gregory the Decapolite. The monastery was restored in 1600 by the Moldavian Prince George Brâncoveanu. Having fallen into ruins, the church was demolished and completely rebuilt by German architects in 1856. An inscription with the name of the original architect, *Mane meşter,* is preserved in the sculptured frame of its main entrance. The abbey had been a great center of Slavic studies and possessed many manuscripts; those preserved are now in the museum of Bucarest.

Bibliography: N. IORGA, *Istoria bisericii românesti,* 2 v. (2d ed. Bucharest 1929–32); and G. BALŞ, *Histoire de l'art roumain ancien* (Paris 1922). *Enciclopedia româniei,* 4 v. (Bucharest 1936–43) 2:305–306, 506.

[T. FOTITCH]

BITTI, BERNARDO, Jesuit painter; b. Camerino, Italy, 1548; d. Lima, 1610. He took up painting at an early age. When he was 20, he joined the Society of Jesus in Rome as a brother. In 1568 the Jesuits went to Peru, where there was a need for religious who were skilled in trades and crafts. When word reached Rome from Lima that a painter was needed, Bitti, who was the best one available, was sent to Peru. He arrived in Lima in 1575 and worked there. In 1583 he went to Cuzco as a painter; and later, to La Paz, Potosí, and Chuquisaca. Most of his work was done in Juli, Peru, a town on Lake Titicaca, where the Jesuits had established their missions to convert the Aymara Indians. Bitti was a representative of Italian mannerism. He painted in tempera with the delicacy of the followers of Michelangelo and Raphael. Line and cool colors predominate in his paintings, which are very fine and are related to Vasari's. Bitti was a great influence in America, especially in Cuzco and in the Audiencia of Charcas (Bolivia). The painters of Peru and Bolivia were faithful to mannerism for many years after that style had disappeared in Europe. Bitti influenced also the Quito school through the Dominican painter Pedro *Bedón. At his death he was esteemed for his virtue and for his talent. Among his surviving works are the canvasses of a retable dedicated to San Ildefonso in the church of San Miguel, Sucre. In Juli there are a number of examples of his painting. There are paintings of the "Coronation of the Virgin" in both Cuzco and Lima. One of his followers was Gregorio Gamarra, who worked in Potosí and Cuzco in the period 1601 to 1628.

Bibliography: J. DE MESA and T. GISBERT, *Bernardo Bitti* (La Paz, Bolivia 1961); *Historia de la pintura cuzqueña* (Buenos Aires 1962). M. S. SORIA, *La pintura del siglo XVI en Sudamérica* (Buenos Aires 1956).

[J. DE MESA; T. GISBERT]

BJÖRNSON, BJÖRNSTJERNE, Norwegian playwright and novelist; b. Österdalen, Dec. 8, 1832;

Björnstjerne Björnson.

d. Paris, April 26, 1910. He was the son of a Lutheran minister and grew up in a scenic farming district with strong cultural traditions. During school years he steeped himself in *Snorri Sturluson and wrote on international politics in the local newspaper. He followed *Ibsen as director of the theater at Bergen (1857–59) and also made his mark as a political speaker. After breaking with "Grundtvigianism" (*see* GRUNDTVIG, NIKOLAI FREDERIK SEVERIN), he turned to social and political problems. His travels took him to the U.S. (1880) and through most of Europe. He returned to Norway (1887) but later went to Paris (1909), where he died.

Björnson early conceived it to be his vocation to promote national culture, mainly by showing the continuity between the age of the *sagas and his own time. In this spirit he wrote the national anthem (1859) and began his "literary rotation of crops": tales of contemporary rural life alternating with historical plays. His prose tales, *Trond* and *Synnöve Solbakken* (1857, The Sunny Hill), *Arne* (1858), *Faderen* (The Father), and *En glad Gut* (1859–60, A Happy Boy), reveal his strong but disciplined will. The dramas *En Fallit* (A Bankruptcy) and *Redaktören* (1875, The Editor) were the first dramas in Scandinavia to treat social problems.

Under the influence of rationalism, Björnson rejected Christianity and adopted an evolutionary philosophy. *Stöv* (1882, Dust) describes the deadening effect of a puritanical faith, and *Over Ævne I* (1883, Beyond Our

Bernardo Bitti, "Virgin with Child and St. John," tempera on canvas, in the church of San Miguel at Sucre, Bolivia.

Power, I), one of his most powerful plays, reveals the dangers of occultism. The novels *Det flager i byen og på havnen* (1884, The Heritage of the Kurts) and *På Guds Veje* (1889, In the Ways of God) express radical views on sex education and on the conflict between science and religion. *Geografi og Kjaerlighed* (1885, Geography and Love) is a sparkling, ironical comedy, and *Paul Lange og Thora Parsberg* (1898) castigates the destructive effect of politics on a sensitive character. Although his dramatic work is uneven and his themes are now dated, he won the Nobel prize in 1903.

Bibliography: *Samlede digter-verker,* ed. F. BULL, 9 v. (Copenhagen 1919–20); *Brev,* ed. H. KOHT, 6 v. (Copenhagen 1912–32); *Artikler og Taler,* ed. C. COLLIN and H. EITREM, 2 v. (Copenhagen 1912–13). H. LARSON, *Björnstjerne Björnson: A Study in Norwegian Nationalism* (New York 1944). **Illustration credit:** The Norwegian Embassy Information Service.

[A. SALVESEN]

BLACK, WILLIAM,

Methodist elder and missionary, known as the Father of Methodism in Nova Scotia, Canada; b. Huddersfield, West Yorkshire, England, 1760; d. Halifax, Nova Scotia, Sept. 6, 1834. In 1775 his parents took him to Nova Scotia, where they settled in the Amherst–Fort Cumberland district. About 1779 a revival began among the Methodists in the district, and William became a convert at 19 and a lay preacher at 20. In this capacity he traveled the length and breadth of Nova Scotia, laying the foundations of organic Methodism. In 1786 at a conference at Halifax, he was placed in charge of the Nova Scotia mission. Three years later at Philadelphia, Pa., where he had visited in 1785, he was ordained deacon and the next day elder. Upon his return to Nova Scotia he was made superintendent of the Methodist societies in British North America. Shortly afterward he made a visit to the Windward Isles and Bermuda. In 1791 he appealed to England for more lay preachers; the response was good and the work of consolidating the missions progressed well. In 1827 Black's first wife and both his children died; he remarried the following year.

Bibliography: M. RICHEY, *A Memoir of the Late Rev. William Black* (Halifax 1839). J. E. SANDERSON, *The First Century of Methodism in Canada* (Toronto 1908).

[J. F. REED]

BLACK DEATH

The name later applied to the wave of plague that swept over Europe in the years 1347 to 1350, and remained endemic, with frequent epidemic outbreaks, into early modern times. Plague is the product of a bacillus, *pasteurella pestis,* and occurs in three major forms: bubonic (attacking the lymphatic glands), septicemic (attacking the bloodstream), and pneumonic (attacking the lungs). All three forms occurred in the first plague of 1347 to 1350, with the bubonic form dominant in warm weather, and the pneumonic common in winter. Only the pneumonic form is readily contagious between humans; bubonic and septicemic plague are passed to men by the fleas of infected rats. The presence of the three forms explains the diversity of reported symptoms.

The plague reached Western Europe by sea late in 1347, and was at its height in the Mediterranean lands in 1348, in England in 1349, and in the Baltic area in 1350. The mortality was immense, being usually estimated at one-quarter to one-third of the population. Had this been a single attack, the loss would have been quickly made good; but severe epidemic recurrences in the following half-century seem to have long held the population well below the preplague level. Russell estimates for England a population decline from 3,750,000

Mass burials during the Black Death, Tournai, 1349. Illumination from a manuscript "Annals" of Giles de Muisit.

in 1347 to 2,000,000 in 1400. After 1400, plague tended to be more localized and urban. The last major outbreak in England was the Great Plague of London in 1665; the last in Western Europe was the violent outbreak in Marseilles in 1720. Disappearance of the plague from Europe seems to have resulted not from advance in sanitation or medical knowledge, but rather from the replacement of the black rat (*rattus rattus*), whose habits and dominant species of flea are highly conducive to plague transmission, by the brown rat (*rattus norwegicus*). Where the black rat has remained common, as in India, plague has remained important.

The demographic consequences of the 14th-century plague in Western Europe seem well-established. Its economic effects have been often exaggerated, and few today would regard plague as a primary factor, though it played a major role in deepening and quickening economic and social trends already apparent. The Church suffered a heavy, though uneven, mortality among the clergy. Since the toll seems to have been especially heavy in the higher age groups, deaths among the clergy must have run well beyond the general average. The mortality of bishops from 1347 to 1350 seems to have been around 35 per cent, and careful study of some English dioceses suggests a loss of clergy approaching 40 per cent in those years. The effort to replace the deceased in both the secular and the regular clergy led inevitably to less rigid standards of ordination and profession, with unhappy results.

The psychological effects of the plague must have been enormous. They are probably reflected in the often remarked tendency toward morbidity in the closing medieval centuries. The plague stimulated medical study, and a considerable literature of plague tractates was produced. Since the nature and transmission of plague were discovered only at the end of the 19th century, these tractates are of major interest only to the medical historian. Though the pneumonic variety was observed to be highly contagious, the greater prevalence of the bubonic form (pneumonic plague was rare in Europe after 1400) helped to protract into the 19th century the ancient miasmic concept of epidemic disease.

Bibliography: A. M. CAMPBELL, *The Black Death and Men of Learning* (New York 1931). J. SALTMARSH, "Plague and Economic Decline in England in the Later Middle Ages," CambHistJ 7 (1941) 23–41. J. C. RUSSELL, *British Medieval Population* (Albuquerque 1948). L. F. HIRST, *Conquest of Plague* (Oxford 1953). E. CARPENTIER, "Autour de la peste noire," *Annales: Economies, Sociétés, Civilisations* 17 (1962) 1062–92; *Une Ville devant la peste: Orvieto et la peste noire de 1348* (Paris 1962). J. M. W. BEAN, "Plague, Population and Economic Decline in the Later Middle Ages," *Economic History Review*, 2d ser., 15 (1963) 423–437. J. STABER, LexThK² 8:312–313. W. M. BOWSKY, "The Impact of the Black Death Upon Sienese Government and Society," *Speculum* 39 (1964) 1–34. **Illustration credit:** Giraudon.
[R. W. EMERY]

BLACKMAN, JOHN, Carthusian biographer of Henry VI; b. Bath and Wells diocese, 1407–08; d. January 1485(?). Blackman was educated at Merton College, Oxford; he was a fellow of the college *c.* 1439, and subwarden *c.* 1443. From 1444 to 1452 he was precentor of Eton College, and in December 1452 was nominated warden of King's Hall, Cambridge. He became an M.A. of Oxford by 1439 and a bachelor of theology by 1452. In July 1457 he resigned his post as warden and subsequently entered the London Charter-house possibly as a *clericus redditus* rather than as a monk. Later he moved to *Witham Charterhouse in Somerset; it is probable he died there. As a secular priest Blackman had been closely associated with *Henry VI and *c.* 1480 he composed a brief essay in praise of the King's virtues. Blackman also owned a large collection of manuscripts, some written in his own hand, consisting of patristic, academic, and devotional texts; he gave most of them to the Witham Charterhouse.

Bibliography: J. BLACKMAN, *Collectarium mansuetudinum et bonorum morum regis Henrici VI*, first printed by Coplande *c.* 1510, ed. and tr. M. R. JAMES, *Henry the Sixth* (Cambridge, Eng. 1919). E. M. THOMPSON, *The Carthusian Order in England* (New York 1930) 316–322. Emden Cambr 670–671.
[R. LOVATT]

BLACKWELL, GEORGE, first archpriest of England; b. Middlesex, *c.* 1545; d. Clink prison Jan. 25, 1612. Although educated at Oxford (M.A., 1567), he left, went to Douai College, and was ordained in 1576. He then worked for 22 years in England. In March 1598, four years after Cardinal William *Allen's death, Clement VIII appointed Blackwell archpriest over the hitherto unorganized seminary priests in England. Though generally approved, he was soon in difficulties from the insubordination of a small minority of priests who reprobated the new office, especially the provision in his instructions for consultation with the Jesuits. He was accused also of misusing his powers. Two appeals were prosecuted in Rome. Though thrice confirmed in office, a brief of Oct. 5, 1602, restricted his powers, and severed Jesuit connections. Despite papal condemnation of the Oath of Allegiance, devised by Parliament after the *Gunpowder Plot, Blackwell advocated that Catholics should take the oath. Having been deposed in 1608, he died without retracting his error. So much unpublished material exists that the following, and other works, should be consulted with caution.

Bibliography: DictEngCath 1:225–231. J. H. POLLEN, *The Institution of the Archpriest Blackwell* (London 1916). T. COOPER, DNB 2:606–608.
[P. RENOLD]

BLAINE AMENDMENT

The Blaine amendment is the common title for a proposed amendment to the U.S. Constitution that would have forbidden the states to devote directly or indirectly any public money or land to schools having any religious affiliation. The history of this amendment shows both the political expediency and bigotry of the men who sponsored it.

One year before the disputed election of 1876, as an opening gun in the campaign to nominate a Republican candidate for the presidency, Pres. Ulysses S. Grant told an encampment of Civil War veterans that the government of the United States had a serious obligation to educate all its citizens to preserve them from the dangers of "demagogery and priestcraft." Between Sept. 29, 1875, when this speech was delivered in Des Moines, Iowa, until the final decision that Rutherford B. Hayes had been elected over his Democratic opponent, Samuel J. Tilden, in March 1877, the issues suggested by Grant remained prominent. Grant's sketchy proposal was incorporated by James Gillespie Blaine, member of Congress from Maine, into a constitutional amendment presented to the House of Representatives on Dec. 14, 1875. Blaine then participated in the maneuvering in Congress while the measure was debated, and wrote to influential editors and politicians to secure support for his proposal.

Education and a Needed Issue. Like Grant, the incumbent President, and Hayes, then governor of Ohio but soon to be the candidate for the presidency, Blaine knew that issues marking a clear distinction between the two major parties were not abundant. The Republican party had emerged as the party of strength (after a brief period of immaturity) only when the Civil War began. Democratic party commitments to attitudes popular in the defeated South had materially decreased that party's effectiveness, but accusations of disloyalty had little impact a decade after the Civil War had ended. The Democrats had shown new strength, moreover, by winning a large number of mid-term elections in 1874. Some states theretofore regarded as certainly Republican had become Democratic; more were showing signs of disaffection from a party that had furnished evidences of corruption during the Grant administrations. The old device of the bloody shirt could hardly be flourished again.

Dissatisfaction of Voters. Republican leaders understood that other appeals, formerly successful in winning large numbers of votes, could no longer be regarded as reliable. Between 1865 and 1875, veterans of the Union Army had returned to their prewar occupations. Their primary interests centered in these activities, in their families, and in local concerns. Impassioned campaign speeches stressing military service of a decade before were proving ineffective in securing Republican victories. Equally disappointing were the efforts aimed at securing votes from an agricultural bloc. Farming regions differed too much, one from the other; the presence of a substantial number of farmers did not argue the existence of any agreement on what should constitute national farm policy. This decade, furthermore, witnessed an extraordinary growth in city dwelling and organization.

Present always in the minds of the party leaders of the 1870s was the possibility that the South might again decide to withdraw from the Union, or might at least participate in some rebellious activity. The "bloody shirt" issue could no longer unite the North and might further disaffect the South; neither veterans' nor farmers' votes could be relied on to ensure a Republican victory. Furthermore, public attention had to be distracted from the sorry record of the Grant years. Some new issue had to be found; and Grant's own speech, together with the letters of leaders within his party, make it clear that the school issue was the one accepted.

Personal Convictions. The unanimity with which Grant, Hayes, and Blaine seized upon this issue was attributable in part to their personal convictions and needs. All three might safely be described as committed to certain policies associated with the American democratic ideal as it was understood in the 19th century. An integral feature of this ideal was the furnishing of educational opportunity to all children in public elementary schools at public expense. Although the concept was introduced into America comparatively late, the idea of universal education had secured widespread support. The three chief figures in the presidential race of 1875 could rely on having chosen a ready-made issue of considerable appeal. Each of them could also associate this issue with his own hopes.

Grant was not yet convinced that a third term might not be his. If he could capitalize on the issues he suggested as vital in his annual message of 1875, he might yet secure sufficient support in the nominating convention to become the first third-term president. Hayes, often defeated for public office during a career of more than 30 years in Ohio politics, needed an appealing issue to carry his name before the national electorate. Neither of these leaders, however, had the deeply personal and strongly political needs of James G. Blaine.

Blaine and Catholicism. Originally a Pennsylvanian, Blaine had won political prominence in his adoptive state of Maine, and had served in the national House of Representatives through three terms. He had secured the speakership and used its then great power to decided effect. In all his actions, he gave evidence not only of great ability but of unusual political ambition. If he could make his name familiar to voters outside his home state, then he might well hope to secure the Republican nomination for the presidency and that office itself. Blaine began to work toward this end almost as soon as the lame duck Congress of 1875 began its sessions, although he must have been aware that a major inconsistency in his proposal could well appear if all the voters knew his entire background.

Family Ties. At a time when nativism continued to be a strong force within state and local politics, when Know-Nothingism frequently called attention to the presence of large numbers of Catholic immigrants in American cities (*see* NATIVISM, AMERICAN; KNOW-NOTHINGISM), Blaine had to keep hidden his affiliations with the Catholic Church or risk alienating his own constituents and possible future supporters throughout the country. Without losing the admiration and affection of his Catholic cousins, Ellen Ewing Sherman, wife of Gen. William T. Sherman, and Mother Angela *Gillespie, CSC, American foundress of her order, Blaine managed to keep hidden his own close connection with their Church. Newspaper stories frequently mentioned Blaine's Catholic mother, Maria Gillespie Blaine, but the vehemence with which Blaine denied any personal allegiance to the Church, together with the reverence he declared he felt for it, since it had been his mother's consolation, preserved him from the political harm he feared.

A Baptized Catholic. In actuality Blaine's ties to the Church were far more binding than he would admit. He had been baptized a Catholic and probably had received some Catholic instruction during early youth. His denial of this charge can hardly be accepted as convincing. He concealed the fact that his father, Ephraim, had been received into the Catholic Church on his deathbed, and had been buried in a Catholic cemetery. If these details became known, Blaine would incur the wrath of the urban Irish-Catholic voters, who would regard him as a traitor to their faith. If he could not maintain his public position as an adherent to some established variety of Protestantism—he claimed both Presbyterian and Congregational ties—he would lose large segments of the voting public elsewhere in the country and would incur, as well, the anger of other Republican chieftains. Hence he pleaded for newspaper stories that would show him as a worshipper in the "church of his fathers," the Presbyterian congregation of Carlisle, Pa.

Amendment and Debate. Blaine's private motives thus gave added urgency to his astute appeals to the electorate during the winter of 1875–76. Without going directly to the voters, since he retained his House membership until July, Blaine could hope to work through his fellow Republicans to secure passage of the proposed amendment. The measure would forbid states to devote public monies or lands to schools under control of any religious sect. A favorable two-thirds vote of each chamber of Congress would send this measure to the states for their consideration. Adoption would mean that Blaine would be most favorably placed for political advancement; even consideration would ensure national political prominence for him.

Goals. Offered originally as a joint resolution, the Blaine amendment capitalized on Grant's message of a week earlier, which had stressed the desirability of such an amendment. The *Congressional Record* discloses that Grant had not only emphasized the need for an amendment, but that three of the five points appearing in the recapitulation of his message mentioned the need for public school education; the desirability of eliminating sectarian influences through the taxation of church properties; and the withholding of public funds from denominational schools, orphanages, hospitals, or other institutions.

Religious Prejudice. The debate touched off by Blaine's proposed amendment included references to nativism, bigotry, treason, and political intrigue. States like New York, Ohio, and Missouri had already adopted constitutional amendments respecting public schools; there was the question now merely of using the most persuasive arguments to place other states in the same column. Hayes had suggested that the Democrats be "crowded" on school and other state issues; Blaine's initial reaction to this suggestion had been to hope that elimination of denominational schools would mean the abolition of all sectarian strife. Since some of his fellow Republicans believed that the growth of the Democratic party was the work of the Roman Catholic hierarchy, however, appeals to religious prejudice as well as to party allegiance might be expected.

Debate over the terms of the amendment centered in conventional issues: the rights of states to determine their own educational policies—a strong Democratic position; the privilege of city-dwellers, many of them Catholics and of foreign origin, to secure religious instruction in schools attended by their children—a popular urban position; and the allegations of politicians distrustful of Blaine's ambitions. The Senate Judiciary Committee reported the amendment to the whole Senate in a fashion that seemed to cast doubts on Blaine's intelligence and honesty. Possibly the clinching arguments against the proposal were that the national government would be left free to give to any private, non-religious corporation any amount of land or money, but could give nothing to any charitable cause, and that the states would likewise be crippled in their efforts to support worthy projects. Such an argument had the added merit of allowing a graceful retreat from support of the bill; it failed to win the necessary two-thirds majority by the middle of August 1876, and never again secured the essential support.

Lasting Effects. Despite this failure, however, the Blaine amendment had performed important services. It had called attention to the flimsiness of earlier political appeals, and pointed out quite accurately that there were deeper issues having greater interest for the electorate. For Blaine himself, it had served to make his name a national one, even though he would wait 8 more years for the presidential nomination. In its own right, the amendment had demonstrated clearly that profound differences of opinion on educational, religious, and political questions existed in divisive fashion among native-white-Protestant and foreign-white-Catholic groups; that the urban and rural voters of the country could be separated into factions or grouped into voting blocs over matters not purely economic; and that a party's choice of an issue combining political with religious and intellectual implications was sure to attract attention. Even in its failure, then, the Blaine amendment proved a potent political force in 1875–76, and surely helped to suggest the similar amendments of the 1890s and 1920s (*see* OREGON SCHOOL CASE).

Bibliography: Archives of The Catholic University of America, Lambert Papers. Library of Congress, Division of Manuscripts, Blaine, Harrison, Hayes, Whitelaw Reid Papers. *Congressional Record,* 44th Congress, 1875–76. A. P. STOKES, *Church and State in the United States,* 3 v. (New York 1950). M. C. KLINKHAMER, "The Blaine Amendment of 1875: Private Motives for Political Action," CathHistRev 42 (Apr. 1956) 15–49; "Historical Reasons for Inception of the Parochial School System," CathEdRev 52 (Feb. 1954) 73–94.

[M. C. KLINKHAMER]

BLAISE OF SEBASTE, ST., bishop and martyr under the Emperor Licinius; b. Sebaste, Armenia; d. c. 316 (feast, Feb. 3). According to legend, during persecution he withdrew from his bishopric of Sebaste

St. Blaise of Sebaste, tempera on a panel by an artist of the Florentine school, 14th century.

to a cave, remaining until he was discovered in a hunt for beasts. Agricolaus, Governor of Cappadocia and Lesser Armenia, had him tortured and later beheaded for his faith. In prison he healed a boy with a fishbone stuck in his throat. Blaise had become the patron of throat diseases in the East by the 6th century, and in the West by the 9th century. He became one of the *Fourteen Holy Helpers. The blessing of throats with candles began in the 16th century, when his cult was at its peak. He is the patron of the city of Ragusa and also of many tradesmen, including woolcarders (the iron comb was an instrument of his tortures). He is invoked to protect animals against wolves and to bring fair weather. His feast day was observed in the West on Feb. 15 until the 11th century; it is celebrated on Feb. 11 in the East, bringing winter to a close.

Bibliography: R. JANIN, DHGE 9:69. P. WIERTZ, LexThK² 2:525–526. M. C. CELLETTI, BiblSanct 3:158–165. **Illustration credit:** Courtesy of the Fogg Art Museum, Harvard University, Gift of Miss Margaret Whitney.

[M. J. COSTELLOE]

BLAKE, WILLIAM

Engraver, painter, and poet; b. London, Nov. 28, 1757; d. London, Aug. 12, 1827. His parents; Catharine Harmitage and James Blake, a hosier, encouraged his talent for visualization; at 10, he was sent to a drawing school in the Strand and at 14 began his apprenticeship (1772–79) to the line engraver James Basire, for whom he copied royal effigies from Gothic tombs. At 21 he began exhibiting historical and poetical watercolors at the Royal Academy. In 1782, he married Catherine Boucher, daughter of a market gardener. A volume of *Poetical Sketches,* superb lyrics and ironic dramatic fragments revealing disapproval of the American war, was printed by friends in 1783. In 1784, he wrote *An Island in the Moon,* a satiric medley showing the author as "Quid, the Cynic," among philosophizing and artistic and egocentric friends, who were interested in Voltaire, Locke, graveyard meditations, Chatterton, the perhaps uncontrollable chemical discoveries of Priestley, and the obtuseness of the Platonizing Thomas Taylor.

In 1788, he began to publish illustrated manifestoes and songs, and prophetic poems by a process of etching he called "illuminated printing." The small tractates *There is No Natural Religion* and *All Religions are One* were probably the earliest; *The Ghost of Abel* (1822) was the last. Dated 1789 were *The Book of Thel* and *Songs of Innocence.*

Blake was now reading *Lavater and *Swedenborg; he attended a London conference of Swedenborgians in April 1789. But soon events in France inspired him to write an epic on *The French Revolution;* of the announced seven parts only the first, printed in 1791, survives. Two great series of illuminated works appeared through 1795: three historical prophecies called *America, Europe,* and *The Song of Los* (comprising "Africa" and "Asia"), which announced a revolutionary apocalypse in Britain to complete those in America and France; and a philosophical series including *The Marriage of Heaven and Hell,* which replaced Swedenborg's vision of a balanced universe with a manifesto of revolutionary Christian humanism; *Visions of the Daughters of Albion,* probing the psychological roots of slavery; and *The Book of Urizen,* with its sequels *Ahania* and *Los,* depicting the imaginative inadequacy and collapse of the exterior and interior worlds of *Newton and *Locke.

Other works of this period include the emblems called *The Gates of Paradise* (1793), *Songs of Innocence and of Experience: Shewing the Two Contrary States of the Human Soul* (1794), and an outpouring of color-printed

William Blake, portrait by Thomas Phillips (1807).

symbolic pictures. For an ambitious edition of Edward Young's *Night Thoughts* in 1797 Blake made 537 drawings, but only 43 were engraved. He next began a symbolic epic, as a unique illuminated manuscript, first entitled *Vala,* later *The Four Zoas,* concerning the generation and regeneration by resurrection of Everyman or "Albion."

Blake was now painting a series of illustrations of the Bible for Thomas Butts. In 1800, he moved to Felpham, Sussex, to work near a new patron, William Hayley, but after 3 years of "slumber" and vexation he returned to London to live out a busy but unprosperous life. The date 1804 on the title pages of *Milton* (etched about 1808) and *Jerusalem* (1818–20) may mark the beginning of his new dedication to the kind of artist's life he considered Jesus to have lived. In 1809, he held an exhibition of 16 "Historical and Poetical" paintings, including "apotheoses" of Lord Nelson and William Pitt as angels of war, the former in contention with a militant Christ. Pictorial series of his late period, each constituting a prophetic work, include his illustrations of *The Grave, The Canterbury Pilgrims,* the Book of Job, *Pilgrim's Progress,* and *The Divine Comedy.* In 1818, a poem of fiercely didactic lyric fragments, *The Everlasting Gospel,* affirmed the essential unity of his life's preaching.

Blake died at 69, to be followed by his devoted wife, at the same age, 4 years later. He was buried in an unmarked grave in Bunhill Fields.

A member of no church, Blake thought of himself as a Christian, but his savior was the creative genius in every man, whose gospel was mutual forgiveness. At his Judgment Day fools perish, the "dark religions" depart, and "sweet Science reigns"—total imaginative consciousness attained through art. As all Blake's literary and philosophical "sources" were transformed to his own idiom, so even the Bible, his greatest source, became in his own painting and poetry a philosophical, psychological, historical prophecy, "the Great Code of Art."

See also MYSTICISM IN LITERATURE.

Bibliography: *Complete Writings,* ed. G. KEYNES (New York 1957–). *The Poetry and Prose of William Blake,* ed. D. V. ERDMAN, commentary by H. BLOOM (New York 1965). *Illustrations to the Bible: A Catalogue,* comp. G. KEYNES (Clairvaux 1957). Color facsimiles are issued by the Blake Trust; color strip films by the Fitzwilliam Museum. A. GILCHRIST, *Life of William Blake* (New York 1942). D. V. ERDMAN, *Blake: Prophet against Empire* (Princeton 1954). N. FRYE, *Fearful Symmetry* (2d ed. Princeton 1958). P. E. FISHER, *The Valley of Vision: Blake as Prophet and Revolutionary* (Toronto 1961). H. BLOOM, *Blake's Apocalypse* (New York 1963). Concordance is in progress (1965), Cornell University Press. **Illustration credit:** National Portrait Gallery, London.

[D. V. ERDMAN]

BLAKELY, PAUL LENDRUM, journalist; b. Covington, Ky., Feb. 29, 1880; d. New York City, Feb. 26, 1943. His parents were Laurie John Blakely, a Confederate officer, and Lily (Hudson Lendrum) Blakely. He was tutored at home until the age of 11, and later attended St. Xavier College, Cincinnati, Ohio. He entered the Jesuit novitiate at Florissant, Mo., on July 30, 1897, and was ordained June 27, 1912. In 1914 he joined the editorial staff of *America,* a weekly review published by the Jesuits. For many years, under three editors in chief, Blakely was the principal editorial writer of the review. It was estimated that he wrote more than 1,100 signed articles and 3,000 short unsigned pieces on the subjects of education, American history, the Federal Constitution, and social problems. In the 1920s he opposed the creation of a Federal department of education (Smith-Towner Bill), and defended the rights of parents in education. His editorials formed part of the background for the U.S. Supreme Court's 1925 decision in the Oregon School Case. Blakely, guided by the encyclicals of Leo XIII, fought against the abuses of capitalism and for the right of labor to organize. In his later years, he became a critic of Franklin D. Roosevelt's administration. His firm belief in states' rights was the basis of much of his writing.

[T. N. DAVIS]

BLANC, ANTHONY, first archbishop of New Orleans, La.; b. Sury, France, Oct. 11, 1792; d. New Orleans, June 20, 1860. He was ordained in Lyons, France, by Bp. Louis W. Dubourg of Louisiana on July 22, 1816, and accompanied the prelate on his return to the U.S. in 1817. First appointed a missionary for Vincennes, he labored in Indiana until February 1820. He spent the next 40 years in Louisiana, first as a parish priest with his brother, Rev. John Baptist Blanc, in Pointe Coupee, the Felicianas, and Baton Rouge (1820–30); then as vicar-general to his immediate predecessor, Bp. Leo de Neckère, with residence in New Orleans (1830–33); administrator of the diocese (1833–35); bishop (1835–50); and finally archbishop (1850–60). During his tenure as ordinary, he saw New Orleans more than triple in population. He established 18 parishes for Creole, German, Irish, and English-speaking congregations in the see city and its environs, and 30 in rural Louisiana. Until Natchez (now Natchez-Jackson)

and Natchitoches (now Alexandria) were created dioceses in 1837 and 1853 respectively, his jurisdiction embraced both Mississippi and Louisiana. For a time (1838–40) he had charge also of the Church in Texas. Lay *trusteeism at St. Louis Cathedral, New Orleans, and elsewhere, the threat of schism, the recrudescence of *Nativism in the 1850s, the anti-Catholic bias of *Know-Nothingism, and the imminence of secession by the South were among his most grievous ordeals. The challenge by the trustees of the bishop's right to appoint pastors was checked by the Louisiana Supreme Court on June 8, 1844, but only after the cathedral had been interdicted (1842). The court decision vindicated the bishop but failed to uproot lay trusteeism in the state. On July 19, 1850, New Orleans became an archdiocese and Blanc, its first archbishop. He received the pallium in St. Patrick's Church on Feb. 16, 1851. Despite a leg fracture suffered while engaged in yellow fever relief work in 1858, he remained active until his death, which came suddenly a few hours after he had offered Mass in his chapel.

Bibliography: R. BAUDIER, *The Catholic Church in Louisiana* (New Orleans 1939).

[H. C. BEZOU]

BLANCHE OF CASTILE, Queen of France and mother of St. *Louis IX; b. Palencia, Spain, 1188; d. Maubuisson, Pontoise, France, Nov. 26, 1252. She was the daughter of Alfonso VIII of Castile. On May 23, 1200, she married the Louis who became Louis VIII of France. After his death she was regent during the minority of Louis IX (1226–34) and during his absence on the Crusade of 1248–52. With papal support the pious and possessive Blanche controlled the unruly barons, suppressed the *Albigenses, and acquired Languedoc for the crown. She helped establish the University at *Toulouse and founded the Cistercian cloister of *Maubuisson. Among her 12 children were Bl. *Isabelle of France, Charles of *Anjou, who ruled Sicily (1266–82); and Alphonse, who married the heiress of Raymond of Toulouse.

Bibliography: É. BERGER, *Histoire de Blanche de Castile* (Paris 1895). M. BRION, *Blanche de Castille* (Paris 1939). J. GONZÁLEZ, *El reino de Castilla en la época de Alfonso VIII,* 3 v. (Madrid 1960).

[D. W. LOMAX]

BLANCHET, FRANCIS NORBERT

Pacific Northwest missioner, first archbishop of Oregon City (now *Portland), Ore., archdiocese; b. St. Pierre, Quebec, Canada, Sept. 3, 1795; d. Portland, June 18, 1883. Son of Pierre and Rosalie Blanchet, whose families had given distinguished leaders to Church and State in Canada, he attended the local parish school and the minor and major seminaries of Quebec. After ordination on July 18, 1819, he was stationed first at the cathedral in Quebec City. In October 1820, in answer to an appeal for a French-speaking priest, he was sent by Bp. Joseph Signay to minister to the Acadians and the Micmac Indians living under primitive conditions in New Brunswick. Early in 1827 he became pastor of St. Joseph de Soulanges parish in Montreal. When Signay was pressed to supply priests for white settlers in the Pacific Northwest, mostly retired Hudson's Bay Company employees, he chose Blanchet as vicar-general for the Oregon country. With

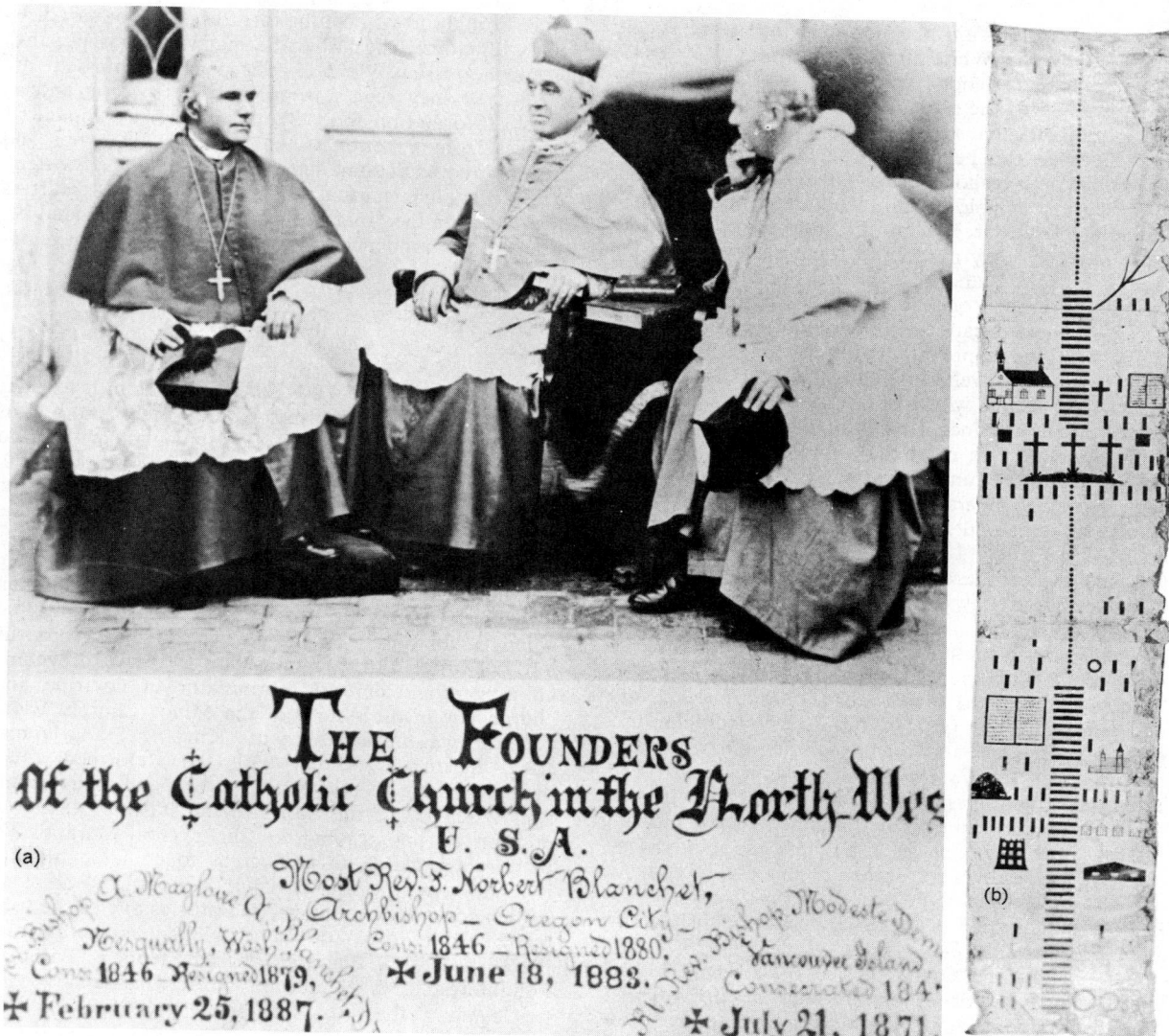

THE FOUNDERS
Of the Catholic Church in the North West
U. S. A.
(a)
Most Rev. F. Norbert Blanchet,
Archbishop — Oregon City
Bishop A. Magloire
Nesqually, Wash.,   Cons. 1846 — Resigned 1880.   Bishop Modeste Demers
Cons. 1846 Resigned 1879,   ✠ June 18, 1883.   Vancouver Island
✠ February 25, 1887.   Consecrated 184
                        ✠ July 21, 1871.
(b)

(a) Bp. Augustine Blanchet, Abp. Francis Blanchet, Bp. Modeste Demers, founders of the Church in the Pacific Northwest. (b) Catholic ladder: bars and dots represent centuries and years; other symbols denote Christian doctrines.

an assistant, Modeste Demers, a Quebec missionary who had worked under Bp. Joseph Provencher at Red River, Blanchet set out in May 1838 with the annual brigade of Hudson's Bay Company, and arrived on November 24 at Fort Vancouver, western headquarters of the company. Eagerly welcomed by whites and Indians, they visited the principal posts of Hudson's Bay Company, established missions at Cowlitz and later among the French Canadians in Willamette Valley, and explored the possibility of working among the Indian tribes. In addition to the difficulties to be expected in a wilderness, they also experienced frustrations and petty opposition from American Methodist missioners who were already well established and had gained converts even among the French Canadians.

In 1842 Blanchet met Pierre Jean De Smet, SJ, and with him and Demers drew up a plan for the ecclesiastical organization of the Oregon country. This plan was eventually approved by the Canadian and American bishops and presented by them to the Holy See. In December 1843, a vicariate apostolic was erected in Ore-

gon with Blanchet at its head as titular bishop of Philadelphia (later changed to Adrasus to avoid confusion with Philadelphia, Pa.). He received the announcement of his appointment in November 1844, and in December he embarked on a long sea journey to Montreal for his consecration by Bp. Ignatius Bourget on July 25, 1845. Before returning to his post he sailed for Europe to seek funds and candidates for the missions. Reaching Rome in January 1846, he had several audiences with Gregory XVI and successfully petitioned the Congregation for the Propagation of the Faith for the erection of an ecclesiastical province from his vicariate, with an archbishop and suffragan bishops, and further divisions to be made as the area developed. He was named archbishop of Oregon City, with his brother Augustin Magloire as bishop of Walla Walla, Wash., and Demers as bishop of Vancouver Island. After leaving Rome he appealed effectively in the major cities of Europe for assistance in his apostolate. When he sailed for home in February 1847, he was accompanied by 21 missionaries, including 8 priests and 7 sisters.

Bright prospects for the new province were rudely shattered by the Whitman massacre, Nov. 29, 1847, which practically ended missionary work among the Indians and was the signal for a new and virulent outbreak of bigotry that strained relations with many whites who clung to the belief, long since refuted, that the priests had been responsible for the massacre. Then, too, the discovery of gold in California drew many French Canadians from Oregon; priests and nuns, deserted by those to whom they ministered, went elsewhere. In the face of all this, Blanchet convened the first Provincial Council of Oregon on Feb. 28, 1848. Again and again during the next decade he sought help for his work. In 1855, with the approval of Rome, he visited South America and was well received in Peru and Bolivia and especially in Chile, where he had published a pamphlet describing his province. He returned home in 1857 with sufficient money to meet the debts of his diocese. In 1859 he collected funds in eastern Canada and brought back 31 more helpers, among them Sisters of the Holy Names of Jesus and Mary to staff his schools. He also attended the First (1852) and Second (1866) Plenary Councils of Baltimore, and in 1869 Vatican Council I, at which he strongly favored the declaration of papal infallibility.

These years were marked by continuous development in Oregon. With the growth of the city of Portland, Blanchet established his residence there in 1862, and chose Immaculate Conception Church for the pro-cathedral. Schools and other facilities opened. A diocesan paper, the *Catholic Sentinel,* appeared in 1870. Even the Indian missions were reopened, though never on the scale that Blanchet had planned. After initiating his coadjutor, Bp. Charles J. Seghers (appointed Dec. 10, 1878), into the work of the archdiocese, he resigned in 1880, retiring to St. Vincent's Hospital.

Essentially a man of action, Blanchet published only his *Historical Sketches of the Catholic Church in Oregon* . . . . (Portland, Ore. 1878). His "Catholic Ladder," a pictorial device for teaching Indians the life of Christ, Christian doctrine, and Church history, was copyrighted in 1859. His interest in the Indians never flagged. His last effort for them was to represent the hierarchy in protesting the injustice of a government policy that placed many Catholic reservations under Protestant control. In the course of protracted controversy, the need for the continual presence in Washington of an authorized representative of Catholic Indian missions became evident, and the Bureau of Catholic Indian Missions was organized in 1874.

Bibliography: L. M. LYONS, *Francis Norbert Blanchet and the Founding of the Oregon Missions, 1838–1848* (Washington 1940). C. B. BAGLEY, *Early Catholic Missions in Old Oregon,* 2 v. (Seattle 1932). H. H. BANCROFT, *History of Oregon,* 2 v. (San Francisco 1886–88). **Illustration credit:** Courtesy of the Oregon Historical Society.

[L. M. LYONS]

BLANDINA OF LYONS, ST.,

martyr at Lyons under Marcus Aurelius in 177 (feast, with the 48 martyrs of Lyons and Vienne, June 2). She was a young slave arrested with her mistress; she showed extraordinary constancy under torture, repeating again and again "I am a Christian, and nothing wicked happens among us." She was later tied to a stake in the amphitheater, but the wild beasts did not touch her. On the last day of the games, she and Ponticus, a boy of 15, were brought to witness the tortures of the other Christians. Blandina, the last to be martyred, was put in a net to be tossed by a bull. The pagans confessed that never had they seen a woman suffer so long and so much. Information about Blandina and her companions derives from a Letter of the Churches of Lyons and Vienne quoted at some length by Eusebius (*Hist. Eccl.* 5.1). Blandina is usually the first of the 48 martyrs mentioned in the *martyrologies. They are included because of the influence Lyons has had on their development.

Bibliography: E. PETERSON, EncCatt 7:1397–98. R. AIGRAIN, *Catholicisme* 2:77–78. H. PLATELLE, BiblSanct 3:202.

[M. J. COSTELLOE]

BLANDRATA, GIORGIO,

physician, lay leader in the anti-Trinitarian Minor Church of Poland and of the Unitarian Church of Transylvania; b. Saluzzo (Piedmont) 1515; d. Gyulafehérvár, *c.* 1588 or 1590. Blandrata (Biandrata) studied in Pavia and became court physician abroad. Returning to Italy, he came under the theological influence of the equivocally anti-Trinitarian jurisconsult Matteo Gribaldi and fled from the Inquisition in 1556, becoming an elder in the Italian Reformed congregation of Geneva. After coming into conflict with Calvin on the doctrine of the Trinity, he left for Zurich (1558), going on to Poland to become an influential elder and formulator of doctrine and church law in the synods of the Minor Church. From 1563 he was physician to the King of Transylvania, John Sigismund, whom, with the Reformed court preacher Franz *Dávid, he won over to anti-Trinitarianism. When Dávid moved on to the still more extreme position of not praying to Christ (non-adorantism), Blandrata urged Faustus Socinus to come to his aid, lest the nascent Unitarian Church in Transylvania, by further innovations, imperil its status as one of the four recognized religions of the religiously and ethnically pluralistic realm. Blandrata, under Stephen *Báthory, lost interest in the Unitarian Church, associated with the Jesuits of the court, but died a Unitarian.

Bibliography: I. RÉVÉSZ, *Magyar református egyhaztörténet,* v.1 (1520–1608) (Debrecen 1938); abr. Eng. tr. G. A. F. KNIGHT, *History of the Hungarian Church* (Washington 1956). E. M. WILBUR, *A History of Unitarianism,* 2 v. (Cambridge, Mass. 1945–52).

[G. H. WILLIAMS]

BLANQUI, ANDRÉS,

Jesuit architect; b. Campioni, near Milan, Italy, Nov. 25, 1677; d. Córdoba, Argentina, 1740. Blanqui, whose name is also found as Bianchi, entered the Society of Jesus in 1716, and went to Rio de la Plata the following year with another young architect, Juan B. *Prímoli. Both completed their novitiate in Córdoba in 1719. From that year until the death of Brother Blanqui, they worked unceasingly on the construction of public and private buildings. They were continually in demand as architects and builders. Successively, not simultaneously, both worked on the many buildings accomplished by them, such as the cathedrals of Buenos Aires and Córdoba; the convents of the Teresas and the Catalinas of Córdoba; the churches of La Recoleta, La Merced, and San Francisco in Buenos Aires; as well as the historic *cabildo* of the capital of Argentina. Although most of the private homes built by them have been replaced by later structures, the public buildings, such as churches, convents, and schools, are still standing. As a general rule, their architectural style was neither classic nor baroque, but eminently functional with sparse but discreet ornamentation.

Bibliography: G. Furlong, *Arquitectos argentinos durante la dominación hispánica* (Buenos Aires 1946).

[G. Furlong]

BLANTYRE, ARCHDIOCESE OF (BLANTYRENSIS),

metropolitan see since 1959, in the Shire highlands, south *Malawi (Nyasaland), southeast Africa. In 1963 it had 19 parishes, 24 secular and 63 religious priests, 21 men in 2 religious houses, 142 women in 15 convents, and 266,500 Catholics in a population of 925,000; it is 7,722 square miles in area. Its five suffragans, which had 179 priests, 278 sisters, and 291,000 Catholics in a population of 2 million, were Chikwawa (1965), Dedza (1959), Lilongwe (1959), Mzuzu (1961), and Zomba (1959). The provicariate of Nyasa (1889) became a vicariate (1897), from which the prefecture of Shire was detached (1903) and made a vicariate (1908) under the Montfort Fathers, who had established the first permanent Catholic mission in the country (1901). The Vicariate of Shire was called Blantyre (1952) when the Vicariate of Zomba was detached from it. Four European congregations of women and the African Servants of the Blessed Virgin (1926), which had 113 members in 1962, work in the diocese, where the Dutch Brothers of the Immaculate Conception have several schools.

Bibliography: *The Catholic Directory of East and West Africa 1961* (Nairobi 1961). AnnPont (1964) 66.

[J. F. O'Donohue]

BLARER

The Blarer (Blaurer) family was prominent in 16th-century Church reform and the politics of Southern Germany and the cantons of Switzerland.

Ludwig, Benedictine, Catholic reformer; b. *c.* 1480; d. Feb. 26, 1544. He became a monk of the Abbey of Saint Gall in Switzerland, where he served as cellarer for some time. In 1528 Clement VII confirmed his appointment as administrator of the Abbey of Einsiedeln and instated him as abbot in 1533, later granting him also the right, because of the religious upheavals, to administer the Sacrament of Confirmation and to consecrate churches. In modern Church history Ludwig is considered a transition figure, who strove to reform the Church from within.

Ambrosius, Protestant reformer in southern Germany and Switzerland; b. Constance, April 4, 1492; d. Winterthur, Dec. 6, 1564. He had entered the Benedictine Abbey of Alpirsbach in the Black Forest, but while pursuing further studies at Tübingen he made the acquaintance of Melanchthon and other humanists. He retained contact with Melanchthon after returning to the monastery. The spirit of Luther's writings impressed him, and he left the abbey in 1522 and returned to Constance, where he preached with zeal for the new movement. He later continued his activities in Württemberg and Switzerland.

Gerwig, Benedictine, Catholic reformer; b. Constance, May 25, 1495; d. Weingarten, Aug. 30, 1567. He made profession in the Abbey of Weingarten in 1513, and then studied Church law in Freiburg im Breisgau, Vienna, and Ferrara. In 1520 he was elected abbot of Weingarten, and in 1547, at the insistence of Emperor Charles V, he became also abbot of Ochsenhausen. Gerwig, always conservatively inclined, not only resisted energetically the efforts of the Protestant Reformers, but also became engaged in conflicts with the Jesuits. The preservation of the Catholic religion in Swabia is in part due to his political activity.

Thomas, politician and Protestant reformer; b. Constance, after 1492; d. Gyrsburg (Thurgau), March 19, 1567. After completing law studies in Freiburg im Breisgau, he studied theology in Wittenberg, where he sided with Luther. He later was influential in inducing his brother, Ambrosius, to leave the monastery. Upon returning to Constance Thomas entered political life, serving as mayor from 1537 to 1547, but was compelled to leave the city in 1548. He also took an important part in the discussions among the Reformers attempting to reach an agreement on the teaching of the Lord's Supper.

Diethelm, Benedictine, religious reformer; b. 1503; d. Saint Gall, Switzerland, Dec. 18, 1564. He became a religious in 1523, and was elected abbot of Saint Gall in 1530. While in exile in Mehrerau, where he became abbot in 1532, he arranged with the civil authorities of Saint Gall to restore the famous abbey. At Mehrerau and Saint Gall he instituted sound spiritual life, and he extended the same spirit to the secular clergy, and effected the restoration of many religious houses for women in Switzerland.

Jakob Christoph, bishop of Basel, Catholic reformer; b. Rosenberg, May 11, 1542; d. Prunktrut (Canton Bern), April 18, 1603. When appointed bishop of Basel in 1575, he found the diocese spiritually and materially impoverished. He resisted the inroads of the Protestant Reformers and carried out the instructions of the Council of Trent; he also erected a Jesuit college in his residential See of Prunktrut. He ranks as one of the foremost figures in the Counter Reformation in Switzerland.

Bibliography: Ludwig. R. Henggeler, *Professbuch der fürstlichen Benediktinerabtei Unserer Lieben Frau zu Einsiedeln,* v.3 of *Monasticon-Benedictinum Helvetiae,* 3 v. (Einsiedeln 1930–34). R. Tschudi, *Das Kloster Einsiedeln unter den Aebten Ludwig II Blarer und Joachim Eichorn 1526–69* (Doctoral diss. unpub. Fribourg U. 1946); LexThK² 2:523. Ambrosius. P. Stärkle, "Zur Familiengeschichte der Blarer," *Zeitschrift für Schweizer Kirchengeschichte* 43 (1949) 100–131, 203–224. O. Feger, NDB 2:287–288. O. Vasella, LexThK² 2:523. Thomas. P. Stärkle, *op. cit.* O. Feger, NDB 2:288. O. Vasella, LexThK² 2:523–524. Gerwig. *Briefe und Akten,* ed. H. Günther, 2 v. (Stuttgart 1914–21). H. Günther, "Abt Georg Blarer von Weingarten und die Gegenreformation," *Festschrift Georg von Hertling* (Kempten 1913) 342–349. R. Reinhardt, LexThK² 2:523. Diethelm. A. Baumann, *Die Fürstabtei St. Gallen unter Abt Diethelm Blarer 1530–64* (Doctoral diss. unpub. Fribourg U. 1948). G. Thürer, *St. Galler Geschichte* (St. Gallen 1953–   ) v.1. O. Vasella, LexThK² 2:524. Jakob Christoph. B. Bury, *Geschichte des Bistums Basel und seiner Bischöfe* (Solothurn 1927). W. Brotschi, *Der Kampf Jakob Christoph Blarers . . . um die religiöse Einheit im Fürstbistum Basel 1575–1608* (Studia Friburgensia, NS 13; Fribourg 1956). A. Chèvre, LexThK² 2:524.

[O. L. Kapsner]

BLASCO IBÁÑEZ, VICENTE

Spanish novelist; b. Valencia, Jan. 29, 1867; d. Menton, France, Jan. 28, 1928. He was graduated in law from the University of Valencia in 1896. He had founded (1891) the newspaper, *El Pueblo,* and kept it well supplied with inflammatory prorepublican articles. Such attacks on the royal government resulted in repeated exile and imprisonment, but in 1897 he obtained immunity by being elected Valencia's representative to the *Cortes*. He served six terms but resigned in 1909. For the next 4 years he unsuccessfully tried ranching

Vicente Blasco Ibáñez.

in the Argentine, but shortly before the outbreak of World War I he settled in France.

Blasco Ibáñez' early stories and novels dealt with his native Valencian region, but each novel handled a different social setting: *Arroz y tartana* (1894), the *bourgeoisie; Flor de Mayo* (1895), Mediterranean fishermen; *La barraca* (1898), farmers of the irrigated Valencian *huerta; Entre naranjos* (1900), an upper-class romance; and *Cañas y barro* (1902), the milieu of fishermen and peasants centering on Valencia's Lake Albufera. Of these, *La barraca* and *Cañas y barro* are works of convincing realism and strong human values. There followed a series of thesis novels about other Spanish cities. Hastily written and heavily slanted works, such as *La catedral* (1903), *El intruso* (1904), *La horda* (1905), and *La bodega* (1905), are of little interest to the modern reader. He attempted the psychological study of an artist and his wife in *La maja desnuda* (1906), and *Sangre y arena* (1908, *Blood and Sand*) ranks as one of the best studies of bullfighting by a Spanish author. *Los muertos mandan* (1909) was occasioned by a visit to the Balearic Islands.

His chief claim to fame, at least within the English-speaking world, is *Los cuatro jinetes del Apocalipsis* (1916, *The Four Horsemen of the Apocalypse*). Despite its strong anti-German bias, the novel's gripping account of noncombatants caught in the toils of war has literary value. *Mare nostrum* (1917) is a melodramatic story of espionage. During his last years he wrote a series of pseudohistorical novels. Two of them deal with Spanish Popes: *El Papa del Mar* (1925) portrays Benedict XIII, and *A los pies de Venus* deals with Alexander VI. Finally, *En busca del Gran Kan* (1929) treats of Columbus, and *El caballero de la Virgen* (1929) concerns the conquistador Alonso de Ojeda.

Blasco Ibáñez' ideals were those of 19th-century French liberalism and his first literary model was the naturalism of Émile *Zola. He was early estranged from the Church. His best work dealt with settings thoroughly familiar to him and was motivated by some form of social protest. He castigates, for example, usurious landlords (*La barraca*), avarice (*Cañas y barro*), militarism (*Los cuarto jinetes*), and the crowd hungering for blood at bullfights (*Sangre y arena*).

Bibliography: *Obras completas,* 3 v. (2d ed. Madrid 1949). J. A. BALSEIRO, *Blasco Ibáñez, Unamuno, Valle Inclán, Baroja: Cuatro individualistas de España* (Chapel Hill 1949). C. PITOLLET, *V. Blasco Ibáñez: Ses romans et le roman de sa vie* (Paris 1921). **Illustration credit:** Embassy of Spain, Washington, D.C.
[D. F. BROWN]

BLASPHEMY

Any expression by word, sign, or gesture that is insulting to the goodness of God. Blasphemy is to be carefully distinguished from *profanity, which is without contempt or insulting intent and does irreverence to God simply by a careless, too frequent, or inappropriate use of sacred names or reference to sacred things. Some theologians list blasphemy among the sins opposed to the virtue of *religion, for it is the object of that virtue to give to God the reverence that is His due, whereas blasphemy, on the contrary, treats Him with positive irreverence and contempt (see B. Häring, *The Law of Christ*, 2.205). The Code of Canon Law also considers blasphemy a sin against religion (CIC c.2323). St. Thomas Aquinas, however, preferred to consider it as a sin opposed to the virtue of faith inasmuch as the blasphemer asserts some error contrary to a truth of faith that he should confess (ST 2a2ae, 13.1). Without doubt blasphemy is an offense against both faith and religion, but to see it primarily in its opposition to faith serves to center attention on what is more radical in the transgression as well as to underline its malice, for, other things being equal, sins against the theological virtues are graver than those against the moral virtues.

Blasphemy is a single species of sin, but it can be committed in many ways. Theologians commonly distinguish between heretical and nonheretical blasphemy. It is heretical if it openly asserts something contrary to faith, as when it denies God's mercy, providence, or justice. It is nonheretical if it openly asserts nothing contrary to faith but consists simply in imprecations or contumelious speech against God. However, even the latter type of blasphemy implicitly contains some error with respect to faith, for it assumes that God is worthy of contumelious treatment. Theologians distinguish also between blasphemy that is directed immediately against God in His person or attributes and that which is directed against His saints, angels, men, or creation generally, in their relations to Him.

Blasphemy has always been considered to be among the gravest of sins from the point of view of objective malice. The degree of subjective malice in any particular occurrence depends on the greater or lesser willful involvement of the blasphemer in the sin. Although every form of blasphemy supposes a malicious will, in its gravest and most "perfect" form it is a deliberate and direct attack upon the honor of God with intent to insult Him. But blasphemy is also possible without a direct intent to insult the divine goodness, as when one gives expression to what does in fact derogate from the divine goodness. In this sense expressions of formal heresy or infidelity are always blasphemous. So also are expressions, commands, or invocations calling upon God to do what is unworthy of Him, such as to curse another or to remove him from the sphere of divine love and favor. Hence if one attends simply to the literal meaning of the words, expressions calling upon God to damn something are objectively blasphemous. But words have meaning in ordinary usage according to the way in which people generally understand them. In many cases they become denatured through overuse and come to have a sense quite different from their literal meaning. The regrettable English expression "God damn" appears to have undergone such a transformation, and its use in ordinary circumstances, when one does not advert to or intend to apply the literal sense, is to be classified as profanity rather than blasphemy.

The Code of Justinian (6th century) prescribed the death penalty for blasphemy, and the crime was listed as capital throughout much of both pre- and post-Reformation Europe. Since the Enlightenment, however, secular authorities have looked upon it as a crime against the sensibilities of citizens rather than against God, and its punishment has been mitigated. Many states still have laws against it. Present Canon Law relegates its punishment to the judgment of the ordinary (CIC c.2323).

Bibliography: CAJETAN, Commentarii in ST 2am2ae 13. Adequate treatments of blasphemy may be found in most handbks. of moral theology, e.g., B. HÄRING, The Law of Christ, tr. E. G. KAISER, v.1 (Westminster, Md. 1961) 205–207. Merkelbach Sum ThMor 1:610–616. J. A. McHUGH and C. J. CALLAN, Moral Theology, rev. E. P. FARRELL, 2 v. (New York 1958) 1:347–356. V. OBLET, DTC 2.1:907–910. G. VIOLARDO, EncCatt 2:1502–03.

[G. A. BUCKLEY]

BLASPHEMY (IN THE BIBLE).

Blasphemy in the OT involved any word or action offensive to God. The Mosaic Law ordered the stoning of anyone who cursed (qillēl) God, or blasphemed [nāqab, connected with qābab, "curse" (?)] His name (Lv 24.10–16; Ex 22.27). The defiant sinner insulted (giddēp) God (Nm 15.30), so also did Israel's rebellion against God (Ez 20.27), and the disparagement of God's power by Israel's enemies (4 Kgs 19.6, 22). Israel's enemies and wicked men are also said to taunt or mock (hērēp) God [Is 37.4, 17, 23; 65.7; Ps 73(74).10, 18; Prv 14.31]. To oppress God's people is to despise or spurn or revile (ni'ēṣ) His name (Is 52.5). Ni'ēṣ appears frequently in connection with God [Nm 14.11; Dt 31.20; 2 Sm 12.14; Ps 9b(10).3, 13; Is 1.4]. Taking the name of God in vain or falsely is a form of blasphemy (Ex 20.7). Later Judaism refrained from even pronouncing God's sacred name, substituting "Heavens," or "the Name," etc.

In the NT βλασφημία (also in verbal and adjectival form) means "revilement," "slander," or "railing" with men as object (Ti 3.2; Rom 3.8; 1 Cor 4.13; 10.30; Acts 13.45; 18.6, Paul's teaching; Ap 2.9; see also the lists of vices in Mk 7.22; Eph 4.31; Col 3.8; Mt 15.19; 1 Tm 6.4; 2 Tm 3.2). It also denotes a sin against God. The Jews take Jesus' claim to the divine prerogative of forgiving sin (Mt 9.3 and parallels) and to be the Son of God (Jn 10.33, 36; cf. 5.18) as blasphemy. The Sanhedrin condemned Him to death for blasphemy [cf. His use of Ps 190(110).1 and Dn 7.13 in Mt 26.63–66 and parallels]. The Jews accused St. Stephen of blasphemy because of his teaching on God, Moses, the Temple, and the Law (Acts 6.11, 13; 7.58; cf. Lv 24.10–16). Unrepentant men blaspheme God (Ap 16.11, 21). His name is also blasphemed (Ap 16.9; 13.6, by the beast of the sea; see also Ap 13.1; 17.3). The Jews by transgressing the Law caused the *name of God to be blasphemed among the Gentiles (Rom 2.24; St. Paul here uses Is 52.5, LXX, with his own inspired purpose). Rebellion of Christian slaves would cause blaspheming of the name of the Lord and His teachings (1 Tm 6.1). Since Christ's miracles are done by the power of the Holy Spirit, to attribute them to the devil is blasphemy against the Holy Spirit. This *sin against the Holy Spirit is unforgivable. A hardened blindness to the coming of the Spirit in power, it totally excludes the divine light of repentance. Other blasphemies, even those against the Son of Man whose divinity is veiled, are forgivable (Mt 12.25–32 and par.; Heb 6.4–6; 10.26–28). Christ is reviled (ἐβλασφήμουν) on the cross (Mt 27.39 and par.). The rich of this world blaspheme His name in their ill treatment of the poor (Jas 2.7). To deny Christ is blasphemy (1 Tm 1.13; Acts 26.11). Immoral conduct leads to blaspheming the Christian message (2 Pt 2.2; Ti 2.5; see also Rom 14.16). Evil men blaspheme angels (2 Pt 2.10; Jude 8, 10).

See also CURSE (IN THE BIBLE); NAME OF GOD.

Bibliography: EncDictBibl 251–253. InterDictBibl v.1.

[J. A. FALLON]

BLASPHEMY (U.S. LAW OF)

The common-law offense of blasphemy is perpetrated through the verbal publication of words calculated to impair or destroy man's reverence for God and religion by maliciously subjecting belief in the deity, Scriptures, or religious doctrines to derision and vilification. If the blasphemous words are written or printed, they constitute blasphemous libel, as do pictorial caricatures which convey a blasphemous meaning.

There appear to be two schools of thought as to the gravamen of blasphemy: one asserts that the intent to detract is sufficient; the other contends that, while the intent is required, the words must be such as tend to lead to a breach of the peace, i.e., a disruption of the public tranquility by any act or conduct that incites to violence or disorder. Historically, an actual affray consequent upon the publication of the blasphemous matter was not an element of the crime; that the words had a tendency to raise such public disturbance was sufficient. If the decencies of controversy are maintained, and no actual or potential breach of the peace is involved, one may question the veracity of any theological dogma without incurring criminal guilt.

Common Law. The crime of blasphemy did not become an offense cognizable under the common law until the early 17th century, at which time the influence of the ecclesiastical courts was rapidly declining. Preceding this transition, jurisdiction over blasphemy had resided in the ecclesiastical courts, judicial tribunals having authority over offenses against religion and morals.

So long as the ecclesiastical courts retained jurisdiction over religious offenses, blasphemy was regarded as a crime directly against God. The onslaught of the Reformation struck the ecclesiastical courts a blow from which they did not recover. The Elizabethan Court of High Commission and the Star Chamber assumed jurisdiction over religious offenses having political overtones. With the introduction of the concept of the monarch as the supreme ruler of both Church and State, there appeared the notion that the expression of an opinion involving either a denial or disparagement of the truths of religion was tantamount to treason, as an offense against both Church and State.

Though there is some indication that inferior common-law courts made incursions into the jurisdiction of the ecclesiastical tribunals during the reigns of Elizabeth and James I (Nokes, 18–20), the first reported prosecution for blasphemy by a common law court occurred in 1617 with *Adwood's Case,* 2 Rolle, Abridgment 78. The *ratio* of the case was that words imputing a lack of orthodoxy to the State-established Anglican religion were *seditious parolls . . . econtre le peace del Realme,* seditious as an attack both upon the King in his capacity as head of the Anglican Church and upon the law by which the church was established; the language was also said to be disruptive of the public order.

In 1641, Parliament abolished both the Star Chamber and High Commission and suspended the coercive power of the ecclesiastical courts. With the Restoration of Charles II, although it was a time of notorious laxity in morals, a general feeling against the expression of atheistic and anti-Christian opinion still prevailed. Since the spiritual censures of the ecclesiastical courts had been rendered innocuous by the abolition of the Star Chamber and High Commission, the King's Bench intervened in an area of offenses that had previously been dealt with by those two tribunals and the ecclesiastical courts. The jurisdiction assumed over unorthodox religious opinions by the court of King's Bench in *Adwood* was reasserted in *R. v. Taylor* (1675), 1 Vent. 293, 86 Eng. Rep. 189. The court propounded the principle that Christianity was part and parcel of the law itself; therefore, anything tending to bring Christianity into disrepute was a violation of the law. The substance of the offense of blasphemy was perceived to be solely the character of the matter uttered, the manner and place of publication being considered irrelevant.

The case of *R. v. Woolston* (1729), 1 Fitzg. 64, 94 Eng. Rep. 655, had the effect of somewhat limiting the scope of the offense; it was concluded that an indictment would lie "only where the very root of Christianity itself is struck at," mere differences of opinion on particular controverted points being considered outside the ambit of the law. The nature of the opinion expressed continued to supply the standard of criminality. The courts went so far as to say that one would not be liable to prosecution for blasphemy in assailing any Christian (or non-Christian) sect other than the established state religion: *R. v. Gathercole* (1838), 2 Lew. C.C. 237, 168 Eng. Rep. 1140.

It should be noted that the common-law concept of blasphemy was broad enough to encompass statements that would have been designated as heretical by the ecclesiastical courts. Because of the lack of a clear line of demarcation between the two offenses, heresy and blasphemy, it appears that the common-law courts treated them as indistinguishable.

However, *Nayler's Case* (1656), 5 How. St. Tr. 801, a proceeding in the House of Commons against the defendant for blasphemous activity in impersonating Christ, made a distinction in the nature of the offenses: "Heresy is *Crimen Judicii,* an erroneous opinion; Blasphemy is *Crimen Malitiae,* a reviling the name and honour of God." Had such a rationalization not been forthcoming and had the defendant been found guilty of heresy, the death penalty might have ensued; for the writ *de haeretico comburendo,* by means of which heresy had been made a capital offense, was still in force. Furthermore, Commons was loath to follow the precedents of what they termed "those bloody, persecuting papists."

With the passage of time, discrepancies in opinion became manifest with reference to the criminality of statements that either lacked defamatory intent or were voiced in such moderate language as to preclude any probability of public disorder. These issues appear to have been settled by *R. v. Ramsay and Foote* (1883), 15 Cox. C.C. 217, 230, when the court concluded that no offense was committed by the profession, in decorous speech, of any religious or irreligious opinion. The intention to shock, outrage, or ridicule the believer was a prerequisite to prosecution. Christianity was no longer to be considered a part of the law of the land. The emphasis was thereby transferred from the matter published to the manner in which the opinion was uttered. Such reasoning was reaffirmed in *Bowan v. Secular Society* (1917), A.C. 406. The most recent prosecution for blasphemy occurred with *R. v. Gott* (1922), 16 C. App. R. 86, where the court, though noting the importance of the intent, placed the greater emphasis upon the possibility of a disturbance of the peace.

American Law. Because of the intimate relationship between the legal institutions of England and those of the U.S., blasphemy, as a common-law offense, found its way into the criminal laws of the colonies and remains on the statute books in a number of jurisdictions of, e.g., Massachusetts, Pennsylvania, New Jersey, and Maryland. Although, in colonial days, blasphemy carried with it a number of corporeal and pecuniary penalties, the character of the punishments, as well as the elements of the offense, have undergone an evolution similar to that in England.

Most of the cases in the U.S. have affirmed the necessity of the defamatory intent and the opprobrious language tending to incite a disorder, *State v. Chandler* [2 Harr., (Del.) 553 (1837)]; *Comm. v. Kneeland* [20 Pick., (Massachusetts) 206 (1838)]; *Updegraph v. Comm.* [11 Serg. & R. (Pennsylvania), 394 (1824)]. The underlying rationale for regarding blasphemy as an indictable offense was that it weakened the foundations of certain moral obligations such as the efficacy of oaths, *People v. Ruggles* [8 John, (N.Y.) 290, 5 Am. Dec. 335 (1811)], *State v. Mockus* [120 Me. 84, 113 A. 39 (1921)]. The courts also concluded that the prohibition of blasphemous language did not limit the free discussion or the undisturbed enjoyment of differing opinions on religious subjects, and therefore was not repugnant to the constitutional guarantees of freedom of speech and religion, *Hale v. Everett* [53 N.H. 9, 16 Amer. Rep. 82 (1868)], *Comm. v. Kneeland, State v. Mockus, People v. Ruggles.*

Thus, the essentials of the offense of blasphemy have come to vary with the temper of the times in which the criminal law was administered. Such an evolution is in keeping with the usual course of the law wherein the inventory of things that are unlawful and criminal is dependent upon public policy. Whereas the ecclesiastical courts maintained that blasphemy is a crime directly against God, the temporal courts subscribed to a modified view, asserting that blasphemy is an offense, not only against the deity, but also athwart the king and society, and therefore subversive of peace and good order.

In modern times, the laws against blasphemy, in those jurisdictions where such an offense continues to exist, are said not to prohibit the fullest inquiry into and discussion concerning religion. This is in consonance with the growing spirit of universal toleration and intellectual freedom; the argument has been tendered indeed that even the existence of such laws inhibits freedom of speech and opinion. Nor are the blasphemy statutes today directed toward restraining those who, in sincerity and good faith, express dissenting or unconventional views in reference to religious matters. In those situations, however, where the motivation is not the pursuit of truth but rather vilification and ridicule, where the language is gross and scurrilous, and where the diatribe is likely to provoke public disorder or to become a public nuisance, a prosecution for blasphemy would probably lie as a reasonable exercise of the police power of the State.

Bibliography: G. D. NOKES, *A History of the Crime of Blasphemy* (London 1928). J. DISNEY, *A View of Ancient Laws against Immorality and Profaneness* (Cambridge, Eng. 1729). H. B. BONNER, *Penalties upon Opinion* (3d ed. rev. and enl. London 1934). J. F. STEPHEN, *History of the Criminal Law of England,* 3 v. (London 1883) 2:396–497. Holdsworth HEL 8:402–420. W. BLACKSTONE, *Commentaries on the Laws of England,* ed. T. M. COOLEY, 2 v. (4th ed. Chicago 1899) 2:1243–62. C. ZOLLMANN, *American Church Law* (Chicago 1933) 31–40. J. BISHOP, *A Treatise on Criminal Law,* ed. J. M. ZANE and C. ZOLLMANN, 2 v. (9th ed. Indianapolis 1923) 2:53–62. R. A. ANDERSON, *Wharton's Criminal Law and Procedure,* 5 v. (Rochester, N.Y. 1957) 2:807–810.

[J. S. CASTELLANO]

BLASTARES, MATTHEW, 14th-century Byzantine canonist and monk. Little is known of his life other than that he was a monk and priest first on Mt. Athos, then in the Isaia monastery at Thessalonika. In 1335 he completed his *Syntagma,* an encyclopedic compilation of ecclesiastical and civil laws to which he added his own and the commentaries of his predecessors, especially Zonaras and the illustrious Theodore *Balsamon. The *Syntagma* groups the laws not according to subject matter but according to the Greek alphabet. Thus there are 24 main headings, and within each main section the items are again arranged in alphabetical order. The work is completed by a short lexicon of Latin legal terms. Widely translated, the *Syntagma* influenced the late Byzantine legal codes and those of the surrounding nations. Blastares also entered the theological controversies of his time, wrote against the Latin use of Azymes, composed a Description of the Error of the Latins (unedited), and a letter to Guy of Lusignan, and probably authored five books against the Jews. Several liturgical tracts and hymns also are attributed to him.

Bibliography: PG 144:960–1400. Beck KTLBR 786–787. L. PETIT, DTC 2.1:916–917. R. JANIN, LexThK² 7:173; DHGE 9:160–161. J. HERMAN, DDC 2:920–925. A. SOLOVIEV, *Studi bizantini e neoellenici* 5 (1939) 698–707.

[H. D. HUNTER]

BLASUCCI, DOMENICO, VEN., Redemptorist clerical student, famed as the Aloysius Gonzaga of the Alphonsian Congregation; b. Ruvo del Monte, Lucania, March 5, 1732; d. Caposele, Avellino, Nov. 2, 1752. He was the younger brother of Peter Paul Blasucci, third superior general of the Redemptorists, and at 18 he was received into the Congregation by (St.) Alphonsus Liguori. He was professed on Feb. 2, 1751. During his religious training he was distinguished for ready obedience, great love of purity, and devotion to the Blessed Sacrament and to the Mother of God. He was once forbidden by his superiors to keep his mind so much on God, but when the strain of this prohibition harmed his health, the order was recalled. Alphonsus styled him angelic, and the austere (Ven.) Paul Cafaro, Redemptorist novice master and superior, attested to the heroic extent of his virtue. The process for his beatification was begun in 1893, and his cause was introduced in Rome on May 23, 1906.

Bibliography: A. M. TANNOJA, *The Lives of the Companions of St. Alphonsus Liguori,* tr. London Oratory (London 1849) 205–227. P. P. LONGARD, *Lebensabriss des Fr. Dominicus Blasucci, Studenten-Klerikers aus der Congregation des allerheiligsten Erlösers* (Regensburg 1887). O. GREGORIO, EncCatt 2:1717–18.

[M. J. CURLEY]

BLENKINSOP

An Irish-American family that contributed to the development of the Church in the U.S.

Peter, publisher; b. Dublin, Ireland, toward the close of the 18th century. He was decended from a Catholic family originally from the north of England and he married Mary Kelly, a sister of Abp. Oliver Kelly of Tuam. In 1826 the family immigrated to America and settled in Baltimore, Md., where Blenkinsop turned to publishing and brought out Charles Constantine Pise's *A History of the Church* (5 v. Baltimore 1827–29). In 1830 he issued the first Catholic monthly in the U.S., the *Metropolitan,* which existed briefly from January to December that single year. Then, he reverted to bookselling. His three children, William A., Peter J., and Catherine, entered religious life.

Peter J., educator; b. Dublin, April 19, 1818; d. Philadelphia, Pa., Nov. 5, 1896. He attended St. Mary's College, Baltimore (1830–33), entered the Society of Jesus at Frederick, Md. (1834), and taught at Georgetown College (later University), Washington, D.C. After ordination (1846) he was assigned to the College of the Holy Cross, Worcester, Mass., where he served as instructor and treasurer and from 1854 to 1857 as its fifth president. He made frequent missionary journeys to the scattered Catholics of central New England, south as far as Norwich, Conn., and west to Springfield, Mass. After pastoral service at St. Joseph's Church in Philadelphia, he returned to Holy Cross in 1873 and cared for the mission at Leicester, Mass., until 1880, when he left for Georgetown. From 1882 until his death, he was stationed at the Church of the Gesu, in Philadelphia.

William A., missionary; b. Dublin, 1819; d. Boston, Mass., Jan. 8, 1892. He studied at St. Mary's College, Baltimore (1833–39), received his M.A. there, and joined the faculty. After ordination in 1843 for the Diocese of Natchez, Miss., he served for 7 years in its missions; became pastor at Chicopee, then part of the Boston diocese; and continued the pioneer labors of Revs. James Fitton and John D. Brady by making monthly missionary trips through an extensive territory in western Massachusetts, including the towns of Holyoke, Ware, Greenfield, and Amherst. In a time of bitterness exacerbated by the excesses of *Know-Nothingism, he fostered an ecumenical spirit between Catholics and Protestants. He built the Church of the Holy Name of Jesus (dedicated 1859) to take care of the expanding Catholic population in Chicopee. In 1864 he was named pastor of SS. Peter and Paul, a parish then embracing the entire area of South Boston.

Catherine, educator; b. Dublin, April 18, 1816; d. Emmitsburg, Md., March 18, 1887. She took the name of Euphemia when she entered the Sisters of Charity of Emmitsburg in 1831. After serving at St. Joseph's school, New York, and at St. Peter's school and St. Mary's Asylum, Baltimore, she was made assistant at the motherhouse in Emmitsburg (1855) and directed the institutions of the Sisters of Charity in the Southern states during the Civil War. In 1866 Mother Euphemia became superior of the Sisters of Charity in the U.S. and in subsequent years opened charitable establishments in various cities.

Bibliography: R. H. LORD et al., *History of the Archdiocese of Boston, 1604–1943*, 3 v. (New York 1944). J. J. McCOY, *History of the Catholic Church in the Diocese of Springfield* (Boston 1900).

[W. J. GRATTAN]

BLESSED. In the language of the Church, "blessed" refers to the just in heaven, those who after a life here below enjoy eternal happiness. St. Paul in 1 Cor 2.9 considers their happiness a mystery. Theologians treat the happiness of the saints in heaven as an aspect of the supernatural, beatific vision, which consists essentially in seeing and loving God without fully comprehending Him. According to Scripture and tradition this happiness is substantially the same for all, but varies according to the merits of the individual.

The title blessed is given by the Church to those whose cause has successfully passed through the process of beatification, which proceeds according to CIC cc.1999–2135. After completion of these proceedings it is established beyond a reasonable doubt that a person practiced heroic virtues and that this fact is confirmed by two miracles. The blessed may be venerated. However, the cult given them is restricted as to persons, places, and acts of worship.

As the translation of the Greek μακάριοι, blessed means happy, fortunate, blissful, and is the opening word of the eight solemn blessings, the Beatitudes (Mt 1.5–10), which are the first part of the Sermon on the Mount.

See also HEAVEN (THEOLOGY OF); CANONIZATION OF SAINTS (HISTORY AND PROCEDURE); BEATITUDES (IN THE BIBLE).

[O. A. BOENKI]

BLESSED SACRAMENT, SERVANTS OF THE, a contemplative congregation of women religious *Societas Ancillarum Sanctissimi Sacramenti* (SS) with papal approval (1871, 1885), founded at Paris in 1858 by St. Pierre Julien *Eymard. The purpose of the community, whose members are cloistered and take perpetual vows, is the perpetual adoration of the Blessed Sacrament and the promotion of that practice among the laity. Retreats for women are conducted in some of the larger convents. When Marguerite Guillot and a small group of ladies came under Eymard's direction, he was able to realize his intention of founding a congregation of sisters similar in scope to that of his *Blessed Sacrament Fathers. The French government's antireligious policy (1903) occasioned the spread of the community to Chicoutimi, Quebec, Canada. In 1947 a convent was opened in Waterville, Maine, and a novitiate was established there. From Waterville the sisters founded convents at Pueblo, Colo., and Melbourne,

Australia. The motherhouse is in Paris, where a superior general rules the congregation. In 1961 there were 471 members in 21 convents. In the U.S. 35 professed sisters (1965) represented the congregation in the Dioceses of Gary, Portland, and Pueblo.

[J. ROY]

BLESSED SACRAMENT, VISITS TO THE. Intervals of prayer in the presence of the Holy Eucharist reserved in Catholic churches or chapels, have become one of the most popular devotions in the Church. In his encyclical *Mediator Dei*, Pius XII wrote: "The churches [should] be entirely at the disposal of the faithful who, called to the feet of their Savior, listen to His most consoling invitation, 'Come to Me all you who labor and are heavily burdened, and I will refresh you.'" The man most responsible for making popular this devotion is St. Alphonsus Liguori whose book *Visits to the Blessed Sacrament* has gone through more than 2,000 editions in 39 languages since 1745. All the details about the origin of this devotion are not known. Before the 12th century any ritual or private honor to the Eucharist outside the time of Mass was impossible because there were no tabernacles visible in the churches. The Sacrament was kept privately for emergencies, as the Holy Oils are kept today. In the 11th century, Berengarius's denial of the Real Presence was the occasion for a deeper study of the Eucharist. The resulting progress in the study of dogma, along with a growing consciousness of the important role of Christ's human nature in man's salvation, caused the faithful to desire to see and adore the consecrated Host. Visits to the Blessed Sacrament were made to honor Our Lord or to pray for special favors. The historian E. Dumoutet claims that this devotion is linked to the practice of burning a lamp before the tabernacle. There is evidence that in the 12th century such visits were being made by the monks in their monastery churches. Thomas Becket told King Henry II that he prayed for him before the Holy Eucharist. At the end of the 14th century private devotion at the place of reservation was common among the monks of Western Europe. It gradually became a practice of lay people. Luther and other reformers objected to this adoration. The Council of Trent in its Decree on the Holy Eucharist, 1551, defended the Feast of Corpus Christi and, in general, the honor and adoration given the Blessed Sacrament. In the next 2 centuries many books were written, in French and Italian especially, advocating devotional visits to the Blessed Sacrament.

Bibliography: H. THURSTON, CE 15:483–484.

[F. COSTA]

BLESSED SACRAMENT CONFRATERNITY

An association for laymen that fosters public worship of the Eucharist. All such confraternities are affiliated automatically with Archconfraternity of the Blessed Sacrament whose headquarters are at the church of S. Maria sopra Minerva in Rome.

The purpose of the confraternity, though varying in particulars from one place to another, is to promote the worship due the Blessed Sacrament by fostering attendance at Holy Mass, reception of Holy Communion, adoration of and visits to the Blessed Sacrament, and care for the decor of churches and altars.

The Confraternity of the Blessed Sacrament was founded by the Dominican Thomas Stella in the church of S. Maria sopra Minerva in Rome and was approved Nov. 30, 1539, by the bull *Dominus Noster Jesus Christus* of Paul III. The Pope not only endowed this organization with many indulgences, but also decreed that all confraternities in existence with the same aim or name, and all those to be created in the future, would be automatically affiliated with the Confraternity of the Blessed Sacrament of the Minerva. On Oct. 2, 1548, the Pope raised the confraternity to the status of an archconfraternity, a title definitively given the organization on Nov. 3, 1606, by Paul V.

The founder of the confraternity, noting that the Blessed Sacrament was often unaccompanied by the Faithful when brought through the streets to the sick, and that altars were frequently found in a state of neglect, established the confraternity to remedy these deficiencies. The society provided candles for churches, and its members promised to accompany the Blessed Sacrament either personally or by a representative from the family. Women members promised at least to pray for the sick who were to receive the Sacrament. Confraternities flourished particularly during the 17th century as a reaction to the Protestant denial of the doctrine of the Real Presence.

The favor that the Confraternity of the Blessed Sacrament enjoys in Church legislation may be seen especially from CIC c.711.2, which states that local ordinaries are to establish the confraternity in every parish (thus making an exception to the prescription of a necessary distance between similar confraternities stipulated in the first paragraph of the canon).

The Code Commission handed down an important decision concerning CIC c.711.2 on March 6, 1927. It stated that instead of the confraternity, a pious union or sodality of the Most Blessed Sacrament may be established. However, these unions or sodalities are not automatically affiliated with the Archconfraternity of the Most Blessed Sacrament of the Minerva in Rome.

There are a number of pious unions of the Blessed Sacrament enjoying favor in the Church. The most widely known is the Confraternity of the Blessed Sacrament with headquarters at the Church of SS. Andrew and Claude in Rome. This pious union was founded by St. Pierre Julien *Eymard at Marseilles in 1859. It was given the honorary title of archconfraternity and its affiliates are called confraternities. (Affiliation is established through canonical erection and petition for affiliation with the headquarters at Rome.) In the U.S. this pious union is called the People's Eucharistic League and has its national headquarters in New York.

The similarity in purpose, organization, customs, regulations, etc., with the Confraternity of the Blessed Sacrament are striking. For this reason it is sometimes mistaken for the archconfraternity. On the other hand, in accordance with the reply of the Code Commission cited above, it is frequently substituted by local ordinaries for the Confraternity of the Blessed Sacrament.

Bibliography: G. BARBIERO, *Le Confraternite del Santissimo Sacramento Primo del 1539* (Vedelago, It. 1944). F. BÉRINGER, *Les Indulgences,* 2 v. (Paris 1925). H. DURAND, DDC 4:128–176. G. VROMANT, *De fidelium associationibus* (Louvain 1932).

[E. R. FALARDEAU]

BLESSED SACRAMENT FATHERS

Founded in France in 1856 by Pierre Julien *Eymard as a religious society of men who would devote themselves entirely to the glorification of the Holy Eucharist. Eymard had been ordained for the Diocese of Grenoble in 1834 and later joined the Society of Mary. After 17 years as a Marist, he founded the Congregation of the Blessed Sacrament (SSS) for which he obtained formal approbation from Pius IX in 1863. At the time of his death in 1868 the society maintained 7 houses, 5 in France and 2 in Belgium, and included 50 religious, of whom 16 were priests. By 1963, membership had grown to more than 1,500 religious, dispersed throughout the world in 100 houses. Eymard was canonized in 1962.

The primary work of the Blessed Sacrament Fathers is the perpetual exposition and adoration of the Blessed Sacrament in its own religious houses. Each religious is bound by rule to make 3 hours of adoration daily before the Blessed Sacrament exposed, and to recite the Divine Office in choir.

The congregation engages also in all forms of apostolate that spread the glory of the Holy Eucharist. The specific works have varied since the days of its foundation. Eymard devoted himself to the preparation of adults for their first Holy Communion, a great need in his day. The fathers have since promoted affiliated societies for different categories of persons who participate in the Eucharistic vocation of the religious themselves.

These societies include the Priests' Eucharistic League, the Eucharistic Fraternity, the People's Eucharistic League, and the Nocturnal Adoration and Catholic Youth Adoration Societies. Members of the Priests' Eucharistic League pledge themselves to a weekly hour of adoration before the Blessed Sacrament. About 25,000 priests in the U.S. belong to this association. The Eucharistic Fraternity requires the same amount of adoration, while the People's Eucharistic League asks for one holy hour a month. The Nocturnal Adoration Society, reserved to men, arranges to continue adoration of the Blessed Sacrament through the night once a month, with each member pledged to adore for 1 hour. This movement, organized in all the churches run by the fathers, has spread also to many parishes throughout the U.S. The Catholic Youth Adoration (CYA), organized by Rev. Joseph Bernier in 1950 for high school boys and girls, has as its aim a monthly public holy hour for its members. Branches of the CYA exist in many parishes, Catholic schools, and colleges. All these societies have their national headquarters at St. Jean Baptiste rectory in New York City. There the Blessed Sacrament Fathers publish two monthly reviews: *Emmanuel* for the members of the Priests' Eucharistic League, and *Eucharist* for the laity.

The congregation was first divided into provinces in 1930. A special province was established for the U.S., with its center at St. Jean Baptiste Church, where the fathers have been active since 1900. By 1960 the American province maintained eight houses, four of which were houses of formation. Besides St. Jean's, the fathers have Eucharistic shrines in Chicago, Ill., Cleveland, Ohio, and Albuquerque, N.Mex. Also attached to this province are churches in Manila, Philippine Islands; in Leicester, England; and in Masaka, Uganda, Africa.

The members of the congregation consist of both priests and lay brothers. Except for recitation of the Divine Office, the brothers lead the same prayer life as the priests. They form about one-third of the total number of religious in the congregation. From 1856 until his death Eymard worked on the constitutions of the congregation. He called this his only book although a collection of his sermons has been published in book form. Definitive approbation for the constitutions was obtained from Rome in 1895.

Bibliography: E. Núñez, ed., *Commentaire des constitutions de la Congrégation du Très Saint Sacrement* (Rome 1958–), with bibliographies. *Centenaire de la Congrégation du Très Saint Sacrement, 1856–1956* (Rome 1956). E. Tenaillon, *Venerable Pierre Julien Eymard* (New York 1914). F. Trochu, *Le Bienheureux Pierre-Julien Eymard: . . . d'après ses écrits, son procès de béatification, et de nombreux documents inédits* (Lyons 1949).

[J. ROY]

BLESSED SACRAMENT SISTERS FOR INDIANS AND COLORED PEOPLE,

a congregation of women religious founded by American-born Katharine Mary *Drexel on Feb. 12, 1891. As defined by the foundress, the special purpose of the Sisters of the Blessed Sacrament for Indians and Colored People (SBS) consists in the total gift of self for the souls of Indians and colored people.

During a personal audience with Leo XIII, Miss Drexel represented the need for sisters to staff schools for Indians and Negroes. In reply the Pope challenged Katharine to give herself as well as her wealth to this cause. In 1889, under the direction of Bp. James O'Connor of Omaha, Nebr., and later under Abp. Patrick Ryan of Philadelphia, Pa., the 31-year-old Katharine began a 2-year novitiate with the Sisters of Mercy of Pittsburgh, Pa.

On July 16, 1890, Leo XIII sent his apostolic blessing to Sister Mary Katharine and her companions, the nucleus of the new congregation. When she made her vows on Feb. 12, 1891, Mother Katharine was named by Archbishop Ryan foundress and first superior of the community. During the construction of a motherhouse, the old Drexel home at Torresdale, near Philadelphia, served as a temporary novitiate. On Dec. 3, 1892, St. Elizabeth's Convent, the new motherhouse, was opened with the offering of the Mass.

The decree of praise for the constitutions came on Feb. 16, 1897; temporary approbation followed on July 11, 1907; and final approval was given by Pius X on May 25, 1913. On June 24, 1961, the Congregation for Religious approved a general revision of the constitutions. In 1963, the congregation's 545 members served the Indian and the Negro in colleges, secondary and elementary schools, clinics, catechetical centers, retreat houses, centers of social service, and one university (Xavier, New Orleans, La.) in 10 archdioceses and 19 dioceses in the U.S.

Mother Katharine did not confine her efforts to her own institute but used the income from the vast family estate to support many other apostolic undertakings. The Drexel family built churches and schools, supported missionary priests and sisters, and gave bountifully to teachers on Negro and Indian missions throughout the U.S. and in many foreign countries. When Mother Katharine survived her two sisters, the congregation she founded enjoyed the benefit of her increased

A Blessed Sacrament Sister assigned to an Indian mission in the Southwest U.S. meets with people of her parish.

income during her lifetime. After her death in 1955, the principal on which Mother Katharine's income had been based was distributed to various charities throughout the U.S.

Bibliography: K. Burton, *The Golden Door: The Life of Katharine Drexel* (New York 1957). **Illustration credit:** *Mission Fields at Home.*

[H. J. SIEVERS]

BLESSING

The OT contains only a few traces of a primitive belief in the magical efficacy of the spoken word, either to bless or to *curse. Some older narratives contain vestiges of superstition, but in their final editing they always make it clear that blessings come ultimately from the Lord. Thus, the *Yahwist indicated that Isaac's blessing of Jacob, which according to the primitive belief could not be annulled, was due ultimately to God's choice of Jacob (Gn 25.23; 27.33–38). The actual formula of blessing is a prayer to the Lord without any suggestion of magical efficacy (Gn 27.28). The narrative about Jacob's struggle with God (Gn 32.24–30) was based upon older material that probably suggested that a blessing had been wrested from a numinous being. In the reshaping of the material, the Yahwist made clear that God imparted His blessing freely (Gn 32.29).

The loyal Israelite had a profound sense of dependence upon the Lord as the source of all blessings. A customary greeting was a prayer to the Lord for blessing (Gn 24.31; Ru 2.4), so that the common verb for "to bless," *bērak*, often meant "to greet" (Gn 47.7, 10; 1 Sm 13.10). God blessed living things with the special power of generation (Gn 1.22, 28). His blessing of Abraham was also connected with generation (Gn 12.2–3). Certain individuals possessed special authority to call down God's blessings upon men: a father, upon his children (Gn 9.26; 27.28; 49.25–26, 28); a king, upon his subjects (2 Sm 6.18; 3 Kgs 8.14, 55–61); and priests, upon the people (Nm 6.22–27).

The conception that one could strengthen one's god by blessing him did not exist in Israel. By blessing Yahweh the Israelite solemnly acknowledged Him as Lord and King and the source of all blessings. In such a context, the verb *bērak* meant to praise or thank

[Gn 24.48; Dt 8.10; Ps 65(66).8; 102(103).1–2] and is the antonym of *qillēl* (to curse), the verb predicated of a man who in his bitterness repudiated his parents, king, or God.

The place of blessing in the NT is typified in St. Luke's Gospel, where Christ ascends to the Father while blessing His disciples and the disciples return to Jerusalem "praising and blessing God" (Lk 24.51–53). These two aspects of the OT blessing, viz, the calling down of God's bounty upon men and thanksgiving returned to God, found their perfect realization in the Eucharist. Christ's blessing at the *Last Supper was both a prayer of thanksgiving to the Father and a calling of His sanctifying power (Mt 26.26; Lk 24.30). The NT term εὐλογέω most often meant to invoke God's blessing, but it sometimes signified to give thanks (e.g., Lk 1.64; 1 Cor 14.16). The word εὐχαριστέω corresponded less perfectly to *bērak* since it meant only to give thanks. The words of the Roman Canon, *Gratias agens benedixit* (giving thanks, He blessed), the result of a conflation of Mk 14.22 and 1 Cor 11.24, accurately describe the double aspect of the perfect Christian blessing.

Bibliography: J. Scharbert, LexThK² 9:590–592. L. De Bruyne, EncCatt 2:1303–04. F. Horst and H. Köster, RGG³ 5:1649–52. EncDictBibl 253–254. S. H. Blank, "Some Observations concerning Biblical Prayer," HebUCAnn 32 (1961) 75–90. A. Murtonen, "The Use and Meaning of the Words *lᵉbarek* and *bᵉrakah* in the O.T.," VetTest 9 (1959) 158–177.

[J. V. Morris]

BLESSINGS, LITURGICAL

The chief sacramental actions of the Church next to the Sacraments themselves are her blessings. As *sacramentals they are sacred signs that, through her impetration, dispose men for the grace of the Sacraments and render holy various occasions in life (Vatican Council II, *Constitution on the Sacred Liturgy* 60). Through the blessings of the Church, benefits, chiefly spiritual but temporal also, come to men, and persons and objects are dedicated to the service of God. For Biblical meaning and use *see* BLESSING.

In the Early Church. There are formulas of blessing in the earliest post-Apostolic documents. Especially significant are those within the celebration of the Mass as seen in Hippolytus's *Apostolic Tradition*. Here we find blessings of oil for the sick, milk, honey and water (to be taken at Communion by the newly baptized), lights, new fruits (5, 6, 21, 25, 32; Botte LQF 19, 57, 65, 78). Serapion attests to the blessing of the people, especially the sick, and that of oil and water (*Euchologion* 4, 6, 8, 17; Funk DidConst 2:163, 165, 167, 179).

The inclusion of such blessings in the Mass itself by the early Church teaches an important truth concerning the relation of blessings to the Eucharist. "But why were the fruits of the earth blessed at this particular point in the Mass? Most likely to show the relationship of such blessings to the greatest of all God's blessings, Christ Himself and His work of redemption" (Miller FundLit 282–283). The point in the Mass here referred to is the conclusion of the Canon.

This connection between the blessings of the Church and her sacrifice is further emphasized by the findings of J. Jungmann in connection with the name of the celebration of the Eucharist that became common in the West, i.e., the Mass. This designation of the Sacrifice had its origin in the dismissal that was accompanied by a blessing. Before sending her children into the world the Church, source of grace and blessing for her members, drew them to herself and imparted a blessing. This was a practice not limited to the Sacrifice but carried out on other devotional occasions as well. It is easy to understand that what at first was used as a term for the conclusion of the liturgy with its blessing came to be applied as the accepted word for the whole rite that is the greatest of all the Church's sanctifying actions, her Sacrifice [see *The Mass of the Roman Rite* (New York 1950) 1:173–174]. Another point of contemporary scholarship bears directly on this matter. This is the fact that the heart of the Mass, the Canon, corresponds to the central action of the Jewish Paschal meal, the blessing (Miller, *Signs* 87).

Theology. This connection between the chief sacramentals, blessings, and the Eucharist strikes at the heart of the theology of these prayers. It shows how clearly what is done in her sanctifying prayers is an extension of what the Church does in her greatest action. At the Eucharist God is blessed (praised and thanked) in union with Christ, and through Him God's saving gifts come to man. In a similar way, always saving the difference, the Church through her impetration does this in her sacramental blessings. In them she specifies her surrender of everything created to the Father in Christ and pleads for continued help for her children in all the vicissitudes of life.

The newly elected Pope Martin V blessing the people attending his coronation at the Council of Constance in 1417, woodcut from the "Concilium Buch" of Ulrich von Reichenthal, printed at Augsburg in 1483.

Because of the fall of Adam there is in the world, a tension described by Scripture as a struggle between God and the powers of Satan. Of course, in Christ God has triumphed, but the spread of His victory to all men and all creation will not be complete until He comes in glory at the end of time. Until then there is conflict between the two kingdoms, the two cities, flesh and spirit. Through her prayerful blessings the Church sanctifies creation, reestablishing under Christ's headship the world redeemed by Him.

This sanctifying action may be looked at as comprising two elements: the expulsion of Satan's power and the taking of possession by God. It is the first of these that explains the exorcisms so frequent in the ritual actions. They are especially significant in the celebration of the Sacrament by which one is initiated into the Christian order, Baptism. In conferring this Sacrament there is also an exorcism of the salt given to the candidate. The various impositions of hands, signs of the cross, and anointings are effective signs of the repossession by God in Christ of the new man.

In this process of reestablishing all things in Christ the Church consecrates certain materials to be used in the sanctification of men and other objects. In so doing she selects matter that in the natural order has a certain aptitude parallel to the supernatural use to which it will be put in the sacramental ministrations of the Church. It is all part of the sign language with which the Church teaches as she sanctifies. Outstanding examples of such are the blessing of baptismal water and the consecration of the holy oils. These are rich sources of knowledge of the Sacraments in which they will be employed.

Blessing of the fishing boats at Fort Myers Beach, Florida by the Bishop of Miami. Each year before the blessing of the individual vessels the bishop celebrates a low Mass aboard a trawler in the Gulf of Mexico.

Some blessings include the proclamation of the Word of God. The saving power of Scripture is thus incorporated into the sacred signs of blessing, as those for the sick members of the Church at various stages of their illness. The almost universal use of holy water in blessings is an obvious reminder of the baptismal foundation of all that we have as members of the Church and a sign of the further purification that her blessings bring.

Types. Among her sanctifying actions some constitute a person or object to service in the Church. These are known as constitutive blessings and result in a permanent deputation to worship. The conferral of clerical tonsure is a constitutive blessing of a person. Some constitutive blessings are more solemn than others, indicated by the use of the holy oils in their celebration; these are called consecrations in contradistinction to simple constitutive blessings. The consecration of an altar, a church, or a chalice are examples of this same type of blessings for objects.

In addition to these there are many blessings that call on God to bless the persons who make use of objects or who are in certain needs. In these the person or object is not permanently changed. They are known as invocative blessings. The prayers seeking God's protection for a home or a sick person are of this class. Since the blessings she imparts consist primarily in her impetration, these (blessings) are what one means first of all in speaking of her sacramentals. The term is used in a secondary sense of the objects to which she gives her blessing.

Minister. Until the provision for laymen as ministers of sacramentals in some cases by Vatican Council II (*Constitution on the Sacred Liturgy* 79) only clerics could fulfill this function. Only bishops are ex officio ministers of consecrations. In the past it has been the practice to limit other blessings to specially designated persons. These have been known as "reserved blessings," but Vatican Council II has ordered that their number be reduced (*ibid.*). In the future such reservation will be made only in favor of bishops or ordinaries. The power of exorcism cannot be exercised except by special and explicit permission of the local ordinary, except for those exorcisms that form part of the ritual of the Sacraments.

Ecclesial Dimensions. Like the Sacraments blessings are acts of worship of the Church. In keeping with the Biblical notion of blessing they have a twofold direction: that of man's praise of God and that of God's sanctifying action on men. It is always the Church that prays in these sacramentals, and if those members who are involved in such specific prayers are to contribute to her praise of the Father and be open to His goodness, each must truly worship. Since complete worship includes interior dedication and external manifestation of this inner sincerity, the recipients, as they are sometimes called, might better be described as participants in the prayers of blessing. The insistence that Vatican Council II places on the fulfillment by each person of his proper role in liturgical celebrations must be carefully observed in this matter (*ibid.* 28). It is often true that the external participation of those other than the minister is materially slight (perhaps no more than "Amen"), but this is no indication that its significance is of minor importance. Any tendency to regard the blessings as affording those who receive them only a passive part reflects a misunderstanding of these actions of the whole Church.

For this very reason, i.e., their ecclesial nature, the blessings of the Church are intended in the first place for her members. This term is not to be interpreted too strictly, however. Catechumens are subjects of blessings; those prior to Baptism are meant directly for them. In addition, those whose relationship to the Church is less than complete may on occasion receive these, e.g., ashes and palms.

Bibliography: A. G. MARTIMORT, *L'Église en prière* (Tournai 1961). J. H. MILLER, *Signs of Transformation in Christ* (Englewood Cliffs, N.J. 1963). Miller FundLit. **Illustration credits:** Fig. 1, Library of Congress. Fig. 2, NCWC Photo Service.

[J. R. QUINN]

BLEULER, EUGEN

BLEULER, EUGEN, outstanding Swiss psychiatrist; b. Zollikon, near Zurich, April 30, 1857; d. there, July 15, 1939. After studies in Zurich and Munich, Bleuler served as professor of psychiatry at Zurich (1898–1927) and directed the Burghölzli University Mental Hospital there. A prolific, widely read author, he produced the textbook *Lehrbuch der Psychiatrie* (1916), which appeared in 1960 in the tenth edition. Bleuler's approach to disease does not stop with the mere enumeration of symptoms. He sought to interpret and explain the reaction types through the application of psychological principles. He early appreciated Freud's contributions, but he evaluated these carefully and did not hesitate to criticize when he felt criticism was warranted.

In his outstanding work *Dementia praecox oder Gruppe der Schizophrenien* (Vienna 1911) Bleuler coined the term "schizophrenia" referring to the splitting of the psychological functions of the mind, characteristic of a group of severe mental diseases. He made contributions to the psychology of emotions and to the psychology of motivation. His works that have been translated into English include: *Textbook of Psychiatry* (New York 1924), *Dementia Praecox or the Group of Schizophrenias* (New York 1950), and *Synopsis* (New York 1952).

Bibliography: R. E. GAUPP, *Zeitschrift für die gesamte Neurologie und Psychiatrie* 168 (1940) 1–35, obit. and bibliog.

[J. BROZEK]

BLIND AND VISUALLY HANDICAPPED, EDUCATION OF

It is estimated that there are from 6,600,000 to 14,000,000 blind persons in the world, and that about 400,000 of this number live in the U.S. Estimates vary because of the lack of a universally accepted definition of blindness. Definitions in current use range from those that limit its meaning to total blindness to those that attribute blindness to all persons who have less than one-tenth normal sight. In the U.S. the definition of legal blindness that is most frequently used is "central visual acuity of 20/200 or less in the better eye, with correcting glasses; or central visual acuity of more than 20/200 if there is a field defect in which the peripheral field has contracted to such an extent that the widest diameter of visual field subtends an angular distance no greater than 20°."

The vast majority of blind persons in the U.S. are adventitiously blinded, not congenitally blind, i.e., they had sight but lost it. More than 50 per cent of the blind in the U.S. are over 65; about 10 per cent are under the age of 21.

Development. Historically treatment of blind persons has included three stages: (1) rejection of the blind person as uneducable, (2) philanthropic and custodial care for the blind, chiefly in segregated settings, and (3) use of modern techniques of special education and rehabilitation that stress the normality and abilities of blind persons and their integration into society as contributing members.

Asylums for the poor and handicapped, which accepted blind persons also, were established under Christian auspices in the 4th century. A refuge exclusively for the blind, a *typhlocomium,* was founded in 630 in Jerusalem. Other asylums were established under Church auspices during the Middle Ages, the most famous of which was the 13th-century Hospice des Quinze-Vingts established in Paris by St. Louis. In the 16th century attempts were made to devise methods of reading for the blind by tracing raised letters on wax, wood, and other materials. Notable among such attempts were those of Francesco Lucas, Pierre Moreau, Girolamo *Cardano, and Francesco Lana-Terzi, an Italian Jesuit who had earlier worked with deaf-mutes. D. Diderot (1713–84) and G. Leibniz (1646–1716) provided some theoretical speculations with regard to education of the blind but did not reduce their theories to practice.

Valentin Haüy (1745–1822), a French teacher of the blind and brother of René Justin *Haüy, succeeded in making practical for the blind as a class what others had advocated or had applied only in individual cases by developing a workable system of letters, printed in relief. These he used to teach a group of blind students in the first day school for the blind, which he established in 1784 in Paris, and which later became a residential school, the Institut des Jeunes Aveugles. Leseur, a blind mendicant, was Haüy's first pupil. The earliest systems of producing tactual reading material for the blind suffered from attempts to make the raised letters appealing visually as well as tactually. A further difficulty was their unsuitability for writing. Louis Braille (1809–52), a blind student at the Institut des Jeunes Aveugles, developed a system of raised dots placed in a "cell" consisting of six points arranged in two vertical rows of three each. He used Barbier's idea, a combination of 12 points arranged in 2 columns. The advantages of Braille include simplicity, tangibility, and the fact that it can be written and adapted for music. Although other raised point systems were later developed, notably the New York point system, Braille (considerably modified by the use of contractions) continues in use as a basic tool for the blind person.

By 1800 four new institutions for the education of the blind were founded in Great Britain, and shortly thereafter schools for the blind were established in most European countries. Although a day school for the blind established in Scotland in 1834 was short-lived, day schools were later successfully operated in Scotland and England.

In the U.S. instruction of the blind was begun at the New York Institute for the Blind and at the New England Asylum for the Blind (now Perkins) in 1832, and at the Pennsylvania Institute for the Instruction of the Blind (now Overbrook) in 1833. By the turn of the century 30 residential schools had been founded in the U.S. The first public day school for the blind started in Chicago in 1900.

Special Programs. Until recently, the majority of blind children were educated in residential schools. Catholic residential schools for the blind in the U.S. include St. Joseph's School for the Blind, Jersey City, N.J., founded in 1900, which, in cooperation with the Mount Carmel Guild of Newark, educates multiple-handicapped blind children, and Lavalle School for the Blind in the Bronx, N.Y., founded in 1904. St Mary's School for the Blind, founded in Landsdale, Pa., in 1922, was closed in 1955 to make way for the establishment of an integrated school of special education: St. Lucy's Day School for the Blind, which opened in Philadelphia in 1955. With the growing awareness of the importance of family life and the social advantages of integrated education of the blind with the sighted, a more recent trend in special education for the blind has been toward placement of blind children in day schools or in more highly integrated educational settings: the resource-room or the itinerant-teacher programs. Since the 1950s the majority of blind children receive their education in the integrated settings.

Under the resource-room program the blind or partially seeing child attends a centrally located school in which there is a classroom with materials, equipment, and teacher to instruct him in special skills. He is gradually integrated into classes with the sighted children, according to his ability and needs. Catholic resource-room programs for the blind have been established in Chicago, Ill. (1953), Portland, Maine (1954), and Newark, N.J. (1960).

The most recent form of integrated education for the blind is the itinerant-teacher program in which children attend local schools, public or parochial, where the regular teacher instructs them in the usual subjects and an itinerant teacher teaches them the special skills needed because of their visual handicap. In this program the itinerant teacher's educational role is combined with that of counseling the blind children, their parents, and the regular classroom teacher. Itinerant-teacher programs for the blind were established in the Diocese of Brooklyn, N.Y., in 1959 and in the Archdiocese of Newark in 1960.

Educators feel that the needs of the individual blind child should determine his placement. There is a continuing need, therefore, for all three settings since no single setting provides for the needs of all blind children. All programs include the teaching of Braille (reading and writing), the use of recorded and tactual materials, typewriting, orientation, and mobility. Braille writing instruction is usually begun on a Braillewriter (a Braille typewriter), which enables the blind child to write from left to right. Since slates, which are lighter and cheaper, require the blind student to learn to write from right to left, instruction is usually postponed until after Braille has been mastered. The Taylor Slate and Cubarithm, both of which involve the manipulation of small, embossed pegs on a board, and the abacus, have been used to teach arithmetic to blind children, but the Braillewriter has begun to supplant these devices. Braille and recorded materials for the blind, which include not only embossed discs but also tape-recorded materials, are produced by publishers and by volunteer organizations throughout the country, many under Catholic auspices. The Library of Congress, division for the blind, supplies both Braille and recorded material free of charge to legally blind persons in the U.S.

Adult Programs. New interest in the rehabilitation of the blind developed after World War II as numbers of blinded veterans returned home. The Veterans Administration conducts the Hines Rehabilitation Center for the Blind in Illinois. St. Paul's Rehabilitation Center for the recently blinded was established in Newton, Mass., in 1954; and the Greater Pittsburgh Rehabilitation Center for the Blind, in Pennsylvania in 1960. As the knowledge of special techniques involved in teaching mobility to blinded persons increases, peripatology (mobility training) has become a speciality with graduate programs established at Boston College, Mass. (1960), and at Western Michigan University, Kalamazoo (1961). Some of the newer techniques of teaching cane travel were developed by Richard Hoover, who worked with veterans blinded during World War II. Guide dogs are used with great success in providing mobility to some blind persons.

Catholic Guilds for the Blind have been established to provide services to blind individuals in the archdioceses of Boston, Chicago, Detroit, Hartford, Conn., Los Angeles, Newark, N.J., New York, Philadelphia, Pa., and Seattle, Wash.; and in the dioceses of Bridgeport and Norwich, Conn., Fall River, Mass., Scranton and Pittsburgh, Pa., Rockville Centre, L.I.

The American Federation of Catholic Workers for the Blind, established in 1954, aids Catholic organizations in the professionalization of services to the blind and provides a forum to discuss such programs specific to Catholic agencies for the blind as Catholic special educational programs or to provide Braille and recorded materials of a spiritual, educational, or catechetical

Blind children examining their own three-dimensional artwork at St. Joseph's School for the Blind.

An instruction session for orientation and mobility, Western Michigan University, Kalamazoo.

nature. Xavier Society for the Blind, founded in 1900 in New York, is the only national Catholic agency for the blind. It publishes and distributes Catholic literature in Braille and recorded form and also maintains a central index of all available Braille and recorded Catholic textbook material.

The only Catholic residence in the U.S. exclusively for the blind persons is St. Joseph's Home for the Blind in Jersey City, N.J., established in 1899. In 1964 St. Raphael's Geriatric Adjustment Center for the Blind and Visually Handicapped was established in a residence formerly occupied by St. Raphael's Home for the Blind in Boston. The American Center for Research in Blindness and Rehabilitation, Newton, Mass., was founded in 1964 to investigate causes and problems resulting from blindness.

Even among well-educated persons there exist misconceptions with regard to blindness, e.g., "miraculous compensation" (that the blind person's remaining senses become more acute), or stereotypes of blind persons as beggars, geniuses, or musically gifted. Such misconceptions and stereotypes may lead to failure to accept the blind as they really are, i.e., as individuals with varying abilities and personality patterns who have suffered a severe traumatic loss but who, with professional assistance, can be helped to reorganize their lives as blinded persons. Education of the public by professional agencies, therefore, plays a major role in society's acceptance of the blind.

Bibliography: T. J. CARROLL, *Blindness, What It Is, What It Does, and How to Live with It* (Boston 1961). T. D. CUTSFORTH, *The Blind in School and Society, A Psychological Study* (rev. ed. New York 1951). W. HATHAWAY, *Education and Health of the Partially Seeing Child*, ed. F. M. FOOTE et al. (4th rev. ed. New York 1959). S. C. ASHCROFT and F. HENDERSON, *Programmed Instruction in Braille* (Pittsburgh 1963). P. A. ZAHL, *Blindness, Modern Approaches to the Unseen Environment* (Princeton 1950; repr. New York 1962). M. E. FRAMTON and E. KERNEY, *The Residential School, Its History, Contributions and Future* (New York 1953). G. L. ABEL, comp., *Concerning the Education of Blind Children* (New York 1959). Amer. Foundation for the Blind, *Itinerant Teaching Service for Blind Children* (New York 1957); *The Pine Brook Report, National Work Session on the Education of the Blind with the Sighted* (rev. ed. New York 1957). G. FARRELL, *Story of Blindness* (Cambridge, Mass. 1956). L. MEYERSON, "The Visually Handicapped," *Review of Educational Research* 23 (1953) 476–491. **Illustration credit:** Fig. 2, News and Information Services, Western Michigan University.

[R. M. MC GUINNESS]

BLOEMFONTEIN, ARCHDIOCESE OF (BLOEMFONTEINENSIS), metropolitan see since 1951, in the Orange Free State, Republic of *South Africa. In 1963 it had 17 parishes, 25 priests, 29 men in 3 religious houses, 88 women in 6 convents, and 35,340 Catholics (33,510 non-Europeans) in a population of 361,580 (264,600 non-Europeans); it is 24,753 square miles in area. Its four suffragans, which had 105 priests, 274 sisters, and 115,000 Catholics in a population of 1,444,000, were Bethlehem, Keimoes, Kimberley, and Kroonstad (all created in 1951). The city of Bloemfontein, founded as a military outpost in 1846, is now an educational center. From the Vicariate of Natal (1850) was detached the Vicariate of the Orange Free State (1886), called Kimberley (1918). In 1951 Kimberley was made a diocese, from which was detached the Archdiocese of Bloemfontein, where there is also an Anglican archbishop. The first Catholic priest to reside in Bloemfontein, a Premonstratensian from Grahamstown (1851), was succeeded by the Oblates of Mary Immaculate (1869), who still care for the see. Keimoes was detached from *Cape Town (1885); Kroonstad, from Kimberley (1923); and Bethlehem, from Kroonstad (1948).

Bibliography: MissCattol 164–171. S. PAVENTI, EncCatt 7: 699–700. AnnPont (1965) 66.

[J. E. BRADY]

BLONDEL, MAURICE

French Catholic philosopher; b. Dijon, Nov. 2, 1861; d. Aix-en-Provence, June 4, 1949. His doctoral thesis, *L'Action* (1893), is a masterpiece of the late 19th century. Blondel completed his studies at the École Normale in 1883, taught for a short time at the University of Lille, and passed the rest of his life at Aix-en-Provence, first as professor of philosophy (1896–1927), and after the onset of blindness, in active retirement until his death. In spite of his affliction, he dictated 10 major volumes between 1929 and 1949, thus entering on a second career at the age of 68, a career more mature but no less brilliant than his earlier one.

L'Action. Blondel uses the term action to characterize the dynamism of *life in all its manifestations. It does not mean simply the deed done, but includes all the conditions, immanent and transcendent, interior and superior, that contribute to the gestation, birth, and expansion of the free act. Therefore, sensation, perception, consciousness, volition, artistic creation, the moral response, and even the divine Action are included in this comprehensive term, itself expressive of the initiative of the *spirit.

Has life a meaning and has man a destiny? By way of answer Blondel examines the various levels of action to determine whether the dynamism of the *will in search of a term equal to its *élan* can be halted or satisfied with the life of sensation, dedication to science, social activity, etc. Having demonstrated against dilettantism and nihilism that the will must will something, Blondel shows that the "something" the primordial will (*la volonté voulante*) seeks is not to be found among the objective values the deliberate will (*la volonté voulue*) pursues in the order of phenomena. But if the whole phenomenal order does not suffice, the action of the deeper will must transcend all the conditions that serve as means for its expansion. Perhaps there is more in the will than the will itself; perhaps the imbalance or lack of adequation between the two phases of the will can be overcome only by the initiative of a superior Action.

For Blondel, it is no longer a question of proving that *God (the Unique Necessary Being) exists, but of determining what attitude a man should take regarding the possibility of a supreme gift that would enable him to share in an infinite Life and Will in which perfect adequation of the real and the ideal is attained. It is not for reason or philosophy to decide whether a supernatural destiny has been offered in fact. Their role is to show the impossibility of proving its impossibility and to indicate the conditions required on the part of man for its reception, should it be offered. One can either adopt a deliberately negative attitude or remain open to the very real possibility by which man's destiny would be to share in the divine Life. This is Blondel's famous "option," and before it man must take a stand: whether to seek God without God or wait in humble expectancy for an initiative that he cannot provoke but that must come entirely from God. Reason and the dialectic of action require this much, and in view of the historic claims of Christianity and man's inability to become, by himself, what he deeply wants to be, the negative option can never be scientifically justified. For it is not for man to decree what can or cannot be. Reason, then, must be as broad as charity and leave open the question of man's supernatural destiny. In this way philosophy, true to its own nature, allows a point of insertion into nature for the supreme vocation.

It is impossible to convey here the dramatic urgency of Blondel's phenomenology of action as it examines the series of means for the expansion of the will. Only the last fifth of *L'Action* deals with the necessary hypothesis of the supernatural, and it would involve a loss of perspective were one to pass over the first 350 pages with their penetrating analysis of action and its role in making possible science, art, and social life. Moreover, Blondel's literary career spanned almost 60 years, and the works that followed the thesis develop the germinal ideas of this original manifesto, making the testament of the Philosopher of Aix one of the most imposing legacies of any modern Catholic thinker.

Other Works. In the *Trilogy* on Thought, Being, and Action (1934–37), Blondel remains true to his original method, which was to indicate the functional duality between two phases of life: the primordial and the elicited. In *La Pensée* he shows that no created thought can equal the need for a Thought that is total and infinite, and in *Être et les êtres* and the revised *L'Action*, being and action receive their full expression only in that Being who is Pure Act.

Beginning with the *Lettre* on apologetic method (1896), the articles on "Monophorism" (1910), *Le procès de l'intelligence* (1921), and *Le problème de la philosophie catholique* (1932) and concluding with the Great Trilogy and the two volumes entitled *La philosophie et l'esprit chrétien* (1944–46), Blondel continued

to refine his thought and to exercise a growing influence on theology. Many of the ideas that have become commonplace in the new theology and apologetics were already clearly outlined in the books and innumerable articles of Blondel written before 1913. When his orthodoxy was challenged during the Modernist crisis, he enjoyed the personal esteem and protection of Leo XIII and (St.) Pius X. But the great vindication of his life's work came with the encomium of Pius XII in a letter from the Vatican secretariat, signed by G. Montini, the future Paul VI, urging the aged philosopher to continue his philosophical investigation, which "you have carried on with a talent equalled only by your faith" [*La Documentation Catholique* 42 (1945) 498–499].

See also ACT; SPIRIT, MODERN PHILOSOPHIES OF; LIFE PHILOSOPHIES.

Bibliography: H. BOUILLARD, "The Thought of Maurice Blondel: A Synoptic Vision," *International Philosophical Quarterly* 3 (1963) 392–402; *Blondel et le Christianisme* (Paris 1961). J. M. SOMERVILLE, "Maurice Blondel, 1861–1949," *Thought* 36 (1961) 371–410; "Action and the Silence of Being," *A Modern Introduction to Metaphysics*, ed. D. A. DRENNEN (New York 1962) 420–431. H. DUMÉRY, *La Philosophie de l'action* (Paris 1948); *Raison et religion dans la philosophie de l'action* (Paris 1963). C. TRESMONTANT, *Introduction à la métaphysique de Maurice Blondel* (Paris 1963).

[J. M. SOMERVILLE]

BLOOD

Life at any level of organization is dependent upon the availability and utilization of certain essential metabolites. Primitive unicellular and multicellular organisms were able to obtain vital chemical requirements directly from their aqueous environment. However, complex marine and terrestrial organisms have had to develop a vascular system through which a specialized nutrient fluid might be transported to each of its cellular components.

Blood consists of both plasma and cellular portions. Dissolved in the plasma are the various blood proteins: albumin, globulin, and fibrinogen, as well as soluble organic and inorganic substances. The cellular portion includes erythrocytes, leukocytes, and thrombocytes.

Since the activity of an organism reflects the activity of its component parts (cells), the blood system, which is in contact with every living cell in the body, in addition to its nutrient function, must serve as the immediate integrator and regulator of cellular processes.

Blood is the medium in which oxygen is transported from the lungs to cells and tissues, and metabolic waste products are carried to the lungs (carbon dioxide) or to the liver and kidneys (nitrogenous compounds) to be eliminated. Moreover, nutrients absorbed from the intestine are transported to cells in the form of simple carbohydrates, amino acids, and fatty acids. Regulatory hormones manufactured by the endocrine glands, antibodies essential for immunologic defense against infectious diseases, and isoagglutinins are found in blood plasma. Blood, because of its 90 per cent water and inorganic salt content, is important in regulating body temperature and normal electrolyte balance.

Erythrocytes. The cellular portion of the blood also serves many highly specialized functions. Erythrocytes (red blood cells), manufactured in the bone marrow, must undergo a process of differentiation and maturation from primitive, undifferentiated "stem" cells before they can be released into the peripheral blood stream as nonnucleated, disclike elements. Since the human red blood cells have an average life span of only 120 days, regulation of their production to maintain a constant circulating population is necessary. Since World War II, much progress has been made in proving the existence of, and isolating this humoral regulator, erythropoietin, which seems to be produced, at least partly, in the kidney. The stimulus for the production of erythropoietin is probably the degree of oxygen saturation in the tissues or in the blood or in both. In addition to erythropoietin, certain dietary and vitaminlike substances are necessary for normal blood cell production.

The principal component of the erythrocyte, and one of the most important functional components of blood generally, is hemoglobin, which serves as an oxygen-binding factor. Any deficit in hemoglobin is classified as an anemia (without blood). Deficiencies in hemoglobin synthesis might result from a lack of iron or a genetically caused defect in protein synthesis. Anemia can result also from hemorrhage or hemolysis (destruction of red cells). Usually the body is able to compensate for its anemic condition because the resulting decreased oxygen tension (caused by a loss of hemoglobin) stimulates the production of erythropoietin and consequently, of more red cells.

On the other hand, an overabundance of erythrocytic elements circulating in the blood stream (polycythemia) may be the result of an abnormally high production of cells in the marrow, which might be due to chronic low oxygen tension or pathologic states of unknown etiology.

Leukocytes. Two principal types of leukocytes (white blood cells), granular and nongranular, are found in the blood. Granulocytes are categorized into neutrophils, eosinophils, and basophils according to their specificity for acidic or basic stains. The leukocytes lacking specific granulation are classified as monocytes or lymphocytes by their morphological characteristics. Granulocytes originate and mature in the bone marrow, while monocytes and lymphocytes are normally produced in lymphatic tissues.

Both granular and nongranular leukocytes are functionally involved in defense against infectious diseases because of their ability to be rapidly mobilized to a site of infection where they phagocytize the infectious agents (this is a property of neutrophils and monocytes), or because of their contribution to antibody production (lymphocytes and eosinophils). The plasma cell, another type of nongranulated leukocyte not usually found in the peripheral blood, also contributes to the antibody response. Since the life span of leukocytes is very short (hours to days), there probably exists a humoral regulator similar to erythropoietin (leukopoietin), which also operates by a feedback mechanism to maintain the normal number of circulating cells.

Thrombocytes. Finally, platelets or thrombocytes, which play a major role in hemostasis, are found in the circulating blood. They originate as cytoplasmic fragments of megakaryocytes, which are found primarily in the bone marrow, although there is evidence that they occur also in the lungs, liver, and spleen.

Normal blood clotting depends on the presence of chemical substances found in both platelets and plasma. Lack of, or subnormal concentrations of, any of these factors will result in prolonged clotting time or complete inhibition of clotting. This condition is known as hemophilia. There are several types of hemophilia. The primary defect may be an absence of certain plasma factors, inability of the platelets to form aggregates that are critical to clot formation, or excessive fragility of blood vessels. Hemophilia is usually inherited by transmission on the female sex chromosome. However, many cases of hemophilia have been reported where there was no previous familial incidence of the disease. Although many questions remain unanswered about it, the success of the research on the problem is attested to by the marked increase in longevity of hemophiliacs.

Other blood dyscrasias also are being treated with greater degrees of success as more is learned about the physiology of blood cell production. X radiation and certain chemical compounds are able to halt excessive proliferation of leukocytes (leukemias) and erythrocytes (polycythemias). Transfusion of platelets or erythrocytes can be administered if the production of these elements falls below normal. Plasma transfusions are effective therapy against sudden hemorrhage.

Blood Types. Along with the advantages of transfusion, there occur many dangers. Transfusion requires a thorough knowledge of blood groups. Only at the start of the 20th century was it discovered that several incompatible blood types exist, so that extreme care must be taken to transfuse only compatible bloods. These blood types are associated primarily with red cells, although white cells also might be involved.

Four blood types of a universal and highly reactive nature have been classified as A, B, AB, and O. Each of these types involves a chemical substance in red cells (agglutinogens A, B, AB, or O) and an antibodylike substance (isoagglutinins A, B, AB, or O) in plasma and tissue fluids. The latter has the ability to cause clumping or agglutination of red blood cells of any type foreign to the individual. For instance, a person with type A blood has A substance in his red cells and anti-B substance in his plasma. Therefore, if he were transfused with type B cells, anti-B substance would cause them to agglutinate, and thus be responsible for a reaction that might be fatal to the patient. Likewise, blood types B, O, and AB have, respectively, anti-A substance, anti-AB substance, and no antibodylike substance.

Since type O blood has no agglutinin, it is often designated as the "universal donor." However, this is often erroneous, since anti-O or anti-H substances have been discovered in persons with A, B, and AB types. The term "universal recipient" may be applied loosely to type AB.

There are several other blood groups, the importance of which in transfusions depends on the "titer" or amount of agglutinins found in the patient's blood. Perhaps the most important of these is the Rh group. Normally, the Rh factor is either present or lacking and has no isoagglutinins associated with it. However, exposure of an Rh negative individual to Rh positive blood causes anti-Rh substance to be produced so that subsequent exposure to positive blood causes a typical agglutination reaction. Successive pregnancies of Rh negative women resulting in Rh positive fetuses or multiple transfusions of a negative individual with Rh positive blood are the usual instances of this phenomenon.

In conclusion, it can be seen from this brief introduction to hematology that within one area of study many different aspects must be considered. Blood, although a functional organ in itself, serves to integrate many bodily functions. Consequently hematology is both a valuable tool for analyzing the general physical condition of an individual and a gratifying research tool for probing deeper into some of the physiological mysteries of life.

Bibliography: L. O. JACOBSON and M. DOYLE, eds., *Erythropoiesis* (New York 1962). H. E. WHIPPLE et al., eds., "Leukopoiesis in Health and Disease," *New York Academy of Sciences: Annals* 113.2 (1964) 511–1092. M. M. WINTROBE, *Clinical Hematology* (5th ed. Philadelphia 1961). G. E. W. WOLSTENHOLME and M. O'CONNOR, eds., *Ciba Foundation Symposium on Haemopoiesis: Cell Production and its Regulation* (Boston 1960).

[P. T. MEDICI]

BLOOD, RELIGIOUS SIGNIFICANCE OF

"Blood" is from a Germanic root with the basic meaning of "bloom." The Greek term αἷμα, in the sense of something which "arouses awe or reverence," belongs much more closely to the vocabulary of religion (see "Blut," ReallexAntChr 2:459).

In Mythology. In Norse myths, the *skalds* characterize blood as an intoxicant on the basis of the myth of Odin's drink of the poets (*Edda, Skáldskaparmál* 27). Blood itself is not personified, probably because, unlike water, it did not appear prominently as a great natural force or power. However, it was brought into numerous mythical relations with other things, and especially with the sun. In Egypt Ra (the Sun) was said to have originated from drops of blood. The association, blood and fire, is self-evident, but in Mexico it plays an especially significant role in Aztec religion. On the other hand, the blood of menstruation turned the imagination to the moon. The Bambuti, for example, call menstrual blood "moon-blood" [P. Schebesta, *Die Bambuti. Pygmäen* (4 v., Brussels, 1938–50) 3:190]. Practically the same idea is present in the Egyptian hieroglyph signifying the blood of Isis. Since this blood was shed to restore the dead Osiris to life, there is a clear association here of blood and life. The ideas of the connection between blood, fertility, and earth are firmly anchored in ancestor-worship. A Papuan group has a myth in which this combination is associated with that of blood and fire. Belief in the vampire is not found in this complex. It has perhaps a special origin, being found to some extent perhaps in animism. E. Rohde made animism the basis for his detailed exposition of the relations between blood and the soul in Greek religion (see E. Rohde, *Psyche,* Eng. tr., H. B. Hillis, London 1925). In totemism, the blood of circumcision is regarded as a totem, at least in isolated instances [see *Zeitschrift für Ethnologie* 76 (1951) 63].

Sociological, Cultic, and Magical Aspects. Incest is generally forbidden even in preethnic groups, the prohibition being based on a feeling of fear or dread. At the same time, in all such groups the duty of blood revenge is already in evidence. It originated out of the barbarous experiences of wanton bloodshed in the kinship group. An extension of the kinship group by the mingling of the blood of men of different family origins—a procedure that may be described as a kind of primitive peace ritual (see König, RelHdbch, "Friedensritualien," 263)—is realized through the blood brotherhood.

The blood dance of the Bushmen has less of the religious in itself than the practice of sprinkling themselves with their own blood found among the Pygmies and the Pomo, for this procedure approaches the central concept of *sacrifice. But in such practices, even if animals are killed to secure blood, as among the Yukaghirs, there is not yet question of a cultic act. It is only when such killing is thought of as an essential part of worship that blood sacrifice, including human sacrifice, especially to the sun, enters upon its development. Blood magic likewise enters only at this stage. It serves especially to give greater strength or power to implements, vessels, actions, or persons, playing a special role in bier ordeals.

See also SACRIFICE.

Bibliography: A. CLOSS, LexThK² 1:537–538. F. ZOEPFL, *ibid.* 1:541–542. W. E. MÜHLMANN, RGG³ 1:1327–28. H. W. ROBINSON, Hastings ERE 1:714–719. J. H. WASZINK, ReallexAntChr 2:459–473. F. RÜSCHE, *Blut, Leben und Seele* (Paderborn 1930). C. M. SCHRÖDER, *Blutglaube in der Religionsgeschichte* (Munich 1936). T. SCHIFNER, *Blutzauber und Anderes* (2d ed. Leipzig 1930). H. TEGNAEUS, *Blood-Brothers* (Uppsala 1951).

[A. CLOSS]

BLOOD, RELIGIOUS SIGNIFICANCE OF (IN THE BIBLE)

The Biblical significance of blood is summed up in Lv 17.11: "The life of a living body is in its blood." This basic principle governs the Biblical theology of blood. Life belongs to God, and so blood belongs to Him. This explains both the moral and the cultic practices in which blood has a part. Some texts that refer to blood evoke also the idea of death. Hence, some scholars make blood the symbol of death. But blood is a sign of death only when it is poured out. This is precisely how blood came to stand for life. Once blood has gone out of a body, death follows. Because of this symbolism, the Biblical concept of blood affected the moral and cultic life of the Israelites.

Moral Life. Men were forbidden to eat the blood of animals (Lv 3.17). Although the prohibition may have had its origin in hygienic considerations of the ancient world, the Mosaic Law assigned it a religious context. Because all life belonged to God, the blood of slain animals had to be poured on the altar, given to God (Lv 17.11). Those who lived too far from the sanctuary expressed their faith in God as the sole Lord of life by pouring the blood on the ground and covering it with earth (Dt 12.24; Lv 17.13).

Men are forbidden to shed the blood of other men. Those "who shed the blood of the innocent" incur bloodguilt, a crime punishable by death (Nm 35.16–34). A "brother's blood" shed unjustly cries to heaven for vengeance (Gn 4.8–16). "Men of blood," i.e., men who unjustly shed blood, are wicked, and the anger of God falls on them. The punishment of the offender rests with the avenger of blood (Nm 35.19; *see* BLOOD VENGEANCE) and with the whole community (Dt 21.8–9). God demands the punishment of the murderer because no one but God has the claim on blood, the life of another.

Cultic Life. Blood held the central place in animal sacrifice. It signified the flow of life between God and man. Poured out on the altar (representative of God), it joined the offerer to God because he had placed his hand on the animal and had become one with it. The blood was not a substitute for that of the offerer but a ritual expression of the total surrender to God. God received the blood and returned it to the offerer in the form of divine life. Thus the desired effect of sacrifice, communion with God, was achieved.

The covenant sacrifice of Sinai was especially significant in underlining blood as the sign of a flow of life between God and man. *See* COVENANT (IN THE BIBLE). There God set up a special bond between Himself and His people. Moses took the blood of the sacrificial victims and sprinkled it partly on the altar and partly on the people, declaring, "This is the blood of the covenant" (Ex 24.8). The blood ratified the covenant and expressed externally what had happened. God and man had been joined together in an agreement of friendship, and the blood sprinkled on the altar and the people was a forceful expression of the union that had taken place.

Closely associated with the covenant of Sinai was the slaying of the *Passover lamb and the sprinkling of the doorposts with its blood (Ex 12.1–13, 21–23). The blood of the lamb saved the Israelites from the death of their firstborn (Ex 12.26–30). The sacrifice of the lamb on the feast of the Passover became a ritual reminder that the people had been redeemed by the blood of the lamb. Thus blood entered the theology of redemption. It became a symbol of liberation (from slavery) and of acquisition (by God). The blood of the paschal lamb was witness to the faith that God does enter into contact with man to bestow the divine favor that the blood ritual signified.

Another significant sacrifice was that of the Day of Atonement (Leviticus ch. 16). The blood rite was especially elaborate on this day. The high priest entered the *Holy of Holies and sprinkled the propitiatory (the top of the *ark) with blood. The altars of incense and of holocausts also were sprinkled. These rites underlined the special power of blood in expiating sin. In fact, its special value in expiatory sacrifices generally came to be highlighted: "It is the blood, as the seat of life, that makes atonement" (Lv 17.11). The blood of the victim should not be viewed as a punishment for sin. It forgave sins because it liberated life. The life poured out on the altar was received by God, who returned it to the repentant sinner in the form of divine life. This restored him to a state of friendship with God.

The blood rite illumines the vocabulary of expiation—propitiation, atonement, justification. Blood is a propitiation for sin because it makes God propitious to the sinner. He looks favorably on him because the blood poured out symbolizes so well the broken heart of the sinner. Blood achieves the justification of the sinner because it makes him just or holy by bringing God's own life to him. Because it restores a relationship of friendship with God, it is blood of "atonement"; the sinner is set "at one" with God. *See* EXPIATION (IN THE BIBLE).

Sacrificial blood played a large part also in the ordination to OT priesthood. The blood was used to anoint the ear, hand, and foot of those ordained (Ex 29.20). The anointing of these extremities of the body together proclaimed that the whole man was dedicated to God. Surely this is the meaning of the final anointing in which the blood mixed with oil was sprinkled on the priests and their vestments. This made them "sacred" (Ex 29.21). The blood was the bearer of God's life to the priests. Ordination made them holy because they were totally immersed in God's own life. *See* ORDINATION.

On the religious significance of blood in the NT, *see* PRECIOUS BLOOD, I.

Bibliography: EncDictBibl 255–258. J. SCHARBERT, LexThK² 2:538–539. K. GALLING, RGG³ 1:1328. T. H. GASTER, InterDict Bibl 4:147–159. L. MORALDI, *Espiazione sacrificale e riti espiatori* . . . (AnalBibl 5; Rome 1956). S. LYONNET, *De peccato et redemptione*, v.2 (Rome 1960) R. DE VAUX, *Les Sacrifices de l'Ancien Testament* (Paris 1964). E. F. SIEGMAN, "Blood in the OT," *Proceedings of the Precious Blood Study Week* (Rensselaer, Ind. 1957) 33–64. L. DEWAR, "The Biblical Use of the Term *Blood*," JThSt 4 (1953) 204–208.

[R. T. SIEBENECK]

BLOOD VENGEANCE, a primitive form of the law of retribution according to which a kinsman must vindicate the rights of a relative whose blood has been shed. Even in civilized societies the force of this primitive law could still be felt. According to the ancient Greek concept every act of bloodshed, even when committed in self-defense, created a certain defilement that required purification (Plato, *Laws* 916). Not only the criminal but his family also was defiled until the slain man's life was appeased by exacting vengeance. The initial crime could easily lead to a series of mutual crimes, a blood feud or vendetta. In primitive societies a whole family or even a whole clan was annihilated for a murder committed by one of its members.

Ancient Israel, too, had the practice of blood vengeance based on the law of talion according to which, to restore the loss suffered by a crime, repayment had to be made strictly in kind: "Life for life, eye for eye, tooth for tooth" (Ex 21.23–25). This law rests on both the principle of the sacredness of blood (Lv 17.14) and that of clan solidarity. In Israel's primitive way of thinking, life resides in the blood; when a man loses his blood, his life is extinguished (*see* BLOOD, RELIGIOUS SIGNIFICANCE OF). Blood, therefore, as the seat of life, belongs to Yahweh, and its wanton shedding demands the life of him by whom it is shed (Gn 9.5–6). Blood spilt on the ground cries to heaven for vengeance (Gn 4.10; Jb 16.18; Ez 24.6–8; 2 Mc 8.3), and an account is demanded from him who shed it (Gn 4.11; 9.6; 2 Sm 4.11; Ez 23.37, 45) by a near relative or avenger acting in Yahweh's name.

Clan solidarity, the second aspect of blood vengeance, is realized in the person of the avenger, who represents the interest of the family or clan of the one slain. The duty of blood vengeance was based on the theory that the family, clan, or tribe was a sacred unity. When the blood of any one member was shed, it was the community's blood that was shed; thus, it fell upon a representative of the community to atone for the crime by shedding the blood of the murderer.

Israel, however, endeavored to restrict the evils connected with blood vengeance. According to Israelite law only the murderer himself, not his family or clan, was to be punished for the crime (Dt 24.16; 4 Kgs 14.6; 2 Chr 25.4). Whereas earlier Israelite custom made no distinction between premeditated and unintentional killing (Gn 9.6), the more benign interpretation of the Deuteronomic law allowed a man who killed another unintentionally to seek refuge in certain designated cities of *asylum (Ex 21.13; Nm 35.9–29; Dt 19.1–13; Jos 20.3–9). If, after a fair trial, the slayer was judged guilty, the punishment was still the prerogative of the avenger of blood (Dt 19.12); he was not free to pardon the slayer or accept a monetary compensation in exchange.

Bibliography: W. E. Mühlmann, RGG³ 1:1331–32. W. Kornfeld, LexThK² 2:546. EncDictBibl 258–259. M. Greenberg, InterDictBibl 1:321; 449–450. J. P. E. Pedersen, *Israel: Its Life and Culture*, 4 v. in 2 (New York 1926–40; repr. 1959) 378–392, 420–425. De Vaux AncIsr 10–12.

[E. J. CIUBA]

BLOSIUS, FRANCIS LOUIS (DE BLOIS),

Benedictine abbot and spiritual writer; b. Donstienne (Flanders), 1506; d. Liessies, Jan. 7, 1566. He was of the lesser nobility and, for a time, a page at the court of the Emperor Charles V, but at 14 he entered the Benedictine abbey of Liessies in the Austrian Netherlands.

Discipline in this abbey was more or less relaxed, in a manner characteristic of the times. Blosius was regarded as an outstanding young man, and his old and well-meaning but weak abbot picked him as his successor. He was made coadjutor abbot in 1527 and in 1530 succeeded as abbot. Blosius found himself faced not with the problem of extirpating grave scandals but with that of revitalizing the whole spirit of the monastic life. Perhaps in his youthful ardor, he demanded too much too soon, but he seems to have come to terms with his community and turned it into a fervent one on the whole.

Blosius belonged to the contemplative tradition of the late Middle Ages; the ideal he held out before the soul was the continual sense, so far as possible, of the presence of God. He did not lay so much stress on the ultimate union that may be achieved, as writers in this tradition usually do, but he was aware of it and described it in terms of Dionysian mysticism as represented by the German school—Tauler and Suso. His program for the soul is meditation in a wide sense, interior conversations with the soul itself and with God; in a word, affective prayer. He knew, of course, what this depended on: detachment from self-will in all its ramifications, and conformity to the will of God. In the contemplative tradition he made mortification consist in this, and his teaching is excellent on that subject. As befits one whose life work was to turn a relaxed into a fervent community, he had an understanding of the weakness of human nature.

Bibliography: *Works,* tr. B. A. Wilberforce, 7 v. (London 1925–30), comprises all his original spiritual writings though he also made florilegia and wrote a few small controversial works. A complete list of the many editions would be lengthy and difficult to compile. ActSS Jan. 1:430–456. G. de Blois, *A Benedictine of the Sixteenth Century: Blosius,* tr. Lady Lovat (London 1878).

[G. SITWELL]

BLOY, LÉON HENRI MARC, novelist and

pamphleteer; b. Périgueux, France, July 11, 1846; d. Bourg-la-Reine, Nov. 3, 1917. He was born of French-Spanish parentage and at an early age was imbued with anticlericalism in the Masonic atmosphere of his home. On moving to Paris, he fell under the influence of the novelist, Barbey d'Aurevilly, and soon, as a young and passionate disciple, joined a coterie of writers who gathered around Villiers de L'Isle-Adam and *Huysmans. A rather obscure mystical experience restored his Catholic faith, of which he claimed to be one of the last loyal defenders. His piety was at the same time humble and haughty, and the violence of his literary language created a void around him: "I travel before my exiled thoughts on a great pillar of silence," he said bitterly. In 1890 he married the convert daughter of a Danish professor. His subsequent life was spent with his family in work and poverty, for his writings won only a limited number of readers. Only after his death did his work become somewhat more widely known.

He was romantic, sometimes mystical and sometimes truculent. At times he wrote of the purest regions of the love of God and of exultant hope. He had a firm pen, and his style was sometimes grandiose, at other times sneering or grave; but he was always original. His temperament drew him to extreme positions. He was not interested in politics, social questions, or science, but he did not hesitate to castigate those he judged inferior to their tasks: the rich, the writers, the priests. His books reveal the need he felt for sanctity, and a horror of spiritual mediocrity. As different and remote as he was from *Péguy, from Francis Jammes, and from *Claudel, Bloy nevertheless made up with them that company of writers who rejuvenated French Catholic literature at the beginning of the 20th century. Besides his two novels, *Le Désespéré* (1887) and *La Femme Pauvre* (1890), he wrote the *Journal* (1892–1917), edited in four volumes with notes by his biographer, Joseph Bollery. Other works are *Le Sang du Pauvre* (1909), *Le Salut par les Juifs* (1892), *Le Pèlerin de l'Absolu* (1914).

Bibliography: J. Bollery, *Léon Bloy,* 3 v. (Paris 1953) contains some unedited documents. M. J. Lory, *La Pensée religieuse de Léon Bloy* (Paris 1951). R. Maritain, *Adventures in Grace,* tr. J. Kernan (New York 1945). H. Colleye, *L'âme de Léon Bloy* (Paris 1930). P. Termier, *Introduction à Léon Bloy* (Paris 1930). P. Arrou, *Les Logis de Léon Bloy* (Paris 1946). A. Béguin, *Léon Bloy: A Study in Impatience,* tr. E. M. Riley (New York 1947).

[P. ARROU]

BLUME, CLEMENS, priest and liturgist, who made

important contributions to the history of the hymn and *Sequence; b. Billerbeck (Westphalia), Germany, Jan. 29, 1862; d. Königstein (Taunus), April 8, 1932. After attending Jesuit schools Blume entered the Society of Jesus at 16. Shortly after his ordination he became a collaborator on the project (initiated in 1886 by Guido *Dreves) of publishing texts of hymns of the Church in a series entitled *Analecta Hymnica* (AnalHymn). For 26 years (1903–29) Blume examined and collected texts and sources of Latin hymns in European libraries, thus helping to establish a broad basis for detailed hymnological research. Upon the death of Dreves (1909), Blume completed his selection from the Anal Hymn and published it as *Ein Jahrtausend lateinisches Hymnendichtung* (Leipzig 1910). An earlier work, *Repertorium Repertorii* (Leipzig 1901), was intended as a practical guide to the diffuse *Repertorium Hymnologicum* of U. Chevalier. In 1929 he became professor of liturgy at Kolleg St. Georgen, Frankfurt-am-Main, a position he held until his death. He had a keen sense of the corporate meaning of liturgy, suggesting in the preface to his final work, *Unsere liturgischen Lieder* (1932), that scientific studies of liturgical sources reach maturity only when their fruits achieve the widest possible currency among the faithful. As an independent scholar he also contributed substantially to liturgical science, but his best known works, including the Anal

Hymn introductions and his articles in the (old) *Catholic Encyclopedia,* deal with the development of the hymn and Sequence.

Bibliography: B. STÄBLEIN, MusGG 1:1947–48. Riemann. Anal Hymn, see introd. to v.53–55. *Catholic Encyclopedia and Its Makers* (New York 1917).

[E. LEAHY]

BLUMHARDT, JOHANN CHRISTOPH,

Lutheran pastor; b. Stuttgart, Germany, July 16, 1805; d. Bad Boll, Germany, Feb. 25, 1880. He studied at Tübingen, taught at a missionary institute in Basel, and in 1838 became a pastor at Möttlingen. His cure of a sick, possibly possessed, girl after a 2-year effort started a movement of penance and prayer that brought great numbers of persons to Möttlingen and after 1852 to Bad Boll, where Blumhardt bought the royal mansion as an asylum for the afflicted. When, after prayer and penance, he laid on his hands in absolution, apparent physical cures often followed. Blumhardt's spirituality won him an influence comparable to that of St. John *Vianney, the Curé of Ars, although he made no attempt to start a school or sect. His son Christoph joined him in his work in 1869, but after the father's death he abandoned prayer and healing to devote himself to the social problems of workers.

Bibliography: F. ZÜNDEL, *Johann Christoph Blumhardt: Ein Lebensbild* (Zurich 1880; 16th ed. Basel 1954). L. RAGAZ, *Der Kampf um das Reich Gottes in Blumhardt, Vater und Sohn* (Zurich 1922). E. JÄCKH and G. MERZ, RGG³ 1:1325–27.

[L. J. SWIDLER]

B'NAI B'RITH,

Jewish service organization, founded in New York City in 1843. The Independent Order of B'nai B'rith ("sons of the covenant") engages in educational and philanthropic programs in the areas of youth work, adult education, veterans' services, civic projects, international affairs, and aid to Israel, among others. Figures (1961) list 1,000 lodges in the U.S. with 185,000 men, 730 lodges with 135,000 women, and youth organizations with 32,000 young men and women. There are also lodges in Latin America, Europe, Asia, and Africa. The Supreme Lodge is located in Washington, D.C. It claims to represent Jewish public opinion in the U.S. because of the breadth of its membership. Its Anti-Defamation League was established in 1913, and the *Hillel Foundations in 1923. Among its publications are *National Jewish Monthly, B'nai B'rith Women's World,* and *Jewish Heritage.*

Bibliography: B. POSTAL, UnivJewishEnc 2:422–427. M. ELLINGER, JewishEnc 3:275–277. A. GOLDSCHMIDT, EncJudaica 4:880–886.

[J. J. DOUGHERTY]

BOBADILLA, NICOLÁS ALFONSO DE,

one of the first companions of *Ignatius of Loyola; b. Bobadilla, León, Spain, *c.* 1509; d. Loreto, Italy, Sept. 23, 1590. He studied rhetoric and logic in Valladolid, philosophy and some theology at Alcalá, and more theology under the Dominicans in Valladolid, then went to Paris in 1533 to complete his studies. He joined Ignatius there and went to Italy, being ordained in Venice on June 24, 1537. In Italy he traveled through more than 70 dioceses as a preacher and missionary. He worked also in Germany (1541–48), in the Valtelline (1558–59), and in Dalmatia (1559–61). As he writes in his autobiography, he had dealings with eight popes, three emperors, numerous electors and German princes, and cardinals and prelates through all of Italy. He was a man of much talent and great contrasts, independent and impulsive, outstanding for both accomplishments and imprudences. The Pope kept him from participating in Jesuit deliberations in Rome in 1539 and 1541, Charles V expelled him from Germany in 1548; after the death of Ignatius, Bobadilla's unsuccessful demands for modifications in the society caused papal intervention. His autobiography is an unburdening of his soul and contains many important notices for the early history of the Jesuits. He left a list of his own works, which are concerned with preaching, exegesis, and theology. His important plan of reform of the Church, presented to Paul IV in 1555, has been studied by P. de Leturia [*Estudios ignacianos,* v.1 (Rome 1957) 447–459]. His work on frequent and daily Communion was the only one of his works published during his lifetime.

Bibliography: J. F. GILMONT, *Les Écrits spirituels des premiers Jésuites* (Rome 1961). M. SCADUTO, *Storia della Compagnia di Gesù in Italia* (Rome 1964). R. BROUILLARD, *Catholicisme* 2:99–100. E. LAMALLE, DHGE 9:270–272.

[I. IPARRAGUIRRE]

BOBBIO, ABBEY OF

Founded by Irish monks, a well-known Benedictine center in the diocese of the same name, Province of Pavia, northern Italy, located on the Trebbia River. St. *Columban, exiled from *Luxeuil, crossed the Alps and founded the abbey with several of his companions. The community was organized under the Rule of St. Columban; it adopted a part of the Benedictine observance in 643, but not until the 10th century did the *Benedictine Rule replace that of the founder. The monastery, soon dedicated to Columban, enjoyed the favor of the Lombard King Agilulf, even though it took a leading part in the struggle against *Arianism in northern Italy. Columban was followed by other outstanding abbots who strengthened the spiritual and temporal resources of Bobbio, especially *Athala, *Bertulf, and Bobolenus (d. 652). Bobbio was the first monastery to be granted papal *exemption (628), and the abbots were given pontifical rights in 643. Emperors from *Charlemagne to *Frederick I Barbarossa made liberal grants of land and revenues to the community, and abbots such as *Wala and Gerbert of Aurillac (the future Pope *Sylvester II) were important figures in their time. In 1014 Emperor *Henry II, on the occasion of his own coronation in Rome, persuaded Pope *Benedict VIII to create Bobbio an episcopal see, and Abbot Petroaldus (d. 1027) became first bishop; for some time his successors were chosen from among the monks and continued to reside in the abbey. The next few centuries saw a gradual decline in the spiritual and intellectual work of the abbey as conflicts arose between the bishops and the monks over jurisdiction. The abbey was a part of the congregation of St. Justina from 1449 until it was seized and secularized by the French army in 1803. What remains of the monastery buildings is used as a school, and the abbey church, with the tomb of Columban, now serves the local parish. The bishopric of Bobbio, also suppressed in 1803, was reestablished by *Pius VII in 1817, and St. Anthony *Gianelli held the see from 1838 to 1846. In 1965 the diocese had

The tomb of St. Columban in the basilica of St. Columban at the Abbey of Bobbio.

about 25,000 Catholics in 70 parishes. It is suffragan to *Genoa.

In the early Middle Ages the abbey was especially well known for its library. Columban brought the traditions of Irish scholarship with him when he came to northern Italy, and later abbots encouraged studies and acquired books. In the middle of the 8th century the learned *Dungal left his library, including the *Antiphonary of Bangor,* to the abbey, and a 10th-century catalogue [ed. L. Muratori, *Antiquitates italicae* (Milan 1740) 3:817–824] shows the broad scope of the library's holdings. It was such libraries as that at Bobbio that preserved much of classical literature during the so-called *Dark Ages. The Bobbio Missal was produced in the monastic *scriptorium in the early 10th century. A great number of the library's books were lost in the 17th and again in the 19th century, although some can still be found in the Ambrosian Library at Milan, the *Vatican Library, and the National Library at Turin.

Bibliography: Sources. C. CIPOLLA, ed., *Codice diplomatico del monastero di S. Colombano di Bobbio . . .,* 3 v. (Rome 1918). G. S. M. WALKER, ed., *S. Columbani opera* (Scriptores Latini Hiberniae 2; Dublin 1957). Literature. Cottineau 1:400–402. A. WILMART, DACL 2:935–962. F. BONNARD, DHGE 9:275–284. C. CASTIGLIONI and T. LECCISOTTI, EncCatt 2:1726–30. P. VERRUA, *Bibliografia bobbiese* (Piacenza 1936). P. COLLURA, *Studi paleografici: La precarolina e la carolina a Bobbio* (Milan 1943); *San Colombano e la sua opera in Italia* (Bobbio 1953). G. PENCO, "Sull' influsso Bobbiese in Liguria," *Benedictina* 9 (1955) 175–181; *Storia del monachesimo in Italia dalle origini alla fine del medio evo* (Rome 1960), *passim,* but esp. 100–110. AnnPont

(1965) 67. **Illustration credit:** Italian Information Center, New York City.

[B. J. COMASKEY]

BOBBITT, FRANKLIN, curriculum designer; b. Mt. Sterling, Ind., Feb. 16, 1876; d. Waldron, Ind., March 7, 1957. Bobbitt earned his A.B. degree from the University of Indiana, Bloomington, in 1901; and a Ph.D. from Clark University, Worcester, Mass., in 1909. From 1902 to 1907 he taught in the Philippine Normal School in Manila, and then in 1909 joined the faculty at the University of Chicago, Ill., where he remained until his death. Along with his teaching assignments, he wrote several books and served as curriculum consultant for the public schools systems of Los Angeles, Calif.; Toledo and Cleveland, Ohio; Denver, Colo.; South Bend, Ind.; and others.

Bobbitt's major concern was curriculum development. The purpose of education, as he saw it, is to bring every child to live and appreciate the "good life"; the educative process is merely what the child does in living the good life; and the teaching process, what teachers do in getting the child to live it. In his *Curriculum of Modern Education,* in which he outlines the areas of the "good life" in educational practice, Bobbitt enlarges upon the ideas of Herbert Spencer's *What Knowledge is of Most Worth.* Education, he states, must bring each human being to live in as practicable a way as possible, and consequently the business of education is to teach growing individuals to perform efficiently those activities that constitute the latest and highest level of civilization.

In school administration, Bobbitt wanted to introduce the same scientific supervision and control that already existed in industry, and he tried to deduce the principles of school administration from so-called scientific industrial administration. Education, he maintained, is a shaping process as much as the manufacture of steel rails.

Since to Bobbitt, a pragmatist, moral education could best be accomplished in the "great school of practical social action and reaction," an act was morally good or bad depending on its effect on society. In his opinion, moral education should be a training in group consciousness, and formal religion was helpful only if it promoted "civic vision." His major works include: *What Schools Teach and Might Teach* (1916), *The Curriculum* (1918), *How to Make a Curriculum* (1924), and *The Curriculum of Modern Education* (1941).

[A. M. FLYNN]

BOBOLA, ANDREW, ST., Polish Jesuit missionary and martyr; b. Palatinate Province of Sandomir, Poland, 1591; d. Janow, May 10, 1657 (feast, May 16). From an old and distinguished family, he was educated in the Jesuit Academy at Vilna (1606–11). He entered the Society of Jesus in 1611 and studied classics and philosophy at Vilna, taught for 2 years at Grunsberg, studied theology at Vilna, and was ordained there in 1622. As pastor at Nieswiez he worked heroically among the plague-stricken in 1624. Except for a period of temporary retirement because of ill health (1643–49), he spent his life in missionary and pastoral work at Vilna and in the countryside, bringing whole villages of Orthodox believers back to communion with Rome. In the political, social, and religious wars between

Poland and Russia involving the Eastern and Western Churches, Bobola was a marked man because of his religious activities. In the devastation of East Poland he was cruelly martyred by Ukrainian Cossacks at Janow. Devotion to Bobola spread rapidly in Poland and Lithuania when his inexplicably incorrupt body was discovered 40 years after burial in the crypt under the ruins of the Jesuit church in Pinsk. The cause of beatification was at first delayed by the suppression of the Society of Jesus and then by the death of Pius VIII who had summoned a congregation for the advance of the cause in 1830. He was beatified in 1853. Marshal Józef Pilsudski sent a postulatory letter for canonization to Benedict XV in 1920. Canonization finally occurred in 1938. Over a period of 280 years the body of Andrew Bobola endured many translations. Having been buried in Pinsk, 1657, the body was removed to Polotsk in White Russia in 1808 and in 1922 taken to Vitebsk and to Moscow where it was concealed by the Bolshevik government until 1923. On the third request of Pius XI it was released and taken to Rome in October 1923. Shortly after canonization, 1938, it was conveyed through Slavic countries via Budapest and Cracow to Warsaw. During the German invasion of Poland in 1939, the body was removed from the cathedral to the Church of St. Andrew Bobola at Mokotow in Warsaw, where it may still be seen. The first church in America named for St. Andrew was consecrated in Dudley, Mass., Diocese of Worcester, Feb. 21, 1954.

Bibliography: C. MARESCHINI, *The Life of Saint Andrew Bobola of the Society of Jesus, Martyr,* tr. and ed. L. J. GALLAGHER and P. V. DONOVAN (Boston 1939); *Santo Andrea Bobòla, martire, della Comp. di Gesù* (Isola de Liri 1938). L. ROCCI, *Vito del B. Andrea Bobòla, martire polacco* (2d ed. Rome 1938). Sommervogel 11:1402–04. P. BERNARD, DHGE 2:1641–44.

[L. J. GALLAGHER]

BOCCACCIO, GIOVANNI

Poet and prose writer; b. probably Florence or Certaldo, Italy, July 1313; d. Certaldo, Dec. 21, 1375. Legend has falsely portrayed the earliest circumstances of his life. Using pseudoautobiographical confidences, vague and mysterious to the point of enigma, that were scattered throughout the youthful works, the 19th century set out to construct an entrancing *vie romancée,* in which Boccaccio was thought to have been born at Paris of the love of a merchant and a gentlewoman, or even a princess, and later to have been the chosen lover of the beautiful illegitimate daughter of King Robert of Anjou, Fiammetta. This is all fantasy; if his father, Boccaccio di Chellino, representative of the powerful trading company of the Bardi, was actually in Paris during 1313, then Giovanni was born of an illegitimate affair of his mother at Certaldo or, more likely, at Florence.

He passed his infancy in the San Pier Maggiore section of Florence, in his father's house, where Margherita de' Martoli had come as wife; she was related to the Portinari (Beatrice's family), and perhaps directly from her or from his first teacher, Giovanni Mazzuoli da Strada, sprang the earliest indications of that Dantean cult that grew throughout his life. When hardly out of boyhood (perhaps about 1325), he was sent into business at Naples with the Bardi Bank, which controlled the finances of the Angevin court. This commercial experience was unhappy and was followed by an equally

Giovanni Boccaccio, detail of a 14th-century fresco by Andrea da Firenze in the Church of Santa Maria Novella at Florence.

disappointing study of Canon Law. Boccaccio thereupon turned completely to literature, under the direction and with the advice of the most learned men of the Neapolitan court (e.g., Paolo *Veneto, Paolo da Perugia, Andalò del Negro) and of such friends as Cino da Pistoia, Dionigi da San Sepolcro, Barbato da Sulmona, and Giovanni Barrili, who held up to him the example of Petrarch. The carefree and lordly life of the Angevin court and city, necessary meeting place of the Italo-French and the Arab-Byzantine cultures, also deeply influenced his formation.

Fiammetta Period. Against such a background, dominated by both avid cultural interests and easygoing pleasure, Boccaccio desired to weave his great romance of love, centering on the fickle and fascinating figure of Fiammetta and the various heady adventures that had brightened his youth. Though Fiammetta is missing from the elegant portrayal of the aristocratic Neapolitan society within the mythological setting in his first poem, *Caccia di Diana* (1334?), and from the flowing ottava rima of *Filostrato* (1335?), which deals with the Troilus-Cressida story, she dominates, directly or indirectly, Boccaccio's other works up to the eve of his masterpiece.

Filocolo, the romantic story of the adventures of Florio and Biancofiore—made all the more valuable by the digressions in which the self-taught young man shows his scholarly enthusiasm, by the autobiographical allusions, and by the storytelling techniques that foreshadow the *Decameron*—appears to have been produced about 1336 at the direct request of Fiammetta. *Teseida* (written about 1340–41, perhaps partly in Florence), which tells the story of the love of Arcita and Palemone for Emilia, inserts lyric motifs and love laments that seem to echo and develop the notes in the dedicatory letter to Fiammetta into his ambitious plan for a first Italian epic poem. The *Commedia della Ninfe* (entitled *Ninfale d'Ameto* by 14th-century scribes and editors) and the *Amorosa visione* (one form in 1341–42 alternating prose and verse, the other in 1342–43 in Dantean *terza rima*) seem to wish to elevate, by the allegorical literary forms of the prevailing Tuscan tradition, the figure of the beloved to a superhuman level. The *Elegia di Madonna Fiammetta* (composed between 1343 and 1344), the first modern psychological novel, inverts the roles of the two lovers and blends the subtlest motivations with the innermost impulses of an enamored feminine heart.

Thus, nearly all the youthful work of Boccaccio (and even more clearly the *Rime* of this period), though patently autobiographical, gives evidence of becoming dominated and almost paralyzed by the experiences of love and enthusiasm for culture. But the immediacy of the first writings gradually gives way to a psychological analysis more detached from the sorrowful matter of love, under an interpretative effort sometimes almost allegorical.

The failure of the Bardi Bank forced Boccaccio to return to Florence in 1340 to meet painful domestic difficulties that are reflected in the laments that crop up in the works and letters of those years. Far from alienating him from literary pursuits, however, these harsh realities put him into immediate contact with his city and the life of the mercantile society to which he belonged. After brief periods in Ravenna at the court of Ostasio da Polenta (1345–46) and at Forlì with Francesco Ordelaffi (1347), he was again at Florence in 1348, where he witnessed the terrible plague described in the introduction to his masterpiece.

The Decameron. Shortly before 1348, Boccaccio had sung in ottava rima in *Ninfale fiesolano* (1344–46?) the story of a fresh and gentle love in the enchanted environs of the Fiesolan countryside. In 1348 he began to prepare and lay out the *Decameron* (1348–51?), the work that splendidly crowns his youthful experiences and sums up his narrative and romantic preludes in a superb *summa* of medieval storytelling. The setting is this: to escape the horrors of the plague of 1348, seven young ladies and three young men retire to a Fiesolan hillside; to pass away the time, each one is to tell a story every day, except Friday and Saturday, on a theme and in the order decreed by the one in charge for that day. A hundred *novelle,* interspersed with depictions of the group's aristocratic way of life, are thus recounted in 10 days. In this powerful and multiform narrative work, Boccaccio displayed the "human comedy" of a society captured in the autumn of medieval civilization, though described at its best in the preceding century when it had achieved its economic conquest of Europe and the Mediterranean world. It is, in other words, the extraordinary epic of Boccaccio's own mercantile class.

According to the most acceptable aesthetic canons of his time, moreover, Boccaccio attached to his varied and iridescent images a didactic value beyond the mere story.

Woodcut from an English edition of the "Decameron" printed at London between 1620 and 1625 under the title "The modell of wit, mirth, eloquence, and conuersation."

Through the 10 days into which his 100 stories are arranged he wished to display the extent of man's capacity for good and evil, almost as in a multicolored legend of Everyman. To this end he pictured man on an imaginary journey that begins with a bitter condemnation of vice (First Day) and concludes with an exaltation of virtue (Tenth Day), after being tested by the three great forces that, as instruments of Providence, are at work in the world (Fortune, Second and Third Days; Love, Fourth and Fifth; Genius, Sixth, Seventh, Eighth; the Ninth Day is a transitional episode).

External Trouble; Interior Growth. His father's death in 1349 plunged Boccaccio even more deeply into family difficulties, but his established literary fame impelled his fellow citizens to entrust him with various civic tasks. In 1350 they sent him as ambassador to the Lords of Romagna and—a more pleasant duty—to present 10 gold florins to Sister Beatrice, the nun daughter of Dante, as indemnity for damages sustained by her family. He was named chamberlain for the commune in 1351 and then representative of the republic (in the negotiations for the acquisition of Prato) and ambassador to Ludwig of Bavaria; in 1354 and 1365 he was ambassador to Innocent VI and Urban V at Avignon and in 1367 presented the homage of Florence to Urban V on his return to Rome. But these honorable missions failed to extricate him from the deplorable condition into which the Bardi bankruptcy had cast him. In the hope of bettering his affairs, and prompted by the pleasant memories of his youthful years and the friendship of Niccolò Acciaiuoli who had become the real arbiter of the Angevin court, he betook himself to Naples in 1355, 1362, and again in 1370–71. Nothing came of these ventures, and he returned disillusioned and embittered to Certaldo, where he had withdrawn probably as early as 1361–62.

The material and temporal circumstances of these years, however, are of far less importance than his humanistic development, his cultural interests, and the religious evolution of his thought. These attitudes were already present in the poems and letters of about 1350, but they emerge clearly after his encounter with *Petrarch, the most fortunate and decisive encounter for Italian and European culture of the 14th century.

Petrarch's Influence. Boccaccio met Petrarch for the first time in 1350, having eagerly gone some miles outside Florence to greet him and invite him to be his house guest. Boccaccio spent weeks of unforgettable, animated discourse at Petrarch's home in Padua in the spring of 1351; he was again his guest in 1359 at Milan, in 1363 at Venice, and in 1368 at Padua. They engaged in a voluminous correspondence, constantly exchanged books and literary information, and from 1350 on were generally *seiuncti licet corporibus unum animo* (though physically separated, one in spirit) as Petrarch wrote. After 1360 especially, Boccaccio's house became one of the chief centers of Italian prehumanism, the retreat wherein Coluccio Salutati, Giovanni Villani, Luigi Marsili, and many other early humanists received inspiration, the scriptorium from which flowed marvelous literary discoveries (from Varro to Martial, from Tacitus to Apuleius) and the new interest in Greek that Boccaccio first, among the literary men of the time, had mastered through his dogged, industrious relationship with Leonzio Pilato (1360–62).

These prehumanistic attitudes continued to characterize the works of his maturity, which he corrected and recorrected to his death, and established in various editions. The *Genealogia Deorum gentilium* (1350–75) is a great dictionary of mythology, a monument of prehumanistic culture; the *Bucolicum carmen* (1351–66?) is a collection of eclogues that are allegorical or allusive to contemporary political events, on the model of Dante and Petrarch. *De montibus, silvis, fontibus* (1355–74?) is an inventory of classical and contemporary geographical culture; *De casibus virorum illustrium* (1356–74?), is designed to show the transience of earthly goods and the ruin in store for those who climb too high, with examples drawn from all epochs. *De mulieribus claris* (1360–75?) sketches the lives of the most noted heroines of antiquity and the Middle Ages up to Queen Giovanna of Naples.

Zeal for the Vernacular. Boccaccio's early humanism, both for these works and in his activity in promoting classical culture, seems less concerned with stylistic and rhetorical principles than does Petrarch's. It is less refined and tends to eclecticism; but it is always supported by a zealous love for poetry, so much so that he feels himself "wholly intended for poetry from as far back as the maternal womb" (*Genealogia*, 15:10). Better than Petrarch, he—the first apostle of the Dantean cult —synthesizes the wonderful and uninterrupted tradition of the intellectual life, of poetry and culture, from antiquity to his own days. Though he was a chief discoverer of the treasures of ancient Hellas, his vision was not confined within the boundaries of the classics; it encompassed Christian authors, certain medieval writers, and poets who wrote in the vernacular. It is not without significance that the *Teseida*, the most ambitious of his youthful works, was modeled both on the great Latin epics and on the typically medieval *cantari*; that in the *Decameron* classical and later sources were drawn upon; that in the description of the plague that opens this masterpiece he mixes Lucretian facts, gained at second hand, with a page from Paolo Diacono; that his prose

rhythms favor Livy more than Cicero, and even more the currently accepted rhetorics and *artes dictandi*.

It is further significant that, as in his youthful years he had constantly juxtaposed experiments in the vernacular with the required employment of Latin, so precisely during the most characteristically prehumanistic years, when he became more directly involved with Greek literature, Boccaccio did not abandon his fond relationship with the muses of the new language and new literature. In witness of this stand the *Epistola consolatoria a Pino de' Rossi*, (1361–62), addressed to a friend exiled for political reasons; that harsh invective against women that stands out in the *Corbaccio* (1366?); the *Trattatello in laude di Dante* (1358–63?); and many vernacular letters to friends. In the same period, too, he undertook to correct and rework the *Amorosa visione* (which occasioned the *Trionfi* of Petrarch) and the final version of the *Decameron* (the Hamilton autograph). All of Boccaccio's activity, whether as writer or as forceful promoter of humanistic studies, is constantly marked by this notable bilingualism that is not merely verbal but mental and cultural, by this vigorous and vital mixture of ancient and contemporary methods and experiments, by this passion, not rhetorical but human, for poetry, for all poetry.

Precisely because of this profound passion, Boccaccio in those years gathered up and defined in the last two books of the *Genealogia Deorum* his aesthetic doctrine, a synthesis of the leading poetic ideas of the Middle Ages and of earlier discussions by the men of the generation before that—discussions that heralded the rapidly approaching debates during the chivalric years between 1300 and 1400. Against the doubts and uncertainties of many, Boccaccio shows the complete propriety and high mission of poetry *ex sinu Die procedens*, of poetry as the *anima mundi*.

Religious Maturity. Tactfully helped by the serene and profound Christianity of Petrarch, Boccaccio during these years also resolved into a firm religious sensibility the emotional instability of his youth. To consecrate this achievement he received minor orders and in 1360 permission to become a director of souls; he dedicated himself enthusiastically to the study of Dante, on whose "sacred poem" he began to lecture at the church of San Stefano di Badia (1373–74). Just as he was publicly exalting the genius of Dante, the death of Petrarch (July 19, 1374) left a void in his heart. All his writings from then on only repeat the lament for the loss of his great friend, for his own spiritual loneliness. Hence, when Boccaccio died, he remained for his contemporaries almost hieratically fixed in the role of last survivor of the "three crowns," the last champion of Italian letters. So he was hymned by Sacchetti, who deplored in Boccaccio's death the death of poetry itself.

Bibliography: *Opere*, ed. V. BRANCA (Milan 1964–); *Decameron*, ed. V. BRANCA (4th ed. Florence 1965); Eng. tr. J. M. RIGG, 2 v. (London 1947); *The Filostrato*, tr. N. E. GRIFFIN and A. B. MYRICK (Philadelphia 1929); *Amorous Fiametta*, tr. B. YOUNG, ed. K. H. JOSLING (London 1929); *The Nymph of Fiesole*, tr. D. J. DONNO (New York 1960); *The Life of Dante*, tr. P. H. WICKSTEED (San Francisco 1922); *Concerning Famous Women*, tr. G. A. GUARINO (New Brunswick, N.J. 1963). Three basic bibliographies are: A. BACCHI DELLA LEGA, *Serie delle edizioni delle opere di Giovanni Boccaccio latine, volgari, tradotte e trasformate* (Bologna 1875). G. TRAVERSARI, *Bibliografia Boccaccesca* (Città di Castello 1907). V. BRANCA, *Storia della critica al "Decameron" con bibliografia boccaccesca* . . (Rome 1939). On the MSS: see V. BRANCA, *Tradizione delle opere di Giovanni*

Boccaccio (Rome 1958); ed., *Studi sul Boccaccio* (Florence 1963–), current bibliog. The biographies by G. BILLANOVICH, *Restauri boccacceschi* (Rome 1945) and V. BRANCA, *Schemi letterari e schemi autobiografici nell'opera del Boccaccio* (Florence 1946) are in strong reaction to the romance built up, on presumed autobiographical confessions, especially by V. CRESCINI, *Contributo agli studi di Boccaccio* (Turin 1887), A. DELLA TORRE, *La giovinezza di G. Boccaccio (1313–1341) proposta d'una nuova cronologia* (Città di Castello 1905), and H. HAUVETTE, *Boccace* (Paris 1914). T. C. CHUBB, *The Life of Giovanni Boccaccio* (New York 1930). C. CARSWELL, *The Tranquil Hearth: Portrait of Giovanni Boccaccio* (New York 1937). A. C. LEE, *The Decameron: Its Sources and Analogues* (London 1909). E. G. PARODI, *Lingua e Letteratura*, 2 v. (Venice 1957). U. BOSCO, *Il Decameron: Saggio* (Rieti 1929). B. CROCE, *Poesia popolare e poesia d'arte* (Bari 1933). V. BRANCA, *Boccaccio medievale* (Florence 1956). H. G. WRIGHT, *Boccaccio in England: From Chaucer to Tennyson* (London 1957). G. GETTO, *Vita di forme e forme di vita nel Decameron* (Turin 1958). A. D. SCAGLIONE, *Nature and Love in the Late Middle Ages: Chiefly an Essay in the Cultural Context of the Decameron* (Berkeley 1963). **Illustration credit:** Fig. 1, Alinari-Art Reference Bureau. Fig. 2, Library of Congress, Rosenwald Collection.

[V. BRANCA]

BOCCHERINI, LUIGI, rococo composer who helped crystallize the classical style, baptized Ridolfo Luigi; b. Lucca, Italy, Feb. 19, 1743; d. Madrid, May 25, 1805. His father, Leopold, a contrabass player, gave him his first violoncello lessons, and Luigi was playing professionally at 13. Further work with local teachers led him in 1757 to Rome, where he was exposed to the

Luigi Boccherini.

Palestrina style. Publication of his first collection of string quartets (1764) and recital tours with violinist Filippo Manfredi so impressed the Spanish ambassador to Paris that in 1768 he was named composer and virtuoso to the Infante Don Luis of Spain. After Luis's death in 1785, Boccherini joined Friedrich Wilhelm II of Prussia, an amateur cellist to whom he dedicated his celebrated Cello Concerto. The King's death (1797) freed him to return to Madrid, where in late 1800 his momentary patron was Lucien Bonaparte, French ambassador. Thereafter he supported his family with such hackwork as scoring his works for guitar *aficionados,* but still maintaining his creative pace undaunted by poverty, intrigues, or family sorrows. He died as he had lived, a gentle Christian. Ceremonial return of his body to Lucca in 1927, plus the onset of longplay recording, triggered a thorough reappraisal of his music. Current research has refuted the "wife of [F. J.]

Haydn" canard, and Boccherini is now regarded as the peer of pre-Mozart classicists. Although he was too much the lyricist and too timidly the contrapuntist to achieve stature as a symphonist, his chamber and other instrumental works reveal a perfection of form, instrumental inventiveness, and a civilized, contemplative beauty that is heightened by its unique infusion of autochthonous Spanish idioms. Of some 370 known works, the religious group includes a Mass for four voices and instruments; a cantata, villancicos, and motets for Christmastide; a pair of oratorios; and a *Stabat Mater* for 3 voices and strings that proves richer and more mature than *Pergolesi's, with which it is often compared.

Bibliography: L. PICQUOT, *Notice sur la vie et les ouvrages de Luigi Boccherini, suivie du catalogue raisonné . . .* (Paris 1851). G. DE SAINT-FOIX, *Boccherini: Notes et documents nouveaux* (Paris 1930), contains and updates Picquot. A. BONAVENTURA, *Boccherini* (Milan 1931). G. DE ROTHSCHILD, *Luigi Boccherini: Sa vie, son oeuvre* (Paris 1962). K. STEPHENSON, MusGG 2:1–6. C. F. POHL, Grove DMM 1:778–779. "Lucca a Luigi Boccherini," *Lucchesia* 5 (Oct. 9, 1927) special issue. A. BONACCORSI, "Boccherini e il *Stabat*," *La rassegna musicale* 19 (April 1949) 92–97. Láng MusWC. **Illustration credit:** Museo Teatrale alla Scala.

[M. E. EVANS]

BOCCIONI, UMBERTO, prominent painter and sculptor of the Futurist movement; b. Reggio Calabria, Oct. 19, 1882; d. Verona, Aug. 16, 1916. After studying in Rome with G. Balla from *c.* 1900, he traveled in France and Germany, absorbing both neoimpressionist technique, and *art nouveau* and German Secession expressive tendencies. In 1909, following the poet Marinetti's futurist manifesto, he joined with other painters in Milan to publish similar manifestoes for artists and to evolve a dynamic art that would effect an identity between spectator and artistic image through the suggestion of speed or overwhelming motion, as in "The City Rises" (1910; Museum of Modern Art, New York). Contact with Picasso's work suggested freer use of form as reflected in his triptych "States of Mind" (1911; Nelson Rockefeller Collection). In 1912 he wrote of Futurist sculpture, a startling manifesto that advocated unconventional materials and stress on dynamic force rather than on static mass. His "Unique Forms of Continuity in Space" (1913; Museum of Modern Art), one of his few surviving sculptures, is among the great lyric achievements of modern sculpture.

See also ART, MODERN EUROPEAN, 3. TWENTIETH CENTURY.

Bibliography: J. C. TAYLOR, *Futurism* (New York 1961). G. C. ARGAN, *Umberto Boccioni* (Rome 1953). R. L. HERBERT, Enc WA 2:539–540. U. BOCCIONI, *Pittura, Scultura futuriste* (ed. Futuriste di "Poesia"; Milan 1914).

[R. J. VEROSTKO]

BÖCKEN, PLACIDUS, canonist, vice chancellor of the University of Salzburg; b. July 7, 1690; d. Salzburg, Feb. 9, 1752. He entered the Benedictine Abbey of St. Peter at an early age and was ordained in 1713. Subsequent to receiving his doctorate in Canon Law and civil law in 1715, he was assigned to Rome (1718–20) and then appointed professor of Canon Law at the University of Salzburg in 1721. In 1729 he was named the University's vice chancellor, but he left in 1741 after falling into disfavor with Prince Archbishop Leopold of Salzburg. He was a pastor for 2 years in Dornback, a suburb of Vienna, but returned in 1743 to Salzburg as superior of Maria-Plain, where he died. At Salzburg he published his valuable *Commentarius in Jus Canonicum universum* (1735–39), which included, in an expanded form, his earlier works on the five books of the Decretals. A reprint of this work appeared in Paris in 1776.

Bibliography: L. JUST, DDC 2:927–928. Hurter Nomencl 4: 1609–10. Schulte 3:170.

[T. F. DONOVAN]

BOCKING, EDWARD, English Benedictine, one of the chief associates of Elizabeth Barton, the Nun of Kent; b. *c.* 1490; d. Tyburn, April 20, 1534. He was educated at Oxford (D.D., 1518), and elected prior of Canterbury College there. Later, he became cellarer at the Benedictine cathedral priory of Christ Church, Canterbury, and in 1525 he headed a commission to inquire into Elizabeth Barton's prophecies. The result favored her, and Bocking was appointed her spiritual adviser after she had joined the Benedictine convent of St. Sepulchre's, Canterbury. The Nun's reputation for sanctity grew, but trouble arose when her prophecies took on a political complexion at the time of the divorce, and the government was forced to take action in 1533. Dr. Bocking, in his dealings with the Nun, had probably acted imprudently, but it is unlikely that he practiced willful deceit. His fate was inevitably linked with hers; and when she was condemned with others by attainder in 1534, after probably having made some sort of confession about her revelations, Bocking suffered with her and the rest. They were all executed at Tyburn on April 20, 1534.

Bibliography: Knowles ROE v.3. H. A. L. FISHER, *History of England 1485–1547* (London 1906).

[J. E. PAUL]

BODEY, JOHN, BL., layman, martyr, b. Somersetshire, 1550; d. Andover, Nov. 2, 1583. The son of a devout Catholic mother and a wealthy merchant and mayor of Wells, he attended Winchester College and New College, Oxford. He received an M.A. in February 1576; that year he was deprived of his Oxford fellowship by Bishop Horne of Winchester because of his Roman Catholicism. He left Oxford and began the study of civil law at Douai, returning to England in February 1578. He seems to have acted as a schoolmaster until 1580, when he was arrested with John Slade and imprisoned at Winchester. Two of the jailers were converted by them, and tradition says that their edifying behavior won many to Catholicism. For some reason not clear, John Slade and John Bodey were tried twice, once at Winchester and then again at Andover in August 1583. They were sentenced to death for denying that the Queen had any supremacy over the Church in England; yet they publicly acknowledged the Queen as their lawful sovereign. Bodey was declared venerable by Leo XIII in 1886, and beatified by Pius XI in 1929.

Bibliography: R. CHALLONER, *Memoirs of Missionary Priests,* ed. J. H. POLLEN (new ed. London 1924). J. H. POLLEN, *Acts of English Martyrs* (London 1891).

[B. C. FISHER]

BODHISATTVA, in Pāli *bodhisatta,* a term meaning "Wisdom Being," first applied to an incarnation of a candidate to Buddhahood, similar to the previous incarnations of Buddha narrated in the *Jātakas* (Birth

"Great Bodhisattva" or *"Bodhisattva Padmapani,"* detail of a fresco of the late 6th or early 7th century, in Cave I at Ajanta, India. Many scholars consider this painting the greatest masterpiece of early Indian art, from both the religious and the artistic viewpoints.

Stories). In early Buddhism only a few zealous and persevering beings could be saved. But from the 1st century A.D., partly under Zoroastrian, Hellenic, and Christian influences, *Mahāyāna made Buddhahood accessible to all conscious beings with a mind for the truth. Thus a bodhisattva became a divine compassionate savior who, upon developing Buddhahood through the practice of the perfections (*pāramitā*) of charity, morality, patience, devotion, meditation, and wisdom, along with accommodation, vows, determination, and understanding, postponed *nirvāṇa* and underwent endless rebirths until all conscious beings who invoked him with faith could be saved. Inspired by this merciful soteriological teaching, all good Mahāyānists strove after the bodhisattva ideal. Above the ordinary bodhisattvas are the great bodhisattvas (mahābodhisattvas), who, on becoming Heavenly Buddhas, save the faithful by the application (*pariṇāma*) of their merit. The most popular Heavenly Buddha is Amitabha, assisted by Avalokiteśvara (Chinese, Kuan-yin; Japanese, Kannon), the God or Goddess of Mercy, Mañjuśri, the Begetter of Wisdom, and Maitreya, the Forthcoming Savior.

See also BUDDHISM; MAHĀYĀNA (GREAT VEHICLE); ZOROASTER (ZARATHUSHTRA).

Bibliography: H. DAYAL, *The Bodhisattva Doctrine in Buddhist Sanskrit Literature* (London 1932). NARADA THERA, *The Bodhisattva Ideal* (Colombo, Ceylon 1944). J. H. CHAMBERLAYNE, "The Development of Kuan Yin, Chinese Goddess of Mercy," *Numen* 9 (1962) 45–52. **Illustration credit:** Photo–Dr. Ananda Coomaraswamy. Courtesy of Prof. Benjamin Rowland and Penguin Books, Ltd., Pelican History of Art.

[A. S. ROSSO]

BODIN, JEAN

French political philosopher; b. Angers, 1530; d. Laon, 1596. He studied at the University of Angers and trained for law at Toulouse. In 1560 he took up the practice of law in Paris but not successfully. His bent was toward jurisprudence and history. In 1566 he published the *Methodus ad facilem historiarum cognitionem*, which foreshadowed the fuller presentation in his *Six livres de la République* (1576) of his theory of the effects of climate on government and society and his theory of progress. In the *Réponse aux paradoxes de M. Malestroit* (1568) he analyzed the cause of the rise in prices that occurred during the 16th century; this, the most original of his studies, earned for him a place of distinction among early economists. Both the *Methodus* and the *Réponse* can be considered preliminary studies for his great work.

In *De la République,* an elaborate treatise in political science, Bodin revealed both prodigious learning and enormous confusion. Facts and arguments were not arranged in logical order. The book was written to serve the interests of France by supplying a principle of political stability for a country torn by religious wars. Its theme concerns the principal end of a "well-ordered republic." Although virtue is formally acknowledged as the principal end of the state (Bodin explicitly disallowed the classical Greek notion of happiness as the end), the emphasis throughout is not on the end of the state as such but on the end of the "well-ordered republic." This end, Bodin argued, is sufficiently achieved by the recognition of *puissance souvraine,* i.e., unlimited power of making law. Nonetheless, he conceived the sovereign to be restricted by those natural-law precepts without which human society could not be maintained—the prohibition of murder, theft, and the like—and by the "fundamental laws" of the land and the obligation to respect the right of private property and the family.

Climate is presented as determining, within limits, the character and potentialities of peoples and their forms of government. Thus, Bodin thought that northern peoples, strong of body and somewhat stupid, tend toward democratic societies; southerners, subtle and contemplative, favor theocracy; and middle-zone populations, balanced and practical, incline toward monarchy (in his judgment the best form of government). Religion he considered also determined by climate.

Bodin exhibited marked caution on the subject of religion. In *De la République* he took the position that religion is desirable as contributing to the well-ordered state and that, if conformity could be had without stirring up civil war, the government should indeed suppress free discussion of religious questions. His profession of tolerance was obviously not related to freedom of conscience but rather to the dictates of the well-ordered state. Later in his life, in the *Heptaplomeres* (1588), he reached the conclusion that for practical purposes one religion is as good as another. By 1593 his religion tended toward an abstract theism that included belief in the immortality of the soul, the existence of angels and demons, and freedom of the will. He was the author of a curious treatise on demonology, *La Démonomanie des Sorciers* (1580).

The year in which *De la République* appeared, Bodin was elected a member of the estate-general of Blois.

In this capacity he opposed the plan of the clergy and the nobility to urge the King to force the Catholic religion on his subjects. He offended Henry III by opposing the King's demand to be allowed to alienate the public lands and royal demesne. In 1588 he joined the Holy League out of consideration for personal safety rather than political conviction, and he repudiated it in 1593.

Bibliography: J. W. ALLEN, *A History of Political Thought in the 16th Century* (3d ed. rev. New York 1957). P. JANET, *Histoire de la science politique* (Paris 1872). H. J. L. BAUDRILLART, *J. Bodin et son Temps* (Paris 1853).

[C. N. R. MC COY]

BOECE, HECTOR (BOYCE, BOETHIUS),

Scottish humanist and chronicler; b. Dundee, *c.* 1465; d. probably Aberdeen, 1536. He studied and lectured at Paris before being appointed first principal of Aberdeen University by its founder, Bp. William Elphinstone (d. 1514), whose life he later wrote in his *Episcoporum Murthlacensium et Aberdonensium vitae* (Paris 1522). His chief work was *Scotorum historiae* (Paris 1527; Scots tr. by John Bellenden, 1536), an elegantly written but uncritical compilation that circulated widely in Europe. It was used by Holinshed in his *Historie of Scotland* (v.2 of the Chronicles) and so gave Shakespeare his plot for *Macbeth.* George *Buchanan made unscrupulous use of this work of Boece in his polemic against Mary, Queen of Scots. Boece, drawing principally on the early chroniclers, had ingenuously incorporated in his history the work of an anonymous forger whose aim was to use bogus history to justify the theory of popular sovereignty. Thomas *Innes (1662–1744) exposed the hand of this forger. He showed also that Buchanan, in selecting Boece as his authority, was "with a formed design and by principle" retailing false history, while Boece himself was imposed upon "out of too great credulity."

Bibliography: A. J. G. MACKAY, DNB 2:759–762. D. IRVING, *Lives of Scottish Writers,* 2 v. (Edinburgh 1839). J. B. BLACK and W. D. SIMPSON, *Quatercentenary of the Death of Hector Boece* (Aberdeen 1937).

[J. QUINN]

BOEHM, JOHN PHILIP,

German Reformed minister; b. Höchstädt, Germany, 1683; d. Whitpain, Pa., April 29, 1749. He was the son of a Reformed minister and was a schoolmaster at Worms, Germany, before coming to the U.S. in 1720. After serving (1725–29) Reformed congregations in Montgomery Co., Pa., as a lay reader, he was ordained at the Dutch Reformed Church in New York City in 1729. In 1730 he became pastor of churches in Philadelphia, Pa., and Germantown, Pa. He resisted the efforts of Count Nicholas Zinzendorf to unite the Reformed congregations with the Moravians from 1741 to 1743. With Rev. Michael Schlatter, Boehm formed in 1747 the Synod of the Reformed Church in Pennsylvania, the first synod of this church in America.

Bibliography: J. P. BOEHM, *Life and Letters,* ed. W. J. HINKE (Philadelphia 1916). H. DOTTERER, *Rev. John Philip Boehm* (Philadelphia 1890).

[R. K. MAC MASTER]

BOEHM, MARTIN,

cofounder of the Church of the United Brethren in Christ; b. Conestoga, Pa., Nov. 30, 1725; d. Conestoga, Pa., March 23, 1812. He was the son of a German-born blacksmith and Mennonite elder. After becoming a Mennonite preacher in 1756, he came under the influence of the Great Awakening through disciples of George Whitefield. In 1767 Boehm met Philip William Otterbein, a minister of the Reformed Church, and their association led to the formation of the Church of the United Brethren. Boehm was also closely associated with Bp. Francis Asbury and other early Methodists, with whose theology he agreed. He was a preacher of religious revival among German settlers in Pennsylvania, Maryland, and Virginia for more than 50 years, and was made bishop of the Church of the United Brethren in 1800.

Bibliography: B. E. FOGLE, *Martin Boehm* (Dayton 1956). H. BOEHM, *Reminiscences . . . of Sixty-four Years in the Ministry* (New York 1866). A. W. DRURY, *History of the Church of the United Brethren in Christ* (Dayton 1924).

[R. K. MAC MASTER]

BOEHMER, JUSTUS HENNING, lawyer and teacher; b. Hanover, Germany, Jan. 29, 1674; d. Halle, Germany, Aug. 29, 1749. He studied at Jena before becoming a professor at the University of Halle in 1701. He was a legal counselor to Frederick I of Prussia. William I named him director of the University of Halle in 1731. He is noted not only for Roman law studies but also for his special interest in the *Decretum* of Gratian. His works include the *Ius ecclesiasticum protestantium,* 5 v. (1714–37); *Ius parochiale* (Halle 1714); and the *Corpus Iuris Canonici,* 2 v. (Halle-Magdeburg 1747). He translated P. de Marca's *De concordia Ecclesiae et imperii* in 1708, and Fleury's *Institutions de droit ecclésiastique* in 1724. The latter work was put on the *Index of Forbidden Books in 1736.

Bibliography: R. NAZ, DDC 2:928.

[T. D. DOUGHERTY]

BOEHNER, PHILOTHEUS HEINRICH, medievalist, philosopher, and botanist; b. Lichtenau (Westphalia), Germany, Feb. 17, 1901; d. St. Bonaventure, N.Y., May 22, 1955. He entered the Holy Cross (Saxonia) Province of the Order of Friars Minor in 1920 and was ordained in 1927. He began his career as a medievalist by translating into German É. Gilson's studies: *Der heilige Bonaventura* (Hellerau 1929), *Der heilige Augustin, Eine Einführung in seine Lehre* (Hellerau 1930), *Die Mystik des heiligen Bernhard von Clairvaux* (Wittlich 1936); and coauthored their *Die Geschichte der christlichen Philosophie* (Paderborn 1937). Majoring in botany and minoring in philosophy at the University of Münster (1929–33), he published as a doctoral dissertation *Über die thermonastischen Blütenbewegungen bei der Tulpe* [*Zeitschrift der Botanik* 26 (1933) 65–107]. He taught philosophy and biology at the Franciscan studium in Dorsten (1933–39); then he went to the Pontifical Institute of Mediaeval Studies (Toronto) to edit the logic of William of Ockham. At the outbreak of World War II, he entered the U.S. and was naturalized. Noted for text editions and studies in 14th-century logic and Ockham's philosophy, he became first director of the Franciscan Institute research center at St. Bonaventure University; there he initiated the new series of *Franciscan Studies* (1941), *Franciscan Institute Publications* (1944), and the *Cord,* a review for Franciscan spirituality (1950).

Bibliography: É. BUYTAERT, "Bibliography of Fr. Philotheus Boehner, O.F.M.," FrancStudies 15 (1955) 321–331. "In Memoriam," *ibid.* 101–105. FranzStud 37 (1955) 292–298. *Cord* 5 (1955) 206–215.

[A. B. WOLTER]

BOETHIUS

Anicius Manlius Torquatus Severinus Boethius, philosopher and statesman; b. Rome, *c.* 480; d. near Pavia, *c.* 524. Educated in Athens and Alexandria, Boethius has been called a founder of the Middle Ages because of his lasting influence on the formation of medieval thought. His father was a consul in 487 under the Arian King of the Ostrogoths, Theodoric the Great (475–526), and in 510 he himself held the consulship. Accused of treason Boethius was later imprisoned and put to death. During his long imprisonment, he wrote the *Consolation of Philosophy,* a work read by every educated man for more than 1,000 years. In it he describes the pursuit of wisdom and the love of God as the true source of human happiness.

Works. While one of his students, *Cassiodorus (*c.* 485–*c.* 580), employed the translator Epiphanius to make the Greek Fathers available to Latin readers, Boethius planned to translate into Latin the entire body of writings by Aristotle and Plato and to show their basic agreement in philosophy. It seems that only a small part of this farsighted project was carried out, however. Still extant is his translation in 510 of Aristotle's *De Interpretatione,* which he explains in two commentaries, one for beginners (511) and one for more advanced students of logic (513). Also still in existence is his translation of Aristotle's *Categories* with a commentary written in 510. Before 505 he had already composed a commentary on Porphyry's *Isagoge,* translated by *Marius Victorinus. Later (509) he decided to make his own translation of the *Isagoge* and comment on it (509–510). He mentions a translation of Aristotle's *Topics* and *Prior Analytics* (PL 64:1173C; 1216D; 1184D), perhaps still extant in MS Oxford, Trin. Coll. 47 (*Topics*) and MSS Chartres 497–498 (excerpts from the *Analytics*). The translations of Aristotle's two *Analytics,* his *Topics* and *Elenchi,* published under Boethius's name (PL 64:639–762; 909–1040), date back to James of Venice (*c.* 1128). Between 513 and 515, he wrote a commentary on Cicero's *Topics,* part of which is lost (PL 64:1039–1174). In addition, Boethius wrote *An Introduction to Categorical Syllogisms* (PL 64:761–94), two books each *On the Categorical Syllogism* (PL 64:793–832) and, in 514, *On the Hypothetical Syllogism* (PL 64:831–876). While the book entitled *De divisione* (PL 64:875–92) is authentic, the *De definitione,* attributed to him (PL 64:891–910) is the work of Marius Victorinus. Also spurious are the attributions to Boethius of the *De unitate et Uno* (PL 63:1075–78), written by *Dominic Gundisalvi, and of the *De disciplina scholarium* (PL 64:1223–38), whose unknown author lived in the 13th century. It is believed that about 520 Boethius composed the *Theological Tractates,* known as *Opuscula sacra,* which were to establish him as a theological authority almost equal to St. Augustine in questions concerning the Blessed Trinity and the Incarnation.

Teaching. Boethius's literary activities began in the field of logic, which is a necessary tool for all the sciences, especially philosophy. The famous definition of *philosophy as "love of wisdom," found in his first commentary on Porphyry's *Isagoge,* is interpreted by

Boethius in his study. Illumination in a mid-12th-century manuscript in the Bodleian Library, Oxford (MS Auct. F.6. 5., fol. 7v.).

him as the quest for God, the root of all being and knowledge (PL 64:10D–11A).

Division of Philosophy. Boethius divides philosophy into two kinds: practical and speculative (or theoretical). Practical philosophy is subdivided into three parts: ethics, which teaches man as an individual how to direct his moral actions; politics, which teaches how the state is to be governed in accordance with the four cardinal virtues; and economics, which concerns the proper conduct of family life (PL 64:11D–12A). Speculative philosophy is likewise subdivided into three parts: natural philosophy, also called physiology, which studies the nature of physical bodies as they exist in reality; mathematics, which deals with the forms of physical bodies by way of abstraction from matter and motion; and theology, which studies forms existing without matter and motion such as God and souls (PL 64:11B–C). Natural philosophy deals with objects as presented by the senses. Mathematics studies the many forms abstracted by the intellect from such objects, to distinguish between the various forms that cause a physical body to be quantitative (large, small) or qualitative (red, warm, soft, etc.). Theology rises above these material objects and contemplates God as the immaterial Form that is the source of all other being, "for everything owes its being (*esse*) to Form" (*De Trin.* 2).

Liberal Arts. To Boethius the Middle Ages owe the transmission of the Roman concept of education comprised in the seven *liberal arts known as the trivium (logic, grammar, rhetoric) and the quadrivium (arithmetic, geometry, astronomy, music), the "quadruple road to wisdom." He himself wrote *On Arithmetic* (PL 63:1079–1168) and *On Music* (PL 63:1167–1300), though not the two works *On Geometry* attributed to him (PL 63:1307–52 and 1352–64).

Universals. From Boethius the Middle Ages inherited a keen interest in the problem of *universals. In his endeavor to reconcile *Aristotelianism and *Platonism, he dealt at length with general ideas or universals as discussed in logic by *Porphyry. It seems that this blend

of two different conceptions accounts for the confusion reflected in the divergent interpretations that divided medieval scholars since the days of *Abelard. Boethius himself leaned toward Plato; the question whether universals are real or simply conceptions of the mind he answered in the sense that universals (*genus, *species) are not only conceived separately from bodies but also exist outside of them.

This view is based on the nature of being as understood by Boethius. Each thing owes its being to a number of forms that determine it to be the kind of thing it is. God is the Supreme Form, a pure form without matter. Lacking all composition, He is absolutely one. Creatures, on the other hand, are composed of parts or of a plurality of forms. An individual thing is a *substance because it underlies accidents. If such a substance is of a rational nature, it is called a *person. What makes a substance be a substance is a subsistence, a term applicable to all created substantial forms. Numerical difference is the result of a variety of accidents.

Theology. It used to be widely disputed whether Boethius was a Christian. The fact that he has been venerated as a Christian martyr at Pavia was officially recognized by Rome in 1883. Doubts were raised in view of the apparent absence of specifically Christian teaching in his most popular and final work, *Consolatio philosophiae.* It is, however, generally admitted that toward the end of his life Boethius turned his attention to theology and produced then the *Opuscula sacra.* He tells us that before writing his first tract *De Trinitate* he had studied the writings of Augustine and that he deliberately adopted "new and unaccustomed words" in the exposition of the mystery. Characteristic of his thoroughness is the analysis of the Aristotelian categories and the statement: "But when these categories are applied to God they change their meaning entirely" (*De Trin.* 4). The explanation culminates in the summary conclusion: "So then, the category of substance preserves the Unity, that of relation brings about the Trinity" (*De Trin.* 6). Boethius addressed this work to his father-in-law and former consul Quintus Aurelius *Symmachus. To John the Deacon he addressed another but shorter tract on the Trinity and a treatise against Eutyches and Nestorius, often called the *Liber de persona et duabus naturis,* in which he clarifies the various meanings of the term nature and defines person as "an individual substance of a rational nature" (*C. Eutych.* 3). More philosophical than these tracts is his brief exposition generally known as *De hebdomadibus.* In it the conclusion is reached that the being of all existing things is good because God, who gave them being, is good. The objection that by parity of reason all things ought to be just because God, who willed them to be, is just, is answered by Boethius in the sense that to be good involves being, while to be just involves an act. In God being and action are identical, but they are not identical in creatures.

There is no general consensus concerning the authenticity of the tract entitled *De fide catholica;* most historians, however, hold that Boethius wrote it. The tract summarizes such doctrines as that of the Trinity and rejects the tenets of Arius, the Sabellians, and the Manichaeans. Speaking of the Church, the author declares: "This Catholic Church spread throughout the world is known by three particular marks: whatever is believed and taught in it has the authority of the

Scriptures, or of universal tradition, or of local and more restricted regulation" (De fide, PL 64:1338A). He teaches that all corruptible things shall pass away, that men shall rise for future judgment, that each shall receive reward according to his deserts, and that the reward of bliss will be the contemplation of the Creator. The author finally speaks of the heavenly city "where the Virgin's Son is King and where will be neverending joy, delight, food, achievement, and unending praise of the Creator" (ibid. 1338B).

Influence. The doctrinal influence of Boethius reached its peak in the 12th century in the commentaries written by scholars of the school of Chartres. But only one of them, *Gilbert de la Porrée, wrote commentaries on all four opuscula sacra (1, 2, 3, 5) generally accepted as authentic. *Thierry of Chartres and his disciple, *Clarenbaud of Arras, are known to have commented on the first and third Tractates. Clarenbaud openly accuses both Abelard and Gilbert of erroneous doctrines based on their misunderstanding of Boethius. The earliest commentary on the first Tractate was written by the Carolingian philosopher *Remigius of Auxerre. Many marginal and interlinear glosses are still found in the libraries of Europe. In the 13th century St. *Thomas Aquinas commented on the first Tractate. The Tractates were first translated into English in 1926 by H. F. Stewart. However, translations of the Consolation have a much longer history. King Alfred the Great (849–899) translated it into Anglo-Saxon. Notker Labeo (c. 950–1022) made the first German translation. The Greek monk Maximos Planudes (1260–1310) translated it into Greek. Well known is the French rendition by Jean (Clopinel) de Meung (c. 1240–c. 1305). While in prison, Albert of Florence (fl. 1323–32) wrote an outstanding Italian translation. Geoffrey Chaucer (c. 1340–1400) translated it between 1372 and 1386. Even Elizabeth, Queen of England (1533–1603), translated what the English historian Edward Gibbon (1737–94) called "a golden volume, not unworthy of the leisure of Plato or of Tully." The English translation in vogue at present dates back to the 17th century. Only the initials (I.T.) of the translator's name are known.

See also SCHOLASTICISM, 1.

Bibliography: A list of editions is found in E. DEKKERS and A. GAAR, SacrErud 3 (1951) 153–156. Dekkers CPL 196–198. Cross ODCC 181–182. Studies and Bibliographies. Gilson Hist ChrPhil. A. A. MAURER, Medieval Philosophy, v.2 of A History of Philosophy, ed. É. H. GILSON, 4 v. (New York 1962–). Copleston 2:101–104. D. KNOWLES, The Evolution of Medieval Thought (Baltimore 1962). H. R. PATCH, The Tradition of Boethius (New York 1935). H. M. BARRETT, Boethius: Some Aspects of His Time and Works (Cambridge, Eng. 1940). P. GODET, DTC 2.1:918–922. M. CAPPUYNS, DHGE 9:348–380. P. COURCELLE, Les Lettres grecques . . . à Cassiodore (rev. ed. Paris 1948); "Étude critique sur les commentaires de la Consolation de Boèce," ArchHistDoctLitMA 14 (1939) 5–140. **Illustration credit:** University Press, Oxford.

[N. M. HARING]

BOETHIUS OF SWEDEN (DACIA), Aristotelian philosopher; b. probably Denmark, first half of the 13th century; place and date of death unknown. The theory that he was of Swedish origin and a canon of the Diocese of Linköping has been seriously questioned by S. S. Jensen ["On the National Origin of the Philosopher Boetius de Dacia," Classica et Mediaevalia 24 (1963) 232–241]. As a secular cleric he taught philosophy in the faculty of arts at Paris, where he was associated with *Siger of Brabant in the Averroist move-ment condemned at Paris in 1270 and 1277. Later he probably became a Dominican of the province of Dacia. Boethius stanchly defended the freedom of philosophy from religion, teaching the eternity of the world and of the human species and denying creation and the Resurrection. However, he did not abandon the Christian faith but tried unsuccessfully to reconcile it with his philosophy. He claimed that faith teaches the truth, though reason sometimes contradicts it. Boethius wrote many commentaries on Aristotle, some of which are lost. His only published works are De summo bono, De sompniis, and De aeternitate mundi.

See also AVERROISM, LATIN.

Bibliography: M. GRABMANN, Neuaufgefundene Werke des Siger von Brabant und Boetius von Dacien (Munich 1924); "Die Opuscula De Summo Bono sive De Vita Philosophi und De Sompniis des Boetius von Dacien," ArchHistDoctLitMA 6 (1931) 287–317; Mittelalterliches Geistesleben, 3 v. (Munich 1925–56) 200–224. G. SAJÓ, "Boetius de Dacia und seine philosophische Bedeutung," Die Metaphysik im Mittelalter, ed. P. WILPERT (Miscellanea Mediaevalia, 2; Berlin 1963) 454–463; ed., De Aeternitate Mundi (Berlin 1964). Gilson HistChrPhil 399–402, 725.

[A. MAURER]

BOGARÍN, JUAN SINFORIANO, Paraguayan archbishop and patriot; b. Mbuyapey, Paraguay, Aug. 21, 1863; d. Asunción, Feb. 25, 1949. Bogarín, son of Juan José Bogarín and Mónica de la Cruz González, was outstanding among the prelates who governed the Church in Paraguay after its independence from Spain, not only for the length (54 years) of his episcopate but especially for the great work of national reconstruction that he accomplished. For 35 years he was the only bishop of the country and was its first archbishop. As a young man he studied in the seminary of Asunción under the Lazarist Fathers; he was ordained Feb. 24, 1887. For several years he was assigned to the cathedral as curate and diocesan secretary and chancellor. Only 7 years after ordination he was appointed bishop of Paraguay by Pope Leo XIII (Sept. 21, 1894) and consecrated on the feast of San Blás (Feb. 3, 1895) by the Salesian Bishop Luis Lasagna. The diocese covered 450,000 square kilometers of territory without means of communication and had barely recovered from the war of the Triple Alliance. The bishop visited the whole diocese at least three times, covering 48,425 kilometers mainly on horseback. In organizing the diocese, he formed a curia and established parishes. He gave the only seminary in the republic strong leadership, a firm spiritual foundation, and an imposing edifice. He brought many religious orders to Paraguay, founded Catholic Action there, and created a Catholic press and radio. In 1899 he participated in the First Plenary Council on Latin America, called in Rome by Pope Leo XIII. He was also named first president of the council of state created by the constitution in 1940. Bogarín lived to the full his episcopal motto—Pro aris et focis. He was an apostle, a tireless preacher, and a patriot. He was his country's outstanding pioneer, builder, spiritual leader, and peacemaker.

[A. ACHÁ DUARTE]

BOGOMILS

Adherents of a medieval Balkan sect that came into being in Bulgaria, but whose origins go back to *Manichaeism via Paulicianism. In the 8th century the Byzantine emperors resettled a number of *Paulicians in

Thrace, and under the influence of these immigrants the heresy called Bogomilism after its founder, Pope Bogomil ("pleasing to God"), was eventually introduced into the Balkans. The first account of this heresy is found in a reply of Patriarch Theophylactus to the Bulgar Czar Peter (c. 950), stating that it was "Manichaeism mixed with Paulicianism" (Μανικαΐσμος γάρ ἐστι, Παυλικιανισμῷ συμμιγής). About 972, the Bulgarian priest Cosmas wrote his *Treatise on the Bogomils,* denouncing these heretics and emphasizing their refusal to obey any authority, civil or ecclesiastical.

For the Bogomils, the world and the human body were works of Satan; only the soul was a creation of God. The true Christian conquered matter by abstaining from all physical contacts, by abstaining from meat and wine, and by forgoing all earthly possessions. This monastic-type ideal was, in practice, possible only for the "Perfect"; the ordinary faithful could sin but they were under obligation to obey the Perfect; they could receive "spiritual baptism" on their deathbeds. The Bogomils accepted only the New Testament and the Psalms, translated into the vernacular. They were Docetists, holding that Christ did not have a human body but only the appearance (δόκησις) of one. Like the Paulicians, they rejected Sacraments, churches, and relics, tithing and church property, but retained a hierarchy of their own.

Bogomilism spread rapidly in the Balkans and even in Asia Minor in the 11th century (as indicated in the *Epistola invectiva* of Euthymius of Peribleptos). At the same time it spread into Italy and in France, where its adherents were called *Patarines or *Cathari (καθαροί; in German, *Ketzer*). Recruits came largely from among the artisans and peasants oppressed by feudalism, but the nobility, in Provence as in Bosnia, also adhered to this "bargain church" that permitted them to appropriate to themselves the goods of the Catholic Church. About 1110, Emperor *John II Comnenus discovered a Bogomil organization in Constantinople headed by a physician, Basil by name, and 12 "Apostles." Basil was burned at the stake, and the monk Euthymius Zygabenus included a description of the heresy in his *Panoplia dogmatica.* In Serbia Prince Stephen Nemania took stern measures against the Bogomils c. 1180, ordering the burning of their leaders and their books. In Bulgaria, the heresy was crushed by Czar Boril, whose *Synodicon* of 1211 censures and condemns the Bogomils. But the movement continued to grow in Dalmatia (where it is mentioned from 1167 on) and in Bosnia, which later became the center of Bogomilism in Europe.

In 1203 the Bogomil leaders of Bosnia allegedly recanted their heresy before the legate of Pope Innocent III (Act of Bolinopolje), but the movement soon spread throughout the entire country, and Pope Honorius III preached a crusade against Bosnia. In 1237 a crusade by Hungarians scored some success, but after the Tatar invasions of Hungary, the whole of Bosnia went into heresy for 2 centuries. With substantial support coming especially from the nobility, Bogomilism became a national religion. Beginning in 1340, however, the Franciscans preached the Catholic faith in Bosnia and founded friaries there. The barons and kings of Bosnia reconverted to Catholicism, but were for a long time unable to combat the heresy, headed by a *dijed* (bishop), and by *gosti* and *starcy* (elders). At length, in 1450 King Thomas required his subjects to accept Catholicism; 40,000 recalcitrants took refuge with their *dijed* in Herzegovina, which remained the final bastion of Bogomilism. But in 1463 the Turks easily took Bosnia and in 1482, Herzegovina. Thereafter many of the local population preferred to abandon their superficial Catholicism and adopt Islam, as they found in it some resemblance to their old faith. Such Islamized Bosnians and Herzegovinians were dubbed *poturi* (those who became Turkish). Some *poturi* preachers worked among the remaining Paulicians in Bulgaria, evidenced by Bulgarian 17th-century Slavic books that had been written in Bosnia. As late as 1660 the *poturi* often read the Gospel side by side with the Koran.

No traces of this heresy remain in the Balkans, except tombstones—quite numerous in Bosnia and Herzegovina—which bear symbolic decorations (sun and moon, Christ the Vine, the anthropomorphic cross) going back to Manichaeism.

Bibliography: M. JUGIE, DictSpirAscMyst 1:1751–54. S. RUNCIMAN, *The Medieval Manichee: A Study of the Christian Dualist Heresy* (Cambridge, Eng. 1947, repr. 1955). D. OBOLENSKY, *The Bogomils: A Study in Balkan Neo-Manichaeism* (Cambridge, Eng. 1948). A. SCHMAUS, "Der Neumanichäismus auf dem Balkan," *Saeculum* 2 (1951) 271–299. A. BORST, *Die Katharer* (Schriften der MGH 12; Stuttgart 1953). E. WERNER, "Die Bogomilen in Bulgarien Forschungen und Fortschritte," StMed 3rd ser. 3 (1962) 249–278. A. V. SOLOVIEV, "Bogomilentum und Bogomilengräber in den südslawischen Ländern," *Völker und Kulturen Südosteuropas* (Munich 1958) 173–199.

[A. V. SOLOVIEV]

BOGOTÁ, ARCHDIOCESE OF (BOGOTENSIS),

see located in the capital of the republic of Colombia; created an archdiocese March 22, 1564. In 1964 it had seven suffragan dioceses: Duitama (1955), Espinal (1957), Facatativá (1962), Girardot (1956), Ibagué (1900), Tunja (1880), and Zipaquirá (1951). In 1902 Leo XIII designated this the primatial see of Colombia.

The site of the city of Santafé de Bogotá, founded in 1538, was in the Diocese of S. Marta. The pleasant climate, the good nature of the Indian inhabitants, and the fertile soil quickly attracted Spanish colonists. In 1540 the bishops of S. Marta began sending priests and religious to the area, the first under Pedro García Matamoros. In 1545 the bishop himself visited the city, and in 1549 he secured a royal order to change the episcopal residence to Santafé. In 1562 Pius IV ordered that the diocesan seat should henceforth be Santafé instead of S. Marta. When the archdiocese was created 2 years later, it covered an immense area: most of modern Colombia and part of Venezuela. Gradually the territory has been limited through the erection of new dioceses until in 1964 it was restricted to the federal district of Bogotá and a few neighboring settlements, with a population of about 1½ million. It has about 150 parishes, most of which have parochial schools attached to them. Larger numbers of religious serve in the archdiocese in parish work and in education. There are a few contemplative orders of nuns, but most women religious are active in schools, hospitals, orphanages, and other service institutions.

Since the erection of the archdiocese there have been 35 archbishops. Archbishop Luis *Zapata de Cárdenas founded the seminary, one of the oldest in the world, in 1581, less than 20 years after the Tridentine decree. At first it was under the direction of the secular clergy. In 1605 it was reorganized by the Jesuits. In 1767 it was returned to the secular clergy. In 1964 it was divided into the major seminary for ecclesiastical studies,

Fig. 1. Bogotá, the church of La Veracruz. An original chapel on the site was built in 1543. The present church was built in 1731 and rebuilt in 1903.

Fig. 2. Bogotá, the interior of the church of San Agustín, built in the colonial period.

Fig. 3. The cathedral of the Archdiocese of Bogotá, begun in 1808 and consecrated in 1823.

directed by the Sulpicians; the minor for the bachelor's degree; and the preseminary. Zapata de Cárdenas also called an archdiocesan council but was never able to convene it. Other archbishops did succeed in holding councils: Fernando Arias de Ugarte in 1625; Agustín Camacho Rojas in 1774; Vicente Arbeláez in 1868 and 1874.

The cathedral of Bogotá is dedicated to the Immaculate Conception. The 16th-century buildings (1556 and 1580) were replaced by the building started in 1808, on the plans of the Capuchin Domingo de Petrez, and consecrated in 1823. It is in the neoclassical style and, since its completion, has been further decorated. Since 1907 it has been a minor basilica. The cathedral chapter associated with it has 11 members.

See also COLOMBIA.

Illustration credits: Fig. 1, Pan American Airways. Figs. 2 and 3, Pan American Union, Washington, D.C.

[J. RESTREPO POSADA]

BOGUMIŁ OF GNIEZNO, ST., archbishop of *Gniezno; date of birth unknown; d. Dubrow, near Koło, Poland, 1092 (feast, June 6). Quite probably he resigned his see in 1080 after 5 years in office and became a hermit till his death 12 years later. There is a puzzling divergence of opinion and lack of accurate information about him. He was venerated as a saint from the Middle Ages, and his cult was approved by the Holy See in 1925.

Bibliography: Z. KOZŁOWSKA-BUDKOWA, in *Polski Słownik biograficzny,* v.2 (Cracow 1936) 200–201. P. DAVID, DHGE 9:417–418. Z. SZOSTKIEWICZ, "Katalog Biskupów obrz. łac. Przedrozbiorowej Polski," *Sacrum Poloniae Millennium,* 1 (1954) 417, 535. For a different version, see Butler Th Attw 2:519–520. B. STASIEWSKI, LexThK² 2:558.

[L. SIEKANIEC]

BOHEMIA MANOR, an important early Jesuit school in Maryland. Around 1741 the growth of religious intolerance in the Maryland colony induced the Jesuits to move the center of their activities, at least for a time, to a remote location in Cecil County, not far from the Pennsylvania border. Here at Bohemia Manor (or Bohemian Manor) they opened a boarding school for boys. Although there is no record of the opening date, among the more likely ones are 1742 and 1745. Thomas Poulton, SJ, under whose jurisdiction the school was established, is mentioned as being at Bohemia Manor in 1742. Other indications make 1745 the more probable opening year. For example, it is believed that one of the school's most outstanding pupils, "Jacky" Carroll, later Abp. John Carroll, was about 11 years old when he came to Bohemia Manor, which would be in 1745 or 1746.

The organization and curriculum of the school at Bohemia Manor was quite simple but no doubt similar to that of its European predecessors. The duration of the school is uncertain; it was probably discontinued shortly after Poulton's death in 1749. According to the financial account of Mr. T. Wayt, the schoolmaster, there were apparently two courses available: a classical course for which he received 40 shillings as tuition, and an English course, probably a type of commercial course, for which he received 30 shillings. On the other hand, there may have been two programs: college preparatory and elementary. The scantiness of the records, however, gives us no complete answer to their exact nature. It would seem that the program was not limited to the three "Rs," for it certainly prepared students to be admitted to St. Omer's College in Flanders on completion of their studies at Bohemia Manor. Besides Carroll, among the early students were the three Neale brothers, Benedict, Edward, and Leonard, founder of the *Georgetown Visitation Convent; James Heath; George Boyes; and Robert Brent.

Whatever the courses offered at Bohemia, the school, like Newtown Manor in St. Mary's County, was of great importance in the early educational endeavors of Maryland. Both schools were of significance to the future of the Church in the U.S., for they were to prepare many students for entrance into European colleges, whence these young men would return to be leaders of the Church in Maryland and the U.S.

Bibliography: T. A. HUGHES, *The History of the Society of Jesus in North America: Colonial and Federal,* 4 v. (New York 1907–17) v.2. J. M. DALEY, *Georgetown University: Origin and Early Years* (Washington 1957).

[J. M. DALEY]

BOHEMIAN BRETHREN

Members of the Unity of Brethren (*Jednota bratrská, Unitas fratrum*) in Bohemia and Moravia, almost all Czech-speaking, and including a later branch in Poland. With the Bible as their rule, interpreted according to the community, they followed a simple, humble life, renouncing violence and recognizing Christ as the only mediator. They held that the sacraments were valid only if administered by a worthy priest to a believer. They denied transubstantiation, having no cult of the Eucharist but admitting the presence of Christ when communion was given. Public faults were to be publicly confessed. The religious songs of the Unity were assigned importance.

The Unity originated in Prague in the early 1450s in the group around the *Utraquist Archbishop-elect John Rokycana and was led by his nephew Řehoř. Rokycana brought the Brethren into contact with Peter Chelčický, who in a number of writings in Czech (e.g., The Net of Faith) called for a return to primitive Christianity. He viewed the functions of ruler, judge, and soldier as incompatible with the Christian calling; and he rejected oaths, serfdom, and town life. His doctrines were taken over by Řehoř's followers, who in 1457–58 settled at Kunvald in northeastern Bohemia. A church discipline was promulgated in 1464. In 1467, at a meeting at Lhotka (near Rychnov), the group broke with the Utraquists when they drew lots to choose three priests from their midst; these were confirmed by a Waldensian elder. The step brought renewed persecution for nearly 150 years.

At first most Brethren were countryfolk or artisans. But in the 1490s pressure from younger, university-educated priests led by *Lukáš of Prague and difficulties due to the Brethren's position toward secular authority caused the Unity to reject this social radicalism. A small minority who split off soon disintegrated.

Lukáš reorganized the Unity, strengthened church discipline, reformulated theology, and wrote constantly in its defense. Soon after his death, Lutheran doctrines found acceptance in the Unity. Their main protagonist was John Augusta. Brethren nobles, who now played an increasingly important role in the Unity, participated in the resistance of the Czech estates in 1547 and provided Ferdinand I with an excuse to suppress the Unity in Bohemia. Some Brethren went into exile in East Prussia and Poland. The Polish Unity worked closely with other Polish Protestants, e.g., the Union of Koźminek (1555) and the Consensus Sandomiriensis (1570). It died out in the 18th century.

In the early 1550s pressure on the Bohemian Unity relaxed. During Augusta's imprisonment (1548–64) John Blahoslav, historian, humanist, and Biblical scholar, rose to prominence. His Czech version of the NT and that of the OT carried out after his death, together known as the Kralice Bible (1579–94), is a landmark in Czech literature. The Brethren had now emerged from their cultural isolation. While Augusta strove for Protestant union, Blahoslav believed the Brethren should preserve an independent testimony. Yet by 1575 the Unity had virtually gone over to a Calvinist doctrinal position. As a result of renewed Catholic activity, Brethren and Lutheran-minded neo-Utraquists drew together and composed a common statement of faith: the *Confessio Bohemica* (1575). In 1609 the Unity obtained full religious freedom with the Letter of Majesty. After the Czech defeat at the White Mountain in 1620, the Unity was suppressed in 1627–28. Among those who went into exile was the theologian John Amos *Comenius. Two bodies claim the heritage of the Unity: the *Moravian Church, whose episcopacy derives from the Unity's Polish branch and whose earliest members included descendants of German-speaking Brethren in Moravia; and the Evangelical Czech Brethren Church in Czechoslovakia.

Bibliography: R. ŘíČAN, *Dějiny Jednoty bratrské* (Prague 1957), abr. as *Die Böhmischen Brüder,* tr. B. POPELÁŘ (Berlin 1961), with bibliog. J. T. MÜLLER, *Geschichte der Böhmischen Brüder,* 3 v. (Herrnhut, Ger. 1922–31). P. BROCK, *The Political and Social Doctrines of the Unity of Czech Brethren . . .* (The Hague 1957). M. SPINKA, "Peter Chelčický, Spiritual Father of the Unitas Fratrum," ChHist 12 (1943) 271–291. M. S. FOUSEK, "The Pastoral Office in the Early Unitas Fratrum," SlEEurRev 40 (1962) 444–457. Y. CONGAR, *Catholicisme* 2:109–111. J. WEISSKOPF, LexThK² 2:563–565. H. RENKEWITZ, RGG³ 1:1435–39.

[P. BROCK]

BOHEMUND I,

Norman Crusader; b. *c.* 1052; d. Canossa, southern Italy, March 26, 1111. The eldest son of the Norman Duke of Apulia and Calabria, *Robert Guiscard, Bohemund fought in his father's unsuccessful war against the Byzantines (1081–85). When Guiscard died in 1085, however, Bohemund was disinherited. In 1096 he raised a force of Norman soldiers in southern Italy to participate in the First *Crusade. Bohemund was active in the Crusaders' battles in Asia Minor but came into prominence during the siege of Antioch. He was largely responsible for the capture of the city (June 3, 1098) and claimed it for himself. Overcoming the opposition of the other crusading princes, he became the first Latin prince of Antioch (*see* CRUSADERS' STATES). In 1100 Bohemund was captured by the Moslems and imprisoned for 3 years. After his ransom he returned to Antioch where he was attacked by the Byzantines in 1104. Later that same year Bohemund went to Europe to raise more troops. In 1107 he attacked Byzantine Dalmatia. Defeated, he made peace with Byzantium in the Treaty of Devol (September 1108) and returned to Apulia. His last years are obscure.

Bibliography: *Gesta Francorum et aliorum Hierosolymitanorum,* ed. and tr. R. HILL (London 1962). R. B. YEWDALE, *Bohemond I: Prince of Antioch* (Princeton 1924). A. C. KREY,

"The Last Judgment," full-page miniature in a manuscript of the Gospels
written and illustrated in Ireland in the mid-8th century (Stiftsbibliothek
Sankt Gallen, MS 51, page 267). The Apostles gaze upward from below.

Dominikus Böhm, interior of the church of Maria Königin, Cologne-Marienburg, 1954, window by Heinz Bienefeld.

"A Neglected Passage in the Gesta . . .," *The Crusades and Other Historical Essays Presented to Dana C. Munro,* ed. L. J. PAETOW (New York 1928). L. BRÉHIER, DHGE 9:484–498.

[J. A. BRUNDAGE]

BOHIC, HENRI, canonist; b. Saint Mathieu (Brittany), 1310; d. 1351. Details of his career are obscure. He was a doctor *in utroque iure,* who studied Canon Law in Paris and Roman law in Orléans. He became clerical counselor of John IV at the time of the agitations that marked the beginning of the Hundred Years' War in the dukedom of Brittany. He taught Canon Law in Paris (1335) and is the author of *Distinctiones,* an excellent commentary, still little known, on the *Decretals of Gregory IX; it was printed at Lyons in 1498 and 1520, and at Venice in 1576 and 1580. In his effort to effect a synthesis between Christian morals and law, Bohic opposed an exclusively technical concept of Canon Law. Being at the confluence of many doctrinal currents, his work is important for analyzing the great conflicts of that century on the constitutional law of the Church: the significance of the sovereignty of the pope, of the role of the universal Church, of the councils, etc.

Bibliography: Schulte 2:266–270. A. LAMBERT, DDC 2:928–929. Van Hove 1:466. B. TIERNEY, *Foundations of the Conciliar Theory* (Cambridge, Eng. 1955) 214–216.

[P. LEGENDRE]

BÖHM, DOMINIKUS, German architect; b. Jettingen, Oct. 23, 1880; d. Cologne, Aug. 6, 1955. He was an important pioneer of modern church architecture in Germany. Although his early work was in a conventional mold and was stated with a certain theatrical flair, in the early 1920s he began to reject the dubious mantle of past styles and create a series of fresh and memorable churches, several of which still proclaim extraordinary maturity and power. His church of Christ the King in Mainz-Bishofsheim (1926) was the first to have a nave construction in poured concrete. His Christ the King in Leverkusen-Küppersteg (1928) and St. Joseph in Hindenburg (1930) are powerfully stated in brick outside and in; these, along with St. Englebert in Cologne-Riehl (1932), which is circular in plan with soaring concrete structure, number among the significant religious buildings of the early 20th century. The positive influence that they exerted throughout Germany and Europe is inestimable. Together with *Perret's heraldic Nôtre-Dame du *Raincy (1922–23), Otto Bartnings's famous steel church for the 1928 Cologne Press exhibition, Karl Moser's St. Antonius in Basel (1928), and Rudolf *Schwarz's Fronleichnam Church in Aachen (1930), the churches of Dominikus Böhm revolutionized Christian architecture. Unfortunately, the forces of evil and reaction in Nazi-dominated Germany stifled progress in all the arts, and from 1933 to the end of the war what is generally called "modern architecture" was banned throughout the Third Reich. Böhm continued to build but in simplified romanesque terms, and in some respects this long-enforced medievalism characterized his work until his death, leaving his greatest contribution in his works of the 1920s. Among his best postwar churches are St. Elizabeth in Coblenz (1953; done with his son Gottfried) and Maria Königin in Cologne-Marienburg (1954), a church whose enormous south wall of stained glass (done with Heinz Bienefield) is one of the loveliest in all religious art.

Bibliography: A. HOFF, et al., *Dominikus Böhm* (Munich 1962). J. PICHARD, *Les Églises nouvelles à travers le monde* (Paris 1960), Eng. *Modern Church Architecture,* tr. E. CALLMANN (New York 1962). G. E. KIDDER SMITH, *The New Architecture of Europe* (Cleveland 1961) 134–135; *The New Churches of Europe* (New York 1964). **Illustration credit:** From *The New Churches of Europe* by G. E. Kidder Smith.

[G. E. KIDDER SMITH]

BÖHM, HANS, shepherd, religious enthusiast; b. near Helmstadt, *c.* 1450; d. Würzburg (lower Franconia), July 19, 1476. Nicknamed Hansel the Drummer or the Piper, he entertained the peasants with kettledrums and bagpipes. Suddenly on Laetare Sunday 1476 (March 24), he burned his drum in front of the pilgrimage church of Niklashausen on the Tauber (Baden) and proclaimed that it was the will of Mary, revealed to him in a vision, that she be especially venerated again at that place. Inspired by stories of St. *John of Capistran's success, the unlearned enthusiast began to preach penance. Eventually he demanded revolutionary social changes that were a combination of radical communism and hatred for the clergy and for the authorities. *Waldensian and *Hussite influences, with which his name is linked, hardly touched him directly; his visions of Mary and Marian devotion are the best proof of that. The influence of some unknown nobles and priests still remains uncertain. His sermons and alleged miracles attracted thousands of people from central and southern Germany. When he called for an armed meeting, Bp. Rudolf of Würzburg, in agreement with the archbishop of *Mainz, had him arrested. After a disorganized attempt of his followers to free him, he was burned as a heretic. The "Niklashausen pilgrimage" lived on in the memory of the people and the church had to be destroyed (1477) to prevent the continuation of the movement, one of many isolated outbreaks antecedent to the *Peasants' War (1524–25).

Bibliography: Sources. *Die Rats-Chronik der Stadt Würzburg,* ed. W. ENGEL (Würzburg 1950), n. 117. Literature. F. A. REUSS, "H. B. und die Wallfahrt nach Niklashausen im Jahre 1476," *Archiv des Historischen Vereines von Unterfranken* 10 (1850) 300–318. A. K. BARACK, *ibid.* 14 (1858) 1–108, basic study. W. E. PEUCKERT, *Die grosse Wende* (Hamburg 1948). A. MEUSEL, *Thomas Müntzer und seine Zeit* (Berlin 1952) 7–40, 185–187. O. GRAF, NDB 2:382. A. BIGELMAIR, LexThK² 2:559. G. FRANZ, *Der deutsche Bauernkrieg* (4th ed. Darmstadt 1956). W. BRÖL, DHGE 9:388–389.

[H. WOLFRAM]

BÖHME, JAKOB, German Lutheran mystic and writer (known also as Boehme, Behmen); b. Alt-Seidenberg near Görlitz, 1575; d. Görlitz, Nov. 17, 1624. His parents were poor peasants who had him apprenticed to a shoemaker at Görlitz. Jakob became a master in 1599 and married the daughter of a master butcher. His wife bore him four sons and two daughters; and he prospered as a shoemaker. As he grew older, the tendencies toward mystical experiences, already apparent in his youth, became more pronounced. Finally, he gave up his business and began to write. About 1612 he published his first work, *Aurora oder die Morgenröthe im Anfang.* Since he attempted here to clarify certain knowledge of God and the universe hitherto unknown, his Lutheran pastor, Gregorius Richter, declared him heretical and had him banished from town. However, the town fathers reversed their earlier decision on condition that Böhme would cease his writing. In the years that immediately followed, he suffered much from the criticisms of the more orthodox of his fellow religionists. After 5 years he began again to publish his ideas only to meet with renewed persecution. In 1624 he went to Dresden where he lived peacefully for a short while, then returned to Görlitz where he died. Though he was given Christian burial by the protesting clergy, the ornate cross placed on his tomb by friends was torn down by one of his enemies.

Böhme was, in spirit, a devout Lutheran who throughout his religious experiences clung to the traditional doctrine of the Trinity, Incarnation, Redemption, and the Sacraments of Baptism and the Lord's Supper. It was in attempting to explain the doctrine of the Trinity that he went astray. When he identified God with heaven, hell, and the material world he was approaching pantheism. When he tried to explain the problem of good and evil, he posited a sort of dualism in the divine nature. He continued to attend church services, although he put much emphasis on the church as it existed in the hearts of men. He believed that by self-renunciation, prayer, and contemplation man can hasten the time of his union with God. Böhme had little formal education, and this deficiency as well as the nature of his writings produced a "dazzling chaos" that has confused even his admirers to the present day. Nevertheless he had an impact not only on religious thinkers, such as George Fox, Antoinette Bourgignon, and Philip Spener, but also on philosophers, such as Hegel and Schelling.

Bibliography: J. BÖHME, *Sämtliche Werke,* ed. K. W. SCHIEBLER, 7 v. (Leipzig 1832–60). J. J. STOUDT, *Sunrise to Eternity: A Study in J. Boehme's Life and Thought* (Philadelphia 1957). H. A. GRUNSKY, *Jakob Böhme* (Stuttgart 1956). P. HANKAMER, *Jakob Böhme* (Hildesheim, Ger. 1960). A. KOYRÉ, *La Philosophie de Jacob Boehme* (Paris 1929). L. LOEVENBRUCK, DTC 2.1:924–926. F. W. DEBELIUS, *The New Schaff-Herzog Encyclopedia of Religious Knowledge,* ed. S. M. JACKSON et al., 13 v. (Grand Rapids 1951–54) 2:209–211.

[H. J. MULLER]

BOHR, NIELS

One of the outstanding physicists of the 20th century; b. Copenhagen, Denmark, Oct. 7, 1885; d. there, Nov. 18, 1962. Bohr came from an academic family; his father, Christian, was professor of physiology at the University of Copenhagen. His younger brother, Harald (1887–1951), was later to be professor of mathematics at the same university that Niels entered after completing high school (1903).

He studied physics and received the gold medal of the Royal Danish Society for a paper on the surface tension of water (1907). His doctoral thesis, presented in 1911, concerned the electron theory of metals. Bohr then spent a year in England studying under J. J. Thomson at Cambridge, and E. *Rutherford at Manchester. The following year (1913) brought the birth of the atomic theory with which Bohr's name is associated. In 1912, Bohr married Margrethe Nørlund.

After holding readerships at Copenhagen (1913–14) and Manchester (1914–16), Bohr returned to Copen-

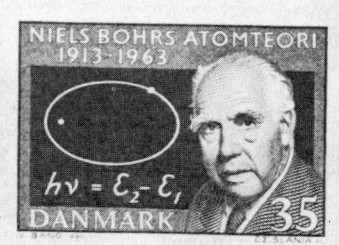

A Danish stamp commemorating the 50th anniversary of Bohr's formulation of his atomic theory.

hagen to assume the chair of theoretical physics that had been created for him. He held this position until his retirement in 1956. In 1921, he founded the Institute of Theoretical Physics in Copenhagen, and acted as director until his death.

In 1922, Bohr was awarded the Nobel Prize in physics. In this decade and in the next, he lectured frequently at European and American universities, and while in the U.S. in 1939, published the theory of uranium fission in collaboration with Professor J. A. Wheeler. Bohr fled the German occupation of World War II, going first to Sweden in 1943 and then from Britain to the U.S., where he assisted in the atomic energy project at Los Alamos. After the war, he returned to Denmark and directed his attention to the peaceful uses of atomic energy and to the development of a spirit of international cooperation aiming at full mutual openness between nations. Bohr was appointed to the Pontifical Academy of Sciences in 1936 by Pope Pius XI.

Bohr's most notable contributions to physics are the quantum theory of atomic structure and radiation (1913), the correspondence principle, the theory of the periodic system (1921–22), the compound theory of nuclear reactions (1936), and the mechanism of nuclear fission (1939). From 1927 onward, Bohr wrote extensively on epistemology, and he developed the principle of *complementarity.

Bohr's papers of 1913 are a landmark in the history of physics. The theory evidently was of a preliminary character, but the application of the quantum idea to atomic structure eventually led to quantum mechanics. Bohr's enunciation of the correspondence principle was basic for the development toward the final formulation of quantum mechanics.

His speculation concerning the epistemological problems presented by quantum mechanics has attracted a large number of followers whose views are usually presented as those of the "Copenhagen School." Bohr's fundamental considerations are expressed in the principle of complementarity, which he tried to extend beyond the realm of physics to other areas of knowledge.

See also ATOMIC THEORY; QUANTUM THEORY.

Bibliography: N. BOHR, "On the Constitution of Atoms and Molecules," *Philosophical Magazine* 26 (1913) 1–25, 476–502, 857–875; *The Theory of Spectra and Atomic Constitution* (Cambridge, Eng. 1922); "Chemistry and the Quantum Theory of Atomic Constitution," *Journal of the Chemical Society* (1932) 349–384; *Atomic Theory and the Description of Nature* (Cambridge, Eng. 1934; reprint 1962); *Atomic Physics and Human Knowledge* (New York 1958); *Essays 1958–62 on Atomic Physics and Human Knowledge* (New York 1964).

[E. RÜDINGER]

BOILEAU-DESPRÉAUX, NICOLAS, poet and critic; b. Paris, Nov. 1, 1636; d. there, March 13, 1711.

Boileau, the 15th son of a clerk of court at the Grand'Chambre du Parlement de Paris, received a solid education at the Collège d'Harcourt and the Collège de Beauvais. He first studied theology and then law, but receiving an inheritance at the death of his father (1657), he abandoned law to devote himself to poetry. His common sense; a flair for the real, the concrete, and the contemporary; and an intelligence prone to see flaws aided his rapid development as a sharp, though necessarily cautious, satirist whose works circulated surreptitiously and were only initialed when published. The legend of an "École de Paris" composed of *Molière, *La Fontaine, Boileau, and *Racine and dating from the outset of their careers has been discredited; and with it, the "formative" influence of Boileau on these writers.

Boileau's reputation as a satirist, at first unsavory and confined to the habitués of certain literary taverns, gradually took on an air of respectability through association with Guillaume de Lamoignon (1617–77) and his Academy, and simultaneously his prestige as a literary critic began to take shape. The *Art Poétique* and his translation of Longinus's *Traité du Sublime* (both 1674) established his literary preeminence and social standing. He was received at court, pensioned, and in 1677, with Racine, made historiographer to Louis XIV. The satirist had made many enemies, and only pressure from the court secured his election (1684) to the Académie Française, then controlled by his enemies.

In 1685 Boileau bought a house at Auteuil where he lived until 1705, last survivor of the generation of clas-

Nicolas Boileau-Despréaux, oil portrait by Dreuet.

sicists whom he had neither "formed" nor greatly influenced; for there is nothing new in his literary tenets, all of which had been expressed by Aristotle, Horace, or more contemporary theorists. In retirement he enjoyed visits of the socially prominent as well as the adulation of young men of letters to whom his vanity and easily aroused vindictiveness were not offensive. Then as always engaged in the struggles of his time, he manifested his lifelong loyalty to the Jansenists in a theological poem *Amour de Dieu* (1698), ridiculing the Jesuits and declaring *Pascal the greatest of the moderns (*see* JANSENISM). On the question of *quietism he aligned himself with *Bossuet. The principal controversy, however, in which he became embroiled was the quarrel of the ancients and the moderns. Against Charles *Perrault he argued for the superiority of the ancients, but was unconvincing. The "legislator of Parnassus" had lost touch with the new generation.

See also NEOCLASSICISM; FRENCH LITERATURE, 3.

Bibliography: *Oeuvres complètes,* ed. C. H. BOUDHORS, 7 v. (Paris 1934–43). G. LANSON, *Boileau* (Paris 1892). R. BRAY, *Boileau: L'Homme et l'oeuvre* (Paris 1942). J. BRODY, *Boileau and Longinus* (Geneva 1958). M. P. HALEY, *Racine and the Art poétique of Boileau* (Baltimore 1938). **Illustration credit:** Archives Photographiques, Paris.

[M. P. HALEY]

BOISE, DIOCESE OF (XYLOPOLITANA)

Suffragan of Archdiocese of Portland, Ore., established Aug. 25, 1893. It embraces the state of Idaho, with a total population in 1964 of 686,969 (46,507 Catholics). The earliest Christian influence in the area came from the fur trappers and especially from the Catholic Iroquois Indians in the employ of the fur-trading companies. Pierre *De Smet, SJ, celebrated the first Mass in Idaho on July 29, 1841, at a spot near Henrys' Lake, near the west end of Yellowstone Park.

St. Joseph's Church, Idaho City. Now a mission church, it was Idaho's first cathedral, built in 1863.

After establishing a Catholic mission in Bitter Root Valley, Mont., De Smet set out for Oregon City to report his presence in the area to Francis Blanchet, the superior of missionaries sent (1838) to Oregon by Bp. J. Signay of Quebec, Canada. On his return journey De Smet visited the Coeur d'Alene Indians in northern Idaho, who begged him to send them "Black Robes." From the Bitter Root mission two Jesuits, Rev. Nicholas Point and Brother Charles Huet, were sent; they set up Sacred Heart Mission (1842) on the St. Joseph River. When the location proved unsuitable because of spring floods, the mission was relocated at Cataldo, Idaho, on April 9, 1846. A year later Bp. A. M. Blanchet, en route to his see at Walla Walla (changed to Nesqually, 1850), Wash., passed through southern Idaho, but because of Indian unrest the government would not permit him to take up residence there.

Archbishop Francis Blanchet at Oregon City (changed to Portland, 1928) administered Idaho south of the 46th parallel, and Idaho north of that parallel passed under the jurisdiction of the bishop of Nesqually (later Seattle) until 1868. In the meantime Archbishop Blanchet sent Rev. Toussaint Mesplie and André Poulin to the Boise Basin in 1863, and they established four parishes there and one in Silver City, Owyhee County. Idaho was made a vicariate on March 3, 1868, and Louis Lootens of San Rafael, Calif., was named vicar apostolic. He resigned in 1876, and the archbishop of Oregon administered the vicariate until 1885, when Alphonse Glorieux of Portland, Ore., was appointed second vicar apostolic. Eight years later, when the Diocese of Boise was erected, Glorieux was appointed first bishop, ruling until his death in 1917. His successors include Daniel M. Gorman (1918–27), Edward J. Kelly (1928–56), James J. Byrne (1956–62), and Sylvester W. Treinen (1962–).

Although priests were few and scattered in the early years of the diocese, their numbers were increased by the arrival of the Salvatorians (1897), the Marists (1903), and the Benedictines (1905). The first synod assembled in St. Mary's Church, Genesee, after the first clergy retreat, Aug. 27, 1904. The subjects of legislation were cathedraticum, salaries, incorporation of properties, uniformity of ceremonies, Forty Hours devotion, mixed marriages, cemeteries, and synodal officers of the diocesan curia. A bishop's residence and chancery (1906) and a cathedral (1907–21) were built. Help was sought and received from the *Catholic Church Extension Society, and chapel cars arrived in 1908. All ecclesiastical societies and confraternities were united (1921) into two councils: the Idaho Council of Catholic Men and the Idaho Council of Catholic Women, both affiliated with the national councils. The diocese was divided into five deaneries in 1929, and vacation schools began in 1931. The correspondence course in catechism was inaugurated in 1935 to care for the religious instruction of children residing in many isolated sections of the diocese; beginning in 1959 a training course for lay catechists was offered in each deanery twice a year. The Confraternities of the Rosary, the Blessed Sacrament, Christian Doctrine, and the Holy Name were canonically erected in every parish. The diocesan paper, the Idaho *Register,* began publication in 1957.

In 1964 the diocese had 56 parishes, 46 missions, and 69 stations, with 97 priests and 440 sisters serving in various capacities in its institutions, including 9

Cathedral of St. John the Evangelist, Boise, Idaho.

general hospitals, 1 orphanage, and 1 home for the aged. Catholic education in Idaho began with the erection of the vicariate, when the Sisters of the Holy Names of Portland opened St. Mary's Academy in Idaho City in 1868. By 1893 there were 5 parish schools and 3 academies; in 1964 there were 1 junior college, 3 high schools, and 27 elementary schools, caring for a total of 7,043 students, with an additional 8,477 students receiving religious instruction under released-time programs.

Bibliography: C. BRADLEY, *History of the Diocese of Boise, 1863–1952* (Caldwell, Idaho 1953). C. J. BROSNAN, *History of the State of Idaho* (5th ed. New York 1948). **Illustration credit:** Fig. 1, Idaho Historical Society.

[C. BRADLEY]

BOISGELIN DE CUCÉ, JEAN DE DIEU RAYMOND DE, archbishop and cardinal; b. Rennes, France, Feb. 27, 1732; d. Angervilliers, Aug. 22, 1804. As a member of an old family of Brittany he entered the service of the Church. Promotion was assured, and at the age of 33 he became bishop of Lavour. Five years later he was nominated to the See of Aix in Provence. As archbishop he was concerned for the material as well as the spiritual well-being of his flock and proved himself an enlightened and effective administrator. His reputation merited for him election to the French Academy in 1776. With the coming of the Revolution the prospects for a new order in France appealed to the archbishop of Aix. He was elected a deputy to the Estates-General and demonstrated his ability as a leader. In the early months of the deliberations of the Assembly he showed that he was willing to accept change. The Assembly honored him by electing him president for a 2-week term. In the months that followed the archbishop joined the opposition when the majority voted for the confiscation of the Church's property and passed the *Civil Constitution of the Clergy. He was a vigorous spokesman in defense of the Church's rights and refused to take the oath sup-

porting the Civil Constitution. For the following 10 years he resided in England. When Napoleon came to power and settled the problem of Church-State relations with the *Concordat of 1801, the archbishop returned to France. In 1802 he was appointed to the See of Tours and received the cardinal's hat from Pope Pius VII. His many contributions to literature have not had much enduring influence.

Bibliography: E. LAVAQUERY, *Le Cardinal de Boisgelin* 2 v. (Paris 1920). C. TESTORE, EncCatt 2.1:1768. C. CONSTANTIN, DTC 2:942–944. P. CALENDINI, DHGE 9:575–576. F. REIBEL, LexThK² 2:566.

[H. L. STANSELL]

BOLAÑOS, LUIS DE, founder of the first reductions in Paraguay; b. Marchena, Spain, c. 1550; d. Buenos Aires, Oct. 11, 1629. Bolaños became a Franciscan in his native town. In 1572, while still a deacon, he left with the Juan Ortiz de Zárate expedition, and he arrived in Asunción in February 1575. With his friend and patron Fray Alonso de San Buenaventura, Bolaños began almost at once to visit the Indians of Guayrá and Villa Rica and to found pueblos, or reductions, which were later transferred to the Jesuits. Since these provinces were later devastated by the fearsome Mamelukes and the territory now belongs to Brazil, there are no records of these pueblos destroyed by the slave raiders from São Paulo. In 1580 he began the Reduction of Pacuyú to the north of Asunción, the first reduction begun by Bolaños of which the name is now known. In 1585, while guardian of the Franciscan friary of Asunción, Bolaños was ordained. In that same year, to the south of Asunción, he founded the famous reductions of San Blas de Itá and San Buenaventura de Yaguarón. Hampered by a lack of help, Bolaños spent the years 1585 to 1607 in caring for the pueblos already founded. In 1607 he began to found another series of reductions to the south of Asunción beginning with San José de Caazapá, still a flourishing city, and ending in 1616 with Baradero near Buenos Aires. In 1623 Bolaños retired to the Franciscan house in Buenos Aires, where he died and where his tomb is still honored.

Bolaños was not only an imaginative missionary but also a true scholar in Indian languages and customs and in theology. His Guaraní catechism, approved by the synod of Paraguay in 1603, was the one used in all the missions of the region, even those of the Jesuits. His grammar and vocabulary in the same tongue were

Autograph of Luis de Bolaños.

considered the best of their kind. As a theologian, Bolaños defended the validity of the Guaraní pagan marriages and defended them against the colonists. His hymns and poems in Guaraní have passed into the common domain of folklore. As a man Bolaños was beloved by all. Perhaps this is his best testimonial. Few regions of Spanish America were beset with more dissensions than Rio de la Plata. Yet Bolaños was esteemed by none more than by the Jesuits, who worked so closely with him.

Bibliography: A. MILLÉ, *Crónica de la Orden Franciscana en la conquista del Perú, Paraguay, y el Tucumán y su Convento del antiguo Buenos Aires, 1212–1800* (Buenos Aires 1961). B. ORO, *Fray Luis de Bolaños, apóstol del Paraguay y Río de la Plata* (Córdoba 1934). R. A. MOLINA, "La obra franciscana en el Paraguay y Río de la Plata," *Missionalia hispánica* 11 (1954), esp. 335–336. **Illustration credit:** Library of Congress.

[L. G. CANEDO]

BOLÍVAR, SIMÓN

Hero in the struggle for Spanish-American independence, known as the Liberator; b. Caracas, Venezuela, July 24, 1783; d. San Pedro Alejandrino, Colombia, Dec. 17, 1830. He belonged to a socially prominent, well-to-do family, but was orphaned before he was 10. He was educated in his own home with such teachers as Simón Rodríguez and Andrés *Bello. Bolívar, anxious to study in Madrid, went there in 1799. He attended

Simón Bolívar.

regular courses at the Academia de San Fernando and had private tutors as well. He was married in Madrid on May 26, 1802, and sailed shortly thereafter for Caracas. At the beginning of 1803 his wife died, and he decided to return to Europe. In Paris in 1804 he met his former professor, Rodríguez. His days in Paris were turbulent, but he did not neglect what was to be the primary goal of his life: the emancipation of Spanish America. His contact with such people as Humboldt, Bonpland, Gay-Lussac, and later, his oath on the Roman hill of Monte Sacro (August 1805) attest to the firmness of his purpose. He returned to Caracas via the U.S. in June 1807. On April 19, 1810, Bolívar was appointed chief of the diplomatic mission to London by the government of Caracas. After the declaration of independence on July 5, 1811, Bolívar commanded the Aragua battalion, and in 1812 he was commander of Plaza de Puerto Cabello, which was lost after an uprising in the garrison. When the first republic failed, Bolívar left for Curaçao and from there went to Cartagena.

His military career actually began in 1813. He initiated the campaign for the reconquest of Caracas, which he entered triumphantly on August 6. The second republic was lost in 1814 to the forces of Boves, and Bolívar emigrated first to Cartagena, and then to Jamaica, where, on Sept. 6, 1815, he wrote his prophetic letter concerning the future of America. He then went to Haiti, returning to the mainland on Dec. 31, 1816, to undertake his campaign through the eastern part of the country. In July 1817 he seized Angostura (today Ciudad Bolívar), organized a government, and continued the struggle for independence. On Feb. 15, 1819, he made an inaugural address to the congress in which he traced his future policies. When he liberated Bogotá that year, he proposed to the congress the creation of the Republic of Colombia (known historically as Gran Colombia), by joining Venezuela, New Granada, and Quito. In 1820 an armistice was signed with the royalist troops, but the war began again. On June 24, 1821, he defeated the Spaniards in the battle of Carabobo, assuring the independence of Venezuela.

Then he undertook the campaign in the south. Quito was liberated in 1822 after the battles of Bomboná and Pichincha. He acquired for Gran Colombia the city of Guayaquil, where in July 1822 he met with *San Martín. In 1823, summoned by the government of Lima, he went to Peru, where he reestablished the republic and organized the army that, after the victory of Junín, sealed the liberty of South America at Ayacucho, Dec. 9, 1824, under the command of Marshall Sucre. On December 7, Bolívar had invited the free republics of America to meet in Panama in 1826, setting a precedent for inter-American cooperation. In August 1825 he created the republic of Bolivia, for whose government he wrote a proposed constitution in 1826.

The Liberator had reached the height of his glory. The last years (1827–30) were lost in bold efforts to avoid civil wars and restrict the lust for power of rivals and local political leaders. He resigned as president of the state on April 27, 1830, and left for Cartagena to retire to private life. The assassination of Sucre, his favorite lieutenant, June 4, 1830, confirmed his decision to abandon everything and go to Europe. In poor health, he stopped at Santa Marta and then at San Pedro Alejandrino, where he died.

In the midst of the whirlpool of his political and military action, he retained profound respect for religious principles as an individual norm and as a unifying element for the society under his command. He said in 1828: "Without religious conscience, morality lacks foundation."

Bibliography: *Selected Writings,* comp. V. LECUNA, ed. H. A. BIERCK, tr. L. BERTRAND, 2 v. (New York 1951). V. LECUNA, *Catálogo de errores y calumnias en la historia de Bolívar,* 3 v. (New York 1956–58). G. MASUR, *Simón Bolívar* (Albuquerque 1948). **Illustration credit:** Pan American Union.

[P. GRASES]

BOLIVAR PONTIFICAL UNIVERSITY

An institution of higher learning founded in Medellin, Colombia, in 1936 by Abp. Tiberio de J. Salazar. The need for a Catholic university in Medellín to offset a growing positivistic spirit in intellectual circles had long been felt and plans for establishing one had been frequently discussed. Definite steps were not taken, however, to put the plans into action until a group of law students from the University of Antioquia in Medellin, convinced that religion should be an integral part of education, approached the archbishop to urge its foundation. Archbishop Salazar, a scholar and a zealous promotor of higher education, gave the project his wholehearted blessing and cooperation.

In keeping with the injunctions of Canon Law that forbids the foundation of a Catholic university without the approval of the Holy See, the archbishop solicited permission for canonical erection, which was granted on Sept. 15, 1936. Shortly thereafter, 70 pioneer students and 25 volunteer, nonsalaried professors, with no fixed locale, libraries, financial backing, or legal support, began classes in the Faculty of Law. In 1937 secondary and commercial schools were added; in 1938 a chair of chemical and industrial engineering, the first to be introduced in Colombia, a Workers's Circle, and a Women's Circle; and in 1943 architecture and city planning and a School of Art and Interior Decoration for women, under the direction of the Religious of the Sacred Heart of Jesus. On Aug. 16, 1945, the institution was raised to the rank of a pontifical university, and in 1946 the School of Economic Sciences was established.

The University, which is under the jurisdiction of the Catholic hierarchy, is governed by a directive council composed of the grand chancellor—the archbishop of Medellin—the *rector magnificus,* who is also president of the council, the deans of Faculties, representatives of the professional staff, and a student representation from each Faculty. Administration officers include the deans of Faculties, Faculty secretaries, and librarians. In 1965 the teaching and administrative staff numbered approximately 105; enrollment totaled 5,034 students, the majority of whom were from various Colombian cities, with a small number from Europe or Central and North America. The main library housed more than 40,000 volumes in addition to special holdings in the Faculty libraries.

The Bolivar Pontifical University comprises (1965) Faculties of Law and Political Science; Chemical, Electrical, and Mechanical Engineering; Architecture and Urban Planning; Philosophy and Letters; Education; Social Science; Fine Arts and Design; Humanities; and Theology; institutes of Commerce and Social Sciences; and a department of commerce. In addition to its academic and professional courses, the University also operates an evening school for adults, which offers basic and practical courses for those who wish to complete their education or improve their economic status. University publications include *Revista Universidad Pontificia, Revista de la Facultad de Derecho,* and *Revista Filosofia y Letras.*

Bibliography: IntHdbUniv. *Prospecto, 1964* (Colombia).

[M. B. MURPHY]

BOLIVIA

The Republic of Bolivia is situated in the central section of South America and is one of the two American nations without a sea coast. It is bounded on the north and the east by Brazil, on the west by Peru and Chile, on the south by Argentina, and on the southeast by Paraguay and has an area of 415,000 square miles. In 1964 the population was 4 million, 55 per cent are pureblooded Indians (Quechua, Aymara, Guarani, and other minor ethnic groups); 25 per cent, mestizos; and

20 per cent, white. The number of people belonging to other races is insignificant.

One-third of the country is traversed by the cordillera of the Andes, and the rest of the land is prairie. The Andean section includes a high and broad plateau, known as the Altiplano Boliviano, and a sierra that is broken by small protected valleys. Here are found the principal centers of population and economic activity: La Paz, the seat of government; Potosí, the famous mining center; Cochabamba; and Sucre. Of greatest economic importance is mining, principally of tin. There is also the kind of agriculture possible in cold and moderate climates and some industry. The plains are in the north and east and are used for tropical farming and forest industries. This region has a rich petroleum field that is exploited by government agencies and American companies. The main center here is Santa Cruz de la Sierra.

The Bolivian nationality originated in the jurisdiction of the Audiencia de Charcas, which lasted almost 300 years under the colonial rule of Spain. In 1809 a revolt against this regime started a bloody war that lasted until 1825. On Aug. 6, 1825, the independence of Bolivia was proclaimed. As a result of the War of the Pacific, Bolivia lost its sea coast to Chile in 1880.

Early Christianization. Catholicism came to this country with the first Spaniards, who were attracted by the rich minerals abounding in the mountainous region and who founded the urban communities of La Plata (today Sucre), Potosí, and La Paz. With them came secular and religious priests, entrusted with the parochial ministry among the Spaniards, and the bringing of the faith among the Indians. It was easy to give religious instruction to the Aymaras and Quechuas, who lived on the Altiplano and in the mountains. Within a few years, priests went into the native communities, learned the languages, and won the natives over to Christianity. Not all the old practices of their primitive religion were uprooted, for a good number of superstitious beliefs remained, and do so, in part, to this day.

The natives on the plains were nomads on the lowest rung of culture. They were warlike and they resisted foreign domination. It took many years to bring them into missions. Prominent among these were the missions among the Moxos and Chiquitos, developed by the Jesuits, and those among the Chiriguanos, cared for by the Franciscans. Among the early missionaries were the Jesuits Pedro Marbán and Cipriano Barace, founders of the Reductions among the Moxos in the middle of the 17th century; José de Arce, first to catechize the Chiquitos, and his successor, Lucas Caballero; the Franciscan brother Francisco del Pilar, who founded missions among the aboriginal Chiriguanos; and the Mercedarian Diego de Porres.

Development of the Missions. About the middle of the 18th century, evangelization among the Moxos and Chiquitos reached its peak with 22 missions, with no less than 60,000 neophytes and catechumens, under the care of 45 missionaries. When the Spanish crown expelled the Jesuits in 1767 and secular priests took charge, the missions declined. Whites and mestizos came to live in the communities, which were transformed into diocesan parishes.

The Franciscan missions among the Chiriguanos reached their acme in about 1800. There were then 16

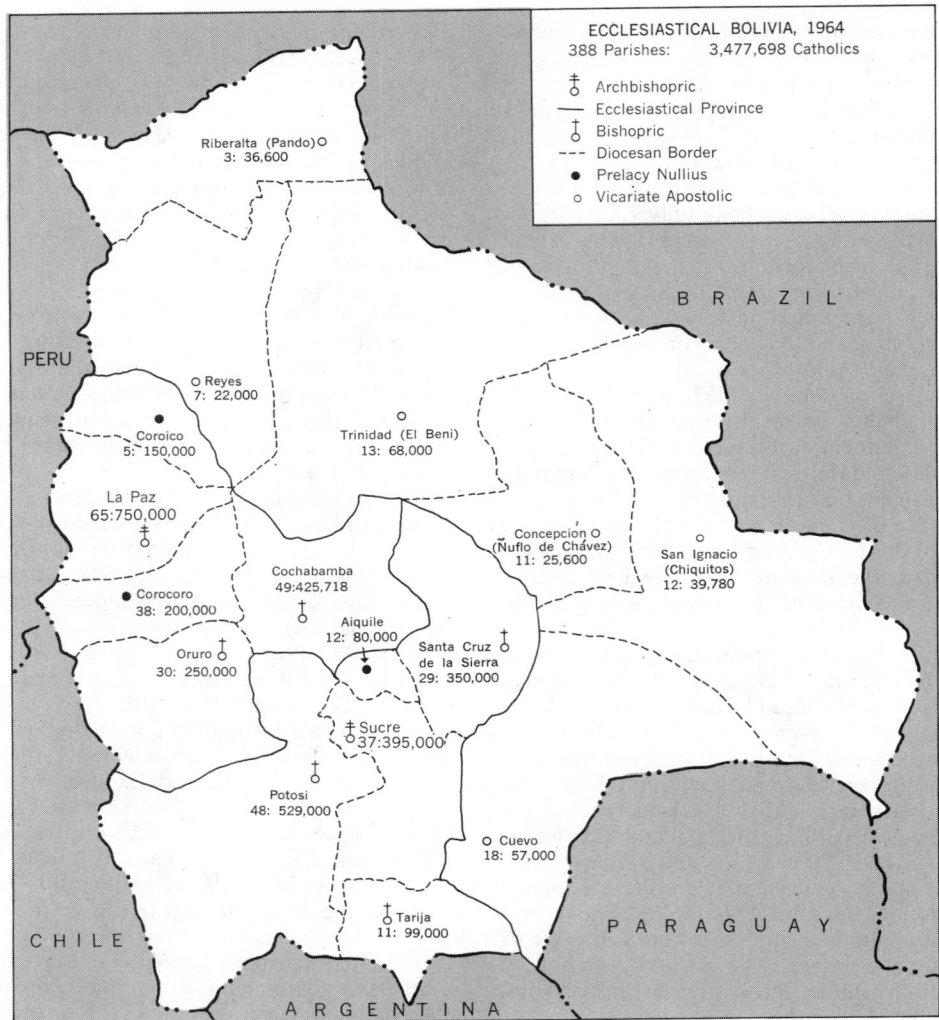

ECCLESIASTICAL BOLIVIA, 1964
388 Parishes: 3,477,698 Catholics

‡ Archbishopric
— Ecclesiastical Province
☦ Bishopric
--- Diocesan Border
● Prelacy Nullius
○ Vicariate Apostolic

Riberalta (Pando) ○
3: 36,600

B R A Z I L

P E R U

○ Reyes
7: 22,000

● Coroico
5: 150,000

○ Trinidad (El Beni)
13: 68,000

La Paz
65: 750,000
‡

Concepcion ○
(Ñuflo de Chávez)
11: 25,600

○
San Ignacio
(Chiquitos)
12: 39,780

● Corocoro
38: 200,000

Cochabamba
49: 425,718
☦

Aiquile
12: 80,000

Santa Cruz
de la Sierra ☦
29: 350,000

Oruro ☦
30: 250,000

‡ Sucre
○ 37: 395,000

Potosi
48: 529,000

○ Cuevo
18: 57,000

Tarija ☦
11: 99,000

C H I L E

P A R A G U A Y

A R G E N T I N A

Fig. 1. Ecclesiastical divisions of Bolivia. The civil capital is La Paz.

towns with 40,000 neophytes. During the war of independence guerrilla bands of patriots, because of their blind hatred for everything Spanish, persecuted the missionaries and destroyed the missions. At the end of that war only two or three missions remained and the diocesan authority converted them into "curatos doctrineros."

The missions among the Chiriguanos were reestablished from 1840 to 1850 by the Franciscans from Spain, Italy, and Austria. They established new missions in the region, bringing about the civilization of thousands of natives. They founded missions also in the territory of the Guarayos and in the regions of the northwest among the Indians of the forest. The mission of the Chiriguanos in the province of Cordillera was secularized in 1915, and the one among the Guarayos in 1937. The sad results were not long delayed. Many natives returned to their native forests, and the old mission towns disappeared. In 1964 the few missions left were attended by the friars of the Austrian province of Tyrol, and the Betica and Tarasconense provinces of Spain. The natives of the forest are yet to be civilized.

Diocesan Organization. The first bishopric was La Plata, erected by Pope Julius III in 1552, with jurisdic-

tion over all of present-day Bolivia and neighboring territories. The first bishop was the Dominican Tomás de San Martín. The Dioceses of La Paz and Santa Cruz were erected in 1605, and La Plata became an archdiocese in 1609. A new ecclesiastical province was formed, which included, besides those mentioned above, the bishoprics of Asunción, Buenos Aires, and Tucumán. The first synod held in the country was convoked by Abp. Arias de Ugarte in 1629. Later, others were held in the same metropolitan see, such as the one of 1771–1773, convoked by Archbishop Argandoña.

Religious Orders. During the period of Spanish rule, monasteries and residences were established by Franciscans, Mercedarians, Dominicans, Augustinians, Jesuits, and the Hospitallers of St. John. The Franciscans and Jesuits worked mainly in the Indian missions. The Mercedarians and Augustinians took care of the parishes among the Quechuas and Aymaras in the cities and rural towns. The Dominicans took as their main work the parishes among the people of European origin. The Religious of St. John of God served in hospitals. Jesuits in urban residences took up the work of education and established the Universidad Mayor de San Francisco Xavier in La Plata (March 27, 1624).

Fig. 2. Bolivia: The portal (a) and the interior (b) of the 17th-century cathedral at Sucre. (c) The interior of the cathedral at La Paz, 19th century. (d) The portal of the 17th-century shrine church at Copacabana.

Fig. 3. Detail of an 18th-century silver frontal in a church in Machaca.

Fig. 4. Sixteenth-century chasuble (cathedral, Sucre).

BOLIVIA

Fig. 5. Eighteenth-century carved wood pulpit in the church of Santa Teresa at Potosí.

Congregations of women were restricted to nuns living the cloistered life, as the Franciscan sisters or Poor Clares, and the Augustinian nuns, who were then called Mónicas. In the 17th century the Carmelites of the Teresan reform came into the country. Convents of nuns were found in the cities of La Plata, La Paz, Potosí, and Cochabamba. Their special function was to provide the churches with furnishings and liturgical vestments, to sew and embroider, and to make fine pastry. In the 18th century some of these congregations took charge of the education of children and the care of orphans. (*See* RELIGIOUS ORDERS OF WOMEN IN COLONIAL SPANISH AMERICA.)

Composition of the Clergy. For the most part, priests, both secular and religious, were of European origin; most were born in Spain but some were Creoles. One exception was the bishop of La Plata Fernando Arias de Ugarte (1626–30), who said he was an aborigine and signed his pastoral documents "Fernando indio arzobispo." Mestizos were usually admitted to religious orders as lay brothers.

Religious vocations were numerous during the colonial period. They diminished to some extent during the first century of independence and even more so in the 20th century, but the 1960s brought a slight increase in the number of ordinations. In 1964, 155 students were preparing for the priesthood. (*See* LATIN AMERICA, CHURCH IN.)

Charitable Institutions. During the colonial period in general, pious associations and confraternities maintained hospitals, orphanages, and homes for the needy. In the 19th century a number of charitable institutions were founded, growing in a century to more than 50. Most are in the charge of religious congregations of women, such as the Sisters of the Good Shepherd, Sisters of St. Vincent de Paul, the Adoration Sisters, the Missionary Crusaders of the Church, and the Servants of Mary.

Lay institutes and religious congregations maintain and administer hospitals, homes for the aged and for foundlings, institutes for the protection of women, and first aid stations. They are sustained by contributions, pious legacies, public collections, and grants from the state and from municipalities. These institutes reach deeply into the life of the country and help negate the appeals of Communism. This is especially true in mining centers, such as Catavi, Llallagua, and Corocoro, where Communist agitation is most active.

Education. Various religious orders of men and women conducted primary and secondary schools during the colonial period, and the Jesuits established their university. The educational activity of the Church has increased notably in the course of the republic, especially in the 20th century. Though there is not a strictly Catholic university in the country, there are 53 secondary schools for students of both sexes, 14 schools for professional training, and 145 primary schools, all conducted by religious orders or congregations, among them Jesuits, Christian Brothers, Franciscans, Sisters of St. Ann, and Sisters of the Sacred Hearts. According to the figures of the ministry of education, in 1964 these schools had some 2,000 teachers, lay and clerical, and more than 40,000 students. Not included in these figures are the four diocesan seminaries, nor the novitiates for religious. Most of the grammar schools are free, particularly those in rural areas for Indians.

Financial Resources of the Church. As in all Latin America, the Church in Bolivia owned much property during the colonial period and in the first years of the republic. It came almost entirely from donations and pious legacies, and only now and then from the generosity of the state. Mission property was originally obtained by small grants from the Spanish crown, which gave also lands and farms. The missionaries managed to increase their goods considerably, transforming them into real wealth. The Moxos and Chiquitos missions were outstanding centers of agriculture, cattle raising, and industry. The wealthiest groups were monastic communities, especially those of women.

In the 19th and 20th centuries the building of churches and schools necessitated the mortgaging or sale of these properties. The last disappeared as a result of the agrarian reform undertaken by the government since 1953. With the exception of some jewels that adorned images and objects of value used in churches, the Church in Bolivia today possesses no riches.

Special Devotions. In colonial times two sanctuaries were prominent in the religious life of the country, and these became centers of national pilgrimage. In the town of Copacabana, situated in the Altiplano on the shores of the historic lake Titicaca, is venerated the image of the Virgin Mary, carved by the Indian Tito Yupanqui in the middle of the 17th century in circumstances that bordered on the miraculous, as popular legend has it. On the eastern plains in the town of Cotoca, a small image of the Mother of God is venerated. Legend says that the image was found in a dense forest within the trunk of a tree by some humble farmers in the middle of the 18th century. Both sanctuaries draw large crowds of the devout, especially on their respective feast days. Though people of all classes come there, the poor and lowly are in the majority.

Intellectual Influence. Not until the 19th century was a press established in La Plata. Even in 1964 the equipment for the religious press was quite modest. The periodical *El Cruzado* was published in Sucre under the direction of eminent religious writers, such as Bishop *Taborga, and *La Cátedra* was edited in La Paz by Rev. Teodosio Sáenz up to the 1930s. Other less important publications, now extinct, were *La Verdad, La Hoja Mensajera,* and *El Domingo* of La Paz; *El Lábaro* of Sucre; *La Cruz Redentora* of Cochabamba; and *El Centinela Católico* and *El Antoniano* of Tarija.

The sectarian and anti-Catholic liberalism, which made its appearance in the late 19th century, was opposed by a vigorous current of Catholic thought, springing from a strong religious and philosophical culture. Among its exponents were Mariano Baptista, who became president of the republic, Donato Vázquez, Aurelio Beltrán, Pedro José Iturri, José Santos Machicao, Luis Paz, José Peredo Antelo, and Abel Iturralde.

Among the ecclesiastical authors of books or pamphlets on religious subjects may be mentioned Juan de Dios Bosque, in theology and Canon Law; Jacinto Anaya, in Canon Law; Francisco María del Granado, famous preacher; and Cayetano de la Llosa, author of commentaries on the devout life. José María Izquierdo in *Carta abierta a Flammarión* refuted rationalism; Primo Arieta wrote a remarkable polemic in defense of religion; Pedro Arístides Zejas was the author of instructive catechisms; and Facundo Quiroga was a famous teacher.

Independence Period. In Bolivia, as in the rest of Spanish America, there was no official pronouncement on the independence movement. In general the hierarchy and the higher ranks of clergymen remained loyal to the Spanish government, while the majority of priests took part in the struggle for independence. The priests José Antonio Medina, José Andrés Salvatierra, and Juan Bautista Oquendo incited the popular movements of 1809 and 1810. Father Muñecas was a leader of a band of guerrillas, and Fathers Polanco and Mercado, and Fray Justo acted as chaplains for the guerrillas.

Relations between Church and State. The erection of the sovereign state of Bolivia did not bring a substantial change in the Church. The *patronato* (*see* PATRONATO REAL), which was exercised by the king of Spain, was passed on to the president of the republic. In the Concordat of 1851 the Holy See recognized the Patronato Nacional and it has continued to operate. Relations have been carried on through diplomatic representatives. In 1925 the papal envoy was raised to the rank of nuncio and Bolivia on its part raised its legation to the rank of an embassy. By right of patronage, the bishops are selected by the president of the republic from nominations by the senate and presented to the Roman Curia for canonical election.

The constitution of Bolivia recognizes as official the Catholic religion and declares that the state will support it. In the national budget, allocations are made for the maintenance of the Church. In the departmental budgets, emoluments are assigned for bishops and ecclesiastical chapters. Religious education is obligatory in primary and middle schools, and the teachers receive special income. The law of Oct. 11, 1911, instituted civil marriage. The law of April 15, 1932, allowed absolute divorce.

The Modern Church. The condition of the Church has improved considerably in these last years, thanks to effective action on the part of the faithful. Besides the pious associations, which are very helpful, the following societies are becoming increasingly active: Catholic Action, the Christian Family Movement, and parish cooperatives. The relations with the state are marked by a respectful deference, and though the Patronato Nacional, which subordinates the Church to the State, is still legal, such subjection is scarcely felt. There is a trend toward the establishment of a free Catholic Church within a free state, which proclaims itself Catholic. The Church, through religious and secular institutions, has succeeded in reasserting its spiritual sway over the people, and is continuously growing in strength. The population is about 95 per cent Catholic, and even among the non-Catholics there is a marked respect for the Church and its representative bodies: schools, colleges, sanitariums, credit and savings cooperatives, periodicals, and radio stations.

Protestant Activity. The activity of dissident Christian churches has increased in these last years. Religious liberty prevails in the country, and Protestant missionaries have entered communities dispensing economic aid and proselytizing. They have gained some hundreds of converts, but since Protestants scarcely number 3 in 100, they have no influence in the life of the country.

Illustration credits: José de Mesa, La Paz.

[H. SANABRIA FERNÁNDEZ]

BOLLANDISTS, a small group of Jesuits in Antwerp, Belgium, organized into a society in the 17th century by Jean Bolland for the critical study and publication of the lives of the saints. Although named after the first of their number, the group got inspiration from the learned Leribert Rosweyde (1569–1629), who conceived the idea of purging the lives of the saints of the innumerable apocryphal and legendary details that encumbered them by the publication of a scholarly *Acta sanctorum*. In a short treatise, *Fastes des saints,* he explained his intention of dealing with the deeds of the saints whose lives are recorded in the MSS collected in Belgian libraries (1607). Rosweyde did not succeed in completing this project, but laid the foundation for the *Acta sanctorum* by editing the oldest texts of the Lives of the Desert Fathers in his *Vitae Patrum* (1615). Charged with continuing the work of Rosweyde, Jean Bolland (b. Julémont, Diocese of Liège, Aug. 13, 1596; d. Antwerp, Sept. 12, 1665) modified both the plan and the method. He decided to deal with all the known saints in the Church's calendar, gathering all the information known about each and publishing it with notes and comments. Each volume of the *Acta* would be furnished with a table of reference and an index. In 1635 Bolland was given Godefroid Henschenius (1601–81), a student of his, as collaborator. Henschenius's suggestions caused him to enlarge the conception of the enterprise, to the extent that he recalled some of his own work that was already in print, and both men turned attention to the saints in the calendar for January. The appearance of the *Acta sanctorum* for January (1643) and February (1658) elicited the admiration of scholars. In 1659 Daniel van Papenbroek, or Papebroch (b. Anvers, 1628; d. 1714), whom H. Delehaye has called "le bollandist par excellence," joined the group and proved to be one of the most learned men of his time, an indefatigable worker, and great discoverer of documents, who combined a firm judgment with the courage of his scientific opinions and was responsible for the publication of 19 volumes. The munificence of Pope *Alexander VII made it possible for the first two companions of Bolland to embark on a journey of study and investigation, the first of a long tradition. They discovered many MSS in Germany, Italy, and France, copies of which were sent to the Bollandist collection.

Papebroch enlarged the field of interest of the *Acta* to include both the chronology of the popes and the evaluation of false documents. This latter study, the fruit of a month of forced leisure at Luxemburg, was based on insufficient evidence and brought him into controversy with the Benedictine scholar Jean *Mabillon, whose representations Papebroch finally accepted. His intellectual honesty and the admirable letter of acquiescence in his opponent's opinion, gained for the Bollandists the friendship of the Benedictine scholar. Since the Bollandists refused to acknowledge the prophet Elias as founder of the Carmelites, they were savagely attacked by certain members of that order. The Bollandists became the victims of a violent pamphlet warfare, and their work was condemned by the Spanish Inquisition; they had to send Father Janninck to Rome to avoid greater difficulties, and Papebroch himself lost much time in refuting the charge of the Carmelite Sebastian de St. Paul. Although condemnation in Rome was avoided, the Bollandists continued to be victims of malevolent insinuations until Pope

*Benedict XIV intervened and put an end to the unfortunate quarrel.

The golden age of the society was constituted by Bolland, Henschenius, and Papebroch, whose successors did not always have their scientific competence. Among them, Du Sollier and J. Stilting showed signs of timidity and prolixity.

With the suppression of the Society of Jesus in 1773, the Bollandist Collection, which had arrived at the third volume for October, was subjected to great difficulty; and although volumes 4 and 5 were published in Brussels (1780, 1786), and volume 6 in Tongerloo (1794), the work had to be abandoned as the result of the disturbance that followed the French Revolution (1789). The library was dispersed and many of its precious MSS lost.

In 1837 the society was reconstituted and began republication of the *Acta* in 1845. V. de Buck (d. 1876), C. de Smedt (d. 1911), A. Poncelet, and H. *Delehaye (d. 1941) brought to their study the assistance of philology and other subsidiary historical disciplines; Delehaye opened new perspectives, and P. Peeters concentrated attention on the hagiography of the Oriental Church.

Besides the *Acta sanctorum,* which now consists of 67 folio volumes (Jan. 1 to Nov. 10), including a Commentary on the Martyrology of St. Jerome (1931) and a *Propylaeum ad Acta SS. Decembris* dealing with the Roman Martyrology (1940), the Bollandists publish a review, the *Analecta Bollandiana,* begun in 1882 and completed with a bulletin of hagiographical publications (since 1891). They produce also a collection of *Subsidia hagiographica* (since 1886) with a control listing of sources for the lives of the saints in alphabetical order, called the *Bibliotheca hagiographica latina* (BHL), the *Bibliotheca hagiographica graeca* (BHG), and the *Bibliotheca hagiographia orientalis* (BHO). In 1964 the work of the scholarly Belgian Jesuits had, since 1950, been directed by Father Maurice Coens, and included B. de Gaiffier, P. Grosjean, F. Halkin, P. Devos, and J. van der Straeten.

Bibliography: B. DE GAIFFIER, LexThK² 2:571–572. H. DELEHAYE, *L'Oeuvre des Bollandistes à travers trois siècles* (Subsid Hag 13a.2; 2d ed. 1958), with bibliog. P. PEETERS, AnalBoll 55 (1937) v–xlix; *Figures bollandiennes contemporaines* (Brussels 1948); *L'Oeuvre des Bollandistes* (new ed. Brussels 1961); Anal Boll 60 (1942) i–lii, Fr. Delehaye. P. DEVOS, *ibid.* 69 (1951) i–lix. R. AIGRAIN, *L'Hagiographie* (Paris 1953) 329–350.

[P. ROCHE]

BOLLIG, JOHANN, Orientalist and theologian; b. Kelz, Germany, Aug. 8, 1821; d. Rome, March 9, 1895. He entered the Roman province of the Society of Jesus as a priest in 1853. In 1855 he became professor of Oriental languages in the Roman College and the Gregorian University. From 1862 to 1864 he taught dogmatic theology at Ghazer, Lebanon. In 1864 he returned to Rome and was appointed a consultor of the Congregation of Propaganda. During Vatican Council I he served as a papal theologian; in 1877 he was appointed prefect of the Vatican Library. He is the author of *Brevis Arabica Christomatia* (Rome 1882) and *Gregor v. Nyssa: Gedichte* (Beirut 1895); together with P. de *Lagarde he edited *Texte des Joh. Mauropus aus Cod. Vat. graec. 676* (Rome 1882).

Bibliography: Koch JesLex 229. Sommervogel 8:1860–61. R. KÖBERT, LexThK² 2:572. B. GULDNER, CE 2:639.

[C. H. PICKAR]

BOLOGNA, GIOVANNI, an Italian mannerist sculptor of Flemish origin, famous for his development of sculpture that can be viewed from all angles; b. Douai, 1529; d. Florence, Aug. 13, 1608. He was born Jean Boulogne, was trained in his native Flanders by the sculptor Jacques Dubroeucq and went to Rome in the 1550s to study from the antique. About 1556 he started homeward, stopping in Florence. There the collector Bernardo Vecchietti offered to support the talented sculptor while he continued his studies in Florence. This city became his lifelong home. His Neptune Fountain in Bologna (1563–66) was the most advanced of its time; all the figures contribute to the water pattern. In "Florence Triumphant over Pisa" (1565–70) and "Samson and a Philistine" (1565–67) he worked toward a unified conception of the multifigured group that reached its climax in "The Rape of the Sabines" (1579–83). The latter two works were planned with an infinity of views, as were his masterly and more manipulable bronze statuettes. The many voids and projecting members overcome the initial solidity of the marble block. His congenital Flemish realism is revealed in his "Monument to Cosimo I" (1587–95), the first equestrian statue cast in Florence, and in the freely expressed physical stresses of "Hercules and the Centaur" (1594–99), his masterpiece. The same realism appears in his religious reliefs. Already in his lifetime his reputation as a sculptor came to rival that of Michelangelo.

Bibliography: J. POPE-HENNESSY, *Italian High Renaissance and Baroque Sculpture* (his *Introduction to Italian Sculpture* 3; New York 1963), bibliog. E. DHANENS, *Jean Boulogne, Giovanni Bologna Fiammingo* (Brussels 1956), bibliog.

[H. V. NIEBLING]

BOLOGNA, ARCHDIOCESE OF (BONONIENSIS)

Metropolitan see since 1582, in Emilia-Romagna, north Italy. In 1964 it had 535 secular and 337 religious priests, 1,250 churches and chapels, 120 minor and 95 major seminarians, 542 men in 61 religious houses, 2,270 women in 252 convents, 9,439 students in 32 schools, 116 parish movie theaters, 96 recreational centers, 68 sports groups, and 850,000 Catholics; it is 1,369 square miles in area. Its two suffragans, which had 486 priests, 874 sisters, and 255,000 Catholics, were *Imola (founded *c.* 370) and Faenza (known in 313), where Protestantism was strong in the 1560s. The city of Bologna, at the foot of the Apennines, is the capital and economic center of Emilia. It had (1964) 120 secular and 285 religious priests, 433 churches and chapels, 490 men in 43 religious houses, 1,530 women in 117 convents, and 26 Catholic schools with 7,929 pupils.

Bologna was the Etruscan *Felsina* in the 7th century B.C. Occupied by Rome in 191 B.C., it was called *Bononia* after the Gallic *Boii,* who had held it from the 4th century. Taken from the Goths by the Byzantines and from the Lombards by the Franks, it was part of Pepin's donation to the papacy (756); but it could not be held. After Charlemagne took it (773), it became part of the Empire until Otto I made it a free city. The thriving commune (established *c.* 1000) resisted Frederick II, but *Guelf-Ghibelline strife and family feuds hurt the city; the Pepoli bankers, the *Bentivoglio family, and the *Visconti of Milan then governed Bologna. Theoretical papal suzerainty was asserted in fact in 1326 and in 1360 (by *Albornoz), but it was Julius II who made

Church of S. Petronio in the Piazza Maggiore, Bologna.

Bologna part of the *States of the Church until it was annexed to the Kingdom of Italy (1506–1859).

Christian origins are unknown. Vitalis, Agricola, and Proculus were martyred during Roman persecutions. Bishop Zama (*c.* 300) was the first bishop. The see was suffragan to *Milan until the 5th century and then became suffragan to *Ravenna (to 1582), from which the bishops began to seek independence in the 9th century. Immediately subject to the Holy See briefly (1106–18), its bishops were named by the popes from 1244. In 1582 Gregory XIII, a native of Bologna, made it the metropolitan of west Emilia; but by 1860 only Faenza and Imola remained as suffragans.

The bishopric grew in the 11th century, when the commune and the university were flourishing. There was a religious renaissance based on monasticism closely associated with the university (11th–13th century). S. Procolo, SS. Nabore e Felice, S. Giovanni in Monte, and S. Maria di Reno were built in the 11th century. Canons Regular, especially Augustinians, were active. The Charterhouse (1334), a religious center in the 15th century, became a public cemetery in 1794. Mendicant orders were active from the 13th century. St. Dominic worked in Bologna and died there (1221). St. Anthony of Padua began and directed the Franciscan *studium* (1223–25). Bologna's religious prestige increased with the conclave that elected Antipope John XXIII during the Western Schism (1410), with the concordat between Leo X and Francis I of France (1515), with the imperial coronation of Charles V by Clement VII (1530), and with sessions 9 and 10 of the Council of Trent (1547–49). Many monasteries disappeared in Napoleonic times and after the Risorgimento. There have been few provincial synods: 1317, 1586, and 1932.

The episcopal list of 115 names (23 archbishops) is complete. St. Felix (397–413) was a friend of St. Ambrose. St. Petronius (431–450) has been the main patron of city and diocese from the 13th century. Bl. Niccolò *Albergati (1417–43), a Carthusian abbot (1407–17), was a reformer. Tommaso Parentucelli (1444–47) became Pope Nicholas V, and Giuliano della Rovere (1483–1502) became Julius II. Lorenzo *Campeggio (1523–25) preceded his son Giovanni (1553–63), who was active in the Council of Trent. Gabriele Paleotti (1566–97), the first archbishop, promoted the Tridentine reform with pastoral visits and founded the seminary (1567) and the episcopal library. Prospero Lambertini (1731–54) became Bene-

dict XIV, and Giacomo della Chiesa (1907–14) became Benedict XV. Carlo Opizzoni (1802–55), imprisoned in *Vincennes by Napoleon, was a conscientious prelate in difficult times. Six popes were natives of Bologna: Honorius II (1124–30), Lucius II (1144–45), Gregory XIII (1572–85), Innocent IX (1591), Gregory XV (1621–23), and Benedict XIV (1740–58). The incorrupt remains of St. *Catherine of Bologna (d. 1463) are venerated in Corpus Domini Church. The layman Giovanni Acquaderni (1838–1922) sponsored several attempts to revive the Catholic laity of Italy.

Bologna is rich in architecture, both secular and ecclesiastical. The most famous is that of S. Stefano (*c.* 950), where Basilian monks may have been as early as 440; the oldest part is attributed to St. Petronius (d. 450), who is said to have planned to restore buildings of Palestine (whence the name *Sancta Hierusalem* from the 9th century). Of seven original churches, four remain, in Lombard Romanesque (11th–12th century). In Gothic are S. Francesco (1236–63); S. Petronio (begun 1390); S. Maria dei Servi; S. Giacomo Maggiore; and S. Domenico (13th century with restorations of 1728) which houses the tomb of St. Dominic and sculpture by Michelangelo. The Cathedral of S. Pietro (16th century) has been frequently restored. The famous shrine on Monte della Guardia overlooking the city, with an icon of the Madonna (attributed to St. Luke) brought from Byzantium in the 11th century, is reached through an arcade more than 2 miles long with 666 arches (1661–1739). Bologna is known for arcades and towers, especially the leaning tower of the Asinelli (318 feet high), built in 1119.

The rich medieval libraries of religious orders were dispersed or appropriated by the state after 1859; in use today are those of the *Archiginnasio,* the university, the archbishop, and the Center of Documentation (an institute of religious studies begun in 1954). The school of music made famous by G. B. *Martini (1706–84) formed masters such as G. *Rossini. For 4 centuries Bologna produced famous paintings.

Many of the archdiocese's 454 parishes have small congregations, and 95 have no pastor. In the city, religious labor in 15 institutes caring for 4,100 children; sisters work in 20 hospitals and rest homes and in 3 homes for the aged; parishes operate 36 asylums and 36 parish movie theaters. Among 18 diocesan publications

The 13th-century church of S. Domenico, Bologna, housing the tomb of St. Dominic.

is the daily, *L'Avvenire d'Italia* (1895). Despite much religious activity, however, many people are influenced by Communist propaganda, which has a very active center in Bologna.

Bibliography: *Corpus Chronicorum Bononiensium,* ed. A. SORBELLI, 4 v. (Città di Castello 1903–28). E. E. C. JAMES, *Bologna: Its History, Antiquities, and Arts* (London 1909). A. HESSEL, *Geschichte der Stadt Bologna von 1116 bis 1280* (Berlin 1910). Kehr ItalPont 5:242–297. G. ROSSI, *Bologna nella storia, nell'arte e nel costume,* 3 v. (Bologna 1924–28). I. B. SUPINO, *L'arte nelle Chiese di Bologna,* 2 v. (Bologna 1932–38). F. BONNARD, DHGE 9:645–660, with list of bishops. A. SORBELLI, *Storia di Bologna dalle origini del Cristianesimo agli albori del comune* (Bologna 1938); et al., EncIt 7:326–350. P. F. PALUMBO et al., EncCatt 2:1792–1806. G. FABBRI, *Bologna, cenno storico artistico* (Bologna 1953). M. FANTI, *San Procolo: La Chiesa, l'abbazia* (Bologna 1963). F. LANZONI, *Cronotassi dei vescovi di Bologna dai primordi alla fine del secolo XIII* (Bologna 1932). T. CASINI, *La diocesi bolognese ed i suoi vescovi* (Bologna 1912). AnnPont (1965) 68. **Illustration credits:** Arthur O'Leary.

[G. D. GORDINI]

A Renaissance cloister of the University of Bologna.

BOLOGNA, UNIVERSITY OF

A coeducational state institution of higher learning in Italy, enjoying administrative autonomy and financially supported by the state and by student tuition.

Early History. The origin of a school at Bologna is so closely linked to the rebirth of the study of law after the 11th century that it is just as impossible to fix a precise date for its foundation as it is to fix a date for the philosophical movements that are identified with it.

The tradition of the commentators (those masters who labored over the interpretation of the text of Roman law—in particular the *Digest,* the most important part of the Justinian collection, which came to their hands by ways no less mysterious than their reasons for meeting in Bologna) refers to a certain Pepo, the predecessor of *Irnerius, who according to tradition headed a school in Bologna around 1080. However, it was only in the first part of the 12th century that the Bolognese school is thought to have assumed, under Irnerius, that distinctive feature that would remain peculiar to it— the isolation of the study of law from the study of the other arts. This was a decisive step in the history of the school, the fame of which was already so widespread at the middle of the 12th century that it attracted the attention of the Emperor Frederick I. He called the four famous Bolognese doctors, Bulgaro, Martino, Ugo, and Jacopo, to Roncaglia to decide the prerogatives of the emperor in regard to the cities. Again, according to tradition, each of the masters had a different approach to philosophy and juridical research. However, if they and their assembly at Roncaglia can be considered as part of the myth that surrounds the Bolognese school, the famous privilege granted to the students there by Frederick I in 1158 is certainly not a myth. This privilege granted students the right to be judged by their masters (*privilegium scholasticum*), a privilege that spread from Bologna and was later inserted in the code of Roman laws, where it is still referred to as the *Habita.*

Organization. By the middle of the 12th century students were flocking to Bologna not only from the various regions of Italy but even from the farthest parts of Europe. The organization of the school, although originally dependent on the name and worth of its masters, really depended on the student organizations, which chose the masters and paid their fees. In its earliest organization the school consisted of groups of students gathered around a master who taught in his home and was recompensed by a collection taken up among his disciples. The city later taking notice of the importance of the school tried to interfere in education— the first step being taken in 1180 when the city of Bologna obliged all masters to swear they would not teach outside the city. The students then organized both to facilitate their living problems and to protect their interests and privileges in dealing with the city and civil authority. In this manner, there arose two great organizations, the so-called cismontanes and the ultramontanes each headed by a rector who was a student. Later the associations subdivided into nations according to the nationality of the single groups. In 1217 the cismontanes (the Italians) split into three groups: Lombards, Tuscans, and Romans, the last of which also included students from Sicily and Campania later called *Illi de regno.* In 1265 the nations of the ultramontanes (the foreigners) were 13 in number with students from France, Spain, Provence, England, Picardy, Burgundy, Poitou, Tours, Maine, Normandy, Cataluna, Hungary, Poland, and Germany. In 1432 with the growth of the school the number of nations increased to 16.

Contrasts and strife between masters and groups of students and between students and the civil authorities led to an increase in the network of new university centers outside Bologna. Universities arose in France, in *Montpellier and Orléans; in Spain, in *Salamanca; and in Italy, in Vicenza (1204), Arezzo (1215), *Padua (1222), Vercelli (1228), Siena (1321), Florence, Pisa, Modena, Perugia, *Rome (1303), *Pavia (1361), Ferrara (1391), Parma, Turin, Messina, and Catania.

Canon and Civil Law. In the meantime, in the mid-12th century, instruction in Canon Law was introduced by Gratian, a monk of the Bolognese monastery of SS. Felix and Nabor. About the year 1140 he worked to unify Canon Law in the *Decretum* that was to be the basis of Church legislation in the 13th century. *See* GRATIAN, DECRETUM OF (CONCORDANTIA DISCORDANTIUM CANONUM). As the genius of Irnerius appeared in the separation of the study of civil law from that of the other arts, so the genius of Gratian was manifested in the distinction he introduced between Canon Law and theology. This work completes and perfects the plan of medieval studies with the union of Roman law and Canon Law in a unique system—*l'utrumque ius,* an ideal form for the new civilization advancing toward the second millennium of Christianity.

These two great branches of 13th-century medieval culture are found distinct at the Bolognese school in two colleges—the *Ius Canonicum* composed of 12 members and the *Ius Civile sive Casesareum,* of 16. These groups gathered together the masters or their representatives from the various colleges for the final examination of a candidate or in exceptional cases held a common meeting.

Expansion. The restoration of Aristotelian philosophy in the 13th century gave a new impulse to the teaching of mathematical, liberal, and mechanical arts, a fact confirmed by the establishment of a third college —*Collegium artistarum et medicorum*—for instruction in philosophical and technical subjects.

These three colleges, which unite the masters, canonists, lawyers, artists, philosophers, and doctors, can be compared to the ancient student organizations of cismontanes, ultramontanes, and nations. The course of study lasted 6 years for Canon Law, 8 years for civil law, and 4 years for arts and medicine. The doctorate was obtained by successfully carrying on a discussion on a topic assigned on the eve by the professors who themselves held the opposition. Those who were successful could obtain the doctorate by giving a lecture in the presence of the academic body, the rectors of the universities, and their colleagues. Since 1219 the formal conferring of the doctorate has been the prerogative of the archdeacon of the Cathedral of Bologna, acting as papal delegate. This formality made the doctorate received at Bologna not simply a *licentia docendi* (an authorization to teach) but rather a *licentia ubique docendi* (an authorization to teach anywhere).

The organization of the University based on three colleges of masters and three "universities" of students remained unchanged until the end of the 18th century. In the late 16th century the various schools were united in one building, the Palazzo dell'Archiginnasio provided by the city, in keeping with the civil authorities' plan to assume authority over the University.

During the French Revolution and especially during the Napoleonic era (1800–15), the ancient organization of the University was transformed. It emerged from this period as a modern state university. The Palazzo dell'Archiginnasio was abandoned, and the University moved to the Palazzo Poggi where it still functions.

The bull of Leo XIII, *Quod divina sapientia,* of Aug. 28, 1824, raised the University of Bologna to the status of a Pontifical University, placing it side by side with the University of Rome with the right to confer both the licentiate and the doctorate. Since 1860 (when it was annexed to the Kingdom of Italy) the University of Bologna has conformed to the organization of institutes of higher learning in the new Italian State.

Modern Development. The University is composed of 11 Faculties: Law (including political science); Economics and Commerce; Letters and Philosophy (including archeology and education); Teacher Training; Medicine (including nursing), Mathematics, Physics and Natural Sciences; Industrial Chemistry; Pharmacy; Engineering (including architecture); Agriculture (including forestry and zoology); and Veterinary Medi-

cine. In addition, there are 10 postgraduate schools affiliated with the Faculties.

Laureate and doctoral degrees are granted in law; economics and commerce; letters; philosophy; modern languages and literatures; education; mathematics; physics; natural sciences; pharmacy; agriculture; and veterinary medicine (4 years); chemistry, industrial chemistry; civil, mechanical, electrical, chemical, mining, and nuclear engineering (5 years); and medicine (6 years). A diploma is given in statistics (2 years) and in postgraduate specialization. The University publishes a quarterly, *Bollettino Ufficiale.*

The governing bodies are the administrative board and the academic senate. Officers are the rector and the administrative director. In 1964 the academic staff numbered 1,200 full-time and 411 part-time professors; student enrollment totaled approximately 16,000 Italian students and 500 foreign students.

Bibliography: I. CECCHETTI, EncCatt 2:1804–06. A. SORBELLI, EncIt 7:347–348. S. D'IRSAY, *Histoire des universités,* 2 v. (Paris 1933–35) v.1. H. RASHDALL, *The Universities of Europe in the Middle Ages,* ed. F. M. POWICKE and A. B. EMDEN, 3 v. (Oxford 1936). *Chartularium studii Bononiensis,* 13 v. (Bologna 1909–40). *Studi e memorie per la storia dell' Università di Bologna,* ser. 1, 18 v. (Bologna 1907–50); NS 1–2 (1956–61). **Illustration credit:** Istituto Italiano di Cultura.

[G. ORLANDELLI]

BOLSEC, JÉRÔME HERMÈS, writer and physician; b. Paris date unknown; d. Lyons, France *c.* 1585. As a Paris Carmelite he was suspected of heresy, and he fled to Italy and the sympathetic protection of Duchess Renée of Ferrara (1545). There he renounced his religious vows and Catholicism, studied medicine, and married. In Geneva by 1550, Bolsec and Calvin differed publicly over predestination. Bolsec maintained that if faith was the consequence rather than the condition of election, God must be charged with partiality. Calvin's position, he said, was illogical and absurd, and manifested a fundamental weakness in the reformer's theological system. Bolsec was arrested, imprisoned, and banished from Geneva. He went to Bern but was soon expelled. In 1551 he returned to France and sought a pastorate from the Reformed Church, but was rejected because of unorthodoxy. In 1563 he sought asylum at Lausanne; but when Theodore *Beza insisted that he first sign the *Confession of Bern* as proof of orthodoxy, Bolsec refused, returned to France, abjured his errors, reembraced the Catholic faith, and retired to Lyons to practice medicine and write. His biographies, *Histoire . . . de Jean Calvin* (1577) and *Histoire . . . de Th. de Beze* (1582), are highly controversial.

Bibliography: A. DI SANTA TERESA, EncCatt 2:1817. C. DE SAINT ETIENNE DE VILLIERS, *Bibliotheca carmelitana,* ed. P. G. WESSELS, 2 v. in 1 (Rome 1927) 637–639. J. DEDIEU, DHGE 9:676–679, bibliog. H. LIEBING, RGG³ 1:1349–50.

[J. W. ROONEY, JR.]

BOLTZMANN, LUDWIG, Austrian theoretical physicist; b. Vienna, Feb. 20, 1844; d. there, Sept. 5, 1906. Boltzmann was educated at Linz and Vienna, obtaining his doctorate from the latter university (1867). He was professor of physics at Graz (1876), Munich (1891), and Vienna (1895). He developed the kinetic theory of gases and established the basic principles of statistical mechanics. Boltzmann's H-theorem attempts to explain the irreversibility of natural processes by showing how molecular collisions tend to increase entropy; any initial distribution of molecular positions and velocities will almost certainly evolve into an equilibrium state, in which the velocities are distributed according to Maxwell's law. The Maxwell velocity distribution law was generalized by Boltzmann to apply to physical systems in which interatomic forces and external fields must be taken into account. He further showed that the entropy of a system in any physical state may be related to its probability, by counting the number of molecular configurations corresponding to that state. This result and the Boltzmann-Stefan formula for the energy of black-body radiation aided Max *Planck in his discovery of the quantum theory in 1900. In the 1890s Boltzmann had to defend the kinetic theory and even the existence of atoms against the attacks of Wilhelm Ostwald, Pierre *Duhem, Ernst *Mach, and others. Boltzmann thought himself to be on the losing side in this battle, and he feared the obliteration of his lifework in science. He committed suicide. However, within a few years of his suicide, the existence of atoms had been definitely established. Since then Boltzmann's methods have been incorporated into modern theoretical physics.

Bibliography: L. BOLTZMANN, *Lectures on Gas Theory,* tr. S. G. BRUSH (Berkeley 1964), with add. nn. and bibliog.

[S. G. BRUSH]

BOLZANO, BERNHARD

Mathematician and philosopher; b. Prague, Oct. 5, 1781; d. Prague, Dec. 18, 1848. At the University of Prague he pursued his early interest in mathematics and philosophy together with the study of theology. After overcoming his father's opposition, Bolzano was ordained in 1805. In the same year he was appointed professor of philosophy of religion at the University of Prague. In 1819, he lost his post by order of the Emperor in Vienna. False charges had been placed against him concerning certain views that he held on matters of civil disobedience, social rank, and war. Even though they were objectionable in the eyes of the Holy Roman Emperor, Bolzano's opinions were not found to be theologically heretical. Through the intervention of the Prince-Archbishop Salm-Salm of Prague, he retained his professorship until 1820, after which his life was spent in studious retirement, first on the estate of his friend J. Hoffman at Lechobuz, and later in the house of his brother at Prague.

Bolzano, a contemporary of A. *Cauchy, K. *Gauss, and N. Abel, was one of the pioneers of greater rigor in the fundamental concepts of calculus. His definition of a continuous function indicated clearly for the first time that the basis of continuity was to be found in the limit concept (1817).

Contrary to J. L. *Lagrange, L. *Euler, and S. Lacroix, he insisted that dy/dx was not to be interpreted as a ratio of dy and dx or as a quotient of zero divided by zero but as a symbol for a single function.

When Charles X of France went into exile, he accepted the hospitality of the government of Prague and was accompanied by Cauchy, a Catholic and a royalist, who was appointed tutor in mathematics to the young Duke of Bordeaux. With this move Cauchy and Bolzano lived near each other from 1833 to 1835. By 1823 Cauchy had published his work on infinitesimal calculus, and Bolzano published no pure mathematics after 1817. All indications are that contributions to

analysis by either man were completely independent of those of the other.

Balzano's Paradox, that infinite aggregates have the property that any part of them can be put into one-to-one correspondence with the whole, anticipated Dedekind's and Cantor's definitions of an infinite set. Though Bolzano failed to recognize what Cantor later called the power of the infinite set of elements, his views of the infinite are substantially those that mathematicians have adopted since the time of Cantor. His works remained largely unnoticed until rediscovered by Herman Hankel more than a half century after his death.

Bibliography: B. BOLZANO, *Paradoxen des Unendlichen,* ed. F. PŘIHONSKY (Leipzig 1851), Eng. *Paradoxes of the Infinite,* tr. and introd. D. A. STEELE (New Haven 1950). J. BAUMANN, "Dedekind und Bolzano," *Annalen der Naturphilosophie* 7 (1908) 444–449. C. B. BOYER, *The History of Calculus and Its Conceptual Development* (pa. New York 1959). R. and D. J. STRUIK, "Cauchy and Bolzano in Prague," *Isis* 11 (1928) 364–366. Copleston 7:256–259.

[T. À K. KLOYDA]

BOMBAY, ARCHDIOCESE OF (BOMBAYENSIS)

Metropolitan see since 1887, in Maharashtra state, west *India. The city of Bombay, an excellent island port on the Arabian Sea, was acquired by Portugal in 1534 and ceded to England in 1661; in 1708 it became the administrative capital of British India. In 1963 the archdiocese, 8,208 square miles in area, had 96 parishes, 228 secular and 189 religious priests, 292 men in 37 religious houses, 620 women in 59 convents, and 348,455 Catholics in a population of 13 million. Its three suffragans, which had 218 priests, 518 sisters, and 186,000 Catholics in a population of 32 million, were Ahmedabad (created in 1949), Belgaum (1953), and Poona (1886).

In 1321 four Franciscans were martyred on Salsette Island, near Bombay, where *Odoric of Pordenone stopped on his voyage to the Far East. On the Portuguese entry into the East, Bombay became part of the See of *Goa, created in 1534 and made an archbishopric in 1558, under the Portuguese padroado. Portuguese Franciscans evangelized the area immediately, aided by Jesuits after the visit of St. Francis *Xavier in 1548 and by native secular clergy later. A vicar-general of the north represented the archbishop of Goa in an area that included Bombay. In 1612 the English settled at Surat, north of Bombay, and in 1661 acquired Bombay in return for protection against the Dutch, who were threatening Portuguese areas elsewhere in the East. Catholic missionary activity declined under the East India Company, whose religious indifference was reflected in its policies.

The Congregation for the *Propagation of the Faith, established in 1622, created the Vicariate of Bijapur (Deccan) in 1637, which was enlarged (1697) and entrusted to Carmelites expelled from Goa for their refusal to take an oath of loyalty to the Portuguese crown (1707). In 1720 the British expelled Portuguese clergy from Bombay, on suspicion of their support of an anti-British movement, and replaced them with Italian Carmelites of the vicariate, now called that of the Great Mogul. The local Marathas seized Portuguese areas around Bombay (1737–40), destroyed much of the work of the missions, and expelled Portuguese clergy; and *Pombal's expulsion of the Jesuits

(1759) brought to an end for a century their missionary work in the area of Bombay. In 1784 the Capuchin Tibet-Hindustan mission was detached from the Vicariate of the Great Mogul. The British in 1789 allowed padroado clergy to work in Bombay, which returned to the jurisdiction of Goa; but local protests led to the restoration of the Carmelite vicariate in 1790. The dispute was resolved a few years later by the division of Bombay's parishes between the padroado and the vicariate. See PATRONATO REAL.

American Protestants opened a mission school in Bombay in 1814. Bombay became a see of the Church of England in 1837, when Scotch Presbyterians also established a church there. Methodists arrived in 1872.

In 1832 the Vicariate of Bombay, under Carmelites, replaced that of the Great Mogul. The padroado clergy protested, and Portugal, which had broken relations with the Holy See in 1828, suppressed religious orders in India in 1834. The papal bull of 1838 specified areas previously under *Goa that were now to be under vicariates but did not mention Bombay. Padroado clergy refused to recognize the bull, and vicariate clergy called them schismatics. The Swiss Capuchin vicar apostolic, Anastasius *Hartmann (1849–58), fostered missionary work in Bombay but failed to make the vicariate prevail over the padroado. The Vicariate of Bombay, taken from the Carmelites, was divided in 1854, the north (Bombay) going to Italian Capuchins and the south (Poona) to German Jesuits. In 1858 Jesuits replaced the Capuchins in Bombay. The Jesuits concentrated on education, founding the College of St. Francis Xavier (1867), affiliated with the British-founded University of Bombay (1857), and extending missionary activity to the north.

The concordat of 1857 between Portugal and the Holy See favored the padroado, creating the padroado Diocese of Damão within the Vicariate of Bombay and leaving padroado churches in Bombay under the jurisdiction of Goa. In 1858 the governing of India was taken from the East India Company and was assumed by the British crown. Differences regarding the padroado were adjusted in a new concordat in 1886, when the ecclesiastical hierarchy of India was established, Bombay becoming an archdiocese with the suffragans Poona, Mangalore, Trichinopoly, Calicut, and Tuticorin. The 1928 concordat suppressed Damão and padroado enclaves, except Diu.

Since 1860 Bombay has expanded with industrialization, and urban problems now combine with nationalism and religious indifference as a barrier to missionary work. In 1922 Spanish Jesuits replaced Germans. Archbishops of Bombay include the Jesuit Alban *Goodier (1919–26) and Cardinal Valerian Gracias (1950–   ), Bombay's first Indian prelate. A National Marian Congress (1954) and an International Eucharistic Congress (1964) were held in Bombay. The latter was honored by the presence of Pope *Paul VI, who took part in several religious services and consecrated six bishops from various continents.

Bibliography: E. R. HULL, *Bombay Mission History,* 2 v. (Bombay 1930). A. VÄTH, *Die deutschen Jesuiten in Indien* (Regensburg 1920). A. HUBLOU, DHGE 9:685–700. A. MEERSMAN, *The Franciscans in Bombay* (Bangalore 1957). J. H. GENSE, *The Church at the Gateway of India, 1720–1960* (Bombay 1960). T. POTHACAMURY, *The Church in Independent India* (Bombay 1961). F. COUTINHO, *Le Régime paroissial des diocèses de rite latin de l'Inde des origines (XVIe siècle) à nos jours* (Louvain 1958). *Catholic Directory of the Archdiocese of Bombay* (Bombay 1960). *The Catholic Directory of India* (Allahabad, India) annual. AnnPont (1965) 69.

[E. R. HAMBYE]

BOMBERG, DANIEL, famous Dutch Christian printer and publisher of Hebrew books; b. Antwerp, Holland, *c.* 1470–80; d. Venice, Italy, 1549. In 1515 he established a printing press at Venice, which published more than 200 Hebrew books. In 1516–17 he published the first Hebrew Bible edited by Felix *Pratensis, which embraced not only the Hebrew text but the Aramaic Targums and Rabbinical commentaries. A second important edition of the Hebrew Bible published by Bomberg was that of Jacob ben Chayyim in 1524–25. In 1519–22, with the permission of Pope *Leo X, Bomberg published the first complete Babylonian *Talmud; his edition of the Palestinian Talmud appeared *c.* 1522–23. During this period law books, grammatical works, and important books on various different rites were also published by Bomberg.

Bibliography: D. W. AMRAM, *Makers of Hebrew Books in Italy* (Philadelphia 1909) 146–148. M. SCHWAB, JewishEnc 3: 299–300. E. KÜMMERER, RGG³ 1:1351. E. L. EHRLICH, LexThK² 2:578.

[C. H. PICKAR]

BOMBOLOGNUS OF BOLOGNA, Italian Dominican theologian; fl. 1265 to 1270. A contemporary of *Thomas Aquinas, although not a Thomist, he lectured on the *Sentences* at the Dominican priory of San Domenico in Bologna. His is the earliest-known commentary on the *Sentences* composed by an Italian Dominican in Italy. The autograph copy containing the commentary on the first book of the *Sentences* is preserved in Bologna, Bibl. Univ. 753. Two other MSS, Bologna, Bibl. Univ. 755, and Assisi, Com. 155, contain his commentary on the third book. Although Parisian influences are not altogether lacking, the work fundamentally represents Italian traditions. Bombolognus upheld universal hylomorphism on the authority of *Avicebron. He described the thesis of the *Immaculate Conception in clear terms, but he himself rejected it in favor of Mary's sanctification before birth. He was familiar with some of the writings of Aquinas, of St. *Bonaventure, and of Peter of Tarentaise (later *Innocent V).

Bibliography: M. GRABMANN, *Mittelalterliches Geistesleben,* 3 v. (Munich 1926–56) 1:339–340. F. PELSTER, "Les Manuscrits de Bombolognus de Bologne, O.P.," RechThAMéd 9 (1937) 404–412. O. LOTTIN, *Psychologie et morale aux XIIe et XIIIe siècles,* v.3 (Louvain 1949) 235–239, 418–421. A. D'AMATO, "B. de Musolinis da B. notizie biografiche e bibliografiche," *Sapienza* 1 (1948) 75–90, 232–252. A. WALZ, LexThK² 2:578.

[P. GLORIEUX]

BON SECOURS, SISTERS OF (CBS), a pontifical institute founded on Jan. 24, 1824, when 12 young women pronounced their vows at Saint-Sulpice in Paris, dedicating themselves to the care of the sick in their homes. Josephine Potel was the first superior. Hyacinthe de *Quélen, Archbishop of Paris, had deliberated long in granting approbation to such an endeavor since it was then a novel form of apostolate. Soon other houses were opened throughout France, and the sisters added the tasks of caring for orphans, operating a school, opening clinics, and providing meeting places for school girls on their days off. The congregation spread to Ireland, England, and later to Scotland.

Through the request of James Gibbons (later Cardinal), three Sisters came to Baltimore, Md., in 1881 for the first U.S. foundation. Night and day they answered the calls of the sick in their homes until a hospital was built in 1919. In the U.S. the sisters operate four general hospitals; one school of nursing; one school of practical nursing; and homes for retired priests, the aged, incurable, and convalescent. These are located in Baltimore, Md.; Philadelphia, Pa.; Washington, D.C.; Detroit, Mich.; Miami, Fla.; Methuen, Mass.; Wildwood, N.J.; and Richmond, Va. The congregation has one foreign mission in Chad, Africa. In 1964 there were more than 600 sisters in the whole congregation, 158 of whom were in the U.S. The American provincialate and novitiate are in Baltimore; the motherhouse is in Paris.

Bibliography: M. BADIOU, *Les Soeurs du Bon Secours de Paris* (Lyon 1958). J. M. HAYES, *The Bon Secours Sisters in the U.S.* (2d ed. Washington 1931).

[M. L. NUGENT]

BONA, ST., patroness of travel hostesses; b. Pisa, Italy, *c.* 1156; d. Pisa, May 29, 1207 (feast, May 29). Distinguished by her piety as a child, she was received as a young woman into the *Canons Regular of St. Augustine, and henceforth lived in a house near the Canons who served St. Martin's church in Pisa. As a result of a vision of Our Lord she made a pilgrimage to the Holy Land. There a hermit Ubald instructed her about the holy places she was to visit and eventually told her when to return to Pisa. On the way home she was wounded by Saracens and molested by robbers. Henceforth she lived as a recluse in Pisa except for her nine pilgrimages to *Santiago de Compostela and frequent visits to St. Peter's tomb in Rome. She is buried in St. Martin's, Pisa. In 1962 Pope *John XXIII named her the patroness of Italian travel hostesses.

Bibliography: ActSS May 7:141–161, 858. BHL 1:206–207. Baudot-Chaussin 5:569–572. F. BARTORELLI, *Santa B. da Pisa* (Bari 1960). B. MATTEUCCI, BiblSanct 3:234–235. ActApS 54 (1962) 707–708.

[M. J. HAMILTON]

BONA, GIOVANNI

Cardinal, Cistercian monk, liturgist, and ascetical writer; b. Mondovi, Piedmont, Oct. 10, 1609; d. Rome, Oct. 28, 1674. He took the habit of a Cistercian monk of the Congregation of Feullants of Italy when he was 16 years old, and after studies in Rome was successively professor of theology (1633–36), prior, abbot, and abbot general of his congregation (1651), and finally was created cardinal (1669).

His liturgical writings, fruit of vast research and sober critical judgment, place him among the founders of modern liturgical studies. The scope of his work on the Divine Office, *De Divina Psalmodia*, is suggested by its earlier title, *Psallentis Ecclesiae harmonia, Tractatus historicus, symbolicus, asceticus de divina psalmodia eiusque causis, mysteriis et disciplina, deque variis ritibus omnium Ecclesiarum in psallendis divinis officiis* (1653). His work on the Mass, *Rerum liturgicarum libri duo* (1671), is simpler and clearer. In explaining the origins of the Mass, its different ways of celebration, its structure and constituent elements, he keeps surprisingly free, for a man of his time, of symbolic interpretation and the polemic tone and leaves to another work, *De sacrificio missae tractatus asceticus* (1658), pious

considerations to help the priest's devotion as he offers the sacrifice of the Mass.

Bona's ascetical works are not original. Drawing from extensive readings in the Fathers, St. Thomas, and more recent spiritual writers, such as St. Francis de Sales and St. Ignatius, his teaching is simple, solid, and traditional. In his *Manuductio ad Coelum* (1658), after explaining the ultimate end of man and insisting on the need of a spiritual director, he treats his subject according to the familiar three ways (*see* WAYS, THE THREE SPIRITUAL). In his *Via compendii ad Deum per motus anagogicos et orationes jaculatorias* (1657), he explains how union with God is perfected in actual loving attention to Him, and proposes ejaculatory prayer as a means to this. His *De discretione spirituum* (1671) is usually discussed in modern treatments of the discernment of spirits.

Bibliography: G. BONA, *Hortus Coelestium Deliciarum,* ed. M. VATTASSO (Rome 1918). H. DUMAINE, DACL 2:992–1002. J. M. CANIVEZ, DictSpirAscMyst 1:1762–66. L. BERTOLOTTI, *Vita Ioannis Bona* (Asti 1677). "Si può sperare la canonizzazione del Cardinale Giovanni Bona?" *Rivista storica Benedettina* 5 (1910) 253–268, 321–364. PIUS X, "Il Cardinale Giovanni Bona a Mondovì," *ibid.* 418–422. A. CORSI, "La feste centenarie di Mondovì pel Cardinale Giovanni Bona," *ibid.* 535–540. A. MICHELOTTI, "Musica e poesia nell'opera del cardinale Giovanni Bona," *ibid.* 6 (1911) 5–35.

[T. BOYD]

BONA MORS CONFRATERNITY, known also as the Confraternity of Our Lord Jesus Christ Dying on the Cross, and of the Most Blessed Virgin Mary, His sorrowful Mother, is a spiritual association founded in Rome in 1648 by Vincent *Carafa, seventh general of the Society of Jesus, known especially for his attentions to the suffering and dying victims of the plague. The association was approved by Innocent X and Alexander VII and raised to the status of an archconfraternity by Benedict XIII in 1729. Benedict authorized the Jesuit general to establish Bona Mors (A Good Death) confraternities in churches of the society. Leo XII, in 1827, extended this authorization to churches not under the direction of the Jesuits.

The purpose of the Bona Mors Confraternity is to prepare each member, through a spiritually disciplined life and a special devotion to Christ's Passion and the sorrows of Mary, for a peaceful death. Instrumental in this preparation for death are the instructions given at public meetings, and the graces and indulgences gained by the member through the union in prayer and good works of the confraternity.

To become a member of this association, one should present himself to his local confraternity director, express a desire for membership, receive a certificate of admission or other outward sign of acceptance decided upon by his chapter, and have his name enrolled in the local register. It is the rule of the association that the interested party present himself for membership. Only in extraordinary circumstances would one be allowed to enroll a person other than himself. This stipulation is set down in a decree of the Congregation of Indulgences. Numerous indulgences have been granted the practices of the confraternity, details of which are contained in the confraternity manual.   [M. MC DONNELL]

BONAL, FRANÇOIS DE, French prelate; b. Bonal, near Agen, France, May 9, 1734; d. Munich, Sept. 5, 1800. He was director general of the Carmelites, and became bishop of Clermont in 1776. He led an austere, apostolic life. He played an important role in the French Revolution. As deputy to the Estates General of 1789, he was named president of the ecclesiastical committee of the assembly and fought anticlerical measures until he was forced to resign. He took the oath of loyalty to the civil constitution in February 1790, but not to the *Civil Constitution of the Clergy in January 1791. His letter of April 1791 advising Louis XVI not to receive the Sacraments from the civil clergy, was introduced later in the trial of the King. Bonal emigrated to Brussels and The Hague (1794). He was captured by French troops, and condemned to deportation. Impoverished, he went to Altona in Prussia, then to Fribourg in Switzerland, and finally to Munich.

In April 1798, he signed the *Instruction sur les atteintes partées à la religion,* published by French refugee bishops in Germany, and before his death he dictated a spiritual testament giving his last instructions to his diocese. He was buried in the Capuchin monastery in Munich.

Bibliography: ABBÉ BOEUF, *Mgr. de Bonnal* (Paris 1910). G. WAGNER, *Catholicisme* 2:120. R. LIMOUZIN-LAMOTHE, Dict-BiogFranc 6:903.

[W. E. LANGLEY]

BONAL, RAYMOND, founder of the Congregation of the Priests of St. Mary (Bonalists); moral theologian; b. Villefranche-de-Rouergue, Aug. 15, 1600; d. Agde, Aug. 9, 1653. His classical, philosophical, theological, and legal studies were done in Cahors at the Jesuit college and at the university. He was ordained at Lombes in 1624, and received a doctorate in theology from the University of Toulouse in 1626.

He exercised the ministry at Villefranche where his spiritual energy attracted other priests to work with him. This was the nucleus of the congregation whose spirit was that of St. Francis de Sales. They followed the common life as early as 1631 at the chapel of Our Lady of Pity in Villefranche. Vincent de Paul, Father Bourdoise, and Jane Frances de Chantal advised Bonal in the drawing up of the Constitutions, which were completed in 1637 and given episcopal approval in 1648. Papal and royal approval came in 1665 and 1678. Mission preaching, retreats for laity and priests, and seminary teaching constituted the congregation's apostolate. The activities of the community spread during the lifetime of Bonal to Foix, Aleth, and Toulouse, where he established a seminary-college called Caraman in 1651. The following year a seminary project at Agde was frustrated by an epidemic. At the same time episcopal approval of his rule was given by Charles Augustus de Sales, third successor and nephew of Francis de Sales.

After Bonal's death in 1653, his work was carried on successfully for another 60 years but vocations became so meager that in 1723 the seminary at Villefranche was entrusted to the Lazarists; the Toulouse seminary suffered the same fate in 1752. This process continued until the congregation was finally absorbed by the Congregation of the Mission.

Bibliography: There is a MS biography of Bonal by a priest of his congregation in the seminary of Sainte-Sulpice. É. M. FAILLON, *Vie de M. Olier* 2 v. (4th ed. Paris 1873) 362–364. L. BERTRAND, *Bibliothèque Sulpicienne* (Paris 1900) 1:214–215. B. MAYRAN, *Raymond Bonal dans les Diocèses de Pamier et d'Alet* (Foix 1914). E. MANGENOT, DTC 2:956–957.

[J. J. SMITH]

BONALD, LOUIS GABRIEL AMBROISE DE

French statesman and social and political theorist, whose writings not only epitomized *traditionalism but also influenced significantly the development of sociological theory; b. Le Monna, near Millau (Rouergue, Aveyron), France, Oct. 2, 1754; d. Paris, Nov. 23, 1840. His family, Catholic and of the "nobility of the robe" (magistrates), had him educated by the Oratorians of Juilly, where he came under the influence of Malebranche's philosophy. He emigrated during the French Revolution but later found favor with Napoleon and returned to France. Under the Restoration monarchy, he was elected to the Académie Française (1816) and named vicomte (1821) and peer (1823). As the leading theorist of the ultraroyalists, he opposed all liberal tendencies. After the Revolution of 1830, he resigned his peerage and retired to Le Monna.

The purpose Bonald set for himself in his writings was to overcome the effects of Enlightenment rationalism by establishing, after the manner of a geometrician proving a series of theorems, the principles upon which a well-ordered society would be founded. To him these included a union of an absolute political power with an absolute religious power in a hierarchical society ordering every aspect of life according to immutable principles arrived at by deduction. Bonald argued first that since man cannot have invented language, God must have revealed it to the first man, and with it all religious, social, and moral truths. It followed that tradition and not individual human reason was the necessary means of attaining truth. The argument embodied all the basic elements of traditionalism, including a failure to distinguish between the natural and supernatural orders of reality, but when the traditionalist position—as a kind of *fideism—was condemned by the Catholic Church, Bonald's works were not specifically included in the condemnation (cf. Denz. 2811–2814, 3026). His principal writings are *La Théorie du pouvoir politique et*

Louis Gabriel Ambroise de Bonald.

religieux (1796), which sets forth his main thesis regarding the nature of society; and *La Législation primitive . . .* (1802) and *Recherches philosophiques . . .* (1818), which together embody most of his arguments.

Bonald's originality lay in his ability to construct an internally consistent system that could treat politics, social organization, religion, the arts, education, and, in theory, all elements in a culture as interacting functions within a closed order. An a priori explanation was applicable to all. His ideas were assimilated in such varied intellectual traditions as those represented by Henri de Saint-Simon, Félicité de Lamennais, Auguste Comte, Hippolyte Taine, and Charles Maurras; the explanation lies principally in the fact that Bonald, grappling with the problem of the relationship between the individual and society, resolved it in favor of man's being, and being only, a product of society. Thus, both the authoritarian and the positivistic implications of Bonald's work have assured it a place in the history of ideas.

Bibliography: *Oeuvres complètes,* ed. J. P. MIGNE, 3 v. (Paris 1859). C. CONSTANTIN, DTC 2:958–961. H. MOULINIÉ, *De Bonald: La Vie, la carrière politique, la doctrine* (Paris 1916). R. SPAEMANN, *Der Ursprung der Soziologie aus dem Geist der Restauration: Studien über L. G. A. de Bonald* (Munich 1959). M. H. QUINLAN, *The Historical Thought of the Vicomte de Bonald* (Washington 1953). **Illustration credit:** New York Public Library, Picture Collection.

[M. H. QUINLAN]

BONAPARTE, CHARLES, prince of Canino and of Musignano, naturalist; b. Paris, France, May 24, 1803; d. there, July 29, 1857. He was the eldest son of Napoleon's brother Lucièn. After marrying his cousin Zenaide (1822), the daughter of Joseph Bonaparte, he came to the U.S. and lived in Philadelphia (1822–28). He established his reputation as a scientist by publishing *American Ornithology: Or, History of Birds Inhabiting the United States Not Given by Wilson* (4 v. Philadelphia 1825–33). He continued his scientific studies after taking up residence in Italy (1828). His most significant work of this period was *Iconografia della fauna italica* (3 v. Rome 1832–41). He entered politics in the Italian Republican party and was vice president of the constitutional assembly (1848). The next year, the failure of the revolution forced him to flee the country. He eventually took up residence in Paris, where he became director of the Jardin des Plantes (1854). Among his 12 children was Lucièn-Louis-Joseph-Napoleon, who was made a cardinal in 1868.

Bibliography: E. DE BEAUMONT, *Notice sur les traveaux scientifiques de Son Altesse le prince Charles-Lucien Bonaparte* (Paris 1866). R. FERRAI, *Il principe di Canino e il suo processo (1847–48)* (Rome 1926).

[N. SCHEEL]

BONAPARTE, CHARLES JOSEPH, U.S. secretary of the Navy, attorney general; b. Baltimore, Md., June 9, 1851; d. there, June 28, 1921. His grandfather was King Jerome, the brother of Napoleon I; his parents were Jerome and Susan May (Williams) Bonaparte. Educated under tutors and in private schools near Baltimore, he graduated from Harvard in 1872 and from its law school in 1874. He married Ellen Channing Day of Hartford, Conn., in 1875. Bonaparte was a Republican who often acted independently of party considerations; his early career was devoted to municipal and civil service reform. When appointed legal adviser to the board of Indian commissioners by Pres. Theodore Roosevelt in 1902, he worked to end corruption among field agents and to obtain Federal funds for Indian mission schools. In 1905 he joined the President's cabinet.

As secretary of the Navy (1905–06), he supported Roosevelt's expansionist naval program; and he prosecuted more than 50 antitrust suits as attorney general (1906–09). Under Roosevelt, Bonaparte was often employed as an intermediary between Church and government leaders, for his advocacy of the separation of Church and State was balanced by insistence on the value of the Church in a self-governing nation. His most notable mediation was in the sale of Church lands in Puerto Rico. Bonaparte left office with Roosevelt in 1909. Although he supported Roosevelt's Progressive campaign in 1912, his chief interests were his law practice in Baltimore and his efforts on behalf of civic reform. He was prominent also as a crusader for Negro rights.

Bibliography: J. B. BISHOP, *Charles Joseph Bonaparte* (New York 1922). E. F. GOLDMAN, *Charles J. Bonaparte, Patrician Reformer: His Early Career* (Baltimore 1943). J. L. PHELPS, "Charles J. Bonaparte and Negro Suffrage in Maryland," *Maryland Historical Magazine* 54 (1959) 331–352. Library of Congress, Charles J. Bonaparte Papers.

[F. W. O'BRIEN]

BONAPARTE, JÉRÔME, youngest brother of *Napoleon I; b. Ajaccio, Corsica, Nov. 15, 1784; d. near Paris, June 24, 1860. He entered the navy and as a lieutenant was sent on an expedition to the West Indies (1801). Taking refuge in the U.S. from the British, he became engaged to Elizabeth Patterson, whom he had met on a previous visit to Baltimore, Md. Although Jérôme was not of legal age under French law and did not have the consent of his one surviving parent, a contract was drafted that ensured a valid marriage. By dispensation the marriage was celebrated on Christmas Eve, 1803, by Bp. John Carroll of Baltimore. Eighteen months later, Jérôme and Elizabeth landed at Lisbon, Portugal. Since Elizabeth was forbidden entrance into France or any of its satellite countries, she traveled alone to London, where she gave birth to a son, Jérôme Napoleon, from whom the American Bonapartes are descended. Meanwhile Jérôme met with Napoleon I at Alessandria, Italy, and agreed to abandon his wife. Napoleon requested an ecclesiastical annulment of the marriage from *Pius VII and threatened to appeal to the "Gallican Church" in case of an adverse decision, but the Pope declared the marriage valid in the eyes of the Church. The French council of state then annulled the marriage, and its decision was ratified in October 1806 by a servile ecclesiastical commission named by the Emperor.

In August 1806 Jérôme, who was a rear admiral in the navy, was named commander of an army corps in Napoleon's campaign against Prussia. Although he demonstrated a complete ignorance of strategy, he was made a general. Negotiations were begun for his marriage to Catherine, daughter of King Frederick William of Württemberg. In July 1807, by the Treaty of Tilsit, Jérôme was recognized as King of Westphalia, and on Aug. 12, 1807, he was married to Catherine by proxy in Stuttgart, according to the Lutheran rite. A civil registration in France and a Catholic ceremony, celebrated by Karl Theodor von Dalberg, Prince-Archbishop of Mayence, followed.

Jérôme was the spoiled child of the Bonaparte family; his administrative and military talents were at best ordinary. He participated in the campaign against Austria (1809) and Russia (1812), both times without distinction. After the Battle of Leipzig, he fled to Paris. Forced into exile from France in 1814, he returned after Napoleon's escape from Elba and was named a peer. After Waterloo, where he held a command and fought bravely, Jérôme resided at Württemberg, Trieste, Rome, and Florence. He returned to France in 1847 and was placed in charge of the Invalides and appointed marshal of France by his nephew, Louis Napoleon, in 1850. Jérôme, named president of the senate in 1852, occupied a position of distinction under the Second Empire.

Bibliography: *Memoires et correspondance du roi Jérôme et de la reine Catherine,* ed. A. DU CASSE, 7 v. (Paris 1861–66). A. H. ATTERIDGE, *Napoleon's Brothers* (London 1909). W. GEER, *Napoleon and His Family: The Story of a Corsican Clan,* 3 v. (New York 1927–29). T. ARONSON, *The Golden Bees: The Story of the Bonapartes* (Greenwich, Conn. 1964).

[R. W. REICHERT]

BONAPARTE, JOSEPH, eldest brother of *Napoleon I; b. Corte, Corsica, Jan. 7, 1768; d. Florence, Italy, July 28, 1844. He began study for the priesthood at the college in Autun, France, but abandoned it and later studied law at Pisa, Italy. He sought refuge from Paoli's Corsican administration in Marseilles, where he married Julie Clary (August 1794). As ambassador to Rome under the Directory (1797), he was enjoined to guarantee the treaty between Napoleon and *Pius VI, but his actual purpose was to sponsor democratic government in Rome. Following a skirmish between French and papal soldiers, Joseph broke relations with the Holy See, and French troops moved in to establish the Roman Republic. In 1801 Joseph served under the Consulate as French plenipotentiary. He negotiated the treaty of Lunéville with Austria (1801). The French *Concordat of 1801 was signed in his Paris townhouse. Joseph also represented France in the discussions that led to the treaty of Amiens with Britain (1802). As grand elector under the First French Empire, he presided over the senate and council of state in Napoleon's absence. Joseph was King of Naples (1806–08) and King of Spain (1808–13). During the campaign of 1814 he acted as lieutenant general of the Empire. After Waterloo Joseph escaped to the U.S. and established himself as a gentleman farmer at Bordentown, N.J., where he remained until he moved to England (1832). He spent his last days in Florence, where his wife, who had refused to share his exile, rejoined him.

Bibliography: R. M. JOHNSTON, *The Napoleonic Empire in Southern Italy and the Rise of Secret Societies,* 2 v. (London 1904). T. ARONSON, *The Golden Bees: The Story of the Bonapartes* (Greenwich, Conn. 1964). A. H. ATTERIDGE, *Napoleon's Brothers* (London 1909). W. GEER, *Napoleon and His Family: The Story of a Corsican Clan,* 3 v. (New York 1927–29).

[R. W. REICHERT]

BONAPARTE, ST.

Doctor of the Church, cardinal bishop of Albano, minister general of the Friars Minor, scholastic; b. Bagnoregio in the vicinity of Viterbo about 1217; d. Lyons, July 15, 1274.

Life. Little is known of his family; his father, John di Fidanza, seems to have been a doctor of medicine and fairly well-to-do; the name Fidanza is that of Bonaventure's grandfather, not a family name. His mother is usually called Maria di Ritello, sometimes simply Ritella. Bonaventure's baptismal name appears to have been John, and this was changed only on his entry into religious life. While still a boy, Bonaventure himself tells us, he fell gravely ill and was saved from death only through the intercession and merits of St. Francis of Assisi (AnalFranc 10.558, 678). The miracle took place, evidently, after the death and canonization of St. Francis. According to Sixtus IV (1482), he received his primary schooling at the friary in Bagnoregio. He then went to Paris about 1234 where he became a master of arts. Bonaventure had made the acquaintance of the Friars Minor at Paris, and developed a great love and admiration for *Alexander of Hales, who is reported to have commented that in him Adam did not seem to have sinned. Bonaventure's early love for Francis and the concrete example of holiness he met in the Paris friars attracted him to the religious life. He entered the Friars Minor at Paris (probably in 1243), but in accordance with regulations current at the time he was considered a member of the Roman province.

As a Franciscan, most likely while still a novice, Bonaventure began the study of theology under Alexander of Hales and *John of La Rochelle. After their deaths (1245) he continued under *Odo Rigaldus and *William of Melitona. He also came under the influence of the Dominican, Guerric of Saint-Quentin, and the secular master, Guiard of Laon. In 1248 Bonaventure became a bachelor of Scripture and lectured on St. Luke and other sacred books. However, not all his commentaries have survived. After giving his commentary on the *Sentences* of *Peter Lombard (1250–52) he was ready to be presented to the chancellor of the University in 1253 to receive the licentiate and doctorate. Since the chancellor acted in the name of the Church, this gave Bonaventure the right to teach not only at Paris but anywhere in the Christian world. Although some authors claim that he was not accepted into the guild or corporation of the masters of the University as a "magister regens" until Oct. 23, 1257, because of the opposition of the secular masters to the mendicants, there is good reason to believe that Bonaventure had status in the University before that date. Between 1253 and his election as minister general, Feb. 2, 1257, Bonaventure gave at least three series of disputed questions, a task proper to a master.

The strife between masters and mendicants flared up anew in 1254, with the appearance of the *Liber introductorius in evangelium aeternum* by Friar Gerard of Borgo San Donnino. The masters hastily extracted 31 errors from it (including a few not found there) and presented the results to Innocent IV, who died without having taken action. The Pope's successor, Alexander IV, submitted the work to a commission of cardinals and condemned it Oct. 23, 1255 [ChartUn Paris 1.257, 297].

These events were to affect the career of St. Bonaventure. Joachimism had found many adherents among the friars, as Salimbene attests, including even the Minister General John of Parma himself (*see* JOACHIM OF FIORE). Hence Pope Alexander secretly commanded John to resign his office [AnalFranc 3.287]. Accordingly, the general summoned a chapter at Rome for late January 1257 and proposed Bonaventure as his successor, because "he knew no one better than him in the whole Order" [*Chronicle of Salimbene,* ed. O. Holder-Egger (Hanover 1905–13) 310]. Bonaventure was elected on February 2.

Bonaventure's first public act as superior general was

to issue an encyclical letter to the Order from Paris, April 23, 1257. He then set out to present himself to the Pope, meeting Alexander IV at Viterbo after May 13. That he then proceeded to Città della Pieve to try Gerard of Borgo San Donnino and John of Parma has not been proved. The condemnation of Gerard took place at Paris, probably in 1258.

In his first years of office Bonaventure visited a great part of the Order to know its problems and needs. In October 1259 he was at La Verna, where he wrote his "Journey of the Mind to God." This visit appears to have had a profound effect on him. Without ceasing to be the scholastic, he became the mystic as he entered more deeply into the inner life of his Seraphic Father whose life he was to analyze in his "Legend of St. Francis." On his return to France he began to prepare for the chapter of Narbonne (1260) by codifying existing ordinances into a new set of constitutions. Since this chapter charged him to write a new biography of St. Francis, Bonaventure went once more to Italy, to visit the scenes of Francis' life and interview those of the early friars who were still living. He interrupted his work to present himself to the new Pope, Urban IV, elected Aug. 29, 1261. Probably Bonaventure was still in Italy early the next year (some say 1263), and was forced to submit John of Parma to a trial at Città della Pieve because of his continued adherence to Joachimism. On April 8, 1263, he was at Padua for the translation of the relics of St. Anthony; at Pentecost, on May 20 he was at Pisa for a general chapter important for the introduction of a series of about 40 liturgical statutes and rubrics that "conclude half a century of intense liturgical activity in the order." Bonaventure presented a copy of his new *Legenda* of St. Francis to each of the 34 provincials present. He was at the papal court in 1264 and 1265, preaching before a consistory of Urban IV, Aug. 31, 1264, and probably delivering his "Sermon on the Blessed Sacrament." He was at Perugia in March 1265, to present himself to Urban's successor, Clement IV. Late that year, November 24, Clement nominated him archbishop of York.

At the general chapter at Paris, May 16, 1266, Bonaventure took measures to correct abuses in the Order, especially in matters of poverty. Among the "definitions" or decrees of this chapter was the famous ruling that since the minister general had provided a new legend of St. Francis, all other legends or biographies were to be destroyed [ArchFrancHist 7 (1914) 678]. A similar regulation had been made in 1260 by the Dominicans after the Master General, *Humbert of Romans, had compiled a new legend of St. Dominic (AnalFranc 10.lxxiii).

Bonaventure remained in residence at a small friary at Mantes-sur-Seine, France, until mid-1268. Some of his ascetical writings probably date from this period. He frequently preached at the University, often touching on some of the religious and philosophical troubles that disturbed faculties and students. In particular, his Lenten conferences of 1267, on the Ten Commandments, and those of 1268, on the gifts of the Holy Spirit, castigated current trends. These sermons bore fruit in 1270, when Stephen Tempier, Bishop of Paris, condemned 16 errors prevalent at Paris. By July 8, 1268, Bonaventure was in Rome, where he received the Archconfraternity of the Gonfalonieri into spiritual communion with the Order [ArchFrancHist 17 (1924) 448–453]. He re-

mained in Italy until the chapter of Assisi, May 12, 1269 [*op. cit.* 7 (1914) 679–680]. On his return to Paris, he was faced with the new attack against the mendicants led by Master Gerard of Abbeville, whose work "Against the Adversary of Christian Perfection" (1269) Bonaventure refuted in "The Apology of the Poor" early in 1270. Before June 12 he was in Lyons for the general chapter, perhaps remaining there until early the next year. In the spring of 1273, his last sojourn in Paris was highlighted by the remarkable "Conferences on the Hexaëmeron," which were never completed.

Gregory X created him cardinal bishop of Albano, when in a consistory before Pentecost he provided for the five vacant suburbicarian sees [for details, see M. H. Laurent, *Le Bx. Innocent V (Pierre de Tarentaise) et son temps,* (StTest 129; 1947) 134–144]. Bonaventure met the Pope at Mugello, north of Florence, after mid-July and proceeded with him to Lyons, the scene of a coming council. Here he was consecrated bishop November 11 or 12, and until May 1274, Bonaventure, as legate *a latere,* helped the Pope prepare for the Second Council of Lyons, which opened May 7. Bonaventure preached at an extraordinary session after the arrival of a letter from the Greek ambassadors, May 28, and again in the actual presence of the Greeks, June 29. He probably presided at several meetings between the Greek delegates and the Latins.

In the midst of such activity Bonaventure died unexpectedly on July 15. He was buried the same day in the Franciscan church, in the presence of the Pope; the next day, at the fifth session of the Council, the Pope ordered all priests of the world to celebrate a Mass for his soul.

The impression Bonaventure made on his contemporaries is summed up in the *Brevis Notitia* of the Council. "At the funeral there was much sorrow and tears; for the Lord had given him this grace, that all who saw him were filled with an immense love for him." Nevertheless, his canonization did not take place until April 14, 1482, a delay occasioned partly by internal strife within the Order, the attitude of the Spirituals, the Western Schism, partly too (as Sixtus IV hints), by lack of interest on the part of the Order and of ecclesiastical and secular princes. Sixtus IV himself took the initiative and after a long process enrolled him "among the saintly confessor Bishops and Doctors," with the Mass and Office of a Confessor Bishop and Doctor. A century later, March 14, 1588, another Franciscan pope, Sixtus V, made a new and solemn declaration on the doctorate of Bonaventure, ranking him among the "primary doctors." St. Pius V had made Thomas the fifth Doctor; Bonaventure was now made the sixth with the title "Doctor Seraphicus." This title was already an old one, though "Doctor Devotus" was even earlier. William of Vaurouillon uses "Doctor Devotus" in his *Sentences* (1429–30) and "Doctor Devotus seu Seraphicus" in his *Liber de anima* (c. 1450). Yet it appears that neither title was known to Thomas of Rossy at Paris in 1373 (BiblFranSchMA 16.31–99).

Theological Doctrine. Although in the prologue to his *Breviloquium* (5.201–208) Bonaventure proposes "the finest program of scriptural study in the 13th century" [M. D. Chenu, *La théologie comme science au xiii° siècle* (Paris 1957) 54], he is primarily a scholastic theologian. Sacred Scripture is never far from his mind, yet his thought and system are within the framework

St. Bonaventure, detail of a wing to an altarpiece by the "Master of the Glorification of Mary," in the Wallraf-Richartz Museum, Cologne, Germany.

and technique of Peter Lombard's *Sentences,* which Alexander of Hales had made the theological textbook at Paris. In keeping with this new trend, Bonaventure is careful to distinguish between the object of faith as such, the *credibile;* that same object as explained

through the authority of Scripture; and the *credibile* as investigated by the use of reason in theology proper. The latter method proceeds by the way of inquiry (*modus inquisitivus*), since to the truth of faith and the authority of Scripture it adds reasons that probe and bolster our belief, helping us understand it and thus delight in it [*S. Bonaventurae Opera Omnia,* 10 v. (Quarrachi 1882–1902) 1.7 and 11; subsequent reference to the *Opera Omnia* will be made simply by volume and page numbers]. In a word, says Bonaventure, "the credible as intelligible" is the subject of the theologian, who uses not only logic but all the profane sciences to penetrate the data of the faith. By reason of such a goal, the theologian borrows from philosophy whatever he may need to give a full account of God, man, and the world as viewed with the eyes of faith (5.205a). The theology that is the result is much broader in content than that which is included under that title today. Philosophy does not stand in contrast to theology, but is incorporated into it, as Bonaventure demonstrates in his consideration of the being of angels and of the human soul (2.97).

While Bonaventure knew something of Platonism and more of Aristotle, neither satisfied for him the demands of Christian theology (5.572a). His conscious choice is the philosophical doctrines provided by Augustine or proposed in his name. But what Bonaventure considered a faithful reproduction and development of the authentic doctrine of Augustine was in reality a specifically scholastic system (*see* AUGUSTINIANISM), a synthesis based not only on the thought of Augustine but also on that of Pseudo-Dionysius, John Damascene, Boethius, Aristotle, Avicebron, and others. The more Bonaventure is considered in the historical context and milieu of the mid-13th century, the more his thought is seen as the flower and fruit of the older scholastic traditions, which he not only adopted but perfected and organized into a fresh synthesis.

Doctrine on God. This trend is immediately evident in Bonaventure's approach to the existence of God and in his theology of the Trinity. The three ways by which he proves that God's existence (*Deum esse*) is undeniable (1.155a; 5.45–51) can be traced back proximately to Alexander of Hales and more remotely to earlier scholastic traditions. By both authority and reason the first way shows that this truth has been impressed on all rational minds: John Damascene, Hugh of Saint-Victor, Boethius, Augustine, and Aristotle are called upon to witness the mind's "natural appetite, knowledge and memory of Him to whose image it has been made" (5.45–46, 49). Even the idolater acknowledges God's existence, while he errs about what God is. The second proof, that "every creature cries out that God is" (5.46b), is derived from an examination of the conditions and properties of finite being. The third is an adaptation both of Anselm's argument in the *Proslogion* and of Augustine's proof from truth. Yet in the final analysis, these three ways are less demonstrations than so many stimuli that make man aware of his almost immediate intuition of God in any knowledge of creatures (5.51a, 325b). Moreover, the whole man, not the intellect alone, is involved in the quest for God. Love is able to penetrate beyond what the intellect attains (3.689a); and far more noble and delightful is the knowledge of God through love than that acquired by mere force of reasoning (3.775a).

The genius of St. Bonaventure as well as his dependence on his predecessors is evident in the theology of the Trinity elaborated at length not only in his commentary on the first book of the *Sentences* but also in a disputed question (5.51–115) and in the *Breviloquium* (5.210–218). Following the tradition of Alexander and Odo Rigaldus, he does not make use of the principles of St. Augustine, as did Peter Lombard before him and St. Thomas after him, but chooses rather the doctrine of Richard of Saint-Victor, itself inspired by the Greek traditions of Pseudo-Dionysius. Accordingly, the Dionysian axiom that the good is self-diffusive (*bonum est diffusivum sui*) leads Bonaventure to conceive of the divine essence as infinitely good and active, an overflowing fountain of life, which gives rise to two processions, one *per modum naturae* (as contrasted to St. Thomas' *per modum intellectus*) in the generation of the Son, the other *per modum voluntatis* in the spiration of the Holy Spirit. The constitution and distinction of the Persons seems to be due more to their origins or processions than to their relations, though Bonaventure is hesitant on this. What makes his synthesis original and influential, however, is the central place given to the idea of *primitas* (firstness), as characteristic of the First Person: the Father is first not only in the sense that He does not proceed from any other, but above all because He is the original source (*plenitudo fontalis*) in whom the other two Divine Persons have their principle, reason, and root (1.470–472; 5.114).

Christology. In Christology Bonaventure advances little beyond his predecessors, at least in the great questions concerning the Incarnation. Yet he does develop at some length the perfections of the human nature in Christ. As the concept of *plenitudo originalis* had played an important role in his doctrine on the Trinity, here the doctrine of the fullness of the special gifts, the *plenitudo charismatum,* in the soul of Christ occupies the center of his thought (5.245). In particular, the question of the human knowledge of Christ receives extraordinary attention. Notable progress is clear between the time of his commentary on the *Sentences* (3.306–317) to his disputed question "On the knowledge of Christ" (5.37–43), and from this to the final though brief statements in the *Breviloquium* (5.246–247). At the same time, the Word Incarnate is the constant theme of many sermons and spiritual treatises, which often present a concrete and practical form of Christology, especially on the inner life of Christ [see A. Sepinski, *La Psychologie du Christ chez S. Bonaventure* (Paris 1948)].

Mariology. Again, Bonaventure's Mariology is traditional, yet reveals his personal touch, especially in his portrayal of Mary's place in the life of a Christian. Her privileges stem from her role as the Mother of God and the spiritual Mother of mankind [cf. E. Chiettini, *Mariologia S. Bonaventurae* (Rome 1941)].

Creator and Creatures. In what may be called his Christian metaphysics Bonaventure is influenced by both Augustine and Pseudo-Dionysius. With Augustine, Bonaventure makes philosophy a step in man's return to God. With Dionysius, he gives a certain cyclic character to his synthesis: "Only then can a man have a true understanding of things when he considers how they originate from God (as their efficient cause), how they are brought back to God as their end, and how God as exemplar cause is reflected in them" (5.343).

Things have come from God alone, without intermediaries, by creation out of nothing, and in time (5.219). Such a truth, which was beyond the ken of the philosophers, is assured us by faith; yet once known by faith, it can be proved by reason (2.16–17). In his confidence in the possibility of rational proof, Bonaventure is much more optimistic than either St. Thomas or John Duns Scotus. Because creation is not emanation, things are radically distinct from God, essentially contingent and dependent, and therefore composed.

For reasons as yet unknown, Bonaventure adopted the theory of a composition of matter and form in all creatures. In the angels (2.89–101) and in the human soul (2.413–416), besides the types of composition advocated by Alexander of Hales and John of La Rochelle, he posited a spiritual, nonextended matter to explain their changeableness and individuation. At the same time, this does not preclude the substantial union of soul and body (2.415b).

Things of creation reflect God because they have been created according to the divine ideas, the eternal forms or exemplars (*rationes exemplares*) in the Word, the eternal "Art" of the Father (5.343, 426). For Bonaventure, "the world of creatures is like a book in which the triune Creator is reflected and made present to us." Creatures are so many stepping stones by which the human mind can rise to the First Principle of all (5.320). Not all creation mirrors God in the same degree; while every creature reflects Him as the Cause of all, man alone is His image, since he alone can have God as the object of his memory, intellect, and will (2.394–395). Long familiar to the followers of St. Augustine, this doctrine allows Bonaventure to attain a "trinitarian" view of the universe and indeed of the whole course of history. As a result, for the man whose eyes are enlightened by faith as well as by reason, the world becomes a path that leads man to God, while through him "all material creation is brought back to its Creator." The full return can be accomplished only by faith and by grace (5.298a), yet reason and philosophy offer partial help in the "Journey of the Mind to God," by the knowledge they give of the sensible world as the "footprint" (*vestigium*) of its Maker, and of the nature of the mind itself, its powers and activities as the image of its Creator. From these preliminary steps the mind can rise to that which is eternal and spiritual, the First Principle, as Being and Goodness (5.297). The dialectic of this return is inspired by Augustine's doctrine of contemplation (see below); its details are drawn in large measure from Richard of Saint-Victor.

Essential to this return, at least in the ultimate steps wherein man reaches the knowledge of God, is the Bonaventuran doctrine of illumination. Convinced that the light of eternal truth, of which Augustine spoke so often (see 5.17–18, 23a, etc.), had a real part to play in man's quest for certitude, Bonaventure elaborated a metaphysics of knowledge in which illumination is considered as the divine concursus or cooperation given the soul precisely when it acts as the image of God (5.24a, 571b–572a). Such illumination is not concerned with the infusion of concepts or with knowledge (*cognitio scientiae*) acquired through the senses (5.572a). It is not required for the lower sciences, for a knowledge of things in themselves that is drawn from things (6.7b). It is required by both the object known and the knowing subject when the mind is searching for immutable truth and certain knowledge. Since created things have being and truth by participation and not by their very essence, their truth or intelligibility, without the presence and support of divine truth, is not sufficient to yield certitude (1.639a; 5.23, 569a). On the other hand, the human intellect, despite its natural light and ability (2.903a), is subject as a creature to a certain instability and fallibility, overcome by the presence and action of the divine ideas (5.24a, 569b). Man is no more conscious of this than he is of God's cooperation with his acts as a "footprint" of God or with his supernatural actions as the "likeness" of God. Nonetheless, the divine "eternal reasons" concur in his actions as image, to stabilize (*regulans*) both object and intellect and to move (*motiva*) the mind to assent to the truth (5.23b). But man's acts as the image of God are primarily those that turn him to God as object (1.83b; 5.304). Illumination, therefore, is to be found precisely in those acts of knowledge whereby the soul rises from the creature to the Creator, as in analyzing the implications of created being (*resolutio plena*) it comes to understand that being through and in the light of the First Being (1.504). "Our intellect does not make a full and ultimate analysis of any single created being unless it is aided by a knowledge of the most pure, most actual, most complete and absolute Being, which is Being unqualified and eternal, in whom are the essences of all things in their purity" (5.304a). Thus to be able to understand the being of creatures in its full significance, the mind needs the regulative and motivating action of the "eternal ratio" of being (*ibid.,* and 308–310), as in the "second way" of showing the existence of God (5.46–47). Briefly, when our intellect by its own light knows a truth drawn from creatures, the uncreated truth assists the intellect by a higher light to reach a more perfect knowledge of that created truth through its eternal principle in God.

Spiritual Life. Even in his own lifetime Bonaventure was regarded as a master of the spiritual life who stirred all Europe by his love of the Passion and by his desire to draw all men to a higher life. His doctrine, which must be pieced together from many writings and sermons, carries the stamp of one who is a mystic himself and knows whereof he speaks. Sometimes his thought is complicated; yet he preached his spiritual doctrine to all, whether to Louis the King (9.69b), to religious, or to the simple faithful (9.269b), in the conviction that, though the heights of mysticism are rarely attained (5.347a), every just man should strive for the contemplative knowledge of God. If God gives something beyond this, such as rapture, it is by special privilege, but contemplation is for all (2.546a).

Role of Grace. Mystical theology is not a separate science but that part of theology which teaches man's return to God and elucidates the role of grace and its ramifications in that return, and the cooperation man must give on the threefold way of purgation, illumination, and perfection (5.298a; 7.349b). For Bonaventure, as for St. Bernard (PL 183:1166), the soul in need of grace is aptly compared to the woman of the gospel (Lk 13.11–13) who "was bent over and utterly unable to look upward" but was "made straight" when Christ laid His hands upon her (9.46a). "Bent over" by original sin, man was delivered to ignorance in mind, rebellion in will, and concupiscence in the flesh (2.3–6; 5.234–235). Only through the grace of Jesus Christ (5.253–254) can man be put in proper order again to God. If

he had been created through the Eternal Word, his re-creation can be effected only by the Incarnate Word.

The grace of Christ is indeed a new creation (5.255a), a new life whereby the soul is made the spouse of Christ, the daughter of the Eternal Father, the temple of the Holy Spirit. By it the soul is purged, enlightened, and perfected; vivified, reformed, and made stable; elevated, made like to God, and joined to Him (2.635a; 5.252a). Many of these effects Bonaventure prefers to attach to what he calls the "ramifications" of grace, viz, the virtues, the gifts, and the beatitudes. The infused virtues "rectify" the powers of the soul, enabling them to act aright: the theological virtues by putting the intelligence, memory, and will in right order to God; the cardinal virtues by directing the reason and the appetites in the fulfillment of man's duties to self and neighbor (5.256b). The gifts of the Spirit are intended to add a certain suppleness to a vigorous practice of the virtues and the Christlife, to achieve an *operatio expedita* (3.741a) in acting and suffering for Christ; while the beatitudes, which are habits like the virtues and the gifts, are for the perfection of the soul, enabling it to act and suffer perfectly (5.258–259). The Sacraments, finally, heal the soul (*sanatio animae*) of all faults and daily defects and help the virtues, gifts, and beatitudes to achieve their effects. In particular, Confirmation and the Eucharist fortify faith and charity, on the firm foundation of which the whole structure of the spiritual life depends (4.176b).

Man's Response. In meriting these graces by His Passion and Death, Christ exercised three "hierarchic" acts, acts which reestablished and ordered man's supernatural life toward God: He purged away our guilt, He enlightened us by leaving us an example, and He perfected us by enabling us to follow in His footsteps (9.296–300, 58a, 388a). In response, the Christian must posit three hierarchic acts by which he will be purged from the malice of sin, enlightened by the word of Christ's teaching, and fed or made perfect by the food of the Eucharist (9.388a) and of contemplation. These are the "three ways," which occupy so central a place in Bonaventure's spiritual theology: "the purgative way, which consists in the expulsion of sin; the illuminative way, in the imitation of Christ; and the unitive way, in the reception of the Spouse" (8.12a). These are not interpreted as successive states of the spiritual life, but are rather three series of acts or spiritual exercises ordered to the acquisition of the three elements of Christian perfection: inner peace of conscience, the perfect following of Christ, and the flowering of grace in mystical union. The practice of such hierarchic acts is required simultaneously at all stages of the spiritual life. They are distinguished less in time than in their respective goals and in the activities and powers of the soul found in each. The prick of conscience (*stimulus conscientiae*) motivates the purgative way, the light of the intellect (*radius intelligentiae*) the illuminative way, and the fine flame of wisdom (*igniculus sapientiae*) the unitive (8.3). In each of the ways the principal exercises will be meditation, prayer, and contemplation.

In the purgative way the Christian is concerned primarily with eradicating the effects of original and actual sin in order to attain inner peace. The illuminative way is more positive in character, as guided by the light of the intelligence the soul seeks to understand and imitate Him who is Truth Incarnate. It is "the way of progress characterized by the imitation of Christ" (5.258b), wherein meditation, prayer, and contemplation are directed to a deeper knowledge and appreciation of the Incarnation and the whole divine economy of salvation. The unitive way is marked by greater activity on the part of grace and passivity on the part of the soul. It is a way attained by the few, not so much because of the extraordinary character of the grace of union as because of a lack of generosity (8.120b). Only the generous man, whose powers of intellect and will are purified, who has detached himself from creatures (5.129b) and become humble, simple, and poor (5.430b), a man of constant ardent prayer (5.297a; 8.502b), is properly disposed to that union which is attained in the contemplation proper to the unitive way.

Bonaventure does not provide a comprehensive definition of contemplation, chiefly because it is found in various forms in each way and is not reserved primarily to the third stage. He recognizes two types coming from two distinct traditions: Augustine teaches an ascent to the peak of contemplation *per viam splendoris,* through the intellectual contemplation of truth; Dionysius, an ascent *per viam amoris,* in experimental knowledge and "tasting" of the divine (7.232a; 8.16b). Intellectual contemplation, rooted in the gift of understanding (3.779a), fills the first chapters of "The Journey of the Mind to God," where in six steps the mind proceeds from the "footprints" of God in things without to the image of God within itself and thence upward "through the light that shines upon our mind" to God Himself. This ascent awakens such admiration and wonder that the soul is caught up in an ecstasy of the understanding (*mentis excessus*) (5.312a) wherein the mind is carried out of itself to the object (5.40a) while the will is inflamed with love (5.427b). The Dionysian contemplation is achieved through the gift of wisdom; partly cognitive, partly affective, it begins in knowledge but is consummated in the affections of the will (3.774). While affirmation marks the Augustinian ascent, sapiential contemplation is primarily negational in character (8.17b), since the soul comes to know God as above all that is sensible, intelligible, existential, and is carried into the "darkness of the mind." Here the mind (or better, the memory as the *apex mentis*) understands not and yet is perfectly illuminated in a certain "learned ignorance" (5.260a, 312–313), in an experiential knowledge of God and most intimate union (3.531b). Beyond such ecstasy is rapture, an extraordinary grace and privilege, in a kind of passing "act of glory," the ultimate union possible in this life (5.348a).

These two traditions do not remain separate and distinct in Bonaventure's mystical theology; they merge at the peak, in ecstasy and the ecstatic knowledge of God (see DictSpirAscMyst 4.2:2120–26). Bonaventure has before him, as a living model, the figure of St. Francis (and to a lesser extent Brother Giles of Assisi), the perfect ecstatic, his "guide and father," whose vision of the Seraph on La Verna "pointed out the way by which the heights of contemplation could be reached" (5.295).

Religious and Franciscan Life. Bonaventure is often called the second founder of the Franciscan Order, not because of any reforms or legislation, but primarily by reason of his theology of religious life, his analysis of the life and ideals of St. Francis, and the practical application he made of those ideals in his writings and in his own life. The *Apologia Pauperum,* for example, is

far less a refutation of the absurd and even heretical opinions of Gerard of Abbeville than a positive theology of the Christian and religious life as the imitation of Christ. To show how Christ is the model of all perfection, Bonaventure has recourse to his theology of exemplarism. As the eternal and uncreated Word of the Father is the exemplar according to which the world is made (5.343, 426), so the Incarnate Word is in His human life and actions the pattern and mirror of all graces, virtues, and merits. From that one eternal Exemplar come all the different natures of creatures. Because no one creature can fully express the perfection of that Model, God has created many species of things that share in diverse ways in that Highest Good. In like manner, from the Word Incarnate as the source of grace and mirror of all holiness and wisdom come the varied states of the Christian life, the grades and orders of the Mystical Body. The perfection of Christ is found in each; yet to no one of them nor to any individual does Christ impart such graces that they can fully reflect His plenitude or imitate Him completely. As a result, there are many degrees in which Christ is imitated (8.242–245). Religious life, whereby "a wayfarer is conformed to Christ by such a habit of virtue that in a supererogatory way he avoids what is evil, does what is good, and willingly and joyfully suffers all for Christ" (8.245), varies within the Church because no one order can fully copy the perfections of Christ. Yet despite the differences, which make for the beauty and variety of the Church (8.250a), each order is a school of perfection that seeks to make its members like Christ in mind and conduct. (8.142–3). Every element of religious life in some way contributes to make the religious conformed to Christ. If Christ took no vows (as William of Saint-Amour had objected), nonetheless the three basic vows are ways of imitating Him: "In Christ there was something more excellent than any vow, His human will confirmed and centered on the Father. In imitation of that will we vow poverty, chastity and obedience, and thus, by binding and strengthening us, the vows make us conformed to Christ" (5.187b).

In the life, rule, and Order of Francis of Assisi Bonaventure found a concrete example of such Christcenteredness. The founder's life had been one of slow growth in likeness to Christ, with the stigmata as the outward sign and fruit of such conformity: "Worthily indeed did this blessed man appear marked with this singular privilege, since his whole life was centered on the Cross." Above all, Bonaventure stresses the mission God gave Francis in the Church. Against the Joachimites among the friars, who saw Francis as the herald of a new Church in the reign of the Spirit, Bonaventure sees him as the "angel [messenger] ascending from the rising of the sun, having the seal of the living God" (Apoc 7.2), who is the herald of a new age of repentance and renewal within the Church (9.593b). This too was the purpose of the Order and the rule. "Filled with the Spirit of God and afire with love of God and neighbor, Francis was possessed of a threefold desire: to imitate Christ as completely as possible in all the virtues, to cleave to God in constant contemplation, and to win to God the souls for whom Christ had suffered and died." But because no existing rule embodied this threefold goal, taught by the Holy Spirit Francis composed a new rule that would direct his sons in the footsteps of Christ in both the apostolic and the contemplative life, in such poverty as would give them freedom of spirit to ascend to the heights of prayer and yet embrace the whole world in their quest for souls (8.338). Given such an approach, Bonaventure himself, as general of the order, was less inclined to stress external regulations than to build up the inner spirit of prayer and devotion and to create right attitudes by holding up before the friars the example of Christ (8.499–503; 9.579a) and of St. Francis (9.580a).

Influence. Among the scholastics of the 13th century Bonaventure exerted an immediate and lasting influence, as is witnessed by the use made of his commentary on the *Sentences* and on other works by *Walter of Bruges, *John Pecham, and *Matthew of Aquasparta, for whom he was model and master even when they sometimes went their own way in clarifying positions he had left unsettled. His influence continued even with the rise of the Scotist school, since many thought they could supplement the metaphysics of John Duns Scotus with the more practical teachings of the Seraphic Schoolman. Later, most Observant Friars were Scotists, while the Conventuals did much to maintain Bonaventure's influence through the Roman College of St. Bonaventure, founded in 1587 by Sixtus V. The Capuchins were inclined from the beginning to follow Bonaventure, first as a Franciscan and mystic, and then as a philosopher and theologian [cf. CollFran 1 (1931) 184–214, 360–374; FrancStudies 6 (1946) 332–349].

In mystical theology Bonaventure has always been regarded as "the prince par excellence who leads us by the hand to God" (Leo XIII). From the 13th century the devout turned to him as guide and teacher of the spiritual life, especially in northern Europe, Germany and the Netherlands. The *Devotio moderna* and the *Imitation of Christ* owe much to him [FranzStud 15 (1928) 294–315]. M. Grabmann and, later, K. Ruh have presented in detail the position Bonaventure occupied in medieval Germany not only among the friars, but also among the Dominicans, Carthusians, Brothers of the Common Life, and many lay people. This was effected partly by the original Latin works but more perhaps through numerous translations, especially of the *De Triplici Via* [K. Ruh, *Bonaventura deutsch* (Bern 1956)].

Bibliography: Works. *Itinerarium mentis in Deum*, tr. as *The Franciscan Vision*, tr. J. O'MAHONEY (London 1937); *The Mind's Road to God*, tr. G. BOAS (New York 1953); *Itinerarium mentis in Deum*, tr. P. BOEHNER (St. Bonaventure, N.Y. 1956); *The Works of Bonaventure*, tr. J. DE VINCK, 2 v. (Paterson 1960) v.1.; *Breviloquium*, tr. E. E. NEMMERS (St. Louis 1946); *De reductione artium ad theologiam*, tr. E. T. HEALY (2d ed. St. Bonaventure, N.Y. 1955). E. R. FAIRWEATHER, ed. and tr., *A Scholastic Miscellany: Anselm to Ockham* (The Library of Christian Classics 10; Philadelphia 1956) deals with question on illumination. Ascetical and mystical works. *De triplici via* in DE VINCK, *op. cit.; Holiness of Life (De perfectione vitae ad Sorores)*, tr. L. COSTELLO (St. Louis 1923); *The Virtues of a Religious Superior (De sex alis Seraphim)*, tr. S. MOLLITOR (St. Louis 1920); *Franciscan View of the Spiritual and Religious Life (De sex alis Seraphim)*, tr. D. DEVAS (New York 1922); *The Life of Saint Francis*, tr. E. GURNEY-SALTER (London 1904); *The Life of St. Francis of Assisi*, tr. MISS LOCKHART (4th ed. London 1898); *Short Life of St. Francis*, abr. A. PRITCHARD (London 1936). Studies. E. H. GILSON, *Die philosophie des heiligen Bonaventura*, ed. P. A. SCHLÜTER (2d ed. Cologne 1960). J. G. BOUGEROL, *Introduction à l'étude de saint Bonaventure* (Paris 1962). S. CLASEN, *Franziskus, Engel des sechten Siegels* (Werl, Ger. 1962) the most recent study of his life and Franciscanism. **Illustration credit:** Rheinisches Bildarchiv, Köln.

[I. C. BRADY]

BONCOMPAGNI, BALTHASAR, Italian mathematician and historian; b. Rome, May 10, 1821; d. Rome, April 13, 1894. Boncompagni, a member of the *Accademia pontificia de' Nuovo Lincei*, became known through his publication of *Scritti di Leonardo Pisano* (Rome 1857–62). His greatest contribution was his *Bulletino di bibliografia e storia scienze mathematische e fisiche* (Rome 1868–87), a collection of a great number of mathematical documents, which he published at his own expense. The *Bulletino* was the first organ of the history of mathematics. It has remained a standard reference and has been reprinted. Its value lies in its use of primary sources and in its precision of documentation.

Before the *Bulletino*, Boncompagni published a number of essays including "Della vita e delle opere di Gherardo Cremonese tradutore del secolo XII" (Rome 1850) and "Dissertazione intorno ad un trattato di aritmetica stampato nel 1478."

Bibliography: R. C. ARCHIBALD, "Outline of the History of Mathematics," *American Mathematical Monthly* 56 (Jan. 1949) pt. 2. F. CAJORI, *A History of Elementary Mathematics* (rev. ed. New York 1917). P. PASCHINI, EncCatt 2:1849–50. G. LORIA, *Storia delle matematiche*, 3 v. (Turin 1929–33). G. SARTON, *The Study of the History of Mathematics* (Cambridge, Mass. 1936). D. E. SMITH, *History of Mathematics*, 2 v. (New York 1951–53).

[T. À K. KLOYDA]

BONDOLFI, PIETRO, founder of the *Bethlehem Fathers; b. Rome, April 10, 1872; d. Immensee (Schwyz), Switzerland, June 27, 1943. Bondolfi, who had been orphaned in 1882, was ordained in 1896 after seminary studies in Chur, Switzerland. He gained a doctorate in Canon Law after studies at Innsbruck and Rome. At Louvain he won a licentiate in economics (1898). He was appointed archivist of the Diocese of Chur, and in 1900 served in the parish of St. Moritz. In 1904 Bondolfi was named canonical visitor of the apostolic school of Bethlehem in Immensee, founded by Peter Barral to educate priests for missions and poor dioceses. During a financial crisis in 1907 Bondolfi was appointed director of the school. In this position he placed the school on a sound financial basis, dedicated it to the Sacred Heart, and infused it with a new spirit. Pius X suggested that the school become a missionary institute, but the plan was not put into effect until 1921, when Bondolfi became the first superior general of the Bethlehem Fathers. He served in this office until his death. Throughout Switzerland he promoted interest in the missions, especially through the monthly periodical *Bethlehem*. In 1924 he sent his first missionaries to China. At his death the institute had four foundations in Switzerland. Bondolfi revealed his spirituality in the booklet *Der Geist des Kindes von Bethlehem* (1938).

Bibliography: *Bethlehem* (1946) 7–87, biog. of Bondolfi; an Eng. monthly issued by the Bethlehem Fathers. A. RUST, *Die Bethlehem-Missionare Immensee* (Fribourg 1961). G. B. TRAGELLA, EncCatt 2:1851–52.

[A. J. BORER]

BONET, JUAN PABLO, Spanish priest, statesman, teacher, and author whose writing on the education of the deaf is still influential; b. Jaca (Huesca), c. 1560; d. c. 1620. He received a thorough, Catholic education and became a courtier, sent abroad by the King on important diplomatic missions. His most significant contribution, however, was in the field of deaf-mute education. His interest was aroused by his deaf-mute brother and by the prevalence of the condition among the aristocracy, where it affected the inheritance of titles and estates. He established the Municipal Institute for deaf-mutes in Barcelona and his book, *Reducción de las letras y arte de enseñar a hablar a los mudos* (Madrid 1620), regarded as the literary foundation of the education of the deaf, was translated into all European languages. Ponce de León (16th century), the first recorded teacher of the deaf, aimed chiefly at speech; Bonet sought complete education and was the first to use lipreading. In 1926 Barcelona erected a monument to both men.

Bibliography: K. W. Hodgson, *The Deaf and Their Problems* (London 1953). A. Gonzalez, *Pérfiles Sociológicos de Sordomudos: El Método Oral* (Madrid 1924).

[S. A. JANTO]

BONET, NICHOLAS, theologian; b. Tours, France, *c.* 1280; d. perhaps Malta, before Oct. 27, 1343. He was a Franciscan, and a disciple of John *Duns Scotus at Paris where Bonet taught for many years. Philip VI made him his private chaplain and authorized him to examine *John XXII's teaching on the beatific vision. Benedict XII sent him as his legate (1338) to Kublai, the Great Khan of the Tartars, and Clement VI named him bishop of Malta (1342). He was not able to complete his term as legate and was bishop of Malta for but a short time. His influence was greatly felt through his writings: *Theologia naturalis* (Venice 1505), *Formalitates in via Scoti* (Venice 1489).

Bibliography: F. O'Briain, DHGE 9:849–852. G. Odoardi, EncCatt 2:1853. T. Barth, LexThK² 7:982.

[G. ODOARDI]

BONFRÈRE, JACQUES, Biblical scholar; b. Dinant, now in Belgium, April 12, 1573; d. Tournai, now in Belgium, May 9, 1642. In 1592 he became a Jesuit, and he taught for many years at Scots College, *Douai, now in France. He wrote commentaries on the Pentateuch (Antwerp 1625) and on Josue, Judges, and Ruth (Paris 1631). In the latter volume he added as an appendix his edition of Jerome's translation of Eusebius's *Onomasticon urbium et locorum S. Scripturae,* which was republished by R. J. de Tournemine in his edition of Menochius's commentary (Paris 1719). The *Praeloquia* (introduction) to his commentary on the Pentateuch, treating of the Bible as a whole, was selected by J. P. *Migne as the most suitable introduction for his *Scripturae S. Cursus* (Paris 1839) 1:5–242. Although scientific methodology was unknown to him and the selection of his topics was largely governed by the current controversies, his erudition was extensive and included a good grasp of Hebrew and Biblical geography. He did not, however, distinguish clearly between inspiration and revelation, and certain ideas of his, e.g., on the possibility of inspiration subsequent to composition, did not find favor with other theologians.

Bibliography: Sommervogel 1:1713–15. Hurter Nomencl 3: 1033–35. A. Poncelet, *Histoire de la Compagnie de Jésus dans les anciens Pays-Bas* (Brussels 1928).

[L. F. HARTMAN]

BONIFACE, ST.

Archbishop of Mainz, apostle of Germany; b. Wessex, England, between 672 and 675; d. Dokkum, Frisia, June 5, 754 (feast, June 5). According to *Willibald of Mainz (*Vita* 1.1), Winfrid (Wynfrid, later Boniface) was entrusted at first to *Benedictines at Exeter as a result of the serious illness of his father and was later sent to Nursling between Winchester and Southampton, where the learned Wynbercht was abbot. Here Winfrid imbibed *Anglo-Saxon monastic ideals: love for learning, for Rome, and for missionary activity (*peregrinatio pro Christo*). He entered the Benedictine monastery at Nursling, was ordained, and became director of its monastic school. Willibald claims that Winfrid was an orator (*ibid.* 1.4), undertook a mission for King *Ine of Wessex (688–725) to Archbishop Berchtwald of *Canterbury (692–731), and was called upon to attend several synods (*ibid.*). Winfrid wrote a Latin grammar and numerous poems (Manitius 1: 149–   ).

Missionary Career. When Winfrid was about 40 he secured the permission of his abbot to evangelize in Frisia (716), a part of the Frankish kingdom since its conquest in 689 by Pepin II. After Pepin's death Frisia became the scene of a revolt led by Duke Radbod and of a widespread rejection of Christianity. *Willibrord of Utrecht, apostle of Frisia (690–739), withdrew temporarily, and it was under these unfavorable conditions that Winfrid attempted an apostolate, even visiting Radbod, who did not actually forbid missionary activity. But Winfrid realized that the time was not ripe and returned to Nursling probably in the same year (716). On the death of his abbot in 717, he was elected to succeed him but relinquished the office in 718 for the purpose of visiting Rome to beg for a mission from the Pope; his request was backed by a letter of recommendation from Bp. Daniel of Winchester. He journeyed from London to La Canche, Quentovic (in Frisia), and thence with a group of pilgrims to Rome, where he was received several times by *Gregory II (715–731). On May 15, 719, the Pope gave him a letter assigning to him broad missionary jurisdiction among the pagans and urging the Roman formula of baptism and recourse to Rome in every difficulty. At the same time Gregory changed Winfrid's name to Boniface in honor of the martyr whose feast had been celebrated the day before. (Willibrord's name had been similarly changed to Clement.)

Boniface went first to Thuringia, where he preached to the leaders of the people and tried to reform the incontinent and partly pagan clergy. The death of Radbod in 719 and Boniface's desire to familiarize himself with Willibrord's missionary methods attracted him again to Frisia, where he worked for several years (719–722?). Willibrord would gladly have made him his auxiliary bishop, but Boniface wanted an independent sphere of activity in view of his Roman commission. Probably in 721 he left Frisia for Hesse, the most pagan area he evangelized. Assisted by two Christian nobles, Dettic and Deorulf, he established a monastery at Amöneburg. Winning the pagan Hessians by his kindness to the unfortunate, he baptized a large number on the Feast of Pentecost 722; his biographer speaks of thousands of converts on this occasion (*ibid.* 1.7). Boniface reported his success to Rome and sought the advice of the Pope on several questions. The Pope invited him to Rome, where he consecrated him bishop (Nov. 30, 722) after receiving his profession of faith. He gave him a collection of canons, probably that of *Dionysius Exiguus, and letters of recommendation to all religious and civil rulers in Germany, including

St. Boniface giving a blessing, enlarged detail of a miniature in a Sacramentary from Fulda, c. 950, preserved in the Göt-tigen University Library (MS 231, fol. 87v, detail); believed to be the oldest picture of the saint.

*Charles Martel. In a letter to the German clergy dated Dec. 1, 722, the Pope summarized the instructions he had given to the new bishop. Boniface went from Rome to Charles Martel, successor to Pepin II as mayor of the palace (714–741), and that prince in 723 granted him a letter of safe conduct, without which Boniface admitted his work would have been impossible.

Return to Germany. The bishop returned for a second mission to Hesse (723–725), where converted Hessians advised him to overwhelm the remaining pagans by felling the sacred oak at Geismar near the Abbey of Fritzlar; Boniface used planks sawn from this tree to erect a chapel to St. Peter. From Hesse he returned to Thuringia (725–735), an area conquered by the Franks under Thierry I and already somewhat Christianized since the recent immigration and the efforts of Frankish and Irish missionaries, such as *Kilian of Würzburg. In 724 Gregory II reproached Gerold of Mainz for his failure to further extend Christianity and to defend his episcopal rights, and the Pope later recommended Boniface to the Thuringians. Boniface's task was complicated by ignorant and even vicious priests, poorly prepared catechumens, and pagan admixtures in Christian ceremonies. His 10-year apostolate, however, was fruitful in conversions and reform. He established a monastery at Ohrdruf, near Gotha.

The Pope died in 731 and was succeeded by *Gregory III (d. 741), to whom Boniface immediately offered his homage and services. Gregory replied in 732 by elevating Boniface to the rank of archbishop, sending him the *pallium, and bidding him consecrate missionary bishops. In 734 Boniface made a short trip to *Bavaria, which had been evangelized earlier by *Rupert of Salzburg with the aid of Irish monks. There Duke Hubert I offered his assistance.

Boniface made his third and last visit to Rome in the fall of 737, remaining there a year. The Pope urged him to evangelize the Old Saxons, a mission dear to Boniface. Gregory also commissioned Boniface to organize the German Church, and he wrote supporting letters to bishops, abbots, and magnates of Hesse, Thuringia, and Bavaria. During this visit Boniface attracted to his apostolate a number of Romans, Franks, and Bavarians, such men as *Winnebald and *Willibald of Eichstätt, who came to him from *Monte Cassino, and probably also at this time *Lull, later bishop of Mainz.

Returning in 738 as papal *legate to Germany, Boniface established three new bishoprics in Bavaria in addition to Passau, already ruled by Bishop Vivolo; they were: *Salzburg, which under Arno was eventually to become an archbishopric in 798, *Regensburg, and Freising. The first Bavarian synod was held in Boniface's presence in 740, and the following year several other dioceses were set up: Buraburg for Hesse under the Anglo-Saxon *Witta, Erfurt for Thuringia under Dadanus(?), *Würzburg for Franconia under *Burchard, a pupil of Boniface in England, and Eichstätt under the Anglo-Saxon Willibald. Nearby Heidenheim was the site of an important abbey, the only double *monastery in Germany, organized and ruled by Winnebald and then by *Walburga, brother and sister of Bishop Willibald. The establishment of bishoprics and abbeys did not solve all problems, for Bishop *Virgilius of Salzburg (745–784) worried

Boniface, who reported what he considered to be his heretical views to the Pope. In 744 Boniface founded the most celebrated of his monasteries at *Fulda. Its purpose, like that of all Boniface's monasteries, was to consolidate the progress already made in the evangelization of upper Bavaria, and it was placed directly under Roman jurisdiction by Pope *Zachary in 751. *Sturmi, a young Bavarian noble who had joined Boniface at Fritzlar, became its first abbot. Fulda was a place of spiritual renewal for Boniface and the center of Germany's religious and intellectual life, where the annual conference of German bishops is still held.

The Reform of the Frankish Church (742–747). The Frankish Church had suffered a decline for over a century largely as a result of lay interference in episcopal elections and consequent worldliness among the clergy, *proprietary churches, exempt monasteries (see EXEMPTION, HISTORY OF), and complete absence of papal control. *Carloman, Austrasian mayor of the palace (741–747), cooperated with Boniface by calling councils to reform the Church in his domain: one, called the *Concilium Germanicum,* was held April 21, 742, at an unknown place, and another, at Liftina or Liptina (modern Estinnes in Hainaut, Belgium) on March 1, 743. Bishops, priests, and lay magnates attended, but final approval of the conciliar decrees was reserved to Carloman, who legislated for annual synods; in 743 and 744 these were held in early March, probably to coincide with the *campus Martius.* In 744 *Pepin III held a council at Soissons that adopted the Austrasian decrees; a council for the whole kingdom, which Boniface probably attended, was held the following year. Archbishops were consecrated for *Rouen, Reims, and *Sens; Rouen received the pallium, but it is not certain whether the other two sees were similarly favored. The council condemned two wandering bishops: the Frank, Aldebert, who claimed to be a saint, and a heretical Irishman, Clement; both escaped imprisonment. Gewiliob, Bishop of *Mainz, was deposed by the council for having killed his father's murderer, and Boniface was appointed to his place, for, although archbishop since 742, he had been assigned neither see nor suffragans. At first he hoped to establish his *metropolitan see in *Cologne, a plan approved by the council of 745 and by the Pope, but he was forced to abandon the idea in face of opposition from the Frankish bishops. Later, in 752, when Boniface resigned, Lull succeeded him, but as a bishop, and Mainz became an archbishopric permanently only c. 781. Implementation of the decrees of 745 was difficult because lay lords opposed the restoration of *Church property, and clerics sometimes resisted reform. In 747 a council was held to which all the bishops of the kingdom were invited, but only 13 attended. Boniface tried to unite them to Rome by professions of faith and loyalty. In the same year Carloman retired to a monastery, and Pepin became sole mayor of the palace. Boniface's authority declined, and it is not certain whether he even attended Pepin's coronation. Boniface feared that his collaborators, mostly Anglo-Saxons, would suffer after his death, so he wrote on their behalf to Fulrad, Abbot of *Saint-Denis.

Last Mission and Martyrdom. Boniface undertook a final mission to the Frisians, accompanied by *Eoban, Archbishop of Utrecht, and others. He was very successful for about a year and was preparing a group of

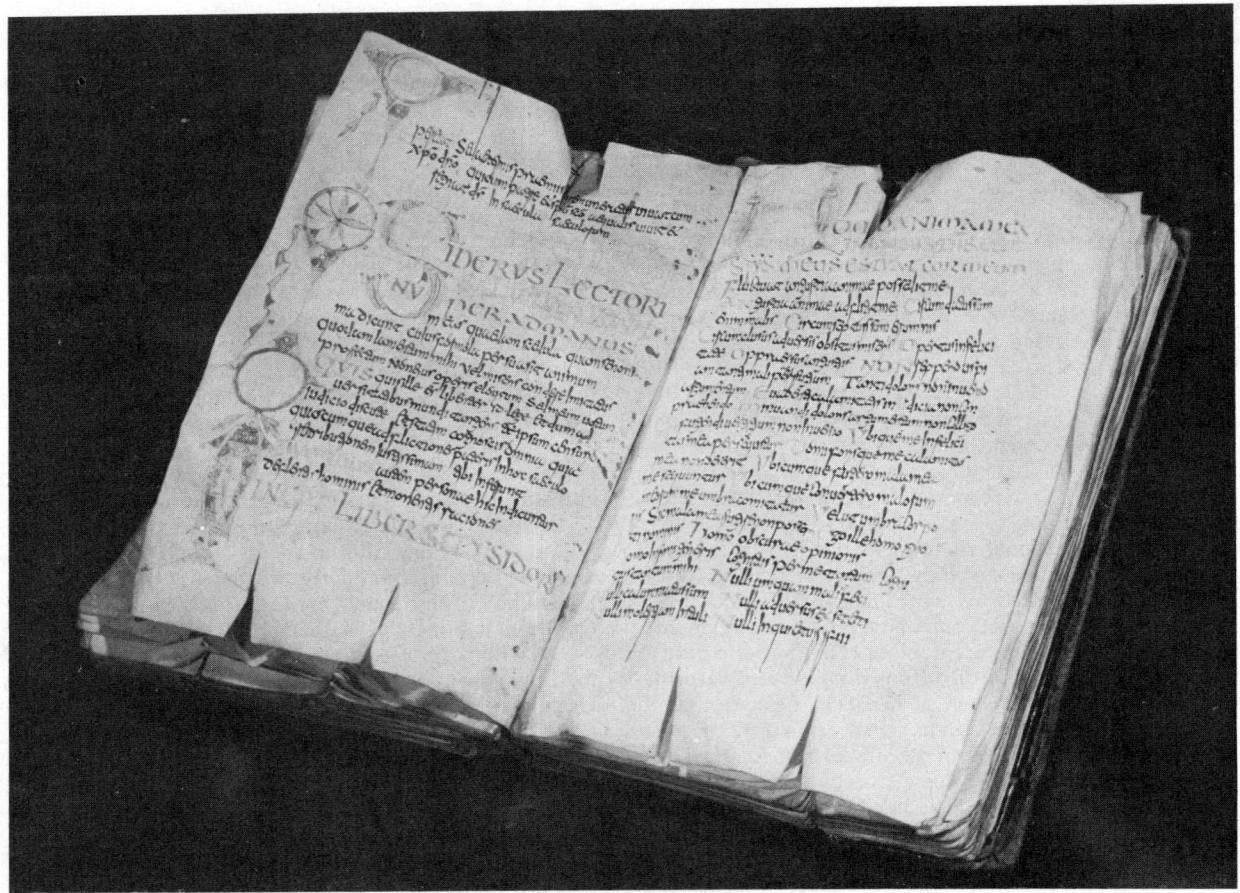

The *"Codex Ragyndrudis,"* preserved in the treasury of the cathedral at Fulda. Tradition states that this is the book held by St. Boniface at his martyrdom, the cuts in the pages being made by the swords of his assassins.

neophytes for Confirmation near Dokkum when attacked at sunrise by pagan Frisians. Boniface would not permit a struggle. An old woman later declared on oath that she saw him protect himself with a Gospel Book (now at Fulda). Boniface and 53 companions were massacred. His remains, which he had asked to have interred at Fulda, rested en route at Utrecht and Mainz, and his cult developed immediately in all three places. Fulda became a center of pilgrimage. Except for the top of his skull, the remains of Boniface are now enshrined in a charming baroque tomb from which the recumbent statue of the bishop appears as emerging with the assistance of two cherubim. Pope *Pius IX extended his feast to the entire Church in 1874.

Characteristics of Boniface's Missionary Activity. Boniface organized the German Church in closest union with Rome, he himself having recourse to the popes for authorization, protection, and guidance. At the same time he depended on his monasteries to give permanence to his work in rural areas. The *ingens multitudo* of Anglo-Saxon monks and nuns who followed him to the Continent peopled his houses and established new ones. Boniface introduced Benedictine nuns into the active apostolate of education, anticipating by many centuries the work of religious women in that field.

Bibliography: *Vita,* ed. W. LEVISON, MGSrerGerm v.57. *Die Briefe,* ed. M. TANGL, MGEpSel v.1. *Die Gedichte,* MGPoetae 1:3–23. H. HAHN, *Bonifaz und Lul* (Leipzig 1883). Hauck 1:418–552. J. M. WILLIAMSON, *Life and Times of St. Boniface* (London 1904). G. F. BROWNE, *Boniface of Crediton and His Companions* (London 1910). WILLIBALD, *The Life of Saint Boniface,* tr. G. W. ROBINSON (Cambridge, Mass. 1916). *The English Correspondence of St. Boniface,* ed. and tr. E. KYLIE (London 1924). W. LEVISON, *England and the Continent in the Eighth Century* (Oxford 1946) 70–93. E. S. DUCKETT, *Anglo-Saxon Saints and Scholars* (New York 1947) 337–455. D. PONTIFEX, *St. Boniface* (London 1954). T. SCHIEFFER, *Winfrid-Bonifatius und die christliche Grundlegung Europas* (Freiburg 1954). *Sankt Bonifatius: Gedenkgabe zum 1200. Todestag* (Fulda 1954). A. ERDLE and H. BUTTERWEGGE, eds., *Bonifatius, Wanderer Christi* (Paderborn 1954). G. W. GREENAWAY, *Saint Boniface* (London 1955). H. LÖWE, "Bonifatius und die bayerisch-fränkische Spannung," *Jahrbuch für fränkische Landesforschung* 15 (1955) 85–127; "Vom Bild des Bonifatius in der neueren deutschen Geschichtsschreibung," *Geschichte in Wissenschaft und Unterricht* 6 (1955) 539–555. Zimmermann KalBen 2:270–277. **Illustration credit:** Bildarchiv Hans Retzlaff.

[S. HILPISCH; C. M. AHERNE]

BONIFACE I, POPE, ST.

Pontificate, Dec. 29, 418, to Sept. 4, 422 (feast, Sept. 4). Boniface was Roman-born, the son of the priest Iocundus, and had been *Innocent I's legate to Constantinople on several occasions.

While Pope *Zosimus was being buried, the archdeacon Eulalius returned to the Lateran where he was acclaimed bishop of Rome. The rest of the presbyterium and the people waited till the next day and elected the aged priest Boniface in the basilica of

Theodora. The following Sunday (Dec. 29) both candidates were consecrated and installed. Boniface was consecrated at St. Marcellus and installed in St. Peter's, because the Lateran was held by the faction of Eulalius. The pagan prefect of Rome, Symmachus, attempted to settle the quarrel, intervening on behalf of Eulalius, but was overruled by the imperial court where Boniface had powerful support. The question was debated inconclusively by several synods.

Meanwhile, both contenders were ordered to leave Rome pending a final solution, and the bishop of Spoleto was delegated to preside at the Easter celebrations (419). Eulalius attempted to prevent this, caused a riot, .and was considered to have forfeited his rights, whereupon Boniface was declared the lawful bishop. When Boniface became ill shortly afterward, he feared a repetition of the schism if he should die and wrote to the Roman Emperor *Honorius in the name of the clergy requesting assurances that peace would be maintained. The imperial rescript replied that if a double election occurred again, the government would remove both candidates and recognize only an election that was morally unanimous.

The case of the African priest Apiarius, who had appealed to Pope Zosimus, was considered at a plenary council in Carthage on May 25, 419, attended by Faustinus and another papal legate. It was decided to verify the acts of Nicaea to which Zosimus had appealed by comparing them with copies kept at Constantinople, Antioch, and Alexandria, since the African version did not correspond to the Roman. Meanwhile the African bishops were willing to abide by the decision of the Pope; Apiarius was to be released from excommunication and transferred to another diocese if he begged pardon for his misdeeds. In their reply to Boniface the African bishops maintained a moderate and dignified tone, though they could not help expressing annoyance at the arrogance of Faustinus.

In dealing with the Pelagians, Boniface left the initiative to Emperor Honorius, who issued an edict (June 9, 419) requiring all the bishops to sign the *Tractoria* of Pope Zosimus; Boniface likewise deferred to St. *Augustine and the African bishops, persuading Augustine to write his *Contra duas epistulas Pelagianorum*. The controversy was prolonged in Italy, however, by a few bishops led by *Julian of Eclanum, who refused to sign the imperial edict.

Under Boniface the vicariate of Gaul, which Pope Zosimus had conferred on Patroclus of Arles, was not renewed. But when the Byzantine Emperor *Theodosius II issued an edict (July 14, 421) ordering the Praetorian prefect for Illyricum not to allow ecclesiastical matters affecting his prefecture to be decided without the knowledge of the bishop of Constantinople "because the latter enjoys the prerogative of Old Rome," Boniface persuaded Honorius to obtain from Theodosius II the revocation of his edict. He wrote to Rufus of Thessalonica as his vicar, and to the other Illyrian and Macedonian bishops insisting that they respect the rules of the vicariate. The law of Theodosius was nevertheless retained in both the Theodosian and Justinian Codes.

Boniface was buried in a chapel or oratory that he built in the cemetery of St. Felicitas on the Via Salaria, the exact location of his tomb being unknown. The date of his death is correctly noted in the *Martyrology of St.

Pope St. Boniface I conducting the last rites for St. Alexius, detail of an 11th-century fresco in the Basilica of S. Clemente at Rome. The meeting of the two saints is a legend that grew out of the dedicating of a church on the Aventine in both their names.

Jerome, but wrongly given as October 25 in the Roman *Martyrology, which follows the Liber pontificalis.

Bibliography: Dekkers CPL 1648–49 and PLSuppl 1:1032–34, editions. PL 20:749–792. Duchesne LP 1:227–229; 3:84. Caspar 1:359–364. H. LECLERCQ, DACL 13.1:1203. P. GOGGI, EncCatt 2:1863–64. R. U. MONTINI, *Le tombe dei Papi* (Rome 1957) 98. G. SCHWAIGER, LexThK² 2:587–588. G. BARDY, DHGE 9:895–897. T. G. JALLAND, *The Church and the Papacy* (SPCK; 1944) 274–277, 288. **Illustration credit:** Alinari-Art Reference Bureau.

[J. CHAPIN]

BONIFACE II, POPE, Sept. 22, 530, to October 532; b. Rome, date unknown; d. Rome, Oct. 17, 532. Boniface, of German lineage, was an archdeacon under Pope *Felix IV, who was determined to avoid contention and schism by designating his successor in the papacy and preferred a cleric who was favorable to the imperial court at Ravenna. Shortly before his death, Felix summoned the Roman clergy and several Roman senators and conferred the pallium of papal sovereignty on Boniface, proclaiming him his successor as pope.

On the death of Felix IV, the majority of the Roman clergy refused to accept Boniface as bishop and proceeded to elect the deacon Dioscorus of Alexandria. Opposition to Boniface stemmed also from the Romans' fear of Ostrogothic domination. Dioscorus and Boniface were consecrated bishops on the same day (Sept. 22, 530), giving rise to the seventh antipapal schism, which lasted only 22 days since Dioscorus died on Oct. 14, 530. Boniface II convened a Roman synod and received the submission of his opponents, who pledged obedience to him as pope (Dec. 27, 530).

In 537, Boniface convoked a second synod, at which he proposed a constitution granting the pope the right to appoint his successor. Since the Roman clergy subscribed and pledged their support, Boniface nominated the deacon Vigilius as his successor; and the choice was ratified by the Roman priests and people. In a short time, however, resentment grew; and after an imperial protest against such action, a third synod was convoked in 531. In the presence of the Roman Senate, Boniface rescinded the former arrangement and personally burned the document.

During his pontificate Boniface II confirmed the acts of the Second Council of Orange (529), which under the leadership of *Caesarius of Arles terminated the controversies over *Semi-Pelagianism. He was esteemed by the populace for his charity, particularly during a famine in Rome. In a jurisdictional dispute in Illyria, Boniface intervened, upholding the election of Stephen of Larissa against the jurisdictional encroachment of Epiphanius of Constantinople. He was buried in St. Peter's, where a fragment of his epitaph is still visible.

Bibliography: A. SCHWAIGER, LexThK² 2:588. A. AMORE, EncCatt 2:1864. Caspar 2:193–198, 767–768. E. STEIN, Cath HistRev 21 (1935–36) 141. Duchesne LP 1:ccliii, cclxi, 281–284. L. DUCHESNE, *L'Église au VIᵉ siècle* (Paris 1925) 142–145. Hefele-Leclercq 2.2:1115–19, 1358–65.

[A. H. SKEABECK]

BONIFACE III, POPE,

Feb. 19 to Nov. 12, 607. A Roman in the service of the Holy See as *primus defensor,* Boniface was appointed *apocrisiarius* to the court of the Byzantine Emperor Phocas in 603 by *Gregory the Great. Boniface was a more successful diplomat than *Sabinian, who had preceded him as *apocrisiarius* as he was to precede him as Pope, and he won the support of the imperial court for the papacy and obtained from Phocas a decree repeating the Novella (CorpIurCivNov 131.2.14) of Justinian, whereby the Roman pontiff was recognized as head of all churches. This pronouncement contradicted the title "ecumenical patriarch" then recently assumed by the Patriarch of Constantinople, *John IV the Faster, and his successor, Cyriacus—a title Pope Gregory had felt challenged the unity of the Church under the pope. The most noteworthy legislation of Boniface's short pontificate was the decree of a Roman council whereby anathema was pronounced on anyone who would propose the successor to a pope or bishop before the 3d day after his death.

Bibliography: Duchesne LP 1:316. *Gregorii Registrum epistolorum* XIII, 41, ed. P. EWALD and L. M. HARTMANN, MGEp v.1–2. Hefele-Leclercq 3.1:247. Mann 1.1:259–267. CMedH² 4.1:440. Jaffé L 1:220; 2:698. Fliche-Martin 5:71, 393.

[P. J. MULLINS]

BONIFACE IV, POPE, ST.,

Sept. 15, 608, to May 8, 615. Boniface proved to be pious, industrious, and devoted to the poor, a worthy successor of *Gregory I. The most remarkable event of his pontificate was the consecration of the basilica Sancta Maria ad Martyres on the site of the Pantheon (609). The Emperor Phocas had acceded to the Pope's request for the conversion of the ancient pagan monument into a Christian church, and Boniface translated there a number of relics from the catacombs. In 610 Boniface held a synod at Rome for the restoration of monastic discipline; *Mellitus, the first bishop of London, was present. He returned to England with the synodal decrees and papal letters to *Lawrence, Archbishop of Canterbury, to King *Ethelbert of Kent, and to the people of England.

During his pontificate the heresy of *Monophysitism was a cause of much ecclesiastical and political confusion. The success of the Persian invasion of many provinces of the Byzantine Empire was aided by the cooperation of heretical bishops. *Heraclius, exarch of Africa, took advantage of the disorder to lead a revolt against Phocas and to seize the throne. Although victorious against the Persians, Heraclius did not succeed in restoring the Monophysites to the unity of the Church.

In northern Italy several of the Lombard bishops persisted in the Istrian schism, which rejected the condemnation of the *Three Chapters by the Second Council of *Constantinople (553). The Irish monk *Columban of Bobbio wrote to the Pope, severely reprimanding him for his support of the Council's action. No reply of the Pope is extant, but subsequent letters seem to indicate that the ill-informed Columban in no wise diminished by this imprudence the relation of his mission to the Holy See.

Bibliography: Jaffé E 1:220–222; 2:698, 739. Duchesne LP 1:317–318. BEDE, *Eccl. Hist.* 2.4. Mann 1:268–279. H. LECLERCQ, DACL 10.2:2062–68; 13.1:1063–67. Caspar 2:517–522. G. SCHWAIGER, LexThK² 2:588–589.

[P. J. MULLINS]

BONIFACE V, POPE,

Dec. 23, 619, to Oct. 25, 625?. A Neapolitan, consecrated pope after the war-torn pontificate of *Deusdedit I, Boniface was noted for his organizing ability. In Rome he endeavored to conform ecclesiastical usage to civil law in the matter of bequests; he established the principle of right of asylum and issued laws over the liturgical function of various orders of clerics. Concerned with England, Boniface sent the *pallium as a symbol of honor and jurisdiction to *Justus, Archbishop of Canterbury, with a letter encouraging him to consecrate other bishops for the spread of the faith in England (624). The Pope also wrote directly to King *Edwin of Northumbria, urging him to study the Catholic faith, and to Queen *Ethelburga, a Christian, encouraging her to procure the Christianization of Edwin and his subjects. Some years later the Queen's confessor, *Paulinus of York, baptized Edwin and founded the Archdiocese of *York. At the opposite end of Christendom, Boniface and his successor witnessed the capitulation of the three ancient Patriarchates of *Jerusalem, *Antioch, and *Alexandria to the rule of *Islam as they became, in effect, "Christian caliphates." Constantinople remained the sole patriarchate of the East (*see* PATRIARCHATE, BYZANTINE).

Bibliography: Duchesne LP 1:321–322. Jaffé L 1:222–223; 2:698. BEDE, *Hist. Eccl.,* v.2. Mann 1:294–303. F. M. STENTON, *Anglo-Saxon England* (2d ed. Oxford 1947).

[P. J. MULLINS]

BONIFACE VI, POPE,

April 896; b. Rome; d. there. He was the son of Adrian, a bishop, and was elected pope almost immediately after the death of his predecessor, *Formosus, on April 4, 896. A struggle for control of Rome was then going on between the partisans of *Arnulf, the German Emperor, and those of *Lambert of Spoleto. In the ensuing popular tumult, the latter group accomplished the election of Boniface, but later a Roman synod under *John IX (898) deplored his election since he had been twice suspended, as a subdeacon and again as a priest, because of unworthy conduct, and had not been canonically reinstated. Afflicted with gout, he died 15 days after his election and was buried in the portico of the popes in the Vatican.

Bibliography: F. BAIX, DHGE 9:899–900. Jaffé L 439. Seppelt 2:341. G. SCHWAIGER, LexThK² 2:589.

[A. J. ENNIS]

BONIFACE VIII, POPE

Pontificate, Dec. 24, 1294, to Oct. 11, 1303; b. Benedict Gaetani, Anagni, c. 1235; d. Rome. His reign is remembered especially for the fierce conflict of *Church and State between the papacy and the French monarchy that broke out in 1296. Boniface has been accused of committing the papacy to novel and extravagant claims in the temporal sphere in the course of that struggle. It is true that he was a pope of grand ambitions, determined to uphold all the prerogatives of his office. He was also a man of autocratic temper, impatient of opposition, given to hot outbursts of rage (which were perhaps caused in part by the painful disease of "the stone" from which he suffered). But it is not true that his own dominating personality led him to propound new doctrines of papal might. The claim that the pope's "plentitude of power" included a right to depose secular rulers and to act in the last resort as a supreme judge set over all men and all their affairs had already been formulated by Boniface's predecessors, especially by *Innocent IV. The defeats that marked Boniface's reign did not, then, result from any aggressive new demands on his part, but rather from his stubborn defense of long-established claims of the *papacy in the political order at a time when they had become totally unacceptable to the new monarchies.

Election. A member of the noble *Gaetani family, Benedict studied Roman and Canon Law at *Bologna

Pope Boniface VIII, bust by Arnolfo di Cambio (d. 1302), in the grotto of the basilica of St. Peter at Rome.

and subsequently entered the service of the Roman Curia, serving in a minor capacity with embassies to France in 1264 and to England in 1265. He became cardinal deacon in 1281 and cardinal priest in 1291. At the Council of Paris in 1290 Benedict played a leading role as papal legate. He vehemently defended the rights of the *mendicant orders against attacks from the secular masters of the University of *Paris and, in the diplomatic sphere, succeeded in negotiating a peace between France and Aragon. In 1294 he was active in persuading the holy but incompetent *Celestine V to relinquish the papal office and was himself elected pope at the conclave that followed. From the beginning Boniface had bitter enemies. His part in encouraging Celestine's abdication earned him the hatred of the Franciscan *Spirituals and their patron, Cardinal James *Colonna, who soon found another motive for opposition in the frank *nepotism that the new Pope displayed in enriching his own Gaetani kin with offices and lands in the Papal States.

Sicily and Northern Europe. Celestine V had been a mere tool of King Charles II of Naples in whose territory he resided. Boniface promptly moved the Curia back to Rome and resumed the conduct of an independent papal diplomacy. There were many problems to claim his attention. The most pressing one was the struggle between *James II of Aragon and Charles II of Anjou for the throne of Sicily. In 1295 Boniface achieved a settlement, which seemed at first a brilliant stroke of diplomacy, by persuading James to relinquish his claim; but the people of Sicily subsequently offered the kingship to James's brother Frederick, and in 1302 Boniface reluctantly had to acknowledge Frederick as independent King of the island of Sicily. Boniface was much concerned with the diplomatic affairs of northern Europe. In 1299 he tried unsuccessfully to mediate between Scotland and England. In 1298 he excommunicated King Eric of Denmark for imprisoning the archbishop of Lund and, in 1303, obtained the King's submission. Boniface at first opposed the election of Albert of Austria as emperor, but in April 1303, at the climax of his conflict with France, he recognized Albert's claim. The Pope took advantage of the occasion to restate the old theory that all national kings were subordinate to the emperor and that the emperor's power in turn came from the pope. (In 1955 *Pius XII referred to this assertion of Boniface as "a medieval conception, conditioned by the period.")

Struggle with Philip the Fair. The great struggle with France began in 1296. *Edward I of England and *Philip IV of France were engaged in a war arising out of feudal disputes and commercial rivalries, and both of them had imposed heavy new taxes on their clergy to help finance the campaigns. A canon of the Fourth *Lateran Council (1215) laid down that clerics were not to be taxed without consent of the pope, but the papacy had acquiesced in such levies in the past, especially when they were intended to support a "just war." In 1296, however, two Christian Kings each claimed to be waging a "just war" against the other, and both were determined to tax the clergy with unusual severity. The situation seemed to Boniface intolerable, and he determined to end it. His bull *Clericis laicos (1296) opened with the assertion that "the laity have always been hostile to the clergy" and went on to describe the recent exactions as an example of this hostility. In the future,

Boniface decreed, any lay ruler who demanded taxes from his clergy without prior papal permission would incur automatic excommunication, and so would any cleric who yielded to such demands. The promulgation of the bull was bitterly resented by the Kings whose policies had provoked it. In England the steadfast *Robert of Winchelsea, Archbishop of Canterbury, bore the brunt of Edward's anger. Philip of France found a way of striking directly at the Pope himself. He issued an order forbidding all export of treasure and negotiable currency from France, a move that created serious financial embarrassment for Boniface, who relied heavily on revenues from the French Church. In September 1296 Boniface sent an indignant protest to Philip (*Ineffabilis amor*), declaring that he would rather suffer death than surrender any of the liberties of the Church; but he explained in conciliatory fashion that his recent bull had not been intended to apply to customary dues from the feudal lands of the Church. He added that Philip was being deluded by evil counselors and that he was rash to pick a quarrel with the papacy, especially when the pope was the rightful judge of the political disputes in which Philip was involved —for the King's enemies alleged that Philip had sinned against them, and judgment on matters of sin belonged to the Roman see.

Struggle with Colonna. Unfortunately Boniface threw away any chance there might have been of carrying the whole issue to a successful conclusion by choosing this time to force a final breach with the Colonna family. In May 1297 a relative of the Colonnas plundered a convoy of papal treasure. Boniface summoned the two cardinals of the family to his presence and commanded that they hand over to him three strategic Colonna castles. The cardinals refused and withdrew to their fortress at Longhezza, where they were joined by *Jacopone da Todi, a leader of the Franciscan Spirituals. From there they issued a manifesto declaring that Boniface was no true pope since the abdication of Celestine V had been illegal. Subsequently they accused Boniface of heresy and simony and also of murdering the aged Celestine, who had indeed died in a papal prison. It was the first public statement of charges—always unproved—that were to harass Boniface to the end of his reign. When Philip IV's minister, Pierre *Flotte, traveled south to negotiate with Boniface, he met with representatives of the Colonnas, and his hand was greatly strengthened by the possibility that Philip might support their charges. In July 1297 Boniface capitulated completely. His bull *Etsi de statu* conceded that in time of necessity the King could tax the French clergy without consulting the Pope and that it was for the King himself to determine when a state of necessity existed.

Resumption of Struggle with Philip. By 1300 Boniface's fortunes seemed to be reviving. To mark the centennial he proclaimed a year of *jubilee, the first such occasion in the history of the Church, and tens of thousands of pilgrims from many lands poured into Rome to worship at the shrines of the Apostles. When the Pope, encouraged by the enthusiastic devotion of the pilgrims, heard of new encroachments on the liberties of the Church in France, he was prepared to challenge Philip again. The occasion of this second dispute was the King's treatment of a French bishop, *Bernard of Saisset. In 1301 Philip accused Saisset of treason and had him arrested, tried before a royal court,

and thrown into prison. In defiance of the universal jurisdiction of the pope over all bishops (*see* IMMUNITY, CLERICAL), Philip was asserting total sovereignty over the persons as well as the property of the French episcopate. Boniface protested in the bull *Ausculta fili* (Dec. 1301), which was considered and approved in a consistory of cardinals. The bull accused Philip of subverting the whole state of the Church in France by abuse of royal rights of patronage and illicit extensions of royal jurisdiction. It declared, "Let no one persuade you that you have no superior or that you are not subject to the head of the ecclesiastical hierarchy, for he is a fool who so thinks." When the bull arrived in Paris, its contents were not publicized, but a crude forgery was put into circulation by the King's agents in which Boniface was alleged to have written, "Know that you are subject to us in spiritualities and in temporalities."

At the end of 1301 Boniface also commanded the French bishops to attend a council to be held at Rome in November 1302 to consider the reform of the French Church. Philip forbade them to attend and in April 1302 summoned an assembly of his own at Paris—a meeting of nobles, burgesses, and clergy. Pierre Flotte harangued this first French Estates-General and apparently accused Boniface of claiming to be feudal overlord of France. The nobles and burgesses then wrote to the cardinals denouncing Boniface and refusing to recognize him as pope. The clergy wrote to Boniface himself addressing him as Pope but protesting against his "unheard-of assertions." When Boniface received the envoys of the French Estates he denied angrily that he had ever claimed to be feudal overlord of France, but he declared that his predecessors had deposed three French kings and that he was quite prepared to depose Philip if necessary.

There was a lull during the summer of 1302. Philip was distracted from his feud against Boniface by a major defeat inflicted on his forces by the Flemings at the battle of Courtrai, in which the King's chief minister, Pierre Flotte, was killed. But Philip still refused to permit his bishops to attend the Pope's council in Rome. When the council met, fewer than half the French bishops were present, and no measures for the reform of the French Church were agreed upon. Immediately after this abortive council (Nov. 1302) Boniface issued the bull *Unam sanctam, the most famous medieval document on spiritual and temporal power. The bull was essentially a theological treatise on the unity of the Church, a unity threatened, as Boniface well saw, when national hierarchies of bishops hesitated between allegiance to their king and obedience to their pope. But it also emphasized, perhaps more explicitly than any earlier papal pronouncement, the power of the pope to "institute" and to judge temporal kings.

Attack on Pope's Person; His Death. Philip's reply to this claim was an extraordinarily brutal and unscrupulous attack on the Pope's reputation and even on his person. At an Estates-General held in March 1303 the King's new minister, Guillaume de *Nogaret, presented a series of accusations against Boniface and demanded that a general council be assembled to sit in judgment on him. The charges were presented in more detail at another meeting held in June. Boniface was accused of usurping the papal office, of heresy, blasphemy, murder, simony, and sodomy. (After all this it is something of an anticlimax to read that "he does not fast on fast days.") Meanwhile Nogaret had left Paris for Italy in an attempt to settle the whole issue by brute force.

In the summer of 1303 Boniface drew up a solemn bull of excommunication directed against Philip (*Super Petri solio*) and moved from Rome to Anagni, from where he intended to promulgate it. Before he could do so (Sept. 7), the little city was seized by a band of mercenaries led by Nogaret and Sciarra *Colonna. After a day of fighting they broke into the papal palace and confronted Boniface, who was waiting for them arrayed in his pontifical robes. Nogaret demanded that Boniface renounce the papacy. When he refused, Sciarra Colonna wanted to kill him on the spot, but Nogaret hoped to carry him off to be condemned by some sort of council. They left Boniface under guard for the night. As he saw the soldiers looting the palace, he murmured only "The Lord gave and the Lord taketh away." On the 2d day Nogaret and Sciarra Colonna still disagreed about their next move. By the 3d day the whole town and countryside was roused against them, and they had to flee from Anagni leaving Boniface at liberty. But the Pope had collapsed after facing Nogaret, and he never recovered in mind or body. He was carried back to Rome and died a few weeks later. Philip continued to hound his memory after his death and succeeded in extracting from a later Pope, *Clement V, an acknowledgment that, in their proceedings against Boniface, Philip and his councilors had "acted out of an estimable, just and sincere zeal and from the fervor of their Catholic faith."

Evaluation of Boniface's Reign. The tragedy of Boniface's reign lies in the disproportion between the ends he set himself and the resources of his own personality. All his diplomacy aimed at establishing peace and concord in a Christendom guided and led by the pope. But his inability to comprehend the new forces of nationalism that were stirring into life, his excessive preoccupation with the advancement of the Gaetani family, his impatient and irascible disposition, all made the attainment of such an end impossible. He was a great lawyer; and the *Liber Sextus*, the third volume of the *Corpus Iuris Canonici*, which was promulgated in 1298 at Boniface's command, stands as a monument to his juristic acumen.

Bibliography: *Les Registres de Boniface VIII*, ed. G. A. L. DIGARD et al., 4 v. (Paris 1884–1939). T. S. R. BOASE, *Boniface VIII* (London 1933). G. A. L. DIGARD, *Philippe le Bel et le Saint-Siège de 1285 à 1304*, 2 v. (Paris 1936). H. DENIFLE, "Die Denkschriften der Colonna gegen Bonifaz VIII. und der Cardinäle gegen die Colonna," Denifle-Ehrle Arch 5:493–529. P. DUPUY, *Histoire du différend d'entre le pape Boniface VIII. et Philippe le Bel* (Paris 1655). H. FINKE, *Aus den Tagen Bonifaz VIII* (Münster 1902). J. RIVIÈRE, *Le Problème de l'église et de l'état au temps de Philippe le Bel* (Paris 1926). R. SCHOLZ, *Die Publizistik zur Zeit Philipps des Schönen und Bonifaz' VIII* (Stuttgart 1903). G. DE LAGARDE, *La Naissance de l'esprit laïque au déclin du moyen âge* (Vienna 1934–   ). L. E. BOYLE, "The Constitution *Cum ex eo* of Pope Boniface VIII," MedSt 24 (1962) 263–302. **Illustration credit:** Alinari-Art Reference Bureau.

[B. TIERNEY]

BONIFACE IX, POPE, Nov. 2, 1389, to Oct. 1, 1404; b. Pietro Tomacelli, Naples, *c.* 1355. Descended from an old Neapolitan family, he was created cardinal deacon of St. George while still a young man, and in 1385, cardinal priest of St. Anastasia by Pope *Urban

Pope Boniface IX, 14th-century statue in the Basilica of St. Paul-Outside-the-Walls, Rome.

VI. Little else is known of his life until his election as pope in Rome in the midst of the *Western Schism. On Urban VI's death, the Avignon antipope, *Clement VII, had hoped that through the diplomacy of King Charles VI of France the 14 Roman cardinals would elect him Urban's successor and end the schism. Instead they elected Tomacelli as Boniface IX. In contrast to his bitter, intolerant, and imprudent predecessor, Urban, the handsome Boniface was amiable, kindly, and practical. Convinced, however, of his papal rights, Boniface immediately excommunicated Clement, declared (1391) sinful the proposal to end the schism through a general council, refused to abdicate (1396–98) despite Anglo-French and German pressure, and rejected (1404) the embassy of Clement's successor at Avignon, antipope *Benedict XIII. Boniface's pontificate had two major problems: the establishment of his political position and the raising of money. Urban had alienated much of Italy. To strengthen his position in Rome, Boniface supported the claims of Ladislaus to the Kingdom of Naples against his Clementine rival, Louis II of *Anjou; won back the allegiance of Rome; and established his authority in the *States of the Church. Although France withdrew its commitment (1398–1403) to his Avignon rival, Benedict XIII, Boniface was unable to increase his European sphere of influence. England remained faithful but disturbed; Sicily and Genoa actually withdrew their allegiance; Boniface was forced to take the side of Prince-elector Rupert of the Palatinate against King *Wenceslas in Germany, and of Ladislaus of Naples against Emperor *Sigismund in Hungary. These essentially secular activities forced Boniface to exploit old sources of revenue and tap new ones. In 1392 he insisted on *medii fructus* from every cleric whom he appointed to a benefice (*see* ANNATES). He gave preferments to the highest bidder, sold exemptions, and in the *Holy Years of 1390 and 1400 used indulgences, especially *ad instar,* for financial gain. He was assisted in his monetary troubles by Baldassare Cossa, later antipope *John XXIII, whom he raised to the cardinalate in 1402. Boniface did not profit personally from these simoniacal practices, but the Church suffered severely. His pontificate was a troubled one; it deserves the phrase "the crooked days of Boniface IX."

Bibliography: Pastor v.1, *passim.* H. HEMMER, DTC 2:1: 1003–05. E. VANSTEENBERGHE, DHGE 9:909–922. J. B. VILLIGER, LexThK² 2:591. **Illustration credit:** Alinari-Art Reference Bureau.

[E. J. SMYTH]

BONIFACE OF MONTFERRAT, marquis, important 'leader of the Fourth *Crusade; b. *c.* 1155; d. 1207. He came from a distinguished line that was closely associated with the Near East. Until his acceptance of the cross, the first 50 years of his life were uneventful; however, following the death of Theobald of Champagne, an assembly of nobles chose him to lead the Fourth Crusade. He prudently arrived in Zara after its surrender; but his influence in diverting the crusaders to attack *Constantinople, although never fully explained, has left him with a shadow of guilt. His role in the events that led to the sack of Constantinople is well known and has caused some historians to class him as an inheritor of the anti-Byzantine ambitions of the Sicilian *Normans. After the fall of the city he aspired to become the first Latin emperor but fulfillment of this ambition was blocked by the Venetians. Following his payment of homage to Baldwin IX of Flanders as emperor, Boniface laid claim to Thessalonica, and this time with Venetian support received the reluctant approval of Baldwin. As King of Thessalonica, Boniface extended his influence as far south as Athens, but the growing power of the Vlacho-Bulgarian state in alliance with the Greeks led to the weakening of Latin hegemony in Greece, and in a skirmish in 1207 with the Bulgarians Boniface lost his life (*see* LATIN EMPIRE OF CONSTANTINOPLE).

Bibliography: L. USSEGLIO, *I Marchesi di Monferrato in Italia ed in Oriente,* ed. C. E. PATRUCCO, 2 v. (Casale Monferrato 1926) v.2. H. GRÉGOIRE, "The Question of the Diversion of the Fourth Crusade," *Byzantion* 15 (1940–41) 158–166. L. BRÉHIER, DHGE 9:958–966.

[J. H. HILL]

BONIFACE OF SAVOY, BL., Carthusian monk, archbishop of Canterbury; b. *c.* 1207; d. Sainte-Hélène, Savoy, July 14, 1270 (feast, July 21; among the *Carthusians, July 15). The son of Thomas I, Count of Savoy, Boniface entered La Grande-Chartreuse at an early age. In *c.* 1232 he became bishop of Belley in Burgundy; serving as administrator of the Diocese of Valence as well in 1239. As uncle of Eleanor of Provence, *Henry III's Queen of England, he was elected archbishop of *Canterbury in 1241 to succeed Abp. *Edmund of Abingdon, but was confirmed only in 1243. In 1244 he arrived in England, was involved in the governmental crisis of that year, and made the first of his two metropolitan visitations. At the Council of *Lyons (1245), he succeeded in gaining for Canterbury province the first fruits, or *annates, of vacant benefices

for the next 7 years. When he returned to England in 1249, he was finally enthroned. Also in 1249 he made his second reforming visitation, during which he was opposed by the chapter of *Saint Paul's Cathedral and the priory of St. Bartholomew in the Diocese of London. This led to excommunications, which Rome annulled in 1251. In 1254 he accompanied Prince Edward I when he married Eleanor of Castile. Boniface was involved in the governmental crises of 1258 to 1265, the so-called Barons' War. In 1258 he compiled constitutions for reform—in the tradition of *Robert Grosseteste— which were later used by Abp. *John Peckham. When his reform measures were published in 1261, Henry III caused Pope Urban IV to refuse them confirmation. In 1263–64 Boniface pleaded for Henry III at the court of *Louis IX of France. Boniface spent his last years in Savoy. His cult was approved in 1838 by Pope Gregory XVI.

Bibliography: MATTHEW PARIS, *Historia Anglorum . . . Historia minor,* ed. F. MADDEN, 3 v. (RollsS 44; London 1866–69) v.3. INNOCENT IV, *Register . . .,* ed. E. BERGER, v.2 (Bibliothèque des Écoles françaises d'Athènes et de Rome, 2d ser.; Paris 1885). C. W. PREVITÉ-ORTON, *The Early History of the House of Savoy* (Cambridge, Eng. 1912). G. STRICKLAND, "Ricerche storica sopra il B. Bonifacio di Savoia," *Miscellenea di storia Italica,* 3d ser. 1 (1895) 349–432. M. CREIGHTON, DNB 2:812–814. F. M. POWICKE, *The Thirteenth Century* (2d ed. Oxford 1962). R. FOREVILLE, "L'Élection de B. de S. au siège primatial de Canterbury . . .," *Bulletin philologique et historique (jusqu'à 1610) du Comitè des travaux historiques et scientifiques* 1 (1960) 435–450.

[V. I. J. FLINT]

BONITUS OF CLERMONT, ST., bishop and ascetic; b. Auvergne, France, *c.* 623; d. Lyons, Jan. 15, 706 (feast, Jan. 15). His life is known through an anonymous contemporary biography by a monk of the abbey of Manglieu in Auvergne. Bonitus was born to a Roman senatorial family and educated in grammar, rhetoric, and Roman law. He was attached to the court of Sigebert III (634–656) and then made rector of the Prefecture of Marseilles under Pepin of Heristal (*see* MEROVINGIANS). He succeeded his older brother, St. Avitus, as bishop of Clermont sometime after 690. Concerned over the form of his election, he resigned (or, as it has been suggested, was forced to resign) and retired to the abbey of Manglieu. After a leisurely pilgrimage to Rome, he returned to France and reached Lyons in 702. The translation of his relics in 712 was accompanied by miracles, and his remains became the object of fervent veneration in Auvergne and surrounding provinces. His feast is celebrated in Clermont, Autun, Lyons, Marseilles, Moulins, and Saint-Flour.

Bibliography: Mabillon AS 3:78–89. MGSrerMer 6:110–139. L. BRÉHIER, DHGE 9:843–847. A. ZIMMERMANN, LexThK² 2: 597. Baudot-Chaussin 1:312–314.

[P. BLECKER]

BONIZO OF SUTRI, bishop, canonist, publicist under Gregory VII (known also as Bonitho, Bonitus); b. perhaps in Cremona, Italy, *c.* 1045; d. probably before 1095, but perhaps as late as 1099. A native Lombard, he devoted his life to the reform of the Church in north Italy and to the *Gregorian reform in general, a program of which he was an extreme and uncompromising advocate. As a subdeacon leading the *Patarines in Piacenza, he came to the attention of Pope *Gregory VII, who made him bishop of the strategic See of Sutri (1075 or 1076) and employed him as legate (1078). In the course of the *investiture struggle he was captured by Emperor *Henry IV (1082), escaped, and took refuge with *Matilda of Tuscany, where he wrote his most famous work, the *Liber ad amicum* (MGLibLit 1:568–620), designed to rally all reformers after Gregory's death in 1085. Partisan, polemical, and panegyric, it is a personal and unreliable memoir of Gregory, though its distortions seem not to be deliberate. About 1086 Bonizo was elected bishop of Piacenza, but the citizens expelled him from the city (1089), whereupon he resigned and devoted his last years to the *Liber de vita christiana* [ed. E. Perels (Berlin 1930)], a compilation of canonistic extracts with commentary. The exact date of his death is unknown.

Bibliography: Fournier-LaBras 2:139–150. L. JADIN, DHGE 9:994–998. E. NASALLI ROCCA DI CORNELIANO, "Osservazioni su Bonizione vescovo di Sutri et di Piacenza come canonista," StGreg 2 (1947) 151–162.

[R. KAY]

BONN

German city 18 miles southeast of Cologne on the Rhine River. The name is Celtic in origin; but the earliest settlement was made under Augustus, who constructed a *castra Bonnensia* (Tacitus, *Hist.* 4.20) or camp for his legions. The city was destroyed by the Franks in the 4th century and abandoned by the Romans. After being slowly rebuilt in the early Middle Ages, it was sacked again, this time by the Normans (9th century).

Archeological evidence is that on the site of the modern city there was a Christian settlement (*c.* 260) and a cult attached to the grave of a martyr, apparently that of SS. Cassius and Florentius, connected by legend with the *Theban legion. A church built *c.* 400 became the focal point of the St. Cassius monastery of canons around which the medieval city arose; its walls were built *c.* 804 and it was called the *civitas Verona* in the 9th century. The original parish church of St. Remigius (*c.* 795) was called the Dietkirche (people's church). The present cathedral, or Münster, begun in 1145 combines late Roman and early Gothic basilica-type architecture, with two choirs, a crosswalk, and late Roman crypt. The bones of the original martyrs were brought there in 1169. Outside the walls was an industrial market place that Abp. Conrad of Hochstaden brought under his control in 1244. The Minorites had possession of the church of St. Remigius from 1274 to 1802, and the parish church was St. Gangolph's. A convent of Augustinian nuns (1323–1794) occupied the Engelthal, while Cistercian nuns had the chapel of St. Gertrude; two smaller convents flanked the chapels of St. Isidore and St. Welrich, which were in the possession of the Beghards and Beguines in the 16th and 17th centuries.

In the 13th century Bonn became the summer residence of the prince archbishops of Cologne, through whose interest the city prospered, and in the 17th century it became a cultural and musical center. During the Reformation, Abps. Hermann of Wied and Gebhard Truchsess of Waldburg defected and attempted to secularize the area; but it was recatholicized by the Kurfürst Ferdinand, whose successors introduced the Jesuits (1590), Capuchins (1618), the Recollect Franciscans (1624), Capuchin nuns (1629), and the Welsh nuns (1664). There was a Cistercian monastery at Grau-

Bonn, the 12th-century Münster on the Münster Platz.

rheindorf (1230–1798) and a pilgrimage center on the Kreuzberg near Poppelsdorf started by the Servites (*c.* 1644) that is now in the charge of the Franciscans. During the French occupation at the close of the 18th century, all the monasteries and convents were secularized.

From 1949 to June 2, 1957, Bonn was the capital of the (West) German Republic (Deutsche Bundes Republik); the capital was officially moved to Berlin with recognition of the republic's complete independence, but Bonn is still the seat of government. Of architectural note is the royal Schloss or castle with its Coblenz tower. Bonn is also the birthplace of Ludwig van Beethoven (Dec. 17, 1770), whose house now serves as a museum.

Begun as the Academy of the Elector of Cologne in 1777 under Prince Max Friedrich, the University of Bonn was recognized by the imperial government in 1786 and served as a center of the *Enlightenment on the Rhine in opposition to the University of Cologne, as well as a rallying point of *Febronianism. Although closed during the French occupation (1798), it was reactivated in 1818 as the Rheinische Friedrich-Wilhelms-Universität with a Catholic and a Protestant faculty. Opposition to the theological doctrines of G. *Hermes (1819–31) caused a grave crisis within the Catholic faculty; and in the *Kulturkampf and aftermath of *Vatican Council I (1870), three of the five ordinary (full) professors joined the *Old Catholic movement but were retained by the government as members of the University. In 1902 special professorships were created for the Old Catholics. The Protestant faculty experienced internal difficulties on ideological grounds during the 19th century, and during the period between the two world wars it turned to a dialectical theology influenced by K. Barth, who served as a professor from 1930 to 1934. The University was almost totally destroyed in World War II; but was rebuilt round the Kurfürsten Schloss and is in flourishing condition.

Bibliography: E. ENNEN and A. FRANZEN, LexThK² 2:598–600. E. SADÉE, *Das römische Bonn* (Bonn 1925). J. NIESSEN, *Geschichte der Stadt Bonn*, v.1 (Bonn 1956). D. HÖROLDT, *Das Stift St. Cassius zu Bonn* (Bonn 1957). M. BRAUBACH, *Kleine Geschichte der Universität Bonn* (Krefeld 1947). T. KLAUSER, ed., *Chronik der Rheinischen Friedrich Wilhelm Universität Bonn* 64 (1949). **Illustration credit:** Arthur O'Leary.

[F. HAUSER]

BONNARD, PIERRE, French painter, etcher, lithographer, book illustrator; b. Fontenay-aux-Roses (Siene), Oct. 3, 1867; d. Le Cannet, Jan. 23, 1947. Bonnard first studied law, then art, at the École des Beaux-Arts and the Académie Julian in Paris. His

Pierre Bonnard.

associations with fellow students there led to involvement with the Nabis and eventually, to the development, with Édouard Vuillard, of a style based on *impressionism and known as Intimism. An important lithograph of 1889, showing the influence of Japanese prints upon the artist, is Bonnard's advertising poster France-Champagne, which allies him with the style known as *art nouveau. His early paintings reflect the influence of *Gauguin of Pont-Aven, whom he came to know through Paul *Sérusier. Bonnard is most famous, however, for his later paintings showing simple settings from daily life—a corner of a dining room or an open window with a view—rendered in a technique and in colors derived from impressionism and characterized by great subtlety and charm. The familiar subject matter (hence the term Intimism) and the beauty of rendering of these compositions have made Bonnard a favorite among the earlier modern masters. In fact, recognition came early; Durand-Ruel organized an exhibition of his work in 1896, when the artist was not yet 30. Bonnard was a prodigious worker, and prints and paintings by him exist in abundance.

Bibliography: J. DE LAPRADE, *Bonnard* (New York 1946). P. SELZ and M. CONSTANTINE, eds., *Art Nouveau* (Garden City 1960), bibliog. Rewald HistImpr, bibliog. M. WALDFOGEL, "Bonnard and Vuillard as Lithographers," *Minneapolis Institute of Arts Bulletin* 52 (1963) 66–81, catalog of the exhibition and bibliog. J. REWALD, *Pierre Bonnard* (New York 1948), extensive bibliog. from 1893 to 1948. J. T. SOBY et al., *Bonnard and His Environment* (New York 1964), bibliog. from 1948 to 1964, extension of the Rewald bibliog. **Illustration credit:** French Embassy, Press and Information Service, New York City.

[R. MARZOLF]

BONNE-ESPÉRANCE, MONASTERY OF, Premonstratensian monastery near Binche, Belgium, in the province of Hainault, Diocese of Tournai; founded 1125 or 1126 by Rainaud de la Croix and his wife Béatrice. The property at Ramignies originally given to St. Norbert proved unsuitable. Odo (d. 1125 or 1126), the first abbot, moved the community to Sart-Richevin and finally to Vellereille-le-Brayeux in 1130. In 1140 a cloister of nuns was erected by Bonne-Espérance (Bona Spes) at Rivreulle as a daughterhouse of the Abbey of *Prémontré. The monastery gained new prominence when the second abbot of Bonne-Espérance, the noted exegete and hagiographer, Philippe de Harvengt (d. 1183), incorporated a number of parishes during his term of office. But the abbey suffered severe damage during the religious wars. It was pillaged in 1543 at the siege of Binche, burned in 1568 by the Prince of Orange and again devastated in 1577, at which time Abbot Jean Trusse (d. 1580) was imprisoned. In 1792, during the Battle of Jemmapses, the abbey was besieged once more, and Abbot Bonaventure Daublain (d. 1797) and his community dispersed. In 1794 it was suppressed, and the buildings, acquired by the Diocese of Tournai, were converted into a seminary.

Bibliography: Backmund MonPraem 2:361–364. A. VERSTEYLEN, DHGE 9:1030–32. É. POUMON, *Abbayes de Belgique* (Brussels 1954). Cottineau 1:424. É. BROUETTE, *Obituaire de l'abbaye de Bonne-Espérance de l'ordre de Prémontré* (Louvain 1964).

[E. D. MC SHANE]

BONNECHOSE, HENRI MARIE GASTON DE, cardinal, archbishop of Rouen; b. Paris, May 30, 1800; d. Rouen, Oct. 28, 1883. He was the son of a Norman of gentle birth and a Dutch Protestant mother, and made his First Communion at the age of 18. After occupying many posts in the magistrature, he studied for the priesthood, was ordained (1833), and was for some time a member of the Society of St. Louis, established by Abbé Louis *Bautain. He became superior of the community at Saint-Louis des Français in Rome (1844), bishop of Carcassonne (1847) and then of Evreux (1854), archbishop of Rouen (1858), and cardinal (1863). As a member of the French Senate from 1863 he intervened perseveringly and eloquently in that body and before Emperor Napoleon III, whom he highly esteemed, in favor of the papal temporal power and in defense of religion. At *Vatican Council I he served on the committee on *postulata* and headed the "third party" among the members, which favored the definition of papal infallibility in a more mitigated form than *Manning and his group sought. During the Franco-Prussian War, Rouen found him a generous protector and an efficacious advocate with the conqueror. He was an energetic and charitable administrator, and continued his religious work diligently under the Third Republic. He was one of the episcopal founders of the Institut Catholique de *Paris.

Bibliography: L. BESSON, *Vie du cardinal de Bonnechose, archevêque de Rouen*, 2 v. (Paris 1882). R. EUDE, *Histoire* religieuse du diocèse de Rouen au XIXe siècle v.1 Les Archevêques de Rouen 1802–1915 (Rouen 1954). C. BUTLER, The Vatican Council, 2 v. (New York 1930). M. PREVOST, Dict BiogFranc 6:996–997. C. LAPLATTE, DHGE 9:1027–28.

[C. LEDRÉ]

BONNEFOY, JEAN-FRANÇOIS,

theologian; b. Laussone (Haute-Loire), France, June 12, 1897; d. Grottaferrata, Italy, May 9, 1958. He entered the Franciscan Order (Aquitaine Province) Aug. 12, 1915, and was ordained July 6, 1924. Despite his delicate health, Bonnefoy earned a doctorate in theology at Toulouse's Institut Catholique, taught theology for many years in both Toulouse and Rome, and engaged in extensive research. Bonnefoy's writings are almost exclusively speculative. Except for a few historical essays, they are devoted to defending and developing the theological doctrines of John *Duns Scotus, particularly the primacy of Christ and the Immaculate Conception. Discarding as insoluble the hypothetical "if Adam had not sinned, would Christ have come?," he compiled scriptural, patristic, and speculative data in support of his view that the Incarnation was not conditioned by Adam's sin. He also felt that this view of God's plan was implied in the solemn definition of the Immaculate Conception. Conceived without sin, Mary had to precede Adam in the creative plan and could not have incurred the debt of sin that many theologians attribute to her. His most important works in this area are Christ and the Cosmos (tr. from La Primauté du Christ selon l'Écriture et la Tradition) and "L'Immaculée dans le plan divin," Ephemerides Mariologicae 8 (1958) 5–61. He also wrote studies on the spirituality of St. Bonaventure, one of which is a classic, Le Saint-Esprit et ses dons selon s. Bonaventure (Paris 1929). In one of his works on the nature of theology, La Nature de la théologie selon s. Thomas d'Aquin (Paris 1939), he held that the methodology of theology as a deductive science differs from mathematics only in the contingency of much of its subject matter.

Bibliography: For a list of Bonnefoy's works, see his Christ and the Cosmos, tr. M. D. MEILACH (Paterson, N.J. 1965).

[M. D. MEILACH]

BONNER, EDMUND

English Reformation bishop and legist; b. probably 1500; d. Marshalsea prison, London, Sept. 5, 1569. Bonner is believed, although it is still debated, to have been the illegitimate son of George Savage, rector of Daneham, Cheshire, and Elizabeth Frodsham, who later married Edmund Bonner, a long-sawyer of Hanley, Worcestershire. At Pembroke College, Oxford, Bonner obtained the baccalaureate in civil and Canon Law (1519) and the doctorate in civil law (1525). He was ordained about 1519. In 1529 he became a chaplain to Cardinal Thomas Wolsey and took part in negotiations between the cardinal and Thomas Cromwell, remaining with Wolsey after his fall from power. Enjoying the favor of Cromwell, Bonner was employed by Henry VIII from 1532 to 1540 on several diplomatic missions on the Continent to Clement VII, Charles V, Francis I, and the Lutheran princes. At Marseilles he argued Henry's case for annulment so truculently before Clement VII as to infuriate him, and on another occasion Bonner's overbearing manner gave offense to Francis I. Although appointed by Henry to the See of Hereford (1538), he was not yet consecrated when he was translated to London (1539), where he was consecrated in April 1540. A vigorous defender of Henry's marriage to Anne Boleyn, he accepted the royal supremacy. He showed his zeal by writing a very antipapal preface to the Hamburg (1536) edition of the De Vera Obedientia, Stephen *Gardiner's defense of Henry's claim to be head of the English Church. Bonner also helped to have Tyndale's Bible printed for distribution in England. Nevertheless, he was just as strongly opposed to Protestant doctrines as Cuthbert *Tunstall and Stephen Gardiner. In later years he openly attributed his acceptance of the royal supremacy to his fear of retaliation by the King.

After Edward VI's accession (1547), Bonner was imprisoned on several charges, such as refusing to recognize the right of the King's Council to make innovations in religion during the royal minority, but essentially for refusing to accept the introduction of Protestantism. As a result of charges brought by John Hooper and Hugh Latimer, and after examination by Archbishop Cranmer, Bonner was deprived of his bishopric in October 1549. Restored by Mary, he took a leading part in the return to the papal allegiance and to orthodox doctrine. As bishop of London he presided over the trials of a great many heretics since his see was the chief center of Protestantism. His position in this connection laid him open to the taunt of having been formerly a belligerent foe of the papacy. He took a more positive attitude to Protestantism by writing and distributing in his diocese A Profitable and Necessary Doctrine for Every Christian Man, a simple statement of Catholic doctrines that Philip Hughes has described as "a singularly warmhearted guide to a better life." For opposing Elizabeth's changes in the Mass and refusing to recognize her claim to supremacy, he was deprived of his see and committed to the Marshalsea in May 1559. His legal acumen enabled him to rebut charges of a more obviously criminal nature, such as the violation of Praemunire, thereby discouraging the government from executing other bishops. He died still in the same prison.

Bonner was accused by Protestant contemporaries, notably John Bale and John Foxe, of being a bloodthirsty persecutor of Protestants, so that his name was reviled in English histories until late in the 19th century. As a result of more objective writings on the Reformation, particularly the works of such (Protestant) scholars as S. R. Maitland and James Gairdner, Bonner's reputation has been freed from this charge. It is now generally agreed that in the light of royal policy and the standards of the time, he was neither cruel nor overzealous in the punishment of heresy.

Bibliography: Hughes RE. L. B. SMITH, Tudor Prelates and Politics (Princeton 1953). G. L. M. J. CONSTANT, The Reformation in England, tr. R. E. SCANTLEBURY and E. I. WATKIN, 2 v. (New York 1934–42). G. E. PHILLIPS, The Truth about Bishop Bonner (London 1910). J. GAIRDNER, DNB 2:818–822. H. O. EVENNETT, LexThK² 2:600–601. C. STARACE, EncCatt 2:1885. DictEngCath 1:260–266.

[M. R. O'CONNELL]

BONNET, JOSEPH,

well-known organist of the French tradition (see ORGAN MUSIC); b. Bordeaux, March 17, 1884; d. Sainte-Luce-sur-Mer (Quebec), Canada, Aug. 2, 1944. His father, Georges Bonnet, was his first teacher; later he studied with A. *Guilmant at the Paris Conservatory and with C. *Tournemire and L. *Vierne. In 1905, after a brilliant competition, he became organist at Saint-Eustache in Paris, and in the following year he took first organ prize at the conservatory. Thereafter until his death he toured the world in concert, presenting neglected compositions of masters of the 17th, 18th, and 19th centuries (later collected in a six-volume edition, *Historical Organ Recitals*). He had completed a performance of Cesar *Franck's three *Chorales* at the Eiffel Tower radio only minutes before the invasion of Paris during World War II. During his last years he headed the organ department at the Eastman School of Music of the University of Rochester (N.Y.), and later at the Conservatoire National of the Province of Quebec. Among his other publications are several collections of organ pieces for concert and study. Bonnet was a Benedictine Oblate; he was buried in the cemetery at Saint Benoît-du-Lac Abbey in Quebec.

Bibliography: N. Dufourcq, *La Musique d'orgue française* (2d ed. Paris 1949). F. A. Raugel, *Les Organistes* (Paris 1923).

[C. BERNIER]

BONNETTY, AUGUSTIN, philosopher and historian; b. Entrevaux, France, April 9, 1798; d. Paris, March 26, 1879. Though he spent 4 years at the major seminary of Digne, he decided not to embrace the priesthood. He went to Paris to live and become part of the circle of Catholic intellectuals including O. P. *Gerbet and H. F. de *Lamennais. In 1830 he founded the review *Annales de philosophie chrétienne*, which he edited until his death. He also collaborated in editing *Université catholique*, begun by Gerbet in 1836, completely assumed its direction in 1840, and in 1855, fused it with his own *Annales*. In these two reviews Bonnetty dedicated his rich talents entirely to the service of the Church, particularly by propagating what he considered to be Christian philosophy.

Unfortunately, he vigorously defended *fideism and *traditionalism. His system, however, was not as extreme as that of Louis G. A. de *Bonald and Louis E. M. *Bautain. Originally he had no intention of discussing the theoretical limits of human reason. He felt it was useless even to pose the question, for according to him man had never been left on a merely natural level; from the very beginning God instructed him in the necessary moral and religious truths. The only problem real to him was: what is the origin of man's rational and religious beliefs? In his opinion, all man's knowledge is traceable to a revelation made by God to our first parents. He went beyond this historical question, however, in maintaining that man is incapable of discovering truth without the help of revelation. This led him to condemn scholasticism, which upheld the demonstrative power of the human intellect. As a result, on June 11, 1855, the Congregation of the Index insisted that Bonnetty subscribe to four propositions (Denz 2811–14) maintaining the distinction but harmony between faith and reason and exonerating scholasticism from the accusation of rationalism. He submitted to the judgment of the Holy See without reserve and remained faithful to the Church.

Besides his many articles in the *Annales*, Bonnetty also published *Morceaux choisis de l'Église*, 2 v. (Paris 1828), which appeared again in 1841 under the title *Beautés de l'histoire de l'Église; Documents historiques sur la religion des romains*, 4 v. (Paris 1867–78); and an annotated translation of the Jesuit De Prémaré's work, *Vestiges des principaux dogmes chrétiens, tirés des anciens livres chinois* (Paris 1879).

Bibliography: E. Dublanchy, DTC 2.1:1019–26. J. Dopp DHGE 9:1058–60. F. Tinivella, EncCatt 2:1886–87.

[J. H. MILLER]

BONOMELLI, GEREMIA, bishop, writer; b. Nigoline di Franciacorta (Brescia), Italy, Sept. 12, 1831; d. there, Aug. 3, 1914. He came of a peasant family, was ordained (1855), and continued theological studies at the Gregorian University, Rome. After teaching at the seminary in Brescia until 1866, he became pastor in Lovere, and then bishop of Cremona (1871–1914). He was a very zealous, pious bishop, deeply interested in pastoral needs, the *Roman Question, social problems, and the reconciliation of science and religion. He was impulsive and intransigent but never a Modernist. When queried by Leo XIII (1882), he suggested that Catholics should participate in political elections; and in 1904 he counseled Pius X to withdraw the *Non expedit*. Convinced that the *States of the Church could not be restored and that a miniature papal state should instead be created, he anonymously wrote a periodical article in 1889, *"Roma e l'Italia e la realtà delle cose,"* soon published separately as a booklet, which was placed on the Index (April 13, 1889). Courageously Bonomelli admitted his authorship and submitted publicly without delay to the judgment of the Holy See. In 1929 the *Lateran Pacts reached a solution along the lines proposed by Bonomelli. He published numerous periodical articles and books on a variety of topics, but mostly on current religious and

Geremia Bonomelli.

socio-economic problems. Many of his pastoral letters, sermons, and conferences also appeared in print. He carried on a very extensive correspondence with many eminent contemporaries. His concern for the difficulties of Italian emigrants led him to found in 1900 the Opera di assistenza agli operai italiani emigranti, better known as the Opera Bonomelli.

Bibliography: P. Guerrini, ed., *Geremia Bonomelli* (Brescia 1939). C. Bellò, *Geremia Bonomelli* (Brescia 1963). G. Astori, "Mons. Geremia Bonomelli: L'opera sua per la conciliazione," *Vita e pensiero* 30 (1939) 574–581; "S. Pio X ed il vescovo G. Bonomelli," RivStorChIt 10 (1956) 212–266. S. Furlani, Enc Catt 2:1887–90. P. Pisani, Mercati-Pelzer DE 1:411–412. Diz BiogItal, s.v. "Bonomelli, Geremia."

[E. A. CARRILLO]

BONONIUS, ST., abbot; b. Bologna, Italy, *c.* mid-10th century; d. Lucedio, Italy, Aug. 30, 1026 (feast, Aug. 30). He first became a *Benedictine monk in the monastery of San Stefano in his native city. Later he set out for Cairo with the intention of becoming a hermit at Mt. *Sinai, and thus he is often called the apostle of Egypt. In 990 he was recalled to Italy by Bp. Peter of Vercelli (d. 997) and became abbot of Lucedio in Piedmont, where he applied himself to the work of monastic reform until his death. He was canonized by Pope *John XIX. There is another tradition concerning the life of Bononius, propagated by the *Camaldolese, in which he is said to have been a student of *Romuald, the founder of that order.

Bibliography: *Vita,* MGS 30.2:1026–30. G. B. MITTARELLI and A. COSTADONI, *Annales Camaldulenses,* 9 v. (Venice 1755–73) 1:396–399. BHL 1:1421–24. A. DE MEYER, DHGE 9:1090–92. AnalBoll 48 (1930) 411–412. H. HOHENLEUTNER, LexThK² 2:602.

[K. NOLAN]

BONSIRVEN, JOSEPH, NT exegete and rabbinic scholar; b. in Lavaur, Diocese of Albi, France, Jan. 25, 1880; d. Toulouse, Feb. 12, 1958. After his education at the Sulpician seminary in Paris, he was ordained Sept. 19, 1903, and immediately thereafter he was assigned to teach Scripture at the major seminary of Albi. In 1906 he studied at the École Biblique under Père Lagrange; in 1909 he received his licentiate in Sacred Scripture from the Pontifical Biblical Commission. The following year his doctoral thesis on rabbinic eschatology, for reasons that had little to do with its scientific merit, was not accepted, and he was forbidden to teach Sacred Scripture. Bonsirven humbly accepted the decision and returned to his diocese for pastoral work, which was interrupted by service and subsequent imprisonment in World War I. While a prisoner of war, he was appointed by Benedict XV to teach dogmatic theology and Sacred Scripture to imprisoned seminarians. After the war he entered the Society of Jesus (Sept. 9, 1919). Following his noviceship and his theological studies, he taught fundamental and dogmatic theology at Enghien, Belgium. In 1928 he finally returned to teaching NT exegesis: in Enghien (1928–40 and 1946–47) and in Lyon-Fourvière, France (1941–46). In 1948 he joined the faculty of the Pontifical Biblical Institute in Rome, where he remained until 1953, when ill health forced him to seek his native climate. Among his numerous published works are: "Bulletins du Judaïsme ancien," in RevScRel from 1929 to 1938; a commentary on Hebrews (Paris 1943); the Johannine Epistles (Paris 1935, 2d ed. 1954) and the Apocalypse volumes for the *Verbum Salutis* Series (Paris 1951); *Le judaïsme palestinien au temps de Jésus-Christ* (Paris 1934–35) in two volumes, later abridged into one (Turin 1950); *Exégèse rabbinique et exégèse paulinienne* (Paris 1939); *Théologie du NT* (Paris 1951); *Textes rabbiniques des premiers siècles chrétiens pour servir à l'intelligence du NT* (Rome 1955); and *Le Règne de Dieu* (Paris 1957).

Bibliography: S. LYONNET, *Biblica* 39 (1958) 262–268.

[S. B. MARROW]

BONVIN, LUDWIG, composer, conductor, protagonist of the *Caecilian movement; b. Siders, Switzerland, Feb. 17, 1850; d. Buffalo, N.Y., Feb. 18, 1939. After pursuing courses in medicine and law, he entered the Society of Jesus in 1874 in Holland and was ordained in 1885 at Liverpool, England. To supplement his irregular musical training, he studied theory, early church music, and Wagnerian composition. From 1887

Ludwig Bonvin.

to 1907 he directed the chorus and orchestra at Canisius College, Buffalo, later concentrating upon composition and historico-musical studies. As a mensuralist (with *Dechevrens and *Jeannin) Bonvin held that the notes in early medieval MSS are definitely of different proportional duration arranged in groups of two to eight beats, such groups constituting measures. His compositions, ending with Op. 168, include liturgical Masses, litanies, Vespers, hymns (notably the collection *Hosanna*), and works for instruments or voice or both; among them were the Symphony in G minor, *Morn on the Northern Coast, Johanna d'arc vor dem Scheierhaufen.*

Bibliography: L. BONVIN, Personal papers and manuscripts, Rosary Hill College, Buffalo, N.Y.; "Liturgical Music from the Rhythmical Standpoint up to the 12th Century," *Proceedings of the Music Teachers National Association* 10 (1915) 215–225; "The 'Measure' in Gregorian Music," MusQ 15 (1929) 16–28. L. BONVIN and A. FLEURY, *Über Choralrhythmus* (Leipzig 1901).

[M. V. BUTKOVICH]

BONZEL, MARIA THERESIA, MOTHER, foundress of the Poor Sisters of St. Francis Seraph of Perpetual Adoration; b. Olpe, Germany, Sept. 17, 1830; d. Olpe, Feb. 6, 1905. Aline was the elder of two daughters of Friedrich Edmund Bonzel, a wealthy industrialist and philanthropist, and Maria Anna (Liese) Bonzel. After studying under the Ursulines at Cologne, she became a Franciscan tertiary (1851) and took the name Theresia, which she retained in religion. Her desire to join the Salesian Sisters was frustrated for more than 5 years after 1852 by her inability to gain her mother's consent and then by a protracted illness. She founded her congregation (July 20, 1863) at Olpe to care for poor and neglected children, an apostolate later extended to the education of children and nursing the sick, especially the poor. During Theresia's lifelong term as superior general, she saw the institute spread to the U.S. (1875) and Austria, and increase to some 700 members (*see* FRANCISCANS—SISTERS).

Bibliography: S, ELSNER, *Mutter Maria Theresia Bonzel und ihre Stiftung* (Werl 1926), Eng. *From the Wounds of St. Francis,* tr. M. F. PETERS and M. H. HAU (Mishawaka, Ind. 1955).

[M. F. PETERS]

BOOK, THE ANCIENT

Books may be discussed with regard to their composition and dissemination. Their composition involves writing materials, book forms, the art of copying, and format of the book; the knowledge of dissemination of books includes their publication, authentication, literary information, and preservation.

COMPOSITION

The composition of the book in antiquity entailed the solution of difficulties no longer met today because of basic techniques developed then.

Writing Materials. The oldest material used for literary purposes and classifiable as a book was the clay tablet, in use in ancient Babylonia and Sumeria. Originally square (but later elongated), smooth on top and concave below, they could be kept in series. The lettering was done while the clay was still soft in one or three columns with a stylus similar to a pencil (Jer 17.1). When baked, the tablet retained its contents indelibly. For cataloguing the tablets the series, number, initial words of the text, and a summary were indicated in captions. These tablets constituted the first attempt to preserve important writings in libraries. More practical were the waxed boards on which characters were engraved with the sharp point of a stylus. The flattened end of the stylus was used to smooth the wax again. Wax tablets were difficult to handle and store but convenient for outlines, bills, letters, and school work, in which they could be corrected and used again (Tibullus 4.7.7; Propertius 3.23; Jerome, *Epist.* 8.1; Augustine, *Epist.* 15.1). In Greece Homer (*Iliad* 6.168) was the first to mention the "folded slate," a wooden tablet covered with a white substance (Euripides, *Alc.* 968), which was used also in ancient Palestine (Ez 37.15–22) and Italy (Gaius, *Inst.* 2.104). In Italy public registers of wood, iron, or ivory were engraved with a heated stylus (Tacitus, *Ann.* 13.28; Jerome, *In Ier.* 3.17; PL 24:786). Authors quoting such documents called them books (Cicero, *Verr.* 1.36).

Papyrus, called βύβλος in Greek, after the Syrian city of Byblos, was made from the pith of the papyrus plant. Extant papyri show that upon a vertical layer of narrow strips was placed a horizontal layer. When these were pressed, the fibers were united by the glue in the plant, or glue added thereto, and formed a smooth writing surface. Different qualities were produced, from packaging material to the fine white paper called *Augustea Regia* (Pliny, *Nat.* 13.74–76, 82; Isidore, *Orig.* 6.10.2). Despite its high cost, four drachmas per roll in the 2d century A.D, many sheets of papyrus had defective strips, bad joinings, or layers that did not stick together firmly. If papyrus was scarce, the writing could be erased with a sponge and the papyrus used again (Martial 4.10). Outlines, notes, letters, records, and literary works of leisure were written on papyrus. Used in Egypt in earliest times, it was exported from there as early as the 11th century B.C., and was sold in Alexandria until the end of antiquity (Jerome, *Epist.* 72.2). From the 7th century B.C., Ionia imported it into the Greek world. Solon's decree that Homer's entire epic be declaimed during the Panathenian feasts led to a more general use, for written copies were made. At the end of the 5th century Aristophanes could affirm that every person of culture possessed books (*Frogs* 1114). The tombs and the dry sands of Egypt have preserved most of the known papyri, some of which are of great value, e.g., the *P 66* (Bodmer 2) of the 2d century, which contains a good part of the Gospel of St. John.

Parchment derives its name, according to an ancient tradition that lasted until the 6th century A.D., from Pergamum, a city in Asia Minor that first flourished *c.* 300 B.C. The material was used for writing in 2000 B.C., however. Although less common than papyrus, parchment was known to the Greek world in the 6th century B.C. (Herodotus 5.58.3), the Dorians being the first Greeks to write on the skins of goats and sheep. Proof for the early use of parchment in Rome is seen in the legend that during the period of the kings, treaties of peace were permanently recorded on the skins of sacrificed animals (Dionysius Halicarnassensis, *Antiq. Rom.* 4.58:4). But as late as the 3d century A.D. it was necessary for Ulpian to determine for jurists that animal skins were as valid for testaments as was papyrus (*Dig.* 37.11:1). Little is known about the preparation of parchment. The hair was scraped off and the hides were dressed and smoothed for long strips, both sides of which could be written upon. Smaller pieces prepared for private and public archives, when stacked on top of one another and fastened together, would later form the "codex," the forerunner of the modern book. Parchment was not prized for literary compositions, because it was crude in comparison with light and elegant papyri, but by the 5th century it had replaced papyrus. It appealed to the circles of Christian ascetics, and Bibles written on it would last longer (Jerome, *Vir. ill.* 113). It was used for correspondence, however,

Fig. 1. Fragments of a clay tablet covered with the cuneiform text of the Babylonian story of the "Creation of Man," found at Nippur.

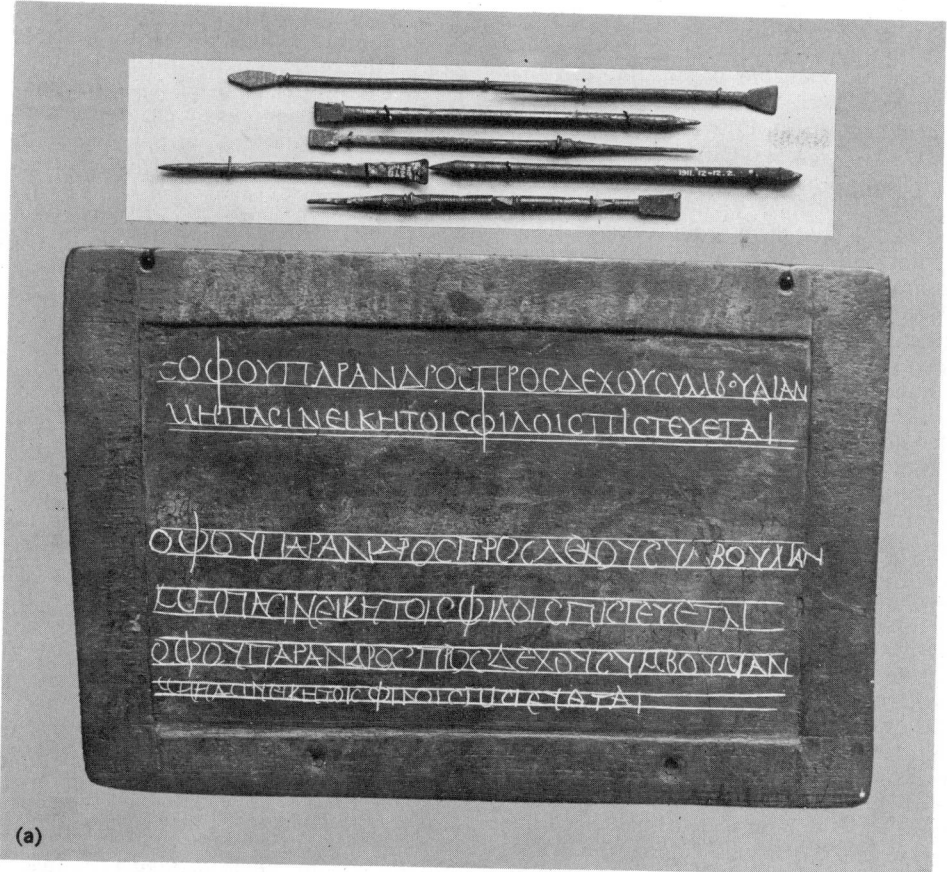

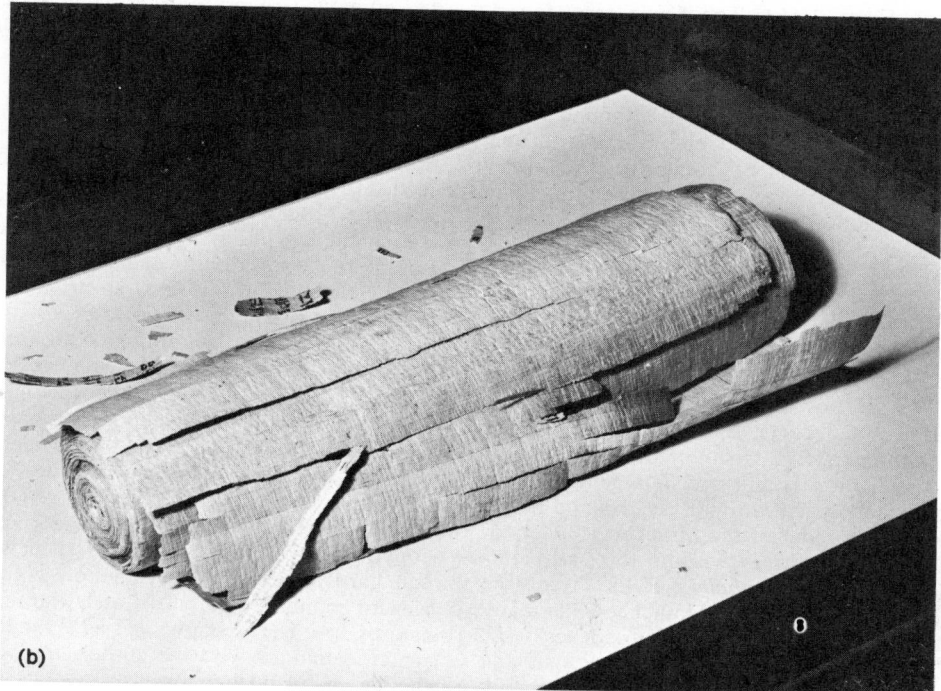

Fig. 2, (a) Wax tablet, one leaf of a diptych that formed a schoolboy's exercise book (Add. MS 34186). The tablet, which probably dates from the 2d century, carries two lines of verse in iambic meter, possibly a quotation from Menander. Above the tablet are various tools used for writing and for smoothing the wax tablets. (b) Papyrus scroll, an Egyptian "Book of the Dead," 3000 years old, still rolled as when found. Unrolled, it is 22 feet long.

only when papyrus became scarce. As a result, the letters published in antiquity, more than any other genre, have perished. Valuable pagan and Christian works have been preserved thanks to Christian writers of the 4th century and after who wrote on parchment.

Book Forms. The scroll (Latin *volumen*, from *volvere*, "to roll") suggests the unrolling of a long MS. The scroll was the usual form for books in Babylonia and Assyria in the 9th century. From there it may have passed to the Phoenicians and Aramaeans. Reference to it in the 7th century B.C. (Jer 36.2) suggests that it was then in common use. Strips of papyrus or parchment already inscribed were overlapped and glued or sewn together. The seams were visible, although great care was taken with them. In Athens the pioneer in the trade of gluing merited a statue, and in Rome an epitaph has immortalized a gluer (DACL 9:1760). Isidore observes that the length of the scroll depended upon the type of composition (*Orig.* 6.12), a small scroll for the lyric, a longer one for epic and history. Very long rolls were rare. Pliny says that "A good book is all the better, the longer it is" (*Epist* 1.20.4), but for him one of Cicero's discourses was a large book. For Martial 300 epigrams was a volume of insufferable length (*Epigr.* 2.1). The four Gospels, even Mark or Luke alone, would constitute a "scroll" (Jerome, *Epist.* 121.6). Even when codices had replaced rolls, Sacred Scripture was often copied on rolls. Copies of the "Exsultet" on great rolls that were annotated and illuminated solemnized the Easter Vigil liturgy until the Middle Ages. The scroll was held in the right hand and unrolled with the left, the text being in perpendicular columns. If, as happened infrequently, the text ran continuously down the scroll, it could be held under the chin and unrolled with both hands (Martial, *Epigr.* 1.66). The *Logia Jesu*, found at Oxyrhynchos (*P. Oxy* 4.454), and the scriptural texts found at Qumran near the Dead Sea are examples of books preserved in scrolls.

The codex or loose-leaf manuscript, although based on the old Oriental device of attaching tablets to one another, seems to have been of Roman origin. It was made of parchment and papyrus, or alternating folia of each, and revolutionized bookmaking. In the 3d century A.D. it was disputed whether codices constituted books according to Roman law. Profane authors would not use them. Of the 3d-century MS fragments extant, there is only one codex for every 15 scrolls. Among Christian writers of the same period there are four codices for each scroll. Christians copied profane works as well as their own works in codices (Rufinus, *Apol. adv. Hier.* 2.8; Jerome, *Epist.* 22.30). Christian calligraphers continued the tradition of artistic ornamentation in gold, purple, and precious gems, particularly in Bibles, in competition with secular and heretical books. Manes, founder of the Manichees, asserted, "The Apostles did not portray wisdom through paintings as I painted her" (*Kephalaia* 154). Augustine speaks of the costly books of the Manichees, "so many and such large and such sumptuous codexes" (*C. Faust.* 13.6). Arians and other adversaries of the Church followed suit. MS *P. Oxy* 30 dates probably from A.D. 100. A few Greek codices date from the 2d century. The 13 codices discovered in Nag' Hammâdi, Egypt, in 1946–47, comprising about 1,000 leaves of papyrus, date from the 3d century to c. 400. Of these leaves, 749 are well preserved. Codex X, measuring 21 by 27 centimeters with 37 lines per page, is the largest and most beautiful of the 13. From the 4th and 5th centuries the codex was the usual book form.

Art of Copying. Black ink (*atramentum*) made of charcoal and gum was used. Red ink (*rubrum*) served for titles. Costly MSS were written in gold letters. The copyist held his parchment or papyrus over a narrow board or inclined table and wrote with a stylus across the column. For the sake of elegance, lines ran continuously down the roll. Each line contained, at most, 18 syllables, a hexameter. To judge from the MSS extant, the number of syllables in a line was not rigidly determined. The columns were narrow enough for the eye to pass from one line to the next without losing the thread of thought. Division into columns (Latin *paginae*, Greek σελίδες) made it possible for Origen to attempt the first critical edition of the Bible, the Hexapla, six texts in parallel columns. Codices Vaticanus and Sinaiticus, both of the 4th century, are in three and four columns, respectively. Normally only one side of the page was written on. Pliny, to prove that his uncle Pliny the Elder wrote prodigiously, asserts that he wrote opisthographs, i.e., he filled both sides of the scroll (*Epist.* 3.5.17). Ironical allusions of the poets indicate that the reverse side served only for outlines and school work (Martial, *Epigr.* 4.86). The Apocalypse, however, refers to the sealed scroll, written within and without (Ap 5.1).

Dictation of their works by authors, classical as well as Christian, and especially public officials, was the rule. The stenographers used three devices: suspension [Anc(ient)], contraction [B(oo)k], and the substitution of conventional signs [&]. In Rome a shorthand system, *notae tironianae*, using 13,000 elements was employed. A professor of stenography in A.D. 301 received a salary 50 per cent larger than that of a teacher on the primary level or a professor of penmanship. In the 5th century a slave skilled in shorthand cost two and a half times more than an unskilled slave (*Cod. Iust.* 6.43.3.1; 7.7.1.5). The stenographic copy was transcribed upon papyrus or upon vellum. No one succeeded, even in the classical period and in the periods of greatest literary production, in establishing an organization for the purely technical task of copying books. But there was training, and schools existed for perfecting the skill of copyists, an art that the Christians preserved. Although the *First Rule* of the cenobitic monks, that of St. Pachomius of the 4th century, does not mention copyists, they were represented before long in the monasteries. Jerome recognized the job of copyist as a means of livelihood and as a stimulus for reading (*Epist.* 125.11). The only evidence that groups of copyists wrote in a workshop while someone dictated to them is a single Egyptian drawing. To say nothing of inevitable errors in dictation, the technical part of copying lent itself very little to team work. A group can hardly trace lines, begin new columns, maintain elegant penmanship, paint, and illumine at the same rate of speed. The copy used as a model, like modern plates, remained with the author, the bookseller, or in the library for further copies.

Format of the Book. "Book," Latin *liber*, originally designated bark on which uncivilized men wrote (Pliny, *Hist. nat.* 13.21.69; Jerome, *Epist.* 8.1). Later it signified a complete literary work or a part thereof. In the first leaf or column appeared the title, index, division, and author's name. These data, indispensable for identification or consultation, sometimes appeared in more complete form at the end of the work where they were better protected. The title could be repeated elsewhere in the work, and the table of contents might appear separately. Many ancient books are known and classified by their initial words, the *incipit,* even in 19th-century editions, just as encyclicals and papal bulls today are identified. Dedications, frequent in pagan and Christian antiquity, might be directed to some divinity, an important person, or a pupil. They included the homage, the first few notes about the book, the author's method, an exposition of difficult points, and at times invectives. Prefaces, ever the same, appear in all periods. To receive a dedication among the ancients was to be immortalized, for they still believed in the immortality of the book. The modern form of chapters and paragraphs were unknown to the ancients although the terms were used. The reader oriented himself by means of brief summaries or captions in the margin of the scroll or page. To cite a passage one referred to these summaries with an indication of its position in the book. Because it might be difficult for the reader to find the passage, or even the work cited, important passages were preferably transcribed or, more often, cited from memory. Critical signs to indicate lacunae, corrections, doubts, and interpolations existed from the days of early Alexandria until the end of antiquity (Isidore, *Orig.* 1.21). Those used by Origen in the Hexapla are well known. To these Jerome added the colon to signify the end of a quotation.

At the end of a book the Hebrews wrote *Amen, Sela,* or *Salom,* "So be it! Pause! Peace!" to confirm the assertions of the book, while promising it survival and expressing joy on the completion of copying (Jerome, *Epist.* 28.4). The Latins, besides *Amen,* used the more functional term *Explicuit* (The End), *Explicit feliciter* (Thank goodness it's finished!), or other phrases expressing the copyist's relief. In the classical period one finds formulas, inherited from the ancient Orient, that guarantee the fidelity of the copy. Jerome has transmitted the formula of St. Irenaeus (d. 202): "You who will transcribe this book, I charge you, in the name of our Lord Jesus Christ and of His glorious Second Coming, in which He will come to judge the living and dead, compare what you have copied against the original and correct it carefully. Furthermore, transcribe this adjuration and place it in the copy" (*Vir. ill.* 35). To prevent papyrus copies from tearing, the ancients reinforced them at both ends of the roll for a width of five centimeters. This part was called significantly *cornu,* "horn." At the end of the reading when the scroll was completely unrolled, it was held by the horns.

DISSEMINATION

The dissemination of the book was laborious and expensive. Forgeries and inaccuracies were difficult to control.

Publication. The terms for publication were in Greek, ἐκδίδωμι, διαδίδωμι; Latin, *librum edere, publicare, divulgare,* and others; *editio* signifies both the process and the result of publication. Unless the author himself provides it, the date of publication can hardly be determined from the various hand-copied MSS. During the classical period publication in large centers normally began with a public reading before friends and distinguished persons. After the session and applause, the book was handed over for distribution. Further advertising, even in handbills and posters, was not neglected (Suetonius, *Ep.* 5.11.3). Authors under the protection of sovereigns or patrons advertised through official channels. This was the procedure with works destined to celebrate great feats or to solemnize religious and civil assemblies or even festive reunions, e.g., the declamations of Homer, Pindar, Herodotus, the Greek tragedies, and until the end of the Roman Empire, the imperial panegyrics. The protection of the poets Vergil, Horace, and Propertius by Augustus and his minister Maecenas was proverbial. Genuine workshops for the dissemination of MSS arose with the libraries of the 5th century B.C. and municipal and court archives, especially with the library at Alexandria c. 300 B.C., which later held 700,000 scrolls. In Pergamum, in the libraries of Augustus and Trajan in Rome, and in the more important cities of the Empire originals were sought for reproduction. Ten copies a year of Tacitus's works were made for the archives by order of the Emperor Tacitus (d. 276). Booksellers, *bibliopolae,* reproduced and sold books of interest to the public. The authors, who received the fame but not the money, frequently made allusions to this exploitation. The copies were expensive, and ordinarily each copy was made as the demand arose, although a few might be kept on hand. The 1,000 copies of M. Regulus's panegyric (Pliny, *Epist.* 4.2.7) were singular.

Influential men maintained their own copyists to meet their needs. St. Clement of Alexandria (d. *c.* 215) indicated Anaxagoras (5th century B.C.) as the first such publisher. Atticus in Cicero's time was another (*Att.* 2.1.2). Among the Christians Origen, Jerome (*Vir. ill.* 61, *Hom. Orig. in Ier.* prologue), and Augustine (*Epist.* 44.2) maintained up to seven copyists for their own works and those of others. Paulinus of Nola, himself an author, disseminated the books of Ambrose (Augustine, *Epist.* 31.8); requested the books of Augustine not only for his personal instruction "but for the good of many churches" (Paulinus, *Epist.* 25.1); and created publicity for Sulpicius Severus (Sulpicius Severus, *Dial.* 3.17 A), Jerome, Rufinus, and others. Generations of monks would later undertake the reproduction of these authors. In the monastery of Martin of Tours this was the only skill allowed (Sulpicius Severus, *Mart.* 10.6). Clerics carried works from India to Alexandria (Jerome, *Vir. ill.* 36), and within their lifetimes Christian authors might be read from one end of the known world to the other (Sulpicius Severus, *Dial.* 1.8).

The author, or others, sometimes published improved, revised, or abbreviated texts, e.g., the longer original text of the Rule of St. Pachomius (*c.* 318) and the shorter text composed after the 5th century. A new edition might offer only the slightest modifications or a complete revision. When an author died his work became public property, and changes were made freely and with impunity. From the 4th to the 6th century the distribution of books without the author's consent became more and more audacious, as did the corruption of texts, the falsification of signatures, and the theft of MSS.

Authentication. Introduced from Syria, authentication by signature appeared in Greece by the 5th century B.C. Signatures to the copy could be forged, however (Jerome, *Epist.* 105.3). Another means of identification was the signet ring possessed by persons of distinction and used on official documents and to authenticate messages, letters, and even entire works. If an authentic copy of a text could be found in an archive or a library, it was easy to authenticate a text in hand. Otherwise authentication had to be accomplished by an internal criticism or by a comparison of data in copies.

Literary Information. In antiquity data about literary works were transmitted with little method. Children in school came to know famous authors through copies of their verses, extant in many papyrus fragments. In the schools of great masters, as in Athens and Rhodes, privileged youths broadened their knowledge of names and books. Once in public life, they kept themselves informed through conversations, meetings, correspondence, and public readings. There were attempts at systematic instruction, similar to modern manuals of the history of literature, such as Plutarch's *Lives* in Greek, Cicero's *Brutus* for Roman eloquence, and especially Suetonius's *De viris illustribus*, which introduced readers to poets, grammarians, rhetoricians, and philosophers. In Christian times Jerome compiled the first manual of literary information in his *De viris illustribus*, a work continued by Gennadius of Marseilles at the end of the 5th century, by Isidore of Seville at the beginning of the 7th, and by Ildefonsus of Toledo (d. 667). The uncertainty of literary information can be seen in expressions like "As someone said recently," "As I myself inquired," and "They say that he produced" (Jerome, *Vir. ill.* 126, 128).

Preservation. When stored, books were bound with leather thongs, *constrictus liber,* and at times inserted into a stronger parchment or papyrus cover, *sittybos.* Scrolls gathered together, especially in a collection, were newly bound and placed in a cylinder or box, Greek κιβωτός or χαρτοφυλάκιον Latin *scrinium, chartarium, arca, armarium, cista, capsa.* The titles were hung outside the container on strips of leather, *pittacia* (Cicero, *Att.* 4.4b.1; Ovid, *Trist.* 1.1.109). Humidity and insects were a real danger. Cedar oil was used against worms and decomposition (Ovid, *Trist.* 1.1.7; Martial 5.6.14). Catalogs antedate the library at Alexandria, but the systematic collecting of books began there. Smaller libraries also assembled books for particular subjects, especially for the divine services (*Acta purgationis Felicis ep. Autumnitani,* CSEL 26).

Precious scrolls were rolled on wooden rods or bones, which were sometimes decorated or gilded. The elaborateness of the internal ornamentation and the external appearance of books were points of pride for amateur book collectors and the newly rich. Wooden chests, boxes of iron or a more precious metal, and even ivory containers, protected literary works for later generations.

See also ABBREVIATIONS; PAPYROLOGY; PALEOGRAPHY, GREEK.

Bibliography: J. DE GHELLINCK, *Patristique et moyen âge,* v.1–3 (Gembloux 1946–   ). F. G. KENYON, *Books and Readers in Ancient Greece and Rome* (2d ed. Oxford 1951). E. ARNS, *La Technique du livre d'après saint Jérôme* (Paris 1953), bibliography. A. BATAILLE, *Les Papyrus* (Paris 1955). W. NEUSS, Lex ThK² 2:746–748. W. MATTHIAS, RGG³ 1:1459–61. ReallexAnt Chr 2:664–772. **Illustration credits:** Fig. 1, The University Museum, The University of Pennsylvania. Fig. 2, Courtesy of the Trustees of the British Museum.

[E. ARNS]

BOOK, THE MEDIEVAL

The medieval book par excellence is the codex, though the rotulus or roll (which must be distinguished from the roll of antiquity) also was in use. The triumph of the parchment codex over the papyrus roll (*see* ROLL AND CODEX), together with the accompanying change in copying procedure of the 4th century, led to the rapid disappearance of papyrus, hitherto dominant. From then on papyrus was used but rarely except for documents (e.g., in the papal chancery into the 11th century). When early medieval codices are compared with the unexcelled quality of the parchment codices of late antiquity (4th to the 6th century), they represent a clear regression, although the method of making them (for which instructions have been preserved from the 8th century) can scarcely have been substantially altered.

Parchment. Parchment was called διφθέρα in Greek and *membrana* in Latin; as early as A.D. 301 there is mention of *membrana pergamena,* and Jerome refers variously to *membrana* and *pergamena.* In the Middle Ages the word *charta,* or charter, was often modified by such words as *ovina, vitulina,* and *pergamena.* The parchment was prepared for writing by a *membranarius, pergamenarius,* etc. The untanned animal skin was first coated with caustic lime for several days, then bleached in limewater. The hair, epidermis, and any remnants of flesh were scraped off. The hide was once again cleaned in a lime bath, stretched on a frame, dried, and finally scraped smooth with pumice. Whiting was then poured over the hide and rubbed in. The inner or flesh side (F) of the parchment and the outer or hair side (H) differed in that the former would be whiter and smoother, the latter rather yellowish or gray, rough, and porous. The difference could be almost eliminated, but only by very special treatment, especially by oxidation. In charters, which usually carried writing on only one side (documents with writing on both sides, called opisthographs, are rare), the difference between F and H is more apparent than in books, since care was taken by bookmakers to render the contrast less noticeable. In southern Europe a finer sort of parchment, whose F is clearly whiter and smoother than its H, was used, whereas in the north a thicker, coarser, and more yellowish parchment predominated. However, it should be noted that the drastic difference between F and H of parchments can be easily discerned only down to the 10th and 11th centuries; from then on both sides tend to be more evenly oxidized. Vellum made from sheepskin by a special method is typical of the British Isles. Southern Europe preferred sheepskins and goatskins; the north often used calfskin as well. The finest parchment came from the skin of newborn or unborn lambs; it was called *charta virginea* or *charta non nata.* The writing surface of deluxe MSS or single pages would sometimes be dyed, generally purple. This ancient custom (used in, e.g., the Codex Argenteus, the Codex Rossanensis, and the Vienna Genesis) came into vogue again under the Carolingians (having been used, e.g., in the Ada MS, the Gottschalk Gospel Book, and the Coronation Gospel Book of Vienna) but died out again in the 11th century. Blue and black parchment is very rare and a collector's item.

Parchment was better suited for repeated use than was papyrus. Hence, when it was in short supply, MSS

Fig. 1. The opening pages of an antiphonary written for the convent of Sainte-Marie at Beaupré in 1290 (Walters MS 759, fol. 1v and 2r). The left-hand page contains a colophon telling for whom the book was made, an anathema against theft, and a benediction for devout use. The MS was probably written at the monastery of Cambron.

that were expendable because their content was out of date, no longer valued, or objectionable, or because the script had become "old-fashioned," were often used again. This happened especially from the 7th to the 9th century, at which time many MSS from the 5th to the 7th century were reused. The original writing was erased by first scraping the parchment with a knife (*rasorium*), then rubbing it with pumice (*pumex,* hence *pumicare*), then soaking it in milk and washing it with a sponge (*spongium* or *peniculus,* hence the German *Pinsel*). When modern scholars first tried to read these twice-inscribed pages (called *palimpsests*), they used reagents (gallnut ink, Gioberti ink) to bring out the original text; but too often this resulted in the total destruction of the text. Today the quartz lamp is used, as is also palimpsest photography. Until the 12th century various European monastic centers—which were the chief consumers—manufactured their own parchment and even sold it. After that time parchment preparation became a secular craft.

Paper. Parchment was employed for books until the 16th or 17th century, but after the 14th or 15th century its use was generally restricted to precious liturgical books and collectors' items. It began to be replaced in the 13th century by paper (called *charta bombycina,* or in 1077 *bambycina,* then *charta papyri* in 1231, and then *papirus* in 1311). Paper had been a Chinese in-

vention dating from the early 2d century B.C., allegedly of the minister of agriculture Ts'ai Lun. It had been used since A.D. 751 by the Arabs, first in Samarkand, and then throughout the Caliphate. In the East, paper replaced papyrus without a transitional parchment stage, but it came to Europe only in the 11th century via Spain, where the oldest paper mill in the West was established in Játiva before 1150, and via northern Italy as an Arab article of trade. In 1276 the first paper mill in Italy was built in Fabriano, in 1337 the first French mill was in Troyes, and in 1390 the first German mill appeared in Nuremberg. Paper first replaced parchment in the chanceries, where it was used for registers, communications, minute books, protocols, letters, etc. It was utilized for books earlier or later according to regions; e.g., in Spain paper was used before 1036, but it was not common before 1300.

Once the rags, the raw material for paper, were chopped into small pieces, they were soaked in water and underwent a decomposition process. The fiber was given more water and was then pulped by a stamping mill into half stuff. This was placed in storage chests and 24 hours later was stamped into paper pulp, or full stuff. The pulp was stored in vats, from which the vat assistant extracted a thin layer with a screen, i.e., a rectangular wooden frame strung with seven bronze wires. Gentle shaking of the screen matted the fibers and drained off the excess water. The leaves of paper thus obtained were then couched, i.e., each leaf was laid between two mats, piled one on top of the other, and pressed so that the water was sucked up by the mat. After a second pressing, this time without mats, the sheets were hung up to dry, often on a clothesline, and then dipped into a solution of glue or gelatinous material, made out of animal offal, to glaze the sheets. Lastly, from the 13th century on, the sheets were always marked with figures, symbols, letters, etc., and together with the imprints of the bottom and binding wire of the frames they formed the "watermark" or filigree. Two journeymen always worked together with a pair of frames: the dipper drew the pulp from the vat with a frame; the coucher pressed the dipped sheet off the frame onto the mat. Further preparation of any codex—as pictured in the 10 medallions on the title page of the 12th-century Michelsberg MS of St. Ambrose in Bamberg—was the business of the scribe.

Assembling the Book. The medieval book was usually of an elongated rectangular shape; some few (of an early date) were almost square, and occasionally an oblique shape appeared (but this was an insular idiosyncrasy). The size, however, varied to an extraordinary degree, depending on contemporary, local, and personal taste, on the book's purpose (e.g., a pocket-size prayerbook, a large choir book), the size of the available hides, the instructions of the client, etc. Thus there are codices of the tiniest size and almost all intervening sizes up to and including the large folio volume. The number of pages likewise varied from that of the slim little volume to that of a ponderous tome.

The scribe first had to cut the parchment given him into the desired size. For this he used a sharp curved knife (*novacula, rasorium*) and a ruler (*regula, linula, norma, canon, praeductale*). The basic unit of any book was the double sheet (*diploma, plicatura,* rarely *arcus*); the single sheet was called a *folium.* The scribe often had to glue tears in the parchment, repair damaged spots, smooth out rough places with the *plana,* and sew up holes with catgut or twine; this was sometimes done in artistic form by skilled women using varicolored silk threads. The trimmed double sheet was then folded together into an individual gathering. If there were a considerable difference between F and H, further care was taken so that similar sides faced each other (F to F, H to H). When the difference was negligible, this rule was less strictly observed. Gatherings were formed by placing folded double sheets inside each other; thus two double sheets formed a binion (II); three, a ternion (III); four, a quaternion (IV); five, a quinternion (V); and six, a sexternion (VI). Until the 12th century, quaternions were most often used in books on the Continent, though often IIs, IIIs, and Vs were intermingled. The Irish (like the ancients) preferred quinternions. From the 13th century on, however, the form and size of the gatherings became irregular, influenced perhaps by the paper codices, in which sexternions often occurred, as did gatherings of up to 10 and more double sheets.

For ruling the page, a compass (*circinus, punctorium*) was used; fine punctures were made at the edge of the sheet at intervals as regular as possible. These punctures are called prickings. A standard scale for ruling seems to have been plotted on the edge of the writing desk, to judge from miniatures. Vertical and horizontal lines were then drawn with a ruler, and a meticulous scribe gave his most careful attention to the accuracy of this operation. Down to the 10th century horizontal lines were ideally framed by double verticle lines; later scribes contented themselves, as a rule, with one vertical line. If there were to be columns, they were similarly separated by vertical lines down the center. In the late Middle Ages the uppermost line (usually not written on) and the bottom line (or several at the top and bottom and occasionally one in the middle) were drawn from the outer left to the outer right edge over both open pages so that the two sheets would not become displaced. Until the 12th century a blunt, or dry, stylus (*stilus, graphium, graphius, graphiarium, ligniculum, sulcare,* i.e., to draw lines) was generally used to make concave and convex "blind" lines on the recto and verso side of the sheet, respectively. By the 12th century, however, the pages were rather generally being ruled with lead pencil or crayon (*plumbum*); and from the 13th century, increasingly with ink. For the earlier, pre-12th century period several variations are worthy of note: in the British Isles, after each gathering had been formed, the folded sheet was punctured with prickings at the inner and outer edge and ruled up; but on the Continent (up to the 10th or 11th century) proper procedure called for the double sheet, not yet folded, to be spread out and then for two, three, or all sheets of the future gathering to be laid on top of it so that when the top sheet was ruled up, the scribe pressed hard enough with the stylus to leave impressions on the sheets below. Only then were the sheets folded and made into a gathering. But from the 12th century on (to some extent even in the 11th) ruling was done after the sheets had been folded into a gathering. Then the two open pages were ruled at a time, skipping the next two, so that in each case the convex impression of the verso side served as lines. Early medieval scribes numbered the gatherings for the bookbinder, generally on the last page of each gathering using Roman numerals, often preceded by a Q (for quaternion). This practice was continued to the 12th century, although most such numbering was lost when the book was trimmed by the bookbinder. In the later Middle Ages the scribe tended to number the first page of the gathering, the last, or both. He might use letters, capital and minuscule, as well as Roman numerals, often with characteristic decoration. A further aid for the bookbinder when putting the gatherings together was the catchword; it guaranteed an accurate sequence of individual gatherings and is still of importance today for arranging the text in its right order. The catchwords were always located on the last page of a gathering, usually at the bottom inside edge. They consisted of the first word or words of the first page of the next gathering. Aside from isolated examples from the 8th and 9th centuries, the catchwords—which were forerunners of the signature marks of old printed books—came into use only in the 12th century. As opposed to the Egypto-Greek and Coptic custom of numbering pages, spaces, or lines, the Middle Ages produced only isolated instances of folio numbering between the 8th and the 12th or 13th century. But in the 12th century, foliation was used in Missals; and by the 13th century, it was already fairly widespread, and was customary by the 14th century. Arabic numbers were used as well as Roman numbers. By contrast, pagination was never generally employed in the Middle Ages. In the 15th century some MSS—like the earlier printed books—numbered only from the first to the middle sheet of the gathering, with letters and figures, e.g., a1, a2, a3, a4 in the first gathering (quaternion), and b1, b2, b3, b4 in the second gathering, etc.

Writing Instruments. After preliminary work of preparing his materials the scribe (Latin, *antiquarius, librarius, scriptor, scriba, notarius, clericus,* etc.) could begin writing—usually copying rather than taking dictation or composing. In addition to the reed pen (*calamus*), the pen (*penna, pennula*) had gained popularity in the Roman Empire (isolated bronze and silver pens have been preserved). From the 4th century the quill pen, made from the tail and wing feathers of geese and swans, competed with the reed pen. This is understandable since parchment was becoming predominant, and the pen wrote better than the reed on parchment. However, since the words *calamus* and *penna* occur side by side and are often synonymous, the exact date at which the reed pen was abandoned cannot be fixed. It is possible that it was used down to the 11th century in individual instances, and it is known that the Renaissance humanists used it again in their antiquarian enthusiasm. The reed pen was kept in a cylindrical holder of wood or metal (Greek καλαμοθήκη, καλαμίς, κανών; Latin *theca calamaria, theca cannarum, calamarium*); the pen was stored in an elongated penholder suited to its shape (*theca libraria,* but also *calamarium*). These containers might also hold an inkwell (*atramentarium, incausterium,* and by metonymy, *calamarium*); but the buckhorn (*cornu*) also was used, one for red and one for black ink, either hung on the wall or placed in an opening of the writing desk. For sharpening both instruments as well as for erasing, the scribe had a broad knife with bowed back (*scalprum librarium, cultellus scripturalis, scalpellum, temperatorium, artavus;* the process was called *acuere, temperare*). It was very important for the writing process (*see* PALEOGRAPHY, LATIN) how the pen was cut, whether symetrically or obliquely, i.e., whether the left or right edge was cut. A pen was tested by the scribe before he began to copy, hence the many *probationes pennae* in medieval MSS, which give interesting clues to the scribe's educational status, etc.

The Ink. Ink used in the Middle Ages was black, but in the course of time it took on shades of brown, gray, and green, by virtue of its chemical composition and atmospheric influences. Codices of late antiquity and generally those of Ireland were written in a deep black ink. Continental codices down to the 11th century often shade from light brown to black; in the 12th and 13th centuries they show deep black tints; in the 14th century, more often green (because of the addition of copper substances); and in the 15th, brown and gray tones, as well as black. The ink was called μέλαν, μελάνιον in Greek, and *atramentum librarium* in Latin, after its black color, to distinguish it from shoeblack, *atramentum sutorium*. When it was manufactured by cooking, it was called *encaustum, incaustum*. Less frequent is the designation *tincta, tingta, tinctura,* from *tingere,* to dye. The earliest inks were made of lampblack and gum and could be washed off with a sponge. Obviously this would not adhere well to parchment, and at least from the 4th or 5th century there was a shift to the manufacture of inks from metallic salts (e.g., iron sulfate or copper sulfate) and from gallnuts dissolved in wine, with

Fig. 2. Back of a book with its original medieval binding. At the top of the leather-covered board cover is the ring with which it was chained.

admixtures of vinegar (or beer) and gum (or water). The metal content in this ink, or acids, or both together have not only caused the ink to turn color but, what is worse, have occasioned serious damage in the older MSS by corrosion (ink erosion). Today research is being devoted to the repair of such damage.

Red ink was made from red lead (*minium*) or cinnabar. It was used by the scribe, an illuminator specialist, or a rubricator to accentuate certain passages, especially at the beginning of a codex, by little red strokes affixed to the letters (red dots in Irish MSS), by writing on top of individual letters or whole lines with red, or by simply writing in red (Latin, *miniare, rubricare*). Red was generally used to decorate and to distinguish any titles, as well as for the *incipit* and *explicit,* for labeling, for initial capitals in chapters and sentences, for initials, etc. With the Carolingian period gold and silver ink was used in writing on purple parchment and in accentuating individual initials and illuminations. For this the scribe used a brush (*peniculus, penicillus*).

The Writing. Writing (Greek γραφεῖν, hence the Latin *graphiare* to the extent that this word is not derived from *graphium* or slate-pencil, or the Greek χαράττειν and Latin *charaxare, scribere;* to make a simple copy or *exemplar* was *exemplare,* but to write elaborately and artistically was *formare,* hence the phrase *littera formata*) was executed by the scribe sitting at a desk with a sloping top (**scriptorium*). Numerous representations show the scribe sitting before the desk, holding the knife in his left hand to erase or to hold down the sheet, while he writes with the pen in his right hand, often with the

Fig. 3. Girdle book, Breviary written in Germany, probably in the monastery of Kastl, near Nuremberg, in 1454.

index and middle finger on the pen and the other fingers under it, without supporting his wrist on the desk. When the scribe was finished with his work, the rubricator or illuminator was called upon to execute any decoration the codex might require.

Bookbinding. When the scribe and rubricator had finished, the MS went to the bookbinder. Several papyrus codices from the 2d and 3d centuries are extant (e.g., the Nag-Hammādi), consisting of one rather large signature made up of many sheets of papyrus, bound in leather-covered boards. For multisignature codices, chain stitching was used in Coptic Egypt, the individual signatures being bound together by loop stitches in such a way that a chainlike pattern—which often served as ornamentation—was formed on the back of the cover, which had been laced to the signatures in the same process. Knowledge of bookbinding technique in late antiquity is very incomplete. The bound codex may have developed out of the *diptych. By the 8th century at the latest (from the earlier periods only the 7th-century, deluxe-bound Theodelinda Gospel Book in Monza, Italy, has been preserved) the signatures were sewn together. But with certain exceptions (including three Fulda MSS), the earliest bindings preserved are

from the 9th century. It is possible that many books before that time were simply wrapped in parchment sheets, as may be seen in codices preserved in *Sankt Gallen. Such MSS encountered in contemporary catalogues are designated as *in quaternionibus* and the like.

The typical method of binding in the Middle Ages was to stitch the individual signatures to several bands or cords running crosswise at the back with whose help the assembled book was laced to the covers. The stitching thread originally ran over the whole length of the back and was allowed to extend out above and below in order to bind the signatures to one another. To prevent the threads from tearing the signatures at top and bottom, a parchment or leather strip was added; this strip was sewn all around and thus formed the headband. After the assembled book had been laced to the cover, the outer edges were cut or planed smooth; in the later Middle Ages the edges were then painted or inscribed, especially if the volumes were displayed with the cut edges facing the user.

Book covers (in contrast to archive volumes, which often had no hard covers) were usually of wood up to the 16th century, but this was gradually supplanted in the Renaissance by pasteboard, which had appeared much earlier in Islamic bindings. Less frequent were covers made of parchment, leather, or woven fabric without boards. Wooden covers were made of beech, maple, or oak and covered with fabric, or more usually with leather made from skins of sheep, goat, deer, antelope, calf, cow, or pig. The leather was stretched moist over the wooden boards. After the boards were covered, the leather that overlapped was glued to the front and back inside cover, and an endpaper was glued over it. Up to the 12th or 13th century the first leaf of the first signature and the last leaf of the last signature of the book were so used, but later wastepaper (parchment or paper) was more often employed. The first free or unattached sheet (often missing at the back) is the end paper in the strict sense, the so-called fly leaf. In older volumes the fly leaf was usually a part of the first signature (i.e., the second sheet of that signature), but later it was often pasted-in wastepaper. Until the 11th century the binding most often had a smooth back, i.e., no back bands were visible; the headband, however, stood out sharply. The leather of the cover was usually decorated only with vertical, horizontal, or diagonal, simple or multiple parallel lines, etc.; only seldom did the cover bear figured ornamentation (cf. the early bindings of Fulda, Sankt Gallen, Schaffhausen, etc.). But from the 12th century book covers began to appear with beveled edges and with metal corner and center pieces (studs, bosses, bands, borders) of iron, copper, or brass, and with decorative and · protective clasps (*clausurae*). Strips of leather, similarly cut and applied, were used, but rarely, in place of these. Metal strips were applied to the outer edges of covers for heavy folio books. Books that were to be chained usually had the chain fastened with a ring through the upper edge of the back cover, though sometimes through the front cover; a ring at the other end of the chain fastened it to a rod on the reading desk. The covers of a book were held together in front by hasps or clasps (*clausurae, fibulae*) made of metal, leather, plaited straps with hinges, etc.

Variations of the simple binding used generally throughout the Middle Ages were the pouch book, the girdle book, and book with jacket, all easy to carry or readily attachable to the belt. The covering material of the pouch and girdle bookbindings was allowed to extend far beyond the bottom edge of the cover (rather than being folded over into the inside of the cover). A book with a jacket binding had another material (leather, silk, velvet) that covered the book's regular binding; since the jacket binding extended some length beyond the edges of the book, it provided protection from dust.

Many bindings incorporated bookmarkers of leather, plaited hemp, or ribbons made of some fabric (*corda, cordula, registrum*), which were fastened to the upper headband. In very large tomes there was sometimes a set of leather bookmarkers fastened to a free, or loose, diagonal strip (*tenaculum*) located on the upper edge. There are some rare volumes that had a wooden box with sliding lid that was affixed to the top edge of the back cover and that contained a wooden reading-stick. Parchment strips called *misericordiae* were often attached to the outside edge of certain pages in the late Middle Ages; sometimes they were dyed red, inscribed, and made to protrude from the edge to facilitate the finding of certain passages or texts. Besides the simple, generally prevalent bindings (*ligatura, coopertorium*), there is also a group of deluxe bindings, many of which date from as early as the 8th century. These are made with ivory covers, exemplified by the consular diptychs of antiquity and by books of Byzantine and medieval western making. Other deluxe bindings were embossed with gold or silver, such as the *Codex Argenteus* and the *Codex Aureus*. Still others were enamel, particularly from Limoges, or adorned with precious stones or filigrees. In the 12th century, leather bindings came to be enhanced with carving (e.g., some Codices of Engelberg), and later, plate and roller stamps were popular.

Fig. 4. German book cover of silver set with carved ivory plaques and a large semiprecious stone, 13th century.

Bookbinding became a secular craft in the 12th or 13th century, and subsequent bindings show that it became a highly developed art form.

See also BOOK, THE ANCIENT; BOOK, THE PRINTED.

Bibliography: S. DAHL, *History of the Book* (New York 1958), revision of original Ger. ed. (1928). E. P. GOLDSCHMIDT, *Gothic and Renaissance Bookbindings,* v.1 (New York 1928). R. DELBRÜCK, *Die Konsulardiptychen* (Studien zur spätantiken Kunstgeschichte 2; Berlin 1929). J. DESTREZ, *La Pecia dans les manuscrits universitaires du XIIIᵉ et du XIVᵉ siècle* (Paris 1935). *Lexikon des gesamten Buchwesens,* ed. K. LÖFFLER and J. KIRCHNER, 3 v. (Leipzig 1935–37). P. LEHMANN, "Blätter, Seiten, Spalten, Zeilen," ZblBiblw 53 (1936) 333–361, 411–442; repr. in *Erforschung des Mittelalters,* 4 v. (2d ed. Stuttgart 1959–61) 3: 1–59. L. W. JONES, "Pricking Manuscripts: The Instruments and Their Significance," *Speculum* 21 (1946) 389–403. *Scriptorium* (Antwerp 1946–). F. G. KENYON, *Books and Readers in Ancient Greece and Rome* (2d ed. Oxford 1951). K. LÖFFLER and P. RUF, "Allgemeine Handschriftkunde," *Handbuch der Bibliothekswissenschaft,* ed. F. MILKAU and G. LEYH, v.1 *Schrift und Buch* (2d ed. Wiesbaden 1950) 106–162. A. BOECKLER and A. A. SCHMID, "Die Buchmalerei," *ibid.* 249–387, with important bibliogs. E. VON RATH and R. JUCHHOFF, "Buchdruck und Buchillustration bis zum Jahre 1600," *ibid.* 388–533. M. J. HUSUNG and F. A. SCHMIDT-KÜNSEMÜLLER, "Geschichte des Bucheinbandes," *ibid.* 782–848. E. KUHNERT and H. WILMANN, "Geschichte des Buchhandels," *ibid.* 849–1004. A. RENKER, "Geschichte des Papiers," *ibid.* 1047–68. D. DIRINGER, *The Hand-produced Book* (New York 1953). G. PICCARD, "Die Wasserzeichenforschung als historische Hilfswissenschaft," *Archivalische Zeitschrift* 52 (1956) 62–115. W. WATTENBACH, *Das Schriftwesen im Mittelalter* (3d ed. Leipzig 1896; 4th ed. repr. Graz 1958). D. DIRINGER, *The Illuminated Book, Its History and Production* (New York 1958). *L'Histoire et ses méthodes,* ed. C. SAMARAN (Paris 1961), with important methodological articles by select authors, with bibliogs. **Illustration credits:** Figs. 1 and 4, Courtesy of the Walters Art Gallery, Baltimore. Fig. 3, Spencer Collection, The New York City Public Library.

[A. BRUCKNER]

BOOK, THE PRINTED

The book printed from moveable type represents a relatively late development in history. In tracing its progress in the West from the 15th century, this article focuses on those aspects of the printed book that are relevant to the fine arts, that is, the effect of its appearance as produced by type face, page design, and illustration.

Printed Books and Manuscripts. Although the printed book can be considered a mechanical product, its physical format in the first stages of development in the 15th century differed little from the medieval manuscript book. Of the similarities between them, perhaps the most significant was the parallel between script and its position on the page and printed type and its position. The decoration of manuscripts, including rubrication, initial lettering, and elaborate marginal treatment, often served as inspiration for similar decoration in the printed book. At first these elements were added by hand; later they were produced by woodcut, metal-cut, and type forms such as printers' flowers. The printers were quick to use woodcut illustrations, which corresponded to the illuminations in manuscript. Finally, common to both the printed book and the illuminated manuscript was the protection provided by binding.

Throughout their history, handwritings in manuscripts assumed characteristic forms that are comparable to styles in the history of art. Beginning with the square capital derived from formal stone-cut letters, such as those on Trajan's Column in Rome, the manuscript letter in Europe underwent various changes in design, resulting finally in the 15th-century gothic pointed letter (called also "black letter") used in the north, and a humanistic rounded letter ("roman"), lighter in weight, that was characteristic of the south. On these two basic MS hands the first type faces were modeled.

A Benedictine Missal printed at Bamberg in 1481 by Johann Sensenschmidt exemplifies the typical gothic type face. The angular letters, somewhat condensed in width, perpendicular and rigid in structure, and black in color, result in a magnificent effect of solemnity, dignity, and formality. This lettering was intended primarily for folio volumes to be used in Offices of the Church. A work such as Cicero's *Epistles,* printed by Nicholas Jenson in Venice (1471), may serve to illustrate the Renaissance round hand. Beautifully designed letters, each in perfect relation to all the others, give a sense of ease and movement in the lines of the page. The two styles of type face corresponded to the prevailing architectural styles of Europe at the time—the pointed Gothic of northern Europe and the round-arched Renaissance style characteristic of Italy.

The Discovery of Printing. How printing was invented in the Western world in the 15th century and who was responsible for it have long been matters of controversy among scholars. It seems to have been a matter of the cumulative solution, at a propitious time, of certain technical problems, rather than the discovery of any new principles. In China moveable wood characters were used for printing by the 11th century, and in Korea cast metal characters were in use in the 14th century. In the West the invention of printing with moveable type has been claimed for Laurens Jansoon Coster from Haarlem in the Netherlands and Procopius Waldfoghel from Avignon in southern France. However, it was Johann *Gutenberg of Mainz, Germany, who first devised the most satisfactory method of printing books, using metal type cast in molds that adjusted to exact dimensions for the separate characters, a workable linseed oil varnish ink, and a press with a sliding bed. Historical records show that Gutenberg was carrying out experiments in printing as early as 1439.

The earliest known example of printing in Germany is a part of a leaf of a Sibylline poem known as the "Fragment of the World Judgment." This work, together with a Latin grammar and an astronomical calendar, were probably printed on an experimental basis in Gutenberg's Mainz workshop between 1444 and 1447. The type face is a pointed gothic letter, not very skillfully handled. The earliest dated piece of printing is a collection of papal indulgences with the date 1454; it contains receipts requested of Pope Nicholas V by the King of Cyprus for donors of money to oppose the invasion of the Moslem Turks and the attendant threat to Christianity. However, the first complete book—and a supreme achievement in printing—is the famous Gutenberg or Forty-two-Line Bible. By 1450 the Bible was being planned by Gutenberg; with the assistance of Peter Schoeffer, a calligrapher and later one of the most skillful of 15th-century printers, he completed it in 1456. The Bible is folio in size, and its 1286 pages are arranged in two columns of type printed in the pointed black letter (*lettre de forme*) similar to the letters in manuscripts written in the Mainz area in the early 15th century. Border and marginal decorations were added by hand. A copy preserved in two volumes in the Bibliothèque Nationale contains an inscription by the rubricator, Heinrich Cremer, a curate of St. Stephen's Collegiate Church in Mainz, stating that it was finished before Aug. 15, 1456. Of the 47 copies known to be in existence, it is thought that the most beautiful is the one in the Library of Congress, Washington, D.C.

Two other important books printed in Mainz have been connected with Gutenberg. The rare Thirty-six-Line Bible was begun *c.* 1450 but not finished until 1460–61. This Bible was probably set up from the printed Forty-two-Line Bible as copy and has perhaps more valid claim to the title "Gutenberg Bible." The *Catholicon,* a Latin dictionary compiled by Joannes Balbus in the 13th century, was printed at Mainz in 1460 in a small rounded gothic type face, with Lombard capitals for initial letters and with the text arranged in two columns to the page. It has been suggested that Gutenberg himself was the author of its colophon (a statement at the end of a book giving information pertaining to its printing).

With the completion of the Forty-two-Line Bible in 1456, Gutenberg seems to have given up his activities in printing, leaving Johann Fust and Peter Schoeffer as the major practitioners. The Psalter of 1457, the first dated and signed book and one of the most beautiful ever printed, is credited to them (*see* PRAYER BOOKS). Its handsome typography is enhanced by red and blue floriated initials printed individually from large metal type after the book was printed, rather than drawn in by hand. Of the 10 copies known to be in existence, that in Vienna is the only one in which the printer's device of the double shield appears in the colophon.

Printing soon flourished in other cities in Germany, such as Strassburg, Bamberg, Augsburg, Nuremburg, and Ulm. The subject matter of the books was primarily religious. In general there came to be three type faces in common use: the *lettre de forme* or pointed gothic letter reserved for formal publications such as service books for the Church; the less formal *lettre de somme* or rounded gothic; and the *lettre batarde,* a cursive-influenced style used chiefly for works in the vernacular. The *lettre de forme* was elaborated in the 16th century with many flourishes into the *fraktur* style, most spectacularly expressed in the *Theuerdanck* printed by Hans Schonsperger in 1517 for Emperor Maximilian. A pure roman type face was first used in Germany by Adolf Rusch at Strassburg in 1464 in the *Rationale divinorum officiorum,* a popular work by Duranti the Elder on the origin and meaning of ecclesiastical ceremonies. In the 16th century, Johann Froben of Basel used a roman face almost exclusively.

Early Printed Illustration. Woodcut illustration became a concern of the 15th-century printer as early as 1460 in the books printed by Albrecht Pfister at Bamberg. Among the most famous of the early illustrated books is the *Nuremberg Chronicle* printed by Anton Koberger in 1493. This volume, compiled by Hartmann Schedel, is a world history up to 1492 in which, obligingly, three pages were left blank for the recording of what might happen after that date. Its 1,809 illustrations, designed chiefly by Michael Wohlgemuth, were made from only 645 separate woodblocks by repeating the same view for many cities and the same portrait for many kings. Stefan Fridolin's *Schatzbehalter,* published by Koberger 2 years before the *Chronicle,* with almost 100 cuts of Biblical subjects, is of

Incipit liber bresith ꝙ nos ge
In principio creauit deus celū nesi dica⁹
et terram. Terra autem erat inanis et
vacua: ⁊ tenebre erant sup faciē abissi:
et spiritus dn̄i ferebatur super aquas.
Dixitqȝ deus. Fiat lux. Et facta ē lux.
Et vidit deus lucem ꝙ esset bona: et
diuisit lucem a tenebris. appellauitqȝ
lucem diem et tenebras noctem. Factū
qȝ est vespere ⁊ mane dies unus. Dixit
quoqȝ deus. Fiat firmamentū in medio aquarū: et diuidat aquas ab a-
quis. Et fecit deus firmamentū: diui-
sitqȝ aquas que erant sub firmamen-
to ab hiis que erant super firmamen-
tum: ⁊ factum est ita. Vocauitqȝ deus
firmamentū celū: ⁊ factum est vespere
et mane dies secundus. Dixit vero deus. Congregentur aque que sub celo
sunt in locum unū et appareat arida.
Et factum est ita. Et vocauit deus ari-
dam terram: cōgregationesqȝ aquaȝ
appellauit maria. Et vidit deus ꝙ esset bonū. et ait. Germinet terra herbā
virentem et facientem semen: et lignū
pomiferū faciens fructum iuxta genus
suū: cuius semen in semetipso sit super
terram. Et factum est ita. Et protulit
terra herbam virentem et facientem semen iuxta genus suū: lignūqȝ faciens
fructū et habēs unūqdqȝ sementē scdm
speciē suā. Et vidit deus ꝙ esset bonū:
et factū ē vespere et mane dies tercius.
Dixitqȝ aūt deus. Fiant luminaria
in firmamēto celi. ⁊ diuidāt diem ac
noctē: ⁊ sint in signa ⁊ tēpora. ⁊ dies ⁊
annos: ut luceāt in firmamēto celi et
illuminēt terrā. Et factū est ita. Fecitqȝ
deus duo luminaria magna: lumiare
maius ut p̄esset diei et lumiare min⁹
ut p̄esset nocti: ⁊ stellas. ⁊ posuit eas in
firmamēto celi ut lucerent sup terrā: et
p̄essent diei ac nocti: ⁊ diuiderēt lucem
ac tenebras. Et vidit de⁹ ꝙ esset bonū:
et factū ē vespere et mane dies quart⁹.
Dixit etiam deus. Producant aque
reptile anime viuentis et volatile sup
terram: sub firmamēto celi. Creauitqȝ
deus cete grandia. et omnē animā viuentem atqȝ motabilem quā produxe-
rant aque in species suas: ⁊ omne volatile secundū genus suū. Et vidit deus ꝙ esset bonū: benedixitqȝ ei dicens.
Crescite et multiplicamini. et replete a-
quas maris: auesqȝ multiplicentur
super terram. Et factū ē vespere ⁊ mane
dies quintus. Dixit quoqȝ deus. Pro-
ducat terra animā viuentem in genere suo: iumenta ⁊ reptilia. ⁊ bestias terre secundū species suas. Factū ē ita. Et
fecit deus bestias terre iuxta species suas: iumenta ⁊ omne reptile terre in genere suo. Et vidit deus ꝙ esset bonū:
et ait. Faciam⁹ hominē ad ymaginē ⁊
silitudinē nostrā. ⁊ p̄sit piscibȝ maris.
⁊ volatilibȝ celi. ⁊ bestiis uniūseqȝ terre:
omīqȝ reptili qđ mouet̄ ī terra. Et creauit deus hominē ad ymaginē et simi-
litudinē suam: ad ymaginem dei creauit illū: masculū et feminā creauit eos.
Benedixitqȝ illis deus. et ait. Crescite
et multiplicamini ⁊ replete terram. et
subicite eam: ⁊ dominamini piscibus
maris. ⁊ volatilibus celi: ⁊ uniuersis
animātibus que mouentur sup terrā.
Dixitqȝ deus. Ecce dedi vobis omnē
herbam afferentem semen sup terram.
et uniūsa ligna que habēt ī semetipis
sementē generis sui: ut sint vobis ī escā.
⁊ cūctis aīantibus terre. omīqȝ volucri
celi ⁊ uniuersis q̄ mouētur in terra. et ī
quibus ē anima vivēs: ut habeāt ad
vescendū. Et factū est ita. Viditqȝ deus
cuncta que fecerat: et erāt valde bona.

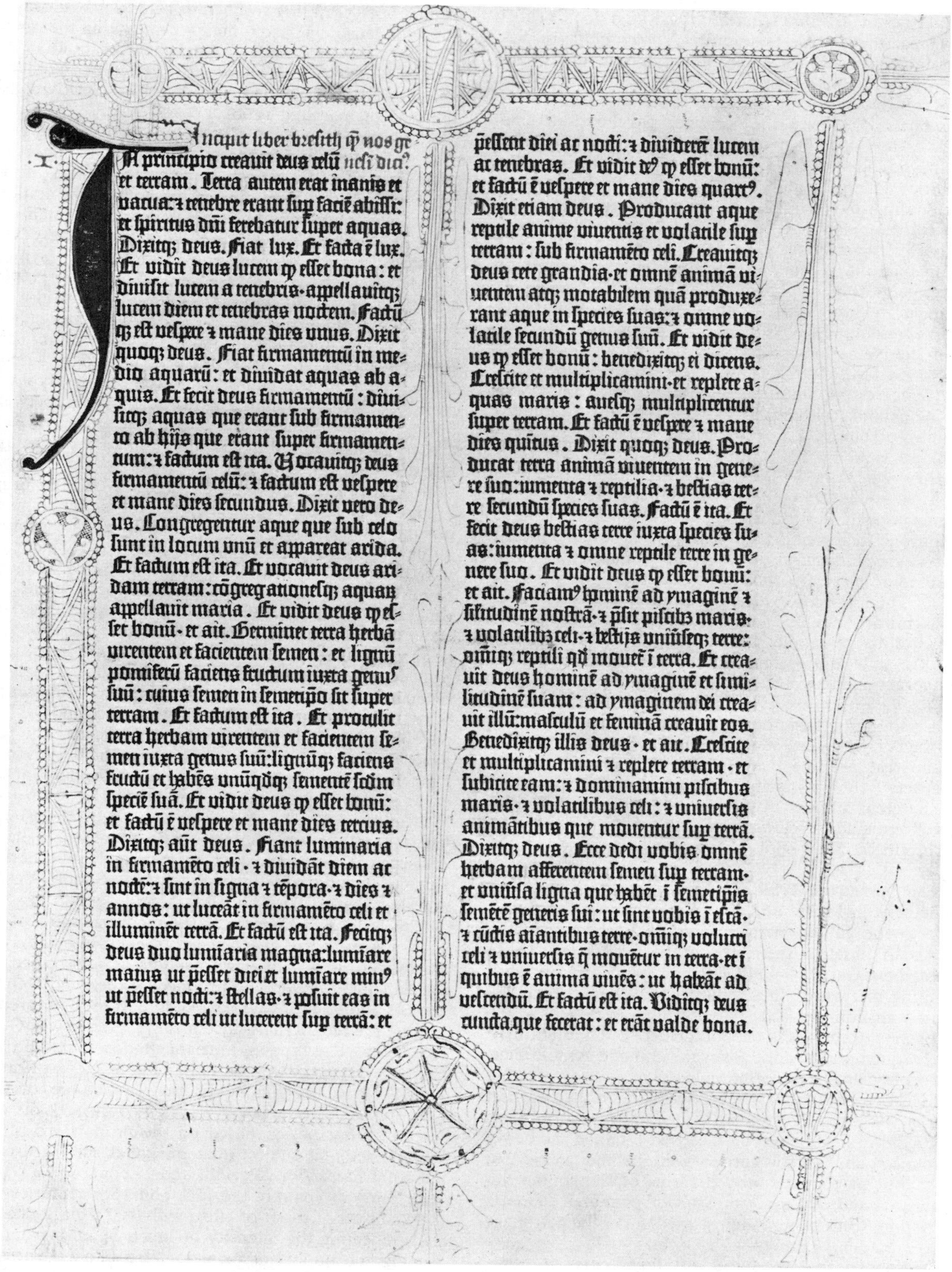

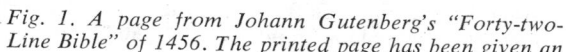

Fig. 1. A page from Johann Gutenberg's "Forty-two-Line Bible" of 1456. The printed page has been given an artistic treatment usual with manuscripts of the period. Initial letter and marginal decorations are hand drawn.

greater aesthetic value. Another illustrated book of importance, the extremely popular *Narrenschiff,* of Sebastian Brant, was printed by Johann Bergmann at Basel in 1494. Albrecht *Dürer is credited with the illustrations of this satire on the foibles of mankind. Both Dürer and *Holbein the Younger gave considerable impetus to book illustration. Of the illustrated Bibles of the period, the Cologne Bible of 1478, printed by Heinrich Quentell, and the Lübeck Bible of 1494 are outstanding. Bernhard Breydenbach's *Peregrinations to the Holy Land* is one of the most interesting of these early illustrated books. The artist Erhard Reuwich accompanied the author on his travels and is thought to have made drawings of scenes as he actually observed them, even though one of the illustrations of animals is a representation of a unicorn. An outstanding work from the Netherlands is the *Chevalier Délibéré,* printed at Gouda (1486–90).

An interesting variation of the illustrated book was the blockbook, with both letter text and illustration cut from wood blocks. Like those of moveable types, blockbooks existed in China long before they made their appearance in the West. The earliest known Chinese example is the *Diamond Sutra* of 868, printed as an aid to popular devotions. Blockbooks became popular in Europe in the mid-15th century and are significant as an early indication of the great social changes that were to result from the development of the printing press. Their purpose was to dramatize pictorially legends, miracle stories, and teachings of the Scriptures for semiliterate people; the printed text played a minor role. In style and design they were derived from contemporary manuscripts. One of the most delightful is the *Canticum canticorum,* illustrating the Song of Solomon as an Old Testament prefiguration of the history of the Virgin (*see* CANTICLE OF CANTICLES). Others of interest are the *Ars moriendi* and the *Biblia pauperum;* the popularity of these two books is attested by the great number of their editions. Blockbooks may have been made as early as 1420, and they continued to be produced after books were printed from moveable type.

The Spread of Printing. As the result of religious difficulties in Mainz and conditions that were unfavorable to the guilds, many printers left that city in the 1460s to practice the newly learned craft elsewhere throughout Europe—Italy, France, Spain, and England. Printing in each of these countries, however, early assumed an unmistakably national character.

In Italy, through the encouragement of Cardinal Juan de Torquemada, Conrad Sweyenheym and Arnold Pannartz of Mainz began printing in the monastery of Santa Scholastica, at Subiaco, near Tivoli. One of their earliest works was St. Augustine's *De civitate Dei,* printed in 1467 in a transitional type face that retained the heavy blackness and narrow proportions of the gothic but also anticipated the rounded forms of the roman humanistic hand. A year later Sweyenheym and Pannartz moved to Rome, where they printed under the patronage of the Massimi family.

Venice became the great printing center in Italy. John and Wendelin de Spire were the first to practice the craft there. Another successful printer, Erhard Ratdolt, specialized in printed decoration. His edition of Appian's *Historia Romana* (1477) shows how readily the printer could adjust his craft to the needs of the printed book. Printing reached its zenith in Venice with Nicholas Jenson, whose roman type has been the model for type faces ever since. An excellent example of his work is Pliny's *Historia naturalis,* printed in 1476. Jenson showed consistently in his work a sensitivity for appropriate marginal ratio.

Aldus *Manutius was, after Gutenberg, perhaps the most famous among printers. He was the inventor not only of a beautiful roman type face but also of the italic letter, which he used for his pocket-size editions of the classics, comparable to Loeb or Everyman editions of recent times. The well-known printing device of Aldus consists of a dolphin, supposedly a symbol of speed and activity, entwined around an anchor, representing firmness and stability. The most beautiful work printed by Aldus was the *Hypnerotomachia Poliphili* (1499), a dream allegory written by the Dominican Francesco Colonna, in a mixture of Italian, Greek, Latin, and Hebrew. This masterpiece of typography is remarkable for the harmonious relationship between outline woodcut illustrations, attributed to various Renaissance artists, and the handsome roman text type and initial letters.

In France the most notable examples of early printing are to be found in the Book of Hours, the layman's manual of devotion. Artists, illuminators, and printers all devoted their skills to this type of book, which was frequently embellished with illustrations of religious scenes, printed from relief-engraved metal plates. In general, early French printing was characterized by elaborate decoration combined with graceful type face designs. A good example is *La Mer des Hystoires,* printed in Paris in 1478 by Pierre La Rouge. This book reflects its derivation from Merovingian manuscripts of the 7th and 8th centuries in the type face and the full-page initials ending in fantastic animal heads. The full-page calligraphic letters, which were characteristic of French printing, may be seen in the title page of another edition of the same book printed in Lyons in 1491 by Jean du Pré. The type face favored by the French was the gothic *lettre batarde,* with a spirited delicacy of design. Other important printers and publishers in France include: Philippe Pigouchet, Simon Vostre, Antoine Verard, and Guy Marchand.

The delight and charm of the medieval spirit of the 15th-century book in France continued into the 16th. There were many scholarly printers as well, especially the Estienne family, who produced Greek and Hebrew classics and scientific works. An important figure representing the new Renaissance ideal in France was Geoffroy Tory. The type and ornamentation of his printed Books of Hours reveal the Italian influence that Francis I had made fashionable at the French court. The *Champfleury,* his greatest work, incorporates his theories of letter design based on the proportions of the human body, a subject that intrigued such artists as Albrecht Dürer, Fra Pacioli, and *Leonardo da Vinci.

Printing in Spain in the 15th and 16th centuries was marked by a splendor of effect with heavy black decoration, reflecting the intensity of much Spanish painting. Among the important printers were Pablos Hurus at Saragossa, Fadrique of Basilea at Burgos, and Lambert Palmart and Nicolaus Spindeler at Valencia.

William *Caxton, the first important English printer, was as much a scholar as a craftsman. He designed several types and produced at least 100 books, some

(a)

(b)

(c)

(d)

Fig. 2. The printed book (specimen pages): (a) Hartmann Schedel's "Nuremberg Chronicle," Anton Koberger, 1493. (b) Sebastian Brant's "Narrenschiff," Johann Bergmann, Basel 1494. (c) Bible, Sweyenheym and Pannartz, Rome, 1471. The marginal decoration is hand drawn. (d) Pliny's "Historia naturalis." Nicholas Jenson, Venice, 1476.

POLIPHILO INCOMINCIA IL SECONDO LIBRO DI
LA SVA HYPNEROTOMACHIA. NEL QVALE PO-
LIA ET LVI DISERTABONDI, IN QVALE MODO ET
VARIO CASO NARRANO INTERCALARIAMEN-
TE IL SVO INAMORAMENTO.

NARRA QVIVI LA DIVA POLIA LA NOBILE ET
ANTIQVA ORIGINE SVA. ET COMO PER LI PREDE-
CESSORI SVI TRIVISIO FVE EDIFICATO. ET DI QVEL
LA GENTE LELIA ORIVNDA. ET PER QVALE MO-
DO DISAVEDVTA ET INSCIA DISCONCIAMENTE
SE INAMOROE DI LEI IL SVO DILECTO POLIPHILO.

E MIE DEBILE VOCE TALE O GRA
tiose & diue Nymphe absone peruenerano &
inconcine alla uostra benigna audiétia, quale
laterrifica raucitate del urinante Esacho al sua-
ue canto dela piangeuole Philomela. Nondi
meno uolendo io cum tuti gli mei exili conati del intellecto, & cum la mia paucula sufficié
tia di satisfare alle uostre piaceuole petitione,
non ristaro al potere. Lequale semota qualúque hesitatione epse piu che
si congruerebbe altronde, dignamente meritano piu uberrimo fluuio di
eloquentia, cum troppo piu rotunda elegantia & cum piu exornata poli
tura di pronútiato, che in me per alcuno pacto non si troua, di cóseguire
il suo gratioso affecto. Ma a uui Celibe Nymphe & ad me alquáto, quan
túche & confusa & incomptaméte fringultiéte haro in qualche portiuncula gratificato assai. Quando uoluntarosa & diuota a gli desii uostri &
postulato me prestaro piu presto cum l'animo nó mediocre prompto hu-
mile parendo, che cum enucleata tersa, & uenusta eloquentia placédo. La
prisca dunque & ueterrima geneologia, & prosapia, & il fatale mio amore
garrulando ordire. Onde gia essendo nel uostro uenerando conuentuale
conspecto, & uederme sterile & ieiuna di eloquio & ad tanto prestáte & di
uo ceto di uui O Nymphe sedule familiare dil acceso cupidine. Et itan-
to benigno & delecteuole & sacro sito, di sincere aure & florigeri spirami-
ni afflato. Io acconciamente compulsa di assumere uno uenerabile auso,
& tranquillo timore de dire. Dunque auante il tuto uenia quae, o bellissi-
me & beatissime Nymphe a questo mio blacterare & agli semelli & terri-
geni, & pusilluli Conati, si aduene che in alchuna parte io incautamente

A

(a)

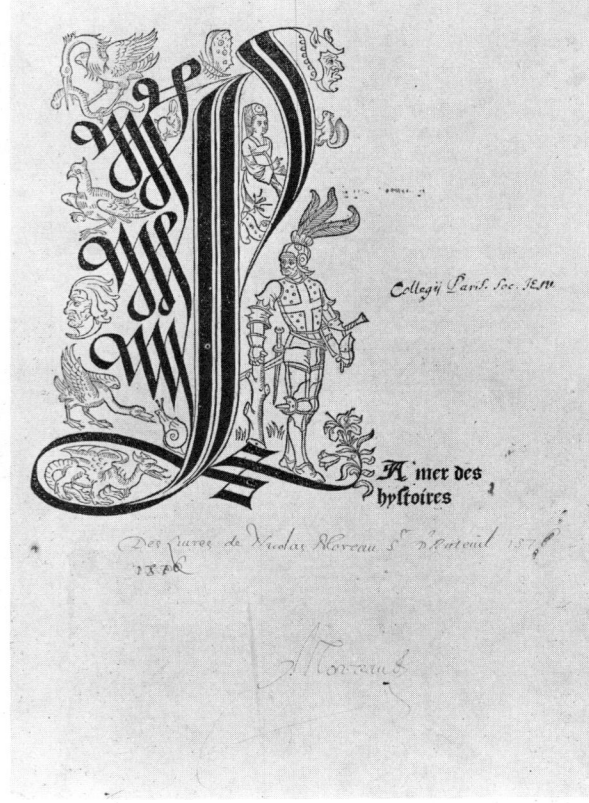

(b)

(c)

(d)

Fig. 3. The printed book (specimen pages): (a) Francesco Colonna's "Hypnerotomachia Poliphili," Aldus Manutius, Ven-
ice, 1499. (b) "La Mer des Hystoires," Pierre La Rouge, Paris, 1478. (c) Oliveros de Castilla's "Historia," Fadrique de
Basilea?, Burgos, 1499. (d) Christine de Pisan's "Fayttes of Armes," Caxton, Westminster, 1489.

juries. And therfore tho two auctoritees that ye han seyd above, been oonly understonden in the juges; for whan they suffren over muchel the wronges and the vileynyes to be doon withouten punysshynge, they sompne nat a man al oonly for to do newe wronges, but they comanden it. Also, a wys man seith: that The juge that correcteth nat the synnere, comandeth & biddeth hym do synne. And the juges & sovereyns myghten in hir land so muchel suffre of the shrewes and mysdoeres, that they sholden by swich suffrance, by proces of tyme, wexen of swich power & myght, that they sholden putte out the juges & the sovereyns from hir places, and atte laste maken hem lesen hire lordshipes.

BUT lat us now putte, that ye have leve to venge yow. I seye ye been nat of myght & power as now to venge yow. For if ye wole maken comparisoun unto the myght of youre adversaries, ye shul fynde in manye thynges, that I have shewed yow er this, that hire condicioun is bettre than youres; and therfore seye I, that it is good as now that ye suffre and be pacient.

FORTHERMOORE, ye knowen wel that, after the comune sawe, It is a woodnesse a man to stryve with a strenger or a moore myghty man than he is hymself; & for to stryve with a man of evene strengthe that is to seyn, with as stronge a man as he, it is peril; and for to stryve with a weyker man, it is folie; and therfore sholde a man flee stryvynge as muchel as he myghte. For Salomon seith: It is a greet worshipe to a man to kepen hym fro noyse & stryf. And if it so bifalle or happe that a man of gretter myght and strengthe than thou art do thee grevaunce, studie & bisye thee rather to stille the same grevaunce, than for to venge thee; for Senec seith that He putteth hym in greet peril that stryveth with a gretter man than he is hymself. And Catoun seith: If a man of hyer estaat or degree, or moore myghty than thou, do thee anoy or grevaunce, suffre hym; for he that oones hath greved thee, another tyme may releeve thee and helpe.

YET sette I caas, ye have bothe myght and licence for to venge yow; I seye that ther be ful manye thynges that shul restreyne yow of vengeance-takynge, and make yow for to enclyne to suffre, and for to han pacience in the thynges that han been doon to yow. First and foreward, if ye wole considere the defautes that been in youre owene persone, for whiche defautes God hath suffred yow have this tribulacioun, as I have seyd yow heerbiforn: for the poete seith, that We oghte paciently taken the tribulacions that comen to us, whan we thynken and consideren that we han disserved to have hem. And Seint Gregorie seith: that Whan a man considereth wel the nombre of his defautes and of his synnes, the peynes and the tribulaciouns that he suffreth semen the lesse unto hym; & inasmuche as hym thynketh his synnes moore hevy and grevous, insomuche semeth his peyne the lighter, & the esier unto him.

Chaucers Tale of Melibee

ALSO ye owen to enclyne and bowe youre herte to take the pacience of oure Lord Jhesu Crist, as seith Seint Peter in his epistles: Jhesu Crist, he seith, hath suffred for us and yeven ensample to every man to folwe & sewe hym; for he dide nevere synne, ne nevere cam ther a vileynous word out of his mouth; whan men cursed hym, he cursed hem noght; and whan men betten hym, he manaced hem noght. Also the grete pacience which the seintes that been in paradys han had in tribulaciouns that they han ysuffred, withouten hir desert or gilt, oghte muchel stiren yow to pacience. Forthermoore, ye sholde enforce yow to have pacience, considerynge that the tribulaciouns of this world but litel while endure, and soone passed been and goone; & the joye that a man seketh to have by pacience in tribulaciouns is perdurable; after that the Apostle seith in his epistle: The joye of God, he seith, is perdurable, that is to seyn, everelastynge.

ALSO troweth & bileveth stedefastly, that he nys nat wel ynorissed, ne wel ytaught, that kan nat have pacience, or wol nat receyve pacience. For Salomon seith: that The doctrine & the wit of a man is knowen by pacience. And in another place he seith: that He that is pacient governeth hym by greet prudence. And the same Salomon seith: The angry and wrathful man maketh noyses, and the pacient man atempreth hem and stilleth. He seith also: It is moore worth to be pacient, than for to be right strong; & he that may have the lordshipe of his owene herte is moore to preyse than he that by his force or strengthe taketh grete citees; and therfore seith Seint Jame in his epistle: that Pacience is a greet vertu of perfeccioun.

CERTES, quod Melibee, I graunte yow, dame Prudence, that pacience is a greet vertu of perfeccioun; but every man may nat have the perfeccioun that ye seken; ne I nam nat of the nombre of right parfite men, for myn herte may nevere been in pees unto the tyme it be venged. And albeit so that it was greet peril to myn enemys to do me a vileynye in takynge vengeance upon me, yet tooken they noon heede of the peril, but fulfilleden hir wikked wyl, and hir corage. And ther-

75

(a)

THE GOSPEL ACCORDING TO S. JOHN

IN the beginning was the Word, and the Word was with God, and the Word was God. The same was in the beginning with God. All things were made by him; and without him was not any thing made that was made. In him was life; and the life was the light of men. And the light shineth in darkness; and the darkness comprehended it not. ¶ There was a man sent from God, whose name was John. The same came for a witness, to bear witness of the Light, that all men through him might believe. He was not that Light, but was sent to bear witness of that Light. That was the true Light, which lighteth every man that cometh into the world. He was in the world, & the world was made by him, & the world knew him not. He came unto his own, and his own received him not. But as many as received him, to them gave he power to become the sons of God, even to them that believe on his name: which were born, not of blood, nor of the will of the flesh, nor of the will of man, but of God. And the Word was made flesh, & dwelt among us, (and we beheld his glory, the glory as of the only begotten of the Father,) full of grace and truth. John bare witness of him, and cried, saying, This was he of whom I spake, He that cometh after me is preferred before me: for he was before me. And of his fulness have all we received, & grace for grace. For the law was given by Moses, but grace and truth came by Jesus Christ. No man hath seen God at any time; the only begotten Son, which is in the bosom of the Father, he hath declared him. ¶ And this is the record of John, when the Jews sent priests and Levites from Jerusalem to ask him, Who art thou? And he confessed, & denied not; but confessed, I am not the Christ. And they asked him, What then? Art thou Elias? And he saith, I am not. Art thou that prophet? And he answered, No. Then said they unto him, Who art thou? that we may give an answer to them that sent us. What sayest thou of thyself? He said, I am the voice of one crying in the wilderness, Make straight the way of the Lord, as said the prophet Esaias. And they which were sent were of the Pharisees. And they asked him, & said unto him, Why baptizest thou then, if thou be not that Christ, nor Elias, neither that prophet? John answered them, saying, I baptize with water: but there standeth one among you, whom ye know not; he it is, who coming after me is preferred before me, whose shoe's latchet I am not worthy to unloose. These things were done in Bethabara beyond Jordan, where John was baptizing. ¶ The next day John seeth Jesus coming unto him, and saith, Behold the Lamb of God, which taketh away the sin of the world. This is he of whom I said, After me cometh a man which is preferred before me: for he was before me. And I knew him not: but that he should be made manifest to Israel, therefore am I come baptizing with water. And John bare record, saying, I saw the Spirit descending from heaven like a dove, and it abode upon him. And I knew him not: but he that sent me to baptize with water, the same said unto me, Upon whom thou shalt see the

111

(b)

(c)

The First Book of Moses, called

GENESIS

CHAPTER I

IN THE BEGINNING GOD CREATED THE HEAVEN AND THE EARTH. ¶2 And the earth was without form, and void; and darkness was upon the face of the deep. And the Spirit of God moved upon the face of the waters. ¶3 And God said, Let there be light: and there was light. ¶4 And God saw the light, that it was good: and God divided the light from the darkness. ¶5 And God called the light Day, and the darkness he called Night. And the evening and the morning were the first day.

¶6 And God said, Let there be a firmament in the midst of the waters, and let it divide the waters from the waters. ¶7 And God made the firmament, and divided the waters which were under the firmament from the waters which were above the firmament: and it was so. ¶8 And God called the firmament Heaven. And the evening and the morning were the second day.

¶9 And God said, Let the waters under the heaven be gathered together unto one place, and let the dry land appear: and it was so. ¶10 And God called the dry land Earth; and the gathering together of the waters called he Seas: and God saw that it was good. ¶11 And God said, Let the earth bring forth grass, the herb yielding seed, and the fruit tree yielding fruit after his kind, whose seed is in itself, upon the earth: and it was so. ¶12 And the earth brought forth grass, and herb yielding seed after his kind, and the tree yielding fruit, whose seed was in itself, after his kind: and God saw that it was good. ¶13 And the evening and the morning were the third day.

¶14 And God said, Let there be lights in the firmament of the heaven to divide the day from the night; and let them be for signs, and for seasons, and for days, and years: ¶15 And let them be for lights in the firmament of the heaven to give light upon the earth: and it was so. ¶16 And God made two great lights; the greater light to rule the day, and the lesser light to rule the night: he made the stars also. ¶17 And God set them in the firmament of the heaven to give light upon the earth, ¶18 And to rule over the day and over the night, and to divide the light from the darkness: and God saw that it was good. ¶19 And the evening and the morning were the fourth day. ¶20 And God said, Let the waters bring forth abundantly the moving creature that hath life, and fowl that may fly above the earth in the open firmament of heaven. ¶21 And God created great whales, and every living creature that moveth, which the waters brought forth abundantly, after their kind, and every winged fowl after his kind: and God saw that it was good. ¶22 And God blessed them, saying, Be fruitful, and multiply, and fill the waters in the seas, and let fowl multiply in the earth. ¶23 And the evening and the morning were the fifth day.

¶24 And God said, Let the earth bring forth the living creature after his kind, cattle, and creeping thing, and beast of the earth after his kind: and it was so. ¶25 And God made the beast of the earth after his kind, and cattle after their kind, and every thing that creepeth upon the earth after his kind: and God saw that it was good.

¶26 And God said, Let us make man in our image, after our likeness: and let them have dominion over the fish of the sea, and over the fowl of the air, and over the cattle, and over all the earth, and over every creeping thing that creepeth upon the earth. ¶27 So God created man in his own image, in the image of God created he him; male and female created he them. ¶28 And God blessed them, and God said unto them, Be fruitful, and multiply, and replenish the earth, and subdue it: and have dominion over the fish of the sea, and over the fowl of the air, and over every living thing that moveth upon the earth.

¶29 And God said, Behold, I have given you every herb bearing seed, which is upon the face of all the earth, and every tree, in the which is the fruit of a tree yielding seed; to you it shall be for meat. ¶30 And to every beast of the earth,

B

1

(d)

de secréter dix ou douze mémoires pour l'Institut. Pieu, Apache ou qui que ce soit, on croit toujours à une présence réelle.

PILATE n'a pas eu besoin de donner un coupe-file à ce cher Apache : il n'a pas quitté l'Homme d'un pas, l'accompagnant de la prison au prétoire, du prétoire à la croix, toujours prompt à lui lancer un coup de pied s'il trébuche, un soufflet s'il perd haleine, dix injures pour un soupir, et pour une larme cent crachats. Le professeur Pieu les recueille à même la sueur d'angoisse, avec le soin merveilleux qu'il a toujours mis à mesurer les atomes de la cellule cérébrale des oursins, comme à compter les battements du cœur des infusoires. — Ils n'en ont pas, dit-il, plein de morgue. — Et vous ?

Fig. 4. The printed book (specimen pages): (a) Chaucer's "Canterbury Tales," Kelmscott Press, 1896. (b) Bible, Doves Press, 1903–05. (c) Bible, designed by Bruce Rogers, Oxford University Press, 1935. (d) Andre Suares' "Passion," published by Ambroise Vollard, Paris, 1939, with wood engravings from blocks drawn by Georges Rouault.

of which were the first books to be printed in the vernacular. Caxton was followed in the 16th century by Wynkyn de Worde and Richard Pynson. Johann Froben was another scholarly printer who worked in Basel. He is remembered for his association with Erasmus and for his employment of Hans Holbein the Younger to decorate many of his publications.

From the 17th Century to the Present. In the 17th century, production of the luxurious book reflected the baroque style of the period. Book design became architectural with the elaboration of bordered title pages, and illustrations were printed from copper line-engravings designed by such artists as Peter Paul *Rubens. The style was exemplified by the *Opera* of Justus Lipsius printed in 1637 at the Plantin-Moretus Press, in Antwerp. Despite the frequent aesthetic deficiencies of the printed book in the 17th century, the period was important for book production. The Imprimerie Royale in France published handsome volumes, its first product being the *De imitatione Christi* of Thomas à Kempis in 1640.

In the 18th century the printed book was marked by the same classical tendencies that one finds expressed in literature, painting, and architecture. John Baskerville in England is important for his type designs and his experiments in papermaking. William Caslon, an English typefounder, designed a handsome old-style type face that has been in continuous use for more than 200 years. The printed book reached its culmination at this time in the simple restrained work of Giambattista Bodoni in Italy and the Didot family in France. Their modern-style type faces, with thick and thin lines sharply defined, and the open spacing of a page resulted in a classical dignity that was also somewhat cold and forbidding. Typical of what may be called the "neoclassical" in printing are the works of Horace printed by Bodoni at Parma in 1793.

In the 19th century, printing underwent a certain decline as a result of innovations in machine-printing. Those who were interested in fine printed books groped for a new aesthetic pattern. At the end of the century an interest in the handpress was revived through the activities of William *Morris. The most impressive and ambitious undertaking of his Kelmscott Press was the printing of the works of Chaucer in 1896. In folio format, the book was printed in one of Morris's gothic types, decorated with elaborate borders and initials designed by him, and illustrated with woodcuts based on drawings by Edward Burne-Jones. Although Morris sometimes violated his own stated principles of good bookmaking in his extravagant decoration and typography, he succeeded in creating a new interest and enthusiasm for fine printing and careful craftsmanship. The private press movement to which he gave impetus has left its mark in raised standards of book design. In this as in other areas, Morris's work was a protest against the ugly, the mediocre, and the indifferent. The first book published by the Kelmscott Press in accordance with the function of the private press as it was originally conceived was one of Morris's own works, *The Story of the Glittering Plain*, printed in his "golden" type. Of the numerous private presses that subsequently came into existence, the most important were the Ashendene, established by C. H. St. John Hornby, and the Doves, founded by Emery Walker and T. J. Cobden-Sanderson. The *Doves Bible* (1903–05) is one of the most beautiful examples of fine printing from any period, marked by a sophisticated simplicity of typography reminiscent of Jenson's work in Venice. Among more recent influential private presses was the late Laboratory Press, established in 1923 at the Carnegie Institute of Technology. This press was experimental in approach; most of its imprints were student projects, worked out as individual solutions to typographical problems posed by the director, Porter Garnett. The private press has flourished also in Germany. The Janus Press, founded by Walter Tiemann, has published works of simple design and high quality. Wilhelm Wiegand's Bremer Press in Munich is especially notable for the use of handsome initial letters designed by Anna Simons. More recent is the distinguished work in type and book design carried out at the *Bauhaus.

Bruce Rogers is the most important figure in fine printing of the 20th century in the United States. His work shows versatility and an instinct for propriety. He has worked with almost impish delight with printers' flowers, yet always in restrained good taste, as in his *Rime of the Ancient Mariner* by Coleridge, printed in 1931. His *Holy Bible,* published by Oxford University Press, is set in the Centaur type face, of Rogers' own creation. In it he has demonstrated the basic tradition of the maker of fine printed books, a sensitivity for the material to be printed.

Considerable interest has been shown in recent times for handsome publications illustrated in fine print media by artists of distinction, such as *Rouault, Odilon *Redon, Picasso, *Braque, and Chagall. The French publisher and art dealer Ambroise Vollard has been an important influence in this area. Similar to the *livre de luxe* of the 17th century, these books show a great freedom of imagination and interpretation for the artist. One of the most impressive is the *Cantiques Spirituels de Saint Jean de la Croix,* illustrated with lithographs by Alfred Manessier, whose style is uniquely expressive of the mysticism pervading the writings of the Carmelite theologian. With the recent emphasis on the artist as illustrator and with the technical knowledge gained over the centuries, the printed book continues in the tradition in which it began, that of being both functional and beautiful.

See also GRAPHIC ART; MANUSCRIPT ILLUMINATION.

Bibliography: *Biblia Latina*, 2 v. (Leipzig 1913–14; repr. New York 1961), fac. ed. of Gutenberg Bible. P. GARNETT, *The Fine Book* (Pittsburgh 1934). F. WEITENKAMPF, *The Illustrated Book* (Cambridge, Mass. 1938). G. P. WINSHIP, *Printing in the Fifteenth Century* (Philadelphia 1940). D. C. MCMURTRIE, *The Book: The Story of Printing and Bookmaking* (3d ed. New York 1943). S. MORISON, *Art of Printing* (New York 1945). P. HOFER, *Baroque Book Illustration* (Cambridge, Mass. 1951). C. EDE, ed., *The Art of the Book* (New York 1951). D. BLAND, *A History of Book Illustration* (Cleveland 1958). D. C. NORMAN, *The 500th Anniversary Pictorial Census of the Gutenberg Bible* (Chicago 1961). S. H. STEINBERG, *Five Hundred Years of Printing* (2d ed. Penguin Bks; Baltimore 1962). R. BELLM, *P. Stephan Fridolin: Der Schatzbehalter,* 2 v. (Wiesbaden 1962). J. C. HARRISON, *Five Hundred Years of the Printed Bible* (Pittsburgh 1964). **Illustration credits:** Figs. 1, 2*b,* 2*d,* and 3*b,* The Pierpont Morgan Library, New York City. Fig. 2*a,* Collection of Monroe H. Fabian. Fig. 2*c,* The Walters Art Gallery, Baltimore. Figs. 3*a,* 3*d,* 4*a,* 4*b,* and 4*c,* Library of Congress, Rosenwald Collection. Fig. 3*c,* In the Library of the Hispanic Society of America, New York City. Fig. 4*d,* Collection of Michael Iampieri.

[V. E. LEWIS]

BOOK CLUBS, CATHOLIC

The practice of organizing societies for book collecting and distribution is at least several centuries old, and is apparently of German origin. While it has had a considerable development in the 20th century, it began with the work of E. Welsser, SJ, who founded (1614) at Munich an organization called Zu dem gulden Almusen, which did effective work for almost 200 years. About 1771 a Catholic convert, A. von Diesbach, founded the Christliche Freundschaft with a similar purpose in view; in 1844, the Borromäusverein was organized at Bonn to encourage the establishment of libraries in individual homes. It was not until 1891 that the Verein der Bücherfreunde was begun.

Various other societies devoted to special interests have published and distributed books to members for more than a century. Among the earliest of such organizations, the Hakluyt Society of London (1846), specializing in source material on geography and exploration, and the Grolier Club of New York (1884), emphasizing rare and unusual publications in fine typography, may be mentioned. These and similar associations, however, are generally of rather limited membership. Book clubs in the modern sense, i.e., organizations that cater to mass membership to whom books are distributed, generally at special prices and frequently with "bonus" books added, are a particular phenomenon of U.S. publishing, though the techniques there developed have spread to some extent to other countries. The Book-of-the-Month Club (1926) and the Literary Guild (1927) were the first U.S. book clubs; by 1964 there were over 50 such clubs, ranging from those that serve teenagers to those that appeal to the interests of farmers, yachtsmen, preachers, history buffs, etc.

In the U.S. The Catholic Book Club, founded (New York 1928) by Francis X. *Talbot, SJ, then literary editor of the weekly Catholic review *America,* was designated to bring superior literature to the Catholic reading public. By 1964, 10 other Catholic clubs were doing similar work. Francis X. Downey, SJ, organized the Spiritual Book Associates (New York 1934) to provide priests, religious, and laity with sound current spiritual reading. Bruce Publishing Company's Catholic Literary Foundation (Milwaukee, Wis. 1943) was the first of the popular-appeal Catholic clubs; 2 years earlier the Thomas More Book Club (Chicago) had been established to provide serious readers with substantial books of mature interest. In 1954 the Catholic Family Book Club, sponsored by Doubleday and Co., Inc. (New York), joined the work of publishing and distributing Catholic books of wide popular appeal. In 1955 two other such clubs were started: the Catholic Digest Book Club (New York) aimed to extend into the book field the editorial concept and policies of the popular *Catholic Digest* magazine (it has a branch in Canada), and the Catholic Youth Book Club (Doubleday) offered to the adolescent biographies of and historical novels dealing with outstanding Catholic figures. The Maryknoll Book Club (Maryknoll, N.Y. 1956), founded to distribute books on missionary activities, ceased operation in 1963. The Franciscan Book Club was founded in Chicago in 1958; the Catholic Know-Your-Bible program (Garden City, N.Y. 1958), founded by the Benedictines of Belmont Abbey, North Carolina, presents great Bible stories as retold by modern authors; the Thomas More Association's Sisters Book League (1959) emphasizes spiritual reading; the Theology Book Club (1963, the Thomas More Association) makes available to members books on the new developments in theology and liturgy. The Catholic Children's Book Club is operated by the Catechetical Guild of St. Paul, Minn. In 1963 more than a million books a year were being distributed by these groups to about 165,000 members.

Abroad. Catholic book clubs have not proliferated in other countries as they have in the U.S., although since 1948 they have developed rapidly, especially in Germany, and to a lesser extent in Austria and Switzerland. The general techniques and ideals, however, operate in the following instances.

Argentina. El Club de Lectores (1936) offers a book a month and selection among fundamental works in theology, philosophy, etc., which the club publishes. Its primary appeal is to the more intellectual reader.

Austria. Welt und Heimat (1955), run by the Pressverein of the Diocese of St. Pölten distributes to members every 3 months a list of 200–300 books from which they choose their selections. The Österreichisches Borromäus-Werk (Salzburg 1946) does not have members of its own, but renders its services to over 1,000 Catholic popular libraries.

Belgium. The organization Davidsfonds distributes editions of fiction for young people (*Jeugdreeks*) and for adults (*Keurreeks*), and awards an annual literary prize.

Canada. A Catholic Digest Book Club operates in Ontario; it is a branch of the U.S. club.

West Germany. The Borromäusverein, which is still very active, sends to members (332,000 in 1963) lists of reviewed books. These lists are distributed by the more than 6,000 parish libraries, and members make their choice therefrom. The club also publishes *Das Neue Buch,* which reviews some 3,000 books a year. The Bonner Buchgemeinde (Bonn), the Herder-Buchgemeinde (Freiburg 1952), which publishes the illustrated Magazine *Der Tip,* and the Michael-Bund (Munich) distribute books to members. Catholics in West Germany appear to prefer Catholic book clubs to those often larger ones sponsored jointly by several religious groups, e.g., the Bertelsmann Lesering, which has 2½ million members, only 36 per cent of them Catholic.

Italy. Club Cattolico del Libro (1963) is an operation of L'Azione Cattolica Italiana; it distributes books and discs to nearly 20,000 members, with special attention to students.

The Netherlands. The Catholic Trade Union operates a book club specializing in books on unionism.

Switzerland. The Schweiser Volks-Buchgemeinde (Lucerne 1942) distributes religious books, fiction, biography, and books for young people to 56,000 members, requiring selection of only 2 a year. Collection Les Trésors du Livre (Geneva 1946) distributes books to members.

[J. J. DELANY; H. C. GARDINER]

BOOK OF LIFE

Term found in both the OT and the NT for an imaginary record of the members of the people of God and of those destined for eternal happiness. The idea of a record or book of names kept by the Lord most likely had its origin in human census lists in antiquity. Sometimes, reference to inclusion in such a book is simply a figurative way of speaking of one's natural life; for example, when the Psalmist adds to the curses upon his wicked persecutors the wish that "they be erased from the book of living" [Ps 68(69).29], he is praying for the death of his enemies. However, those whose names appear on the Lord's census lists are His elect, His intimate friends, or at least His people.

In the Old Testament. The first use of the term is found in Ex 32.32. After the Israelites had sinned by worshiping the golden calf, Moses pleaded with the Lord for their forgiveness in words similar to those that St. Paul would later use when he wrote, "I could wish to be anathema myself from Christ for the sake of my brethren" (Rom 9.3). With great boldness Moses demanded, "If you will not [forgive the sin of the people], then strike me out of the book that you have written." In the ancient Near East, a man's name was more than a label suitable for distinguishing him from others. In Egypt, e.g., a man's name, his *ren,* was an essential part of him; to blot it out was equivalent to destroying the man himself. This view explains the zeal shown by the native Egyptian kings in erasing the names of the hated *Hyksos invaders from every monument in Egypt after their expulsion. The notion that obliteration of the name meant devastation to the one named was shared by the Israelites, a fact that makes Moses' act of generosity all the more magnificent.

Isaia, speaking of the messianic blessings of the future under the figure of a lush harvest, announces their possession by the *remnant of Israel, which will consist of those "marked down for life in Jerusalem" (4.3), i.e., God's list of his chosen ones. Malachia speaks of a "record book . . . of those who fear the Lord" (Mal 3.16). Daniel says that "everyone who is found written in the book" shall escape in the "time of unsurpassed distress" (Dn 12.1–2). In Ps 138(139).16 the book is envisioned as one that contains not only names but deeds that constitute material for judgment, an idea found also in the NT Apocalypse.

In the New Testament. The notion that God keeps a record in the "book of life" of those who are destined for heaven is found in Phil 4.3 (Paul's "fellow workers whose names are in the book of life"; cf. Lk 10.20; Heb 12.23). But the figure is especially frequent in the Apocalypse: in 3.5 it is said of him "who overcomes" that Christ "will not blot his name from the book of life"; in 13.8 the book is called the "book of life of the Lamb"; in this passage and in 17.8 those not destined for salvation are called those "whose names have not been written in the book of life"; in 20.12, 15 "anyone not found written in the book of life" is cast into the pool of fire; in 21.27 the inhabitants of the heavenly Jerusalem are those "who are written in the book of life of the Lamb."

See also LIFE (IN THE BIBLE); PREDESTINATION (IN THE BIBLE).

Bibliography: EncDictBibl 261–263. C. KOPP, LexThK² 2:738–739. J. DUPONT, *Essais sur la christologie de saint Jean* (Bruges 1951), 157–162. L. KOEP, *Das himmlische Buch in Ankike und Christentum* (Bonn 1952).

[W. N. SCHUIT]

BOOK OF THE COVENANT

The collection of laws extending from Ex 20.22 to 23.19 is so named because of the designation in Ex 24.7; it is generally attributed to the *Elohist (E) tradition of the *Pentateuch. This law code, undoubtedly

Israel's oldest after the Decalogue, is presented in its present literary context as part of the terms of the Sinai Covenant (Exodus ch. 19–24).

General Character. The laws of the covenant code point, like the Decalogue, to man's duty toward God, his fellow man, and society as a whole; but they follow no orderly plan of presentation. Enclosed between an initial cultic section (20.22–26) and a final exhortation (23.20–33) are laws regulating cult (22.28–29; 23.10–19), determining man's moral responsibility to God and neighbor (22.15–27), and upholding the interests of justice within society (21.1–22.14; 23.1–9). The form of the laws themselves is twofold: casuistic, a type commonly found in ancient law codes, using a conditional clause ("if," "when," "whoever") to express the case, followed in the main clause by the determined sanction or action to be pursued, e.g., 21.26–27; and apodictic, a type more specifically Israelite, expressing the law succinctly either as a positive command (22.30; 23.11–12) or as a prohibition (22.17, 20; 23.1–3); *see* LAW, MOSAIC.

Date and Background. Despite evidence of some editing done as late as the 8th century B.C., the substance of the code reflects the period of Israel's transition from a seminomadic to a settled agricultural existence during the period immediately preceding or concomitant with the occupation of Palestine at the end of the Late Bronze Age, with at least some of its laws attributable to Moses himself. The time of its codification, according to scholars favoring this early date, ranges from the period of the Transjordanian sojourn before entrance into the Promised Land (Dt 28.69) to the time of Josue's assembly of the tribes at Sichem (Jos 24.25–26). Its clearly premonarchical tone argues against any date later than the time of the Judges, a period favored by some scholars.

A comparison of the covenant code with the more ancient Mesopotamian codes, e.g., those of Lipit-Ishtar, Eshnunna, Hammurabi (*see* LAW, ANCIENT NEAR-EASTERN), while warranting no conclusions regarding direct dependence, gives ample evidence of a common legal milieu. The fact of the Israelites' Mesopotamian origins coupled with the spread of the Sumero-Babylonian culture in the Oriental world of the 2d millennium makes this wholly understandable. In addition, the code evidences Assyrian and Hittite influences. But what makes the Exodus laws truly distinct is the sacred character with which they are permeated, their intimate connection with the covenant that they are intended to safeguard, and above all, their being presented as given by God Himself.

While granting the code's antiquity, critical scholarship generally maintains that it has been linked artificially with the actual Sinai event. One cannot overlook its concern with the cares of a recently settled community. Moreover, references in Deuteronomy to the covenant law clearly refer to the Decalogue alone (Dt. 4.12–14; 5.2–22). If the code is to be identified with the final stages of the Israelite journey, it may have originally stood where Deuteronomy now stands. Displaced by the more developed Deuteronomic Code, it was then incorporated into the covenant account.

Contents. The worship laws of the code were those in force during the early period of tribal federation. Monolatry is strongly emphasized (20.22–23; 23.13b); altar construction at local sanctuaries is specified (20.24–26), with directives given for the firstborn and first-fruit offerings (22.28, 29; 23.19), the observance of the weekly *Sabbath, the *Sabbath year, and the three pilgrimage feasts, viz, Unleavened Bread, Weeks, and Booths (23. 10–17). *See* FEASTS, RELIGIOUS; BOOTHS (TABERNACLES), FEAST OF; PASSOVER, FEAST OF; PENTECOST, HEBREW FEAST OF.

Moral precepts (22.15–27) regulate conduct toward God (v. 19, 27a), tribal chiefs (v. 27b), unmarried women (v. 15–16), resident foreigners (vv. 20–23), and fellow Israelites (v. 24–26). In the matter of justice, an unbiased attitude is required of a witness or judge in a lawsuit, and respect must be shown for the property of others (23.1–8).

The book's central section (21.1–22.14), comprised mainly of casuistic laws, designates the rights of slave and master, setting limits on the former's length of service (21.1–11), and it indicates the penalty to be meted out to those inflicting personal injury (21.12–32). Restitution is demanded for property damages (21.33–22.5); it is to be noted that the "gored ox" case (21.35–36) is closely paralleled in the centuries older Code of Eshnunna (par. 53). Restitution is to be made also for the loss of entrusted goods, the amount to be restored depending on the degree of guilt (22.6–14).

Bibliography: H. CAZELLES, *Études sur le code de l'alliance* (Paris 1946). A. ALT, "Die Ursprünge des israelitischen Rechts," *Kleine Schriften zur Geschichte des Volkes Israel* v.1 (Munich 1953) 278–332. De Vaux AncIsr 143–163. J. VAN DER PLOEG, "Studies in Hebrew Law," CathBiblQuart 12 (1950) 248–259, 416–427; 13 (1951) 28–43, 164–171, 296–307. G. E. MENDENHALL, "Ancient Oriental and Biblical Law," BiblArchaeol 17 (1954) 26–46.

[R. J. FALEY]

BOOK OF THE DEAD

A body of Egyptian texts on death and the afterworld, written on papyrus and placed in the tombs. The name Book of the Dead is generally applied to the texts of the New Kingdom and later, but their origin can be traced back to the mortuary literature of earlier periods: the Coffin Texts and Pyramid Texts.

The Pyramid Texts are the oldest heterogeneous compositions inscribed on the walls of the inner chambers of the Fifth- and Sixth-Dynasty pyramids for the benefit of the deceased kings. They include rituals, mythological allusions, incantations, and magical spells. Most of them are associated with the solar cult center at Heliopolis, but some reflect the basically different Osirian complex, and others can be explained only as remnants of predynastic *fetishism. Some sections of the Pyramid Texts were later included in the mortuary texts of Egyptian nobility of the Middle Kingdom and were inscribed on coffins; hence they are known as the Coffin Texts. Through the Coffin Texts these sections made their way into the New Kingdom Book of the Dead, which was considered beneficial to anyone who could afford to purchase a copy and place it in his tomb.

The Book of the Dead contains, according to the different recensions, from about 150 to 190 chapters, not all of equal value, equal popularity, or equal length. They include: magical spells of much variety; prayers and hymns to the gods *Ra (Re), Osiris, etc.; ritual recitations with instructions for priests; theological instructions; and a guidebook to the other world. Almost every chapter had its own title, such as, Chapters of Coming Forth by Day (ch. 1–2), Chapter of Opening of the Mouth (ch. 23), Chapter of Not Dying for a Second Time (ch. 44), Chapter of Not Being Tripped

Up in the Underworld (ch. 51), Chapter of Changing into a Divine Hawk (ch. 78).

Among the most important and interesting are chapters 17 and 125. Chapter 17 consists of questions and answers on theological subjects, such as:

> "I am the great god who came into being by himself." Who is he? "The great god who came into being by himself" is water; he is Nun, the father of the gods. Another version: He is Ra . . . .
> "I am yesterday, while I know tomorrow." Who is he? As for "yesterday," that is Osiris. As for "tomorrow," that is Ra on that day on which the enemies of the All-Lord are annihilated and his son Horus is made ruler . . . . [Translation of J. A. Wilson.]

Chapter 125, which concerns the judgment of the soul before Osiris and 42 divine judges, includes the so-called Negative Confession or, more correctly, Declaration of Guiltlessness, containing statements such as these:

> I have not made anyone weep . . . . I have not killed . . . . I have neither increased nor diminished the grain measure . . . . I have not taken milk from the mouths of children . . . . [Translation of J. A. Wilson.]

The Book of the Dead was primarily a book of rituals, as has been recently demonstrated; it often mentions the reciting priest and the ritual objects. The kind of ritual was generally indicated in the title of each chapter. However, it was apparently intended, not for the priests, but for the deceased, so that his soul could participate in his own funerary service. A large portion of these rituals had to be performed in front of the eternal gods by the soul itself in the netherworld.

Beyond the ritual requirements and overwhelming magic, employed here as a protective force, the Book of the Dead contains the fundamental belief in personal responsibility of each soul before the divine judgment and in ultimate justice in the afterlife.

Bibliography: Pyramid Texts. K. H. SETHE, *Die altägyptischen Pyramidentexte,* 4 v. (Leipzig 1908–22); *Übersetzung und Kommentar zu den altägyptischen Pyramidentexten,* 6 v. (Hamburg 1935–62), no more pub. S. A. B. MERCER, *The Pyramid Texts in Translation and Commentary,* 4 v. (New York 1952). Coffin Texts. A. DE BUCK, *The Egyptian Coffin Texts,* 7 v. (Chicago 1935–61), the Egyptian text without tr. Book of the Dead. E. A. T. W. BUDGE, tr., *The Book of the Dead: The Hieroglyphic Transcript of the Papyrus of Ani . . .* (London 1895; repr. New Hyde Park, N.Y. 1960), somewhat out of date. T. G. ALLEN, ed., *The Egyptian Book of the Dead: Documents in the Oriental Institute Museum . . .* (Chicago 1960). C. MAYSTRE, *Les Déclarations d'innocence: Livre des morts, chap. 125* (Cairo 1937). J. A. WILSON, *The Burden of Egypt: An Interpretation of Ancient Egyptian Culture* (Chicago 1951) 116–118. Pritchard ANET² 3–4, 10–12, 34–36. For an illustration of the Book of the Dead, *see* EGYPT, ANCIENT, 3.

[B. MARCZUK]

BOOKS, PROHIBITION OF

Forbidden books are those that are declared such by competent ecclesiastical authority or by ecclesiastical law, and that cannot be read because, in the judgment of the Church, they are dangerous to faith and morals. It is within the sphere of the Catholic Church's teaching authority to exercise such control over objectionable literature because she is the divinely appointed guardian and teacher of the revealed word of God and has both the right and the duty to protect the deposit of faith. Only those who are members of the Church are obliged to follow her judgments on the prohibition of certain books.

The Church exercises control in this matter in two ways. First, there is a previous censorship of writings that pertain to faith and morals. Second, the Church forbids the reading of works already published but which are judged to be offensive. Formerly certain books were forbidden by name and placed on the *Index of Forbidden Books. At present, Church law prohibits only general categories of books that cannot be read without ecclesiastical permission (CIC c.1399).

Authority to Prohibit. The supreme ecclesiastical authority forbids books throughout the universal Church. This is usually done through the Congregation of the Holy Office. Books thus condemned are to be considered as forbidden everywhere in the world and in whatever language they may appear. Local ordinaries can forbid books for their subjects within the territory of their jurisdiction. While it is the duty of all the faithful and more especially of clerics, ecclesiastical dignitaries, and those noted for learning to report to local ordinaries or to the Holy See books that they consider pernicious, this obligation pertains more particularly to legates of the Holy See, local ordinaries, and rectors of Catholic universities.

Effects of Prohibition. Prohibition means that unless the required permission has been obtained, the forbidden books may not be published, read, retained, sold, translated into another language, or communicated in any way to other persons. Communication includes the giving, lending, and reading of the forbidden book to another. A librarian does not violate this obligation by keeping or retaining forbidden books as long as he leaves them in the library and does not give them to those who have no permission to read them. Booksellers shall not have such books for sale without having obtained the required permission from the Holy See, nor shall they sell them to anyone unless they can prudently judge that the buyer has permission to read them. Neither shall dealers sell, lend, or keep books that professedly treat of obscene matters.

Books Forbidden by Common Law. Some books are explicitly forbidden by name and are eventually inserted into the new edition of the Index. But by no means are all forbidden books to be found in the Index. The Code of Canon Law (c.1399) lists 12 broad categories of books forbidden by the law itself:

1. Editions of the original text and of ancient Catholic versions of Sacred Scripture published by non-Catholics. Also, all translations of Sacred Scripture into any language made and published by non-Catholics. The reason: serious danger of inaccuracies or the elimination of genuine texts.

2. Books that propound or promote heresy or schism, or that in any way attempt to undermine the very foundation of religion. (The word "book" is to be taken in a broad sense and applies to daily publications, periodicals, and other published works of any kind, unless the contrary is evident.) Included under this heading are works proposing false philosophies of man and the universe, e.g., materialism, atheism, skepticism, rationalistic positivism, etc. To be condemned, books of this nature must treat of the subject in a deliberate and systematic manner, in an attempt to persuade the reader.

3. Books that professedly and purposely attack religion or good morals, either religion in general or Catholicism in particular. Writings trying to disprove God's existence, the possibility of divine revelation, or the inspiration of the Bible are banned.

4. Books by any non-Catholics that treat professedly of religion, unless it is certain that they contain nothing against the Catholic faith. The usual presumption is that non-Catholic works such as theological treatises and textbooks do contain doctrinal errors.

5. If published without previous censorship the following books are forbidden:
   a. Books of Sacred Scripture, annotations and commentaries on them, and translation of Scripture into the vernacular. Here there is the question of Catholic editions of the Bible. We are reminded by CIC c.1391 that translations of the Sacred Scriptures into the vernacular may not be printed, unless they have been approved by the Holy See or unless published under the supervision of the bishops; accompanying annotations should be from the works of the holy Fathers of the Church and from learned Catholic writers. Annotations pertaining to archeology, ethnography, or other natural sciences may also be taken from sound non-Catholic authors.
   b. Books that deal with divine Scripture, sacred theology, church history, Canon Law, or other religious or moral subjects. Also, books and booklets of prayer, devotion, or instruction that tell of new apparitions, revelations, visions, prophecies, and miracles, or that introduce new devotions.

6. Books that attack or ridicule any of the Catholic dogmas, or that defend errors condemned by the Holy See; books tending to diminish the fervor of divine worship or striving to undermine ecclesiastical discipline; books that purposely insult the ecclesiastical hierarchy, the clerical or religious state.

7. Books that teach or approve of any kind of superstition, fortunetelling, divination, magic, spiritism, and other such practices.

8. Books that hold dueling, suicide, or divorce to be licit, or which, when treating of masonic sects and other similar societies, contend that they are useful and not harmful to the Church and civil society. Books, periodicals, daily papers, or leaflets promoting communism are included in this category.

9. Books that professedly treat of, narrate, or teach lascivious or obscene matter. Among these are books with the intrinsic tendency to arouse sexual passion. All salacious and pornographic literature is included here.

10. Editions of liturgical books approved by the Holy See in which anything has been changed so that they do not agree with the authentic editions approved by the Holy See.

11. Books containing indulgences that are apocryphal or that have been forbidden or revoked by the Holy See.

12. Pictures, howsoever they may be printed, of Our Lord Jesus Christ, of the Blessed Virgin Mary, of the angels and saints, or of any other servants of God, that are foreign to the mind and decrees of the Church.

Permission to Read Forbidden Books. Canon 1400 of the Code of Canon Law contains a permission in favor of students of Scripture and theology. The use of non-Catholic editions of the original text of the Bible, of all translations of the Bible made by non-Catholics, and of translations published without the requisite permission, is permitted only to persons who are in some way engaged in theological or scriptural study, provided that the books are faithfully and completely edited, and that their introductions or annotations do not attack Catholic dogmas. Lay persons studying these subjects in school or privately have the same privilege with the same conditions.

For a justifying reason, one can obtain permission from his ordinary (bishop) to read forbidden books. Since Nov. 30, 1963, bishops have ordinary power to grant this permission to their subjects either personally or through other prudent and worthy men to whom the bishop may confide the concession of this power, e.g., pastor, confessor, rector of a Catholic institution, or chaplain of the Newman Club. Bishops can concede permission to read and to retain prohibited books and magazines, but with care, lest they fall into the hands of others. Books and magazines that professedly propose heresy or schism or that advocate the overthrow of the very foundation of religion are not excepted from this power of the bishop. But this concession may be conceded only to those who need to read prohibited books or magazines either to refute them or to fulfill properly their own office or to pursue lawfully a course of studies.

Finally, a restriction resulting from the natural law itself should always be kept in mind. No matter from whom the permission has been obtained, no one is exempted from the prohibition of the natural law that forbids one to read books that place him in proximate spiritual danger.

See also INDEX OF FORBIDDEN BOOKS; CENSORSHIP OF BOOKS (CANON LAW).

Bibliography: *Index librorum prohibitorum* (Rome 1948). R. A. BURKE, *What Is the Index?* (Milwaukee 1952). H. C. GARDINER, *Catholic Viewpoint on Censorship* (New York 1958; rev. ed. Image Bks. 1961). Bousc-Ellis. J. M. PERNICONE, *The Ecclesiastical Prohibition of Books* (CUA CLS 72; Washington 1932).

[N. J. SOJAT]

BOOLE, GEORGE, English logician and mathematician, whose writings laid the systematic foundations for later theories of logic and probabilities; b. Lincoln, Nov. 2, 1815; d. Ballintemple, Ireland, Dec. 8, 1864. He was appointed professor of mathematics in Queen's College, Cork, Ireland (1849). Apart from his technical publications in mathematics, his most important work is *An Investigation of the Laws of Thought* (London 1854). Boole's logic, which was a development and systematization of work begun by A. *De Morgan, was later completed in the system of E. *Schröder (1890). Boole made extensive, if not excessive, use of arithmetical symbolism and formal laws. This overarithmetization is responsible for the two major defects of his system, viz, the definition of disjunction as exclusive rather than inclusive and the absence of any well-defined concept of inclusion. Perhaps the most distinctive characteristic of Boole's logic lies in its susceptibility of two distinct interpretations, classical and propositional.

See also LOGIC, HISTORY OF; LOGIC, SYMBOLIC.

Bibliography: R. HARLEY, "George Boole, FRS," *British Quarterly Review* 87 (1899). W. KNEALE, "Boole and the Revival of Logic," *Mind* 57 (1939) 149–175. A ser. of commemorative papers in *Proceedings of the Royal Irish Academy* 57 (1955) 63–121.

[G. L. FARRE]

BOONEN, JACQUES, archbishop of Malines (Belgium) and protector of Jansenism in its initial stages; b. Antwerp, Oct. 11, 1573; d. Brussels, June 30, 1655. He was born into a family of jurists, studied law at the University of Louvain, received his licentiate, and became a lawyer at the Council of Brabant in 1596. He then entered upon an ecclesiastical career. He became a canon in 1604 and was ordained in 1611. He was made *officialis* of Malines in 1608; ecclesiastical counselor to the Great Council in 1611; dean of the cathedral of Malines in 1620; member of the Estates of Brabant in 1621; and counselor to the Council of State in 1626. He generously served the interests of his country and the Church. Boonen, imbued with the spirit of Charles *Borromeo, was one of a succession of prelates who fought for the application of the decrees of the Council of Trent and the restoration of the Church. He was a rigorist who fought laxism in all its forms. Some of the propositions censured by the University of Louvain at his command were afterward condemned by Rome. As a friend and admirer of his suffragan Cornelius *Jansen, he petitioned Rome untiringly, even calling upon the good offices of the King of Spain, in order to bring about a reversal of Rome's condemnation of Jansenism. He was misunderstood and severe censures were imposed upon him; however, these were soon lifted (1653). His historical reputation continues to be controversial.

Bibliography: P. CLAESSENS, *Histoire des archevêques de Malines,* 2 v. (Louvain 1881) v. 1. L. CEYSSENS, "La Publication officielle de la bulle 'In eminenti,'" *Augustiniana* 9 (1959) 161–182, 304–338, 412–430; 10 (1960) 77–114, 245–296, 365–423; "Les Dernières années de Boonen," *ibid.* 11 (1961) 87–120, 320–335, 564–582. V. SEMPELS, DHGE 9:1144–60.

[L. CEYSSENS]

BOOTH, LAWRENCE, archbishop of York, chancellor of England; b. Lancashire; d. Southwell, May 19, 1480. He became master of Pembroke Hall, Cambridge, in April 1450, a position he held for life. Soon after succeeding his half brother William *Booth as chancellor to *Henry VI's wife, Queen Margaret, in 1452, he received rapid preferment with court patronage, becoming archdeacon of Richmond (1454) and dean of St. Paul's, London (November 1456). On Aug. 22, 1457, he was provided to the See of *Durham and on September 25, consecrated. As keeper of the privy seal from September 1456 to July 1460, he was closely associated with the Queen and the court party in Henry's later years, but the political importance of his northern palatinate brought him into favor with the Yorkist King, Edward IV, to whom he became confessor (1461). His loyalty was later suspected, his temporalities were confiscated (December 1462 to April 1464), and he seems to have lived chiefly in his Cambridge college between 1462 and 1466. Restored to favor in 1471, he was chancellor of England from July 1473 to May 1474. In July 1476, he was provided to the archbishopric of *York, which he held until his death. Little is known of his diocesan administration, but it is doubtful whether he was an active pastor, politics being his chief concern.

Bibliography: Emden Cambr 78–79. A. H. THOMPSON, DHGE 9:1164–65.

[C. D. ROSS]

BOOTH, WILLIAM, archbishop of York; b. Lancashire; d. Sept. 12, 1464. Booth was one of the few English prelates of his age not to receive a university education, but had as a young man practiced law at Gray's Inn, London. He became a prebendary of Southwell (York diocese) in 1416, chancellor of St. Paul's, London (1421–23), and archdeacon of Middlesex (1429–41). He first became prominent in 1445 as chancellor to *Henry VI's queen, Margaret of Anjou, and court influence procured his provision to the See of Coventry and Lichfield on April 26, 1447, and his subsequent succession to Cardinal John *Kemp at *York, by papal bull of July 21, 1452. His half-brother, Lawrence *Booth, succeeded William as chancellor. Although less active in politics thereafter and holding no high office under the crown, William still did not turn his energies to pastoral work. In January 1450 Pope *Callistus III had dispensed him for life from personally making the episcopal *visitation of his diocese, and the diocesan administration of York remained in the hands of competent subordinates. His contemporary Thomas *Gascoigne criticized somewhat unfairly the avarice, lack of learning, and nepotism of this *indignus episcopus Cestriae.* Booth undoubtedly promoted the advancement of his kinsmen, three of whom became bishops, but they seem to have been men of ability. At York he was remembered as a benefactor of the lesser clergy.

Bibliography: A. H. THOMPSON, DHGE 9:1166–67. MS Register in Borthwick Institute, St. Anthony's Hall, York.

[C. D. ROSS]

BOOTH, WILLIAM, founder of the *Salvation Army; b. Nottingham, England, April 10, 1829; d. near London, Aug. 20, 1912. He was of laboring-class, partly Jewish origin, and had an unhappy youth. As a pawnbroker's apprentice (1842), he learned urban misery. He abandoned nominal Anglicanism for Methodism at 15, when he was stirred by Feargus O'Connor

William Booth.

and experienced "conversion." At 17, influenced by an American evangelist, Booth preached in the Nottingham slums. He went to London (1849), worked as a pawnbroker's assistant to support his mother, and acted as a lay preacher. Disliking the individualism of the Wesleyans and the doctrine of predestination of the Congregationalists, whom he thought of joining, he entered

Catherine Booth.

the Methodist New Connexion (1854). After brief attendance at a London seminary, Booth became an outstanding evangelist; he was ordained in 1858. In 1855 he married Catherine Mumford (1829–90), who shared his outlook. Their preaching success intensified Booth's view that God intended them to be roving revivalists. When ordered to a pastorate (1861) he left his denomination, became an independent evangelist, and gained some financial support. In 1865, while preaching in a tent in London, Booth began the movement that in 1878 became the Salvation Army. For the remainder of his life he was its general. Horrified by the plight of the homeless, he collaborated with W. T. Stead and wrote *In Darkest England and the Way Out* (1890). Booth sought the material rehabilitation of the poor to effect their spiritual regeneration. In this, as in his evangelizing, Booth met opposition, but by his persistence he triumphed. He died a national hero. Booth was a Biblicist, and stressed the sacrifice of Christ, instantaneous conversion, and Christian perfection.

Bibliography: ST. JOHN G. ERVINE, *God's Soldier: General William Booth,* 2 v. (New York 1935). H. C. STEELE, *I Was a Stranger: The Faith of William Booth* (New York 1954). **Illustration credit:** Figs. 1 and 2, The Salvation Army, National Information Service, New York City.

[E. E. BEAUREGARD]

BOOTHS (TABERNACLES), FEAST OF

An agricultural feast of Canaanite origin celebrated at the conclusion of harvest and, upon adoption by the Israelites, soon transferred to local sanctuaries and ultimately to Jerusalem, where it became the greatest of the three pilgrimage feasts. With the passage of time, the Feast of Booths was "historicized" by symbolic connection with the desert sojourn of the Exodus. It also became an occasion for reading the Law to the assembled people. This article treats the Feast of Booths in its origins, in the OT, in Rabbinic literature, in its messianic symbolism, in the NT, and in the Christian Era.

Origins. The Hebrew appellation of the feast, *ḥag hassukkôt,* indicates a "pilgrimage feast" (*ḥag*) that is "of the booths" (*hassukkôt*). The term "booths" (Lat.

tabernacula, hence Eng. Tabernacles) signified originally the temporary, leafy structure, supported by branches, built in the vineyard or field to accommodate the busy farmer during the harvest season (Gn 33.17; Jb 27.18; 38.40; Is 1.8). Jews call the feast simply "Sukkot." Evidence indicates that Booths was, in its origins, an agricultural feast connected with harvest booths. It has always been celebrated during Tishri (Sept.–Oct.) in connection with the grape and olive harvest. Its most ancient appellation is the "feast of ingathering" (*'āsîp;* Ex 23.16; 34.22); and it is noteworthy that the Gezer calendar mentions with this same word the season of "ingathering." (See EPIGRAPHY, HEBREW.) The "hut" feature, plainly agricultural, has never been dropped from the solemnities of the feast. Finally, the texts show a confusion in fixing the date for the celebration of the feast, partially because in Palestine, as elsewhere, the harvest season varies slightly from place to place and from year to year [Ex 34.18–23 (J); Ex 23.14–17 (E); Dt 16.13–15 (D); Lv 23.33–36, 39–43 (P); see also De Vaux 498–500]. Although S. Mowinckel agrees that the Feast of Booths had its harvest aspect, according to his hypothesis it was not a simple harvest feast that later became historicized, but rather the great, ancient New Year's Festival that in preexilic times had the enthronement rites of Yahweh as king, analogous to Babylonian cult; also, this great feast began with purification rites that were later separated to form the distinct cultic celebration of Yom Kippur. H. J. Kraus sees the origin of the feast in an ancient, nomadic "feast of tents" that celebrated a covenant renewal; this nomadic feast assimilated the indigenous Canaanite harvest feast. G. MacRae discusses and concedes the plausibility of Kraus's hypothesis. However, R. de Vaux rejects both Mowinckel's hypothesis of the elaborate New Year's enthronement feast and the hypothesis of nomadic origins. He considers the feast purely agricultural in its origins, pointing out that in the earlier sources the feast is always connected with the *sukkâ* (booth), while only in later, secondary sources is it connected with the desert tent of the Exodus (Lv 23.43) or with the Sabbatical-year reading of the Law (Dt 31.9–13).

In the Old Testament. The feast was originally celebrated in the vineyards at the conclusion of the grape and olive harvest, accompanied by dancing, merrymaking, and even some licentiousness (Jgs 9.27; 21.19; see also the prophetic censures in Am 5.21–27; Os 9.1; Is 28.7–8). Unlike the feasts of *Passover and *Pentecost, which were connected with such farm work as mowing and threshing, Booths was held after the harvest. This leisure facilitated the eventual transfer of the festivities to neighboring and more decorous sanctuaries. *Silo (Shiloh) assumed a certain importance in connection with this feast (1 Sm 1.3). The celebration at the sanctuaries may, later on, have included a covenant-renewal ceremony; the reading of the Law every 7th year in connection with Booths was prescribed in Dt 31.10–12. Solomon dedicated his Temple on the occasion of this feast (3 Kgs 8.1–3, 65–66; 2 Chr 5.2–7.10), and Jerusalem became more and more the center for Booths, as well as for the other feasts. The meaning of the feast shifted accordingly, and as it became more a Temple festivity, new and more complicated rites were introduced. After the destruction of the Temple, some people continued to come up to the ruined city to keep the feast (Jer 41.5). The Jews who returned after the Exile restored the ancient feast (Neh 8.13–18; cf. Ezr 3.4) in keeping with the prescription of Dt 31.10–13.

In Rabbinical Literature. According to the Talmud the feast lasted 7 days (15th to 21st of Tishri), with an 8th "day of conclusion" (*š⁽ᵉ⁾mînî 'ăṣeret;* cf. Neh 8.18) added. And rabbinical custom added a 9th day, "the joy of the Law" (*śimḥat tôrâ*), on which the yearly cycle of Scripture readings was completed. The tractate *Sukkah* of the Talmud, which treats of this feast, delineates the salient characteristics of the celebration that prevailed around the time of Our Lord. The hut had to be of a temporary nature, and the participants were to eat and sleep in the hut during the celebration. Together with myrtle and willow branches, the *lûlāb* (palm) and *'etrôg* (citron) were carried in procession (see LULAV). These two items, as important to Sukkot as the evergreen is to Christmas, have remained prominent to the present day. Two other features of the Temple celebration, water-drawing and illumination, are treated in the Talmud. The priests went each day to the pool of Siloe, where they drew water in large silver ewers. Upon their returning in joyous procession through the Water Gate to the Temple confines, a libation was poured on the southwest corner of the altar. Rain comes to Jerusalem from the southwest, and a primitive rain-making rite is perhaps at the basis of this ceremony. On the eve of the first day of the feast, a massive illumination was held in the women's court of the Temple and the huge candelabra were witness to joyful dancing and much festivity. The 7th day featured the singing of the great Hosanna (cf. Jn 7.37; "the great day of the festival"). Booths, accepted as the greatest of all feasts, was often referred to simply as "the Feast" (Lv 23.39; Ez 45.25; Josephus, *Ant.* 8.4.1). Rabbinical tradition considered Booths the "time of our joy."

Messianic Symbolism. The great feast acquired messianic overtones, and the Prophets taught that its observance by the faithful "remnant" and the Gentiles would herald messianic days (Za 14.16; 8.20–23; Mi 4.1–3; Is 56.6–7). Zacharia especially stresses the messianic details of the coming feast. The illumination aspect will blossom into perpetual light (14.7), and the water-drawing will evolve into the eschatological streams of living water that will flow from Jerusalem to the ends of the earth (14.8).

In the New Testament. In John ch. 7, Jesus is presented as going up to Jerusalem for the feast of σκηνοπηγία (literally, "booth-building"; Jn 7.3), i.e., Booths. A messianic discussion develops, and Jesus says, "If anyone is thirsty, let him come to me and drink . . . I am the light of the world" (Jn 7.37; 8.12). Note also the three booths and the bright cloud in the Transfiguration accounts (Mt 17.1–8; Mk 9.2–13; Lk 9.28–36), as well as the palm and hosanna details of the triumphant entry into Jerusalem for the Passover (Lk 19.35–38). The description of the New Jerusalem in the Apocalypse juxtaposes water and light once again in a messianic context (21.23–26 and 22.1–2). Finally, it is of interest that light and water figure prominently in the Easter vigil service, the messianic feast par excellence, although a relationship of dependence upon Booths is improbable here.

In the Christian Era. Post-Biblical Judaism has considered the hut that is erected for the feast a tearful reminder of the splendrous Temple. Orthodox Jews, who build their booths in their gardens or yards, keep

Jewish family in Israel (Tel Aviv, Oct. 1959) building a booth in their yard for the Feast of Sukkot.

the 1st, 2d, 8th, and 9th days of the feast as full holidays, while the Reformed Jews observe only the 1st and 8th in this way. The Reformed also stress, once again, the agricultural aspects of the feast. This is the approach (somewhat secularized) to the feast also in the modern state of Israel. The Passover has overshadowed Sukkot in importance since the period of the second Temple, but the note of deep joy and messianic expectancy has proved durable and surrounds the feast to this day.

Bibliography: De Vaux AncIsr 495–502. InterDictBibl 1:455–458. EncDictBibl 265–270. H. J. KRAUS, *Gottesdienst in Israel: Studien zur Geschichte des Laubhüttenfestes* (Munich 1954). H. SCHAUSS, *The Jewish Festivals* (Cincinnati 1938; repr. New York 1958). J. VAN GOUDOEVER, *Biblical Calendars* (2d ed. Leiden 1961). G. W. MACRAE, "The Meaning and Evolution of the Feast of Tabernacles," CathBiblQuart 22 (1960) 251–276.

[W. F. BARNETT]

BORDA, ANDRÉS DE, Mexican theologian; b. Mexico City, date unknown; d. there, 1723. The problems that accompanied the conquest and conversion of Mexico in the 16th century challenged the philosophers and theologians to produce books of enduring value. The humanistic revival of 18th-century Mexico called forth works that are prized in the 20th century because of the similarity in point of view prevalent in the 2 centuries. Mexican authors of the 17th century are ignored not because they were less learned, but because there is little interest in their problems and solutions. Andrés de Borda is one of these authors, greatly appreciated in his lifetime and almost completely forgotten in the 20th century. He was trained in the Franciscan houses of study of Mexico City. As the first Franciscan to receive a doctor's degree from the University of Mexico (1697), he ended a period of estrangement begun at the time of the founding (1553), when the Franciscans were intent on building a university for the Indians at their college of Santa Cruz de Tlaltelolco. In 1688 he had been given the Scotistic chair at the University of Mexico, and he retained it until his retirement in 1711. In 1701 he was named to go to Spain to defend the University against the pretension of the Colegio de los Santos. In 1708, with Juan Ignacio de Castorena y Ursúa, later editor of the *Gaceta de México,* he drew up the official response to the 14 doubts presented to the university by the Bethlehemites. After re-

tirement from the university, Borda became theological consultant to the Inquisition of Mexico City and prepared the verdict in the important case, pending since 1702 against Francisco Figueroa, disciple of the ex-Jesuit Francisco Davi. At the request of the university, Borda wrote also a series of philosophical treatises that remain in manuscript. All his works show that he was an author of his time; yet, he was calm; he searched for the truth, and prized the value of human dignity; and he had an objective sense that gave him an advantage over his contemporaries. Most highly valued among his spiritual works is his *Práctica de confesores de monjas* (1708), a work marked by its clarity, kindness, and objectivity.

Bibliography: J. M. BERISTAIN DE SOUZA, *Biblioteca hispano americana septentrional,* 5 v. in 2 (Colección Daniel; 3d ed. Mexico City 1947).

[R. BECERRA]

BORDEAUX, ARCHDIOCESE OF (BURDIGALENSIS)

Metropolitan see in southwest France, corresponding to Gironde department (4,141 square miles in area). In 1961 it had 623 parishes, 450 secular and 174 religious priests, 375 men in 28 religious houses, 1,642 women in 118 convents, and 900,000 Catholics in a population of 950,000. The six suffragans, which had 2,727 parishes, 2,775 priests, 4,534 sisters, and 2,346,-500 Catholics, were: *Agen, *Angoulême, *Périgueux, *Poitiers, Luçon (a Benedictine monastery founded in 675; a diocese since 1317 except 1801–22, occupied by *Richelieu), and La Rochelle (founded in 1648 as a bulwark against *Huguenots by transferring the See of Maillezais). The City of Bordeaux (population 258,000), on the left bank of the Garonne River, is the capital of Gironde department.

Bordeaux, capital of the Gallic *Bituriges Vivisci* and a Gallo-Roman *civitas,* was destroyed in 267 by Germans. Orientalis, who attended the Council of *Arles (314), is the first known bishop. *Ausonius and St. *Paulinus of Nola were born and studied in Bordeaux, which had famous schools in Gallo-Roman times. The Visigothic conquest (412) led to a persecution of Catholics under King Euric (466–484); but there was a renaissance after *Clovis's victory (507), and several basilicas were built. In the 11th century, under the dukes of Aquitaine, the temporal power of the bishops grew. Aquitaine was part of the domain of the Plantagenets (kings of England) from 1152 to 1453 and so belonged to the Roman obedience during the *Western Schism. From the 15th century to the Revolution (1789), Bordeaux was the capital of Aquitaine (Guyenne).

The 5th-century bishops SS. Amandus and Severin have legendary vitae. Bertrand de Got (1300–05) became Pope Clement V, the first pope of *Avignon. Bl. Pierre Berland (1430–57) founded the University of Bordeaux (1441). François d'Escoubleau de Sourdis (1600–28), a Tridentine reformer, created diocesan commissions, held synods, and governed strictly. Many religious houses were established in the 17th century. Archbishops *Cheverus (1826–36), Donnet (1837–82), Guilbert (1883–89), Lecot (1890–1909), Andrieu (1909–35), and Richaud (1938–   ) were cardinals.

In the 5th century, when ecclesiastical provinces were organized, Bordeaux, the civil province of *Aqui-*

Saint-André Cathedral, Bordeaux, 13th to 14th century.

tania II, was an ecclesiastical metropolitanate with the suffragans Agen, Angoulême, *Saintes, Poitiers, and Périgueux. In the 6th century it gained territory from the *civitas Boiatium,* which disappeared. Bordeaux and *Bourges long disputed the ecclesiastical primacy of Aquitaine, until Clement V bestowed the title on both bishops, who still use it. Newly created suffragans were added in 1317, and by 1789 Dax, *Limoges, Luçon, La Rochelle, and Sarlat had joined the original suffragans. The *Concordat of 1801 reduced these to Angoulême, La Rochelle, and Poitiers. Until 1905 French colonial sees were suffragan to Bordeaux. Councils held in Bordeaux or under its jurisdiction include those of 384 (which judged the heretic *Priscillian), 1079 (*Gregorian reform), 1080 (which judged the heretic *Berengarius), 1088, 1093, 1149, 1582 (reform after the Council of *Basel), and 1624 (the most important, reform after the Council of *Trent).

In the city of Bordeaux are Saint-Croix Church (12th–13th century) with a Romanesque façade, Saint-André Cathedral (13th–14th), and Saint-Seurin Church (12th–14th). The archdiocese includes the former episcopal See of Bazas, 11 men's abbeys, and 5 chapters. The pilgrimage shrine of Verdelais is the most important of several shrines of Our Lady.

Bibliography: G. LOIRETTE, DHGE 9:1182–99. E. JARRY, *Catholicisme* 2:161–164. C. HIGOUNET, ed., *Histoire de Bordeaux,* 2 v. (Paris 1962–63). P. BROUTIN, *La Réforme pastorale en France au XVIIᵉ siècle,* 2 v. (Tournai 1956). AnnPont (1965) 70. *Annuaire des Instituts de religieuses en France* (Paris 1959). **Illustration credit:** French Embassy, Press and Information Division, New York City.

[E. JARRY]

BORDONI, FRANCESCO, theologian, canonist, historian; b. Parma, April 25, 1595; d. Aug. 7, 1671. At the age of 15 he joined the Franciscan Third Order Regular. He studied philosophy and theology in the Studium Parmense where he received the doctorate and taught theology for 20 years. He was chosen master of novices, prior, and provincial in the Province of Bologna; from 1653 to 1659, he governed the Order as minister general. His first literary production appeared in 1630, and from then until his death his writing was prolific. Forty-one printed works and almost as many unprinted works remain extant. The most important are: *Sacrum Septenarium Immaculatae Conceptionis* (Palermo 1644), *Propugnaculum Opinionis Probabilis* (Lyon 1666), *De Miraculis* (Parma 1703), *Contraversiae Morales* (Lyon 1665–66), *Cronologium Fratrum et Sororum Tertii Ordinis S. Francisci* (Parma 1658), and the *Archivium Bullarum Tertii Ordinis* (Parma 1658).

Bibliography: R. PAZZELLI, *Il Terz'Ordine Regolare di S. Francesco* (Rome 1958). F. O. MANCINI, *Brevis historia gestorum P. Francisci Bordoni Parmensis* (Parma 1703).

[V. PETRICCIONE]

BORGESS, CASPAR HENRY, bishop; b. Addrup, Oldenburg, Germany, Aug. 1, 1826; d. Kalamazoo, Mich., May 3, 1890. At 12 he immigrated to the U.S. with his parents; he entered St. Mary's Seminary, Cincinnati, Ohio, and was ordained Dec. 8, 1845. After 11 years as pastor of Holy Cross parish, Columbus, Ohio, and a year at Immaculate Conception parish, Cincinnati, he was appointed chancellor of that archdiocese (1860). On Feb. 14, 1870, Pius IX named him coadjutor and administrator of *Detroit, Mich., a diocese left vacant by the departure for Germany of Frederic Résé, its first bishop. Borgess was consecrated titular bishop of Calydon on April 24 in the Cincinnati cathedral, and he arrived in Detroit on May 8, 1870; he succeeded to the see at Résé's death the following year. During his administration he worked to develop an indigenous clergy; to reduce nationalistic tensions among

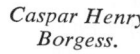
Caspar Henry Borgess.

immigrant groups; to extend Catholic education, especially by inviting the Jesuits (1877) to establish what later became the University of Detroit; and to improve the administrative structure of the diocese. In 1881 he petitioned the Holy See for a division of his see; a year later the Diocese of Grand Rapids was established, reducing Detroit to the 29 counties of southern Michigan. Ill health, aggravated by several unpleasant experiences with recalcitrant priests, caused Borgess to resign April 16, 1887, 3 years before his death. A hospital and nursing school in Kalamazoo were named in his honor.

Illustration credit: The Burton Historical Collection of the Detroit Public Library; Joseph Klima, Jr., photographer.

[F. X. CANFIELD]

BORGHESE

A Sienese patrician family noted from the start of the 13th century for its jurists and municipal officials. *Agostino* was made a knight by Emperor Sigismund (1410–37) and granted the privilege of carrying the eagle on his escutcheon. During the pontificate of Leo X (1513–21), *Pietro* served as a Roman senator. *Giambattista* defended Clement VII (1523–34) during the sack of Rome (1527) by the mutinous imperial army of Charles V. *Niccolò* is remembered for his biography of Catherine of Siena, whom he claimed to be a Borghese. *Galgano* represented Siena at the Roman court of Nicholas V (1447–55) and later became ambassador to Naples (1456).

Upon the election of *Camillo* Borghese (1552–1621) as *Paul V (1605–21), the family acquired great wealth and distinction. Paul's cousin, *Camillo,* was made bishop of Castro (1594) and Montalcino (1600), and archbishop of Siena (1607). One of the Pope's nephews, *Marcantonio,* on whom the continuation of the family line would depend, was created Prince of Sulmona (1610), then married to Princess Camilla Orsini (1619), and the next year appointed general of the Church. Another nephew, *Scipione* (1576–1633), son of Francesco Caffarelli and Ortensia Borghese, sister of Paul V, was invested as cardinal of San Grisogono (1606), given the Borghese coat-of-arms, and made cardinal nephew (secretary of state). He was also appointed legate to Avignon (1607), archpriest of the Lateran, prefect of the Congregation of the Council, and abbot of San Gregorio on the Coelian (1608); librarian of the Roman Church (1609); head of the Grand Penitentiary and archbishop of Bologna (1610); and *Camerlengo* of the Roman Church and prefect of Briefs (1612). Through his large annual income (90,000 scudi in 1609; 140,000 scudi in 1612) Scipione was able to buy extensive estates in Latium and the suburbs of Rome and become a generous patron of the arts. Affable, indulgent, but shrewd, he lived as a Maecenas in the Villa Borghese, which he built outside the Porta Pinciana to house his great collections of art and books and to serve as a setting for fêtes and theatrical performances. At Paul V's death, his prominence in Roman public life decreased, but his building projects and his renovation of Roman monuments continued until his own death.

Among other prelates bearing the Borghese name are: *Ippolito,* a Benedictine monk who became abbot general of the Congregation of Olivetans (1617–18), and then bishop of Montalcino (1619) and Pienza (1636); *Pier Maria,* grandnephew of Paul V, created cardinal of Santa Maria in Cosmedin (1626) and San Grisogono (1633); *Enrico,* prior general of the Servites (1652), then bishop of Alife in the Kingdom of Naples (1658); *Girolamo,* Benedictine scholar and bishop of

The main portal of the Borghese Palace at Rome.

Pienza (1668); *Lucio,* Bishop of Chiusi (1682); *Francesco,* titular Archbishop of Trajanopolis (1728), Cardinal of San Pietro in Montorio (1729), San Silvestro in Capite (1732), Santa Maria in Trastevere (1743), Bishop of Albano (1752), and Bishop of Porto (1759); *Scipione, maestro di camera* of Clement XIII (1766), Archbishop of Theodosia (1766), created cardinal of Santa Maria della Minerva by Clement XIV (1770); *Tiberio,* Bishop of Soana in Tuscany (1762) and Archbishop of Siena (1772).

In the 19th century the Borghese were prominent in the politics affecting the Papal States. *Camillo* (1775–1832) married Marie Pauline, sister of Napoleon Bonaparte and widow of Gen. Jacques Leclerc. He was made a brigadier general, the duke of Guastalla (1806), and governor of the French provinces of Piedmont and Genoa. When he died childless, the princely Borghese title passed to his brother *Francesco* (1776–1839). Because of previous intermarriage, the Borghese by this time also carried the family names of the Salviati and Aldobrandini. Accordingly, Francesco divided the titles among his three sons; Marcantonio (1814–86) as first-born was Prince Borghese, and married Catherine Gwendolyn, daughter of the last Catholic Duke Talbot-Shrewsbury. Both were known for their humanitarian interest in supporting schools, asylums, and bettering the lot of the underprivileged; *Camillo* (Borghese) Aldobrandini (1816–1902) became a colonel of the papal guard (1848) and war minister in the cabinet of Giacomo *Antonelli; *Scipione* (Borghese) Salvati (1823–92) married Arabella Fitz-James and after 1870 was a leader of Catholic interests in the strained relations of the Church with the Italian State. Together with his wife, he founded the hospital of the Child Jesus in Rome. The Borghese line was again divided by Marcantonio for his two sons: *Paolo* (1845–1920) with the cognomen Borghese, and the title of prince of Montecompatri, prince of Vivaro, duke of Bomarzo, and prince of Nettuno; *Giulio* (1847–1914) with the cognomen Torlonia, prince of Fucino, duke of Ceri, and marquis of Romavecchia.

The splendor of the Borghese family came to an abrupt halt with the great bankruptcy of 1891, when their wealth fell into the hands of speculators. The palace of Paul V became an emporium and housed a Freemason's lodge. The art collection and library were auctioned. Leo XIII bought the MSS and the family archives for 300,000 francs. The MSS (300) are in the Vatican Museum; the archives, known as the *fondi Borghese,* became part of the Secret Vatican Archives. In 1902 the state acquired the Villa Borghese and converted it into a public park.

Bibliography: For the early history see G. GIGLI, ed., *Diario Sanese* 2 v. (Lucca 1723) v.1. J. H. DOUGLAS, *The Principal Noble Families of Rome* (Rome 1905). P. E. VISCONTI, *Città e famiglie nobili e celebri dello stato pontificio,* 3 v. (Rome 1847) 3:913–985. E. RE, EncIt 7:468–469. Pastor v.25. G. WAGNER, *Catholicisme* 2:167–68. P. DALLA TORRE and E. GERLINI, Enc Catt 2:1903–06. Moroni 6:37–45. P. PASCHINI, DHGE 9:1213–17. **Illustration credit:** Alinari-Art Reference Bureau.

[E. D. MC SHANE]

BORGIA (BORJA)

A number of persons with the surname Borja (later Italianized as Borgia), originally from the Aragonese city of that name, settled in the kingdom of Valencia after the reconquest in 1238. In the 14th century there was a branch of the Borjas, of the lesser nobility, living in Valencia and Alzira with a manor house in Xàtiva. Gonçal-Gil de Borja was military magistrate (*jurat militar*) in 1346. He was the father of Rodrigo-Gil (testament 1375) who, after his marriage with Francesca Fenollet, had two children, Rodrigo-Gil, junior, and Francesc (?) de Borja. The latter became the father of two children also, Francesca and Francesc de Borja. But this last Francesc has been considered since the 16th century to have been the illegitimate son of Alfons de Borja, who later became Pope *Callistus III. Francesc was bishop of Teano and archbishop of Cosenza and was elevated to the cardinalate in 1500 by Pope *Alexander VI.

Rise to Prominence. The Borjas' social standing dated from the War of Union between Pedro IV of Aragón and the feudal nobles, when the Borjas fought on the King's side. Rodrigo-Gil, junior, married Sibília (d'Oms). From this union were born Joan-Gil; Rodrigo, Bishop of Barcelona (d. 1478); Galceran-Gil (testament 1435); Joana, childless wife of Bartomeu Serra; and Jofré-Gil de Borja, Master of Adzeuva and Albuixa (testament 1430). Another branch of the family included Domingo, Master of Canals, who was father of Catarina. She married Joan del Milà, Baron of Masalavès. Their children were Joan-Lluís del Milà, cardinal under Callistus III and founder of the line of the counts of Albaida; Joana, who married Bartomeu Martí and left no children; Alfons (Callistus III); and Isabel. Isabel married the Jofré-Gil mentioned above. Their son Rodrigo de Borja became Alexander VI. Their other children were Pere-Lluís, Duke of Spoleto under Callistus III (d. 1458 without heirs); Tecla (d. c. 1462); Beatriu (d. 1503), and Joana, who in her second marriage with Pere-Guillem Llançol de Romaní, Baron of Vilallonga (d. 1489) had a son, Jofré de Borja-Llançol. This son changed the order of his last names, married Joana de Montcada, and went to Rome. His children all served Pope Alexander VI: Rodrigo as a military man;

Joan as bishop of Melfi, governor of Perugia, archbishop of Capua and Valencia, and cardinal in 1496 (d. 1500); Pere-Lluís as his brother's successor as archbishop of Valencia and cardinal in 1500 (d. 1511); their sister Jeronima was married first to Fabio Orsini and then to Tiberio Carafa; the other sister, Angela, married to Alessandro Pio, was lady-in-waiting to Lucrezia in Ferrara (see below). Alexander VI's nepotism gave the cardinal's hat to other Borjas: in 1492 to Joan de Borja, senior, son of Galceran, who in turn was the son of the above mentioned Galceran-Gil and Tecla Navarro d'Alpicat; in 1493 to his own son Cesare (see below); in 1503 to Joan Castellar, son of Bernadona de Borja (who was the daughter of the same Galceran-Gil) and her husband, Galceran de Castellar, Master of Picassent; and finally to Francesc de Lloris, son of Isabel de Borja (sister of Cardinal Joan de Borja senior) and Ximèn Pérez de Lloris. Other relatives of the Pope also made cardinals were Giuliano Cesarini (named in 1493), Bartomeu Martí, the Catalan Joan de Castro (1496), and Jaume Serra (1500). Family friends included the Valencians Joan Llopis, datary (1496), Joan de Vera (1500), Jaume Casanova (1503), and another Catalan, Francesc Remolins (1503). The cardinals Luigi d'Aragona, illegitimate son of Ferrante I of Naples (1494), and the Sicilian Pietro Desvalls or d'Isvaglies (1500) were of Catalonian-Aragonese origin. The only Castilian cardinals were Bernardino López de Carvajal (1493) and Diego Hurtado de Mendoza (1500).

Children of Rodrigo Borgia. Critical value is lacking in the pseudo-apologetic efforts made to deny Alexander VI's paternity of a number of children. The mothers of the first three children are unknown. The children were Pere-Lluís (see below); Girolama (d. c. 1484), who married Gianandrea Cesarini in 1482 but left no children; and Isabella, who married Piergiovanni Mattuzzi (d. 1519). The other four children (see below), Cesare, Joan, Lucrezia, and Jofré, were born of Vannozza Cattanei, possibly from Mantua, who was married successively to Domenico d'Arignano, Giorgio de Croce, and Carlo Canale, all employees of the Roman Curia. It has not been proved that Alexander VI was the father of Orsino Orsini or Laura Orsini (b. 1492), daughter of Giulia Farnese, who was the mistress of Rodrigo de Borja at the end of his cardinalate. Giulia was married to Orsino Orsini, who was the son of Ludovico Orsini and Adriana del Milà, daughter of Pere del Milà, brother of the above-mentioned Cardinal del Milà. However, it is certain that Alexander VI was the father of Joan de Borja, Duke of Camerino and Nepi (1498–1546). The documents are contradictory as to whether Lucrezia was Joan's mother. Also sufficiently proved was Alexander's paternity of Rodrigo de Borja (b. 1502 or 1503), whose mother is unknown.

Pere-Lluís, first Borgian duke of Gandia; b. Rome, c. 1468; d. Rome, 1488. He was the son of Cardinal Rodrigo de Borja (Alexander VI). In 1483 his father gave him 50,000 ducats and the barony of Llombai and sent him to Spain. He was arrested in 1484 by Ferdinand II, King of Aragón because of dissension between the King and the cardinal. Pere-Lluís took part in the seizure of Ronda and on May 28, 1484, the King recognized his nobility along with that of his younger brothers Cesare, Joan, and Jofré. On December 3 Ferdinand, acting as procurator for his son Don Juan de Aragón sold Pere-Lluís the city and lands of Gandia and

Cesare Borgia, portrait by Giorgione in the Pinacoteca Comunale at Forlì, Emilia, Italy.

the next day gave him the title of duke. In 1486 the Duke became engaged to María Enríquez, first cousin of the King. Before the marriage could take place, the Duke died in Rome in August 1488, leaving his holdings to his brother Joan.

Cesare, cardinal and condottiere; b. Rome, Sept. 1475; d. Viana, Navarre, March 12, 1507. He was the son of Cardinal Rodrigo (Alexander VI) and Vannozza Cattanei. Ferrante I legitimized him in 1481. The year before Sixtus IV had dispensed his illegitimacy so that he could obtain ecclesiastical benefits. After having received only the tonsure, he was successively apostolic protonotary, canon of Valencia, archdeacon of Xàtiva, sacristan of Cartagena, bishop of Pamplona in 1491, and archbishop of Valencia in 1492. In spite of all that, Ferrante I of Naples offered his illegitimate daughter Lucrezia d'Aragona to Alexander VI as a wife for either Cesare or Jofré. On Sept. 20, 1493, Cesare was made a cardinal. Although he had received the diaconate on March 26, 1494, his unrestrained life and his ambitions took him back to the lay state, on the grounds of reverential fear of ordination (1498). Alexander VI forbade him to marry Carlotta d'Aragona, daughter of Federico III, of Naples, but accepted for Cesare the hand of Charlotte d'Albret, sister of Juan II, King Consort of Navarre. Named duke of Valentinois by Louis XII of France, Cesare saw in the campaign against Milan in 1499 the chance to establish a feudal state in Romagna with small feudal holdings belonging to the Holy See. Cesare took over Forlì, Cesena, and Faenza, plotted with Giovanni Bentivoglio of Bologna, called himself master and duke of Romagna, invaded Tuscany, and

took over Piombino. In the War of Naples in 1501, which ended in the division of the kingdom between Ferdinand the Catholic and Louis XII, Cesare fought on the side of the King of France. He attacked Urbino, Camerino, and Senigaglia and invaded Umbria in 1503. But the death of Alexander VI prevented Cesare's keeping his holdings. Cesare, taken prisoner by Julius II, escaped and fled to Naples. When this kingdom was conquered by Ferdinand, Cesare was arrested, sent to Spain, and imprisoned in the Castillo de la Mota (Medina del Campo). Escaping to France, he went into the service of the King of France in his wars against Ferdinand. Cesare died in the Battle of Viana.

Joan (Juan), second duke of Gandia; b. Rome, 1476; d. Rome, July 14 or 15, 1497. He was the son of Cardinal Rodrigo de Borja (Alexander VI) and Vannozza Cattanei. In 1493 he married María Enríquez, who had been betrothed to his brother Pere-Lluís, from whom he inherited the dukedom. Joan stayed in Valencia and Gandia and consolidated his holdings, although Ferdinand and Isabella did not make good their promises to him. Named captain-general of the Church, he returned to Italy. His military losses in the war against Charles VIII of France and his allies drove him back to Rome, where he was assassinated and thrown into the Tiber. It is uncertain whether his brother Cesare was the instigator of the crime.

Lucrezia (Llucrècia), duchess of Ferrara; b. Subiaco, April 1480; d. Ferrara, June 24, 1519. She was the daughter of Cardinal Rodrigo de Borja (Alexander VI) and Vannozza Cattanei. She lived in Rome with her relatives Adriana del Milà and Joana de Montcada. After unsuccessful plans for marriage with Querubí de Centelles, Gaspar de Próxita, and the Count of Prada,

Detail of the fresco "La disputa di Santa Caterina," by Pinturicchio, in the Sale Borgia, Vatican Palace. It is thought Lucrezia Borgia modeled for this figure.

she was betrothed by Alexander VI in 1492 to Giovanni Sforza, Count of Cotignola and Master of Pesaro, in order to consolidate an alliance with the Sforzas of Milan. Later the alliance of Charles VIII of France with Milan brought about a divorce on the grounds that the marriage had not been consummated. In 1498 Lucrezia, having given birth to an illegitimate son, was prevailed upon by Alexander for political reasons to marry Alfonso d'Aragona, Duke of Bisceglie, who was the illegitimate son of Alfonso II of Naples (d. 1495). The couple had a son, Rodrigo d'Aragona (1499–1512). On Aug. 18, 1500, Alfonso was assassinated in Rome by a henchman of Cesare. On Dec. 30, 1501, Lucrezia married Alfonso d'Este in the Vatican. He was the son and heir of Hercules II, Duke of Ferrara (d. 1504). In spite of her secret affairs with Pietro Bembo and with her brother-in-law Francesco Gonzaga, Duke of Mantua, and of the scandals involving her lady-in-waiting Angela Borja, Lucrezia was seriously religious, especially in her later years. She gave her husband Alfonso seven sons, three of whom died in infancy. The survivors included the future Hercules III, Cardinal Ippolito, and Francesco.

Jofré, prince of Squillace; b. Rome, 1481; d. Squillace, 1517. He was the son of Cardinal Rodrigo de Borja (Alexander VI) and Vannozza Cattanei. Alexander, although he legitimized Jofré, doubted that he was really Jofré's father. In 1494 Jofré married Sancha d'Aragona, sister of the Duke of Bisceglie. Alfonso II of Naples gave Jofré and Sancha the principality of Squillace, which gift was confirmed by Ferdinand the Catholic in 1502. When Sancha died after an irregular life, leaving no children, Jofré married Maria del Milà. Their children were Lucrezia, Marina, and Francesco, heir to the title.

Bibliography: Sources. M. OLIVER, "D. Rodrigo de Borja," BolRealAcHist 9 (1886) 402–447. "S. Franciscus Borgia," Mon HistSJ 1 (1894), *passim.* J. BURCHARD, *Liber notarum,* Eng. tr. G. PARKER (London 1963). M. MENOTTI, *Documenti inediti sulla famiglia e la corte di Alessandro VI* (Rome 1917). J. SANCHIS Y SIVERA, *Algunos documentos y cartas privadas que pertenecieron al segundo Duque de Gandía, don Juan de Borja* (Valencia 1919). P. DE ROO, *Material for a History of Pope Alexander VI, His Relatives and His Time,* 5 v. (New York 1924). M. BATLLORI, *Epistolari dels B.* (Barcelona 1966); and L. CERVERÓ, *Genealogía documentada de los B.* (Rome 1967). Literature. F. A. GREGOROVIUS, *Lucrezia Borgia* (4th ed. Stuttgart 1906), Eng. *Lucrezia Borgia,* ed. L. GOLDSCHEIDER, tr. J. L. GARNER (London 1948). C. E. YRIARTE, *Les Borgia: César Borgia* (Paris 1889), Eng. *Cesare Borgia,* tr. W. STIRLING (London 1947). P. D. PASOLINI DALL'ONDA, *Caterina Sforza,* 4 v. (Rome 1893–97). F. FERNÁNDEZ DE BÉTHENCOURT, *Historia genealógica y heráldica de la monarquía española,* 10 v. (Madrid 1897–1920) 4:3–389. W. H. WOODWARD, *Cesare Borgia* (London 1913). M. BELLONCI, *Lucrezia Borgia,* tr. B. and B. WALL (New York 1957). G. PEPE, *La politica dei Borgia* (Naples 1946). M. BATLLORI, *Vuit segles de cultura catalana a Europa* (2d ed. Barcelona 1959) 51–83; "De ortu Iohannis, tertii ducis gandiensis, sancti Francisci Borgiae patris, monumenta quaedam," ArchHistSoc Jesu 26 (1957) 199–211. A. LUZIO, "Isabella d'Este e i Borgia," *Archivio storico lombardo,* 5 ser. 1 (1914) 469–553; 5 ser. 2 (1915) 115–167, 412–464. M. MENOTTI, *I Borgia, storia ed iconografia* (Rome 1917). **Illustration credits:** Alinari-Art Reference Bureau.

[M. BATLLORI]

BORGIA, FRANCIS, ST.

Third general of the Society of Jesus; b. Gandía, Spain, Oct. 28, 1510; d. Rome, Sept. 30, 1572 (feast, Oct. 10). He was the first son of Juan Borja, third Duke of Gandía, and of Joanna of Aragón. At the age of 10, after the death of his mother, he was sent to

Zaragoza, where his uncle Juan of Aragón was archbishop. Later he went to Tordesillas as page to the sister of Emperor Charles V, Princess Catherine, who in 1525 became the wife of John III of Portugal. In 1528 Francis was in the service of the Emperor at the Court of Spain. In the next year he married Leonor de Castro, and they had eight sons. On July 7, 1530, his barony of Lombay was raised to the category of marquisate by Charles, and he was nominated first hunter of the court and head of the stables of the Empress Isabella. His wife became her lady-in-waiting. Deeply moved by the death of the Empress on May 1, 1539, he accompanied her remains to Granada and assisted at the ceremonies of identification and burial on May 17. On June 26 of that year, Francis was named viceroy of Catalonia, an office that he kept until 1543. After his father's death on Dec. 17, 1542, he went to Gandía to claim his inheritance and his rights as successor in the dukedom. In Barcelona he had met the Jesuits Antonio de Araoz and (Bl.) Peter *Faber (Lefèvre), and determined to build them a college in Gandía. Faber laid the cornerstone of this first college of the society on May 4, 1546. Pope Paul III elevated it to the rank of university on Nov. 4, 1547.

In 1546, after the sudden death of Doña Leonor, Francis took his first vows in the society; he made his solemn profession on Feb. 1, 1548. He kept this a secret and continued to wear secular clothes in order to administer his estates and settle his children. He also studied theology at his new university, receiving a doctorate on Aug. 20, 1550. On the 26th of the same month Francis started a pilgrimage to Rome ostensibly

St. Francis Borgia.

to gain the Jubilee indulgences of the Holy Year but mainly to arrange with (St.) Ignatius for his official entrance into the Society. He remained in Rome until Feb. 4, 1551, and on May 23, he was ordained in Oñate, saying his first Mass at Loyola on August 1. Following his ordination he preached and taught catechism to children throughout Guipúzcoa and practiced severe austerities until curbed by his superiors. On April 1, 1554, he became commissary general of the society in Spain, and in the following year he went to Tordesillas to assist Queen Joanna in her last illness. *Charles V, who in 1556 abdicated and retired to Yuste, often relied on Borgia for advice and made him and Philip II the executors of his will. In 1559 a book entitled *Las Obras del Duque de Gandía* was placed on the list of forbidden books for Spain. It included some treatises of his but also writings not of his authorship. In order to avoid further embarrassment, Borgia retired to Portugal until called to Rome by Pope Pius IV in 1561. There he was received kindly and 3 years later was appointed Assistant General for Spain and Portugal.

In 1565, after the death of the General Diego *Laínez on January 19, Francis was nominated vicar-general, and on July 2 of that year he was elected general of the society. His 7 years of office were noted for activity and the expansion of the Society of Jesus. He started new missions in the Americas, strengthened the organization of those already existing in the East Indies and Far East, and furthered the training of priests at the German College in Rome for the lands lost to Protestantism. He established new colleges in France, erected the province of Poland and planned others. The Roman College continued to receive his special interest, and the Gesù, the church of Sant' Andrea, and a novitiate were erected. He is noted, too, for his interior mystical life, which seems to have thrived in the surroundings of business. He was beatified on Nov. 24, 1624, by Urban VIII, and canonized on April 12, 1671, by Clement X.

Bibliography: His writings are ed. by C. DE DALMASES and J. F. GILMONT, ArchHistSocJesu 30 (1961) 125–179; *Evangelio meditado,* ed. F. CERVÓS (Madrid 1912); *Meditaciones sobre los evangelios para las fiestas de los santos,* ed. J. M. MARCH (Barcelona 1925); *Monumenta Borgiae,* 5 v. (MonHistSJ; Madrid 1894–1911); *Tratados espirituales,* ed. C. DE DALMASES (Barcelona 1964). Literature. P. SUAU, *St. François de Borgia 1510–1572* (Paris 1905). O. KARRER, *Der Heilige Franz von Borga 1510–1572* (Freiburg 1921). H. DENNIS, *St. Francis Borgia* (Madrid 1956). Sommervogel 1:1808–17, 8:1875–76. B. SCHNEIDER, LexThK² 4:235–236. **Illustration credit:** Jesuit Archives, Rome.

[C. DE DALMASES]

BORIS I OF BULGARIA, 852 to 889, first Christian ruler of Bulgaria; d. May 7, 907. During his reign Christianity was introduced among the *Slavs and Bulgars of *Bulgaria and the Bulgarian Church was first established. An ambitious and energetic ruler, Boris realized the importance of bringing his people within the community of Christian nations, but hesitated to accept Christianity from the Byzantine *patriarchate under the auspices of the Byzantine Empire, the traditional rival of Bulgaria. He wanted instead to secure complete independence from the jurisdiction of Constantinople for the Bulgarian Church, and with this in view he began negotiations with Rome and the Frankish Empire. However, in 864, Byzantine military pressure

compelled him to accept Baptism from Constantinople with the Emperor *Michael III as godfather. But Constantinople's refusal to grant autonomy to the Bulgarian church prompted Boris to turn to Pope *Nicholas I in Rome in 866, asking for bishops and missionaries. In 870, however, he returned to Constantinople. Then in 880 Rome and Constantinople reached an agreement that recognized Roman jurisdiction over the Bulgarian Church. Political events, however, and the remoteness of the area prevented Rome from exercising effective authority over missionary activities there, and they remained largely in the hands of the Byzantine clergy. In 885 Boris welcomed to Bulgaria the clergy of the Slavic rite expelled from Moravia after the death of Methodius in 884 (*see* CYRIL AND METHODIUS, SS.). Their missionary work, conducted in the vernacular, was very successful among the Bulgarian Slavs and was an effective counterpoise to Byzantine influence. In 889 Boris resigned the throne in favor of his son Vladimir (889–893), but the pagan reaction with which Vladimir seems to have been in sympathy forced Boris to return to power. Having suppressed the rebellion and deposed Vladimir, he replaced him with his other son Symeon (893–927). After that Boris returned to his monastery, where he died in 907.

Bibliography: V. N. ZLATARSKI and N. STANEV, *Geschichte der Bulgaren,* 2 v. (Leipzig 1917). S. RUNCIMAN, *A History of the First Bulgarian Empire* (London 1930). F. DVORNIK, *Les Slaves, Byzance et Rome au IXᵉ siècle* (Paris 1926); *The Slavs: Their Early History and Civilization* (Boston 1956).

[O. P. SHERBOWITZ-WETZOR]

BORROMEO, CHARLES, ST.

Cardinal, archbishop of Milan, and prominent figure in the Tridentine Reform; b. Rocca d'Arona, near Lago Maggiore, Oct. 2, 1538; d. Milan, Nov. 3, 1584 (feast Nov. 4). The second son of Count Giberto Borromeo

St. Charles Borromeo, portrait by Giovanni Battista Crespi, in the Galleria Ambrosiana at Milan.

and Margherita de' Medici, sister of Pius IV, he was intended for the service of the Church, and received the clerical tonsure and the title of the abbacy of San Gratiniano when 12 years old. He was tutored at Milan by Francesco Alciati, and studied law at the University of Pavia (1552–59), where he earned a doctorate *in utroque.* Three weeks later (Dec. 25, 1559) Cardinal Gian Angelo de' Medici succeeded Paul IV, taking the name of *Pius IV. The new Pope called his young nephew to Rome and advanced him rapidly through a brilliant ecclesiastical career.

Curial Responsibilities. Borromeo held several posts in the Roman Curia, and was created a cardinal in 1560 with the title of SS. Vitus and Modestus (changed in 1564 to St. Praxedes). He was cardinal protector of Portugal, the Low Countries, and the Catholic cantons of Switzerland, and of six religious orders (Franciscans, Carmelites, *Humiliati, Canons Regular of the Holy Cross of Coimbra, Knights of Malta, and Knights of the Holy Cross of Christ in Portugal); administrator of the Legations of Bologna, Romagna, and the Marches; and commendatory abbot of several monasteries. His most responsible office as cardinal nephew was that of prefect of the Secretariate of State, in which he was his uncle's most valued assistant, especially during the third period of the Council of *Trent (1562–63). Grief at the death of his elder brother, Federigo, on Nov. 19, 1562, turned him to a more austere manner of living as well as to his ordination to the priesthood (July 17, 1563). The literary academy of the *Noctes Vaticanae,* which he had founded, was transformed and adopted for its meetings spiritual rather than literary and philosophical themes. He took steps to raise the moral tone of the people of Rome by promoting the *Catechismus romanus ad parochos* and collaborating in projects for the completion of the work of the Council of Trent, such as the Roman Seminary, reforms in the Missal, Breviary, and sacred music, and the edition of the writings of the Church Fathers.

Archbishop of Milan. In the year of his promotion to the cardinalate, Borromeo was named also perpetual administrator of the Archdiocese of Milan, of which he would be titular archbishop for the remainder of his life. Because of his multiple duties in Rome, he was at first represented by a vicar-general, Niccolò Ormaneto, but in October 1565 he came to Milan to preside over the first provincial council and from April 1566 he remained in permanent residence. His pastoral activities during these years were of considerable influence upon the whole Catholic world and affected the many important facets of the post-Tridentine Church. To his credit are: (1) the reorganization of diocesan administration into subordinate offices and functions; (2) the calling of 6 provincial councils and 11 diocesan synods; (3) regular and systematic pastoral visits to all parts of his diocese; (4) the opening of a seminary entrusted to the Jesuits (1564–79) and later to the Oblates of St. Ambrose, as well as similar institutions for candidates for the priesthood (Collegio Helvetico); (5) a considerable use of existing religious groups, as the Jesuits and Capuchins, and the foundation of a new diocesan religious society, the *Oblates of St. Charles (1578), for which he wrote the *Institutiones* (1581); (6) various cultural and social institutions that include the Collegio Borromeo at Pavia (1564–68), the University of Brera at Milan (1572), shelters for

wanderers, homes for neglected or abandoned wives (Casa del Soccorso), refuges for reformed women, orphanages, *montes pietatis* (lending houses), and hospitals; and (7) the noteworthy promotion of the Confraternity of Christian Doctrine for the teaching of catechism, which in 1595 had grown to more than 20,000 pupils.

Pastoral Ideal. Borromeo's pastoral awareness was inspired by his high ideal of the responsibility of a bishop. To him, each pastor was obliged to have a detailed knowledge of the conditions of his flock. This ideal made astonishingly severe demands in its successful implementation and showed constructive characteristics that were hierarchic, systematic, kerygmatic, and sacramentarian. The amazing results are described in the *Acta ecclesiae Mediolanensis,* whose many editions published since 1582 have become the patrimony of the whole Church. There are found the records of the provincial councils and diocesan synods; numerous instructions, edicts, decrees, pastoral letters; and the rules and constitutions for a score of congregations, confraternities, and other charitable, cultural, or pious groups that Borromeo founded or encouraged. These documents treat the subjects regarded by Borromeo as most useful in promoting religious renewal in his archdiocese along the lines of the Council of Trent. They include preaching, reception of the Sacraments, presence at Mass, liturgical feasts, funerals, the exercise of Eucharistic devotion, exact clerical deportment, the building and equipping of churches, meetings of the diocesan clergy, Lenten regulations, relations with heretics, and preparation of the *Liber status animarum* and similar tracts on parochial administration. Much was written in Italian and certain rules were prescribed for pulpit reading at least once a year. A great part of Borromeo's effectiveness and popularity was due to his interest in social problems. A well-known episode, frequently illustrated by artists, is the plague of 1576 (Plague of St. Charles) during which he proved his heroic dedication.

Reform and Opposition. Borromeo's resolve to promote Catholic reform and to protect the prerogatives of his office brought opposition both from the civil power over questions of jurisdiction and from clerical communities over his disciplinary demands. He struggled with the Spanish governors of Milan, Gabriel de la Cueva, Duke of Alburquerque, Luis de Requesens, and Marquis Antonio di Ayamonte; peace was restored only through the intervention of Philip II and the Pope. Twice his life was endangered. The first occasion involved his right to episcopal visitation of the collegiate church of Santa Maria della Scala, which claimed an exemption from the jurisdiction of the archbishop of Milan granted by Clement VII in 1531. The exemption had been given but was provisional upon the consent of the archbishop, which had not been obtained. When Borromeo attempted to enter the church in September 1569, he was prevented by the canons, and by soldiers of the Duke of Alburquerque who opened fire and damaged the cross in his hands. Again in October 1569 he was in danger. Some of the Humiliati resisted his reform programs and conspired to take his life. A hired assassin, Girolamo Donato, known as "Farina," fired at him point-blank while he knelt in prayer with his household. The wound was slight, but civil authorities later condemned Farina to death by hanging.

Borromeo also undertook reform activities outside his diocese. He made apostolic visits to the Dioceses of Cremona (1575), Bergamo (1575), and Brescia (1580), and four missionary journeys into pastorally neglected Alpine valleys, where he worked vigorously against sorcery and the infiltration of Protestantism. Three times he traveled even into German areas of Switzerland (Altdorf, Unterwalden, Zug, Sankt Gallen, Schwyz, and Einsiedeln), where his influence led to the establishment of a papal nunciature at Lucerne. Other trips took him to Rome, to Loretto, to the Holy Shroud of Turin, and to his favorite place of pilgrimage at the Sacro Monte at Varallo. At the end of October 1584, on his return from Milan after making the Spiritual Exercises, he was stricken with fever. He was brought into the city on a stretcher, and died on November 3. He was canonized by Paul V on Nov. 1, 1610. His body rests at the foot of the main altar in the cathedral of Milan. His popular cult spread rapidly, especially in Italy, Germany, and the Spanish Netherlands. A statue, 100 feet tall was erected on a hill near his birthplace, and many works of art recall episodes in his career of reform. Several cultural and religious associations were founded under his patronage. One of the last acts of Cardinal Giovanni Battista Montini before he left Milan to become Paul VI was the creation of the "Accademia di san Carlo Borromeo" to promote scientific research and study of the life and writings of this saint.

Bibliography: Manuscript sources. The principal collections are found in Milan (Archiepiscopal Curia, Ambrosian Library and the archives of the Borromeo family), Rome (Archives of the Vatican and Congregation of Rites, and the Library of the Barnabites), and Brussels (Library of the Bollandists). Printed sources. *Opere complete di S. Carlo Borromeo,* ed. G. A. SASSI, 5 v. (Milan 1747); 2d ed., 2 v. (Augsburg, 1758). *S. Caroli Borromaei Orationes XII* (Rome 1963), ed. at request of Paul VI for the Fathers of Vatican Council II. A. RIVOLTA, "Epistolario giovanile di S. Carlo Borromeo," *Aevum* 12 (1938) 253–280; "Corrispondenti di S. Carlo Borromeo," *ibid.* 556–619; 13 (1939) 65–116. G. GALBIATI, *I duchi di Savoia Emanuele Filiberto e Carlo Emanuele I nel loro carteggio con S. Carlo Borromeo* (Milan 1941). A. G. RONCALLI [JOHN XXIII] and P. FORNO, comp., *Gli atti della visita pastorale di S. Carlo Borromeo a Bergamo, 1575,* 5 v. (Florence 1936–57). *Acta Ecclesiae Mediolanensis,* ed. A. RATTI [PIUS XI] (Milan 1890–92) v.2–3. Contemporary biographies. A. VALIERO, *Vita Caroli Borromaei* (Verona 1586). C. BASCAPÉ (Basilica Petri), *De vita et rebus gestis Caroli card. S. Praxedis* (Ingolstadt 1592; Brescia 1610). G. P. GIUSSANO, *Istoria della vita, virtu, morte e miracoli di Carlo Borromeo* (Milan 1610), annotated copiously by B. OLTROCCHI (Milan 1751) tr. into Eng. with pref. by H. E. MANNING, 2 v. (London 1884). Recent biographies. More than 60 exist, of which the principal are A. SALA, *Biografia di S. Carlo Borromeo,* 3 v. (Milan 1857–61), numerous documents. C. SYLVAIN, *Histoire de St. Charles Borromée,* 3 v. (Lille 1884). L. CELIER, *St. Charles Borromée* (Paris 1923). C. ORSENIGO, *Vita di S. Carlo Borromeo* (Milan 1929), Eng. tr. R. KRAUS (St. Louis 1943). A. RIVOLTA, *S. Carlo Borromeo, note biographiche. Studio sulle sue lettere e suoi documenti* (Milan 1938). M. YEO, *A Prince of Pastors: St. Charles Borromeo* (London 1938). P. GORLA, *S. Carlo Borromeo* (Milan 1939). G. SORANZO, *S. Carlo Borromeo* (Milan 1944). A. DEROO, *Saint Charles Borromée, Cardinal réformateur, docteur de la pastorale* (Paris 1963), bibliog. See also S. A. RIMOLDI, BiblSanct 3:812–850, with bibliog. Butler ThAttw 1:255–262. F. VAN ORTROY, AnalBoll 39 (1921) 338–345. A. DUVAL, *Catholicisme* 2:992–994. C. CASTIGLIONI, Dict SpirAscMyst 2:692–700, with bibliog. Réau IAC 3.1:298–300. G. GALBIATI, EncCatt 3:853–861, iconogr. *Storia di Milano* (Milan 1953–) 10:119–302, 351–495; 11:283–331. R. MOLS, DHGE 12:486–534, with bibliog. **Illustration credit:** Anderson-Art Reference Bureau.

[R. MOLS]

BORROMEO, FEDERIGO, cardinal and leader of Catholic reform; b. Milan, Aug. 18, 1564; d. there, Sept. 22, 1631. Federigo, son of Giulio Cesare and Margherita Trivulzio, was orphaned early in life and oriented toward an ecclesiastic career by his renowned cousin, Charles *Borromeo, in whose footsteps he followed. Having completed his studies at Bologna and Pavia with a doctorate in theology (1585), he resided in Rome in the service of Sixtus V, who made him a cardinal (December 1587). He was friendly with Caesar *Baronius, Robert *Bellarmine, *Joseph Calasanctius, and Philip *Neri. After being appointed to the See of Milan, he resided there as a leader of reform and patron of learning from 1601 until his death. He held a provincial council and 14 diocesan synods, made regular visits to the parishes, constructed churches, established colleges and academies, and built a picture gallery, and above all, the Ambrosian library (1609). At the conclave of 1623, he received 18 votes but was opposed by the Spanish party. His interest in mystical problems and his correspondence with certain sisters, for example, Caterina Vannini, a former courtesan who entered the convent, caused diverse comment. Borromeo was highly regarded because of his courage and generosity during the famine of 1627–28 and the plague of 1630. His writings, though unpublished, are listed by C. Cantù, *La Lombardia nel secolo XVII* (Milan 1832, appendix D).

Bibliography: F. RIVOLA, *Vita di Federigo Borromeo* (Milan 1656), contemporary and detailed. P. BELLEZZA, *Federigo Borromeo* (Milan 1931). M. PETTROCHI, *Omaggio a Federigo Borromeo: L'uomo e la storia* (Bologna 1940). P. MISCIATTELLI, *Caterina Vannini: Una cortegiana convertita senese e il card. Federigo Borromeo alla luce di un epistolario* (Milan 1932), and the reply by A. SABA, *Federigo Borromeo e i mistici del suo tempo. Con la vita e la corrispondenza inedita di Caterina Vannini da Sienna* (Florence 1933). G. GALBIATI, *Federigo Borromeo, studioso umanista e mecenate* (Milan 1932); EncIt 7:512–513, with bibliog. F. CASOLINI, EncCatt 2:1927–30. Moroni 6:60–62. Eubel HierCath 3:52, 240; 4:237. P. PASCHINI, DHGE 9:1281–83.

[R. MOLS]

BORROMINI, FRANCESCO, original and controversial architect of the *baroque in *Rome; b. Francesco Castelli (the name Borromini was adopted c. 1628) at Bissone, Lake Lugano, Sept. 25, 1599; d. Rome, Aug. 2, 1667. Francesco, the son of an architect,

The façade of the church of S. Agnese, Rome, designed by Francesco Borromini and constructed between 1645–50.

went to Rome in 1616 to work first under his kinsman *Maderno and later under *Bernini. His genius shows itself in the unprecedented designs for S. Carlo alle Quattro Fontane, with its restless interior and undulating façade; S. Ivo alla Sapienza, with its star-hexagon plan; S. Agnese a Piazza Navona (after *Rainaldi); S. Philip Neri; the Collegio di Propaganda Fide; and renovations in St. John Lateran. He enjoyed the patronage of Virgilio Spada, almoner to Innocent X, and was created a knight of the Order of Christ in 1652. Though his designs, animated by the tormented restlessness of his spirit, have been attacked by academic purists as perversions of classical correctness, he is considered a creative artist of high rank. He died of a wound self-inflicted in a fit of melancholy.

See also CHURCH ARCHITECTURE, 7.

Bibliography: R. WITTKOWER, *Art and Architecture in Italy, 1600 to 1750* (PelHArt; 1958). T. H. FOKKER, *Roman Baroque Art* (London 1938). G. C. ARGAN, *Borromini* (Milan 1952). P. PORTOGHESI, EncWA 2:547–570. **Illustration credit:** Alinari-Art Reference Bureau.

[J. M. SHELLEY]

BOSBOOM-TOUSSAINT, ANNA LOUISA GEERTRUIDA,

Dutch novelist; b. Alkmaar, Dec. 16, 1812; d. 's Gravenhage, April 13, 1886. She is the best-known Dutch author of historical novels in the tradition of Walter Scott, but the passion that gave Scott his impulse to tell stories in relation to a historic past was not hers. Hers was a passion to recapture religious experiences, especially in times of great spiritual and social upheaval, e.g., the rise of the Reformation in the Netherlands. The historical facts, diligently researched and often given too much in detail, serve only as the background for emotional involvement. The attractiveness of the dominant characters in her best novels is striking, e.g., Paul in *Het Huis Lauernesse* (1840, The House of Lauernesse); Gideon Florensz in the *Leycester Cycle* (1846–56); Jan Jacobsz in *De Delftsche wonderdokter* (1870, The Wonder-doctor of Delft). They are well-balanced people who, passionately devoted to the new religious ideas, stimulate others to emulate their high religious ideals. These ideals are the author's own and are based on an evangelical belief in the Bible. Bosboom-Toussaint was prejudiced against Catholicism, as represented by Capuchins, Dominicans, and Jesuits in her novels, but dealt with Catholics sincerely and honestly in daily life. Her novels are frequently ambiguous because she tried to combine the techniques of the picaresque novel with those of the novel of character. Her peculiar talent, and so her best achievement, lies in the second field, wherein she exhibits deep psychological insight. This develops in her later novels, and reaches a peak in the best, *Major Francis* (1874), a psychological study of a most unconventional young woman molded into a fine character by love.

Bibliography: A. L. G. BOSBOOM-TOUSSAINT, *Romantische Werken*, 25 v. (The Hague 1885–88). G. KNUVELDER, *Handboek tot de geschiedenis der Nederlandse letterkunde van der aanvang tot heden*, 4 v. ('s Hertogenbosch 1948–53). J. M. C. BOUVY, *Idee en werkwijze van Mevrouw Bosboom-Toussaint* (Rotterdam 1935).

[P. LUKKENAER]

BOSCARDIN, MARIA BERTILLA, ST.,

nursing sister; b. Brendola, near Vicenza, Italy, Oct. 6, 1888; d. Treviso, Oct. 20, 1922 (feast, Oct. 22). Baptized Anna Francesca, as a young girl she was pious, obedient, and quiet. She suffered because of her father's excessive drinking. At school, where she was diligent but slow to learn, she was derisively called "the goose." In 1901 she took a private vow of virginity, and in

St. Maria Bertilla Boscardin.

1905 she joined the *Dorotheans, at Vicenza. While a novice, she was sent to the local hospital in Treviso to work as a kitchen maid. When she made her religious profession (1907), she took the name Maria Bertilla. Returning to the hospital at Treviso, she cared for children stricken by diphtheria. Outwardly her life was not out of the ordinary. During the bombardment of Treviso after the collapse of the Italian troops at Caporetto (1917), however, her courage sustained the wounded soldiers. The advance of the German troops forced the transfer of the hospital to Viggiù, near Como, but after the armistice she returned to Treviso. She was beatified June 8, 1952, and canonized May 11, 1961.

Bibliography: ActApS 44 (1952) 522–527; 53 (1961) 289–295. L. CALIARO, *La Beata M. B. B.* (Vicenza 1952). E. FEDERICI, *Santa M. B.* (Vicenza 1959). L. X. AUBIN, *Ste. Marie Bertilla* (Montreal 1963). C. DE VITO, *The Cinderella of the Gospel* (Bombay n.d.) Butler Th Attw 4:161–162.

[F. G. SOTTOCORNOLA]

BOSCH, HIERONYMUS (HIERONYMUS VAN AEKEN),

Dutch painter noted for his bizarre visual imagination; b. 's Hertogenbosch (Bois-le-Duc), c. 1450; d. 's Hertogenbosch, 1516. Little is known of his early life and artistic training; the records of the Confraternity of Notre Dame in 's Hertogenbosch, where he apparently spent his entire life, list him as a member from 1480 to 1512. His early paintings show some similarity to the work of Dirk *Bouts and Roger van der *Weyden. The pictures of his maturity appear to be unique in their extreme elaboration of visual fantasy. In the 16th century Philip II of Spain was an ardent collector of Bosch's works, and many of his most important compositions remain in Spanish museums.

His paintings are unusual in conception, style, and iconography; the last still has not been adequately explained. The world they depict seems beset by the forces of evil, perhaps a reflection of the painter's experience of the deep unrest in the pre-Reformation north. In "The Adoration of the Magi" (Prado, Madrid), the tattered thatched eave above the Virgin and Child is scarcely sustained by a crooked branch, while the Three Wise Men in the foreground are ambiguously repeated in a trio of unsavory figures peering from a dark doorway. In his "St. John the Baptist in the Wilderness" (Museo Lázaro, Madrid), Bosch represents the figure of the saint reclining by the side of a fantastic article of vegetation that supports a huge egglike fruit cracking open to spill its contents. The symbol of the egg, which is derived from alchemy, appears under a multiplicity of forms in Bosch's most remarkable work, "The Garden of Delights" (c. 1500; Prado, Madrid). Its two side panels represent the Garden of Eden, just after the creation of Eve, and the torments of hell. The central panel contains masses of miniature naked figures ostensibly partaking of delights. Here the distinctions between human and bestial, animal and vegetable, and animate and inanimate realms of existence are obliterated. Nevertheless, there is no haziness in the plastic quality of the picture. Details are painted in bright, vivid colors and with a ruthless realism. It is a strange world in which horror, brilliantly illustrated, is treated as a virtual commonplace.

Bibliography: C. DE TOLNAY, *Hieronimus Bosch* (Basel 1937), bibliog. J. BALTRUŠAITIS, *Le Moyen âge fantastique* (Paris 1955). C. A. WERTHEIM AYMÈS, *Hieronymus Bosch: Eine Einführung in seine geheime Symbolik* (Amsterdam 1957). J. COMBE, Enc WA 2:570–580. **Illustration credit:** MAS, Barcelona.

[L. P. SIGER]

BOSCO, JOHN, ST.

Founder of the *Salesians and the *Salesian Sisters, and commonly referred to as Don Bosco; b. Becchi, near Turin, Italy, Aug. 16, 1815; d. Turin, Jan. 31, 1888 (feast, Jan. 31). His father died in 1817 and John was reared in poverty by his pious, hard-working mother, Margaret (Occhiena) Bosco. St. Joseph *Cafasso encouraged the boy's ambition to become a priest and to work with youths and directed him to enter the major seminary in Turin (1835), where John was ordained (1841). On Dec. 8, 1841, his main work began when he met, in the sacristy of Cafasso's Institute of St. Francis, a poor orphan, Bartolomeo Garelli, and decided to prepare him for his first Communion. Soon he gathered a group of young apprentices to teach them the catechism. Through Cafasso he was introduced to the Marchesa di Barola and became chaplain at her hospice of St. Philomena for working girls. In order to devote himself completely to working with boys, he opened, in the Valdocco section of Turin, his own hospice, which grew into the Oratory of St. Francis de Sales. His mother served as housekeeper until her death. Don Bosco gained powerful patrons, such as Abp. Franzoni of Turin and Count Camillo Cavour. By 1850 two workshops for shoemaking and tailoring were added to the hospice, and by 1856 there were 150 boys in residence. Later Don Bosco obtained a printing press, and he wrote and printed catechetical and pious pamphlets for youths. His reputation as a preacher became widespread, and miracles were attributed to his intercession. So successful was his work among homeless youth that even the bitterly anticlerical politician Urbano Rattazzi encouraged him.

Don Bosco experienced so much difficulty in retaining the services of young priests that from 1850 he began training his own helpers. By 1854 a group of these bound themselves together informally under the patronage of St. Francis de Sales. With Pious IX's encouragement, Don Bosco gathered 17 of them and founded in 1859 a religious congregation, which received papal approval in 1868. The Salesians spread quickly throughout Italy. When the founder died, there were 1,039 members and 57 houses in Italy, Spain, France, England, Argentina, Uruguay, and Brazil. The apostolate came to include work on the missions as well as the education of boys. Together with St. Maria *Mazzarello, Don Bosco founded in 1872 the Salesian Sisters for a similar apostolate among girls. In 1964 there were more than 40,000 Salesian priests, lay brothers, and sisters in all parts of the world. Don Bosco established also a kind of third order, the Salesian Cooperators, to assist in this work.

Don Bosco was preeminently an educator, whose characteristic approach is known as the Salesian preventive system of education. It rejected corporal punishment and strove to place youths in surroundings that removed them from the likelihood of committing sin.

Hieronymus Bosch, "Adoration of the Magi," center panel of a triptych, 53¾ by 28⅞ inches, in the Prado.

St. John Bosco, portrait by G. Rollini, 1888.

Frequent confession and Communion, thorough catechetical training, and fatherly guidance were the pillars of this system of spiritual formation, which sought also to unite the spiritual life of youths with their study, work, and play. Don Bosco's insistence that boys be taught trades made him a pioneer in modern vocational training.

Don Bosco had special devotion to Mary Help of Christians, and was responsible for the construction of a basilica in Turin with that title (1868). He also began the erection of the Basilica of the Sacred Heart in Rome and traveled to France in 1883 to raise funds for it. Pius XI, who as a young priest had known Don Bosco, beatified him June 2, 1929, and canonized him April 1, 1934. He has been named patron saint of Catholic publishers and of young apprentices.

Bibliography: A. AUFFRAY, *Bl. John Bosco,* tr. W. H. MITCHELL (London 1930). H. GHEON, "The Secret of Don Bosco," *The Secrets of the Saints,* tr. F. J. SHEED and D. ATTWATER (New York 1944). N. BOYTON, *The Bl. Friend of Youth, St. John Bosco* (2d ed. New York 1943). F. A. M. FORBES, *St. John Bosco* (Tampa, Fla. 1941). L. C. SHEPPARD, *Don Bosco* (Westminster, Md. 1957). E. B. PHELAN, *Don Bosco, A Spiritual Portrait* (Garden City, N.Y. 1963).

[E. F. FARDELLONE]

BOSCOVICH, RUGGIERO GIUSEPPE

Mathematician, astronomer, and natural philosopher; b. Ragusa (Dubrovnik), Dalmatia, May 18, 1711; d. Milan, Feb. 13, 1787. He was the eighth of the nine children of Nicholas Boscovich, a native of Herzegovina and an Orthodox Serb who became a Catholic on settling in Ragusa.

Having completed his primary and higher school education at the Jesuit grammar school of his native city, Boscovich entered the novitiate of the Society of Jesus in Rome on Oct. 31, 1725. He attended the Collegium Romanum and completed with great distinction the usual course of rhetoric, philosophy, and theology, as well as physico-mathematics. After that, he spent 5 years (1733–38) as a teacher of languages and poetics at various schools and subsequently became professor of mathematics at the Collegium Romanum itself.

Boscovich's literary activity began in 1736 with his scientific treatise in verse, *De solis et lunae defectibus,* and almost every year after that he published scientific treatises on various mathematical, physical, and astronomical subjects. In 1744 he was ordained a priest in the Society of Jesus, and the following year he published his first philosophical treatise, *De viribus vivis,* in which he put forth, for the first time, a new theory of matter. In 1754 he published a second more detailed treatise on the same subject, *De continuitatis lege et consectariis pertinentibus ad primae materiae elementa eorumque vires.* In 1755 and 1757 he published still further treatises on the same subject; finally in 1758 he produced his chief work, *Theoria philosophiae naturalis redacta ad unicam legem virium in natura existentium.* Boscovich held that bodies could not be composed of a continuous material substance, not even of contiguous material particles, but of innumerable "point-like structures" whose individual components lack all extension and divisibility. An infinitesimal repulsion, due to certain endowed forces of the elements, exists between them, which force cannot vanish without compenetration taking place. It tends to become infinite when the elements are in close proximity, whereas within certain limits it diminishes as the distance is increased and finally becomes an attractive force.

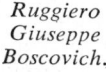

Ruggiero Giuseppe Boscovich.

The three principal points set forth in this theory are: (1) The ultimate elements of matter, the "atoms," are real, indivisible points. (2) The atoms are centers of forces. (3) Force varies both qualitatively and quantitatively in proportion to distance. Boscovich's work antedates by more than 100 years the birth of modern atomic theory.

Boscovich became known all over Europe and was recognized by the foremost scientific bodies. During a stay in England (1760) he was made a Fellow of the Royal Society of London.

Pope Benedict XIV commissioned Boscovich and his fellow Jesuit Le Maire to carry out several meridian measurements. In October 1750 the two Jesuits left Rome and worked for 2 years measuring 2½ degrees of the meridian Rome-Rimini; their work appeared in 1752.

The Royal Society of London proposed to send Boscovich in charge of a 1769 scientific expedition to California to observe the transit of Venus, but, unfortunately, the opposition manifested everywhere to the Society of Jesus made this impossible. After the suppression of the Jesuits by Clement XIV (1773), Boscovich went to Paris at the invitation of the King of France and became Director of Optics for the Marine, an office he held for 9 years, after which he returned to Italy for reasons of health. He superintended an issue of his works in Latin in five volumes, which appeared in Bassano in 1785: *Rogerii Josephi Boscovich opera pertinentia ad opticam et astronomiam . . . in quinque tomos distributa,* the last important work from the pen of this active man.

Streets in Rome, Milan, and Dubrovnik, as well as a crater on the moon, have been named after Boscovich. Sommervogel's *Bibliography of the Society of Jesus* devotes 12 pages to an account of his many publications.

Bibliography: H. V. GILL, *Roger Boscovich, S.J.* (Dublin 1941). W. T. KELVIN, *Baltimore Lectures on Molecular Dynamics and the Wave Theory of Light* (London 1904). Koch JesLex 1:236–237. B. PETRONIEVICS, *Slav Achievement in Advanced Science* (London 1917). L. L. WHYTE, ed., *Roger Joseph Boscovich* (New York 1962). Microfilms of principal works in Pius XII Library, St. Louis University, Mo.

[M. M. FITZPATRICK]

BOSO, CARDINAL, papal chamberlain; d. Rome, 1178. He was probably an Englishman making a career for himself at the papal Curia. A Bologna necrology calls him English (the sole evidence for this), though it has been argued that he was of Lombard origin. A papal clerk and scriptor, he was made a chamberlain by *Adrian IV in 1154–55. In this office he was responsible for the Lateran treasury and the papal finances, and he drew up a revision of an earlier book of dues, the *Liber Censuum. He became a cardinal in 1156, was sent by Adrian on a mission of uncertain purpose to Portugal, and in the disputed papal election of 1159, he held the *Castel Sant' Angelo in Rome for *Alexander III against the antipope Victor IV. He wrote useful biographies of Adrian and Alexander.

Bibliography: F. GEISTHARDT, *Der Kämmerer Boso* (Berlin 1936). G. ALBION, DHGE 9:1319–20. M. PACAUT, *Alexandre III* (Paris 1956). J. SYDOW, LexThK² 2:621.

[H. MAYR-HARTING]

BOSRA AND HAŪRĀN, ARCHDIOCESE OF (BOSTRENUS ET AURANENSIS), archbishopric of the *Melchite rite in south *Syria. In 1962 it had 22 parishes, 18 secular and 4 religious priests in 2 convents, 15 women in 4 convents, 1,800 pupils in 8 schools, and 13,200 Catholics in a population of 275,000; it is 3,861 square miles in area. Bosra, a village with ancient origins near Jebel ed Druz in the Haūrān, came under Rome in A.D. 106 (when the era of Bosra begins) and was metropolis of the province of Arabia. Roman ruins are still noteworthy. The city continued to be a fortress and trade center under the Arabs (634) but declined under the Ottomans (1516).

According to legend, Timon, one of the Disciples, was the first bishop of Bosra. Eusebius calls *Beryllus "bishop of the Arabs around Bosra." Christianity therefore existed among the neighboring Arabs as well as in the Greek city. *Titus (c. 378) and Antipater (457) also occupied the see. Bosra had some 20 suffragan sees as a metropolitanate under the Patriarchates of *Jerusalem and, after 431, *Antioch. *Jacobite "bishops of Arabia" (783–956) were probably bishops of Bosra, but it is unlikely that they resided in the city. Held briefly by Crusaders, Bosra had a Latin bishop, who, like the Greek metropolitan, was under Jerusalem rather than Antioch; Bosra is still a titular Latin archbishopric.

There was no bishop of Bosra when the Melchite Patriarchate of Antioch split into Catholic and Greek Orthodox patriarchates (late 17th century), although there were probably many Christian Arabs there. The see was restored in 1687; its first prelates were mostly titular (1763–1836). Patriarch *Maximos III Mazlūm visited the area, and from 1836 the prelates, mostly monks, became resident. The title Bosra and Haūrān dates from 1881. In 1932 Philadelphia, once suffragan to Bosra, was restored and united with *Petra as the archdiocese for Jordan under the Patriarchate of Jerusalem.

Bibliography: C. KOROLEVSKIJ, DHGE 9:1399–1405. W. DE VRIES, EncCatt 2:1952–53. L. GROLLENBERG, LexThK² 2:622. F. SCHMIDTKE, *ibid.* 1040–41. OrientCatt 247–272. AnnPont (1964) 70–71.

[J. A. DEVENNY]

BOSSI, MARCO ENRICO, organist, composer, and recitalist who strongly influenced modern Italian church music; b. Salo (Brescia), Italy, April 25, 1861; d. Feb. 20, 1925. Study at Bologna (1871–73) and Milan (1873–81) prepared him for a long career as organist of Como cathedral (1881–89); professor of organ and harmony, Naples Conservatory (1889–96); professor of organ and composition, Liceo B. Marcello, Venice (1896–1902); and director, Liceo Musicale, Bologna (1902–12), and of the music school of Santa Cecilia Academy, Rome (1916–23). He died aboard the SS *DeGrasse* en route home after a successful recital tour in the U.S. His *Metodo di Studio per l'organo moderno* (1893) laid the foundations for the reform of Italian organ technique, performance, design, and pedagogy. His compositions include Masses, motets, sonatas, organ concerti, orchestral suites, *Fantasia sinfonica* for organ and orchestra, choral works, oratorios. All are written in a style that is a blend of 19th-century Teutonic symphonic idioms and Italian lyricism and expressiveness.

See also ORGAN MUSIC.

Bibliography: G. C. PARIBENI et al., *M. E. Bossi* (Milan 1934). L. BOSSI, MusGG 2:149–152. J. A. FULLER-MAITLAND, Grove DMM 1:831. Baker 187–188.

[C. A. CARROLL]

BOSSUET, JACQUES BÉNIGNE

French bishop and orator; b. Dijon, France, Sept. 27, 1627; d. Paris, April 12, 1704. He was the seventh child of Bénigne Bossuet, a judge in the parliament of Dijon, and Madeleine Mochet. For more than half a century his ancestors, both paternal and maternal, had occupied judicial posts. He began his classical studies at the Jesuit college in Dijon and, when his father was appointed to the parliament of Metz, remained in Dijon under the care of an uncle. He made remarkable progress, at the same time becoming thoroughly acquainted with the Bible, which always remained his principal source of inspiration. Destined for the Church, he received the tonsure at the age of 8 and at 13 obtained a canonicate in the cathedral of Metz. Moving to Paris in 1642, he continued his classical studies adding philosophy and theology, at the Collège de Navarre. He offered his first thesis (*tentativa*) in 1648, was ordained subdeacon the same year, deacon the next, and began to preach at Metz. His second thesis (*sorbonica*) was defended in 1650, after which he prepared for the priesthood under St. Vincent de Paul (1576–1660). He was ordained March 18, 1652, and received the degree of doctor of divinity a few weeks later. He then resided at Metz for 7 years, engaged in preaching, study of the Bible and the Fathers, discussion with Protestants, and activities as a member of the Assembly of the Three Orders. He was associated also with the Compagnie du Saint-Sacrement.

Jacques Bénigne Bossuet, portrait by H. Rigaud in the Louvre, Paris.

In 1659 Bossuet returned to Paris on business for his chapter, but was induced to remain there as a preacher, largely through the influence of Vincent de Paul and the Queen Mother, Anne of Austria. He retained his connection with Metz and was appointed dean when his father, a widower, became a priest and canon at the same cathedral. In 1670 Bossuet was consecrated bishop of Condom. Although he was not obliged to reside in his diocese, his convictions in this matter caused him to resign a year later, at which time also he was elected to the French Academy. He was named tutor to the Dauphin in 1670 and threw himself energetically into his functions, even composing books for his pupil's instruction (see below). After the Dauphin's marriage in 1681, Bossuet was assigned to the bishopric of Meaux. He administered his see in residence, following the Assembly of the French Clergy in 1682, but was called away more and more frequently to Paris or to wherever the court might be staying. His health was failing by 1700, but he continued to defend his principles to the end, dictating letters and polemical essays to his secretary from his bed.

Court Orator. Bossuet's eminence as an orator is uncontested. He has been called the voice of France in the age of Louis XIV and is a perfect exemplar of the period's classicism. His simple but facile vocabulary well served the intensity of his thought, often expressed in the deep sonority of periodic sentences. His thought turned normally to terms of universality, majesty, balance, order, and *raison* in the 17th-century sense. He was passionately devoted to unity and considered its attainment possible only in absolutism. He believed in the divine right of kings and in a hierarchy involving both Church and State; and if he was himself somewhat authoritarian, this resulted probably from his conviction that it was his duty to demand from inferiors and those he directed the same obedience that he himself must render to superiors. Yet he was remarkably human, and, until his last years, conciliatory to the point of being accused of weakness.

With unfailing courage—and with some success—he preached and counseled against the King's adulterous liaisons. When Louis bridled, insisting that monarchs are above the law of men, Bossuet conceded this much but insisted that even kings are not above the law of God. Although this stand was clearly taken, Bossuet continued to admire the great ruler who, with all his faults, could unify and glorify France. Inspired by St. Vincent, Bossuet pleaded the cause of the poor against the extravagance of the court, but at the same time he felt that the proper discharge of his own role demanded a certain wealth, used with detachment of spirit. He also frankly enjoyed position and power, but most biographers find no justification for the charge that he actively sought them. He remained at court probably because he was convinced that his presence there acted as a Christian leaven in the midst of corruption.

Bossuet was physically and mentally robust and usually convinced that he was right. He was sometimes sanguine to the point of naïveté. Thus he approved the revocation of the Edict of Nantes (1685), while neither approving nor expecting the use of force, because he was convinced that Protestants would be amenable to the new ruling and would collaborate for Christian unity. (*See* NANTES, EDICT OF.)

Writer and Preacher. Bossuet's first published work, *Réfutation du catéchisme du sieur Paul Ferry, ministre de la religion prétendue réformée* (1655), was directed against a Protestant pastor at Metz. During this early period he began also to compose and preach panegyrics on the saints. Those on St. Francis of Assisi (1652), St. Bernard (1653), St. Paul (1657), and the Apostle Peter (1661) are among the best. The studies served as bases for moral lessons; he employed the same tactic in his masterpieces, the *Oraisons funèbres*. The first of these was preached at Metz, but the more highly perfected ones came later, notably those for Henriette de France (1669), for Henriette d'Angleterre (1670), and for le Prince de Condé (1687).

Bossuet's ordinary sermons, not composed for publication, were scattered in manuscript and note form and have been recovered only gradually and incompletely. His greatest preaching period extended from 1659 to 1670. He was invited to give the Lenten sermons at the Louvre in 1662 and his stern commentary on the wicked rich, the efficacy of Penance, death, and so on, sometimes leveled at the King personally, and accompanied by threats of damnation, was little calculated to improve its author's welcome, although it was recognized that a genuine orator had emerged from a host of preachers. Soon, however, he became involved in the Jansenist controversy (*see* JANSENISM). The degree of his sympathy with *Port-Royal is debated. While he undoubtedly favored the austere Jansenist morality and condemned what he considered the "easy devotion" of the Jesuits, he agreed with full conviction that five propositions drawn from *Augustinus* were to be found in Port-Royal doctrine and should be condemned. His own spirituality was Bérullian (*see* BÉRULLE, PIERRE DE), influenced by St. Vincent de Paul and by the works of St. Francis of Sales (1567–1622).

Three of Bossuet's most important works were composed primarily for the instruction of the Dauphin: *Traité de la connaissance de Dieu et de soi-même* (1677), *Politique tirée de l'Écriture Sainte* (1679), and the *Discours sur l'histoire universelle* (1681). He considered the *Discours* his most important written work; he published two revisions, and was working on another at the time of his death. In what was one of the first "philosophies of history," Bossuet conceived the whole of history as directed by Providence, and in relation to a single event, the Incarnation. In philosophy as such, Bossuet was partially Thomist, but he taught the Dauphin the ideas of Descartes, which he later repudiated. In the Assembly of the Clergy called by the King to deal with jurisdiction over vacant episcopal sees, the whole question of papal authority and the rights and liberties of the Gallican church came up for debate (*see* GALLICANISM). Although Bossuet was Gallican by family tradition and patriotism and did not believe in papal infallibility, he had no thought of renouncing due submission to Rome. He sought a compromise and was chosen to draw up the Four Articles (1682) that Pope Innocent XI rejected. An act of submission from the French bishops in 1693 ended the troubles, and it was chiefly Bossuet's loyalty and spirit of moderation that recalled France from the brink of schism.

Severity of His Later Years. To the period of Meaux belongs his *Histoire des variations des églises protestantes* (1688); in 1691 he began a correspondence with *Leibniz, a kindred spirit who, from the Protestant point of view, also dreamed of a Christian unification of the world. Their rapprochement failed and their hopes were soon abandoned. So many reverses in Bossuet's grandiose plans began to weaken the patience that had always characterized him, and a certain harsh and sometimes unjust insistence marked his final controversies. He was a ruthless foe of any innovations in Biblical criticism. He began furiously to blame the classics and the theater for relaxed morality, and condemned all poetry and amusement. These ideas are expressed in his *Traité de la concupiscence* (1693) and *Maximes sur la comédie* (1694). Most 17th-century moralists tended to frown upon the theater, but Bossuet's frown was as grim as the Jansenists'. In this period the great quarrel over *quietism arose (especially *c.* 1694–1700). Bossuet, neither conversant with mysticism nor drawn to it by temperament, worked hard to grasp its meaning when asked to examine Mme. *Guyon, whom *Fénelon defended. Bossuet recognized in Mme. Guyon an unbalanced personality and a false mysticism. He had a hand in the Articles of Issy that condemned propositions drawn from Mme. Guyon's writings. The articles were agreed to by all parties, but their interpretation involved a series of explanations and counter-explanations that really constituted the quarrel over them. Bossuet wrote during this affair the *Instruction sur les états d'oraison* (1696) and *Relation sur le quiétisme* (1698). His remaining years were peaceful and his death reflected the calm and majesty of his great works.

Bibliography: *Oeuvres complètes*, ed. E. N. GUILLAUME, 10 v. (Bar-le-Duc 1877); *Oeuvres oratoires*, ed. J. LEBARQ et al., 7 v. (Paris 1922–27); *Correspondance*, ed. C. URBAIN and E. LEVESQUE, 15 v. (Paris 1909–25). J. CALVET, *Bossuet: L'Homme et l'oeuvre* (Paris 1941); *Histoire de la littérature française*, v.5 (Paris 1939) 259–319, good bibliography 450–453. A. RÉBELLIAU, *Bossuet* (Paris 1900). J. TRUCHET, *La Prédication de Bossuet* (Paris 1960), A. LARGENT, DTC 2:1049–89. P. DUDON, Dict SpirAscMyst 1:1874–83. E. K. SANDERS, *Jacques Bénigne Bossuet: A Study* (SPCK; New York 1922). W. J. SIMPSON, *A Study of Bossuet* (New York 1937). D. O'MAHONY, ed., *Panegyrics of the Saints: From the French of Bossuet and Bourdaloue* (St. Louis 1924), also contains parts of other works of Bossuet. **Illustration credit:** Archives Photographiques, Paris.

[L. TINSLEY]

BOSTE, JOHN, BL., one of martyrs of Durham (feast, July 24); b. Dufton, Westmoreland, *c.* 1543; d. Dryburn, near Durham; July 24, 1594. John Boste (Boast, Bost) was educated at Queen's College, Oxford, and after receiving his M.A. took the Oath of Supremacy. However, he was converted to Catholicism in 1576 and 4 years later began his studies for the priesthood at the English College at Rheims. He was ordained in 1581 and returned to England to an active apostolate among the English Catholics. Traveling disguised as a servingman in the livery of Lord Montacute, he visited Norwich, Maidenhead, Colnbrook, and Gloucestershire. Most of his missionary years were spent in the northern counties—Westmoreland, Cumberland and the Border, Durham, and Yorkshire. Because of his energy and success, he was sought after by both his Catholic friends and the English government. He was betrayed by a Catholic apostate, Francis Ecclesfield, and arrested near Durham, September 1593. He was conveyed to York, and thence to the Tower of London. Several times he was tortured in an effort to make him reveal his associates and was finally sent back to Durham for trial in July 1594, together with Father John Ingram and George Swallowell, both later beatified. Boste was charged under the statute of 1585 with having been ordained abroad as a Roman priest and with having returned to England to further the Catholic faith. He refused to plead to the indictment, saying he would not have a jury guilty of his blood. When accused of having had foreknowledge of the attempt at a Spanish invasion he answered: "It is our [priests'] function to invade souls, and not to meddle with these temporal invasions." He was condemned for high treason and sentenced to be hanged, drawn, and quartered. His trust and tranquility in the face of death inspired Swallowell, who in his fear was near apostatizing, to persevere. Boste endured his martyrdom with heroic resolution, joy, and fortitude, forgiving his executioners and inspiring a multitude of spectators. He was beatified in 1929 as one of the Forty Martyrs whose cause for canonization was opened in 1960. (*See* MARTYRS OF ENGLAND AND WALES.)

Bibliography: R. CHALLONER, *Memoirs of Missionary Priests,* ed. J. H. POLLEN (new ed. London 1924). J. MORRIS, ed., *The Troubles of Our Catholic Forefathers Related by Themselves,* 3 v. (London 1872–77) v.3. CathRecSoc 1 (1905); 5 (1908). T. COOPER, DNB 2:884.

[A. M. C. FORSTER]

BOSTIUS, ARNOLD, Carmelite theologian and humanist (known also as Arnold van Vaernewijck); b. Ghent, 1445; d. Ghent, April 4, 1499. Bostius, subprior and possibly prior at Ghent, served as a spiritual director to Carmelite nuns. He was greatly influenced by the Carmelite reformer Bl. John *Soreth (d. 1471). Keenly interested in the humanistic movement, Bostius promoted classical studies within his order and was in contact with such leading humanists as *Erasmus, *Trithemius, Sebastian *Brant, Robert *Gaguin, and Bl. *Baptist of Mantua. He was a proponent of the Immaculate Conception and wrote about the Virgin Mary's patronage of the Carmelites (*De patronatu et patrocinio Virginis Mariae*). Bostius also composed works on the history of his order (*De illustribus viris; Speculum historiale;* and *Breviloquium tripartitum*).

Bibliography: "Epistolae Arnoldi Bostii Gandavensis," *Monumenta historica Carmelitana,* ed. B. ZIMMERMANN (Lérins 1907) 511–522. P. S. ALLEN, "Letters of A. B.," EngHistRev 34 (1919) 225–236. C. DE VILLIERS, *Bibliotheca carmelitana* (Orléans 1752); ed. G. WESSELS, 2 v. in 1 (Rome 1927) 1:198–200. A. DE SAINT PAUL, DHGE 4:555–558. G. MESTERS, LexThK² 1:892–893. E. R. CARROLL, *Doctrina Mariologica Arnoldi Bostii, 1445–1499* (Doctoral diss. unpub. Pontifical Gregorian U. 1951); *The Marian Theology of Arnold Bostius, O.Carm., 1445–1499* (Rome 1962).

[K. J. EGAN]

BOSTON, ARCHDIOCESE OF (BOSTONIENSIS)

Metropolitan see of eastern Massachusetts, extending over the five counties of Suffolk, Essex, Middlesex, Norfolk, and Plymouth (with the towns of Mattapoisett, Marion, and Wareham excepted, in order to connect Cape Cod and the Islands with the mainland portion of the Fall River Diocese). In this area of 2,465 square miles there were (1963) 1,733,620 Catholics in a total population of 3,335,895. The diocese was formed April 8, 1808, as one of four subdivisions of the original U.S. Diocese of Baltimore, and was raised to the rank of archdiocese in 1875. Suffragans of Boston include the sees of Burlington, Vt., Manchester, N.H., Portland,

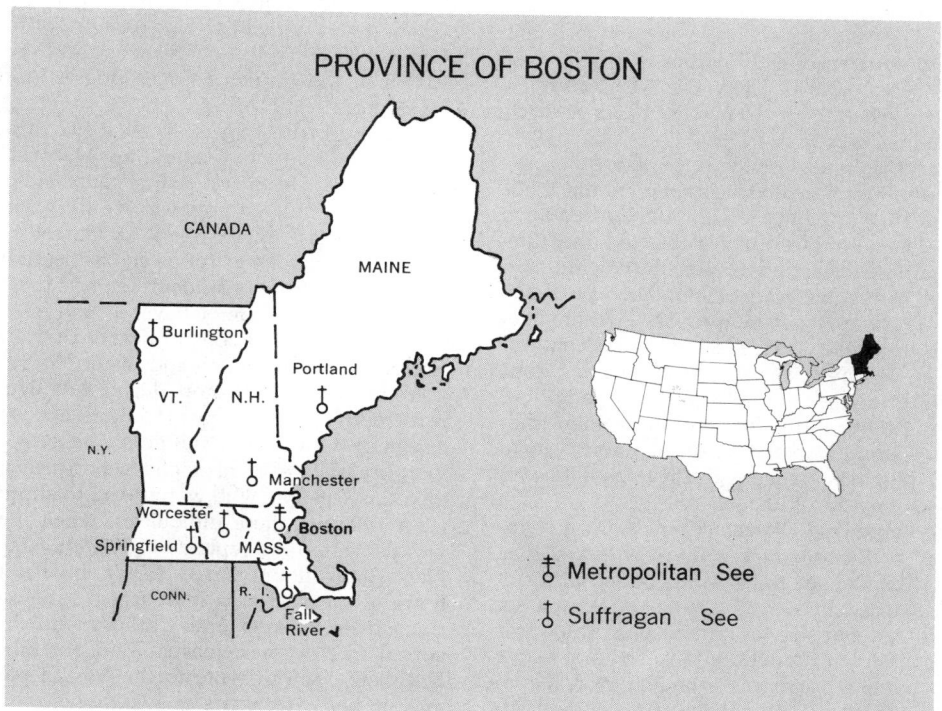

Fig. 1. Province of Boston comprises the Archdiocese of Boston, called the metropolitan see, and six dioceses, called suffragan sees. The archbishop has metropolitan jurisdiction over the province.

Maine, and Fall River, Springfield, and Worcester in Massachusetts.

COLONIZATION TO ERECTION OF DIOCESE

The explorer Samuel de *Champlain mapped the coast of New England in two successive voyages, 1604 and 1605, while he was a colonist at Sainte Croix, Maine; there a priest named Nicholas Aubry was chaplain for the colony established in 1604. In this same period an Englishman named Waymouth also planted the cross in the region in preparation for the attempt under Lord Thomas Arundel to establish an English Catholic colony, a venture that proved unsuccessful. The French colonists were attacked by the English from Virginia in 1613, and all but a few left Sainte Croix for Cape Sable. On Nov. 3, 1620, the English crown granted a patent for a colony between 40 and 48 degrees North Latitude in the region to be called New England. Plymouth was settled in 1620, and Salem and Boston in the following decade.

Colonial Anti-Catholicism. The only priests at the time were beyond the Kennebec River. Although the Massachusetts Bay Colony had passed a law in 1647 to ban the presence of any priest in the colony, Gabriel Druillettes, SJ, was allowed to visit Boston in December 1650 to discuss trade proposals between Canada and the English colony. The antipriest law was reenacted in 1700, with a penalty of life imprisonment for offenders and death for a priest who might escape confinement. From 1685 the observance of Pope's Day (November 5) gave public expression to hatred of the Catholic Church. Recurring battles between the colonists and the combined French and Indian forces to the north culminated in the Norridgewok raid on Aug. 23, 1724, and the death, among others, of the Indians' chaplain, Sebastian *Rale, SJ. The victorious Boston captain brought the priest's scalp and those of 27 Indians to Boston to claim the bounty of £100 from the Massachusetts Council. A peace treaty signed Aug. 6, 1726, assured the Indians religious freedom.

Meanwhile Massachusetts maintained a hostile attitude toward Catholicism, evidenced in the annual Dudleian Lectures at Harvard and the continued observance of Pope's Day. The latter custom was checked only during the Revolution by the action of General Washington, who deprecated its bigoted purpose. On the eve of the Revolution the Quebec Act, which in 1774 granted religious freedom in Canada, was resented in Boston, but hostility had to give way to the practical considerations of trying to win the cooperation of Canada. In addition, the aid given by France in the war and the valiant military service of Catholics in the cause of liberty led to the granting of religious freedom in the Massachusetts constitution of June 15, 1780.

Beginning of Organized Church. French naval chaplains said Mass in Boston during the war years. The French officer Chevalier de St. Sauveur, killed in a riot in Boston, was buried in King's Chapel in September 1778, and before a parish was established Mass was offered by the occasional French visitors. The first native Bostonian to become a priest was John *Thayer, a convert in 1783 from Congregationalism and a Yale graduate, who was ordained in Paris, June 2, 1787. The first foundation of the Church in Boston was the work of a renegade French naval chaplain, Claude Florent Bouchard, who called himself Abbé de la Poterie. Born in

Fig. 2. St. Augustine's Chapel and cemetery in 1828.

1751 at Craon and ordained for the Diocese of Angers in 1777, he served two terms as a naval chaplain before leaving the fleet when it sailed from Boston, Sept. 28, 1788. He offered the first public Mass in Boston, Nov. 2, 1788, in a church formerly used by Huguenots and Congregationalists. The relic of the true cross brought to Boston by the abbé is still preserved in the Cathedral of the Holy Cross. The superior of the Catholic Church in the U.S., John Carroll, extended faculties to Poterie until, after several months, the abbé's debts, troubles with the French consul, and damaging letters from French ecclesiastical authorities dictated that he be suspended. To replace the abbé, Carroll sent Father Louis de Rousselet, who found it difficult to work in harmony with Thayer. The latter's pastorate in Boston (1790–92) was troubled by controversies with Protestants as well as by disputes with Rousselet that led to open schism. The situation was settled by the departure of both under the direction of Carroll, now bishop, and the assignment to Boston of the French refugee priest, Francis Anthony *Matignon.

Arriving in Boston, Aug. 20, 1792, Matignon found only a few Catholics attending Mass because of the factional strife of the preceding years. He quickly healed the division, and Catholics in New England soon numbered 500. His appointment as Carroll's vicar-general for New England was followed by the arrival on Oct. 3, 1796, of his former student Jean Lefebvre de *Cheverus. Like Matignon, Cheverus had refused the oath supporting the civil constitution of the clergy in France and had escaped to England, where he received Matignon's invitation to Boston. There he aided the pastor in constructing Holy Cross Church according to plans drawn up by Charles Bulfinch. Cheverus was subjected to court trials over his right to perform marriages and to counsel people who were taxed to support local ministers. Despite these difficulties, when the new church was dedicated on Sept. 29, 1803, the Catholic flock in New England numbered 1,000. Indefatigable mission tours of the vast area invigorated religious life and attracted Protestants and Catholics alike. The English consul in Boston requested Baptism on his deathbed. Elizabeth *Seton wrote to the Boston priests for guidance in her early years as a Catholic.

DIOCESE

On April 8, 1808, Pope Pius VII erected a diocese for New England, which was to be a suffragan of Baltimore, and named Cheverus the first bishop of Boston.

Cheverus. The consecration of the new bishop was delayed for 2 years by the blockade of Papal States' ports. After authentic copies of the bulls reached Baltimore, he was solemnly consecrated there on Nov. 1, 1810. He then conferred with his brother bishops, visited Mother Seton at Emmitsburg, and returned to Boston. The War of 1812 impaired the commerce of the city and hurt Cheverus's efforts to establish schools. Catholic groups helped build fortifications when the city was threatened by British troops. A legacy of Thayer, who died in Ireland, Feb. 17, 1815, provided for the foundation of an Ursuline school in the city. By 1820 the first nuns had arrived. Cheverus suffered a crushing loss in the death of Matignon on Sept. 19, 1818, a loss scarcely lightened by the tributes of the newspapers and the signs of public mourning.

Immigration brought Catholics to all parts of New England, where by 1820 political liberty for Catholics was fully realized. In 1823, although he had refused to accept nomination to the See of Montauban, Cheverus was commanded by the King of France to return. With great reluctance and over the protests of Catholics and Protestants in New England, he departed on Sept. 26, 1823. In 1826 he was named archbishop of Bordeaux and shortly before his death (July 19, 1836) was raised to membership in the College of Cardinals. Boston, numbering 5 priests and 4,000 Catholics, was administered by William Taylor vicar-general, until a successor was named.

Fenwick. The second bishop of Boston, Benedict Joseph *Fenwick, was a native American of a Colonial Maryland family, who entered the Society of Jesus and was ordained June 11, 1808. Thereafter he served in New York for 9 years, was twice president of Georgetown College, vicar-general for Georgia and the Carolinas, and pastor in Maryland. He was consecrated on Nov. 1, 1825, in Baltimore by Abp. Ambrose Maréchal and took possession of his diocese on December 4. He found that the number of priests had fallen to 3, the number of Catholics had increased to 7,000, and that he had only 8 churches in addition to the cathedral to serve them.

The bishop set about building more churches to meet the needs of immigrants attracted to New England by the development of manufacturing centers and the building of canals and railroads. In 1826 he moved the Ursuline school to Mount Benedict in Charlestown. He brought students into his own house to prepare them for the priesthood. Meanwhile, at Claremont, N.H., the convert Barber family led a flood of conversions. New churches sprang up to the south of Boston and in Vermont, with continued attention given to the Indians in Maine. Cheap rates of passage brought great numbers of Irish to New Brunswick and thence to New England. In 1833 Bishop Fenwick began his Catholic colony at Benedicta, Aroostook County, Maine, planning to have mills, homes, and schools. Two members of the new community of the Sacred Hearts of Jesus and Mary were obtained for the Indians. Aid for the growing diocese came from the Society for the *Propagation of the Faith and the Austrian *Leopoldine Society.

In 1843 Hartford was made a diocese, encompassing Connecticut and Rhode Island. Plagued by such troubles as *trusteeism, nationalism, and bigotry (see NATIVISM), Fenwick continued to expand his diocese. At his death

in 1846 there were 39 priests, 48 churches, and 70,000 Catholics. He took special pride in the foundation of the Jesuit College of the Holy Cross at Worcester, Mass., June 21, 1843. To him goes the credit for the first clergy retreat in Boston and the first synod in 1842; regular catechism for the children of the diocese (4 hours weekly); the establishment of homes for orphan boys and girls (the latter cared for by Sisters of Charity from 1832); the inauguration of a Catholic newspaper in 1829 (first called the *Jesuit;* continued as the *Pilot* in 1836); approximately 2,000 conversions; and a significant role in the first five Provincial Councils of Baltimore. His death on Aug. 11, 1846, after an episcopate that was the turning point in the history of the Catholic Church in New England, was followed by a procession through the streets of Boston.

Fitzpatrick. Fenwick had consecrated his successor, Boston-born John Bernard Fitzpatrick, March 24, 1844, in the chapel of the Visitation nuns at Georgetown. During his 2 years as coadjutor of Boston, Fitzpatrick made visitations to Maine and Vermont and administered Confirmation in all parts of the diocese, where his charity made him a beloved figure, known to all as Bishop John. Gifted and urbane, he won entry also into the society of the Cabots and the Lodges. Five trips to Maine and two to Vermont led him to propose the separation of the northern states into two new dioceses in 1853, Burlington for Vermont, and Portland for the states of Maine and New Hampshire. This division gave 8 churches to Burlington and 24 to Portland, leaving Boston with 63 churches. Fitzpatrick's schoolmate, Louis de Göesbriand, was named first bishop of Burlington, and until the choice of a bishop for Portland was settled in 1855, Fitzpatrick administered that dio-

Fig. 3. Cathedral of the Holy Cross, 1803.

cese. He opposed as premature the proposal that Boston be raised to an archdiocese.

In 1854 he was the first Boston bishop to make the *ad limina* visit. In Rome he discussed with the Jesuit general and his council his hope of opening a college in Boston; and in Paris he obtained a renewal of aid from the Society for the Propagation of the Faith. With 57 priests in the diocese by 1854, the bishop named as the first chancellor and secretary, Father James Healy (later bishop of Portland). A clergy society was formed to aid sick and aged members of the clergy, and to parish life were added such new organizations as the Sodality, Propagation of the Faith, and the Association of the Holy Childhood. Liberal contributions were made to relieve famine victims in Ireland, and the generosity of Yankee neighbors increased the total to $150,000. At home the needs of increasing numbers of immigrants were met. Hundreds of homeless children were sheltered in St. Vincent's Orphan Asylum and the House of the Angel Guardian. Through the generosity of Andrew Carney, the hospital that bears his name was opened (1863). Schools multiplied, and *Boston College was established by the Jesuits in 1863.

During the Civil War three priests of the diocese served as military chaplains, and the patriotism of Boston Catholics, particularly in the 9th and 28th Regiments at Bull Run, Antietam, Gettysburg, and the Wilderness, scored a victory over bigotry in Massachusetts. In 1861 Harvard University conferred an honorary doctor of divinity degree on Fitzpatrick. Under his supervision plans were drawn by Patrick Keeley for a new cathedral; however, it could not be constructed until after the war. Fitzpatrick, an invalid during his last years, died Feb. 13, 1866, 4 days after the papal bulls arrived naming John J. *Williams his coadjutor with right of succession.

Williams. The fourth bishop of Boston and its first archbishop had served as pastor of St. James in Boston and vicar-general before his nomination as coadjutor *cum iure* Jan. 8, 1866. During the 40 years following his consecration (March 11, 1866, at St. James Church) churches and schools multiplied beyond any expectation. Diocesan synods were held in 1868, 1872, 1879, and 1886; the last was mistakenly numbered the fourth, when in fact it was the fifth synod in Boston. At Vatican Council I, Abp. Martin J. Spalding's proposal for a compromise solution of the debate on infallibility was endorsed by Williams. At his suggestion the Diocese of Springfield was created June 14, 1870, embracing five counties of central and western Massachusetts and taking from Boston 52 churches, 40 priests, and 100,000 people. Two years later, when Rhode Island was separated from the Diocese of Hartford as the Diocese of Providence, Williams gave up four counties in southeastern Massachusetts and three towns in Plymouth County to assure sufficient population for the new diocese. Fifteen churches, as many priests, and 30,000 Catholics were affected by this transfer.

ARCHDIOCESE

The rapid growth of the Church in New England was recognized on Feb. 12, 1875, when the New England states were constituted a province, with Boston as the archdiocesan see. Williams received the pallium from Cardinal John McCloskey May 2, 1875. Following the dedication of the new Cathedral of the Holy Cross Dec. 8, 1875, the archbishop built St. John's Seminary, Brighton, blessing the first building on Sept. 18, 1884, and staffing it with Sulpicians headed by the Abbé John Baptist Hogan. A second building was opened in 1890, and the Romanesque chapel was completed in 1899. In response to the constant growth of his flock, which now included immigrants from Portugal (the Azores and Cape Verde Islands), Poland, Lithuania, Germany, Italy, and the Near East, Williams set up a matrimonial tribunal in 1893 and named a superintendent for archdiocesan schools in 1897. Through its branches of the Society for the Propagation of the Faith, Boston by 1904 led the entire world in its contributions to the missions.

Carmelites were brought to Boston in 1890 and Franciscan Poor Clares, in 1899. The Little Sisters of the Poor established their apostolate, the Sisters of St. Joseph undertook teaching duties, and the Sisters of the Good Shepherd came with their protective mission. Hospitals were built in Cambridge (Holy Ghost), Lowell (St. John's), and Boston (St. Elizabeth's). When he was 82, Williams asked for a coadjutor with the right of succession. In 1906 Rome named Bp. William H. *O'Connell of Portland, Maine, who became second archbishop of Boston at Williams's death, Aug. 30, 1907.

O'Connell. Boston's fifth ordinary and second archbishop brought to his task not only experience as an ordinary in Portland, but Roman training and a worldwide comprehension of the Church. During his 37-year rule he undertook the reorganization of the archdiocese, an intensification of apostolic activities, and an adjustment of relations with the community. The centenary of the diocese was observed in 1908, the fifth synod was held Feb. 11, 1909, the duties of the chancellor were broadened, 32 new parishes were set up in 4 years, and annual retreats for the clergy ordered. The *Pilot* was purchased as a diocesan journal, Boston College moved to a new campus in Newton, and the seminary was transferred from Sulpician to diocesan management. Several institutions were saved from bankruptcy. Father James Anthony Walsh was released to found Maryknoll, the American foreign mission society. Passionists and the Religious of the Cenacle came to Boston to direct retreats. On Nov. 27, 1911, O'Connell was created cardinal priest, with the title church of St. Clement; he took part in the election of Pius XII in 1939, having failed twice before to arrive in Rome in time to vote in the conclaves that ended in the elections of Benedict XV and Pius XI. During World War I he issued frequent messages in behalf of the war effort and gave over diocesan facilities in the influenza epidemic of 1918. The sixth synod, April 7, 1919, resulted in the naming of rural deans, synodal judges, and a diocesan building commission. Between 1907 and 1944, the number of churches grew from 248 to 375; parishes, from 194 to 322; priests, from 598 to 1,582; brothers, from 140 to 356; and sisters, from 1,567 to 5,469. Religious communities of men increased from 13 to 21; those of women, from 29 to 44. O'Connell remained well and active, without need of a coadjutor or more than one auxiliary bishop, until his death April 22, 1944.

Cushing. At O'Connell's death, his auxiliary, Richard James Cushing, was named administrator and became archbishop of Boston Sept. 25, 1944. Born in Boston Aug. 24, 1896, he attended Boston College and St. John's Seminary, was ordained May 26, 1921, and con-

Fig. 4. Cathedral of the Holy Cross, 1963.

secrated bishop June 10, 1929. He was raised to the College of Cardinals Dec. 15, 1958, as cardinal priest, with the title church of Santa Susanna. Under his direction the number of colleges in the archdiocese doubled, from three to six: Boston (Newton), Cardinal Cushing (Brookline), Emmanuel (Boston), Merrimack (Andover), Regis (Weston), and Newton College of the Sacred Heart (Newton). By 1963, 13 new central secondary schools had increased the total to 100, caring for 24,259 students. Elementary schools, both parochial and private, had increased to 241, with 118,000 students. Social works were inaugurated to meet the needs of the aged, the handicapped, and the homeless. The vast building program reached every corner of the archdiocese, from seminary and chancery to hospitals, schools, catechetical centers, churches, convents, and rectories. An ecumenical committee was organized in 1963 to promote dialogue with Protestants and Jews. The Sacramental Apostolate of the Archdiocese offered lectures and information on liturgical topics. The Holy Name Society, the Sodality of Our Lady, and the Confraternity of Christian Doctrine expanded their influence to all parishes. The program of lending priests to other dioceses, which Cushing began soon after his installation, developed into the Pious Society of St. James the Apostle. Once founded by the cardinal in July 1958, the Society sent more than 100 priests to Latin-American mission fields, principally Peru and Bolivia. Cushing's apostolate includes recitation twice daily of the Rosary by radio, televised Mass on Sunday, the first television channel allotted to a diocese in the U.S. (WIHS), local and long-distance pilgrimages, and personal visits to Protestant and Orthodox audiences. In 1952 the seventh synod was held. A year later the separation from Hart-

ford left Boston a province with six suffragans. The Sons of Mary, a medical mission community of diocesan status, was founded by Edward Garesché, SJ, at Framingham in 1952. The first national seminary for delayed vocations, named for Pope John XXIII, with a capacity of 100 seminarians opened in Weston, Mass., in 1964.

Notable Clergy and Laity. Among outstanding priests were James *Fitton, for 50 years a missionary in all parts of New England; William Wiley (b. N.Y., 1803 or 1804), converted after Harvard President Kirkland took him in from the streets, a pioneer like Fitton; John *Bapst, SJ, Maine missionary who was tarred and feathered by a wild mob because of their hatred of Catholicism; William Henry Hoyt, converted from the Episcopal ministry and ordained in 1877 after the death of his wife; George Haskins, founder of the House of the Angel Guardian; Robert Fulton, SJ (b. Alexandria, Va., June 28, 1826), once a Senate page, twice president of Boston College, and close friend of Oliver Wendell Holmes; and Bp. James Anthony *Walsh, founder of the Catholic Foreign Missionary Society of America (Maryknoll) with Father Thomas F. *Price.

Distinguished laymen include those who made the *Pilot* a newspaper of high merit—Patrick *Donahoe, the publisher, and among the editors, Thomas D'Arcy *McGee and John Boyle *O'Reilly. Andrew *Carney was a philanthropist without peer. George *Healy painted portraits of the greatest personages of the 19th century. The ranks of New England statesmen include Edward *Kavanagh, congressman and governor of Maine in the 19th century, and David I. *Walsh of Massachusetts, U.S. senator, and John F. *Kennedy, 35th President of the U.S., in the 20th century.

Conversions have been a strong point of New England Catholicism. Bishop Cheverus knew Dr. Stephen Cleveland Blyth of Salem, who after extensive travels and study of religions was baptized in 1809, followed by Thomas Walley in 1814. The *Barber family of Claremont, N.H., were responsible for scores of conversions, leading with their own turning to the Faith and religious life. Fenwick's era counted many physicians as converts, such ministers as George Haskins, William Hoyt, and Augustine *Hewit; the Russian consul, Peter Kielchen; the artist David Claypoole Johnston; Joshua Moody Young, who became second bishop of Erie; Ruth Charlotte Dana; and such members of the Brook Farm colony as Isaac *Hecker and Mrs. George Ripley. Orestes *Brownson was a distinguished convert of the age, and Bishop Fitzpatrick served as guide for Emma Forbes Cary; George M. *Searle, later Paulist general and director of the Vatican Observatory; and Paul Revere's grandson, Gen. Joseph Warren Revere. Nathaniel Hawthorne's daughter, Rose; Longfellow's niece, Marion; and Dr. Thomas *Dwight of the Harvard faculty became Catholics during Archbishop Williams's time. In Cardinal O'Connell's era the writer Daniel Sargent, the diplomat Gardiner Howland Shaw, and the Harvard history professor Robert Howard *Lord (later ordained and named domestic prelate) became Catholics.

Opposition to Catholicism. The favor enjoyed by Bishop Cheverus among the members of the Boston community did not outlive his departure without diminution. The revival of evangelical Protestantism after 1820 brought attacks on the Church, both verbal and physical. Immigration of large numbers of Irish Catholics was another cause. Boston witnessed street riots in the 1830s and 1840s and the burning of the Ursuline Convent on Aug. 11, 1834. Educational conflicts were frequent in the decades that followed, with some instances of Catholic children being whipped in public schools for refusing to read from a Protestant version of the Bible. A lengthy campaign was necessary to win freedom for priests to enter public institutions to minister to Catholics. In more recent times a controversy centered on the St. Benedict Center in Cambridge, where Leonard Feeney, SJ, and his followers taught a doctrine that only Catholics could be saved. This error was the subject of the letter *Suprema haec sacra,* issued by the Holy Office at the Vatican, Aug. 8, 1949, presenting an explicit explanation of the teaching of the Catholic Church on salvation.

Present Status. By 1963 there were 403 parishes (including 10 Eastern rite), 20 missions, and 18 chapels, including those at the airport, railroad station, and shrines; a total of 2,428 priests, of whom 1,034 were religious; the number of sisters had increased to 5,896; brothers, to 362; and diocesan seminarians, to 550. Hospitals numbered 12; protective institutions, 7; juvenile court chaplains, 44; and homes for the aged, 11.

Bibliography: R. H. LORD et al., *History of the Archdiocese of Boston . . . 1604 to 1943,* 3 v. (New York 1944; Boston 1945). W. H. O'CONNELL, *Recollections of Seventy Years* (Boston 1934). A. M. MELVILLE, *Jean Lefebvre de Cheverus, 1768–1836* (Milwaukee 1958). J. E. SEXTON and A. J. RILEY, *History of St. John's Seminary, Brighton* (Boston 1945). D. G. WAYMAN, *Cardinal O'Connell of Boston* (New York 1955).

[T. F. CASEY]

BOSTON COLLEGE

A Jesuit coeducational university in Chestnut Hill, Mass., on the borderline of Newton and Boston. It had a 1964 total enrollment of nearly 10,000 students in its 12 schools and colleges; it is situated in a metropolitan area outstanding for the richness of its intellectual and cultural environment.

The historic role of the Society of Jesus in Massachusetts was inaugurated in 1825 when Benedict Joseph Fenwick, SJ, was named bishop of Boston. In 1847 Fenwick's successor, Bp. John B. Fitzpatrick, invited members of the Jesuit society to take charge of St. Mary's Church in Boston's North End. Boston was one of the principal East-Coast cities inundated, during the late 1840s and early 1850s, with Irish Catholic immigrants seeking sanctuary from the potato famine and from political oppression. Since the majority of these newcomers had little formal education and the demands of a hostile community frequently caused hardship to many young students, there was pressing need for parochial schools in Boston.

While Fitzpatrick's most immediate concern was for elementary schools, John McElroy, SJ, at St. Mary's, was considering the possibility of a Catholic college in the city. Following his appointment by Pres. James K. Polk as a chaplain in Zachary Taylor's army during the Mexican War, in 1847 McElroy was assigned to Boston where he continually urged the establishment of a Catholic college. Although the difficulties involved in establishing, financing, and staffing such a college made the prospects discouraging, McElroy pressed forward with determination.

After a long struggle, McElroy finally obtained a tract of land in a residential area in Boston's South End. Here he constructed the Church of the Immaculate Conception and the first red-brick building that was the nucleus of Boston College. In March 1863, while the Civil War was at its most critical phase, the Massachusetts Legislature approved the University charter; and on April 1, 1863, John A. Andrew, the Bay State's famous wartime governor, signed it. When in September 1864 Boston College was formally opened as an institution of advanced learning, the first president, John Bapst, SJ, presided over a faculty of 6 Jesuits and a student body of 22 young Bostonians.

Boston College remained in Boston's South End until the turn of the century, when the city's changing patterns and the steadily growing student body made it necessary to acquire more spacious quarters. The modern history of Boston College begins in January 1907 with the appointment of Thomas I. Gasson, SJ, as its 13th president. Shortly after his accession he began the search for a new location, and finally chose the Lawrence farm, a rolling hillside overlooking the Chestnut Hill Reservoir.

The architect Charles Donagh Maginnis laid elaborate plans for a campus to be constructed in the English Collegiate Gothic style. From a single building, completed in 1913—the Gasson tower building, which continues to dominate the campus—Boston College has expanded to some 200 acres, involving three campus levels.

The upper campus is the site of 14 dormitory buildings and a student chapel that serves the 1,500 male resident students. From a small, commuting city college, Boston College has been transformed into a major university that draws its student body from every state and from many foreign countries.

The main campus, composed of 10 buildings grouped around Gasson tower, comprises the library, the admin-

Boston College, with Gasson Tower in background.

istration building, and most of the 12 schools and colleges constituting the University. The College of Arts and Sciences (for men), the Graduate School (coeducational), the College of Business Administration (for men), the School of Education (coeducational), and the Nursing School (for women) all function in the central portion of the campus. The School of Social Work (coeducational) is in downtown Boston. The Liberal Arts College, at Lenox, Mass., and the Schools of Theology and Philosophy, at Weston, Mass., are limited to members of the Society of Jesus.

The University library, which in 1964 numbered more than 600,000 volumes, is housed in the Bapst Library. Of special interest to scholars is the Irish collection, composed of rare Irish first editions and manuscripts, as well as works of art by contemporary Irish artists. Of even greater fame is the Thompson Collection, which contains a major part of the manuscripts of the poet Francis Thompson. In addition to this main library, there are smaller libraries throughout the University pertaining to specialized fields of science, business administration, education, nursing, and law.

The lower campus, located around Ławrence Reservoir, is the site of the University Church of St. Ignatius Loyola and the Law School (coeducational), which publishes *The Annual Survey of Massachusetts Law* and the *Boston College Industrial and Commercial Law Review*. Roberts Center, McHugh Forum, Alumni Stadium, and athletic playing fields occupy the southeastern area.

As a Catholic university, associated in objectives with the 28 other Jesuit colleges in the U.S., Boston College continues the 400-year-old tradition of education according to the principles of the Jesuit *Ratio Studiorum. In addition to the basic core of liberal arts courses in philosophy, theology, science, mathematics, history, English, and languages, Boston College provides the student with a strong undergraduate foundation in a major field of concentration of his own choosing.

In addition to the regular academic opportunities available to all students, all divisions of the University maintain offices of special programs in order to allow the superior student to undertake more challenging courses of study. These offices maintain close contact with secondary schools in order to foster the development of advanced placement, sophomore standing, and early admissions programs. Boston College has also made it possible for sophomores, both men and women, in good standing in any of the undergraduate schools, to complete their junior year abroad. Provided he has the necessary language preparation, a student is free to choose the country and the university and to fulfill the requirements for a field of concentration and a degree.

In 1958, Michael P. Walsh, SJ, took office as the 22d president of Boston College. The rapid physical expansion of the University under his direction (three academic buildings, an arena, an auditorium, and six residence halls in 6 years) was matched by the energy with which he carried the university's tradition of "liberal studies liberally pursued" into fresh areas of teaching. Honors divisions in the College of Business Administration and in the School of Education were inaugurated after the pattern of the successful honors

seminar, which had been functioning in the College of Arts and Sciences since 1958. Interdepartmental programs in Russian, Asian, and Latin American studies were organized; scholarship grants given by the University increased fourfold; and the average salary of lay members was doubled.

The increase in professional staff has accompanied the University's growth. The original faculty of 6 Jesuits had become 140 by 1964, with more than 500 lay professors who participate in the teaching assignments and share deanships and departmental chairs in most of the 12 schools of the University. They hold 213 doctoral, 117 professional, and 195 master's degrees. Twenty-three departments offer fields of specialization for the baccalaureate; and the Graduate School offers degree programs leading to the Ph.D., Ed.D., M.A., M.S., M.Ed., and M.A. in teaching.

Bibliography: D. R. DUNIGAN, *A History of Boston College* (Milwaukee 1947). W. E. MURPHY, "The Story of Boston College," *The Catholic Contribution to Religion and Education* 249–259, v.5 of W. S. BENSON et al., *Catholic Builders of the Nation*, ed. C. E. McGUIRE, 5 v. (Boston 1923). L. P. KELLOGG, DAB 1:583–584. R. J. PURCELL, *ibid.*, 7:179; 12:36–37. E. BOYLE, *Father John McElroy, the Irish Priest* (Washington 1878). R. H. LORD et al., *History of the Archdiocese of Boston in the Various Stages of Its Development, 1604–1943*, 3 v. (New York 1944). O. HANDLIN, *Boston's Immigrants, 1790–1880: A Study of Acculturation* (rev. ed. Cambridge, Mass. 1959). M. L. HANSEN, *The Atlantic Migration, 1607–1860* (Cambridge, Mass. 1940). M. P. HARNEY, *The Jesuits in History* (Chicago 1962).
[T. H. O'CONNOR]

BOSWELL, JAMES.

Scottish man of letters; b. Edinburgh, Oct. 29, 1740; d. London, May 19, 1795. He was the eldest son of Lord Auchinleck, of an old and staunchly Presbyterian family. Though he studied law and was admitted to the bar, he was always more attracted to literature. He visited

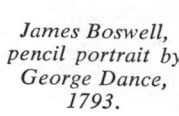

James Boswell, pencil portrait by George Dance, 1793.

Corsica in 1766 and first distinguished himself as a writer with his *Account of Corsica* (1768) and *Essays in Favour of the Brave Corsicans* (1769). Hero-worship stimulated his best writing and was the inspiration of his famous *Life of Samuel Johnson* (1791). (*See* JOHNSON, SAMUEL.) As Johnson's guide he made the tour through Scotland that provided material for *Tour to the Hebrides* (1785). His copious journals, unpublished during his life, were discovered 135 years after his death.

SANDRO
BOTTICELLI

Fig. 1. Self-portrait, detail of the fresco of the "Punishment of Korah, Dathan and Abiram" in the Sistine Chapel, Rome.

Fig. 2. "Madonna and Child," the so-called "Corsini Madonna," tempera, 29⅞ by 21⅞ inches.

Fig. 3. "The Last Communion of St. Jerome," tempera, 13½ by 10 inches, painted probably c. 1495.

Boswell was an eccentric and remarkable character, often vehemently attacked for his sycophancy, his conceit, and his immorality. His severest critics, however, are constrained to praise the charm and lucidity of his style and his gift for capturing the personalities of his acquaintances and the flavor of their conversations. Shrewd judgment and conscientious art underlie the deceptive ease of his narration. His writing is full of humor and captures unique pictures of life in Scotland and London in the 18th century.

At the age of 17 Boswell ran away to London and was received into the Catholic Church. As a Catholic in penal times he would have been prevented from following any professional career and from succeeding to the family estates. He accordingly concealed his conversion and did not live as a Catholic, though his journals contain many references to attending Mass. He avoided any formal abjuration of his beliefs and on occasion argued with Dr. Johnson in defense of them. He left in his will a request for prayers for his soul, but this was suppressed by his heirs, who held no belief in purgatory.

Although devoted to his wife, Boswell was frequently unfaithful to her. He constantly expresses contrition for his marital lapses and for his bouts of drunkenness; he laments his weakness of character, which plunged him into periods of terrible despondency. He writes even of his own conceit and pretentiousness with candor and humility. The affection he inspired in men of high principle and discrimination is a tribute to his capacity for loyalty and friendship.

Bibliography: J. BOSWELL, *Note Book, 1776–1777*, ed. R. W. CHAPMAN (London 1925); *Private Papers of J. Boswell from Malahide Castle*, ed. G. SCOTT and F. A. POTTLE, 18 v. (London 1928–34); *Letters*, ed. C. B. TINKER, 2 v. (London 1924); D. B. WYNDHAM LEWIS, *The Hooded Hawk* (London 1946). The Yale edition of the Private Papers of James Boswell, ed. F. A. POTTLE et al. (New York): *London Journal, 1762–1763*, ed. F. A. POTTLE (1950); *Boswell in Holland, 1763–1764* (1952); *Boswell on the Grand Tour* 2 v. (1953–55); *Boswell in Search of a Wife, 1766–1769* (1956); *Boswell for the Defence, 1769–1774* (1960); *The Ominous Years, 1774–1776* (1963). **Illustration credit:** National Portrait Gallery, London.

[G. SCOTT-MONCRIEFF]

BOTTICELLI, SANDRO

Florentine painter; b. Alessandro di Mariano Filipepi (called Botticelli), in Florence, 1445; d. there, 1510. He is buried in the church of Ognissanti (All Saints). He was the son of a leather tanner and studied under Filippo *Lippi and *Verrocchio; he was influenced also by A. Pollaiuolo. In 1470 he began work independently, participating in the decoration of the Palazzo dell'Arte in Mercanzia. He painted also in Pisa, executing several frescoes of the Camposanto in 1474; in Rome where in 1481 he executed three historical subjects and several fresco figures of popes in the Sistine Chapel; and in Volterra where he executed work for the Villa dello Spedaletto (c. 1483). But his major work was done in Florence where he rapidly rose to fame and counted among his patrons important personages, such as Sixtus IV and Lorenzo the Magnificent. Nevertheless, it appears that in his old age both his fame and success diminished.

He possessed poetic imagination, fantasy, melancholy elegance, and a typical Renaissance capacity for finding inspiration both in classic fables and in Christian religious themes. These qualities joined to his individual technique, in which he allied an almost medieval stiffness of design to a softness of light and skillful use of perspective, place Botticelli among the most important of the artists of the Quattrocento. These qualities and the fact that he was "Leonardesco" before Raphael and Michelangelo, made him the preferred artist of the Pre-Raphaelites.

His principal works on mythological themes are the celebrated masterworks the "Primavera" (1477–78), "Pallas and the Centaur" (1481), and "The Birth of Venus" (1483–84, Uffizi, Florence). There are many Madonnas among his paintings on religious themes. The best known of these are: the "Madonna Corsini" (National Gallery, Washington, D.C.), the "Madonna Duveen" (Metropolitan Museum, New York), the "Madonna Chigi" (Gardner Museum, Boston), the "Madonna della Melagrana" (Uffizi Gallery, Florence), and the "Annunciazione Lehman" (Metropolitan Museum, New York). He is also renowned for the exquisite "Adoration of the Magi" (Uffizi Gallery), his portraits of the Medici (c. 1490, Uffizi Gallery; 1481, National Gallery, Washington, D.C.), and the solemn "Nativity" of London (1501?). Botticelli had been deeply affected by Savonarola's preaching, and the resulting spiritual crisis seems to have led him in his later painting to renounce pagan aesthetic pleasures in favor of an abstract linear formalism, redeemed, however, by the winged sweep of angelic figures.

See also RENAISSANCE ART.

Bibliography: B. BERENSON, *The Florentine Painters of the Renaissance* (London 1896). H. ULMANN, *Sandro Botticelli* (Munich 1894). H. P. HORNE, *Alessandro Filipepi: Commonly Called Sandro Botticelli* (London 1908), fundamental. A. SCHMARSOW, *Sandro del Botticello* (Dresden 1923). Y. YASHIRO, *Sandro Botticelli*, 3 v. (Boston 1925; rev. ed. in 1 v. 1929). A. VENTURI, *Botticelli* (London 1927). L. VENTURI, *Botticelli* (2d ed. London 1949). S. BETTINI, *Botticelli* (Bergamo 1942; 2d ed. 1947). G. C. ARGAN, *Botticelli*, tr. J. EMMONS (New York 1957). **Illustration credits:** Fig. 1, Anderson-Art Reference Bureau. Fig. 2, National Gallery of Art, Washington, D.C., Mellon Collection. Fig. 3, The Metropolitan Museum of Art, New York, Bequest of Benjamin Altman, 1913.

[E. N. ORENGO]

BOTUCATÚ, ARCHDIOCESE OF (BOTUCATUENSIS),

located in the state of São Paulo, Brazil; created a diocese in 1908; raised to an archdiocese in 1958. In 1964 it had five suffragan sees: Lins (1926), Assis (1928), Marília (1952), Presidente Prudente (1960), and Bauru (1964).

Lúcio Antunes de Sousa (1908–23) organized the diocese, established a major and a minor seminary and a diocesan high school for boys and one for girls, built the episcopal residence, and put the finances of the diocese on a sound basis. He traveled constantly through his vast diocese. In 1922 he began systematic catechizing of Japanese immigrants. His successor, Carlos Duarte da Costa (1925–37), began his administration well and started building the cathedral. However, he was removed for poor administration and intemperate actions; he subsequently apostatized (1945). He then founded the Brazilian Catholic Apostolic Church. Before his death in 1960, "Dom Maura," as he was known, consecrated 20 bishops and ordained 100 schismatic priests, but his church has declined steadily since then. Bishop Luís Maria de Santana (1938–46) had to reorganize the diocese more firmly after that episode. The cathedral was finally completed in 1964 during the administration of Abp. Henrique H. Golland Trindade.

1964 STATISTICS

Area	Population	Parishes	Clergy Sec.	Clergy Reg.
Botucatú	452,000	41	53	67
Lins	600,000	35	33	39
Assis	636,959	40	17	46
Marília	670,000	45	26	42
Presidente				
Prudente	350,000	17	13	15
Bauru	210,000	17	14	33

In 1964 among the religious orders serving in the province were Capuchins, Missionaries of the Sacred Heart, Salesians, Jesuits, Pallottine Fathers, Augustinians, Holy Ghost Fathers, Josephites, Missionaries of Milan, Franciscans, Stigmatine Fathers, and more than 600 sisters of various congregations. In 1961 a group of secular priests from Canada went to the Diocese of Marília to help in parish work.

Bibliography: L. CASTANHO DE ALMEIDA, *São Paulo, filho da Igreja* (Petrópolis, Brazil 1955); *Dom Lúcio, bispo de Botucatú* (Petrópolis 1956). F. DUBOIS, *O Ex-Bispo de Maura e o bom senso* (Petrópolis 1945).

[O. VAN DER VAT]

BOTULPH OF ICANHOE, ST., abbot and monastic founder; fl. 7th century (feast, June 17). Very little is known about him, for the *Anglo-Saxon Chronicle* states merely that in 654 "Botulf began to build a minster at Ycean-ho," and the anonymous *Historia abbatum,* once mistakenly attributed to *Bede, mentions him as "a man of distinguished achievement and learning, dedicated to the spiritual life," who was already famous in his own lifetime. It was only in the 11th century that Folcard, Abbot of *Thorney, recorded the historically unreliable and legendary life. According to this legend, Botulph was the brother of St. Adulph, an alleged bishop of *Utrecht, of whose existence at Utrecht there is no record. The two brothers left their native England to become monks on the Continent, but Botulph returned and founded a *Benedictine monastery at Icanhoe, a location now generally identified with Boston (Botulphstown). He is said to have died c. 655 and to have been buried with Adulph in the sanctuary of his foundation, which, however, was destroyed in the Danish invasions. His cult was widespread, especially in Norfolk, and the brothers share the same feast day in most calendars.

Bibliography: Sources. "The Anglo-Saxon Chronicle," ed. H. PETRIE et al., in *Monumenta historica britannica* (London 1848) 1:312. "Historia abbatum auctore anonymo," in *Venerabilis Baedae opera historica,* ed. C. PLUMMER, 2 v. (Oxford 1896) 1:389. Mabillon AS 3.1:3–7. ActSS June 4:324–330. Literature. F. WORMALD, ed., *English Kalendars before A.D. 1100,* v.1 (Henry Bradshaw Society 72; London 1934) 161, 203, 245, 259. F. S. STEVENSON, *Proceedings of the Suffolk Institute of Archaeology and Natural History* (Ipswich 1922) 29–52. Zimmermann KalBen 2:322, 324–325. F. O'BRIAIN, DHGE 9:1433–34. S. BRECHTER, LexThK² 2:625–626.

[J. BRÜCKMANN]

BOTURINI BENADUCI, LORENZO

Historian and collector of Mexican antiquities; b. Sondrio, Lombardy, Italy, 1702; d. Madrid, Spain, apparently in 1755. Little is known of his early life. He studied in Milan and spent some time in Vienna and Lisbon. In Madrid he met the Countess of Santibáñez, a descendant of the Aztec Emperor Montezuma, who in 1735 ceded to Boturini a yearly stipend of 1,000 pesos paid her from the royal treasury of Mexico City. By February 1736 he was in Mexico City collecting the pension. Boturini became interested in the pilgrimages to the shrine of Our Lady of *Guadalupe at Tepeyac and in the tradition that the Virgin Mary had appeared there in December 1531. To find documentary evidence of this miracle, he began intensive research into the Indian past. He learned Nahuatl so he could converse with the Indians in their own tongue and collected Indian codices of historical events. In his enthusiasm he accumulated during 6 years a fine collection of documents, even though few of them bore direct testimony to the apparitions. By then he planned to use the material to write a new history of colonial Mexico.

In the meantime he wished to contribute to the devotion to Our Lady of Guadalupe by placing a golden crown over her head on the miraculously painted image. In July 1740 he obtained permission from ecclesiastical authorities in Rome to do so and he began to solicit funds for the coronation. Late in 1742 the new viceroy, the Count of Fuenclara, ordered an investigation, and on November 28 Boturini was charged with both coming to the colony and promoting devotion to Our Lady of Guadalupe without royal authorization. He was accused of collecting alms without the necessary permission and of including on the crown the coat of arms of the Vatican as well as that of a noble Italian family that had contributed toward the coronation. On Feb. 4, 1743, he was imprisoned, and his collection of documents and antiquities was seized by local authorities. His answers to the charges, sent to officials in Spain April 16, 1743, were to no avail. In the Archives of the Indies, Seville, are letters of 1743 in which Viceroy Fuenclara wrote in great detail to Philip V of the Boturini affair. Boturini was sent to Spain under special vigilance at the end of 1743 but was put ashore at Gibraltar by English corsairs who had plundered and sunk his vessel, the "Concordia." At the beginning of 1744 he arrived in Madrid penniless and found assistance from the Mexican historian Mariano Veytia. The Council of Indies exonerated Boturini of all charges. He was given a yearly pension and on July 10, 1747, was named official chronicler and historian of the New World.

Boturini never returned to Mexico and therefore did not repossess his collection of antiquities. He did, however, attempt to write the history of the Indies and by April 1749 finished the first volume of *Historia general de la América septentrional.* It was an account of the physical features of the valley of Mexico, of its indigenous tribes, their customs, and way of life. Even though approved by the crown, the work was never published. In a letter of March 6, 1755, Boturini reminded officials of this and asked that his stipend be increased to 5,000 pesos yearly so he could return to Mexico and continue the writing of the other volumes. Apparently Boturini died shortly afterward; no further documentation is found concerning the petition or his work. In Madrid and in Mexico his personal papers and collection of ancient MSS, amounting to some 40 volumes, disappeared in time. However, copies of many of the documents are to be found mainly in archives and libraries of Spain, Mexico, and the U.S. Besides writing his *Historia general,* Boturini outlined the general division of New Spain's history in the *Idea de una historia general de la América septentrional* (Madrid 1746). This was reedited in Mexico in 1871. It contains an appendix, *Catálogo del Museo Histórico Indiano,* which lists some of the materials the author had gathered when he lived in Mexico. Boturini wrote also a short treatise in Latin on the apparitions of Our Lady of Guadalupe.

Bibliography: J. García Icazbalceta, *Diccionario universal de historia y de geografía,* 10 v. (Mexico City 1853–56) 1:676–677. J. Torre Revello, "Lorenzo Boturini Benaduci y el cargo de cronista de las Indias," *Boletín del Instituto de Investigaciones Históricas* 5 (Buenos Aires 1926–27) 52–61.

[N. F. MARTIN]

BOTVID, ST., active in evangelizing Sweden; d. *c.* 1120 (feast, July 28). The exact dates of his birth and death are unknown, but his legend seems fairly reliable. Botvid, a native of Sweden, was a pious layman, and he was killed by a foreign slave whom he had converted and freed. His relics were honored, probably from 1129 and translated in 1176. Two offices are known; the older was found in a 13th-century MS and is composed partly in prose, partly rhythmically, with a sequence *Almi patris merita.* The later was composed by Bp. Nicolaus Hermanni (d. 1391) as a *historia rhythmica,* with the sequence *Celi chorus esto gaudens.* The church and village of Botkyrka (Botvidskyrka) are named for him. In iconography he is symbolized by the ax and the fish.

Bibliography: *Scriptores rerum Suecicarum medii aevi,* ed. E. M. Fant et al., v.2 (Uppsala 1828) 377–387. AnalHymn 25:179–181; 42:180–181; 43:104–105. I. G. A. Collijn, *Redogörelse för på uppdrag af Kungl. Maj:t i Kammararkivet och Riksarkivet verkställd undersökning angående äldre arkivalieomslag* (Stockholm 1914); ed., *Acta et processus canonizacionis beate Birgitte* (Uppsala 1924–31) 81, 486, 619, issued in 10 pts. Bridget of Sweden, *Revelationes,* Extravagantes, ch. 72. T. Schmid, "Eskil, Botvid och David," *Scandia* 4 (1931) 102–114. H. Jägerstad, LexThK² 2:626. Butler Th Attw 3:204.

[T. SCHMID]

BOUCHARD, JAMES, missionary, orator; b. Muskagola, near Leavenworth, Kans., *c.* 1823; d. San Francisco, Calif., Dec. 27, 1889. His mother, surnamed Bouchard, was of French ancestry; she had been captured by Indians and adopted into the Delaware Tribe with the name of Monotowan (White Fawn). Her marriage to a Delaware brave called Kistalwa resulted in the birth of a son whose tribal name was Watomika (Swift Foot). After his father's death in a skirmish with the Sioux in 1834, Watomika was taken by a Protestant missionary to Marietta College, Ohio, where he studied for the Presbyterian ministry. While visiting St. Louis, Mo., in late 1846 or early 1847, he was converted to Catholicism by a Jesuit missionary, Arnold Damen. Bouchard entered the Jesuits at Florissant, Mo., on July 29, 1848, and was ordained on Aug. 5, 1855, in St. Francis Xavier's College Church, St. Louis. He was the first American Indian to be ordained in the U.S. After several years of ministry in the Middle West, he was assigned to California. He arrived in San Francisco on Aug. 16, 1861, and was soon in demand as a retreat master, pulpit orator, and lecturer. He was asked to preach at the dedications of St. Vibiana's Cathedral, Los Angeles (1876), and the Cathedral of the Blessed Sacrament, Sacramento (1889), and spoke also on such public issues as the Chinese question in California. In addition to his speaking engagements, he devoted himself to missionary activity in the mining camps and towns of the Mother Lode section of California.

Bibliography: J. B. McGloin, *Eloquent Indian: The Life of James Bouchard, California Jesuit* (Stanford 1949).

[J. B. MC GLOIN]

BOUCHER, PIERRE, governor of Trois Rivières, Canada; b. Lagny, France, 1622; d Boucherville, Canada, April 19, 1717. He arrived in Canada with his father in 1635; spent 4 years with the Jesuits in the Huron territory, where he studied Indian languages;

Pierre Boucher.

and upon his return to Quebec (1641), served as garrison interpreter. He took part in several expeditions against the Iroquois. In 1645 he settled in Trois Rivières, and became the chief interpreter; he was later named governor (1652). Boucher was sent to France in 1661 to obtain reinforcements, and returned with a group of colonists and a title of nobility. Although uneducated, he wrote (1664) a history of the customs and products of New France, which became an authoritative source on the subject and was reprinted four times in Paris. As a reward for having saved Trois Rivières from an Iroquois attack, he was granted the seigniory of Boucherville (1667), where he later died. His first marriage (1649) was to a Huron, Marie Chrestienne; his second (1652), to Jeanne Crevier, by whom he had 15 children.

Bibliography: S. Marion, *Pierre Boucher: Un pionnier canadien* (Quebec 1927). L. Conan in *Revue Canadienne* (Montreal 1913). M. Leland, *Encyclopedia Canadiana* 2:30. **Illustration credit:** Château de Ramezay Museum, Montreal.

[G. CARRIÈRE]

BOUDON, HENRI MARIE, spiritual writer; b. La Fère, France, Jan. 14, 1624; d. Évreux, Aug. 3, 1702. After early schooling at Rouen, he went to Paris in 1644 to study philosophy and theology. In 1655 he was named archdeacon of the Diocese of Évreux and was ordained shortly thereafter. The diocese was then in a deplorable condition, and Boudon worked zealously to restore order and ecclesiastical discipline. His efforts to eradicate abuses, ensure proper clerical appointments, and improve the spiritual and moral tone of the diocese aroused opposition, especially on the part of the Jansenists, to whom Boudon was opposed. He became the victim of false accusations and scandalous calumnies. When Bp. Henri de Maupas went to Rome in 1664 for the canonization of St. Francis de Sales,

Boudon was given complete charge of the diocese, and the charges against him increased. Eventually, he was suspended from his office. Boudon bore these trials in patience and resignation, and in 1674 De Maupas affirmed Boudon's innocence and restored him to good favor. In the last years of his life, Boudon traveled and preached extensively in Lorraine, Bavaria, and Flanders. He enjoyed a wide reputation for great personal sanctity, and the process for his canonization was opened at Évreux in 1885, although it was never carried through.

Boudon was the author of numerous spiritual works, many of which enjoyed extraordinary success and were translated into Latin, Italian, Spanish, German, and other languages. The principal idea of his spiritual doctrine is the pure love of "God alone"—a phrase that opened all his letters and written work. One of his important treatises, *Dieu seul o l'association pour l'intérest de Dieu seul* (Paris 1662), which enjoyed the approval of Bousset at the time of its publication, was many years later used by the quietists to support their position and for that reason was consigned to the Index in 1688. Devotion to Our Lady was another important theme in Boudon's spirituality. His *Le Saint esclavage de l'admirable Mère de Dieu* (Paris 1674) was not condemned but was not looked upon with favor by the Holy See because of the possible abuse inherent in that kind of terminology. This disapproval was a contributing factor in the long delay of the publication of Grignion de Montfort's *Traité de la vraie dévotion*. Boudon's writings were collected and published by J. P. Migne, *Oeuvres complètes de Boudon* (3 v. Paris 1856–57).

Bibliography: C. MATHIEU, *Vie nouvelle de M. Henri-Marie Boudon* (Besançon 1837). Bremond 4:240–266. P. POURRAT, *Catholicisme* 2:193–194. R. HEURTEVENT, DictSpirAscMyst 1: 1887–93.

[J. T. KELLEHER]

BOUILLON, EMMANUEL THÉODOSE DE LA TOUR D'AUVERGNE,

French diplomat, prelate; b. Turenne, Aug. 24, 1643; d. Rome, March 2, 1715. He was educated at the College of Navarre in Paris, and received the doctorate in theology at the Sorbonne in 1667. In 1669 he was created a cardinal at the request of Louis XIV, and 2 years later was named Louis's chief almoner. However, he became involved in court intrigue through his efforts to further his family's fortunes, and was removed from office and exiled to the abbey of Cluny by the King in 1685. Eventually he was back in favor and for a time was the royal representative in Rome. Again Bouillon irritated Louis XIV by failing to demand the condemnation of Fénelon at Rome and by refusing to answer the King's summons back to France. Despite the royal displeasure, Bouillon functioned in Rome as dean of the cardinals, and directed the conclave that elected Clement XI. Finally he submitted and accepted retirement, first at Cluny (1701–09), and then in Holland (1709–13). In 1713 he returned to Rome, died there, and was buried at the Jesuit novitiate.

Bibliography: L. DE ROUVROY SAINT-SIMON, *Mémoires,* ed. A. DE BOISLISLE, 41 v. (Paris 1879–1928) v.7, 26. F. REYSSIÉ, *Le Cardinal de Bouillon, 1643–1715* (Paris 1899). A. DE BOISLISLE, "La Désertion du cardinal de Bouillon en 1710," RevQuestHist 84 (1908) 420–471; 85 (1909) 61–107, 444–491.

[C. B. O'KEEFE]

BOULAINVILLIERS, HENRI DE,

French historian and philosophical writer; b. Saint-Saire, Normandy, Oct. 11, 1658; d. Paris, Jan. 23, 1722. Henri, son of François de Boulainvilliers and Suzanne de Mannville, first took up a career with the royal musketeers, but he left military service after his father died in order to assume responsibility for the family affairs. In attempting to investigate complications in the family estate, Henri became interested in the study of history and politics. In his search for the origin of French institutions, he grew to admire the feudal regime and proceeded to attack the absolute monarchy of Louis XIV, on the one hand, and popular government, on the other. His political and historical writings trace what he considered to be the decline of the French state from rule by individual nobles to absolute monarchy. The policy of conquest pursued by the Capetians increased the power of the kings disproportionately and transformed the nobles into servants rather than peers of the king. With this new strength, the monarchs emancipated the communes and granted seats in the Estates-General to plebeians. The nobility also lost prestige by having to sell much of their land to plebeians creating a new "ignoble" and corrupt nobility. Because of his rationalist approach to history, the empiricism in his *L'Idée d'un système général de la nature,* and his attempts at the study of comparative religions in such works as *Vie de Mahomet* and *Histoire des Arabes,* Boulainvilliers is considered by some as a precursor of the 18th-century *philosophes.* He is that in fact, but not in intention. He held Christian dogmas unassailable in his philosophical writing and entered the field of comparative religions only to show that other religions either derived their dogmas from the true religion of Christ or were purely human in origin. Finding that Henri's surname appears as Boulainviller in the signature of the epitaphs of his family in the crypt of the Church of Saint-Saire, R. Simon has accepted this as the preferred spelling.

Bibliography: R. SIMON, *Henry de Boulainviller: Historien, politique, philosophe, astrologue* (Paris 1941); *Un Révolté du Grand siècle: Henry de Boulainviller* (Garches 1947). C. LAPLATTE, DHGE 10:50–53.

[J. W. BUSH]

BOULAY, CÉSAR ÉGASSE DU (BULAEUS),

educator, historian; b. Saint-Elier (Mayenne), *c.* 1600; d. Paris, Oct. 16, 1678. His early career was that of teacher of humanities and rhetoric at Poitiers and then at the College of Navarre. In 1661 he was named rector of the University of Paris. In 1662 he was made registrar of the University, a position of great responsibility that required a thorough knowledge of the complicated organization of the University. He is best known as a historian of the University of Paris. Between 1665 and 1673 he published in Latin a six-volume history of the University, entitled *Historia Universitatis Parisiensis,* covering the period from its origins to the time of its reformation by Henry IV. Boulay wrote also an abridged version in French, *Histoire de l'université,* as well as seven separate works in French on the organization and history of the University. His work is less a conventional history than a collection of documents to support his interpretation of the origins of the University. According to Boulay the University was founded by Charlemagne and consisted originally only of the faculty of arts and the four nations. This interpretation, which gave to the faculty of arts exclusive right to name the rector and to the four nations equal status with the faculties of theology, medicine, and law, was challenged by the interested parties. He was also accused of misappropriating funds for the writing of his books. He died before the latter charge was investigated.

Bibliography: *Biographie universelle,* ed. L. G. MICHAUD, 45 v. (Paris 1843–65) 5:231–232. C. CONSTANTIN, DTC 2.1:1092–93. Hurter Nomencl 2:241.

[J. W. BUSH]

BOUQUILLON, THOMAS JOSEPH,

educator, moral theologian; b. Warneton, Belgium, May 16, 1842; d. Brussels, Belgium, Nov. 5, 1902. He had a brilliant career as a student in the Collège of Saint-Louis in Menin, and later in the preparatory seminary at Roulers and the major seminary at Bruges, Belgium. He entered the Capranica in Rome and was ordained in 1865. Two years later he received the doctorate from the Gregorian University and returned to the seminary in Bruges, where he was appointed professor of moral theology. In 1877 he was appointed to the Catholic University of Lille, France, where he taught moral theology until 1885. He spent 4 years (1885–89) with the Benedictines of the Abbey of Maredsous, Belgium, and then accepted the invitation of Bp. John J. *Keane, first rector of The Catholic University of America, Washington, D.C., to join the original faculty as professor of moral theology.

Bouquillon's theological knowledge was exceptionally wide, encompassing more than is usually included within the limits of moral theology. He was an expert on the theologians of 16th- and 17th-century Spain and the Netherlands. His influence was considerable on the academic development of the new university in Washington, where he planned and selected a basic theological library of 30,000 volumes. He cultivated in his students a critical sense of history as the context for their theological understanding. A prodigious author and commentator on the subjects of the day, he published a pamphlet on education (1891) that aroused great opposition throughout the U.S. and Europe (*see* BOUQUILLON CONTROVERSY). In addition to more than 50 scholarly articles in several languages in such journals as *Revue des sciences ecclésiastiques, Nouvelle revue théologique, Revue bénédictine, American Catholic Quarterly Review,* and *The Catholic University Bulletin,* his published works include *Theologia Moralis Fundamentalis* (1903), *De Virtutibus Theologicis* (1890), and *De Virtute Religionis* (2 v. 1880). He had completed but did not publish three other works: "De Justitia et Jure," "De Eucharistia," and "De Penitentia." He edited and added critical notes to the following: *De Magnitudine Ecclesiae Romanae* of Thomas Stapleton (1881), *Leonis XIII Allocutiones, Epistolae, Aliaque Acta* (first 2 v. 1887), the *Catechismus ad Parochas* (1890), the *Dies Sacerdotalis* of Dirckinck (1888), *L'Excellence de la très sainte eucharistie* of Luis de Granada, and *Synopsis Cursus Theologiae* by Platel. In June 1902 Bouquillon left Washington for Europe, where he became ill and died in Brussels.

Bibliography: J. FORGET, DTC 2.1:1093–94. *The Catholic University of America Bulletin* 9 (1903) 152–163. C. G. HERBER-MANN, "The Faculty of the Catholic University," AmCathQRev 14 (1889) 701–715. J. T. ELLIS, *The Formative Years of the Catholic University of America* (Washington 1946).

[J. P. WHALEN]

BOUQUILLON CONTROVERSY

An educational dispute precipitated in the U.S. in 1891 by the *Faribault Plan, a compromise school arrangement effected by Abp. John Ireland with the public school boards of Faribault and Stillwater, Minn. Its name came from Rev. Thomas *Bouquillon, professor of moral theology at The Catholic University of America, Washington, D.C., whose theory granting the state a special and proper right to educate engendered contradictory reactions.

Cause. Concomitant with the rise of the public school system in the U.S. between 1820 and 1870 was a growing tendency to secularize tax-supported schools. The American hierarchy, urged by the Congregation of Propaganda Fide in 1875, passed laws at the Third Plenary Council of Baltimore in 1884 discouraging attendance at public schools and pressing the construction of parochial schools. The hierarchy, however, were not unanimous in the execution of the laws. In 1890 Archbishop Ireland of St. Paul, Minn., and other bishops pleaded poverty as an excuse from building and maintaining parochial schools, and proposed giving daily religious instructions to Catholic students in public schools outside class hours as an alternative solution. Abp. Michael A. Corrigan of New York and certain Jesuit writers championed parochial schools as envisioned by the decrees of the Third Plenary Council of Baltimore.

In the midst of this practical debate over constructing parochial schools, Bouquillon published his pamphlet, *Education: To Whom Does It Belong?* Although he claimed that his tract was "a purely abstract exposition of principles independent of circumstances of time and country," the arguments presented so buttressed the position championed by Ireland and his party that Bouquillon was accused of knowingly offering the theoretical basis for Ireland's solution to the school question. The publication date, Nov. 18, 1891, 10 days before the American hierarchy was to meet in St. Louis, Mo., to debate the issue, seemed to confirm that suspicion.

Bouquillon held that education "belongs to the individual, physical or moral, to the family, to the state, to the church; to none of these solely and exclusively, but to all four combined in harmonious working . . .." By ceding this right to an individual and equating the rights of the family, the State, and the Church, Bouquillon offered a new view for Catholics on the right to educate.

Regarding the State's power in this area, moreover, he maintained that "the state has been endowed by God with the right of founding schools that contribute to its welfare." Based on this prerogative, therefore, the State has the further right to pass compulsory education laws, determine the minimum of obligatory instruction, establish schools, appoint capable teachers, prescribe branches of knowledge, and inspect hygiene and public morality.

The Rejoinder. It was incumbent on Catholic educators favoring establishment of parochial schools to answer these arguments, especially the seeming equality of State and Church in conducting schools. René Holaind, SJ, Professor of Ethics at the Jesuit seminary, Woodstock College, Md., prepared an answer within a week of Bouquillon's publication and before the bishops' meeting. Holaind's main objections were: (1) teaching is essentially the duty of the Church and the parents; the State, which has no proper right to educate, enters the field of education at the bidding of the family and/or the Church; (2) the State enters the field of education only when it is entirely necessary and not merely when it is useful to contribute to the State's welfare; (3) the State has no right to control instruction in non-State schools since this would abrogate the rights and duties of parents and Church to open schools and control instruction.

Ecclesiastical Intervention. The two pamphlets generated such a heated public discussion in the religious and secular press that both sides appealed to Rome to settle the problem. In November 1892 Abp. Francesco Satolli, a special representative of Rome, presented to the assembled hierarchy "Fourteen Propositions Designed for the Settling of the School Question," which, since they were more practical than theoretical, left the basic issue unsolved. Rome, in fact, had intended that the hierarchy debate the propositions secretly among themselves, and then by majority vote, reach an agreement emanating from Catholic principles. The propositions, however, were leaked to the secular press and the controversy could not be solved in the heat of the ensuing public debate.

In view of this impasse, Leo XIII asked all the bishops to submit their views to Rome and permit the Holy See to settle the question. On May 31, 1893, Leo XIII addressed his answer to Cardinal James Gibbons for the American hierarchy, stating that the Holy See supported the propositions of the Third Plenary Council of Baltimore and encouraged the construction of Catholic schools, but granted to the local ordinary the power to decide under what conditions Catholics might attend public schools. The meeting of the American hierarchy in September 1893 unanimously adopted a resolution declaring that the controversy over the "School Question" had ended. Privately both sides claimed victory, although the problem is still unsolved.

Bibliography: D. F. REILLY, *The School Controversy, 1891–1893* (Washington 1943). T. BOUQUILLON, *Education: To Whom Does It Belong?* (Baltimore 1891); *Education: To Whom Does It Belong? A Rejoinder to Critics* (Baltimore 1892); *Education: To Whom Does It Belong? A Rejoinder to the Civiltà Cattolica* (Baltimore 1892). R. I. HOLAIND, *The Parent First* (New York 1891). F. SATOLLI, *For the Settling of the School Question and the Giving of Religious Education* (Baltimore 1892).

[E. G. RYAN]

BOURASSA, HENRI, politician and journalist; b. Montreal, Canada, Sept. 1, 1868; d. Outremont, Quebec, Canada, Aug. 31, 1952. He was the son of Napoleon Bourassa, painter, architect, and writer, and Azélie (Papineau) Bourassa; and the grandson of Louis-Joseph Papineau, French-Canadian leader of the 19th century. After private education by tutors, Bourassa became a journalist, first with *L'Interprète,* published in Clarence Creek, Ontario, then as contributor to *Le Nationaliste,* Montreal, and finally as founder and editor in chief of the Montreal Nationalist daily, *Le Devoir* (1910–32). He entered politics as an independ-

ent Liberal and was elected to the House of Commons for Labelle County, 1896. A man of strong impulses, he resigned in 1899 "in order to vindicate his position on the constitutional aspect of the participation of Canada in the South African War." Reelected by acclamation in 1900, he sat until 1907. In 1903 his adherents founded the Ligue Nationaliste, under the presidency of J. F. Olivar Asselin, one of the best French-Canadian journalists of his time. Bourassa was the moving spirit of the Ligue, though not himself a member. For nearly 30 years he was leader of the Nationalists and an outstanding political figure in French Canada, although he never attained cabinet rank.

In 1907 he resigned his seat in the Commons to contest Bellechasse against the Hon. Adelard Turgeon in the Quebec provincial election and was defeated. He was elected in 1908 for two counties and chose to sit for St. Hyacinthe. The Liberal defeat of 1911 marked the climax of his long duel with Sir Wilfred Laurier, whom he considered too British-minded. Bourassa returned to the House of Commons for Labelle (1925–35) and participated actively in the constitutional struggle of 1926. In 1932, having broken with many of the Nationalists, he resigned from *Le Devoir.* He returned to prominence during World War II, delivering a few speeches on behalf of the Bloc Populaire. He published many pamphlets and lectures in French and English on political questions; his most important books were *Que devons nous à l'Angleterre?* (1915) and *Hier, aujourd'hui, demain* (1916), which includes a partial list of his publications. In 1905 he married Josephine Papineau, a cousin; they had eight children, two of whom became Jesuits.

Bibliography: P. ALLEN et al., *La Pensée de Henri Bourassa* (Montreal 1954). R. RUMILLY, *Henri Bourassa: La Vie publique d'un grand canadien* (Montreal 1953). *Canadian Who's Who 1948.* W. S. WALLACE, *The Macmillan Dictionary of Canadian Biography* (3d ed. New York 1963).

[R. DUHAMEL]

BOURDALOUE, LOUIS

French Jesuit preacher, who brought the classic sermon to its most perfect oratorical technique; b. Bourges, France, Aug. 20, 1632; d. Paris, May 13, 1704. Bourdaloue, of a distinguished though not wealthy family, entered the Society of Jesus in 1648 at the age of 17. Early in life he manifested penetrating intelligence, tireless diligence, and devotion to religious discipline. Having completed his studies, he became a professor of philosophy and later, of moral theology. When, unexpectedly, he showed special talent for oratory, he was asked to dedicate himself to preaching. He began in Amiens in 1665 and later went on to Orléans and Rouen. In 1669 he was sent to Paris where he preached for 34 consecutive years with a success that was greater each year until the end of his life.

In eloquence he ranked with the great masters of style in the most splendid part of Louis XIV's reign. He was hailed as the "king of orators and the orator of kings." In fact he preached before the court five courses of Lenten sermons and seven Advent series. He was often invited to preach at ceremonies for the taking of the religious habit and at religious professions, and upon every other kind of religious occasion.

He adhered strictly to the traditional doctrine of the Church, which he expounded and defended with great

Louis Bourdaloue.

an audience that, though irresponsive to other appeals because of its worldliness, frivolity, etc., showed great esteem for reason.

His personal saintliness and gentleness contributed to his influence. While always duly respectful to the great, he was also simple and devoted to the poor. He was always ready to hear confessions and exerted a wonderful power at the deathbed, especially that of hardened sinners.

Bourdaloue won for himself a place in French literature. Fénelon said that his style "had perhaps arrived at the perfection of which our language is capable in that kind of eloquence." Sainte-Beuve wrote: "He was a good orator and is a good writer." Voltaire claimed that he was superior to Bossuet.

Bibliography: L. BOURDALOUE, *Sermons,* ed. F. BRETONNEAU, 16 v. (Paris 1707–21); *Pensées,* ed. F. BRETONNEAU, 2 v. (Paris 1734), together the authoritative source of Bourdaloue's complete works. They were published together in 4 v. (Bar-le-Duc 1864). C. A. SAINTE-BEUVE, *Causeries du lundi,* 15 v. (Paris 1851ŗ62). H. CHÉROT, *Bourdaloue inconnu* (Paris 1898); *Bourdaloue: Sa correspondance et ses correspondants* (Paris 1899); DTC 2.1:1095–99. A. A. L. PAUTHE, *Bourdaloue, d'après des documents nouveaux: Les maîtres de la chaire en France au XVIIᵉ siècle* (Paris 1900). C. H. BROOKE, ed. and tr., *Great French Preachers,* 2 v. (London 1904), sermons of Bourdaloue. E. BYRNE, *Bourdaloue moraliste* (Paris 1929). R. DAESCHLER, *Bourdaloue: Doctrine spirituelle* (Paris 1932). T. J. CAMPBELL, CE 2:717–719.

[R. B. MEAGHER]

lucidity, becoming a very able controversialist against Protestants, Jansenists, and quietists. As were many others of his time he was perhaps overly inclined to favor the crown in the dispute about the Gallican Articles.

Bourdaloue used two exordiums: the first, more general, beginning adroitly with the text of the subject matter of the sermon and ending with a Hail Mary, the second, more detailed and specific, presenting the doctrine in three different manners. The body of the discourse was divided into three points: exposition of the doctrine found in Scripture and the Fathers of the Church, the moral to be drawn from the doctrine, and the portrayal of worldly Christians whose lives were at variance with the moral doctrine with which he was concerned. Each of the three points was further subdivided into three parts. Fénelon and La Bruyère vigorously criticized his method as rigidly and arbitrarily mechanical but admitted that it was useful as a memory aid for the speaker and the listeners. However heavy the plan may appear, Bourdaloue used it artfully, and its use brought him great success.

Bourdaloue was most effective in his moral sermons in which he manifested a remarkable delicacy of balance. For him Christian morality was just as free from excessive rigors as it was from any culpable indulgence. Sainte-Beuve considered his sermons the best refutations of Pascal's *Lettres Provinciales.*

He was masterly in his analysis of the human heart and was able to draw strikingly true word portraits. No doubt the 17th century taste for a moral analysis accounted for much of his success. His reasoning was rigorous, and he habitually sought to convince his auditors. Actually in this also he was adapting himself to

BOURDEILLE, ELIAS OF, Franciscan, archbishop of Tours and cardinal; b. château of Agonac, Perigord, France, 1413; d. château of Artannes, near Tours, France, July 5, 1484. He was the son of baron Arnaud I and Jeanne of Chamberlhac, and in 1423 he became a *Franciscan at Perigueux. In 1432 he presented his thesis at Toulouse and taught and preached at Mirepoix. As bishop of Perigueux (1437–68) he attended the Council of *Florence. He was a pious prelate, austere and zealous. In 1468 he became confessor to *Louis XI and was promoted to the archbishopric of *Tours. His influence on the King was extensive as he obtained the repeal of the Pragmatic Sanction and defended the rights of the pope and the bishops against *Gallicanism. *Sixtus IV raised him to the cardinalate in November 1483. He was buried in his diocese, where his tomb was desecrated in 1562. Inquiries toward his *canonization were held at Perigueux in 1527; proceedings were undertaken again at Tours in 1913. For this purpose his writings were investigated (*Acta ordinis Minorum* 76:142); they include *Consideratio super processu et sententia contra Ioannam prolata* (1452 or 1453), a justification for the beatification of *Joan of Arc (ed. P. Lanery d'Arc, Paris 1898), as well as an important work opposing the Pragmatic Sanction, entitled *Contra impiam Gallorum sanctionem cui Pragmatice nomen est* (Rome 1486). The latter work was at first rather poorly received in France, but it later gained popularity there and was reprinted several times following the concordat of 1516.

See also PRAGMATIC SANCTION.

Bibliography: B. T. POÜAN, *Le Saint cardinal Hélie de Bourdeille . . .,* 2 v. in 1 (Neuville-sous-Montreuil 1887–1900), with contemporary vita by P. DE BOIS-MORIN. BiblSanct 3:374–375. E. GRAU, LexThK² 2:630 P. CALENDINI, DHGE 10:148–149. E. LONGPRÉ, *Catholicisme* 4:15.

[J. CAMBELL]

BOURGCHIER, THOMAS (BOURCHIER), archbishop of Canterbury, cardinal; b. *c.* 1410; d. Knole manor, Kent, England, March 30, 1486. A younger son of William Bourgchier, Count of Eu, by Anne, daughter of Thomas, Duke of Gloucester, his high birth marked him out for rapid advancement. An M.A. of Oxford (by 1433) and chancellor of the University (1434–37), he was made dean of St. Martins-le-Grand, London, before taking orders and held canonries in Lichfield, Wells, Lincoln, and York (1428–35). In 1433 Cardinal Henry *Beaufort and the court party pressed him on Pope Eugene IV for the See of *Worcester, although the Pope had already provided Thomas *Brouns, notwithstanding Bourgchier's lack of canonical age. The dispute lasted until March 9, 1435, when he was appointed by a reluctant Pope. By 1437 Bourgchier had become a royal councilor, and he spared little attention either for Worcester or for *Ely, whither he was translated on Dec. 20, 1443. On June 21, 1454, he succeeded Cardinal John *Kemp as archbishop of Canterbury. Prominent as a mediator in the party struggles between 1452 and 1458, he supported the Yorkists in 1460 and became a loyal servant of King Edward IV, who persuaded Pope Paul IV to make him a cardinal in September 1467. Bourgchier held high office only briefly (as chancellor of England, March 1455–October 1456), but was active in the court and council of Edward IV. As archbishop he crowned Edward IV in 1461, *Richard III in 1483 (albeit with reluctance), and *Henry VII in 1485. He was not regarded as a mere time-server, but won his contemporaries' respect. His busy political life made him a negligent archbishop: in 32 years as primate he performed no ordinations and relied heavily on suffragans and officials in his diocesan administration.

Bibliography: *Registrum Thome Bourgchier,* ed. F. R. H. Du Boulay, 2 v. (Canterbury and York Society 54; Oxford 1957). C. L. Scofield, *The Life and Reign of Edward the Fourth,* 2 v. (New York 1923). Emden 1:230–232.

[C. D. ROSS]

BOURGEOYS, MARGUERITE, BL., foundress and first superior of the Sisters of the *Congregation de Notre Dame; b. Troyes, France, April 17, 1620;

Marguerite Bourgeoys.

d. Montreal, Canada, Jan. 12, 1700. She was the daughter of a prosperous merchant and grew up in a quiet corner of Champagne. In 1653, after several unsuccessful attempts to enter the cloister, she sailed for Canada with Paul de C. *Maisonneuve, Governor of Montreal, a frontier garrison in New France, founded only 12 years before. There in 1658 she opened the first school in Montreal in an abandoned stone stable. Within a few years she had established a school for Indians, an Indian mission, a boarding school for the daughters of merchants, and a training school for the poor. As the scope of her work grew, she brought assistants from France; later, Canadian-born girls and two Indians joined her in her work. The group developed into a new kind of religious community, not bound to the cloister, but free to go, dressed in the costume of the poor, wherever their zeal and the needs of the people demanded. In 1698, 2 years before her death, the Congregation de Notre Dame won ecclesiastical approval.

The foundress consistently refused endowments, dowries for her companions, and gifts of money that would have made her life less directly dependent on God. She and her religious supported themselves by sewing, living frugally so that they could give alms to the poor. They began needed buildings without the money to complete them and offered the work of their hands in exchange for the services of carpenters and masons. After a disastrous fire in December 1683, the community was left destitute. As soon as the ground thawed in the spring, they began, totally without resources, the construction of a new school. With alms, Marguerite built a chapel as a place of pilgrimage to Our Lady, Notre Dame de Bon Secours; she and her companions carried stones and poured mortar for the masons. Marguerite Bourgeoys was beatified in 1950 by Pius XII, who said of her role in the flowering of Catholicism in Canada that "her boundless influence has not ceased to make itself felt during the three centuries which have elapsed since her lifetime. In the space of a few years, God sent to New France heroic missionaries. Yet even in this firmament in which there shine such holy and illustrious personages, Marguerite Bourgeoys is still a figure resplendent in her humility: teacher, traveling missionary, foundress of a Congregation of secular women, in whom she realized the dream cherished for France by Saint Francis de Sales. . . ."

Bibliography: M. Bourgeoys, *Les Écrits de Mère Bourgeoys. Autobiographie et testament spirituel* (Montreal 1964). E. Montgolfier, *La vie de la vénérable Marguerite Bourgeoys dite du Saint-Sacrement, institutrice, fondatrice* (Montreal 1818). É. M. Faillon, *Vie de la soeur Bourgeoys,* 2 v. (Villemarie 1853). A. Jamet, *Marguerite Bourgeoys,* 2 v. (Montreal 1942). Y. Charron, *Mère Bourgeoys,* tr. Sister St. Godeliva (Montreal 1950). K. Burton, *Valiant Voyager* (Milwaukee 1964).

[V. M. COTTER]

BOURGES, ARCHDIOCESE OF (BITURICENSIS)

Metropolitan see comprising the civil departments of Indre and Cher (whose capital is the city of Bourges) in central France. In 1963 the archdiocese, 5,440 square miles in area, had 506 parishes, 355 secular and 50 religious priests, 115 men in 5 religious houses, 500 women in 70 convents, and 500,000 Catholics. Its five suffragans, which had 1,889 parishes, 1,754 priests, 4,030 sisters, and 1,563,770 Catholics were: Clermont (founded *c.* 300, with 12 early bishop saints), Le Puy (4th century), *Limoges, Saint-Flour (1317, with the nearby Abbey of *Aurillac), and Tulle (1317, from a 7th-century Benedictine monastery).

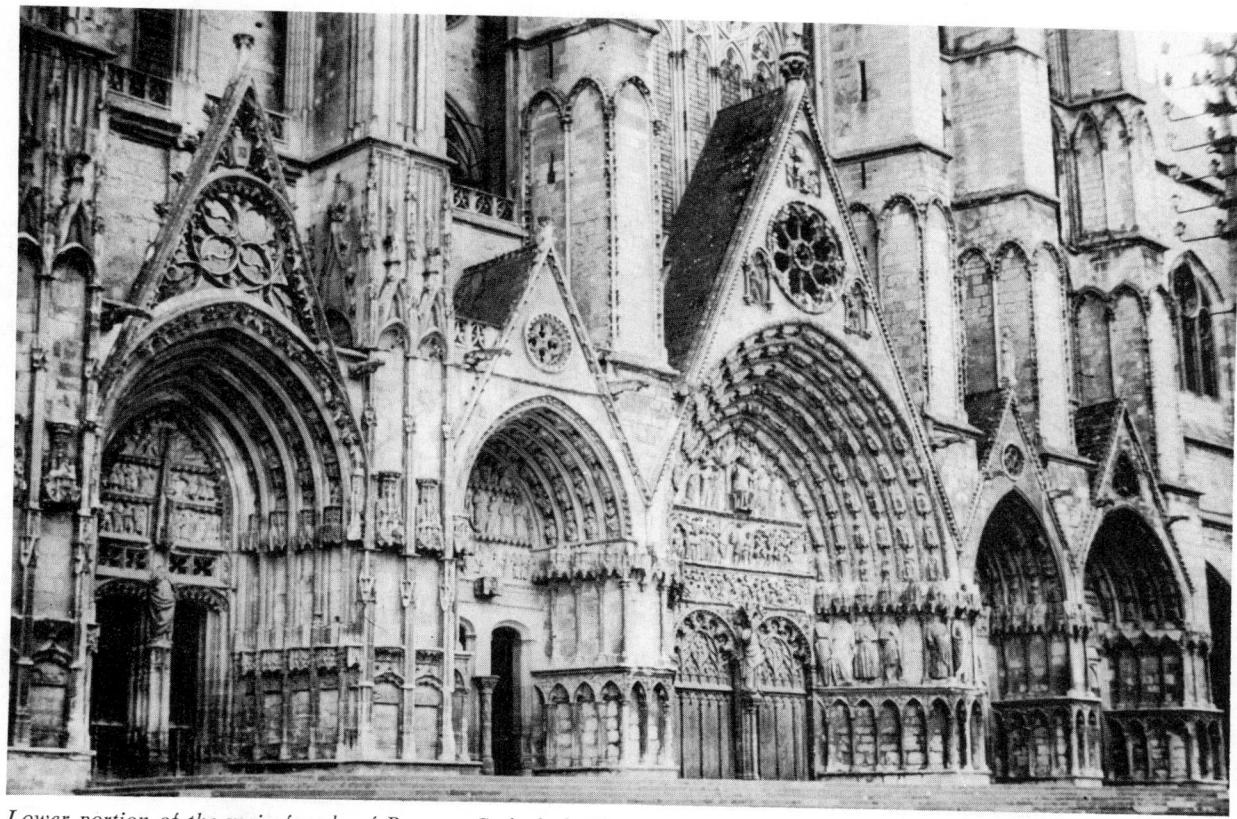

Lower portion of the main façade of Bourges Cathedral. The five portals reflect the five-nave interior.

In Gallic times Bourges was the powerful capital of the *Bituriges* (Celto-Latin *Avaricum*). Conquered by Caesar in 52 B.C., it became a Gallo-Roman *civitas* and in the 3d century capital of *Aquitania I*. Unreliable traditions attribute the first evangelization to disciples of the Apostles. According to *Gregory of Tours (d. 593), the first bishop was St. Ursinus (*c.* 250), who was sent from Rome; but the Church of Bourges did not venerate him as founder before the 6th century. The see was probably founded *c.* 300, becoming a missionary center. The first bishop to whom a definite date can be assigned (453) is 12th in the episcopal list. Ursinus's disciple, Leocadius, is credited with the building of the first church, on the location of which stands the present cathedral (12th–14th century, with five naves and perhaps the most beautiful stained glass in France). Bourges had four abbeys: Saint-Ambroix (8th century), Saint-Sulpice (7th), Bussières (moved to Bourges in 1625), and Saint-Laurent (Benedictine, 7th century?). Some of Bourges' 7 chapters of canons derived from abbeys, the most famous being that of Sainte-Chapelle, founded by Duke John of Berry (1405); its church was demolished in the 18th century. On the eve of the French Revolution, Bourges, capital of the province of Berry, had 15 religious establishments. The present city, with 53,900 inhabitants, has 7 parishes, the most recent being Sainte-Barbe, the seat of an international archconfraternity of St. Barbara. The university of 1463 was abolished in the Revolution.

Bourges has been a metropolitanate since these sees were first organized. Its suffragans were the sees of *Aquitania I:* Clermont, Rodez, *Albi, Cahors, Limoges, Javols-Mende, and Saint-Paulien-Le Puy. Bishops of Merovingian times (5th–8th century) were of Gallo-Roman origin. In Carolingian times they were the protégés of the emperors, and to the late 10th century they came from the noblest families of Berry. After 987 they had close ties with the *Capetians. Bourges was added to the royal domain in 1101, and Berry was an appanage of royal princes in the 14th and 15th centuries. The province suffered in the *Wars of Religion; Protestants, who established themselves solidly, organizing 6 churches, pillaged and devastated. Application of the decrees of the Council of *Trent was followed in the 17th century by a religious revival marked by clerical reform and the activity of Jesuits, Capuchins, Minims, Oratorians, and other religious. In 1317–18 Bourges received four newly created suffragans: Saint-Flour, Tulle, Castres, and Vabres. Albi became a metropolitan see in 1676 and took several suffragans from Bourges, which in 1789 had as suffragans Clermont, Limoges, Saint-Flour, and Tulle—Le Puy being immediately subject to the Holy See. The See of Bourges covered the area of the old *civitas,* which the Revolution made into the departments of Cher and Indre (which received a constitutional bishopric at Châteauroux). The *Concordat of 1801 and the agreements of 1817–22 gave Bourges as territory Cher and Indre (the former Berry), with Limoges, Clermont, Le Puy, and Tulle as suffragans.

Councils in Bourges have dealt with important matters: in 452 with ecclesiastical jurisdiction; in 472, under *Sidonius Apollinaris of Clermont, with the election of the archbishop of Bourges; in 841 and 1031; in 1145, attended by *Louis VII, with Crusade problems; in 1225 with the *Albigensian heresy and crusade; in

1276, 1280, 1286, and 1336 with ecclesiastical discipline; in 1438 an assembly of prelates and delegates named by *Charles VII to regulate reform and to determine the statutes of the Church of France concluded with the famous royal edict called the *Pragmatic Sanction of Bourges, the basis of *Gallicanism, never to be accepted by Rome; in 1528 Luther's errors were condemned; in 1584 the decrees of Trent were applied. In 1800 Bourges's juror bishop sought to restore the constitutional church but was thwarted by the Concordat of 1801.

Archbishop *Sulpicius II the Good (615–647), venerated as a saint, founded the abbey that bears his name. St. Raoul (840–866) was involved in major religious events of his time. The relics of St. *William (1150–1209), whose vita was written by a canon of Bourges, were almost all burned by Huguenots. *Giles of Rome (1295–1316), theorist of papal theocracy, and Jean Coeur (1447–83), son of an entrepreneur in the Levant trade (Jacques), both were prelates of Bourges. The reform prelate Renaud of Beaune (1581–1602) received the abjuration of *Henry IV. Pierre d'Hardivilliers (1638–49) founded the seminary (1644). Cardinal Léon Potier of Gesvres (1694–1729) combatted Jansenism and had a dispute regarding the papal bull *Unigenitus. Cardinal F. de La Rochefoucauld (1729–57), ambassador of France to the Holy See, reformed Bourges's liturgical books. Berry's patroness is the 10th-century St. Solangia.

Bourges disputed the primacy of Aquitaine with *Bordeaux from the 11th to the 14th century, when Clement V, once archbishop of Bordeaux, bestowed the title on both prelates. Bourges archdiocese had 25 men's abbeys and 5 women's, the most famous being *Chezal-Benoît; Saint-Cyran, where the Jansenist Jean *Duvergier de Hauranne was commendatory abbot; Plaimpied, with an admirable Romanesque church; Noirlac, a masterpiece of Cistercian architecture almost intact; and Olivet. The see also has several pilgrimage shrines.

Bibliography: A. GANDILHON, DHGE 10:178–211. M. DE LAUGARDIÈRE, *L'Église de Bourges avant Charlemagne* (Bourges 1951). E. JARRY, *Catholicisme* 2:210–214. AnnPont (1964) 72. **Illustration credits:** Fig. 1, R. V. Schoder, SJ. Fig. 2, Archives Photographiques, Paris.

[E. JARRY]

BOURGET, IGNACE

Second bishop of Montreal, Canada; b. Saint-Joseph-de-Lévis, Canada, Oct. 30, 1799; d. Montreal, June 8, 1885. He attended secondary school at Quebec and began his work in theology there, finishing it at Montreal under J. J. Lartigue, the auxiliary bishop to whom he was secretary. When Montreal became a diocese (1836), he was named vicar-general; the following year he was consecrated coadjutor bishop, and in 1840 he succeeded to the see. His first concern was to obtain for Montreal the priests and institutions needed. He entrusted the direction of its Grand Seminary to the Sulpicians. In 1841 he went to Europe and obtained the services of several Oblates of Mary Immaculate (1841), Jesuits and Sisters of the Sacred Heart (1842), and nuns of the Good Shepherd from Angers (1844). He also made arrangements for the coming of other religious institutes: the Clerics of St. Viator and the Fathers, Brothers, and Sisters of the Holy Cross (1847). He founded two institutes of charity: the Sisters of Providence (1843) and the Sisters of Mercy; and two institutes of instruction, the Sisters of the Holy Names of Jesus and Mary (1844) and the Sisters of St. Anne (1848); and he welcomed into the diocese the Brothers of Charity of Gand (1865). Although a man of action himself, Bourget was a great believer in prayer; he collaborated in the foundation of a Canadian contemplative institute, the Sisters of the Precious Blood (1861), and he established the Carmelites of Reims in Montreal (1875). His zeal was not limited to his own diocese, and he sent out to the poorest of the dioceses, and especially to the missions of the Pacific Coast, numerous secular priests, monks, and nuns. "The best means of preserving the Faith," he used to say, "is to propagate it far and wide."

With many bishops of his time, he favored *ultramontanism, or papal supremacy, and he had to withstand heavy attacks from liberals and the supporters of *Gallicanism of the period. Ten years after the foundation of Laval University at Quebec (1852) he tried to obtain an independent Catholic university for his episcopal city. Although his 15-year effort was unsuccessful, he advanced all the arguments that ultimately led to the establishment of the independent University of Montreal (1920). No less important was the struggle he waged for the spiritual well-being of Montreal. By virtue of a privilege dating from the 17th century, which he himself had confirmed in 1843, the Seminary of Montreal was empowered to minister, in perpetuity, to the entire city as a single parish. Because of the rapid increase in the city's population (to 100,000 in 1860), this privilege became more burdensome than useful. In 1865 Rome granted Bourget the right to establish new

"St. Mary of Egypt Leaving for Jerusalem," detail of a 13th-century stained-glass window in Bourges Cathedral.

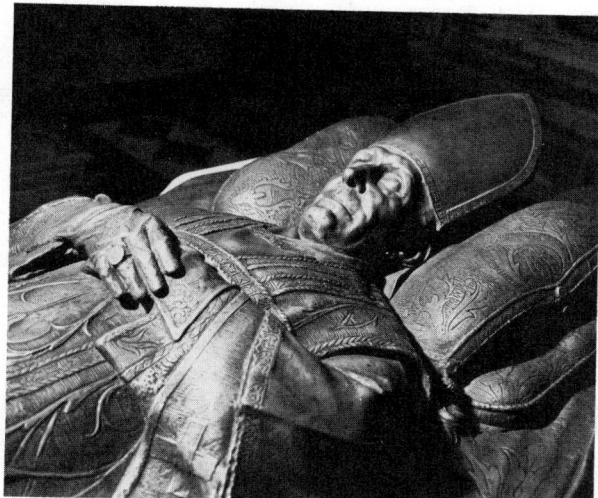

Ignace Bourget, effigy on his tomb in the bishops' funeral chapel of the cathedral at Montreal.

parishes in the city in accordance with the needs of the faithful, thus enabling the Diocese of Montreal to progress during the second half of the 19th century at the same rate as the rest of the country. The prestige and the reputation for sanctity that accrued to him during his lifetime did not cease with his death; in 1903 a monument was erected to him in front of the basilica. His remains are interred in a marble tomb in the center of the bishops' funeral chapel.

Bibliography: A. LEBLOND DE BRUMATH, *Monseigneur Bourget, archévêque de Marianapolis ancien, évêque de Montréal* (Montreal 1885). F. LANGEVIN, *Mgr. Ignace Bourget, deuxième évêque de Montréal* (Montreal 1931). L. POULIOT, *Monseigneur Bourget et son temps,* 2 v. (Montreal 1955–56), v.3–4 in prep. **Illustration credit:** Armour Landry, Montreal.

[L. POULIOT]

BOURGOING, FRANÇOIS, Oratorian spiritual writer; b. Paris, March 18, 1585; d. there, Oct. 28, 1662. Born of a noble family, he was the *curé* of Clichy until 1611, when he resigned the position in favor of Vincent de Paul and became one of the first six priests of the Oratory founded by Pierre de *Bérulle. He taught in various seminaries, including those of Paris, Rouen, and Nantes, and also preached extensively in Auvergne, Brittany, and Lyons. In 1626 at the request of the archbishop of Malines, he went to Flanders and established Oratorian houses in Louvain, Maubeuge, and Mons. He preached the funeral oration for Cardinal De Bérulle at Louvain, and then presided at the assembly of the Oratory that elected Charles de *Condren as De Bérulle's successor. Bourgoing returned to France in 1630, and on Condren's death in 1641, became the third superior general of the Oratory. He initiated vigorous regulations for his community and drew up a plan of studies for seminaries. His subordinates criticized him for his authoritarian manner, and the assembly of 1661, by legislating that no superior could accept a position at court, indirectly reproached him for accepting the office of confessor to the Duke of Orleans. Nevertheless the prosperity of the Oratory under his direction proved his wisdom and competence as an administrator. In 1656 he suffered a stroke, from which he never fully recovered, and after 1660 his health and

spirit failed. Bousset preached the funeral oration for Bourgoing.

A close disciple of Bérulle, Bourgoing was a fierce opponent of Jansenism and one of the leading figures in the religious renaissance in France in the 17th century. A prolific writer, he published many works of piety that went through numerous editions and were translated into other languages. Among his principal works are *Lignum vitae* (Mons 1629), *Institutio spiritualis ordinandorum* (Paris 1639), *Méditations sur les vérités et excellence de Jésus Christ* (6 v. Paris 1636), and *Exercises de retraites* (4 v. Paris 1648). Along with other collections of homilies on the gospel and meditations on the Blessed Virgin and the saints, he also edited the works of De Bérulle.

Bibliography: C. E. CLOYSEAULT, *Généralats du P. François Bourgoing,* 2 v. (Paris 1880) 2:1–26. L. BATTEREL, *Mémoires domestiques pour servir à l'histoire de l'Oratoire,* 5 v. (Paris 1903–11) 2:285–329. A. MOLIEN, DictSpirAscMyst 1:1910–15. E. LEVESQUE, DHGE 10:226–228.

[J. T. KELLEHER]

BOURGUEIL-EN-VALLÉE, ABBEY OF, former Benedictine house in the former Diocese of Angers, now Indre-et-Loire, France (patron, St. Peter). It was founded in 989 by Emma, wife of Count William IV of Poitiers, and confirmed by Pope John XV in 990 and by King Hugh Capet in 994. The first abbot, Gausbert, ruled simultaneously the Abbeys of Bourgueil, Saint-Julien of Tours, *Marmoutier, and La Couture at Le Mans. *Baudry of Bourgueil, the seventh abbot (1079–1107), was the most notable prelate to come from the abbey. He was archbishop of Dol in Brittany and one of the most important Latin poets of the 12th century. At its height the abbey directed 42 priories and 64 parish churches; it had properties throughout western France, as well as some important vineyards in the Loire Valley. The abbey was placed under commendatory abbots after 1475 but was reformed by the *Maurists in 1630. It was suppressed in 1791. The buildings, which were mostly destroyed during the French Revolution, included the Gothic church (built 1246–93), a cloister of the 15th century, and the conventual dwellings dating from 1658 to 1672.

Bibliography: There is a copy of the unedited cartulary of Bourgueil at the Bibliothèque Municipale of Tours, MS 1338, 1339. GallChrist 14:654–667. P. CALENDINI, DHGE 10:229–234. L. MUSSET, "Les Plus anciennes chartes normandes de l'abbaye de B.," *Bulletin de la société des antiquaires de Normandie* 54 (1957–58) 15–54; "Deux nouvelles chartes normandes de l'abbaye de B.," *ibid.* 56 (1961–62) 5–41. M. DUPONT, "Monographie du cartulaire de B., des origines à la fin du moyen âge" (Mémoires de la soc. archéol. de Touraine 56; Tours 1962).

[L. MUSSET]

BOURNE, FRANCIS, cardinal, fourth archbishop of Westminster, England; b. Clapham, London, England, March 23, 1861; d. Westminster, Jan. 1, 1935. He was the son of Henry, a convert and post office clerk, and Ellen (Byrne) Bourne. He was educated in England at Ushaw College, Durham; St. Edmund's, Ware; and Hammersmith. After completing his theological studies at Saint-Sulpice, Paris, he was ordained (June 11, 1884). He held several brief curacies before becoming rector of a house of studies at Henfield Place, Sussex (1889), and of the diocesan seminary at Wonersh (1891). In 1896 he was consecrated as coadjutor to the bishop of Southwark, whom he succeeded the same year. In 1903 he was transferred to the Archdiocese of *Westminster, where he was elevated to the cardinalate (1910). His achievements as archbishop included a successful defense of Catholic voluntary schools against

Cardinal Francis Bourne.

government restriction, organization of the International Eucharistic Congress in London (1908), and progress in the construction of Westminster Cathedral, consecrated in 1910.

Bibliography: E. OLDMEADOW, *Francis Cardinal Bourne*, 2 v. (London 1940–44). W. J. WOOD, DNB (1931–40) 92–93.

[D. MILBURN]

BOURNE, GILBERT, last Catholic bishop of Bath and Wells, noted orator and disputant; b. place and date unknown; d. Silverton, Devonshire, Sept. 10, 1569. His father was Philip Bourne of Worcestershire. Gilbert entered the University of Oxford in 1524, and was a fellow of All Soul's College in 1531. In 1541 he became prebendary of the King's new foundation at Worcester. Dr. Bourne must have conformed to the religious changes under Edward VI as he was prebend at St. Paul's, London; rector of High Ongar in Essex; and archdeacon of Bedford. However, he remained loyal to his patron, Bishop Edmund *Bonner, during the latter's trial in 1549. With Mary's accession, Bourne returned to the old religion. His great gifts as a preacher were used by Mary. As royal preacher, he caused a tumult among the enraged reformers with a sermon in defense of Catholic doctrine and Bonner, delivered Aug. 13, 1553, at Paul's Cross, London. His eloquence and courage, together with the influence of his uncle, Sir John Bourne, principal secretary of state, won him election as bishop of Bath and Wells, March 28, 1554. After his consecration by Bishop Bonner, Bourne zealously restored Catholic practices and worship.

He was noted, however, even among Protestants, for his kindness. There is no record of any executions in his diocese. Queen Mary showed her esteem by appointing him lord president of the Council of Wales, from which office he was removed by Elizabeth in 1558. His refusal to participate in a commission for consecrating Matthew Parker, Archbishop of Canterbury, and to take the oaths of supremacy and allegiance (Oct. 18, 1559) brought his deprivation and imprisonment in the Tower. In September 1563 he was removed to house arrest, first with the bishop of Lincoln, then with Dean Carey of Exeter, where he died.

Bibliography: W. M. BRADY, *The Episcopal Succession in England, Scotland, and Ireland, A.D. 1400 to 1875,* 3 v. (Rome 1876–77). H. TOOTELL, *Dodd's Church History of England,* ed. M. A. TIERNEY, 5 v. (London 1839–43). Hughes RE. W. HUNT, DNB 2:936–937.

[J. D. HANLON]

BOUSSET, WILHELM, Protestant NT scholar; b. Lübeck, Germany, Sept. 3, 1865; d. Giessen, Germany, March 8, 1920. He taught Scripture at Göttingen from 1896 to 1916 and at Giessen from 1916 to his death. At Göttingen he was one of the cofounders of the school of comparative religion, and together with W. Heitmüller he successfully applied its method in the field of NT studies. He opened new paths with his commentary on the Apocalypse [*Offenbarung Johannes* (*Meyer Kommentar* 16; Göttingen 1896, 6th ed. 1906)], his *Die Religion des Judentums im ntl. Zeitalter* [Göttingen 1902; rev. ed., H. Gressmann, ed., *Die Religion . . . im späthellenistischen Zeitalter* (Göttingen 3d ed. 1926)], his *Die Hauptprobleme der Gnosis* (Göttingen 1907), and his chief work, *Kyrios Christos* (Göttingen 1913, 4th ed. 1935; new ed. in preparation in 1965). In these works he endeavored to show that so-called late Judaism was influenced by Iranian and especially Hellenistic ideas and that Hellenistic *Gnosticism borrowed religious concepts from the Near East. While A. von *Harnack regarded the history of dogma as a history of the Hellenization of Christianity, according to Bousset primitive Christianity had been deeply influenced by Hellenism, and the decisive turning point in the history of Christianity lay not at the end of the NT period, but was the transitional period when the faith of the primitive Judeo-Christian community of Palestine in the Son of Man with its expectation of His Parousia changed into the faith of Gentile Christianity of the Hellenistic world with its veneration of Kyrios already present. Thus the inner bond between the theology of the NT and that of the early Church could be explained. Bousset's ideas continued to affect NT scholars in the 20th century, particularly R. Bultmann and his disciples.

Bousset founded the *Theologische Rundschau* (1897), which he edited together with W. Heitmüller until 1917. With H. *Gunkel he published the *Forschungen zur Religion und Literatur des Alten und Neuen Testamentes* (1901–20). With Heitmüller he prepared the third edition of *Die Schriften des Neuen Testaments neu übersetzt und für die Gegenwart erklärt* (Göttingen 1917–19).

Bibliography: H. GUNKEL, *Evangelische Freiheit* 42 (1920) 141–162. L. THOMAS, DBSuppl 1:989–992. H. SCHLIER, LexThK² 2:632. E. KAMLAH, RGG³ 1:1373–74.

[O. KAISER]

BOUTRAIS, CYPRIEN MARIE, Carthusian author; b. Paris, June 10, 1837; d. Vedana, Italy, Aug. 18, 1900. He was baptized Jules Hippolyte. He entered the Redemptorist order and was ordained in 1863 but 7 years later decided to join the Carthusians at the Grande-Chartreuse; he made solemn profession in 1875. He became manager of the Carthusian printing offices at Montreuil-sur-Mer (1885–88). He held the office of prior, successively, at La Valsainte (Switzerland), Glandier (France), and Vedana.

Dom Cyprien Marie published: a life of Bl. Ayrald, Carthusian bishop of Maurienne (Montreuil 1880); *La Grande Chartreuse par un Chartreux* (1881), frequently reprinted, and in 1950 brought up to date (ed.

B. Arthaud, Grenoble); and a history of the Charterhouse of Glandier (Montreuil 1886). He had earlier completed two books revealing the part Carthusians played in the development of devotion to the *Sacred Heart of Jesus: *Lansperge-le-chartreux et la dévotion au Sacré-Coeur* (Grenoble 1878) and *Semaine du Sacré-Coeur de Jésus par Dom Innocent Le Masson, Général des Chartreux.* In the third edition of the latter (Toulouse 1886), he added *Un Mois du Sacré-Coeur et des prières par d'anciens auteurs Chartreux.* The 1955 English edition, *Ancient Devotions to the Sacred Heart by Carthusian Monks of the XIV–XVII Centuries,* is still available at Parkminster Charterhouse, Horsham, Sussex, England.

[B. DU MOUSTIER]

BOUTROUX, ÉTIENNE ÉMILE MARIE

French philosopher of science; b. Montrouge, July 28, 1845; d. Paris, Nov. 22, 1921. Boutroux succeeded J. *Lachelier as conference master at the Ecole Normale, and exercised a great influence over a whole generation of French philosophers and philosophers of science, including H. *Bergson, M. *Blondel, P. *Duhem, and J. Henri *Poincaré.

His doctoral dissertation, *De la contingence des lois de la nature* (1874), was hailed as a landmark in the philosophy of nature. It was an attack on the doctrinnaire determinism of academic rationalists and positivists who allowed no contingency in the laws of nature. Scientific laws are abstract figures of an ideal necessity that can never be fully equated with the concrete, physical reality they symbolize; first, because one can never know all of the influences that condition a fact or event, and secondly, because the human mind, due to its limitations, necessarily eliminates differences in order to stress what is common. Hypotheses, then, are but partial views that are reformable, and in no sense absolute or necessary. They tell little about nature itself, whose behavior is unpredictable and not subject to the scientific formulas man invents to describe it. It is a mistake, then, to absolutize nature or man's way of thinking about nature.

In addition, quite apart from the multiplicity of external factors that condition scientific facts, the constructions of science are influenced by, and in turn have only a limited application to, human life, thought, and freedom. In sympathy with E. Zeller, whose lectures he heard in Germany, Boutroux extended his criticism of determinism in his later works to those neo-Hegelians who viewed history as a deductive science subject to iron laws of necessity. Man's freedom breaks into the closed world of historical and scientific determinism, resisting all attempts to subject the course of progress to an absolute rule.

Yet, man's quest for an absolute and his attachment to the noncontingent reveal a deeper necessity whose complement lies in the area of morality and religion. He is confronted with the fact of duty and the need for a faith, and science itself shows the importance of cooperative enterprise that should engage all men in the common task of wresting from nature her secrets and working toward the universal brotherhood of man. It is the Christian Gospel that outlines what should be the fullest realization of unity among men. Not only does it offer the hope of reconciling freedom and necessity, and the aspirations of the person with the needs of the commu-

nity, but it also places science and history within the larger framework of a reality that transcends the limits of the contingent order of creation.

See also SCIENCE, PHILOSOPHY OF.

Bibliography: Major works translated into English. *Science and Religion in Contemporary Philosophy,* tr. J. NIELD (London 1909); *Historical Studies in Philosophy,* tr. F. ROTHWELL (London 1912); *William James,* tr. A. and B. HENDERSON (London 1912); *Natural Law in Science and Philosophy,* tr. F. ROTHWELL (London 1914); *The Contingency of the Laws of Nature,* tr. F. ROTHWELL (London 1916). Studies. A. P. LA FONTAINE, *La Philosophie d'É. Boutroux,* v. 1 of *La Culture française,* 3 v. (Paris 1920–26). M. SCHYNS, *La Philosophie d'Émile Boutroux* (Paris 1924). A. BAILLOT, "La Philosophie et la religion selon Émile Boutroux," RevThom 39.1 (1934) 313–352. J. BENDA, *De quelques constantes de l'esprit humain* (Paris 1950).

[J. M. SOMERVILLE]

BOUTS, DIRK, early Netherlandish painter; b. Haarlem, *c.* 1415; d. Louvain, 1475. Bouts (Thierry) was of Dutch descent; he married (*c.* 1448) the daughter of a wealthy Flemish family of Louvain, where in 1468 he was made the official city painter. Though drawing upon the art of Jan van *Eyck and Roger van der *Weyden, Bouts did not continue their highly symbolic style. He introduced a new psychological intensity in his figures (see illustration) and, with the aid of focal point perspective, a new coordination between figures and extensive landscape setting. His interest in recording an atmospheric environment may be seen in such works as the "St. Erasmus Altarpiece" or the landscapes on the wing panels of the "Altarpiece of the Blessed

Dirk Bouts, self-portrait, detail of the central panel of the "Altarpiece of the Blessed Sacrament," 1464 to 1467, in the church of St. Peter at Louvain, Belgium.

Sacrament," both of which were painted between 1464 and 1467 for the church of St. Peter in Louvain.

Bibliography: W. SCHÖNE, *Dieric Bouts und seine Schule* (Berlin 1938). M. J. FRIEDLÄNDER, *Dierick Bouts und Joos van Gent,* v.2 of *Die alterniederländische Malerei,* 14 v. (Berlin 1924–37). K. M. BIRKMEYER, "The Arch Motif in Netherlandish Painting of the 15th Century," ArtBull 43.1–2 (1961) 1–20, 99–112. **Illustration credit:** Copyright A.C.L., Brussels.

[S. N. HOPPS]

BOUVET, JOACHIM, mathematician and missionary; b. Le Mans, France, July 18, 1656; d. Peking, China, June 28, 1732. At the age of 17 he entered the Society of Jesus. One of six Jesuits selected by Louis XIV to further French influence in China by the advancement of religion and science, Bouvet arrived at Peking, Feb. 7, 1688, where he was received and retained at court as royal mathematician by the Emperor K'ang-Hsi. He made a visit to France from 1697 to 1699 to carry presents between Emperor and King and to recruit more Jesuits for the mission. From 1708 to 1715, he prepared a geographical survey of China. His services to the Emperor did much to facilitate the religious ministry of the Jesuits. He cooperated with four fellow missionaries to obtain from K'ang-Hsi an official pronouncement that certain Chinese ceremonies in honor of Confucius and the dead were without religious significance. Besides his works on mathematics, he compiled a Chinese dictionary. His unpublished letters include correspondence with Leibniz. His most known work, *Portrait historique de l'Empereur de Chine* (Paris 1697), was subsequently translated into English, Dutch, German, Italian, and Latin, the last by Leibniz in 1699.

Bibliography: Sommervogel 2:54–58; 8:1896; 12:970. A. DE BIL, DHGE 10:275–276. A. H. ROWBOTHAM, *Missionary and Mandarin: The Jesuits at the Court of China* (Berkeley 1942). C. CARY-ELWES, *China and the Cross: A Survey of Missionary History* (New York 1957). K. S. LATOURETTE, *A History of Christian Missions in China* (New York 1929).

[J. V. MENTAG]

BOUVIER, JEAN BAPTISTE, bishop and theologian; b. Saint-Charles-la-Forêt, Mayenne, Jan. 16, 1783; d. Rome, Dec. 29, 1854. The son of a carpenter, he entered the seminary of Angers in 1805 and was ordained in 1808. After teaching philosophy at the College of Château Gonthier, he became professor of philosophy and moral theology at the seminary of Le Mans in 1811 and was made rector there in 1819. After 1820 he was vicar-general of the diocese until he was consecrated bishop of Le Mans in 1834. During his episcopate he was known for his learning, piety, and apostolic zeal. The Sisters of Providence of St. Mary-of-the-Woods (Ind.) are particularly indebted to Bouvier for his support and assistance in the foundation of their community. Pius IX held him in such high esteem that he invited Bouvier to be present at the definition of the dogma of the Immaculate Conception.

The principal work among his many writings was the *Institutiones theologicae* (Le Mans 1817), which went through 15 editions and was used in almost all the seminaries of France, the U.S., and Canada. First issued in separate theological treatises comprising 13 volumes, the work was reduced to 6 volumes in 1834. Although Bouvier tried to improve his work in the course of succeeding editions, he never succeeded in removing completely the traces of Gallicanism that had influenced

Jean Baptiste Bouvier.

his early formation. He readily submitted to the corrections of the theologians selected by Pius IX. Their revision resulted in the eighth edition (1853). After Bouvier's death, the professors at Le Mans seminary eliminated many imperfections not noted by the papal revisers.

As a manual, the *Institutiones theologicae* was well adapted to the period of transition (1830–70) in ecclesiastical studies, during which they were recovering ground lost in the Gallican and Jansenist disturbances in the French Church. A mélange of history, liturgy, canon and civil law, and casuistry, the work contained serious weaknesses. However, clerical studies had become so disorganized in the course of the 18th century that the reestablishment of a solid curriculum was a very difficult problem. Moreover, the scarcity of vocations, the urgent need for priests, and limited financial resources had reduced seminary training to 3 years. Despite its faults, Bouvier's work served to free clerical education from the errors and the lethargy of the preceding period, and thereby opened the way to reforms achieved during the latter part of the 19th century.

Bibliography: A. L. SÉBAUX, *Vie de mgr. J. B. Bouvier, évêque du Mans* (2d ed. Paris 1889). F. DESHAYES, DTC 2.1:1117–19. L. CALENDINI, DHGE 10:276–277. M. B. BROWN, *History of the Sisters of Providence of Saint-Mary-of-the-Woods,* v. 1 (New York 1949).

[F. C. LEHNER]

BOVA, ST., Benedictine abbess, 7th century (feast, April 14). She was the first abbess of Saint-Pierre, Reims, where she introduced the *Benedictine rule. According to *Flodoard of Reims, she was the daughter of *Sigebert, King of Austrasia, and therefore would have been the sister of St. Baudry of Montfaucon, but the place and date of her birth are not known. Her feast is observed with that of her niece, Doda, who became a religious in the same monastery and probably succeeded her as abbess.

Bibliography: ActSS April 3:285–293. J. BOUETTE DE BLÉMUR, *L'Année bénédictine,* 6 v. (Paris 1667–73). P. DE BEAUVAIS, *Le Tableau . . . de sainte Bove et sainte Dode* (Reims 1655). Baudot-Chaussin 4:615–616. W. GRUNDHÖFER, LexThK² 2:633. A. D'HAENENS, BiblSanct 3:377–378.

[O. L. KAPSNER]

BOVILLUS, CAROLUS (CHARLES DE BOUELLES), humanist, philosopher, and theologian; b. Saucourt near Amiens, *c.* 1470; d. Noyon, *c.* 1553. A disciple of Jacques *Lefèvre d'Étaples, Bovillus traveled widely and came to know many of the intellectuals of his day. Some time after ordination, he became canon and professor of theology at Noyon. His interests were almost universal; he composed valuable works on geometry, physics, linguistics, philosophy, theology, and spirituality. His most important and most characteristic philosophical work is *De sapiente* [new ed. in E. Cassirer, *Individuum und Kosmos in der Philosophie der Renaissance* (Leipzig 1927)], a typical Renaissance document placing the concept of man at the center of reality. In his philosophico-theological system, Bovillus unites elements from the Aristotelian-traditional school, from *Pico della Mirandola, and from *Nicholas of Cusa. He is particularly indebted to Nicholas not only for his writings on philosophy and theology, but also for his works on spirituality. On the subject of prayer, Bovillus emphasized the necessity of internal dispositions [*De indifferentia orationis* (Paris 1529)] and the importance of the element of praise. He explained ecstasy as the overflow of the soul into God and the overflow of God into the soul. Though not immune from a certain rationalism, his synthesis, founded on the principles of Nicholas of Cusa, is Catholic in spirit.

Bibliography: F. STEGMÜLLER, LexThK² 2:627. A. VANSTEENBERGHE, DictSpirAscMyst 1:1894–95.

[M. A. ROCHE]

BOWET, HENRY, archbishop of York, civil servant; b. probably *c.* 1350; d. Cawood Castle, Yorkshire, Oct. 20, 1423. He was a doctor of canon and civil law by 1386. As a young man of knightly family he accompanied Henry *Despenser, Bishop of Norwich, on his crusade to Flanders (1382). From *c.* 1385 to the mid-1390s he was an official of the Roman Curia. During the parliamentary crisis under *Richard II, Bowet was accused by the Appellants in 1388 and was excluded from pardon. But with the restoration of Richard II to real power, he was back in the royal grace. Through John of Gaunt's good offices, he was made constable of Bordeaux (1396). When Bolingbroke (later King Henry IV) was banished, Bowet joined him in exile. Although he was subsequently condemned to death by a parliamentary commission set up by Richard II, his sentence was later commuted to perpetual exile and confiscation of all domains and benefices. But upon Henry IV's return to England and coronation, Bowet's possessions were returned, and Henry added new benefices. An integral part of the new regime, Bowet was made bishop of *Bath and Wells in 1401 and was briefly treasurer of England (1402). He was charged to defend Carmathen during Owain Glyndwr's rebellion. In 1407, despite his mismanagement of the Diocese of Bath and Wells (he left debts to his successor), he was translated to the archbishopric of *York, succeeding the executed Abp. Richard *Scrope. After his appointment to York, his interest and involvement in state matters declined. In 1411 the King remitted Bowet's debts in consideration of his diplomatic and state services.

Bibliography: Register from Bath and Wells, ed. T. S. HOLMES (Somerset Record Society 13; London 1899). T. F. TOUT, DNB 2:971–973. A. H. THOMPSON, DHGE 10:304–306. A. STEEL, *Richard II* (Cambridge, Eng. 1941; repr. 1963). A. H. THOMPSON, *The English Clergy and their Organization in the Later Middle Ages* (Oxford 1947). Emden Cambr 83–84.

[V. MUDROCH]

BOY BISHOP, the name given in the Middle Ages to the leader of the revels of the choirboys on Holy Innocents' Day (Dec. 28). The revels can be traced to the 10th century; their initial motive seems to have been the exaltation of the innocent and lowly. For the duration of the festival, the choirboys took over the senior positions in all the cathedral ceremonies and offices except the Mass. In these activities they were led by a boy bishop, or *episcopus puerorum,* whom they elected well in advance, often on December 6, the Feast of St. Nicholas. The custom, originally confined to the cathedrals, spread to large monastic and scholastic establishments, and to nearly all parishes throughout Europe, flourishing particularly in France, Germany, and England. In England the feast proved far more popular and enduring than the *Feast of Fools. It is amply recorded from the 13th century to the 16th, with full details for the ministry of the boy bishop provided by the Sarum breviary and processional. *See* RITES, ENGLISH MEDIEVAL.

The central rite was the great procession between Vespers and Compline on the Eve of Holy Innocents, after which the boys took the higher stalls and kept them until Vespers of the feast. On the Continent, at First Vespers, the *baculus* (staff of office) was handed over to the boy bishop while the *Deposuit potentes* of the Magnificat was being sung. In various places in England the boy bishop preached at Mass. Several church councils attempted to abolish or to restrain the abuses, which crept in probably through contamination by the revels of the subdeacons. The boy bishop was, however, less subject to criticism than the lord of fools, and the feast certainly preserved for a longer period the integrity of the original religious tradition. The custom was prohibited by the Council of Basle in 1435, but was too popular to be entirely suppressed. In England it was finally abolished by Elizabeth I; on the Continent traces of the feast survived into the 19th century.

See also FEAST OF ASSES.

Bibliography: E. K. CHAMBERS, *The Medieval Stage,* 2 v. (Oxford 1903) 1:336–371, 2:282–289. K. YOUNG, *The Drama of the Medieval Church,* 2 v. (Oxford 1933) 1:106–111, 552.

[M. N. MALTMAN]

BOYCOTT, the concerted withholding of, or inducing to withhold, social intercourse, custom, or services in order to exert pressure on the person against whom the boycott is directed. It is occasionally employed to coerce a third person who is in some way dependent upon the custom or services of the person boycotted. The word came into use in Ireland and derives from the name of Captain Charles Cunningham Boycott (1832–

97), a land agent for the Earl of Erne. When Boycott refused to meet the demands of his tenants in regard to their rent, they threatened him and his servants and interfered with his property. "Boycott" then came to be applied to group action intended to affect adversely the economic interests of another to obtain an economic, social, or political goal of the boycotting group.

Although occasionally it has been effectively used to promote some general social reform—e.g., the bus boycott in Montgomery, Ala., to achieve desegregation of the municipal bus system—the boycott in the U.S. has generally been associated with labor disputes. The courts have called strikes boycotts because a strike consists of a withholding by employees of services from the employer to achieve better wages, hours, or other working conditions. In labor-relations literature, however, strikes are rarely called boycotts. The term usually designates either a concerted withholding of purchase or custom, or a concerted refusal of employees, who perform all their other normal duties, to handle the products of certain concerns. Thus, employees who strike against their employer may also boycott his products. Other employees who have no dispute with their own employer may refuse to handle in the course of their work—that is, may boycott—goods or materials coming from the plant on strike.

An English statute enacted in 1800 (39, 40 George III 106) made illegal a combination of workmen for the purpose of obtaining higher wages, and to engage in such a combination was deemed a felonious conspiracy. A boycott could be enjoined by a court of equity if interference and coercion could be shown. The Pullman strike of 1894 was so enjoined, and the injunction was upheld by the U.S. Supreme Court (*In re Debs,* 158 U.S. 564). The Clayton Act was framed to alleviate this situation, but the boycott met the same fate under that law [*Duplex Printing Press Co. v. Deering,* 254 U.S. 443 (1921)]. Finally, the Norris-LaGuardia Act of 1932 deprived the Federal district courts of the power to issue such injunctions.

The Taft-Hartley Act (1947) and the Landrum-Griffin Act (1959), however, have made some labor boycotts illegal and permit the proscription of others by Federal injunction. Thus, today, the legality of a labor boycott must be determined by reference to statute law and relevant court decisions.

See also LABOR LAW, U.S.

[J. J. KINSELLA]

BOYLE, ROBERT, one of the founders of experimental science; b. Lismore Castle, Ireland, Jan. 25, 1627; d. Oxford, Dec. 30, 1691. His father was Richard Boyle, second Earl of Cork. Robert studied at Eton until age 14 and spent the next 14 years in Europe because of political strife in England. He was in Florence the winter Galileo died. After returning to Oxford, Boyle's writings and extensive experiments made him a founder of the new science. His collected works form seven volumes (ed. by Birch, 1744). Boyle's work in chemistry included development of a "corpuscular theory," which was a precursor of Dalton's atomic theory; experiments on flames and calcination; and one of the first clear definitions of a chemical element. In physics he extended Otto von Guericke's studies of air pressure. Boyle's Law describes the inverse relationship of volume and pressure. Boyle's presence at the found-

Robert Boyle, copy of a 17th-century portrait by the Dutch artist J. Kerseboom.

ing of the Royal Society in 1660 was politically important because of the connection of his family with the court. He was appointed to the first council of the Royal Society, and for the first 30 years of the society's existence Boyle was its chief scientist. Boyle was also an amateur theologian and student of medicine.

Bibliography: J. F. FULTON, *A Bibliography of the Honourable Robert Boyle, Fellow of the Royal Society* (2d ed. Oxford 1961). L. T. MORE, *Life and Works of the Honourable Robert Boyle* (Oxford 1944). M. BOAS, *Robert Boyle and 17th Century Chemistry* (Cambridge 1958). M. S. FISHER, *Robert Boyle, Devout Naturalist: A Study in Science and Religion in the 17th Century* (Philadelphia 1945). **Illustration credit:** National Portrait Gallery, London.

[M. A. J. JUNGBAUER]

BOYLE, ABBEY OF, former Cistercian abbey on the river Boyle, within the Diocese of Elphin, County Roscommon, Ireland (Latin, *Monasterium Buellense;* Gaelic, *Mainistir na Búille*). Originally the Celtic foundation Áth Da Loarg of Bishop Mac Cainne, it was taken over by *Cistercian monks from *Mellifont (in 1161), who had first established themselves at Greallach Da Iach in 1148. Many of its abbots became bishops; four of its monks died for the faith between 1580 and 1585. There is no evidence that the famous poet Donnchadh Mór Ó Dálaigh was abbot there. From it were founded Assaroe (1178) in the Diocese of Raphoe and Knockmoy (1190) in the Diocese of Tuam. At the time of its suppression (before 1569) it consisted of a church (consecrated in 1218), a belfry, a cloister, a hall, a dormitory, a cemetery, and a round tower (a survival of the Celtic foundation), and extensive lands (frequently mentioned in state papers dating from the end of the 16th and the beginning of the 17th centuries).

Bibliography: J. M. CANIVEZ, DHGE 10:315–316. M. V. RONAN, *Irish Martyrs of the Penal Laws* (London 1935) 199,

201. M. O'FLANAGAN, ed., *Letters Containing Information Relative to the Antiquities of the County of Roscommon,* 2 v. in 1 (Bray, Ire. 1927) 1:204–206, 224–236. G. MacNIOCAILL, *Na manaigh liatha in Éirinn, 1142–c.1600* (Dublin 1959).

[C. MC GRATH]

BRACKEN, THOMAS

BRACKEN, THOMAS, New Zealand poet, politician, and journalist; b. Clones, Ireland, Dec. 21, 1843; d. Dunedin, New Zealand, Feb. 16, 1898. Born of Irish Protestant parents, Thomas Bracken was orphaned at the age of 9. In 1855 he went to Melbourne, Australia, where he worked successively on an uncle's farm, as a chemist's apprentice, and as a sheep-shearer. He moved to Dunedin in 1869 and entered journalism. In 1875, he helped establish and edit the *Sunday Advertiser,* whose popularity depended largely upon his own contributions, signed "Paddy Murphy." "God Defend New Zealand," adopted later as the country's national song, and "Not Understood," his best-known poem, first appeared in the *Advertiser.* From 1885 to 1890, he edited the *Dunedin Evening Herald.*

Bracken became the most popular 19th-century New Zealand versifier, treating commonplaces in simple language. His collection *Behind the Tomb* (1871) was followed by several others, the most ambitious being the sumptuously produced *Musings in Maoriland* (1892), dedicated to Lord Tennyson and prefaced by the Governor General, Sir George Grey. Bracken also published volumes of political and social comment in the manner of Finley Peter *Dunne's "Mr. Dooley": *Paddy Murphy's Annual* (1886) and *Tom Bracken's Annual* (1896–97). He served two terms in Parliament as Member for Dunedin Central (1881–84, 1886–87).

Bracken was a kindly, somewhat Bohemian figure. (On one occasion he lightened proceedings in Parliament with a comic song.) His later years were clouded by financial troubles. He gave stimulus to New Zealand literature by his encouragement of writers in the various journals he edited. He was reared a Protestant and was for a time a Freemason, but his Irish ancestry gave him a particular sympathy for New Zealand Irish Catholics. As a Member of Parliament he campaigned for assistance to Catholic schools, and in 1887 he moved a resolution supporting Irish Home Rule. When Bp. Moran founded the *New Zealand Tablet* in 1873, Bracken canvassed for shares with conspicuous success. He became a Catholic in 1896, and died in the faith. (*See* CATHOLIC PRESS, WORLD SURVEY, 20.)

Bibliography: G. H. SCHOLEFIELD, *Dictionary of New Zealand Biography* (Wellington, N.Z. 1940).

[J. C. REID]

BRACTON, HENRY DE

English cleric and jurist (known also as Henry of Bratton); b. Bratton Fleming, Devon, England, *c.* 1210; d. by September 1268. He came of a well-to-do family from Devon and quite possibly studied at the University of *Oxford. He was in orders and held various ecclesiastical *benefices, becoming canon, prebendary, and eventually (1264) chancellor of the Diocese of *Exeter. Bracton was trained in law and devoted much of his career to its administration and study, first entering the service of a noted judge, William Raleigh (d. 1250). When Raleigh was nominated bishop of Norwich in 1239, Bracton transferred to the service of King *Henry III and became a judge himself in 1244, serving for the most part in the southwestern counties.

He was a member of the King's Council in 1255–56 and after the Barons' War was named a special commissioner to settle the claims of the disinherited supporters of *Simon de Montfort in February, 1267. He was buried in the nave of Exeter Cathedral, where he founded a chantry for two chaplains.

Bracton's fame rests chiefly on his writings, *De legibus et consuetudinibus Angliae* (ed. G. E. Woodbine, New Haven 1915– , 4 v. to date) and a *Note Book* (ed. F. W. Maitland, 3 v. London 1887), which together form one of the most important attempts to organize and rationalize English medieval *common law, which had evolved from classical prototypes. The *De legibus et consuetudinibus Angliae* may have been begun as early as 1239, and Bracton was still revising it at the time of his death. Surviving MSS are often corrupted by interpolations of later editors. It begins with an analysis of the principles of English law and then cites some 450 cases exemplifying the practice and procedure of the courts. The *Note Book* contains some 2,000 cases that Bracton heard during his years on the bench. The complex interrelationship of *rex* and *lex,* king and law, is treated but not completely resolved. The work of this English churchman had an impact on later constitutional development, especially with regard to appeal to legal precedent. Not until Blackstone was there a more comprehensive treatment of common law.

Bibliography: H. U. KANTOROWICZ, *Bractonian Problems* (Glasgow 1941). C. H. McILWAIN, "The Present Status of the Problem of the Bracton Text," *Harvard Law Review* 57 (1943) 220–240. F. SCHULTZ, "Critical Studies on B.'s Treatise," *Law Quarterly Review* 59 (1943) 172–180; "A New Approach to B.," *Seminar* 2 (1944) 41–50; "B. on Kingship," *EngHistRev* 60 (1945) 136–176. G. POST, "A Romano-Canonical Maxim *Quod omnes tangit* in B.," *Traditio* 4 (1946) 197–251. G. T. LAPSLEY, "B. and the Authorship of the *addicio de cartis,*" *EngHistRev* 62 (1947) 1–19. S. J. T. MILLER, "The Position of the King in B. and Beaumanoir," *Speculum* 31 (1956) 263–296. Holdsworth HEL 2:239–290. E. KANTOROWICZ, *The King's Two Bodies* (Princeton 1957) 143–192. Emden 1:240–241. T. F. T. PLUCKNETT, *Early English Legal Literature* (Cambridge, Eng. 1958) 61–79. B. TIERNEY, "B. on Government," *Speculum* 38 (1963) 295–317. H. G. RICHARDSON, "Tancred, Raymond and B.," *Eng HistRev* 59 (1944) 376–384; "Azo, Drogheda and B.," *ibid.* 22–47; "Studies in B.," *Traditio* 6 (1948) 61–104; *Bracton: The Problem of his Text* (Seldon Society Supplementary Series 2; London 1965).

[B. J. COMASKEY]

BRADFORD, WILLIAM

BRADFORD, WILLIAM, Pilgrim father and governor of Plymouth Colony, Mass.; b. Austerfield, Yorkshire, England, 1590; d. Plymouth, 1657. Although he was only 16 years old when the Puritans organized their church at Scrooby, his piety and knowledge soon made him one of the leaders of the congregation. With the rest of the Scrooby congregation he went to Holland (1609–20), where he developed a deep knowledge of theology. He arrived in Plymouth (1620) on the "Mayflower" and, following the death of the first governor, was elected his successor (April 1621), remaining governor for 30 of the next 36 years. Although Calvinist in theology, he was in practice quite liberal for the period. He took part in legislation against the Quakers, but declared "it is too great arrogance for any man or church to think that he or they have so sounded the word of God to the bottom." His famous *History of Plymouth Plantation,* not intended for publication but probably only for the use of his family, was begun in 1630 and completed probably in 1650. It was printed in full for the first time in 1856, although the manuscript was available to historians before that time.

Bibliography: V. H. PALTSITS, DAB 2:564–566. P. G. E. MILLER and T. H. JOHNSON, eds., *The Puritans,* 2 v. (New York 1938; pa. 1965). B. SMITH, *Bradford of Plymouth* (Philadelphia 1951).

[E. DELANEY]

BRADLEY, DENIS MARY, bishop; b. County Kerry, Ireland, Feb. 25, 1846; d. Manchester, N.H., Dec. 13, 1903. His mother brought the family to Manchester after the father's death in Ireland. Denis was taught by Thomas Cochran, a pioneer Catholic educator, and in 1864 entered Holy Cross College, Worcester, Mass. He subsequently attended Georgetown College (now University), Washington, D.C., and St. Joseph's Seminary, Troy, N.Y. After ordination on July 3, 1871, he was appointed curate at the cathedral in Portland, Maine, and he later became chancellor of the diocese and rector of the cathedral. His interest in the temperance movement gained him support from the non-Catholics of Portland. In 1884, after serving as pastor of St. Joseph's church in Manchester, he was appointed to the new Diocese of *Manchester and consecrated by Abp. John J. Williams of Boston, Mass. Bradley helped to revitalize Catholicism in New Hampshire. In addition to administering his diocese and sponsoring a building program, he dealt successfully with problems created by *nativism and labor dissatisfaction. He also helped to promote the growth of Catholic schools in the state.

Bibliography: M. H. DOWD, *Life of Denis M. Bradley* (Manchester, N.H. 1905).

[J. L. MORRISON]

BRADLEY, FRANCIS HERBERT

A major English philosopher of the post-Hegelian school of monistic idealism; b. Clapham, Jan. 30, 1846; d. Sept. 18, 1924. Bradley was the fourth child of Rev. Charles Bradley, a popular evangelical preacher, by his second wife, Emma Linton. A. C. Bradley, the noted literary critic and scholar, was F. H. Bradley's younger brother.

Life. Bradley was educated at Cheltenham (1856–61) and Marlborough (1861–63), where his half-brother, George Granville Bradley, was headmaster. In 1865 he went to University College, Oxford, where he achieved a first in classical moderations in 1867 but dropped to a second class in *literae humaniores* in 1869. This reversal may have been due to his increasing disenchantment with the empiricist orthodoxy, stemming from J. *Locke, G. *Berkeley, and D. *Hume and continued in J. S. *Mill, which then dominated philosophical England and Oxford and whose hegemony Bradley was to overthrow during his lifetime. In spite of the 1869 setback, the next year saw him appointed to an exclusively research fellowship at Merton College, Oxford, with no teaching or lecturing duties, which he held for the rest of his life. In 1871 Bradley was the victim of a kidney inflammation, which became chronic; for the remainder of his long life he was never fully well and was often in pain. He wintered usually on the Riviera or the English coasts, but conscientiously returned to all college meetings. Chronic illness and later deafness combined to make Bradley something of a recluse, although within a small circle of friends he was both liked and a little feared. He is said to have been intolerant of stupidity; indeed, he became one of the greatest masters of philosophical polemic in history. The poet T. S. Eliot considered him one of the most perfect stylists in the English language. The increasing influence of his writings led to many honors, both at home and abroad, culminating in the Order of Merit in 1924.

Thought. Bradley's first book, *Ethical Studies,* was published when he was 30. It is an all-out attack against the reigning doctrines of English *utilitarianism, especially in the famous criticism of *hedonism in the third essay. *Ethical Studies* is the most Hegelian of Bradley's works, not only in its exploitation of the notion of the "concrete universal" but in its dialectical structure, ranging particular and partial moral views against each other as theses and antitheses and seeking their correctives in higher viewpoints. For Bradley, morality is self-realization, and the inadequacies in this respect of hedonism, of the Kantian identification of self-realization with activity of a purely formal will, and even of the self as equated with the social organism, are all exposed. Bradley goes on to maintain that morality involves a collision between self-assertion, in the interest of comprehensiveness and system, and self-sacrifice, in the interest of higher ends. The contradictory demands of morality call for transcendence in religion, in the assertion of a higher divine will. But Bradley is unwilling to identify God, understood as personal, with ultimate, Absolute Reality. Thought about God, like all thought, is inexorably relational, and to be in relationship is to have only a compromised, an appearance mode of existing that, when analyzed, exhibits contradiction.

The later works of Bradley develop, in the contexts of logic, epistemology, and metaphysics, the schism between appearance and reality. Negatively, Bradley was devoted, like *Parmenides and *Zeno of Elea, to showing the self-destructive implication of any pluralism, whether of externally or internally related entities. Beginning with a felt unity of experience beneath relations, thought, separating always the "what" and the "that," seeks hopelessly to reunite existence and formal content by endlessly extending the system of relations. Bradley's idealism does not identify thought and reality, but it finds Absolute Reality in an experience that transcends thought and that is beyond all relation. The content of the experience that is Absolute Reality is not other than the content of the experience of finite centers that appear only, but the mode of synthesis or fusion is nonrelational.

The absolute monism of Bradley's doctrine is clearly unacceptable to Christian theists. But the dialectical power of his thought can teach all philosophers much.

See also IDEALISM.

Bibliography: Works. *Ethical Studies* (Oxford 1876; 2d ed. 1927); *The Principles of Logic,* 2 v. (London 1883; 2d ed. rev. New York 1922); *Appearance and Reality* (London 1893; 2d ed. 1897); *Essays on Truth and Reality* (Oxford 1914); *Collected Essays,* 2 v. (Oxford 1935), detailed bibliography of Bradley's writings in v.1.
Study. R. WOLLHEIM, *F. H. Bradley* (Penguin Bks. Baltimore 1959).

[L. J. ESLICK]

BRADY, MATTHEW FRANCIS, bishop and educator; b. Waterbury, Conn., Jan. 15, 1893; d. Burlington, Vt., Sept. 20, 1959. He was the son of John and Catherine (Caffrey) Brady. After early education in the public schools of Waterbury, he attended St. Thomas Seminary, Bloomfield, Conn.; the American

College, Louvain, Belgium; and St. Bernard Seminary, Rochester, N.Y. He was ordained in Hartford, Conn., on June 10, 1916, and served as assistant pastor at Sacred Heart, New Haven, until 1922, except for 8 months as U.S. Army chaplain during World War I. From 1922 to 1932 he taught English, French, and Sacred Scripture at St. Thomas Seminary, Bloomfield, returning then to pastoral work at St. Rita's, Hamden. In 1934 he was appointed to the archdiocesan staff of Hartford, where, as director of the Confraternity of Christian Doctrine (CCD), he organized the Fourth National Catechetical Congress, held in Hartford in October 1938.

Appointed bishop of Burlington on July 30, 1938, he was consecrated in his cathedral on October 26 by Abp. Amleto Cicognani, then U.S. apostolic delegate. In Burlington, Brady established the CCD, a diocesan school department, a bureau of information, the Catholic Boy Scouts, and the Junior Catholic Daughters of America. He gave strong leadership to Catholic Charities and was host to the First New England Regional Congress of the CCD, which was held in Burlington. During World War II he established centers for servicemen and women. On Nov. 11, 1944, Brady was transferred to the See of Manchester, N.H., as fifth ordinary. Besides founding Catholic Charities (1946) and a diocesan labor institute, he established 30 parishes, built 47 churches, 11 grammar schools, 5 high schools, 3 homes for the aged, 2 large summer camps, 11 convents, 29 rectories, and 18 parish halls.

On the national level, Brady served as episcopal chairman of the department of education, National Catholic Welfare Conference (1950–56), and president general of the National Catholic Educational Association (1957–58). In 1945 he became a member of the episcopal committee of the CCD, and at the death of Abp. E. V. O'Hara, replaced him as its chairman (October 1956), an office Brady held until his own death 3 years later.

[W. H. PARADIS]

BRADY, NICHOLAS FREDERIC, financier, philanthropist; b. Albany, N.Y., Oct. 25, 1878; d. Philadelphia, Pa., March 27, 1930. He was the son of Anthony Nicholas and Marcia (Myers) Brady. After his education at Albany Academy and at Yale University, New Haven, Conn., he entered the public utilities business founded by his father. In 1906 he became a Catholic and in the same year married Genevieve Garvan, of Hartford, Conn. At his father's death he was left in control of the family fortune, which he soon doubled. As a financier Brady displayed skill in merging public utility companies and in the management of diversified corporations; during his career he became director of more than 100 concerns. As a pioneer in labor relations he advocated extended security benefits for employees. In 1929 he received the Ordine Supremo del Christe, in recognition of his numerous charities and for his contributions to the study of the moral problems of capitalism; he was the first U.S. citizen to receive this papal award. He contributed the funds for the construction of the Jesuit novitiate at Wernersville, Pa.; among his many other beneficiaries were Yale University and the Vatican.

Bibliography: J. J. DALY, *Nicholas Frederic Brady* (New York 1935).

[J. L. MORRISON]

BRADY, WILLIAM MAZIERE, Irish ecclesiastical historian; b. Dublin, Ireland, Jan. 8, 1825; d. Rome, March 19, 1894. Brady, who came from a distinguished Protestant-Irish family, entered Trinity College, Dublin (1842), and received there an M.A. (1853) and a D.D. (1863). After taking orders in the Church of *Ireland (1848), he served as curate in Maynooth and then as rector and vicar in the Dioceses of Dublin, Limerick, Cloyne, and Meath. He served also as chaplain to liberal lords lieutenant of Ireland such as Clarendon, St. Germans, Carlisle, and Spencer. In 1851 he married a widow, Frances (Walker) O'Reilly. Brady published *Clerical and Parochial Records of Cork, Cloyne and Ross* (3 v. 1863–64), the preparation of which convinced him of the unhistorical nature of the Church of Ireland's claim to continuity from Celtic times. Later works, notably *The Alleged Conversion of the Irish Bishops at the Succession of Queen Elizabeth* (1866) and *State Papers concerning the Irish Church* (1868), received a hostile reception from his coreligionists. His argument for the disestablishment of the Church of Ireland, which appeared in books and in articles in *Fraser's Magazine* and *The Contemporary,* contained massive factual information that materially assisted William *Gladstone in carrying disestablishment through Parliament (1869–71). Brady pursued his researches on the Irish Church in the Vatican Archives in Rome, where he and his wife were received into the Catholic Church (1873). Subsequent publications included *Episcopal Succession in England, Scotland and Ireland* (3 v. 1867–77), a work impressive in its day, but lacking in meticulousness by present standards. Brady's studies and publications altered substantially the accepted English identification of the Church of Ireland with the early Irish Church and strengthened the links between Irish national tradition and the Roman Church. But his later works, notably *Rome and Fenianism* (1883) and *Anglo-Roman Papers* (1890), were uncritical in sifting sources. Pius IX and Leo XIII honored Brady by making him a private chamberlain.

[R. D. EDWARDS]

BRAGA, ARCHDIOCESE OF (BRACHARENSIS), metropolitan see since 1101, in north *Portugal. In 1963 it had 832 parishes, 820 secular and 165 religious priests, 336 men in 21 religious houses, 928 women in 70 convents, and 947,250 Catholics; it is 1,907 square miles in area. Its seven suffragan sees, which had 2,008 secular and 288 religious priests,

The "Old Convent" in the city of Braga, Portugal.

2,357 sisters, and 3,405,000 Catholics, were: Aveiro (1774–1881, 1938), Bragança (created in 1545), Coimbra (restored in 1080), Lamego (restored in 1147), Porto (restored in 1112), Vila Real (1922), and Viseu (restored in 1147). The city of Braga (present population 41,000), as *Bracara Augusta,* was the Roman administrative center of north Lusitania.

The acts of the first Council of Toledo mention a Bishop Paternus during the *Priscillianist controversy. Braga was still important when St. *Martin (d. 579) converted the *Suevi, who made it their capital. Until 650 its episcopal jurisdiction extended south of the Douro, but with the invasion of the Moors (8th century) and raids by Northmen (10th–11th century) its bishops resided in Lugo, until Bishop Peter restored the diocese (1070). From 1101, when St. *Gerald made Braga a metropolitan see, until 1199, it sought, against *Santiago de Compostela, which had succeeded *Mérida as metropolitan, to preside over all Portuguese sees. Of eight suffragan sees in 1199, Porto, Coimbra, Viseu, Tuý, Orense, Mondoñedo, Lugo, and Astorga, the last five became independent in the *Western Schism. Braga struggled to gain primacy in the peninsula also from *Toledo until a papal bull imposed silence on both sides in 1218; but the matter was raised again at the Council of Trent. From 1122 to 1790 the bishops were invested by the kings with temporal authority, but from the 13th to the 16th century the bishops had conflicts with kings and the cathedral chapter.

Bishops of the "Portuguese Rome" include: St. *Fructuosus (656); the Cluniac Maurice Burdin (antipope Gregory VIII, 1118–21); John Peculiar (1138–75); *Peter of Spain (1273, later Pope *John XXI); Fernando da Guerra (1416–67); the administrator and builder Diogo de Sousa (1505–32); the spiritual author and historian Bartolomeu dos Mártires, OP (1559–81), who founded the seminary in 1571; the historian Rodrigo da Cunha (1627–36); Caetano Brandão (1790–1805), who protected agriculture and industry; and Manuel Vieira de Matos (1915–32), who promoted church activities and revived the liturgy of Braga.

The Romanesque cathedral, consecrated in 1089 and 1592, was restored in the 18th century. Other monuments are the 7th-century Church of St. Fructuosus, the 16th-century chapel of the Coimbras, the neighboring 11th-century Benedictine monastery of Tibães, and the nearby shrine of Our Lady of Sameiro. Provincial synods were held at Braga in 561, 572, 675, 1148, 1262, 1426, and 1566.

Bibliography: J. A. FERREIRA, *Fastos episcopaes da igreja primacial de Braga,* 4 v. (Braga 1928–35). M. MARTINS, *Correntes da filosofia religiosa em Braga nos s. IV a VII* (Porto 1950). A. DE J. DA COSTA, *O bispo D. Pedro e a organização da diocese de Braga,* 2 v. (Coimbra 1959). *Bracara Augusta* (1950–   ). *O distrito de Braga* (1961–   ). A. PIMENTA, DHGE 10:352–361. AnnPont (1965) 73. **Illustration credits:** Photos, "SNI-YAN."

[J. MATTOSO]

BRAGA, RITE OF

This rite takes its name from the city and archdiocese in Portugal where it is found. It is limited to the diocese itself; all seven suffragan sees of Braga follow the Roman rite. The origins of the rite are very obscure; it is most difficult to trace the history of any particular practice or custom. Little is known of liturgical practices before the 6th century when Bishop Profuturus consulted Rome about the rite of Baptism, the formula of Consecration, and the date of Easter. Even though there exists documentation of Pope Vigilius's (6th century) reply touching Baptism and the Canon of the Mass according to the Roman usage, it is not known to what extent the Roman usages were subsequently followed at Braga. Vigilius sent only suggestions; he did not impose the Roman usage. A century later the Mozarabic liturgy became common in most of the Iberian peninsula, prescribed as it was by the Visigoths. In contrast, the Roman rite was imposed by Rome in the 11th century. But since the Roman rite was brought to the peninsula at this time by the monks of Cluny, it was well mixed with Gallican customs. The rite of Braga is rooted in this varied background and there is no evidence with which to relate with certitude its special practices to any historical moment. The ancient roots and character of the rite have always been stressed by official documents confirming its continuance. Nevertheless, through the years the Roman rite often threatened to overtake it in practice, especially for private usage, as in the low Mass and the Office. As late as 1918 it was necessary for a diocesan synod to insist that the liturgical books of the rite were of obligation. A new edition of the Breviary was approved by the Holy See in 1919, and a new Missal in 1924. The rite of Braga was one of the exceptions cited by Pius V in 1570 in the bull *Quam primum* imposing the Roman Missal on the churches of the West.

There are few particulars to be pointed out concerning the rite of Braga. Marian devotion is strong; the preparations for Mass and the final prayer after Mass

The Basilica of Our Lady of the Olive Tree at Guimarães in the Archdiocese of Braga, Portugal.

include Marian elements. The Calendar is close to that of the Roman rite, the greatest variations being in the feasts of the saints. In the Mass ritual, the chalice is prepared with wine and water before the introductory prayers at the low Mass, while at the sung Mass it is prepared between the Epistle and Gospel at the bench. If there are offerings by the people, they are received after the incensations in the Offertory rite. The rubrics prescribe the sermon at the same place, between the incensations and the washing of the hands. There are three Elevations, one after the Consecration, a second at the beginning of the Our Father, and a third just before the Communion of the celebrant. It is not difficult to see the rite of Braga as a mere variant of the Roman rite.

The most reliable sources for the rite of Braga are the Missal of Mateus, discovered in 1925, and a Pontifical that dates from the 12th century. The Missal of Mateus is of 15th-century usage and dates probably from the 10th or 11th century.

Bibliography: A. A. King, *Liturgies of the Primatial Sees* (Milwaukee 1957) 155–285. J. A. Ferreira, *Estudos histórico-litúrgicos: Os ritos particulares das Igrejas de Braga e Toledo* (Coimbra 1924). A. G. Ribeiro de Vasconcelos, *Notas Litúrgico-Bracarenses: Congresso litúrgico nacional* (Braga 1927) 177–255.

[R. F. LECHNER]

BRAHE, TYCHO, most accurate astronomical observer from the time of Hipparchus to the invention of the telescope; b. Knudstrup, Scania, Denmark, Dec. 14, 1546; d. Prague, Bohemia, Oct. 24, 1601. The son of Otto and Beate (Bille) and a member of the nobility, Tycho attended the University of Copenhagen from 1559 to 1562, when he was sent to that of Leipzig. Except for two short trips to Denmark, he remained away until 1570, visiting Leipzig, Rostock, Wittenberg, Basle, and Augsburg.

Pursuing astronomical interests aroused at Copenhagen, he soon realized the need for continuous, precise observations. To ensure accuracy, he built huge instruments with divisions for each minute of arc, later applying transversal divisions. A supernova in Cassiopea in 1572 permanently focused his attention on the heavens. He lectured at the University of Copenhagen before revisiting foreign countries.

In 1576 the King of Denmark granted him an island, on which Tycho built two observatories, a printing press, and a paper mill. There he observed the comet of 1577 and six later ones, star positions (for a catalogue), the moon (discovering the third inequality), planets, and meteorologic phenomena. He was visited by scholars and nobility and carried on a vast correspondence.

Although convinced of the untenability of the Aristotelian system of the universe because he found the star of 1572 and the comets supralunar and because the observed motions of the comets necessitated discarding the notion of crystalline spheres, Tycho rejected the Copernican doctrine because of Scripture and because he could not conceive of a universe so large that his accurate observations would not have detected an apparent displacement of the fixed stars if the earth moved. He suggested a system in which the planets circled the sun while the sun in its motion circled the stationary earth.

After disagreement with the Danish ruler, Tycho left Denmark in 1597, finding refuge under Emperor Rudolph II in Prague, where he died in 1601, shortly after being joined by a young assistant, Johann *Kepler, who later used Tycho's observations to derive the laws of planetary motion.

Bibliography: *Opera omnia*, ed. J. L. E. Dreyer, 15 v. (Copenhagen 1913–29). J. L. E. Dreyer, *Tycho Brahe: A Picture of Scientific Life and Work in the 16th Century* (Edinburgh 1890; pa. New York 1963). C. D. Hellman, "Was Tycho Brahe as Influential as He Thought?" *British Journal for the History of Science* (1963) 295–324.

[C. D. HELLMAN]

BRAHMAN, meaning originally "sacred utterance," came to signify the "sacred power" believed to reside in the ancient Vedic sacrifice in Hinduism, and then by a natural transition of thought the sacred power that sustains the universe. In the Upanishads and in all later Hindu thought the word is used to signify the Supreme Being or the Absolute. The Brahman is conceived as pervading the universe in such a way that it can be said, "All this [world] is Brahman." Again, it is said, "As a spider comes out with its thread or as small sparks come forth from a fire," so all this world comes forth from the Brahman. But at the same time, lest this should be taken in a material sense, it is said, "Brahman is not this, not this" (*neti, neti*); it is beyond all material forms. It is described as "consisting of nothing but knowledge," and again, as "knowledge and bliss." Hence, in later philosophy it came to be defined as "being-knowledge-bliss" (*saccidānanda*). Conceived as knowledge and bliss, Brahman is not the object of thought but the subject; it is "that by which all things are known"; it is the "Knower," the "Ruler within," the "immortal Person" (*puruṣa*). Thus, Hindu philosophy was led to its great affirmation: "The Brahman is the Atman," or Self. That is, the ultimate ground of the soul or self is identical with the ultimate ground of the universe. This, in one form or other, is the basic doctrine of Hindu philosophy.

See also INDIAN PHILOSOPHY; HINDUISM.

[B. GRIFFITHS]

BRAHMS, JOHANNES

Eminent composer of the late 19th century; b. Hamburg, Germany, May 7, 1833; d. Vienna, April 3, 1897. The standard biographies have traced the influences of poverty and sordid childhood circumstances on the composer's youth, character, and creative intuitions. It is clear that his lifelong friendships and correspondence with Clara Schumann (*see* SCHUMANN, ROBERT) and the music *amateur* Theodor Billroth, among others, testify to his capacity for warm personal loyalties; and that in matters of musical opinion he remained true to the inner necessities of personal conviction, despite strong opposition from partisans of *Liszt, R. *Wagner, and *Bruckner. (Brahms was championed by the critic Eduard Hanslick, whose reviews kept the musical world of that day in a lively ferment of pro- and anti-Brahms debate.) From a religious point of view, however, still to be settled are (1) the relation, if any, between Brahms's "form-consciousness" and his ethical background, and (2) the influence of his type of Protestant piety on such works as *A German Requiem*, a non-liturgical setting of texts from Luther's translation of the Bible (1857–63). "The chaste Johannes," as Wag-

Johannes Brahms, portrait by Karl Jagermann after a photograph made in 1866 or 1867.

ner called him, may, in rejecting the Symphonic Poem of Liszt and the Music Drama of Wagner, have been motivated by ethical convictions that favored the "orderliness" of Beethovenian sonata-form over the more amorphous cyclic utterances of *Berlioz and Liszt, although the *idée fixe* of Berlioz and the "motivic cell" of Liszt, like the *leitmotiv* of Wagner, led to a "formlessness" that was more apparent than real. Brahms, too, offered a contemporary and personal yet basically traditional solution to the problem of form in his four symphonies, four concertos (of symphonic proportions), and some two dozen major works in varying chamber combinations, as well as in more than 250 songs and a rich legacy of piano pieces. It may perhaps still be argued whether he should be labeled as a "classical romanticist" or a "romantic classicist" within his own compellingly expressive but rigorously disciplined personal idiom. Schoenberg saw in Brahams's epic-lyric mastery of structural techniques a "development of the musical language" unequaled since Mozart.

The mid-20th-century attitude of professional musicology toward the philosophical discipline of aesthetics hardly admits, yet, of a style-critical analysis that could "prove" the point of Brahms's Protestant piety as a tangible factor in the *Requiem*. One may instinctively sense, nevertheless, not only the presence of the elegiac, but also of the pessimistic in this and corresponding works, noting with Geiringer that in the *Requiem* "all mention of the name of Christ is expressly avoided." An early *Missa canonica* (c. 1855) survives in only

its brief *Benedictus*. Settings of *O bone Jesu, Adoramus te,* and *Regina coeli* (Opus 37) are among the composer's somewhat unjustly neglected minor works. Eleven Chorale Preludes for Organ (Opus 122) brought his *oeuvre* to a close (1896) with a setting of "O Welt, ich muss dich lassen" (Oh world, I must leave you).

See also MUSIC, SACRED, HISTORY OF, 7.

Bibliography: *Briefwechsel,* ed. Deutsche Brahms-Gesellschaft, 16 v. (Berlin 1907–22). E. EVANS, *Historical, Descriptive, and Analytical Account of the Entire Work of Johannes Brahms,* 4 v. (London 1912–36). M. KALBECK, *Johannes Brahms,* 4 v. (Berlin 1904–14). K. GEIRINGER, *Johannes Brahms: His Life and Work,* tr. H. B. WEINER and B. MIALL (2d ed. New York 1947). P. C. LANDORMY, *Brahms* (Paris 1948). P. MIES, "Brahms und die katholische Kirchenmusik," *Gregoriusblatt* 53.4 (Düsseldorf 1930). S. KROSS, *Die Chorwerke von Johannes Brahms* (Berlin 1958). A. SCHOENBERG, "Brahms the Progressive," in *Style and Idea* (New York 1950). R. GERBER, MusGG 2:184–212; "Das Deutsche Requiem als Dokument Brahmscher Frömmigkeit," *Deutsche Musikleben* (1959) No. 7–10. P. F. RADCLIFFE, Grove DMM 1:870–903. Young ChorTrad. Láng MusWC. **Illustration credit:** Historishche Museum der Stadt Wien.

[F. J. BURKLEY]

BRAIN

The simplest form of the nervous system occurs in invertebrate animals in which only a few nerve cells form simple chains and nerve nets. In more complex animals the nervous system becomes more and more highly developed, with specialization into a central portion consisting of the brain and spinal cord and a peripheral part that connects with all parts of the body. The vertebrate animals are characterized by the presence of a more complicated nervous system that develops from a hollow tube of tissue in the embryo and retains a system of cavities in the adult condition. The head end of this tube becomes enlarged into the brain, with its internal cavities or ventricles. Within the vertebrate group there is an ascending complexity of the brain, culminating in man.

Brain Structure. Located in the cranial portion of the skull, the brain is surrounded by coverings or meninges and further protected by the shock-absorbing cerebrospinal fluid. Specialized tissue in the ventricles produces the cerebrospinal fluid, which then finds its way out to the space surrounding the brain. The brain is composed of nerve cells and their processes and of supporting nervous tissue called neuroglia. Functionally and anatomically the brain may be divided into three main parts: the brainstem, the cerebellum, and the cerebrum.

The brainstem is the direct upward continuation of the spinal cord. Most of the cranial nerves arise from the brainstem, which has many pathways for nerve impulses connecting with the spinal cord, cerebellum, and cerebrum. Long pathways through the brainstem connect the cerebrum and spinal cord. Central control for many body functions, including respiration and the regulation of the heart, and many reflexes for muscular movements involve areas located here. Developmentally and anatomically, the brainstem is subdivided into the medulla oblongata, the pons, the midbrain or mesencephalon, and the diencephalon. The diencephalon is surrounded by the very large cerebrum. Two important parts of the diencephalon are the thalamus and the hypothalamus. The thalamus consists of a pair of oval-shaped masses of nerve cells that form an important part of the pathways for sensory impulses from nearly every part of the body. The hypothalamus is the main center

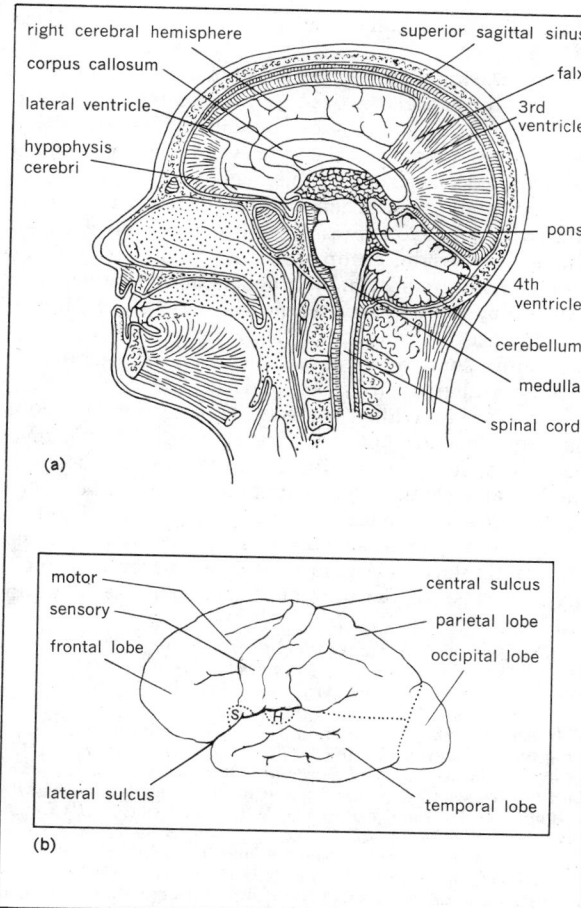

threefold by broad ridges and grooves called gyri and sulci, respectively. Each cerebral hemisphere is subdivided into five incompletely separated lobes: frontal, parietal, occipital, temporal, and insular. Functions of the cerebrum include the initiation of muscular movements and the reception of incoming sensory impulses. It is generally agreed that most sensations become conscious only when they reach the cerebral cortex although pain and possibly the affective aspect of other sensations enter consciousness from the thalamus. Deep in the cerebral hemispheres are masses of nerve cells known as the basal ganglia, which aid in the regulation of muscular movements in conjunction with the cerebellum and the cerebral cortex.

Size, Localization of Function. The size of the adult brain varies widely. Kuntz lists the brain weights of certain distinguished individuals as being between 1,207 and 2,012 g with an average weight for the adult white male of 1,360 g and for the adult white female of 1,260 g. There is apparently little correlation with intelligence, provided that the brain is at least minimum size.

How the mind functions through the brain is perplexing. Injuries or deficiencies of specific parts of the brain often result in deficiencies of specific mental functions. Loss of memory of the immediate past is common in the aged. Probably this results from impairment of the blood supply. Various kinds of aphasia result from lesions to areas of the parietal lobe. Loss of vision follows injury to the occipital lobe. Much of the frontal lobe cortex is concerned with muscular movements of the body, and destruction of the front part of the frontal lobe results in personality changes.

Bibliography: H. A. CATES and J. V. BASMAJIAN, *Primary Anatomy* (4th ed. Baltimore 1960) ch. 10, "Nervous System." A. KUNTZ, *A Textbook of Neuro-Anatomy* (5th ed. Philadelphia 1950). **Illustration credits:** Figs. *a* and *b* after H. A. Cates and J. V. Basmajian, *Primary Anatomy.*

[R. H. WEBBER]

(a) Brain in situ in sagittal section. Cut-away window shows part of medial aspect of right cerebral hemisphere. (b) Lateral aspect of left cerebral hemisphere, with centers for hearing (H) and speech (S) bordering lateral sulcus.

for controlling the visceral or autonomic functions of the body. An important endocrine gland, the hypophysis or pituitary body, is attached to its lower side.

The cerebellum comprises about one-tenth of the total brain weight in man. It is a much folded structure with a layer of nerve cells immediately beneath the surface forming the cerebellar cortex. Deep in the cerebellum are other masses of nerve cells forming the cerebellar nuclei. The cerebellum functions in balance and in the regulation of muscular movements. The part of the inner ear concerned with balancing or orientation of the individual in relationship to space and to gravity sends information into the cerebellum, which is then integrated with sensory impulses from other parts of the body. Information from muscles, tendons, and joints indicating the position of parts of the body and the state of muscular contractions forms an important part of the entering sensory impulses. Regulation of muscular movements by the cerebellum is correlated with conscious and volitional control originating from the cerebrum.

The highest levels of nervous activity occur in the cerebrum. This largest part of the brain is divided into two nearly equal halves, the cerebral hemispheres. Several layers of nerve cells immediately beneath the surface form the cerebral cortex, which is very highly developed in man. The surface area is increased about

BRAINWASHING

A prolonged, calculated, psychological process, used by Communist countries, designed to distort and erase an individual's past belief and concepts and to substitute new ones, without his consent. The expected result is an inducement of passive acceptance and obedience, and, if possible, the creating of active approval and conversion to the Communist political socioeconomic doctrine. The term was popularized by the journalist Edward Hunter as a translation of *hsi nao* (literally "wash brain"), a Chinese colloquialism. The Chinese Communists have a program, called *szu-hsiang kai-tsao* (translated as "ideological reform," "ideological remolding," or "thought reform"), of directed attempts to change the "mentation" and "bourgeois ideas" of non-Communists. Brainwashing is also termed "menticide," "coercive persuasion," and a "technique of group political indoctrination."

Thought reform has been applied to (1) the Chinese population as a whole, (2) the Chinese intellectuals, and (3) Westerners, both non-military and military. The Chinese Communists established thought reform programs in special centers, but to varying degrees applied these principles to university, labor, business, and government groups and to the peasants also. Its application to prisoners of war in the Korean War (1950–53) aroused great popular interest when false confessions of germ warfare and of change of political allegiance by American soldiers were reported. American prisoners were subjected only to group indoctrination to obtain military information and collaboration, to secure propaganda, and to attempt to undermine their faith and trust in their country, government, and leaders. This was not brainwashing in its extensive form.

Method. Brainwashing has two immediate basic goals, confession and reeducation. There are two major modern developers of persuasive coercion—the Russian and the Chinese Communists. The methods of both groups are the same; they differ only in technique.

Eastern European or Russian System. Testimony has revealed that a political prisoner in Russia is subjected to a certain regimen. The KGB, which is the state police, determines who threatens the party or the state. Once a person is arrested, he is deemed to be guilty. There is no hope for acquittal or vindication, as under this system judgment of his guilt is made prior to his arrest. His case cannot be settled until a confession has been prepared, which must be signed by both the prisoner and the interrogating officer.

The following is a typical timetable for an individual accused of a political crime: (1) suspicion; (2) accumulation of evidence by surveillance and informers—4 weeks; (3) arrest and detention, resulting in isolation and interrogation—7 or 8 weeks; (4) confession (12th week); and (5) punishment.

The Russian system allocates a period of a few weeks to several months, during which time the interrogator must obtain a confession from the prisoner. The emphasis in Russia is placed on interrogation and not on indoctrination as it is in the Chinese system.

Chinese System. Under the Chinese system the timetable is quite different, as there is an attempt to produce a long-lasting change in the basic attitude and behavior of the prisoner. Hence indoctrination plays a very important part in the Chinese methods. The prolonged isolation used in Russia is not used in China. The Chinese emphasis is on group interaction, and therefore a prisoner is generally kept in a cell with six or eight other political prisoners. The Chinese use public self-criticism and group criticism for indoctrination, as well as diary writing.

Psychology of Brainwashing. The implication that *psychiatry and psychology provide the basis for brainwashing has no factual basis. There have been serious claims by psychiatrists and others that scientific knowledge was the foundation of menticide and that the ideas of I. *Pavlov are its principal source, but this is more speculation than fact.

R. J. Lifton distinguishes a series of operations at work on the individual during the brainwashing process: (1) annihilation of identity (taken from own group); (2) establishment of guilt·(inner pain experienced as guilt); (3) conflict with an inflexible environment (only he is wrong); (4) adaptational solution (leniency when he admits guilt); (5) confession compulsion (everyone urges it); (6) channeling of guilt (guilt anxiety becomes attached to acts seen as subversive from the peoples' viewpoint); (7) coercive confabulation (final confession-submission); (8) broadening of guilt (guilt is expanded to include major elements in his identity); (9) adaptional rewards (later participation in a "togetherness"); (10) working through (living the principle of thought reform); (11) recoding

of reality (alters values and identity; serves to reinterpret the past).

Brainwashing is not dependent on drugs, *hypnotism, or any other special procedure devised by scientists.

The psychological forces encountered in brainwashing are not unique to the process. They represent an exaggerated expression of elements present in varying degrees in all social orders. Every culture makes use of somewhat analogous pressures of milieu control—guilt, shame, confession, group sanction, loading of language —in order to mold common beliefs and identities. In a democracy there is an attempt to limit the pressures.

Comparisons have been made between the process of brainwashing and *psychotherapy, propaganda, education, religious training, and advertising. In these systems, the individual is given the opportunity to compare multiple concepts and to accept or reject whatever he wishes. In brainwashing the process continues until the leader feels that the desired change has taken place to the already established point, without benefit of comparison with other concepts or with other people. Where similarities are present, they become insignificant because of the ultimate moral purpose of brainwashing.

Bibliography: R. J. LIFTON, *Thought Reform and the Psychology of Totalism: A Study of Brainwashing in China* (New York 1962). U.S. Dept. of the Army, *Communist Interrogation, Indoctrination and Exploitation of American Military and Civilian Prisoners of War* (Washington 1956). R. A. BAUER and E. H. SCHEIN, eds., "Brainwashing," *The Journal of Social Issues* 13.3 (1957) 3–55. *Methods of Forceful Indoctrination: Observations and Interviews,* Groups for the Advancement of Psychiatry, symposium No. 4 (New York 1957). W. W. SARGANT, *Battle for the Mind: A Physiology of Conversion and Brainwashing* (New York 1957). E. HUNTER, *Brainwashing in Red China: The Calculated Destruction of Men's Minds* (New York 1951). "Communist Methods of Interrogation and Indoctrination," *Bulletin of the New York Academy of Medicine* 33 (1957) 599–653. E. H. SCHEIN, "The Chinese Indoctrination Program for Prisoners of War: A Study of Attempted *Brainwashing*," *Psychiatry* 19 (1956) 149–172. L. E. HINKLE and H. G. WOLFF, "Communist Interrogation and Indoctrination of Enemies of the State," *A.M.A. Archives of Neurology and Psychiatry* 76 (Aug. 1956) 115–174. P. A. SANTUCCI and G. WINOKER, "Brainwashing as a Factor in Psychiatric Illness," *ibid.* 74 (1955) 11–16. U.S. Dept. of Defense, Report of Secretary of Defense's Advisory Committee on Prisoners of War, *Power Fight Continues after Battle* (Washington 1955). H. A. SEGAL, *Observations of Prisoners of War Immediately Following Their Release,* U.S. Army Medical Service Graduate School. Recent Advances in Medicine and Surgery, v.2 (Washington 1954) 403. J. SEGAL, *Factors Related to the Collaboration and Resistance Behavior of U.S. Army PW's in Korea* (Washington 1956). L. J. WEST, "Psychiatric Aspects of Training for Honorable Survival as a Prisoner of War," AmJ Psych 115 (1958) 329–336.

[P. A. SANTUCCI]

BRAMANTE, DONATO, leading architect of the High Renaissance in Italy; b. near Urbino, 1444; d. Rome, 1514. Only one important example of his early activity as a painter remains, the "Christ at the Pillar" (c. 1490; Brera, Milan). A noted engineer of domes, Bramante carefully studied Roman ruins for building techniques. From c. 1480 he worked as an architect in Milan, where the domed east end of S. Maria presso S. Satiro, his first commission in Milan (1480–90), includes a false choir illusionistically painted to suggest additional space. Bramante went to Rome in 1499, where his Tempietto of S. Pietro in Montorio (1502) is the first and most perfect High Renaissance building. Bramante planned to surround this small circular chapel, like a reliquary in form and function, with a

Donato Bramante, fresco portrait by Giovanni Santi.

circular colonnade. His projects for St. Peter's date from 1505 until his death. The most famous, an intricate Greek-cross plan in keeping with the Renaissance preference for the circle and square, would have located the tomb of the Apostle directly beneath the great dome, but only the huge crossing piers were completed. A medal struck by Caradosso in 1506 shows the projected elevation, a monumental grouping of barrel-vaulted arms flanked by towers leading up to the hemispherical dome. Bramante's Belvedere Courtyard in the Vatican (begun 1505) was based on the Roman ruins at Palestrina and the Palatine Hill. Always reliant upon precise knowledge of ancient Roman architecture, Bramante nevertheless created according to the spirit rather than the letter of classical antiquity.

Bibliography: O. H. FÖRSTER, *Bramante* (Vienna 1956). J. S. ACKERMAN, *The cortile del Belvedere* (Vatican City 1954). **Illustration credit:** The Photographic Archives of the Vatican Museums.

[M. M. SCHAEFER]

BRAMBACH, WILHELM, scholar, historian who put library science and philology at the service of musicology; b. Bonn, Germany, Dec. 17, 1841; d. Karlsruhe, Feb. 26, 1932. Brambach's early formation was in classical philology and musicology. Later he perfected himself in library science at the Bonn university library, where he worked from 1862 to 1866. After 6 years as professor of classical philology at Freiburg im Breisgau he was district librarian at Karlsruhe for 32 years. There he uncovered early liturgical books among the uncatalogued MSS of the ancient abbey of *Reichenau, which were at that time housed at Karlsruhe. This new evidence filled lacunae in the history of Gregorian chant between *Boethius and *Guido of Arezzo and emphasized the role played by the abbey in the unfolding of this history. Brambach concerned himself particularly with the writings of *Berno and *Hermannus Contractus, two famous medieval theoreticians. Some of his works are *Das Tonsystem und die Tonarten des christlichen Abendlandes im Mittelalter* (1881), *Die Musikliteratur des Mittelalters bis zur Blüte der Reichenauer*

Sängerschule (1883), and *Gregorianisch; bibliographische Lösung der Streitfrage über den Ursprung des gregorianisches Gesang* (1895).

Bibliography: H. HÜSCHEN, MusGG 2:212–213. Riemann.

[E. LEAHY]

BRAMMART, JOHANNES, theologian; b. Aachen, *c.* 1340; d. Cologne, Sept. 8, 1407. After joining the Carmelite Order, he was sent to Paris for study but finished his course at Bologna probably because of the *Western Schism. From 1384 till 1404 he was provincial of the German Carmelite province. He cooperated in the foundation of the University of Cologne. In theology he followed *voluntarism and showed clearly the influence of *nominalism; however, he remained in line with traditional *realism in treating the relation between faith and intellect. This ambiguous position led to confused solutions for such doctrinal questions as the demonstration of God's existence. His main work *Lectura super I Sententiarum* survives only in two unpublished manuscripts.

Bibliography: B. M. XIBERTA Y ROQUETA, *De scriptoribus scholasticis saeculi XIV ex ordine Carmelitarum* (Louvain 1931) 414–452.

[H. SPIKKER]

BRANCATI, LORENZO, theologian; b. Giovanni Francesco in Lauria, Calabria, Italy, April 10, 1612; d. Rome, Nov. 30, 1693. He entered the Conventual Franciscans in 1630, taking the name Lorenzo. After his profession in 1631, he studied at Lecce, Bari, and the Roman College of St. Bonaventure; he was ordained in 1636, and awarded the doctorate in theology in 1637. He taught at Aversa, Naples, and was regent of studies for his order in Florence, Ferrara, and Bologna. Later, he was professor at the Sapienza University, Rome,

Lorenzo Brancati.

where he earned his great reputation as a Scotist; and for many years he was prefect of studies at the Propaganda, Rome. From 1655 he held numerous posts in the Roman Curia as consultor to 10 Congregations, and was prefect of the Vatican Library. In 1681 he was created cardinal by Innocent XI (d. 1689), and was named librarian of the Holy Roman Church. Brancati also played a considerable role in the Jansenist and quietist controversies of his day.

His chief work is the *Commentaria in III et IV Librum Sententiarum J. D. Scoti* (8 v. Rome 1653–82). With the 12 volumes of the *Sacrae Theologiae Summa* of A. *Vulpes, Brancati's commentary forms one of the most complete expositions of Scotus's teaching. This work treats nearly all subjects pertaining to special dogmatic theology. Part of the tract "De Fide" of the commentary is devoted to a treatise on the missions. The first part is a historical survey of the missionary activity of the Church to the 16th century. The second part is doctrinal and concerns the missionary vocation, its requisites, purpose, and the methods to be employed by the missionary. By formulating the general principles of the missionary apostolate Brancati made a distinctive contribution to mission science. Publication of the treatise by the Propaganda is indication that the mission doctrine of the author was in conformity with the mind and practice of the Congregation at that time.

His penchant for positive theology is apparent in the commentaries on the third book of Scotus's Sentences, as well as in his *Opuscula Tria de Deo* (Rome 1687). As a result of his teaching experience at the Propaganda College, he was the first and for a long time the only theologian to include a systematic study of the missions as an integral part of theology. His *Opuscula Octo de Oratione Christiana* (Rome 1685), written because of the quietist controversy, remains a classic. Benedict XIV (d. 1758) drew much on Brancati in the composition of his work on beatification and canonization of saints. In general, Brancati was a faithful disciple of Scotus, except on questions of grace, in which he followed St. Augustine.

Bibliography: Hurter Nomencl 4:351–355. É. d'Alençon, DTC 9.1:13–15. J. Heerinckx, DictSpirAscMyst 1:1921–23. R. Hoffman, *Pioneer Theories of Missiology* (Washington 1960). C. Testore, EncCatt 3:23. Sbaralea v.3:267–268.

[P. D. Fehlner]

BRANCH THEORY OF THE CHURCH

A theoretical, ecclesiological teaching devised by theologians of the 19th-century *Oxford movement in the Church of England that, while excluding communion with the Roman Catholic Church, attempted to explain the meaning of the *unity of the Church and the relation of this unity to different Christian bodies fulfilling the definition of Catholicism as understood by Anglicans. The classical formula of this teaching was set down by William Palmer of Worcester College, Oxford (1838). It became more general and popular later through the writings of Edward B. *Pusey (1800–82), who in 1865 wrote his famous letter to John Keble, *Eirenicon: The Church of England a Portion of Christ's One Holy Catholic Church, and a Means of Restoring Visible Unity.* However, one finds a sign of this teaching in the writings of the 16th-century Catholic Henrician Bp. Stephen *Gardiner (c. 1490–1555), as well as in the theory of James I, distinguishing between "the Church" and "communions." This position is still held today, although with slight adjustments of categories and labels that emphasize the pragmatic nature of the theory.

Accordingly, the Catholic Church is alleged to be one through a deep unity of life and profession of the faith of the Apostles in the one, original, undivided Church, while maintaining the apostolic order and succession of its bishops, celebrating the same Sacraments, and adhering to its ecclesiastical institutions. Through schism the Church is *de facto* although not *de jure* divided as to belief and ecclesiastical communion into three great bodies separated from one another: the Eastern Church, the Roman Church, and the Anglican Church. The proponents of the branch theory do not identify their teaching with the constitution of the Church, but with the vital unity underlying its divisions in its actual state. The substantial unity of the Church is that of a family bound by a common life and a common origin. Confessional differences and breaches of ecclesiastical communion do not involve the *esse* of the Church and hence are normal and inevitable. The unity is not broken by this schism: the same Catholic Church is Anglican in England, Gallican in France, Roman in Italy. These particular Churches are but one Catholic Church, indeed one visible body, and although the *diversum sentire* creates external barriers, yet it is united by the essential principles of its oneness (*salvo jure communionis;* cf. Rosenthal's distinction between unity and union). This is actually the basis of the Anglican Reformation as seen in *The King's Book* (1543). Consult therein "The Creed, Article 9." Similarly compare *The Anglican Canons of 1603,* revised in 1865.

These schismatic branches, according to the theory, will eventually be united into the future "ecumenical" Church, a synthesis of all of the confessional Churches at present separated in practice but united in origin and substance with the reality of apostolic Catholicism. (See *The Lambeth Appeal,* pars. 4 and 9.) This ecumenical Church will be one in essentials although, in the Anglican mystique, broadly diversified as to doctrine and discipline in nonessentials all broadly conceived in relation to "fundamental doctrines." This would permit the variety of the customs and rites and dogmatic formulas as already expressed by the Roman, Greek, Anglican, Lutheran, and Presbyterian liturgies no less than the confessions of each particular Church—e.g., the *West-minster Confession, the Confession of *Augsburg, the Formula of *Concord. All these would be considered as valid differentiations of the one Christian revelation.

See also ANGLICANISM; UNICITY OF THE CHURCH; UNITY OF FAITH.

Bibliography: T. Sartory, LexThK² 2:643–644. W. Palmer, *A Treatise on the Church of Christ,* 2 v. (New York 1841). E. B. Pusey, *An Eirenicon,* 3 v. (Oxford 1865–70). J. H. Newman, *Parochial and Plain Sermons,* 8 v. (new ed. London 1877–88) 3:191–192. "The Lambeth Quadrilateral (1888–1920)," in *Documents on Christian Unity,* ed. G. K. A. Bell, 2 v. (London 1924–30) 2:47–49, The Lambeth Appeal (1920). G. D. Rosenthal, *The Unity of the Church: Report of the Anglo-Catholic Congress 1930* (London 1930). Denz 2885–88. Y. M. J. Congar, *Chrétiens désunis* (Paris 1937) 218–247, with best criticism. A. Gatard, "Anglicanisme," DTC 1.2:1298–1302.

[A. H. Amadio]

BRANCO, MANUEL ALVES, Brazilian political figure, legislator, and cabinet officer; b. Salvador, Bahia, June 7, 1797; d. Niterói, near Rio de Janeiro, July 13, 1855. He received his bachelor's degree from the University of Coimbra in 1823. During his stay in Portugal he frequented an important literary circle whose principal figure, Almeida Garret, must have influenced his philosophic ideas. Alves Branco served as a magistrate in Bahia and in Rio de Janeiro. When elected a deputy in the second legislature (1830–33), he showed himself a parliamentarian of the first rank, sympathetic to the distinguished group led by his fellow representative Antonio Ferreira França. The latter was the author of a plan that would permit the marriage of the secular clergy, the abolition of the regular clergy (1827), an inter-American meeting (1830), and finally, the extinction of the monarchy and the election of the chief of state (1831, 1835). But Alves Branco was primarily a legal expert. His great parliamentary contribution was the drafting of the Code of Criminal Procedure (1832), a liberal legislative monument, complementary to the Criminal Code (1830), and a high point of the achievement of his Liberal party. In 1831 along with José Bonifácio de *Andrada e Silva, he signed a bill for an electoral law that represented a great advance. It even permitted women to vote when they became heads of households. When he left the chamber of deputies, he devoted himself to public finance and was comptroller general and a member of the treasury tribunal. In this capacity he drafted the general accounting regulations of the empire. In 1837 his name was on the list of three for filling a vacancy in the senate caused by the death of the first Viscount, Marquis of Caravelas, who was his mother's uncle. He was selected by the Emperor for the seat and later received the title of second Viscount of Caravelas. He was also, from 1842, a councilor of state. He held various ministerial posts. As minister of justice in 1835, he signed the law that abolished entailed estates and conditional inheritances. His most important term in the government was in 1844, when he held the post of minister of finance. He then laid the foundations for the new monetary system and, in particular, approved new customs tariffs initiating the protectionist policy that was to permit the rise of industry. He also drafted a rather bold plan for a court of accounts. After 1848 he held no more posts in the executive branch, restricting himself to the functions of senator and councilor. Alves Branco was characterized by austerity of habits and by an honesty that was, in the words of a biographer, "carried to the degree of madness." His few writings consist mainly of legislative and administrative documents.

[A. J. LACOMBE]

BRANCUSI, CONSTANTIN, considered by many the greatest sculptor of the 20th century; b. Pestisani Gorj, Rumania, Feb. 21, 1876; d. March 16, 1957. He attended the local school of arts and crafts in Craiovia and then the Academy of Fine Arts in Bucharest, where he graduated in 1902. After making his way slowly across Europe, Brancusi arrived in Paris in 1904; he remained there and became a French citizen in 1957. Although Brancusi worked briefly at the Académie des Beaux-Arts in the studio of Antonin Mercié, the strongest influence on his early work was Auguste Rodin. In 1906, however, Brancusi refused to become Rodin's assistant and elected instead a life of hardship but artistic independence. This early decision was characteristic of his dedication and concentration.

Brancusi's work gradually became widely known; first through single pieces shown in large exhibitions such as the Salon des Indépendants, Paris, and the famous Armory Show, New York (1913), then in one-man shows at the Brummer Gallery, New York (1926, 1933), and finally in a major retrospective exhibition at the Guggenheim Museum (1955–56). He traveled

Constantin Brancusi, "The Miracle," marble, 43 inches high, 1936.

to America three times and in 1937 to India and Rumania, but the center of his life remained his studio (now reconstructed in the Musée d'Art Moderne, Paris).

Brancusi's sculpture, his sketches, and his rare paintings are based on a few apparently simple themes: the human head and figure, birds, fish, and animal forms. Working with infinite patience and meticulous skill, he obtained faultless purity in such classic statements as "The New-Born," "Mlle. Pogany," "Bird in Space," "Endless Column," and "The Seal." All these exist in many versions, differing in date and materials, as he constantly sought to achieve the most perfect solution to any formal problem. His works, more than merely formal statements, always seem invested with his own profound philosophical convictions and his sense that in his art he was searching for a form of absolute truth. Brancusi was stimulated in this search by the writings of an 11th-century Tibetan monk, Milarepa. He was moved also by the Gregorian chants he sang in the Rumanian Orthodox church in Paris.

Bibliography: D. LEWIS, *Brancusi* (New York 1958). C. GIEDION-WELCKER, ed., *Constantin Brancusi,* tr. M. JOLAS and A. LEROY (New York 1959). I. JIANOU, *Brancusi* (New York 1963). **Illustration credit:** The Solomon R. Guggenheim Museum.

[E. BARTON]

BRANDES, GEORG MORRIS COHEN

Danish literary critic; b. Copenhagen, Feb. 4, 1842; d. there, Feb. 19, 1927. Brandes's parents belonged to the Jewish community in Copenhagen, but seem to have been rather indifferent to religion. His own religious instruction was deficient, and he never understood sincere religious feelings. Further, his attitude toward Christianity was always unsympathetic, and often arrogant. After a few years as a law student, he received his

M.A. degree (1864) and devoted himself to literature. In the late 1860s he wrote two collections of essays still classed among his finest works, and in 1870 he earned his doctor's degree with a dissertation on modern French

Georg Morris Cohen Brandes.

aesthetics (*Den franske Æsthetik i vore Dage*), an evaluation of Hippolyte *Taine's critical methods. The next year he traveled in Europe and made the acquaintance of Taine, Ernest Renan, and John Stuart Mill.

Returning to Denmark, Brandes gave a series of lectures on European literature in the 19th century; these are regarded as the beginning of a new era in Scandinavian literature. They and the following series were published as *Hovedstrømninger i det nittende Aarhundredes Litteratur*, 6 v. (1872–90), translated as *Main Currents in Nineteenth-Century Literature*, 6 v. (London 1901–05). Brandes had undeniably proved himself among the most gifted literary critics of his day, and it was expected (also by himself) that the chair of aesthetics in the University of Copenhagen (left vacant at the death of the poet Carsten Hauch) would be offered him. Prejudice against him, however, was too strong, and he never received a regular university position. His influence on contemporary writers (among them Henrik *Ibsen) was formidable, and he was regarded as the leader of the naturalistic movement in Danish literature during the 1870s.

Brandes's often radical views did not win favor in the conservative milieu of Copenhagen, and after 1877 he preferred to live in Germany (his wife was German), until a group of his followers and admirers invited him back 5 years later and gave him an annual salary equivalent to that of a university professor. In 1902 he was appointed professor by the government, with a salary from the state but without any duty to lecture. Politically, Brandes was always a liberal, though a highly individual one, but never a democrat in the true sense of the word; his inclinations were at times rather aristocratic. He was willing to offer his opinion on almost any contemporary problem and wrote passionately, for instance, against war during World War I. Among his more important books are an essay on Ludvig Holberg (1884), and books on Benjamin Disraeli (1878) and Ferdinand Lassalle (1881). From a later period are the books on Shakespeare (1895–96; tr. as *William Shakespeare: A Critical Study*, London 1898, several times reprinted), Goethe (1914–15), Voltaire (1916–17), and Julius Caesar (1918). These books, highly individualistic in outlook, typify Brandes's interest in persons rather than ideas in this period. His attitude, often labeled hero-worship, was probably somewhat in-

fluenced by his friend *Nietzsche, on whose philosophy he wrote an essay in 1889. *Sagnet om Jesus* (1925; tr. as *Jesus, a Myth,* London and New York 1926, 1927) from Brandes's last years clearly shows his limitations. In it, he adapted features from contemporary rationalistic Biblical criticism and used them with an almost innocent ignorance of what religion is.

Brandes was a bone of contention for more than 50 years, and was never afraid to fight for his ideas. He seemed to draw his strength from a constant conviction that he was fighting every kind of halfheartedness. His importance lies in the fact that he introduced European ideas into Denmark, often with a badly needed electrifying effect. He is still widely read by compatriots who regard him as the central figure in modern literary criticism, while his international audience has dwindled. The backbone of his brilliant and often beautiful style was a never-failing faith in himself, which sometimes sank to a quite formidable personal arrogance.

Bibliography: G. M. BRANDES, *Samlede Skrifter*, 18 v. (Copenhagen 1899–1910); *Levned*, 3 v. (Copenhagen 1905–08). C. S. PETERSEN and V. ANDERSEN, *Illustreret dansk Litteraturhistorie*, 4 v. (Copenhagen 1924–34) v.4. *Dansk skønlitterært fofatterleksikon 1900–1950* (Copenhagen 1959–60) v.1. **Illustration credit:** Gyldendalske Boghandel Nordisk Forlag.

[H. BEKKER-NIELSEN]

BRANDSMA, TITUS, Carmelite philosopher, historian of mysticism, martyr for the freedom of Catholic press; b. Oegeklooster (Friesland), Holland, Feb. 23, 1881; d. Dachau, Germany, July 26, 1942. He was of Catholic Frisian origin. Titus Brandsma (Anno Sjoerd) entered the Carmelite Order in 1898 and was ordained June 17, 1905. After obtaining his doctorate in philos-

Titus Brandsma in the academic dress of rector magnificus at Nijmegen.

ophy at the Gregorian University, Rome, he lectured at the Carmelite major seminary in Oss.

Meanwhile, he started writing articles on sociology and religion; he began a Dutch translation of St. Teresa of Avila (1918–26); from 1919 to 1923 he edited the local paper in Oss and founded a Catholic library. He founded high schools at Oss and Oldenzaal and was president of the Catholic board of secondary schools. In 1923 he was nominated professor at the Catholic University of Nijmegen, and in 1932 became rector. He distinguished himself especially in the study of the medieval mysticism of the Netherlands. In 1935 he lectured in the U.S. Besides these activities, he dedicated himself to the study of the Frisian language and culture, and to the apostolate for the reunion of Oriental Churches. In 1935 he was nominated spiritual director of the union of Dutch Catholic journalists. After the Nazis occupied Holland in 1940, he vigorously defended the Catholic schools, refusing moreover to dismiss Jewish children from these schools. In the name of the hierarchy, he induced Catholic newspaper editors to reject Nazi propaganda. On Jan. 19, 1942, he was taken prisoner. After a stay in various prisons and concentration camps, he was put to death in Dachau. In 1964 the process of his beatification was awaiting introduction in Rome.

Bibliography: B. MEIJER, *Titus Brandsma* (Bussum 1951). H. W. F. AUKES, *Het leven van Titus Brandsma* (Utrecht 1961). J. ALZIN, *A Dangerous Little Friar* (Dublin 1957). E. RHODES, *His Memory Shall Not Pass* (New York 1958). R. WELCH, "A Prophet for our Times," CrossCrown 15 (1963) 294–308.

[A. STARING]

BRANGWYN, SIR FRANK, painter, etcher, lithographer, book illustrator; b. Bruges, Belgium, May 13, 1867; d. Ditchling, Sussex, England, June 11, 1956. Brangwyn was a Catholic. His father, an ecclesiastical architect of Welch-English descent, had returned to London with his family in 1875. At 15 Brangwyn worked for William *Morris designing textiles. The Royal Academy accepted a picture for exhibition (1885), but then Brangwyn took to the sea (1888), visiting Africa, Asia Minor, and Spain, sometimes paying his way with drawings.

Sir Frank Brangwyn, drawing by Philip William May.

In painting Brangwyn captured the exotic colorfulness of the Orient, whereas in his prints he gave attention to the human figure—often depicting workers in worn clothes and people in the street. Today the hard, exposed limbs, tattered garments, and active attitudes in prints and drawings appear more interesting than his vast extravagant paintings for public spaces. Brangwyn admired the French painters Delacroix and Millet, and he must have looked hard at prints by Piranesi, whose dark, large-scale architectural forms he echoes in his skillfully composed prints.

He was elected associate of the Royal Academy (1904) and made a fellow in 1919. He received the gold medal of honor from the Emperor of Austria, was knighted in 1941, and was the first living artist to have a retrospective show at the academy (1952).

His war memorial compositions for the royal gallery in the House of Lords (initiated 1925) were rejected; in 1933 the work was accepted for the assembly hall of the civic center in Swansea, Wales. Notable of his interior decorations are: "The Empress of Britain," Canadian Pacific liner (1930); Skinner's Hall, London; Houses of Parliament, Ottawa; Radio City, New York City.

Bibliography: H. E: A. FRUST, *The Decorative Art of Frank Brangwyn* (London 1924). P. MACER-WRIGHT, *Brangwyn* (London 1940). V. GALLOWAY, *The Oils and Murals of Sir Frank Brangwyn 1867–1956* (Leigh-on-Sea, Eng. 1962). Vollmer Allg Lex 1:298–299. **Illustration credit:** National Portrait Gallery, London.

[P. F. NORTON]

BRANLY, ÉDOUARD, French physicist, inventor of the coherer employed in wireless telegraphy; b. Amiens, Oct. 23, 1844?; d. Paris, March 24, 1940. After he had received his early education at the Lycée of Saint-Quentin, his scientific studies were begun at the Lycée Henri IV at Paris, and in 1865 he became licentiate in mathematics and physical science. He occupied a professor's chair at the Lycée of Bourges, and was made director of the laboratory of instruction in the department of physics at the Sorbonne in 1873. Branly obtained his medical degree in 1882.

Branly is best known for his research in electricity, and particularly for his invention of the coherer, which first made *Marconi's system of wireless telegraphy possible. Other researches include studies relating to the effect of ultraviolet light upon positively and negatively charged bodies (1890–93), and the electrical conductivity of gases (1894). Branly became Commander of the Order of St. Gregory the Great in 1899; he was nominated Chevalier of the Legion of Honor in 1900, and, in the same year received the *grand prix* at the Paris exposition. In 1903, with M. *Curie, he received the *prix Osiris* from the Syndicate of the Press. Branly's papers were published chiefly in the *Comptes Rendus*. He also wrote a *Cours élémentaire de physique* and *Traité élémentaire de physique*.

Bibliography: *Larousse du XXᵉ ·Siècle*, 6 v. (Paris 1928) 1:845–846.

[H. M. BROCK]

BRANN, HENRY ATHANASIUS, writer; b. Parkstown, County Muth, Ireland, Aug. 15, 1837; d. New York City, Dec. 28, 1921. His parents brought him to the U.S. in 1849, settling in Jersey City, N.J., where Brann attended public and parochial schools. He graduated from St. Francis Xavier College, New York

City, in 1857; studied at St. Mary's Seminary, Wilmington, Del., and at Issy, France; and entered the North American College in Rome in October 1860. On June 14, 1862, he was ordained for the Diocese of Newark, N.J., and he became vice president and professor of metaphysics (1862–64) at Seton Hall College (now University), South Orange, N.J. Following pastorates in Jersey City and Fort Lee, N.J., he became director (1868) of the diocesan seminary in Wheeling, W.Va. In 1870 he went to New York, where Abp. John McCloskey assigned him to form St. Elizabeth's parish in the Fort Washington area. He built a church there in 1871 and one at Kingsbridge in 1877. From January 1890 until his death he was pastor of St. Agnes Church, New York City, where he built a school, church, and rectory; bought a convent; and raised funds to endow a boys' high school. In 1910, he was made a domestic prelate by Leo XIII. Brann was a popular speaker and an ardent controversialist. He contributed regularly to leading Catholic newspapers and periodicals, and was noted for the articles against the *Faribault Plan that he wrote in support of Abp. Michael A. Corrigan's position during the school controversy in 1897. Among his published works are: *Age of Unreason* (1880), a reply to Robert Ingersoll and other rationalists; *Life of Archbishop Hughes* (1892); and *History of the American College, Rome* (1912).

[F. D. COHALAN]

BRANT (BRANDT), SEBASTIAN, German humanist author and satirist; b. Strassburg, 1457; d. there, May 10, 1521. He was the son of an innkeeper and entered the University of Basel (1475), where he taught Roman and Canon Law (1489–99). When Emperor Maximilian I ceded Basel to Switzerland, Brant

Sebastian Brant, engraving of the 17th century.

returned to his birthplace and through the intercession of Geiler von Kaisersburg (1445–1510), a famous scholar and powerful preacher, became Syndikus (1500) and 3 years later city clerk of Strassburg and was named an imperial councilor and Count Palatinate. Although born in a time of transition, Brant adhered to the old faith and to the medieval traditions of the German Empire.

Apart from judicial treatises, Brant wrote religious and politicohistorical poems; he translated Vergil, some writings of the Church Fathers, the complete works of Petrarch, and Latin hymns and aphorisms by Cato, Facetus, and others. He also reedited Freidank's (d. *c.* 1233) didactic *Bescheidenheit* (1508). None of these works, however, attained the fame of his first work, *Das Narrenschiff* (1494), which was reprinted, reedited, revised, plagiarized, imitated, and translated many times. A Latin version by Jacob Locher, *Stultifera navis* (1497), was translated into English by Alexander Barclay (1509). The original had been composed in Brant's native Alsatian dialect at a time when most chanceries and individual authors used modern High German, and the language—in versification as well as in the choice of expression—betrays clumsiness, but the theme and its verse treatment apparently charmed readers of that time.

Das Narrenschiff is a satire on all the sins, crimes, and foibles of mankind, which are treated, after the humanist fashion, with ridicule as being follies. There are 112 categories of "fools" on board the ship that is to take them to Schlaraffenland (Utopia) on their way to Narragonia. But the ship is wrecked and all perish. Brant's treatment of an old theme is new in that he does not gravely judge and admonish his readers, but holds a mirror up to them (the text was accompanied by explanatory woodcuts) so that they may recognize themselves, be ashamed, and abjure the evil that springs from a lack of self-knowledge. His gentle hints are fortified by learned allusions to the Bible, Vergil, Ovid, the Fathers of the Church, and the *Corpus Iuris,* and to idioms and popular proverbs. Thus the satire becomes a treasure trove of practical wisdom. This first bourgeois satire received high praise: Brant's friend Geiler modeled more than 100 sermons on the different categories of fools, and another contemporary, the Swiss Franciscan Thomas *Murner (*c.* 1475–1537), an outspoken adversary of Martin Luther, followed its style in his *Die Narrenbeschwörung* and *Die Schelmenzunft* (1512).

Bibliography: S. BRANT, *Das Narrenschiff,* ed. F. SCHULTZ (Strassburg 1913), new fac. ed. with an epilogue. W. KOSCH, *Deutsches Literature-Lexikon,* 4 v. (2d ed. Bern 1947–58) 1:210, with bibliog.

[S. A. SCHULZ]

BRAQUE, GEORGES, French painter; b. Argenteuil, near Paris, May 13, 1882; d. Paris, Aug. 31, 1963. After completing formal art studies, Braque, in 1906–07, under the influence of Pierre Matisse, Othon Friesz, and others, adopted the Fauve style, which employed extremely bright, antinaturalistic colors for expressive effects. From 1908, influenced by Cézanne and working in close association with Pablo Picasso, Braque was a pioneer of *cubism. For about 4 years the two artists explored the possibilities of "analytical cubism," a style they had developed in which natural form is "analyzed" into small facets painted within a limited brown-gray

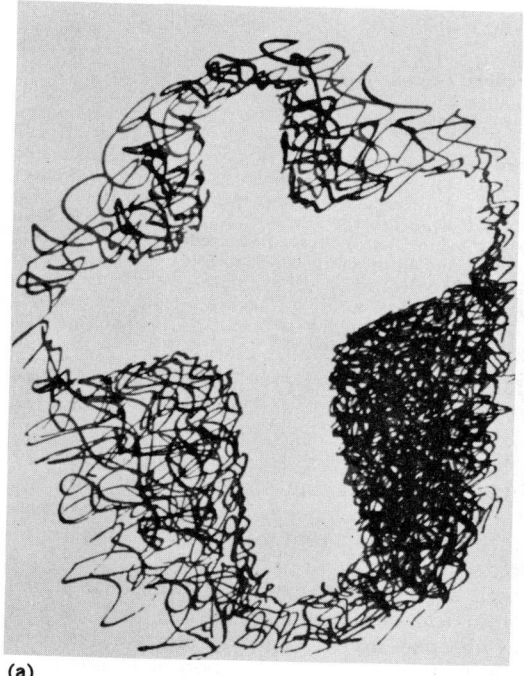

(a)

(b)

Fig. 1. (a) and (b): Devotional cards designed for Club des Nou-
velles Images.

BRAQUE

Fig. 2. "Musical Forms," 1918, collage on paper, 30⅛ by 38 inches.

Fig. 3. Georges Braque.

color scheme. The works of Braque and Picasso from 1908 to 1912—very similar in appearance—are of fundamental importance for the history of 20th-century art. In 1912 and 1913 the two artists developed "synthetic" cubism in which forms became larger, colors more varied, and the total effect more decorative. This new style was stimulated by the technique of *collage,* which introduces pieces of paper or other foreign elements into paintings and drawings; the discovery of *collage* is sometimes attributed to Braque.

At the outbreak of World War I, Braque was mobilized, sent to the front, wounded (1915), and discharged (1916) after convalescence. After the war, Braque, no longer collaborating with Picasso, continued to paint variations of the synthetic cubist style, his work alternating between an intricate linearity and a manner of drastic reduction and simplification. The latter method became increasingly prominent toward the end of his career. In addition to his paintings, the artist produced woodcuts, etchings, color lithographs, and a small body of sculptures.

Among Braque's few works of specifically religious subjects are the designs he executed for the Club des Nouvelles Images. Through the efforts of Father A. Ayfre (d. 1964) and J. Blanc, these were issued (1958, 1961) in editions for popular devotional use. Braque also designed stained glass windows for the chapel of the Maeght Foundation at Saint-Paul-de-Vence (1962) and for the parish church at Varengeville, the Norman

village where the artist often lived and where he is buried.

Bibliography: *Le Jour et la nuit: Cahiers, 1917–1952* (Paris 1952), popular ed. of *Cahier de Georges Braque: 1917–1947* (Paris 1948) and suppl. to 1955 (1956); *Nouvelles sculptures et plaques gravées,* ed. C. ZERVOS (Paris 1960). H. R. HOPE, *Georges Braque* (New York 1949). M. GIEURE, *Georges Braque* (New York 1956), with bibliog. J. RUSSELL, *Georges Braque* (London 1959). J. RICHARDSON, *Georges Braque* (London 1961). J. LEYMARIE, *Braque,* tr. J. EMMONS (New York 1961), with bibliog. EncWA 2:612–616. **Illustration credits:** Fig. 3, French Embassy, Press and Information Division, New York City. Fig. 2, Philadelphia Musuem of Art, The Louise and Walter Arensberg Collection. Fig. 1, Courtesy of Club des Nouvelles Images.

[D. DENNY]

BRASÍLIA, ARCHDIOCESE OF (BRASILIA-POLITANUS),

created an archdiocese Jan. 16, 1960, without having been a diocese. The territory, that of the Federal District, an enclave in the state of Goiás, was taken from the Archdiocese of Goiânia. In 1964 it had no suffragan sees but the military vicariate, located in Rio de Janeiro since 1950, was transferred to it.

On April 21, 1960, the capital of Brazil was transferred from Rio de Janeiro to Brasília and on that same day the new archdiocese was erected. The first archbishop was the former archbishop of Diamantina, Dom José Newton de Almeida Batista. Unfortunately, the planners of the new capital had not paid enough attention to provisions for religion. The government donated 22 sites for as many parishes. The archbishop proposed a plan, since put into execution, of establishing 14 parishes along each of the north and south wings of the airplane design of the city, with the idea that the 28 parishes would become an eventual 35. By 1964, 24 parishes had been established. Each parish is a community center, including the church, school, high schools for boys and girls, and various kinds of social action groups. The population was increasing rapidly and in that year reached about 300,000. Eight secular priests, three of them American, and 50 religious priests served the diocese. In 1962 a minor seminary was opened under the direction of the Vincentians. The cathedral, planned by Oscar Niemeyer, was begun

The chapel of the President's Palace at Brasília, built in 1958 by the architect Oscar Niemeyer, is typical of the contemporary architecture of the archdiocese.

before the erection of the archdiocese. When it is finished, it will be the largest cathedral in Brazil and one of the largest in the world. The archbishop has founded Catholic Action, Vincentian Conferences, and various other charitable and social works such as Casa dos candangos for the help of the proletariat. Among the religious orders working in the archdiocese are Franciscans from the Holy Name province in New York, whose church of Santo Antônio serves as temporary cathedral, Marists, Salesians, and 29 communities of women. A Catholic university to be administered by Dominicans is planned.

Bibliography: *Brasília. Um ano de arquidiocese* (Brasília 1961). M. Penido Burnier, *Brasília, a cidade que tem alma* (Belo Horizonte 1964). **Illustration credit:** Copyright by Marcel Gautherot.

[O. van der Vat]

BRASK, HANS, Swedish bishop and opponent of Lutheranism; b. 1464; d. Danzig, July 30, 1538 or 1539. He studied in Rostock and Griefswald. In 1510 he was provost of the cathedral and then (1513) bishop of Linköping, where he was exceptionally able and zealous, promoting scholasticism, and writing chronicles (now lost). In the national revolt against Denmark he supported Gustavus Vasa, but he opposed the introduction of Lutheran doctrines by the Petersson (Petri) brothers. In 1522 he threatened to excommunicate anyone bringing in Luther's writings, in 1523 he accused Olaus *Petri of heresy, and he continued to denounce the Petri, despite the King's displeasure. After breaking with Rome over annates (1524), the impecunious Gustavus in 1526 attacked church property, particularly Brask's wealthy see, and he gave Uppsala's press to Petri. The climax came at the diet of Västerås (1527). As spokesman for the bishops Brask refused to surrender clerical properties or to authorize a doctrinal disputation. Nevertheless, the diet deprived the bishops of power and property, subjected the Church to royal control, and virtually established Lutheranism. Brask preferred exile at Danzig to submission.

Bibliography: *Svenskt biografiskt lexikon,* ed. J. A. Almquist et al. (Stockholm 1917–) 6:45–65. H. Jägerstad, LexThK² 2:653.

[J. T. Graham]

BRASSEUR DE BOURBOURG, CHARLES ÉTIENNE, French priest and expert in the prehistory of Central America; b. Bourbourg (about 9 miles from Dunkirk), 1814; d. Nice, 1874. His ecclesiastical studies were made in Rome, where he was ordained in 1845. In that same year he traveled to Canada, where he taught for a brief period in the seminary at Quebec, and thence to Boston, Mass., where he is said to have been vicar-general for a brief time in 1846. There he had occasion to read Prescott's *Conquest of Mexico,* which, he said, aroused his interest in the pre-Hispanic cultures of the Americas. To satisfy this new interest, Brasseur went back to Europe in 1846 and devoted 2 years to study in the Vatican Library and went to Mexico via the U.S. in 1848. The position of chaplain of the French embassy (until 1851) gave him an opportunity to become acquainted with the codices in the Biblioteca Nacional of Mexico City. In 1854 he went to Central America, where diplomatic friends introduced him to the Archbishop of Guatemala, Francisco de Paula

García Peláez, and to Juan Gavarrete, both students of Central American prehistory. Peláez not only gave Brasseur valuable manuscripts but also appointed him pastor in areas where he could learn Quiché. Gavarrete introduced him to the works of the celebrated Dominican Francisco Ximénez, the Quiché scholar. Brasseur spent also the years from 1859 to 1861 in Central America, where he served as pastor in San Juan Sacatepéquez to perfect his knowledge of Cacchiquel.

Brasseur was a self-taught expert, whose works helped to arouse interest in a scientific study of Central American prehistory. The publication of the French translation of *Popol-Vuh* (1861), a sacred book of the Quiché Indians, and of Diego de Landa's *Relación de las cosas de Yucatán* (1864) were noteworthy in this regard. However, Brasseur's enthusiasm for his subject frequently carried him away, and later scholars dispute many of his findings, such as his method of decipherment published in *Le manuscrit Troano, étude sur le système graphique de la langue des Mayas* (1869–70) and his theory that the center of Western culture was situated in America. To his credit, Brasseur never resented the correction offered by other scholars.

[L. Lamadrid]

BRATISLAVA

Capital of Slovakia, south central *Czechoslovakia; a trade center and port on the left bank of the Danube where the river flows through the Little Carpathians, 30 miles east of Vienna. It was called Pressburg until 1918; the Hungarian name is Pozsony. The city of 242,000 (1961), which formerly belonged to the See of *Esztergom (Hungary), has been under the apostolic administrator of Trnava since 1922.

Settled by Celts before the time of Christ, Bratislava and Devin (6 miles west of Bratislava) were occupied by Roman legions from the 1st to the 4th century; *Marcus Aurelius fought the Quadi there (173). Slavs and Avars settled the area (6th–8th century), which was a stronghold of the princes of Great Moravia (840–894), evangelized by SS. *Cyril and Methodius, before it became a margravate. *Stephen I of Hungary (997–1038) annexed Bratislava and made the castle parish a *praepositura* with quasiepiscopal jurisdiction. New settlers in the 12th century broke feudal ties and gained an autonomy based on German city rights. After its destruction in a Tatar raid (1241) Bratislava was fortified and received a town charter (1291); there were two settlements, a feudal settlement around a castle and a walled free town. A Franciscan church (1297) and a collegiate church of St. Martin (1350–1452) were built. Privileges were obtained from Emperor *Sigismund (1411–37), who fortified Bratislava against Hussites. *Matthias Corvinus in 1465 founded the university (Academia Istropolitana).

When the Turks took Budapest, Bratislava became the capital of Hungary (1541–1784); Hapsburgs were crowned kings of Hungary in the Gothic cathedral (1536–1791); and the Hungarian Diet met in Bratislava until 1848, after which the city lost much of its importance to Vienna. After Esztergom fell to the Turks (1543), archbishop and chapter moved to Bratislava, where Abp. Miklós *Oláh held a synod (1548) that established a seminary at Trnava (1566). Protestant religious freedom in Slovakia, regulated by the Diet of 1608, was revoked after a Protestant alliance with the Turks; Protestant leaders were tried, and churches were returned to Catholics (1673). A synod of 1682 repudiated Gallicanism. Under Maria Theresa Bratislava became the residence of a governor general, who built baroque palaces and churches. *Joseph II established a seminary in Bratislava to replace those in Trnava and elsewhere (1781). Napoleon concluded the treaty of Pressburg (1805) in the baroque primatial palace, built in 1781.

Hieronymus *Noldin, Ludwig *Lercher, and Josef *Donat taught at the Jesuit college (1854–1911) before they went to *Innsbruck. Mátyás Bél (1684–1749), A. Bernolák (1762–1813), József Bajza (1804–58), and L'udovít *Štúr (1815–62) were patriot scholars of Bratislava who fostered Slovak nationalism.

Austria promoted industrialization in the late 19th century, and Bratislava flourished as part of Czechoslovakia (from 1918) and as capital of independent Slovakia (1939–45), when it was the residence of President Jozef *Tiso and became the most modern town in Slovakia.

Bibliography: E. LAZIŠT'AN, *Bratislava* (3d ed. Bratislava 1959). F. HRUŠOVSKY, *History of Slovakia* (Turčiansky Svaty Martin 1940). F. BOKES, *History of Slovakia and the Slovaks* (Bratislava 1946). M. SPRINC, ed., *The Republic of Slovakia, 1939–1949* (Scranton, Pa. 1949). J. KVAČALA, *History of the Reformation in Slovakia (1517–1711)* (Liptovsky Svaty Mikuláš 1935). J. PAPIN, *Bratislava: Center of the Scholars of the 19th Century* (Rome 1959). L. ZACHAR, *St. Cyril and Methodius* (Trnava 1928). *Slovak Bratislava* (Bratislava 1948–). J. KÁLMÁN, *Bratislava's Castle* (Bratislava 1960). The above titles are in Slovak. E. PORITISCH, *Geschichte der Stadt Pressburg* (Bratislava 1939). J. PAPIN, "Trnava," LexThK² v.10.

[J. PAPIN]

BRAUER, THEODOR, labor economist and Catholic leader in social thought, educator, writer; b. Cleve, Germany, Jan. 18, 1880; d. St. Paul, Minn., March 19, 1942. Although he was the son of a German shoe manufacturer, his mother tongue was Dutch, and his high school education in Belgium was in French. Proficient in languages, he worked as the foreign correspondent and later as the assistant manager of a grain firm. He joined a union for salaried employees, and while supervising its health insurance fund, he was brought in touch for the first time with the Catholic social movement. In 1907 he became the assistant director of the Catholic People's Union (München-Gladbach) and, in 1908, staff assistant at the headquarters of the German Federation of Christian Trade Unions in Cologne. From 1914 to 1919 he was editor of the Federation's "Central Organ," and later of its monthly, *Deutsche Arbeit*. In 1919 he received a Ph.D. degree in economics from the University of Bonn; and in 1923 accepted the post of professor of economics at the Baden Institute of Technology, Karlsruhe. In 1928 he became a director of the Institute for Social Research and professor of labor economics and social legislation at the University of Cologne and, simultaneously, after 1930 directed the Labor School of the Christian Trade Unions in Königswinter. Having been dismissed from both directorships by the Nazis in 1933, he was arrested and jailed. When released he resumed his close cooperation with the Cologne headquarters of the *Kolping Society (Association of Catholic Journeymen's Guilds). At the invitation of Archbishop John G. Murray, he joined the department of

economics of St. Thomas College, St. Paul, Minn., in 1937, and 2 years later became its chairman. With the exception of H. Pesch, SJ, he was the most prolific German writer in the Catholic social movement.

Bibliography: An almost complete list of all publications is to be found in L. H. A. GECK and B. RIDDER, eds., *Theodor Brauer: Ein sozialer Kämpfer* (Cologne 1952). Publications in English. T. BRAUER, *The Catholic Social Movement in Germany* (Oxford 1932); *National Economy: A Discussion of the Bases for the Science of Economics* (St. Paul, Minn. 1939); *Economy and Society* (St. Paul, Minn. 1940); EncSocSc 2:683; 8:589. T. BRAUER et al., *Thomistic Principles in a Catholic School* (St. Louis 1943).

[F. H. MUELLER]

BRAULIO, ST., bishop and writer; b. probably in Saragossa, Spain, *c.* 585; d. Saragossa, *c.* 651. (feast, March 26). A student of *Isidore of Seville, Braulio succeeded his brother John as bishop of Saragossa in 631, and played a part in the national Councils of *Toledo in 633, 636, and 638, answering the charge of laxity that Pope *Honorius I had brought against the Spanish bishops. He wrote the biography of St. Aemilian and also a poem in his honor. His collection of 43 letters is an invaluable source of information about the Church and State in Visigothic Spain, and also reveals his bibliophile tendencies. He encouraged Isidore of Seville to write his *Etymologies* and is responsible for the present division of the subject matter into 20 books. In a preface to Isidore's *De viris illustribus* Braulio listed almost all the writings of the author with a brief examination of their contents. Braulio became blind in the closing years of his life. He is honored as the patron of Aragon.

Bibliography: BRAULIO, *Epistolario*, ed. J. MADOZ (Madrid 1941), critical edition. Z. GARCÍA VILLADA, *Historia eclesiástica de España*, 3 v. in 5 (Madrid 1929–36) 2.1:189–191, 271–274. C. H. LYNCH, *Saint Braulio, Bishop of Saragossa* (Washington 1938; Span. ed. rev. P. GALINDO, Madrid 1950). H. RAHNER, LexThK² 2:654.

[S. J. MC KENNA]

BRAUN, JOSEPH, archeologist and liturgist; b. Wipperfürth, Rhineland, Jan. 31, 1857; d. Pullach near Munich, July 8, 1947. He was ordained in 1881 and

Joseph Braun.

entered the Society of Jesus in 1890. After much travel and study, he taught archeology and the history of art in the theological scholasticates of his order at Valkenburg, Frankfurt, and Pullach. He was for a long time a collaborator on the *Stimmen aus Maria Laach*. Without opening essentially new vistas of knowledge, he produced many voluminous works basic to a knowledge of Christian archeology, iconography, and liturgy; they are indispensable to students because of their massive material and their description of literary sources. The monumental two-volume *Der christliche Altar in seiner geschichtlichen Entwicklung* (Munich 1924) is without doubt his most significant contribution to modern scholarship. His other works, however, are not less important: *Die liturgische Gewandung im Occident und Orient nach Ursprung und Entwicklung, Verwendung und Symbolik* (Freiburg 1907), *Sakramente und Sakramentalien* (Regensburg 1922), *Liturgisches Handlexikon* (2d edition, Regensburg 1924), *Das christliche Altargerät in seinem Sein und seiner Entwicklung* (Munich 1932), *Die Reliquiare des christlichen Kultus und ihre Entwicklung* (Freiburg 1940), *Tracht und Attribute der Heiligen in der deutschen Kunst* (Stuttgart 1943).

Bibliography: E. KIRSCHBAUM, EncCatt 3:47–48. H. SCHADE, LexThK² 2:655. NDB 2:553.

[B. NEUNHEUSER]

BRAUN, PLACIDUS, Benedictine historian; b. Peiting near Schongau in Upper Bavaria, Feb. 16, 1756; d. Augsburg, Oct. 23, 1829. He made his religious profession in the Abbey of SS. Ulrich and Afra in Augsburg and was ordained in 1779. As librarian and archivist, he organized the library book collection and published catalogues with accurate descriptions of its printed books (3 v. 1787) and of its MSS (6 v. 1791–96). The ravages of the French Revolution led to the occupation and dissolution of the abbey in 1806. Braun then devoted himself to historical studies and parish work in Augsburg. His published works thereafter deal mainly with the history of the Diocese of Augsburg and suppressed religious houses in the diocese.

Bibliography: U. BERLIÈRE, "Le P. Placide Braun, Bénédictin de Saint Ulric d'Augsbourg," RevBen 16 (1899) 1–13, lists Braun's numerous publications. P. VOLK, DHGE 10:456. R. O. AUSENDA, EncCatt 3:48–49. F. ZOEPFL, LexThK² 2:655–656.

[O. L. KAPSNER]

BRAUNS, HEINRICH, German political leader and minister of labor in the Weimar period; b. Cologne, Jan. 3, 1868; d. Lindenburg (Allgäu), Oct. 19, 1939. He was the son of a tailor. He studied theology from 1885 to 1889 and after ordination served as a curate from 1890 to 1900. In the latter year he joined the staff of the *Volksverein at München-Gladbach, and in 1903 became head of its department of organization and director of courses in political economy that had widespread influence upon Catholic social education. At the same time he completed a doctorate in political science at the University of Freiburg (1905). He became active in industrial disputes as an arbitrator for the Christian trade unions. As a delegate to the National Assembly at Weimar in 1919, and a member of the Reichstag as well as minister of labor from 1920 to 1928 (in 13 successive cabinets), he sought to promote, so far as the difficult times permitted, the social policies developed by the *Center Party under the influence of Franz *Hitze. His constant concern for the welfare of the whole people, despite his deep ties to labor, won wide recognition. Especially important achievements of his ministry were the enactment of the Labor Tribunal

Law (1926) and the establishment of unemployment insurance (1927). His more important writings include *Christliche Gewerkschaften oder Fachabteilungen in katholische Arbeitervereinen?* (Cologne 1904), published under the pseudonym Rhenanus; *Die Gewerkschaftsfrage* (Vienna 1912); *Das Betriebsrätegesetz* (München-Gladbach 1920); and *Lohnpolitik* (München-Gladbach 1921).

See also SOCIAL MOVEMENTS, CATHOLIC, 3.

[P. JOSTOCK]

BRAUWEILER, ABBEY OF, former *Benedictine monastery near Cologne, Germany, Archdiocese of Cologne (patrons, SS. Nicholas and Medard). It was founded in 1024 by the Count Palatine Erenfrid (Ezzo) of Lorraine and his consort Matilda. Abbot *Poppo of Stavelot supplied the first monks; the first and third abbots, Ello and Bl. *Wolfhelm (1065–91), came from Sankt Maximin at Trier. The abbey sided with the Emperor in the *investiture struggle. It is thought that Wolfhelm may have adopted the *Cluniac reform from *Fruttuaria-Siegburg, but the reform may have been introduced later on. Monks from Brauweiler collaborated with Count Burkhard, who wanted to convert his castle into a monastery, and thus was founded the Abbey of Komburg, which also took St. Nicholas as patron. In 1467 monks from St. Martin the Great in Cologne went to Brauweiler, which then became part of the *Bursfeld reform congregation. In 1802 Brauweiler was secularized. The abbey church, a late Romanesque columned basilica whose west towers and nave date from *c.* 1140 and whose east end and choir are early 13th century (six towers in all), is now a parish church. Its portals are richly sculptured with signs of the zodiac. Today the monastery buildings

Abbey church of Brauweiler, view from the sanctuary.

(dating from 1760–80 except for the chapter room, which has late 12th-century Biblical frescoes) serve as the provincial house of correction.

Bibliography: P. CLEMEN, ed., *Die Kunstdenkmäler der Rheinprovinz,* v.4 (Düsseldorf 1897). Cottineau 1:480. W. BADER, *Die Benediktinerabtei Brauweiler bei Köln* (Berlin 1937). P. VOLK, DHGE 10:457–458. P. SCHMITZ, *Histoire de l'Ordre de Saint-Benoît,* 7 v. (Maredsous, Bel. 1942–56). K. HALLINGER, *Gorze-Kluny,* 2 v. (StAnselm 22–25; 1950–51). E. WISPLINGHOFF, in *Jahrbuch des kölnischen Geschichtsvereins* 31–32 (1956–57) 62–73. **Illustration credit:** German Information Center, New York City.

[G. SPAHR]

BRAVO, FRANCISCO, Spanish physician, author of the first book on medicine printed in America; b. Osuna, Spain, *c.* 1530; place and date of death unknown. He completed his medical training in Osuna in 1553 and practiced medicine in New Spain during the second half of the 16th century. It is known that before he left Spain he practiced in Seville, where, as he himself related, he gave his services during an epidemic of spotted fever. On the press of Pedro Ocharte in Mexico in 1570 he published a book entitled *Opera medicinalia,* now very rare and famous. The book is written in Latin in a technical style and is a work of great erudition. The author revealed his profound knowledge, and disputed and criticized the ideas of Nicolás Monardes. Bravo was active in New Spain and enjoyed considerable prestige. His name appears frequently in documents of the period in connection with other contemporary intellectuals such as Cervantes de Salazar, who is known to have been his friend, and the mayor of Tlaxcala, Constantino de Lagunas, who was his relative.

Bibliography: J. GARCÍA ICAZBALCETA, "Los médicos de México en el siglo XVI," *Bibliografía mexicana del siglo XVI,* ed. A. MILLARES CARLO (new ed. Mexico City 1954) 223–242.

[G. SOMOLINOS]

BRAZIL

The largest and most populous country in South America and the largest Catholic nation in the world, covering an area of 3,288,240 square miles. The population in the 1960 census was 70,960,000. The official estimate of Sept. 1, 1963, placed the number at 77,000,000. Of this number more than 90 per cent declared themselves to be Roman Catholics. The history of the Church in Brazil began on April 22, 1500, with its discovery by Pedro Álvares *Cabral, then commanding the second Portuguese expedition to India. With Cabral were a few diocesan priests and 15 Franciscans under the leadership of Frei Henrique de Coimbra, who celebrated the first Mass on Brazilian soil on April 26. When the fleet proceeded on its way to the Orient, none of the priests remained in Brazil.

Very little was made of this discovery by the Portuguese for years. The only activity was almost purely commercial—expeditions in search of the brazilwood for making dyes. Trading and storage forts were set up along the coast, but only a few of these (e.g., Pôrto Seguro) had resident priests. In 1530 the King divided the land into captaincies, to be administered in a semi-feudal manner by donataries, each with absolute power in his region, subordinate only to the monarch. There was no centralized government in the colony and only sporadic priestly activity.

The Indian culture and religion made the work of conversion extremely difficult. The Tupí Indians were of marginal and silvan culture. They had a strong sense of religion based on a naturalistic pantheism with vague vestiges of monotheism. They were extremely well adapted to their environment, and from them the Portuguese learned many culture traits, the most significant being the use of manioc as food, the hammock as a bed, and the slash and burn system of cultivation. The Brazilian Indians had many good qualities, such as love of children and hospitality, but they were also burdened with some vices, especially polygamy, some cannibalism, excess in drinking alcoholic beverages, continuous wars of vengeance, and a general lack of constancy.

COLONIAL PERIOD

Owing to the paucity of historical records, it is difficult to establish the early ecclesiastical history of Brazil. There seems little doubt, however, that some Franciscan friars were present at various places in Brazil before 1549. Between 1500 and 1521 some Portuguese Franciscans were present at Pôrto Seguro, where, after some time, they and the other white colonists were captured and eaten by the natives. Other visitations by Franciscans occurred about 1538, at the founding of the captaincy of Pôrto Seguro. At nearly the same time Father Bernardo de Armenta and some Spanish Franciscan companions worked in the region of Santa Catarina on the boundaries of Paraguay, in what was then considered Spanish territory. The Franciscan Frei Pedro Palacios, a Spanish member of the Portuguese province, after helping the Jesuits catechize the Indians for some time, founded the sanctuary of Penha in modern Espirito Santo sometime in the 1560s. The early Jesuits, especially José de *Anchieta, speak of Indians so well catechized by these early friars that they spontaneously presented themselves as Christians to the Jesuits when the latter arrived in 1549.

Political and Ecclesiastical Organization. With the failure of the captaincy system to colonize Brazil, the Portuguese king John III created a central government in 1549, naming Tomé de Sousa as governor-general and Salvador as the capitol. Four Jesuit priests and two lay brothers, under the direction of Manuel da *Nóbrega, accompanied the governor to the New World. Some secular priests also were sent, but details have come down to us only concerning a very few, such as Manoel Lourenço, in Salvador, Bahia.

The Jesuits fell to work immediately, both among the colonists and among the Indians. The first governor placed his prestige and power behind their efforts. After founding a church and school in Salvador, the Jesuits extended their apostolate into the neighboring Indian villages, and through the help of trained native and Portuguese boys, converted some of the Indians. Within 6 months about 600 were ready for Baptism. Within a year the number had risen to about 1,000. Soon the Jesuits were able to compose crude grammars and catechisms in the so-called "lingoa geral" a sort of lingua franca more or less understood by most of the Indians in the region. (*See* ALDEIAMENTO SYSTEM IN BRAZIL.)

From 1514 to 1551 Brazil was under the nominal jurisdiction of the bishop of Funchal, but he made no effort to exert his authority over the new colony. By the bull "Super specula militantis ecclesiae" of Feb.

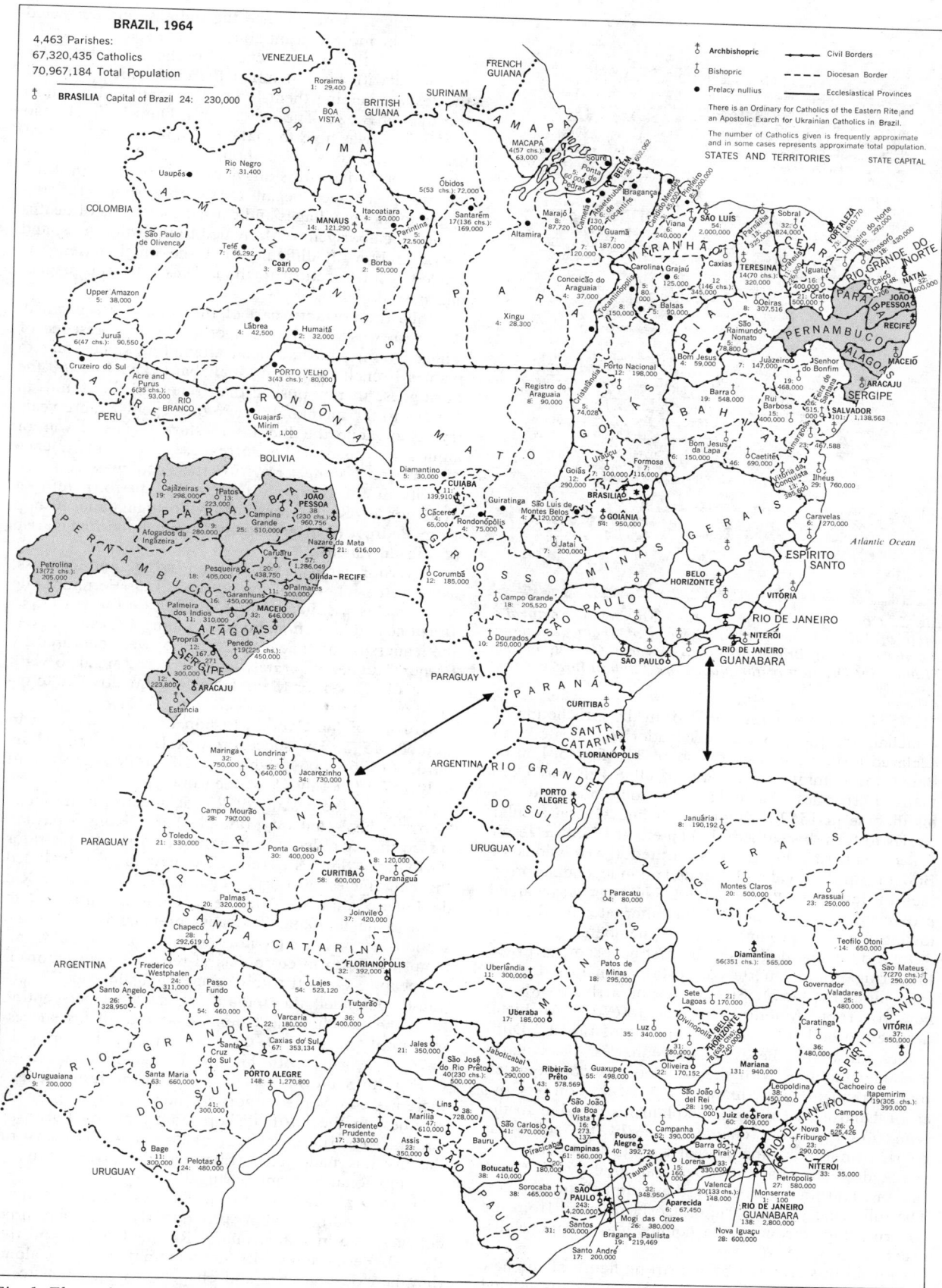

BRAZIL, 1964

4,463 Parishes:
67,320,435 Catholics
70,967,184 Total Population

✠ **BRASILIA** Capital of Brazil 24: 230,000

Fig. 1. The ecclesiastical divisions of the United States of Brazil in 1964.

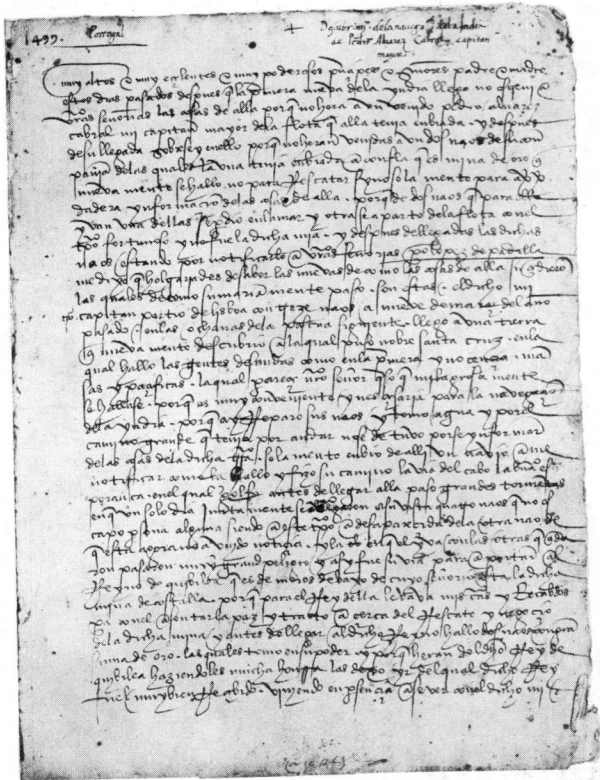

Fig. 2. Contemporary copy of King Manuel of Portugal's letter of 1500 to the King and Queen of Spain describing the discovery of Brazil by Pedro Álvarez Cabral, in the Manuscript Division of the New York Public Library.

central government, pacified the Indians, and corrected some of the most flagrant abuses of the colonists, which had caused the Indian revolts in the first place. He promoted with his full might the catechetical work of the Jesuits, helping them to erect schools and missions throughout Brazil. The new bishop, Dom Pedro Leitão (1559–73), was able to make a canonical visitation of the area and to baptize thousands of Indians in the *aldeias,* or Indian mission villages. However, in 1563 various pestilences began to sweep through the unhygienic Indian villages and caused thousands of deaths among the aborigenes. Many fled to the wilderness, and it was only with difficulty that the missionaries persuaded them to return to the *aldeias* after the plagues had passed.

While the northern part of the colony was pacified, the south was rendered dangerous by the presence of Villegaignon, who had been attempting since 1555 to plant a French colony in Guanabara Bay. In 1560 the Portuguese merely pushed the French off the islands in the bay to the mainland, where they spent 7 more years trying to incite the Indians to start a general war of annihilation against the Portuguese. As a consequence of the French danger, in 1567 the Portuguese founded the city of São Sebastião do Rio de Janeiro, naming it in honor of King Sebastian of Portugal, and Bishop Dom Pedro Leitão personally founded the first parish of Rio de Janeiro.

Governor Mem de Sá, broken by age and sickness, asked to be relieved of his position. Luis Fernandes de Vasconcelos was named in 1570, but on the voyage to Brazil he and his companions, including 40 Jesuits under the leadership of Inácio de Azevedo, were captured by French Huguenot pirates, and 39 were forced to walk the plank. Governor Mem de Sá consequently had to remain at his post until his death in 1572.

Growth of the Church. Bishop Pedro Leitão died in October 1573. His successor was Dom Antônio Barreiros (1576–1600), who arrived in Pernambuco in May 1576. On July 19 of the same year Pope Gregory XIII created the prelacy of Rio de Janeiro, in the brief "Novi Orbis," and on May 11, 1577, King Sebastian signed the royal letter nominating as first administrator Bartolomeu Simões Pereira. The new prelacy included the captaincies of Pôrto Seguro, Espirito Santo, Rio de Janeiro, and São Vicente, extending southward to the Rio de la Plata. The new prelate visited all the sections of his vast territory and began at once to attempt a reform in customs and religious instruction of his people. Unfortunately, since he openly and strenuously defended the Indians, he suffered persecution from the slaveholding colonists, as did all his successors until the time of the creation of a bishopric in 1676. Disgusted with his lot, Father Pereira retired to Espirito Santo in 1591 and died at the Jesuit college there in 1603. Some authors say he was poisoned by his enemies. In the north Bishop Dom Antônio Barreiros had a successful episcopacy of 24 years. The work of the missions made great strides with the advent of many new missionaries from Portugal.

Work of Religious Orders. The Jesuits by this time had expanded their labors prodigiously. They had three colleges, one in Bahia, one in Rio de Janeiro, and the third in Pernambuco. In the captaincy of Bahia alone they had 62 churches and chapels, 16 of which were

25, 1551, Brazil was separated from the jurisdiction of Funchal, and the Diocese of Salvador was created and declared a suffragan see of Lisbon. The first bishop of Bahia and commissary general of all Brazil was Dom Pedro Fernandes *Sardinha, who took possession of his diocese in 1552, bringing with him several secular clerics to form his cathedral chapter. In 1553 the Jesuit general superior in Rome separated the missions of Brazil from Portugal and founded an independent province of Jesuits in the new land. Nóbrega was named provincial; and Luis de Grã, his alternate. By the following year the province had 26 members.

In 1553 Tomé de Sousa, the first governor, returned to Portugal, and Duarte da Costa was named to succeed him (1553–57). Sixteen Jesuits arrived with the new governor. Among them was José de *Anchieta, destined to be known as the "Apostle of Brazil." Difficulties arose for the Jesuit missionaries, particularly misunderstandings with the new bishop, compounded by the frequent wildly immoral acts of the son of Governor Duarte da Costa. To explain his position to the King and to answer charges made by the Jesuits at court, Bishop Sardinha set sail for Portugal, was shipwrecked off the coast of Brazil, captured by the Caeté Indians, and finally eaten by the cannibalistic savages. The following year Duarte da Costa resigned from the governorship, throwing the colony into complete disorder.

Control was restored by the strong figure of the new governor, Mem de Sá (1557–72). He soon consolidated

parishes. Anchieta claims that the number of baptized rose to over 100,000. Other religious orders now began their apostolate in Brazil. In 1584 the Franciscans began organized work. At the petition of Jorge de Albuquerque Coelho, the donatary of Pernambuco, the minister general of the order decreed the creation of the custody of St. Anthony and nominated the first *custos,* Frei Melquior de Santa Catarina. Pope Sixtus V confirmed the founding by his bull "Piis fidelium votis" in 1586. Frei Melquior and his confreres established themselves in Olinda and soon were invited to enter other provinces of Brazil: Bahia in 1587, Iguaraçu in 1588, Paraíba in 1589. Within 70 years the Franciscans had more than 20 monasteries, with many Indian missions. The Benedictines, headed by Dom Antônio Ventura, founded their first abbey in Salvador in 1584. They soon had monasteries also in Rio de Janeiro (1589?), Olinda (1596), Paraíba do Norte (1596), São Paulo (1598), Santos (1650), and Sorocaba (1660). Normally they did not accept Indian missions. The Carmelites arrived in Pernambuco in 1589 under the command of Frei Domingos Freire. They soon spread to Salvador, Santos, São Paulo, and Rio de Janeiro. They cared for many Indians in their missions, especially in the Amazon region.

Expansion into the Amazon Region. At the end of the 16th century there began the push to the north of Brazil toward the Amazon. This move was made partly to combat the French efforts to colonize there after their defeat in the south and partly in response to the desire of restless adventurers who wanted to conquer new lands. The first French attempt in 1594 failed to found a settlement on the island of Maranhão, but in 1612 the French returned. With them came four French Capuchins under Claude d'*Abbeville. Seventeen more Capuchins arrived in 1614. The Capuchins made valuable efforts to study and write about the Indians and their customs, but French efforts were doomed almost at once by a concerted drive of the Portuguese to expel them. In 1615 the French were defeated by a force of Indians and Portuguese under command of Jerônimo de Albuquerque and Alexandre de Moura and were immediately expelled from the country. With them went the Capuchins. Their work was taken over by Jesuits

Fig. 3. The church of São Francisco, Salvador, Brazil.

and Franciscans. The latter were more active and spread northward to Pará in 1617, led by the missionary and linguist Frei Antônio de Marciana.

In 1624 the long-planned division of Brazil into two states was carried out, with the respective capitals at Salvador and São Luiz. With the new governor came Frei Cristóvão de *Lisboa, who was sent with quasi-episcopal powers, with 18 companions, 5 of them Brazilians who knew the Indian languages, to the newly named state of Maranhão e Grão Pará. The King had first thought of sending a bishop to the area but finally decided to send a Franciscan with episcopal and inquisitorial powers. This was much less of a drain on the royal treasury. Frei Cristóvão made a zealous attempt to set up orderly Indian-white relations, only to come up against instant colonist fury and disobedience. Results of these efforts, therefore, were meager.

Obstacles to Church Development. Throughout Brazil missionaries and bishops encountered opposition from the colonists and government officials. Feliciano de Coelho, Governor of Paraíba, expelled both the Jesuits (1593) and the Franciscans (1596). Some years later Governor General Diogo de Botelho (1602–07) asked for authority to forbid the founding of any new monasteries in Brazil. Both he and his successor, Diogo Menezes (1607–12), were involved in almost continual quarrels with Bishop Dom Constantino Barradas (1600–18) and with the religious, mainly because of the always touchy question of Indian protection. Affairs were just being regularized when the next great crisis struck the colony.

One consequence of the Dual Monarchy of Spain and Portugal (1580–1640) was that the Dutch resolved to conquer part of Brazil. Bahia was taken after token resistance on May 9, 1624; Governor Diogo de Mendonça Furtado, with all the Jesuits, Benedictines, and Franciscans there, was taken to Holland under guard. The rest of the religious fled by sea to Pernambuco. Other priests and Bishop Dom Marcos Teixeira went into the interior. Only Frei Vicente do *Salvador, the Franciscan historian, was allowed, after a short imprisonment, to remain in the city. The cathedral was transformed into a Calvinist temple, the college of the Jesuits was used as a barracks, and the other churches were turned into warehouses. The Portuguese retook Salvador on May 1, 1625, but the Dutch returned to the attack in 1630. They secured Olinda and Recife in Pernambuco and built a colonial empire extending northward to Pará. Legally, religious freedom was guaranteed to the Catholic population; but actually there was much repression and bigotry. Forty Franciscans were allowed to stay in four of their six monasteries; ten Carmelites remained in the only one of their ten monasteries left to them; Jesuits continued to be forbidden altogether. When seditious letters of the Franciscans and Carmelites were intercepted by the Dutch, this short period of tolerance ended, and the priests were made to suffer privations and imprisonment. A new Dutch governor, Count Maurice of Nassau, ended the persecution for a short time and restrained the Calvinist ministers in their anti-Catholic zeal, although he later exiled and killed friars who were working in favor of their mother country. After two battles of Guararapes in 1648 and 1649 crushed the power of the badly divided Dutch, the Brazilians forced them to sign a capitulation in 1654, ending the strongest Protestant threat to colonial Brazil.

Although the Portuguese revolted successfully against Spanish rule in 1640, a peace treaty between Spain and Portugal was not signed until 1668. This had important results for the Church in Brazil, since it had been impossible to organize the Church during the Dutch supremacy and the war with Spain. Now Pope Innocent XI, by the bull "Inter pastoralis officii curas," raised the Diocese of Bahia to the rank of an archdiocese, with suffragan sees in Rio de Janeiro, Olinda, and Maranhão.

Protection of the Indians. It was especially in the Amazon region that the question of protecting the Indians came to be important. In other parts of Brazil the coming of Negro slaves freed the Indians from the slave hunters to a large extent. Not so in the north, where the colonists were usually too poor to pay the exorbitant prices charged for Negro slaves. The whole question resolved around one problem: who was to administer and control the Indians, laymen or religious? Frei Cristóvão de Lisboa had difficulties in 1624, when he tried to end lay administration of the aborigines and to put into effect Franciscan control. Such was the strength of the opposition that the crown was forced to suspend the execution of the law of 1624 brought to Brazil by the Franciscan prelate. So began the long series of vacillations of the Portuguese crown: sometimes the laws protected the Indians and gave them to the religious for Christianizing; at other times the colonists were more powerful and retained control. Perhaps the most militant figure of the 17th century in the north was the Jesuit Antônio Vieira, who, because of his influence at court, was able to obtain adequate authority to missionize and protect the Indians to a greater extent than ever before. However, insurrection in Maranhão (1661) forced the Jesuits to leave the country. Effective missionizing began again only in 1680, when a new series of laws again gave control of the Indians to the missionaries, at the same time forbidding any enslavement of the Indians. Application of the laws of 1680 caused a local revolt in São Luiz, Maranhão, in 1684, led by the wealthy plantation owner Manuel Beckmann, or Bequimão.

There were still to be vacillations and weaknesses shown by the government in the face of lobbyists for Indian enslavement, but for the most part the principle of freedom for the Indians was maintained until the time of Pombal. The golden age of the missions in the Amazon region was 1680 to 1750. Jesuits, Franciscans, Carmelites, and (to a lesser extent) Mercedarians, all had *aldeias*.

The boundaries between Portuguese and Spanish America in the La Plata region remained fluid during the centuries after Tordesillas. Spanish Jesuits working out of Paraguay founded in the 17th century a series of *reductions along the banks of the Paraná, Paraguay, and Uruguay Rivers. In 1585 the first bishop of Tucumán, Fray Francisco Vitoria, OP, invited Portuguese Jesuits to work in his diocese. Four of them actually arrived there, but no permanent settlements were founded. The territory did impinge on Portuguese territory in what is today Santa Catarina and Rio Grande do Sul. The Portuguese claim to the La Plata region was maintained along the coast by small villages and by the fortified town called Colônia do Sacramento, across the estuary from Buenos Aires. These settlements had parish priests or chaplains most of the time but only occasional visits from missionaries.

The Church in the 18th Century. This was a century of immense difficulties for the Church in Brazil. Among the Portuguese and Brazilians all religious idealism was lost in the gold and diamond fever that swept the colony. Ecclesiastics also were infected. The irreligious spirit in the philosophies of the time culminated in the suppression of the Society of Jesus in 1782 and in the ensuing control over education by the state.

Expulsion of the Jesuits. The treaty of Madrid of 1750 gave present-day Uruguay (Sacramento) to Spain, while Spain ceded to Portugal the Jesuit missions, in the present state of Rio Grande do Sul, which had a population of 30,000 Guaraní Indians. It seems certain that some of the Jesuits there disregarded the command of the Jesuit general to abide by the treaty. In any case, the Marquês de Pombal, Minister of State in Portugal (1750–77), seized upon this evidence of noncompliance to start his campaign against the society. A joint Spanish-Portuguese expedition defeated the Indians and expelled them by force in 1756. When the governor of Rio de Janeiro refused to take over the mission lands or to cede Colônia do Sacramento, the whole treaty was annulled, and the Indians were allowed to return to their ruined villages in 1761. Next Pombal used the delimiting expedition in the Amazon region, under command of his brother, Francisco Xavier de Mendonça Furtado, with the bishop of Belém Dom Miguel de Bulhões as his willing ally, to attack the Jesuits. For real or imagined insults to the royal prerogative, the Jesuits in the north were successively deprived of their royal salary, their missions, their lands, and finally their freedom. They were sent under guard to Portugal, where many of them spent long years in prison. Any ecclesiastic or layman who defended them was subjected to government displeasure and even exile.

The loss of almost 500 Jesuits at one time was a blow from which the Church in Brazil was not to recover until well into the 20th century. Many religious of other orders were also exiled from Brazil at the same time. Those who stayed and tried to continue work among the Indians were powerless, after the so-called "law of liberation of 1755," to stop depredations against their Indian parishioners, since all temporal power was taken away from the padres, and they became merely parish priests in parishes the size of European countries. There was in the late 18th century a growing move to repress religious orders of both sexes, generally through the very effective means of controlling or prohibiting the reception of novices for years at a time.

Effects of Regalism on Church Organization and Secular Clergy. Regalism kept the number of dioceses and bishops in Brazil small. The government wanted to avoid the onus of supporting new dioceses and paying clerics' salaries. Besides Salvador (1551) and Rio de Janeiro (1676), only five more dioceses were created during the entire colonial period: São Luiz do Maranhão (1677), Olinda-Recife (1678), Belém do Pará (1719), São Paulo (1746), and Mariana (1748). Even with this small number of dioceses, the government did not support seminaries for each. Although the Portuguese government had accepted without modification the decrees of the Council of Trent that made diocesan seminaries obligatory, the results were meager. Bahia possessed a short-lived seminary in 1569 and again in 1608, but

Fig. 4. Brazil: (a) The 18th-century church of Our Lord of Bomfim at Bahia. (b) The church of São Alexandro, Belém, begun in 1616. (c) Panoramic view of Belém (founded 1613), near the mouth of the Amazon River.

the first quasi-conciliar seminary was begun in Rio de Janeiro only in 1739, by Bp. Antônio de Guadalupe. Later others were founded in Belém (1749), Mariana (1750), Olinda (1800), and Salvador (1815). Most of these did not endure long. What was worse, the majority of the students, especially in the preparatory seminaries, were really not destined for the priesthood but simply were taking advantage of the only institutions of higher learning in Brazil. There was not one university in Brazil until the 19th century. The only attempt to found one was made by the Franciscans in 1776, with some graduate courses for lay students in their monastery in Rio de Janeiro.

At the end of the colonial period the principle that priests were civil servants had been firmly established. Education was completely under governmental control, and the so-called "Reforms of Coimbra," which stressed the positive sciences at the expense of scholastic or spiritual philosophy, were taught in every school, even in the primary grades. The texts used in philosophy and theology were controlled by the state, and Jansenist and regalist texts predominated. The paucity of bishops and the immense distances they had to travel within their dioceses made inspection difficult, and ecclesiastical subjects had the right of recourse to the civil courts. This made discipline difficult to uphold. Energetic bishops were not lacking at times, but little could be done against the all-pervading *padroado.* (*See* PATRONATO REAL.) Many churchmen became politicians. However, it remained for the empire after independence (1822–89) to perfect the regalistic control over the Church and in the process to bring the Church to the lowest condition it ever suffered in Brazil.

Religious Orders of Women. Because of royal restrictions issued in 1603, 1609, and 1683, convents of nuns were not founded in Brazil until late in the colonial period. Ursulines of the Sacred Heart of Jesus, of the Roman Union, founded the Colégio das Mercês (1735) and the Colégio da Soledade (1739) in Bahia and later expanded their work to the south. The Carmelites of St. Theresa established themselves in Rio de Janeiro in 1742. Conceptionist sisters entered Bahia in 1744, founding first a retreat house and then the monastery of Lapa. In 1750 they founded the monastery of Ajuda in Rio de Janerio in the institution originally established by Capuchin sisters in 1705. The retreat house of the Macaúbas, Santa Luzia do Rio das Velhas in Minas Gerais, founded in 1715, eventually became a Conceptionist monastery (1933) as did a number of similar foundations. In 1720 there was also a convent of Poor Clares in Bahia. The social contribution of these cloistered communities was principally educational for they usually conducted boarding schools.

THE CHURCH IN INDEPENDENT BRAZIL

Under pressure from Napoleon, the royal family fled Portugal and arrived in Rio de Janeiro on March 7, 1808. The colony now became the metropolis of the Portuguese Empire until in 1822 independence from Portugal was declared by Brazil. Although the Church officially did not take sides in the struggle for independence, many churchmen played prominent parts. Freemasonry, making its own the ideas of independence and republicanism, found many adherents, lay and ecclesiastic. An unsuccessful republican revolution in Pernambuco in 1817 had so many priests among the

agitators that it has been called the "revolution of the padres." Most of the churchmen and laymen involved in this revolution had been educated in the seminary of Olinda, founded in 1800 by Bp. José Joaquím da Cunha Azeredo Coutinho. This seminary taught the special species of Jansenistic regalism inculcated by Pombal in his reform of the University of Coimbra. The influence of this seminary continued to be felt through most of the century.

The constituent assembly of 1823 was dominated by ultraliberal republican ideas. With few exceptions, the 23 clergymen representatives expressed uniformly regalistic ideas. However, the constitution unilaterally promulgated by the King, after he dissolved the constituent assembly, proclaimed that Catholicism would continue to be the official state religion. The restraint with which the Catholic religion was treated was owing mainly to the efforts of José da Silva *Lisboa, who led the Catholic cause.

Further diocesan organization was undertaken. The prelacies of Goiás and Cuiabá, created but hardly implemented on Dec. 6, 1745, were in 1826 raised to the category of bishoprics. In 1828 the Dioceses of Maranhão and Pará were separated from the Archdiocese of Lisbon and became suffragan sees of Salvador, Bahia. In 1826 an apostolic nunciature also was created, but in 1832 it was reduced to the rank of a simple internunciature.

During the reign of Pedro I (1822–31) and the regency (1831–40) regalism was rampant. Pontifical messages required the imperial placet; religious orders were subjected to unwarranted interference, even in internal affairs, as were dioceses and diocesan seminaries. The government suppressed the Augustinians in Bahia in 1824, and the Discalced Carmelites and Capuchins in Pernambuco in 1830. Hundreds of permissions were given by the civil government to religious, male and female, to reside outside the convents for long periods of time, thus fostering decadence in the religious orders. The regency period saw the introduction of many anti-Church and antireligious measures, inspired by liberalism and freemasonry. Frequently the bishops complained of the flood of decrees that restricted their liberty and independence of action.

The questions of the confirmation of bishops and of celibacy muddied the relations with the Holy See for many years. A noted antipapal ultraregalist priest, Antônio de *Moura, was deliberately proposed by the government as bishop of Rio de Janeiro. The Holy See refused to accept this nomination. Father Diogo *Feijó, the regent, was so incensed that he resolved in the name of the government (July 18, 1836) to deny permission to any Brazilian to have recourse to the Holy See until the bulls of confirmation for Moura were granted. The stalemate finally terminated when Moura withdrew his candidacy. The government showed ever more clearly its tendency to control the economy of the Church and to reduce it to a department of civil administration. Happily a champion arose finally in the chamber of deputies: Dom Romualdo Antônio de *Seixas, Archbishop and Primate of Bahia.

Decline of the Religious Orders and Brotherhoods. The state of monastic life in the 19th century sank to its lowest possible level. Some religious communities died out completely. Others were forced to sell monastic property and convents to support themselves. All suffered from lack of new members and from the growing ease with which the civil government and the papal internuncios gave briefs of exclaustration or secularization to religious. It was determined by the government that it would take over the property of the orders upon the death of the respective last member. The crowning blow came on May 19, 1855, when José Tomás Nabuco de Araújo, Minister of Justice, decreed that no novices could be accepted in any religious order "until a concordat about to be presented by the government to the Holy See be resolved." No concordat was presented during the rest of the empire, although a few half-hearted attempts were made. Cynically, the government continued to speak piously of the "reform" of the religious orders.

The Franciscans, who had tried to take the place of the Jesuits in the missions after 1759, found themselves without any power to protect the Indians after the secularization. Soon even this work was impossible for them as their numbers decreased and no new members were allowed. Instead, Italian Capuchins were called in for work among the Indians in 1825 and continued through the years of the empire. The very government that was trying to extinguish Brazilian religious orders paid for foreign friars to do the same work the local orders had been doing when they had sufficient numbers. A few Vincentians, Salesians, Redemptorists, and Sisters of Charity also were allowed to come into the country during this century, but their numbers were too small to stem the tide of religious decadence.

A feature of religion in Brazil from colonial times was the ecclesiastical brotherhoods (irmandades), founded along class lines for social, economic, and religious purposes. These built their own churches and were always difficult for the local bishops to control. In the 19th century Freemasonry penetrated these confraternities. Papal bulls condemning Freemasonry had never been published in Brazil, and this gave rise to the common opinion that Brazilian Masonry was different from world Masonry, was favorable to religion, and was therefore open even to clergy memberships. The clergy joined the lodges with distressing regularity.

The Religious Question (1872–75). The antagonism between the Church and Masonry broke out into the open in 1872, when the Bishop of Rio de Janeiro Dom Pedro María de Lacerda suspended Almeida Martins, who was going to celebrate a solemn Mass of Thanksgiving on the anniversary of the founding of the local Masonic lodge. The Viscount Rio Branco, Minister of State and Grand Master of the Grand Orient of Lavradio, decided to "smash the episcopate with a double condemnation, civil and religious," so that never again would a Catholic bishop dare to question the rights of all Brazilians to be Freemasons and Catholics at the same time. The other local lodge, the Grand Orient of the Vale dos Beneditinos, joined in the attack on Bishop Lacerda, who allowed the suspension to stand but was afraid to take any more steps.

Only two of the bishops of Brazil entered the lists openly in this battle against regalism: Dom Vital María *Gonçalves de Oliveira, Bishop of Olinda, and Dom Antônio de *Macedo Costa, Bishop of Belém. Both bishops were convinced that Brazilian Masonry was identical with that of Europe and said so in pastorals. Brotherhoods in these dioceses published lists of members, including priests, who were Masons and members

in good standing in the brotherhoods. When the two bishops ordered priests to sever all connection with these brotherhoods, the clergy obeyed with only one or two exceptions. When the brotherhoods would not expel Masonic members, the bishops placed them under interdict. This was the edict that was appealed to the crown. The Emperor, following the advice of Minister Rio Branco, sent a message to the bishops ordering them to lift the censures. They refused.

The government, hoping to gain a double condemnation of the bishops by both Church and State, in August 1873 sent the Baron of Penedo as special envoy to Rome. In talks with the Secretary of State Cardinal Antonelli, he stressed the extreme urgency of restoring peace to the Church in Brazil and insinuated that the conflict could have been avoided if the bishops had acted with less precipitation. He made no mention of the fact that the bishops had already been apprehended. Both Pius IX and Cardinal Antonelli appear to have believed the envoy and without further verification dispatched a letter on Dec. 18, 1873, to be given by the internuncio Monsignor Sanguigni to the two bishops. The letter praised the zeal of the bishops but mildly censured them for the rapidity of their actions; it ordered them to lift the interdict and then to take care of the purification of the brotherhoods. Within a few days after the envoy left Rome, word reached the Eternal City of the imprisonment of the bishops, who had in fact been awaiting trial while the talks were going on.

Meanwhile the letter to the bishops arrived at the internunciature, and Monsignor Sanguigni still gave the letter to the bishops. The two bishops, however, did not publish the letter; the government had to spread the word of the Pope's censure of the two "hotheads." The two bishops never wavered, being certain that the Holy Father had been badly informed. On trial before the supreme court, they refused to defend themselves since they did not recognize the competence of the secular tribunal. Three distinguished Catholic laymen, Zacarías de Góis e Vasconcelos, Cândido Mendes de Almeida, and Antônio Ferreira Viana, came forward voluntarily to present the defense. The arguments they presented were brilliant, but both bishops were condemned to 4 years at hard labor. The Emperor refused amnesty, although he reduced the sentence to simple imprisonment for 4 years.

A flood of protests reached the Emperor from every side. Pope Pius IX wrote a personal letter to Pedro II, decrying the violence and duplicity of the government and approving all the acts of the two bishops. He also reiterated the condemnation of Brazilian Masons. The Holy Father also ordered the nuncio to destroy the "fatal letter" of Cardinal Antonelli.

Even after their sentence to prison the two bishops did not lift their interdicts. Their substitutes in the two dioceses, some of whom went to prison, also refused to do so. The Brazilian bishops were belatedly united as never before. A real Catholic revival set in. Churches were crowded with people pledging their allegiance in writing to the two condemned bishops. It was partially owing to the intransigence of Baron Rio Branco in this question that his ministry fell in 1875. The Emperor invited the Duque de Caxias to form a new ministry, and Caxias accepted only on condition, it is said, that the Emperor would grant amnesty to the bishops. Pedro

II was forced to accede and signed their pardon on Sept. 17, 1875.

The victory, although great, was not complete for the Church. Pius IX, in a communication to the bishops, commanded them to lift the interdicts immediately upon their release. They did so but could not then insist on the purification of the brotherhoods. The bishops' control over the more influential brotherhoods even today is somewhat tenuous, although priests are no longer members of the Masonic lodges.

Abolition Movement. Slavery was an important question in 19th-century Brazil. The movement for abolition grew strong after 1870 and was sponsored especially by the rising, new republican party. Clergymen seem not to have had much to do with this movement, although some religious orders and bishops freed all their slaves many years before abolition. Decrees in 1871, 1885, and 1888 destroyed slavery gradually, but even so the "golden law" of 1888 was a severe blow to the plantation economy. It will long be a moot point whether the religious question or the slavery question contributed more to the overthrow of the empire. In any case, Pedro II submitted peacefully to the republican authority on Nov. 15, 1889, and went quietly into exile. On Jan. 7, 1890, the provisional government declared "extinct all patronage with all its institutions, recourses and prerogatives."

The Church in the Republic. The new constitution of 1891, positivistic in the extreme, decreed the complete separation of Church and State in Brazil. It also decreed complete liberty of cults, secularization of cemeteries, the laicization of education in public schools, civil marriage as the only legal marriage, denial of all political rights to religious, exclusion of Jesuits, and the absolute prohibition against new convents of religious. The mode of attack was different, but the purpose was still the same: the empire smothered the Church, and the new republic completely ignored her, but both wanted to keep her powerless.

Urged by the new internuncio, Monsignor Spolverini, the bishops issued the celebrated Collective Pastoral Letter of March 19, 1890, which solemnly protested the new decrees and succeeded in blunting many of the new measures. They obtained their freedom of government of the Church and had the law against Jesuits abolished. Although the positivists continued their attacks in newspapers and pamphlets, the official government persecution ceased. Permission was obtained for foreign members of religious orders then extant in Brazil to revivify these venerable groups. The Franciscans, Carmelites, and Benedictines were able to rebuild their provinces. Jesuits and Redemptorists came in numbers.

New Dioceses. With separation of Church and State, it was at last feasible to create the necessary new bishoprics that the imperial government had so long denied. The country was divided by Pope Leo XIII into two provinces: Bahia, with seven suffragan sees, and Rio de Janeiro, with nine. Pius X raised the number of archbishoprics to seven and created many new bishoprics and prelacies. Benedict XV, Pius XI, and Pius XII continued to increase the number of dioceses, until in 1960 Brazil counted 25 archdioceses, 87 suffragan dioceses, 30 prelacies *nullius*, and 1 abbacy *nullius*, all these in a country that in 1889 had but 12 dioceses.

Relations with Rome continued to improve after 1890. In 1901 the internunciature was elevated to the rank of nunciature. Four years later the first cardinalate was given to Brazil in the person of Dom Joaquím *Arcoverde de Albuquerque. In 1919 Brazil's representation at the Holy See was raised to the rank of embassy.

Education. Because of the secularistic contents of the 1891 constitution, the Church had very little influence in the public schools. Little by little the prohibition against the teaching of religion in public schools broke down. Minas Gerais became the first state to introduce religious education into the schools; it was followed by the state of São Paulo. A strong fight against these changes was made by the ultraliberals and Freemasons, but in the constitution of Nov. 10, 1937, it was ordained that the teaching of religion be allowed if the parents so wished. This law is still being followed throughout the country.

Beginning in 1901 some of the hierarchy met periodically (five times before 1916) to discuss common problems and write collective pastorals. A national plenary council was urgently needed, however, especially after the new Code of Canon Law in 1917 modified or annulled many of the provisions of the earlier pastoral letters. In 1939 the first Brazilian council of bishops was held, coinciding with the opening of the Catholic University of Rio de Janeiro. The council opened on June 1, 1939, with 98 members present, and ended on June 20. The report of this council spoke frankly of the 20th-century problems facing the Church. It stressed especially the lack of learned and saintly priests. There were many seminaries, it was true. Since 1929 the Brazilian College in Rome had been functioning separately from the *South American College, but there were not sufficient worthy students. Because of the lack of priests, parishes were much too extensive, and many of them lacked pastors.

Problems of the Mid-20th Century. Brazil lacks a strong Catholic press. Only in 1930 was the first Catholic newspaper in Portuguese published. Today most dioceses have some publications, but often they are poorly edited and of small circulation. An exception is the popular and influential *O Diario* of Belo Horizonte, Minas Gerais. An excellent monthly magazine for clerics is the *Revista eclesiastica brasileira.*

High illiteracy (about 50 per cent) and poor living conditions for thousands pose a special challenge to the Church's social ideas, programs, and conscience. Vocations to the priesthood and the religious state have never really become sufficient. The majority of the clergy even today are still foreigners. Spiritism, appealing to the overemotionalism of rich and poor, colored and white, has made inroads among Catholics, even among the better educated. However, there has been considerable growth in vitality in the last 75 years. In 1958 there were in Brazil 6,256 members of 82 male religious orders. The Franciscans, Capuchins, Salesians, and Redemptorists were most numerous. There were also 1,706 members of nonclerical male religious orders, the majority being Marists and Brothers of the Christian Schools. There were over 35,000 sisters in 216 congregations. Partial statistics for 1960 showed 4,270 diocesan priests, 6,255 religious priests, 91 male religious orders and congregations, and 237 female religious congrega-

Fig. 5. The church of São Francisco, Pampulha, Belo Horizonte, Brazil, by the noted architect Oscar Niemeyer.

tions. In 1960 there was an average of 16,120 persons in each parish, about 6,127 Catholics for each priest. There is an increasing unity and cooperation between the religious orders represented in their conferences and the yearly national conferences of the bishops. Next to that of the U.S., the Brazilian hierarchy is the largest in the world.

[M. C. KIEMEN]

Spiritism. In 1964 about 30 per cent of the Brazilian population was connected with Spiritism in one way or another. By "espiritismo" is meant a pretended communication, perceptive and provocative, with the departed spirits, either to receive their news or to consult them (necromancy) or to place them at the service of man (magic) to do good (white magic) or to do evil (black magic). As a religious-moral system, Spiritism originated in France with Allan *Kardec in 1857. This French Spiritism, also called "Kardecismo," began its propaganda in Brazil in 1865. Various religious groups united in 1884 in the Federação Espírita Brasileira, which since then has directed the Brazilian Spiritist movement through local organizations in all the Brazilian states. By the pact of 1949 the federalized societies promised to adopt the doctrinal orientation contained in the works of Kardec (which is characterized by the principle of reincarnation). In 1952 they officially declared the practice of Spiritism as a religion. In the census of 1940 this Kardecistic group had 463,400 professed practitioners; in 1950 there were already 824,553. Along with Kardecism arose other numerous spiritist movements and independent spiritualists, who also accept the reincarnation doctrine, which is basically contrary to Christian belief. These people are often called "Kardecistas."

Another movement, entirely independent of Kardecism, is called Espiritismo de Umbanda. It is impossible to indicate the exact date of its appearance. Popular movements of clearly African origin, with Christian façades but strongly paganized and directly influenced by spiritist practices, little by little were brought together and continue to be amalgamated to form "Umbanda" (a word of Bantu origin meaning a "bewitcher"). The "batuque" of the Sul, the "macumba" from Rio de Janeiro, the "candomblé" of Bahia, the "xangô" of Pernambuco, the "catimbó" of Nordeste, the "nagô" of Maranhão, the "pajelança" of the Amazonia are the varied materials of this new type of Spiritism, the most widespread and popular in Brazil among all types of peoples, including the whites. The Federação Espirita Brasileira, in an official declaration of 1953, granted to the Umbandistas the right to qualify as "espiritas," since they claim to practice communication with the spirits of the dead, although they do it in a boisterous way and with ceremonies unknown among the Kardecists.

No one knows definitely how many Spiritists (Kardecists and Umbandistas) exist in Brazil. In the small state of Guanabara (formerly the Federal District) there are more than 10,000 sites (centers and "terreiros") known by the government where this "religion" is practiced. In São Paulo, also, locations are numbered in the thousands, as in Rio Grande do Sul, Minas Gerais, Bahia, from north to south of the nation. There are 162 periodicals (reviews and newspapers) of spiritist propaganda in Brazil. There is also much propaganda through books and the radio (radiophonic stations being exclusively spiritist). The majority of those who frequent spiritist centers continue to call themselves Catholics. Earnest, uneducated people, by tradition devoted to the saints, through too much ignorance are devoted to consecrated articles to which they attribute infallible and magic powers. They confuse the Sacraments of the Church with amulets, charms, and other preservatives. Credulous and religious, they are not qualified to distinguish the truth from error. In part they have been religiously abandoned by the shortage of clergy, abandoned in their sickness and misery, deceived, moreover, by hypocritical declarations, fallacious promises, and untrue façades. They are naturally inclined toward wonderful manifestations and, with an immense longing for their dead, are ready to give up everything to aid their departed ones and to receive some sign from them. As a result, the people succumb in a truly alarming degree to the temptation of necromancy and magic.

In 1953 the conference of Brazilian bishops declared that, of all the doctrinal deviations, Spiritism was the most dangerous for Brazil. Spiritists claim to be able to summon the wisest spirits, powerful leaders and doctors. They present themselves to the suffering people as having the power to resolve pangs of love, difficulties of work, questions of health, in fact, all problems. It is, above all, through quackery that Spiritism makes its principal propaganda in Brazil. If, however, religious ignorance and misery are the principal causes of the diffusion of Spiritism in Brazil, the remedy is in the intensification of religious instruction and social assistance; and much intensive work of this type is being done throughout Brazil.

[B. KLOPPENBURG]

See also RELIGIOUS ORDERS OF MEN IN LATIN AMERICA; MISSIONS IN COLONIAL AMERICA, II (PORTUGUESE MISSIONS); LATIN AMERICA, ART AND ARCHITECTURE IN; BELÉM, ARCHDIOCESE OF; OLINDA-RECIFE, ARCHDIOCESE OF; SALVADOR, ARCHDIOCESE OF.

Bibliography: F. A. DE VARNHAGEN, *História geral do Brasil,* 5 v. (4th ed. São Paulo 1948–53). R. SOUTHEY, *History of Brazil,* 3 v. (London 1810–22). J. L. MECHAM, *Church and State in Latin America* (Chapel Hill 1934). H. VAN DER VAT, *Princípios da igreja no Brasil* (Rio de Janeiro 1952). J. DORNAS, *O padroado e a igreja brasileira* (São Paulo 1938). F. DE AZEVEDO, *Brazilian Culture,* tr. W. R. Crawford (New York 1950). G. FREYRE, *The Masters and the Slaves,* tr. S. PUTNAM (2d ed. New York 1956). C. HARING, *Empire in Brazil* (Cambridge, Mass. 1958). C. R. BOXER, *The Dutch in Brazil, 1624–1654* (Oxford 1957). M. C. KIEMEN, *The Indian Policy of Portugal in the Amazon Region, 1614–1693* (Washington 1954). R. DE OLIVEIRA, *O conflito maçônico-religioso de 1872* (Rio de Janeiro 1952). F. GUERRA, *A questão religiosa do segundo império brasileiro* (Rio de Janeiro 1952). B. KLOPPENBURG, *O espiritismo no Brasil* (Petrópolis 1960); *A umbanda no Brasil* (Petrópolis 1961); *O reencarnacionismo no Brasil* (Petrópolis 1961). D. KALVERKAMP and B. KLOPPENBURG, *Acão pastoral perante o espiritismo* (Petrópolis 1961). C. P. DE CAMARGO, *Aspectos sociológicos del espiritismo en São Paulo* (Fribourg 1961). **Illustration credits:** Fig. 3, The Library of the Pan American Union. Fig. 4, Pan American Airways. Fig. 5, Marcel Gautherot.

[M. C. KIEMEN; B. KLOPPENBURG]

BRAZILIAN LITERATURE

The literature of Brazil is written in the Portuguese language. It is related to continental Portuguese literature in approximately the same way that French, Spanish, and English writing in the Western Hemisphere are related to their European counterparts. The literatures of Brazil and Spanish America, particularly, offer striking parallels because of cultural affinities between the Spanish and Portuguese of the Iberian Peninsula and because of their analogous experiences in colonization and later historical evolution. The artistic development of both can be examined within a framework of periods of art history that apply equally to Europe: Middle Ages, Renaissance, baroque, neoclassicism, romanticism, realism, symbolism, and Modernism (*Modernismo). The process of racial and cultural amalgamation of Indian, Negro, and European began in the 16th century. Distinctively Brazilian fruits began to emerge in literature in the late 18th and have flowered in the 20th century in a unique synthesis.

Lacking the freedom of the musical composer or creator in the plastic arts, the literary artist of Brazil has been obliged to work with a language that is only in a few subtle linguistic features different from that of Portugal; accordingly, originality must be expressed principally in shades of psychological variation indicative of a new spirit, in the use of American themes, and in the adaptation and blending of motifs from African, Indian, and European folklore. In his customary lyricism (a trait widely recognized as inherited from the Portuguese, whose literature is also known for a similar melancholy and nostalgic quality called *saudade*), the Brazilian contrasts markedly with his fellow Latin American writers, though he may share with them an attraction for Europe and sometimes the U.S., with implications of originality sacrificed through imitation.

However, New World culture, so far from being purely imitative, is characterized by its capacity for adaptation, interpretation, and assimilation of currents of thought and creativeness from the world at large into its own new and distinctive synthesis.

Period of Colonization. The theme that since the first colonization has most consistently occupied American and specifically Brazilian writers is that of America itself, in all its beauty, variety, and strangeness; even today Brazil has captured the world's imagination as the "land of the future," the home of the "cosmic race." The first European to write about Brazil was the scribe Pero Vaz de Caminha in his letters of the first voyage of discovery in 1500. Besides accounts of French, Italian, and German travelers, there are chronicles by the Portuguese Jesuits Manuel de *Nóbrega, João de Azpilcueta Navarro, José de Anchieta, and Fernão Cardim; by the navigator Pero Lopes de Sousa; and by the colonists Pero Magalhães *Gandavo and Gabriel Soares de *Sousa, among others. Representative is Soares de Sousa's *Tratado Descritivo do Brasil em 1587,* a careful inventory of the flora and fauna, with valuable insights into the nature of indigenous society. Such writing may be linked with the literature of exploration, to which the Portuguese made important contributions; however, though they betray the wakening spirit of Renaissance men, in form their writings are derived from the modest chronicle of the Middle Ages. Indeed, it is proper to say that Brazil enjoyed no *Renaissance and that its literary history leaps from the Middle Ages to *baroque.

The dominant figure, in the widest cultural as well as literary sense, is the Jesuit missionary José de *Anchieta. Both the essentially medieval poetry and religious drama of this apostle of Brazil were subservient to his task of catechizing, in both the Tupi and the Portuguese languages, the natives of the wild regions of São Vicente (later to be called São Paulo). In his Latin poetry of humanistic bent, Anchieta is a transitional figure between the medieval and the baroque in art.

Beginnings of Baroque. This style, allied with the Counter Reformation, was transported to Brazil by the Jesuits who came after Anchieta, particularly to the cultural centers of Bahia, Olinda, Rio de Janeiro, and São Paulo. The colonial churches, with their delicate but dynamic façades and their sumptuous interiors, are perhaps the real monuments of baroque art in 17th-century Brazil. A commanding figure in the pulpits of such churches was Antônio *Vieira (1608–97), a Jesuit orator of world renown during his century and influential in affairs of state both in Portugal, where he was born, and in Brazil, where he received his early education. His sermons are clear examples of the baroque in their conceptual ingenuities, though their author remained innocent of cultist obscurities. His defense of his adopted land and his relatively enlightened spirit of racial tolerance identify him as close to the Brazilians in temperament.

Baroque poetry in Brazil owes much to the sensuous refinements and conceptual subtleties of the Spaniards *Góngora and *Quevedo and of their Portuguese counterpart, Francisco Manuel de *Melo. By this time, Portuguese Renaissance forms had evolved in the direction of intricacy, complexity, and greater appeal to the senses. The baroque was a literature of tensions and contrasts between exaltation and disillusionment. Some of these characteristics are found in the most engaging poet of the 17th century, and, some would say, the founder of Brazilian poetry, Gregório de *Matos. He was a law student who, like all aspirants to higher education, had to journey to the Portuguese University of Coimbra for further training; during his bohemian career he shuttled back and forth between colony and mother country and once went into exile in Africa. His poetry offers themes of mundane alongside divine love, of idealism against sensuality, and of a picaresque temperament capable of deep religious feeling. His excoriation of every social estate from the depths of the racial cauldrons of Bahia to the venal representatives of the crown won him many enmities and the sobriquet "The Mouth of Hell." His aggressiveness and rebelliousness mark him as the first really Brazilian personality to emerge in literature.

If one excludes as an essentially Portuguese work Bento Teixeira's panegyric *Prosopopéia* (Lisbon 1601), a poem largely influenced by the golden octaves of *Camões, honors for the first Brazilian poetry to be published must go to Botelho de Oliveira (1636–1711) for his *Música do Parnaso* (1705). He published his work in Lisbon, as did all writers of the colonial era, because of the lack of a printing press until the 19th century. His book is a curious collection of varied literary forms, including two plays in the manner of the Spanish *comedia*. This aristocratic poet wrote poems in Portuguese, Spanish, Italian, and Latin that betray an admiration for the involutions and surface brilliance of Góngora and the Italian Marini (1569–1625), particularly in sonnets that allow him to escape into a "garden reserved for the few." His well-known *silva* to the "Isle of Maré," with its glimmering of pride in the luxuriance of the Brazilian landscape, illustrates the cultivated baroque at its best. A kindred work of the 18th century is the Franciscan Friar Manuel de Santa Maria Itaparica's *Descrição da Ilha de Itaparica* (Lisbon 1769), a poetic inventory whose culminating scene is a whale hunt stylized in royal octaves.

An example of the baroque or euphuistic prose style that carries over into the 18th century is the *História da América Portuguêsa* (Lisbon 1730) of Sebastião da Rocha Pita (1660–1738), written under the aegis of the Academia Brasileira dos Esquecidos, founded in 1724. The Brazilian academies were pallid imitations of the Portuguese, and their existence was transitory; but in their dedication to literature, history, and science they gave signs of increasing cultural maturity in the life of the colony.

Arcadianism. In the second half of the 18th century the capital was moved from Bahia to Rio de Janeiro, and there was a consequent shift of literary activity to the south. An admirable group of poets is associated with the province of Minas Gerais, the new center of the mining industry, and particularly with an incipient revolt there against Portuguese rule, which was discovered and crushed in 1789. Alvarenga Peixoto and Tomás Antônio Gonzaga were sent into exile, and the poet Cláudio Manuel da Costa committed suicide in prison. Their art is unified within the style of *Arcadianism, an aspect of neoclassicism expressing revolt against the baroque and advocating a return to more transparent forms. The poets, posing as shepherds in the tradition of Greco-Roman bucolic poetry, find much inspiration in nature. Rigid adherence to neoclassical precepts is lacking, and in several of the poets of the "Minas school" there is a

preromantic subjectivity. Cláudio Manuel da Costa (1729–89) is at best an elegant sonneteer showing some features of the earlier euphuism. The poems of Alvarenga Peixoto (1744–93) were probably confiscated at the time of his imprisonment; the few that remain place him among the Arcadians in taste and technique.

The most talented of the revolutionary poets was Tomás Antônio *Gonzaga, whose *Marília de Dirceu* (1792) consists of love poems that have had more editions than any work in the Portuguese language except Camões's *Os Lusíadas*. Master of a variety of impeccable verse forms, Gonzaga sings of love in settings that are often those of Minas Gerais itself rather than the conventional idyllic backgrounds. An anonymous satire, now firmly attributed to Gonzaga and indicative of revolutionary ferment, is the *Cartas Chilenas,* whose Chilean locale was merely a disguise under which the poet might express his vituperation against the royal Portuguese administrator. Two other poets associated with the Minas group are Silva Alvarenga (1749–1814) and Caldas Barbosa (1738–1800), both mestizos who represent a transition between Arcadianism and romanticism. These two musician poets enjoyed much acclaim in Portugal: the former for his spontaneous and personal idiom, as seen in the delicate lyrics of *Glaura* (1799); and the latter, for poems that were refreshingly humble and popular in spirit and were often set to music that owed much to African folksongs transplanted to Brazil.

Close to the epic genre but without its moral sense and national scope are two narrative poems of the period, Basílio da Gama's *Uraguai* (1769) and Friar Santa Rita Durão's *Caramuru* (1781). Both are of interest for their treatment of the Indian theme. In his narrative extolling a Spanish and Portuguese expedition in 1752 against the Jesuit missions, Basílio's natives display the virtues and beauties attributed to the noble savage in 18th-century Europe. Basílio da Gama (1740–95) is by far the better poet of the two; he uses the supple blank decasyllable and prefers not to follow the Camonian model chosen by his compatriot Santa Rita Durão (1722–84). The latter's *Caramuru* deals with the adventures of a Portuguese sailor, shipwrecked on the Bahia coast in the 16th century, who lived among aborigines idealized as were those of "Uraguai." In their relative directness and simplicity of language, these two poems reflect the Arcadian rather than the baroque tradition.

Romanticism. Important events of the early 19th century were the arrival of King João VI from Portugal, fleeing Napoleon, and in 1822 Brazil's independence from colonial status. Into a climate propitious to its development came the new style of *romanticism, introduced by the Brazilian poet and dramatist Gonçalves de Magalhães (1811–82), who published his *Suspiros Poéticos e Saudades* in Paris in 1836 during a journey to Europe, where he absorbed notions of the new aesthetic from such writers as Chateaubriand, Lamartine, Victor Hugo, and Byron. Romanticism, with its tenets of artistic freedom from neoclassical authority, accorded well with the nationalistic aspirations of poets, novelists, and dramatists, each of whom could feel that he was helping to create a new Brazilian literature. Their reliance on France for inspiration was great, but this does not detract from a really impressive achievement during the early decades of a benign and stable empire, especially by poets such as Gonçalves Dias and Castro Alves and the novelist José de Alencar (1829–77), who more than any other fought to break the hegemony of classical Portuguese in favor of a more Brazilian idiom.

Gonçalves Dias (1823–64)—it is significant that he was of mixed blood—reflected the national pride in its Indian heritage in his lyric poems and later in his epic *Os Timbiras* (1857), in which the Indian is idealized, to be sure, but presented with an ethnographer's interest in setting and detail. An experimenter with freer forms of versification, Dias also handled the range of other themes favored by his contemporaries: patriotism, slavery, nature, and love. His melancholy tones bespoke a tragic outlook. Indeed, tragedy pursues all the noteworthy poets of romanticism; they were out of harmony with society, led disordered lives imbued with the passion of Byronic heroes, and all died young. Alvares de Azevedo (1831–52), in his *Lira dos Vinte Anos* (1853), writes in anguish of a bohemian existence filled with taunting erotic visions. The great popular favorite of his day, Casimiro de Abreu (1839–60), seems placid in comparison as he recalls with appealing ingenuousness his loves, his longings, and the simple scenes of his childhood. Junqueira Freire (1832–55), in his *Inspirações do Claustro* (1855), reveals the heart of a monk without a calling who, after 3 impossible years, must retire from the monastery, where he sought faith and tranquillity.

Two figures of a final generation of romantic poets are Fagundes Varela (1841–75) and Castro Alves (1847–71), who because of their lofty flights of imagination and heightened lyric tone (precisely the qualities they admired in Victor Hugo) have been called "Condor poets." Both defied social conventions, and both championed the rights of the Negro during the abolitionist campaign in which, more than any other, Castro Alves distinguished himself as the ardent and, at the same time, technically brilliant poet of the final phases of romanticism.

Early Novels. The earliest Brazilian novels, based on the historical novels of Walter Scott or on French models and of scant artistic interest, appear *c.* 1840. Four years later, however, with *A Moreninha,* Joaquim Manuel de Macedo (1820–82) found in the atmosphere of imperial Rio de Janeiro the setting for a poetic and sentimental love story with moral overtones that is still a favorite example of the romantic novel, designed above all to entertain a then-expanding reading public. The best feature in Macedo's early novels is their representation of city life, though one may complain of exaggeration and lack of verisimilitude in plot and character. An author of romantic novels who excelled in all their thematic variations was José de Alencar (1829–77), who undertook to project a vast panorama of Brazilian life, in the jungles, the pampas, the backlands, the cities, stretching in time from the 16th century to his own day. His desire for divorce from all things Portuguese led him to begin as a novelist of the Indian with *O Guarani* (1857) and to follow with the poetic *Iracema* (1865). The historical novel is well represented by his *Minas de prata* (1865) and the regional by *O Gaúcho* (1870), along with novels of urban life. No other 19th-century writer did more to help create the Brazilian novel.

Bernardo Guimarães (1825–84) lacked the popular style of Macedo and Alencar but enjoyed a following in his day for such works as *O Garimpeiro* (1872), based on his own experiences in the *sertão,* or backlands, and especially for the abolitionist novel *A Escrava Isaura* (1875). Another novelist of the *sertão* was Escragnolle Taunay (1843–99), an engineer and geographer as well as an artist, who anticipates realism in the carefully observed backlands setting of the novel *Inocência* (1872); here the heroine has, however, all the charm and moral rectitude proper to most heroines of romantic literature. An important exception is constituted by the one novel written by the journalist Manuel Antônio de Almeida (1831–61), *Memórias de um Sargento de Milícias* (Rio de Janeiro 1854–55, but serialized earlier in newspaper form). The characters seem almost to be sketched from the Spanish picaresque, and the settings of Rio de Janeiro under João VI have an authenticity that recalls Balzac.

Drama. Of the romantic writers already mentioned, Gonçalves Dias, Gonçalves de Magalhães, Alencar, and Macedo were dramatists as well in this period, which saw the rise and apogee of a national theatre. This, unfortunately, never managed to build a strong tradition even to the present. The actor and producer João Caetano (1808–63) helped give impetus to the fledgling genre, and Martins Pena (1815–48), creator of a drama of customs and social satire, ranks as the outstanding figure of the 19th century, along with his successor França Júnior (1838–90).

Emergence of Realism. About 1880, and even a bit earlier, there were signs of a new orientation in intellectual life, notably in the positivistic thought of Tobias Barreto (1839–89) at Recife and in his so-called "scientific poetry," which was influenced by German philosophy. The prestige of French science, thought, and literature (especially of Flaubert and later of Émile Zola) had never been so high. Under such influences authors became more objective, less impassioned in their study of man in his environment, more universal in their values, and more concerned with giving a finished form to their writing. This last tendency is seen in the so-called Parnassian poetry (an aspect of the period style of realism) in the last 2 decades of the 19th century (*see* PARNASSIANISM). Alberto de Oliveira (1859–1937), Raimundo Correia (1860–1911), and Olavo Bilac (1865–1918), among others, reflect the care for form through painstaking versification, new vocabulary and rhyme, and experimentation with French meters, particularly the Alexandrine, although Brazilian exuberance, for example in the love sonnets of Bilac, went counter to the impersonality and impassiveness of the French masters Théophile Gautier, Leconte de Lisle, and José Maria Heredia. Correia's *Primeiros Sonhos* (1879) and *Sinfonias* (1883), in which the poet records his impressions of the Brazilian landscape, are pessimistic in tone. Alberto de Oliveira, in *Meridionais* (1884) and later work, is also inspired by nature to create brilliant visual images that reveal a refined temperament. The dominant figure among the Parnassians, Olavo Bilac, established himself in his earliest work, *Poesias* (1888), as the master of sensual, ardent love lyrics that typify the more biological concept of sex appearing in the literature of realism; the lapidary sonnet was the favorite form of this poet, who gave great dignity to "art for art's sake."

The most respected writer of the 19th century and, in fact, of all Brazilian literature is *Machado de Assis, whose work as poet, dramatist, critic, and also founder of the Brazilian Academy of Letters, is far exceeded in importance by his novels, several of which have won for him a major reputation in world literature. Possessor of an unusually broad culture extending from classical antiquity to contemporary European (especially French and English) literatures, Machado was the largely self-educated son of a mulatto father and Portuguese mother, but was fortunate to acquire much of his literary education under the tutelage of the publisher Paula Brito, also a man of color. Machado's *Memórias Póstumas de Braz Cubas* (1881) narrates the futile, apparently meaningless, and therefore to Machado wryly humorous life of a well-to-do gentleman of the empire; its artistic charm lies in its spare but beautifully proportioned form. *Dom Casmurro* (1900) states Machado's deterministic philosophy less abstractly by analyzing the ineluctable forces that would tend to make Dom Casmurro's magnificently instinctive wife an adulteress; the superb art of the novel is in the hint that these forces may not have operated after all. His other novels and his later short stories have the same formal perfection, but it is their universal validity that has impelled readers throughout the world to call him "classic."

The sociological, as opposed to the predominantly aesthetic, aspect of realism is represented by Aluízio de Azevedo (1857–1913). His best-known novels are *O Mulato* (1881), *Casa de Pensão* (1884), *O Homem* (1887), and *O Cortiço* (1890). Exemplifying the scientific and naturalistic pretensions of the *roman experimental*, they are well made and are particularly valuable for their documentary presentation of social strata and related problems in the second half of the 19th century. A similar orientation is evident in the bitter reminiscences and often crude realism of *O Ateneu* (1888), in

Fig. 2. Aluízio de Azevedo.

which Raul Pompéia (1863–95) criticized an important type of educational establishment. *A Carne* (1888) by Júlio Ribeiro (1845–90) and *O Missionário,* published by Inglês de Sousa (1853–1918) in the same year, maintained shocking theses and are well remembered for the controversy they aroused, although the two novels are not outstanding for their artistry.

Symbolism. This movement, which has commonly been associated with only a few figures of a poetic reaction to Parnassianism beginning in 1893 with the publication of João Cruz e Sousa's *Broquéis,* has recently been the subject of an important revision (*see* SYMBOLISM, LITERARY). Antônio Soares Amora dates symbolism from approximately the time of the establishment of the First Republic in 1889 to about 1920, and thus includes a variety of poets, novelists, and essayists who had hitherto somewhat unsatisfactorily been linked with the dying phase of realism. For example, the prose style of Euclides da *Cunha is now better understood in the light of attitudes and aesthetic preoccupations comprehended by symbolism. In this period there was a reaction to the preceding materialism and a new idealism and spiritual awakening that sought to reappraise, without the cynicism of the realists, the nature of Brazilian reality. Artists were especially interested in the psychology of the unconscious as it affected their fantasy and their use of language to express, less logically than before, their inner states.

Free verse is one important result of greater freedom of form. Many of these advances are apparent in the poetry of João Cruz e Sousa (1861–98), the son of Negro slaves, whose master provided him with an education. The supreme unhappiness of this aristocratic spirit, doomed to sarcasm, persecution, and family misfortune during his brief life, pervades Cruz's poetry. After refining out the Baudelarian spleen and satanism shown in *Broquéis,* he was able in later poetry, written between 1893 and 1898 and published posthumously, to sublimate his hatred and anguish. Of great interest are his symbols, especially that of the color white, with which he finally expresses a mystical and radiant love. A distinguished follower of Cruz e Sousa was Alphonsus

Fig. 1. *Illustration by Brazilian artist Candido Portinari for the 14th chapter of Machado de Assis' "Memórias Póstumas de Braz Cubas."*

de Guimarães (1870–1921), who is noted for his religious poems and whose *A Catedral* is representative of the nebulous atmosphere in which he projects private symbols of chaos and despair. Symbolism is also the epoch style of a group of poets of such varied tendencies as those of Augusto dos Anjos, B. Lopes, Emiliano Perneta, and of several younger writers who appeared between 1910 and 1920, among them Manuel Bandeira, Olegário Mariano, Alvaro Moreira, Ronald de Carvalho, and Ribeiro Couto, who were all to make their literary reputations in the era of Modernism.

Symbolism in the novel is characterized by aestheticism, fantasy, impressionism, and dazzling rhetorical effects. This is the moment of such prose stylists as the orator Rui Barbosa (1849–1923), the social historian Euclides da Cunha, and the novelist Coelho Neto (1864–1934). An objective view of Coelho Neto's production of more than 100 volumes, in which novels and short stories excel, must make clear that he is one of the country's outstanding writers, although his virtuosity of language and his stylistic refinements may have made him seem to be over the heads of some of his countrymen and out of contact with the realities of his time. However, such objections are ill founded in the light of his knowledge of the most divergent aspects of Brazil's make-up, which he couples with extraordinary powers of imagination. In 1902 his contemporary Graça Aranha (1868–1931) published his world-renowned *Canaã*, a searching and prophetic novel of cultural conflicts between New World and Old in this "land of Canaan." It departs radically from the techniques and spirit of the older realism in art, especially in its optimistic conclusions concerning the future of the Brazilian nation.

A work of similar impact, appearing in the same year, but even more important because of its unique vision of backlands society expressed in an incomparable combination of rhetorical, scientific, and poetic writing, is Euclides da Cunha's *Os Sertões,* the real monument among several thought-provoking interpretations of Brazil during this period. It centers on the government's suppression of fanatical *sertanejos* in the backlands of Bahia (1894–96). A final novelist, in this selection of the chief prose writers of the symbolist era, is Lima Barreto (1881–1922), who, though he lacks the outward brilliance of the others, breaks with realism in such novels as *Recordações do Escrivão Isaías Caminha* (1909) and *Vida e morte de M. J. Gonzaga de Sá* (1919). This break can be seen in his intensely subjective but knowing presentation of the quality of existence at the turn of the century among humble and especially colored Brazilians struggling up through the social layers of Rio de Janeiro.

The Watershed of 1922. The contemporary period of Brazilian literature dates from a few years prior to the world-famous Modern Art Week, held in São Paulo in February 1922. From it derives the term designating in Brazil a variety of social, political, philosophical, and aesthetic tendencies unified by their common spirit of renovation in all walks of national life, rejection of much of the past (including the European), and above all a search for deeper meanings in all things Brazilian. Stagnation and disillusionment following World War I and specifically the vanguardist movements in literature and art in Europe—though it may seem paradoxical—were the tripwires leading to the explosion of Modern Art Week. Symptomatic of unrest were the political dissatisfactions expressed in the minor revolutions of 1922 and 1924, culminating in the overthrow of the First Republic in 1930.

Early Modernism. Under the leadership of Mário de Andrade and Oswald de Andrade, the poets of the early or destructive phase of Modernism smashed the molds of all previous poetry, seeming to enjoy immensely the atmosphere of anarchy. But soon positive advances could be noted in the liberation of verbal forms, and many poets delightedly embraced the vernacular in the further probing of that seemingly inexhaustible theme of national reality and consciousness. A few important works in this vein are *Paulicéia Desvairada* of Mário de Andrade (1893–1945), *Cobra Norato* of Raul Bopp (1898–), *Tôda a América* of Ronald de Carvalho (1893–1935), *Juca Mulato* of Menotti del Picchia (1892–), *Novos Poemas* of Jorge de Lima (1895–1953), *Libertinagem* of Manual Bandeira (1886–), *Martim Cererê* of Cassiano Ricardo (1895–), and *Noroeste e Outros Poemas do Brasil* of Ribeiro Couto (1898–).

Perhaps the most thoroughgoing revolution in Brazilian letters since romanticism, Modernism becomes attenuated only toward the mid-20th century. Its most important later poets are Augusto Frederico Schmidt (1906–65), who early refused to ally himself with the exclusively nationalistic writing in favor of more universal themes; Cecília Meireles (1901–64), Brazil's most distinguished woman poet, who sought in simplicity and reserve the expression of her emotion; Carlos Drummond de Andrade (1902–), thoughtful and satirically humorous author of the important collection *Fazendeiro do ar e poesia até agora* (1954); and Vinícius de Morais (1913–), who pictures the fleshly poet hard beset to preserve the ideals of traditional religion and morality.

Prominence of the Novel. In the period 1922 to 1945, the novel was the genre most equal to the demands of the moment and hence it enjoyed the greatest popularity. In the 1920s a group of São Paulo modernists experimented with novelistic form (e.g., Mário de Andrade's *Amar, Verbo Intransitivo*) in works dealing with urban life in that great industrial community. However, the main impetus for the new novel came not from the south but from the northeast, with the publication by José Américo de Almeida (1887–) of his *A Bagaceira* in 1928. Modern in technique and regional in the locale of its grim clash between littoral and backlands, the book is nevertheless national in its implications of the need for reform at all levels of Brazilian life. The sociologist and cultural historian Gilberto Freyre (1900–) had already begun to exert an influence on his countrymen with his far-ranging interpretations of national reality in terms of his region, the northeast. The result in literature was the regional novel that all Brazil read avidly, in the works of a small group of talented writers who may be said to have dominated the literary capital of Rio de Janeiro as late as 1950.

José Lins do Rego (1901–57), in his *Sugar-Cane Cycle* and later novels, gave a panorama of life in the patriarchal slaveholding society of the northeast as it rose and declined. A similar achievement is that of Jorge Amado (1912–) in his novels of the city of Bahia and of the cacao groves to the south, picturing the social unrest among the lowly that is his special, politically motivated theme. The four novels of Graciliano *Ramos, *Caetés, São Bernardo, Angústia,* and *Vidas Sêcas,* all dealing with environmental determinism as observed in acute psychological studies of character, show the novel of the northeast in its most artistic form.

Fig. 3. Jorge Amado.

Also of importance are the psychological and sociological novels of Rachel de Queiroz (1910–), who brings to Brazilian literature a moving interpretation of the role of woman in the northeast. Novelists of other regions have contributed to the generation's major undertaking of presenting Brazil in all its diversity, and special recognition must be accorded Erico Veríssimo (1905–) of Rio Grande do Sul, master of the fullest range of modern narrative techniques as his *roman fleuve, O Tempo e o Vento* (1949–62), attests. He has also written urban novels dealing with the tensions and conflicts of modern life, as have Otávio de Faria (1908–), José Geraldo Vieira (1897–), and Marques Rebelo (1907–).

Postmodernist Era. Trends from 1945 to the mid-1960s (sometimes called the postmodernist era) make clear that the modernist movement has been the capital event in Brazilian literature in the 20th century. The effects of this creative movement are still being felt, especially on the literary language, which is more than ever based on the spoken idiom of Brazil. The modernists' early concern with the whole of Brazilian reality has been intensified not only by social scientists and other scholars but by poets, novelists, and playwrights as well.

In the novel the regionalism of the northeasterners, of a José Lins do Rego, for example, has been given a different form, thanks to the abandonment of 19th-century realism in favor of more introspective techniques. Jorge Amado (1912–), Brazil's most widely read novelist, has himself evolved in the same direction, in *Gabriela, Cravo e Canela* (1958) and *Os Velhos Marinheiros* (1961). Others representing this more poetic approach to regionalism are Adonias Filho (1915–), Mário Palmério (1916–), and António Callado (1917–). The most original of all is João Guimarães Rosa (1908–), a diplomat by profession, whose short stories and especially the novel *Grande Sertão: Veredas* (1956) derive from the experimentalism of the modernists. In the judgment of many, his

stylistic innovations will henceforward mark a precise watershed between the Portuguese and Brazilian literary languages. He reminds one somewhat of James *Joyce in his creation of a fresh, private, and sometimes even hermetic idiom in which to project his epic vision of the people of the backlands of Minas Gerais. Clarice Lispector (1922–) is also a vanguardist and experimentalist; her poetic and sometimes philosophical novels are rich in symbols and often lack precise geographical settings. Both Guimarães Rosa and Lispector have an international following, thanks to European translations.

Theater. A significant event in the Brazilian theater was Nelson Rodrigues's *Vestido de Noiva* (1943), a poetic though morbid play of intricate structure that was directed by the Polish refugee Zbigniew Ziembinski. He brought to it his vast knowledge of expressionistic staging and assembled a group of players and technicians whose impact on dramatic production was to endure. Though 50 years late, this international style caught on. The leading playwrights, however, Jorge Andrade (1922–), Ariano Suassuna (1927–), Gianfrancesco Guarnieri (1934–), Nelson Rodrigues (1912–), prefer Brazilian social and political themes. Of all the genres, drama is the one most involved in current issues and ideology. Its existence is also the most precarious: underdeveloped since colonial times, the theater is still struggling for life, though individual works, such as Vinícius de Morais's *Orfeu da Conceição* (1956) and Dias Gomes' *O Pagador de Promessas* (1960), have captured the world's fancy through cinematographic adaptations.

Poetry. Contemporary poetry shows how benefit is still being derived from the apparently unlimited possibilities opened up by Modernism. Of the older modernists the major influences today are those of the theorist Mário de Andrade and of the poets Jorge de Lima, Carlos Drummond de Andrade, Cecília Meireles, Augusto Frederico Schmidt, and Manuel Bandeira. The leader of a creative group calling themselves the "Generation of 1945" and including Mauro Mota (1912–), Paulo Mendes Campos (1922–), Lêdo Ivo (1924–), Marcos Konder Reis (1922–) and others, was João Cabral de Melo Neto (1920–), cerebral and inventive, who works within a framework of traditional and popular metres that convey startling images. Most of the later poetic developments can be comprehended under the liberating tenets of the earlier Modernism.

Since 1960 a fruitful dialogue has been established between the poets and critics of the São Paulo journal *Noigandres,* who call themselves concretists and their opposite numbers associated with the journal *Tendência* in Belo Horizonte. The former write poems that are valued as nondiscursive objects and that have graphic or spatial as well as acoustical dimensions. The word is more important than the phrase; sound is more prized than syntax. The poets and critics of *Tendência* have contended that such poems are excessively intellectualized and are relatively lacking in social context; they argue for the conventional collective use of language and seek through art to win independence, autonomy, and above all, self-affirmation for Brazil. Because of their implications for all literature, these opposing positions can be expected to continue the age-old dialogue between so-called pure art and art that possesses social implications.

Journalistic Essay. A widely practiced subgenre, thus far unmentioned, is the so-called *crônica* or journalistic essay on the passing scene. Its notable practitioners, such as Rachel de Queiroz (1910–   ), Rubem Braga (1913–   ), Paulo Mendes Campos (1922–   ), and Fernando Sabino (1923–   ), are of undisputed literary importance. Literary history and criticism has been intensively cultivated, especially since World War II. Such studies have been published not only in books and scholarly journals but also in the nation's press, notably in the larger cities, where newspapers are an important vehicle for criticism as well as for creative writing. Suggestions as to the quality and scope of critical writing can be gathered from the Brazilian works in the appended bibliography.

As the Brazilian nation has grown more complex not only through expansion of its population and changes in its social structure but also through such processes as urbanization, industrialization, and diversification of the economy, writers have been challenged to interpret the new phenomena. Theirs is, in general, a confident spirit that tries to know and to improve all aspects of national life and that seeks above all to affirm the national character. They are producing and will continue to produce what has appropriately been called "the literature of development."

Bibliography: M. DE ANDRADE, *Aspectos da literatura brasileira* (His *Obras completas* v.10; São Paulo 1950), includes his famous essay on the modernist movement. M. BANDEIRA, *Apresentação da poesia brasileira* (3d ed. Rio de Janeiro 1957), standard anthology with critical notes by a major poet. M. DA S. BRITO, *Antecedentes da semana de arte moderna*, v.1 of *História do modernismo brasileiro* (São Paulo 1958–   ), well-documented study of the background of the 1922 upheaval in art. J. B. BROCA and G. DE SOUSA, *Introdução ao estudo da literatura brasileira* (Rio de Janeiro 1963), valuable introductory study of literary criticism in Brazil, with a new bibliog. of bibliog., anthologies, genre studies, regional studies, and varied basic works of literary history and criticism. L. DA CAMARA CASCUDO, *Literatura oral* (Rio de Janeiro 1952), the authority on Brazilian folklore. O. M. CARPEAUX, *Pequena bibliografia crítica da literatura brasileira* (3d ed. Rio de Janeiro 1964). R. DE CARVALHO, *Pequena história da literatura brasileira* (11th ed. Rio de Janeiro 1958). J. A. CASTELO, *Aspectos do romance brasileiro* (Rio de Janeiro 1960). A. COUTINHO, ed., *A literatura no Brasil* (Rio de Janeiro 1955–   ), broad in scope and with a long list of foremost contributors, it is notable also for its fundamentally aesthetic approach to literary history. F. P. ELLISON, *Brazil's New Novel: Four Northeastern Masters* (Berkeley 1954). J. D. M. FORD et al., *A Tentative Bibliography of Brazilian Belles-lettres* (Cambridge, Mass. 1931). I. GOLDBERG, *Brazilian Literature* (New York 1922). A. A. LIMA, *Introdução à literatura brasileira* (2d ed. Rio de Janeiro 1957); *Quadro sintético da literatura brasileira* (2d ed. Rio de Janeiro 1959), introductory works by Brazil's leading Catholic intellectual and an important critic of the early phase of Modernism. W. MARTINS, *A crítica literária no Brasil* (São Paulo 1952), perhaps the best history of Brazilian literary criticism by a younger critic. A. C. MELLO E SOUZA, *Formação da literatura brasileira*, 2 v. (São Paulo 1959), challenging new interpretation of the origins of Brazilian literature in the 18th century and later development. L. MIGUEL PEREIRA, *Prosa de ficção de 1870 a 1920* (Rio de Janeiro 1950), fundamental study of Brazilian prose writing. O. MONTENEGRO, *O romance Brasileiro* (2d ed. Rio de Janeiro 1953), essays on the principal Brazilian novelists. D. DE A. PRADO, *Apresentação do teatro brasileiro moderno: Crítica teatral, 1947–1955* (São Paulo 1956). S. PUTNAM, *Marvelous Journey: A Survey of Four Centuries of Brazilian Literature* (New York 1948). S. ROMERO, *História da literatura brasileira*, 5 v. (3d ed. Rio de Janeiro 1943), indispensable reference with sociological and nationalistic orientation. R. S. SAYERS, *The Negro in Brazilian Literature* (New York 1956). E. VERISSIMO, *Brazilian Literature: An Outline* (New York 1945), a charming introduction for the non-specialist, by a leading novelist. J. VERISSIMO DE MATTOS, *História da literatura brasileira* (3d ed. Rio de Janeiro 1954), comparable in importance to work of S. Romero but less indebted to sociology. N. W. SODRE, *História da literatura brasileira, Brasileira: Seus fundamentos econômicos* (3d ed. Rio de Janeiro 1960), complements other more aesthetically oriented histories with its emphasis on the economic and social background. **Illustration credits:** Figs. 1 and 2, Marcel Gautherot. Fig. 3, Sascha Harnisch.

[F. P. ELLISON]

BRAZZAVILLE, ARCHDIOCESE OF (BRAZZAPOLITANUS), metropolitan see since 1955, in south *Congo Republic (Brazzaville), central Africa. In 1962 it had 14 secular and 56 religious priests, 81 men in 22 religious houses, 111 women in 13 con-

Church of St. Anne of the Congo, Brazzaville.

vents, and 135,000 Catholics in a population of 300,000; it is 14,073 square miles in area. Its two suffragan sees, Fort-Rousset and Pointe-Noire, both created in 1955, had 165,000 Catholics. The city of Brazzaville, founded in 1880 on the northwest shore of Stanley Pool (part of the Congo River) across from *Léopoldville, is the capital of the Congo Republic; it is connected by rail with its seaport, Pointe-Noire.

In 1883 a mission was founded at Linzolo, near Brazzaville. The Vicariate of the French Congo (1886) was formed from territories of the Prefecture of the Portuguese Congo, the Vicariate of the Two Guineas (1842), and the mission of the Congo (Léopoldville). In 1890 this vicariate was divided into the Vicariate of the Lower (Pointe-Noire) and the Upper French Congo, called Ubangui (1894). In 1909 the Prefecture of *Bangui (*Central African Republic) was detached from the Vicariate of Ubangui, called Middle Congo (1909), and Brazzaville (1922). In 1950 the Vicariate of Fort-Rousset was detached from that of Brazzaville, which became an archdiocese in 1955. After some 15 years the labors of the first vicar apostolic of Brazzaville, the missionary-explorer Prosper Augouard, among savage tribes addicted to cannibalism and slavery were rewarded by a sudden acceptance of Christianity (c. 1905).

The archdiocese has major and minor seminaries. In Brazzaville is the Secretariat of Catholic Organizations for Congo Republic, Gabon, Central African Republic, and Chad, which distributes publications in the four countries, especially *La Semaine africaine* (12,000 circulation). About 15 per cent of the population of the ecclesiastical province is Protestant, mostly around Pointe-Noire, deriving from the labors of Swedish Lutherans (1909) and the Salvation Army (1937). About 3 per cent of the natives belong to the racist sects of Matsouaism, founded by André Matsoua (d. 1942), Kimbanguism, founded by Simon Kimbangu (d. 1951), and the African Prophetic Religion, founded c. 1950 by Zéphirin Lassy.

Bibliography: MissCattol 128. G. B. Tragella, EncCatt 3:50. *Bilan du Monde* 2:261–264. AnnPont (1965) 74.

[J. LE GALL]

BREAD, LITURGICAL USE OF.

By divine institution, bread is one of the two essential elements of the Eucharist. The Eastern Churches for the most part make use of leavened bread, while the Western Churches, since the 11th century, have used unleavened bread. Only bread made of wheat is recognized by the Catholic Church as a valid element of the Eucharist. In the beginning, the faithful took bread from their domestic supply and brought it for divine service; consequently, the Eucharistic bread did not differ from the shape of bread used for domestic purposes. The altar breads assumed a round form of moderate thickness; and, in the Western Church, they took the light, wafer-like form now so common.

The Eucharistic bread aptly signifies the effect conferred upon the communicant by the Eucharist. The Council of Florence (1438–45) said "What material food and drink do for the life of the body—sustaining and strengthening it, restoring it to health and giving pleasure—, this the sacrament [of the Eucharist] does for the life of the soul" (Denz 1322).

Another liturgical use of bread is the distribution of blessed bread, the *eulogiae*, which survives even today in certain Eastern liturgies and in France. At the end of the liturgy, bread that has been specially blessed is distributed to the faithful who are present. Centuries ago, this blessed bread was considered to be a substitute for Holy Communion and was distributed only to noncommunicants. However this conception gradually disappeared; the blessed bread is distributed to all, whether noncommunicants or communicants.

In the Roman rite, the newly consecrated bishop at his consecration presents to the consecrator, along with other gifts, two loaves of bread. Two loaves of bread are offered to the pope in the solemn canonization of saints. At the ordination of a priest, the bishop presents to the newly ordained priest a paten on which there is a host, in order to signify that power has been given to the priest to change bread into the Body of Christ. The Roman Ritual contains several blessings for bread.

Bibliography: J. A. Jungmann, *The Mass of the Roman Rite*, tr. F. Brunner, 2 v. (New York 1951–55) 2:31–37, 452–455. A. Molien, DTC 11.2:1731–33. Miller FundLit 203. F. Cabrol, DACL 1.2:3254–60. **Illustration credits:** Fig. 1, Trinity Missions. Fig. 2, Byzantine Catholic World.

[E. J. GRATSCH]

BREAKING OF BREAD,

an early technical term used in Acts 2.42, 46; 20.7, 11; 1 Cor 10.16 for the celebration of the Eucharist. The Jews were accustomed

Bread on paten at Offertory of Roman Mass.

Arrangement of breads on diskos in Byzantine Rite.

"Breaking of Bread," wood sculpture by the contemporary German artist Heinrich Gick, height 13½ inches.

to begin their common meals with a prayer of grateful praise to God (the Semitic idea behind εὐχαριστία, εὐλογία) spoken over a loaf of bread, which was then divided among the participants (see, e.g., *Berakhot* 46a–b). Although foreshadowed at least linguistically in the OT (Is 58.7; Jer 16.7; perhaps Lam 4.4), this breaking of bread, as a special rite with fraternal and religious significance, was unknown in the Greek and Roman world; *fractio panis* is itself an expression of Christian Latinity. (*See* MEAL, SACRED.)

Jesus had used this ordinary Jewish rite during the meals of His public ministry (Mk 6.41 and parallels). The accounts of the *Last Supper in Mk 14.22 (and parallels) and 1 Cor 11.24 indicate the place the rite had in the institution of the Eucharist and why the *Judaeo-Christians used the breaking of bread as a technical term to describe the reenactment of the *Lord's Supper. In Acts 2.42–47 the breaking of bread is mentioned as parallel to temple worship in a liturgical context: the Christians of the primitive Jerusalem community were faithful to fraternal union, the breaking of bread, and common prayer—all characteristic of a liturgically communal life (Acts 4.32). The sorrow of the Last Supper had given way to the joy of the meals eaten with the risen Lord (Acts 2.46; Lk 24.30, 41–43; Jn 21.9–13). As in the *Didache (14.1), the Christians of the Pauline church at Troas met on Sunday precisely for the breaking of bread (Acts 20.7–11). Paul's words (1 Cor 10.16; 11.23–29) related the breaking of bread to the Body of the Lord, conceived of as a sacred meal.

In Lk 24.13–35, the two disciples at Emmaus recog-

nized Jesus in the breaking of bread. Although this phrase might not signify an actual celebration of the Eucharist, Luke apparently used it with a Eucharistic meaning. Perhaps his intention was to show that, while the Scriptures lead to Christ, only the Eucharist permits Christians to recognize and possess Him fully. A similar purpose can be discerned in Acts 27.33–38: Paul's action in taking ordinary food is described in Eucharistic terminology (took bread; gave thanks to God; broke it) to remind the readers that the Eucharist is the true "food for your safety" (or "salvation," σωτηρία has both meanings). Writing about 25 years later, St. Ignatius of Antioch described the broken bread as "the medicine of immortality" (*Ephesians* 20.2). The multiplication of loaves in Jn 6.1–13 not only served as a prelude to the great discourse on the bread of life, but like the Synoptic accounts (Mk 6.41; 8.6 and parallels) was described in terms reminiscent of the Last Supper, thus showing how the early Church saw in this miracle a foreshadow or type of the Eucharistic banquet.

See also EUCHARIST (BIBLICAL DATA).

Bibliography: EncDictBibl 276–277; 697–702. J. GEWIESS, Lex ThK² 2:706–707. A. PIOLANTI, EncCatt 5:1564–65. J. DUPONT, "Le Repas d'Emmaüs," LumetVie 6 (1957) 77–92. **Illustration credit:** Courtesy of Deutsche Gesellschaft für Christliche Kunst.

[C. BERNAS]

BREASTPIECE OF THE HIGH PRIEST, an object worn by the high priest over the *ephod. It is described twice: in the instructions of the Lord to Moses on how it should be made (Ex 28.15–30; see also 25.7; 35.9, 27) and then in the description of how it was actually made for Aaron, the first high priest (Ex 39.8–21). It was made of fine linen embroidered with threads of gold, violet, purple, and scarlet yarn and, like a liturgical burse, was a square of one span (*c.* 10 inches) and doubled to form a pocketlike receptacle. On the front were mounted, in gold filigree work, four rows of precious stones, three to a row, and on each stone the name of one of the twelve tribes was engraved. These gems were rendered with various Hebrew words, some of which are conjectural even in the Greek translations. *See* PRECIOUS STONES (IN THE BIBLE). At each of the four corners were golden rings. Through the two upper ends gold cords were fastened to the shoulder straps of the ephod. Through the two lower ends violet ribbons passed through the rings of the ephod and fastened the breastpiece below the arms. Inside the breastpiece were placed the *Urim and Thummim. The Septuagint translated the Hebrew word *ḥōšen* (breastpiece) by λογεῖον (oracular instrument), which was poorly rendered in the Vulgate as *rationale,* whence the old English term "rational" as the name of this object.

Bibliography: H. THIERSCH, *Ependytes und Ephod* (Stuttgart 1936). F. NÖTSCHER, *Biblische Altertumskunde* (Bonn 1940) 309–310.

[J. E. STEINMUELLER]

BRECHT, BERTOLT

German dramatist and essayist; b. Augsburg, Feb. 10, 1898; d. East Berlin, Aug. 14, 1956. After the National Socialists came into power in 1933, he and his family went into a voluntary exile that brought him, by way of Vladivostok, to the U.S. in 1941. In 1948 he settled in East Berlin, where he organized his own theatrical company, the Berliner Ensemble, in which his wife, Helene Weigel, took prominent roles. He was a loyal supporter of the Communist-dominated regime.

From the beginning Brecht was identified as an activist among expressionistic dramatists. The early

Bertolt Brecht.

dramas of social satire include *Baal* (1922), *Trommeln in der Nacht* (1922), *Im Dickicht der Städte* (1924), and *Mann ist Mann* (1927). *Die Dreigroschenoper* (1928, The Threepenny Opera), which won considerable acclaim in Europe and the U.S. as drama, opera (with a musical score by Kurt Weill), and film, is based on Gay's *The Beggar's Opera* (1728) but is updated to a mordant satire of capitalism; a treatment of the same theme in novel form is found in *Dreigroschenroman*

(1934). The culture of our great cities is satirized in *Aufstieg und Fall der Stadt Mahagonny* (1929), also set to music by Kurt Weill. Marxist propaganda is apparent in the play *Badener Lehrstück* (1929) and in some of the subsequent plays. In *Die Massnahme* (1931) a Communist comrade makes a "confession" before his execution. A modern *Joan of Arc in the person of a Salvation Army girl dies in *Die heilige Johanna der Schlachthöfe* (1932) because she fails in her mission to improve the lot of stockyard workers in Chicago.

In the first play completed during his self-imposed exile, *Der gute Mensch von Sezuan* (1941), Brecht argues that man can live in a purely capitalistic society only through assuming a dual existence. *Mutter Courage und ihre Kinder* (1941), with music by Paul Dessau, which takes its principal character at least nominally from *Grimmelshausen's *Simplicissimus* (1668–69), shows an old camp follower who ekes out a living from the profits of the degradation of war. The original version of *Leben des Galilei* (1938–39) is a treatment of progress and knowledge in conflict with the authority of Church and State; an altered script in English, however, staged in 1947 with Charles Laughton in the title role, interprets Galileo's vision in social terms. *Der kaukasische Kreidekreis* (1947) purports to prove that social ties are above those of blood relationship. *Herr Puntila und sein Knecht Matti* (1948) treats of a hopeless master-servant relationship in which the master reveals human qualities only when he is drunk.

Brecht explained his dramatic technique in essays called *Versuche*. Several of his plays exemplify his principle of epic realism, which is an illusion-shattering use of devices to interpret the action of a play to the audience. In addition to this he formulated the so-called doctrine of alienation (*Verfremdung*) that entails the

A scene from Bertolt Brecht's play "Saint Joan of the Stockyards" as played by the Schauspielhaus, Hamburg.

counter development of one action by another. His lyric poetry shows the influence of Rimbaud and Villon. Collections of his poems include *Hauspostille* (1927), *Lieder, Gedichte, Chöre* (1934), *Hundert Gedichte* (1950), and *Gedichte und Lieder* (1956).

Bibliography: J. BITHELL, *Modern German Literature: 1880–1950* (London 1959). P. DEMETZ, ed., *Brecht* (Englewood Cliffs, N.J. 1962). R. GRIMM, *Bertolt Brecht* (Stuttgart 1961), with extensive bibliog. J. WILLETT, *The Theatre of Bertolt Brecht* (New York 1959). **Illustration credits:** Fig. 1, German Information Center, New York City. Fig. 2, Rosemarie Clausen—German Information Center.

[J. E. BOURGEOIS]

BRÉHIER, LOUIS, Byzantine scholar; b. Brest, France, Aug. 5, 1868; d. Reims, Oct. 13, 1951. Bréhier studied at the Sorbonne, where he received the licentiate in 1890, was declared agrégé in 1892, and received the doctorate in 1899. After teaching in four lycées, he was appointed to the chair of ancient and medieval history at the University of Clermont-Ferrand in 1898, remaining there until his retirement in 1938. Bréhier lived and worked in isolation at Clermont-Ferrand and, after his retirement, at Reims. An extraordinarily prolific scholar, he wrote some 30 books and hundreds of articles. His interests centered on the history of Greek-Latin relations during the Middle Ages. The first of his published studies was *Le Schisme oriental du XIᵉ siècle* (Paris 1900). His essay on the papacy and the Crusades, *L'Église et l'Orient au moyen âge*, has passed through many editions and is one of his best-known works. Bréhier wrote much on the history of art, including *L'Art chrétien* (Paris 1918), *L'Art byzantin* (Paris 1924), *La Sculpture et les arts mineurs byzantins* (Paris 1936), and *Le Style roman* (Paris 1946). His crowning achievement was a three-volume synthesis of Byzantine history and civilization, *Le Monde byzantin* (Paris 1947–50).

Bibliography: P. LEMERLE, RevHist 208 (1952) 380–382. R. DUSSAUD, *Syria* 28 (1951) 362–363. P. GUILLAND, *Byzantinoslavica* 12 (1951) 287.

[J. A. BRUNDAGE]

BREMEN-HAMBURG, ANCIENT SEE OF

Former medieval German archdiocese and ecclesiastical province (Latin, *Brema, Hamburgum*). In 787 *Charlemagne had the Anglo-Saxon *Willehad consecrated bishop and then gave him the mission of converting the pagan Frisians and *Saxons who lived at the mouth of the Weser River. Two years later Willehad consecrated his cathedral church (St. Peter's) in Bremen. But the Diocese of Bremen was definitively constituted only under his successor, Willerich (805), at which time it was assigned to the ecclesiastical *province of *Cologne. Then in 831 Emperor *Louis I the Pious erected the Diocese of Hamburg for all mission territory north of the Elbe River and entrusted it to *Ansgar (consecrated bishop in 832). Pope Gregory IV made Ansgar both archbishop and, together with *Ebbo of Reims, papal legate for the mission to the unbaptized Danes, Swedes, and Slavs. When Hamburg (including the cathedral of Our Lady) was destroyed by the *Normans in 845, King *Louis the German gave Ansgar (847) the then-vacant See of Bremen. Subsequently, Pope Nicholas I, after a long struggle, removed the combined See of Bremen-Hamburg from the jurisdiction of Cologne (864) and confirmed Ansgar as archbishop of Hamburg and bishop of Bremen. Pope Sergius III later ratified the union of the two dioceses under Archbishop *Adalgar (888–909) for as long as the Hamburg archdiocese would have no suffragan sees of its own. In fact, the union was permanent; the archbishop resided in Bremen.

Archbishop Ansgar (d. 865) and his successors, especially *Rembert (865–888), *Unni (918–936), and *Adaldag (937–988) developed a far-reaching missionary network in the north. Under Adaldag, the Danish suffragan Dioceses of Schleswig, Ribe, Aarhus, and Odense were founded; in 967 or 968 Oldenburg diocese in Holstein was created as the base for the mission to the Wends. It was destroyed in 985, but in 1160 it was again erected, this time in Lübeck. The other suffragan dioceses of Bremen-Hamburg were Mecklenburg (diocesan see in Schwerin after 1160) and Ratzeburg, both formed from the older Diocese of Oldenburg. Bremen-Hamburg was at the peak of its glory under Archbishop Bezelin (1035–1043) and then under Emperor *Henry IV's mentor, *Adalbert of Bremen (1043–72), who envisioned a Nordic patriarchate. However, in 1104—despite the bitter resistance of the Bremen-Hamburg archbishops, who continued to claim *metropolitan rights over the whole of Scandinavia (i.e., Denmark, Sweden, Norway, Iceland, Greenland, the Orkneys, the Faeroes)—the ecclesiastical Province of *Lund was erected and the northern Province of Bremen-Hamburg dissolved. Thereafter the metropolitan See of Bremen-Hamburg included only the suffragan Dioceses of Lübeck, Ratzeburg, and Schwerin.

During the later Middle Ages, when both cities of Bremen and Hamburg were principal members of the *Hanseatic League, the see's many able archbishops included Giselbert of Brunkhorst (1274–1306), Burchard Grelle (1327–44), the pious Otto of Brunswick (1395–1406), John Slamstorp (1406–20), who implemented the *Windesheim reform in the monasteries of the archdiocese, and John Rode (1497–1511). In 1522, under the worldly Abp. Christopher of Brunswick (1511–58), the Lutheran Reformation penetrated Bremen-Hamburg, where a former Augustinian, Henry von Zütphen, was especially responsible for its spread. By 1558 both the archdiocese and the cathedral chapter were almost entirely Protestant. Christopher's brother and successor, Abp. George of Brunswick (d. 1566), was still outwardly Catholic, but subsequent archbishops were all Protestant. The last archbishop, Prince Frederick of Denmark, was driven out by the Swedes in 1644. By the Peace of *Westphalia (1648) all territorial possessions of the Sees of Bremen-Hamburg and Verden passed as a secular duchy to Sweden, later to Denmark, to Hanover, and to Prussia, among others. But the city of Bremen itself remained, as did Hamburg, a free imperial city. In 1645 the Catholic Bishop of Osnabrück, Franz Wilhelm von *Wartenberg, was appointed *vicar apostolic for Bremen; in 1669 the former ecclesiastical province, now containing only a few Catholics, was placed under the jurisdiction of the apostolic vicariate for the Nordic missions. In 1946 the area that had originally been within the confines of the archdiocese became part of either the Free Cities of Bremen and Hamburg or of the states of Lower Saxony and Schleswig-Holstein in the German Federal Republic. In 1929 religious jurisdiction over even the non-Prussian parts of the former Archdiocese of Bremen-

Hamburg, the East-West Road; in the background, the church of St. Michael, at the right, the ruins of the church of St. Nicholas.

Hamburg passed to the Diocese of Osnabrück, and one section of Hamburg went to the Diocese of Hildesheim. Since 1958 Hamburg has been the seat of a suffragan bishop.

Bibliography: Sources. ADAM OF BREMEN, *Gesta Hammaburg. eccl. pontificum,* ed. B. SCHMEIDLER, MGSrerGerm (3d ed. Hanover 1917); fac. ed. of the *Codex Havniensis,* ed. C. A. CHRISTENSEN (Copenhagen 1948); Eng. tr. F. J. TSCHAN (New York 1959). O. H. MAY and G. MÖHLMANN, *Regesten der Erzbischöfe von Bremen,* 2 v. (Hanover 1928–53). Literature. G. DEHIO, *Geschichte des Erzbistums H.-B. bis zum Ausgang der Mission,* 2 v. (Berlin 1877). C. JOPPEN, DHGE 10:506–518. B. SCHMEIDLER, *H.-B. und Nordosteuropa vom 9.–11. Jahrhundert* (Leipzig 1918). G. MÖHLMANN, *Der Güterbesitz des Bremer Domkapitels* (Bremen 1933). G. APEL, *Die Güterverhältnisse des hamburg. Domkapitels* (Hamburg 1934). H. KOCH, *Den danske Kirkes Historie,* v. 1 *Den aeldre middelalder indtil 1241* (Copenhagen 1950). H. SCHWARZWÄLDER, *Entstehung und Anfänge der Stadt Bremen* (Bremen 1955). H. FUHRMANN, "Studien zur Geschichte mittelalterlicher Patriarchate," ZSav RGKan 41 (1955) 95–183, esp. 120–170, 177–178. F. OTTO, *Die rechtlichen Verhältnisse des Domstiftes zu Hamburg von 1719 bis 1802* (Diss. Göttingen 1958). E. WEISE, LexThK² 2:665–667. G. GLAESKE, *Die Erzbischöfe von Hamburg-Bremen als Reichsfürsten, 937–1258* (Hildesheim 1962). W. GÖBELL, "Die Christianisierung des Nordens und das Werden der mittelalterlichen Kirche bis zur Errichtung des Erzbistums Lund (1103)," *Österreich. Archiv für Kirchenrecht* 15 (1964) 8–22, 97–102. **Illustration credit:** German Information Center, New York.

[G. SCHWAIGER]

BREMOND, HENRI

Spiritual writer; b. Aix-en-Provence, France, 1865; d. Arthez d'Asson, France, Aug. 17, 1933. He received his early education at Aix-en-Provence, and in 1882 entered the Society of Jesus. He was sent for his novitiate and studies to England, where he spent 10 years.

During this time he "discovered" John Henry *Newman, who, after Maurice *Blondel, had the greatest influence on his thought. Bremond was ordained in 1892. Though a professor and an editor of *Études,* he still found time to devote to extensive research, unwittingly preparing himself for the great work he was to publish from 1916 to 1933. During this earlier period his books, characteristically, were studies of religious thought: *L'Inquiétude religieuse* (1900); *Ames religieuses* (1902); *Thomas More* (1904); *Newman: Essai de biographie psychologique* (1906); *Gerbet* (1907); *La Provence mystique au XVIIème siècle* (1908); *Nicole* (1909); and *Apologie pour Fénélon* (1910), a book that, though brilliant, was unfair to Bossuet.

Bremond's chief work is *L'Histoire littéraire du sentiment religieux en France, depuis la fin des guerres de religion jusqu'à nos jours.* The title indicates that he intended to study religious thought not in the actions that provokes, but in the literary expression that men of talent had given it. He did not include the Middle Ages, because his purpose was the study of the religious life of modern man, the product of the Renaissance. He intended to extend his investigations to works of the 20th century, but at his death his study had progressed only to the end of the 17th century. His central idea was that French religious thought in the 17th century had been revivified by the influence of the Italian, Spanish, and Flemish mystics, thus reaching a sort of perfection of its own and becoming a truly original expression. The French had ignored the riches of their spirituality: the studies of Bremond were for them a revelation.

The writing of this work did not keep Bremond from making literary excursions according to his fancy. He explored widely, returning always, as to a focal point, to the thought of Pascal: "God is apprehended and felt by the heart, which has its reasons that the mind knows not of." Thus he came to relate mysticism with poetry, not to confound them, but to show that they spring from the same faculty "outside of reason." In the course of these researches he coined the term "pure poetry," which had immediate popularity and which represented poetry stripped of its rational elements and reduced to its essence. Among his works should be mentioned: *Poésie et prière* (1925), *Dans les tempêtes* (1926), *Introduction à la Philosophie de la prière* (1929), *Divertissements devant l'Arche* (1930), and *La Poésie pure* (1933).

In 1904 Bremond left the Society of Jesus "because of incompatibility of temperament," as he said. He had a volatile and independent nature, which he showed by maintaining his friendly relations with George *Tyrrell and Alfred *Loisy, even to the point of compromising himself and throwing doubt on the sincerity of his own faith, which was, however, incontestable. He was elected a member of the French Academy in 1923. He spent little time in Paris, making his home at Arthez d'Asson, near Pau, in the Pyrenees.

Bibliography: A. AUSTIN, *Henri Bremond* (Paris 1946). J. DE GUIBERT, DictSpirAscMyst 1:1928–38. A. BREMOND, "Henri Bremond," *Études* 217 (1933) 29–53. J. JACQUEMET, *Catholicisme* 2 (1948) 239–242. H. HOGARTH, *Henri Bremond: The Life and Work of a Devout Humanist* (London 1950).

[J. CALVET]

BRENDAN, SS. The name of several Irish saints: Brendan of Clonfert, Irish abbot, patron of the Diocese of Kerry; b. Annagh on Tralee Bay, *c.* 486; d. 578

St. Brendan's Island, marked on a map by Pizzigani, 1367.

(feast, May 16). He is said to have been fostered by St. *Ita of Killeedy before further studies with Bishop Erc at St. Finian's Clonard and with St. Jarlath of *Tuam. Later, Brendan took charge of the monastery at Ardfert, making a number of new foundations in both Ireland and Scotland. Of these his principal monastery was Clonfert, County Galway, founded in 561. Brendan was a great traveler—he is mentioned in the Hebrides with *Columba of Iona (Colmcille) in *Adamnan's biography of Columba; he may also have visited Wales and perhaps Brittany. He is associated with Mt. Brandon, County Kerry, Ireland's second highest mountain, on the summit of which a ruined oratory and cells are claimed to mark the saint's hermitage. It was once among the most famous places of pilgrimage in Ireland. Probably in the first half of the 10th century, an unknown Irish resident on the Continent chose Brendan of Clonfert as the hero of a voyage romance. Such romances were an Irish literary form, conveniently linking adventures on several islands into a unified story. Of these, the *Voyage of Brendan* is the most famous and has been translated into all the languages of Europe. St. Brendan's Island continued to be marked on charts into the 18th century. The author drew on what he knew of world geography, and on mythological and adventure themes from many sources. C. Selmer considers the work to be a deliberately Christianized Aeneid. Voyage romances were also attached to other Irish saints beside Brendan, but they have not been preserved in their entirety. Any idea that Brendan's voyage represents a historical reality, happening to a historical person, must be dismissed.

Brendan of Birr, Irish abbot (feast, Nov. 29). He was a contemporary of Brendan of Clonfert, known only from references to him in accounts of other saints. He would appear to have been an important individual, famous enough to be called "the chief of the prophets of Ireland." His principal monastic foundation was at Birr, County Offaly.

Bibliography: BRENDAN, *Navigatio sancti Brendani Abbatis,* ed. C. SELMER (Notre Dame, Ind. 1959). Kenney 1:406–420. F. O'BRIAIN, DHGE 10:532–534. C. PLUMMER, comp., *Vitae sanctorum Hiberniae,* 2 v. (Oxford 1910) 1:98–151; 2:270–294; ed., *Bethada náem nÉrenn,* 2 v. (Oxford 1922) 1:44–102; 2:44–98. L. GOUGAUD, *Les Saints irlandais hors d'Irelande* (Louvain 1936). K. HUGHES, "On an Irish Litany of Pilgrim Saints Compiled c. 800," AnalBoll 77 (1959) 305–331. G. A. LITTLE, *Brendan the Navigator* (Dublin 1945). G. ASHE, *Land to the West: St. Brendan's Voyage to America* (New York 1962).

[D. D. C. POCHIN MOULD]

BRENNAN, CHRISTOPHER JOHN, Australian poet; b. Sydney, Nov. 1, 1870; d. there, Oct. 5, 1932. Brennan, of Irish Catholic descent, was educated at parochial schools, and at two Jesuit colleges—St. Kilda's, Woolloomoolloo, and St. Ignatius, Riverview—before matriculating at the University of Sydney, where he majored in literature and philosophy. After teaching at St. Patrick's College, Goulburn, he won a scholarship for study overseas and went to Berlin. Returning without a degree, he was employed first as a librarian in Sydney, later gave lectures at the university, and eventually (1920) he became professor of German and comparative literature. He lost this post in 1925 and supported himself by tutoring and writing. He ceased to be a practicing Catholic in his youth, but returned to the faith toward the end of his life. Brennan's first publications were *XVIII Poems* and *XXI Poems: Towards the Source* (both 1897); most of these were gathered into *Poems 1913* (actually 1914), which contains the core of his work—the three sequences "Towards the Source," "The Forest of Night," and "The Wanderer." Other less important writings are found in two volumes (1960–62) edited by A. R. Chisholm and J. J. Quinn, which collect Brennan's verse and prose; the verse volume contains also an illuminating biographical introduction by Chisholm. Brennan's poetry is allusive and rhetorical, sonorous, and at time obscure. Unlike other Australian verse, his owes little to the local landscape. Brennan was a good linguist, widely read in the literatures of Greece and Rome, France, Germany, and Italy; his writings reveal a multiplicity of influences from his reading. Much attention has been paid to his debt to the French Symbolist poets, especially *Mallarmé with his notion of the *livre composé,* but Brennan was deeply affected also by Swinburne and other Victorian English poets. Though not widely read, he was for a long time regarded as Australia's finest poet; of late this reputation has begun to suffer.

Bibliography: G. A. WILKES, *New Perspectives on Brennan's Poetry* (Sydney 1953). J. McAULEY, *Christopher Brennan* (Melbourne 1963).

[G. K. W. JOHNSTON]

BRENT, CHARLES HENRY, Protestant Episcopal bishop and pioneer in the ecumenical movement; b. Newcastle, Ontario, Canada, April 9, 1862; d. Lausanne, Switzerland, March 27, 1929. He received his B.A. (1884) from Trinity College, Toronto, Canada, and was ordained in 1887. After serving in several parishes he was elected bishop of the Philippines in 1901, a post he held until 1918, when he became bishop of western New York. In 1926 he was chosen bishop-in-charge of the Episcopal churches in Europe for a term of 2 years.

Brent's experience as a missionary in the Philippines convinced him of the need for Christian unity. In 1910 he attended the World Missionary Conference at Edinburgh, Scotland, considered the beginning of the modern *ecumenical movement. The harmony and zeal evidenced at the Edinburgh meeting convinced him that cooperation among the various denominations was possible, and he urged an international meeting for the discussion of religious differences. En route to the Philippines, he attended the 1910 general convention of the American Episcopal Church in Cincinnati, Ohio, where his words in praise of the Edinburgh meeting resulted in the formation of a commission for the purpose of organizing an international meeting of Christian churches. World War I and its aftermath delayed the planning, but representatives of 108 churches finally met at Lausanne in 1927 under the presidency of Bishop Brent. Doctrinal differences were discussed, and a continuation committee was appointed to meet annually with Brent as chairman. From these and other independent meetings later developed the *World Council of Churches.

Charles Henry Brent.

Brent believed in a religious unity analogous to the unity that bound together the dissimilar sections of the British Empire, i.e., a unity of essential principles that would at the same time respect the traditions of the various groups. He looked to a future united church to which every Christian communion would contribute something from its own particular insight or experience.

Bibliography: A. ZABRISKIE, *Bishop Brent: Crusader for Christian Unity* (New York 1948). G. WEIGEL, *A Catholic Primer on the Ecumenical Movement* (Westminster Md. 1957). **Illustration credit:** Library of Congress.

[E. DELANEY]

BRENT, MARGARET, Maryland pioneer; b. England, 1601(?); d. Virginia, 1671(?). Her parents, Richard, Lord of Admington and Larkstoke, Gloucester, England, and his wife, Elizabeth (Reed), had 13 children. With her sister Mary and her brothers Giles and Foulke, Margaret immigrated to St. Mary's, Md., in November 1638, bringing letters from Lord Baltimore ordering Gov. Leonard Calvert to grant them as large a portion of land and as great privileges as had been given to the first settlers. To the initial grant of 70½ acres of townland and 1,000 acres outside the town, Margaret gradually added extensive holdings; she was the first woman in Maryland to hold land in her own right, and she played an important part in the affairs of the colony. During Claiborne's rebellion she raised a small body of volunteers in defense of the Calvert government and property. Subsequently, as executrix of Governor Calvert and as attorney for the proprietary interests, she engaged in a multiplicity of lawsuits. In January 1648 she asked the Maryland assembly to give her voice and vote in her double capacity as executrix and attorney. Although her request was refused, the assembly later came to her defense, when the heirs contested her handling of the Calvert estates. Her brother Giles, an ardent royalist, made over his Maryland property to her (1642); and when he moved

to Virginia (1646), he made her his attorney. Margaret stayed in Maryland until 1650, when, having made George Manners attorney for her own and her brother's interests, she joined Giles in Virginia. Her will, dated Dec. 26, 1663, and admitted to probate May 19, 1671, left her land in Maryland and Virginia to her brother Giles and his heirs.

Bibliography: Maryland Historical Society, *Transcripts from the Public Records: References to Mistress Margaret Brent, 1638–1644. Archives of Maryland* (1883–) v.1, 4, *passim.* W. B. CHILTON, "The Brent Family," *Virginia Magazine* 13–21 (1903–13), *passim.* A. REPPLIER, "The Elusive Lady of Maryland," *Catholic World* 138 (1933–34) 660–669.

[J. DE L. LEONARD]

BRENTANO, CLEMENS MARIA, German Romantic author; b. Ehrenbreitstein, Sept. 8, 1778; d. Aschaffenburg, July 28, 1842. The parentage of a prosperous merchant of Italian descent in Frankfurt am Main and Maximiliane (née La Roche) meant both financial security and friendship with the intellectually and socially prominent members of his mother's circle. His years as a student at Halle, Jena, and Göttingen resulted chiefly in his marriage to the divorced Sophie Mereau, ended by her death in 1806, and the beginning of his close personal and literary association with Achim von Arnim, with whom he collected and published the important collection of folk songs, *Des Knaben Wunderhorn* (1806). Returning to the Church in 1817, he spent the next 7 years practically at the bedside of a stigmatized nun in Westphalia, Anna Katharina *Emmerich, a devotion that led him largely to forgo secular writing in favor of recording this experience. The remainder of his life was spent quietly in Koblenz, Frankfurt, and Munich.

Some principal works are: the novel *Godwi* (1801); the historical drama *Die Gründung Prags* (1815); the story *Geschichte vom braven Kasperl und dem schönen Annerl* (1817); the fanciful tale *Gockel, Hinkel und Gackeleia* (1838); *Die Märchen* (1846); a long unfinished poem *Die Romanzen vom Rosenkranz* (1852), treating the origin of the rosary; *Das bittere Leiden unsers Herrn Jesu Christi* (1833), based on his Westphalian experience; and many religious and secular poems. It is in the poems that Brentano probably made his chief contribution to German literature; in mood and technique, they are often reminiscent of Heine and *Eichendorff.

See also GERMAN LITERATURE, 5; ROMANTICISM, LITERARY.

Bibliography: C. BRENTANO, *Gesammelte Schriften*, ed. C. BRENTANO, 9 v. (Frankfort 1852–55); *Werke*, ed. M. PREITZ, 3 v. (Leipzig 1914). R. GUIGNARD, *Un Poète romantique allemand* (Paris 1933).

[H. TUCKER, JR.]

BRENTANO, FRANZ

German philosophical psychologist influential in the development of *phenomenology; b. Marienberg, near Boppard, June 16, 1838; d. Zürich, Switzerland, March 17, 1917. Brentano's parents were devout Catholics; his uncle, Clemens *Brentano, was a noted romantic poet; his brother, Lujo, was a political economist and professor at the University of Munich. Franz entered the Dominican Order in his youth but left as a novice. In 1864 he was ordained and in the same year was attached to the University of Würzburg, first as a lecturer in philosophy, later as a full professor (1872). Though he was deep in doubt concerning certain dogmas of the

Church, he was asked to prepare a brief on papal infallibility for a meeting of the German bishops before *Vatican Council I. When the dogma of infallibility was proclaimed, Brentano resigned his professorship and abandoned his priesthood. In 1874 the University of Vienna offered him a professorship, which he surrendered in 1880 when he married. He remained in Vienna for 15 years as an unsalaried lecturer, until approaching blindness forced him to retire. He spent his remaining years traveling in Italy and Switzerland.

Thought. Three major influences were operative in Brentano's thinking. First, he became acquainted with the philosophies of Aristotle, St. Thomas Aquinas, and the scholastics during his seminary training. From these Brentano adopted many principles, as well as his orderly, analytic approach to philosophy. Second, he refused to accept the a priori principles of German idealists, being opposed to any form of dogmatism. Third, impressed with the discoveries of the physical sciences, he attributed progress in science to empirical methodology and urged that such methodology be adopted by the philosopher. Under these influences, Brentano set out to construct a "scientific" philosophy that would start with no "categories" or "forms." On the analogy of mathematics' being basic to the physical sciences, he sought to determine a similar science that would be basic to philosophy, and settled upon psychology.

Arguing that psychological phenomena can be objectively studied only in their proper setting, which is experience, Brentano proposed to construct a "psychology from an empirical standpoint." He avoided the subjectivist extreme of studying experience through introspection alone; rather, he proposed that in each man there is an experience of "inner perception," an awareness that is both immediate and infallible. By analyzing this "inner perception," Brentano hoped to describe and categorize the contents of experience.

For Brentano, all psychological phenomena possess an "intentionality," a property not found in physical phenomena. His was not the Thomistic theory of an idea's "intentional inexistence" in the mind (see INTENTIONALITY; SPECIES, INTENTIONAL). Instead, Brentano merely stated that psychological phenomena have a "reference-to-an-object"; ideas, desires, feelings are essentially concerned with things external. By his "inner perception," man is immediately aware that each psychic phenomenon refers to or "intends" an outside object. Thus every such phenomenon must be conscious; unconscious phenomena are self-contradictory.

In Brentano's view, psychic phenomena are of three types: (1) mere representations, (2) judgments, and (3) feelings of love and hate. These phenomena are not static concepts; Brentano saw them all as "activities" that refer differently to objects. An analysis of each type uncovers a basic truth. (1) Representations are the primary phenomena; thus every psychological phenomena is, at least originally, a representation. (2) Judgments are objectively true or false; yet certain judgments are experienced by all men as self-evident. (3) All acts of love and hate possess the value of good or evil; analogously, certain of these volitional acts are experienced as naturally good or evil. It was on this analogy of self-evident value that Brentano based his ethics.

Influence. Brentano prepared the ground for phenomenology by enlarging the scope of empiricism: man not only viewed the elements of experience; he was aided by a certain intuition. His notion of "intentional reference" is his most important contribution to the philosophy of E. *Husserl, who called Brentano "my one and only teacher in philosophy." His analogue of self-evidence applied to moral philosophy is at least indirectly reflected in the value-qualified beings of M. *Scheler. However, his impact on philosophy was as a teacher, not as an author. His major works are *Psychologie des Aristotles* (1867), *Psychologie vom empirischen Standpunkt* (Leipzig 1874), and *Vom Ursprung sittlicher Erkenntnis* (Leipzig 1889).

Bibliography: C. Rosso, EncFil 1:796–799. A. Scholz, Lex ThK² 2:670. C. Fabro, EncCatt 3:58–59. H. Spiegelberg, *The Phenomenological Movement* (The Hague 1960–) v.1. A. Kastil, *Die Philosophie Franz Brentanos* (Bern 1951).

[C. P. SVOBODA]

BRENZ, JOHANN, Lutheran reformer of Württemberg; b. Weil der Stadt, 1499; d. Stuttgart, Sept. 11, 1570. Brenz saw Luther at Heidelberg in 1518 and became his follower. For 24 years he served as an evangelical minister in Schwäbisch-Hall, writing a small catechism for youth in 1529, composing an influential order of service, and publishing sermons and scriptural commentaries. In the Sacramentarian controversy with the Swiss *Reformed Churches, he held to the doctrine of the real presence of Christ, his *Syngramma suevicum* being one of the best statements of the Lutheran doctrine. As the Protestant reformer of Württemberg he assisted Duke Ulrich, after his restoration in 1534, and his successor Duke Christopher. Brenz fled to Switzerland during the Schmalkaldic War when the imperial chancellor Antoine Perrenot De *Granvelle put a price on his head. In Württemberg he established schools, orphanages, homes for the poor, and proseminaries; helped reform Tübingen University; and developed a church order (1559), used as a model in other parts of the empire. He even composed a "Swabian Confession" for the Council of Trent, which was, however, flatly rejected.

Bibliography: J. Hartmann and K. Jäger, *Johann Brenz*, 2 v. (Hamburg 1840–42). G. Bayer, *Johannes Brenz, der Reformator Württembergs* (Stuttgart 1899). A. Brecht, *Johannes Brenz* (Stuttgart 1949). W. Köhler, *Bibliographia Brentiana* (Berlin 1904; repub. Nieuwkoop 1963). H. Fausel, RGG³ 1:1400–01.

[L. W. SPITZ]

BRESCIA, the second city of Lombardy, north central Italy, 52 miles east of Milan, at the foot of the Alps. The chief city of the Gallic *Cenomani* became a Roman strongpoint beyond the Po and was sacked by Attila (452). Lombard dukes gave way to Carolingian counts, whose authority passed to bishops from local feudal families in the 9th and 10th centuries. *Arnold of Brescia appeared in the long political-religious struggle between bishops and the commune (established 1120–27), which joined the *Lombard Leagues. After 200 years of *Guelf-Ghibelline conflict, Brescia was ruled by the *Scaligers and *Visconti before it came under Venice (1426–1797). It was part of the Cisalpine Republic and the kingdom of Lombardy-Veneto (1815–59) before the unification of Italy.

Brescia was probably the first see to be detached from that of *Milan (early 4th century), to which it is still suffragan. The first known bishop, Ursicinus, attended the Council of Sardica (342). Until 680 all Brescia's bishops were venerated as saints, notably St. Filastrus (d. 397), whose *Diversarum hereseon liber* was used by St. Augustine, and his successor, St. *Gaudentius. Rampert built the cathedral (836–838) and *c.* 840 founded the Benedictine monastery of SS. Faustinus and Jovita (early Christian martyrs in Brescia who became patrons of the see). Adelman of Liège, probably an imperial appointee (1059), opposed *Berengarius of Tours, with whom he had studied at Chartres. The first prior of the Dominicans in Brescia (1221), *Guala, became bishop (1229–44). Under Bernard Maggi (1275–1308), who held spiritual and temporal authority, Brescia enjoyed a period of peace. The diocese declined in the 14th century under foreign absentee bishops; Venetians served as prelates frequently from 1442. Several of Brescia's prelates were cardinals; Pietro Ottoboni (1654–64) became Pope Alexander VIII. Cardinal Angelo M. Quirini (1727–55) founded Brescia's library (1743). St. Angela *Merici founded the Ursulines in Brescia (1535).

Roman ruins include a bronze statue of Winged Victory. Many buildings of artistic interest have been built since the 12th century. The new cathedral (1604–1825) was built onto the old Romanesque rotunda cathedral (11th century). Brescia produced a number of famous musicians from the 15th to the 18th century.

Bibliography: H. LECLERCQ, DACL 2:1139–57. P. GUERRINI, *Memorie storiche della diocesi di Brescia,* 2 v. (Brescia 1930–42); EncCatt 3:62–66. F. BONNARD, DHGE 10:549–555. H. JEDIN, LexThK² 2:672. AnnPont (1964) 74. *Brixia sacra* (1910–25).

[E. P. COLBERT]

BRESCIA COLLEGE, a coeducational liberal arts college directed by the Ursuline Sisters of Mt. St. Joseph in Maple Mount, Ky. It had its beginning in 1874 when a Kentucky missionary, Rev. Paul Joseph Volk, invited the Ursuline Sisters to establish Mt. St. Joseph, an academy for girls, at St. Joseph, Ky. (now Maple Mount, Ky.). Mt. St. Joseph Academy was incorporated by the Legislature of Kentucky under a charter granted in 1880, and was empowered "to confer such academic diplomas and degrees as are conferred by the colleges of the U.S." Mt. St. Joseph Junior College for women was opened on the Maple Mount campus in September 1925. In 1947 a division of St. Joseph Junior College in Maple Mount began a full-time coeducational program in Owensboro, Ky. A rapid increase in enrollment prompted the administration to expand the facilities in Owensboro and to establish an independent institution there. At this time, the name was changed from St. Joseph to Brescia College, in honor of St. Angela Merici who founded the Ursuline Order in Brescia, Italy, in 1535.

The College was affiliated with The Catholic University of America, and upper-division courses leading to a baccalaureate degree were added to the curriculum in 1951. The senior college was admitted to membership in the Southern Association of Colleges and Secondary Schools in 1957. Brescia College is accredited by the Kentucky State Department of Education and is a member of the Kentucky Association of Colleges and Secondary Schools, Association of American Colleges, and National Catholic Educational Association.

The curriculum offers major fields in the liberal and fine arts; social, natural, and political sciences; modern languages; and business. The College offers preprofessional courses in law, medicine, dentistry, engineering, and pharmacy; and prepares students for certification in elementary, secondary, and special education. An ex-perimental course in Christian femininity was introduced in 1963.

The library, which has a potential of 100,000 volumes, in 1964 had 30,000 volumes and received 317 periodicals. It also houses a collection of printed Kentuckiana materials. A reading and speech center serves as a psychological testing bureau for four county school systems and provides a program for teacher certification in the special areas of mental retardation, speech, and hearing.

Brescia College is governed by a board of trustees consisting of the superior general and the councilors of the Ursuline Order of Mt. St. Joseph, Maple Mount. A board of community trustees chosen from lay civic leaders assists the president's development program. The bishop of Owensboro heads the administrative officers as chancellor. The 55-member teaching staff in 1964 consisted of 39 sisters, 2 priests, and 24 laymen. They held 15 doctorates and 30 master's degrees. Student enrollment totaled 900. College revenue accrues from student tuition and fees and from the contributed services of the religious community. Subsidies and grants have been conferred by private and Federal educational foundations and commissions.

[M. DE C. WHELAN]

BREST, UNION OF

An agreement concluded in 1596 uniting the Ruthenian Orthodox and Roman Catholic Churches of Poland. The Union had both political and religious aspects. Fearing the continued influence and danger arising from the independent Orthodox Patriarchate of Moscow founded in 1589, the Polish government was eager for the elimination of Russian religious and political institutions and traditions. The Orthodox clergy in Ruthenia (the Polish Ukraine) were at this time engaged in an effort to reform and revive the religious, moral, and social life of their discouraged coreligionists. A number of leading Orthodox nobles also supported reform, among them Prince Constantine Ostrogski, who favored reunion with Rome as well. The idea of reunion with the Latin rite along the lines of the Union of Florence (1439) gained strength among members of the Ruthenian hierarchy. Led by Michael Rahosa, Metropolitan of Kiev, and the bishops of Łuck (Terlecki), Lvov (Balaban), Prźemyśl (Kopýstenski), Pinsk (Pełczyński) and Chelm (Zbirujski), the first overtures were made to Catholic authorities. Among the latter, King Sigismund III, John Zamoyski, Chancellor of the Kingdom, John Solikowski, Archbishop of Lvov, Bishop Bernard Maciejowski of Łuck (later bishop and cardinal of Cracow), and members of the Jesuit Order, especially Piotr *Skarga and Antonio *Possevino, were most favorable to reunion. In 1590 Metropolitan Rahosa convoked an Orthodox synod at Brest. A few days before it opened on June 24, Bishops Terlecki, Balaban, Pełczyński, and Zbirujski drew up a document agreeing to "submit their will and intelligence to the Pope of Rome." The synod subsequently approved this statement, which was secretly sent to King Sigismund, who promised to grant the Ruthenians the rights and privileges enjoyed by the Latin rite. Progress was slow, however; finally, in June 1594, the Ruthenian hierarchy once again advanced the proposals of 1590. A year later Rahosa, assisted by three bishops, met at Brest and drew up two petitions, one to Clement VIII and one to

Sigismund III, requesting a reunion based on the Union of Florence, except for the retention of Eastern rites and customs. After Ruthenian consultations with royal delegates and the papal nuncio, King Sigismund on Aug. 2, 1595, proclaimed equal rights, privileges, and guarantees for both Ruthenian and Latin Churches, pending papal sanction. Eventually Clement VIII issued *Magnus Dominus et laudabilis nimis,* confirming and approving the rites, customs, and Julian calendar of the reunited Ruthenian Church.

Despite the devious behavior of Rahosa, who now attempted to hinder the Union, and Prince Ostrogski, who denounced and opposed it, the reunion movement proceeded. In keeping with the Pope's request, a synod was held at Brest in October 1596. Although there was opposition and division, a majority of the Ruthenian bishops led by Rahosa accepted the Union proclaimed at Brest. Bishops Balaban and Kopýstenski dissented, however, and were deposed and excommunicated. Ostrogski became the leader of the opposition, which won strong support among the lower clergy and peasantry. The optimistic expectations of both parties failed to materialize. Rome believed that the Union would be a stepping stone toward unity with Moscow, but the strong opposition in Ruthenia itself portended the failure of this hope. Instead of a united Church based on peace and cooperation resulting, distrust and fear created hostile and separated brethren.

Bibliography: E. LIKOWSKI, *Die ruthenisch-römische Kirchenvereinigung, gennant Union zu Brest,* tr. P. JEDZINK (Freiburg 1904). J. WOLINSKI, *Polska Kościol prawoslawny* (Lvov 1936), Poland and the Orthodox Church. *The Cambridge History of Poland,* ed. W. F. REDDAWAY et al., 2 v. (Cambridge, Eng. 1941–50). G. OLŠR, EncCatt 10:1483–85. J. OSTROWSKY, DHGE 10: 615–618.

[F. J. LADOWICZ]

BRETHREN, a term used in the names of several Protestant denominations, signifying fellowship and the unity of the believing Christians in Christ and with one another. The name originated, in most cases, from the circumstances of a small persecuted group, forced to rely on its own inner spiritual resources and sense of community. The followers of John *Hus represented such a group in Moravia. Under the patronage of Count Nicholas Zinzendorf, a remnant of the *Hussites was invited to settle on the Count's estate at Herrnhut in southern Germany. From this nucleus, the *Unitas Fratrum,* or Church of the Moravian Brethren, developed. The present *Moravian Church in America grew from the settlements made by Zinzendorf at Bethlehem, Pa., in 1741. The *Anabaptist movement in Germany and Switzerland in the 16th century resulted in the dispersion of all but a few minority groups, the Swiss Brethren, the *Hutterites, and the *Mennonites, who continued to insist on faith before baptism. Despite intermittent persecution, a number of Hutterian communities (*Bruderhofs*) developed in Moravia, Hungary, and Transylvania. Persecution drove the Hutterian Brethren to Russia and finally to the U.S. (1874–77). Two other small groups of German immigrants to Pennsylvania were spiritual descendants of the Anabaptists. The *Church of the Brethren (Dunkers) was formed in 1708 at Schwarzenau, Germany, and a majority of its members had settled in Pennsylvania by 1729. A similar group of German origin had settled in York County, Pa., along the banks of the Susque-

hanna River. From this circumstance, their fellowship became known as the *River Brethren. A religious revival among the Mennonite and Reformed churches in Pennsylvania resulted in the formation of a church of essentially Methodist faith and polity among the German settlers. It took its name from the phrase used by M. *Boehm and P. W. *Otterbein on their first meeting in 1767 ("We are brethren") and is now known as the *Evangelical United Brethren Church. The *Plymouth Brethren share the common note of origin as a small group met for fellowship and prayer, but otherwise have nothing in common with the other groups of brethren. Their congregations, formed (1827) in Plymouth, England, are only centers of Bible study and do not form a separate church in the eyes of their adherents.

Bibliography: J. T. HAMILTON, *A History of the Moravian Church* (Bethlehem, Pa. 1901). J. HORSCH, *The Hutterian Brethren, 1528–1931* (Goshen, Ind. 1931). D. F. DURNBAUGH, comp. and tr., *European Origins of the Brethren* (Elgin, Ill. 1958). F. MALLOTT, *Studies in Brethren History* (Elgin, Ill. 1954). M. G. BRUMBAUGH, *A History of the German Baptist Brethren in Europe and America* (Mt. Morris, Ill. 1899; new ed. North Manchester, Ind. 1961).

[R. K. MAC MASTER]

BRETHREN OF THE COMMON LIFE

A religious society in the Netherlands from the 14th to the 16th century; it differed from religious orders in that its members did not take vows. During the lifetime of Gerard *Groote (1340–84) the first community of Brethren of the Common Life, priests and laymen, lived in the house of Florent Radewijns in Deventer. They led a life in community without specific religious vows or joining any definite religious order, although they did renounce the world. The task the Brethren set themselves was to live in the presence of God a life of total dedication to Him and to prepare themselves for eternal life. They also strove to arouse true and fervent religious life in others by means of pastoral care and preaching. It was the preaching of Gerard Groote that had inspired the organization of such a free community.

Origin. It is still a question how the first community in Deventer actually came into being. A theory based on information furnished by *Thomas à Kempis seems most probable: that the community developed gradually because of the fact that men, sympathetic with the efforts of Gerard Groote, met regularly in the house of Groote's fellow worker, Florent Radewijns, and that some of them stayed there and lived from the revenues accruing from their work as copyists, which they put into a common fund. Florent Radewijns took over the direction after Gerard Groote's death (1384). Among the earliest Brethren were John of Höxter, John Brinckerinck, John Vos of Heusden, Amilius van Buren, Gerard Zerbolt of Zutphen, and several others. Their way of life, as described in shorter or longer vitae, was presented to later members of the community as an example worthy of imitation. These biographies, written in Latin or occasionally in the vernacular, aimed at a lively picture of pious predecessors whose lives had been filled with fervent love for Christ and the desire to imitate him; they may be found in the *Chronicon Windeshemense* of John Busch, in Rudolph Dier of Muiden, Thomas à Kempis, Peter Hoorn, in the *Narratio de incohatione domus clericorum in Zwollis* of James de

Voecht, and in the anonymous Frenswegen manuscript. It may be assumed that they were read to the Brethren during mealtimes.

Growth and Expansion. The Deventer community became an example for houses of the Brethren in other cities, and later the Brethren settled also outside the cities in solitary places of the countryside.

In the Netherlands. During Gerard Groote's lifetime a community was started in Zwolle itself, but as the Brethren soon moved to the monastery of Mount St. Agnes in the neighborhood of Zwolle, a second foundation was launched in Zwolle, the St. Gregory House. Together with the Deventer House it became an important center of the *Devotio Moderna and a base for new foundations in the neighborhood, e.g., Albergen (1406) and Hulsbergen (1407). Houses were founded also in Hoorn (1384), Amersfoort (1395), and Delft (1403). Although some of these establishments had little or no success, others were founded throughout the 15th century, in Brussels (1422), 's Hertogenbosch (1424), Doesburg (1426), Groningen (1435), Harderwijk (1441), Gouda (1446), Geerardsbergen (1452), Emmeri (1467), Nijmegen (1470), Utrecht (1475), Berlicum (1482)—all in the Netherlands.

In Germany. The Brethren of the Common Life spread also into the neighboring German regions. From Deventer Henry of Ahaus founded a house in Münster (1401), with which were associated foundations in Osnabrück (1410), Osterberg (1410), Cologne (1417), Herford (1426), Wesel (1435), and Hildesheim (1440). In the second half of the 15th century, the Brethren spread to southern Germany. Some of the German houses amalgamated into the *Colloquium* of Münster (1431). Outside Westphalia and the Rhenish territories, several German houses were of an intermediary sort, somewhat resembling monasteries of Canons Regular, in which, under the influence of the Devotio Moderna, the common life of the canons was revived after it had been abandoned during the High Middle Ages. Most of the houses of the Brethren in the Netherlands confederated into the *Colloquium* of Zwolle, but it is not known exactly which ones these were.

Decline. The development was rather slow; some communities collapsed, and others constituted themselves as monasteries soon after their foundation. The number of houses of the Brethren that were founded in the course of a century and managed to maintain themselves was not very large, and the number of Brethren in each house was also often very modest. In Albergen, for example, there were only about five brothers at the outset, and this number increased somewhat only later. Exactly the same situation prevailed in Emmerich and several other houses; only in such houses as Deventer, Zwolle, and Münster was the number larger. There were many reasons for this: first, the Brethren were by no means desirous of exerting much pressure to build up their houses. Furthermore, they were initially regarded with suspicion and were even opposed later on, especially by the mendicant orders.

Opposition was aroused among the regular clergy by the fact that the Brethren united into a common life without forming a monastic community and that they gave to these free (i.e., canonically unrecognized) communities a certain organization. Groote had recognized this problem, admitted it, and prepared a solution: the foundation of a monastery to which the Brethren could retire if it became impossible for them to continue living in a free community.

The Monastery of Windesheim. As early as 1387 the Deventer Brethren founded the monastery of *Windesheim (near Zwolle), which associated itself with the *Canons Regular of St. Augustine and soon became the center of the Windesheim congregation, which spread very rapidly; it was a sort of complement to the houses of the Brethren in that many men who favored the Devotio Moderna had been accepted into the monasteries associated with it. To Windesheim's existence is traceable the fewness of the free communities of the Brethren. Among the houses of the Windesheim congregation, the monastery of Frenswegen was an important center for the spread of the Devotio Moderna in Westphalia. It was also a focal point for religious contacts between the eastern Netherlands and Westphalia.

Scriptoria of the Brethren. An important occupation of the Brethren was the copying of manuscripts of various sorts: vitae of the saints, theological works, liturgical books. Their books were often illuminated and beautifully bound. The Deventer community, especially before the invention of printing, depended principally on the revenues from the copying of manuscripts and also on simple handicrafts. Other communities founded elsewhere on the model of Deventer derived most of their income from copying work also. The monasteries of the Windesheim congregation, a product of the Devotio Moderna, had *scriptoria where members of the community copied Bibles, Missals, prayer books, and other ecclesiastical books, sometimes by commission; they had a good market. The Brethren wrote for their own use the biographies of Gerard Groote and the men who had been leaders in the society. Their work was unusually legible (*rotunda, fractura*); their scripts, generally used in MSS destined for divine service, for private prayer, and for reading in the refectory, are well exemplified in the two 1447 folios from the workroom of the master copyist Hermanus Strepel, who belonged to the Münster House of the Brethren.

Customaries. In the few *Consuetudines* that have been preserved, copying is specifically stressed as a necessary work, supplementing religious practices:

> Concerning the work of copying, note that you should order the work of your hands to the end that it may lead you to purity of heart, because you are weak and cannot be always at spiritual exercises and for this reason was handiwork instituted. Wherefore you ought to attend in your copying to three things, to wit, that you make the letters properly and perfectly, that you copy without error, that you understand the sense of what you are copying, and that you concentrate your wandering mind on the task.

There is also the regulation: "Twice a week they [the Brethren] write for one hour in the evening for the poor, to wit from six to seven." Not only do the *Consuetudines* regulate the *horarium* and duties of the Brethren; they also contain description of the hours of the Divine Office and state how the members of the house are to conduct themselves externally and interiorly during Mass and what special prayers they are to add to those generally prescribed. In the *Consuetudines* are to be found the combination of individual practice and common custom. A closer investigation of the *Consuetudines* and their relation to the Devotio Moderna are problems still to be treated.

Schools and Residences. Recent research has shown that the Brethren of the Common Life concentrated on pastoral work and taught only rarely; usually the students from large city schools lived in residences managed by the Brethren or with lay families formed by the Devotio Moderna. Only in Gouda, Utrecht, and Liège did the Brethren have schools of their own c. 1500. Of these the school of St. Jerome in Utrecht was by the 16th century the most important. The pastoral care and religious training of the young entrusted to them in their residences was generally the proper task of the Brethren.

Bibliography: Sources. J. BUSCH, *Des Augustinerpropstes Johannes Busch Chronicon Windeshemense und Liber de reformatione monasteriorum,* ed. K. L. GRUBE (Halle 1886). THOMAS À KEMPIS, *The Founders of the New Devotion, Being the Lives of Gerard Groote, Florentius Radewin and Their Followers,* tr. J. P. ARTHUR (London 1905); *The Chronicle of the Canons Regular of Mount St. Agnes,* tr. J. P. ARTHUR (London 1906). J. T. DE VOECHT, *Narratio de inchoatione domus clericorum in Zwollis,* ed. M. SCHOENGEN (Amsterdam 1908). G. GROOTE, "The Original Constitution of the Brethren of the Common Life at Deventer," ed. A. HYMA in his *The Christian Renaissance: A History of the "Devotio Moderna"* (New York 1925) 440–474. W. J. ALBERTS, ed., *Het Frensweger Handschrift* (Groningen 1958); *Consuetudines fratrum Vitae Communis* (Groningen 1959); *Consuetudines domus fratrum Embricensis* (Groningen 1965).

Literature. E. BARNIKOL, *Studien zur Geschichte der Brüder vom Gemeinsamen Leben* (Tübingen 1917). R. R. POST, "Studiën over de Broeders van het Gemeene Leven," *Nederlandsche Historiebladen* 1 (1938) 304–335; 2 (1939) 136–162; *De Moderne devotie* (2d ed. Amsterdam 1950). A. HYMA, *The Brethren of the Common Life* (Grand Rapids, Mich. 1950). S. AXTERS, *Geschiedenis van de vroomheid in de Nederlanden* 4 v. (Antwerp 1950–60) v.3: *De moderne devotie 1380–1550* (1956). C. VAN DER WANSEM, *Het ontstaan en de geschiedenis der Broederschap van het Gemene Leven tot 1400* (Louvain 1958). T. P. VAN ZIJL, *Gerard Groote, Ascetic and Reformer, 1340–1384* (Washington 1963).

[W. J. ALBERTS]

BRETHREN OF THE CROSS

During the era of the Crusades, as a reflection of European reverence for the Holy Land, the site of Christ's life, death, and Resurrection, several religious communities known as bearers of the cross or brothers of the cross (*cruciferi, crucigeri*) were founded.

Order of the Holy Cross. The most renowned of these communities was the *Ordo sanctae Crucis,* canons regular of St. Augustine frequently referred to as the *Crosier Fathers. According to traditions not yet critically studied (LexThK² 6:619; DictSpirAscMyst 2.1:2562), the founder, Theodore of Celles (1166–1236), had participated in Frederick Barbarossa's ill-fated *crusade. Upon returning to Europe, he received a canonry in the cathedral of St. Lambert at Liège. Choosing to live in community, he and his four original companions took vows in the presence of the bishop of Liège on the feast of the Exaltation of the Holy Cross, Sept. 14, 1211. Their first home was the church of St. Theobald at Clair-Lieu, near Huy, a gift of the bishop. Pope Innocent III gave his blessing to the community; and Pope Honorius III, his formal approbation. Peter of Walcourt, the second superior of the order, adopted in large measure the constitutions of the *Dominicans and secured the approval of Pope Innocent IV on May 3, 1248. During the 13th century the Crosiers spread rapidly through Belgium, Holland, France, England, and Germany. Some participated in the mission to the pagan Livonians, while others, it is said, preached the gospel to the *Albigenses, heretics in southern France, and established a house in Toulouse,

the heart of the affected region. *Joinville, the biographer of St. Louis IX of France, reports that the King gave the Crosiers a house in Paris on the "street of the Holy Cross." In 1318 Pope John XXII granted the Crosiers the privileges enjoyed by the *mendicant orders. The Crosiers flourished in the 14th and 15th centuries, but they suffered greatly during the Reformation. Their houses in England and Holland were closed, and during the French Revolution they were expelled from France and Belgium. A revival commenced in the middle years of the 19th century. Today the order has three provinces, with missions in Indonesia, the Congo, and New Guinea. The master general was elected for life and since 1630 has enjoyed the privilege of using pontifical insignia. The habit consists of a white tunic and a black scapular, mantle, and hood. A cross of white and red is embroidered on the scapular.

Italian Cruciati. In Italy the former crusader Cletus of Bologna founded a community of canons regular of St. Augustine, known as *cruciferi* or *cruciati.* In 1169 Alexander III gave his approval. In 1591 they received the privileges of the mendicant orders. At its greatest extent the congregation had five provinces, viz, Bologna, Venice, Rome, Milan, and Naples, with 200 houses. Pope Alexander VII suppressed the congregation in 1656.

Portuguese Canons Regular of the Holy Cross of Coimbra. In Portugal, Tello, the archdeacon of the cathedral of Coimbra, founded the canons regular of the Holy Cross in 1131. Four years later Pope Innocent II confirmed them, and they soon spread through Portugal and Spain. The prior of Coimbra was also chancellor of the university of *Coimbra. The canons played an important role in the spiritual and political life of Portugal throughout the 16th century, but in 1833 the congregation was suppressed.

Bohemian Military Order of the Cross with a Red Star. In Bohemia the *Ordo militaris crucigerorum cum rubea stella,* or Knights of the Cross with the Red Star, was devoted principally to the care of the sick, though it also claimed to be a military order. In 1233 Princess *Agnes of Bohemia gave the brethren the church of St. Peter and the hospital of St. Francis in Prague. Pope Gregory IX in 1237 approved the congregation under the rule of St. *Augustine. In 1250 the papacy allowed the brothers to wear a red cross with a six-pointed red star. From their house in Breslau in Silesia the brothers established numerous hospitals. They especially distinguished themselves during the Hussite Wars and the Reformation. In the course of the Thirty Years' War the brothers fought against the Protestants, thus justifying their claim to be a military order. A general reform of the order was effected during the late 17th century. Although in 1810 the Prussian government suppressed the house in Silesia, the order still exists in Czechoslovakia, with headquarters in Prague.

Order of the Holy Cross with the Red Heart. A military order organized in 1250 with its headquarters at Cracow developed especially in the 16th century. It spread into Poland, Lithuania, and Bohemia, continuing in Lithuania into the first half of the 19th century.

Bibliography: C. R. HERMANS, *Annales canonicorum regularium s. Augustini ordinis s. Crucis,* 3 v. ('s Hertogenbosch

1858). R. Haass, *Die Kreuzherren in den Rheinlanden* (Bonn 1932). F. Jacksche, *Geschichte des ritterl. Ordens mit dem roten Stern* (Prague 1904). A. van de Pasch, LexThK² 6:619–621. P. A. Ceyssens, DDC 4:799–814. M. Vinken, DictSpir AscMyst 2.2:2561–76; DHGE 13:1042–62.

[J. F. O'CALLAGHAN]

BRETON, VALENTINE MARIE (HENRI), Franciscan spiritual writer; b. Besançon, Nov. 18, 1877; d. Paris, July 6, 1957. Breton (baptized Henri) entered the Franciscans at Amiens, Nov. 16, 1899. Because of the persecution of the religious congregations in France (1903) he was obliged to emigrate to Canada. He was ordained in Quebec, July 25, 1907. In 1920 he returned to Paris where he remained until his death at the service of the Franciscan church of Rue Marie-Rose. In Canada as well as in France his life was dedicated to preaching, writing, and spiritual direction both in and outside of the confessional. His writings were inspired by SS. Francis and Bonaventure and by Duns Scotus. Franciscan spirituality, according to Breton, is Christocentric both in theory and in practice. Of his works the following have been translated into English: *The Community of Saints* (by R. E. Scantlebury, St. Louis 1934); *Franciscan Spirituality* (by F. Frey, Chicago 1957); and *Lady Poverty* (by P. J. Oligny, Chicago 1963).

Bibliography: Y. Bougé, *Frère Mineur, Père Majeur: Le Père Valentin–M. Breton, 1877–1957* (Mulhouse 1958). M. ab Alatri, CollFran 29 (1959) 543–544, review with bibliog.

[G. GÁL]

BREUIL, HENRI ÉDOUARD PROSPER, French prehistorian, pioneer of paleolithic studies; b. Mortain, Normandy, Feb. 28, 1877; d. L'Isle-Adam, Aug. 14, 1961. He was educated at the lycée of Claremont and at the seminary of Issy-les-Moulineaux, where he became interested in prehistoric archeology. The then most famous French prehistorians, E. Piette and D'Ault de Mesnil, introduced him to the problems of paleolithic research. After his ordination to the priesthood in 1900, he was authorized to make prehistoric

Henri Breuil at Lascaux, 1940.

scholarship his full-time work. Primarily interested in the Old Stone Age, he developed the tentative ideas of culture sequences of G. Mortillet and firmly laid the foundations of west European prehistory. But his spec-

tacular contribution concerned the art of Stone Age man. With tremendous energy he exercised his scientific sense of accuracy and his gifts as an artist by copying and tracing the pictures found on the walls of French and Spanish caves and on the rocks of eastern Spain. Thanks to Prince Albert I of Monaco, volume after volume of his classical monographs appeared with splendid color reproductions. His eminent scientific achievements brought him successively to professorial appointments in prehistory at Fribourg, Switzerland; the Institut de Paléontologie Humaine; the Sorbonne; the Institut de France; the Collège de France; and the Institut de France. Universities, academies, and learned societies of many nations bestowed on him membership and honors. Wide travels took him to the Far East and to Africa, especially to South Africa, where he studied and copied the art of old Bushmen. The immense corpus of his scientific publications comprises about 27 books, mostly of monumental size, and 878 articles.

Bibliography: A. H. Brodrick, *Father of Prehistory: The Abbé Breuil* (New York 1963). **Illustration credit:** Hutchinson & Co., Ltd., London, and William Morrow & Co., Inc., New York.

[J. MARINGER]

BREVIARY, ROMAN

A book of convenience containing but a seasonal part of the Liturgical Year's Divine Office. It emerges in history as the fruit of a long, slow process inseparable from the development of the Divine Office itself. As a condensed tome it could appear only after the contents and form of this liturgical prayer were more or less fixed and widely used and after the obligation of daily recitation was regarded as resting upon individual persons rather than upon a religious community or local church.

In general, by the 7th century the Roman Divine Office was more or less fixed in form and content; Carolingian Europe, with its liturgical imports from Rome and its own traditions, had its Office firmly molded by the 10th century. Fixed in content, this Office rendered by community, monastic or diocesan, was solemn in form and required many books and several ministers; the congregation participated without books by reciting Psalms and responses from memory or responding to the Psalms with refrains.

The first Breviaries were choir books that gathered the Office material from many books into one. These began to appear as early as the 11th century. Portable Breviaries did not develop until the obligation devolved from the community to the individual. The first real need for the portable Breviary arose with the appearance of the mendicant orders, groups of religious who in their apostolate did not reside in a community yet desired to remain united in prayer. The need became acute with the rapid expansion of the Franciscan Order in the 13th century.

Innocent III had already approved a shortened version of the Office for the members of his curia. It was this convenient book that the Franciscans adopted. Further revised by Haymo of Faversham, general of the order in 1240, the Breviary was spread throughout Europe by his friars. And the printing press later made it easily available on a large scale, whereas the printing on a small scale of local Offices, non-Roman Breviaries, had become prohibitive.

Fig. 1. Folio from a Breviary for the Diocese of Dijon, A.D. 1287. An example of an early Breviary for a particularly local use, its calendar suggests that it was written and illuminated for the monastery of St. Benigne.

Fig. 2. Folio containing the Office of St. Michael the Archangel according to the Roman usage, illustrating the acceptance of that usage outside Rome. This Breviary, c. 1398 to 1412, was made for Franciscans at Rouen, France.

Fig. 3. Title page of an early printed edition of the Roman Breviary printed at Venice in 1507 by L. de Guinta.

Before the reforms of Trent this same Breviary grew cumbersome with new saints' feasts; these feast days vied with one another for prominence, obscuring the centrality of the mysteries of Christ. Pius V in 1568, in accord with the reform of the Council of Trent, imposed this Breviary universally, ruling out any Office not 200 years old. Piecemeal revisions since Trent have brought the Breviary to the threshold of a new era, making apparent the need for a thoroughgoing reform.

The 20th-century liturgical movement is attracting the laity to the richness of the Office, formerly the reserve of clerics and religious. In fact, Vatican Council II encouraged the laity to recite the Divine Office (*CSL* 100). Also available is a short Breviary following the hours of the day and the liturgical year. There are at least four such Breviaries in English: *A Short Breviary* (1941), edited by the Benedictines of Collegeville, Minn.; *The Divine Office* (1959), a translation of a lay Breviary promoted by the Fulda Conference of German bishops; *The Book of Hours* (1956), from the French Benedictines of Encalcat; *The Little Breviary* (1957), from a Dutch original offered by the Stanhope religious of England.

See also DIVINE OFFICE; BOOK, THE MEDIEVAL; BOOK, THE PRINTED.

Bibliography: F. CABROL, CE 2:768–777. M. BOUCHÈRE, *Catholicisme* 2:253–258. H. LECLERCQ, DACL 2.1:1262–1316. J. PASCHER, LexThK² 2:679–684. S. J. VAN DIJK and J. H. WALKER, *The Origins of the Modern Roman Liturgy* (Westminster, Md. 1960). P. SALMON, *The Breviary through the Centuries*, tr. D. MARY (Collegeville, Minn. 1962). S. BÄUMER, *Histoire du Bréviaire*, 2 v. (Paris 1905). H. A. SCHMIDT, *Introductio in* *liturgiam occidentalem* (Rome 1960). **Illustration credits:** Figs. 1 and 2, Courtesy of the Walters Art Gallery, Baltimore. Fig. 3, From the Lessing J. Rosenwald Collections, Library of Congress.

[R. T. CALLAHAN]

BREVIARY, SHORT

Several shortened forms of Divine Office have been published in English. These breviaries retain most of the elements of the Roman Office, but do not schedule all 150 Psalms of the Psalter for recitation in 1 week. They usually emphasize the temporal cycle of the liturgical year and include only the major feasts.

For religious and lay people of the Roman rite who were not bound to the recitation of the full Roman or Monastic Office, it had long been customary either to recite the Day Hours alone, omitting Matins, or to use the *Little Office of the Blessed Virgin Mary.* The need was felt, however, for a shortened form of Office that would include all the Hours and would provide a wider range of Psalms and a closer adherence to the liturgical calendar than did the *Little Office of the Blessed Virgin.* The shortened breviaries were published in order to fill this need.

The only original American composition, *A Short Breviary,* was edited by William G. Heidt, OSB (3d ed. Collegeville, Minn. 1962). While it contains 95 Psalms in the regular edition, the complete edition adds the rest of the 150 Psalms to be recited during the course of 4 weeks at Matins. It has been adopted for both communal and private recitation by numerous religious communities.

The *Little Breviary* was composed originally in Dutch by T. Stallaert, CSSR. It was translated into English by the Benedictine nuns of Stanbrook Abbey (Westminster, Md. 1957). This book uses 109 Psalms and includes all the feasts of the Roman calendar.

The *Book of Hours* was composed in French by the Benedictine monks of Encalcat Abbey. A Latin-English edition was prepared by the monks of Worth Priory and the nuns of Talacre Abbey (Notre Dame, Ind. 1956). It covers all 150 Psalms in a 4-week cycle, with a selection of Old Testament canticles for the occasional 5th week. A supplemental lectionary and martyrology are included only in the English edition.

The *Divine Office* was originally composed in German by Hildebrand Fleischmann, OSB, and translated into English by Edward A. Malone, OSB (New York 1959). It arranges 128 Psalms over a 2-week cycle, with the option of reciting all in 1 week.

An enlarged edition of the *Little Office of the Blessed Virgin Mary* was prepared by Cardinal Augustin Bea, SJ, with an English translation by Aurelian Scharf, OFM (Westminster, Md. 1954). It provides more variation for the liturgical seasons and the principal feasts of the year than did the older edition. The number of Psalms remains, however, at 32.

New status was given these shortened Offices by the Vatican Council II in its *Constitution on the Sacred Liturgy,* December 1963. Paragraph 98 specifies that members of any institute dedicated to acquiring perfection are performing the public prayer of the Church, if in virtue of their constitutions, they recite any parts of the Divine Office or any short Office, provided the shortened Office follows the pattern of the Divine Office and is duly approved.

[L. J. DOYLE]

BREVICOXA (JEAN COURTECUISSE), theologian; b. Haleine (Orne), France, mid-14th century; d. Geneva, May 4, 1423. He began his theological studies at the University of Paris in 1367, taught there from 1389, and was dean of the theological faculty from 1416 to 1421. His eloquence and knowledge earned for him the title Doctor Sublimis. He played an important role in bringing the Great Schism of the West to an end. Because of this Charles VI of France in 1395 and 1396 named him ambassador to the rulers of England and Germany in order to enlist their efforts toward putting an end to the rule of the two rival pontiffs. Courtecuisse was met by a peremptory refusal when he asked Benedict XIII to abdicate. In 1398, he became partisan to a movement to withdraw obedience to Benedict. He took part in the Council of Pisa in 1409 and in that of Rome in 1412. His panegyric of the Duke of Orléans (Jan. 10, 1414) drew upon him the hatred of the Duke of Bourgogne, and this led him to join the ranks of the Armagnacs. His election as bishop of Paris was confirmed by Martin V (June 16, 1421) contrary to the wishes of the English crown, which supported another candidate. The hostility of the King of England toward him was such that he had to be transferred to the see of Geneva (June 12, 1422). In his *Tractatus de fide et ecclesia, de Romano pontifice et concilio generali,* he teaches the superiority of the council over the pope.

Bibliography: A. COVILLE, "Recherches sur Jean Courtecuisse," BiblÉcChartes 65 (1904) 469–529. N. VALOIS, *La France et le grand schisme d'Occident,* 4 v. (Paris 1896–1902) v.3–4. A. COVILLE, *Jean Petit* (Paris 1932). A. BIGELMAIR, LexThK² 5:1011–12. E. MANGENOT, DTC 3.2:1984–85. G. MOLLAT, DHGE 13:953–954.

[G. MOLLAT]

BŘEZINA, OTOKAR, Czech poet and essayist; b. Počátky, Sept. 13, 1868; d. Jaroměřice, Czechoslovakia, March 26, 1929. By profession a grammar school teacher, living constantly in small towns of western Moravia in complete isolation from contemporary Czech literary and artistic society, Březina (whose real name was Václav Jebavý), combined two rather opposed interests—the inquisitiveness of a scientist and the mysticism of a contemplative. His poetical work is characterized not only by a conspicuous lack of dramatic and historical elements, but, above all, by a complete absence of the very notion of historical time. Where he does employ the word "time," he means by it an analytical, artificial representation of things eternal and therefore, to him, truly real. His prose, especially in his published correspondence, is noble and meditative, but he was at his best in his slow, majestic verse. A literary perfectionist, he repolished his poems for years before entrusting them to print. The result was a few collections of a most melodious and rhythmically majestic poetry, formally one of the most perfect literary accomplishments in all Slavic literature.

In contrast to Paul *Valéry, whose equally polished verse is perhaps the best counterpart in Western literature to Březina's work, the Czech poet was profoundly influenced by the Christian traditions of his people. Not only did Catholic liturgy furnish him with numerous parables and images, but in its very essence his poetry was concerned with a Christian vision of mankind as an immense brotherhood assembled around Golgotha. The physical universe, viewed through the prism of modern scientific discoveries, occupied a large part of his vision. But everything in that vision, from the wonders of the subatomic microcosm to the immense distances of outer space, appeared more or less "hominized," centered on man and the mysterious ties that bind human hearts to one another and to God.

Březina's two most famous collections, *Tajemné dálky* (1895, Mysterious Horizons), and *Svítání na západě* (1896, Dawn in the West) appeared in the 1890s. He wrote and published little during the last 3 decades of his life. But his vision grew more and more optimistic—not in the pragmatist, "progressive" sense, but rather in that which a Christian derives from his faith. During his lifetime Březina influenced contemporary painters and sculptors, and his thought and imagery later played an important role in the development of *Zahradníček.

Bibliography: O. Králík, *Otokar Březina, 1892–1907* (Prague 1948). F. Chudoba, *A Short Survey of Czech Literature* (New York 1924).

[B. CHUDOBA]

BRIAN BORU, King of Ireland, 1002 to 1014; b. County Clare, Ireland, 941. He was born Brian Bóroimhe or Brian mac Cennédigh of the relatively unimportant Dál Cais. He became king of Munster in 978 and then the high king of Ireland in 1002 solely by his exceptional ability. A rare combination of soldier and statesman, he was successful because of his bravery and outstanding powers of conciliation. He consolidated his claim to universal political rule in *Ireland by allying himself with *Armagh's claim to ecclesiastical supremacy over the island. Though fully occupied with affairs of state, he found time to promote the arts and learning and to repair the damage done to ecclesiastical buildings by the Norse. The last and greatest of his battles was fought at Clontarf on Good Friday, April 23, 1014, when he was slain, in the hour of victory, by the fleeing Broðir. Recent historians hold that the battle had not the importance formerly claimed for it, i.e., a victory of Christianity over heathendom that stemmed the resurgence of the Norse to power. There were, in fact, Norse on both sides, and not all Brian's allies were Christians just as not all his opponents were heathens. About two-thirds of the vanquished army (led by Máel Mórdhai of Leinster) were Irish and Christian.

Bibliography: A. S. Green, *History of the Irish State to 1014* (London 1925). J. Ryan, "The Battle of Clontarf," *Journal of the Royal Society of Antiquaries of Ireland* 68 (1938) 1–50. A. J. Goedheer, *Irish and Norse Traditions about the Battle of Clontarf* (Haarlem 1938).

[C. MC GRATH]

BRIAND, ARISTIDE, French statesman; b. Nantes, March 28, 1862; d. Paris, March 7, 1932. Adopting socialist views as a law student in Paris, he helped to found the moderate Parti Socialiste Français and the socialist newspaper, *L'Humanité.* In 1902 he was elected to the Chamber of Deputies, where he supported the Bloc des Gauches in the *Waldeck-Rousseau government. He played an important role as *rapporteur* in the passage of legislation separating Church and State (1905) and ending the *Concordat of 1801. He braved strong Vatican opposition to this law while minister of education and religion in the Sarrien and Clemenceau cabinets; but his application of the law was sufficiently moderate to placate many French Catholics. He was premier 11 times between 1909 and 1929 and also held important ministerial posts under other premiers. His reputation in foreign affairs and peace endeavors grew with his roles in the Washington Naval Conference

Aristide Briand, by Marcel Baschet, 1916.

(1921), the Lacarno Pact (1925), and the Briand-Kellogg Peace Pact (1928). In 1926 he received the Nobel peace prize. Resumption of French diplomatic relations with the Holy See was another of his accomplishments (1921), along with the exemption of Alsace from the application of the law separating Church and State. Briand's *anticlericalism was motivated by a belief that the Church should be removed from all influence in State affairs. In this, as in international problems, he was a moderate, an improvisor and conciliator, eager for the least distasteful solutions.

Bibliography: A. Léger, *Briand* (Aurora, N.Y. 1943). G. Saurez, *Briand: Sa vie, son oeuvre, avec son journal et de nombreaux documents inédits,* 6 v. (Paris 1938–52). W. Schurer, *A. Briand und die Trennung von Staat und Kirche* (Basel 1939). L. V. Méjan, *La Séparation des Églises et de l'État* (Paris 1959). L. Capéran, *Histoire contemporaine de la laïcité française,* 3 v. (Paris 1957–61). E. Franceschini, Dict BiogFranc 7:269–273. E. Kordt, StL 2:173–176. **Illustration credit:** French Embassy, Press and Information Division, New York City.

[D. R. PENN]

BRIAND, JEAN OLIVIER, seventh bishop of Quebec, Canada; b. Plérin, France, Jan. 23, 1715; d. Quebec, June 25, 1794. He was educated in his native Diocese of Saint-Brieuc, ordained there in 1739, and immigrated to Canada, arriving in 1741 with Bp. H. M. Pontbriand, his predecessor in the See of Quebec. Named canon, he became the bishop's assistant, confessor to the sisters, and then vicar-general. He dedicated himself to these duties during the siege of Quebec (1759) and, through his loyal obedience, gained the good graces of the new English masters. After lengthy negotiations and despite British law, he was recognized as "Superintendent of the Roman Church." This permitted his private consecration as bishop in France in 1766. By his zeal and diplomacy he was able to repair the damages sustained by religious institutions during the war. To replenish his decimated clergy he ordained 90 priests during his episcopate. He consolidated the Church's situation with the English authorities and in return exacted from his own people a deep loyalty to the British during the American Revolution. He resided at the Seminary of Quebec, contributing generously to its development. He composed a new catechism for the diocese. With approval from London, he chose L. P. d'Esglis as coadjutor with the right of succession, and in 1784 turned over the administration of the diocese to him. (Illustration below.)

Bibliography: H. Têtu, *Les Évêques de Québec* (Quebec 1889). A. H. Gosselin, *L'Église du Canada après la conquête*, 2 v. (Quebec 1916–17). F. Porter, *L'Institution catechistique au Canada français, 1633–1833* (Washington 1949). M. Trudel, *L'Église canadienne sous le régime militaire, 1759–1764*, 2 v. (Montreal 1956–57). **Illustration credit:** Public Archives of Canada.

[H. PROVOST]

BRIANT, ALEXANDER, BL., English Jesuit martyr; b. Somerset, *c.* 1561; d. Tyburn, Dec. 1. 1581 (feast, Dec. 1). While an undergraduate at Hart Hall, Oxford, in 1574, Briant was reconciled to Catholicism. He left Oxford for studies at Douai, arriving there on Aug. 11, 1577. He was ordained on March 29, 1578, and returned to England on March 3, 1579. In his native Somerset, he reconciled many to the Church, including Robert *Persons' father. This drew Father Persons and Briant together and indirectly led to his own arrest in April by pursuivants looking for Persons. He was imprisoned first in the Counter and then in the Tower, and endured intense torture rather than disclose Persons' whereabouts. Starvation, detention in an unlit dungeon, the scavenger's daughter, the thumbscrew, and needles under the nails were of no avail. One of his torturers declared that "this is an evident miracle, but it is a miracle of undauntable pertinacity in this Papish priest; I would not on any account anyone were here present who was not well and solidly grounded in our faith."

Jean Olivier Briand, after the portrait by Louis Chrétien de Heer, Archiepiscopal Palace, Quebec.

He was handed over to Thomas Norton (d. 1584), the notorious rackmaster, and racked mercilessly. Although Norton boasted that he had made him "a foot longer than God made him," Briant never spoke except in prayer. Even Elizabethan England was shocked. In 1583, 2 years after his death, the government felt it was necessary to reply in a pamphlet (ascribed to Lord Burghley) that "a horrible matter is also made of the starving Alexander Briant; how he should eat clay out of the walls. . . . Whatsoever Briant suffered in want of food, he suffered the same willfully and of extreme impudent obstinacy." Briant had written from prison to the Jesuits in England, begging admission to their society; although his formal entry was not possible, he was counted as a member. On November 21, with six other priests, he was tried at Westminster Hall. Carrying aloft a rough cross he had made, he entered the court room. Charged with a fictitious plot and found guilty, Edmund *Campion, Ralph *Sherwin, and Alexander Briant were drawn to Tyburn on Dec. 1, 1581. Briant was the last to die. He was beatified by Leo XIII on Dec. 29, 1886.

See also MARTYRS OF ENGLAND AND WALES.

Bibliography: Butler Th Attw 4:469–470. B. Camm, ed., *Lives of the English Martyrs Declared Blessed by Pope Leo XIII in 1886 and 1895* (London 1905) 2:397–423. H. Foley, ed., *Records of the English Province of the Society of Jesus*, 7 v. (London 1877–82) 4.2:343–367. R. Challoner, *Memoirs of Missionary Priests*, ed. J. H. Pollen (rev. ed. London 1924). DictEngCath 1:293–294. P. de Rosa, *Blessed Alexander Briant* (Postulation pamphlet; London 1961).

[G. FITZ HERBERT]

BRIAR CLIFF COLLEGE

Briar Cliff College of Our Lady of Grace, Sioux City, Iowa, is a 4-year liberal arts college for women. It was established in 1930, at the request of Bp. Edmond Heelan who donated the 70-acre property to the Sisters of the Third Order of St. Francis of the Holy Family. Begun as a junior college, Briar Cliff first awarded bachelor's degrees to 16 candidates in 1938. The college has shown steady growth in plant and enrollment with 749 students in 1964. Plans anticipate 800 students with 425 in residence by 1973. The college is accredited with powers to grant B.A., B.M., and B.S. degrees by the North Central Association of Colleges and Secondary Schools, State University of Iowa, and the Iowa State Department of Public Instruction for Certification of Teachers. It holds membership in the American Association of University Women and other educational associations. The local bishop is honorary chancellor of the administrative organization. The board of trustees is composed of the mother general, the College president, and 6 sister-members of the general council; a 10-member board of lay advisors and 6 administrative officers. In 1964 the faculty and staff included 44 Franciscan sisters, 20 lay persons, a chaplain, and 2 priests, of whom 9 held doctorates and 33 held master's degrees. The teacher-student ratio was 1 to 11.

The College receives periodic grants from business and industry but has no other subsidy. The income provides 60 per cent of the annual budget (exclusive of developmental funds). The remaining 40 per cent consists of the contributed services of the religious faculty. Besides the Alumnae Association scholarship endowment fund, scholarships and grants, including the National Defense Education loan are available to students.

The curriculum is organized into six broad divisions: fine arts, language and literature, philosophy and religion, science, social science, and professional arts. Adult education classes are held in the late afternoon and evening on radio and television, and in summer session. The ecumenical movement is promoted by parish-student catechetical cooperation and specific training for extension. An honors program has also been implemented. Special programs include speech correction in collaboration with *Marquette University, medical technology affiliated with two Catholic hospitals, and teacher education at the Mt. St. Francis Branch. In 1964, the library had 40,000 of its 65,000 volume capacity and received 321 periodicals regularly. The Alumnae Association, an affiliate of the International Federation of Catholic Alumnae and the American Alumni Council, has active chapters in 20 metropolitan areas. Alumnae are employed in a wide range of professional occupations.

Bibliography: M. E. MOUSEL, *They Have Taken Root* (New York 1954) 331–347.

[M. M. JOHANSON]

BRIBERY

A bribe is a gift or favor, given or promised, for the purpose of influencing the official decisions or conduct of a person in a position of trust. Bribery is the act or practice of giving such gratuities or the acceptance of them.

Where a public official is corrupted, bribery involves the violation not only of legal but also of commutative justice: of legal justice because it involves, presumably, the transgression of just laws and is damaging to the common good; of commutative justice, because the corrupted official is induced to violate the contractual obligation to the community that he took upon himself in accepting office. He fails to provide the public service for which he is paid. In some cases, commutative justice is also violated with respect to a private individual who suffers harm by the official's dishonesty. For example, if a judge, induced by a bribe, renders an unjust decision, he does an injury to the one who loses the case, and in compensation for this injury the loser is entitled to *restitution. If the winner of the judgment refuses to restore his unjust gain to the injured man, the judge is bound to do it in his stead, even if this means giving up a greater sum than came to him through the bribe. His responsibility extends to the whole of the damage actually done by his unjust act. A similar obligation of restitution to persons suffering loss would arise in the case of a public building inspector who under influence of bribery permits inferior materials or substandard procedures to pass without correction. Other applications of the same principle are to be found in similar violations of trust.

The degree of guilt is greater where a person is induced to perform an act contrary to the duties of his office; it is less grave if it is intended as compensation for an act already performed.

In modern society it is sometimes customary for policemen and other officials to accept gifts from merchants or others who have benefited from their services. Although this practice is open to abuse, gifts of this kind are not bribes provided that they are not understood as payment for services rendered and that the citizens are not made to feel that they will not receive these services unless they make their contribution.

In cases of bribery in which no one suffers harm, it is disputed whether a dishonest official may keep money he has taken as a bribe. Some moralists hold that he may, because his act has caused no injury to others. Others hold that he has violated commutative justice and hence may not retain the money. Still, the violation of justice has been done to the community, which is paying the official for a service that he has failed to perform, and this wrong cannot be righted by restoring the bribe to the donor. If restitution is necessary, it should be made to the community.

Generally speaking, the giver and the taker of a bribe share equally in the malice of the act. If the taker violates his trust and possibly his oath of office, the giver participates in this malice by inducing him to commit the act. It sometimes happens, however, that honest individuals cannot enjoy the benefit of ordinary public services or obtain appointment to public office without paying a bribe. If the conditions necessary for permissible material cooperation are fulfilled, a person cannot be accused of sin if he pays what is demanded. He is a victim of extortion rather than a formal violator of justice.

Bibliography: F. J. CONNELL, *Morals in Politics and Professions* (Westminister, Md. 1946) 34–35, 58–61, 69–74.

[T. CRANNY]

BRICE OF TOURS, ST., 5th-century monk and bishop; b. Touraine, France, *c.* 370?; d. Tours, 444 (feast, Nov. 13). A disciple of St. *Martin of Tours at Marmoutier, Brice was at first noted for his violence and indocility. On the death of Martin in 397, Brice was elected bishop of Tours. His previous irregularities caused him to be delated before several local synods by Lazarus, later bishop of Aix (Jaffé K 330–331), but both the Council of Turin in 401 and Pope *Zosimus (2 *Epist.* dated Sept. 21 and 22, 417) upheld Brice. Dispossessed of his see on a morals charge (see Sid. Apoll. *Epist.* 4.18), he was replaced by Bishop Justinian, then by Armentius. In 430 he pleaded his cause in Rome and in 437 was restored. He was buried in the chapel of St. Martin, which he had constructed. In the Middle Ages his cult spread throughout the West, particularly because of his biography by *Gregory of Tours.

Bibliography: GREGORY OF TOURS, *Historia Francorum*, ed. W. ARNDT, MGSrerMer 1.1:36–38; Eng. *The History of the Franks*, tr. O. M. DALTON, 2 v. (Oxford 1927). SULPICIUS SEVERUS, *Dialogus III*, PL 20:220–222. S. HANSSENS, DHGE 10:670–671. Duchesne FÉ 2:303. A. PONCELET, AnalBoll 30 (1911) 88–89. H. DELEHAYE, *ibid.* 38 (1920) 124–125. R. AIGRAIN, *Catholicisme* 2:262–263. W. BÖHNE, LexThK² 2:685. *Saint Martin et son temps: Mémorial du XVIᵉ centenaire des débuts du monachisme en Gaule* (Rome 1961).

[A. DANET]

BRICEÑO, ALONSO, Chilean philosopher and theologian; b. Santiago, Chile, 1587; d. Trujillo, Venezuela, Nov. 15, 1668. In January 1605 Briceño received the Franciscan habit in Lima and soon acquired renown as a teacher of theology. He became guardian of the Franciscan convent where he had been educated, and later, definitor of the province of the Twelve Apostles, commissary and visitor of the province of San Antonio de los Charcas and of that of Chile, and finally, vicar general. In 1636 he was sent to Spain as procurator of the province of Twelve Apostles and was named by the Holy Office to the sensitive post of censor. Between 1638 and 1642 he published in Spain two large volumes (963 and 968 folios) of interpretations of the doctrines of Duns Scotus, the first time such material was published in Europe by an American. Briceño's study *Prima pars celebriorum controversiarum in Primum Sententiarum Joannis Scoti doctoris subtilis . . .* was praised for its keen penetration and understanding of Scotist thought. The first volume is an apology for Scotus's doctrines; the second treats "de scientia Dei et ideis" and mentions a companion volume on "voluntate et potentia Dei, de praedestinatione et Trinitate complectens caeteris controversias ad primum Sententiarum atinentes." In 1639 Briceño took part in the general chapter of the order at Rome, where he presided at the solemn theological convocation dedicated to Cardinal Albornoz. By special order of the minister general, he was named *Lector bis jubilatus* in theology. While in Rome he was also active in the beatification proceedings of Francis *Solano. Briseño was appointed Bishop of Nicaragua and took possession of his diocese in December 1646. In August 1649 he was transferred to Caracas.

[G. LOHMANN VILLENA]

BRIÇONNET, family name of three French churchmen of the 15th and 16th centuries.

Robert, prelate and statesman remembered for his improvement of the French fiscal system; place and date of birth uncertain; d. Moulins, June 3, 1497. Through the influence of his younger brother Guillaume (d. 1514) he received important appointments to ecclesiastical and secular positions. After serving as canon of St. Aignan and abbot of St. Vaast, he was appointed archbishop of Reims in 1493. Charles VIII made him chancellor of France (1495), an office he fulfilled until his death.

Guillaume, cardinal of Saint-Malo and principal adviser to Charles VIII; b. Tours, 1445?; d. Narbonne, Dec. 14, 1514. Guillaume entered the religious life after the death of his wife, and became bishop of St. Malo (1493), archbishop of Reims (1497) and Narbonne (1507). He accompanied Charles VIII on his Italian expedition in 1494–95, at which time he was created a cardinal by Alexander VI. In 1498 he crowned Louis XII king of France in the cathedral at Reims. During the pontificate of Julius II he led a movement among the cardinals, culminating in the council of Pisa-Milan, to force the Pope to undertake reform. Julius summoned him to Rome, where he was stripped of his office and excommunicated. When Leo X became pope (1513) the censure was lifted and Guillaume was restored to his cardinalate.

Guillaume, bishop and advocate of church reform; b. Tours, 1472; d. Saint-Germain-des-Prés, Jan. 24, 1534. He was the son of Guillaume, the cardinal. Briçonnet served as bishop of Lodève (1504) and director of the Abbey of Saint-Germain-des-Prés (1507), where he began a series of reforms. He carried out missions to Rome for both Louis XII and Francis I. Upon his appointment as bishop of Meaux (1516) he supported a reform movement through a group of intellectuals known as the "Meaux reformers." Some of its members turned too favorably toward the Lutheran movement, and Guillaume was accused of heresy. The group was dispersed in 1535. Briçonnet successfully defended himself against the charge of heresy and died a Catholic.

Bibliography: P. IMBART DE LA TOUR, *Les Origines de la réforme,* 4 v. (Paris 1905–35) v.3. A. RENAUDET, *Préréforme et humanisme à Paris pendant les premières guerres d'Italie, 1494–1517* (2d ed. Paris 1953). G. BRETONNEAU, *Histoire généalogique de la maison de Briçonnet* (Paris 1620). Fliche-Martin v.15. GallChrist v.6, 9. M. LECOMTE, DHGE 10:677–682. A. DUVAL, *Catholicisme* 2:263–265.

[W. J. STEINER]

BRICTINIANS, a congregation of hermits named from the hill of Brettino near Fano, Italy, on which their first monastery was built. Founded apparently between 1200 and 1215, they later (1228) adopted the Rule of St. *Augustine as one of those permitted by the Fourth *Lateran Council and as best suited to their purpose. Their constitutions, approved in 1235, reveal a way of life stressing bodily mortification and poverty. It was often charged that a similarity in their form of dress to that of the Franciscans occasioned their obtaining alms that would otherwise have gone to the Friars Minor. Their rapid growth in numbers seems traceable mainly to the attractive simplicity of their life; priest members of the congregation were engaged in apostolic works. In the Great Union of 1256, they and other existing hermit congregations were joined together into one Order of Hermit Friars of St. Augustine (*see* AUGUSTINIANS).

Bibliography: Sources. "Bullarium ordinis eremitarum S. Augustini: Periodus formationis, 1187–1256," ed. B. VAN LUIJK, *Augustiniana* 12 (1962) 161–195, 358–390; 13 (1963) 474–510; 14 (1964) 216–249. Literature. F. ROTH, "Cardinal Richard Annibaldi: First Protector of the Augustinian Order, 1243–76," *ibid.* 2 (1952) 26–60, 108–149, esp. 132–138.

[J. E. BRESNAHAN]

BRIDEL, BEDŘICH, Czech poet; b. Vysoké Mýto, 1619; d. Kutná Hora, Bohemia, Oct. 15, 1680. Little is known about the life of this priest of the Society of Jesus. As a poet he belongs, together with Luis *Góngora and Friedrich von Spee, among the best lyric poets of his time. The words of one of his carols, "Veselé vánoční hody" (The Merry Feast of Christmas), have been heard for generations in the churches of his native country, but his books had either been destroyed during the Josephite purges at the end of the 18th century or had lain forgotten in the less-frequented libraries. His name was hardly ever mentioned in literary histories by 19th-century scholars.

Only in the 1920s did Professor Vašica of Charles University locate them and, in his wake, other historians have realized the true stature of Bridel. Since then, several collections of his verse have been discovered and published and are now an essential part of the Czech literary heritage. The neglect of Bridel's work may have been caused partially by the elements of early *baroque, from which its outstanding features were derived: the predominance of the musical over the literary and the concentration on the visual, dramatic image. Bridel weighed every line for its sound effect: the soft as well as the harsh sounds of the Czech idiom were used like the keys of an organ. Grammatical structure and individual words were frequently contorted in an effort to express the inexpressible. *Co Bůh? co člověk?* (1658, What God? what man?), an astonishing vision of the human situation, is perhaps his best meditative poem. There, as well as in *Jesličky* (The Manger), a collection of hymns and prayers, the visual reference challenges the reader with sharply contrasting images and forces him to reach beyond their ordinary meaning. Bridel also wrote several legends, among them *Život sv. Ivana* (Life of St. Ivan) and *Jiskra slávy svatoprokop-*

ské (A Sparkle of the Glory of St. Procopius of Sázava). His influence, evident in the work of *Mácha, disappeared from late 19th-century Czech literature, but was to play a prominent role again in the style of some eminent modern Czech authors, above all that of Jaroslav *Durych.

Bibliography: A. NOVÁK, *Die tschechische Literatur*, 3 pts. (Potsdam 1931–32).

[B. CHUDOBA]

BRIDGEBUILDING

Bridges in the Middle Ages enjoyed a prestige that they have never had before or since. The name of a town was frequently taken from that of a local bridge, and the Pont des Tourelles at Orléans was described in the 15th century as the most beautiful jewel of the town. Moreover, the building of bridges, a boon to townsmen and travelers, was considered a pious work; and frequently a bridge had its own chapel and many times its own hospital.

Roman and Carolingian bridges had been much neglected before the year 1000, but considerable reconstruction was undertaken shortly thereafter: at Angers, Tours, Blois, and elsewhere bridges were rebuilt by the great feudatories. Moreover, many new structures were undertaken—as, for example, at Albi (*c.* 1035) and at Toulouse (*c.* 1130), where bridges resulted from the initiative of lay and ecclesiastical authorities and the cooperation of the inhabitants. In the 13th century a number of towns multiplied their bridges, so that Metz, which had only one at the beginning of the century, had four at the end. Typical bridges of the period were timber structures; but great stone spans were begun at London (*c.* 1176) and at Avignon (1177).

After the middle of the 12th century, and in conformity with the view of bridges as charitable works, papal and episcopal indulgences encouraged construction, legacies to bridges became common, and bridgebuilding brotherhoods were formed. There seem to have been only three societies, mutually independent, which could with certainty be called bridgebuilding brotherhoods—one at Avignon, begun *c.* 1181; one at Lyons, *c.* 1184; and one at Pont-Saint-Esprit, *c.* 1277. Each consisted of laymen organized, after construction had begun, to forward the completion and maintenance of the local span. At Lyons the brothers seem to have supervised construction, whereas at Avignon and Pont-Saint-Esprit they were engaged chiefly in the solicitation of funds. There seems to be no evidence that the brothers of the bridge were artisans, despite legends representing them as such. By the early 14th century each of the three societies of *fratres pontis* had disappeared or had been transformed into a hospital order of oblate brothers and sisters.

In the 13th century the concept of the bridge as a public work gained ground. The Pont-Saint-Esprit (under construction 1265–*c.* 1307) was among the last of the prominent bridges financed by charity, and it was able to maintain free passage only because, after 1328, it received the proceeds of a special tax on salt. In general, the problems of maintenance were such that gradually almost all bridges came to be supported by tolls and taxes, responsibility generally falling—especially in England, France, and Italy—on the neighboring town, or less frequently, on the inhabitants of the

region. Bridgebuilding continued actively during the 14th and the 15th centuries. Medieval masons contributed the ogival arch to bridgebuilding, but their piers lacked solidity and required constant upkeep. Nevertheless, the special esteem in which bridges were held persisted into the modern period. Thus London Bridge was a national wonder, and despite the nursery rhyme, had an enviable record of maintenance and continued usefulness.

Bibliography: W. EMERSON and G. GROMORT, *Old Bridges of France* (New York 1925). G. C. HOME, *Old London Bridge* (London 1931). G. DUPRÉ, *Un Pont au moyen-âge: Le Pont de Pont-Saint-Esprit* (Pont-Saint-Esprit 1947). F. ZOEPFL, LexThK² 2:712–713. M. N. BOYER, "The Bridgebuilding Brotherhoods," *Speculum* 39 (1964) 635–650.

[M. N. BOYER]

BRIDGEPORT, DIOCESE OF (BRIDGEPORTENSIS),

suffragan of the metropolitan See of *Hartford, comprises all of Fairfield County in southwestern Connecticut, an area of 633 square miles. The diocese, formerly a part of the Hartford jurisdiction, was established on Aug. 6, 1953, at which time Hartford was raised to an archdiocese. St. Augustine's parish church was chosen as cathedral, and Lawrence J. Shehan, Auxiliary Bishop of Baltimore, Md., was named Bridgeport's first ordinary. In 1961 he returned to Baltimore as its archbishop, and Walter W. Curtis, Auxiliary Bishop of Newark, N.J., was transferred to Bridgeport, September 23.

In 1963 Catholics in the diocese numbered 295,123 in a total population of 697,900 and were organized in 84 parishes and 7 missions. Nineteen of the parishes were national in character, serving French, German, Hungarian, Italian, Lithuanian, Polish, Slovak, and Slovene ethnic groups; two of the missions were Puerto Rican, and one Portuguese. There were also two parishes of Oriental rite, one Melkite and the other Maronite,

Cathedral of St. Augustine, Bridgeport, Conn.

subject to the bishop of Bridgeport; five parishes of the Byzantine-Slavonic rite were subject to bishops of their own rite. The presence of so many ethnic groups within so small a territory is explained by the number of industrial centers throughout Fairfield County. The diocese contained *Fairfield University (1942), conducted by the Jesuits for men; *Sacred Heart University (1963), Bridgeport, administered and staffed by Catholic laymen; and 13 high schools and 58 elementary schools under Catholic auspices. Also serving the diocese were two general hospitals, one in Bridgeport conducted by the Daughters of Charity of St. Vincent de Paul, and the other in Stamford conducted by the Sisters of St. Joseph of Chambery; and St. Joseph's Manor, a home for the aged in Trumbull, opened in 1960 by the Carmelite Sisters for the Aged and Infirm. There were four retreat houses, one conducted by the Holy Ghost fathers for laymen at New Canaan, one for men by the Jesuits at Ridgefield, and two for women under the auspices of the Bernardine Sisters of the Third Order of St. Francis at Stamford and the Bridgettine Sisters at Darien. The Congregation of the Missions (Vincentians) conducts a novitiate at Ridgefield, and the Holy Ghost fathers conduct a novitiate at Ridgefield and a seminary at Norwalk. The Glenmary Home Missioners have a preparatory seminary at Fairfield. Since 1953 five religious communities have established provincialates within the diocese: Holy Cross Fathers, the Sisters of Notre Dame de Namur, the School Sisters of Notre Dame, the Bernardine Sisters of the Third Order of St. Francis, and the Sisters of St. Thomas of Villanova. The four latter communities have established novitiates also. The number of priests totaled 349, of whom 142 were religious, representing 7 communities of religious men. There were about 1,000 sisters from 35 religious communities working in the diocese.

Illustration credit: Corbit's Studio Bridgeport.

[L. J. SHEHAN]

BRIDGET OF SWEDEN, ST., patron saint of Sweden and foundress of the *Bridgettines; b. Upland, principal province of Sweden, 1302 or 1303; d. Rome, 1373 (feast, Oct. 8). The daughter of Birger, Governor of Upland, and his second wife, Ingeborg, she married Ulf Gudmarsson when she was about 14 years of age. One of their eight children was St. *Catherine of Sweden. Bridget was for 2 years lady in waiting to Blanche of Namur, wife of King Magnus II, and attempted to win the young royal couple to holiness. After Ulf's death in 1344, she lived as a penitent near the Cistercian monastery at Alvastra. Visions and revelations, which she had first experienced in childhood, became more frequent and began to be written down. In 1346 Magnus endowed a double monastery at Vadstena, where she established her order. Urban V confirmed the rule of her congregation in 1370. Bridget went to Rome in 1349, and for the rest of her life remained there, except for traveling on various pilgrimages in Italy and for a long journey to the Holy Land undertaken in 1371. Her canonization by Boniface IX (Oct. 7, 1391) was confirmed in 1415. To an Englishwoman, Margery Kempe, Bridget's maid confided that her lady had been "kind and meek to every creature and that she had a laughing face."

Along with her penitential practices and her charitable works for the poor and humble, she devoted her-

St. Bridget of Sweden writing of her visions, German woodcut of the 15th century.

self to urging reforms within the Church. She denounced abuses of bishops and abbots and advised princes and kings on political matters. She was especially concerned for the return to Rome of the Avignon popes, and for 20 years she admonished them to do so. Revelations and prophecies frequently supported her various causes. Because of their celebrity, the written accounts and subsequent editions of her revelations have been the subject of much theological examination and textual criticism.

Bibliography: P. DEBONGNIE, DHGE 10:719–728. J. JØRGENSEN, *Saint Bridget of Sweden,* tr. I. LUND, 2 v. (New York 1954). Butler Th Attw 4:54–59. F. VERNET, DictSpirAscMyst 1:1943–58. **Illustration credit:** National Gallery of Art, Washington, D.C., Rosenwald Collection.

[M. S. CONLAN]

BRIDGETT, THOMAS EDWARD, author; b. Derby, England, Jan. 20, 1829; d. Clapham, London, Feb. 17, 1899. He came from an Anglican family, and was educated at Tonbridge School (1845–47) and at St. John's College, Cambridge. In 1850 he left the College without graduating in order to avoid taking the required oath recognizing the royal supremacy over the Church of England. After attending John Henry Newman's lectures on "Anglican Difficulties," he was received into the Catholic Church at the London Oratory, June 12, 1850. He joined the Redemptorists a few months later. After studying theology at Wittem, Netherlands, he was ordained (1856) and spent the rest of his life in various offices of his congregation in England and Ireland, and made his name as a missioner. From 1871 until his death he was at Clapham, where for some time he was rector. Of his books, which were

Thomas Edward Bridgett.

mainly controversial, the two most important are: *Our Lady's Dowry* (1875), an account, based on historical and literary sources, of devotion to the Blessed Virgin in Great Britain from the introduction of Christianity to the Reformation; and *The History of the Holy Eucharist in Great Britain* (1881), which studied this subject over the same period of time. Both books give evidence of Bridgett's considerable learning. He wrote also *The Life of Blessed John Fisher* (1888), *Blunders and Forgeries* (1890), and *The Life of Blessed Thomas More* (1891).

Bibliography: C. RYDER, *Life of Thomas Edward Bridgett* (London 1906). A. F. POLLARD, DNB 22:267.

[L. C. SHEPPARD]

BRIDGETTINES

The Order of the Most Holy Saviour (OSsS), commonly called the Bridgettine Sisters, is an order of semi-cloistered nuns founded by the medieval mystic (St.) *Bridget of Sweden and first approved by Urban V in 1370. They follow the Augustinian Rule (*see* AUGUSTINE, RULE OF ST.).

Bridget felt that she had been commanded by Christ to found a new religious congregation for the reform of monastic life. In order to fulfill this divine summons, she left Sweden for Rome. She was compelled to remain there for 25 years while urging the return of the Popes from Avignon and, while awaiting the full approval of her order, she died in Rome in 1373 before her mission was fully realized. Her religious foundation, however, continued to grow. Shortly after her death, her daughter (St.) *Catherine of Sweden became the first abbess of the original monastery in Vadstena, Sweden, begun by Bridget about 1346. Other monasteries followed, none numbering more than 60 nuns. Attached to each of them was a monastery for monks who shared the same liturgical life under the government of the abbess (*see* MONASTERIES, DOUBLE). The discipline of the new order stressed humility and simplicity in contrast to the pride and pomp of many clerics of the

period. The Bridgettines contributed greatly to the culture of Scandinavia. One of the first printing presses was established in Vadstena Abbey.

Prior to the Reformation the order numbered about 80 houses, located throughout Europe. In 1595, however, the motherhouse at Vadstena was confiscated and the order was officially banished from Sweden. From the 16th century onward, the European houses were further reduced by suppression and confiscation. In modern times no Bridgettine monks survive, but there still exist four autonomous houses of nuns: Syon Abbey in Devonshire, England; Weert and Uden in Holland; and Altomünster in Bavaria. These houses follow the original rule.

In 1911, Elisabeth Hesselblad, a Swedish convert, founded a new branch of the old order. With only two postulants, she began her work of renewal in a small apartment in St. Bridget's former house in Rome, whose possession the order did not regain till 1931. In 1923 she led the Bridgettines back to Sweden, after more than 300 years of exile. During her lifetime (1870–1957) she established houses in Italy, Sweden, Switzerland, India, England, and the U.S. In 1964 the order had about 200 members, 6 of whom had established the first house in the U.S., in Darien, Conn. (1957).

The order is essentially contemplative, and aims at the fullness of liturgical worship. Its members offer themselves to God in prayer and reparation, working thus for the reunion of all Christians, and in particular for the return of Scandinavia to the Catholic Church. Each Bridgettine monastery maintains a guest house to which members of all faiths are welcomed. Though ancient in its history, the order is modern both in its role in the monastic revival and in its ecumenical concern.

Bibliography: H. JÄGERSTAD, LexThK², 2:486–487. P. DE-BONGNIE, DHGE 10:728–731, esp. biblio g. B. WILLIAMSON, *The Bridgettine Order* (London 1921). O. EKLUND, *A Faith Stronger than Death: The Life of Mother M. Elisabeth Hesselblad* (Rome 1962).

[A. J. ENNIS]

BRIDGEWATER, JOHN, Catholic theologian, known also as Aquapontanus; b. Yorkshire, 1532?; d. probably at Trèves, 1596?. He was admitted to Brasenose College, Oxford, on Feb. 4, 1552 (N.S.; 1551, O.S.), and supplicated as a B.A. of Cambridge on Feb. 21, 1555 (N.S.; 1554, O.S.). He received the degree of B.A. at Oxford on March 13, 1555 (N.S.; 1554, O.S.) and the M.A. 2 years later. He was the recipient of several ecclesiastical appointments that included St. Austell, Cornwall, in 1550; Yelling, Huntingdonshire, in 1554; Aldeburgh, Suffolk, in 1554; the archdeaconry of Rochester in 1560 (N.S.; 1559, O.S.); Columb Major, Cornwall, in 1559; Luccombe, Somerset, in 1563; Porlock, Somerset, in 1565; Prebend of Combell in 1564; and Compton Bishop in the Cathedral of Wells in 1572. On April 14, 1563, he was elected rector of Lincoln College, Oxford, but resigned this and his other preferments in 1574 and went abroad. It is unlikely that he ever returned to England. Pedro de Ribadaneira, Nathaniel Southwell, and Henry Foley claim him as a member of the Society of Jesus, but this is questioned. His two polemical works of theology are, *Confutatio virulentae disputationis theologicae, in qua Georgius Sohn, professor academiae Heidelbergensis, conatus est docere Pontificem Romanum esse antichristum a prophetis et apostolis praedictum* (Trèves 1589) and *Con-*

certatio ecclesiae catholicae in Anglia adversus Calvino-papistas et Puritanos sub Elizabetha regina quorundam hominum doctrina et sanctitate illustrium renovata et recognita (Trèves 1589–94).

Bibliography: Douai, English College, *The First and Second Diaries of the English College Douay*, ed. Fathers of the Congregation of the London Oratory (London 1878) 99, 119, 128, 130, 146, 408. DictEngCath 1:294–295. DNB 2:1232–33. H. FOLEY, *Records of the English Province of the Society of Jesus*, 7 v. (London 1877–82) 4:485–488.

[C. W. FIELD]

BRIDGIT, ABBEY OF, a former foundation of *Bridgettines, situated on Lake Vättern, Östergötland, Sweden, in the former Diocese of Linköping. It is the mother abbey of the Bridgettine Order and was built according to the directions of St. *Bridget *c.* 1365 on the royal estate of Vadstena, which was willed to her in 1346 by King Magnus Eriksson. The first abbess was Bridget's daughter, St. *Catherine of Sweden, who reestablished the community in 1374. The work was favored by a special fee, Our Lady's pence, and in 1384 the abbey was consecrated by the diocesan bishop. According to Bridget's plan the abbey should have a nuns' and a monks' convent under an abbess as the common leader, with a general confessor at her side and visitation rights granted to the bishop of Linköping. Bridget's corpse was moved from Rome to the site in 1374, and in the later Middle Ages the tombs of the saint and her daughter became the main destination for pilgrims in Sweden. With its more than 900 estates, Vadstena was the richest abbey in Scandinavia; a large income was further derived from the Vincula (feast of St. Peter in Chains), the *Portiuncula, as well as the *Jubilee *indulgences, title to which the abbey had acquired. This foundation had one of the largest libraries in Scandinavia, from which about 450 volumes are extant, housed in the University Library of *Uppsala and the Royal Library at Stockholm. Among these there may be mentioned the *Diarium Vazstenense* for the years 1344 to 1545 (Codex Ups. C 89) and a copy book preserved in the State Archives in Stockholm. Great literary and artistic impulses emanated from Vadstena, and the abbey, dedicated to the Virgin Mary, became a center for the Marian devotion in Sweden. The originator of the weekly ritual of the nuns, the *Cantus sororum ordinis Sancti Salvatoris*, was Magister Petrus Olavi (d. 1378), a man of saintly reputation. The house in Rome where Bridget died was purchased by the abbey and used as a hospital for pilgrims. When the Protestant *Reformation reached Sweden the importance of the abbey ceased, and in 1595 it was formally dissolved. The church is now used as the town church of Vadstena, and parts of the former buildings, among them the original royal estate, are still preserved.

Bibliography: R. GEETE, ed., *Jungfru Marie örtagård* (Stockholm 1895). E. NYGREN, ed., *Diarium Vadstenense* (Copenhagen 1963). H. CNATTINGIUS, *Studies in the Order of St. Bridget of Sweden* (Stockholm 1963–). T. HÖJER, *Studier i Vadstena klosters och Birgittinordens historia intill midten af 1400-talet* (Uppsala 1905). A. LINDBLOM, *Johann III och Vadstena nunnekloster* (Lund 1961); *Kult och konst i Vadstena kloster* (Stockholm 1965). L. A. NORBORG, *Storföretaget Vadstena kloster* (Lund 1958). T. NYBERG, *Birgittinische Klostergründungen des Mittelalters* (Lund 1965). **Illustration credit:** Swedish Information Service, New York City.

[O. ODENIUS]

BRIEFS TO PRINCES, SECRETARIATE OF

The Secretariate of Briefs to Princes is one of the offices of the Roman Curia and its first Latin secretariate at the direct service of the pope (CIC c.264; ClerSanc c.210). For many years after its more or less official establishment in the 15th century, it existed and functioned first as part of the Apostolic Secretariate and then as part of what was initially the Secretariate of State. When Innocent XI, with the bull *Romanus Pontifex* of April 1, 1678, reorganized the latter office, he also detached from it the Secretariate of Briefs to Princes—which thus acquired its present autonomous form and somewhat independent status. No changes were made in this regard by either Pius X's constitution *Sapienti consilio* of June 29, 1908, or the Code of Canon Law.

The purpose of this office, which works in close conjunction with the Secretariate of State, is the preparation of the Latin text of letters to be sent by the pope to heads of state and high Church prelates, as well as that of encyclicals, consistorial allocutions, papal homilies on the occasion of canonizations, and other pontifical documents and letters of major import. This Secretariate once had the faculty to grant matrimonial dispensations to heads of state and members of their families; but the faculty to grant such dispensations to all the faithful without distinction is now reserved to the Congregation of the Sacraments and the Supreme Congregation of the Holy Office. By the constitution *Sapienti consilio*, the Secretariate of Briefs to Princes was deprived also of all faculties that it enjoyed by virtue of Benedict XIV's bull *Gravissimum* of Nov. 26, 1745—which faculties were given instead to the third section (charged with the expediting of apostolic briefs) of the Papal Secretariate of State.

The Secretariate is presided over by a prelate, called the secretary of briefs to princes, who, as required by the nature of his task, is always a proficient Latinist. He belongs to the noble pontifical anticamera. In the performance of his work as chief Latinist of the Holy See, the secretary of briefs to princes is assisted by a num-

Fifteenth-century church of the Abbey of Bridgit, now the parish church at Vadstena, Östergötland, Sweden.

ber of officials, also skilled in the knowledge and use of Latin. To him, as a rule, is assigned also the task of announcing in Latin the solemn proclamation of new saints during the ceremonies of canonization and that of delivering the sermon concerning the election of a new pope (*oratio de eligendo Summo Pontifice*) immediately after the celebration of the votive Mass of the Holy Spirit just before the opening of the conclave.

Bibliography: A. BACCI, EncCatt 9:247. N. DEL RE, *La Curia Romana* (2d ed. Rome 1952). C. BERUTTI, *De Curia Romana* (Rome 1952) 81–82.

[J. A. ABBO]

BRIEUC, ST., monk, founder and patron of the town of St. Brieuc, Brittany (Côtes-du-Nord); b. Cardigan, Wales, 410; d. St. Brieuc, 502 (feast, May 1). Born of pagan parents, Brieuc was converted at Verulam by (St.) Germanus of Auxerre and in 429 followed him to Gaul, where he was ordained. On returning to Wales, Brieuc worked among his compatriots, but in 480 had to flee before the Saxon invasion. With about 100 Christians he crossed La Manche and established himself in Armorican Brittany not far from Tréguier. There he converted a rich chieftan, Conan, and founded at Brieuc a monastery around which the town rose. If he was consecrated a bishop, he remained a bishop-abbot in the Celtic tradition, without administering the diocese. His relics were transported to St. Sergius in Angers during the Norman invasions, but were returned to St. Brieuc in 1210. Because of his charity, he is the patron of pocketbook makers. The city was erected into an episcopal see *c.* 848 by Nominoë, King of the Bretons; its cathedral was built in the 13th century over the foundations of the chapel Brieuc erected.

Bibliography: ActSS May 1:93–97. F. PLAINE, AnalBoll 2 (1883) 161–190. H. WAQUET, DHGE 10:712–713. Duchesne FE 2:255, 262–263, 300–301. G. H. DOBLE, *Saint Brioc* (Cornish Saints 17; Long Compton, Eng. 1928). R. AIGRAIN, *Catholicisme* 2:267–268.

[A. DANET]

BRIGGS, CHARLES AUGUSTUS, Presbyterian Biblical scholar; b. New York City, Jan. 15, 1841; d. there, June 8, 1913. He was educated at the University of Virginia, Charlottesville, and after military service in the Civil War, at Union Theological Seminary, New York City. His study at the University of Berlin (1865–70) under Emil Rodiger and Isaac A. Dorner gave him a firm grounding in the methods of the higher criticism. Upon returning to the U.S., Briggs served as pastor of a Presbyterian church in Roselle, N.J., until 1874, when he became professor of Hebrew at Union Theological Seminary.

In 1880 Briggs became editor of the *Presbyterian Review*. His articles in this periodical, republished as *Biblical Study* (1883) and *Messianic Prophecy* (1886), advocated a moderate stand between rationalistic criticism and reactionary conservatism in Biblical scholarship. He opposed the Calvinist scholasticism of the Princeton school and argued against it in *Whither?* (1889), a work which directly influenced the efforts at revision of the Westminster Confession at the general assembly in 1890. In *The Bible, the Church and Reason* (1892), his inaugural address as professor of Biblical theology at Union in 1890, Briggs held that theories of verbal inspiration were barriers to church unity and committed Protestantism to a superstitious bibliolatry. The immediate result was his trial for heresy, which

culminated in Briggs's suspension from the ministry in 1893. He remained at Union, however, and in 1899, over the protests of Anglo-Catholics, was ordained a priest of the Protestant Episcopal Church. In 1904 he became professor of symbolics and irenics at Union.

In his later years, Briggs worked for reunion of Catholics and Protestants. He had an audience with Pius X in an effort to stave off the decrees of the Biblical Commission, which he later criticized in *The Biblical Commission and the Pentateuch* (1906). His doctrinal position was that of traditional Christianity, and he met the attacks of Modernists and rationalists in *The Incarnation* (1902), *The Virgin Birth* (1909), and *The Fundamental Christian Faith* (1913). His principal work was the *Commentary on the Book of Psalms* (1906), which he contributed to the *International Critical Commentary on the Holy Scriptures,* of which he was the general editor.

Bibliography: Union Theological Seminary, Library, his correspondence and works. L. A. LOETSCHER, *The Broadening Church* (Philadelphia 1957); "C. A. Briggs in the Retrospect of Half a Century," *Theology Today* 12 (1955) 27–42.

[R. K. MAC MASTER]

BRIGHTMAN, EDGAR SHEFFIELD, philosopher, leading American exponent of *personalism; b. Holbrook, Mass., Sept. 20, 1884; d. Newton, Mass., Feb. 25, 1953. The son of a Methodist minister and himself an ordained Methodist minister, Brightman studied at Brown University, at Boston University, and at the Universities of Berlin and of Marburg. His life as a professor and scholar, after early teaching at Nebraska Wesleyan University (1912–15) and at Wesleyan University in Middletown, Conn. (1915–19), was spent at Boston University (1919–53). Between 1925 and 1953 he wrote 14 books, more than 200 articles, and 300 book reviews on metaphysics, religion, ethics, and education. His scholarly and personal concern for his students was remarkable; an unusual proportion of his disciples became college presidents, deans, productive scholars, teachers, and pastors in America and elsewhere.

In B. P. Bowne's personalism Brightman found the synthesis of what had attracted his earlier loyalties to J. *Royce and W. *James. Brightman grounded the theistic, pluralistic idealism that Bowne had developed from Berkeleyan, Lotzean, and Kantian roots in what he believed to be sounder experiential foundations. He argued that metaphysical, theological, and ethical hypotheses should be reasoned explanations of data immediately given in irreducible personal experience. The person, which he conceived as a complex unity of activities and capable of self-consciousness, moral purpose, and religious sensitivity, in his view should replace the scholastic notion of *soul. The person is not a part of the personal God who created him free within limits. By contrast, physical and organic nature exist as the order of God's active Will, guided by reason and love. God Himself is omnitemporal, not eternal, and His power is limited. He is a personal Creator whose goodness and reason are the ideal guides of His will as He exerts continuous, if somewhat incomplete, control throughout cosmic evolution over the nonrational factors within His own nature.

Although Brightman's critics urged that this finitistic view of God did not meet the demands of religious experience and faith, Brightman questioned the unanimity of genuine religious experience on this point. Critics urged also that God's nature was dichotomized, but Brightman held that His metaphysical unity was not in fact jeopardized. In any case, he said, God's purpose is realized as persons actualize their individual potential in a free communitarian society that treats persons and God as ends in themselves and never as means only.

See also PERSONALISM; AMERICAN PHILOSOPHY.

Bibliography: E. S. BRIGHTMAN, *Introduction to Philosophy* (New York 1925; 3d ed. R. N. BECK, 1963); *The Problem of God* (New York 1930); *The Finding of God* (New York 1931); *Moral Laws* (New York 1933); *A Philosophy of Religion* (New York 1940; reprint Englewood Cliffs, N.J. 1958); *Person and Reality: An Introduction to Metaphysics,* ed. P. A. BERTOCCI et al. (New York 1958).

[P. A. BERTOCCI]

BRIGID OF IRELAND, ST., early Irish monastic foundress and saint; b. Offaly, Ireland *c.* 460; d. Kildare, *c.* 528 (feast, Feb. 1). Brigid came from the Fotharta Airbrech people near Croghan Hill. Her mother was a slave-girl; but the child was acknowledged by her father and given to a foster mother to rear. Having been instructed in letters and the accomplishments of embroidery and household duties, she was sought in marriage by an eager suitor whom she rejected on the ground that she had vowed "her virginity to the Lord." After paternal objections were overcome she took the veil, the symbol of the religious state; she founded in the Liffey plain a church called Cill Dara (Kildare)— "the church of the oak"—and associated with herself a pious hermit, Conleth, who lived alone in a nearby solitude. The house for men, which he ruled as bishop

St. Brigid of Ireland is invested with the religious habit, miniature in the 15th-century Breviary of the Duke of Bedford (Bib. Nat. MS Lat. 17294, fol. 410 v.).

and abbot, was so near the convent of women that both communities could use the same church. Kildare was thus a *double monastery, the only institution of its kind in Ireland. The Life of St. Brigid written in the 7th century represents her as a new type of Irish woman—the Christian saint. Her likeness to modern missionary sisters is remarkable; she often left Kildare in her chariot, doing the work of the Lord's charity in distant parts. To her countrymen she was "the Mary of the Gael," and when they went as missionaries and pilgrims to the Continent of Europe they spread devotion to her wherever they settled. St. Brigid, St. *Patrick, and St. Colmcille are the three patron saints of Ireland.

Bibliography: COGITOSUS, *Vita S. Brigidae,* ActSS Feb. 1:135–155. M. A. O'BRIEN, tr. and ed., "The Old Irish Life of St. Brigit," *Irish Historical Studies* 1 (1938–39) 121–134, 343–353. C. PLUMMER et al., eds., "Vita Brigitae," *Irish Texts* 1 (1931) 2–16. J. F. KENNEY, *The Sources for the Early History of Ireland* (New York 1929) 1:356–363. **Illustration credit:** Bibliothèque Nationale, Paris.

[J. RYAN]

BRIGIDINES, or congregation of St. Brigid (CSB), a community of women religious with papal approval (1845, 1907), founded at Tullow, County Carlow (Ireland), in 1807 by Daniel Delaney (1747–1814), Bishop of Kildare and Leighlin. The sisters profess simple perpetual vows and devote themselves to Christian education. They are governed by a superior general who resides at the motherhouse in Tullow. Bishop Delaney, aware of Ireland's educational deficiencies, and himself a "graduate" of that country's famous "hedge schools," formed the congregation with a group of six catechists whom he trained in the religious life, based on the Rule of St. Augustine. The community adopted the episcopal motto, *Fortiter et suaviter.* The sisters are organized in three provinces, one for Ireland and Great Britain and two for Australia and New Zealand. Since 1953 the congregation has been in the U.S., where a novitiate was established in San Antonio, Tex. (1960). In 1964 some 800 sisters (16 in the U.S.) in 60 convents staffed 76 grade schools with about 20,000 students; 32 high schools with about 8,000 students; and a teachers' training college.

Bibliography: M. M. DUNNE, *Watching for the Dawn* (Dublin 1963).

[M. V. DOBSON]

BRINDISI, ARCHDIOCESE OF (BRUNDUSINUS), metropolitan see since the 10th century, in Apulia, south Italy. Since 1821 it has had the perpetual administration of its only suffragan, Ostuni. An old Greek colony occupied by Rome in 266 B.C., and tied to Rome and *Benevento by Roman roads, it was the base of Rome's expansion to the East. Christianity probably came there very early, but the first known bishop was St. Leucius under Emperors Theodosius I (379–395) or II (408–450); his vita, however, is legendary. Byzantium successfully contested the port against Goths and Lombards and rebuilt it after Emperor Louis II (855–875) razed it. In 886 Saracens destroyed Brindisi, and the bishops moved inland to Oria, which remained under their jurisdiction until 1591. Until the Norman Guiscard took Brindisi from Byzantium in 1060 and the bishopric was restored there, the city and the coast had been under the Byzantine Greek Church, although without a Greek bishop.

The widespread Greek liturgy declined under the Normans but was still followed in the 13th century and even revived with later Greek immigration. In 1088 Urban II consecrated the cathedral, which was rebuilt after an earthquake in 1743. Brindisi has enjoyed considerable expansion since 1861. Its notable archbishops include G. P. Caraffa (1518–24) later Pope Paul IV, G. *Aleandro (1524–41), F. Aleandro (1541–60), G. Bovio (1564–70), and A. Sersale (1743–50). Benedictines built the church of San Benedetto with a Romanesque cloister in 1080; the Romanesque San Giovanni al Sepolcro may be older. Santa Lucia (11th–12th century) has three naves with ogives built over a Romanesque crypt with Byzantine paintings. The black and white designs characteristic of medieval Brindisi decorate the façades of the 13th-century Church of Christ and the 14th-century Santa Maria del Casale; the latter is Romanesque-Gothic with rich contemporary frescoes.

In 1963 the archdiocese had 226,065 Catholics in 42 parishes, 123 secular and 36 religious priests, a major and minor seminary, 40 men in 9 religious houses, and 411 women in 45 convents; it is 607 square miles in area.

Bibliography: Gams. Eubel HierCath. F. BONNARD, DHGE 10: 744–748, with list of bishops. N. C. SCIPIONI and M. LUCERI, EncCatt 3:101–103. A. FRANCO, LexThK² 2:695–696. AnnPont (1964) 76, 1414.

[G. A. PAPA]

BRINKLEY, STEPHEN, printer, translator, and confessor; parentage and date and place of birth and death unknown; lost to view after 1586. Brinkley was a matriculated pensioner at St. John's College, Cambridge, in 1562, and received the LL.B. in 1570. As "James Sancer," he dedicated his translation of Gaspare Loarte's *Exercise of a Christian Life* at Paris, June 20, 1579, which was a deliberate subterfuge, since the book was really printed in London by William Carter. In 1580 a spy listed him among alleged papal pensioners "now in England." Brinkley offered his services to Edmund *Campion and Robert *Persons after their landing in June 1580, and he organized and supervised their secret press at Greenstreet House, East Ham. The betrayal and torture of a servant caused the press's disbandment after completing (November to December 1580) Persons's *Brief discours* and two other books. Brinkley reassembled it to print Persons's *Brief censure* (January 1581) in a house lent by Lord Montague's brother, Francis Browne. Three more books were printed before the press was moved to Stonor Park, Henley, where Campion's *Rationes decem* was finished during June. With other work at press, Stonor was raided on the Privy Council's orders; Brinkley and four workmen were seized (August 8) and committed to the Tower. Brinkley was released on June 24, 1583. He went abroad and visited Rome with Persons and later assisted Persons's secret press at Rouen. Books issued there included his translation of Loarte—then (1584) "newly corrected by the translatour"—which had inspired Persons's *Christian Directory*. Persons suggested (September 1585) that Brinkley should become the Duke of Savoy's intelligencer at Paris. He was last described (December 1586) as a "factor for all the Jesuyts."

Bibliography: DictEngCath 1:298–300. CathRecSoc v.2, 4, 39, 53. A. C. SOUTHERN, *Elizabethan Recusant Prose, 1559–1582* (London 1950). A. F. ALLISON and D. M. ROGERS, *A Catalogue of Catholic Books in English . . . 1558–1640,* 2 v. (London 1956). W. R. TRIMBLE, *The Catholic Laity in Elizabethan England 1558–1603* (Cambridge, Mass. 1964).

[D. M. ROGERS]

BRISACIER, JACQUES CHARLES DE, director of the seminary of the *Paris Foreign Missionary Society; b. Blois, France, Oct. 18, 1642; d. Paris, March 23, 1736. He came of an illustrious family. After his ordination he became commendatory abbot of Saint-Pierre de Neuvilliers and chaplain to Queen Marie Thérèse. Entering the seminary of the Paris Foreign Mission Society c. 1670, he was superior there almost continuously from 1681 to 1736. He built the church of the society in 1683, and the seminary buildings in 1732. The regulations of 1700 for the society were modified in 1716 to give the seminary a separate organization. While Brisacier was superior, 49 missionaries were sent to the Far East. He entered the controversy over the *Chinese rites, taking a stand with the Dominicans and Franciscans against the Jesuits and the Sorbonne. Through Mme. de *Maintenon, whom he counseled regarding regulations for her college of Saint-Cyr, he became involved in the dispute over *quietism. He was esteemed by his contemporaries for his intelligence, piety, and skill in spiritual guidance.

Bibliography: A. LAUNAY, *Mémorial de la Société des missions-étrangères, 1658–1913,* 2 v. (Paris 1912–16) 2:95–98. H. SY, DHGE 10:758–759. M. PREVOST, DictBiogFranc 7:349–350. R. CHALUMEAU, *Catholicisme* 2:275–276.

[H. PROUVOST]

BRISBANE, ARCHDIOCESE OF (BRISBANENSIS), metropolitan see of the State of Queensland, *Australia; diocese (1859), archdiocese (1887), whose suffragans are Cairns, Rockhampton, Townsville, and Toowoomba. Permanent colonization began when the region, originally a convict station known as the Moreton Bay District, was opened to free settlers (1842). The first priests for the immigrants were two Irish missionaries, Fathers McGinnety and Hanly, who arrived in 1843. The first mission to Australian aborigines was undertaken (1843) by four Italian Passionist fathers on nearby Stradbroke Island, but was abandoned in 1846. James O'Quinn, first bishop (1859–81), built St. Stephen's Cathedral, established a Catholic newspaper, and laid the foundations of a Catholic education system. With government approval, he also established the Queensland Immigration Society and brought out 10 shiploads of Irish settlers; but, because of sectarian opposition, the society was dissolved in 1865. Robert Dunne, bishop (1882–1917), who consolidated and extended the work of his predecessor, was a distinguished scholar and secretary to the Plenary Council of Australasia (1885). Sir James Duhig, Archbishop (1917–65), was the first Catholic Australian ecclesiastic to be knighted by the British Sovereign. (*See* AUSTRALIA for statistics and map.)

Bibliography: *The Official Year Book of the Catholic Church of Australasia* (Sydney). AnnPont (1964) 76.

[J. G. MURTAGH]

BRISSON, LOUIS ALEXANDRE, religious founder; b. Plancy (Aube), France, June 23, 1817; d. there, Feb. 2, 1908. He was the second and sole-surviving child of Marie Savine (Corrard de la Noue) and Toussaint Brisson, a grocer. After studying at the minor and major seminaries in Troyes from 1831, he was ordained (1840). He then taught at the major seminary and also served as chaplain at the local convent of the *Visitation Nuns, where he came into contact with Maria *Chappuis, the superior and mistress of novices. At her urging he founded the *Oblate Sisters of St. Francis de Sales (1866) and the *Oblates of St. Francis de Sales (c. 1871). He also directed a successful society to promote the spread of the faith in mission territories. His spirituality was modeled on that of St. *Francis de Sales. Brisson's sole extant writings are those preserved by his followers. The *Decretum super scripta* in his cause for beatification was issued in 1955.

Bibliography: K. BURTON, *So Much, So Soon: Father Brisson, Founder of the Oblates of St. Francis de Sales* (New York 1953). P. DUFOUR, *Le Très Révérend Père Louis Brisson* (Paris 1937); DictSpirAscMyst 1:1962–66.

[E. J. CARNEY]

BRISTOW, RICHARD, theologian; b. Worcester, England, 1538; d. Harrow, near London, Oct. 21, 1581. He went to Oxford in 1555, received the B.A. degree in 1559, and the M.A. in 1562, being a member of Christ Church College. A brilliant scholar and speaker, he was chosen, with Edmund Campion, to debate before Queen Elizabeth I on her visit in 1566. He was a fellow of Exeter College in 1567. In his refutation of Lawrence Humphrey, he revealed his Catholic tendencies. He withdrew to Louvain and later joined William *Allen (later cardinal) at the English College of Douay in 1569, and was its first student to be ordained (1573). There he was prefect of studies, pro-rector in Allen's absence and daily lecturer on Holy Scripture. With Allen he revised and corrected Gregory Martin's translation of the New Testament in 1581. Allen and others wanted him for rector of the English College in Rome. But strain and fatigue compelled him to rest, so he went to Spa and then to Harrow, where he died shortly after his arrival. Bristow's chief writings are *A briefe treatise . . . conteyning sundry worthy motiues unto the Catholic faith* (Antwerp 1574), later called his *Motives* (new ed. 1599); *Demaundes to bee proposed of Catholickes to the heretickes* (1576); *A reply to William Fulke in Defence of M. D. Allen's Scrole of Articles and Booke of Purgatorie* (Louvain 1580).

Bibliography: DictEngCath 1:300–303.

[H. E. ROPE]

BRITAIN, EARLY CHURCH IN

The Christian faith was introduced into England and Scotland probably by commercial and military contacts between Britain and Gaul. Irenaeus in his *Adversus Haereses* (1.3), written c. 176, does not mention Britain in a list of Christian lands that includes the regions of the Celts. *Tertullian, writing shortly after 200, spoke of "the places of the Britons not reached by the Romans but subject to Christ" and adds that "Christ's name reigns" there (*Adv. Judaeos* 7). This is the first concrete reference to the existence of Christianity in Britain, though Tertullian probably exaggerated the extent and social influence of the faith there at that time. The controversial legends of the Glastonbury mission of *Joseph of Arimathea (allegedly in A.D. 63) and the request of King Lucius of the Britons to Pope *Eleutherius (c. 167) for missionaries are without historical value.

There is 6th-century evidence (Gildas, *De excidio Britanniae* 10; 11; Bede, *Eccl. hist.* 1.4; 5.24, using

Fig. 1. Celtic stone head, probably of 2d- or 3d-century workmanship. The object is a complete sculpture and not a fragment. It may be a votive object from one of the pagan Celtic shrines obliterated by Christianity.

Gildas) of a persecution of Christians either in the middle of the 3d century or at the beginning of the 4th century; but there is strong evidence against its being an integral part of the Diocletian repression, since both Eusebius (*Hist. eccl.* 8.13) and Lactantius claim that Constantius I as emperor of the West (293–306) took no part in the *Diocletian persecution. The most famous martyr mentioned for this period is St. *Alban (Gildas, *loc. cit.;* Constantius, *Life of Germanus*); he was already reverenced as a martyr in Britain in 429.

After the so-called Edict of *Milan (313) the Church in Britain developed in security and sent three bishops to the Council of *Arles (314): Restitutus of London, Eborius (probably quite simply his title) of York (Eboracum), Adelphius (of Lincoln or Caerleon). The conciliar decisions that bishops were not to invade dioceses other than their own and that ordinations were to be performed by a minimum of three bishops indicate that the British Church, like all those represented at Arles, was by this time a full-fledged episcopal and diocesan organization.

There is no conclusive evidence that any British bishops attended the Councils of Nicaea (325) or Sardica (343); but at least three attended Ariminum (360); according to Sulpicius Severus they were the only three to take advantage of Emperor Constantius' offer to pay bishops' travel expenses from imperial funds.

This same year (360) saw the beginning of the barbarian irruptions that were to involve Britain in the general decline and eventual collapse of the Roman Empire. The Picts and Scots attacked heavily along the northern frontier and in 367 were joined by the Saxons.

Hadrian's Wall was breached and Britain's security rendered precarious. After a temporary containment of the barbarian invaders by *Theodosius I, the great Roman withdrawal began in 401 under Stilicho. By 409 the Britons had been told by Emperor *Honorius I to provide their own defense. In a barbarian raid by the Irish (c. 405) *Patrick was carried off to Ireland.

About the same point another young Briton, *Pelagius, began (c. 400) to teach a doctrine in Rome that developed into a denial of original sin. There is no record of the return of Pelagius himself to Britain after his Roman stay (405–410), but *Pelagianism was probably introduced into Britain by his disciples expelled from Rome in the reign of Pope *Celestine I (422–432). A second-rate Pelagian, Agricola, son of the Pelagian bishop Severianus, fled to Britain and seems to have been the main instrument for the introduction of heresy into the Church there. The consequent laxity became so widespread within a decade that an appeal was made to Rome, resulting in the famous missions of the Gaul St. *Germain (429 and 447).

During the first 3 decades of the 5th century St. *Ninian preached to the Picts of Galloway and can be called the first known missionary to Scotland; after his death in 432 his converts among the Picts fell away from the faith.

The Anglo-Saxon invasions of the second half of the 5th century brought a heathen agglomeration into southern and eastern Britain, and the British Church as a hierarchically organized institution ceased to exist in the more densely populated portions of the country. Many British Christians were slaughtered by the continental invaders; others fled to Brittany; and some were fired with missionary zeal and the desire for monasticism that could better be realized abroad. A remnant in the Welsh and Cornish mountains maintained close contact with Gaul.

This remnant welcomed the newly spreading phenomenon of monasticism. C. J. Godfrey's remark is cogent: ". . . its fervent spirit was welcomed by the defeated and displaced Britons, who found in specialized

Fig. 2. A section of the Roman Wall near Housesteads, Northumberland, built by Hadrian in the 2d century A.D.

Fig. 3. Interior view of the early minster at Brixworth, Northants., England, constructed in the 7th century.

'religion' a compensation for their temporal losses." Important monastic foundations were that of Illtud at Hodnant or Llanilltud (c. 500), where a school was founded to train men for monasticism, but which also offered a liberal education; that of David at Menevia (c. 560); of Cadoc at Llancarvon; of Kentigern (Mungo) at a Strathclyde site named for his "dear family" of disciples, Glasgu (c. 580).

The Welsh Christians evangelized the pagan or apostate Picts and maintained constant spiritual commerce with Ireland and Brittany, but hated the Anglo-Saxon invaders for their crime of total dispossession to an extent that precluded all missionary activity to them. When *Augustine of Canterbury in his mission in 597 appealed to the Celts for charity to the Angles, the reply of Abbot Bangor was: "We will never, never, preach the faith to this cruel race of foreigners who have so treacherously robbed us of our native soil" (PL 80:21–24).

Bibliography: Bede, *A History of the English Church and People,* tr. L. Sherley-Price (Penguin Bks. Baltimore 1955). A. Plummer, *The Churches in England before A.D. 1000,* 2 v. (London 1911–12). M. Deansley, *The Pre-Conquest Church in England* (New York 1961). H. Williams, *Christianity in Early Britain* (Oxford 1912). S. N. Miller, "The British Bishops at the Council of Arles," EngHistRev 42 (1927) 79–80. C. R. Peers, "The Earliest Christian Churches in Britain," *Antiquity* 3 (1929). C. J. Godfrey, *The Church in Anglo-Saxon England* (New York 1962). **Illustration credits:** Fig. 1, Courtesy of the Cleveland Museum of Art. Gift of Dr. and Mrs. Jacob Hirsch. Fig. 2, British Travel Association, New York City. Fig. 3, National Buildings Record, London.

[A. G. Gibson]

BRITHWALD OF CANTERBURY, ST., Benedictine monk, archbishop of Canterbury; b. c. 650; d. probably Jan. 13, 731 (feast, Jan. 9). Neither his family nor birthplace is known but his training, presumably at the Canterbury school, earned him a reputation for ecclesiastical learning. Before 679 Brithwald (Bertwald, Beorhtwald) became abbot of the new monastery at Reculver, Kent; for in that year there is a charter—the earliest Anglo-Saxon charter in contemporary text—that records a gift of land by King Hlothhere of Kent to Brithwald and his monastery. Having been elected Theodore's successor (*see* THEODORE OF CANTERBURY, ST.) as archbishop of *Canterbury on July 1, 692, and consecrated by Abp. Godwin of Lyons on June 29, 693, he was enthroned Aug. 31, 693. As archbishop he participated in several great councils and presided over those dealing with *Wilfrid of York. His tenure of office for 37½ years, the longest in Canterbury's history, is particularly noteworthy as a period of diocesan reorganization. He was buried in the church of SS. Peter and Paul, Canterbury (*St. Augustine's Abbey).

Bibliography: BEDE, *Eccl. Hist.* 5.8, 19, 23–24. WILLIAM OF MALMESBURY, *Gesta pontificum Anglorum*, ed. N. E. S. A. HAMILTON (RollsS 52; 1870) 7, 53–55, 235–242, 376. Hefele-Leclercq 3.1:587, 591–596. W. R. W. STEPHENS, DNB 2:1251–52. F. M. STENTON, *Anglo-Saxon England* (2d ed. Oxford 1947) 142–145.

[R. D. WARE]

BRITHWALD OF WILTON, ST., abbot, bishop; d. April 22, 1045 (feast, Jan. 22). Brithwald (Beorhtweald) became monk and then abbot of *Glastonbury, and was elected bishop of Wiltshire (or Ramsbury) in 995. Despite his long episcopacy, there is almost no direct information on his life and work. He was remembered as a generous benefactor to both *Malmesbury and Glastonbury, where he was buried, but is chiefly famous for a reputed vision in which was foretold the succession of Ethelred II's son, *Edward the Confessor, to the dynasty of Canute. Under his successor Hereman, the See of Ramsbury was united with Sherborne, and in 1078 the seat was permanently established at *Salisbury.

Bibliography: WILLIAM OF·MALMESBURY, *De gestis pontificum Anglorum*, ed. N. E. S. A. HAMILTON (RollsS 52; 1870) 182; *De gestis regum Anglorum*, ed. W. STUBBS, 2 v. (RollsS 90; 1887–89) 1:272. FLORENCE OF WORCESTER, *The Chronicle . . . with the Two Continuations*, tr. T. FORESTER (London 1854) 111, 146. *The Life of King Edward . . .*, ed. and tr. F. BARLOW (London 1962) 8–9. G. HILL, *English Dioceses* (London 1900).

[R. D. WARE]

BRITISH COUNCIL OF CHURCHES, an organization established in England in 1942 to promote common action among the Christian Churches of Great Britain. It seeks to facilitate common evangelical action among the Churches, to promote international friendship, to stimulate a sense of social responsibility, to guide youth work, to assist in the growth of ecumenical consciousness, and to promote Christian unity. Various conferences and groupings of the *Free Churches had previously existed, but the British Council brought together the established Churches of England and Scotland and the Nonconforming Churches. The 112 delegates, distributed roughly according to the size of the membership of the constituent Churches, meet at least twice a year. Beginning with William *Temple, the presidents of the Council have been the archbishops of Canterbury. The British Council includes the Church of England, the Episcopalians of Scotland, Ireland, and Wales, the English Presbyterians, the Presbyterian Church of Scotland, the Methodists, the Congregationalists, the Churches of Christ, the Baptists, the Quakers, the Unitarians, and the Salvation Army. Asso-

ciated with the council are also interdenominational societies such as the YMCA, the YWCA, the Student Christian Movement, the Christian Auxiliary Movement, and the Conference of British Missionary Societies. Up to 1965 the Catholic hierarchies of the British Isles had remained aloof from the council.

Bibliography: G. K. A. BELL, ed., *Documents on Christian Unity*, 3d ser., 1930–48 (New York 1948), No. 187, contains the articles of amalgamation. Cross ODCC 199.

[W. HANNAH]

BRITISH HONDURAS

Coextensive with the Diocese of Belize, it is bound on the north by Mexico; on the south by the River Sarstoon; on the east by the Caribbean; and on the west by Guatemala, where the frontier extends from the rapids of Gracias á Dios on the Sarstoon, through Garbutt's Falls on the Belize River, and then due north to the Mexican border. The most important exports of the country are forest products, sugar, and citrus; there are good possibilities for industrial development. The country unites peoples from almost every part of the world. The Mayas, the original inhabitants, are now a minority, and the majority of the people are descendants of early European settlers. English and Spanish are the most common languages.

Catholicism under the Vicariates. The country received its first Catholic settlers in 1830, and a Franciscan, Fray Antonio, was the first of several priests to serve them. During this time the country was roughly included in the vicariate of Trinidad. In 1836 it became part of the vicariate of Jamaica. In 1851 Benito Fernández, a Franciscan and the first vicar apostolic, provided two Jesuit missionaries for the refugees of the Indian revolt in Yucatán. James Dupeyron, SJ, suc-

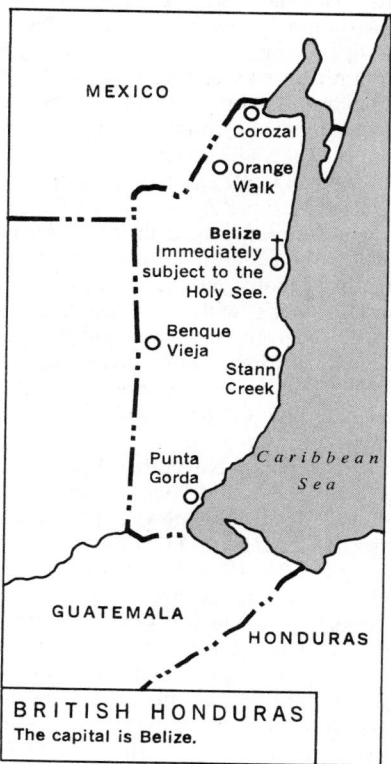

MEXICO
Corozal
Orange Walk
Belize
Immediately subject to the Holy See.
Benque Vieja
Stann Creek
Punta Gorda
Caribbean Sea
GUATEMALA
HONDURAS

BRITISH HONDURAS
The capital is Belize.

ceeded to the vicariate and visited the mission several times before retiring in 1871; Joseph Wollett, SJ, became provicar apostolic for Jamaica; he was followed by Thomas Porter, SJ, who died in office in 1888.

In the same year British Honduras became a prefecture apostolic because of communication difficulties with Jamaica. The mission superior, Salvador DiPietro, SJ, was appointed prefect apostolic and later consecrated bishop. In 1893 the mission was made a vicariate apostolic and put under the direction of the Jesuits of the Missouri province. In the 1890s Sisters of Mercy, who now number 37, opened St. Catherine Academy for girls; the Jesuits started the secondary school that is now known as St. John's College. The Sisters of the Holy Family came to Stann Creek, and today 10 of them continue to conduct three elementary schools and Austin High School for girls. Bishop DiPietro died in 1898; a little over a year later, Frederick Hopkins, SJ, was consecrated bishop. During his long term in office, which saw great progress, the Pallottine Sisters opened a convent at Benque Viejo. Bishop Hopkins was drowned during his annual visitation in 1923, and Bishop Joseph Murphy was named the new vicar apostolic. The blessing of the novitiate for the Pallottine Sisters, who now total 74, occurred in 1931, the same year as the hurricane that devastated the city of Belize and took the lives of 11 Jesuits. Many of the mission's buildings, including those of St. John's College, were destroyed, although generous benefactors enabled the mission to continue.

Afflicted by ill health and advanced in years, Bishop Murphy retired in 1938. Bishop William A. Rice succeeded him in 1939. Three hurricanes struck the country during his brief administration; in 1941, Stann Creek was hit; in 1942, Corozal and Orange Walk; in 1945, Punta Gorda. He was therefore obliged to undertake a large reconstruction program. Bishop Rice died suddenly in 1946, and for 2 years David Hickey, SJ, served as provicar until he was named vicar in 1948. A program for the training of teachers was begun in July 1947. An extension of St. John's College was established in 1947, and St. John's Teachers' College in 1954. The Lyman Agricultural College, established in 1954, anticipated the United Nations' *Development Plan for British Honduras,* which stressed agricultural improvements as the solution for the economic problems of the country. In 1951 Brother Jacoby, SJ, was awarded an honorary M.B.E. for his work with the Boy Scouts; Marvin O'Connor, SJ, received the same honor in 1953, and the O.B.E. in 1959 for his long efficient service to education. In 1955 hurricane Janet destroyed many northern towns, including Corozal, which necessitated another reconstruction program.

Diocese of Belize. In November 1956, the vicariate was raised to a diocese, and Hickey was named the first bishop of Belize. The following year poor health caused him to retire, and Marvin O'Connor administered the diocese until June 26, 1958, when Robert Hodapp, SJ, was consecrated the second bishop of Belize.

Of the population of 98,500 (1963), Catholics number 62,000 and about 60 per cent practice their religion. Most of the people are poor and concubinage is common. To serve these people, there are a bishop, 5 diocesan priests, 30 Jesuits, 121 sisters (half were recruited locally), 10 parishes, and 75 chapels. The poor are helped by the St. Vincent de Paul Society and Catholic Relief Services. Jesuit fathers started credit unions, and the labor unions have Catholic leaders. Organizations such as the Retreat Movement, Sodalities of Mary, and the Legion of Mary aid in pastoral work.

Education. The main contribution of the Church in British Honduras has been in the field of education. There are 91 Catholic elementary schools with 14,800 students and 560 teachers; 91 teachers (mostly foreign) instruct the 1,500 students in the 10 high schools. St. John's College offers opportunities for post–high school work. At the grade school level the government ordinarily pays teachers' salaries and 50 per cent of building and maintenance costs. In every branch of education, but particularly in the secondary field, the diocese is aided by the professional help of Papal Volunteers and some members of the Peace Corps.

Relations between Church and State. Relations between Church and State are amicable. Divorce, although legal, is rare; absolute freedom of worship prevails, and no established church exists. The achievement of self-government and the movement toward independence are encouraged by the Church.

Bibliography: A. C. S. WRIGHT et al., *Land in British Honduras* (Gt. Brit., Colonial Office Research Pub. 24; London 1959). S. L. CAIGER, *British Honduras: Past and Present* (London 1951). J. H. PARRY and P. M. SHERLOCK, *Short History of the British West Indies* (New York 1956). E. O. WINZERLING, *The Beginning of British Honduras, 1506–1765* (New York 1946; 1960). F. C. HOPKINS, "The Catholic Church in British Honduras, 1851–1918," CathHistRev 4 (1918–19) 304–314.

[R. F. O'TOOLE]

BRITISH MORALISTS

The term "English moralists" has become current in recent years as the title of a "paper" at Cambridge University and of a course of lectures connected with it. The phrase is imprecise, and could cover a large number of writers on man's moral nature and conduct. A more accurate term is "British moralists," since Irish thinkers such as Francis Hutcheson and Edmund *Burke, Scots such as David *Hume and others, and Bernard Mandeville, a Dutch physician who lived in England and wrote in English, must be included in an acceptable list. Although certain medieval scholastics, such as 16th-century thinkers as St. Thomas *More and Richard *Hooker, and numerous 20th-century writers belong among British moralists, the term is here restricted to philosophers living in Great Britain in the 17th, 18th, and 19th centuries, writing in English, and making distinctive contributions to moral theory.

Chief among 17th-century moralists are Thomas *Hobbes and Ralph Cudworth (*see* CAMBRIDGE PLATONISTS), Hobbes as an innovator and Cudworth as spokesman for traditional doctrine. Because of his materialistic mechanism, his concept of man, and his theory of society and the state, Hobbes had an immediate and lasting effect on ethics. For him, each man in the state of nature possessed the supreme right of self-preservation and with it all other rights; hence society, the state, and justice result from positive agreement among men. In the controversy occasioned by *Leviathan,* Shaftesbury stressed that the chief issue should be Hobbes's ethics and his defective picture of man as dominated by "only one Master-Passion, Fear, which has in effect devour'd all the rest, and left room only for that infinite Passion towards *Power after Power,* Natural (as he affirms) to *All Men, and never ceasing but in Death.*" Cudworth argues for an objective and natural distinction between good and evil and for man's power to choose between them. Another Cambridge Platonist, Henry More, tries for originality in his *Enchiridion Ethicum* but offers little more than use of the geometric method, an inferior arrangement of virtues and vices, and a theory of conscience as the "boniform faculty."

Despite his religious interests, writings on the state and education, and pervasive influence on philosophy, John *Locke can hardly be classed as a moralist. In *The Fable of the Bees*: *or, Private Vices, Publick Benefits,* Mandeville (1670–1733) shows the influence of Locke and especially of Hobbes. Claiming to be a realist concerned with what man is rather than what he ought to be, he describes man as "a compound of various Passions, that . . . govern him by turns, whether he will or no." By nature unsociable, man has qualities such that he can be made sociable by rulers using force and cunning. Acts contrary to his natural impulses, whereby he strives to help others and conquer his passions out of a rational ambition to be good, are virtuous. Mandeville gives a repellent but effective statement of what follows from Hobbes's doctrine, and finds that debauchery, luxury, avarice, fraud, and the rest of the "private vices" serve the common good. Anthony Ashley Cooper, third Earl of Shaftesbury (1671–1713), author of *Characteristicks of Men, Manners, Opinions, Times,* advances a refined Stoicism. An optimist, he finds that man is naturally disposed to virtue, which is its own reward and reflects the order instituted by God throughout the universe. Love of beauty is helpful to virtue, and man posseses a moral sense, a faculty partly rational and partly aesthetic, whereby he recognizes and loves what is good. He was criticized by George *Berkeley, who was particularly critical in his *Alciphron.*

A follower of Shaftesbury, founder of the Scotch school and forerunner of Bentham and the utilitarians, Hutcheson (1694–1746), in his *Inquiry into the Original of Our Ideas of Beauty and Virtue* and elsewhere, elaborates the doctrine of a moral sense, equates virtue with benevolence, and makes universal happiness the norm of morality. Joseph Butler (1692–1752) is important for his *Analogy of Religion,* where he is a powerful opponent of *Deism, and for his sermons on moral subjects. A cautious thinker, he settles for probability as the guide of life. While there are "natural appearances of our being in a state of degradation," man is disposed to condemn obvious vices and to approve other deeds in themselves and apart from consideration of which is "likeliest to produce an overbalance of happiness or misery." Hume's greatest work, the *Treatise of Human Nature,* applies Locke's method to morality or, better, is an introduction to such application, and by it and other works he made his great impact on conduct as well as on thought. Morality is the object of feeling rather than of thought. The "mere survey" of certain mental qualities gives pleasure and of certain others pain; hence he calls one class virtues and the other vices. Man has a power of unselfish benevolence, and moral approbation is "humanity," "a feeling for the happiness of mankind." Hume's analysis is never deep or thorough. Greatest of British empiricists, he describes certain things that are but never gets at what ought to be and why. Far higher in value are Burke's doctrine of man as a social and political being and moral agent and the shrewd and solid teachings of Samuel *Johnson.

Among later thinkers Jeremy *Bentham, greatest of the utilitarians; John Stuart *Mill, who refined the utilitarian doctrine; and Herbert *Spencer, the philosopher of evolution, are the most important. Basically a utilitarian, Spencer regarded his ethics as his greatest achievement. Moral realities are subject to evolutionary laws, and "absolute ethics" will arrive when man and his environment are completely evolved. At the same time, he limits the powers of state and society and puts supreme value on the individual man. Henry Sidgwick (1838–1900), author of *The Methods of Ethics* and partly a follower of Mill, the idealists T. H. Green (1836–82) and F. H. *Bradley, and Joseph *Rickaby, SJ, a neoscholastic notable for his learning, grasp of principles, originality and sureness of thought, and clarity of presentation, may also be named.

A study of the classical British moralists ends largely in disappointment. The most influential among them offer nothing to compare with the doctrines of the great Greeks and Latins, the schoolmen, and leading Renaissance thinkers. A verdict on them is seen in the wide-

Anthony Ashley Cooper, third Earl of Shaftesbury, portrait by J. Closterman, 1702.

spread contemporary British acceptance of ethical relativism and a permissive morality.

Bibliography: Copleston. B. WILLEY, *The English Moralists* (New York 1964). W. R. SORLEY, *History of British Philosophy to 1900* (Cambridge, Eng. 1965). **Illustration credit:** Collection: Earl of Shaftesbury, Wimborne, St. Giles, Dorset.

[J. K. RYAN]

BROAD CHURCH, a term applied originally to those members of the Church of England in the second half of the 19th century who, having no organized party, agreed in interpreting the religious formularies of *Anglicanism in their widest sense to enable men of varied religious views to continue membership in the Church. Thomas Arnold (1795–1842), classical scholar and famed headmaster of Rugby, was a powerful influence in forming this school of thought. Broad Churchmen stressed moral rectitude and tolerance of heterodox views, but decried hierarchical organization and ritualism as unimportant. They freely accepted whatever scientific opinion seemed to say about religion and the Bible. The latter they considered a source of teaching on righteousness rather than a guide to belief. The publication by seven authors of *Essays and Reviews* (1860) made such views widely known and caused a general outcry in the Established Church. The book was officially condemned and two of the essayists were punished. Their successors in the 20th century are generally referred to as modernists, but many are more easily recognizable as members of the Modern Churchmen's Union, founded in 1898 for the promotion of theological *Liberalism in the Church of England. They advocate a continuing reformulation of Anglican beliefs as the exigencies of the times may seem to require, even when this involves discarding beliefs usually thought fundamental to Christianity.

See also HIGH CHURCH; LOW CHURCH.

Bibliography: J. A. T. ROBINSON, *Honest to God* (Philadelphia 1963). Cross ODCC 91, 199, 287–290, 463, 910.

[E. MC DERMOTT]

BROCH, HERMANN JOSEF, Austrian poet and philosopher; b. Vienna, Nov. 1, 1886; d. New Haven, Conn., May 30, 1951. He was of Jewish descent, attended a school of technology in Vienna and the textile college in Mulhouse in Alsace, and began work in his father's textile factory. He studied philosophy, mathematics, and psychology at the University of Vienna (1928–31). He was arrested by the Nazis in 1938, but managed to emigrate to the U.S., where he received support from the Overland Trust and the Guggenheim, Bollingen, and Rockefeller Foundations. He was appointed (1949) honorary faculty member of the German Department at Yale University.

The novel-trilogy, *Die Schlafwandler: Pasenow oder die Romantik* (1888), *Esch oder die Anarchie* (1903), *Huguenau oder die Sachlichkeit* (1918; *The Sleepwalkers: A Trilogy,* 1931–32), was not designed as a chronicle of German history between 1888 and 1918, but rather as a depiction of three stages in the decay of ethical values. The characters who group themselves around the protagonist of each volume represent certain attitudes of mind, which are defined by the concepts romanticism, anarchy, and objectivity. In *Der Versucher* (1953), Broch portrayed in poetic fashion the invasion of an apparently redeemed community by a Proteus-like savior, Marius Ratti, and the susceptibility of men to this false prophet, whom they follow in their unconscious behavior. Immune to this demoniacal magician, however, is Mother Gisson, who is able to transmute the religious impulses of her soul into contact with the Absolute and thus to shape her own life and the world. In *Der Tod des Vergil* (1945), which originated as a radio play, there emerges from the latent threat of death through Nazism, and as a kind of "private preparation for death," a vision, couched in the poetic expression of Vergil's return to the "pure word," and of his intentional union with the Absolute. It suggests a personal apocalypse on the part of the author. Woven into this death theme is a probing into the creative significance of the true poet who, through the self-renunciation of his reason, is prepared for each new reception of the truth through intuition. He thus becomes the seer and singer, whose task it is to awaken the human intellect to transcendence. In *Die Schuldlosen* (1950), a novel in 11 tales, the question of guilt is of central importance for Broch. Andreas, benumbed by a personal indifference, which his stunted morality regards as innocence and his existential ethics regards as heavy guilt, is, in meeting a beekeeper facing death, the "primitive companion," brought to judgment and thus reawakened to a "flash of absoluteness."

Broch's philosophical essays range from theories of knowledge and logic through a theory of value, and from mob psychology to a philosophy of history. His work in general depicts the end of a decay of values and the reform of the Western intellect.

Bibliography: *Gesammelte Werke,* 10 v. (Zurich 1952–61); *Die Entsühnung,* ed. E. SCHÖNWIESE (Zurich 1961); *The Sleepwalkers: A Trilogy,* tr. W. and E. MUIR (Boston 1932; new ed. New York 1947); *The Unknown Quantity,* tr. W. and E. MUIR (New York 1935); *The Death of Vergil,* tr. J. S. UNTERMEYER (New York 1945). H. J. WEIGAND, "Broch's Death of Vergil: Program Notes," PMLA 62 (1947) 525–554. F. MARTINI, "H. B. und 'Der Versucher'," *Deutsche Rundschau* 80 (1954) 468–474. C. VON FABER DU FAUR, "Der Seelenführer in Brochs 'Tod des Vergil'," in *Wächter und Hüter: Festschrift für Hermann J. Weigand zum 17 Nov. 1957,* ed. C. VON FABER DU FAUR et al. (New Haven 1957). K. W. JONAS and L. E. ZEIDLER, "H.B.: Eine bibliographische Studie," *Philobiblon* 6 (1962) 291–323. E. KAHLER, *Die Philosophie von Hermann Broch* (Tübingen 1962). K. R. MANDELKOW, *Hermann Brochs Romantrilogie "Die Schlafwandler": Gestaltung und Reflexion im modernen deutschen Roman* (Heidelberg 1962). T. ZIOLKOWSKI, *Hermann Broch* (pa. New York 1964).

[W. F. SOMM]

BROCKELMANN, CARL, Orientalist and Semitist; b. Rostock, Germany, Sept. 17, 1868; d. Halle, Germany, May 6, 1956. In 1895 he published a *Lexicon Syriacum* and shortly thereafter his Syriac grammar. In 1902 he completed the *Geschichte der arabischen Literatur,* a systematic review of the range of Arabic literature. Supplementary volumes followed in 1937 and 1938 and again in 1942. Sucessive editions followed his initial revision of Albert Socins' Arabic grammar for the *Porta linguarum orientalium* series. His *Geschichte der islamischen Völker und Staaten* was translated into several languages. In the area of Turkish studies he made the lexicographical material of the *Dīwān lugāt at-Turk* by Maḥmūd al-Kāšġarī accessible to scholars through his *Mitteltürkischer Wortschatz* (1928). He later published an *Osttürkische Grammatik der islamischen Litteratursprachen Mittelasiens* (1951–

54). In his *Grundriss der vergleichenden Grammatik der semitischen Sprachen* (1913), by using comparative and historical principles to review language and dialect, he made a notable advance in the science of comparative Semitics. In the succeeding years he published other valuable studies in Semitics. Professor Brockelmann was attached to faculties of the Universities of Königsberg, Breslau, Halle, and, briefly, Berlin.

Bibliography: O. Spiess, *Verzeichnis der Schriften von Carl Brockelmann* (Leipzig 1938). *Wissenschaftliche Zeitschrift der Martin Luther Universität, Halle-Wittenberg* (Gesellschaftswissenschaftliche Reihe) 8.4 (1957–58).

[T. W. BUCKLEY]

BROEDERLAM, MELCHIOR,

Flemish painter of the international Gothic style of Ypres, dates unknown; fl. 1381–1409. He is first found as court painter to Louis de Male, Count of Flanders. By 1384 he was working for Philip the Bold, Duke of Burgundy, and was his *valet de chambre* (1385–c. 1401). Subsequent references at Ypres (1406) and Courtrai (1407) concern nonducal commissions. His ducal work involved the painting of furniture, banners, standards, and tournament harnesses. The wings he painted to go with a carved altarpiece destined for the Chartreuse de Champmol (Dijon) are his only surviving documented work. These wings, commissioned by Duke Philip in 1392 and delivered in 1399 (Musée des Beaux Arts, Dijon), are remarkable for the skillful way in which Broederlam filled an awkward shape, and for the evident Italianism (Siena and Lombardy) of his style. Since nothing further can be attributed to him with confidence, the

Melchior Broederlam's "Presentation of Christ" and "Flight into Egypt," wing of an altarpiece completed 1399.

sources of this style are obscure; it is unlikely that they could have been found in his native Ypres. In their naturalism and spatial treatment, these altar wings represent an important step toward later artistic developments in Flanders.

Bibliography: L. Dimier, ed., *Les Primitifs français* (Paris 1911). Panofsky ENethPaint. Dupont-Gnudi. P. Durrieu, Thieme-Becker 5:48. **Illustration credit:** Musée des Beaux Arts, Dijon.

[A. MARTINDALE]

BROGLIE, ALBERT DE,

French statesman, publicist, historian; b. Paris, June 13, 1821; d. there, Jan. 19, 1901. Jacques Victor Albert, Duke de Broglie, was the son of Duke Victor de Broglie, who was a member of the Chamber of Peers, minister several times, and president of the Council under Louis Philippe. His mother was the daughter of the famous Mme. de Staël. After completing legal studies in Paris, Albert soon made his mark as a publicist. During the 1850s he was an editor of *Le Correspondant*. His frequent contributions to this and to other periodicals defended Catholic interests, the monarchy, and moderate constitutional liberalism. As a prominent member of the National Assembly (1871–75) and of the Senate (1875–85), De Broglie opposed *Thiers and later the anticlerical leaders of the Third Republic, but he alienated his fellow legitimists by attempting to reconcile their differences. He emerged as the leader of the Orleanists and strove to establish an aristocracy of birth, wealth, and talent in a constitutional monarchy. During these years he served for a time as ambassador to London, president of the Council of Ministers, foreign minister, minister of the interior, and premier (1877). De Broglie championed religious liberty, Catholic education, and ultramontanism.

De Broglie's prolific pen was active until the end of his life and produced numerous articles and books on a diversity of topics, especially on literature, morals, and history. His most notable book, *L'Église et l'empire romain au IVe siècle* (6 v. 1855–66; 5th ed. 1867), won him a seat in the French Academy (1862) but roused considerable controversy because it rejected the thesis of Edward *Gibbon and asserted that Christianity's victory over paganism did not result from official protection or from opposition to Roman civilization but from its own moral superiority and the influence of Christian truth on men's minds.

Bibliography: *Mémoires du Duc de Broglie* (Paris 1942). C. T. Muret, *French Royalist Doctrines since the Revolution* (New York 1933). J. Dedieu, DHGE 10:808–813, with list of Broglie's writings. R. d'Amat, DictBiogFranc 7:398–400.

[M. H. QUINLAN]

BROGLIE, MAURICE JEAN DE,

Bishop of *Ghent; b. Broglie (Normandy), Sept. 5, 1766; d. Paris, July 20, 1821. Despite his illustrious military ancestry, Prince de Broglie chose an ecclesiastical career. After studies at the Seminary of Saint-Sulpice, Paris, he went to Germany (1790), was ordained at Trier (1792), and became a provost at Posen. Upon his return to France (1802), his candor, piety, distinction, and renowned family name won him the favor of Napoleon I. He became almoner at the imperial court (1803), then bishop of Acqui, in Piedmont (Nov. 17, 1805). When delicate health forced him to abandon this diocese, he was promoted to the See of Ghent (March

1807). At first he manifested there a certain amount of deference to Napoleon; later he opposed him at the time of the founding of the imperial university and still more during the French national synod (1811). This led to his imprisonment at Vincennes, exile to Beaune, resignation of his episcopal charge, the suspicion of his maintaining relations with the diocesan curia at Ghent, and his further incarceration at Île Sainte-Marguerite. After Napoleon's death Broglie returned to his diocese (May 28, 1814), which was henceforth incorporated into the Low Countries. He organized diocesan education, and in his *Jugement doctrinal* (1815) opposed the Fundamental Law of this kingdom, because of an unwillingness to admit the freedom of worship inscribed in it. For this he was hailed before the Court of Assizes, and condemned to deportation (Nov. 8, 1817). He fled to France, going first to Amiens, then to Paris.

Bibliography: F. CLAEYS BOUUAERT, DHGE 10:813–818.

[A. SIMON]

BROGNE, ABBEY OF, former *Benedictine monastery in Saint-Gérard, Namur, Belgium, Diocese of Namur, originally the Diocese of Liège. It was founded by *Gerard of Brogne, who had been trained at *Saint-Denis-en-France. He transferred the relics of St. Eugene to Brogne and was abbot there from 923 until his death (959). The discipline of the new community attracted attention: the Duke of Lorraine asked Gerard to restore Saint-Ghislain in Hainaut; Count Arnold of Flanders solicited him to do the same for Saint-Bavon and Saint-Pierre in Ghent, for *Saint-Bertin and *Saint-Amand. Gerard's disciple Mainard restored the Norman monasteries of *Fontenelle, *Mont-Saint-Michel, and *Saint-Ouen in Rouen. Gerard, however, founded no new congregation; he only introduced his "observance" into older houses. In 992 Emperor *Otto III came to Brogne with Bp. *Notker of Liège to meet his old teacher, Abbot Heribert. Bishop Nithard of Liège consecrated the abbey church on Nov. 14, 1038. The simoniacal abbot Guiremond, monk of Saint-Jacques (Liège), bought Brogne from Bishop Othbert, thus incurring stern reproaches from *Rupert of Deutz. In 1131 Alexander of Juliers, Bishop of Liège, exalted the relics of St. Gerard (MGS 4:22). Material and spiritual decline set in later; wars between Burgundy and Liège (*c.* 1425) and the conflict between the Count of Namur and the Dinantais (*c.* 1475) hurt Brogne. The Germans (1525) and the French (1554) ravaged the abbey, which, soon after the creation of the Diocese of Namur, was made part of the episcopal *mensa* (income) in 1566 and was governed by a prior who had a 3-year term of office. Thus began the interminable conflict between the bishops of Namur and the monks. In 1645 the abbot of *Liessies, Dom Gaspar Roger, restored Brogne, whose community had been reduced to 6 religious; he imposed the statutes of Francis Louis *Blosius, which were replaced in 1656 by those of *Bursfeld. In 1686 King Louis XIV issued an edict that accorded the monastery a third of its revenues, the other two-thirds going to the bishop; but in 1731, the bishop of Namur had Emperor Charles VI annul this edict. The French Revolution completely destroyed the abbey, which then had 12 monks.

Brogne is one of the few monasteries in Belgium for which there is a catalogue of books prior to 1200 (MS 46). It is now in the major seminary of Namur, which contains other notable Brogne codices (MSS 43–50). Dom Eugène Massart (d. 1736), a *Maurist, was the last chronicler of the abbey.

Bibliography: Cottineau 1:510–511. F. BAIX, DHGE 10:818–832. U. BERLIÈRE, "L'Abbaye de Saint-Gérard," in *Messager des fidèles* 5 (1888) 169–181, 216–223; "L'Abbaye de Brogne ou de Saint-Gérard," in *Messager de Saint-Benoît* 7 (1905). É. SABBE, "Étude critique sur la biographie et le réforme de Gérard de Brogne," in *Mélanges Félix Rousseau* 8 (1958) 497–524. *Saint Gérard de Brogne et son oeuvre réformatrice* (Maredsous 1960), also in RevBén 70 (1960).

[J. DAOUST]

BROLLO, BASILIO, vicar apostolic to China; b. Gemona, Italy, March 25, 1648; d. San-yüan, China, July 16, 1704. He became a friar at Bassano in 1666 and a priest in 1674. He followed Bp. Bernardino *Della Chiesa to the Orient in 1680 and landed in Kuang-chou, China, on Aug. 27, 1684, assuming the name Yeh Tsun-hsiao. Between 1685 and 1700, acting as Della Chiesa's provicar, he was by his initiatives and writings the main instrument by which were established the vicariates apostolic to rid the missions of the obsolescent Portuguese and Spanish patronage. Despite continual illness, Brollo, with the bishop, visited and attended the missions of Chiang-hsi and Fu-chien (1686), Che-chiang (1687), and Hu-kuang and Chiang-nan (1689); he took up residence at Nan-ching in 1692. Named vicar apostolic of Shăn-hsi (Shensi), he left for his see in June 1700. Arriving at Hsi-an with Antonio Laghi, OFM, in May 1701, he began to visit the missions of Hsi-an and San-yüan and Han-chung and he opened new stations at Mei-hsien and Feng-hsiang. In 1703 he moved to San-yüan to establish his headquarters there, but he fell ill and died. He was truly great for his learning, wisdom, zeal, and supreme charity. He left numerous mission letters, reports, and essays as well as five Chinese works: *T'ien-chu-chiao Yao Chu-lüeh* (Compendium of Catholic Prayers and Doctrine, 1687); *Chien-cheng Sheng-shih Kuei-i* (Confirmation's Notion and Rite, MS, author's preface 1689); *Han Çu Si Ie [Han Tzu Hsi I* (a Chinese-Latin dictionary arranged by radicals, MS 1694]; a Chinese-Latin dictionary alphabetically arranged by transliterated phonetics (MS 1699), a model much followed and plagiarized; and *Brevis Methodus Confessionis Instituendae,* published in transliterated Chinese by Pedro de la Piñuela, OFM, in his edition of Francisco Varo, OP, *Arte de la Lengva Mandarina* (1703).

Bibliography: *Sinica Franciscana,* v.6, ed. G. MENSAERT (Rome 1961). A. S. Rosso, *Apostolic Legations to China of the Eighteenth Century* (South Pasadena, Calif. 1948); "Pedro de la Piñuela, O.F.M., Mexican Missionary to China and Author," FrancStudies 8 (1948) 250–274.

[A. S. ROSSO]

BROMYARD, JOHN OF, English Dominican preacher; from the name Bromyard it is conjectured that he was born in Herefordshire, England; d. 1352(?). Probably a student at Oxford, he was licensed to hear confessions in the Hereford diocese from 1326 to 1352. He prepared his *Opus trivium,* or *Distinctiones Bromyard,* a compilation from the divine, canonical, and civil laws, as a handbook for preachers. A revised and augmented version of this work, entitled *Summa praedicantium,* was a voluminous source of moral and anecdotal sermon materials arranged in alphabetical form. The *Summa* was highly esteemed during the later Middle

Ages. It was multiplied in manuscripts and went through many printed editions (the first, at Basel, 1474), and served for years as a manual for preachers. The prologue to the *Summa* indicates its relationship to the *Opus trivium*. Bromyard further prepared notes for sermons, entitled also *Distinctiones*. The *Summa* was formerly ascribed to another John Bromyard (d. after 1397), who was at one time chancellor of Cambridge, prior of the Dominican priory of Hereford, and member of the 1382 London Black Friars council, which condemned the errors of John *Wyclif. From internal textual evidence, contemporary allusions in the *Summa*, and a sermon of Bp. John de *Shepey of Rochester preached in 1354, it is now clear that the later Bromyard was not the author.

Bibliography: Emden 1:278. G. R. Owst, *Preaching in Medieval England* (Cambridge, Eng. 1926); *Literature and Pulpit in Medieval England* (2d ed. New York 1961) 224, 595.

[A. DABASH]

BRONDEL, JOHN BAPTIST, first bishop of *Helena (Mont.) Diocese; b. Bruges, Belgium, Feb. 23, 1842; d. Helena, Nov. 3, 1904. He was taught by the Xaverian Brothers and attended the Episcopal Institute of St. Louis, Brussels, for 10 years. Deciding to prepare for the missions, he entered the American College in Louvain, Belgium. After his ordination on Dec. 17, 1864, at Mechlin, Belgium, he joined Bp. Augustin M. A. Blanchet in the Diocese of Nesqually (now Seattle Archdiocese), Washington Territory, in November 1866, and was appointed pastor at Steilacoom (Steilicom) on Puget Sound. From this base he organized parishes in Olympia and Tacoma, and did missionary work in Walla Walla until he was appointed bishop of Vancouver Island (now Victoria) on Dec. 14, 1879.

On April 7, 1883, he was named administrator of the vicariate apostolic of Montana and established his residence at Helena, the territorial capital. When the Diocese of Helena was created on March 7, 1884, Brondel became its first bishop. Besides transforming his territory from missionary to diocesan status, he promoted the building of schools, hospitals, and asylums; increased the number of churches from 7 to 56; and added the Sisters of the Good Shepherd to the communities already staffing diocesan institutions. Development outside the city kept pace with that within: 49 churches, 4 hospitals, 5 academies, and 7 parochial schools were established throughout the diocese during his episcopate. On behalf of the Indians he made fund-raising tours in the East and founded a mission among the warlike Cheyenne. At his request the eastern two-thirds of Montana was separated from the Helena jurisdiction in 1904 to form the Diocese of Great Falls.

Bibliography: L. B. Palladino, *Indian and White in the Northwest* (2d ed. rev. Lancaster, Pa. 1922). DAB 3:67–68.

[W. J. GREYTAK]

BRONISŁAWA, BL., Polish contemplative; b. Kamien, Silesia, 1203; d. Aug. 29, 1259 (feast, Aug. 30). Her father was Stanislaus, Count of Prandata-Odrowaz; her mother Anna, of the noble family of Jaxa-Okolski. St. *Hyacinth and Bl. *Ceslaus of Silesia were her first cousins. At 16 she entered the convent of *Premonstratensian nuns of Zwierzyniec near Cracow. Her biographers picture her as a model of mortification and of heroic virtues. It is claimed that she had a vision of Mary bearing the body of St. Hyacinth,

who had just died, from his Dominican priory to heaven. This experience intensified her contemplative life, and pious custom labels the hill near her convent where she retired to pray Mt. St. Bronisława. She died 2 years after Hyacinth. Her body, buried in the convent church, was lost during the Swedish invasion of Poland, but was rediscovered in the 17th century. Her convent was rebuilt and it became a center of prayer for the Polish nation. Cracow has always considered her a saint. In 1839 Pope Gregory XVI approved her cultus. She was known as the patroness of a happy death and of a good reputation. Cardinal Hlond (d. 1948), the Primate of Poland, encouraged the Poles to ask Bronisława, who had saved them from various plagues, to protect them from the danger of the worse contagion of atheism and immorality.

Bibliography: J. Chrząszcz, *Drei schlesische Landesheilige* (Breslau 1897). A. Gonet, *Novena in Honor of Bl. B.* (Lyndora, Pa. 1936). P. David, DHGE 10:841.

[L. L. RUMMEL]

BRONTË, CHARLOTTE AND EMILY JANE

Sister novelists, the most gifted of the six children of Maria Branwell and Patrick Brontë, an Anglican curate of Haworth in Yorkshire who had apparently changed his name from Brunty to hide his lowly Irish origin. Charlotte, b. Thornton, England, April 21, 1816; d. Haworth, March 31, 1855. Emily Jane, b. Thornton, July 30, 1818; d. Haworth, Dec. 19, 1848. Their mother died in 1821, when all six children were less than 8 years old. In 1824 the four older girls attended the Clergy Daughters' School at Cowan Bridge, but Charlotte and Emily left after Elizabeth and Maria contracted fatal illnesses there. At various times thereafter the

Anne, Charlotte, and Emily Brontë, oil on canvas, 35 by 29½ inches, by their brother Patrick, c. 1835.

girls (Charlotte, Emily, and Anne) boarded at a school in Roe Head, and Charlotte became a teacher there in 1835. By 1838 they were residing at Haworth. Emily and Charlotte went to Brussels in 1842 to study languages. Their stay was brief, but Charlotte returned to Belgium to teach until 1844. In that year the Brontë girls advertised a school in their home, but no students applied.

The children began very early to write plays, poems, and stories. Charlotte said that she composed 22 volumes between April 1829 and August 1830. Their brother's wooden soldiers stimulated the girls' imaginations; and they began a cycle of stories centered on the imaginary lands of Angria and Gondal.

In 1846 Charlotte arranged for publication, at the girls' expense, of a volume of poems by Ellis, Acton, and Currer Bell (Emily, Anne, and Charlotte). Although the volume was a financial failure, Emily's poems still survive in anthologies of Victorian verse. The girls then turned to novels, working in the same room. Emily wrote *Wuthering Heights;* Charlotte, *The Professor;* and Anne, *Agnes Grey.* In 1847 Newby accepted Emily's novel, which was not truly appreciated until a century after its publication. The presentation of its wild and terrible characters, skillfully filtered through two commonplace minds, is now seen as a notable expression of the Romantic movement (*see* ROMANTICISM, LITERARY). Charlotte could not find a publisher for *The Professor* in 1847. She then wrote *Jane Eyre,* which Smith Elder accepted immediately; it actually appeared 2 months earlier than Emily's novel. *Jane Eyre,* a partly autobiographical novel, was an immediate success. Its heroine's claim to economic independence was antithetic to 19th-century British custom; and her demand for emotional freedom shocked the reading public. In 1849, still using her pseudonym, Charlotte published *Shirley,* which enjoyed a small measure of success. On June 29, 1854, Charlotte married Arthur Bell Nicholls, her father's curate. Her last work, the fragment *Emma,* appeared posthumously.

Although the Brontë sisters remained conventionally Protestant all their lives, their novels are peculiarly godless. Emily's passionate characters in *Wuthering Heights* struggle in an amoral universe; Charlotte's characters work out their salvation outside any supernatural dimensions, and her novels are marked by anti-Catholicism. Their letters, however, are evidence that in their brief and tragic lives both Charlotte and Emily were supported by a profound Christian faith.

Bibliography: *The Shakespeare Head Brontë,* ed. T. J. WISE and J. A. SYMINGTON, 19 v. (Oxford 1931–38). E. J. BRONTË, *Wuthering Heights,* ed. W. M. SALE (New York 1963), best text. P. E. BENTLEY, *The Brontë Sisters* (New York 1950). L. L. HINKLEY, *The Brontës: Charlotte and Emily* (New York 1945). F. E. RATCHFORD, *The Brontë's Web of Childhood* (New York 1941). L. and E. M. HANSON, *The Four Brontës* (New York 1949). **Illustration credit:** National Portrait Gallery.

[C. T. DOUGHERTY]

BRONZES

A term for statuary and liturgical objects made of bronze and also for articles made of brass. Bronze is an alloy of copper and tin; the blending of copper and zinc yields brass. Copper usually forms 90 per cent of bronze and 70 per cent of brass. Bronze is brownish-red in color, brass is golden yellow. The surfaces of both these metals can be colored with ease. Bronze can be molded

into any shape desired and has the advantage of being highly resistant to weather. The Christian church took over the use of bronze from the ancient world and has employed it in almost all periods for the production of statues and objects for which precious metal was not specifically prescribed.

Early Christian. Practically no large bronze statuary has been preserved from the Early Christian period. There are documentary references, however, to a fountain with the Good Shepherd in Constantinople and to a group with Christ and the woman with an issue of blood in Panaea (Cana). Smaller utensils such as oil lamps, chandeliers, candlesticks, and thuribles and amulets, rings, and pectoral crosses have been preserved in great numbers. These were produced and disseminated primarily in the countries of the eastern Mediterranean.

Byzantine and Romanesque. The most important medieval examples of large-scale bronze casting are doors, monuments, baptismal fonts, and candlesticks. The 9th-century church doors of St. Sophia in Constantinople have no decoration except archaicized profiles or lion heads, but seven Byzantine portals from the 11th century in Italian churches have panels with the figures of individual saints in silver. The oldest doors with relief representations date from the early 11th century (Hildesheim, Augsburg). In Italy nine 12th-century doors, most of them signed by their creators, have been preserved (Pisa, Verona, Troia, Trani, Ravello, Monreale, Benevento). From the same period are the doors with relief decoration in Gniezno and Novgorod. The few 12th-century funeral monuments that survive show the picture of the deceased. The monumental tablet of Rudolf of Swabia in Merseburg dates from the 11th century; the tablets of Archbishops Friedrich and Wichmann in Magdeburg belong to the 12th century. There are a few isolated examples of monumental crosses and crucifixes (Werden, Minden). The fine baptismal font in Lüttich is probably the work of *Renier of Huy; other fonts are in Salzburg, Hildesheim, and Bremen.

Among the outstanding bronzes of this period are the great seven-branched candelabra, the oldest of which, in Essen, is almost entirely devoid of decorative figures. The 12th- and 13th-century specimens in Reims, Prague, and Milan are heavily adorned with human figures, animals, and foliage. In the 12th century it became the custom to place upon the altar a cross and two or more candlesticks; many bronzes of this type have been preserved, and they are of high artistic value. The 12th and 13th centuries also produced thuribles decorated with beautiful scrollwork and lavabos in the form of lions and other animals. A few figured pails for blessed water also survive.

Gothic. The shape of bronzes in the later Middle Ages was conditioned by forms taken over from architecture. There is a plethora of objects still in existence, especially in Belgium, Holland, Germany, and the Scandinavian countries: altar candlesticks of various sizes, monumental paschal candelabra, chandeliers, eagle lecterns, tabernacles, choir and chapel lattices, and especially baptismal fonts and bells. Fountains and free-standing monuments, such as that in Prague, are less common. Bronze monuments to clerics and laymen occur in central Europe (Cologne, Augsburg, Lübeck), but they are found more frequently in England (London, Canterbury, Warwick) and France (Paris, Amiens, Saint-Denis). More widespread are the carved brass funeral

(a)

(b)

(c)

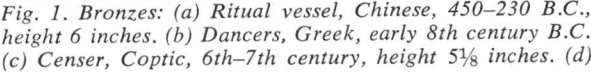

(d)

Fig. 1. Bronzes: (a) Ritual vessel, Chinese, 450–230 B.C., height 6 inches. (b) Dancers, Greek, early 8th century B.C. (c) Censer, Coptic, 6th–7th century, height 5⅛ inches. (d)

"The Charioteer of Delphi," from the Sanctuary of Apollo at Delphi, c. 470 B.C., now in the Museum at Delphi, Greece, height 71 inches.

(b)

(c)

Fig. 2. Bronzes: (a) Tomb relief of Rudolph of Swabia, German, 11th century, in the cathedral at Merseberg. (b) "Madonna and Child with Four Angels," medallion at- *tributed to Donatello, 15th century, diameter 8⅔ inches. (c) Altar portrait of a dead king, Nigeria, Benin, probably 17th century, height 11¾ inches.*

Fig. 3. Bronzes: (a) Jacques Lipchitz, "Notre-Dame-de-Liesse," 1955, in the church at Assy, France, height about 6 feet. (b) Alberto Giacometti, "Quatre Figurines sur un Socle," 1950, height 31 inches. (c) Jean Antoine Houdon (1741–1828), "The Countess Thelusson as a Vestal Virgin," height 33 inches.

tablets from Flanders, with the picture of the deceased set in an architectonic frame of figures of saints.

Renaissance. After the Middle Ages, altar appurtenances were no longer made of bronze but rather of silver and gold or gilt copper. The art of bronze casting flourished in Italy, where in the first half of the 14th century, A. *Pisano made a door for the Florence baptistery. In the early 15th century two magnificent doors were added by L. *Ghiberti, who also made statues and shrines in Florence and worked on reliefs for the baptismal fonts in Siena, as did Della *Quercia and *Donatello. The high altar in the Chiesa del Santo in Padua was richly adorned with statues and reliefs by Donatello, who did also the chancels and doors in S. Lorenzo in Florence. The bronze treasures of Rome include monuments to several popes by eminent artists: Martin V (G. Ghini), Sixtus IV and Innocent VIII (A. *Pollaiuolo), Paul III (G. della *Porta), Innocent X (A. Algardi), and Urban VIII (L. *Bernini). There are bronzes by the Sansovini and by T. Aspetti, A. Lombardi, and A. Riccio in Venice, Padua, and other cities. Members of the Leoni family worked in Lombardy and Spain. Belgium also has important monuments in Antwerp and Bruges. In Germany, the output of brass monuments was dominated by the Vischer family, resident in Nuremberg; they created especially fine monuments in Magdeburg, Cracow, and Wittenberg. Their masterpiece is the Sebaldus Tomb in Nuremberg. The Vischer foundry also collaborated on the most impressive bronze monument of the time, the Emperor Maximilian monument in Innsbruck. Although, from the 17th century on, bronze was supplanted generally by stone and plaster, the remarkable "Madonna columns" were still being erected in public squares in south Germany and Austria.

Bibliography: Technical. L. AITCHISON, *A History of Metals*, 2 v. (New York 1960). H. LÜER, *Technik der Bronzeplastik* (Leipzig 1902). A. J. G. VERSTER, *Brons in den tijd* (Amsterdam 1956). F. SCHOTTMÜLLER, *Bronze Statuetten und Geräte* (2d ed. Berlin 1921).
Historical. Medieval. A. GOLDSCHMIDT, *Die deutschen Bronzetüren des frühen Mittelalters* (Marburg 1926). H. LEISINGER, *Romanesque Bronzes: Church Portals in Medieval Europe* (London 1956). O. VON FALKE and E. MEYER, *Romanische Leuchter und Gefässe* (Berlin 1935). P. BLOCH, *Siebenarmige Leuchter in christlichen Kirchen* (Cologne 1962). A. BOECKLER, *Die Bronzetüren des Bonanus von Pisa und des Barisanus von Trani* (Berlin 1953). W. F. CREENY, *A Book of Facsimiles of Monumental Brasses* (London 1884). Renaissance. L. PLANISCIG, *Piccoli bronzi italiani del Rinascimento* (Milan 1930). W. VON BODE, *The Italian Bronze Statuettes of the Renaissance,* tr. W. GRÉTOR, 3 v. (London 1908–12). E. F. BANGE, *Die deutschen Bronzestatuetten des 16. Jahrhunderts* (Berlin 1949). **Illustration credits:** Fig. 1*a,* The Minneapolis Institute of Arts, Bequest, 1950, Alfred J. Pillsbury. Fig. 1*b,* National Archaeological Museum, Athens. Fig. 1*c,* Courtesy of the Brooklyn Museum. Fig. 1*d,* Hirmer Verlag München. Fig. 2*a,* Marburg-Art Reference Bureau. Fig. 2*b,* National Gallery of Art, Washington, D.C., Samuel H. Kress Collection. Fig. 2*c,* The Cleveland Museum of Art, Dudley P. Allen Fund. Fig. 3*b,* Collection of Museum of Art, Carnegie Institute, Pittsburgh. Fig. 3*c,* Courtesy of the Detroit Institute of Arts.
[E. MEYER]

BRONZINO, ANGELO, or Agnolo, Florentine painter and poet, whose fame rests on a portraiture distinguished for the elegance and hauteur of his sitters; b. Monticelli, 1503; d. Florence, 1572. His known teachers were Raffaellino del Garbo and Jacopo da *Pontormo, whom he assisted in the decorations of the Certosa del Galluzzo (1522–25) and the Medicean villas at Careggi and Castello (1536–42). Bronzino also executed easel paintings of religious and allegorical

Bronzino, portrait of Guidobaldo da Montefeltro, oil on canvas, in the Galleria Palatina at Florence.

subjects and cartoons for tapestries. His style, which has been described as mannerist, was acquired essentially from Pontormo, but there is in it also a cold and sedate reflection of Michelangelo. It is characterized by a clarity and firmness of drawing tending toward relief, a simplification of planes and volumes, and, with rare exceptions, a disinterest in the representation of space, the emphasis being on the human figure. In color, it is pallid and almost frigid .

See also MANNERISM.

Bibliography: Vasari. H. G. A. VOSS, *Die Malerei der Spätrenaissance in Rom und Florenz,* 2 v. (Berlin 1920) 1:208–231. A. McCOMB, *Agnolo Bronzino: His Life and Works* (Cambridge, Mass. 1928). L. BECHERUCCI, *Manieristi toscani* (Bergamo 1944) 42–51. C. H. SMYTH, "The Earliest Works of B.," ArtBull 31 (1949) 184–210; *Bronzino Studies* (Doctoral diss. unpub. Princeton U. 1955). A. EMILIANI, *Il Bronzino* (Busto Arsizio 1960). **Illustration credit:** Alinari-Art Reference Bureau.
[L. P. LEITE]

BROOK FARM, a religious experiment in communal living (1841–47) at West Roxbury, near Boston, Mass. It was founded by George Ripley, a Boston Unitarian minister and Transcendentalist, and his wife, Sophia Dana Ripley, to manifest in miniature the Transcendental belief in a new world in which each man might develop his own talents according to the norms of individualism and self-reliance. Each member was to enjoy complete freedom as long as he did not trespass on the rights of others. Although it is not certain that the new association was consciously socialistic, it is clear that the founders did envisage a new attitude toward manual labor and the creation of a utopian society. As one of the Brook Farm students expressed it: "No Adventist ever believed more absolutely in the coming of Christ than we in the reorganization of society on a fraternal basis."

At Brook Farm all domestic work was divided among the members of the society. At first farming occupied most of the men, but when the land proved unproductive because of the lack of tools and skills, the community turned to manufacturing. Carpenters, shoemakers, and printers plied their trade, and Isaac *Hecker worked for a while as a baker. All labor was paid at the rate of $1 per day. Room, board, and clothing were supplied practically at cost. The work week was 48 hours during the winter and 60 hours in summer. But it was in the field of education that Brook Farm truly excelled. The curriculum of the community school was well organized and included mathematics, classics, history, literature, modern languages, philosophy, botany, drawing, dancing, and music. Faculty and students lived together, with frequent contacts between teacher and pupil. There were no specific study hours, emphasis being put on the need for personal responsibility. Each student worked at least 2 hours a day at manual labor, and all were called upon to work in the kitchen or wait on table. Famous visitors, including Ralph Waldo Emerson, Margaret Fuller, Orestes Brownson, Robert Owen, Horace Greeley, and Elizabeth Peabody, furthered the students' education by informal conversations, lectures, and dialogues. Many of the New England intelligentsia sent their sons there after the Harvard faculty especially recommended the Brook Farm school as an excellent place to prepare for college.

If it had concentrated on education, Brook Farm might have prospered, but its founders were more interested in universal reform. When the works of Charles Fourier, the French Socialist, were published in the U.S., Brook Farm turned itself into a Fourierist phalanx (1844), with little change in its original constitution. For the next 4 years it published the *Harbinger*, an important socialist paper that kept the community in debt. Meanwhile, the school was neglected as missionaries went out to teach socialism. After a fire destroyed a new and uninsured central building (March 1846), the community decided to disband and to auction all its assets to pay the heavy debts.

Bibliography: E. R. CURTIS, *A Season in Utopia* (New York 1961). K. K. BURTON, *Paradise Planters: The Story of Brook Farm* (New York 1939). A. F. TYLER, *Freedom's Ferment* (Minneapolis 1944).

[E. DELANEY]

BROOKES, JAMES (BROOKS), Roman Catholic bishop of Gloucester (1554–59); b. Hampshire, May 1512; d. Gloucester, February 1560. Brookes, educated at Oxford, received his doctor of divinity degree in 1546 and the following year was made master of Balliol College. He served also as chaplain and almoner of Stephen Gardiner, Bishop of Winchester. He was appointed bishop of Gloucester, replacing the deposed John Hooper in 1554. As papal subdelegate in the trials of *Cranmer, *Ridley, and *Latimer, he refrained from degrading the last two, although he zealously supported their conviction and execution. He was an eloquent preacher, a number of whose sermons appear in Foxe's *Acts and Monuments*. With the accession of Elizabeth in 1558, Brookes was deprived of his see because he refused to take the oath of royal supremacy over the Church. He was cast into prison, where he died. Since

Gloucester was created a see in 1541 by Henry VIII, Brookes was the first and last bishop of Gloucester in communion with Rome.

Bibliography: T. COOPER, DNB 2:1346–47. P. HUGHES, *Rome and the Counter-Reformation in England* (London 1942). L. B. SMITH, *Tudor Prelates and Politics* (Princeton 1953). DictEng Cath 1:315–316.

[M. R. O'CONNELL]

BROOKLYN, DIOCESE OF (BROOKLYNIENSIS)

Suffragan of the metropolitan See of New York, embracing the boroughs of Brooklyn and Queens in New York City. It has an area of 179 square miles and a total population (1964) of about 4½ million, of whom approximately 34 per cent were Catholics. The diocese, originally including the four counties of Long Island, was established by Pius IX on July 29, 1853. The area had previously been under the successive ecclesiastical jurisdiction of London, Baltimore, and New York. In 1957 the Diocese of Rockville Centre, embracing the two eastern counties of Long Island, was created and the Brooklyn Diocese was thus limited to the two western counties.

Early History. The first Mass in the area may have been celebrated by Philip Lariscy, an Irish-born Augustinian, probably in 1821, in a private house owned by William Purcell. Until then, Catholics in the village of Brooklyn crossed the East River to New York to attend Mass. In 1822 a group of Catholic tradesmen, led by Peter Turner, organized the Roman Catholic Society, purchased ground for a church and cemetery, and invited Bp. John Connolly, of New York, to consecrate the Gothic edifice they had erected. The church, consecrated on Aug. 23, 1823, was dedicated to St. James and was the sixth Catholic church in New York State and the third in what is now the City of New York. After the establishment of the Diocese of Brooklyn, it became the procathedral.

Diocese. After Connolly died, Brooklyn was subject to the jurisdiction of his successor, Bp. John Dubois, until his death in 1842, and then to Bp. John Hughes, who presided over the affairs of the Church in the area until 1853 when Brooklyn was made a diocese. The first bishop of Brooklyn was John *Loughlin, who died in 1891; he was succeeded by a New York priest, Charles E. McDonnell, in 1892. When McDonnell died in 1921, he was succeeded by his auxiliary, Thomas E. *Molloy, who died in 1956. Molloy was granted the title of archbishop *ad personam* in 1951. In 1957 Bp. Bryan J. McEntegart became the diocese's fourth ordinary; he received the personal title of archbishop in 1966. Two American cardinals, Abp. John *McCloskey of New York and Abp. George W. *Mundelein of Chicago, had Brooklyn associations: Cardinal McCloskey was born there, and Cardinal Mundelein lived there as a young man and became a priest and auxiliary bishop of the diocese. Others who served as auxiliaries include Raymond A. Kearney, John J. Boardman, Edmund J. Reilly, Charles R. Mulrooney, and Joseph P. Denning.

Since Brooklyn is on New York harbor, port of entry for millions of immigrants, the population of the diocese has always been racially diverse. In each period the varied ethnic groups have required the services of priests capable of speaking their languages. While some priests accompanied the immigrants from their home countries,

Bishop John Loughlin.

the bishops of Brooklyn attempted to supplement their ministrations by calling on foreign language provinces of religious communities. In addition, clergy native to the diocese have learned the languages of their congregations.

Growth. The rapidly rising population required an ever increasing supply of priests. In 1891 Loughlin established St. John's Seminary, staffed by priests of the Congregation of the Mission (*see* VINCENTIANS). This institution served the diocese until Molloy opened the Seminary of the Immaculate Conception in Huntington, N.Y., in 1930. McDonnell established a preparatory seminary, Cathedral College, in 1914. However, these institutions were supplemented by numerous other seminaries both in Europe and the U.S. By the 1960s the diocese had 1 diocesan priest for every 1,600 Catholics. In addition, there were 10 communities of religious priests, many of whom were engaged in teaching or other extraparochial work. In the same period, more than 500 brothers and 4,000 sisters worked in the diocese.

Although parish schools had existed previously, the diocesan educational system began with the appointment of the first inspector of schools in 1893. The constantly increasing population demanded a corresponding expansion in schools, so that by the second half of the 20th century the diocese had the second largest parochial elementary school system in the U.S. This was followed by an increasing emphasis on high school construction that reached a climax in 1960 when approximately $40 million was raised in a diocesan fund drive, largely for secondary education. *St. John's University, under the Vincentians, was opened as a high school and college in 1870 and received its university charter in 1933. *St. Francis College, a Franciscan institution, opened as an

academy in 1859 and was empowered to grant degrees in 1884. *St. Joseph's College for Women, conducted by the Sisters of St. Joseph, opened in 1916 and received its permanent charter in 1929.

The diocese long manifested a deep interest in the foreign missions by supplying numerous vocations to the missionary communities. In the quarter century following 1935, Brooklyn Catholics also contributed more than $30 million to the Society for the *Propagation of the Faith.

In 1908 the *Tablet* was founded in the diocese as a Catholic weekly. Its circulation reached 165,000 by 1960, and its readers included thousands of subscribers outside the diocese. Diocesan priests also published an Italian language newspaper called *Il Crociato*. The Confraternity of the Precious Blood issued a series of liturgical and devotional books in compact, inexpensive format. The troops in World War II helped to popularize "Father Stedman's Sunday Missal," and in 3 decades the organization had distributed over 36 million copies of its publications.

Bibliography: J. K. SHARP, *History of the Diocese of Brooklyn, 1853–1953,* 2 v. (New York 1954).

[F. E. FITZPATRICK]

BROOKS, PHILLIPS, Protestant Episcopal Bishop of Massachusetts; b. Boston, Mass., Dec. 13, 1835; d. Boston, Jan. 23, 1893. He was educated at Boston Latin School, Harvard University, and the Virginia Theological Seminary, Alexandria, Va., and was ordained in 1860. He served as rector of Holy Trinity Church, Philadelphia, Pa., before accepting a call to Trinity Church, Boston, in 1869. During this period he combated racial prejudice and advocated full citizenship rights for Negroes. At Trinity Church he won renown as a pulpit orator and frequently preached in churches of other denominations. In his sermons and particularly in the Bohlen lectures, published as *The Influence of Jesus* in 1879, Brooks stressed personal devotion and regarded dogmatic questions as of little importance. His views incited considerable opposition when he was consecrated bishop of Massachusetts in 1891.

Bibliography: A. V. G. ALLEN, *Life and Letters of Phillips Brooks,* 2 v. (New York 1900). W. LAWRENCE, *Life of Phillips Brooks* (New York 1930).

[R. K. MAC MASTER]

BROSIG, MORITZ, church composer and teacher; b. Fuchswinkel, Upper Silesia, Oct. 15, 1815; d. Breslau, Lower Silesia (now Poland), Jan. 24, 1887. After schooling in the Breslau Gymnasium, he began organ and harmony studies with Joseph Wolf in the Breslau cathedral. He became cathedral music director in 1853, and was appointed to the faculty of the University of Breslau in 1871. Meanwhile there developed around him a following of Silesian composers who reacted against Caecilian restrictions on instrumentally accompanied church music (*see* CAECILIAN MOVEMENT) and attempted to exploit 19th-century sonorities and techniques in their own creative work. His concern for the sung Propers of the Mass is apparent in his 7 volumes of Graduals and Offertories. He also published 7 concerted Masses and 20 volumes of organ pieces consisting of preludes, fugues, and chorale preludes. Among his theoretical works are a *Modulations theorie* (1866), *Handbuch der Harmonielehre und Modulation* (1874,

1879), and *Über die Alten Kirchen Kompositionen und ihre Wiedereinführung* (1880).

Bibliography: M. Brosig, *Ausgewählte Orgel-compositionen,* ed. P. Claussnitzer, 5 v. (Leipzig 1905). Kornmüller. Riemann 1:234. Fellerer CathChMus.

[F. J. MOLECK]

BROTHER, RELIGIOUS. According to the original and most generic meaning of the term, a professed member of an institute of religious men. In the beginnings of monasticism, both in the East and West, the notion of brotherhood or fraternity was paramount. The distinction between cleric and noncleric was little emphasized, since among the *monks the minority were priests, sufficient usually for the spiritual needs of the community.

With the rise of the *mendicant orders in the 13th century, this notion of brotherhood was retained since all the members of the first order were *fratres.* However, since the majority of the *friars either were priests or were destined for the priesthood, the distinction between the clerical and nonclerical groups assumed a greater importance, the latter retaining the title of brother or laybrother. The same distinction was adopted by clerical institutes established in subsequent centuries.

In common usage and in the most restricted meaning, the term religious brother designates a professed male religious who is a member of a lay community, i.e., one in which none or at the most a minority of the members are priests or aspirants to the priestly state (CIC c.488n4). The members of these institutes are true religious in the canonical sense of the term, but they are designated as "lay" to distinguish them from an essentially clerical community.

An institute of religious brothers may be established as an order wherein the members take solemn vows or as a congregation in which simple vows are professed (CIC c.488n2). An example of the former is the Hospitaller Order of St. John of God founded for the care of the sick and infirm. In this order, according to the needs of the community, some of the members are advanced to the priesthood. The greater number of institutes of religious brothers, however, are congregations dedicated to some specific apostolate, such as the work of education by the Brothers of the Christian Schools and the Brothers of St. Francis Xavier, or the care of the sick by the Brothers of Mercy and the Alexian Brothers.

Bibliography: T. Schäfer, *De religiosis ad normam codicis iuris canonici* (4th ed. Rome 1947).

[W. B. RYAN]

BROTHER IN CHRIST, an appellation referring to the specifically Christian unity, of which Christ Himself is the center and criterion and to which the Synoptic tradition witnesses (Mk 3.31–35; 10.29–30). It is by *faith and the doing of the Father's will that one becomes a brother of Jesus (Mt 12.46–50; 21.28–32). By His death and Resurrection Jesus has become in the fullest sense "the firstborn among many brethren" (Rom 8.29; see FIRSTBORN), reconciling divided humanity in His Body on the cross (Eph 2.11–18). It is the risen Lord who calls His Apostles truly His "brothers" (Mt 28.10; Jn 20.17), and in them all men without exception. This Christian concept of brotherhood is found in a strongly

ecclesial context in Matthew, ch. 18 (see especially v. 15, 21, 35). To live as a brother is the specifically Christian way to live as a part of the community, to share in its common life. Brothers in Christ must show one another a tender, devoted love modeled on the sacrificial love that Christ showed His own (Jn 13.1, 15, 34–35; 15.12–13; 1 Jn 2.10–11; 3.10, 16, 17; 5.16; Rom 14.10, 13, 15; 1 Cor 6.6, 8; 8.11–13). Although the love of a Christian brother must take in all men without exception (1 Thes 3.12; 2 Pt 1.7), the visible community of the Christian brotherhood is the special field for that privileged form of love called *philadelphia* (φιλαδελφία: Rom 12.10; 1 Thes 4.9; Heb 13.1; 1 Pt 1.22–23; 2 Pt 1.7).

The early Christians soon adopted the term brother as their usual mode of addressing one another (30 times in Acts and 130 times in Paul), and the name remained in common use among Christians in general until late in the 3d century, when its use was gradually restricted to clerical and monastic circles.

See also MYSTICAL BODY OF CHRIST; SOCIETY (IN THEOLOGY); UNITY OF FAITH; UNITY OF THE CHURCH; EXCOMMUNICATION.

Bibliography: K. H. Schelkle, "Bruder," ReallexAntChr 2: 631–640. J. Ratzinger, *Die christliche Brüderlichkeit* (Munich 1960).

[F. X. LAWLOR]

BROTHERS AND SISTERS OF THE FREE SPIRIT, a name given in the 13th century to certain followers of idealistic pantheism. This ancient inheritance had received a rejuvenating impetus from the works of the Neoplatonist *Proclus and of *John Scotus Erigena, and found adherents in practically every Christian country throughout the Middle Ages. The name in the above title was widely used by pantheistic groups in Central Europe between the 12th and 15th centuries. In Italy, too, the name was known, as is evident from the early 14th-century investigation conducted by *Ubertino of Casale in Tuscany, Spoleto, and Ancona. The link sometimes indicated between the "brethren" and the followers of *Amalric of Bène and Ortlieb of Strasbourg (see ORTLIBARII) is doubtful. But they shared in common the central idea of the "Free Spirit," i.e., a licentious intellect, incapable of any wrong, and bearing the spark of an all-pervading divinity. *Albert the Great, while serving as bishop of Regensburg, compiled a list of the main tenets of the group: all creatures are identical with the Creator; man is capable of becoming God; there is no resurrection from the dead; man transformed into God is incapable of sin. They were opposed by J. *Tauler, *Henry Suso, J. *Ruysbroeck, G. *Groote, and Jean *Gerson. The doctrines of the brethren were never extinguished in some parts of the Netherlands, Germany, and Bohemia, and they may have been the origin of the teachings of the *Anabaptists in Germany in the early 16th century.

Bibliography: R. Allier, *Les Frères du libre esprit* (Paris 1905). H. Grundmann, *Religiöse Bewegungen im Mittelalter* (Berlin 1935). F. Vernet, DTC 6.1:800–809. G. Mollat, *Catholicisme* 4:1630. O. Rühle, RGG³ 1:1433–34.

[B. CHUDOBA]

BROTHERS OF CHRISTIAN INSTRUCTION OF PLOËRMEL, sometimes called La Mennais Brothers (*Institutum Fratrum Instructionis Christianae de Ploërmel*, FIC), a religious congregation with papal approval (1891, 1910) that emerged from the union in 1820 of a group in Brittany founded by Gabriel *Deshayes in 1816 at Auray with another started by Jean de *La Mennais in 1819 at St. Brieuc. La Mennais administered the congregation until his death (1860), when the direction passed to a superior general and six assistants. The original apostolate of teaching in elementary schools was later extended to include agricultural, commercial, and nautical education. Secondary education was undertaken, and eventually college instruction. Missions were undertaken by 1837. In 1860 membership numbered 937, and in 1903 was 2,200. French laic laws then reduced membership in France to 500, and total membership dropped to 1,030. In 1963 there were more than 2,200 brothers, who staffed 285 schools with 85,430 students in France, Tahiti (since 1859), Haiti (1864), Canada (1886), Spain, England, U.S. (1903), Italy (1921), Uganda and Tanganyika (1926), Argentina (1933), Seychelles Islands (1950), Uruguay and Japan (1951). The first school in the U.S. opened in Plattsburgh, N.Y. (1903). Twenty brothers assisted the Jesuits in their work on the Indian reservations of Idaho, Montana, and Alaska from 1903 to 1910. In 1963 junior and senior high schools, enrolling more than 2,000 students, were staffed by 120 brothers in Plattsburgh, N.Y.; Fall River, Mass.; Biddeford and Sanford, Maine; Detroit, Mich.; and Canton, Ohio. *Walsh College was founded in Canton, Ohio, in 1960. In 1946 a separate American province was organized with headquarters at Alfred, Maine. The generalate was in Ploërmel, France, from 1824 until 1904, when it was transferred to Jersey, in the Channel Islands.

Bibliography: A. P. LAVEILLE, *Jean-Marie de La Mennais, 1780–1860*, 2 v. (Paris 1903). H. C. RULON and P. FRIOT, *Un Siècle de pédagogie dans les écoles primaires, 1820–1940* (Paris 1962).

[E. G. DROUIN]

BROTHERS OF CHRISTIAN INSTRUCTION OF ST. GABRIEL,

or Brothers of St. Gabriel (*Institutum Fratrum Instructionis Christianae a Sancto Gabriele*, FSG), a religious congregation devoted to education. For a long time there was question whether Gabriel *Deshayes merely restored a group that had been started in 1705 by St. Louis *Grignion de Montfort or founded a new institute in 1821 at Saint-Laurent-sur-Sèvre (Vendée), France. A study by the historical section of the Congregation of Rites supported the latter conclusion [ActApS 39 (1947) 240–241]. Until 1853 members were known as the Brothers of the Holy Ghost. In France, when Justin Émile *Combes caused the closing of schools run by religious (1903), the bishop of Luçon suppressed the Brothers of St. Gabriel, still a diocesan congregation. After subsequent reorganization it became a papally approved institute (1910). The original apostolate of teaching in elementary schools soon came to include instruction for the deaf, mute, and blind, especially in France. Later the brothers engaged in secondary education and in teacher training. The congregation spread to Canada (1888), Belgium and Gabon (1900), Thailand (1901), England, Spain, Madagascar, and India (1903), Italy (1904), Congo (Léopoldville, 1928), Malaysia (1952), Senegal (1954), Congo (Brazzaville, 1955), Republic of South Africa (1957), U.S. (1958), Colombia (1961), and Peru (1962). In 1963 the congregation had 1,720 professed brothers, 217 schools, and 93,630 students. Four members resided in the U.S., at Des Plaines, Ill.

Bibliography: A. BLAIN, *Institut des Frères de l'Instruction Chrétienne de St-Gabriel* (Poitiers 1897). E. GOUIN, "Les Frères de St-Gabriel au Canada, 1888–1913," *La Revue Canadienne* NS 12 (Sept. 1913) 193–206. *Nova inquisitio super dubio: An B. Ludovicus M. Grignion de Montfort historice haberi possit uti fundator . . . Fratrum Instructionis Christianae a S. Gabriele* (S. Rituum Congregatio, Sectio Historica 66; Vatican City 1947). G. Löw, EncCatt 5:1706–07.

[E. G. DROUIN]

BROTHERS OF JESUS

There are various places in the NT where reference is made to the relatives of Our Lord. "Is not this the carpenter, the son of Mary, the brother of James, Joseph, Jude, and Simon? And are not also his sisters here with us?" (Mk 6.3; cf. Mt 13.55–56). In Jn 2.12; 7.3,5,10; and Acts 1.14 mention is made of "His brethren." St. Paul calls James "the brother of the Lord" (Gal 1.19). The Synoptics speak of "His mother and His brethren" who came to see Him as He was preaching (Mt 12.46–50; Mk 3.21–25; Lk 8.19–21; see also 1 Cor 9.5). In all languages the words "brother," "brethren," and "sister" are used in the strict sense of blood relatives as well as in the broader sense of some one or ones united in a religious or other common bond. The same is true of the Sacred Scriptures. Our Lord Himself used the terms in reference to those who are united to Him through the fulfillment of the will of God (Mt 12.46–50). Paul and his group "greeted the brethren," that is, the Christians, at Ptolemais (Acts 21.7). In the OT the word "brother" is used by Abraham in reference to his nephew Lot (Gn 14.14). While the names of the so-called "sisters" are not given in the NT, four "brothers" are named: James, Joseph, Jude, and Simon. Three of these names occur in the list of the Apostles (Mt 10.2–4; Mk 3.14–19; Lk 6.12–16; Acts 1.13), with one, namely, that of James, being given twice. There is little doubt that "James of Alphaeus, and Simon called the zealot; Jude the brother of James (Lk 6.14–16)" are the ones called the brothers of Our Lord. Paul's reference to "James the brother of the Lord" (Gal 1.19) is most likely to the Apostle, James of Alphaeus. *See* JAMES (SON OF ALPHAEUS), ST.

Of these listed, James and Joseph are called the sons of Mary, one of the women mentioned in the story of the passion, death, and resurrection of Our Lord (Mt 27.56,61; 28.1; Mk 15.40,47; Lk 24.10). This Mary cannot be the Mother of Jesus; some, however, identify her as "His mother's sister" who stood at the foot of the cross (Jn 19.25). She may thus be the same as the "Mary of Cleopas" mentioned in this text, as some scholars hold. It is possible that *Cleopas, or Clopas, is another spelling of Alphaeus. If so, then the conclusion is that James and Joseph, as well as Simon and Jude (although there is more doubt about these two), are the sons of Mary and Cleopas, otherwise known as Alphaeus. Another opinion would make Cleopas the brother of Joseph, the foster father of Our Lord. There is no probability to the theory of the *Protoevangelium Jacobi*, Origen, and Ambrosiaster (PL 17:344–345) that "the brothers of Jesus" were the children of Joseph by an earlier marriage. The variety of opinions is an indication that the texts in the NT mentioning "brothers and sisters and brethren" of Our Lord cannot be used to pinpoint their relationship.

Sacred Scripture is very definite about Mary being a virgin when she conceived Jesus (Mt 1.18–25; Lk 1.26–27; 2.7). He is the firstborn, a term meaning the first "to open the womb" without any implication of other children to follow. The very definiteness with which Our Lord is called "the son of Mary" (Mk 6.3) would seem to point to an only son. From the cross Our Lord charged John, the beloved Apostle, with the care of His Mother, which would have been a strange action if she had other sons.

The NT writings are the products of men who were the first members of the Church established by Christ. They are inspired in their teaching and preaching; they reflect what the early Church believed. It is by placing these writings into the background of the Church that we are able to understand them and interpret them; in this way light is thrown on the NT text concerning the problem of the "brothers of Jesus," which involves the perpetual virginity of Our Blessed Mother, a doctrine of the Church. The Church from its earliest days taught that Mary was always a virgin. In view of this, then, there can be no doubt that Mary did not have any other children; therefore the "brothers and sisters" mentioned in the NT cannot be the blood brothers and sisters of Our Lord.

Bibliography: F. PRAT, "La Parenté de Jésus," RechScRel 17 (1927) 127–138. J. BLINZLER, "Zum Problem der Brüder des Herrn," TrierThZ 67 (1958) 129–145, 224–246. M. J. LAGRANGE, *Évangile selon S. Marc* (4th ed. Paris 1947) 79–93. J. J. COLLINS, "The Brethren of the Lord and Two Recently Published Papyri," ThSt 5 (1944) 484–494.

[G. H. GUYOT]

BROU, ALEXANDRE, Jesuit spiritual writer and historian of the missions; b. Chartres, April 26, 1862; d. Laval, France, March 12, 1947. He entered the Society of Jesus in 1880, and after completing his studies, made for the most part in England, he taught literature at Canterbury (1894–97, 1907–10, 1920–23), on the Isle of Jersey (1902–06, 1911–19), and at Laval (1899–1901, 1924). He was a man of broad and scholarly interests, but his most outstanding writings were in the fields of the mission history of the Far East and Ignatian spirituality. He wrote numerous articles on St. Francis Xavier and Matteo Ricci for *Les Études,* with whose editorial staff he was associated until his death. His monograph *S. François Xavier: Conditions et méthodes de son apostolat* (Bruges 1925) illustrates his basic insight in relating spiritual principles and practical method in mission apostolate. An earlier study, *S. François Xavier* (2 v. Paris 1914), was a landmark in accurate hagiography. The same happy blend of sound scholarship and historical sense is likewise found in Brou's writings on Jesuit spirituality. His study of the Jansenist controversy, for example, in *Les Jésuites de la légende* (Paris 1906–07), is a mine of historical information. Notable among his other works are: *Les Exercices spirituels de S. Ignace, histoire et psychologie* (Paris 1922); *La Spiritualité de S. Ignace* (Paris 1914), tr. W. Young, *The Ignatian Way to God* (Milwaukee 1952); *S. Ignace, maître d'oraison* (Paris 1925), tr. W. Young, *Ignatian Methods of Prayer* (Milwaukee 1949).

Bibliography: M. SCADUTO and E. LAMALLE, ArchHistSocIesu 16 (1947) 223–225, with complete chronological bibliog. of his works. *Index bibliographicus Societatis Iesu,* ed. J. JUAMBELZ (Rome 1938–), for works 1937–50.

[T. J. JOYCE]

BROUILLET, JOHN, Indian missionary; b. near Montreal, Quebec, Canada, Dec. 11, 1813; d. Washington, D.C., Feb. 5, 1884. He was educated at St. Hyacinth College, Quebec, and was ordained Aug. 27, 1837. Ten years later he joined Bp. Augustine M. Blanchet in establishing the Diocese of Walla Walla in Oregon Territory. As vicar-general he began his long missionary career at Nesqually and established the mission of Umatilla. He was in the vicinity of Marcus J. Whitman's Presbyterian mission among the Cayuse Indians when they massacred the minister and his family in 1847. Whitman's associate, Henry H. Spalding, was spared the same fate by Brouillet's timely warning. Spalding, nevertheless, accused Brouillet and other Catholics of being responsible for the attack. A national controversy ensued; Brouillet was not fully vindicated for many years, in spite of his own authoritative book on the matter.

Blanchet and his brother, the bishop of Oregon City, named Brouillet to settle difficulties arising from Pres. U. S. Grant's peace policy, which began in 1868. Brouillet called attention to the inequities to Catholic missions in governmental assignments and the lack of free access to Catholic Indians by their missionaries. In 1872 he went to Washington as legal representative of the two bishops and early became an adviser to Gen. Charles Ewing, Catholic commissioner for Indian affairs. The Grant policy was soon revised in favor of Brouillet's views. Shortly before his death he became director of the Bureau of Indian Missions, largely his own creation. Previous to this he had fostered various missionary aid associations, often in the face of apathy and militant opposition. In 1879 at Rome he won from Leo XIII a recommendation to the American bishops for the bureau's unified program. When the Third Plenary Council of Baltimore authorized an annual collection in all dioceses, continued existence of the bureau was assured.

Bibliography: P. J. RAHILL, *The Catholic Indian Missions and Grant's Peace Policy 1870–1884* (Washington 1953).

[T. O. HANLEY]

BROUN, MATTHEW HEYWOOD CAMPBELL, author; b. Brooklyn, N.Y., Dec. 7, 1888; d. New York City, Dec. 19, 1939. He was the son of Heywood Cox and Henriette (Brosé) Broun. After study at the Horace Mann School, New York City, he attended Harvard until 1910, when he embarked upon a career as a reporter with the New York *Morning Telegraph.* He joined the New York *Tribune* as a sportswriter (1912), and was later sent to France as a war correspondent (1917). Upon his return to the U.S. (1919), he served as the *Tribune's* literary and drama critic until 1921, when he joined the staff of the New York *World.* Broun's daily column in the *World,* "It Seems to Me," dealt with such highly controversial issues as the Socialist Eugene V. Debs, the *Ku Klux Klan, and the Sacco-Vanzetti Case. His defense of Sacco and Vanzetti, Italian anarchists whose execution (1927) aroused worldwide sympathy demonstrations, led to Broun's dismissal, but he continued his column in Roy Howard's New York *World-Telegram* after 1931. The year before he had joined the Socialist party, running unsuccessfully for Congress. Three years later he organized the newspaper employees' union, the American Newspaper Guild, which he served as president. Following the death (1934) of his first wife, Ruth Hale, Broun married Connie Madison, a dancer. He subsequently decided to become a Catholic, and he was baptized by Rev. (later Bp.) Fulton J. Sheen on May 23, 1939. Broun's publications include *Seeing Things at Night* (1921) and *Pieces of Hate* (1922), selections from his newspaper columns; *The Boy Grew Older* (1926), an autobiographical novel; *The Sun Field* (1923); *Gandle Follows His Nose* (1926); and studies of censorship, *Anthony Comstock* (1927); and of anti-Semitism, *Christians Only* (1931).

Bibliography: D. KRAMER, *Heywood Broun* (New York 1949); *Heywood Broun as He Seemed to Us* (New York 1940). I. DILLIARD, DAB 22:67–69.

[J. L. MORRISON]

BROUNS, THOMAS, English bishop, jurist and administrator; b. *c.* 1381; d. Hoxne, Suffolk, England, Dec. 6, 1445. He was the son of William Brouns, a military tenant of the Courtenays in Sutton Courtenay, Berkshire. Thomas took the master's degree at Oxford in 1404, the licentiate in laws in 1411, and later, the doctorate. He owed his early advancement to Bp. Philip *Repington of Lincoln, who made him sub-dean of the cathedral (1414), a canon of Lincoln and prebendary of Welton Westhall (1416), and archdeacon of Stow (1419). He was also given the prebends of St. Botolph's (1419) and Langford Manor (1423). Then Abp. Henry *Chichele brought him into the court of Canterbury as auditor of causes and chancellor (1425–29), in which capacity he was prominent in the Southern Convocation. In 1420 Brouns began his series of diplomatic missions on behalf of Kings Henry V and *Henry VI. In 1433–34 he was one of the King's representatives at the Council of *Basel and stayed on to be a member of the second English delegation to the council. In 1435 he was provided by Pope Eugene IV to the See of *Worcester, but the King's Council preferred the young Thomas *Bourgchier. Brouns was made bishop of *Rochester in 1435, and the following year accepted *provision to *Norwich, but had to apologize for receiving the bull without the royal assent, later given. At Norwich he was a zealous and methodical diocesan, much concerned with securing orthodoxy and liturgical uniformity. Despite the ill-will of the Norwich citizens, who attacked his palace and the priory in 1443, he remained a good friend of the municipality, interceded for it twice with Henry VI, and left money to help it pay taxation. In his will he also left a sum for maintaining six boys to study grammar and logic at Oxford.

Bibliography: Norwich Register in Norwich Public Library, Institution Books, 10; Rochester Register preserved in the Rochester Diocesan Registry. M. ARCHER, ed., *The Register of Bishop Philip Repingdon, 1405–19* (Lincoln Record Soc., 57–58; Hereford 1963). *The Register of Henry Chichele, Archbishop of Canterbury*, ed. E. F. JACOB, 4 v. (Canterbury and York Soc.; Oxford 1937–47) v.3, 4. Emden 1:281–282. E. F. JACOB, "T.B., Bishop of Norwich 1436–1445," *Essays in British History: Presented to Sir Keith Feiling*, ed. H. R. TREVOR-ROPER (London 1964).

[E. F. JACOB]

BROUWER, CHRISTOPH, historian; b. Arnheim, Holland, Nov. 10, 1559; d. Trier, Germany, June 2, 1617. After studying humanities at the Jesuit college at Cologne, he entered the Society of Jesus on March 12, 1580. At the completion of his courses in philosophy and theology, he was ordained and subsequently taught philosophy at Trier until he was named rector of the college at Fulda. He then became rector of Trier and made this archiepiscopal see the major field of his historical research. Under the patronage of Johann VII of Schönberg and later Lothar of Metternich, Archbishops of Trier, he undertook an annalistic history of the archdiocese to the year 1600, entitled *Antiquitates et annales Trevirenses et episcoporum Trevirensis ecclesiae suffraganorum*. It grew to 26 books. Because of his historical objectivity, he did not omit details that were unflattering to the archbishops, and was accused of presenting a partisan view, especially in the conflict of the Prince Elector, Abp. Philippe Christoph de Soetern with the abbot of St. Maximin. The curial advisors of the archbishop succeeded in stopping the publication, confiscating the first 18 books already in print, and in 1626 preparing a greatly altered version. Mutius Vitelleschi, sixth general of the Society of Jesus, threatened to expose this mutilation of the original text. The Jesuits at Trier managed to obtain a copy of the first printing and the remaining manuscripts, and sent them to France. There they were enlarged by Jacob Masenius, SJ, to include events up to 1652. They were printed in their entirety in 1670 at Liège. Brouwer published also an edition of the poems of Venantius *Fortunatus, *Venantii Honorii Clementiani opera* (Mainz 1603), and of *Rabanus Maurus, *Hrabanus Maurus poemata* (Mainz 1617); an account of the lives of some German saints, *Sidera illustrium et sanctorum virorum* (Mainz 1616); and the *Antiquitatum Fuldensium libri 4* (Mainz 1612).

Bibliography: Sommervogel 2:218–222. B. DUHR, *Geschichte der Jesuiten in den Ländern deutscher Zunge*, 4 v. in 5 (St. Louis 1907–28) 2.2:424–428. E. LAMALLE, EncCatt 3:126. A. DE BIL, DHGE 10:865–866. Koch JesLex 267–268.

[E. D. MC SHANE]

BROWE, PETER, theologian and historian; b. Salzburg, Dec. 22, 1876; d. Baden-Baden, May 18, 1949. He entered the Society of Jesus in 1895 and dedicated himself to research in medieval moral and pastoral theology. He taught these subjects in the Society's houses of study at Maastricht, Valkenburg, Frankfurt, and Immensee. In time his interest turned to the medieval religious folklore. With unflagging research he achieved an uncommon knowledge of the sources. Of lasting value are his numerous works on the historical development of Eucharistic devotion: *De frequenti Communione in Ecclesia occidentali usque ad annum circa 1000* (Rome 1932), *De Ordaliis* (2 v. Rome 1932–33), *Die Verehrung der Eucharistie im Mittelalter* (Munich 1933), *Die häufige Kommunion im Mittelalter* (Münster 1938), *Die eucharistischen Wunder des Mittelalters* (Breslau 1938), *Die Pflichtkommunion im Mittelalter* (Münster 1940). It is precisely because of his calm objectivity that his purely scientific works are of such significance, even for the practical consequences of a timely theology and liturgy of the Eucharist. He also wrote *Beiträge zur Sexualethik des Mittelalters* (Breslau 1932), and *Die Judenmission im Mittelalter und die Päpste* (Rome 1942).

Bibliography: H. TÜCHLE, NDB 2:639. A. STENZEL, LexThK[2] 2:710.

[B. NEUNHEUSER]

BROWN, GEORGE, first Anglican archbishop of Dublin; b. England?, *c.* 1500; d. Dublin, *c.* 1559. Little is known of his life before 1532. As prior of the London Austin friars, Brown (Browne) leased property to

Thomas *Cromwell on May 16, 1532. He was appointed provincial by Henry VIII after the breach with Rome and acted for Cromwell as one of the visitors general of all the mendicants. In 1534 Oxford awarded him the degree doctor simpliciter. After the Geraldine revolt (1534) against the new English policy and the reconquest of the Dublin area by the King's viceroys, William Skeffington and Leonard Gray, he assisted in securing the enactment by the Irish Parliament of Reformation legislation and successfully imposed on Ireland an external acquiescence to royal supremacy and the exclusion of papal jurisdiction. After the killing of Abp. John Allen of Dublin by the Irish, Brown was elected by royal direction and consecrated by Abp. Thomas Cranmer (1536). Under Edward VI he reluctantly accepted Protestantism, and he secured the primacy from Armagh when George *Dowdall abandoned the temporalities of his see rather than substitute the communion service in the Book of *Common Prayer for the Mass. Under Queen Mary I, Brown was deprived of his see for contracting marriage; the primacy was restored to Armagh, and Hugh Curwen was appointed archbishop of Dublin. After evidence was offered in his behalf that he had been hostile to the Edwardian changes in Eucharistic doctrines, and after his marriage was declared invalid, Cardinal Reginald *Pole, as papal legate, rehabilitated Brown and dispensed him so that he could hold a benefice in the diocese.

The weakness of English power in Ireland necessitated political compromises in the Reformation even under Henry VIII. The Irish reaction to the destruction of venerated shrines and monasteries deprived Brown of any chance of permanent achievement. He was reproved personally by Henry VIII for slowness in forwarding the royal supremacy. He quarreled with the only other Reform bishop, Edward Staples of Meath, and received little support from secular authorities against the general passive resistance of the people. Later, John Bale, Protestant bishop of Ossory under Edward VI, called Brown apathetic. While prepared to use the Eucharistic controversy to defeat secular opponents, he himself was accused of opposing those who preached against transubstantiation. He attempted to save his cathedrals from secularization by advocating the foundation of a royal university.

Bibliography: R. D. EDWARDS, *Church and State in Tudor Ireland* (New York 1935). G. V. JOURDAN, "The Breach with Rome, 1509–1541," in *History of the Church of Ireland*, ed. W. A. PHILLIPS, 3 v. (New York 1933) 2:169–227; "Reformation and Reaction, 1541–1558," *ibid.* 228–291. H. J. LAWLOR, *The Fasti of St. Patrick's, Dublin* (Dundalk 1930). M. V. RONAN, *Reformation in Dublin 1536–1558* (New York 1926). F. ROTH, *History of English Austin Friars, 1249–1538*, 2 v. (New York 1961). R. W. DIXON, DNB 3:43–45.

[R. D. EDWARDS]

BROWN, WILLIAM ADAMS, Presbyterian theologian; b. New York City, Dec. 29, 1865; d. there, Dec. 15, 1943. He was the son of John Crosby Brown, a prominent banker, and Mary E. Adams, daughter of a New York minister. After study at Yale University, New Haven, Conn., Union Theological Seminary, New York City, and the University of Berlin, he was ordained a Presbyterian minister in 1893. He then began a long career as a teacher and author at Union Theological Seminary. Friedrich *Schleiermacher, Albrecht *Ritschl, and other German thinkers inspired Brown's theological and ethical views. By adopting also the pragmatic realism of William James, he developed a distinctive evangelical-liberal position. His eclecticism served to mediate between Protestant Modernism and more traditionally orthodox thought. Brown was active in the ecumenical movement and was a proponent of the moral values of democracy. His most influential book, *Christian Theology in Outline* (1906), revised the earlier manual of William Newton Clarke, inserting a fuller doctrine of the church and more historical material.

Bibliography: K. CAUTHEN, *The Impact of American Religious Liberalism* (New York 1962).

[E. C. BIANCHI]

BROWNE, CHARLES FARRAR (ARTEMUS WARD), author, humorist; b. Waterford, Maine, April 26, 1834; d. Southampton, England, March 6, 1867. As a youthful apprentice on various New England newspapers, he published his first burlesque in the Boston *Carpet Bag* in 1852. After he had moved to the Middle West as a journeyman-printer and editor, he earned a local reputation as a humorist with stories in the Toledo *Commercial*. The character of "Artemus Ward," created for the *Cleveland Plain Dealer* in 1858, was a grotesquely misspelling itinerant showman. The Ward essays were immensely popular and led to Browne's appointment as editor of *Vanity Fair* in 1859. In 1861 he went on the road as "Artemus Ward," lecturing on such repertory titles as "The Babes in the Wood," "Among the Free Lovers," "Sixty Minutes in Africa," and "Among the Mormons." Although tuberculosis barred him from military service, he was a strong supporter of the Union, and his "High-Handed Outrage at Utica" was read by Pres. Abraham Lincoln to the Cabinet before submission of the Emancipation Proclamation. Browne influenced Bret Harte and Mark Twain, and was instrumental in launching Twain in New York by arranging for publication of "The Celebrated Jumping Frog." In 1866 he went to England where he received an impressive welcome and became a favorite contributor to *Punch*, a member of the Savage Club, and a lecturer at Egyptian Hall in London. He was attended in his last illness by a Catholic priest, Rev. Robert Mount.

Browne's mild social criticism exposed human absurdities through typically American hyperbole. His platform technique anticipated the "free association" method of Robert Benchley, a mélange of solemnity and nonsense uttered hesitantly and incoherently only to collapse in the confusion of dawning self-discovery. Along with "Josh Billings" and "Petroleum V. Nasby," he raised American humor to something approaching a national type. His works' permanent appeal is jeopardized by his dependence upon eccentricities and his essentially oral style.

Bibliography: C. F. BROWNE, *The Complete Works of Artemus Ward* (New York 1903); *Artemus Ward: His Travels* (New York 1865); *Artemus Ward: His Book* (New York 1862). D. C. SEITZ, *Artemus Ward: A Biography and Bibliography* (New York 1919).

[H. G. FAIRBANKS]

BROWNE, ROBERT, first post-Reformation separatist from Church of England, claimed by Congregationalists in England and America as first exponent of their principle of church government; b. Tolethorpe, Rutland, 1550; d. Northampton, 1633. Browne was influenced at Cambridge by Thomas Aldrich and Thomas Cartwright, leaders of a strong puritan, presbyterian party there, and took to preaching, fervently and effectively, in London and Cambridge, without episcopal license. He denounced ordination, all Church government, and everything remotely connected with popery. For him, the Christian Church was in no sense catholic, but exclusive to the chosen few with no call to convert the wicked. Putting theory into practice, he preached in Norwich and Bury St. Edmunds to small groups calling themselves "the church" and known as Brownists. For this "schism" Browne was imprisoned, but was freed by order of Secretary Cecil, a kinsman, whose campaign at that moment to check Jesuit and Catholic activities led him to leniency toward Protestant sects. Browne and his Norwich "church" migrated in 1581 to Middelburg in Holland where he published *A Book which sheweth the Life Manner of all True Christians* and *A Treatise Of Reformation without Tarrying for Any.* This violently dictatorial man soon quarreled with his flock and left for Scotland (1583), where he carried on his denunciation of everything ecclesiastical. Having been jailed by the Kirk, Browne was suddenly and unexplainably released, and he left for England. He was again imprisoned for his subversive writings, again released at Cecil's personal intervention, but he was excommunicated for contempt of the Established Church. Making a complete *volte-face,* at least outwardly, Browne submitted, was episcopally ordained (1591), and became rector of Achurch, Northants, till his death in Northampton jail, where he was sent for assaulting a police constable. Despite his mental unbalance, he had considerable influence on the development of Congregationalism.

Bibliography: C. BURRAGE, *The True Story of Robert Browne* (London 1906) with full list of his writings. A. PEEL, *The First Congregational Churches* (Cambridge, Eng. 1920). Cross ODCC 201–202. A. JESSOPP, DNB 3:57–61.

[G. ALBION]

BROWNING, ROBERT AND ELIZABETH BARRETT

Robert. English poet, b. Camberwell, London, May 7, 1812; d. Venice, Italy, Dec. 12, 1889. He was the son of Robert Browning, a comparatively well-to-do banker interested in the arts and literature, and of Sarah Anna Wiedemann, a Scottish gentlewoman of German descent, gently pious (a Congregationalist) and an amateur pianist. Robert's formal schooling ended when he was 14, but he read widely in his father's library, rapidly acquiring a precocious and sometimes eccentric erudition. He was guided by his father in the classics, and by private tutors in French, Italian, and music. By his own account, he wrote verse from the age of 5. In 1828 he enrolled in the newly opened University of London to study languages, but left in less than a year.

Browning began publishing with *Pauline* (1833), and *Paracelsus* (1835). In 1835 he interrupted the writing of *Sordello* (1840) to visit Italy for the first time, and to try drama with *Strafford* (1837). He began his series *Bells and Pomegranates* with *Pippa Passes* (1841), and wrote several plays. On his second return from Italy in 1844, he read the recently published poems of Elizabeth Barrett and in January 1845 began a correspondence with her that rapidly developed into the famous love match. They were secretly married on Sept. 12, 1846, and left for Italy a week later. There Browning produced *Christmas Eve* and *Easter Day* (1850), and *Men and Women* (1855). Elizabeth died in 1861, and

Browning and their son returned to England. He published *Dramatis Personae* (1864) and began work on *The Ring and the Book* (1868–69). Eight volumes followed; the last, *Asolando,* was published on the day of his death.

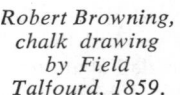
Robert Browning, chalk drawing by Field Talfourd, 1859.

Philosophical and Religious Bases. To his contemporaries, Browning was a great philosophical and religious teacher whose doctrines were willfully obscured in presentation. Whatever the psychological roots of his obscurity (or rather, obliquity), it was part of his theory of art and life. He saw life essentially as a process whereby a soul realizes itself, in fact forms itself, by moral choice. If moments of choice (and occasionally of illumination) are acted upon, one discovers some of life's meaning; if they are rejected, one becomes a moral cipher. The flash of recognition of their love by himself and Elizabeth Barrett, and their bold decision to marry and elope, was such a critical moment. It gave their whole lives meaning, the same meaning that he finds in the stories of Perseus and Andromeda, of St. George, and of *The Ring and the Book*—"do and dare."

The sense of life as an individual, almost solitary, affair is one of the most characteristic notes of Browning's serious poetry and is probably the most persistent effect of his Protestant inheritance. It underlies the last part of *Christmas Eve* and of *Easter Day,* all of *La Saisiaz* (1878), and much of *A Death in the Desert* (1864). In *La Saisiaz* in particular it leads to an ironic note, as it does also in the final book of *The Ring and the Book.* For it involves the paradox implicit, as Browning recognized, in the common view of the poet as a religious and philosophical teacher. Those who look to the poet for facile solutions are trying to evade responsibility and are mistaking the function of art, which is to "do the thing shall breed the thought." When Browning, in so many poems, explores the nature and grounds of his religious belief, he is thrashing out his own problems, not offering his own particular solutions to anyone else.

Browning's system is progressively expounded from *Paracelsus* through *Christmas Eve* and *Easter Day, Saul* (1845, 1855), *Bishop Blougram's Apology* (1855), *A Death in the Desert, The Ring and the Book* (especially book 10), *La Saisiaz,* and *Ferishtah's Fancies* (1884).

After a youthful flirtation with Shelleyan atheism, followed by a period of rather vague theism, Browning returned in 1850 to a fully committed Christianity, evident in the basic theme of *Christmas Eve*. This poem does not pose the choice of a form of worship (dissenting chapel or Catholic Church), but the choice of a doctrine of the nature of Christ. The very title suggests this—what does Christmas Eve mean? For Browning it meant the Incarnation, as evidence of God's love. This doctrine led him by 1864 (in *A Death in the Desert*) to the complete development of the analogy between God's infinite power, knowledge, and love as revealed in the Trinity and man's finite power, knowledge, and love. Through this analogy Browning finally worked out for himself the full meaning of human finiteness in its relation to God and His providence.

Catholic Implications. In working out his own theology, Browning approached the Catholic position and his attitude toward Catholicism itself underwent some change. He never fully overcame the popular prejudices of his time and upbringing, but in *Christmas Eve* the expression of Low-Church prejudice against popery is almost certainly ironic and is preceded by a passage on the Consecration of the Mass that is totally sympathetic, at least imaginatively. Five years later, in *Bishop Blougram's Apology*, it is clear that Browning is on the bishop's side, and as Cardinal Wiseman himself noted, in a review in the *Rambler,* "There is an undercurrent of thought that is by no means inconsistent with our religion." Finally, in *The Ring and the Book* (book 10), the Pope is presented as the most profoundly wise and religious of the characters.

Browning's extreme individualism, however, allows no place for the conception of a church, and there is nowhere in his work a recognition of the meaning of Sacraments, except for the short passage on the Mass mentioned above. The doctrines of the atonement and of original sin are mentioned, and apparently accepted, in *Easter Day* and *Gold Hair* (1864), respectively, but do not form part of Browning's developed theology. It

Elizabeth Barrett Browning, chalk drawing by Talfourd, 1859.

is, in fact, wholly consonant with his basic philosophy that his theology should be personal and eclectic.

Elizabeth Barrett. English poet; b. Durham, March 6, 1806; d. Florence, June 30, 1861. She is best known for her sequence of love sonnets (1850) to Robert Browning, *Sonnets from the Portuguese* (Browning called her his "little Portuguese"). In her own day, however, her fame rested on *Poems* (1844), *Poems* (1850), *Casa Guidi Windows* (1851), the long narrative poem *Aurora Leigh* (1856), and *Poems Before Congress* (1860). The third and fifth of these are, as their titles suggest, concerned with the cause of Italian liberation; the volumes of *Poems* and *Aurora Leigh* show much concern for social injustice. The sonnets have a simple directness and an ease of style that make them among the very best of their period.

Bibliography: *Works,* ed. F. G. KENYON, 10 v. (London 1912), the standard Centenary Edition. W. C. DEVANE, *Browning Handbook* (2d ed. New York 1955), invaluable reference work, best bibliographical guide. W. H. GRIFFIN, *The Life of Robert Browning,* ed. H. C. MINCHIN (3d ed. London 1938), standard biography. W. O. RAYMOND, *The Infinite Moment* (Toronto 1950). F. R. DUCKWORTH, *Browning: Background and Conflict* (New York 1932). C. W. SMITH, *Browning's Star-Imagery* (London 1941). W. WHITLA, *The Central Truth: The Incarnation in Robert Browning* (Toronto 1964), the most complete exposition of Browning's religious views.
E. B. BROWNING, *Complete Works,* ed. C. PORTER and H. A. CLARKE, 6 v. (New York 1900), standard edition. V. WOOLF, *Flush* (New York 1933), an unusual biography. K. E. INNES, *Elizabeth Barrett Browning and Her Poetry* (London 1918). **Illustration credits:** National Portrait Gallery, London.

[F. E. L. PRIESTLEY]

BROWNSON, JOSEPHINE VAN DYKE,

teacher, author; b. Detroit, Mich., Jan. 26, 1880; d. Grosse Pointe, Mich., Nov. 10, 1942. She was the youngest child of Henry Francis and Josephine (Van Dyke) Brownson, and the granddaughter of Orestes A. Brownson. After being educated by the Religious of the Sacred Heart, she completed her training at Detroit Normal School and the University of Michigan, Ann Arbor. She began teaching in Detroit at the Barstow School in 1914, transferring 10 years later to Cass Technical High School. In 1930 she resigned to concentrate on the Catholic Instruction League, which she had organized in 1916 for the benefit of children attending public schools. She outlined her method of teaching religion in *Stopping the Leak* (1926); her *Catholic Bible Stories* (1919), *Living Forever* (1928), and *Learn of Me* (1936) became standard books for catechists. In 1939 the Catholic Instruction League was incorporated into the Detroit Archdiocesan Confraternity of Christian Doctrine. That same year she was awarded the Laetare medal by the University of Notre Dame, Ind., and was named a member of the American Social Service Mission to Venezuela. She had been earlier (1933) honored by the papal decoration *Pro Ecclesia et Pontifice* and the LL.D. degree from the University of Detroit.

Bibliography: W. ROMIG, *Josephine Van Dyke Brownson* (Detroit 1955).

[M. A. FRAWLEY]

BROWNSON, ORESTES AUGUSTUS

Preacher, journalist, editor, philosopher; b. Stockbridge, Vt., Sept. 16, 1803; d. Detroit, Mich., April 17, 1876. His spiritual and intellectual odyssey, which found him successively a Presbyterian, a Universalist preacher, a Unitarian minister, and an evangelist for his own "Church of the Future," brought him finally, at the age of 41, into the Catholic Church. During his Catholic years he became, chiefly through his editorship of *Brownson's Quarterly Review,* one of the most influential Catholic laymen of the 19th century. (*See* CATHOLIC PRESS, WORLD SURVEY, 27). Yet his significance is by no means solely historical. As a protestant, Brownson was a leader in various movements for social reform. He developed an incisive and cogent criticism of the Transcendentalist movement and discussed with profundity both the foundations of authority in democratic government and the problems of an emerging industrial society. As a Catholic, he wrote essays on *Church and State, on civil and religious freedom, on Catholic education, on the philosophy of science, and on the conflict between conservative and progressive forces in the Church. These observations not only retain their relevance but were often prophetic in their vision. *See* TRANSCENDENTALISM, LITERARY; FREEDOM, INTELLECTUAL; FREEDOM, POLITICAL; FREEDOM, SPIRITUAL; FREEDOM OF RELIGION; EDUCATION, I (HISTORY OF), 9; SCIENCE, PHILOSOPHY OF.

Brownson and his twin sister were the youngest of Sylvester and Relief Metcalf Brownson's six children. His father died when Orestes was a child, and poverty forced his mother to send him to live for several years with guardians in nearby Royalton. The family was reunited in 1817 and moved to Ballston Spa in northern New York, where Orestes attended the local academy and worked as a printer's apprentice. At the age of 19, he joined the Presbyterian Church. Two years later he became a Universalist and taught school in Elbridge, N.Y.; there he met Sally Healy, whom he married in June 1827.

Early Writing. From 1826 until 1831 Brownson preached in New Hampshire, Vermont, and New York, and for a time edited the *Gospel Advocate,* the chief publication of the Universalists. He soon turned to Unitarianism, and from 1832 to 1834 was a Unitarian minister in Walpole, N.H. He gave Lyceum lectures

Orestes Augustus Brownson, portrait by G. Healy, 1863.

in Boston and in 1834 became the Unitarian minister at Canton, Mass. In 1836 he organized in Boston "The Society for Christian Union and Progress" to promote his "Church of the Future" and brought out his first essay, *New Views of Christianity, Society, and the Church.* In the same year he joined Alcott, Emerson, Hedge, Ripley, and others in the discussion group later referred to as the Transcendental Club.

In 1838 Brownson founded the *Boston Quarterly Review,* and for 5 years personally wrote the greater part of each issue. His long, two-part essay, *The Laboring Classes* (1840), reviewing Carlyle's *Chartism* but going far beyond Carlyle's views, condemned in the strongest terms the injustices of industrialism. The essay created a sensation; in the presidential campaign of 1840, Whig politicians used it as evidence of the socialistic leanings of the Democratic party, since Brownson had come out for Van Buren, the Democratic candidate.

The outcry against his essay led Brownson to reexamine his entire intellectual position. His Unitarian and transcendentalist assumptions gradually gave way. His study of Pierre Leroux gave him a sense of hierarchy and the doctrine of life through communion. By April 1844 he had decided that "either there is already existing the divine institution, the church of God, or there are no means of reform" (*Works* 4:511). Terminating the *Boston Quarterly Review* in 1842, Brownson wrote chiefly for J. L. O'Sullivan's *Democratic Review* until he revived his own review as *Brownson's Quarterly* in January 1844.

The Catholic Journalist. Brownson began taking instruction in the Catholic faith from Bp. John B. Fitzpatrick of Boston in May of 1844 and entered the Catholic Church on October 20. Although Brownson at first considered abandoning his *Review* to study law, Bishop Fitzpatrick urged him to continue as a Catholic journalist to bring Catholic principles to bear on the great questions of the day. Agreeing, Brownson studied St. Augustine, St. Thomas, and manuals of scholasticism, and renounced entirely the eclectic modes of thought that had led him to the door of the Church. Having been in the mainstream of American Protestantism, and a leading figure in "the movement party" of New England, he entertained hopes of winning many of his former associates and readers to a sympathetic consideration of Catholicism. Unlike his friend and fellow convert, Isaac *Hecker, he adopted a militant tone and strategy of which he was later critical. A letter of general approbation and encouragement from the American bishops appeared in his *Review* from 1849 to 1855, and Pope Pius IX favorably recognized his work in 1854. Late in 1853 Newman invited him to join the faculty of the new Catholic University at Dublin but withdrew the invitation because of the feeling aroused in Ireland by Brownson's views on the issue of *Americanism.

In October 1855, because of disagreements with Bishop Fitzpatrick, Brownson moved to New York with his *Review.* He defended the Union cause vigorously during the Civil War, but in the 1864 presidential race would have preferred to support General John C. Frémont rather than Lincoln. The disappointment at Frémont's withdrawal from the campaign, together with his own failing eyesight and the death of his two sons, led Brownson to suspend his *Review* in

1864. He revived it from 1873 to 1875. He died April 17, 1876, and was buried in Detroit; 10 years later his remains were moved to a crypt in the Sacred Heart Church on the campus of the University of Notre Dame.

Brownson's Achievement. As a journalist and controversialist, Brownson brought a penetrating intelligence to bear on temporal and spiritual issues. His style was vigorous and lucid, if rarely graceful. As a general critic, he wrote voluminously on religion, philosophy, society and politics, literature, and education. The central concern of his Catholic years was to clarify the relation between Christianity and civilization, and between Church and State, and to define the limits of freedom and authority. *The American Republic* (1866) is of central importance as a summation of his political philosophy. While he had rejected transcendentalism prior to his conversion to the Catholic Church, he did not abandon his reliance on intuition, and it is generally agreed that from 1842 to 1844 he was an ontologist in the sense rejected by the Catholic Church in 1861 (*see* ONTOLOGISM). Scholarly opinion remains divided whether he was an ontologist after his conversion (see Raemers and Farrell, bibliography).

Any just evaluation of the Catholic Brownson as a political and social thinker must recognize the fundamental changes of emphasis in various periods. From 1844 to 1854 Brownson's emphasis was conservative and traditional. In repudiating his earlier vision of an earthly Utopia, he seemed also to abandon any attempt at mediating between the Church and contemporary society. From 1855 to 1864, however, he increasingly sympathized with those European Catholic thinkers whose political and social views were liberal, as his essays on *Lacordaire and Catholic Progress* (1862) and *Civil and Religious Freedom* (1864) make abundantly clear. His return, from 1865 until his death, to a conservative position is largely accounted for by his belief that the Syllabus of Errors, published with the encyclical *Quanta cura* in December 1864, was a condemnation of such views as he had expressed for the previous 10 years. Weary and in failing health, Brownson accepted the interpretation given the Syllabus by his severest critics, and for the rest of his life did penance for his liberal period.

While Brownson at various periods of his life was denounced by liberals for his conservatism and by conservatives for his liberalism, the real task of criticism is to evaluate the dialectical relation between the conservative and liberal elements in his thought and to see both in historical context. As journalist and critic, Brownson tried to bring enduring principles into a dynamic relation with the great issues of his time. Yet he saw the Church as tied to no social or political forms merely because they were old; he stressed the Church's constant mission of renewal and the responsibilities of Catholics on the level of culture and civilization.

The Brownson papers are available to scholars in the library of the University of Notre Dame. The same university awarded its Laetare Medal to Brownson's son and first biographer, Henry F. Brownson, in 1892, and to his granddaughter, the author and catechist Josephine Van Dyke Brownson, in 1939.

Bibliography: *The Works of Orestes A. Brownson,* ed. H. F. BROWNSON, 20 v. (Detroit 1882–1887). H. F. BROWNSON, *Orestes Augustus Brownson . . . Life . . .,* 3 v. (Detroit 1898–1900). B. FARRELL, *Orestes Brownson's Approach to the Problem of God* (Washington 1950). T. MAYNARD, *Orestes Brownson: Yankee, Radical, Catholic* (New York 1943). P. MILLER, ed., *The Transcendentalists: An Anthology* (Cambridge, Mass. 1950). F. L. MOTT, *History of American Magazines,* 3 v. (New York 1930–38). S. A. RAEMERS, *America's Foremost Philosopher: O. A. Brownson* (Washington 1931). A. S. RYAN, "Orestes A. Brownson: The Critique of Transcendentalism," *American Classics Reconsidered,* ed. H. C. GARDINER (New York 1958); ed., *The Brownson Reader* (New York 1955). A. M. SCHLESINGER, JR., *Orestes A. Brownson: A Pilgrim's Progress* (Boston 1939). **Illustration credit:** University of Notre Dame Archives.

[A. S. RYAN]

BROWNSVILLE, DIOCESE OF (BROWNSVILLENSIS),

established in July 1965 as suffragan of the metropolitan See of San Antonio and comprising four counties in the lower Rio Grande Valley (an area of 4,226 square miles) taken from the Diocese of *Corpus Christi, Tex. The former auxiliary of Corpus Christi, Bp. Adolph Marx, was transferred to Brownsville as its first ordinary. Brownsville had served (1874–75) as the residence of the first vicar apostolic of the area until he transferred his residence to Corpus Christi. In 1965 the Brownsville diocese had the services of the Oblates of Mary Immaculate, who had arrived in 1849 to do missionary work in southern Texas and the left bank of the Rio Grande; they were joined later by diocesan priests, Holy Family Missionary fathers, and Salesians. Religious communities of women included the Sisters of Divine Providence, Holy Cross, Incarnate Word and Blessed Sacrament, and Mercy, and the Sister Servants of the Holy Ghost and Mary Immaculate, Salesian sisters, Missionary Sisters of Jesus, Mary, and Joseph, and the Sisters of Mary of the Catholic Apostolate. After Marx's sudden death (Nov. 1, 1965), Humberto Medeiros of Fall River, Mass., was named (April 1966) Brownsville's second ordinary.

Bibliography: C. E. CASTAÑEDA, *Our Catholic Heritage in Texas, 1519–1936,* 7 v. (Austin 1936–58). B. DOYON, *The Cavalry of Christ on the Rio Grande, 1849–1883* (Milwaukee 1956).

[M. P. CARTHY]

BRUCE, a family of American Catholic publishers. William George, b. Milwaukee, Wis., March 17, 1856; d. there, Aug. 13, 1949. William George, the son of Augustus Bruce, a Great Lakes sailor, became a cigar maker at the age of 12 after childhood illness had limited his education to completion of the sixth grade. He later entered newspaper work and founded the *American School Board Journal* (1891) and *Industrial Arts and Vocational Education* (1914). His firm was then incorporated as the Bruce Publishing Company. About 1927, William George turned over active management to his two sons and devoted the remainder of his life to civic activities. He was an early proponent of the St. Lawrence Seaway; for 39 years he headed the Milwaukee Harbor Commission, in addition to providing active leadership in other Milwaukee community affairs. He was named a Knight of St. Gregory (1921) and awarded the Vercelli and Laetare medals as an outstanding Catholic layman.

William C. (1882–) and Frank M. (1886–1953), sons of William George, joined the firm in 1902 and 1906, respectively, and established it as a major Catholic publishing house in the 1930s. Expansion continued with the founding of the magazine *Hospital Progress* (1920) in collaboration with the *Catholic

Hospital Association, and with the purchase of the *Catholic School Journal* (1929). The firm's first Catholic books appeared in the 1920s and a program of Catholic publishing in both textbooks and trade books was set up in 1930. The *Highway to Heaven* series was a new approach to teaching religion on the elementary level. The *Science and Culture* series (1932) was a "university in print." More than 300 titles, including works in biography, history, literature, education, natural science, Scripture, religion, and many other fields were published during the next 25 years. A Catholic book club, the Catholic Literary Foundation, began operation in 1943 (*see* BOOK CLUBS, CATHOLIC).

Frank M. was also a founder and first president of *Serra International and president of the National Association of Publishers and Church Goods Dealers. By the time of his death the firm had become one of the largest Catholic publishing houses in the U.S.

William C. was active in founding the National Catholic Educational Association and a pioneer in the field of modern school construction. He received an honorary LL.D. degree from Mt. Mary College, Milwaukee and an honorary Lit.D. degree from Marquette.

In 1964 a third generation, William George II (1912–   ), Frank M., Jr. (1913–   ), and Robert C. (1918–   ), sons of Frank, Sr., also directed publishing activities with William C. Bruce.

[H. SMITH]

BRUCHÉSI, LOUIS JOSEPH PAUL NAPO-LÉON,

second archbishop of Montreal, Quebec, Canada; b. Montreal, Oct. 29, 1855; d. there, Sept. 20, 1939. After early studies with the Sulpicians in his native city, he continued them at Issy and Paris in France and Rome, Italy, receiving a doctorate in theology. With his illustrious fellow student Jacques Della Chiesa (later Benedict XV), he was ordained at St. John Lateran Dec. 21, 1878. He taught dogma at the Grand Seminary of Quebec, was assigned to the department of parochial affairs, and became secretary to Abp. Edouard C. Fabre of Montreal, whom he succeeded in 1897. During his episcopate the 21st International Eucharistic Congress was held at Montreal (1910), and the branch of Laval University established in Montreal (1876) became independent as the University of Montreal (1920). Bruchési was a noted theologian and orator, known for his lofty and rich thought and elegant style. The last 15 years of his life were ones of inactivity and suffering.

Bibliography: *Mandements des évêques de Montréal*, v.13–16. "Éloge funèbre par son successeur Mgr. Georges Gauthier," in *La Semaine Religieuse de Montréal* 98 (1939) 614–624. J. BRUCHÉSI, "La Vocation sulpicienne de Monseigneur Bruchési," *Mémoires de la Société royale du Canada* (1941); *Témoinages d'hier* (Montreal 1961) 225–301.

[L. POULIOT]

BRÜCK, HEINRICH,

ecclesiastical historian; b. Bingen, Germany, Oct. 25, 1831; d. Mainz, Nov. 5, 1903. After his ordination (1855), he made postgraduate studies under Johannes *Döllinger in Munich (1856—57). In 1857 he began teaching Church history at the seminary in Mainz and became a full professor in 1862. In 1885 he became professor of Canon Law there also. He was consecrated bishop of Mainz in 1899. Brück was a productive scholar and one of the first Catholic historians to study the 18th and 19th centuries methodically and comprehensively.

Since this period was marked in many countries by a decline of Catholic rights and influence and by a struggle for their maintenance, a defensive attitude crept into his books. The *Kulturkampf provided him with scholarly leisure by closing the Mainz seminary, but it also heightened the apologetical tone in his writings. His first book, *Die rationalistischen Bestrebungen im katholischen Deutschland* (1865) shaped the Catholic outlook on the theological and pastoral implications of the *Enlightenment in Germany into the 20th century. His *Geschichte der katholischen Kirche in Deutschland im 19. Jh.* (5 v. 1887–1905) and *Die Kulturkampfbewegung in Deutschland, 1807–1900* (2 v., 1901–1905) exhibit an acute awareness of the importance of current problems, but are now outdated except for the source materials contained in them. Brück's textbook on Church history, *Lehrbuch der Kirchengeschichte* (1874; 9th ed. 1906) was translated into French and Italian; it appeared in English as *History of the Catholic Church* (1884). Brück lacked warmth in human contacts, but he had a strong energetic personality.

Bibliography: G. ALLEMANG, DHGE 10:882–883. A. P. BRÜCK, NDB 2:654. L. LENHART, "Dr. Heinrich Brück, 1831–1903: Der Kirchenhistoriker auf dem Mainzer Bischofsstuhl 1900–03," *Archiv für mittelrheinische Kirchengeschichte* 15 (1963) 261–333.

[V. CONZEMIUS]

BRUCKNER, ANTON,

distinguished symphonist and organist of the late 19th century; b. Ansfelden, Upper Austria, Sept. 4, 1824; d. Vienna, Oct. 11, 1896. His father, a schoolmaster, died when Anton was 13, and the boy was sent to the Augustinian monastery of St. Florian to continue his education. St. Florian became his spiritual home and, as he wished, his body rests under the great organ there. After a succession of lesser positions, he became organist at Linz cathedral in 1856. There the conductor Otto Kitzler introduced him to Richard *Wagner's music—a revelation that stimulated his development as a symphonist. In 1868 he moved to Vienna, where he was successful as teacher and organist but had difficulties as a composer, for he was violently opposed by Eduard Hanslick, Vienna's most influential critic, because of his Wagnerian partisanship. By the time of his death, however, he enjoyed recognition even in his own country, and through the line of descent Bruckner-Mahler-Schoenberg his influence was transmitted to composers of the later 20th century.

Bruckner's religion was the center of his life. With sincere piety he dedicated his Ninth (unfinished) Symphony to his *Lieber Gott*. Of his specifically sacred music, the D-major Mass (1864), generally considered his first extended masterwork, utilizes a full symphony orchestra. In contrast, the E-minor Mass (1866; revised 1885), uses only wind and brass accompaniment (nonobligatory in the *Kyrie*). The F-minor Mass (1867–68, revised in 1890) represents his most triumphant essay in the symphonic Mass style. The *Te Deum* (1881), which begins and ends in an unrestrained blaze of glorious C major, Bruckner considered a testimony to his faith. Memorable also is *Psalm 150,* with its moving violin solos and impressive fugue theme. Although fascinated by plainsong and Palestrinian tradition, he could not completely accept the viewpoint of the Caecilians, whose goal was to return church music

Anton Bruckner, portrait by Ferry Beraton, 1889.

to Palestrinian purity and eliminate the vivid orchestra of the Viennese classical Mass (*see* CAECILIAN MOVEMENT).

See also MUSIC, SACRED, HISTORY OF, 7.

Bibliography: H. F. REDLICH, *Bruckner and Mahler* (rev. New York 1963). D. NEWLIN, *Bruckner, Mahler, Schoenberg* (New York 1947); "Bruckner's Three Great Masses," *Chord and Discord* 2.8 (1958) 3–16; "Bruckner's *Te Deum*," ibid. 71–75. F. BLUME, *MusGG* 2:342–382. Láng MusWC. Fellerer Cath ChMus. M. AUER, *Anton Bruckner als Kirchenmusiker* (Regensburg 1927). Grove DMM 1:969–976. **Illustration credit:** Historische Museum der Stadt Wien.

[D. NEWLIN]

BRUEGHEL, also Bruegel or Breughel, a Flemish family famous for its several generations (16th and 17th centuries) of genre and landscape painters. The most important and eldest was *Pieter the Elder,* called also "Peasant Brueghel" and "the Droll"; his satire and close observation of nature joined to his depictions of religious subjects and fantasies were often symbolic and held moral implications. He had two sons. The first, *Pieter the Younger* (c. 1564–1638) called "Hell Brueghel" because of his hell paintings; he frequently copied his father's work and presumably taught his own son, a third Pieter (1589–1638 or 1639?) who was a mediocre artist. The second son of Pieter the Elder was *Jan the Elder* (1568–1625), called "Velvet Brueghel" and "Flower Brueghel," the first of the Flemish little masters. His work, landscape and genre with figures and animals, often confused with that of his father, was executed with meticulous care and elicited the admiration of his contemporaries. Born in Brussels, he had come early to Antwerp, where he studied with Pieter Goetkind and became a friend and collaborator of Rubens; except for short visits to Italy (1574, 1596), he remained active in Antwerp. His first son, *Jan the Younger* (1601–78), was his pupil, a painter of religious subjects, landscapes, and flowers; his second son, *Ambrose* (1617–75), also a painter, imitated the father. Jan the Elder (Velvet)

had also three daughters who married painters. Jan Brueghel the Younger had five sons, all of whom were painters but not of great merit. Of these, *Abraham,* called Rhyngraeft and Il Napolitano, painted still life in an Italian-Flemish style, and *Jan Baptist* (1670–1719), called Meleager, painted flowers and fruits. The Abraham Brueghels continued to produce artists for several generations.

Bibliography: C. VAN MANDER, *Dutch and Flemish Painters,* tr. C. VAN DE WALL (New York 1936). A. MICHELL, *Histoire de l'art depuis les premiers temps chrétiéns jusqu'à nos jours,* 8 v. in 17 (Paris 1905–29) v.5. M. FRIEDLÄNDER, *Die altniederländische Malerei,* 14 v. (Berlin 1924–37) v.14. H. GERSON and E. H. TER KUILE, *Art and Architecture in Belgium, 1600 to 1800,* tr. O. RENIER (PelHArt Z18; 1960). Wilenski FlemPaint 1:514–516. F. GROSSMANN, EncWA 2:632–651. V. DENIS et al., EncWA 5:417–418.

[R. J. VEROSTKO]

BRUEGHEL, PIETER, THE ELDER

Flemish painter; b. probably at Antwerp, *c.* 1525–30; d. 1569. Although long thought to have been a countryman by birth who produced amusing scenes of peasant life, Brueghel is now believed to have been an educated townsman who had learned friends among the humanists of his day. While his works are hard to interpret and little is known of his life, he appears to have been a rather skeptical Christian freethinker who turned a sharp and often satirical eye upon the world.

Though he had traveled in Italy, Brueghel derived his style from Netherlandish sources—mainly from the moralistic works of *Bosch and the landscapes of Patinir. Landscape had emerged as an independent

Pieter Brueghel the Elder, "The Painter and the Patron," drawing, c. 1520.

Pieter Brueghel the Elder, "The Tower of Babel," version of 1563, *oil on panel,* 3 *feet* 8⅞ *inches by* 5 *feet* 1 *inch.*

genre only during Brueghel's lifetime. By its means he could affirm the centrality of the individual who possesses his own standpoint from which to grasp and assess the world. Brueghel's attitude is illustrated in his large "Tower of Babel" (1563): within an immense landscape one sees a Flemish port city like Antwerp, in the midst of which there is being erected, at the behest of a king before whom the city's artisans must grovel, a titanic building that reaches to the clouds. The artist probably intended a satirical reference to the overweening ambitions of Philip II of Spain, who, in alliance with Rome (perhaps alluded to in the Tower's resemblance to the Colosseum), was then trying to create a European empire for himself and, in so doing, was imposing an oppressive government on the Low Countries.

From 1564 comes "Christ Carrying the Cross." Except for the holy figures in the foreground, everyone is in modern dress and holiday mood. The burghers come forth from an unmistakably Flemish Jerusalem on the left, move across the center of the picture (ignoring the inconspicuous figure of Christ, who has fallen under His cross), and mount the hill to the right, where the site of the Crucifixion is already surrounded by a circle of eager spectators. Plainly Brueghel meant to liken the brutal public executions of 16th-century Europe to those of Roman times—to mock the hypocrisy and indifference with which men still rejected Christ, even as they had in the 1st century.

Probably the best known of Brueghel's works are the five "calendar" landscapes of 1565—great, sweep-

ing scenes in which the recurrent activities of the farmer's year are depicted. Here the artist seems to declare his conviction that man does well to root his life in the constancies of nature, to live simply and in accord with the necessities that nature imposes. Brueghel did not idealize the peasant but celebrated the earthy goodness of a world that was far removed from the vagaries of urban fashion. In "The Census-Taking at Bethlehem" (1566) and "The Adoration of the Magi in the Snow" (1567) he showed the Nativity taking place among the farmhouses of a little Flemish village. By contrast, he had satirized the city in "Children's Games" (1560) as a place where everyone is occupied with private childish occupations.

Bibliography: G. GLÜCK, *Les Tableaux de Peter Bruegel le vieux au Musée impérial à Vienne* (Brussels 1910); *Bruegels Gemälde* (6th ed. Vienna 1953); *Das Bruegel Buch* (Vienna 1936), Eng. *Peter Brueghel, the Elder* (6th ed. New York 1952). F. GROSSMANN, EncWA 2:632–651; ed., *Bruegel: the Paintings* (London 1955–). C. G. STRIDBECK, *Bruegelstudien,* tr. F. HORB and G. ELMER (Stockholm 1956). **Illustration credits:** Fig. 1, Fonds Albertina, Vienna. Fig. 2, Kunsthistorisches Museum, Vienna.

[N. K. SMITH]

BRUGES

Capital of West Flanders province in Belgium. Bruges received *c.* 1190 from the Count of Flanders its own constitutional statute. In the 13th century it was a center of the wool trade, especially with England, and became a member of the Hanseatic League (1300). In the early 14th century it attained the peak of its political power, and in the 14th and early 15th century, of its economic prosperity; it then gave way to *Antwerp for diverse reasons. The Order of the Golden Fleece was founded in Bruges (1429) under the Burgundian Dukes (1384–1477). Under the Spanish Kings, Bruges was seized by Calvinists (1578–84). It suffered an economic depression in the 17th and 18th centuries but has expanded since the late 19th century. It is famous in art for its buildings and paintings.

In 1963 the Diocese of Bruges (*Brugensis*), 1,247 square miles in area, suffragan to *Mechelen-Brussels, had 394 parishes, 1,508 secular and 412 religious priests, 973 men in 59 religious houses, 8,630 women in 653 convents, and 1,020,500 Catholics.

St. *Eligius, Bishop of *Noyon-Tournai, preached Christianity in Bruges c. 650. Count Baldwin I built a chapel in his castle and after the Norman invasions translated there the relics of St. Donatian, Bishop of Reims. St. Salvator became the parish church of the port under the castle walls. A third church, Notre-Dame, was built outside the walls as Bruges grew. The constantly growing population of "the Venice of the North" in the 13th century had parishes of St. James and St. *Walburga, dependent on St. Salvator; and St. Giles and St. Catherine (now Sainte-Madeleine), dependent on Notre-Dame. Count Charles the Good, later venerated as a saint, was murdered in St. Donatian (1127). Count Diederik (Thierry) of Alsace

brought back from a crusade in the Holy Land a relic of the Precious Blood.

Bruges, part of the medieval See of Tournai, was made a diocese by Paul IV in 1559, with St. Donatian as the cathedral. The first two bishops, Pierre de Corte and Remi Drieux, suffered from the religious troubles of the time, when Bruges was held by Calvinists. French Revolutionaries destroyed the cathedral, and the *Concordat of 1801 suppressed Bruges as a see, uniting it with Ghent. Bruges was restored in 1834 with St. Salvator as the cathedral. Half the population of 52,000 (almost entirely Catholic) attended Mass when a count was made on one Sunday (October 1962). In 1963 Bruges had 13 parishes, 251 priests, 51 brothers, and 772 sisters. Its Catholic schools had 2,038 children (ages 3 to 6), 4,931 pupils (6 to 12), 4,063 humanities and 4,625 technical students (12 to 18). Catholics also directed 3 clinics with more than 242 beds caring for 6,000 patients a year, 3 homes for the aged with 208 beds, 4 medical-pedagogical institutes caring for 450 infirm, 2 psychiatric institutes with 820 patients, and 8 family homes with 455 orphans.

Bruges la Morte has never recovered from the decline it suffered when Antwerp replaced it as the port for the Low Countries. Tortuous streets, picturesque canals, houses—many relics from the 15th to 17th centuries—recall the past. Near the market is the Markethall (13th century) with its massive tower and belfry (c. 1500). The City Hall (c. 1400) was somewhat

View of the Steenstraat in the city of Bruges. In the background is the tower of the cathedral of St. Salvator.

deformed in a late 19th-century restoration. The cathedral (13th–14th century) has Gothic chapels (1480–1511) around the choir. Notre-Dame, with five naves, a lower part from *c.* 1250, and a 15th-century tower 400 feet high, houses the tombs of Charles the Bold and his daughter Marie of Burgundy and Michaelangelo's statue of the Madonna in white marble. The Gothic St. James (14th–15th century) has beautiful 17th-century choir stalls, and the Gothic St. Giles has a remarkable pulpit. St. Walburga is typical baroque. The Gothic Holy Sepulcher has Byzantine elements, such as its tower. The Basilica of the Precious Blood (Gothic on top of 12th-century Romanesque) houses its relic in a shrine more than 4 feet high; its annual procession has attracted crowds since 1303. St. John hospital, in part 13th-century, has in the former chapter hall six paintings by Memling, including the Mystical Marriage of St. Catherine and the Shrine of St. Ursula. Gruuthuse (15th century) has a museum of Bruges lace, and the Palais de Justice has the Renaissance chimney of the Frank of Bruges. In the town museum are works of Jan van Eyck, who lived in Bruges (1425–41), of Hans Memling, Gerard David, and others.

Just south of Bruges are the Benedictine abbeys of Saint-André and Steenbrugge. The former Augustinian abbey of Eeckhout is now a town museum; and the former Cistercian abbey of Ter Duinen, moved from Furnes to Bruges (1628), is now a seminary. Amid the troubles of the 16th century Cistercian nuns took refuge in Bruges from their abbeys of Spermalie and Hemelsdael, the one now a boarding school and the other a deaf and dumb institution. The *Beguine house of La Vigne (1242) is still in Bruges, impressively silent, but occupied by Benedictine nuns.

Bibliography: M. H. LETTS, *Bruges and Its Past* (London 1929). *Bruges, City of Art. Illustrated Guide* (Bruges 1930). É. DE MOREAU, DHGE 10:889–906; *Histoire de l'Église en Belgique* 7 v. (Brussels 1945–52). H. VAN WERVEKE, *Brugge en Antwerpen. Acht eeuwen Vlaamsche handel* (Brussels 1944). T. LUYKX and J. L. BROECKX, *Brugge* (Antwerp 1943). *West-Vlaanderen* (Roesalare 1952–   ). AnnPont (1964) 77. **Illustration credit:** Arthur O'Leary.

[M. DIERICKX]

BRUMEL, ANTOINE, Renaissance composer of sacred music; b. Flanders or France, *c.* 1460; d. *c.* 1525. After substituting for Mureau at Chartres (1483), he was at Notre Dame in Paris from 1498 to 1500, which he left to serve the Duke of Sora at Lyons. In 1505, or sometime thereafter, he became maestro at the court of Duke Alfonso I of Ferrara, where he may have spent the rest of his life. He was among those addressed by the poet Molinet in the *Déploration* on the death of *Okeghem (1495), set to music by *Desprez. *Petrucci published a volume of his Masses in 1503 and included motets in later collections. His *Missa Et ecce terrae motus* handles 12 voices skillfully; his *Missa de Beata Virgine,* according to *Glareanus, was written in competition with Desprez's work of the same name. His motet *Mater Patris,* which makes some notable use of imitation, became the basis of a path-breaking parody Mass by Desprez; his *Laudate Dominum,* preserved in a MS dated 1507, is one of the earliest approximately datable examples of a Psalm text in a genuine motet setting.

See also MUSIC, SACRED, HISTORY OF, 4.

Bibliography: *Opera Omnia,* ed. A. CARAPETYAN, 2 v. (Corp MensMus 5.1–2; Rome 1951–1956). J. SCHMIDT-GÖRG, MusGG

2:398–402. C. VAN DEN BORREN, *Études sur le XVᵉ siècle musical* (Antwerp 1941). Reese MusR. Roland-Manuel v.1.

[C. V. BROOKS]

BRUNEAU, JOSEPH, Sulpician educator; b. Saint-Galmier, France, April 18, 1866; d. Evian-les-Bains, Haute-Savoie, France, Aug. 26, 1933. He studied at the seminaries of Saint-Jodard, Alix, Lyons, and Issy, and at the Institut Catholique, before being ordained on July 15, 1889. In 1894, he was sent to the U.S., where he taught for 2 years at St. Mary's Seminary, Baltimore, Md. He was appointed superior of philosophy at St. Joseph's Seminary, Dunwoodie, N.Y., in 1904, and held the same position at Boston, Mass. (1906–09), and Baltimore (1909–33). In addition to teaching his courses in philosophy, dogmatic theology, and Scripture, he served as director of the seminary choir at Baltimore. He gave early encouragement to the Maryknoll Missioners of his close friend Bp. James A. Walsh. Bruneau's writings included *Harmony of the Gospels* (1898), *Our Priesthood* (1911), and *Our Priestly Life* (1928). As a translator, he put into French Patrick A. Sheehan's *My New Curate,* Bp. John C. Hedley's *Retreat,* and Basil W. Maturin's *Self-Knowledge and Self-Discipline;* and into English, Prosper G. Boissarie's *Healing at Lourdes* and Frédéric Ozanam's *Bible of the Sick.*

[E. I. VAN ANTWERP]

BRUNELLESCHI, FILIPPO, Italian architect and pioneer of Renaissance architecture; b. Florence, 1377; d. Florence, April 15, 1446. He began his artistic career as a silversmith and sculptor. His excellent training in mathematics led him to the discovery of the scientific laws of linear perspective, which played so decisive a role in the development of Renaissance art. He erected without the aid of scaffolding the most daring construction of his time—the cupola of S. Maria del Fiore (1421–36). Its beauty derives from the brilliant application of scientific laws of construction and the architect's sense of classical proportion. Brunelleschi's achievement was extremely influential on his contem-

Filippo Brunelleschi, interior view of the church of S. Lorenzo, Florence, begun in 1423.

poraries. The open arcade motif of the Loggia of the Foundling Hospital (1421–24) also enjoyed great popularity with later Florentine architects. The combination of dark *pietra serena* and white walls in the interior of the Old Sacristy (1420–28) and Pazzi Chapel (1429–44) resulted in an unprecedented clarity of structural logic and architectonic space. His persistent concern with the surface of walls rather than volumes, that is, with pictorial rather than sculptural properties, is manifest in the unfinished façade of the same chapel. By means of the linear perspective that governs the rows of columns and the other architectural elements, the vast space in the interiors of S. Lorenzo (1423) and S. Spirito (1432; *see* CHURCH ARCHITECTURE, 6) is so rationalized that the viewer, from any point within, feels himself clearly related to and fully in control of the space in which he is immersed. Brunelleschi's concern for the capacity of the human occupants of his buildings to encompass their architectural surroundings contributed to the humanistic quality of his art.

Bibliography: R. WITTKOWER, "Brunelleschi and Proportion in Perspective," *Journal of the Warburg and Courtauld Institutes* 16 (1953) 275–291. P. SAMPAOLESI, *Brunelleschi* (Milan 1962), bibliog. **Illustration credit:** Alinari-Art Reference Bureau.

[I. GALANTIC]

BRUNHILDE, QUEEN OF AUSTRASIA,

reigned 566 to 613; b. Spain, *c.* 534; d. Renève (Côte-d'Or), 613. A Visigothic princess, she married *Sigebert I, King of Austrasia, *c.* 566, and was regent for her son, grandsons, and great-grandsons (575–613). A feud broke out (*c.* 569) among the Merovingian royalty when Chilperic I of Neustria, at the instigation of his concubine, *Fredegund, murdered his wife, Galswintha, who was Brunhilde's sister. Chilperic then married Fredegund, and bloody fighting continued until Chlothar II (Fredegund's son) cruelly executed Brunhilde with all of Sigebert's descendants in 613. *Gregory of Tours (d. 591) portrays Brunhilde in positive to neutral tones. She is regarded as execrable by later authors—possibly as a result of her conflict with *Columban—even being considered as a persecutor of the Church. Actually, like all Merovingian rulers, she was generous toward churchmen and assisted the redoubtable Irishman—at least at first—and, at the request of Gregory the Great, protected *Augustine of Canterbury by a safe-conduct through her territories.

Bibliography: GREGORY OF TOURS, *The History of the Franks,* ed. and tr. O. M. DALTON, 2 v. (Oxford 1927), bks. 4–10. JONAS OF BOBBIO, *Vita sancti Columbani,* ch. 18–19, ed. B. KRUSCH, MGSrerGerm 35 (1905) 186–200. FREDEGARIUS, *Chronicon,* ed. B. KRUSCH, MGSrerMer 2:108–118, 128–142. G. KURTH, "La Reine Brunehaut," *Études franques,* 2 v. (Paris 1919) 1:265–356. E. EWIG, "Die fränkischen Teilungen und Teilreiche (511–613)," *Akademie der Wissenschaften und der Literatur, Mainz. Geistes- und Sozialwissenschaftliche Klasse. Abhandlungen* (1952) 9: 676–715. J. M. WALLACE-HADRILL, *The Long-Haired Kings and Other Studies in Frankish History* (New York 1962) 195–206.

[W. GOFFART]

BRUNI, LEONARDO ARETINO, Italian hu-

manist and historian; b. Arezzo, *c.* 1369; d. Florence, March 9, 1444. He was a pupil of Giovanni da Ravenna, and a protégé of Coluccio *Salutati, the Florentine secretary and humanist, who guided his career. In 1397 Manuel *Chrysoloras arrived in Florence and from him Bruni quickly mastered Greek. In 1405 he was appointed secretary to *Innocent VII; but his sensitive nature was repelled by the ecclesiastical squabbles of

the *Western Schism, and in 1410 he returned to his native Florence as secretary to the *Signoria.* For a brief period, 1412 to 1414, he served again in the papal Curia, this time under antipope *John XXIII, whom Bruni accompanied to the Council of *Constance. He devoted the last years of his life to his *The Twelve Books of Florentine History or the History of Florence.* This work, upon which his fame rests, has been criticized by modern scholars because of its excessive imitation of the Greek and Roman rhetorical style and its rejection of the intellectual *milieu* of the Middle Ages. The writing of the *History,* over a period of 30 years was frequently interrupted by his official duties for the Republic of *Florence and by several diplomatic missions. Bruni's historical work covers Florentine history to 1404 and was completed in 1415. It is a strongly prejudiced history, but is still important in the development of historiography since it evaluates the whole history of Florentine culture, dissipates many legends, and interjects the human and psychological aspects of his city's history. Throughout this work, Bruni stressed the importance of the struggle for liberty over the forces of tyranny. Although Bruni was not critical of his sources, his work marks a significant departure from previous historical writing. The *History* brought him immediate fame and the chancellorship of Florence. His other works include Latin translations of St. Basil, Plutarch, Aristotle, Plato, and Xenophon, in addition to lives of his early idols, Petrarch and Dante. Bruni's Latin translation of *Basil's *To Young Men* was originally printed in Venice, *c.* 1470. He employed the treatise as a defense of humanism, and at least 19 editions appeared before 1500, attesting to its influence in the history of Renaissance education.

Bibliography: L. A. BRUNI, *Historiarum Florentini populi* in Muratori RIS² 19.3. H. BARON, *The Crisis of the Early Italian Renaissance,* 2 v. (Princeton 1955); ed., *Leonardo Bruni Aretino* (Leipzig 1928). L. BERTALOT, "Zur Bibliographie der Übersetzungen des L. Br.," QuellForschItalArchBibl 27 (1936–37) 178–195. A. DE MEYER, DHGE 10:944–946. G. FALLANI, EncCatt 3:146–147. E. GARIN, ed., *Prosatori Latini del Quattrocento* (Milan 1952).

[C. L. HOHL, JR.]

BRUNINI, JOHN B., lawyer; b. Vicksburg, Miss.,

Dec. 25, 1868; d. Vicksburg, Nov. 8, 1954. He studied law at the University of Virginia, Charlottesville, and was admitted to the Mississippi bar in 1891. Establishing the firm of Brunini and Hirsh in Vicksburg, he was attorney for the Sisters of Mercy in the Botto case, which he carried successfully to the Supreme Court of Mississippi. The court's decision established the right of a nun in Mississippi to inherit property and led to the repeal of a state law prohibiting bequests to religious institutions. Brunini acted also for more than 40 years as legal adviser to the bishops of Natchez, Miss. Although he held only one political office, that of Vicksburg city attorney (1898–99), he was politically active as an adviser to Mississippi senators and governors and became a power in the Mississippi Democratic party. He served as chairman of the Mississippi State Highway Commission and director of the Delta Council, and was an active member of the American and Mississippi State bar associations, the Catholic Committee of the South, the Newcomen Society, and the Knights of Columbus. In 1928 Brunini became the first Mississippian to be named a Knight of St. Gregory, and in 1951 he was awarded an honorary doctorate of laws by Georgetown University, Washington, D.C.

[A. PLAISANCE]

BRUNNER, FRANCIS DE SALES, founder of the American province of the Society of the *Precious Blood; b. Mümliswil, Switzerland, Jan. 10, 1795; d. Schellenberg, Liechtenstein, Dec. 29, 1859. After early training at home he was sent to the Benedictine school at Maria Stein in 1809. He entered the *Benedictines, changing his baptismal name Nicholas to Francis de Sales; was ordained March 6, 1819; and then spent 10 years teaching and doing missionary work in neighboring areas. Because of personal spiritual problems, he left the Benedictines (1829) and joined the *Trappists at Oelenberg, Alsace. When the revolution of 1830 forced his removal from French territory, he returned to Switzerland, gradually separated himself from the Trappists, and began working as a missionary in eastern Switzerland under the direction of the papal nuncio at Lucerne.

In 1838, after a chance meeting with members of the Precious Blood Society at Cesena, Italy, Brunner joined the newly founded institute. He was sent to make a foundation in Switzerland, and he gathered around him several young men at Castle Loewenberg near Llanz in Canton Graubünden, where 4 years earlier he and his mother had established the *Precious Blood Sisters. In 1843, after a brief training period and ordination, Brunner and his companions immigrated to the New World. There John Baptist Purcell, then bishop of Cincinnati, Ohio, assigned the newly arrived missionary group to north central Ohio with headquarters first in Huron and then in Seneca County. During the next 16 years Brunner succeeded in firmly entrenching the Society of the Precious Blood in Seneca, Putnam, and Mercer counties. He established nine religious houses, all except one in Ohio. Brunner made several highly

Francis de Sales Brunner.

successful journeys to Europe to gather recruits from German-speaking areas; in 1858 he returned to establish a convent and a recruiting center for America in Schellenberg. His remains are buried in a crypt in the church there.

[P. J. KNAPKE]

BRUNNER, SEBASTIAN, Austrian priest, publicist; b. Vienna, Dec. 10, 1814; d. there, Nov. 26, 1893. The son of a silk manufacturer, he studied at the Schottengymnasium and the University of Vienna and was ordained (1838). Active in parish work and close to Anton *Günther, he attracted the attention of *Metternich, with whom he collaborated (1843–48). The revolution of 1848 convinced him of the need for a Catholic revival in the Austrian Empire that would take full account of the new forces at work in society. His main contribution to this revival was his activity as a writer and controversialist. As founder (1848) and editor (1848–65) of the *Wiener Kirchenzeitung* and as author of numerous books, Brunner conducted a witty, often violent campaign against *Josephinism, Prussianism, Protestantism, and (in strongly anti-Semitic tones) against Austrian liberalism. His principal books were his autobiographical *Woher? Wohin?* (1855), *Die theologische Dienerschaft am Hofe Joseph II* (1868), and *Die Mysterien der Aufklärung in Österreich* (1869). Brunner has been called a latter-day *Abraham of Sancta Clara, with a similar crusading spirit, popular touch, and baroque tendency to excess.

Bibliography: J. SCHEICHER, *Sebastian Brunner* (2d ed. Vienna 1890). *Österreichisches biographisches Lexikon* (1954–) 1: 121–122. NDB 2:683–684.

[W. B. SLOTTMAN]

BRUNO THE CARTHUSIAN, ST.

Founder of the *Carthusians; b. Cologne, before 1030; d. Santa Maria, La Torre, near Catanzaro (Calabria), Oct. 6, 1101 (feast, Oct. 6). He was of an unknown noble family; the Hartenfausts are cited, but without foundation. The 12th-century chronicle *Magister* calls him "Master Bruno." Nothing of his childhood is known except that his education was carefully supervised. The chronicle says he was well-versed in letters, both profane and divine. He began his studies at St. Cunibert in Cologne and completed them at the famous schools of Reims. There is nothing to prove that he went to Paris or was ever a disciple of Berengarius of Tours. He became a canon of Reims, where he taught the "arts" and theology, becoming master of the schools (1056), and finally chancellor of the archdiocese (*c.* 1075). His students, notably the future *Urban II, praised him as an incomparable teacher.

Bruno was not content to bask in his comfortable social position and intellectual achievements. At the height of his career he chose to side with *Gregory VII in his fight against the decadence of the clergy. At Reims itself the simoniacal Archbishop *Manasses I had reached the point of openly courting scandal. It was as much through Bruno's efforts as through the zeal of the legate, *Hugh of Die, that Manasses was finally removed (1080). Bruno had no secular ambitions, and when the cathedral see was offered him, he refused it.

Before the end of this conflict, he had vowed to leave the world and live the life of the *pauperes Christi* or Christ's poor, the name given to groups of hermits who withdrew into the solitude of the forests to live a contemplative life of poverty and penance. Drawn to the "desert," Bruno left Reims *c.* 1082 with two companions, although his friend Ralph refused to go. At first, with the advice of *Robert of Molesme, he established himself at Sèche-Fontaine (Diocese of Langres), not far from *Molesme. But Bruno was not drawn to a cenobitic vocation; he set out once more in the spring of 1084 to find greater solitude. His journey brought him into the Alps, to the heart of the Chartreuse, where

St. Bruno the Carthusian (by Houdon, S. Maria degli Angeli, Rome).

Bishop *Hugh of Grenoble helped him to establish himself. With a few clerics and laymen, he lived an eremetic life for 6 years in this small valley 3,500 feet above sea level, surrounded by rugged mountains and possessed of a severe climate—a site well suited to guarantee silence, poverty, and small numbers. He wrote no rule for the Carthusians and did not intend to found an order. The observance of the first Carthusians harmonized the cenobitic framework with the solitary life, without reference either to the Benedictine or to the Camaldolese practice.

In 1090 Urban II unexpectedly called his former teacher to his side. Bruno obeyed, leaving Landuin in charge at La Grande Chartreuse. Urban II and Bruno were obliged to flee Rome that summer and went to southern Italy, then under Norman rule. While there, Bruno again refused the miter (he had been elected to the See of Reggio). But with the material assistance of *Roger of Sicily he founded the hermitage of Santa Maria of La Torre. The eulogies of Bruno's mortuary rolls described him as an extraordinary soul as well as a revered teacher, a man "with a profound heart." His extant works include two letters, which are veritable ascetical treatises; an authentic commentary on the Psalter; and a less certain commentary on the Epistles of St. Paul, as well as the profession of faith he dictated just before he died.

Bruno's body, buried in the hermitage cemetery (1101) of Santa Maria of La Torre, was later transferred to the church there, and still later (1193) to the church of S. Stefano. In 1514, Leo X canonized Bruno viva voce. His feast was introduced into the Roman liturgy in 1623. (See illus. on following page.)

Bibliography: Sources. *Lettres des premiers chartreux,* with the profession of faith (SourcesChr 88; Paris 1962) 28–93. *Expositiones* (*Psalter,* etc.) in PL 152:633–1420; 153:11–568. A. WILMART, "La Chronique des premiers chartreux," *Revue Mabillon* 16 (1926) 77–142. Funeral eulogies in PL 152:555–606. Literature. C. LE COUTEULX, *Annales ordinis cartusiensis,* 8 v. (Montreuil 1887–91) 1:iii–cxviii. H. LÖBBEL, *Der Stifter des Carthäuser-Ordens* (Münster 1899). B. SMALLEY, *The Study of the Bible in the Middle Ages* (2d ed. New York 1952). B. BLIGNY, *L'Église et les ordres religieux dans le royaume de Bourgogne aux XIe et XIIe siècles* (Grenoble 1960). *Aux sources de la vie cartusienne* (Saint-Pierre-de-Chartreuse, France 1960). Baudot-Chaussin 10:164–175. Butler Th Attw 4:40–45. S. AUTORE, DTC 2.2:2274–82. Y. GOURDEL, DictSpirAscMyst 2.1:705–776. R. AIGRAIN, *Catholicisme* 2:291–293. H. WOLTER, LexThK² 2:730–731. **Illustration credit:** Fig. 1, Alinari-Art Reference Bureau. Fig. 2, Wallraf-Richartz Museum, Cologne.

[B. BLIGNY]

BRUNO OF COLOGNE, ST., archbishop of Cologne (953–965); b. 925?; d. Reims, Oct. 11, 965 (feast, Oct. 11). He was the youngest son of Henry I of Germany and St. Mathilde. He was educated under Bishop Balderich in the cathedral school of Utrecht, then in the court of his brother Otto (later Emperor *Otto I), where he met the most prominent scholars of the age. In 940 he became Otto's chancellor and sometime after receiving the order of deacon in 940 (or 941) was appointed abbot of the monasteries of *Lorsch near Worms and of *Corvey on the Weser. He was ordained priest in 950 and in 951 accompanied Otto on the latter's first trip to Italy. He seems to have been named archchaplain in the same year. In 953, for his loyalty to his brother during the troublesome early years of Otto's reign, especially during the revolt of Ludolf, Otto's oldest son, and of Conrad, Duke of Lorraine, Bruno received the administration of the Duchy of Cologne and at Otto's wish was elected archbishop of *Cologne, being consecrated on Sept. 25, 953. During Otto's second trip to Italy (961–965) Bruno, with his half-brother William, Archbishop of Mainz, was coregent of the kingdom and guardian of Otto's infant son. Renowned for his personal sanctity, Bruno successfully exercised both spiritual and secular authority without prejudice to either. As abbot and bishop, he insisted on a strict observance of monastic rule and devoted himself untiringly to the religious and moral training of clergy and people. He is said to have made three foundations in Cologne (St. Pantaleon, where he was buried; St. Martin; and St. Andreas) and to have been a generous benefactor of many other churches and monasteries in his archdiocese. As statesman, he worked closely with Otto in shaping imperial policy and reformed the imperial chancery, making it a fruitful source of able administrators, especially of those prince-bishops whose loyalty to the throne made them effective instruments in the government of the Empire; he established peace not only within the Duchy of Lorraine but frequently also in France. He died while returning from Compiègne, where he had gone to restore amicable relations between his two nephews, Lothaire III and Hugh Capet (*see* CAPETIANS). The *Vita*

St. Bruno the Carthusian with a kneeling donor, wing of a triptych by the 15th-century German painter called "The Master of the Holy Kindred." This painting is the oldest known representation of the saint and is evidence of a popular cult before his canonization in the 16th century.

Brunonis, written shortly after Bruno's death by his disciple Ruotger, is, despite its bombastic style, one of the best extant medieval biographies.

Bibliography: ActSS Oct 5 (1863) 698–790, *Vita* by Ruotger, 765–788. MGS 4:252–275. H. SCHRÖRS, *Annalen des historischen Vereins für den Niederrhein* 87–89 (1910) 1–95; 90 (1911) 61–100; 100 (1917) 1–42, German text of Ruotger's *Vita,* annotated and with critical bibliog. I. SCHMALE-OTT, LexThK² 2:731. W. NEUSS, ed., *Geschichte des Erzbistums Köln* (Cologne 1964) 1:165–172. Hauck 3:41–46. G. ALLEMANG, DHGE 10:956–957, with bibliog. Wattenbach-Levison 1:321–323, 360–361.

[M. F. MC CARTHY]

BRUNO DE JÉSUS-MARIE, Carmelite writer and pioneer in the field of religious psychology; b. Bourburg, France, June 25, 1892; d. Paris, Oct. 16, 1962. Born Jacques Froissart, he entered the Discalced Carmelitès in 1917, but poor health, which marked his early life, forced him to leave. After studying philosophy and theology at Rome for 2 years, he reentered the order in 1920 at Avon-Fontaine. From 1921 to 1925 he continued his theological studies at the Catholic University of Lille, and he was ordained in 1924. He was appointed editor of *Études Carmélitaines* in 1930, a position that he held for the rest of his life. This review became his forum for arousing interest in religious psychology, then a new field of intellectual activity. Along with his editorial work he organized the first Congress of Religious Psychology. The congress included philosophers, theologians, and psychiatrists and, except for the war years (1940–45), continued to meet annually. He also gave a series of lectures at the Universities of Vienna and Salzburg in 1935 and at that of Cairo in 1950. Among honors accorded him were the presidency of the Académie Septentrional in 1948 and the award of the Rose d'Or bestowed by the Rosati de Flandres in 1957.

His most important writings were in the fields of biography and religious psychology. They include: *Saint Jean de la Croix* (1929, with later editions and translations); *La Vie d'amour de St. Jean de la Croix* (1944); *Madame d'Acarie, épouse et mystique* (1937); *Le Sang du Carmel* (1954); and *Le Livre d'amour* (1961). His *Les Faits mystérieux de Beauring* (1933) and *L'Espagne mystique au XVIᵉ siècle* (1947) were done in collaboration. He also edited an important work under the title *Satan* (English translation, 1951).

Bibliography: A. PLÉ, "Le Père Bruno Jésus-Marie," VieSpirit, suppl. 63 (1962) 523. LUCIEN-MARIE DE ST. JOSEPH, "Le Père Bruno de Jésus-Marie, Directeur des *Études carmélitaines,*" *Foi vivante* 3 (Brussels 1962) 169–175. P. Fr. Bruno a Jesus Maria, OCD, in *Acta Ordinis fratrum carmelitarum discalceatorum* 9 (Rome 1964) 176–182, necrology. *Le Père Bruno de Jésus-Marie* (Paris 1964) 49–53, bibliog., various authors.

[O. RODRIGUEZ]

BRUNO OF MAGDEBURG, chronicler; d. after 1084. He was probably a cleric at the court of Abp. Werner of Magdeburg (leader of the Saxon uprising and vigorous opponent of *Henry IV). In 1082, while in the entourage of Bp. Werner of Merseburg, Bruno dedicated to him his *Liber de bello Saxonico,* covering the period from 1073 to 1081. Nothing else is known about Bruno's life. As a historian, he is not always reliable. He clearly favors the Saxons against Henry IV (as a reward for his partisanship, he may have been made chancellor to the rival king, Hermann of Salm). His work, written in retrospect, is often inexact; it is valuable, however, both for its vivid portrayal of contemporary events, especially as they pertain to Saxony, and for the letters and papers of the Magdeburg and Merseburg bishoprics, which it preserves unaltered.

Bibliography: Bruno of Magdeburg, *De bello Saxonico,* ed. G. H. Pertz, MGS 5:327–384. Wattenbach-Holtzmann 1.3:592–594. Manitius 3:398–402. G. Allemang, DHGE 10:966–967. F. J. Schmale, LexThK² 2:732.

[M. F. MC CARTHY]

BRUNO OF QUERFURT, ST., bishop, monk,

martyr; b. Saxony, *c.* 970; d. Prussia, Feb. 14, 1009 (feast, Oct. 15, June 19). Born into the family of the feudal lords of Querfurt in Saxony, he was educated at the cathedral school at *Magdeburg under the care of St. Adalbert, first archbishop of Magdeburg and missionary to the *Slavs. A man of piety and ability, Bruno was made a canon of the Magdeburg cathedral while still young and was attached to the court of the Emperor *Otto III, his close friend and, possibly, his relative. In 996 he accompanied the Emperor to Rome, where he met *Adalbert of Prague and became closely associated with the Benedictine Abbey of SS. Alexius and Boniface. After Adalbert's martyrdom (997), Bruno decided to follow in his steps and to dedicate his life to missionary work among the Slavs and the Baltic peoples. He entered monastic life under the guidance of St. *Romuald, founder of the *Camaldolese, at the monastery of Pereum, near Ravenna. Pope *Sylvester II, the Emperor *Otto III, and Romuald all supported his missionary plans. In 1004, after having been consecrated *archiepiscopus gentium* and having received the *pallium, Bruno (or Boniface, his name in religion) was ready to begin his mission, but the war between Boleslas I of Poland and the Emperor *Henry II, Otto's successor, forced him to divert his activities temporarily to Hungary and later, in 1007, to Kievan Russia, where the ruler *Vladimir welcomed him. He worked for several months among the heathen Patzinaks in the steppes between the Don and the Danube. In 1008 Bruno went to Poland and there wrote a letter to the Emperor trying to bring peace between the Poles and the Germans. At the end of the same year he and 18 missionaries went across the Polish border into the country of the Prussians, where he met a martyr's death with all his companions. The bodies of the martyrs were ransomed by Boleslas of Poland. Bruno was an outstanding hagiographer, author of a life of Adalbert of Prague (MGS 4:596–612), and of the martyrdom of the so-called Five Polish Brothers (MGS 15:709–738), a group of two Camaldolese monks and their Polish companions, slain by the heathens near Gniezno, Poland, in 1003.

Bibliography: Thietmar of Merseburg, *Chronicon,* MGSrer GermNS 9. H. G. Voigt, *B. von Q.* (Stuttgart 1907). *Cambridge History of Poland,* ed. W. F. Reddaway et al., 2 v. (Cambridge, Eng. 1941–50) v.1 Butler Th Attw 2:585–586. F. Dvornik, *The Making of Central and Eastern Europe* (London 1949).

[O. P. SHERBOWITZ-WETZOR]

BRUNO OF SEGNI, ST., bishop, abbot; b.

Solero (Piedmont), *c.* 1040 or 1050; d. Segni, Italy, July 18, 1123 (feast, July 18). Bruno was canon of Siena *c.* 1073–79. His friendship with the reforming Pope *Gregory VII, who appointed him bishop of Segni in 1079, resulted in his imprisonment by Emperor *Henry IV in 1082. He was librarian of the Roman Church under Pope Victor III (1086–87), and later counselor (1088–99) to Pope *Urban II, whom he often accompanied on his journeys, notably to the Council of Clermont-Ferrand (1095–96), and by whom

he was entrusted with various missions. He was also a confidant of Urban's successor, *Paschal II. In 1103 he became a monk at *Monte Cassino and was elected abbot, November 1107. He publicly condemned the Concordat of Sutri (1111), signed between Paschal II and Henry V of Germany. The Pope was displeased with his action and obliged him to return to Segni, where he died. He was canonized at Segni by *Lucius III (1183). His scriptural commentaries mark him as an eminent representative of medieval exegesis and monastic theology.

Bibliography: Works. PL v.164–165. MGLibLit 2:546–562. *Spicilegium Casinense* 3 (1897) 1–204. Literature. B. Gigalski, *Bruno . . . sein Leben und seine Schriften* (Münster 1898). A. des Mazis, DHGE 10:968–970. Butler Th Attw 3:140–141. R. Grégoire, *Bruno de Segni, exégète médiéval et théologien monastique* (Spoleto 1965).

[R. GRÉGOIRE]

BRUNO OF WÜRZBURG, ST., bishop and im-

perial counselor; b. *c.* 1005; d. Persenbeug, near Linz, May 27, 1045 (feast, May 17). Bruno, son of Conrad I of Carinthia and cousin of Emperor *Conrad II, was probably educated in Salzburg. He was a member of the royal chapel, the imperial chancellor of Italy (1027–34), and an intimate adviser of Conrad II and Emperor *Henry III, before being elected bishop of *Würzburg (1034). Bruno rebuilt the cathedral, constructed new churches, and improved education, to which purpose he composed an exegesis on the *Psalms,* and various catechetical writings (PL 142:39–568). Under his direction the cathedral school flourished. Bruno died accidentally, en route to Hungary with Henry III, and was buried in Würzburg cathedral crypt. His cult spread in Germany, and though never formally canonized, he appears in the martyrology of 1616.

Bibliography: J. Baier, *Der Heilige Bruno . . . als Katechet* (Würzburg 1893). G. Allemang, DHGE 10:972. Butler ThAttw 2:339–340. T. Kramer, LexThK² 2:733.

[D. ANDREINI]

BRUNO, GIORDANO

Philosopher and poet; b. Nola, 1548; d. Rome, Feb. 17, 1600. A Dominican priest, Bruno lived until 1576 in various priories in the kingdom of Naples, where he acquired a vast knowledge of philosophy, theology, and science, and became well versed in Latin and Italian letters. He conceived culture as a single common tradition containing all religious and profane doctrines, the authentic understanding of this tradition being possible only through a philosophical interpretation reserved to dominant personalities. An impetuous and intolerant love for knowledge led him to attack the supine ignorance of the unlearned and the pedantic, whom he regarded as deforming the true meaning of teachings through grotesque attempts at interpretation. His violent and imprudent criticisms against every doctrinal profession not illumined by philosophical and personal knowledge, his rejection of all authority other than reason itself, and his independent and rebellious position made him an object of condemnation and persecution in many countries and led to a tragic end.

Life and Works. Bruno fled his priory in 1576 to avoid a trial for heresy consequent upon his disrespect for current religious opinions and wandered for 15 years through many European states, testing contemporary cultures as well as various religious positions. After traveling through northern Italy in 1579, he vainly sought refuge in Calvinistic Geneva, where he was pursued by a penal lawsuit. He successfully commented upon Aristotle at the University of Toulouse from 1579 to 1581. During his consequent sojourn in Paris (1581–82), he published his first important group of writings, wherein he delineated a new method for memorization and tried to develop the combinative art projected by R. *Lull. After an unsuccessful attempt at teaching at Oxford, he continued his abundant literary activity in London from 1583 until 1585.

In his *Cena delle Ceneri* (London 1584) Bruno originated a completely new cosmological conception based upon the Copernican criticism of geocentricity: space is infinite, without an absolute horizon or center. This concept is amplified in his *De l'infinito, universo e mondi* (London 1584): innumerable heavenly bodies move through interminable space, and various living forms populate the stars. The universal meaning of life in Bruno's conception of the universe is the soul; his cosmological teaching relies upon a metaphysics of living and generating nature, which, as an image of and emanation from God, divinely forms and gathers all things into one organic totality. This manifests itself in each living thing, in which it interiorly acts and guides, as the soul does in relation to the body. The dialogue *De la causa, principio e uno* (London 1584) explains the principal concepts upon which his unitary view of life hinges. In *Spaccio della bestia trionfante* (London 1584), *Cabala del cavallo pegaseo* (London 1585), and *Asino cillenico* (London 1585), Bruno astutely used symbols to criticize positive religions by citing superstitious aspects and advancing the idea of a purely rational interpretation of traditional teachings. In another Italian dialogue, entitled *Gli eroici furori* (London 1585) he exalted Platonic love, which enables the soul of the philosopher to rise to the contemplation of God through wisdom.

Upon returning to Paris in 1586, Bruno advanced a series of criticisms against Aristotle's philosophy in his 120 articles *De Nature et Mundo adversus Peripateticos* and in his *Camoeracensis Acrotismus* (Wittenberg 1588). Leaving Paris to avoid the resentment aroused by some disputes, he went into Lutheran Germany, where after a vain attempt at Marburg, he gained acclaim at the University of Wittenberg. While pursuing his researches relevant to the Lullian art, he continued to study Aristotle until 1588. In 1589 he made a short visit to Prague and benefited from the liberality of Rudolph II of Hapsburg. Then he stayed at Helmstädt, where his independent conduct soon brought on an excommunication enforced by the Lutheran religious authorities of the city. His sojourn at Frankfurt am Main from 1590 to 1591 enabled him to compose a series of poems in classical Latin. These, published in Frankfurt in 1591 as *De minimo, De monade,* and *De innumerabilibus sive de immenso,* manifest the power of his imagination in reference to metaphysics. Here, starting with original interpretations anent the meaning of geometric figures and mathematical functions, he tried to explore what is infinitely great and what is infinitely small in the cosmos. The metaphysical synthesis entitled *Summa terminorum metaphysicorum ad capessendum logicae et philosophiae studium* he composed at Zurich; this was published there by one of his disciples in 1595.

Condemnation and Critique. Bruno's speculative work was interrupted by a tragic event. Invited to Venice by the patrician Giovanni Mocenigo, who wanted to learn the mnemonic and Lullian arts, Bruno

Giordano Bruno.

was betrayed by his host and in 1592 given over to the Inquisition. Accused of heresy and incarcerated in Venice, then in Rome, he refused to retract his teachings and was burned at the stake in the Roman Campo dei Fiori.

Bruno's teaching cannot be separated from his impetuous, genial, and confused personality, wherein a generous love for wisdom hid under a violent and intolerant temperament. He did not know how to assume social responsibility during an era that was painfully disturbed by complex changes, during which Europe gradually overcame the torment of a religious and moral crisis. It is difficult, then, to synthesize his teaching in brief formulas, inasmuch as it is involved with polemics and affected by personal and historical circumstances. Later the name of Giordano Bruno was unduly used as a symbol for movements against the Church, and he was called the precursor of immanentistic, romantic, and scientist positions hardly reconcilable with the historical truth about him.

Bibliography: Works. *Opere italiane,* ed. G. GENTILE and V. SPAMPANATO, 3 v. (Bari 1907–09); *Opera latine conscripta,* ed. F. FIORENTINO et al., 3 v. (Naples 1879–91).
Literature. Copleston v.3. A. GUZZO, EncFil 1:807–820. V. SALVESTRINI, *Bibliografia di Giordano Bruno (1582–1950)* (2d ed. Florence 1958). V. SPAMPANATO, *Vita di Giordano Bruno, con documenti editi e inediti,* 2 v. (Messina 1921–23); *Documenti sulla vita di Giordano Bruno* (Florence 1933). A. MERCATI, *Il sommario del processo di Giordano Bruno* (Vatican City 1942). F. A. YATES, *Giordano Bruno and the Hermetic Tradition* (Chicago 1964). I. L. HOROWITZ, *The Renaissance Philosophy of Giordano Bruno* (New York 1952).

[A. PUPI]

BRUNSCHVICG, LÉON, French idealist philosopher and historian of philosophy; b. Paris, 1869; d. Aix-les-Bains, 1944. He was professor at the Sorbonne (1909), president of the Academie des sciences morales et politiques (1932) and of the Société française de Philosophie (1936), and founder of the Societas Spinoziana. Between the two world wars Brunschvicg served as the official representative of French philosophy at international conferences and on cultural missions. His doctrine is an *idealism with a strong historical orientation and with epistemological emphases. Brunschvicg viewed philosophy in close relation to the history of culture and of science, devoting much attention to physics, mathematics, and metaphysics. Philosophy, for him, is the integrating principle of knowledge and not a means of extending knowledge materially; it is intellectual activity that takes complete account of itself. Only in its critical activity can reason and science free themselves and realize themselves.

As a historian, Brunschvicg gained distinction especially through his studies of Spinoza (1894 and 1924) and of Pascal (1924). In both he saw his ideal of total mediation realized under different forms; in Spinoza through the elevation of reason to the role of total mediating principle; in Pascal through an appeal to mediating principles that outrange, without denigrating, abstract intellect.

See also SPIRIT, MODERN PHILOSOPHIES OF; IDEALISM.

Bibliography: Works. *L'Idéalisme contemporain* (2d ed. Paris 1921); *Les Étapes de la philosophie mathématique* (3d ed. Paris 1929); *Le Progrès de la conscience dans la philosophie occidentale* (Paris 1927). Studies. J. MESSAUT, *La Philosophie de Léon Brunschvicg* (Paris 1938). M. DESCHOUX, *La Philosophie de Léon Brunschvicg* (Paris 1949), extensive bibliog. C. ROSSO, EncFil 1:820–821.

[A. R. CAPONIGRI]

BRUSSELS

City of 172,000 (in 1964) on both banks of the Senne River, in central *Belgium, of which it has been the capital since 1830; capital of the Province of Brabant; and an archbishopric, with *Mechelen, since 1961; it is known for its medieval buildings. Brussels was the scene of strife between aristocratic landowners and bankers, and merchant guilds seeking representation in the government from c. 1200 until 1421, when a constitution was framed that lasted to the 18th century. Trade taken from Louvain and the manufacture of luxury goods replaced the wool trade that had been lost to England in the Hundred Years' War. In the 11th century the dukes of Brabant moved their capital from Louvain to Brussels, which from 1530 was the capital of the Spanish Netherlands and later of the Austrian Netherlands.

Christianity was preached in Brussels by St. *Géry (Gaugericus) of Cambrai (d. 625), who is supposed to have built a chapel on a river island, which c. 900 was called *Broucsella* (dwelling in the marsh). Charles of Lotharingia (977–993) is the first known duke of a fortress on the island, where there was a castle chapel dedicated to St. Géry. Relics of the Merovingian St. *Gudula, patroness of Brussels, were translated in 1047 to the parish church (St. Michael) of a community on the bank of the Senne; until 1962 the Gothic church (1220–1653), with rich stained glass, was called SS. Gudule et Michel. St. Géry became the second parish church when the castle was moved and rebuilt with a new chapel of St. James. Notre-Dame-de-la-Chapelle became an autonomous parish (1210); and St. Catherine, a "quasiparish" (1461). St. Nicholas and St. James did not become parish churches until 1622.

Medieval Brussels, part of the See of *Cambrai, had an archdeacon. Since 1559 it has been part of the See of Mechelen. The city was in the hands of Calvinists (1578–85).

The Cathedral of St. Michael, with three naves, is a synthesis of 13th–16th-century Gothic. The Pulpit of Truth is the work of Hendrick Verbrugghen, and several statues of the main nave were done by François Duquesnoy (1594?–1642) and Luc Faid'herbe. The chapel of the Blessed Sacrament, where are kept the miraculous hosts that are said to have bled after profanation by Jews (1370), has four magnificent stained-glass windows after the designs of Bernaert van Orley (1492?–1542) and Michiel van Coxcie (1499–1592). St. Nicholas, begun in the 11th century, has Gothic pillars and a baroque main altar. La-Chapelle has a Romanesque nave, a choir and transept in early Gothic, and a flamboyant Gothic tower. Sablon (Zavelkerk), from the 15th–16th century, has statues by Faid'herbe, Jérôme Duquesnoy, and Artus Quellinus (1609–68). Saint-Jacques-sur-Coudenberg (18th–19th century) was built in French classical by Guimard and Montoyer. St. Catherine (14th century, rebuilt in 1850) has famous paintings, including an Assumption attributed to Rubens. The Basilica of the Sacred Heart of Koekelberg in Greater Brussels, a parish church and national shrine, was built by Belgian Catholics in gratitude after World War I.

The famous Grande Place is of unusual beauty. The City Hall, built after the plans of Jean van Ruysbroeck (1402–54), has a tower 374 feet high. The Broodhuis (Hall of the Bakers), also called Maison du Roi, and some 40 houses, including former guild houses, were rebuilt after the French bombardment of 1695. European and exotic styles meet in the gigantic Palais de Justice (1866–83), after the plans of Joseph Poelaert (1817–79). Brussels also has rich museums, old houses, great palaces, and famous statues, such as that of Egmont and Hoorne.

Greater Brussels (19 communes) had 1,023,000 inhabitants in 1964, of whom 97 per cent were Catholic,

The façade of the cathedral of St. Michael, Brussels.

25 per cent practiced their faith regularly, 63 per cent had married in the Church, and 89 per cent had Catholic burials. There were 96 parishes, 723 secular and 345 religious priests, 237 brothers, and 2,408 sisters. In 658 Catholic schools there were 15,869 children (ages 3 to 6), 41,209 pupils (6 to 12), and 21,733 humanities and 12,938 technical students (12 to 18). The University Faculty of Saint-Louis had 380 students in 1964. In 13 Catholic clinics, with 1,729 beds, 45,000 sick were cared for; 16 homes for the aged had 730 beds; 3 medical-pedagogical institutes cared for 700 infirm; a psychiatric institute had 53 mental patients; 930 orphans were in 14 family homes.

Bibliography: A. HENNE and A. WAUTERS, *Histoire de la ville de Bruxelles*, 3 v. (Brussels 1845). H. DE BRUYN, *Trésor artistique des églises de Bruxelles* (Louvain 1882). A. VAN GELE, *Bruxelles et ses faubourgs* (Brussels 1910). H. VELGE, *La Collégiale des Saints-Michel-et-Gudule à Bruxelles* (Brussels 1925). H. HYMANS, *Bruxelles* (Paris 1927). G. DES MAREZ, *Guide illustré de Bruxelles*, 2 v. (3d ed. Brussels 1928). L. VERNIERS, *Bruxelles: Esquisse historique* (Brussels 1941). M. VANHAMME, *Histoire de Bruxelles* (Brussels 1945). É. DE MOREAU, *Histoire de l'Église en Belgique*, 5 v. (Brussels 1945–52). R. MARTENS, *Brussel* (Brussels 1950). R. MOLS, *Bruxelles et les bruxellois* (Louvain 1961). F. HOUTART, *Les Paroisses de Bruxelles, 1803–1951: Législation, délimitation, démographie, équipement* (Brussels 1956). **Illustration credit:** Official Belgian Tourist Office, New York City.

[M. DIERICKX]

BRUTÉ DE RÉMUR, SIMON WILLIAM GABRIEL

First bishop of Vincennes, Ind. (now Archdiocese of *Indianapolis); b. Rennes, Brittany, France, March 20, 1779; d. Vincennes, June 26, 1839. He was the son of Simon Bruté de Rémur, overseer of the royal domains in Brittany, and Jeanne Renée Le Saulnier de Vauhelle Vatar. Left fatherless as a child, Bruté attended local schools and then trained for the printing works inherited by his mother. During the French Revolution, young Bruté, according to his own diary, made frequent visits to imprisoned priests and nobles, smuggling messages and even the Blessed Sacrament to them. From 1796 intermittently to 1803 he studied medicine in Paris, graduating first in his class of more than 1,000. Instead of practicing, however, he entered the Sulpician seminary in Paris, and upon ordination on June 11, 1808, joined the Society of Saint-Sulpice. In 1810, while teaching theology in the Rennes seminary, he met Bishop-elect Benedict J. Flaget of Kentucky, who was seeking recruits for the American missions; that June they sailed for the U.S. together.

For the first 2 years, Bruté taught philosophy at St. Mary's Seminary, Baltimore, Md., devoting the summer of 1812 to missionary work in Maryland's Talbot and Queen Anne Counties. That September he was transferred to Mt. St. Mary's College, Emmitsburg, Md., where for another 2 years he taught and served as pastor to the Catholics of the countryside. Here, too, he met Mother Seton, whose spiritual director he was until her death in 1820. In 1815 he was appointed president of St. Mary's College in Baltimore, but returned to Emmitsburg in 1818 and remained until 1834. He was then named bishop of the new See of Vincennes and consecrated by Bishop Flaget in St. Louis on Oct. 28, 1834.

The new diocese was a frontier mission field embracing all of Indiana and a large part of eastern Illinois,

with two priests, an unplastered building for a cathedral, and a widely scattered flock of about 25,000. One of Bruté's prime needs was a seminary. He visited France in 1835, gathering funds from the Propagation of the Faith, and recruiting 20 priests and seminarians. His 5-year episcopate was one of unrelieved hardship: constant journeying through his diocese, preaching, teaching, composing expositions of the faith, writing to his priests when he could not visit them, and administering the Sacraments. He attended the Third Provincial Council of Baltimore (1837), but never fully recovered from the effects of the hard, wintry trip from Indiana. Although he published nothing, his memoranda, diaries, and letters are of historical significance, the more so since they involve prominent persons in France and America, among them H. F. R. de Lammenais, whom he tried unsuccessfully to reconcile with the Church.

Bibliography: J. W. RUANE, *The Beginnings of the Society of St. Sulpice in the United States, 1791–1829* (CUA StudAm ChurchHist 22; Washington 1935). L. F. RUSKOWSKI, *French Émigré Priests in the United States, 1791–1815* (CUA StudAm ChurchHist 32; Washington 1940). M. S. GODECKER, *Simon Bruté de Rémur* (St. Meinrad, Ind. 1931). J. H. SCHAUINGER, *Cathedrals in the Wilderness* (Milwaukee 1952).

[J. J. TIERNEY]

BRUYÈRE, JEANNE HENRIETTE CÉCILE,

first abbess of Sainte-Cécile de Solesmes; b. Paris, Oct. 12, 1845; d. Ryde, Isle of Wight, March 18, 1909. Prepared for her first Communion by Prosper *Guéranger, abbot of Solesmes, she remained under his fatherly direction. When he decided to establish Benedictine nuns at Solesmes, he appointed Cécile Bruyère superior of the first group of postulants. After a period of novitiate, they took vows Aug. 14, 1868. Two years later Bp. Fillion of Le Mans, obtained from Pius IX the right of an abbess for the new monastery and conferred the abbatial blessing upon Mother Cécile. Under her long rule of 38 years, two new foundations were made. Exiled by the French anticlerical laws, in 1901 she settled at Ryde on the Isle of Wight. Her book on prayer, written for her daughters in Solesmes, is based on the teaching of Guéranger. Well-known and valued in monasteries in Germany and England, it was printed at Saint-Pierre de Solesmes in 1899 as *La Vie spirituelle et l'oraison d'après la Sainte Écriture et de la tradition*.

Bibliography: *Dom Guéranger, abbé de Solesmes*, 2 v. (8th ed. Paris 1909–10) 2:18–19. J. DE PUNIET, DictSpirAscMyst 1:1972–74.

[M. M. BARRY]

BRYENNIOS, JOSEPH,

Byzantine preacher and theologian; b. c. 1350; d. apparently c. 1438. Little is known of his origin and career. He was sent to Crete in 1381 to defend the Orthodox position against Roman propaganda on the part of the Venetians who then governed the island. Twenty years later he was forced to leave as a result of his criticism of the local clergy, and he became a monk at the Studion monastery outside Constantinople. In 1405 he went to Cyprus to recall the Catholic Uniates to Orthodoxy and presided over a local synod. A strong opponent of union with the Roman See, he criticized the negotiations between the Emperor *Manuel II and Pope *Martin V aimed at reunion. After a final break with policies of John VIII Palaeologus, he set sail for Crete (1431) and disappeared effectively from subsequent history.

A preacher of renown and a redoubtable polemicist, he was known for his erudition, but he did not produce original theological thought. In his controversies he restated the complaints of his predecessors against the Latin filioque and use of azymes. His extant writings consist mainly of homilies and controversial tracts: 21 homilies on the Trinity, 3 treatises on the procession of the Holy Spirit, a discourse on the union of the Churches, and reflections on the return of the Cypriots to Orthodoxy. His writings had been forgotten until Eugenius *Bulgaris published some of them in 1768. A. Papadopulos-Kerameus (1885) discovered the acts of the synod in Cyprus over which he presided.

Bibliography: P. MEYER, ByzZ 5 (1896) 74–111, life. Hugie TheolDogm v.2. A. PALMIERI, DTC 2.1:1156–61. Beck KTLBR 749–750.

[P. ROCHE]

BRYENNIOS, PHILOTHEUS, Orthodox metropolitan and patristic scholar; b. Constantinople, 1833; d. Constantinople, 1914. Philotheus studied at Leipzig, Berlin, and Munich, and from 1861 taught Church history at Chalki. He became the director of the Ecclesiastical Academy at Constantinople in 1867, and metropolitan of Serres in Macedonia in 1875 and of Nicomedia in 1877. He represented the Orthodox Church at an assembly of Old Catholics in Bonn in 1875. His fame rests on his discovery in the library of the hospital of the Holy Sepulcher in Constantinople and publication (1883) of a Greek (1056) parchment codex that contained the text of the hitherto unknown *Didache, the Epistle of *Barnabas, and the Letter of *Clement I of Rome to the Corinthians.

Bibliography: N. TURCHI, EncCatt 3:163. Quasten Patr 1:30. J. R. HARRIS, ed., The Teaching of the Twelve Apostles (Baltimore 1887).

[F. X. MURPHY]

BUBWITH, NICHOLAS, bishop, ambassador, treasurer of England; b. Menthorpe, near Bubwith, Yorkshire; d. Wookey, Somersetshire, England, Oct. 27, 1424. During his career he was distinguished as a royal official and as a genuinely resident bishop. He began as a chancery clerk (c. 1380). He soon became such a notable provisor (Emden 1:295) that in 1399 he had to secure a pardon for obtaining *papal provisions without the royal license. Under King Henry IV he received canonries and prebends in Exeter (1399), Wells (1399), and York (1400), and the archdeaconry of Richmond (March 16, 1402, which he exchanged two days later for the prebend of Driffield in York), as well as canonries in Salisbury (1400), Chichester (1402), Lincoln (1403), and Saint Paul's (1406). These offices he held while he was secretary to Henry IV (1402); he was also custos rotulorum (1402–5) and keeper of the privy seal (1405–06). He was provided to the bishopric of *London on May 19, 1406. A year later he became treasurer of England (1407–8), then bishop of *Salisbury (June 22, 1407), but he was moved to allow for Robert *Hallum, who had been provided to the archbishopric of York but had been denied the title by the King and Council. Bubwith was provided to *Bath and Wells on Oct. 7, 1407. While bishop of the latter see he was appointed an envoy to treat with Scotland May 22, 1412; in 1414 he was one of the King's ambassa-

dors at the Council of *Constance, returning in August 1418. At Constance he and Bp. Robert Hallum induced Giovanni Bertoldi da Serravalle, Bishop of Fermo, to translate the Divine Comedy into Latin verse, with a Latin commentary. Bubwith was generous with his wealth, which was considerable. Wylie (Henry IV, 3: 131) states that he often returned to the Exchequer sums that he might legitimately have claimed, not least as a member of the Council (£200 a year). He built the western tower and altered the walls of the church of Bubwith, Yorkshire; at Wells he contributed to poor churches and built the northern tower of the west front of the cathedral and the library above the east cloister. He also founded the Bishop Nicholas Almshouse.

Bibliography: J. H. WYLIE, History of England under Henry IV, 4 v. (London 1884–98) v.3, 4. The Register of Henry Chichele, ed. E. F. JACOB and H. C. JOHNSON, 4 v. (Canterbury and York Society 42, 45–47; London 1937–47) 2:298–302, for his will. Emden 1:294–296.

[E. F. JACOB]

BUCCERONI, GENNARO, Jesuit theologian; b. Naples, April 22, 1841; d. Rome, Feb. 18, 1918. He entered the Society of Jesus Sept. 7, 1856, but was forced to leave Italy during the political upheavals of 1860. He then studied philosophy and theology in Belgium. He was recalled to Rome and taught moral theology at the Gregorian University from 1884 until his death. He was a consultor to various congregations and a member of the commission for writing the Code of Canon Law.

Bibliography: Obituary in Collegium Germanicum Hungaricum 27 (1918) 62–63. E. LAMALLE, EncCatt 3:165. L'università Gregoriana del Collegio Romano (Rome 1924) 149–150. G. CELI, "Le nuove edizioni delle opere morale del R. P. Bucceroni, S.I.," CivCatt 68 (1917) 1:604–607.

[R. M. BUSH]

BUCELIN, GABRIEL (BUZLIN), Benedictine church historian; b. Diessenhofen, Switzerland, Dec. 27, 1599; d. Weingarten, Germany, June 9, 1681. After early schooling, he studied at Weingarten Abbey in 1612 and became a monk there in 1617; further studies at Dillingen led to his ordination on April 23, 1624. During 1625 he was novice master at St. Trudbert's in Feldkirch; and for 5 years, at Weingarten, where his first writings, ascetical and historical, appeared. Swedish armies threatened Weingarten from 1632 on, and Bucelin made several journeys (1632, 1633, 1634) from the abbey for safety or to help the monastery. He worked amid war threats at Weingarten but had to flee (1646) to Switzerland and to Admont, where he could return to his writing. As prior of St. John's Priory (1651–81) Bucelin continued his studies. After 1676 his health and eyesight failed, and in March 1681 he returned to Weingarten. Among Bucelin's monastic, profane, and church history writings are Historiae Universalis Nucleus (Augsburg 1658) and Germania topo-chrono-stemmato graphica sacra et profana (4 v. Augsburg 1655–78).

Bibliography: T. STUMP, "Gabriel Bucelin" in Festschrift zur 900-Jahr-Feier des Klosters, 1056–1956, ed. G. SPAHR (Weingarten, Ger. 1956) 370–395. P. LINDNER, "Verzeichniss von P. Gabriel Bucelins Druck- und Handschriften" in Studien und Mitteilungen aus dem Benediktiner- und Zisterzienserorden 7 (1886) 84–91. KELCHNER, ADB 3:462. T. STUMP, LexThK² 2: 737–738.

[D. MC ANDREWS]

BUCER, MARTIN (BUTZER)

Protestant reformer of Strassburg; b. Schlettstadt in Alsace, Nov. 1, 1491; d. Cambridge, England, Feb. 28, 1551. At 15 he left his poor parents to enter the Dominican house at Schlettstadt. Ten years later he was sent to study at the University of Heidelberg, where he joined the humanist movement and came to admire *Erasmus. When in April 1518 *Luther defended himself against Dominican opponents in a disputation at Heidelberg, Bucer was won to Lutheran theology. He obtained a papal dispensation from vows and in 1521 became a secular priest. In 1524 he was already a chief champion of Protestant divinity at Strassburg and well known as a leading reformer in Germany. As pastor at Strassburg for 25 years, he helped to introduce Protestantism into Hesse, Ulm, Augsburg, and other cities, and was as strong an antagonist of the Anabaptists as of the Catholics. In 1522 he married Elizabeth Silbereisen, a former nun; it was one of the first marriages of a priest. She died of the plague in 1541. A year later he married Wolfgang *Capito's widow; she survived Bucer.

His chief work was *De regno Christi,* published posthumously in 1557. All his life he was a diligent writer, voluminous to a fault. A lack of brevity and clarity prevented him from leaving any book of lasting influence. But his original and powerful mind inspired several Protestant divines, including John *Calvin and *Peter Martyr Vermigli. He was a peaceable man with a strong pastoral sense laying much emphasis upon catechetical instruction. He strove to give the church authorities a due independence of the secular magistrates in spiritual things and helped to introduce the system of discipline by pastors and elders that Calvin brought to a more highly organized state in Geneva. Calvin worked as his lieutenant in Strassburg from 1538 to 1541. All his life Bucer sought to reconcile Luther with the Swiss, especially in the theology of the Real Presence. He was the chief theologian of the mediating theology known broadly as "receptionism," whereby the Body and Blood of our Lord are believed to be received by faith "with" though not "in" or "under" the elements of bread and wine. In this irenic office he expended tireless energy. He was present at the fruitless Marburg meeting of 1529 between Luther and Zwingli, and attained his main success in the Wittenberg Concord of 1536, which reconciled Luther and the Protestant churches of Upper Germany, though it was repudiated by the Swiss Protestants. These mediating efforts gained him no popularity with stern Protestants on either side. He was present at the Colloquy at the Diet of Regensburg in 1541, when Cardinal Gasparo *Contarini sought formulas of reconciliation with the more moderate Protestants. Bucer drafted important formulas for the Cologne reformation of 1543 when Abp. Hermann of Wied tried vainly to make the archbishopric a Protestant territory. When *Charles V enforced the Augsburg Interim of 1548, the situation of many non-Lutheran divines in south Germany became untenable. Bucer sought refuge in England. Through the influence of Archbishop *Cranmer he was made regius professor of divinity in the University of Cambridge. His criticism of the first English Prayer Book of 1549 caused Cranmer to make many alterations in the second Prayer Book of 1552. Under Queen *Mary I his bones were burned in the market square at Cambridge. Three years later, after the accession of *Elizabeth I, the remains were solemnly reburied in Great St. Mary's Church.

See also REFORMATION, PROTESTANT (IN THE BRITISH ISLES); CONFESSIONS OF FAITH, PROTESTANT; COMMON PRAYER, BOOK OF.

Bibliography: *Opera omnia,* ed., R. STUPPERICH (Gütersloh 1960–); *Martin Bucer: Études sur la correspondance,* ed. J. V. POLLET (Paris 1958–). R. STUPPERICH, "Bibliographia Bucerana," H. BORNKAMM, *Martin Bucers Bedeutung für die europäische Reformationsgeschichte* (Gütersloh 1952); RGG[3] 1:1453–57. H. EELLS, *Martin Bucer* (New Haven 1931). C. HOPF, *Martin Bucer and the English Reformation* (Oxford 1946). P. POLMAN, DHGE 10:1015–19. E. ISERLOH, LexThK[2] 2:845–846.

[W. O. CHADWICK]

BUCHANAN, GEORGE, Scottish humanist, Protestant propagandist; b. Killearn, Stirlingshire, *c.* Feb. 1, 1507 (N.S.), d. Edinburgh, Sept. 28, 1582. After studies at Paris and St. Andrews, he taught humanities in France, Scotland, and Portugal. Upon returning to Scotland finally in 1560 or 1561 as a declared Calvinist,

George Buchanan, oil on panel by an unknown artist.

he became "instructor" to *Mary Queen of Scots and later, to her son, James VI. He was appointed principal of St. Leonard's College, St. Andrews, in 1566. His *De jure regni apud Scotos* (1579) and *Rerum Scoticarum historia* (1582) provided intellectual respectability to the political revolution of 1567, which deposed Mary Queen of Scots. He had in consequence a European reputation as political theorist and historian until Father Thomas *Innes's *Critical Essay* (1729) exposed his unscrupulous falsification of history, and his studied viciousness against Mary, especially in the legend of the Casket Letters, first made public in Buchanan's *Detectio Mariae Reginae Scotorum.* Buchanan was one of the greatest postclassical Latin stylists, but his achievement, though unique in his day, appears less phenomenal with the gradual rediscovery of contemporary Scottish humanism.

Bibliography: G. BUCHANAN, *The Tyrannous Reign of Mary Stewart,* ed. and tr. W. A. GATHERER (Edinburgh 1958). P. H. BROWN, *G. Buchanan, Humanist and Reformer* (Edinburgh 1890). A. M. MACKENZIE, *The Scotland of Queen Mary and the Religious Wars, 1513–1638* (London 1936). A. J. G. MACKAY, DNB 3:186–193. **Illustration credit:** National Galleries of Scotland.

[J. QUINN]

BUCHAREST, ARCHDIOCESE OF (BUCURESTIENSIS)

Latin archbishopric since 1883 and metropolitan see since 1930, in south central *Rumania. In 1948 (date of the latest reliable statistics) it had 51 secular and 14 religious priests, 24 men in 3 religious houses, 340 women in 7 convents, and 60,000 Catholics in a population of 7 million; it is 35,567 square miles in area. Its four suffragans, which had 784 secular and 227 religious priests, some 1,400 sisters, and 1,134,000 Catholics in a population of 9,300,000, were: Alba Iulia (established in 1932, successor to the See of Transylvania founded in 1103); Iași (1884); Timișoara (1930); and Satu-Mare (1804) and Oradea Mare (1077), united from 1930 to 1941 and since 1948. Bucharest is also the seat of the Rumanian Orthodox patriarch and of an episcopal vicariate for Catholics of the *Rumanian rite. Oradea Mare is also a suffragan of the Rumanian-rite Archdiocese of *Făgăraș and Alba Iulia. Persecution by the Communist government and the emigration of many Latin Catholics (for the most part Hungarians, Germans, and Bulgarians) have radically altered the condition of the Latin Church since 1948.

The city of Bucharest, on both banks of the Dâmbovița River, 25 miles north of the Danube, is the capital of Rumania. It was founded c. 1400 as a fortress for the Walachian capital of Târgoviște (45 miles northwest of Bucharest) and became the capital of Walachia (1698) and Walachia-Moldavia or Rumania (1859). In the 18th century most of the population was composed of Phanariot Greeks from Constantinople. Bucharest was occupied by Russia (1828–34, 1848–51, 1854, and 1877) and by Austria (1854–56). The university was founded in 1864. In 1960 the population of the city was 1,384,916.

Christianity entered the area early, probably in the Latin rite and perhaps under the Archbishopric of *Thessalonica. St. *Nicetas of Remesiana (366–414), a Latin author, evangelized the region. Bulgars conquered the area and under their rule the Rumanians adopted the Byzantine rite. Latin Catholicism was preached to the newly immigrant Cumans, for whom the See of Milcov was founded (1227–41); but the see disappeared in the Tatar invasion. The Sees of Severin (1380) and Argeș (1381), established by Hungarians, also were short-lived. Dominicans and Franciscans were missionaries, the latter becoming very popular. In the 16th century most Catholics became schismatic or Protestant. Bucharest came under the Latin See (archbishopric in 1642) of Sofia (Bulgaria) from 1610 to 1728. Conventual Franciscans from Constantinople cared for German, Italian, and Dalmatian merchants, and (after 1688) for Bulgarian refugees in Bucharest. From 1728 to 1883 Bucharest was under the bishops of Nikopol (Bulgaria), resident in Bucharest from 1792.

After Rumanian independence (1859) Bucharest became a Latin archbishopric for Walachia and Dobruja, immediately subject to the Holy See (1833); Iași became a bishopric for Moldavia. Ignace Paoli (d. 1885), a Passionist, founded the seminary and built the Cathedral of St. Joseph. The Benedictine scholar Raymond Netzhammer (bishop 1905–24, d. 1945) resigned in the nationality difficulties after World War I; Alexander Cisar (1924–54), a naturalized Rumanian, built a new episcopal residence and seminary. In accordance with the Rumanian concordat, the Metropolitanate of Bucharest was created in 1930. After World War II, the Communist regime suppressed the archdiocese and two suffragans, leaving only the Sees of Alba Iulia and Iași (1948). Archbishop Cisar was held in confinement until his death. For some years Rumania had only one

Latin bishop, of Alba Iulia. In late 1965 a bishop of Iași was consecrated. Bucharest is vacant. The Communist changes have not been recognized by the Holy See.

Bibliography: *Schematismus archidioeceseos romano-catholicae Bucarestiensis* (Bucharest 1933). R. Janin, DHGE 10: 1010–13; LexThK² 2:762–763. M. Baffi and F. Tailliez, Enc Catt 3:163–165. AnnPont (1965) 77.

[M. LACKO]

BUCHEZ, PHILIPPE JOSEPH BENJAMIN, important contributor to the formative ideas of Christian socialism in 19th-century France; b. Matagne-la-Petite, March 31, 1796; d. Rodez, Aug. 12, 1865. Buchez became a doctor of medicine in 1824 but was more interested in revolutionary activity. In 1821 he founded with Armand Bazard *le Charbonnerie française,* which sought the overthrow of the Bourbons and the convocation of a national constitutional assembly. He was at first a disciple of C. H. de *Saint-Simon, but was converted to Catholicism in 1829. He was never a practicing Catholic, because he hoped by his nonobservance to be more successful in reaching republicans with his message of social Christianity. As a philosopher, historian, economist, socialist, and deputy, he believed that the ideals of the *French Revolution were a development of the fundamental truths of Christianity and especially of the call to the disinterested service of one's fellow man.

His ideas were expressed in numerous publications, especially in the journals *L'Européen* (1831–32, 1835–38), *Revue Nationale* (1847–48), *L'Atelier* (1840–50); in the prefaces of the 40 volumes of his *L'Histoire parlementaire de la Révolution française* (1833–38); and in *L'Essai d'un traité complet de philosophie au point de vue du catholicisme et du progrès* (1838–40). He complemented his critique of the industrial system with proposed remedies, including associations of workingmen and credit facilities; these ideas were influential during the Revolution of 1848 and the Second Republic, a period in which Buchez served briefly as first president of the National Assembly.

Bibliography: A. Cuvillier, *P.-J. Buchez et les origines du socialisme chrétien* (Paris 1948). J. B. Duroselle, *Les Débuts du catholicisme social en France, 1822–1870* (Paris 1951).

[E. T. GARGAN]

BUCHMAN, FRANK NATHAN DANIEL, founder of movement known variously as Oxford Group, *Moral Re-Armament (MRA), and Buchmanism; b. Pennsburg, Pa., June 4, 1878; d. Freudenstadt, Germany, Aug. 7, 1961. After receiving his M.A. from Muhlenberg College, Allentown, Pa., Buchman was ordained in the Lutheran ministry (1902) and did parish work for 3 years in Philadelphia, Pa., where he subsequently directed a hostel for homeless boys. During a trip abroad he experienced a "conversion" while listening to a sermon in an English village church. From this experience he formulated ideas that constituted a basic part of his movement: a Christian renaissance based on absolute love, honesty, purity, and unselfishness. For 5 years he did evangelistic work among the students of Pennsylvania State College. He spoke at youth conferences and traveled in the U.S., Europe, and the Far East. Convinced that men must be approached individually in order to be converted to God, he introduced "house parties" at which men might, in an informal setting, be induced to amend their lives. The first important house party was held at Oxford in 1921, hence the name Oxford Group. Buchman described the movement as a "Christian revolution . . . the aim of which is a new social order under the dictatorship of God." In 1938 he renamed it Moral Re-Armament, calling it a "God-guided campaign to prevent war by a moral and spiritual awakening." The activities of MRA, diminished during World War II, gained new popularity after 1945. MRA has been praised for its insistence on sincere devotion and personal commitment, and denounced for its lack of emphasis on Christ. Buchman wrote extensively; among his publications are *Moral Re-Armament* (1938), *Remaking the World* (1948), and *The World Rebuilt* (1951).

Bibliography: F. E. MAYER, *The Religious Bodies of America* (4th ed. St. Louis 1961). W. G. SCHWEHN, *What is Buchmanism?* (St. Louis 1940). W. H. CLARK, *The Oxford Group: Its History and Significance* (New York 1951).

[E. DELANEY]

BUCHNER, ALOIS, theologian; b. Murnau, Bavaria, April 20, 1783; d. Passau, Aug. 29, 1869. He was a Benedictine novice at the time of the suppression of his monastery; J. M. *Sailer allowed him to continue his priestly studies at Landshut. He was ordained in 1806. After teaching dogma at Dillingen (1818), Würzburg (1824), and Munich (1827), he became rector of the theological faculty at Passau (1840–57). Among his chief works are the following: *Summa theologiae dogmaticae* (4 v. Sulzbach 1838–39). *Enzyklopädie und Methodologie der theologischen Wissenschaft* (Sulzbach 1837).

Bibliography: Hurter Nomencl 5.1:1095. H. LAIS, LexThK² 2:748.

[M. SCHMAUS]

BÜCKERS, HERMANN JOSEPH, Scripture scholar; b. Uedem, Niederrhein, Germany, Feb. 23, 1900; d. Hennef, Sieg, near Cologne, May 6, 1964. He became a Redemptorist in 1921 and was ordained in 1926. After his seminary studies at Hennef, he made graduate studies in Scripture at the *Pontifical Biblical Institute (1927–30), where he obtained the licentiate (1930) and the doctorate (1937) in Sacred Scripture. His doctoral dissertation on the doctrine of the immortality of the soul in the Book of Wisdom caused quite a stir because of his arguments to prove that the rational thinking of the OT author and the influence of contemporary Hellenism on Jewish wisdom literature formed the basis for the origin of the doctrine of immortality. In the field of OT exegesis, which he taught at Hennef for most of his life after 1930, he produced many scholarly books and learned articles. His terms of office as rector of the seminary at Hennef and as provincial of the Cologne province of the Redemptorists (1952–62) bore much good fruit. During the last years of his life he collaborated on a new translation of the OT in German authorized by all the German-speaking bishops. His principal works were: *Die Unsterblichkeitslehre des Weisheitsbuches: Ihr Ursprung und ihre Bedeutung*, ATAbh 13.4 (Münster 1938); *Die Makkabäerbücher, Das Buch Job*, Herder-Bibel 5 (Freiburg 1939); *Die biblische Lehre vom Eigentum* (Bonn 1947); *Die Bücher der Chronik*, Herder-Bibel 4.1 (Freiburg 1952); *Die Bücher Esdras, Nehemias, Tobias, Judith und Esther*, Herder-Bibel 4.2 (Freiburg 1953).

[W. PESCH]

BUCKFAST, ABBEY OF, Benedictine abbey in Devonshire, southwest England. Although it has been alleged that a Celtic cloister existed there from St. Pectroc's time (6th-century), Buckfast actually was founded by Earl Aylward and endowed by King Canute (1018). The Domesday Book lists its possessions in detail (1086). Stephen attached it to *Savigny (1136), and it thus became affiliated with *Cîteaux (1147). A new abbey was then built. Buckfast was suppressed in the general dissolution of monasteries under Henry VIII (1538); its property was alienated, and church and abbey fell into ruin. French Benedictines from La-Pierre-qui-Vire purchased the site (1882); they were joined by German Benedictines. Buckfast became an abbey under a German abbot (1902). Under the second abbot, Anscar *Vonier (1906), the rebuilding of the abbey on its ancient foundations was undertaken. The church was consecrated in 1932.

Bibliography: A. HAMILTON, *A History of St. Mary's Abbey of Buckfast* (Buckfast 1906). J. STÉPHAN, *Buckfast Abbey* (Buckfast 1923). J. M. CANIVEZ, DHGE 10:1034–36. A. SCHMITT, LexThK² 2:751. Cottineau 2:525. Kapsner BenBibl 2:193.

[J. STÉPHAN]

BUCKLAND, ABBEY OF, former *Cistercian abbey on the river Tavy, Devon, England, Diocese of Exeter. Buckland, or *Locus s. Benedicti de Bochland* (*Boclan, Buglanda*), was founded by Amicia, countess of Devon, in 1278 with monks from *Quarr, Isle of Wight. Because Walter Bronescombe, Bishop of *Exeter, had not been consulted about the foundation, he placed it under interdict, releasing it only on the intervention of Queen Eleanor, May 27, 1280. The Abbey had two mills, one for corn, the other for fulling, but it was never rich. During the 14th century the abbots were appointed collectors of the tenth and were asked to assist the supervisors of the king's mines in the providing of fuel for smelting and to collaborate in the defense of the coast near Dartmouth. This did not free them from subsidies demanded for the marriage of Edward III's sister Eleanor to Reginald, Count of Gueldres, and for the war against France. Buckland's history was uneventful except for the quarrel between Thomas Oliver and William Breton for the abbacy, a struggle which dragged out for 7 years (1467–73). At the dissolution John Toker, the abbot, was given a pension of £60, and 12 monks, sums of £5 or £3 according to their status.

Bibliography: Dugdale MonAngl 5:712–715. G. OLIVER, *Monasticon dioecesis Exoniensis* (Exeter 1846). *Calendar of the Close Rolls Preserved in the Public Record Office, London* (*1279–1477*). *Calendar of the Patent Rolls Preserved in the Public Record Office, London* (*1272–1494*). C. GILL, *Buckland Abbey* (rev. ed. Plymouth, Eng. 1956).

[C. H. TALBOT]

BUCKLE, HENRY THOMAS, English cultural historian; b. Lee, Kent, Nov. 24, 1821; d. Damascus, Syria, May 29, 1862. Because of frail health, he received little formal education. Hence his mother, a strict Calvinist, and his father, a well-to-do conservative, strongly influenced his early life. From 1840 to 1844 he visited Europe, acquired a knowledge of several languages, and discarded his previous intellectual background to become a freethinker and a radical. He was a rapid, omnivorous reader, possessed of a good imagination and an excellent memory. Chess, his chief recreation, won him recognition in public tournaments by the age of 20. Buckle's most lasting achievement was his two-volume *History of Civilization in England* (1857–61), which consisted of an extended introduction to the subject. His study reflected the Victorian optimism in *progress, in man's ever-increasing knowledge and control of nature, and in English *empiricism. He contended that "the progress of every people is regulated by principles . . . as certain as those which govern the physical world"; these would be uncovered by a scrupulous inductive examination of history. Written in a masterly style, his *History* contains many imaginative ideas and insights. Although aware of the early writings of Charles Darwin and Herbert Spencer, Buckle was too early to assimilate their teachings on evolution. He lacked a knowledge, understanding, and sympathy for ancient and medieval history. His many glittering generalities, truisms, and paradoxes reveal his lack of professional historical training. He was a brilliant amateur, not a true scholar. His *History* created much controversy immediately after its publication, and popularized the notion that scientific and mathematical techniques could be applied to history.

See also HISTORY, PHILOSOPHY OF.

Bibliography: H. T. BUCKLE, *Miscellaneous and Posthumous Works,* ed. H. TAYLOR, 3 v. (London 1872). G. ST. AUBYN, *A Victorian Eminence: The Life and Works of Henry Thomas Buckle* (London 1958). L. STEPHEN, DNB 3:208–211.

[J. KUTOLOWSKI]

BUCKLER, REGINALD, Dominican spiritual writer; b. London, Feb. 14, 1840; d. Grenada, West Indies, March 18, 1927. Both Buckler's father and grandfather were topographical artists and architects of distinction. His three elder brothers became Catholics, two of them Dominicans, before he entered the Church in 1855. The following year he entered the Order of Preachers at Woodchester and was given the name Reginald (he had been called Henry at birth). He was ordained in 1863, and during the 63 years of his priestly life he was stationed at various Dominican houses and assigned to various duties. In 1903 he received Robert Hugh Benson into the Church. He received his last assignment at the age of 71 when he volunteered for the mission in Grenada in the West Indies. Twice he held the office of novice master at Woodchester (1895–98, 1908), during which times he wrote two works on the religious life. His first and most important book, *The Perfection of Man by Charity,* a spiritual classic, was published in 1889. This was republished under the title *Spiritual Perfection through Charity* (1912), but was later published again under the earlier title (London 1954). His other principal works were: *A Spiritual Retreat* (London 1907 and 1924); *Spiritual Instruction on Religious Life* (London 1909); and *Spiritual Considerations* (New York 1912), which was later republished under the title *An Introduction to the Spiritual Life* (London 1957).

Bibliography: C. M. ANTONY, *Father Reginald Buckler O.P., 1840–1927* (London 1927). W. GUMBLEY, *Obituary Notices of the English Dominicans from 1555–1952* (London 1955).

[S. BULLOUGH]

BUDDE, KARL FERDINAND REINHARDT, OT scholar; b. Bensberg, near Cologne, Germany, April 13, 1850; d. Marburg, Jan. 29, 1933. He was educated at Bonn, Berlin, and Utrecht and taught OT in Bonn, Strassburg, and Marburg (1900–21, emeritus). As an exegete, he contributed frequent commentaries to various series. A leading representative of the school of Biblical literary criticism, he was highly regarded both in Europe and in America as one of the founders of modern OT studies. His analyses were characterized by razor-sharp distinctions. His minute analysis of the J (*Yahwist) tradition in the *Pentateuch into several subdivisions started a trend that was continued by other scholars. This type of analysis is also in the analytical and critical character of his other commentaries. As an historian of religion he wrote on Biblical prehistory and the religion of Israel to the Exile. He lectured extensively in the U.S. on this subject in 1898. The Society of Biblical Literature and Exegesis made him an honorary member. His biography and collection of the complete works of Adrian Ludwig Richter, the painter, graphic artist, and illustrator (published in 1922) are highly regarded.

Bibliography: T. H. ROBINSON, ExposTimes 46 (1934–35) 298–301. JBiblLit 55 (1936) ii–iii. E. WÜRTHWEIN, NDB 2:714–716. E. KUTSCH, RGG³ 1:1468–69.

[L. A. BUSHINSKI]

BUDDHISM

The complex of religious beliefs and philosophical ideas that has developed out of the teachings of the Buddha (in Sanskrit, "the Enlightened One"), the honorific title of the founder of Buddhism, the North Indian prince Siddhārtha Gautama. Beginning as a discipline for human deliverance from pain, it came to embrace various cults and sects. Two main branches flourished side by side for many centuries: the *Hīnayāna* (Little Vehicle) and the *Mahāyāna* (Great Vehicle). Buddhism is not a strictly logical dogmatic system of beliefs and practices in the Western sense. Its adherents require of religion not that it be true rather than false, but that it be good rather than bad. The characteristic symbol of Buddhism is the "Wheel of the Law" (*Dharma-Cakra*). The most complete extant collection of early Buddhist teachings, the "Buddhist Scriptures," is the *Pali Canon, which was given written form in Ceylon in the 1st century A.D. In modern times, in part under the impact of Western thought, the rise of theosophic neo-Buddhism is to be noted. The geographic expansion of Buddhism coincided with its ideological evolution. Since the Buddhism of each country assumed various forms and characteristics, it is practically necessary to treat it on a regional basis.

INDIA

In the 6th century B.C., the masses believed in the hymns of the *Vedas, collections of chants and prayers to divinities, and in their pantheon of gods and ghosts, the immortality of the good in heaven and the punishment of the wicked by hell and extinction, and the fatality of suffering and the deliverance from it. The intellectuals upheld the pantheism of the *Vedānta* essays, the certain consequence of actions (*karma*), the reward of heaven for those who became one with Brahman or divine essence and Ātman the unchanging Self, atonement in a kind of purgatory for those who had not yet achieved such oneness, and endless rebirths for the wicked.

Buddha. When the intellectual revolt, set forth in the *Vedānta,* or Upanishads, had resulted in disintegration of thought and life, many wandering masters offered

Fig. 1. Buddha in the state of nirvana, detail of a frieze of scenes from the life of Buddha carved in high relief on dark gray-blue slate, Indian, Gandhara, c. A.D., 150. The influence of Hellenistic art is clearly evident.

a way of salvation. According to tradition one of these was Siddhārtha, the son of Śuddhodana and Māyā Gautama (c. 563–c. 483 B.C.), born at Lumbinī in the Nepāl Valley. He was publicly proclaimed the sage of the Śākya clan (Śākyamuni) and the "Enlightened" (Buddha). At 29 he renounced his wife and child to seek deliverance from pain and rebirth. In 5 years of asceticism he reached the stage of emptiness and, meditating under the "wisdom-tree" (Bo tree, bodhidruma, pippala) at Gayā in Mahagda, attained "Enlightenment" (Buddhahood) by understanding pain and the way to conquer it.

Before his death at Kuśinagara, Buddha formulated his doctrine and the rules for orders of monks and nuns. He taught that pain could be conquered by the knowledge and practice of the "Four Truths"; (1) Human existence is pain, which (2) is caused by desire, and (3) can be overcome by victory over desire (4) by means of the "Eightfold Path." The Path consists in (1) right knowledge of the Four Truths; (2) right resolve to curb malice; (3) right speech, true and kind; (4) right behavior respecting life, property, and propriety; (5) right occupation; (6) right effort to free the mind of evil qualities and to retain the good; (7) right control of sensations and ideas; (8) right contemplation in four steps: isolation resulting in joy, meditation causing inner peace, concentration producing bodily happiness, and contemplation rewarded with indifference to happiness and misery.

Buddha's doctrine of nonself (anatta) implied that self is not an eternal entity distinct from the one life permeating all beings, but a compound of sensations, ideas, and volitions. Inconsistently enough, this impermanent nonself is subject to the principle of moral cause and effect (karma) and is responsible for the consequences of conduct, becoming good by good deeds and bad by bad deeds. Good men, who have extinguished desire and attachment, enjoy a state of liberation and eternal bliss (nirvāṇa).

Early Order and Councils. Any male who was not sick, disabled, a criminal, a soldier, a debtor, or a minor lacking parental consent could enter the order as a monk. The initiation ceremony comprised the renunciation (pabbajja), the arrival, and the pledge to keep the four prohibitions against sexual intercourse, theft, harm to life, and boasting of superhuman perfection. The initiated was bound to observe the 10 abstentions, i.e., from killing, stealing, lying, sexual intercourse, intoxicants, eating after midday, worldly amusements, using cosmetics and adornments, luxurious mats and beds, and from accepting gold or silver. Initiation, abstentions, and vows did not bind a monk for life, but only for the time he remained in the order. Daily exercises of the monks comprised morning prayers, recitation of scriptures, outdoor begging, a midday meal followed by rest and meditation, and evening service. Fortnightly exercises consisted in observing a day of fast and abstinence (*uposatha*) and in making a public confession of sins (*pratimokṣa*).

At the entreaty of his foster mother, Mahāprajāpatī, Buddha founded a second order for nuns. Moreover, he established a third order, this one for lay people, who were obliged only to abstain from killing, stealing, lying, intoxicants, and fornication. But they were exhorted to practice kindness, clean speech, almsgiving, religious instruction, and the duties of mutual family and social relations.

According to traditional sources the primitive doctrine lapsed into heresy, and hence a council was held at Rājarha, where the authorized version of the sayings of the Master, the *Vinaya* and the *Dhamma*, were fixed. A hundred years later a second council took place at Vaiśālī to settle 10 questions concerning monastic discipline.

Asoka, Apostle of Buddhism. Conscience-stricken at the horrors of a war for the unification of Northern India, King Asoka (273–231 B.C.) embraced Buddhism. He then abolished the royal hunt and meat at his meals, engraved his precepts on stone, issued a series of edicts embodying Buddhist rules of conduct and justice, spread the Buddhist faith, governed with piety and wisdom, and convened a third council at Pāṭaliputra in 247. In 240 he became a monk, but without abdicating his royal office. He required his officials to give moral training to their subordinates, to promote piety among people of all sects, and to prevent unjust punishments. He sent his brother (or son) Mahinda and other missionaries to spread the faith in Ceylon and another group to Western Asia, Macedonia and Epirus. Only the mission in Ceylon was successful, but Buddhists elsewhere subsequently exerted some influence on the Gnostic and Manichaean sects. Asceticism and missionary movements left an enduring mark in India, whence Buddhism spread throughout Eastern Asia.

Rise of Mahāyāna. Northern Buddhist tradition holds that a fourth council, ignored by Pāli sources, was held at Jālandhara about A.D. 100 and authorized the addition of Sanskrit commentaries to the canon. In the first 2 centuries of the Christian era Buddhist believers sought a more emotional piety and more personal deities by syncretizing their faith with polytheistic Vedism, monistic Vedantism, and ritual Yoga. They also felt the influence of Zoroastrian, Gnostic, and Hellenic elements brought by Persian, Parthian, Kushan, and Greek invaders. Thus, the ideal of the *bodhisattva*, the one who sacrifices himself to save others in a long chain of rebirths, replaced that of *Arhat*, the one who attains *nirvāna* by his own virtue. Gautama was regarded as only one of the earthly manifestations of cosmic Buddha who did and will incarnate himself countless times. Buddhas and *bodhisattvas* were considered superbeings and deities. Hence, the adherents of the new doctrine called it *Mahāyāna*, the Great Vehicle to salvation, to distinguish it from the conservative *Hīnayāna* or Little Vehicle.

In the 2d century A.D. Nāgārjuna founded the School of the Mean (*Mādhyamika*) to develop the Great Vehicle and taught that individuals and their constitutive elements (*dharma*) were unreal and that existence was but a screen of illusory phenomena whose continuity could be broken only by the knowledge of their basic unreality. *Nirvāna* consisted in reaching the end of the chain of phenomena. The Yogācāra School, founded by Asaṅga and Vasubandhu in the 4th century, propounded that all phenomena originate in the mind through eight kinds of awareness that reveal the illusion that there is an objective world and cause men to acquire the wisdom whereby they unite with the ultimate. Aśvaghoṣa developed the system in a form that greatly influenced China and Japan. For him the essence of things consists in the oneness of the totality of things; ignorance of the totality results in the illusory phenomenal world, while recognition of it actualizes the only true reality, which is *nirvāna*. "Personality" is triple: the absolute in itself (*Dharmakāya*), the absolute as embodied in earthly Buddhas (*Nirvāṇakāya*), and the absolute as realized in heavenly Buddhas (*Sambhogakāya*). Salvation is attained by faith in the Buddha Amitābha ("having infinite light").

Decline. Buddhism became mixed with the worship of deities (*deva*), dragons and snakes (*nāga*), and Siva's consort (Devi, Durgā, Kālī, Śakti), who was confused with Tārā, Avalokita's consort. This erotic mysticism was further compounded with Tantrism, a magic ritual of spells, diagrams, sorcery, erotics, and temple prostitution borrowed from China. In the 11th century Buddhism was still strong in Kashmir, Crissa, and Bihar, but with the establishment of the Moslem power in 1193, it disappeared from Northern India, its cradle. In Western India it vanished at about the mid-12th century under the rising tide of Hinduism.

Internal and external causes account for the decay of Buddhism in India. Although Buddha taught salvation through personal effort without dependence on any god, he neither denied the existence of the Hindu

Fig. 2. The faithful worshiping the Wheel of the Law, stone relief from Bharhut, India, Sunga period, 185–72 B.C.

gods nor forbade their worship or the rites connected with birth, marriage, and death. Under the influence of Hinduism the *Mahāyāna* sect evolved a pantheon of Buddhas and Bodhisattvas and a metaphysics of a pantheistic world soul complicated by Yoga and Tantra practices. Arising as a variation of Hinduism, this sort of Buddhism was naturally reabsorbed by it, for Hinduism, which had deeper and stronger roots in the Indian soul, in time developed a caste system with impassable social and religious barriers. This was incompatible with classless Buddhism.

CEYLON

When Mahinda, brother (or son) of King Asoka, introduced Buddhism into Ceylon about 250 B.C., he met King Devanampiya Tissa at a place since called Mahindatale (now Mihintale), near the capital Anurādhapura. Having been moved by sermons and portents, the King and his subjects embraced the faith. Some days later the minister Avittha and his brothers joined the order; when Mahinda's sister arrived from India, she validly admitted many Ceylonese ladies to the order of nuns. In his capital King Tissa then erected shrines and monasteries, notably the Mahāvihāra or Great Monastery, which remained the stronghold of orthodoxy for centuries. In compliance with Mahinda's directives, in order to give the faith a firm foundation, he convened the council of Thuparama so that the sacred books might be committed to memory and in turn taught by native monks.

The invasion of the Tamils from Southern India had arrested the civil and religious progress furthered by the Buddhist kings, Uttiya (207–197 B.C.), Mahāsiva (197–187), and Suratissa (187–177). The kingdom returned to normal only under Dutthagamani (101–77 B.C.), who expelled the invaders, reorganized the island, spread the faith, and built the Lohapasada and Mahāthupa monasteries, where a golden image of Buddha and statues of Māra, Brahmā, and many other Hindu gods were displayed. There ensued a period of Tamil aggression, famine, and uprisings that forced many monks to flee to India and Malaya. When the monks returned to their monasteries under King Vattagamani Abhaya (29–17 B.C.), they began to show more interest in learning than in piety. The King built the Abhayagiri monastery for Mahātissa and his monks, who had helped to repulse the Tamil aggression, but the monks of the Mahāvihāra reproved Mahātissa for his familiarity with laymen, and a schism was enkindled in the order.

Canon and Commentaries. The monks of the Mahāvihāra feared that Buddha's teachings, thus far committed only to memory, could perish with the monks in wars and the attendant miseries, or be altered through heterodox leanings in some monks. At the rival Abhayagiri monastery, in fact, the rise of a *Mahāyāna* school presaged heresy and corruption. Accordingly 500 monks convened on neutral grounds at the Aluvihāra near Matale to write down in Pali the *Tripiṭaka* (Three Baskets): *Sutta Piṭaka* (Buddha's sermons), *Vinaya Piṭaka* (monastic rules), and *Abhidhamma Piṭaka* (treatises), the whole being known as the canon of the *Theravāda* or Elders' Tradition school. The writing of the canon away from the capital and from the King bespeaks the disciplinary and doctrinal rift between the two rival monasteries. The appearance of the written canon caused controversies, the compilation of Sin-

halese commentaries, and a deeper cleft between the two schools. A dispute between the two groups over the interpretation of the *Vinaya*, presided over by King Bhatiya (A.D. 38–66) and settled by a polyglot minister, gives evidence that the *Mahāyāna* school at the Abhayagiri was already using Sanskrit versions of the canon embellished with heterodox legends. Under Voharatissa (A.D. 269–291) the schismatics upheld the *Vaipulya Piṭaka* as containing the true teaching of the Buddha, but the King thought otherwise and had their books burned. During the reign of Mahanaman (412–434) Buddhaghoṣa wrote the *Visuddhimagga* (The Way of Purification), a thorough exposition of *Hīnayāna* Buddhism, and translated most of the Sinhalese commentaries on the canon into Pali.

The Tamils resumed their incursions and finally drove the native dynasty and its religion from the northern tip of Ceylon. But in the 11th century King Vijaya Bahu restored the dynasty and requested the Burmese Buddhists to validate initiation in Ceylon to their order. In 1165 his successor called a council to stamp out schism and heresy, but again after his death the Tamils took the country. Subsequent occupations by the Portuguese (1505) and Dutch (1658) damaged the position of Buddhism, and in the 18th century the order died out. Once again it revived when the king obtained 10 Thai monks to validate the succession and establish the Thai school. Finally, before the British displaced the Dutch in 1802, the Amapura school was founded through valid initiation in Burma.

Beliefs, Order, and Cult. Unlike the ethical system of the canon, which has been kept through the centuries, the religious system has become a blend of many ingredients of the rebirth tales of the late Buddhist tradition (*jātaka*) and belief in many universes, heavens, and hells on the one hand, with Hindu polytheism and demonism on the other. The Brahmās are the highest Buddhist deities recorded in the canon. Sakka of the Pali commentaries is the same god as the Indra of the Vedic pantheon. The world is protected by the Four Kings (*lokapāla*) who rule the six heavens above the world of men (*mānuṣaloka*). Yama rescues people born in hell, a realm of eight divisions, each subdivided into many sections, whereas Māra, the impersonation of evil, prevents people from doing good. Four evil destinies (*apāya*) are realized in the underworld: hells, animals, hungry ghosts (*petaloka*), and giant demons (*asura*). Above man's world of sense-desire there is the abode of the Brahmās, gods in material body, and the world of no-form, which is the abode of the immaterial Brahmās, is supreme. This hybrid system began to be undermined by Christian influence after 1505 and by public education in the 20th century.

The backbone of the Buddhist faith is the order of monks. Postulants may enter the novitiate at the age of 12 through the ceremony of tonsure and investiture of the yellow robe (*pabbajja*). At 20 they make a temporary profession (*upasampada*). They spend the day in domestic work, reading the canon, meditating, begging for food, instructing children in the scriptures, healing the sick by charms and chants, and reciting protection *sūtras* (*Paritta*) to ward off the malevolence of the goblins.

The cult includes many forms of popular worship. Objects of veneration are the relics and images of Buddha. Religious celebrations are marked by offerings (*pūjā*) to Buddhist and Hindu deities and goblins and by the propitiatory recitation of the canon. Modern educated Ceylonese associate Buddhism with the greatness of Ceylon's past and the national prestige of the present. Their theosophic Buddhism is only one more step away from the original path of Siddhārtha (Buddha). Buddhism, though still strong, began in the 20th century to lose ground to Christianity, indifferentism, and communism.

BURMA

A Burmese tradition relates that Theravāda Buddhism, later known as *Hīnayāna* or Little Vehicle, was introduced into Burma by two of Asoka's missionaries from India. Centuries later heretical Indian teachers came via Nepal and Tibet to spread a mixture of *Mahāyāna* and *Tantra*. King Anawrahta (A.D. 1044–77), who unified Burma, adopted *Hīnayāna* as the state religion, curbed the heretic sect, inaugurated the era of temple-building, and appointed his religious adviser as superior general of the order. Although disorganized by the Mongol occupation of 1287 and subsequent Shan raids, the order was revived by Dammazedi (1472–92), who sent monks to Ceylon to secure valid admission. In 1871 King Mindon Min convened the fifth Buddhist council in Mandalay, but with the British annexation of Upper Burma in 1885, Buddhism ceased to be the state religion.

Belief. The Burmese and the Shan believe in the "Four Noble Truths," the requital of actions, the acquisition and sharing of merits, rebirth and *nirvāṇa*, the canon, impermanence, and impersonality. Inconsistently enough, they combine atheism with the animism of the hill tribes and believe in the spirits (*nat*) of the six Buddhist heavens and the spirits of nature. They propitiate the spirits of their ancestors and hostile goblins and heed good and ill omens. The Burmese, instead of adopting pure Buddhism as a philosophy of life and as an outlet for some form of social activity, take refuge in the warmer and more personal contact with the spirits to satisfy their deeper religious sense of dependence, need, and survival. Their religion is animism with a coating of Buddhism.

Order and Cult. Burmese monachism is organized according to that of Ceylon. Any male of over 7 years of age may join the order as a novice (*koyin*). After initiation (*upazin*) a monk must observe the 227 monastic rules. Every morning young monks and novices go out to beg their daily food. The monks perform certain daily exercises, assemble fortnightly for their confession chapter (*uposatha*), and in the lenten season (*wa*) make their annual retreat.

Burmese Buddhism has neither a formal head nor a centralized organization. Every village has a monastery (*kyaung*) with a monk (*pongyi*) in charge and a nearby pagoda. Worship at the shrines is reverential and apart from a few community exercises it is individual. Intellectual monks pray to nobody and for nothing. Many laymen make private petitions to the Buddha, though this is inconsistent with the theory that he is in *nirvāṇa* beyond all touch of change. Some people pray hoping for a blessing in return, and others repeat Buddha's words with a pure heart as an infallible means of acquiring merit. The worship of images, relics, and spirits is popular. The New Year Feast (*Thin-gyan*) celebrates the annual visit of the king of the spirits, Thagyamin.

The beginning of the lenten season is marked by devotions, floats of *nats* (spirits), and a show of Buddha's birth-stories (*zat*). The end of the season commemorates Buddha's return from the Tawadeintha heaven.

Despite the lack of a central leadership and organization, most Burmese are devout Buddhists deeply attached to the order.

THAILAND

Theravāda Buddhism was introduced probably by Asoka's missionaries some time after 245 B.C. and superimposed on the native animism. In the first centuries A.D. the country was Hinduized and it later fell under the influence of Tantric *Mahāyāna*. Since 1057, however, a modified *Hīnayāna* has prevailed over *Mahāyāna*, at least among the educated. The stele of King Rama Kamheng of 1292 records two *Hīnayāna* schools. About 1360 Rama Thibodi, founder of the Ayuthia monarchy, believing that it was necessary to get a validation of monastic initiation, sent an abbot to Ceylon to enter the order and thus secure the valid succession. King Boromoraja II captured Angkor, the Cambodian capital, and brought back its statesmen and brahmans (1431). Twenty-nine years later his successor used these Cambodian leaders to reorganize the national administration and ceremonial and to establish himself as the divine Buddhist king (*Buddharājā*), after Cambodia's divine Hindu kings (*Devarājā*). Buddhism remained the state religion, but it exhibited the marked influence of Hinduism and animism. After the fall of the Thai kingdom in 1767, its restorer, Rama I (1782–1809), upheld the national religion, showed devotion to the order, displayed zeal in temple building, promoted the revision of the canon, and published the legal corpus, *Phra Dharmaśāstra*. In its first volume appeared the Indian Code of the patriarch and seer Manu, dealing with the creation of the world, the state of the soul after death, and the customary law concerning religion, caste, and society. Rama IV (1851–68) strove to rid *Hīnayāna* of animistic, Mahayanistic, and Brahmanic accretions and reorganized the order. Rama VII (1925–35) established an ecclesiastical board within the ministry of education, and was made "Upholder of the Faith" by the constitution of 1932, a title reaffirmed by subsequent constitutional drafts.

Order and Cult. Although Thai monachism had derived inspiration, instruction, and valid succession from the order of Ceylon, the order had not been centralized because of the Hinduization of the country and the political absolutism dating back to 1460. However, Rama IV, initiated into Western scholarship by Catholic and Protestant missionaries, introduced a hierarchical structure into the order, patterning it after Catholic monachism. Accordingly, authority was vested in a patriarch assisted by 15 councillors, forming together the supreme chapter. Four leaders were provided for the Mahānikaya school and four for the Dharmayuthika school, and under each there were four subdivision leaders. For each of the 10 circles there was an administrator, and provincials served the 70 provinces. Superiors were constituted for the 407 districts, abbots for the precincts, and priors for the temples and monks.

Boys of 12 or more could enter the monastery as pupils. Novices were admitted at any age and for any length of time, but could not become monks before 20. Monks were exempt from military service. They received jurisdiction to initiate others, as well as titles of their own from the ecclesiastical board. Most of the temples had a monastery, and both were generously endowed by the faithful and the government. The initiation rite showed a combination of *Mahāyāna, Hīnayāna,* and animistic elements. Upon initiation each monk received a credential booklet marked with his name; in this he was to keep his own vital statistics, right thumbprint, his picture, the name of his parents, initiator, and teachers, and the records of his transfers, examinations, positions, legal charges, and laicization.

Public worship was conducted by the monks. They were to reserve the morning service to themselves, except on the four *uposatha* days set for the laity. In formal services a leader addressed an invocation to the *devatas* (minor deities) and *nāgas* (serpents) borrowed from Hinduism. The rainy season retreat (*vassa*) was marked with rites and pageantry of Buddhist and Hindu flavor. Some of the life-cycle rites (birthday, tonsure, wedding, and funeral) contained Brahmanic features but were conducted by Buddhist monks with charms, amulets, invocations for good fortune, and the sprinkling of magic water. Despite the orthodox doctrine of impermanence and impersonality, most people believed that their good deeds and Buddha's grace could be applied for the repose of the souls departed. Rites celebrating national holidays were conducted by Brahmans and Buddhists in a mixture of Hinduism and Buddhism.

Buddhist Action. Thai Buddhism, which is well organized and state supported, has at its disposal the school, the press, and the state broadcasting system. It freely borrows methods of action from other religions, especially Catholicism. In 1928 the King sanctioned the *Buddhamāmaka* oath, an adaptation of Catholic confirmation, to be taken by students going abroad. The ritual, although inspired by Catholicism, is a mixture of Buddhism and Hinduism. In 1929 Buddhist religious instruction was introduced into all state schools. The Young Buddhists Association (1933), the Buddha Dharma Association (1934), and similar societies promote Buddhist action among the laity. Buddhism is rooted in Thai history, culture, and psychology and remains the soul of the nation.

CAMBODIA

After centuries of rivalry with Hinduism, the religion of the Buddha became established in Cambodia. By the 1st century A.D. the inhabitants, known as the Khmers, had been Hinduized under rulers of Indian and Indonesian descent. But *Hīnayāna,* the conservative Buddhism of Burma, was accepted by the Khmers in the 3d century and flourished along with sects worshipping the Hindu deities Siva and Vishnu. Moreover, according to an inscription of 791 recording the erection of an image of the Buddhist Lokeśvara (Avalokiteśvara), *Mahāyāna* had been introduced into Cambodia, probably tinged with *Vajrayāna* Tantric mysticism and the influences of various Hindu cults. Jayavarman II (802–854), the founder of a kingship at Angkor, called his realm Kambudja, established the cult of the divine king (*Devarāja*), deriving his authority from Siva, and, at the expense of Buddhism, upheld a form of Hinduism based on the *Purāṇas,* or treatises on cosmogony.

Spread of Buddhism. Hinduism continued to be strong when Indravarman (877–889) began the con-

struction of a magnificent capital at Angkor, Siva's *linga,* a phallic symbol in stone of his divine authority. His son and successor Yasovarman I (889–900) built temples for the various sects of Siva, Vishnu, Brahmanic Yoga, and *Mahāyāna.* This religious eclecticism gradually disappeared when Jayavarman VII (1181–c. 1200), a devout Mahayanist, turned the *Devarāja* cult into that of the *Buddharāja,* the divine Buddhist ruler. In Ceylon his son studied *Hīnayāna,* which he introduced into Cambodia. Because of its popular appeal and the monastic school system, *Hīnayāna* eventually became the predominant religion. After 1350 the religious life was so disrupted by Thai invasions that in 1423 Cambodian monks repaired to Ceylon to be reinvested, to ensure valid succession and reorganization of the order in accord with orthodox Buddhism. When in 1460 Cambodia lost its independence to Thailand, *Hīnayāna,* largely because of Thai influence, remained the dominant religion.

Belief, Order, Cult. Cambodian Buddhism is a fusion of the predominant *Hīnayāna* with pristine ancestor and ghost worship, Brahmanism, and *Mahāyāna.* Its Hindu cosmogony, detailed in the sacred books *Trey-Phet* and *Kampi Preas Thomma Chhean,* comprises *Prohm* (*Brahmā*), the eternal, uncreated, and uncreating absolute; the universe of countless triads of worlds (*chakralaveal*) and stars that are worshipped as deities; three categories of paradises; and great and small purgatories where the departed atone for their faults and are reborn on earth or in paradise. The pantheon contains four major Buddhas, including Gautama; *Mettrey* (*Maitreya*), the Buddha that will come at the end of time; countless Brahmanic deities; and all the heavenly beings. The universe is full of ghosts and fantastic animals that are invoked and propitiated by the Cambodians in time of need or fear. Although the core of Cambodian Buddhism is *Hīnayāna,* the monks tend toward a godless monism, and the people, while longing for a transcendent theism, syncretize all religions that have crossed the land.

The order is territorially divided into two regions and subdivided into provinces, each with from 10 to 20 monasteries and temples, under the jurisdiction of a superior general. The monastic rules, exercises, and privileges are the same as those found in the Thai order. The monastery, where most Cambodian males spend some time in study and meditation, forms the center of religious and social activities. Each village has its temple. The cult includes court ceremonies, holiday rites, private devotions, propitiations, exorcisms, and conjurations against sickness and evil.

The Buddhism of Vietnam and Laos exhibits the same characteristics as that of Cambodia.

CHINA

The Chinese, unsatisfied with the ancestral, Confucian, and Taoist ways of life, welcomed the Buddhist message of mercy, hope, and paradise, so tradition says, about A.D. 67, though there are evidences of earlier contacts.

Ching-t'u. The doctrine of Ching-t'u (Skr. Sukhāvatī, Pure Land), the oldest *Mahāyāna* school, was first expounded in the *Wu-liang Shou Ching* (Skr. *Sukhāvatīvyūha Sūtra,* Infinite Life Sūtra), and *Wu-liang Ch'ing-ching Ching* (Infinite Purity *Sūtra*), put into Chinese by An Shih-kao (fl. 148–186). They tell how Buddha

Amitābha became the savior of the world, vowing that sinners who had lost their way might invoke his name with faith and be reborn at death into the Pure Land. Ambitābha was the final object of the cult (*Amidism), but almost all requests were made and granted through the mediation of Kuanyin (Avalokiteśvara). In accommodating Amidism to native ancestor worship, Fa-hu (Dharmarakṣa, fl. 266–317) put into Chinese the "All Souls" service (*Ullambanapātra Sūtra*) to free from purgatory and endless rebirths those who died without invoking Amitābha. Hui-yüan, a disciple of Tao-an, had adopted Buddhism and in 386 founded the first Amidist community; he spread the invocation so common in East Asia, "Hail, Amita Buddha" (in Chinese, *Nan-wu, A-mi-t'o Fo*). For the faithful, Amitābha was a supreme being of mercy and love, attended by innumerable Buddhas and *bodhisattvas*. His cult is the purest and highest form of worship the Chinese have ever known outside of Christianity.

Ch'an. This form was probably founded by Chu Tao-sheng (fl. 397–434) as a Chinese version of the Indian *Dhyāna* (Meditation) and developed by Bodhidharma, an Indian mystic (fl. 520–529). This intuitive school held that the only reality is the buddhaship in the heart of every man, discovered by a sudden intuition that cannot be taught, learned, or implored. Hence, study, prayer, asceticism, and works of mercy are of no avail. Most monks followed this doctrine, which harmonized with the Upanishads, the ancient philosophical and mystical systems found in the Hindu scriptures of India, and Taoism, an Indian doctrine, contemporary with the Upanishads, adopted to a Chinese movement of nonconformity to traditional institutions.

San-lun. The Three Śāstra (Mādhyamika, or Middle Way) school was founded in India by the logician and poet Nāgārjuna (2d century A.D.), and was established in China as the San-lun sect by Chia-hsiang under Emperor An of the Eastern Chin (397–419). The Three Śāstra, or treatises, written by Nāgārjuna—translated into Chinese by Kumārajīva (404–409)—expounded the unreality of all phenomenal existence, but admitted a spiritual realm beyond human conception.

T'ien-t'ai and Other Schools. In 575 Chih-i first came to Mt. T'ien-t'ai in Che-chiang province and established his school based on one of the *Mahāyāna* scriptures known as the *Saddharma-puṇḍarīka Sūtra* (Chin. *Fa-hua Ching,* Lotus of the Good Law). Chih-i strove to reconcile the doctrines of all the schools and sects, asserting that Buddha had presented different teachings in different periods of his life. To realize the buddhaship present in all living beings, men ought to study and apply all Buddha's teachings. During the T'ang dynasty (618–906), which marked a period of alternate favor and persecution of the faith, T'u-shun (556–640) established the Hua-yen (*Avataṁsaka*) sect based on another of the scriptures, the *Buddhāvataṁsaka Sūtra* (Chin. *Hua-yen Ching*), professing a *Mahāyāna* realistic monism. The Chinese scholar and monk Hsüan-tsang (620–664), on his return from a pilgrimage to Afghanistan and India (629–645), introduced the Fa-hsiang (*Dharmalakṣana*) sect, propounding a *Mahāyāna* subjective idealism. In 716 Subhakara introduced the esoteric *Chen-yen* or True-Word sect variously called *Yogācāra, Vijñānavada, *Vajrayāna,* or *Mantrayāna* according to the particular feature stressed in it. This system combined pure idealism, in which the whole universe had no objective reality and existed only in the mind of the perceiver, with Yoga, polytheism, and Tantrism. Subhakara set aside its philosophical intricacies and turned it into a cult of countless deities of his own invention to be propitiated by spells and charms. Vajrabodhi (671–741) popularized it further, and his successor Amogha (c. 704–744) borrowed from Nestorian Christianity, then flourishing in North China, the service for the dead and particularly the Mass; he also composed a ritual, *Yü-lan Sheng-hui,* for the "All Souls" festival, held on the 15th of the 7th moon, when Masses were said by Buddhist monks and offerings were made to the Buddhist Trinity to release from purgatory the souls of those who died on land or sea.

Syncretism of Religious Heritage. In the Northern Liao empire (907–1125) Buddhism absorbed more Nestorian elements. In the South the cultural movements of the peace-loving Sung dynasty (960–1279) were inspired largely by Buddhism. Popular writers produced numerous pseudoreligious tales that added a new demonism to the native religious heritage. According to this religion of fear, the world was governed by a supreme being attended by *Kuan-ti,* the god of war, and the patrons of the cities, villages, and homes. In criminal cases the Thunder Ghost (*Lei Kung*) executed the culprit. The judges (*yen-wang*) issued a warrant to apprehend the souls condemned to hell and rebirth. The world was populated by a myriad of maleficent goblins. Man was believed to have two souls. After passing through hell the superior soul was reincarnated, while the inferior vanished after the decomposition of the body or, surviving for a time, became a dreadful vampire. The dead behaved like the living, might even have sexual intercourse with them, and were capable of performing the most fantastic feats. Geomancy and other forms of divination were practiced by almost everyone. Even inanimate objects were thought to be transcendent, intelligent, animated, and usually maleficent. Animals could assume human guise and behavior. This hybrid religion was believed almost universally and all but eclipsed the consoling faith, hope, and love of the Pure Land.

Order and Temples. Most monks were of humble origin and belonged to the intuitive Ch'an sect, while the remainder came from the upper classes and followed T'ien-t'ai. The activities of the monks comprised daily devotions, meditation, religious reading and lectures, holiday celebrations, rain and drought processions, exorcisms, burials and remembrances of the dead, and pilgrimages to famous shrines. The pantheons in the temples suggest the extent of syncretization undergone by Chinese Buddhism.

Neo-Buddhism. In 1915 the monk T'ai-hsü inaugurated a revival of missionary zeal to spread the faith and reform the monasteries through national seminaries, libraries, learned societies, literature, lectures, and social service. This movement, promoted by a group of lay and religious intellectuals, was a kind of atheistic Unitarianism that generally did not affect the 263,000 temples and 738,000 monks dedicated to Buddha.

Seminaries and institutes were established in the major cities. They sponsored the translation of the Buddhist texts, notably Tibetan books, into Chinese, and some into English. However, around 1949 organized Buddhism began to be crippled by the Communist domination of China.

TIBET AND MONGOLIA

Nature worship and magic were practiced freely until *Mahāyāna* entered the Tibetan court of Sroṅ-brtsan-sgam-po (A.D. 639–650). The new faith was bitterly opposed by the Bon-po aristocracy and was eventually proscribed, until King K'ri-lde-gtsug-brtsan Mes-ag-ts'oms (755–797) invited Indian monks and scholars to come and spread the Indian faith and culture.

Spread of Buddhism. The Indian mystic Padmasaṁbhava under royal patronage built a monastery at bSam-yas, accommodating Tantric Buddhism to the native Bon cult, and he established the rÑiṅ-ma-pa or Red Hat sect, thus founding *Lamaism. The king sanctioned Buddhism as the state religion and at the council of Don-mkhar (792–794?) chose to follow Indian rather than Chinese Buddhism. Toward A.D. 1000 Tibetan Buddhism enjoyed a period of revival and growth. In 1042 the Bengalese Atīsha came to preach *Mahāyāna Pāla.* About 1050 his disciple Broṅ-ston organized the bKa'-gdams-pa sect to restore monastic discipline and celibacy, while Mar-pa (1012–97) organized the bKa'-rgyud-pa sect, which held marriage to be compatible with asceticism and Yoga. In 1261 P'ags-pa, Abbot of Sa-skya, converted the Mongols of Central Asia to Lamaism, and when he converted Kublai Khan, he was granted the sovereignty of Tibet (1275). About 100 years afterward monastic laxity prompted the learned bTsoṅ-k'a-pa (1357–1419) to reform the bKa'-gdams-pa into the dGe-lugs-pa or Yellow Hat sect and to commission the printing of a gigantic collection of *sūtras,* the *bKa' agyur,* at Pei-ching *c.* 1411. The third incarnated head of the sect, bSod-nams-rgya-mts'o, in 1577 converted a large part of Mongolia to the faith and was nominated Dalai Lama by Altan Khan.

Doctrine, Orders, and Ritual. Lamaism is a syncretism of the Bon and Shamanist cults. Tantric charms and Indo-Tibetan demonolatry were combined with *Mahāyāna* tenets and rites. Its immense pantheon contains innumerable deities, demons, and goblins. In this religion without a creator, the monks were in the position of priests to a host of deities and devils, holding the key of hell and heaven and maintaining that without a lama available to the faithful there was no salvation. The laity undertook no business of importance without first offering prayers and sacrifices. Suggestions of Nestorian and Catholic influence were evident in their baptism, confession, eucharistic dispensation of bread and wine for longevity, devotion to the "Goddess of Mercy," the "Trinity," and Māyā the "Virgin Mother" of the Buddha, litanies, beads, censers, bells, celibate and tonsured monks, and nuns. On the other hand, their use of astrology, divination, sorcery, and necromancy, was characteristically pagan. The monasteries,

divided into sects, were the strongest influence in Tibet. The Dalai Lama, head of the dGe-lugs-pa sect, was supreme temporal and spiritual ruler.

In 1924 Mongolia became a Soviet satellite. While the older generation remained attached to the old religion, the young were perverted to Communism and irreligion. In 1951 the Chinese Communists invaded Tibet and in 1959 completed the extermination of its social and religious system by executions, desecrations, confiscations, forced labor, and exactions.

KOREA

The early Korean cult of the sun-god, of heaven or the king of heaven, and of ancestors was mingled, after the Chinese invasion of the country in 108 B.C., with Confucianism and Taoism. The kingdom of Koguryŏ in the north received *Mahāyāna* Buddhism in A.D. 372, that of Paekche in the southwest, in 384, and that of Silla in the southeast, in 424.

Spread of Buddhism. In the Silla period (670–935) Buddhist life and art flourished, and the following Koryŏ period (935–1392) witnessed a still greater progress of Buddhism. Eventually Buddhism emerged as the dominant power in religion and in politics. However, its very power and splendor induced laxity, impoverishment, disintegration of the family, corruption of the order, and heterodoxy through Lamaism and Chu Hsi's materialistic statism that had been brought by the Mongol invaders (from 1231). The revolution of 1392 was in part a rebellion against the excessive power of the Buddhist monks, who were accordingly forbidden to enter the new capital under pain of death. In 1405 the 13 Buddhist sects were ordered to merge into 7, and eventually into 2: the *Sun,* based on intuition, and the practical *Kyo.* Confiscation of monastic properties and the banning of monks from monasteries and schools in towns and villages (1397) were followed by prohibitions against joining the order without royal permission (*c.* 1450) and by the abolition of the Buddhist official examinations, which were replaced by Confucian civil service tests (1507). Left without monks, teachers, temples, and rituals, most Koreans gradually abandoned their religion, the intellectuals holding to the tenets of Confucian ethics and the masses relapsing into nature worship. Particularly after the Confucian persecution of 1849, Buddhism died out except in the magnificent shrines hidden in remote valleys and hills. Modern attempts at central organization of the monasteries and temples have failed.

Order and Ritual. Of the 900 monasteries and temples only a few are near the cities. Monks and nuns, even those who live under the same roof, may belong to either sect, *Sun* or *Kyo.* They uphold the "Four Noble Truths," the "Eightfold Path," the requital of the good with heaven, and of the evil with hell, instead of rebirth and *nirvāṇa,* and all hold in highest reverence Amitābha,

Fig. 3. Leaf from the Dhammacakka-pavattana Sutta (MS Egerton 764) engraved on silver plates, probably 18th century. The segment reproduced here discusses the "five groups of grasping" and the "Eightfold Path," *the course that Buddhists believe leads to elimination of all ills. The text is engraved in the Sinhalese script.*

Śākyamuni, and Avalokiteśvara, or the Goddess of Mercy.

The temples display the combined pantheons of Buddhism, Taoism, Confucianism, Brahmanism, and animism. Public worship consists mainly of mere repetition of personal spells (*dhāraṇī*) and of communal ones (*mantra*), in Sanskrit, a language largely unknown to the clergy and laity. Community devotions, retreats, holidays, and pageants follow the traditional pattern. Where Christian influence is strong, the Buddhist monks conduct Sunday services, weddings, and funerals; some of them practice magic, fortunetelling, cures by charms according to the instructions of the *Milkyo Chip,* and crystal gazing as explained in the *Yoji Kyung.* Even before the war of 1937–45, Korean Buddhism was on the wane, but the Allied occupation and division of the country in 1945, the attack of the North against the South in 1950, the armistice of 1953, and the systematic eradication of all religion in the North by the Communists damaged it irreparably. In the South Buddhism began to lose ground to irreligion on the one hand and to Christianity on the other.

JAPAN

In A.D. 552 Buddhism was introduced to the Emperor of Japan by Paekche in southwest Korea only to meet violent opposition; but according to the *Nihongi* (Chronicles of Japan), in 587 Emperor Yōmei embraced Buddha's law (*Buppo*), revering at the same time the "Way of the Gods" (*Shintō*). However, by his constitution of 604 and by his enlightened promotion, the real founder of Japanese Buddhism was Prince-Regent Umayado [(573–621), posthumous title, *Shotoku Avataṁsaka Sūtra* (Chin. *Hua-yen Ching;* Jap. *Taishi,* Prince Imperial "Holy Virtue"]. Soon after his death various Buddhist sects entered the country.

Sanron and Jōjitsu. In 625 the Korean monk Ekan established three sects: the Sanron of "Three Śāstra" (Skr. *Mādyamika;* Chin. *San-lun*), founded in India by Nāgārjuna; the Jōjitsu (Skr. *Satya-siddhi;* Chin. *Ch'eng-shih*), based on the *Satya-siddhi Śāstra* by Harivarman; and the Keikyō (Skr. *Sautrāntikāḥ;* Chin. *Chin-liang*). The last upheld the reality of phenomena, the emptiness of self and of all things, and the word of Śākyamuni (on these and following sects see the corresponding Chinese sects above).

Hossō and Kusha. From China the Hossō (Skr. *Dharmalakṣaṇa;* Chin. *Fa-hsiang*) sect was brought by Dōshō in 654. According to him all things are monads aiming to discover the essence of cosmic existence and to realize their basic nature in Buddhahood. The doctrine lent itself to an accommodation with the native religion that since 587 had been called Shintō. From China came also the Kusha (Skr. *Kośa;* Chin. *Chü-she*) sect (658), based on the *Abhidharma-kośa Śāstra* by Vasubandu and holding the unreality of self and the reality of the law (*dharma*).

Kegon and Ritsu. While Shintō evolved further into an official cult during the period when the emperors resided at Nara (710–784), Buddhism dominated court life and in 736 imported from China the Kegon (Skr. *Avataṁsaka;* Chin. *Hua-yen*) sect, based on the *Kegonkyō*) and teaching the immanence of Buddha's essence in all things. The court's support of both Shintō and Buddhism began to disturb officials and commoners. By way of conciliation the Buddhist monk Gyōgi (670–

749) developed the notion that the two religions were merely two aspects of the same belief. In 754 the Ritsu (Skr. *Vinaya;* Chin. *Lü:* Discipline) sect was established. It was at that time a *Hīnayāna* system of attaining Buddhahood by the observance of the monastic rules of the *Tripiṭaka* revised by Dharmagupta.

Tendai. In 805 Saichō (Dengyō Daishi, 767–822) brought from China the T'ien-t'ai (Jap. *Tendai*) sect, based on the *Saddharma Puṇḍarīka Sūtra* (Chin. *Fa-hua Ching;* Jap. *Hokkekyō*). To resolve the divergences and contradictions in Buddhist scriptures, schools, and tenets, the Tendai held that Buddha's teaching was progressive over five periods of his life. The limitless eclecticism of the Tendai sect came to regard the scriptures, tenets, pantheons, and practices of all schools as varying manifestations of the same universal Buddha. Even Shintō deities were accommodated in its pantheon. Despite strong opposition from the other sects, Tendai came little by little to such prominence as to become the mother of all subsequent sects.

Shingon. The Mantrayāna (Chin. *Chen-yen;* Jap. *Shingon:* True Word or Magic Formula) sect, based chiefly on the *Mahāvairocana Sūtra* (Chin. *Ta-erh Ching;* Jap. *Dainichi-kyō*), imported from China by Kūkai (Kōbō Daishi, 774–835) in 806, was a cosmotheism according to which the universe was considered the body of Buddha Vairocana (Jap. *Dainichi,* Great Sun). Mystical absorption in the Infinite was attainable by spells, charms, trance, and hand positions. To the Buddhistic system Kūkai added the theory of 10 stages of asceticism, the initiation to Buddhahood by sprinkling (*kanchō;* Skr. *abhiṣecana*), and the fusion of Shintō, by identification of the native gods with Buddhist deities, all being manifestations of the primordial Buddha. This doctrine, which popularized Buddhism, was called Dual Shintō (Ryōbu-Shintō) by Emperor Saga (809–823).

Jōdo. To spread the faith among the masses the monk Kūya (903–972) toured the country, dancing in the streets and invoking Buddha thus: "Hail, Amita Buddha" (*Namu Amida Butsu;* Skr. *Namaḥ Amita Buddha*). But Amidism came into its own with the introduction (1175) of the Jōdo (Skr. *Sukhāvatī;* Chin. *Chin-t'u*) or Pure Land sect by the monk Hōnen (1133–1212).

Shin and Ji. Shinran (1173–1262) carried Hōnen's doctrine of salvation by faith to its logical conclusion in founding the "True Pure Land" (*Jōdo Shin*) on the principle that faith in Amida is a gift from him and the only requisite for salvation. Partly as reaction to Shin, Ippen (1239–89) established the Ji sect in 1276, holding that faith was useless for salvation, but that the invocation of Amida was essential. Shintō gods were but manifestations of the Buddhas in the superior synthesis of the Dual Way of the Gods. Dual Shintō thus reached its peak and subsequently permeated the most religious beliefs and rites.

Zen. This, the Chinese Ch'an system of meditation, came to Japan in the 7th century, but did not become solidly established until several centuries later, when it appeared in three branches: the Rinzai (1191), Sōtō (1236), and Obaku (1654). Zen has neither god, hereafter, soul, nor ritual. It assumes the inner purity and goodness of man; its aims are to discipline the mind by an insight into its proper nature and to acquire a new viewpoint for perceiving the essence of things.

Nichiren. In 1261 Nichiren formulated the principles of a Buddhist revival based on the Buddhist scripture *Saddharma Puṇḍarīka* (*Lotus Sūtra*) and Śākyamuni (the Buddha) as the supreme being. His religious patriotism appealed to the young and made them organize into a well-knit sect named after him.

Ryōbu-Shintō. By the 13th century Buddhism completed the absorption of Shintō, syncretizing the entire Japanese religious heritage into a sort of "Unitarianism" that was to prevail for centuries. In this popular religion most believers were satisfied to revere Amida and any other deity, spirit, shrine, scripture, relic, likeness, and statue, regardless of denominational differences. This Dual Shintō, however, maintained the definition of spheres of life. The interests of everyday living were entrusted to the Shintō gods, while the affairs of the hereafter were assigned to the Buddhas. Soon after birth a child was presented at a Shintō shrine and marriage and holidays were associated with Shintō symbolism. Divination, exorcism, and ancestor worship were common to both religions, but the services for the dead were conducted according to a Buddhist rite.

Buddhism declined in the Ashikaga period (1336–1568), and was eclipsed by Neo-Confucianism during the Tokugawa period (1600–1868). It lost its privileged position as a state religion in the 19th century, when the Emperor moved to Tōkyō and Japan became a world power (from 1868). Furthermore, it suffered government restrictions that culminated in the Religious Bodies Act of 1939 ordering a merger of Buddhist sects. However, after World War II the merged subsects regained their autonomy. Except for a few puritan Buddhists and Shintoists, Christians, and those without religion, the masses profess a Unitarian Amidism resulting from the syncretism of the various schools of Buddhism with Shintō. Intellectuals follow Neo-Buddhism, a materialistic atheism that believes in degrees of truth and reality and denies individuality and a substantial soul.

THE WEST

Buddhism entered Hawaii with the first Chinese and Japanese immigrations of 1852 and 1868 respectively. While the Chinese contingent remained rather small and scattered, the growing and well-knit Japanese community fostered the zeal of the *Jōdo Shin* (True Pure

Fig. 4. Worshipers at the Zenkoji, a venerable Buddhist temple in Nagano, Japan. A nun with a shaved head and a young monk face the enshrined Buddhist scriptures and read prayers to the assembled faithful.

Fig. 5. Main building of Taisoji temple of Jodo sect, Tokyo. The temple, founded in 1668, was several times destroyed by fire. The present building, designed in 1961, is unique so far as the use of modern architecture for Buddhist temples is concerned.

Land) sect. Its missioners established a mission (1897), the Women's Buddhist Association (1898), the Y.M.B.A. (1900), a Sunday school (1902), and the Honpa Hongwanji Mission headquarters in charge of 21 stations and Sunday schools (1907), which had increased to 33 by 1916. World War II greatly reduced the membership and activity of the sect. Despite efforts to accommodate itself to the Christian surroundings, the sect began to lose ground with the advance of Christianity.

U.S. On the continent, Buddhism was established in 1899 by Japanese-American faithful. It supervised branches of the Y.M.B.A. and Y.W.B.A.A., bilingual papers and periodicals, Sunday schools, and social service agencies. The few Buddhists of Chinese origin were scattered and disorganized. Efforts were made to establish Buddhism, particularly Dhyāna (Ch'an, Zen), among Westerners in San Francisco, Los Angeles, Philadelphia, and New York. A Buddhist Mission of North America was organized in 1914 and incorporated under the name of Buddhist Churches of America in 1942. Buddhism, however, has made little progress in the U.S.

Europe. Before 1914 the efforts of the Pāli Text Society and the Buddhist Society of Great Britain and Ireland paved the way for the spread of Buddhism in the United Kingdom. The Buddhist Lodge, founded in London in 1924, became the Buddhist Society in 1943. It is nonsectarian, and studies all phases of Buddhism, but stresses the Dhyāna approach of sudden intuition. A parallel movement was started by the Anagarika Dharmapāla of Calcutta, which founded in London the British Maha Bodhi Society. These movements are theosophical and tend to fuse the various schools into a Western Buddhism. Similar societies and movements, inaugurated in Germany, France, Denmark, and other countries, met with limited success.

Bibliography: C. REGAMEY et al., LexThK² 2:752–759. H. HÄRTEL et al., RGG³ 1:1469–91. C. H. HAMILTON, *Buddhism in India, Ceylon, China and Japan: A Reading Guide* (Chicago 1931). H. VON GLASENAPP, *Der Buddhismus in Indien und im Fernen Osten* (Berlin 1936). E. CONZE, *Buddhism: Its Essence and Development* (New York 1951). N. DUTT, *Early Monastic*

Buddhism (Calcutta Oriental Series 30; Calcutta 1941). A. BAREAU, *Les Premiers Conciles bouddhiques* (Paris 1955). G. APPLETON, *Buddhism in Burma* (Burma Pamphlets 3; London 1943). G. COEDÈS, *Les États hindouisés d'Indochine et d'Indonésie* (Histoire du monde 8.2; Paris 1948), 2d ed. of author's *Histoire ancienne des états hindouisés d'Extrême-Orient*. K. E. WELLS, *Thai Buddhism: Its Rites and Activities* (Bangkok 1960). M. GRANET, *La Religion des Chinois* (2d ed. Paris 1951). E. ZÜRCHER, *The Buddhist Conquest of China,* 2 v. (Sinica Leidensia 11; Leiden 1959). A. B. GOVINDA, *Foundations of Tibetan Mysticism, According to the Esoteric Teachings of the Great Oṁ Maṇi Padme Hūṁ* (New York 1960). F. R. MORAES, *The Revolt in Tibet* (New York 1960). D. SUZUKI, *Manual of Zen Buddhism* (New York 1960). J. FINEGAN, *The Archeology of World Religions* (Princeton 1952). C. REGAMEY, "Der Buddhismus Indiens," König Christus 3:229–305. M. EDER, "Die Religionen der Chinesen, *ibid.,* 3:319–373. F. K. NUMAZAWA, "Die Religionen Japans," *ibid.* 3:393–436. On the relations between Buddhism and Christianity, see the systematic bibliog. in E. BENZ and M. NAMBARA, *Das Christentum und die nicht-christlichen Hochreligionen* (Beihefte der Zeitschrift für Religions- und Geistesgeschichte 5; Leiden 1960) 53–66. H. DE LUBAC, *La Rencontre du Bouddhisme et de l'Occident* (Paris 1952); *Aspects of Buddhism* (New York 1954). H. DUMOULIN, *A History of Zen Buddhism,* tr. P. PEACHEY (New York 1963). W. T. DE BARY et al., eds., *Introduction to Oriental Civilizations,* 3 v. (Records of Civilization 54–56; New York): *Sources of Japanese Tradition* (54; 1958); *Sources of Chinese Tradition* (55; 1960); *Sources of Indian Tradition* (56; 1958). **Illustration credit:** Fig. 1, Courtesy of the Smithsonian Institution, Freer Gallery of Art, Washington, D.C. Fig. 2, Indian Museum, Calcutta. Fig. 3, Courtesy of the Trustees of the British Museum. Figs. 4 and 5, Japan Travel Bureau, Tokyo.

[A. S. ROSSO]

Guillaume Budé, portrait by Jean Clouet (active 1516, d. 1540), tempera and oil on wood.

BUDÉ, GUILLAUME, the great revivalist of Greek studies; b. Paris, Jan. 26, 1467; d. there, Aug. 20, 1540. He studied at Paris and Orléans and became proficient in Greek, philosophy, law, theology, and medicine. He owes much of his success in Greek studies to the encouragement of John *Lascaris. Budé belonged to the early humanist tradition and, like John Colet and Erasmus, turned to the study of the ancient languages for their own sakes, remaining free from the corruption by heathen antiquity to which the later humanists of Germany and Italy fell prey. Budé's abilities were recognized by King Louis XII of France, who sent him as his ambassador to Rome for the coronation of Pope Julius II in 1502. On his return he became the King's secretary until 1515, when he was again sent to Rome on a mission to Pope Leo X but was recalled at his own request. Shortly after his return to France, Budé was appointed royal librarian by the new King, Francis I, to whom he suggested the creation of a college for the study of Greek, Latin, and Hebrew. As a result, he was empowered to ask Erasmus to take charge of the proposed institution. He was not successful, and the founding of the college was delayed until 1530, when it opened as Collège Royal, later known as Collège de France. At this time Budé prevailed upon Francis I not to ban the printing press as recommended by the Sorbonne.

For a while, Budé was suspected of leanings toward Calvinism as shown by his correspondence with Erasmus. After his death, however, these suspicions were disproved, and his orthodoxy declared. Budé was undoubtedly the best Greek scholar of his day, not excepting even Erasmus; his *Commentarii linguae graecae* (1529) greatly advanced the study of Greek literature. His greatest title to distinction, however, is the foundation of the Collège de France, which marked an epoch in the revival of classical studies in France and restored to the University of Paris something of its lost prestige. Literary France also owes to Budé's efforts the foundation of the Bibliothèque de Fontainebleau, later known as the Bibliothèque Nationale. Among his writings are: *Annotationes in XXIV pandectarum libros* (1508), *De asse et partibus eius libri V* (1515), *De contemptu rerum fortuitarum libri III* (1521–26), *De philologia libri II* (1530), *De transitu hellenismi ad christianismum libri III* (1534), and the *Epistolae,* containing 160 letters written to Thomas More, Erasmus, Sadoleto, Bembo, Rabelais, and Vives.

Bibliography: *Opera omnia,* ed. C. S. CURIO, 4 v. in 3 (Basel 1557). J. PLATTARD, *Guillaume Budé (1468–1540) et les origines de l'humanisme français* (Paris 1923). J. BOHATEC, *Budé und Calvin* (Graz 1950). A. ROERSCH, DHGE 10:1040–41. A. FINGERLE, LexThK² 2:759. A. PRATESI, EncCatt 3:182–184. H. R. GUGGISBERG, RGG³ 1:1494. Sandys 2:170–173. **Illustration credit:** The Metropolitan Museum of Art, Maria De Witt Jesup Fund, 1946.

[M. I. C. DUFFEY]

BUENOS AIRES, ARCHDIOCESE OF (BONAËRENSIS), see including only the city of Buenos Aires and Martín García Island. It had in 1963 an area of 202 square kilometers, but a population of almost 4 million. The diocese was established by Pope Paul V on March 30, 1620; it was made an archdiocese on March 5, 1865, by Pope Pius IX. From the first bishop, Pedro Carranza (1621–32), to Cardinal Antonio Caggiano, 25 prelates governed the territory that in 1620 included an area that in 1963 comprised 26 dioceses and 5 archdioceses, some of which are now in the Republic of Uruguay. In 1963 the suffragan sees of Buenos Aires were Mercedes (1934), Morón (1957), Nueve de Julio (1957), San Isidro (1957), and San Martín (1961). Before the start of the war for independence from Spain in 1810, the following bishops were appointed to the diocese: Pedro Carranza (1620–32), Cristóbal de Aresti (1636–

Cathedral of the Archdiocese of Buenos Aires.

38), Cristóbal de la Mancha y Velazco (1641–75), Antonio de Azcona (1676–1700), Gabriel de Arregui (1713–16), Pedro Fajardo (1717–29), Juan de Arregui (1731–36), José de Peralta (1741–46), Cayetano Marsellano y Agramont (1751–59), José Antonio Basurco (1760–61), Manuel Antonio de la Torre (1765–76), Sebastián de Malvar y Pinto (1778–84), Manuel Azamor y Ramírez (1788–96), and Benito Lué y Riega (1803–12). Bishop Mariano Medrano y Cabrera (1830–51) took over the diocese after independence. He was followed by Mariano José Escalada (1854–70), Federico Aneiros (1873–94), Uladislao Castellano (1895–1900), Mariano Antonio Espinosa (1900–23), José María Bottaro (1926–32), Santiago Luis Copello (1932–56), Fermín E. Lafitte (1956–59), and Cardinal Caggiano (1959–   ). All these bishops were interested in increasing vocations to the priesthood, which unfortunately remained far below the level of need for the growing city. In 1959 there were 5 auxiliary bishops, 355 diocesan priests (84 not attached to the diocese), and 539 belonging to religious communities. The latter had charge of 49 of the 137 parishes. There were 144 seminarians, of whom 74 were in the major seminary and 67 in the minor. An additional 131 seminarians were from other dioceses. Forty-nine religious orders of men and 107 religious communities of women are represented, occupying 95 houses and 246 convents respectively. The total of religious in the archdiocese reached 3,720. Buenos Aires was the site of the Pontifical University (the Pontifical Seminary of Villa Devoto), the Catholic University of Buenos Aires, and the University of El Salvador. There were also 23 secondary and 42 primary schools for boys, 63 secondary and 131 primary for girls—all operated by religious—as well as 3 parochial secondary schools and 21 grade schools. There were 96 kindergartens under religious and 19 established in parishes. College students could choose among 35 residences for male students and 34 for women. The sisters staffed 24 rehabilitation centers, 10 homes for the aged, 27 hospitals, 17 clinics and sanitariums, and 6 visiting nurse centers. In 1959 there were 10 athletic centers and 5 retreat houses.

See also ARGENTINA.

Illustration credit: Pan American Union.

[G. FURLONG]

BUFALO, GASPARE DEL, ST., founder of the Society of the *Precious Blood (CPPS); b. Rome, Jan. 6, 1786; d. there, Dec. 28, 1837 (feast, Oct. 21). He was educated at the Collegio Romano and while yet a seminarian he catechized, visited hospitals, and reactivated the Santa Galla hospice for homeless men. After ordination (1808) he took as spiritual director Canon Francesco Albertini, known for his devotion to the *Precious Blood, and assisted him in establishing a pious union of the Precious Blood in the church of San Nicola in Carcere. As a canon of the church of San Marco, Gaspare was summoned to swear allegiance to Napoleon I when the latter gained control of the *States of the Church. For his refusal he spent about 4 years (1810–14) in exile and prison. Returning to Rome, he was assigned by Pius VII to preaching missions in the Papal States. Encouraged by the Pope, Cardinal Cristaldi, and others, he established the Society of the Precious Blood (Aug. 15, 1815) and opened its first house in the monastery of San Felice in Giano (Umbria). He also advised Bl. Maria De *Mattias to found the *Precious Blood Sisters. The rest of his life was devoted to preaching, spiritual direction, and defense of his society against the sharp objections that were made because of its title. Outstanding was his missionary activity in the bandit-infested areas of the Papal States and the Kingdom of Naples. Among his friends were SS. Vincent *Pallotti and Vincenzo *Strambi. He was beatified Dec. 18, 1904, and canonized June 12, 1954. Pope John XXIII called him the greatest apostle of the Precious Blood. *See* PRECIOUS BLOOD, III (DEVOTION TO).

Bibliography: G. DE LIBERO, *S. Gaspare de Bufalo romano e le sua missione nel sangue di Cristo* (Rome 1954). V. SARDI, *Herald of the Precious Blood: Gaspar del Bufalo,* tr. E. G. KAISER (Minneapolis 1954).

[A. J. POLLACK]

BUFFALO, DIOCESE OF (BUFFALENSIS)

Established April 23, 1847; suffragan of the metropolitan of New York, comprising the New York State counties of Erie, Niagara, Genesee, Orleans, Chautauqua, Wyoming, Cattaraugus, and Allegany, an area of 6,357 square miles. In 1963 the Catholic population numbered 887,928 in a total population of 1,754,163.

Early History. During the 17th and early 18th century, French missionaries labored successfully within this territory until it passed to the English. In the post-Revolutionary period, the area was visited by itinerant priests as early as 1808, when the see city was still a small village. Following completion of the Erie Canal in 1825 the rapid increase of population in western New York, especially in the Buffalo area, caused concern to Bp. John *Dubois of New York City whose diocese then comprised the whole state. The impulse to organized Catholicism in western New York may be traced to a visit in 1828 of Kentucky missionary Stephen *Badin, who, remaining 6 weeks with the leading Catholic layman of Buffalo, Louis LeCouteulx, successfully urged him to donate land for a church, school, rectory, and cemetery. In October 1829 Rev. J. Nicholas Mertz, a native of Luxemburg, arrived as first resident priest. The first parish church, made of logs and ready for use in 1832, was dedicated to "The Lamb of God"; later structures were dedicated to St. Louis to honor the donor of the land.

In his visitations of the surrounding settlements where Mass was offered in private homes, Mertz was assisted by transient priests including (Bl.) John N. *Neumann (later fourth Bishop of Philadelphia); Alexander Pax, Mertz's successor as pastor of St. Louis parish; and Matthias Alig, CSSR. In 1836, at the age of 72, Mertz retired to East Eden, N.Y., where he died on Aug. 10, 1844.

Diocese from 1847. When the diocese was established on April 23, 1847, it included all 20 counties west of Lake Cayuga, almost one-third of the state; in 1868 Rochester was formed from eight of the eastern counties, and in 1896 four more were cut off and added to Rochester. John *Timon, visitor general of the Congregation of the Missions (Vincentians) and Texas missionary, was consecrated Buffalo's first bishop on Oct. 17, 1847. There were 16 priests, 16 churches, less than 10 schools, almost all of very primitive construction. A few Redemptorists (in Rochester and Buffalo) constituted the only religious congregation in the diocese. Within 1 year, however, six Sisters of Charity from Emmitsburg, Md., opened the first Catholic hospital and orphanage, and the first Jesuits arrived from Canada for parochial, mission, and teaching service.

During Timon's episcopate 2 seminaries were started, St. Bonaventure's at Allegany, by Franciscans, and Our Lady of the Angels, near Niagara Falls, by Vincentians; 13 communities of sisters were introduced, 2 of which, however, discontinued their work in the diocese; Oblates of Mary Immaculate, Passionists, and the Christian Brothers came to assist in the education of young men; and following the cholera epidemic of 1849, Brothers of the Holy Infancy, founded by Timon, took charge of an orphanage for boys at "Limestone Hill," the modern Lackawanna. The first cathedral, dedicated to St. Joseph, patron of the diocese, was begun in 1852 and dedicated, though not completed, on July 1, 1855.

At Timon's death in 1867, Stephen V. Ryan, like his predecessor a visitor general of the Vincentians, was consecrated on Nov. 8, 1868. His tenure of 28 years concentrated on development of new parishes and parochial schools. During the next 60 years, Buffalo was occupied by a succession of prelates under whom steady progress continued to be made. James E. Quigley, a diocesan priest, was consecrated on Feb. 24, 1897, to succeed Ryan. Six years later when Quigley was transferred to the archdiocese of Chicago, Charles H. Colton of

Altar of reconstructed chapel at Old Fort Niagara. Original structure built in 1726 as first permanent house of worship in present Buffalo Diocese.

New York City was consecrated fourth bishop of Buffalo, Aug. 24, 1903. During his episcopate a new cathedral was begun nearer the residential area of the city, dedicated, as the first one had been, to St. Joseph. The cornerstone was laid June 9, 1912, and the building was scarcely finished when Colton died, May 9, 1915. His funeral was the first public service in the new cathedral.

Colton was succeeded by Dennis *Dougherty, who was transferred to Buffalo from the Diocese of Jaro, Philippine Islands, Dec. 6, 1915. In May 1918 he was promoted to the Archdiocese of Philadelphia, to be succeeded in Buffalo by William *Turner, professor and librarian at The Catholic University of America, Washington, D.C. Turner was consecrated on March 30, 1919, and ruled until his death on July 10, 1936. He was followed on April 14, 1937, by Bp. John A. Duffy of Syracuse, Buffalo's seventh bishop, whose 7-year tenure terminated with his death on Sept. 27, 1944. On March 10, 1945, Bp. (later Cardinal) John F. *O'Hara, military delegate of the armed forces of the U.S., was transferred to the Buffalo diocese. Upon his election to the Philadelphia archdiocese in 1951, he was succeeded, Feb. 7, 1952, by Joseph A. Burke, a Buffalo priest, who died suddenly 10 years later while attending Vatican Council II. On Feb. 12, 1963, Bp. James A. McNulty of Paterson, N.J., was transferred to the Buffalo Diocese as ordinary.

Institutional Growth. The steady growth of Catholicism in the diocese is exemplified by the institutions of Lackawanna known nationally as "Father Baker's Homes of Charity," which include a large hospital, grade and high school, a protectory for homeless boys, a residence program for younger children, an infant home, and the National Shrine of Our Lady of Victory, which is also the church of a flourishing parish. Originating in Timon's orphanage of 1856 at "Limestone Hill," the project was greatly expanded by the efforts of Msgr. Nelson H. Baker.

Catholic Charities Corporation, organized by Turner Oct. 30, 1923, finances 35 institutions and numerous subsidiary agencies by its annual appeal for funds. The missionary apostolate, begun in 1940 by Duffy, serves the sparsely populated southern part of the diocese. Its purposes are to extend full parochial life into areas remote from established parishes and to develop in newly ordained priests a recognition of pastoral and missionary needs, good habits of parish administration, and zeal for souls.

The diocese has its major seminary at East Aurora; its minor seminary in Buffalo; and one regional seminary. Its 12 colleges and universities, including St. Bonaventure and Niagara universities and Canisius, D'Youville, and Rosary Hill colleges, had a total enrollment (1963) of 9,441. By 1963 there were 38 high schools with 17,891 students and 194 elementary schools with 79,023 students. Expansion of adult education programs, under the guidance of the Catholic Family Life department, penetrated even to remote areas. The importance of the Catholic press was recognized as early as 1853, when Timon founded the *Catholic Sentinel,* which continued until 1864. In 1872 the *Catholic Union* became the official weekly. In 1914 a second weekly, the *Echo,* began publication. Though not official, it proved of great influence, especially among those of German descent, and, under capable lay editors, attained a wide circulation. In 1939 Duffy arranged the merger of the two papers, to form the present *Catholic Union and Echo.*

Bibliography: C. G. DEUTHER, *Life and Times of the Rt. Rev. John Timon, D.D.* (Buffalo 1870). M. P. GALLAGHER, *The History of Catholic Elementary Education in the Diocese of Buffalo, 1847–1944* (Washington 1945).

[C. G. ZIMPFER]

BUFFIER, CLAUDE, French philosopher; b. Warsaw, May 25, 1661; d. Paris, May 17, 1737. His French parents moved to Normandy when he was a child. He studied at Rouen, entered the Jesuits on Sept. 9, 1679, and taught literature at Paris and philosophy and theology at Rouen. He was exiled in 1696 for disputing the Jansenist recommendations of his archbishop (*see* JANSENISM), but he justified himself in Rome and returned to Paris in 1701 to work on the *Journal de Trévoux* until 1731. He wrote widely on religion, philosophy, history, philology, and pedagogy, and was an original, analytical, and penetrating thinker. In his *Traité des premières verités* (Eng. tr. 1780) he shows the influence of *Descartes, *Locke, and *Malebranche, but does not follow them. For Buffier, first truths are propositions so evident that they cannot be proved, or refuted, by others more evident. These truths are perceived by the *common sense that nature has put in men so that they will judge in a uniform manner. French eclectic philosophers in the 19th century rediscovered Buffier through Thomas *Reid and the *Scottish School of Common Sense. Buffier's successful French grammar (1709) was translated into several languages. The *Encyclopedists excerpted extensively from his *Cours des sciences* (1732) without acknowledgment.

Bibliography: P. BERNARD, DTC 2.1:1167–73. A. DE BIL, DHGE 10:1083–87. P. MAGNINO, Mercati-Pelzer DE 1:446. Koch JesLex 277.

[M. MARTIN]

BUFFON, GEORGES LOUIS LECLERC DE, French writer and scientist; b. Montbard, Sept. 7, 1707; d. Paris, April 16, 1788; remembered for his extensive writing on natural history; the first investigator of the earth's history to stress the development of living creatures. His father was a councilor in the Burgundian parliament, and Buffon's formative years were spent in an atmosphere of wealth and cultural interests.

While studying law at the Jesuit college in Dijon, he made the acquaintance of Lord Kingston, a young Englishman, and his tutor, a student of natural history. They traveled the Continent together, and it was during this tour that Buffon's interest in nature matured. He was then elected a fellow of the Royal Society, and settled in England for a year of scientific study. Upon his return to France, he translated Sir I. *Newton's *Fluxions,* and S. Hales's *Vegetable Staticks,* two works that presaged his own investigations. In 1739 Buffon was appointed keeper of the Jardin du Roi and its adjoining museum, where, utilizing a research grant from Louis XV, he collected data for his 44-volume *Histoire naturelle,* a work that exerted extensive influence on the scientific world. The first volumes appeared in 1749, and others followed during the ensuing 50 years. In 1753 Buffon was elected to the Académie Française.

In the *Histoire naturelle,* Buffon expressed his idea of nature as one whole, all of whose forces intertwine and whose manifestations stand in mutual causal connection. He held that although the primary cause of nature is concealed from the scientist, he must observe, compare facts, and attempt to find a regular course of events. Buffon's basic evolutionary ideas, which preceded those of *Lamarck and *Darwin, dissatisfied French theologians, although he personally held no animosity toward religion and recognized man's spiritual as well as his biological nature.

In total perspective, the *Histoire naturelle* was the first attempt at anthropology in the modern sense, and opened the door to further study along similar lines.

Bibliography: A. M. DUCLAUX, *The French Ideal* (London 1911). DictBiogFranc 7:629–631. E. NORDENSKIÖLD, *The History of Biology* (New York 1935).

[L. P. COONEN]

BUGENHAGEN, JOHANN, Lutheran churchman, known as "Dr. Pommer"; b. Wollin, Pomerania, June 24, 1485; d. Wittenberg, Saxony, April 20, 1558. Bugenhagen, a Premonstratensian canon, became rector at Treptow (1504), was ordained (1509), and became

Johann Bugenhagen.

a lector in Scripture and patrology at Belbuck (1517). Converted by Luther's treatise "Babylonian Captivity" (1520), he fled to Wittenberg in 1521 and studied theology. After his marriage (1522), he served as city pastor (1523–57), and held a professorship from 1535. Next to Philip Melanchthon, Bugenhagen was the most influential member of Luther's intimate circle: a lifelong friend, confessor, adviser, and lieutenant, endowed with Melanchthon's moderation and Luther's firmness. His works include commentaries, a Low German translation of the NT (1524) and the Bible (with colleagues, 1533), as well as polemical works against Catholics, Zwinglians, and Anti-Trinitarians. He established Lutheranism in North Germany and Denmark upon request of authorities there, writing church orders between 1528 and 1544 for Brunswick (city), Hamburg, Lübeck, Pomerania, Denmark, Holstein, Brunswick-Wolfenbuettel, and Hildesheim; these emphasized good schools, good administration of church property, good ministers, and liturgical conservatism. In 1537 he went to Denmark where he crowned King Christian III, consecrated seven men as "bishops" or superintendents of the Danish church, and reorganized the University of Copenhagen.

Bibliography: J. BUGENHAGEN, *Sechs Predigten,* ed. G. BUCHWALD (Halle 1885); *Katechismuspredigten, gehalten 1525 und*

1532, ed. G. Buchwald (Leipzig 1909) sermons; *Briefwechsel,* ed. O. Vogt (Stettin 1888), letters. E. Sehling, ed., *Die Evangelischen Kirchenordnungen des 16. Jahrhunderts,* 5 v. (Leipzig 1902–13). H. Hering, *Doktor Pomeranus, Johannes Bugenhagen* (Halle 1888). W. Rautenberg, *Johann Bugenhagen* (Berlin 1958). E. Wolf, *Peregrinatio* (Munich 1954), with sketch and bibliog. O. Thulin, RGG³ 1:1504. J. Allendorf, LexThK² 2:761. C. Crivelli, EncCatt 3:188–189. **Illustration credit:** New York Public Library Picture Collection.

[R. H. FISCHER]

BUGLIO, LUDOVICO, missionary and author; b. Mineo, Sicily, Jan. 26, 1606; d. Peking, China, Oct. 7, 1682. He was a Jesuit by 1622, and he arrived in China in 1637. He was joined in Szechwan in 1642 by Gabriel de Megalhaens, but their missionary work was interrupted in 1643 when the bandit Chang Hsien-chung desolated the province and made them prisoners. From 1647 to 1651 they were imprisoned by the Emperor in Peking as collaborators of Chang. After further difficulties from 1659 to 1669, Buglio at last resumed missionary work. He translated much of Aquinas's *Summa theologica* into Chinese (30 v., Peking 1654–79, 2d ed. 1930), wrote a treatise of moral theology in Chinese, and translated several liturgical works into Chinese. He delighted the Emperor with paintings done in perspective and taught the technique to Chinese artists.

Bibliography: A. de Bil, DHGE 10:1090–93. E. Lamalle, EncCatt 3:189–190. J. Schütte, LexThK² 2:762. G. H. Dunne, *Generation of Giants* (Notre Dame, Ind. 1962).

[B. LAHIFF]

BUKAVU, ARCHDIOCESE OF (BUKAVU-ENSIS), metropolitan see since 1959, in Maniema province, east *Congo Republic (Léopoldville), central Africa. In 1963 it had 101 priests, 10 sisters, and 223,000 Catholics in a population of 619,000; it is 3,403 square miles in area. Its five suffragans, 97,044 square miles in area, which had 255 priests, 373 sisters, and 629,000 Catholics in a population of 2,033,000 were: Beni (created in 1959), Goma (1959), Kasongo (1959), Kindu (1959), and Uvira (1962). There were 19,000 Protestants and 332,000 pagans in the archdiocese and 124,000 Protestants and 1,057,000 pagans in the suffragan sees. Beni, Kindu, and Uvira were abandoned in 1964 because of the difficulties accompanying Congo independence. The city of Bukavu, at the south end of Lake Kivu near the *Rwanda border, was called Costermansville until 1954. From the Vicariate of the Upper Congo (1887) was detached that of Kivu (1929), called Costermansville (1952), and Bukavu (1954), an archdiocese in 1959. Another Vicariate of Kivu (1912), to the east, became the Vicariates of Rwanda and Urundi (1922).

Bibliography: C. Corvo, EncCatt 7:712–714. MissCattol 141–142. AnnPont (1964) 79.

[L. JADIN]

BUKHTĪSHŪʻ

A Christian Nestorian family prominent in medicine and in the service of the *ʻAbbāsid caliphs and their successors from the second half of the 8th to the second half of the 11th century. Their public roles and academic interests were characteristic of physicians in their day. The following 10 are identified and described in the literature.

Jūrjīs (George) ibn Jibrīl (Gabriel) ibn Bukhtīshūʻ (d. after 769) was the director of the hospital of Jundishāpūr, Iran, an institution going back to Sassanian

times. He was summoned to Baghdad in 765 to cure the Caliph al-Manṣūr (754–775). His success won him the Caliph's favor. Like many of the family, he knew Greek, Syriac, and Arabic. For the Caliph he translated from Greek into Arabic. Works of his own written in Syriac were later translated into Arabic. After a few years in Baghdad he returned and died in Judishāpūr.

Bukhtīshūʻ ibn Jūrjīs (d. 801), son of the former, continued the direction of the Jundishāpūr hospital. He was twice summoned to court. Intrigue blocked his stay the first time, but the second time, in 787, he was named by the Caliph Hārūn al-Rashīd (786–809) physician in chief, and he kept his post until he died.

Jabrīl ibn Bukhtīshūʻ (d. 828), son of the preceding, had a checkered 22 years of service to the court under three caliphs. He was replaced for a while by his son-in-law. New Syriac translations of Galen were placed at his disposal, and he wrote in Arabic on medicine and logic.

Bukhtīshūʻ (d. 870), son of Jibrīl, succeeded his father and served the Caliph al-Maʾmūn (813–833). Exiled to Jundishāpūr by the Caliph al-Wāthiq (842–847) and recalled too late to cure this Caliph, he served under the Caliph al-Mutawakkil (847–861), only to be exiled again. He had the translation of Galen continued, and he himself wrote a text on bloodletting.

ʻUbaid Allāh, probably son of the preceding, was a financial official but died, leaving a son Jibrīl, who followed the family tradition. The date of his death is unknown.

Yuḥanna, illegitimate son of Bukhtīshūʻ, was at first physician of the brother of the Caliph Al-Muʻtamid (870–892). In 893 he became bishop of Mosul, and he was twice an unsuccessful candidate for the office of patriarch. The date of his death is unknown.

Bukhtīshūʻ ibn Yaḥya cannot be more particularly identified than as a member of the family. He served the Caliph al-Rāḍī (834–940) and was held responsible for the death of Prince Hārūn in 936. The date of his death is unknown.

Jibrīl ibn ʻUbaid Allāh (d. 1006), son of ʻUbaid Allāh, learned medicine in Baghdad. He served the Buwayhid Caliph ʻAḍud al-Dawla (949–983) in Shiraz, Iran, and returned to Baghdad. He went on a pilgrimage to Jerusalem. He declined the invitation to Cairo from the Fāṭimid Caliph al-ʻAzīz (975–996) but accepted that of the Marwānid at Maiyāfāriqīn (in modern eastern Turkey). He died there at the age of 85.

Abu Saʻid ʻUbaidallah ibn Jibrīl (d. 1058), son of the preceding, lived in Maiyāfāriqīn, a contemporary and friend of Ibn Butlan (d. *c.* 1063). His scholarly work was concerned with medicine, love, and the translation from Syriac of church law on inheritance.

ʻAlī ibn Ibrahim ibn Bukhtīshūʻ, the last of the family to write, was concerned with ophthalmology. The date of his death is unknown.

Bibliography: Graf GeschChArabLit 2:109–112, with abundant ref. to mod. literature in Arab. and Western lang. D. Sourdel, EncIslam² 1:1298. C. Brockelmann, EncIslam¹ 1:614–615. E. Hammerschmidt, LexThK² 2:551.

[J. A. DEVENNY]

BULGAKOV, MACARIUS, one of the most influential 19th-century Russian theologians and church historians; b. Kursk, Russia, 1816; d. Moscow, 1882. In the world he was called Michael Petrovich, but he took the name of Macarius when he received the monastic tonsure. As the son of a country priest from the region of Kursk, he studied at the Ecclesiastical Academy of Kiev. Upon completion of his studies, he was appointed to the chair of history then recently created at the academy. In 1842 he was called to the Ecclesiastical Academy of St. Petersburg to teach theology, and he became its rector in 1850. Four years later he was elected a member of the Imperial Academy of Sciences, and until his death he remained one of its most active members. He was consecrated bishop of Tambov in 1854 and was transferred to Kharkov in 1859. In 1868 he became bishop of Lithuania, and in 1879, metropolitan of Moscow. He traveled widely and expended his resources in helping students and scholars.

Besides numerous articles for religious periodicals, Macarius wrote (1843) a dissertation on *The History of the Ecclesiastical Academy of Kiev*. In 1847 the publication of his *Introduction to Orthodox Theology* earned him the title of doctor in divinity, which was rarely conferred in Russia. This was the first of six volumes of a complete course of Orthodox theology that appeared during the following years. At the same time, he was writing his history of the Russian Church. Twelve volumes were completed during his lifetime; the thirteenth was published by his brother after his death. In 1868 he published a condensed course of theology in one volume for seminarians. Besides these works, he left a *History of the Russian Schism of the Old Believers* and three volumes of sermons.

In keeping with the Eastern tradition, Macarius's theology is predominantly positive; he indulges little in speculation. He takes some inspiration from Catholic writers, particularly P. Perrone, but on controversial questions such as the procession of the Holy Spirit, purgatory, divorce, and satisfaction in the Sacrament of Penance, his views are decidedly not Catholic. Although his historical works do not always meet the standards of modern criticism, they are nevertheless a treasury of often unpublished historical documents. His compendium of theology has been translated into French and several Eastern European languages. As a consequence, his influence in the Orthodox world has been considerable.

Bibliography: M. JUGIE, *Catholicisme* 2:306–307; DTC 9.2: 1443–44. Jugie TheolDogm 1:612–613; v.2–4, *passim*. J. B. FRANZELIN, *Examen doctrinae Macarii Bulgakov . . . de processione Spiritus Sancti* (Rome 1876).

[P. MAILLEUX]

BULGAKOV, SERGEĬ NIKOLAEVICH,

Russian economist, philosopher, and theologian; b. Livny, Orel Region, central Russia, July 16, 1871; d. Paris, July 13, 1944. He came of a family of Orthodox priests. He studied at the seminary in Orel until a religious crisis caused his transfer to a school in Elcy, where he completed his secondary education. In 1890 he entered the University of Moscow as a convinced Marxist. But his master's dissertation (written in Russian, as were almost all his works), *Capitalism and Agriculture* (2 v. 1900), questioned Marx's basic thesis because agricultural development did not substantiate it. While professor of political economy at the Kiev Polytechnic Institute (1901–06) he experienced a second spiritual crisis as described in his *From Marxism to Idealism* (1903). He transferred in 1906 to the Commercial Institute of Moscow, where he became intimately friendly

with Pavel *Florenskiĭ and Nicholĭ *Berdíaev. His doctoral dissertation, *Philosophy of Economics* (1912), showed the influence of the doctrine of Sophia or Divine Wisdom derived from Vladimir *Solov'ev and Florenskiĭ. *The Unfading Light* (1917) terminated Bulgakov's purely philosophical writing. Thereafter he concentrated on theology. In 1918 he became an Orthodox priest. When the Bolshevists forced him to relinquish his professional chair, he moved to the Crimea. The government caused him to flee to Prague in 1922. From 1925 until his death he served as dean of the Russian Orthodox Theological Institute of St. Sergius in Paris. Although he steeped himself in the Fathers of the Church, he interpreted them in a very liberal fashion and was greatly influenced by German *idealism. His principal theological works were: *The Burning Bush, The Friend of the Bridegroom,* and *Jacob's Ladder,* which form the "small trilogy" (1927–29); and *The Lamb of God, The Comforter,* and *The Bride of the Lamb,* which constitutes his "large trilogy" (1933–46). His writings frequently assailed Catholic doctrines. His own doctrine on Divine Wisdom caused so much controversy among the Russian Orthodox by seeming to postulate a fourth divine person that it was condemned by the Synod of Karlovci, Yugoslavia, and by Patriarch Sergeĭ of Moscow (1935). Bulgakov submitted to Metropolitan Eulogius of Paris and declared his belief in all Orthodox dogmas. His "sophiology" was, he said, merely his personal interpretation of these beliefs. A popular exposition of his doctrines appeared in English as *The Wisdom of God* (1937).

Bibliography: V. V. ZENKOVSKY, *History of Russian Philosophy,* tr. G. L. KLINE, 2 v. (New York 1953) 2:890–916. N. O. LOSSKY, *History of Russian Philosophy* (New York 1951). L. ZANDER, in *Irénikon* 9 (1946) 168–185. B. SCHULTZE, *Russische Denker* (Vienna 1950); EncCatt 3:193. I. H. DALMAIS, *Catholicisme* 2:307–309.

[J. PAPIN]

BULGARIA

European country, 42,830 square miles in area, in the Balkans, bordered by Turkey, Greece, Yugoslavia, Rumania, and the Black Sea. In 1962 its population of 8,000,000 included 450,000 Turks, 150,000 Gypsies, 30,000 Armenians, and 6,000 Jews. Sofia, the capital, had 718,000 inhabitants. Ethnically the Bulgarians, who moved into the lower Danube basin at the beginning of the 7th century, belonged to Turco-Tartar stock (*see* BULGARS). Despite their small numbers they founded in 679 a large, powerful state. Intermarriage with their Slav subjects, who had previously settled there, caused the Slav strain eventually to predominate. After a long period under Turkish domination Bulgaria became a principality (1878) and then an independent kingdom (1908). Since 1946, with the Communists in power, it has been known as the Bulgarian People's Republic.

Christian Origins. Christianity clearly entered the region of modern Bulgaria early, since in 343 a famous council met in Sardica (modern Sofia). This primitive Christianity almost disappeared when the Slavs and other peoples migrated into this area. Present-day Christianity traces its origin to the conversion (864–865) of *Boris I, who was baptized by the clergy of Constantinople. Soon after his conversion, Boris (reigned 853–889), who was eager for a status of equality with the Byzantine emperor, sought to have a patriarchate created for

Bulgaria, showing the ecclesiastical subdivisions and points important in the development of the Church.

the Bulgarian Church. When Photius, the Patriarch of Constantinople, refused this request, Boris sent a delegation to Rome (866). As a result Pope Nicholas I sent to Bulgaria as legate Bishop (later Pope) Formosus and promised to appoint an archbishop for the country later. Dissatisfied with the papal solution, Boris took his case to the Council of Constantinople IV (869–870). At this ecumenical synod the Byzantines decided to submit Bulgaria to the jurisdiction of Constantinople, despite the Pope's protest. This question was one of the chief issues in the controversy between Rome and Constantinople during the 9th century. Bulgaria remained under Constantinople's jurisdiction and, as a result, part of the Byzantine rite and within the orbit of Byzantine civilization (*see* CONSTANTINOPLE, PATRIARCHATE OF; BYZANTINE RITE; BULGARIAN RITE; BYZANTINE CIVILIZATION).

Orthodox Church. In 917 King Simeon the Great (893–927) proclaimed himself emperor and named the archbishop of Preslav as patriarch of Bulgaria. In 927 Constantinople recognized the first Bulgarian patriarchate, which lasted until 1018. After the Byzantines overthrew the first Bulgarian Empire (971), the patriarch left Preslav and resided in Ohrid, Macedonia. When Byzantium occupied Macedonia (1018), the Bulgarian patriarchate was reduced to the rank of autocephalous archbishopric until 1767.

With the regaining of independence Bulgaria established its second empire (1186–1396), with Trnovo as capital. Opposition to Constantinople motivated renewed

contacts with Rome. Emperor Kalojan (1197–1207) asked Pope Innocent III to acknowledge him as emperor and to recognize the archbishop of Trnovo as patriarch. The Pope granted the kingly crown to Kalojan and the title of primate to the archbishop, who received also the pallium from Rome. Union with Rome lasted until 1235, when Emperor John Assen II (1218–41) allied with the Greeks against the Latin Empire in Constantinople. In 1235 he obtained from the Byzantine patriarch recognition of the second Bulgarian patriarchate, which endured until Turkish occupation of Trnovo (1393). Thereafter the Bulgarian Church was reincorporated into the Orthodox Church of Byzantium (*see* ORTHODOX CHURCHES).

Bulgarian national consciousness awoke in mid-19th century and caused renewed strife between Greeks and Bulgarians. The Greeks refused to allow the Bulgarians their own hierarchy. When the Turkish government granted an independent Bulgarian exarchate (1870), the patriarch of Constantinople excommunicated the Bulgarian Church. This ban lasted from 1872 to 1945. Controversy broke out again in 1953 when the Bulgarian Church, without Constantinople's permission, established the third patriarchate and elected Cyril (Markov) as patriarch. In 1961 Constantinople agreed to this change and settled the dispute.

Catholic Church. Some Catholics in Bulgaria belong to the *Latin rite, some to the Bulgarian rite. Most Latin-rite Catholics are descended from heretical Pauli-

Emperor John Alexander of Bulgaria (1331–71) and his family, from the Emperor's Gospel Book (Add. MS 39627).

cians and *Bogomils, who were converted by Franciscans in the 17th century. Since the 18th century, Capuchins have been caring for Catholics residing in the Plovdiv region, and Passionists, for those in the Danube area.

Bulgarian-rite Catholics stem from the reunion movement of mid-19th century. When the patriarch of Constantinople refused to permit a national hierarchy for Bulgaria, appeal was made to the Holy See, resulting in a formal union between Rome and several groups in Thrace and Macedonia (1859–60). Joseph Sokolski was consecrated archbishop by Pius IX in Rome (1861) but shortly after his return to Constantinople, he was seized and taken to Russia. In 1881, when the faithful totaled about 70,000, the Holy See created one vicariate apostolic for Macedonia (with its seat in Salonika) and another for Thrace (with its seat in Constantinople). Later misfortunes reduced the numbers of Bulgarian-rite Catholics. In 1964 Bulgaria, Yugoslavia, and Greece had about 10,000 Catholics descending from the union of the 19th century. Most of those dwelling in Bulgaria came from Greek Thrace after the Balkan wars (1912–13). *See* EASTERN CHURCHES.

Christianity in 1964. When the Communists seized power in 1945, they immediately forbade religious instruction in schools. The constitution of 1947 separated Church and State. In 1948 the government confiscated all Catholic schools and institutions and banished all religious who were not Bulgarians. The apostolic delegate was expelled in 1949. In 1952 Ivan Romanoff, Vicar Apostolic of Plovdiv, died in prison. In 1964 there was a Bulgarian-rite bishop for the Apostolic Exarchate of Sofia residing in the capital and a Latin-rite bishop for the Vicariate Apostolic of Sofia and Plovdiv living in the latter city. Both were permitted limited activity, but each of them attended Vatican Council II.

The Latin-rite Catholics have one diocese and one vicariate. The Diocese of Nikopol, established in 1789, has its seat in Ruse and is served mostly by Passionists. Bishop Eugene Bosilkoff was condemned to death in 1952; in 1965 the see still remained vacant. According to the latest available statistics (1952), it had 19 parishes, 4 secular and 10 regular priests, and 22,000 Catholics. The Vicariate Apostolic of Sofia and Plovdiv, created in 1758, has its seat in Plovdiv and is served mainly by Capuchins. Its 13 parishes had 10 secular and 39 regular priests and 28,000 Catholics. Bulgarian-rite Catholics pertain to the Apostolic Exarchate of Sofia, founded in 1926. In 1963 its 17 parishes had 6 secular and 13 regular priests, 35 religious women, and 7,000 Catholics. No Catholic seminary or institutions existed.

The Orthodox Church constitutes an autocephalous patriarchate, with its seat in Sofia. It has 11 dioceses in Bulgaria and 1 in North America (with its episcopal residence in New York). Residential bishops follow the Greek custom of using the title of metropolitan. The estimate of 7,250,000 faithful may be excessive after 2 decades of Communist persecution. About 10,000 Bulgarian-rite Orthodox dwell in the U.S. and Canada. One theological faculty is open in Sofia and two seminaries.

As a result of Turkish occupation, Islam has about 600,000 followers, 450,000 of whom are Turks, the rest being Bulgarians (called Pomaks).

Bibliography: K. J. JIREČEK, *Geschichte der Bulgaren* (Prague 1876). S. VAILHÉ, DTC 2.1:1174–1236. E. REINHARDT, *Die Entstehung des bulgarischen Exarchats* (Lucka 1912). G. SONGEON, *Histoire de la Bulgarie depuis les origines jusqu'à nos jours* (Paris 1913). F. DVORNIK, *The Slavs: Their Early History and Civilization* (Boston 1956); *The Slavs in European History and Civilization* (New Brunswick, N.J. 1962); *Les Slaves, Byzance et Rome au IXe siècle* (Paris 1926). S. RUNCIMAN, *A History of the First Bulgarian Empire* (London 1930). M. SPINKA, *A History of Christianity in the Balkans* (Chicago 1933). R. JANIN, DHGE 10:1120–94. D. SLIJEPČEVIĆ, *Die bulgarische orthodoxe Kirche 1944–56* (Munich 1957). M. ZAMBONARDI, *La Chiesa autocefala bulgara* (Gorizia 1960). I. SOFRANOV, *Histoire du mouvement bulgare vers l'Église catholique au XIXe siècle* (Rome 1960). M. MACDERMOTT, *A History of Bulgaria 1393–1885* (London 1962). OrientCatt 191–198. *Bilan du Monde* 2:175–179. **Illustration credit:** Courtesy of the Trustees of the British Museum.

[M. LACKO]

BULGARIAN ART

Around 650 the Khazars, displaced from their homesteads on the Caspian Sea by fresh Altai-Arabic hordes, invaded the habitats of the Bulgars north of the Azov and Black Seas. Some of these Bulgars remained in their original habitats, acknowledging the Khazar rule. Another part moved north following the river Don, then east to the Volga, and established there the Khanate of the Volga-Bulgars. But one horde of the Bulgars, under the leadership of Asparuch (Isperuch), moved west, crossed the Danube Delta, and settled south of it on what is now Dobrudja, on Byzantine territories. Constantine IV granted them the right to remain on the occupied lands (679). From here the invaders soon moved south into Thrace and began trade with the empire under Theodosius III. The able Khans Omurtag (815–831) and Malamir (831–852) expanded the territories westward and into northern Macedonia; the Czar Symeon (893–927) expanded it to the Adriatic in the west, the Black Sea in the east, the Danube in the north, and Thrace in the south.

A century earlier the same territories were settled by the agricultural Slavs, whom the Bulgars, a people with social and economic forms of higher nomadism, at first had subjugated. But in the course of history, and particularly because of the struggle between the khans and the tribal Bulgarian aristocracy, the Slavs prevailed. The Bulgars lost their language, and the Slavs their name. Under Czar Boris (852–889) the Bulgars as well as the Slavs were converted to Christianity.

The new homesteads of the Bulgaro-Slav peoples were on territories of a rich and varied racial, political, social, and cultural history. Of prime importance for the future artistic development were the Greco-Roman traditions; Greco-Hellenistic civilization existed on the shores of the Black Sea and south of the Balkan Mountain range in central Thrace, and Western, Roman civilization north of the Balkans and along the Danube. Between the 4th and 7th centuries, Christianity took deep roots in lands that were later to be Bulgarian, and, with the division of the empire, Bulgaria became more or less a province of the eastern half. Macedonia became the cradle of the Old Slavonic language and also a great center of art.

This article considers first the artistic monuments of the early Christian period preceding the Christianization of the Bulgars and then the successive periods of artistic production from Christianization to the Byzantine occupation; the Bulgarian state from 1186 to 1396 and the consequent long period of Turkish rule; and finally modern Bulgarian art from 1878 to the present.

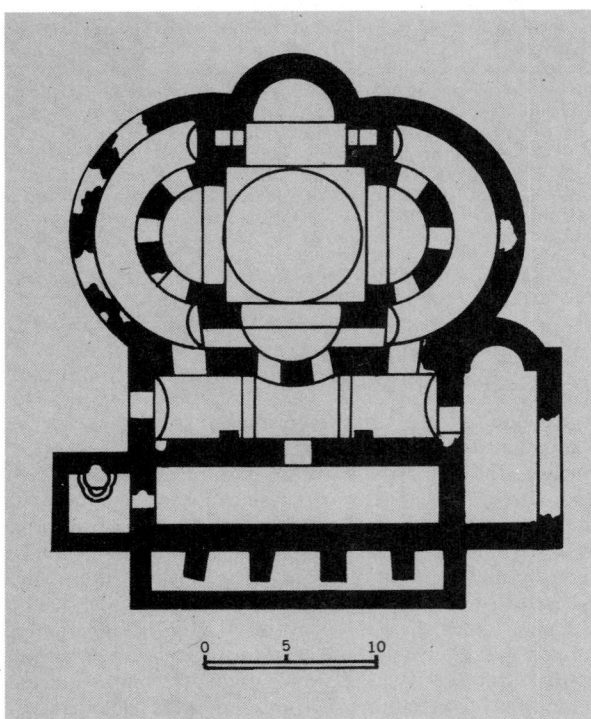

Fig. 1. Ground plan of the Red Church at Peruštica.

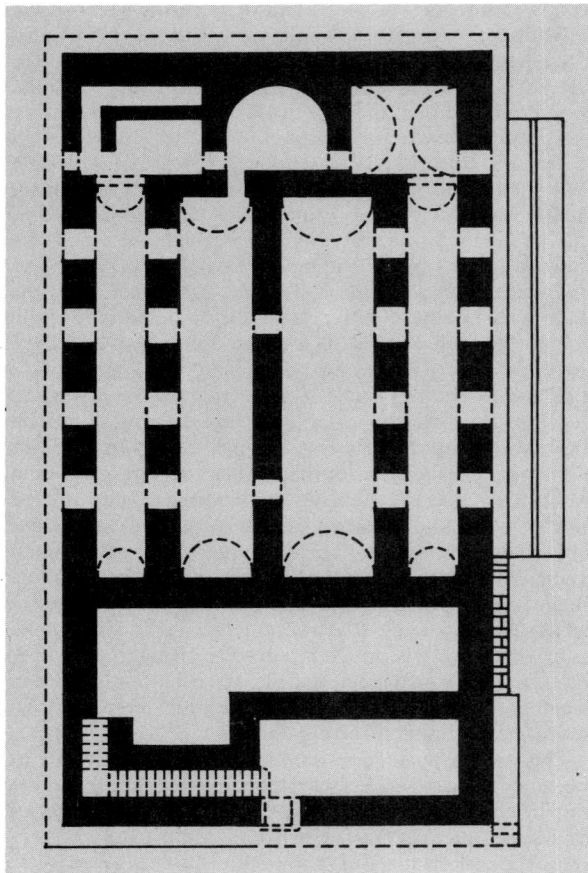

Fig. 2. Ground plan of the Throne building at Pliska.

Early Christian. A remarkable number of churches were built in early Christian times. These were basilica-type structures with apses, narthex, and one nave, sometimes with side aisles, and covered with either flat roofs, as found at Buhovo, Hissar, near Plovdiv, and Nessebur, or vaulted ones as in Goljamo Belovo and Sofia (St. Sophia). The apses are projected at the nave terminal, generally have a semicircular articulation on the interior, and are polygonal on the exterior. The domed basilica also was constructed during this period. The one at Pirdop, early 6th century, has columns separating the nave from side aisles with the elaboration of galleries above the aisles. The better known church at Peruštica, called the Red Church because it is built of red brick, has a dome resting on pendentives over a square base; semicircular conches with ambulatories emerge from the sides of the square base, and the front of the church has a double narthex. Similar in structure are Hadrian's Stoa in Athens and S. Lorenzo in Milan. The St. George Church in Sofia (in the courtyard of the Hotel Balkan), a round plan, originally a Roman bath with rotunda (3d century), was later converted into a church (5th century).

Proto-Bulgarian Times. The residence of the khans and capital of the state before the conversion to Christianity was Pliska (near Aboba, Šumen district). Here, within a fortress with inner and outer walls, two palaces were built under Khan Omurtag. The so-called Little Palace had two oblong halls flanked on the sides by corridors divided into compartments; walls were of stone, vaults of brick. The second, or the Great Palace, also called the Throne building, replaced a structure built by Khan Krum and destroyed (811) by Nikephoros. The lower of its two stories had the same design as the Little Palace; the upper story had a portico leading to the foreroom and from there into the large hall or nave, which ended in a semicircular apse flanked by a rectangular compartment on each side. The plan of the upper floor is related to the plans of the praetorium churches and basilicas. Filov explained this Proto-Bulgarian architecture as a creation of the Sassanian art, on the assumption that the Bulgars were of Irano-Sassanian extraction. However, the Great Palace is a copy of the Audience Hall of the Magnaura. It was erected with antique materials employing local traditions and the skilled help of masons who were, for the most part, slaves from Asia Minor. The khans were certainly great builders; inscriptions tell of palaces built by Krum with the aid of captive architects, of one built by Omurtag on the river Tiča and another on the Danube, of Omurtag's mausoleum located halfway between these two rivers, and of an aqueduct built by Malamir.

Stone reliefs of this period from Stara Zagora show figures of legendary animals from Oriental sources and are related to similar relief sculpture in the Greek and Byzantine world. The most famous monument is the rock carved relief known as the Horse Rider of Madara. It rises some 75 feet above ground and probably depicts Khan Omurtag hunting; it is similar in style and structure to the Sassanian rock reliefs in Bishapur and Naqsh I Rustem (3d century). The famous treasure of Nagy-Szent-Miklos (7th to 9th centuries) is ascribed by some authors to the Hungarian focus of the Proto-Bulgarian period. Apparently the treasury was executed in the workshops of migrating

Fig. 3. "The Horse Rider of Madara," plaster cast of the 9th-century rock relief, National Museum at Sofia.

tribes who were strongly influenced by late and post-Sassanian goldsmiths' art. The inscription on one of the gold cups in Greek characters, but in a Caucasian dialect, reads that the donor of the cup is Župan Buila from the lower Tisa, son of Župan Buta from Tagroga. The treasure of Nagy-Szent-Miklos is stylistically eclectic.

Christianization (865) to End of First State (1018). With Malamir's son, Czar Boris (852–889), the golden age of the Old Bulgarian culture began. In Pliska he erected the Great Basilica, one of the seven cathedrals said to have been built by him. This basilica features three apses, nave with side aisles, atrium, and alternating pillars and columns; on the outside, stone bands are alternated with every five rows of bricks. This basilical form, modestly conservative by comparison with contemporary architecture in Constantinople, was partially continued under Boris's successor, Symeon (892–927), who was educated in Constantinople and called "half Greek." Symeon transferred the capital to Preslav, where his two-story royal palace and residence were built within the fortress. The main monument of Symeon's reign is the Golden or Round Church of Preslav, a rotunda with 12 semicircular niches, of which the eastern one is elongated to form an apse and accommodate the altar: it has a tripartite narthex, a tower in each corner of the façade, and a large atrium. Twelve monolithic columns of marble in front of the niches support the dome, and 14 limestone columns form the colonnade of the atrium. The architectural style of the Church is a reflection of the classicist ideals of the Czar. Contemporary Byzantine in-

fluence emerges more strongly in the churches in Čupkata, in Bjal Brjag in Preslav, in Patleina, and in the St. John the Baptist Church in Nessebur. All these are built on a domed cruciform plan.

Painting of pre-Bulgarian times, represented by the frescoes in the Red Church of Peruštica, was early Byzantine in both iconography and style. Although many churches in Preslav were decorated with frescoes during this first Bulgarian period, the most remarkable surviving decorations are fragments of ceramic slabs, found particularly in Preslav, Tuzlalka, and Patleina. These show ornamentation with figures, such as one finds on the ceramic icon from Patleina, composed of several tiles and representing the figure of St. Theodor Stratilatos. Kilns found *in situ* indicate that these painted ceramics were made locally, and they are referred to as Preslav ceramic. Skilled craftsmen, many of them slaves who were natives of Asia Minor, South Central Asia, and the Middle East, were employed all over the Byzantine world and most probably were engaged in the ceramic production.

Byzantine Interlude (1018–1186). In 1018 the whole Bulgarian state was recaptured by the Byzantines under Basilios II, Bulgaroktonos; the Patriarchate of Ohrid was suspended, a Greek archbishop was installed, and Byzantine government officials were appointed to the administration. One of them, the Georgian Gregorios Bakurian, great servitor of the Byzantine army, founded the monastery and the church in Bačkovo (1083). This church served as his mausoleum and was built with a lower-level crypt. The upper-level chapel, a vaulted single nave with apse, was built in the

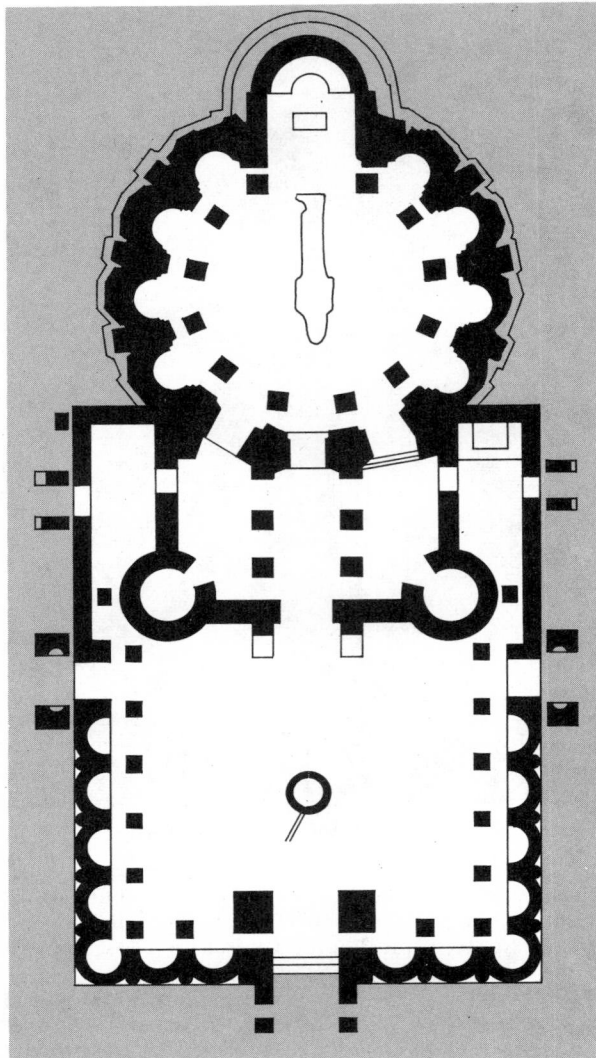

Fig. 4. Ground plan of the Round Church at Preslav.

churches, the seat of the patriarch, and also residential areas; the Trapezica side includes the homes of the boljars (lower nobility) and innumerable small churches and chapels. In this period Trnovo became a center of Bulgarian art that also felt strong Byzantine influence.

Architecture. Two common types of church made their appearance. The first was a nave church with a dome over the central compartment supported by wall pillars. The best known of these is the church of the Virgin in Assen's fortress (Assenovgrad, Stanimaka), a two-story mausoleum church with crypt below and chapel above. Arches over the built-in piers carry the low tambour and the dome, and the central section of the nave is marked outside by an arch extending to the base of the tambour; a new feature is the tower over the narthex. This church in its mountainous terrain preserves a rugged beauty. Of the same type is the Archangel Gabriel Church in Nessebur, and of the same class if not exactly the same type, is the Kalojan church in Bojana (1295), which is an adaptation of the Bojana I church (the St. Nicholas) from the 11th century. The Bojana II or Kalojan church is another example of the chapel-crypt two-story combination. The second type of church in this period was cruciform with a dome on free piers. Examples are: SS. Peter and Paul in Trnovo, the Pantokrator church in Nessebur, and particularly the church of St. John the Divine (Aleiturgitos) in the same town, the most elaborate of all Bulgarian churches. The most common church of small dimensions had one nave without a dome, such as St. Dimiter in Trnovo.

Churches were usually built with stone and brick. In the church at Stanimaka, bands of broken stones in triple lines alternate with triple bands of brick in the lower story, and triple rows of hewn stones alternate with triple bands of brick in the upper story. Endless variations are achieved with the colored marble and the rich white mortar seams. Bricks are composed in geometrical forms, along with glazed and multicolored ceramic tubular tiles that are trefoil or quatrefoil. The outside of the walls shows a diversified system of blind niches, arcades, and arches, often superimposed in several rows and used in a purely decorative way. The patterned incrustation reduces the structural function of the material. This style of surface ornamentation, similar to but richer than the Macedonian, culminated in the St. John Aleiturgitos Church in Nessebur, where it developed. Following this achievement the Nessebur school declined.

Mural Painting; Illumination. The most important murals of the period are in Bojana. They were executed in 1259 for Sevastokrator Kalojan and adorn the first church and the tomb chapel. The cycle in the church is theological in content and follows a Byzantine iconographic program. The tomb murals mix symbolism with historical record. The tomb chapel has portraits of Kalojan and his wife Desislava (left of the arcosolium) and of Constantine Assen and his wife Irene (right of it). These portraits, exceptional in the articulation of color values and individualization of the model, are the culminating point of Bulgarian medieval painting. Other frescoes include figures of St. John of Rila and of Sveta Nedelja. They are undoubtedly the work of Bulgarian artists of the school of Trnovo. In a rock church in Rusenski Lom, near Ivanovo, the

Georgian tradition with the arcades of the niches on the outside extending almost to the roof. The apse and arch of the upper floor and the apse of the ossuary were decorated with frescoes, painted by the Georgian painter Yoan *c.* 1100. The hieratic form and composition are stylistically related to 12th-century mosaics in Constantinople. A distinctive individuality emerges in the expression of the figure of the Virgin in the Deësis fresco of the lower apse. Somewhat earlier are the frescoes of St. Sophia in Ohrid, painted under Archbishop Leo, before 1056. They are close to the style of the mosaics in Greece (Salonika). The paintings in the village church of Vodoča continue an antique tradition of outlining the contours and modeling of the form. These frescoes have been dated from the late 10th century to the 13th century.

Second Bulgarian State (1186–1396). In 1186 John and Peter Assen broke from Byzantine rule and proclaimed independence in Trnovo, the new capital of the Bulgarian czardom. The Jantra River divides the two hills of the city. The Carevec side, surrounded by walls, includes the palace and residence of the czar,

murals, also the work of the Trnovo painters, reveal Hellenistic elements; this work is believed to have been connected with a local group of the Hesychasts. The quality of Bulgarian fresco painting declined in the 14th century, as can be seen in Berende or in St. George in Sofia, both somewhat Byzantine in style and program. The same applies to the frescoes in Zemen (*c.* 1350), where new elements appear that are of Western origin. The realism in the scene of nailing Christ on the cross suggests an influence from the West of late Gothic realism. The book illumination shows two different styles: one vernacular and conservative, the other official. The Tetraevangelion of the priest Dobrejša ("Dobrejša Gospel," *c.* 1221) and the Psalter of Ohrid, now in Bologna, are of the first type. Interlace ornament with zoomorphic motifs and human figures are conservative in style and close to western European pre-Romanesque illumination. It is assumed that Dobrejša himself made the illumination. The second group is exemplified by the Chronicle of Manasses (*c.* 1356–62, Vatican) and the Tetraevangelion of Czar Ivan Alexander (from *c.* 1356, London; *see* BULGARIA) written by the monk Symeon. These two manuscripts were probably written and illuminated in Trnovo; they contain interesting historic and topographic details from the town and show several distinctly Slavic features in interpretation of ornament and presentation of narrative.

Period of Turkish Rule (1393–1878). Artistic activity under Turkish rule did not come to a complete standstill, though activity before the 19th century was relatively restricted.

Architecture. At first, building activity was confined to small churches in populated areas and relatively larger ones in remote mountainous terrains (Boboševo, Dragalevci, Poganovo). The cruciform church with dome, as in Poganovo (*c.* 1390), exhibits the modest and simple appearance of these churches, while the cathedral in Bačkovo monastery (1604) shows more elaboration with side choirs of the Athonite type. The trend was toward a simple aisleless church with one apse and semicylindrical vault (Dragalevci, Kremikovci). In Arbanassi an interesting L-shaped narthex was added on the west and north side, transforming what was originally an open colonnade. The building of churches increased after the peace of Adrianople (1829), which granted religious freedom to all Christians of the Turkish Empire. Of the many churches built between 1830 and 1860, the church of the Holy Virgin in Tatar-Pazardjik (1832) is typical: the nave and two aisles under the same roof (pseudobasilica) have the same sense of spaciousness as in the St. Nicholas Church of Sopot, even though they are of different heights. This is achieved by maintaining the same height of nave and aisles (hall church). Commensurate with this spatial volume is the size of the iconostasis. Baroque elements are present in the churches in such parts as the empories projecting with their curves into the naves (Sopot) and in efforts to create illusionistic effects of spaciousness with different heights of columns, varying interwalls between them, and converging orders. The baroque elements are seen in the St. George Church in Jambol, the metropolitan church in Samokov, and others. The most important monument of the period is the Rila monastery and cathedral. It was founded in the 10th century and restored in the 14th by Prince Hrelj; the Hrelj tower was erected in the court in 1335. After its destruction by fire in 1833, the Rila monastery was again restored and completed in 1860. In the courtyard next to the tower is the cathedral, built on a basilica plan with a dome over the intersection of the nave and the transept,

Fig. 5. *Exterior view of the apse of the Church of St. John the Divine (Aleiturgitos) at Nessebur.*

Fig. 6. *Eastern portion of the narthex of the church at Bojana with a view of the 13th-century frescoes.*

(a)

(b)

Fig. 7. Bulgarian art, the Bojana murals, A.D. 1259: (a) The Descent of Christ into Hell. (b) Head of Christ, detail of the fresco of the Transfiguration. (c) Sevastokrator Kalojan, donor of the frescoes, detail of his full-length portrait. (d) Czar Constantine Assen and Czarina Irene, fresco in the tomb chapel of the church.

(c)

(d)

and with side chapels of the Athos type flanking the iconostasis on either side.

The new trends accompanying the Enlightenment and mercantilism found expression in the architecture of cities and towns; the clock tower typified Bulgarian urban settlements (Berkovica, Trjavna, Botevgrad), and the urban house developed a new architectural interest. At the end of this period stand the works of two Bulgarian builders, Nikola Fičev (1800–81) and Genčo Kunev (1825–90). Fičev's main church buildings are the Holy Trinity in Svištov (1865–67) and the SS. Constantine and Helen Church in Trnovo (1872–74). He is well known for designing the stone bridge over the Jantra River in Bjela (1865–67) and the covered wooden bridge in Loveč (1872–73). Slavic baroque elements present in his work became more academic and conventional in the church and administration buildings of Kunev.

Painting. Mural painting flourished throughout the period of the Ottoman rule, though many monuments were later destroyed either by the Turks themselves or by the great earthquake in 1913. The earlier frescoes of note are found at: SS. Peter and Paul in Trnovo (dated now second half of the 15th century), the monastery of Dragalevci (15th century), Kremikovci (1493), and Poganovo (*c.* 1500). After a gap of more than a century, frescoes of note were executed at St. George in Trnovo (1616), Nedobarsko in East Macedonia (1614), Bačkovo (1643), Arbanassi (church of Christ, completed 1649), and Vidin (1643). Mural painting of the 18th century was carried on at St. George (1710) and St. Archangel in Arbanassi (1760).

Among the new iconographic themes to appear were the Font of Wisdom, John of Rila, pictorial calendars, and representations of the ecumenical councils, with particular stress on that of Chalcedon in 451. A picture of Mt. Athos with its monasteries (Dragalevci) and such portraits as donor Radivoj and his family in Kremikovci (1493) are also of interest for their subject matter.

The painters were apparently traveling fellows, mostly Bulgarians, who drew their program and inspirations from the Athos monasteries. In subject matter and form they adhered rigidly to Byzantine principles and aesthetics. The work gradually became more and more impersonal and assumed the character of workshop production, though many painters signed their frescoes (either in Greek or in Bulgarian). These painters laid foundations for painting in the following period, which produced a Bulgarian renaissance. This was initiated by four local schools: Trjavna, Bansko (better known as the school of Razlog), Debar, and Samokov, all of them active in fresco, icon painting, carving, and, at times, graphics and portraits. The more important of these schools were those of Razlog and Samokov. The school of Razlog was founded by Toma Višanov (*c.* 1790), who had trained in Vienna; the school of Samokov was founded by Christo Dimitrov, who studied fresco painting first at Athos and later in Vienna (*c.* 1770). His son, Dimiter Christov, also known as Dimiter Zograph (1796–1860), was father of Zahari Zograph (1823–76), the best-known representative of the group, who went to Russia (1851), studied in Kiev and Odessa, and then in Petersburg (1857). Zahari won a gold medal and changed his name to Stanislav Dospevski. The Samokov school executed

frescoes in Pleven, Trnovo, Trojan, Athos, and Rila. Zahari, who painted portraits and landscapes, executed a self-portrait mural in Rila. With Zahari and his contemporaries Nikola Pavlovič, Christo Cokev, and Dimiter Dobrovič, Bulgarian painting made the transition from the era of *obrazopisci* (painters of icons and religious pictures) to the modern era of the creative artist searching for new values. All of them received training abroad in either Austria, Germany, Italy, or Russia.

From 1878 to the Present. The shortage of art teachers in the Bulgarian public schools brought many foreign painters to the land; foremost among them were the Czech Ivan Mrkvička and Jaroslav Vešin. Mrkvička worked in a descriptive ethnographic genre with stress on drawing and dramatic effects ("The Peasant Dance"). Vešin painted with an accent on the spaciousness and atmosphere of the landscape ("Crossing the Erkene River"). Anton Mitov (1862–1930), teacher at the academy in Sofia, is known for his genre paintings, portraits, and frescoes (in the Alexander Nevski Cathedral). Ivan Angelov exemplified a close relationship to contemporary work in Western Europe through his plein-air painting ("Harvest"). The portraits of Stefan Ivanov, Ceno Todorov, Nikola Marinov, and particularly Nikola Mihajlov and Boris Mitov, were moderate and academic in style, expressing not so much likeness as sentiment and mood; Mihajlov and Mitov composed their portraits in fine decorative arrangements. Impressionist elements appeared in the landscapes of Athanas Michov and Nikola Petrov, both of whom were students of Vešin. A realistic narrative style dominated the landscapes of Peter Morozov and the seascapes of Alexander Mutafov. Approaching a more expressionistic landscape were scenes from the Pirin Mountains executed by Konstantin Štarkelov. For a short time after World War I, Bulgarian painters turned to historic and national subjects with a kind of *Heimatkunst;* their repertory ranged from the colorful and figuratively symbolic compositions of Vladimir Dimitrov to the rhapsodic war scenes of Boris Denev ("Before the Storm"). This spirit was soon dominated by Western European influence both in painting and sculpture. However, the Munich trained Žeko Spiridonov, Marin Vasiljev, and their few followers (Andrej Nikolov, Ivan Lazarov, Marko Markov, Alexander Andrejev, etc.) maintained the idea of artwork as primarily an expression of the mood (the *Stimmung*) created with elements employed by the visual faculty. In this, Bulgarian art was closely related to Russian art.

Minor Arts and Woodcarving. The art of metal work in gold, silver, and bronze flourished during the Turkish period. One of the centers was Čiprovci, to which is attributed a silver gilt bowl (1644, now in Bačkovo) and a silver cross (National Museum). It is assumed that the Čiprovci goldsmiths learned the trade from the Saxons. The treasure of the monastery in Bačkovo, dating from the 17th century, shows Turkish-Persian elements in ornaments and probably originated from southern Bulgaria (Plovdiv or Tatar-Pazardjik). A large number of Gospel covers have been preserved, including one from Krupnik (1577, now in the Rila monastery), one from Štip (1596), and another from Philippopel (1743). The inscriptions and signatures are Bulgarian: Master Matthias of Sofia made the Krupnik cover; Master Ivan Janov, the cover of Sucava (1656,

Fig. 8. Silver gilt bowl, 1644, from the Bačkovo monastery.

Rila monastery); and Master Kostadin, the cover now in the Sofia National Museum.

Activity of Macedonian woodcarvers from the 12th to the 13th century is evident in the doors of St. Nicholas Church in Ohrid; the carving is related to that of the famous chest in Terracina, Italy. A masterpiece of early Bulgarian woodcarving is found in a door of the Rila monastery (14th century). The open work and interlace ornamentation is probably the work of the artist who executed the wooden throne of Hrelj in the same monastery. The style is continued in the door of Slepča (15th century). From the 15th to the 17th century, doors were carved for St. Clement (Ohrid), St. Petka, (Trnovo), and the church of Christ (Arbanassi); all show distinctly local Bulgarian features in style. The highest achievement in the art of woodcarving emerges in the carved altar screens (iconostasis). To the school of Debar are attributed the screens in St. John in Bigor (early 19th century), in the Holy Redeemer in Skopje (1824), and in the church of the Virgin in Tatar-Pazardjik (1832). The masters of Samokov made the monumental screen in the cathedral church of Rila (early 19th century) and the side wings of the screen in the church in Samokov. The latter were made by Athanas, a Greek who in turn instructed Bulgarian carvers in this art. The school of Debar invariably included figural scenes in ornamental frames. That of Samokov concentrated on ornament and its minute execution.

Bibliography: B. D. FILOV, *Early Bulgarian Art* (Bern 1919); *Geschichte der altbulgarischen Kunst bis zur Eroberung des bulgarischen Reiches durch die Türken* (Berlin 1932); *Geschichte der bulgarischen Kunst unter der türkischen Herrschaft und in der neueren Zeit* (Berlin 1933). A. GRABAR, *La Peinture réligieuse en Bulgarie,* 2 v. (Paris 1928). G. FEHÉR, *Les Monuments de la culture protobulgare et leurs relations hongroises* (Budapest 1931). A. PROTICH, *Pedeset' godini bŭlgarsko iskustvo,* 2 v. (Sofia 1933–34). N. MAVRODINOV, *Le Trésor protobulgare de Nagyszentmiklós* (Budapest 1943); *Modern Bulgarian Art,* tr. M. MINKOV (Sofia 1946); *Izkustvoto na bŭlgarskoto vŭzrazhdane* (Sofia 1957), the art of the Bulgarian renaissance, summaries and indexes in Fr., Ger., and Russ. A. ALFÖLDI, "Études sur le trésor de Nagyszentmiklós," *Cahiers archéologiques* 5 (1951) 123–149; 6 (1952) 43–53; 7 (1954) 61–67. W. SAS-ZALOZIECKY, *Die byzantinische Baukunst in den Balkan Ländern und ihre Differenzierung unter abendländischen und Islamischen Einwirkungen* (Munich 1955). K. KHRISTOV et al., *The Rila Monastery: History, Architecture, Frescoes, Woodcarvings,* ed. A. G. CHRISTOPHOROV, tr. B. ATHANASSOV and A. GOSPODINOV (Sofia 1959). M. BICHEV, *Architecture in Bulgaria from Ancient Times to the Late 19th Century,* tr. A. RIZOV (Sofia 1961). K. MIYALEV, *The Bojana Murals* (Dresden 1961). M. TSONCHEVA, *Bŭlgarsko vŭzrazhdane: Zivopis i grafika* (Sofia 1962), Bulgarian renaissance, summaries in Russ., Fr., Eng., and Ger. United Nations Educational, Scientific and Cultural Organization, *Bulgaria: Medieval Wall Paintings* (Greenwich, Conn. 1962). W. MOLÈ, *Sztuka Słowian boludniowich* (Wrocław 1962). Galerie Charpentier, *Trésors des musées bulgares depuis le Xᵉ siècle avant Jésus-Christ* (Paris 1963). *Medieval Bulgarian Culture,* tr. M. ALEXIEVA et al. (Sofia 1964), fifteen essays with bibliogs. *Kunstschätze in bulgarischen Museen und Klöstern* (Essen 1964), catalogue of Villa Hügel exhibit covering all periods. **Illustration credits:** Figs. 3 and 8, Reproduced from Filov, *Early Bulgarian Art.* Fig. 5, Courtesy, UNESCO. Figs. 6 and 7, Reproduced from Miyatev, *The Bojana Murals.*

[R. LOŽAR]

BULGARIAN LITERATURE

The 19th-century Bulgarian *vŭzrazhdané* (renaissance) and sense of nationhood, which was stimulated by and reflected in modern literature, was based on a culture and literature rooted in the 9th-century work of St. Cyril (827–869), his brother St. Methodius (*c.* 827–885), and their pupil St. Clement (840–916), Bishop of Ohrid. *See* CYRIL (CONSTANTINE) AND METHODIUS, SS.

Old Literature. They devised *kirilitsa,* the cyrillic alphabet of Bulgarian and other southern and eastern Slav languages, which enabled them and their followers, St. Naum (*c.* 820–910), Bishop Konstantin of Preslav (*c.* 830–?), and Bishop Ioan (*c.* 860–?), to contribute to Czar Simeon I's golden age of Preslav (892–927) a corpus of Christian texts translated from Greek into this new written Slavic. Despite much opposition, which was demolished in the monk Hrabr's work *O pismenekh* (On Letters), Cyril got his Slavic liturgy approved by Pope Adrian II in 869.

Christianity was established as the state religion by Czar Boris I in 864. Old Bulgarian literature remained dedicated to it in its hagiography; its condemnation of heresy, e.g., *Slovo na eretiki* (Sermon against the *Bogomils) by Presbyter Kozma (d. 960); and its devotion to orthodox theology. This orthodoxy was always under the authoritative influence of Greek Byzantium, which, however, crushed the czardom from 1018 until Asen I restored it in 1186. This hieratic literary tradition was reaffirmed at Tŭrnovo, the new court, where papal influence—Pope Innocent III's nuncio attended Kaloyan's coronation in 1197—waned with the establishment of a Bulgarian patriarchate by Asen II in 1235. The striking developments in "middle Bulgarian," which still distinguish the Bulgarian language from other Slavic ones, were shunned and expurged in the *zhitiya* (saints' lives), chronicles, translations, and other Tŭrnovo texts of this time in favor of pristine Slavic forms and the Byzantine canon. The reigns of Ioan Alexandŭr (1331–71) and his son Shishman saw this school's fruition in the work of Teodosy of Tŭrnovo (*c.* 1300–63) and Eftimy (*c.* 1330–1403), the last Tŭrnovo patriarch (1375–1403), who, with his pupils Grigory Tsamblak (1364–1420), Konstantin Kostenechky (*c.* 1500–?), Bp. Ioasaf Bdinski of Vidin, and Vladislav Gramatik (*c.* 1420–?), witnessed the beginning of the Turkish yoke that was to last for 5 centuries.

Literature under Turkish Occupation. Through this long dark age, the Bulgarian monastery—an institution founded by St. Ioan of Rila in the 10th century—became the repository of Bulgaria's literary heritage: it was from Mt. *Athos that Father Paisy (*c.* 1722–?) of Chiliandar was to sound the call to national rebirth in his *Istoriya slavyanobolgarskaya* (1762, Slavobulgarian History). There were also other literary lifelines. Besides an unbroken oral tradition of folklore (tales, songs, and epics on such medieval heroes as Krali Marko), there survived in the *zhitie,* homily, apocrypha, and classical legend a tradition of the popular miscellany running from Simeon I's 9th-century *Sbornik* to the *damaskini* collections of the 16th to the 18th century. From the 17th-century Bosnian Franciscan mission, based at its seminary at Chiprovets and raised by a papal bull of June 2, 1624, to the status of Custodia Bulgaria, came the first printed (in Rome) Bulgarian book, the *Abagar* (1651) of Filip Stanislavov (*c.* 1610–?), Catholic Bishop of Nikopol. Petăr Bogdan (1651–?), Catholic Archbishop of Bulgaria, wrote a 10-chapter history of Bulgarian Catholicism, translated St. Bonaventure's *Meditations on Our Lord's Passion* (Rome 1638), and left an account of his tour of Bulgaria (*Opisanie na Bulgaria,* 1640), a historical document of inestimable value. With the razing of Chiprovets in reprisal for its revolt in 1868, the Turks expelled the Franciscans, thus ending a mission responsible, at this low ebb of Bulgarian cultural life, for sound schooling, for contact with western Europe, and for such Catholic Bulgarian patriots and writers as Stanislavov, Bogdan, and P. Parchevich.

Vŭzrazhdané. Out of this initially brilliant past, a new national literature grew during the final century of Turkish rule. With the *Zhitie i stradaniya* (1804, Life and Sufferings) of Bp. Sofrony of Vratsa (*c.* 1739–?) and the *Mati Bolgariya* dialogues (1811, 1844, Mother Bulgaria) of Neophyte Bozveli (*c.* 1784–1848, the last of the militant Bulgarian monks), the long ecclesiastical domination of literature ended, though the didactic attitude remained. Paisy's admonition to his countrymen to desist from aping the Greeks and to "know your stock and your own tongue" set a style of utilitarian writing dictated by the times. Like journalism, ethnography, or education, literature was dedicated to the *vŭzrazhdané* ideals of national consciousness, religious autonomy, and political independence.

This cultural awakening was marked by such pioneer work as P. Beron's pedagogical *Riben bukvar* (1824, Piscine Primer); V. Aprilov's school at Gabrovo (1835) under Neophyte Rilski (*c.* 1793–1882), his grammar (1835), and his translation of the New Testament (1840); Haji Teodosy's Bulgarian printing press (Salonica 1838); K. Fotinov's periodical *Filologiya* (1842–46, Philology); I. Bogorov's newspaper *Bŭlgarski orel* (1846–47, Bulgarian Eagle); and K. and D. Miladinovs' collection *Bŭlgarski narodni pesni* (1861, Bulgarian Folk Songs).

A reading public was being created. To reach and hold it required a living literary language untrammeled by Grecomania or ecclesiastical archaism and invigorated by the vernacular of the current dialects—in effect by the eastern Bulgarian dialects of most writers. Despite doubts of a Russian apologist of the *vŭzrazhdané,* Y. I. Venelin, this challenge was met in the verse of D. Chintulov (1822–86), G. Rakovski (1821–67),

and N. Gerov (1823–1900), the compiler of the first and still famous Bulgarian dictionary.

The new literary language was finally confirmed in works of sustained literary merit by P. R. Slaveykov (1827–95, father of Pencho, see below); L. Karavelov (1837–79); and H. Botev (1848–76). Each of these was in both life and letters a typical protagonist of the *vŭzrazhdané.* Slaveykov, a self-made versatile poet, teacher, and journalist, pursued both in his homeland and Tsarigrad (Constantinople) the cause of education and religious autonomy (won with the establishment of the Bulgarian exarchate in 1870); his many works include a translation of the Bible for Dr. A. Long of the American Bible Society (Constantinople 1864). Karavelov and Botev worked abroad as students in Russia in the 1860s and in Rumania among *émigré* revolutionaries, whose hopes and frustrations inspired the fiery genius of Botev's poems. Karavelov recalled his "forgotten Slav brothers across the Danube" in ethnographical sketches, creating in Gogolesque prose his *Bŭlgare ot staro vreme* (Bulgarians of a Former Time), prototypes of the patriarchal peasant eccentric often met in the later literature. Frustrated by the betrayal of the revolutionary leader V. Levski in 1873, Karavelov turned to educational journalism in his *Znanie* (1875–79, Knowledge). The *Periodichesko spisanie* (1870, Periodical) of the Bulgarian Literary Society (precursor of the Academy of Sciences) began to explore the scope and standards of the new literature, which N. Bonchev (1839–78), "the first Bulgarian literary critic," set himself to define.

Independent Bulgaria: Liberation to the Wars. Liberation in 1878 led to an uneasy transition from Turkish vassaldom to a national state and parliamentary democracy. The attention of the new generation of writers, who initially devoted themselves to public and cultural affairs in Plovdiv, capital of East Rumelia (technically still a province of Turkey until the union of 1885), turned back not so much to the Russo-Turkish War of Liberation as to the preceding abortive Bulgarian risings. Through such "eyewitness accounts" as the *Zapiski po bŭlgarskite vŭzstaniya* (1884–92, Records of the Bulgarian Risings, 1870–76) by Z. Stoyanov (1851–89), the new writers created the heroic national legend, chronicling the feats of the revolutionaries and the events of the brutally quelled April Rising of 1876.

The disillusionment at the new society's pettiness and corruption felt by these writers of the "Vazov circle" turned to bitterness at S. Stambolov's *Diktatura* (1886–94); the poet K. Velichkov (1885–1907) fled to Italy and Vazov to Odessa. The scathing satire of S. Mihaylovski (1856–1927) was matched by pained irony in the stories of provincial and village life by *Vazov and M. Georgiev (1852–1916). In this "sad reality" A. Konstantinov (1863–97) created the best-known character of Bulgarian literature, Bay Ganyu, a tragicomic *parvenu,* pictured peddling his rose attar and rugs in foreign settings so piquantly sketched in the same author's *Do Chicago i nazad* (1893, To Chicago and Back). The social and economic wreckage of peasant life occupied also the *narodnik* (populist) writers, who included most of the young talents of the time, e.g., P. Yavorov (1878–1914), P. Todorov (1879–1916), and Elin Pelin (1877–1949). To cure this malady by education was the aim and devoted practice of many, notably T. G. Vlaykov (1865–1943), who sacrificed to social and public duty a literary vocation evident in his stories of village life and insufficiently appreciated autobiographical trilogy, *Prezhivyanoto* (1934–42, Experiences). The *narodnik* predicament was poignantly stated by A. Strashimirov (1872–1937) in his novel *Krǔstopǔt* (1904, Crossroad).

The turn of the century saw the revolt against utilitarian and "social content" literature by a *pléiade* of "individualist" writers associated with *Misǔl* (1892–1908, Thought), the famous periodical of K. Krǔstev and Pencho *Slaveykov. The latter, with his illustrious antagonist Vazov, dominated the literary scene between the liberation and the wars. Committed to standards of excellence found in the widest European and classical context, writers were free as never before to explore the full potentialities of their own spiritual and aesthetic heritage. The result may be assessed in the subtle imagery of Todorov's prose idyls, the elemental tragic rhythms of Yavorov's poetry, the uninhibited lyrical skill of K. Hristov (1875–1944), and the further wave of neoromantic or symbolist writing by T. Trayanov (1882–1945), N. Raynov (1889–1954), N. Liliev (1885–1960), H. Smirnenski (1898–1923), and others. Enriched and refined, the Bulgarian language had become a literary instrument capable of evoking the inner world of intuition and feelings through a whole range of semantic and musical overtones.

Between the World Wars. The Balkan Wars, World War I, and the civil upheavals of 1923 were a period of disaster and defeat, a national trauma not easily lived down. Literary traditions only gradually revived. Vazov's and Raynov's retrospect into old Bulgarian history continued in the novels of S. Zagorchinov (1889–) and F. Mutafova (1902–); the 1,000th anniversary of Czar Simeon I was celebrated in 1827. To the genre literature of village life developed by Karavelov and the *narodnik* writers, Elin Pelin, author of the prose poems *Cherni rozi* (1928, Black Roses) and the stories *Pod manastirskata loza* (1936, Under the Monastery Vine), imparted a new human breadth and mellow humor in his *Razkazi* (Stories, I, 1904, and II, 1906). This tradition now came to full maturity in the story cycles and novels of *Iovkov and has continued to be represented by K. Petkanov (1891–1952), A. Karaliychev (1902–), G. Karaslavov (1904–), S. Daskalov (1909–), and others. Among many literary reviews, the worthiest successor to *Misǔl* was V. Vasilev's *Zlatorog* (1920–43), a veritable symposium of *belles lettres*. The modern world, its materialism and automata wittily satirized by S. Minkov (1902–) in his *feuilleton* stories, was challenged in the poetry of E. Bagryana (1898–) with a defiant humanity and tenderness, characteristic also of M. Isaev (1907–) in his war poems on the Allied air raids; of the resistance martyr-poet N. Vaptsarov (1909–42); and of the Tǔrnovo poetess B. Dimitrova (1922–).

Contemporary Literature. Since World War II the historical tradition has again been revived by K. Zidarov (1902–) with his tragedy *Ivan Shishman,* and by the Macedonian D. Talev (1898–) in a trilogy of novels on his own unhappy land's *vǔzrazhdané.* After Sept. 9, 1944, the Stalin-Zhdanov era inevitably produced a state-committed cliché literature, little related to the variety and wealth of original talent with its promise of a revival in the field of Bulgarian literature (*see* SOCIALIST REALISM).

Bibliography: M. P. ARNAUDOV, ed., *Bǔlgarski pisateli,* 6 v. (Sofia 1929–30). B. PENEV, *Istoriya na novata bǔlgarska literatura,* ed. B. YOTSOV, 4 v. (Sofia 1930–36). G. KONSTANTINOV, *Nova bǔlgarska literatura,* 2 v. (Sofia 1943). Bǔlgarska Akademiya na Naukite, Institut za Literatura, *Istoriya na bǔlgarska literatura* (Sofia 1962–). G. KONSTANTINOV, *Bǔlgarski pisateli: Biografski i bibliografski danni* (Sofia 1947). G. KONSTANTINOV, et al., *Bǔlgarski pisateli: Biografii, bibliografiya* (Sofia 1961). C. A. MANNING and R. SMAL-STOCKI, *The History of Modern Bulgarian Literature* (New York 1960). V. PINTO, *Bulgarian Prose and Verse* (London 1957).

[V. PINTO]

BULGARIAN RITE

In the strict sense, one of 18 canonical *rites that are recognized as such by the Church. In its origin, it can be considered a branch of the patriarchate of *Constantinople, but the differences are greater than the resemblances. In fact, the two rites are distinct, because they were created by two peoples profoundly different in race, language, character, and dress, as well as historical development.

HISTORY OF THE RITE

In the 6th century the tribe known as the Bulgars, nomads of Hunnish origin, whose warriors roamed through eastern Europe, were united by Kubrat (585–642) into a vast and powerful state, which the Byzantines called "Great Bulgaria on the Volga" and which extended northward from the sea of Azov between the Volga and the Dniester. After the death of Kubrat, his five sons divided the kingdom, and one of them, Isperich (643–701), left the bank of the Volga with his tribe, and headed for the Danube. After several wars Isperich succeeded in occupying a considerable part of the Byzantine Empire, specifically ancient Parva Scythia and Moesia Inferior. In 679 Emperor *Constantine IV, having been defeated by Isperich, accepted a treaty of peace that marked the beginning of present-day Bulgaria. After rapid expansion, especially during the reign of Krum (802–814) and that of Simeon the Great (893–927), the new Bulgarian state comprised almost the whole Balkan peninsula, separating the Eastern and the Western Roman Empires. Thanks to its location, Bulgaria was frequently decisive in politicoreligious relations between the old and new Rome. On the other hand, Bulgaria also necessarily suffered the frequently tragic consequences of the constant tension between these great powers.

The Bulgarians had their first contacts with the Church in the remnants of the Christianity that had flourished before their arrival in the territory they occupied. These contacts increased, especially in the 8th and 9th centuries, through Bulgarian expansion into Byzantine territory and as a consequence of commercial dealings with the Franks. In 813 Krum (the Terrible) had 30,000 prisoners, including entire families, transported from Thracia into Bulgaria. All of them were Christian; many never left Bulgarian territory. It is obvious that the religious practices of so many Christians, not a few of whom underwent martyrdom, could not pass unnoticed. History also points out the promotion of Christianity by the Franks, through their merchants, and through the efforts of several Germanic or Byzantine missionaries.

Rome or Constantinople. Boris I (852–888) became speedily convinced that Bulgaria could not long remain a pagan enclave in the midst of Christian powers; that Christianity had brought his people the advantages of the Christian culture of the neighboring peoples; and last but not least, that a national Church, after the pattern of those times, would assure him the title of king, and perhaps even of emperor. From the outset of his reign he showed a certain sympathy for Christianity and seemed to incline somewhat toward the Roman Church as the result of a letter from Pope Nicholas I. The perspicacious *Photius, Patriarch of Constantinople, and the Emperor Michael III, disturbed by the possibility of a Bulgarian movement toward Rome (and therefore from a political viewpoint toward the West), inserted into the peace treaty forced upon Boris by the Byzantines in 863 a clause imposing on him the introduction of Christianity into his country. In 864 Boris and his court accepted Baptism, opening the door to Byzantine missionary activity.

The Byzantine Christianization of Bulgaria had been under way hardly 2 years when Boris requested of Photius the erection of a Bulgarian hierarchy in the form of a patriarchate. Receiving a negative reply and discovering that the Byzantine missionaries were involved in political activity, Boris reacted in character, quickly and forcefully; he broke with Constantinople and turned again toward Rome. In 866 his legates delivered to Pope *Nicholas I a letter in which Boris asked Rome's viewpoint on the multiple problems recently arisen between pagans and Christians in Bulgaria; moreover, he requested the Pope to send Latin missionaries, liturgical books, and a civil code; finally he asked the portentous question: could Bulgaria have its own patriarch?

The Pope's answer was contained in the famous "Reply of Pope Nicholas I to the Bulgarians." The Latin liturgical books and the civil code were brought to Boris by *Formosus, Bishop of Porto, accompanied by Paul, Bishop of Populonia. They were to replace the Byzantine missionaries and introduce the Latin rite. Satisfied, Boris "swore perpetual allegiance to St. Peter" and gave his full support to the work of the Latin missionaries, who preached, celebrated the Latin liturgy, and built churches and schools in the principal towns. Their evangelization proceeded so successfully that Boris, after 2 years, thought it opportune to apply again, this time to the new Pope, *Adrian II, for the institution of a national hierarchy, as it had been foreseen by Nicholas I.

A first disillusionment came from the slowness with which Rome treated his request, and a second from the refusal of the Pope to name as head of the Bulgarian hierarchy one of the persons favored by Boris, viz, Formosus, the Apostolic Delegate Marinus, or some other renowned individual who would offer a sure guarantee of the success of the evangelization of Bulgaria. The new Pope, uninformed of the situation in Bulgaria and unaware of the impulsive character of Boris, not only did not accept his suggestions, but, yielding to certain intrigues against Formosus, recalled him to Rome and sent as his replacement a certain subdeacon named Sylvester.

This decision, which seemed destined to hinder rather than help the evangelization of Bulgaria, provoked an immediate reaction from Boris. He quickly rejected the unwanted subdeacon, and breaking with Rome, turned anew toward Constantinople. A Bulgarian delegation appeared unexpectedly at the Council of *Constantinople IV (870), inquiring whether Bulgaria was dependent on the jurisdiction of Constantinople or of Rome. The question disrupted anew the peace that had hardly been reestablished between the two Churches. The Byzantines hastily replied in their own favor; and despite the protests of the Roman legates the Patriarch of Constantinople, St. *Ignatius, sent Boris the desired archbishop and several bishops, who resumed the introduction of the Byzantine rite into Bulgaria.

In vain Adrian and his successors tried, now with paternal exhortations and now with threats, to reduce Boris to obedience to Rome, enjoining Constantinople to withdraw its jurisdiction from Bulgaria. Constantinople obeyed, but all the efforts of Rome were shattered by the obstinacy of the Bulgarian King. Consequently, neither the Byzantine nor the Roman rite could assert itself, and the evangelization of Bulgaria, isolated from a mother Church, came practically to a halt for several years.

Autonomy. In this grave crisis affecting both ecclesiastical unity and the infant Bulgarian Church, the work of SS. *Cyril and Methodius was providential. Having composed the Slavic alphabet and translated the Holy Scriptures and the Byzantine liturgical books into Slavic, they initiated the difficult work of Christianizing the Slavs in Moravia. The success of their work, of major importance in the evangelization of the Slavic people, was due in great part to Bulgaria. Pope Adrian II had approved the Slavic liturgy, but following new intrigues, Stephen V had prohibited it. Thereupon Clement, Naum, Angelar, and other disciples of Methodius, expelled from Moravia, took refuge in Bulgaria. Boris, foreseeing the importance of their work for his people, who were mostly Slavs, received them and gave his full approval to their activity.

At this point, with the new Byzantine-Slav rite, began the real conversion of Bulgaria. There soon arose the two great missionary centers of Devol and Titcha, directed by Clement and Naum, where translations of the Byzantine ecclesiastical books were completed and recopied; here also, thousands of priests, monks, catechists, and scribes were trained and then sent far and wide to teach the people and to build churches, monasteries, and schools. Christianity visibly transformed the land and its people. In 893, after the harsh repression of the revolt instigated by Prince Vladimir and the pagan boyars against the Christians, the national assembly proclaimed Christianity the state religion, officially adopted the Slavic language, and ordained that the Byzantine books be replaced by those of the new Slavic rite. The assembly also placed on the throne the other son of Boris in place of the apostate Vladimir. Thus opened the era of Simeon the Great (893–927), which by reason of political and economic growth and developments in ecclesiastical life, literature, and the arts, is justly called the "golden age" of Bulgarian history.

The political, religious, and cultural ideas of this period gave life and strength to the renaissance of the Bulgarian people. Educated at Constantinople, where he had observed the arts, the glory, and the decline of the Empire, Simeon was well versed in the encyclopedic knowledge of the time and in the diplomacy and strategy of Byzantium. Because of his education, the Byzantines referred to him as "half-Greek." In reality he became one of the most dangerous enemies of the Byzantine Empire. Under Simeon Bulgaria attained its greatest limits—from the Transylvanian Alps almost to the Mediterranean, from the Black Sea to the Adriatic. He merited the title "Great" all the more for powerfully promoting cultural and ecclesiastical activity; ordering the building of numerous churches, monasteries, and schools; and directly participating in the editing of literary works. The convent of Patleina, built possibly by Boris, was enlarged and transformed into a national academy, under Simeon's direction, for the training of translators, copyists, artists, teachers, and writers. Here were assembled the greatest experts in literature and calligraphy, to whom were entrusted the translation or editing of the outstanding works of Byzantine literature. Thus was Bulgarian literature born: a long catalogue of works, few of them original, in theology, philosophy, history, legends, lives of the saints, and homilies.

From the copies extant today, found mostly in other countries (due to the destruction wrought by the Greek clergy), it is evident that this rich heritage passed to Russia and Rumania and had a great influence on the literature of Serbia. From the 10th to the 15th century, Russia received from Bulgaria missionaries, liturgical books, scholars, and artists. The first Rumanian liturgical and historical books were written in the Old Slavic language. All this indicates the Bulgarian origins of Old Slavic literature.

Simeon also reorganized the ecclesiastical hierarchy, replacing Greek bishops with bishops of Slavic origin and erecting the Bulgarian patriarchate of Preslav. The first Bulgarian bishop was Clement, consecrated bishop of Velica, followed by Constantine, bishop of the region of Titsha. Then the Church of Constantinople rose in opposition to the new Bulgarian rite, upholding in its own interests the theory of the "three liturgical languages." The monk Chrabâr, interpreting the common conviction of the Bulgarian clergy, rejected in a brilliant and spirited pamphlet the pretensions of Constantinople. The new rite was finally approved definitively. Bulgaria had a national hierarchy and clergy, a liturgy and religious practice of its own.

Subjection to Constantinople. The further development of the Bulgarian Church was especially trying. Czar Peter (927–969) was a pious King, but a miserable statesman. He abandoned the anti-Byzantine policies of his father and sought to maintain good relations with both Constantinople and Rome. Leading a semimonastic life, he especially favored monasticism, which then had its greatest development. Putting the accent on the interior life, monasticism gave ecclesiastical life an imprint of mysticism. But the ineptitude of the King in political matters opened the door to the perennially dangerous influence of Constantinople. Foreseeing disaster, the traditional anti-Byzantine party instigated several revolts against the government; these finally enervated the country and split it into two camps.

Constantinople did not miss its opportunity; invading Bulgaria, it occupied first the eastern part (972), then the western part (1018). The occupation lasted until 1186. The patriarchal see, recently transferred to Dorostol, was subjected to the patriarch of Constantinople and apparently replaced by the "patriarchate" of Ochrida, which in reality became an important center of Hellenization in Bulgaria. The archbishop-primate of Ochrida, appointed by Constantinople, was Greek, as were eventually almost all the bishops. And the Slavic liturgical language was replaced by Greek.

In 1054 the *Eastern Schism between Constantinople and Rome occurred. It is noteworthy that Leo, then primate of Ochrida, was among the most tenacious supporters of *Michael Cerularius, and it was he who dragged Bulgaria into the Greek schism. The most noted of the archbishops of Ochrida was *Theophylactus, a worthy and intelligent pastor even though, being Greek, he was not loved by the people. Strenuously defending his archdiocese against the ecclesiastical meddling of Constantinople, he struggled against the abuses of the clergy and wrote several historical, exegetical, and polemic works, in which he displayed an irenic attitude toward the confrontations with Rome.

The inclination to mysticism in ecclesiastical life, the comfortable life of the clergy, and especially the lack of contact between the Greek hierarchy and the lower clergy permitted the upsurge of the *Paulicians and *Bogomils, both founded on the dualist doctrine of the White God, principle of good, and the Black God, principle of evil. Some Paulicians went over to Bogomilism and some were converted to Catholicism in the 17th century. Bogomilism, founded by the priest Bogomil, became widespread, possibly because of its politicosocial character. It combatted the abuses of the clergy and preached anarchy against the political activity of the Greek hierarchy. The sect nevertheless contributed through its polemical works to the sustaining of the national spirit and language during the period of Byzantine dominance. In the 12th century it spread into the West.

Relations with Rome. A general revolt (1186) marked the end of Byzantine domination and the beginning of the second Bulgarian Kingdom, which Ivan Assen II (1218–41) brought to its greatest political expansion and which disappeared in 1396. The new capital, Tyrnovo, was also the residence of the archbishop. The first important event in this period was the return of Bulgaria to communion with the Holy See (1204) after its sad experience with Constantinople. According to the agreement between Kaloian, Archbishop Basil, and Pope Innocent III, Bulgaria returned to Catholic unity, keeping its own rite, while the Pope granted Kaloian the title of king and Basil that of primate of Bulgaria. This title corresponded to the Oriental title of patriarch, since Basilio, invested with the pallium, obtained the right to crown the Bulgarian kings, consecrate chrism, and install metropolitans.

The union with Rome lasted until 1235. At that time relations with Constantinople (Nicaea) having been restored and those with Rome having deteriorated because of the Latin Empire of Constantinople, the Bulgaro-Byzantine Council of Blasherna was convoked, which proclaimed the autonomy of the Bulgarian Church in communion with Nicaea and separated from Rome. Bulgaria thus definitively entered the Byzantine sphere and the union effected by the Ecumenical Councils of Lyons and Florence was rendered even less stable than it had been before.

The national synod (1211), which condemned Bogomilism and promulgated the *Synodicon of King Boril* (Collection of Decrees and Instructions of the Council), gave new impulse to ecclesiastical life. The hierarchy was reorganized, new churches and monasteries sprang up, and literary activity was renewed, fostered by requests for books on the part of Russia and other Slavic peoples. The promoters of monasticism in this period were Theodosius, founder of the great monastery of the Trinity, and Evtimi, who transformed it into an important center of literary activity and spiritual life. Becoming patriarch (*c.* 1375–94), Evtimi wrought a fundamental revision of the liturgical books and wrote and directed other works, which constitute the bulk of medieval Bulgarian literature.

Turkish Domination. In the full flowering of its ecclesiastical, cultural, and social development, Bulgaria was struck by a new disaster—Turkish political domination (1396–1878), to which was joined Byzantine spiritual domination. This was the saddest period in Bulgarian history, when the people were reduced to actual slavery. The Patriarchate of Phanar, preserving a certain autonomy as mediator between the "Sublime Portal" (Turkish government) and the subject Christian people, devoted itself to the exploitation and Hellenization of the Slavic population. The Bulgarian bishops were gradually replaced by Greeks, and the Bulgarian language by Greek in schools and churches. The "Phanariots" did not hesitate to destroy even the most ancient libraries and archives.

In 1767 the Archdiocese of Ochrida, which had continued to "represent" the autonomous Bulgarian Church, was officially subjected to the jurisdiction of Constantinople. For almost 5 centuries the Bulgarian Church and state did not exist, while the people lived in the most profound ignorance and misery. Many Bulgarians were either Hellenized or totally oblivious of their national origins. The liturgy was celebrated in Bulgarian only in monasteries hidden in the mountains.

Independence. The first signs of rejuvenation came from the Catholic bishops Partehevitch, who carried on a tireless diplomatic activity, exhorting the Western powers to free Christianity from the Turks, and Stanislavov, who composed a booklet in the New Bulgarian language. The father of the Bulgarian revival, the monk Paissi, wrote the Bulgaro-Slavic History (1762), in which he implored the Bulgarians, "a nation of kings and saints," not to forget the glorious past of their land and their Church. His ideas, taken up by Spiridon, Sofronius (Bishop of Vratsa), and others, stirred up a vast national movement.

The difficult struggle against Constantinople for ecclesiastical independence was caused by two currents: the one, guided by Tsankov, proposed the union of Bulgaria with Rome, but because of the opposition of Russia, only a small group returned to the Catholic Church; the other, guided by Makaripolski, succeeded in creating an Orthodox exarchate (1870) recognized by the Turks but excommunicated by Constantinople. With the coming of political independence to Bulgaria (1878), the Church was finally able to reorganize, consolidate, and become a state Church. The present Communist regime has restricted its liberty, but its hierarchy has remained; it has a seminary and two official publications; and is therefore in better condition than the Catholic minority. Despite all this, its impact on public life is more apparent than effective.

STRUCTURE AND LIFE

During the reign of Boris I ecclesiastical organization was quite confused because of the repeated changes of rite. Relations between the first archbishop, Joseph, and the bishops, as well as territorial jurisdiction, were not clearly defined; and the first properly organized hierarchy was not erected until the reign of Simeon.

History of Ecclesiastical Organization. With the definitive introduction of the Slavic rite, the Greek bishops in Bulgaria were gradually replaced by Bulgarians. About 904 the first Bulgarian archbishop was appointed (John Esarca, who resided at Preslav). The Patriarchate of Preslav was created, probably at the national synod of 918, then later transferred to Dorostol; its first incumbent was Leontius. His successor Damian was recognized by Rome in about 927 and by Constantinople at the end of the same year. By the end of the first kingdom there were 40 dioceses and metropolitans subject to the Patriarchate of Dorostol; the most important were Provat, Tomi, Apollonia (Sozopol), Adrianopolis, Philippopolis (Plovdiv), Serdica (Sofia), Bregalnitsa, Ochrida, Strumitsa, Belgrade, and Bononia (Vidin). One peculiarity that distinguished the Bulgarian ecclesiastical organization from the Byzantine was the existence of exempt dioceses, that is, those depending on the patriarch not through an intermediary metropolitan, but directly. In this way the government of the Church became more centralized.

Under the second kingdom, the first patriarch, Basil, who resided in the capital (Tyrnovo), was recognized by Rome, with whom he entered into communion in 1204; but the recognition of Constantinople (1235) again disrupted relations with the Holy See. The jurisdiction of the patriarch of Tyrnovo was noticeably extended by the conquests of Ivan Assen II. Ochrida, which by decree of Basil II became the seat of the archbishop-primate of Bulgaria during the Byzantine domination, succeeded in maintaining its independence from Tyrnovo. During the Turkish domination the archbishops of Ochrida resumed the title of primate or patriarch of Bulgaria, which lasted until their subjection to Constantinople in 1767. After almost 5 centuries of suppression, the Bulgarian hierarchy was reestablished in the form of an exarchate in 1871.

At the third national synod (1950) the patriarchate was solemnly restored according to Bulgaro-Byzantine law. The official documents extol the "benevolent consent of the Patriarchate of Moscow" and of the Communist government, which had permitted this major change in the Bulgarian Church. The patriarch of Constantinople, who was merely informed of the move, at first protested, then resigned himself to recognizing the new patriarchate. Its organizational structure, like that of the Bulgarian rite in general, follows the form of the Church of Constantinople.

Canon Law. If we exclude the various civil and ecclesiastical codes sent to Boris by Pope Nicholas I and the Greek *nomocanon,* which the respective rites, Latin and Byzantine, followed for a short time in Bulgaria, the origin of Bulgarian Canon Law may be traced to the introduction of the rite of Cyril and Methodius (after 885). At that time the *nomocanon* was replaced by the Slavic elaboration *Zakonu Pravilo* (Collection of Laws), which was followed at the beginning of the 10th century by *Zakon sudni liudiam* (Judiciary Law), drawn from the *Ecloga* of Leo the Isaurian and Constantine V. From the second kingdom there are the *Sinodicon of King Boril* (collection of conciliar decrees), which is not of an exclusively juridic character, since it contains historical notes and other teachings.

During the two long periods in which the primates of the Bulgarian Church, residing in Ochrida, were appointed by Constantinople, Greek Canon Law was in effect in Bulgaria. It stifled any development of a national law. Modern law, based on the ancient Byzantine-Slavic legislation, began with the resurgence of the Bulgarian Church. At the first national synod in Constantinople (1871) the first ecclesiastical constitution was approved. This was corrected in 1895 and the form finally accepted was called *Ekzarchijski Ustav* (Rule of the Exarchate). It was restored in 1950 and today provides the basic church constitution. A compilation called *Pravilata na Svyatata Pravoslavna Crkva* (Regulations of the Holy, Orthodox Church) contains in two volumes all the canons of past Councils and accepted writings of the Holy Fathers with commentaries by John Zonaras (last of 12th century), Alexius Aristenus (c. 1180), and Theodore Balsamon (after 1195). New church legislation is published officially in the ecclesiastical journal *Cărkoven Vestnik*.

The political instability of Bulgaria (as witness the treaties of San Stefano and Berlin, and World War I), which frequently altered the territory of the exarchate; internal agitations; continual changes of often anticlerical governments; and finally, rapid social and cultural development—all necessarily resulted in several revisions of the constitution. The first was approved by Parliament in 1883, but rejected by the ecclesiastical authorities. A second revision was prepared by a special commission, composed of the foremost Bulgarian jurists, such as the noted Stefan Tsankov, and was approved by the second national synod (1922) and by Parliament (1923). This revision, more thorough and fundamental, is known as the second constitution. It is substantially preserved in the third constitution, which was necessitated by the particular circumstances in which the Bulgarian Church found itself under the Communist regime. It was approved by the third national synod (1950).

After this evolution the Bulgarian Church presented the following juridic structure. An autonomous and democratic Church, its supreme legislative authority is a national synod for general laws and the diocesan synod for provincial laws. The supreme administrative authority is the permanent synod (holy synod), composed of all the bishops under the presidency of the patriarch. To this corresponds the permanent diocesan synod, composed of the bishop (as president), with two clerics and two laymen elected for 4 years. For business that is not strictly ecclesiastical (education, finances, charitable organizations), the permanent synod is assisted by a supreme council, under the presidency of the patriarch, or on the diocesan level, the bishop. All these administrative bodies are recognized by the state as moral persons, and about half of their members (with the exception of the holy synod) are laymen.

The patriarch is elected for life (but can resign or be deposed) by a two-thirds vote of the national synod, which is composed of the holy synod, three clerics and

four laymen from each diocese, representatives from the principal monasteries and ecclesiastical institutions, and special delegates of the government; the third national synod had 107 members. For the election of the patriarch, three candidates from among the bishops are proposed by the holy synod with the previous consent of the government. Bishops are chosen from a list of candidates proposed by the holy synod; the electoral body in each diocese selects two of them, and between these the holy synod makes the final choice. The hierarchical order corresponds to that of the Byzantine rite.

Under the Communist regime the Church has been separated from the state and its liberty severely restricted. The Church's property having been confiscated, the principal source of income for the clergy is the contributions of the faithful. However, the state appropriates an annual sum for the holy synod, which distributes it among the clergy. The economic problems of the Orthodox clergy, who are generally married, constrain them, especially today, to find some secular employment, to the detriment of their apostolic ministry. There is also a growing lack of priests; the only seminary in operation in 1964 housed only 100 candidates for the priesthood and diaconate.

The Orthodox Bulgarian patriarch rules over an estimated 6,500,000 faithful in 11 dioceses in Bulgaria and 1 diocese in the U.S. which has 8,000 faithful (*see* BULGARIA).

Catholics of the Bulgarian Rite. The formation of a small group of Catholics of the Bulgarian rite dates from the middle of the 19th century. Bulgarians in the Macedonian cities of the Kilkis Province sent a petition in 1859 to the apostolic delegate in Istanbul to be admitted into the Catholic Church. In the following year another group of Bulgarians similarly petitioned the Catholic Armenian archbishop of Istanbul. Joseph Sokolski was consecrated archbishop and received help from the Assumptionist and Resurrectionist Fathers who adopted the Bulgarian rite. He was captured by Russian spies and was imprisoned in Kiev where after 18 years he died. Raphael Popov succeeded Sokolski and administered the Bulgarian Catholic exarchate from 1865 to 1876. At this time there were about 80,000 Catholics of the Bulgarian rite. The growing progress was halted due to a lack of clergy, a Russian persecution and the defection of the Catholic Bishop Lazzarus Mladenov. Many thousands returned to the Bulgarian Orthodox Church. World War I crushed any further growth. An apostolic administrator was appointed in 1923 and in 1926 an exarchate was formed with Cyrill Kurteff appointed as the apostolic exarch. After World War II Bulgaria became a satellite of the Soviet Union and the Church today has gone in hiding. The last statistics available (from 1948) list the Catholic faithful of the Bulgarian rite as 9,480. There were then 20 parishes, 20 churches or chapels, 15 secular priests, 30 religious priests, and 40 religious nuns of the Oriental rite.

Liturgy. The Bulgarian liturgy is substantially the Byzantine translated into Slavic, as mentioned above. The current edition of the liturgical books is generally the revision made by the Patriarch Evtimi in the 14th century, known as the Tyrnovo edition. One peculiarity is the use of the vernacular for the rubrics and the modern scale for musical notation. *See* BYZANTINE RITE, CHANTS OF.

The liturgical calendar features the feasts of saints especially venerated in Bulgaria, such as SS. Cyril and Methodius and their disciples; St. Ivan Rilski (d. 946), whose sanctuary is the most frequently visited; St. Theodosius and St. Evtimi of Tyrnovo, who lived in the 14th century; and finally the popular monk Paissi, canonized by the holy synod in 1962.

The Mass, celebrated three or four times a week, occupies the principal place in the liturgical life of the faithful. For the rest, the veneration of icons, prayers for the dead, severe fasting, and other traditional practices more frequently take the place of reception of the Sacraments. Private confession is almost unknown, and general absolution is given only on certain occasions. Holy Communion and preaching are also rarities.

Monasticism. The origins of monasticism also are found in the work of the disciples of Cyril and Methodius in the 9th century. The first monasteries were those of Ochrida and Titsha. Simeon the Great favored the monastic organization and life, which reached its greatest development, never again duplicated, in the time of Czar Peter.

In the Middle Ages, the kings (e.g., Ivan Assen II) and the nobility loved to demonstrate their piety by building and supporting monasteries. Between the 10th and 12th centuries their number grew to 100, including those of Zografou (Athos) and Ivan Rilski, which formed part of a group of monasteries near Sofia, called "The Little Holy Mount." In the 14th century monastic life flourished because of the influence of the great monastery of the Trinity at Tyrnovo, founded by Theodosius, which was subsequently reorganized by Evtimi.

During the Turkish domination, many monasteries were destroyed and very few built, such as that of Batshkovo (17th century). Those that escaped Hellenization transmitted the ancient ecclesiastical tradition to succeeding generations. Toward the end of the 19th century monasticism gave signs of revival, but in mid-20th century it was in a steady decline. In 1890 there were about 100 monasteries with 184 monks and 346 nuns. In 1936 (the most recent official statistics), there were 105 monasteries, of which 79 were for men with 99 monks, and 26 for women with 212 nuns (an average of 3 persons per establishment). The only monasteries strictly so-called are the three large ones at Rila, Troian, and Batshkovo and about 10 monasteries of nuns. The monastic discipline is based on the ancient Byzantine rule.

See also BULGARIA.

Bibliography: J. B. BURY, *A History of the Eastern Roman Empire From the Fall of Irene to the Accession of Basil I, A.D. 802–867* (London 1912). M. SPINKA, *A History of Christianity in the Balkans* (Chicago 1933). S. RUNCIMAN, *A History of the First Bulgarian Empire* (London 1930). C. GERARD, *Les Bulgares de la Volga et les Slaves du Danube* (Paris 1939). G. SERGHERAERT, *Syméon le Grand, 893–927* (Paris 1960). V. N. ZLATARSKI, *Istoriā na Bŭlgarskata Dŭrzhava*, 3 v. in 4 (Sofia 1918–40), basic work. D. TSUKHLEV, *Istoriā na Bŭlgarskata Tsŭrkva*, 2 v. (Sofia 1910–). S. TSANKOV, *Die Bulgarische Orthodoxe Kirche seit der Befreiung bis zur Gegenwart* (Sofia 1939). I. SOFRANOV, *Histoire du mouvement bulgare vers l'Église catholique au XIXᵉ siècle* (Rome 1960). A. CRONIA, *Saggi di letteratura Bulgara antica* (Rome 1936). S. VAILHÉ, DTC 2.1: 1174–1236. COSMAS, *Theologia antibogomilista*, ed. J. GAGOV (Rome 1942).

[I. SOFRANOV]

BULGARIS, EUGENIUS, the most important Greek Orthodox theologian of the 18th century; b. Corfu, Aug. 10 or 11, 1716; d. St. Petersburg, May 29 or June 10, 1806. Bulgaris (baptized Eleutherius) studied philosophy and theology at Padua, then lectured at Janina, Greece, and entered the monastery of Vatopedi on Mt. Athos (1749) and taught there and at the Patriarchal School of Constantinople. When dismissed from his teaching assignment because his methods differed from the Oriental tradition, he migrated to Leipzig, Germany, where he encountered the Russian Marshall Theodore Orlov, who recommended him to the Czarina *Catherine II. She brought him to St. Petersburg and gave him charge of her library (1771). He was ordained a priest in 1775, and named archbishop of Kherson (Oct. 1, 1776). There he pursued his literary activities, but he soon resigned his bishopric, returned to St. Petersburg, and composed a series of exegetical and polemical works. In 1802 he retired to the monastery of St. Alexander Nevski.

A polyglot, Bulgaris served as editor, translator, and biographer and wrote on theology, philosophy, philology, history, physics, and mathematics. He was considered a champion of Oriental Orthodoxy by his coreligionists, since he disputed both the Catholic and the Protestant positions. When the Catholics of eastern Poland were forced into Orthodoxy, he protested in favor of tolerance. One of his principal works is a dogmatic theology composed in Scholastic fashion (Venice 1872).

Bibliography: Jugie TheolDogm 1:526–527. B. KOTTER, LexThK² 2:766. A. PALMIERI, DTC 2.1:1236–41. R. JANIN, DHGE 10:1195–98. E. Wolf, RGG³ 1:1509.

[B. SCHULTZE]

BULGARS

A Turko-Mongol race akin to the *Huns, *Avars, Patzinaks, and the Cumanians; together with the Slavic tribes of the northeastern Balkans and the lower Danube region, they compose the population of Bulgaria. They originally inhabited the area between the Ural Mountains and the Volga. In the late 7th century a group of Bulgar tribes led by Asperuch, presumably a son of Khan Kubrat and the first historically known Bulgarian ruler, migrated to the West, crossed the Danube (679), and invaded the eastern Balkans. Having defeated the forces of the *Byzantine Empire in 680, the Bulgars settled in the area between the Balkans and the Danube and formed a powerful state with a capital at Pliska. From the beginning they were a menace to any Byzantine control of the Balkans. On several occasions the Bulgarian armies advanced to the very gates of *Constantinople, and during the reign of Khan Krum (808–814) the Bulgarian state extended from Adrianople to the Carpathian foothills and from Sardica in the central Balkans to the Black Sea.

Christianity was introduced in Bulgaria during the reign of Khan *Boris I (852–889), but he preferred not to accept Christianity from the *Patriarchate of Constantinople under the auspices of the Byzantine Empire. He therefore began negotiations with Rome. Pope *Nicholas I (858–867) received his appeal favorably, especially since a Bulgarian Church under Rome's direct authority might facilitate the restoration of the Holy See's jurisdiction over Illyricum, which had been detached from Rome by the Byzantine emperors of the iconoclastic period (*see* ICONOCLASM). Boris insisted on patriarchal dignity for the head of the Bulgarian Church and independence of the Bulgarian Church from Constantinople. This conflict over Bulgaria and the vacillating policy of Boris further strained relations between Rome and Constantinople and contributed to the Photian Schism (*see* PHOTIUS, PATRIARCH OF CONSTANTINOPLE). Byzantine pressure compelled Boris to accept Baptism from Constantinople in 864, but in 866 he again appealed to Rome asking for Latin-rite bishops and priests. Then in 870 he turned to Constantinople. Finally, in 880 an agreement was reached between Rome and Constantinople recognizing Roman jurisdiction over Bulgaria. Political events, however, and the remoteness of the area prevented the Holy See from exercising effective control over missionary activity in Bulgaria, and it remained largely in the hands of the Byzantine clergy until Boris and his successors offered asylum to the clergy of the Slavic rite expelled from Moravia after the death of Methodius in 884 (*see* CYRIL AND METHODIUS, SS.). The missionary work of Methodius's disciples *Clement the Bulgarian, Gorazd, Naum, and others was conducted in the vernacular and had such great success among the Balkan Slavs that it served as a counterpoise to the Byzantine influence. Clement was appointed bishop of Ochrida in Macedonia and laid the foundations of an important center of religious and cultural activity. After 893 Slavonic was the official language of the Bulgarian Church.

Under Czar Symeon (893–927), the son of Boris, the Bulgarian state reached the zenith of its power. Its new capitals, Preslav in eastern Bulgaria and Ochrida in western Bulgaria, became great centers of political and cultural life. In 913 Symeon assumed the title of Czar (emperor) and in 924 established an autocephalous Bulgarian patriarchate, forcing Byzantium to recognize both offices. Only the skillful diplomacy of Constantinople and the military energy of the Emperor *Romanus I Lecapenus prevented the establishment of Bulgarian control over the empire itself. The rapid decline of Bulgaria under Symeon's immediate successors was due to the exhaustion following a long period of wars, the devastating inroads of the Magyars and the Patzinaks, and the revolt of the Serbs and Croatians. After 967, the situation was further aggravated by the Russian invasion led by the Kievan Prince Sviatoslav. The internal stability of the Bulgarian realm was greatly weakened by the spread of the *Bogomils, a heretical sect of Manichaean origin. Taking advantage of the situation, the Byzantines occupied eastern Bulgaria in 972, and after the abdication of Czar Boris II (969–972) incorporated it into the empire. Western Bulgaria, with its center in Ochrida, succeeded in maintaining its independence under Czar Samuel (976–1014), but in 1014 the Emperor *Basil II annihilated the Bulgarian armies and all of Bulgaria was divided into several Byzantine provinces. The restoration of Bulgarian independence under the Asen dynasty (1185–1257) with a capital at Tirnovo in the central Balkans was short lived: the conquest of the Balkan Peninsula by the *Ottoman Turks put an end to Bulgarian independence. In 1393 it was incorporated into the Ottoman Empire. Under the Turks, the Bulgarian Church was placed under the jurisdiction of the Patriarchate of Constantinople, and it has since remained under the complete domination of the Greeks.

See also BULGARIA.

Bibliography: K. J. JIREČEK, *Geschichte der Bulgaren* (Prague 1876). V. N. ZLATARSKI and N. STANEV, *Geschichte der Bulgaren,* 2 v (Leipzig 1917). S. RUNCIMAN, *A History of the First Bulgarian Empire* (London 1930). R. JANIN, DHGE 10: 1116–20. F. DVORNIK, *Les Slaves, Byzance et Rome au IX*ᵉ *siècle* (Paris 1926); *The Slavs: Their Early History and Civilization* (Boston 1956).

[O. P. SHERBOWITZ-WETZOR]

BULLA

A lead seal used for authenticating documents, which for durability replaced the older wax seals. It is apparently of Byzantine origin and was used by the papal chancery from the 6th century. It was likewise employed by the royal chancelleries of Europe, with gold or silver replacing the lead on more important documents. Silken or hemp cord bindings, which became less common after the 12th century, held the document together. These cords were themselves immersed in the leaden globule, which was then impressed on the document with a circular stamping device that imprinted a double image. On one side was the signature of the pope (as this side remained empty before his coronation ceremony, such a bull was called a "half-bull"); on the other side was imprinted the papal motto and, since the end of the 11th century, the embossed facial features of the Apostles Peter and Paul, with the corresponding abbreviations S.PE and S.PA for St. Peter and St. Paul respectively.

After the 13th century the documents that were equipped with such seals were themselves called bulls. Although the expression was never officially adopted in the Papal Chancery, it gave rise to an inaccurate but common term for all documents stamped with a leaden seal.

One class of documents, called in earlier times *bullae majores* and later *privilegia,* concerned the bestowal or corroboration of rights without time limitation. In addition to the solemn preamble and conclusion ending with the monogrammed *Benevalete* as the salutation, these documents contained the signatures of the pope and cardinals. This type of bulla was discontinued in the 14th century.

A second class of documents, called *litterae* (or in earlier times *bullae minores*), dealt with matters of lesser importance. After the 12th century these less important documents were classified as: rescripts, to grant favors and promulgate decisions; or executive documents, which contained precepts and ordinances. The

Obverse (a) and reverse (b) of the lead seal, or bulla, of Pope Callistus III.

The original of the papal bull of Pope Honorius III, Nov. 29, 1223, approving the Third Rule of St. Francis, preserved in the treasury of S. Francesco of Assisi. The original lead seal is still attached to the document.

string bindings of such bulls were of silk or of hemp.

The dating of the bulls included the locality and the date of issue according to Roman calculation. For papal letters, usually only the year of the pontificate was given. Since 1908 the reckoning of the year, month, and day has been given according to the civil calendar.

The material on which papal bulls were written was papyrus until the end of the 10th century, but since the 11th century parchment (vellum) has been used exclusively. The language of papal bulls is Latin, and the script up to the 12th century was the so-called "curia-type writing"; from the 12th to the 14th century, the Gothic cursive script, and from the 16th to the 19th century a variation of Gothic script was employed. In the pontificate of Pope Leo XIII modern Latin script was introduced.

The different types, such as consistorial, curial, cameral, common, and secret bulls and briefs, arise from the place of origin, the classification, or the style and form of composition.

Since 1878 the leaden seals for bulls have been discontinued except for the more solemn ones. For all the other bulls, letters, and papal documents a red ink stamp with the name of the pope encircling the heads of St. Peter and St. Paul is used. Bulls are quoted or cited with the first words of the text, as encyclicals, e.g., Pope Boniface VIII's bull *Clericis laicos*.

Bibliography: J. P. KIRSCH, DACL 2.1:1334–50. F. C. BOÚÚAERT, DDC 2:1126–32. G. BATTELLI, EncCatt 2:1778–81. A. STICKLER, LexThK 2:767–768. W. M. PLÖCHL, *Geschichte des Kirchenrechts*, 3 v. (Vienna 1953–59) 2:65–66. **Illustration credits:** Fig. 1, Archivio Segreto Vaticano. Fig. 2, Leonard von Matt.

[A. H. SKEABECK]

BULLA CRUCIATA

A papal bull or letter conceding various privileges to those who participated in or contributed to the war against the Moslems. Historically, the first concessions were issued to promote the Reconquest in Spain, the earliest known grant being that of *Alexander II to Ramiro of Aragon in 1063. *Urban II followed with a concession to the Count of Barcelona in 1089. Successive popes, e.g., Gelasius II (1118), Callistus II (*c.* 1123), Eugene III (1152), and Innocent III (1212) renewed the privileges for Spain. Whereas Urban II, in granting a plenary indulgence for the First *Crusade to the Holy Land (1095), may have been influenced by previous procedures applicable to Spain, *Callistus II, who renewed Urban's indulgence for the East at *Lateran Council I (1123), granted to Spanish crusaders the same privileges offered to crusaders to the orient. These privileges were more clearly defined in what is commonly regarded as the first formal crusade bull, the *Quantum praedecessores* (1145), issued for the Second Crusade by *Eugene III; it included a plenary indulgence, protection of family and property, and a moratorium on interest for debts. Alexander III reissued Eugene's bull in 1165, and Innocent III's *Qui major* (1213) extended the indulgence to contributors

Eugene III's bull "Quantum praedecessores" German MS, 12th or 13th century (Clm. 22201, fol. 257r).

who were unable to participate personally. Thus the Holy Land privileges became the standard for application elsewhere, not only in Spain, but for wars against the *Albigenses (Innocent III), and against the Pope's political enemies in Europe (Innocent III and IV).

As crusades to the East and in Europe waned, the *bulla cruciata* (*cruzada*) came to apply exclusively to Spain or Spanish territory. A series of bulls was granted to Ferdinand and Isabella, and the bull of Gregory XIII (1573), with somewhat extended privileges, was reissued, with constant modifications, by his successors down to the present. Following the conquest of Granada (1492), the emphasis was placed on the offerings of the faithful to be used to promote various enterprises originally growing out of the Reconquest, e.g., restoration of damaged churches or building new ones, and eventually including works generally conducive to the promotion of religion. In the course of time the original requirements of support for the crusade were commuted to other religious acts, e.g., visits to specified churches and prayers. Privileges granted in lieu of the original plenary indulgence have been modified and expanded to include various dispensations for clergy and laity, notably from fast and abstinence. The bull came to apply equally to Spanish dominions, including Naples and Sicily, Latin America, and Portugal (with certain limitations), and to resident foreigners in these countries. The most recent renewals of the bull, those of

Benedict XV (1915) and Pius XI (1928), were designed to bring greater precision, in harmony with the Code of Canon Law.

Bibliography: J. FERRERES, *La nueva bula de cruzada y sus extraordinarios privilegios según la concessión de Benedicto XV* (Madrid 1916). N. PAULUS, *Geschichte des Ablasses im Mittelalter*, 3 v. (Paderborn 1922–23). E. CASPAR, "Die Kreuzzugsbullen Eugens III," *NeuesArch* 45 (1924) 285–305. U. SCHWERIN, *Die Aufrufe der Päpste zur Befreiung des Heiligen Landes*, ed. E. EBERING (Berlin 1937). G. CONSTABLE, "The Second Crusade as Seen by Contemporaries," *Traditio* 9 (1953) 213–279. A. WAAS, *Geschichte der Kreuzzüge*, 2 v. (Freiburg 1956). J. G. GAZTAMBIDE, *Historia de la Bula de la Cruzada en España* (Vitoria 1958). J. A. BRUNDAGE, *The Crusades: A Documentary Survey* (Milwaukee 1962). **Illustration credit:** Staatsbibliothek, Munich.

[M. W. BALDWIN]

BULLFIGHTING

A spectacle in which men excite and fight with bulls in an arena for the entertainment of the public. Introduced into Spain by the Moors, it rapidly became a source of rivalry between Spanish nobility and Moorish chieftains. In spite of official Catholic opposition it rapidly became popular and in time became a part of most important national celebrations. The 18th century witnessed the introduction of the custom of fighting the bull on foot with a sword and muleta, a small red cloth draped over a stick used by the matador to attract the bull's attention.

In Spain and Latin America the bullfight is held in an open-air arena called the *plaza de toros*. A colorful parade precedes the release of the bull into the arena, where it is first assailed by picadors. Mounted on decrepit horses protected by mattress armor, the picadors wound the bull with steel-pointed lances to weaken its neck muscles. The *banderilleros* then plant steel-pointed darts ornamented with colored paper flags into the neck of the bull. At this point the matador enters the ring alone on foot with sword and muleta. He manipulates the bull into a favored position and tries to plunge his sword between the shoulder blades and spine of the animal, thereby causing instant death. In Portugal, a bloodless form of bullfighting, consisting chiefly of tests of horsemanship, is popular.

In 1567 Pius V condemned bullfighting, punishing participants and spectators with excommunication. A few years later, Gregory XIII restricted the penalties to clerics in major orders. The rules of bullfighting were not well established at that time. Fights were sometimes held in the streets and marketplaces. Excessive cruelty to animals and serious injury to life and limb of both participants and spectators often resulted.

Theologians do not consider bullfighting intrinsically wrong. When it involves unjustifiable risk of serious injury, excessive cruelty to animals, or inordinate satisfaction of the cruel impulses of either spectators or participants, then the sport is immoral. Animals may be used by man for amusement and sport, provided there is no excessive cruelty. Hunting and fishing have never been considered to be abuses of the moral law per se, even though practiced merely for diversion.

Aficionados regard bullfighting as an aesthetic spectacle, a moral drama, a work of art justifying some animal suffering, affirming that the rigid rules for professional bullfighting provide the beast with protection from excessive cruelty. They consider bullfighting to be not a cowardly pleasure in the suffering of animals or man, but rather a psychological match between man's intelligence and the bull's untamed brute force; a display of man's valor, skill, and graceful mastery over the animal's power, ferocity, and instinctive courage. Some authorities consider danger to the life of participants to be minimal in properly organized professional bullfighting, a danger comparable to that involved in mountain climbing.

The introduction of the sport among peoples not culturally prepared for its violence would probably give offense and stir up general feelings of outrage and disgust. In such circumstances the sport would be, by reason of its effect, immoral.

See also CRUELTY TO ANIMALS.

Bibliography: J. PEREDA, "La iglesia y los toros," *Razon y Fe* 130 (1944) 505–524; "La moral y los toros," *ibid.* 132 (1945) 105–115, 291–304.

[B. RIEGERT]

BULLINGER, HEINRICH

Swiss Reformer, successor to Huldrych *Zwingli; b. Bremgarten, Swiss Canton of Aargau, July 18, 1504; d. Zurich, Sept. 17, 1575. Bullinger's early schooling with the Brethren of the Common Life at Emmerich was followed by a humanistic training at the University of Cologne. His acceptance by the humanistic circle there brought him under the influence of Erasmus and of the new Reformation ideas of Calvin, Luther, and Melanchthon. Dissatisfaction with scholasticism led him to the critical study of the Scriptures, Origen, Ambrose, Augustine, and John Chrysostom. Upon his return to Switzerland, he taught at the Cistercian monastery near Cappel (1523–29). In 1528 he heard Zwingli preach at Zurich, was converted to his theology, and accompanied him to the disputations at Bern during that year. Bullinger succeeded his father as pastor of Bremgarten in 1529, and married a former nun, Anna Adlischwiler, by whom he had six sons and five daughters. On Dec. 9, 1531, he was chosen pastor of the Great Minster of

Heinrich Bullinger.

Zurich to succeed Zwingli, who died in the battle of Cappel, Oct. 11, 1531. In this position, which he held until his death, Bullinger became an important voice in theological debate, particularly in his efforts to find doctrinal solutions to disputes over the Real Presence in the Eucharist that were dividing the Reformers. Together with Oswald *Myconius and Simon Grynaeus (1493–1541), both of Basel, he composed the First Helvetic Confession (Zwinglian in tone, but with Lutheran elements) in 1536. This was accepted by the Protestant cantons with the exception of Strassburg and Constance. The second Helvetic Confession (Calvinistic in tone with Zwinglian elements) was also the work of Bullinger and appeared in 1566 at the instance of the Calvinist Elector Palatine, Frederick III (the Pious). It was accepted in the Protestant cantons of Switzerland, Hungary, Scotland and France. (*See* CONFESSIONS OF FAITH, PROTESTANT.)

During his leadership in Zurich Bullinger offered hospitality to refugees fleeing from France after the terror of the massacre of *St. Bartholomew's Day (Aug. 24, 1572); from Italy through fear of the Inquisition; and from England during the reign of Mary Tudor (1553–58). His special interest in England appears in his support of Lady Jane Grey in her abortive attempt to succeed to the throne (1553); his advice to Elizabeth in her opposition to the *Puritans; and his dedication of the third and fourth of his *Decadi* to Edward VI. Bullinger's theological beliefs shifted sharply away from *Zwinglianism to *Calvinism, especially after he collaborated with Calvin in formulating the *Consensus Tigurinus* in 1549. Bullinger was a prodigious writer, composing more than 150 works and 12,000 letters. Among his writings are a biography of Zwingli; the edition of the reformer's books; polemical treatises; the *Zürcher Chronik* and the *Diarium,* both works of historical value; and the *Hausbuch,* a popular collection of sermons and articles of faith. He was less active after the plague of 1564–65, which left him in poor health and which brought death both to his wife and to his daughters.

Bibliography: A complete collection of his writings does not exist. *Heinrich Bullingers Diarium (Annales vitae),* ed. E. EGLI (Basel 1904); *Zürcher Chronik,* ed. J. J. HOTTINGER and H. VÖGELI, 3 v. (Frauenfeld 1838–40); *Korrespondenz . . .,* ed. T. SCHIESS, 3 v. (Basel 1904–06). *The Decades of Henry Bullinger,* ed. T. HARDING, 4 v. (Cambridge, Eng. 1849–52). G. W. BROMILEY, ed. and tr., *Zwingli and Bullinger* (Library of Christian Classics 24; Philadelphia 1953), contains tr. "On the Catholic Church." Literature. F. BLANKE, *Der junge Bullinger* (Zurich 1942). A. BOUVIER, *H. Bullinger, réformateur et conseiller oecuménique, le successeur de Zwingli, d'après sa correspondance avec les réformés et les humanistes de langue française* (Neuchâtel 1940), bibliog. T. SCHIESS, "Der Briefwechsel Heinrich Bullingers," *Zwingliana* 5 (1933) 396–409. P. WALSER, *Die Prädestination bei H. Bullinger im Zusammenhang mit seiner Gotteslehre* (Zurich 1957), bibliog. G. WOLF, *Quellenkunde der deutschen Reformationsgeschichte,* 3 v. (Gotha 1915–23), bibliog. P. SCHAFF, *Bibliotheca symbolica ecclesiae universalis. The Creeds of Christendom,* 3 v. (6th ed. New York 1919). R. PFISTER, NDB 3:12–13. P. POLMAN, DHGE 10:1210–11. O. E. STRASSER, RGG³ 1:1510–11. **Illustration credit:** Courtesy of the Trustees of the British Museum.

[E. D. MC SHANE]

BUNDERIUS, JAN (VAN DEN BUNDERE),

theologian; b. Ghent, Belgium, 1481; d. Ghent, June 8, 1557. After joining the Dominicans at Ghent in 1507, he studied theology at Louvain. He taught theology for a while at Ghent and served as prior of the house there for three terms (1529, 1550, 1553), and once as provincial vicar (1550). He was appointed inquisitor for the Diocese of Tournai in 1542. He is famous for his polemics against the reformers. Among other works, he wrote the *Compendium dissidic quorumdam haereticorum atque theologorum* (Paris 1540).

Bibliography: P. MANDONNET, DTC 2.1:1263–64. E. FILTHAUT, LexThK² 2:779. M. H. LAURENT, DHGE 10:1215.

[J. H. MILLER]

BUNSEN, CHRISTIAN KARL JOSIAS VON,

Prussian diplomat, publicist, Protestant lay theologian, and liturgist; b. Korbach (Waldeck) Prussia, Aug. 25, 1791; d. Bonn, Germany, Nov. 28, 1860. Supporting the union of Lutheran and Reformed Churches in Prussia established by Frederick William III in 1817, Bunsen became the chief liturgist of the new church. As Prussian ambassador to the Holy See (1832–39) he played a leading role in the *Cologne mixed marriage dispute and was, as a result, removed from Rome. He was ambassador to Bern (1839–41) and to London (1841–54). In furtherance of his desire for a rapprochement with the Anglicans, he was largely instrumental in creating the joint Anglican and Prussian Protestant bishopric in Jerusalem (1841). John Henry Newman confessed in his *Apologia* that his alienation from Anglicanism was decisively affected by this event. Despite his shortcomings as a diplomat, Bunsen served as an intellectual bridge between Germany and England. He helped impregnate Protestant theology with liberal thought. His own theology was liberal but amateurish, with a fondness for liturgy and sentiment, and a pronounced anti-Catholicism. Bunsen's books were numerous, verbose, and rarely of enduring value, ranging over such diverse fields as art history, Egyptology, patrology, ecclesiastical history, and religious philosophy. They include: *Das evangelischen Bisthum zu Jerusalem* (1842); *Allgemeines evangelisches Gesangbuch* (1846); *Gott in der Geschichte* (3 v. 1857–58); and *Die Zeichen der Zeit* (2 v. 1855).

Bibliography: F. BONSEN, *A Memoir of Baron Bunsen*, 2 v. (London 1868). R. PAULI, ADB 3:541–552, detailed but tendentious. W. HÖCKER, *Der Gesandte Bunsen als Vermittler zwischen Deutschland und England* (Göttingen 1951). R. A. D. OWEN, *Christian Bunsen and Liberal English Theology* (Montpelier, Vt. 1924). W. BUSSMANN, NDB 3:17–18.

[S. J. TONSOR]

BUNSEN, ROBERT WILHELM, chemist and

spectroscopist; b. Göttingen, March 31, 1811; d. Heidelberg, Aug. 16, 1899. Bunsen was a pioneer spectroscopist who, with G. R. Kirchhoff (1824–87), predicted the use of spectral analysis to discover elements present in minute quantities or too difficult to separate from other elements. His almost immediate discovery of rubidium and cesium confirmed this prediction. Bunsen studied at Heidelberg and was professor at Kassel, Marburg, and Breslau before succeeding L. Gmelin (1788–1853) at Heidelberg in 1852. Though Bunsen studied cacodyl compounds extensively and was able to increase the efficiency of blast furnaces, his interests were primarily in inorganic and analytical chemistry. He was the first to prepare analytically pure compounds of potassium, sodium, lithium, barium, strontium, calcium, and magnesium. His study of burning magnesium (1852) led to his interest in photochemistry. He developed many common laboratory tools, such as the nonluminous burner that bears his name (1855), the filter pump (1868), the ice calorimeter (1870), and the vapor calorimeter (1887). Early in his career Bun-

Robert Wilhelm Bunsen, by Willhem Trübner, 1908.

sen developed an antidote to arsenic poisoning that is still used today (freshly precipitated hydrated ferric oxide). He wrote only one book, *Gasometrische Methoden* (1857), but published many articles.

Bibliography: G. LOCKEMANN, *R. W. Bunsen: Lebensbild eines deutschen Naturforschers* (Stuttgart 1949). **Illustration credit:** Photo Deutsches Museum München.

[M. A. J. JUNGBAUER]

BUNYAN, JOHN

Puritan author and preacher; b. Elstow, England, November 1628; d. London, Aug. 31, 1688. His father was a tinker, a descendant of propertied yeoman farmers. Thus John (like William Langland before him) became a rightful spokesman of "the common man" when he later wrote religious allegory in terms of his own life experience. His boyhood was made up of a little schooling, much hard work, games, and church-going. Village society was then becoming conscious of its political powers, while Puritanism struggled with the Established Church. When the Civil War between King and commoners broke out, Bunyan served in the parliamentarian army at a garrison in Newport Pagnell (1644–47). He then married and settled in a small house at Bunyan's End.

Bunyan had until then led what he called a "dissolute" life; he now turned to an intensely prayerful study of the Bible, seeking "the conviction of salvation." After 5 years of spiritual anguish he found peace in the Baptist congregation in nearby Bedford, and, while working as a tinker, became one of the many "mechanic preachers" who spread the Gospel through the countryside. He also published controversial or devotional pamphlets, such as *Gospel Truths Opened* and *A Few Sighs from Hell.* In 1685 his wife died and he married again.

The Puritans, who had enjoyed freedom under the Commonwealth, were again persecuted after the Restoration. Bunyan refused to attend the Anglican Church services, was arrested in 1660 for preaching without a license, and, on refusing to desist, spent 12 years in Bedford prison. After his release he was named pastor of the Baptist congregation. In 1677 he was again imprisoned for 6 months. He died as a result of exposure while performing an act of charity, and was buried at Bunhill Fields.

Bunyan's works as a whole belong, in form and subject matter, in the flood of controversy of his day, but the best of them are marked by the observation, insight, and style of the born writer. They owe nothing to the university or to the coffeehouse, and very little to reading. From the Bible Bunyan drew doctrinal content, figures of speech, and a cadence that elevated his simple vocabulary; in his youth he had reveled in romantic chapbooks; his wife's dowry had brought him two books: the allegorical *Plain Man's Pathway to Heaven* and the devotional *Practice of Piety.* All these shaped his thought. Yet one authentic literary source, of which Bunyan was probably unconscious, may be found in pre-Reformation allegories. Their influence reached him through the living word of the pulpit tradition. G. R. Owst has shown ("Scripture and Allegory," *Literature and Pulpit in the Middle Ages,* Cambridge, Eng. 1933) that sermon figures from the poetical works of the 14th century spanned the gap made by the coincidence of Reformation and Renaissance in England, and reached the Bedford tinker through sermons then still heard in rural pulpits (*see* SERMON LITERATURE, ENGLISH MEDIEVAL).

Literary Achievement. Of Bunyan's 60 printed works 4 are capital. *Grace Abounding to the Worst of Sinners* (1660) recounts his conversion. *The Life and Death of Mr. Badman* (1680) relates the sad end of a sinful life in the form of a dialogue between Mr. Wiseman and Mr. Attentive concerning "this deep judgement of God, . . . enough to stagger a whole world." The book exposes the evils of small-town society in a tone that anticipates the 18th-century novel. *The Holy War* (1682) is an elaborate allegory, in which the town of Mansoul is recaptured from Diabolus by Emmanuel. The grandiose theme is vivid with memories of the Civil War.

The Pilgrim's Progress, Part 1 (written in prison and published in 1677) is a dream allegory in forthright prose. It has the tonal unity of a great poem and the human variety of a novel of character. It tells of the journey of Christian through "the wilderness of this world" to Sion, threatened by the Slough of Despond, the Valley of the Shadow of Death, Vanity Fair, and Doubting Castle, refreshed in the Palace Beautiful and the Delectable Mountains. Along the way he discourses with lively personifications of every human attitude. When he passes through the Waters of Death into the Golden City, "they shut up the gates, which when I had seen I wished myself among them," says the dreamer. In Part 2 (1684) Christiana follows the same road and at last joins her husband.

The Pilgrim's Progress has been translated into almost

every language; its archetypal story has a supranational theme and its psychology is perennially familiar. It spread through Europe before the end of the 17th century, and was subsequently carried by Protestant missionaries to Africa, Asia, and Oceania. Through the colonial pilgrims it entered deeply into the orthodox New England consciousness. Its most appealing interpretation may be found in the first chapter of the American classic, *Little Women,* when Marmee says: "We are never too old for this . . . . Our burdens are here, our road is before us, and our longing for goodness and happiness is the guide that leads us through many troubles and mistakes to the peace which is the true Celestial City." This is the basic ethical relevance of Bunyan's greatest work.

Theological Relevance. This has been both attacked and defended. Much in the book is obviously "antipapist"—the views of an uneducated Puritan conditioned by his historical place at the storm-center of an embittered religious warfare. His picture of "Old Man Pope" biting his nails because he cannot get at the pilgrims passing his cave is probably as sincere as it is ludicrous. There are other repellent elements, such as the condemnation of Ignorance to Hell. A rather extreme criticism of these and other features has been voiced by Alfred Noyes ("Bunyan Revisited," *The Opalescent Parrot,* New York 1929). But scholarly study and popular opinion alike form a constant tradition that recognizes these elements merely as limitations due to Bunyan's times and to his upbringing. The book is almost universally placed among the classic expressions of the Christian imagination. R. M. Frye (*God, Man, and Satan,* Princeton, N.J. 1960) claims that *The Pilgrim's Progress* has as much

John Bunyan, portrait by T. Sadler, 1684.

to contribute to contemporary Christian thought as that thought has to contribute to an understanding of the book itself.

Bunyan's "Christian" is perennially important; he is guided by Evangelist, he is freed from sin by the Cross of Christ, and cries in return: "To tell you the truth, I love Him." Bunyan is a writer whose private experience finds a place in the long *confessio* tradition begun by St. Augustine; his universal vision follows the journey of Everyman through successive lifetimes to an abiding city.

See also ALLEGORY; PURITANISM AND LITERATURE.

Bibliography: J. BUNYAN, *The Works of That Eminent Servant of Christ, John Bunyan,* ed. G. OFFOR, 3 v. (London 1862), the only complete edition; *The Pilgrim's Progress,* ed. J. B. WHAREY, rev. R. SHARROCK (2d ed. Oxford 1963) definitive edition; *Grace Abounding and The Pilgrim's Progress,* ed. J. BROWN (Cambridge, Eng. 1907); *Life and Death of Mr. Badman and The Holy War* (Cambridge, Eng. 1905). J. BROWN, *John Bunyan, His Life, Times and Work,* ed. F. M. HARRISON (Tercentenary ed. London 1928). R. SHARROCK, *John Bunyan* (London 1954). W. Y. TINDALL, *John Bunyan, Mechanick Preacher* (New York 1934). O. E. WINSLOW, *John Bunyan* (New York 1961), good bibliography. **Illustration credit:** National Portrait Gallery, London.

[M. WILLIAMS]

BUONACCORSI, FILIPPO, known also by the pseudonym Callimaco Esperiente, humanist, philosopher, and political figure; b. San Gimignano (Siena), Italy, 1437; d. Cracow, Poland, November 1496. With Pomponio Leto, he founded the Roman Academy. He took part in the plot against Pope Paul II (1468) with other members of the Academy. Later exiled, he took refuge in Poland, where he became secretary to Casimir IV, for whom he performed various delicate missions (e.g., as delegate to Constantinople, Rome, Venice, etc.). He left historical works, discourses, letters, and poetry in which he gives evidence of a vast humanistic culture. He denied the immortality of the soul, called into question the distinction between soul and body, affirmed the complete independence of morality from religion, and defended the absolute sovereignty of the state. In his *Consilium Callimachi* (ed. R. Nsetecka, Cracow 1887), he went so far as to consider religion a political instrument, thus anticipating N. *Machiavelli.

Bibliography: A. SAPORI, "Gl'Italiani in Polonia nel medioevo" in ArchStorIt 3 (1925) 156. G. AGOSTI, *Un politico italiano alla corte polacca nel sec. XV* (Turin 1930). G. SAITTA, *Il pensiero italiano nell'umanesimo e nel Rinascimento* 3 v. (Bologna 1949–51) 1:485–490.

[G. PANTEGHINI]

BUONAIUTI, ERNESTO, Modernist, writer; b. Rome, June 25, 1881; d. there, April 20, 1946. After ordination (1903), he taught philosophy in Rome at the Urbanian University (Pontificia Università Urbaniana de Propaganda Fide). At the Apollinaris in Rome he taught ecclesiastical history (1904–06) and acted as archivist (1906–11). Meanwhile he became active in *Modernism and was reputedly the author of the anonymous *Il programma dei modernisti* (1907), which was placed on the Index March 17, 1908, and was translated into English by George *Tyrrell. This book, the best known of all Italian Modernist writings, endeavored to reply to *Pascendi, Pius X's encyclical condemning the movement. Buonaiuti maintained the Modernism was based on the results of recent Biblical and historical criticism and that its primary purpose was to reconcile Catholicism with these scientific findings. According to

him, the Modernists abandoned *scholasticism because it possessed no further value as a method of apologetics. Buonaiuti was presumed to be the author of *Lettere di un prete modernista* (1908; 2d ed. 1942), to which he referred in his autobiographical *Pellegrino di Roma* (1945) as "a sin of my youth." From 1905 until it was placed on the Index (Sept. 7, 1910), he was editor of the *Rivista storico-critica delle scienze teologiche,* a periodical that published articles on the history of dogmas and of the Church. While director of the bimonthly review *Nova et Vetera* (1908), Buonaiuti published his own articles under the pseudonym "P. Vinci." After the Holy Office condemned (April 12, 1916) the *Rivista di scienza della religioni,* a periodical started shortly before this by Buonaiuti, he subscribed to the oath against Modernism prescribed by Pius X. He failed to observe this and later submissions and was suspended *a divinis* in 1921. *Ricerche religiose,* a periodical he edited, was placed on the Index (Jan. 28, 1925) soon after it began publication. Buonaiuti was excommunicated *vitandus* (1925) and was forbidden to wear clerical garb (1930). In 1931 he was relieved of his post at the University of Rome as professor of the history of Christianity, which he had held since 1915, because he refused to take an oath supporting *fascism. Another of his numerous works, *Storia del cristianesimo,* also was put on the Index (Dec. 16, 1942). All his works, *Opera et scripta omnia,* were condemned to the Index on three occasions (March 24, 1924; Jan. 28, 1925; June 17, 1944). On his deathbed Cardinal Francesco Marmaggi visited him but did not succeed in reconciling him, although Pius XII had authorized the cardinal to do so without requiring a retractation, provided the dying man expressed his belief in the Church's teachings and his disapproval of all that the Church reproved.

Bibliography: M. RAVÀ, *Bibliografia degli scritti di Ernesto Buonaiuti* (Florence 1951), with preface by L. SALVATORELLI. E. ROSA, "Il caso Buonaiuti," CivCatt (1925) 2:229–243; 3:220–238. D. GRASSO, *Il Cristianesimo di E. B.* (Brescia 1953). V. VINAY, *E. B. e l'Italia religiosa del suo tempo* (Rome 1956). V. CERESI, EncCatt 3:218–219.

[F. M. O'CONNOR]

BUONPENSIERE, ENRICO, theologian; b. Terlizzi, near Bari, Oct. 26, 1853; d. Rome, Feb. 18, 1929. Having become a Dominican in 1869, he followed the courses of Tommaso Zigliara (later cardinal) at the College of St. Thomas, Rome. There he obtained the doctorate, taught many different subjects, and was rector (1897–1909). He then taught dogma at the Lateran University until 1925, and was a consultor for various Congregations. His published commentaries on almost all the dogmatic tracts of St. Thomas show him to have been one of the most qualified Thomists at the turn of the century.

Bibliography: A. D'AMATO, EncCatt 3:222.

[I. GROSSI]

BURCHARD OF WORMS, bishop and canonist; b. Wesse, c. 965; d. Aug. 20, 1025. Burchard was a member of the noble family of Hesse. He studied at several schools, the most important of which was the Benedictine school at Lobbes in the Diocese of Cambrai. He entered the service of Archbishop Willigis of Mainz, who ordained Burchard to the diaconate. Burchard held the positions of first chamberlain and primate (judge) of the city of Mainz. His discretion and impartiality in fulfilling these offices brought him to the attention of Emperor Otto III, and the result was Burchard's being appointed by Otto III as bishop of Worms in the year 1000. Burchard was then ordained to the priesthood and consecrated bishop by Archbishop Willigis at Seligenstadt.

As bishop of Worms, Burchard first had to establish his authority. The rival power of an important family, supported by the Saxon dynasty, had been in complete control and were hostile to the interests of the Church. Burchard labored tirelessly for the temporal and spiritual welfare of his diocese. He erected several monasteries and churches and undertook the reconstruction of the Cathedral of Worms in 1016. He also paid special attention to the education and formation of his clerics in his cathedral school. In the interest of diocesan ecclesiastical reform he conducted several diocesan visitations and synods.

Burchard was a leading figure in the general ecclesiastical reform taking hold in Germany at the beginning of the 11th century. He attended several provincial councils: at Thionville (1002–03), over which Henry II presided; at Frankfurt (1007); and at Seligenstadt (1023). This latter council was particularly noteworthy for its reform decrees.

Burchard is also the author of one of the most important canonical collections of the Middle Ages, namely, his *Decretum collectarium* (known later as the *Brocardus*). He compiled this collection between the years 1007 and 1014 with the aid of Oldbert of Gembloux. Between the years 1023 and 1025 he promulgated a celebrated body of laws known as the *Leges et statuta familiae S. Petri Wormatiensis*. These laws were concerned principally with the impartial administration of justice, and they are a useful source for customs and conditions of the feudal society of that period (they may be found in *Monumenta Germaniae Historica I Constitutiones* 639–644).

Shortly after Burchard's death one of his clerics wrote his biography, providing valuable historical details of his life and of the period (cf. *Vita Burchardi;* PL 140:507–   ). Apparently Burchard was highly esteemed by his people, but there does not appear to have been any public cult given to him after his death.

Bibliography: G. ALLEMANG, DHGE 10:1245–47. J. PÉTRAU-GAY, DDC 2:1141–57. K. WEINZIERL, LexThK² 2:783–784. Fournier-LeBras 1:364–421.

[J. M. BUCKLEY]

BURCHARD OF WÜRZBURG, ST., bishop;

b. England; d. Germany, 753 or 754 (feast, Oct. 14). When already a *Benedictine monk Burchard was attracted by the great apostolate of his countryman St. *Boniface and left England, probably c. 735, to become a disciple and collaborator of the Apostle of Germany. When Boniface established the hierarchy in Thuringia, he made Burchard the first bishop of Würzburg in 741 or 742. On April 21, 743, Burchard attended the first German synod and in 747 the general synod of Franconia, and he went to Rome in 748 to report on the state of the Church in Franconia. He enjoyed the esteem of *Pepin III, who sent him in 750–751 with Fulrad of Saint-Denis (d. 784) to Rome regarding the deposition of *Childeric III, last of the *Merovingians, and recognition of Pepin's claim to be

St. Burchard of Würzburg, wood reliquary figure by German sculptor Tilman Riemenschneider (c. 1460–1531).

king of the Franks. At his death, Burchard was buried in the cathedral of Würzburg, but Bishop Hugo (d. 990), on Oct. 14, 983, translated his relics to the monastery of St. Andrew, founded by Burchard in 752. The account of his abdication (vita II) seems to be mere legend.

Bibliography: Sources. *Vita Burchardi* I, unreliable 9th-cent. life, and *Vita* II, 12th cent., both ed. O. HOLDER-EGGER in MGS 15.1:47–62. *Vita Sancti Burkardi, Die jüngere Lebensbeschreibung des hl. Burkard,* ed. F. J. BENDEL (Paderborn 1912). E. ULLRICH, *Der hl. Burkardus erster Bischof von Würzburg* (Würzburg 1877). BHL 1:1483–85. Zimmermann KalBen 3:177–180. P. F. PALUMBO, EncCatt 3:226. W. LEVISON, *England and the Continent in the Eighth Century* (Oxford 1946). **Illustration credit:** National Gallery of Art, Washington, D.C., Samuel H. Kress Collection.

[P. L. HUG]

BURCHARD, DECRETUM OF

Burchard of Worms wrote his *Decretum* (*Liber Decretorum, Brocardus*) between 1007 and 1015. He profited from the help of Walter, Bishop of Spire, and Olbert of Gembloux, who was a monk of the Abbey of Lobbes. The *Decretum* is composed of 1,758 chapters divided into 20 books: the first 18 contain a complete outline of canonical prescriptions followed in that time. Book 19 (*Corrector sive Medicus*) is penitential, and the 20th (*Liber Speculationum, Speculator*) treats of dogmatic questions especially on eschatology.

Sources. The sources for the *Decretum* are mainly the Collection of *Regino of Prüm (600 texts), the *Anselmo dedicata (300 texts), the *Dionysio-Hadriana,* the *False Decretals, the councils of the 9th century, the episcopal *Capitula* (Theodolph of Orléans, Haito of Basel, Herard of Tours), the Collectio *Hibernensis* and some penitentials (Theodore, *Rabanus Maurus, Halitgaire), and finally, extracts of works of SS. Gregory the Great, Isidore of Seville, and Augustine. Texts of Roman law are rare; on the other hand, almost 90 fragments come from authentic Carolingian capitulars or from apocrypha of *Benedict the Levite.

Burchard used his sources very freely; he modified almost 600 inscriptions and even, at times, altered the substance of the documents, to adapt them to contemporary discipline or to promulgate his own ideas for reform.

Contents. Burchard's central idea is that necessary reforms must be worked out by the episcopate, aided in its task by secular power. Toward the Holy See, occupied at that time by the energetic Benedict VIII (1012–24), Burchard has the greatest respect; he recognizes pontifical primacy and the role of the pope as legislator, guarantor of councils (1.42, 179), and guide of Christianity. But this deference for principle does not prevent Burchard from defending the rights of bishops; he pretends to ignore monastic exemptions (8.66) and does not admit that the faithful have recourse to Rome to defeat the decisions of their bishops (2.80). The bishop, head of the local church, may not be judged by the secular power; it is the provincial council (not only the metropolitan one) and, on appeal, the pope, who judges such matters.

The bishop must promote the dignity of life of his clergy. Burchard condemns the marriage of clerics who have taken major orders, but does not ask the faithful to boycott the Sacraments of married priests (2.108). He condemns all forms of simony and avarice but readmits guilty clerics to the functions of their order after they have done penance and have returned to a worthy life (19.42).

Burchard attempts to ensure the morality of the Christian people by proclaiming the indissolubility of marriage (he admits, however, some cases of remarriage after divorce: 17.10, 11; 19.5). He condemns private vengeance, drunkenness, and superstition. True guide of confessors, his *Corrector* contributed to refining the moral sense and individualizing penance: *diversitas culparum diversitatem facit paenitentibus medicamentorum* (19.8).

The *Decretum* of Burchard, signed with the seal of pastoral realism, conservative and conciliating, had a large and rapid diffusion. Through the collections of *Ivo of Chartres, his work entered the *Decretum* of *Gratian.

See also BURCHARD OF WORMS.

Bibliography: Fournier-LeBras 1:364–421. J. PÉTRAU-GAY, DDC 2:1142–57. P. FOURNIER, "Études critiques sur le Décret de Burchard de Worms," NouvRevHistDrFranÉtr 34 (1910) 41–112, 291–331, 564–584; "Le Décret de Burchard de Worms: Ses caractères, son influence," RHE 12 (1911) 451–473, 670–701. O. MEYER, "Ueberlieferung und Verbreitung des Dekrets des Bischofs Burchard von Worms," ZSavRGKan 24 (1935) 144–180.

[C. MUNIER]

BURCKHARDT, JAKOB

Historian; b. Basel, Switzerland, May 25, 1818; d. there, Aug. 8, 1897. Son of a Calvinist pastor, he studied theology, history, and philology at the University of Basel and later attended the Universities of Berlin and Bonn. From 1845 until his death he was professor of history in Basel, except for 3 years (1855–

58) spent teaching in Zurich. Burckhardt favored a society dominated by a true elite. Opposed to what he called the destructive, Jacobin, and vulgar tendencies of his own nationalistic, industrial age, he predicted a

Jakob Burckhardt.

despotism of the masses and a 20th century of triumphant authoritarianism. His views on contemporary society affected his characterization of 4th-century civilization, described in his book *Die Zeit Konstantins des Grossen* (1852; Eng. tr. *The Age of Constantine the Great*) as an age of ignorance, insecurity, and desire for novelty. His belief that the only worthwhile fight was that for culture against barbarism pervades his *Cicerone* (1855; Eng. tr. *Cicerone: A Guide to the Works of Art in Italy*).

His fame rests mainly on the brilliant, frequently-translated *The Civilization of the Renaissance in Italy* (1860), which for the first time treated the history of an era as an integral whole based on "its inner principle." Dramatically it pictured Italy of the *Renaissance as a highly self-conscious, creative, independent culture, secular and individualistic, the birthplace of modern man. Its theme and emphases admittedly sprang from the author's values and yearnings for his own era. The book viewed medieval and Renaissance man as opposites, the former "dreaming or half awake beneath a common veil . . . woven of faith, illusion and childish prepossession . . . conscious of himself only as a member of a race, people . . . or corporation"; the latter throwing off that veil to permit "an objective treatment . . . of all the things of this world," but retaining a "subjective side" permitting him to become a spiritual individual and to recognize himself as such. Political factors in 13th-century Italy, the rediscovery of classical antiquity, and "the genius of the Italian people," according to Burckhardt, brought about these changes. He claimed also that medieval asceticism and religiosity declined in the excitement of discovering nature, man's psychological self, the world at large, and beauty. The perception and elaboration of all this was determined, he wrote, by the rediscovery of classical antiquity and the genius of the Italian people.

Since the 1920s Burckhardt's thesis has been severely criticized, but much of this opposition was based on exaggerated or misconstrued views. Burckhardt attempted to isolate the dominant spirit of an age that was, by his own testimony, dynamic and elusive. It seems valid to say that in dealing with later medieval civilization Burckhardt appeared unaware of its diversity and maturity, neglected its philosophical and theological concerns, misjudged its moral, ethical, and religious temper, and presented a false antithesis between northern Europe and Italy. In treating Renaissance Italy, he described science in cursory, distorted fashion, failed to discuss the fine arts or to relate them to the general history of the era, and greatly underrated their Christian content and feeling. His masterful synthesis has not, however, become outmoded, although it needs emendations and additions. Recently Burckhardt's reputation as a philosophical historian of profound insight has risen to notable proportions.

Bibliography: Works. *Gesamtausgabe,* 14 v. (Stuttgart 1929–34); *Griechische Kulturgeschichte,* 4 v. (Berlin 1898–1902); *Force and Freedom,* ed. J. H. NICHOLS (New York 1943); *Judgments on History and Historians,* tr. H. ZOHN (Boston 1958). Literature. W. KAEGI, *Jacob Burckhardt,* 2 v. (Basel 1947–50); *Europäische Horizonte im Denken Jacob Burckhardt* (Basel 1962). E. GRISEBACH, *Jacob Burckhardt als Denker* (Bern 1943). A. VON MARTIN, *Nietzsche und Burckhardt* (4th ed. Munich 1947); *Die Religion Jacob Burckhardts* (2d ed. Munich 1947). W. K. FERGUSON, *The Renaissance in Historical Thought* (Boston 1948). Symposium on the Renaissance, University of Wisconsin, Milwaukee, 1959, *The Renaissance: A Reconsideration . . . ,* ed. T. HELTON (Madison 1961). Central Renaissance Conference, University of Kansas, 1960, *Jacob Burckhardt and the Renaissance: 100 Years After* (Lawrence 1960). D. HAY, "Burckhardt's Renaissance: 1860–1960," *History Today* 10 (1960) 14–23.

[W. J. PETRY, JR.]

BUREAU, PAUL, French sociologist and moralist; b. Elboeuf (Seine-Maritime), Oct. 5, 1865; d. Paris, May 7, 1923. After completing secondary school at Rouen, he made study tours to England in 1884 and San Francisco in 1885 and then studied law at Rouen and at the Institut Catholique of Paris. He argued few cases as an attorney. In 1891 he took charge of the course in Roman law at the Institut Catholique and then became professor of international law in 1902. He also occupied a chair of sociology at the Sorbonne.

As a sociologist, Bureau was a disciple of Frédéric *Le Play, adhering at first to the school of La Science sociale, led by Henri de *Tourville, from which he later withdrew. He was interested in perfecting its method, treating social facts objectively (*comme des choses*) on the condition that their character as psychological facts was respected. To the social factors considered by Tourville (geography, work), Bureau added *Weltanschauung,* thus avoiding sociological determinism and emphasizing the role of individual initiative in social development. Against Émile *Durkheim, he refused to attribute to collective consciousness a reality anterior and superior to individual life. He prolonged the influence of Gabriel Tarde and prepared the way for Henri *Bergson. For Bureau, sociology as a science was both necessary and insufficient. He proposed the necessity of a social art, i.e., the ordering of institutions from the point of view of the reform of morals, in a period in which the reconstruction of morality was sought by rationalism and positivism. Bureau was an exacting moralist, disquieted by the sexual indiscipline and conjugal dissolution he observed. His most important works include *La Crise morale des temps nouveaux* (Paris 1907), *L'Indiscipline*

des moeurs (Paris 1920), and *Introduction à la méthode sociologique* (Paris 1923).

Bibliography: G. DE LANZAC DE LABORIE et al., *Paul Bureau* (Paris 1924).

[G. JARLOT]

BUREAU OF CATHOLIC INDIAN MISSIONS

The Church's representative to the U.S. government in matters pertaining to Indian missions and the agency entrusted with promoting the apostolate among the Indians in the U.S. The bureau was created (1874) to protect and advance Indian missionary work, then under severe stress. The success of its efforts led the Third Plenary Council of Baltimore (1884) to make it a permanent institution of the Church. It has played an important part in the development of Indian mission work. Its first director, Rev. J. B. A. *Brouillet (1874–83), secured recognition of the constitutional rights of Catholic missionaries and of Catholic Indians in the face of steady sectarian and political opposition; he obtained for Catholic Indian schools the same assistance from the government that Protestant schools enjoyed.

During the short-lived period of Federal patronage, Catholic mission schools increased from 7 in 1874 to 59 in 1896. Means to build these schools were obtained from the Catholic laity, mainly through the efforts of Rev. Joseph A. Stephan, second director of the bureau (1884–1900), who also induced religious orders of men and women to staff them. A resurgence of anti-Catholicism during the 1890s influenced the Congress to curtail aid to mission schools and to end it in 1900. Meanwhile, missionary and pastoral work also had been fostered by the bureau. Sites for more than 100 mission posts had been secured and assistance provided for building and maintaining chapels on them.

Upon the withdrawal of Federal aid, unpromising schools were discontinued. The resourcefulness of Rev. William H. *Ketcham, third director of the bureau (1901–21), was taxed to maintain the others. He secured tribal funds to aid some of these, contributions from the laity to support others, and considerable indirect Federal aid permissible under the law, e.g., rations for children in Indian mission schools. New mission schools were established and missionary work was further expanded. Within a decade, more Indian children were in Catholic schools than ever before, and the number of missions and of Catholic Indians had steadily increased. Amicable relations with the Congress and Federal officials had been reestablished. The Catholic laity was more widely informed of mission activities and needs, and induced to lend more generous aid.

His successors, Fathers William Hughes and J. B. Tennelly, have followed a similar program of promoting the interests of the missions and the welfare especially of the Catholic Indians. Mission chapels increased from fewer than 40 in 1874 to 401 in 1965; mission schools from 7 caring for 400 children to 53 with 8,636 pupils; and Catholic Indians from less than 25,000 in 1874 to a reported total of 130,122 in 1965. The bureau consists of a board of directors, composed of the archbishops of New York, Baltimore, and Philadelphia and an executive director, secretary, and treasurer. Its office is in Washington, D.C.

Bibliography: Bureau of Catholic Indian Missions, *Reports of the Director* (Washington 1883–1910); *Annals of the Catholic*

Indian Missions, 2 v. (Washington 1877–79). *The Indian Sentinel* (Washington 1902–   ). P. J. Rahill, *The Catholic Indian Missions and Grant's Peace Policy 1870–1884* (Washington 1953).

[J. B. Tennelly]

BUREAUCRACY

The term refers loosely to the people, materials, and equipment that any modern large-scale organization uses to coordinate its work activities and to accomplish its defined purposes, whether these be the maintenance of national defense, the dispensing of insurance benefits, the manufacture of automobiles, or the collection of funds for charitable causes. The term is derived from two words: the French *bureau,* originally a writing table or desk, applied by extension to any place where work desks were installed, and, finally, to the work itself; and the Greek word κρατός, meaning dominion or power, having a governmental or public character. In English-speaking countries and in most of Europe, bureaucracy in its popular usage has a clearly derogatory, although not always consistent, meaning. It connotes dullness of mind, arbitrariness, rigidity, officiousness, aggressiveness, and contrariness, timidity, caution, and conservatism. It suggests also a disposition toward routine; strict procedural regularity and consistency; "red tape"; or, to use the more descriptive French term, *la paperasserie.* Bureaucracy, however, has a more precise and, correspondingly, a less emotional meaning for scholars and social scientists.

Weber's Concept. Max *Weber (1864–1920) was the first modern writer to describe and analyze systematically the essential characteristics of bureaucratic organization, whether public or private. His "ideal-type" evidenced 10 basic characteristics: (1) bureaucratic officials, while personally free, must discharge their official duties according to defined rules and regulations; (2) they are organized hierarchically; (3) they are selected on the basis of technical competence, which may be ascertained by competitive examination or by the production of an appropriate diploma that certifies the completion of the required amount of technical training; (4) they are remunerated in money, generally through fixed salaries; (5) they do not own, but use, the means of administration and production; (6) they are subject in their official actions to close supervision, discipline, and control; (7) each bureaucratic office has a clearly defined sphere of legal competence that attaches to it; (8) it is filled through individual tacit or formal contracts; (9) it is the sole or primary occupation of the incumbent; and (10) it constitutes the professional career of the functionary.

Origins. Opinion differs as to the conditions that gave rise to bureaucratic organization in different historical epochs, a problem in which Weber stimulated interest. A money economy, which permits fixed salaries, favors the growth of bureaucratic organization. Apparently it is not an indispensable requirement, however; the bureaucracies of Egypt, China, and Rome not only were based on remuneration in kind but also were characterized by a number of feudal and patrimonial features. The pressure of an insurmountable problem of human survival may encourage bureaucratic development. Thus, the evolution of Egyptian bureaucracy was at least partially a response to the flooding of the Nile and the need to construct and maintain an elaborate network of waterways and irrigation canals. In this con-

nection, the bureaucratization of land armies on the European Continent earlier and more rapidly than in England can be explained partially by the fact that England, as an insular power, did not require large land forces to guard its frontiers. Arnold Toynbee provides a comparative account of the role of professional military and civil services in his *Study of History* (London 1954, 7.6).

The most fully developed theories concerning the development of bureaucracy are rooted in two conflicting interpretations of the evolution of modern capitalism. Some theorists, like Franz Neumann, say that contemporary bureaucracy grew out of monopoly capitalism. Improved technology and the efficiency of large-scale production encouraged the concentration of economic power and the growth of private bureaucracies. To protect their massive investments and to eliminate free and cutthroat forms of competition, monopoly capitalists induced the government to regulate the economy. While the risks of investment were reduced, regulation gradually led to the development of governmental bureaucracies that rivaled private bureaucracies in size and power. On the other hand, many economists, like Friedrich von Hayek, contend that the willful or thoughtless interference of government in the economy is the instrumental cause of bureaucratic growth. Regulation undermines the free play of economic forces. Its major consequence is the expansion of governmental bureaucracies, which, it is argued, eventually results in the bureaucratization of all aspects of economic, social, and political life. Neither theory, taken alone, is very satisfactory. Each stresses elements that the other ignores. Historical research is moving in the direction of an explanation that combines the essential features of both viewpoints.

Contemporary Problems. Three separate, though overlapping, trends can be distinguished in contemporary social science studies of bureaucracy. First, writers criticize the adequacy of Weber's description of the internal structure and operation of modern bureaucracies. Second, they point to a number of serious flaws in Weber's argument that bureaucracy is the most efficient form of human organization. Third, they focus on a number of possible sources of conflict between bureaucratic organization and democratic values that emphasize popular rule and individual freedom.

Chester I. Barnard, in *The Functions of the Executive* (Cambridge, Mass. 1938), claims that formal authority is not necessarily hierarchically arranged in a bureaucracy and that, paradoxically, authority ultimately rests in the hands of those persons to whom orders are directed, and not in the issuing authority. Barnard bases his argument on the fact that, before a person acts, he must accept the order that has been communicated to him as authoritative. If, for example, he finds his fundamental interests in conflict with the order, he is likely not to obey it. Herbert Simon, in his *Administrative Behavior* (New York 1957), has noted that efficiency in administration is as much a product of rational decision making as it is a function of aptly employed methods and processes. Individuals are limited not only by their ability to perform certain specific tasks, but also by their capacity to make proper judgments. Others have observed that informal group relations within a larger bureaucratic framework are often crucial to its effective operation. Still others have pointed to a subtle process of displacement of goals within a bureaucracy, in which the original or announced objectives are gradually subordinated to a narrow conformity to the explicit regulations that govern the internal operations of the organization. Rigidities develop and the organization is increasingly unable to adapt to new situations.

Bureaucracies, moreover, may themselves breed inefficiency through what Thorstein Veblen describes as "trained incapacity." Training and skills that were once applicable to certain external conditions may be inapplicable, even harmful, when applied to changed circumstances. Officials, nevertheless, may continue to respond to new conditions in terms of their previous training and instruction. The maladjustments that occur may in the long run undermine the general capacity of the organization 'to cope with its new environment. The impersonality that is deliberately bred in bureaucracies to encourage the impartial application of regulations may have the effect, too, of corroding the bureaucrats' contacts with the public, and may diminish the effectiveness of the organization in achieving its goals. Bureaucracies also tend to grow in size, even when their actual functions may be diminishing. C. N. Parkinson satirized this point in his *Parkinson's Law and Other Studies in Administration* (Boston 1957), which coins the novel proposition that in a bureaucracy "work expands so as to fill the time available for its completion."

The rise of bureaucratic organizations poses a twofold challenge to democracy. There is, first of all, a growing problem of maintaining popular control and free expression within private associations, such as labor unions, businesses, professional and trade organizations, religious bodies, charitable institutions, and political parties, which have large bureaucratic organizations to carry out their respective objectives. Second, the growth of these organizations and the corresponding growth of government bureaucracies may challenge democratic procedures and values within the larger political order. The root of the problem is essentially the same at each level. The knowledge and expertness possessed by bureaucratic officials is a source of power that may conceivably tempt them to seize control of the private or public associations in whose interests they act and to perpetuate themselves in office. The task of resolving conflicts between bureaucracy and democracy constitutes one of the major problems facing Western societies in the 20th century.

Bibliography: M. WEBER, *From Max Weber: Essays in Sociology,* tr. and ed. H. H. GERTH and C. W. MILLS (New York 1958) 196–244. R. K. MERTON et al., eds., *Reader in Bureaucracy* (Chicago 1952). P. M. BLAU, *Bureaucracy in Modern Society* (New York 1956). M. E. DIMOCK, *Administrative Vitality* (New York 1959). R. V. PRESTHUS, *The Organizational Society* (New York 1962). C. S. HYNEMAN, *Bureaucracy in a Democracy* (New York 1950). S. M. LIPSET et al., *Union Democracy* (Chicago 1956). R. MICHELS, *Political Parties,* tr. E. and C. PAUL (Chicago 1949). F. J. ROETHLISBERGER and W. J. DICKSON, *Management and the Worker* (Cambridge, Mass. 1939).

[E. A. KOLODZIEJ]

BURGOA, FRANCISCO DE, Mexican Dominican chronicler; b. Antequera (today Oaxaca), *c.* 1600; d. Zaachila or possibly Teozapotlán, 1681. He was the son of Ana de Porras, but his father's name is unknown. Burgoa was a descendant of the conquistadores of Oaxaca and was related to prominent families there. He took the habit in 1618 and made his profession in Ante-

quera in the Dominican province of San Hipólito (1620); he was ordained in 1625. Burgoa taught theology for many years and worked in various parishes. He mastered the Zapoteca and Mixteca languages, which enabled him to learn the traditions and legends of the natives of the province. He was provincial in 1649 and was named procurator of his province to the Holy See and to the master general. Eager to improve the culture of his country, he visited many libraries, museums, cultural centers, and convents while in Europe. In Rome he attended the general chapter of his order (1656) and was named definitor, officer of the Inquisition in New Spain, inspector of libraries, censor of books, and vicar-general. On his return to Mexico, he was again made provincial (1662). After his term of office, Burgoa went to the convent of Zaachila, where he wrote two of his best literary works: *Palestra historial de virtudes, y exemplares apostólicos* (1 v.) and *Geográfica descripción de la parte septentrional, del polo ártico de la América, nveva iglesia de las Indias Occidentales y sitio astronómico de esta provincia de predicadores de Antequera Valle de Oaxaca . . .* (2 v.). Both these works were published in Mexico City (1670 and 1674). They were reissued by the Mexican government in 1934, along with a biography of Burgoa and a bibliography of his published and unpublished works. The *Palestra historial* is a chronicle beginning with the arrival of the Dominicans in Mexico City in 1526 and emphasizing their work in the area of Oaxaca. It is largely biographical. The *Geográfica descripción* is concerned mainly with histories of the monasteries. While Burgoa's style is extravagant and tedious, his works are irreplaceable sources for the history of Oaxaca.

[E. GÓMEZ TAGLE]

BURGOS, ARCHDIOCESE OF (BURGENSIS)

Metropolitan see since 1574, in north *Spain. In 1963 it had 990 parishes, 712 secular and 260 religious priests, 973 men in 31 religious houses, 1,383 women in 83 convents, and 385,628 Catholics; its area of 5,351 square miles covers the civil province of Burgos. Its four suffragans, which had 1,982 secular and 729 religious priests, 6,102 sisters, and 1,316,365 Catholics, were: Bilbao (created in 1949); Osma-Soria (restored in 1088), with a university founded by Bp. J. *Palafox y Mendoza (1654–59); Palencia (*c.* 200?, restored in 1035), whose university of 1212, the first in Spain, gave way in 1243 to that of *Salamanca; and Vitoria (1861).

Early History. Burgos had no history before the Reconquest of Spain from the Moors, and its importance in Spanish history declined from the late 15th century, when the Reconquest was terminated and the Americas were discovered. The See of Burgos, located in the watershed of the Douro River, was founded in 1075 as the successor of Oca, in the watershed of the Ebro River, a see existing (589–*c.* 693) under the Visigoths. The area has no history under the Moors, who left no vestiges. In the 10th and 11th centuries there were bishops of Oca who resided temporarily in Valpuesta and Muñó.

Strong counts made Burgos the capital of a country of castles. On the southern pilgrimage route to *Santiago de Compostela and on the road from the Meseta to either the Ebro valley or the port of *Santander, Burgos *c.* 1000 became a capital of the Reconquest, until Toledo assumed that role *c.* 1100. Both *Toledo and *Tarragona claimed Burgos as a suffragan see, but Urban II made it immediately subject to the Holy See (1095).

Mozarabic refugees and Jews appeared in Castile *c.* 950; Benedictines entered later, supported by the Council of Coyanza (1050). Many monasteries were founded then in and near Burgos; four of these had saintly Benedictine abbots who were contemporaries of the Cid: Arlanza (St. García), Cardeña (St. Sisebut), Oña (St. Iñigo), and *Silos (St. *Dominic). Burgos, known for its many MSS in Visigothic script of *Smaragdus's commentary on the Benedictine rule and of the Mozarabic liturgy, was a meeting place of these two ecclesiastical cultures. The Roman rite, introduced into Castile and Galicia in 1076 at the expense of the Mozarabic, was solemnly imposed at the Council of Burgos (1085), the acts of which are lost. Burgos's oldest monastery, Santa Colomba, became a Cluniac priory (1081–1476).

The bishops of Burgos, with close ties to the kings of Castile, had great political and economic power. In the period of the city's greatest prosperity (1130–1300), when pilgrims and commerce made it wealthy, the cathedral, monasteries, and hospitals were built. Royal marriages took place in Burgos in 1219, 1237, and 1269. Important cortes dealing with royal and national affairs met there frequently. That of 1169 gave the king control of the government; it was noteworthy for the attendance of ordinary citizens as well as counts, prelates, and knights. Of four councils held in Castile (1379–1437) which dealt inconclusively with papal allegiance in the *Western Schism, that of Burgos in 1379 was the most important. In 1367 Burgos chose as count Henry of Trastamara, a family that came to rule Aragon as well as Castile. In 1385 the bishops of Burgos, Toledo, Santiago, and Seville were named ex officio to the royal council of 12 members. In 1493 the bishops ceased to be elected and were appointed by the sovereign. The first patriarch of the West Indies (1526) was the bishop of Burgos. From the 14th to the 16th century, numerous synods were held for the reform of the clergy, of which there were more than 12,000 seculars in 1565. Philip II secured the establishment of the archbishopric (1574). Burgos's diocesan constitution of 1576 lasted until 1905. Religious institutions in and around Burgos suffered serious damage from the French occupation (1808–12) and from secularization (1835).

Great Personages; Artistic Treasures. Burgos has had distinguished bishops. Mauritius (1213–38) built the cathedral and organized the cathedral chapter. Juan Cabeza de Vaca (1407–13) composed important synodal constitutions. Paul of Santa Maria (1415–35), a converted rabbi, was a famous spiritual author; his son Alfonso of Cartagena (1435–56) was a diplomat, jurist, and author. Luis de Acuña (1456–95) was an important reformer. Cardinal Francisco de Mendoza y Bobadilla (1551–66) applied the Tridentine reform and founded a seminary (1563). Five popes came from Burgos: Gregory XI, Alexander VI, Adrian VI, Clement VII, and Paul V. Burgos's early saints include *Adelelm (Lesmes), patron of the diocese, and *Julian, Bishop of Cuenca. Among persons of recent times who

have been noteworthy for sanctity were Pedro Barrantes Aldana and his sister Jacinta in the 17th century; the Franciscan Bl. Manuel Ruiz y López (d. 1860) one of the martyrs of *Damascus; and the pedagogue of *Granada, Andrés Manjón (d. 1923), founder of the schools of Ave Maria, whose cause for beatification has been introduced.

The archdiocese has some 200 churches that are Romanesque in whole or in part and even more that are Gothic. The cloister of Silos began a Romanesque style peculiar to Castile. The main Gothic monument is the Cathedral of the Assumption, begun in 1221, a minor basilica since 1921. The basic example of French Gothic in Spain, though erected on a Romanesque foundation (1075–96), it is a museum of architectural work, medieval sacred gold work, marvelous statuary, Flemish tapestries (62), and paintings by Memling, Michelangelo, and Da Vinci. Among artists who worked on the cathedral were Master Henry (d. 1277), builder of the cathedral of *León; John of Cologne, brought back from the Council of Basel by Bp. Alfonso de Cartagena (1431); and Juan de Vallejo, who constructed the vault (1539–67) under which the remains of the Cid were buried after translation to Burgos (1919). Each chapel is a work of art in itself. The Cistercian monastery of Las *Huelgas (1187) and the Charterhouse of Miraflores (1454), with the famous tombs of John II and Isabella of Portugal, are near Burgos. The Gothic church of St. Dorotea (Canonesses of St. Augustine) has a prone statue of St. Juan de Ortega.

The Consulado de Burgos, a source of funds for kings in the 14th century, had trade relations with the

The 13th-century cathedral of the Assumption, Burgos.

*Hanseatic league and with Flanders (especially in wool) in the 15th century and was a center of maritime insurance and capitalism in the 16th. It declined *c.* 1600 as Bilbao and Seville took trade from Burgos and came to an end in 1829. Its rich archives (Archivo de Castilla) contain important documents for the history of maritime trade of northern Spain from the 14th to the 18th century. The archives of the cathedral and of several nearby monasteries are also rich in old documents.

Burgos has three seminaries (established in 1563, 1898, and 1920), the last founded by Canon Villota to train priests for South America and converted into a seminary for foreign missions by Cardinal Benlloch. Diocesan pastoral problems in the mid-20th century derived mainly from emigration to industrial centers.

Bibliography: I. García Rámila, *Bibliografía burgalesa* (Burgos 1961). N. López Martínez, in *Burgense* 3 (1962) 433–456. J. Pérez Carmona, in *Boletín de Instituto Fernán González* 41 (1962) 265–298. M. Martínez Añibarro y Rives, *Intento de un diccionario biográfico y bibliográfico de autores de la provincia de Burgos* (Madrid 1889). L. Ruiz and J. García Sainz de Baranda, *Escritores Burgaleses* (Alcalá 1935). L. Serrano, *El obispado de Burgos y Castilla primitiva desde el siglo V al XIII,* 2 v. (Burgos 1935). F. B. Deknatel, "The Thirteenth Century Gothic Sculpture of the Cathedrals of Burgos and León," ArtBull 17 (1935) 243–289. M. Martínez Burgos, *Guía turística de Burgos* (Burgos 1955). S. Ruiz, DHGE 10:1271–1351. Espasa 9:1453–76. *Burgense* (Burgos 1960–). Flórez EspSagr 27. AnnPont (1965) 81. **Illustration credit:** Embassy of Spain, Washington, D.C.

[N. López Martínez]

BURGUNDIANS, an East German tribe that established an independent kingdom in southeastern Gaul and was incorporated under Frankish rule in 534. During the 1st and 2d centuries they migrated along the Vistula; by the 3d century they turned westward into the Main valley with the ultimate intention of entering Roman lands south of the frontier. As the Alamanni had preempted this region, they drove the Burgundians back (278–280). Then, on the heels of the Vandals, King Gundahar led the Burgundians farther west. By 409 to 412 they established a kingdom on the left bank of the middle Rhine, with Worms as a capital. The Romans recognized them as *foederati.* During their 30-year sojourn here, they accepted Arian Christianity; *Orosius erroneously calls them Catholics at this time. In 435 they attempted to seize more land but the Roman general Aetius checked them; he then summoned an army of Huns who slaughtered Gundahar and many of his people. The *Nibelungenlied* immortalized the story.

In 443 Aetius transferred the surviving Burgundians into Sapaudia, south of Lake Geneva, probably to block the expansion of the Alamanni. As the Roman Empire weakened, the new Burgundian kingdom under Gundioc (437–474) expanded southward along the Rhone and acquired Lyons as a capital. Of Gundioc's four sons— Gundomar, Gundowech, Godigisel, and Gundobad— the last-named survived to reign from 474 to 516. His chief accomplishment was to fend off *Clovis and the Franks who, failing to defeat the Burgundians (*c.* 500), accepted them as allies. Gundobad's policy of good relations with his Roman subjects, who vastly outnumbered the Burgundians, caused him to promulgate for them the *Lex Romana Burgundionum;* his own people received the Germanic law of the *Lex Gundobada.* At about this time the Burgundians accepted Catholicism. They had long been subjected to the pressure of public

opinion and the apostolic zeal of individuals such as Bishop *Avitus of Vienne. Gundobad died an Arian, but his daughters became Catholics and his son King Sigismund (516–523) officially renounced Arianism. Sigismund and his brother Gundomar (523–532) fought a series of wars against the aggressive Franks who were led by Clovis's sons; the wars ended in 534 and Burgundy passed into Frankish control. During the Merovingian period, Burgundy enjoyed a special status under Frankish rule.

Bibliography: *The Burgundian Code,* tr. K. Fischer (Philadelphia 1949). E. Schwarz, *Germanische Stammeskunde* (Heidelberg 1956). E. Ewig, LexThK² 2:790–791.

[R. H. Schmandt]

BURIAL, I (IN THE BIBLE)

In the Bible there is no complete account of burial customs. They are set out here on the basis of data gathered from isolated Biblical passages and from archeological finds. The limitations of this material must be kept in mind; much valuable information has been gathered from the several thousand graves and tombs that have been found and excavated, but only a small fraction of the millions of bodies buried in Bible lands have been brought to light.

Inhumation, Not Cremation. In Syria and Palestine during the Biblical period the common manner of disposal of dead bodies was inhumation, not cremation. Passages that speak of burning refer to ceremonial offerings of aromatic spices (2 Chr 16.14; 21.19; Jer 34.5) or to criminals or enemies (Gn 38.24; Jos 7.25; Lv 20.14; 21.9), whose remains could also be interred (Dt 21.23; Jos 8.29; 10.27). Bodies were deposited in their tombs garbed in the clothes used in life (1 Sm 28.14; Ez 32.27); the use of special burial clothes is late (Jn 11.44; Mk 15.46 and parallels). The corpse was either drawn together, knees to chin, and laid on one side, usually the left, or stretched out on its back; it was surrounded by deposits of articles used in life: dishes, bowls, pitchers, lamps, pieces of furniture, weapons, amulets, and articles of adornment.

Location of Burial Places. The place of burial was outside the inhabited area (as in the necropolises at *Jericho, Mageddo, Gabaon, and Lachis), without a preconceived plan in the layout of the graves, whether on even terrain or in tombs excavated in rocky hillsides. However, graves of individuals have been found in cities and villages and such burials are mentioned in the Bible; e.g., Samuel was buried in his house at Ramah (1 Sm 25.1), and Manasse in Jerusalem (2 Chr 33.20). Individual graves outside the inhabited area are exceptional (Gn 35.8; 1 Sm 31.13); the more common practice was the reuse of family tombs for new burials, in some cases over hundreds of years.

Historical Sequence of Grave Forms. From the Neolithic Period to the transition from Middle Bronze to Late Bronze, the most common forms of tombs are single or connected natural caves, sometimes reshaped to better suit their use for burials. The access was direct, from above, and could be blocked by a stone and refill [see illustration (*a*)].

Typical of Middle Bronze and continuing into Late Bronze is the shaft grave [see illustration (*b*)]; here the access to the sepulchral chamber is a small opening at the bottom of a perpendicular or stepped, circular

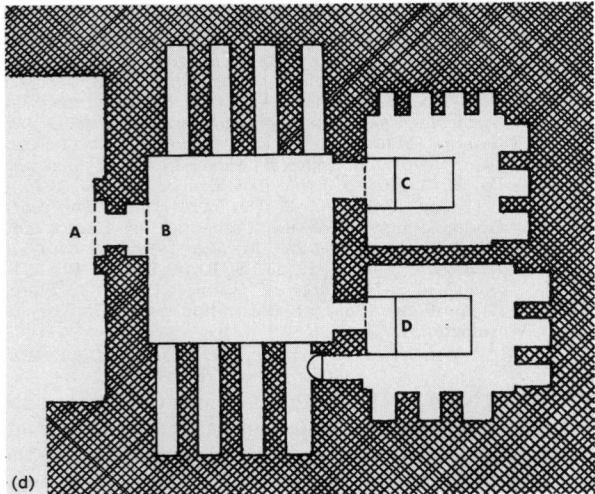

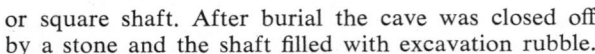

Various forms of graves in ancient Palestine: (a) Reshaped natural cave with access from above. (b) Shaft grave. (c)

Tomb with burial ledges. (d) Tomb with several chambers, each provided with niches.

or square shaft. After burial the cave was closed off by a stone and the shaft filled with excavation rubble.

The transition from Late Bronze to the Iron Age is marked by the development of burial ledges in the sepulchral caves [see illustration (*c*)]; on reuse, the defleshed bones were gathered and deposited in an ossuary pit or in a specially prepared bone cavern.

The last development in burial chambers comes in the Greco-Roman period [see illustration (*d*)]; a vestibule gives access to a series of burial chambers provided with niches, dug at waist height or lower, perpendicularly into the rock. These niches could be closed off by plain or inscribed coverings. When the niche was to be reused, the defleshed remains were gathered into bone boxes known as *ossuaries. Some graves have longitudinal, arched niches in which the bodies could be placed.

The use of sarcophagi of stone, wood, clay, or lead throughout the Biblical period was an exception made in favor of especially prominent persons, no doubt because of the great cost of preparing such containers. The six so-called sarcophagi of Abraham and Sara, Isaac and Rebecca, and Jacob and Lia beneath the ḥaram in Hebron are cenotaphs erected many centuries after the burials of these people. Monuments above ground calling attention to the presence of buried bodies are late, like the Machabean mausoleum at Modin (1 Mc 13.27–30). In earlier centuries the effort seems rather to have been to conceal the place of burial.

Interpretation of Burial Customs. The deposit of articles of daily life and, at least in the earliest period, of food and drink may indicate that, in the belief of non-Israelites, the dead were thought to live in the tombs and to have need of and use for these goods. There is nothing to show that Israelites shared this view. In their burial customs they followed the practices they found in vogue as part of the ritual of decent burial and respect for the dead, allowing themselves to be guided in their beliefs by the affirmations of their religion (*see* AFTERLIFE, 2). The late custom of collecting the defleshed bones from the niches in which they had lain and depositing them in individual ossuaries, often inscribed with the name of the dead person, may reflect the belief in bodily resurrection that arose in the 2d pre-Christian century (for illustration, *see* AZARIA, KING OF JUDA).

See also MOURNING CUSTOMS (IN THE BIBLE).

Bibliography: J. VAN DODEWAARD, LexThK² 2:117. H. SCHMID, RGG³ 1:961–962. De Vaux AncIsr 56–61. Galling BR. F. NÖTSCHER, *Biblische Altertumskunde* (Bonn 1940) 97–104. A. G. BARROIS, *Manuel d'archéologie biblique* (Paris 1939–) 2:274–323. G. E. WRIGHT, *Biblical Archaeology* (rev. ed. Philadelphia 1963) 289, index s.v. Burial of Dead. K. M. KENYON, *Archaeology in the Holy Land* (New York 1960) 321, index s.v. Burial Customs; *Digging up Jericho* (New York 1958) 272, index s.v. Tombs. J. B. PRITCHARD, *The Bronze Age Cemetery at Gibeon* (Philadelphia 1963); *Gibeon, Where the Sun Stood Still* (Princeton 1962). L. Y. RAHMANI, "A Jewish Tomb on Shahin Hill, Jerusalem," IsrExplorJ 8 (1958) 101–105. R. DE VAUX, "Fouille au Khirbet Qumrân," RevBibl 60 (1953) 83–106.

[M. A. HOFER]

BURIAL, II (EARLY CHRISTIAN)

In the primitive Church, burial customs continued Jewish practices, as is attested by the Acts of the Apostles. As Christianity spread, however, the rites were adapted to local usages that were gradually modified by Christian belief in the Redemption, salvation, and eternal life. Christian burial stressed reverence for the body as the creation of God, the coinstrument of the soul that shared life in Christ and was destined for a glorious resurrection both personal and ecclesial. The most profound theology of burial is in Augustine's work *On the Care of the Dead*, while the most developed burial liturgy is found in the *Ecclesiastical Hierarchy* of *Pseudo-Dionysius the Areopagite.

Laying Out of the Body. Upon ascertainment of death, the eyes and mouth were closed. In pagan funerals this was the occasion for the *conclamatio* or violent outcries of mourning. Christians attempted to curb this practice by singing psalms. Augustine mentions the chanting of Psalm 100, which speaks of God's mercy and judgment. After this came the washing of the body; this is attested to by the Acts of the Apostles in the case of the body of Dorcas. Tertullian witnesses to the continuation of this practice in his defense of the Christians: "When I die I can become stiff and pale as death after being washed." Egyptian Christians occasionally adopted embalming, a practice witnessed to by John *Cassian, St. Anthony, and St. Augustine, as well as by archeological remains that bear the Chi-Rho monogram or the Good Shepherd. Ordinarily, the body was anointed to preserve it before burial, a custom the pagans criticized as recorded in Minucius Felix: "You do not grace your body with perfumes, you reserve unguents for funerals." Frequent mention is made of myrrh and of Arabian and Sabean spices. This anointing is not to be confused with the anointing of the deceased during the church service, as described by Pseudo-Dionysius. This was a completion of the Baptismal anointing and signified that the deceased had waged a victorious struggle.

The clothing of the dead followed the anointing. The body was wrapped in linen, since the linen of burial, like that of Baptism, signified immortality. Then the body was clothed in the toga and the outer cloak or in the garments of the deceased's state in life, e.g., emperor or monk. Usually the outer garment was dark, violet being the usual color. Constant denunciations by Eastern and Western Fathers indicate that Christians also employed precious apparel of silk or gold as burial robes and that they were berated for vain display and urged to concentrate on the garment of immortality, the resurrection. Sixth-century canonical legislation indicates that the body was wrapped in or covered with palls and cloths used for divine services. In pagan funerals, the deceased was crowned. Christianity at first rejected this custom because of its idolatrous association with the crowning of the gods; but it gradually was interpreted as presenting the crown of victory.

Wake. Whenever possible there was a wake before burial, held at times in the home of the deceased. When burial occurred on the same day as death, a 3-day watch was often held at the grave. The wake for one who was buried the following day took the form of a night vigil, which at times was celebrated in the church and was an occasion for friends to condole the relatives and to pray for the deceased. This custom was greatly influenced by monastic practices. The body was surrounded with candles, symbolizing the *lux perpetua* to which the deceased was called, and priests read scriptural passages dealing with death, the resurrection, and life everlasting.

Procession. The Christian funeral procession was more a triumphal march. This applied to the simple burials of the early martyrs and to the more solemn funerals after the Peace of the Church. The body, covered with an outer covering, was carried on the funeral bed, with the head raised and exposed. The Acts of the Apostles mentions special young men deputed to carry the corpse. Later there were official *lecticarii* to perform this work. Frequently, relatives acted as pallbearers. For the funerals of outstanding persons, bishops and priests carried the body, and normally it was followed by the family and friends. In the more solemn funerals, acolytes led the procession, and deacons carrying torches escorted the corpse. In some cases the participants were arranged in such a way that the women marched with the nuns and the men with the monks. The main feature was the triumphal spirit, a feature that amazed the pagans. Pagan practices— instrumental music, hired mourners, actors and buffoons—were excluded. The entire group joyfully sang Psalms, the reason for which is given by St. John Chrysostom: "Is it not that we praise God and thank Him that He has crowned the departed and freed him from suffering, and that God has the deceased, now freed from fear, with Himself?" The favorite Psalms were 22, 31, 100, 114, and 115.

Eucharistic Celebration. A distinctive feature of Christian burial was the celebration of the Eucharistic sacrifice and partaking in the Eucharistic banquet. With the pagans, there was a sacrifice offered to the departed, and often a fish was used. Christianity had its own ΙΧΘΥΣ, Jesus Christ, and the sacrifice of Christ was offered for the deceased. The apocryphal *Acts of John* (c. A.D. 150–180) mentions the celebration of the Eucharist at the grave on the 3d day. The casual manner in which this is mentioned indicates that it was the accepted practice to offer Mass at funerals. The Eucharist was celebrated at the grave or in the church. The Mass for *Constantine I and for St. *Monica was celebrated at the grave. St. Ambrose's Mass was that of Easter. St. Zeno of Verona and Pseudo-Dionysius speak of celebrating Mass in the church before the burial.

Interment. The funeral oration, if not previously delivered in the church, was spoken by a relative or friend at the grave. This was meant not only to eulogize the deceased, but to offer consolation drawn from Christian beliefs. Those of SS. Gregory of Nazianzus, Gregory of Nyssa, and Ambrose are the most famous. The relatives then approached the corpse to impart the final kiss, which was given also before leaving the house; but Pseudo-Dionysius speaks of the kiss as part of the liturgical service in the church. It indicated natural affection and the Christian belief in the sacredness of the body. This was a Christian practice, since contemporary religions considered contact with a corpse as a ritual defilement. The body, after being wrapped in linen, was placed in the grave in a lying position. The hands were extended alongside the body or folded across the chest. The body was buried facing the east,

Tomb slab of the sculptor Eutropos, c. 300, Galleria Nazionale delle Marche, Urbino. Left, a figure raises the cup in the funeral meal toast to the departed. Also shown are the father and son working on a sarcophagus and a sarcoph- *agus with the inscription "Eutropos." The Greek inscription reads "The holy and pious Eutropos, in peace. His son made this. The laying to rest took place on the tenth day before the calends of September."*

awaiting the Parousia, the second coming of Christ in glory.

From the beginning Christians practiced earth burial and not cremation. In so doing, they imitated the burial of Christ and followed the Jewish practice. Originally, there was no intrinsic link between earth burial and resurrection. However, St. Paul speaks of the body being sown in corruption and rising in incorruption. Hostile pagans regarded the Christian earth burial as linked with the resurrection and often prevented burial by burning the bodies of Christians or exposing them to vultures. Through earth burial, Christianity and the resurrection became interchangeable concepts. The Christians frequently affirmed that no human intervention could thwart the divine work of the resurrection. Otherwise, Christians professed indifference to being buried or not. This was a radical change, for in contemporary non-Christian religions the proper carrying out of the funeral was regarded as vital for the repose of the soul in the land of the dead, lest the deceased become a restless and vengeful ghost. Before leaving the cemetery the participants pronounced the last farewell. The pagan departure ceremony was *vale*, a final farewell; that of the Christians was *vivas*, a prayer that the departed might live in God and intercede for the living.

Visits to the grave were frequent, and the special days for commemorating the dead were the 3d, 7th or 9th, 30th or 40th, and the anniversary. After the paschal mystery celebrated in the Eucharist, the first liturgical feasts of the saints evolved from these anniversary celebrations, which were considered prolongations of the paschal mystery, life and death in Christ being unique because of the Resurrection. In the words of St. Augustine, "it is this belief alone that distinguishes and separates Christians from all other men."

Bibliography: A. C. RUSH, *Death and Burial in Christian Antiquity* (Washington 1941), bibliog. Centre de pastorale liturgique, *Le Mystère de la mort et sa célébration* (Lex orandi 12; Paris 1956). H. LECLERCQ, DACL 5.2:2705–15; 15.1:1266–72. J. KOLLWITZ, ReallexAntChr 2:208–219. **Illustration credit:** M. Arceci, Urbino.

[A. C. RUSH]

BURIAL, CANON LAW OF

The reverence and devotion bestowed upon the body of the departed Christian are founded upon the doctrine of the resurrection of the body, according to which the body is destined, with the soul, to enjoy eternal happiness in heaven. Moreover, as the temple of the Holy Spirit and the tabernacle of the Eucharist, it is fitting that it be honorably and reverently buried in a safe and becoming place.

The Christian manner of burial is, therefore, a religious act, an ecclesiatical rite, and as such it has come down substantially unchanged through the centuries.

Christian burial has traditionally consisted of three parts: the escorting of the body to the church or cemetery; religious rites at the house, the church, and the cemetery; and burial in the ground set aside by the authority of the bishop for the interment of the faithful. This form has been retained in present legislation (CIC c.1204).

Right to Christian Burial. As to who may receive Christian burial, CIC c.1239.3 states that all the baptized may and must be given it. Obviously, the law concerns baptized Catholics, since baptized non-Catholics are excluded by the provision of CIC c.87, which speaks of the obstacles that impede their full communion with the Catholic Church. An exception to this rule would be the infants of Catholic parents who have died before they could be baptized. Provision is made for their burial in an unblessed part of the Catholic cemetery or, with the ordinary's permission if he sees sufficient reason, in a family plot in the blessed cemetery. No rites are necessary since they died in their innocence and are without sin and need of prayers.

The Code of Canon Law (c.1239.2) makes provision for the granting of full Christian burial also to those catechumens who are under instruction and die before Baptism. They are said to have baptism of desire.

Denial of Christian Burial. With regard to those who may not be given Christian burial, CIC c.1239.1 states that the unbaptized may not be given it, and CIC c.1239.3 adds that it must not be given to those Catholics to whom the law expressly forbids it.

The law expressly forbids Christian burial to six classes of Catholics who are enumerated in CIC c.1240:

(1) "Notorious apostates from the Christian religion." The canonical writers emphasize here that the *apostasy must be total. The mere denial of one or another dogma does not constitute total defection, sinful though it may be. Nor does mere indifference to, or neglect of, one's religious duties place him in this category, although, if carried far enough, it might constitute him a public sinner and exclude him under CIC

c.1240.1n6. This same section of the canon forbids Christian burial also to "notorious members of heretical, schismatical or masonic groups, or societies of a similar nature." This includes the female auxiliaries of all such societies.

The word "notorious" in the text deserves special attention. In law, a notorious offense is one that is public not only as to fact, but public also as to guilt. Thus, one who joined such societies in ignorance would not incur the penalty if he left them after being warned.

(2) "Those who have been excommunicated or interdicted by sentence." This would not, per se, include those who had incurred automatic *excommunication, although they, too, might fall under the category of public sinners and, if so, be excluded from Christian burial by CIC c.1240.1n6.

(3) "Those who, in full possession of their faculties, have killed themselves." In modern practice, and according to most medical authorities, a person who commits suicide is considered deprived at least temporarily of the full possession of his faculties. Psychiatrists and medical examiners regularly issue a certificate to this fact, and it is considered sufficient proof by most ecclesiastical authorities. Doubtful cases are considered below.

(4) "Those who have died in a duel or from a wound therein received." Duels, in the ordinary sense of the word, are either no longer practiced or, if they are, are very unlikely to be fatal since the contestants desist as soon as their "honor" is satisfied by a touch or any sign of blood. Owing largely to ecclesiastical law, this evil practice has practically been eradicated. However, the German university duels come under this proscription by an express condemnation of the Congregation of the Council in 1925. It was decreed that, while these duels lack the malice and evil intent of a real duel, they are but a preparation for later duels in the real sense, and as such, are included in this number.

(5) "Those who have commanded that their body be cremated."

(6) "Other public and manifest sinners." "Public" and "manifest" are terms that express the idea of "notorious" as explained in reference to number (1). Such people are those whose lives are an open scandal, disgrace, and offense to society, such as gangsters, dope peddlers, outlaws, or murderers. Divorced persons who are remarried may or may not come under this heading. In a completely Catholic community they certainly would be included, but in our pluralistic society, they might not. Each case must be judged on its own merits or demerits.

Doubtful Cases. The Code of Canon Law c.240.1 and 2 make two very merciful provisions for these six cases. If the deceased has given any sign of repentance, he regains his lost right. If there is any doubt about the case, either as to guilt or as to sign of repentance, the doubt is to be submitted to the ordinary if there is time. If the doubt persists, the deceased is to be given Christian burial, but in a way that avoids scandal. Those who have committed suicide and persons remarried after a divorce often come under these provisions. Scandal is sometimes avoided by having a less solemn funeral or a burial at an odd hour, and by the omission of publicity. *See* FUNERAL.

Bibliography: R. NAZ, DDC 5:353–354, 928–930. Abbo 2: 1203–42. Beste 1203–42. Bousc-Ellis 607–631. Woywood-Smith 1235–70. M. CONTE, *De locis et temporibus sacris* (Turin 1922) 125–133, 150–151, 253–268. C. KERIN, *The Privation of Christian Burial* (CUA CLS 136; Washington 1941). A. BERNARD, *La Sépulture en Droit Canonique* (Paris 1933).

[C. A. KERIN]

BURIAL WITH CHRIST

"For you were buried together with him in Baptism" (Col 2.12). "But if we have died with Christ, we believe that we shall also live together with Christ" (Rom 6.8). "It is now no longer I that live, but Christ lives in me" (Gal 2.20). St. Paul thrusts the Christian into the theme of death and burial with Christ. One is faced with the paradox: unless he dies with Christ he will not live with Him. This incorporation into the death of Christ is initiated by the Sacrament of Baptism, through which the Christian experiences a death to sin, punishment, and the spirit of the old Adam.

The death of the old man was strikingly symbolized in the ancient rite of Baptism. The catechumen descended into the waters of the baptismal pool. While he was immersed, the words of Baptism were pronounced over him. At that moment a wonderful spiritual effect took place: sin and allegiance to sinful humanity died, just as they died with Christ's crucifixion and death. This immersion was immediately followed by an emersion, symbolic of the risen Christ.

In the 4th century, Cyril of Jerusalem reflected patristic thought when he addressed fellow Christians: "After that you were led to the holy font of divine Baptism, as Christ was brought from the cross to the sepulcher, which is before your eyes. . . You made the saving confession and descended three times into the water and came up again, here also recalling by a symbol the three-days burial with Christ" (*Catech.* 2.4; PG 33:1080).

By combining Pauline and Johannine texts, Cyril concluded that the baptismal waters serve as grave and mother. ". . . you died and were born at the same time. . . . And what Solomon spoke of others will suit you also; for he said 'There is a time to bear and a time to die' [Eccl 3.2]. But with you it is the opposite. The time to die is also the time to be born. One and the same season brings about both of these, and your birth went hand in hand with your death" (*ibid.*; PG 33:1080–81).

The scholastic theologians of the Middle Ages preserved and elaborated upon this Christian theme of burial with Christ. Aquinas, for example, reiterated that through Baptism the Christian is incorporated into the Passion and death of Christ. The newly baptized is cleansed from all sin, orginal and actual, as well as all punishment. "Hence it is clear that the Passion of Christ is communicated to every baptized person, so that he is healed just as if he himself had suffered and died" (ST 3a, 69.2). But do the other effects of sin remain after Baptism: the wounds of sin, sickness, suffering, and death? The Angelic Doctor responds: ". . . these defects will not be taken away until the ultimate restoration of nature through the glorious resurrection" (ST 3a, 69.3 ad 3).

Such views were relatively unchallenged until the Reformation, when Martin Luther proposed that grace did not change the basic sinfulness of man. The old Adam did not and could not die, even in the waters of Baptism. Did the grace of Christ really touch man? Yes, but rather like a garment hiding the leprosy of sin. This view prompted the Council of Trent to reassert: "If anyone denies that by the grace of Our Lord Jesus Christ, which is conferred in Baptism, the guilt of original sin is remitted, or even asserts that the whole of that which has the true and proper nature of sin is not taken away . . . let him be anathema" (Denz 1515).

Current theories on justification by some Protestant theologians appear closer to traditional Christian understanding. Karl Barth, for example, in commenting on Rom 6.4 says: "Baptism is a representation of Christ's death in the midst of our life. It tells us that when Christ has been dead and buried, we too have been dead and buried, we the transgressors and sinners. As one baptized you may see yourself as dead" [*Dogmatics in Outline,* tr. G. T. Thompson (New York 1959) 151]. Yet, in Barth's thought the Christian never becomes completely incorporated in Christ. Rather, this "inherent depravity" of man is dismissed as of no account in view of Christ's death.

Contemporary Catholic theologians, such as K. Rahner and E. H. Schillebeeckx, speak of the encounter with Christ. Christian rebirth paradoxically involves the process of encountering Christ in His death and Resurrection. This encounter ordinarily occurs in the historical Church through the life-giving Sacraments. Baptism plunges the initiate into Christ. Yet even reborn man needs the sacrificial encounter present in the Eucharist: "For as often as you shall eat this bread and drink the cup, you proclaim the death of the Lord, until he comes" (1 Cor 11.26). Since baptismal innocence can be lost, there is need for "a second baptism" to re-create and reinforce the original encounter with the Savior in His immolation through the Sacrament of Penance.

The Church's liturgy at the Easter Vigil echoes the yearnings of today's Christian to die and be buried with Christ as he prepares to renew his baptismal vows: "But since as the Apostles teach we have been buried with Christ by Baptism into death, we also must walk in the newness of life, just as Christ has arisen from the dead, knowing that the old man in us has been crucified with Christ, so that we may no longer serve sin. Therefore, let us realize that we are dead to sin, but alive unto God, in Christ Jesus Our Lord."

See also BAPTISM (LITURGY OF); BAPTISM (THEOLOGY OF); INCORPORATION IN CHRIST; REBIRTH (IN THE BIBLE); REBIRTH (IN THEOLOGY).

Bibliography: G. BAREILLE, DTC 2.1:196–200. E. DELAYE, Dict SpirAscMyst 1:1218–30. Quasten Patr 3:372–375. F. PRAT, *The Theology of St. Paul,* tr. J. L. STODDARD, 2 v. (London 1926–27; repr. Westminster, Md. 1958) 1:221–222; 2:257. K. RAHNER, *On the Theology of Death,* tr. C. H. HENKEY (Quaestiones disputatae 2; New York 1961) 64–88.

[F. W. MC GUIRE]

BURIGNY, JEAN LÉVESQUE DE, French scholar; b. Reims, 1692; d. Paris, Oct. 8, 1785. He came to Paris in 1713 and acquired an immense erudition in ancient and modern history, philosophy, and theology, and a knowledge of Latin, Greek, and Hebrew. He and his brothers formed an academy that compiled a 12-volume encyclopedia in MS. In 1720 they went to The Hague and worked with Saint-Hyacinthe on the journal *Europe savante* (1718–20). Almost all of Burigny's writings deal with religious matters and have a Gallican, even Presbyterian, slant. His treatise on the authority of the Pope (4 v. in 12, 1720) is a good example of his doctrine and method. He also wrote two volumes on pagan theology (1724), a noteworthy two-volume history of Sicily (1745), three volumes on Byzantine revolutions (1750), and biographies of Plotinus, Grotius,

Erasmus, Bossuet, and Cardinal J. Du Perron. In 1756 he was made a member of the Académie des Inscriptions et Belles-lettres.

Bibliography: C. CONSTANTIN, DTC 2.1:1264–65. J. CARREYRE, DHGE 10:1375–76.

[W. E. LANGLEY]

BURKE, EDMUND

British statesman and author whose writings are a main source of modern Anglo-Saxon political thought; b. Dublin, probably Jan. 12, 1729, N.S.; d. Beaconsfield, Buckinghamshire, July 8, 1797. As children of a Protestant attorney father and a Catholic mother, Edmund and his brothers were raised as Anglicans, their sister as a Catholic. Jane Nugent, whom Burke married in 1756, may have been a Catholic like her father; she conformed to the Church of England on marrying Burke.

Burke attended Trinity College, Dublin, from 1744 to 1750. He began to study law at the Middle Temple in London in 1750, but soon abandoned it to follow a literary career. In 1756 he published two works that attracted attention: *A Philosophical Inquiry into the Origin of Our Ideas of the Sublime and Beautiful* expressed a rather crudely sensistic psychology, but had an influence on aesthetic theory in England and on the Continent; *A Vindication of Natural Society* was a parody of Bolingbroke satirizing the individualistic rationalism that Burke was to combat all his life. In 1757 he became editor of Dodsley's *Annual Register,* a review of the outstanding events of each year.

In 1765 the Marquis of Rockingham, who had become first lord of the treasury, made Burke his private secretary. In the same year Burke got a seat in the

Edmund Burke, studio of Joshua Reynolds, 1771.

Commons from Lord Verney's pocket borough of Wendover. For almost 30 years he sat in Parliament, almost always in opposition after 1766 since the Rockingham Whigs were not in favor with George III. He was elected from Bristol in 1774, an occasion he used in his *Speech to the Electors at Bristol* to expound a theory of representation that has become classic. Feeling that an attempt at reelection in 1780 was useless, he withdrew and was then made member for Rockingham's nomination borough of Malton. He held that seat until his retirement in 1794.

Position in British Politics. Burke was the philosopher and spokesman for the Whig aristocracy. His *Thoughts on the Cause of the Present Discontents* (1770) exposed what the Whigs regarded as a dangerous increase in the royal power. His administrative reform plan, which he introduced in 1780, was designed to reduce crown influence in Parliament by eliminating part of the royal patronage. The East India Bill of 1783, of which Burke was at least part author, had the same object among its purposes. At the same time Burke opposed reform of the representation in the House of Commons. Centuries of failure to reapportion representation had produced a system that allowed decayed villages to continue sending two members to Parliament while thriving new towns had none. Burke saw any change as a threat to his ideal of a constitution that maintained a careful balance among the crown, the great landowners, and a random sample of the gentry and merchants. The natural-rights ideology in terms of which parliamentary reform was usually advocated did nothing to commend reform to him, as can be seen in his *Speech on the Reform of the Representation in the House of Commons* (1782).

Generally, however, Burke was a moderate reformer who advocated criminal law reform, relaxation of the *penal laws against Catholics and debtors, and the gradual abolition of the slave trade. He never favored the dissolution of the British Empire. Rather, he sought to bind the American colonies and the Kingdom of Ireland to Britain by ties of fair treatment and mutual interest. In his great speeches on *American Taxation* (1774) and *Conciliation with the Colonies* (1775) he upheld Britain's right to tax the colonies but denounced the attempt to exercise that right as folly. Burke's policy in regard to India was influenced by considerations of party politics and by the financial interests of his relatives. But a genuine moral indignation grew in him as he delved more deeply into Indian affairs. The impeachment of the governor-general of India, Warren Hastings, with Burke as chief prosecutor, failed. But Burke's flaming oratory inspired the British public's concern for the fate of colonial peoples in the 19th century.

Opposition to the French Revolution. Burke showed his *conservatism most fully in his attack on the *French Revolution, which he distrusted almost from its beginning. His masterpiece, *Reflections on the Revolution in France*, appeared in February 1790. That work and the subsequent *Appeal from the New to the Old Whigs* (1791) contain the heart of Burke's philosophy. Together with *Thoughts on French Affairs* (1791), *Remarks on the Policy of the Allies* (1793), and *Letters on a Regicide Peace* (1796–97), they made him a leader not only of British but also of European public opinion against the Revolution. Burke saw the Revolution less as a revolt against intolerable conditions than as the overthrow of the social and political order by the doctrinaire devotees of an abstract theory of the rights of man. But for all his denunciations of "theory" and "metaphysics" in politics, Burke had a social and political theory and it implied a metaphysic.

Political Philosophy. His conception of a divinely founded universal order, of which the state is a part, sprang from a basically Catholic philosophy. He received the medieval doctrine of *natural law through the Anglican tradition. But he insisted that although principles are necessary, they are not enough; they must be applied by *prudence. Here Burke's thought is strikingly similar to the Aristotelian and Thomistic doctrine of practical reason.

He was also keenly aware of history. A good constitution cannot be struck off at a given time by the brain and purpose of man. According to Burke, "it is made by the peculiar circumstances, occasions, tempers, dispositions, and moral, civil and social habitudes of the people, which disclose themselves only in a long space of time" ["Speech on the Reform of the Representation . . . ," *Works* (London 1812) 10.97]. This idea is said to have influenced the historical school in Germany and to have made Burke a forerunner of G. W. F. *Hegel.

Burke saw human nature as realizing itself through an evolving and organic social order (a concept with which his laissez-faire economic theory seems inconsistent). Society, government, law, and rights satisfy natural human needs. But in themselves they are products of convention, framed not according to a blueprint furnished by an abstract law of nature but by practical reasoning and long experience. Once established, however, they have a prescriptive force and may not be abolished by appealing to a radically individualistic theory of popular sovereignty. Reform, therefore, must be accomplished by the gradual adjustment of a complex social organism to new situations, not by social revolution and only in extreme cases by political revolution.

Burke's writings are magnificent examples of the great period of British political rhetoric. Sir Philip Magnus has called them "the finest school of statecraft which exists." The frequency with which they are still quoted today is evidence both of Burke's wisdom and of his style.

Bibliography: Sources. *Works*, 12 v. (Boston 1901); *Speeches of the Right Honorable Edmund Burke*, 4 v. (London 1816); *The Correspondence of Edmund Burke*, ed. T. W. COPELAND et al., 10 v. (Chicago 1958–), 5 v. pub. to date. A. P. I. SAMUELS, *The Early Life, Correspondence and Writings of the Rt. Hon. Edmund Burke* (Cambridge, Eng. 1924).

Literature. D. BRYANT, *Edmund Burke and His Literary Friends* (St. Louis 1939). F. P. CANAVAN, *The Political Reason of Edmund Burke* (Durham, N.C. 1960). C. B. CONE, *Burke and the Nature of Politics*, 2 v. (Lexington, Ky. 1957–64). T. W. COPELAND, *Our Eminent Friend Edmund Burke* (New Haven 1949). R. J. S. HOFFMANN, *Edmund Burke, New York Agent* (Philadelphia 1956). J. MacCUNN, *The Political Philosophy of Edmund Burke* (London 1913). T. H. D. MAHONEY, *Edmund Burke and Ireland* (Cambridge, Mass. 1960). J. MORLEY, *Burke* (New York 1879; repr. 1928). P. J. STANLIS, *Edmund Burke and the Natural Law* (Ann Arbor 1958). The best source of complete and recent bibliographical information is *The Burke Newsletter* (Detroit 1959–). H. C. MANSFIELD, *Statesmanship and Party Government: A Study of Burke and Bolingbroke* (Chicago 1965). **Illustration credit:** National Portrait Gallery, London.

[F. P. CANAVAN]

BURKE, JOHN, politician, judge; b. Keokuk County (Harper), Iowa, Feb. 25, 1859; d. Rochester, Minn., May 14, 1937. He was one of three sons of John and Mary (Ryan) Burke. He moved to Dakota Territory in 1888 and married Mary Kane in 1891; they had four children.

Burke was elected county judge in 1889, then county attorney, state representative, and state senator. In 1906 he was elected first Catholic governor of North Dakota, and was the only Democrat reelected twice (1907–13). Under his leadership a broad liberal program was enacted; it included an act against corrupt practices, a lobbying law, the first primary law, a pure food law, public utilities control, and the creation of several important commissions.

Burke was his state's favorite son candidate at the Democratic convention of 1912; he received 386½ votes for the vice-presidential candidacy. President Wilson appointed him treasurer of the U.S. (1913–21). Afterward Burke resumed the practice of law. In 1924 he was elected to the supreme court of the state, and was chief justice from 1929 to 1931 and from 1935 until his death. He was North Dakota's first representative in the Statuary Hall of Congress; the ceremony accepting the heroic statue of him by Dr. Avard Fairbanks, of Salt Lake City, Utah, was held in the rotunda of Congress June 27, 1963.

[J. H. SCHAUINGER]

BURKE, THOMAS, Dominican preacher; b. Galway, Sept. 8, 1830; d. Tallaght, Ireland, July 2, 1882. Burke entered the Order for the Irish Province in Perugia, Italy, Dec. 29, 1847. While still a deacon studying in Rome, he was appointed (1852) novice-master at Woodchester, England, by Master General Jandel. He was ordained March 26, 1853, and then went to Ireland to open a novitiate at Tallaght. As a result of a sermon on Church music, which he delivered at Our Lady, Star of the Sea, Sandymond, Sept. 4, 1859, he acquired a reputation as an orator that he maintained throughout his life. Burke was prior at Tallaght (1863), and rector of San Clemente, Rome (1864). He returned to Ireland in 1867. Acting as theologian to Bishop Leahy of Dromore, he attended Vatican Council I in 1870. As visitor to the American Dominican Province of St. Joseph (1871), he gave many sermons and a notable series of lectures refuting James Anthony Froude, who sought to justify English occupation of Ireland. In 1873 Burke returned to Ireland, where he continued preaching until his death. He is buried in the church at Tallaght.

Bibliography: W. J. FITZPATRICK, *The Life of the Very Rev. Thomas N. Burke, O. P.,* 2 v. (New York 1886). *Le Père Thomas Burke, Dominicain,* tr. P. CAVALONNE (Brussels 1899).

[J. HALADUS]

BURKITT, FRANCIS CRAWFORD, Orientalist, exegete, and Church historian; b. London, Sept. 3, 1864; d. Cambridge, England, June 5, 1935. Although he received his degree in mathematics at Cambridge University (1886), he soon became interested in the study of Hebrew. In 1903 he began his university career at Cambridge as instructor in paleography and religion. In 1905 he was elected a member of the British Academy. By then he had made Syriac his special field of study and was the first to recognize the importance of the Syriac *palimpsest from the Monastery of St.

Catherine at Mt. Sinai, which he published under the title *Evangelion da-Mepharreshe* (Cambridge 1904). *See* BIBLE, IV (TEXTS AND VERSIONS), 12. Although he also devoted himself to the study of the OT, his more important contributions were concerned with the NT. In this field he was one of the pioneers in England of the new trend in Biblical studies, particularly by his book *The Gospel History and its Transmission* (Edinburgh 1906; 3d ed. 1920). He made important contributions also in the field of Church history, especially in that of Franciscan studies. Finally, his works on *Manichaeism and *Gnosticism are still of considerable value. The list of his numerous publications takes up 10 pages of fine print in the *Journal of Theological Studies* 36 (1935) 337–346.

Bibliography: A. SOUTER et al., JThSt 36 (1935) 225–254. J. F. BETHUNE-BAKER, DNB (1931–40) 124–125.

[J. M. SOLA-SOLE]

BURLINGTON, DIOCESE OF (BURLINGTONENSIS)

Suffragan of the metropolitan See of Boston, Mass., comprising the state of Vermont, an area of 9,135 square miles, which had previously been part of the Diocese (later Archdiocese) of *Boston. The diocese was established July 29, 1853, and Louis de *Goesbriand appointed first bishop. During his episcopate the rapid growth of Catholics in Vermont led to the need for a cathedral, which was begun in 1863 and completed in 1867. It was consecrated December 8 of that year and dedicated to Mary under the title of the Immaculate Conception. De Goesbriand increased the number of priests from 5 to 52, the number of churches from 10 to 78; he established 8 academies and 16 parochial schools and brought 7 congregations of nuns

Cathedral of the Immaculate Conception, Burlington, Vt.

to the diocese. At his death Nov. 3, 1899, John Stephen Michaud, Vermont's first native priest, who had been consecrated coadjutor of Burlington in 1892, succeeded to the see. Michaud was largely responsible for the founding of Fanny Allen Hospital at Winooski Park, Vermont's first Catholic hospital, in honor of the convert daughter of Ethan Allen (*see* ALLEN, FRANCES MARGARET, SISTER). In 1899 Bishop Michaud welcomed to Vermont the Society of St. Edmund, a religious community of men who were exiles from France. They founded *St. Michael's College in 1904 at Winooski Park, the only Catholic college for men in Vermont. When Michaud died, Dec. 22, 1908, there were 95 parishes and missions, 88 secular priests, and 14 religious priests in the diocese.

Michaud's successor, John Rice of Northridge, Mass., was consecrated April 14, 1910. Three high schools were erected during his episcopate, and *Trinity College for women was opened (1925) by the Sisters of Mercy in Burlington. Rice also directed the building of De Goesbriand Memorial Hospital (1923) and placed it under the direction of the Religious Hospitalers of St. Joseph. To succeed Rice, who died on April 1, 1938, Matthew Brady, of Hartford, Conn., was consecrated Oct. 26, 1938. Brady organized the Vermont Catholic Charities and established a diocesan branch of the National Council of Catholic Women, the Catholic Boy Scouts of America, the Junior Catholic Daughters, and the Catholic Youth Organization. He directed the construction of 12 new churches in towns that until then had never had churches of their own. When Brady was transferred to Manchester, N.H., Nov. 11, 1944, Edward Francis Ryan was appointed Burlington's fifth bishop and consecrated Jan. 3, 1945.

Ryan reorganized the Holy Name Societies throughout the diocese, set up a Catholic camp for boys on Lake Champlain, established the Don Bosco School for Boys at Burlington (1945), initiated the Vermont edition of *Our Sunday Visitor* (1946), and gave Vermont its own Catholic weekly, the *Vermont Catholic Tribune* (1956). He introduced eight religious communities of men and women, opened a new school in Rutland, and planned a central Catholic high school in Burlington. Under the bishop's direction a new wing was added to the De Goesbriand Memorial Hospital, and 23 churches were built in small towns and villages throughout the state. Ryan died Nov. 2, 1956, and Robert F. Joyce, who had been consecrated his auxiliary July 14, 1954, was installed as sixth bishop Feb. 26, 1957. Under Joyce the central Catholic high school was completed in 1958 and named the Rice Memorial High School in honor of Bishop Rice. The Newman clubs throughout the state were built up and each given a permanent chaplain. Another wing was added to De Goesbriand Memorial Hospital. Joyce also sponsored the establishment of the Papal Volunteers for Latin America and the Oblates of St. Joseph, a lay institute, and brought several new religious orders to Vermont. He instituted a diocesan Confraternity of Christian Doctrine and set up a diocesan board to work with pastors to help retarded children.

In 1963 the diocese numbered more than 130,250 Catholics in a total population of 390,880, organized in 96 parishes, 43 missions, and 6 stations. They were served by 267 priests, including 81 religious; 29 brothers; and 598 sisters, representing 18 communities. There

Interior of the Cathedral of the Immaculate Conception.

were 4 colleges—*St. Joseph the Provider, for women (1960), Rutland, and St. Joseph Commercial, Bennington, both under the Sisters of St. Joseph; St. Michael's; and Trinity—10 high and 26 elementary schools; 2 general hospitals; 2 schools for nurses; 3 homes for the aged; and an orphanage. Among the religious communities of men were the Vincentians, Redemptorists, Carthusians, Oblates of Mary Immaculate, Benedictines, Holy Cross, and St. Edmund fathers, Servants of the Holy Paraclete and the Xaverian brothers.

Bibliography: V. B. MALONEY and J. K. DURICK, eds., *1853–1953: One Hundred Years of Achievement by the Catholic Church in the Diocese of Burlington, Vermont* (Burlington 1953). **Illustration credits:** Kirk Studio.

[G. E. DUPONT; J. SULLIVAN]

BURMA

Country in southeast *Asia, situated on the Bay of Bengal and bordered by *Thailand, *Laos, *China, *India, and East *Pakistan, 261,000 square miles in area. Burma was formed in the 16th century out of the kingdoms of Ava and Pegu; it annexed Arakan in the 18th century. It was occupied by the British (1824–85) and administered as part of India until 1937. The Union of Burma regained its independence as a republic in 1948. The population in 1963 was estimated at 23 million. *Buddhism, the religion of about 85 per cent of the populace, was made the state religion in 1961. The remainder of the inhabitants adhered in approximately equal numbers to *Hinduism, *Islam, paganism, and Christianity. Protestants reported a total community of 1,137,000 in 1962, of whom 464,000 were full members.

Christianity was introduced into Burma *c.* 1500 by Portuguese merchants who visited the ports and established themselves in the commercial centers. Portuguese priests (seculars, Franciscans, and Jesuits) ministered to them. The first to evangelize the Burmese was a French Franciscan, whose efforts (1554–57) were unsuccessful. In 1666 Burma had one priest, who resided in the city of Ava with 70 Catholics and who visited twice yearly 970 other Catholics dwelling in 11 localities. When the Vicariate Apostolic of Siam, Ava, and Pegu was created (1669), Bishop Laneau of the *Paris Foreign Mission Society (MEP) became the

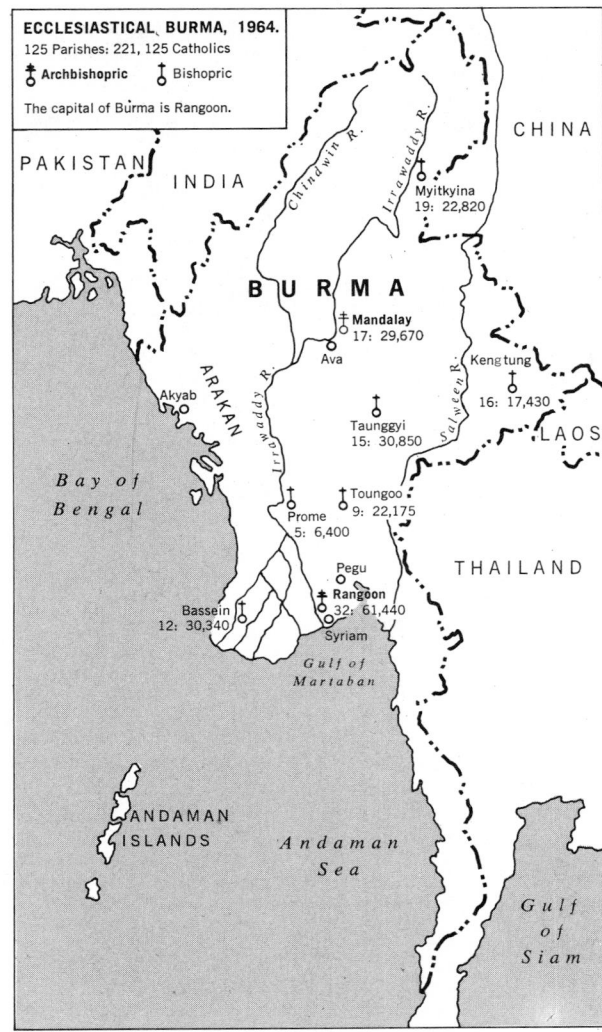

ECCLESIASTICAL BURMA, 1964.
125 Parishes: 221, 125 Catholics
✠ Archbishopric   ☨ Bishopric

The capital of Burma is Rangoon.

Bishop Paul Bigandet, vicar apostolic (1856–93), was the real organizer of the Church in Burma. The hierarchy was established in 1955 when *Mandalay and *Rangoon became archdioceses and metropolitan sees for the two ecclesiastical provinces. In 1963 Mandalay had as suffragan dioceses Kengtung (created in 1955) and Myitkyina (1961). The Dioceses of Bassein (1955), Prome (1961), Taunggyi (1961), and Toungoo (1955) were suffragan to Rangoon. Burma had 191,000 Catholics, one Burmese archbishop (at Mandalay), two native bishops (at Bassein and Toungoo), 94 Burmese among the 187 secular and 65 religious priests, 39 seminarians, 100 brothers, 688 sisters, and 75,000 students in 367 Catholic schools. In 1966 all foreign missionaries were expelled.

Bibliography: L. GALLO, *Storia del cristianesimo nell 'Impero birmano* 2 v. (Milan 1862). P. BIGANDET, *An Outline of the History of the Catholic Burmese Mission, 1720–1887* (Rangoon 1887). H. HOSTEN and E. LUCE. *Bibliotheca catholica birmana* (Rangoon 1915). E. PAPINOT, "L'Apostolat des Barnabites en Birmanie (1722–1829)," RevHistMiss 11 (1934) 270–286; DHGE 8:1533–36. V. BA, "The Early Catholic Missionaries in Burma," *The Guardian* (Rangoon; Aug. 1962–May 1964). *Bilan du Monde* 2:144–149. AnnPont has annual data on all dioceses.

[J. GUENNOU]

BURNETT, PETER HARDEMAN, governor, jurist; b. Nashville, Tenn., Nov. 15, 1807; d. San Francisco, Calif., May 17, 1895. Burnett spent his early life in Tennessee and Missouri, where he worked at odd jobs, edited a newspaper, and eventually studied law. In 1842 he crossed from Independence, Mo., to the Oregon Country, where he was elected to the territorial legislature and appointed justice of the Oregon supreme court. In the California gold rush of 1849, Burnett led the first wagon train from Oregon to the California gold fields and became a leader in the movement for California statehood. In November 1849 he was chosen the state's first governor, serving until Jan. 9, 1851. Following a term on the California supreme court (1857–58), he became a founder and first president (1863) of the Pacific Bank in San Francisco. Burnett had joined Alexander Campbell's Church of the Disciples in the 1830s, but his beliefs were altered by Campbell's debate with Bp. John B. Purcell of Cincinnati, Ohio, and in June 1846 he became a convert to Catholicism. He told the story of his conversion in *The Path Which Led a Protestant Lawyer to the Catholic Church* (1860); he wrote also *Recollections and Opinions of an Old Pioneer* (1880), a source for California and Oregon history.

Bibliography: W. J. GHENT, DAB (1957) 2.1:300–301.

[K. MELLON, JR.]

BURNING BUSH, traditional term applied to a thorn bush of uncertain species (Heb. s^eneh) in the desert near Mt. *Horeb that appeared to Moses to be on fire without burning up and by which Moses became aware of the presence of God (Ex 3.1–4; Acts 7.30; see also Mk 12.26). The historical and scientific details of the apparition are irrelevant in the author's attempt to recount the *theophany. The importance of this event is to be found in its theological dimension. Fire is used frequently as a symbol of the manifestation of God, as well as of His holiness, His protection, and His action on earth. All of these notes are prominent on this occasion as is evidenced in the unfolding of the dialogue: Moses must remove his shoes because it is a holy place; Yahweh has witnessed the affliction

Vicar Apostolic, but he lacked the personnel to staff the mission. The two missionaries whom he sent to Pegu (1687) were brought to Ava (1693), enclosed in a sack, and cast into the river to drown. Evangelization of the pagans was not undertaken again until 1721, when Carlo *Mezzabarba, the papal legate, took the initiative and sent to Ava and Pegu two Italian priests, one a Barnabite, the other a secular. In 1722 the Vicariate of Ava and Pegu was formed and confided to Italian Barnabites. They enjoyed some success in Ava, Pegu, Syriam, and Toungoo, the principal cities, despite the massacre of Bishop Gallizia and two priests (1745). Paolo Nerini continued the work alone until he shared their fate (1756). New missionaries arrived in 1760, but all of them soon died except Father Percotto, an outstanding vicar apostolic (1768–76). Rangoon had 3,000 Catholics, 2 parishes, and several schools *c.* 1790. The Barnabite missionaries were withdrawn, however, as a result of the invasion of Italy by the armies of the French Revolution. The Congregation for the Propagation of the Faith sent other priests without delay, but wars between England and Burma ruined the mission. Oblates of Mary the Virgin came in 1842 from Turin, but in 1855 they were replaced by the MEP, to whom the mission was entrusted.

of His people and will rescue them. The figure of fire in the burning bush is intrinsically linked to the self-revelation of Yahweh to Moses. Modern attempts at a natural or a miraculous explanation of the burning bush ignore the literary genius of a man groping to communicate a supernatural experience.

Bibliography: B. W. ANDERSON, *Understanding the OT* (Englewood Cliffs, N.J. 1957). W. G. WILLIAMS, InterDictBibl 1:476–477. EncDictBibl 290–291. G. RINALDI, EncCatt 10:1417–18. **Illustration credit:** R. V. Schoder, SJ.

[E. ROESSLER]

BURNS, JAMES ALOYSIUS, educator; b. Michigan City, Ind., Feb. 13, 1867; d. Notre Dame, Ind., Sept. 9, 1940. He entered the vocational school at the University of Notre Dame, Ind., to learn the printer's trade, but in 1883 he transferred to the college department and in 1888 entered the novitiate of the Congregation of the Holy Cross. In 1889 he was sent to Watertown, Wis., where he spent 2 years in teaching and theological study. He returned to Notre Dame for more theology, and was ordained on July 21, 1893. Thereafter, as a teacher of chemistry at Notre Dame, he noted the general lack of preparation among Catholic college instructors and argued that they should pursue advanced studies before starting to teach. Burns did not have a major role in promulgating this idea until 1900, when he was appointed superior of Holy Cross College, Washington, D.C., the house of studies for seminarians of the Congregation of the Holy Cross. There, in addition to directing the seminarians, he continued his own research. The Catholic University of America, Washing-

ton, D.C., awarded him the Ph.D. degree in 1906. He was instrumental in founding the National Catholic Educational Association in 1904 and became its first vice president. During his 19 years in Washington, he

James Aloysius Burns.

wrote three basic studies of Catholic education in the U.S.: *Principles, Origin and Establishment of the Catholic School System* (1908), *Growth and Development of the Catholic School System* (1912), and *Catholic Education—A Study of Conditions* (1917). In these works he sought to promote the concept of quality in Catholic education.

In 1919 Burns was elected president of the University of Notre Dame. He closed its preparatory (high school) department; reorganized the university into the four distinct colleges of arts and letters, science, engineering, and law; appointed deans and department heads in the colleges; and raised the salaries of lay professors. After increasing the enrollment, he inaugurated a campaign to match funds offered to the university by the Rockefeller Foundation and the Carnegie Foundation. In 1922 he was named president emeritus, but he continued to direct the fund raising activities of the university. In 1926 Burns was returned to the office of superior of Holy Cross College in Washington, D.C., and, in 1927, was appointed provincial of the Indiana Province of the Congregation of the Holy Cross. He was elected first-assistant superior general of the congregation in 1938.

[E. J. POWER]

BURNS, ROBERT

Scottish poet; b. Alloway, near Ayr, Jan. 25, 1759; d. Dumfries, July 21, 1796. He was the eldest son of a gardener turned small tenant farmer who wrote for his family's guidance "a manual of religious belief." The severe conditions of the times and the poor soil of successive farms combined to ruin and then kill the father. His sons were forced to labor beyond their strength, a circumstance that left a permanent mark on Robert's constitution. As wage earners with their father, the children secured enough to resettle the family in Mossgiel. This was to be the continuous pattern of Burns's life: struggle, crisis, and temporary relief. *Poems, Chiefly in the Scottish Dialect* (1786) was the beginning of an extraordinary fame and an astonishing output. Burns came to a conscious artistry at the culmination of a revival in the Scots' poetic tradition. The acrimony of incessant

Chapel on the traditional site of the Burning Bush, Greek Orthodox monastery of St. Catherine, Mt. Sinai.

Robert Burns, mezzotint engraving by William Walker and Samuel Cousins from Alexander Nasmyth's portrait.

religious squabbling had subsided but the Kirk had reached a crossroad, pulled in one direction by the doctrine of predestination and in the other by the new enlightenment. This division and disagreement and the resultant ludicrous situations met Burns's shrewd observation and brought the scathing effects of his comic satire. *The Holy Fair, The Ordination, The Kirk's Alarm, Address tae the Deil,* and *Holy Willie* are all poems of keen comic insight and relevant comment. Certain poems, verses, and epitaphs constitute buffoonery, but his sense of the comic triumphs when the matter is straightforward and the words unfeigned. The songs, written throughout his career as farmer and excise officer at Ellisland and Dumfries, were contributed to Johnson's *Scots Musical Museum* (1787–1803) and Thomson's *Select Collection of Original Scottish Airs* (1793–1805). Of his longer poems the rollicking *Tam o' Shanter* is considered his masterpiece; *The Twa Dogs* and certain of the *Epistles* are of lasting value. A study of *The Jolly Beggars, A Cantata* helps to a full understanding of his spiritual and intellectual position. No innovator, he drew together the ends of a tradition, which he strengthened with his keen folk sense. Burns made little sustained intellectual effort, depending on the occasion for inspiration. His apparent lack of real critical awareness now makes him the object of some strictures, but his genius tends to elude any rigid scale of academic values. Spiritually he was deeply conscious of disinheritance, but the tenets of a faith rejected could not be readily replaced by a true seriousness when the foundations were lacking and his genius dazzled all, including, at times, himself.

Bibliography: R. BURNS, *Poetry*, ed. W. E. HENLEY and T. F. HENDERSON, 4 v. (Centenary ed. Edinburgh 1896–97); *Works*, ed. W. SCOTT DOUGLAS, 6 v. (Edinburgh 1877–79); *Songs*, ed. J. C. DICK (London 1903; reprint 1963). H. HECHT, *Robert Burns*, tr. J. LYMBURN (2d rev. ed. London 1950). D. DAICHES, *Robert Burns* (New York 1950). T. CRAWFORD, *Burns: A Study of the Poems and Songs* (Stanford 1960). R. D. THORNTON, *James Currie, the Entire Stranger, and Robert Burns* (London 1963). **Illustration credit:** National Gallery of Art, Washington, D.C., Rosenwald Collection.

[M. JAMIESON]

BURNT OFFERING

Translation of the Greek ὁλοκαύτωμα and some similar forms, "wholly burnt (sacrifice)," the Septuagint (LXX) equivalent of the Heb. *minhâ 'ōlâ*, "offering that is caused to ascend (in smoke)." A related older term is *kālîl*, "wholly burnt" (Dt 33.10; cf. 1 Sm 7.9), denoted *sacrifices, other than animal, completely consumed on the altar [Lv 6.15–16; Ps 50(51).21; Sir 45.14; cf. Dt 13.17). Similar offerings were known before Moses, but no cognate term seems to have originated in other Semitic languages. The ceremony is described in the Priestly Code (Lv 1.3–17). Perfect animals (bulls, cows, calves, sheep, lambs, goats, kids), or birds (pigeons, doves) for the poor, were selected. In the tabernacle, after the laying-on-of-hands, they were killed, cut, and placed on the altar by the one offering the sacrifice, or by the priest (assisted perhaps by *Levites), if it was a public sacrifice. (*See* PRIEST AND PRIESTHOOD, ISRAELITE.) The blood was then sprinkled around the altar. The victim was completely consumed by fire; the hide was given to the priest.

There were eight obligatory burnt offerings:

1. Daily burnt offering, at the 3d and 9th hour, of a yearling lamb or a kid; part of morning and evening prayer, accompanied by a cereal offering and wine libation. (This was the *tāmîd*, "routine": Ex 29.38–42; Nm 28.3–29.39; Ez 46.13–15; Dn 8.11–14; 11.31; 12.11.)
2. Sabbath burnt offering, double the daily offering (Nm 28.9–10).
3. Feast day burnt offerings, celebrated at the New Moon, Passover, Pentecost, Trumpets, Day of Atonement, Tabernacles; here the number of victims was increased (Nm 28.11–29.39).
4. Consecration of a priest (Ex 29.15; Lv 8.18; 9.12).
5. Purification of women after childbirth (Lv 12.6–8).
6. Cleansing of lepers after their cure (Lv 14.19–20).
7. Removal of ceremonial defilement (Lv 15.15, 30).
8. Atonement offered by a Nazirite whose vow was broken (Nm 6.11, 16).

Voluntary burnt offerings could be made on special occasions (Nm 7; 3 Kgs 8.64). Gentiles, forbidden to offer other sacrifices, were allowed to make this one. Josephus says war with Rome began when Eleazar forbade Roman rulers the usual sacrificial offerings (*Bell. Jud.* 2.17.2). Burnt offerings (*'ōlâ*) were part of Canaanite cult (3 Kgs 18; 4 Kgs 5.17; 10.18–27). The price list of Marseilles (Punic inscription found at Carthage) mentions three sacrifices: *kālîl* (expiatory sacrifice), *sewa't* (communion sacrifice), and *šelem kālîl* (holocaust). Ras Shamra may have known burnt offerings (*šrp*). Its symbolism was recognized by theologians: "This kind of sacrifice was offered to God especially to show reverence to His majesty, and love of His goodness; it typified the state of perfection as regards the fulfillment of the counsels. Wherefore the whole was burnt up: that as the whole animal by being dissolved into smoke soared aloft, so it might denote that the whole man, and whatever belongs to him, are subject to the authority of God, and should be offered to Him" (ST 1a2ae, 102.3 ad 8; cf. St. Augustine, PL 37:1775; St. Gregory the Great, PL 75:577).

See also HOLOCAUST.

Bibliography: A. A. DE GUGLIELMO, "Sacrifice in the Ugaritic Texts," CathBiblQuart 17 (1955) 196–216. DE VAUX AncIsr. W. B. STEVENSON, "Hebrew 'ōlāh and zebach Sacrifices" in *Festschrift für Alfred Bertholet* (Tübingen 1950). L. ROST, "Erwägungen zum israelitischen Brandopfer," *Von Ugarit nach Qumran* (Festschrift Eissfeldt; Berlin 1958).

[K. SULLIVAN]

BURROWS, ERIC NORMAN BROMLEY, Orientalist; b. Ramsgate, Kent, England, March 26, 1882; d. in Oxfordshire, June 23, 1938. After completing his B.A. at Oxford, he was received into the Roman Catholic Church in December 1904, and entered the Society of Jesus the following September. He studied Oriental languages at St. Joseph's University, Beirut, from 1912 to 1914, and Sumerian and Akkadian under Anton Deimel at the Pontifical Biblical Institute in Rome from 1920 to 1922. From 1924 to 1930 he served as epigraphist for archeological expeditions to Kish and to Ur in Iraq, which resulted in his major contribution to the Oriental field, a study of the oldest written documents found at Ur: *Ur Excavations, Texts, II: Archaic Texts* (London 1935). After his untimely death, the result of an automobile accident, several of his papers on Biblical subjects were published: *The Oracles of Jacob and Balaam* (London 1939) and *The Gospel of the Infancy and other Biblical Essays* (London 1940).

Bibliography: R. CAMPBELL THOMPSON, JRoyAsSoc (1938) 644. G. R. DRIVER, ArchOr 12 (1937–39) 311.

[J. A. BRINKMAN]

BURRUS, PETRUS, neo-Latin poet and theologian; b. Bruges, Belgium, June 4, 1430; d. Amiens, France, April 25, 1507. No definite information on his youth is extant, though it is claimed that he studied at the University of *Paris and acquired a licentiate in Canon Law. He lived many years in Paris, devoting himself to the education of boys committed to his charge, for he was highly regarded as a tutor by families of the upper class. He was an excellent poet and a thorough scholar, interested in the writings of Christian and pagan antiquity. In 1495 he became a canon in *Amiens and there spent the last years of his life. His literary compositions in prose and verse were collected in two volumes published in Paris in 1503 and 1508, but it is not certain that they are complete.

Bibliography: P. BURRUS, *Moralium . . . carminum libri novem* (Paris 1503); *Paenes quinque festorum divae Virginis Mariae* (Paris 1499). A. SANDERUS, *. . . de Brugensibus eruditionis fama claris libri duo* (Antwerp 1624) 65. Chevalier BB 1:734–735. J. F. FOPPENS, *Bibliotheca belgica*, 2 v. (Brussels 1739) 2:959. G. ELLINGER, *Geschichte der neulateinischen Lyrik in den Niederlanden*, v.3 of *Geschichte der neulateinischen Literatur Deutschlands in sechzehnten Jahrhundert*, 3 v. (Berlin-Leipzig 1929–33) 3–7. F. BRUNHÖLZL, LexThK² 2:795. J. N. PAQUOT, *Mémoires pour servir à l'histoire littéraire des dix-sept provinces des Pays-Bas de Principauté de Liège . . .*, 18 v. (Louvain 1763–70) 14:256–259. *Biographie nationale de Belgique* 4:851–852.

[M. MONACO]

BURSE, a container for carrying the corporal to and from the altar. It came into use during the 11th century when the corporals, formerly large, were reduced in size. Originating probably at Reims, the use of the burse gradually spread throughout Europe. When it is employed for Mass, the burse is carried with the folded corporal inside it, on top of the veiled chalice; it is used also for Communion outside Mass and for Benediction. The burse is square, made of two cloth-covered stiff cards hinged along one edge; the corporal is placed between these. At least the upper side of the burse must be of the same color as the other Mass vestments. The name "burse" is given also to a small bag, of leather or other strong material, in which the priests of some countries carry the pyx containing the Blessed Sacrament when they are taking Communion to the sick.

[C. W. HOWELL]

BURSFELD, ABBEY OF, former *Benedictine abbey on the Weser River, about 8 miles from Münden (Hanover), Germany, Diocese of Mainz (patrons, SS. Thomas and Nicholas). Bursfeld or Bursfelde was founded in 1093 by Count Henry the Fat of Northeim, its first monks coming from *Corvey. Emperor Henry IV accorded it his imperial protection and the right of coinage; Abp. Ruthard of Mainz confirmed the foundation. The abbey church, a *Hirsau-type structure of the 12th century, was restored in 1433 and 1589, but was drastically altered in the process; it was again restored in 1846 and shows traces of successive decoration. In 1574 a fire destroyed all the early monastic buildings. Popes Eugene III and Boniface VIII confirmed all Bursfeld's possessions and privileges. Under Abbots Henry II (d. 1334) and John II (d. 1339) discipline deteriorated, and in 1433 it was necessary for the zealous reformer Johann Dederoth, Abbot of Clus, to renew and revive the impoverished and almost extinct monastery at the insistence of Duke Otto (the One-eyed) of Brunswick. Under his successor several other monasteries amalgamated with Bursfeld into a Bene-

The interior of the Abbey church of Bursfeld.

dictine reform congregation; hence the beginning of the Bursfeld Congregation. Bursfeld itself flourished until the Reformation; Abbot Melchior Böddeker (d. 1601) became a Protestant. The Restitution Edict brought back two Catholic abbots (1629–80), but Protestant abbots continued to rule side by side with them. Since the 19th century the head of the Protestant Theological Faculty of the University of Göttingen has always been titular abbot of Bursfeld and receives revenues from that office. The abbey church is used for Lutheran services.

The Bursfeld Congregation was a 15th-century development. Johann Dederoth, Abbot of Clus, took over Bursfeld in 1433, uniting it in his person with Clus. On a journey to Rome he had become acquainted with the Benedictine Reform of S. Giustina (Padua), and from Abbot Johann Rode of Sankt Matthias in Trier he received two monks each for Clus and Bursfeld to initiate the new reform. Reinhausen, Huysburg, and Cismar soon joined what was to become a real reform movement. Dederoth's successor at Bursfeld, Abbot Johann von Hagen, (d. 1469) received much help and inspiration from the canon regular Johann Busch. The first general chapter of the Bursfeld Congregation as such was held from May 1 to 16, 1446, at Bursfeld, which was to remain head of the congregation until the abbey itself would become Protestant. (Clus could not lead the reform movement, as it was a proprietary monastery of the Convent of *Gandersheim.) Meanwhile, Pope Pius II approved the congregation in 1459, and it grew rapidly. By 1780 there were 111 abbeys (excluding convents) united in the congregation; the acts of the general chapters from 1458 to 1780 are extant. Bursfeld had its own seminary for monastic priests from 1616 to 1740 at the University of Cologne. The Bursfeld Congregation, or Union, came to an end with the secularization of 1802–03.

Bibliography: Cottineau 1:534–535. P. VOLK, LexThK² 2:796–798, including list of congregation members; ed., *Die Generalkapitels-Rezesse der Bursfelder Kongregation*, v.1 (Siegburg 1955) 1–5. **Illustration credit:** German Information Center, New York City.

[P. VOLK]

BURTSELL, RICHARD LALOR, civic leader, canonist; b. New York City, April 14, 1840; d. Kingston, N.Y., Feb. 5, 1912. His parents, John Low and Dorothea (Morrogh) Burtsell, were both members of old New York Catholic families. After attending Catholic schools in New York, he began his theological studies in the Sulpician Seminary in Montreal, Canada. In 1857 he went to Propaganda College in Rome, where he obtained doctorates in philosophy (1858) and theology (1862), and was ordained Aug. 10, 1862. From 1862 to 1868 he was assistant to T. S. *Preston, vicar-general and pastor of St. Ann's, New York City. There, Thomas Farrell (1823–80), pastor of St. Joseph's, Waverly Place, exercised a lasting influence on him and a small group of his young priest friends.

Burtsell founded Epiphany parish (1867) and was responsible for establishing St. Benedict the Moor parish (1883), the first in the New York archdiocese for Negroes. From 1887 to 1892 Burtsell was canonical advisor and advocate for his friend, Rev. Edward *McGlynn, supporter of the controversial single-tax theory of Henry George. At least indirectly as the result of his association with McGlynn, Burtsell was deprived in 1889 of his parish, the Epiphany. He won his appeal in Rome, and in 1890 was appointed pastor of St. Mary's in Kingston, where he remained until his death.

In the last quarter of the 19th century, Burtsell was one of the few canonists of note in the eastern U.S. As an effective parish administrator, he cleared the debt on both Epiphany and St. Mary's churches and had them consecrated. Burtsell was a contributor to the old *Catholic Encyclopedia* and wrote regularly for scholarly journals. He was also more civic minded than most pastors of his time, and was a member of the Kingston Board of Trade, a founder and onetime president of the City of Kingston Hospital, trustee of the Kingston Library, and probably the most highly esteemed citizen of the city. He was named papal chamberlain in 1905, and appointed a domestic prelate in November 1911.

Bibliography: *Burtsell Diaries (1865–1912)*, Archives, Archdiocese of New York. F. J. ZWIERLEIN, *Life and Letters of Bishop McQuaid*, 3 v. (Rochester 1925–27); *Letters of Archbishop Corrigan to Bishop McQuaid and Allied Documents* (Rochester 1946). C. A. BARKER, *Henry George* (New York 1955). S. BELL, *Rebel, Priest and Prophet: A Biography of Edward McGlynn* (New York 1937), partial to McGlynn and largely undocumented but with pertinent factual information. HistRecStud 6.2 (1912) 171, 300.

[E. H. SMITH]

BURUNDI, an inland constitutional monarchy, densely populated and agricultural, near the equator in east central *Africa, 10,747 square miles in area. The Nile-Congo divide runs through Burundi, which is bordered by Lake Tanganyika, the *Congo Republic (Léopoldville), *Rwanda, and *Tanganyika (Tanzania). The capital, Bujumbura (Usumbura), is a port of 50,000 on Lake Tanganyika. The Tutsi kingdom, established in the 16th century, was part of German East Africa (1898-1916) and was then administered by Belgium as part of Ruanda-Urundi until independence was gained (1962). The mwami (ruler) has a prime minister and a council of ministers; a legislative assembly of 64

members is elected for 6 years by universal suffrage. Kirundi, a Bantu language, and French have official status. In a population of 2,644,000 in 1963 there were 1,460,000 Catholics and 133,600 catechumens, 111,-000 Protestants, 25,000 Moslems, and 820,000 animists. Almost all education is in Catholic schools, which had some 90,000 students in 1963; the state university at Bujumbura (1960) has a board composed of government members and clergy.

White Fathers arrived at Rumonge (1879) but abandoned the mission when three members were slain (1881). The first permanent post was established at Muyaga (1898). The Vicariate Apostolic of Kivu (created in 1912) split into the Vicariates of Rwanda and Burundi (1922). After Bukoba was detached from it (1929), the Vicariate of Burundi split into the Vicariates of Kitega and Ngozi (1949). In 1959 *Kitega became a metropolitan see with the suffragans Ngozi and Bujumbura; Bururi became a suffragan in 1961. In 1925 the first Burundi priests were ordained, and in 1930 began the multitude of conversions (1,000 baptisms a week in 1935) that has made Burundi and Rwanda the most flourishing Catholic mission area in the world. By 1949 Burundi had 609,000 Catholics. Conversions are based on a well-organized catechumenate of 4 years in a population well-disposed toward Catholicism and on an active lay apostolate that works closely with the hierarchy. In Bujumbura 74 per cent of Easter duties were made; in Kitega, 91 per cent (1963). There is a major seminary at Burasira (Ngozi) and six minor seminaries. Two Burundi congregations of sisters have developed and, at a slower rate, one congregation of brothers. Belgian, Spanish, and Italian secular priests assist several European men's and women's religious orders in missionary work. Bujumbura gained a Burundi bishop in 1959 and Ngozi in 1961.

German, Belgian, English, Danish, American, and Swedish Protestant missions formed the Protestant Alliance of Rwanda and Burundi (1936); after 1962 they were coordinated in the Protestant Alliance of Burundi.

Bibliography: J. R. Clément, *Essai de bibliographie du Ruanda-Urundi* (Bujumbura 1959). J. Perraudin, *Naissance d'une Église. Histoire du Burundi Chrétien* (Bujumbura 1963). *Ruanda-Burundi* (Bujumbura 1963). *Bilan du Monde* 2:179–183. Ann Pont (1965) 217.

[J. PERRAUDIN]

BURY, JOHN BAGNELL

British classical scholar and Byzantine historian; b. Monaghan, Ireland, Oct. 16, 1861; d. Rome, June 1, 1927. His father, an Anglican clergyman, taught him Latin and Greek at an early age, and he had a brilliant career at Trinity College, Dublin, his principal teacher being the famous classical scholar J. P. Mahaffy. He graduated from Trinity in 1882, was made a fellow in 1885, was elected to the professorship of modern history in 1893, and was appointed regius professor of Greek in 1898. In 1902 he became Lord Acton's successor as regius professor of modern history at the University of Cambridge, a post that he held until his death. By 1891 he had acquired a knowledge of Sanskrit, Hebrew, Syriac, and several modern languages, including Russian and Hungarian. His classical training and love of ancient classical literature had a profound affect on his later work and outlook. He regarded later Roman and Byzantine history as essentially the continuation

of ancient, and particularly Hellenic, civilization. Although influenced by the philosophy of G. W. F. Hegel, he was more Hellenic than Hegelian in his rationalism, opposition to revealed religion, and theory of contingency in history. In 1889 he published his *History of the Later Roman Empire from Arcadius to Irene* (2 v. London); and shortly afterward, his excellent edition of the *Odes of Pindar* (2 v. London 1890–92). Between 1896 and 1900, he produced his scholarly edition of *Gibbon's Decline and Fall* (7 v. London), with introduction, notes, and appendices, which has remained standard. His *History of Greece to the Death of Alexander* (1st ed. London 1900, 2d ed. 1913) was long regarded as the best one-volume work in its field. His *Life of St. Patrick and His Place in History* (London 1905), inspired by his interest in the influence of Roman civilization, marks an epoch in critical Irish hagiography. His *Ancient Greek Historians* (New York 1909) retains a high place in Greek historiography.

Bury's profound knowledge of Byzantine constitutional history is exhibited especially in *The Constitution of the Later Roman Empire* (Cambridge, Eng. 1909) and *The Imperial Administrative System in the Ninth Century, with a Revised Text of the Kletorologion of Philotheos* (London 1911). His detailed *History of the Eastern Roman Empire from the Fall of Irene to the Accession of Basil I* appeared a little later (London 1912). Preoccupation with philosophical questions led to the writing and publication of *A History of Freedom of Thought* (London 1913) and *The Idea of Progress: An Inquiry into Its Origin and Growth* (London 1920), both books revealing a marked rationalistic bent. His last significant work was the *History of the Later Roman Empire from the Death of Theodosius I to the Death of Justinian* (2 v. London 1923). He planned the *Cambridge Medieval History,* and the first six volumes of the *Cambridge Ancient History* carry his name as one of the main editors.

Bury was one of the greatest of modern scholars in the Byzantine field. He was primarily concerned, however, with political, constitutional, and administrative history, showing too little interest in social history—and even less in religion as such. His failure to perceive the significance of religion as a dynamic and guiding force in ancient and Byzantine civilization is a weakness, above all, in his works on Byzantine history, that must be recognized.

Bibliography: N. H. Baynes and H. Last, DNB (1922–30) 144–147. J. W. Thompson and B. J. Holm, *History of Historical Writing,* 2 v. (New York 1942) 2:527–529. N. H. Baynes, *A Bibliography of the Works of J. Bury . . . with a Memoir* (Cambridge, Eng. 1929).

[M. R. P. MC GUIRE]

BURY-ST.-EDMUNDS, ABBEY OF,

former Benedictine monastery in the town of Bury-St.-Edmunds, Suffolk, England, Diocese of Norwich. Founded by King *Canute (1020) at the shrine of King St. *Edmund the Martyr, the abbey was England's chief center of pilgrimage until Thomas *Becket's murder (1170). Colonized from *Ely and richly endowed with lands and churches, Bury ranked among England's wealthiest and most influential monasteries throughout its existence. Bishops of Norwich failed to gain control of it, and its *exemption was confirmed (*c.* 1100). Its great abbots included Baldwin (1065–98), physician and builder; Anselm (1121–48), *Anselm of Canter-

The Abbey of Bury-St.-Edmunds, remains.

bury's nephew; *Samson (1182–1211), the subject of *Jocelin of Brakelond's chronicle; and Samson's successor, Hugh II of Northwold, who played an important part at the Fourth *Lateran Council (1215) and became bishop of Ely (1229–54). Since the town of Bury was a monastic borough, the abbey was continuously involved in town affairs; and since it held of the king by a service of 40 knights, the abbey often quarreled with both king and tenants. Dependencies included *Thetford Priory (dissolved 1160) and six hospitals in Bury. Important persons were buried at the abbey; kings paid visits and sent abbots on missions; the abbot sat in Parliament, which sometimes convened there. The number of monks rose from 20 (1020) to 80 (c. 1260). Bury's library had about 2,000 books, including such rarities as Caesar's *Commentaries* and Plautus. The Bury Bible at Corpus Christi College, Cambridge, and the *Life of St. Edmund* in Pierpont Morgan Library, New York, are outstanding productions of its *scriptorium. Bury monks wrote annals and hagiography and started a school of monastic history (14th century); they numbered among their authors John Lydgate, the poet (1370?–1451?). Bury sent monks to Oxford, fostered the cult of Mary in England, and was a center of musical life. When *Henry VIII dissolved the abbey in 1539, there were 43 monks in the community and little sign of decay. Substantial building had taken place in the 15th century, but today little remains at the Abbey site, which is designated an ancient monument.

Bibliography: *Memorials of St. Edmund's Abbey*, ed. T. ARNOLD, 3 v. (RollsS 96; 1890–96), including Jocelin of Brakelond's chronicle. Dugdale MonAngl 3:98–176. M. R. JAMES, *On the Abbey of St. Edmund at Bury: I. The Library. II. The Church* (Cambridge, Eng. 1895). R. GRAHAM, *English Ecclesiastical Studies* (New York 1929) 146–187, 271–301. Knowles MOE. Knowles ROE. Knowles-Hadcock 61, 250. **Illustration credit:** National Buildings Record, London.

[R. W. HAYS]

BUS, CÉSAR DE, VEN., priest, catechetical apostle, founder of Fathers of Christian Doctrine (Doctrinaires); b. Cavaillon (Comtat), Feb. 3, 1544; d. Avignon, April 15, 1607. After studies at Avignon and a worldly life, Bus was influenced by several devout persons and began seriously to serve God in 1574. He

was ordained in 1582, having already taught catechism around Cavaillon. This apostolate, needed because of the pastoral neglect and ignorance attending the wars of religion, became his main work. In it he was imitated by his convert cousin J. B. Romaillon, who was ordained in 1588. Forceful and spiritually gifted, Bus adopted a method that added to his effectiveness; it consisted of simple lively explanations for children and clearly divided dialogue instructions for adults based on the Council of *Trent's catechism. As coworkers joined the cousins, there grew up an association of catechists, influenced by the community ideals of (SS.) Charles *Borromeo and Philip *Neri. Bus directed its formal union of 1592 and the first foundation at Avignon in 1593; papal confirmation came in 1598. Despite outside criticism, the group worked well until c. 1600 when Bus and Romaillon differed over its structure. A painful but charitable split came in 1602. Romaillon and five others opposed to forming an institute with vows continued their work under the bishop of Aix, uniting in 1619 with the Oratory of Pierre de *Bérulle. Bus and the rest remained at Avignon and took the vow of obedience; they soon received papal approval. Though ill and blind, Bus launched the Doctrinaires so vigorously that they survived both this split and his death in 1607 to become quite numerous and extensive. Both he and Romaillon helped establish the *Ursulines in France. As an aid for effective preaching by his disciples, he wrote the *Instructions familières . . .* (5 v. Paris 1666; last French ed. 1867). On Dec. 8, 1821, Pius VII declared Bus Venerable.

Bibliography: P. BROUTIN, *La Réforme pastorale en France au XVIIe siècle*, 2 v. (Tournai 1956) 2:139–154. P. GILOTEAUX, *Le Vénérable César de Bus: Fondateur de la Congrégation des Prêtres de la Doctrine Chrétienne 1544–1607* (Paris 1961), lacks documentation. A. RAYEZ, "Spiritualité du Vénérable César de Bus," RevAscMyst 34 (1958) 185–203. Brémond 2:9–31. P. CALENDINI, DHGE 10:1408–09. A. DUVAL, *Catholicisme* 2:332–333. L. CRISTIANI and P. BAILLY, DictSpirAscMyst 3:1501–12.

[W. H. PRINCIPE]

BUSAEUS (DE BUYS)

Family name of two brothers who played important roles in defense of the Church in the 16th century.

Petrus. Jesuit theologian and editor of the catechism of Peter *Canisius; b. Nijmegen, Netherlands, 1540; d. Vienna, April 12, 1587. In 1561 he entered the Cologne novitiate of the Society of Jesus and 6 years later was appointed novice master. He undertook to complete the catechism of Peter Canisius, adding, with the author's approval, the full texts of all scriptural and patristic references cited in order to demonstrate to the reformers the agreement of the catechism with the doctrine of the ancient Church. The first edition appeared in Cologne and was entitled *Authoritatum sacrae scripturae et sanctorum patrum, quae in summa doctrinae christianae doct. Petri Canisii . . . citantur, et nunc primum ex ipsis fontibus fideliter collectae, ipsis catechismi verbis subscriptae sunt . . .* (4 v. 1569–70). The favorable reception of this work necessitated subsequent editions. Unaccountably missing from the 1571 edition by the renowned press of Aldus Minutius in Venice was the fourth volume. In 1577 the catechism was reissued at Cologne in a folio volume revised by Jean Hase, another Dutch Jesuit, under the title *Opus catechisticum, sive de summa doctrinae . . . Petri Canisii.* In 1571 Busaeus went to Vienna to lecture on Scripture in the university and teach Hebrew in the Jesuit college. He went to Rome in 1584, one of a six-member commission entrusted with drawing up a plan of studies for the entire Society of Jesus. Upon his return to Vienna he held until his death the position of rector of the College of Nobles.

Bibliography: J. BRUCKER, DTC 2.1:1265–66. Sommervogel 2:439–442. A. DE BIL, DHGE 10:1414–15.

[M. S. CONLAN]

Johannes, Jesuit author and theologian; b. Nijmegen, Netherlands, April 14, 1547; d. Mainz, Germany, May 30, 1611. A younger brother of Petrus Busaeus he entered the *Jesuits in 1563. He studied theology at Rome and then taught that subject successfully at Mainz for 22 years; he was also responsible during that time for the spiritual guidance of the sodality (*see* SODALITIES OF OUR LADY). Initially he produced polemic works against *Protestantism: a dissertation on fasting in answer to Martin *Chemnitz, another on the person of Christ directed against the supporters of *Ubiquitarianism, a defense of the Gregorian calendar (*see* CALENDAR REFORM), two articles on the *rosary and several replies to Stephen Gerlach of Tübingen on the person of Jesus. To all of these works he imparted an irenic tone rare in that age. After 1595, forsaking controversy, he edited ascetical works, such as the meditations of Fathers Bruni and Pinelli and Father Androtius's treatise on frequent Communion. Busaeus himself composed, among other works, the *Enchiridion piarum meditationum* (1st ed. Mainz 1606, numerous later editions and translations); πανάριον, *hoc est Arca medica . . . adversus animi morbos* (Mainz 1608); and *Viridarium christianarum virtutum* (Mainz 1610). Busaeus also published editions of ecclesiastical writers, most notably *Peter of Blois (Mainz 1600), *Hincmar of Reims (Mainz 1602), the *Vitae romanorum pontificum* of *Anastasius the Librarian (Mainz 1602), which he erroneously attributed to *Liutprand of Cremona, the works of Johannes *Trithemius, and an abridgement of *Abbo of Fleury.

A third brother, Gerard (1538–96) was also a theologian.

Bibliography: J. N. PAQUOT, *Mémoires pour servir à l'histoire littéraire des dix-sept provinces*, v.1 (Louvain 1763) 72–80. Sommervogel 2:416–439; 8:1949–51, complete list of works of Busaeus. Hurter Nomencl 3:421. B. DUHR, *Geschichte der Jesuiten in den Ländern deutscher Zunge*, 4 v. in 5 (2d ed. Freiburg 1907–28). A. DE BIL, DHGE 10:1414. J. BRUCKER, DTC 2.1:1265. A. RAYEZ, LexThK² 2:799.

[J. DAOUST]

BUSENBAUM, HERMANN

Jesuit moral theologian; b. Nottuln, Westphalia, 1600; d. Münster, Jan. 31, 1668. He taught the humanities, philosophy, theology, and particularly moral theology, in various colleges, and is best remembered for his teaching at Cologne. Socius of his provincial, rector of the colleges of Hildesheim and Münster, confessor and adviser of the Prince Bishop of Münster, Christoph Bernhard von Galen, Busenbaum was known for his ardent piety, his prudence, his keen knowledge in directing souls, and his talent for teaching.

He wrote two works: *Lilium inter spinas,* written in German and dedicated to virgins consecrated to God but living in the world (Cologne 1659); and *Medulla Theologiae Moralis facili ac perspicua methodo resolvens casus conscientiae ex variis probatisque authoribus*

concinnata (Münster 1650). The *Medulla* immediately achieved great popularity. During Busenbaum's life there were 40 editions; in 1670 the 45th edition appeared in Lisbon; and from 1670 to 1770, there were 150 editions published in the different countries of Europe.

By its clarity, its precision, and its methodical arrangement the *Medulla* became the classic type of manual for moral theology as taught in seminaries. The great commentaries written after the model of the *Medulla* further extended its influence. One example of such a commentary was the *Theologia Moralis* of Claude *Lacroix, SJ (Cologne 1707–14). In 1757 F. A. *Zaccaria, SJ, brought out the most complete edition of it. St. Alphonsus Liguori wrote his *Theologia Moralis* as a kind of commentary on the *Medulla* (Padua 1737). The last great commentary on it was that of Antonio *Ballerini, the revision of which, the *Opus theologicum morale in Busenbaum medullam* (7 v., Prato 1889–93) was the work of D. *Palmieri.

Sources. Busenbaum made frequent use of the manuscript "summae" of cases of conscience written by his confreres, Hermann Nünning and Friedrich Spe, professors of moral theology. He also used the work in manuscript of Maximilien Buchier, SJ. In addition to these immediate sources, all the authors of practical moral theology who had written since the middle of the

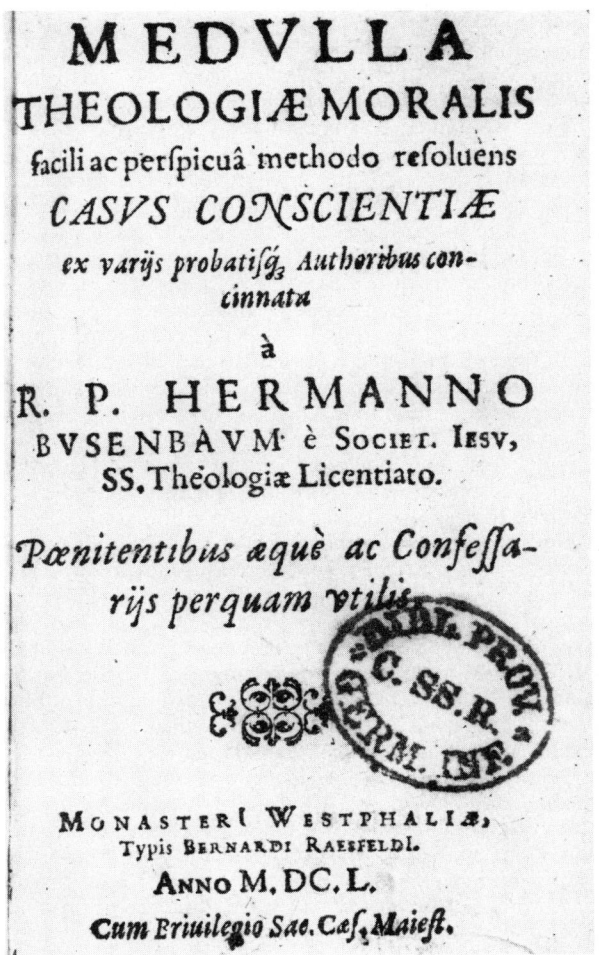

Frontispiece of first edition of the "Medulla," 1650.

16th century are to be encountered in the *Medulla*. It was Busenbaum's merit to have been able to discern in the mass of opinion found in his sources the views that deserved to be regarded as having permanent value. In including them in his manual, which was destined to exert so wide an influence, Busenbaum contributed effectively to the stabilization of theological opinion on a number of critical points.

Method. Busenbaum's method was strictly casuistic and analytical. It was also more rationalistic than theological, for he regarded the Decalogue as making explicit the obligations of the natural law. There is also a notable emphasis upon the idea of obligation in his writing, and this is no doubt a consequence of the purpose he had in mind in writing, which was the practical formation of confessors. Moral theology, as he saw it, was particularly necessary to enable the priest to fulfill his office of judge in the Sacrament of Penance. It is his duty to pronounce sentence, approving what is good and condemning what is not. A professional moralist should not be expected, therefore, to write a treatise on moral perfection but should content himself with producing something to help the ordinary confessor in the exercise of his judicial function.

False Accusations. There was nothing startling to be found in Busenbaum's moral doctrine. A small number of his opinions were condemned as laxist by Alexander VII and Innocent XI, but there is nothing surprising in this if one considers the enormous number of matters upon which he passed judgment. Certainly he fared no worse than other reputable moralists, and his teaching on the whole is unquestionably orthodox. Nevertheless, he was vigorously denounced at one time for his teaching on two points: tyrannicide and the doctrine that the end justifies the means.

As to tyrannicide, Busenbaum actually wrote: "In order to safeguard his life or the integrity of his members, it is even permitted for a son, a religious, a subject, to defend himself, going so far even as to kill his father, his abbot or his prince, if need be, unless the death of the latter would bring about serious consequences, such as wars. . . ." (*Medulla* 3.4.1.38). This was no more than the application to a particular case of the teaching on legitimate self-defense propounded by St. Thomas Aquinas, St. Antoninus, D. Soto, D. Concina, St. Alphonsus Liguori, and many others. However, the fear of having this text exploited against them caused the French Jesuits in 1669 to ask the general of the society to have it suppressed. In numerous editions of Busenbaum's work, therefore, this proposition is missing. Opposition to the moral theology of Busenbaum reached its height in 1757 at the time of the attempted assassination of Louis XV, King of France, by Damiens. The *Medulla* was condemned and burned by the Parlement of Toulouse in 1757; it was condemned by the Parlement of Paris in 1763 and was burned in the public square. Impartial authors have recognized the falsity of the accusations cast against the *Medulla*.

As to his supposed doctrine that the end justifies the means, Busenbaum did no more in fact than affirm a truth of common sense. When a person has a right to do something, he has by that very fact the right to use the legitimate means necessary for its performance. Busenbaum himself expressly excluded violence, injustice, and, in general, the use of means intrinsically bad (*op.*

cit. 4.3.7.2). M. Reichmann has retraced the history of the controversies raised by this formula.

Bibliography: Sommervogel 2:444–455. WERNER, ADB 3:646–648. T. B. BARRETT, CE 3:86–87. A. DE BIL, DHGE 10:1417–18. J. BRUCKER, DTC 2.1:1266–68. C. TESTORE, EncCatt 3:243. J. C. PILZ, LexThK² 2:801. E. SCHWARZ, Herzog-Hauck PRE 3:581. L. FENOT, RGG³ 1:1534. A. BROU, *Les Jésuites de la légende* (Paris 1907). B. DUHR, *Jesuiten-Fabeln* (Freiburg 1904); *Geschichte der Jesuiten in den Ländern deutscher Zunge*, 4 v. in 6 (v. 1–2 Freiburg 1907–13; v. 3–4 Regensburg 1921–28) 2.2:389–390. M. REICHMANN, *Der Zweck heiligt die Mittel* (Freiburg 1903).

[L. VEREECKE]

BUSHNELL, HORACE, Congregationalist minister and theologian; b. Bantam, Conn., April 14, 1802; d. Hartford, Conn., Feb. 17, 1876. After attempts at teaching and journalism he turned to the study of law,

Horace Bushnell.

but a conversion experience in 1831 led him to the ministry. In 1833 he began a long career as Congregationalist pastor of the North Church in Hartford. In this position he developed a religious outlook that led to the preaching of the *social gospel, and shaped the development of American Protestant theology during the second half of the 19th century. Bushnell adapted a contextual view of reality from German philosophic idealists, especially Friedrich *Schleiermacher. This led him in his best known work, *Christian Nurture* (1847), to argue that the church is not a collection of adult individuals converted by revivals, but a community of the faithful, including children who should be educated as Christians from the time of their baptism. Bushnell believed also that men exist only in the context of social interaction, that all men are involved in the guilt of the human community, that the supernatural is consubstantial with but distinguishable from the natural, and that fallen man could not be regenerated without the moral influence of Christ's atonement. Among his writings are *God in Christ* (1849), *Christ in Theology* (1851), *Nature and the Supernatural* (1858), *The Vicarious Sacrifice* (1866), and *Sermons on Living Subjects* (1872).

Bibliography: M. B. CHENEY, comp., *Life and Letters of Horace Bushnell* (New York 1880). B. M. CROSS, *Horace Bushnell: Minister to a Changing America* (Chicago 1958). **Illustration credit:** Connecticut Historical Society.

[R. MATZERATH]

BUSINESS ADMINISTRATION, CATHOLIC SCHOOLS OF

Collegiate education for business as a profession began with the establishment of the Wharton School of Finance and Economy at the University of Pennsylvania, Philadelphia, in 1881. In 1898 the University of Chicago, Ill., and the University of California, Los Angeles, established Colleges of Commerce. With these exceptions, schools of commerce, business, and finance did not exist in either public or Catholic higher education until the early 20th century. Although commercial courses were available in most Catholic colleges since the early 19th century, these were essentially high school courses offered as vocational subjects. E. J. Power, in his study of Catholic higher education, reports that although business schools were the last of the professional schools to be organized in Catholic colleges, they achieved such popularity that by the late 1920s they outnumbered all other types of professional schools in Catholic higher education. By 1930, he points out, there were 20 such schools, all of which have continued to retain their numeral superiority in the 1960s. In 1955 there were 23 Catholic universities with schools of business administration or commerce and finance; in 1964 there were 29.

Catholic business schools in general offer the following courses, leading to the bachelor's or master's degree: accounting, business, public and international administration; finance, banking, insurance, and real estate; personnel, production, foreign, and office management; business education, trade, merchandising, marketing, and transportation; labor and industrial relations; economics, statistics; and secretarial science.

The American Association of Collegiate Schools of Business (AACSB) was organized in 1916 for "the promotion and improvement of higher business education in North America." Membership is limited to independent degree-granting units that exercise autonomy in curriculum, budget, and faculty and possess an acknowledged curricular excellence, with a core program in specific business subjects. Member schools must have a highly qualified, professional full-time faculty and administrative staff holding terminal degrees and teaching a restricted load, and maintain adequate library and laboratory facilities. Membership numbered 13 schools in 1916 and 108 in 1963.

Marquette University, Milwaukee, Wis., was the first Catholic university admitted to the AACSB (1928). Other Catholic member schools include: Fordham University, Bronx, N.Y. (1939); St. Louis University, Mo. (1948); Creighton University, Omaha, Nebr. (1949); the University of Detroit, Mich. (1949); Loyola University of New Orleans, La. (1950); the Universities of San Francisco and Santa Clara, Calif. (1953); Loyola University of Chicago, Ill. (1955); Boston College, Chestnut Hill, Mass. (1956); DePaul University, Chicago, Ill. (1957); Duquesne University, Pittsburgh, Pa. (1961); and University of Notre Dame (1962).

In 1962 the Association started accrediting Master of Business Administration programs. Of the 53 schools accredited, five were Catholic universities: DePaul, Detroit, Duquesne, Marquette, and Santa Clara.

Bibliography: AACSB, *Constitution and Standards for Membership* (St. Louis 1962). J. H. S. BOSSARD and J. F. DEWHURST, *University Education for Business* (Philadelphia 1931). E. J. POWER, *A History of Catholic Higher Education in the United States* (Milwaukee 1958).

[L. V. RYAN]

BUSINESS ETHICS

The study of the moral rightness and wrongness of the acts involved in the production, distribution, and exchange of economic goods and services. It develops secondary principles and criteria for their application to concrete cases involving, among others, the relationships of employer and employee, buyer and seller, firm and industry, industry and the nation. Business ethics is therefore not identical with law, trade practices, or codes of various business associations, but goes beyond these to the morality of both individual and social relationships. In its narrowest sense, business ethics concentrates on those moral problems that arise from the very nature of business, since general ethics has already established the obligations that the businessman has as a man and as a member of a specific society. Business ethics is concerned with the particular obligations of truthfulness, justice, and charity that a man assumes when he enters business either as an employee or an employer, buyer or seller.

Basic Obligations. Because business decisions have repercussions in many areas of human life, the businessman has an obligation to consider both the direct and indirect effects of his acts on both groups and individuals. Although many of these effects have not been considered by ethicians, moralists, economists, or students of business, they still have moral implications if they help or harm human beings. After the businessman has prepared for the formation of his conscience by a careful consideration of his concrete situation, he must make a prudent judgment about the morality of the act under consideration. The principle of double effect (*see* DOUBLE EFFECT, PRINCIPLES OF) will have wide application in such judgments, since most business acts have unintended and harmful side effects that can be permitted only for a proportionate reason. Often the correct application of the principle will require consultation with experts who alone can foresee and weigh all the factors involved. In view of all these warnings, the principles and areas mentioned below are necessarily only illustrations.

Obligations of Employees. Employees are bound in justice to give a fair day's work for a fair day's wage. In addition, they must protect the property and interests of the employer by all reasonable means. Not only bribery but gift-taking can give rise to a conflict of interests that violates either the implicit or explicit terms of his employment contract. In the absence of permission from the proper authorities, employees may not take company property or claim income that they have not actually earned. Thus, it is unjust to submit an expense account voucher for money not actually spent on behalf of the firm unless proper authority has authorized such an application with full knowledge of the situation.

Obligations of Employers. The employer is bound to pay a wage that is fair by industry scales and to work for the payment of an adequate wage where such is not being paid due to the financial position of the company. He must see to it that dangers to health or morale resulting from working conditions are eliminated or reduced as much as possible. In short, the employer may never use the worker as a mere means to economic gain. At the same time, he may not refuse to employ men except for factors relevant to work performance. In cases where factors such as color or race have temporary relevance because of the prejudice of the public or of other workers, the employer as a citizen must work for the removal of such obstacles to rational and therefore ethical hiring. The discharging of workers must be based not only on work performance at the time but on past services to the firm and such factors as employee morale and long-run prospects of the firm.

Obligations of Producer and Distributor. As a producer, the businessman is obliged to use all nonhuman resources in such a way as to produce the greatest economic utility at the smallest cost. This obligation to avoid waste is reinforced by the fact that unless he does this, he cannot fulfill his obligations to his workers and stockholders and to the general society. When applying these principles to concrete cases it should be recalled that economic utility extends beyond the satisfaction of merely biological needs. Further, some waste can be justified by the need to protect workers, stay in business, or supply an urgently needed good.

The producer and distributor, whether wholesale or retail, have an obligation to see that the consumer is not exposed to any unnecesary risks. They therefore must give reasonable warning about possible dangers and information about the safe use of a product or service. This duty does not fall equally on all involved in production and distribution, but in general it may be said that it falls more heavily on the ultimate seller who is servicing the consumer. Producers and intermediate distributors, are obliged, of course, to inform their customers of the dangers involved.

Buying and Selling. In exchange the seller must not deliberately exploit the customer by the use of power or fraud or the creation of ignorance or passion. The reason is that a just exchange implies free informed choice on the part of both buyer and seller. False and misleading advertising, as well as forms of price fixing, whether prohibited by law or not, represent exploitation by the use of fraud or power or a combination of these. Advertising that seeks to distract from relevant buying motives or to create unreasonable desires exploits through ignorance and passion. In practice, where the ignorance and passion already exist and cannot be removed at a reasonable cost, the seller may have a proportionate reason for permitting some harm to result from the customer's own negligence. Buyers and consumers have obligations similar to those of the seller. In addition, they have not only an individual but a social obligation to buy carefully, since a disregard of price and quality can lead to harmful increases in the price level and the encouragement of dubious procedures on the part of both manufacturers, wholesalers, and retailers. In short, there is an obligation to see that the buying process is rational and minimizes harmful effects.

Competitors may not be deliberately injured by selling below cost in order to gain mastery of the market and of future prices. However, harm to competitors resulting from price cuts based on real efficiency may be permitted since this is to the best interests of customers and of the economic efficiency of society. In general, competition will be fair when it is based on real economic efficiency and the service of the customer and not on methods that serve a given company without affording corresponding benefits to society as a whole.

Management. Managers and directors must reconcile the best interests of all parties involved in their business. Though they are legally only representatives of stockholders, they are morally in charge of a society that has obligations to a variety of individuals and groups. Because the firm has not always been recognized as a society of which the workers as well as managers and stockholders are members and not merely hired hands, exact principles for determining priorities have not been worked out. In general, however, the need for the continued existence of the firm as a means of livelihood would appear to take precedence over the demands of any group—workers, stockholders or managers—for a merely useful good. Ordinarily, since stockholders, unlike most wage earners, do not depend on the firm for their entire income, the necessities of workers would in some circumstances appear to take precedence over the interests of stockholders.

The Firm and Society. The broader social obligations of the firm, of the industry, and of business as a whole are difficult to define. In the first place, the theory of social obligations has not kept up with the changing reality of business. Secondly, economic theory has not supplied tools that give an adequate understanding of the complex factual reality of business. Yet, because both individual and collective decisions of business have important effects on the economic, social, and political orders, firms, industries, and business as a whole are obliged to consider these effects in evaluating the morality of their acts.

In the concrete these obligations will vary with the power of the group in question, the importance of the good to be obtained and the evil avoided, as well as with the availability of means for discharging the obligation. Since most of the social obligations of business cannot be discharged in isolation from organized labor and the government, business is obliged to cooperate with them. This obligation is a serious one, for without such cooperation society will tend to weaken liberty by continuous appeal to the government for the fulfillment of social needs that should be satisfied by lesser groups insofar as is possible. Such an obligation to cooperate exists in the following areas.

The relative stability of the economy is necessary for orderly development and the prevention of waste and of both human and economic injury to workers. Such stability cannot be obtained without some form of planning and control, whether public, private, or a combination of these, in the areas of investment, wages, prices, and technological innovation that has far-reaching effects on employment. Without such planning it is difficult if not impossible to protect the incomes of older people and the purchasing power of those with fixed salaries or wages. In addition, in the absence of such planning, it is difficult to see how the satisfaction of public needs can be integrated with the workings of the market economy.

The larger corporations, like large unions, act as pace setters for large segments of the economy. They would appear to have special obligations since they have power over great resources, both human and economic. In particular, their financial power, resulting from both credit and retained earnings, makes it possible for them to devote large sums to research and development. There would seem to be some obligation to use these resources, which have been extracted from society, for the good of society. For example, there may well be an obligation to use the funds for the development of new job opportunities.

The Business Community. Business leadership is obliged to work for the establishment of an economic order, which will enable it to satisfy the need for both individuals and society. In particular, business leaders should not seek legislation that gives business freedom at the expense of the general society or of consumers. Some tariffs and *fair-trade laws seem to protect particular businesses without corresponding returns to the public good. This may be true also of oil depletion allowances and government subsidies in some areas. A question might arise about a patent system that would enable a company to have a quasi monopoly of a particular good. Further, it is difficult to see how business operates in a socially responsible manner when it fights all attempts at laws governing packaging, labeling, and affirmative disclosure of pertinent product information. Of course, the business community can and should work to make sure that laws are reasonable and realistic, but they are not justified in countering the public interest merely because this would change traditional ways of doing business.

As the international society grows in importance, both the larger corporations and the business community as a whole will have social obligations that extend beyond national boundaries. As yet the relationship between national and international needs is not clear enough to indicate the exact character of these obligations. However, they will almost certainly involve cooperation of both private and state agencies for the financing and staffing of business in underdeveloped nations and for the stabilization of the prices for raw material. This is to say that here as elsewhere the rapid changes in both business and society will continue to create new needs and new obligations that transcend the present statement of business responsibility.

See also CONSUMPTION, ECONOMICS OF; EMPLOYERS, MORAL OBLIGATIONS OF; EMPLOYEES, MORAL OBLIGATIONS OF; ECONOMIC JUSTICE; FAIR-TRADE LAWS.

Bibliography: T. M. GARRETT, *Ethics in Business* (New York 1963). H. JOHNSTON, *Business Ethics* (New York 1956). H. J. WIRTENBERGER, *Morality and Business* (Chicago 1962). L. S. WOELFEL, *Catholic Thoughts in Business and Economics,* 2 v. (Austin, Texas 1959–61).

[T. M. GARRETT]

BUSNOIS, ANTOINE, Renaissance composer and poet (family name, De Busne); b. France, date unknown; d. Bruges, Belgium, Nov. 6, 1492. His name is first found in historical documents about 1465; he served as chaplain at the Burgundian court from 1467, but spent his final years in Bruges. He wrote Masses, motets, and Magnificats, which, although of high quality, were technically less forward looking than his elegant and sophisticated chansons. One of these, *Fortuna desperata,* was used by *Desprez and *Obrecht as the basis for Masses, and others served Obrecht, *Agricola, and *Isaak. Obrecht based his *Missa L'Homme armé* almost directly on Busnois's Mass of that name. In one motet, *Victimae paschali,* Busnois extended the musical range upward as, in his chansons, he had ex-

tended it downward. Another, *Antoni usque limina,* dedicated to his patron saint, Anthony Abbot, includes a part for a bell (Anthony's symbol). He used much imitation (comparatively new at the time), and was extraordinarily resourceful in his treatment of rhythm. Busnois composed the texts for several of his works and corresponded in verse with the Burgundian court poet Molinet. *Tinctoris dedicated an important treatise jointly to Busnois and *Okeghem.

See also MUSIC, SACRED, HISTORY OF, 4.

Bibliography: A. BUSNOIS, *Missa super L'Homme armé* in *Monumenta polyphoniae liturgicae,* v.1, fasc. 2 (Rome 1948). Compositions in DenkmTonköst 14. G. THIBAULT, MusGG 2: 515–520. G. PERLE, "The Chansons of Antoine Busnois," MusRev 11 (1950) 89–97. C. VAN DEN BORREN, *Études sur le XVᵉ siècle musical* (Antwerp 1941). Roland-Manuel, v.1. Reese MusR.

[C. V. BROOKS]

BUSS, FRANZ JOSEPH VON, a pioneer of the German Catholic social movement; b. Zell am Harmersbach (Baden), March 23, 1803; d. Freiburg im Breisgau, Jan. 31, 1878. Despite his humble origins, he completed doctorates in medicine, law, and political science, and became a *Privatdocent* in 1829 and a professor of political science and law at Freiburg in 1833. He was a member of the Baden legislature from 1837 to 1840 and from 1846 to 1848, and a delegate to the German national assembly of 1848 at Frankfurt and to the Reichstag in 1873. He was highly gifted and more interested in general learning and politics than in scientific research; he made his strongest impression as a popular orator. Although at first a liberal, influenced by Karl von Rotteck and others, and somewhat of a freethinker in religion, he assumed in the 1830s a more conservative and strongly Catholic position. His concerns always included social problems and welfare as well as the political union of Catholics. The first German Katholikentag of 1848 chose him as its president. During his service in the Landtag of Baden in 1837 he became the first to advocate social legislation in a German parliament. The Emperor Franz Josef knighted him in 1863 for his services to Austria, and the separation of Austria from Germany in 1866 shook him so that he was hardly able to work thereafter. He published a great number of works on contemporary problems.

See also SOCIAL MOVEMENTS, CATHOLIC, 3.

Bibliography: A. RETZBACH, *Franz Josef Ritter von Buss: Zu seinem 50. Todestag* (Mönchengladbach 1928), social political program of 1837. R. LANGE, *Franz Joseph Ritter von Buss und die soziale Frage seiner Zeit* (Freiburg 1955).

[P. JOSTOCK]

BUSTAMANTE, CARLOS MARÍA, Mexican politician, newspaperman, historian, and editor in the independence and republican era (1805–48); b. Oaxaca, Nov. 4, 1774; d. Mexico City, Sept. 21, 1848. After being educated in Oaxaca, Mexico City, and Guadalajara, he practiced law (graduated, 1801) and became a journalist (1805). After the initiation of the independence movement, he joined Morelos in the south and later suffered many privations and imprisonments. Although he accepted a Spanish amnesty offer in 1817, he escaped and was caught and imprisoned in San Juan de Ulúa and elsewhere until *Iturbide's triumph in 1821. Soon his opposition to Iturbide, in his paper *La Abispa de Chilpancingo,* again brought imprisonment, but from 1824 until his death Bustamante served almost continuously in congress as a deputy from Oaxaca. The Jesuit historian Mariano Cuevas has written of him: "The Church can be especially grateful to him for the defense he made of her rights, of the Society of Jesus,

Carlos María Bustamante.

and of the Guadalupan Apparition" (*Historia de la Iglesia en México* 5:370). A faithful Catholic all his life, Bustamante fought for the return of the Jesuits to Mexico. He was a prolific but disorderly writer who published some 107 works of various kinds, including *Cuadro histórico de la revolución mexicana* (1843–46), *Historia del Emperador D. Agustín Iturbide* (1846), and *El Nuevo Bernal Díaz o sea historia de los anglo-americanos en México* (1847). The latter title is said to reflect the depression and sadness he felt at the victory of the Americans in the war with Mexico and their occupation of the capital of the country. His editions of the historical works of Gómara, of the Jesuits Cavo and Alegre, and of Sahagún's *Historia general de las cosas de la Nueva España,* 3 v. (1829–30), the only edition of this fundamental work available for more than a century, mark him as a pioneer in modern Mexican historiography and letters.

Bibliography: C. GONZÁLEZ PEÑA, *Historia de la literatura mexicana* (Mexico City 1940; 7th ed. 1960), Eng. *History of Mexican Literature,* tr. G. B. NANCE and F. J. DUNSTAN (rev. ed. Dallas 1945). **Illustration credit:** Archivo Fotográfico, Instituto Nacional de Antropología e Historia, Mexico.

[P. V. MURRAY]

BUSTAMANTE Y SEPTIEM, MIGUEL DE, botanist and scientist, influential in the Mexican scientific revival after Independence; b. Guanajuato, Mexico, 1790; d. Mexico City, 1844. He was a member of a family that had already produced distinguished men in mineralogy. He studied in the seminary of his native city and during the first years of the 19th century went to the Real y Pontificia Universidad de México, but apparently never received a degree. Later he was a pupil of Don Vicente Cervantes, botanist of the scientific expedition of New Spain led by Sessé. For many years he worked at the Botanical Garden of Mexico. From 1826 he substituted for his teacher as professor of botany there; in 1829, upon Cervantes's death, he was given the chair permanently. In 1833 the government assigned him to plan and execute the new Botanical Garden that was beginning to take shape in the Hospice of Santo Tomás. He belonged to various scientific societies and was a member of the Sociedad Mexi-

cana de Geografía y Estadística from its foundation, contributing to its development with a number of works, many of them still unpublished. Among his outstanding professional publications are: "Sobre el Guaco," *Revista Mexicana,* 1:182–183 (1835), *Memoria instructiva para colectar y preparar para su transporte los objetos de historia natural* (Mexico City 1839), and *Curso de botánica elemental* (Mexico City 1841).

Bibliography: N. LEÓN, *Biblioteca botánico-mexicana* (Mexico City 1895).

[G. SOMOLINOS]

BUTIN, ROMANUS, b. Saint-Romain d'Urfé, France, Dec. 3, 1871; d. Dec. 8, 1937. After studying at the Petit Séminaire de Saint-Jodard, he pursued his priestly studies at Dodon, Md., and was ordained a Marist in 1897. He obtained his Ph.D. in Semitic languages and literatures at The Catholic University of America, where he taught from 1912 till his death in 1937. He was the 1926 annual professor and acting director of the American School of Oriental Research in Jerusalem and a member of the 1930 Harvard–Catholic University expedition to Sinai. As an orientalist, Butin made his main contribution in placing the study of the Proto-Sinaitic inscriptions on a solid basis for the investigation of the origins of the alphabet. His doctoral dissertation was an explanation of the enigmatic "extraordinary points" of the Pentateuch. Among his other contributions were 3 books, 38 articles, and 21 book reviews. The founding of the Catholic Biblical Association of America was due largely to his initiative.

Bibliography: J. A. GRISPINO and R. T. COCHRAN, "Rev. Romain François Butin, S.M.," CathBiblQuart 24 (1962) 383–393.

[J. GRISPINO]

BUTLER, ALBAN, English hagiographer; b. Appletree, Northamptonshire, Oct. 10, 1710; d. Saint-Omer, France, May 15, 1773. His parents died when he was a child, and he was sent first to Ladywell School near Preston and then to *Douai in France,

Alban Butler, engraving by William Finden.

where after distinguished study he was ordained in 1735. He remained at Douai as professor of philosophy and theology. In 1745 he accompanied the Earl of Shrewsbury and his brothers, the future bishops James and Thomas Talbot, on a tour of France and Italy, and then returned to Douai to continue teaching. In 1749 he returned to England to do missionary work in the Midlands and Warkworth. Bishop *Challoner appointed him chaplain to the Duke of Norfolk and tutor to the duke's nephew, Edward Howard. He accompanied his pupil to Paris, where Howard died of a sudden illness.

After 30 years' labor, Butler completed in Paris his *Lives of the Saints*, published anonymously (4 v. London 1756–59). The work contains the lives of about 1,600 saints and has influenced English Catholics and non-Catholics. It was thoroughly revised by H. *Thurston (1926–38) and by D. Attwater (1956). In 1766 Butler was chosen president of the English College at Saint-Omer, France, from which the French Jesuits had been expelled. The bishops of Amiens and Boulogne assured him that he could with good conscience accept the office, which he held until his death. He was buried at Saint-Omer. His other works include *Life of Mary of the Cross* (1767), *Moveable Feasts and Fasts* (1774), and *Meditations and Discourses on Sublime Truths* (1791–93). He collected much material on the lives of SS. John Fisher and Thomas More. His nephew Charles Butler wrote his biography in 1799.

Bibliography: D. ATTWATER, "Lives of the Saints," *Commonweal* 66 (1957) 349–351. T. COOPER, DNB 3:495–496. P. J. CORISH, "New edition of Butler's *Lives of the Saints*," IrEcclRec 89 (1958) 195–198. H. THURSTON, "Alban Butler," *Month* 172 (1938) 52–63. A. DES MAZIS, DHGE 10:1439–40. **Illustration credit:** Library of Congress.

[R. J. BARTMAN]

BUTLER, CHARLES, English Catholic lay leader; b. London, Aug. 14, 1750; d. there, June 2, 1832. He was the son of a merchant and the nephew of Alban *Butler the hagiographer. After studying in France at Esquerchin and *Douai, concentrating on rhetoric (1759–66), he returned to England for legal studies (1769–75). Since Catholics were banned from full participation in the courts, he practiced law as a conveyancer. After the Catholic Relief Act of 1791, he became the first Catholic lawyer to be called to the bar

Charles Butler.

since 1688. In 1830 he was appointed king's counsel. Butler was active in the movement for Catholic *emancipation, beginning in 1782 when he was named secretary to the committee of Catholic laymen formed to promote abolition of the *penal laws: Butler's approach

to the emancipation question was a controverted one, because he consistently took the position that only through concessions to the government, especially by permitting it a power of veto over the appointment of bishops, could full emancipation be attained. In this stand he met vigorous opposition from Bp. John *Milner, Daniel *O'Connell, and the Irish hierarchy. In 1792 Butler helped to organize the Cisalpine Club, which sought to thwart the prelates who opposed compromise and favored waiting until complete freedom of religion seemed likely to be granted. After the passage of the Catholic Emancipation Act (1829), Butler retracted publicly some of his earlier statements and admitted their unorthodoxy. Throughout his life he was a devout, ascetic Catholic. Butler's writings ranged over a wide area. He published studies of Roman law, lives of 17th-century Catholic writers, and critiques of Mohammedan and Hindu literature. His best-known work was the *Historical Memoirs of the English, Irish and Scottish Catholics since the Reformation* (4 v. 1819–21).

Bibliography: B. N. WARD, *The Dawn of the Catholic Revival in England, 1781–1803*, 2 v. (New York 1909); *The Eve of Catholic Emancipation*, 3 v. (London 1911–12). F. C. HUSENBETH, *The Life of the Right Rev. John Milner* (Dublin 1862). E. BONNEY and M. HAILE, *Life and Letters of John Lingard* (London 1911). DictEngCath 1:355–364, for Butler's writings. T. COOPER, DNB 3:497–499.

[A. J. BANNAN]

BUTLER, EDWARD CUTHBERT, Benedictine abbot and scholar; b. Dublin, May 6, 1858; d. Clapham, London, April 1, 1934. His father was professor of mathematics in the Irish university organized by John Henry (later Cardinal) Newman. After his school days at Downside he entered the Benedictine novitiate (1876) and later studied and taught in the priory school at Downside. He took a leading part in a controversy in the English Benedictine Congregation that issued in the conversion of a unitary congregation devoted to missionary work into one of fully autonomous abbeys. In 1896 he became first head of the Downside house of studies at Cambridge and produced a study and text of the *Lausiac History of Palladius* (1898, 1904). He was recalled in 1904 and succeeded Dom Edmund Ford as second abbot of Downside in 1906. As abbot he was an apostle of the liturgy and an advocate of mental prayer; his lifelong guide was Augustine Baker's *Holy Wisdom*. In 1922 the frustration of his endeavors to diminish the parochial commitments of Downside led to his resignation; he moved to Ealing Priory, where he remained until his death. He produced a valuable Latin edition of the Rule of St. Benedict (1912), and *Benedictine Monachism* (1919), a series of studies on every aspect of Benedictine history, polity, and spirituality. In retirement he published *Western Mysticism* (1922), his *Life and Times of Bishop Ullathorne* (1926), and *History of the Vatican Council* (1930). Much of his work still retains its value and reflects a scholar of wide learning, sane judgment, and powerful mind. Butler lacked the common touch and some of the qualities of leadership, but his unassuming piety and patent sincerity won universal respect.

Bibliography: D. KNOWLES, "Abbot Butler: A Memoir," DownRev 52 (1934) 347–440, reprinted in *The Historian and Character*, ed. C. N. L. BROOKE and G. CONSTABLE (New York 1963) 264–341.

[M. D. KNOWLES]

BUTLER, JOSEPH, English theologian and bishop of Durham; b. Wantage, Berkshire, England, May 18, 1692; d. Bath, June 16, 1752. Butler was the eighth and youngest child of a linen draper who reared him a Presbyterian; he joined the Episcopal Church later and entered Oriel College, Oxford, in 1715, transferring to Cambridge on Sept. 30, 1717. He received the B.A. degree in 1718, was ordained deacon and priest in 1721

Joseph Butler.

by Bp. William Talbot at Salisbury, and was appointed preacher at the Rolls Chapel, whence he delivered his famous "Sermons on Human Nature" (1726). In 1721 he received the B.C.L. degree and became prebendary of Salisbury. When Bishop Talbot was transferred to Durham, he gave Butler the rectory of Houghton-la-Skerne (1722) and the wealthy rectory of Stanhope (1725). In 1736 Butler was appointed clerk of the closet to Queen Caroline, who recommended his promotion in the church. In 1737 Caroline died, and George II arranged with Walpole for Butler's appointment to the impoverished See of Bristol. The sharp yet courteous letter of acceptance to Walpole indicated Butler's resentment. Butler was presented to St. Paul's attractive deanery in 1740, and made clerk of the closet to George II in 1746. He declined the primacy in 1747, explaining "it was too late to support a falling church," but in 1750 accepted the bishopric of Durham, where, after delivering a remonstrance, he urged the maintenance of churches and regular services. Earlier he had offered a plan for establishing Episcopal sees in the American colonies, but it remained unheeded.

Butler's *Analogy of Religion, Natural and Revealed, to the Constitution and Course of Nature* (1736), serving as a retaliation against deistic writers who were attacking traditional theology, is widely accepted as the most solid defense of revealed religion during the 18th century. Cardinal J. H. Newman claimed that it "formed an era in his religious opinions." But others, such as John Stuart Mill, regarded the *Analogy* as a retort, not an exposition, and therefore skeptical in essence.

Bibliography: *Works,* ed. W. E. GLADSTONE, 3 v. (London 1896); *The Analogy of Religion,* notes W. FITZGERALD (Dublin 1849), with introd. E. C. MOSSNER (New York 1961). A. E. BAKER, *Bishop Butler* (London 1923). E. C. MOSSNER, *Bishop Butler and the Age of Reason* (New York 1936). A. E. TAYLOR, *Philosophical Studies* (London 1934). Y. M. J. CONGAR, *Catholicisme* 2:336. J. HOMEYER, LexThK² 2:844. Cross ODCC 211. L. STEPHEN, DNB 3:519–524.

[M. A. FRAWLEY]

BUTLER, MARIE JOSEPH, MOTHER, religious superior, educator; b. Kilkenny, Ireland, July 22, 1860; d. Tarrytown, N.Y., April 23, 1940. After being educated by the Sisters of Mercy, she entered the Congregation of the Sacred Heart of Mary at Beziers, France, at the age of 16. Before taking her first vows, she was sent to Portugal. She was recalled in 1903 to head the congregation's second American foundation, in Long Island City, N.Y. For the next 37 years she planned an expansion program that produced 14 American schools, including 6 Marymounts (3 of them colleges) and a New York novitiate, and 23 foreign institutions, including a novitiate in Ireland and Marymount schools in Rome, Paris, and Canada. She was foundress of an international educative program. Mother Butler's cause for canonization was officially opened in 1948. Her remains rest in the crypt at Marymount, Tarrytown.

Bibliography: K. BURTON, *Mother Butler of Marymount* (New York 1944). J. K. LEAHY, *As an Eagle: The Spiritual Writings of Mother Butler, RSHM* (New York 1954).

[F. DE S. BORAN]

BUTLER, PIERCE, attorney, Associate Justice of the Supreme Court of the U.S.; b. Northfield, Minn., March 17, 1866; d. Washington, D.C., Nov. 16, 1939. He was the sixth of Patrick and Mary (Gaffney) Butler's eight children born on a Minnesota farm. His parents, emigrants from County Wicklow, Ireland, sent the children to local schools, and managed to secure for Pierce admission to the preparatory school of Carleton College, a Congregational institution. After graduation with a B.S. degree in 1887, Pierce read law in St. Paul, was admitted to the bar in 1888, and settled down to the practice of law in his native state.

Associate Justice Pierce Butler.

Almost immediately after forming a law partnership with Stan Donnelly, son of Ignatius Donnelly, author and politician, Butler determined to seek political experience. He was elected to three consecutive terms as assistant county attorney of Ramsey County, Minn., between 1891 and 1897, but was then defeated for state senator on the Democratic ticket. Withdrawing from politics, Butler began to act as counsel in important cases then testing the application of the Sherman Antitrust Act and similar legislation in the states. Butler acted as one of the national government's counsel in *Swift v. United States,* but his chief clients during the period from 1898 to 1921 were railway corporations in the U.S. and Canada. Large business interests of other types also sought his counsel, and he established a reputation as an indefatigable, forceful, aggressive counsel, always prepared with formidable arrays of facts. His 900-page brief in the *Minnesota Rate Cases* became famous.

Nominated to the Supreme Court by Pres. Warren G. Harding and confirmed as associate justice in 1922, Butler spent 16 years in judicial service, writing more than 300 majority opinions and 140 dissents. From 1933 until his death, Butler was the leader of the conservative bloc, opposed on principle to the legislation of the New Deal and determined to find constitutional reasons to cast it aside. Although he was one of the chief targets of the court-packing scheme (1936–37), Butler's composure remained as monumental as his physical appearance.

He married Annie Cronin in 1891, and they had eight children. He exhibited a continuing interest in education, serving on the board of regents of the University of Minnesota and as a member of the board of trustees of The Catholic University of America. His contributions to the Supreme Court were his carefully reasoned presentations of the conservative attitude toward the law (*United States v. Schwimmer; Panhandle Oil Company v. Mississippi*). The death of Pierce Butler in 1939 brought to a close an important era in the Supreme Court.

Bibliography: F. J. BROWN, *The Social and Economic Philosophy of Pierce Butler* (CUA Stud. in Sociol. 13; Washington 1945). "Pierce Butler," *Georgetown Law Journal* 28 (1939) 163–164. **Illustration credit:** Harris and Ewing.

[M. C. KLINKHAMER]

BUXTEHUDE, DIETRICH,

baroque organ virtuoso and composer; b. Oldesloe, Holstein (then a Danish possession), *c.* 1637; d. Lübeck, Germany, May 9, 1707. Buxtehude studied organ with his father and played in Denmark until he succeeded Franz Tunder as organist at the Church of St. Mary, Lübeck, in 1668. In 1673 he initiated the soon celebrated *Abend-Musiken,* twilight musical services held on the five Sundays preceding Christmas. Both J. S. *Bach and *Handel journeyed to Lübeck to hear him play. He was a leader of the North German school of organ composition, with its presupposition of virtuoso technique, and his organ works exerted great influence on Bach's early compositions. Buxtehude's best organ works are those in "free" form, i.e., toccatas (or preludes) and fugues; his chorale preludes are not outstanding musically. His many church cantatas, some based on chorales, others freely composed, are a treasure of concerted church music. The cantatas, because of the great variety in their music, as well as the finesse with which their texts are set, are possibly even more important historically than his organ works.

See also ORGAN MUSIC.

Bibliography: Published music. *Sämtliche Orgelwerke,* ed. P. SPITTA, 2 v. (Leipzig 1876–77); *Complete Organ Works,* ed. J. HEDAR, 4 v. (London 1952–54). Many cantatas are pub. in modern editions. A. PIRRO, *Dietrich Buxtehude* (Paris 1913). W. STAHL, *Dietrich Buxtehude* (Kassel 1937). W. E. BUSZIN, MusQ 23 (1937) 465–490. F. BLUME, MusGG 2:548–571.

[W. C. HOLMES]

BUXTORF, Protestant family, originally from Westphalia, Germany, that produced several illustrious Hebraists at Basel, Switzerland, in the early post-Reformation period.

Johannes the Elder; b. Kamen, Westphalia, Dec. 25, 1564; d. Basel, Sept. 13, 1629. After his studies, especially at Marburg and Herborn, he was appointed instructor (1588–91) and professor (1591–1629) of Hebrew at the University of Basel, where he specialized in rabbinical literature. His friendly relations with the Jews and his participation in some of their ceremonies brought him into temporary difficulties with the authorities of Basel. His *Lexicon Hebraicum et Chaldaicum* (Basel 1607), especially as revised by his son (Basel 1639), and his great rabbinical Bible, *Biblia Hebraica cum paraphasi Chaldaica et commentariis rabbinorum* (Basel 1618–19), served as indispensable reference works until the 19th century. In his *Tiberias* (Basel 1620), an otherwise scholarly commentary on the Masoretic Text of the Bible, he opposed the correct view that the vowel points were added to the consonantal Hebrew text by the Masoretes of Tiberias about the 8th Christian century; in the interests of the current Protestant belief in the absolute reliability of the Masoretic Text, he claimed that even the vowel points went back to the inspired authors, or at least to Ezra.

Johannes the Younger, son of the preceding; b. Basel, Aug. 13, 1599; d. there, Aug. 17, 1664. He became a student at the University of Basel at the age of 12 and received the degree of master of arts when 16 years old. In 1630 at this university he succeeded his father in the chair of Hebrew, which he held until his death. In 1647 he received also a professorship of theology, created especially for him, but in 1654 he relinquished this for the professorship of OT studies, which had then become vacant. He continued and completed his father's works, besides publishing several of his own, particularly a *Lexicon Chaldaicum et Syriacum* (Basel 1622). He likewise defended his father's opinions on the antiquity of the current Masoretic Text; this brought him into a celebrated dispute with the Protestant scholar L. Cappel (1585–1658), who correctly held that the Masoretic vowel points were added to the Hebrew text in the early Middle Ages and also showed that the script of the Samaritan Pentateuch was older than the "square" script of the Hebrew Bible.

He was followed in his chair of Hebrew at Basel by his son, Johannes Jakob (1645–1704), and the latter was succeeded by his nephew Johannes (IV) Buxtorf (1663–1732). The Buxtorf family, therefore, taught Hebrew at Basel through four generations over a period of 140 years.

Bibliography: A. BERTHOLET and W. BAUMGARTNER, RGG³ 1:1556–57. A. BERTSCH, LexThK² 2:846–847. E. F. KAUTZSCH, *Johannes Buxtorf der Ältere* (Basel 1879). G. H. SCHNEDERMANN, *Die Kontroverse des L. Cappellus mit den Buxtorfen über das Alter der hebräischen Punktation* (Leipzig 1879).

[L. F. HARTMAN]

BUYING AND SELLING, MORAL ASPECTS OF.

The contract of buying and selling (or purchase and sale) is a contract whereby two persons agree to exchange a commodity for a certain price. This contract is essentially the same as barter, but differs from it because money is used as the medium of exchange. According to natural law, the expression of agreement between buyer and seller seals the contract. However, the civil law may require certain formalities even for the validity of the contract.

Since the seller supplies goods and services and since their value is more mutable than the monetary price paid for them, the seller's obligations are more detailed than the buyer's. The seller assumes the following moral obligations: (1) He must own the object he sells. Articles belonging to another, whether stolen or held by mistake, cannot be validly sold. A seller in bad faith must stand the loss, both refunding the price to the buyer and returning the property to the true owner. (2) He must manifest hidden defects. If the defect is substantial (i.e., materially affecting the quality of an article or rendering it useless for the purpose for which it was purchased), the attention of the buyer must be expressly called to it. Otherwise there is no true agreement between the parties about the article, and therefore no contract. Minor or accidental defects, as long as they are reflected in a suitably lower price, need not be revealed unless the buyer raises questions about them. If asked, the seller must answer truthfully. (3) The seller must deliver to the buyer the identical article designated or, depending on the nature of the transaction, one of the same kind. The goods must be transmitted to the buyer at the time, place, and in the manner called for by the contract of sale. Unless there is an agreement to the contrary, the seller is responsible for any damages until delivery and must repair any loss to the buyer because of delayed delivery.

The *buyer* assumes the following moral obligations: (1) He must accept on delivery the goods contracted for. (2) He must pay for what he has purchased at the time, place, and in the manner determined by the contract—according to custom or law. In the absence of other arrangements, he must pay for the purchase when he receives it. Failure to pay the agreed price when payment is due is a violation of commutative justice and obliges to restitution. (3) Though he need not inform the seller of the use he will make of the property or the profit he expects from it, he must assure himself that the seller knows the nature of the goods, even if buyer and seller differ as to their estimate of the value.

Both buyer and seller, though they are not morally bound to assist each other in making a good bargain, are morally obliged to ascertain that the contract is valid according to the norms set down for contracts in general. They are also bound to see that justice is done; therefore, they must agree on a just price.

See also JUST PRICE.

Bibliography: Thomas Aquinas, ST 2a2ae, 77. A. Michel, DTC 15.2:2623–35. H. J. Wirtenberger, *Morality and Business* (Chicago 1962).

[D. LOWERY]

BUYL, BERNAL (BOYL), first vicar apostolic of the New World; b. near Tarragona, Spain, 1445; d. place and date unknown. The name is variously spelled as Buyl, Boyl, Boil, etc. As a youth he entered the Benedictine monastery of Montserrat, and he was ordained in 1481. He became involved with governmental business and was known to King Ferdinand, serving

him in various capacities, including that of ambassador to France in 1488. During much of his life as a Benedictine, Boyl lived as an anchorite in the garden and not in the monastery itself. Sometime after 1488 he left the Benedictine Order and in France joined the Order of *Minims founded by Francis of Paula. This change in religious order gave rise to much confusion about the identity of the first vicar apostolic until Fita discovered documents on the matter. In October 1492 King Ferdinand granted Boyl permission to found the new order in Spain and in the spring of 1493 donated to it a hermitage in Málaga. However, the King also had other plans for Boyl and on June 25, 1493, secured a papal bull appointing him vicar apostolic in the Indies. Boyl left Cádiz for America on Sept. 25, 1493, in the second expedition of Columbus; probably a dozen or more priests accompanied him. In Española Boyl quarreled with Columbus over the Admiral's harsh treatment of the colonists and the Indians. Since he considered the situation quite impossible, Boyl left for Spain while Columbus was on an expedition to Cuba and Jamaica. He arrived there Dec. 3, 1494. Even though nothing came of his assignment in America, Boyl had not lost the confidence of the King. At the end of the century he spent 3 years in Rome acting as a special ambassador, at times for the King of Spain, at others as the representative of his superior, Francis of Paula. Nothing is known about the last years of his life.

Bibliography: E. W. Loughran, "The First Vicar-Apostolic of the New World," AmEcclRev 82 (1930) 1–14. F. Fita, a series of articles in *BolRealAcHist* 19 (1891) 173–233, 267–348, 354–356, 557–560; 20 (1892) 160–178, 179–205, 573–615.

[J. HERRICK]

BYBLOS

Greek name of an ancient Phoenician seacoast town about 20 miles north of Beirut. The Greek name Βύβλος, from which the word *Bible is derived, comes from the Canaanite (*Phoenician) name *gublu* (mountain, hill), with assimilation of the g to the following b. In the Hebrew Bible the name (with faulty vocalization?) appears as $g^e bal$ (Ez 27.9; see also Jos 13.5). The modern Lebanese villagers have tenaciously preserved the ancient name in the modern Arabic diminutive form Jubayl (little mount), the name of the pretty town of some 4,000 inhabitants, mostly Maronite Catholics, directly north of the ancient ruins.

Early Period. Excavations begun by the Egyptologist P. Montet (from 1921 to 1924) showed that Byblos, called *kbn* or *kpn* by the Egyptians, was a genuine Asiatic enclave of the pharaos from the earliest times. He discovered inscriptions of Nekba-Khasekhemwi of the Second Dynasty and, among the thousands of votive offerings in the Ba'al (or Ba'alat?) temple and attached rooms, scarabs of Cheops (Fourth Dynasty) and earlier pharaos (now in the Beirut Museum). Superstitious veneration of the site was perhaps connected with legends of the "blood of Tammuz-Adonis" at seasons when the fallen leaves turned to red the water that gushed down nearby from the famous 'Afqa spring in the mountains. In the hieroglyphic inscriptions the "Count [*hatya*] of Byblos" was the title of a recognized government official [see P. Newberry, JEgyptArch 14 (1928) 109]. In the Sixth Dynasty the traffic in cedars of Lebanon that were shipped from Byblos to Egypt

Ruins and archeological excavation at ancient Byblos.

was so flourishing under Snefru that the Egyptian word for a Mediterranean ship was a *kbnyt* (Byblos) ship. The *Admonitions* [ed. A. Gardiner (Leipzig 1909) 3.6] from the Middle Kingdom (*c.* 2040–1660 B.C.) lamented that there were no longer (after the time of Pepi II of the Sixth Dynasty) any convoys to bring back from Byblos cedars for mummy cases.

M. Dunand, who continued the excavations at Byblos from 1925 to 1966, showed that there had been a settlement on the site even from neolithic times. It was characterized by smooth plaster floors like those of neolithic Jericho and by herringbone-incision pottery like that of Sha'ar-ha Golan, as well as by other ceramic and architectural features thought to be chalcolithic [but see R. North, *Ghassul: 1960 Excavation Report* (Rome 1961) 70].

The temple of Ba'al (or Ba'alat?) suffered a catastrophic conflagration *c.* 2100 B.C. Above it, after a lethargy of some 400 years, was raised another temple of similar proportions, but this structure had its cult area filled with standing obelisks 5 to 7 feet high. The excavators dismantled the later temple and reconstructed it a short distance away; they thus made it possible for visitors today to see it in its integrity, but also in striking comparison with the ground plan of the temple that had preceded it. According to Dunand a second temple for the consort divinity was built further west, and the immemorial spring of the town was allowed to gush up and form a sacred lake between the two buildings.

Four royal tombs that were discovered by Montet in 1922–23 have been shown by W. F. Albright [BullAm SchOrRes 176 (December 1964) 38–46] to date from the beginning to the end of the 18th century B.C.; they reveal the close ties that Byblos had with Egypt (*see* EGYPT, 2) throughout this century. From about this

time comes a West-Semitic inscription that uses 114 hieroglyphic signs that have not yet been successfully deciphered. Quite different is the alphabetic inscription on the sarcophagus of King Ahiram of Byblos (now in the Beirut Museum), dated by Albright as *c.* 1000 B.C. (rather than Dunand's 1300). It represents one of the earliest stages of the Phoenician *alphabet, from which all modern alphabets are derived.

Amarna and Biblical Periods. It is strange that Byblos shows no trace of the *Hyksos, who were Asiatic rulers in Egypt (*c.* 1660-*c.* 1570), unless the sloping stone rampart is to be recognized as their handiwork. Among the *Amarna letters, however, there are 60 cuneiform letters from Rib-Addi of Byblos, from which important conclusions can be drawn regarding the *Habiru (Habiri) marauders in Syria and Palestine in the 14th century B.C. These documents are of prime importance also for the modern knowledge of the Canaanite language as then spoken, of which the *Hebrew language is a later dialect. [See W. Moran, "The Hebrew language in its Northwest Semitic Background," *The Bible and the Ancient Near East,* G. E. Wright, ed. (Garden City, N.Y. 1961) 63.] The practices of the myth religion of the Canaanites in this period (*see* CANAAN AND CANAANITES) were, according to the much later *Philo of Byblos, as brutal as those of nearby *Ugarit (*see* UGARITIC-CANAANITE RELIGION).

A century after the wide-eyed visit of the Egyptian Wen-Amun to Byblos (*c.* 1060 B.C.; for the story of his journey, see Pritchard ANET² 25–29) the town furnished cedars and architects for the building of *Solomon's temple (if the reading in 3 Kgs 5.32 is correct). However, this episode is linked rather with King *Hiram of *Tyre (see also 3 Kgs 5.15), who was not the same man as Ahiram of Byblos, although they bore the same name in slightly variant forms. Thereafter Byblos was eclipsed by Tyre and *Sidon, and according to Ez 27.9 the shipwrights of Byblos were the servants of the Tyrians.

In the Greco-Roman period Byblos again came into prominence as an import-export center of papyri (*see* PAPYROLOGY) so that papyrus was called ἡ βύβλος or βίβλος (i.e., Byblos material) in Greek. In the Roman epoch the city was one of renewed splendor, from which a theater and a colonnade survive. The north wall of the ancient city was used by the Crusaders as the castle-crowned axis of their settlement (called Gibellet) to the north. Their cathedral of St. John is a chief surviving masterpiece, which is now used for Maronite and Latin Catholic worship.

Bibliography: L. HENNEQUIN, DBSuppl 3:451–468. A. BEA, EncCatt 2:1620–21. R. NORTH, LexThK² 2:847. EncDictBibl 292–293. P. MONTET, *Byblos et l'Égypte* (Paris 1928). M. DUNAND, *Fouilles de Byblos* (Paris 1937–); *Byblia grammata* (Beirut 1945); RevBibl 57 (1950) 583–603; 59 (1952) 82–90; *Bulletin du Musée de Beyrouth* 9 (1950) 53–74; 12 (1955) 7–23; 13 (1956) 73–86. W. F. ALBRIGHT, "Some Oriental Glosses on the Homeric Problem," AmJArch 54 (1950) 162–176, esp. 165; *Ensiqlopediya Miqra'it,* v.2 (Jerusalem 1954) 404–411, in Heb. **Illustration credit:** Matson Photo Service, Los Angeles, Calif.

[R. NORTH]

BYRD, WILLIAM, Elizabethan Catholic composer and organist; b. Lincolnshire, 1543; d. Stondon Massey, Essex, July 4, 1623. He was organist of Lincoln Cathedral at 20 and in 1572 joined Thomas *Tallis as co-organist of the Chapel Royal, London. He had been appointed a Gentleman of the Chapel in 1570, and retained this office to the end of his life. He is important in the history of English music because of his many influential developments. Solo song, virginal music, fantasias for viols, the verse anthem, and other music for the Anglican church all benefited from his keen musical mind and unusually diversified talents. His greatest contribution, however, was to Catholic church music, which included three collections of *Cantiones sacrae* (1575, with Tallis; 1589; 1591), two books of *Gradualia* (1605, 1607), and three Masses (*c.* 1611).

As a faithful Catholic, Byrd was seldom free from worry, and an impression of his personal plight seems to emerge from the frequently despondent and penitential nature of the texts of certain of his motets. On the other hand, his professional life appears to have elicited a marked degree of respect and tolerance. Byrd is not known to have traveled abroad, and although he knew the work of some of his Continental contemporaries, his style retains a few parochial features. Yet he was a superbly capable contrapuntist, and ever sensitive to the needs of a liturgical text. His early motets include settings of hymns, responsories, and antiphons based on Sarum chants (*see* SARUM RITE, CHANTS OF); later works exhibit an almost exclusive concern with the *Roman rite, although Catholic services could be held only in strictest privacy.

Bibliography: *Collected Works,* ed. E. H. FELLOWES, 20 v. (London 1937–50). E. H. FELLOWES, *William Byrd* (2d ed. New York 1948). P. C. BUCK et al., eds., *Tudor Church Music,* 10 v. (New York 1922–29) v.2, 7, 9. J. KERMAN, "Byrd's Motets: Chronology and Canon," JAmMusSoc 14 (1961) 359–382. J. L. JACKMAN, "Liturgical Aspects of Byrd's Gradualia," MusQ

Title page, with a decorative woodcut, of Byrd's "Psalmes, sonets, & songs of sadnes and pietie," first edition (1588).

49 (1963) 17–37. **Illustration credit:** Edinburgh University Library.

[D. STEVENS]

BYRNE, ANDREW, bishop; b. Navan, County Meath, Ireland, Dec. 3?, 1802; d. Helena, Ark., June 10, 1862. In 1820 he arrived in the U.S. from the diocesan seminary at Navan as a volunteer to work in the

Andrew Byrne.

newly created Diocese of Charleston, S.C. After finishing his studies under the tutelage of Bp. John England, he was ordained at Charleston Nov. 11, 1827. He worked as a missionary until 1830, when he was made pastor of St. Mary's Church, Charleston. For several years he was vicar-general of Charleston, and he served as England's theologian at the Second Provincial Council of Baltimore (1833). Because of a disagreement with England, Byrne moved in 1836 to New York, where he held, successively, pastorates in several parishes. When the Diocese of *Little Rock, comprising the state of Arkansas and the Indian Territory, was created in 1843, Byrne was named its first bishop. He was consecrated on March 10, 1844, in New York by Bp. John Hughes. With fewer than 1,000 Catholics in Arkansas, Byrne became active in promoting immigration to the Southwest. Twice he went to Ireland to seek co-workers for his diocese, and in 1851 he welcomed the Sisters of Mercy from Dublin. He took part in both the Sixth Provincial Council of Baltimore (1846) and the First Provincial Council of New Orleans (1856).

Bibliography: *The History of Catholicity in Arkansas* (Little Rock 1925). R. H. CLARKE, *Lives of the Deceased Bishops of the Catholic Church in the U.S.,* 4 v. (New York 1872–89) v.2. J. D. HACKETT, *Bishops of the United States of Irish Birth or Descent* (New York 1936).

[A. A. MICEK]

BYRNE, EDMUND, archbishop of Dublin; b. probably Ballyback, near Borris, County Carlow, *c.* 1656; d. Ireland, 1723 or 1724. He was a member of Gabhal Raghnaill branch of the O'Byrnes and a descendant of Fiach MacHugh. He entered the Irish College in Seville (1674), where he was ordained on March 18, 1679, and remained until 1681, acquiring the Spanish equivalent of D.D. At St. Nicholas outside Dublin he served as parish priest (1698). Appointed archbishop March 15, 1707, he was consecrated Aug. 31, 1707, in Newgate Jail, Dublin, by Dr. O'Donnelly,

Bishop of Dromore, in times of appalling difficulty. He was the first archbishop actually resident since Russell's death in 1692. Although constantly fleeing the notorious priest catchers Garzia and Tyrell, he succeeded in holding a diocesan synod in 1712 to continue a precarious discipline under penal conditions. A patron of a school of Gaelic learning, he is commemorated in its versifications; he took part by his writings in public religious controversy. His difficulties were increased by the interference of the Primate, Hugh McMahon, Archbishop of Armagh. He encouraged the Dominican and Poor Clare Sisters to return to the diocese and led acceptance of Clement XI's constitution *Unigenitus* (1713) against Jansenists.

Bibliography: N. DONNELLY, *History of Dublin Parishes* (Dublin n.d.) 2:35–36, 38–48. J. J. MEAGHER in *Reportorium Novum* (Dublin n.d.) 3:378–386.

[J. J. MEAGHER]

BYRNE, PATRICK JAMES, Maryknoll missioner, first apostolic delegate to Korea; b. Washington, D.C., Oct. 26, 1888; d. Ha Chang Ri, Korea, Nov. 25, 1950. He was the 7th of 10 children of Patrick and Anna (Seales) Byrne, and was born on the site of the present Supreme Court Building, which he referred to with typical drollery as his "family homestead." He attended St. Charles College, Catonsville, Md., and St. Mary's Seminary, Baltimore, and was ordained June 23, 1915, for the Baltimore Archdiocese. A week later, however, he entered the Catholic Foreign Mission Society (*see* MARYKNOLL MISSIONERS), the first priest to do so. After various administrative assignments he founded a Maryknoll mission in north Korea in 1923. Four years later he became the prefect apostolic of Pyongyang, with headquarters at Pengyang. He relinquished this post in 1929 when he was elected vicar-general of the society.

In 1935 he opened Maryknoll's first Japanese mission, which was soon designated the prefecture apostolic of Kyoto. He resigned from this in 1940 in favor of Rev. Paul Furuya Yoshiyuki, later first bishop of Kyoto. Byrne remained in Japan during World War II, though his mission activity was curtailed. His postwar apostolate in Japan came to an end in 1947, when he was appointed apostolic visitor, and later first apostolic delegate to Korea.

He was consecrated in Seoul as titular bishop of Gazera, June 14, 1949. With the invasion of South Korea by Communists a year later, Byrne stayed at his post,

Patrick James Byrne.

was arrested July 16, 1950, and taken to Pengyang, the Communist capital, where he was held prisoner until October 21. On that day he began a "death march," with 700 other prisoners, to the Manchurian border, 100

miles north. On the way he died of exhaustion and pneumonia in the village of Ha Chang Ri, and was buried in the land of his first mission.

Bibliography: R. A. LANE, *The Early Days of Maryknoll* (New York 1951); *Ambassador in Chains* (New York 1955). G. D. KITTLER, *The Maryknoll Fathers* (New York 1961). **Illustration credit:** Maryknoll Fathers.

[W. J. COLEMAN]

BYRNE, WILLIAM, educator, author; b. Kilmessan, County Meath, Ireland, Sept. 8, 1833; d. Boston, Mass. Jan. 9, 1912. After immigrating to the U.S. in 1853, he attended St. Mary's College, Wilmington, Del., and Mt. St. Mary's College, Emmitsburg, Md., where he received his M.A. (1861) and taught mathematics and Greek. He was ordained on Dec. 31, 1864, for the Diocese of Boston, and was named diocesan chancellor (1866) and rector (1874) of St. Mary's Church, Charlestown, Mass. During this period, he began his lifelong activity on behalf of penal reforms, founded the Boston Temperance Missions, and edited the *Young Crusader*. At the request of Cardinal John McCloskey and Abp. (later Cardinal) James Gibbons, Byrne was elected in 1881 as the 12th president of Mt. St. Mary's College. As president and treasurer, he successfully rescued the institution from the financial difficulties that had threatened to close its doors. In 1884 he returned to Boston as rector of St. Joseph's Church, but he continued until his death as a member of the college's governing council. Byrne contributed frequently to both the secular and Catholic press, and he wrote several religious manuals in addition to a *History of the Catholic Church in the New England States* (1899). Georgetown College (now University), Washington, D.C., awarded him a doctor of divinity degree in 1881, and the library of Mt. St. Mary's College is named in his honor.

Bibliography: M. M. MELINE and E. F. X. McSWEENEY, *The Story of the Mountain: Mount St. Mary's College and Seminary,* 2 v. (Emmitsburg, Md. 1911).

[H. J. PHILLIPS]

BYZANTINE ART

Byzantine art is the art of the Byzantine Empire. The formation and general development of Byzantine art was influenced by Roman imperial statecraft, Greek culture, and the Christian religion. Its roots lay in the complex amalgam of early Christian, Roman, and Hellenistic art. Its authentic and independent nature was articulated largely within the walls of the imperial capital of Constantinople and in response to tasks set by the Byzantine imperial court and the Greek Church. Diplomacy, trade, and missionary zeal carried Byzantine art well beyond the borders of the empire, while the survival of Greek Christianity guaranteed its life after the catastrophe of 1453. Essentially the art of the Greek Middle Ages, Byzantine art provides a bridge from antiquity to modern times. *See* HELLENISTIC ART; CHURCH ARCHITECTURE, 3; ART, EARLY CHRISTIAN; LITURGICAL ART, 9; ICON; MOSAICS; BASILICA; RAVENNA; YUGOSLAVIAN ART; ARMENIAN ART; GEORGIAN LITERATURE AND ART.

CHARACTER OF BYZANTINE ART

The unique location in space and time of Constantinople (ancient Byzantium, modern Istanbul) provided Byzantine art with an unbroken Roman imperial tradition, a Hellenistic Greek ambience, and a Christian millennium. These are the principal factors, combined here as in no other Mediterranean city, that contributed to the formation of the essential characteristics of Byzantine art.

Constantine inaugurated his city in 324 and dedicated it on May 11, 330, with pagan rites and games and a Christian procession chanting the *Kyrie eleison*. From Rome he brought the Palladium and Tyche; he gave the city its official name, Second Rome (Δευτέρα Ῥώμη), which, from the middle of the 5th century, ecclesiastical authorities transformed into New Rome (Νέα Ῥώμη). Within one century the image of ancient Rome was re-created in the new city even to the number of hills (seven), districts (fourteen), and triumphal columns with spiral reliefs (two), not to mention imperial bronze equestrians and a rich collection of Greek, Hellenistic, and Roman statuary that filled the streets, fora, and public buildings. In this setting the presentation and representation of Roman imperial majesty were elaborated to an astonishing degree in the long history of the city. The court pressed the artisan into service, provided him with costly materials, demanded of him a high order of craftsmanship, set him challenging commissions, published his fame abroad through distribution of his works as gifts, and made his work the trademark of majesty in general. High quality and the aura of majesty, therefore, are immediately recognizable attributes of Byzantine art (Figs. 6a, 13).

The site of the new Roman capital was on a Greek peninsula; its citizens called themselves Romans but did so in Greek (Ῥωμαῖοι). In their new environment the imported Roman Latin forms of statecraft, written and representational, were eventually transformed into Byzantine Greek. Greek classics were studied and copied, often from ancient manuscripts whose illustrations, along with other antique sources, supplied Byzantine illuminators and other craftsmen with a rich supply of Hellenistic architectural and landscape backgrounds, as well as ancient figure types. These the artists excerpted, codified into pattern or model books in the ateliers, and quoted liberally as they carved mythological scenes on an ivory box (Fig. 9), or surrounded an Old Testament Prophet with the romantic nostalgia of a Hellenistic setting (Fig. 8).

Byzantine absorption with its Greek past, however, went beyond the adventitious quotation of ancient examples to grasp the essentials of Hellenic form. The Hellenic artist had preserved at all costs the organic shape and coherence of living creatures, giving them dignity and importance in two ways: by isolating them from nature (in contrast to most Hellenistic and Roman art) and by investing them with grace and a slow measured rhythm. The result in ancient Greek art was a timeless world of heroic dimension. The Byzantine artist, particularly during the Comnenian period, re-created this vision in his own terms with such obvious mastery and consistency as to convince some observers that "not before the tenth or eleventh century are we in the presence of a Byzantine art fully constituted, enjoying a complete autonomy both in form and in spirit" (Fig. 12). Byzantine art shared the Hellenic feeling for refined forms in graceful, rhythmic motion. These are the marks that identify it to be the art of the Greek, not the Latin, Middle Ages. Byzantine art never abandoned entirely the ancient Hellenic devotion to organic coherence, though it devised its own scale and proportion for the human figure and allowed its own rhythms to predominate, on occasion, over the facts of human anatomy. Both ancient and Byzantine Greek art are a mimesis of living forms, neither a copy nor an abrupt departure from them; but the Byzantine mimesis is Neoplatonic and Christian in character. In its supreme creations, the mosaic programs of church decoration, Byzantine art created its own timeless world, cosmic, noetic, and intensely spiritual (Figs. 13–17).

Constantine's city was granted a millennium during which the forms of Roman majesty and Greek thought were adapted to the needs of Christian theology and worship. The union of classical and Christian elements determined the procedure of Byzantine artisans. It ensured the representation of Christ in imperial terms and drew His image into the forefront of Christological and iconoclastic controversy, from which it emerged as the Pantocrator of a cosmos at once Greek and Orthodox. The plain Gospel narrative of the life of Christ was carefully excerpted and organized into a liturgical cycle, whose chief points were emphasized by great feasts. These scenes especially, such as the Annunciation, Nativity, Transfiguration, and Ascension, had to be imbued with a theological meaning and a spiritual power that could lift them above the level of simple historical narrative and confer upon them the iconic quality of an action eternally present. The talents and techniques of Byzantine craftsmen were expanded to meet these challenges as they moved from close description of a narrative text (Fig. 3) to the portrayal of an inner spiritual response (Figs. 2, 8, 16b, 17b) and to the presentation of the Incarnate Logos as the Lord of All, commanding the entire church interior though made of tiny cubes pressed swiftly into drying mortar (Figs. 13, 15). In and through the representation of his assigned subjects, the Byzantine artist was able to suggest visually the evidence of things not seen.

PERIODS OF BYZANTINE ART

Two severe crises divide Byzantine history and art history into three broad periods. The first of these crises occurred in the 8th and early 9th centuries when the empire had to wage a desperate struggle for survival against both Arabs and Bulgars while it was internally rent by the iconoclastic controversy. *See* ICONOCLASM. Religious images, but not secular scenes, were ordered destroyed and were banned between 730 and 787, and again between 815 and 843.

Leo III (717–741), who had first preached openly against the use of religious images in 726, decreed their destruction Jan. 17, 730. Patriarch Germanos refused to assent and was deposed. Constantine V (741–775) intensified the attack on religious images, wrote treatises advancing Christological arguments against their use, convoked a council in 754 that decreed that Christ could not be represented, banned images of the *Theotokos and the saints, and ordered the destruction of all icons of religious content. This Emperor also removed a Christological mosaic cycle from the church at Blachernae and replaced it with a decoration of plants, animals, and birds. A standing figure in mosaic of the Virgin was removed from the apse of the church of the Dormition, Nicaea, and replaced by a large cross. Similar large crosses in mosaic were placed in the apses of St. Irene, Constantinople, and Hagia Sophia, Thessalonica.

The first iconoclastic period was ended by the Council of Nicaea II in 787, which repudiated the *acta* of the iconoclastic council of 754 and sanctioned the use of religious images, carefully distinguishing their veneration from the worship due to God alone. This first restoration, however, ended in 815, when a Constantinopolitan synod, convoked under Leo V, the Armenian (813–820), repudiated the *acta* of Nicaea II and again ordered the destruction of religious images. The ban against them was finally lifted in March 843 by a synod held early in the reign of Michael III (842–867), the Empress Theodora being Regent. (The only surviving Byzantine figural mosaic of the iconoclastic period may be seen in the chapel of St. Zeno at S. Prassede, Rome, 817–824.)

Iconoclasts generally attacked the images on the grounds that they had become objects of idolatrous worship and that images of Christ were heretical, since it was not possible to represent His divine nature. The only image of Christ was the bread and wine of the Eucharist. Iconodules defended the image as a vehicle through which veneration was paid to its prototype and justified the figural representation of Christ by the doctrine of the Incarnation. To deny His image was to deny this doctrine. Moreover, pictures, when faithful to the Gospel account and orthodox belief, were held to transform worshipers from auditors into eyewitnesses of the deeds themselves, excelling verbal teaching by far in speed and clarity of instruction (Nicephorus in 817, *Antirrhetus III*, PG 100:381–384). "Sight," declared Photius in a homily on the newly restored image of the Virgin in Hagia Sophia, "having touched and encompassed the object through the outpouring of optical rays, sends the essence of the thing seen on to the mind . . . . Before our eyes stands motionless the Virgin, carrying the Creator in her arms as an infant, depicted in painting as she is in writing and visions, an interceder for our salvation and a teacher of reverence to God, a grace of the eyes and of the mind, carried by which the divine love in us is uplifted to the intelligible beauty of truth" (*Hom.* 17, March 29, 867, tr. C. Mango).

What emerged from the Christological debate over the images was a refined theory and definition of the character and role of religious art and an elaborate, comprehensive, and ordered system of iconography. In this way the iconoclastic controversy serves to divide the late antique (Figs. 1–5) from the medieval phase (Figs. 6a–15) of Byzantine art.

The second major crisis in the history of Byzantium was the conquest of Constantinople in 1204 by the Crusaders, whose Latin kingdom ruled there until 1261. This abrupt hiatus in Byzantine rule at Constantinople forced the main line of development of Byzantine art to continue elsewhere, exposing it to new demands. What emerged was a new style, still Byzantine, but possessed of a far wider range of emotional expression, compositional daring, and painterly vision. Thus the Latin conquest may stand as the division between the high medieval phase of Byzantine art and its final flowering (Figs. 16a–17b).

The physiognomy of the three broad periods of Byzantine art (4th to 8th century, 9th through 12th, and 13th to mid-15th) is emerging in the work of Kitzinger, Weitzmann, Lazareff, and Demus, not to mention the earlier magisterial studies by Kondakov, Ainalov, Millet, and Grabar.

Fig. 1. "High Official," from Aphrodisias, marble, 5th century, height 5 feet 11¼ inches, Archeological Museum, Istanbul.

The 4th to the 8th Century. Constantinopolitan sculpture of the late 4th century exhibits a supple modeling and serene outlook that reflect its Hellenistic heritage. The qualities are apparent in the flying angels on the Child's Sarcophagus (*c.* 370s) and in the marble statue of Valentinian II (*c.* 390), both in the Archeological Museum, Istanbul. However, in official life and art, bodies soon retreated beneath the robe of office (chlamys), whose long folds covered, concealed, and overcame them. An early 5th-century statue of an official from Aphrodisias (Fig. 1) is dominated by the chlamys, which encases the figure, contracts the left shoulder, and expands the right; the head, a thoughtful portrait, emerges off-center, and the right knee is an interruption of drapery folds rather than an organic joint in a leg. The slab of marble is thin, the back unworked; the conception is that of high relief, not of a figure fully in the round. Plastic qualities of ancient sculpture are being eroded by a new pictorial vision; ancient concern for weight and support is surrendering to a rhythm and pattern externally imposed; the nude body is no longer the basis for the robed figure. The true successor of this figure appears a century later in *mosaic, among the officers accompanying Justinian in San Vitale, Ravenna.

Mosaic. The new vision ruled out large-scale sculpture, transformed architecture, and led to an unprecedented development of the monumental wall mosaic. The mosaic medium consists of small cubes, or tesserae, varied in color and material (marble, terra cotta, shell, vitreous paste), fixed to a cement covered wall. For the process, one should imagine the master mosaicist swiftly sketching his design directly on to the wet cement setting bed. Assistants quickly laid in the tesserae of the background, coming up to the bold outlines of the figures, whose draperies were set by more experienced aides. Heads, hands, and feet were the work of the master himself. Of the many outstanding examples preserved from this period in Rome, Milan, Ravenna, Salonika, and St. Catherine's monastery on Sinai, only a few may be mentioned here.

In St. George, Salonika, remains of a late 4th-century mosaic frieze encircle the 80-foot dome built in about 305 by Galerius. Paired saints of the Greek calendar flank columnar octagons sheltering a Gospel Book resting on an altar. Behind them, against a gold background, two-storied columnar structures rise in Hellenistic perspective. Peacocks, crosses, altars, and the lavish use of gold transform a late Pompeian scheme of wall decoration into a "Hellenistic" celestial city inhabited by saints. To turn from this Theodosian mosaic to one in the apse of St. David's, Salonika (second half of the 5th century), is to turn from a serene eternity to a startling Epiphany. A youthful, beardless Christ faces the observer from the center of the apse. He is seated upon a rainbow (Gn 9.8–17 and Ap 4.3) set in a large circular aureole of transparent light, white around the blue robe of Christ, with green and white rays (Ap 4.5) leading to the circumference. This light alters the tones but not the shapes of the winged man, lion, bull, and eagle (Ap 4.9), which it partially covers. The whole apparition hovers above a river teeming with fish, at which two Prophets on the shore stare in amazement. The right arm of Christ is raised in proclamation, while the left holds a scroll bearing a free paraphrase of Is 25.9–10. The opening words, "Behold our God," set the tone. As Grabar has shown (*Martyrium II* 198–   ), this mosaic presents a theophanic vision of the New Jerusalem, prophetic (Ez 47.1, 9; Za 14.8) and apocalyptic (Ap 4.3–9).

Two Modes of Byzantine Mosaic. The two contrasting modes and aims represented in these Salonikan mosaics persisted through the period. The first relied heavily on Hellenistic motifs and principles of composition, often developed from Theodosian models. This is clear from the lower zone of mosaics in the dome of the Orthodox baptistery (*c.* 458) and the Good Shepherd mosaic in the "Tomb" of Galla Placidia (*c.* 450) in Ravenna, and from nine silver plates showing scenes from the life of David (Fig. 5) found in Cyprus but made in Constantinople (613–630). This Hellenistic strain in Byzantine art should be distinguished from certain works that seem to skip the intervening centuries and make direct contact with Hellenistic models. Pagan subjects, sketchy treatment, and lively action characterize these works, though they generally fail to recapture Hellenistic scale and spatial illusion. Two famous manuscripts should be cited here: the Vienna Dioskurides (512; from Constantinople) and the Milan *Iliad,* which has been attributed to the city at about the same time. Refined examples occur among the silver plates of the 4th to the 7th century published by Matzulewitsch and Dodd.

The second mode, an early stage of which occurs in St. David's, Salonika, sought to transcend description of Biblical visions and miracles in an effort to convey their numinous, spiritual quality. To this end a flat, abstract style was developed, made intense by bold colors contained in decisive, linear contours and patterns. The impetus for representing figures in complete frontality lay in the growing cult of the icon, described by Kitzinger, and in the cult of the Holy Places in Palestine, whose impact on Byzantine art has been assessed by Ainalov (*Hellenistic Origins* 224–   ) and Grabar (*Martyrium II* ch. 4, 6). Both factors constituted a steady pressure on the artist to emphasize the spiritual content of his compositions. The results may be seen in many works of the 6th and 7th centuries: Passion mosaics, S. Apollinare Nuovo, Ravenna, early 6th century; Transfiguration mosaic, St. Catherine, Sinai, *c.* 560; the "Riha Paten" (Fig. 2); the Rabbula Ascension (Fig. 4) and the Crucifixion fresco in S. Maria Antiqua, Rome, 8th century; and votive mosaic panels, St. Demetrius, Salonika, after 630.

Synthesis. The court art of Justinian, not untouched by the aims that led to these divergent styles, rose above them to achieve a remarkable synthesis, the last creative statement of Roman imperial art. The mosaic panels of Justinian and Theodora in San Vitale, Ravenna (*c.* 547), recall the majestic splendor of the Theodosian saints in St. George, Salonika, but the figures are more sharply defined and are set in bolder colors more daringly juxtaposed. The classic, almost blank, beauty of Theodosian portraiture has been replaced, in the principal figures especially, by a powerful modeling of facial anatomy. The tesserae, varied in shape, are set like successive strokes of a blunt brush in rows obedient to the anatomy; the colors fuse at a distance in well-defined highlights and shadows. The result is a mosaic portraiture as sculptural in its solidity as it is Roman in character. The ateliers in Constantinople, from which came the model for the panels in San Vitale, demonstrate in these works their unbroken contact with ancient Roman imperial art and their capacity to transcend their heritage and create an authentic, integral style. The entire apse, indeed, is a single composition into which the imperial panels are carefully fitted. The figure of Justinian marks the point where the apse begins to curve; directly over his head rises the border of the mosaic in the conch, where, above the windows, a youthful Christ is seated upon the globe of the cosmos. The celestial landscape overlaps the imperial procession, defining the relation between the realm of Christ and of Justinian. This integration of architectural and mosaic composition made articulate the meaning of architec-

Fig. 2. *"The Communion of the Twelve Apostles" on the "Riha Paten," silver gilt, 565–578, diameter 13¾ inches.*

Fig. 3. *"The Last Supper and the Washing of Feet," in the Rossano Gospels, folio 3, 6th century, archiepiscopal treasury, Rossano, Italy.*

BYZANTINE ART

Fig. 4. *"Ascension," in the Rabbula Gospels, 586, Florence, Biblioteca Laurenziana (MS Plut. I. 56).*

Fig. 5. *"Introduction of David to Saul," silver plate, 613–30. diameter 10½ inches.*

(a)

Fig. 6. (a) "Christ Enthroned and the Emperor Leo VI," mosaic of the late 9th century over the "Imperial" door in the narthex of the church of Hagia Sophia, Istanbul. (b) Detail of the head of Christ.

(b)

Fig. 8. "David's Repentance," in the Paris Psalter, early 10th century, Paris, Bibl. Nat. (MS gr. 139, fol. 136v).

Fig. 7. "The Transfiguration," in the Homilies of Gregory of Nazianzus, c. 880, Paris, Bibliothèque Nationale (MS gr. 510, fol. 75r).

Fig. 9. Two of the panels on the side of the "Veroli Casket," ivory, late 10th century, length 16 inches.

tural surfaces and spaces, clearly distinguishing the celestial from the terrestrial. It insured the monumentality of the mosaic figures designed to fill them; as a result, Byzantine art never lost sight of the life-sized and more than life-sized figure.

The 9th through the 12th Century. After the political and religious crises of the 7th and 8th centuries, a medieval Byzantine state emerged as the eastern remnant of the Christian Roman Empire of late antiquity and maintained its own position between the Islamic Near East and the Latin West. Byzantine art of this period is marked by an individual rhythm, space, light, and expression, which make it medieval rather than ancient, Greek rather than Latin in character. This character comes most sharply into focus in the greatest achievement of Byzantine painting, the comprehensive ecclesiastical mosaic program, with its unique relation between the image and the beholder.

When the last iconoclastic emperor, *Theophilus, died in 842, the way was open again for imperial patronage of religious art. His widow, *Theodora, shortly after 843 restored a famous image of Christ to its position at the entrance of the imperial palace. This act publicly proclaimed her orthodoxy in respect to images, for the removal and destruction of the original of this image in 730 and of its replacement in 814 had announced each outbreak of iconoclasm. Sometime after 856 Michael III reintroduced sacred images into the throne room of the palace (*Palatine Anthology I* 106, 107). A still more important step was taken in 864 when the church of the Pharos, in the center of the palace, received a mosaic program that consisted of a throng of angels set in a ribbed dome at whose summit a medallion framed a bust portrait of Christ, "overseeing the world" (Photius, *Hom. 10,* tr. C. Mango). In the apse was a figure of the Virgin, standing and orant; elsewhere, a band of Prophets, Apostles, martyrs, and Patriarchs was arrayed in hierarchical order. There was no cycle of the life of Christ; it was a severely theological program, dedicated to the Incarnate Ruler of the cosmos and the organization of His Church. Each figure addressed the worshiper directly.

The Program of Hagia Sophia. Similar to this was the theme of the most ambitious mosaic program ever attempted, the decoration of *Hagia Sophia, Constantinople (Istanbul). Planned and begun toward the end of the reign of Michael III (842–867), the program was carried forward by Basil I (867–886), the founder of the Macedonian dynasty, and most likely by Leo VI (886–912) as well. Leo VI is now generally recognized as the emperor kneeling before the enthroned Christ in the dedicatory mosaic over the imperial door (Fig. 6a). Work began in the apse in 867 with a standing figure of the Virgin holding the Child (Photius, *Hom 17,* tr. C. Mango). The accompanying inscription indicated that this replaced images that "the impostors had cast down here." A large figure of Christ was set in the medallion, some 35 feet in diameter, centered in the vast dome 180 feet above the floor. Seraphim occupied the 60-foot pendentives; 16 Prophets and 14 bishops (three of which are preserved), ranged on the north and south tympanum walls, completed the program in the nave. Except for a representation of the Savior's Baptism in the north gallery, there were no scenes of the life of Christ. Later restorations in the apse (enthroned Virgin and Child still preserved) and in the dome (an enormous

Pantocrator bust set in 1355, last seen in 1652) and later additions in the galleries (imperial portraits and a Deësis; Figs. 16a, 16b) did not alter the basic program.

The mosaic programs of the Pharos, the palatine church, and of Hagia Sophia, the greatest church of the empire, presented independent figures, set against gold backgrounds, entering the sanctuary, as it were, from all sides of the domed centralized structure. There was no narrative thread to follow, no dramatic unity to seek, but rather a timeless theology to comprehend, clarified by a hierarchical order. The program as a whole recalls Hebrews ch. 1. The mosaic figures, majestic and motionless, were scaled to the upper walls and curving surfaces of domes and vaults, which conferred on them an architectural movement. To Photius it seemed "that everything is in ecstatic motion and the church itself is circling round." The gold ground denied them a pictorial spatial setting; rather, they projected into the space of the sanctuary the presence of their archetypes. Mesarites described the mosaic of the Pantocrator in the central dome of Holy Apostles', Constantinople, as "leaning and gazing out as though from the rim of heaven" (see Fig. 13).

Other Liturgical Programs. This severely iconic program maintained a tension between worshiper and image unrelieved by narrative scenes. The typical program, however, included mosaics of major events in the life of Christ, treated as monumental icons of the liturgical year rather than as illustrations of the Gospel text. They were disposed in the middle zone of the typical cross-in-square church, below the domes reserved for the Pantocrator, Ascension, and Pentecost; and above, or in more prominent places than the spaces reserved for images of saints and martyrs. The beginnings of this development under Basil I have been lost (see *Palatine Anthology I* 109–117 and the descriptions of the church of the Holy Apostles by Constantine of Rhodes, early 10th century, and by Mesarites, c. 1200). The full program can be ascertained from mosaics remaining in three monastic churches of the 11th century: Hosios Loukas in Phocis, first half of the century; Nea Moni on Chios, 1042 to 1056; and the church of the Dormition at Daphni, near Athens, c. 1100. Each of these was dominated by mosaics of the Pantocrator in the central dome, preserved only at Daphni (Fig. 13), and of the enthroned Virgin and Child in the apse, fully preserved only at Hosios Loukas. The liturgical cycle of the life of Christ expanded from 9 scenes at Hosios Loukas to 14 at Nea Moni and 19 at Daphni, where 5 were devoted to the life of the Virgin. The basic program was restricted almost exclusively to the Twelve Feasts of the Byzantine rite. The program begins in the naos, in the squinch vaults or apsidioles under the dome, and concludes in the narthex, except at Hosios Loukas, where the Pentecost mosaic was placed in the smaller dome above the altar. Far from forming a contiguous series as on the long flat walls of early Christian or Western medieval churches, these scenes were fitted into distinct architectural units of the highly articulated structure, each addressing the beholder as an independent icon. The later history of this program exhibits a steadily expanding number of narrative scenes and picturesque details that diminishes the iconic and liturgical character dominant in 11th-century examples (programs at Monreale, San Marco in Venice, and in the narthex at the Kariye Djami, Istanbul).

Fig. 10. "Deësis with Apostles," detail of the outer container for a reliquary of the true cross, c. 960, in the cathedral treasury at Limburg an der Lahn, Germany; height of detail is approximately 8 inches.

The style of these programs is remarkably varied, considering the fact that they shared common aims, technical problems, and a common faithful adherence to accepted prototypes for each scene. The mosaics of Hosios Loukas and Nea Moni are indebted in varying degrees to an Eastern Christian monastic tradition evident also in contemporary frescoes in Cappadocia. The tradition, whose roots lay in Syria and Palestine, favored the expression of an emotional intensity height-

ened by an abstract use of color and line. This is particularly noticeable at Nea Moni, where only two shades of each color were employed, skillfully handled for dramatic effects both of linear pattern and bold massing of contrasting color areas.

The mosaics at Daphni, except for the powerful bust of the Pantocrator, stand in the Greek and Hellenistic tradition, firmly embedded in the art of the Macedonian and Comnenian periods. Classic ideals of beauty and

Fig. 11. *"Arrival of the Body of John Chrysostom at Constantinople,"
in the Menologion of Basil II, c. 1000, Rome (MS Vat. gr. 1613, fol.
353, detail).*

BYZANTINE ART

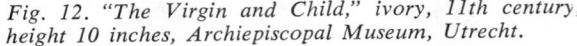

Fig. 12. *"The Virgin and Child," ivory, 11th century,
height 10 inches, Archiepiscopal Museum, Utrecht.*

Fig. 13. *"The Pantocrator," mosaic, c. 1100, in the dome of the
monastery church at Daphni,
Greece.*

grace govern many of these figures, whose mosaicists employed five or six tones of each color to produce subtle effects of plastic modeling. A comparison of the Crucifixion scenes in each church reveals their distinctive character, perhaps no more strikingly than in the figure of John, awkwardly standing in helpless sorrow at Hosios Loukas, dully staring at the ground in somber despondency at Nea Moni, and at Daphni, the image of grace and poise, gently inviting the compassion of the onlooker. Though each program has its own tone created by an anonymous group of artists, yet in the mosaics of the Pantocrator and Passion scenes in the narthex at Hosios Loukas, and in the masterpiece of the Pantocrator in the dome at Daphni, one can recognize the hand of superior artists, who stand out from their fellow craftsmen.

The Expansion of Byzantine Art. Byzantine monumental painting continued to flourish and expand beyond the borders of the Byzantine state, unaffected by territorial losses and declining fortunes in the 11th and 12th centuries. In Sicily, Italy, the Balkans, and southern Russia, Byzantine artists continued to set mosaics and paint frescoes for foreign patrons. Their activity not only met the current needs of provincial centers for skilled craftsmen, but by training local artists in Byzantine techniques they laid the basis for local "dialects" of Byzantine art. Byzantine art became an international koine throughout the Orthodox world and beyond, in which provincial and metropolitan factors mingled.

Certain mosaics, however, stand out as clearly Comnenian in style: those in the apse at Torcello (Apostles, *c.* 1100; solitary Virgin Hodegetria in the gold conch, 12th century); in the Palatine chapel, Palermo (the Pantocrator in the dome and in the south transept, the Greek Church Fathers on the nave wall, 1143); and at Cefalù, 1148 (*see* CEFALÙ, CATHEDRAL OF), where Greek mosaicists successfully adapted the traditional image of the Pantocrator to fit the conch of the apse, there being no dome in this Western basilica. At Nerezi, near Skoplje, Yugoslavia, the usual classic reserve of Comnenian art gave way to an overt and powerful expression of emotion in the fresco of the Pietà (Fig. 14). The fact that these frescoes were commissioned by a member of the Comnenos family suggests a reflection here of Constantinopolitan art.

A further release of energy, from perhaps a similar source, led to the swinging movements, exaggerated postures, and turbulent draperies in frescoes of the Communion of the Apostles and of the Ascension in Holy Apostles', Perachorio, Cyprus (1160–80). Their baroque style is not typical of 12th-century frescoes on Cyprus and may be the product of a master from the capital. These provincial monuments indicate that dynamic figure composition was a major development in the reign of Manuel I (1143–80). In the vast mosaic program at Monreale (1180–90) this power and verve seem lacking, though the mosaicists were aware of current developments in Comnenian style. The total effect of the interior, however, remains overwhelming. In San Marco, Venice (late 11th to late 13th century), the uneven dialogue between Byzantine and local Venetian style can be followed from the Ascension in the central cupola, where the former is dominant, to the last cupola in the narthex (Life of Moses), where

a confident fusion of both Byzantine and Venetian seems to have been effected.

Manuscript Illumination. The text of the Bible as well as the interior of the church was liberally and sumptuously illustrated by Byzantine painters. *See* MANUSCRIPT ILLUMINATION. Hellenistic editors had profusely illustrated the Greek classics, and many of their manuscripts survived into Byzantine times to offer the miniaturist a variety of methods and a full repertoire of figures, personifications, scenic backgrounds, and picturesque details. Full use was made of these manuscripts by miniaturists of the 6th through the 10th century. Miniatures in the Vienna Genesis, the Paris Gregory, the Paris Psalter, the Bible of Leo the Patrician, and the Joshua Roll in the Vatican contain a rich array of classical motifs, disposed to serve the illustration of Biblical texts. In addition, the sumptuous edition of the sermons of St. Gregory of Nazianzus, made for Emperor Basil I about 880, exhibits among its 46 large miniatures a pictorial compendium of the sources of Byzantine illumination, embracing preiconoclastic miniature cycles and contemporary wall paintings (Pentecost on fol. 301; the Transfiguration, Fig. 7). The miniatures of the Paris Psalter, richly framed, are more consistently classical. The figures in both are modeled with great subtlety and are firmly planted on the ground. The Joshua Roll, done in the manner of a colored sketch, recalls the reliefs on Roman imperial columns and seems to be no more than a retouching of an ancient prototype.

Toward the end of the 10th century a new style appears in which a gold ground displaces the Hellenistic setting, the drawing tightens, the highlights sharpen and become abstract, and the proportions of the figure elongate. The antique atmosphere disappears before the advance of an authentic Byzantine setting. This new style appears in the Menologion of Basil II (Fig. 11), to each of whose 430 miniatures the scribe attached the name of the painter (there were eight in all). Here a new formal unity firmly subordinates architectural backdrops to the figures, many of which suggest ties with icons. In the course of the 11th and 12th centuries a more ascetic ideal developed, noticeable first in the more intense expression in the faces. The figures soon submit to a more taut outline, within which the modeling becomes severe and abstract (Paris, Bibl. Nat., MSS grec. 64 and 74). Yet, as this trend develops, it comes into harmony and balance, strangely enough, with the classical tradition and issues in such masterpieces as the four dedicatory miniatures of the Emperor Nicephorus Botaniates, which preface the manuscript of the sermons of St. John Chrysostom (Paris, Bibl. Nat., Coislin 79, 1078–81). This high moment in Comnenian art may be observed also in ivories of John the Baptist in the Victoria and Albert Museum, London, and of the standing Virgin and Child at Utrecht (Fig. 12). The Comnenian artist succeeded in infusing a spiritual awareness into a purified classical form.

The 13th through the 15th Century. The Latin conquest and occupation of Constantinople (1204–61) cut the Byzantine artist adrift from his professional center but did not stop the production of Byzantine art. On the contrary, it was a fruitful period for Byzantine painting, particularly in Serbia, Macedonia, and Greece.

Final Sylistic Development. The frescoes at Milesevo (*c.* 1235) show that the abstract drapery, the

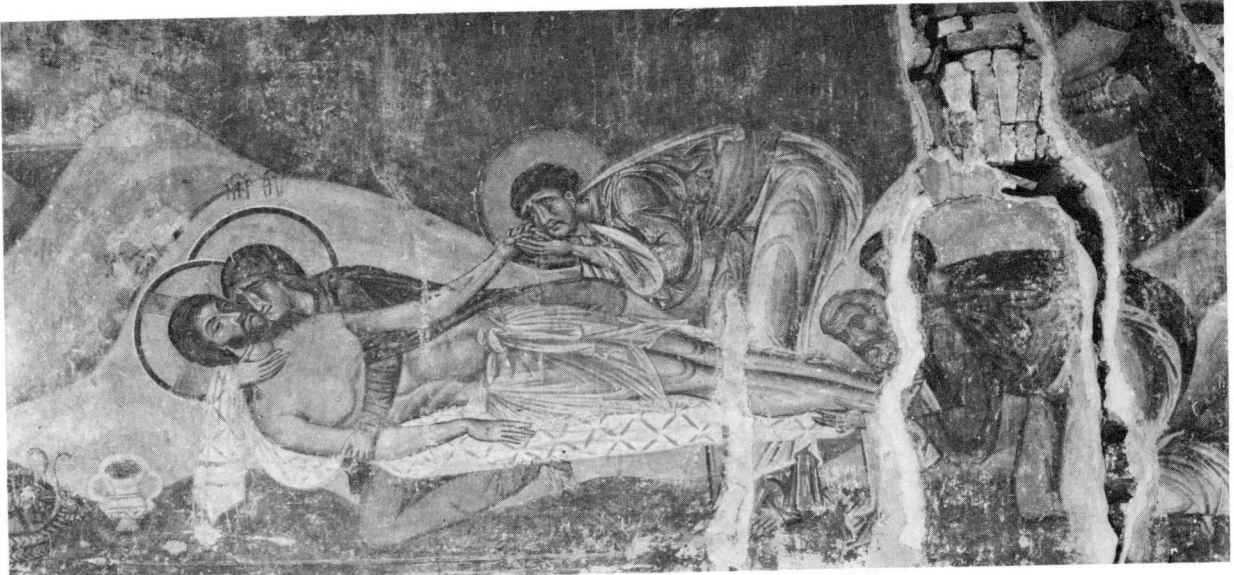

Fig. 14. "The Lamentation over the Dead Christ," fresco, 1164, in St. Panteleimon, Nerezi, Yugoslavia.

Fig. 15. "The Pantocrator," mosaic, 12th century, in the apse of the cathedral at Monreale, Sicily.

(a)

(b)

BYZANTINE

ART

Fig. 16. (a) "The Deësis," mosaic, 13th century, in the south gallery of Hagia Sophia. (b) Detail, head of St. John the Baptist.

(a)

BYZANTINE

ART

Fig. 17. (a) "The Anastasis," fresco, 1310–20, in the apse of the Parecclesion, Kariye Djami, Istanbul. (b) Detail of the head of Adam.

(b)

intense emotion, and dynamic weightlessness of the figures at Nerezi (Fig. 14) were no longer current. The drapery has given up its linear independence to lie more easily on fuller, more plastically modeled figures. This results in a greater emphasis on weight and volume. The figures become ponderous and massive, the modeling being broad and general, the proportions classic. At Sopočani (c. 1265) the figures acquire greater volume, in part because of the verve with which the drapery plays more freely around the figure in sweeping folds and tends to billow. The figures are modeled in broad simple areas of subtly blending tones. Something akin to this is found in the mosaic of the Deësis in Hagia Sophia (Figs. 16a, 16b), set after the return of the Paleologi to Constantinople. Luminous modeling, produced by the most delicate grading of tones in the tesserae, is apparent in the face, neck, and hand of Christ and in the face of the Virgin. The face of the Baptist (Fig. 16b) is lined more heavily to indicate his ascetic character. The panel emerges as one of the most refined and assured of all Byzantine mosaics. The proportions of the Paleologan figure continued to rise, however, to become high and mannered both at Gračanica (c. 1320) and in the mosaics of the life of the Virgin in the narthex of the Kariye Djami (c. 1310). The full cycle, replete with scenes from the Apocrypha, is a masterpiece of narrative depiction on a grand scale in which every nuance of the story is presented.

Kariye Djami. The most striking masterworks of the Paleologan period are the frescoes in the Parecclesion of the Kariye Djami. A remarkable series of full-length portraits of Church Fathers and saints line the walls below the cornice. The apse contains the Anastasis with Christ in the center, clad in white in front of a white *mandorla*, literally pulling Adam and Eve from their tombs (Figs. 17a, 17b). In the domical vault above is the Second Coming, whose various elements spread out onto the walls, the entire composition being quite unique in the history of Byzantine art. Here and at Mistra in the Peloponnese, during the final century of its long career, Byzantine art was at its most resourceful, as it strove to image the things that are not seen.

Bibliography: Sources. Texts and translations. A. N. Didron, *Christian Iconography,* tr. E. J. Millington, completed by M. Stokes, 2 v. (London 1886), based on *Manuel d'iconographie chrétienne grecque et latine* (Paris 1845), Fr. tr. of the Mount Athos Painters' Guide, an 18th-century compilation containing earlier materials; Ger. tr. G. Schaefer (Trier 1855); Gr. text, P. Kerameus (St. Petersburg 1909). F. W. Unger and J. P. Richter, *Quellen der byzantinischen Kunstgeschichte,* 2 v. (Quellenschriften für Kunstgeschichte u. Kunsttechnik des Mittelalters u. der Renaissance 12, NS 8; Vienna 1878, 1897), texts in Unger describe Constantinople and its secular buildings; texts in Richter describe churches, monasteries, palaces, and other public buildings. W. R. Lethaby and A. Swainson, *The Church of Sancta Hagia Sophia, Constantinople* (London 1894) 35–65, extensive tr. of the descriptive poem of Paulus Silentiarius. T. Preger, ed., *Scriptores originum Constantinopolitanarum,* 2 v. (Leipzig 1901–07) 1:74–108, Gr. text of *Description of the Construction of Hagia Sophia* (not later than the 10th century and quotes earlier sources); v.2: Gr. text of *Patria Constantinopoleos* by an anonymous late 10th-century writer, Pseudo-Codinus; 2.3:214–283: *On Buildings;* 2.4:284–289: *On Hagia Sophia.* W. R. Paton, tr., *The Greek Anthology,* 5 v. (LoebCl Lib; New York 1927–60), bk. 1 "Christian Epigrams," (many refer to Byzantine Churches); bk. 16 "Planudian Anthology," (a number refer to Byzantine official portraits and other works of art). H. B. Dewing and G. Downey, eds., *Procopius,* 7 v. (LoebClLib; Cambridge, Mass. 1914–40) v.7 *On Buildings.* A. Dupont-Sommer, "Une Hymne syriaque sur la cathédrale d'Édesse," *Cahiers archéologiques* 2 (1947) 29–39. G. Downey,

Nikolaos Mesarites (Transactions of the Amer. Philosophical Society, NS 47.6; Philadelphia 1957), Gr. text with Eng. tr., commentary, and introd. C. Mango, tr., *The Homilies of Photius* (Cambridge, Mass. 1958), homily 10, 184–190, descriptive sermon on the inauguration of the Palatine Church, Our Lady of the Pharos, c. 864. C. Mango and J. Parker, "A Twelfth Century Description of St. Sophia," DumbOaksP 14 (1960) 233–245.

Studies of sources. V. Grecu, "Byzantinische Handbücher der Kirchenmalerei," *Byzantion* 9 (1934) 675–701. A. Grabar, "Le Témoinage d'une hymne syriaque sur l'architecture de la cathédrale d'Édesse au VIᵉ siècle et sur la symbolique de l'édifice chrétien," *Cahiers archéologiques* 2 (1947) 41–67. R. Janin, *Constantinople byzantine* (Paris 1950) xv–xxvii. J. Schlosser, *La letteratura artistica,* tr. F. Rossi (3d ed. Florence 1964) 15–25, 709– . A. Frolow, "Deux églises byzantines d'après des sermons peu connus de Léon VI, le Sage," *Études byzantines* 3 (1945) 43–91.

Literature. Encyclopedias. G. Millet, "L'Art byzantin," in A. Michel, *Histoire de l'art,* 8 v. in 17 (Paris 1905–29) 1.1:127–301. *Larousse Encyclopedia of Byzantine and Medieval Art,* ed. R. Huyghe (New York 1963). K. Wessel, ed., *Reallexikon zur byzantinischen Kunst* (Stuttgart 1963–).

Journals and bibliographical studies. *Byzantinische Zeitschrift* (Leipzig-Munich 1892–). *Byzantion* (Brussels 1924–). *Cahiers archéologiques* (Paris 1945–). *Corso di cultura sull' arte ravennate e bizantina* (Ravenna 1955–). *Jahrbuch der österreichischen byzantinischen Gesellschaft* (Vienna 1951–). *Seminarium Kondakovianum,* 11 v. (Prague 1927–40). F. Dölger and A. M. Schneider, *Byzanz* (Bern 1952), critical survey of bibliog. 1938–50. *Kunstgeschichtliche Anzeigen,* ed. K. M. Swoboda, NS 5 (Graz-Cologne 1961–62), critical survey of Byzantine bibliog. 1950–61.

Collections. G. Mendel, *Catalogue des sculptures grecques, romaines, et byzantines,* v.2 (Constantinople 1914). M. H. Longhurst, *Catalogue of Carvings in Ivory,* v.1 (London 1927). H. Schlunk, *Frühchristlich-byzantinische Sammlung* (Berlin 1938). N. Firatli, *A Short Guide to the Byzantine Works of Art in the Archaeological Museum of Istanbul* (Istanbul 1955). G. Soteriou, *Guide du Musée byzantin d'Athènes* (Athens 1955). M. C. Ross, *Catalogue of the Byzantine and Early Medieval Antiquities in the Dumbarton Oaks Collection,* 2 v. (Washington 1962–65).

Exhibition catalogues. *Early Christian and Byzantine Art* (Walters Art Gallery; Baltimore 1947). G. Muzzioli, *Mostra storica nazionale della miniatura* (2d ed. Florence 1954). J. Porcher, *Byzance et la France médiévale* (Paris 1958). D. T. Rice, *Masterpieces of Byzantine Art* (Edinburgh 1958). *Byzantine Art, an European Art* (2d ed. Athens 1964), large and comprehensive exhibition; full bibliog. keyed to objects; essays by leading scholars.

General. D. V. Ainalov, *The Hellenistic Origins of Byzantine Art,* tr. E. and S. Sobolevitch (New Brunswick, N.J. 1961). O. M. Dalton, *Byzantine Art and Archaeology* (Oxford 1911; repr. New York 1961). O. K. Wulff, *Altchristliche und byzantinische Kunst,* 2 v. (Berlin 1914–18; Bibliographisch-kritischer Nachtrag, Potsdam 1935). A. Grabar, *L'Empereur dans l'art byzantin* (Paris 1936); "Plotin et les origines d'esthétique médiévale," *Cahiers archéologiques* 1 (1945) 15–34; *Martyrium,* 2 v. and portfolio (Paris 1943–46); *Byzance: L'Art byzantin du Moyen Âge* (Paris 1963). W. Koehler, "Byzantine Art in the West," DumbOaksP 1 (1940) 60–87. H. Bloch, "Monte Cassino, Byzantium and the West in the Earlier Middle Ages," *ibid.* 3 (1946) 163–224. K. Weitzmann, *Greek Mythology in Byzantine Art* (Princeton 1951). E. Kitzinger, *Byzantine Art in the Period between Justinian and Iconoclasm* (Munich 1958); "The Hellenistic Heritage in Byzantine Art," DumbOaksP 17 (1963) 95–115. D. T. Rice, *The Art of Byzantium* (New York 1959), photos by M. Hirmer. J. Beckwith, *The Art of Constantinople* (London 1961). C. Mango, "Antique Statuary and the Byzantine Beholder," DumbOaksP 17 (1963) 53–75. G. Matthew, *Byzantine Aesthetics* (New York 1964).

Painting and mosaic. E. Diez and O. Demus, *Byzantine Mosaics in Greece: Hosios Lucas and Daphni* (Cambridge, Mass. 1931). C. Diehl, *La Peinture byzantine* (Paris 1933). A. Frolow, "La Mosaïque murale byzantine," *Byzantinoslavica* 12 (1951) 180–209. G. and M. Soteriou, *The Basilica of St. Demetrios, Thessalonica,* 2 v. (Athens 1952), in Gr. T. Whittemore, *Mosaics of Hagia Sophia at Istanbul,* 4 reports (Byzantine Institute of America; Oxford 1933–52). O. Demus, *Byzantine Mosaic Decoration* (London 1948); *The Mosaics of Norman Sicily* (London 1950). G. Mathew, *Byzantine Painting* (London 1950). K. WEITZMANN, *The Fresco Cycle of S. Maria di Castelseprio* (Princeton 1951), reviewed by M. SCHAPIRO, Art Bull 34 (1952) 147–163. C. R. MOREY, "Castelseprio and the Byzantine 'Renaissance'," *ibid.* 173–201. A. GRABAR, *Byzantine Painting,* tr. S. GILBERT (Skira; New York 1953). S. PELEKANIDIS, *Kastoria* (Thessalonica 1953–   ), Byzantine wall paintings; title and pref. in Gr. P. UNDERWOOD, "The Deësis Mosaic in Kariye Camii," in *Late Classical and Medieval Studies in Honor of Albert Mathias Friend, Jr.,* ed. K. WEITZMANN (Princeton 1955) 254–260; "Preliminary Reports on the Restoration of the Frescoes in the Kariye Camii . . .," DumbOaksP 9–10 (1955–56) 253–288; 11 (1957) 173–220; 12 (1958) 235–265; 13 (1959) 185–212; "Paleologan Narrative Style and an Italianate Fresco of the 15th Century in the Kariye Camii," in *Studies in the History of Art, Dedicated to William E. Suida on His Eightieth Birthday* (London 1959) 1–9. O. DEMUS, *Die Entstehung des Paläologenstils in der Malerei* (Munich 1958). P. VERZONE et al., EncWA 2:752–840. D. OATES, "A Summary Report on the Excavations of the Byzantine Institute in the Kariye Camii," DumbOaksP 14 (1960) 223–231. E. KITZINGER, *The Mosaics of Monreale* (Palermo 1960). A. GRABAR and M. CHATZIDAKIS, *Greece: Byzantine Mosaics* (UNESCO; Greenwich, Conn. 1960). C. MANGO, *Materials for the Study of the Mosaics of St. Sophia at Istanbul* (DumbOaks Studies 8; 1962). A. XYNGOPOULOS, *The Frescoes of St. Nicholas Orphanos, Thessalonica* (Athens 1964). Gr. with Fr. summary. P. UNDERWOOD, ed., *The Kariye Djami,* 4 v. (New York 1966).

Manuscript illumination. N. P. KONDAKOV, *Histoire de l'art byzantin considéré principalement dans les miniatures,* tr. F. TRAWINSKI, 2 v. in 1 (Paris 1886–91). G. MILLET, *Recherches sur l'iconographie de l'Évangile aux XIVe, XVe et XVIe siècles* (Paris 1916). J. EBERSOLT, *La Miniature byzantine* (Paris 1926). H. GERSTINGER, *Die griechische Buchmalerei* (Vienna 1926). A. M. FRIEND, "The Portraits of the Evangelists in Greek and Latin MSS," *Art Studies* 5 (1927) 115–147. H. A. OMONT, *Miniatures des plus anciens manuscrits grecs de la Bibliothèque Nationale du VIe au XIVe siècle* (Paris 1929). C. R. MOREY, "Notes on East Christian Miniatures," ArtBull 11 (1929) 4–103. K. WEITZMANN, *Die byzantinische Buchmalerei des 9. und 10. Jahrhunderts* (Berlin 1935). P. BUBERL, *Die byzantinischen Handschriften: Der Wiener Dioskurides und die Wiener Genesis* (Leipzig 1937). H. BUCHTHAL, *The Miniatures of the Paris Psalter* (London 1939). E. T. DEWALD, *Illustrations in the Manuscripts of the Septuagint,* v.3. *Psalms and Odes,* pt.1, *Codex Vaticanus Graecus 1927,* pt.2, *Codex Vaticanus Graecus 752* (Princeton 1941–42). K. WEITZMANN, *Illustrations in Roll and Codex* (Princeton 1947). A. GRABAR, *Les Peintures de l'Évangéliaire de Sinope* (Paris 1948). O. PÄCHT, *Byzantine Illumination* (Oxford 1952). R. BIANCHI BANDINELLI, *Hellenistic-Byzantine Miniatures of the Iliad* (Olten 1955). C. CECCHELLI, ed., *The Rabbula Gospels* (Olten 1959). E. WELLESZ, *The Vienna Genesis* (New York 1960). S. DER NERSESSIAN, "The Illustrations of the Homilies of Gregory Nazianzus: Paris Gr. 510," DumbOaksP 16 (1962) 195–228. I. SEVCENKO, *The Illuminators of the Menologium of Basil II,* *ibid.* 243–276.

Sculpture and the minor arts. J. EBERSOLT, *Les Arts somptuaires de Byzance* (Paris 1923). L. MATZULEVICH, *Byzantinische Antike* (Berlin 1929). R. DELBRUECK, *Die Consulardiptychen und verwandten Denkmäler* (Berlin 1929). A. GOLDSCHMIDT and K. WEITZMANN, *Die byzantinischen Elfenbeinskulpturen des 10.-13. Jahrhunderts,* 2 v. (Berlin 1930–34). G. BRUNS, *Der Obelisk und seine Basis auf dem Hippodrom zu Konstantinople* (Istanbul 1935). L. BRÉHIER, *La Sculpture et les arts mineurs byzantins* (Paris 1936). C. CECCHELLI, *La Cattedra di Massimiano ed altri avori romano-orientali,* 7 v, (Rome 1936–44). J. KOLLWITZ, *Die oströmische Plastik der theodosianischen Zeit* (Berlin 1941). A. GRABAR, "Le Succès des arts orientaux à la cour byzantine sous les Macédoniens," *Münchner Jahrbuch der Bildenden Kunst* 2 (1951); *Les Ampoules de Terre Sainte* (Paris 1958); *Sculptures byzantines de Constantinople, IVe–Xe siècle* (Paris 1963). M. SCHAPIRO, "The Joseph Scenes of the Maximianus Throne in Ravenna," *Gazette des beaux-arts* 40 (1952) 27–38, 72–76. W. F. VOLBACH, *Elfenbeinarbeiten der Spätantike und des frühen Mittelalters* (2d ed. Mainz 1952). E. KITZINGER, "A Marble Relief of the Theodosian Period," DumbOaksP 14 (1960) 17–42. G. BECATTI, *La colonna coclide istoriata* (Rome 1960), column of Theodosius, 63–150; column of Arcadius, 151–288. E. C. DODD, *Byzantine Silver Stamps* (Washington 1961).

Image-Icon-Iconoclasm. D. T. RICE, *The Icons of Cyprus* (London 1937). G. B. LADNER, "The Concept of the Image in the Greek Fathers and the Byzantine Iconoclastic Controversy,"

DumbOaksP 7 (1953) 1–34. E. KITZINGER, "The Cult of Images in the Age before Iconoclasm," *ibid.* 8 (1954) 83–150; "On Some Icons of the 7th Century" in *Late Classical and Medieval Studies in Honor of Albert Mathias Friend, Jr.,* op.cit. 132–150. W. FELICETTI LIEBENFELS, *Geschichte der byzantinischen Ikonenmalerei* (Lausanne 1956). G. and M. SOTERIOU, *Eikones tēs Monēs Sina,* 2 v. (Athens 1956–58), Gr. text with Fr. résumé. A. GRABAR, *L'Iconoclasme byzantin: Dossier archéologique* (Paris 1957). H. SKROBUCHA, *Von Geist und Gestalt der Ikonen* (Recklinghausen 1961). W. NYSSEN, *Das Zeugnis des Bildes im frühen Byzanz* (Freiburg 1962). R. LANGE, *Die byzantinische Reliefikone* (Recklinghausen 1964). **Illustration credits:** Figs. 1, 3, 7, 8, 10 and 12, Hirmer Verlag München. Fig. 2, Courtesy of the Dumbarton Oaks Collections. Figs. 4 and 15, Alinari-Art Reference Bureau. Fig. 5, The Metropolitan Museum of Art, Gift of J. Pierpont Morgan, 1917. Figs. 6, 16, and 17, Courtesy of the Byzantine Institute. Fig. 9, Courtesy of the Victoria and Albert Museum, London. Fig. 11, Biblioteca Apostolica Vaticana. Figs. 13 and 14, Josephine Powell, Rome.

[W. C. LOERKE]

BYZANTINE CHURCH, HISTORY OF

The term Byzantine Church, as used here, designates exclusively the official Church of and in the Byzantine Empire from the death of Justinian (565) to the fall of Constantinople (1453), not its Slavic offshoots or the Melchite Patriarchates of Antioch and Alexandria. The key to its history is the idea of the Christian World State, which may best be described as a Christianization of the *pax romana*. Rome, in conquering the Mediterranean basin, had brought peace, law, and prosperity to its variegated peoples and attempted to weld them into one by worship of the ruler, an age-old formula. In the new Rome of Constantine the Great, Christ, the Prince of Peace, was to unite all mankind in the bond of charity, and to crush all resistance and all discord. Wherever Eternal Rome went, Christianity was to go hand in hand until all the world was gained to Christ. In the practical sphere this conception had a tendency to make the emperor the superior and to degrade the Church to an instrument of imperial policy. In any case, State and Church were never separate in Byzantium; an ecclesiastical difference became a political division, and vice versa. A state that made itself independent of Byzantium had necessarily to make its Church autonomous. This mentality dominated all Europe for many centuries.

This article is divided as follows: from the death of Justinian I (565) to the accession of Leo III the Iconoclast (717); from the accession of Leo III to the Feast of Orthodoxy (717–843); from the Feast of Orthodoxy to the death of Michael Cerularius (843–1059); from the death of Michael Cerularius to the death of Michael VIII Palaeologus (1059–1282); and from the death of Michael VIII to the fall of Constantinople (1282–1453).

FROM JUSTINIAN I TO ACCESSION OF LEO III
565–717

With the death of Justinian I (565), medieval Byzantium rapidly assumed its characteristic features. The Jacobite Monophysites consolidated their hold on Egypt and Syria and began to break away from the empire (*see* MONOPHYSITISM). The papacy and Italy were thrown more and more on their own resources. The Slavs were settling down in the Balkans. Efforts to win back the Monophysites of Egypt and Syria by a compromise creed had begun with Zeno's *Henoticon, and they were continued under Heraclius (610–641)

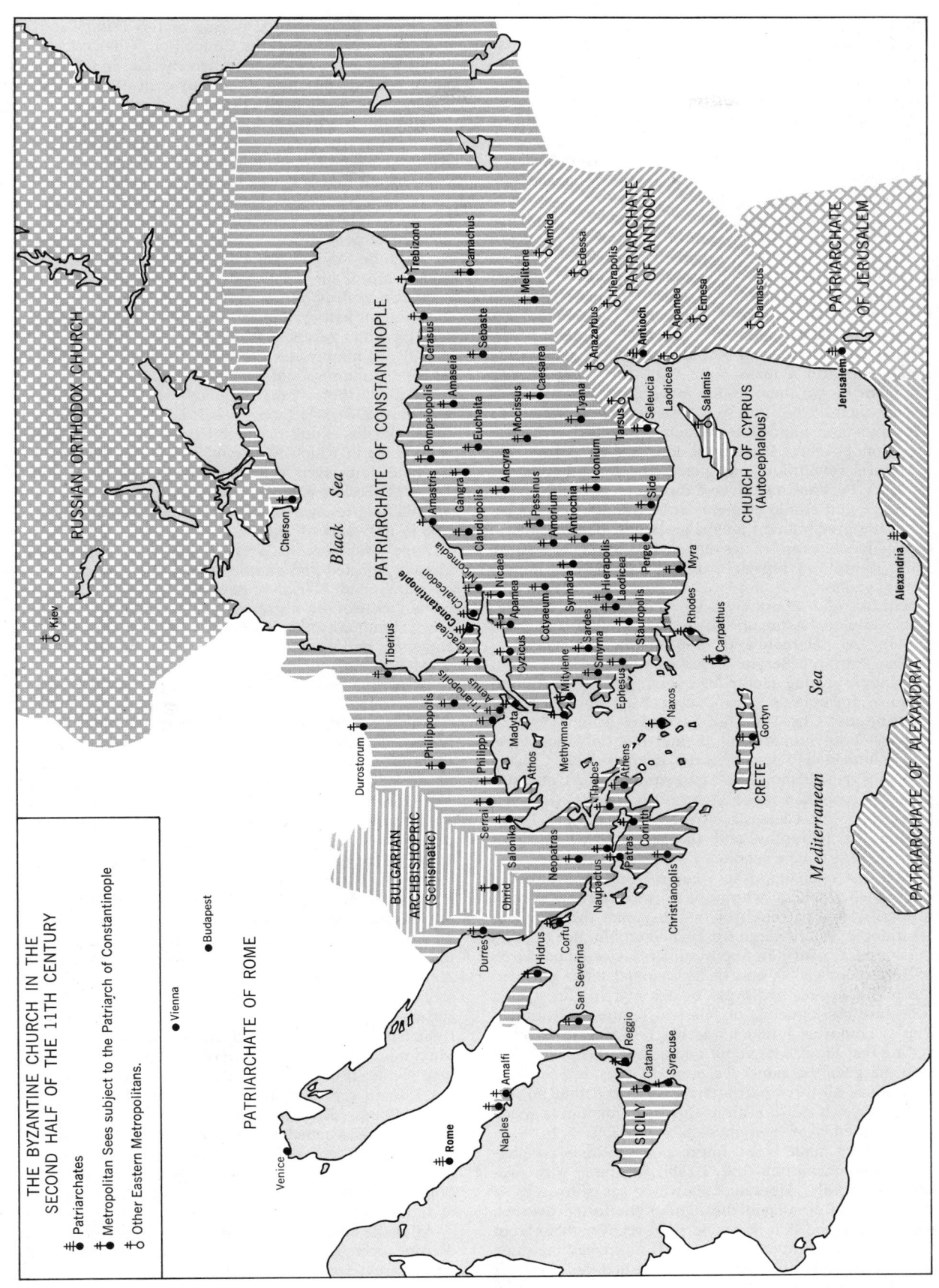

THE BYZANTINE CHURCH IN THE
SECOND HALF OF THE 11TH CENTURY

⊞ Patriarchates

☩ Metropolitan Sees subject to the Patriarch of Constantinople.

☩ Other Eastern Metropolitans.

● Vienna   ● Budapest

PATRIARCHATE OF ROME

RUSSIAN ORTHODOX CHURCH

☩ Kiev

Black Sea

☩ Cherson

PATRIARCHATE OF CONSTANTINOPLE

☩ Trebizond   ● Camachus   ○ Amida
● Cerasus   ● Melitene   ○ Edessa   PATRIARCHATE OF ANTIOCH   PATRIARCHATE OF JERUSALEM
● Amaseia   ● Sebaste   ○ Hierapolis
● Pompeiopolis   ● Caesarea   ● Anazarbus   ● Antioch   ○ Damascus
● Euchaita   ● Mocissus   ● Tyana   ● Laodicea   ○ Apamea   ○ Emesa
● Amastris   ● Ancyra   ● Tarsus   ● Seleucia   ☩ Jerusalem
● Gangra   ● Pessinus   ● Iconium   ○ Salamis
● Claudiopolis   ● Amorium   CHURCH OF CYPRUS
● Tiberius   Nicomedia   ● Antiochia   (Autocephalous)   ● Alexandria
● Nicaea   ● Hierapolis   ● Side
Heraclea   Chalcedon   ● Apamea   ● Laodicea   ● Myra
Constantinople   ● Cyzicus   ● Synnada   ● Perge   ● Rhodes   ● Carpathus
● Cotyaeum   ● Sardes   Stauropolis   Mediterranean
Tiberius   ● Mytilene   ● Smyrna   ● Ephesus   Sea
Tiranopolis   Madyta   ● Naxos   CRETE   Gortyn
☩ Philippopolis   ● Methymna   ● Thebes   Gortyn
☩ Durostorum   Athos   ● Athens
☩ Philippi   ● Corinth
BULGARIAN   ☩ Serrai   ☩ Neopatras   ☩ Patras   Christianopolis
ARCHBISHOPRIC   Salonika   Naupactus
(Schismatic)   ☩ Ohrid   ● Christianopolis
☩ Durrës   ☩ Hidrus   ☩ Corfu
☩ San Severina   SICILY
☩ Reggio
● Rome   ☩ Catana   ☩ Syracuse
Venice   Naples   Amalfi   PATRIARCHATE OF ALEXANDRIA

and Constans II (641–668). The last phase consisted of the formula of one will and one operation in Christ, devised by Patriarch Sergius I (610–638), but condemned by the Sixth General Council (680–681), and briefly revived by Emperor Philippicus (711–713).

Monophysitism, Monoenergism, and Monothelitism. The reorganization of the Jacobite Church occurred on the eve of the Persian and Arab invasions and shaped the whole course of Christianity in the Near East. At the death of Justinian, the Monophysites were thoroughly demoralized by persecution and their own disagreements; they had split into more than 20 sects. But during the years of toleration granted by Emperors Tiberius I (578–582) and *Maurice (582–602), they reconstituted their hierarchy; and by the end of the 6th century, Syria and Egypt were overwhelmingly Monophysite. The Monophysites had never thought of defecting from Byzantium before, but savage persecution under Emperor Phocas (602–610)—in contrast with the favor shown them by the invading Persians—disaffected them. The Persians drove out the orthodox Melchites and handed over their sees and parishes to the Monophysites. During the long enemy occupation, a cultural revolution took place. By depopulating the land, the Persians had given a mortal blow to the Greek language and ethnic element; and Aramaic rapidly became the predominant language. A new national literature of Jacobite tendencies replaced the Hellenic culture. Later, Syria and especially Egypt went over willingly to the Arabs.

Sergius and Heraclius. The cooperation of anti-Chalcedonian *Armenia was indispensable to the grand strategy of *Heraclius (610–641) for the defeat of Persia. Patriarch Sergius I, practically coruler of Constantinople during Heraclius's reign, proposed a compromise formula by introducing Monoenergism, the doctrine that Christ did not have two distinct types of activity, both human and divine, but only one type, divine-human. He won a recruit in the sincere Chalcedonian Cyrus, Bishop of Phasis, south of the Caucasus. By 633 Cyrus had made numerous converts to Monoenergism in cis-Caucasia, Armenia, Syria, and Egypt among the hierarchy and the monasteries, but not among the ordinary people.

The first open opposition came from Sophronius, a monk of Bethlehem, who went to Alexandria to protest to Cyrus, now patriarch of that city, and then to Constantinople, where Sergius prevailed on him not to press the matter any further. Sophronius was elected patriarch of Jerusalem (634) and in his synodal letter affirmed the two energies, two types of activity, in Christ as a necessary consequence of His two natures. Meantime, Pope *Honorius I had made his response to Sergius, stating that the debate about one or two energies should stop; he gave the same decision to Cyrus and Sophronius. Since all three patriarchs now agreed that no one should discuss the question, this agreement was made law in an edict of Heraclius (634 or 635).

This edict made a bad impression on the Monophysites, and meantime the Arab conquest was proceeding rapidly. Heraclius, however, as shown by a proclamation circulated throughout the lost provinces, took for granted that he would soon recover them from the Arabs, and Emperor Constans II nourished the same hope. Consequently Heraclius published his *Ecthesis* (638), or exposition of the faith, a creed elaborated by

Sergius. It presented the dogma of the Trinity and Incarnation according to the Council of *Chalcedon, prohibited the expression one or two energies in Christ, and affirmed one sole will, without any confusion of the two natures, for each nature kept its properties in a sole person, the Word made Flesh. *Monothelitism was thus substituted for Monoenergism. The expression "one will" was taken from the letter of Honorius, who, however, meant that in Christ there was no conflict between reason and the flesh. This doctrine was generally accepted by the Eastern Church and the Melchite patriarchs, but not by Coptic Egypt. It was condemned by Pope *John IV, and Heraclius wrote to him disclaiming authorship of the edict.

Maximus the Confessor. After the death of Heraclius, the religious battleground shifted to Africa, where Syrian and Egyptian refugees from both Persians and Arabs, mostly Monophysites, were proselytizing zealously. There *Maximus Confessor first took up the defense of orthodoxy; there, too, Sergius's successor, Patriarch Pyrrhus (638–641; January to June 654) had gone into exile after his expulsion from Constantinople. A debate took place in which Maximus convinced Pyrrhus, and the latter journeyed to Rome to make his submission to Pope *Theodore I. This abjuration of error by a patriarch in the presence of the pope had a tremendous reaction in Italy and Africa.

Pope Theodore in a letter to Constantinople had already rejected and anathematized the *Ecthesis.* Now, he summoned Patriarch Paul II (641–653) to abjure Monothelitism; on his refusal, he excommunicated him. He excommunicated also Pyrrhus, who, taking refuge in Ravenna, had written to the Pope that he had returned to Monothelitism.

Emperor Constans II, to avoid a rupture with Rome and to settle the religious difficulties once for all, took down the *Ecthesis* from the place in which it had remained publicly posted, and issued his *Typos* or Decree (647, not 648), which forbade all discussion of one or two energies or of two wills. Pope *Martin I, Theodore's successor, took action on the *Typos* by summoning a council at the Lateran (649), which condemned both the *Ecthesis* and the *Typos* and professed the faith in two wills and two operations corresponding to the two natures in Christ.

Constans II arrested the Pope, tried him for treason at Constantinople, and exiled him to Cherson, where he died of the cruelties and privation to which he was subjected. Maximus Confessor and two of his companions, Anastasius the Disciple and Anastasius the papal representative, were likewise arrested in Rome (653) and suffered severe hardship and cruelties for 9 years. Their right hands were lopped off and their tongues cut out. Maximus Confessor and Anastasius the Disciple both died while in exile in Lazica, cis-Caucasia, in 662; the Roman representative survived until 666. Finally, under Popes *Eugene I and *Vitalian, a tacit understanding was reached; the latter sent his synodical letter to the patriarch and abstained from any condemnation of the *Typos,* while Constans II presented the Pope with rich gifts and a perfectly orthodox confession of faith.

After the courageous stand of Maximus Confessor, a division occurred in the Byzantine Church. He awakened a great many to a realization of the importance of the issue and the true solution, and henceforward discord persisted among the clergy between the followers of Maximus and the Monothelites. The latter took the offensive when Patriarch Theodore (677–679; 686–687) asked the Emperor for authorization to strike the name of Pope Vitalian from the diptychs. The Pope had died in 672, and neither of his successors had been added to the diptychs. Constantine IV (668–685), recognizing that Syria and Egypt were lost to the empire, not only rejected this suggestion but determined to effect a final settlement of the question by calling the Council of Constantinople III in conjunction with Popes *Donus, *Agatho, and *Leo II. The council condemned Monoenergism and Monothelitism, but in the process listed Pope Honorius among the heretics condemned.

Quinisext Synod. Justinian II summoned what is known as the *Quinisext Synod to make general laws for the Church, since the Fifth and Sixth General Councils had dealt with dogma, not with discipline. It is acknowledged as ecumenical by the Greeks, but not by the Latins. Its legislation, which is basic to Greek Canon Law, is characterized by open hostility to particular customs of both the Roman and Armenian Churches. Pope *Sergius I (687–701) repudiated the synod, and Justinian's effort to arrest him was balked by the militia of Ravenna. The Emperor then appealed to Pope *John VII and, as he was anxious to have papal approval, finally invited Pope *Constantine to Constantinople. The sources are vague as to the details of the ultimate settlement worked out principally with the future Pope Gregory II. Monothelitism was briefly revived by Emperor Philippicus (711–713). But Pope Constantine rejected his heresy and would not recognize him.

Other Issues. Medieval Italy began to emerge after Justinian's death. The popes still regarded themselves as subjects of the empire. Gregory I (590–604) wanted a truce made with the Lombards to spare the people useless suffering, but he could not induce Emperor Maurice to accept this proposal. To save Rome in 593, Gregory concluded an armistice himself, for which he received an angry rebuke from Maurice. This episode is typical of the clash of policy that ultimately caused the total secession of the papacy. The Holy See and the Italian population became gradually more independent of Byzantium. The growth of national sentiment is dramatically high-lighted by the fact (already noted) that, while Emperor Constans II did violence to Pope Martin in 653, Justinian II was prevented by a mutiny of the Ravenna militia from arresting Pope Sergius for disapproving of the Quinisext Synod (692).

Friction between Pope Gregory and Maurice developed over the title, Ecumenical Patriarch, regularly used in addressing Patriarch *John IV the Faster. Pope *Pelagius II had objected strongly and ordered his representative in Constantinople not to concelebrate the liturgy with John until the practice was abandoned. Gregory also carried on a tireless campaign against the title. Although he did not consider the issue important enough to make a break over it, he was displeased when Maurice refused to forbid the title. Later, Emperor Phocas did forbid it, but without permanent result. Scholars differ as to the significance of the issue, but it remained a bone of contention between Rome and Constantinople for centuries.

Another difference between Maurice and the Pope occurred over an imperial law of 592 forbidding public functionaries to accept ecclesiastical office and barring municipal officials and soldiers from entering a monastery. The issue was ultimately resolved by a compromise: municipal officials could not become monks until they had quit themselves of their obligations, and soldiers would have to serve 3 years.

The primacy of Rome is taken for granted throughout this period in both dogma and discipline. When Gregory, Patriarch of Antioch, was tried at Constantinople by the synod attended by the five patriarchs or their legates, the acts were forwarded to Pope *Pelagius II for his approval as a matter of course. The papacy remained the center of the whole controversy over Monoenergism and Monothelitism. Maximus Confessor ranks among the great champions of the primacy. For him, Rome is the center of the true faith; it has dominion over all the Churches of God that are in the whole world, and the gates of hell do not prevail against it; and he denies that the emperor has any role in the definition of a dogma.

Gregory the Great exercised veritable supervision over the patriarchates; he censured both Alexandria and Jerusalem for tolerating *simony. He rebuked Patriarch John the Faster for mistreating two priests accused of heresy. He was consulted by Kyrion of Georgia, cis-Caucasia, on the validity of Nestorian baptism. In 571 John of Jerusalem kept Abas, the Catholicus of Albania, east of Georgia, from becoming a Monophysite by writing him that Rome repudiated Monophysitism. Nevertheless, Rome does not seem to have had much influence on the Byzantine hierarchy.

FROM ACCESSION OF LEO III TO FEAST OF ORTHODOXY 717–843

At the beginning of his reign, Emperor *Leo III the Iconoclast rendered a great service to Christendom. He saved it from being overrun by Islam, repulsing a massive attack of the Arabs from the walls of Constantinople. But, convinced that he was both priest and king, head of both State and Church, he thought it his duty to cleanse the Church of images, thus setting off the iconoclast or image controversy.

This had a decisive influence on the history of Europe and of the Byzantine Church itself. It occasioned the division between eastern and western Europe that exists to the present day. The Byzantine Empire thought of itself as the Roman Empire; of its rulers as the legitimate successors of Augustus; of its citizens as Romans, *Romaioi;* in its own eyes it was the universal empire. The iconoclast controversy precipitated the secession of the papacy and the ultimate creation of the Western Roman Empire of Germanic kings with its direct challenge to Byzantine supremacy. Whether the political division also caused the religious schism is debatable, but Leo III's transfer of large territories from the Patriarchate of Rome to that of Constantinople gave rise to great bitterness between the sees. *Iconoclasm brought about a profound change in the Byzantine Church itself by impelling the monks into ecclesiastical leadership.

Iconoclasm. The iconoclast conflict lasted well over a century (726–843). An attack on the veneration of images was bound to cause bitter strife. *Icons, a special type of religious picture, had become universal in Byzantium not only in churches but also in public places and in widespread private use. Contemporary sources blamed the origin of iconoclasm on Moslem influence, specifically dating it from a decree issued by Caliph

Yezid II in 723 (some modern scholars ascribe it to Omar II in 720); the decree ordered the destruction of icons in all Christian churches. Some historians, however, point to a tradition against images from the 4th century and to the sentiment against them in Asia Minor, where several bishops, including the heresiarch Constantine of Nacolea in Phrygia, were iconoclasts even before Leo III. Other historians combine both the ancient and the modern views. Still others hold that there is no satisfactory explanation of the origin of iconoclasm. The iconoclasts themselves constantly cited the Old Testament prohibition of images.

The first period of iconoclasm (726–780) culminated in the Synod of Hieria, which was held in 754 and made iconoclasm the state religion. Leo III (717–741) opened his campaign in 726; whether by edict or not is disputed. He was opposed by Patriarch Germanus I and Pope *Gregory II; his most famous antagonist, *John Damascene, who developed the orthodox theology of images, lived in the Caliphate beyond his reach. However, Leo III won over enough of the hierarchy to obtain a synodal decision against images, deposed Germanus, and proceeded to systematic violence against both icons and their venerators.

His successor, Constantine V (741–775), was an even more rabid iconoclast; he determined to get the backing of a general council, recruited the soldiery from iconoclastic Asia Minor, filled the episcopal sees with iconoclasts, and obtained a decree that the cult of icons was idolatry from a synod of 338 bishops held at Hieria (754), which called itself the Seventh General Council. It condemned all who made, honored, or maintained an icon in church or at home. Empowered by this conciliar decree, Constantine waged a fanatical war, not only against icons, but against relics and the intercession of the Blessed Virgin Mary and the saints. As the episcopate, almost to a man, proved false to its trust, the faithful turned to the monks, who offered heroic resistance. Their first leader, St. Stephen, was martyred.

Ecumenical Council of Nicaea II. Leo IV (775–780), in his brief and milder reign, temporized on the question. Irene, widow of Leo IV and regent for the 10-year-old Constantine VI, favored icons. She invited Pope Adrian I and the Eastern patriarchs to send representatives to a general council, and *Tarasius was made patriarch of Constantinople. The Seventh General Council, *Nicaea II, was the last acknowledged by the Byzantine Church. It met in 787, anathematized the enemies of icons, and clarified the theology of the cult of the Blessed Virgin, the saints, and their pictures.

Pope Adrian had assumed that the council would return to Rome the territory taken from it by Leo III, namely, Sicily, South Italy, and the Balkans. But Tarasius had simply suppressed this statement in the Greek translation of the Pope's letter to the council. This act occasioned lasting bitterness between the Sees of Rome and Constantinople. Pope Gregory I had conditioned his allegiance to Byzantium on its defense of the papacy and Italy. But when iconoclasts attacked and confiscated papal estates, Pope Stephen II, presumably, felt himself no longer bound to the Byzantine Empire, and he made an alliance with Pepin and the Franks. To Byzantium his action was an enormity. The loss of Rome, mother city of the empire, must have been a profound shock. Whether all this caused Constanti-

nople's refusal at the council to restore Illyricum, South Italy, and Sicily, there is no way of knowing, but Pope Adrian resented the failure to do so.

The acts of this council seem never to have been submitted to Rome for approval. Tarasius had sent the Pope a summary of events, and 7 years later (784) the Pope had still not answered. The Franks themselves did not believe in the cult of religious pictures; they regarded them as purely educational. Moreover, they had received a badly garbled Latin translation of the acts, which at times conveyed the opposite of the original meaning. They resented, too, the arrogance of the Byzantines in giving the name of a general council of the Church to a local Greek synod with no representatives of the West present. They reacted violently and rejected the definition of the council in favor of their own doctrine.

*Charlemagne demanded that Pope Adrian repudiate the council, but the Pope, who had received an authentic copy of the acts, easily answered all objections and stanchly defended the cult of icons. However, he was so dissatisfied over the Byzantine retention of papal possessions that he offered, if Charlemagne wished, to inform the Eastern Emperor that he would hold back approval of the council until restitution was made, and, if that were not done, he would declare the Emperor heretical for persisting in this error. Whether such a step was ever taken is not known.

The Filioque and the Studite Monks. The term *filioque first became a controversial issue at the council, which used the Nicene Creed for its profession of faith, recording it in the minutes. The Eastern Church had kept the original wording, without the filioque, which is an addition and was first made in the West in Spain. The Franks, eager to prove that the Greeks were heretics, accused them of holding that the Holy Spirit proceeds from the Father alone. Pope Adrian, by quoting statements from the great Fathers, showed that the omission of filioque did not necessarily have any such implication.

Another epoch-making change took place at the Seventh General Council with the entrance of the monks into the government of the Church in the East. Monastic figures had taken over the leadership of the faithful during the iconoclast controversy in default of the episcopate, and this new role was now organized and consolidated in the Studite reform, to which most of the monks adhered. The leading monastery was that of the *Studion in Constantinople, and the leading spirit was its abbot, St. *Theodore, who strove to imbue not only the Church but also the state, layman as well as cleric, with the highest Christian ideals. To attain this end, he took the diametrically opposite pole to the iconoclastic rulers' claim to both priesthood and royalty. Theodore held that the Church had to enjoy absolute independence in both dogma and discipline. Against the whole Byzantine theory and practice, he maintained that the civil ruler had no competence in matters of faith, morals, or ecclesiastical government and law. The only true head of the Church was the pope, and the papal primacy was the best safeguard of the Church's freedom. To purify society he insisted upon the strict and impartial application of the ecclesiastical canons without respect of persons.

The reform was soon put to the test in the *Moechian controversy. In 795 Emperor Constantine VI (780–

797) made an adulterous marriage with his mistress that was blessed by Joseph, an abbot and high official of the patriarchate, and Patriarch Tarasius permitted the guilty pair to receive Holy Communion as if nothing improper had been done. The Studites condemned the Emperor and broke off communion with the patriarch. Thus began the Moechian controversy, which persisted until the reign of Michael I (811–813).

Attitude toward the West. The coronation of Charlemagne on Christmas Day, 800, caused a profound change in the Byzantine attitude toward the West. Whatever the intention of Charlemagne and Pope Leo III, it was taken for granted within a few years that the Western Roman Empire represented the true heir of Eternal Rome, that it was the Universal Empire destined to conquer and unify the world. Byzantium was but a Greek state doomed ultimately to be absorbed into the providential world state. Henceforward, the Eastern empire regarded every advance of the Latin Church as an advance of the Frankish kingdom.

Even before the coronation, had any change taken place in the attitude of the Eastern Church when the papacy had seceded from the empire? Some historians believe that in translating Adrian's letter for the Seventh General Council, Tarasius had suppressed every suggestion of the primacy of Rome and even of the primacy of Peter. Others maintain that the patriarch merely substituted older usage, by referring to both Peter and Paul as founders of the Roman See, and not Peter alone, as a precaution. The Byzantines were not sure what the Romans meant by the newer expressions.

There is no doubt about the stand of Emperor Nicephorus I (802–811), Irene's successor; he forbade Patriarch *Nicephorus I (806–815) to notify the Pope of his accession because, as the Emperor said explicitly, the Pope had broken away from the true Church. On the other hand, the patriarch did write to Rome of his own accord in the succeeding reign. His letter seems equivocal on the primacy, though he firmly supported it 6 years later; bitter experience had taught him the necessity of some independent check on the Emperor's interference in Church affairs.

Revival of Iconoclasm. Although iconoclasm had been violently suppressed by Irene, it continued strong in the empire. Most of its adherents were firmly convinced that the military calamities of the times were the direct result of its suppression. A representative of this party, Leo V (813–820), next gained the throne and decided to bring back iconoclasm. Patriarch Nicephorus called a synod at Constantinople. When a debate was proposed between both sides in the presence of the Emperor, *Theodore the Studite denied absolutely the competence of the civil ruler in religious matters and asserted the exclusive authority of the Church in dogma and discipline. The Emperor had to dissolve the synod. He deposed Nicephorus, who resigned, and had a new patriarch chosen, Theodotos Melissenos Cassiteras (815–821).

Cassiteras called a synod that annulled the Seventh General Council and reinstated the Synod of Hieria and its decrees. Violent persecution raged once more; orthodox metropolitans, bishops, abbots, and monks were jailed, exiled, and subjected to great hardships. St. Theodore was deported to Smyrna. The savagery continued for 5 years until Leo's death. Though many

defected, a goodly number remained faithful, so that the Byzantine Church could afterward celebrate its heroic resistance.

Michael II (820–829) granted a general amnesty but refused to reestablish the cult of icons, for at heart he was an iconoclast. He proposed a council in which both friends and foes of images would exchange their views, but the orthodox bishops and abbots declared it impossible: "If there remained in the mind of the emperor any doubt not settled by the patriarchs, he had only to submit it to the judgment of Rome, as tradition prescribed." When it became apparent that Michael would not restore images, the Studites passed over to positive hostility, and Theodore went into voluntary exile in Bithynia, where he died in 826 without seeing the triumph of the cause for which he spent his life. Michael, alarmed by a dangerous rebel who posed as a champion of icons, engaged in persecution especially of monks. Anxious to restore peace to his country, he enlisted the Franks on his side (824) and asked Louis the Pious to send an embassy to accompany his own envoys to Rome to win over the new Pope, *Eugenius II (824–827), to a compromise with the iconoclasts. The Frankish doctrine was to provide the basis of agreement. Nothing further is known about this episode.

Michael's successor, Theophilus (829–842), resumed wholesale persecution, but shrank from bloodshed; he made no martyrs but numerous confessors, the most famous being Lazarus, the painter, and two brothers called the *Grapti,* or Inscribed, into whose foreheads were burnt with hot needles some verses deriding their folly. The second iconoclasm had no real vigor and was kept alive artificially. Everybody realized that a change waited only for the death of the sickly sovereign. Theodora, regent for Michael III (842–867), saw to the appointment of an orthodox patriarch, *Methodius I. A synod was called that renewed the decisions of the seven general councils, declared the cult of images legitimate, and excommunicated the iconoclasts. This triumph of the true doctrine was sealed by a solemn and joyful celebration on the first Sunday of Lent. This first Feast of Orthodoxy (March 11, 843) marked the birthday of the Holy "Orthodox" Church, the Church of the Seven Councils.

The Pentarchy. The rule of the five patriarchs called the Pentarchy gained great favor in Byzantium during this period. According to this theory, the college of the five patriarchs of Rome, Constantinople, Alexandria, Antioch, and Jerusalem, in that order of precedence, governed the Church as successors to the college of the Apostles with Peter as their *coryphaeus,* or head. From the end of the *Acacian Schism, Constantinople had begun to feel its lack of apostolicity a handicap in comparison with Rome. Consequently, it welcomed the pentarchy theology, in which all the patriarchal sees were apostolic in the sense that the patriarchal college succeeded to the apostolic college.

The iconoclastic emperors had regarded themselves as both kings and priests, heads of the Church by divine right. The Studites fought for the absolute independence of the Church from the State. The Studites won to the extent that no subsequent ruler used the title of priest. Otherwise, the emperors continued to interfere as much as ever in ecclesiastical matters.

FROM FEAST OF ORTHODOXY TO DEATH OF CERULARIUS 843–1059

It is during this period that the Byzantine Church broke away from the Roman. Neither Church ever formally excommunicated the other. They drifted apart; and there were steps taken at different times by which the Eastern Schism may be said to have begun: (1) when the Greeks repudiated belief in the Roman primacy, (2) when they excluded the Pope's name from the commemoration in the Liturgy (Mass), etc. Yet L. Bréhier has maintained that despite friction and occasional breaks between the ecclesiastical or civil rulers of East and West, the ordinary faithful of both rites got along very well until shortly after the Cerularius incident, when they began to regard each other as enemies —and that this was the real schism. Many modern Byzantinists would accept Brehier's view in principle, but in fact they would date the rise of real antipathy—and, therefore, of the true schism—to the time of the Fourth Crusade.

The Photian Affair. Shortly after the Synod of Orthodoxy occurred the celebrated affair of *Photius. Michael III (842–867) exiled Patriarch *Ignatius (858), who was not deposed; he may have resigned, but it was under duress and invalid, as even his enemies tacitly admitted when they finally deposed him 3 years later in the synod of 861 for uncanonical promotion to the see (after he had occupied it, universally recognized, for 11 years). Photius was duly elected to succeed him, and he chose as one of his co-consecrators Gregory Asbestas, who was under a ban from the Holy See. Photius's election thus had two defects: the see was not vacant and he was consecrated by a suspended bishop.

Strife soon broke out between the backers of Photius and supporters of Ignatius (Studites), who included a popular following and most of the monks. When Photius sent his synodal letter to Pope *Nicholas I (858–867), Michael III invited the Pope to send legates to a general council for a second condemnation of iconoclasm. The Holy See could not participate in an affair in which Photius acted as patriarch without thereby acknowledging him as legitimate. To do so would have gone a great way toward breaking down the opposition to Photius, since the Studites had the highest respect for Rome. Many scholars think iconoclasm was just a pretext for calling the council and gaining Rome's tacit approval of Photius. Nicholas accepted the invitation to the council but, dissatisfied with the treatment of Ignatius, insisted on reviewing the case, reserving judgment to himself, and empowering his legates only to take evidence. He also requested the restitution to Roman control of the Balkans, South Italy, and Sicily. Despite his explicit instructions, the legates deposed Ignatius on the ground that he had been uncanonically elevated to the see, and pronounced Photius the lawful patriarch. Nicholas disavowed this action immediately without, however, censuring his legates. And he let it be known that he regarded Ignatius as the legitimate patriarch until proof to the contrary should be presented by Photius. There was no answer.

Pope Nicholas I. In 862 or 863 a supporter of Ignatius appeared in Rome to present an appeal. Nicholas heard his version, waited a full year to give Photius a chance to reply, and then at a synod (863) stripped Photius of his dignity since he had been consecrated by a suspended

bishop. The Pope likewise censured him for trying to bribe the legates and disqualified all those consecrated or ordained by him. He also reinstated Ignatius and his followers. Rome abided by this decision and never recognized Photius's first term. Nicholas excommunicated also one of the legates to the synod of 861. The other was absent on a mission and was punished later. The verdict against Photius, however, was provisional since it had been rendered only by default, and the way was still left open for a fair trial at Rome with both parties present either in person or by proxy—an offer that was repeated on several occasions and to which no answer was ever made.

The Bulgarian Question. F. Dvornik holds that Nicholas's whole conduct up to this point had been guided by the desire to obtain restitution of Bulgaria as part of the jurisdiction taken away by Leo the Iconoclast. P. Stephanou denies this.

At the request of Boris, King of Bulgaria, Photius had sent Greek clergy to instruct that nation. Boris wanted an autonomous Church with an independent patriarch to crown him czar, and as Photius refused this arrangement, the Bulgarian King turned to Rome in 866. Latin missionaries superseded the Greeks. Boris took a great fancy to the leader of the group, Bishop Formosus, and in 867 he decided that he wanted him named archbishop of Bulgaria without delay. But Nicholas refused.

The evangelization of Bulgaria by the papacy seemed to Byzantium to bring the Franks to their back door, and, as the Byzantines could not conquer the country by force, they decided on a religious offensive. Photius invited the Eastern patriarchs to a general council in a famous encyclical that proposed to condemn the papal incumbent without repudiating the see. Photius rejected the filioque, affirming that the Holy Spirit proceeds from the Father alone. The synod met in the summer of 867 and excommunicated Nicholas I for exceeding his authority; but the Pope died in November without ever hearing of the action taken.

In September, *Basil I (867–886) assassinated Michael III and assumed the purple; he brought back into favor the Studites, deposed Photius, reinstated Ignatius, and restored communion with Rome. He likewise offered to accept Nicholas's offer of a fair trial in Rome for Photius and Ignatius as if the antipapal council of 867 had never existed, and he sent representatives of both prelates with his embassy to submit the affair to the judgment of the Holy See. *Adrian II (867–872), Nicholas's successor, could hardly overlook the antipapal council; he decided that Photius and all the bishops consecrated by him should be deposed, that those consecrated by Methodius and Ignatius who had gone over to Photius should be pardoned only after signing a *libellus* that professed the primacy and condemned Photius and his adherents, and that the signatories to the acts of the council of 867 would be pardoned but would have to apply to the Holy See for absolution.

Photius's representative had died before the trial, but Adrian II nevertheless condemned Photius presumably because he had excommunicated a pope and his guilt was clear from the acts. As a general council was being prepared in Constantinople, Adrian determined to impose his verdict on it and instructed his legates to that effect.

The Emperor, however, knew that Photius's supporters would seize upon the fact that he had been condemned without a hearing and would continue the factional strife throughout the empire. His own hold on the throne was not secure, and he was equally determined to have some sort of trial. Hence he decided to proceed with the council.

Council of Constantinople III. The Eighth General Council was held in Constantinople (869–870) and became a conflict of wills between the Roman legates and Basil's representative. With tempers running high, the dictatorial conduct of the legates alienated even the pro-Studite bishops, the Pope's warmest supporters. In the end, however, the council finally submitted to Pope Adrian's will, but it caused further dissension between the Churches. (The Eastern Church does not recognize this council.)

At the last session, a Bulgarian embassy arrived; for Boris had turned back to Constantinople when the Pope refused to give him Formosus as archbishop. The determination of the jurisdiction to which Bulgaria belonged was left to the judgment of the pentarchy, and the three Eastern patriarchs pronounced in favor of Constantinople. Though formally forbidden by the legates to interfere in Bulgaria, Ignatius, on their departure for Rome, consecrated an archbishop and later 12 bishops for that country. Ignatius was about to be excommunicated by Pope *John VIII (872–882) when he died; he was succeeded by Photius, who was now acceptable to all parties.

Peace was made between the two sees in the Synod of Constantinople (879–880). John VIII agreed to recognize Photius if he apologized to the assembled bishops for his past misconduct, became reconciled with his enemies, and gave up Bulgaria. Photius refused to apologize but satisfied the other demands. It was agreed that Bulgaria should remain in the Byzantine rite, but under Roman jurisdiction. Finally John VIII absolved Photius from all censures and synodal decrees against him, including the disciplinary decrees of the Eighth General Council. The authenticity of the acts of the last two sessions, which deal with the filioque, has been questioned; both parties, according to the present text, came to terms on the basis of the *status quo ante,* i.e., that the addition should not be made to the Creed. However, because Photius later quoted this as proof that John VIII taught that the Holy Spirit proceeds from the Father alone, and since papal legates could not have subscribed to that, one wonders just what action was taken. At all events, the two sees were in union at the end of Photius's patriarchate (886), though their relations in the interval did not always remain cordial. Whether minor breaks between the sees occurred under Pope *Formosus or Pope *Stephen VII is a matter of dispute.

Photius is a controversial figure. Older scholars held that he was the chief author of the Eastern Schism. But Dvornik has demonstrated that though his works became a source book for writers against the Latins, nobody singled him out as leader of schism until centuries after his death. Some maintain that he was a loyal son of the Church despite mistakes. Others, however, for various reasons think that he tried deliberately to make the Byzantine Church independent of Rome.

Photius instituted the missions to the Slavs, which won so many peoples for the Church of Constantinople. The most famous mission was the sending of *Cyril (Constantine) and Methodius to the Moravians. He also began the evangelization of the Rhos of Kiev and tried to win over their neighbors, the Khazars, to Christianity. The real conversion of the Rhos, however, came with the baptism of Vladimir of Kiev and his marriage to Anna, Basil II's sister, in 989. Bulgaria was taken over by the Byzantine hierarchy after 1025, and the Church of Kiev, in 1037. Patriarch *Nicholas I Mysticus sent an archbishop to the Alans, north of the Caucasus, and kept him there by his encouragement.

Photius was forced to resign (886) by Emperor *Leo VI (886–912), who wished to appoint his brother Stephen. The Studites returned to power once more but objected to the new patriarch because he had been ordained a deacon by Photius. They believed that Photius had been consecrated invalidly (or illicitly—they were not clear about the distinction), and that therefore all orders administered by him were invalid (or illicit). They were willing to recognize Stephen if Rome granted a dispensation to all those promoted by Photius, and therefore appealed. The affair dragged on until Pope *John IX (898–900) reaffirmed the previous papal decisions, that the correct patriarchal line was Methodius, Ignatius, Photius, Stephen, Anthony; i.e., Photius's first term did not count, but his second did. Most of the Studites accepted this settlement and were thus finally reconciled both to Rome and Patriarch Anthony II Cauleas (893–901), who had the happiness of receiving them back in a solemn Synod of Union (899), perhaps in the presence of the papal legates and the representatives of the Eastern patriarchs.

Dispute over the Tetragamy. Peace lasted less than 10 years, after which the Church was torn asunder by the quarrel over the fourth marriage (tetragamy) of the Emperor. It is possible to give only a provisional account of this affair, because newly discovered sources dealing with it have not yet been published (1966). The Byzantine Church had remained faithful to the early Christian attitude toward the unity of marriage; its Canon Law imposed a penance for a second marriage, very severe penalties for a third marriage, and absolutely forbade a fourth. In fact this legislation had been strengthened by Emperor Leo himself. However, after the death of his third wife left him without male issue, he took as mistress Zoe, and in 905 she bore him a son out of wedlock, the future Constantine VII (913–959). Patriarch Nicholas I Mysticus had kept on cordial terms with the Emperor, paying no attention to the love affair. He himself baptized the infant with all the pomp befitting a *Porphyrogenitus* (one born in the Purple Chamber of the palace while his father was emperor); this act amounted virtually to a legitimation of the child. He set one condition—that Leo and Zoe should separate. However, 2 days after the baptism, Leo brought Zoe back to the palace and shortly thereafter crowned her queen; they were married by a priest, Thomas. The patriarch then forbade them to attend the liturgy or receive the Sacraments while he considered whether or not he could dispense them. Despite the confusing nature of the sources, it seems that Leo had already appealed to the pentarchy, and chiefly to Rome—at the patriarch's suggestion, according to Nicholas's own statement.

The Emperor was firmly convinced that the patriarch was engaged in treasonable dealings with a rebel in

Asia Minor, and he resolved to depose Nicholas at the first opportunity, despite the patriarch's large popular following in Constantinople. Nicholas was almost convinced that he could dispense the royal pair, but suddenly reversed his position. Several influential bishops, notably Arethas, metropolitan of Caesarea, were inalterably opposed to a dispensation, and the patriarch made the members of the Synod take a solemn oath to resist the Emperor's attempt at tetragamy even to death, if need be. At last the verdict of Rome and the other patriarchs arrived. It showed the utmost respect for Byzantine usage: Pope *Sergius III (904–911) stated that a fourth marriage was against Byzantine Canon Law and propriety; however, the dispensation was granted out of consideration for the good of the state. To those who objected that a fourth marriage was adultery, Rome pointed to its own practice in this regard and the texts of St. Paul but did not thereby intend to foist its customs on the Eastern Church. Backed by the decision of the pentarchy, Leo determined to break the resistance of the patriarch. Nicholas resigned despite the urging of Arethas and others opposed to the dispensation. Arethas thereafter always despised Nicholas, who had with great bravado led them into battle and then, by resigning, deserted them at the first sign of danger. The synod voted to accept the pentarchy's verdict, but Arethas and his companions stood their ground.

The synod then elected *Euthymius I, a saintly man. He accepted only on condition that the patriarchal representatives repeat their decision in his presence. He reconciled Arethas to the dispensation. He degraded Thomas, the priest who had performed the marriage, and refused to crown Zoe in church or to put her name in the diptychs. Not everybody shared Arethas's low opinion of Nicholas. Very many regarded him as the hero of Christian marriage, who had resigned rather than debauch it, and they formed the Nicholaites, who were opposed by the Euthymians. The government persecuted the former, and once more strife raged.

On the death of Leo, his brother Alexander (912–913) deposed Euthymius and reinstated Nicholas. It is debated whether Leo himself may have repented and recalled Nicholas before his death. Nicholas took savage vengeance on Euthymius and severely punished his party, particularly those who had sworn to stand by Nicholas and then changed over. Nicholas maintained that he had not resigned, and, even if he had, the resignation had been motivated by fear. As Arethas put it, he had the impudence to demand that the bishops suffer anything rather than admit the validity of the resignation by which he had himself evaded what he was asking them to endure. Nicholas turned on the Pope, protesting the deep humiliation inflicted upon his Church; and he pretended that he had never thought of granting the dispensation himself. He berated the Holy See for approving of adultery by permitting a fourth marriage in order to curry favor with the Emperor, and he demanded that the Pope make an example of the legates guilty of such an enormity. Then he erased the Pope's name from the diptychs. Yet in 917 Nicholas was reconciled with Euthymius and attempted to bring peace between the Euthymians and the Nicholaites. He succeeded partially at a synod in July 920. The two parties agreed not to condemn those who had contracted a fourth marriage and to settle the Canon Law on mar-

riage by stating that a second marriage was on a par with a first, that a third was subject to stringent restrictions, and that a fourth marriage was equivalent to living in sin. An apparently strong minority demanded the intervention of the Pope, however, and Nicholas finally persuaded (923) the Holy See to send legates to repeat the decision made originally by Pope Sergius III. A few Euthymians resisted and were reconciled finally under Patriarch Nicholas II (979–991) or his successor, Sisinnius II (996–998).

In 933 Emperor Romanus I desired to put his son Theophylactus in the patriarchal see, although he was only 16 years old. Despite local opposition, he prevailed on the Pope to send legates, who assisted at the consecration and enthroned him.

This incident is interesting as the last testimony of the Eastern Church to the prestige of the Holy See before the formal break. Up to this point there existed a group in the Byzantine Church that believed in the primacy of Rome, a strong group that had to be reckoned with. Within the next 75 years all belief, all memory even, of the papal primacy disappeared without a trace. How or why it did so remains a mystery.

Formal Schism under Sergius IV. The formal break with Rome came in 1009, when Patriarch Sergius II (1001–19) dropped the name of Pope *Sergius IV (1009–12) from the diptychs. Even a contemporary, Peter, later patriarch of Antioch, did not know why this was done. Later Byzantine statements that it was because the Pope had sent a creed containing the filioque must have been conjectures. As the Pope's name was never restored to the diptychs, this is the only official beginning of the schism; yet, as already mentioned, neither Church ever formally excommunicated the other.

The pentarchy had developed into a theory that negated the supremacy of Rome. Peter of Antioch expounded the ecclesiology of the period in one of his epistles to Dominic, Patriarch of Venice. Peter took pains to point out that there was ńo such thing as a patriarch of Venice; that a sixth patriarchate was unheard of; and that just as there were five senses so there were five patriarchates, Rome, Constantinople, Alexandria, Antioch, and Jerusalem. He described the pentarchy as a committee of five equals in which the majority rules. This was unequivocal; the patriarchs are all independent and the only head of the Church is its invisible Head, Christ. Peter took for granted that this was the doctrine held universally. He mentioned it incidentally as the self-evident proof for the impossibility of a sixth patriarchate, and though his correspondent was a Latin bishop, he had no doubt that they both agreed. Furthermore, Peter did not believe in the inerrancy of the Holy See; it was not only capable of error, but actually in error.

In 1024, according to a Western writer, the proposition was made to the Pope by Emperor *Basil II, "whether with the Roman Pontiff's consent, the Church of Constantinople might be entitled, within its own limits, to be called, and treated as, ecumenical, as Rome was ecumenical throughout the world." The proposal was rejected. Some authorities maintain that this report is unreliable and the event did not occur at all; others think that it did occur, but disagree as to the meaning of the offer. If it happened, it was the first effort at reunion.

Patriarch Michael Cerularius. In 1042 *Michael Cerularius became patriarch, but the famous incident with which his name is connected began only in 1052, the year in which the Byzantines, whose position in South Italy was desperate, made an alliance with Pope *Leo IX (1049–April 19, 1054) against the Normans. It was taken for granted that as a preliminary to the political treaty, religious unity would be reestablished. But Leo, Byzantine Archbishop of Bulgaria, supposedly incited by Cerularius, wrote a letter to a bishop of southern Italy, addressed through him to the Pope and the whole Western Church. He argued, while condemning many lesser points such as fasting on Saturdays, that unleavened bread was not valid matter for the Holy Eucharist. The writer assumed that only Constantinople had the true faith and the true sacrifice, and that every other Church had to learn from her. Constantinople claimed Rome's own prerogative. To the Byzantines of the 11th century, the title "Holy Orthodox Church" meant what it said, and Orthodox was equivalent to infallible. This idea had been formulated clearly in Photius's encyclical of 867, and the Synod repeated his words in its excommunication of the papal legate, Cardinal Humbert, which closed the Cerularian episode. Though Constantinople subscribed in theory to the equality of the patriarchs in the pentarchy, in fact she regarded herself as the first see. The foundation for this belief was based upon a revision (ascribed by some to Photius) of the ancient Constantinian *translatio imperii,* the claim that both the civil and the religious leadership had been transferred by Constantine from the Old (decrepit) Rome to Constantinople, New (vigorous) St. Andrew, the "first-called" of the Apostles, had established the See of Byzantium.

Cerularius had been raised in this belief and apparently had never heard of the papal primacy. When the papal legates acted as his superior, he thought that they were out of their minds. However, Leo IX was one of the great reform popes, and he would not give ground. The normal reaction in Byzantium called for the Emperor to bend the patriarch to his will, or have him resign; but Cerularius had no intention of compromising his convictions or of resigning. His great asset was the enormous popularity he enjoyed with the common people of Constantinople, while his adversary, Emperor *Constantine IX (1042–55), was quite unpopular.

The letter of Leo of Ochrida gave rise to a lively literary polemic. Patriarch Michael closed the Latin churches in Constantinople, after desecrating their hosts to demonstrate that they were invalidly consecrated. He likewise began an intensive campaign to rouse the populace.

The papal embassy, headed by Cardinal Humbert, arrived in Constantinople to negotiate the treaty. The conditions for reunion of the Churches were the restitution of the Balkans, South Italy, and Sicily to Roman jurisdiction and the acknowledgment of the primacy. In June, 2 months after the Pope's death, in the presence of the Emperor, Humbert insisted that one of his literary opponents, *Nicetas Stethatos, repudiate his own work and in addition deliver a clear anathema against all those who denied that Rome was the first church or questioned its orthodox faith. Cerularius averred that the legates were impostors and refused to meet them, except in the patriarchal palace surrounded by the synod. The legates in the Church of *Hagia Sophia, crowded for the morning liturgy, laid a document of excommunication on the high altar. It anathematized Michael, the patriarch, and his followers; and it condemned as heretical the special features of the Greek rite. In this way, though intended only against Cerularius, the anathema was applied to the whole Byzantine Church and aroused strong opposition. The legates had to flee for their lives, and the Emperor was forced to a humiliating surrender to the patriarch. On July 24, 1054, the Synod met, condemned Humbert and his companions as impostors, repudiated the filioque, following word for word Photius's encyclical, and defended the beards and marriage of the Byzantine priests. They made very clear that they were not excommunicating either the Pope or the Western Church. The silence on unleavened bread was a stinging rebuff to Cerularius, who, after all, had commanded one of his officials to trample on the Latin consecrated hosts. Nevertheless, Michael reached a pinnacle of power never attained by any other ecclesiastic in the history of Byzantium.

This incident was not the beginning of the Eastern Schism. Popes had excommunicated patriarchs before, and Humbert's excommunication of Cerularius was of doubtful value, since the Pope had died before it was proclaimed. The Byzantines made clear that they were not excommunicating the Western Church. Actually, the episode was an attempt at reunion, as M. Jugie maintains, but, as he adds, the reunion, if made, could not have endured. It did awaken the Western Church to the fact that Constantinople had drifted into schism and there was need for reunion.

FROM DEATH OF MICHAEL CERULARIUS TO DEATH OF MICHAEL VIII PALAEOLOGUS 1059–1282

This period is marked by the succession of efforts at reunion of the Churches, culminating in the Council of *Lyons. The attempts provoked a vigorous polemic over the differences between Byzantine and Latin liturgy and theology. A number of other theological controversies occurred during the time of the Comneni.

John Italus and Psellus. The case of *John Italus came to a head early in the reign of *Alexius I Comnenus (1081–1118) and is of extraordinary interest. His trial seems an isolated event, but it really constitutes the last act of the conflict between the Byzantine Church and the classics. It was not John Italus himself who was attacked but through him the celebrated humanist Michael *Psellus, who was his teacher and whom he succeeded in the chair of philosophy at the university as consul of philosophers, or head of the school. While *Symeon the New Theologian was busy sustaining the thesis of the exclusive preeminence of the gifts of the Holy Spirit over all science and all authority, Psellus with his pupil Italus launched the idea that all human knowledge is a step toward God, and that dogma should be interpreted in the light of rational principles, a sort of scholasticism. This contradicted the attitude adopted by the monks since the Studite reform in the 9th century. For them the object of knowledge was revelation; all else was valueless. The only science was the insight inspired by the Holy Spirit, which comes from prayer.

Psellus had returned to the Neoplatonism of *Proclus, not to Plato; Italus favored *Plotinus, but he also learned much from *Origen. Together with their contemporaries, they represented a revolutionary and rationalistic tendency, and their age had a remarkable affinity with the later Western Renaissance. In 1076–77 the movement was condemned by the Synod, which mentioned no particular theologians but anathematized doctrines close to modern rationalism. One excommunicated group denied the miracles of Our Lord, the Blessed Virgin, and the saints; another considered profane literature the repository of truth to which all else must be reduced directly or indirectly. They thus placed reason above faith. Neither Psellus nor Italus held such extreme views, but their lectures were open to the public and, as they encouraged free discussion, this gave rise to serious misunderstandings. In a synod of 1082, John Italus's teaching was rejected explicitly. Actually, the judgment was passed by Emperor Alexius I Comnenus. Byzantium was at a crisis and could not afford to risk factional strife by antagonizing the monks. After the synod, John Italus disappeared from history. He seems to have been entirely orthodox, but misunderstood. One of Italus's pupils, Eustratius of Nicaea, was suspended for life after 1117, and the use of dialectic in theology was condemned. Italus's excommunication occasioned a change in the function and meaning of the Sunday of Orthodoxy. The anathemas against him and his followers were appended to the *Synodicon,* and this practice was continued with later heresies. The *Synodicon* became the expression of the beliefs of the Orthodox Church.

Other Controversies under the Comneni. Leo of Chalcedon accused Alexius I Comnenus of iconoclasm when, in order to save the state, he melted the gold and silver attached to icons and particularly medals stamped with the image of Christ or a saint. In 1086 the Synod condemned and deposed him. Eustratius of Nicaea, who had opposed Leo, and who, like Italus, believed in a union of theology and philosophy, fell into an error approximating *Nestorianism during a controversy with the Monophysite Armenians. He was condemned by the synod and recanted. Nilus, an unlearned but upright monk with a large following among the Armenians of Constantinople, unwittingly became a Monophysite. After the death of Alexius, the Synod condemned both him and the Monophysites to perpetual anathema (1087).

The contest between the empire and the sects of Manichaean character seems to have reached a crisis under Alexius. The *Paulicians, a group that first appeared in the 7th century, had rejected the hierarchy, sacraments, and cult, and opposed images. Subject to sporadic persecution, they were favored by the early iconoclastic emperors and spread all over Asia Minor. Large numbers were transplanted to Thrace by Constantine V to counterbalance the sentiment there in favor of icons. These were reenforced by another group brought over by Emperor *John I Tzimisces (969–976). Their center was Philippopolis. By the 12th century they were absorbed into a similar sect, the *Bogomils, who are presumed to have developed from the Paulicians in the 10th century in Bulgaria, and who by the 12th century had won great popular support in Constantinople and throughout the empire. Alexius led a special expedition against Philippopolis in order to convert the heretics; two of the high officials were imprisoned for life, and the leader, Basil the Physician, was burned at the stake. Under John Comnenus (1118–43), the works of the monk Constantine Chrysomallus, which were tainted with Manichaean errors, were discovered circulating in several monasteries and were burnt by order of the Synod in 1140. In the reign of *Manuel I Comnenus (1143–80), two bishops were found guilty of upholding certain Bogomil tenets; Patriarch Cosmas II Atticus (1146–47) was involved and deposed, though perhaps unjustly.

During Manuel's reign two interesting discussions arose. The first concerned the meaning of a passage in the liturgy, "You are the offerer and the offered, and the receiver." Soterichus Panteugenus decided that Christ's sacrifice was offered only to God the Father and God the Holy Spirit, and not to God the Son, since he held that Christ could not offer something to Himself. This view was condemned in a synod of 1157. Soterichus taught also that the Mass was not a sacrifice but merely a solemn and dramatic recall of Christ's Passion and death. This doctrine was repudiated. The other controversy dealt with the meaning of Christ's words, "The Father is greater than I." At least five different interpretations were proposed; the debate became embittered, and some of the views were clearly unorthodox. It required eight sessions of the synod in 1170–71 to dispose of the difficulties. Even then the Emperor's interference prevented a thorough examination of the issues, and the forced solution proved unsatisfactory. However, an attempt at revision of the synod's decisions by Patriarch Michael IV Autorianus (1208–14) was blocked by opposition within the Church.

In the reign of Alexius III and Patriarch *John X Camateros (1198–1206), Michael *Glycas proposed the theory that Christ's body in the Holy Eucharist is mortal from the Consecration to the Communion, just as it was at the Last Supper, but incorruptible immediately after it had been absorbed by the communicant, as it was in the Resurrection. The Synod took no positive action but simply forbade any one to read either Glycas or his opponent.

Efforts at Reunion. Once the Cerularius incident had disclosed the rent between Rome and Constantinople, efforts at reunion began almost immediately. For the East, the initiative was taken by the emperor due to the special place of the civil ruler in the Byzantine Church. As a result of this situation, the popes, even when their principal end was reunion, had to negotiate politically, not religiously, and they never bypassed the monarch to treat directly with the patriarch. The popes seem to have taken for granted that once they had won the emperor, he could make the Church do anything he pleased. But this was never true of Cerularius.

These political compromises belong to the history of the Byzantine state, not the Church, which often was not even consulted. Only two such episodes seem worthy of note. The more interesting involved Pope Urban II. He complained to Alexius I Comnenus that his name had been removed from the diptychs uncanonically and asked to have it restored. A synod summoned by the Emperor had to concede the justice of the complaint and decided that, for the time being, the Pope would be commemorated if he submitted a satisfactory confession of faith and accepted the Quinisext synod (which had condemned clerical celibacy). Whether the Pope took any further interest in reunion is not known, but he won the fast friendship of Alexius I and detached him from his alliance with Henry IV, the enemy of the Holy See. The uncompromising attitude of the Greek Church is shown not only by the impossible conditions laid down by the synod, but also by a letter ascribed to the patriarch exhorting his confrere of Jerusalem not to yield on the primacy, filioque, and azymes.

The second episode, also revealing, was a supposed(?) synod at Constantinople in 1171 or 1176. According to the source, Emperor Manuel Comnenus proposed that the primacy of the pope be acknowledged, but Patriarch Michael III of Anchialus replied that it was impossible to have communion with heretics; the primacy had been lost to Rome when the pope had become a heretic (filioque!), and had been transferred to Constantinople; the pope was nothing but a layman.

The Emperor and the synod then broke off all relations with the Latins but did not excommunicate them. The constant assumption behind such statements is the infallibility of the Holy "Orthodox" Church, as mentioned before. Some scholars regard the foregoing account as apocryphal, others do not; still others think of it as a dressed-up version of an actual event. True or false, the incident does reflect faithfully the bitter feelings that had grown up during the age of the Comneni against the Latins and especially against the papacy.

The Crusades. This rancor was increased by the followers of *Peter the Hermit, who looted their way across Europe in the First *Crusade, and by *Bohemund's seizure of Antioch, which established the Normans, the deadliest enemy of Byzantium, on both its flanks. The Byzantine Church, particularly, resented its humiliating position in the Holy Land. Meantime, the ears of the West were filled with calumnies about Byzantine perfidy principally by the Normans. The Second and Third Crusades, with their threat to Constantinople itself, strained relations almost to the breaking point. The Venetians, using their trading privileges ruthlessly, were driving Byzantines out of business in their own country and making themselves everywhere detested. Emperor Manuel I Comnenus had favored the Latins, and the Greeks saw Latins displacing themselves in high government positions. The mounting fury was unleashed in a massacre of the Latins all over the empire in 1182. By this time Latin hatred of the Greeks was also intense. The climax came in the sack of Constantinople in the Fourth Crusade, when for 3 days the soldiers pillaged and murdered, and desecrated nuns and the altars of refuge, as well as the Sacred Species.

The Byzantine Church and Empire took refuge in Asia Minor, rallying around Theodore I Vatatzes (1208–22), who gathered the scattered elements of both in Nicaea. He invited Patriarch John X Camateros to join him but was refused. In 1206 Camateros died, and in 1208 Theodore assembled all available Byzantine bishops and suggested that they elect a new patriarch. Michael IV Autorianus (1208–14) was chosen, and he crowned Theodore emperor in Holy Week of 1208. Nicaea thus became the rallying point and new hope of the eastern Greeks. It had a rival, however, in the Despotate of Epirus, the cultural and political center of the western Greeks.

Innocent III. Though shocked at the outrage to Constantinople, Pope Innocent III acquiesced in the *fait accompli* and regarded the conquest as a providentially designed reunion of the Churches.

The Venetians gained control of Hagia Sophia, and so of the patriarchate, and selected Thomas *Morosini as Latin patriarch of Constantinople; the Pope had no choice but to approve. Naturally it angered the Byzantines exceedingly to have any other than a Greek patriarch. Despite the long existence of Eastern rite churches and monasteries in Rome itself and in other parts of Italy under papal control, Innocent III planned the absorption of the Greek rite by the Latin. This was his idea of union of Churches. But he pursued a policy of limited tolerance. When early conferences (1205–07) of Byzantine representatives with the legate Cardinal Benedict made it clear that they would not adopt the filioque, unleavened bread, or other Latin customs, the Pope did not force them. He did insist on the oath of canonical obedience to the Pope and the Latin patriarch of Constantinople. If the bishops demurred, every effort was to be made to win them over before deposing them and appointing a Latin in their stead. However, no new bishop was to be consecrated in any rite but the Latin; hence the Byzantine hierarchy was doomed to die out with the existing generation.

Despite all this, the Byzantine Church maintained itself. Cardinal Benedict had a winning personality, and he induced a good many clerics, though a minority, to take the oath of obedience. They felt that they were yielding nothing essential and their flock would still have shepherds. When some who were willing to submit to the Pope found it abhorrent to recognize the Latin patriarch, since they regarded the patriarch at Nicaea as the true one, Cardinal Benedict dispensed them. The majority refused to take the oath. To those who resigned and went into voluntary exile, the empire of Nicaea offered a refuge. To those who stood their ground, it held out hope and encouragement. Many never had to take the oath because the Latin rulers refused to carry out the law, some out of sympathy and some out of cupidity, pocketing income that should have gone either to the Latin bishop or the Holy See. Intending to put a stop to these abuses and to win over the rest of the Byzantines, Innocent III dispatched a new legate, Cardinal Pelagius, in 1213 or 1214. Acting entirely contrary to the spirit of his orders, Pelagius started a persecution, manacling and imprisoning those who refused the oath of canonical obedience, sealing up churches, and driving monks from their monasteries. The Latin Emperor Henry, who dealt fairly with the Greeks, released them from jail and made a compromise, according to which they need not mention the Pope in the diptychs if they acclaimed the Latin emperor as political ruler after the service when they used to acclaim the Byzantine emperor. Pelagius also had been commissioned to treat with the empire of Nicaea on reunion and for political ends, and when he did that he had to stop the persecution.

Yet reunion via a general council was still possible. Among those Byzantines who had remained in the Latin-held territory was a group who believed with Innocent III that the conquest had providentially brought together under one power the two previously divided peoples. It had not, however, achieved a spiritual union of the Churches. In a letter to the Pope they proposed that they should be permitted to elect a Greek patriarch who shared their views, and that then it would be possible to settle the religious differences in a general council. This move was made, apparently, with the approval of Nicaea. Innocent III would not hear of it and held to his own policy; he had proclaimed the union of Churches, and to permit a general council would be to confess that the union was illusory. As a result, the conciliatory party turned its back on the Latin empire and gave its allegiance to Nicaea. The episode is variously dated 1206–07 or 1213–14.

Innocent IV. The most promising attempt at reconciliation ever made was that between Pope *Innocent IV and Emperor *John III Vatatzes in 1253–54. The immediate successors of Innocent III continued his policy, but Innocent IV abandoned it completely. He proposed that John restore Constantinople in exchange for a reunion of the two Churches. Patriarch *Manuel II (1244–54), who sincerely desired an end to the schism, suggested a compromise formula, "the Holy Spirit, who proceeds from the Father through the Son," instead of ". . . and the Son," a formula entirely acceptable to the Latins. He succeeded in winning over the Greek Church to the following agreement: if the Pope yielded the throne of Constantinople to the Greek emperor and its see to the Greek patriarch, the Greek Church would acknowledge the primacy by restoring his name to the diptychs and would take the oath of canonical obedience. Innocent accepted these terms and also consented to a general council on Greek territory to ratify the agreement. But all the principal personalities died, Innocent IV, John III Vatatzes, and Patriarch Manuel. John's successor, Theodore II Lascaris, rejected the whole plan.

Council of Lyons. Though official efforts at reunion had little success, informal exchanges between scholars contributed to a better understanding. The Latins were represented during the age of the Comneni by *Peter Grossolano (Chrysolanus, to the Greeks), Archbishop of Milan, and Bishop *Anselm of Havelberg, a Premonstratensian, who both had occasion to visit Constantinople, and *Hugo Eterianus, councilor and official theologian to Manuel I Comnenus. The Byzantines relied on Photius's work *Mystagogy*, which was written in his old age and is far from his best work. Photius taught that the Holy Spirit proceeded from the Father alone. Eterianus's three books on the Procession of the Holy Spirit, published in both Greek and Latin, forced on the Photians a notable revision of their patristic material. The discussions of Grossolano and Anselm induced some of the Byzantines to consider the formula "through the Son," instead of "from the Father alone," and led others to admit the validity of the Latin position. Most of the Comnenian theologians, however, held to the Photian doctrine, and the Fourth Crusade hardly gained friends for the Western views. A turn came with the work of *Nicephorus Blemmydes during the Nicaean period. He accepted the Latin argument that unless the Son is involved in the procession of the Holy Spirit, no distinction between Son and Holy Spirit could be established. He abandoned the Photian teaching entirely. It was principally to Blemmydes and partially to Hugo Eterianus that Patriarch *John XI Beccus, the union patriarch under *Michael VIII Palaeologus, owed his conversion to the Latin position. Beccus himself made the important point that "through the Son" was in the best Greek tradition and Photius had not done it justice.

On July 6, 1274, at the Second Council of *Lyons, the union between Rome and Constantinople was sealed. Letters from Michael VIII, his son and coemperor

*Andronicus II, and the Byzantine hierarchy were read. The Emperor recognized the primacy in a formula worded by Pope *Gregory X himself. He accepted the filioque and the validity of consecration of unleavened bread. The Byzantine hierarchy acknowledged the primacy as it had existed before the schism and affirmed their entry into the Church, but did not repeat the formula of faith contained in the Emperor's letter. A plea of the hierarchy was put into the Pope's hands before they returned to Byzantium: they asked the Pope to permit the Greek hierarchy to exist side by side with the Latin, and for a guarantee in writing that Greek customs would not be disturbed. The latter request was made a condition for acceptance of the union.

Michael VIII had been impelled to negotiate with the Pope as the only way of saving Byzantium from destruction by Charles of Anjou. The Emperor had to use pressure, but ultimately he got most of the hierarchy to sign. Patriarch Joseph I preferred to resign, and John XI Beccus succeeded to the patriarchal see. Beccus had greatly aided the Emperor's efforts. At first a determined foe of the filioque, he had been imprisoned and his reading of Blemmydes and study in jail had converted him to the Latin view.

The union was successful for a time politically, but a failure religiously. The people bitterly opposed it. To gain the throne, Michael VIII had blinded the legitimate ruler, John IV Lascaris, and had been excommunicated by Patriarch *Arsenius Autorianus. He succeeded in deposing the latter, but the Arsenites formed a schism and fought against both the Emperor and reconciliation with Rome. After the union of Lyons, the country was divided into two hostile camps. Michael had to enforce the union to keep Charles of Anjou at bay, and he had recourse to persecution. Finally, Pope *Martin IV, a friend of Charles of Anjou, excommunicated Michael VIII as a heretic (1281). Byzantium was saved by the *Sicilian Vespers (1282). The union died with Michael; it was solemnly repudiated by his son, Andronicus II (1282–1328). The Arsenite Schism ended only in 1310.

FROM DEATH OF MICHAEL VIII PALAEOLOGUS TO FALL OF CONSTANTINOPLE 1282–1453

The high points of this period are the Hesychast movement and the Council of Florence. The latter had no influence on the Byzantine Church. However, the agreements made at the council have ever since served as the basis for reunion, e.g., with the Melchites.

The discussions between scholars on the filioque continued and bore fruit. The Dominicans founded houses in Constantinople and elsewhere in the Latin kingdoms and kept up a vigorous offensive with influential publications in Greek. The union of Lyons had stimulated considerable polemic; and the controversy took a new turn with the translation into Greek of important Latin works, particularly Augustine's *On the Trinity* by Maximus *Planudes, a celebrated humanist, in the reign of Michael VIII, and of the *Summa contra gentiles* and *Summa theologiae* of Thomas Aquinas by Demetrius *Cydones (1355–58), completed by his brother Prochorus. These works were used extensively in the controversy over Hesychasm. Disciples and successors of Demetrius continued this activity. Manuel Calecas translated Boethius's *De trinitate* and Anselm's *Cur Deus Homo*; he died a Dominican in 1410. Maximus

Chrysoberges (d. 1430) entered the Dominicans *c.* 1390; his younger brother, known as Andrew of Crete, also a Dominican, devoted his life's work to missionary activity for union. Several Byzantines were won over to the Catholic cause at the Council of Florence, notably *Isidore of Kiev and *Bessarion. Most of these scholars, beginning with Demetrius Cydones, found life too difficult at Constantinople and sought refuge in Italy; they were forerunners of those who revived Greek in the West and reunited the two cultures after centuries of isolation. Theodore of Gaza, a translator of Aristotle, was a follower of Bessarion. John Argyropolus, founder of Greek philology in Italy, was famous among scholars deriving from Cydones. Both Theodore and John were stanch supporters of Florence.

The papal primacy constituted an insuperable barrier to union. To acknowledge the primacy was to admit the pope's prerogative to abolish the Byzantine rite at will. This was just what Innocent III and his successors had hoped to do. The Byzantine Church could never concede this possibility; at Lyons and Florence the unionists restricted their acceptance of the primacy correspondingly, and the popes tolerated the restriction.

Differences arose with respect to purgatory in the 13th century, and over the *epiclesis in the 14th. The Greeks objected to the idea of a purgatorial fire, for which they could find no proof in Scripture or the Fathers. It was the Latins who raised the question about the epiclesis, a prayer to the Holy Spirit in the Greek Liturgy after the Consecration: "Send down thy Holy Spirit . . . and make this bread the Precious Body of thy Christ, and that which is in this chalice the Precious Blood of Thy Christ, transmuting them by Thy Holy Spirit." How could this petition be made after the Consecration? Neither of the objections, however, became prominent in polemic; the energies of the Greeks were entirely absorbed with the filioque and the Hesychastic controversies.

The debate on the azymes, which raged so hotly starting with Cerularius and continuing through the 12th century, gradually subsided thereafter. Both sides realized that the argument was of its nature incapable of settlement. Furthermore, moderate Greek churchmen found it too abhorrent to believe that the Latin Church had been deprived of the Eucharist for centuries.

Hesychastic Controversy. *Hesychasm, following a traditionally Byzantine school of mysticism that reached its most complete development with Simeon the New Theologian, became associated on Mount *Athos with a special technique for inducing ecstasy, apparently already in vogue in the 12th century. When by a life of mortification and prayer the monk had arrived at the contemplative stage, to make further progress he should adopt the following practice: sitting in the corner of a quiet cell, he should bend his head so as to rest his chin on his chest, fix his eyes on his navel, hold his breath, and repeat the *Jesus Prayer, "Lord Jesus Christ, Son of God, have mercy on me." Gradually sinking into ecstasy, he would see himself bathed in a supernatural light, the Increate Light that the Apostles beheld in the Transfiguration on Mount Thabor. This method had only mild opposition till its orthodoxy was challenged by the monk *Barlaam of Calabria, who, besides ridiculing the peculiar procedure, contested the notion of an uncreated light: what is uncreated must be God, and how could God be seen?

Gregory *Palamas came to the defense of the monks. He accepted as fact the visionaries' belief that they saw the Increate Light of Mount Thabor and thus came into direct union with God. This new revelation made to them was implied in the New Testament as the Trinity was implied in the Old. To reconcile this doctrine with the traditional teaching about the incommunicability and invisibility of the Divine Essence, Palamas, during his debates with Barlaam, enunciated a special theory, but one incapable of logical proof, since it involved a mystery, such as the Trinity.

The Palamite controversy convulsed the Byzantine world for many years. Gregory was challenged by such scholars as *Gregorius Akindynos, who argued from the Church Fathers according to the true Byzantine method, and Prochorus *Cydones, who used the scholastic type of reasoning. When the question became inextricably embroiled in politics, Palamas and the monks prevailed through the backing of Emperor John VI Cantacuzenus (1347–54), who presided over a great synod at Constantinople in 1351 that condemned all opposition to Palamas. *John V Palaeologus (1341–91), after the expulsion of Cantacuzenus, permitted free discussion but did not prevent the Church from imposing spiritual penalties on the anti-Palamites. The Synod of Constantinople in 1368 closed the affair so far as the Church was concerned by suspending Prochorus Cydones for life and canonizing Gregory Palamas.

True union between Latins and Greeks had by now become impossible. Occasionally explorations were made by the Churches themselves, as in the conversations in 1367 between the papal legate, the imperial family, the ex-emperor Cantacuzenus, three high-ranking metropolitans of the synod, and representatives of the patriarch, in which it was agreed that a general council should debate the issues between the Churches. But the Pope refused this suggestion as it seemed to put in doubt the teaching defined at the Council of Lyons. Besides, Cantacuzenus had made modifications in Palamas's theology that the Palamites themselves would never have admitted. Generally, however, negotiations centered on the political question of the peril to Byzantium from the Turks, and as time went on the chance of success diminished. In 1369 John V Palaeologus went to Rome and became a Catholic. Pope *Urban V, and after him *Gregory XI, a true friend of the Greeks, made a ringing appeal to Europe to come to the aid of the now Catholic Byzantine Emperor; but the plea fell on deaf ears. The Byzantine people became convinced that even if they changed their religion they would get no effective military help. It got to the point where schism made no real difference; the Latin principalities in Greece were by then in grave danger, and coalitions including schismatics had to be made for mutual protection. Finally, the one really strong Western effort, the Crusade of Nicopolis, collapsed.

Council of Florence. Nevertheless, *John VIII Palaeologus (1425–48) decided to bring his people and the Greek clergy into union with Rome; early in 1438, on the invitation of Pope *Eugene IV, he arrived in Ferrara for the General Council of Ferrara-*Florence. After a thorough discussion of each point, agreement was reached on the filioque, azymes, purgatory, the enjoyment of the beatific vision by the blessed before the Last Judgment, the primacy, and the order of the patriarchs, Constantinople being named second after Rome. Compromises were reached: nothing was said about purgatorial fire since the Greeks did not teach it; the Pope's right to call a general council was not specifically stated owing to the objection of the Emperor; but the Pope was acknowledged as head of the Church without prejudice to the rights and privileges of the Eastern patriarchs; and finally, the Pope waived the question of the distinction between God's substance and operations, which had been the subject of the controversy between the Palamites and the anti-Palamites. This question was too explosive to reopen, since it was threatening to cause a civil war in Byzantium.

The only consistent dissenter among the Greeks was Mark *Eugenicus, Bishop of Ephesus, who alone did not sign the council's decrees. Most of the other Greek prelates agreed to the union, but with varying degrees of assent. Patriarch Joseph II, who had contributed much to the outcome of the debate on the filioque, died before the end of the council. On the night of his death he left a note professing his faith in the filioque, purgatory, and the primacy.

The Council of *Florence was never accepted by the Byzantine monks and lower clergy. John VIII vacillated about proclaiming its decrees, and many of the prelates who agreed to the union revoked their assent in the hostile atmosphere of Constantinople shortly after their return. But the new emperor, Constantine XII, a Catholic, determined to carry out the union, and Cardinal Isidore, formerly of Kiev, as papal legate, solemnly proclaimed it in Hagia Sophia on Dec. 12, 1452, despite the herculean efforts of the antiunionists to prevent it. At that moment, however, the Sultan was determined to take the city by storm, and neither argument nor impassioned plea could avail against the grim fortress of Rumeli Hissar, built earlier that year by the Turks a few miles above Constantinople, which cut off help from the north. Six months later, May 29, 1453, Constantinople fell to Mohammed the Conqueror.

See also BYZANTINE THEOLOGY; BYZANTINE CIVILIZATION; BYZANTINE EMPIRE.

Bibliography: Fliche-Martin v.4–8. CMedH 2:222–235, 245–248, 398–405. CMedH² v.4. Beck KTLBR. J. PARGOIRE, *L'Église byzantine de 527 à 847* (Paris 1905). L. DUCHESNE, *L'Église au VIᵉ siècle* (Paris 1925). Grill-Bacht Konz 2:179–192. R. PARET, RevÉtByz 15 (1957) 42–72, Maurice. P. SHERWOOD, *An Annotated Date-List of the Works of Maximus the Confessor* (St Anselm 30; 1952). Ostrogorsky. A. A. VASILIEV, *A History of the Byzantine Empire, 324–1453* (2d Eng. ed. Madison 1952). F. DVORNIK, *The Idea of Apostolicity in Byzantium* (Dumbarton Oaks Studies 4; Cambridge, Mass. 1958); *Byzance et la primauté romaine* (Paris 1964); *The Photian Schism* (Cambridge, Eng. 1948). P. J. ALEXANDER, *The Patriarch Nicephorus of Constantinople* (Oxford 1958). F. MASAI, *Byzantion* 33 (1963) 191–221, the Isaurians. W. OHNSORGE, "Das Kaisertum der Eirene und die Kaiserkrönung Karls des Grossen," *Saeculum* 14 (1963) 221–247. R. MAINKA, *Ostkirchliche Studien* 13 (1964) 273–281, Nicephorus I. V. GRUMEL, RevÉtByz 18 (1960) 19–44, Leo V. W. NORDEN, *Das Papsttum und Byzanz* (Berlin 1903). J. M. HUSSEY, *Church and Learning in the Byzantine Empire* (Oxford 1937; repr. New York 1963). M. JUGIE, *Le Schisme byzantin* (Paris 1941). P. STEPHANOU, OrChrPer 134 (Rome 1949), John Italus. D. J. GEANAKOPLOS, *Emperor Michael Palaeologus and the West, 1258–1282* (Cambridge, Mass. 1959). S. RUNCIMAN, *The Sicilian Vespers* (Cambridge, Eng. 1958). P. L'HUILLIER, in *Akten des XI. Internationalen Byzantinistenkongresses, München 1958*, ed. F. DÖLGER and H. G. BECK (Munich 1960) 314–320, Crusades. W. DE VRIES, *Ostkirchliche Studien* 12 (1963) 113–131, Innocent IV. M. LEHMAN, *ibid.* 132–156, Lyons. P. WIRTH, *ibid.* 61–63, Soterichos Panteugenos. J. M. HUSSEY, in *A History of the Crusades*, v. 2, ed. K. M. SETTON (Philadelphia 1962) 123–151. E. H. MCNEAL, *ibid.* 152–185. R. L. WOLFF, *ibid.* 186–233. B. ROBERG, *Bonner Historische Forschungen* 24 (Bonn 1964), Lyons. W. DALY, MedSt (Toronto) 22 (1960) 43–91, Crusades. D. M. NICOL, *Proceedings of the Royal Irish Academy* 63 (Dublin 1962); in *Medieval Studies Presented to Aubrey Gwynn* (Dublin 1961) 454–480, Lyons; JEcclHist 13 (1962) 1–20, 11th century. M. LEHMAN, *Ostkirchliche Studien* 12 (1963) 295–313. J. MEYENDORFF, in *Akten des XI. Internationalen Byzantinistenkongresses, op. cit.* 363–369; DumbOaks Papers 14 (1960) 149–177. J. GILL, *The Council of Florence* (Cambridge, Eng. 1959). V. LAURENT, RevÉtByz 20 (1962) 1–60; 18 (1960) 45–54, 136–144, 145–162. J. DARROUZÈS, *ibid.* 19 (1961) 76–109. G. T. DENNIS, *Jahrbuch der österreichischen Byzantinischen Gesellschaft* 9 (1960) 51–55, John Calecas. P. JOANNOU, OrChrPer 27 (1961) 38–45, Calecas. M. A. SCHMIDT, ChHist 30 (1961) 35–49, Florence. I. DUJČEV, RevÉtByz 19 (1961) 333–339. A. ESSER, *Ostkirchliche Studien* 9 (1960) 26–46, Photius. C. TOUMANOFF, "Moscow the Third Rome: Genesis and Significance of a Politico-religious Idea," CathHistRev 40 (1954–55) 411–447. P. CHARANIS, in *A History of the Crusades*, ed. K. M. SETTON, v.1 (Philadelphia 1955) 207–219. F. DÖLGER, *Byzanz und die europäische Staatenwelt* (Ettal 1953), 83–105, *translatio imperii.* S. RUNCIMAN, *A History of the Crusades*, 3 v. (Cambridge, Eng. 1951–54) 1:93–105; 3:107–131. P. KARLIN-HAYTER, *Byzantion* 25–27 (1955–57) 757–763, 764, 767; 34 (1964) 49–67. R. J. JENKINS, DumbOaksP 16 (1962) 233–234, Nicholas Mysticus. F. DVORNIK, "The Patriarch Photius in the Light of Recent Research," *Berichte zum XI. Internationalen Byzantinistenkongress 1958* (Munich 1958) pt. 3.2. P. STEPHANOU, "1. Korreferat," *ibid.* 17–23. K. BONIS, "2. Korreferat," *ibid.* 24–26. *Diskussionsbeiträge* (Munich 1961) 41–54, contributions by Dvornik, Stephanou, Bonis, Grumel, Spuler.

[M. J. HIGGINS]

BYZANTINE CIVILIZATION

The term Byzantine civilization includes the period from the founding to the fall of Constantinople. The civilization is dealt with here in regard to (1) historical background, (2) imperial and administrative tradition, (3) Church and monasticism, (4) social and economic life, and (5) education and art.

HISTORICAL BACKGROUND

The roots of the Byzantine Empire go far back into the Greco-Roman world, but its true beginnings may be dated from the formal inauguration of the capital at Constantinople on May 11, 330. Long after Rome and the Western provinces had been lost, the eastern half of the Roman Empire stood as the bulwark of Christendom. The Byzantine cultural and administrative tradition bore witness to the empire's close links with the Greco-Roman world. But it was also a Christian empire. In 313 *Constantine the Great had proclaimed his adoption of Christianity, which, apart from the short interval of the pagan Emperor Julian's reign (361–363) henceforth remained the faith of the imperial house. By the end of the 4th century, it had become the only permitted religion, though paganism lingered on for centuries. Constantine, with his predecessor *Diocletian, had effected significant administrative and financial reforms. He himself further assisted imperial stability after the troubles of the 3rd century by his successful personal resumption of power, and by his establishment of the strategically placed eastern capital *Constantinople. After the death of *Theodosius I the Great in 395, the empire, though in theory a single whole, was for practical purposes split into an eastern and a western half, ruled by two imperial colleagues. In the West, political life was increasingly disrupted as the Roman provinces disappeared before the incoming Vandals, whom the ineffectual western emperors failed to check. But in contrast life in the East went on normally; legal codes were revised, the University of Constantinople was founded in 425, and the menace of

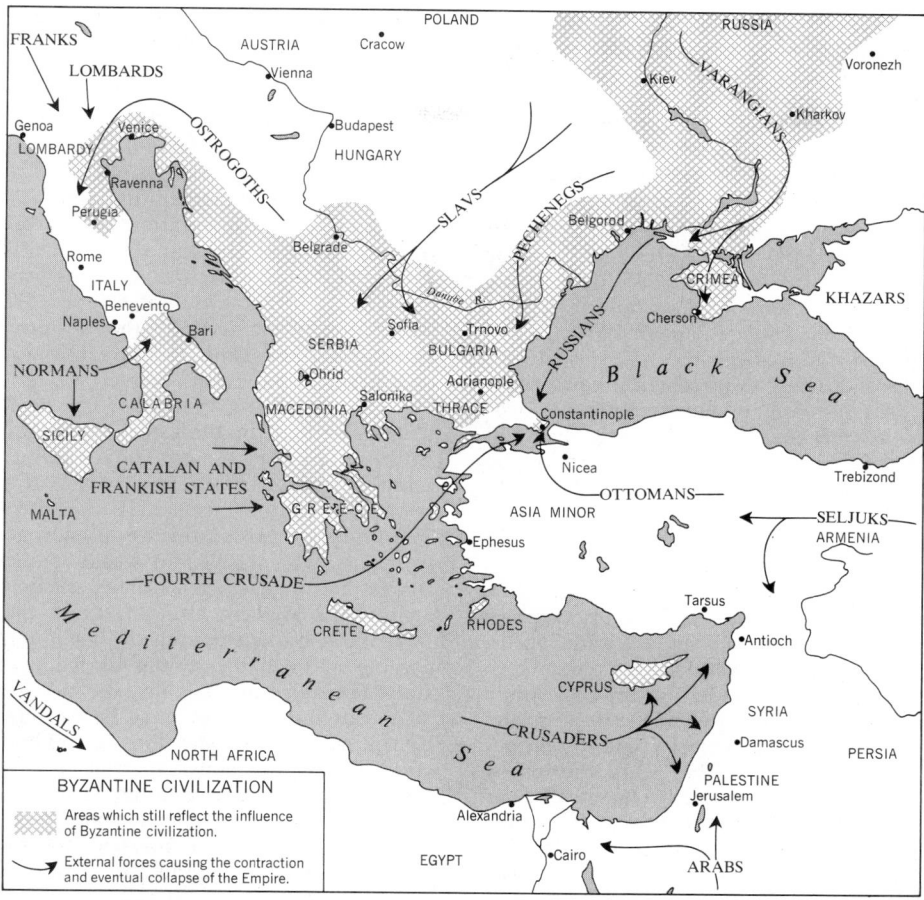

BYZANTINE CIVILIZATION

Areas which still reflect the influence
of Byzantine civilization.

External forces causing the contraction
and eventual collapse of the Empire.

barbarian infiltration was brought under control. The
wisdom of Constantine's choice of a capital was shown,
for from Constantinople it proved possible to defend
the eastern frontier against the growing power of the
Persians (Sassanians) and to enlist native soldiers from
Asia Minor as a counterbalance against rebellious barbarian recruits and *foederati*. The problem posed by
fullscale migrations across the Danube into the Balkans
was temporarily solved by the directing of the incoming
Ostrogoths away from Constantinople into Italy, where
they set up the Ostrogothic kingdom, which *Theodoric
ruled as viceregent for the Byzantine emperor. Probably the most acute problem of Constantinople at this
time was the growing separatist feeling in the outlying
eastern provinces, Egypt, Syria, and Palestine. Here
hatred of imperial government was accompanied by
rapid developments in native cultures and languages, as,
for instance, in Coptic and Syriac, and also by views
on Christological doctrine that were not in accordance
with the orthodox teaching of the Church as confirmed
in the general councils of the 5th century (*see* MONO-
PHYSITISM; NESTORIANISM).

Justinian. The last major attempt at reestablishing
full Roman control over the provinces lost to the Germanic peoples, particularly Italy and North Africa, was
made by *Justinian I (527–565). He destroyed the
Ostrogothic and Vandal kingdoms and reincorporated
these into the empire; he also stabilized the Byzantine
position in the Caucasus region, keeping control of the
eastern end of the Black Sea. But he could not safeguard

the Balkans from the invading Slav tribes. Though the
legal and architectural achievements of his reign remained a glorious memorial to his name, he failed to
revive the late Roman Empire.

During the 150 years after Justinian's death territorial and ethnical changes took place that brought into
being the medieval Byzantine Empire. The Lombards
settled in northern and central Italy, the Arabs surged
into the southern and eastern Roman provinces, as well
as into the lands of Byzantium's old enemy Persia. By
the end of the 7th century North Africa, Egypt, Syria,
Palestine, and parts of Italy were lost. But the Heraclian
dynasty whose members ruled during this period did at
least save Asia Minor, Greece, and most of the islands.
Thus political continuity centering in Constantinople
was maintained in the essential core of the Greco-
Roman world. Further, the southern provinces of Italy
were retained until the late 11th century, and Ravenna
with the duchies of Rome and Perugia was kept until the
second half of the 8th century. But in the Balkans during
the 7th and 8th centuries significant racial changes took
place when the Slavs flooded in and set up their own
principalities.

Isaurian Emperors. The dynasty of the North Syrian
(the "Isaurian") emperors fought valiantly to keep the
Moslems out of Asia Minor and to check the Slavs in
the Balkans. Their foreign policy was accompanied by
an internal crisis in the Church brought on by widely
supported but unsuccessful attempts to forbid the use
of icons, or holy pictures. Thus fully occupied at home

as well as on the northern and eastern frontiers, the North Syrian rulers were unable to send adequate help to defend Ravenna and central Italy against the aggressive *Lombards. Consequently the papacy turned to the *Franks, and the *Carolingian rulers took the opportunity to place under their own, and papal control those parts of northern and central Italy that had previously been either Lombard or Byzantine. This strengthened ties between the pope and the Frankish ruler, and in 800 Charlemagne was crowned emperor in Rome by Pope Leo III. The emergence of a "western" empire was a bitter blow to Constantinople, but it actually corresponded to an incipient cleavage between the Greek and Latin worlds.

Although Byzantium, despite its remaining provinces in South Italy, had lost forever any real control over the western half of the old Roman Empire, the solid work of its Heraclian and north Syrian rulers in the 7th and 8th centuries bore fruit. From the mid-9th century to the days of the Crusades, the Byzantine Empire became a factor of first importance, not only in the east Mediterranean, but in the Christian world. In the East, the Moslems were pushed back and Byzantine control was once more established in the Taurus regions in southeast Asia Minor, as well as in Crete and Cyprus, and in 969 the stronghold of Antioch was recaptured. In the Balkans, after a struggle lasting for more than 100 years, the Bulgarian empire was subdued and split into Byzantine provinces. In Italy the Byzantines made no territorial advance, but they were courted by the German rulers who were powerful in north Italy and in Rome. The Saxon *Otto II married a Byzantine noblewoman, Theophano, and Otto III, who died young in 1002, was betrothed to a princess of the imperial Macedonian house.

The successes of distinguished generals abroad were paralleled by the effectiveness of statesmen, churchmen, scholars, and artists. The legal code was revised, and the Greek *Basilica,* newly issued in *Leo VI's reign, was to become the cornerstone of the medieval Byzantine legal system. The central authority of the state was maintained as far as possible in the face of ever-expanding, powerful, landed families. The Church played a leading role in bringing Christianity to the South Slavs and Russian Kievans, and it worked closely with the Byzantine state in the Balkans in introducing the young principalities to the highly organized statecraft and mature civilization of Byzantium.

In spite of the apparent strength of the Byzantine Empire in the early years of the 11th century, it rapidly lost ground after the death of the astute military emperor *Basil II (1025). From 1025 to 1081 the state was rent by struggles between the civil aristocracy in Constantinople and the military aristocracy entrenched in the provinces. This clash, combined with a rapid succession of ineffective rulers and the presence of aged Macedonian empresses in the background until 1056, made impossible any consistently reasonable financial and military policy. At the same time the Byzantine frontiers were restive, and Slav vassals ready to give their support to the highest bidder. The Turkic Pecheneg tribesmen were constantly crossing the Danube and pushing their raids deep into the countryside. On the eastern frontier other Turkic tribes from central Asia (of whom the Seljuks are the best known) were already established in the caliphate of Baghdad and

were attacking the Byzantine provinces in Asia Minor and advancing toward the sea of Marmara. In the West the *Normans, having conquered the Byzantine provinces in south Italy, were threatening western Greece.

Comnenian Dynasty. This was the situation that faced *Alexius I in 1081. A brilliant member of the military aristocracy, both soldier and diplomat, he established the Comnenian dynasty (1081–1185) and staved off the disintegration of the empire for more than a century. He came to terms with the Seljuk Turks. He allied with the naval power of Venice and drove the Normans out of Greece. But the situation was radically changed by the western *Crusades because the Latins and the Greeks had different aims and needs. The Latins wanted to go directly to the Holy Land and to gain independent principalities, while it was essential for the Greeks to begin by driving the Turks out of Asia Minor. The temporary success of the Latin crusaders in setting up small states in Palestine and Syria further weakened the Byzantine Empire. The Greeks regarded this as an encroachment on their preserves, while the Latin world retaliated by making Byzantium the scapegoat for its failure to hold its own against the Moslem attack. During the 12th century, Byzantium battled courageously though it was almost completely encircled by the Christian powers of south Italy, Hungary, the Balkans, and the crusader states, as well as by the rising forces of Islam. Internally the main Byzantine problem was the weakening of the central authority by the constant granting of privileges and the consequent increase in the power of local landlords, both lay and ecclesiastical. There was also a marked separatist tendency manifested by the secession of *Cyprus and Trebizond. In 1185 the Comnenian dynasty lost the throne to the less able Angeli family. Meanwhile with the failure of the Third Crusade in 1189 the Latin crusaders retained little territory in Syria and Palestine. The West was now ready to attack Constantinople itself, long envied for its wealth.

It suited Venetian policy to make the most of the growing rift between the Churches of Constantinople and Rome (often dated from 1054; see below) and to stress the need for Latin control of the Byzantine Empire before proceeding against Islam. In reality *Venice wanted to safeguard her trade against Italian competition and Byzantine hostility. The feudal nobles from the West were more ready to carve up the Byzantine Empire into principalities for themselves than to embark on a hazardous war against the infidel. Thus in 1204, for the first time since its inauguration, Constantinople was successfully stormed. Out of the wreckage, the Byzantines salvaged only three small Greek kingdoms, Epirus in northwest Greece, Trebizond on the far shores of the Black Sea, and Nicaea in northwest Asia Minor.

Palaeologi Emperors. After competing with Epirus and Bulgaria, the Byzantine rulers of Nicaea regained Constantinople in 1261 and for nearly 250 years it was ruled by the Palaeologi emperors. But Byzantine power was broken. The Latins were never completely driven out of the Aegean. New principalities had risen in the Balkans, first *Bulgaria, and then the short-lived Serbian empire of Stephan Nemanja (d. 1346). The Byzantines struggled on, rent by civil wars in the 14th century and unable to come to terms with the West. A new Moslem foe was thus able to take advantage of a divided Christendom and to subdue alike Greeks, Latin intruders, and Balkan principalities. Among the various small Turkish emirates that had grown up in Asia Minor after the 13th-century Mongol raids were the Ottomans in Bithynia opposite Constantinople. They gradually infiltrated into neighboring Turkish emirates as well into the Byzantine European lands. In 1453 they crowned their work by conquering Constantinople—a disaster for Christendom. But at least the last 250 years of bitter struggle had something to offer on the credit side, as the story of Byzantine learning and art shows.

BYZANTINE IMPERIAL AND ADMINISTRATIVE TRADITION

Byzantium could never have survived for so long but for its tenacious hold on tradition. Though there was frequent change in administrative detail, certain basic principles survived to the end. It always remained an empire with "universal" claims (in theory at least) and it was governed by a monarch. Its ruler was God's viceregent and the imperial authority was the reflection on earth of the divine power. The emperor was an autocrat and he alone directed policy at home and abroad; he was the supreme lawgiver, judge, administrator, and commander in chief. But this autocracy was tempered by certain factors. Efficiency was a condition of self-preservation in an empire constantly facing external attack. If defenses broke down usurpers might appear and the most competent usually won and established his own dynasty. If the emperor were a minor, or perhaps a scholar with little interest in active politics, a more military minded associate or coemperor might be chosen. In origin the imperial office was elective and the choice was made by the senate (or the aristocracy), the army, and the people. In practice the support of the army was often the deciding factor. From the 5th century onward it became customary for the emperor to be crowned by the patriarch of Constantinople. Popular feeling for legitimacy grew and fostered the continuity of an established house. The emperor usually designated his successor from his own family. Such was the case with the 7th-century *Heraclius, or the 12th-century Comnenian dynasty. The only way to get rid of an emperor was by revolution unless he chose to abdicate of his own free will.

Civil Administration. There were always strong links between Church and State. In the emperor's coronation oath (known from the 9th century onward) he made his profession of orthodoxy and promised to maintain the traditions of the Church. The spheres of Church and State were closely integrated: the emperor no less than the patriarch had his essential part to play in promoting the well-being of the Church. This integration was indeed symbolized by the liturgical element, which permeated the ceremonial accompanying every aspect of daily court life. Surviving records such as the 10th-century *Book of Ceremonies* make it possible to reconstruct procedure in the complex of buildings that formed the Great Palace, adjacent to the church of the *Hagia Sophia in *Constantinople, the very heart of the empire.

Law and General Administration. Roman legal principles, through the 6th-century corpus of Justinian and more especially through the late 9th-century Greek compilation called the *Basilica,* were a formative influence in Byzantine law. Other influences also, both Oriental and Christian, can be discerned. From the 7th century onward physical mutilation as punishment for crime was increasingly used, though this and the death penalty were sometimes mitigated by substituting banishment to a monastery. Culprits could often claim rights of *asylum, though the sanctuary was not always respected and was in any case denied to traitors and heretics. The imperial court was the supreme court of appeal and in the later Middle Ages was composed of both laymen and clerics. The Church had its own courts with competence in the first instance over certain cases and persons.

Civil and ecclesiastical law were closely interwoven, as is shown by the growth of a body of law known as the *nomocanons, i.e., secular law or *nomoi* and the Church rulings or *canones.* Legislation was effected by means of imperial edict, or in the case of the Church by patriarchal rulings and the decisions of synods, whether general councils (applying to the whole of Christendom), or the local synods of each patriarchate and province. As in the West, a judge's directions might give either a different emphasis or a different interpretation to the law.

During the period of nearly 900 years between Justinian's death in 565 and the fall of Constantinople in 1453 there were naturally administrative changes. In comparison with those of the late Roman Empire, such departments of the central government as the exchequer, the judiciary, the secretariat, or the imperial household were controlled by an increasing number of officials responsible directly to the emperor. There was an elaborate system of court titles conferring rank and precedent upon the holders. Some titles were honorary and conferred by investiture; some were attached to important offices, such as that of the grand chamberlain in the 10th century and these were conferred by imperial edict. Titles of officeholders changed in the course of the Middle Ages as departments were reorganized or became differentiated. Below the heads of departments there was a well-trained bureaucracy drawn from an educated laity, and from time to time the emperor tried to ensure that adequate, and often free, higher education was available, particularly in the field of legal training. Even after the capture of Constantinople by the Latins during the Fourth Crusade, the Byzantines, upon regaining the capital in 1261, were able to reconstruct something of the former civil service and to maintain some semblance of government until 1453.

Provincial Organization. In provincial organization one difference between the late Roman and the medieval periods was the concentration from the 7th century onward of supreme military and civil provincial authority in the hands of the same man, thus emphasizing military needs. This process of reorganization seems to have been accompanied by the settling of soldiers on the land in Asia Minor in return for their military service, the rights to land passing from the father to the eldest son. After the precarious days of the 7th and 8th centuries the well-known medieval provinces, or themes as they were called (from the name of an army corps, the *thema*), began to emerge, first in Asia Minor, and then, as the Slavs began to settle down, in the European lands of the empire. The military origin of the themes is reflected also in the title of many of the governors who were called "general" (*strategos*).

Defense and Diplomacy. The Byzantine capacity for organization was used to good effect in the mustering of its resources for defense. The empire was almost always at war and its army and navy as well as its diplomatic corps were therefore of first concern.

Army corps (*themata*) were regularly stationed in each province; frontier regions, strengthened by forts and signal stations, were organized into districts called "passes" (*kleisurai*). Troops were stationed in and around Constantinople, including the guards composed of mercenaries. In the early 11th century the Varangian, or Russo-Scandinavian, imperial bodyguard became famous, from the 11th century onward recruiting many Anglo-Saxons. A number of military handbooks have survived showing how seriously the Byzantines took the art of war. Their mailclad heavy and light cavalry and infantry, and their military engineering and its mobile artillery and gunners, made them a formidable enemy. They made a science of studying their opponents and aimed to avoid battle if it were possible by outwitting the enemy by other means.

A navy also was essential for an empire with so extensive a seacoast as that of Byzantium. Certain maritime provinces in Asia Minor and the Aegean (and afterward also the European coastal themes) were charged with the provision of sailors and ships and the fleet was based off these provinces. There was an additional imperial fleet stationed off Constantinople, which in the 10th century was of considerable strength. The fleet had its failures, as the Moslem conquest of Crete, or of Sicily, shows, but in the middle Byzantine period it played a vital role in stemming the Arab attacks.

Decline of the Defense System. In the 11th century both fleet and army suffered from neglect as a result of the unfortunate policy of the civil bureaucracy in Constantinople. This party may perhaps have felt comparatively secure after the successful offensive of the previous 150 years, but its main concern was to undermine the power of the provincial military aristocracy. This was fatal because it weakened resistance to new enemies, particularly the *Seljuk Turks. From the end of the 11th century Constantinople was forced to draw all too often on the naval resources of the Italian cities, particularly Venice and Genoa, paying a heavy price in the trading privileges that it had to grant them in return. Mercenaries, always an important element in the army, became the rule as the small native soldier-farmer gradually disappeared, as a result partly of the encroachments of the powerful landowners and partly of substantial losses of land in Asia Minor to the Turks. Some indigenous military forces appear to have been provided in return for grants of proprietary rights (*pronoia*) bearing a superficial likeness to the feudal holdings of the West.

Diplomacy. Diplomacy had always been an art at which Byzantium excelled. Its principles are admirably outlined in the 10th-century handbook *De administrando imperio,* drawn up by Emperor *Constantine VII for his son and perhaps of more use to the inner circle · of the foreign office than to the lighthearted young prince Romanus II. As resources diminished, particularly after 1204, the Byzantines had to rely on their diplomacy, though it could no longer be backed up by such lavish streams of gold as in the heyday of the empire. At every point Byzantium sought to impress its neighbors by its superior civilization. The magnificent reception of foreign visitors in the Great Palace at Constantinople; the splendid embassies bearing priceless works of art from the imperial ateliers as presents; the lavish subsidies to encourage allies and to ward off enemies; the well-informed intelligence service drawing on every source of information from merchants and missionaries to minor frontier officials; the coveted prize of a marriage alliance held out to appease or win over some foreign power—all these practices were deployed to buttress the state and to safeguard it against the actual outbreak of hostilities.

THE CHURCH AND MONASTICISM

The Church played an important role in the Christian Byzantine polity, which regarded itself as the avowed champion of orthodoxy, dedicated to the evangelization of neighboring peoples. Following the example of Constantine the Great, the Emperor took the lead in calling general councils to discuss doctrine and discipline. After the loss of Antioch, Jerusalem, and Alexandria to the Arabs the ecclesiastical leaders of Christendom were Rome and Constantinople. During the Middle Ages the Greek and Latin worlds unhappily drew apart and various attempts failed to heal the formal schism of 1054 between the two Churches, though in the 14th and 15th centuries it was literally a matter of life and death to Constantinople and the Balkan principalities.

Patriarchate of Constantinople. The patriarch of Constantinople, virtually appointed by the emperor, normally worked closely with him, though it was also his duty to reprove him if necessary; there are instances when the patriarch refused coronation or Communion until the emperor had amended his conduct. After all, episcopal authority was derived not from an imperial, but from an apostolic mandate. But, generally speaking, the two authorities worked well together and the use of the term "caesaropapism" to describe relations between the Byzantine Church and State is misleading.

The patriarchate of Constantinople was served by the normal ecclesiastical hierarchy. Metropolitans and bishops were responsible for the provinces and dioceses. They, like the patriarch, had their households, their synods, and their ecclesiastical courts. At the bottom of the scale was the priest or *pappas* who in Greek lands was a married man. Village folk often used monastery churches, and the supply of parish churches, as distinct from that of the private chapels of the rich, was probably somewhat inadequate. Big cathedrals, such as the Hagia Sophia in Constantinople, had their splendid sung services in magnificent surroundings and were in part financed by imperial donations. Churches associated with venerated relics would be thronged with streams of pilgrims from all over the Christian world. Such was the church of St. Demetrius in Thessalonica or the cathedral of Euchaita in northern Asia Minor dedicated to another warrior martyr, St. Theodore.

The splendid work of the early Church councils with their triumphant vindication of the Church's Trinitarian and Christological teaching and the brilliant exposition of outstanding patristic fathers is well known. But the Church was not always successful in fighting heresies, partly because doctrinal and political differences went hand in hand. The eastern provinces disliked being ruled by Constantinople and vernacular literatures grew up in Syriac and Coptic accompanied by tenacious adherence to unorthodox Christological teaching. This created "separated" churches regarded as heretical by Greek and Latin alike. They reciprocated the scorn of their opponents and went their own ways, keeping their identity under Islamic rule. Another widespread heresy that the Greeks, unlike the Latins, failed to eradicate, was the dualist teaching of a sect known as the *Bogomils from its 10th-century leader's name. It flourished in the Balkans side by side with acute criticism of social conditions and of Greek political and ecclesiastical dominance and it lingered on until the Ottoman conquest when some of the Bogomils became Moslem. But the greatest failure of Christendom was in respect to Islam. Moslems were regarded as heretics and it was rare to hear of a conversion; by the end of the Middle Ages Christianity in the east Mediterranean had receded.

Missionary Activity. In certain fields the medieval Greek Church had far-reaching missionary and other achievements to its credit. Its missionary bishops and priests were largely successful in planting the seeds of the Christian faith among the Hunnic peoples who moved from central Asia via the steppes of south Russia to the Hungarian plains. From the 7th century onward similar work was in progress in the Balkans among the Slavs. This work was extended north of the Black Sea to the kingdom of Kiev.

Diplomat and missionary worked side by side, and the acceptance of Christianity, quite apart from what the Church had to give in its own right, resulted also in the Slavs' introduction to the Byzantine way of life. The Slavs' debt to Byzantine statecraft was as marked as their debt to the Greek Church. Slav rulers borrowed from Byzantine administration and law and sent their children to be educated in the court circles of Constantinople. From the 10th century onward they married into Byzantine imperial and noble families. Above all, they were profoundly influenced by the Byzantine conception of a Christian and monarchical society.

This aspect of the Byzantine world was stressed at every turn and it clearly inspired the lesser rulers of the political hierarchy at whose apex the majestic imperial figure reigned preeminent. But it was not the mainspring of the Church's life. The last Greek emperor died in 1453 and for 4 centuries Byzantine lands were ruled by the infidel. Yet the Church survived. The source of its life lay partly in its monastic life, partly in the daily devotion of its humble priests and laity. Behind imperial politics or ecclesiastical ambitions had always lain the more profound essentials of the Christian life, made available through two channels—the Sacraments and the special spiritual gifts (*charismata*) of holy men and women.

Monastic Life. Monasticism had a special place in the Orthodox Church, whether of Greek, Slav, or other rite. Hermit life, or cells grouped around a proved ascetic, or life under a common roof, were not mutually exclusive in the east Mediterranean and it was possible to pass from one to the other and perhaps back again, although generally speaking, the eremetic way was considered to be far the more advanced. Unlike Western medieval monasticism, the Eastern and Slav Churches showed no differentiation into clear cut "orders." Some of the classics of this spirituality, as the *Ladder of Heavenly Ascent* written by the 6th-century

*John Climacus of Mount Sinai, or the sermons and mystical hymns of the 11th-century *Symeon the New Theologian, or the more homely saints' lives, help to explain monastic aims and influence.

The monk far advanced in the contemplative life might have passed beyond the ordinary sacramental channels, but for the most, whether lay or monastic, these were the mainspring of their spirituality, centering in the public worship of the divine liturgy, "to which the name of Eucharist is most fitly given, since this is the most perfect and intimate of our conversations with God, the sacrament of Communion," as the 14th-century Nicolas *Cabasilas wrote in his commentary on the Communion service. Byzantines had a strong sense of the "interplay" of time and eternity. Their artists painted frescoes showing the liturgy being celebrated by Christ and angels and the very plan of the interior decoration of their churches aimed at representing both heaven and earth, Christ and the angelic host, present together with the faithful.

BYZANTINE SOCIETY: SOCIAL AND ECONOMIC LIFE

The Byzantine Empire was a multiracial society bound together by its pride in a common political and religious tradition and by Greek civilization. But the overwhelming predominance of its Hellenic heritage did not insure its entire immunity from the influence of provinces and neighbors with different cultural roots, as Armenia or Syria, or later the young Slav peoples. Native languages persisted in Asia Minor until at least the 6th century, perhaps longer. Armenian and Georgian languages flourished in the Caucasus. The Balkan Slavs steadily clung to the use of their own language. But Greek was the lingua franca and the citizens of Byzantium who had other native tongues had to be bilingual.

The road to advancement was open to all without discrimination of race. *Justinian I came from a peasant family in the west Balkans; *Leo III was probably of North Syrian stock; Michael II was a rough soldier from Phrygia in Asia Minor. A particularly prominent role was played by Armenians: in the army they proved excellent fighting men and they were a dynamic influence in politics, but they were never very popular among the Greeks. Though of diverse racial origin and upbringing, the men who rose to the top positions adapted themselves in a remarkable way to the close-knit hierarchical system that dominated Byzantine society, accepting the demands of court ceremonial and taking pride in the imperial and administrative traditions of Byzantium.

Constantinople. As a capital, Constantinople was famous in both civilized and barbaric circles. The magnificent walled fortifications, the Golden Horn with its cosmopolitan throng of chants, the shipping, the churches with their venerated relics, the imperial palace, the senate and the hippodrome seemed to impress even the most hardened diplomat. The city was a magnet to traders and soldiers of fortune alike; even men of royal blood such as Harold Hardraga of Norway were found fighting in the ranks of the Byzantine army. The *Russian Primary Chronicle* tells how in 987 the Kievans who visited the churches of Tzarigrad, as they called Constantinople, did not know whether they were in heaven or on earth, and were unable to forget the beauty of what they saw. Those privileged to be received in the innermost imperial circle told of magnificent music and spectacular mechanical reproductions of growling lions that ushered the visitor into the sacred presence of the emperor. When the 10th-century ambassador *Liutprand of Cremona was there, he saw the splendid formal imperial presentation of the annual honorarium to dignitaries and officials robed in their ceremonial vestments.

Agriculture. For the majority outside the big cities, land and agriculture were all-important. This was equally true of the state since the land tax formed one of its main sources of revenue. In the production of bare essentials both large estates and small farms and villages could be self-sufficient, growing their grain, wheat or barley, and oats for cattle, as well as vegetables, olives, and vines, and supplementing their diet by fish. The wealthy household, whether in town or country, would have in its store-cupboards many extra delicacies and spices. The middle-class family in the cities seems to have fared better than the subsistence farmer of the countryside whose life was an unending struggle against the elements and the taxcollector. A bad season and no reserves must have led many a small farmer to turn to a less hazardous life as a tenant under the protection of a landed magnate. A legal code called the *Farmer's Law* dating probably from the late 7th or early 8th century provides information about life in a free village community of small farmers, describing the usual country hazards, such as loss of oxen to marauding wolves or hired shepherds who surreptitiously milked their master's cattle. The central government was anxious to preserve the independence of the small rural proprietor, who might also be one of the soldier-farmers settled on the land, but this proved a losing battle. The treasury was naturally interested in those farmers who made payments directly to the fisc and it tried to limit the migration of such men to the large lay or ecclesiastical estates. In the early 11th century the responsibility for taxes from uncultivated land was removed from the village community and placed on the shoulders of the "powerful," but once *Basil II's strong hand was removed this arrangement was short-lived. After the Turkish invasion of Asia Minor in the 11th century large areas passed out of Byzantine control. Villagers no doubt adapted themselves as best they could to Moslem rule, but the great estates of the Asian provinces no longer remained in Christian hands. Henceforth the Byzantines had to rely on their European lands and here the nobles still retained great wealth in trade, industry, and cattle, particularly in Thessaly and Macedonia.

Trade. Judged by medieval standards the more important Byzantine cities were large and the towns comparatively plentiful. Late 7th-century conciliar lists record from 174 to 211 bishops from towns mostly in Asia Minor, for at this period ecclesiastical life had been disrupted in the Balkans by the Slav invasions and the eastern provinces had been lost to the Arabs. There is reason to believe that economic life continued in a number of towns apart from the important centers such as Constantinople and Thessalonica, which never fell to the Slavs. Ephesus, Nicaea, and Trebizond in Asia Minor, Anchialus on the western shores of the Black Sea, and Cherson to the north were such towns. In Greece Thebes and Corinth became such renowned centers of the silk industry that in the 12th century

they roused the envy of the Norman ruler of Sicily who raided them and kidnaped their silk-workers. Industry and trade were controlled by the state. The 10th-century *Book of the Prefect* describes the city regulations and the guild system then in force in Constantinople. The export of certain goods, for instance the best brocades, was strictly controlled, but not to the detriment of Byzantine trade, which indeed flourished. Byzantine industry specialized in exquisitely designed and magnificently woven materials and other luxuries, such as jewelry and enameled cloisonné, gold and silver plate and church ornaments and vases, and finely worked ivories. There was a ready market for its products both within the empire and without. And there were of course the more homely articles and commodities. Foodstuffs and raw materials from all parts of the empire and from outside sources found a sale in the larger cities as well as in the capital. Merchants journeying over the Russian waterways brought honey and furs. Fields outside the walls of Constantinople in the 9th century produced grain which, after supplying the city's own needs, could be shipped to Thessalonica. Some slave labor was used throughout the Middle Ages and slaves were considered to be an acceptable kind of import.

Constantinople and the other ports of the empire were admirably situated for international as well as internal trade. Byzantine merchants were the middlemen of East and West and it was a profitable role. Their success was partly due to a stable gold coinage, which was not seriously debased until the 11th century. When in the 7th century the Arabs cut off supplies of gold from Nubian sources, the Byzantines could still look to the mines of Asia Minor and the Caucasus lands. Custom dues together with land taxes formed the main items in the Byzantine budget, and when from the 11th century onward the Italian cities gained strongholds and concessions within the empire, they deprived the empire of one of its main sources of revenue. Even so, compared with contemporary Western countries, Byzantium was still wealthy, and it was certainly envied by its Latin neighbors.

Although life was always hard for the small farmer and for hired labor in the cities, there were certain compensations and amenities. In the larger towns there were public races and entertainments, imperial processions, and, on occasion, imperial largesse. In the countryside there was excitement and often profit to be gained from the throngs of pilgrims visiting a shrine on a popular saint's festival. There were the big annual fairs in town and countryside; one of the most famous was held in Thessalonica on the feast of the city's patron, St. *Demetrius. These were all accompanied not only by vendors but by troops of entertainers and musicians. In need and sickness, the pauper might receive help and sometimes even burial from the neighboring monastic house. All monasteries included almsgiving as part of their daily function, and some were by their charter tied to particular duties of this nature. Imperial and princely patrons sometimes attached to their foundation a home for old people, or an orphanage, or a hospital. Medical and nursing staffs were provided and the monks were charged with general supervision. In the countryside the humble small monastery was equally ready to help its village neighbors, as innumerable saints' lives record.

EDUCATION AND ART

Continuity with the Greco-Roman world was nowhere more marked than in Byzantine learning. Byzantium was an educated society, at least in the middle and upper reaches. Even when the empire was broken up in 1204, the little scattered Greek kingdoms set store by their libraries and harassed rulers could still find the time to read voraciously. Thus education was never the monopoly of the Church; moreover, it could be enjoyed by girls as well as boys. A secular education based on Greek literature and rhetoric was conducted at the lowest level in the village school and at the highest in centers of learning such as Constantinople, or, in the very early period, *Beirut or *Gaza, the one famous for legal, the other for philosophical, studies.

Higher Education. Until 1204 Constantinople was understandably a particularly favored center for higher education and the resort of scholars. The state university, founded in 425, was reorganized under imperial patronage in the mid-11th century and it offered free facilities for legal studies, essential for civil servants; for the arts the faculty of philosophy was under the direction of the distinguished scholar Michael *Psellus. There were also ecclesiastical schools run by clerical staffs. But many a monk or ecclesiastic had been grounded in the disciplines of Greek education before he entered the Church or monastery, where he could apply his techniques to a study of the Fathers or to spiritual and theological problems, as is reflected in countless catechetical sermons or Biblical commentaries or indeed in their openly secular activity. For instance, Abp. Eustathius of Thessalonica in the 12th century was a cultured man of the world with wide interests and, in addition to his writings on religious topics, he left a moving and graphic account of the sack of Thessalonica in 1185 and well known commentaries on classical authors, particularly Homer. It was not essential to attend a university. Young, and perhaps penniless, scholars could find their training in the households of wealthy patrons who themselves would often take part in learned discussions and read far into the night though they were at the same time carrying heavy ministerial responsibilities. Such was Theodore Metochites, the grand chamberlain in the early 14th century. He furthered the arts as well as sciences, as is shown in his restoration of the church of the Chora (Kariye Djami) with its splendid mosaics and frescoes.

Literature. In this educated society there was constant demand for copies of handwritten books. The *scriptorium, or copying room, was the printing press of the Middle Ages and to it we owe not only Byzantine secular and ecclesiastical literature but such classical texts as the tragedies of Euripides, which the medieval Greeks read. To meet current needs the essential tools such as dictionaries and encyclopedias were produced. There was a spate of material on a wide range of practical subjects, including veterinary surgery, beekeeping, military engineering, and optics. There were commentaries on philosophers such as Aristotle and Plato. But the finest products of Byzantine secular literature were its histories (as distinct from biographies and chronicles), which were generally contemporary history written by men of the world nourished in the twin traditions of classical learning and Christian religion. Almost every age produced historians of distinct individuality. Despite their vaunted objectivity, they stand self-revealed in their writings, e.g., the vain, shrewd, observant scholar and "emperor maker" Psellus; the proud, self-conscious, arrogant princess Anna Comnena; the touchy humanist Nicephorus Gregoras, with his partiality for astronomy; and the likable, detached former emperor Cantacuzenus. In execution and method their histories were superb, quite apart from their brilliant content. Among surviving Byzantine prose works there is a vast body also of occasional pieces, panegyrics, and letters written in the florid style fashionable in Byzantine circles.

The language of literature was an imitation of the Attic style of classical days, differing from both medieval demotic or popular Greek as spoken and the koine or "common" Greek used in ecclesiastical works from New Testament days and earlier. There are traces of the usages of demotic or vernacular Greek even in writers in the classical or "pure" language, but these slipped in unawares. Nevertheless, by the end of the Middle Ages there was only a slender output of literature written entirely in this vernacular idiom for it was not generally regarded as a literary medium appropriate for an educated man.

Theological and religious writings have survived in abundance: polemic against heretics, Biblical commentaries, doctrinal exposition, ascetical handbooks, as well as saints' lives and liturgical works. Byzantine spirituality is in a class by itself. Noted for acumen and psychological insight is St. John Climacus (of the Ladder), so-called because of his book *The Ladder of Heavenly Ascent.* Byzantines seem to have found lyrical outlet in their writings on spirituality. The 11th-century monk Symeon the Young described his experiences in his *Hymns of the Divine Love,* in nonclassical meter having a syllabic stress.

Some Byzantine poetry (both secular and religious) was written in the old classical quantitative meters. There are long descriptive pieces, such as that on the newly built cathedral of Hagia Sophia in Constantinople or on the Emperor Heraclius's campaigns; there are also epitaphs, love songs, and short descriptive poems. One of the finest surviving secular poems, the epic *Digenis Akrites,* is in syllabic meter. This popular poem, based on folk tales and meant to be recited in banquet halls, tells of the exploits on the eastern frontier of a marcher-lord born of two races. Religious poems written in nonclassical meter are legion. Many of these fill supplementary hymnbooks for monastic use; some were incorporated into the divine liturgy and are still in the service books. Short hymns, such as " O joyful light," gradually developed into something more elaborate. The kontakion was a kind of dramatic exposition, often of fine poetic quality, based on syllabic stress with frequent rhyme. The *canon,* written and elaborated from the 7th century onward, consisted of nine short hymns each referring to one of the great Biblical canticles, and sometimes they were bound together by an acrostic.

Music. Byzantine church music, of which a considerable body survives, was closely related to the words of these hymns. Both poets and musicians followed tradition in imitating patterns or referring to Biblical songs. Medieval church poetry and music at their best are among the highest of Byzantine achievements and are still part of a living tradition.

Arts and Crafts. Byzantine raciness and relish in secular occupations was paradoxically linked with a deep concern for Christianity. This combination is reflected in their art. Their genius for design and craftsmanship is displayed in exquisitely designed jewelry and silks, which were used both in their households and in their churches. The same ability is displayed in their architecture and mural decoration, which rank among their highest achievements. Their genius showed itself in their fusion of existing architectural traditions into the domed church of which the supreme example is Hagia Sophia in Constantinople built in Justinian's day. Here the magnificent cupolas and rich interior decoration create a sense of infinity that remains unsurpassed. Other surviving churches also, though on a smaller scale, show a plan of interior decoration, which was carefully related to the architecture and was designed to be part of the liturgical worship. In the great days of Byzantium the medium of interior decoration was mosaic; later, after 1204, it was more usually fresco. Disaster did not dim Byzantine art, and some of the most striking work was created in the 14th century. Such was the dynamic figure of Christ rising triumphant over Satan and reclaiming Adam and Eve from Limbo (the Anastasis), which dominates the east wall of the mortuary chapel in the church of Kariye Djami in Constantinople. Secular architecture was doubtless as magnificent and impressive as ecclesiastical, but practically nothing after the 6th century has survived. It was the Church that outlived the empire and remained the center of Greek aspirations under Ottoman domination.

The Byzantine achievement is something more positive and creative than the preservation of ancient Greek literature or the defense of the medieval Latin world against the onslaught of Islam. It stands in its own right. It was above all a way of life, woven of a dual thread, the ascetic other-worldly and the humanist, and this Christian and Hellenic tradition was a formative influence not only in the medieval Greek-speaking lands, but in the young South Slav countries and Russia.

See also BYZANTINE EMPIRE; BYZANTINE LITERATURE; BYZANTINE THEOLOGY.

Bibliography: N. H. BAYNES, *The Byzantine Empire* (London 1925; rev. ed. 1943); *Byzantine Studies and Other Essays* (New York 1955). N. H. BAYNES and E. A. S. DAWES, trs., *Three Byzantine Saints* (Oxford 1948). N. H. BAYNES and H. ST. L. B. MOSS, eds., *Byzantium* (Oxford 1948). L. BRÉHIER, *Le Monde byzantin*, 3 v. (Paris 1947–50) v.1. J. B. BURY, *A History of the Eastern Roman Empire from the Fall of Irene to the Accession of Basil I, 802–867* (London 1912); *A History of the Later Roman Empire from Arcadius to Irene, 395–800*, 2 v. (New York 1889); 2d ed. . . . *from the Death of Theodosius I to the Death of Justinian, A.D. 395–565*, 2 v. (London 1923). CMedH (new ed. 1966). v.4. C. DIEHL, *Byzantium: Greatness and Decline*, tr. N. WALFORD, ed. P. CHARANIS (New Brunswick, N.J. 1957). *Dumbarton Oaks Papers* (Cambridge, Mass. 1941), this now appears almost every year and contains studies on nearly all aspects of Byzantine civilization. G. EVERY, *The Byzantine Patriarchate* (2d ed. London 1962). R. M. FRENCH, *The Eastern Orthodox Church* (London 1951). D. J. GEANAKOPLOS, *Emperor Michael Palaeologus and the West, 1258–1282* (Cambridge, Mass. 1959). K. M. SETTON, ed., *A History of the Crusades* (Philadelphia 1955–). J. M. HUSSEY, *Church and Learning in the Byzantine Empire, 867–1185* (Oxford 1937); *The Byzantine World* (London 1961). Ostrogorsky. S. RUNCIMAN, *Byzantine Civilisation* (London 1933); *A History of the Crusades*, 3 v. (Cambridge, Eng. 1951–54); *The Sicilian Vespers* (Cambridge, Eng. 1958). D. T. RICE, *The Byzantines* (New York 1962). A. A. VASILIEV, *History of the Byzantine Empire*, tr. S. RAGOZIN, (2d ed. Madison 1952).

[J. M. HUSSEY]

BYZANTINE EMPIRE

The Byzantine Empire may be defined as the continuation of the later Roman Empire in the East. Byzantinists tend to begin Byzantine history with the foundation of Constantinople by Constantine the Great (A.D. 330), or even with the accession of Diocletian (A.D. 284; e.g., E. Stein). However, it is hardly just to speak of a Byzantine Empire in any strict sense before the separation of the Roman Empire into two halves after the death of *Theodosius I (A.D. 395), or of a Byzantine Empire in an exclusive sense before *Justinian I the Great (527–565). For the history of the Later Roman Empire, including the collapse of the western half of the empire, *see* ROMAN EMPIRE. This article deals with the early Byzantine Empire (395–641), the middle Byzantine Empire (641–1081), and the late Byzantine Empire (1081–1453). The treatment is primarily political, as there are separate articles on other phases.

EARLY BYZANTINE EMPIRE (395–641)

This age was characterized by the transformation of the eastern half of the later Roman Empire into the fully developed Byzantine state in both the political and religious spheres; by Justinian's attempt to recover the West; by the far-reaching reforms of Heraclius; and by the successful defense of Constantinople against Islam.

Arcadius and His Successors (395–527). Theodosius I divided the government of the empire, giving the East to *Arcadius (d. 408) and the West to *Honorius (d. 423), but there was continual rivalry between the generals and regents of Arcadius and the German General Stilicho, who controlled the West for Honorius. The *Visigoths under Alaric invaded the Balkans, and, despite the growth of an anti-German party in Constantinople, the Goths and Germans formed an indispensable element in the Byzantine military to the 7th century. Under *Theodosius II (408–450) the Theodosian Code was promulgated (438) in East and West alike; and despite a practical separation, a generally peaceful relationship prevailed. War with Persia was activated because of the persecution of the newly flowering Armenian Christianity, and the *Huns under Attila ravaged both the Balkans and Italy, where chaos reigned after the murders of General Aetius (454) and Valentinian III (455).

The theological disputes that followed the Council of *Chalcedon (451), called by Emperor *Marcian and Empress Pulcheria with the consent of Pope *Leo I (440–461), led to uprisings in Egypt, Syria, and the East, and the formation of the Monophysite Church (*see* MONOPHYSITISM), while the *Nestorians gradually emigrated to the East through Persia. Under *Leo I the Isaurian (457–474), who was the first emperor to be crowned by the patriarch of Constantinople, an attempt was made to free the throne from the control of Aspar the Alan and the Ostrogoths. Aspar was assassinated in 471. Following the sudden death of Leo II (474), son of General Zeno the Isaurian, who had married Ariadne, daughter of Leo I, Zeno himself obtained the imperial throne (474). He was deposed and replaced by *Basiliscus the following year, but again obtained the imperial office and held it despite plots and civil war for 15 years (476–491). Then in 482 he published the *Henoticon*, which occasioned the *Acacian Schism. He solved the Gothic problem in the East by encouraging *Theodoric

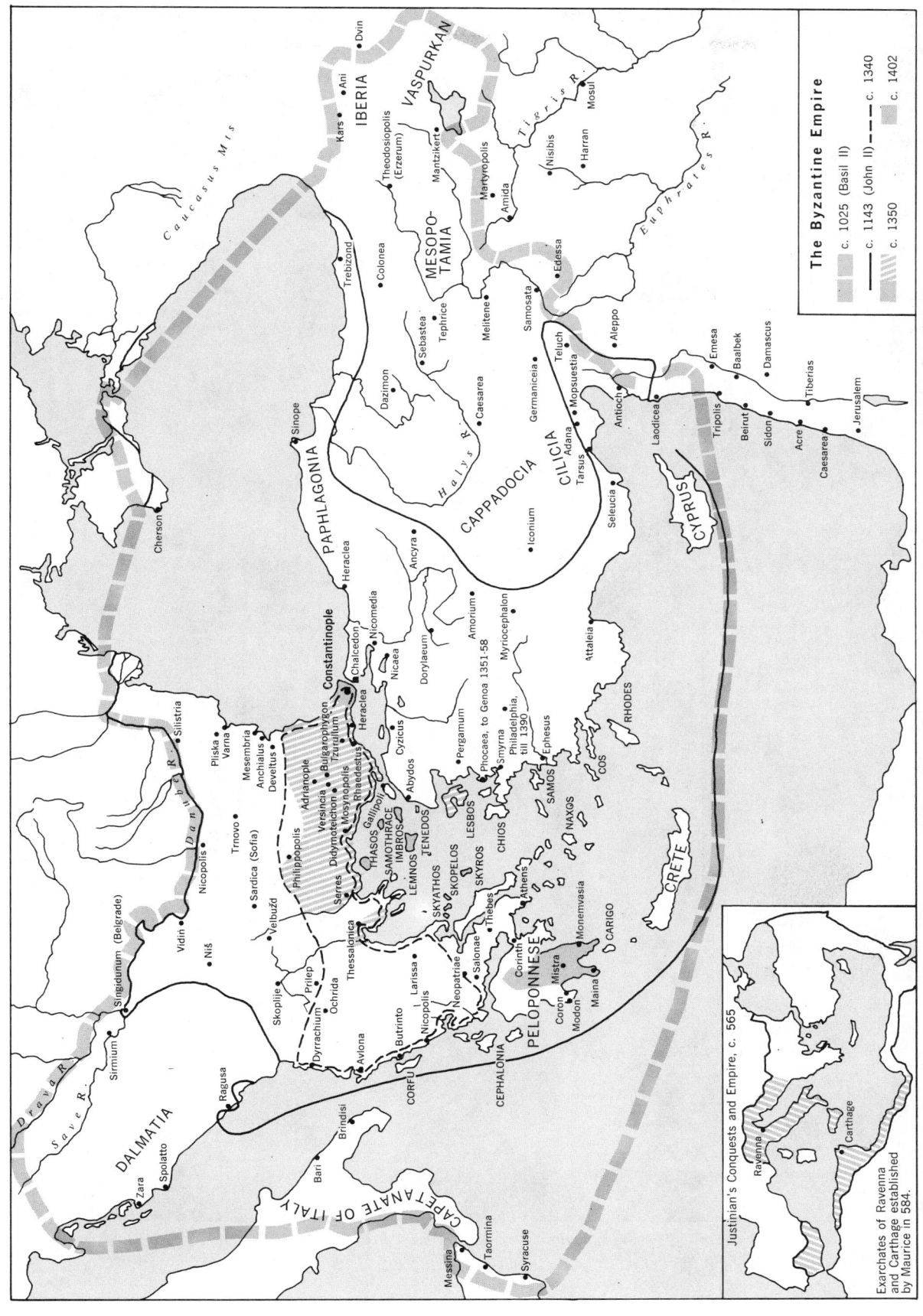

The Byzantine Empire

c. 1025 (Basil II)   —— c. 1340
c. 1143 (John II)   ---- c. 1402
                          c. 1350

Justinian's Conquests and Empire, c. 565

Exarchates of Ravenna
and Carthage established
by Maurice in 584.

Fig. 1. The Byzantine Empire in the more important stages of its history.

Fig. 2. The Emperor Anastasius I (491–518) on the "Bar-
berini Diptych," 6th century, in the Musée du Louvre. In
the bottom panel barbarians bring tribute, and an embassy
from India brings ivory and beasts to the court.

the Great to attack Odoacer in Italy and thus had a part in the establishment of a new Ostrogothic kingdom in the West.

On his death, Ariadne married the elderly courtier Anastasius (491–518), who, though a pious Monophysite, proved to be a good administrator, in particular by his stabilization of the monetary system. Nevertheless he was faced with a rebellion of the Blues, and could not achieve an effective religious or imperial policy. (In Byzantine history the circus factions, especially the Blues and Greens, were aggressive and influential organizations in politics.) His successor, *Justin I (518–527), was a Latin from Thrace who reasserted the unity of the empire by ending the Acacian schism through agreement with the Pope and began a series of reconquests in the West.

Justinian I. His nephew *Justinian I the Great (527–565) reconquered North Africa, Italy, and Spain; but this victorious action had required the neglect of the Danube area and a slackening of the struggle with the Persians. In 532 the bravery of Empress *Theodora (1) saved the throne for Justinian in the Nika riots. While she favored the Monophysite party and frequently acted contrary to the Emperor's religious policy, the imperial couple lived a simple pious life. Justinian attempted to solve religious dissensions, condemned Origenism (see ORIGEN AND ORIGENISM), held colloquies with the Monophysites, exerted strong pressure on Pope *Vigilius, whom he forced to come to Constantinople to support his views, and convoked the Council of *Constantinople II (553). He attempted to complete the suppression of paganism, crushed Samaritan and Jewish revolts in ruthless fashion, took stern measures against Arians and, above all, against Manichaeans, and encouraged missionary activity, particularly in the Orient. But his costly military operations and indecisive administrative reforms, despite the great codification of Roman law carried out under his direction (see ROMAN LAW, 4), did not pacify the political factions within or deal successfully with the converging enemies of the empire from without.

His successors, *Justin II (565–578), Tiberius Constantine (578–582), and *Maurice (582–602), despite the loss of Italy to the Lombards (568) and Spain to the Visigoths (584), finally defeated Persia and brought most of *Armenia into the empire. Maurice the most distinguished emperor in this group, was responsible for the victory over the Persians. In the West, he regrouped the remnants of Justinian's conquests in the exarchates of Carthage and Ravenna. In his years of campaigning he was unable, however, to destroy the Slavic power in the Balkans and was deposed and murdered in a revolt led by the general, Phocas, who replaced him as emperor (602–610). Under the tyrannical Phocas, who was supported by the Blues, a reign of terror convulsed the empire. The slaughter of representatives of the high aristocracy was answered by aristocratic conspiracy against the tyrant. Phocas's one positive achievement was his edict addressed to Pope *Boniface III in which he recognized the apostolic Church of St. Peter as head of all the Churches. On the verge of ruin, the empire was saved by the action of the exarch of Carthage, Heraclius, who dispatched his son, also called Heraclius, with an army and fleet to Constantinople where he was crowned emperor (Oct. 5, 610). Phocas and his followers were massacred.

Heraclius and His Organization of Themes. *Heraclius (610–641), one of the greatest of all Byzantine emperors, reorganized the administration and defence of the empire on the principle of large military zones called themes under control of a *strategus,* or general. Soldiers were settled in these zones and were given inalienable grants of land provided that they should furnish hereditary military service. Having established the four primary themes in Asia Minor, the Emperor carried through a complete reorganization of the central administration. The praefectorian system was replaced by a number of financial departments headed by officers called logothetes. The reorganization of the army and the adoption of new tactics and his personal leadership made possible the Emperor's brilliant victories over the Avars and Persians. He was greatly aided by a renewal of religious fervor under Patriarchs *Sergius I (610–638) and *Pyrrhus (638–641), whom he appointed regents in his absence. In 628, after his victories, the Persian dynasty collapsed, and Heraclius took possession of Armenia, Mesopotamia, Syria, Palestine, and Egypt. On March 21, 630, Heraclius restored the Holy Cross to Jerusalem—it had been taken to Ctesiphon by the Persians after their sack of Jerusalem in 614—as a symbol of the first great holy war of Christendom. He put an end to the official use of Latin, making Greek the official language of the empire, and gave impetus to a renewal of culture.

Adopting the old Greek title of *Basileus,* he cooperated with Patriarch Sergius in an attempt to restore religious unity by publishing an *Ecthesis* that established *Monothelitism (638) as the official Christology of the realm. *Sophronius, Patriarch of Jerusalem, vigorously opposed this doctrine, and when the Mohammedans conquered Syria and Palestine (638), the futility of the imperial religious policy became apparent (see MOHAMMED; ISLAM). The persecutions of Syrians and Copts by the Byzantine Empire for their religious belief led them to take—initially at least—a friendly attitude toward the new conquerors. The reign of Heraclius marks the end of the first major period in Byzantine history and the beginning of the second—a beginning that was already affected by the sudden rise and amazingly rapid conquests of Islam and their consequences for Byzantium.

THE MIDDLE BYZANTINE EMPIRE

It is characterized by the consolidation of the reforms of Heraclius, by the menace of Islam and the defense of Constantinople, by the iconoclastic controversy, the codification of Byzantine law, and the flowering of Byzantine civilization under Leo VI, but subsequently by the disintegration of the internal administration and by the disastrous defeat at Manzikert (1071) in Armenia and the loss of Bari in Italy in the same year.

The Successors of Heraclius and the Menace of Islam. Following the death of Heraclius, Empress Martina, his niece and second wife, who was bitterly hated by the people, failed despite all her efforts to become regent for her son Heraclonas. Heraclius Constantine, the son of Heraclius by his first wife, was elected emperor as Constantine III, but died 3 months later. His son, a boy of 11 years, was chosen emperor as *Constans II (641–668). In later life he was nicknamed *Pogonatus,* "the bearded." Despite defeats by the newly created Arab sea

Fig. 3. The Virgin and Child enthroned between the Emperors Constantine I (306–337) and Justinian I (527–565), late 10th-century mosaic in the south vestibule of Hagia Sophia. The Emperors symbolically present the Church.

power, he profited by internal strife among the caliphs and made peace in the East (659). He then carried on successful campaigns against the Slavs. A decade earlier, he found it necessary to deal with religious revolt within the empire. To achieve religious peace, he issued his *Type* (648), forbidding any discussion of the problem of the divine will as well as the problem of the divine energy.

At the Council of the Lateran held under Pope *Martin I (October 649)—whose election (July 5) had not been sanctioned by the exarch of Ravenna—both the *Ecthesis* and the *Type* were condemned and Patriarchs Sergius I, Paul II, and Pyrrhus I were excommunicated. On June 15, 653, the Pope was taken prisoner, transported to Constantinople, condemned for treason by the Senate, and maltreated publicly. He died in exile at Cherson (656). Probably in 653 also, *Maximus the Confessor was arrested, tried, and condemned; after exiles in various places, he died in Lazica (Aug. 13, 662). Maximus had challenged the Emperor's right to decide religious questions on the ground that he was a layman and that this right belonged to the Church alone. The idea was not new but Maximus gave it a clear—and quotable—foundation. In 663 Constans, in order to strengthen the position of the empire in the West, rather than because of the hatred of the people of Constantinople, established himself during the last 5 years of his life at Syracuse, but no full-scale transfer of government from Constantinople to the West was carried out.

His campaigns against the *Lombards failed, and he was assassinated in his bath (668).

The reign of his son, *Constantine IV (668–685), was a decisive one not only for Byzantine but for world history as well. The Arabs ravaged Asia Minor repeatedly from 663 on, and by 670 Cyprus, Rhodes, Cos, Chios, and the peninsula of Cyzicus were in their hands. In 672 Smyrna and the coasts of Lycia and Cilicia were occupied. Constantinople itself was attacked for 4 years in succession (674–678), but the use of Greek fire—invented by the Greek architect Callinicus and employed for the first time—played a decisive role in the repulse of the Arabs.

This defeat of the Arabs proved a turning point in their bid for world dominance. In fact, it was the first and most important of the great Christian victories that halted or repelled the advance of Islam. Avars and Slavs asked for peace and friendship, but Constans was unable to halt the penetration of the Bulgars into the Balkans. Religious peace within the empire remained a pressing problem. Accordingly, after consultation with the Pope, Constans summoned the General Council of *Constantinople III (Nov. 7, 680–Sept. 16, 681) with the hope of reestablishing religious unity and peace. The council defined the doctrine of the two wills and two energies in Christ; it condemned Monothelitism and excommunicated Patriarchs Sergius, Paul, Pyrrhus, Peter of Constantinople, and also Cyrus of Alexandria, Theodore of Pharan, and Pope Honorius.

Constans, who died at the early age of 33, was followed by his son *Justinian II (685–695 and 705–711), who had an exalted concept of his office and wished to emulate the achievements of his great namesake. He was successful in a large-scale campaign against the Slavs, and he continued the colonization policy of Heraclius. He strengthened the manpower of the themes, creating the new theme of Hellas. He encouraged the development of free peasantry by the Farmer's Law (Νόμος γεωργικός), which apparently belongs to his reign. A devout ruler, he presided over the *Quinisext Council in Trullo (691–692), which drew up a series of disciplinary canons that the previous general councils (the fifth and sixth) had neglected to provide. When the Pope objected to certain of these canons, the Emperor took steps to apprehend him for trial, but on this occasion the imperial officer had to ask protection from the Pope.

Justinian's high-handed measures at Constantinople led to revolt and to his deposition, mutilation (his nose was cut off; hence his nickname Rhinometus), and exile. His successors, Leontius, elected through the Blues (695–698), and Tiberius II (698–705), elected largely through the rival faction of the Greens, made no headway against the Arabs. North Africa was lost in 697, and the Arabs entered Spain in 711. Meantime, Justinian escaped from exile in Cherson, married Theodora, the daughter of the Khazar ruler, and by his fantastic boldness and resourcefulness regained both the throne (705–711). The Emperor indulged his vengeance with such savagery that the power of the empire was badly damaged. However, the dispute over the canons of the Quinisext Council was settled, and Pope *Constantine I, on the invitation of the Emperor, visited Constantinople in 710 and was received with great pomp. In 711 an Armenian, Philippicus Bardanes, was proclaimed emperor. Justinian and his infant son were murdered, thus ending the house of Heraclius. Under this dynasty the whole organization and outlook of the Byzantine Empire underwent a radical transformation. As Ostrogorsky puts it epigrammatically, "it had become an Empire of soldiers and monks" (129).

The Age of Iconoclasm. Philippicus Bardanes (711–713) had Monothelite leanings. He canceled the decisions of the Council of Constantinople III and destroyed the inscription that commemorated the council in the imperial palace. Papal reaction took the form of refusing to impress the Emperor's portrait on coins, and his name was omitted from prayers and official documents. In addition, the Pope had representations of the first six ecumenical councils put up in St. Peter's. When the Arabs and Bulgars advanced on Constantinople, Philippicus was deposed and blinded (June 3, 713). The new Emperor, Anastasius II (713–715), rescinded the Monothelite decrees of his predecessor. Despite the danger of Arab invasion, civil war broke out, and Anastasius was replaced by the weak Theodosius III (715–717). The latter in turn was soon forced out of office by the North Syrian Leo, *strategus* of the Anatolian theme, who was crowned emperor as *Leo III (717–741) and who founded the Syrian dynasty (717–802).

Leo had to defend the city immediately against an Arab siege. Thanks to a pestilence in the enemy camp and Bulgar aid, the blockade was lifted (Aug. 15, 718). Constantinople was saved a second time from Arab conquest, and further Arab depredations were halted

through an alliance of Byzantium with the *Khazars (733). Leo developed further the system of themes and theme administration. His legal manual, the *Ecloga* (726), marks an epoch in Byzantine legal history. It updated or supplemented the Justinian legislation with the practical needs of judges as the primary concern in its selection and presentation of legal matters. It reflects the greater influence of Canon Law and also that of Oriental customary law (*see* ROMAN LAW, 5).

*Iconoclasm, however, became the central issue in Leo's reign. In 726 the Emperor revealed his design to curb the veneration of icons in keeping with the feelings of the eastern provinces of the empire. His edict of 730 against images caused fanatical opposition in Constantinople and the other large cities of the empire, and his policy was opposed by both Patriarch *Germanus I and Pope *Gregory II. When Pope *Gregory III condemned iconoclasm in two Roman synods (731), Leo treated his legates shamefully. He seized the opportunity to detach Sicily, Calabria, and Illyricum from Roman control and placed them—along with their revenues—under the Patriarchate of Constantinople. The Emperor thus extended his own control in ecclesiastical affairs, for he believed that he could exert pressure much more easily on the patriarch of Constantinople than on the Pope. The Pope, on the other hand, was led under the circumstances to turn to the West for military and political support. The cleavage between East and West now became much more marked in the consciousness of both.

The accession of *Constantine V (741–775), son of Leo III, was disputed by the anti-iconoclast Artabasdus, *strategus* of the Armenian theme, who was crowned emperor by Patriarch *Anastasius and who restored the icons. However, Constantine V regained Constantinople (Nov. 2, 743), exposed Artabasdus to public ignomy, and punished the patriarch but retained him in office. A greater military leader and more violent iconoclast than his father, Constantine owed his victories over the Arabs and Bulgars to his calculating strategy and personal courage. He destroyed an Arab fleet (747), reconquered Armenia and Mesopotamia, and died during a campaign against the Bulgars in 775. Through his neglect of Italy, however, Ravenna was taken by the Lombards (751). This marked the end of the Byzantine exarchate in central and northern Italy and gave a new incentive to the Pope to seek Frankish aid against the Lombards.

Constantine had played a leading part in the attack on icons, composing 13 theological tracts in which he emphatically condemned the representation of Christ as idolatry. In the packed council held in the palace of Hieria on the Bosporus (Feb. 10, 754), with a final session in the church of the Blachernae in Constantinople (August 8), 338 bishops subscribed to iconoclasm. Despite the absence of papal legates and the patriarchs at the council, the Emperor then embarked on a ruthless destruction of ecclesiastical and pietistic art. Abbot Stephen of Mt. Auxentius in Asia Minor died a martyr's death as a leader of the opposition (November 765), monasteries were closed, and a number of public officials were executed. The monastic opposition was strongest of all. Hence the persecution of the monks was especially violent.

The short reign of Leo IV (775–780) brought comparative peace to the religious situation, particularly through the influence of his wife, *Irene, whose son

Constantine VI (780–797) was supported by the army following the premature death of his father (Sept. 8, 780). In 784, Irene as regent forced the iconoclast Patriarch Paul to resign and, having assembled the populace of Constantinople, had Tarasius consecrated as the new patriarch (784–806).

On agreement with Rome a new Council of Constantinople was convoked in July 786, but it was interrupted by the military and reassembled as the Council of *Nicaea II in May 787. It received the former iconoclast bishops into communion upon their abjuration of heresy, despite the opposition of the monks, and, following the teachings of St. *John Damascene, linked the veneration of images with the theology of salvation. In 790, after Constantine VI rebelled against her tutelage, Irene attempted to have herself proclaimed as senior coruler but failed. In 793, however, Constantine divorced his wife, Maria, and married his mistress, Theodote. This act occasioned the *Moechian controversy (from μοιχεία, adultery) and its repercussions. Constantine soon lost both orthodox and iconoclast support, and in 797 his mother had him blinded and deposed. Irene (797–802) was supported by the monks and, through a relief in taxation, won over the people. Foreign and financial policy was badly handled under Constantine VI and Irene. The Byzantines were defeated in battle by the Arabs, and a heavy tribute had to be paid as the price of peace. Irene's repeal of certain taxes and reduction of import and export duties practically ruined the finances of Byzantium.

The Council of Nicaea II had condemned iconoclasm but had not yielded to the demands of Rome regarding papal prerogatives. Pope *Hadrian I's letter to the council was read, but the passages containing papal claims were omitted. Hence Hadrian's successor, Pope *Leo III, confirmed the alliance made by Pope *Stephen II and Hadrian between the papacy and the Carolingian kingdom by a revolutionary act, the crowning of *Charlemagne as emperor at Rome on Dec. 25, 800. In 802, legates from both Pope and Emperor arrived in Constantinople to secure Charlemagne's recognition by the Byzantine ruler, but, owing to the palace revolution (Oct. 31, 802), in which Irene was deposed and replaced by Nicephorus, former logothete of the treasury, no action could be taken at this time.

Administrative Reform and the End of Iconoclasm (802–843). Nicephorus I (802–811) was an able ruler, although happier in his civil reforms than in the religious field. His appointment of the learned layman *Nicephorus I as patriarch of Constantinople after the death of Tarasius (806) caused a deep resentment that was increased by the revival of the Moechian controversy and the Emperor's recognition—in defiance of the canons—of the marriage of Constantine VI and Theodote. As a former financial official, he carried through a sweeping and badly needed reform of public finances, including a general reassessment and the establishment of new taxes, especially the hearth tax, a kind of poll tax. He reformed the system of landholdings in the themes in order to make available a larger number of men liable for military service. His elaborate colonization program was intended to protect exposed areas and, again, to increase manpower for military service.

In 805 he defeated the Slavs who had invested Patras, and the people ascribed the victory to the miraculous intervention of St. Andrew the Apostle. The event restored Byzantine power in the Peloponnese after 200 years of Slav control. But the destruction of the Avars by Charlemagne unleashed Bulgar forces under a powerful leader, Krum. In 811 Nicephorus defeated them at Pliska, but his army was destroyed in the mountain passes (July 26, 811), and he himself was killed. The disastrous defeat and death of the Emperor in battle was a heavy blow to Byzantine prestige and foreign policy. Although his son Stauracius escaped and recovered from his wounds, Michael I Rangabe, the brother-in-law of Nicephorus, was proclaimed emperor (Oct. 2, 811) and crowned by the patriarch; but he ruled only 2 years. He broke with the economic policy of Nicephorus, supported the veneration of icons, and employed *Theodore the Studite as a revered advisor in civil as well as religious affairs.

In 812 Byzantine legates in Aachen recognized Charlemagne as *Basileus,* thus admitting *de facto* the existence of two empires. Michael was defeated by the Slavs at Versinicia, near Adrianople, on June 22, 813, and deposed. On July 11, *Leo V the Armenian (813–820) became emperor.

Leo V determined to imitate his great predecessors as generals and iconoclasts. In autumn 813 he defeated the Bulgars at Mesembria. However, Krum's march on Constantinople the next year was halted only by his sudden death (April 13, 814), after which a 30-year peace was signed with his successor, Omurtag. Leo then pursued an iconoclast policy, despite his written promise to Patriarch Nicephorus at the start of his reign that he would not change the religious situation in the empire. The Emperor relied on the theology of *John Grammaticus as his chief advisor in iconoclasm, while Theodore the Studite, the champion of the icons, and many other monks were exiled. Patriarch Nicephorus was deposed, and Theodotus Melissenus was installed in his place (April 1, 815). A synod repudiated the Council of Nicaea II, recognized the acts of the iconoclast council of 754, and ordered the destruction of the restored icons. The movement lacked dynamism, however, and on Christmas Day 820 Leo was assassinated at the services in Hagia Sophia by the followers of the uncultured officer Michael the Amorian.

Michael II (820–829), founder of the Amorian dynasty (820–867), attempted to restore religious peace by recalling the exiles, but temporized in canceling the iconoclastic decrees. He feared collusion between the iconodules, or venerators of images, and Rome. Hence he grossly maltreated the papal messenger Methodius. His reign was challenged by Thomas, a Slav from Asia Minor, who posed as a protector of the poor and fomented a social and even racial revolution. Thomas was crowned emperor at Antioch with the consent of the Arab Caliph and invested Constantinople (December 821), but Michael, with the help of Omurtag, Khan of the Bulgars, forced Thomas to raise the siege in the spring of 823. He was captured, tortured, and finally executed. The civil war had grave consequences. Apparently, a large number of the small landholders in Asia Minor were ruined, and there was a rapid rise of great estates. *Crete was lost to the Arabs (823–828), who from 827 began to occupy Sicily. The Byzantines were now paying heavily for the long neglect of their fleet.

Michael's son Theophilus (829–842), who had had John Grammaticus as his teacher and was clearly influenced by Moslem art and culture, was a convinced iconoclast. He organized the κλίματα, or Byzantine possessions on the Black Sea, into a theme, with Cherson as its center. He was defeated in the battle of Dazimon (July 22, 838) by the Arabs under Caliph Mutasim, who then stormed Amorium, the strongest fort in the Anatolian theme. In 837 John Grammaticus was made patriarch, and he attacked the monks who rejected iconoclasm, resorting to branding and other cruelties. But the death of the Emperor (Jan. 20, 842) marked the permanent collapse of the iconoclastic movement.

The new ruler, *Michael III (842–867), was a minor. His mother, *Theodora (2), acted as regent and governed with the aid of her brothers Bardas and Petronas, the *magister* Sergius Niceticates, and, in particular, Theoctistus, Logothete of the Drome. John Grammaticus was deposed as patriarch, and *Methodius I (843–847) was installed. On the first Sunday of Lent (March 843) a synod proclaimed the victory over iconoclasm and other heresies. This became an annual festival known as Orthodox Sunday. Theoctistus dominated the regency and favored a great cultural revival; but the Studite monks turned against the new patriarch, and on his death the monk *Ignatius, son of the former Emperor Michael Rangabe, was appointed patriarch. Suppressive measures were taken against the Paulician heretics, war was declared on the Slavs in Thrace, and the Arab campaigns were pursued.

In 856 the young Emperor Michael and his uncle Bardas overthrew the regency. *Bardas was made Caesar and organized a university in the Magnaura palace. He assembled a number of outstanding scholars, headed by Leo the Mathematician, nephew of John Grammaticus, and among them *Photius, who soon replaced Ignatius, who had been forced to resign on Dec. 25, 858, as patriarch. Immediately two parties arose, one supporting the deposed Ignatius, and the other, Photius. The new patriarch sent his *synodica* to Rome for papal recognition. Pope *Nicholas I (858–867), however, on appeal from Ignatius, disavowed the actions of his legates, who had recognized Photius at the Synod of Constantinople (861), and in a synod at the *Lateran (863) the Pope declared Photius deposed.

Meanwhile Michael and Bardas, although unable to stem the Arab advance in Sicily, pursued a successful military policy against the Arabs in Asia Minor and on Sept. 3, 863, achieved a great victory in Amisus. Byzantium was now free to deal with the problems presented by new and powerful Slavic attacks from Russia and Moravia. The Russians had invested Constantinople in 860, and the people ascribed deliverance to a miracle worked by the Virgin Mary. Photius sent Constantine (Cyril) of Thessalonica on a religious mission to the Khazars, and subsequently, Constantine (Cyril) and his brother Methodius, at the request of the Moravian Prince Rastislav, as missionaries to Moravia (*see* CYRIL AND METHODIUS, SS.). Constantine (Cyril) invented the so-called Galgolithic alphabet, translated the Bible into Slavonic, and introduced the liturgy in that tongue. Under Byzantine pressure, the Bulgarians were induced to give up their alliance with the Franks and to receive their Christianity from Byzantium. The Bulgarian King *Boris was baptized Michael, with the Emperor as his sponsor (864), and the Greek clergy, on orders from Photius, organized the new church. As Boris desired a church under its own patriarch, and not under the patri-

arch of Constantinople, he appealed to Pope Nicholas I, who sent Roman missionaries. This further enkindled trouble between Photius and the Pope. The Emperor wrote to Nicholas I demanding recognition of Photius as patriarch, while Photius drew up a list of complaints against what he regarded as heretical practices of the Roman Church in liturgy and discipline. In particular, he objected to Latin teaching on the procession of the Holy Spirit from the Father and the Son, emphasized by the introduction of the *filioque in the Creed on the part of the Carolingians. A synod at Constantinople (867), with the Emperor as president, excommunicated the Pope, declared Roman doctrine on the filioque heretical, and rejected Roman interference in Byzantine church affairs.

The Macedonian Period (867–1056): The Byzantine Golden Age. Michael III was overthrown by his former ally Basil the Macedonian (Sept. 23–24, 867), who obtained the imperial office by duplicity and murder. Basil I (867–886), the founder of the Macedonian dynasty (867–1056), deposed Photius, reinstated Ignatius as patriarch (Nov. 23, 867), and resumed relations with Rome. The Council of *Constantinople III (869–870), with the legates of Pope Hadrian II present, excommunicated Photius. However, Ignatius considered direct papal control in Bulgaria contrary to Byzantine interests. With the consent of the representatives of the three Eastern patriarchs, he consecrated an archbishop for the Bulgarians, thus giving Boris a semi-independent church, but one recognizing the supremacy of Constantinople.

Basil's fleet prevented an Arab conquest of the Dalmatian coast. This area was then organized into a theme, and missionaries were sent to Christianize not only the whole coastal region but the interior as well. Ecclesiastically, Moravia came under the control of Rome; but Serbia, Bulgaria, and Macedonia, under that of Constantinople. After consolidating the Byzantine position in Asia Minor by the defeat of the *Paulicians (872) and extending the eastern frontiers, Basil attempted to restore Byzantine control in Sicily. The Arabs had made steady gains in this whole area, seizing the strategic island of Malta (870). They captured Syracuse also (878), but the general *Nicephorus Phocas was able to restore Byzantine rule in southern Italy. Nevertheless, the Arabs still remained masters of the Mediterranean.

In 875 Photius returned from exile and was charged with the education of the Emperor's sons. On the death of Ignatius (Oct. 20, 877) he succeeded him as patriarch and was recognized by Pope *John VIII. In the synod of November 879, the papal legates officially confirmed the recognition. Basil not only encouraged education and culture but inspired the production of a new collection of law books, particularly the *Procheiron* and the *Epanogoge,* which were published in his reign. These works, along with others that remained uncompleted, formed the foundation of the great *Basilica* published by his successor, Leo VI. The *Epanogoge* includes a treatment of the Byzantine concept of the relations of Church and State. This section was written probably by Photius (*see* ROMAN LAW, 5).

Leo VI the Wise. Leo VI the Wise (886–912) devoted himself primarily to the internal affairs of the empire. He replaced Photius as patriarch with his own brother Stephen. As a former pupil of Photius, Leo was a prolific writer in theology, sprinkling his dogmatic sermons and treatises with classical references. In addition to the *Basilica* in 60 books, he published a collection of 113 new decrees known as the Novels, a term that echoes the last phase of Justinian's legislation. The Novels revoked formally the ancient rights of the municipal, *curiae* and Senate. The Emperor was absolutely supreme in all spheres, except the religious. In the religious sphere, the patriarch of Constantinople was supreme in theory, but in practice the Emperor appointed the patriarch and exercised wide powers and controls in ecclesiastical legislation. However, the Emperor had, in theory at least, no power to evoke or change the decisions of Church councils. The state was administered by the Emperor's military and bureaucratic machine. The themes were given their practically final form of organization and administration. The elaborate bureaucratic machinery, with its long list of grades and titles, is described in detail in the *Cletorologion* of Philotheos, while the *Book of the Eparch* furnishes specific information on economic life, and particularly on the guild system of Constantinople. Despite the absolutism of the Emperor, there was a steady growth in the prestige of the aristocracy and in its acquisitions of peasant lands. A feudal system was already exhibiting steady development.

Leo's foreign policy was weak and the empire suffered severe blows. Conflict with the new and able Bulgarian ruler Symeon culminated in the decisive victory of the Bulgarians (896) and tribute as the price of peace. Sicily was lost to the Arabs (902), and Thessalonica was sacked by them with terrible slaughter (904). Leo incurred the enmity of the monks and people by marrying, as his fourth wife, his mistress, Zoe, although he had strengthened the legislation against a third marriage in his revision of the law code. The marriage was opposed also by Patriarch Nicholas I, whom the Emperor then deposed (*see* NICHOLAS I, PATRIARCH OF CONSTANTINOPLE).

Following the death of Leo (May 12, 912), his irresponsible brother Alexander became emperor. On Alexander's death (June 6, 913), Nicholas, whom Alexander had restored as patriarch, became regent for the 7-year-old Constantine VII. The regent had to deal with Symeon of Bulgaria, who appeared before Constantinople and demanded that he be recognized as coemperor. He was actually crowned emperor by Nicholas, but most probably as *Basileus* of Bulgaria, not coemperor of the Byzantine Empire. The humiliating concessions made by Nicholas to Symeon were soon repudiated, and Symeon invaded and devastated Byzantine territories. Following repeated defeats at the hands of the Bulgarians, Romanus Lecapenus, a man of Armenian peasant origin who had risen high in the imperial service, became coemperor (Dec. 20, 920).

Romanus I. *Romanus I Lecapenus (920–944) introduced an Armenian dynasty. The war with Symeon involved the whole Balkans. Symeon conquered the Serbs (924), but after his severe defeat by the Croats (926), peace was made, with the Pope as intermediary. Symeon died on May 27, 927, and a decade of peace followed between the two powers. Meantime, Byzantine influence increased steadily in Bulgaria. Economically, however, internal conditions were bad. Ecclesiastical and lay estates increased steadily, and there was growing misery and unrest among the masses. Under the circumstances the *Bogomil movement spread with amazing rapidity in Bulgaria and far beyond its borders.

Following the decision at the synod of 920 respecting the four marriages of Leo VI, amical relations were established between Romanus and Patriarch Nicholas, who gave the Emperor his fullest support in the war against Symeon. Nicholas (d. 925) was followed by two weak patriarchs. Then on Feb. 2, 933, Romanus had papal legates consecrate his 16-year-old son Theophylactus (933–956) as patriarch despite local opposition. As Romanus apparently desired, Theophylactus remained completely under his domination. The patriarchate of Theophylactus thus marks a date in the decline of the authority of the Byzantine Patriarchate.

Romanus took strong measures to prevent the absorption of the small landholders by the aristocracy, since the payment of taxes and military services depended on the security and independence of the peasant class. In his novels of 922 and 934 he censured the rapacity of the aristocracy, yet he found himself opposed in part by the small-holders themselves, who complained of the great tax burdens. Despite the great successes of his brilliant General John Curcuas against the Russians and Arabs, including the recovery of the great Christian relic, the sacred Mandylion, preserved at Edessa, Romanus was deposed by his sons (Dec. 10, 944) and died in exile as a monk on the Island of Prote (June 15, 948).

Constantine VII. *Constantine VII Porphyrogenitus (913–959), despite the plots of the sons of Romanus, assumed control of the state as sole emperor and devoted himself mainly to cultural pursuits, to the stimulation of education and learning. Among his own writings mention must be made especially of his *Book of Ceremonies,* a kind of encyclopedia, which is of the greatest value as a historical source (*see* BYZANTINE LITERATURE). He enforced and supplemented the agrarian policy of Romanus. On the military side, the situation took a definite turn for the better in the last years of his reign under Generals Nicephorus Phocas and John Tzimisces. John took Samosata in 958, and Nicephorus recovered Crete in 961 and won a great victory

Fig. 4. Constantine VII (913–959) and Romanus II (959–963) on the obverse of a gold solidus of their joint reign.

at Aleppo in 962. Constantine inaugurated a series of diplomatic missions to the Arab states and to the court of *Otto I the Great (962–969). The Russian Princess Olga, who had been recently converted to Christianity, taking Helena as her baptismal name, was received in 957 at Constantinople with great pomp. Her visit gave a stimulus to closer relations with Byzantium and to missionary effort in Russia. Romanus II (959–963), son of Constantine VII, was a weak character who was dominated by his wife, the beautiful but unscrupulous and ambitious Theophano.

Nicephorus II Phocas and John I Tzimisces. On the death of Romanus, General Nicephorus Phocas became emperor as *Nicephorus II Phocas (963–969). He married Theophano and—at her suggestion—made the eunuch Basil, an illegitimate son of Romanus Lecapenus, the head of the civil government. John Tzimisces, greatest general of the age, was given supreme military command in the East. Nicephorus favored the aristocracy against the peasants in a law of 967. Yet by an earlier edict (964) he had attempted to prevent the growth of the ecclesiastical and monastic estates. He regarded war against Islam as a sacred mission, considering death in battle against Islam as martyrdom. He conquered Cilicia and much of Syria, including Aleppo, and was able to enlist the Russians as allies. In the West, however, he had to accept the fact that Otto I the Great had conquered and became master of much of Italy, and had assumed the imperial crown. The proposal of a marriage alliance made by Otto through his ambassador Bp. Liutprand of Cremona was scornfully rejected. Through the treachery of his wife, Theophano, who had become the mistress of John Tzimisces, the aged Emperor was murdered by John Tzimisces and a group of fellow conspirators.

Before *John I Tzimisces (969–976) could be crowned, he was required by Patriarch Polyeuctes to do penance, expel Theophano, and punish his fellow conspirators. A member of the high aristocracy, Tzimisces married Princess Theodora, daughter of Constantine VII. He conquered the Bulgarians under Svjatoslav, and annexed their country. Their patriarchate was abolished. He gave his kinswoman Theophano in marriage to *Otto II, who married her in Rome (April 14, 972). In the East he renewed the war, reconquering the coast of Palestine and Syria from the Moslems. He contracted a fatal illness on campaign and died at Constantinople Jan. 10, 976.

Basil II. Although the two sons of Romanus II, Constantine and Basil, were now old enough to rule, Constantine proved frivolous, and, the elder (he was 18), *Basil II (976–1025), took control. The revolt of Bardas Sclerus was put down by General Bardas Phocas (May 24, 979). Six years later (985) Basil rid himself of his great-uncle, the all-powerful counselor Basil the eunuch, who had begun to plot against him. Basil II, after being defeated in battle (986) by a new Bulgarian leader, Samuel, who was attempting to build up a large independent Balkan state with Macedonia as its nucleus, had to face a civil war in which Bardas Sclerus and Bardas Phocas opposed him. Basil appealed for aid to the Russian Vladimir, Prince of Kiev. Six thousand Varangians were sent, and with this force Basil defeated the rebels at Chrysopolis (988). The rebellion was finally broken by his victory at Abydus (April 13, 988). As a reward for his assistance, Vladimir was promised

the hand of a Byzantine princess, Anna, the Emperor's sister, on condition that he and his people be baptized. The conversion of Kiev to Christianity was of the greatest importance for the history of Russia. Furthermore, the new Russian Church was under the supreme control of the Patriarchate of Constantinople and was governed during its early years by Greek metropolitans from Constantinople.

Basil II, who never married, devoted his whole interest to the affairs of state. He resumed antiaristocratic policies in favor of the peasantry, and in a novel of 996 he decreed that all property—including large ecclesiastical and, in particular, monastic holdings—acquired from the poor from the time of the edict of Romanus Lecapenus (922) should be restored without compensation. Furthermore, he made the rich landholders responsible for paying the *allelengyon* (τὸ ἀλληλέγγυον), or community taxes, of the small landholders. Despite the opposition of Patriarch *Sergius II (1001–09) to the restoration of ecclesiastical property, he persisted in this financial policy. War was renewed against Samuel and the Bulgars. After many years of campaigning, Basil annihilated the main Bulgarian forces near Struma (July, 1014) and was hailed as *Bulgaroctonos,* "Slayer of Bulgarians." He treated his captives in savage fashion, having them blinded by the thousands. Samuel, who survived the battle of the Struma, died a few months later (October 1014). In 1018 Basil entered the Bulgarian capital, Ochrida, in triumph. The conquered regions were reorganized into themes, the theme of Bulgaria being the most important. The patriarchate of the Bulgarians was abolished and replaced by an archbishopric at Ochrida, but one with special privileges. The archbishop was appointed by the Emperor and was under his jurisdiction and not under that of the patriarch of Constantinople.

In Asia Minor he extended Byzantine control to Armenia and northern Mesopotamia and incorporated the newly conquered areas into the empire. The great Emperor was in the midst of preparations to recover Sicily from the Arabs when he died (Dec. 15, 1025). He left an empire that stretched from the Adriatic to the Euphrates and included the whole region south of the Drave and the Danube.

Constantine VIII, Romanus III, Michael IV, Zoe and Theodora (1025–42). The last rulers of the Macedonian dynasty were weak. Lulled into security by the prestige of Basil's conquests, they neglected to build up strong frontier defenses, indulged in lavish spending, and, above all, failed to curb the feudal nobility. There was a resulting rapid decline of military small holdings, which undermined the foundations of the whole system of imperial military defence and taxation. In the end, the feudal civil and military aristocracy became masters of the Byzantine state.

Basil was succeeded by his aged brother Constantine VIII (1025–28), who was more concerned with the pomp and pleasures of the Hippodrome than with affairs of state. He had no sons, but his two daughters, Zoe and Theodora, although past middle age, were destined to play important political roles during the 25 years following his accession. Constantine on his deathbed arranged a marriage between Zoe and the eparch Romanus Argyrus, who became Emperor Romanus III Argyrus (1028–34). A vain and visionary character who had no capacity for government, partly through acquies-

Fig. 5. Christ enthroned between the Emperor Constantine IX Monomachus (1042–55) and the Empress Zoe (1028– 50), in the south gallery of Hagia Sophia. The main portion of the mosaic is dated between 1028 and 1034.

cence and partly through neglect, he gave free reign to the ambitions of the great landholders. Without the enforcement of Basil's laws and strong imperial protection, the free small holdings of the peasants and soldiers were absorbed into the estates of the landed nobility. The danger of an Arab invasion of Syria was met by the able General George Maniaces, who drove back the Arabs and captured Edessa (1032).

The relations between Zoe and Romanus became increasingly strained. With the aid of the capable but unscrupulous eunuch John the Orphanotrophus, Zoe, who had fallen in love with John's young brother Michael, had Romanus murdered (April 11, 1034). On the same day she married Michael, who ascended the throne as Michael IV (1034–41). The actual administration was carried on by John, who restored the old centralized bureaucracy. He even gained the support of the civil nobility of the capital and was able to exercise some restrictions on the rival feudal and military nobility in Asia Minor. A revolt in the Balkans, occasioned by John's oppressive taxation, was put down (1041) after several years of fighting, but Stephen Vorslav of Zeta maintained his independence from Byzantium. Michael

(d. Dec. 10, 1041) was succeeded by the incompetent and profligate nephew of John the Orphanotrophus, Michael V Calaphates (1041–42). One of his first acts was to banish his uncle, the man to whom he owed the imperial dignity. He was deposed and blinded a few months later (April 20, 1042) and was replaced by the two sisters Zoe and Theodora as joint empresses (1042).

Constantine IX Monomachus and the Break with Rome. Zoe soon married Senator Constantine Monomachus, who as coemperor ascended the throne as *Constantine IX Monomachus (1042–55). His reign inaugurated a brilliant—if in part dissipated—court life and lavish spending of imperial revenues. But it was an age also that saw the flowering of Byzantine literature and learning. Scholars were employed as imperial counselors, and a university was established at Constantinople in 1045.

The civil administration in the capital under Constantine took no effective measures against the growth of large secular and ecclesiastical estates. On the contrary, the great landowners were granted increasing privileges and immunities from taxations. The so-called *pronoia* was introduced whereby for service rendered, prominent Byzantines were given properties to administer with the accompanying right to their entire revenue. Tax farming was adopted on a major scale, and its typical abuses soon followed. Owing to its hostility to the military, the civil authority deliberately reduced the armed forces in various ways. The original purpose of the themes and their contribution to the defense of the empire were largely destroyed. As in the days before Heraclius, mercenaries—chiefly Normans—were employed instead of native soldiers in regiments of the imperial guard. The reduction of the armed forces was carried through the more easily because of a sense of false security. The victories of George Maniaces in the East had enabled Constantine even to annex the kingdom of Ani. The splendid initial success of General Maniaces in Sicily, however, was nullified by his removal from command and his subsequent revolt. Unrest in Macedonia was reflected in the formidable rebellion of Leo Tomaces and his siege of Constantinople in 1047. In the following year, the Patzinaks, a people from the Russian steppes, crossed the Danube and plundered as they went. Since they could not be driven back, Constantine eventually had to permit them to settle in imperial territory and had to flatter their leaders with high-sounding titles.

Finally, in the last years of Constantine's reign, the long tensions between the Churches of Rome and Constantinople culminated in the great schism beginning in 1054. The background and detailed accounts of the events and personages involved in the schism are covered in other articles (*see* EASTERN SCHISM; MICHAEL CERULARIUS; LEO IX, POPE; HUMBERT OF SILVA CANDIDA). The schism was destined to have a much more profound effect on the subsequent history of Christendom than was or could be even dimly envisioned by the main participants in the fateful break between the two Churches.

Theodora, Michael VI, and Isaac Comnenus (1055–59). Following the death of Constantine IX (Jan. 11, 1055), Theodora, the last of her dynasty, ruled as empress until her death in September of the following year. Her successor was her nominee, a revered high official belonging to the civil nobility, Michael VI Stratioticus (1056–57). With the powerful aid of Patriarch Michael Cerularius, Michael VI was forced to abdicate, and General Isaac Comnenus, who had been proclaimed emperor by his troops in Asia Minor, became emperor (1057–59). In order to build up the badly depleted treasury, the new Emperor seized secular and ecclesiastical lands that had been in part illegally acquired and in so doing incurred the sharp opposition of the civil aristocracy and Patriarch Cerularius. Plots were organized against him in which the scholar Michael *Psellus most probably took part. In 1058 Isaac exiled Cerularius, who died while the synod called to depose him was in session. The following year Isaac resigned the throne (December 1059) and became a monk.

The Collapse of the Middle Byzantine Empire (1059–81). Michael Psellus, with the support of the civil aristocracy and of the new patriarch, *Constantine III Leichudes, succeeded in having his friend Constantine Ducas, husband of Eudocia Macrembolitissa, the niece of Michael Cerularius, raised to the imperial throne. He himself was the new Emperor's chief advisor in all public affairs and the tutor of his son. Constantine X Ducas (1059–67) concentrated his attention on strengthening the position of the civil nobility of the capital. The extension of the civil service, a corresponding rise in the cost of government, and lavish court spending exhausted the finances of the state. The gross neglect of the army, as Psellus acknowledged later, was a fatal mistake. From 1059 the Normans under *Robert Guiscard were carrying all before them. In 1064 the Hungarians seized Belgrade, and in the same year the Balkans were overrun and devastated by the Uzes, a people from the Russian steppes who fled southward under the pressure of the Cumans. But a much more formidable and lasting menace faced the empire in the East. With lightening speed, the Seljuk Turks made themselves masters of the Near East as far as the Byzantine frontiers and the borders of Egypt. In 1065 they occupied the kingdom of *Ani (Armenia) and devastated Cilicia, and in 1067 they captured *Caesarea of Cappadocia.

Following the death of Constantine X (May 1067), Eudocia became regent and was assisted by Psellus and the Caesar John Ducas. However, to meet the dangers threatening the empire, Patriarch *John VIII Xiphilinus, despite the opposition of Psellus and John Ducas, urged Eudocia to marry the Cappadocian noble and able general, Romanus Diogenes, and the latter was raised to the imperial throne. Romanus IV Diogenes (1068–71), with an army made up largely of mercenaries, attempted to drive the Turks from Asia Minor. After some initial successes his army was destroyed by the Seljuk Sultan Alp Arslan at the Armenian town of Manzikert (August 1071), and he was taken prisoner. The defeat resulted from the undisciplined character of his troops, but also from the treachery of Andronicus Ducas, son of the Caesar John Ducas. The agreements that he made with the Seljuks were repudiated at Constantinople. He was deposed and blinded by his enemies, the chief of whom was Psellus, and replaced by his eldest son and pupil of Psellus, *Michael VII Ducas (1071–78). In the same year (1071) Robert Guiscard's conquest of Bari marked the end of Byzantine rule in Italy.

Michael was a weak ruler, dominated at first by Psellus, but soon by the unscrupulous Logothete Nicephorus. Despite the all-important need of defending the frontiers, Nicephorus continued to neglect the army and attempted to strengthen the central civil bureaucracy and to make the wheat trade a state monopoly. The financial affairs of the state were thrown into confusion, aggravated by a rapid rise in prices. Revolts broke out within the empire, and the Turks and other external enemies took full advantage of the situation to invade and seize Byzantine territory.

In 1078 Nicephorus Botaneiates, a member of the military aristocracy of Asia Minor, did not hesitate to use Turkish help to win the imperial office. He was proclaimed emperor as Nicephorus III (1078–81) and was crowned by the patriarch (March 24, 1078). He married the Empress Maria, although her first husband, the deposed Michael, was still living. The short reign of the aged ruler was characterized by the collapse of the central civil government in the midst of revolts and civil war, and by the steadily increasing economic and financial crisis that was made worse by the devaluation of the currency.

Power was now in the hands of the military, and it was simply a question of which of the rival commanders would obtain the imperial office and maintain his position against further aspirants. In the meantime, the

Fig. 6. The Emperor Nicephorus Botaneiates (1078–81) and the Empress Maria, miniature in an 11th-century manuscript of the homilies of St. John Chrysostom (Paris, Bibliothèque Nationale MS Coislin 79, fol. 2).

Turks had conquered Asia Minor from Cilicia to the Hellespont and established the Sultanate of Rūm, with Iconium, and later Nicaea (1092), as its capital, and in 1075 they took Damascus and Jerusalem from the Fatimid caliphs. Alexius Comnenus, the ablest of the generals and a man of superior political gifts, had married Irene, the grand-daughter of the Caesar John Ducas, and had been adopted by Empress Maria. He entered Constantinople at the head of his troops. After 3 days of rioting, Nicephorus abdicated, and Alexius was crowned emperor on Easter (April 4) 1081. The government of the empire thus passed into the hands of the military aristocracy, in which the provincial element was dominant.

THE LATE BYZANTINE EMPIRE

This period is characterized by the formation of a new feudal aristocracy with military obligations, by the increasing Turkish power and conquests, by the involvement in the Crusades and the States of the Crusaders, by the sack of Constantinople and the establishment of the Latin Empire in the East, by the restoration of the Byzantine Empire, but also by the steady decline resulting from internal weaknesses and external pressures, and finally by the collapse culminating in the capture of Constantinople by the Turks in 1453.

Alexius I Comnenus (1081–1118), Founder of the Dynasty of the Comneni (1081–1204). Alexius had to restore an empire that was now limited in territory and limited in internal resources. Hence he could not hope —nor did he try—to be a second Heraclius. He worked prudently within the framework of the possible. In foreign policy in the East, he accepted the fact that most of Asia Minor was lost to the Turks, and he made peace with the Sultan Suleiman. His immediate concern was the Norman threat. Robert Guiscard, master of southern Italy, was besieging Dyrrachium (Durazzo) and clearly intended to seize Constantinople. By pawning the vessels of the altar, Alexius built up a mercenary force and appealed for aid to Pope Gregory VII and the Republic of Venice. The support of Venice was secured at the cost of granting the Venetians extraordinarily broad trading rights and privileges throughout the Byzantine Empire, but especially at Constantinople itself (1082). Nevertheless, Robert took Durazzo, and his Normans pushed through Epirus into Macedonia and southward into Greece as far as Larissa. However, the Venetians defeated the Norman fleet near Corfu (1085) and retook Durazzo. Robert suddenly died of plague the same year, and the Norman danger was temporarily ended. From 1086 to 1091 Alexius was engaged in suppressing the revolt of the Bogomils in Thrace and Bulgaria, who were joined by the Patzinaks. The Patzinaks, in alliance with Tzachas, Emir of Smyrna, besieged Constantinople, but with the help of the Cumans, another people from the Russian steppes, the Patzinaks were slaughtered to the last man at the battle of Mt. Levunion (1091). In 1094 Constantine Diogenes, who hoped with his army of Cumans to seize the imperial throne, was defeated, and the Cuman bands were scattered.

Byzantium and the Crusading Movement. Alexius was soon faced with the problems that the Crusades presented to the Byzantine Empire. (For the history of the Crusades, *see* CRUSADES. Nevertheless, a few observations are necessary here to clarify Byzantine attitudes and reactions.) For many centuries the Byzantines had been defending their territories against Islam and in so doing had been protecting the West against Mohammedan conquest. They regarded Asia Minor, Syria, Palestine, and Egypt, to say nothing of North Africa, Sicily, and southern Italy, as lost provinces of their empire. Alexius and his successors, however, were unrealistic in thinking that they could recover even Asia Minor and Syria alone or that Westerners would be altruistic enough to recover their lost territory for them. The Crusaders came to the East to recover the Holy Places for all Christendom. At the same time, against the background of feudal tradition, they believed that lands conquered from the infidel—even if once possessed by the Byzantines—could be claimed as their own by right of conquest. Hence the kingdoms and principalities of the Crusaders in the East, although bitterly resented by the Byzantines, were regarded as legitimate in the eyes of the West (*see* CRUSADERS' STATES). Material considerations were also present—in some cases to a high degree. Thus, from the outset, the Venetians were certainly more concerned with promoting their rising and lucrative trade and commerce than with the defense of Byzantium or with the Crusades. Finally, the tragedy of the schism underlies all the mutual suspicions and bitter tensions between East and West throughout the whole period to the fall of Constantinople.

Alexius was able to persuade the leaders of the First Crusade to restore the western coast of Asia Minor to Byzantine control after their victories at Nicaea and Dorylaeum (1097), but the capture of Antioch by *Bohemund I and his refusal to recognize Byzantine control led to a long conflict (1098–1108). Alexius recovered Antioch, only to lose it to *Tancred 3 years later (1111). In a successful campaign against the Seljuks in Asia Minor (1110–17), the Emperor won back the whole region west of a line Sinope-Ancyra-Philomelium.

Alexius' Internal Reforms. Side by side with Alexius' extension of the frontiers went his internal reorganization of the state. He created a whole series of new titles to describe more precisely the functions—in part old and in part new—of the numerous officials in the central administration and in the themes. But his major concern was the restoration of the armed forces, stabilization of the currency, and increasing the revenues. He stabilized the debased gold coinage by fixing its worth at one third of its original value. Then a series of supplementary taxes were introduced in which the government took advantage of the debasement itself. Alexius, however, did not abolish tax farming or the immunities given to landowners, so that the tax burden became heavier than ever for the masses of taxpayers. Perhaps the most important innovation was the transformation of the *pronoia* into a military system. The holder of a *pronoia* was now required to furnish military service himself as a mounted knight and at his own expense, and, according to the value of his *pronoia,* to supply a prescribed number of light-armed troops. The peasants living on the *pronoia* were required to pay taxes and render other services to the holder of the *pronoia* as their feudal lord. Thus it is evident that Western feudalism was exercising its influence in the East.

Alexius tried in various ways to obtain revenues from monastic property or at least to restrict its growth, but in the face of strong opposition he abandoned this policy. In general, Alexius worked in close harmony with the Church. As protector of orthodoxy, he suppressed heresy by the sword, took an active part in the condemnation of the philosopher John Italus, and gave special rights and immunities to the reforming monk Christodoulus and his community on the island of Patmos. As already mentioned, it was solely under the pressure of dire necessity that he granted Venice the extensive privileges and concessions that gave the Venetians such a dominant commercial and naval position in the eastern Mediterranean. (*See* ALEXIUS I COMNENUS.)

John II and Manuel I Comnenus. *John II Comnenus (1118–43), despite family intrigue against him in which his sister Anna, who later became distinguished as a historian, took a leading part, established himself firmly on the throne and is to be regarded as the greatest of the Comneni. Like his father, he pursued policies within the framework of the possible. His attempt to free Byzantium from the concessions made to Venice failed (1122–26), and he had to renew the treaty of 1082. But he crushed a new invasion of Patzinaks in the Balkans and settled a large number of survivors in imperial territory or impressed them into his army (1122). Furthermore, he brought Serbia under Byzantine control and reached a peaceful agreement with the Hungarians. In the East he conquered Cilicia and was then able to push into Syria and again established Byzantine sovereignty over Antioch (1137–38). A master diplomat, he succeeded in getting the German Emperors Lothair III and Conrad III, along with the city-state of Pisa, to enter into an alliance against Norman expansion in southern Italy. He died of a hunting wound as he was planning to recover Antioch, which had revolted (1142). To his youngest son and successor, Manuel, he left a larger and stronger empire than he had inherited from his father Alexius.

*Manuel I Comnenus (1143–80) was a gifted general and diplomat. His court was brilliant, and through marriage and alliances he was in close contact with the West and was an admirer of Western chivalry. He was com-

pletely Byzantine, however, in his basic policies. Unlike his two predecessors, he failed to give proper consideration to the limitations of the possible. Even before his accession he had dreamed of the restoration of the Roman Empire of the days of Justinian and, following religious union, of the reestablishment of universal spiritual and political authority, with the pope and the emperor supreme in their respective spheres. His wars against the Normans, in particular against Roger II of Sicily, in which he was aided by the German Emperor and Venice, were marked by some successes, but also by many losses, and ended in failure—as was acknowledged by the peace of 1158. Meantime, he had been inevitably involved in the Second Crusade (1147–49) and was blamed by many for its disastrous ending. The schism, as already noted, entered into all relationships between East and West, intensifying mutual cultural and political antipathies.

In 1152–54 and again in 1163–68 he brought the Hungarians under imperial control, and several years later Bela III (1173–96) ruled his kingdom as a Byzantine vassal. In 1172 Stephan Nemanja, the Grand Župan of Rascia, was likewise forced to accept Manuel as the overlord of the Serbian kingdom. The Venetians were alienated by Byzantine occupation of Dalmatia. The Byzantines, on their side, took drastic action against the Venetians, at Constantinople especially. Through the superiority of their naval forces the Venetians were victorious in the war between the two states, and by the peace of 1176 the Byzantines were required to restore all the old trade privileges and to pay a heavy indemnity. Affairs in the East turned out better for Manuel. Despite the Turkish victory at Myriocephalon (1176), the Byzantines succeeded in driving back the Turks the following year. One of Manuel's greatest triumphs was the reduction of the *Crusaders' States to Byzantine vassalage (from 1158).

His attempt to recover the West had placed a much too heavy strain on Byzantine resources. During his

Fig. 7. The Virgin and Child flanked by Emperor John II Comnenus (1118–43) and Empress Irene, mosaic, c. 1118, in the south gallery of Hagia Sophia. The figure on the adjoining pilaster is Alexius Comnenus.

Fig. 8. Marble roundel relief of an emperor, late 12th century. It probably represents Manuel I Comnenus (1143–80) or Andronicus Comnenus (1182–85).

reign the *pronoiai* of the military type had to be greatly extended. In fact, the military class had become so dominant and the burden of taxation so heavy on the civil population that men sought in one form or another to enter military service or to obtain military status. Owing to the failure of Manuel's policy in the West, the weakness of the Byzantine Empire had become clearly revealed.

Andronicus I Comnenus, Isaac II Angelus, and Collapse. The regency of the Empress Maria of Antioch, widow of Manuel I, for her 12-year-old son, Alexius II (1180–83), aroused deep resentment because of her Latin origin and employment of Latin officials. With the announcement of the imminent coming of Andronicus Comnenus, a cousin of Manuel I and an able but absolutely ruthless leader and anti-Latin in policy, to the capital, a terrible massacre of foreigners, especially Latins, was perpetrated by the city mob (May 1182). Andronicus entered Constantinople in triumph and was proclaimed emperor (1183–85). He carried through a number of excellent reforms: sale of offices was abolished, competent officials were chosen, bribery was reduced through the payment of adequate salaries, the landowners were forced to treat their peasants with justice, abuses in tax collecting were suppressed by severe penalties, and the plundering of wrecked ships was punished with death. On the other hand, the opposition of the nobility was crushed with wholesale killings, and this violence was met with counterplots. By striking

down the landed aristocracy, he crippled the military strength of the state. In the midst of civil strife, the Hungarians and Serbs invaded the empire, and the Serbians under Stephen Nemanja established their independence (1183). Two years later the Normans captured Dyrrachium and, pushing on to Thessalonica, stormed that great city (Aug. 24, 1185). Large numbers of the inhabitants were killed or tortured in retaliation for the massacre of Latins at Constantinople (1182). The inhabitants of the capital now turned against Andronicus with fury, deposed him, and tortured him to death.

His successor, Isaac II Angelus (1185–95 and 1203–04), gave free reign to all the old abuses, squandered public revenues on his court, and neglected frontier defense. The weakness of the central government was encouraging the development of practically independent feudal principalities in the provinces. The victory of General Alexius Branas over the Normans at Dimitrica (1185) led to their expulsion from the Balkans (1191). On the other hand, the Bulgarians, provoked by corrupt Byzantine fiscal officials, revolted under Peter and John Asen (1186) and founded the Second Bulgarian Empire (1188). In 1187 Jerusalem fell to *Saladin and occasioned the Third Crusade. On his way to the East by land the German Emperor *Frederick I Barbarossa captured Adrianople and forced the Byzantines to give him passage and transport from Gallipoli to the Asian shore. In 1191, Cyprus, which had been ruled as an independent principality for some years by Isaac Comnenus, a namesake of the Emperor, was conquered by Richard the Lion-Hearted and remained in Latin hands until taken by the Turks nearly 4 centuries later (*see* CYPRUS).

Following his unsuccessful campaigns against the Bulgarians (1190–94), Isaac was deposed and blinded by his brother Alexius, who ascended the throne as Alexius III (1195–1203); he was a weak ruler under whom internal collapse continued. When the German Emperor Henry VI (d. 1197) fell heir to Norman possessions, Alexius had to pay a heavy annual tribute to prevent Henry's seizure of the territory between Dyrrachium and Thessalonica. The hated German tax (τὸ ἀλαμανικόν) had to be raised in part by the seizure of the precious ornaments from the imperial tombs in the Church of the Apostles (1197). In 1201 Alexius made peace with the Bulgarians, but only at the price of leaving them the larger part of the eastern Balkans.

The so-called Fourth Crusade brought catastrophe. The astute doge of Venice, Enrico Dandolo, in the interests of establishing Venetian commercial supremacy in the eastern Mediterranean on a more secure basis, transformed the crusading forces into a military expedition against Constantinople. An excellent opportunity for intervention in Byzantine affairs had been given by the appeal for help by Alexius, son of the deposed Isaac, to restore his father to the throne. The Western forces broke into Constantinople in 1203. Isaac recovered his throne, and his son was made coemperor as Alexius IV (1203–04). The latter was killed in a popular revolution and replaced by Alexius V Ducas (1204), who refused to pay tribute. Constantinople was stormed and sacked (April 12, 1204), and a Latin Empire established.

The Latin Empire and the Byzantine Restoration (1204–82). For a detailed treatment of the Latin Empire, *see* LATIN EMPIRE OF CONSTANTINOPLE. It will suffice here to record the following facts by way of summary. Baldwin of Flanders was elected emperor and was assigned one-fourth of the imperial territory, including Thrace, northwestern Asia Minor, and several islands. Of the remaining territory, Venice received half, and the other half was assigned to the knights as fiefs. *Boniface of Montferrat, after violent disagreement with the distribution, seized Thessalonica and made himself king of the adjacent territories of Thrace and Macedonia. Venice obtained possessions that were especially valuable for her maritime expansion and defense: three-eighths of Constantinople, the chief ports on the Hellespont, Adrianople, Coron and Modon in the Peloponnesus, most of the Ionian islands, and Crete. Byzantine feudalism, viz, the *pronoia*, was easily adapted to the Western type. On the religious side, the Venetian Thomas Morosini was made Latin patriarch, and a Latin hierarchy replaced the Greek throughout the territories held by the Latins. In the light of all the events mentioned, any voluntary abandonment of the schism or reunion of the Latin and Greek Churches was impossible. The history of the Latin Empire was marked by failure to defend Thrace and Macedonia from the Bulgarians and, above all, by failure to appreciate the importance of Asia Minor or to prevent the development of the Empire of Nicaea.

The Empires of Trebizond, Nicaea, and the Despotate of Epirus. Even before the sack of Constantinople, David and Alexius Comnenus had taken Trebizond and set up an independent state, which, despite the loss of much territory to the Empire of Nicaea, lasted until it was conquered by the Turks in 1461. Following the conquest of Constantinople, Theodore I Lascaris (1204–22) gradually built up an independent Byzantine state in northern Asia Minor, the Empire of Nicaea. Michael Autorianus was appointed patriarch, and he crowned Theodore as emperor (Holy Week 1208). Henceforth the Empire of Nicaea represented politically and religiously in Greek minds the legitimate continuation of the Byzantine Empire. Lascaris, by an alliance with *Leo II of Armenia, was able to ward off a possible attack by the Sultan of Rūm (Iconium) and make peace with the Latin Empire. At his death the Empire of Nicaea was a small but strong and prosperous state. In this same period, Michael Angelus (1204–15) and his half brother Theodore Angelus (1215–30) built up a Greek empire or despotate in Epirus. Theodore strengthened his power and won great prestige by his conquest of Thessalonica (1224), the former kingdom of Boniface of Montferrat (d. 1207).

The Rise of the Empire of Nicaea. *John III Ducas Vatatzes (1222–54), having established himself as the successor of Theodore I Lascaris, defeated the Latin Emperor at Poimanenon and became master of Asia Minor and the islands of the adjacent coast. He was prevented only from seizing Adrianople, by his rival Theodore of Epirus. John Asen II of Bulgaria (1218–41) defeated Theodore at the battle of Klokotnica (1230), and Theodore was captured and blinded. In 1236 a combined attack of John Asen and John Vatatzes on Constantinople failed when the Venetians and the Duke of Achaia came to the aid of the city. The Nicaeans sanctioned the establishment of the Bulgarian Patriarchate with the provision that the Bulgarian patriarch had to recognize the primacy of the patriarch of Nicaea (1235). John Vatatzes and the blinded Theodore, who had been freed by the Bulgarians, failed to take Thessalonica (1242), but John, despot of Thessaly, was forced to recognize John Vatatzes as his overlord.

The Mongol invasion (1244) reduced the Empire of Trebizond and the Sultanate of Iconium to a tributary status, but the diplomacy of Vatatzes helped not only to save Nicaea but also to strengthen its position in Asia Minor. In 1246 the Emperor of Nicaea, taking advantage of the weakness of Bulgaria, conquered northern Macedonia and also captured Thessalonica, deposing its despot, Demetrius Angelus. Michael II of Epirus (1237–71) was defeated by Vatatzes in 1254 and had to recognize his suzerainty. Negotiations between Vatatzes and Pope *Innocent IV for the union of the Churches of Rome and Nicaea broke down in their final stages. John carried out a number of needed reforms in the administration and defence of the Empire of Nicaea, giving special attention to agriculture. He strove to make his state self-supporting by forbidding the purchase of foreign luxury articles and by encouraging the development of native crafts. At his death he left a strong, well-organized state, double its size at the beginning of his reign.

Recovery of Constantinople. Under Theodore II Lascaris (1254–58), a pupil of the distinguished scholar Nicephorus Blemmydes, the Empire of Nicaea experienced a great cultural revival. Theodore was an able but austere ruler who ignored privileges of rank. He appointed the monk Arsenius, a strict ascetic, as patriarch (1255–60) and revealed a cold attitude to union with

Rome. In 1255 he defeated a Bulgarian army under Michael Asen, but was himself defeated the following year by Michael II of Epirus, who had revolted against him. His hostility toward the nobility was reciprocated, and on his death (August 1258) his choice of regent, George Muzalon, was repudiated. General Michael Palaeologus, a representative of the high aristocracy, was appointed as regent for John IV Lascaris (1258–61), and then coemperor (1259).

*Michael VIII Palaeologus (1259–82) had to face a coalition consisting of Manfred of Sicily, Michael II of Epirus, and William Villehardouin of Achaia that planned to destroy the Empire of Nicaea. However, John Palaeologus, Michael's brother, inflicted a crushing defeat on the forces of the coalition in the valley of Pelagonia in Macedonia (autumn 1259). To offset the danger of Venetian attack, Michael formed a military alliance with Genoa against Venice, the price of which was special trading concessions to the Genoese. By a sudden attack Michael's general, Alexius Strategopulus, captured Constantinople, July 25, 1261, and on August 15 Michael himself took solemn possession of his city, where he was later crowned a second time by the patriarch in the Church of the Holy Wisdom (Hagia Sophia). Michael's little son Andronicus was proclaimed *Basileus* as heir to the throne, but John IV Lascaris was deposed and blinded.

The Byzantine Empire was restored, but it was a small and relatively weak state as compared with the empire of Heraclius or that of Basil II. Michael had to resort so far as possible to diplomacy to prevent aggressive action from the West in order to be free to restore Byzantine rule over the Despotate of Epirus and in the areas still held by the Latins. He seized the southeastern Peloponnesus (Morea), with Mistra as its chief center (1261), and within the next 4 years he reduced Michael II of Epirus to dependent status and incorporated much of his territory into the empire (1265). In the same period, in campaigns against the Bulgars, a portion of Macedonia was recovered. A treaty with Venice (1265) and a renewed treaty with Genoa, despite the exclusive trading privileges granted, gave Michael the assurance of naval help and also an opportunity to play off one rival power against the other. Despite heavy defeats by the Tatars (1264 and 1271), Michael was able to make a treaty with the great Tatar leader Nogaj (1272). Stephen of Hungary was his ally, and he was on friendly terms with the Mamelukes of Egypt.

But the primary concern of Michael's foreign policy was, by means of his military alliances, diplomatic missions, and acceptance of union with Rome, to prevent Charles of Anjou, the powerful king of Naples and Sicily (1266–83), from carrying out his avowed purpose, the conquest of the Byzantine Empire. Michael's negotiations with the popes on union culminated in his solemn acceptance of the papal conditions at the Council of *Lyons (1274). However, despite his own efforts, including resort to arrests and imprisonments, to enforce the union, the majority of his clergy and people rejected it. Pope *Martin V, an adherent of Charles of Anjou, condemned Michael, and a Western alliance was formed against him. Michael, however, had won the support of *Peter III of Aragon against Charles, and imperial agents spent Byzantine gold freely in Sicily to arouse its badly oppressed people to open rebellion. Thus, Michael had a hand in the *Sicilian Vespers (1282), which de-stroyed the power of Charles of Anjou and saved Constantinople from almost certain conquest.

Michael VIII's Immediate Successors and John VI Cantacuzenus. Under *Andronicus II Palaeologus (1282–1328) the tremendous strain on the resources of the empire in the process of its reestablishment were manifest. Feudalization reached its fullest development, while excessive taxation and debasement of the coinage weakened the financial system. Andronicus was compelled by internal religious dissension to repudiate the union with Rome, and *John XI Beccus, a strong supporter of union, was deposed as patriarch and replaced by Joseph (1268–75; 1282–83), who had been deposed by Michael. The monks of Mt. Athos were placed under the control of the patriarch of Constantinople, and the diocesan structure of the empire was reorganized. Andronicus had temporary success in dealing with Epirus, and a treaty with the Serbians laid the foundation for the spread of Byzantine religious and cultural influence in the Serbian area. He himself was a cultured ruler who employed scholars among his most trusted advisers. But the defense system of Asia Minor had collapsed under attack from the Turks, and by 1300, apart from some strongholds on or near the coast, almost all of Asia Minor was held by the Ottoman Turks. To meet the Turkish crisis, Andronicus took Roger de Flor and his Catalan Grand Company (6,500 mercenaries) into his service. But after a victory against the Turks, the mercenary army turned to plundering, attacked Constantinople, and caused enormous damage in Thrace and Macedonia, finally seizing the Duchy of Athens and establishing themselves there (1302–11). Asia Minor was permanently lost to the Turks, Nicomedia being captured in 1328.

In this same year a devastating civil war broke out between Andronicus II and his grandson and coemperor Andronicus III (1322–28). The latter was strongly supported by the Grand Domestic John Cantacuzenus. Andronicus II was eventually forced to abdicate in favor of *Andronicus III Palaeologus (1328–41), a brave but erratic ruler who left the administration largely in the hands of John Cantacuzenus. Andronicus recovered Thessaly, a part of Epirus, Chios, and Lesbos (1329–36), but the Serbian advance in the Balkans had begun. Despite attempts to reform the juridical system and reestablish Byzantine naval power, and despite the aid derived from an alliance with the Seljuk Turks, the situation of the Byzantine Empire was weak internally and externally.

On the death of Andronicus III (June 1341), John Cantacuzenus was made regent, as John V was only 9 years old. The regent was opposed from the outset by the Empress Anne of Savoy and the Patriarch *John XIV Calecas (1334–47).

Civil War, Hesychasm, and the Zealots. Another civil war broke out that was destined to be much worse than the previous one, as new and in part radical movements led to sharp cleavages among intellectuals in Church and State and to mass revolution and widespread loss of life and destruction of property. In the absence of John Cantacuzenus from the capital, Alexius Apocaucus, a former supporter of Andronicus III, seized the regency. Cantacuzenus then had himself proclaimed emperor as *John VI Cantacuzenus (October 1341) and got military support in Thrace. It was precisely at this time that *Hesychasm rose to great importance as a religious movement. It was warmly supported by the theologian Gregory *Palamas and was as strongly opposed by the monk *Barlaam of Calabria. In the new civil war, Hesychasm inevitably played a political as well as a religious role, and the radical movement of the Zealots had an opportunity that it could not have had otherwise. The miserable plight of the masses in city and country-side made them ripe for revolution. John Cantacuzenus was an adherent of Hesychasm; Anne and the Patriarch John Calecas opposed it, while Alexius Apocaucus exploited the Zealots to serve his own ends.

The Zealot revolution broke out in Thessalonica with all its fury. The Zealots became masters of the city (1342). There and elsewhere they carried out their radical program of attack on the aristocracy and expropriation of their lands, as well as those belonging to churches and monasteries. Both Cantacuzenus and his opponents turned to the Slavs for help. Cantacuzenus, furthermore, did not hesitate to enlist the aid of the Ottoman Sultan Orchan or make an alliance with him (1344–45). By the summer of 1345, Cantacuzenus had won back all Thrace, and his opponents suffered a heavy blow through the assassination of Alexius Apocaucus in the capital (June 1345). The reign of terror continued in Thessalonica, but Cantacuzenus could now be crowned emperor at Adrianople (May 1346), and he entered Constantinople (Feb. 3, 1347). Only the day before, as an overture, the Empress Anne had released Gregory Palamas from prison, deposed John Calecas, and appointed the latter's friend Isidore as patriarch in his place.

Disastrous Effects of the Civil War. The weakness of the Byzantines was only too obvious to their rivals and enemies. The Serbians under Stephen Dušan seized most of Macedonia—half of all remaining Byzantine territory. Despite an alliance with the Venetians, the Emperor could not prevent the Genoese from retaining their favored trading privileges and holdings. However, he was able to make the Greek Morea an independent despotate and to install his second son Manuel as despot (1348). But the economic and financial situation was deplorable. For the time being, no appreciable revenue could be raised through taxation. The gold sent by the Grand Duke of Moscow to restore Hagia Sophia (c. 1350) was used to pay Turkish mercenaries. The great plague struck Constantinople in 1348 and then spread through Europe. In 1354 the *Ottoman Turks crossed into Europe and seized Gallipoli. In his last years as emperor, Cantacuzenus's foreign and domestic enemies embarrassed him by giving increasing support to the young and legitimate Emperor John V Palaeologus (1341–91). His attempt to make his elder son, Matthew, coemperor and to set aside *John V Palaeologus failed. He was forced to abdicate (November 1354) and enter a monastery. As the monk Joasaph he spent the rest of his life (d. 1383) writing his history and theological works.

The Later Palaeologi and the End of the Byzantine Empire. The decline of the empire was beyond remedy. The governmental machinery had disintegrated, and with a small and constantly shrinking territory no adequate sources of revenue existed. Intrigue and civil war, however, as well as external pressures, afflicted the state to the end. The sudden death of Stephen Dušan (1355) saved Byzantium from a Serbian conquest, but the collapse of the Serbian Empire only made Turkish advance easier, as the Byzantines did not have the power to recover their lost territories. The Turkish menace led John V, whose mother, the Empress Anne of Savoy, was a Catholic, to seek papal aid and to agree to accept unconditional union. But it was soon evident that he could not speak for the majority of his people, including the intransigent Patriarch Callistus I (1350–54; 1355–63), and the appeal for Roman help failed. The Turks overran Thrace and captured Adrianople (1359–61). On his way to Hungary to seek help, John was captured by the Bulgarians, but he was subsequently liberated by Amadeus of Savoy, who forced the Bulgarians to surrender the cities of Mesembria and Sozopolis to John. In 1369 John appeared before Pope *Urban V at Rome and joined the Catholic Church, but his personal conversion did not change the strained relations between the two Churches. Nothing could indicate more clearly the low state of Byzantine prestige than the arrest of John at Venice as an insolvent debtor. Following the Turkish victory over the Serbians on the Marica (1371), John became practically a vassal of the Turkish Sultan. Dethroned by his own son Andronicus IV Palaeologus (1374–79) with the help of the Genoese, John recovered the imperial office with Turkish support and as a Turkish vassal.

Division of the Empire among the Palaeologi and the Reign of Manuel II. The Byzantine Empire was then divided among the members of the Palaeologi dynasty, John retaining Constantinople, Andronicus IV receiving the cities on the Sea of Marmora, *Manuel II receiving Thessalonica, and Theodore I, the Morea. The Turks advanced steadily, and after the decisive defeat of the Serbians at the battle of Kosovo (June 15, 1389), they were masters of a large portion of the Balkans. With the aid of the Sultan Bajezid I (1389–1402), John VII Palaeologus, son of Andronicus, seized the imperial throne, deposing the aged John V (1390). The following year, however, Manuel II Palaeologus (1391–1425) recovered the throne for himself and his father, John V. Both, however, were now vassals of the Sultan and subjected to various humiliations.

Manuel was a gifted ruler and a noble character who won the respect of his Turkish overlord. In 1393 the Bulgarian Empire was conquered by the Turks, and in 1396 the Christian army, assembled from the West to answer Hungary's appeal for help against the infidel, was disastrously defeated at the battle of Nicopolis. Constantinople had been blockaded from 1391 but continued to maintain its defenses. Furthermore, despite Turkish raids, the Despotate of the Morea maintained its independence and was a flourishing center of Hellenic culture. Manuel spent 3 years visiting European capitals seeking aid, but from the military point of view, as distinct from the cultural, his mission was a failure. Temporary salvation for Constantinople came from an unexpected source: Bajezid was decisively defeated and captured by the great Mongol conqueror Timur (Tamerlane) at the battle of Angora (July 28, 1402). Timur's withdrawal from Asia Minor and rivalries among the Ottoman princes gave Byzantium respite for some years, especially under the reign of Muhammed I (1413–21), who was occupied with the internal consolidation of his own empire.

The accession of Muhammed's son Murad II (1421–51) ended the respite. When Murad defeated the pretender Mustafa, who had received support from Manuel's son, *John VIII Palaeologus (made coemperor in 1421), he besieged Constantinople; but, faced with another threat to his throne, he broke off the siege (1422). Andronicus transferred Thessalonica to the Venetians (1423), but in 1430 Murad attacked and captured the city. Following the death of Manuel II, John became sole emperor (1425–48) over an empire that was confined practically to the city limits of Constantinople, as the other areas of Greek rule were independent. Of these, the most important, as noted earlier, was the despotate of the Morea. It was ruled by John's three brothers, Theodore, Constantine, and Thomas. By 1432 the whole Peloponnesus, with the exception of the Venetian ports, was incorporated, largely through the efforts of Constantine, into the despotate. In 1437 John VIII, leaving Constantine of the Morea as regent, went to Italy seeking aid. The question of union was taken up at the Council of *Florence. On July 9, 1439, the union was solemnly proclaimed in the cathedral of Florence by Cardinal Julian Cesarini and John *Bessarion, Archbishop of Nicaea. However, the majority of the Byzantines refused to accept the union, and the Russian Church decided to choose its own metropolitan. At the request of the Pope a crusade against the Turks was organized, but after some initial successes the crusading army was destroyed by Murad II at the battle of Varna (Nov. 10, 1444). The Morea was ravaged by the Turks (1446–48), and its despot was reduced to a vassal status.

Constantine XI and the Fall of Constantinople. On the death of John VIII (October 1448), *Constantine XI Palaeologus (1449–53) became the last emperor of Byzantium. The new sultan, Murad II's son Muhammed II (1451–81), prepared to take Constantinople. Constantine again sought help in the West, and again the union was proclaimed by the legate Cardinal Isidore, the former Greek metropolitan of Russia, in Hagia Sophia (Dec. 12, 1452). But the bitterness of the majority toward union remained to the end. It received epigrammatic expression in the declaration of an imperial official: "I would rather see the Moslem turban in the midst of the city than the Latin mitre" (Ducas, 264). A small but excellent contingent of Genoese troops (700 men) under John Giustiniani joined the defenders a short time before the siege. The attack on Constantinople began on April 7, 1453, and despite the conspicuous bravery of Giustiniani and the Emperor himself and the tenacious courage of their limited forces, the city was taken in the general assault on May 29. The Emperor was killed, fighting to the end. For 3 days the Sultan's troops were allowed to plunder the great city as they willed. Constantinople became the capital of the Ottoman Empire, and the Church of the Holy Wisdom, Hagia Sophia, was made a Mohammedan mosque. In 1460 the Turks conquered the Morea, and in 1461, the remnants of the Empire of Trebizond.

For Byzantine civilization, art, literature, theology, and related matters, *see* CHURCH, HISTORY OF, I (EARLY); CHURCH, HISTORY OF, II (MEDIEVAL); BYZANTINE ART; BYZANTINE CHURCH, HISTORY OF; BYZANTINE CIVILIZATION; BYZANTINE LITERATURE; MONASTICISM, 4. ORIENTAL; BYZANTINE RITE; BYZANTINE THEOLOGY, I; CONSTANTINOPLE; CONSTANTINOPLE, PATRIARCHATE OF; CRUSADES; CRUSADERS' STATES; EASTERN SCHISM; HESYCHASM; JERUSALEM, KINGDOM OF; LATIN EMPIRE OF CONSTANTINOPLE; NORMANS; ROMAN EMPIRE; ARMENIA; GEORGIA, CHURCH IN ANCIENT; SLAVS; UNION OF SOVIET SOCIALIST REPUBLICS (early sections); ARABIA, 1; ARABS, HISTORY OF THE; ISLAM; OTTOMAN TURKS.

Bibliography: E. STEIN, "Introduction à l'histoire et aux institutions byzantines," *Traditio* 7 (1949–51) 95–168. Stein-Palanque HistBEmp. G. OSTROGORSKY, *History of the Byzantine State* (Oxford 1956; New Brunswick, N.J. 1958), basic and comprehensive, with indication of the sources. A. A. VASILIEV, *A History of the Byzantine Empire 324–1453* (2d Eng. ed. Madison, Wis. 1952). CMedH, v.4 *The Eastern Roman Empire 717–1453.* CMedH² v.4 (1966) *The Byzantine Empire. Part I, Byzantium and Its Neighbors,* with copious bibliog. E. GIBBON, *The History of the Decline and Fall of the Roman Empire,* ed. J. B. BURY, 7 v. (London 1896–1900; repr. 1923). J. B. BURY, *A History of the Later Roman Empire from Arcadius to Irene, 395–800,* 2 v. (London 1889); 2d ed. *A History of the Later Roman Empire from the Death of Theodosius I to the Death of Justinian, 395–565,* 2 v. (London 1923); *A History of the Eastern Roman Empire from the Fall of Irene to the Accession of Basil I, 802–867* (London 1912); *The Imperial Administrative System in the Ninth Century,* with a rev. text of the *Kletorologion of Philotheos* (London 1911). Fliche-Martin v.4–8. N. H. BAYNES and H. ST. L. B. MOSS, eds., *Byzantium* (Oxford 1948). L. BRÉHIER, *Le Monde byzantin,* 3 v. (Paris 1947–50). J. M. HUSSEY, *Church and Learning in the Byzantine Empire, 867–1185* (Oxford 1937). W. NORDEN, *Das Papsttum und Byzanz* (Berlin 1903). H. G. BECK, *Kirche und theologische Literatur im byzantinischen Reich* (Munich 1959). F. DVORNIK, *Byzance et la primauté romaine* (Paris 1964). R. GROUSSET, *Histoire des Croisades et du royaume franc de Jérusalem,* 3 v. (Paris 1934–36). S. RUNCIMAN, *A History of the Crusades,* 3 v. (Cambridge, Eng. 1951–54); *The Sicilian Vespers: A History of the Mediterranean World in the Late 13th Century* (Cambridge, Eng. 1958). K. M. SETTON, ed., *A History of the Crusades* (Philadelphia 1955–); *Catalan Domination of Athens, 1311–1388* (Cambridge, Mass. 1948). C. TOUMANOFF, "Moscow the Third Rome: Genesis and Significance of a Politico-Religious Idea," CathHistRev 40 (1954–55) 411–447. The following journals, esp. the first, furnish current systematic bibliog.: *Byzantinische Zeitschrift, Byzantion, Revue des Études byzantines.* **Illustration credits:** Figs. 2 and 6, Hirmer Verlag München. Figs. 3, 5, and 7, Courtesy of the Byzantine Institute. Fig. 4, Division of Numismatics, Smithsonian Institution, Washington, D.C. Fig. 8, Courtesy of the Dumbarton Oaks Collections.

[M. R. P. MC GUIRE; F. X. MURPHY]

BYZANTINE LITERATURE

The importance of the contribution the Byzantines made to modern civilization by creating a new kind of art and by protecting western Europe from barbarian invaders for more than 1,000 years is universally recognized. In appraising Byzantium as a cultural force, however, emphasis is usually laid on what the Byzantines did rather than on what they wrote. The customary verdict is that Byzantine literature is more significant for the information it contains than for its own sake. This judgment, though valid in general, is not altogether unassailable, and leaves out of account a number of significant facts, which are reviewed in this article.

INTRODUCTION

It should be noted at once that, except for a large number of fragments on papyrus and the *Persians* of Timotheus (which has been preserved almost intact on a papyrus nearly contemporary with its author), virtually all of our texts of the ancient Greek classics were literally saved from destruction by the diligence of the Byzantine scholars who studied them and laboriously transcribed them. If it had not been for this Byzantine interest, the pagan Greek classics would have perished

Fig. 1. Discorides at work in his study, miniature in a MS of his works written at Constantinople for Juliana Anicia, granddaughter of Valentinian III, c. 512 (Vienna, National Library Cod. Med. Gr. 1, fol. 5v).

long ago, and the whole shape of modern life would have been profoundly altered. Moreover, the Byzantines achieved aesthetic distinction of a high order in some areas, especially in the liturgy and in historiography.

Scope of Byzantine Literature. Strictly speaking, Byzantine literature includes the entire literary production, in all genres, of the occupants of the *Byzantine Empire from the beginning of the reign of Diocletian (284) to the fall of the empire on May 29, 1453. Hence, in a survey of Byzantine literature one should presumably consider texts written not only in Greek but also in Latin, Syriac, and Arabic. Accordingly, a strong case could be made for the inclusion under this rubric of such Latin writers as *Lactantius (fl. c. 317), who was the tutor of Crispus, Emperor *Constantine I's eldest son.

Similarly, it would not be inappropriate to discuss here such works as the *Corpus Iuris Civilis,* despite the fact that only one of its four major divisions (the so-called *Novels,* Νεαραί) was written in Greek. For the other three parts of this extraordinary code of laws, though derived directly from preexisting Latin texts and codifications of the law, represent Byzantine legal thought and practice as reflected in the additions, omissions, and emendations made by Tribonian, Emperor *Justinian I's chief adviser in such matters, and the other jurisconsults of his staff.

Nevertheless, for the sake of simplicity, this article is limited to the materials written in Greek, which was the dominant language of the empire, at least from the time of Justinian I. Even Emperor Constantine I, whose native language was Latin, used Greek in addressing the bishops at the first ecumenical council (*Nicaea I, 325). Still, Latin persisted in the eastern portions of the empire as late as the time of Emperor *Heraclius I (610–641), who apparently was the first to make Greek the official language of the Byzantine court and chancery, as it had always been of the Greek Churches in the East, which were the direct descendants of the Greek-speaking communities that had produced the New Testament, carried the Gospels to the West, and left their mark upon Rome through the first popes, all of whom had written and spoken in Greek until the time of *Victor I (c. 189–198).

Byzantine Greek. The form of the Greek language that the Byzantines used varied greatly. The standard of most serious writers was the usage that prevailed in ancient Athens. That is, they were Atticizers. But not even the most determined classicists were able to reproduce this ancient language with complete fidelity, and their use of the Attic idiom invariably fell short of their ideal. Moreover, new vocabulary and usages, which are always associated with a living language, turned up regularly not only in the nonliterary texts of the years following upon the death of Alexander, but also with even greater frequency in the Christian period as a result of the birth and growth of the Christian Church.

In general, however, the intelligentsia clung to the traditional language of antiquity, so far as it was possible for them to do so. But inevitably in their hands the language underwent great changes, marked principally by the simplification of syntax that resulted from such phenomena as the disappearance of the dative case, the loss or misunderstanding of the optative and subjunctive moods of the verb, and the breaking down of the more complicated conjugations and declensions.

These transformations were unavoidable. At the same time, however, the determined classicism of the Atticizers, aided by the concentration of authority in *Constantinople, the major cultural center of the empire, had a unifying effect linguistically, and succeeded in eradicating the ancient non-Attic dialects, which now had almost completely disappeared. Provincialisms of various kinds were always to be found, but they rarely penetrated into literary circles. Nor did they ever become truly separate types of speech that could be described as dialects.

What is called the κοινὴ διάλεκτος (the "common language") was essentially the neo-Attic type of Greek that resulted from the strenuous but never altogether successful efforts of writers to reproduce the idiom of ancient Athens. In the course of its history, this Atticizing language had to make concessions on a large scale to modernisms of many sorts (originating in the speech of the people, the army, imperial chancery, etc.). But the resulting changes affected syntax and vocabulary rather than morphology.

Besides their success in eliminating the non-Attic dialects, the Atticizers won another fundamental victory, for the influence of the imperial court and of the liturgy (which was always under the domination of the Atticizers), as well as the patriotic instincts of the people, served to keep the Greek language as such alive, and prevented its disintegration into new linguistic creations like the Romance languages of the West (Italian, Spanish, Portuguese, and French), which came into being during the Middle Ages. Indeed, in the last 3½ centuries of its history, the very period during which the Byzantine national existence was gravely threatened (by the Crusaders and foreign enemies of all sorts who invaded and occupied its territories), the common language was strengthened by new and vigorous classical revivals. Naturally, the common language was not the language of the people, but the latter never had the strength to drive out the former. In the West, on the other hand, popular usage corrupted classical Latin and made of it what was called Vulgar Latin, which then, sometime between the 7th and 10th centuries, disappeared entirely (except for the survival of the ancient idiom in the Roman liturgy and in the works of scholars), and was supplanted as a spoken tongue by the new Romance languages. In Byzantium the metamorphosis of the Vulgar form of Greek into anything resembling Romance never took place. Instead, there was, and remains to this day in modern Greece, a duality of languages: the "common" or literary language (of the Atticizing writers now known as the καθαρεύουσα) and, over against this, the popular or "demotic" language of the people. But both were, and are recognizably Greek in form and structure. *See* GREEK LANGUAGE, EARLY CHRISTIAN AND BYZANTINE.

GENERAL CHARACTER OF BYZANTINE LITERATURE

Though it is rarely prudent to generalize concerning an entire people, there are a few traits of Byzantine literature as a whole that may be regarded as characteristic. Above all, the medieval Greeks, like their ancient ancestors, whose literature they cherished, had a fierce sense of national pride that left its mark in every phase of their activity. Their emperor, who was, according to them, chosen by God himself, was the ruler of the whole of the inhabited world; and the *Byzantine Church was in their sight the divinely appointed custodian and champion of the only true faith, just as their language was the sole respectable medium for communication.

In some important respects the Byzantines were the heirs of the Hellenistic age, i.e., of the Greek culture that flourished for 600 or 700 years between *c.* 350 B.C. and the middle of the 4th century of the Christian Era. It is from this period, from the school of *Alexandria, that the Byzantines inherited their flair for scholarly works of all kinds—for the transcription, critical revision, and excerpting of the ancient texts; for the compilation and collection of literary materials of every description; for philological studies; for their predilection for the *ekphrasis* (a description, long or short, in prose or verse, of a person, place, object, work of art, etc.); and for the annotation, exegesis, and appraisal of ancient literature of all kinds.

Dominance of Rhetoric. Probably also of Alexandrian origin was the addiction to rhetoric, which colored everything the Byzantines said and wrote. They avoided ordinary and customary words, invented a bewildering array of new sesquipedalian monstrosities with the aid of prefixes of various kinds, and constantly strained after novel modes of expression. The result is that the modern reader has often to cut his way through all but impenetrable thickets of bombast and tangled webs of tortuously constructed sentences, which are not always fully comprehensible.

Fortunately, a great many writers, especially in the earlier centuries, were untainted by this passion for rhetorical embellishment. St. Athanasius, for example, and most of the theologians of the period of the ecumenical councils cultivated a simple, unadorned style that usually offers no difficulties, and was often uninfluenced by classical standards. But more erudite authors, the chief partisans of the common language, men such as Photius and Psellus, struggled so earnestly to write in the elevated manner that they became all but unintelligible.

Lack of Originality. Paradoxically, despite these frantic efforts to achieve originality of form, the Byzantines had no abhorrence of plagiarism, and uninhibitedly paraphrased or even copied out whole paragraphs and pages from the works of other authors without acknowledgment or fear of censure for so doing.

The Byzantine lack of sensitivity in such matters is probably to be explained by a characteristic docility before authority, imperial and ecclesiastical, and also by the traditional convention of imitation. An emperor's decree or the dogma formulated by one of the ecumenical councils might be copied, annotated, or discussed. It could not be altered. This attitude of obeisance was transferred to literary, philosophical, and scientific texts, and is reflected in the innumerable Byzantine compendia, anthologies, excerpts, and paraphrases. Euclid, for example, or the ancient philosophers could be expounded or, very rarely, emended.

But no one felt the need to begin afresh or to develop a new system of thought and belief. Even the neopagan George Gemistos *Plethon (*c.* 1355–1452), who sought to overthrow the Christian religion, confined himself in his scheme for a new pagan state to summarizing

and weaving together a great variety of sources, mostly Platonic and Neoplatonic. He never for a moment contemplated creating something entirely original or departing from the paths laid down in the ancient tradition.

Hence, even when they fail to cite the authors whom they copy or follow, it is doubtful that many Byzantine writers had any intention to deceive. Thus, *John Damascene in the *Fountain of Knowledge* (Πηγὴ γνώσεως) disarmingly confesses that he was wholly dependent upon his authorities, and had made no attempt to present ideas of his own.

Being overpowered by the weight of tradition and predisposed to follow models of one sort or another, the Byzantine writers felt free to write in as many media as they chose. Before the Hellenistic Age, no writer (except Ion of Chios in the 5th century B.C., and possibly Plato, if the poems attributed to him are genuine) expressed himself in more than one literary genre. The historian confined himself to history, the lyric poet to lyric poetry, the dramatist to drama, and the philosopher to philosophy. But in Byzantium many writers tried their hands at a variety of styles, and wrote in every conceivable literary form: history, philosophy, mathematics, and poetry. As a result, the novelty they achieved was usually in expression rather than in ideas.

THEOLOGY

The whole of Byzantine civilization turned around two foci: the Church and the emperor. There is hardly a phase of Byzantine activity that can be considered apart from these two vital factors. Though the emperor dominated all phases of Byzantine life and even exerted control over the Byzantine Church, the Byzantines felt no special urge to write about political theory or on the relation between Church and State. There are, of course, important Byzantine treatises on this subject, but they are greatly outweighed in both bulk and number by the works of the theologians, who concerned themselves with all the major problems of theology, especially those involved in the *Trinitarian and *Christological controversies. These were the principal subjects on the agenda of the seven ecumenical councils (Nicaea I, 325; *Constantinople I, 381; *Ephesus, 431; *Chalcedon, 451; *Constantinople II, 553; *Constantinople III, 680–681; *Nicaea II, 787) that produced the official creeds of the Church. *See* COUNCILS, GENERAL (ECUMENICAL), HISTORY OF.

These documents, especially the so-called *Nicene Creed (more technically described as the Niceno-Constantinopolitan Creed, to distinguish it from that of 325, which it closely resembles) and the Creed of Chalcedon provide the basic definitions of the doctrines of the Trinity and of the person of Christ, respectively, as these are understood in most of the Christian Churches throughout the world—Roman, Greek Orthodox, and Protestant.

From the point of view of the enormous influence of these creeds on the entire history of the Christian world, therefore, the theologians who drafted, expounded, and defended them deserve a place in intellectual history hardly, if at all, below that of the ancient Greek philosophers. Aesthetically and liturgically, as well as theologically, the creeds themselves merit careful study.

Moreover, on the evidence of the New Testament, in which Christ is represented both as a divine being (i.e., one who performed miracles, conquered death, and rose to heaven) and as a true man (who ate, drank, slept, wept, etc., like other men), the theological definitions contained in these creeds are logically inevitable. In other words, the heretics were not condemned because they made use of pagan philosophy, terminology, and logic, as some contend, but primarily because, in one way or another, they failed to take adequate account of the New Testament portrayal of Jesus Christ.

Antiheretical Polemics. The reasoning by which the doctrines set forth in these creeds were evolved becomes a matter of the highest interest. The earliest monuments of this doctrinal development (after the New Testament itself, the writings of the *Apostolic Fathers, of the *Apologists, of Pope *Dionysius I and *Dionysius of Alexandria, and of theologians such as *Irenaeus, *Clement and *Origen of Alexandria, and *Tertullian of Carthage), fall outside of the chronological limits of this essay.

Within our scope, however, comes *Alexander, Patriarch of Alexandria, and, even more significantly, his successor, St. *Athanasius (bishop, 328–373), the chief defender of the Nicene theology in the first half of the 4th century, to whom we owe three *Orations Against the Arians,* as well as letters and other treatises that rank among the chief sources for our knowledge of the transactions of the first ecumenical council and of much of the subsequent development down to 381. In addition, Athanasius occupies a place of importance in the history of monasticism for his *Life of St. Anthony* (251–356), the first of the great hermits and one of the spiritual ancestors of Byzantine asceticism (*see* ANTHONY OF EGYPT, ST.).

In the next phase of the Arian controversy, down to and including the second council (381), the chief authorities were the three Cappadocians, St. *Basil of Caesarea in Cappadocia (d. 379), his younger brother *Gregory, Bishop of Nyssa (d. 394), and their friend Bishop *Gregory of Nazianzus (d. 389 or 390).

In his letters as well as in his works *Against Eunomius* and *On the Holy Spirit* Basil refuted the arguments of the Arians. His major contribution was the formulation and dogmatic defense of the Trinitarian formula, μία οὐσία ἐν τρισὶν ὑποστάσεσι: one substance (or essence, i.e., one divinity) in three hypostases (i.e., three persons). Moreover, Basil was the founder of Byzantine monasticism, his regulations for which exerted influence also in the West. His nine homilies on the *Hexaemeron* (the Biblical account of creation) are noteworthy as a statement of Christian principles of cosmology, which drew freely upon pagan authorities, such as Plato, Aristotle, Poseidonius and *Plotinus. Gregory of Nyssa carried on the attack against the Eunomians and the Macedonians (*see* SABELLIANISM; MONARCHIANISM), continued his brother's study of cosmology with a treatise *On the Creation of Man* (*De Opificio hominis*), and produced a host of works on other subjects. He relied extensively upon Plato. Gregory of Nazianzus, known as "the Theologian" because of his five theological orations, was less prolific than Gregory of Nyssa. He wrote some 400 poems and, among other things, a bitter treatise against Emperor *Julian.

Another, but still virtually unstudied, refutation of Julian's polemic against the Christians was that of *Cyril of Alexandria (bishop, 412–444), whose chief importance, however, lay in his interpretation of the relation of the two natures (the divine and the human) in Christ. Actually, his famous Christological formula, μία φύσις τοῦ Θεοῦ Λόγου σεσαρκωμένη [one incarnate nature of God the Word (Logos)], was taken over from Apollinaris (the heretic, *c.* 310–390) in the mistaken belief that it had been enunciated by Athanasius (*see* APOLLINARIANISM). The "strict" Chalcedonians, including *Theodoret of Cyr (d. *c.* 466) and *Nestorius (fl. 428), objected that this phrase was Monophysitic and signified that Christ had only one nature instead of two. The Cyrillian theologians, in turn, insisted that, by stressing the fact that the "one nature" was "incarnate," this formula fully safeguarded the integrity and reality in Christ of two natures, as orthodox theology required.

The chief defenders of the strictly Chalcedonian dyophysite Christology were *Hypatius of Ephesus (fl. 532) and *Leontius of Byzantium (fl. 543), the latter of whom wrote against both the Nestorians and the Monophysites.

Taking a position midway between the strict Chalcedonians and the Monophysites were the so-called Neochalcedonians, who attempted to reinterpret the creed of 451 in Cyrillian terms. The most interesting as well as the most powerful of the theologians of this group was Emperor Justinian I (527–565), who, besides several pronouncements in the *Corpus Iuris Civilis* on theological matters, is credited in the manuscripts with three erudite doctrinal dissertations. His chief aim was to vindicate the theology of Cyril against its critics. This he succeeded in doing at the Council of 553 by interpreting Cyril's Christological formula and other aspects of the Cyrillian system, which the Chalcedonians had found objectionable, in harmony with the creed of 451.

At the same time, however, the Neochalcedonians continued to attack the Monophysites despite the fact that many modern critics fail to find much difference between Neochalcedonianism and the so-called "*Monophysitism" of Bp. *Severus of Antioch (512–538), who devoted his considerable talents to the defense and exposition of the Cyrillian position. For this reason, many have doubted whether he can be properly classified as a Monophysite. Nevertheless, the orthodox prejudice against him was so great that very little of what he wrote is extant, save in Syriac translation. His chief offense, perhaps, was that he polemized against the Creed of Chalcedon, which he took to be Nestorian. On the other hand, another Monophysite of the 6th century, *Julian of Halicarnassus, is not easily defended, and was attacked even by Severus of Antioch for Aphthartodocetism.

In the conflict with Monenergism and *Monothelitism, the great champion of the doctrine that Christ had two energies and two wills (as set forth eventually by the sixth ecumenical council), was *Maximus the Confessor (580–662), the author of numerous dogmatic and polemical treatises and letters on various theological subjects, including commentaries on the Pseudo-Dionysius, an allegorical interpretation of the liturgy, and a series of so-called *Centuries*. At the end of the 7th century the struggle against heresy was continued by *Anastasius Sinaita (d. *c.* 700), who polemized against the Monophysites in his *Hodegos* (Guide), and wrote a commentary on the Biblical account of creation.

Despite their condemnation at the Councils of 451, 553, and 680 to 681, the Monophysites persisted in the struggle to obtain an ecumenical decision in their favor, and in the 8th and 9th centuries sought to circumvent the strict dyophysitism of 451 by calling for the condemnation of the images of Christ, Mary, and the saints, which they deemed sacrilegious (*see* ICONOCLASM). The iconoclasts were led by Emperors *Leo III (717–741), *Constantine V (741–775), and *Leo V (813–820), but in the end they were defeated, largely through the efforts of Empresses *Irene (in 787) and *Theodora (in 843). The chief defenders of the images were Patriarch *Germanus I of Constantinople (715–730; d. 733), John Damascene (the greatest theologian of his day; d. *c.* 753), Patriarchs *Tarasius (784–806) and *Nicephorus I (806–815) of Constantinople, and *Theodore the Studite (759–826).

John Damascene is celebrated not only for his *Three Orations Against the Iconoclasts,* a number of Biblical commentaries, and some liturgical poems of high merit, but above all for his great theological encyclopedia, the *Fountain of Knowledge* (Πηγὴ γνώσεως). John exerted great influence on theology both in Byzantium and in the Latin West (to which parts of the *Fountain* were made available in Latin translations of the 12th and 13th centuries). But he made no claim to originality and was slavishly dependent upon his sources, pagan and Christian, which in truly Byzantine fashion he often copied verbatim.

In the second iconoclastic period (815–843), the leading figure was Theodore the Studite, an uncompromising champion of images, whose intransigence on this subject thrice drove him into exile. Besides his polemical

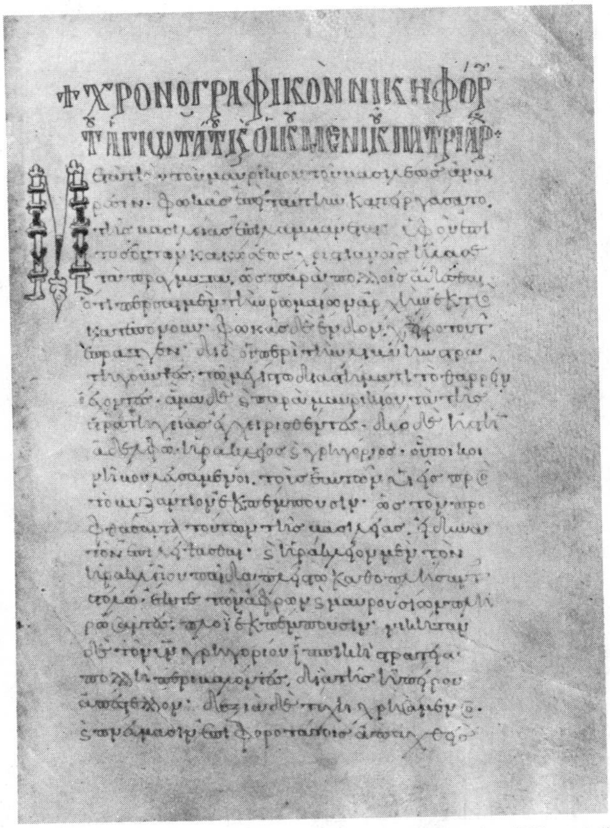

Fig. 2. Page from a late 9th-century MS of the "Historia" of Nicephorus, Patriarch of Constantinople (Br. Mus. Add. MS 19390, fol. 24r).

writings in favor of images, he is known for two collections of *Catechetical Precepts* (on the duties of monks), an extensive correspondence, homilies, panegyrics, his epigrams (see below), and a notable group of liturgical poems.

Mystical Theology. Hardly less characteristic of Byzantium than the dogmatic decrees of the ecumenical councils was the Byzantine interest in mystical theology, which is closely connected with ascetical practices of various kinds. Alongside the early Biblical type of mystic union with Christ as set forth in the Pauline Epistles, the early Fathers, and Basil of Caesarea, there was the more intellectual type, which was dependent upon philosophical sources, mediated by Origen (*c.* 185–254) and *Evagrius Ponticus (346–399). This latter form of mysticism is best known in its most developed form as presented by the *Pseudo-Dionysius the Areopagite (fl. 500), who was deeply influenced by *Proclus, the Neoplatonist, and served as one of the major channels by which Neoplatonic ideas were transmitted to the later Middle Ages (*see* NEOPLATONISM). Apart from heterodox variations of mysticism like that of the Messalians [combated by *Diadochus of Photice (d. before 486)], the Byzantine tradition was best represented by *John Climacus of Sinai (d. *c.* 670), Maximus the Confessor (580–662), Theodore the Studite (759–826), *Symeon the New Theologian (949–1022), and *Nicetas Stethatos (fl. 1054). Finally, in the 14th century, differences of opinion on various aspects of mystical theology led to the Hesychast controversy, which ended in the triumph of the Hesychasts, such as Gregory *Palamas and Emperor *John VI Cantacuzenus, against their opponents, *Barlaam of Calabria, *Nicephorus Gregoras, and others (*see* HESYCHASM).

After the final settlement of the iconoclastic controversy in 843, the most fruitful period in the history of Byzantine theology came to an end. The production of theological works continued as in the past. But the questions discussed after 843, though often hotly contested, were not so significant as the dogmas of the Trinity and the Incarnation, to the definition of which the ecumenical councils had addressed themselves. Even some of the earlier questions had reverberations in the later centuries, and Photius, for example, near the end of the 9th century, still found it necessary to polemize against the iconoclasts. Similarly, *Manichaeism rose up in new forms (*Paulicians and *Bogomils) which called forth new refutations.

But the interests and literary activity of the theologians of the later period were most actively engaged in dealing with the question of the proposed union of the Churches of Rome and Byzantium, the problem of Hesychasm, and the polemic against Islam. The proponents of union with Rome were greatly aided by the Greek translations of Latin theological masterpieces that were made by Demetrius *Cydones (*c.* 1324–1397 or 1398). The most important of these were of Thomas Aquinas's *Summa contra Gentiles* and *Summa theologiae* (the latter of which was completed by Demetrius's brother Prochorus), the *Donation of Constantine,* and Anselm's *De processione spiritus sancti.*

In the middle of the 15th century the leading theologian, next to *Bessarion (the Greek champion of union with Rome) and Abp. Mark of Ephesus (a resolute foe of the union), was George Scholarius (Patriarch *Gennadius II of Constantinople, 1454), who was mildly in

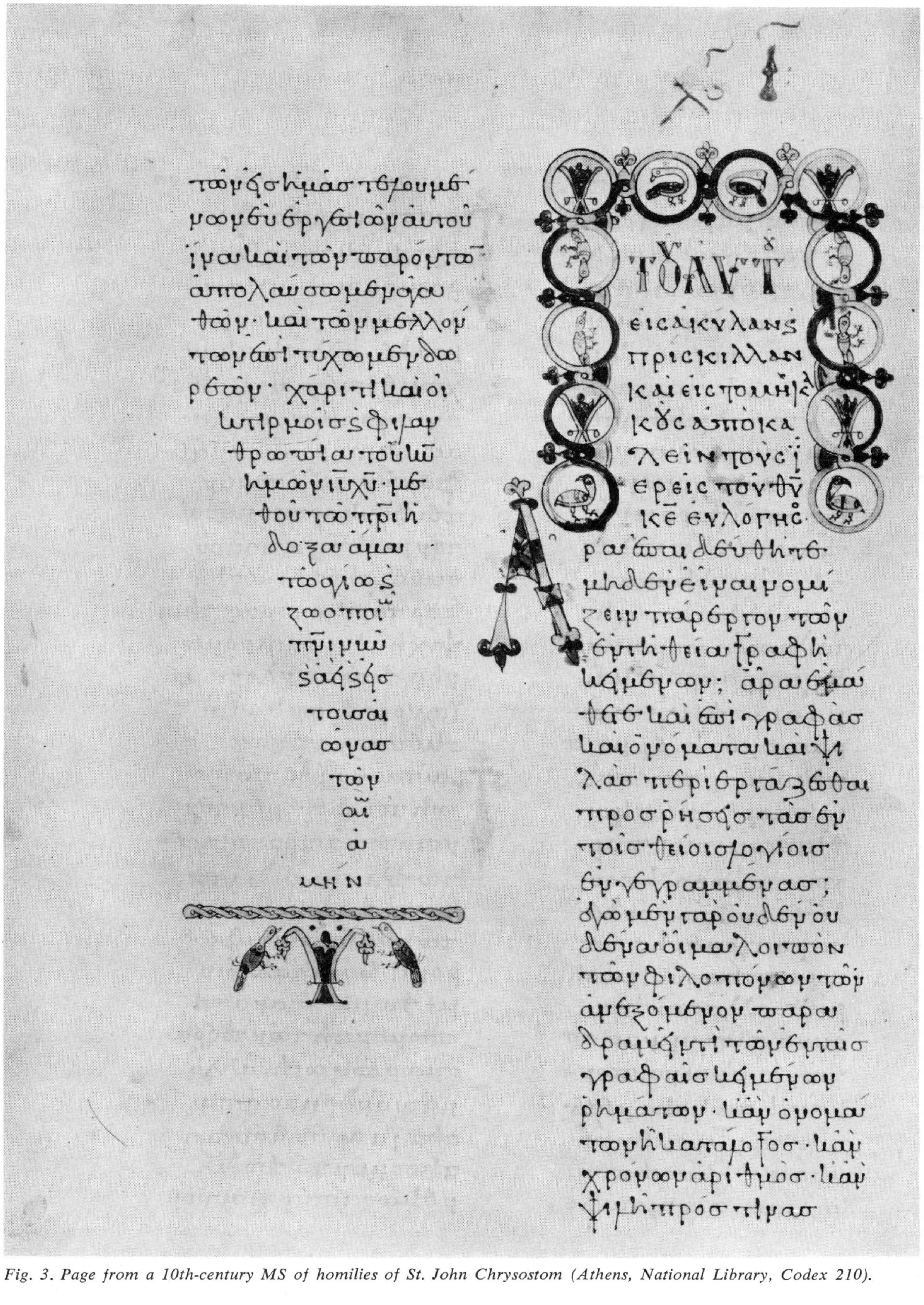

Fig. 3. Page from a 10th-century MS of homilies of St. John Chrysostom (Athens, National Library, Codex 210).

favor of union with Rome until 1443 or 1444, when he began to polemize against it. He defended the Palamites, wrote against the Jews and Plethon, and produced a number of valuable Greek translations of Latin theological classics.

Theological Encyclopedias. Appearing as compendia of the total Byzantine effort, theological encyclopedias were a favored form of synthesis, and several of them were remarkably successful. The Byzantines found this type of scholarly activity particularly congenial, and many theologians had devoted a great deal of energy to encyclopedic résumés or analyses of various kinds. (See for the earlier period, the *Stromata* of *Clement of Alexandria, Eusebius of Caesarea's *Praeparatio* and *Demonstratio,* *Epiphanius of Constantia's *Panarion,* Theodoret's polemic against the pagans, and the great theological encyclopedia of John Damascene.)

In the later period the most noteworthy example of this genre was the *Dogmatic Armory* (Πανοπλία δογματική) of Euthymius *Zigabenus, which was written to please Emperor *Alexius I Comnenus, and to serve as an arsenal for orthodox theologians in their debates against the heretics. The first 22 sections are taken up with a consideration of early heresy with special emphasis on the post-Nicene era. In this section Zigabenus is dependent entirely upon quotations from the leading theological authorities of early times (Athanasius, the Cappadocians, John Damascene, Photius, etc.). But the concluding portions (bks. 23–28) in which he treats the heretics of his own time (the Armenians, Paulicians, Messalians, Bogomils, and Moslems) have independent value as historical source. Zigabenus is known also for his commentaries on the Psalms and the Gospels.

Of similar scope but different plan is the *Holy Arsenal* (Ἱερὰ ὁπλοθήκη) of Andronicus Camaterus, dedicated to Emperor *Manuel I, c. 1170–75. The first division of this *Arsenal* begins with a dialogue between the Emperor and the Roman *Kardenalioi* (cardinals) on the procession of the Holy Spirit, in which the Byzantine doctrine on the "single" procession is supported by quotations from the Bible and the Fathers, and fortified by syllogisms taken from the writings of earlier Byzantine opponents of the Latins. The second part of the work is directed against the Armenians, whom the Byzantines condemned as Monophysites, and is made up of an attack on heretical views of a Monophysitizing tendency (i.e., not only on Monophysitism itself, but also on Monotheletism, the theopaschite doctrine, and aphthartodocetism). Only a small part of the *Arsenal* has been published.

A third theological encyclopedia following those of the Comnenian period, the *Treasury of Orthodoxy* (Θησαυρὸς ὀρθοδοξίας), came from the pen of the historian *Nicetas Choniates (brother of Michael Choniates), who supplemented the *Panoplia* of Zigabenus, and concentrated on a survey of the older heresies, which the latter had not discussed. It is probably to be assigned to the years between 1204 and 1210, when Nicetas was in Nicaea. (See history below.)

Homiletics. The Byzantines produced a vast number of sermons, which are marked by their fondness for rhetorical display; many of the major theologians have left large homiletic collections. The best known of the Byzantine preachers is the archbishop St. *John Chrysostom of Constantinople (d. 407), one of the most prolific authors of the Byzantine period (the author of 18 volumes in the *Patrologia Graeca*), the greater part of whose extant writings consists of sermons usually delivered in the form of commentaries on various books of the Bible. Chrysostom suffered for his outspokenness as censor of morals. But he was enormously popular with the people of Constantinople, who were so captivated by his oratory, that, to his annoyance, they often interrupted him by applause.

Of interest also in this genre, to choose only one example out of many, was Abp. Michael Choniates (Acominatus) of Athens (*c.* 1175–1204; d. *c.* 1220), whose sermons and letters illuminate the literary and cultural history of Athens in this period. Michael deplored the low state of learning in the Athens of his day, the cultural level of which had fallen so low, he complained, that his style had been corrupted as a consequence.

HISTORY

In the field of history, the Byzantines continued the ancient Greek tradition with notable success, and produced a great historical literature. The extant texts are of two types: (1) the history and (2) the chronicle.

Historians and Chroniclers. The chroniclers and historians differed from each other in many respects. The former were usually men of humble station and far less ambitious than the latter. With few exceptions the chroniclers were members of the clergy, and looked upon history as a kind of homiletical exercise, by which they were enabled to justify the ways of God to man. Their chief concern was to champion their own brand of orthodoxy and to deliver themselves of pious sentiments. They had little taste for real historical research or criticism, and made use of the most convenient sources at hand, which they excerpted freely or even reproduced verbatim, with special emphasis upon the bizarre and the unusual. They had a special fondness for miracles, ice storms, comets, floods, and other phenomena that might provide interesting or edifying material for the common people.

Since the writers of the chronicles were not connected with the imperial court and centers of culture, most of them wrote in the popular idiom; and their works thus often preserved specimens of the vernacular language of their period. Though less critical than the historians, the chroniclers are by no means devoid of significance. Many reported events at firsthand as eyewitnesses, or covered subjects, persons, and places ignored by the historians; and several have proved to be the only available sources for the information that they supply. Moreover, not a few of the chronicles, like that of *John Malalas, for instance, which deals primarily with the history of *Antioch, preserve local information and traditions, concerning which the Constantinopolitan writers were uninformed.

The chroniclers set out to cover the entire history of the world from the creation on, and prefixed to the treatment of their own special period a section on the creation of the universe, together with a survey of ancient history, Biblical and classical. After this introductory sketch of early times, the chroniclers then went on to deal with the events of their own day. The historians, on the other hand, except for Laonicus Chalcocondyles and Ducas, made no place for the history of their remote forbears and concentrated, instead, on their own times.

Fig. 4. St. John Climacus pointing the way to the "Heavenly Ladder," miniature in a 12th-century MS of the 7th-century saint's work of the same title (Princeton University Library, Garrett MS 16, fol. 194r).

Fig. 5. Miniature illustrating an episode in the life of Emperors Tiberius II and Maurice in a 14th-century Slavic MS of the "Chronicle" of Constantine Manasses (Cod. Vat. slav. 2, fol. 117r, detail).

Moreover, most, but not all, of the chroniclers contented themselves with a very cursory summary of each period of Biblical or ancient history, and with a short paragraph, often not exceeding a few sentences in length, for each year of later history.

In contrast with this simple, pedestrian, unsophisticated method, the historians gave lengthy and detailed accounts of the eras with which they were primarily concerned. Most of them were laymen of high social position and excellent education, who either were themselves active participants in the events they described or were indirectly involved as ambassadors, generals, or members of the royal household. They wrote for people like themselves, often at the emperor's command, and had access to the best sources: letters, archival material of various kinds, and texts in many languages, as well as the testimony of eyewitnesses. They prided themselves on their disinterestedness and undertook, like the ancient models they imitated, to investigate and expatiate upon the causal relations of the facts they reported.

The historians resembled professional scholars, and were strongly influenced by the great historical writers of antiquity (Herodotus, Thucydides, Xenophon, and Polybius), whom they constantly sought to emulate in language, style, and method. For this reason, they usually avoided contemporary nomenclature and have confused modern students by insisting upon the geographical designations current in the ancient writers [e.g., Scythians, rather than the current name, Rosoi (οἱ Ῥῶς or Ῥῶσοι) for Russians].

Similarly, in the effort to reproduce the manner and syntax of their ancient models, the Byzantine historians often used words and constructions that they did not fully understand, with the result that many sentences are so twisted and garbled as to defy analysis. Since they lacked adequate lexica and grammars, their attempted emulation of ancient rhetoric led them into many errors and ambiguities.

Not all of the great corpus of Byzantine historians is extant. But from the histories that have been preserved it can be seen that the historians provided what is almost a continuous, uninterrupted account of the Byzantine world from the time of Diocletian (284–305) until the fall of Constantinople in 1453. Normally, one historian took up the thread of the narrative where his predecessor left off. Usually, there was one historian for each period, and only one. Hence, except as noted below (in the 14th and 15th centuries, in which special conditions prevailed), there were no rival historians, and we have only one major authority among the historians for each chronological division.

The interpretation of history thus presented would be extremely one-sided if it were not possible, as it usually is, to compare the views of the historians with contemporary chronicles, legal documents, theological treatises, the *typika* (foundation charters of monasteries, etc.), letters, and the historical works of non-Byzantine writers (Arabic, Syriac, Armenian, Latin, and others). This generalization is applicable only to the portions of each history upon which the historian concentrated as his own special province, not to the introductory sections in which he reviewed the events of preceding years by way of preface.

Since the historians were all men of high station and intimately connected, in one way or another, with the imperial court, it is possible that they were chosen by the emperor himself to serve as official historians. Under such circumstances few would have dared to oppose their version of history to that of the emperor's personally selected scrivener.

Ecclesiastical History. One of the fields in which the Byzantine historians excelled was ecclesiastical history.

Eusebius. The first and greatest representative of the historians was *Eusebius of Caesarea in Palestine (c. 263–340), who exerted an enormous influence on subsequent writers in this genre, despite his leanings toward *Arianism and iconoclasm. His chief works were his panegyric on, or, as it is usually designated, the biography of, Constantine I and his invaluable history of the early Church (from the beginning to 324). The former (in four books), when allowances are made for its adulatory tone, is an absolutely indispensable key to the understanding of Constantine's reign, and in recent times has been strongly defended against the attacks certain modern critics had made against it.

The latter, in 10 books, which is no less monumental in significance, preserves in excerpt a mass of historical records that otherwise would have perished. Eusebius is memorable also as the first to have popularized, on the basis of the efforts of Ammonius of Alexandria, an elaborate scheme for tabulating the parallel passages in the Gospels (where two or more Gospels are similar or identical) and the material peculiar to each of them by dividing the Gospels into numbered sections, which he listed under rubrics or headings, now known as the Eusebian canons or sections. These canons, which were taken over by Jerome in the Vulgate translation, are found in many medieval Gospel Books and New Testaments (both Greek and Latin), and are usually adorned with handsome representations of animals, flowers, arcades, arches, columns, and with decorative patterns of many types.

Of his numerous other works on related subjects, special interest attaches to his *Praeparatio evangelica* (*Preparation for the Gospel*), in 15 books, which is an elaborate and erudite refutation of pagan religion and mythology (based on hundreds of quotations from the classics) and a glorification of the teaching of the Old Testament. In the *Demonstratio evangelica* (*Proof of the Gospel*), originally written in 20 books, of which 10 and a fraction are extant, Eusebius explained why the Christians accept the Old Testament (in which he found numerous prophecies of the appearance of Christ) but reject the Mosaic Law.

Eusebius's *Ecclesiastical History* served as the model for later Church historians in the Greek East as well as in the Latin West. *Rufinus (d. 410) rendered it into Latin and expanded it with certain, not always felicitous, additions of his own (which carried the history down to 395). More successful was St. *Jerome's (d. 419 or 420) translation of the *Chronicon* (Eusebius's *Chronicle*), to which he added some new material and

a supplement on the period from 324 to 378. Eusebius's work was not free from weaknesses and defects; his style is dry, humorless, and far from inspiring. Nevertheless it is doubtful whether any of his medieval successors ever attained the high standard of historical research that he set.

His Successors. His history was continued in the following century by *Socrates the Historian, *Sozomen, and Theodoret, who dealt with the periods 305 to 439, 324 to 439, and 325 to 428, respectively. Some 100 years later, at the suggestion of *Cassiodorus (d. c. 583), the renowned scholar, theologian, and adviser to King Theodoric, these three works were put into Latin and woven into a continuous narrative entitled *Historia ecclesiastica tripartita* by a certain Epiphanius. This tripartite history, in 12 books, though ineptly translated from the Greek, and unskillfully plaited together, was the principal Latin handbook of early ecclesiastical history, and circulated widely in the West throughout the Middle Ages and the Renaissance.

Epiphanius's text represents the orthodox point of view, as does Gelasius of Cyzicus, who in the last quarter of the 5th century produced an *Ecclesiastical History of the Constantinian Period,* which has little independent value except for the use of two illuminating but otherwise unknown sources.

On the heterodox side of the great theological debates of this era, however, there is not much information. Except for a few scraps, most of the heretical apologiae have fallen victim to the intolerance of the Byzantine government, which ordered them destroyed and meted out stern punishment to theologians temerarious enough to try to evade imperial proscription. Thus, for the Arian version of the Trinitarian controversy, we are reduced to the few remaining fragments of the *Ecclesiastical History* (on 300–425) by the radical Arian *Philostorgius.

Similarly, the history of Christology seen through the eyes of Nestorius's allies and written by Irenaeus of Tyre (c. 450–457) has survived only as quoted by the Orthodox Rusticus Diaconus (565) in his so-called *Synodicon adversus tragoediam Irenaei.* Despite this loss, we are, so far as Nestorius is concerned, the beneficiaries of the accident that has preserved the so-called *Bazaar of Heracleides,* Nestorius's minutely detailed defense of his position against Cyril, the Greek original of which was struck down by imperial decree. What we have is the Syriac version that happily found a haven in a Nestorian community, and has thus come down to the present day virtually intact.

Among the victims of imperial persecution were the valuable ecclesiastical histories of the Monophysites John Diacrinomenus (John the Heretic) and Basil of Cilicia, the former of which covered the years 429 to 518, and the latter, c. 450 to 540. In addition, time and accident, not the orthodox or imperial relentlessness, are responsible for the loss of many precious sources, such as *Theodore Lector's *Historia tripartita* (of which two out of four books have disappeared) and the same author's *Ecclesiastical History* (on the years 450–527), which circulated in a popular *Epitome* of the 8th or 9th century.

In the midst of all these losses, we are fortunate to have the Syriac translation of *Zachary the Rhetor's *Ecclesiastical History* (in the original Greek, on 450–491), which (in Syriac) extends to 568 or 569.

Zachary, who ended his days as bishop of Mytilene (d. before 553), was a convert from Monophysitism to Neochalcedonianism, and the author of a biography of Severus (the Monophysite bishop of Antioch) as well as a polemic against the pagan doctrine of the eternity of the universe. The *Life of Severus* is preserved only in Syriac; but the polemic is extant in Greek.

Evagrius Scholasticus. The fullest and best history of the Church in this period (431–593), however, is that of *Evagrius Scholasticus, a Syrian Greek. Despite a tendency toward prolixity, Evagrius's *Ecclesiastical History* is well written (in Greek), and imitates the ancient Greek historian Thucydides. It is a history, not a chronicle, and treats extensively of secular affairs (like the Persian wars of its times).

After Evagrius, ecclesiastical history as such seems to have disappeared almost entirely, save for that from the pen of Nicephorus Callistus *Xanthopulus (*c.* 1320), who used the best sources available to him but did not, in the extant portion of his work, get beyond 610. For the later history of the Church, therefore, we have to depend upon chronicles, secular histories, the acts of councils, letters, archival records, and similar materials.

Secular History. In secular history, however, the materials are more abundant.

Early Period. For the earliest period, we have the pagan Eunapius of Sardis, whose *Lives of the Sophists* (on 270–404) is extant complete. But only fragments remain in his *Historical Memoirs* (on 270–404), as of the works by the pagan Olympiodorus of Thebes in Egypt (on 407–425), the pagan(?) Priscus of Thrace(?) (on *c.* 411–472), the Christian sophist Malchus from Philadelphia in Palestine (on the period 306 to 480), and the Christian Candidus from Isauria (on 457–491). In addition, a few extracts have survived from the *Chronicle* of Hesychius Illustrios of Miletus, who was apparently a pagan; the *Chronicle* recounted events of the period from the Babylonian Bel to 518.

More interesting is the *Historia nova* of Zosimus, an imperial fiscal officer (fl. *c.* 450–501), who set out to prove that the fall of the Roman Empire was to be ascribed to the neglect of the ancient pagan religion. The villain in this drama was Emperor Constantine I, because he granted toleration to Christianity, and the hero was Emperor Julian (361–363), who had attempted to restore paganism. Zosimus did not fail to touch upon the great Greek victories over the Persians at Marathon (490 B.C.) and Salamis (480 B.C.). But his chief emphasis was on Roman history from the victory of Augustus Caesar (31 B.C.–A.D. 14) in the battle of Actium in 31 B.C. to the accession of Diocletian in 284 (bk. 1), and from 284 to 410 (bks. 2–6).

Procopius. The best known and most important of the Byzantine writers of history was *Procopius (from Caesarea in Palestine), the historian of the age of Justinian I (527–565), the most glorious era of the Byzantine Empire. Since he was (from 527) adviser and secretary to the great general *Belisarius, it was natural that Procopius should have occupied himself seriously with the *History of the Wars* (against the Persians, Vandals, and Goths: in eight books, principally on 527–553). But he did not neglect internal history and, in his six books *On Buildings,* which he intended as a panegyric, reviewed the unparalleled program of new buildings and engineering projects of every description,

which Justinian devised and brought to completion throughout the empire. In the *Anecdota* ("Unpublished Documents"), however, Procopius abandoned adulation for vituperation and gave himself up to paroxysms of rage, in which he heaped abuse on Justinian and Empress *Theodora. He not only blamed them personally for earthquakes, floods, and other natural disasters, but also berated them for all manner of debauchery and vice. Procopius's reasons for this astounding *volte face* can only be conjectured. His style, though dominated by the customary classicizing tendencies and marred by the usual errors, is forceful and clear.

Agathias, Menander Protector, and Theophylactus. Procopius was followed by two historians of importance, Agathias, who put out five books on the years 552 to 558, and Menander Protector, of whose history on the period from 558 to 582 only fragments have been preserved. Agathias, whom Menander and many later writers imitated, wrote in a pompous style, overburdened with poetic language and rhetorical conceits. An even greater offender of this kind was *Theophylactus Simocatta, whose eight books on the reign of Emperor *Maurice (582–602) are marred by fanciful language and rhetorical extravagances that make him a 7th-century forerunner of euphuism and Marinism. Despite these stylistic defects, his history was highly esteemed by later Byzantine writers for its accuracy and objectivity.

The historical continuity was broken after Theophylactus, from 602 to 813; and the sequence of historical books was not resumed until Joseph Genesius, a historian at the court of Emperor Constantine VII (reigned 912–959), picked up the thread once again in his history of the empire from the time of Leo V to the death of *Leo VI (813–886). The reason for the interruption in the historical record between 602 and 813 has not been determined. It may perhaps be attributable to the Persian wars, the Arab invasions, or the iconoclastic controversy, which took place during this interval. But this is by no means certain; and it is not at all inconceivable that new sources may eventually come to light that will fill this gap, at least partially.

Constantine VII and the Golden Age of Byzantine Historiography. In the 10th century, however, formal historical research flourished as never before in the Byzantine Empire. The inspiration for this outburst of activity came from Emperor *Constantine VII Porphyrogenitus, who was in his own right a classicist and historian of note. During the years that he was excluded from actual power by his father-in-law, Emperor *Romanus I (920–944), he set his subordinates the task of assembling, excerpting, and summarizing documents, while he and his most trusted collaborators collected intelligence from ambassadors, merchants, and spies. These were the materials that formed the basis for the great historical compendia he and his aides produced.

He himself probably was the author of the *Life of Basil I* (867–886). Since Constantine was writing of his grandfather, this work, although constituting a valuable source, must be used with caution because it was an encomium rather than a critical biography. More significant is his *De administrando imperio,* a manual on foreign and domestic policy intended by him for the guidance of his son and successor, Romanus II

(959–963). It is a great treasury of geographical, ethnological, and historical information, written in a popular style, and therefore more comprehensible than many of the Atticizing historical works. It may be compared to a modern summary of foreign intelligence, and was undoubtedly reserved for private circulation among the most reliable members of the imperial court.

Equally official but less confidential in nature was the imperial book of ceremonies (De ceremoniis), an invaluable description of the rituals, religious and secular, of the imperial court. A third unit in this historical series, On the Themes (De thematibus), in two books, which outlined the geographical boundaries of the military and administrative districts into which the empire was divided, is somewhat disappointing because it was taken not from the latest information available in the imperial archives, but almost verbatim, in the typically Byzantine manner, without acknowledgment, from the geographical works of Stephen of Byzantium (fl. probably 5th century) and Hierocles (6th century). But Constantine himself (c. 933–934), the compiler of the first book, and an unknown hand in the second (c. 998) added the names of the frontiers as they were known in the 10th century.

In addition, Constantine's staff put together a vast historical encyclopedia of 53 volumes of excerpts from books of history. Constantine believed that an abridgment of this kind was necessary in order to simplify the study of history, the bulk of which, he felt, had grown to such enormous proportions that it was impossible for any ordinary person to encompass or understand it. Unfortunately, most of this great anthology has disappeared, except for 24 of the 53 titles and two printed volumes On Embassies (De legationibus), two On Virtue and Vice (De virtutibus et vitiis), one On Plots against the Emperors (De insidiis), one On Opinions (De sententiis), and a few fragments of some others. Many of the excerpts preserve valuable texts, ancient and medieval, which otherwise would have perished.

Besides engaging in these herculean projects, Constantine's associates expanded the great legal code, the Basilica, which was based upon the Digest, Codex, and Novels of Justinian, as compiled in the time of Basil I (867–886) and Leo VI (886–912). Their editorial activity was expended also, c. 950, on the Geoponica (a treatise on agronomy, based upon materials of the 4th, 5th, and 6th centuries); and Theophanes Nonnus, a physician at Constantine VII's court, turned out a medical handbook based upon the Epitome, which Oribasius had compiled c. 350.

None of the extant historians fills the gap between the years 886 and 959 except in part through John Cameniates's eyewitness description of the capture of Thessalonica in 904 by Leo of Tripoli. After Constantine's death, the historical series was taken up again by *Leo Diaconus, who in 10 books related the history of the empire between 959 and 976, on the basis, as he says, of his own experiences and the reports of authorities close to the events portrayed. The style resembles that of Agathias and Theophylactus.

Michael Psellus and 11th-century Historiography. After Leo Diaconus came Michael *Psellus, one of the greatest of the Byzantine polymaths (1018–c. 1096), to whom we are indebted for a fascinating portrait of the

emperors and the court from 976 to 1077. In large part, Psellus drew upon his own reminiscences of his association with the emperors, all of whom, from 1028 to 1077, were his close personal friends. He had nothing to say about foreign affairs, but compensates for this serious omission by full and accurate reporting of the lives and characters of the emperors and their families. In spite of his intimate association with the members of the royal entourage, he managed to retain his objectivity, except in regard to his pupil, Emperor *Michael VII Parapinakes (1071–78), whom he could not find it in his heart to criticize.

But concerning *Constantine IX (1042–55), whom he had intended to eulogize, he allowed himself to make some unfavorable observations, especially with regard to what he considered the Emperor's prodigality in utilizing the empire's resources. He did not refrain from calling attention, also, to Constantine's eccentric behavior in introducing his mistress Sklerena into the palace, crowning her empress, and persuading his wife Zoe not only to remain in the palace in the bedchamber next to his, but also to give written consent to this ménage à trois in a document witnessed by the senate.

Psellus seems not to have overlooked the tragicomic overtones in these somewhat bizarre details in the life of the Empress, who, in these unpleasant surroundings, was nevertheless able to console herself by gathering herbs and brewing fragrant unguents, while her younger sister, Theodora, who had been joint empress with her for 3 months in 1042, and was to be sole ruler of the empire (1055–56), amused herself, as did Zoe herself, by collecting gold coins. Psellus was one of the most brilliant of the Byzantine historians, none of whom had greater narrative power than he. But his brand of the Atticizing style is not easy to read, and his memoirs of life at the court, though scintillating and in their way unexampled, need to be supplemented at many points by other sources.

From the 11th century we have the Strategikon of Cecaumenus (c. 1071), the advice of a father to his son on how to pursue a career in the army and the imperial service. Then, after another brief interruption, the historical continuum was taken up once again by Michael Attaliates (from Attalia in Pamphylia), who wrote on the period between 1034 and 1079. His work was colored by the rhetorical, poetizing style that had become fashionable in historiography since the time of Agathias, but he was a skilled and reliable historian.

Anna Comnena. A new era in historical writing began with the accession of Alexius I Comnenus (1081–1118) to the throne. The Emperor's son-in-law, Nicephorus Bryennius, wrote a personal, romanticized sketch of Alexius's life from 1070 to 1079. But the court historian par excellence of the day was Alexius's daughter, and Nicephorus's wife, *Anna Comnena, whose Alexiad, though an unabashed panegyric of her father and family (on the years 1069–1118), presents a gripping account of Alexius's rise to power and of the relations between the Byzantines and the Latins during his reign. Her style, which is heavy, pedantic, and pretentious, is often extremely difficult to unravel. Notwithstanding her passionate Byzantine patriotism and contempt for the Latins, she did not distort the facts. Nor did she minimize the victories and triumphs of the "barbarians." Her zeal for the truth, which shines through in spite of her national prejudices, her sense of drama, and her narrative skill make the *Alexiad* a masterpiece of medieval literature that ranks with the best.

Anna's Successors in the 12th and 13th Centuries. Anna's story was continued by John Cinnamus in his *Epitome,* which carried the history of Byzantium from 1118 to 1176. He had intended to devote his principal attention to the reign of Emperor *Manuel I (1143–80), for whom he had great admiration, but he seems never to have reached the end of his tale. He was extremely conscientious in all matters, and did not allow himself, because of his dislike for the Latins, to misrepresent the facts. He was less learned than Anna, but his style is clearer and more intelligible.

More significant were *Nicetas Choniates's 21 books on 1118 to 1206, which are notable, among other things, for a vivid description of the sack of Constantinople by the Crusaders in 1204 (bk. 19) and a whole book (21) on the statutes of Constantinople. (See theological encyclopedias above.)

The *Chronike Syngraphe* of George Acropolites (1217–82) has as its theme the history of Constantinople from the time the Crusaders attacked the city in 1203 until its recovery by the Byzantines in 1261 (*see* LATIN EMPIRE OF CONSTANTINOPLE). A great part of his narrative depends on his own personal observation as a general and high imperial official. He gave an objective, unvarnished account of his period in a simple if somewhat pompous style.

The continuation of Acropolites we owe to George *Pachymeres (1242–1310), who rose to high rank in the imperial service, and carried the narrative from 1261 (in part from 1255) to 1308. A man of great learning and versatility, he was the author, among other things, of a *Quadrivium* (*Syntagma ton tessaron mathematon;* i.e., on arithmetic, music, geometry, and astronomy), and an outline of the philosophy of Aristotle. He was one of the great polymaths of his age. He used many transliterations from Latin and non-Greek terms, such as κομμέρκιον and φρέριος (from *frères*). At the same time he carried pedantry so far as to use the Attic names of the months instead of the customary Christian designations.

Nicephoras Gregoras and the Last Historians of Byzantium. The next century produced the greatest scholar of the last 2 centuries of the Byzantine Empire. This was *Nicephorus Gregoras (1295–c. 1359), who spared only 7 out of the 37 books of his *Roman History* for the years 1204 to 1320, and lavished 30 on the 40 years from 1320 to 1359. Throughout, he focused attention upon theological questions, especially upon Hesychasm, of which he was a determined but unsuccessful opponent. He experimented with every form of literary medium and not only wrote on nearly every conceivable subject, but even, in his astronomical work, anticipated Pope *Gregory XIII's reform of the Julian calendar (in 1582). *See* CALENDAR REFORM.

Emperor *John VI Cantacuzenus (1347–54) was a partisan of Palamism and the Hesychasts against Gregoras, for whose defeat and discomfiture he was responsible. But, when in 1354 he was forced to abdicate by Emperor *John V (1341–76), whom he had himself dethroned, he retired to a monastery, as the monk Ioasaph, and there busied himself with scholarly works. The chief fruit of this activity was his four books of history (on 1320–56, with some references extending as far as 1362). He confined himself to matters that he

knew at first hand, and castigated his predecessors (especially Gregoras) for deliberate suppression of the truth.

Actually, Gregoras and Cantacuzenus must at all points be supplemented by each other, not only for correction of bias but also in subject matter, since Cantacuzenus (who was an Aristotelian) limited himself to domestic history, while Gregoras (a Platonist) was concerned with foreign affairs as well. Cantacuzenus wrote clearly and forcefully. But he and his friends always occupied the center of the stage, and his history was in effect an elaborate *apologia pro vita sua.*

In 1422 Murad II laid siege to Constantinople but was unable to enter the city. His defeat was attributed to the intervention of the Virgin Mary, as we learn from John Cananus, who left an account of the siege and the repulse of the Turks in this year. In 1430, however, the Byzantines were less fortunate, and lost Thessalonica. The fall of this, the second city of the empire, was described at some length in the usual literary style of the Atticizing historians by John Anagnostes, who is to be contrasted in this respect with Cananus. The latter wrote in the idiom of the people, in simple, naive language, with few concessions to the classical mannerisms in which the professional historians delighted.

The last unhappy days of the Byzantine Empire, culminating on May 29, 1453, in the collapse of Constantinople, and of the Byzantine Empire, formed the subject for four excellent historians, each of whom wrote from a different point of view. The first of these, Laonicus Chalcocondyles, was one of the few Athenians who figured prominently in Byzantine history. He paid scant attention to chronology as such but sought instead, on the basis of Turkish and Greek sources, to explain how it was that the Turks rose to power. In his 10 books (on 1298–1463), to which, like the chroniclers, he prefixed a summary of universal history, it is the Turkish Empire, not Byzantium, which occupies the center of the stage. This was a most unusual approach for a Byzantine, as was also his conclusion that the Turks took Constantinople to avenge themselves for the fall of Troy. Chalcocondyles consciously imitated Herodotus and Thucydides, and in so doing sedulously avoided using foreign words and place names, which he either ignored altogether or tried to translate into the appropriate ancient equivalents.

Byzantium returned to the center of attention in the history of Ducas, who, however, like Chalcocondyles, opened with a sketch of universal history from Adam to the Palaeologi. He then paused to consider the expansion of the Ottoman Empire down to 1402. But he skimmed rapidly over these matters and the history of the second half of the 14th century in order to pass on to a more extended treatment of the reigns of the last three emperors (from 1391–1453) and of the capture of Lesbos in 1462 by Mohammed II, with which he brought his history to a close. He wrote in the popular language, avoided rhetorical excesses, and strove after accuracy. He had a flair for the dramatic, and was able because of his own close observation to give a moving account of the empire's last days.

The third of the historians, George Sphrantzes, had been taken prisoner by the Turks in 1453 and led away with his family into captivity. He ended his days as the monk Gregorius on the Island of Corfu, on which in 1477 he completed his *Chronicon* in four books (on the years 1258–1476), the most important of which are the second (on 1425–48), the third (on 1448–53), and the fourth (on the struggles of the Palaeologi in the Peloponnesus). He wrote from deep, personal knowledge and with considerable passion against both the Turks and the Latins, the latter of whom, he complained, regarded the fall of Byzantium as punishment for heresy, although political history, in his opinion, had nothing to do with orthodoxy. He closed with an examination of ancient prophecies on the duration of the Turkish Empire. Standing stylistically between the artificial archaisms of Chalcocondyles and the simple, unadorned prose of Ducas, Sphrantzes had a fluent, easy style. He made occasional concessions to the popular language of his day, without abandoning altogether the traditional Atticizing manner of the historians.

Apparently before 1470, the fourth of the historians in this group, Critobulus, a Greek of good family from the Island of Imbros, composed a panegyrical history of the Sultan Mohammed II from 1451 to 1467. He imitated Thucydides as far as he was able in style and in the arrangement of his material, but was notable chiefly because of his subservience to the Turks. Since Critobulus, alone of the four historians, lived under Turkish jurisdiction at the time he wrote his history, it is perhaps understandable that he felt called upon to flatter the sultan and adopt the Turkish point of view.

Chronicles. The chroniclers are here listed by name, with a brief note on the extent of each chronicle:

Chronicler	Extent of Chronicle
John Malalas (491–578) of Antioch in Syria	Creation to 563 (probably originally went to 565 or 574)
John of Antioch (in fragments)	Creation to 610
Chronicon Paschale	Creation to c. 627
*George Syncellus (d. 810/811)	Creation to 284
*Theophanes Confessor	284–813 (continuation of G. Syncellus)
Theophanes Continuatus	813–961
Nicephorus (d. 829) *Historia syntomos* (the *Brevarium*) and *Chronographikon syntomon*	602–769
Georgius Monachus	Creation to 829
*Symeon Metaphrastes and Logothete–continued by Leo Grammaticus to 1013 (Theodosius Melitenus)	Creation to 842
John Skylitzes (unpublished)	Creation to 948
*George Cedrenus	811 to 1079
John *Zonaras	Creation to 1057
Constantine Manasses (in political verse)	Creation to 1118
Michael *Glycas	Creation to 1081
Joel	Creation to 1118
Synopsis chronike (of Sathas)	Creation to 1204
Ephraem (in iambic trimeters, c. 1313)	Creation to 1261
Michael Panaretus of Trebizond	Julius Caesar to 1261
Chronicon breve de Graecorum imperatoribus, ed. R. J. Loenertz [in *Epeteris Hetaireias Byzantinon Spudon,* 28 (1958) 204–215]	1204 to 1426
	1341 to 1453 (and in part to 1470)
Chronicle of the Morea (see romance, below)	

POETRY

The meters of classical poetry had been based upon quantity, i.e., upon the length of vowels and of syllables. Some Byzantine poets followed the ancient prosody, mostly in iambic trimeters, less commonly in hexameters, elegiac distichs, or anacreontic verse. But even the writers who accommodated themselves to these norms took many liberties in the observance of quantity and caesura (pause), liberties which would not have been tolerated by the best poets of antiquity. They also introduced innovations, like putting the stress accent on the 11th syllable of the iambic trimeter, which in the classical form of this meter was always unaccented.

In addition, Byzantine poets created a number of new vehicles of their own. In most liturgical poetry they abandoned the quantitative system altogether and introduced rhythm on the basis of accent. They also ignored the classical insistence on fixed limits on the length of the lines. The liturgical poets had great freedom in this respect, and imposed restraints only through the use of the *heirmos* ($\epsilon\iota\rho\mu\dot{o}\varsigma$) or model strophe, which could assume almost any shape the poets wished, but which, once it was chosen, determined the pattern of all the strophes it governed; every strophe had to be identical with it, not only in the number of lines, but also in musical mode (*echos,* $\mathring{\eta}\chi o\varsigma$), in the number of syllables per line, and in the position of the accents and caesura in each line. Thus, all strophes in a poem based upon and following the *heirmos* had to conform with it in every respect. Deviations from this arrangement of syllables and accents were not normally tolerated, and occurred infrequently.

Perhaps the most common and characteristic form of Byzantine poetry was the 15-syllable "political" verse:

$$\cup\underline{\perp}\mid\cup\underline{\perp}\mid\cup\underline{\perp}\mid\cup\underline{\perp}\parallel\cup\underline{\perp}\mid\cup\underline{\perp}\mid\cup\underline{\perp}\mid\overline{\cup}$$

with permissible substitution of $-\cup$ at the beginning of each half line. The political verse was once believed to have originated in the 12th century, but has been traced back at least as far as the beginning of the 7th; there is no agreement as to whether it developed out of the iambic scheme ($\cup-$), the trochaic ($-\cup$), or a combination of both.

Liturgical Poetry. The practice of singing hymns in the Christian service, which began in the earliest times and made an impression on the pagans, as we learn from the Younger Pliny's famous letter to Emperor Trajan, is undoubtedly to be traced to Jewish customs. Similarly, the structure of the later Byzantine liturgical hymns is said by some to have been derived from Semitic prototypes. Hymns of various kinds are attested from every age of the Church, but in this article attention is focused on those that were built around the troparion ($o\mathring{\iota}\kappa o\varsigma$ i.e., stanza) in the Byzantine liturgy (*see* HYMNOLOGY).

Romanus Melodus. The greatest and most renowned of the Byzantine liturgical poets was *Romanus Melodus, who was born in Emesa in Syria. According to legend, he was a convert to Christianity from Judaism, and went to Constantinople during the reign of Anastasius I (491–518). He was said to have invented the kontakion and was alleged to have composed "thousands" of poems of this type. The kontakion, as we know it from the extant kontakia ascribed to him, consists of from 18 to 30 or more troparia. Each troparion varies in length from 3 to 13 lines, and all of the troparia of each kontakion follow the pattern of a model stanza (the *heirmos*).

At the beginning of each kontakion stands a separate troparion, which is metrically and melodically independent of the *heirmos* (and thus of all the other troparia of the kontakion). This separate troparion is known as the *prooimion* or *kukulion,* and is connected with the kontakion by means of the refrain (*ephymnion*) with which each of the stanzas ends, and by the musical mode (*echos*). The stanzas of the kontakion are linked together by means of an acrostic or by the successive letters of the alphabet. That is, the initial letters of the first line of each of the stanzas form a sequence either in regular alphabetical order (from alpha to omega, etc.) or spell out an acrostic. Thus, in the *Akathistos Hymnos* (the hymn sung unseated, i.e., standing), the most celebrated of all the kontakia, and one which many authorities ascribe to Romanus, each of the troparia begins with a letter of the alphabet from alpha to omega.

Romanus's kontakia deal with the Nativity, the massacre of the Innocents, the presentation in the Temple, Epiphany, the woman of Samaria, the man possessed by devils, the woman with an issue of blood, Pentecost, the Last Judgment, etc.

The kontakion was a melodic homily and was crowded out of the liturgy from about the end of the 7th century by the *kanon,* the first example of which was said to have been composed by *Andrew of Crete (*c.* 660–740). The *kanon* is made up of nine odes, each of which at first consisted of from six to nine troparia (i.e., stanzas). Later on, only three of the troparia of each ode were sung in the liturgy; and there are odes of four, three, or two troparia. The nine odes of every *kanon* were patterned upon the Nine Canticles from the Scriptures, and were intended as hymns of praise or exaltation. The *kanons* usually have a different *heirmos* (or model strophe) for each ode, i.e., a total of eight or nine *heirmoi* for each *kanon.* This scheme made for great variety of structure within each *kanon,* as contrasted with the greater rigidity of the kontakion, in which all the troparia were based upon the same *heirmos.*

The most famous of the *kanons* is the *Great Kanon* of Andrew of Crete, which has 250 troparia divided into four sections. After Andrew, the leading composers of *kanons* were the theologian John Damascene (*c.* 675–753) and his foster brother *Cosmas the Melodian of Jerusalem, also described as "of Maiuma" in Phoenicia because of his being made bishop of that city in 743. John Damascene and Cosmas were less passionate in language and more obscure than Romanus. John delighted in elaborate poetic structure and reverted, in part, to quantitative verse in the iambic trimeters he wrote for his *kanons* on Christmas, Epiphany, and Pentecost. At the time of the second iconoclastic controversy flourished Joseph the Hymnographer (*c.* 816–886), who was born in Sicily and was then driven by circumstances all over the Mediterranean world. An earlier contemporary of his, Methodius of Syracuse, was the last poet to write a *kanon* on the basis of 12-syllable iambics.

Other Liturgical Poets. In the 9th century the great center for liturgical poetry was the monastery of *Studion in Constantinople, with which a number of important liturgical poets were associated, notably *Theodore the Studite (759–826) and the brothers Theodore and Theophanes, known as "the branded" or "inscribed" (γραπτοί). The two brothers were so designated because Emperor *Theophilus (829–842) was said to have punished them for their resistance to iconoclasm by having 12 iambic trimeters branded

upon their foreheads. When he issued the order for this outlandish punishment, the Emperor is reported to have said, "Don't worry if the verses are no good." The poems of the two poets themselves were not of the highest quality and were characterized by a bombastic manner and a fondness for neologisms created by tacking on prefixes and suffixes to ordinary words.

More distinguished than they was the poetess Kasia (b. *c.* 810), who, on being rejected as a candidate for his hand by Emperor Theophilus because of her pertness and lack of docility, founded a convent, and composed a number of poems that found their way into the service books.

After the end of the 10th century, only a few writers continued to compose hymns, since the liturgy was fixed and was generally closed to new compositions. But the church historian Nicephorus Callistus Xanthopulus wrote a liturgy for the Virgin that was admitted into the *Pentekostarion.* A curiosity of the later period was a *kanon* on St. *Thomas Aquinas, called Thomas Ἀγχίνους (the regular Greek translation for Aquinas, i.e., the "sharp-witted").

As inspiration and opportunity for the production of hymns declined, the commentators rushed in to fill the gap. Bishops Cosmas of Maiuma and *Nicetas David expounded upon the poems of Gregory of Nazianzus, and John Damascene produced a commentary on the *Trisagion. Most of these exegetical efforts were expended upon the more obscure poets, while hymnographers like Romanus Melodus, whose works offered no special difficulty, were rarely commented upon. Commentaries of one kind or another on liturgical poetry have been attributed to Theodore Prodromus (who at least regarded himself as a poet), the philosopher *Nicephorus Blemmydes, and Abp. Eustathius of Thessalonica.

The modern critic is occasionally repelled by the tediousness of some liturgical poetry, its repetitiousness and artificiality of manner. But these defects arise in part from the convention that required the poet to stretch his poetic fancy over 24 or more strophes, all of which dealt essentially with the same subject. All in all, it must be conceded that the best of the poets showed great ingenuity in adapting themselves to these requirements and commendable inventiveness in finding in the few bare facts with which tradition supplied them sufficient material for the construction of the hundreds of poems the liturgy contains on the religious festivals of the Church and the exploits of the saints.

Secular Poetry and Nonliturgical Religious Poetry. Although Byzantine literary production rarely, if ever, reached the level of the great classical writers, this was not because of lack of excellent training in ancient literature. Many Byzantine scholars acquired an intimacy with the classical texts that would put even our best classicists to shame and knew Homer and the tragic poets almost by heart.

The theologian Gregory of Nazianzus (*c.* 330–*c.* 390) was the author of more than 400 poems, some of which are of great interest historically. But none of them has any unusual metrical, lyrical, or melodic distinction.

On the other hand nine or ten hymns of *Synesius (*c.* 370–*c.* 413), the Neoplatonizing Christian bishop of Ptolemais, the author of treatises *On Kingship, On Baldness, On Dreams,* and of 156 letters, were in classical meters that exhibit intense religious feeling and a lyrical spirit of high order, expressed in a mélange of pagan and Christian symbolism.

*Nonnus (b. *c.* 400) of Panopolis, another pagan poet from Africa, who was later converted to Christianity, composed while he was still a pagan, a work called the *Dionysiaca* in hexameters. It contains 48 books (i.e., as many as the *Iliad* and *Odyssey* combined) and is the longest extant poem in Greek. It was written in Alexandria, and describes the mythical journey of the god Dionysus to India. It is very probable that the author was the same Nonnus who became a Christian and then wrote, again in hexameters, a *Paraphrase of the Gospel according to St. John* (in 21 books).

Somewhat later, Empress Eudocia (d. *c.* 460), daughter of the Athenian philosopher Leontius, and originally named Athenais ("Maid of Athens"), but baptized Eudocia at the time of her marriage to Emperor *Theodosius II (408–450), produced a most extraordinary Homeric canto. She had such control over the text of Homer that, working on materials assembled by others, she composed a poem of some two thousand lines, each of which was taken almost intact from the *Iliad* and *Odyssey*. She made only minimal changes, but, nevertheless, out of the Homeric lines she had stored in her head, she wove together an impeccably orthodox treatise on theology. Her poem is divided into 50 parts: Paradise and the serpent, the Annunciation, the birth of Christ, the star and the shepherds, the Magi, Herod, the flight into Egypt, John the Baptist, the betrayal, the burial, the Resurrection, the doubting Thomas, etc.

Virtuosity of this sort with ancient Greek verse was common in Byzantine imperial circles. Psellus (1018–96) had committed the whole of the *Iliad* to memory when he was 14; Anna Comnena made effective use of quotations from Homer; and Eustathius, Archbishop of Thessalonica (1175–*c.* 1194), wrote a huge commentary of seven volumes on the Homeric poems.

George of Pisidia. The best secular poet of the Byzantine period was George of Pisidia, deacon of the church of *Hagia Sophia, who flourished in the reign of Emperor *Heraclius (610–641), and celebrated the latter's exploits in iambic trimeters of Byzantine style. He was so skilled in the use of iambics that in the 11th century critics could ask whether he or Euripides was the greater poet. His three historical poems dealt with (1) Heraclius's successful campaign against the Persians; (2) the Byzantine victory over the Avars, who stormed the gates of Constantinople in 626, and the Virgin Mary's protection of the city during this crisis; and (3) Heraclius's final triumph over the Persian king Chosroes (628). Of much greater length is his commentary on the Biblical account of the creation, a theological work in which, however, he found opportunity for many allusions to contemporary events. He also wrote a hexameter poem, *On Human Life.*

The Greek Anthology. In addition to the better poems of the liturgy, special mention must be made of the Byzantine compilation known as the *Greek Anthology,* which now amounts to 16 books, containing some 4,000 epigrams and approximately 25,000 lines, extending in date from the 6th century B.C. to the 10th century of the Christian Era. The Byzantine epigrams are both in the conventional ancient form (consisting of alternate dactylic hexameters and pentameters, in the so-called elegiac couplet) and in iambic trimeters.

The first major collection of poems of this kind was made by Meleager of Gadara (*c.* 60 B.C.), who brought together some of the choicest bits of ancient poetry (from the works of Archilochus, Anacreon, Sappho, Simonides, etc.). Meleager had many successors in the Hellenistic and Byzantine periods. In the age of Justinian, for example, appeared a number of epigrams by *Paulus Silentiarius, who, however, was more celebrated for his two *ekphraseis* (mostly in hexameters), one on the church of Hagia Sophia and the other on its ambon. More productive in this genre was Paul's contemporary Agathias the Historian who not only wrote hexameter poems and about 100 epigrams, but also put together a collection of contemporary epigrammatists.

Of the later editions of epigrammatic poems the most indispensable for the constitution of the text of the *Greek Anthology* in its present form were those of Constantine Cephalas (*c.* 900, known from a later recension of *c.* 980, the famous *Anthologia Palatina,* so-called from the Bibliotheca Palatina in Heidelberg in which the manuscript containing it was housed) and Maximus *Planudes (*c.* 1260–1310). Cephalas arranged the poems according to subject, and Planudes carried this division still further. The modern editions of the *Greek Anthology* consist of the *Palatine Anthology,* plus the "Planudean Appendix" (bk. 16) of 388 additional poems, which were derived principally, it seems, from lost MSS of Cephalas's recension and of the *Palatine Anthology.* Apart from a host of anonymous pieces (*adespota*), some 364 poets are represented by compositions primarily in epigrammatic verse but also in a great variety of other meters.

Representative successors of George of Pisidia. Some 200 years after Agathias, the epigram was revived by Theodore the Studite (759–826) in a series of poems (mostly in iambic trimeters) on the monastic life, in which he celebrated the monastic calling itself, and did not disdain to mention individually not only the *hegumenos* (the abbot) of the monastery but also the tailor, the shoemaker, the monk who awakened the brethren in the morning, the doorkeepers, the cells of the monks, the hospice for wayfarers, etc. In choice of theme and freshness of treatment Theodore was strikingly original. More conventional, but also interesting, are his epigrams on the parts of a church (in which he called attention to the altar, the gate of the narthex, the shrine, etc.), on icons, on various saints, and on himself.

Unpoetic, but historically noteworthy iambic trimeters on the state of the empire, on the Roman months, on animal fights in the circus, etc., are ascribed to Emperor *Leo VI (886–912), who is said to have been the author also of peculiar palindromes, which he called crabs (καρκίνοι) because they could be read either backward or forward, like: ὦ γένος ἐμόν, ἐν ᾧ μέσον ἐγώ.

Not long after the death of Leo, Constantine of Rhodes, who held high posts in both State and Church, wrote (between *c.* 931 and 944) an *ekphrasis* in which he described the no-longer extant Constantinopolitan Church of the Holy Apostles and its mosaics. The verses themselves, in iambic trimeter, are of little account and far inferior to the poetic *ekphrasis* of Paulus Silentiarius. Constantine was endowed with neither expository nor lyric skill, but his poem is an altogether unique source, highly prized by archeologists.

More distinguished than Constantine of Rhodes was his contemporary John Kyriotes (known also as John the Geometer), who composed trimeters, hexameters, elegiac distichs, and hymns on poets, politicians, philosophers, historians, theologians, and saints, not to mention cities, historical events, myths, etc. He often managed to achieve poetic imagery of high order, but also suffered from the usual Byzantine addiction to plays on words and the ornate style.

One of the most elegant of the Byzantine poets was Christopher of Mytilene (c. 1000–50), from whose hand we have 145 poems (14 in hexameters, the rest in iambic trimeters) addressed to the chief personages of the Byzantine court of his day, on ants, sparrows, the four seasons, the baptism of Christ, the saints, a bronze statue of a horse in the Hippodrome, a painting of the 40 martyrs, etc. His inscriptions for gravestones and riddles are better than ordinary. He even had a sense of humor, as can be seen in the complaints he made against the mice that scampered all over his house and devoured everything edible they could find, not excluding his books and papers. It was in retaliation for his verses on this subject, we may suppose, that the same creatures, or their descendants, ate up one half of the sole surviving manuscript of his poems.

In the later centuries, the most famous (one would hardly say distinguished) poets were "Beggar-poets," such as Theodore Prodromus (or Ptochoprodromus: "poor" Prodromus) and John Tzetzes, both of whom lived (hardly "flourished") in the middle of the 12th century. They were learned men, although not so erudite as they fancied themselves to be. They were constantly complaining of their poverty and begging the Emperor or some patron for financial assistance. (For Tzetzes, see section below on Byzantine scholarship and philosophy.)

Prodromus's chief work is a verse romance in 4,614 iambic trimeters entitled *Rodanthe and Dosicles* (on which see romance and satire below). In another work of his, the *Battle of the Cat and the Mice* (*Galeomyomachia*), a parody in 384 trimeters of the Homeric *Batrachomyomachia*, the mice, led by their King Kreillos and Queen Tyrokleptes ("Cheese-thief"), snatched victory from certain defeat, when a beam fell suddenly from the ceiling and slew the all but triumphant cat.

His poems in political verse were devoted to seriocomic recitations of how he suffered at the hands of his nagging wife and of two abbots in the monastery to which he had fled to find peace. He bewailed his unhappy lot as a teacher and cursed the day he first went to school.

Very similar to Theodore Prodromus in lively language, grim humor, and passionate complaints about poverty was Michael Haplucheir, who flourished at the end of the 12th century and was responsible for a so-called *Dramation* in 122 iambic trimeters, in which a rustic, a wise man, fate, the muses, and a chorus were the dramatis personae.

One of the most prolific of the Byzantine poets was Manuel Philes (c. 1275–1345), who confined himself, as did very few others, almost exclusively to this medium. Nearly all of his more than 20,000 verses were iambic trimeters, in which he sedulously avoided hiatus. In addition to poems *On the Characteristics of Animals,* and a short description of an elephant, he wrote three poems in dialogue form (two of them to console

families that had suffered bereavement, one a panegyric), several on theological subjects, a number of epigrams on works of art (a marble statue of St. George, an equestrian statue of Emperor Justinian I), and a host of occasional poems soliciting favors, and expressing gratitude for gifts to leading officials and churchmen. In general Philes was a Palaeologan reincarnation of Theodore Prodromus, whom he resembled in choice of subjects, method of treatment, and preoccupation with what he deemed his sad lot.

Approximately at the end of the 13th century appeared a moralizing poem in 3,060 political verses, written by a certain Meliteniotes, and dedicated to Moderation (*sophrosyne*), personified as the poet's guide on a long and perilous journey to a magic palace set in the midst of a fabulously beautiful garden (Paradise). The entrance to the palace was barred by seven obstacles, which represented the snares that block the path to virtue. The journey gave opportunity for all kinds of miscellaneous learning, mineralogical, mythical, and historical, which the author sedulously collected from his sources.

Romance. Parallel with the romances of the West were a number of Byzantine romantic tales, some of which seem to have been produced without Latin influence. The most noteworthy of these, the *Digenes Akrites* (or *Akritas*), an epic poem in political verse, was written sometime during the reign of Emperor Constantine IX Monomachus (1042–55), and records romantic episodes that were conceived of as having taken place along the Arab-Byzantine frontier c. 860 to 960. The *Digenes Akritas* is untouched by Western influences but shows contact with the Arab world.

In the 12th century, besides Theodore Prodromus's *Rhodanthe and Dosicles,* appeared Nicetas Eugenianus's *Drosilla and Charicles,* which owes much to Prodromus's romance in structure and meter. Both of these are in nine books and in iambic trimeters, and are closely related to the contemporary *Hysmine and Hysminias* (in 11 books), a romance in prose by Eustathius Macrembolites. All three, crude adaptations from the works of Heliodorus, Achilles Tatius, and Longus, have similar plots involving lovers who were separated, became involved with pirates, and eventually were reunited. The coarseness and unimaginativeness of these tales repel the modern reader.

Much more interesting are the romances of the later period. In *Callimachus and Chrysorrhoe* (in political verse), for example, dating from the 14th century, the hero and the heroine, after a series of adventures with a magic apple (which could kill or raise from the dead), a dragon, and a sorceress, finally triumph over adversity.

In *Belthandros and Chrysantza,* first composed in the 13th century (also in political verse), but reworked in the 15th, Belthandros came upon an enchanted palace built of sardonyx and there, in the Castle of Love, was by magic informed that he was destined to fall in love with Chrysantza, daughter of the King of Antioch. Later on, he found her, and discovered that she was the girl to whom in the Castle of Love he had presented the prize for beauty. Caught after his first tryst with her, he pretended that his intention was to pay court to her maid, whom he was then required to marry. Under cover of this marriage, he continued to make love to Chrysantza, and escaped with her to Constantinople, where they were married by the patriarch. *Lybistros and Rhodamne* (in political verse), which dates from the 14th century, was apparently influenced by both *Callimachus and Chrysorrhoe* and *Belthandros and Chrysantza,* or by their sources.

Very different from these three in originality and execution were Byzantine paraphrases of Western tales like *Phlorios and Platziaphlora* and *Imberios and Margarona,* both of which were written in political verse. The former, a free Greek version of the Provençal romance of *Flore and Blanchefleur,* of which several versions exist in French and Italian, dates from the late 14th century or the early 15th. Similarly, the second of these, which was derived from the old French romance *Pierre de Provence et la belle Maguelonne,* exists in several versions, both unrhymed (15th century) and rhymed (16th century).

On the other hand, the three above-named romantic epics, though apparently at several points influenced by the French *Chansons de geste,* have points of contact with Oriental poetry; and there are many features that are obviously Greek in origin. This mélange of characteristics is what might be expected of poetry produced in the latter part of the Byzantine period, when the Greeks lived in close contact with the Crusaders and their descendants, on the one hand, and with the Moslems, on the other.

This same blend of culture is illustrated by the *Chronicle of the Morea,* especially in the Greek version, which was composed in the popular, nonliterary idiom, and indicates that by *c.* 1388 or so, the date of its composition, many Latins in the Morea had become Hellenophones. This *Chronicle,* which was written in political verse and exists in French, Spanish, and Italian, as well as in Greek, gives a summary of the history of the first *Crusade and of the capture of Constantinople in 1204, but devotes its principal attention to the Peloponnesus from 1205 to 1292. The major Greek translation, which was intended for Latins who spoke Greek, is anti-Greek in tone and includes some data on the 14th century.

SATIRE

The Byzantines were far less interested in satire, which was undoubtedly inhibited by the absolutistic character of the imperial power. But this genre was not altogether neglected. For example, in the *Philopatris,* a satire cast in the form of a dialogue, there is an exchange of views between a Christian and a pagan. The unknown author wrote *c.* 969, and was so successful in imitating the ancient satirist Lucian that the *Philopatris* was once included among the latter's works.

Another imitation of Lucian, the *Timarion,* which is also anonymous, dates from about the middle of the 12th century. Taking Lucian's *Necyomantia* as his model, the author described his death, journey to the underworld, and conversations with Emperors Theophilus (829–842) and Romanus IV Diogenes (1068–71), with Michael Psellus, and many others. The *Timarion* reveals a sense of humor, which is exceedingly rare in Byzantine literature. Both the *Philopatris* and the *Timarion* direct some of their satirical shafts at the Church.

A third Byzantine imitation of Lucian, *Mazaris's Journey to Hades,* was written by a certain Mazaris (*c.* 1414–16). It is coarser and less elegant than the *Timarion,* but nevertheless a useful source for the early years of the 15th century.

BYZANTINE SCHOLARSHIP AND PHILOSOPHY

The Byzantines were the best scholars of the Middle Ages. If they themselves did not produce creative works that, aesthetically considered, rival Homer and the other great monuments of ancient literature, they at least were uniquely responsible for all that have survived. They not only avidly collected these texts, but also, as we easily forget, rescued them from the fragile papyrus on which they had originally been written by copying them to the more substantial parchment. Every classical text made its debut in an edition prepared by some Byzantine editor, who corrected the errors he saw or thought he saw in the work of his predecessors.

In the early centuries, many of the best scholars were pagans. Among the rhetoricians, the late offspring of the ancient orators and the Alexandrian grammarians, cross-fertilized by Greek philosophy, were Libanius, Himerius, and Themistius, all three of whom flourished in the 4th century. Close to this circle was Emperor Julian (361–363), who made an unsuccessful attempt to revive the pagan religion, and wrote an anti-Christian polemic (*Against the Galilaeans*), as well as a number of orations and letters.

Platonism and Neoplatonism. Greater significance attaches to the successors of *Plotinus (*c.* 205–270), the Neoplatonist philosophers *Porphyry (d. *c.* 304), *Iamblichus (*c.* 250–325), and *Proclus (410 or 412–485), who were important thinkers both in their own right, and because of the influence they exerted upon medieval philosophy in general. The *Platonism of the Middle Ages was thoroughly Neoplatonized, and Proclus was the model for the Pseudo-Dionysius's mystical theology. The latter, in turn, was so widely read in Byzantium as well as the West (to which it was available through four medieval translations) that mysticism as a whole, medieval, Renaissance, and modern, has a Neoplatonic coloration.

The Byzantine interest in Platonism, especially in the 4th, 5th, 6th, 11th, and 15th centuries, was an important factor in the survival of the text of *Plato. Similarly, much of the credit for the preservation of *Aristotle belongs to the great Byzantine commentators and philosophers of the 6th century, especially to Olympiodorus, Simplicius, and *John Philoponus, the last of whom was a Christian, not a pagan, and the author of a number of important theological treatises. Actually, Platonic and Aristotelian studies were pursued virtually without interruption through the whole of the Byzantine period.

An aberrant member of this learned circle, *Cosmas Indicopleustes by name, repudiated the cosmological and astronomical notions of the ancient Greeks in favor of the Mosaic concept of the universe. According to this Biblical scheme, Cosmas believed, the earth lay at the bottom of a cosmos, which resembled a two-storied house, and in which night and day, as well as lunar and solar eclipses, were caused by a high range of mountains to the north.

John Stobaeus. Scholarly activity of a somewhat different nature is associated with the name of John Stobaeus (fl. *c.* 500?), who was one of the most extraordinary anthologists in history. He was a native of Stobi (hence his name) in Macedonia and compiled a huge collection of excerpts in four books known variously as the *Eclogae* or the *Anthologion*. Only about a half of this work (which originally contained 208 chapters of varying length divided into four books) has survived but this portion of it fills five stout volumes in the modern edition, and preserves countless texts and authors (ranging in date from Homer to Themistius) that would, but for Stobaeus, have disappeared.

Each of the chapters deals with a separate topic, and many of the topics are examined from several points of view. For example, in the section on marriage (4.22), passages are collected to show that marriage is best (4.22.1), that it is not good to marry (4.22.2), and that in marriage one should not seek high position or wealth but character (4.22.6). Stobaeus was fond of paradoxes, and he concluded his survey of this subject by reproducing a number of passages (4.22.7) that are sharply critical of the female sex, many of which were culled from Menander (342–291 B.C.), the poet of the New Comedy, who, to judge from his plays and the gnomic utterances attributed to him, was one of the most irreconcilable misogynists of all time.

The philosophical and scientific production of the school of *Alexandria had continued into the 7th century under Stephen, the astronomer and polymath. Reference should be made also to Paul of Aegina and Theophilus Protospatharios, the *diadochoi* in the 7th century of ancient Greek medicine, which had been well represented by Oribasius, Emperor Julian's physician, in the 4th century, as well as by Aetius of Amida and Alexander of Tralles, in the 6th. Still, the 7th century was for the Byzantine Empire a period of tragedy, frustration, and defeat. The 8th century brought revival under the iconoclastic emperors, the importance of whose military exploits against the Arabs even the orthodox historical writers grudgingly admitted. The reverses suffered in the West at the same time, culminating in the fall of Ravenna in 751 and the loss of north Italy, seem not to have affected literary production.

Photius. The most brilliant scholar of the Byzantine period was Patriarch *Photius (858–867, 877–886), whose importance in the history of literature is wholly independent of his polemical writings against the popes and the Paulicians. He was a learned exegete, a prolific epistolographer, and an erudite preacher, even if his congregation must at times have had difficulty with his highly ornate style. But he is chiefly memorable for his so-called *Myriobiblon* or *Bibliotheke* (Library), a huge corpus of Greek texts arranged in 279 sections (called codices), which contain excerpts from authors both pagan and Christian, many of whom are otherwise unknown. The *Bibliotheke* is therefore of inestimable value to students of both ancient and medieval literature, all the more interesting because of Photius's trenchant critiques of the writers from whom he made excerpts.

Almost every conceivable kind of writing except poetry, is discussed. Photius's reading was so encyclopedic, so deep, and so varied that, at nearly every turn he provides data otherwise unavailable. Of the 31 historians whose works he analyzed, for example, approximately 20 are known to us either solely or largely because of the *Bibliotheke,* and only 9 of the 31 whose histories Photius had before him in their entirety and discussed in the *Bibliotheke* are extant in full today. Not more than four of the codices deal with philosophy as such, but Photius frequently referred to Plato and Aristotle, and was himself an Aristotelian.

A companion volume to the *Bibliotheke* was the *Lexicon,* which had hitherto been inadequately published. But a manuscript that has recently been discovered in Thessalonica will throw light on both Photius's scholarly methods and the history of Byzantine lexicography in general.

Photius's disciple, *Arethas, Archbishop of Caesarea in Cappadocia (c. 850–944), is noted for his rich library of classical authors, and for the interesting information he provided on the cost of transcribing papyrus codices (in uncials) to parchment (in the miniscule hand). *See* PALEOGRAPHY, GREEK. In addition, he was, together with a certain Oecumenius (6th century) and Andrew (an earlier archbishop of Caesarea, c. 563–614), one of the few Byzantine exegetes to write a commentary on the Apocalypse attributed to St. John.

The Suda. One typical kind of literary activity to which the Byzantines were much addicted was the compilation of learned works and encylopedias. The best of the encyclopedias, properly so-called, as contrasted with the anthologies and collections of excerpts, is that of the so-called *Suda*, once thought to have been a proper name, *Suidas. Silvio G. Mercati conjectured ingeniously that "Suidas" was a south-Italian scribe's misunderstanding of the late-Latin *Guida* (guide), but others hold that "suda" (meaning ditch, "catch-all" and thus encyclopedia) is the correct form. Aside from brief notices on lexicographical and etymological questions, often of great interest, the *Suda* includes articles on literature, history, philosophy, and science, the most significant of which, often in the form of biographies, provide data not to be found in other sources on ancient and medieval authors and their works. The *Suda* fills many gaps in our knowledge and is indispensable for the student of Greek literature.

Michael Psellus. In the 11th century, the most active of the classical scholars was the polymath Michael Psellus (1018–c. 1096), who, though he complained that men of learning were scarce in his day, nevertheless succeeded in locating an excellent teacher, named John Mauropus, who proved to be a thoroughly competent classicist. Psellus was a Platonist, but his works reflect a wide classical learning; and his universal encyclopedia, the *De omnifaria doctrina,* offers information on a great variety of subjects drawn from the major classical authorities. Similar materials can be found in other encyclopedias of the 11th century, such as the *Anonymi logica et quadriuium* and Symeon Seth's *Conspectus rerum naturalium* and *De utilitate corporum caelestium.*

The philosophical tradition also was ably represented by *John Italus, Psellus's successor as dean of the School of Philosophy (ὕπατος τῶν φιλοσόφων), who, however, in 1082 was removed from his post because, his enemies charged, he had lapsed into paganism. Actually, John Italus was a well-trained Hellenist and an Aristotelian in orientation. But there is no evidence that either he or his student, Eustratius of Nicaea (who commented on Aristotle and defended the Platonic theory of ideas), ever apostasized.

John Tzetzes and Eustathius. In the next century, the two major classicists were John Tzetzes (c. 1112–85) and Eustathius (fl. 1175–95), both of whom, in contrast to most of the authors considered above, were concerned with poetry rather than prose. The former and less distinguished of the two was a man of insupportable vanity, who spent great energy heaping praise upon himself and denigrating his rivals. Like his contemporary, Theodore Prodromus, he overburdened his works with references to his poverty ("My head is my library, and I am too poor to buy books": *Allegory on the Iliad,* 15.87), with interminable complaints against the universe, which had failed to recognize his enormous talents, and with abject, servile flattery of the patrons who befriended him. Nevertheless, he had had an excellent education, and he cites most of the major ancient authors.

Unfortunately, not all the references in his letters and poems are trustworthy, despite his modest avowal that no man had ever had a more tenacious memory than he (*Chiliades,* 1.277). He wrote a prose *Exegesis* of the *Iliad,* a whole volume of political verses on the allegorical interpretation of both the *Iliad* and the *Odyssey,* hexameter poems on other Homeric subjects, a long prose commentary on Hesiod's *Works and Days,* and a poem in political verse on the traditional pagan *Theogony.* Of his numerous scholia on various other authors, including some 1,700 iambic trimeters on Porphyry's *Eisagoge to the Categories of Aristotle,* the most important are the elaborate introductions and annotations he wrote on the comedies of Aristophanes.

Most astounding of all are his *Chiliades,* a poem of 12,674 political verses, which he wrote as a commentary on his own letters, and then reissued with marginal annotations in prose and verse, dedicatory letters, and supplementary poems of abuse directed against his enemies. Pompous and arrogant as he was, Tzetzes is not altogether devoid of merit and deserves further study.

Far superior to Tzetzes in every way was Eustathius (*c.* 1125–1193 or 1198), who rose to be archbishop of Thessalonica. In the history of scholarship he is chiefly noted for his huge commentary in seven printed volumes (six of text, one of indexes) on Homer. In addition, he produced exegetical works on Pindar and Dionysius Periegetes. The most valuable part of the material he assembled is his extracts from the earlier scholia and from texts that would otherwise have been lost.

His learned works were written in Constantinople before he went to the metropolitanate of Thessalonica, in which he distinguished himself as a reformer of lax monastic discipline. He was subjected to much abuse by his enemies on this account, but showed himself fearless and resolute both against his personal opponents and against the *Normans, who captured Thessalonica and held it briefly in 1185.

Though it would be difficult to withhold praise from Eustathius for his courage and enterprise, many are disdainful of the compilations he made of scholia and excerpts, as if labors of this kind amounted to nothing more than a mechanical exercise. It cannot be denied that he made mistakes of various kinds and that he occasionally misunderstood his texts. Nonetheless, the collection of so vast a corpus of materials from hundreds of codices and authors was a triumph of industry and ingenuity. Modern scholars operate very much in the

same way, and it may be doubted that many even of the best of them deserve to be ranked in the same class with Eustathius in the knowledge and appreciation of the Homeric poems.

Nicephorus Blemmydes and Maximus Planudes. In the next century flourished Nicephorus Blemmydes (*c.* 1197–1272), a philosopher and theologian who wrote a lengthy handbook in two books on logic and physics, a treatise favoring the Latin doctrine of the double procession of the Holy Spirit, two short geographical essays, two autobiographical sketches, and several poems, one of them a very spirited and vituperative reply to slanderous charges made against him by one of his students.

But he never lost the devotion of his most celebrated tutee, Emperor Theodore II Lascaris (1254–58), who was himself an accomplished scholar and the author, among other things, of a treatise on the underlying unity of nature despite appearances to the contrary, eight discourses on Christian theology, a polemic against the Roman doctrine of the Holy Spirit, and *kanons* on the Virgin Mary.

More memorable than Blemmydes was Maximus (born Manuel) *Planudes (*c.* 1260–1310), who wrote poems on theological and secular subjects, essays on grammar, an *Encomium of Winter,* and an idyll in 270 hexameters in the form of a dialogue between two farmers, Cleodemus and Thamyras. Apart from his commentaries on Euclid's *Elements* and Diophantus's *Arithmetica,* his *Psephophoria* (a mathematical treatise in which he makes use of zero and the nine so-called Arabic numbers, which had occurred in Byzantium for the first time about 50 years previously), and his poems on Ptolemy's *Geography,* his major contribution was as scholiast, editor, and translator. He annotated Sophocles, Euripides, Hesiod's *Works and Days,* and Aesop's *Fables.* Of his critical editions, the most celebrated was that of the *Greek Anthology,* which he augmented and improved by the use of manuscripts that are no longer accessible.

Likewise of great interest are his critical editions of Theocritus's *Idylls* and Nonnus's *Dionysiaca.* But he himself prized above all the work he did in establishing the text of Plutarch's *Moralia,* which he published in three editions. The most sumptuous of these (*Parisinus Graecus* 1672) contains all 23 of Plutarch's *Parallel Lives* (i.e., 46 in all: 2 × 23) and the 78 *Moralia* (including all that is extant of this collection except for some fragments). He was the best Latinist of his times in Byzantium, as can be seen in his Greek versions of Augustine's *De trinitate,* Pseudo-Augustine's *De duodecim abusionum gradibus,* Boethius's *De consolatione philosophiae,* Cato's *Dicta,* Macrobius's *Commentum in somnium Scipionis,* and Ovid's *Metamorphoses* and *Heroides.*

Highly as we prize the learning and acumen of the Byzantine textual critics of the 13th, 14th, and 15th centuries, it must be admitted that in their enthusiasm they often made changes that were arbitrary, unnecessary, and erroneous. Many of their emendations indicate ignorance rather than subtlety. The scholars of the previous centuries, on the other hand, were more restrained in their methods and frequently, therefore, better witnesses to the original reading than their successors. Nevertheless, the classicists of the Palaeologan

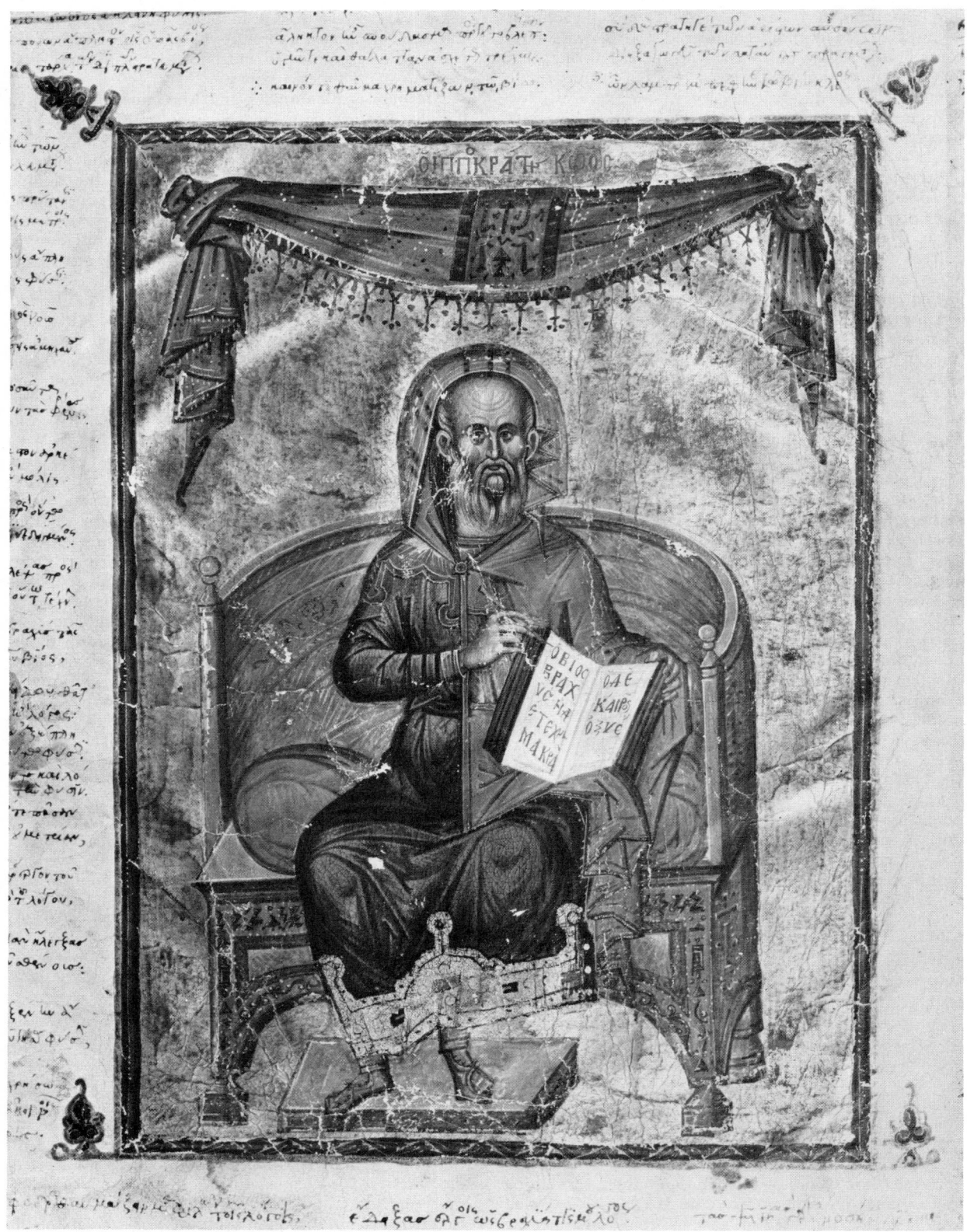

Fig. 6. Hippocrates, miniature in a MS of his works written and illuminated at Constantinople, c. 1342, for Apocaucus, prefect during the minority of John V Palaeologus (Paris, Bibl. Nat. MS Gr. 2144, fol. 10v).

period (1261–1453) made important contributions, both in the exegesis of texts and in the preservation of materials, which otherwise would have been inaccessible.

Theodore Metochites, Demetrius Triclinius, and Plethon. The most important member of this group was Theodore Metochites (d. 1332), one of the leading statesmen of his day until the fall of his patron, *Andronicus II in 1328. His major work was the *Miscellanea philosophica et historica*, which contains 120 essays on philosophical, ethical, political, aesthetic, and historical subjects, drawn for the greater part from ancient history and philosophy. He was very much interested in mathematics and astronomy, on which he wrote a number of treatises. Most of these have not yet been published, and only the Latin translation of his paraphrase of Aristotle is available in print. Metochites's contemporary Nicephorus Chumnus (c. 1250–1327) also deserves mention among the classicists of this period.

The best philologist and textual critic of the Palaeologan era was Demetrius Triclinius (c. 1280–1340), who devoted himself to the principal poets of antiquity (Hesiod, Pindar, Aeschylus, Sophocles, Euripides, Aristophanes, and Theocritus), whom he studied, annotated, and edited. Triclinius was responsible for many misguided emendations, but he nevertheless deserves the esteem of classical scholars for his great erudition and tireless activity.

Of the numerous contemporaries of Triclinius who devoted themselves to classical studies, the most noteworthy were Manuel Moschopulos and Thomas Magistros, both of whom compiled lexica of Attic usage.

In the next century, on the eve of the collapse of the empire, Byzantine classical scholarship rose to an even higher level. Manuel *Chrysoloras (d. 1415), the most influential of the Byzantine professors who taught Greek to the Latins, was an avid collector of Greek manuscripts and initiated the Western humanists in the art of translating from Greek into Latin.

The greatest of the classicists in this period were George Gemistus Plethon, an indefatigable excerpter, teacher of many of the leading scholars of his day, and Bessarion, his disciple, who became a partisan of union with Rome and was made a cardinal (1439). Plethon visited Italy (1438–39) during the Council of Ferrara-*Florence, and was credited by Cosimo de *Medici with having inspired him with the project of founding the Platonic Academy of Florence. In the great debates on the relative merits of Plato and Aristotle, Plethon championed Plato, and was bitterly attacked for so doing by *George of Trebizond, a partisan of Aristotle. Bessarion then joined the fray with his *In calumniatorem Platonis*, in which he took a mediating position in the controversy, and rebuked George of Trebizond for his abusive tone.

Bibliography: General. Altaner. E. BARKER, ed. and tr., *From Alexander to Constantine* (Oxford 1956); *Social and Political Thought in Byzantium from Justinian I to the Last Palaeologus* (Oxford 1957). Beck KTLBR. H. G. BECK, *Theodoros Metochites* (Munich 1952). L. BRÉHIER, *Le Monde byzantin*, 3 v. (Paris 1947–50), v.3 *La Civilisation byzantine*. W. BUCHWALD et al., eds., *Tusculum-Lexikon griechischer und lateinischer Autoren des Altertums und des Mittelalters* (2d ed. Munich 1963). DACL. DTC. DHGE. LexThK². ReallexAntChr. F. FUCHS, *Die höheren Schulen von Konstantinopel im Mittelalter* (Leipzig 1926). H. HUNGER, *Byzantinische Geisteswelt* (Baden-Baden 1958). B. KNÖS, *L'Histoire de la littérature néo-grecque* (Stockholm 1962).

Krumbacher. G. MORAVCSIK, *Byzantinoturcica*, 2 v. (2d ed. Berlin 1958), v.1. Quasten Patr. S. RUNCIMAN, *Byzantine Civilisation* (London 1933). M. V. ANASTOS, *The Mind of Byzantium* (in preparation). On the Renaissance, see the numerous studies of G. MERCATI, *Notizie di Procoro e Demetrio Cidone . . .* (St Test 56; 1931); *Opere minori*, 5 v. *ibid.* 76–80; 1937–41). Many of the major Byzantine writers can be found in Pauly-Wiss RE. Translations of many of the historians have been published in *Byzantinische Geschichtsschreiber*, ed. E. VON IVÁNKA (Graz 1954–). For the Renaissance and the knowledge of Greek in the West, see K. M. SETTON, "The Byzantine Background to the Italian Renaissance," ProcAmPhilS 100 (1956) 1–76. For the activity of Byzantine textual critics, see the numerous publications of A. TURYN on the text tradition of Pindar, Sophocles, Euripides, etc.

Prose. G. CAMMELLI, *I dotti bizantini e le origini dell'umanesimo*, 3 v. (Florence 1941–54). J. DANIÉLOU, *Platonisme et théologie mystique* (rev. ed. Paris 1954). J. DARROUZÈS, ed., *Épistoliers byzantins du Xᵉ siècle* (Archives de l'Orient chrétien 6; Paris 1960). J. DRÄSEKE, "Byzantinische Hadesfahrten," *Neue Jahrbücher für das klassische Altertum, Geschichte und deutsche Literatur* 29 (1912) 343–366. A. J. FESTUGIÈRE, ed., *Les Moines d'orient* (Paris 1961–). R. GUILLAND, *Essai sur Nicéphore Grégoras: L'Homme et l'oeuvre* (Paris 1926). J. M. HUSSEY, *Church and Learning in the Byzantine Empire, 867–1185* (Oxford 1937). *Ioannes Italos, Quaestiones Quodlibetales*, ed. P. JOANNOU (Ettal 1956). E. VON IVÁNKA, *Plato Christianus* (Einsiedeln 1964). K. KARLSSON, *Idéologie et cérémonial dans l'épistolographie byzantine* (Uppsala 1962). P. JOANNOU, *Christliche Metaphysik in Byzanz*, v.1, *Die Illuminationslehre des Michael Psellos und Joannes Italos* (Ettal 1956). F. MASAI, *Pléthon et le platonisme de Mistra* (Paris 1956). L. MOHLER, *Kardinal Bessarion als Theologe, Humanist und Staatsmann*, 3 v. (Paderborn 1923–42). B. RUBIN, *Das Zeitalter Justinians* (Berlin 1960–). ChrSch Stäh GeschGL. I. ŠEVČENKO, *Études sur la polémique entre Théodore Métochite et Nicéphore Choumnos* (Brussels 1962). J. SIRINELLI, *Les Vues historiques d'Eusèbe de Césarée durant la période prénicéenne* (Dakar 1961). B. TATAKIS, *La Philosophie byzantine*, suppl. 2 of *Histoire de la philosophie*, ed. É. BRÉHIER (Paris 1959). J. W. TAYLOR, *Georgius Gemistus Pletho's Criticism of Plato and Aristotle* (Menasha, Wis. 1921). C. TRESMONTANT, *La Métaphysique du christianisme et la naissance de la philosophie chrétienne* (Paris 1961). M. TREU, "Mazaris und Holobolos," ByzZ 1 (1892) 86–97. J. VERPEAUX, *Nicéphore Choumnos* (Paris 1959). C. ZERVOS, *Un Philosophe néoplatonicien du XIᵉ siècle, Michel Psellos* (Paris 1919). S. V. POLIÁKOVA, "The Byzantine Satire *Timarion*," Vizantiiski Vremennik 6 (1953) 357–386, in Russ.

Poetry and romances. H. BECKBY, ed. and tr., *Anthologia Graeca*, 4 v. (Munich 1957–58). W. VON CHRIST and M. PARANIKAS, eds., *Anthologia Graeca carminum Christianorum* (Leipzig 1871). *Anthologie grecque. Anthologie palatine*, ed. and tr. P. WALTZ et al., 6 v. (Paris 1928–60). R. CANTARELLA, *Poeti bizantini*, 2 v. (Milan 1948). *Digenes Akrites*, ed. and tr. J. MAVROGORDATO (Oxford 1956). Εὐχαριστήριον: *Franz Dölger zum 70. Geburtstage* (Salonika 1961), including a new ed. of "Byzantinische Dichtung in der Reinsprache" (1948). P. FRIEDLÄNDER, ed., *Johannes von Gaza und Paulus Silentiarius: Kunstbeschreibungen justinianischer Zeit* (Leipzig 1912). A. C. GIDEL, *Études sur la littérature grecque moderne* (Paris 1866). A. S. F. GOW, *The Greek Anthology* (London 1958). R. HELM, *Der antike Roman* (2d ed. Göttingen 1956). S. IMPELLIZZERI, "La Morte di Digenis Akritas," *Atti del Museo Pitrè* (Palermo 1950) 1:5–42. E. KRIARAS, ed., *Byzantine Romances of Chivalry* (Athens 1955), in Gr. S. KYRIAKIDES, "Forschungsbericht zum Akritas-Epos," *Berichte zum 11. Internationalen Byzantinisten-Kongress* (Munich 1958). E. VON NISCHER-FALKENHOF, "Belthandros und Chrysantza. Ein byzantinischer Minnesang aus dem 13. Jht., dem griechischen Urtexte nachgedichtet," *Jahrbuch der österreichischen byzantinischen Gesellschaft* 8 (1959) 87–122. T. NISSEN, *Die byzantinischen Anakreonteen* (Munich 1940). M. PICHARD, ed. and tr., *Le Roman de Callimaque et de Chrysorrhoé* (Paris 1956). G. REICHENKRON, "Zu den ersten Beziehungen zwischen Byzanz und den ältesten französischen Chansons de Geste," *Südost-Forschungen* 15 (1956) 160–166. E. ROHDE, *Der griechische Roman und seine Vorläufer* (3d ed. Leipzig 1914). H. SCHREINER, "Der geschichtliche Hintergrund zu Imberios/Pierre de Provence und Margarona/La Belle Maguelonne," ByzZ 44 (1951) 524–533. A. SIGALAS, "Methodological Problems: The Romance of Belthandros and Chrysantza and its Restoration," *Mélanges offerts à O. and M. Merlier* 2 (Athens 1956) 355–377, in Gr. G. SOYTER, ed., *Byzantinische Dichtung*

(Athens 1938); ed. and tr., *Griechischer Humor* (2d ed. Berlin 1961). G. Spadaro, "Studi introduttivi alla *Cronaca di Morea*," *Siculorum gymnasium* NS 12 (1959) 125–152; NS 13 (1960) 133–176; NS 14 (1961) 1–70. P. Maas and C. A. Trypanis, eds., *Sancti Romani Melodi Cantica*, v.1, *Genuina* (New York 1963). *Scholia in Aristophanem Jo. Tzetzae commentarii*, ed. L. Massa Positano et al., 4 v. (Groningen-Amsterdam 1960–64). A. Veniero, *Paolo Silenziario* (Catania 1916). Wellesz ByzMus. G. T. Zōras, *Byzantine Poetry* (Athens 1956), selections and introds. in Gr.

On the romances, etc., see above all H. E. Lurier, *Crusaders as Conquerors* (New York 1964), a tr. of the *Chronicle of the Morea*. O. Mazal, "Der griechische und byzantinische Roman in der Forschung von 1945 bis 1960," *Jahrbuch der österreichischen byzantinischen Gesellschaft* 11–12 (1962–63) 9–55; 13 (1964) 29–86 (to be concluded). E. Trapp, "Specimen eines Lexikons zum Akritasepos," *ibid.* 13 (1964) 13–27. **Illustration credits:** Fig. 1, Picture Archives, Austrian National Library. Fig. 2, Courtesy of the Trustees of the British Museum. Figs. 3 and 6. Hirmer Verlag München. Fig. 4, Princeton University Library. Fig. 5, Biblioteca Apostolica Vaticana.

[M. V. Anastos]

BYZANTINE RITE

Of all the Eastern rites, the Byzantine is the most important in regard both to the number of Christians belonging to it and to its widespread diffusion. It was the rite of the ancient Byzantine Empire, which spread its ritual influence not only throughout all of the Eastern base of the Mediterranean but also to the countries of the lower Danube and Balkan Peninsula and up into all of the Slavic countries. Through immigration the rite has been brought to all parts of Europe and North and South America, counting more than 100 million Christians, both Orthodox and Catholics of various races and languages.

History

The rite is called Byzantine rather than Greek to distinguish it from other Greek rites that have disappeared and to allow for liturgical tongues other than Greek; but especially to center the point of elaboration of the rite from the 4th to the 10th century. The rite did not in fact originate in the capital of the Byzantine Empire but had its liturgical roots in an involved evolution from liturgies that were in use in Palestine, Antioch, and Cappadocia. In dealing with the sources the leading role of St. Basil the Great in this transformation will be pointed out, but it must be kept in mind that its evolution was gradual and took its inspiration from various sources. These developments were usually furthered under the instigation of saints, such as Basil, John Chrysostom, John Damascene, Romanos, Andrew of Crete, and Cosmas the Melodius. They guaranteed its doctrinal soundness and aesthetic richness and produced a rite of majesty and universal appeal.

Its expansion was intimately connected with the political ambitions of the Byzantine emperors, eager always to spread their influence throughout the Balkan and Russian lands, to Syria, the Holy Land, Egypt, and even the coasts of Italy. As Constantinople grew in power, other independent ecclesiastical centers, such as Antioch and Alexandria, diminished. This soon made for one rite and one language within the vast confines of the Byzantine Empire and left the non-Byzantine rites, such as the Antiochene (Syrian) and Coptic, to develop only among heretics and schismatics who modified the doctrinal content and substituted their own national languages. Outside the empire, the rite of Constantinople spread to other embryonic nations while

allowing other liturgical languages. Thus Byzantine influence penetrated to the Iberian Peninsula of Caucasian Georgia in the 4th century. From the 9th to the 11th century missionaries were sent from Constantinople into the Slavic countries, but old Slavonic was used as the liturgical language in place of Greek. Rumania translated the rite into its national tongue when the displaced Latin soldiers and colonists of Trajan formed into a non-Slavic nation. Western Syrians, no longer speaking Greek, used their own Syrian language from the 11th to the 17th century and then adopted Arabic. The Russian Church followed the same principle of vernacular liturgical languages in its missions in Estonia, Latvia, and Germanic areas in the Baltic states; among the Eskimos and Indians of Alaska and western America; and among the Chinese and Japanese.

Churches Using Rite. With the use of national languages and the destruction of Constantinople (1453) by the Turks, there developed the principle of *phyletism*, according to which, autonomous and autocephalous churches arose for each nation, to be independent of the ecclesiastical control of the Patriarchate of Constantinople. One might divide the churches using the Byzantine rite according to liturgical languages used. Those among the Orthodox that employ pure Greek are the Patriarchal Church of Constantinople, the Synodal Church of Greece, and the autocephalous archbishopric of Cyprus. Four churches use both Greek and Arabic: the Patriarchates of Alexandria, Antioch, and Jerusalem and the autocephalous Archdiocese of Mount Sinai. Pure Greek is the language of the Catholics in Turkey and Greece, and of the Italo-Greeks of southern Italy (Calabria) and Sicily, while the Catholic Melchites of Syria, Egypt, and Lebanon use both Greek and Arabic. Among the Orthodox employing the Slavonic liturgical language are the three Patriarchates of Moscow, Bulgaria, and Serbia and smaller autonomous churches in Poland, Latvia, and Czechoslovakia. Originally founded as missions of the Russian Church but now autonomous and using their own vernaculars are the churches of China, Finland, and Estonia. The Rumanians, Hungarians, Georgians, and Albanians also celebrate in their own languages. The accompanying table gives in a summary form the relative sizes of these national churches of both the Orthodox and the Catholic groups. The statistics are those compiled by the Oriental Congregation and published in the volume *Oriente Cattolico: Cenni storici e statistiche* (Vatican City 1962).

Melchite. The word Melchite properly speaking designates Christians of the Byzantine rite, either Catholic or Orthodox, of the Patriarchates of Alexandria, Antioch, and Jerusalem. The word comes from the Syriac *malka* or the Arabic word *malek* or *melek* meaning king or emperor. The term was first coined by the Monophysites in derision of those Christians who remained faithful to the Byzantine emperors in their attempt to impose the Christology taught by the Council of Chalcedon (451). But today, in its popular and limited sense, the word refers to the Orthodox of the Byzantine rite using both Greek and Arabic who through the centuries became reconciled with Rome. If now all Melchites are of Arabic speaking extraction, their history was not always of such unity. Between the 5th and 12th centuries some were of Greek extraction, others of Syrian, others Egyptian. Originally they followed the Antiochene, Alexandrian, or Jerusalem rites, but with

NATIONAL CHURCHES OF THE BYZANTINE RITE

Ethnic Group	Orthodox	Catholic	Catholic bishops
Albanian	255,000	400	
Bulgarian	6,500,000	9,480	1
Georgian	750,000	10,000	
Greek	10,000,000 (3 groups)	2,872	1
Hungarian	30,000	250,000	1
Italo-Albanian		70,000	2
Melchite	605,000	397,611	23
Rumanian	16,300,000	1,572,979	3
Russian	54,000,000	3,000	1
Ruthenian	450,000	778,555	3
Slovak	50,000	305,645	
Ukrainian	In Russia, see above; abroad 500,000	4,340,000	15
White Russian	In Russia, see above; Poland 400,000; abroad 300,000	35,000	1
Yugoslavian	7,000,000	56,000	2

time and the centralization forced upon them by Byzantine emperors they adopted the Byzantine rite exclusively. They are now centered in three patriarchates: Alexandria, Antioch, and Jerusalem. Through the centuries, especially in the Patriarchate of Antioch, an active movement of reconciliation with Rome was developed. Beginning with the Catholic patriarch, Cyril VI (1724–59), there was an uninterrupted line of Catholic Melchite patriarchs. This movement spread into the other two patriarchates by immigrants chiefly from Syria and Lebanon. Melchite Catholics (1962) number 397,611 and have 23 bishops, the largest episcopal representation among the Eastern Catholics. The Orthodox number 605,000 and have three patriarchs residing in Alexandria, Damascus, and Jerusalem; the one Catholic patriarch resides at Damascus (with a vicar-patriarch at Cairo) and bears the title "Patriarch of Antioch and of all the East" and the personal titles of the patriarch of Alexandria and Jerusalem. In the U.S. the Catholic Melchites center mostly around New York and in New England and number about 40,000 subject to the local bishop.

Italo-Albanians. Three different movements are accountable for the origins of the Italo-Albanian Catholics' adoption of the Byzantine rite. Greek colonists first immigrated to Sicily and southern Italy even before Christianity was founded. The second wave of Greeks to Italy came shortly after the sacking of Constantinople by the Turks in 1453. The third migrating group was composed of Albanians. When their kingdom passed into the hands of the Turks after the death of their leader Skanderbeg (d. 1463), many fled to Italy and Sicily where they found the same Byzantine rite of their homeland. Today these Italo-Albanian Catholics are organized into two eparchies. Lungro in southern Italy has its own Italo-Albanian bishop with 40,000 faithful. The other eparchy, set up in 1937, has its see at Piana dei Greci and is administered by the apostolic administrator, the archbishop of Palermo, and an auxiliary bishop empowered to ordain priests for the Greek

Byzantine rite. The faithful number about 30,000. The famous Oriental Catholic monastery that has never known schism, St. Mary's of Grottaferrata, outside of Rome, has about 50 monks of this rite and ministers to parishes in southern Italy and Sicily besides printing the liturgical books for Catholic Oriental rites, especially in Greek and church Slavonic.

Russian. The Christian faith came to pagan Russia through the Byzantine rite when Prince Vladimir in 989 received Baptism from Greek missionaries and then set about to convert his Kievan kingdom to the same rite. Because the hierarchy was made up predominantly of Greeks, the estrangement of the See of Constantinople from Rome was accepted also in Russia. No specific date can be set as the point of final separation. The last Greek metropolitan of Kiev, Isidore, participated in the Council of Florence and accepted union with Rome, but both he and union were rejected by the Czar Basil II. In 1459 Metropolitan Jona was recognized as the head of the autocephalous church of Russia. Eagerly seeking to make Moscow the third Rome after the fall of Constantinople to the Turks (1453), the Russians sought and obtained from the Greek Patriarch of Constantinople, Jeremias II, recognition of the Russian Church as an independent patriarchate and of Job (1586–1605) as the first "Patriarch of Moscow and of all Russia." Various internal dissensions arose, chief among which was the schism of the Old Believers (Raskolniki) who opposed the reforms of Patriarch *Nikon (1654–67). They split off from the Russian Church into two groups, the Popovtsi (with priests) and the Bezpopovtsi (without priests); today they are reduced in number and importance. Peter the Great in 1721 suppressed the patriarchate, which was later restored as a result of the overthrow by the revolutionists of the czarist regime in 1917. Then, although the Communists suppressed it, Stalin restored it again in 1943 when he most needed the patriotic support of the religious peasant class. The Orthodox Church in Russia is undergoing bitter persecution, but it is roughly estimated that there are still some 50 million believers. Abroad the Russian Orthodox are split into various jurisdictions. The patriarch of Moscow directs three exarchates for Central Europe, Western Europe, and North America. Another Western exarchate with its see in Paris depends upon the patriarch of Constantinople while another, the Russian Church in Exile, formerly with its see in Karlovci, Yugoslavia, now in Jordanville, N.Y., has parishes spread throughout the world. The Russian-American Church is independent of either patriarchate and stems from the original Russian mission to Alaska and California. The Russians abroad total about 1 million, with about 600,000 in the U.S. Catholic Russians of the Byzantine rite number only about 3,000 and owe their beginnings to the embryonic Russian Catholic Church of the Byzantine, begun in Russia in the first quarter of the 20th century under Exarch Leonid Feodorov (1879–1935).

Ukrainians and Ruthenians. Much confusion through the centuries has been caused by the terminology for designating the Christians of the Byzantine rite who inhabited the area west and southwest of Russia in eastern and western Galicia, Podcarpathia, Hungary, and certain districts of Czechoslovakia and northern Rumania. These people prefer to call themselves Ukrainian, White-Russians, Ruthenians, and Slovaks, although for many years the official ecclesiastical term Ruthenian was used to include all of them. In the *Annuario Pontifico* of 1960 they are designated as "Ruteni," but since 1962 this general ecclesiastical term has been dropped, and the terms Ukrainians, or Galicians, and Ruthenians are employed. As both groups exhibit a different language and cultural development it would be better to view each separately in its historical development.

The Ukrainians may well claim to be the original Russians, as the nation known as Russia today first developed in Kiev, the present-day capital of the modern Ukrainian Republic. After Russia centralized its power around the duchies of Moscow, Vladimir, and Kazan, Kiev became known as the center of Little Russia, especially for the 5 centuries when it was subject to Poland and Lithuania. Here a reunion of the Orthodox with Rome was effected through the Synod of Brest-Litovsk (1595–96), which set up the largest branch of Eastern Catholics in the Church. No doubt there were many factors, political, social, and cultural, that prompted this reunion. In 1620 an Orthodox hierarchy was established that paralleled the greater Catholic group numbering about 12 million. The Ukrainians in the West, centered in the province of Galicia, after having been under the control of Poland, came under the power of the Austrian Empire in the 19th century and were granted more freedom than their Eastern Ukrainian brethren under Great Russia. One of the great names among the Galician Ukrainians is that of Metropolitan Andrew Sheptitzky who from 1900 until his imprisonment by the Soviets in 1944 ruled the See of Lvov as the primate of the Galician Ukrainians. He did much to strengthen his fellow Ukrainians amid great persecution from the Soviets and to instill in them an equal fidelity to Rome and to their Byzantine rite. Great numbers of these Ukrainians migrated to America in two groups, the first from 1880 to 1914 and the second group during World War II. The first immigration was that of Catholics from Galicia; the second, of Western and Eastern Ukrainians. The Catholics in the Ukraine number approximately 4,340,000 according to the last available statistics of 1943 before the complete destruction of the Ukrainian Catholic Church took place. Of these there are 270,500 in the U.S., divided into the dioceses of Philadelphia, Stamford (Conn.), and Chicago.

Ethnically a different race from the Ukrainians and with a different language, the Ruthenians are called also Podcarpathian Rusins. For many centuries the area they inhabited belonged to the Hungarian Empire, but they were Slavic. After World War I, Podcarpathia Rus was made a part of the Czechoslovakian Republic, and in 1939 it was proclaimed the Independent Republic of the Carpathian Ukraine. It was briefly returned to Hungary (1939–44) but is now part of Soviet Ukraine. The majority of its Christian inhabitants became Catholics in the Union of Uzhorod (1646), and in 1771 the eparchy of Musachevo was established. In the latest statistics before its dissolution by the Soviets in 1944, there were 461,555 Catholics with 450,000 Orthodox. In America (1963) in the two Dioceses of Pittsburgh and Passaic they numbered, along with the Hungarian, Slovak, and Croatian Catholics, 312,000 Catholics.

There is no Ruthenian rite distinct from the Russian Byzantine rite properly so-called, but in time certain usages have been recognized either as vestiges from the more ancient Slavonic Missals, which Patriarch Nikon in the 17th century had changed, or as modifications introduced by the Ukrainian clergy in the Synod of Zamosc (1720). These changes were sufficiently numerous to cause the rite used both by the Ukrainan and Ruthenian Catholics to be called the Ruthenian rite and to have its own edition of liturgical texts. Some of these modifications were: the addition of the Filioque to the Creed, changes in the preparation (Proskomide) by way of shortening the commemorations, the introduction of a "low" Mass, and the practice of keeping the royal doors open during the entire Liturgy with no veil or curtain drawn. A decided Latin influence is seen in the special bowing of the head during the singing of the second antiphon (*Edinorodny Syne:* O only begotten Son) and the Creed (He became man), the covering of the chalice with a pall, the striking of the breast three times before receiving Holy Communion and the holding the veil of aër aloft during the singing of the Creed with no accompanying movement. An ablution of the fingers before the Communion prayer was added, but the pouring of hot water into the chalice after the division of the Host was abolished along with the use of the sponge. The clergy usually follow the Western rule of shaven priests and tend to favor Roman clerical dress.

Rumanian. The beginnings of Christianity are not clear in Rumanian history. It seems that in the early centuries evangelization was first carried on by Latin missionaries among the descendants of the Roman colonisers sent there by Emperor Trajan. When the Bulgars conquered Rumania, they brought with them the Byzantine rite, using the Old Slavonic language in the liturgy. After the fall of the second Bulgarian Empire the Greek patriarch of Constantinople held the religious jurisdiction and imposed the Greek language and culture. Only in 1881 was Rumania finally formed into a single state consisting of Moldavia and Vallachia whose religion was of the Byzantine rite, using Rumanian as the liturgical language. After World War I Transylvania, Bessarabia, and Bucovina were added to Rumania. In 1947 Rumania became a republic under the Russian Soviets.

A movement started in the 17th and 18th centuries came to a climax when a large part of the Orthodox Rumanian Church was reunited with Rome (1701). With the dissolution of the Austrian-Hungary Empire in 1918, the Rumanian Catholics found themselves along with their Orthodox brethren in a united Rumania. The Catholic clergy and people were well organized and instructed and grew constantly in number until the Popular Republic, set up in 1947, put an end to the Catholic Church's organization. Before they were swallowed up through a mandate of the state by the Orthodox Church, the Catholic Rumanians in 1948 numbered about 1,600,000. An estimated 10,000 have immigrated to the U.S. where 16 priests administer to them. The Rumanian Orthodox Church was established in 1925 as a patriarchate with an estimated 14 million faithful. In the U.S. it is divided into three different jurisdictions. The Rumanian Orthodox Church and the Canonical Episcopate of America, dependent on the patriarch of Rumania, numbers 20,000 faithful, and has Detroit as its see; the Rumanian Orthodox Episcopate of America has about 60,000 and is under the jurisdiction of the Russian American Catholic Orthodox Church; the last and smallest, the Rumanian Orthodox

Episcopate of the Western Hemisphere, is under the jurisdiction of the Russian Church in Exile (Jordanville) and includes about 5,000.

Greek. Once Constantine had built his "New Rome" along the shores of the Bosphorus, Byzantium grew from a small suffragan See of Heraclea in Thrace into the mighty ecclesiastical center for the patriarchate, which jurisdictionally coincided with the limits of the Byzantine Empire. In the Councils of Constantinople (381), Ephesus (431), and Chalcedon (451) the See of Constantinople was recognized, because it was the "New Rome," as having first place of honor after the venerable See of Rome. In time, especially through heresies and the ravages of the Arab conquests, Alexandria and Antioch were reduced to nothing, and Constantinople stood indisputably as the head of all the Byzantine Churches. At the time of the rupture of relations with ancient Rome the jurisdiction of this patriarchate extended over all Christians using the Byzantine rite in northern Africa, Asia Minor, the Balkan States, through all the Eastern Slavic countries as far as the Baltic Sea. In the 11th century more than 600 episcopal sees looked to the See of Constantinople for spiritual leadership. It was a relatively easy task for Patriarch *Michael Cerularius in 1054 to break off all further relationships with the pope and to take with him the millions of Christians using the same Byzantine rite to an estrangement that was to last for 9 centuries. The Crusaders and their sacking of Constantinople in 1204 furthered the cleavage between the East and the West, which various unionistic councils, such as the Council of Lyons (1274) and of Florence (1439) tried in vain to mend. Today the Orthodox, designated by the term Greek Byzantine Church, number about 10 million faithful scattered throughout the Patriarchate of Constantinople, the Synodal Autocephalous Church of Greece, and the Archbishopric of Cyprus. In 1829 Greek Catholics were freed from the civil jurisdiction of the Orthodox patriarch, preparing the way for the formation of a Greek Catholic Church of the Byzantine rite. This movement started under John Marango (d. 1885) in Constantinople and was transplanted to northern Greece in Thrace at the turn of the century. These Greek Catholics in Greece number 2,872 under the leadership of one bishop, an apostolic exarch who resides in Athens. The few Greek Catholics in Turkey are under an apostolic administrator.

Bulgarian. The Bulgars were originally a Turco-Finnish race that settled in the Balkans in the 7th century. They fused with the Slavs who surrounded them and accepted their Slavic language. They received Christianity through the Byzantine rite of the missionaries sent by Constantinople on request of the Bulgar Czar Boris (853–889). In 917 Czar Simeon declared the Bulgarian Church an independent patriarchate, but in 1019 it was suppressed by the Byzantine Emperor Basil II. A second Bulgarian patriarchate was set up at Trnovo in 1186 but it was destroyed under Ottoman persecution in 1393. In 1870 the Bulgars obtained from the Turkish Sultan the decree to set up their own national church free of Greek influence. The Greeks excommunicated the Bulgarian Church in 1872, but the other Slavic Churches recognized it. Only in 1961 did the patriarch of Constantinople recognize it as an independent patriarchate. Today the Bulgarian Church (Orthodox) numbers about 6,500,000.

A Catholic Bulgarian Church of the Byzantine rite began slowly in 1859, but the Balkan War (1912–13) and World War I crushed the movement. It began again, only to be throttled during World War II. An apostolic exarch for the Bulgarian Catholics of the Byzantine rite resides in Sofia, and according to the last available statistics (1948) the faithful numbered 9,480. There are no Bulgarian Catholic Byzantine parishes in the U.S., but the Orthodox Church has one diocese with a total of 8,000 faithful.

Georgian. The early history of Christianity in Georgia is very obscure. Christianity is said to have been brought there by St. Nina, a Christian prisoner, who converted King Miriam about 320. The first missionaries came from the patriarchate of Antioch and exercised jurisdiction until the 8th century. Byzantine missionaries entered Georgia in the 6th century, and the Georgians readily accepted the Byzantine rite and thus freed themselves from the Syrian and Armenian Monophysite error. Through the succeeding centuries Georgia became the prey of conquering armies of Persians, Byzantines, Arabs, Turks, Mongols, and finally Russians. It was annexed to Russia by Czar Alexander in 1801, and from then until the Russian Revolution of 1917 the Georgian Church was under the domination of the Russian Orthodox Church, which tried in vain to force out the native language used in the Byzantine rite. The Communists took complete control, annexing Georgia to the Soviet Union in 1925, and the Georgian Church had its autocephaly recognized by the Moscow Patriarchate.

The actual number of Georgian Orthodox of the Byzantine rite is not known, but it is estimated to be about 750,000. Before World War I Latin Catholics numbered only about 50,000 mainly because the Russian law enforced in Georgia until 1918 prohibited the practice of religion by Catholics of the Byzantine rite. After its quasi-freedom, some Georgian Catholics of the Byzantine rite banded together, but they never numbered more than 10,000.

Estonian and Latvian. Linguistically the Estonians belong to a Finnish ethnic race. From the 16th century nearly all of them were Lutheran. During the period from 1830 to 1848 about 75,000 Estonians and Latvians, through various pressures, became Orthodox under the Moscow Patriarchate. In 1923 they sought and obtained their autonomous metropolia from the patriarch of Constantinople. However, in 1940 the Soviet Union annexed Estonia and Latvia; the Moscow patriarch, considering the autonomy granted these two churches by the patriarchate of Constantinople, assumed them under his own jurisdiction. There are about 8,000 Estonian Orthodox abroad, mostly in Sweden, while in Soviet Estonia there are about 100,000. The Latvian Orthodox are mostly of Russian nationality and number about 150,000. There are no Catholic Estonians or Latvians of the Byzantine rite.

Albanian. Christianity came to Albania from two directions, bringing the Latin rite to the northern part and the Greek Byzantine rite to the southern part. After the 15th century with the occupation of the Turks, Christianity was in part suppressed, making Islamism the prevalent religion in Albania. The Orthodox of the Byzantine rite (1962) using Albanian as the liturgical language, add up to about 255,000 of whom 5,000 are in the U.S. Catholics of the Byzantine rite were reduced by persecution to a mere 400 according to the latest statistics, which were reported in 1945.

Finnish. The Finns belong ethnically to the same group as the Estonians and Hungarians. In 1917 they were declared independent of Russia, but after World War II they were forced to cede a part of their southern territory to the Soviet Union. More than 96 per cent of the Finns are Lutheran; there are only 72,000 Orthodox. The Finnish Church received its autocephaly from the patriarch of Constantinople in 1923, an autonomy that was recognized only in 1957 by the Russian patriarch. The liturgical language is Finnish. One Catholic priest of the Byzantine rite labors in Rekola, but there is no substantial group of Catholic Finns of the Byzantine rite.

Sources. The evolution of the Byzantine rite shows that the Eastern rites did not develop in a vacuum. They were the fruit of a long and gradual formation through centuries from earlier existing rites.

St. Basil's Work. Tradition in the Byzantine Church ascribes to St. Basil (d. 379) the oldest of its two Liturgies. It is quite certain that Basil reformed the Liturgy in use in Cappadocia. He wrote to his clergy in Neocaesarea about the complaints leveled against him because he permitted the new antiphonal way of singing the psalms (*Epist.* 207.3; PG 32:763). Gregory of Nyssa, his brother, compared Basil to Samuel because he had given a new form to the liturgical service (*Oratio funebris;* PG 46:808). An evolved form of the Antiochene Liturgy must have been used in Neocaesarea during the time of St. Basil, and it was this that he reformed by shortening it considerably. One ancient Antiochene Liturgy is extant, that of St. James. It seems to be the basis for Basil's order and to have prayers nearly identical with his in content and position. The oldest form of the Liturgy of St. Basil in manuscript form, located in the Barberini Library, dates from the 9th century (MS III, 55; Brightman 309–344). The text shows that from the Anaphora to the Communion the Liturgy is of his redaction; the Mass of Catechumens and the Offertory prayers came after Basil's lifetime.

Reform of St. John Chrysostom. The next point in the evolution of the Byzantine rite is its reform under St. John Chrysostom (d. 409). The reformed Liturgy of St. John is found in its earliest manuscript in the same Barberini manuscript that contains the 9th-century text of the Liturgy of St. Basil (Brightman 309–344). There is a tradition that St. John, when he came from Antioch to Constantinople to be its patriarch in 397, composed a shortened form of Liturgy from the Liturgy of St. Basil. Pseudo-Proclus [*Tract. de traditione div. missae* (written not before the 7th century); PG 65:851] says: "He [Chrysostom] left out a great deal and shortened all the forms so that no one . . . would stay away from this apostolic and divine institution." A comparison of the two texts shows that the same order is followed, but abbreviations occur mainly in the Anaphora.

Brightman has attempted a reconstruction of the Liturgy as St. John Chrysostom revised it by bringing together bits and pieces from the saint's homilies. His Liturgy must have lacked the present Preparation of the Gifts (Proskomide), the Little and Great Entrances, and the recitation of the Creed. The Liturgy began with the bishop greeting the faithful with "Peace

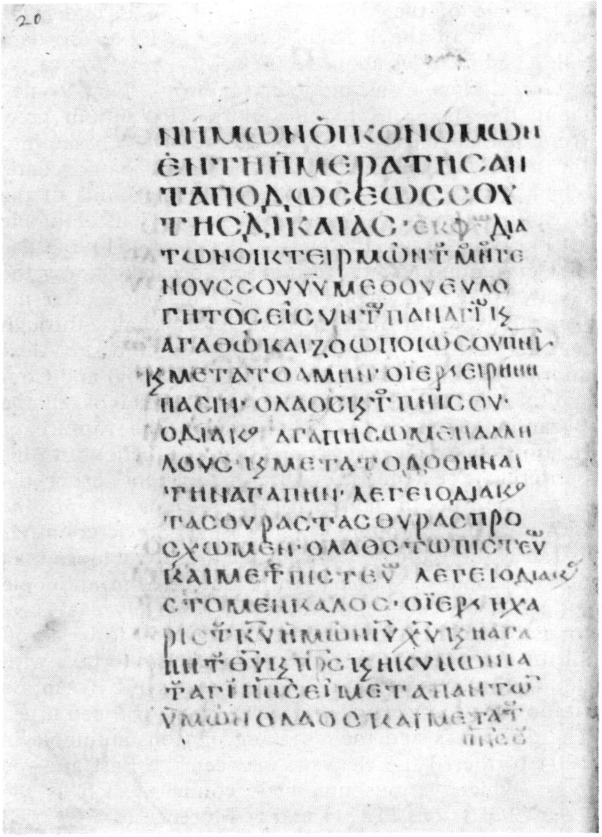

Fig. 1. Page from the 9th-century manuscript of the Liturgy of St. Basil (Cod. Barb. gr. 336) in the Vatican Library. The text reproduced here gives the conclusion of the Offering Prayer, the Kiss of Peace, the Creed, and the beginning of the Anaphora.

to all." There followed readings from the Prophets, the Epistles, and the Gospels. A homily was delivered and a prayer said over the catechumens who were then dismissed. Chrysostom mentions a new Offertory ritual in which the bishop carried bread and wine from the prothesis to the main altar in solemn procession, but Brightman claims that the present Great Entrance and the Hymn of the Cherubim evolved much later (Brightman 532). One should note that the doxology after the Our Father, "For thine is the kingdom . . ." was found in the New Testament codex used by St. John Chrysostom (*In Matt. hom.* 19.6; PG 57:282). Since it was in Antioch that St. John preached most of the homilies from which we can reconstruct the reformed Liturgy, it is possible that he had already shortened the Liturgy of St. Basil then in use throughout the Eastern world and brought this version to Constantinople. Various additions found their way into the Liturgy in succeeding centuries. The Trisagion was supposedly revealed to St. Proclus of Constantinople (patriarch, 434–447); the Cherubim Hymn was added by Justinian II, and the Creed was ordered by him to be recited in each Liturgy (Brightman 532).

The third Byzantine liturgical service, the Liturgy of the Presanctified, is no real Liturgy, as it consists mainly in a Communion service preceded by Vespers and celebrated with a Host consecrated in a previous Liturgy.

Legend attributes it to St. Gregory the Great. The real author of this liturgical service is unknown.

Divine Office. The sources of the Divine Office and the administration of the Sacraments and sacramentals are more difficult to discover. The basic structure probably came from Antiochene usage. It has already been seen that St. Basil introduced a new way of singing Psalms, which must have affected the Divine Office. In a letter to the clergy of Neocaesarea, he gave an outline of the monastic Office consisting of a nocturnal penitential watch and at dawn the reciting of Matins (*Epist.* 207.1, 4; PG 32:762, 764). A peculiarity found in Byzantine Matins, the singing of the Gloria in Excelsis, came from popular Antiochene usage. The evening vesper hymn, Phôs Hilarón, is quoted by Basil (*Liber de Spiritu S.* 28.73; PG 32:205). John Cassian in his *Institutiones* (3.4; PL 49:131) attributes the addition of Prime to the monks of Palestine, and Basil refers to Compline as the final evening prayer of the monks (*In psalmum* 114:1; PG 29:484). The Antiochene usage of the Office was introduced into the Byzantine rite by St. John Chrysostom, at least as far as the recitation of the canonical hours went (*In Epist. 1 ad Tim. 5 Hom.* 14.4; PG 62:575–577). The long, complicated canons of unmetrical hymns introduced into Matin were the compositions of various hymnographers, such as Cosmas, Romanos the Melodius, John Damascene, and St. Theodore of Studion. SS. Sabas (d. 532) and John Damascene (d. *c.* 780) are accredited with having arranged the Office for the entire year, although even after their time the Divine Office underwent further changes.

CHARACTERISTICS OF RITUAL

Here will be discussed the Mass, called by Eastern Catholics the Liturgy, the Divine Office, calendar, Sacraments, sacramentals, the church building, sacred vessels and vestments, and the liturgical books.

The Liturgy. For the most part the Byzantine liturgical text remains fixed for the whole year. There were formerly many varying Anaphoras, but through the centuries, due primarily to the centralization imposed by Constantinople, these were reduced to the two Liturgies of SS. Basil and John Chrysostom and the Liturgy of the Presanctified of St. Gregory the Great. The scriptural readings, mostly from the Epistles and Gospels, differ each day with continuous reading of Gospels or Epistles more or less in their canonical order. Thus in one liturgical year the whole NT is read publicly. There are small sung portions that change, such as the commemorations for each saint or feast day, known as troparia and kontakia, along with seasonal antiphons and hymns to Our Lady for special feasts. Now the longer Liturgy of St. Basil is celebrated only 10 times a year: for his feast on January 1, the Sundays of Lent (except for Palm Sunday), Holy Thursday, Holy Saturday, and the Vigils of Christmas and Epiphany. It is only in the Anaphora or Canon that there is a change to longer prayers; these are more beautiful in their poetry and theological depth than those expressed in the Liturgy of St. John Chrysostom. The Liturgy of the Presanctified can be celebrated each day during Lent except Saturday and Sunday; however it is usually employed on Wednesday and Friday, whereas the Divine Office is recited on the other days. For the other Sundays the priest celebrates the Liturgy of St. John. To show the chief characteristics, the Liturgy of

St. John Chrysostom will be taken as most representative, for it contains all of the audible, external parts of the Liturgy of St. Basil.

It is divided into three parts: preparation, Liturgy of the Catechumens, and the Liturgy of the Faithful.

Preparation. The priest and deacon prepare themselves individually for celebrating the Liturgy by reciting prayers before the iconostasis. Entering into the sanctuary, they kiss the altar, Gospel book and cross, then they proceed to vest. They begin the initial Offeratory at the side altar called the prothesis where the fermented bread and wine are prepared for the liturgical sacrifice. The bread is much larger than the Latin host and thicker. It has a special form with a mark stamped on its top. This consists of a square with a cross passing through the middle. Along the arms of the cross are printed the letters IC, XC, and below NI, KA, Jesus Christ triumphs. This square, called the lamb (amnos), is cut out and placed on the paten. With the lance the priest pierces the left side of the lamb saying: "A soldier pierced His side and out poured blood and water" (Jn 19.34). The deacon pours wine into the chalice, adding a few drops of water, while the priest arranges beside the lamb various particles: first, one to the left symbolizing the Blessed Lady and nine in three rows of three to the right in honor of the angels and various groups of saints. Below these the priest places further particles, commemorating in the first row the living and in the second the dead. The

Fig. 2. Byzantine priests celebrating the Liturgy at the Council of Constance, woodcut from the "Concilium Book" of Ulrich of Reichenthal, printed at Augsburg in 1483.

Fig. 3. Byzantine Liturgy: (a) Service of preparation, priest pierces host and recalls the soldier's piercing Christ's side with a lance. (b) Priest pours wine and water into the chalice. (c) Priest incenses the prepared oblation. (d) Little Entrance with Gospel book through north door; procession halts before royal door.

asterisk is incensed and placed over the paten, then the two veils likewise are incensed and placed over the paten and chalice, and the whole offering is covered by a large veil. The priest recites a final prayer of offering, and the deacon begins to incense the altar, icons, and faithful as he recites Psalm 50.

Liturgy of the Catechumens. The priest begins the Liturgy by making the sign of the cross with the Gospel book, and the deacon leads the faithful in the "Peaceful Litany," so-called from its various petitions for peace in the world and in the churches. After each petition sung by the deacon, the faithful or choir responds with "Kyrie eleison." A series of three antiphons sung alternately by two choirs is interspersed by two short litanies, and the priest and deacon then make the Little Entrance, in which the Gospel book is carried in solemn procession. Great respect is shown the Gospel book as representing the Divine Word, Jesus Christ Himself. When the deacon arrives at the royal doors after having passed in solemn procession accompanied by acolytes carrying candles and followed by the celebrant, he sings out in a loud voice: "Wisdom; let us stand erect." With a proper bow to the Gospel as to Christ Himself the deacon, followed by the priest, goes into the sanctuary where the Gospel is placed on the altar. The troparia and kontakia commemorating the feast of the saints of the day are chanted, followed by the solemn singing of the Trisagion: "Holy God, Holy Strong One, Holy Immortal One, have mercy on us." During the reading of the Epistle by the lector, the deacon incenses the altar and the people. The priest blesses the deacon, who brings the Gospel to the ambo and reads it solemnly to the people. Several litanies follow with petitions for all present, all the living, the dead, and the catechumens and end with the ancient dismissal of the catechumens.

Liturgy of the Faithful. Two short litanies with two prayers for the faithful assisting at the liturgical sacrifice are sung. The Liturgy suddenly assumes a dignified solemnity with the singing of the Hymn of the Cherubim. During this singing the priest reads a very long prayer asking to be deemed worthy by God to assist at this sacrifice for "it is really You who offer and are offered." The so-called Great Entrance is the procession during which the priest carries solemnly before the faithful the holy gifts of bread and wine. He blesses the faithful and carries the gifts solemnly through the royal doors to place them on the main altar. The doors are closed and the curtain drawn, thus creating the atmosphere of impending mystery and solemn reverence. The deacon standing before the royal doors leads the faithful in more litanies, ending with the drawing of the curtain and the solemn chanting of the Nicene-Constantinople Creed, in which, contrary to Latin usage and that of some Oriental Catholics, the Filioque phrase is omitted. A Preface, always the same, begins with the same exhortation as in the Western Mass: the priest urges the faithful to lift up their hearts and give thanks to God. The choir answers by singing the Sanctus. A very short prayer of thanks for the salvation brought by Jesus Christ leads into the account of the Last Supper with the priest singing in a loud voice the words of Institution, first over the bread, then over the wine. The deacon crosses his hands above him, holding the paten and the chalice aloft while the priest sings: "We offer You Your own from what is Yours, in all and for all." The Epiclesis or prayer asking the descent of the Holy Spirit on these gifts to change them into the Body and Blood of Jesus Christ is said, and the gifts are blessed with the sign of the cross by the priest. Other litanies commemorating the living and the dead are climaxed by the solemn singing of the Our Father. After the priest raises the consecrated bread with the command "Holy things to the holy," he proceeds to break the Host into four parts. One part, bearing the mark IC, is placed into the chalice while the others are cut into smaller pieces for distribution at Communion. The deacon pours a few drops of warm water into the chalice signifying that in the Blood of Christ there is warmth and life; also that fervor is proper in those participating. The priest and deacon communicate, first under the species of bread, then from the chalice. The consecrated particles are placed into the Precious Blood and presented to the people with the invitation chanted by the deacon: "Approach with faith and in the fear of God." After Communion, the priest blesses the people with the Sacred Species and brings them to the prothesis while the hymns and litanies of thanksgiving are sung by the deacon and faithful. After a prayer sung by the priest before the iconostasis, the priest gives the final blessing with the concluding prayer, the Apolysis, which commemorates the feast or saint celebrated in that Liturgy. While the deacon consumes at the side altar the remaining Sacred Species, the priest gives the cross to the faithful to be kissed and distributes antidora, blessed particles of bread. Thus terminates the Byzantine Liturgy of St. John Chrysostom.

Divine Office. The canonical hours are the same as those of the Latin rite. The Office consists mainly of Psalms and liturgical hymns, so that all can be sung according to the eight tones of Byzantine music. Each week the entire Psalter is chanted. It is divided into 20 parts called kathismata, which include from seven to eight Psalms each. The normal Office is actually twofold, at least for Matins and Lauds, and includes the Office of the day of the week and the Office of the saints of that day. The ferial office includes three parts: that of Lent (Triod); that of Paschal time (Pentekostarion) and the time after Pentecost (Octoechos). The Office begins with Vespers celebrated the evening before; then Compline, Matins, Lauds, Prime, Terce, Sext, and None; the Liturgy is celebrated between Terce and Sext.

Calendar. The majority of the Orthodox and some Eastern Catholics use the Julian Calendar (called the Old Style), which is 13 days behind the Gregorian. September is the beginning of the new liturgical year. The feasts are divided into four cycles. The weekly cycle commemorates each day a different mystery or group of saints: the Resurrection on Sunday; the angels on Monday; John the Baptist on Tuesday; the Holy Cross on Wednesday and Friday; the Apostles, wonder-workers, and bishops, especially St. Nicholas on Thursday; and confessors, martyrs, all the saints and the dead on Saturday. The Blessed Mother of God is commemorated each day, but in a particular way on Sunday, Wednesday, and Friday in connection with the mystery of the Redemption. The cycle of the 8 weeks, Octoechos, according to the eight modes of music, begins with the week of St. Thomas immediately after Easter and every 8 weeks repeats the same eight modes. The annual cycle of movable feasts gravitates around the feast of Easter.

It includes the 18 weeks: 10 of preparation before Easter (the period of the Triod) and the 8 weeks after Easter until the week of All Saints (the period of the Pentekostarion.) The annual cycle of fixed feasts begins with September 1 and ends with August 31.

Sacraments. Texts for the administration of the seven Sacraments are found in the liturgical book called the Euchologion. Baptism is conferred by immersion. After the child has been anointed all over its body with blessed oil, it is immersed three times in water over its head while the priest says the formula: "The servant of God, N., is baptized in the name of the Father, Amen, and of the Son, Amen, and of the Holy Spirit, Amen." Confirmation follows immediately, and the priest is the usual minister, not the bishop as in the Latin rite. After the priest anoints with a specially prepared oil all the senses and limbs and the whole body, he recites the simple formula: "The seal of the gift of the Holy Spirit. Amen."

The Eucharist is usually given under two species with a spoon. However, among Catholic Melchites, the priest dips slender oblong pieces into the consecrated wine with his fingers and thus distributes it to the faithful.

Among the Orthodox there is the tradition of confessing before each reception of Holy Communion. Among the Orthodox a general accusation has become the accepted custom, whereas among Catholics there is greater frequentation and more intelligent preparation. Except among some Eastern-rite Catholics who use the Latin confessional, there is usually no box used. The penitent approaches the priest who stands before a table on which is found the Gospel book and the cross. Either standing or kneeling, he confesses, and the priest places the ends of his wide stole over the head of the penitent as he recites the formula of absolution.

Extreme Unction is called the Anointing of the Sick. A special oil used for the anointing oftentimes contains wine in memory of the Good Samaritan and is blessed before the priest performs the anointing. It is given sometimes even in the church on the vigil of a feast as a preparation for Holy Communion, especially on Wednesday of Holy Week. The priest anoints the senses and limbs, reciting the formula: "Holy Father, You, the Physician of souls and bodies, who sent Your only Son, Our Lord Jesus Christ, who heals from every sickness and saves from death, heal your servant, N., of the bodily and spiritual sickness of which he is afflicted and give him the fullness of life through the grace of Your Christ."

There are fewer degrees of Holy Orders than in the Latin Church. Lector and subdeacon are the only two minor orders; the major orders are deacon, priest, and bishop. Orders are given in a very simple but moving rite by the bishop's imposing his hands.

Marriage is called the "crowning" because the spouses are crowned with two nuptial crowns with the formula: "The servant of God, N., and the servant of God, N., are crowned in the name of the Father and the Son and the Holy Spirit. Amen."

Sacramentals. These are of various kinds. Antidora are blessed particles of bread, distributed immediately after reception of Holy Communion and after the final blessing. At the vigils of solemn feasts a special anointing occurs during Matins with an oil usually taken from a lamp that has been burning before a holy icon. Another blessed bread, the kolyba, is blessed and eaten in honor of some saint or in memory of the dead. A solemn blessing of water takes place on Epiphany. There are blessings for all sorts of things, the formulas of which are found in the Euchologion. The priest usually wears for such sacramental blessings the epitrakelion and the kalimavkion (the black cylindrical hat) with the phelonion.

Church Building. The Byzantine churches are usually constructed in the shape of a Greek cross with four arms of equal length. The Russians, besides the one central cupola above the middle of the cross, place four other cupolas over the ends of the cross, surmounted on the outside by onion-shaped bulbs covered by copper or gold gilding. The building is divided into three parts, each distinct from the others: the sanctuary (bema), the nave (naos), and the vestibule (narthex). The sanctuary and nave are separated by the iconostasis. This is a partition of wood or marble, usually high and richly decorated with images or icons of Our Lord, Our Lady, and various saints, and set facing the nave. The iconostasis is pierced by three doors, one in the middle and one at each side. The more ornate set of doors in the middle is called the royal doors. The faithful and clerics below a deacon cannot pass through these doors. Stretching behind the royal doors is a curtain that is pulled aside at certain moments of the Liturgy. The door on the right is called the south door and usually is adorned with an icon of St. Stephen, the first martyred deacon; on the left or north door, there is an icon of St. Michael. Through these pass the clerics inferior to a deacon.

Fig. 4. Interior of the cathedral of the St. Nicholas Diocese in Chicago for the Ukrainians. The arrangement of the iconostasis and of mural decorations is typical of that found in the churches of the Byzantine rite.

Behind the royal doors is the altar. It is a flat square of wood or stone, resting on four legs. There is no altar stone as in the Latin rite, but the relics are sewed into the antimension, a type of corporal, painted or stamped with the entombment of Our Lord. Only the bishop can consecrate an antimension, which is never washed but, when soiled, is burned. The Gospel book and a hand cross always rest on the altar. The Blessed Sacrament may be reserved in a tabernacle on the altar or in a silver or golden dove suspended above it. Usually one or more pieces of fermented consecrated bread, tinctured with a few drops of the Precious Blood, are reserved for Viaticum. Before giving it in Holy Communion, the priest dips it into unconsecrated wine. The Blessed Sacrament is renewed by many of the Orthodox only once a year on Holy Thursday.

The sanctuary continues in front of the iconostasis by means of an elevated platform above the nave, called the solion or soleas. Here the deacon chants the litanies, and the faithful receive Holy Communion. The ambo at the left of the altar is the place from which the gospel is chanted. Usually pews are not known, except for members of the clergy and the sick and aged; others usually stand. However, in the West among the Greeks and many Eastern Catholics pews are used. In the nave there is a small table on which the image of the saint of the day or the patron of the church is placed for veneration. The nave connects with the vestibule through several doors. In ancient churches a double division separated the vestibule into two parts, the exterior and the interior vestibule. In the interior, the monks recite canonical hours except for Lauds and Vespers; here also is kept the baptismal font. In countries not under Turkish domination, bell towers are found, but carillonning is employed rather than the western clanging. The Mussulman government in the name of the Koran forbade the use of bells, which were replaced by wood, hit by a mallet. Such a device called a simandron is still used in monasteries of the Near East. The interior of churches are ornately decorated with frescoes painted in the Byzantine style with themes proper to each part of the church. Above the altar in the cupola of the apse is usually found a fresco of the Blessed Virgin holding the Child Jesus, while in the central cupola there is a painting of Christ the Pantocrator (the Almighty).

Vessels. The chalice is the same shape as in the West. The paten, called the diskos, is longer and often rests on a base. The lance or knife and the asterisk or star are peculiar to the Eastern rites. The lance, symbolizing the spear by which the centurion pierced the side of the Savior, is used to cut the fermented bread. The asterisk is made of two pieces of curved metal superimposed to form a cross. At the point of juncture a small star or sometimes a cross hangs down over the host on the paten. The asterisk is used to prevent the covering over the paten from touching the bread. Another covering is used over the chalice, and a large veil, the aër, covers the whole Eucharistic offering. These veils or covers symbolize the linen clothes and the tomb of Our Lord.

The zeon is a small metal container from which hot water is poured into the chalice before receiving Holy Communion. A spoon is used to distribute Holy Communion. A small sponge is employed for purifying the fingers and the paten, but Catholic Melchites, Italo-Greeks, Ukrainians, and Ruthenians use the Latin

Fig. 5. Byzantine-rite liturgical vessels: a diskos with asterisk, a chalice, and a communion spoon.

purificator or a small ball of cotton wrapped in a sack of silk.

A ripidion is a round disk made of metal fixed on a wooden pole with the painted image of the seraphim with six wings. The deacon waves it over the Holy Species at certain moments after the Consecration. During the processions two or more ripidia accompany the cross. In pontifical Liturgies the bishop holds the dikirion, a two-branched candlestick, in his left hand and the trikirion, a three-branched candlestick, in his right hand when blessing the faithful. Usually behind the altar is a seven-branched candelabra.

Vestments. While he is not celebrating the Liturgy, the priest wears the anterion, a cassock of two pieces meeting in the middle and held by a cincture or hemmed in tightly at the sides. It is generally black, but for the secular clergy no color is prescribed; often it is gray, brown, or purple. Over it is worn the conton, a shorter habit going down to the knees with larger sleeves than the anterion. Over this, or directly over the anterion, is the rason, with ample sleeves; it is usually pleated and touches the ground, giving an air of dignity when the priest walks. Priests and deacons and sometimes lower clerics wear the kalimavkion or kamilavkion, a black cylindrical hat. Monks, archimandrites, bishops, and patriarchs cover the kalimavkion with a black veil, called an epanokalimavkion, that falls over the shoulders. Among the Slavs and Rumanians, priests and lower clerics often wear a cap called the scoufa. The Catholic Ukrainians, Ruthenians, and Rumanian priests of the Byzantine rite have adopted the Latin custom of shaving and cutting their hair.

Vestments worn during the Liturgy are colorful and ornate. Inferior clerics wear a loose tunic of varying color without a cincture. The deacon wears a stikarion, a long vestment that touches the ground and is usually of a clear color with large sleeves. He wears the orarion, a long and narrow cloth placed over the left shoulder. The front end he holds in his right hand as he prays, while the other end falls back over his shoulder to the ground. After the chanting of the Our Father the deacon crisscrosses the orarion over his back. There are five distinct vestments for the celebrating priest. The stikarion corresponds to the Latin alb; it can be of different materials, usually very light. Over it he wears

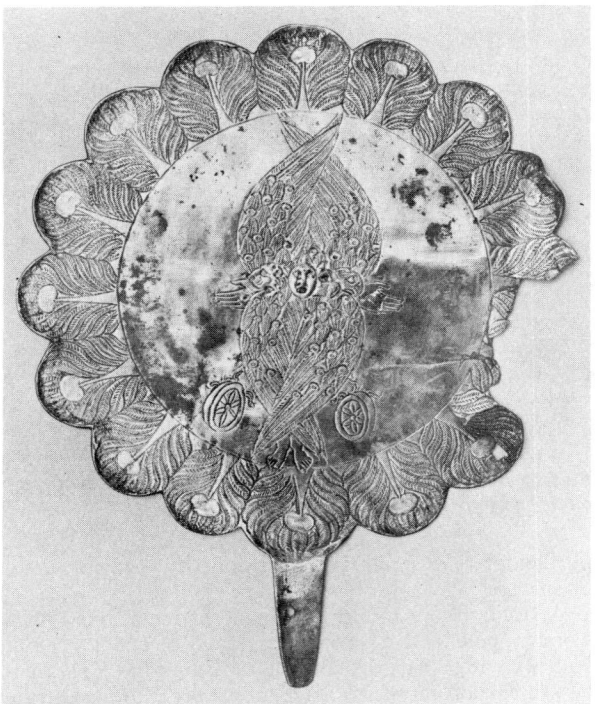

Fig. 6. Ripidion, or liturgical fan of silver, probably made at Constantinople between the years 565 and 578.

the epitrakelion, a wide stole adorned with crosses; it fits over the head and falls·down the front almost to the ground. It is held by the cincture (zoni), which is fastened around the waist. Cuffs are worn from the wrists to midway forearm to keep the loose flowing sleeves of the stikarion in place. The phelonion or chausuble is of ample and supple material; it is long in front and must be folded back onto the arms for certain ceremonies. The stole, cincture, cuffs, and chasuble are of the same material and color. Archimandrites, bishops, metropolitans, and patriarchs wear the epigonation, a stiff, square material with a cross or image embroidered on the center. The priest wears it under the phelonion suspended to the height of his knees by a band from the left waist, while the bishop wears it over the sakkos, fixed by a button.

Generally the bishop wears the same vestments as a simple priest, but the phelonion is replaced by the sakkos, a short tunic with half sleeves, richly embroidered and loosely buttoned on the sides or tied by ribbons. Small bells are attached to the sleeves or sides in imitation of the high priest of the Jews. Over the sakkos, the bishop wears the omophorion, which corresponds to the Latin pallium. It is worn around the neck, forming an angle on the breast with one end falling to the ground. On the chest the bishop wears an oval medallion called the enkolpion, one or two pictures of Our Lord and Our Lady, along with a pectoral cross. The headdress, or mitra, is not the usual Latin miter, but a crown, made of rigid material and adorned on top with a cross and various small pictures or icons. The pastoral staff or scepter terminates in two intertwined serpents, surmounted sometimes by a cross or the image of a saint. In assisting at, or before actually celebrating, the Divine Liturgy, the bishop wears the

mantle called the mandyas. It is very ample with the two parts attached in front at the neck and bottom. Along the border is rich embroidery and small bells.

From ancient times the Byzantine priests employed three liturgical colors in the celebration of the Liturgy: black for the Liturgy of the Presanctified, red for Lent and funerals, and white for all other occasions. But in modern times except perhaps among the Russians, the rules of color are not maintained with rigor. For the normal celebration of the Liturgy any color that would not shock is admissible.

Books. Many heavy books are used in the performance of the liturgical services. The Euchologion contains the text for the three Liturgies as well as the ritual for the administration of the Sacraments and sacramentals. The Evangelion contains the readings for each day of the gospel, and the Apostolos, the corresponding epistles. In the Psaltirion the Psalms are divided into 20 groups called kathismata. The Triodion includes the offices for Lent, and the Pentekostarion, those of Easter up to the first Sunday after Pentecost. The Octoechos or Paraklitiki have offices from the first Sunday after Pentecost to the Sunday of the Pharisee and Publican before Septuagesima Sunday. It contains the tropars or collects for Vespers, Compline, Matins, and Lauds divided into eight parts, each to be sung for a week according to one of the eight tones of Byzantine music.

The Menaia contain the offices of the saints for the whole year and are divided into 6 or 12 volumes. The Horologion has parts of the office that never change, also the ecclesiastical calendar, the apolitikia or dismissal prayer, and the kontakia or collects for each day. The Typikon is a type of directory of rules to be observed for the Liturgy and Office for all the feasts.

The Archieratikon corresponds to the Roman Pontifical and provides for the liturgical functions of a bishop.

Fig. 7. Archbishop of the Byzantine rite blessing the cornerstone of a new church. He is vested in mitra, omophorion, and mandyas.

The Theotokarion is a collection of chants in honor of the Mother of God (Theotokos) divided into eight groups according to the eight musical tones. The Hirmologion is made up of strophes and melody types used as basic rhythms for hymns found in other liturgical books unaccompanied by musical notation. Finally, the Hagiasmatarion is a collection of prayers, blessings, and offices that the priest has most need of in daily ministrations to the faithful.

Bibliography: D. Attwater, *The Christian Churches of the East*, 2 v. (rev. ed. Milwaukee 1961–62). F. E. Brightman, *Liturgies Eastern and Western*, 2 v. (Oxford 1896) v.1. J. M. Hanssens, *Institutiones liturgicae de ritibus orientalibus* (Rome 1930–32) v.2, 3. A. A. King, *The Rites of Eastern Christendom*, 2 v. (London 1950). *Oriente Cattolico: Cenni storici e statistiche* (Vatican City 1962). P. de Meester, DACL 6.2:1591–1662. **Illustration credits:** Fig. 2 Library of Congress, Washington, D.C. Fig. 6 Courtesy of the Dumbarton Oaks Collections, Washington, D.C.

[G. A. MALONEY]

BYZANTINE RITE, CHANTS OF

The expression commonly designates Greek ecclesiastical music of the Eastern imperial period—a repertory some of which long survived the fall of Constantinople in 1453. Included under this heading, though not part of a church service, are the acclamations addressed to the emperor and his family as a matter of courtly ceremony. These acclamations are religious in character: of purely secular Byzantine music no evidence exists save in literary references. The same may be said of instrumental music. Though instruments might accompany the imperial acclamations, they were altogether excluded from the church service proper; Byzantine musical notation, presumably the invention of clerics, was developed for the sole purpose of recording the melodies of a monophonic and unaccompanied chant. Even in this domain, the oldest surviving Byzantine musical documents can scarcely be earlier than 10th century— by which time virtually all the texts that were to figure henceforth in the standard Byzantine ritual had taken their place there, and the order of service itself had, at least in large part, assumed definitive shape. Hence, while it is reasonable to suppose that many Byzantine melodies are much older than the earliest sources preserving them, one can speak with assurance only of the textual forms of Byzantine hymnody during the period of its greatest poetical creativity.

In Eastern ritual as in Western, the intonation of scriptural lessons and the chanting of Psalms and canticles (Psalmlike texts from other books of the Bible) always played an important part. The Byzantine rite, however, tended to accord a prominence to original (i.e., non-Biblical) hymnography, which the hymns, tropes, and Sequences of the Latin world never achieved. Scattered examples of hymn texts from the early centuries of Greek Christianity still exist. Some of these employ the metrical schemes of classical Greek poetry; but the evolution of pronunciation had rendered those meters largely meaningless, and with rare exceptions when classical forms were imitated, Byzantine hymns of the following centuries are prose poetry—unrhymed verses of irregular length and accentual patterns. The common term for a short hymn of one stanza, or one of a series of stanzas, is troparion (this may carry the further connotation of hymn interpolated between psalm verses). A famous example, whose existence is attested as early as the 4th century, is the Vesper hymn Φῶς ἱλαρόν (Gladdening Light), still a part of the Orthodox Evening Service; another, Ὁ μονογενὴς υἱός (The Only-Begotten Son), ascribed to Justinian I (527–565), figures in the introductory portion of the Byzantine Divine Liturgy, or Mass. Perhaps the earliest set of troparia of known authorship are those of the monk Auxentios (first half of the 5th century), recorded in his biography but not preserved in any later Byzantine order of service.

Development of the Kontakion. At the end of the 5th and beginning of the 6th century came the development of the first large-scale form of Greek hymnody, which only at a much later date received the special name kontakion (literally, scroll). This has been described as a kind of poetical sermon, in general setting forth the narrative theme of one of the great feasts with much rhetorical embellishment. Modern scholars have traced the derivation of the genre from Syriac prototypes. Formally, the kontakion consists of 20 to 30 or more stanzas (oikoi, literally, houses), all metrically identical (though of the characteristic irregular meter), so that each might be sung to the same music—the whole series prefixed by a metrically independent stanza known as prooimion or koukoulion. (Not only were succeeding oikoi within a given kontakion modeled on the first; it became common practice to borrow the metrical structure of a preexisting kontakion for a new poem, perhaps with the object of making use of an already well-known melody.) The stanzas were further linked together by the occurrence of a short refrain (ephymnion) at the end of each, and by an acrostic formed of the initial letters of each stanza, which might spell out the author's name, the alphabet, etc. (both devices are characteristic of Semitic poetry). The most illustrious composer of kontakia was Romanos (called the "melodist"), a Syrian Jew converted to Christianity and active at Constantinople in the first half of the 6th century; to him some 80-odd poems are ascribed. But the most celebrated example of the genre itself is the anonymous *Akathistos hymn, the only kontakion to persist in the Office through later Byzantine and modern times intact with all its stanzas. Other kontakia suffered drastic abridgment with the declining popularity of the genre: by the 10th century they had by and large been cut down to the prooimion and a single oikos. Some new kontakia were written even at this late date, but in the truncated form to which the old ones had been reduced.

Development of the Kanon. It was in fact the second of the two large-scale forms of Byzantine hymnography that seems to have supplanted the kontakion in liturgical favor: the kanon, which first appeared in the second half of the 7th century. For an indeterminate time before this, a central position in the Morning Service (*Orthros*) had been occupied by the chanting of a group of nine Biblical canticles: (1) and (2) those of Moses (Exodus ch. 15 and Deuteronomy ch. 32), (3)–(6) those of Anna (1 Kings ch. 2), Habacuc (ch. 3), Isaia (ch. 26), and Jona (ch. 2); (7) and (8) the Canticle of the Three Youths, in two parts (Daniel ch. 3); and (9) the Magnificat (Luke ch. 1). The kanon had its origin in the practice of interpolating a certain number of troparia between verses of these canticles, so that to each there corresponded a set of hymns, newly composed, but showing their relation to the original by textual quotation or allusion (and often combining this reference with references to the feast of the day). In time these new compositions came largely to supplant the canticles themselves in the service; and the term "ode" ('ωδή)—at first simply the equivalent of "canticle"—was applied as well to the set of stanzas corresponding to any individual canticle. The term kanon designates the resulting non-Biblical hymnodic complex: thus a kanon has, in principle, nine odes (in fact, the second is usually omitted outside of the Lenten season); an ode in turn consists typically of three or four stanzas or troparia (several early kanons survive in which the number of troparia to an ode is much greater). Further, in each ode the successive stanzas are exact metrical reproductions of the first, so that the same music will fit all equally well; however, the model-stanzas for the different odes are, save in a few exceptional cases, metrically dissimilar. The Greek term for such a model-stanza is *heirmos,* from which derives the name of the collection containing model-stanzas (texts and, in general, music as well) for a given repertory of kanons: the Heirmologion, one of the principal types of source-book for Byzantine music. Tradition attributes the invention of the kanon to Andrew of Crete (*c.* 660–*c.* 740). While there is reason to suppose that examples of the form existed before the period of his activity, he is probably the earliest known poet to whom kanons are ascribed by the sources. Certain aspects of his work belong to the early history of the genre, e.g., the composition of an ode in a large number of short troparia: his famous "Great Kanon" of mid-Lent contains in sum 250 stanzas. Younger contemporaries and successors of Andrew as kanon-writers were men associated with the monastery of St. Sabas (between Jerusalem and the Dead Sea), notably John of Damascus (d. *c.* 750) and Cosmas of Maiuma. John's celebrity as hymn-writer rivals his preeminence as codifier of theology. Outstanding among his works are the Easter kanon Ἀναστάσεως ἡμέρα (Day of Resurrection) and the kanons in iambic meter for Christmas, Epiphany, and Pentecost; in general the kanons ascribed to "John the Monk" have a leading place among the heirmoi in each of the 8 modally-divided sections of the Heirmologion. (Indeed, so numerous and varied are the kanons with this attribution in the manuscripts that a number of them must be the work of authors other than John Damascene himself.) In the 9th century the center of hymnography was no longer Palestine but Constantinople, and in particular the monastery of Studion, a bastion of the anti-iconoclastic struggle. The principal representative of this school is the Abbot Theodore (759–826), writer of kanons, kontakia, etc., who in collaboration with his brother Joseph composed many of the hymns of the Lenten season. Prominent also among the Studite hymnographers are two Sicilians: Methodios (d. 846), who was to become patriarch of Constantinople after the triumph of Orthodoxy; and Joseph (d. 883), known with special emphasis as "the Hymnographer"—his kanons remaining today in printed Greek service-books number in the hundreds. There are a few 9th-century hymn-writers not of the Studion group who are worthy of commemoration, such as the nun Kasia, of whose work there survives a kanon for Holy Saturday and several hymns.

Other Hymn Forms. Though these hymnographers have been mentioned chiefly as writers of kanons, they composed also shorter, monostrophic hymns, some of which have considerable prominence in the service. Such troparia have a variety of denominations, specifying their liturgical function (e.g., *hypakoë* designates a short troparion of the Morning Office preceding the Gradual Antiphons, or *anabathmoi*) or their subject matter (e.g., *theotokion* designates a hymn in praise of the Mother of God). These categories are too numerous to list in detail. The most important class, in number and in variety of liturgical use, bears the name sticheron (στιχηρόν), deriving from *stichos* (psalm-verse) and showing the origin of such a hymn as appendage to a verse of a Psalm, or intercalation between verses. Thus attached to selections from the Psalter, the stichera generally occur in groups, of which the principal, throughout the year, are those accompanying the fixed set of Psalms toward the beginning of Vespers (Psalms 140, 141, 129, 116), those at the end of Vespers (called aposticha), and those accompanying the Psalms of Lauds toward the end of the Morning Service (Psalms 148–150). By the time the hymnology of the Office had reached its full development, there were proper stichera serving these functions for all the feast days of the year, for the Sundays and weekdays of Lent, and for the recurrent cycle of 8 weeks in the order of the modes beginning with Easter. The music book containing these sets of stichera, together with certain other sets of troparia (such as those for special solemnities of the year, e.g., the Great Hours of Good Friday), was known as the Sticherarion; this compilation as such—unlike the Heirmologion—exists only in medieval manuscripts. If the metrical pattern and melody of a sticheron were original with itself, it was called idiomelon; if borrowed from another sticheron, prosomoion; an idiomelon, which had thus served as a model for later stichera, received the special name *automelon.* Most important among the stichera prosomoia are those in the collection composed by Theodore and Joseph of the Studion for the Lenten Office.

Significant additions were made to the Byzantine Office after this 9th-century generation of hymnographers: e.g., the eleven morning hymns (*heothina*) by Emperor Leo VI (886–912), and the eleven Resurrection hymns (*exaposteilaria*), also for the Morning Service, by his son Constantine VII Porphyrogennetus (913–959). But in general, with the 10th century the composition of new hymns within the Eastern Empire went into decline; and by the end of the 11th it had all but ceased. Hymnography flourished a while longer in the Italo-Greek world, and notably at the Byzantine-rite Abbey of Grottaferrata (near Rome)—today a leading center for the study of Byzantine music and liturgy.

The Later Byzantine Chant. With the cessation of new poetical composition, Byzantine chant entered its final period, devoted largely to the production of more elaborate musical settings of the traditional texts: either embellishments of the earlier simpler melodies, or original pieces in highly ornamental style. This was the work of the so-called "masters" (*maistores*), of whom the most celebrated was John Koukouzeles (active *c.* 1300), compared in Byzantine writings to John Damascene himself as an innovator in the development of chant. The multiplication of new settings and elaborations of the old continued in the centuries following the fall of Constantinople, until by the end of the 18th century the original musical repertory of the medieval MSS had

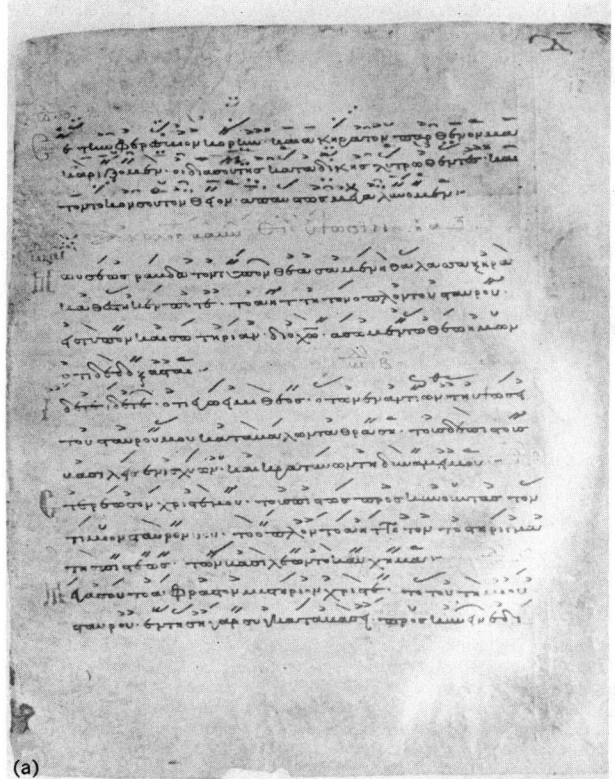

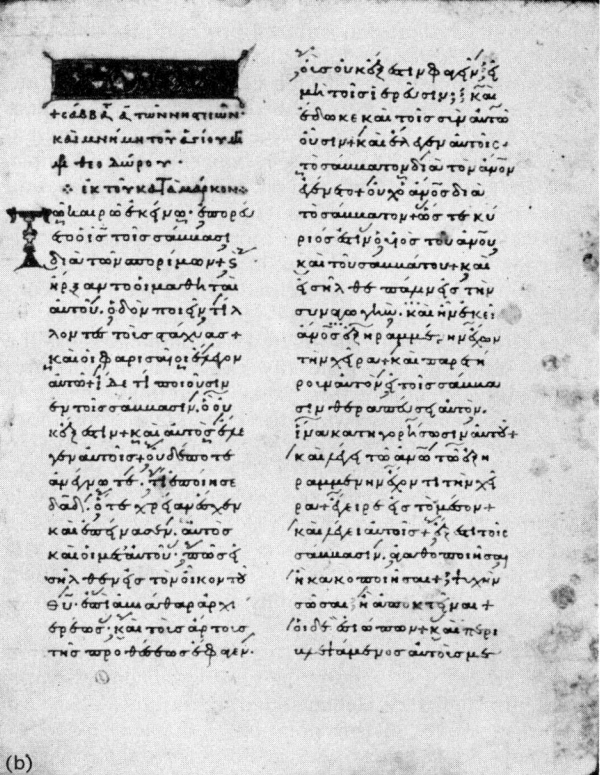

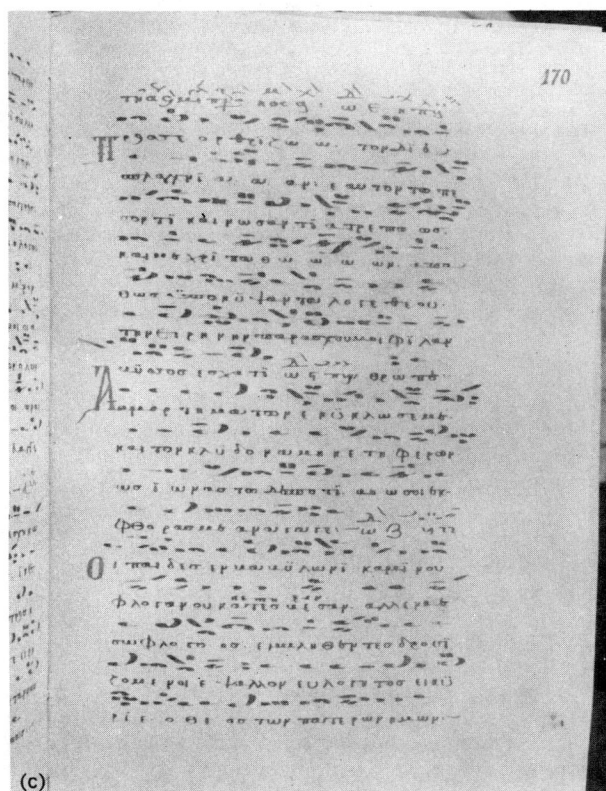

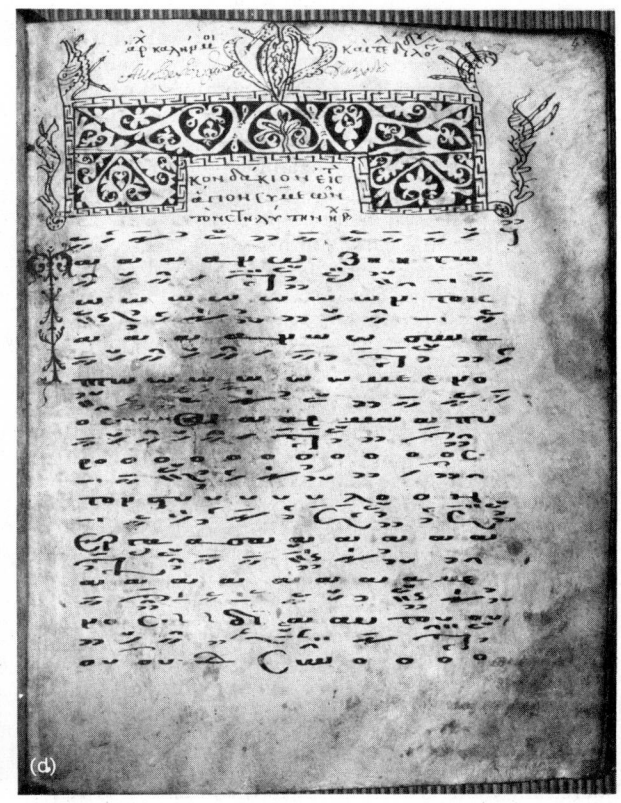

Byzantine rite chants (specimens of medieval notation): (a) Tenth or 11th century (Jerusalem, Library of the Patriarch, MS Saba 83, fol. 17r). (b) Twelfth century (Edinburgh, Reid Music Library). (c) A.D. 1281 (Grottaferrata, MS E.γ II). (d) A.D. 1289 (Florence, Laurenziana, Codex Ashburnham 64, fol. 45r).

been quite replaced by later compositions, and even the basic modal system had suffered profound modification under Near-Eastern influences.

To a still greater extent than Latin plainchant, Byzantine chant, as shown even in the early MSS, is formulaic in structure. Each mode is characterized by a limited number of musical formulas, ranging in length from a few notes to an entire phrase, which recur time and again, in more or less invariable form, throughout the repertory of pieces within that mode. (The greatest variation tends to occur in the middle of phrases; the most stereotyped formulas are the cadential ones.) Depending upon the literary and liturgical genre of a piece, its musical style may be more or less complex; thus, the kanons and stichera generally exhibit a simple, predominantly syllabic setting, the Communion verses a more ornamented one, while the kontakia are still more elaborate. Yet the principle of formulaic construction remains present in each style. The period of the *maistores,* however, saw the development of a new style known as "kalophonic," highly florid, not reliant on the traditional preexisting formulas (though observing melodic conventions of its own), and applicable to almost all the liturgical genres—kanons and stichera as well as kontakia, etc.

It is generally agreed that Byzantine musical notation derives from the Greek phonetic signs (accents, breathings) introduced by Hellenistic grammarians. The most primitive variety of this notation is that employed by lectionary books (those with readings from the Bible for liturgical use) dating from the 9th to the 15th century. Over that period it remains essentially unchanged—a small set of signs that occur as couples (one at the beginning of a phrase, one at the end), and which presumably call for various sorts of simple cantillation formula. This notation, of which nothing more definite can confidently be said, has been named "ekphonetic" by modern scholars (see Fig. *a*). Almost as rudimentary are the earliest surviving examples—10th century or later—of hymn notation (see Fig. *b* lower portion, which shows several heirmoi of kanons with archaic notation). Like the early Latin neumes, these signs do not have unambiguous pitch meaning. Yet by the beginning of the 13th century, the system had been developed to the point of expressing all pitch relationships unequivocally: each sign shows the intervallic distance, up or down, from its predecessor; and a key-signature (*martyria*) shows the degree of the mode on which the piece begins. (See Fig. *b,* top three lines, in which the archaic notation has been revised to conform to the later system; Figs. *c* and *d* show, respectively, heirmoi and a kontakion in the fully developed notation.)

This article has dealt solely with the hymnology of the Greek Church; but that of the Slavic Church as well might be included under the heading "Byzantine." Slavic hymnology, as with liturgy in general, is in all but exceptional details simply a faithful adaptation of the Greek; even the medieval Slavic musical notation is directly based upon an early state of Greek Byzantine notation. And if specific examples of parallelism between Byzantine and Latin chant are far more the exception than the rule, nonetheless such examples in increasing number have come to the attention of scholars. Further comparative study of these relationships will be a major endeavor of future scholarship, building on the pioneering work of Wellesz and Tillyard in the Byzantine field.

Bibliography: Wellesz ByzMus. E. WELLESZ, ed., *Trésor de musique byzantine,* 2 v. (Paris 1934); *The Music of the Byzantine Church* (Cologne 1959). H. J. W. TILLYARD, *Byzantine Music and Hymnography* (London 1923); in Grove DMM 1:1068–78. L. TARDO, *L'Antica melurgia bizantina* (Grottaferrata 1938). J. QUASTEN, *Musik und Gesang in den Kulten der heidnischen Antike und christlichen Frühzeit* (LiturgQuellForsch 25; 1930). A. BAUMSTARK, *Comparative Liturgy,* rev. B. BOTTE, tr. F. L. CROSS (Westminster, Md. 1958); "Hymns (Greek Christian)," Hastings ERE 7:5–16. C. HÖEG, "The Oldest Slavonic Tradition of Byzantine Music," *Proceedings of the British Academy* 39 (1953) 37–66. O. STRUNK, "The Tonal System of Byzantine Music," MusQ 28 (1942) 190–204; "Intonations and Signatures of the Byzantine Modes," *ibid.* 31 (1945) 339–355; "The Notations of the Chartres Fragment," *Annales musicologiques* 3 (1955) 7–37; "The Byzantine Office at Hagia Sophia," DumbOaksP 9–10 (1955–56) 175–202. K. LEVY, "A Hymn for Thursday in Holy Week," JAm MusSoc 16 (1963) 127–175. M. VELIMIROVIĆ, "Liturgical Drama in Byzantium and Russia," DumbOaksP 16 (1962) 349–385. E. KOSCHMIEDER, *Die ältesten Novgoroder Hirmologien-Fragmente* (AbhMünchAk, Philos.-Hist. Klasse, NS 35, 37, 41; 1952–58). B. DI SALVO, "L'essenza della musica nelle liturgie orientali," *Bollettino della Badia Greca di Grottaferrata,* NS 15 (1961) 173–191; "Asmatikon," *ibid.* 16 (1962) 135–158; "Stichera Antiphona," *ibid.* 17 (1963) 37–55. The principal publication for sources and studies is the series *Monumenta musicae byzantinae,* ed. C. HÖEG et al. (Copenhagen 1935–): I. Facsimilia: v.1 *Sticherarium* (1935); v.2 *Hirmologium Athoum* (1938); v.3 *Hirmologium Cryptense* (1950); v.4 *Contacarium Ashburnhamense* (1956); v.5 *Fragmenta Chiliandarica palaeoslavica,* 2 v. (1957); v.6 *Contacarium palaeoslavicum Mosquense* (1960); v.7 *Specimina notationum antiquiorum* (1965). II. Lectionaria: v.1 *Prophetologium,* ed. C. HÖEG and G. ZUNTZ, 4 fasc. (1939–60). III. Transcripta: v.1 *Die Hymnen des Sticherarium für September,* transcr. by E. WELLESZ (1936); v.2 *The Hymns of the Sticherarium for November,* transcr. H. J. W. TILLYARD (1938); v.3 and 5 *The Hymns of the Octoechus,* transcr. *id.* (1940–49); v.4 *Twenty Canons from the Trinity Hirmologium,* transcr. *id.* (1952); v.6 and 8 *The Hymns of the Hirmologium,* pt. 1 and 3.2, transcr. A. AYOUTANTI and M. STÖHR (1952–56); v.7 *The Hymns of the Pentecostarium,* transcr. H. J. W. TILLYARD (1960); v.9 *The Akathistos Hymn,* introd. and transcr. E. WELLESZ (1957). IV. Subsidia: v.7, fasc. i, H. J. W. TILLYARD, *Handbook of the Middle Byzantine Notation* (1935); fasc. ii, C. HÖEG, *La Notation ekphonétique* (1935); v.2, E. WELLESZ, *Eastern Elements in Western Chant* (1947); v.3, R. PALIKAROVA VERDEIL, *La Musique byzantine chez les Bulgares et les Russes . . .* (1935); v.4, M. VELIMIROVIĆ, *Byzantine Elements in Early Slavic Chant* (1960). **Illustration credit:** (*b*) From MS in Edinburgh University Library.

[I. THOMAS]

BYZANTINE THEOLOGY, I (TO 1500)

The orthodox development of Christian doctrine in the Byzantine Church continued in conformity with the Christological teaching of the Council of *Chalcedon, in contradistinction to *Nestorianism and *Monophysitism. Byzantine theology developed during the period from the end of the patristic age to the fall of Constantinople in 1453, when it became a Greek or Hellenistic theology.

NATURE AND SOURCES

Byzantine theology remained faithful, generally speaking, to the dogmas defined by the first seven ecumenical councils and had great reverence for the writings of the *Fathers of the Church. It recognized the same Sacraments and the same ecclesiastical organization and was presided over by bishops whom the Roman Church acknowledged as true successors of the Apostles. Nevertheless, Byzantine and Latin theology are profoundly different. While they treat of the same matters, they deal with them diversely. What differentiates and even divides Latin from Byzantine theology is not so much the objects of belief as the manner of dealing with them. It is a question of mentality or *esprit*.

Spiritual Platonism. The Byzantine approach to theology is primarily influenced by a spiritual *Platonism that considers the world as an epiphany or appearance of a superior world. The Gospel of John and the Platonizing Fathers of the first 5 centuries formed Oriental and Byzantine Christian thought. This thought insists on the separation between the visible world and the invisible world. What one sees here below are the changing, imperfect things. Behind these beings there is the true unchanging Being that the soul will contemplate happily in immortal life. The hereafter is the sole end of man's destiny and of all worldly activity.

Visible creation is admired as the work of the Divinity, but this vision will never fully satisfy the ineffable desire of the human spirit. As long as the soul is confined to the body, it will not attain that of which it is capable. Thus, Byzantine theology considers the corporeal envelope of the senses as a prison; with the Apostle Paul it groans for liberation from the body and considers death as an accomplishment or gain. The Fourth Gospel and the Apocalypse express this tension of the soul in striving after Him who is the way, the truth, and the life.

The Platonizing method of Byzantine theology does not look for immanent ideas in things or a rational explanation after the fashion of the Aristotelian method; for this reason, supernatural reality, with which revelation is concerned, is enveloped in mystery. It is something spiritual, and consequently not comprehensible to the soul immersed in the material as in a prison. Byzantine theology does not seek out reasons to justify the intelligibility of the supernatural in the natural order; it does not attempt to build the supernatural upon nature, nor does it consider the human spirit as naturally Christian. Speculative Byzantine theology is therefore not highly developed or systematic. It is rather mystical, liturgical, scriptural, patristic, and eclectic.

As human reason is incapable of comprehending the supernatural, or the divine side of the Christian mystery that is revelation, there are few dogmas in Byzantine theology, few rational explanations of revealed truths. There are *theologoumena*, or truths that can be accepted without being clothed with dogmatic value to be imposed as the faith for all. Byzantine theology does not admit of a well-determined, proximate rule of faith and leaves much room for belief. There is a tendency simply to identify dogma with revelation, the human and contingent expression of the revealed truth with the revealed truth itself.

In Byzantine theology revelation is a determined sum of supernatural truths fixed from all eternity; there is little dogmatic progress in the theological science of revealed doctrine. According to Bulgakov, dogmas are the markers or limits beyond which orthodox doctrine should not strive to pass. Not having a permanent, living magisterium, Byzantine theology does not try to penetrate the revealed truths received from tradition through reason; but it tries to live them in a mystical and liturgical atmosphere. This is why Byzantine theology has not produced a powerful rational synthesis, but rather, particular treatises dealing with controverted questions, frequently merely repeating the arguments of others. *Aristotelianism had more success among the Nestorians and Monophysites in the Orient. Despite his greatness, *John Damascene, who was actually a Syrian Melchite of Damascus, did not exercise an influence on Greek Byzantine thought in any way comparable to that of *Thomas Aquinas on Western theology.

Sources of Byzantine Theology. The Byzantines admit in general two sources of their theology: Scripture and tradition. Recent Greek, rather than Byzantine, theology seems to speak of but one sole source of revelation; this reflects the influence of Cyril Lucaris. For the canon of the Scripture, the Byzantine theologians followed the third and fourth synods of Carthage and the Council of Trullo (Quinisext 691), which with very little exception admitted Catholic teaching on both the NT and the Apocalypse and on the Deuterocanonical books of the OT. They attributed an infallible authority to all the books of Sacred Scripture, particularly as regards faith and morals, and taught that the Church is charged with the interpretation of Scripture by means of tradition. They speak of an active tradition, by which they mean the consent of the Church, or of the piety and liturgical sense, as well as the universal consciousness of the Church. Modern authors developed and emphasized this point.

Passive tradition comprises: the *creeds or symbols of faith, including the Nicene-Constantinopolitan, the Athanasian, and Apostles' Creeds; the *Apostolic Constitutions; the first seven councils before the separation of the Churches, to which are added the Quinisext of 691 and, usually, the Photian Council of 879–880. The doctrinal authority of the councils is infallible. Some moderns, including *Khomiakov, also attribute this infallibility to the Church "as already instructed." According to Bulgakov the councils are merely the expression of this infallibility. The Byzantines attribute dogmatic value also to certain synods, to the Apostolic canons, the *acts of the martyrs, the Liturgy, the usage of the ancient Church, the Fathers, and certain confessions of faith in recent theology, such as those of Dositheus and Peter *Moghila. Among the Fathers of the Church they venerate in particular the old, post-Nicene theologians: Athanasius, the Cappadocians, Maximus the Confessor, Pseudo-Dionysius, and John Damascene; and among the Latins, Pope Leo I and Augustine. They consider them as witnesses to tradition, and their consensus as a definite sign of the truth.

Christology. The *Apostolic Fathers, such as *Ignatius of Antioch, occupy the particular attention of the Byzantines in the discussion concerning the reality of Christ's humanity in controversy against the Docetists (*see* DOCETISM). In the 4th century it was the divinity of Christ that had to be defended against the Arians (*see* ARIANISM) leading to a deepening of the doctrine of the hypostatic union through definitions at the Councils of *Ephesus (431) and of *Chalcedon (451).

After the constitution of the great patriarchal churches of Constantinople, Alexandria, Antioch, and Jerusalem, these patriarchal centers were at rivalry not only for ecclesiastical supremacy but also for doctrinal control. The theological school of *Antioch, by stressing the twofold nature of Christ, provided a foundation for *Nestorianism; while the school of *Alexandria favored the divinity of Christ, and gave a foothold to

Fig. 1. Saints Basil the Great and John Chrysostom, a pair of iconostasis doors painted at Novgorod, c. 1450.

Monophysitism. The Alexandrian theologians, with their Platonizing tendencies under the guidance of Pantaenus, Clement, and Origen, attempted to reconcile Neoplatonism with an allegorical interpretation of Scripture; they tended to confuse the unity of the person in Christ with the two natures.

The school of Antioch, with its Aristotelianism and its teachers such as *Lucian of Antioch, *Dorotheus, *Paul of Samosata, and *Diodore of Tarsus, tried to reconcile Aristotelianism with a literal exegesis of Scripture, and not only tended to establish a division between the double nature in Christ, but introduced this division into the person of the Savior. The schools of *Edessa and of *Nisibis were attached to Antioch. Constantinople did not develop its own theological school; only under Emperor *Theodosius II was a school of philosophy founded to replace the pagan academies of the Greeks.

THE AGE OF JUSTINIAN

In the Justinian age, Byzantine theology was engaged in a battle against two excesses: Monophysitism and Nestorianism. *Proclus, the Patriarch of Constantinople (434–446), had begun this controversy and inspired a group of defenders of orthodoxy in the East. He gave an orthodox explanation of the hypostatic union in his Tome to the Armenians and in his Marian homilies. *Leontius of Byzantium (485–543) began as a Nestorian, then combatted both Nestorianism and Monophysitism, leaning in part on Origenism (see ORIGEN AND ORIGENISM). His principal works, the Three Books against the Eutychians and Nestorians and his Diversa Opuscula et Scholia, employed the Neoplatonic dialectic against the Aristotelian heresiarchs and established the orthodox relations between the human nature of Christ and His divine hypostasis or person. The human nature is a true and real nature belonging to the divine hypostasis.

The concepts of nature and of hypostasis or person were finally clarified by John Damascene. Meanwhile, Byzantine writers, and particularly Emperor *Justinian I (527–565), the fervent caesaropapal ruler and theologian, based their doctrine on *Cyril of Alexandria and attacked the Monophysites; Justinian rejected Origenism and condemned the *Three Chapters as Nestorian, using his own authority and that of the ecumenical Council of *Constantinople II (553), finally bending Pope *Vigilius to his will in this matter. While the Emperor admitted the doctrine of the Roman primacy, in practice he proclaimed the ruler's right to make doctrinal and ecclesiastical decisions. His *caesaropapism, particularly in ecclesiastical legislation, had a great influence on Byzantine Church development, in hierarchical structure and in disciplinary decrees for clerics and monks, as well as on matrimonial law. By inserting the famous canon 28 of the Council of Chalcedon concerning the privileges of the See of Constantinople as the second Rome, Justinian sowed the seed of discord between the churches of the Orient and that of Rome.

Patriarchal Rights. The Council of *Nicaea I (325) had recognized the patriarchal rights of the Sees of Alexandria and Antioch. The Council of *Constantinople I (381) changed the order of the sees established by Nicaea I and attributed the first rank and the "same privileges of honor" to Constantinople after Rome. The fathers at Chalcedon (451), despite their assertion that

Fig. 2. Pope St. Leo I, 14th-century fresco at Mistra, Greece, a rare Eastern depiction of the Latin saint.

they respected the sense of canon 3 of the Council of Constantinople I, actually gave Constantinople true jurisdiction over the Dioceses of Pontus, Asia, and Thrace; they suppressed the term "of honor" and added as justification the fact that old Rome enjoyed a primacy because it was the political capital. In itself the sense of canon 28 was disciplinary and canonical; but it could easily be employed in an abusive interpretation, to concede to the See of Constantinople the same powers over the East that Rome enjoyed in the West. Hence the papal legates and Pope Leo I rejected this canon. Before Justinian, canon 28 did not actually prevail in Byzantine theology; he gave it the attribute of law, and after him the Council in Trullo (691) and later Byzantine writers accepted it as such.

Monothelitism. Theological deviation appeared at this epoch in the guise of *Monothelitism that admitted but one, unique theandric operation in Christ. This doctrine was taught by the Patriarch of Constantinople, *Sergius I (610–638), and was adopted gradually by the Copts, Syrians, and Armenians. *Sophronius, Patriarch of Jerusalem (d. 638), was the first effective adversary of Monothelitism; he was aided by *Maximus the Confessor (d. 662), who during his journeys and by his contacts in Jerusalem and in Rome, particularly with Pope *Martin I, combatted both Monophysitism and Monothelitism. In his Florilegium he shows the influence of *Pseudo-Dionysius and Leontius of Byzantium, as he employed Neoplatonic philosophy and dialectic to combat these errors; he employed them also to explain the double will of Christ.

The doctrine of Maximus triumphed finally at the Council of *Constantinople III (681). Another Byzantine Melchite, John Damascene (d. 749), achieved a reputation as a great theologian in the 8th century. He is properly called the Thomas Aquinas of the East. He composed a series of ascetical, dogmatic, polemic, and poetic works. His *Fons cognitionis* (Πηγὴ τῆς γνώσεως) is a learned compilation of patristic authors, systematized in an Aristotelian, logical structure; it dealt with problems that later became matters of contention between the Latins and the Byzantines, such as the Immaculate Conception, the epiclesis, and purgatory. In the Christological domain he gave clear and orthodox testimony regarding the hypostatic union, the Eucharist, and the notions of nature and person, in his *De fide orthodoxa*. John achieved eminence also with his *Three Orations on Images,* in which he defended sacred icons against the iconoclastic Byzantine emperors of the Syrian dynasty. He distinguished between the worship of latria due to God, and the worship of dulia, due to the saints and their representations in images. In this cult, it is not the material of the image that is venerated but the person of the one who is depicted.

Council of Nicaea III. Under Empress *Irene, the veneration of images was vindicated with the Council of *Nicaea III (787). At the Synod of Constantinople (843), held under *Theodora (2) and Michael III (842–867), iconoclasm was definitively vanquished. As a souvenir of this event the Sunday of Orthodoxy was established. *Theodore the Studite, founder of the Studite monastery at Constantinople (798) and an ascetical and poetic writer, defended the Roman primacy and the cult of images with the same arguments as those used by John Damascene.

Carolingian Controversies. In the Carolingian age the Western theologians took an interest in the iconoclastic controversy of the Byzantines. Under Alcuin they opposed the iconophile doctrine defined at the Council of Nicaea III. In the collective work called the Carolingian Books (*Libri Carolini*) they attempted to achieve a *via media;* while they repudiated the exaggerations of the iconoclasts, they did not agree with the iconophiles that images were to be worshiped with the cult of dulia. This stemmed from a misunderstanding. Actually, for the Westerner the cult given to images is a relative worship, going directly to the person represented; while for the Oriental, the cult given to images is an external veneration or *proskynesis* that differs from the worship rendered to God and that given to the saints. Images, in the thought of John Damascene, possess a superior virtue because of their consecration and their quality as instruments by which God works miracles.

The Carolingian theologians also complained that the Council of Nicaea III had employed a formula proposed by Patriarch *Tarasius of Constantinople concerning the procession of the Holy Spirit "from the Father through the Son." They charged that this was a vague and even equivocal expression, giving the impression that the Holy Spirit was a creature. They defended the *filioque formula and accused Tarasius of dogmatic error. Pope Adrian came to the defense of the patriarch by showing that the formula "through the Son" was well founded among the Greek fathers. Thus the filioque dispute changed terrain and became a quarrel between the Carolingians and the Romans. At the behest of Charlemagne, Alcuin defended the filioque in his *Libellus de processione Spiritus Sancto.*

The Filioque. This difficulty was increased between the Byzantines and the Carolingians in 809, at a synod of Aix-la-Chapelle, when the formula "filioque" was introduced into the Creed in the Latin sung Mass. The Carolingians also supported the Latin monks on Mt. Olivet in Jerusalem, who defended the filioque against the Greek monks in the monastery of St. Sabas. For ecumenical reasons Pope Leo III did not approve the use of the filioque in the Mass. "Why approve the use of this formula without necessity," he asked, "when such an addition will favor a division between the East and the West?"

Another question that came to the fore at this time was the doctrine of the pentarchy. The defenders of images were in favor of a moderate pentarchy in attributing to the five patriarchs supreme power in the Church. By this they desired to prove that the Iconoclastic Synod, presided over by only one patriarch, was not legitimate. Their chief, Theodore the Studite, recognized the full powers of the five patriarchs in an ecumenical council but did not desire to downgrade the Roman primacy, which, according to him, was of divine right and was provided with the charism of infallibility and the principle of unity. For the defenders of the pentarchy, the Pauline idea of the Mystical Body of Christ suggested a concept of the Church in which all the members, with their head, the Roman sovereign pontiff, are united among themselves by the intermediary of the patriarchs, who hold a rank midway between the Roman pontiff and the bishops in the direction of the Church. However, in the 9th century, the Byzantines abused this interpretation of the Church to assert that it was not reconcilable with the monarchic structure defended by the Latins, and that as a consequence all the patriarchs were equal in dignity and power, including the Roman patriarch of the Latin Church.

THE PHOTIAN PERIOD: 9TH AND 10TH CENTURIES

After the suppression of the Ecumenical Academy in 726 by the iconoclastic Emperor Leo III, Michael III and his minister Bardas founded in 863 the University of the Imperial Palace of Constantinople. Profane sciences were taught at the university, and the professors were all laymen. Theology was cultivated by the monks of the Studite monastery, particularly under Theodore. Among the renowned lecturers at the university were Leo the Philosopher, Photius, and Constantine (Cyril), later the apostle of the Slavs. In the West, the secular and theological sciences were cultivated in the Carolingian Empire and in northern Italy. At Rome these studies were almost totally neglected. It was only under the Greeks in flight from the iconoclastic persecution that sacred studies began to flourish in Rome.

Photius became patriarch of Constantinople under Emperor Michael III in 858 in place of the deposed Ignatius. Because of his controversy against the Roman primate, as well as for his knowledge and virtue, Photius is held in great veneration by the Byzantine Orthodox Church. It should be remarked, however, that the knowledge of Photius was more encyclopedic than profound, and that his integrity was tarnished by his intrigues against Patriarch Ignatius and the Roman See.

Responsibility of Photius. More recently F. Dvornik has attempted to diminish the responsibility of Photius in the break between the two Churches. In his opinion

Photius would have opposed the Pope only in the beginning; and his reinstallation in the patriarchal see after the resignation of Ignatius would have been approved by the Pope. Likewise, in Dvornik's view, Photius lived in peace with the Church of Rome until his death. As regards his doctrine, Photius admitted the inspiration of the Deuterocanonical books; he interpreted the Sacred Scriptures in a literal and historical sense. The Fathers of the Church, from whom he omitted the pre-Nicaeans, the Latins, and even John Damascene, are in his estimation the authentic interpreters of the Bible and witnesses to tradition. He used Aristotelian dialectic adroitly in his polemics against the Latins, particularly in the subtle questions of the procession of the Holy Spirit, not hesitating to reverse himself when the Roman-Byzantine relations took a more favorable turn for him.

In his writings before his break with the Latins (867), as in his letters to Zachary of Armenia, to King Boris Michael of Bulgaria, to Pope Nicholas I (860; containing his profession of faith), and in another letter to the same Pope in 862 with his apology for his election to the patriarchate, he taught nothing contrary to the faith of the Roman Church, even though he mentioned diverse liturgical and disciplinary uses. In these letters Photius also clearly admitted the primacy of St. Peter.

Primacy of Rome. As for the primacy of the Roman pontiffs there is nothing explicit. While he rejected the Synod of Sardica (c. 13) quoted by Pope Nicholas, it seems that Photius was merely refuting the argument against the legitimacy of his own election. Besides, the allusions in the writings of Photius during this period and his whole attitude toward the Pope show how much he prized papal approbation of his election. This must be said against those who would interpret his actions as tactical rather than dictated by conviction. But Photius tried in vain to convince the Pope to confirm his election, and this certainly disposed him against the Roman See. Yet he did not immediately break with Rome. The occasion arose in the course of the conflict over Bulgaria.

Boris of Bulgaria was conquered by the Byzantines in 865 and baptized by them, but he turned toward Rome, despite the fact that Photius as patriarch sent him a dogmatic letter on the Christian faith and believed that the Byzantine Church should exercise jurisdiction over Bulgaria. Boris was motivated by political resentment against Byzantium. He maltreated and expelled the Byzantine missionaries and addressed himself to Pope Nicholas. The latter wrote his famous *Letter to the Bulgarians*. Photius in furious reaction convoked the Synod of 867, which condemned the Latins and addressed an *Encyclical Letter to the Oriental Thronos* inviting them to an ecumenical council called in Constantinople that same year. This council excommunicated the Latins and deposed Pope Nicholas as illegitimately elected. But immediately afterward, Emperor Michael was assassinated and his successor, Basil I the Macedonian, reestablished peace between the two Churches, reinstated Ignatius as patriarch, and expelled Photius.

After the death of Ignatius (878), Photius resumed the patriarchate until his exile in 886. During this period a relative peace existed between Byzantium and Rome. Photius had not changed in his resentment, nor in his doctrine regarding the procession of the Holy Spirit, as is evident, for example, in his *Mystagogia*, written at this time. It is probable that he had at least a fragmentary knowledge of the Latin replies to his attacks, even though he knew no Latin. But he passed over the recriminations against the liturgical and disciplinary usages in silence and his older arguments against the Roman primacy. He made an indirect attempt to weaken the primatial authority of Rome.

The Ecumenical Council of 869–870 anathematized Photius for favoring new dogmas and for deceit. He had had predecessors who in word and deed had acted independently of the Roman See and admitted the Roman primacy when it pleased them. Before Photius no Byzantine employed the phrase "from the Father alone" of the Holy Spirit, but said rather "from the Father through the Son." The doctrine of Photius on the active inspiration of the Father alone is certainly contrary to the tradition of the Fathers with the exception of one or other who used the Alexandrian formula "from the Father through the Son," but limited the function of the spiriting principle to the Father, and understood "through the Son" as including only the temporal mission of the Holy Spirit. Duns Scotus came close to this Byzantine opinion on the procession "through the Son" in his work *De divisione naturae*.

Photius to Michael Cerularius. There is little evidence for the relations between Rome and Byzantium during this period. Basil I considered the quarrels between the two churches as an internal affair of the clergy and the partisans of Ignatius and Photius. Patriarch *Nicholas I Mysticus anathematized Emperor Leo VI (912), who was already dead, and with him, all who had admitted the legitimacy of the Emperor's fourth marriage, among whom was the Pope, Sergius III. Although the Photian attacks were not repeated, his doctrinal attitudes prevailed. As the Byzantine Empire was then at the apex of its influence, the Church propagated its doctrine among the Slavs and Arabs. However, the 10th century produced no Byzantine theologian of renown, despite the writings of Arethas of Caesarea, Nicetas of Byzantium, George of Nicomedia, and particularly Emperors *Leo VI the Wise and *Constantine Porphyrogenitus with their homilies, as well as Patriarchs Eutychius of Alexandria and the saintly Euthymius (d. 917) of Constantinople. These authors held the procession of the Holy Spirit "from the Father through the Son" and favored the prerogatives of Constantinople against Rome. Yet there were Byzantine authors in this period who admitted the Roman primacy, including Nicholas of Paphlagonia, a student of both Arethas and Photius. The Byzantines were interested in defending Christianity against the Mohammedans and Jacobites. Among them were those who bore excellent witness to the Mother of God (*Theotokos), whom the Byzantines exalted by literary and rational arguments rather than by a profound search of revelation. In their Marian homilies they went back to the ancient theses of the Marian feasts: her perpetual virginity, her bodily assumption, her mediation through intercession, and her holiness at the moment of her conception.

THE BREAK WITH ROME

After the formal break between the Churches of Rome and Byzantium under Patriarch *Michael Cerularius (1042–59), tension grew. During this period many popes, including Alexander II, Gregory VII, and Urban II, tried to reestablish unity, but in vain. The

Fig. 3. The Virgin and Child with two saints, Byzantine ivory statuette of the second half of the 10th century.

lower clergy and the monks in particular were opposed, as also were the Patriarchs *John VIII Xiphilinus and *Nicholas III, who made use of the title "Ecumenical Patriarch" and tried to turn the Melchites, Nestorians, and Monophysites of the Diaspora against Rome. With the *Crusades and the founding of the Latin Kingdom of Jerusalem (1099), matters worsened between the two Churches.

Spread of the Schism. Question was raised concerning the validity of the excommunication hurled at *Michael Cerularius and his followers by Cardinal Humbert on July 16, 1054, since Pope Leo IX (d. April 19, 1054) was

dead at this time. The mutual excommunications themselves were directed at the persons and not the Churches, but unhappily the schism that resulted spread to the other patriarchates of the East, and it was further fomented by the schools. The university founded at Constantinople in 1045 by *Constantine IX Monomachus had faculties of philosophy and law and exercised an influence on Byzantine thought. There was also a patriarchal school for theology that held a middle position between the university and the monastery schools. In the latter two, theology was taught in a positive fashion, while at the university Michael Psellus tried to apply hellenistic philosophy to the revealed doctrines. Michael Cerularius had contributed to the separation of the churches not only by his hostile attitude toward the papal legates in his *Edictum Synodale,* read to the people on July 20, 1054, in Hagia Sophia, but also by his writings (such as his *Epistula ad Petrum Antiochenum*) on the errors of the Latins, by his *Panoplia,* and by his *Epistula Leonis Achridensis.* Michael accused the Latins of liturgical deviations and dogmatic errors concerning the azymes or unleavened bread, the Saturday fast, abstinence, Baptism, the veneration of images, lack of respect for the Greek Fathers, the filioque, and the Roman primacy; 22 accusations in all, which were repeated by contemporary writers.

Hostile Influences. The Studite monk *Nicetas Stethatos, called Pectoratus (d. after 1054), left a number of works on spiritual theology and on controversy with the Jews, Armenians, and Latins (such as his *Spiritual Paradise* and *De fermentato et azymo contra armenios et latinos*). Leo of Ochrida, the Bulgarian archbishop, accused the Latins, in a letter to John of Apulia, of liturgical deviations, such as not chanting the Alleluia during Lent. The Patriarch of Antioch, Peter III, in his *Epistula ad Dominicum Gradensem* and in other writings, also brought up these questions, particularly that of the azymes. But he seemed to act as a supporter of peace, saying that he would absolve the Latins of all abuses if they would leave the filioque out of the Creed.

An anonymous *Contra francos aliosque latinos* in the second half of the 11th century brought the number of accusations to 28; this had great influence on the hostile mentality of the Byzantines and led Michael Cerularius to consider the filioque as heretical. Michael did not attack the Roman primacy directly but insisted on breaking with the Pope, whom he considered in heresy, and said it was not traditional to remain in communion with heretics, even the head of a Church. If the head of the fish is rotting, he asked, how can the body be salutary? Peter of Antioch, who deplored the schism, actually held for the pentarchy, according to which the church under one head alone, Christ, was governed by the five patriarchs as equals. But the question of unleavened bread was principal at this period. The Byzantines maintained that when Christ instituted the Eucharist, the Jews did not have unleavened bread.

Michael Psellus. Among the Byzantine theologians who tried to apply a Platonizing philosophy to the dogmas of the Trinity and Christology was Michael *Psellus the Younger (d. 1078). He was a poet, historian, and philosopher. Only part of his works have been published, but he used both an Aristotelian and Platonizing approach to the Trinity and Christology and was accused by the monastic schools of Neoplatonizing. He admitted the procession "from the Father alone," a certain material essence in the angels, the holiness of the Mother of God at her conception, and her mediatorship. *John Italus (d. 1084), of Calabria, succeeded Psellus as rector of the university. But he had to resign his professorial chair due to the accusation of Hellenization made by the monks under Emperor Alexius Comnenus. Eleven anathemas were brought against Psellus in the *Synodicon* of the first Sunday of Lent (1082), called the Sunday of Orthodoxy. This gave a death blow to speculation in Byzantine theology.

These theologians were accused of attempting to rationalize the mysteries of the Trinity and the Incarnation. In the same current were Theodore Prodromus, a humanist rather than theologian, Euthymius *Zigabenus, who in the second section of his *Panoplia dogmatica* furnished rational expositions for the service of theology that were fairly profound; John Mauropus, the master of Psellus; and Michael Italicus.

One of the better theologians of the time was Theophylactus, Metropolitan of Bulgaria (d. 1108), disciple of Psellus and lecturer in the patriarchal school at Constantinople. Among his writings were his *Enarrationes in 4 Evangelia; Commentaria in V. et N. Testamenta;* and *Vita St. Clementis Bulgaris.* His opuscule *De üs quorum Latini incusantur* gives an exact idea of the problems being disputed between the Latin and Greek churches. He differed with those who accused the Roman Church of heresy. He appeared to reject the Roman primacy but admitted the primacy of Peter. He said the deficiency of the Latin language was responsible for their confusion on the filioque between the "eternal procession" and the "temporal sending" of the Holy Spirit. He would allow the filioque in private usage if the Son were not considered a *principium,* or cause.

Positive Theologians. Concerning the two principal doctrines of the Trinity and Christology, the positive theologians had a better position after the condemnation of Psellus and his school. Along with Euthymius Zigabenus, whose *Panoplia dogmatica* was a new version of the Photian *Libellus* with attention to the opinions of the Greek Fathers and some of the Latins, were Andronicus Camateros, with his *Sacrum Armentarium,* and Nicetas Acominatus and his *Thesaurus Orthodoxiae,* who both followed the official doctrine of Constantinople in the dispute with the Latins. John Phurnensis, Eustratius of Nicaea, A. Demetrakopoulus, Nicetas Seides, and Nicholas of Methone did likewise, although through their interest in the Fathers they departed from the attitude of Photius.

Nicetas of Maronia, in his *Dialogues on the Holy Spirit,* affirmed that the Holy Spirit proceeded immediately from the Son and through the Son from the Father as from a primary and original cause. He hoped to arrive at a compromise by requesting the Latins to suppress the filioque in the Creed if the Greeks would admit that the Holy Spirit proceeds from the Father through the Son, or even from the Father and the Son, understanding the *ex filio* in accord with the Fathers as *ex principio immediato,* and not *ex principio carente principio.* During all this period, however, these authors repeated the old Cerularian accusations.

Pentarchy. The Byzantine concept of the pentarchy had evolved at the end of the 12th century into a system against the Roman primacy. The canonist Theodore *Balsamon (d. after 1195) contributed to this development with his *Commentary on the Canons* and in his *Responsum de Patriarcharum privilegiis,* in which he dealt with the origin, privileges, and equality in dignity of all the patriarchs. He admitted the apostolic origin of the three Patriarchates of Jerusalem, Antioch, and Alexandria. The Patriarchate of Rome had its origin with Constantine I, and that of Constantinople with the Council of Constantinople I (381). This theory was sustained by the Byzantines and the Slavs up to the 17th century with few exceptions. The other questions agitated during this period were the cult of images, as something absolute, a position sustained by Leo of Chalcedon, but who was condemned for this reason; and the sacrifice in the Liturgy of the Mass, that is not offered to the

Fig. 4. *Abraham and the Three Heavenly Visitors, Russian icon of the 14th century. In Eastern art, the Holy Trinity is usually symbolized by this Old Testament event.*

Word (Christ offers and is offered), a position sustained by Soterichus Panteugenus of Antioch, Eustathius Dyrrachiensis, and Michael of Thessalonica, all of whom were condemned at the Synod of Constantinople of 1157. The Synod of 1166 gave an explanation of the words "the Father is greater than I" (Jn 14.28), which refer to Christ as man, and not solely to the humanity in Christ.

The Council of Lyons. Byzantine theology in the 13th century gravitated around the Council of Lyons (1274), as a preparation or a consequence, with one nuance before the Latin occupation of Constantinople (1204–61) and another nuance after the occupation. During the Latin Empire of the East (1204–1393) the controversy with the Latins became acute under the brothers John and Nicholas Mesarites, the first a monk and exegete, and the other the metropolitan of Ephesus. The two engaged in conferences with the Latins in which the question of the Roman primacy was discussed and combatted by the Byzantines with new arguments. It was asserted that Peter was not the first bishop of Rome, but Linus; and that it was not Rome but Jerusalem or Antioch that should enjoy the primatial right. This idea is found in John Camateros (d. 1206) of Constantinople in his *Letters to Pope Innocent III.*

Many authors taught the Photian doctrine on the procession of the Holy Spirit. At this period the problem of purgatory appeared for the first time. Georgius III Bardanes, Metropolitan of Corfu, denied the fire of purgatory (1231) for venial sins not expiated on earth, and also denied immediate retribution after death. This idea became a common Byzantine teaching. The Franciscan Bartholomeus answered Georgius, and Pope Leo IV took up the question of purgatory in his letter to the legate in Cyprus (1254); Leo also brought up the problem of fornication, which the Greeks did not consider a mortal sin.

Principal Arguments. The Tract against the Errors of the Greeks of the Dominican Bartholomew of Byzantium (1252) gave a résumé of the principal Greek arguments and the Latin responses. After the transfer of the imperial government from Nicaea back to Constantinople under Michael Palaeologus in 1261, two tendentious factions controlled the religious thought of the capital: the zealot monks and the learned courtiers and courtesans. Michael persecuted the *zealots, who, with the deposed patriarch Arsenius, violently opposed the Emperor's efforts to approach Rome.

The writings of the monk *Nicephorus Blemmydes (d. 1272) contributed to the cause of union, particularly in clarifying the question of the procession of the Spirit. Nicephorus did not approve the addition of the filioque in the Creed. His teaching deviated from that of Photius far enough, however, to admit the procession "from the Father and Son" or "through the Son," admitting that the Holy Spirit was the Spirit of the Son for he pertained to the Son essentially. His critics said that the formula *per filium* in Blemmydes' thought signified the mediation of the Son in the eternal procession of the Spirit. This mediation was essential but not actual, according to V. Grumel, while Gordillo sees it as an active principle of the Holy Spirit in so far as the Son receives it from the Father. Blemmydes' doctrine, at once positive, patristic, and catholic, on the procession, had great influence on many Byzantines, including the Patriarch *John XI Beccus, and helped prepare a mentality that would affect the discussion of union at the Council of Lyons.

Rejection of the Roman Primacy. It was precisely the charge that the Latin Church taught heresy in this matter that occasioned the rejection of the Roman primacy. The council under Pope *Gregory X and Michael Palaeologus favored the Byzantine approach. Although its acts have been lost, it condemned extreme positions and decreed that the Holy Spirit proceeded not from two principles, or two spirations, but from the Father as principle, and from the Son through spiration. Accord was reached in regard to purgatory, the immediate retribution after death, and the Sacraments; mention was also made of the unleavened bread for the Eucharist and the Roman primacy.

This reunion was not brought about solely by external political pressure. Gregory Acropolites, who taught after the Council, sincerely held the Roman doctrine on the Holy Spirit and the primacy, as his homily on the Apostles Peter and Paul clearly indicates. However, the monks and lower clergy, as well as certain members of the imperial family, rejected the union despite the efforts of the Emperor. Pope *Martin IV felt constrained on Nov. 18, 1281, to excommunicate the refractory Byzantines, and a synod at Constantinople under Emperor Andronicus II declared the union at an end in 1283. Andronicus expelled John Beccus from the patriarchate. Besides Beccus, Constantinus Melitiniotes, George *Metochites, and the Dominican theologians living in Byzantium had written in favor of the union; George Moschabarus, a professor at the ecumenical Didascaleion, Patriarch Gregorius II, Maximus *Planudes, and the followers of Arsenius had vigorously opposed it. There had been falsifications of the texts of the Fathers in the course of the controversy. Gregorius II in his *Tomus fidei* even said he had found a patristic text justifying "an eternal illumination which the Spirit received from the Son, and reflected in having his Being from the Father."

Between the Councils of Lyons and Florence. A number of theological academies were organized in the 13th and 14th centuries, of which the more important was that at the monastery of Chora founded by Nicephorus *Gregoras. In the patriarchal school and university at Constantinople, under the stimulus of Andronicus III and Manuel II, along with jurisprudence and philosophy, theology was taught in a fashion affected by Western methods. The works of Thomas Aquinas, translated into Greek by the *Cydones brothers in the 14th century, and especially by George (*Gennadius) Scholarius in the 15th, had considerable influence. Meanwhile, the question of Palamism became a burning issue. Besides the official theology, a current of ascetical and spiritual ideas were fomented in the monasteries. One of these manifestations could be traced back at least to the writings of John Climacus in the 6th century, author of the *Ladder of Paradise,* and a monk on Mt. Sinai. He described the rise of the soul toward God in a series of steps after the 30 steps of Jacob's Ladder. The 29th step resembles stoic impassibility and describes a state in which through asceticism the flesh has been incorruptible in the sense that all sensation has been subordinated to the reaching after transcendent Being. John is an important link binding later Byzantine spirituality to Neoplatonism as well as to the *Desert Fathers and the *Fathers of the Church. This current of spirituality included the works of Dionysius the Areopagite (*see* PSEUDO-DIONYSIUS), whose mystical thought was preserved in the monasteries, and the commentary on the Books of Solomon by an anonymous 8th-century author inspired by the Neoplatonism of Maximus, the disciple of Dionysius; and it was related to the thought of *Symeon the New Theologian, who maintained that mystical contemplation was incompatible with life in the world. It lead directly to Palamism.

Palamism. Gregory *Palamas (d. 1359), a noble Asiatic educated at the imperial court, who became a monk on Mt. Athos, taught a real distinction between the divine essence and the divine operation. This doctrine occasioned a strange form of asceticism and *Hesychasm, in which the soul liberated from the passions could arrive at the sight of divine light, such as that which surrounded Christ in the transfiguration on Mt. *Thabor. Under the influence of *Gregory Sinaites, author of *Quietude and Two Methods of Prayer,* of Nicephorus Haghiorita in the 14th century, and of the commentaries of Symeon the New Theologian, who wrote tracts on *Prayers and Practical Theological Chapters,* as well as *Books of Divine Love,* Hesychasm underwent a degenerating influence. Palamas maintained that the Taborite light was distinct although inseparable from the Divine Essence. It was the Divine energy or opera-

tion whose contemplation was a form of deification due to grace and the beatific vision. Barlaam of Calabria, Gregorius Akindynos, and Nicephorus Gregoras opposed the Palamite theology, and Palamism was condemned by the Patriarch *John XIV Calecas in 1344. The Patriarch Callistus, the homily writer, condemned Barlaam in 1351, and Palamism was restored as an authentic form of Byzantine theology; Palamas himself became archbishop of Thessalonica. The condemnations against Barlaam were added to the *Synodicon* read each year on the Sunday of Orthodoxy, and Palamas was considered a saint after 1368.

Disciples of Palamas. Among the disciples of Palamas were David *Dishypatos, author of a *Dialogue,* Nilus *Cabasilas (d. 1363), successor to Palamas in the See of Thessalonica and author of *Regula theologica, De causis dissensionum in Ecclesia, De papae imperio,* and long treatises on the procession of the Holy Spirit; *Philotheus Coccinus (d. 1376), first abbot on Mt. Athos, then metropolitan of Heraclea, and finally patriarch of Constantinople, who wrote *Contra Nicephorum Gregoram, Three Dissertations* on Palamite doctrine, an *Encomium* of Gregory Palamas, and other liturgical works (he canonized Palamas in 1368); and Theophanes, Metropolitan of Nicaea (d. 1381), author of *A Sermon in Honor of the Theotokos, Five Books on the Living Light of Mt. Tabor, Seven Books against the Jews, Against the Latins . . ., On the Procession of the Holy Spirit,* and numerous letters.

*John VI Cantacuzenus (d. 1383), the emperor, wrote against the adversaries of Palamas. Nicolas *Cabasilas, the nephew of Nilus Cabasilas, was the author of two well-known tracts, *Seven Books on the Life of Christ* (a remarkable ascetical work) and an *Interpretation of Sacred Liturgy;* he wrote also a pamphlet *Against the Ravings of Gregoras,* and also three Marian homilies. Matthew Angelus Panaretus was a determined adversary of the Latins in the 14th century, who wrote some 18 works against them. Simeon of Thessalonica (d. 1429) was a writer of irenic tendencies, and was attached to tradition; he composed a *Dialogue* against heresy and an *Exposition of the Divine Temple and the Sacred Liturgy.* He denied the infallibility of the pope but admitted the Roman primacy. Demetrius Chrysoloras (d. 1430), a friend of Michael Palaeologus, wrote some 100 letters against the enemies of Palamas and a series of dialogues (unedited). Joseph *Bryennios (d. c. 1435), a monk of Crete and of the Studion, also proved a determined adversary of reunion. He wrote some 49 chapters on various theological, philosophical, and moral questions.

Anti-Palamites. Of the anti-Palamite theologians *Barlaam of Calabria (d. 1348), a monk who lived in Constantinople and enjoyed imperial favor, was charged with various diplomatic and religious missions. He was an adversary of Nicephorus Gregoras and Gregory Palamas. After his condemnation in 1341, he returned to his own country as a bishop and became a Catholic. In his earlier writings he had zealously opposed the Latins and later used the same zeal and courage against the Palamites. He was the author of an *Adversus umbilicanimos* and *Adversus Messalianos* and other minor writings and letters in favor of the Roman faith. Among the other adversaries of Palamas were *Gregorius Akindynos (d. c. 1350), who wrote against both Barlaam and Palamas and was condemned with Barlaam;

and Nicephorus Gregoras (d. 1360), who wrote *Eleven Orations against Gregory Palamas, Historia Byzantina,* Marian homilies, and on the reform of the calendar. Prochorus *Cydones (d. *c.* 1368) translated the works of Thomas Aquinas and Augustine and wrote on the Divine Essence and operation and on the divine light of Mt. Thabor. He suffered much because of his ideas against Palamas. Demetrius *Cydones (d. 1400) also translated part of the *Summa* and the *Contra Gentiles* of Aquinas and wrote *On Contempt of Death.* John Cyparissiota, called the Wise, was one of the principal adversaries of Palamas and composed *Four Books of Palamitic Transgressions,* to which he added a fifth book against Nilus Cabasilas, and an elementary exposition of theology. Manuel Calecas (d. 1410) was a Byzantine Dominican and author of *On the Principle of the Catholic Faith, On the Procession of the Holy Spirit,* and *Four Books against the Greeks.* Maximus Chrysoberges (d. after 1410), also a Dominican, wrote on the procession of the Holy Spirit.

While the adversaries of Palamism utilized theological information and the distinctions found in the works of Aquinas, the Palamite group repudiated this type of theological argument. In the controversy over the Holy Spirit, they refuted the Thomistic arguments in favor of the filioque. Barlaam and Nilus Cabasilas maintained that Latins could not demonstrate the procession of the Holy Spirit by dialectical methods and appealed to the doctrine of *Duns Scotus. Nilus searched for new arguments against the Roman primacy, but recommended the convocation of a general council to put an end to schism.

Nilus distinguished two phases of papal power; that which the pope held as the bishop of Rome, and that which he held as the legitimate successor of Peter. He enjoyed power as *primus episcoporum,* which the conciliar fathers and the emperors, not Christ or St. Peter, had conferred on him. Peter had indeed received the primacy by divine right, but he had not transmitted these extraordinary powers to his successors, since he enjoyed them as a personal privilege. The bishop of Rome is the successor of St. Peter in the same manner in which other bishops are the successors of the Apostles without inheriting apostolic powers. Nilus added that the Roman pontiffs are fallible in questions of faith, as history demonstrated, and that other sees had had recourse to Rome for a testimony of mutual charity and to preserve order and unity.

Epiclesis. During this period the controversy over the Epiclesis arose. After the words of Consecration in their liturgy, the Byzantine rite employed a prayer in which the Father was asked to send the Holy Spirit to change (*transmutare*) the holy gifts into the body and blood of the Savior. According to more recent research the words *ea transmutans* in the liturgy of St. John Chrysostom are not found in the ancient Armenian translation of this liturgy (5th century) or in the codex of Grottaferatta. These words would seem to have been added in the Athens codex in the 15th or 16th centuries. However, in the 13th century an Armenian, Vartanus Magnus, mentioned the question; and in the second half of the 14th century a Latin writer approached the Byzantines for the employment of the words of the Epiclesis in the liturgy. Nicholas Cabasilas was the first Byzantine writer to defend the legitimacy of the Epiclesis, and after Nicholas, this subject became a regular anti-

Orthodox recrimination. At first Byzantine theologians defended its place in the canon of the liturgy; later they attributed a consecratory power to the Epiclesis as completing the words of the Savior. In his book on the *Exposition of the Sacred Liturgy* (ch. 29), Nicholas Cabasilas, in answer to the Latins, said that this prayer was legitimate and useful in the liturgy, on a par with the other prayers and the other Sacraments. He claimed that the *Supplices rogamus* of the Latin liturgy was an Epiclesis. Besides, he maintained, it was necessary, because the words of the Savior achieved the Consecration not in so much as pronounced by the priest in a narrative fashion but by the priest as such provided with sacerdotal power; and this power is the grace of the Holy Spirit. It is only when the priest pronounces the Epiclesis after the words of the Savior that one becomes aware that the priest desires to use the sacerdotal power, that is, the power of the Holy Spirit who makes him a minister of the sacred mystery. While Nicholas did not enter into the problem of the exact moment in which the Consecration takes place in the liturgy, Simeon of Thessalonica, in his *Exposition of the Divine Temple,* maintained that the sign of the cross and the inclination after the Epiclesis was an indication that the Consecration took place during the Epiclesis, and he quoted the Liturgy of St. Basil as supporting this theory (ch. 87). Thus the way was open for the Byzantines at the Council of Florence; they maintained that Consecration came with both the Epiclesis and the words of the Savior; or even through the Epiclesis alone, as the Byzantines and Greeks thought after the 17th century.

Byzantine Mariology. Since the time of Photius at least, Marian questions had been treated in homilies. The 14th century became the golden age for Byzantine Mariology. Theophane of Nicaea (d. 1381), in his *Oration for the Most Holy Theotokos,* taught that the Mother of God from the first moment of her existence possessed all creaturely perfections, particularly in the supernatural order, with the plentitude of graces. She is thus the source of man's salvation, the mediatrix between God and man. But as a Palamite, Theophane exaggerated in speaking of the relations between the Mother of God and the Divine Persons. He maintained that the Palamites excelled in extolling the privileges of Mary, such as the Immaculate Conception, the divine maternity, the perpetual virginity, the universal mediation through intercession, her bodily assumption, and her royalty.

The Byzantines taught that Marian mediation implied the cooperation of Mary in the work of man's deification. The privilege is extended to all intelligent creatures, men and angels, to whom the gifts and privileges of the "new creature" were accorded. With the exception of Nicholas Cabasilas, Byzantine theology did not enter into the question of the coredemption. The historian Nicephorus Callistus, in his *Synaxaria,* expressed certain doubts on the Immaculate Conception. In his explanation of the Marian hymn in the liturgy that she is worthy of all praise, he added that the Mother of God had been purified of original sin by the Holy Spirit at the Incarnation, but no one imitated him until the 16th century. On the contrary, Byzantine theologians had excluded Mary from the taint of original sin, imitating the Franciscans who maintained that as a consequence of her original purity she was created in the state of original justice.

Fig. 5. The Dormition of the Virgin, icon painted by an artist of the school of Moscow in the 16th century.

The Council of Florence. In preparation for the Council of *Florence, the Emperor had assembled several theologians in Constantinople under Patriarch Joseph, for example, *Bessarion, *Isidore of Kiev, and Marcus *Eugenicus of Ephesus; to the council, with representatives of all the metropolitans, he brought the lay theologians George Scholarius (later Patriarch Gennadius II) and Gemistos *Plethon for lack of well-trained ecclesiastics. Joseph's opinion before departing for the West was naïve; he felt that the Greeks would simply demonstrate the Latin errors for the Roman theologians, and that because the Orthodox teaching faithfully represented the tradition of the Fathers of the Church, their adversaries could not but be convinced.

When the debate proved otherwise at the council, Joseph showed heroic forbearance, and with the advice of Bessarion, Isidore, and George Scholarius, little by little the Greeks conceded that the two positions on the processions of the Holy Spirit, on purgatory, and on the Consecration of the Eucharist could be harmonized. The papal primacy was accepted with the provision that nothing would be done to interfere with the Oriental rites and customs. Nothing was said of moral issues such as marriage and divorce. The only dissenter at the council was Mark Eugenicus. After his return he began a violent campaign against the union and produced innumerable theological tracts that prevailed among the lower clergy and the monks. The union was defended by Bessarion and Isidore of Kiev and some of the Byzantine refugees in the West after the fall of *Constantinople (1453). But with that catastrophe, Byzantine theological production as such ended.

See also PHOTIUS, PATRIARCH OF CONSTANTINOPLE; BYZANTINE CHURCH, HISTORY OF.

Bibliography: Denz. CSCO. DTC, Tables générales 1:1898–1919. H. G. BECK, LexThK² 2:860–863. E. A. VOETZSCH and H. G. BECK, RGG³ 1:1573–78. M. JUGIE, EncCatt 2:1696–99; *Theologica dogmatica christianorum orientalium*, 5 v. (Paris 1926–35). M. GORDILLO, *Theologia orientalium cum latinorum comparata* (OrChrAnal 158; 1960); *Mariologia orientalis* (ibid. 141; 1954). A. PALMIERI, *Theologia dogmatica orthodoxa*, 2 v. (Florence 1911–13). J. MEYENDORFF, *Orthodoxie et catholicité* (Paris 1965). Krumbacher. Beck KTLBR. J. GILL, *The Council of Florence* (Cambridge, Eng. 1959). S. RUNCIMAN, *Byzantine Civilisation* (New York 1933; pa. 1956). Important articles or studies have been pub. over many years in: *The Christian East* (London 1920–   ). ÉchosOr. Irénikon. OrChrPer. RevÉtByz. DumbOaksP. **Illustration credits:** Fig. 3, Courtesy of the Dumbarton Oaks Collections. Fig. 2, R. V. Schoder, SJ. Figs. 1, 4, and 5, George R. Hann Collection, Sewickley Heights, Pennsylvania.

[V. MALANCZUK]

BYZANTINE THEOLOGY, II (FROM 1500 TO PRESENT)

On May 29, 1453, when the Moslem Turks captured Constantinople and put an end to the Byzantine Empire, the development of Byzantine theology ceased. From 1500 on theology was written by Greek-speaking Orthodox and Uniate Catholics inhabiting what had been the Byzantine Empire. It is this body of material that is designated Byzantine theology. A more exact term would be Greek theology of the Byzantine tradition.

This article deals with Greek theology: (1) from 1500 until the patriarchate of Cyril *Lucaris (1612); (2) from Cyril Lucaris to the Synod of Constantinople (1723); (3) from 1723 to the constitution of the autocephalous Church of Greece (1833); (4) from 1833 until 1923; and (5) from 1923 to the present.

First Period: 1500 to 1612. Even though the patriarchal school continued to function in Constantinople under the guidance of Matthaeus Kamariotas during the reign of Mohammed II, theological centers of learning were gradually suppressed. Among the Orthodox, the Slavs, especially in Kiev and Moscow, utilized their independence of Constantinople and began to develop their own Slav theology (*see* RUSSIAN THEOLOGY). Greek students migrated to theological universities in the West, especially in Germany, Italy, and England. Their initiation into non-Orthodox theology resulted eventually in grouping into three types of theologian depending upon one or another emphasis: (1) the conservative, rigid followers of early Byzantine theology who would accept no influence from the West and as-

sumed a polemical attitude in the attempt to preserve their traditional Orthodoxy; (2) those who came under the influence of Protestant doctrines and incorporated them into Oriental theology; and finally (3) those who favored Latin theology and strove to introduce Latin concepts and terminology into Orthodoxy.

The abortive attempt made by the Council of Florence (1439) to heal the schism between the Western and Eastern Churches had prepared the ground for fresh, anti-Latin writings. Catholic missionaries entered Orthodox countries intent on proselytizing to bring about unity of faith and practice particularly in the Near East and in the Polish kingdom. The reunion of *Brest-Litovsk (1595), which united millions of Orthodox Ukrainians with Rome, further stiffened Greek opposition to Latin theology. From the middle of the 16th century many Byzantine writers who had studied in Italy and Germany manifested interest in Catholic as well as Protestant theology. This development was looked upon with disfavor by the conservative Greek theologians.

Augsburg Confession. Early Protestant leaders, beginning with *Melanchthon, had sought the friendship of the Orthodox. The Reformers were eager to obtain Greek approval of their *Augsburg Confession. When Patriarch Joasaph II sent his deacon Demetrius Mysos to Wittenberg to investigate the newly reformed Christianity, Melanchthon gave him a Greek version of the Augsburg Confession, but the patriarch quickly rejected its teaching (1559). In 1573 the professors of the University of Tübingen, through Stephan Gerlach, tried to obtain approval for their doctrines from Jeremias II. Three documents sent by way of response, in 1578, 1579, and 1581, completely rejected the Lutheran Confession. These were the first Greek writings to sound the alarm at Protestant infiltration.

The principal author of these responses was Patriarch Jeremias, but others collaborated, such as Joannes and Theodosius Zygomalas, Leonarus Mindonios, Damascene the Studite, and probably Gabriel Severus. The Council of *Trent's doctrine was upheld in the Orthodox presentation of their teaching on justification and free will, on the Sacraments, on the invocation of the saints, and on the monastic life. However, with regard to procession of the Holy Spirit, the *filioque doctrine was rejected. In general, the fundamental tenets of the Augsburg Confession were repulsed with an exhortation that the Protestants return to the doctrine of the Church Fathers and the definitions of the first seven ecumenical councils.

Meletius Pigas. Catholic influence is seen more in the Orthodox theologians after Jeremias, who remained up to his death strongly anti-Catholic and attacked the Roman authorities for their forceful tactics in bringing about the union of Brest. But many of the Greek theologians who had studied at the University of Padua openly accepted Catholic teachings. The first Greek theologian of note to study in Italy was Meletius Pigas (1601). He was born on the island of Crete, and after completing his studies at Padua he took the monastic habit and began to preach and teach. He was made patriarch of Alexandria in 1590.

After the union of Brest Pigas turned from his earlier Catholic sympathies and began to write sharply against Roman teaching. "Concerning the Primacy of the Pope in the Form of Letters" was his first polemical attack.

Three of these letters were sent to the Ukrainians living in the Polish kingdom, urging them to repudiate the union of Brest, while the fourth was directed to the Orthodox faithful on the island of Chios where there was a similar movement in favor of reunion with Rome. Little originality is shown by Pigas, who repeated the standard objections of his Byzantine predecessors against the primacy of the pope, filioque, Communion under one species, purgatory, fasting on Saturday, and use of unleavened bread. His main theological works are "The Orthodox Christian," a long discussion on the procession of the Holy Spirit, Penance, and purgatory (published at Vilna in 1596 and later at Jassy, Rumania, 1769), and "Concerning the True Catholic Church and Its Genuine and True Head and Concerning the Primacy of the Pope of Rome" (1585). His archdeacon Maximus of Peloponnesus followed in his footsteps leaving among his other anti-Latin writings an "Enchiridion against the Schism of the Papists" in which, like Pigas, he attacked the doctrine of the primacy, procession of the Holy Spirit from the Son, and the use of unleavened bread. But both Pigas and Maximus follow the Catholic position in presenting the Sacraments.

Two other alumni of Padua University were Maximus Marguinios (1602) and Gabriel Severus (1616). Maximus had disputed with Gabriel Severus at Venice in favor of the Catholic doctrine expressed in the word filioque. He presented his arguments in three treatises, which he sent to the Patriarch Jeremias II in 1683, and staunchly supported Jeremias II against Protestant influences in Orthodoxy. Gabriel Severus, Metropolitan of Philadelphia, spent most of his writing career in Venice where he was in charge of the Greek Orthodox church of St. George. In his "Brief Tract on the Holy Sacraments" (Venice 1600) he used terminology borrowed chiefly from the Latin scholastics to describe the theology of the Sacraments in a refutation of the doctrines of the Protestants.

Second Period: 1612 to 1723. The 17th century was a period of controversy both within the Greek Orthodox Church itself and on the part of Catholics and Protestants who fought to draw the Orthodox to themselves. The Protestants seemed to have had the first success in attracting Cyril Lucaris to Calvinistic doctrines, which he expressed in his *Confession* of 1629; but soon both Russian and Byzantine theologians reacted strongly, and, in various synods and confessions of faith, the Orthodox rejected Protestant errors.

Cyril Lucaris. Of the theologians sympathetic to Protestantism, Cyril Lucaris was the most influential. Born in 1572 on the island of Crete, Cyril studied at Padua and Venice where he became proficient in Latin and Italian. Meletius Pigas in 1584 sent him to the Ukraine where he took part in the Council of Brest. He became patriarch of Alexandria in 1601 and held this office until 1620. In various letters to Calvinists he showed his sympathy toward their doctrine, especially in the matter of the Eucharist, free will, and justification. He was elected patriarch of Constantinople in 1620, a dignity he held on and off six different times, until, by order of the Turkish ruler, he was drowned in the sea.

In violation of the traditional teaching of the Orthodox Church, his *Confession* (1629, augmented 1633) accepts Calvinistic teaching: Holy Scripture is the only rule of faith (art. 2); justification comes by faith alone

(art. 13); free will is abolished (art. 14); predestination is presented according to the teaching of Calvin (art. 3); consequently a false concept of the Church is taught (art. 11). He admitted only two Sacraments, Baptism and Eucharist, and believed that Christ is present only at the time of Holy Communion (arts. 15, 17). He rejected purgatory (art. 18), the cult of images (q. 4), and the deuterocanonical books of the Old Testament (q. 3). Some Orthodox, such as Chrysostomos Papadopoulos, claimed that Cyril was not the author of the *Confession*. But his correspondence with Calvinist theologians demonstrates his sympathies toward their doctrines, and an extant autographed codex leaves little doubt that Cyril Lucaris was its author.

Lucaris gave the impetus to other Orthodox theologians who openly proclaimed their Protestant teachings. Theophilus Corydalleos, Zacharias Gerganos, Joannes Caryophyllos, Maximus Callipolita, and *Metrophanes Critopoulos all followed this example. Critopoulos was a pupil of Lucaris, who sent him to universities in England, Germany, and Switzerland. In his travels he strove to bring about a union of Orthodox and Protestants. On his return to Greece he was created patriarch of Alexandria and abstained from manifesting Protestant tendencies. He even took part in the Synod of Jassy (1642), which condemned the *Confession* of Lucaris. His adherence to Protestantism is clear, however, from his *Confession of Faith of the Catholic and Apostolic Oriental Church,* composed in Helmstadt in 1624 but printed only in 1661. There has been much discussion about the *Confession*. A. Palmieri maintains that it is a clear expression of Lutheran faith; others, with I. Mihalcescu, concede that in some points Critopoulos deviated from common Orthodox opinion. Finally there are those who hold it as one of the chief symbols of Orthodox faith and quite genuinely in keeping with the Byzantine theological tradition.

A synod held in 1925 on Mt. Athos vindicated Critopoulos and his *Confession*. Yet an influence from Protestant theology cannot be denied, e.g., in his definition of the Church, in his treatment of the Sacraments, in his accepting only three (Baptism, Eucharist, and Penance), and in his rejection of the deuterocanonical books. Critopoulos's *Confession* is valued highly by contemporary Greek theologians who accept his Protestant opinions and his arguments against Roman Catholicism concerning the filioque, the Immaculate Conception, and the Roman primacy. They favor the mystical concept of the Church, which is derived mostly from Protestant sources.

Polemicists. A chief characteristic of Greek theology in the 17th century was the role played by polemical writings against both Catholics and Protestants. Meletius Syrigos (d. 1667) had studied both at Padua and Venice and was commissioned by Parthenios I, Patriarch of Constantinople, to correct the *Confession* of Peter *Moghila and translate it into modern Greek. It was his corrected version that was accepted as a confession of faith for all the Orthodox in the Council of Jassy (Romania) in 1642. Moghila had protested the changes made in his original Latin text by Syrigos, and the Greek text was not edited until 1667, after the death of Moghila. D. Balanos claims that the original *Confession* of Moghila was a compendium of the *Catholic Catechism* of St. Peter *Canisius. But Syrigos removed most of the Tridentine doctrine found in the original text and brought it into closer harmony with the Greek thinking of his day. His chief theological work was a polemical monograph against Calvinist doctrine: *Orthodox Refutation of the Chapters and Questions of the Confession of Cyril Lukaris*. Except for the chapter concerning the procession of the Holy Spirit, most of this work is consonant with Catholic theology. Both Greek and Latin Fathers as well as Scripture are quoted frequently.

Dositheus of Jerusalem. Syrigos was employed by Dositheus, Patriarch of Jerusalem (d. 1707), one of the leading Byzantine figures in the polemics against non-Orthodox groups. His own *Confession* proved of great importance in checking Protestant infiltration into Orthodoxy when it was accepted at a synod in Jerusalem (1672) by all the Orthodox patriarchs. More intent on fighting Calvinistic errors than Latin Catholicism, Dositheus demonstrated his dependence on Latin theology, not only in the opinions expressed but even in terminology, particularly in the theology of the Sacraments where words never before used by Byzantine theologians, such as confirmation, satisfaction, and transubstantiation, were introduced into Greek theology. As expressed in the *Confession,* his doctrine on free will and predestination (decrees 3, 14), on justification and good works (decree 13), and on the seven Sacraments (decree 15) is in perfect harmony with the teaching of the Council of Trent. He did not use the word purgatory, yet he holds a third state between heaven and hell that would correspond to Catholic teaching on purgatory. Dositheus is the author of *An Enchiridion against the Errors of Calvinism* (Bucharest 1690); he established a printing press at Jassy, Rumania, to spread the polemical works of both earlier and contemporary Byzantine writers against Calvinism and the Roman Church.

Other theologians include George Coressios (d. 1641), who studied medicine in Pisa and returned to Greece to write polemical tracts against both the Protestants and the Catholics; and Paisy Ligarides (d. 1678), who embraced Catholicism as a boy in Rome but later left the Church to become a sharp controversialist against Protestant and Catholic theological doctrine. Nectar, Patriarch of Jerusalem (d. 1676), wrote a tract *Concerning the Primacy of the Pope,* which Dositheus printed at Jassy. The two Lichudes brothers, Joannes (d. 1717) and Sophronius (d. 1730), both studied in Venice and Padua. Dositheus sent them as instructors to the seminary of Moscow where they wrote polemical tracts attacking the theological school of Kiev for its Catholic tendencies. Sevastus Kymenites (d. 1702), Elias Meniates (d. 1714), and Nicolaus Kerameos (d. 1672) must also be listed among the polemicists of this period.

Catholic Sympathizers. Amidst so many Greek theologians dedicated to polemics, a few with Catholic sympathies wrote works that never became popular. Agapius Landos, with his ascetical writings printed at Venice, was the most esteemed of this group. Among his writings are: *Salvation of Sinners* and *New Paradise* (lives of the saints taken from Symeon Metaphrastes), and *Eklogion* and *New Eklogion* (more selected lives of the saints). Gregorius of Chios published a compendium of the *Divine and Sacred Dogmas of the Church* (Venice 1635). Nicolaus Kursulas (d. 1652), an alumnus of St. Athanasius Greek College founded in Rome

by Pope Gregory XIII to bring about concord between the West and East, wrote a *Synopsis of Sacred Theology* using the scholastic method and permeated by a Catholic mentality. Nicolaus the Bulgar studied in Padua and edited his *Sacred Catechism* (Venice 1681), which has been used by more recent Greeks in an effort to correct errors in later Orthodox speculation.

Two outstanding Byzantinists, also alumni of St. Athanasius College, Rome, were Peter Arcudius (d. 1633) and Leo Allatius (d. 1669), who held various offices in the Vatican and used their Oriental background in the service of the Church. Arcudius was mainly responsible for effecting the union of Brest while Allatius collected innumerable Greek and Syrian manuscripts under Pope Gregory XV, thus preserving in the Vatican Library an important Eastern heritage that otherwise would have been lost.

Third Period: 1723 to 1833. The nadir of modern Greek theology, the period from 1723 to 1833 was typified by an increase in theological compendia, polemical writings against Roman Catholics, and synopses of Byzantine spirituality. In the 18th century many Christians of the Antiochene patriarchate united with Rome and constituted the Uniate Church of Catholic Melchites. Hatred against Catholics mounted. In 1755 the Ecumenical Patriarch Cyril V declared Baptism by infusion, as administered by the Latins, invalid. The chief theologian of the period was Eugenius the Bulgar, even though he showed no great talent. His main writing, a theological compendium called *Theologikon,* was printed in Venice in 1872. Other authors who collected the past theological traditions into compendia were Vincent Damodos (d. 1752), Antonius Moschopoulos (d. 1788), Joannes Kontones (d. 1761), and Theophilus Papaphilos (d. c. 1785).

The chief compiler of Byzantine spiritual writings was Nicodemus, the Hagiorite of Mt. Athos (d. 1809). Together with Agapius Leonardos he compiled the *Pedalion* (Rudder), which today is the most famous Byzantine collection of commonly accepted (in the Greek-Slavic Churches) canons from ancient ecumenical or local councils. The two authors also provided commentaries on the canons. But Nicodemus is more popularly known as the editor of the *Philokalia,* a 5-volume collection of ascetical writings, drawn mostly from the spiritual writers of the Hesychastic tradition. This was first printed in Venice in 1782; a third edition was printed in Athens in 1957.

Fourth Period: 1833 to 1923. There followed a period chiefly of eclecticism. Political freedom had been won in 1833, and the Greeks were able to form their own nation. This brought them freedom to have their own universities and faculties of theology. The University of Athens' theology faculty was founded in 1837. Theology in the other Orthodox patriarchates of Antioch and Alexandria was practically nonexistent, due again to Moslem oppression. The theology that did develop in the newly liberated Greece was not very original but came under the influence of three principal sources: some theologians favored positions held by Protestant theologians; others, those of Catholics; while a third group became followers of the more creative Russian theologians, especially of the Khomiakovian school. Thus their eclecticism brought about many diverging opinions. Meanwhile, from 1867 onward, many sought reunion with the Anglicans.

Count Protasov. In 1833 Greece won autocephaly for its own Church and took as its model the independent Church in Russia. Protestantism had been spreading, but, recognizing the possibility of having its own theology schools, the Greek Church, like the Russian Church under Count Protasov, the procurator of the Holy Synod of Moscow, began to react against the infiltration of Protestant thinking in Orthodox theology. In 1836 Patriarch Gregorios VI of Constantinople issued an encyclical in which he condemned the errors of Luther, Zwingli, Calvin, and followers. The Greek Orthodox faithful were forbidden to read Protestant books and, above all, to read the Protestant versions of the Holy Scripture.

Encyclical of the Four Patriarchs. A document that exacerbated relations with the Catholics was the *Encyclical of the Four Patriarchs* of 1848. On Jan. 6, 1848, *Pius IX in his encyclical *In Suprema Petri Apostoli Sede* had addressed himself to the Orientals, inviting them to reunion with the Roman Church. In May 1848 the four chief Greek-speaking Orthodox patriarchs, Anthimus VI of Constantinople, Hierotheus II of Alexandria, Methodius of Antioch, and Cyril II of Jerusalem, along with 29 metropolitans, signed the *Encyclical of the Four Patriarchs*. The author of this document was Constantius I, Patriarch of Constantinople, who several years before (1834) had written an anti-Latin document as M. Popescu has shown. The contents of this encyclical summarized all the main points of the polemical literature of the prior centuries. Papism is claimed as a heresy that embraces several errors: that expressed by the word filioque; Baptism by aspersion; the defect of an epiclesis; Communion under one species; and the use of unleavened bread. The chief difficulty was the confusion of religious with civil power, which the Roman pontiffs abused by imposing an intolerable yoke on others. Thus the encyclical appeared more as a violent diatribe against the Roman pontiff than an answer to Pius IX.

Another document that became the source of authority for polemical writers of the period was the *Encyclical of Anthimus VII*. Pope Leo XIII, who was respected by many Orthodox for his zeal in promoting unity, sent to the Orientals his encyclical *Praeclara gratulationis* (June 20, 1894). Anthimus VII, Patriarch of Constantinople, answered at the end of 1894 with a long list of denunciations against the innovations of Latin Catholics. The list repeated the charges of the former 1848 Orthodoxy encyclical and added an attack on the idea of the fire of purgatory, immediate retribution, the newly defined dogma of the Immaculate Conception (1854), and that of the primacy of the pope and his infallibility, which had been declared dogma in the Vatican Council of 1870.

Theological Compendia. Russian theologians at this time excelled in theological manuals, and many of these were translated into Greek and used by the Greek Faculties. Popular Russian compendia that had great use in Greece included that of Antony Amphiteatrov, rector of the Academy of Kiev, *Dogmatic Theology of the Eastern Catholic Church* (Kiev 1848), and that of Macarius Bulgakov, *Introduction to Orthodox Theology* (St. Petersburg 1847). It was not long, however, before the Greek theologians were producing their own compendia. Nicolaus Damalas, Zikos Rhosis, Crestos Andrutsos, K. J. Dyovuniotis, D. S. Balanos, I. Mesoloras,

Nectarios Kephalas, and Nicolaus Ambrazis all made useful compendia for use in Greek-speaking seminaries.

Meanwhile, during this period internecine controversies arose among the Greeks concerning the relation of the newly liberated Church and State in Greece and the primacy of the patriarch of Constantinople in ruling this Church. The Greek Orthodox divided into two factions: those, led by Theoclitus Pharmakides (d. 1860), who favored full ecclesiastical autonomy and autocephaly rendering the Church subject to the State in all that pertained to external administration and jurisdiction; the others, led by Constantinus Economos (d. 1857), who favored complete independence of the State and submission in all Church jurisdiction to the ecumenical patriarch of Constantinople. These two factions quarreled among themselves concerning the use of Protestant Bibles. In 1823 Protestant Bible societies began to disseminate Bibles printed in the modern Greek tongue. Pharmakides and Neophyte Vamvas (d. 1855) upheld the usefulness of these versions, while Economos argued theologically that the Protestant translations from the Hebrew had many discrepancies from that of the Septuagint, which alone he held to be infallible.

Theosevia. A new religion appeared in Greece about this time, a mystical rationalism promulgated by Theophilus Kairis (d. 1853). It was a type of the *Modernism later condemned in the West by Pius X. The Synod of Greece condemned this so-called *Theosevia* religion as heretical, and Kairis was expelled in 1841. He returned only to be imprisoned by the state and soon died.

Theological journals began to appear as a greater spirit of creative speculation awoke among the Greek theologians. The Constantinople patriarchate published *Ekklesiastike Aletheia* (Church Truth), which was suppressed in 1923 when the majority of Greeks emigrated from Turkey. It was replaced by *Orthodoxia* in 1925 and *Apostolos Andreas,* the latter being the official voice of the ecumenical patriarch; but it printed theological articles also. Both of these periodicals were suppressed in 1964 by the Turkish government. Holy Cross Seminary in Jerusalem prints *Nea Sion;* the former *Ekklesiastikos Pharos* by the Alexandrian Patriarchate has been replaced by *Pantaios.*

Fifth Period: 1923 to the Present. The modern era has witnessed a renaissance in Greek theology. Under the inspiration of two leading archbishops of Athens, Meletius Mataxakis and Papadopoulos, theological studies and learning among the clergy and laity were fostered. Yet much of this modern Greek theological literature displays certain common defects. The majority of the older professors studied abroad, particularly in Germany. They mastered the critical techniques of the German schools of theology of the latter part of the 19th century, but because of nationalistic circumstances they had little contact with the more relevant theology developed in the 20th century among the Russian Orthodox *émigrés* and the Western Catholic world. They produced a theology almost wholly academic, confined to manuals and bearing little relation either to the spiritual contempory world or to the patristic tradition of the past.

Contemporary Development. Paradoxically, in the 1950s and early 1960s the professors of the two leading theological faculties in Greece were almost exclusively laymen. They include Chrestos Androutsos, P. N. Trembelas, P. I. Bratsiotis, A. Alivisatos, B. Vellas, I. N. Karmiris, B. Joannides, C. Bonis, G. Konidaris, and Archimandrite Jerome Kotsonis, all of whom teach in the theological faculties of the universities of Athens and Salonika, and have produced many serious theological writings.

A suspicion grew among the monks and pastors of souls as well as among the members of new movements such as *Zoe* (Life), *Aktines* (Action), and the two *Apostoliki Diakonia* (Apostolic Services) of Athens and Salonika, that this academic theology was irrelevant for confronting the materialism of modern Greece. A gradual change is now noticeable among these contemporary Greek theologians, especially with the impetus received from the *Zoe* movement, which is known also as the "Brotherhood of Theologians." This was started by Father Eusebius Matthopoulos in 1907 as a semimonastic order whose members remain celibate but take no formal vows. A quarter of the brothers are monks, the rest are laymen. Through their teaching of theology in the two faculties of Greece and in their innumerable printed works, they are making theology less academic and more Biblical, liturgical, and relevant for modern men in a rapidly changing society.

Ecumenical Interests. Active participation in the various ecumenical discussions launched throughout Europe in the 20th century, especially in the World Council of Churches from the very first assembly of 1948 in Amsterdam, has brought closer contact with Protestants and Roman Catholics. Present-day Greek theologians have thus sought to emerge from the national narrowness in an attempt to understand forms of Christianity other than their own. Thus the second half of the 20th century has witnessed in Greek theology a flexible approach to theology, a return to the Bible, the Eastern liturgies, and the writings of the early Fathers. The new Greek theology aims for relevance to the modern Christian developments.

Bibliography: C. ANDROUTSOS, *Dogmatic Theology of the Orthodox Eastern Church* (2d ed. Athens 1956), in Greek. Beck KTLBR. P. I. BRATSIOTIS, "Greek Theology in the Last 50 Years," *Theologia* 19 (1941–48) 83–112, 271–286, in Greek; ed., *Die orthodoxe Kirche in griechischer Sicht*, 2 v. (Stuttgart 1959–60). F. GAVIN, *Some Aspects of Contemporary Greek Thought* (Milwaukee 1923). Jugie TheolDogm v.1. E. S. KIMMEL, *Monumenta fidei ecclesiae orientalis*, 2 v. (Jena 1850). Krumbacher. A. PALMIERI, *Theologia dogmatica orthodoxa*, 2 v. (Florence 1911–13). D. SAVRAMIS, ed., *Aus der neugriechischen Theologie* (*Das östliche Christentum*, Neue Folge 15; Würzburg 1961).

[G. A. MALONEY]

C

CABALA

A system of occult theosophy based on a mystical interpretation of the Scriptures, common not only among the Jews of the Middle Ages but also with some influence on certain medieval Christians. This article considers its rise and spread, its principal literary works, particularly the *Bahir* and the *Zohar,* and its later development, especially in Lurianic circles.

The term comes from the Hebrew word *qabbālâ,* which etymologically means a "receiving, accepting," but which is used also in the sense of "tradition," both actively, as a "handing down" of traditional lore, and passively, as the lore itself thus handed down. In rabbinical writings it is used both of the post-Mosaic Scriptures and of the traditional Talmudic law. In modern Israeli Hebrew it even has the sense of "receipt." But ordinarily it is used in the technical sense of the Jewish mystic lore of the Middle Ages, and this is the meaning in which the term is employed here.

Early Period. The cabala is basically a development of Jewish *Gnosticism. As a historical phenomenon it arose toward the end of the 12th century in Provence (southern France). From here it spread at the beginning of the 13th century to Spain, where it passed through its first classical period. It arose, therefore, in Christian surroundings; only after three generations did it take root in regions of Moslem culture. Its first centers were at Lunel, Narbonne, and Posquières—all in southern France. From there it was brought by students of the Provençal Jewish scholars to Burgos, Gerona, and Toledo, and from these cities it spread to the rest of Spain.

Provençal Cabala. In the 12th and 13th centuries Provençal Judaism reached a cultural zenith. In Provence the Tibbonide family (*see* IBN TIBBON), the greatest translators of Arabic religious-philosophical works into Hebrew, were active. In this region Jews lived at the meeting place of Moslem and Christian cultures and in the immediate vicinity of the seething currents among Christians that led to the agitation for Evangelical poverty among the *Waldenses and to the Gnostic movements of the *Cathari and the *Albigenses. It was not by accident that the Jews who lived in such surroundings gladly welcomed ascetical tendencies and mystic-Gnostic traditions that were at that time latent in Judaism itself. The intermediaries of these tendencies and

traditions were the Ashkenazic Ḥasidim (pious men), who were very influential in Jewry from the middle of the 12th century to the beginning of the 13th. There is evidence that in the circles of certain Provençal scholars people were having peculiar mystical experiences known as "revelations of Elia." Such revelations were said to have been received by Abraham ben Isaac (d. 1179), the Abh Beth Din (head of the Jewish court) in Narbonne; by his son-in-law, Abraham ben David (d. 1198) of Posquières; by Jacob ha-Nazir of Lunel, a contemporary of Abraham ben David; and by Isaac Saggi Nehor (Isaac the Blind), Abraham ben David's son, who lived till the 1230s in Posquières or Narbonne. The last-mentioned was the most important personality in Provençal cabalism, and he was already using the terminology of the *sephirot* that would henceforth be customary in cabala. Thus the union of Jewish religious philosophy with Gnostic tendencies and mystical experiences among Provençal scholars led to the concrete phenomenon of cabala.

The Bahir. The first important work of the cabala was the *Book of Bahir* (Heb. *bāhîr,* taken here to mean "bright," although in Jb 37.21, which is the first Biblical quotation in the book and which thus gave the book its name, the word really means "obscured"). The work was already known by this name around A.D. 1200, but it was spread also under the names of *Haggadah, Yerushalmi,* and *Midrash* of Rabbi Neḥunya ben Hakana, who is mentioned in the first section of the work as a bearer of the tradition. The text, as it has come down to us, is a collection of various literary units from different periods, some of them showing elements from an otherwise lost Jewish Gnosticism, others containing typical teachings of a date not earlier than the 12th century. Certain motifs in the *Bahir* are also found in the writings of the Ashkenazic Hasidim. One of the important sources that the author or editor of the book thus received and used was a book with the significant title of "The Great Mystery" or "The Great Secret"—known at first in the Orient by the Aramaic title, *Raza Rabba,* but later given the Hebrew title, *Sepher ha-Sôd ha-Gadôl.* As early as the 9th century the *Raza Rabba* was known in the East as a work concerned with divine names, angelology, and magic. Typical of the 12th century are many of the ideas that have been taken over into the *Bahir* from Judeo-Spanish religious philosophy. Thus, for instance, the influence of the teachings of Abraham bar Ḥiya can be seen in *Bahir* 2.9–10. He was the first to interpret the tohu and bohu of Gn 1.2 as meaning matter and form, and the same idea appears in *Bahir* 2.9–10. Since Abraham bar Ḥiya died around the middle of the 12th century, the *Bahir* must have been composed in Provence around A.D. 1200.

The concept of God in the *Bahir* is theosophic-Gnostic. God is the bearer of cosmic forces, which He causes to flow into the cosmic tree. The God of the *Bahir,* therefore, is similar to the God of the Gnostic myth, even though the book adheres to the principle of pure monotheism. In ch. 14 it is emphatically stated that the angels were created on the second day of creation so that they might not claim that they assisted in the creation of the heavens and the earth. In this sense, *mî'ittî,* "Who was with me [when I created the world]?" in Is 44.24, is taken, as in *Midrash Rabba* on Gn 1.4, to be mê 'ittî, "from me, by my own power." Moreover, the *Bahir* is acquainted with the concept of the golem—a legendary human figure made of clay (ch. 136) and the doctrine of the transmigration of souls [see G. Scholem, "Seelenwanderung und Sympathie der Seelen in der jüdischen Mystick," *Eranos* 24 (1956) 55–118], which is used for solving the problem of theodicy (ch. 135).

Spanish Cabala. An important center of the early cabala in Spain was the city of Gerona, where from 1215 to 1265 many influential cabalists were active. Most of these men had studied in the Jewish schools of Provence. Some of them are known to have been disciples of Isaac Saggi Nehor. The most important one was Azriel of Gerona, who, together with other disciples of Isaac Saggi Nehor, was interested in "Platonizing" the Gnostic material contained in the *Bahir.* A sort of cabalistic catechism of his has been preserved under the title, *Sha'ar ha-Shô'ēl* (Gate of the Inquirer), later called the *Perush 'Eser ha-Sephirot* (Explanation of the Ten Sephirot) and printed as the introduction to the edition of Meir ben Gabbi's *Derekh 'Emûnâ*—"Way of Faith" (Berlin 1850). The influence of Neoplatonism can clearly be seen in this work. Another important cabalist in Gerona was Moses *Nahmanides (1194–1270), who was likewise famous as a physician, philosopher, Talmudist, exegete, and poet. Cabalistic influence is unmistakable in his works, particularly in his commentary on the *Book of *Yeṣirah (Jesira)*, since this commentary, in contrast to his other books, was primarily intended for readers interested in cabalism. The concept of God that is presented here is influenced both by the Neoplatonic doctrine of emanations and by the Gnostic doctrine of the aeons. The *'Ên Sôph* (Infinite One), as the Furthest Removed, is not the personal God of the Bible; the latter becomes manifest only through the *sephirot,* to which the divine attributes correspond.

The Zohar. The most important cabalistic work is the *Zohar* ("Illumination," a term taken from Dn 12.3). About 100 years of development lie between the *Bahir* and the *Zohar.*

Authorship. The alleged author of the *Zohar* is Simeon bar Yochai, a Tanna (*see* MISHNAH) of the 2d century, of whom it is said, in the Mishnah tractate *Sabbath* 33b, that he hid in a cave in order to escape the persecution of the Romans. This legendary anecdote is introduced into the *Zohar* in connection with its alleged authorship. Actually, the work was composed by the cabalist Moses de Leon, who was active in Spain during the last quarter of the 13th century. The whole corpus of the *Zohar* consists of five books, of which the first three are the most important. These three books contain midrashim (*see* MIDRASH; MIDRASHIC LITERATURE) on the Pentateuch: Book 1 on Genesis, Book 2 on Exodus, and Book 3 on Leviticus, Numbers, and Deuteronomy. Book 4, called *Tiqqunē Zohar* (Emendations on the *Zohar*), is a literary unit by itself, and Book 5, called *Zohar Hadash* (New Zohar), is made up of sections of the first four books that were missing in the manuscripts used for the first printed edition (Mantua 1558–60). With the exception of Book 4, the work consists of numerous small literary units. It is written in an artificial Aramaic, only the part called *Midrash ha-Ne'lam* (Interpretation of What is Hidden) being written partly in Hebrew. The parts called *Ra'ya Mehemna* (The True Shepherd) and *Tiqqunē Zohar* were not written by Moses de Leon, but were added by some other cabalist shortly after A.D. 1300.

From the very beginning opinions were divided on the question of the origin of the *Zohar.* Clear evidence for it comes from the information supplied by Isaac of Accho, who migrated to Spain when the Moslems captured Accho in 1291. According to this man, Moses de Leon had indeed sworn that Simeon bar Yochai had composed the work and that he himself had merely made a copy of it; but, according to Isaac of Accho, Moses de Leon's wife had stated after his death (1305) that her husband had written the *Zohar* "out of his own head, his own heart, his own knowledge, and his own understanding." This statement of Moses de Leon's wife deserves the fullest confidence, for modern research has established with certainty the pseudepigraphic character of the *Zohar.* Moreover, the writings of Moses de Leon show that, in any case, he took a decisive part in the spread of the work; his own writings contain numerous Zoharic expressions at a time when the *Zohar* itself was hardly known.

The earliest citations from the *Zohar* are found in the cabalistic literature written toward the end of the 13th century. These quotations show that the writers who cited the *Zohar* at that time were acquainted only with certain parts of it. This confirms the statement of Isaac of Accho that Moses de Leon gradually spread the work in the form of separate fascicles. Quotations of greater length and from all parts of the complete *Zohar* are first made in the 3d decade of the 14th century. Many other arguments can be adduced to show that the *Zohar* could not have been composed at the time of Simeon bar Yochai in the 2d century. Thus, the generations of the Talmudic rabbis are frequently confused, and many Talmudic statements are wrongly understood. The author of the *Zohar* knew Palestine only from literature, and even this he at times misunderstood. The artificial Aramaic of the *Zohar* depends on the Aramaic of the Babylonian Talmud and of the Targums [*see* BIBLE, IV (TEXTS AND VERSIONS), 11], and it is also influenced by the Hebrew of the 13th century. Besides, clearly in evidence is the philosophical terminology of the Hebrew philosophical literature of the 12th and 13th centuries. From the *Zohar's* frequent changes of the modifications of the verbal roots it is clear that, for its author, Aramaic was no longer a living language. Moreover, the many later sources that are used in the *Zohar* prove that it could not possibly have been composed as early as the 2d century. Such sources are the Targums, both Talmuds, various midrashic works, *Avicebron's *Keter Malkuth,* *Judah al-Ḥarīzī, *Judah ben Samuel ha-Levi, Abraham bar Hiya, *Maimonides, *Rashi, etc. Even the *Hekhalot* literature, the *Book of Yeṣirah,* the *Book of Bahir,* and the cabalistic literature from the end of the 12th and from the 13th century are used in the *Zohar.* These reasons, as well as the testimony of Isaac of Accho, justify the conclusion that the *Zohar* was composed and circulated by Moses de Leon between 1275 and 1290.

Contents. The concepts of God and creation in the *Zohar* are based upon those of the *'Ên Sôph* (the Infinite) and the 10 *sephirot.* The idea of the *sephirot* and of their number, 10, comes from the *Book of Yeṣirah.* In the *Yeṣirah* the term *sephirot* (numbers) refers to the elements of creation. In cabala this term received an entirely new meaning. Under the influence of Neoplatonic philosophy the *sephirot* became the intermediaries and bases of all existence in God, yet without losing their original character as dynamic powers. In the *Zohar,* however, the term *sephirot* is found but seldom; the author, for the sake of protecting his anonymity, substitutes numerous symbolic expressions for them. The current names for the 10 *sephirot* are: (1) *Keter,* "Crown"; (2) *Hokhmah,* "Wisdom"; (3) *Bînah,* "Understanding"; (4) *Ḥesed* or *Gedullah,* "Grace" or "Greatness"; (5) *Dîn* or *Gebhurah,* "Judgment" or "Strength"; (6) *Raḥamîm* or *Tiph'eret,* "Mercy" or "Majesty"; (7) *Neṣaḥ,* "Eternity"; (8) *Hôd,* "Splendor"; (9) *Yesôd* or *Ṣaddîq,* "Foundation" or "the Just Man"; (10) *Malkhût,* "Kingdom."

The *'Ên Sôph* is the Hidden God (*Deus absconditus*) who reveals Himself through the *sephirot.* These are not intermediate degrees between God and creations in the sense of the purely Neoplatonic degrees of emanation, but rather the self-revealing Deity Itself is jointly acting dynamic powers. Although the *Zohar* speaks of the *sephirot* as degrees in the figurative sense, they are only gradations in God Himself. Thus, in *Zohar* 3.70a it is said, as similarly in *Yeṣirah* 1.7, "Come and see. The Holy one (praised be He!) brought forth ten crowns, holy crowns, above. He crowned Himself with them and bedeckt Himself with them, and He is they, and they are He, as the flame is one with burning coal, and there is no separation at all." The *sephirot,* therefore, do not form a fixed ontological hierarchy, as the Neoplatonic degrees of emanation do, but they are all in equal proximity to their source and unite with one another in syzygies unto mystic glory as they move up and down in the divine Organism. Very frequently the relationship of the *sephirot* to one another is presented under the form of sexual symbolism. One and the same *sephirah* can be both feminine in relationship to its source of power, and masculine in relationship to the *sephirah* depending on it. The *sephirot* are also likened to doorways through which man, by means of the right intention in his prayers and keeping of the commandments, can enter into the apprehension of the divine mysterium. Man is capable of this (only *Keter* and *Hokhmah* being too subtle for a direct knowledge of God) because he, like the rest of the world, has been created in the likeness of the *sephirot* and because the

sephirot pour themselves forth as creative powers on the lower world. Thus man, like the rest of creation, becomes an image of the divine essence manifesting itself in the *sephirot.*

In the history of the cabala the *sephirot* were often portrayed in the representation of a figure, e.g., in the form of the heavenly "protoman." This idea is already found in embryo in the *Abhot de Rabbi Nathan* 31, and it is met with in the later cabala (especially after Isaac Luria) in the form of *Adam Qadmon* (earlier man). For the idea of the heavenly protoman the *Zohar* uses the symbol of *Adam Dal'ela* or *Adam Ila'a* (Upper Man). Besides being portrayed in human form, the *sephirot* are presented in the form of a tree or of a circle.

The doctrine of creation out of nothing was understood to mean that the "nothing" was a highest "something," the first externalization of God. The "nothing" therefore received a positive significance. It is the first *sephirah, Keter,* and thus emanated as the first activity directly from the *'Ên Sôph.* It is a "nothing" only subjectively from the viewpoint of the creature. It is the bridge between the transcendence of the *'Ên Sôph* and the divine creative power that reveals itself in the *sephirot.* In *Zohar* 2.239a it is said:

> Only the earliest nothing [*Keter*] brings forth a beginning [*Hokhmah*] and an end [*Malkhût*]. What is the beginning? It is the highest point [*Hokhmah*] that is the beginning of all things, that is hidden, and that has existence within thought. This achieved an end, which is then called the end of the thing. But there, in the *'Ên Sôph,* there is neither will, nor lights, nor lamps. All these lamps and lights depend on It, but It Itself is not known. That which the *'Ên Sôph* knows and also does not know is nothing else than the highest will, the most hidden of all, the nothing.

Under the symbol of the lamps and the lights the *sephirot* are meant.

The *sephirot* were thought of as three columns: to the right, the column of divine grace and love; to the left, that of divine rigor and judgment; in the middle, that of mercy. The *sephirah* *Tip'ert,* the first *sephirah* after *Keter* in the middle row, is therefore also called *Raḥamîm* (Mercy). In this way a reconciliation is made between God's goodness and His severity. Thus also, in the representation of the *sephirot* tree, the *sephirah* *Tiph'eret* is symbolized by the trunk; in the representation of the *Adam Qadmon,* it is symbolized by the trunk of his body. The place for hell is at the left side (*Zohar* 1.17a), an idea already present in embryo in *Bahir* 109. Evil is thus a consequence of God's power of judgment and punishment; it is God's *sitrā ăḥērā* (other side), which comes into play only when it loosens itself from the state of intercommunion with God's love and mercy and so acts on its own. As long as man does not sin, God's "other side" can have no power over him. If man's sin would not disturb the harmony in the *sephirot* world, the "other side," the *sephirah* *Gebhurah,* could not develop as an evil power, but would be suspended in its quality as an evil power because of its intercommunion with love and mercy. The last *sephirah, Malkhût,* should, as the "tree of knowledge," be in union with *Tiph'eret,* the "tree of life." But man's sin destroys this unity and lets the powers of the "other side" have the upper hand. When this happens, the function of *Malkhût* as the "tree of knowledge" is changed into the function of a "tree of death."

By its position at the end of the emanation series, *Malkhût* has a double function. On the one hand, it is the last member of the *sephirot* world; on the other it is the forms that lie below it. It is thus both the channel by which the divine creative power descends to the world below and the doorway by which man can ascend to the contemplation of the *sephirot* world above. In the *Zohar*, *Malkhût* is frequently called *Shekinah, God's presence, and as the mother of the lower world, especially as the mother of Israel, it is called *Matronita* (Matron). In relation to the upper mother in the *sephirah* world—the *Sephirah Bînah*, which is the "upper" Shekinah, *Malkhût* is also the "lower" Shekinah. Because Israel stands directly under the faithful protection of the Shekinah, *Malkhût* is also called, in the *Zohar*, the "Community of Israel," and thus it is also the mystical archetype of Israel.

The procedure of the creation and conservation of the world within the *sephirot* corresponds to the procedure of the divine emanation and is, in particular, the work of the last *sephirah, Malkhût.* In *Zohar* 1.240b it is said, "The act of creation proceeds on two levels, one above and one below; that is why the Torah begins with the letter Beth [the numerical value of which is two]. The lower corresponds to the upper. The one [*Bînah*] is effective in the upper world [of the *sephirot*], the other [*Malkhût*] in the lower world [of creation]." The principal, original part of the Zohar does not present a well-developed picture of the forms of existence below the *sephirot.* But around A.D. 1300 (already in the *Ra'ya Mehemna* and the *Tiqqunim*) there appeared the doctrine of the four regions, although it was only after 1500 that its importance grew. These four regions are: (1) the world of *Aṣîlut* (noblest) emanation, which is the world of the *Sephirot;* (2) the *Ber'îah* (creating) world, which is the world of God's throne and *Merkabhah* ("chariot" of Ez 1.4–28); (3) the *Yeṣîrah* (forming) world, in which are the angels and the celestial spheres; (4) the *'Aśîyah* (making) world, the material world. (The names of the last three regions are taken from Is 43.7: *bᵉrā'tîw yᵉṣartîw 'ap-'aśîtîw*, "I have created it, I have formed it, I have made it.")

Later Cabala. After the Jews were driven from Spain in 1492, there was a strong upsurge of interest among them in the cabala. Only mysticism could give them an answer to the burning questions, why the coming of the messianic times should be so long delayed and why Jewry seemed destined for unending oppression. The center of the cabala in the 16th century was the city of Safed in Upper Galilee, which was also the home at this time of the great scholar of Jewish law Joseph *Caro. The two outstanding leaders of the cabala in this period were Moses Cordovero and Isaac *Luria. Cordovero (1522–70) was the greater systematizer, who collected the products of the old cabala and arranged them in logical order. Luria (1534–72) was the more original thinker, who gave to the cabala a new impetus. Even the first major work of Cordovero, the *Pardes Rimmônîm* (Garden of Pomegranates), which was completed in 1548, was a systematic standard work on cabalism; in his later writings, too, he knew how to use his special talent for systematizing.

Lurianic Cabala. Very few of the authentic writings of Isaac Luria are preserved. Immediately after his arrival at Safed in 1569 he became a disciple of Cordovero. After the latter's death he wrote a commentary on

the beginning of the *Zohar,* but most of his new teachings he set forth merely in oral fashion. His intellectual legacy was handed down by his disciple, Hayyim Vital (1543–1620), in the latter's two major works, *'Eṣ Hayyim* (Tree of Life) and *Sepher Ha-Gilgûlîm* (Book on Transmigration of Souls).

If, according to Luria, the *'Ên Sôph* is really infinite or "without end" (as the term literally means), outside the *'Ên Sôph* there is no place left for any emanation or any created universe. If something is to go out of the absolutely Infinite One, He must first set aside, out of Himself, a region for the finite. This self-limiting of the *'Ên Sôph* is called *Ṣimṣûm* (contraction) in the Lurianic cabala. Of His own free will God has, so to say, drawn back from an unlimited infinity to a limited infinity, and what is left over is the realm of evil, in fact, evil itself. Creation therefore necessarily presupposes the existence of evil. Yet in drawing back, God left something of His essence in the vacated space —a small remnant, which Luria calls *Reshîmô* (His trace), like the few drops left in a bottle when it is emptied. Luria describes this in his commentary on *Zohar* 1.15a, on which he must have worked shortly before his death [see G. Scholem, *Kiryath Sepher* 19 (1943) 184–199, esp. 197]. The later cabalists did not concern themselves much with the problem of the *Reshîmô.*

As man was conceived of as a microcosm (an epitome of the whole world), so God was regarded as a "macro-anthropos" (man on an infinite scale). When the *Adam Qadmon,* the protoman of the *sephirot,* drew back into the *Ṣimṣûm* region, the lights of the *sephirot* were forced out of his eyes, ears, nostrils, and mouth. At first they were a unit, without any differentiation. In order to give to each *sephirah* its proper place, vessels were needed for receiving the emanations of the *sephirot.* The vessels of the first three *sephirot* were able to hold the light that emanated from these *sephirot,* but the vessels of the lower *sephirot* broke to pieces. Thus the divine light mixed with the nondivine, the divine light was caught and held in the "cups" of the extradivine. The rays of the divine light that are in the cups are "in exile." Not only Israel, but God Himself is in exile. Corresponding to Israel's exile here below is an exile of the Deity in the cosmos.

Therefore, because the vessels of the *sephirot* were broken, and the divine rays emanated out of the broken vessels into the extradivine and mixed with it, there is need of the so-called *Tiqqûn,* "restoration," of the original order. By means of the *Tiqqûn* the rays are brought back from their scattered and banished state. Since God was thought of as a macroanthropos, there was need of man here below in order to complete the process of the *Tiqqûn.*

Man's decision in favor of the good is *Tiqqûn,* but by committing sin he causes a further intensification of the exile of the divine rays and sparks of light under the "cups." The first Adam did not fulfill his task of completing the *Tiqqûn;* on the contrary, he committed sin and thereby again banished under the "cups" the sparks of light that were already on their way back. The task that Adam did not complete is now laid upon Israel, whose dealings through the covenant with God become relevant in the sense of the *Tiqqûn.* Here there is a cabalistic modification of the idea that is frequently attested to in the OT and the Talmudic literature, that Israel's fidelity brings on the eschatological consummation, whereas its sins delay it.

Israel has failed and sinned. Consequently, Israel must also bear the lot of exile, so that in the Diaspora among the Gentiles it can do its work in the sense of the *Tiqqûn*. Israel's exile corresponds to man's exile from paradise and the exile of the divine rays of light that have fallen under the "cups." Because of the task that is laid on Israel in the *Tiqqûn*, it is directly entrusted with the messianic task also. The appearance of the Messiah is nothing else than the visible sign that Israel has fulfilled the task of the *Tiqqûn* that was laid on it. Israel's existence and sufferings thus received an eschatological character. In this total picture there is also a place for the trait of the transmigration of souls. Every soul receives a new existence after death until it has done its duty and completed its *Tiqqûn*.

Post-Lurianic Cabala. The two messianic movements that were founded respectively by Shabbatai Zevi (*see* SHABBATAIISM) in the 17th century and by Jacob *Frank in the 18th were, in a certain sense, consequences in the political sphere of Lurianic cabalism. Both movements were sparked by the thought that at last the period of the *Tiqqûn* was coming to an end and that the messianic age was about to dawn. Both movements were concerned with messianic attempts to break out of the agelong Jewish destiny. On account of the widespread popularization of the Lurianic teachings, east European *Hasidism succeeded in controlling the messianic activity and giving the idea of the *Tiqqûn* real significance for the life of the Hasidic community.

Bibliography: A. FRANCK, *La Kabbale ou la philosophie religieuse des Hébreux* (new ed. Paris 1889). E. MÜLLER, *Der Sohar und seine Lehre* (Vienna 1932); *History of Jewish Mysticism,* tr. M. SIMON (Oxford 1946). D. NEUMARK, *Geschichte der jüdischen Philosophie des Mittelalters,* 2 v. in 3 (Berlin 1907–28). G. G. SCHOLEM, *Das Buch Bahir* (Leipzig 1923); *Bibliotheca Kabbalistica* (Leipzig 1927); *Die Geheimnisse der Schöpfung* (Berlin 1935); *Major Trends in Jewish Mysticism* (3d rev. ed. London 1955); *Zohar, the Book of Splendor* (New York 1949); *Zur Kabbala und ihrer Symbolik* (Zurich 1960); *Ursprung und Anfänge der Kabbala* (Berlin 1962). *The Zohar,* tr. H. SPERLING et al., 5 v. (London 1931–34). G. VAJDA, *Introduction à la pensée juive du moyen-âge* (Paris 1947). R. J. Z. WERBLOWSKY, "Philo and the Zohar," *Journal of Jewish Studies* 10 (1959) 23–44, 112–135. E. BENZ, *Die christliche Kabbala* (Zurich 1958).

[K. SCHUBERT]

CABALLERO, ANTONIO, founder of the modern Franciscan missions in China; b. Baltanás, Spain, 1602; d. Kuang-chou, China, May 13, 1669. He became a friar in 1618, was ordained in 1626, and entered China from Manila in 1633. He worked in Fu-chien and Chiang-nan but was forced back to Manila. After receiving the decrees appointing him prefect apostolic of China (1643) and forbidding certain Chinese rites as superstitions (1645), he returned to China with two companions (1649). Settling in Chi-nan, Shan-tung, he opened his first church and established stations and churches in various towns and villages, baptizing over the years some 3,000 converts and working in perfect harmony with Jean Valat, SJ. In the general persecution of 1665, he was banished with the Jesuits and Dominicans to Kuang-chou. He wrote a number of reports, essays, and books. Of his Chinese books the following, written in 1653, have been published: (1) *Wan Wu Pen Mo Yo Yen* (Compendium on the Origin and End of All Things), published before 1667 and reprinted at Chu-chiang (Kuang-chou): Yang-jen Li,

Fu-yin-t'ang, n.d.; (2) *T'ien Ju Yin* (Catholicism and Confucianism Compared), with editor's preface, 1664, published at Chi-nan: Hsi-t'ang, n.d.; and (3) *Cheng Hsüeh Liu Shih* (True Science's Touchstone), with editor's preface, 1698, published posthumously.

Bibliography: *Sinica franciscana,* v.2, ed. A. VAN DEN WYNGAERT (Quaracchi-Florence 1933). M. COURANT, *Catalogue des livres chinois . . . de la Bibliothèque Nationale,* 3 v. (Paris 1910–12) v.3. A. S. ROSSO, *Apostolic Legations to China of the 18th Century* (South Pasadena 1948) 104–122.

[A. S. ROSSO]

CABALLERO Y GÓNGORA, ANTONIO, Spanish archbishop of Bogotá and viceroy of New Granada; b. Priego, Córdoba, 1723; d. Córdoba, March, 1796. He studied at the University of Granada. After ordination he was canon of Córdoba. He was consecrated bishop of Mérida, Yucatán, Mexico, in 1775. When transferred to Bogotá in 1778, he brought several young men from Yucatán with him to be educated there. He brought also his very rich library and a number of works of art, including paintings by Rubens and Murillo. During his archiepiscopate the insurrection of the Comuneros occurred (1781). The insurgents resolved to march to the capital to demand their objectives, almost all of which were of an economic nature (the repeal or reduction of certain taxes). Bogotá was defenseless. The archbishop arranged for both sides to sign capitulations that provided that the insurgents would disband and return to their homes. The viceroy, who was in Cartagena, failed to observe the terms and ordered the capture of some of the leaders who had been offered guarantees. The archbishop has been accused for not protesting these actions. Some have seen this as a betrayal on his part. However, as a Spaniard who had sworn fidelity to the King, he was acting in accordance with his principles. When Viceroy Torrezar Díaz Pimiento died, the archbishop was placed in charge of the viceroyalty. His zeal for science was responsible for the establishment of a botanical expedition, a scientific commission, headed by the priest José Celestino *Mutis, that studied the flora of New Granada. About 1784 the viceroy moved his residence to Cartagena to defend the city from attack and from British armies. At that time he requested from the Holy See an auxiliary bishop to whom he entrusted the ecclesiastical administration. An earthquake occurred in 1785, and he gave generously of his own funds for the reconstruction of the churches. About 1787 he resigned from the see and the office of viceroy. Appointed bishop of Córdoba, he left South America in 1789.

Bibliography: J. M. PÉREZ AYALA, *Antonio Caballero y Góngora* (Bogotá 1951). P. E. CÁRDENAS ACOSTA, *Los Comuneros* (Bogotá 1945). G. ARCINIEGAS, *Los Comuneros* (new ed. Santiago 1960).

[J. RESTREPO POSADA]

CABANILLES, JUAN BAUTISTA JOSÉ, Spanish organist and composer of the baroque period; b. Algemesí, province of Valencia, Sept. 4, 1644; d. Valencia, April 29, 1712. Cabanilles was a pupil of Jerónimo de la Torre, whom he succeeded as organist of the cathedral of Valencia in 1665. He was ordained priest in 1668. His works show the typical Spanish features of skill in writing variations on sacred and secular themes, and a maximum of musical expression through a minimum of technical device. He composed prolifically but apparently most of his music was not published during his lifetime, and much still remains unedited.

Bibliography: *Works,* ed. H. ANGLÈS (Barcelona 1927–); three *tientos* in *Historical Organ Recital Series,* ed. J. BONNET, 6 v. (New York 1940), v.6. F. PEDRELL, ed., *Antología de organistas clasicos españoles,* v.1 (Madrid 1908). Buk MusB 175. Baker 238. H. ANGLÈS, Grove DMM 2:2. J. SUBIRÁ, MusGG 2:595.

[A. DOHERTY]

CABASILAS, NICOLAS

Byzantine theologian, liturgist, and spiritual writer; b. Thessalonica, *c.* 1320; d. before 1391. Nicolas's surname was Chamaetus, but he preferred to use his mother's family name, Cabasilas. His uncle, Nilus *Cabasilas, Archbishop of Thessalonica, was his teacher. Nicolas served at the court of Emperor John VI Cantecuzenus in 1350, apparently as a layman; and in 1354 he was one of the three candidates for the Patriarchate of Constantinople. He was not selected, however, and remained a layman; the view that he succeeded his uncle in the See of Thessalonica is false. He is not to be identified with Michael Cabasilas, the sacellarius, nor was he a partner of *Nicephorus Gregoras in controversy.

Of his more important writings, *A Commentary on the Divine Liturgy* is an explanation of the Byzantine Mass; it is unexcelled as a profound and devout tract on the Eucharistic sacrifice. In spite of an anti-Latin section (cc.29–30) that deals with the dispute concerning the words of *consecration, the work has been well received in the West and was used at the Council of Trent during the deliberations on the Mass as a witness to Catholic tradition. Nicolas dealt with the spiritual life in his *Life in Christ,* composed of seven books; it is a major work on Christian asceticism. The first five books treat of the divine activity in the spiritual life, the last two, of man's cooperation. God's activity is seen to take place within the sacramental life. Thus the first book treats of Baptism, Confirmation, and the Eucharist. Man's activity is seen as a submission to the will of God, which is accomplished by prayer and meditation on the life of Jesus.

Nicolas exhibited a keen awareness of the social revolution affecting the Byzantine Empire, and particularly Thessalonica. He wrote a tract against usury and directed a memorandum to the Empress concerning the rate of interest. He opposed the policies of the religious zealots in regard to ecclesiastical property, and wrote a consideration concerning the cultivation of learning on the part of virtuous men (unedited). He wrote also a treatise on skepticism directed against the influence of Sextus Empiricus on his contemporaries.

His preaching, particularly because of its theological quality, was greatly appreciated. Among his writings are sermons on the Ascension, on the Annunciation, and on other feasts of the Blessed Virgin Mary; sermons on the sufferings of Christ; encomiums for St. Demetrius, St. Theodora, and St. Nicholas, James the Younger, and on the Three Hierarchies. He engaged in mild polemics with the West and took some part in the Hesychast controversies. He wrote religious poetry of some value and left a considerable amount of correspondence. Nicolas Cabasilas represents the tradition of the Byzantine lay theologian at its best.

Bibliography: PG 150:368–772. M. JUGIE, ed. and tr., PatrOr 19.3 (1925) 456–510, sermons. R. GUILLAUD, ByzZ 30 (1929–30) 96–102. V. LAURENT, *Hellenicá* 9 (1936) 185–205. R. J. LOENERTZ, OrChrPer 21 (1955) 205–231, letters and chronology. *A Commentary on the Divine Liturgy,* tr. J. M. HUSSEY and P. A. McNULTY (SPCK; 1960). Beck KTLBR 780–782. S. SALAVILLE, Catholicisme 2:339–340; DictSpirAscMyst 2:1–9. J. GOUILLARD, DHGE 11:14–21. F. VERNET, DTC 2.1:1292–95. H. M. BIERDERMANN, LexThK² 7:988. G. HORN, RevAscMyst 3 (1922) 20–45. M. I. LOT-BORODINE, *Un Maître . . . Nicolas Cabasilas* (Paris 1958).

[H. D. HUNTER]

CABASILAS, NILUS, 14th-century Byzantine theologian and apologete, metropolitan of Thessalonica; b. Thessalonica, *c.* 1298; d. *c.* 1363. Nilus served at the court of John VI Cantecuzenus and in 1361 was consecrated metropolitan of Thessalonica, although he never took possession of the see. He was the revered professor of his nephew Nicolas *Cabasilas and of Demetrius *Cydones. At first Nilus appears to have been either neutral or inclined against the Palamite teaching. He was consulted by Demetrius Cydones for clarification of the doctrines in dispute between the Latin and Greek Churches and favored efforts at reunion. He became an admirer of the writings of *Thomas Aquinas and encouraged Cydones in his translation of the *Summa contra gentiles.* Apparently at the request of the Emperor he took an interest in the Hesychastic controversies and eventually sided with Palamas, attempting to win Nicephorus *Gregoras to the Palamite position. With the Patriarch Philotheus Coccinus, Nilus composed the Palamitic tome of the Synod of 1351 and wrote an *Antigramma* against Gregoras. Realizing that the works of Aquinas posed a threat to Byzantine theology, he set about to refute the arguments of the *Summa contra gentiles* and made free use of the works of *Barlaam of Calabria in his "On the Procession of the Holy Spirit." Finally, he produced several other anti-Latin writings, including a refutation of the Thomistic use of the syllogism in theology, which seems originally to have been part of the work on the Holy Spirit, and tracts on the causes of the schism, another on the primacy of the pope, and one on the synod of 879–880. A work on purgatory attributed to him actually belongs to Mark *Eugenicus. His considerations on the procession of the Holy Spirit were influential at the Council of Florence.

Bibliography: PG 148:1328–1435, *Adversus Gregoras Nicephorus;* 149:683–730, schism and primacy; 151:707–764, tome of the synod. E. CANDAL, OrChrPer 9 (1943) 245–306, Procession of the Holy Spirit; *ibid.* 23 (1957) 237–266, Palamite theology; ed., *Nilus Cabasilas et theologia S. Thomae de processione Spiritus Sancti* (StTest 116; 1945). F. VERNET, DTC 2.1:1295–97. H. BECK, DivThomF 13 (1935) 1–22, Thomism. Beck KTLBR 727–728. M. RACKL, *Xenia Thomistica,* ed. S. SZABÓ, 3 v. (Rome 1925) 3:363–389. L. PETIT, PatrOr 15 (1927) 5–168. G. SCHIRO, *Studi Bizantini* 9 (1957) 362–388.

[H. D. HUNTER]

CABASSUT, JEAN, theologian and priest of the Oratory; b. Aix, 1604; d. Aix, 1685. He taught Canon Law at Avignon, and was companion and confessor to the Archbishop of Aix, Cardinal Grimaldi, when the latter became Pope Alexander VII. He was well known for his writings on ecclesiastical history and was considered an authority on Canon Law and moral theology. In moral theology he was a probabiliorist and was highly esteemed by St. Alphonsus. His main works were: *Notitia Conciliorum* (Lyons 1668); *Notitia ecclesiastica historiarium, conciliorum . . .* (Lyons 1680), considered an authoritative work on the history of councils; and *Juris canonici theoria et praxis* (Lyons 1660), which went through many editions.

Bibliography: J. RAFFALLI, DDC 2:1185. Hurter Nomencl³ 4:508. L. BATTEREL, *Mémoires domestiques pour servir à l'histoire de l'Oratoire,* ed. A. INGOLD and E. BONNARDET, 5 v. (Paris 1903–11) 2:396–412. Van Hove 1:541.

[J. M. BUCKLEY]

CABEZÓN, ANTONIO DE, eminent Renaissance organist and composer; b. Castrillo de Matajudíos, near Burgos, Spain, March 30, 1510; d. Madrid, March 26, 1566. Although blind from childhood, he was appointed court organist to Isabel, consort of Charles V, in 1526 and settled in Ávila, where he married Luisa Núñez. In 1548 he became court organist to Philip II, whom he accompanied on journeys to Italy, Germany, France, England, and the Netherlands. He moved to Madrid in 1560 and remained there until his death. His son Hernando (1541–1602) succeeded him as court organist and published the most important source of his works, the *Obras de música* . . .. It contains keyboard arrangements of hymn-tunes and motets, variations (*diferencias*) on popular tunes, and *tientos,* short pieces similar in style to the Italian canzona and ricercar, all written in Spanish keyboard tablature. His music exhibits in a purely instrumental style a mastery of counterpoint and genius of conception that foreshadows Bach and ranks Cabezón among the great composers for keyboard instruments.

Bibliography: Works. *Obras de música para tecla, arpa, y vihuela,* ed. H. DE CABEZÓN (Madrid 1578); *Hispaniae schola musica sacra,* ed. F. PEDRELL, 8 v. (Barcelona 1894–98) v.3, 4, 7, 8, only complete modern ed. of *Obras* . . .; selected organ pieces in Edition Schott, 1621, 4826, 4948, and in *Historical Organ Recital Series,* ed. J. BONNET, 6 v. (New York 1940) v.1, 6. Literature. S. KASTNER, Grove DMM 2:3–4; *Antonio de Cabezón* (Barcelona 1952). H. ANGLÈS, MusGG 2:595–602. G. CHASE, *The Music of Spain* (rev. ed. New York 1959). Reese MusR. W. APEL, "Early Spanish Music of Lute and Keyboard Instruments," MusQ 20 (1934) 289–301. A. C. HOWELL, "Cabezón: An Essay in Structural Analysis," MusQ 50 (1964) 18–30. For a possible kinship of Cabezón and Cavazzoni, see the following: T. DART, "Cavazzoni and Cabezón," MusLett 36 (1955) 2–6. K. JEPPESEN, "Cavazzoni–Cabezón," JAmMusSoc 8 (1955) 81–85. T. DART, *ibid.* 148, a reply to Jeppesen.

[A. DOHERTY]

CABOT

John, explorer who established English claims to North America; b. Genoa, Italy, *c.* 1450; d. Bristol?, England, 1498. In 1476 he became a naturalized citizen of Venice. While trading with the Levant, he developed an interest in finding an all-water route to the East. About 1484 he went to England seeking financial support for such a voyage. He may have lived in Bristol earlier, *c.* 1472, and his son Sebastian may have been born there. In March 1496 after the voyages of Columbus were known, Henry VII issued letters patent to Cabot and his sons Lewis, Sebastian, and Santius for a voyage of exploration. They left Bristol May 2, 1497, and arrived at Cape Breton Island June 24. Cabot thought the island was a part of the northeastern coast of Asia and took possession of it in the name of the English king. He returned to Bristol in August. In May 1498, with new letters patent, he crossed the Atlantic again, exploring the coasts of Greenland. Hoping to find Japan, he sailed South along the eastern coast of North America as far as the 38th parallel. He died shortly after his return to Bristol in the autumn of 1498.

Sebastian, navigator and cartographer, son of John; b. Bristol or Venice; *c.* 1476; d. Bristol?, 1557. Recent scholarship favors the tradition that he was born in Bristol. He accompanied his father on the voyages to North America in 1497–98.

He established a reputation as a skilled cartographer, and in 1512 he was employed by Ferdinand of Spain in that capacity. In 1519 Charles V appointed him pilot major and official examiner of pilots. In 1526, while commanding an expedition to Brazil, he explored the La Plata region. On his return to Spain in 1530 he was arrested and imprisoned, charged with mismanagement of the expedition. By 1533, however, he was reinstated in his former position as examiner of pilots. In 1547 he returned to England, where he was granted (1548) a life pension by Edward VI. Despite efforts on the part of Charles V to bring him back to Spain, he remained in England. He was instrumental in setting up the Company of Merchant Adventurers, which he served as governor.

Bibliography: J. B. BREBNER, *The Explorers of North America, 1492–1806* (New York 1933). C. H. COOTE, DNB 3:618–623. G. P. WINSHIP, *Cabot Bibliography, With an Introductory Essay on the Careers of the Cabots* . . . (New York 1900). *The Northmen, Columbus and Cabot, 985–1503,* ed. J. E. OLSON and E. G. BOURNE (New York 1906). G. ROSSO, EncCatt 3:263–264.

[E. A. CARRILLO]

CABRAL, PEDRO ÁLVARES, Portuguese navigator, discoverer of Brazil; b. Belmonte, *c.* 1467; d. Santarém, between 1518 and 1520. Very little is known about his life, except for his voyage to India, in the course of which he discovered Brazil. He was known as one of the best sailors of his time, and in 1500 King Manuel appointed him to command a fleet of 13 ships sailing from Lisbon to Calcutta, India, thus to repeat the voyage of Vasco da Gama. The expedition set sail from Lisbon on March 9, 1500. What really determined its landing on the coast of Brazil is not known. Was it a storm? Was it a desire to escape the calmness of the African coast? Was it done deliberately, under orders of King Manuel, to find out lands that the Portuguese believed existed west of the Cape Verde Islands? Arguments can be provided for each one of these hypotheses; but in any case, Cabral landed in Brazil April 21, 1500. After taking possession of the new land, which he called Land of the Holy Cross, Cabral sent a ship back to Portugal with a letter describing the land, written by the fleet's chronicler Pero Vaz de Caminha, and proceeded on to India. A storm around the Cape of Good Hope sank four ships, and Cabral had to stop in Mozambique to repair the other vessels. He continued then to India by way of Madagascar, and was well received by the ruler of Calcutta. Later, however, some of the Portuguese were massacred. Cabral explored the various points of the Indian coast and the island of Ceylon. On his return journey he lost two other vessels and arrived in Lisbon on July 31, 1501. Another ship of his fleet had already reached the Tagus on June 23, 1501. King Manuel received the admiral with great celebration; the precious cargoes more than covered the expenses of the expedition. In 1502 Cabral was again indicated to command another fleet to India, but circumstances prevented him from carrying out the plans, and he was replaced by Vasco da Gama. He then retired to his family lands and received a high pension from the King. The date of

Miguel Cabrera's "St. Joseph," oil on canvas (detail), in the Museo de Chapultepec, Mexico City.

his death is uncertain, but he was still alive in 1518. Pedro Álvares Cabral was first to cross the South Atlantic, first to lead a fleet from America to Asia, and the first European to touch Madagascar. His voyage added much to man's knowledge of the Atlantic Ocean and the southern hemisphere.

Bibliography: J. R. McClymont, *Pedraluarez Cabral: His Progenitors, His Life and His Voyage to America and India* (London 1914). W. B. Greenlee, *The Voyage of Pedro Álvares Cabral to Brazil and India* (London 1938). J. Cortesão, *A Expedição de Pedro Álvares Cabral e o descobrimento do Brasil* (Lisbon 1922).

[T. BEAL]

CABRERA, MIGUEL, famous painter of the colonial period in Mexico; b. Oaxaca (then Antequera), 1695; d. Mexico City, 1768. There is little known about his early life. He was reared by a charitable relative and taken to Mexico City where he became an apprentice in the studio of Juan Rodríguez Xuarez, one of the most renowned painters of the period. His natural gifts and the quality that he imparted to his paintings made him within a few years the most celebrated artist of the viceroyalty. His style was influenced by Murillo, and he knew how to combine beauty of physiognomy, nobility of attitude, and softness of coloring.

This type of painting exactly suited the taste of Mexican society of the 18th century. Consequently, he was given countless commissions, both by individuals and by organizations, for portraits and religious scenes. In his workshop were produced separate paintings and large series, such as the "Life of St. Dominic" intended for the cloister of the monastery of that name, or the "Life of St. Ignatius" done for the Casa Profesa of the Jesuits. The second of these two series is partially preserved. The great demand for his paintings was prejudicial to their quality, since many were executed by his students according to drawings prepared by Cabrera. His fame persisted throughout the 19th century among Mexican writers and foreign travelers, who termed him "the Mexican Murillo." Even today his paintings are highly esteemed and bring high prices, although there are innumerable forgeries dating from the end of the 18th century. His work may be seen in Mexico City in the Pinacoteca de San Diego, in the Museo de Historia at Chapultepec, and in San Ignacio Church (Polanco).

Bibliography: M. Toussaint, *Arte colonial en México* (2d ed. Mexico City 1962). A. Velázquez Chávez, *Tres siglos de pintura colonial mexicana* (Mexico City 1939). **Illustration credit:** Instituto Nacional de Antropología e Historia, Mexico.

[G. OBREGÓN]

CABRERA, PABLO, Argentine priest, historian, ethnographer, archeologist, and musician; b. San Juan, Cuyo, Sept. 12, 1857; d. Córdoba, Jan. 29, 1936. While still very young, he began his work in the ministry and in historical research. In Córdoba, where he lived from childhood, he was acquainted with all public and private archives, and he made an unusually thorough study of their documents. He published 450 books, monographs, and articles, in all of which he surpassed his predecessors. He corrected many errors in the fields of ethnography and archeology, and in the civil as well as the ecclesiastical history of western and central Argentina. He was a self-taught scholar; but he contributed an enormous amount of material that is still useful, and he revealed the insight of genius. With regard to colonial culture, he was the first to publicize the deep concern for general, efficient public instruction that was common to Spanish colonizers. His principal books are: *Ensayos de etnografía argentina* (1910), *Tesoros del*

Pablo Cabrera.

pasado argentino (1911), *Universitarios de Córdoba* (1916), *Córdoba de la Nueva Andalucía* (1917), *Los aborígenes del país de Cuyo* (1929), *La segunda imprenta de Córdoba* (1930), *Misceláneas* (1930), *Los*

Comechingones (1931), *Etnología argentina* (1931), *Espigando en el pretérito cordobés* (1932). His kindly, generous personality, his equal treatment of rich and poor, and his lack of egotism made him universally loved and admired as a priest and a man of science.

Bibliography: E. Martínez Paz, *Monseñor Pablo Cabrera* (Córdoba, Argen. 1928); *Elogio de Mons. Pablo Cabrera* (Córdoba 1936). G. Furlong, *Monseñor Pablo Cabrera: su personalidad, su obra, su gloria* (Buenos Aires 1945). **Illustration credit:** Library of Congress.

[G. FURLONG]

CABRINI, FRANCES XAVIER, ST.

Foundress; b. Sant' Angelo Lodigiano, Lombardy, Italy, July 15, 1850; d. Chicago, Ill., Dec. 22, 1917. She was the last of 13 children of Agostino and Stella (Oldini) Cabrini. She completed the primary grades

St. Frances Xavier Cabrini.

under her sister Rosa, the village schoolmistress, and at 13 Francesca went to the Daughters of the Sacred Heart in Arluno where, at 18, she secured a teacher's license with highest honors. At this time the annual, private vow of virginity, which she had taken for 6 years, became permanent. Having been a victim of smallpox in 1872, she was refused entrance to the Daughters of the Sacred Heart because of frailty, and taught at Vidardo where, in 1874, Don Antonio Serrati persuaded her to begin charitable work at the House of Providence orphanage in Codogno. Here she took the religious habit and made her vows in September 1877.

When Bp. Domenico Gelmini closed the orphanage in 1880 he made her prioress of an Institute of *Missionary Sisters of the Sacred Heart formed from seven of the orphanage girls. The foundation was formally approved by Rome on March 12, 1888. Between 1882 and 1887 seven houses had been opened in northern Italy, and in the latter year a free school and nursery were founded in Rome. Although she had hoped from childhood to do mission work in China, Mother Cabrini nevertheless surrendered to the insistence of Leo XIII and Bp. Giovanni Battista Scalabrini of Piacenza that she go to the U.S., and on March 23, 1889, she sailed for New York with six sisters.

In New York Mother Cabrini worked among the Italian immigrants for whom she established orphanages, schools, adult classes in Christian doctrine, and

Columbus Hospital, which gained state approval in 1895. In 1909 she became a naturalized citizen and in 1910 was elected superior general for life. She founded convents, schools, orphanages, and hospitals throughout the U.S. and in South America and Europe. Always frail in body, she nevertheless crossed the sea 30 times and within 35 years established 67 houses with more than 1,500 daughters. She died of malaria in Columbus Hospital, Chicago; her body is preserved in the chapel of Mother Cabrini High School in New York City.

On Nov. 8, 1928, Cardinal George Mundelein ordered an informative hearing on the merits of her cause; it was introduced by Pius XI on March 30, 1931. She was pronounced venerable on Oct. 3, 1933, and was beatified on Nov. 13, 1938. At her canonization on July 7, 1946, Pius XII said, "Although her constitution was very frail, her spirit was endowed with such singular strength that, knowing the will of God in her regard, she permitted nothing to impede her from accomplishing what seemed beyond the strength of a woman."

Bibliography: *Frances Xavier Cabrini,* by a Benedictine of Stanbrook Abbey (London 1944). P. Di Donato, *Immigrant Saint: The Life of Mother Cabrini* (New York 1960). J. Mary, *Mother Cabrini* (Derby, N.Y. 1955). T. Maynard, *Too Small a World: The Life of Francesca Cabrini* (Milwaukee 1945). R. J. Purcell, DAB 21:146–148. **Illustration credit:** Missionary Sisters of the Sacred Heart of Jesus—Mother Cabrini High School, New York City.

[A. M. MELVILLE]

CABRINI COLLEGE

A Catholic, 4-year, liberal arts institution for young women, chartered by the Commonwealth of Pennsylvania in 1957, and empowered to grant degrees. The College, accredited by the State Department of Public Instruction and affiliated with The Catholic University of America, is dedicated to the educational principles of St. Frances Xavier *Cabrini, first American citizen to be canonized, who founded the Missionary Sisters of the Sacred Heart who administer the College. Cabrini College was granted full regional accreditation by the Middle States Association of Colleges and Secondary Schools in June 1965.

The College, which occupies a 116-acre campus (the former Dorrance estate) in Radnor, Pa., attracts resident students mainly from New York, New Jersey, Pennsylvania, Delaware, and Connecticut. Of the total population of 320 students in 1964, about 25 per cent commute daily from Philadelphia and suburban areas.

Cabrini College curriculum is designed to carry out the liberal arts aims of the institution. Curricular patterns provide a degree sequence that enables students to fulfill the general education requirements in theology, philosophy, humanities, and social and natural sciences. Teacher preparation, an important part of the program, engages the majority of the students. Majors in biology, chemistry, education, English, history, and mathematics and psychology offer an intensive area study; the minor either supports the major or provides a professional orientation to teaching. Curricular offerings are flexible and designed to satisfy both student and technological needs. To this end in 1964 radiation biology and radiochemistry were included in the science area; and Russian history, in the social science program.

In 1964 the 33-member faculty was composed of 6 priests, 7 sisters, and 20 laymen, holding 12 doctorates

Main building and residence hall, Cabrini College, Radnor.

and 15 master's degrees. Membership in professional organizations, publication in scholarly journals, and research projects manifest a continuing intellectual activity among the members.

The Cabrini College library, which has a capacity of 60,000 volumes, is constantly expanding its facilities to keep pace with its academic program. In 1965 the library housed 22,000 volumes and subscribed to 150 periodicals. Library facilities are supplemented by nearby libraries open to the students—Villanova University, Bryn Mawr College, Eastern Baptist College, and the Philadelphia Public Library. Other campus buildings and facilities include: Cabrini Hall, a dormitory for upper classmen; Sacred Heart Hall, an all-purpose building; the Bruckmann Chemistry laboratory; the Jablonski Collection; the Bruckman Memorial Chapel; a language laboratory; and athletic facilities.

Campus academic life is complemented by a varied extracurricular and intercollegiate activity program as well as area cultural opportunities. Students attend the college-sponsored Cardinal Newman Lecture Series, concerts, panels, and planned excursions; participate in activities offered by the many other institutions of higher learning in the area; and take advantage of Philadelphia's wide choice in cultural and historical experiences, such as the Pennsylvania Academy of Fine Arts, Independence Hall, and Franklin Institute, Philadelphia Museum of Art, and the Academy of Music.

Students' organizations, which include departmental clubs, publications, and activities sponsored by the Student Government Association, meet campus spiritual, recreational, and social needs. Religious practices are approached as a way of life.

[M. U. LAWRENCE]

CABROL, FERNAND, Benedictine, from 1877 popular author on the liturgy; b. Marseilles, France, Dec. 11, 1855; d. St. Leonard's-on-Sea, England, June 4, 1937. He was ordained at Le Mans in 1882 and taught Church history at *Solesmes, where he was prior, 1890 to 1896. In June 1896 he became prior of the newly founded St. Michael's at Farnborough, England, and from 1903 until his death was abbot, relinquishing actual rule to an abbot coadjutor in 1924. The abbey soon became known as Cabrol, and his fellow monks, especially H. *Leclercq, continued the liturgical tradition of Solesmes. In 1900–02 Cabrol and Leclercq began the *Monumenta ecclesiae liturgica,* a collection of texts pertaining to the liturgy from Apostolic times to Constantine. Volumes 2, 3, and 4 are lacking, but M. *Férotin of Farnborough published as volumes 5 and 6 the *Liber ordinum* (1904) and the *Liber sacramentorum* (1912), texts and studies of the Mozarabic liturgy based on several MSS. In 1903 Cabrol and the monks of Farnborough agreed to undertake the *Dictionnaire d'archéologie chrétienne et de liturgie* (DACL), planning to make generally available exhaustive and definitive studies on archeology to c. 800 and on the liturgy to modern times. In 1913 Leclercq assumed major responsibility, and after his death the work was completed (1953) by H. Marrou. The *Monumenta* and the DACL have both contributed to the continuous advance of scholarship. Cabrol did a study (1895) of the liturgy in Jerusalem as seen in the *Peregrinatio Aetheriae* (c. 400). His *Livre de la prière antique* (1900) has been edited and translated many times. Although his writings are not definitive, they promoted popular interest in the liturgy and its history.

Bibliography: H. THURSTON, *Month* 170 (1937) 267–270. J. WARRILOW, IrEcclRec 50 (1930) 364–369. L. GOUGAUD, RHE 33 (1937) 919–922. M. HARVARD, *Revue grégorienne* 22 (1937) 201–213; 23 (1938) 1–6. T. DE MOREMBERT, DictBiogFranc 7:773–774.

[E. P. COLBERT]

CACCIAGUERRA, BONSIGNORE, spiritual writer; b. Siena, 1494; d. Rome, June 30, 1566. As a young man he became a very successful merchant in Palermo and devoted his life to luxury and pleasure. An apparition of Christ on the cross and a series of personal misfortunes finally brought about his conversion. He disposed of his wealth, left Palermo and all its associations, and as a penitent visited the shrine of Santiago de Compostela and various cities in Italy. In 1545 he went to Rome and was ordained there 2 years later. His close friend and confessor, St. Philip Neri, helped Cacciaguerra secure a position as chaplain at S. Girolamo della Carità and encouraged him in what proved to be his particular apostolate, the fostering of frequent reception of the Holy Eucharist. While neither a learned theologian nor a profound thinker, he possessed a deep spiritual insight characterized by prudence and fervor. His writings were widely read, much admired by St. Francis de Sales, and repeatedly edited and translated into other languages. They include *Trattato della comunione* (Rome 1557), *Trattato della tribolazione* (Rome 1559), *Lettere spirituali* (2 v. Rome 1564–75), and others.

Bibliography: L. PONNELLE and L. BORDET, *St. Philip Neri and the Roman Society of His Times,* tr. R. F. KERR (New York 1933). P. AUVRAY, DictSpirAscMyst 2.1:10–14. C. TESTORE, EncCatt 3:266.

[J. C. WILLKE]

CÁCERES, ARCHDIOCESE OF (CACERENSIS), metropolitan see since 1951, on Bicol peninsula, southeastern Luzon, *Philippines. In 1963 it had 113 secular and 21 religious priests, 17 men in one religious house, 65 women in 11 convents, and 980,000 Catholics in a population of 1,053,000; it is 2,889 square miles in area. Its two suffragan sees, Legaspi and Sorsogon, both created in 1951, had 160 secular and 13 religious priests, 96 sisters, and 1,247,000 Catholics in a population of 1,307,500. The Spanish settlement of Cáceres (1573), later Nueva Cáceres, was absorbed in 1948 when Naga became a city, the name Cáceres continuing only in the name of the see. Naga is at the confluence of the Naga and Bicol Rivers 5 miles from San Miguel Bay. The local vernacular is Bikol. Augustinian missionaries were joined by Franciscans (1578), and Cáceres became a see, suffragan to *Manila (1595–1951). The first bishop was Luís Maldonado. The first Filipino bishop, Jorge Barlín, was bishop of Cáceres (1905–09).

Bibliography: D. ABELLA, *Bikol Annals* (Manila 1954–) v.1. *Catholic Directory of the Philippines, 1963* (Manila 1963). Ann Pont (1964) 81–82.

[D. ABELLA]

CADOUIN, ABBEY OF,

CADOUIN, ABBEY OF, former French Cistercian abbey, in the Diocese of Périgueux. It was founded in 1115 by Gerard of Sales, a disciple of *Robert of Arbrissel. In 1119, however, it was acquired by the *Cistercians of Pontigny. It became famous as the shrine of Christ's Holy *Shroud, deposited there by the Crusaders. Between 1123 and 1175, Cadouin founded Gondon, Bonnevaux, Ardorell, La Faise, and Saint-Marcel. The monastery was magnificently remodeled by the generosity of King Louis XI (d. 1483). Cadouin declined rapidly under commendatory abbots. It joined the Cistercian Strict Observance (*see* TRAPPISTS) in 1643 and regained some of its earlier prosperity but declined again in the 18th century. The abbey was suppressed by the French Revolution (1791). Its remarkable Romanesque church and late Gothic cloister serve the local parish.

Bibliography: R. DELAGRANGE, *Cadouin: Histoire d'une relique et d'un monastère* (Bergerac 1912). J. SIGALA, *Cadouin en Périgord* (Bordeaux 1950). J. M. CANIVEZ, DHGE 11:118–122. Cottineau 1:548–550. R. GAZEAU, *Catholicisme* 2:348–349.

[L. J. LEKAI]

CAECILIAN MOVEMENT

A proposed reform of church music, originating in Germany during the second half of the 19th century. The adjective is used also to designate the style in which the advocates of the reform composed, namely, a style polyphonic in texture, frequently unaccompanied in imitation of Renaissance polyphony but highly influenced by romanticist harmonies.

Background. The immediate roots of Caecilianism lay in church-music activity during the early decades of the 19th-century. Prevalent at that time were two aesthetics and styles of composing: *stile moderno,* which became in the late 18th century a symphonic orchestral approach; and *stile antico,* the careful adherence to academic contrapuntal rules (*see* MUSIC, SACRED, HISTORY OF, 4, 5, 6). The symphonic emphasis was especially prevalent in Germany, while the *stile antico* was represented in Rome, notably in the *Sistine Choir tradition. Chief among the Italian composers were Zingarelli (1752–1837), Raimondi (1786–1853), and Pietro Alfieri (1801–63). Their enthusiasm for the Renaissance ideal found support in Germany and Austria also and included Aiblinger (1779–1867), Schiedermayer (1779–1840), and Assmayer (1790–1862). In their concern to write in the pure style of *Palestrina, composers turned scholars and launched investigations into the actual music of the 16th century. Aiblinger traveled extensively throughout Italy

collecting works of Italian masters. The publications of Giuseppe *Baini (1775–1844) and the music collection of Fortunato Santini (1778–1862), now housed in Münster, Germany, did much to enhance the prestige of Renaissance musical art—especially that of Palestrina and the Roman school—and to encourage performances of these works. Alexander *Choron (1771–1834), through his *École de chant* for the study of church music and his writings, especially *Principles de composition* (1808) and *Encyclopédie musicale* (1836–38), helped bring the Renaissance ideal to France. R. J. Von Maldeghem (1810–93), another pioneer musicologist, concentrated on Flemish vocal polyphony and gave currency to much early choral music in his 29-volume *Trésor musical* (Brussels 1865–93).

It was Germany, however, that gave the movement its greatest practical impetus. Karl *Proske (1794–1861) had made three trips to Italy collecting the works of Renaissance masters. Regensburg, where his library was kept, became the center of diffusion for Germany. Here Joseph *Schrems (1815–72) developed the cathedral choir into a highly proficient group and a means of implementing the polyphonic revival. Extensive work was done also by Kaspar *Ett (1799–1847) in Munich; and F. Commer (1813–87), a tireless scholar and musical leader in Berlin, published several valuable collections of old music, notably his 28-volume *Musica sacra* and 2-volume *Cantica sacra*. Concern for liturgical propriety brought about a revaluation of the role of chant in the celebration of the liturgy. In the early 19th century there were thus some attempts to produce a feasible version of the chant. Among the first was Ett's *Cantica sacra* (1827; last ed. New York-Cincinnati 1906), with its simplified melodies and accompaniments. His efforts were followed by those of Schiedermayer and Alfieri.

Reform Movement. It is small wonder that the contrast between the tasteless orchestral style that had predominated in Germany and the resuscitated Renaissance repertory should have moved many musicians (among them *Liszt and R. *Wagner) and clergymen to seek reform. In Regensburg Bishop *Sailer's reform writings and teachings found a well-prepared soil. The entire milieu collaborated to bring about reform and revival in the establishment of the Caecilianverein by F. X. *Witt (1839–80) in 1868. There had been agitation for reform before this, and Witt himself had sought unsuccessfully to win approval of such an organization at a general meeting of the Catholic Society of Germany at Innsbruck in 1867. At a meeting of the same society the next year, however, his ideas received more sympathy. The general objective of his movement was to improve the quality of the church music performed in Germany (and elsewhere as well). Unaccompanied polyphonic works of the Renaissance were looked on as the consummate ideal, but the reform embraced also the use of chant, the composition of new unaccompanied works, organ and instrumentally accompanied works, and the vernacular hymn. There was no attempt to proscribe altogether the use of instruments in church, and even Witt and his colleagues continued to provide instrumental accompaniment. *A cappella* polyphony remained, however, the goal to be reached by the composer. The organization was set up under the patronage of St. Cecilia. Named to its executive body were a cardinal-protector, a general president, and local officers. The reforms were promulgated rapidly, first in Germany, then in Europe, and very vigorously in the U.S. *See* MUSIC, SACRED (U.S.); MUSIC SOCIETIES IN THE U.S. Witt disseminated his principles in the periodicals *Fliegende Blätter für Katholische Kirchenmusik* (later renamed *Caecilienvereinsorgan,* or CVO) and *Musica sacra* (which included frequent music supplements) so thoroughly that both the cathedral and the country parish quickly adopted Caecilian reforms. Pope Pius IX gave it official sanction on Dec. 16, 1870, in the brief *Multum ad movendos animos.*

Effects of Reform. Adherence to Caecilian standards produced a copious amount of new music intended for liturgical use. By copying polyphonic devices, cadences, and chordal declamation, composers found a stock of formulas for turning out sacred music in quantity. The rigidity of such technique brought forth many unimaginative works that produced an effect opposite from that originally intended. Whenever Caecilian reforms were spread, they were carried with somewhat dictatorial tones that triggered some opposition, such as that on the part of J. E. Habert (1833–89) in Austria, who in 1875 voiced his objection to the absolutism of the Caecilian Society. The reactionaries against Caecilian dictates favored closer collaboration with current aesthetics and a lightening of the restrictions on concerted music. M. *Brosig (1815–87) attempted a reconciliation of concerted music and Caecilian principles. In spite of such dissatisfaction, Caecilianism grew in influence, and societies based on Witt's constitution flourished everywhere. Under the patronage of Abp. John Henni of Milwaukee, John *Singenberger (1848–1924) formally established the American Caecilian Society, which became one of the largest in the world. Its official organ, *Caecilia,* first appeared in 1874 and was still published until its merger with the *Catholic Choirmaster* in 1964.

As mentioned earlier, one of the chief objectives of the Caecilians was the restoration of Gregorian chant. Books of chant accompaniment, such as the *Enchiridion Chorale* (1853) by J. G. *Mettenleiter, perpetuated Renaissance harmonic principles with little imagination. An edition of the chant itself was prepared by F. X. *Haberl (1840–1910) from the Medicaean version. His *Gradualia* (1871) and *Antiphonaria* (1878), however, were based on inaccurate scholarship and were supplanted by the Vatican edition of 1903 (*see* CHANT BOOKS, PRINTED EDITIONS OF). The disqualification of this edition from the Church's liturgical books proved to be one of the death blows to Caecilianism as a society. Its reforming function, however, was fulfilled in St. Pius X's *motu proprio* on sacred music (1903). Caecilianism had generated and maintained interest in reforming church music, in reviving the Renaissance masters, in promoting Gregorian chant, and in unifying liturgical practice—the points conspicuously emphasized in the *motu proprio.*

In the 20th Century. Since the society's goal had been reached, its usefulness as an organization ceased, but the style peculiar to its adherents remained. Composers such as *Ravanello (1871–1938), *Goller (1873–1953), and *Yon (1886–1943) were composing well into the 20th century in a style directly linked with Caecilianism, although strong romanticist sonorities predominate. Polyphonic devices frequently became nothing more than rows of clichéd patterns in the later

Caecilian composers. The works of *Haller (1840–1915), early *Griesbacher, and Goller are among the best written in the style. Chromaticism and leitmotiv principles introduced by Griesbacher (1864–1933) created in the harmony a tendency toward Wagnerian sentimentality. In general, the "established" Caecilian spirit created a unique ecclesiastical style and formed a framework that, by its own inflexibility, condemned itself. The style cramped creative effort relevant to its own age, and almost none of the later efforts show originality. The spirit of the reform, however, may still be felt in the absence of orchestras in the celebration of the liturgy, the fact of a uniform edition of the chant, and the general awareness of the need for constant surveillance of the musical activity of the Church.

Bibliography: L. W. ELLINWOOD, *The History of American Church Music* (New York 1953). Fellerer CathChMus. K. G. FELLERER, MusGG 2:621–628. Ursprung. E. TITTEL, *Oesterreichische Kirchenmusik* (Vienna 1961). R. SCHLECHT, *Geschichte der Kirchenmusik* (Regensburg 1871), esp. 184–215. A. SCHARNAGL, *Die Regensburger Tradition* (Cologne 1962). G. REESE, "Maldeghem and His Buried Treasure," *Music Library Association, Notes* 6 (1948) 75–117. See also the complete files of *Musica Sacra* 1–21 (Regensburg 1868–88), NS 1–58 (1889–1928), *Caecilienvereinsorgan* 1–68 (Regensburg 1866–1937), and *Caecilia* 1–91 (Milwaukee 1874–1964).

[F. J. MOLECK]

CAEDMON, first English poet whose name is known; fl. *c.* 670. His story is told in one of the great chapters of *Bede's *Ecclesiastical History* (5.24). He was a cowherd on lands of the monastery of Streanes Healh, usually identified with Whitby. In rustic feasts at Streanes Healh, the company used to entertain one another by singing poems to the music of the harp. Caedmon had grown old and had never been bold enough to take his turn; when the harp, passed from hand to hand, approached him, he used to steal away from the feast. One night as he slept after deserting the festival, an angel appeared to him and told him to sing of the beginning of things. "He began at once to sing lines in praise of God the Creator, verses he had never heard before." Here Bede gives a Latin paraphrase of Caedmon's Creation Hymn. On awakening, Caedmon found he could compose other verses. His miraculous talent was called to the attention of the learned monks of Streanes Healh. Thereupon, they instructed him from Scripture in the events of sacred history. He meditated and composed verses until he had versified the principal events in the Old and New Testaments. Many imitated Caedmon, but none could equal him. Bede clearly regarded him as the father of vernacular Christian poetry in England (*see* ENGLISH LITERATURE, 1).

Of Caedmon's apparently very extensive composition in English, only the Creation Hymn (nine lines) is extant. A version in Northumbrian English is found in the oldest MS of Bede's *Historia Ecclesiastica*. The translation of Bede's *Historia* made in King Alfred's time (849–899) contains a related version in West Saxon. The Biblical poems of the Junius Manuscript, *Genesis, Exodus,* and *Daniel,* can no longer be regarded as the work of Caedmon. The older portions of the poems—*Genesis,* at least, is certainly composite—may be later developments of the kind of composition based on Scripture that Caedmon introduced. In that sense, they are of his school, Caedmonian.

Bibliography: E. V. K. DOBBIE, *The Manuscripts of Caedmon's Hymn and Bede's Death Song* (New York 1937), detailed account of the versions of the Creation Hymn. G. P. KRAPP, ed., *The Junius Manuscript* (New York 1931), ed. of the Caedmonian poems. C. W. KENNEDY, tr., *The Caedmon Poems* (New York 1916). C. L. WRENN, *The Poetry of Caedmon* (London 1947), best study of significance of the Creation Hymn in the tradition of early English poetry.

[C. J. DONAHUE]

CAEDWALLA, KING OF WESSEX; b. *c.* 659
of the stock of Cerdic; d. Rome, *c.* April 20, 689. Caedwalla became King of the West Saxons in 685 or 686, resigning in 688. Under his brief but fierce rule, Wessex rose to prominence and power, Sussex was subjugated, Surrey and Kent were reduced to dependency. He also conquered the Isle of Wight and extirpated its inhabitants, the last adherents of Anglo-Saxon heathenism. Probably influenced by his friend St. *Wilfrid, he abdicated to go to Rome, the first of several Anglo-Saxon kings to make that pilgrimage. He was baptized by Pope *Sergius I on Easter eve, April 10, 689; he died a few days later, and was buried in St. Peter's, Rome, on April 20.

Bibliography: BEDE, *Eccl. Hist.* 4.12, 15–16; 5.7. J. EARLE and C. PLUMMER, eds., *Two of the Saxon Chronicles Parallel*, 2 v. (Oxford 1892–99) 2:31–32. W. BRIGHT, *Chapters of Early English Church History* (3d ed. Oxford 1897). F. M. STENTON, *Anglo-Saxon England* (2d ed. Oxford 1947) 68–70.

[R. D. WARE]

CAELESTIS AGNI NUPTIAS, a hymn written
by Francesco Lorenzini of Florence for the office of St. Juliana *Falconieri (d. 1341), who was canonized in 1737. In 1738 the hymn was inserted in the Breviary for the Vespers and Matins of her feast (June 19). It consists of four strophes in iambic dimeter, plus the doxology. It reflects the baroque style of the period and resembles strongly the hymn *Regis superni nuntia* in the office of St. Teresa of Avila, from which it borrows (though the converse also is possible). Both hymns are based on events in the lives of the heroines.

Bibliography: A. MIRRA, *Gli inni del breviario romano* (Naples 1947). S. MATTEI, EncCatt 3:273. B. STÄBLEIN, LexThK² 2:880–881. J. CONNELLY, ed and tr., *Hymns of the Roman Liturgy* (Westminster, Md. 1957).

[J. J. GAVIGAN]

CAELESTIS AULAE NUNTIUS, a hymn of
five strophes in iambic dimeter, composed apparently by the Dominican, E. Sirena (d. 1796), although others attribute it to his confrere A. Ricchini (d. 1779). In remembrance of the victory over the Turks at Lepanto (1571), Gregory XIII instituted the feast of the Holy *Rosary, extended by Clement XI to the universal Church after another victory over the Turks in Hungary (1716). In the 18th century, either Sirena or Ricchini composed the hymns in honor of the Rosary, which were inserted in the Dominican Breviary in 1834. Finally, in 1888, under Leo XIII, a new Office was adopted and the hymns of Sirena (or Ricchini) were employed; this hymn on the five joyful mysteries was assigned to the first Vespers.

Bibliography: A. MIRRA, *Gli inni del breviario romano* (Naples 1947). S. MATTEI, EncCatt 3:273. Chevalier RepHymn 3448, 24710. J. CONNELLY, ed. and tr., *Hymns of the Roman Liturgy* (Westminster, Md. 1957).

[J. J. GAVIGAN]

CAELESTIS URBS JERUSALEM, a hymn
of nine strophes, now in iambic dimeter after revision under Urban VIII of the original hymn in trochaic dimeter. The author is unknown, but MSS of the earlier form, the *Urbs beata Jerusalem*, prove that it was composed no later than the 8th century, and perhaps one or two centuries earlier. It was employed in the 8th century in Poitiers as a hymn (then in eight strophes) for the procession to the baptismal font on Holy Saturday. In the 10th century (with 9 to 12 strophes) it was used as a hymn for the dedication of churches. Today it is found in the Roman Breviary as part of the common for the Dedication of a Church. At Vespers, four strophes plus a doxology are sung. The hymn considers the church built on earth with her human members as a symbol of heaven. Though somewhat abstract in tone, it weaves in many references from the Old and New Testaments to present the Church militant as the bride of Christ, destined to lead her members to Him.

Bibliography: A. MIRRA, *Gli inni del breviario romano* (Naples 1947). S. MATTEI, EncCatt 3:273–274. H. LAUSBERG, LexThK² 2:881. AnalHymn 51:110. Chevalier RepHymn 20918, 3461 (20920, 34237 for further adaptations). J. CONNELLY, ed. and tr., *Hymns of the Roman Liturgy* (Westminster, Md. 1957).

[J. J. GAVIGAN]

CAELI DEUS SANCTISSIME, hymn of un-
known authorship, sung at Vespers on Wednesday in the ferial Office. Written in iambic trimeter, the hymn, in a manner appropriate for the hour of Vespers (the evening Office), draws a poetic picture of the varying phases caused by the Creator in the coming and going of celestial light. Each of the four strophes plays its part in the usual style of Vesper hymns, i.e., mention is made of the original creation of all things, followed by an appropriately associated divine attribute manifested therein; in this case, sanctity and the orderly arrangement of creation are celebrated. With simple beauty the hymn refers in the first strophe to the creation of light. The second, following the account of Gn 1.14–19, describes the forming on the 4th day (Wednesday) of the "glowing wheel" of the sun, and the assignment of their ordered movement to the moon and stars. The third strophe notes the use of sun and moon to begin and close the day, and to point out the beginning of the new month. The fourth makes the typical application of such hymns by asking God to expel darkness (sin) from men's hearts and minds, and to free them from the slavery of their sins.

Bibliography: A. MIRRA, *Gli inni del breviario romano* (Naples 1947). AnalHymn 51:37. *Monumenta monodica medii aevi*, ed. B. STÄBLEIN (Kassel 1956–). Connelly Hymns 38–39.

[J. J. GAVIGAN]

CAELITUM JOSEPH DECUS, opening line of a
hymn of unknown authorship, consisting of five sapphic strophes, found in the Roman Breviary at Matins on the feast of St. *Joseph, March 19. Its earliest occurrence is in a *Benedictine Breviary of 1580. It is not employed in the new feast of St. Joseph the Artisan because of a desire to use in that feast a hymn that puts more emphasis on daily physical labor. The older hymn presents Joseph from the viewpoint of his historical and theological position. Hence, he is called "certain hope of (eternal) life," a reference to his importance as intercessor; "spouse of the Virgin"; and the man chosen by the Creator "to be called the father of the Word," in which his historical importance is evident. His place as patriarch at the end of the Old Testament and the beginning

of the New is beautifully brought out in the third strophe. His rank as father of the Holy Family, in which the King of Kings obeyed him, is the teaching of the fourth strophe. The fifth and last is a doxology, quite different from the usual type; for it not only contains the normal praise of the three Divine Persons, but is also presented as a prayer, asking for eternal life by the intercession of St. Joseph.

Bibliography: A. MIRRA, *Gl'inni del breviario romano* (Naples 1947) 198–199. S. MATTEI, EncCatt 3:274. Szövérffy AnnLat Hymn 2:450.

[J. J. GAVIGAN]

CAEN

Capital city of Calvados, Normandy, France; population 100,000 in 1964. First mentioned in a document of 1026, *Cadomum,* formed of four villages at the confluence of the Orne and the Odon, grew up around the Abbey of Saint-Etienne (*aux hommes*) built by William the Conqueror in 1077 and the Abbey of La Trinité (*aux dames*) built by his wife Matilda in 1066 to make amends for their marriage of kinship. *Lanfranc consecrated Saint-Etienne, which shows Lombard architectural influence, and Matilda is buried in the church of La Trinité. Philip II took Caen in 1204, and the English pillaged it in 1346 and occupied it during the Hundred Years' War (1417–50). The university founded in 1432 by the Duke of Bedford, the English regent, still exists. In the 17th century Caen was noted for the Hermitage, a spiritual retreat of the *Compagnie du Saint-Sacrement, to which belonged St. John *Eudes, the founder of the seminary in Caen (1664). The French Revolution suppressed religious communities of long standing in Caen: Carmelites (1228), Jacobins

The church of Saint-Pierre at Caen, France.

(1234), Cordeliers (1236), Crosiers (before 1238), Capuchins (1575), Jesuits (1612), Oratorians (1615), Eudists (1643), Carmelite nuns (1616), Ursulines (1636), Benedictines of Good Help (1644), Sisters of Charity (1651), Sisters of the Holy Redeemer (1731), who began a new method for the education of the deaf and dumb, and the Daughters of Charity (*c.* 1750). The *Concordat of 1801 left only a few communities of sisters, to which several have been added since. Caen, with seven parishes, is in the Diocese of *Bayeux. There were 200 students in its minor seminary in 1961, and Catholic school enrollment was 6,250. Pilgrimages to Notre Dame de la Délivrande remain popular.

The churches of Caen were happily spared in World War II or have been restored since. Saint-Etienne with a 12th-century nave, was damaged by Protestants in 1562 and restored shortly after 1600. The buildings of the abbey, now the town hall, were rebuilt (1704–44) by Guillaume de la Tremblay in an excellent style. The façade of La Trinité was not so well restored in the 19th century. The buildings of its abbey now house an old men's home. Saint-Pierre, rebuilt in 13th-century Gothic and completed in 1535, has a noteworthy Renaissance apse. Other churches also deserve mention: Saint-Jean in 15th-century flamboyant; the late 17th-century Jesuit chapel, Notre Dame de la Gloriette; the 14th–16th century Holy Redeemer; and the 11th-century Romanesque St. Nicholas, no longer in use.

Bibliography: H. PRENTOUT, *Caen et Bayeux* (Paris 1909). *Le Diocèse de Bayeux-Lisieux aux environs de l'an 1960* (Bayeux 1961).

[J. GOURHAND]

CAESAREA, SCHOOL OF

An offshoot of the theological school of *Alexandria, stemming from the same doctrinal tradition. The school of Caesarea in Palestine possessed the most important library in Christian antiquity.

Origen. Banished from Alexandria by Bp. Demetrius (231–233) after his ordination by Bp. Theoctistus of Caesarea, *Origen settled in that city and began to lecture. A short while later *Gregory Thaumaturgus and his brother Athenodorus became his disciples. Gregory's farewell address (*In Gratitude to Origen*) traced the program and pedagogic method of his master.

Teaching was given according to the divisions of the philosophy of the time. Logic, a mixture of dialectics and criticism, followed the Socratic method. Physics, which meant above all geometry and astronomy, demonstrated the work of God in His creation. Moral doctrine gave a knowledge of oneself and one's purpose in the study of virtues. Finally, theology was taught in two fashions: by readings in the philosophers and poets of all the schools except the atheists, to form a critical sense in avoiding systematic and exclusive attachments; then by the study of Scripture, for it was thought that one should attach himself only to the word of God. This method had a strong spiritual orientation, and Origen stressed the practice of virtue. Certain of Gregory's expressions that are confirmed by two fragments of letters (from Origen on Ambrose according to the 11th-century Byzantine antiquarians, George Kedrenos and Suidas; of Ambrose to Origen according to Jerome, *Epist.* 43, to Marcella) suggest a community life of the master with his Maecenas, Ambrose, and his students in prayer, the reading of Scripture, and intellectual activities.

At Jerusalem (then called Aelia) Bishop Alexander, a friend of Origen, had founded a Christian library (*see* LIBRARIES, ANCIENT). That of Caesarea contained from the beginning the books possessed by Origen and his own writings, particularly an original copy of the *Hexapla,* which Jerome consulted and which seems never to have been reproduced in its entirety; but the text of the *Septuagint that it contained was copied constantly. The group of copyists that the affluent Ambrose supported for Origen followed the latter from Alexandria to Caesarea. The letter preserved in Kedrenos and Suidas shows Origen and Ambrose making a collation of the texts and verifying copies.

Pamphilus. Was the school continued after the death of Origen under the direction of an able disciple from Caesarea, possibly Theotecnus? It is not possible to affirm this. However, the library was preserved, and 40 years later (*c.* 290) *Pamphilus was installed at Caesarea by the new bishop, Agapius, after having been the disciple of Pierius, who was nicknamed Origen the Younger, in the Didascalion of Alexandria. Ordained by Agapius, Pamphilus remained faithful to the method of Origen, taught him by Pierius. Two students, Apphianus and Aidesius, are known to have lived with him in a community together with Eusebius (*De mart. Pales.* 4.6; 5.2). The only writing of Pamphilus is his *Apologia* for Origen.

Pamphilus paid particular care to the library, which he enriched considerably (Eusebius, *Hist. eccl.* 6.33), and in the lost biography he wrote of Pamphilus, *Eusebius of Caesarea had transcribed a catalogue of the works of Origen and other ecclesiastics, which his master had assembled; the list of Origen's writings was reproduced in part by Jerome (*Epist.* 33, *ad Paulam*). He had likewise gathered a collection of more than 100 scattered letters of Origen (*Hist. eccl.* 6.36.3).

Pamphilus also employed a group of copyists to reproduce MSS that were in poor condition or those he could not acquire otherwise, as well as to furnish copies of his own holdings for others. Among the copyists was the young slave Porphyry, whom Pamphilus had brought up as a son and who desired to suffer martyrdom with him (*De mart. Pales.* 11.1.15–19). Certain MSS of the *Hexapla* Septuagint show traces of the corrections made by Pamphilus in the volume that served as a model for the copyists; thus, in the *Sinaiticus* after II Esdras there is a note: "Antoninus has made the collations; I, Pamphilus, have corrected it."

According to an interesting hypothesis of C. Martin ["Le Testamonium Flavianum: Vers une solution définitive?", *Revue belge de philologie et d'histoire* 20 (1941) 409–465], a copyist of Pamphilus and his corrector were guilty of error in respect to the testimony of Flavius Josephus (*Ant.* 18.63–64) on Jesus. Origen presents this testimony definitely as that of an unbeliever (Origen, *Contra Cels.* 1.47). Sixty years later Eusebius cited the passage in Josephus as a profession of Christian faith (*Hist. eccl.* 1.11.7–9), basing his position on the reading of the text of Josephus that he had—and which is the extant text—containing these clauses: "if he is really to be called a man," "he was the Christ," and "he appeared to them the third day, alive again, the divine prophets having foretold these wonderful things and many others about him." Martin suggests that these clauses were marginal notes, perhaps made even by Origen himself, and that between the time of Origen

and Eusebius they were inserted into the text of Josephus by a careless copyist. The rest of the text of Josephus regarding the rise of Christianity is to be regarded as genuine.

Eusebius. The spiritual son of Pamphilus, Eusebius returned to Caesarea after the persecution and became its bishop, perhaps in 315. Acacius of Caesarea is supposed to have written a life of Eusebius referring to him as his master (*didascalos*), which would seem to imply that Eusebius taught at Caesarea. In any case, Eusebius used for his erudite works the libraries at Jerusalem and Caesarea, the latter of which he developed through the use of his own group of copyists. Constantine demanded 50 copies of the Bible from him for his new capital (*Vita Const.* 4.36).

Acacius and Euzoius. According to Jerome (*De vir. ill.* 113; *Epist.* 34, *ad Marcellam*), these successors of Eusebius had all the volumes recopied from papyrus onto the more durable parchment, a fact that MSS mention. Jerome frequently speaks of the library at Caesarea, where he had labored and received a good part of his learning. Regarding a visit by *Hilary of Poitiers and *Eusebius of Vercelli during their exile in the East there is no certain evidence. *Isidore of Seville speaks of 30,000 volumes there (*Etymol.* 6.6). The destruction of the library by either the Persians or the Arabs in the 7th century was a great loss. Many of the MSS of the Bible or of Christian antiquity now known go back through copies to a volume or codex of the library of Origen and Pamphilus at Caesarea.

Bibliography: A. EHRHARD, "Die griechische patriarchal Bibliothek von Jerusalem," RömQuartalsch 5 (1891) 217–263; 6 (1892) 329–331. F. CAVALLERA, *Saint Jérôme,* 2 v. (SpicSacLov; 1922) 2:88–89. R. CADIOU, "La Bibliothèque de Césarée," Rev ScRel 16 (1936) 474–483. Ghellinck Patr 2:259–268.

[H. CROUZEL]

CAESAREA IN CAPPADOCIA, Mazaca, capital of the kings of Cappadocia, heirs of the last Persian satrap. The area was Hellenized in the 2d century B.C. and became Eusebeia (*c.* 160), later Caesarea (12–9 B.C.) before it was annexed to the Roman Empire. The region was backward, with a primitive tribal and village economy and a few Greek-type cities, all in the south, requiring, in addition to the bishops, many *chorbishops. Until the reign of Diocletian, the governor of Cappadocia had hegemony over Armenia Minor and the Pontic districts; and the See of Caesarea enjoyed a certain primacy over the central and eastern portion of Asia Minor. The Council of *Chalcedon transferred these rights to the See of Constantinople, leaving to Caesarea the title of *protothronus* (or first see). The city commanded the roads to *Armenia and the upper Euphrates Valley; its strategic importance is reflected in its missionary activities toward the northeast, including work among the *Goths, in the 3d century. Legend states that the see was founded by Longinus, the centurion at the Crucifixion. Christians in Cappadocia are mentioned already in 1 Pt 1.1; some of them were in Rome and elsewhere in the 2d century. Bishop *Firmilian of Caesarea (235–256) supported St. *Cyprian of Carthage and was a representative of the theology of *Origen. Under Leontius I (285) there was missionary activity in Armenia. From that point on, there exists an almost certain picture of the episcopal succession. Caesarea's prestige attained its acme in the time of St. *Basil (370–379). Another great bishop was *Arethas (907–*c.* 932), a scholar and commentator on the Apocalypse. The city was taken by the Turks in 1064, and its importance in the Church declined. There was a massacre of Armenians there in 1895; and the Greek population was deported after the Treaty of Lausanne (1923). Besides the Greek metropolitanate, it had an Armenian see and a Uniate Armenian see from 1850 to 1938.

Bibliography: R. JANIN, DHGE 12:199–203. A. H. M. JONES, *The Cities of the Eastern Roman Provinces* (New York 1937) 175–182.

[J. GRIBOMONT]

CAESAREA IN PALESTINE,

a city originally called *Straton's Tower* (*Stratonos Pyrgos*) and probably founded by Straton, King of Sidon. The city came under Roman rule with Pompey and Caesar; and Augustus gave the city to Herod the Great, who improved its excellent harbor, adorned it with magnificent buildings, erected a temple to Augustus, and renamed the city Caesarea (Josephus, *Ant. jud.* 15.217). About a decade before the beginning of the Christian era it became the administrative headquarters of the Roman procurators and of the Roman garrison in Palestine. Caesarea's contacts with Christianity begin with the Apostles: Peter preached here and baptized Cornelius the centurion (Acts 10). Paul was imprisoned here under the procurators Felix and Porcius Festus until he appealed to the tribunal of Caesar (Acts 23.22–26.32). Yet the first known bishop of Caesarea is Theophilus, a contemporary of St. *Irenaeus, who presided at a council in 195 that determined that Easter must be celebrated on a Sunday (Eusebius, *Hist. Eccl.* 5.23). Shortly after 230 *Origen left Alexandria where he had incurred the displeasure of Bishop Demetrius; he arrived at Caesarea and founded the famous school where such great men as St. *Gregory Thaumaturgus and St. *Basil came to study. Here, too, was the celebrated library that contained among other treasures Origen's *Hexapla,* one of antiquity's most significant works in scripture studies. Pierius and *Pamphilus, Origen's successors at the school, expanded the library holdings to 30,000 rolls (*see* LIBRARIES, ANCIENT). This collection provided rich source material for the *Historia Ecclesiastica* of *Eusebius of Caesarea but was destroyed during the Arab invasion in 638.

Caesarea was the metropolitan see of *Palestina Prima* and the scene of many councils summoned to combat *Arianism. Until the Council of Chalcedon (451) raised Jerusalem to the dignity of a patriarchate, Caesarea was the ranking see in Palestine. Surviving the *Diocletian persecution, the Church in Caesarea flourished until the inroads of the Persians in 612, and of the Arabs in 638. A brief period of reconstruction came during the crusades, notably under *Baldwin, King of Jerusalem, but by 1265 the glory of Caesarea was once more in ruins.

Bibliography: I. BENZINGER, Pauly-Wiss RE 3.1 (1897) 1291–94. R. JANIN, DHGE 12:209–211. Robert-Tricot 1:626–628, 697–699. K. HONSELMANN, LexThK² 2:417. G. BÖING, ibid. 5:1244.

[H. DRESSLER]

CAESAREA PHILIPPI,

a city of Roman times on an ancient site long associated with fertility cults, both Canaanite and Greek. A sizeable river, the Banyasi, one of the main sources of the Jordan, issues from a nearby cave. In the 3d century B.C. the grotto was dedicated by the predominantly Greek population to Pan and the Nymphs; hence, the nearby city was called Paneas (Panion). Herod the Great received the territory in 20 B.C. from Augustus. Under his son, *Philip the Tetrarch, the city was rebuilt, including, on the old sanctuary site, a new marble temple in honor of the Emperor. The city was known as Caesarea Philippi or Philip's Caesarea (to distinguish it from several other Caesareas) until *Agrippa II altered the name to Neronias (*Ant.* 20.9.4). Coins from the following centuries call the place Caesarea Paneas. The old Greek name survives in its Arab form, Baniyas, the present-day village.

The city is mentioned in the first two Gospels as the site where Peter professed his belief in the messiahship and divinity of Jesus (Mt 16.13–20; Mk 8.27). According to an ancient tradition, known through Eusebius, this was the town of the woman who had been suffering from hemorrhage and was miraculously cured by touching the edge of Jesus' cloak (Mt 9.20–22). In the early Christian era, the city was a suffragan of Tyre. After its recapture by the Crusaders (*c.* 1132), it became a Latin see. Ruins of columns, capitals, hewn stones, and a city gate are still witness to the splendor it had in Greco-Roman times.

Bibliography: D. BALY, *The Geography of the Bible* (New York 1957) 194–196. C. KOPP, *The Holy Places of the Gospels,* tr. R. WALLS (New York 1963) 231–235.

[P. HORVATH]

CAESARIA, SS.,

the name of two abbesses of Saint-Jean in Arles, France.

Caesaria the Elder; b. *c.* 465; d. after 524 (feast, Jan. 12). She came of a Gallo-Roman family in the territory of Chalon-sur-Saône, and was educated at Marseille. Later she became first abbess of the convent of Saint-Jean, founded at Arles by her brother, St. *Caesarius of Arles, and dedicated on Aug. 26, 512. The rule Caesarius composed for the community [ed. G. Morin, *Florilegium patristicum* 34 (1933)] provided for common ownership of goods, strict enclosure, and a communal life of prayer and good works. Caesaria governed the flourishing community for more than 10 years in its work of educating girls, caring for widows, orphans, and the poor. Both *Gregory of Tours and Venantius *Fortunatus mention her with praise.

Caesaria the Younger, second abbess of the convent of Arles, probably a relative of Caesaria the Elder; d. *c.* 559. Little is known about her life. She was instrumental in inducing *Cyprian of Toulon to compose the life of Caesarius of Arles, and had many holy books, including the sermons of Caesarius and St. Augustine, copied at Arles and disseminated throughout Gaul. A treatise on religious vocation and true asceticism (MG Ep 3:450–453) is often ascribed to her.

Bibliography: ActSS Jan. 2:11–19. C. F. ARNOLD, *Caesarius von Arelate und die gallische Kirche seiner Zeit* (Leipzig 1894). A. MALNORY, *Saint Césaire, évêque d'Arles* (Paris 1894). *Vita s. Caesarii* in MGSrerMer 3:433–501. G. DE PLINVAL, DHGE 12: 212–216. M. C. MCCARTHY, *The Rule for Nuns of St. Caesaria of Arles: A Translation with a Critical Introduction* (Washington 1960).

[M. F. MC CARTHY]

CAESARIUS OF ARLES, ST.

Archbishop of Arles (502–542); b. Chalon-sur-Saône, 469 or 470; d. Aug. 27, 542. Caesarius was tonsured in his 18th year by Bp. Sylvester of Chalon (*c.* 486–518 or 523) and 2 years later became a monk at Lérins, where he was appointed cellarer (*Vita* 1.4–6).

In ill health he was sent by Abbot Porcarius to Arles. There his relative Bishop Eonius (before 494–502) ordained him a deacon and then priest (no earlier than 499 or 500) and made him abbot of a suburban monastery (*Vita* 1.7–13), probably at Trinquetaille. Eonius sought him as a successor, and on his death (Aug. 16, 502?) Caesarius was consecrated archbishop of Arles, apparently in August or September 502 (*Vita* 1.13–14). Though Caesarius was a Burgundian subject, his election was approved by the Visigoth Alaric II (485–507), in whose domain Arles lay.

On charges of conspiring to deliver Arles to the Burgundians, Alaric summoned Caesarius to Bordeaux *c.* 505, only to acquit him (*Vita* 1.21–24). After Alaric's defeat by the Franks (507), Arles fell to the Ostrogoths of Italy, who finally ceded it to the Franks in 536. The transfer to Ostrogothic rule entailed the seige of Arles (508 or 510) by the Franks and the Burgundians, and Caesarius practiced an heroic charity in the ransoming of captives (*Vita* 1.28–34). In 513 he was called to Ravenna by King *Theodoric (475–526) on suspicion of Burgundian sympathies, but once again he won exculpation (*Vita* 1.36–38; Ennodius in Morin 2:3–4). He then visited Rome, where Pope *Symmachus (498–514) received him warmly and on Nov. 6, 513, granted him the pallium (*Vita* 1.38, 42). The same pope named Caesarius his vicar for Gaul and Spain on June 11, 514, and succeeding pontiffs continued him in this office. Caesarius presided over synods at Agde in 506, at Arles in 524, at Carpentras in 527, at Orange and Vaison in 529 and at Marseilles in 533 (Morin, *Opera* 2:36–89). Of these synods, Agde is renowned for its canonical code; Orange, for its teaching on grace, approved by Pope *Boniface II (530–32) on Jan. 25, 531 (Morin 2:67–70), thus vindicating Caesarius's Augustinianism against his detractors (Vita 1.60); Vaison for its provision for the training of clerics; and Marseilles for its censure of Bishop Contumeliosus of Riez (before 518–533) because of his many irregularities. Caesarius was buried in the basilica of St. Mary at Arles (*Vita* 2.46–50). A portion of his tomb may still exist.

The saint was loved for his holiness (*Vita* 1.45, 46; 2.5, 6, 35) and great benevolence. Faithfully he visited his outlying parishes, instituted a full Divine Office in his cathedral of St. Stephen, and authorized the preaching of his deacons and priests. He founded a nuns' convent at Aliscamps, to the southeast of the city, and after its destruction during the siege reestablished it at the side of the cathedral, where it was dedicated on Aug. 26, 512, with his own sister, Caesaria, as abbess. To this in 524 he added the basilica of St. Mary (Conc. Arles, 524; *Vita* 1.57). For a male community, under his nephew, the priest Teridius, he composed a *Rule for Monks*.

Preeminent among works of Caesarius are 238 *Sermons* edited monumentally by Dom Morin (*Opera omnia* v.1, reproduced in *Corpus Christianorum,* v.103–104), though others will surely be substantiated as his. A portion of his correspondence is preserved (Morin, *Opera,* 2:3–32; 125–27; 129–48). So also are the texts of the councils at which he presided; his *Rules for Nuns and Monks,* with annexed documents; *Opusculum de gratia; De mysterio S. Trinitatis; Breviarium adversus hereticos; Expositio de Apocalypsi;* and *Testament.* While in 1894 A. Malnory thought Caesarius the au-

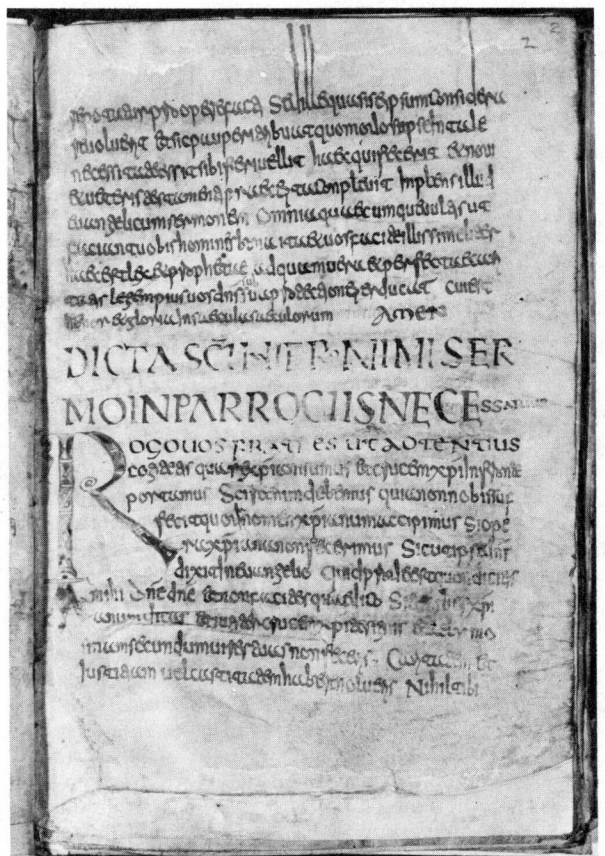

Page of an 8th-century MS of Caesarius of Arles's "Sermo in Parrociis Necessarius" (Morgan MS 17, fol. 2r).

thor of the *Statuta ecclesiae antiqua,* modern scholarship regards them as antedating the saint and as perhaps the composition of *Gennadius of Marseilles. The *Vita Caesarii* was completed by Bp. Cyprian of Toulon and four other disciples of Caesarius prior to 549 and is the most authoritative of Merovingian lives of saints.

Caesarius's *Sermons,* popular in his own time, have proven a most revealing source for Church life in 6th-century France. Recent investigators have plumbed his teaching on the Trinity, the Redemption, divine grace, penance, purgatory, monasticism, and the Christian attitude toward the state. Though his theology is not original, his constant pastoral concern places him among the truly relevant writers of the patristic age.

Bibliography: Works. *Opera omnia,* ed. G. MORIN, 2 v. in 3 (Maredsous, Bel. 1937–42); rev. ed. of v.1.1–2, *Sermones,* 2 v. (CorpChrist 103–104; 1953), suppl. in preparation; Eng. *Sermons,* tr. M. M. MUELLER, FathCh 31 (1956), 47 (1964), in progress; *S. Césaire d'Arles: Sermons choisis,* ed. and tr. A. BLAISE (Namur 1962); *The Rule for Nuns,* ed. and tr. M. C. McCARTHY (Washington 1960). Dekkers CPL 1008–19a.
Literature. ActSS Aug. 6:50–83. C. F. ARNOLD, *Caesarius von Arelate und die gallische Kirche seiner Zeit* (Leipzig 1894). A. MALNORY, *Saint Césaire, évêque d'Arles* (Paris 1894). M. CHAILLAN, *Saint Césaire* (Paris 1912). J. FASSY, *Saint Césaire d'Arles* (Paris 1909). G. DE PLINVAL, DHGE 12:186–196. P. LEJAY, *Le Rôle théologique des C. d'Arles* (Paris 1906). E. GÖLLER, ArchKathKRecht 109 (1929) 3–126, penance. S. CAVALLIN, *Literarhistorische und textkritische Studien zur Vita s. Caesarii Arelatensis* (Lund 1934). A. D'ALÈS, RechScRel 28 (1938) 315–384, sermons. F. HOPPMANN, *Die christliche Frömmigkeit bei Caesarius* (Breslau 1942). G. BARDY, RevHistÉgl

France 29 (1943) 201–236, preaching; *ibid.* 33 (1947) 241–256, political attitude. J. RIVIÈRE, *Bulletin de littérature ecclésiastique* 45 (1944) 3–20, redemption. K. BERG, *Die Werke des heilige C. von Arles als liturgiegeschichtliche Quelle* (Munich 1946). H. G. J. BECK, *The Pastoral Care of Souls in South-East France during the 6th Century* (AnalGreg 51; 1950); AmEcclRev 127 (1952) 321–329; 133 (1955) 6–15, sermons 179 and 13. C. VOGEL, *La Discipline pénitentielle en Gaule, des origines à la fin de VIIᵉ siècle* (Paris 1952). M. DORENKEMPER, *The Trinitarian Doctrine and Sources of St. C. of Arles* (Fribourg 1953). P. JAY, RechTh AMéd 24 (1957) 5–14, purgatory. M. SUVÉE, *Fondements et notions essentielles de la morale dans la prédication de s. C. d'Arles* (Lille 1958). M. C. McCARTHY, *Month* NS 26.1 (1961) 140–154, spirituality. C. GINDELE, *RevBén* 69 (1959) 216–236, penance. **Illustration credit:** The Pierpont Morgan Library, New York City.

[H. G. J. BECK]

CAESARIUS OF HEISTERBACH, Cistercian ascetical writer and historian; b. *c.* 1180; d. Heisterbach, Germany, *c.* 1240. He was educated in Cologne at St. Andrew's and at the cathedral school (1188–98). On meeting Gevard, second abbot of *Heisterbach (S. Petrus de Monte) in 1198, he was moved to enter religious life. After delaying his entrance to go on pilgrimage to Our Lady of Rocamadour (Quercy in the Limousin), he became a monk at Heisterbach (*c.* 1199), where with a few interruptions he served as master of novices or as prior until his death.

Caesarius himself tells us the number and character of his writings. In the *Epistula catalogica,* prefaced to his homilies [ed. A. Hilka, *Die Wundergeschichte des C. von H.* 1 (Bonn 1933) 2–7], he enumerated for Peter, Abbot of Marienstatt, 36 items of which today only 17 are extant. His writings include: (1) theological works, viz, homilies, *Sermones* and *Expositiones* [ed. A. Coppenstien, *Fasciculus moralitatis C. von H.* (Cologne 1615); A. Hilka 1:63–188, 3:381–390; J. H. Schütz, *Summa Mariana* (Paderborn 1908) 687–

716; other works unedited]; (2) narratives, viz, *Dialogus miraculorum* [composed *c.* 1219–23; ed. J. Strange (Coblenz 1850)], *Index nominum* [ed. J. Strange (Coblenz 1857); 2d ed. 1922], and *Libri VIII miraculorum* (composed *c.* 1225–27, ed. A. Hilka 3:15–222); and (3) historical works, viz, *Catalogus archiepiscoporum Coloniensium* (composed *c.* 1225–38; MGS 14:332–347), *Vita s. Elisabethae* (written *c.* 1226–37 for Conrad of Marburg, ed. A. Huyskens in Hilka 3:17–50), and *Vita s. Engelberti* [written *c.* 1226–37 for Henry of Molenark; ActSS Nov. 3 (1910) 644–81; Hilka 3:234–328].

From the theological and ascetical point of view the *Dialogus miraculorum* is important as a reflection of contemporary beliefs, customs, and folklore and as a continuation of the Cistercian tradition of *exempla.* Written as an exhortation to Christian perfection for his fellow religious, it presents definitions of virtues and vices, followed by supporting *exempla.* In this, Caesarius follows in the footsteps of such predecessors as Herbert de Torres and *Jacques de Vitry. For modern tastes, these stories, culled from far and wide, along with his original contributions are "robust." The homilies, really meditations, since only the introduction and conclusion are in the oratorical manner, reflect medieval piety and belief. The purpose of the *Libri VIII miraculorum* (only three books extant) is to stir devotion to the Eucharist, confession, and the Blessed Virgin Mary. The historical works, in general, are of high quality, even by modern standards. While the *Vita s. Elizabethae* is primarily a work of edification, the *Catalogus,* when dealing with contemporaries, and the *Vita s. Engelberti* are thoroughly reliable in fact and judgment.

Bibliography: *The Dialogue on Miracles, 1220–1235,* tr. H. VON E. SCOTT and C. C. S. BLAND, 2 v. (London 1929). J. T. WELTER, *L'Exemplum dans la littérature religieuse et didactique du moyen âge* (Paris 1927). J. M. CANIVEZ, DictSpirAscMyst 2:430–432. G. BAADER, LexThK² 2:965. **Illustration credit:** Library of Congress.

[J. M. MARIQUE]

Caesarius of Heisterbach at prayer, reproduced from a facsimile of an initial in a manuscript in the Stadtbibliothek, Düsseldorf, Germany (Cod. misc. `D, fol. 2r).

CAESARIUS OF NAZIANZUS, ST., 4th-century physician; b. probably Arianzus, 330; d. Bithynia, 369 (feast, Feb. 25; Greek, March 9). Caesarius, the son of (St.) Gregory, Bishop of Nazianzus (modern Nenizi) and (St.) Nonna, and the brother of (St.) Gorgonia and *Gregory Nazianzus, received a religious and literary formation at home with his brother, and was sent to Alexandria to complete his scientific education and study medicine. In Constantinople, during his journey home, he met his brother Gregory returning from Athens, and they traveled together to Nazianzus (354). On a second visit to Constantinople, Caesarius became a friend and physician to the Emperor *Constantius II (337–361). During the persecution of *Julian the Apostate he was relieved of his position at court and he returned home (363). Recalled by Valens (364), he was made quaestor in Bithynia (368) and on miraculously escaping an earthquake in Nicaea, decided to follow the ascetical life, but after receiving Baptism, he died suddenly. His body was buried in the family vault in the presence of his parents, and (St.) Gregory of Nazianzus preached the funeral oration, which is the source of Caesarius's biography. He was soon honored as a saint (Nicephorus, *Hist. Eccl.*

10.19). The four dialogues that are attributed to Caesarius are certainly spurious.

Bibliography: GREGORY OF NAZIANZUS, PG 35:755–788. ActSS Feb. 3:501–507. F. S. PERICOLI-RIDOLFIN, EncCatt 3:1354. Bardenhewer 3:174. G. BARDY, Catholicisme 2:844.

[F. CHIOVARO]

CAESARIUS OF SPEYER,

preacher and Franciscan founder; b. Speyer, Germany, second half of the 12th century; d. Italy c. 1239. After having studied theology in Paris under Conrad of Reisenberg, he became a famous Lenten preacher in *Speyer. There he effectively promoted new forms of religious life for women, an apostolate that led him into many difficulties. He was accused of heresy. In 1217, when he was probably already a subdeacon, he joined the Fifth *Crusade and met St. *Francis of Assisi in the Holy Land. There *Elias of Cortona won him over to the *Franciscans. Early in 1220 St. Francis took him to Italy and commissioned him to incorporate Holy Scripture into the *Regula non bullata* of the Franciscans; a third of the completed text is Caesarius's work. Toward the end of September 1221, as provincial, he accompanied a group of friars going to Germany, where he established the Franciscan Order. In 1223 he asked to be released from his duties as provincial and returned to Italy. He was present at the death of St. Francis (1226). The account of his imprisonment by Elias and death at the hands of an overzealous guard is based on *Angelus Clarenus's account, which is not trustworthy.

Bibliography: *Chronica Fratris Jordani*, ed. H. BOEHMER (Paris 1908) 8–32. L. HARDICK, ed., *Nach Deutschland und England* (Werl 1957) 45–68. C. EUBEL, *Geschichte der oberdeutschen Minoriten-Provinz* (Würzburg 1886) 3–6. W. LAMPEN, "De textibus S. Scripturae allegatis in opusculis S. P. N. Francisci," ArchFranchHist 17 (1924) 443–445. L. OLIGER, EncCatt 3:1354–55. A. VAN DEN WYNGAERT, DHGE 12:197–198.

[L. HARDICK]

CAESAROPAPISM

This term expresses the conception of government in which supreme royal and sacerdotal powers are combined in one lay ruler. Although the term itself is a more recent coinage, the concept is very old and applied particularly to the kind of government exercised by the emperor at *Constantinople. The reason for the emergence of this kind of government lay in the conception of the Roman emperor that he as supreme head of the Christianized Roman Empire had to take care of all the issues affecting it. Christianity had imparted to the Roman Empire a great strength of coherence and given it a force that bonded the various heterogeneous elements together. This consideration, together with the special functions that priests in a Christian community had, explains the efforts made by the emperors from the 4th century onward to control the Christian body politic by ordaining the faith for their subjects and by appointing and dismissing higher ecclesiastical officers, notably patriarchs and bishops.

Caesaropapism was, basically, nothing less than the transplantation of the function of the ancient Roman emperor as *pontifex maximus* to the Christian Roman emperor. The fundamental idea underlying caesaropapism was that the emperor as the divinely appointed vicegerent of divinity on earth, that is, of the *pantokrator,* was the *autokrator* who alone considered himself called upon to provide unity, peace, and order within the Christian empire. Just as only one being in the celestial order combined all power, so in the terrestrial order there was to be only one monarch.

Although signs of caesaropapism became ever clearer throughout the 5th century, it entered the sphere of practical politics in the *Henoticon of the Emperor Zeno (482), in which he unilaterally and in disregard of the Council of *Chalcedon ordained the faith for his subjects; at the same time began imperial appointments and dismissals of prelates. Caesaropapism reached its highest point in the government of *Justinian I (527–565) who, imbued with the idea of monarchy, acted to all intents and purposes as king and priest. In his time it could truly be said that there was "one state, one law, one Church."

Caesaropapism remained, with modifications, the governmental principle of Byzantium throughout the millennium of its existence. The breach between the *papacy and Constantinople was to a very large extent due to the caesaropapal form of the imperial government. It was obvious that the papacy, as custodian of the Christian idea of government, could not acquiesce in this state of affairs. Although in the West European Middle Ages caesaropapism was hardly a doctrinal possibility, the Byzantine brand of caesaropapism was continued in Czarist *Russia; evidence of caesaropapism could also be detected among Protestant princes, when *cuius regio, eius religio* came to be applied. Similar observations can be made about *Josephinism, *Febronianism, and partly also about *Gallicanism, where the principle was adopted that the ruler had a *jus maiestatis circa sacra.*

Bibliography: K. JÄNTERE, *Die römische Weltreichsidee*, tr. I. HOLLO (Turku 1936). V. MARTIN, *Les Origines du gallicanisme*, 2 v. (Paris 1939). H. BERKHOF, *Kirche und Kaiser* (Zurich 1947). J. GAUDEMET, *L'Église dans l'empire Romain* (Paris 1958). O. TREITINGER, *Die oströmische Kaiser- und Reichsidee* (2d ed. Darmstadt 1956). H. RAAB, LexThK² 6:289–295. H. RAHNER, *Kirche und Staat im frühen Christentum* (Munich 1961).

[W. ULLMANN]

CAFASSO, JOSEPH, ST.,

moral theologian, preacher, and spiritual director; b. Castelnuovo d'Asti, Piedmont, Jan. 15, 1811; d. Turin, June 23, 1860 (feast, June 23). Born of peasant stock, he entered the diocesan seminary at Chieri and became a priest in 1833. After ordination he studied at the Institute of St. Francis in Turin, which had been founded somewhat earlier by Luigi Guala for the education of young priests. Guala's teaching was strongly influenced by the doctrine of St. Alphonsus Liguori and was aimed at combating the continuing Jansenist tendencies in north Italy. Cafasso learned from his master well, and the same orientation characterized all his later work. After completing his studies he became lecturer in moral theology at the institute, and upon Guala's death in 1848, he was made rector. Thereafter he labored for the intellectual and moral improvement of the young clergy from various dioceses and left his influence upon innumerable spiritual protégés. One of these was St. John *Bosco, whose spiritual progress Cafasso guided and whose vocation for the education of boys Cafasso aided and encouraged. His work also extended to tireless efforts among the laity, preaching, conducting retreats, hearing confessions, and giving spiritual direction. He was particularly noted for his concern and care for those imprisoned or condemned to death. His writings include *Meditazioni e instruzioni al clero* (Turin 1892). He was beatified in 1925 and canonized in 1947.

Bibliography: N. DI ROBILANT, *Vita del ven. G. Cafasso,* 2 v. (Turin 1912). B. C. SALOTTI, *La perla del clero italiano* (3d ed. Turin 1947). Butler Th Attw 2:628–631. L. CASTANO, EncCatt 6:818–819.

[J. C. WILLKE]

CAGAYAN, ARCHDIOCESE OF (CAGAYANUS),

diocese (July 1933), metropolitan see (June 29, 1951), whose suffragans are the Diocese of Surigao and the prelatures *nullius* of Cotabato, Davao, Marbel, Ozamis, and Tagum. Located in northern Mindanao, the second largest island of the *Philippines, the archdiocese comprises the provinces of Misamis Oriental and Bukidnon and the subprovince of Camiguin, an area of 4,616 square miles. It was first evangelized by Jesuits and Augustinian Recollects from Spain. American Jesuits began replacing Spanish in 1921, while Sacred Heart Missionaries from Holland joined and gradually replaced Spanish missionaries in Surigao and Agusan. Irish Columban Fathers replaced those in Misamis Occidental and Lanao. Fully organized parishes are being turned over to Filipino secular priests. In 1960 the archdiocese had a total population of 641,576, and a Catholic population of 578,800. The non-Christian population of the ecclesiastical province is chiefly Moslem in Lanao, and pagan in Surigao, Agusan, and Bukidnon, populated by primitive peoples practicing an animistic religion. There is a well-developed system of parochial schools, elementary through high school, in the principal towns. The Jesuit Xavier University is in the city of Cagayan de Oro. Besides conducting an agricultural school, Xavier University trains a significant percentage of the teachers for both public and private schools in the area and is helping to establish credit and marketing cooperatives throughout the territory. The archdiocese has a minor seminary.

Bibliography: H. DE LA COSTA, *The Jesuits in the Philippines, 1581–1768* (Cambridge, Mass. 1961). *Catholic Directory of the Philippines* (Manila annual). AnnPont (1964) 82–83, 1421.

[H. L. DE LA COSTA]

CAGLIARI, ARCHDIOCESE OF (CALARITANUS),

metropolitan see since *c.* 500, in south *Sardinia. In 1963 it had 186 secular and 146 religious priests, 214 men in 22 religious houses, 911 women in 128 convents, and 398,000 Catholics; it is 1,892 square miles in area. Its three suffragans, which had 200 secular and 41 religious priests, 458 sisters, and 335,000 Catholics, were: Iglesias (5th-century Sulcis, moved to Iglesias 1503, united with Cagliari 1513, restored 1763), Nuoro (12th-century see, suppressed 1496–1779), and Ogliastra (1824). The city of Cagliari, capital of Sardinia, on the Gulf of Cagliari, was founded by Phoenicia and taken from Carthage by Rome. Vandals held it until it was retaken by Justinian (485–533). Local kings (687) were replaced by judges in the 10th century. *Pisa took Cagliari (1052) and was replaced by Aragon (1324); Spanish rule lasted to 1714. Austria ceded the island to the Dukes of Savoy, who became the Kings of Sardinia (1720), resident in Cagliari (1798–1814).

A very early Christian community has left 3d-century catacombs. Several early bishops seem to have been martyrs. Quintasius attended the Council of Arles (314).

*Lucifer (d. 370), rigorist opponent of Arianism, was exiled several times. Pope Gregory I (d. 604) reproved Januarius for personal faults and asserted a role in the ecclesiastical affairs of Sardinia, where papal possessions were considerable. Later popes copied him, despite strong Byzantine influence in Cagliari; Boniface VIII transferred Sardinia from Pisa to Aragon (1297). Saracen raids, beginning in 709, isolated Sardinia. Of seven 6th-century sees, Cagliari (metropolitan of Sardinia and the Balearics) was one of four to last to the 9th century, still a metropolitan. The Archbishop of Pisa became apostolic legate (1176), and the Aragonese Archbishop of Cagliari laid claim to his title of primate of Sardinia and *Corsica (1490). In the 15th and 16th centuries the archdiocese comprised a fourth of the island, as other sees were united to it. Antonio de Gastilleyo (1558) took part in the Council of Trent. The seminary was approved in a synod of 1576. Seven diocesan synods have been published. Under Tommaso Natta (1759–63) a revival of studies took place.

The Romanesque cathedral built by Pisans (1257–1312) was redone in baroque (1676). The shrine of Our Lady of Bonaria, in baroque, derives from a Mercedarian foundation (*c.* 1330). The university founded in 1626 had faculties of theology, philosophy, and law; science and medicine were added in 1764. Suppressed in 1848, it reopened as a state university in 1862.

Bibliography: R. CIASCA, *Bibliografia sarda,* 5 v. (Rome 1931–34). D. SCANO, *Codice diplomatico delle relazioni diplomatiche fra la S. Sede e la Sardegna* (Cagliari 1940–41). D. FILIA, *La Sardegna cristiana,* 3 v. (Sassari 1909–29). M. PINNA, *L'archivio del duomo di Cagliari* (Cagliari 1899). A. SOLMI, *Le carte volgari dell'archivio vescovile di Cagliari* (Florence 1905). M. SCADUTO, EncCatt 3:288–293. A. DE MAZIS, DHGE 11:167–174. AnnPont (1965) 1065.

[F. RAFFAELE]

CAGLIERO, JUAN,

missionary, bishop, and cardinal; b. Castelnuovo Don Bosco, Jan. 11, 1838; d. Rome, Feb. 28, 1926. From the age of 13, he was a favorite pupil of St. John *Bosco in Turin. He became seriously ill in 1854, and on that occasion Bosco had two visions that foretold the future of the young boy. He recovered, joined the Salesians that same year, and was ordained in 1862. He was a music teacher and composer. In 1875 he led the first 10 Salesians who came to America and founded five houses in Argentina and Uruguay in less than 2 years. In 1877 he returned to Italy and there became spiritual director for both branches of the Salesian Society. In 1883 he was chosen vicar apostolic of Patagonia and made titular bishop of Magida. In 1885 he went to Patagonia, where he served as a missionary until 1904, when he was named titular archbishop of Sebaste and diocesan visitor in Italy. In 1908 the Pope sent him to San José de Costa Rica as apostolic delegate to Central America. He found 5 bishops there and raised the number to 20. In 1915 he was made a cardinal, and in 1921 he accepted the Diocese of Frascati.

Bibliography: R. A. ENTRAIGAS, *El Apostol de la Patagonia* (Rosario, Argentina 1956).

[R. A. ENTRAIGAS]

CAHENSLY, PETER PAUL,

lay leader; b. Limburg an der Lahn, Rhine province of Nassau, Germany, Oct. 28, 1838; d. Dec. 25, 1923. He was the youngest of four children of a mercantile wholesale grocery family. As preparation to succeed his father in the firm, he traveled throughout Germany, Switzerland, France, England, Belgium, and Holland, studying freight and shipping techniques. In the ports of those countries and on ships, he saw the conditions of the emigrants from Europe to the American countries during the 19th century. As an active member of the St. Vincent de Paul Society, Cahensly became a pioneer and strong advocate of welfare and care for these emigrants. He collected data regarding conditions on ships, as well as in ports of exit and entry; spoke at the annual *Katholikentage* of German Catholics; initiated social action programs to alleviate conditions; established missions and chapels at ports; and addressed petitions to governments and bishops to control the chicanery of emigration agents, lodging proprietors, local police, ticket agents, ship lines, and money changers. In 1871 the *St. Raphael's Society for the protection of German Catholic emigrants was established and was later broadened to include Italian, Belgian, French, and other European representation. Cahensly was first secretary and then president (1899) of this pioneer 19th-century lay Catholic organization, which was without clerical membership or direction and was supported by annual dues. Despite opposition from governments and vested interests, as well as from the liberal and antireligious press, the movement gained momentum. Cahensly also served in local, regional, and national political positions, including membership in the Prussian House of Delegates (1885–1915) and the Reichstag (1898–1903), where he caucused with the Center party.

A daughter branch of the St. Raphael's Society was established (1883) in the U.S.; 8 years later a turmoil broke out among American Catholics concerning the rights of Catholic immigrants to their native language and customs that was termed "Cahenslyism" by opposition partisans. The controversy stemmed from a petition to Leo XIII in 1890, signed by 51 members of European boards of directors of the St. Raphael's Society from seven nations, requesting separate churches for each nationality, appointment of priests of the same nationality as the faithful, parochial schools where the mother tongue would be taught, and representation in the American hierarchy of the immigrant races. The petition, unacceptable to the Americanizing members of the Catholic Church in the U.S., was discredited in an extended journalistic and pamphlet exchange. This Lucerne memorandum was never acted upon by the Holy See, although it continued as a partisan factor in the tension leading to the *Americanism controversy in the Church of the U.S. at the end of the 19th century. Cahensly was eventually personally vindicated and recognized internationally, with honors from Church and state, under the title of "Father of the Emigrant."

[C. J. BARRY]

CAIN AND ABEL, the first two sons of Adam, the elder a fratricide, the younger a martyr. The redactor of Genesis sees in them the eponymous ancestors of the nomad and the seminomad (Gn 4.1–24). Cain's name (Heb. *qayin*) is explained in the sacred text by folk etymology that links it to *qānâ* (to give birth to; Gn 4.1; cf. Prv 8.22), though it is noteworthy that it is similar to *qānā'* (to be jealous). The word *qayin* means smith, and in Nm 24.21–22 Cain may be re-

God accepts the sacrifice of Abel, 12th-century carved Romanesque capital from Moutier-Saint-Jean, France.

garded as the eponymous ancestor of the *Cinites (see Gray, "The Sacrifices of Cain and Abel," 19), a nomadic tribe with an obscure relationship to metalworking (Gn 4.22). There is no etymological explanation of Abel's name (Heb. *hābel*) in the sacred text; at various times it has been linked to *hebel* (breath, transitoriness), *'ābēl* (meadow), *'ābēl* (mournful), and even the Sumerian *ibila* and the Akkadian *aplu* (son).

Cain was a tiller of the soil, while Abel was keeper of flocks (Gn 4.2). Urged on by jealousy and anger because God preferred the sacrifice of Abel, Cain slew his younger brother. After the fratricide, Cain was condemned to the life of the nomad, and God put a sign on his forehead signifying that blood revenge will be exacted if he is killed. The narrative utilizes the theme of gratuitous election, gives sanction to the desert law of blood revenge, and seeks to demonstrate the proliferation of evil after the original sin. Presupposing the existence of the cultures of the nomad, seminomad, and farmer, the story weaves into the narrative etiological hints of their origin.

Later writers presume ethical or religious qualities that distinguish Abel from Cain, whence God accepts the younger and rejects the older. In the NT, Abel is extolled for his righteousness (Mt 23.35) and faith (Heb 11.4) and is looked upon as a type of Christ (Heb 12.24), and so the Canon of the Roman Mass see a symbol of Christ's sacrifice in that of Abel's. On the other hand, the Christian who does not love his brother is "like Cain, who was of the evil one" (1 Jn 3.10–12).

Bibliography: L. HICKS, InterDictBibl 1:4, 482. EncDictBibl 4–5, 297–298. De Vaux AncIsr 11, 13–14, 42–43. E. PALIS, DB 1.1:28–30. K. G. KUHN, Kittel ThW 1:6–7. C. A. KELLER, RGG³ 3:1089–90. H. JUNKER and J. KESSELS, LexThK² 1:13; 5: 1240–41 (see the latter for iconography). G. B. GRAY, "The Sacrifices of Cain and Abel," *Expositor* 10 (1915) 1–23; "Cain's Sacrifice: A New Theory," *ibid.* 21 (1921) 161–182. **Illustration credit:** The Fogg Art Museum, Harvard University.

[E. H. PETERS]

CAIPHAS (CAIAPHAS), Joseph, Jewish high priest, appointed A.D. 18 by the Roman Procurator Valerius Gratus and deposed in 36 by the governor of Syria, Vitellius. He owed his office to his father-in-law, *Annas, who continued to dominate the high-priestly clan so firmly that in the Lucan and Johannine traditions he was considered to be, in effect, high priest (Lk 3.2; Jn 18.13, 24). In Jn 11.49–53 Caiphas is singled out as the one who definitively decides to have Jesus put to death lest the Romans should come and destroy what was left of Jewish independence, then controlled by the high priests. John sees here a prophetic utterance of which Caiphas was completely unaware but which he gave as the result of his charismatic office as high priest, namely, that Jesus' death would bring about the salvation not only of Israel but of all the scattered children of God. True to his previous decision, Caiphas, as the head of the *Sanhedrin, evokes from Jesus a confession of His messiahship and His office as the *Son of Man coming to establish God's final kingdom; accuses Him of the capital offense of blasphemy; and, with the Sanhedrin, condemns Him to death (Mk 14.60–64). With Peter (Acts 3.17) one may well excuse Caiphas for having acted his part in the divine drama in ignorance. Nothing is known of his subsequent history.

[E. J. HODOUS]

CAIRD, EDWARD AND JOHN, brothers, Scottish scholars.

Edward, philosopher; b. Greenock, Renfrewshire, Scotland, March 22, 1835; d. Oxford, England, Nov. 1, 1908. The brother of John Caird, he was educated at Glasgow University and at Balliol College, Oxford. In 1864 he was elected fellow and tutor of Merton College, Oxford. Two years later he was appointed professor of moral philosophy at Glasgow. He was master of Balliol College, Oxford, from 1893 until his resignation in 1907. He expounded neo-Hegelianism in *Hegel* (1883), in *The Critical Philosophy of Immanuel Kant* (1889), and in his Gifford lectures, *The Evolution of Religion* (1893). *See* HEGELIANISM AND NEO-HEGELIANISM.

John, theologian, philosopher, preacher; b. Greenock, Renfrewshire, Scotland, Dec. 15, 1820; d. Greenock, July 30, 1898. After being educated at Glasgow University, he began his career as a parish minister in 1845. In 1855 he preached his famous sermon "Religion in Common Life" before Queen Victoria; Dean Stanley described it as the greatest single sermon of the century. In 1862 Caird became professor of divinity at Glasgow University. From 1873 to 1898 he was principal there. His publications, which set forth his neo-Hegelian interpretations of Presbyterian theology, included *An Introduction to the Philosophy of Religion* (1880) and *Spinoza* (1888).

Bibliography: Edward. H. JONES and J. H. MUIRHEAD, *The Life and Philosophy of Edward Caird* (Glasgow 1921). DNB (1901–11) 1:291–295. John. E. C. CAIRD, "Memoir," in J. C. CAIRD, *The Fundamental Ideas of Christianity*, 2 v. (Glasgow 1899) v.1. C. L. WARR, *Principal Caird* (Edinburgh 1926).

[J. QUINN]

CAIUS, JOHN, physician, annalist, antiquarian; b. Norwich, England, Oct. 6, 1510; d. London, July 29, 1573. Caius received a bachelor of arts degree from Cambridge in 1533, and 2 years later began studies for the master's degree. In 1539, he went to Padua, where he studied medicine under J. Montanus and A. *Vesalius. Caius received his M.D. (1541); left Padua (1542) to travel extensively in Italy, Germany, and France; and returned to England in the winter of 1544–45.

He then lectured in anatomy for the next 17 years in London and gave anatomical demonstrations to the barber surgeons (1546–63). In 1547 he was elected a fellow of the College of Physicians, and subsequently was elected president of the College for 9 terms. Caius was physician to King Edward VI, Queen Mary, and Queen Elizabeth. In 1557, he refounded Gonville Hall, Cambridge, as Gonville and Caius College, of which he became master in 1559. He resigned this post in 1573 after a period of troubles caused partly by his restrictive measures and partly by his staunch Catholicism. Of his medical writings, the most important was the treatise *A boke or counseill against the disease called the sweate* (1552), the first original description of a disease to be written in English. Further works were a history of the University of Cambridge, and the compilation of the annals of the College of Physicians, 1518 to 1572.

Bibliography: *The Works of John Caius,* ed. E. S. ROBERTS (Cambridge, Eng. 1912), with a memoir of his life by J. VENN.

[C. D. O'MALLEY]

CAJETAN, ST. (GAETANO DA THIENE), the leading founder of the *Theatines; b. Vicenza, near Venice, October 1480; d. Naples, Aug. 7, 1547 (feast, Aug. 7). He was the son of Count Gaspare da Thiene. He studied law in Padua and in 1505 became *prothonotary apostolic to Julius II; he was ordained on Sept. 30, 1516, and joined the Oratory of Divine Love in Rome, a group devoted to piety and charity. In 1518 he returned to Vicenza and continued his charitable activities, going to Venice in 1520 and founding a hospital for incurables (1522). He returned to Rome in 1523 and on Sept. 14, 1524, with three companions, Gianpietro Caraffa (later Pope *Paul IV), Bonifacio da Colle, and Paolo Consiglieri, founded the *Clerici regulares,* priests who took religious vows but lived in the world working for a truly Christian reform of society. By example and by exhortation they were to inspire the rest of the clergy. They were called Theatines after Chieti (Teate), the episcopal see of their first superior, Caraffa. Cajetan and the Theatines escaped from Rome in the sack of 1527 and found refuge in Venice, continuing their work. In 1533 Cajetan was made superior of a new foundation in Naples, where he labored till his death, except for a term (1540–43) as superior in Venice. In Naples he opposed the heretics Juan *Valdes and Bernardino *Ochino and founded a *monte di pietá* (see MONTES PIETATIS) that has become the Bank of Naples. He is buried in S. Paolo Maggiore, where he resided in Naples. He was beatified on Oct. 8, 1629, by Pope Urban VIII, and canonized on April 12, 1671, by Pope Clement X.

Bibliography: P. CHIMINELLI, *San Gaetano Thiene, cuore della Reforma Cattolica* (Vicenza 1948). A. VENY BALLESTER, *San Cayetano de Thiene* (Barcelona 1950). P. PASCHINI, EncCatt 5:1844–46. P. H. HALLETT, *Catholic Reformer* (Westminster, Md. 1959). H. RAAB, LexThK² 2:874–875. G. JACQUEMET, Catholicisme 4:1694–95. **Illustration credit:** Photo MAS, Barcelona.

[A. SAGRERA]

St. Cajetan, by Andrea Vaccaro, Museo del Prado, Madrid.

CAJETAN (TOMMASO DE VIO)

Thomistic theologian; b. Gaeta, Italy, Feb. 20, 1469; d. Rome, Aug. 10, 1534.

Life. Although he was to be popularly known by the place of his birth (Gaietanus), he was baptized James de Vio. At the age of 16 he entered the Dominican Order at Gaeta, receiving the religious name of Thomas. After studying philosophy at Naples and theology at Bologna, he was sent to Padua, where he lectured on metaphysics in the priory and on the *Sentences* at the university (1493). At the general chapter of the Order at Ferrara in 1494, he held a disputation with Giovanni Pico della Mirandola. On this occasion, though only 25 years of age, he was promoted to master in sacred theology at the request of Hercules, Duke of Ferrara. At the invitation of Duke Sforza he taught at Pavia (1497–99), lecturing on the *Summa* of St. Thomas. From 1501 to 1508 he taught at the Sapienza University in Rome and served as procurator general of his Order. During this time he had occasion to preach for Alexander VI and Julius II. On the death of the master general, John Clérée, in 1507, he was appointed vicar-general by Julius II. As master general of the Dominicans (1508–18), he stressed reform, study, and the common life; settled certain difficulties involving devotees of *Savonarola; sent the first Dominican missionaries to the New World; and defended the mendicant orders at the Fifth Lateran Council (1512–17).

From 1508 until his death he was deeply involved in ecclesiastical affairs. When consulted about the pseudo-Council of Pisa (1511), he urged Julius II to convoke a legitimate council. Forbidding his own friars to support the schismatic council, he sent trusted friars to the scene to win over the secular clergy to the Pope's cause, and he wrote an important treatise on papal authority against French conciliarists, *De comparatione auctoritatis papae et concilii* (1511). At the Fifth Lateran Council, convoked in 1512, he defended papal supremacy, urged ecclesiastical reform, and participated in discussions on *Averroism and the *Immaculate Conception. He was made a cardinal priest of St. Sixtus on July 6, 1517, and was sent to Germany the following year as legate of Leo X to arouse interest in a crusade against the Turks. While there he represented the Holy See in discussions with Luther at Augsburg (1518)—which proved unsuccessful—and in the election of the new German emperor in 1519. In the latter assignment he succeeded, getting the Pope's candidate, Charles V, elected. On March 14 of that year Thomas was appointed bishop of Gaeta, his native city. He took part in the consistory of 1520, which condemned Luther, and in the conclave of 1522 which elected Adrian VI. In the following year he was made legate to Hungary, Poland, and Bohemia in the hope that he could obtain support for a crusade. After the death of Adrian (Sept. 14, 1523), he was recalled by Clement VII. Disappointed with Clement's lack of interest in reform and the crusade, Thomas devoted full time to study, writing, and examining the question of Henry VIII's divorce. During the last illness of Clement (1534) many considered Cajetan a likely successor, but he himself was gravely ill and died on the morning of Aug. 10, 1534, at the age of 66. He was buried according to his wishes at the entrance of the Dominican church of Santa Maria sopra Minerva so that the faithful might walk over his grave, but since 1666 his remains have been preserved in the sacristy.

Cajetan was a man of deep prayer and devotion to study; simple and exacting with regard to himself; broad-minded and generous with regard to others; and profoundly conscious of the needs of the Church, particularly in Biblical studies and ecclesiastical reform.

Writings. Over 150 works, long and short, came from the pen of Cajetan (see Groner 57–73). Most of them can be dated accurately from his habit of indicating year, day, and place of completion together with his own age and occupation. Apart from acts and official documents, his writings may be grouped under three headings: philosophical, theological, and exegetical.

Philosophical. The commentaries and treatises were the fruit of his teaching at Padua, Pavia, Milan, and Rome between 1493 and 1507. They include commentaries on Porphyry's *Isagoge* (1497); Aristotle's *Praedicamenta* (1498), *Peri Hermeneias* (1496), *Posterior Analytics* (1496), *De Anima* (ed. 1509 from earlier notes), and *Metaphysics* (1493?); St. Thomas's *De ente et essentia* (1494–95); and five treatises, the most important of which is *De nominum analogia* (1498).

Theological. Between 1507 and 1524, while Cajetan was master general and papal legate, he wrote theological works. The most important are the commentary on the

Cardinal Cajetan; antique engraving after a lost portrait.

Sentences (1493–94, unpublished), the influential commentary on the *Summa theologiae* of St. Thomas (I, completed in 1507; I–II, completed in 1511; II–II, completed in 1517; III completed in 1520), and treatises on papal authority, confession, the Eucharist, Matrimony, Holy Orders, religious life, social questions, and Protestant errors.

Exegetical. This work filled the years from 1524 until his death. Using the Greek text of Erasmus and the latest methods of exegesis, he examined carefully the claims of Protestant reformers. In 1527 he dedicated to Clement VII a new translation of the Psalms from the Hebrew. His commentaries on the Gospels (1527–28), Epistles (1528–29), Pentateuch (1530–31), historical books (1531–32), Job (1533), and Ecclesiastes (1534) provoked much opposition, even from his own brethren. Cajetan insisted that the Latin Vulgate was insufficient for serious Biblical studies. He expressed strong doubts about the literal meaning of Canticles and the Apocalypse; the authenticity of Mk 16.9–20 and Jn 8.1–11; and the authorship of Hebrews, James, 2 Peter, 2 and 3 John, and Jude. Some of his views were censured by Ambrogio Catarini, Bartholomew Medina, Melchior Cano, and "many theologians" of the Sorbonne (1533, 1544).

Doctrine. Cajetan stands out as one of the most gifted and influential thinkers of the Thomistic tradition. Coming at the beginning of "second Thomism," he not only helped to replace the *Sentences* of Peter Lombard by the *Summa* of St. Thomas in the schools of theology, but he also managed to influence the whole of Thomism with his views. The importance of his commentary on the *Summa* was so great that Pius V ordered its publication with the complete works of St. Thomas in 1570 (minus certain heterodox opinions expressed in the Third Part). Leo XIII ordered it to be published with the critical edition of St. Thomas's *Summa* (1888–1906). Little is known about Cajetan's intellectual formation. In his own day he was a pioneer in Thomistic studies. Undoubtedly his polemics with Averroists, Scotists, and Protestants, his sympathy for Renaissance humanism, and his involvement in practical affairs did much to shape his philosophical and theological outlook. The Thomism that he lived was not simply a restatement of St. Thomas but a Thomistic approach to problems of his day. Many of the opinions he held are not to be found in St. Thomas but are the insights that were a result of his own genius. *See* SCHOLASTICISM.

In philosophy Cajetan stressed the Aristotelianism of St. Thomas, often to the detriment of St. Thomas's originality. Constantly attacking Scotist views of being and abstraction, he presented a concept of being, which though analogical, might be considered too realistic and formalistic, depending as it does on the pseudo-Thomistic *Summa totius logicae.* In his doctrine of analogy he overemphasized the importance of proper proportionality. Thus for Cajetan the proper subject of metaphysics is attained by "formal abstraction" from all matter. In the metaphysical constitution of person Cajetan posited a special modality (*subsistentia*) to terminate the essence prior to existence. His doctrine of psychological abstraction, while basically Thomistic, was explained in terms of extrinsic illumination of the phantasms by the active intellect, which operates also within the thinking intellect.

The most conspicuous of Cajetan's unique positions rests on his personal view that the immortality of the human soul cannot be demonstrated by reason. In a discourse given in Rome in 1503, 5 years after departing from the Averroist university of Padua, Cajetan demonstrated the immortality of the human soul from the spirituality of intellectual and volitional functions, much as St. Thomas had done. Commenting on the *Summa* (1a, 75.2) in 1507, he confirmed the validity of St. Thomas's reasoning. But when preparing his *De anima* for publication in 1509, he admitted with Averroës that Aristotle had denied the immortality of the thinking intellect because of its dependence on phantasms; consequently only the active intellect is immortal and separated. However, Cajetan maintained that the immortality of the soul could be demonstrated from Aristotelian principles. Commenting on Matthew, ch. 22, in 1527, he flatly asserted that the immortality of the soul is not rationally demonstrable. He repeated this opinion in his commentary on Romans, ch. 9, in 1528, listing the doctrine of immortality with knowledge of the Trinity and Incarnation. Commenting on Ecclesiastes, ch. 3, in 1534, he asserted that no philosopher has ever demonstrated the immortality of the soul, and that this truth can be known only through Christian revelation. The reason for Cajetan's change of view is still far from certain. What is certain is that Thomists after Cajetan have unanimously rejected it as incompatible with the teaching of St. Thomas and Christian tradition.

In his commentary on the *Summa* Cajetan is a faithful expositor of St. Thomas. In the first two parts his principal adversaries are Duns Scotus, Henry of Ghent, Gregory of Rimini, Peter Aureole, and Durandus of St. Pourçain. In sacramental theology it is principally the errors of Luther and Zwingli that are criticized. The passages which Pius V had suppressed from the Third Part in no way touched the basic principles of Thomism. Rather, they were minor points which might have added coals to rampant heresies. Here his concern was to find areas of agreement between Catholic theology and Protestantism.

In Biblical exegesis Cajetan represents the best humanist tradition, faithful to the Church and to the spirit of St. Jerome; much of his criticism was far in advance of his time. While his farsightedness in Biblical theology and ecclesiastical reform were little appreciated by his contemporaries, his scholastic theology found immediate response in Italy and Spain. Even today he is found a stimulating and illuminating guide to the basic doctrines of St. Thomas; on many moral and social issues he is a very modern teacher.

Bibliography: Quétif-Échard 2.1:14–21. A. COSSIO, *Il Cardinale Gaetano e la riforma* (Cividale, Italy 1902). D. A. MORTIER, *Histoire des maîtres généraux de l'Ordre des Frères Prêcheurs,* 8 v. (Paris 1903–20) v.5. RevThom 39.2 or NS 17.2 (1934–35). *Angelicum* 11 (1934) 405–608. RivFilNeosc 27.2 (1935). J. HEGYI, *Die Bedeutung des Seins bei den klassischen Kommentatoren des heiligen Thomas von Aquin* (Pullach-Munich 1959). Stegmüller RB 5:8207–32.9. J. F. GRONER, *Kardinal Cajetan* (Fribourg 1951). **Illustration credit:** Library of Congress.

[J. A. WEISHEIPL]

CAJETAN, CONSTANTINO,

Benedictine writer of the Cassinese Congregation, also known as Cajetani, Gaetani, Gaetano; b. Syracuse, Italy, 1560; d. Rome, Sept. 17, 1650. He was of noble birth and made his profession in the Monastery of San Nicolò d'Arena at Catania, Oct. 29, 1586. Constantino devoted his life to scholarship and secured a prominent position in the Vatican Archives. He was named abbot of San Baronzio in the Diocese of Pistoia and prior of Santa Maria Latina in Sicily. The Gregorian College of St. Benedict, the first Benedictine college in Rome, was founded by him. It was a hostel for Benedictine travelers in Rome and a study center for young clergy. Gregory XV issued the bull of establishment on May 18, 1621, naming Cardinal Peretti Montalto as protector and Dom Constantino as president. When other sources failed him, Constantino requested assistance for this college from Richelieu and Mazarin. Its magnificent library was eventually dispersed, and enriched, among others, the libraries of Propaganda, the Sapienza, and the Biblioteca Alessandrina. Constantino is credited with writing 26 books and about 60 manuscripts. He glorified in the achievements of the Benedictines and listed among their number St. Columbanus, St. Isidore, and even Jean Gerson, to whom the *Imitation of Christ* was often attributed. He also questioned the authorship of St. Ignatius's *Spiritual Exercises*. The writings of St. Peter Damian, edited by Constantino, were published in Rome in 1606, and in Paris in 1642. It is his finest contribution to scholarship and was reproduced by Migne. Constantino was buried in the Church of San Benedetto in Piscinula in Trastevere, Rome.

Bibliography: P. SCHMITZ, DHGE 11:146–147. M. VILLER, DictSpirAscMyst 2.1:15–16. M. ARMELLINI, *Bibliotheca Benedictino-Casinensis,* 2 pts. (Assisi 1731–32) 1:123–136. J. M. BESSE, "Une Question d'histoire littéraire au XVIᵉ siècle: L'Exercice de Garcia de Cisneros et les Exercices de S. Ignace," RevQuestHist 61 (1897) 22–51.

[B. EGAN]

CALANCHA, ANTONIO DE LA,

historian and chronicler of colonial Peru; b. Chuquisaca (now Sucre), Bolivia, 1584; d. Lima, Peru, March 1, 1654. At the age of 14 he joined the Augustinians and later, at the University of San Marcos in Lima, he earned the doctorate in theology. Among the offices that he occupied in his order were those of rector of the Colegio San Ildefonso in Lima and prior of the monasteries in Arequipa, Trujillo, and Lima. His fame as a preacher was considerable. Some half dozen works have been attributed to Calancha; best-known among them is the *Corónica moralizada del orden de San Agustín en el Perú, con sucesos egemplares en esta monarquia* (pt. 1 Barcelona 1638; pt. 2 Lima 1653). Part 1, the longer and more valuable volume, contains not only a history of the Augustinians in the period 1551 to 1597, but also an interesting compilation of information about the Peruvian Indians, their religion, and their customs. Part 1 was later printed in an abridged form in Latin (tr. Joachim Brulius, OSA, Antwerp 1651) and in French (translator unknown, Toulouse 1653); selections from part 1 were published also in Italian (Genoa 1645) and in Spanish (Madrid 1659, Mexico City 1763, and La Paz 1939). Calancha's work, though not scientific by modern standards, is a valuable source for both history and ethnology. Another of his writings, *Historia de la Universidad de San Marcos hasta el 15 de julio de 1647,* was edited by L. A. Eguiguren (Lima 1921).

Bibliography: G. DE SANTIAGO VELA, *Ensayo de una biblioteca ibero-americana de la orden de San Agustín,* 7 v. in 8 (Madrid 1913–31) 1:487–494. A. PALMIERI, DHGE 3:764–765.

[A. J. ENNIS]

CALAS, JEAN

French Calvinist executed for the murder of his son in the controversial "Calas case"; b. Claparède, near Castres (Dept. of Tarn), March 19, 1698; d. Toulouse, March 10, 1762. From his marriage in 1731 to Rose Anne Cicibel, an Englishwoman of French Protestant origin, he had four sons and three daughters. Calas became a successful cloth merchant of Toulouse and reared his family in the Calvinist faith. Sometime in 1760 Louis, his second son, was converted to Catholicism and left his home because of his father's hostility. When Louis complained to the magistrate, Saint-Florentin, that he had been abandoned without support because of his religious views, Calas was obliged to pay the debt of 603 livres incurred by his son (Feb. 7, 1761). Then his eldest son, Marc Antoine, 28, announced his intention of renouncing Calvinism and on Oct 13, 1761, was found hanged in his father's storehouse. The funeral became an occasion for explosive anti-Calvinist feeling. Penitents marched in procession, and the Dominicans placed a skeleton on the catafalque with a martyr's palm in one hand and the document of abjuration in the other. Jean Calas was arrested for murder, and the members of his family were accused as possible accomplices. In the interrogations (October 1761 to February 1762) Calas was often silent or involved himself in contradictions, alleging that Marc Antoine had committed suicide or was strangled by an assassin. He was found guilty by the votes of 7 of the 8 town councilors and 11 of the 13 members of the parlement of Toulouse, and on March 9 was sentenced to be tortured on the rack and burned. Calas suffered with courage and to the last protested his innocence. The family property was confiscated. The young girls were sent to a convent of the Visitation; the widow and her sons sought refuge in Geneva.

Opposition to the sentence grew, and when Voltaire heard of the case, he used his influence to have the judgment reversed and the family reinstated. He wrote his friend Charles Argental to acquaint the Duke Étienne de Choiseul, then powerful at court, of this *horrible aventure*. He also began a pamphlet campaign, wrote the *Sur la tolérance à cause de la mort de Jean Calas* (1763), and called Calas's widow to Paris to plead for justice. By June he had the support of Jean d'Alembert, Aimar Nicholaï, Chancellor Jérome Maurepas, and Mme. de Pompadour. On June 4, 1764, the Royal Council annulled the sentence passed by the tribunal at Toulouse and on March 9, 1765, declared Jean Calas innocent. The property was restored and gifts of money were sent to Rose Anne Calas by Louis XV. David Baudigné, one of the magistrates at the trial at Toulouse, became demented and committed suicide. The Calas case became celebrated not only through the writings of Voltaire, but through dramas, such as T. Lemierre's *Calas ou fanatisme* (1790) and F. L. Laya's *Jean Calas* (1790), and through more than 100 books. During the French Revolution the Convention voted to erect a commemorative pillar to Calas in Toulouse (25 Brumaire II). Historians have weighed the evidence, examined the qualifications of the judges, and arrived at opposing verdicts. Some are convinced that Marc Antoine committed suicide; some that if Calas were innocent, his contradictions and behavior at the trial led inevitably to condemnation; others that a solution escapes the judgment of history.

Bibliography: D. D. BIEN, *The Calas Affair* (Princeton 1960). M. CHASSAIGNE, *L'Affaire Calas* (4th ed. Paris 1929). L. LABAT, *Le Drame de la rue des Filatiers* (1761): *Jean Calas* (Toulouse 1910). A. LEFRANC, *La Grande Encyclopédie*, 31 v. (Paris 1886–1902) 8:853–854. J. DEDIEU, DHGE 11:340–344.

[E. D. MC SHANE]

CALATRAVA, ORDER OF, Spanish military and religious order, founded January 1158 by King Sancho III of Castile, who ceded the fortress of Calatrava, in the modern Province of Ciudad Real, to Raymond, abbot of the Cistercian monastery of *Fitero, "to defend against the pagans, the enemies of the cross of Christ." Many of the warriors who came to assist in the defense assumed the monastic habit. In this way the military Order of Calatrava came into being. Six years later the order, then under the direction of its first master, obtained a *vivendi forma* from the *Cistercian general chapter and a bull of confirmation from Pope Alexander III. In 1187 the order was affiliated to the Cistercian Abbey of *Morimond, whose abbots were authorized to visit Calatrava annually, to appoint the prior and to confirm the election of the master as well.

In return for its services in the Reconquest the order acquired extensive properties, especially in the central and southern regions of Castile, and also in Aragon (*see* SPAIN, 2). The loss of Calatrava to the Moslems in 1195 was a grievous blow to the order, which established its headquarters at Salvatierra until it also

The badge of a knight of the Order of Calatrava.

was lost in 1211. The recovery of Calatrava and the Moslem defeat at Las Navas de Tolosa in 1212 repaired the order's fortunes and opened the road to Andalusia. Sometime before 1221 the order moved its seat to the castle known thereafter as Calatrava *la nueva*. From this vantage point the knights were able to render significant services in the conquest of Andalusia.

Governed by a master elected for life, the order was composed of knights and conventual brethren, observing the three monastic vows and an ascetic regimen based upon that of Cîteaux. The fundamental sources concerning the order's organization and customs are the statutes enacted by the abbots of Morimond or their delegates. The military Order of *Aviz, the *Knights of Alcantara, and the *Knights of Montesa were all affiliated with Calatrava.

As the Reconquest slowed to a halt, the order became involved in domestic politics, participating in the civil wars of the 14th and 15th centuries. To prevent the order's resources from being used against the monarchy, King *Ferdinand V and Queen *Isabella, with papal consent, assumed the administration of the order in 1489. Pope *Adrian VI in 1523 annexed the mastership to the crown in perpetuity. The order was gradually transformed into an honorary society of noblemen, although the conventual brethren continued to adhere to the monastic observance until the dissolution of all the Spanish military orders in the 19th century. Today the nuns of Calatrava maintain the traditional monastic spirit in their convent in Madrid.

Bibliography: F. DE RADES Y ANDRADA, *Chronica de las tres ordenes y cavallerias, de Sanctiago, Calatrava y Alcantara*, 3 v. (Toledo 1572). J. F. O'CALLAGHAN, "The Affiliation of the Order of Calatrava with the Order of Cîteaux," AnalOCist 15 (1959) 161–193; 16 (1960) 3–59, 255–292. **Illustration credit:** MAS, Barcelona.

[J. F. O'CALLAGHAN]

CALCIDIUS, Neoplatonic philosopher; fl. *c.* A.D. 400. His translation of, and commentary on, the *Timaeus* of Plato is addressed to Osius, who was probably the Milanese patrician appointed, at first, chief administrator of the imperial demesne and later, head of the imperial treasury. Although Calcidius's work shows a superficial knowledge of a few Hebrew and Christian documents, it is hardly probable that he was a Christian.

The translation and commentary covers only one-third of the *Timaeus* (31C–53C). The translation is, at times, very literal; at others, little more than a paraphrase. The commentary is expository in style and often lacks depth. It is eclectic and contains many references from Adrastus, Numenius, Galen, Porphyry, Jamblichus, Albinus, and *Origen (Commentary on Genesis). Aristotle is quoted with respect, especially his definition of the soul. Calcidius did not hesitate to criticize the philosophers whom he cited; usually the criticisms are in Plato's favor. The commentary is, for this reason, a valuable source of information about current philosophical interpretations. Some authors have thought Posidonius to have been the basic source of Calcidius; this, however, is unlikely.

Calcidius's influence was considerable. He is responsible for the term *silva* in place of *hyle,* or Aristotelian ὕλη. He was also an important source of Platonic doctrine throughout the Middle Ages. The authors of the hexaemeral literature of the school of Chartres make use of Calcidius in an attempt to explain philosophically and scientifically the origins of the universe. There is no evidence to show whether the commentary was an original composition of Calcidius or whether he merely translated from the Greek an already existing commentary. There are 144 known extant manuscripts of the work, most of which are complete; eight different editions have been published, the earliest in 1520.

Bibliography: J. H. WASZINK, ed., *Timaeus, a Calcidio translatus commentarioque instructus* (Corpus platonicum medii aevi. Plato latinus 4; London 1962). J. C. M. VAN WINDEN, *Calcidius on Matter, His Doctrine and Sources* (Leiden 1959). T. GREGORY, *Platonismo medievale: Studi e ricerche* (Rome 1958). R. KLIBANSKY, *The Continuity of the Platonic Tradition During the Middle Ages* (London 1939). J. H. WASZINK, "Die sogenannte Fünfteilung der Träume bei Chalcidius und ihre Quellen," *Mnemosyne* 9 (1941) 65–85. W. H. STAHL, "Dominant Traditions in Early Medieval Latin Science," *Isis* 50 (1959) 95–124. J. R. O'DONNELL, MedSt 7 (1945) 1–20. A. C. VEGA, *Ciudad de Dios* 152 (1936) 145–164; 155 (1943) 219–241.

[J. R. O'DONNELL]

CALCULUS

Calculus is a division of mathematical science consisting of two principal parts, *differential* and *integral* calculus. Isaac *Newton (1693) collected, used, and extended the basic ideas of infinitesimal analysis (fluxions) that Napier, *Kepler, *Galileo, *Pascal, *Fermat, his teacher Isaac *Barrow, and Wallis had developed. Newton lived at a time when the groundwork had been laid, and his ability enabled him to construct almost at once a complete calculus.

Differential Calculus. Differential calculus differed from infinitesimal calculus only in its notation, which is credited to *Leibniz (*c.* 1677; published 1684) about 9 years before Newton's earliest printed account.

Two problems engaged the attention of the mathematicians of the 16th and 17th centuries: the problem of tangents to a curve, which is the fundamental problem of differential calculus; and the problem of quadra-

tures (to determine the area within a given curve), the fundamental problem of integral calculus. The fact that these two problems were interrelated was the important discovery of Newton and Leibniz.

For several centuries, scientists had been studying phenomena of motion and variability. The Latin words *fluxus* and *fluens* were used in this connection. Newton spoke of a variable mathematical quantity as a *fluent,* and called its rate of change a *fluxion.* Apparently he saw no need for a definition of the notion of fluxion and was satisfied to make a tacit appeal to one's intuition of motion. He contributed to the development of the concept of *limit, which enabled others following him to put the new ideas on a more rigorous foundation. The concept of limit had evolved from an appeal to geometrical intuition, the foundation for which was laid 30 years earlier by Descartes (*see* GEOMETRY, ANALYTIC). Almost at the same time the method of *indivisibles* was introduced to determine areas, volumes, and positions of centers of mass by summation in a manner analogous to that presently effected by the methods of integral calculus.

Barrow's lectures on geometry had contained some new ways, suggested by Fermat, of determining areas and tangents to curves; these led to the methods of differential calculus. To illustrate this, let T be where the tangent line to a curve at P meets the x axis (see illustration *a*). Let M be the foot of the perpendicular from P upon the x axis. Then $OM = x$ and $MP = y$. Fermat had observed that for a smooth curve the tangent at a point P on a curve was determined if one other point besides P on it, say T, were known. Barrow suggested considering another point Q on the curve close to P; let N be the foot of the perpendicular from Q upon OX, then ON and NQ are the x and y coordinates of Q on the curve. Let PR parallel to OX meet QN in R. Then the small triangle PQR was called by Barrow the *differential* triangle because its sides RQ and RP were the differences of the ordinates and of the abscissas of P and Q. Leibniz called the triangle PQR the *characteristic* triangle. The closer Q is to P, the more nearly will the differential triangle be similar to the triangle TMP. Thus the relationship $PM/MT = QR/PR$ is true as Q becomes coincident with P. To find QR/PR Barrow assumed the coordinates of Q to be $(x + h, y + k)$ so that $h = PR$ and $k = QR$. Since Q lies on the curve, its coordinates $(x + h, y + k)$ must also satisfy the equation of the curve. Thus two equations are available to obtain an expression equal to the ratio k/h in terms of x, y, h, k, which gives the slope or direction of the secant line PQ. As the new differential triangle becomes smaller due to the eventual coincidence of Q with P, h

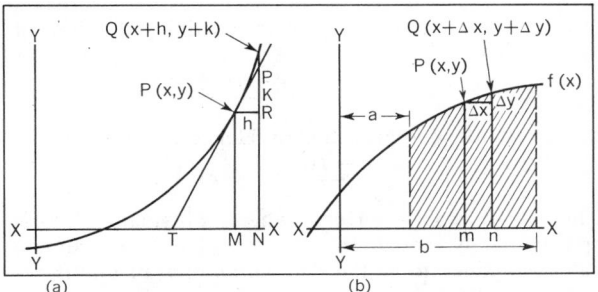

(a) *Development of the derivative as the slope of a curve.*
(b) *Development of the integral as the area under a curve.*

and k simultaneously become smaller and approach zero, thus giving the slope or direction of the curve at point P.

The mathematics of Barrow and Wallis were the starting points from which Newton, with a greater degree of ingenuity, moved onward. His *Method of Fluxions* was first translated by J. Colson from the original Latin in 1736, about 65 years after it was written. In it Newton lays the foundations for abstract calculus by considering the solution of the following two problems in mechanics: (1) "The length of curve described being given continually, to find the velocity of the motion at any time." (2) "The velocity of the motion being continually given to find the length of the curve described at any given time."

We illustrate Newton's first problem. Essentially it says that if the distance s covered is known in terms of the elapsed time t, i.e., as a function of time t, we may say $s = f(t)$. Now for a change Δt (increment t) in time there is a corresponding change Δs in the distance. Thus the new distance $s + \Delta s$ is given by

$$s + \Delta s = f(t + \Delta t)$$

The change in distance Δs is therefore

$$f(t + \Delta t) - f(t)$$

The *average* velocity along the curve then, in distance units per unit of time, is

$$\frac{\Delta s}{\Delta t} = \frac{f(t + \Delta t) - f(t)}{\Delta t}$$

The instantaneous velocity at any given time t then becomes the limiting value of this expression as the time increment Δt is made smaller and eventually becomes zero. Here we have essentially the same analysis that Barrow had used to find the slope of a tangent line to a curve at a given point. Thus Newton conceived the fundamental concept of the absolute calculus, viz, if $y = f(x)$ we have the concept of the limiting value of

$$\lim_{\Delta x \to 0} \frac{\Delta y}{\Delta x} = \lim_{\Delta x \to 0} \frac{f(x + \Delta x) - f(x)}{\Delta x}$$

By definition this limit is the *derivative* of the function $f(x)$ with respect to x; it is designated by dy/dx, a notation due to Leibniz. Direct substitution of $\Delta x = 0$ in the expression for $\Delta y/\Delta x$ gives the anomalous expression $0/0$, which has no meaning; however the limiting process can be carried out. The complete process is called *differentiation* of $f(x)$ with respect to x; if $y = f(x)$ is represented graphically as a curve in Cartesian rectangular coordinates, then

$$\frac{dy}{dx} = \lim_{\Delta x \to 0} \frac{f(x + \Delta x) - f(x)}{\Delta x}$$

is the slope of the curve at the point (x,y).

So far $f'(x) = dy/dx$ has not been regarded or treated as a fraction. It has been a symbol defining the limit of the fraction

$$\frac{f(x + \Delta x) - f(x)}{\Delta x}$$

as Δx is made to approach zero. Hence we may write

$$\frac{f(x + \Delta x) - f(x)}{\Delta x} = f'(x) + \xi$$

where $\xi \to 0$ as $\Delta x \to 0$. Hence when Δx is small, $\Delta f(x)$ is approximately equal to $f'(x)\Delta x$. This approximate value is defined to be the *differential* of $f(x)$ and is denoted by $df(x)$, i.e. $df(x) = f'(x)\Delta x$. In particular when $f(x) = x$, we have $dx = \Delta x$. Hence when x is the

independent variable, $dx = \Delta x$. This yields $dy = df(x) = f'(x) \, dx$, thereby justifying the treatment of dy/dx as a fraction.

Integral Calculus. Integral calculus deals with integration, an operation which is the inverse of the operation of differentiation.

Consider the area under a curve $y = f(x)$ bounded by the curve, the x axis, and two ordinates whose equations are $x = a$ and $x = b$, $a < b$ (see illustration b). We assume $f(x)$ to be single-valued and continuous between $x = a$ and $x = b$. Choose some point P on the curve between the two ordinates and let M be the foot of the perpendicular from P upon OX. Then we may consider the area as generated by the ordinate MP moving from $x = a$ to $x = b$; thus the area up to the ordinate MP depends on $x = OM$; this defines the area as a function of x. Call it $A(x)$. When $x = a$, $A(a) = 0$. Now apply the differentiation process to $A(x)$. Let Q be a point near P so that Q has coordinates $(x + \Delta x, y + \Delta y)$; then $\Delta x = MN$ where N is the foot of the perpendicular from Q upon OX. Then the increment of area $\Delta A =$ area $MNQP = y_m \, \Delta x$ where y_m is some ordinate between PM and QN. Then $\quad \dfrac{\Delta A}{\Delta x} = y_m$

As Δx approaches zero, y_m becomes $PM = y$; i.e.,

$$\frac{dA}{dx} = y = A'(x)$$

Hence $dA(x) = A'(x) \, dx = y \, dx = f(x) \cdot dx$. The area $A(x)$ is therefore that function of x whose derivative is $f(x)$; call it $\varphi(x)$. This operation of finding $\varphi(x)$ such that $\varphi'(x) = f(x)$ is called integration. This is designated by the symbol $\int f(x)dx$.

Since $\quad \dfrac{d}{dx} [\varphi(x) + C] = \varphi'(x)$

(where C is an arbitrary constant; the derivative of a constant being zero), one should write $A(x) = \varphi(x) + C$, which gives the area under the curve from $x = a$ to the ordinate MP. Now $A(a) = \varphi(a) + C = 0$; hence $C = -\varphi(a)$. Thus

$$A(x) = \int f(x)dx - \varphi(a) = \varphi(x) - \varphi(a)$$

And

$$A(b) = \varphi(b) - \varphi(a)$$

which is designated by

$$\int_a^b f(x) \, dx$$

It is effected by finding the function $\varphi(x)$, whose derivative is $f(x)$, evaluating $\varphi(b)$ and $\varphi(a)$ and subtracting. In case the curve $y = f(x)$ crosses the axis of OX, the area below will be negative. Hence the integral

$$\int_a^b f(x) \, dx$$

gives the algebraic sum of the areas above and below the x axis between the ordinates $x = a$ and $x = b$.

The area under the curve $y = f(x)$ between the x axis and the ordinates $x = a$ and $x = b$ can be approximated using a method quite similar to the method of "indivisibles" used by Galileo and *Cavalieri. The method is as follows: the interval $x = a$ to $x = b$ on the x axis is subdivided into a number n of small subintervals Δx_i, $i = 1, 2, 3, \ldots, n$; ordinates are erected at each point of subdivision and each strip of the area under the curve is replaced by a rectangle whose altitude is an ordinate f(x'_i) where $x_i < x'_i < x_{i+1}$, somewhere between the greatest and least ordinate in that strip. The area sum of these rectangles gives an approximate value for the area A under the curve, between the x axis and two ordinates, $x = a$ and $x = b$. The value of this approximation will be better the larger the number of rectangles and the smaller the width of each rectangle. The area can then be represented as the limit of a sum of rectangular approximations, as long as the width of the widest rectangle tends to zero as the number n of rectangles increases indefinitely. Moreover, this limit is independent of the way in which the sequence of subareas is chosen, as long as the width of each approximating rectangle tends to zero. This area is the same as the area obtained above by the process of integration. Hence

$$A = \lim_{n \to \infty} \sum_{i=1}^{i=n} f(x_i)\, \Delta x_i = \int_a^b f(x)\, dx$$

where $a = \lim x_1$, $b = \lim x_n$ as n tends to infinity. This result is known as the fundamental theorem of the integral calculus.

Calculus is the threshold of higher mathematics including subjects such as differential equations, calculus of variations, and functions of a complex variable.

Bibliography: F. CAJORI, *A History of Mathematics* (New York 1895). W. W. BALL, *A Short Account of the History of Mathematics* (4th ed. reprinted London 1935). C. B. BOYER, *The Concepts of Calculus* (New York 1949). R. COURANT and H. ROBBINS, *What is Mathematics?* (New York 1954). E. T. BELL, *Men of Mathematics* (New York 1937).

[O. J. RAMLER]

CALCUTTA, ARCHDIOCESE OF (CALCUTTENSIS)

Metropolitan see since 1887, in West Bengal state, northeast *India. The city of Calcutta, on the left bank of the Hooghly River, was founded in 1690 by Job Charnock of the East India Company. Retaken by Robert Clive in 1757, it was the capital of British India from 1773 to 1912. In 1963 the archdiocese, 31,102 square miles in area, had 27 parishes, 29 secular and 120 religious priests, 202 men in 11 religious houses, 450 women in 34 convents, and 68,000 Catholics in a population of 28 million. Its seven suffragans, which had 350 priests, 760 sisters, and 264,000 Catholics in a population of 54 million, were: Darjeeling (created in 1962); Dibrugarh (1951); Dumka (1962); Jalpaiguri (1952); Krishnagar (1886); Patna (1919), which includes *Nepal; and Shillong (1934), which includes *Bhutan.

Part of the See of *Goa in 1534 and part of the See of Cochin, suffragan of Goa, in 1558, Bengal became part of the new See of Mylapore in 1606 (*see* MADRAS). Portuguese settled in the area *c.* 1571, and Augustinians, with Jesuits in a secondary role, soon evangelized from Hooghly. Christian numbers increased with Portuguese refugees from the Dutch elsewhere in the East, and the present cathedral church was built in 1697. The Augustinians, to whom the area was entrusted, did not accept native candidates for the clergy, and the lack of qualified priests combined with difficult social conditions to produce some decadence of the Catholic communities. From 1606 to 1834 Bengal was visited once by the bishop of Mylapore (1712), and his efforts for reform were fruitless. Protestants, who entered in 1758, were better organized than Catholics, and *c.* 1800 founded several well-endowed schools.

In reply to a petition from Catholics of Bengal for a bishop, the Vicariate of Bengal was detached from Mylapore and entrusted to English and Irish Jesuits (1834). But Augustinians and other Catholics under the Portuguese padroado would not recognize the vicars, one of whom died after a short stay in the unhealthy climate. The Vicariate of East Bengal (1850) and the mission of central Bengal (1855) were detached from the Vicariate of Bengal, which also ceded territory to the new Vicariate of Vizagapatam (1852) and entrusted Assam to the *Paris Foreign Mission Society (1853). English Jesuits had left Calcutta in 1846, but in 1859 Belgian Jesuits returned, since it was impossible to recruit a local clergy. There were then less than 10,000 Catholics in the vicariate, almost all in the city. When the Catholic hierarchy was established in India in 1886, Calcutta became an archdiocese, with *Dacca and Krishnagar as suffragans from 1887. In 1928 the last traces of the padroado came to an end in Calcutta. The first Indian prelate was V. A. Dyer (1960–62). P. Johanns and George *Dandoy were important figures for the Catholic-Hindu dialogue.

Bibliography: H. JOSSON, *La Mission du Bengale occidentale ou archidiocèse de Calcutta,* 2 v. (Bruges 1921); DHGE 11:356–361. N. KOWALSKI, "Die Errichtung des apostolischen Vikariates Kalkutta nach den Akten der Propagandaarchivs," ZMissRel 36 (1952) 117–127, 187–201; 37 (1953) 209–228. T. POTHACAMURY, *The Church in Independent India* (Bombay 1961). *The Catholic Directory of India* (Allahabad, India). AnnPont (1965) 86.

[E. R. HAMBYE]

CALDARA, ANTONIO, baroque vocal composer; b. Venice, *c.* 1670; d. Vienna, Dec. 28, 1736. His early life is obscure, but it has been established that he was a pupil of *Legrenzi. By 1690 he was composing operas to *Metastasio librettos and oratorios to texts by Apostolo Zeno. After travels in Spain and Italy he settled in Vienna in 1716 as assistant chapelmaster to J. J. *Fux under Charles VI, retaining this post until his death. Although during his early period he was esteemed as a cellist and string composer, he is known primarily for his vocal writing, particularly his mangificent 16-part *Crucifixus,* and has been favorably compared to *Lotti in this sphere. In his works, which include many Masses, cantatas, and other sacred compositions, he unites the lyrical Italian cantilena with impeccable contrapuntal technique and utilizes indigenous elements that produce a valid and individual expression of the Austrian baroque. His canonic writing as exemplified in the *Missa in contrapunto canonico . . .* was said to be especially admired by Fux.

Bibliography: A. CALDARA, *Kirchenwerke,* ed. E. MANDYCZEWSKI (DenkmTonkOst 26); *Kammermusik für Gesang Kantaten, Madrigale, Kanons,* ed. E. MANDYCZEWSKI (*ibid.* 75). B. PAUMGARTNER, MusGG 2:645–650. Eitner QuellLex. Baker 241–242. C. GRAY, "Antonio Caldera," *Musical Times* 70 (1929) 212–214. Fellerer CathChMus. Buk MusB. Young ChorTrad.

[M. CORDOVANA]

CALDAS, FRANCISCO JOSÉ DE, Colombian physicist, astronomer, and naturalist; b. Popayán, Cauca, 1768; d. Bogotá, Oct. 29, 1816. He was shot for his activities in the cause of national independence. He dedicated his life to the sciences—mathematics, geography, and astronomy—for which he had great aptitude, and he contrived to make the instruments necessary for his observations. In 1802 the erudite German traveler, Humboldt, considered him "a prodigy in astronomy" and admired him as a real genius. Because of his almost encyclopedic knowledge, he became a protegé of the learned priest José Celestino *Mutis, who made it possible for him to dedicate himself fully to the sciences. He was appointed a member of the botanic expedition and made head of the Astronomic Observatory, founded by Mutis in Bogotá in 1802.

The greatest accomplishments of Caldas were in geography and physics. His basically intuitive genius led him to the most famous discovery made in the Spanish America of his day: the principle of the hypsometer. Caldas was the inventor, in the exact meaning of the word, of the process of measuring altitude by the boiling point of water. He conceived the method by himself, tested it, and deduced the physical laws governing it. A scientific memorandum, written in 1802, gives indisputable proof of his discovery. At the beginning of the war for national independence (1810) Caldas enlisted in the engineers, in which he was a colonel and the director of the first cadet school in his country. His literary fame derives from the publication of the celebrated *Semanario del Nuevo Reino de Granada* (1808–11), a scientific periodical unsurpassed anywhere in America. In it he published his best works and revealed himself a forerunner of anthropo-geography with his study *Del influjo del clima sobre los seres organizados*.

[G. HERNANDEZ DE ALBA]

CALDERÓN DE LA BARCA, PEDRO

Spanish dramatist; b. Madrid, Jan. 17, 1600; d. there, probably May 25, 1681. He was the son of Diego Calderón de la Barca and María Henao y Riaño. At the age of 8 or 9 he entered the Colegio Mayor de los Jesuitas, where he began the study of classical languages and the Holy Scriptures. His mother died in 1610, and in October 1614 he entered the University of Alcalá, but his father's death in November 1615 brought him back to Madrid. The next 5 years seem to have been divided between the universities of Alcalá and Salamanca. Records indicate that he studied Canon Law at Salamanca and left there in 1620 with the *bachillerato*. In 1622 he won third prize in a poetic competition held during the celebrations of the canonization of St. Isidore and earned some vague praise from Lope de *Vega. His first play, *Amor, honor, y poder* (1623), was well received by the public in Madrid. With this and other literary successes, Calderón's name became well known. He appears to have been with the army in Italy between 1624 and 1628, perhaps even in Flanders.

By 1630 Calderón had completed 15 plays, some of them notable successes. His fame had become so well established that when Lope de Vega died in 1635, Calderón was named to succeed him as director of theatrical functions at court. Two years later the King made him Knight of the Order of Santiago. He continued to turn out plays, and the period that followed was the most fruitful of his life. In 1640 he took part in the expedition to put down the Catalonian rebellion, and in 1646 joined the household of the Duke of Alba. He resigned his position at court, entered the Third Order of St. Francis, and was ordained probably on Oct. 16, 1649. In 1653 he was appointed to a chaplaincy in

Pedro Calderón de la Barca, an antique engraving.

Toledo, which he held until 1663, when the King persuaded him to return to his court post. Here he remained until his death.

In spite of his Gongoristic manner, Calderón was the continuator of the *comedia nueva* as defined by Lope de Vega (*see* GONGORISM). Every type of play invented by Lope is found in Calderón's theater. His historical plays, inspired by antiquity and late European history, show less regard for historical verity than interest in the dramatic possibilities of incident and situation. Plays like *La gran Cenobia* (1635), set in the Orient; *Las armas de la hermosura* (1652); and *La cisma de Inglaterra* (1634), dealing with Henry VIII and Anne Boleyn, seem almost to mock historical accuracy. Better in this respect are his semihistorical dramas such as *El alcalde de Zalamea* (c. 1642), which he borrowed from Lope and made one of his masterpieces.

Tragedy and "Honor" Plays. The nearest thing to real tragedy in Spanish theater are his "honor" plays. Their use of the *pundonor* (point of honor) was full of complexities and casuistries that lent themselves well to the requirements of the baroque drama, with its fondness for subtleties of rhetoric and plot. The denouement was always bloody and too often required the sacrifice of innocent beings. In spite of the cruelty of their "justice," they achieved tragic heights, if not sublimity. The best, as well as the most typical, are *A secreto agravio, secreta venganza* (1635), *El mayor monstruo, los celos* (c. 1634), *El médico de su honra* (1635), and *El pintor de su deshonra* (c. 1648–50). (*See* BAROQUE, THE.)

More a theologian than a philosopher, Calderón wrote the best religious dramas of Spain, employing them as vehicles for Catholic dogma. Though some of the problems discussed may have less dogmatic interest today, these plays are still moving because they are projections of human struggle with superior forces. *La vida es sueño* (1635), probably the greatest of them, uses the ancient Oriental theme of the awakened sleeper and deals with the apparent conflict between free will and predestination. It argues that man by the exercise of his will may better himself in this life, which is a dream, and thus prepare himself for the real life that is to come. The conception is lofty, the language is noble, and the execution is superb. Another masterpiece is *El mágico prodigioso* (1637), built on the legend of St. Cyprian of Antioch. *El príncipe constante* (1628) is based on the ill-fated crusade (1437) of Prince Ferdinand of Portugal against Tangier, in which the Prince sacrificed himself as a hostage; it contains one of the finest sonnets in Spanish, the one beginning:

> Estas que fueron pompa y alegría
> despertando al albor de la mañana,
> a la tarde serán lástima vana,
> durmiendo en brazos de la noche fría.

La devoción de la cruz (1633) was of such universal appeal that it enjoyed great popularity even in the Protestant countries of Northern Europe.

Calderón and Comedy. Calderón was a master of the *comedia de capa y espada*. His plays in this manner are dramas of intrigue rather than comedies of manners. Their complicated plots, skillfully resolved, show consummate dramatic architecture. More than the plays of any contemporary, his responded to the demands of the baroque stage. The plots are exercises in ingenuity, the language sparkles with conceits, and the action is fast and complicated. However, the characters are types, not individuals, and the social customs depicted are limited. Excellent examples of this genre are *La dama duende* (1629), *Casa con dos puertas mala es de guardar* (1629), and *Mañanas de abril y mayo* (1632).

Among writers of **autos sacramentales* Calderón was supreme. In them he clothed a prodigious inventive talent with the rich splendor of his poetic genius. He drew their plots from the Bible, from the lives of the saints, and from sacred lore. If the story was profane, allegory made it sacred. Many of his *autos* have weathered changes in time and taste. The profound concepts of *La vida es sueño* find simpler, but nobler, expression in the *auto* of the same title (1673). Others of great lyric power are *El gran teatro del Mundo* (c. 1645–50) and *La cena del Rey Baltasar* (1632), with its sublime monologue of Death. After 1666 Calderón ceased almost wholly to write plays for the public but continued to turn out two *autos sacramentales* a year for the municipality of Madrid; and when he died, leaving behind more than 100 plays and some 70 *autos,* the golden age of Spanish literature came to an end.

See also SPANISH LITERATURE, 2.

Bibliography: *Obras completas,* ed. A. VALBUENA PRAT and A. VALBUENA BRIONES, 3 v. (Madrid 1952–59). A. L. CONSTANDSE, *Le Baroque espagnol et Calderón de la Barca* (Amsterdam 1951). E. FRUTOS CORTÉS, *Calderón de la Barca* (Barcelona 1949). H. H. HILBORN, *A Chronology of the Plays of D. Pedro Calderón de la Barca* (Toronto 1938). S. DE MADARIAGA, *Shelley and Calderón, and Other Essays on English and Spanish Poetry* (London 1933). F. DE S. MCGARRY, *The Allegorical and Metaphorical Language in the Autos Sacramentales of Calderón* (Washington 1937). M. MENÉNDEZ Y PELAYO, *Calderón y su teatro* (Madrid 1881). A. A. PARKER, *The Allegorical Drama of Calderón* (New York 1943). A. E. SLOMAN, *The Dramatic Craftsmanship of Calderón* (Oxford 1958). A. VALBUENA PRAT, *Calderón: Su personalidad, su arte dramático, su estilo y sus obras* (Barcelona 1941). L. E. WEIR, *The Ideas Embodied in the Religious Dramas of Calderón* (Lincoln, Neb. 1940). **Illustration credit:** Hispanic Society of America.

[P. ROGERS]

CALDEY, ABBEY OF, Cistercian house, on Caldey Island, which lies southwest of Tenby, a small town on the Pembrokeshire coast of south Wales. Celtic monks settled this abbey in the 6th century. During the reign of Henry I it became a cell of the abbey of Tironian Benedictines (*see* TIRON, ABBEY OF) then recently founded at Saint Dogmaels, near Cardigan, Wales. In July 1534 Caldey acknowledged the royal supremacy and passed at once to lay ownership. It was purchased in 1906 by a community of Anglican Benedictines, the greater number of whom submitted to Rome in 1913. The *Trappists bought it in 1928, and the Benedictines moved to *Prinknash Park, Gloucestershire.

Bibliography: P. F. ANSON, *The Benedictines of Caldey* (London 1940). Dugdale MonAngl 4:129–131. W. D. BUSHELL, "An Island of the Saints," *Archaelogia cambrensis* 6 ser. 8 (1908) 237–260. Knowles-Hadcock 102. J. M. CANIVEZ, DHGE 11:375–376.

[A. BYRNE]

CALDWELL, MARY GWENDOLINE, philanthropist who was instrumental in inaugurating The Catholic University of America, Washington, D.C.; b. Louisville, Ky., 1863; d. New York City, Oct. 10, 1909. Mamie, as she was called, was the daughter of Mary Eliza (Breckenridge) and William Shakespeare Caldwell. She and her younger sister, Mary Elizabeth (later the Baroness Moritz von Zedtwitz), moved to New York City with their father after the death of their mother. In 1874 their father died, leaving his daughters a considerable fortune. They attended the Academy of the Sacred Heart, New York City, where they first made the acquaintance of Father John Lancaster Spalding, a fellow Kentuckian on leave from the Diocese of Louisville, who was then assistant pastor of St. Michael's Church in New York and later the first bishop of Peoria, Ill. Through her friendship with Bishop Spalding, Mamie became interested in the idea of a university or higher school where Catholic clergy could be educated.

At the Third Plenary Council of Baltimore in 1884, Miss Caldwell's offer of $300,000 for the founding of a national school of philosophy and theology was made known to, and accepted by, the bishops in council, with the stipulation of the young heiress that she was to be considered the founder of the institution. Thus was inaugurated the work that later led to the establishment of The *Catholic University of America.

In 1896 Miss Caldwell married the Marquis Jean des Monstiers-Merinville in Paris, with Bishop Spalding officiating. Three years later the University of Notre Dame, South Bend, Ind., awarded its Laetare medal to the Marquise. However, on Oct. 30, 1904, the world learned through an Associated Press announcement that the former Miss Caldwell had renounced Catholicism. The Marquise, who died in her stateroom on the North German liner, the *Kronprinzessin Cecile,* as it lay anchored outside New York, was buried in Louisville.

[D. F. SWEENEY]

CALDWELL COLLEGE FOR WOMEN

Situated in Caldwell, N.J., Caldwell College for Women is the only women's college in the Newark Archdiocese. It was opened Sept. 19, 1939, by the Dominican Sisters of the Congregation of the Sacred Heart, under the direction of Mother M. Joseph. The College is accredited by the Middle States Association of Colleges and Secondary Schools, the Department of Education of the State of New Jersey, and the Regents of the University of the State of New York. It is affiliated with The Catholic University of America.

Religious of the Congregation constitute the majority of the board of trustees. The archbishop of Newark is the president, and the mother general, chairman. These, with the general council of the Congregation, are ex officio members; others are elected annually. The board determines the administrative, educational, and financial policies of the College. In 1964 there were 8 administrative and 65 faculty members, including priests, sisters and laymen. They held 10 doctorates, 4 professional degrees, and 43 master's degrees. Although the Ford and the Kellogg Foundations have made grants to the College, financial support depends in large measure on tuition and on the contributed services of the religious.

For the purpose of coordinating the fields of learning, the departments are organized in four divisions: theology and philosophy, humanities, natural sciences and mathematics, and social sciences. Eleven departments, embracing the humanities, physical and social sciences, and modern languages, offer fields of concentration that lead to B.A. or B.S. degrees. All students follow the general curriculum—theology, philosophy, humanities, and natural and social sciences—for the first 2 years. In the junior and senior years, opportunity is offered for intensive study in a field of concentration. Methods of instruction include lectures, laboratory work, discussions, research, and independent study. Directed reading in the junior year and the seminar in the senior year add breadth and depth to the student's knowledge. Plant experimentation and cancer research are carried on, the latter by the Caldwell College unit of the Institutum Divi Thomae, a research center founded in Cincinnati, Ohio, by Abp. John T. *McNicholas. Preprofessional programs include medicine, nursing, and law. A teacher-training program prepares students to teach in the public schools of New Jersey and neighboring states.

Caldwell is the only undergraduate institution in its vicinity that offers courses in library science. Besides full-time students, adults attend evening classes to become more efficient in public library work. In 1960 the College inaugurated an honors program whose members are designated as Siena Scholars. In the freshman year, focus is on right reasoning and creative thinking. Sophomores concentrate on the world's great literature. Junior and senior Siena Scholars pursue independent study under the guidance of their faculty advisors. A library erected in 1952 provides space for approximately 60,000 books besides periodicals and audiovisual materials. In 1964 the collection numbered 33,148 bound volumes and received 315 periodicals. The library affords practical training in all processes for students enrolled in the library science program.

To the original five buildings erected on the 100-acre campus, Raymond Hall (1960) and Mother Joseph residence hall (1961) have been added to accommodate the increasing enrollment. From 41 students in 1939, the College in 1964 reached a full-time enrollment of over 600. Part-time students raised the total to 834.

An annual College survey by which 5-year studies are made keeps the College in close touch with its alumnae. Graduates have been successful in business, industry, and education. Approximately 400 alumnae staff, public elementary and secondary schools. Many have pursued graduate study and research in specialized fields, frequently by means of grants, fellowships, or assistantships. Most become homemakers.   [M. A. RAHER]

CALEB, son of Jephonne and eponymous ancestor of the Calebites. Among the 12 spies sent from Cades to reconnoiter the land of Canaan (Nm 13.6), Caleb alone remained confident of dispossessing the native inhabitants (Nm 13.30; Jos 14.6–14). For his confidence in Yahweh Caleb was allowed to enter the Promised Land with Josue (Nm 26.65; 32.12; Dt 1.36). The clan of Caleb, along with other extraneous clans, helped the tribe of Juda conquer southern Palestine (Jos 15.15–19; Jgs 1.11–20), and, after the defeat of the *Enacim (Anakim), they received, according to the promise of Moses (Jgs 1.20), the city of *Hebron (Jos 14.6–15; 21.11–12; Jgs 1.20; 1 Chr 2.42). The story of Caleb's role as spy, sent from Cades northward to scout out southern Palestine, may reflect, in etiological fashion, the way the Calebites came into the possession of Hebron. The OT traditions about Caleb are wavering and uncertain. An early tradition calls him a Cenezite (Nm 32.12; Jos 14.6, 14); another tradition makes Cenez (Kenaz) his brother (Jos 15.17; Jgs 1.13; 3.9); and a late tradition makes Cenez his grandson (1 Chr 4.15) while giving Caleb a strict Judaite genealogy (1 Chr 2.9, 18, 24, 42, 48). Since Genesis represents Cenez as an Edomite (Gn 36.11, 15, 42), it is probable that the clan of the Calebites was closely related to both the Cenezites and Edomites. With the passage of time the Calebites, like the Simeonites, Othonielites, *Cinites (Kenites), and Jerameelites—all originally non-Israelite clans of the far south of Palestine—became incorporated into the tribe of Juda.

Bibliography: InterDictBibl 1:482–483. EncDictBibl 299. R. DE VAUX, "Mambré," DBSuppl 5:753–758. M. NOTH, *The History of Israel,* ed. and tr. P. R. ACKROYD (2d ed. New York 1960).
                              [A. L. BARBIERI]

CALENDAR, CHRISTIAN

Although from the beginning of the Christian Era, the Christians followed the Julian solar calendar of 46 B.C. for general purposes and with it adopted the Roman usage of counting the days of the month in a continuous series in relation to nones, ides, and kalends, they also evolved a specifically Christian calendar, the center of which was the day of the Resurrection (*see* CHRONOLOGY, ANCIENT; CHRONOLOGY, MEDIEVAL).

Easter. Since the majority of the early Christians were Jewish converts, it is understandable that from the outset the Christian calendar was governed by the fact that the death and Resurrection of Christ had taken place at the time of the chief Jewish feast, the Pasch, or Passover, celebrated on the 14th day of the month of Nisan, i.e., at the full moon following the Spring equinox (*see* CALENDARS OF THE ANCIENT NEAR EAST). However, rather than literally follow the Jewish Passover, since this would necessitate the commemoration of the Resurrection on a different day of the week each year, Christian custom (sanctioned at the Council of *Nicaea I in 325; ConOecDecr 2–3, n.6) fixed the anniversary of Christ's Resurrection on the actual day of the week (the first day) on which the Resurrection had taken place. As a result, Easter falls on the first day of the week (Sunday) after the first full moon following the spring equinox, and thus can be as early as March 22 and as late as April 25.

The Christian Week. Adopting also from the Jews the 7-day divisions of the year known as weeks, the Christians divided their week much as the Jews did, but with some striking differences. Since Christ had died on the eve of the Passover Sabbath and had risen from the dead on the first day of the week following that Sabbath, the sacred character of the Jewish Sabbath (the last day of their week) was now transferred, in memory of the Resurrection, to "the first day of the week" (Acts 20.7), "the Lord's Day" (Ap 1.10), "the day named after the sun" (St. Justin, *First Apology*, ch. 67; *c.* 150). Likewise the Jewish tradition of a day of rest was transferred from the Sabbath to Sunday, becoming law in the 4th century. Again, the traditional Jewish fasts on Tuesday and Thursday were advanced by a day to Wednesday (the day of the betrayal of Christ in Passover week) and Friday (the day of the Crucifixion). Apart from the first day of the week, however, all the days of the week retained in Christian usage their Jewish designations, thus the second day (Monday) became *feria secunda* and the Sabbath became *Sabbathum* (Saturday).

Movable Feasts. By the mid-4th century there was a cycle of commemorations that had evolved about the feast of Easter, again paralleling Jewish usage. Thus Pentecost, the celebration of the descent of the Holy Spirit, was related to Easter much as was the Jewish Pentecost (Feast of Tabernacles, or First-Fruits) to the Passover, and at the same interval of 50 days. Again the penitential period before Easter, said by *Leo I (d. 461) to be of apostolic institution, was modeled on that observed by the Jews before the Passover. Ascension Day, however, was determined by the fact that, as the Acts of the Apostles testify (Acts 1.3), the event had taken place 40 days after the Resurrection.

Computation of Easter. Both the adoption of a movable Easter and the rejection of a variable day of the week for Easter Day was to involve the early Church in the so-called *Easter controversy. If various computations of the lunar cycle were current (e.g., those of Alexandria and Rome), the matter was further complicated by the adherence of some Christians (Quartodecimans) to the variable weekday. The Council of Nicaea, however, imposed Sunday as the fixed day of the commemoration of the Resurrection; the universal acceptance of the Alexandrian 19-year cycle or *computus of Easter is due to the Scythian monk *Dionysius Exiguus at Rome in 526, although the Celtic Church still clung to the Roman computation until 664 (*see* WHITBY, ABBEY OF). The introduction of a chronological Christian Era is also the work of Dionysius; for, when continuing the Easter tables of *Cyril of Alexandria for another 95 years, he counted for the first time the years from the birth of Christ, which, however, he wrongly dated to 754 A.U.C., some 4 years, at least, too late.

The Christmas Cycle. A second cycle of feasts, this time a fixed one, was introduced some time after the movable Easter cycle. The earliest mention of an anniversary of the birth of Christ on Christmas Day (December 25) is in the so-called Philocalian Calendar, in which the entry, which may be dated to 336, reads: *VIII.kal. Ian. natus Christus in Betleem Iudeae.* Probably the date was chosen to offset the imperial feast of the *Natalis solis invicti* (the birthday of the unvanquished sun), with its Mithraic overtones. The *Christological controversies of the 4th and 5th centuries doubtless contributed to the growth in importance of the feast; it aided also in a lessening of the originally more important feast of the *Epiphany to a point at which it became part of the Christmas cycle, which, evolving in Africa some time between 380 and 530, passed into Spain, and thence to Italy. *Advent, which now prefaces the cycle, appears to have been introduced at Rome by Pope *Simplicius or Pope *Gelasius I in the 2d half of the 5th century.

Other Fixed Commemorations. In Asia Minor from the end of the 2d century and at Rome from at least the 3d, the anniversary of a martyr's death was kept as a feast, with a liturgical celebration at his tomb (*see* ASIA MINOR, EARLY CHURCH IN). This day was the *dies natalis* of the martyr, possibly meaning his "heavenly birthday." These commemorations, together with a brief indication of the time, place, and circumstances of the martyr's death or burial, were often entered into registers roughly known as *calendars or *martyrologies (*see* CALENDAR OF THE EARLY SAINTS). The oldest extant compilation of this nature occurs in a commonplace book of Furius Dionysius Filocalus. Begun at Rome in 336 and completed in 354, it contains an invaluable list of Popes (*Depositio episcoporum*) and martyrs (*Depositio martyrum*), together with indications of other Roman commemorations, e.g., Christmas. From an examination of the three most ancient martyrologies (Philocalian; Syrian, 411; Carthaginian, *c.* 450) and of other martyrologies such as the Hieronymian, the Gallican of Polemius Silvius, the Mozarabic, and the Andalusian, it may be concluded: (1) that although the celebrations of martyrs were occasioned initially by local cultus, the more celebrated of these martyrs soon obtained favor outside their own localities; (2) that from an early date feasts were granted to the Apostles; (3) that feasts of Our Lady (*see* MARIAN FEASTS) were not general until *c.* 650, although the *Purification of Mary was kept locally at Jerusalem on Feb. 14 (later Feb. 2) from *c.* 350.

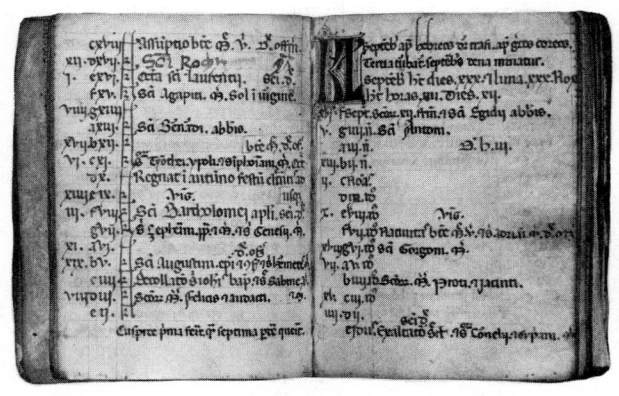

Calendar in a manuscript written in the Marches of Italy, c. 1330 (Boston Pub. Lib. MS 1554).

Reforms and Revisions. The multiplication of lists of martyrs (to which in time nonmartyrs were added) and the emergence of *liturgical books (of the Roman rite) such as *sacramentaries, lectionaries, and Gospel books contributed greatly to the decline of the ferial day, especially during the Carolingian period, when continuators of the classic martyrology of *Bede (d. 735) rushed to fill in every blank space. The inclusion of new saints and new devotional interests led, well before the end of the Middle Ages, to overcrowded and chaotic calendars. A greater uniformity throughout the Church was ensured by the reformed calendar of *Pius V (1568–70), inasmuch as all churches and religious orders that could not prove a prescription of 200 years were obliged to conform to the new disposition of the calendar. An instruction of the Congregation of Rites of Feb. 14, 1961 [ActApS 53 (1961) 168–180], reducing considerably the commemoration of saints, now allows the ferial day much of its original Paschal connotation. The Gregorian reform of the Julian solar calendar under *Gregory XIII in 1582 relates only incidentally to the Christian calendar (*see* CALENDAR REFORM).

Bibliography: The three earliest martyrologies in H. LIETZMANN, ed., *Die drei ältesten Martyrologien* (Bonn 1903). See additional bibliog. under MARTYROLOGIES, MARTYROLOGY, ROMAN, MARTYROLOGY OF ST. JEROME. L. DUCHESNE, "La Question de la Pâque au concile de Nicée," RevQuestHist 28 (1880) 5–42. N. NILLES, ed., *Kalendarium manuale utriusque ecclesiae, orientalis et occidentalis,* 2 v. (Innsbruck 1896–97). F. CABROL, *Les Origines liturgiques* (Paris 1906). W. H. FRERE, *Studies in Early Roman Liturgy,* 3 v. (Oxford 1930–35) v.1. B. BOTTE, *Les Origines de la Noël et de l'Épiphanie* (Louvain 1932). H. DELEHAYE, *Les Origines du culte des martyrs* (2d ed. Brussels 1933). F. WORMALD, ed., *English Kalendars Before A.D. 1100* (London 1934–); ed., *English Benedictine Kalendars After A.D. 1100* (London 1939–). E. FOCKE and H. HEINRICHS, "Das Kalendarium des Missale Pianum vom Jahre 1570 und seine Tendenzen," ThQschr 120 (1939) 383–400, 461–469. G. DIX, *The Shape of the Liturgy* (2d ed. London 1945). M. ALAMO, "Les Calendriers mozarabes d'après Dom Férotin," RHE 39 (1943) 100–131. H. STERN, *Le Calendrier de 354* (Paris 1953). A. A. McARTHUR, *The Evolution of the Christian Year* (London 1953). P. JOUNEL, "Le Sanctoral romain du 8e au 12e siècles," Maison-Dieu 52 (1957) 59–88. N. M. DENIS-BOULET, *The Christian Calendar,* tr. P. HEPBURNE-SCOTT (New York 1960). H. LECLERCQ, DACL 2.2:1585–93; 8.1:623–667. R. LESAGE, *Catholicisme* 2:381–383. M. BAFFI, EncCatt 3:355–360. G. LÖW, *ibid.* 3:364–372. W. BÖHNE, LexThK² 5:1257–58. **Illustration credit:** By courtesy of the Trustees of the Boston Public Library.

[L. E. BOYLE]

CALENDAR, FRENCH REVOLUTIONARY,

a calendar adopted by the National Convention (Nov. 24, 1793) and used in France to date the period from Sept. 22, 1792, until Dec. 31, 1805. The decree (Oct. 5, 1793) abolishing the Gregorian calendar was intended to disassociate the newly born Republic from both the monarchy and Christianity and to substitute a new chronology based on the decimal system and in harmony with astronomical and other natural phenomena. This unique calendar remains a tribute to the ideals motivating its composition and to the energy and enthusiasm expended on it. It began the year at midnight Sept. 21–22 to coincide with the autumnal equinox. It counted 360 days in 12 months, each with 30 days, and added 5 complementary days (*sans-culottides,* Sept. 17–21); the additional day of the traditional leap year remained and was called the Day of the Revolution. Each month was divided into three periods of 10 days (*décades*) with the 10th day (*décadi*) a hol-

iday in place of Sunday. The years were marked in Roman numerals with 1792 as the year I. Each 4-year period was termed the *franciade.*

Considerable imagination was displayed in coining names for the months and days. The months, beginning with September 22 (or September 23, between 1799– 1805), were: *Vendémiaire* or month of vintage; *Brumaire,* month of fog; *Frimaire,* month of frost; *Nivôse,* month of snow; *Pluviôse,* month of rain; *Ventose,* month of wind; *Germinal,* month of buds; *Floréal,* month of flowers; *Prairial,* month of meadows; *Messidor,* month of reaping; *Thermidor,* month of heat; and *Fructidor,* month of fruit. Each of the 360 days of the year had its distinctive name drawn from either flora, fauna, or agricultural tools. The new calendar rejected names referring to saints or liturgical feasts.

Besides its lack of universal applicability, the calendar was doomed to an early demise because it disrupted days for markets and fairs and other economic traditions. Its nomenclature was burdensome, its days of rest were too few, and it was accepted by few people outside government circles. Catholics abhorred its anti-Christian intent. The *Concordat of 1801 augured the restoration of the Gregorian calendar. A decision of the Senate (Sept. 9,1805) restored the Gregorian calendar effective Jan. 1, 1806.

Bibliography: J. H. STEWART, *A Documentary Survey of the French Revolution* (New York 1951). P. CARON, *Manuel pratique pour l'étude de la Révolution française* (Paris 1947). J. GODECHOT, *Les Institutions de la France sous la Révolution et l'Empire* (Paris 1951). A. KESSEN, *Le Calendrier de la République française* (Paris 1937). All works containing chronological tables devote a section to the French Revolutionary Calendar.

[R. J. MARAS]

CALENDAR OF THE EARLY SAINTS

A calendar is essentially a list of feasts arranged in chronological order. During the first centuries of Christianity there was a gradual growth of such lists, first of a local, then of a regional, and finally of a universal character. From the secular calendar of Rome the early Christians derived their system of reckoning time and marking anniversaries. Upon this they imposed the Jewish 7-day week, which was necessary for the observance of the Lord's Day and movable feasts, such as Easter. The discussion that Polycarp had with Pope Anicetus in Rome over the date of the latter points up a discrepancy in these early lists. The oldest extant calendar is one found in the Roman *Chronographer of 354.* This "Philocalian Calendar" is divided into two parts, a *Depositio episcoporum,* giving the dates of burial of 12 popes of the 3d and 4th centuries, and a *Depositio martyrum.* In addition to giving the anniversaries of the more famous Roman martyrs of these same 2 centuries, it includes three martyrs of Carthage, SS. Cyprian, Perpetua, and Felicitas, the feast of St. Peter's Chair on February 22, a commemoration of St. Peter *in Catacumbas* and of St. Paul on the Ostian Way for June 29, and the Nativity of Christ on December 25. In A.D. 362 at Maiuma and Gaza in Palestine the anniversaries of bishops and martyrs were also kept on separate lists (Sozomen, *Eccl. Hist.* 5.3). Evidence of the celebration of the *dies natalis,* or anniversary, of a martyr's death is already found in the East by A.D. 156 (*Martyrium Polycarpi* 18.2). The absence of known Roman martyrs of the 2d century from the Philocalian Calendar may indicate that no special cult was offered

Fragment of a Gothic calendar of the saints, early 5th century (Ambrosiana MS S. 36. sup., fol. 196).

to the martyrs this early at Rome. In A.D. 251 St. Cyprian ordered the names of the Christian confessors dying in the prison at Carthage to be recorded so that their anniversaries could be kept with those of the martyrs (*Ep.* 12.2).

The earliest calendars contained little more than dates, names, and places of burial. Later lists incorporated more details, particularly with respect to the manner of a martyr's death. These fuller accounts came to be known as "martyrologies," though it is obviously difficult to distinguish them adequately from the simpler "calendars." The most important of these later records are the Syriac Martyrology of A.D. 411, which lists also some saints of the West; the 4th- and 5th-century Calendar of Carthage, which includes a number of saints from Italy, Sicily, and Spain; and the *Martyrologium Hieronymianum,* compiled in Southern Gaul between 592 and 600. A fragment of a Gothic calendar from the beginning of the 5th century is preserved in the Ambrosian Library in Milan. St. Gregory of Tours has preserved for us another used in the late 5th century at Tours. Part of a late 5th- or early 6th-century calendar is preserved in an inscription found in 1909 at Carmona near Seville. More recent still has been the discovery of a fragment of a 6th-century calendar from Oxyrhynchus in Egypt.

Bibliography: H. LECLERCQ, DACL 8.1:624–667. R. AIGRAIN, *L'Hagiographie* (Paris 1953) 11–31. P. TESTINI, *Archeologia cristiana* (Rome 1958) 17–21. **Illustration credit:** Biblioteca Ambrosiana, Milano.

[M. J. COSTELLOE]

CALENDAR REFORM

The calendar introduced by Julius Caesar in 45 B.C. was based on a tropical year of 365.25 days. It was known already during the Middle Ages that the length of the year was less than this, and that the calendar was getting more and more out of step with the seasons.

Gregorian Reform. The Church had at various times considered plans of reform, such as those proposed in the 15th century by *Peter of Ailly and *Nicholas of Cusa. *Sixtus IV sought the advice of *Regiomontanus, the leading astronomer of the day, but the latter died soon after. Finally *Gregory XIII appointed a commission to study the question and founded the Vatican Observatory to provide the necessary astronomical data. It was decided to drop 10 days from the calendar to bring the vernal equinox back to the date it had in the time of Caesar. The leap year was omitted in century years, except when the year is divisible by 400, so that the average length of the year became 365.2425 days, which is very close to the length of the tropical year. In fact the difference will not amount to a day until *c.* 4500. The Gregorian calendar was promulgated in 1582, when the day after October 4 became October 15. In Protestant countries there was strong opposition to the reform. England (and the American colonies) did not adopt the new calander until 1752. It was introduced in Russia in 1918 (by Lenin); in Rumania and Greece in 1924; and in Turkey in 1927.

Proposals have been made to alter the leap year rules to adjust the calendar year even more closely to the tropical year; but alteration of the present rules seems unnecessary. In one respect the Gregorian calendar is even more accurate than its designers knew. Not until 8000 will the vernal equinox begin to deviate systematically by as much as half a day from its present date.

Easter. In the early centuries the diversity of rules for observing Easter was the cause of much strife among the churches (*see* EASTER CONTROVERSY; COMPUTUS). In 525 *Dionysius Exiguus drew up a list of Easter dates using the Alexandrine 19-year cycle, and this scheme was adopted everywhere by the end of the 8th century (*see* CHRONOLOGY, MEDIEVAL; CALENDAR, CHRISTIAN). The Dionysian cycle was universally followed until the Gregorian reform, which altered the cycle so as to predict the date of full moons more accurately. Belief in the Nicene origin of the Dionysian cycle was one reason for opposition to the Gregorian reform by the Orthodox Churches, which still use the old cycle (so that their Easter sometimes differs by as much as 5 weeks from that of the Latin Church). The full moon computed by the Gregorian cycle may differ from the date of the astronomical full moon, so that occasionally the Gregorian Easter differs from that determined astronomically (as in 1962). This was well known to the authors of the reform and is inherent in any form of cyclical computation. It could be avoided by using the astronomical full moon. But this solution was rejected, for it would bring its own difficulties; e.g., full moon may fall on different days on either side of the date line.

If Easter were freed from its dependence on the moon, the present oscillation of 5 weeks in the date would be reduced to 1 week. This would have obvious social and economic advantages. *Vatican Council II (*Constitution on the Liturgy, Appendix*) has declared that it is in no way opposed to the fixing of Easter on a definite Sunday, provided that agreement is reached with the separated brethren.

Perpetual Calendar. Many schemes have been proposed to make each date fall always on the same day of the week. The plan that has received most support is that of the World Calendar, which would drop 1 day each year from the sequence of weeks and 2 days in leap year; the length of the months also would be changed, so as to make the quarters of equal length. This plan, which would have obvious advantages, has met with strong opposition from orthodox Jews, Moslems, and some Protestants. At various times it has been considered, and rejected, by the United Nations (the last time in 1954). Vatican Council II has stated that it is not opposed to a perpetual calendar, provided the sequence of the weeks remains intact. Such a break in sequence would be considered by the Holy See only for the gravest reasons.

Bibliography: C. Clavius, *Romani Calendarii a Gregorio XIII restituti explicatio* (Rome 1603). F. K. Ginzel, *Handbuch der mathematischen und technischen Chronologie*, 3 v. (Leipzig 1906–14) v.3. J. Hartmann, "Der gregorianische Kalender . . .," *Memorie della pontificia accademia delle scienze Nuovi Lincei*, 2d ser. 11 (1928) 191–214. J. de Kort, "Astronomical Appreciation of the Gregorian Calendar," *Acta pontificia academia scientiarum* 13 (1949) 55–62. D. J. O'Connell, "Easter Cycles in the Early Irish Church," *Journal of the Royal Society of Antiquaries of Ireland* 66 (1936) 67–106. League of Nations, *Report on the Reform of the Calendar . . .* (Geneva 1926); *Classification and Summary of Proposals for Calendar Reform . . .* (Geneva 1927). E. Achelis, *The Calendar for the Modern Age* (New York 1959). P. Grosjean, "La Date de Pâques et le concile de Nicée," *Académie royale des sciences . . . de Belgique, classes des sciences bulletin*, 5th ser. 48 (1962) 55–66.

[D. J. K. O'CONNELL]

CALENDARS, GREEK AND ROMAN

The calendars of the Greeks and Romans, in common with those of the Near East, were lunar or soli-lunar in origin and were primarily concerned with maintaining the regular celebration throughout the year of a cycle of religious feasts intimately connected with agriculture and fertility. The months in part received numerical names and in part names based on those of gods or religious feasts. The names are really adjectives, the word for month in Greek or Latin being understood. Owing to the marked differences in the political development of the Greeks and Romans, the world of originally independent Greek states exhibits great diversity in its calendar, while Rome presents essentially one calendar.

Greek Calendar. The lunar month consisted of 29½ days, but the Greeks divided their months into "hollow" months of 29 days and "full" months of 30 days, respectively. They ordinarily reckoned the day itself from sunset to sunset. The lunar year of 354 days is 11 days shorter than the solar year. Accordingly, the Greeks had to adjust their calendar constantly so that it would be in harmony with the natural seasons of the solar year and thus indicate the proper time for the celebration of agricultural feasts. At Athens—and elsewhere—an intercalary month was inserted in the calendar every 3 years. The Athenians repeated their month of Poseideon (December) and called the new month Second or Latter Poseideon. Greek mathematicians worked out first an 8-year cycle (*oktaeteris*) to bring the lunar calendar and the necessary intercalations into more exact correspondence with the solar year. Subsequently, the astronomer Meton (432 B.C.) developed a better cycle of 19 years, but later the old 8-year cycle was revived.

The Greeks divided their months into 3 decads or groups of 10 days each. The first and last decads were called the "rising" and "vanishing" month, respectively. The days were named according to their place in each decad. However, it was customary to number the days of the last decad backward.

There was a wide variety in the names of the months and in their order in Greek calendars. Furthermore, Greek states had different dates for the beginning of their calendar and civil years. At Athens, the calendar year began on the summer solstice, and the civil year, about July. In Delos, Olympia, and Thebes the year

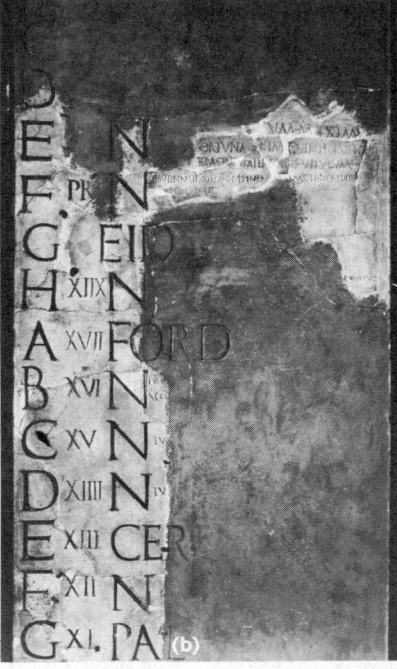
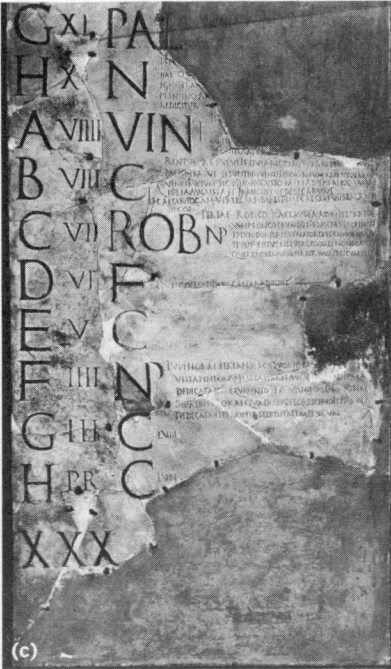

Fragments (a), (b), (c) of April, Calendarium of Praeneste, c. A.D. 4–10, Museo delle Terme at Rome.

began on the winter solstice, and at Sparta, on the autumnal equinox. Greek calendar and civil years, accordingly, all cross a given year in the Julian and modern Western calendars, and the Greek months normally cross present-day months, i.e., a given Greek month corresponds to the last half and first half of two Western months. Thus at Athens the first month, Hekatombaion, occupied approximately the last half of present-day July and the first half of August.

Among the early Greek calendars that of Athens is best known, but, despite long scholarly investigation, it still presents problems, especially in regard to the Athenian civil year. The Macedonian calendar was a Greek calendar that assumed great importance following the conquests of Alexander the Great and the establishment of the kingdoms of his successors. It was widely used in Asia Minor, Syria, Palestine, and Babylonia. In the course of its dissemination it exhibited considerable variation in the names of the months and in their order. The Macedonian year began in the autumn. J. Finegan (*Handbook of Biblical Chronology*) has compiled a series of tables illustrating the use of the Macedonian calendar throughout the Near East into the early centuries of the Christian era. His correlations in these tables of the Macedonian with the Jewish, Babylonian, Egyptian, and Roman calendars are especially valuable.

The native Egyptian calendar was a solar calendar from the outset. Under the Ptolemies it became a Greek calendar. Ptolemy III Euergetes perfected it by introducing a leap year, and his reformed calendar was made official by his decree of 238 B.C. It is this calendar that was later adopted by the Romans.

Roman Calendar. The Roman calendar was in the charge of the college of pontiffs. At first, the Roman months March, May, *Quintilis,* and October had 31 days, February had 28, and the remaining months 29. This lunar year of 355 days required constant intercalating to keep the seasons in proper relation to the solar year. A month of 22 or 23 days, called *Intercalaris,* was inserted between February 23 and 24. As the name December indicates, the Roman year began originally in March. In 153 B.C., chiefly for military reasons, the date of the beginning of the civil year was changed to January 1. The intercalations were repeatedly carried out badly by the Romans, and their calendar was often 2 or 3 months in advance of the solar year. In the period of the Civil War (49–46 B.C.) there was a difference of 3 months. Accordingly, Julius Caesar in his capacity of *Pontifex Maximus* carried out a radical reform of the calendar that still bears his name (Julian). The solar calendar was introduced from Alexandria and a year of 365 days was adopted, with the provision for adding a full extra day every 4 years. The minor error involved in Caesar's calendar was corrected by the Gregorian reform in 1582. The days in the Roman months were increased to give the required total of 365 days. March, May, *Quintilis,* and October retained 31 days, and February 28, but January, *Sextilis,* and December were increased to 31 days, with 30 days being given to April, June, September, and November. *Quintilis* was renamed *Iulius* (July) in honor of Caesar, and *Sextilis* was later renamed *Augustus* (August) in honor of Augustus.

The Roman month had 3 major divisions, the Kalends (the 1st), the Nones, and the Ides. In March,

May, July, and October the Nones and Ides fell on the 7th and 15th respectively; in the other months, on the 5th and 13th. The Romans counted their days backward from each of these major divisions, including the starting point in their calculation. The Roman day began at midnight. Roman calendars indicated market days (*nundinae*) at 8-day intervals by successive lists of the letters A to H. The symbol C was employed to indicate *Comitialis,* a day on which assemblies were to be held, F (*Fastus*), a day on which court could be held, and N (*Nefastus*), a day on which it was forbidden to conduct any form of public business. Finally, the extant remains of Roman calendars often carry brief statements of great historical or religious interest.

Bibliography: H. J. ROSE, OxClDict 155–156. L. WHIBLEY, ed., *Companion to Greek Studies* (4th ed. Cambridge, Eng. 1931) 589–591. J. E. SANDYS, *A Companion to Latin Studies* (4th ed. Cambridge, Eng. 1931) 91–100, 169–172. E. F. BISCHOFF, Pauly-Wiss RE 10:2 (1919) 1568–1602. W. KUBITSCHEK, *Grundriss der antiken Zeitrechnung* (Munich 1928). K. LATTE, *Römische Religionsgeschichte* (Munich 1960), esp. the table "Der römische Festkalender," at the end of the book. B. D. MERITT, *The Athenian Year* (Sather Lectures 32; Berkeley–Los Angeles 1961). J. FINEGAN, *Handbook of Biblical Chronology: Principles of Time Reckoning in the Ancient World and Problems of Chronology in the Bible* (Princeton 1964), with tables and bibliog. **Illustration credit:** Gabinetto Fotografico Nazionale, Rome.

[M. R. P. MC GUIRE]

CALENDARS OF THE ANCIENT NEAR EAST

All methods of calculating time in antiquity were founded upon the periodic revolutions of the moon, the apparent movements of the sun, or both. Yet together these norms are incompatible, for a solar year comprises approximately 365¼ days, while 12 appearances of the moon occupy approximately 354⅓ days. The resulting difficulties are still reflected in the complicated formulas for fixing the date of the Christian Easter. (*See* EASTER AND ITS CYCLE.)

The history of the calendar in the ancient Near East is that of an effort to develop a system that would reconcile both the solar and the lunar elements. In all systems, ancient and modern, the basic unit is the day, but in ancient times days were not always counted in a uniform manner. The earliest standard for devising and for using calendaric systems was the annual agricultural cycle, and for agricultural purposes a latitude in intercalating days was permissible. The rise of such institutions as civil reigns, periodic religious festivals, periodic taxes, and contracts demanded a more stable method of reckoning the calendar.

Egyptian and Assyro-Babylonian Calendars. In Egypt the oldest calendar was a lunar one that counted 12 lunations, or lunar months, beginning with the heliacal rising of the star Sirius, that is, its first rising after invisibility. An extra lunar month was intercalated when it became necessary to rectify the system according to the solar or agricultural year. Around the beginning of the 3d millennium B.C. a solar calendar was introduced, at least for civil purposes. Starting with the same new year's day, the year contained 12 months of 30 days each, with 5 "intercalated days" [($\dot{\eta}\mu\acute{\epsilon}\rho\alpha\iota$) $\dot{\epsilon}\pi\alpha\gamma\acute{o}\mu\epsilon\nu\alpha\iota$]. No allowance was made within the system for the quarter-day discrepancy from the true solar year until the calendaric reform of Julius Caesar. Months were at first designated by numbers, but were later named after the feast days that occurred in them. The 7-day week was unknown in Egypt, where days were reckoned from morning to morning.

In the long history of Mesopotamia, a succession of different calendars was in use, all of them basically lunar, with some sort of intercalation to reconcile them with the solar year. From the earliest times the Sumerians and then the Akkadians used a calendar with 12 months of 29 or 30 days, each month beginning when the new moon was sighted and proclaimed; the names for these months differ in each of the major cities of the period. The *Nippur calendar became standard during the golden age of ancient Babylonia under *Hammurabi (late 18th century B.C.), and Babylonian names of the months were used. Tiglath-Pileser I of Assyria (c. 1116–1078 B.C.) replaced the various Assyrian calendars with the Babylonian calendar, which predominated in Mesopotamia into Hellenistic times. The Babylonian year began at the spring equinox in the month of Nisānu, though there is evidence that it had once begun at the autumn equinox (e.g., the name of the 7th month, Tašrītu, means "beginning"). Every 2d or 3d year an intercalary month was added by doubling the 6th (Ululu) or the 12th month (Adāru). Until the 4th century B.C. this process was governed by official decree; thereafter it was calculated according to a 19-year cycle. There were no 7-day weeks, and days were counted from evening to evening.

Early Palestinian Calendar. There is little certainty regarding the earliest calendars used in Syria-Palestine. Since a mixture of Egyptian, Hurrian, and Phoenician month names is known to us, it would seem that native systems did exist but that these gave way to borrowed ones during periods of foreign domination. These were probably all lunar systems with solar rectification. In Biblical times the earliest attested calendar was lunar (the Hebrew words for month were first *yeraḥ*, "moon," and then *ḥōdes*, "new moon"), with alternate months of 29 and 30 days. Four of these Canaanite month names occur in the Bible: Ethanim (1st), Bul (2d), Abib (7th), and Ziv (8th). There must have been intercalation, but it is not mentioned in the Bible. The year began in the autumn (as the festival calendars of Exodus ch. 23, 34 suggest). A 7-day week of uncertain origin (perhaps traceable to the approximate phases of the moon or to the popularity of the number 7) was observed with the entirely original Israelite feature of a sacred day of rest on the 7th day (the *Sabbath). Days were reckoned from morning to morning (Jer 33.25). There is evidence that along with the use of this civil and religious calendar there was a more popular way of identifying time. The famous limestone calendar tablet from *Gazer (Gezer) of the late 10th century B.C. contains a listing of the months with names derived from the agricultural functions performed in them, e.g., harvest, sowing, late sowing (*see* EPIGRAPHY, HEBREW). Some of these expressions occur also in the Bible, e.g., in Jgs 15.1; Ru 1.22; 2.23.

Later Jewish Calendar. Following the reign of King Josia (c. 640–609 B.C.), and especially after the Babylonian Exile, a number of significant and enduring changes occurred in the Israelite calendar, showing that the Jews gradually adopted the Babylonian calendar of the time. The civil year now began in the spring, though the religious observance of the autumn new year persisted. The months were simply designated by ordinal

Gazer (Gezer) calendar of late 10th-century B.C. *Limestone tablet with Hebrew inscription in ancient Hebrew characters listing the farm work done in four single and four double months of the solar-lunar year.*

numbers until after the Exile, when the Babylonian names were adopted.

The reason for the delay was perhaps opposition to the religious connotations of the names. These names are still in use and appear in transliteration as: Nisan, Iyar, Sivan, Tammuz, Ab, Elul, Tishri, Heshvan (or Marcheshvan), Kislev, Tebet, Shebat, and Adar. The 7-day week persisted despite its failure to divide evenly either the month or the year. The day, however, was counted from evening to evening, after the Babylonian fashion (Dn 8.14). The intercalation of an extra month to rejoin the solar cycle remained, for a long time, a matter of observation and official decree. It was probably only in early Christian times, after the destruction of the Temple, that the method of calculating intercalary months according to the Babylonian 19-year cycle was adopted. The only month repeated, however, was and is Adar (called Second Adar, or Veadar).

Arabic and Other Calendaric Systems. In pre-Moslem Arabia the customary type of lunar-solar calendar was in use. Mohammed, however, changed this to a purely lunar calendar, still employed by the Moslems, in which every year has only 12 lunar months, totaling 354 or 355 days. Thus the month of *Ramadan, the annual period of fasting in Islam, gradually advances through the solar year. (For the complication in medieval chronology that this shorter year creates, *see* ERAS, HISTORICAL.)

Two other calendaric systems should be mentioned here. The first, the "pentecontad" calendar, involving

HEBREW MONTHS AND ANNUAL FEASTS

Postexilic names of Hebrew months and no. of days[a]	Order of Hebrew months		Annual Hebrew feasts	Preexilic names of Hebrew months	Corresponding Babylonian months	Corres. Macedonian mos.[b]	Corres. modern months
	With 1st of Nisan as New Year's Day	With 1st of Tishri as New Year's Day					
Nisan, 30	1	7	The Passover, eve. of 14th–15th. Feast of Unleavened Bread,[c] 15th–22d	Abib[d]	Nisānu	Ἀρτεμίσιος	March–April
Iyar, 29	2	8		Ziv[e]	Ayāru	Δαίσιος	April–May
Sivan, 30	3	9	Feast of Weeks (Pentecost),[f] 7th day		Simānu	Πάνεμος	May–June
Tammuz, 29	4	10			Du'ûzu	Λῷος	June–July
Ab, 30	5	11	Fast day of Ab,[g] 9th day		Abu	Γορπιαῖος	July–Aug.
Elul, 29	6	12			Ulūlu	Ὑπερβερεταῖος	Aug.–Sept.
Tishri, 30	7	1	New Year's Day,[h] 1st. Day of Atonement,[i] 10th. Feast of Booths (Tabernacles),[j] 15th–22d	Ethanim[k]	Tašrītu	Δῖος	Sept.–Oct.
Heshvan, 29 or 30	8	2		Bul[l]	Arahsamnu	Ἀπελλαῖος	Oct.–Nov.
Kislev, 29 or 30	9	3	Feast of the Dedication of the Temple,[m] 25th, lasts 8 days		Kislīmu	Αὐδυναῖος	Nov.–Dec.
Tebet, 29	10	4			Tebētu	Περίτιος	Dec.–Jan.
Shebat, 29	11	5			Šabātu	Δύστρος	Jan.–Feb.
Adar, 29 or 30	12	6	Feast of Purim,[n] 14th		Adāru	Ξανθικός	Feb.–March
Veadar, 29	13	7					March

[a] The number of days in each Hebrew month was first fixed by Rabbi Hillel II c. A.D. 360. Previously, any Hebrew month might have 29 or 30 depending on actual observation of the new moon. [b] Some time after A.D. 31 Ἀρτεμίσιος was equated with Adar, Δαίσιος with Sivan, etc., and Ξανθικός with Nisan; so that for the years after A.D. 31 the name of each Macedonian month in this column corresponds with the Hebrew name one line lower. [c] Ex 23.14–15, Lv 23.4–8. [d] Ex 13.4, 34.18; Dt 16.1. [e] 3 Kgs 6.1, 37. [f] Ex 23.16, 34.22; Lv 23.15–16; Dt 16.16. [g] Za 7.5, the anniversary of the Babylonian capture of Jerusalem; cf. Jer 52.6–7. [h] Lv 23.24, Nm 29.1. [i] Lv 16.29, 23.27–28; Nm 29.7. [j] Ex 23.16, 34.22; Lv 23.39; Dt 16.16. [k] 3 Kgs 8.2. [l] 3 Kgs 6.38. [m] 1 Mc 4.59, 2 Mc 1.18, Jn 10.22. [n] Est 9.19, 21, 26.

a sequence of 50-day periods, is proposed by some as the ancestor of the modern custom among the peasants of Palestine of the year of "7 fifties." Its proponents find it used in Assyria, Babylonia, and ancient Israel. The system is built on 7 periods of 7 weeks, with an added feast day in each period. The total is 350 days, to which a 15-day period was added annually.

The second, and possibly related, calendar is the solar one described in the apocryphal Book of Jubilees. Its year contains 364 days, 52 weeks, 4 quarters of 13 weeks each, 12 months of 30 days with an extra day added to every third month. Such a calendar is perpetual: the same date falls on the same day of the week each year. Although the system falls behind the real solar year by 1¼ days annually, the sources mention no method of intercalation. Several of the fragments discovered among the *Dead Sea Scrolls indicate that this calendar was actually in use among later sectarian Jews. It is not, however, generally accepted that either

the pentecontad system or the Jubilees calendar was ever actually used in early Israel or that either underlies the older strata of the Bible.

Bibliography: De Vaux AncIsr 178–194. H. M. CHADWICK, Hastings ERE 3:61–141. S. LANGDON, *Babylonian Menologies and the Semitic Calendars* (New York 1935). R. A. PARKER, *The Calendars of Ancient Egypt* (Chicago 1950). J. B. SEGAL, "Intercalation and the Hebrew Calendar," VetTest 7 (1957) 250–307. On the pentecontad and Jubilees calendars, see H. and J. LEWY, "The Origin of the Week and the Oldest West Asiatic Calendar," HebUCAnn 17 (1942–43) 1–152c. A. JAUBERT, *La Date de la Cène: Calendrier biblique et liturgie chrétienne* (ÉtBibl; 1957). J. MORGENSTERN, "The Calendar of the Book of Jubilees: Its Origin and Its Character," VetTest 5 (1955) 34–76, with bibliog. **Illustration credit:** Museum of the Ancient Orient, Istanbul, Turkey.

[G. W. MAC RAE]

CALÉNUS, HENRI, "first of the Jansenists"; b. Beringen, Belgium, 1583; d. Brussels, Feb. 1, 1653. Henri Calénus (Van Caelen) completed his studies at Louvain, where he established a friendship with Cornelius *Jansen, future bishop of Ypres. From 1609 to 1624, Calénus served the parish of Asse, near Brussels, as an exemplary pastor, and was also active as dean of the deanery of Alost (1613–24). After his transfer to Brussels as pastor of Sainte-Catherine and dean of the city, he displayed remarkable zeal. Having maintained close contact with Jansen, he collaborated with him and the Abbé de Saint-Cyran in introducing Bérulle's Oratory into the Low Countries. As canon (1637) and later archdeacon (1642) in Malines, he became the close collaborator of Archbishop *Boonen, and was made vicar-general.

Shortly before Jansen died, he asked Calénus to work with Libert Froidmont, a professor at Louvain, in preparing a correct edition of his work, the famous *Augustinus. In accordance with Jansen's wishes, Calénus devoted himself to this work from 1638 to 1640. After its publication (1640) and its condemnation by Rome, he continued to defend it, and strove to obtain a revision of Rome's condemnation, especially with a view to safeguarding Augustinian doctrine. In 1644, the King of Spain appointed him to the episcopal see of Ruremonde, but he was unable to obtain confirmation from Rome despite his anti-Jansenistic oath. He renounced the episcopal title in 1648; his last years were marked by illness.

Bibliography: L. CEYSSENS, "Henri Calénus, évêque manqué," *Bulletin de la Commission royale d'histoire* 127 (1961) 33–128, with extensive bibliog.

[L. CEYSSENS]

CALEPINO, AMBROGIO, Latin lexicographer; b. June 2, 1435; d. Nov. 30, 1511. Ambrogio, the son of the Count of Calepio, Italy, became an Augustinian at Bergamo in 1451 and devoted himself to humanistic studies. His Latin dictionary (Reggio Emilia 1502), a *Cornucopia* of many years' labor, was revised by him in 1505 and 1509. Humanists reprinted and revised the work almost constantly, especially in France and Italy where *calepin* and *calepino* were added to the vocabulary. Non-Latin words were gradually added until the Basel edition of 1590 contained 11 languages. Many Latin-English dictionaries depended on Calepino's work, as did almost all Latin dictionaries before *For-cellini's great lexicon in 1771. Calepino's vita of St. *John Bonus of Milan (ActSS, Oct. 9:693–885) is unreliable. He wrote a *De Venetiarum civitatis laude* (see P. Foresti, Supplementum chronicarum, Bergamo 1483).

Bibliography: D. A. PERINI, *Bibliographia Augustiniana*, 4 v. (Florence 1929–38) 1:166–169. Sandys 2. D. T. STARNES, *Renaissance Dictionaries* (Austin, Tex. 1954) 51–57. É. VAN CAUWENBERGH, DHGE 11:386. Cosenza DictItHum 1:781–783.

[F. ROTH]

CALÈS, JEAN, Jesuit exegete; b. Larzac (Dordogne), France, Aug. 6, 1865; d. Vals-près-Le-Puy, Haute-Loire, Aug. 1, 1947. He taught OT exegesis at the Jesuit college of Vals, where, for almost 40 years, he collaborated with the renowned NT scholar Ferdinand *Prat, whose Biblical work he described in *Un Maître de l'exégèse contemporain, le P. Fernand Prat, S.J.* [Paris 1942; see J. Curran, ThSt 8 (1947) 316–319]. His *Le Livre des Psaumes traduit et commenté* (2 v. Paris 1936) was well received [see J. Vaccari, *Biblica* 19 (1938) 80–82]. His scholarly articles include "Le Code de Hammourabi d'après une *introduction* et

un *commentaire* récents," published in RechScRel 30 (1940) 356–365.

Bibliography: DTC Tables générales 1:499.

[B. F. SARGENT]

CALIFORNIA

A state in west U.S., admitted to the Union (1850) as the 31st state. It is bounded on the north by Oregon; on the east by Nevada and Arizona, from which it is separated by the Colorado River; on the south by Mexico; and on the west by the Pacific Ocean. Sacramento is the capital, and Los Angeles, San Francisco, Oakland, and San Diego are the largest cities and major seaports.

History to 1840. Although it had been discovered by Juan Rodríguez Cabrillo in 1542 and revisited by Sebastián Vizcaíno in 1602, California was not colonized until 1769, when the Church was established in the territory. The conquest, ordered by José de Gálvez, Spanish visitor-general in Mexico (New Spain), had for its purpose the protection of Mexico's northern borders against possible Russian aggression. Spain desired a bloodless conquest and from the very beginning enlisted the Franciscan missionaries of the Apostolic College of San Fernando, Mexico City, then laboring in Lower California (Mexico), to cooperate spiritually and to implant the mission system among the native Indians. Gálvez and Junípero *Serra, OFM, president of the Lower California Missions, worked out relationships between the military and the missionaries in the southern peninsula. San Fernando was to supply the missionaries. The *Pious Fund, which had been created by the Jesuits and administered by the government after their expulsion in 1767, was used to defray the expenses of founding missions and to pay the salaries

Fig. 1. Junípero Serra's library-office as restored at Mission Carmel, California.

of the missionaries. Two military and naval expeditions were sent to occupy the ports of San Diego and Monterey. Gaspar de Portolá was named military leader. All forces reached San Diego by July 1, and on July 16, 1769, Serra established the first mission at San Diego.

Franciscan Missionaries. Between 1769 and 1823, 21 missions were established in California, 9 under Serra, 9 more under Fray Fermín Francisco de Lasuén, and the last 3 under his successors. They were San Diego (1769); San Carlos, Monterey-Carmel (1770); San Antonio and San Gabriel (1771); San Luis Obispo (1772); San Francisco and San Juan Capistrano (1776); Santa Clara (1777); San Buenaventura (1782); Santa Barbara (1786); Purísima Concepción (1787); Santa Cruz and Soledad (1791); San José, San Juan Bautista, San Miguel, and San Fernando (1797); San Luis Rey (1798); Santa Inés (1804); San Rafael (1817); and San Francisco Solano (1823). Several submissions, such as San Pedro y San Pablo, Santa Margarita, and San Antonio de Pala, were established also. Four presidios, each with a chapel, were founded at San Diego, Monterey, San Francisco, and Santa Barbara. Three civilian colonies were established at San Jose (1777), Los Angeles (1781), and Branciforte (1797). These missions, presidios, pueblos, and intervening ranches were the only Christian settlements in California between 1769 and 1840. All were administered spiritually by the Fernandino missionaries. Serra, called the Apostle of California, experienced misunderstandings and altercations with the military authorities. Disputes arose over church asylum, clerical appointments, military guards, postal frankage, Indian *alcaldes* (overseers), immorality of soldiers, and a host of minor questions. The history of the missions in California between 1769 and 1840 is understandable only in the light of the royal patronage of the Indies granted to the Spanish kings by Popes Alexander VI and Julius II and the accompanying abuses that grew out of the exercise of that grant in later times (*see* PATRONATO REAL). During the 18th century especially, Carlos III and IV tended toward state absolutism in ecclesiastical affairs.

Serra's successors were Fermín Francisco de Lasuén (1785–1803), Estevan Tapis (1803–12), José Señan (1812–15, 1820–23), Mariano Payeras (1815–20), Narciso Durán (1824–27, 1830–36), José Bernardo Sánchez (1827–30), and José Joaquín Jimeno (1839–53). In 1812 the office of commissary prefect was established whereby jurisdiction was divided between him and the president. The former was assigned the duty of transacting the business affairs of the missionaries with the territorial government, while the president attended to the disciplinary matters relating to the missionaries. Thus the commissary-prefect ranked with the president in matters pertaining to Indian missions, while the president held the position of vicar forane of the bishop and as such was head of the Church in the territory. The office of commissary-prefect was held by Vicente Francisco de Sarriá (1812–18, 1824–30), Mariano Payeras (1818–23), Narciso Durán (1836–46), and José Joaquín Jimeno (1846–53). Beginning in 1833 the northern missions of California were administered by the Franciscan missionaries of the Apostolic College of Our Lady of Guadalupe, Zacatecas, while the southern missions were retained by the missionaries of San Fernando College. The first commissary-prefect of the Zacatecan missionaries was Francisco *García Diego y

Fig. 2. Mission San Luis Rey de Francia, founded in 1798 by the Franciscan fathers of the College of San Fernando of Mexico City.

Moreno, OFM, who in 1840 became the first bishop of California; the first president was Fray Rafael Moreno.

When California was first missionized, the territory belonged to no diocese; the nearest bishops resided at Guadalajara and Durango, Mexico. On May 7, 1779, Pius VI created the Diocese of Sonora, which included the districts of Sonora, Sinaloa, and both Californias. Antonio de los Reyes, OFM, was appointed the first bishop of the extensive territory on Dec. 12, 1780. Consecrated in 1782, he arrived in Sonora in 1783 and made his headquarters at Alamos. Neither he nor any of his successors visited Upper California. Lasuén was the first mission president who had ecclesiastical relations with the Sonoran bishops. From these bishops Lasuén and his successors received the powers of vicar forane and military vicar until 1840.

The California missions were manned by 146 Franciscans until 1840, two serving at each mission. The great majority were Spaniards, the rest of Mexican birth. The missionaries were required to give 10 years of service, though many served longer. All were volunteers. Traveling expenses and supplies for the journey were paid for from the royal exchequer. Two of the missionaries, Luis Jayme at San Diego, and Andrés Quintana at Santa Cruz, were murdered by the Indians. Four more, Francisco Garcés, Juan Barreneche, Juan Diaz, and Matías Moreno, of the Apostolic College of Santa Cruz, Querétaro, were massacred along the Colorado River at Yuma in 1781. Those Colorado missions, founded a short time before, were not revived.

Indians and Mission System. The Indians among whom the missions were founded belonged to a class of people described by anthropologists as lower nomads or marginal people, preagricultural and preliterate, who lived by hunting, fishing, and seed gathering. Between San Francisco and San Diego six distinct languages were spoken. Along the Santa Barbara coast somewhat greater progress was noted among the Chumash in their well-ordered towns, their dextrously made and skillfully handled canoes, their greater vivacity and industry. The Indians about Monterey were noted for their lack of spirit, those about San Diego for their treachery. The missionaries sought to attract these Indians from their native villages by kindness and gifts to Christian villages built alongside the missions, where they lived for a period as catechumens, later permanently as neophytes. Having accepted Christianity, they were required to remain at the missions and to accept the orderly regime. If they became runaways they were sought out and brought back.

At the missions the Indians were entirely under the jurisdiction of the missionaries except in certain criminal matters when the military took over. The Franciscans were in charge of both their spiritual and temporal formation, and by decree of Viceroy Bucareli in 1773 they held the place of parents over their children. The missionaries were to instruct, educate, and punish their charges. The law envisaged a complete transformation in 10 years, when the mission towns would become pueblos of freed, formed Indians after the pattern of the civic entities of the whites. In California, because of the low cultural status of the natives, such a transformation was realized—and then only partially—only after half a century. The practical working out of mission affairs was determined at three levels: locally between the governor and the mission president; at the intermediate level between the viceroy and the guardian of the College of San Fernando; and at the highest level between the commissary-general of the Franciscans at Madrid and the king and his royal Council of the Indies. Throughout the period of missionization everything was done on a cooperative basis between Church and State at all levels, and thus little independent action was allowed the missionaries. The system resulted in frequent misunderstandings, conflicts, and disputes. Thus the time, the place, and the manner of founding a mission were decided both by the civil and religious arms. The name of the mission was bestowed by the viceroy.

In the beginning the missions were crude, frontier settlements composed of buildings in log-cabin style, with grass or earthen roofs and dirt floors. These originals were followed by adobe structures with tile roofs and floors. In some cases stone churches, such as those at Carmel and Santa Barbara, resulted in the final stage of building. In several cases the site of a mission was changed in favor of better economic conditions or to separate it from too close proximity to a presidio. Because of growth in the number of Christians or because of damage to a mission by physical factors, such as earthquake, a number of succeeding churches appeared, including four at Santa Barbara and seven at Carmel. Usually a mission was built in quadrangular shape to form a compound, which included the church, the missionaries' residence, a dormitory for single girls and women, workshops, and storage rooms. At first the natives, turned Christians, built their new villages by the missions in the traditional manner of native huts, which were followed by sturdier structures in the Spanish fashion. Thus at Santa Barbara there were 252 family dwellings made of adobe with tile roofs, with a door and window, built along straight streets. A mission

took from 30 to 40 years to reach its final perfection. Usually it took about that same period of time to gather into the Christian fold all the Indians of the mission territory, which at times extended far inland to the mountains for 50 miles and more. Missionaries at times accompanied military expeditions into the interior of the great valleys contacting new tribes of Indians, baptizing the sick and dying, keeping diaries, and looking for new mission sites. Such a new line of missions was prevented from developing by the revolt of Mexico against Spain.

The average day at a mission—and all were governed in the same manner—was regulated according to the system that had been followed earlier in Texas and in the Sierra Gorda of Mexico. The natives rose at dawn and attended Mass, during which they recited the *doctrina,* a set form of the principal prayers and articles of faith, after which breakfast was served and the work of the day apportioned. Work in the morning lasted about 3 hours, that of the afternoon, 2 or 3 hours. The noonday meal was followed by a siesta; afternoon work was followed by prayers in church. Evenings were free for rest or amusements. There were no formal schools in the modern sense at the missions. The schools were primarily of a practical nature, where pupils learned by doing. It has been estimated that about 50 trades were taught, the principal occupations being farming and animal husbandry. Next came the making of adobes and tiles, spinning and weaving, stonecutting and setting, tanning, shoe and harness making, the fashioning of candles and soap, and the exercise of other trades and crafts that tended to make a mission self-sustaining. Most important at each mission was the irrigation system, bringing water for domestic and agricultural purposes to the mission and its fields, by which the waters of a nearby stream were harnessed by dams, aqueducts, reservoirs, filters, and fountains. Extensive remains of such systems may be seen today at San Diego, Santa Barbara, and San Antonio. Music and choral singing were cultivated at the missions, bands of musicians being formed and taught by the padres, a type of activity to which the natives took readily. Fray Narciso Durán of San José and Santa Barbara was the greatest of the friar musicians. Other missionaries, such as Buenaventura Sitjar of San Antonio and Felipe Arroyo de la Cuesta of San Juan Bautista, became expert linguists, while Gerónimo Boscana became the ethnologist of Mission San Juan Capistrano. Francisco *Palóu of San Francisco was California's first historian and biographer. All the missions had their libraries; the central archive was at Mission San Carlos, Carmel, which later was transferred to Santa Barbara.

Besides participating in the functions of the liturgical year, wherein Corpus Christi and Holy Week were colorfully celebrated, the Indians at Christmastide produced the *Pastores,* the traditional Christmas play of Mexico. They were given frequent vacations, being allowed to visit their pagan relatives in their native towns, and were permitted to scour the mountains for wild berries and seeds. At the missions whatever was produced was conserved for the common good and apportioned out by the missionaries according to need. Physical punishment such as the lash, stocks, and shackles was given for the serious infraction of laws. Men were punished by the soldiers with permission of the missionaries. Women were chastised in the women's quarters by a matron.

Early in the 19th century the missionaries reported that the number of deaths of Christian Indians exceeded that of births because of the Indians' lack of immunity to the white man's diseases, particularly social disease. On the spiritual side, between 1769 and 1845 the missionaries baptized about 99,000 persons in California, the great majority being Indians. They blessed 28,000 marriages and gave Christian burial to 74,000 persons.

Secularization of Missions. When Mexico became independent of Spain in 1821, California became part of the republic. Meanwhile the condition of the missions deteriorated since they had to supply the military with food and clothing during the struggle and afterward, a burden that became oppressive both to the missionaries and the Indians. The missions were secularized in 1833 by the Mexican Congress; temporal control was placed in the hands of lay commissioners, and the Indians were emancipated. Conditions worsened until finally the missions, except for the churches and direct church property, were sold.

After 1840. On April 27, 1840, Gregory XVI created the Diocese of Both Californias (Upper and Lower) and appointed as bishop Francisco García Diego y Moreno, OFM, who was consecrated Oct. 4, 1840, at the national shrine of Our Lady of Guadalupe, Mexico City. Arriving in San Diego on Dec. 11, 1841, he decided to establish himself at Santa Barbara, where he resided until his death in 1846. The annexation of California to the U.S. by the Treaty of Guadalupe-Hidalgo (1848) completely changed territorial and ecclesiastical matters in the territory. The same year brought the discovery of gold and touched off the California gold rush. After heated debate over statehood, California entered the Union under the Compromise of 1850. In that year Joseph Sadoc *Alemany, OP, arrived in San Francisco on Dec. 6, 1850, with the title of Bishop of Monterey in Upper California. Between the death of the Franciscan bishop and the arrival of his Dominican successor, the administration of ecclesiastical affairs in both Upper and Lower California had been in the hands of another Franciscan, José Maria de Jesus Gonzalez Rubio (1804–75), who had ruled the vacant see with the title of Governor of the Mitre. Alemany alternated between his see city and San Francisco until July 29, 1853, when Rome appointed him the first archbishop of the newly created Archdiocese of *San Francisco. In 1859 Rome decreed a change of title for the See of Monterey, which was known as Monterey–Los Angeles until 1922, when Pius XI established *Los Angeles as a separate diocese (archdiocese 1936) and created a new Diocese of *Monterey–Fresno. Another significant change affecting Catholicism in California came in 1936 with the erection of the Diocese of *San Diego in the southernmost part of California. In northern California the Vicariate Apostolate of Marysville was created in 1860; it became the Diocese of Grass Valley (1868–86), which was later (1886) changed to the Diocese of *Sacramento. In February 1963 three additional jurisdictions were created in California, with see cities at *Oakland, *Santa Rosa, and *Stockton.

Population. Between 1941 and 1961 California more than doubled its population with a rise from 7 million to more than 16 million, with corresponding attempts to match the state's religious advance. In 1952 Catholics constituted 22.1 per cent of the total state population of 10,586,223; Protestants accounted for 14.6 per cent;

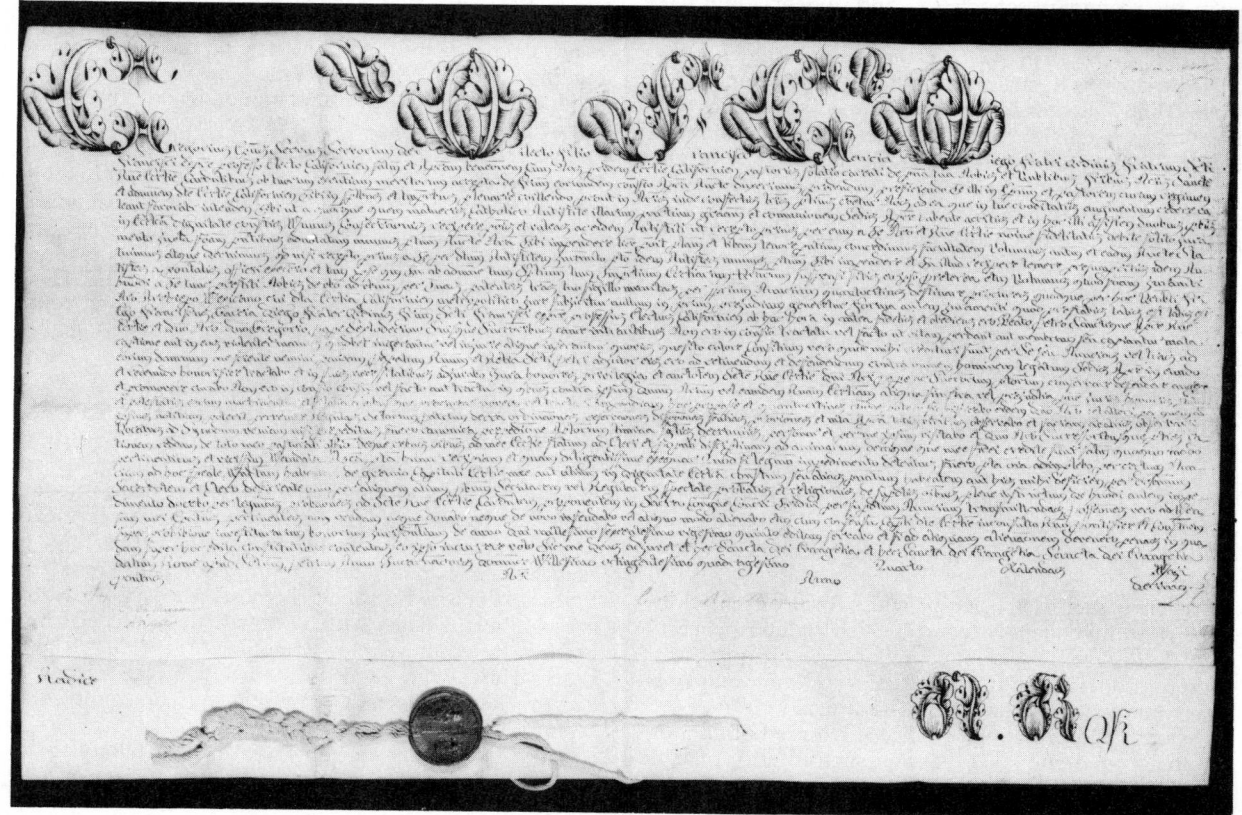

Fig. 3. Original document of the bull for the erection of the Diocese of Both Californias, promulgated in 1840.

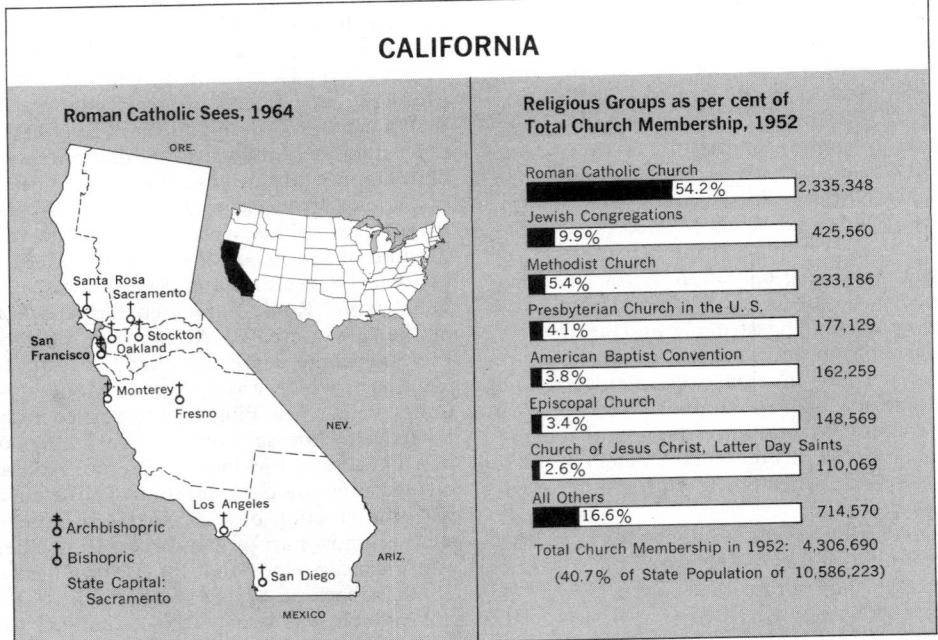

CALIFORNIA

Roman Catholic Sees, 1964

ORE.

Santa Rosa
Sacramento

Stockton
San Francisco   Oakland

Monterey
Fresno   NEV.

Los Angeles

✝ Archbishopric
♟ Bishopric

State Capital:
Sacramento   San Diego   ARIZ.

MEXICO

Religious Groups as per cent of Total Church Membership, 1952

Religious Group	Per cent	Members
Roman Catholic Church	54.2%	2,335,348
Jewish Congregations	9.9%	425,560
Methodist Church	5.4%	233,186
Presbyterian Church in the U. S.	4.1%	177,129
American Baptist Convention	3.8%	162,259
Episcopal Church	3.4%	148,569
Church of Jesus Christ, Latter Day Saints	2.6%	110,069
All Others	16.6%	714,570

Total Church Membership in 1952: 4,306,690
(40.7% of State Population of 10,586,223)

Fig. 4. Church-membership statistics were compiled by the Bureau of Research and Survey of the National Council of the Churches of Christ in the U.S.A.

Jews, 4 per cent, and all others 59.3 per cent (*see* CHURCH MEMBERSHIP, U.S.). By 1964 Catholics numbered nearly 3,718,000 in the state's total population of 17,642,975.

Education. In 1964 the state's 19 Catholic universities and colleges enrolled more than 18,000 students. There were 146 secondary schools (71,560 students) and 628 elementary schools (277,010 students) under Catholic auspices; more than 421,400 additional students received religious instruction under released-time programs. The 8 diocesan seminaries and 32 seminaries and novitiates for religious orders of men had an enrollment of more than 3,300. More than 3,500 priests, 780 brothers, and 9,300 sisters served the Church in California.

Church-State Relations. References to and provisions affecting religion are incorporated in the state constitution and in acts of the legislature and the judiciary.

Constitution. California is governed by the Constitution of 1879, as amended. The preamble states that the people are "grateful to Almighty God."

Article 1, sec. 4, provides for liberty of conscience; "no person shall be rendered incompetent to be a witness or juror on account of his opinions on matters of religious belief; but the liberty of conscience hereby secured shall not be so construed as to excuse acts of licentiousness or justify practices inconsistent with the peace or safety of this state."

Public aid for sectarian purposes is prohibited (art. 4, sec. 30).

Article 8, sec. 1 (a, b, c), provides for tax exemptions for nonprofit college property; burial plots; property used for religious, hospital, and charitable purposes; church property; church parking lots; and buildings under construction for such institutions.

An oath or affirmation of office is required of all public officials and employees, except such inferior officers and employees exempted by law (art. 20, sec. 3).

Marriage and Divorce. The statutes fix no age under which persons may not lawfully marry. The consent of parents is required for men under 21 and women under 18. A license and blood test are required. Certain public officials and clergy may perform the ceremony. Common-law marriages are valid if consummated before 1895.

Marriages are void if either party is bound by a prior subsisting marriage; if the parties are related by blood in any degree of the direct line, and up to but not including first cousins. Marriages may be annulled on the grounds of nonage, unsound mind, fraud, force, and physical incapability.

The grounds for absolute divorce are: adultery; extreme cruelty; willfull desertion or neglect; habitual intemperance; conviction of a felony if the action is commenced within 2 years of completion of the sentence or pardon; incurable insanity for at least 3 years with a 3-year confinement preceding the action. There are no restrictions on remarriage after the final judgement. The court may restore to the wife her maiden name. Support of an insane spouse is required. *See* MARRIAGE, U.S. LAW OF; DIVORCE (U.S. LAW OF).

Abortion, Birth Control, Sterilization. The law forbids *abortion unless it is necessary to save the life of the mother. Any person providing, supplying, or administering to a woman any medicine, drug, or substance, or employing any instrument or other means whatever with the intent to procure the miscarriage of such woman is punishable by imprisonment from 2 to 5 years. Those who solicit or those who submit to the use of abortifacients with an intent to produce a miscarriage are punishable by imprisonment for 1 to 5 years. Those who advertise abortion or the means to accomplish an abortion or miscarriage are guilty of a felony.

The law restricts *birth control. It is a felony to advertise the means for the prevention of conception (*see* CONTRACEPTION).

The penal code allows punitive *sterilization. California is one of two states allowing this as a punishment in certain cases involving carnal abuse of a female under the age of 10. Sterilization is permitted on persons, who while prisoners are found to be moral or sexual degenerates or perverts. Sterilization is permitted on persons in state homes or hospitals who are afflicted with mental disease that may have been inherited and is likely to be transmitted to descendants, those with various degrees of mental deficiency, and those with marked departures from normal mentality. Certain safeguards are required to afford the prisoner a proper hearing and appeal.

Property and Taxation. Religious societies and charitable associations may incorporate under the nonprofit corporation statutes. Carrying on business at a profit as an incident to the main purpose of a corporation and the distribution of assets to members on dissolution is not forbidden. But under the section dealing with charitable organizations distribution of assets on dissolution is forbidden. Under the nonprofit corporation statutes a corporation sole with perpetual existence may be formed by a bishop or other presiding officers of the church for the purpose of administering and managing its affairs, properties, and temporalities. Religious and charitable corporations are authorized to invest in common trust funds.

Real and personal property of religious societies and charities not run for profit are exempt from taxation.

No real or personal estate may be bequeathed or devised to any charitable or benevolent society or left in trust for them by a testator who leaves a spouse, brother, sister, nephew, niece, descendant, or ancestor surviving him, who under the will or laws of succession would otherwise have taken the property unless the will was duly executed at least 30 days before the death of the testator. In any event it may not exceed one-third of the testator's estate. However, the rule does not apply if the will is executed at least 6 months prior to the death of a testator who leaves no spouse, child, grandchild, or parent; or when all of such heirs, by a writing executed at least 6 months prior to testator's death, have waived the restriction.

California's fund-raising statute does not deal with the solicitation of money but with the acquisition of salvageable personal property. It is not allowed except to associations exempt under the Revenue and Taxation Code; religious and charitable institutions fall under this. An occasional rummage sale or bazaar sponsored by a fraternal, social, political, or service organization is permitted if it does not constitute a major part of the organization's activities.

Prisons and Reformatories. The court held [*In re Ferguson* 361 P (2) 417] that the admitted discriminatory treatment of the Black Muslims in prison was necessary as a disciplinary matter and was not such an extreme or unreasonable deprivation as would justify relief on Federal constitutional grounds.

Holidays and Sunday Observance. Sunday, Christmas and New Year's Day, Labor Day, Thanksgiving Day, Good Friday from noon to 3 P.M., general election day, February 12, February 22, May 30, July 4, September 9, October 12, and November 11 are legal holidays. When a holiday falls on Sunday, the next day is a holiday. The sale, giving away, or furnishing of liquor during the hours the polls are open on a state election day

is a misdemeanor. Daily closing hours are 2 to 6 A.M.

Morality, Public Health, and Safety. No state condones polygamy. The willful disturbance of a religious meeting is a misdemeanor. Although the competency of a witness is not affected by his religious sentiments or convictions or lack of such, the credibility of the witness may be in question. The provisions of the chapters on cancer, venereal disease, and tuberculosis do not apply to any person who depends exclusively upon prayer for healing in accordance with the teachings of a bona fide religious sect. But the provisions and rules regarding the reporting of communicable diseases and the quarantine of such diseases, and those concerning the callings in which a person with venereal disease may not engage, do apply.

In the case of *Pencovic v. Pencovic* 287 P (2) 501 (1955), involving divorce and child support payment, the court held that although freedom of conscience and belief is absolute, the freedom to act is not; the constitution does not compel the subordination of the statutory duty of a parent to support his child to a rule of religious conduct prohibiting gainful employment.

In August 1964 the California supreme court reversed a decision involving Indians who were arrested for using peyotl in a religious ceremony and convicted of illegal possession of narcotics. The court held that "since the defendants used the peyotl in a bona fide pursuit of a religious faith, and since the practice did not frustrate a compelling interest of the state, the application of the (narcotics) statute improperly defeated the immunity of the first amendment of the Constitution of the U.S."

Various Constitutional Freedoms. A municipal ordinance prohibiting distribution of commercial advertising matter upon public streets and thoroughfares but not prohibiting the distribution of handbills upon religious, political, and scientific subjects was found not unconstitutional as denying right of freedom of press, speech, due process, or equal protection of the laws. The court held that there is a real basis for distinction between the exercise of constitutional rights of free speech and free press in connection with ordinary business activities and the exercise of the same rights in relation to public expressions of opinion on political, religious, social, and economic questions so far as regulation and control thereof under police power is concerned [*Pittsford v. City of Los Angeles* 122 P (2) 535].

Freedom of thought includes freedom of religious belief and embraces the right to maintain theories of life and death and the hereafter that are rank heresy to followers of orthodox faiths and precludes the putting to proof of religious doctrines or beliefs (*U.S. v. Ballard* 64 Sup. Ct. 882).

Bibliography: Early Church Period. The two principal centers for original MS material are Archives, Santa Barbara Mission; and Archives, Archdiocese of San Francisco. These are supplemented by Archivio General de la Nación, Mexico City.

Printed works. F. PALOU, *Historical Memoirs of New California,* tr. H. E. BOLTON, 2 v. (Berkeley, Calif. 1926); *Life of Fray Junípero Serra,* tr. and annot. M. J. GEIGER (Washington 1955). M. J. GEIGER, *The Life and Times of Fray Junípero Serra,* 2 v. (Washington 1959). J. SERRA, *The Writings of Junipero Serra,* ed. A. TIBESAR, 4 v. (Washington 1955–60). Z. ENGELHARDT, *The Missions and Missionaries of California,* 4 v. (San Francisco 1908–15). H. H. BANCROFT, *History of California,* 7 v. (San Francisco 1888–90).

American Period. Archives, Archdiocese of San Francisco. Archives, Archdiocese of Los Angeles. Archives, Historical, University of San Francisco. There is a dearth of literature on this period of Roman Catholicism in California. The most complete bibliog. listing and evaluation of pubs. to 1949 appears in J. B. McGLOIN, *Eloquent Indian: The Life of James Bouchard, California Jesuit* (Stanford 1949); *California's Pioneer Archbishop: The Life of Joseph Alemany, O.P., 1814–1888* (New York 1965), a complete biog. study. F. J. WEBER, *A Biographical Sketch of the Right Reverend Francisco García Diego y Moreno* (Los Angeles 1961). H. L. WALSH, *Hallowed Were the Gold Dust Trails: The Story of the Pioneer Priests of Northern California* (Santa Clara 1946). *West's Annotated California Codes* (St. Paul 1954–   ). *West's California Digest, 1850 to Date* (St. Paul 1951–   ). **Illustration credits:** Figs. 1 and 2, Academy of American Franciscan History. Fig. 3, David Marshall.

[M. GEIGER; J. B. MC GLOIN]

CALIPH

A title (from the Arabic *khalīfa,* meaning successor, lieutenant, deputy) applied to the successors of the Prophet Mohammed. The first caliph was Abū Bakr (A.D. 632–634), and the last, the Ottoman Abdul Mejid (1923–24), the Ottoman caliphate being abolished in 1924 by Kemal Ataturk. Very early in the political history of *Islam, controversy over the office of the caliphate brought into being the schismatic sects of the Khārijites (1 per cent of Islam) and the *Shiïtes (9 per cent), who broke away from the "orthodox" *Sunnites (90 per cent).

The Sunnite theory of the caliphate was that the office was an elective one, thus following the custom of pre-Islamic tribes. But the candidate had to be of the tribe of Quraysh, the tribe of the Prophet Mohammed. The Khārijites opposed this limitation, holding that the election should be truly democratic, allowing for the election of any person, even "an Ethiopian Negro." The Shiïtes opposed the very principle of election, holding that God Himself made the appointment of their *Imām, whom they regarded as impeccable.

The duties of the caliph were to preserve the religion according to the principles established by the Fathers of the Moslem community; to establish equity; to maintain public order; to maintain penal sanctions; to equip armies for guarding the frontiers; to lead the holy war (*jihād*) against those who refused to accept Islam until they either did so or entered into the status of protection (*see* DHIMMI); to collect the alms; to divide the booty; to employ trustworthy men and appoint good advisers; and to attend personally to the supervision of the conduct of government. In order to qualify for the caliphate a person had to be an adult male of the tribe of Quraysh, of good character, free from mental and physical defects, with administrative ability, knowledge of the law, and the courage to defend the territory of Islam.

The Prophet Mohammed died without making provisions for a successor. His sons had died before him. Abū Bakr was the first caliph, followed by three others, all of whom were elected democratically. These four caliphs, Abū Bakr, 'Umar, 'Uthmān, and 'Alī, are referred to as the "rightly guided caliphs" (*al-khulafā' al-rāshidūn*). Their combined reign extended from 632 to 661, a period referred to as that of the Orthodox Caliphate, the seat of which was in *Mecca, one of the two holy cities of Islam, the other being *Medina. The succeeding period was that of the Umayyad Caliphate (661–750). Its founder was Mu'āwiya (661–680), who moved the seat of government to Damascus (*see* UMAYYADS). Henceforth, the caliphate became hereditary, though the representatives of the community still expressed their consent

through the institution of the *bay'a,* symbolized by a handshake with the caliph and denoting recognition of his authority and obedience to him. This dynasty had 14 caliphs and was succeeded by the 'Abbāsid dynasty, which numbered 37 (*see* 'ABBĀSIDS). The capital of this dynasty was in Baghdad, and its downfall came with the sacking of the city by the Mongols in 1258. In Spain, the Umayyad Caliphs of Cordova reigned from 756 to 1031 (followed by minor Spanish dynasties until 1492). The dissenting Fātimid Caliphate of Egypt, representing the Shiïte minority in Islam, numbered 14 caliphs who reigned from 909 to 1171 when the dynasty was overthrown by the famous Sultan *Saladin, champion of the Sunnite majority (*see* SULTAN). The Ottoman claim to the caliphate was based on an alleged nomination of the Sultan Selim I (1515–20) by the last member of the 'Abbāsid dynasty, who died in exile in 1539 in Egypt. But Selim did not fulfill the necessary qualification of belonging to the Prophet's tribe of Quraysh, hence the anomaly in the Ottoman Caliphate until it was abolished. The caliphate, one of the most central features of the Moslem state, is still a living issue.

Bibliography: T. W. ARNOLD, *The Caliphate* (London 1924). H. LAOUST, ed., *Le Califat dans la doctrine de Rasīd Ridā* (Beirut 1938). L. GARDET, *La Cité Musulmane: Vie sociale et politique* (Paris 1954).

[G. MAKDISI]

CALIX SOCIETY, a group organized in 1947 to assist Catholic alcoholics in overcoming their addiction. It was founded by five alcoholics, with the approval of Abp. John Gregory Murray of St. Paul. Its object has not been to become a Catholic rival to the nondenominational *Alcoholics Anonymous (AA). On the contrary, it accepts the AA program and intends only to bring to bear the spiritual resources available to Catholics in implementing the eleventh of AA's Twelve Steps, namely, "We sought through prayer and meditation to improve our conscious contact with God as we understand Him, praying only for knowledge of His will for us and the power to carry that out." Calix works for total abstinence of those with a drinking problem and seeks to bring about the spiritual development of its members through worship at Mass, the reception of the Sacraments, and prayer. Where a unit is established there is a program of a monthly Mass at which the members receive Communion (although to protect anonymity, they do not sit together), a Communion breakfast, a conference with the chaplain, a discussion of problems, a monthly Holy Hour, and an annual weekend retreat. The members are encouraged to engage in the corporal and spiritual works of mercy. In 1963 there were 37 separate units in the U.S., Canada, India, and Scotland. Each unit has its own officials and a priest to act as spiritual director. There are also international officials. International headquarters is located in Minneapolis, Minn. The society publishes a newsletter called the *Chalice.*

Bibliography: R. GRIBBEN, "The Calix Society," *The Priest* 16 (1960) 37–40.

[R. D. DICKINSON]

CALIXTUS, GEORG

Professor of theology and propagator of theoretical and historical bases of ecumenism; b. Medelby, Schleswig-Holstein, Dec. 14, 1586; d. Helmstedt, March 19, 1656. At 16 Calixtus (Callisen), son of a Lutheran pastor, entered Helmstedt University, where *Philippism was protected. Among his professors were the humanist Johann Caselius (1533–1613) and the Aristotelian Cornelius Martini (1568–1621). With this background, his principle that "mind is godlike and logic divine" spelled an approach to theology in large part disdained by contemporary Lutheran theologians. Although personally devoted to the *Augsburg Confession (1530), he believed a man could be saved though a Calvinist or Roman Catholic. In his concern for reunion, Calixtus appealed to spokesmen of an irenic tradition, such as St. *Vincent of Lerins (d. before 456), Desiderius *Erasmus, Philipp *Melanchthon, George *Cassander, Georg *Witzel, Marcantonio de Dominis. In such irenicists he found support for the idea of all churches measuring their creeds by the Apostles' Creed and the Fathers.

Calixtus's writings, though prolific, do not present a systematic theology. They consist mainly of elaborately reasoned proposals for interdenominational meetings, conciliatory tracts aiding reunion, a vast and varied correspondence, and polemical brochures. His reunion proposals were generally well received especially by the Calvinists, partly through their wish for equal status with Lutherans within the Empire, partly because of their experience in France and the Lowlands, partly because of a lingering force of humanism. He corresponded on Protestant reunion with Franciscus Junius (1545–1602), David Pareus (1548–1622), Isaac *Casaubon (1559–1614), Hugo *Grotius, John Durie (1596–1680), Gerhardus Johannes Vossius (1577–1649), Ludwig Crocius (1586–1655), Johannes Bergius (1587–1658), and Moïse *Amyraut, as well as with the Mt. Athos monk Metrophanes Kritopoulos (d. c. 1640), with whom he discussed his proposals in regard to Greek Orthodoxy.

Efforts at reunion with Catholicism foundered on the differences in the conception of the Church as a visible and continuous entity, the Petrine doctrine, Tridentine authority, and the nature of heresy. Calixtus urged Catholics to recognize man's obligation toward reason and the benefits of dialogue in mitigating bitterness. Vitus Erbermann (1597–1675), Valeriano *Magni, Johannes C. von Boyneburg (1622–72) were among the Catholic scholars to whom Calixtus submitted his proposals. The strict orthodox Lutherans also resisted his efforts, and the conflict that ensued between them and Calixtus and his school was called the "syncretistic controversy." Beginning in 1645 it continued to the end of the century. The orthodox included Coelestinus Myslenta (1588–1653), Johannes Behm (1578–1648?), Michel Behm (1610–88), and particularly Abraham *Calov. Conrad Horney the philosopher (1590–1649), Herman Conring the jurist (1606–81), and Johannes Latermann (1620–82)—all Calixtine students—defended their master's arguments. After his death, the influence of Calixtus was further extended by his student Gerard Wolter Molanus (1633–1722) and the philosopher G. W. *Leibniz.

See also CONFESSIONS OF FAITH, PROTESTANT; GNESIO-LUTHERANISM.

Bibliography: Works. *Epitomes theologiae moralis pars prima una cum Digressione de arte nova* (Helmstedt 1634); ed., *Sancti . . . Augustini De doctrina christiana libri IV: De fide et symbolo liber unus* (Helmstedt 1655); *Disputatio theologica de auctoritate antiquitatis ecclesiasticae* by J. HENICH (Helmstedt 1639). E. L. HENKE, ed., *G. Calixtus Briefwechsel: In einer Auswahl aus Wolfenbüttelschen Handschriften* (Halle 1833); *Commercii literarii Calixti* (Marburg 1835–40) fasc. 2–3. Literature. E. L. HENKE, *Georg Calixtus und seine Zeit,* 2 v. (Halle 1853–56), still definitive. J. T. MCNEILL, *Unitive Protestantism* (rev. ed. Richmond, Va. 1964). W. C. DOWDING, *. . . Life and Correspondence of G. Calixtus* (London 1863). R. PREUS, *The Inspiration of Scripture: A Study of the Theology of the 17th Century Lutheran Dogmaticians* (Edinburgh 1955). P. PETERSEN, *Geschichte der aristotelischen Philosophie im protestantischen Deutschland* (Leipzig 1921). H. SCHÜSSLER, *Georg Calixt, Theologie und Kirchenpolitik: Eine Studie zur Ökumenizität des Luthertums* (Wiesbaden 1961). H. SCHMID, *Geschichte der syncretistischen Streitigkeiten in der Zeit des Georg Calixt* (Erlangen 1846). O. RITSCHL, *Dogmengeschichte des Protestantismus,* 4 v. (Leipzig-Göttingen 1908–27). F. LAW, RGG³ 1:1586–87.

[Q. BREEN]

CALLAHAN, PATRICK HENRY, industrialist, reformer; b. Cleveland, Ohio, Oct. 15, 1865; d. Louisville, Ky., Feb. 4, 1940. He was the son of John Cormic and Mary Anna (Connolly) Callahan. After attending St. John's High School and the Spencerian Business College in Cleveland, he had a brief career in professional baseball as a member of the Chicago White Stockings (now White Sox) organization. After leaving baseball in 1888, he worked for the Glidden Varnish Company in Cleveland and Chicago, and on Jan. 20, 1891, he married Julia Cahill of Fremont, Ohio. The couple moved the following year to Louisville, where Callahan became manager, and later president, of the Louisville Varnish Company. In 1915 he and Rev. John A. Ryan formulated a profit-sharing plan for the company, under which surplus revenues were divided between stockholders and workers. Callahan lectured and wrote extensively on behalf of this plan. He was also active as chairman (1914–16) of the Knights of Columbus Commission on Religious Prejudices, founder (1916) of the Catholic Laymen's Association of Georgia, chairman (1917–18) of the Knights of Columbus Committee on War Activities, and helped to organize (1926–27) the Catholic Association for International Peace. After World War I he became one of the directors of the Catholic Conference on Industrial Problems (1923) and an ardent champion of prohibition, serving as general secretary of the Association of Catholics Favoring Prohibition and chairman of the Central Prohibition Commission. In 1925 he came to the aid of William Jennings Bryan in the Scopes evolution trial. He favored New Deal legislation, which he helped to administer in Kentucky, and served as a trustee of the National Child Labor Commission and vice president of the Kentucky Interracial Commission. Callahan was named to the Order of St. Gregory the Great in 1922 and awarded the Illinois Newman Foundation's honorary medal in 1931.

Bibliography: Archives, The Catholic University of America. A. I. ABELL, DAB (1957) 11.2:86–88.

[R. J. BARTMAN]

CALLAN, CHARLES JEROME, author and theologian; b. Lockport, N.Y., Dec. 5, 1877; d. Milford, Conn., Feb. 26, 1962. He received his early education in the public schools of Niagara County, N.Y., and then attended Canisius College in Buffalo. Entering the Order of Preachers at St. Rose Priory, Springfield, Ky., he was professed on Oct. 23, 1900. After ordination at Somerset, Ohio, June 29, 1905, he was sent to Fribourg, Switzerland, for further theological studies. He returned to the U.S. in 1909, and was appointed to the teaching staff of the Dominican House of Studies, Washington, D.C., as professor of philosophy and Scriptural exegesis. He held that post until 1915, when he was sent to teach the same subjects at the newly opened major seminary of the Maryknoll Fathers, Maryknoll, N.Y. In 1916 he became co-editor with Father John A. McHugh of the *Homiletic and Pastoral Review*. The two collaborated not only in editorial work but in other writing as well. Together they wrote 16 works on theology, Sacred Scripture, and the liturgy. In addition to the works in collaboration with McHugh, Callan wrote or compiled seven books of his own, and two in collaboration with Father Thomas Reilly, on the Dominican liturgy. In 1931, Callan received the Dominican degree of Master of Sacred Theology, and in 1940 he was appointed by the Holy See as consultor of the Pontifical Biblical Commission.

Bibliography: W. ROMIG, ed., *The Book of Catholic Authors*, 2d ser. (Detroit 1943). *Dominicana* 16 (1931) 148–149; 25 (1940) 246–247; 40 (1955) 284–285.

[J. COFFEY]

CALLAN, NICHOLAS, scientist, inventor; b. Darver, Dundalk, Ireland, Dec. 20, 1799; d. Maynooth, Ireland, Jan. 14, 1864. Callan was a member of the extensive Catholic family of Dromiskin of County Louth, the son of Denis and Margaret (Smith) Callan. He was educated at Dundalk Academy, run by William Neilson, a Presbyterian minister and philomath, and Navan seminary. He entered Maynooth College (1816) and was ordained (1823) while a Dunboyne scholar in physics (1822–24). He received a D.D. degree from the Sapienza University in Rome (1826) and returned to Maynooth where he was appointed professor of physics. Callan invented the induction coil (1836) and discovered the principle of the self-induced dynamo (1837). His demonstration of his pioneer apparatus for high-voltage electricity at the London Exhibition in 1837 aroused great interest and spurred further investigations. In the 1840s, Callan wrote numerous religious publications, one of which influenced Newman's conversion. The last 12 years of his life were spent in scientific research, while also acting as confessor to students and colleagues.

Bibliography: P. J. McLAUGHLIN, "Dr. Callan of Maynooth," *Studies* 25 (1936) 253–269; *Nicholas Callan: Priest Scientist* (Dublin 1963).

[P. MC LAUGHLIN]

CALLES, PLUTARCO ELÍAS

Mexican revolutionary leader and persecutor of the Catholic Church; b. Guaymas, Sonora, Mexico, Jan. 27, 1877; d. Mexico City, Oct. 19, 1945. Calles, a descendant of Sephardic Jews from Almazán, Soria, Spain, was a natural son of Plutarco Elías Lucero and María de Jesús Campuzano. When he was 4, his father died and his mother married J. B. Calles, whose last name young Plutarco took. On completing his primary education, he worked as an assistant elementary teacher. Finding this incompatible with his impulsive and authoritarian personality, he worked next in the municipal treasury of Guaymas until a small embezzlement left him jobless. After administering a hotel owned by his brother, he finally went into business for himself. The revolution of Francisco I. Madero did not affect him. However, as a commissioner of Agua Prieta—a position that he held for the benefit of his business—

Calles, together with Alvaro Obregón, joined the revolution headed by Venustiano Carranza, Governor of Coahuila, when the president was assassinated. Obregón had previously fought Pascual Orozco when Orozco

Plutarco Elías Calles.

betrayed Madero. Calles, a captain, undertook his first attack against Naco; it was so unsuccessful Calles fled when the first shots rang out. Later he was more fortunate, and in a short time he rose to the rank of general. The revolution removed Victoriano Huerta from office and degenerated into anarchy. Since the ambitions of the *caudillos* did not bring peace to the republic, the principal revolutionary chiefs convoked a convention to find remedy. The convention, held in Aguascalientes in mid-1915, disowned Carranza and Carranza disowned the convention. Pancho Villa, in open rebellion against the commander-in-chief, was defeated by General Obregón, while Calles obtained power and influence. In August 1915 Venustiano Carranza appointed Calles governor and military commander of Sonora. There he remained 9 months during which time he first indicated his propensity toward the destruction of the Catholic Church. In Querétaro, on Feb. 5, 1917, the Constitutional Congress promulgated the new constitution in which there were included antireligious articles that served as a legal base for Calles' unleashing, as president of the republic, the most cruel religious persecution.

Carranza appointed Calles secretary of industry and commerce, a position that he left early in 1920 to follow Obregón in a new revolutionary adventure. Adolfo de la Huerta, also from Sonora, initiated the Plan of Agua Prieta, disavowing Carranza. He was seconded by a large part of the army, and the president was assassinated in a hut in Tlaxcalaltongo. Huerta became provisional president while the elections were held. Álvaro Obregón won; he took office Dec. 1, 1920, and appointed Calles secretary of war. In 1922 Calles became secretary of the interior. When Obregón's term came to an end, his secretary of the treasury, Adolfo de la Huerta, was prevented from becoming president and provoked a bloody rebellion. He was defeated and Calles became president on Dec. 1, 1924.

The first 2 years of his government revealed his socializing tendencies; among other things he constructed highways and irrigation projects, reorganized the army, and founded the Bank of Mexico. A man of strong passions, he first tried to divide the Catholic

Church by promoting the establishment of a Mexican national church. That failing, he enforced Article 130 of the constitution and promulgated the Decree of Reforms on Transgressions of the Common Order. This meant limitation of the number of priests, prohibition of religious teaching in the schools, state control over the clergy, and suppression of religious orders. The bishops protested through the legal means at their disposal but with no effect; they were forced to suspend the public worship in churches after Aug. 1, 1926. In some states, uprisings broke out, and for 3 anguished years, the Mexican Catholics gave their blood to the cry of "Long live Christ the King!" At the end of his presidential term, two early revolutionaries, friends of Calles and Obregón, became candidates, but both were cut down by bullets. Obregón, without an opponent, was then elected, but José de León Toral assassinated him.

Calles remained chief of the revolution. Portes Gil, the provisional president, bent to his will. He imposed Ortíz Rubio as president against the wishes of the people who were in favor of José *Vasconcelos. He withdrew Ortíz Rubio and replaced him with Gen. Abelardo Rodríguez. He raised also Lázaro Cárdenas to the presidency, using the official political party created by him to guarantee the continuation of the revolutionary group in power. Calles, objecting to Cárdenas's policies, tried to intervene once more, but this time his protegé turned on him and exiled him to the United States. When in 1941, during the presidency of Manuel Ávila Camacho, he returned to Mexico, Calles remained apart from all political activity.

Bibliography: F. MEDINA RUIZ, *Calles: Un destino melancólico* (Mexico City 1960). A. RIUS FACIUS, *Méjico cristero: Historia de la ACJM, 1925 a 1931* (Mexico City 1960).

[A. RIUS FACIUS]

CALLEWAERT, CAMILLE,

historian of liturgy; b. Zwevegem, Belgium, Jan. 1, 1866; d. Bruges, Aug. 6, 1943. Callewaert studied at the episcopal college of Courtrai and took his philosophy at the seminary at Roulers. He never finished the usual course of theology at the major seminary of Bruges because his bishop sent him to study for a degree in Canon Law at Louvain. Here he also enrolled in the faculty of philosophy, studied historical criticism under A. Cauchie (1860–1922), and followed B. Jungmann's (1833–95) course in Church history. In the meantime, he was ordained on June 15, 1889.

In 1893 Callewaert was recalled to Bruges and named assistant at the cathedral. The following year he was appointed professor of Church history at the major seminary; in 1903 he was given the chair of liturgy. He was rector from 1907–34. Meanwhile, he was also professor of liturgy at the University of Louvain from 1910 to 1921. In 1929, Pius XI made him a domestic prelate, and upon his retirement he was named archpriest of Bruges. His last years were devoted entirely to study.

A historian of the first order, Callewaert made his rubrics lectures a genuine study of liturgy; they were eventually published as *Liturgicae Institutiones*, 3 v. (Bruges 1919–37). But he was not interested only in liturgical science. Conscious of the liturgy's role in the people's spiritual life, he started a liturgical study group at Bruges in 1907, an institution that was soon imitated all over Belgium. At the request of L. *Beauduin,

Callewaert organized the Dutch liturgical week of which he retained the presidency for years.

Bibliography: The long list of his works was published in SacrErud 1 (1948) 353–379. The greater part of his articles were reprinted in the volume *Sacris Eruditi* (Steenbrugge 1940). C. VAN HULST, EphemLiturg 58 (1944) 319–321.

[N. HUYGHEBAERT]

CALLIÈRE, LOUIS HECTOR DE,

governor of New France; b. Cherbourg, France, 1646; d. Quebec, Canada, May 26, 1703. He was the son of Jacques, Governor of Cherbourg, and Madeleine (Potier) de Callière. After a career in the army, where he became captain of the regiment of Navarre, he went to Canada, serving as governor of Montreal (1684–98) and governor of New France (1698–1703) during a period of almost constant warfare with both the English and the Iroquois Indians. In 1687, after building defense bastions at Montreal and reinforcing Ft. Frontenac (Kingston, Ontario), Callière launched an expedition against the Iroquois nations. Although only moderately successful, the attack enabled the French to retain their hold on the western fur trade against the opposing efforts of the Iroquois and English. Three years later he led his men to relieve the siege of Quebec by the British, and in 1691 he routed an attack from Albany under Maj. Peter Schuyler. From 1692 to 1696 the French took the offensive in the struggle. Small war parties emanating from Montreal harried the outlying English settlements and larger forces decimated the Indians. By 1701 Callière succeeded in concluding a peace treaty with the warring factions. Despite great suffering from gout and, in his later years, from dropsy, he served France with energy. He was made a chevalier of St. Louis in 1694.

Bibliography: B. SULTE, "La Famille de Callières," *Trans. Royal Soc. of Canada* (1890). F. M. BIBAUD, *Le Panthéon canadien* (rev. ed. Montreal 1891). W. J. ECCLES, *Frontenac: The Courtier Governor* (Toronto 1959).

[F. BOLAND]

CALLIERGIS, ZACHARIAS,

Byzantine humanist in the West; b. Rethymnon, Crete, 1473; d. *c.* 1524. One of the numerous post-Byzantine humanists who emigrated to the West during the *Renaissance, Calliergis made his principal contributions through his copying, editing, and printing of Greek texts in Venice and later in Rome, where he established the first Greek press.

Early in his life Calliergis established the first Greek-operated press in Venice (it may even have preceded that of Aldus), and devoted it exclusively to the publication of Greek works. Calliergis's first edition (1499) was the *Etymologicum magnum,* largest of the existing Greek dictionaries. There followed the *editio princeps* of the *Commentary of Simplicius on the Categories of Aristotle,* which influenced the Renaissance interpretation of the original Greek text of Aristotle. During his stay in Venice, Zacharias maintained close contacts with the Aldine circle of scholars, which included *Manutius, Pietro *Bembo, and Marcus *Musurus, and *Erasmus, during the period he spent there.

From 1509 to 1515 Calliergis dropped out of sight, to appear again only when he set up the first Greek press in Rome. His initial publication was the celebrated edition of Pindar, which for 3 centuries was to remain the vulgate version of both text and scholia. Another of his

Roman publications was the first edition of the Greek Sophist Phrynichus, published in 1520, which constitutes a significant contribution to the knowledge of Atticistic style. His last publication was the Greek dictionary of Varinus Favorinus (1523); there is no record of Calliergis after 1524.

Because of his endeavors to publish editions of high quality, his introduction of the art of Greek printing to Rome, and his work as editor and calligrapher of numerous classical and Byzantine texts, Calliergis deserves a higher place than is usually accorded to him in the dissemination of Greek learning to the West.

Bibliography: A. FIRMIN-DIDOT, *Alde Manuce et l'hellénisme à Venise* (Paris 1875), outdated sketch. E. L. J. LEGRAND, *Bibliographie hellénique*, 4 v. (Paris 1885–1906; repr. Brussels 1963) 1:cxxv–cxxx. D. J. GEANAKOPLOS, *Greek Scholars in Venice: Studies in the Dissemination of Greek Learning from Byzantium to Western Europe* (Cambridge, Mass. 1962) 201–222, with bibliog., the only full-length monograph on his career.

[D. J. GEANAKOPLOS]

CALLINICUS, PATRIARCH OF CONSTANTINOPLE,

693 to 705 (feast, in the Eastern Church, Aug. 23, 24, or 30). His origin is unknown, but he had served in an important post at the Blachernae Church in the royal quarter of the capital city before he succeeded Paul III as patriarch of Constantinople, and frequently opposed the brutality and interference of the Byzantine Emperor, *Justinian II. When the patrician Leontius mounted a revolt that resulted in the mutilation and banishment of the Emperor in 695, Callinicus supported the conspiracy and crowned Leontius as the new monarch. Another revolution placed Apsimar-Tiberius II on the imperial throne in 698. Meanwhile, Justinian was preparing a return from exile and in 705 he laid siege to Constantinople with a formidable army of Slavs and Bulgars. A surprise raid won Justinian's restoration. In the reign of terror that followed, Callinicus was blinded and exiled to Rome. The choice of Rome seems to have been dictated by reasons of security rather than of religious intrigue. Hagiographic sources report that Callinicus was immured alive—probably a typical exaggeration of the fact of his imprisonment.

Bibliography: J. GOUILLARD, DHGE 11:415. M. V. BRANDI, BiblSanct 3:673–675.

[R. J. SCHORK]

CALLISTUS I, POPE, ST.

Pontificate, *c.* 217 to 222 or 223 (feast, Oct. 14). According to the Liber pontificalis, Callistus was a Roman by birth; his father, Domitius, was from the district of Trastevere. Originally an imperial household slave of Carpophorus, Callistus is said to have engaged in banking and was accused of peculation; he was condemned to the mines of Sardinia (*c.* 186–189). Through the influence of Marcia, the concubine of Emperor Commodus, he was released and lived in Anzio on the bounty of Pope *Victor I. Under Pope *Zephyrinus he became deacon and was apparently given charge of the cemetery of S. Callisto. A majority elected him to succeed Zephyrinus (*c.* 217). Later, *Eusebius of Caesarea assigned a length of 5 years to his pontificate (*Hist. Eccl.* 6.21). The followers of *Hippolytus of Rome, however, were not prepared to accept Callistus and elected their own leader as bishop, thus making Hippolytus the first *antipope in a schism that lasted until 235. On Oct. 14, 222, or 223, in Rome, Callistus was martyred, probably

in a local disturbance in Trastevere, since there is no record of a formal persecution under Emperor Alexander Severus (222–235). He was buried in the cemetery *iuxta Callistum*, possibly on the site of an earlier oratory connected with him (*titulus Callisti*).

Callistus is credited with having stabilized the Saturday fast, three times a year, decreeing abstention from food, oil, and wine according to the prescription of Za 8.19. This is thought to be a source of the *Ember days.

From the *Philosophumena* (9.11–12; 10.27) of Hippolytus, a prejudiced but factually correct source, we have considerable information about Callistus. His dispute with Hippolytus was primarily doctrinal. Callistus began by condemning Sabellius, the chief exponent of *Monarchianism that tended to overemphasize the unity of persons in the Blessed Trinity. This did not, however, reconcile him with Hippolytus, since Callistus apparently could not accept Hippolytus's theory of the Logos, which seemed to exaggerate the distinction between Father and Son and thus savored of ditheism. Since Callistus had condemned Sabellius for heresy, it is difficult to believe that he embraced the Monarchian position as asserted by Hippolytus (*Philos.* 9.12). Undoubtedly the dispute was due, in part, to inconsistencies in theological terminology, a defect that was remedied only in the course of time. Callistus also introduced a number of disciplinary changes that brought the ire of Hippolytus upon him. He authorized the ordination of men who had been married two and even three times; he recognized the validity of marriages between free women and slaves; and he maintained that the Church had authority to absolve from all sins, and should adopt a policy of mercy toward the *lapsi* who had compromised their faith by temporary apostasy, but had repented. The last decision became a matter of controversy in the Church for years, dividing the clergy and faithful into two factions: the so-called laxists and the rigorists.

It is probable that *Tertullian's famous sarcasm concerning a peremptory edict did not refer to Callistus: "I hear that an edict has been published, and a peremptory one: the bishop of bishops, that is the Pontifex Maximus, proclaims: I remit the sins of adultery and fornication for those who have done penance" (*De*

Pope St. Callistus I, gold glass of the 4th century in the Cabinet des Médailles, Bibliothèque Nationale.

pudicitia 1). This decision came to be known as the Edict of Callistus; many historians maintained that it had reference to Pope Callistus, and contained a sarcastic allusion to the *primacy. Contemporary scholars generally believe that it was aimed at the bishop of Carthage, but no text has survived.

Callistus is the first pope, except for Peter, whose name was commemorated as a martyr in the oldest martyrology of the Roman Church, the 4th-century *Depositio Martyrum* (c. 354). A late tradition alleged that his relics were transported to France, while another maintained that they were deposited in the crypt of S. Maria in Trastevere under Pope *Innocent I (401–417). His tomb in the cemetery of Calepodius, on the Via Aurelia, was discovered in 1960 in the remains of an oratory erected there by Pope *Julius I in the 4th century, and described by the 7th-century *Salzburg Itinerary*. The crypt is decorated with paintings depicting his martyrdom. The name and picture of Callistus also appear on a piece of gold glass, now in the Cabinet des Médailles in Paris.

Bibliography: Duchesne LP 1:141–142; 3:73–74. C. CECCHELLI and E. JOSI, EncCatt 3:386–391. FLICHE-MARTIN 2:101–103, 404–415. E. CASPER, *Primatus Petri* (Weimar 1927). Caspar 1:22–47, 572–575. C. CECCHELLI, *Tre deportati in Sardegna* (Rome 1939) Quasten Patr 2:233–235. C. DALY, TU 3:176–182, edict. G. FERRETTO, BiblSanct 3:681–689. K. BEYSHCLAG ThZ 20 (1964) 103–124. U. FASOLA, LexThK² 6:20–24, tomb. **Illustration credit:** Hirmer Verlag München.

[J. CHAPIN]

CALLISTUS II, POPE

Pontificate, Feb. 2 to Dec. 14, 1124; b. Guido, date unknown. The fifth son of Count William of Burgundy, he was related to several royal houses of Europe. A member of the Church-reform party, he became archbishop of Vienne in 1088. When appointed papal legate in France by *Paschal II, who apparently also made him a cardinal, Guido strenuously opposed Paschal's "Privilege," extorted by *Henry V, which would have surrendered most of the political positions held by Church officials in the Empire. After protesting the "Privilege" at the Lateran synod of 1112, he called and presided over a synod of French and Burgundian bishops at Vienne that denounced lay *investiture of the clergy as heretical, and excommunicated Henry V as hostile to the welfare of the Church. When *Gelasius II, who succeeded Pascal, refused to confirm the "Privilege," the angry Henry V set up Archbishop Burdinus of Braga as antipope Gregory VIII and installed him in Rome. Gelasius was forced to spend his brief harassed pontificate in exile and died at Cluny within a year. Some of the cardinals who had come to Cluny now elected Guido, who was crowned in Vienne on Feb. 9, 1119.

Callistus took immediate steps to establish peace with the imperial government, since both sides were tired of the long *investiture struggle. Henry V favorably received a papal embassy and temporarily withdrew his support from Gregory VIII. A meeting between Pope and Emperor was arranged for Mousson. After presiding over a synod at Toulouse (1119), which was mainly concerned with reform of the French Church, Callistus proceeded to Reims, where he held a great council (1119), attended by some 400 prelates and by Louis VI of France. Negotiations with Henry V broke down after he came to Mousson with a large army, and papal plans to meet with the Emperor were abandoned. The Em-

peror was excommunicated again (October 1119).

Callistus then went to Rome, where he was enthusiastically received by the people, who had meanwhile driven out the antipope. He allied himself with the Normans, who aided in the capture of Gregory VIII. Gregory, who had taken refuge at Sutri, was held prisoner, and subsequently other enemies of the Pope in Italy were overcome. The Pope then sent a new embassy to Henry V. A preliminary understanding with a truce was arranged at Würzburg in 1121. The following year, the famous Concordat of *Worms (1122) was arrived at in a synod held in that city. Because of the Pope's patience and perseverance, the Concordat was a reasonably satisfactory arrangement for both sides, though a complete victory for neither, bringing peace to both Empire and Church, to the great relief of Christendom. The first *Lateran Council (1123), convoked by Callistus, solemnly confirmed the Concordat of Worms and issued decrees against clerical marriage (*see* CELIBACY) and *simony. It provided penalties against violators of the Truce of God (*see* PEACE OF GOD) and against forgers of ecclesiastical documents, and renewed indulgences for crusading.

During his pontificate Callistus also secured from *Henry I of England the acceptance of his candidate *Thurstan for the archbishopric of York, transferred metropolitan rights in Spain from the ancient See of Merida (Emerita) to the popular See of *Santiago de Compostela, and settled the old French rivalry over metropolitan rights between *Arles and *Vienne in favor of the latter.

Bibliography: Jaffé L 1:780–821. U. ROBERT, ed., *Bullaire du pape Calixte II*, 2 v. (Paris 1891); *Histoire du pape Calixte II* (Paris 1891). Hefele-Leclercq 5.1:568–592, *passim*. Fliche-Martin 8:378–395. É. JORDAN, DHGE 11:424–438. P. F. PALUMBO, EncCatt 3:391–393. Haller 2:505–512, 623. T. SCHIEFFER, LexThK² 2:884.

[D. D. MC GARRY]

CALLISTUS III, POPE

Pontificate, April 8, 1455, to Aug. 6, 1458; b. Alfonso de *Borgia, Játiva (near Valencia), Spain, Dec. 31, 1378; d. Rome, Italy. Born in the year the *Western Schism began, he studied and taught law at the University of *Lérida, where he was a cathedral canon before he became a jurist in the service of his King, Alfonso V of Aragon. Pope Martin V made him bishop of Valencia in 1429 for having obtained the resignation of antipope Clement VIII (Gil S. Muñoz, who succeeded *Benedict XIII) in Peñíscola; Eugene IV created him a cardinal for his services in separating Alfonso V from the supporters of the Council of *Basel. A man of austere life who possessed the mind of a medieval canonist, he was elected pope as a neutral, since it was impossible to elect anyone from the *Colonna or *Orsini camps. He was not a dedicated patron of *humanism, as his predecessor *Nicholas V had been, but neither was he its enemy. The policy of a balance of power in Italy that he followed had been begun by Nicholas with the Peace of Lodi, resulting in the Italian League (1454–55) of Venice, Milan, Florence, Rome, and Naples. His main goal, a crusade, made urgent after the fall of *Constantinople to the Turks (May 29, 1453), depended on peace in Italy. Hence in 1455–56 he opposed by spiritual and military means the Sienese conquests of the condottiere Giacomo Piccinino, who was protected by Al-

Pope Callistus III, bronze medal by Andrea Guacialoti.

fonso V of Aragon and (after 1442) of *Naples. On Alfonso's death (June 27, 1458), Callistus asserted the rights of the Holy See to the Kingdom of Naples, which had been left by Alfonso to his natural son, Ferrante I.

The *crusade against the Turks was Callistus' greatest achievement. The papal legate to the *Holy Roman Empire and to *Hungary, Cardinal Juan de *Carvajal, won the promise of aid from Emperor Frederick III and the complete support of King Ladislaus V of Hungary and Bohemia. John *Hunyadi, exregent of Hungary, and St. *John Capistran, who preached the crusade, led the troops that forced the Turks to raise the siege of *Belgrade. Confronted with opposition to this enterprise from German princes and prelates, who regarded the tithes to be levied as a burden on the German Church, Callistus turned to *Scanderbeg (George Castriota), Prince of Albania, and to Alfonso V. After the defeat of the Turkish fleet at Metelino by the papal-Aragonese fleet under Cardinal Scarampo and after the land victory of Scanderbeg at Tomorniza (both in 1457), the Pope formed an alliance with Stephen Thomas, King of Bosnia, and with *Matthias Corvinus (Hunyadi), the new King of Hungary, as he was not able to rely for aid on Germany, Burgundy, France, Castile, or Portugal. At the same time, he was reconciled with the new King of Bohemia, George *Poděbrad. The Turkish threat kept Callistus from the needed reform of the Church, but his excessive nepotism was a contributing factor. The swarm of Valencians and Catalans at his court can be explained only by the animosity and ill-will shown by Italians at the election of a foreign pope and by the presence of numerous Spaniards in Naples after its occupation by Alfonso V. Some of them, however, e.g., Abp. Pedro de Urrea of *Tarragona and Antoni Olzina, were more loyal to the King than to the Pope.

Callistus' nephews Rodrigo de Borgia (later Pope *Alexander VI), bishop of Gerona, Oviedo, and Valencia and vice-chancellor of the States of the Church, and Lluís Joan del Milà (bishop of Segorbe), cardinals in 1456, were known for loose and worldly lives. Rodrigo's brother Pere Lluís (duke of Spoleto and captain general

of the States of the Church) had to flee Rome on the day of Callistus' death, and he himself died in nearby Civitavecchia when the Italians vented their hate against the Catalans. Callistus died on the Feast of the *Transfiguration, which he had instituted to commemorate the victory at Belgrade.

Bibliography: Sources. POGGIO BRACCIOLINI, *Vitae quorundum pontificum* in Duchesne LP 2:546–560. Cf. C. DA CAPODIMONTE, "Poggio Bracciolini autore delle anonime *Vitae quorundam pontificum,*" RivStorChIt 14 (1960) 27–47. *Magnum bullarium Romanum a beato Leone Magno usque ad S. D. N. Benedictum XIII.,* 8 v. (new ed. Luxembourg 1727) v.1. F. FITA, "Restos mortales de C. III y Alejandro VI," BolRealAcHist 18 (1891) 159–166. L. VON PASTOR, ed., *Ungedruckte Akten,* v.1 (Freiburg 1904) 37–91. F. MARTORELL, "Un inventario della biblioteca di C. III," *Miscellanea Francesco Ehrle,* v.5 (StTest 41; 1924) 166–191. J. RIUS SERRA, "Un inventario de joyas de C. III," AnalSac Tarracon 5 (1929) 305–320; ed., *Regesto ibérico de C. III,* 2 v. (Barcelona 1948–58). O. RAYNALDUS, *Annales ecclesiastici,* ed. J. D. MANSI, 15 v. (Lucca 1747–56) 10:13–157.

Literature. J. STEIN, *C. III et la comète de Halley* (Rome 1909). J. B. ALTISENT JOVÉ, *Alfonso de Borja en Lérida* (Lérida 1924). Pastor 2:315–495. J. SANCHIS SIVERA, "El obispo de Valencia, Don Alfonso de Borja (C. III), 1429–1458," BolRealAc Hist 88 (1926) 241–313. J. RIUS, "Catalanes y Aragoneses en la corte de C. III," AnalSacTarracon 3 (1927) 193–330. P. PASCHINI, "La flotta di C. III, 1455–1458," *Archivio della Società romana di storia patria* 53–55 (1930–32) 177–254. L. GÓMEZ CANEDO, *Un español al servicio de la Santa Sede, Don Juan de Carvajal* (Madrid 1947). F. BABINGER, *Mehmed der Eroberer und seine Zeit* (Munich 1953). G. HOFMANN, "Papst Kalixt III. und die Frage der Kircheneinheit im Osten," Misc Mercati, 6 v. (StTest 121–126; 1946) 3:209–237. A. M. ALBAREDA, "Il bibliotecario di C. III," *ibid.* 4:178–208. C. M. DE WITTE, "Les Bulles pontificales et l'expansion portugaise au XVᵉ siècle," RHE 51 (1956) 413–453, 809–836. P. BREZZI, "La politica di C. III," *Studi romani* 7 (1959) 31–41. **Illustration credit:** National Gallery of Art, Washington, D.C., Samuel H. Kress Collection.

[M. BATLLORI]

CALLISTUS I, PATRIARCH OF CONSTANTINOPLE, 1350–54 and 1355–63, Byzantine preacher and hagiographer; d. 1363. He was a monk at Iviron on Mt. *Athos, companion of Gregory *Palamas, and disciple of *Gregory Sinaites, the principal proponent of *Hesychasm in the skete of Magula. Callistus signed the Hagiorite *Tome* of 1341 as a hesychastic *manifesto.* In March 1342 he joined the Athonite delegation in Constantinople to negotiate peace between *John VI Cantacuzenus and the court of Anne of Savoy; on June 10, 1350, he succeeded his former student Isidore I as patriarch of Constantinople. He presided over a synod in Blachernae palace (May–June 1351), which canonized Palamite doctrine. He was deposed after 1353 for refusing to crown Matthew Cantacuzenus Emperor.

After the abdication of John Cantacuzenus in 1354 he regained the patriarchal throne. He reorganized the parochial system under the surveillance of an exarch, excommunicated the Serbian Czar, Stephen Dušan, and attempted to regroup the various Orthodox churches, particularly the Hungarian, under his patriarchate. He spread Palamite doctrine, particularly through biography, and wrote a life of Gregory the Sinaite; a life of St. Theodosius of Tirnovo; a panegyric on John the Faster, renovator of the Prodromos-Petra monastery; and many homilies, a number of which have been recently discovered.

Bibliography: O. VOLK, LexThK² 5:1263. M. JUGIE, *Catholicisme* 2:391–392; DTC 11.2:1789–92. Beck KTLBR 774. J. MEYENDORFF, *Introduction a l'étude de Grégoire Palamas* (Paris 1959).

[I. H. DALMAIS]

CALLISTUS II XANTHOPULUS, PATRI- ARCH OF CONSTANTINOPLE in 1397, and Byzantine spiritual writer. His surname indicates that he was from the monastery of Xanthopulus. With another monk, Ignatius Xanthopulos, Callistus composed the important *Century,* a tract of 100 sections on the ascetical practices of the Hesychastic monks; it was incorporated in the *Philokalia* of Nicodemus the Hagiorite and had a great influence on Orthodox spirituality. The *Century* avoided the Palamite controversy; it confined itself to practical directives based on the teachings of the Greek fathers, such as Evagrius, Maximus the Confessor, and John Climacus. At the start of his spiritual life, the monk must seek a director who will lead him to the perfection of his baptismal graces in a life of faith, hope, and charity. Obedience to the director eliminates self-will and leads to fulfillment of the commandments of Jesus. A life of continual prayer, strict self-discipline, and practice of the bodily activities of the Hesychasts are prerequisites as is the Prayer of the Heart or the *Jesus Prayer. These means are, however, subordinate to the action of Divine Grace (c.24). Callistus seems to have used the work of Callistus Angelicudes as a basis for this compilation. A series of Texts on Prayer is also attributed to Callistus in the *Philokalia.* Several rescripts and a confession of faith have been preserved from his reign as patriarch. The homilary attributed to him in a MS of the Chilandar monastery is not of his authorship.

Bibliography: PG 147:635–812. E. KADLOUBOVSKY and G. E. H. PALMER, trs., *Writings from the Philokalia on Prayer of the Heart* (London 1951) 162–273. Beck KTLBR 774, 784–785.

[H. D. HUNTER]

CALLISTUS ANGELICUDES, 14th-century Palamite and mystical writer, probably identical with Angelicudes Melenikeotes, recognized as the founder of a monastery through a patriarchal seal of 1371. He is known in Byzantine literature also as Callistus Meliteniotes or Callistus Telicudes. A. Ehrhard attributed to the authorship of Meliteniotes 30 *Logoi hesychastices paracleseos;* and to Telicudes, a tract on the *hesychastices tribes.* The latter, however, seems to be merely an abbreviated section of the first-named

treatise. Both works are apparently parts of a handbook of Hesychastic doctrine.

Bibliography: Beck KTLBR 784. G. MERCATI, "Callisto Angelicudes Meliniceota," *Bessarione* 31 (1915) 79–86, repr. in his *Opere minori,* v.3 (StTest 78; 1937) 415–552.

[F. X. MURPHY]

CALLOT, JACQUES, Europe's first major etcher, combined Renaissance stylistic elegance with realistic and grotesque subjects; b. Nancy, France, 1592; d. Nancy, March 24, 1635. At the Medici court from 1614 to 1621, although trained as an engraver, he adopted etching, portraying with finesse images of the Florentine theater. Callot's etchings of court masques, rural fairs, *commedia dell'arte* actors, beggars, gypsies, and comic dwarfs are famous. Similar popularizations were religious prints that revived gothic fantasy, e.g., "The Temptation of St. Anthony," "The Martyrdom of St. Sebastian." From 1621 to 1635 he worked independently in Nancy, an artistic *honnête homme* working in the spirit of middle-class Catholic reform. His style in his late etchings became stoic, as in his chilling cycles of war, and morally rationalistic, as in his "L'Enfant prodigue."

Bibliography: F. BALDINUCCI, *Notizie de'professori del disegno . . .,* 6 v. in 3 (Florence 1681–1728). A. FÉLIBIEN, *Entretiens sur les vies et les ouvrages des plus excellens peintres . . .,* 5 v. (Paris 1666–88). Illus. catalogs. J. LIEURE, *Jacques Callot,* 5 v. (Paris 1924–29), prints. P. MAROT, *Jacques Callot d'après des documents inédits* (Paris 1939); "L'Apprentissage de Jacques Callot," in *Mélanges . . . Félix Grat,* 2 v. (Paris 1946–49). E. DE T. BECHTEL, *Jacques Callot* (New York 1955). D. TERNOIS, *L'Art de Jacques Callot* (Paris 1962), exhaustive bibliog.; comp., *Dessins de Jacques Callot* (Paris 1962). **Illustration credit:** National Gallery of Art, Washington, D.C. (Baumfeld Collection).

[O. J. ROTHROCK]

CALLUS, DANIEL ANGELO PHILIP, Dominican medievalist; b. Malta, Jan. 20, 1888, the son of Paul Callus-Azopardi and Theodora née Vella; d. Malta, May 26, 1965. He joined the order as a young man and studied at Malta, Fiesole, and Florence, where he took the degree of lector in theology and philosophy and followed university courses in palaeography, history of arts, and Semitic languages. He was ordained and did postgraduate work at the Angelicum in Rome, after which he taught as professor of theology at the Theological College of Malta from 1914 to 1921. Then

Jacques Callot, "Pillaging of a Convent," etching from "The Large Miseries of War," worked between 1633 and 1635.

came his first visit to England, where he was to make his home. He taught at the Dominican House of Studies at Hawkesyard, Staffordshire, from 1921 to 1923 and returned in 1931. He spent the intervening years as

Daniel Callus.

regent of studies, first at Viterbo and then in Malta. He took his degree as master of theology in 1924. In 1932 he settled permanently at the Oxford Blackfriars. Father Bede Jarrett, OP, had planned to make Blackfriars a center of scholarship that would be closely linked to the university: in Callus he found the man to realize his hopes. Callus worked under the supervision of the late Sir Maurice Powicke, then Regius Professor of Modern History, and himself became the center of a group of colleagues and pupils interested in medieval thought and learning. He received the degree of doctor of philosophy in 1938. Henceforward he regularly lectured, supervised, and examined and attended faculty meetings in the university; in addition he held the regency of studies at Blackfriars from 1942 to 1954. He read papers at many international congresses, made lecture tours in the U.S., and was visiting lecturer at the Angelicum for the last few years of his life. His researches into the history of early scholasticism took him to libraries all over Europe. The University of Malta honored him with a degree. His busy life as priest and teacher did not prevent him from publishing extensively, from 1917 onward. He was the acknowledged expert on the early history of the Oxford schools, especially of Aristotelian studies and of Thomism there. A bibliography of his published work up to 1963, with an appreciation of his life and writings, is to be found in *Oxford Studies Presented to Daniel Callus* [Oxford Historical Society, New Series 16 (Oxford 1964)].

[B. SMALLEY]

CALLY, PIERRE, Cartesian philosopher and theologian; b. Mesnil-Hubert, near Séez, date unknown; d. Caen, Dec. 31, 1709. His principal work, *Universae philosophiae institutiones* (Caen 1695), is a presentation and defense of the philosophy of Descartes. In the same year he published a copiously annotated edition of the *De consolatione philosophiae* of Boëthius. He was named professor of philosophy and eloquence at the University of Caen in 1660 and president of the *collège des arts* in the same city in 1675. In 1684 he was named pastor of the parish of St. Martin in Caen. He gave many conferences attempting to dispel the prejudices of

Protestants and for their benefit wrote a book on the Eucharist that caused him much trouble and embarrassment. Relying on Cartesian principles, he denied the possibility of transubstantiation, holding that the matter of bread became at the Consecration the matter of the body of Christ. He ordered 60 copies printed for private distribution to scholars, but his printer put 800 copies on general sale. The bishop of Bayeux, after consulting Bossuet, condemned the book. Cally submitted. Though it was not required of him, he publicly read the condemnation from his own pulpit, and he made efforts to dispose of existing copies. He published also a homiletic work on Christ as He appears in the Gospels, *Discours en forme d'homélies sur les mystères* (Caen 1703).

Bibliography: Hurter Nomencl³ 4:665–666. E. MANGENOT, DTC 2.2:1368–69. G. MARSOT, *Catholicisme* 2:392.

[A. ROCK]

CALMET, AUGUSTIN (ANTOINE), exegete and historian; b. Ménil-la-Horgne (Meuse), France, Feb. 26, 1672; d. Senones, France, Oct. 25, 1757. After his early studies at Breuil and the University of Pont-à-Mousson, he entered the Benedictine Abbey of Saint-Mansuy in Toul and was professed there, Oct. 23, 1689. He studied philosophy at Saint-Evre in Toul and theology at Munster in Alsace and was ordained, March 17, 1696. He became in turn professor at Moyen-Moutier (1698), subprior at Munster (1704), professor at Paris (1706), titular prior of Laye-Saint-Christophe (1716), abbot of Saint-Leopold in Nancy (1718), visitator of the Benedictine Congregation of St. Vanne and St. Hydulphe (1719), president of this congregation (1727), and abbot of Senones (1728).

Calmet was one of the best Catholic exegetes of the 18th century. He endeavored to adhere to the literal sense at a time when the influence of J. B. *Bossuet had made the spiritual and mystical interpretation of Scripture supreme. Yet his exegetical works are merely conscientious compilations and lack true critical judgment. These works include his *Commentaire littéral sur tous les livres de l'Ancient et du Nouveau Testament* (26 v. Paris 1707–16) and *Dictionnaire historique . . . de la Bible* (Paris 1719). Of much greater value is his *Histoire ecclésiastique et civile de la Lorraine* (3 v. Nancy 1728).

Bibliography: P. SCHMITZ, DHGE 11:450–453. G. RINALDI, EncCatt 3:397. P. AUVRAY, *Catholicisme* 2:392–393. P. VOLK, LexThK² 2:886. E. KUTSCH, RGG³ 1:1587. J. E. MANGENOT, DB 2.1:72–76. F. BECHTEL, CE 3:189.

[M. STRANGE]

CALOV, ABRAHAM, Lutheran dogmatic theologian and polemicist; b. Mohrungen, East Prussia, April 16, 1612; d. Wittenberg, Feb. 25, 1686. He studied at Königsberg (1626–32), received his doctorate at Rostock (1637), and became rector of the gymnasium at Danzig (1643) and pastor of Trinity church. From 1650 until his death he lived in Wittenberg, holding various academic and ecclesiastic positions. While a delegate to the Thorn Conference (1645), he came in contact with Georg *Calixtus. From that time on, he devoted himself to polemical activity directed against what he termed the syncretism of Calixtus and his followers. In his *Historia syncretistica* (1682) he attempts, as the outstanding champion of the controversial Lutheran orthodoxy of the 17th century, to show the erroneous agreements between the doctrines of Calixtus and those of Roman Catholics, Calvinists, Arminians, and Socinians. His work in theology, *Systema locorum theologicorum* (12 v. 1655–77), is considered one of the most important productions of the period. Here, as in his *Biblia illustrata* (4 v. 1672–76), he defends Lutheran orthodoxy against the intellectual forces that were preparing the way for the Enlightenment.

Bibliography: E. L. T. HENKE, *Georg Calixtus und seine Zeit,* 2 v. (Halle 1853–56). F. A. G. THOLUCK, *Der Geist der lutherischen Theologen Wittenbergs* (Hamburg 1852). F. LAU, RGG³ 1:1587. R. BÄUMER, LexThK² 2:886.

[C. J. BERSCHNEIDER]

CALUMNY, the blackening of an absent person's good name by telling a deliberate lie about him. This is sometimes called slander. The term "blackening" better describes the effects of calumny than do the more general terms "unjust violation" and "injury." Just as one's good name bestows a certain luster on a person, calumny either partially blackens or totally obscures this luster. Scripture tells us that "a good name is more precious than great riches" (Prv 22.1). In calumny a person steals part or all of another's good name, a good to which the person possesses a right in strict justice. Besides being a violation of the virtue of justice, calumny has the added malice of a lie.

Calumnious remarks can be slight offenses; thus one who tells a lie that does only slight harm to a person's reputation would be guilty of a venial sin. If a lie seriously blackens a person's reputation, the offense is grave. In any actual instance, the extent of the harm done to a person's reputation depends on the esteem in which the calumniated person was held by his fellow men, the crime, sin, or defect falsely attributed to him, and also the credibility of the calumniator. If the person calumniated is held in high esteem, one who falsely attributes a serious crime, sin, or defect to him is guilty of a serious violation of the person's rights. If, on the other hand, the calumniated person does not enjoy a good reputation, the damage to his reputation is slight.

If the calumniating person has a name for lying or notably exaggerating, his listeners probably do not believe him anyway. In this case, however, the calumniator's evil intention makes his action seriously sinful.

Because calumny blackens a person's good name, the offender is obliged to repair the damage he has done. If other damage, e.g., monetary damage, has been caused and this was foreseen, the calumniator is obliged to repair this also. Theologians agree that a blackened reputation can never be fully restored. The calumniator, however, is obliged to do all he can to restore the person's good name; hence he must first of all withdraw his false statements. He must also speak in a friendly manner about the person, show deference to him, etc. The awareness that a blackened good name can never be adequately restored should serve as an added deterrent to calumnious speech.

See also DEFAMATION; GOSSIP; DETRACTION; REPUTATION, MORAL RIGHT TO.

Bibliography: Merkelbach SumThMor 2:423–432. K. B. MOORE, *The Moral Principles Governing the Sin of Detraction* . . . (Washington 1950).

[K. B. MOORE]

CALVARY, the site of the Crucifixion of Jesus, identified with Golgotha and the Place of the Skull (Mt 27.33; Mk 15.22; Jn 19.17). The Greek equivalent is κρανίου τόπος, which in Lk 23.33 is given as the name of the Crucifixion site without mention of the Aramaic form Golgotha (skull). It is not known why the place was so called. Jerome suggested that the skulls of criminals lay about unburied; according to an early Christian tradition cited by Origen, it was believed that the skull of Adam was buried under the cross. But more probably the name is connected with the skull-like shape of the hill or rock.

Calvary was located outside Jerusalem (Mt 27.32; Mk 15.20; Heb 13.12) near a garden, where at least one tomb was located (Jn 19.41–42); it was a conspicuous place near the city (Jn 19.20), easily seen from a

Altar in the Church of the Holy Sepulcher at Jerusalem, marking the traditional site of the hill of Calvary.

distance (Mk 15.40; Lk 23.49), and probably near a country road (Mt 27.39; Mk 15.29). The traditional site of the Crucifixion dates back to the 4th century, when the Emperor Constantine (324–337) laid bare the rock and erected there the church of the Holy Sepulcher and the Resurrection. Calvary or Golgotha is located today within the compound of the Holy Sepulcher. Until A.D. 43, this site lay outside the northern wall of Jerusalem. Under the Emperor Hadrian (A.D. 117–138), Jerusalem was rebuilt and renamed Aelia Capitolina; the Calvary or Golgatha area and the Holy Sepulcher were covered with rubble and formed part of the forum of the new city. Today, sections of the original walls of the city, whose exact line has not yet been traced, can be seen. The small, modern chapel of the Holy Sepulcher is built over the bedrock on which the original tomb of Christ once stood.

See also SEPULCHER, HOLY.

Bibliography: C. KOPP, LexThK² 4:1046–47; *The Holy Places of the Gospels,* tr. R. WALLS (New York 1963) 374–388. U. HOLZMEISTER, EncCatt 3:400–401. EncDictBibl 887–888; 1021–23. L. H. VINCENT and F. M. ABEL, *Jérusalem nouvelle,* v.2 of *Jérusalem,* 2 v. in 4 (Paris 1912–26). A. PARROT, *Golgotha and the Church of the Holy Sepulcher,* tr. E. HUDSON (New York 1957). J. SIMONS, *Jerusalem in the OT* (Leiden 1952). **Illustration credit:** R. V. SCHODER, SJ.

[S. MUSHOLT]

CALVERT

The Calvert family played a prominent role in the establishment of an English colonial settlement that welcomed Catholics. Maryland was the center of Catholic life and culture in the 13 colonies at the time of the formation of the U.S.

George. First Lord Baltimore, founder of Maryland; b. Yorkshire, England, *c.* 1580; d. April 13, 1632. Leonard, a gentleman, and Alice (Crosland) Calvert, both Catholics, were his parents. During George's childhood, Leonard conformed to the Church of England under the pressure of penalties and the threatened arrest of his wife. At about the age of 12, George was placed under the instruction of an Anglican clergyman and was later graduated from Trinity College, Oxford, in 1597. Leonard won public office, thus opening the way for his son's subsequent career. George married Anne Mynne. After leaving college he became secretary to Sir (later Lord) Robert Cecil, then clerk of the privy council, to which office he soon succeeded. He served in Parliament from 1609 to 1624. In 1617 he was knighted and 2 years later became one of the principal secretaries of state, a sign of his friendship with the ruling House of Stuart. He was raised to peerage in 1625 and named Baron of Baltimore in the County of Longford in Ireland. His interests and services to the King included a commission for securing the religious pacification of Ireland through conformity; a Latin translation of the King's tract against a Dutch theologian; and support of the Spanish marriage for Prince Charles, to which some Catholic noblemen looked for relief from disabilities.

By 1620 Baltimore had become involved in colonizing activities with two Catholic families, the Arundells and the Howards. In 1628 he brought his family to his own chartered colony of Avalon in Newfoundland, and the following year visited Virginia. Baltimore's return to Catholicism had occurred not later than 1625 so his reception in Virginia was hostile. The King eased the ensuing hardships, acceding to Baltimore's desire for a colony free of religious oppression. The Maryland Charter reflected the flexibility of Baltimore in Church-State matters. He had earlier demonstrated this attitude when he signed a Catholic Remonstrance of Grievances stating that Catholics in England need not conform to what was purely disciplinary in the practices of Catholic states. The broad meaning of the charter did not require the application of discriminatory English statutes to the new colony.

Cecil. Eldest son of George, second Lord Baltimore, colonizer and proprietor of Mayland; b. London, 1606; d. London, Nov. 30, 1675. He was graduated from Oxford in 1621 and 8 years later, himself a Catholic, he married the Catholic Lady Anne Arundell of Wardour. Within a decade of his father's death, Cecil had successfully planted a colony of diverse faiths in Maryland. Before the departure for Maryland of the "Ark" and the "Dove" in 1633, he issued a memorable pamphlet, "Objections Answered," which justified his experiment with the principles of religious toleration and pluralism. Baltimore commissioned his brother, Leonard Calvert (1610–47), governor of the colony, enjoining him to enforce an "Instruction" designed to prevent religious disputes.

Baltimore did not succeed in providing the basic laws for Maryland. The colonists themselves had set about this work shortly after their arrival in America. John Lewger, secretary of the council, then tried to impose Baltimore's own code of laws. Like similar ones in England it made reference to penalties for blasphemy and to other religious matters. Thomas Cornwallis successfully led the assembly opposition, which was also defending its right to initiate legislation. The dominantly Catholic assembly adopted the *Toleration Act of 1639, which contained none of the controversial religious references of Baltimore's code. Instead, emphasis was put on the rights of Englishmen, whether Christian or not, and the state relaxed its authority over religion, in keeping with the views of English Catholics unsympathetic to the confessional-state theory.

A controversy between Baltimore and the Jesuits arose over matters related to these Church-State considerations. The original core of contention was the Jesuit title to land grants from the Indians. When the Jesuit, Thomas Copley, made dubious applications of Church law and teaching to this question, Calvert invoked the principle of the Remonstrance of the first Lord Baltimore. Henry More, the major Jesuit superior, did not support Copley's contentions and Baltimore did nothing about the legitimate basis of grievance originally stated by the Jesuits.

Although Baltimore, as a Cavalier, inevitably became an opponent of Parliamentarians and Puritans, he was not bitterly partisan. Amid the discriminatory measures that came into law during Puritan control in England, he secured passage of the *Toleration Act of 1649 in Maryland. Peace did not entirely return, however, until 1660 when Baltimore's half-brother, Philip Calvert, assumed the governorship.

Charles. The third Lord Baltimore, last Catholic proprietor; b. London, 1629; d. Epson, Surrey, Feb. 20, 1715. He was the eldest son of Cecil and Anne (Arundell) Calvert and married Jane Lowe, widow of Henry Sewall of Maryland. To them was born Benedict Leonard, fourth Lord Baltimore and first Protestant proprietor of Maryland. Charles served as governor

George Calvert, first Lord Baltimore.

from 1661 to 1684, became lord proprietor in 1675, and interpreted proprietary authority and privilege strictly. He required property holding for membership in the lower house of the assembly, which had challenged his aristocratic rule. The policy affected Catholic freemen, who nevertheless saw in a strong proprietary party a defense of their religious freedom.

A Protestant revolution in England in 1688 was all that was needed to induce anti-Catholic feeling to support the overthrow of the Calverts in Maryland. It was effected by Coode's Rebellion and a royal colony was created, the Church of England established, and in 1718 an estimated 10 per cent of the population were disfranchised for their Catholicism. Baltimore's son Benedict Leonard conformed to the Church of England and thereby qualified for the proprietorship in 1715. Neither father nor son seemed to possess the character of the first two Barons of Baltimore. But the third Lord Baltimore had brought Charles *Carroll to Maryland during these troubled times as his attorney general, thus ensuring the continuation of Catholic tradition in Maryland's public life. Benedict Leonard survived his father by only a few months and his son Charles assumed the proprietorship while still in his minority.

Bibliography: W. H. BROWNE, *George Calvert and Cecilius Calvert, Barons Baltimore of Baltimore* (New York 1890). T. O. HANLEY, *Their Rights and Liberties: The Beginnings of Religious and Political Freedom in Maryland* (Westminster, Md. 1959). J. M. IVES, *The Ark and the Dove* (New York 1936). **Illustration credit:** Maryland Historical Society.

[T. O. HANLEY]

CALVET, JEAN, French critic and literary historian; b. Castelnau-Montratier, department of Lot, Jan. 17, 1874; d. Sèvres (Seine-et-Oise), Jan. 26, 1965. He was of peasant birth, but his family included municipal judges in Toulouse. His studies in French, Latin, and Greek literature were begun at the Montfaucon minor seminary and completed at the Cahors major seminary and the Institut Catholique of Toulouse. He was ordained in 1896, received an arts degree the following year, and after 3 years at the Institut Catholique of Paris was qualified to teach in the lycées. Having refused an official position at the Lycée of Vannes, he taught at the Institut Catholique of Toulouse (1904–07) and at the Collège Stanislas of Paris (1907–21). He became professor of literature at the Institut Catholique of Paris in 1921 and dean of the institute in 1934. At the request of Cardinal Emmanuel *Suhard, he was made acting rector following the death of Cardinal Henri *Baudrillart. Although nominated as rector (1945), he resigned before receiving confirmation of his appointment from Rome. In recognition of his outstanding services, Pius XII expressed his gratitude to him in a letter while Monsignor Calvet was rector emeritus. From then on, he lived alternately in Sèvres, a suburb of Paris, and on his Vernède estate in Sauveterre, department of Tarn-et-Garonne.

Calvet's works include *Manuel de littérature* (1920), highly praised by Henri *Bremond; *Bossuet* (1941); *Polyeucte* (1944); *Molière est-il chrétien?* (1950); *Les Types universels dans la littérature française* (1928); *L'Enfant dans la littérature française* (1930); *Le Bestiaire de la littérature française* (1954); *Saint Vincent de Paul* (1948); and *La Littérature religieuse de François de Sales à Fénelon* (1938). This last work was included in the 10-volume *Histoire de la littérature française,* which was published under his direction in collaboration with professors from the Sorbonne and the Catholic institutes: "the Calvet workshop," as Albert Thibaudet put it.

Further works were the literary sketches *Les Témoins de la conscience française* (1943); *Visages d'un demi-siècle* (1958); lively accounts of the native soil, *Contes de la vieille France* (1925), under the name of Jean Quercy; and two collections of meditations, *La Trame des jours* (1955) and *La Lumière de complies* (1960). In addition, he contributed authoritative articles to the *Catholic Encyclopedia.* His sound judgments, balanced thought, and firm, temperate, picturesque style commanded attention.

[L. CHAIGNE]

CALVIN, JOHN

After Martin Luther the most important Protestant reformer and theologian; b. Noyon, France, July 10, 1509; d. Geneva, May 27, 1564. Calvin, influenced by Luther, with whom his background and temperament are in sharp contrast, gave Protestant doctrine its most incisive and systematic formulation. His *Institutes of the Christian Religion,* which first appeared in 1536, is early Protestantism's greatest theological work. Calvin's thought and influence, emanating from Geneva, where he lived without interruption from late 1541 to his death, dominated Protestantism in France, the Netherlands, and Scotland. Calvinism also became a strong movement in England and in parts of Germany and central Europe.

John Calvin, 16th-century portrait by an anonymous artist.

Early Years. Calvin's family background was middle class. His father, Gérard Cauvin (Calvin is the Latinized form), had settled in 1481 in the episcopal town of Noyon in Picardy, where he became a solicitor and fiscal agent for the diocese, a secretary to the bishop, and a procurator of the cathedral chapter. His mother was Jeanne Le Franc, the daughter of a retired innkeeper from Cambrai. John was the second of four sons and two daughters. His father's close relations with the bishop and with the cathedral chapter opened the way toward ecclesiastical careers for Calvin and his brothers. "My father intended me as a young boy for theology," he writes in the autobiographical preface to his *Commentary on the Psalms* (1557). His early schooling was in the local Collège des Capettes where he proved a serious and able student. In 1521 he received a cathedral benefice by way of endowment for his studies; in 1527 he was given a second benefice.

Training at Paris. When he was 14, Calvin was sent to Paris with three young members of the noble Hangest family—Charles de Hangest was Bishop of Noyon—to continue his studies. For a short time he attended the Collège de la Marche, where he studied grammar and rhetoric under the humanist Mathurin Cordier and began a lifelong friendship with this scholar, who years later joined him in Geneva. He soon transferred to the austere Collège de Montaigu for theology. There he was introduced to nominalist theology under the auspices of John Major and apparently undertook the study of the early Fathers, especially St. Augustine. In these formative years he became intimately acquainted with the

family of Guillaume Cop, the scholarly physician of Francis I, and formed a close association with a humanist cousin, Pierre Robert *Olivétan, who had already been influenced by the Lutheran teachings. In 1528 Calvin received his master of arts degree at Paris, but about this time his father had a change of mind about theology and directed him to the study of law, which he deemed more lucrative. This change of mind has been linked to a dispute that Calvin *père* was having with the cathedral chapter in Noyon over the closing of an estate and that resulted in his excommunication. In obedience to his father Calvin proceeded to the University of Orléans, where he studied under the famous French jurist Pierre de l'Estoile. The following year, attracted by the reputation of the Italian jurist Andrea Alciati, he went on to Bourges. At both Orléans and Bourges he also pursued his humanist studies and interests, learning Greek from the German Lutheran scholar Melchior Wolmar.

The illness and death of his father in May 1531 occasioned Calvin's hurried return to Noyon and terminated his studies in law. Free now to devote himself to the literary scholarship that most interested him, he returned to Paris and attended the new Collège de France, recently founded by Francis I. He continued his Greek with Pierre Danès and studied Hebrew with François Vatable. In April 1532, he published at his own expense his first book, a commentary on Seneca's *De clementia,* a treatise in the tradition of Erasmus and Budé, intended to launch the young humanist on his scholarly career.

The Sudden Conversion. Humanist study was not to be Calvin's life work, or long remain his chief preoccupation. Sometime in late 1533 or early 1534 he underwent, in his own words, a "sudden conversion" and embraced the doctrines of the Protestant reformers. Neither the time nor the circumstances are known with exactness. (Discussion in Wendel, 37–44.) One event closely connected with this great turn in his life was the inaugural address that his friend Nicholas Cop, the son of the royal physician and the new rector of the University of Paris, delivered on All Saints Day, 1533. The address, borrowing passages from Erasmus and Luther, brought speedy action by the Parlement of Paris against Cop, who fled to Basel, and the others suspected of harboring heretical ideas. Calvin, who for a time was thought to have been the author of the discourse, was threatened with arrest and took refuge with a friend, Louis du Tillet, at Angoulême. There in temporary retirement, with a large library at his disposal, he gathered his thoughts and perhaps arrived at the great decision to break with the Church and devote himself wholly to the cause of Protestant reform. During these critical days he visited the famous Lefèvre d'Etaples, the humanist and scriptural scholar, then living under the protection of Marguerite of Angoulême at her court at Nérac. In May 1534 he returned to Noyon to surrender his ecclesiastical benefices, and at the end of the year, as a result of the stringent measures being taken against heretics, he left France for haven in Protestant Basel.

Publication of the Institutes. It was in Basel that his career as reformer and theologian began. In contact and correspondence with Protestant leaders in the Swiss and Rhenish cities, he undertook a formulation of the new theological ideas under debate. *See* CALVINISM; PREDESTINATION (IN NON-CATHOLIC THEOLOGY); INFRALAPSARIANS (SUBLAPSARIANS); SUPRALAPSARIANS; AR-

MINIANISM; JUSTIFICATION, 3. IN PROTESTANT THEOL-
OGY; CONFESSIONS OF FAITH, PROTESTANT.

These ideas he published in March 1536 in *Institutio religionis Christianae* (*Institutes of the Christian Religion*), the first edition of his master work, which was to reappear in several enlarged revisions and translations during the course of his life. The *Institutes*, prefaced by a bold letter to Francis I of France, was originally intended to be a statement and defense of the beliefs of the French Protestants then being persecuted. About the time that the treatise appeared Calvin paid a visit to Ferrara to see the Duchess Renée, daughter of the former Louis XII of France and a woman sympathetic to the Protestant movement. He returned to Paris to settle some family business and in June 1536 set out again for asylum abroad. His intention was to go to Strassburg, but war between the French and Emperor Charles V obliged him to take a detour through Geneva. He planned to spend but a night in that town. However, his fellow countryman Guillaume *Farel, who had been working in Geneva to implant the new Gospel, pleaded with him to remain and help in the task. Calvin yielded to Farel's forceful entreaty and made Geneva henceforth the scene of his active ministry.

Protestantism in Geneva. When Calvin came to Geneva, he found a city of 13,000 inhabitants engaged in a struggle to maintain municipal independence against the Duke of Savoy in league with the ousted Bishop of Geneva. The neighboring city of Berne, militantly Protestant since 1528, had aided Geneva, and it was under its auspices that Protestant preachers had entered Geneva as early as 1532. Farel was the most important of these missionaries. In the months prior to Calvin's arrival he had won the city government's acceptance of the new reforms, as well as the proscription of Catholicism, but the task of firmly establishing and organizing the new Genevan church remained. This task Calvin made his own. In January 1537 he submitted a memorandum on church government to the town councils. This was followed by a *Confession of Faith* and a *Catechism*. From the start Calvin envisaged a strict unity of belief and practice and a close supervision of conduct that included the excommunication of recalcitrants.

Exile at Strassburg. The uniformity and discipline that Calvin sought evoked opposition from Catholics as well as from those alarmed at the rigid, theocratic character of the new reforms. In early 1538 the Genevan government passed into the hands of those hostile to Calvin, and in April the town councils, as a result of a dispute over liturgical forms, banished Farel and Calvin from the city. From April 1538 to September 1541 he settled in Strassburg, at the invitation of Martin *Bucer, and took charge of a church for French Protestant refugees. Under Bucer's influence he developed his own liturgy in the French language, revised and published in 1539 a new edition of the *Institutes*, lectured on Holy Scripture, and in 1540 published the first of many volumes of scriptural *Commentaries*. He also attended the colloquies at Worms in 1540 and at Regensburg in 1541, convened by Emperor Charles V in an effort to end the religious schism. In 1540 he married the widow of one of his converts, Idelette of Buren, who bore him a son who died soon after birth. She herself died in 1549.

Ecclesiastical Ordinances. Meanwhile, in Geneva there continued division and contention, in the midst of which Calvin's supporters urged his recall. In October

1540, with the city government again controlled by the pro-Calvin faction, an embassy was sent to Strassburg to invite him to return. After hesitation Calvin agreed, and in September 1541 he reentered the city on Lake Leman to remain there for the rest of his life. In November he submitted to the town authorities a new constitution, the *Ecclesiastical Ordinances*, which was approved with modifications to safeguard their own civil jurisdiction. These *Ordinances* were the groundwork of the so-called theocracy in Geneva and became the charter of all future Calvinist church polity. They provided for four ministries or offices—pastors, teachers, elders, and deacons—and for a consistory of elders and pastors to maintain strict discipline in the community. Under the close and constant supervision of this latter body Geneva was intended to become a saintly city, a "kind of huge convent for laity." The *Ordinances* were supplemented in 1542 by the adoption of a new liturgical formula, modeled after that of Strassburg, and the drafting of a new *Catechism* for the instruction of the young.

Conflicts and Executions. A long struggle to reach Calvin's stern ideal ensued. One of the many conflicts was the quarrel with Sebastian *Castellio, whom Calvin had made schoolmaster in Geneva. A dispute on certain minor doctrinal points led in 1545 to Castellio's banishment from the city. Jacques Gruet, a more extreme critic of Calvin and the consistory, was found guilty of blasphemy in 1547 and beheaded. In 1551 Jérôme *Bolsec, a former Carmelite who attacked Calvin's doctrine of predestination and defended free will, was imprisoned and subsequently banished. The most famous of all these cases is that of Michael *Servetus (Michael Served y Reves), Spanish physician and anti-Trinitarian. In flight from France, he passed through Geneva, August 1553, was arrested on Calvin's demand, tried for heresy and blasphemy, and burned alive. Calvin faced political opposition also during these years. From 1546 the "libertines," headed by Ami Perrin, a former supporter of Calvin, criticized the ecclesiastical police system and resisted the encroachments of a theocratic regime. They were overcome in 1554–55 when stanch Calvinists gained full control of the municipal government and affirmed the consistory's right of excommunication. Perrin escaped to Berne, but four other leaders, less fortunate, were caught and beheaded.

Last Years. Although polemical disputes continued with the Lutherans and Italian anti-Trinitarians, Calvin's dominance was secure. Large numbers of refugees flocked to Geneva, and efforts of evangelization abroad, particularly within Calvin's native France, were made. In 1559 the Academy of Geneva was founded at Calvin's suggestion, and Theodore *Beza, later designated as his successor, was made rector. Calvin suffered gravely from ill health in his last years, but he continued the direction of his church and the preaching of the Word as he so sternly conceived it up to the end.

Bibliography: Works. *Joannis Calvini opera quae supersunt omnia*, ed. G. BAUM et al., 59 v. (CorpRef 29–87; 1863–1900); *Institutes of the Christian Religion*, tr. J. T. McNEILL, tr. F. L. BATTLES, 2 v. (Philadelphia 1960); *Theological Treatises*, tr. J. K. S. REID (Philadelphia 1954); *Commentaries . . .*, tr. J. HAROUTUNIAN and L. P. SMITH (Philadelphia 1958) includes autobiographical preface 51–57; *Tracts and Treatises . . .*, ed. T. F. TORRANCE, tr. H. BEVERIDGE, 3 v. (Grand Rapids 1958) includes short life of Calvin by T. BEZA.
Literature. É. DOUMERGUE, *Jean Calvin*, 7 v. (Lausanne 1899–1927), the classic life. F. WENDEL, *Calvin . . .*, tr. P. MAIRET (New York 1963). Q. BREEN, *John Calvin: A Study in French*

Humanism (Grand Rapids 1931). J. T. McNeill, *The History and Character of Calvinism* (New York 1954). G. E. Harkness, *John Calvin: The Man and His Ethics* (New York 1958). A. Lanz, EncCatt 3:402–417. P. Imbart de La Tour, *Les Origines de la réforme,* 4 v. (Paris 1905–35). A. Ganoczy, *Calvin, théologien du ministère et de l'Église* (Paris 1964). A. Baudrillart, DTC 2.2:1377–98. O. E. Strasser and O. Weber, RGG³ 1:1588–99. **Illustration credit:** Archiv für Kunst und Geschichte, Berlin.

[J. C. Olin]

CALVINISM

Calvinism is the theological system elaborated by the French reformer, John *Calvin, chiefly in the *Institutes of the Christian Religion* (1536–59). *See* INSTITUTES OF CALVIN. This synthesis, which justifies his title as the "theological genius of the Reformation," was the first systematic presentation of Protestantism as well as the doctrinal background for most non-Lutheran churches of the Reformed tradition. This article treats Calvinism under the headings: (1) Calvinism as a system, (2) doctrinal structure, (3) historical development, (4) geographical expansion.

Calvinism as a Theological System

Although Calvinism is a systematic synthesis, it is not a system properly so-called with a central idea, an articulated development, and a rigid harmony such as that of Aristotelianism, Thomism, or Kantianism.

A Qualified System. Calvin was 27 when he published the first edition of his *Christianae Religionis Institutio.* His intention, as he declared in the "Epistle to the King" (Francis I, 1515–47), which prefaced the work, was to write an exposition, as simple as possible, of Christian doctrine by which "those who are touched with any zeal for religion might be shaped to true godliness" (*Library of Christian Classics,* 20:9). Throughout the rest of his life, up to the time of the definitive Latin edition (1559) and its French translation (1560), Calvin amplified his treatise, revised and polished it, until it became a complete presentation and an authoritative statement of Calvinism. The training in logic Calvin had received at the Collège de Montaigu and his legal education from the jurists of Orléans and Bourges are evident in the construction of his theological thought. Nevertheless, neither the *Institutes* nor any of his other writings are the work of a logician. Calvin's dogmatic formulation cannot be compared in power of reasoning to the *Metaphysics* of Aristotle, the *Summa Theologiae* of St. Thomas, or the *Ethics* of Spinoza, not because of a lack of logical concentration but because of his particular dogmatic conviction that the Scriptures are the necessary and sufficient source of man's knowledge of God for salvation. Since all that is required for salvation is in the Scriptures and in them alone, Calvin in presenting his thought had to follow a method of systematizing the teaching of the Bible into a coherent whole.

The content of the Bible is not like a set of basic principles upon which a thoroughly unified philosophy can be erected by means of rigorous logic. Its many themes allow for coherence but not for rigid dogmatic systematization. Therefore, insofar as Calvin remained faithful to the Biblical foundations of his theology, Calvinism can be called a system only in a qualified sense.

Central Idea. In the past the tendency has been to regard predestination as the focal point of Calvin's theology. Then the sovereignty of God, and more recently, the divinity of Christ, was proposed as the constitutive principle of Calvinism. What appears the better view today, however, is that Calvinism is not a closed system that revolves around one central idea. Rather than build his system around one pivotal abstract notion, Calvin seems to have preferred to draw together a number of Biblical ideas. As he developed each, he tried to fit it into a harmonious exposition of doctrine. While his attempts at this reconciliation of ideas were often ingenious and valid, sometimes they did not succeed, but became contrived and resulted in what are called "the paradoxes of Calvin."

Sources. The first and indisputable source of Calvin's theological system was the Bible. Calvin read and knew the Bible thoroughly, producing commentaries on almost every book. Perhaps no other reformer had such a remarkable knowledge of the Old Testament. What is significant about this knowledge for Calvin's dogmatic system is that, while he did indicate that the Old Testament promises what the New Testament offers in Christ (*Inst.* 2.11.4), Calvin had little or no idea of progressive revelation. This factor influenced him to see the church everywhere in Scripture, for example, and to attribute to texts from the Psalms or Isaia or Malachia applicability equal to that of the New Testament to the life of the church for all time. The weakness of this approach appears particularly in Calvin's treatment of ethics. It also tended to make the Bible a book of texts in which it was necessary to find confirmation for dogmatic positions. The Fathers of the Church form an important background for Calvin's system. He probably made contact with them for the first time at the Collège de Montaigu, and all his life he deepened his knowledge of their Greek and Latin writings (see the exhaustive index of references made in the *Library of Christian Classics,* 21:1592–1634). Though St. John Chrysostom seemed to have been his favorite at one time, St. Augustine's influence was predominant and unique. Calvin read St. Augustine constantly, quoted him frequently, and felt that he was in substantial agreement with him.

Calvin knew and drew upon scholastic authors as well. He was acquainted with the works of St. Anselm, Peter Lombard, and St. Thomas Aquinas. But it is to Duns Scotus and William of Ockham that he appears to have been particularly attracted. A number of authors have traced the Calvinist concept of God to Duns Scotus, and while this view has been questioned by E. Doumergue, A. Lecerf, and others, still the resemblance between Calvin's doctrine on God (e.g., *Inst.* 3.23.2) and Scotus's teaching is too strong to be ignored. The nominalist influence on Calvin's giving primacy to the will of God manifests itself also in his making the efficacy of the Passion of Christ (*Inst.* 2.17.1), the transmission of the sin of Adam (*Inst.* 2.1.8), and the nature of the Mediator as God and man (*Inst.* 2.12.1), all depend upon the decree of God.

Calvin was in full agreement with Luther on the fundamental doctrines of justification, the total perversion of man, original sin, Christ the unique Savior, and the appropriation of salvation through the Holy Spirit, the Word, and the sacraments. After 1536, however, Calvin parted with Luther over the question of the Lord's Supper, and gradually, as Calvin developed his system, differences appeared also on matters of the canon of Scripture, predestination, the church, Christ, and the sacraments. Such differences, while making Calvinism distinct from Lutheranism, are less important than the fundamental agreement on the doctrine of justification by faith.

Philipp Melanchthon, especially through his *Loci Communes* (1531), must be looked upon as one of the sources of Calvin's thought. Calvin wrote the preface to the French translation (Geneva 1546). He, moreover, signed the Confession of Augsburg (1530) and considered that he was in full agreement with it, although he differed with Melanchthon on free will and predestination, as he declared in the preface to Melanchthon's book.

Martin Bucer and Calvin were personal friends and the accord is evident in their works. The influence of Bucer on Calvin is seen particularly in his doctrine of predestination. Calvin adopted Bucer's point of view on the definitive character of predestination and on the part played in it by vocation, justification, and glorification. At the same time, he affirmed the distinction between predestination and foreknowledge whereas Bucer fused them together (*Inst.* 3.21.5).

DOCTRINAL STRUCTURE

An initial general summary of Calvin's doctrines will give perspective to the more detailed study of the Reformer's principal tenets: true wisdom consists in a knowledge of God and of ourselves. Only in the light of the knowledge of God can true self-knowledge be found. God makes Himself known in a twofold revelation; as Creator through the visible universe and as Redeemer, i.e., as the saving knowledge of God, through Scripture alone. Scripture points to Christ, the sole Mediator, by whom salvation is achieved. Salvation is ours through the secret operation of the Holy Spirit and faith. Faith is necessary since by Adam's fall all men are under the blight of sin and divine judgment. Salvation is due to God's mercy, which is extended to those whom in His inscrutable will He has eternally chosen to receive it; others are justly excluded from the operation of His saving grace and suffer the consequences of their sin. Justification is by faith alone, but because of our ignorance and sloth we stand in need of such external helps as the preaching of the Gospel in His church and the administration of the sacraments of baptism and the Lord's supper. The church is both invisible and visible: the invisible church consists of all those who, by confession, example, and participation in the sacraments, profess God and Christ; the visible church has as its marks: the preaching and the hearing of the Gospel and the administration of the sacraments.

The Sovereignty of God. The *Institutes* begins with the statement: "Nearly all the wisdom we possess, that is to say, true and sound wisdom, consists of two parts: the knowledge of God and of ourselves" (*Inst.* 1.1.1.). To set forth all relations between God and man is the task of Calvin's entire theological structure. As Luther before him, the Genevan reformer declared that "our very being is nothing but subsistence in the one God" (*ibid.*). Whether Calvin intended to counteract Lutheran preoccupation with man or whether through his own firm conviction, he went beyond Luther's idea of gratuitous salvation to that of the complete sovereignty of God. God is all in the order of ends as well as of

means; everything tends toward His glory. This doctrine colors his viewpoint concerning rational inquiry into the nature of God. For Calvin it is futile and even presumptuous to ask "Quis est Deus?" because "His essence is incomprehensible; hence his divineness far escapes all human perception" (*Inst.* 1.5.1.).

Thus Calvin conceives of God in terms of His supreme will that is absolute law, ". . . the truly just cause of all things" (*Inst.* 1.17.1). From it comes every decree by which all is ordered: God has "decreed what he was going to do, and now, by his might, carries out what he has decreed" (*Inst.* 1.16.8). Nor may this decree be questioned. Calvin declares: "God's will is so much the highest rule of righteousness that whatever he wills, by the very fact that he wills it, must be considered righteous. When, therefore, one asks why has God so done, we must reply: because he has willed it" (*Inst.* 3.23.2). Calvin's view of God is also connected with his view of the Bible. No one, according to Calvin, can attain to the knowledge of God unless he is taught by the Holy Scriptures (*Inst.* 1.6.2), which must be read with faith and under the enlightenment of the Holy Spirit, viz, "Therefore Scripture will ultimately suffice for a saving knowledge of God only when it certainly is founded upon the inward persuasion of the Holy Spirit" (*Inst.* 1.8.13).

The Depravity of Man. When man looks at God through the Scriptures he arrives at a knowledge of the complete sovereignty of God. When he looks at himself through the Scriptures, he sees his own total depravity. The Bible gives us this view of man's condition in the story of the Fall, where the image of God in man was not utterly destroyed, ". . . yet it was so corrupted that whatever remains is frightful deformity" (*Inst.* 1.15.4). By total depravity Calvin means the complete inability of man to institute or maintain a right relation with God by his human activity alone. Calvin's emphasis is on the order of salvation and on man's total dependence on God for justification. When Calvin turns momentarily in the *Institutes* (2.2.13) to those interests of man that belong to the present life, such as political doctrine, the mechanical arts, philosophy, and the liberal arts, he readily grants that man can do many wonderful things.

Man's will, however, is bound by the slavery of sin. If the question is raised, "Is man bound to commit sin?" Calvin answers that if man commits sin, he does so voluntarily; he has a strong propensity to sin, but he is not coerced (*Inst.* 2.3.5). Calvin also distinguishes what seems to be a denial of free will. Man's will is not destroyed, according to Calvin, but he cannot of himself will faith: ". . . free will is not sufficient to enable man to do good works, unless he be helped by grace" (*Inst.* 2.2.6). The reformer's point is that God brings justification by His activity and not man by his. Through justification the sinner is accepted even though he is a sinner, since man is inevitably a sinner.

Faith in Christ. Man in his sinful state needs a saving contact with God. This he obtains in Christ, the sole Mediator, but he does not initiate this movement toward union with Christ. "Faith is the principal work of the Holy Spirit" (*Inst.* 3.1.4). It is "a firm and certain knowledge of God's benevolence toward us, founded upon the truth of the freely given promise in Christ, both revealed to our minds and sealed upon our hearts through the Holy Spirit" (*Inst.* 3.2.7). Even faith, however, of itself has no power nor worth. "We say that faith justifies," explains Calvin, "not because it merits righteousness for us by its own worth, but because it is an instrument whereby we obtain free the righteousness of Christ" (*Inst.* 3.18.8). Here again Calvin insists on the complete power of God and the corresponding impotency of man to do anything of himself to gain salvation. The faith that is received by man from the Holy Spirit unites him to Christ and that union is a precondition whereby ". . . we principally receive a double grace: namely, that being reconciled to God through Christ's blamelessness, we may have in heaven instead of a Judge a gracious Father; and secondly, that sanctified by Christ's spirit we may cultivate blamelessness and purity of life" (*Inst.* 3.11.1). The first of these gifts Calvin calls justification or righteousness and the second, regeneration or sanctification.

By regeneration Christ becomes man's living Lord; he is grafted into the body of Christ. The consequence of this union is that man lives by the spirit of Christ. No longer is life to be lived apart from God; the Christian life ". . . consists in the mortification of our flesh and of the old man, and in the vivification of the Spirit" (*Inst.* 3.3.5). The doctrine of justification, for Calvin, is the "main hinge on which religion turns" (*Inst.* 3.11.1). He views it under the figure of a court trial. The accused is freed or "justified" if he has a witness to affirm his righteousness. "We are sinners and therefore deserve to be condemned, but because of our communion with Christ through faith, we receive His righteousness with him" (*Inst.* 3.11.10). We are not made righteous, but simply are clothed with Christ's righteousness. God, seeing us in Christ, or rather, seeing Christ's righteousness, makes a judgment of "justification." This judicial act has two parts: the forgiveness of sins and the imputation of Christ's righteousness (*Inst.* 3.11.2). These parts are not successive, but are rather like two sides of the one action. Justification, however, is not a single act. If it were, the good works of the once-justified sinner would condemn him again since all man's works are contaminated by sin. God, therefore, not only justifies the sinner but also justifies the justified in his works so that they are not imputed to him as sins. This is Calvin's doctrine of double justification (*Inst.* 3.17.5).

Predestination. Calvin's doctrine of double predestination to election or reprobation is the result of both his logic and his doctrinal principles. Given his conviction on the absolute sovereignty of God and on man's complete inability to contribute to his salvation, the doctrine of predestination is a necessary foundation stone in his system. But practical reasons also entered into its formulation. Only by placing salvation in the divine will could the believer be freed from placing trust in merits and works for salvation. Moreover, such a doctrine was needed for Calvin's ecclesiology. "We call predestination," Calvin explains, "God's eternal decree, by which he determined with himself what he willed to become of each man. For all are not created in equal condition; rather, eternal life is foreordained for some, eternal damnation for others" (*Inst.* 3.21.5). This decree of God is so absolute that it is independent of God's foreknowledge, and a fortiori cannot be thwarted by anyone. Grace is irresistible. Just as sinful man necessarily wills evil, so the elect or the justified man necessarily conforms to God's desires. Commenting

on St. Augustine's treatise, *De correptione et gratia ad Valentinum* (PL 44: 935, 939, 943), Calvin declares: ". . . it is . . . grace which forms both choice and will in the heart, so that whatever good works then follow are the fruit and effect of grace; and it has no other will obeying it except the will that it has made" (*Inst.* 2.3.13). Calvin felt obliged to affirm the doctrine of reprobation. It appalled him, but with invincible candor as well as logic he maintained that the decree of reprobation is incomprehensible but absolutely just. The reprobate is condemned justly (*Inst.* 3.21.7). The ultimate reason of the *decretum horribile* is to manifest the glory of God in the very mystery in which it is veiled.

The Church and the Sacraments. Because of man's ignorance and sloth, he stands in need of external helps to sustain and confirm his gift of faith. Therefore, declares Calvin, God, in accommodation of this infirmity, has established the church and the two sacraments of baptism and the eucharist. The church, which Calvin calls "mother" from St. Cyprian (*De catholicae ecclesiae unitate* 6; CSEL 3.1.214), is a divinely constituted institution and therefore is necessary. There is no salvation outside it: ". . . away from her bosom one cannot hope for any forgiveness of sins or any salvation" (*Inst.* 4.1.4.). The church is both visible and invisible. Under its visible aspect it is the Christian community; the invisible church includes all the elect of God and coincides with both the communion of the saints and with the body of Christ. The visible church, because it includes reprobates in its midst, is to that extent not the body of Christ. But it does not follow that two churches exist. Rather, it is one church under two aspects: invisible insofar as it is an object of faith, or as God sees it; visible as it is an object of experience and as it appears to men (*Inst.* 4.1.7). To judge the presence of the true church, Calvin, as Luther before him in the Augsburg Confession (art. 7), sets forth two objective criteria: "Whenever we see the Word of God purely preached and heard, and the sacraments administered according to Christ's institution, there, it is not to be doubted, a church of God exists" (*Inst.* 4.1.9).

Calvin defines a sacrament as "an outward sign by which the Lord seals on our consciences the promises of his good will toward us in order to sustain the weakness of our faith; a testimony of divine grace toward us, confirmed by an outward sign, with mutual attestation of our piety toward him" (*Inst.* 4.14.1). In Calvin's doctrine, the sacraments do not contain or confer grace but mirror the reality that they symbolize. The reality, promised by Christ and made effective by Him, is given at the same time that the material symbols of the sacraments are received. Thus Calvin says in regard to the eucharist: "Now, if it be asked nevertheless whether the bread is the body of Christ, and the wine his blood, we should reply that the bread and wine are visible signs, which represent to us the body and the blood; but that the name and title of body and blood is attributed to them, because they are as instruments by which our Lord Jesus Christ distributes them to us." Calvin continues: "It is a spiritual mystery, which cannot be seen by the eye, nor comprehended by the human understanding. It is therefore symbolized by visible signs, as our infirmity requires, but in such a way that it is not a bare figure, but joined to its reality and substance" (*Short Treatise on the Lord's Supper*, 2. *Library of Christian Classics*, 22:147). Thus the effects of the sacraments are given because of the promise of Christ, are received by faith, are gained by the elect alone, and are sealed by the outward signs. They bring man into communion with Christ, from whom he receives everything that Christ gained by his death and resurrection. What are these benefits? Calvin summarizes: "Baptism attests to us that we have been cleansed and washed; the Eucharistic Supper, that we have been redeemed" (*Inst.* 4.14.22). In short: ". . . redemption, righteousness, sanctification, and eternal life" (*Inst.* 4.17.11).

HISTORICAL DEVELOPMENT

Calvinism as a doctrinal system inevitably evolved not only into a structure of church order (generally called *Presbyterianism) but also into a particular way of life, as exemplified in Calvin's reign over the city of Geneva. In this growth, Calvinism underwent structural and doctrinal modifications.

Doctrinal Disputes. The first break in the rigor of Calvinistic doctrine came in Holland. Holland had become solidly Calvinistic after the successful fight against Philip II by William of Orange, who declared himself a Calvinist in 1573. But the very strength of the uniformity Calvinism exacted brought a reaction. The successor to Calvin, Theodore *Beza, had added to the doctrine of predestination by a position known as supralapsarianism (*see* SUPRALAPSARIANS), in which the decree of election preceded the fall of man, so that the fallen state was part of the eternal plan of God. Dirck *Coornhert, a Dutch theologian, challenged Beza's position with a doctrine of conditional predestination, or *infralapsarianism, that made the divine decree succeed the fall rather than precede or determine it. To the strongly orthodox Calvinists of Holland both of the positions differing with Beza's were heretical. In 1589 they invited Jacob *Arminius (Hermandszoon), once a student of Beza, to refute Coornhert and the infralapsarians. Arminius, however, found that as he studied the question, he could not defend the orthodox position and instead developed a doctrine that differed from both supralapsarianism and infralapsarianism.

Arminius was attacked by Franciscus *Gomarus, a strong supralapsarian, and had to defend himself against the charges of Pelagianism and Socinianism. In 1610 the followers of Arminius presented a remonstrance to the government for protection against the orthodox Calvinists. In the petition the *Remonstrants set forth five theses concerning their view of predestination. The government authorities summoned a national synod at Dort (Dordrecht) from Nov. 13, 1618, to May 9, 1619, through 154 formal sessions. It was attended not only by Dutch theologians but also by delegates from Switzerland, Germany, Scotland, and England. The synod, which took on the nature of an ecumenical council for the Reformed Church, decided against the Remonstrants. It set forth its resolutions, upholding the orthodox position on predestination, in 93 canons divided into five chapters that corresponded to the five theses of the Arminians. The synod asserted: (1) unconditional election; (2) limited atonement, i.e., Christ died for the elect alone; (3) total depravity of man; (4) irresistibility of grace; and (5) final perseverance of the saints. [Text in P. Schaff, *The Creeds of Chris-*

tendom (1877) 3.550–580]. *See* CONFESSIONS OF FAITH, PROTESTANT; INFRALAPSARIANS (SUBLAPSARIANS).

Covenant Theology. Other difficulties concerning Calvin's doctrine arose, especially over a visible and invisible church, the irresistibility of grace, and an authoritarian civil government whose theocratic duty was to "cherish and protect the outward worship of God, to defend sound doctrine of piety and the position of the church" (*Inst.* 4.20.2). Of the new movements that modified Calvin's doctrine in seeking an answer to what seemed like intractable rigidity, the most significant was the Puritans' *covenant theology. Puritanism (*see* PURITANS) first appeared in the middle of the 16th century as a protest against the prescribed vestments and liturgical customs in the Church of England. The movement was essentially Calvinistic in doctrine but its main thrust was a type of piety. Concerned with man's right relation to God as a way of life and at the same time fully accepting the predestination of God as all-determining, the Puritans developed the idea of covenant. They discovered that all of salvation history had been a series of covenants between God and man. Even the government that protected the church had a covenant.

The significance of the covenants was that, while theologically upholding the absolute sovereignty of God, they made God's absolutism tractable to man's ability to conform. Man's duty was to fulfill his contract with God. Since God had made the contract, in the image of the legal and trade agreements of the time, His demands

Monument at Geneva, Switzerland, to the Calvinist reformers. The figures are those of Farel, Calvin, Beza, and Knox.

were reasonable and humanly possible of fulfillment. Thus, Calvin's God of predestination and irresistible condemnation became a Puritan God who could be served by righteous living and who would thereby consider those so living among the elect. Puritanism in this way marked the midpoint between orthodox and liberal Protestantism, between voluntarism and rationalism, between the sovereignty of God and the sovereignty of man.

GEOGRAPHICAL EXPANSION

Calvinism triumphed first in Geneva where, under Calvin's leadership from 1541 to 1564, the city became the most thorough example of a community welded into a total Calvinistic society. Geneva was governed in both civil and ecclesiastical affairs by the elect.

Church Government. Basing his view on Scripture (Eph 4.11; Rom 12.7; 1 Cor 12.28) and on the practice of the early church, Calvin declared in his *Ecclesiastical Ordinances:* "There are four orders of office instituted by our Lord for the government of his Church. First, pastors; then doctors; next elders; and fourth deacons" (*Library of Christian Classics* 22:58). Thus, the pastors preached and administered the sacraments. To the doctors belonged the duty of teaching, a function that under Calvinistic encouragement blossomed into schools and universities. The elders shared in the enforcement of discipline; and the deacons took care of the sick and the poor. The Consistory, made up of ministers and laymen, was responsible for the corporate religious life of the city and under Calvin it became chiefly a tribunal of morality. Whenever necessary, its decisions were enforced by the Council of Geneva whose responsibility included not only the promotion of civil order but also the welfare of the Reformed Church. Geneva, under Calvin, not only became a model city to which Calvinists looked as an ideal, but also a haven for Protestant refugees through whom Calvin's ideas spread far and wide.

Switzerland. In Switzerland, Heinrich *Bullinger, the successor to Zwingli, signed a formula of faith (*Consensus Tigurinus*) with Calvin in 1549. This paved the way for the general acceptance of Calvinism throughout the cantons. In 1566 the Second Helvetic Confession, drawn up by Bullinger but heavily Calvinistic in doctrine, was published in the name of all the Swiss cantons except Basel and Neuchâtel and had wide popularity. Today about half the population in Switzerland belongs to the Reformed Church.

Germany. In Germany, Calvinism spread mostly in the Rhine region where the fierce repression of the Peasant Revolt (1524–26) cost Luther many adherents. Reformed Protestantism also appealed to the free cities, particularly Strassburg, Memingen, Lindau, and Constance. Calvinism attained great influence in the Palatinate under the Elector, Frederick III (1515–76). During his regime, the University of Heidelberg became a center of Calvinism, and a confession of faith, the Heidelberg Cathechism, was compiled in 1562 by two professors, Zacharias *Ursinus and Caspar Olevianus (1536–87). This Calvinistic document became the creed of the Reformed churches in Germany, and Reformed churches in Poland, Bohemia, Hungary, and Moravia were influenced by it. Today, the largest of these churches is in Hungary and has a total membership of about 2 million.

France. In France, the Calvinists, who were called *Huguenots, were opposed from the time of their origin almost constantly, although various edicts such as the Edict of January 1562 and the Edict of *Nantes in 1598 gave some official toleration. Many Huguenots fled to Holland, Switzerland, America, England, and Prussia. Finally, in 1802 full legal standing was given to the Reformed Church. Today, there are about 600,000 Huguenots in France.

Netherlands. In the Netherlands, the Calvinists were not strong until about 1560. They gained the favor of William of Orange (1533–84) who became a Calvinist in 1573. After the declaration of independence (July 26, 1581), the Reformed Church became the established church in the northern region (Holland). In the 19th century, it became independent of the state. About 40 per cent of the population now belongs to the Dutch Reformed Church.

Scotland. Scotland is the only country where the majority of the people presently belong to the Reformed Church. Nowhere else has Calvinism triumphed so well, although its history since the time of John *Knox has been one of struggle. Knox was a personal friend of Calvin and received the Genevan reformer's warm encouragement and support. In 1900 the Free Church of Scotland merged with the United Presbyterian Church to form the United Free Church of Scotland. The resulting church merged with the Established Church to form the Church of Scotland in 1929.

England. In England the Calvinist doctrine brought about a divisive struggle within the Church of England toward the end of the 16th century. One group emerged as Presbyterians with their characteristic type of ascending series of governing bodies called synods and with a confession of faith, the Westminster Confession of 1648. A further group were the Separatist and Non-Separatist Congregationalists who migrated to New England as Puritans. Today there are various free churches in England that have been influenced by Calvinism and also a relatively small Presbyterian Church.

North America. Contingents from many of the European Reformed Churches went to North America during colonial times. A number of these groups fled from persecution. In the New World they influenced the shaping of a new nation and at the same time were influenced in their religious thinking. The strict orthodoxy of old world Calvinism was slowly modified by contacts in a pluralistic society, as well as by the demands of colonial life, trade, the Revolutionary War, a new government, and a new civilization. The modification, particularly in the 18th and 19th centuries, placed more and more emphasis on man and on his power for initiative and independence. Denominations proliferated across the U.S. Today, under the stimulus of the ecumenical movement, the modification has taken a new turn toward church mergers and under the pressure of a mechanized, materialistic age, toward the sovereignty of God once again (*see* REFORMED CHURCHES; REFORMED CHURCHES IN NORTH AMERICA).

What has been the contribution of Calvinism to the religious life of Western Christianity and especially to Protestantism? No one today accepts Calvinism as a complete system. During the 400 years of its existence, however, Calvinism as an aim and tendency has contributed significantly to man's understanding of his relation with God: a radical acceptance of the will of

God, an insistence on the lowly state of man before God, an insight into the power of grace, a powerful stimulus toward Biblical faith in Christ, and most of all, a stern but exalted and even mystical appreciation of the sovereignty of God, the knowledge of whom is "true and sound wisdom" (*Inst.* 1.1.1).

Bibliography: J. CALVIN, *Opera quae supersunt omnia,* ed. G. BAUM et al., 59 v. (CorpRef 29–87); *Institutes of the Christian Religion,* ed. J. T. McNEILL tr. F. L. BATTLES, 2 v. (Philadelphia 1960); *Theological Treatises,* tr. J. K. S. REID (Philadelphia 1954); *Concerning the Eternal Predestination of God,* tr. J. K. S. REID (London 1961). J. T. McNEILL, *The History and Character of Calvinism* (New York 1954). W. KRUSCHE, *Das Wirken des Heiligen Geistes nach Calvin* (Göttingen 1957). E. A. DOWEY, *The Knowledge of God in Calvin's Theology* (New York 1952). A. M. HUNTER, *The Teaching of Calvin* . . . (2d ed. London 1950). P. SPRENGER, *Das Rätsel um die Bekehrung Calvins* (Neukirchen 1960); F. WENDEL, *Calvin* . . ., tr. P. MAIRET (New York 1963). J. H. FORSTMAN, *Word and Spirit* . . . (Stanford 1962). J. MACKINNON, *Calvin and the Reformation* (New York 1962). G. P. HARTVELT, *Verum corpus: Een studie over een centraal hoofdstuk uit de Avondmaalsleer van Calvijn* (Delft 1960). L. SMITS, *Saint Augustin dans l'oeuvre de Jean Calvin* (Assen 1957). W. NIESEL, *The Theology of Calvin,* tr. H. KNIGHT (Philadelphia 1956). V. RULAND, "The Theology of New England Puritanism," Heythrop 5 (1964) 162–169. M. NEESER, *Le Dieu de Calvin d'après l'institution de la religion chrétienne* (Neuchâtel 1956). L. BOUYER, *The Spirit and Forms of Protestantism* (Westminster, Md. 1956). W. E. STUERMANN, *A Critical Study of Calvin's Concept of Faith* (Tulsa 1952). A. GANOCZY, *Calvin, théologien du ministère et de l'Église* (Paris 1964). O. WEBER, RGG³ 1:1593–99. E. W. ZEEDEN and J. MARLET, LexThK² 2:891–898. A. BAUDRILLART, DTC 2.2:1398–1422, earlier bibliog. Y. CONGAR, *Catholicisme* 2:421–424. J. QUINN, Davis CDT 1:313–317. **Illustration credit:** Swiss National Tourist Office.

[R. MATZERATH]

CALVO, CARLOS

Argentine internationalist and diplomat; b. Montevideo, Feb. 26, 1822; d. Paris, May 3, 1906. He was educated in Argentina, where he remained until 1845. During the last years of the Rosas regime he traveled through Europe and lived in Brazil for some time. He returned to Argentina in 1852 with the fall of Rosas and entered the diplomatic service. He held the posts of vice consul, consul general, and chargé d'affaires in Montevideo. He represented Paraguay in England and undertook special missions to the Holy See on behalf of the government of Argentina that led to the resumption of diplomatic relations between Argentina and the Vatican. He was minister plenipotentiary and envoy extraordinary in Germany, Vienna, and St. Petersburg; he also represented Argentina in France, Belgium, and the Holy See. In 1874 he was one of the founders of the Institut de Droit International, and he became associate member of the Academy of Moral and Political Science of Paris (1892). He was made *gran oficial* of the Legion of Honor (1888) and held the German Red Eagle among other decorations.

His important legal and historical writings were produced in a span of more than 30 years of extraordinary activity. Most were published in French, and some in Spanish and French, as was his most famous work, *Derecho internacional teórico y práctico de Europa y América* (Spanish ed., 1868; French ed., 1870; 5th French ed., 1896). This was even translated into Chinese and exerted considerable influence on the development of international law. Other works included *Manuel de droit international public et privé* (Paris 1881; Montreal 1901; there is also a Spanish edition) and *Le Dictionnaire du droit international public et privé* (Berlin 1885).

Calvo Clause. This is the designation given to the clause that is inserted in certain contracts made between a government and a foreign concessionary by which the latter renounces national diplomatic protection and submits to the jurisdiction of the contracting state. The validity of this clause has not always been conceded, for example in cases of denial of justice.

Calvo Doctrine. In general terms, this doctrine declares improper the use of military force or diplomatic pressure against one state by another to obtain the payment of claims made by its nationals for losses suffered as a result of civil war, internal disturbances, etc. Calvo justified his doctrine on the ground that to concede the opposite would be (1) an abuse of force of powerful states against weak states; (2) the establishment of an unjustifiable inequality between nationals and foreigners; and (3) an attack on one of the basic elements of the independence of nations, i.e., their territorial jurisdiction. When Germany, Great Britain, and Italy intervened in Venezuela in 1902, Calvo contributed to the formulation and defense of the Drago doctrine, which is a special and limited form of his own doctrine.

See also DRAGO, LUIS MARÍA.

Bibliography: A. V. FREEMAN, "Recent Aspects of the Calvo Doctrine and the Challenge to International Law," *American Journal of International Law* 40 (1946) 121–147. D. R. SHEA, *The Calvo Clause: A Problem of Inter-American and International Law and Diplomacy* (Minneapolis 1955). U.S. State Dept., Office of Public Affairs, Div. of Hist. Policy Research, *The Calvo Clause in American Policy and Practice* (Washington 1947).

[J. QUERO MOLARES]

CAMAIANI, PIETRO,

bishop of Ascoli Piceno and papal nuncio; b. Arezzo, June 1, 1519; d. Ascoli Piceno, March 27, 1579. From 1539 he was in the service of Duke Cosimo of Florence, and in 1546 he became his agent at the Council of Trent. In 1551 Pope Julius II took the able diplomat into the service of the Curia. As nuncio to Charles V (1552–53) and as nuncio at Naples (1554–55) he mediated in critical situations arising out of papal and Hapsburg policies. As bishop of Fiesole he was present at the third session of the Council of Trent. From 1566 till his death, as bishop of Ascoli Piceno, he promoted successfully the letter and the spirit of the Tridentine reforms. During his episcopate he acted as nuncio extraordinary at the court of Philip II at the request of Pope Pius V. His life and character bear witness to the movement away from the tradition of Renaissance diplomacy to the new pastoral idea of Catholic reform.

Bibliography: Short biography in *Nuntiaturberichte aus Deutschland,* Abt. 1, v.12, ed. G. KUPKE (1901) xxvi; v.13, ed. H. LUTZ (1959), his reports from the imperial court. P. VILLANI, "Origine e carattere della nunziatura di Napoli," *Annuario dell' Istituto Storico Italiano per l'età moderna e contemporanea,* 9–10 (1957–58) 315ff, 411ff. Pastor 8:286–289, 345–347. L. SERRANO, *Correspondencia diplomatica entre España y la Santa Sede durante el pontificado de S. Pio V,* 4 v. (Rome 1914). H. JEDIN, "La politica conciliare di Cosimo I," *Rivista Storica Italiana* 62 (1950) 345–374, 477–496. G. FABIANI, *Ascoli nel Cinquecento* (Ascoli Piceno, Italy 1957).

[H. LUTZ]

CAMALDOLESE

The Congregation of Monk Hermits of Camaldoli (ErCam or BCam), commonly known as the Camaldolese, is an offshoot of the Benedictine Order (*see* BENEDICTINES). The spirit and purpose of the order are predominantly contemplative. St. *Romuald, while remaining a Benedictine monk, imparted a unique spirit to his followers and to the many monasteries that he reformed, so that from the very beginning they began to form a separate family or institution. Romuald, however, never intended to found an eremitic order separate from the Benedictine monastic order, and the Camaldolese always pronounced their profession according to the Rule of St. Benedict.

Internal Development. Romuald's activity, begun in Italy in the early years of the 11th century, was a part of the reform movement of the 11th and 12th centuries that sought to restore the more ancient monastic tradition, according to which Benedict had formulated his rule. Monasticism, since the Carolingian era, had become overladen with formalism. The movement found different forms of expression, but most of them had a more or less pronounced tendency toward primitive eremitism, that is, greater penitential austerity, more separation from the world, and greater freedom to converse with God. Following the teaching and example of Romuald, the Camaldolese added to the Benedictine rule special regulations or customs. These were later compiled by (St.) *Peter Damian at *Fonte Avellana, and especially by (Bl.) Rudolf (d. 1089) at *Camaldoli about 1080.

Romuald organized the eremitic life by reuniting the anchorite with the monastery. In this he kept in mind the traditions of the Fathers and, in particular, the Palestinian *lauras of SS. *Euthymius and *Sabas. His monastic institution was based on the following ideas. The monastery and the hermitage form one unit and complement each other. Unity is composed of three elements: rule, under a single superior; members, forming a single family; and goal, which is the ascent by degrees toward the highest summits of perfection and contemplation. Beginners reside in the monastery; the proficient and the more perfect, in the hermitage. The function of the monastery in this scheme is to prepare the monk for the solitary life. All must aspire to this, but the superior alone is to determine the suitability of the monk and the length of the preparation. He must exhort and, at the proper moment, summon the candidate to the hermitage. One may not enter the solitary life without the abbot's approval. The monastery also serves the purposes of administration, reception of guests, care of the sick and the aged, and instruction of novices. In the hermitage, the monk devotes himself solely to contemplation. Romuald summed up the rule for hermits in three things: fasting, silence, and solitude. Manual labor is encouraged to a limited degree, in conformity with the contemplative ideal.

The superior, whether abbot or prior, is the father of both hermits and cenobites (those living together in the monastery). The cenobitic family must venerate its hermit brothers, but the latter are warned against pride. In the Camaldolese tradition, the hermitage and the monastery thus take on a special character. The monastery loses some of its inflexible cenobitism, which, in Romuald's day particularly, did not allow the monk freedom to converse alone with God; the hermitage, in turn, is no longer the dangerous desert of the anchorites, but a laura where, along with the advantages of solitude, the hermits enjoy brotherly help and, above all, the blessing of obedience that preserves them from illusions and makes every good work valid. Finally, when

the hermit monk has attained the highest degree of perfection, he may aspire to the apostolate of preaching the Gospel among the pagans, where he may hope to offer to Christ the supreme homage of martyrdom. This ideal union of hermitage and monastery did not prove to be possible everywhere. At times Romuald founded hermitages and monasteries that were independent of one another. In such a case, the hermits were recruited from any monastery or even directly from the laity, if such candidates were sufficiently mature for the solitary life. Peter Damian also used this procedure at Fonte Avellana.

External Development. Camaldolese monasticism developed around the two principal centers in Italy, Camaldoli and Fonte Avellana. Many monasteries—some were new foundations, while others were existing monasteries that became identified with the new movement—adopted the Camaldolese rule and customs. The juridic ties between the dependent houses and the principal monasteries varied greatly, so that many monasteries were practically autonomous. The two principal centers were themselves juridically independent of one another until united by papal decree during the 16th century reform. Fonte Avellana, although it had flourished under the leadership of Peter Damian and his successors, later underwent a change in its eremitical character. Many of its monks were called to fill bishoprics in the Marches of Ancona and in Umbria. In 1325 it was converted into an abbey; the hermitage thus ceased to exist. Thereafter, the abuse of the *commenda*, whereby the abbey became the benefice of a secular cleric, hastened the decline of the monastery until Pius V, in 1569, reconstituted Fonte Avellana, and its dependent monasteries, by subjecting them to Camaldoli.

Throughout the history of the Camaldolese Order, Camaldoli itself remained the chief center of vitality. Fortified by many privileges, both papal and imperial, it extended its influence over hundreds of monasteries, especially in the period between the 11th and the 13th centuries. The form of government within the order developed slowly and suffered from numerous conflicts. The chief source of difficulty lay in the very nature of Camaldolese monasticism, that is, in the tension between the twofold objective of the order, cenobitic and eremitic. The general chapter was introduced into the government of the order in the 13th century; the first chapter met at Padua in 1239. As with the other religious orders, the Camaldolese suffered from the unfavorable circumstances of the 14th and 15th centuries. In the 15th century, several reform efforts, initiated both inside and outside the order, were undertaken. One such effort, promoted by Eugene IV, was earnestly advanced by (Bl.) *Ambrose Traversari, the noted Camaldolese humanist who was elected superior general in 1431.

Effective reform was not realized, however, until the following century, when the Congregation of Camaldoli and San Michele di Murano (Venice) was formed. The leaders in this movement were the then superior general, Pietro *Delfino, superior from 1480 until his death in 1525, (Bl.) Paolo *Giustiniani, and Pietro Querini (1479–1514). Giustiniani, whose ideas were more radical than those of his confreres, led a further reform movement that came to be known as the Congregation of Monte Corona (Umbria). This congregation, autonomous since 1523, still exists. Under the impetus of these movements the Order of Camaldoli experienced a new vitality, but the tension between the cenobitic and eremitic ideals remained. In the 17th century the cenobites separated themselves from the hermits, forming an independent group (1616). Further divisions resulted from the formation of congregations in Piedmont and in France, but both of these disappeared during the French Revolution. Finally, on July 2, 1935, the Holy See reunited the cenobites with the hermits at Camaldoli, thus reconstituting the ancient order of Romuald.

The Camaldolese have enjoyed a reputation for holiness. Their recognized saints and blesseds, however, are generally persons who became known by reason of some activity outside the hermitage, such as, SS. Peter, Archbishop of Pisa (d. 1120); John, Cardinal Bishop of Ostia (d. 1134); and *Bogumil of Gniezno. Among many blesseds, two are remembered as martyrs: Daniel of Ungrispach (d. 1411) and Angelo of Mussiaccio (d. 1485). The Camaldolese have made notable contributions to various fields of learning and of the arts. A tradition of scholarship was begun by Jerome of Prague (Johannes Silvanus, d. 1440) and the above-mentioned Ambrose Traversari. From an earlier period, however, the names of *Guido of Arezzo, the musician, and *Gratian, the author of the *Decretum,* are remembered. The prior general Pietro Delfino was an outstanding humanist, and the monastery in Florence, Santa Maria degli Angeli (1294), became the meeting place for the great Florentine humanists of the 15th century. Nicolò Malermi (d. 1481) published in 1471 the first complete translation of the Bible in Italian. Fra Mauro (d. *c.* 1459) was a cosmographer of note. The historian, Giovanni *Mittarelli, published the *Annales Camaldulenses* (9 v. 1755–73). The Order of Camaldoli gave to the Church many bishops, several cardinals, and one pope, Gregory XVI.

In the U.S. the Camaldolese began, in 1958, a promising foundation called New Camaldoli at Big Sur, Calif. In 1964 the community had 29 members. The Congregation of Monte Corona established (1959) a hermitage at McConnelsville, Ohio. Throughout the world the order numbered 296.

Bibliography: A. DES MAZIS, DHGE 11:512–536, esp. bibliog. P. ROBERT, DictSpirAscMyst 2:50–60. G. B. MITTARELLI and A. COSTADONI, *Annales camaldulenses,* 9 v. (Venice 1755–73). A. GIABBANI, *L'eremo, vita e spiritualità eremitica nel monachismo Camaldolese primitivo* (Brescia 1945). A. PAGNANI, *Storia dei Benedettini Camaldolesi* (Sassoferrato 1949). W. FRANKE, *Romuald von Camaldoli und seine Reformtätigkeit zum Zeit Ottos III* (Berlin 1913). M. BEDE, *The Hermits of New Camaldoli* (Big Sur, Calif. 1958).

[A. GIABBANI]

CAMALDOLI, ABBEY OF, the name of (1) the cénobitical monastery, lying at a height of 2,680 feet in the Tuscan-Romagnese Appenines, commune of Poppi, civil province and Diocese of Arezzo, and (2) of the eremitical monastery, 2 miles farther up (3,610 feet) in the midst of forest land. Both monasteries were built by St. *Romuald, founder of the *Camaldolese congregation, on land granted by Count Maldoli to Romuald (1012–15), the name Camaldoli being formed from *Campus Maldoli.* The hermitage, with its characteristic separation of the monks' dwellings from each other by small cultivated plots of ground, served as the model for other Camaldolese eremitical foundations. Consecrated in 1027, its Romanesque-style church was almost entirely rebuilt in 1220; the present baroque form dates from 1658. The once-great library was destroyed in the

Napoleonic and Italian suppressions. The archives are now preserved almost intact in the state archives in Florence. The monks continue to lead a strict life of almost continuous prayer and rigorous penance and observe complete silence. The monastery proper was, like the hermitage, built by St. Romuald *c.* 1015. Originally it was a hospice and guest house. In order that the hermit-monks might devote themselves entirely to the contemplative life, it was later organized into a cenobitical monastery. Today it consists of a 16th-century church with works by Vasari, a cloister with monks' quarters, and a section reserved for lay retreats. There is a printing press, a pharmacy, and since 1946 a workshop for the restoration of books and incunabula.

Bibliography: G. B. MITTARELLI and A. COSTADONI, *Annales camaldulenses,* 9 v. (Venice 1755–73). Kehr ItalPont 3:171–185. Cottineau 1:567–569. A. GIABBANI, *L'eremo* (Brescia 1945).

[S. OLIVIERI]

CAMBODIA

Country in southeast Asia bordering on the Gulf of Siam, Thailand, *Laos, and *Vietnam, 69,000 square miles in area. Cambodia became a French protectorate in 1863 and part of French Indochina. It became a constitutional monarchy in 1946, an autonomous state in the French Union in 1949, and fully independent in 1953. The population in 1964 was estimated at 5,750,000, of which 90 per cent were Khmers. There were significant minorities of Vietnamese, Chinese, and Thais, but Europeans numbered only a few thousand. About 90 per cent of the inhabitants adhered to *Buddhism, which had 53,450 monks. Islam claimed about 2 per cent of the populace and Catholicism about half that percentage.

Fernando Mendez Pinto, a Jesuit, visited Cambodia in 1554, but the first attempt at evangelization was by the Dominican Gaspar da Cruz in 1555. Some Portuguese Dominicans and Franciscans came from Malacca. One of them, Silvestro de Azevedo, OP, was put to death (1576). These early Portuguese efforts seem to have had no lasting success. From the Philippines came two Spanish Dominicans, one of whom, Father Bastide, was slain (1588). Jesuits and priests from Goa, India, also labored in the area. When Louis Chevreul, a priest of the *Paris Foreign Mission Society (MEP), arrived in 1665, he found the Portuguese ecclesiastical "governor" Paul d'Acosta at Colompé (Phnom Penh), where he was caring for 400 Portuguese who had been driven from Makassar by the Dutch. Across the river was a group of 600 refugees from Cochin China, 50 of whom were Christians. Chevreul also encountered Charles Della Rocca, SJ, at Udong, where he was occupied with 100 Portuguese and a village of 500 or 600 pagan Cochin Chinese (Vietnamese). In 1670 Chevreul was seized by a Portuguese commander, imprisoned at Macao on charges of violating Portugal's rights of *padroado, tried by the Inquisition of Goa, and finally released. Bishop Louis Laneau, MEP, the first vicar apostolic of Siam (1673–96) and administrator general of the missions in Indochina, sent one MEP to Cambodia in 1680 and two more in 1682. All three suffered greatly because of intrigues and wars, and departed for Cochin China or Siam in 1685.

Nearly all the efforts of the missionaries for 2 centuries concentrated on the Portuguese and Cochin Chinese. Nicholas Levasseur, MEP, was the first to specialize in the apostolate to the Cambodians, or Khmers. Between 1768 and his death in 1777 he translated into their tongue a catechism and various books. Unfortunately he had no successors. By 1842 Cambodia had only 222 Catholics and 4 churches. After being attached to the Vicariate Apostolic of Cochin China since 1658, Cambodia, along with part of Laos, became the Vicariate of Cambodia (1850), which then numbered 600 Catholics. The French, who had established themselves in Cochin China in 1859, extended their protectorate to Cambodia in 1863. In 1865 the Vicariate of Cambodia gained jurisdiction over eight "provinces" of Cochin China, which then had 5,000 Christians. Thenceforth mission activity centered around the Vietnamese in these eight "provinces," or around the numerous persons who were attracted to Cambodia from Cochin China by commerce and by the vast rice fields, whose value increased under the French protectorate. The name of the vicariate was changed in 1924 to Phnom Penh, which early in 1955 had among its 4,500,000 inhabitants 126,000 Catholics (of whom 123,000 were Vietnamese and 3,000 Cambodians), 25 MEP priests and 77 Vietnamese priests, 17 major and 49 minor seminarians, 50 religious men (mostly Vietnamese), and 517 religious women (almost all Vietnamese).

The eight Vietnamese "provinces" were then separated (September 1955) to form the Vicariate of Cantho (diocese in 1960), and the territorial limits of Phnom Penh were made coterminous with those of the kingdom of Cambodia. In 1964 the vicariate, whose bishop belonged to the MEP, reported 55,000 Catholics, 70 priests (including 40 MEP and 11 Vietnamese and 3 Khmer seculars), 12 major and 65 minor seminarians (52 Vietnamese, 13 Khmers), 50 brothers, 293 sisters, and 59 Catholic schools with 11,400 students. (For map, *see* VIETNAM.)

Bibliography: J. PIANET, *Histoire de la Mission du Cambodge* (Hong Kong 1929). B. BIERMANN, "Die Missionen der portugiesischen Dominikaner in Hinterindien," ZMissRelw 21 (1931) 305–327; "Die Missionsversuche der Dominiker in Kambodscha," *ibid.* 23 (1933) 108–132. MissCattol 270–271. *Bilan du Monde* 2:183–185. AnnPont (1965) 762.

[J. GUENNOU]

CAMBRAI, ARCHDIOCESE OF (CAMERACENSIS)

Metropolitan see since 1559, in Nord department, north France. In 1963 the archdiocese, 1,254 square miles in area, had 459 parishes, 642 secular and 38 religious priests, 23 men in 4 religious houses, 1,160 women in 121 convents, and 983,214 Catholics. Its two suffragans, Arras and Lille (with a Catholic university since 1875), had 1,392 parishes, 2,878 priests, 5,371 sisters, and 2,135,927 Catholics.

Cambrai's diocesan borders have changed several times, according to the political fortunes of the region, which is on France's border with the German world. At the end of the Roman Empire the see corresponded to the *civitas Nerviorum* in *Belgica II*. It had no bishop after the German invasions of the early 5th century. St. *Remigius, Bishop of Reims, made St. *Vedast (d. *c.* 540) bishop of the *Nervii;* but he resided in Arras. His second successor, Vedulphus, who moved the see to Cambrai, was followed by St. *Géry (d. *c.* 625). Until 1094 Arras and Cambrai had a common bishop, who

usually resided in Cambrai. Bordered on the west by the Schelde River, the diocese expanded, along with evangelization, as far north as Antwerp.

Charles V abdicated in 1558, and Philip II moved to Spain in 1559 after the Peace of Cateau-Cambrésis. To combat Protestantism better, *Mechelen and *Antwerp were in 1559 detached as dioceses from Cambrai, which, previously suffragan to *Reims, became a metropolitan with Tournai, Arras, Saint-Omer, and Namur as suffragans. In 1790 the *Civil Constitution of the Clergy reduced Cambrai to a suffragan of Reims. It was restored as a metropolitan without authority over its former Belgian suffragans by the agreements of 1822, but no archbishop was appointed until after the death of Bishop Belmas (1841), last of the constitutional prelates. Cambrai then encompassed all Nord department, part of which was detached to create the See of Lille in 1913.

The bishops of Cambrai, who had regular and good relationships with the Carolingian emperors, became more powerful when the emperors gave them the *comitatus* (rights of a count) over part of the episcopal *civitas* (*c.* 941) and then (1007) over the whole county. Thus they became temporal and spiritual lords with a role in Church history under the German (Holy Roman) Empire. Trouble with the bourgeoisie caused the bishop to cede some of his rights to the commune in 1185. Under Burgundian rule (1384–1477) the bishops, who came from the highest nobility and even from the ducal family, favored the popes of Avignon in the *Western Schism; *Peter of Ailly (1396–1411), a prolific author,

The church of Notre-Dame at Douai (Nord) in the Archdiocese of Cambrai.

had a strong influence in scholastic and ecclesiastical circles. When France annexed Cambrai (1678), *Louis XIV gained from the cathedral chapter the right to appoint bishops. Cambrai then followed the fortunes of France. François Salignac de la Mothe *Fénelon (1695–1715) was an outstanding prelate, and Auguste *Gratry (d. 1872) was a noteworthy theologian.

A rich land, the diocese has had many abbeys since the 7th century: Benedictines (11 men's and 5 women's), Augustinian (4 and 4), and Cistercians (2 and 6); 4 Premonstratensian abbeys were important in the 12th-century reform. (See AFFLIGEM; GROENENDAEL; LOBBES; SAINT-BERTIN; and SAINT-VAAST.) There were also many houses of the mendicant orders, a Jesuit college (1563), and a university at *Douai to train priests for England (William *Allen's English College, 1568). Wars have left few monuments in good repair; the cathedral has been almost destroyed. Of note are the abbey churches of Saint-Géry, Vaucelles, and Oisy-le-Verger; and the churches of Avesnes-lès-Aubert and Saint-Géry in Valenciennes. The main pilgrimages are to Our Lady in Cambrai and in Valenciennes. The diocese, rural as well as industrial, is thriving, thanks to good parishes, schools, and divers groups.

Arras's first resident bishop seems to have been Diogenes, perhaps a missionary, slain in the Vandal invasion (407). Early monasteries were associated with the expansion of Irish monasticism c. 700. The temporal power of Arras's 9th-century chapter in the *civitas* (the area around the cathedral) suffered from nearby Saint-Vaast Abbey, around which grew up a prosperous community. Normans destroyed both Arras and Cambrai (879–885). When the counts of Flanders began to reside in Arras in the 10th century, the temporal power of the bishops (in Cambrai) suffered. A dispute over the episcopal succession (1092) led to the creation of the See of Arras (1094). In the 13th century, as Arras grew rich, there was a movement for evangelical poverty, and rich bourgeois founded houses of the mendicant orders. Part of Burgundy in 1369, Arras came to France in the Peace of the Pyrenees (1659); but neither its clergy nor those of Cambrai took part in the French Assembly of the Clergy. Bishop Gui Scève de Rochechouart (1670–1724) founded the seminary.

See also ARRAS, MARTYRS OF; ARRAS, COUNCILS OF.

Bibliography: C. J. DESTOMBES, *Les Vies des saints et des personnes d'une éminente piété des diocèses de Cambrai et d'Arras,* 4 v. (4th ed. Lille 1889). F. VERCAUTEREN, *Étude sur les civitates de la Belgique seconde* (Brusseles 1934). É. DE MOREAU, *Histoire de l'Église en Belgique* (2d ed. Brussels 1945–); DHGE 7:519–756, *passim.* M. CHARTIER, *ibid.* 11:547–565. E. JARRY, *Catholicisme* 1:860–864; 2:427–434. M. DIERICK, "La Réorganisation de la hiérarchie ecclésiastique des Pays-Bas par la bulle 1559," RHE 59 (1964) 489–499. AnnPont (1965) 88. **Illustration credits:** French Embassy, Press and Information Division, New York City.

[E. JARRY]

CAMBRIDGE, UNIVERSITY OF

The origins of the University of Cambridge go back to the 13th century. There may have been schools in the town before 1200, and scholars may have come from Oxford in 1209. The University is certainly mentioned in documents of 1231.

Development. The University of Cambridge was recognized as a *studium generale* by Pope John XXII in 1318. The medieval masters and students were mostly

St. John's College, Cambridge University.

secular clerks, but the regular clergy, both Franciscans and Benedictines, were important until the Reformation. The first college, Peterhouse, was founded by the Benedictine monk, Hugh de Balsham, Bishop of Ely, in 1284, although few students were members of colleges until the 16th century. Among the more important college foundations were King's (1441), St. John's (1511), and Trinity (1546). By 1600, however, all teachers and students were members of one of the 16 colleges then existing. In fact, between that date and the 19th century the University was little more than a loose federation of colleges.

The chief promoter of the "new learning" in Cambridge was its chancellor, John *Fisher (d. 1535), who probably brought *Erasmus to Cambridge. The Reformation was strong there, for English Protestantism was preeminently a Cambridge movement. Under Elizabeth I theology played a more prominent part in university studies than it had done in the Middle Ages. Puritanism was flourishing, and in the following century Cambridge men played an important part in the foundation of New England and of Harvard College. During the English Civil Wars (1642–52) the sympathies of the University were largely Royalist and many of the heads and fellows of colleges were expelled by the victorious Parliamentarians. In academic studies Aristotelian and scholastic ideas remained predominant all through this period, until a new interest in scientific and mathematical studies appeared, the greatest name here being that of Isaac Newton, who was working on the theory of gravity in the 1660s. In the following century the ancient disputations were gradually replaced as the means of qualifying for a degree by a written examination in mathematics, later called the mathematical tripos.

The 18th century was not a prosperous period in Cambridge. There were, however, some distinguished men, such as the classical scholar Richard *Bentley. After 1815 reforms were gradually introduced, although pressure from Parliament was necessary to bring about radical changes. After the appointment of a royal commission of enquiry in 1850 and the consequent reform of the university and college statutes a new age of expansion began. Numbers rose; new studies, in particular the natural sciences, were fostered; colleges for women were founded (Girton 1869, Newnham 1871), though women did not become full members of the university until 1948. The main obstacle to expansion in the later 19th century was lack of money, for although the colleges had large endowments, these were fully committed and the University had very little available for new developments. Eventually the University (and indirectly the colleges) came to depend on government grants, the first general grant being given in 1919–20. As a result another royal commission of enquiry was appointed, and new university and college statutes were made between 1926 and 1928, by which Cambridge is still governed.

Organization. The University is a common-law corporation by prescription, consisting of a chancellor, masters, and scholars. Its incorporation was confirmed by Act of Parliament in 1571. Each of the colleges is itself a self-governing body, the control of its affairs resting in the hands of its own head and fellows. There are now 20 colleges—18 for men and 2 for women. Churchill College (1960), which ranks as an approved foundation, and Fitzwilliam House for noncollegiate students (1869) both approximate very closely to colleges of the normal type as does New Hall (1954), a recognized institution for women. The self-government of both university and colleges is limited only by the fact that the authority of the Queen-in-Council must be obtained for the amendment of their statutes. The interconnection between the University and its colleges is so close that one cannot be thought of without the other. It is in general not possible to be a member of one without being a member of the other, and many university officers hold college offices and vice versa. All undergraduates and research students must first obtain admission to a college; this control over admissions gives the colleges their distinctive position in the structure.

The main gatehouse and the chapel of King's College, Cambridge University.

After 1871 when all religious tests for the University degree were withdrawn, residences for Catholic students attending the various colleges were established. Among these were Fisher House, named in honor of St. John Fisher, the martyred Bishop of Rochester, which serves as the Catholic chaplaincy and provides a program of religious and social activities for Catholics associated with the University; St. Edmund's House, a residence for secular priests, seminarians, and laymen attending the University; and Benet House, reserved as a residence for members of the Benedictine Order. Other religious orders maintain residences for their own members, and Lady Margaret Hall is a hostel for Catholic women students, mainly foreign students residing in the city.

Administration. The ultimate governing body of the University is the senate, which consists of doctors and masters in all faculties, and of bachelors of divinity, whether resident or not. The senate has the right to confer degrees and to elect the chancellor, who is the supreme university officer but whose position is largely formal. The effective government of the University lies in the hands of the Regent House, which decides major matters of policy and consists of university and college teachers, and administrative officers who are resident in Cambridge. There is no permanent executive head like an American university president. One of the heads of colleges acts as vice-chancellor for a period of 2 years, and as such presides over the three main administrative bodies: the council of the senate, the general board of the faculties, and the financial board. The first, elected by the Regent House, is responsible for the general oversight of affairs and for the presentation of reports on matters of policy on which the Regent House may subsequently vote. The second is responsible for advising the university on educational policy, teaching, and research; and the third, for the regulation of expenditure.

Research and teaching are handled by 20 faculties and other independent departments. In 1963–64 there were 97 professors and a large number of lecturers who shared the responsibility of research and public teaching. The most ancient chair, the Lady Margaret professorship of divinity, was established in 1502. Other chairs, since introduced, cover the humanities, sciences, classical and modern languages, agriculture, engineering, medicine, and Oriental and veterinary studies. In the 1850s the teaching of undergraduates was done by the colleges and private tutors, but since the early 1900s it has become more and more centralized in the University itself, particularly as a result of the rapid growth of the scientific departments. The colleges retain responsibility only for the individual teaching of their own members by college supervisors, a system that has developed during the 20th century. Many of these supervisors, but not all, are fellows of colleges, who may often hold university lectureships. The most important college officials from the undergraduate point of view are the tutors who are responsible for the welfare and discipline of the men under their charge. Although in modern times the University has become more important at the expense of the colleges, college tutoring and supervision are still regarded as very important parts of the Cambridge system.

Degrees and Examinations. All students in all subjects take the B.A. as their first degree. In the 1850s less than half the undergraduates took honors, the only road to which was through the mathematical tripos (the word "tripos" refers to a three-legged stool used in university ceremonies, and the word came eventually to be applied, by a devious course of events, to the honors examinations themselves). In the 19th century new tripos examinations were created in classics (1822) and in moral and in natural sciences (1848), and subsequently new triposes have been founded which cover all the main subjects of academic study, including music, architecture, and fine arts. For the B.A. degree nine terms' residence is required, and for an honors degree the appropriate standard must generally be reached in two tripos examinations. The majority of the triposes are divided into two parts, the first being taken at the end of the 1st or 2d year and the second at the end of the 3d year after a course of more specialized study. It is possible, unlike the system in most British universities, for the two tripos examinations to be taken in different subjects. Honors are classified into first, second, and third class. Within each class the arrangement is alphabetical; until 1909 mathematical honors were graded in order of merit, the first man on the list bearing the ancient title of senior wrangler. Almost all undergraduates now take honors degrees; pass degrees still exist, but they are of very little importance.

Until the 1890s there was no organized provision for graduate study. Any B.A. may be admitted to the M.A. degree without further examination after 6 years have elapsed from the end of his first term. The M.A. confers membership of the senate and certain privileges in the use of the University library and other institutions, but it does not represent any additional academic qualification. In the later 19th century the University began to give graduates of other universities certain credits toward the B.A. degree (at present graduates of many other universities may obtain the B.A. after obtaining honors in one tripos examination and keeping six terms' residence). In 1895 it was for the first time made possible for graduate students from other universities to obtain the B.A. by thesis, a step that inaugurated the "research student" in the modern sense. The Ph.D. degree was established in 1919, its supporters urging that after World War I many students, especially Americans, who had previously gone to Germany for their research work would come to England if a doctorate were available for them. The graduate studies of the University have developed with great rapidity since World War II, especially in the scientific departments. Graduate students come to Cambridge from all over the world, and in 1964 there were more than 1,000 graduate students as compared with about 7,500 undergraduates. In both groups men form a large majority.

Library and Finance. Among the chief university institutions is the University library, which contains about 2,000,000 books, 10,000 MSS and 350,000 maps. It is entitled under the Copyright Acts to a copy of every book published in the United Kingdom. There are other faculty and departmental libraries, and each college has a library of its own, many of these containing important MSS and printed collections. The university and college buildings are scattered throughout the city. The income of the University is derived largely from the Treasury grant, and also from endowments, fees, and contributions from the colleges. In 1962–63 the total recurrent income of the University was £6,204,-937. Of this the Treasury grant was £3,921,110; apart from this the other principal items were grants for research and contributions for services rendered (£829,-223), fees (£582,752), and endowments (£507,913). The colleges all have their own endowments and vary greatly both in their wealth and in the number of their fellows and undergraduates.

Bibliography: *The Student's Handbook to the University and Colleges of Cambridge, 1962–63* (1963); *The Annual Register, 1962–63* (1963); *Statutes of the University of Cambridge . . .* (1961); *The Historical Register of the University of Cambridge . . . to the Year 1910*, ed. J. R. Tanner (1917), with suppls.; *Alumni Cantabrigienses*, comp. J. and J. A. Venn, 10 v. (1922–54). Emden Cambr. *Cambridge University Reporter* (1870–), weekly in term. (All published by Cambridge University Press.) J. P. C. Roach, ed., *The City and University of Cambridge* (*Victoria History of the County of Cambridgeshire . . .*, v.3; London 1959). C. H. Cooper, *Annals of Cambridge*, 5 v. (Cambridge 1842–1908). R. Willis, *The Architectural History of the University of Cambridge . . .*, ed. J. W. Clark, 4 v. (1886). D. A. Winstanley, *The University of Cambridge in the 18th Century* (1922); *Unreformed Cambridge* (1935); *Early Victorian Cambridge* (1940); *Later Victorian Cambridge* (1947). (All published by the University Press.) T. D. Atkinson, *Cambridge Described and Illustrated* (London 1897). **Illustration credits:** British Travel Association, N.Y.C.

[J. P. C. ROACH]

CAMBRIDGE PLATFORM, or the Platform of Church Discipline, was framed by a synod held in Cambridge, Mass., in 1648. Representatives of the Puritan churches in the four New England colonies gathered to take steps against interference by unfriendly authorities in England and to formulate a common church polity based on Scripture. The *Westminster Confession had proposed a national church on a Presbyterian pattern, and the clergy of New England— not seeking freedom from English political rule—were determined to maintain the autonomy of their own churches. Though recognizing a bond through the covenant of grace, the leaders wanted to ensure the right of each congregation to elect and ordain a minister of its own choosing and to regulate its affairs without direction by any higher authority.

The 17 chapters of the Platform, mainly the work of Richard Mather, described carefully a system of church discipline that would regularize the practices of the New England churches, with each item supported by texts from Scripture. The synod used the word Congregational and provided for the free election of church officers by the church members. Although each church was to be distinct, the Platform recommended consultation among neighboring churches. The support of the churches by local taxation was taken for granted, but the civil authorities were to have no control, except in cases of heresy, blasphemy, profanation of the Lord's Day, and open disturbance of worship.

The Cambridge Platform established a new church order, a type of government that served the *Congregationalists for 200 years. Its principle of the autonomy of the local church was adopted by the *Baptists, the *Universalists, and other groups, so that nearly half of American Protestants belong to churches that are congregational in practice (*see* PROTESTANTISM IN THE U.S.).

Bibliography: F. L. Fagley, "The Narrative of the Cambridge Synod," in *Cambridge Platform of 1648: Tercentenary Commemoration . . .*, ed. H. W. Foote (Boston 1949). H. W. Foote,

"The Significance and Influence of the Cambridge Platform of 1648," *ibid*. Bibliog. of editions of the Platform, *ibid*. 115–119.

[W. D. HOYT, JR.]

CAMBRIDGE PLATONISTS

A group of 17th-century English Protestant thinkers, so named because of their connection with Cambridge University and the presence of certain Platonic elements in their teaching. In religion they were "latitude-men," standing, as Matthew Arnold says, "between the sacerdotal religion of the Laudian clergy . . . and the notional religion of the Puritans," and in their theology they emphasized conduct rather than doctrine. Since some of them continued to hold office at the University during the time of the Commonwealth, they were considered suspect after the return of the Stuarts in 1660. However, as a contemporary account given by "P.S." (Symon Patrick?) puts it, "they were glad to conform to the Church after the Restoration." The same author also defends their attitude toward rites and ceremonies since "they do highly approve that virtuous mediocrity which our Churches observe between the meretricious gaudiness of the Church of Rome, and the squalid sluttery of fanatic Conventicles," adding that they subscribed to the Thirty-nine Articles, were attacked by both Papists and Presbyterians, and were unjustly accused of "liberty of conscience," that is, licentiousness in their private lives. "But there is another crime, which cannot be denied, that they have introduced a new philosophy; Aristotle and the schoolmen are out of request with them," since they had taken up with the atomical or Cartesian doctrine.

The principal representatives of the school are Benjamin Whichcote, who is generally regarded as its founder, John Smith, Henry More, and Ralph Cudworth.

Benjamin Whichcote. Whichcote (1609–1683) entered Emmanuel College, a Puritan foundation, in 1626, was ordained an Anglican priest, and held high places in the University under the Puritans. After he was deprived of the provostship of King's College in 1660, he spent his remaining years as a rector, first in country places and later in London. His *Select Sermons* were published with a notable introduction by Shaftesbury in 1698, and *Several Discourses* by John Jeffrey (4 vols., 1701–07). In "The Malignity of Popery" he gives the essence of "the reformed religion" by way of contrast to asserted doctrines and practices of the Church of Rome. In various other sermons he presents what may be called a theory of natural religion, writing that "the State of Religion lyes, in short, in this; *A good Mind, and a good Life*. All else is *about* Religion, and hath but the place of Means or an Instrument." He advances the teleological and moral arguments for God's existence and shows in various ways that "it is more Knowable that there is a God, than any thing else is knowable." For Whichcote "the great Rights" are: (1) God is to be worshiped and adored; (2) There is a difference between good and evil; and (3) Good is to be done, evil avoided. Elements of scholasticism are plentiful in his work, as evidenced by many particular terms, ideas, and axioms, and his theories of truth, objective morality, faith and reason, intellect and will, and freedom.

John Smith. A philosophically more important and appealing figure is John Smith (1616–52), a student of Whichcote's at Emmanuel and later dean of Queens'

College. His full development as a thinker and writer was cut off by an early death, but his posthumous *Select Discourses* (1659) show him to have been a man of wide learning, considerable intellectual power, originality of thought and expression, genuine spiritual perception, and great sincerity. He stands apart from Whichcote, More, and Cudworth because of the absence of bigotry and intolerance from his writing, and especially from More because of his sane and rational attitude toward superstitious beliefs and practices. More truly Platonic than others in the group, Smith's cast of mind may also be described as Plotinian and Augustinian. Accordingly, he gives particular attention to the soul and advances four arguments for its immortality, viz, (1) from its incorporeity, indivisibility, powers, and operations; (2) from the distinction between man's free and "automatical" actions; (3) from mathematical notions, which are "the true characters of some immaterial being, seeing that they were never buried in matter, nor extracted out of it: and yet these are transcendently more certain and infallible principles of demonstration than any sensible thing can be;" and (4) from man's clear and stable ideas of truth.

On the existence and nature of God, Smith's doctrine is both ambitious and original, since he holds that he would "not so much demonstrate that He is, as what He is." From a study of his own being man can arrive at conceptions of "the most perfect mind and understanding," and God's omnipotence, "almighty love," eternity, omnipresence, and absolute freedom. Smith has many fine passages on God's nature and relations to the universe and man, and on "the Excellency and Nobleness of True Religion." One of the best of these is on man's true happiness as found in God. He has, or should have, a place in the history of English prose; his works are filled with memorable phrases, and he may be regarded as a pioneer in the aphoristic style of writing and preaching that has been popular in more recent times. In addition to Scripture, he cites innumerable authors—Greek, Roman, patristic, and medieval, as well as contemporary—and the influence of others, e.g., St. *Francis de Sales, is apparent.

Henry More. More (1614–87) ranks with Cudworth as the most famous of the Cambridge Platonists. Although raised a Calvinist, he rebelled against predestinarianism while a student at Eton. At Christ's College he was a fellow student of John Milton and became an M.A. and fellow in 1639. His studies of Aristotle, Julius Scaliger, G. Cardano, and others ended, he says, in "mere scepticism" and he turned to "the Platonic writers, Marsilius Ficinus, Plotinus himself, Mercurius Trismegistus, and the Mystical Divines." After taking Anglican orders, he received two benefices but gave them to friends; later he declined two bishoprics, and the deanery of St. Patrick's and provostship of Trinity College, Dublin, preferring to spend his life in Cambridge. He had a wide circle of friends and many correspondents, among them Descartes, the younger Van Helmont, William Penn, John Norris, Baron Knorr, and Joseph Glanvill. He was a voluminous writer on philosophy and theology and produced some verse.

Philosophy. To a basic philosophy derived from Aristotle and the scholastics More added elements drawn from Plato, the Neoplatonists, and other sources. Making an early acquaintance with Descartes, he first had an extravagant admiration for his doctrine, but later showed himself to be anti-Cartesian in metaphysics, and finally doubted that there is anything mechanical in nature. Incorporeal substance is for him the object of metaphysics; the universe is "one huge Animal," or if it lacks sense, which lack is not proved, "one monstrous Plant"; all nature, he says, is pervaded by "the spirit of nature," or "a plastical power"; space is an objective reality endowed with divine attributes. At the same time, he advances a doctrine of monads: bodies are composed of indivisible physical monads, and can be dissolved back into them by God's power, while spiritual substance is a "metaphysical monad."

In psychology and epistemology More labors to refute Hobbes and other materialists and to establish the reality of the soul, which has both preexistence and immortality. At death the soul leaves its "terrestrial vehicle," "glides into the free air," and enters first into an "aereal" and later into an "aethereal or celestial vehicle." The mind is never a *tabula rasa* but possesses innate ideas; the secondary qualities of bodies are in the perceiver rather than in things. In ethics More develops a doctrine of conscience under the name of "the boniform faculty," which he says is "the best and divinest part . . . the celestial particle of the soul," but here as elsewhere in his ethics he has nothing new that is of value.

Theology. More's theodicy is elaborate but unreliable. Leaving undeveloped the basic proofs for God's existence, he gives first place to his statement of the *ratio Anselmi* and advances so extravagant a statement of the proof from order as to discredit teleology. Further arguments are adduced from man's innate idea of God, the nature of the soul, morality, "miracles," viz, accounts of ghosts, witchcraft, demonism, and the like, and man's religious instincts. In religion More is important chiefly for his strong Protestantism, in which he holds that treason against any Protestant prince or opposition to Protestantism is both civil treason and religious heresy. The Church of Rome is the kingdom of anti-Christ and "the mystery of iniquity." In his attack More spares nothing: the Church's doctrine, history, claims, morals, ceremonial, members, leaders, and head were all assailed. So savage is his hatred that he was found extreme even in an age when like attacks were common among such diverse groups as Anglicans, dissenters, and *freethinkers.

More must be rated low both as a philosopher and a theologian. His work is marred by such intense bigotry and superstition as to bring injury on various valid doctrines, especially in theodicy and rational psychology. His attempts at novelty are abortive, and his work must be characterized as a mélange of doctrines taken from the Greeks, the scholastics, Jewish cabalists, Protestant theology, Sacred Scripture, and contemporary science. His books were read in colonial New England and helped to prepare the way for the sordid events at Salem.

Ralph Cudworth. Cudworth (1617–1688), a student and later fellow of Emmanuel College, had prestige and power under Cromwell but promptly wrote verses welcoming Charles II back home. His chief works were *The True Intellectual System of the Universe,* finished in 1671 but delayed in publication by opposition at court until 1678; and the posthumously published *Confutation of the Reason and Philosophy of Atheism* (1706); *Treatise concerning Eternal and Immutable Morality* (1731); and *Treatise of Freewill* (1838). The *True Intellectual System* is a vast work, itself a part of a vaster unfinished project, worthy—in conception at least—of comparison with some of the great systematic works of earlier centuries. It may be divided into: (1) a refutation of atheism, (2) the true idea of God, (3) proofs for the existence of God, (4) the natural distinction between good and evil, and (5) freedom of will. First giving the arguments for atheism, he perhaps, as Dryden says, states them better than he refutes them. Although he rejects the Anselmian and Cartesian arguments, he gives one based on the idea of God and others from contingency, order, and the character of knowledge.

Famous for his theory of a plastic nature, Cudworth describes it as a lower faculty of some conscious soul, or itself a kind of inferior life or soul, an immaterial, incorporeal substance that is the divine art embodied in nature, a shadowy imitation of mind and understanding, analogous to mental causality, acting for ends but unconscious of them. It is an instrument used by God, and it operates according to laws imposed by him. Analogies to ancient theories of a *world soul and to later doctrines like those of Schopenhauer, Bergson, and E. von Hartmann are evident. Certain anticipations of Kantian doctrines in theodicy, and on space and time as mental forms, the categories, and the unknown "thing in itself" may also be found in Cudworth.

Cudworth is almost a great philosopher. Along with pronounced intellectual abilities and immense learning, he unites many past and contemporary strains, makes some contributions of his own, and anticipates certain future developments. His purposes are good, but he fails in some of his means since his great learning is often uncritical, and he overuses his authorities, and he is at times too severe in his judgments. Instances of these defects may be found in his account of atomistic philosophy, which he traced back to Moses. If he had advanced an extremist doctrine, as did Hobbes and Spinoza in his time, he would have been a more famous and influential, but less able, thinker. As it is, Cudworth ranks with Bacon, Hobbes, and Locke in 17th-century English philosophy, and in certain respects is superior to them.

Related Thinkers and Influence. Other thinkers sometimes, but incorrectly, associated with the Cambridge Platonists are Nathaniel Culverwel (1615/18–1650/51), George Rust (d. 1670), Symon Patrick (1626–1707), Joseph Glanvill (1636–80), John Hales (1584–1656), John Norris (1657–1711), and Richard Cumberland (1631–1718). In addition to their relation to Kant and Locke, the Cambridge Platonists influenced particularly the third Earl of Shaftesbury (1671–1713). In religion the effects of their teaching were away from traditional doctrine and toward *rationalism and a nondogmatic religion of morality. In philosophy they were dualists concerned with fundamental things—God, the soul, natural morality, free will, and the epistemological problem. In some areas, they prepared the way for more radical doctrines of the 18th century.

See also BRITISH MORALISTS; ENLIGHTENMENT, PHILOSOPHY; PLATONISM; PROTESTANTISM.

Bibliography: Sources. J. SMITH, *Select Discourses,* ed. H. G. WILLIAMS (4th ed. rev. Cambridge, Eng. 1859). H. MORE, *Opera omnia,* 3 v. (London 1675–79). R. CUDWORTH, *The True Intellectual System of the Universe,* tr. J. HARRISON, 3 v. (London 1845).

Literature. Copleston 5:52–66. J. TULLOCH, *Rational Theology and Christian Philosophy in England in the Seventeenth Century,* 2 v. (2d ed. Edinburgh 1874). J. K. RYAN, *The Reputation of St. Thomas Aquinas Among English Protestant Thinkers of the Seventeenth Century* (Washington 1948); "John Smith, 1616–1652: Platonist and Mystic," NewSchol 20 (1946) 1–25. E. CASSIRER, *The Platonic Renaissance in England,* tr. J. P. PETTEGROVE (Austin 1953). B. WILLEY, *Seventeenth Century Background* (New York 1950). J. A. PASSMORE, *Ralph Cudworth* (Cambridge, Eng. 1951).

[J. K. RYAN]

CAMDEN, DIOCESE OF (CAMDENSIS)

Suffragan of the metropolitan See of Newark, established Dec. 9, 1937, from the six southernmost counties of New Jersey—Camden, Gloucester, Salem, Cumberland, Atlantic, and Cape May—formerly part of the *Trenton diocese and earlier under the jurisdiction first of *Philadelphia and then of *Newark.

The area's Catholic history goes back to 1740, when four pioneer Catholic families settled near the Salem glass works. Because the Jerseys did not then enjoy freedom of worship, Jesuit missionaries from St. Joseph's, Philadelphia, Pa., secretly served the scattered Catholics from Salem to New York, making regular visits throughout the area. When iron works, saw mills, and shipbuilding in Pleasant Mills, Waterford, and Port Elizabeth brought more settlers, Philadelphia priests built the first church, St. Mary's, Pleasant Mills (1826), and the first full-time parishes, Gloucester (1848) and Salem (1852). In 1853 the Newark diocese was created, including the entire state, and five new parishes developed: Immaculate Conception (1855) and SS. Peter and Paul (1867), Camden; Millville (1864), Egg Harbor (1866), and Swedesboro (1872). By 1894 South Jersey's shipbuilding, glass works, paper and textile mills, foodstuffs, and fertile farmlands had attracted still larger numbers and the total number of parishes there had grown to 17.

In 1937, when Camden became a diocese, a New Yorker, Bartholomew Eustace (1887–1956), was named first ordinary. A scholarly, mild, dignified man, the new bishop, a former seminary professor, faced four major problems: a priest shortage, debts, impending war, and the remnant of anti-Catholic feeling. Immaculate Conception, Camden, became his cathedral. During his 19-year episcopate, he added 32 parishes, 19 elementary schools, 6 high schools, 115 priests, 242 seminarians, and 2 hospitals to his diocese. His successor Justin McCarthy (1900–59) had grown up in Elizabeth, N.J.; he was ordained in Rome (1927), consecrated auxiliary of Newark (1954), and transferred to Camden on March 19, 1957. There he directed the expansion of high school facilities, and established five parishes, eight elementary schools, and the Puerto Rican apostolate before his sudden death 2 years later. The third bishop, Celestine J. Damiano, was born in Dunkirk, N.Y. (1911), ordained in Rome (1935), consecrated titular archbishop of Nicopolis in Epiro (1953), and served as apostolic delegate to South Africa and member of the Preparatory Commission for Vatican Council II. He was installed as archbishop-bishop of Camden on May 3, 1960.

Geographically, the Camden diocese forms three sections: a northern, consisting of Camden city with mushrooming suburbs, bounded by an extensive belt of farmlands with scattered towns and industry; a central, stretching through Bridgeton, Millville, and Vine-

St. Mary's, Gloucester, N.J., where the first parish in the Camden diocese was established (1848).

land to Hammonton, with industry surrounded by truck farms; and a southern, with pines and farms, sprinkled with small towns and encompassed by coastal communities from Cape May to Atlantic City, with their resorts and limited industry. Damiano adopted a policy of expansion and centralization. He created 20 parishes, enlarged the educational system, appointed 41 priests to graduate studies, increased the chancery and Catholic Charities staffs, and inaugurated a mission in Brazil with 4 Camden priests. By 1964 the number of Catholics had increased to more than 263,000 in a total population of about 962,000; there were 108 parishes, 11 missions, and 16 stations; 352 priests, of whom 48 were religious; 12 high schools, and 62 elementary schools; and 2 hospitals, 1 nursing school, and 2 homes for the aged.

[M. L. PANCZYK]

CAMERA, APOSTOLIC

The Apostolic Camera administers the property and guards the temporal rights of the Holy See, especially during its vacancy (CIC c.262; ClerSanc c.208). The word "especially" here is really a euphemism, for at other times the administration is entirely in the hands of a pontifical commission established in 1891 and still functioning. The Camera's chief officer is called the camerlengo.

Duties. During a vacancy of the Holy See the camerlengo has such grave and urgent responsibilities that if the office itself is vacant a successor must be elected as soon as possible by the cardinals at the first general congregation preparatory to the conclave. During the short interval before this can be done the dean of the Sacred College acts in his place.

Concerning the duties of the camerlengo during a vacancy, canon 262 declares that "he shall observe exactly the provisions of the apostolic constitution of Pius X, *Vacante Sede Apostolica,* of 25 December 1904." That document is now supplanted by the constitution of Pius XII, *Vacantis Apostolicae Sedis,* Dec. 8, 1945, as amended by the motu proprio of John XXIII, Sept. 5, 1962. Hence these are now the duties of the camerlengo, during the vacancy only: he has charge of the property and temporal rights of the Holy See, assisted by the senior cardinals of each of the three orders (bishop, priest, and deacon); upon receiving notice of the death of the pontiff he must proceed immediately to take possession of the apostolic palace of the Vatican (and also, by deputies, of the Lateran and Castel Gandolfo); he must make a juridical verification of the death, inform the cardinal vicar of Rome, and affix seals to the pope's private apartments. He alone can give permission for photographs or recordings to be made there.

With the three heads of orders, he decides the time for the first general congregation preparatory to the conclaves. He may give permission for individual cardinals to have more than one conclavist, and he sees to it that the conclavists take the prescribed oath in due time before the conclave. After the conclave is closed within and without, the camerlengo with the three other senior cardinals mentioned must examine the hidden corners of the conclave to see that no one not admissible remains. Notes taken by the cardinals on the results of the voting, instead of being burned with the ballots as formerly, must be delivered to the camerlengo, or to one of the other three, to be sealed and deposited in the archives. Finally, when the conclave is finished, the camerlengo draws up a report, to be approved by the three heads of orders, declaring the result of the balloting at each session. The sealed envelope containing this report is kept in the archives and may not be opened by any one without the express permission of the pope.

The personnel of the Apostolic Camera consists of the cardinal chamberlain, a vice chamberlain, an auditor, a treasurer, five *chierici di Camera,* and two other officials.

History. The *camerarius* (chamberlain, camerlengo) dates from the end of the 11th century, when he appears as the chief financial administrator of papal properties and revenues. In the 13th and 14th centuries he acquired also judicial functions not only in fiscal matters but also in other civil and penal cases. The Camera thus became an extremely important administrative office and judicial tribunal. The senior assistants of the *camerarius* were the *clerici Camerae.* Several special assignments, branching off from the office of the chamberlain, subsequently developed into independent offices. The vice chamberlain became the *gubernator urbis* or governor of Rome; the general treasurer remained in charge of financial administration; the auditor general was a strictly judicial officer with a tribunal of prelates and doctors of laws at his disposal. The highest court was the *Tribunal plenae Camerae,* with appellate jurisdiction; its judges were the *clerici Camerae* already mentioned. Since the events of 1870 and the end of the Papal States, there remains only a trace of all this activity.

Bibliography: Abbo 1:262. E. HESTON, *The Holy See at Work* (Milwaukee 1950). Wernz-Vidal 2. J. RAFFALLI, DDC 2:1275–78. B. OJETTI, *De Romana Curia: Commentarium in constitutionem apostolicam "Sapienti consilio"* (Rome 1910).

[T. L. BOUSCAREN]

CAMERARIUS, JOACHIM, classical philologist, Lutheran humanist, and biographer, known also as Kammermeister; b. Bamberg, April 12, 1500; d.

Leipzig, April 17, 1574. A student at Leipzig in 1512, he joined the Erfurt circle of humanists in 1518, and then went to Wittenberg (1521), where he became a favorite pupil of Philipp Melanchthon. He taught in Nuremberg (1526) and was a deputy of the city at the Diet of *Augsburg (1530). As professor in Tübingen (1535) he helped reorganize the university, and in 1541 he led in the reorganization of the University of Leipzig. Besides a large correspondence, he left several biographies, including those of Eobanus Hessus (1533), Duke George of Anhalt (Lutheran bishop of Merseburg, 1555), and Philipp Melanchthon (1566); many philological, pedagogical, and historical works; editions of ancient classics; and an edition of Albrecht Dürer's works. "Peaceable and learned," he exercised a moderating and irenical influence for Lutheranism at the Augsburg Diets of 1530 and 1555, in the Osiandrian controversy, and in discussions with Francis I (1535) and Maximilian II (1568) regarding the possibility of Catholic-Protestant reunion.

Bibliography: H. HELBIG, *Die Reformation der Universität Leipzig im 16. Jahrhundert* (Gütersloh 1953). F. STÄHLIN, *Humanismus und Reformation* (Leipzig 1936). F. LAU, RGG[3] 1:1602. E. ISERLOH, LexThK[2] 2:903–904.

[R. H. FISCHER]

CAMERINO, ARCHDIOCESE OF (CAMERINENSIS), metropolitan see immediately subject to the Holy See since 1787, in the Apennines, the Marches, central Italy. In 1963 it had 146 secular and 31 religious priests, 240 women in 34 convents, and 74,000 Catholics; it is 475 square miles in area. Christian origins, as in all the Marches, are obscure. The first known bishop is Gerontius (465). Under the Lombards and Carolingians the see grew. The County of

The Cathedral of Camerino, Italy, built in 1832.

Camerino, under the dukes of *Spoleto, had its own duke in the 10th century, and Camerino was capital of a march (10th-12th century) until it became part of the *States of the Church, with which it had had special ties. It was ruled by the Varano family as a papal fief (c. 1250–1545). The diocese lost territory to Macerata (1320), Tolentino and Sanseverino (1586), Fabriano (1728), and Matelica (1787). The cathedral still has the wooden casket of Bishop St. Ansovinus (840). In the 11th century St. *Romuald founded several monasteries and inspired others in the diocese with his Camaldolese rule; he died at S. Salvatore in Val di Castro, no longer in the diocese. Abbot St. Amicus lived in S. Maria di Rambona (Macerata). The Church of S. Venanzio is dedicated to a Dalmatian martyr, the account of whose martyrdom is legendary. The spiritual author Bl. Battista Varano (1458–1527) died in the monastery of Poor Clares that she founded in her native Camerino. Paolo da Camerino, a Jesuit, accompanied Francis Xavier to Goa (1541) and died there (1560).

Bibliography: B. FELICIANGELI, *Cronotassi dei più antigui vescovi di Camerino* (Camerino 1921). F. LANZONI, *Le diocesi d'Italia dalle origini al principio del sec. VII,* 2 v. (Faenza 1927) 2:487–489. EncIt 8:533–534. L. JADIN, DHGE 11:594–600. S. PRETE, EncCatt 3:432–433. AnnPont (1965) 88. **Illustration credit:** Arthur O'Leary.

[S. PRETE]

CAMERLENGO. Although there is a camerlengo of the *Sacred College and of the Roman clergy, this title usually refers to the camerlengo of the Holy Roman Church, whose office is to supervise the property and temporal rights of the Holy See, especially *sede vacante.* As head, *sede vacante,* of the Sacred College he verifies the death of the pope and makes preparations for the *conclave, which he directs. He is appointed by the pope or, if the office is vacant at the pope's death, by the Sacred College.

See also CARDINAL, I (HISTORY OF); CARDINAL, II (CANON LAW OF); CURIA, ROMAN; POPES, ELECTION OF.

Bibliography: CIC cc.262, 160, as modified by PIUS XII, "Vacantis apostolicae sedis" (apostolic constitution, Dec. 8, 1945), ActApS 38 (1946) 65–99, and by JOHN XXIII, "Summi pontificis" (motu proprio, Sept. 5, 1962), ActApS 54 (1962) 632–640.

[B. FORSHAW]

CAMERON, JOHN, Scottish theologian, a leading divine of the French Huguenot Church; b. Glasgow, 1579; d. Montauban, France, 1625. He was educated at the University of Glasgow. In 1600 he went to France where his abilities as a classical scholar won him a professorship at the Protestant University of Sedan. From 1604 to 1608 he studied theology at Paris, Geneva, and Heidelberg. In 1608 he published the first of a series of theological tracts (*De triplici Dei cum homine foedere*), which were to make him a controversial figure in Calvinist circles. In retrospect, Cameron's theological intentions seem quite clear. He, like the Dutchman Jacobus *Arminius, was trying to resolve the dilemma implicit in orthodox Calvinist theology as to whether Christ had died for all men or for the elect only. Arminius, unlike Calvin, insisted that the atonement was for all—believers and nonbelievers, elect and reprobate alike. If Christ died for all, anti-Arminians charged, then nonbelievers were the victims of divine caprice and the unregenerate had a voluntary power to resist grace. In either case, significant attributes of the divine nature were impugned. Cameron contended by way of compromise that Christ's death was a universal sacrifice but that nonbelievers did not therefore have a choice of accepting or resisting grace. According to Cameron, the will of man is determined by the judgment of the mind. Men do good or evil as a result of knowledge infused into them by God, who does not move the will physically but only morally as a consequence of its dependence on human judgment. Thus Cameron believed he had removed God's ultimate responsibility for sin, preserved the irresistible nature of grace, and explained how it was that some men could seemingly accept or deny the consequences of Christ's sacrifice.

Despite his ambivalent position, Cameron held the chairs of divinity at Saumur (1618–20) and Glasgow (1622–23). Never popular with the strong Presbyterian party in the Scottish Church, he ended his days in France where he taught briefly at the University of Montauban before his death.

Bibliography: T. F. HENDERSON, DNB 3:747–748. Cross ODCC 223.

[S. A. BURRELL]

CAMERON, JOHN, bishop, educator; b. South River, Antigonish County, Nova Scotia, Canada, Feb. 16, 1826; d. Antigonish, April 6, 1910. He was the youngest son of John Cameron. After attending St. Andrew's grammar and normal school, he pursued his ecclesiastical studies at the Urban College of the Propaganda, Rome, was ordained July 26, 1853, and received the doctorate of philosophy and theology. On his return to Canada he served as professor and director of a school at Arichat, Nova Scotia. In 1855 he was assigned as parish priest to St. Ninian's, Antigonish, where he served also as rector and professor of philosophy and theology in the newly established St. Francis Xavier College (later University) and directed its progress for more than a half-century. He was appointed to the cathedral at Arichat (1863), and was named vicar-general (1865), and coadjutor (1869). He was consecrated titular bishop of Titopolis (in Isauria) at Rome on May 22, 1870, and succeeded to the see July 17, 1887, becoming Arichat's third bishop. On Aug. 23, 1886, the episcopal see was transferred from Arichat to Antigonish. There Cameron opened new parishes, institutions, and religious schools; and under his guidance St. Francis Xavier College became the center of Catholic learning in the Maritime Provinces. In May 1885 he was sent as papal delegate to Three Rivers, Quebec, to investigate the division of the diocese. He was regarded as one of the ablest Catholic spokesmen in Canada.

Bibliography: D. J. RANKIN, *A History of the County of Antigonish, Nova Scotia* (Toronto 1929).

[J. T. FLYNN]

CAMERONIANS, the most uncompromising Presbyterian communion in Scotland (known also as the Reformed Presbyterian Church). Though numerically small, the group is historically important. The Cameronians take their origin from those *Covenanters who refused to follow their brethren in accepting the Revolution Settlement of the Church of Scotland (1689–90). Their reason was that the Settlement ignored the perpetual obligation incurred by the Scottish nation in the National Covenant of 1638, and by the whole of Great Britain in the Solemn League and Covenant of 1643. The name Cameronian derives from that of the principal preacher of these dissenting Covenanters, the youthful extremist Richard Cameron (1648–80), who fell in the skirmish at Aird's Moss near Auchinleck. His followers organized themselves in local societies, mainly in Ayrshire and Lanarkshire (1681). Though their three ministers entered the national church of the Revolution Settlement in 1690, the greater part of the sect, numbering several thousand, refused to conform; 16 years later (1706) they obtained a new minister, John Macmillan, whose intensive, itinerant missionary activity so strengthened the movement that the sectarians were often called Macmillanites. Under his leadership in 1743, a presbytery, known as the Reformed Presbytery, was set up, and the Reformed Presbyterians increased their numerical strength in Scotland; their ideas had considerable effect on Scottish communities overseas. They maintained, into the 19th century, the principle of "political dissent," refusing to swear allegiance to the British Constitution or to take part in any way in civil government. In 1863 a majority of the Reformed Presbyterian Synod decided to refrain from taking disciplinary action against those who exercised the franchise or took part in the civil government of an "uncovenanted" nation. In 1876 this majority joined the Free Church and were finally merged in the Established Church of Scotland in 1929. The minority, however, continues as the Reformed Presbyterian Church, and it consists of a synod, organized in two presbyteries, in the Lowlands of Scotland. In all there are eight congregations, whose diminishing total membership was estimated in 1960 as about 600.

Bibliography: M. HUTCHISON, *The Reformed Presbyterian Church in Scotland, 1680–1876* (Paisley, Scot. 1893). W. J. COUPER, *The Reformed Presbyterian Church in Scotland* (Edinburgh 1925). J. HIGHET, *The Scottish Churches* (London 1960). Cross ODCC 223.

[D. MC ROBERTS]

CAMEROON

Tropical, largely agricultural country in West *Africa bordering on the Gulf of Guinea, 182,000 square miles in area. From 1844 to 1916 it was a German colony. After World War I the French and British held it as a mandate territory. The United Nations administered it as trust territory (1944–60). In 1960 the French trusteeship became an independent republic in French Community. The southern region of the former British trusteeship voted in 1961 to unite with it. The population was estimated in 1964 at 4,000,000, with 17,000 Europeans. About one-third of the populace was Christian, including 550,000 Protestants (250,000 being full members). Moslems comprised approximately a sixth of the inhabitants, concentrated in the northernmost areas. The remaining half of the inhabitants were pagans.

The Portuguese landed on the coast as early as 1472, but methodical evangelization did not begin until 1890, when the area was detached from the Vicariate Apostolic of the Two Guineas, and the Prefecture Apostolic (vicariate, 1904) of Cameroon was created and entrusted to German Pallottines. The northern section was detached in 1914 to form the Prefecture Apostolic

of Adamaoua, which was confided to the German province of the Priests of the Sacred Heart. During World War I all missionaries, except French military chaplains, were expelled. After 1922 the Vicariate of Cameroun was staffed by French Holy Ghost Fathers. The Prefecture of Adamaoua was transferred to Foumban (vicariate, 1934), and Sacred Heart Fathers from France replaced those from Germany. Mill Hill Missionaries took charge of evangelizing the British mandate territory, where in 1923 the Prefecture of Buea was created (vicariate, 1939). Thereupon the mission experienced a rapid growth: 60,000 Catholics in 1920; 110,000 in 1925; 280,000 in 1935; 360,000 in 1940; 500,000 in 1950; 700,000 in 1960. In 1931 the Vicariate of Cameroon was divided into the Vicariate of Yaoundé and Prefecture of Douala (vicariate, 1932). In 1947 the Oblates of Mary Immaculate were given charge of the newly created Prefecture of Garoua (vicariate, 1953) in the extreme north with jurisdiction over some territory in Chad until 1956. In 1949 the Vicariate of Doumé was separated from Yaoundé and was given to the Holy Ghost Fathers.

The hierarchy was established in 1955, when *Yaoundé became an archdiocese and metropolitan see for the entire country. Its seven suffragan dioceses in 1964 were Buea, Douala, Doumé, Garoua, Mbalmayo, Nkongsamba, and Sangmélima. In 1965, the Prefecture of Bafia was detached from the Yaoundé diocese. In 1935 the first African priests were ordained in Cameroon, and in 1955 the first African bishops were consecrated. Jean Baptiste Zoa became in 1961 the first African archbishop of Yaoundé. Cameroon had four other African bishops (1964). In 1963 there were about 900,000 Catholics, 105,000 catechumens, 550 priests (166 Africans), 54 seminarians, 178 brothers, 572 sisters (175 Africans), and 5,900 catechists. The mission has placed stress on education. Catholic elementary schools enrolled 211,000 pupils (45 per cent of all students in these grades), 7,570 in secondary schools (40 per cent of the total), and 1,400 in technical schools (25 per cent of the total). The mission publishes a weekly newspaper and several periodicals.

Bibliography: *Bilan du Monde* 2:186–193. AnnPont (1965) 78, 137, 162, 269, 304–305, 492, 1255, statistics on all dioceses. For additional bibliography, *see* AFRICA.

[J. BOUCHAUD]

CAMILLIANS, popular name of the Order of St. Camillus (OSCam), whose official title is the Order of Clerics Regular, Servants of the Sick. The order was founded in Rome by (St.) *Camillus de Lellis about 1582 and given final approval as an order with solemn vows in 1591. To the usual three vows of religion was added a fourth, that of serving the sick, including the victims of the plagues so common at that time. This vow is still made by all members of the order. Camillus composed his rule with this specific character of the order in view.

The first Camillians rendered their services by visiting the hospitals of Rome, bringing the patients both physical and spiritual assistance. In 1594, however, they began founding communities housed within the hospitals, where the religious took the place of the chaplains and of the servants who were hired for nursing. Establishing itself in Naples in 1588, the order grew rapidly. At the time of the founder's death in 1614 there were 330 professed members in 15 cities of Italy. After the death of Camillus the religious began caring for the sick in their homes, gradually giving up the communities within the hospitals. By the end of the 18th century they were exercising this form of apostolate not only in Italy, but also in Hungary, Spain, Portugal, and several parts of Latin America. The Order of St. Camillus, like other religious orders, suffered greatly from the suppressions and confiscations of the 19th century. At one point it was reduced to about 100 members, all of them in Italy. In the 20th century, however, they experienced a recovery, so that by 1964 membership had risen to about 1,350. The Camillians are located in 11 countries of Europe, in the U.S. and Canada, in South America, Formosa, and Thailand. The order is ruled by a prefect general and his four consultors, all of whom reside in Rome.

In the course of its modern expansion the order has returned to exercising most of its apostolate in hospitals. In 1964 the Camillians owned and operated 36 hospitals, clinics, and nursing homes. The great majority of the lay brothers were engaged in nursing in these institutions. Camillian priests, besides holding administrative posts and being chaplains in the order's own hospitals, were chaplains in 121 other hospitals and charitable institutions. They were also active as directors of Catholic associations of nurses and of nursing sisters in Italy, Germany, and Austria. In the U.S. the first foundation was made in Milwaukee, Wis., in 1924. In 1964 there were four houses, three of which served the sick and aged. These houses, located in the Archdiocese of Milwaukee, and in the Dioceses of Madison, Wis., and Worcester, Mass., constituted a province with about 40 members.

Bibliography: H. DAMMIG, LexThK² 5:1269. M. VANTI, Enc Catt 8:1040–42.

[P. TUTWILER]

CAMILLUS DE LELLIS, ST.

Copatron with St. John of God of hospitals, nurses, and the sick, founder of the Order of *Camillians; b. Bucchianico (Abruzzo), Italy, May 25, 1550; d. Rome, July 14, 1614 (feast, July 18). His mother, Camilla de Compellis, was nearly 60 at his birth and died when he was a child. His father, Giovanni, who served as a captain in both the French and Neapolitan armies, neglected the child's own education. As a youth, his own inclinations were already strongly turned to the military life and to gambling. His enrollment in the army was delayed by the outbreak of an ulcer on his right foot; in 1571 it obliged him to seek medical care at the hospital of San Giacomo in Rome. When he was sufficiently healed, he stayed on as a servant in the hospital, but was dismissed for card playing. From 1571 to 1574 he fought in various campaigns of the Venetian army against the Turks. After gambling away his possessions in the winter of 1574–75, he accepted employment at the Capuchin monastery of Manfredonia (Puglio).

A friar stirred him to repentance on Feb. 2, 1575. He was accepted by the Capuchins as a lay brother but was dismissed from the novitiate when the old wounds irritated by the coarse garb would not heal. Camillus then returned to San Giacomo for treatment and again stayed on as a servant. He reentered the Capuchins in 1579, but the wound again opened and led to his final rejection from the order. This ailment persisted during the next 35 years of his life. Welcomed back to the hospital, Camillus was made Maestro di Casa (superintendent). He now determined to devote his life to the sick, and on the advice of his friends and his spiritual guide, Philip Neri, he began his studies for the priesthood at the Jesuit College in Rome. He was ordained in 1584 and gathered followers to share his work. He founded an order, known then as Ministers of the Sick, or Fathers of a Good Death; as first superior general he spent much of his time in the direct spiritual and bodily care of the infirm. He resigned the generalship in 1607 and devoted the final years of his life exclusively to such personal service. He died after establishing several houses throughout Italy. His body lies in the church of St. Mary Magdalen in Rome.

St. Camillus is known more for his charity toward the sick than for contributions to the technique of their care. Yet, his insistence on hospital cleanliness and the technical competence of his religious deserves mention. Notable also was his method of instructing his patients, rather than constraining them, to receive the Sacraments.

Benedict XIV beatified Camillus in 1742 and canonized him 4 years later. In 1886 Leo XIII declared St. Camillus and St. John of God patrons of the sick and of hospitals and inserted their names in the litany of the dying. In 1930 Pius XI extended their patronage to all nurses and to all Catholic nursing associations.

Bibliography: M. VANTI, *S. Camillo de Lellis ed i suoi ministri degli infermi* (2d ed. Rome 1958); EncCatt 3:438–439, full bibliog. S. CICATELLI, *Vita del P. C. de Lellis* (Rome 1624); this early life is tr. by W. FABER, *St. Camillus de Lellis* (Milwaukee 1926). M. FISCHER, *Der hl. Kamillus von Lellis* (Freiburg 1940). C. C. MARTINDALE, *Life of Saint Camillus* (New York 1946). Butler Th Attw 3:134–136. BullRomCon 1:175–176.

[P. TUTWILER]

CAMISARDS,

French Protestant zealots who revolted against the government of Louis XIV early in the 18th century. They were provoked to revolt by the brutal repression of all public practice of their faith following the revocation of the Edict of Nantes (1685), and by the apocalyptic writings of certain Protestant intellectuals, notably Pierre Jurieu. They were led by a number of ecstatic, uneducated "prophets" convinced of their own direct inspiration and of the imminent end of the world. Their first great act of violence was the assassination in 1702 of an archpriest, François de Langlade du Chayla, a leader in the suppression of Protestantism in the Cévennes. Immediately thereafter the Camisards organized armed bands to resist government punitive action in rural parts of the southern French provinces of Dauphiné, Vivarais, and, above all, the Cévennes. They found an effective amateur military leader in Jean Cavalier and won some sympathy and a little support from Protestant nations. They fought with fanatic ferocity but were no match for the armies of Louis XIV. The revolt had been effectively crushed by 1704, when many of its leaders fled into exile abroad. Later flare-ups of violence were easily contained by government troops. The movement was repudiated by the more responsible Protestant leaders in France, notably Antoine Court, and some of its characteristic claims, particularly of direct revelation, were condemned by a secret provincial synod of the French Reformed Church of the Cévennes (1715). But the Camisards' excesses provided an excuse for continuing sporadic persecution of French Protestantism throughout much of the rest of the 18th century.

See also NANTES, EDICT OF.

Bibliography: H. M. BAIRD, *The Huguenots and the Revocation of the Edict of Nantes*, 2 v. (New York 1895) v.2. A. DUCASSE, *La Guerre des Camisards* (Paris 1946). C. ALMERAS, *La Révolte des Camisards* (Paris 1960). F. VERNET, DTC 2:1435–43. R. VOELTZEL RGG³ 1:1603–04. P. CHIMINELLI, EncCatt 3:439–440.

[R. M. KINGDON]

CAMÕES, LUÍS DE

The most famous of Portuguese poets; b. Lisbon or Coimbra, 1524; d. Lisbon, 1580. Facts about his colorful life in Portugal, North Africa, and the Orient are meager, and biographers often resort to interpretation of apparent biographical references in his writings. His family was possibly an old Galician one that had moved to Portugal in 1370. He certainly studied in the university city of Coimbra, then lived in Lisbon in and around the court, and served as a soldier in Ceuta, Morocco, where he lost an eye. Back in Lisbon, he is said to have lived riotously, and was thrown into prison as the result of a street fight. He was pardoned and volunteered to serve his King in India. He sailed for Goa in 1553 and spent some 16 years in the East. His personal headquarters would have been Goa, the Portuguese political and ecclesiastical capital on the west coast of India, and he evidently sailed the waters farther east. His poetic ability was obviously widely known, for the first major book published in Goa (Garcia d' Orta's *Coloquios dos simples, e drogas he cousas mediçinais da India*, 1563)

Luís Vaz de Camões, a portrait in red pigment, 6 by 9 inches, painted c. 1558 by Fernando Gomes. This is the only portrait of Camões known to have been painted during his lifetime. Unknown until 1925, it was discovered in the effects of the famous collector of Camoniana, Dr. Carvalho Monteiro. It is now in the Academy of Sciences at Lisbon.

contains a dedicatory ode by him, his first published work.

In 1567 he arrived in Mozambique and 2 years later returned at last to Lisbon. He had been in Portuguese India after the peak of its splendor, at a time when corruption signaled the beginning of its long decline. Significantly, the Inquisition had been introduced into Goa in 1560. Camões returned to an unstable Portugal to learn of King Sebastian's defeat and death (1578) at Alcázarquivir (El Qsar el Kbir) in Morocco. His epic poem *Os Lusíadas* (1572), had been published and had earned a modest pension from the King. The day of his death—June 10, according to report—has become virtually a national holiday, *o Dia da Raça.*

Motivation of Os Lusíadas. Camões, well-educated, sincerely Christian, and patriotic in the best sense of the term, was both shocked at the state of Portuguese affairs in the Indies and inspired by the heroic deeds of lesser Portuguese, the minor officials and lower-class workers who accomplished much in spite of inept leadership. His extensive reading at Coimbra of glorious Portuguese exploits at home and abroad may ultimately have fired his resolve to sing of the Portuguese collectively, emphasizing their virtues but never glossing over or failing to censure severely their human weakness. *Os Lusíadas* is the result, an epic celebration of the "sons of Lusus." (Lusus was the mythological founder of Lusitania, that is, Portugal.)

The poem is written in ottava rima, in 10 cantos averaging 110 stanzas each, and employs, among other devices, the juxtaposition of Christian God and pagan deities. Extensive critical discussion has arisen from this theme and device. Ironically, perhaps no more perceptive statement of the poem's subject and of the role of mythology in its elaboration has been made than that of the ecclesiastical censor of the original text, Bartolomeu Ferreira, OP, whose opinion is included in the first edition (Lisbon 1572):

> At the command of the Holy and General Inquisition I have examined these ten Cantos of *Os Lusíadas* of Luís de Camões concerning the valorous feats of arms which the Portuguese accomplished in Asia and Europe, and I have found nothing scandalous in them, nor contrary to faith and morals. I do feel constrained to warn readers, however, that the Author, in order to emphasize the difficulties experienced by the Portuguese in sailing to and entering India, makes use of a fictitious device involving the pagan gods. And even though St. Augustine in his *Confessions* confesses having referred to the Muses as gods in the books which he composed *De Ordine*, nevertheless, as this is poetry and pretense, and inasmuch as the Author, as a poet, claims to do no more than embellish his poetic style, we have not found this fable about gods improper in the work, for it is recognized as such, and the truth of our holy faith which affirms that all the gods of the pagans are demons always remains intact. Wherefore the book appeared to me to be worthy of publication, and the Author exhibits in it much ingenuity and considerable knowledge of the humanities.

Stature of Camões's work. *Os Lusíadas* is a masterpiece by a great poet, and should be read as poetry. Unfortunately, it has too often been used by special pleaders to support one or another doctrine or thesis, whereas in reality no single point of view can find consistent support in the epic. It has also been used by scholars as an example of erudition—of the study of flora and fauna, nautical science, naval architecture, and countless other disciplines—whereas in fact its author was simply a man of the Renaissance, of broad culture and interests, capable of taking up either pen or sword. This breadth of content surely accounts for the many translations, including eight different English verse versions and one in English prose.

Most critics agree that Camões's lyrics alone would rank him among the world's great poets. The sonnets, *redondilhas*, odes, *canções*, elegies, eclogues, and other poems first appeared in the collection *Rhythmas* (1595). The determination of the exact authorship of many poems attributed to Camões has puzzled editors and scholars ever since, but there is no doubt that the author of *Os Lusíadas*—itself a poem replete with lyric passages—wrote the greatest of them, including a moving adaptation of Psalm 136 ("By the Streams of Babylon"), *Sôbolos rios que vão*.

Camões wrote also three plays, *Os Enfatriões*, *Filodemo*, and *El-rei Seleuco*, the first two published as early as 1587, the last in the 1645 edition of the *Rimas*. A few of his letters survive.

Bibliography: Works. *The Lusiads*, tr. L. BACON (New York 1950); *Rimas*, ed. A. J. DA COSTA PIMPAO (Coimbra 1953); *Obras completas*, ed. H. CIDADE, 5 v. (Lisbon 1946–47). Literature. A. F. G. BELL, *Luis de Camões* (Oxford 1923). G. LE GENTIL, *Camoëns: L'oeuvre épique et lyrique* (Paris 1954). H. H. HART,

Luis de Camoëns and the Epic of the Lusiads (Norman, Okla. 1962). H. CIDADE, *Luís de Camões* (Lisbon 1961). **Illustration credit:** Copyright 1962, University of Oklahoma Press.

[F. M. ROGERS]

CAMPANA, EMILIO, theologian; b. Signora (Val Colla, Ticino), 1874; d. Lugano, June 8, 1939. He completed his early education at Pollegio and Lugano. He was sent to Rome for higher studies at the Urban (Propaganda) College and won doctorates in both philosophy and theology. His teacher Alexis Lépicier (later cardinal) encouraged his pursuit of Mariological studies. After his ordination in 1897, he returned to the major seminary at Lugano to teach dogmatic theology, holding the post until his death. In 1914 he was appointed official theologian of the bishop of Lugano. From 1927 until 1932 he served as rector of the seminary at which he taught. He is known principally for his two works in the field of Mariology: *Maria nel dogma cattolico* (Turin 1923) and *Maria nel culto cattolico* (2 v., Turin 1933). The former work has been highly acclaimed by theologians throughout the world. It has gone through five Italian editions and has been translated into several languages. Besides these works Campana left two incomplete studies: one on Mary in art and the other a dogmatic-historical treatise on Vatican Council I. In addition to these monographs he published a number of articles in various theological reviews.

Bibliography: A. PIOLANTI, EncCatt 3:449.

[C. R. MEYER]

CAMPANELLA, TOMMASO

Dominican philosopher; b. Stilo, Calabria, Italy, Sept. 5, 1568; d. Paris, May 21, 1639.

Campanella entered the religious life at an early age and was educated in the houses of studies of his order. Becoming dissatisfied with the Aristotelian teachings of his day, he favored instead the naturalistic views of B. *Telesio, whom he undertook to defend against his opponents. In 1599 he was arrested by order of the Spanish authorities and taken in chains to Naples, where he had to stand trial on charges of heresy and conspiracy. Although subjected to physical torture, he never confessed to crime or heresy, and even resisted by feigning insanity. In 1602 he was sentenced to perpetual imprisonment, and, whether rightly or not, spent a total of 27 years in a Neapolitan dungeon. Released in 1626, he was again arrested and brought before the Holy Office in Rome. After regaining his freedom, he spent some time at the Dominican priory of Santa Maria sopra Minerva, but fearing further persecution, he followed the advice of Pope Urban VIII and fled to France in 1634. The 71-year-old friar ended his troubled days in the quiet of the priory of Saint-Jacques in Paris.

Campanella was an extremely prolific writer, and the critical edition of his works (ed. L. Firpo, Milan 1954–   ) will fill many volumes. He antedated Descartes as the first philosopher to assert the need of positing a universal methodic doubt at the beginning of his system and to state the principle of self-consciousness as the basis of knowledge and certitude. His philosophy was an attempt to fuse, into a new original synthesis, the naturalistic doctrines of his time and the traditional scholastic teaching; it showed a marked tendency toward Platonic *Augustinianism. Campanella conceived being as a transcendental composition of power, knowledge, and will, which are its "primalities" or essential principles. This panpsychic conception of reality is matched by his theory that being and nonbeing are the metaphysical constituents of all creatures, which are thus

Tommaso Campanella.

distinguished from God who is pure being. For Campanella, to know is to be (*cognoscere est esse*), a principle that underlies his complex theory of knowledge. The central idea of his theology is Christ as universal reason. In politics he advocated a universal monarchy headed by the pope. *The City of the Sun,* his best-known work, is a political dialogue in the tradition of Plato's *Republic* and St. Thomas More's *Utopia.*

See also RENAISSANCE PHILOSOPHY.

Bibliography: Works. *Del senso delle cose e della magia,* ed. A. BRUERS (Bari 1925); *Epilogo magno,* ed. C. OTTAVIANO (Rome 1939); *Atheismus triumphatus* (Paris 1636); *Disputationum in quatuor partes suae philosophiae realis libri quatuor* (Paris 1637); *Philosophiae rationalis partes quinque* (Paris 1638); *Universalis philosophiae seu metaphysicarum rerum iuxta propria dogmata, partes tres, libri XVIII* (Paris 1638); *Theologicorum libri XXX,* ed. in part R. AMERIO (Milan 1936–); *Aforismi politici,* ed. L. FIRPO (Turin 1941); "The City of the Sun," tr. W. J. GILSTRAP, in *The Quest for Utopia,* ed. G. R. NEGLEY and J. M. PATRICK (New York 1952). Literature. R. AMERIO, EncFil 1:866–874. N. PICARD, LexThK² 2:907. L. FIRPO, *Bibliografia degli scritti di Tommaso Campanella* (Turin 1940). G. DI NAPOLI, *Tommaso Campanella, filosofo della restaurazione cattolica* (Padua 1947). B. M. BONANSEA, *The Theory of Knowledge of Tommaso Campanella, Exposition and Critique* (Washington 1954); "The Concept of Being and Non-Being in the Philosophy of T. C.," NewSchol 31 (1957) 34–67; "The Political Thought of T. C.," *Studies in Philosophy and the History of Philosophy,* ed. J. K. RYAN, v.2 (Washington 1963) 211–248. **Illustration credit:** Italian Information Center, New York City.

[B. M. BONANSEA]

CAMPANI, GIUSEPPE, Italian astronomer and optical instrument maker; b. Castel San Felice, near Spoleto, 1635; d. Rome, July 28, 1715. He moved to Rome (*c.* 1651) and in 1656, with his two older brothers, invented a silent night clock for Pope Alexander VII. He became noted as an inventor and maker of lenses of superior quality for telescopes of great focal lengths. In 1663–64, Campani invented the composite lens type of eye-piece and developed a telescope with four lenses, consisting of a triple ocular and an object lens. In 1664 he invented the first lens-grinding lathe, with which he ground and polished lenses without first casting them in molds. G. D. *Cassini used and pre-

ferred Campani's lenses and instruments to all others, and the Royal Observatory at Paris acquired Campani telescopes of 100 and 136 feet focal length among others. Campani made significant astronomical observations of the satellites of Jupiter and the rings of Saturn in 1664–65. He also pioneered in the development of the compound microscope, and invented a screw-barrel type of instrument that permitted greater precision of adjustment than was previously possible. In 1747 the equipment of Campani's optical workshop was purchased by Pope Benedict XIV for the Istituto delle Scienze at Bologna.

Bibliography: M. DAUMAS, ed., *Histoire de la science des origines au XXᵉ siècle* (*Encyclopédie de la Pléiade* 5; Paris 1957).

[S. A. BEDINI]

CAMPBELL, ALEXANDER, founder of the Disciples of Christ; b. Ballymena, County Antrim, Ireland, Sept. 12, 1788; d. Bethany, W.Va., March 4, 1866. He was the son of Rev. Thomas Campbell, a Presbyterian minister, and was educated in his father's school. After attending Glasgow University, Scotland, he joined his father's Christian Association of Washington, Pa., and was. ordained in 1812. His theological views, spread by preaching tours, induced congregations in Kentucky, Ohio, Indiana, West Virginia, and Tennessee to separate from the Baptists. Campbell united these churches with the Christian churches organized by Barton Stone to form the Disciples of Christ in 1832. Denominational organization was not completed until the first national convention of the Disciples in 1849. While advocating a simplistic theology, Campbell saw the need for an educated ministry and founded Bethany College, W.Va., in 1840. He engaged in numerous debates on religious topics, including a controversy with Bp. John B. Purcell of Cincinnati, Ohio, in 1830. Besides his published debates, his thought is found chiefly in his book, *The Christian System* (1835), and in his periodicals, *The Christian Baptist* and *The Milennial Harbinger.* He held that baptism and ac-

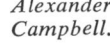
Alexander Campbell.

knowledgment of Jesus Christ as Messiah were the only requisites of Christianity.

Bibliography: J. KELLEMS, *Alexander Campbell and the Disciples* (New York 1930). W. E. GARRISON and A. T. DEGROOT,

The Disciples of Christ: A History (rev. ed. St. Louis 1958). H.
K. Rowe, DAB 3:446–448. **Illustration credit:** Disciples of Christ
Historical Society.

[R. K. MAC MASTER]

CAMPBELL, JAMES, judge, politician, postmaster
general of the U.S.; b. Southwark, Pa., Sept. 1, 1812; d.
Philadelphia, Pa., Jan. 27, 1893. He was the son of
Irish-Catholic parents, Anthony Campbell, a prosperous
merchant, and Catherine McGarvey. After reading law
in a Philadelphia office, he was admitted to the Pennsylvania bar on Sept. 14, 1833. He soon gained influence
in local and state politics as a leader of the growing
Irish immigrant minority. Campbell was a justice of the
Philadelphia court of common pleas for 10 years
(1840–50), during which time he experienced the hostility of the Know-Nothing Movement. Changing his
party allegiance from Whig to Democrat, he ran for
election to the state supreme court in 1851. The entire
Democratic ticket was elected except for Campbell, who
fell victim to Know-Nothing opposition. Gov. William
Bigler, however, appointed him state attorney general in
1852, and thereafter Campbell's influence was of national significance. In the presidential election of 1852,
he supported Franklin Pierce, who appointed him to the
cabinet as postmaster general. During his 4 years
(1853–57) in this office, he negotiated agreements to
lower foreign postal rates, inaugurated the registry system, and initiated economy measures. In 1856 Campbell
delivered the Pennsylvania Irish vote to James Buchanan, a vital factor in Buchanan's election. Campbell
ran unsuccessfully for the U.S. Senate in 1861, after
which he retired from politics. Returning to his legal
practice, he served as president of the board of trustees
of Jefferson Medical College, vice president of St.
Joseph's Orphan Asylum, and member of the Philadelphia County board of trusts.

Bibliography: J. M. CAMPBELL, "Biographical Sketch of Hon.
James Campbell," RecAmCHSPhila 5 (1894) 265–303. J. F.
COLEMAN, "The Public Career of James Campbell," *Pennsyl-
vania History* 29 (1962) 24–39.

[R. J. OARD]

CAMPBELL, ROYSTON DUNNACHIE IGNATIUS

Poet of Scottish extraction; b. Durban, Natal, South
Africa, Oct. 2, 1901; d. Setubal, Portugal, April 23,
1957. Son of S. G. Campbell, a Presbyterian doctor
he was educated at Durban High School but failed in
1918 to qualify for Oxford. Instead, he mixed with bohemian writers and artists in London, being strongly influenced by D. B. Wyndham Lewis. In 1922 he married
Mary Garman (whose piety influenced his conversion
to Roman Catholicism in 1935) and in 1924 published
The Flaming Terrapin, a short humanistic epic based on
the Noah story, which immediately made him famous.
Returning to Natal, he edited a monthly review, *Voor-
slag* (Whiplash), but his liberal views alienated local
opinion, so he returned to Europe and published two
satires, *The Wayzgoose* (1928) and *The Georgiad*
(1931); in these his mordant wit pilloried, respectively,
South African cultural pretensions, the "Bloomsbury"
minor poets and "advanced" intellectuals.

Between 1928 and 1936 he lived in Provence and
Spain. *Adamastor* (1930) and *Flowering Reeds* (1933)
contain such classic lyrics as "Tristan da Cunha," "The
Zulu Girl," "Horses on the Camargue," and "Choosing
a Mast"; in them the spiritual power of physical beauty

and activity is conveyed in rich imagery. In 1937 he
was war correspondent for the *Tablet* (London) with
Franco's forces, but soon retired to Portugal to write
Flowering Rifle (1939), a satirical, violently pro-Franco
"epic of the Spanish Civil War." He served in the British Army in East Africa from 1942 to 1944. From 1946
to 1949 he was a talks producer at the BBC, London,
and in 1952, after the demise of the Catholic review,
Catacomb, of which he was joint editor, he moved to
Portugal, where he was killed in a car accident.

Campbell's poetic genius was never doubted by such
authorities as T. S. Eliot, Edith Sitwell, and Edmund
Blunden; but his early "fascist" views (see *Broken Record,* 1934) and his ruthless lampoons on the former
"Communist" poets (see *Talking Bronco,* 1946) made
him unpopular in England. Though his work was uneven in quality, as in *Mithraic Emblems* (1936), his
fame rests securely on *Collected Poems* (3 v., 1949–60)
and on his superb translations: *Poems of St. John of
the Cross* (1951), Baudelaire's *Les Fleurs du Mal*
(1952), and *Six Spanish Plays* (ed. E. Bentley, 1959).
His lively prose works include *Taurine Provence* (1932),
Light on a Dark Horse (autobiography mixed with
fantasy, 1951), *Lorca* (1952), and *Portugal* (1957).

Bibliography: W. H. GARDNER, "Voltage of Delight," *Month*
19 (1958) 5–17, 133–147. A. PATON, "Roy Campbell: Poet and
Man," *Theoria* 9 (1957) 19–31. G. M. MILLER and H. SERGEANT,
A Critical Survey of South African Poetry in English (Cape-
town 1957).

[W. H. GARDNER]

CAMPBELL, THOMAS JOSEPH, author, educator; b. New York City, April 29, 1848; d. Monroe,
N.Y., Dec. 14, 1925. He was educated in New York
City in the public schools and at the College of St. Francis Xavier, where he received his M.A. in 1867; he entered the Jesuit novitiate at Sault-au-Recollet, Canada.
In 1870 he was sent to St. John's College, later Fordham University, New York, where he taught classical
literature for 3 years. After studying philosophy and
science at Woodstock, Md., he returned in 1876 to St.
Francis Xavier College to teach rhetoric. He then went
to Louvain University, Belgium, where he studied
French literature and ecclesiastical history in addition
to theology. He was ordained in 1881, returned to the
U.S., and spent his 3d year of probation at Frederick,
Md., after which he became president of St. John's College. In 1888 he was appointed provincial of the Jesuits'
Maryland–New York Province, a post he held until
1893. Under his administration colleges were expanded,
missionary work among Italian immigrants was undertaken, a laymen's retreat movement was started, and
plans were begun for a national Jesuit magazine (*America*). Campbell served briefly (1893) as vice-rector of
St. Francis Xavier College, devoted 2 years to giving
missions and retreats, and was for 5 years president of
Fordham University. In August 1900 he was attached
to the staffs of the Apostleship of Prayer and the *Messenger of the Sacred Heart* as preacher, editor, and
writer. After serving from 1910 to 1914 as editor of
America, he went to Canada for historical research and
published the results in *The Pioneer Priests of North
America* (3 v. 1908–19) and *The Pioneer Laymen of
North America* (2 v. 1915). After filling posts at St.
Francis Xavier Church (1916) and at St. Joseph's
Church, Philadelphia, Pa. (1917), he returned to New
York as lecturer on American history at the Fordham
University Graduate School. He also completed *The*

Jesuits, 1534–1921 (1921), before retiring in 1925.

[V. C. HOPKINS]

CAMPEGGI, CAMILLO, theologian; b. Pavia or Piacenza, unknown date; d. 1569. He joined the Dominicans, and after teaching theology he was inquisitor at Pavia, Ferrara, and Mantua. He was the Pope's theologian at the Council of Trent (1561–63), and became bishop of Nepi and Sutri in 1568. Besides his *De mundi fallaciis* (Venice 1562; Brescia 1563), a sermon he preached at the Council before 1561, he published only editions of texts: *De potestate papae et concilii generalis* (Rome 1563), Jean de Torquemada's sermon at the Council of Florence; and *Tractatus de haereticis* (Mantua 1567; Rome 1579) by Zanchino Ugolini (14th century). The treatise, *De primatu romani pontificis contra Matthaeum Flacium Illyricum,* which is doubtfully attributed to Campeggi, was published by J. T. Rocaberti in his *Bibliotheca maxima pontificia,* 7 (Rome 1696) 133–264.

Bibliography: Quétif-Echard 2.1:201–202.

[A. DUVAL]

CAMPEGGIO, LORENZO, cardinal and presiding judge at the court trial of Henry VIII and Catherine of Aragon, legate at the Diets of Nürnberg and Augsburg; b. Milan, Italy, 1472; d. Rome, July 25, 1539. Born of a Bolognese family that traced its ancestry to 1220 and was famous for its many lawyers, writers, and prelates, Lorenzo became a professor of law at the University of Bologna. Though a father of five children, he embraced the ecclesiastical state after the death of his wife in 1509. His advancement was rapid. He was auditor of the Rota in 1511, bishop of Feltre in the next year, nuncio to Emperor Maximilian I in 1513, and cardinal, July 1517. His first major diplomatic assignment came in 1518, when he was sent to the court of Henry VIII by Leo X to secure English support in a crusade against the Turks. Thomas Wolsey blocked his entry into England, until he himself was appointed colegate. Although the mission failed, Campeggio won honors from Henry—including a mansion (built by

Seal of Lorenzo Campeggio on a document, April 17, 1584.

Bramante) in Rome, the charge of English affairs in Rome, and the bishopric of Salisbury.

Ten years later, when the annulment of Henry's marriage was being petitioned, Wolsey requested Clement VII to appoint Campeggio as judge of the legal proceedings, because of his learning and tractability. Hoping that the King's interest in Anne Boleyn would wane with time, Campeggio delayed his arrival with a convenient attack of gout. Once in England he failed to reconcile the royal couple and failed in his later attempts to induce Queen Catherine's retirement into a convent. After a series of sessions, he adjourned the proceedings of the trial, giving as his reason that the time for summer vacation had arrived. Henry's chagrin resulted in Wolsey's dismissal from Court and Campeggio's loss of prestige. As he was leaving England his baggage was ransacked at Dover, in defiance of his diplomatic immunity, for evidence of bribes from the Emperor Charles V, nephew of Catherine of Aragon, or for a decretal bull defining conditions of the divorce.

Campeggio represented Rome at the diets of Nürnberg in 1524 and Augsburg in 1530. Although he opposed any council meetings with the Protestants, believing that they could be controlled only by imperial authority, he was sent by Paul III in 1538, together with cardinals Giacomo Simonetta and Girolamo Aleandro, to convene a council at Vincenza. He died on his return to Rome in the next year and was buried in Bologna.

Bibliography: J. S. BREWER and J. GAIRDNER, eds., *Letters and Papers of the Reign of Henry VIII,* 21 v. (London 1862–1910). M. FERNÁNDEZ DE NAVARRETE, *Colección de documentos inéditos para la historia de España,* Eng. tr. and summary in *Calendar of State Papers, Spanish* (London 1856). G. FANTUZZI, *Notizie degli scrittori bolognesi* (Bologna 1783) 3:47–61. C. SIGONIO, *De Vita L. Campegi cardinalis* (Bologna 1581). J. GAIRDNER, DNB 3:850. H. LIEBING, RGG³ 1:1606. E. V. CARDINAL, *Cardinal Lorenzo Campeggio: Legate to the Courts of Henry VIII and Charles V* (Boston 1935). A. D'AMATO, EncCatt 3:470–471. G. CONSTANT, DHGE 11:633–640. Hughes RE v.1. *Nuntiaturberichte aus Deutschland,* Abt. 1, suppl. 1 *Legation Lorenzo Campeggios 1530–1531 und Nuntiatur Girolamo Aleandros 1531,* ed. G. MÜLLER (Tübingen 1963). **Illustration credit:** Vatican Library.

[E. V. CARDINAL]

CAMPIN, ROBERT, now generally identified with the Master of *Flémalle, was the first major painter of the Northern Renaissance and teacher of Jacques Daret and Roger van der *Weyden; b. possibly in Valenciennes, *c.* 1378; d. Tournai, 1444. In 1410 Campin acquired citizenship in Tournai and in 1423 was elected dean of the painter's guild. His early works such as the "Dijon Nativity" or the "Salting Madonna" (*c.* 1420–25) appear highly naturalistic both in the accuracy of handling individual objects and in the logical rendering of three-dimensional space. Specific objects and often the spatial organization comprise a subtly disguised symbolic system. His most famous work, the "Mérode Altarpiece" (see illustration), shows the profound Mystery of the Incarnation as taking place within a humble 15th-century bourgeois setting. In Campin's later works of the 1430s, in such panels as "St. Veronica" and the "Virgin" in Frankfurt, he relinquished his extensive use of symbolism. His style and his representation of spiritual concepts in concrete physical form greatly influenced early Netherlandish painting. (For illustration, see following page.)

Bibliography: C. DE TOLNAY, *Le Maître de Flémalle et les Frères Van Eyck* (Brussels 1939). Panofsky ENethPaint. T. ROUSSEAU, JR., "The Mérode Altarpiece," *Bulletin of the New York Metropolitan Museum of Art,* NS 16 (Dec. 1957) 117–129. M. B. FREEMAN, "The Iconography of the Mérode Altarpiece," *ibid.* 130–139. W. SUHR, "The Restoration of the Mérode Altarpiece," *ibid.,* 140–144. **Illustration credit:** The Metropolitan Museum of Art, The Cloisters Collection, Purchase.

[S. N. HOPPS]

Robert Campin, "Annunciation with Donors and St. Joseph" (the so-called Mérode Altarpiece), oil on wood, left wing 25⅝ *by* 10¾, *center panel* 25³⁄₁₆ *by* 24⅞, *right wing* 25⅝ *by* 10¹⁵⁄₁₆ *inches.*

CAMPINAS, ARCHDIOCESE OF (CAMPINENSIS),

located in the state of São Paulo, Brazil; created a diocese in 1908; raised to an archdiocese in 1958. In 1964 it had three suffragan sees: São Carlos (1908), Bragança Paulista (1925), and Piracicaba (1944).

1964 STATISTICS

Area	Population	Parishes	Clergy	
			Sec.	Reg.
Campinas	686,838	61	79	64
São Carlos	517,396	40	48	42
Bragança Paulista	*219,496	19	22	16
Piracicaba	266,557	25	25	24

*This figure includes Catholics only.

Even before it was created a diocesan see, Campinas was the second largest city in São Paulo and an important Catholic center. The diocese was organized by João Batista Corrêa Neri (1908–20). During that time a schismatic sect arose in Itapira, which, although it died out by 1938, gave rise to other schismatic churches such as that of Dom Salomão Ferraz. Bishop Francisco de Campos Barreto (1920–41) founded in 1928 the Congregation of Missionary Sisters of Jesus Crucified. These women assist the clergy in parishes and missions and frequently administer vacant parishes. They have spread throughout Brazil and by 1964 the congregation was organized into four provinces with 100 houses and 1,500 members. In 1964, among the orders serving in the province, in addition to the sisters mentioned, were Missionaries of the Sacred Heart, Salesians, Jesuits, Franciscans, Claretians, Benedictines, Premonstratensians, Passionists, Redemptorists, Fathers of the Divine Word, Augustinians, Missionaries of

Milan, Stigmatine Fathers, and more than 1,700 sisters of various congregations.

Bibliography: L. CASTANHO DE ALMEIDA, *São Paulo, filho da Igreja* (Petrópolis 1955). J. C. A. NOGUEIRA, *Elogio histórico de D. João Neri* (Rio de Janeiro 1945); *D. Francisco de Campos Barreto, homenagem póstuma* (Campinas 1941).

[O. VAN DER VAT]

CAMPINAS, CATHOLIC UNIVERSITY OF,

a coeducational institution of higher learning in Campinas, in the state of São Paulo, Brazil. The University was founded in 1941 as a Faculty of Philosophy and in 1955 was officially raised to university level by the federal government. In 1956 it was canonically erected as a pontifical university by the Holy See. In 1941 Dom Francisco de Campos Barreto, second Bishop of Campinas, assigned the task of organizing the Catholic University in Campinas to Msgr. Emílio José Salim. Shortly after the bishop's death, the institution opened in 1942 with Salim as dean.

The bishop of Campinas serves as president of the University, which is governed by the University council and the University assembly. In 1964 the academic staff consisted of approximately 300 members, priests and laymen. Enrollment totaled more than 2,700 men and women from Campinas and other cities in the state of São Paulo, as well as Minas Gerais, Paraná, and Mato Grosso; and from Bolivia, Perú, and Venezuela. The central library on campus housed more than 25,000 volumes.

The University comprises the Faculties of Philosophy, Science, and Letters; Economics, Dentistry, Law, and Social Service; Schools of Librarianship, Nursing, a choral conservatory; and departments of educational orientation and domestic science (teacher training). In 1963 the University college, Pius XII, was established.

The Catholic University of Campinas confers the bachelor's degree in economics, and social science and law; and the licentiate in philosophy. It grants the doctorate in letters, and after 2 years' additional study, in

Façade of the Catholic University of Campinas, São Paulo.

science; and confers the professional title of surgeon-dentist. The academic year is divided into 2 semesters, March to June and August to November.

The University biannually publishes the *Revista da Universidade Católica de Campinas* and the *Notícia Geomorfológica* and maintains an anthropological museum on campus.

In 1964 plans for university expansion included a building program and the addition of an engineering school.

[C. A. CASTANHO]

CAMPION, EDMUND, BL.

English martyr; b. London, *c.* 1540; d. Tyburn, London, Dec. 1, 1581. His father, a bookseller, sent him for his education to Christ's Hospital (some say St. Paul's); at age 15 he was awarded a scholarship at St. John's College, Oxford, where 2 years later he was appointed a junior fellow. He was an outstanding orator and was chosen to speak before Queen Elizabeth when she visited Oxford in 1566; as a schoolboy he had read an address of welcome to Queen Mary on her entry into London in 1553. He won the patronage of the Earl of Leicester, and Queen Elizabeth and William Cecil both expressed interest in his future. Brilliant, popular, and the leader of an influential group, he became the most notable figure in the Oxford of his day: Cecil later referred to him as a "diamond of England."

In August 1569 Campion crossed to Dublin to assist in the foundation of a university. After writing his *History of Ireland,* a superb piece of literature (first published in Holinshed's *Chronicles,* 1587), he returned to London in 1571, witnessed the trial of Dr. John Storey and then crossed to Douai, where he was reconciled to the Church—he had taken the Oath of Supremacy and deacon's orders according to the Anglican Ordinal (1553). He was ordained subdeacon at Douai in 1573, and went as a pilgrim to Rome, where he was admitted into the Society of Jesus by Father Everard Mercurian. After his novitiate at Brünn in Moravia, he was assigned to teach in the Jesuit school in Prague, where he was ordained in 1578. At the end of the following year Campion, with Father Robert *Persons, was chosen by Mercurian, at the instigation of Cardinal William *Allen, to inaugurate a Jesuit mission to England. Campion set out from Rome in the spring of 1580, visiting on his way Cardinal Charles *Borromeo at Milan and *Beza at Geneva; he landed at

Dover in the guise of a jewel merchant on June 25. On reaching London, where he visited Catholic prisoners, he wrote hurriedly his "Challenge to the Privy Council" (commonly called "Campion's Brag"), in which he proclaimed the purpose of his mission, namely, "of free cost to preach the Gospel, to minister the Sacraments, to instruct the simple, to reform sinners, to confute errors—in brief, to cry alarm spiritual against foul vice and proud ignorance, wherewith many [of] my dear countrymen are abused."

Campion's winning personality, saintliness, and eloquence gave fresh heart to Catholics throughout England, but he was pursued by agents of the crown and more than once narrowly escaped capture. He wrote to Mercurian, describing his labors in Lancashire, Yorkshire, and the Midlands: "I ride about some piece of country every day. The harvest is wonderful great . . . I cannot long escape the hands of the heretics . . . I am in apparel to myself very ridiculous; I often change it and my name too." At Stonor Park, Oxfordshire, he wrote and secretly printed his *Decem Rationes,* in which he openly challenged Protestant divines to dispute with him the grounds of Catholicism. On June 27, 1581, some 400 copies of this book were secretly distributed in University Church, Oxford, at the service of "Commemoration."

Blessed Edmund Campion, German engraving of the 16th century, the only known impression of which is in the British Museum. Although not a portrait from life, the likeness corresponds well with the near-contemporary portrait formerly in the Church of the Gesù at Rome.

Three weeks later, at Lyford Grange, Berkshire, Campion was betrayed, arrested, and taken to the Tower of London. Attempts were made to bribe him into apostasy. He was racked several times, forced into theological debate, and finally on November 14, together with Ralph Sherwin, Luke Kirby, and others, condemned to death. Before sentence he addressed the court: "In condemning us you condemn all your own ancestors—all the ancient priests, bishops, and kings—all that was once the glory of England . . . God lives; posterity will live; their judgment is not so liable to corruption as that of those who are now going to sentence us to death." On December 1, with Sherwin and Alexander Briant, he was hanged, drawn, and quartered at Tyburn. Campion was beatified by Leo XIII on Dec. 9, 1886.

See also MARTYRS OF ENGLAND AND WALES; OATHS, ENGLISH POST-REFORMATION; RECUSANTS; RECUSANT LITERATURE.

Bibliography: H. FOLEY, *Records of the English Province of the Society of Jesus,* 7 v. (London 1877–82) *passim.* R. SIMPSON, *Edmund Campion* (new ed. London 1896). E. WAUGH, *Edmund Campion* (New York 1935). **Illustration credit:** Courtesy of the Trustees of the British Museum.

[P. CARAMAN]

CAMPO SANTO TEUTONICO

The oldest of the German national foundations in Rome. It comprises a church, a college for priests, and a cemetery and is situated left of St. Peter's, in the area of *Nero's circus. According to legend, Empress St. *Helena had brought some of the soil of Mt. Calvary to Rome and scattered it in the area of Nero's circus, thus the name Campo Santo (Holy Field). Under *Charlemagne the *Schola Francorum* was founded there (799) with a church, a pilgrim's hospice, and a cemetery, where Frankish priests took care of their countrymen and buried their dead.

The Augustinian Johannes Golderer, later auxiliary bishop of Bamberg, founded (*c.* 1450) the All Souls *Confraternity for his German countrymen in Rome; its statutes were approved by Pope Pius II in 1461. In 1519 Pope Gregory XIII raised this association to the rank of an archconfraternity with headship over all other similar confraternities. It is still in existence and is the juridical body for Campo Santo.

Today the archconfraternity (*Arciconfraternità di Santa Maria della Pietà dei Teutonici e Fiamminghi*) is made up of German-speaking men and women of every class and country living in Rome. They participate in regular church services wearing their national costume. They are especially devoted to assisting at Masses for the poor souls. In the 19th century guilds of German bakers and shoemakers were included in the archconfraternity. In a small cemetery with its cypress and palm trees are graves of many famous persons, e.g., Anton de *Waal. It is visited annually by thousands of tourists from Germany, Austria, Switzerland, Luxembourg, and the Netherlands. Here likewise German Catholics of Rome celebrate the Feast of Corpus Christi, a celebration in which the papal Swiss Guard joins. November 1 is the major feast of the archconfraternity of the poor souls.

A cruciform hall church was consecrated in 1501. The paintings of the old winged altar are still preserved and are hanging in the choir. The main altar with the

Cemetery of the Campo Santo Teutonico, Rome.

Pietà is the creation of Wilhelm Achtermann (d. 1884), as is the marble Resurrection altar on the left side chapel. The tombs of the Swiss Guards who died in 1527 defending Pope *Clement VII are in the Resurrection chapel. In the 19th century the church was repainted in the *Nazarene style. The church has been enriched by various patrons: Franz Joseph of Austria (windows), Emperor Wilhelm II (organ), Pope Leo XIII (candelabra), and Pope John XXIII (a chalice). In 1959 the President of the German Republic, Theodore Heuss, donated a bronze door, which was made according to the design of E. Hillenbrand.

A college for priests was founded in 1876 by De Waal, mainly for young clerics who came to Rome to study Church history and Christian archeology. A special library of 30,000 volumes serves this purpose. In 1888 the Roman Institute of the *Görres-Gesellschaft was founded. It provides scholarly training for the new generation and publishes source material from the *Vatican archives (e.g., Acts of the Council of *Trent, papal nunciature reports). In conjunction with the college it also edits the *Römische Quartalschrift für christliche Altertumskunde und Kirchengeschichte,* with supplementary issues.

The museum houses a collection of Christian antiquities, assembled originally by De Waal. It contains small articles of early Christian art, sarcophagi, inscriptions, lamps, Coptic textile fabrics, Roman imperial coins, and paintings of the Middle Ages. The association Villa Hügel in Essen arranged for the cataloguing of the museum. Displays of its holdings have been held in Essen, Mainz, Mechlin, Utrecht, and Vienna.

Bibliography: P. M. BAUMGARTEN, *Cartularium vetus Campi Sancti Teutonicorum de Urbe,* RömQuartalsch 16. Suppl. Heft (1908). E. DAVID, *Vorgeschichte und Geschichte des Priesterkollegiums am Campo Santo* (Freiburg 1928). W. KUHN, *Frühchristliche Kunst aus Rom. Katalog,* ed. Verein Villa Hügel (Essen 1962). A. SCHUCHERT, LexThK² 2:912.

[J. E. GUGUMUS]

CAMPRA, ANDRÉ, composer of opera and church music who ranks with *Lully and *Couperin among the masters of the French baroque; b. Aix (Provence), Dec. 4, 1660; d. Versailles, June 29, 1744. His first post was music director at Toulon cathedral in 1680. After holding a number of similar positions, he was appointed *maître de chapelle* at Notre Dame in 1694. He resigned in 1700 to devote himself more exclusively to operatic composition, since his operas were fast becoming successful. Among his important church works are five books of motets (1695–1720), a Mass (1700), and two books of psalms (1737–38). Most of these settings have orchestral accompaniment, and he is credited with having introduced stringed instruments into the services at Notre Dame. His church style can be described as a mixture of declamatory French and florid Italian techniques. As a composer of operas he is justly considered the chief link between Lully and Rameau.

Bibliography: M. BARTÉLEMY, *André Campra* (Paris 1957). R. GIRARDON, MusGG 2:730–740. A. H. WODEHOUSE et al., Grove DMM 2:36–39.

[W. C. HOLMES]

CAMUS, ALBERT

French novelist, essayist, and playwright; b. Mondovi, Algeria, Nov. 7, 1913; d. in an automobile accident, Sens, France, Jan. 4, 1960. His 1957 Nobel prize citation extolled his literary art for having illuminated "the problems of the human conscience of our time." His childhood was marked by poverty. He studied at Algiers University where he wrote a thesis on Plotinus and St. Augustine for his *diplôme d'études supérieures;* however, poor health forced him to abandon a projected teaching career. He early combined a commitment to social justice with his literary talents, helping to found a workers' theater, L'Equipe (for which he adapted Aeschylus's *Prometheus Bound*) and reporting the economic misery of the Berbers. He continued his newspaper career in Paris in 1939. During the Nazi occupation of France, he wrote his *Lettres à un ami allemand* for the Resistance paper *Combat,* and as editor after the liberation, he espoused the democratic left wing's program of political renewal through social justice, though he rejected Marxism and the popular front movement. His editorials, including many written after his dissociation from any paper after 1947, were republished under the title of *Actuelles.*

World of the Absurd. In *L'Envers et l'endroit* (1937) and *Noces* (1938), semiautobiographical narratives and lyrical, imagistic descriptions of Mediterranean landscapes, Camus reveals his consciousness of being born as a man uprooted from routine experiences and alienated from himself in an inhuman, foreign world; he calls this state "man's dual consciousness of his desire for duration and his fate to die"; it is a neoprimitivistic atheism that denies immortality but fosters pity for others. *Le Mythe de Sisyphe* (1942) crystallizes these experiences into the notion of the "absurd," born when man's need for meaning and unity encounters the world's irrationality. Absurd man, lucidly accepting this dilemma as his situation, rejects both nihilistic despair and transcendant "evasions" (e.g., *Kierkegaard's existentialism) as philosophical suicide, and purports to find happiness in the living of an intense life that is both devoid of supernatural hope and in constant rebellion against his contingent nature. Assuming the absurd frees man completely, for all experience has equal value.

L'Etranger (1942) makes of a condemned murderer an exemplar of absurd man; Mersault, the socially estranged, unreflective hero, is unable to manifest conventional responses, either grief at his mother's funeral or remorse at his unpremeditated killing of an Arab, and is judged guilty because he fails to satisfy society's logic. He achieves absurd awareness in prison when he refuses the chaplain's explanation of man's fate, rejects both his guilt and eternal salvation, and rebels against a death that deprives him of the earthly happiness he knows. Awareness of living beyond any rational appeal brings peace.

Plays: Tragedy and Solution. In two plays Camus dramatizes the absurd as tragedy. In *Le Malentendu* (1944) Marthe hangs herself to attest to the world's irrationality after she and her mother, failing to recognize their brother and son, Jan, who has been absent for 25 years, have murdered him. In *Caligula* (1945) the tyrant, discovering that men are unhappy, becomes the pedagogue of the absurd, teaching through arbitrary terror the valuelessness of all, until he himself is killed by a patrician rebellion.

La Peste (1947) offers a humanistic solution to the absurd. Suffering, becoming collective, creates solidarity among those who rebel against the plague. Dr. Rieux, rejecting Father Paneloux's belief that the plague is punishment for guilt and Tarrou's quest for sanctity without God, opposes fate in human terms for human ends, and achieves a noble altruism without absolutes. Together with Rambert, who discovers that there may be shame in being happy alone, Rieux finds in the common human rebellion against evil the only alternative to grace.

A modern morality play, *L'Etat de Siège* (1948), dramatizes the plague's imposition of a totalitarian rule on Cadiz; only a fearless, selfless man can break the plague's power by sacrificing his life for the city's freedom. *Les Justes* (1949) portrays Kaliayev's refusal to commit injustice in order to advance a utopian justice. Having assassinated a duke, he refuses religious consolation so as to preserve revolutionary fellowship, but is reconciled with his fate by accepting his own death.

L'Homme révolté (1951) opposes absurd freedom to

Albert Camus, novelist, Nobel prize winner.

a revolutionary philosophy of permitted limits of action, which has been evolved through meditation on metaphysical and historical rebellion. Revolt rejects injustice and affirms human solidarity, whereas historical revolution, having "killed God," became God in order to legitimize murder. Camus chooses moderation in which the antinomies of such a tension as justice-freedom mutually limit the universality of each. In *L'Eté* (1954) he reaffirmed his commitment to live without despair.

The Essential Artist. Camus tended after 1956 to adapt foreign literature to the stage, e.g., Faulkner's *Requiem for a Nun* (1956), and Dostoyevsky's *The Possessed* (1959). He also experimented anew with fiction in *L'Exil et le Royaume* (1957) and *La Chute* (1956), an ironic monologue by the lawyer Jean-Baptiste Clamance, who confesses loss of confidence in his own virtue because he failed to save a woman. He is both judge and penitent at the same time.

Essentially an artist and not a philosopher, Camus renewed the tradition of writer as *moraliste,* interpreting man's anguish anew. As a consummate stylist, he disciplined a lyrical exuberance to varied narrative styles and logical exposition. Though his efforts to create tragedy had only qualified success, he gave new dimensions to the novel and the reflective essay.

See also EXISTENTIALISM IN LITERATURE; LITERARY REVIVAL, CATHOLIC.

Bibliography: A. CAMUS, *Notebooks,* ed. and tr. J. O'BRIEN (New York 1963–). G. BRÉE, *Camus* (New Brunswick, N.J. 1959). J. CRUICKSHANK, *Albert Camus and the Literature of Revolt* (New York 1960). A. MAQUET, *Albert Camus: Ou L'Invincible été* (Paris 1956). R. QUILLIOT, *La Mer et les prisons* (Paris 1956). P. THODY, *Albert Camus: A Study of His Work* (London 1957). R. DE LUPPÉ, *Albert Camus* (Paris 1951). T. HANNA, *The Thought and Art of Albert Camus* (Chicago 1958). **Illustration credit:** French Embassy, Press and Information Division, New York City.

[G. E. GINGRAS]